CONCISE ENCYCLOPEDIA OF SOCIOLINGUISTICS

Edited by

RAJEND MESTHRIE
University of Cape Town, South Africa

Consulting Editor

R. E. ASHER
University of Edinburgh, UK

2001

ELSEVIER

AMSTERDAM – NEW YORK – OXFORD – SHANNON – SINGAPORE – TOKYO

Elsevier Science Ltd, The Boulevard, Langford Lane,
Kidlington, Oxford OX5 1GB, UK

Copyright © 2001 Elsevier Science Ltd

All rights reserved. No part of this publication may be reproduced, stored in any retrieval system or transmitted in any form or by any means: electronic, electrostatic, magnetic tape, mechanical, photocopying, recording or otherwise, without permission in writing from the publishers.

Library of Congress Cataloging-in-Publication Data
Concise encyclopedia of sociolinguistics / edited by Rajend Mesthrie ; consulting editor, R.E. Asher.
   p.cm.
  Based on the 10-volume: The encyclopedia of language and linguistics / R.E. Asher, editor-in-chief. 1994.
  Includes bibliographical references.
  ISBN 0-08-043726-5 (HC : alk. paper)
  1. Sociolinguistics--Encyclopedias. I. Mesthrie, Rajend. II. Encyclopedia of language and linguistics.

P40 .C564 2001
306.44'03--dc21

                                                      2001054486

British Library Cataloguing in Publication Data
A catalogue record for this book is available from the British Library.

ISBN 0-08-043726-5 (HC)

∞™ The paper used in this publication meets the minimum requirements of the American National Standard for Information Sciences—Permanence of Paper for Printed Library Materials, ANSI Z39.48–1984.

Typeset by Macmillan India, Bangalore, India.
Printed and bound in Great Britain by Polestar Wheatons, Exeter.

Contents

Editor's Preface and Biographical Note   xxvi

Introduction
Sociolinguistics: History and Overview   1
R. Mesthrie

Section I. Foundations of Society and Language
Anthropological Linguistics   5
E. Keating

Attitudes and Behavior   6
W. S. Bainbridge

Bilingualism, Individual   10
F. Grosjean

Bilingualism, Societal   16
M. H. A. Blanc

Communication   22
K. L. Berge

Communicative Competence   29
A. Duranti

Ecology of Language   30
J. M. Y. Simpson

Language   31
J. M. Y. Simpson

Language as a Social Reality   34
T. Pateman

Language in Society: Overview   36
M. L. Apte

Multiculturalism and Language 48
J. R. Edwards

Pragmatics and Sociolinguistics 50
J. L. Mey

Prescriptive and Descriptive Grammar 58
C. Cullen

Role Theory 59
R. H. Turner

Sapir–Whorf Hypothesis 65
O. Werner

Saussurean Tradition and Sociolinguistics 73
J. E. Joseph

Social Psychology 80
W. S. Bainbridge

Socialization 87
C. B. Cazden

Sociolinguistics of Sign Language 89
C. Lucas

Sociology of Language 92
W. S. Bainbridge

Speech Community 105
B. B. Kachru

Section II. Language and Interaction

Antilanguage 109
P. A. Chilton

Audience Design 109
A. Bell

Conversation Analysis 110
P. Drew

Conversational Maxims J. Thomas	116
Cooperative Principle J. Thomas	121
Deaf Community: Structures and Interaction J. G. Kyle	125
Dialogism T. A. Marshall	127
Discourse A. McHoul	133
Discourse in Cross-linguistic and Cross-cultural Contexts M. Clyne	145
Doctor–Patient Language M. Lacoste	152
Ethnography of Speaking G. Philipsen	154
Ethnomethodology G. Psathas	160
Identity and Language R. Mesthrie & A. Tabouret-Keller	165
Kinesics A. Kendon	169
Kinship Terminology E. L. Schusky	172
Language in the Workplace B. Holmqvist & P. B. Andersen	177
Narrative, Natural M. Toolan	179
Phatic Communion D. Abercrombie	186

Politeness G. KASPER	187
Speech Accommodation H. GILES	193
Speech Act Theory: An Overview K. ALLAN	197

Section III. Language Variation: Style, Situation, Function

Advertising M. L. GEIS	209
Blessings B. G. SZUCHEWYCZ	211
Business Language G. RASMUSSEN	212
Code, Sociolinguistic U. AMMON	214
Context U. M. QUASTHOFF	218
Diglossia A. HUDSON	226
Discourse Analysis and the Law D. EADES	231
Formulaic Language F. COULMAS	233
Genre T. THREADGOLD	235
Institutional Language S. SARANGI	239
Literary Language R. CARTER	243

Media Language and Communication — 246
K. C. Schrøder

Medical Language — 256
J. Maclean & J. C. Maher

Register — 259
W. Downes

Religion and Language — 262
J. F. A. Sawyer

Slang: Sociology — 265
I. L. Allen

Speech and Writing — 270
J. E. Miller

Speech Play — 276
M. L. Apte

Style — 280
M. Short

Taboo Words — 283
M. L. Apte

The Internet and Language — 287
C. Thurlow

Verbal Duel — 289
R. Ackerman

Section IV. Language Variation and Change: Dialects and Social Groups

Accent — 293
J. M. Y. Simpson

Adolescent Peer Group Language — 297
R. L. Taylor

Chain Shifts — 303
G. J. Docherty & D. J. L. Watt

Contents

Class and Language — 307
F. GREGERSEN

Dialect and Dialectology — 310
S. ROMAINE

Dialect Humor — 319
M. L. APTE

Ethnicity and the Crossing of Boundaries — 321
B. RAMPTON

Ethnicity and Language — 324
E. F. KOTZÉ

Forensic Phonetics and Sociolinguistics — 329
P. FOULKES & J. P. FRENCH

Gay Language — 332
W. L. LEAP

Gender and Language — 336
K. M. MCCORMICK

Language Change and Language Acquisition — 345
E. L. BAVIN

Maps: Dialect and Language — 350
J. M. KIRK

Social Class — 362
M. W. MACY

Social Networks — 370
A. L. MILROY

Sociolinguistic Variation — 377
R. MESTHRIE

Sociolinguistics and Language Change — 389
J. MILROY

Sociophonetics — 391
S. WRIGHT. Revised by C. M. SANGSTER

Sound Change 396
J. J. OHALA

Subcultures and Countercultures 401
R. L. TAYLOR

Syntactic Change 407
N. VINCENT

The Atlas of North American English: Methods and Findings 412
S. ASH

Urban and Rural Forms of Language 418
A. M. HAMILTON

Vernacular 420
R. MACAULAY

Section V. Language Contact

Areal Linguistics 423
J. M. Y. SIMPSON

Bilingualism and Language Acquisition 430
C. LETTS

Borrowing 432
J. HEATH

Code-mixing 442
R. MESTHRIE

Code-switching: Discourse Models 443
P. AUER

Code-switching: Overview 447
K. M. MCCORMICK

Code-switching: Sociopragmatic Models 454
S. GROSS

Code-switching: Structural Models 456
R. M. BHATT

Contact Languages . . . 461
S. G. THOMASON

Endangered Languages . . . 465
L. A. GRENOBLE & L. J. WHALEY

English as a Foreign Language . . . 467
G. ABBOTT

Ethnolinguistic Vitality . . . 472
H. GILES

Foreigner Talk . . . 474
M. CLYNE

Interlanguage . . . 475
E. TARONE

Intertwined Languages . . . 481
P. C. MUYSKEN

Jargons . . . 483
P. MÜHLHÄUSLER

Koinés . . . 485
R. MESTHRIE

Language Enclaves . . . 489
K. MATTHEIER

Language Loyalty . . . 492
R. MESTHRIE

Language Maintenance, Shift, and Death . . . 493
R. MESTHRIE

Language Spread . . . 498
R. MESTHRIE

Language Transfer and Substrates . . . 499
T. ODLIN

Lingua Franca . . . 503
M. BAROTCHI

Migrants and Migration — A. M. Pavlinic — 504

Missionaries and Language — P. Lewis — 509

Native Speaker — A. Davies — 512

New Englishes — B. B. Kachru — 519

Pidgins and Creoles: An Overview — L. Todd — 524

Pidgins and Creoles: Models — J. Aitchison — 530

Pidgins and Creoles: Morphology — F. C. V. Jones — 536

Sociolinguistic Area — J. D'Souza — 538

Section VI. Language, Power and Inequality

Critical Language Awareness — J. L. Mey — 541

Critical Sociolinguistics — G. Kress — 542

Discrimination and Minority Languages — T. Skutnabb-Kangas & R. Phillipson — 545

Hegemony — G. Mininni — 550

Honorifics — M. Shibatani — 552

Ideology — A. Luke — 559

Language Conflict . . . 563
D. P. Pattanayak

Linguicide . . . 567
T. Skutnabb-Kangas & R. Phillipson

Linguistic Imperialism . . . 570
R. Phillipson & T. Skutnabb-Kangas

Manipulation . . . 574
N. Fairclough

Marxist Theories of Language . . . 575
G. Mininni

Minority Languages . . . 579
J. M. Y. Simpson

Politicized Language . . . 580
A. Davies

Politics and Language . . . 584
P. A. Chilton

Power and Language . . . 591
N. Fairclough

Power Differentials and Language . . . 597
P. L. van den Berghe

Representation . . . 604
R. Fowler

Semilingualism . . . 606
J. Cummins

Stereotype and Social Attitudes . . . 608
M. L. Apte

Symbolic Power and Language . . . 610
C. B. Vigouroux

The Linguistic Marketplace . . . 612
I. Gogolin

Section VII. Language Planning, Policy, Practice

Academies: Dictionaries and Standards — 615
L. C. Mugglestone

Artificial Languages — 616
A. Large

Heritage Languages — 619
J. Cummins

International Languages — 620
U. Ammon

Language Adaptation and Modernization — 626
S. Bowerman

Language Development — 630
H. R. Dua

Language Diffusion Policy — 634
C. G. MacLean

Language Planning: Models — 644
A. Deumert

Linguistic Census — 648
L. M. Khubchandani

Linguistic Habitus — 650
I. Gogolin

Multilingual States — 652
D. D. Laitin

National Language/Official Language — 657
C. M. Eastman

Nationalism and Language — 662
L. Greenfeld

Orthography — 669
M. Sebba

Prescription in Dictionaries — 672
L. C. Mugglestone

Reversing Language Shift 673
J. A. FISHMAN

School Language Policies 679
D. J. CORSON

Standardization 681
E. HAUGEN

Statistics: Principal Languages of the World (UNESCO) 683
J. M. Y. SIMPSON

Verbal Hygiene 688
D. CAMERON

Section VIII. Language and Education

Applied Linguistics and Sociolinguistics 691
D. R. PRESTON

Bilingual Education 696
M. E. BRISK

Black English in Education: UK 700
M. DALPHINIS

Child Language: An Overview 703
S. STRÖMQVIST

Ebonics and African American Vernacular English 708
J. BAUGH

Education and Language: Overview 710
K. PERERA

Educational Failure 714
J. R. EDWARDS

English Grammar in British Schools 723
A. M. PHILP

Gender, Education, and Language 735
J. SWANN

Home Language and School Language 737
M. MacLure

Literacy 739
C. J. Daswani

Oracy 746
A. M. Wilkinson

Pidgins, Creoles, and Minority Dialects in Education 747
J. Siegel

Spoken Language in the Classroom 749
N. Mercer

Standard English and Educational Policy 753
M. Farr & A. Ball

Teaching Endangered Languages 757
L. Hinton

Section IX. Methods in Sociolinguistics

Attitude Surveys: Question–Answer Process 761
H. Schuman

Corpus Linguistics and Sociolinguistics 765
M. Sebba & S. D. Fligelstone. Revised by W. A. Kretzschmar Jr.

Data Collection in Linguistics 769
J. E. Miller & R. Cann

Field Methods: Ethnographic 772
M. L. Apte

Field Methods in Modern Dialect and Variation Studies 776
K. Hazen

Fieldwork and Field Methods 779
U. Canger

Fieldwork Ethics and Community Responsibility 781
B. Johnstone

Contents

Interactional Sociolinguistic Research Methods N. Berenz	784
Literacy: Research, Measurement, and Innovation D. Wagner	787
Multidimensional Scaling W. C. Rau	793
Observer's Paradox A. Davies	802
Observing and Analyzing Classroom Talk A. D. Edwards & D. P. G. Westgate	803
Reliability/Validity E. Babbie	809
Salvage Work (Endangered Languages) N. C. Dorian	813
Scaling E. Babbie	816
Small Group Research W. S. Bainbridge	821
Sociometry W. S. Bainbridge	827
Statistics in Sociolinguistics D. Sankoff	828

Section X. The Profession

Institutions and Resources

Endangered Languages Projects (An Inventory) L. A. Grenoble & L. J. Whaley	835
Internet Resources for Sociolinguistics A. Deumert	838

Professional Associations — 840
R. MESTHRIE

Sociolinguistics Journals: A Critical Survey — 842
N. COUPLAND

Profiles of Sociolinguists

Ammon, Ulrich (1943–) — 844
A. DEUMERT

Bakhtin, Mikhail M. (1895–1975) — 845
J. M. WEIR

Bamgbose, Ayo (1932–) — 846
R. MESTHRIE

Baugh, John (1949–) — 847
R. MESTHRIE

Bernstein, Basil (1924–) — 848
K. RAJAGOPALAN

Bickerton, Derek (1926–) — 849
G. G. GILBERT

Blommaert, Jan (1961–) — 850
K. MARYNS

Boas, Franz (1858–1942) — 851
R. DARNELL

Bourdieu, Pierre (1930–) — 852
C. B. VIGOUROUX

Bright, William (1928–) — 853
B. B. KACHRU

Cameron, Deborah (1958–) — 854
S. S. MCRAE

Coates, Jennifer (1942–) — 855
S. S. MCRAE

Contents

Cooper, Robert Leon (1931–)   855
B. Spolsky

Cummins, Jim (1949–)   856
C. Baker

Das Gupta, Jyotirindra (1933–)   857
L. M. Khubchandani

DeCamp, David (1927–79)   858
R. Le Page

Dittmar, Norbert (1943–)   859
P. Schlobinski

Dorian, Nancy (1936–)   860
S. Romaine

Edwards, John Robert (1947–)   861
W. F. Mackey

Emeneau, Murray Barnson (1904–)   862
W. Bright

Fairclough, Norman (1941–)   862
H. Janks

Fasold, Ralph W. (1940–)   863
W. Wolfram

Ferguson, Charles A. (1921–98)   864
J. A. Fishman

Firth J. R. (1890–1960)   865
F. R. Palmer

Fishman, Joshua A. (1926–)   867
B. Spolsky

Foucault, Michel (1926–84)   868
J. C. Maher

Giles, Howard (1946–)   869
J. Bradac

Gilliéron, Jules (1854–1926) — 870
T. Hill

Goffman, Erving (1922–82) — 871
R. L. Schmitt

Görlach, Manfred (1937–) — 872
E. W. Schneider

Gramsci, Antonio (1891–1937) — 873
N. Helsloot

Grierson, Sir George Abraham (1851–1941) — 874
J. C. Wright

Gumperz, John J. (1922–) — 875
N. Berenz

Hall, Robert A. Jr (1911–97) — 876
M. Danesi

Halliday, Michael Alexander Kirkwood (1925–) — 877
J. Fine

Haugen, Einar (1906–94) — 877
N. Hasselmo

Heath, Shirley Brice — 878
C. B. Cazden

Hesseling, Dirk Christiaan (1859–1941) — 879
G. G. Gilbert

Hill, Jane (1939–) — 881
V. Santiago-Irizarry

Hymes, Dell Hathaway (1927–) — 882
N. H. Hornberger

Jaberg, Karl (1877–1959) — 882
T. Hill

Kachru, Braj B. (1932–) — 883
R. V. Pandharipande

Contents

Khubchandani, Lachman M. (1932–)   884
R. K. Agnihotri

Kurath, Hans (1891–1992)   885
T. Hill

Labov, William (1927–)   885
D. Sankoff

Lakoff, Robin Tolmach   887
J. Bennett

Lambert, Wallace E. (1922–)   888
G. R. Tucker

Le Page, Robert (1920–)   889
A. Tabouret-Keller

Lewis, E. Glyn (1920–94)   890
D. Brown

Malinowski, Bronislaw Kaspar (1884–1942)   891
A. T. Campbell

Mazrui, Ali A. (1933–)   891
A. M. Mazrui

McDavid, Raven Ioor, Jr (1911–84)   892
T. Hill

Milroy, Lesley (1944–)   893
Li Wei

Mufwene, Salikoko S. (1947–)   894
R. Mesthrie

Mühlhäusler, Peter (1947–)   895
P. Baker

Muysken, Pieter Cornelis (1950–)   896
A. Bruyn

Myers-Scotton, Carol   897
S. Gross

Nida, Eugene Albert (1914–)   898
R. E. LONGACRE

Paulston, Christina Bratt (1932–)   899
M. SWAIN

Platt, John T.   900
M GÖRLACH

Poplack, Shana   901
G. VAN HERK

Quirk, Professor Sir (Charles) Randolph (1920–)   901
J. ROBERTS

Reinecke, John E. (1904–82)   903
G. G. GILBERT

Rickford, John Russell   904
J. BAUGH

Romaine, Suzanne (1951–)   905
C. M. SANGSTER

Sacks, Harvey (1935–75)   905
G. PSATHAS

Sankoff, Gillian (1943–)   906
C. SUREK-CLARK

Sapir, Edward (1884–1939)   907
R. DARNELL

Saville-Troike, Muriel   908
R. V. PANDHARIPANDE

Schegloff, Emanuel (1937–)   909
J. HERITAGE

Schiffrin, Deborah (1951–)   910
S. HUNT

Schuchardt, Hugo (1842–1927)   911
G. G. GILBERT

Contents

Shuy, Roger W. (1931–)   912
J. Kreeft Peyton

Spolsky, Bernard (1932–)   913
R. Mesthrie

Srivastava, Ravindra Nath (1936–92)   914
R. K. Agnihotri

Street, Brian (1943–)   914
M. Prinsloo

Tannen, Deborah   916
J. Bennett

Trudgill, Peter John (1943–)   916
P. Kerswill

Tucker, G. Richard (1942–)   918
J. Crandall

Valdman, Albert (1931–)   919
B. Spolsky

Van Name, Addison (1835–1922)   919
G. G. Gilbert

Voloshinov, Valentin Nikolavic (1895–1936)   920
D. Brown

Weinreich, Uriel (1926–67)   921
T. Hill

Wenker, Georg (1852–1911)   922
T. Hill

Whorf, Benjamin Lee (1897–1941)   923
J. H. Stam

Williams, Glyn (1939–)   924
D. Brown

Wodak, Ruth (1950–)   925
C. Anthonissen

Wolfram, Walt (1941–) C. T. ADGER	926
Alphabetical List of Articles	927
List of Contributors	941
Name Index	953
Subject Index	983

Editor's Preface

Ever since its publication in 1993 the *Encyclopedia of Language and Linguistics* has been an invaluable reference to my students, colleagues, and myself. The entries dealing with sociolinguistic and applied sociolinguistic topics were invariably accessible, informative, and thought provoking. If I had one reservation, it was that of having to work through ten volumes to access entries of sociolinguistic relevance, well alphabetized and indexed though the encyclopedia was. When the chance came to edit a single-volume spin-off for sociolinguistics, suitably revised, updated and extended, whilst retaining as many original articles as possible, I grabbed it with both hands. I trust the present spin-off, *Concise Encyclopedia of Sociolinguistics* (*CESO*) will prove as valuable a resource as the parent encyclopedia was. Debts incurred in producing *CESO* are numerous. Above all I thank the contributors, especially those who produced new articles within very tight deadlines, and those who revised earlier entries within even tighter deadlines. I am most grateful to Elsevier Science Limited for acting as host to this the first encyclopedia of sociolinguistics. In particular I thank Chris Pringle, Senior Publishing Editor, and Helen Collins, Editor, for the initiatives relating to planning of the work; Tamson Morley for her helpful and speedy support on e-mail as editorial assistant in the first part of the project; Ros Fane and the other members of the production team who turned a massive and slightly raw manuscript into a reference work. In Cape Town I incurred many debts in the process of editing: to the University of Cape Town for allowing me short periods of leave in 2001 that enabled me to work with the press at first hand at key stages; to Roger Lass who allowed me unlimited access to his office to consult or borrow his 10 volumes of the parent encyclopedia; to Sean Bowerman who assisted me in many ways to meet my teaching and administrative commitments when I was immersed in editorial duties; to Rowan Mentis, Germain Kouame, and Ginny Kerfoot who assisted with the very necessary chores of photocopying, checking of references, and the like; and most of all to my research assistant, Sarah Johnson, who instilled new admiration in me for the cheerfulness, efficiency, and computer-savvy of the young.

This volume is dedicated to the four individuals who labored over the original ten-volume encyclopedia, whom I was lucky enough to meet during a brief visit to Edinburgh a decade ago, and on whose editorial shoulders I have metaphorically stood: Ron Asher; Seamus (JMY) Simpson, Alison Bowers and Colin MacLean.

Biographical Note

Rajend Mesthrie was born in Umkomaas, a rural part of KwaZulu-Natal, and went to school there. His first university degree (in English, Mathematics, and Education) was at the University of Durban-Westville, a racially segregated university, as was customary at the time. He taught English and Mathematics at his old high school in Umkomaas, before embarking on a year of graduate education (Honors) in English Language at the University of Cape Town, where the inspirational teaching of J. M. Coetzee and others confirmed his desire for a career in Linguistics. An Anglo-American scholarship took him to the University of Texas (Austin) where he pursued his interests in General and Historical Linguistics as an MA student. The Linguistics Society of America's summer institute of 1980 at the University of New Mexico inculcated an abiding interest in Sociolinguistics in general and Variation and Contact Linguistics in particular. He has since taught English Language at the University of Durban-Westville and Linguistics at the University of Cape Town. His PhD was on the transformation of Bhojpuri in South Africa. Mesthrie has remained a 'contact sociolinguist with variationist leanings' whilst interfacing with the more 'applied' concerns of South African research. He has worked on the contact sociolinguistics of three of the major families in South Africa: the Indic (chiefly Bhojpuri); the Bantu (chiefly Fanakalo pidgin and initial Bantu-Germanic contacts); and the Germanic (chiefly English interlanguages and non-standard dialects; and early contact and code switching between Afrikaans and English). This has led to his being invited as keynote speaker at all the societies involved in southern African language studies: the Linguistics Society; Applied Linguistics Society; African Languages Association; Indological Association and the English Academy. Mesthrie has been involved in a small way in the process of political transformation in South Africa; and sees educational development as an important part of his duties. He is currently head of the Linguistics Section (of the department of Linguistics and Southern African

Languages) and deputy director of CALSSA (Centre for Applied Language Studies and Services in Africa) at the University of Cape Town; and President of the Linguistics Society of Southern Africa. He was a visiting fellow at the University of Pennsylvania on an Educational Opportunities Fellowship in 1989 and Visiting Scholar at Berkeley in 1998. He is married to Uma Mesthrie, a historian at the University of the Western Cape and is the proud father of an eight-year-old daughter, Sapna Mayuri Mesthrie.

Introduction

Sociolinguistics: History and Overview
R. Mesthrie

1. Language

The Concise Encyclopedia of Sociolinguistics (*CESO*) is intended to give a comprehensive overview of the main topics in an important branch of language study, generally known as Sociolinguistics. Linguistics may be somewhat blandly defined as the study of language. Such a characterization leaves out the all-important formulation of how such study is to be conducted, and where exactly the boundaries of the term 'language' itself lie. Broadly speaking, different branches of linguistics are concerned with language structure, acquisition, and use.

The term 'language' is generally accepted to refer to a system of arbitrary symbols used for human communication. Having 'human communication' as part of the definition of language makes it impossible to study language comprehensively without due regard to social contexts of speech. This emphasis was not always explicit in linguistics.

2. Sociolinguistics' Antecedents

While Sociolinguistics as a specially demarcated area of language study only dates to the early 1960s (see e.g., Paulston and Tucker (1997) and Shuy (1997: 23) who cite the summer of 1964 as a crucial time), attention to the social was implicit in many earlier studies. It is possible that just as most linguists accept that scholarly linguistics was first practiced in ancient India, culminating in Pāṇini's *Astādhyāyī* (ca. 500 BCE), he may prove a pioneer of sociolinguistics too. The suggestion has been made that Pāṇini's rules are, *inter alia*, 'sophisticated attempts at capturing the stylistic preferences among variants which are characteristic of any living language' (Kiparsky 1979: 1). In terms of a continuous lineage for modern sociolinguistics, however, four western traditions have been most influential: historical and comparative linguistics; anthropology; rural dialectology; and the study of mixed languages.

Historical and comparative linguists became interested in modern speech forms (or 'dialects') for the possible light they could shed on theories of language change previously based on written materials. Two branches of what is now called sociolinguistics had strong nineteenth-century antecedents: the study of rural dialects in Europe and contact between languages that resulted in new 'mixed languages.' Schuchardt and Hesseling produced their first major works on mixed languages in 1882 and 1897, respectively. But it is in the earlier, recently rediscovered work of an American librarian, Van Name (1869–70) that we find descriptions and analyses of mixed languages which reach a level of theoretical sophistication.

Even de Saussure (1857–1913), who is most frequently associated with modern structuralism, stressed in his work that language was a 'social fact,' i.e., it belonged to a realm larger than that of the individual. A society is not just the lowest common denominator of its individuals. For de Saussure, the concrete data of language (what he called *parole*) are produced by individual speakers, but 'language is not complete in any speaker; it exists perfectly only within a collectivity' (1959: 14).

In the early twentieth century, structuralists in the USA were partly motivated by the need to describe rapidly eroding American Indian languages before they became extinct. Becoming acquainted with the cultural patterns of societies that were novel to them led scholars like Franz Boas, Leonard Bloomfield and Edward Sapir to establish the foundations for studies of language, culture, and cognition. Such an anthropological perspective on language was a forerunner to some branches of sociolinguistics, especially the ethnographical approach.

The term 'sociolinguistics' appears to have been first used in 1952 by Haver Currie, a poet and philosopher who noted the general absence of any consideration of the social in the linguistic research of his day. Significant works on sociolinguistics appearing after this date include: Weinreich's influential *Languages in Contact* (a structural and social account of bilingualism) of 1953; Einar Haugen's two volume study of the social history of the Norwegian language in America (1953); and Joos (1962) on the dimensions of style.

3. Emphases in Sociolinguistics

Chomsky's insistence in the 1950s and 1960s on abstracting language away from everyday contexts

Introduction

ironically led to the distillation of a core area of sociolinguistics, opposed to his conception of language. In a now infamous passage Chomsky (1965: 3) argued that linguistic theory should be concerned primarily with an ideal speaker-listener, in a completely homogeneous speech community, who knows its language perfectly and who is unaffected when applying his knowledge of the language in actual performance. Whilst such an approach brought significant gains to the theory of syntax and phonology, many scholars felt that abstracting away from society served limited ends which could not include an encompassing theory of human language. This period marked a break between sociolinguists with an interest in language as a communicative tool within human societies and the generativists with their interest in an idealized, non-social, psycholinguistic competence. Whereas the Chomskyan framework focused on what could be generated in language and by what means, the social approach tries to account for what can be said in a language, by whom, to whom, in whose presence, when and where, in what manner and under what social circumstances (Fishman 1971, Hymes 1971, Saville-Troike 1982). For the latter group the process of acquiring a language is not just a cognitive process involving the activation of a pre-disposition in the human brain, it is a social process as well, that only unfolds in social interaction. The child's role in acquiring its first language is not a socially passive one, but one which is sensitive to certain 'environmental' conditions, including the social identity of the different people with whom the child interacts.

Dell Hymes (1971) was the principal objector to the dominance of Chomsky's characterization of what constituted the study of linguistic competence. He suggested that a child who might produce any sentence whatever without due regard to the social and linguistic context would be 'a social monster' (1974: 75) who was 'likely to be institutionalized.' Hymes coined the term *communicative competence* to denote the human ability to use language appropriately in different settings. Hymes' interest was not just in the production of sentences but in characterizing the more social-bound aspects like the amount and volume of talk in different communities, acceptability of silence, rules for turn-taking, amount of simultaneous talk, etc. There are, in this view, rules of use without which the rules of grammar are, at best, abstractions (at worst, Hymes says, 'useless'). William Labov (1972: xiii), whose name features prominently in the discipline, expressed uneasiness about the term sociolinguistics, since in his view there can be no linguistics that is not social. Still others are slightly suspicious of the term since it privileges the linguistic over the social. One distinction that is sometimes made is that between sociolinguistics (proper) and the sociology of language. Some scholars believe that the former is part of the terrain mapped out in Linguistics, focusing on language in society for the light that social contexts throw upon language. For these scholars, the latter (Sociology of Language) is primarily a sub-part of Sociology, which examines language use for its ultimate illumination of the nature of societies. One writer (Fasold 1984, 1990) has attempted to capture this formulation by writing two scholarly books, one devoted to *The Sociolinguistics of Society* and the other to *The Sociolinguistics of Language*. Whilst there is some basis for such a partition, and something to be gained by it, in practice the boundaries between the two areas of study are so flexible as to merit one cover term. *CESO* tries to give equal coverage to both areas. Sometimes the distinction between the two orientations is expressed by the terms *macro-* and *micro-sociolinguistics*. As in other subjects, notably economics, macro-studies involve an examination of interactions at a broader level (the focus is broad, as in the study of multilingualism, or language attitudes in a community). Micro-studies examine finer patterns on a local level (e.g., conversational structure or accents in a particular community).

4. Branches of Sociolinguistics

To a large extent the sections within *CESO* cover the main concerns of the discipline: Interaction; Variation; Culture; Power and Ideology; Language Contact; Applications of Sociolinguistics. Like most editors in this series I have agonized over whether to present entries in sections or as a straight alphabetical list. It is hoped that the choice of entries within sections rather than a straight alphabetical list gives a better sense of the subject, without getting in the way of looking up specific entries.

The first section *Foundations of Society and Language* is concerned with defining and approaching the key concepts language and society, from the vantage points of the parent disciplines of Linguistics, Sociology, Anthropology, and Social Psychology. Sociolinguists have learned to live with the situation that, after extensive research and debate, key terms like 'language,' 'native speaker,' and 'society' are still fuzzy concepts. The next section covers the subfield that I believe has gained the most ground in the last 20 years, viz. the study of *Language and Interaction*. Here the emphasis lies on the principles of conversation, the ways in which people make adjustments in speech when interacting with others and the ways in which societies differ in their assumptions about, expectations for, and use of language. The next two sections of the encyclopedia cover what is for many the heartland of the discipline: a close attention to the ways in which a language may vary. The first of these, *Language Variation: Style, Situation, Function* deals with the

SECTION I
Foundations of Society and Language

Anthropological Linguistics
E. Keating

Anthropological linguistics, or as it is sometimes called, linguistic anthropology, is a cross-disciplinary and cross-cultural approach to the study of language. The goals are understanding and describing the important ways that language organizes social life and cultural ways of thinking, including the interpretation of others' utterances and behavior. Anthropological linguistics is an area of research concerned particularly with the social production and negotiation of meaning, including both an exploration into relationships between linguistic structures and an exploration into the role of context in communicating and understanding them. Linguistic anthropologists study a wide range of phenomena, including relationships between language and status, who can say what to whom and in what context, language genres, language and gender, language and institutions, language and the transmission of knowledge, the acquisition of language, multilingualism, identity, creolization, linguistic ideologies, literacy, linguistic borrowing, language change, the social valuing of particular language practices, the esthetics of language production, notions of the self as produced through language, cognition, gesture, the role of space in communication, as well as what constitutes competence, performance, participation, and even language itself. There is thus a considerable overlap with the field of sociolinguistics.

The study of language within particular contexts has always been recognized as a crucial means to understand linguistic structures. However, for those linguists working within the Chomskyan perspective, the social parameters of language use have not been considered important to theorizing meaning production. This situation has resulted in the further development of the field of Anthropological Linguistics as a center for research into theories of meaning production that include social context. The study of language has always been important to anthropologists, particularly those anthropologists whose tradition follows from the work of the German-born Franz Boas on Native American languages (see *Boas, Franz*).

Anthropological Linguistics is an approach that recognizes meaning as a process negotiated between interactants rather than as something that exists within the individual or language structures. As argued by Wittgenstein, 'meaning is use' (1958: paragraph 43), and utterances are only understandable in relation to activities. To anthropological linguists, language is assumed to be not only a rule-governed system with its own internal logic (learned by every child in the community), but also a system of tools for the constitution of social life. This includes language structure, language practice, visual codes, the interface between verbal and visual codes, and relationships to habitual modes of thought. In all societies children develop concepts of a 'socioculturally structured universe' through their participation in language activities and acquisition of language (Ochs 1988: 14). To engage in an act of communicating is 'to take up a position in a social field in which all positions are moving and defined relative to one another' (Hanks 1996: 201). Talk is designed and interpreted as meaningful in relation to particular sequences and contexts. For example, in a courtroom in the US the meaning of a particular utterance is dependent on its sequential placement in ongoing discourse, on the participants, and on how conventional interpretations of meaning are manipulated, confirmed, or resisted by those authorized to speak in order to shape meanings. In Samoan political meetings participants similarly negotiate how to define and assign responsibility for socially disruptive acts, a process that involves linguistic strategies. Ways in which agency is grammatically expressed in such contexts are connected not only to different points of view, but to local political practices (Duranti 1994). Ethnographic accounts of communicative events cross culturally have repeatedly shown the importance of context in understanding language practices. Utterances and actions are context-shaped and certain features of language invoke contextual assumptions. Indexical relations are an important area of research, since interpretation of deictics is impossible outside of a particular context (see *Context*).

There are several important methodological and theoretical paradigms that influence work in

Anthropological Linguistics. These include the view of language as social action developed by John Austin, where language is a 'force' and in the production of an utterance a speaker performs an action (e.g., reminding, denying, criticizing, pledging, swearing, urging, demanding, apologizing, greeting, and so on), a view now expanded beyond the individual's single utterance to include how each turn at talk makes relevant some next action by another. Anthropological linguists have been influenced by Wittgenstein's notion of language as a game with numerous strategies available to participants, Goffman's work on social situations and the production and maintenance of understanding, and Garfinkel's studies of the tacit procedures members of a society use to make sense of everyday actions. The work of Bakhtin (see *Bakhtin, Mikhail M.*) investigating relationships between past and present utterances and the facility of language for presenting multiple perspectives has been important to many linguistic anthropologists, as well as the work of Bourdieu (see *Bourdieu, Pierre*) on the importance of habitual, embodied, everyday practices, Foucault's (see *Foucault, Michel*) ideas on the evolution of relationships between individuals and institutions, and the work of Vygotsky on the development of human cognition from interactions with others and with tools. Anthropological linguistics draws on ideas developed by the Prague school of linguistics, particularly Jakobson's formalizations of inquiry into relationships between form and content as consequential to meaning, for example, how poetic patterns can create semantic relations. The work of discourse analysts on texts and the work of conversation analysts on talk-in-interaction have been influential, in order to understand how language is manipulated and how language activities are locally managed moment-by-moment, including recipient design of utterances, code-switching, and the role of participation frameworks. Work in the paradigm known as the ethnography of speaking (Gumperz and Hymes 1972) has also been influential in studying communication as a cultural practice (see *Ethnography of Speaking*). Anthropological linguists typically combine ethnography with a number of other methods described above, including linguistic analysis at the phrase and morpheme level.

Anthropological linguistics has a close affinity to sociolinguistics, a field also concerned with the social uses of language. It is also related to studies being conducted in communication, ethnomusicology, sociology, applied linguistics, linguistics, sociology, psychology, education, cognitive science, and performance studies. Language is a pervasive aspect of daily life. Scarcely any society has not felt the effects of new communicative technologies. These new tools have been extremely important in the practice of Linguistic Anthropology, in terms of providing rich new opportunities for data collection and analysis, and enhancing our understanding of language.

Bibliography

Austin J L 1962 *How to Do Things With Words*. Oxford University Press, Oxford, UK
Bakhtin M 1981 *The Dialogic Imagination*. University of Texas Press, Austin, TX
Bauman R, Sherzer J 1974 *Explorations in the Ethnography of Speaking*. Cambridge University Press, London
Bourdieu P 1977 *Outline of a Theory of Practice*. Cambridge University Press, Cambridge, UK
Duranti A 1994 *From Grammar to Politics*. University of California Press, Berkeley, CA
Duranti A 1997 *Linguistic Anthropology*. Cambridge University Press, Cambridge, UK
Foley W 1997 *Anthropological Linguistics: An Introduction*. Blackwell, Oxford, UK
Foucault M 1972 *The Archaeology of Knowledge*. Pantheon Books, New York
Garfinkel H 1967 *Studies in Ethnomethodology*. Prentice Hall, Englewood Cliffs, NJ
Goffman E 1967 *Interaction Ritual: Essays on Face-to-Face Behavior*. Doubleday, Garden City, NY
Gumperz J 1982 *Discourse Strategies*. Cambridge University Press, Cambridge, UK
Gumperz J, Hymes D (eds.) 1972 *Directions in Sociolinguistics: The Ethnography of Communication*. Blackwell, New York
Hanks W F 1996 *Language and Communicative Practices*. Westview Press, Boulder, CO
Levinson S 1983 *Pragmatics*. Cambridge University Press, Cambridge, UK
Ochs E 1988 *Culture and Language Development: Language Acquisition and Language Socialization in a Samoan Village*. Cambridge University Press, Cambridge, UK
Sacks H, Schegloff E, Jefferson G 1974 A simplest systematics for the organization of turn-taking for conversation. *Language* **50**: 696–735
Vygotsky L 1962 *Thought and Language*. MIT Press, Cambridge, MA
Wittgenstein L 1958 *Philosophical Investigations*. Blackwell, Oxford

Attitudes and Behavior
W. S. Bainbridge

Between words and deeds there is a gap; the attitudes people express often seem contradicted by the behavior in which they engage. The problem has been examined intensively within sociology and social psychology, yet it is of great importance for linguistics. If what people say is very different from what they do, how can we know what they really mean?

1. The Problem

In the early 1930s, Richard La Piere conducted an influential study that cast serious doubt on the trustworthiness of verbal responses to questionnaires. In the company of an English-speaking Chinese couple, he sought service at 251 American hotels and restaurants, and on only one occasion was it refused. Later, he sent a brief survey to the places they had visited, asking, 'Will you accept members of the Chinese race as guests in your establishment?' Of the 128 that replied fully, 118 said no. As measured by a questionnaire item, the respondents appeared to have strong antipathy to the Chinese, but as measured by actual behavior, they did not. La Piere argued that 'social attitudes are seldom more than a verbal response to a symbolic situation. For the conventional method of measuring social attitudes is to ask questions (usually in writing) which demand a verbal adjustment to an entirely symbolic situation.'

DeFleur and Westie (1963) note that social scientists have never agreed what the word 'attitude' means and, while widely used, it is a highly unsatisfactory scientific concept. In the seventeenth century, they say, 'attitude' was the physical positioning of an artist's subject with respect to the background, but the meaning was gradually extended to include the mental positioning of a person toward any issue. It is a fact of language that terms originally with physical meaning often come to refer to emotional and mental situations. For example, someone who has a positive attitude toward political party X is positively inclined toward it, wants to go in the same political direction, and is very far from the position taken by party Y. Social philosophers adopted 'attitude' in the nineteenth century, and by the 1930s batteries of questionnaire items had been developed that supposedly measured various attitudes. Shunning more subtle definitions, some operationalists decided that attitudes were simply whatever these scales measured.

DeFleur and Westie distinguish two more refined approaches: probability conceptions and latent process conceptions. The probability conception avoids any discussion of what might be going on inside the mind of a respondent, but focuses instead on the consistency of his or her behavior, including verbal utterances. To say that a person has an attitude is merely to note a measure of consistency in some particular sphere of behavior. For example, anti-Mexican prejudice would be revealed in consistent rejection of Mexicans, consistently expressing discomfort in the presence of Mexicans, and utterance of anti-Mexican epithets.

The more ambitious latent process conception says an attitude is a somewhat coherent constellation of cognitive events and structures, within the mind of the respondent, that shape behavior of all relevant kinds. Thus, an attitude cannot be directly observed but must be inferred. An attitude concerning a class of objects is the meaning that class has for the person, with a stress on how the individual evaluates the class, whether positively or negatively. Some versions of this conception hold that attitudes are encoded verbally in the brain, and that when people say how they feel about something they are merely giving voice to words already held within their minds. Clearly, the concept of attitude is deeply implicated in debates over the importance of language in shaping human behavior.

Despite the definitional problems, attempts have been made to summarize the conclusions of many research studies to see how often behavior is congruent with attitudes. Richard Hill (1981) examined several of these summaries and concluded that many research studies that were careful in conceptualization and research methodology showed a substantial positive correlation between attitudes and behavior. While we cannot assume that any particular attitude will strongly predict the logically related behavior, in general the connection is far from insignificant. The question then becomes: What factors give strength to the relationship between attitudes and behavior, and what factors weaken it?

2. Sources of Congruence and Incongruence

Several things can intervene between verbal attitudes and overt acts, thus reducing the congruence between them. One is time; a person can favor one candidate when the pollster knocks at the door, but another candidate several days later when the election is held. The congruence may be greatest if the verbally expressed attitude and overt behavior are at the same level of generality; a person may usually favor one political party, but may occasionally vote for a particular attractive candidate from another party. Behavior may be influenced by multiple attitudes about different aspects of it; a voter may oppose some policies of a candidate and favor others, so the pollster will have to ask about several different attitudes, and find some method of weighting them in the proper combination before a perfect prediction of voting behavior can be expected.

Speech itself is a kind of behavior, and people often use words to achieve something with their listeners, rather than to express inner thoughts and feelings directly. Put baldly, people may lie. Christie and Geis (1970) have given deceitful interaction strategies a more elegant and scientific cloak by calling them *Machiavellianism*, after the Italian social philosopher who advocated that rulers follow such policies, Niccolò Machiavelli. Less blatantly, people may possess *response sets*, habitual ways of interacting that have the effect of distorting expression. For example, *acquiescence* is the tendency to agree with what another person says, and *social desirability bias* is the tendency to limit one's utterances to those that are socially accepted. When verbally expressed attitudes concern topics about which the community and the listener have strong feelings, they are unreliable gauges of behavior.

Apparent discrepancies between attitudes and behavior may also arise when researchers force people to express attitudes on matters about which they know and care nothing. Howard Schuman and Stanley Presser (1980) showed that this problem can be explored by experimenting with 'don't know' responses in telephone interviews. In one survey, they presented a forced-choice question about the obscure Agricultural Trade Act of 1978 in two forms. When asked merely if they favored or opposed the act, 69 percent of respondents volunteered that they did not know, but when explicitly offered a 'don't know' response, fully 90 percent of them took it, a difference of 21 percentage points. In a replication study, similar results were obtained about the little-known Monetary Control Bill of 1979. Both studies revealed that respondents' level of education shaped reported attitudes when the 'don't know' response was not offered, educated people being significantly more likely to volunteer that they did not have an attitude. Thus, spurious attitudes elicited by poorly designed questions may introduce serious biases into research. (See *Attitude Surveys: Question–Answer Process*).

Problems are not limited to the validity of verbal attitude measures, and, as Allen Liska (1974) notes, equal problems plague measures of behavior. Many research studies ask respondents for verbal reports about their own behavior. But, just as respondents may misrepresent or be confused about their feelings, they may distort their behavior, often in unpredictable ways. Teenagers responding to questions about delinquent behavior may conceal their illegal deeds from an adult interviewer, but within a peer group that confers status for bravery, they may magnify them. Respondents may not use the same definitions of behavior as did the authors of a questionnaire. For example, children often engage in trivial fights with each other, and the maturing teenager may be quite uncertain whether he or she has been guilty of 'assault.' A famous questionnaire written by criminologist Travis Hirschi told the teenage respondents not to count fights with a sister or brother, but let them include fisticuffs with a first cousin or close friend.

Among the most hotly debated discrepancies between self-reported and externally observed behavior concerned the correlation several social variables have with rates of crime. For example, members of lower social classes are disproportionately represented among inmates of prisons, while several self-report studies of juvenile delinquency in the general population show no social class differences. Hindelang et al. (1979) argue that the offenses of the two groups are simply not comparable, the prisoners being incarcerated for very serious crimes, while the delinquency questionnaires concern trivial violations likely to have been committed by substantial fractions of the population.

One factor that can increase the correspondence between attitudes and behavior is social support, as research on alcohol drinking by Rabow et al. (1987) demonstrated. Research subjects' attitudes were evaluated by agree–disagree survey items like, 'Social occasions seem more pleasant when people are drinking,' and behavior was measured by self-reports of how many drinks had been imbibed in the previous month. Social support for drinking was measured by items like, 'Nearly everybody I know expects me to offer alcoholic beverages when they are guests in my home.' Pro-alcohol attitudes were associated with actual drinking, as was social support for drinking, and there seemed to be a complex interaction between attitudes and social support, with social support perhaps strengthening the connection between attitudes and behavior.

To bridge the gap between words and deeds, a number of investigators have postulated an intervening variable, *behavior intention*. A person may possess a variety of attitudes relevant to a particular behavior; for example, voting in an election will be shaped by attitudes toward the candidates, the parties, the particular issues emphasized in the campaign, and the political orientations of the voter's friends and family. All these combine in a complex way to determine how the person intends to vote. Barring some mistake in the voting booth, this is how the person will vote. But many kinds of behavior not only depend on intentions; resources and opportunities may also be important. A good example, studied by Christian Ritter (1998) is illegal drug use. Obviously, a person cannot make good on an intention to use a particular drug if the drug is not available, and Ritter's research indicates that availability interacts in a complex way with other factors in determining the connection between attitudes and behavior.

3. The Rhetoric of Attitude–Behavior Congruence

Several writers have pointed out that people may engage in various mental gymnastics to justify the inconsistencies between their verbal attitudes and their overt behavior. In a highly influential essay, Gresham Sykes and David Matza (1957) explored five techniques of neutralization which youth may employ to justify commission of delinquent acts while professing adherence to conventional morality. Indeed, several studies had indicated that juvenile delinquents frequently express verbal support for the very norms they violate. Sykes and Matza note that norms generally are not categorical imperatives, but highly conditional upon social circumstances. Thus, there is room for rhetoric to separate the word from the deed.

First, the delinquent can 'define himself as lacking responsibility for his deviant actions,' perhaps by invoking 'accident,' the actions of others, or unavoidable conditions, saying, in effect, 'I didn't mean it.' Second, the delinquent can deny that real injury took place, for example, by redefining auto theft as 'borrowing.' Third is denial of the victim, often through claims that the deed was a form of rightful retaliation or punishment of someone who 'asked for it.' Fourth, the delinquent may condemn his condemners, asserting that courts and police are corrupt, thus changing 'the subject of conversation in the dialogue.' And fifth, the delinquent can appeal to higher loyalties, invoking, for example, the claims of friendship over those of law to 'never squeal on a friend.' Sykes and Matza assert that these five techniques of norm neutralization substantially lessen the effectiveness of social controls and produce delinquent behavior.

A very different rhetorical problem that has fascinated researchers is the difficulty of understanding a person's true attitudes when the norms concerning expression of feelings change. For example, modern societies have recently and quickly decided to prohibit not only racial slurs, but also sober public statement of views that races differ in qualities like intelligence. Polite public discourse, therefore, has no room for overt racism. However, a few public issues concerning race have remained discussable, and some social scientists argue they have become vehicles for *symbolic racism*. For example, a public issue for several years in the USA was the busing of pupils across cities for purposes of achieving racial balance in the schools. A racist could no longer directly disparage members of another group, but socially acceptable attitudes against the policy of busing could give voice to the suppressed bigotry.

As Lawrence Bobo (1983) has argued, however, racial attitudes are not mere prejudice, but may reflect very real economic, social, and political conflict. Many social scientists used to believe, perhaps out of a naive sense of optimism, that racial and ethnic antagonism reflected little more than ingrained prejudice, unreasonable ideas, and feelings transmitted from one generation to the next. Supposedly, once members of different groups have been taught to be tolerant of each other, the prejudice would melt away. Public campaigns promoting liberal ideologies were supposed to help achieve this attitudinal change, but this strategy ignored the possibility that the groups were locked in inescapable competition for scarce resources. Thus, an important but scientifically questionable part of the concept of attitudes was that purely symbolic appeals could transform human behavior because the attitudes that were believed to shape behavior were mere symbols in the minds of the populace.

4. The Case of Religion

Perhaps the classic example of a system of symbols that is supposed to shape behavior powerfully is religion. In church sermons, we are told to love our neighbor and to obey the ten commandments. Anticrime attitudes are presumably supported by the belief in the Devil and the fires of Hell, taught by many churches. Travis Hirschi and Rodney Stark (1969), authors of the most famous study on the topic, noted that religion might strengthen moral values, instill the belief that one's fellows deserve fair and just treatment, and promote acceptance of legal authority. But when Hirschi and Stark examined the questionnaire responses of thousands of California high school students, they found no evidence for these propositions. Students who believed in the existence of the Devil and the afterlife, and students who attended church frequently, were no less likely than their irreligious peers to have committed acts of juvenile delinquency. Thus, the societal institution reputed to be most directly responsible for instilling good attitudes, the church, had apparently failed in its task. Or, possibly even more shocking, verbally transmitted attitudes just do not matter in determining behavior.

Many sociologists quickly accepted the findings of this study, perhaps because they themselves are irreligious, and textbooks on criminology and juvenile delinquency seldom mention religion at all. But in the 1970s, a series of research findings and theoretical arguments began to add significant complexity to the picture. Replications of the Hirschi and Stark research gave different results depending upon where they were done: studies performed in the Pacific region of the USA showed no capacity of religion to deter delinquency, while studies done elsewhere revealed a significant religion effect. The key study was done by Stark and two of his graduate students, who were able to examine a massive survey dataset that came from questionnaires administrated to clusters of high school students across the USA. It not only verified the geographic differences, but connected them to the general level of religiousness in the community. Where most young people attend church and possess religious faith, religiousness correlates negatively with delinquency. But in highly secular communities where only a minority are religious, religion does not deter delinquency. Thus, the importance of social support as a variable intervening between attitudes and behavior was confirmed.

Other factors turn out to be important as well. Burkett and White discovered that religion continues to affect behavior, even in irreligious communities, if the behavior involves 'victimless crimes,' which may be better defined as hedonistic acts that are dangerous primarily to oneself: illegal drug use and heavy alcohol drinking. Hoge and De Zulueta (1985) suggest that the salience of the particular kind of behavior for religion is also important, religion having its most robust effects on attitudes about family life, sexuality, and personal honesty. However, the reader should not assume that research has cleared up all the mysteries, and sociologists are very far from a full understanding of how religiously transmitted attitudes affect behavior. One thing is quite clear, however. Without support from other social and psychological factors, religiously-instilled attitudes lack power to prevent people from taking actions they think may benefit them, even in defiance of societal norms. Thus, words alone cannot control deeds.

See also: Attitude Surveys: Question–Answer Process; Social Psychology; Sociology of Language.

Bibliography

Albrecht S L, Chadwick B A, Alcorn D S 1977 Religiosity and deviance: Application of an attitude–behavior contingent consistency model. *Journal for the Scientific Study of Religion* **16**: 263–74

Block J 1965 *The Challenge of Response Sets*. Appleton-Century-Crofts, New York

Bobo L 1983 Whites' opposition to busing: Symbolic racism or realistic group conflict? *Journal of Personality and Social Psychology* **45**(6): 1196–210

Burkett S R, White M 1974 Hellfire and delinquency: Another look. *Journal for the Scientific Study of Religion* **13**(4): 455–62

Christie R, Geis F L 1970 *Studies in Machiavellianism*. Academic Press, New York

DeFleur M, Westie F R 1963 Attitude as a scientific concept. *Social Forces* **42**: 17–31

Deutscher I 1973 *What We Say/What We Do*. Scott Foresman, Glenview, IL

Edwards A L 1967 The social desirability variable: A review of the evidence. In: Berg I A (ed.) *Response Set in Personality Assessment*. Aldine, Chicago, IL

Hill R J 1981 Attitudes and behavior. In: Rosenberg M, Turner R H (eds.) *Social Psychology: Sociological Perspectives*. Basic Books, New York

Hindelang M J, Hirschi T, Weis J G 1979 Correlates of delinquency: The illusion of discrepancy between self-report and official measures. *American Sociological Review* **44**: 995–1014

Hirschi T, Stark R 1969 Hellfire and delinquency. *Social Problems* **17**: 202–13

Hoge D R, De Zulueta E 1985 Salience as a condition for various social consequences of religious commitment. *Journal for the Scientific Study of Religion* **24**: 21–38

La Piere R T 1934 Attitudes versus actions. *Social Forces* **13**: 230–7

Liska A E 1974 Emergent issues in the attitude–behavior consistency controversy. *American Sociological Review* **39**: 261–72

Rabow J, Neuman C A, Hernandez A C R 1987 Contingent consistency in attitudes, social support and the consumption of alcohol. *Social Psychology Quarterly* **50**: 56–63

Ritter C 1988 Resources, behavior intentions, and drug use—A 10-year national panel analysis. *Social Psychology Quarterly* **51**(3): 250–64

Schuman H, Johnson M P 1976 Attitudes and behavior. *Annual Review of Sociology* **2**: 161–207

Schuman H, Presser S 1980 Public opinion and public ignorance: The fine line between attitudes and nonattitudes. *American Journal of Sociology* **85**(5): 1214–25

Stark R 1989 *Sociology*. Wadsworth, Belmont, CA

Stark R, Kent L, Doyle D P 1982 Religion and delinquency: The ecology for a 'lost' relationship. *Journal of Research in Crime and Delinquency* **19**(1): 4–24

Sykes G M, Matza D 1957 Techniques of neutralization: A theory of delinquency. *American Sociological Review* **22**: 664–70

Bilingualism, Individual

F. Grosjean

Few areas of linguistics are surrounded by as many misconceptions as is bilingualism. Most people think that bilingualism is a rare phenomenon found only in such countries as Canada, Switzerland, and Belgium and that bilinguals have equal speaking and writing fluency in their languages, have accentless speech, and can interpret and translate without any prior training. The reality is in fact quite different: bilingualism is present in practically every country of the world, in all classes of society and in all age groups; in fact, it has been estimated that half the world's population is bilingual. As for bilinguals themselves, the majority acquired their languages at various times during their lives and are rarely equally fluent in them; many speak one of their languages less well than the other (and often with an accent) and many can only read or write one of the languages they speak. Furthermore, few bilinguals are proficient interpreters and translators.

In this article many facets of the bilingual individual will be discussed; the focus will be on the stable bilingual adult, that is the person who is no longer in the process of acquiring a second or third language. First the bilingual person in terms of language knowledge and use will be described. Then, the bilingual's linguistic behavior when communicating with monolinguals and with other bilinguals will be examined. A certain number of issues in the psycholinguistics and neurolinguistics of bilingualism will be discussed, and the article will end with a brief overview of the attitudes, behaviors, and personality of the bilingual individual.

1. Describing the Bilingual

Although a few researchers have defined bilinguals as those who have native-like control of two or more languages, most others agree that this position is not realistic. If one were to count as bilingual only those people who pass as monolinguals in each of their languages, one would be left with no label for the vast majority of people who use two or more languages regularly, but who do not have native-like fluency in each. This has led researchers to propose other definitions of bilingualism, such as: the ability to produce meaningful utterances in two (or more) languages, the command of at least one language skill (reading, writing, speaking, listening) in another language, the alternate use of several languages, etc. This article will define as bilingual those people who use two (or more) languages (or dialects) in their everyday lives. (Throughout this entry, dialects are subsumed under the term 'language.') Thus, this definition includes people ranging from the migrant worker who speaks with some difficulty the host country's language (and who cannot read and write it) all the way to the professional interpreter who is totally fluent in two languages. In between is found the foreign spouse who interacts with friends in his or her first language, the scientist who reads and writes articles in a second language (but who rarely speaks it), the member of a linguistic minority who uses the minority language only at home and the majority language in all other domains of life, the deaf person who uses sign language with her friends but a signed form of the spoken language with a hearing person, etc. Despite the great diversity that exists between these people, all share a common feature: they lead their lives with two (or more) languages. (Bilinguals who are no longer using their different languages but who have retained knowledge of them will be termed 'dormant bilinguals.')

The reasons that bring languages into contact and hence foster bilingualism are many: migrations of various kinds (economic, educational, political, religious), nationalism and federalism, education and culture, trade and commerce, intermarriage, etc. These factors create various linguistic needs in people who are in contact with two or more languages and who develop competencies in their languages to the extent required by these needs. In contact situations it is rare that all facets of life require the same language (people would not be bilingual if that were so) or that they always demand two languages (language A *and* B at work, at home, with friends, etc.). In fact, bilinguals acquire and use their languages for different purposes, in different domains of life, with different people. It is precisely because the needs and uses of the languages are usually quite different that bilinguals rarely develop equal fluency in their languages. The level of fluency attained in a language (more precisely, in a language skill) will depend on the need for that language and will be domain specific. It is thus perfectly normal to find bilinguals who can only read and write one of their languages, who have reduced speaking fluency in a language they only use with a limited number of people, or who can only speak about a particular subject in one of their languages. This explains in part why bilinguals are usually poor interpreters and translators. Not only are specific skills required, but interpretation and translation entail that one has identical lexical knowledge in the two languages, something that most bilinguals do not have. Certain domains and topics are covered by the lexicon of one language, others by the lexicon of the other language, and some few by the two. Interpreting and translating when one lacks the appropriate vocabulary and the necessary skills is thus something that bilinguals find difficult.

The failure to understand that bilinguals normally use their languages for different purposes, with different people, and in different domains of life has been a major obstacle to obtaining a clear picture of bilinguals and has had many negative consequences: bilinguals have been described and evaluated in terms of the fluency and balance they have in their two languages; language skills in bilinguals have almost always been appraised in terms of monolingual standards; research on bilingualism has in large part been conducted in terms of the bilingual's individual and separate languages; and, finally, many bilinguals evaluate their language competencies as inadequate. Some criticize their mastery of language skills, others strive their hardest to reach monolingual norms, others hide their knowledge of their 'weaker' language, and most simply do not perceive themselves as being bilingual even though they use two (or more) languages in their everyday lives.

Researchers are now starting to view the bilingual not so much as the sum of two (or more) complete or incomplete monolinguals but rather as a specific and fully competent speaker–hearer who has developed a communicative competence that is equal, but different in nature, to that of the monolingual. This competence makes use of one language, of the other, or of the two together (in the form of mixed speech; see below) depending on the situation, the topic, the interlocutor, etc. This in turn has led to a redefinition of the procedure used to evaluate the bilingual's competencies. Bilinguals are now being studied in terms of their total language repertoire, and the domains of use and the functions of the bilingual's various languages are being taken into account.

It should be noted finally that as the environment changes and the needs for particular language skills also change, so will the bilingual's competence in his or her various language skills. New situations, new interlocutors, and new language functions will involve new linguistic needs and will therefore change the language configuration of the person involved. Extreme cases of restructuring are language forgetting and a return to functional monolingualism, be it in the person's first, second, or third language.

2. The Bilingual's Linguistic Behavior

One of the most interesting aspects of bilingualism is the fact that two (or more) languages are in contact within the same person. This phenomenon, which has led to a vast body of research, can best be understood if one examines the bilingual's various language modes. In their everyday lives, bilinguals find themselves at various points along a situational continuum which induce different language modes. At one end of the continuum, bilinguals are in a totally monolingual mode in that they are communicating with monolinguals of one—or the other—of the languages that they know. At the other end of the continuum, bilinguals find themselves in a bilingual language mode in that they are communicating with bilinguals who share their two languages and with whom they normally mix languages (i.e., code-switch and borrow; see below). For convenience, this article refers to the two end points of the continuum when speaking of the monolingual or bilingual language modes, but it should be kept in mind that these are end points and that intermediary modes do exist. This is the case, for example, when a bilingual is speaking to another bilingual who never mixes languages, or when a bilingual is interacting with a person who has limited knowledge of the other language. It should also be noted that bilinguals differ among themselves as to the extent they travel along the continuum; some rarely find themselves at the bilingual end whereas others rarely leave this end (for example, bilinguals who live in tight-knit bilingual communities where the language norm is mixed language).

2.1 The Monolingual Language Mode

In this mode, bilinguals adopt the language of the monolingual interlocutor(s) and deactivate their other language(s) as completely as possible. Bilinguals who manage to do this totally and, in addition, who speak the other language fluently and have no foreign accent in it, will often 'pass' as monolinguals. Although such cases are relatively rare, it is precisely these that have led people to think that bilinguals are (or should be) two monolinguals in one person. In fact, deactivation of the other language is rarely total as is clearly seen in the interferences bilinguals produce (these are also known as between-language deviations). An interference is a speaker-specific deviation from the language being spoken due to the influence of the other 'deactivated' language. Interferences can occur at all levels of language (phonological, lexical, syntactic, semantic, pragmatic) and in all modalities (spoken, written, or sign) (see *Language Transfer and Substrates*). They are of two kinds: static interferences which reflect permanent traces of one language on the other (such as a permanent accent, the meaning extensions of particular words, specific syntactic structures, etc.) and dynamic interferences which are the ephemeral instrusions of the other language (as in the case of the accidental slip on the stress pattern of a word due to the stress rules of the other language, the momentary use of a syntactic structure taken from the language not being spoken, etc.) Examples of interferences produced by a French person speaking English are as follows. At the phonetic level, pronouncing *Sank evven for dees* instead of *Thank heaven for this*; at the lexical level, using *corns* (from French *cornes*) instead of *horns* in *Look at the corns on that animal!*; at the syntactic level, saying *I saw this on the page five* (instead of *on page five*), and in writing, misspelling *adress* or *appartment* (based on the French *adresse* and *appartement*).

In addition, if one of the bilingual's languages is mastered only to a certain level of proficiency, deviations due to the person's interlanguage (also known as within-language deviations) will also occur. These include overgeneralizations (for example, taking irregular verbs and treating them as if they were regular), simplifications (dropping pluralization and tense markers, omitting functions words, simplifying the syntax, etc.) as well as hypercorrections and the avoidance of certain words and expressions. Between- and within-language deviations are clearly observable when bilinguals are in a monolingual language mode but they also occur in the bilingual language mode (see below). It should be noted finally that both types of deviations, although sometimes quite apparent (such as a foreign accent), usually do not interfere with communication. This is because bilinguals develop their languages to the level of fluency required by the environment. Deviations in bilingual speech are thus of the same nature as slips of the tongue and hesitation phenomena. They are present but do not usually affect communication.

2.2 The Bilingual Language Mode

In this mode, bilinguals interact with one another. First they adopt a language to use together, what is known as the 'base language' (also the 'host' or 'matrix' language). This process is called 'language choice' and is governed by a number of factors: the interlocutors involved (i.e., their usual language of interaction, their language proficiency, language preference, socioeconomic status, age, sex, occupation, education, kinship relation, attitude toward the languages, etc.); the situation of the interaction (location, presence of monolinguals, degree of formality and of intimacy), the content of the discourse (topic, type of vocabulary needed), and the function of the interaction (to communicate information, to create a social distance between the speakers, to raise the status of one of the interlocutors, to exclude someone, to request something, etc.). Language choice is a well-learned behavior (a bilingual rarely asks the conscious question, 'Which language should I be using with this person?') but it is also a very complex phenomenon, which only becomes apparent when it breaks down. Usually, bilinguals go through their daily interactions with other bilinguals quite unaware of the many psychological and sociolinguistic factors that interact to help choose one language over another. The base language can change several times during a single conversation if the situation, topic, interlocutor, etc., require it.

Once a base language has been chosen, bilinguals can bring in the other language (the 'guest' or 'embedded' language) in various ways. One of these ways is to code-switch, that is to shift completely to the other language for a word, a phrase, a sentence. (For example, *Va chercher Marc and bribe him avec un chocolat chaud with cream on top* (Go get Marc and bribe him with a hot chocolate with cream on top).) Code-switching has long been stigmatized, and has been given a number of pejorative names such as Franglais (the switching between French and English) or Tex–Mex (the switching between English and Spanish in the southwestern part of the USA). The consequence of this has been that some bilinguals never switch while others restrict it to situations in which they will not be stigmatized for doing so. During the late 1980s and early 1990s code-switching has received considerable attention from researchers (see *Code-switching: Overview*). For example, sociolinguists have concentrated on when and why switching takes place in the social context. Reasons that have been put forward are: to fill a linguistic need, to continue the last language used, to quote someone, to specify the addressee, to exclude someone from the conversation, to qualify a message, to specify speaker involvement, to mark group identity, to convey emotion, to change the role of the speaker, etc. Linguists, on the other hand, have sought to study the types of code-switches that occur (single words, phrases, clauses, sentences, etc.) as well as the linguistic constraints that govern their appearance. Although there is still considerable controversy over this latter aspect (are constraints universal or language specific? how broad can a constraint be?) it is now clear that switching is not simply a haphazard behavior due to some form of 'semilingualism' (see *Semilingualism*) but that it is, instead, a well-governed process used as a communicative strategy to convey linguistic and social information.

The other way bilinguals can bring in the other, less activated, language is to borrow a word or short expression from that language and to adapt it morphologically (and often phonologically) into the base language (see *Borrowing*). Thus, unlike code-switching which is the juxtaposition of two languages, borrowing is the integration of one language into another. Most often both the form and the content of a word are borrowed (to produce what has been called a loanword or more simply a borrowing) as in the following examples taken from French–English bilinguals: '*Ca m'étonnerait qu'on ait <u>code-switché</u> autant que ça*' (I can't believe we code-switched as often as that) and '*Maman, tu peux me <u>tier</u>/taje/mes chaussures?*' (Mummy, can you tie my shoes?). In these examples, the English words 'code-switch' and 'tie' have been brought in and integrated into the French sentence. A second type of borrowing, called a loanshift, consists in either taking a word in the base language and extending its meaning to correspond to that of a word in the other language, or rearranging words in the base language along a pattern provided by the other language and thus creating a new meaning. An example of the first kind of loanshift would be the use of *humoroso* by Portuguese–Americans to mean 'humorous' when the original meaning is 'capricious.' An example of the second kind is the use of idiomatic expressions that are translated literally from the other language, such as '*I put myself to think about it*' said by a Spanish–English bilingual, based on '*Mepuse a pensarlo.*' It is important to distinguish idiosyncratic loans (also called 'speech borrowings' or 'nonce borrowings') from words which have become part of a language community's vocabulary and which monolinguals also use (called 'language borrowings' or 'established loans'). Thus, in the following text, every third or fourth word is an established loan from French which has now become part of the English language: 'The <u>poet</u> lived in the <u>duke's</u> manor. That day, he <u>painted</u>, played <u>music</u> and wrote <u>poems</u> with his <u>companions</u>.' Research in the late twentieth century has examined, among other things, the differences and similarities that exist between code-switches and borrowings (and within the latter, between idiosyncratic borrowings and established borrowings), as well as the impact of the two on language itself, such as first- and second-language restructuring.

3. The Psycholinguistics of Bilingualism

The psycholinguistics of bilingualism studies the processes involved in the production, perception, comprehension, and memorization of the bilingual's languages (spoken, written, or signed) when used in a monolingual or a bilingual language mode. The emphasis has, until the early 1990s been put on the independence of the bilingual's languages (how does the bilingual keep the two languages separate? does the bilingual have one or two lexicons?) to the detriment of issues such as the on-line processing of language, be it in a monolingual or in a bilingual language mode. Much research was conducted, for example, on the coordinate–compound–subordinate distinction. According to it, there are three types of bilinguals: coordinate bilinguals who have two sets of meaning units and two modes of expression, one for each language (this means that the words of the two languages are totally separate entities); compound bilinguals who have one set of meaning units and two modes of expression ('equivalent' words in different languages have the same meaning); and subordinate bilinguals who have the meaning units of the first language and two modes of expression: that of the first language and that of the second, learned by means of the first (here the bilingual interprets words of the weaker language through the words of the stronger language). Despite the inherent appeal of this distinction, no amount of experimentation has brought conclusive evidence that bilinguals can be classified as coordinate, compound, or subordinate.

Another area of considerable investigation has been whether bilinguals possess one or two internal lexicons. Proponents of the one-lexicon view (also referred to as interdependent storage) state that linguistic information is stored in a single semantic system. Words from both languages are organized in one large lexicon, but each word is 'tagged' to indicate the language it belongs to. Other researchers have claimed that bilinguals have two lexicons (the independent storage view), and that the information acquired in one language is available in the other only through a translation process. Again, despite a large number of studies, no clear-cut results have been found. In fact, it has been proposed that bilinguals have *three* stores, one conceptual store corresponding to the bilingual's knowledge of the world and two language stores, one for each language.

A third issue of interest has been the ability of bilinguals to keep their two languages separate in the monolingual mode. Researchers have postulated the existence of a language switch which allows bilinguals to block out the other language, and experimental studies have been conducted to find evidence for this proposal. The results obtained have been inconclusive or, at the very least, questionable, and currently it is felt that no switch, be it psycholinguistic or neurolinguistic, exists in bilinguals. Rather, it has been proposed that bilinguals are probably using various activation and deactivation procedures to keep their languages separate in the monolingual mode and to make them interact in the bilingual mode.

It is more generally accepted in the early twenty-first century that the bilingual is not two monolinguals in one person, but a unique speaker–hearer using one language, the other language, or both together depending on the interlocutor, situation, topic, etc. (see above). Current psycholinguistic research is trying to understand the processing of language in the bilingual's different language modes. Researchers are studying how bilinguals in the monolingual mode differ from monolinguals in terms of perception and production processes, and they are investigating the actual interaction of the two languages during processing in the bilingual mode. This latter issue has produced some interesting findings. For example, in the recognition of 'guest' words (borrowings and code-switches) the phonotactics of the word (whether it is marked clearly as belonging to one or the other lexicon), the presence or absence of a base language homophone, the language phonetics of the word (the pronunciation of the guest word in one language or in the other), and the language that precedes the word (the base language context), all play a role in the recognition process. Actual models of bilingual processing are now being proposed to account for the data obtained. Thus, an interactive activation model appears to accommodate the word recognition results just presented. In the production domain, researchers are attempting to explain the underlying processes involved in the on-line production of code-switches and borrowings and a number of models are also being proposed.

4. The Neurolinguistics of Bilingualism

Neurolinguists have long been interested in describing how language is organized in the 'bilingual brain' and how this organization differs from that of the monolingual. One approach has been to observe and test bilingual aphasics in order to better understand which languages have been affected by brain injury and which factors best account for the different patterns of recovery of the languages. Another approach has been to study normal bilinguals to ascertain whether language processing occurs mainly in the left hemisphere of the brain (as it appears to do in monolinguals) or in both hemispheres.

As concerns aphasia, researchers have observed various recovery patterns of the bilingual's two or more languages after injury (they have been labeled parallel, differential, successive, antagonistic, selective, mixed) and they have tried to account for the factors that seem to play a role in non-parallel recovery (that is, when the languages are not all recovered together at the same rate). Currently, no single factor has emerged to explain the different types of recovery patterns, and it is not known whether recovery significantly differs following therapy in one language, in the other or in both. It would appear, though, that if a language is not recovered, it is not that it is lost, but simply that it is inhibited, temporarily or permanently.

On the topic of language lateralization, it is now a well-known fact that the left hemisphere of the brain in monolinguals is dominant for language. The question has been whether bilinguals also show strong left-hemisphere dominance for language. Until a few years ago, and based on case studies of bilingual aphasics and on experimental results, some researchers proposed that bilinguals use the right hemisphere in language processing more than monolinguals. However, after further studies that were better controlled, there appears to be clear evidence that monolinguals and bilinguals do not differ at all in hemispheric involvement during language processing. As concerns language organization in the bilingual brain, most researchers agree that the bilingual's languages are not stored in completely different locations. In addition, it would appear that bilinguals have two subsets of neural connections, one for each language (each can be activated or inhibited independently) while at the same time possessing one larger set from which they are able to draw elements of either language at any time. This said, the bilingual brain is still very much terra incognita, and only further experimental and clinical research will tell how similar it is to the monolingual brain and in what ways it may be different.

5. The Bilingual Person

This last section will discuss the attitudes and feelings bilingual and monolinguals have towards bilingualism, various mental activities in bilinguals, the interaction of language and emotion, and the personality of bilinguals.

5.1 Attitudes and Feelings about Bilingualism

It would appear from various surveys that have been conducted that either bilinguals have no strong feelings about their bilingualism (it is simply a fact of life!) or that they see more advantages than inconveniences in having to live with two (or more) languages. Most appreciate being able to communicate with people from different linguistic and cultural backgrounds, others feel that bilingualism gives them a different perspective on life, that it fosters open-mindedness, allows one to read and often write in a different language, makes learning other languages easier, gives more job opportunities, etc. As for inconveniences, these are less numerous and involve such aspects as mixing languages involuntarily, having to adjust to different cultures, feeling one is losing one of the languages one possesses (usually a minority language) or having to act as a translator on various occasions. It is interesting to compare these reactions to the attitudes and feelings that monolinguals have towards bilingualism. These are extremely varied, ranging from very positive attitudes (such as wonder at the fact that some bilinguals can speak and write two or more languages fluently) to very negative attitudes (such as surprise that many bilinguals do not master their two languages perfectly, that they cannot translate automatically from one language to another, etc.). It should be noted that most of the views that monolinguals have about bilinguals are usually based on socioeconomic and cultural bilinguals are usually based on socioeconomic and cultural considerations rather than on linguistic factors.

5.2 Mental Activities, Emotion, and Stress

Little is known about the languages used by bilinguals in their mental activities or how bilinguals react when under stress or in an emotional situation. It does seem to be the case that many mental operations are language specific. Thus, bilinguals usually count and pray in the language in which they learned these behaviors. Thinking or dreaming also seem to be language specific and depend on the person, the situation, and the topic involved (see above). When tired, angry, or excited, bilinguals will often revert back to their mother tongue or to whatever language they usually express their emotions in. Stress may also cause more interference, problems in finding the appropriate words, and unintentional switching. In addition, it has been reported that bilinguals wish that the monolinguals closest to them (spouse, companion, friends) were also bilingual.

5.3 Personality and Bilingualism

Some bilinguals report that when they change language they change attitudes and behaviors. This has been alluded to quite frequently in the literature: some bilinguals seem to hold slightly different views depending on the language they are speaking; some others are more authoritarian in one of their languages; others still are more reserved or gentle, etc. Is it possible to conclude from this that there is some truth to the Czech proverb, 'Learn a new language and get a new soul?' (see *Sapir–Whorf Hypothesis*) Some would answer in the affirmative and go as far as to say that the bilingual has a split personality. In fact, there appears to be no real evidence that bilinguals suffer any more from mental disorders than monolinguals. In fact, what is seen as a change in personality is simply a shift in attitudes and behaviors corresponding to a shift in situation or context, independent of language. As was seen above, bilinguals will choose a language according to the situation, the interlocutor, the topic, and the intent of the conversations. These factors trigger different attitudes, impressions, and behaviors (just as they do in monolinguals who modify the content and form of their discourse depending on the context), and thus what is seen as a personality change due to language shift may really be a shift in the situation and interlocutor. In a word, it is the environment as a whole that causes the bilingual to change languages, along with attitudes, feelings, and behaviors—and not language as such. The main difference between monolinguals and bilinguals in this respect is that bilinguals often shift languages (and hence appear to be different people) whereas monolinguals do not. In addition, bilinguals are often switching from one culture to another in their interactions (many are bicultural) whereas monolinguals usually remain within the same culture.

6. Research in the Twenty-first Century

Despite what is already known about the bilingual individual, much more research needs to be conducted on the topic. The emergence of a holistic view of bilingualism is encouraging researchers to move away from the monolingual yardstick and develop a true linguistics of bilingualism. However, many issues require further study: the structure and organization of the bilingual's different languages; the various processing operations involved in the perception, production, and memorization of language when the bilingual is in the monolingual or the bilingual language modes; the linguistic and psycholinguistic differences (and similarities) between code-switches, borrowings and interferences; the organization of the bilingual brain; and finally, the psychology of the bilingual and bicultural person.

See also: Bilingualism, Societal; Code-switching: Overview; Language Transfer and Substrates.

Bibliography

Baetens-Beardsmore H 1986 *Bilingualism: Basic Principles*. Multilingual Matters, Clevedon, UK
Baker C, Prys Jones S 1998 *Encyclopedia of Bilingualism and Bilingual Education*. Multilingual Matters, Clevedon, UK
de Groot A, Kroll J (eds.) 1997 *Tutorials in Bilingualism: Psycholinguistic Perspectives*. Lawrence Erlbaum, Mahwah, NJ
Fabbro F 1999 *The Neurolinguistics of Bilingualism*. Psychology Press, Hove, UK
Grosjean F 1982 *Life with Two Languages: An Introduction to Bilingualism*. Harvard University Press, Cambridge, MA
Grosjean F 2001 The bilingual's language modes. In: Nicol J (ed.) *One Mind, Two Languages: Bilingual Language Processing*. Blackwell, Oxford, UK
Hakuta K 1986 *Mirror of Language: The Debate of Bilingualism*. Basic Books, New York
Haugen E 1969 *The Norwegian Language in America: A Study in Bilingual Behavior*, 2nd edn. University of Indiana Press, Bloomington, IN
Li Wei (ed.) 2000 *The Bilingualism Reader*. Routledge, London
Muysken P 2000 *Bilingual Speech: A Typology of Code-mixing*. Cambridge University Press, Cambridge, UK
Paradis M 1989 Bilingual and polyglot aphasia. In: Boller F and Grafman J (eds.) *Handbook of Neuropsychology*, vol. 2. Elsevier, Amsterdam
Poplack S 1980 Sometimes I'll start a sentence in Spanish Y TERMINO EN ESPAÑOL: Toward a typology of code-switching. *Linguistics* **18**: 581–618
Romaine S 1995 *Bilingualism*, 2nd edn. Blackwell, London
Vaid J (ed.) 1986 *Language Processing in Bilinguals*. Lawrence Erlbaum, Hillsdale, NJ
Weinreich U 1968 *Languages in Contact*. Mouton, The Hague

Bilingualism, Societal
M. H. A. Blanc

Societal bilingualism or multilingualism refers to the co-existence of two or more languages used by individuals and groups in society. It should be distinguished from the contact of different languages within the individual, which is sometimes called bilinguality, defined as 'the psychological state of the individual who has access to more than one linguistic code as a means of communication' (Hamers and Blanc 2000) and is outside the scope of this article (see *Bilingualism, Individual*). Societal bilingualism does not necessarily imply that all members of the society are bilingual. In fact, paradoxically, a majority of the members of an officially multilingual country may be monolingual, because the different language groups are territorially separated by more or less fixed and secure boundaries, as is the case in Belgium and Switzerland (territorial bilingualism). Societal bilingualism is a widespread phenomenon, the vast majority of nation-states in the world having more than one language used indigenously within their borders; indeed, this must be the case since the total number of languages has been estimated at around 5000, while there are only some 200 states. The impression that unilingual states are the norm comes from the nineteenth-century concept of 'one nation-one language' and from confusion between language and official language, confusion perpetuated by geolinguistic maps. Moreover, language and state are not necessarily coterminous: the same language may be spoken in several different countries. For example, English and French are official in countries the world over, whether spoken as a first or a second language, by majorities or minorities. German is the majority official language in Germany and Austria, one of the official languages of Luxembourg and Switzerland, and spoken as a language or dialect by minorities in Belgium, Czechoslovakia, Denmark, France, Hungary, Italy, Poland, Romania, and Russia, to name only European countries.

1. Origins of Societal Bilingualism

Societal bilingualism develops from a variety of contact, both between and within countries and communities. It is found in border areas between states, either because of constant interchange through visits, trade, work or wars, or because a geographical dialect continuum has been interrupted by more or less arbitrary political frontiers. One example is the West Romance language continuum in Europe, which cuts across the national borders of Portugal, Spain, France, Belgium, Luxembourg, Switzerland, and Italy. Although the standard varieties of Portuguese, Spanish, French, and Italian are mutually unintelligible, the rural dialects of these languages are linked by a chain of mutual intelligibility, such that speakers on either side of the political borders have few problems understanding each other. Moreover, these people are bilingual, since they speak the official national language as well as the regional or local language/dialect. For example, many Galicians in northwest Spain speak Gallego (a variety of Portuguese) and Castilian; a majority of Catalans speak Catalan and Castilian. In the Valle d'Aosta many Italians speak French as well as Italian, while a majority also speak a Franco-Provencal dialect which has recently received some official status. Political events may divide people speaking the same language or bring together people speaking different languages. The first pertains in many African and Asian countries previously under colonial rule, where the colonial powers drew arbitrary frontiers regardless of ethnolinguistic realities. Conversely, alloglots may be brought together, whether voluntarily or by force. In the former case, we have free federations, like Switzerland or the European Community; in the latter case we have more or less enforced federations, like the former USSR or the former Yugoslavia. Annexations and invasions, migrations and mass deportations also bring groups from different cultural and linguistic backgrounds together, as can be seen by the many shifts of borders in Central and Eastern Europe in the nineteenth and twentieth centuries, with resulting new language contacts and conflicts. Economic factors can also bring alloglots into contact, whether voluntarily (e.g., the European Community) or from necessity (e.g., immigrants to North America) or by force (e.g., the slave trade). Religion can be a reason for different linguistic groups who share the same faith to live together, whether temporarily (e.g., pilgrimages) or permanently (e.g., the Indian subcontinent, Israel). Conversely, different religious groups may divide a country along linguistic and religious lines. For example, at the time of partition in 1947 the Indian subcontinent split up along religious lines, thereby dividing a common lingua franca, Hindustani, into two distinct official languages, Hindi used by the Hindu community, and Urdu used by the Muslim community. Lastly, a society may decide to make a second language official alongside the indigenous official language in order to gain access to wider markets or information. An example is the increasing use of English as an official or semi-official language in many countries of the world, and its use as an international auxiliary language. But whatever the reasons for societal bilingualism, it always involves languages in intergroup relations.

2. Sociolinguistic Variations in Language Contact Situations

In a situation of societal bilingualism the status of each of the languages in contact varies as a function of, on the one hand, intergroup power relations and, on the other hand, the perception that speakers form of these relations. When intergroup relations change, status relations and perceptions, attitudes and uses also change. It is important to stress that it is not so much the languages that vary as their speakers, who select from a variety of possible models, which are socially marked. As Le Page points out, change only takes place when the social values attached to the models change and the behavior of the speech community also changes (Le Page and Tabouret-Keller 1985) (see *Identity and Language*).

2.1 Speech Repertoires in Multilingual Communities

In a multilingual speech community a whole range, or repertoire, of languages is available to speakers, who use some of them in their linguistic interactions to perform particular social roles. Note that the term *repertoire* is also used to refer to the range of language varieties, such as dialects, registers, and styles typical of a unilingual community of speakers for whom the choice of one variety rather than another can have the same social value as code selection in a multilingual community (Gumperz 1971). Repertoire applies to both the speech community and the individual. No bilingual speaker controls the whole range of codes that constitute a speech community's repertoire continuum but only a number of these (his verbal repertoire). An illustration of a complex multilingual repertoire is that provided by Juillard (1995) who has investigated the urban area of Zinguinchor in West Africa, situated at the cross-roads of three states: Senegal (official languages: Wolof and French), Gambia (English) and Guinea-Bissau (Portuguese), and of numerous ethnic groups and languages: eight African, three ex-colonial, and one creole. Speakers in Zinguinchor classify their repertoire in three ways: languages of identity, of cross-communication, and of culture. In the wider educational domain, boys use French, girls use Wolof. Speakers vary from a trilingual farmer who uses Diola (the majority language) and Mandinka with men and Wolof with his mother and sister, to a high school boy who declared speaking 20 languages and used eight daily. In the market place Peul (Kpelle) is the language of transactions, Wolof the language of bargaining power, and French is used to conclude a bargain. An example of how a multilingual speaker uses the different codes in his repertoire is that of an Indian businessman dealing in spices and living in the suburb of Bombay described by Pandit (1979). His mother tongue and home language is Kathiawari, a dialect of Gujarati; he reads his daily newspaper in standard Gujarati; in the market place he uses a colloquial variety of Marathi, the state language; at the railway station he speaks Hindustani, the pan-Indian lingua franca; the language of business is Kachchi; in the evening he will relax watching a TV film in Hindi or English, or listening to a cricket-match commentary in English. (For a typology of speech/verbal repertoire, see Kachru 1982.)

What roles does each of the different languages play in a speech community? These various codes are neither used nor valued in the same way: if they were, all but one would become redundant. They usually fulfill different functions in the sense that each is used according to interlocutor, domain, topic, and role, the choice of one code involving an 'act of identity' (Le Page and Tabouret-Keller 1985) on the part of the speaker (see *Identity and Language*; *Role Theory*).

2.2 Diglossic Bilingualism

When two or more different varieties or languages co-occur throughout a speech community, each with a distinct range of social functions in complementary distribution, we have a situation of diglossia (see *Diglossia*). Originally developed by Ferguson (1959) to describe two functionally different varieties of the same language, one called the high variety (H), reserved for formal uses and formally learned, the other the low variety (L), used in informal situations (example of diglossia: classical (H) and colloquial (L) Arabic). The concept of diglossia has been extended to cover multilingual situations. Examples of diglossic bilingualism range from simple binary contexts, e.g., Guaranì (L) and Spanish (H) in Paraguay, to double-overlapping diglossia, e.g., African vernacular (L), Swahili (L and H) and English (H) in Tanzania (the last two are second languages), or double-nested diglossia, with L and H having each an L and an H variety, e.g., Khalapur in North India, to linear polyglossic situations characteristic of Singapore and Malaysia (see *Diglossia*).

One of the most complex polyglossic situations is found in Northern India (Khubchandani 1979). At the local level dialects vary from village to village to such an extent that they quickly become mutually unintelligible: when a villager visits a neighboring town he must use a less localized variety in order to be understood. This is how local trade languages developed and became regional dialects. Above them is one of the official state languages. Each state language comprises a colloquial and a standard form. Over and above these are the two official national languages, Hindi and English. Hindi is also a regional language extending over several states and diversified into a number of dialects. The Hindi-Urdu-Panjabi geolinguistic area of Northern India comprises 46 percent of the total Indian population and is a vast polyglossic continuum where languages and dialects complement, or merge or compete with one another according to domains, functions, social group, and religious affiliations.

Diglossia does not remain stable but evolves and changes. It is said to 'leak' when one language/variety invades the domains and functions previously reserved for the other: this is a sign of an incipient breakdown in the diglossic relationship which reflects changes in power relations between the groups in the society. The result is either a blend of the two former H and L varieties or a language shift.

2.3 Language Shift

When members of an ethnolinguistic group start using the language of another for domains and functions hitherto the preserve of their own language (L1), the process of language shift is under way. Typically, language shift takes place over three generations: the first is either unilingual or dominant in L1; the second is variably bilingual (L1/L2); the third dominant or unilingual in L2. The shift also takes place in synchrony: at a given point in time the first generation is still monolingual in L1 while the last is already monolingual in L2. Throughout this process L1 is affected by L2; its forms and uses are reduced; its speakers borrow heavily from it, mixing, and switching between, the two codes (see de Bot and Clyne 1994). In extreme cases a group's language may cease to be spoken at all: this is an example of language death. A number of factors account for language shift, the most important being changes in the way of life of a group, which weaken the strength of its social networks (e.g., urbanization, education);

changes in the power relations between the groups; negative attitudes towards the stigmatized minority language and culture; or a combination of all these. Language shift has been studied from various perspectives: sociological and demographic at the macro-level (see, for example, Tabouret-Keller 1968); social psychological (see Landry et al. 1996); and ethnographic at the micro-level (see, for example, Gal 1979 and Kulick 1992), each approach using specific research methods which are complementary. Language shift and language death adversely affect the state of societal bilingualism in the world and should be better understood if languages and cultures in pluralist societies are to be maintained (Fishman 1991) (see *Language Maintenance, Shift, and Death*).

2.4 Lingua Francas, Pidgins, and Creoles
In language shift one language is abandoned for another and may die. But there is a situation in which a new language is born out of languages in contact: this process is known as pidginization. When speakers with different mother tongues want to communicate with each other they use a lingua franca when one is available; it is a natural contact language, like, for example, a trade language (e.g., Hausa in West Africa, Swahili in East Africa). A pidgin is a contact language, which has no native speakers and is the product of a multilingual situation in which people must develop a new language to be able to communicate. One distinguishes between endogenous pidgins, which are born from the contact of a native population with foreign traders, and exogenous pidgins which develop from contact between non-indigenous populations speaking mutually unintelligible languages, as in the case of slaves or indentured laborers on the plantations and their masters. Typically, a pidgin evolves out of low-status substrate languages spoken as L1s (e.g., the African languages of slaves) in contact with a high-status superstrate, or base language (e.g., English, French, Dutch, or Portuguese). A pidgin is an L2, which results from an incomplete learning of the superstrate owing to a quantitatively and qualitatively restricted input. It is a mixed language, which borrows from both substrates and superstrate: the forms of the lexical items are derived from the latter, while the syntactic and semantic properties of these lexical items follow the rules of the former (see, for example, Mühlhäusler 1986).

When a pidgin has to fulfill new, more numerous and complex social functions, it develops new and complex forms and structures, until adults begin to use it as the main language of communication and children learn it as their mother tongue (nativization process): the pidgin has become a creole, which is a relatively stable language, though in constant interaction with the base language (see, for example, Jourdan and Keesing 1994). Sometimes, because of economic, social and cultural pressures, the creole evolves in the direction of the base language by a process called decreolization (Bickerton 1975). Pidgins and creoles are real languages, suited to the needs for which they are developed. Some even become official national languages, like Tok Pisin in Papua New Guinea. Their study enables linguists to witness their birth and development; their variety and relative speed of transformation provide new insights into language change and behavior (see also *Lingua Franca*).

2.5 Theoretical Implications of Societal Bilingualism
When different linguistic groups come into contact their languages come into contact. These languages may either converge or diverge, or converge and diverge at one and the same time. This is because the degree of variation in intra- and inter-lingual uses depends on the relative strength of two tendencies in society: the tendency to reduce intergroup differences (convergence) and the tendency to accentuate these differences (divergence). Convergence is found where speakers are in close and constant contact and there is consensus on the norms of language behavior; it characterizes small communities with dense and multiplex social networks (see *Social Networks*) as well as societies where a standard written language is imposed as the legitimate norm on a nation or group of nations (e.g., French, English and Classical Arabic, as national and international languages). Divergence, on the other hand, prevails in situations where there are no imposed norms and social networks are loose, leading to wide variations in usage. Language creativity is then at its highest, as in pidginization. Sometimes both convergence and divergence are at work, as the following examples show.

The 3000 inhabitants of Kupwar in South India between them speak four different languages, Marathi and Urdu (both Indo-European), Kannada and Telugu (both Dravidian). The village is divided into clearly distinct castes, each identified by its language. As they need to communicate, they, especially the men, learn each other's languages. Over centuries their syntaxes have converged and become more similar than they are in other parts of the Indian subcontinent (the convergence is essentially towards Marathi, the state language). However, they are still distinct in their respective vocabularies, which serve as a powerful symbol of each group's ethnic identity and distinctiveness (Gumperz and Wilson 1971).

In Nairobi, Kenya, at a time of great social change, children from four different ethnic and language backgrounds speak Swahili in the streets but, as adolescents they divide into two camps, each one identifying with either Swahili or English, each symbolizng their different social allegiances. As adults, however, they return to their original ethnolinguistic groups through endogamy, but all also use Swahili, while some are capable of speaking English. Here there are successively acts of convergence and divergence expressed by allegiance to different groups and languages at different times (Parkin 1977).

Mixed languages are in-group languages, usually with their grammatical structure taken from one language and their lexicon from another, e.g., Maltese (Arabic with heavy borrowings from Italian and English) or Media Lengua (Quechua and Spanish). A very unusual mixed language is Michif in Western Canada and North Dakota (Bakker 1994). The internal structure (phonology, lexis, morphology, and syntax) of the noun group is essentially French (dialect), while that of the verb group is essentially Cree (an Algonquian language). Is Michif a case of code switching? The answer must be no, since in code-switching speakers are more or less competent in the two languages and most Michif users speak neither French nor Cree. Is it a pidgin? But Michif is the mother tongue of its speakers and is a fully developed language. Then is it a creole? In so far as a creole is a development from a pidgin, then Michif is not a creole. Moreover, Michif is an in-group language, while creoles are developed for communication across languages. Thus Michif poses a real puzzle for linguistic theory: what is its syntax? What do categorial rules look like, since French and Cree have very different rule systems? How should its lexis be organized? Are there one or two phonologies? These are some of the theoretical questions which linguists have to answer (see *Intertwined Languages*).

Thus, variation and change are the essence of language, because language is at once the expression, symbol, and instrument of a group's identity and of its dynamic relations to other groups in a society. A language is not a homogeneous, static entity; it varies along multidimensional continua and its speakers identify with some of the varieties and their verbal repertoire is an expression of these identities.

3. Language Planning in Multilingual Societies

Confronted with many different languages within its boundaries, how does a state solve its communication problems, given the complexity of ethnolinguistic group relations? Historically, the state has imposed one language, usually the dominant legitimized language of the ruling group, upon the other linguistic groups, thus either reducing the latter's languages to minority status or eradicating them by assimilating its speakers through education or coercion. For example, the French State, in its pursuit of national unity, has succeeded in imposing the Parisian sociolect on the whole of its population at home and on the elites of its colonies overseas, thus making French the official language of the French-speaking world (francophonie).

Today, however, the state uses the much subtler instrument of language planning, which is a species of economic planning (Grin 1996). Language planning is of two kinds, internal (or corpus planning) and external (or status planning). Corpus planning, a form of linguistic engineering, is the same in multilingual as in unilingual societies. Status-planning means interfering with the existing status relations between the languages and their speakers and using one or more languages for official purposes. As the status of languages is a function of the relative economic, demographic, social, cultural and political power of the various linguistic groups and of the subjective perceptions of these power relations, status planning will necessarily reflect the power structure in society (Fishman 1994). Two main approaches confront each other: nationism and nationalism (Fishman 1968). In the nationist solution a language is selected for reasons of national efficiency (e.g., English and French as official languages in most former British and French colonies). In the nationalist solution language acts as a powerful symbol and instrument of ethnic identification, and the different ethnolinguistic groups resist acculturation by maintaining or reinforcing their language (e.g., Catalan in Spain, Flemish in Belgium, French in Canada). But most cases in the world fall between these two solutions, especially in multilingual states. Usually, one or more regional languages are given national status together with a national or international language. A comparison between Singapore and Malaysia will illustrate the difference between the nationist and the nationalist option.

Both Singapore and Malaysia are multiethnic, multireligious, and multilingual societies. It is noteworthy that, while these states have evolved along similar historical lines and are composed of roughly the same ethnic mix—though in different proportions—they have chosen very different approaches to language planning. Malaysia has opted for a nationist (or 'depluralization') solution: divided along geographic, political, linguistic, ethnic, religious, and economic lines, it has followed the path of cultural assimilation with the adoption of Bahasa Malaysia (Malay) as the sole official language of the country. In Singapore, by contrast, the traditional cultural values of each major group have been fostered, a policy of cultural integration (as opposed to assimilation) has been pursued, and the four main languages (Malay, Mandarin, Tamil, and English) have been made official. But this policy is not one of strict nationalism, since, while encouraging the three ethnic languages as a foundation for the maintenance of traditional values, it has at the same time emphasized the functional importance of English as the basis for a supra-ethnic Singaporean identity (Ward and Hewstone 1985).

One of the key issues in language planning, particularly in the West, is that between the personal and the territorial solution to the problems of the multilingual state. The personal solution is based on enforcing individual rights throughout the state; these include the right to understand and be understood in public life, to be educated in one's own language, and the right to one's own identity. By contrast, the territorial solution consists of separating the different language populations by fixed boundaries. There are several models of territoriality, of which the Swiss, the Belgian, and the Canadian are examples: all show tensions between the territorial and the personal solution. In the former Soviet Union the dominant Russian group used the territorial solution on the one hand to protect minorities and, on the other, to protect and promote its own interests. All the republics, with the exception of the Russian Federation, were officially bilingual, Russian being in every case one of the official languages. Russian-speaking minorities had the right to use their mother tongue, while the other ethnolinguistic groups had to learn Russian as well as their own language. But in the Russian Federation only Russian was official. The principle of territoriality led to an asymmetrical, non-reciprocal bilingualism (see *Language Planning: Models*).

A presumed link has been suggested between multilingual societies and national underdevelopment: does the fact that a country is culturally and linguistically diverse and heterogeneous cause that country to be economically disadvantaged? Are nation-states more stable than multinational ones? Pool (1969) tried to show that linguistically diverse countries tend to be underdeveloped, while highly developed countries have considerable linguistic uniformity. However, other researchers have challenged Pool's methodology and findings; they argue that both linguistic diversity and economic disadvantage are the legacy of colonialism (Liberson and Hansen 1974). Moreover, are not some of the most advanced and dynamic countries and cities in the world, such as the US, Canada, Australia, Hong Kong and Singapore, among the most ethnically and linguistically heterogeneous? As Weinreich pointed out as long ago as 1953, the greater the linguistic diversity of a country, the greater the degree of biliguality and bilingualism. Where there are many people who speak many different languages, they will learn each other's languages. In other words, individual and societal bilingualism compensates for linguistic diversity (see *Language Development*).

4. Education in Multilingual Societies

Education is one of the tools of language planning. One of the most intractable yet urgent problems of language planning worldwide is that of ensuring at least functional literacy, that is, a level of literacy that will enable people to function in a given society. This is not so much a technical as a social issue, since illiteracy is an obstacle to informed citizen participation in decision-making and to national development. Illiteracy is a problem not only for the Third World but also for developed post-industrial countries, which have recently known a sharp rise in illiteracy rates, owing to the marginalization of immigrant communities and the rise of unemployment. Unfortunately, both status and corpus language planning are not adequate instruments for tackling these wider social issues. The limited success of large-scale state measures would suggest that small-scale solutions with multiple literacy programs at all levels are preferable (Tabouret-Keller et al. 1997).

What of bilingual education and the teaching of the mother tongue to linguistic minority children? Two important contextual aspects in the development of these children must be borne in mind: firstly, they usually come from a devalued linguistic background and, secondly, because they often come from socially deprived communities, their literacy-oriented skills are less developed than those of the children from the dominant language group. They suffer from a double handicap when they are schooled with the children of this latter group: they have to develop literacy skills in a language they either do not know, or only know for communicative purposes, and cannot fall back on their first language for literacy functions. The poor academic achievement of these children is then attributed by the educational system to a cognitive deficit. Cummins (1984) has given a critical review of the use made of academic assessment tests to demonstrate the deficit of minority schoolchildren. He shows that there is strong experimental evidence that valorizing the first culture of these children and introducing literacy skills in their first language enhance both linguistic and academic achievement. Experiments in bilingual education, that is, where the first and the second language are used as media of instruction demonstrate how the subtractive situation in which minority schoolchildren find themselves can be turned into an additive bilinguality. By valuing the first language and culture of these children, and motivating them to learn through their mother tongue, their linguistic and cognitive abilities are enhanced (Hamers and Blanc 2000) (see *Cummins, Jim*).

Unfortunately, the majority of bilingual programs for linguistic minority children are transitional ones, which have been decided by the dominant group. The ultimate aim is the assimilation of the subordinate groups who will, in the long run, be at best dominant, at worst monolingual, in the second language, and be acculturated or assimilated. So, even if bilingual education appears to be a necessary condition for the maintenance of minority cultures and languages and the academic achievements of minority children, it is not a sufficient one. Only a strong ethnolinguistic vitality, allegiance to the cultural group, and the use of the mother tongue in the home and the speech community will ensure cultural and linguistic survival (see *Ethnolinguistic Vitality*). For of all the domains it is the family network that most resists the penetration of the dominant language and perpetuates societal bilingualism.

See also: Bilingual Education; Minority Languages.

Bibliography

Bakker P 1994 Michif. In: Bakker P, Mous M (eds.) *Mixed Languages: 15 Case Studies in Language Intertwining*. Institute for Functional Research into Language and Language Use, Amsterdam, pp. 130–3

Bickerton D 1975 *Dynamics of a Creole System*. Cambridge University Press, Cambridge, UK

Cummins J 1984 *Bilingualism and Special Education: Issues in Assessment and Pedagogy*. Multilingual Matters, Clevedon, UK

de Bot K, Clyne M. 1994 A 16-year longitudinal study of language attrition in Dutch immigrants in Australia. *Journal of Multilingual and Multicultural Development* **15**: 17–28

Ferguson C A 1959 Diglossia. *Word* **15**: 125–40

Fishman J A 1968 Nationality-nationalism and nation-nationism. In: Fishman J A, Ferguson C A, Das Gupta J (eds.) *Language Problems of Developing Nations*. Mouton, The Hague

Fishman J A 1991 *Reversing Language Shift: Theoretical and Practical Foundations of Assistance to Threatened Languages*. Multilingual Matters, Clevedon, UK

Fishman J A 1994 Critiques of language planning: A minority languages perspective. *Journal of Multilingual and Multicultural Development* **15**: 91–9

Gal S 1979 *Language Shift: Social Determinants of Linguistic Change in Bilingual Austria*. Academic Press, New York

Grin F (ed.) 1996 Economic approaches to language and language planning. *International Journal of the Sociology of Language* **121**

Gumperz J J 1971 *Language in Social Groups*. Stanford University Press, Stanford, CA

Gumperz J J, Wilson R 1971 Convergence and creolization: a case from the Indo-Aryan/Dravidian Border in India. In: Hymes D H (ed.) *Pidginization and Creolization of Language*. Cambridge University Press, Cambridge, UK

Hamers J F, Blanc M H A 2000 *Bilinguality and Bilingualism*, 2nd edn. Cambridge University Press, Cambridge, UK

Jourdan C, Keesing R 1994 From Fisin to Pijin: Creolization in process in the Solomon Islands. *Language and Society* **26**: 401–20

Juillard C 1995 *Sociolinguistique Urbaine. La Vie des Langues à Ziguinchor (Sénégal)*. CNRS, Paris

Kachru B B 1982 The Bilingual's Linguistic Repertoire. In: Hartford B, Valdman A, Foster C R (eds.) *Issues in International Bilingual Education*. Plenum Press, New York

Khubchandani L M 1979 A demographic typology for Hindi, Urdu, Punjabi speakers in Northern India. In: McCormack W C, Wurm S A (eds.) *Language and Society*. Mouton, The Hague

Kulick D 1992 *Language Shift and Cultural Reproduction: Socialization, Self, and Syncretism in a Papua New Guinea Village*. (Studies in the Social and Cultural Foundations of Language, **14**). Cambridge University Press, Cambridge, UK

Landry R, Allard R, Henry J 1996 French in South Louisiana: Towards language loss. *Journal of Multilingual and Multicultural Development* **17**: 442–68

Le Page R B, Tabouret-Keller A 1985 *Acts of Identity: Creole-based Approaches to Language and Ethnicity*. Cambridge University Press, Cambridge, UK

Lieberson S, Hansen L K 1974 National development, mother tongue diversity, and the comparative study of nations. *American Sociological Review* **39**: 523–41

Mühlhäusler P 1986 *Pidgin and Creole Linguistics*. Blackwell, Oxford, UK

Pandit P B 1979 Perspectives on sociolinguistics in India. In: McCormack W C, Wurm S A (eds.) *Language and Society*. Mouton, The Hague

Parkin D 1977 Emergent and stabilized multilingualism: Polyethnic peer groups in PP urban Kenya. In: Giles H (ed.) *Language, Ethnicity and Intergroup Relations*. Academic Press, London

Pool J 1969 National development and language diversity. *La Monda Lingo-Problemo* **1**: 140–56

Tabouret-Keller A 1968 Sociological factors of language maintenance and shift: a methodological approach based on European and African examples. In: Fishman J A, Ferguson C A, Das Gupta J (eds.) *Language Problems of Developing Nations*. Wiley, New York

Tabouret-Keller A, Le Page R B, Gardner-Chloros P, Varro G (eds.) 1997 *Vernacular Literacy: A Re-Evaluation*. Clarendon Press, Oxford, UK (Oxford Studies in Anthropological Linguistics)

Ward C A, Hewstone M 1985 Ethnicity, language and intergroup relations in Malaysia and Singapore: a social psychological analysis. *Journal of Multilingual and Multicultural Development* **6**: 271–96

Weinreich U 1953 *Languages in Contact*. Mouton, The Hague

Communication

K. L. Berge

The content and use of the term 'communication' is even by humanistic standards extremely ambiguous, and it has therefore often been difficult to use in practical, empirical work. The most exact use of the term has been standardized in Shannon and Weaver's information theory. Within the tradition of semiotics, the value of communication as a term has been questioned, and in linguistics the term has sometimes been used as a synonym or part-synonym with more exactly defined terms such as use, parole, text, behavior, and performance. In spite of this, certain theorists—often those with a background in cybernetics—have used 'communication' as a generic term for all theories about man, in the same way as semioticians have defined the domain of semiotics.

A very simple and general, but neither unproblematic nor uncontroversial, way of defining communication is to view it as an information process going on between at least two human communicators (not necessarily two persons as long as one can communicate with oneself) embedded in a context (see *Context*), and a situation. More specifically, communication can be defined as a generic term covering all messages uttered in different contexts and situations.

A message can be divided into sign-vehicle and meaning. The sign-vehicle then covers all possible variants on the expression plane of linguistic utterances, and meaning covers all possible variants on what is called, in the glossematic school, the content plane. In this way, communication is used as a sociological term, and language is viewed as a primarily social fact (see *Sociology of Language*).

Furthermore, communication can also be conceived of as inherent in the linguistic message. The situation, the context, and the communicators involved in communication make their mark on the content and expression planes of the message. This definition is neutral with regard to the different traditions in linguistics which divide language for instance into 'langue' or 'system' on the one hand, and 'parole' or 'behavior' on the other (see *Saussurean Tradition and Sociolinguistics*).

1. 'Communication': Different Models and Metaphors

One possible way of bringing order into the rather chaotic world of the different approaches to the study of communication in linguistics, is to differentiate between the various trends in communication-relevant research. These trends can be classified according to the basic models of communication they have adopted. Or rather, according to the different metaphors that linguists use in order to try to illustrate or make explicit the phenomenon of communication.

1.1 The Linear, Conduit Model

The simplest model of communication has been called the conduit model (Reddy 1979) because of its underlying assumption that language functions as a sort of channel, or tool for transferring a linguistic message from a source (or sender) to a destination (or hearer). This idea of communication has some of its roots in information theory. To separate what they call information from communication, certain philosophers of language (e.g., Grice) have advocated the idea that communication proper is characterized by intentional communication, or what Grice calls 'non-natural meaning'. The idea is that the addresser ('sender') intends that the message (or utterance) will cause what is called an effect in the addressee ('receiver'). The only necessary condition is that the addressee recognize this intention. In spite of the differences between these approaches, they are basically teleological models of communication, and this makes them closely related to perhaps the oldest theory of communication, namely that of classical rhetoric. Rhetoric can be defined as a theory of communication that seeks to find the quality which makes it possible for an addresser to persuade or convince his addressee about something.

The most problematic aspects in these models are the notion of effect, or perlocution on the addressee's side, and the notion of intention on the addresser's side. How are we to build a theory of communication on such vague terms, and how are we to find out what is/was the intention in a message and how are we to distinguish between the different effects? Other problematic aspects are the basically individualistic and monological views of communication that advocates of such models implicitly accept. Such views are seriously challenged in the three following communication models.

1.2 The Circular, Dialogic Model

The basic idea in what is here called the circular or dialogic model (see *Dialogism*), is that for communication to take place, it is not sufficient that an addresser manifests his intention in a message which results in an effect in the addressee. It is also necessary to give the addressee a more active role in communication.

First, this active part is the more or less conscious interpretation process that the addressee must be involved in for the intended message to get through.

Second, a more or less expressed manifestation of the intended effect in the form of a response, answer, action, etc. from the addressee is necessary for the addresser to understand that his message has been received—in fact, *is* a message. Without a response of some sort, the addresser would be left in a situation where he is at best talking to himself, at worst is indulging in a monologue more typical of madness. Thus, the interpretation requirement is not restricted to the addressee alone. The addresser, too, has to identify some sort of signal in the addressee's message which can be interpreted as a response or reaction to the intended message.

In this way, communication can be seen as a system of questions and answers, or as a sort of cooperation where the communicators are actively organized in the construction of the message. It is not necessary that the addresser's intended meaning is identically reproduced by the addressee. If such an interpretation is at all possible, it is certainly limited to extremely restricted contexts, e.g., when certain logicians communicate solely with the help of logical formulas. The prototypical communication between humans is in fact characterized by the opposite: a partial, or limited understanding, or even misunderstanding, on the part of the addressee, which has to be clarified by further messages. Communication is not only the transfer of intentions with language as its tool. It is a constructive process going on in time. The message is constructed through the mutual activity of the actors. In this way, communication is a creative dynamic process. In fact, if communication did not have these qualities, a great deal of quite normal linguistic activity, like small talk during a lunch break, would be meaningless.

What is retained in this model from the conduit communication model, is the notion of intention. For dialogue to take place, it is necessary that the communicators intend to take part in the conversation, that they accept some sort of honesty principle, etc. Such principles are described in theories of conversational implicatures or of pragmatic universals (see *Pragmatics and Sociolinguistics*).

1.3 The Feedback, Interaction Model

The third model of communication distinguishes itself from the dialogical model by doing away with the notion of intention altogether. In this model, communication is viewed in a much more general way than in the two previous ones. Communication would include all those processes by which human beings influence one another. In its most extreme form, this model entails that all behavior can be said to be communicative. The interaction of human beings is characterized by the necessity to communicate; this necessity is superior to the notion of intention, which is based not only on the will to communicate, but also the will to interpret. Communication is thus part of perception; attention to and interpretation of communication are part of the process of perceiving.

What remains in this model are the principles of mutuality and reciprocity as basic requirements for communication to take place. However, those principles are not governed by normatively colored principles, such as Grice's conversational implicatures and Habermas's universal pragmatic consensus principles. In those frameworks, communication is a certain mutual tuning which necessarily must involve a certain moral commitment, that one believes what one says to be true, that one intends that which one says, and that the addressee necessarily takes for granted that the addresser follows these and similar principles (see *Cooperative Principle*). Communication, in the feedback model, is not characterized by a search for what could be called mutual knowledge, consensus, or intersubjective understanding. Rather, the opposite is the case, namely that to communicate is to experience such principles as ideal goals: one cannot share other people's experiences or mental worlds, or truly understand the intentions of other communicators. The reason is that these principles of general reciprocity and mutuality are subject to societal power relations (see *Power and Language*). Such relations are neither intended to be recognized in the message, nor perhaps even intended to be a part of the meaning of the message at all. But as sociologists insist on telling the naive linguist, power relations are inherent in every communicated message (see *Manipulation*). There is no society in existence without social hierarchies of some sort; a powerless utopia is at best a pastoral idyll, at worst a totalitarian goal.

The basic problem in the feedback model is how to distinguish communication from information. As long as neither the addresser's nor the addressee's intentions are preconditions to communication, how are we to discriminate between all the incoming information, both on the content and expression planes of a message—an amount of information which, according to certain theorists, is infinite? It seems that this problem can be solved only by defining communication as involving both information (in the sense of information theory), the conveyed message, and the understanding of the message. Advocates of this model focus on the temporal nature of communication; communication is viewed as an enduring process which imposes meaning upon disturbances and noise, through the selective processes of information, message conveyance and understanding. Such a selection process is, of course, determined by the internalized language of the communicators, and is governed by other semiotic systems as well.

1.4 The Self-regulatory (Autopoesis) Model

The autopoesis model appears to be a radicalized version of the feedback model, in the sense that the model seems to have done away with what have been called the principles of reciprocity and mutuality. The autopoesis model is therefore something as seemingly paradoxical as a solipsistic model of communication. In this model, the communicators (or as they are called, the 'emitters' and 'receivers') do not communicate in order to transfer and create a message (as in the conduit and dialogue models), or even to create some information, a conveyed message, and an understanding, but simply to integrate elements from the communicative situation (the environment) which can contribute to the communicators' so-called self-regulation and self-creation (hence the term 'autopoetic'). This self-regulation and self-creation is an individual, idiosyncratic version of an interaction input. A basic goal of this self-regulation or autopoesis is to create a difference with respect to all other (real or potential) communicators. In this sense, communication is necessary for the individual in order to be constituted as an individual. The communicators are seen as closed systems, insofar as nothing can be integrated which is not specified in the system's own structure. It is important to note that the system is not a static structure, but rather a process. Communication is self-reflection, characterized as an unceasing search for functional substitutes.

Interestingly enough, this model allows for another, more advanced view of linguistic messages, such as written texts, than is normal in the linguistic tradition (see *Speech and Writing*). Instead of being viewed as inferior reproductions of the prototypical or even 'natural' linguistic communication, namely verbal conversation, written messages are viewed as more communicative and creative, in that they not only allow for a finer distinction between the individual communicator and his communicative environment, but also for more permanent self-referential and autopoetic activity on the part of the individual communicator. Oral dialogue is thus reduced to one type of communication among others.

2. The Relation Between Communication and 'Language'

So far, the fundamental problem of the relation between communication and language has not even been superficially touched upon. Language is what most linguists recognize as the one and only object of linguistics; however, its relation to communication is a matter of continuous controversy: in fact, it is not even clear that the phenomenon of communication is at all relevant for the study of languages, and of language as such (see Sect. 3, below).

Still, most linguists are willing to accept a division of the phenomenon of language. On the one hand, it is seen as a kind of stable, over-individual structure, or type-schema, which for the sake of simplicity may be called a 'signification system.' On the other hand, it can be viewed as a set of tokens somehow belonging to such a schema, these may be called 'utterances.' This opposition between a system of signification and its associated utterances has many names, e.g., langue–parole (Saussure), schema–usage (Hjelmslev), code–behavior (Halliday), competence–performance (Chomsky), to name just a few of the most influential. The status of communication varies depending on, first, which opposition one considers most relevant, and second, which element in the opposition one chooses as most fundamental for the study of language.

The latter alternative allows us to distinguish between what the Soviet philosopher of language V. N. Voloshinov (see *Voloshinov, Valentin Nikolavic*) called 'abstract objectivists' on the one hand, and on the other, a heterogeneous group (consisting of behaviorists, empiricists, nominalists, 'socio'-linguists, processualists; etc.) called 'skepticists.' These groups will be dealt with in the following.

2.1 The Abstract Objectivist View

The abstract objectivist view can, in the light of the history of modern linguistics, be considered the traditional way of seeing things. The prototypical abstract objectivist sees language as a relatively stable, finite, and invariant system of signification, that is either as a unifunctional, adult-type system which is the goal of socialization, or as a social institution (Saussure's 'langue'), or as a universal innate mental grammar (Chomsky's 'competence'), or even as a pure form (Hjelmslev's 'schema'). The relation between signification system and utterances is seen as an either–or opposition: either one studies language systematically (i.e., as a signification system), or one doesn't study it at all. In this view, language is then something which precedes communication.

It does this in two different ways: First, as a generic term for language utterances, and therefore as a synonym of performance, behavior, usage, and parole. Second, communication can be viewed as the context (see *Context*) where language is used between communicators uttering tokens belonging to the signification schema, i.e., the language system.

In both these views, language is seen as a pre-condition to communication, either as a structuring grammar of utterance tokens, or as a common code (see *Code, Sociolinguistic*) of some sort, defining the difference between what has meaning and what is meaningless. The code is necessary for communicators transferring a message, as in the conduit model (see above, Sect. 1.1), accomplishing a dialogue, as in the circular model (see Sect. 1.2), interacting with one another, as in the feed-back model (see Sect. 1.3), or reaching a state of autopoesis, as in the self-regulatory model (see Sect. 1.4).

2.2 The Skepticist View

Common to the skepticist view is the radical critique of the abstract objectivist opposition between the system of signification and the utterances derived from the system.

The skepticists challenge this opposition in three different and not necessarily compatible ways. In all three, communication plays a more important role in research and reflection on language than in the abstract objectivist tradition.

2.2.1 Language as Communicative Behavior

The skeptics' first option is to get rid of the opposition altogether. Language as a signification system is viewed as a mentalistic abstraction from a heterogeneous mass of data. This mentalistic abstraction is considered as type–schema product created by the analyst. Language is, then, a generic term for communicative behavior. This view is typical of the nominalist and the radical descriptivist. A prominent group of philosophers of language embracing these ideas are the so-called 'analytic philosophers' in the Anglo–American tradition (e.g., the later Wittgenstein, Strawson, Grice, Quine, Goodman). Meaning of linguistic messages in communication can only be said to belong to a signification system as an arbitrary classification of intentional (or habitual) acts having some sort of common similarity, the so-called 'family concepts.' An abstract objectivist theory of meaning, such as the (Saussurean) structuralist theory of semantic components and fields is in principle impossible, since in any case, message meaning is determined by an infinite number of components in a steadily changing communication situation, where intention, contextual setting, contextual restriction and other situational components play a major role.

2.2.2 Communication as Determining Language

The second option turns the abstract objectivist view upside down. It claims that communication (as a set of messages, not utterances) precedes, and is a precondition of, the signification system, not the other way round. Communication is viewed as determining language. Language is a message structure (Rometveit) embedded in time, which at the same time structures, constructs, and creates meaning as the result of an ongoing dialogic process. This view of language is closely related to the circular communication model (see above, Sect. 1.2), but it can also be seen as related to the nonintentional search for a common code which makes communication work in the interaction model (see Sect. 1.3), and to the notion of consensual domains as a prerequisite for the process of communication in the autopoesis model (see Sect. 1.4).

Many linguists involved in a sociological description of language choose this option (see *Sociology of Language*; *Language as a Social Reality*). Approaching language from the corpus of messages, and not from a hypothetical, abstract system, one is struck by the heterogeneity of the data. Not only is communication a multidimensional semiotic, where verbal and written language play a subordinate role (as in phenomena of the 'double bind' type), but communicators may use different signification systems simultaneously, or even systematically break such systems' unconscious normative rules. This heterogeneity in communicative activity could be interpreted as a process of signification whose variation is an index of the conflicts between different, incompatible signification schemes.

An example of how such a linguistic heterogeneity and flexibility in verbal communication can be legalized as the norm of a national written language is furnished by the two standards of written Norwegian. These standards represent two languages, in fact two competing conceptions of what constitutes 'Norwegian.' Since these conceptions are socioculturally determined, the languages could be called written sociolects (see *Language in Society: Overview*). In each language, a great number of morphemic and lexemic variants are admitted. For instance, the following are all possible determiners of the singular substantive *bok* 'book': *bok-en, bok-a, bok-i* 'the book.' On the lexical level, variation is allowed, where other written languages normally would have only one lexeme. For instance, two variants of the lexeme 'language' are possible: *sprog, språk*. Morphological variants such as these have different social, political, stylistic, regional, etc., meanings dependent on context and genre; these different meanings are familiar to every relatively language-competent Norwegian. For a descriptive, synchronic grammar of written Norwegian which pretends to be exhaustive, it is thus necessary to allow for situational rules, sociological parameters, and the like. It is not in principle possible to reduce the morphemes *-en, -a, -i* to a single abstract archimorpheme, or the lexemes *sprog, språk* to one and only one invariant ideal. In fact, the history of written Norwegian at the beginning of the twenty-first century is characterized by a willingness on the part of the language planners to accept a great many variants, because of these variants' different meanings in different contexts and situations. Interestingly enough, this sociologically determined multidimensionality seems to be one of the crucial factors that explains why Norwegians generally are much better at understanding their closely related neighbors, the Swedes and the Danes (who use written codes of the more unifunctional type), than the other way round (see *Sociolinguistics and Language Change*).

2.2.3 Communication and Language as Complementary Phenomena

The third alternative to the abstract objectivist view of language and communication is to claim that the elements in the opposition are complementary to each other. Language is *both* a signification system *and* communication (understood as a set of messages); this relation cannot be understood as an either–or. Therefore, language phenomena are conceived of as a process (i.e., communication of messages) and a product (i.e., a signification system), both at the same time. Which aspect one focuses upon is determined by one's theoretical model and one's more or less explicit interests in the study of verbal messages.

As a signification system, language is viewed as an open system or semiosis. The system is not finite, but as a social reality, it is open for modifications of different kinds, such as restructuring and creativity during communication. The signification system thus has the form of a variation grammar, a system of multifunctional potentialities, allowing for orderly variation and flexible regularities. These regularities can be described not in the form of abstract 'rules,' 'principles,' and the like, but as social norms or even potential 'resources,' i.e., arbitrary conventions grounded in communication. More specifically, grammar is conceived of as a network of relations: a systemic network, not a system of rules.

From the communication angle, language can be viewed as some socially controllable elaboration and/or modification of an earlier established reality, i.e., an already internalized system. But communication-as-language can also be conceived of as the creation of such a system. One consequence of this language conception is seen in our understanding of the language acquisition process. In this process, the child is not interpreted as a passive agent, but as an active and meaning-seeking organism trying to adapt itself during either the dialogue, interaction, or self-regulation process, towards an environment and other communicators in the environment.

Furthermore, this conception neutralizes one of the classical oppositions in the abstract, objectivist conception of language, namely that between diachronic and synchronic. As a communication process, language seeks a stability that can never be achieved. Diachronicity is an inherent quality of language; the synchronic is merely a fixation of this diachronic quality, necessitated uniquely by the conscious rationalization of a supposed mutual intelligibility, by the need for an abstract, objectivist description of language, or by the language planner's urge for codification; for all of these, translating process to product is an essential demand.

3. Linguistics and Communication

The phenomena of communication have often been thought of as peripheral in linguistic research. This view is a result of the strong hold the abstract objectivist language conception has had on modern linguistic thought. Most workers in this tradition share (implicitly or explicitly) the idea that the essence of language is to represent some intellectual structure; thus, they reduce communication to a subordinate place amongst the possible functions of language.

Some linguistic schools have advocated a more communication-relevant approach to language; here, one could name the Prague School, and different versions of linguistic functionalism. This low status attributed to communication is similarly challenged by different pragmatic approaches to language (see *Pragmatics and Sociolinguistics*), as well as by language-relevant research in related disciplines such as sociology, poetics, psychology, or anthropology. Only some of the more important and coherent attempts of such communication-relevant approaches to language will be mentioned here.

3.1 Soviet Semiotic Dialogism

In the pre-Stalin era of Soviet intellectual life, a group of scholars emerged with a more or less common view of language, cognition, and communication; the language philosopher V. N. Voloshinov (see *Voloshinov, Valentin Nikolavic*), the psychologist L. S. Vygotsky, and the literary critic M. M. Bakhtin (see *Dialogism*; *Bakhtin, Mikhail M.*; *Marxist Theories of Language*). All these scholars launched an attack on the basic ideas of abstract objectivism. For political reasons, it took a long time before their ideas reached the western world, but since the late 1960s, their approach to humanistic studies has come to play an increasingly important role in a great number of humanistic disciplines such as psychology, sociology, poetics, philosophy, semiotics, and linguistics.

The basic idea of these scholars is that language is essentially dialogic. This dialogicity is not to be mistaken for a possible external, instrumental use of language; it is dialogic in its most radical sense, i.e., that of the inner dialectic quality of the language sign. The addresser and the addressee are integrated as part of the nature of language. Language never exists as a unifunctional, closed system: rather, it is a process of communication. This process is furthermore characterized by the notions of multiaccentuality, heterogeneity, polyphony, intertextuality and in particular 'voicing' (see *Dialogism*), all referring to the social nature of language. In communication, language never appears as single-voiced: the situation, the tradition, the power relations between the communicators, and so on, all place their mark in the message. Thus, language really is this multivoiced message or speech process.

The Soviet dialogists see the nature of language as fundamentally social. The study of the content plane of linguistic messages becomes part of the study of ideology (see *Ideology*), whereas the object of study of the expression plane are the so-called speech genres. Consequently, even cognition is interpreted as a communication process, or, as it is called: 'inner speech.' Cognition or 'thought' is only possible through language; language is this multiaccentuated interaction process.

It remains to be seen whether the ideas of the Soviet dialogists can stimulate the traditional study of languages and language in the same way as they have influenced psychology and text linguistics. But one linguistic theory has emerged which partly seems to have been inspired by this school: namely the theory of enunciation and polyphony, developed above all by the French linguist Oswald Ducrot. This theory not only focuses on the self-referential aspects of language, such as deictic elements and shifters, but also on the fact that each message may have more than one source, and therefore may represent several points of view. These qualities are grammaticalized in language, for instance in the system of modalities. One consequence of the theory is that the monolithic notion of the addresser's integrity is suspended.

3.2 The Prague School and Functionalism

The Prague School was a linguistic school which did not limit its study of language to isolated utterances in so-called 'normal' situations. Quite the contrary: its focus was on a number of different types of human communication where language was used as a tool, such as literature and film. The school's basic relevance for the study of communication lies in the Prague linguists' development of a process theory of syntax, based on the notions of *theme* and *rheme*. Theme and rheme refer to the different linguistic qualities in the message which, in the communication process, signal already given meaning as 'theme,' and introduce new meaning as 'rheme.'

An even more important contribution to a communicative approach to language study is the Prague School's development of different taxonomies of so-called communicative functions. These taxonomies play an important role in Trubetzkoy's phonological theory. Another linguist (who is often associated with the Prague school), André Martinet, also challenges the traditional view of the basic function of language as representation. To Martinet, language is an instrument for communication. Martinet's stance appears to stem (at least in part) from his view on language as serving the need for mutual understanding. This 'sociological' attitude may also be prompted by Martinet's interest in what he calls the 'vocal basis' of language and by his studies in diachronic phonology. This basic communicative function of language could, e.g., explain why certain phonemes do not merge, and why the distinctive values of a language system are retained, even though its substance is fundamentally changed.

Like the Soviet dialogists, but perhaps in a less radical fashion, the Praguians refuse to reduce the essence of language's functions to intellectual representation. To them, language is a polyfunctional potential: its different functions are grammaticalized at different strata in the language system. Moreover, each individual utterance of a language is seen as a potential which in the interpretation process is reduced and given a coherent structure. Interpretation thus happens according to a more or less conscious choice of what is called a 'dominant': among the possible functions of an utterance in a specific communicative situation, the one is picked that is felt to be the most important for the message. It was in this way that Roman Jakobson explained the poetic quality of language: not as something extrinsic, but as an inherent quality.

3.3 Rommetveit's Message Structure Theory

The Norwegian psycholinguist Ragnar Rommetveit developed his theory of message structure over the years 1968–90, often in opposition to dominant paradigms in American linguistic research, such as Generative Grammer and Montague Grammar. The theoretical basis for his theory is a combination of experimental psychology (e.g., experiments with word associations), G. H. Mead's symbolic interactionism, and the European hermeneutic tradition. In fact, Rommetveit has made a point of being a methodological pluralist.

Rommetveit's basic idea is that language is embedded in a social matrix or context (see *Context*). Language can never be studied in isolation from the interaction of context. The analysis of interaction and communication is then related to the actual needs, feelings, intentions, and understanding of the subjects involved and their life worlds. Therefore, meaning is necessarily bound to context. Rommetveit attacks all ideas about 'literal' meaning, minimal semantic universals, etc., as fantasies based on theories of language that are in reality theories of written, formal language. On the content plane, messages are considered to be so-called 'meaning potentials.' Rommetveit, without being a nihilist, advocates a theory of perspectival relativity, in keeping with the sociological perspective of his theory. The social nature of language is guaranteed by so-called 'drafts of contracts.'

Contracts are seen as a process of negotiating tacit agreement and a shared world of discourse (see *Discourse*); the process is characterized by the notion of *message structure*. In the process of structuring a message, the communicators try to build a temporarily shared social reality (see *Language as a Social Reality*). The message structure consists of cyclic patterns of nesting new (or, as it is called, 'free') information into given (or 'bound') information.

To the theoretical-oriented linguist, Rommetveit's theory appears to be somewhat limited, as it seldom focuses on what the theory means in terms of the grammar. It is basically an interaction theory which focuses on the content plane of messages, not on the structure of the sign vehicle.

3.4 Halliday's Socio-semiotic Theory of Language

As a student of the English linguist J. R. Firth (see *Firth J.R.*), M. A. K. Halliday (see *Halliday, Michael Alexander Kirkwood*) was also influenced (albeit indirectly) by the anthropologist Malinowski (see *Malinowski, Bronislaw Kaspar*). Consequently, he has referred to his theory as an 'ethnographic or descriptive grammar.' Language, or as it is called, the combination of a 'semantic,' a 'lexico-grammatical,' and a 'phonological system,' is studied as the product of a social process, a *social reality* is schematized (or 'encoded') as a semantic system. However, among the systems that construct culture (the *semiotic* systems, as they are called), language is just one, even though it has a privileged place: most other semiotic systems are obligatorily mediated through language and its system. The product of the social process is the 'code' (see *Code, Sociolinguistic*); human behavior is essential for its explanation. In Halliday's words the 'system is determined by the process.'

Typical of Halliday, then, is the endeavor to explain the structure of language as a consequence of some dialogue, of which it is in some way an abstraction. As this dialogic process is determined by the exchange of commodities, language is both determined by the nature of the commodity (such as 'goods and services' versus 'information'), and by the rules defined for the commodity exchange (such as 'giving' and 'demanding'). However, this is not a monolithic process: language develops characteristic realizations at its different levels in accordance with what Halliday calls 'congruence patterns.'

Thus, Halliday's theory of language is structured as a system network, where the expression plane is conceived of as manifestations of meanings chosen from a semantic system (the encoded social reality). While the notion of 'choice' is central to Halliday's theory, it should not be mistaken for a conscious act of choosing, but understood as a term referring to the processual nature of the socio-semiotic system of language.

4. Future Work

A great deal of what has been discussed above is often classified as belonging to the domain of 'pragmatic' in linguistics. But if pragmatics is conceived as a superficial attribution to, or even as a 'waste-basket' for the more systematic, and therefore more prestigious, studies of syntax and semantics, this is a misrepresentation (see *Pragmatics and Sociolinguistics*). Among the fundamentally radical views that some of the most important communication-oriented linguists share not least the four 'schools' explicitly mentioned here have inspired, or are still systematically searching for such an alternative. For the linguist who is skeptical about most of the traditional conceptions in linguistics associated with what has been referred to here as 'abstract objectivism,' there exists several research alternatives.

See also: Halliday, Michael Alexander Kirkwood; Bakhtin, Mikhail M.; Voloshinov, Valentin Nikolavic.

Bibliography

Bakhtin M M 1981 *The Dialogic Imagination*. University of Texas Press, Austin, TX
Bourdieu P 1982 *Ce que parler veut dire*. Libraire Arthème Fayard, Paris (1991 *Language and Symbolic Power*. Polity Press, Cambridge, UK)
Ducrot O 1984 *Le dire et le dit*. Les Editions de Minuit, Paris
Gagnepain J 1981 On language and communication. *Language and Communication* **2/3**: 149–54
Habermas J 1984–87 *The Theory of Communicative Action*. Vol. 1. Beacon Press, Boston, MA, Vol. 2, Polity Press, Cambridge, UK
Halliday M A K 1984 Language as code and language as behaviour. In: Fawcett R P, Halliday M A K, Lamb S M, Makkai A (eds.) *The Semiotics of Culture and Language*. Printer, London, Vol. 1
Halliday M A K 1985 *An Introduction to Functional Grammar*. Edward Arnold, London
Köck W K 1980 Autopoesis and communication. In: Benseler F, Heilj P M, Köck W K (eds.) *Autopoesis, Communication and Society*. Campus, Frankfurt, Germany
Linell P 1982 *The Written Language Bias in Linguistics*. Studies in Communication 2. Linköping University, Linköping, Sweden
Martinet A 1964 (trans. Palmer E) *Elements of General Linguistics*. Faber and Faber, London
Reddy M J 1979 The conduit metaphor—A case of frame conflict in our language about language. In: Ortony A (ed.) *Metaphor and Thought*. Cambridge University Press, Cambridge, UK
Rommetveit R 1974 *On Message Structure*. Wiley, London
Ruesch J, Bateson G 1951 *Communication: The Social Matrix of Psychiatry*. Norton, New York
Steiner P (ed.) 1982 *The Prague School. Selected Writings, 1929–46*. University of Texas Press, Austin, TX
Todorov T 1984 (trans. Godzich W) *Mikhail Bakhtin: The Dialogical Principle*. University of Minnesota Press, Minneapolis, MN
Vachek J (ed.) 1964 *A Prague School Reader in Linguistics*. Indiana University Press, Bloomington, IN
Voloshinov V N 1986 *Marxism and the Philosophy of Language*. Harvard University Press, Cambridge, MA
Wertsch J V 1991 *Voices of the Mind*. Harvard University Press, Cambridge, MA

Communicative Competence
A. Duranti

The notion of 'communicative competence' was introduced by Dell Hymes in the late 1960s to express the idea that the ability to speak a language requires more than the knowledge of grammatical rules (Hymes 1972, 1984). Children grow up in the midst of verbal interactions in which they need to pay attention not only to grammatical form (e.g., the order of words and their inflection) but also to the implications, for themselves and other participants, of what is said. To the extent to which linguistic research is concerned with the association between forms and meanings, it should recognize that any linguistic expression is associated with and often reproduces a set of attitudes, values, and beliefs about the world. To be a fluent speaker means to be able to recognize and exploit such attitudes, values, and beliefs. Furthermore, language is often only one of the codes used for communication. Speakers complement, refine, and sometimes neutralize or even contradict the meaning of words they use by relying on gestures and eye gaze, and by the use of tools and other material resources around them. The notion of communicative competence was also meant to encourage the study of different codes and modes of communicating within and across situations. Although the term 'competence' echoes Chomsky's (1965) use of the same word, the addition of the adjective 'communicative' broadens the object of inquiry. Furthermore, while Chomsky's notion of competence refers to an abstract set of (typically unconscious) rules—based on an innate language faculty and independent of actual usuage—Hymes' notion of competence refers to the knowledge necessary for adequately communicating in real-life situations. Hence the attention to what speakers actually do with language that is implicit in the notion of communicative competence is not only a methodological but also a theoretical concern. That is, it not only allows us to start from what people do with language in order to infer what they need to know, but also recognizes that knowledge of language is gained from participation in actual communicative events, implying the simultaneous reliance on a number of semiotic resources and the collaboration of other participants. In this sense, Hymes' notion of competence is not separate from the notion of performance—the use of language—as it is in Chomsky's model.

The introduction of the notion of communicative competence was consistent with Hymes' (1964) earlier call for a new interdisciplinary field, the 'ethnography of communication' (sometimes called the 'ethnography of speaking') (see *Ethnography of Speaking*). This field is dedicated to the empirical study of patterns of speaking in different communities around the world. Theoretically, it draw from a number of traditions, most notably Roman Jakobson's functionalism as represented in his 'speech event' model (Jakobson 1960), from which Hymes derived his notion of 'communicative event,' which is a unit of analysis conceived for the study of communicative competence (see *Ethnography of Speaking*). In this framework, speaker competence is no longer defined exclusively in terms of their knowledge of grammatical rules, but is also defined in terms of the range of communicative events in which they can participate. Such a range defines person's 'repertoire' within a given community.

The term communicative competence is also used in other disciplines by authors such as Habermas (1970), albeit with different theoretical implications from the ones discussed above (see also *Hymes, Dell Hathaway*).

Bibliography

Chomsky N 1965 *Aspects of the Theory of Syntax*. MIT Press, Cambridge, MA

Habermas J 1970 Toward a theory of communicative competence. In: Dreitzel H P (ed.) *Recent Sociology No. 2*. Macmillan, New York, pp. 114–48

Hymes D 1962 The ethnography of speaking. In: Gladwin T, Sturtevant W C (eds.) *Anthropology and Human Behavior*. Anthropological Society of Washington, Washington, DC, pp. 13–53 (Reprinted in Fishman J A 1968. *Readings in the Sociology of Language*. Mouton, The Hague, pp. 99–138)

Hymes D 1964 Introduction: Toward ethnographies of communication. In: Gumperz J J, Hymes D (eds.) *The Ethnography of Communication*. American Anthropologist (Special Issue), Washington, DC, pp. 1–34

Hymes D 1972 On communicative competence. In: Pride J B, Holmes J (eds.) *Sociolinguistics*. Penguin, Harmondsworth, pp. 269–85

Hymes D 1984 *Vers la compétence de communication*. Hatier, Paris

Jakobson R 1960 Closing statement: Linguistics and poetics. In: Sebeok T A (ed.) *Style in Language*. MIT Press, Cambridge, MA, pp. 398–429

Ecology of Language

J. M. Y. Simpson

The 'ecology' of an organism is the set of relationships between that organism and its environment. The term 'ecology of language' was introduced by the Norwegian—American linguist Einar Haugen (see *Haugen, Einar*) to describe the relationships between a variety of language and its surroundings. Such surroundings include geographical entities, human beings, and other varieties of language. The investigation of the ecology of a language therefore deals with such topics as where the language is spoken, by whom it is spoken, and what other varieties of language are spoken in the same region; furthermore, it studies any observable interactions among the language, its speakers, and other languages.

The articles in Section 6 are those most closely concerned with the ecology of language, strictly defined, together with certain of those in Sections 5, 7, and 8. However, it has to be said that almost every article in this Encyclopedia could be regarded as revealing some aspect of the ecology of language.

Bibliography

Haugen E 1972 *The Ecology of Language*. Stanford University Press, Stanford, CA

Language
J. M. Y. Simpson

'Language' has two different yet related meanings, related in that both are concerned with human behavior of a particular kind. The difference in meaning correlates with a grammatical difference, namely whether the word is used as a mass noun ('language') or as a countable noun ('a language'). In this article these two meanings are examined in turn.

1. The Term 'Language'

The mass noun 'language' is in fact used in several ways. It may be used of human behavior on a particular occasion when an individual speaks or writes or signs: he or she may be said to be 'communicating in language.' This ability is often held to be the distinguishing mark of the human race and it makes possible the existence of human society. Such behavior is of course not random but takes place in accordance with a system or, more precisely, with an intricate complex of systems. This particular use of 'language' is central to this Encyclopedia in that every article deals with some aspect of such human behavior and its role in society.

'Language' may also be used to refer to the biological faculty of the human mind which makes the above behavior possible—this is the sense in which it is frequently used in psycholinguistics, one area of which studies the 'language acquisition device' of the human mind which enables an infant to learn how to communicate in language. This is also the sense in which it is used by neurolinguists when they identify 'language areas' of the human brain.

'Language' may also be used to refer to all systems of speaking and writing, as in the sentence 'Human language can talk about an infinite number of topics.' A great amount of effort has gone into the investigation of the properties that characterize all these systems, in other words into the defining properties of human language.

A particular type of speaking or writing felt to be typical of, or appropriate to, a given type of situation may also popularly be called 'language,' as in the phrase 'scientific language.'

In popular usage 'language' is also extended to systems of human communication other than speaking, writing, and signing, as in phrases such as 'body language' and 'the language of gesture.' Computer scientists, logicians, and mathematicians for strictly limited purposes construct notational systems which they call 'languages.' And it is common in some quarters to refer to 'animal language.' None of these systems would be described by linguists as 'language,' on the grounds that they do not possess the defining properties of human language.

2. The Term 'A Language'

The countable noun 'a language' is used to refer to an abstract system underlying the behavior in speech, writing, or signing of an entire community; to put it more simply, 'a language' is regarded as a system of speaking, writing, or signing common to a group of people. Thus French is thought of as 'a language spoken by Frenchmen' or American Sign Language as 'a language used in the USA.' This interpretation of 'a language' is probably the most common in contexts outside linguistics. Unfortunately, it is by no means easy to define what 'a language' might be.

2.1 The Twofold Fallacy of 'A Language'

A common assumption is that languages are separate entities. It is assumed, for example, that Arabic, Dutch, English, French, German, Italian, and Scottish Gaelic are seven 'languages' and this assumption is supported by the facts that teaching-grammars are on sale for all seven and that various educational and political institutions recognize them as 'languages.' Moreover, certain atlases include maps with captions such as 'Languages of the World,' in which the geographical distribution of such 'languages' is indicated by areas of different colors; one block of color does not merge into an adjacent block of a different color: the change between them is quite abrupt (see, for example, *The Times Atlas of the World: Comprehensive Edition*, London 1967, 5th edn. 1975, rev. 1977: Plate 6 'World Mankind, Languages'). Thus it is easy for the layman to assume that languages are distinct from one another (because of such maps) and that each represents a homogeneous system (because of teaching-grammars which reveal this system). However, both parts of this assumption are false.

2.2 Languages Can Merge into One Another

In the first place, some languages do merge into others, unlike the areas of different colors in maps. Dutch and German are held to be two different languages, as has been indicated, and admittedly the comparison of a newspaper written in Standard Dutch with one written in Standard German would seem to bear this out. Yet standard languages are abnormal varieties of language, in the sense that they come into being by deliberate intervention on the part of society; 'on the ground' there is no sharp break between so-called 'Dutch' dialects and so-called 'German' ones.

To take one very simple example: the Standard Dutch form meaning 'I do' is *ik maak* (also found in certain Dutch dialects) and the Standard German is *ich mache* (also found in certain German dialects); but in the dialect of Düsseldorf the form is *ich make*, representing a kind of halfway house between the two other forms. Copious other examples of similar phenomena can be found, affecting not only consonants and vowels but also grammatical features and vocabulary. Indeed it is possible to travel down the River Rhine from an area where a Swiss German dialect is spoken to a Dutch-speaking area on the North Sea without encountering any sharp linguistic break; at the extremes. Swiss German and Dutch are mutually incomprehensible, but it is safe to say that on the Rhine the inhabitants of any one town can understand without difficulty those of the next town upstream and those of the next town downstream. Such an area can be referred to as a 'dialect continuum.' Instead of the two linguistic areas 'German' and 'Dutch' which a simplistic map of languages shows, there is one linguistic area composed of related varieties and in this one area not everyone can understand everyone else.

A very selective set of linguistic features illustrating these gradual linguistic changes met with on a journey down the Rhine are shown in Fig. 1; this illustrates only differences in sounds and it ignores differences in grammar and vocabulary.

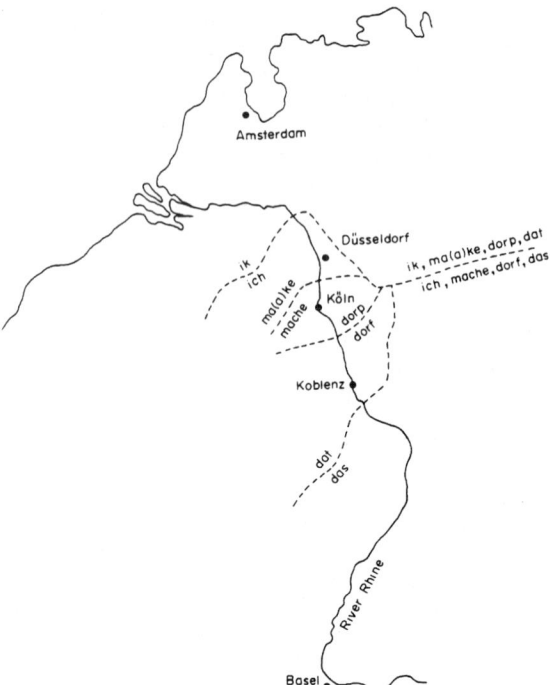

Figure 1. This map illustrates how, along the River Rhine, there is a gradual transition in German–Dutch dialects from an area in the north in which the words for 'I,' 'do,' 'village,' and 'that' are pronounced *ik, ma(a)ke, dorp*, and *dat* to an area in the south in which they are pronounced *ich, mache, dorf*, and *das*.

Such merging of one language into another is not peculiar to German and Dutch. French dialects merge into Italian ones, so that there is another large linguistic area that stretches from Normandy to Sicily; indeed since French dialects also merge into Spanish ones, and Spanish ones into Portuguese ones, this linguistic area must be expanded to include the Iberian peninsula. A similar situation is seen in the gradual transition between dialects of Czech and of Slovak, and of Czech and of Polish; the latter in turn merge into dialects of Belorussian, Ukrainian, and ultimately Russian. A fourth linguistic area of this kind in Europe is that in which dialects of the mainland Scandinavian languages—Danish, Norwegian, and Swedish—are spoken. Dialect continua are by no means a phenomenon peculiar to Europe, another celebrated example is afforded by the Indo-European varieties in Northern India.

To return to the particular case of 'German' and 'Dutch' dialects, there is no reason for considering any one difference between them as being more important that any other and there is therefore no linguistic reason for postulating a boundary where

'German' ends and 'Dutch' begins. Any such division is made on political grounds, between 'dialects spoken in The Netherlands and Belgium' and 'dialects spoken in the Federal Republic of Germany, Austria, Liechtenstein, and Switzerland.'

Allusion was made above to the popular view of *a language* as 'as a system of speaking or writing common to a group of people'; but in the case of each dialect continuum mentioned above no single ystem *is* discernible. It will be apparent that one has no independent, universally applicable linguistic criterion by which one 'language' can be singled out as opposed to another, genetically related, one. Linguistics cannot tell what 'a language' is and so the meaning of what would appear to be one of the basic terms has, so to speak, disappeared. There is no precise definition of *a language* available.

2.3 'A Language' Is Not a Homogeneous System

The second aspect of the above-mentioned fallacy concerning languages was that each represents a homogeneous system. But in fact something that is widely recognized as 'a language' need not be a homogeneous system: Standard English, for example, exhibits all sorts of variations in pronunciation, in grammar, and in vocabulary.

For instance, most Scotsmen will pronounce the word *pay* with a monophthong, a vowel of unchanging quality, whereas Londoners (and indeed the majority of Englishmen) will pronounce it with a diphthong, a vowel of continuously changing quality; to Scottish hearers the Londoner will sound as though he or she were trying to say *pie*. Not only the pronunciation of individual sounds may vary, the number of sounds at the disposal of speakers may be different. American and English speakers make a distinction between *pool* and *pull*, Scottish speakers do not. Conversely, most English speakers do not distinguish between *wail* and *whale*, Scottish speakers do. There are hundreds of such differences in the English-speaking world (Wells 1982) as well as additional differences in intonation patterns and in voice quality.

Differences of grammar within Standard English are fewer, but they exist: for example, Scottish and North American speakers can utter a sentence such as *The cat wants out*; the English version is *The cat wants to go out*. A Scotsman may remark *The woodwork needs painted*, a sentiment that an Englishman renders as *The woodwork needs painting*. In fact, Trudgill and Hannah (1982) devote some 25 pages (out of a total book-length of 130 pages) to grammatical differences between English English and North American English.

Vocabulary differences are much more numerous than differences of grammar. The same word may have a different meaning in two varieties: *homely* (of a person) in British English means 'warm and domesticated in manner or appearance' but in United States English it means 'ugly.' Alternatively, the same item may have different names in different varieties: a British car-owner will have a *silencer* on his vehicle but an American will have a *muffler* on his; an Australian child may ruin his teeth by eating *lollies*, a British one by eating *sweets*. Such differences amount to several hundreds and can lead to confusion.

The last three paragraphs have dealt with regional differences. But differences within English and other 'languages' may correlate with non-regional factors, such as social class, caste, tribe, sex, religion, occupation, or even political allegiance. Moreover, differences in the types of situation in which 'the language' is used (for example, an informal conversation, a formal lecture, a religious ceremony, a news report, a poem), or the role of a speaker or writer in such situations, may impose the selection of particular styles of speaking or writing.

Most importantly, individuals may not always exhibit complete uniformity in speaking (or indeed in writing). They may vary their linguistic behavior according to their partner in conversation (see *Speech Accommodation*) or for reasons that are not immediately discernible.

Variation of the above types seems to be a vital factor in perhaps all instances of human linguistic behavior and the identification of it, the reasons for it, and the implications of it, are a crucial area of sociolinguistic investigation (see the articles in Sections 4 and 5). The study of such variation within 'a language,' though by and large ignored by general linguistics until the 1960s, is now seen to be a vital component in our understanding of how 'language' works.

2.4 'A Language': A Useful Term Nevertheless

The conclusion is that 'a language' is not definable in linguistic theory. No firm boundary can necessarily be drawn between one language and another and one language may contain vast differences of pronunciation, grammar, and vocabulary. The question now arises why the term 'a language' is so widely used and why it is undeniably so useful. There are various answers to this question.

In the first place it may be that a given group of speakers feel that in spite of regional or other differences they all speak 'the same language.' This can be observed in writings by Germans from the earliest period: Otfrid in the ninth century tells us that he is writing 'in German' (his Latin term is *theotisce*, his German phrase *in frenkisga zungun*). In the subsequent history of German, it is never questioned that there is one 'German language,' in spite of extreme dialectal differences. This 'German' includes Plattdeutsch spoken in the north of the country, and 'German' is felt to be something different from Dutch. From the point of view of a descriptive linguist, however, Plattdeutsch resembles Standard Dutch more closely than it does Standard German. In this particular instance, political considerations have underpinned the popular view in modern times. By the same token, tribal affiliations may influence popular judgments on what are different languages.

A second answer is that a given standard language (see *Standardization*) is held to be *the* language and related varieties, which may or may not be intelligible to the speaker of the standard, are held to be dialects of the standard. But again there may be differences of opinion on how close this relationship must be before a variety can be regarded as a dialect of one language or how distant the relationship must be before a variety is regarded as a different language. Sardinian for example, is variously held to be either a dialect of Italian or a language distinct from Italian. On the other hand, Danish, Norwegian, and Swedish are so similar that they could quite easily be held to be three dialects of the same language; however, since Danish and Swedish are standard languages (while Norwegian has two standards), there is never any question of regarding them as anything other than 'languages' in their own right.

A third possible answer is that 'a language' is a convenient label attached by a scholar to name a variety of language in which he or she is interested. He or she may indeed leave the question open whether or not this variety is subsequently to continue to be regarded as one language or a group of related languages.

Teaching grammars that will allegedly teach one to speak and write a 'language' such as 'Arabic,' 'Albanian,' 'French,' and so on in fact purvey abnormally restricted varieties of language with few (if indeed any at all) of the variations noted above. These books do not reflect reality. Nevertheless, they are useful, indeed indispensable, for beginners would find the complexities of native language-behavior quite bewildering. In this connection it is relevant to point out that one does not expect an obvious language-learner to have a native mastery of all the variations in a variety of language and one may, in fact, talk to a learner in a nonnative manner (see *Foreigner Talk*).

It will be obvious that the impossibility of defining 'a language' as a technical term in linguistic theory does not prevent the widespread use of the phrase, especially in popular speaking or writing. But within linguistics, and especially in sociolinguistic investigation, the term tends to be avoided and the neutral description 'variety' or 'variety of language' is used instead.

Bibliography

Bloch B, Trager G L 1942 *Outline of Linguistic Analysis*. Linguistic Society of America/Waverley Press, Baltimore, MD
Hall R A 1968 *An Essay on Language*. Chilton Books, Philadelphia, PA
Hudson R A 1980 *Sociolinguistics*. Cambridge University Press, Cambridge, UK
Keller R E 1961 *German Dialects: Phonology and Morphology with Selected Texts*. Manchester University Press, Manchester, UK
Lyons J 1981 *Language and Linguistics: An Introduction*. Cambridge University Press, Cambridge, UK
O'Donnell W R, Todd L 1980 *Variety in Contemporary English*. Allen and Unwin, London
Robins R H 1979 *General Linguistics: An Introductory Survey*, 3rd edn. Longman, London
Ross A S C 1954 Linguistic class-indicators in present-day English, *Neuphilologische Mitteilungen* **16**: 171–85
Sapir E 1921 *Language*. Harcourt Brace, New York
Trudgill P, Hannah J 1982 *International English: A Guide to Varieties of Standard English*. Edward Arnold, London
Wells J 1982 *Accents of English*, 3 vols. Cambridge University Press, Cambridge, UK

Language as a Social Reality
T. Pateman

A social reality is any causally efficacious system, structure, or mechanism which can exist independently of any particular historical individual, but cannot exist independently of some group of individuals somehow linked together in sustaining or reproducing that reality from day to day (Bhaskar 1979, Durkheim 1982, Giddens 1979). So French is an existing social reality which preexists any infant born into a French-speaking society and which is causally efficacious in bringing it about, all other things being equal, that the infant ends up speaking French. In contrast, Cornish—like every other dead language—is not a social reality. It is not now sustained as a living language by any group of individuals, nor is it causally efficacious in producing any new speakers of Cornish by the usual mechanisms of language development, whatever those are. Cornish is merely an object of linguistic study.

Individuals may sustain (reproduce) a language from day to day without knowing that is what they are doing, or needing to have as a goal or intention that they do it. Someone may use British Sign Language without having the belief or knowledge that they are using it—they may believe no more than that they are signing. Someone may speak English, knowing that they do so, but careless of whether their actions reproduce English in any particular form. Linguistic prescriptivism requires the reflexive monitoring (Giddens 1979) of speech and writing by individuals with the objective of ensuring that a language (their own or, for example, their pupils') is reproduced in some particular, valued form. Because of the tendency to change inherent in all language use, prescriptivism is essential to language maintenance (Pateman 1987). This is very obvious in the case of written forms, but is equally true for spoken ones.

Any discussion of language as a social reality will soon encounter the problem of the identity conditions for a language, which troubled Saussure (1983) and others since. How can the same thing (say, English) be different over time? In all probability I learnt to speak from people who learnt to speak from people who...spoke Anglo–Saxon. Some consequences of language change are catastrophic (in the sense of catastrophe theory): despite the unbroken chain, I do not understand Anglo–Saxon. There is a breakdown of mutual intelligibility. On the other hand, Danish, Norwegian, and Swedish are counted as separate languages despite a high degree of mutual inter-intelligibility (Haugen 1972). Pateman (1987) has put forward the view that languages are best regarded as social facts (realities) which are not linguistic facts, developing Chomsky's distinction between E(xternal) and I(nternal) languages (Chomsky 1986), which is a distinction between languages as a social reality and language as a psychological reality. (For further discussion see Chomsky 2000.)

As already implied, coordination of speakers' actions on a common target language is by no means necessary to successful communication. There are both centrifugal and centripetal forces at work in language learning and language use. Centripetal forces do lead to mutual adjustment towards a regularity which can then become normative as a standard of right and wrong. The emergence of norms in this way is explored in Ullman-Margalit 1977, drawing on the pioneering work by Lewis (1969 though for a critical discussion of Lewis, see Gilbert 1989). Such mechanisms are distinct from, and prior to, conscious planning and prescription.

If French is a social reality and Cornish is not, at least in the required sense, this implies that a language can be described without invoking a social reality for it. This is a necessary condition of the possibility of autonomous linguistics, though not a sufficient condition, since some other kind of reality (e.g., psychological) might still have to be invoked (Katz 1981, 1985.) However, it is arguable that dead and living languages are different in that whilst a dead language can in principle be fully described by a grammar, this is not even in principle possible for a living language. It has been argued that living languages are open-ended and, specifically, never fully conventionalized social realities or fully determinate psychological realities. There is always scope for individuals using 'a language' to create new forms which were not already implicit in social conventions or internal psychological rules. On this view (for which see Croce 1967, Harris 1981, Matthews 1979, Sampson 1979, 1980), there can be true intuitions of grammaticality which do not derive from preexisting rules just as there can, on a view deriving from Kant, be true judgements of beauty which do not derive from rules of beauty (Mothersill 1984, Pateman 1997). Such intuitions are not in the requisite sense obviously social: they may be distributively shared by individuals, but they are not socially derived. This view is anathema to 'strong' social reductionists, such as Bourdieu 1991 and, perhaps, Itkonen 1978. Equally, it raises doubts about the possibility of an autonomous linguistics, this time from the side of individual psychology.

Language is, however, clearly a social reality when its resources—its symbolic powers—are used by speakers in efforts to affect other social realities. So, for example, in hypercorrection language is being used to affect perceived social status relationships and all that then follows from the estimation of those realities. Such phenomena have been studied by both linguists and sociologists, operating within different scientific traditions, exemplified by Labov (1966) and Bourdieu (1991).

See also: Sociology of Language; Representation.

Bibliography

Bhaskar R 1979 *The Possibility of Naturalism*. Harvester Press, Brighton, UK
Bourdieu P 1991 *Language and Symbolic Power*. Polity Press, Cambridge, UK
Chomsky N 1986 *Knowledge of Language: Its Nature, Origin and Use*. Praeger, New York
Chomsky N 2000 *New Horizons in the study of Language and Mind*. Cambridge University Press, Cambridge, UK
Croce B 1967 *Aesthetics as Science of Expression and General Linguistics*. Peter Owen, London
Durkheim E 1982 *The Rules of Sociological Method*. Macmillan, London
Giddens A 1979 *Central Problems in Social Theory*. Macmillan, London
Gilbert M 1989 *On Social Facts*. Routledge, London
Harris R 1981 *The Language Myth*. Duckworth, London
Haugen E 1972 The Scandinavian languages as cultural artifacts. In: *The Ecology of Language*. Stanford University Press, Stanford, CA
Itkonen E 1978 *Grammatical Theory and Metascience*, Benjamins, Amsterdam

Katz J 1981 *Language and Other Abstract Objects*. Blackwell, Oxford, UK
Katz J (ed.) 1985 *Philosophy of Linguistics*. Oxford University Press, Oxford, UK
Labov W 1966 *The Social Stratification of English in New York City*. Center for Applied Linguistics, Washington, DC
Lewis D 1969 *Convention*. Princeton University Press, Princeton, NJ
Matthews P 1979 *Generative Grammar and Linguistic Competence*. George Allen and Unwin, London
Mothersill M 1984 *Beauty Restored*. Oxford University Press, Oxford, UK
Pateman T 1987 *Language in Mind and Language in Society*. Oxford University Press, Oxford, UK
Pateman T 1997 Language, Art and Kant. In: Wolf G, Love N (eds.), *Linguistics Inside Out. Roy Harris and his Critics*. Benjamins, Amsterdam, pp. 226–8
Sampson G 1979 *Liberty and Language*. Oxford University Press, Oxford, UK
Sampson G 1980 *Making Sense*. Oxford University Press, Oxford, UK
Saussure F de 1983 *Course in General Linguistics*. Duckworth, London
Ullman-Margalit E 1977 *The Emergence of Norms*. Oxford University Press, Oxford, UK
Pateman T 1997 Language, Art and Kant. In: Wolf G, Love N (eds.), *Linguistics Inside Out. Roy Harris and his Critics*. Benjamins, Amsterdam, pp. 226–8

Language in Society: Overview
M. L. Apte

It is axiomatic that language is an essential and significant part of the concept of culture and that it enables human beings to form stable social–structural aggregates. While the nature of language has been studied in depth for more than two thousand years going back to the Greeks and Indians and manifesting the results in such remarkable achievements as Pāṇini's Sanskrit grammar, the development of linguistics in the twentieth century has been primarily achieved due to the separation of language from its sociocultural moorings. Yet this very embedding of language in society and culture has been the focus of intense and sustained research efforts since the 1960s.

The aim of this essay is to provide an overview of these theoretical and methodological developments and the resulting insights that have been achieved concerning the multitudinous nature of the relationship of language to society and culture. In this endeavor, the fundamental concepts relevant to the development of sociolinguistic theories will be discussed and the important areas of significant research highlighted.

A crucial aspect of the human sociocultural evolution has been the development of language. While communication occurs among various animal and insect species, human communication is probably the most complex. Human language is evolved to such a degree that for many social scientists it is the sole criterion separating humans from the rest of the animal world (Chomsky 1965). Scholars (Hockett 1960) have systematically tried to delineate those properties of the human communication system that separate it from others.

1. Anthropological and Linguistic Origins

As anthropologists are interested in investigating all aspects of human existence, language is a major topic in their research. It is well-recognized that culture is transmitted over time through language. Linguistics and the study of language were inseparable from anthropological and folklore studies in America before the twentieth century; note, for example, that the founders of the American Folklore Society, American Ethnological Society, and American Anthropological Association were determined to classify Native Americans on the basis of their languages.

In Europe, language was studied as part of logic, rhetoric, and philosophy throughout the ancient and medieval periods. From the beginning of the eighteenth century, linguistic studies became comparative and historical in nature, focusing on the origin and evolution of language. Contemporary European languages were traced to their common ancestor(s) through comparative methods. The discovery that Sanskrit, the classical language of India, was structurally and lexically similar to Greek and Latin, the classical languages of Europe, accelerated this emphasis on historical and comparative linguistics. The study of the Indo–European language family became the most important task and the Indo–European model was used for writing the grammars of non-Indo–European languages.

This situation began to change at the start of the twentieth century. The linguist Ferdinand de Saussure developed revolutionary ideas about the nature of language, and Boas, Sapir, and Bloomfield laid the foundation of modern linguistic science in the USA. The scope of linguistic inquiry was narrowed so that language was studied in and of itself. Language was increasingly seen as a system with a structure.

The objective of linguistics became not only the writing of structural descriptions of as many languages as possible, but also the developing of a universal conceptual and theoretical framework which could be the foundation of language-specific grammars. This orientation led to the development of a universal system for transcribing speech sounds—the International Phonetic Alphabet—and the creation of such universal linguistic concepts as phoneme and morpheme. Structural descriptions of individual languages were presented in terms of phonological, morphological, and syntactic units and their relationships. Sentence was considered the largest, and speech sound the smallest, unit of analysis. Formalism was emphasized because of the so-called scientific perspective of empiricism, and rigorous methodology was developed for systematically eliciting linguistic data while doing fieldwork. Discovery procedures became the basis of fieldwork. The emphasis changed to describing language as spoken rather than as written. Prescriptive attitudes were replaced by descriptive orientation.

The first half of the twentieth century witnessed an extraordinary growth of linguistic theory, the gathering of linguistic data, and structural analyses of diverse and so-called 'exotic,' unwritten languages. Phonological analyses of these unwritten languages were used in adopting the Roman script for writing them.

Although the emergence of generative-transformational theory shifted the emphasis from fieldwork and the earlier conceptual framework based on structuralism, linguistics did not move away from the study of language in isolation. It became even further abstracted, focusing on the linguistic competence of the ideal speaker–listener (Chomsky 1965: 3–4) formalized by way of rule-oriented grammars of languages without considering the linguistic performance of the average language speaker in a sociocultural context.

While both the structuralist and the generative–transformational theories with their focus on language in isolation dominated the field of linguistics in the twentieth century, there had existed a small coterie of influential linguists such as Boas, Sapir, and Whorf who investigated not only the psychological and cognitive aspects of language but also its multitudinous linkages with the rest of the human sociocultural system (Carroll 1956; see *Sapir–Whorf Hypothesis*).

It was not until the 1960s, however, that attention began to be focused on language variation, use, and function, to understand the nature of the relationship between society and culture on the one hand and language on the other. Increasingly language, was being studied as a social and cultural institution. In part, this focus was also a reaction to the isolationist tendencies of generative–transformational linguists. Their emphasis on the abstract nature of language and their focus on the linguistic competence of the ideal speaker–listener meant that there was no room for the individuals' socioculturally influenced linguistic performances in everyday life. Thus began the development of the fields of inquiry that came to be known as sociolinguistics.

Sociolinguistics as a field of inquiry includes all aspects of the relationship between language on the one hand and society and culture on the other. Even psychologically and politically oriented investigations of language have occasionally been subsumed within this field. Such nomenclature as ethnolinguistics, psycholinguistics, language and politics, linguistic anthropology, sociology of language, as and when used, primarily suggest either disciplinary or topical focus within the broad field. Several edited and single author textbooks with titles such as *Sociolinguistics, Introduction to Sociolinguistics* (Gumperz and Hymes 1972, Pride and Holmes 1972, Trudgill 1974a, Mesthrie et al. 2000) present the field with the broadest possible scope.

2. Culture, Meaning, and Context

A study of the relationship of language to culture and society necessitates an understanding of the fundamental concepts of culture, meaning, and context. The most prominent emphasis in sociolinguistic research in recent years has been on developing theories to explain the nature and function of these concepts and their importance in understanding language.

2.1 Culture

There exists a large body of literature in anthropology delineating the concept and various theories of culture (Kroeber and Kluckholm 1952, Keesing 1974, Schneider 1976, Shweder and LeVine 1984). A major theoretical orientation is to consider culture as a system of symbols and meaning (Schneider 1976; Sherzer 1987). Human beings create symbols by which an element, be it an object, action, event, person, etc., is arbitrarily associated with a specific meaning. For Schneider (1976) 'culture places disparate parts of the social system together into a meaningful whole.' Culture is also viewed as a system having a separate and independent existence from that of the individuals who manifest it in their behavior. This view is in some ways comparable to the language/speech (*langue/parole*) dichotomy of Ferdinand de Saussure, who maintained that language (*langue*) was a social institution with an independent existence over and above its acquisition by individuals who manifested it in their speech (*parole*).

Despite a century of efforts to define culture adequately, there is no agreement among anthropologists regarding its nature. This is not surprising, as most basic concepts in a discipline are refined repeatedly as new knowledge, ideas, and paradigms replace old ones (Kuhn 1970). The change in cultural anthropology since the 1960s has primarily been one of a new perspective. Rather than viewing culture as uniform, largely static, holistic, and deterministic, the new orientation is to view culture as complex, varied, and dynamic in nature.

Culture has also been perceived in terms of a model *of* and *for* reality, the underlying assumptions of which motivate human action (Geertz 1973). Individuals internalize this model without necessarily being aware of doing so. There is also an emphasis on formalizing the nature of culture by trying to develop models presumably internalized by individuals and groups. Just as in linguistics considerable research has been devoted to understanding the nature of language acquisition, so research efforts in cultural anthropology have been directed towards understanding how individuals acquire culture and, once acquired, how they retain it, use it, and add to it.

If culture is viewed as a symbolic and meaningful system, certain fundamental questions arise: How can its symbols and meanings be extrapolated? How can they be adequately analyzed and described? By what techniques can meanings and symbols be identified, and what methods can be used towards this objective? What are the ways, if any, of independently verifying constructs of cultural systems that are associated with particular human aggregates as being true? These are important questions for cognitive scientists and anthropologists interested in discovering the role of cognition in cultural investigation, and in endeavoring to answer them they have increasingly focused on language, which combines form and meaning in numerous ways and shapes the natural world for its speakers. The aim, then, is to construct theories of both culture and meaning.

2.2 Meaning

In the development of structural linguistic theory and in its application for writing grammars of individual languages, meaning, however the concept was understood, did not have a central position. Bloomfield's most influential work does include a chapter on meaning (Bloomfield 1933: 139–57), but his theoretical approach is based on the notion that 'The statement of meanings is...the weak point of language-study, and will remain so until human knowledge advances very far beyond its present state.' A similar note of caution pervades later structuralist works. Gleason (1961: 172), for instance, speaks of the 'difficulties...in making clear statements about language on the basis of meaning.' A result of these tendencies was that the study of meaning in language was for a time primarily the concern of linguistic philosophers. This situation changed, however, with the advent of generative–transformational theory; for linguists of this school, an essential part of a grammar of a language was a separate, though integrated, semantic component.

For many researchers, the study of meaning and the study of culture are inseparable. Therefore, there is an increasing focus on including the concept of meaning as part of the cultural and linguistic systems (Basso and Selby 1976). The objective is to understand how cultural encyclopedic knowledge is acquired and expressed by individuals, enabling them to participate in social interactions and to communicate their thoughts, ideas, intentions, motivations, and emotions, and the underlying cultural values and ideologies. There is no single or uniform approach to the study of meaning. Although, traditionally, meaning was considered to be the domain of semantics (Leech 1981), more recently meaning has been the object of multidisciplinary and interdisciplinary research. Philosophy, psychology, linguistics, literary criticism, and anthropology all claim to be interested in studying meaning, though for different purposes and with different orientations.

Extensive research efforts have been aimed at finding answers to such questions as the following: What are the underlying principles of human cognition? Is cultural knowledge systematized and, if so, how is it organized? Do different models of cultural knowledge exist for different kinds of activity, such as talking or doing things? If so, how are they related? Are these models reflected in or represented by language and can they, therefore, be articulated? How do humans formulate their experiences into concepts and what is the nature of the human conceptualization process in its broadest sense? Do the processes of language acquisition and cultural acquisition go hand in hand? How do the conceptual categories labeled by cultural symbols get organized as part of the mental model? How are these categories reflected or represented in language? Are there cultural models of reality as reflected in language and thought?

There is a long tradition in linguistics going back to Boas, Sapir, and Whorf, who concerned themselves in understanding the linkages between language and cognition. This concern received an additional input from psychologists in the 1950s (Brown and Lenneberg 1954, Hoijer 1954).

Human beings' ability to comprehend the meaning of any linguistic communication depends in large part on how their cognitive maps are set up and how they understand the natural and social world around them. The reverse is also true, that is, human beings' ability to understand the natural and social world around them develops through their acquisition of language. Both these processes lead to internalizing encyclopedic cultural knowledge including types of meanings. Meaning is itself a multifaceted and multipurpose concept. Research in semantics has concentrated on lexical and syntactic meaning, while anthropological and sociolinguistic research has focused on the ways in which the meaning of linguistic discourse is influenced and/or shaped by sociocultural factors.

For an average speaker of a language, the most relevant meaning is the referential one whereby s/he grasps the connection between the sound sequence uttered and the human, animal, or inanimate object in the empirical world. However, in semantic studies various types of meanings are recognized, such as conceptual, connotative, social and affective, reflected and collocative, associative, and thematic; Leech (1981: 9–23) refers to these collectively by the phrase 'communicative value.' Interestingly, all these meanings exists in an individual's communicative repertoire and are used in social interaction, though s/he may not always be conscious of them unless her/his attention is drawn to them; metamessages, that is, messages about linguistic messages, are heavily laden with them (Tannen 1990)

Meaning is also presented in terms of: (a) oppositional pairs, such as synonymy and homonymy, denotation and connotation, core and peripheral meaning, lexical and grammatical meaning, abstract and concrete meaning, analytic and synthetic meaning, and referential and metaphorical meaning; and (b) presuppositions underlying any conversational interaction.

2.2.1 Theories of Prototype and Metaphor

In the quest for an understanding of the relationship between meaning and culture, theories of prototype and metaphor have gained considerable saliency. The basis of all cultural and meaning systems is considered to be concept formation. According to prototype theory (Rosch 1976), concepts can best be viewed as prototypes. A 'bird' for example, is not best defined by reference to a set of features that refer to such aspects as wings, egg-laying capacity, two legs, warm-bloodedness, ability to fly, etc., but, rather, by reference to typical instances, so that a prototypical bird is something more like a sparrow or a crow than it is like a turkey, penguin, or ostrich. The whole idea behind this proposition is to find out how people classify objects of various kinds according to what they regard as being typical instances rather than categorizing them by a set of defining features.

A major advantage of prototype theory is the degree of flexibility it allows in understanding how people acquire concepts and use them in their language. Prototype theory predicts that in people's use of language some concepts are necessarily 'fuzzy,' which allows speakers to be creative or to be deliberately ambiguous in their linguistic usage.

Prototype theory can be applied to social situations in which speech occurs. When participants hear a new linguistic item, they generally associate it with the typical context in which it occurs or with the person who uses it. Only a few instances are needed to enable participants to carry out such a task. This is generally the manner in which individuals acquire their competence in the social use of language.

Another major effort to understand the relationship between meaning and culture in the late twentieth century has been through the study of metaphor. While tropes in general have been intensively studied in philosophy and literature, the emphasis, during the second half of the twentieth century has been on understanding how metaphors contribute to the cognitive process and how they constitute the foundation of a culture-specific worldview. The study of Lakoff and Johnson (1980) is a significant contribution in this direction.

Lakoff and Johnson claim that metaphors can never be comprehended independently of their experiential basis; nor can they ever be adequately represented without such a basis. On the basis of extensive linguistic evidence from American English, they demonstrate the following significant aspects of metaphors: (a) metaphors are based on human spatial orientation such as up–down, in–out, and front–back, yet such spatial orientation can lead to the formation of different metaphors across cultures; (b) metaphors are 'ways of viewing events, activities, emotions, ideas, etc., as entities and substances' (p. 25); (c) some metaphors are more basic and dominant than others, and the metaphors which are dominant vary from culture to culture; and (d) metaphors are pervasive in everyday language and thought. The theories of prototype and metaphor described above are illustrative of the current multidisciplinary efforts at developing universal theories of meaning within the context of language and culture (Austin 1962, Basso and Selby 1976, Black 1962, Searle 1969).

2.2.2 Worldview and Linguistic Relativity

In his introduction to the *Handbook of American Indian Languages*, Boas (1911) alluded to the unconscious nature of language proficiency in relation to the rest of the sociocultural system. In their writings, both Sapir (Sapir 1921) and Whorf (Carroll 1956) explored the nature of the relationship between linguistic structure and cultural worldview. They expressed the view that the greater the structural and lexical differences between languages, the more the diversity in the worldview of their speakers. This view became known variously as the linguistic relativity principle and the Sapir–Whorf hypothesis (see *Sapir–Whorf Hypothesis*). This hypothesis is most explicitly stated in Whorf's essay *Science and Linguistics*. Whorf tried to demonstrate the validity of this hypothesis by writing several articles on Hopi, a Native American language, emphasizing how the concept of time was perceived differentially by speakers of Indo–European languages and those of the Hopi language. He also focused on covert grammatical categories which he claimed influenced much of the thinking of language speakers.

Linguistic influence on cognition is, however, at the unconscious level, without the speakers being aware of it. During the enculturation and socialization processes, individuals internalize the ready-made categories available to them by way of lexical items and grammatical structure and learn to relate them to external reality.

Since the early 1950s the Sapir–Whorf hypothesis has been discussed extensively (Hoijer 1954, Schaff 1973) and continues to be tested through experimental studies and through varied interpretations and applications (Kay and Kempton 1984, Lucy and Shweder 1979). Sherzer, for example, has demonstrated by analyzing examples from different cultures that an equally beneficial way to explore language–culture relationships is through discourse which 'creates, recreates, modifies, and fine tunes both culture and language and their intersection' (1987: 296).

A major development related to the Sapir–Whorf hypothesis that occurred in the 1960s was the emergence of the anthropological theory variously known as ethnoscience, ethnosemantics, componential analysis, folk taxonomy, or new ethnography. The fundamental premises of this theory were: (a) semantic domains in a language are systematically structured and this structure is reflected in hierarchical and/or paradigmatic arrangements of lexical items within the semantic domains; (b) such an arrangement of lexical items in semantic domains reflects the speakers' cognitive categorization of the universe; (c) it is possible to discover this arrangement by asking questions of native speakers in systematic and rigorous ways and to present it in a formal way; and (d) such a formal presentation reflects what goes on in the speakers' heads and represents their psychological reality.

Numerous formal analyses of lexical terms in various semantic domains of several languages were carried out. These included kinship, color, disease, animals, pronouns, plants, etc. Among them the domain of color received the most attention. Early studies (Conklin 1955, Ray 1952) demonstrated that the systems of color terminology differed widely and unpredictably in the way the 'color spectrum' was perceived in different languages, thereby supporting the linguistic relativity principle. A study based on laboratory research of more than 40 languages by Berlin and Kay (1969) demonstrated, however, the universality and linear evolution of basic color terms. Berlin and Kay demonstrated that there was a limited universal set of 11 color categories, that identification of color foci was universal, and that there was a historical sequence in which languages acquired additional color terms in increasing their basic color terminology.

Since the Berlin and Kay study, there have been claims and counterclaims regarding the language-specificity versus universality of color cognition and the nature and degree of correlation between color differentiation and terminological color categorization in individual languages (Burgess et al. 1983, Kay and Kempton 1984, Lucy and Shweder 1979).

There appears to be a general agreement among scholars regarding the following points: (a) 'languages differ semantically but not without constraint' and 'linguistic differences may induce non-linguistic cognitive differences but not so absolutely that universal cognitive processes cannot be recovered under appropriate contextual conditions' (Kay and Kempton 1984); and (b) Sapir and Whorf probably overstated their case in emphasizing absolute linguistic determinism and linguistic relativity.

2.3 Context

In sociolinguistic studies context is a key concept for understanding the nature of communication in general. While several levels of context are recognized, the primary distinction appears to be between linguistic versus sociocultural context.

Concerning the linguistic context, the analytical focus is no longer restricted to the unit of the sentence, but has been extended to linguistic texts, including naturally occurring dialogues in everyday social interaction. To participants engaged in social interaction in which language plays a significant part, it is important to know the linguistic context in terms of sequentiality, which permits them to determine the overall coherence of communication. Linguistic context also includes the phonological and grammatical features that is, phonological and prosodic cues, affixes indicating grammatical categories and morpheme classes, word order and concordal affixes, etc., that are essential for producing grammatical and meaningful sentences.

The sociocultural context can be as broad as a speech community or as narrow as an interpersonal interaction. It is varied and includes: social aggregates such as community, group, network, socio-economic class, voluntary association, and neighborhood; cultural factors such as shared knowledge, beliefs, and values; demographic and social factors such as age, sex, education, socioeconomic class, and residence; and regional, ethnic, or national identity. Awareness and/or knowledge of these aspects allows participants to connect the linguistic utterances to empirical and social reality and aids them in comprehending and interpreting the linguistic texts. Therefore, participants always look for such contextual cues, which vary cross-culturally since each culture develops its own contextualization conventions (Gumperz 1982). Depending on the size and cultural complexity of a community, such conventions may also vary intraculturally and in some instances even interpersonally. A primary objective of the studies of language in a sociocultural context is to make the implicit sociocultural knowledge and values explicit, and to discover how various aspects of the nonlinguistic context influence the nature of linguistic communication. Native speakers of a language already possess this knowledge, albeit unconsciously, and it enables them to participate successfully in social and linguistic interaction.

Hymes (1974) discusses three main orientations for those investigating language in its sociocultural context: (a) the social as well as the linguistic; (b) socially realistic linguistics; and (c) socially constituted linguistics. The objective of those with the first orientation is to investigate language in itself, but also as it pertains to education, minority groups, politics of language and so on, in other words, practical uses of language. Scholars of the second orientation are concerned with traditional linguistic problems, such as the nature of linguistic rules and the nature of sound change, and with developing new methodologies which can result in new findings. Scholars of the third orientation are 'concerned with social as well as referential meaning, and with language as part of communicative conduct and social action' (Hymes 1974: 196–7). Hymes contrasts two fundamental approaches based on these orientations, namely, striving toward a theory of grammar as opposed to a theory of language. The structuralist and generative–transformational theoretical schools in linguistics have been concerned primarily with the former, while sociolinguistics has been oriented towards the latter.

An important issue is the extent to which sociolinguistic contexts can be formalized. Lavandera (1988: 5) mentions three important and contrasting positions regarding the problem of formalization: those of, Labov (1972), Hymes (1974), and van Dijk (1977). Labov shares the assumptions regarding formalization inherent in mainstream generative grammar and believes that his own theory regarding variable rules contributes to it. Hymes makes explicit the nature of rules that would be necessary to formalize the communicative competence of speaker–hearer. Van Dijk extends rule formulation to cover many aspects of linguistic and nonlinguistic discourse.

3. Language in Society and Culture

Perhaps the most significant consequence of sociolinguistic studies has been the awareness that language, like other sociocultural elements of human existence, needs to be viewed as having not only structural regularities but also regularities of usage; it has to be a vehicle for conveying not only information in communication but also self-expression in terms of motives, emotions, desires, knowledge, attitudes, and values.

Sociolinguistic research undertaken with the objective of pursuing the sociocultural nature of language has branched out in numerous directions. While it is difficult to demarcate clearly these divergent pursuits because of much overlapping, the sections in the remainder of this essay briefly outline the issues and discuss the relevant concepts and theories that have been proposed for the following recognized subareas of inquiry: (a) cultural patterns of language usage; (b) discourse analysis; (c) conversational analysis; and (d) correlational studies focusing on the relationship between language and social class, language and gender, and language and race.

3.1 Cultural Patterns of Language Use

One of the most important developments in sociolinguistics has been the focus on analyzing communicative competence which implies not only knowledge of language structure, but also cultural knowledge of language usage. The way to understand the nature of individuals' communicative competence in specific cultures is to analyze their linguistic performances in varied social situations and interactions. As sociolinguists and anthropologists have increasingly become interested in discovering how members of a culture know what to say to whom, when, where, and how, they have started concentrating on discovering how cultural knowledge of appropriate language usage is acquired and how specific cultural patterns of language use could be analyzed.

The theoretical model labeled the 'Ethnography of Speaking' (Hymes 1964, 1972, 1974) can be applied for delineating cultural patterns of language usage. The basic units of analysis are speech community, speech event, and speech act. While the first concept has been much discussed, criticized concerning its usefulness, and modified (see *Speech Community*), the concepts of speech event and speech act have been much more central to this model. The focus of this approach is on linguistic performance and its sociocultural constraints, especially its appropriateness as judged by the participants in specific social interaction.

The components of a speech act (Hymes 1964) are: time and place; participants and their backgrounds in terms of age, sex, education, class/caste, residence, and so on; channel, code, topic, message, and cultural norms of interactions and expectations. Such functions of speech act as expressive, directive, referential, contextual, contact, poetic (stylistic), metalinguistic and metacommunicative have been identified. This theoretical model has been revised over a period of several years (Hymes 1972) and now an acronym SPEAKING represents the components of speech acts, that is, setting, participants, ends, act sequences, keys, instrumentalities, norms of interaction, and genres. Several ethnographic studies have been carried out in the last 25 years applying this framework. They present analytical descriptions of culture-specific speech genres in terms of their components, functions, and norms of appropriateness of usage (Bauman and Sherzer 1974, Philipsen and Carbaugh 1986).

The ethnography of speaking framework is etic in nature. Analyses resulting from its application provide insights only into emic patterns of language usage and rule-governed speech behavior. However, the model has not developed into a general theory of the possible relationship among the various components at the universal level. Part of the problem may be that discerning patterns of language usage involves concrete culture-specific ethnographic information with regard to both the nature and the relationships of components and functions. Such ethnographic data and analyses are not amenable to abstraction for universalization, unlike the situation in structural or generative linguistic theory. Speech genres are cultural-specific constructs dependent on linguistic and sociocultural knowledge.

3.2 Discourse Analysis

Discourse analysis (see *Discourse*), though primarily a field of inquiry in linguistics, has now become multidisciplinary in nature and the object of inquiry may mean different things to sociolinguists, anthropologists, psychologists, and computational linguists, especially those interested in artificial intelligence. The main focus in all such investigations is on the linguistic text with varying degrees of sociocultural context taken into consideration. The basic issue, then, is one of demonstrating how extralinguistic knowledge as reflected in cognitive and/or social structures and independent of communication is brought into the speech situation so as to convey the participants' intentions and purposes in linguistic interaction (Brown and Yule 1983, Coulthard 1985, Gumperz 1982, Sherzer 1987).

It is clear that discourse involves both text and context. The focus, therefore, could be on either or both and in this respect it analyzes, like the ethnography of speaking, language usage. A major problem in discourse analysis is the elusive nature of the object of inquiry. Discourse as a linguistic text constantly emerges and re-emerges, is created and recreated in keeping with the appropriate sociocultural context. Although a discourse text may consist of a single sentence, it is generally assumed that it involves a continuous text consisting of several sentences and could be in the nature of a narrative, dialog, discussion, political speech, question–answer sequence, poetry, verbal duel, magical chant, and the like.

Despite the changing nature of discourse, research has indicated that there are some general properties that characterize most linguistic discourse. Primarily, discourse is interactional or transactional in nature, since one of the basic functions of language is to transmit information, be it factual or propositional. Discourse analysis focuses on what the participants in a social situation must know in order to identify and interpret various types of linguistic utterances such as questions, suggestions, requests, and statements. Discourse is also used for negotiating relationships among participants based on their respective roles, for emphasizing group cohesion and solidarity, for opportunities to take a turn in speaking and expressing one's views, for apologizing or face-saving, for beginning or ending social interaction, and so on. Linguistic discourse, then, is the primary tool for social interaction.

Despite the varied functions of linguistic discourse, analysts consider the concepts of 'coherence' and 'relevance' as crucial for the interpretation of any discourse text. Speakers and listeners both depend on linguistic and nonlinguistic contextual assumptions which are necessary to construct their models of the state of affairs and the events that are described in discourse. In humorous discourse, the goal is to make participants aware that the coherence aimed at in the discourse is other than the one they are likely to understand initially. Since such an interpretation does not suit the overall situation, they are forced to look for another kind of coherence and relevance. The linguistic text has to be sufficiently ambiguous for this to happen, and therein lies the creativity aspect of humor (Apte 1987).

3.2.1 Communicative and Discourse Strategies

Strategies used by individuals in any social interaction involving speech are important in understanding the nature of speech acts. Individuals often attempt to manipulate a social situation to their advantage while remaining within the rule-governed cultural norms of appropriateness. The means of speech available to do this are the totality of distinct language varieties, that is, dialects and styles employed in a community and an individual's linguistic repertoire dependent on his/her ability to use varied registers, styles, dialects and languages, code-switching and code-mixing, and linguistic creativity. These strategies often shape the nature of speech events and determine what form a speech act will take, and constitute a legitimate part of linguistic discourse in social life.

Various discourse strategies used by participants constitute a fundamental aspect of any discourse. Analysts attempt to replicate the comprehension process and interpretation strategies of participants in speech interaction. Such an interpretation relies on grammatical knowledge, and linguistic and extra-linguistic presuppositions. Additionally, participants look for coherence and relevance in the linguistic text and, drawing on their knowledge of the world, attempt to interpret utterances in context by drawing inferences. Contextualizing cues are all-important in such interpretation and both the speaker and listener use them, which makes such cues a major part of discourse strategies.

Gumperz (1982) (see *Gumperz, John J.*) has analyzed linguistic discourses in English between native English speakers in England and South Asian immigrants to England, and between White and Afro-American individuals in the US. In these instances, because they speak the same language, the participants assume a common base in terms of cultural knowledge, presuppositions, and strategies, including contextualization cues. However, as Gumperz has demonstrated, the participants have different sets of extralinguistic knowledge, assumptions, and expectations, leading to misinterpretations. It is evident that lack of cultural knowledge, of shared presuppositions, and of appropriate contextualizing cues can result in miscommunication or no communication at all, despite a shared purely linguistic competence. Tannen (1990) has demonstrated the differences in discourse strategies based on sexual identity. In North American culture, men and women are socialized into using different strategies for participation in interpersonal and social conversation.

Code-switching (see *Code-switching: Overview*) and code-mixing are also important discourse strategies. Code-switching, as the term suggests, involves changing a code in the middle of linguistic discourse, that is, switching from one language, dialect, style, or register to another. Such a strategy may be undertaken by a speaker for a variety of reasons and intentions, such as: belief about the appropriateness of a code to a particular domain and/or situation—called situational code switching; for broaching or discussing a specific topic; for reinforcing a message in terms of solidarity; use of a specific code commensurate with the listener's social background; or simply the lack of mastery over a specific code in contrast to another. Such code-switching is quite common among bi- and multilingual speakers, who may have definite notions as to which language is appropriate for particular domains and/or topics. Code-mixing generally results from inadequate code-switching, so that grammatical and lexical features of more than one code, be it a language or dialect, are juxtaposed within a single sentence. The most common code-mixing is of the lexical type.

3.3 Conversational Analysis

The objectives of conversational analysis (see *Conversation Analysis*) are similar to those of discourse analysis except that the focus is on studying the process *per se* without making any *a priori* assumptions about the social and cultural backgrounds of participants. Thus, conversational analysis is strictly linguistic in nature. Most conversational analysis research has focused on naturally occurring actual conversations in social interactions. The primary goal is to identify, describe, and explain the numerous processes through which participants engaged in conversation create joint meanings (Goodwin 1981, Jefferson 1978, Sacks et al. 1974, Schiffrin 1987, 1988, Tannen 1990).

Such concepts as turn-taking, sequentiality, conversational inference, speech routines, dialogic pairs, and opening and closing conversations are fundamental to conversational analysis. Of these, turn-taking has been considered the most crucial and refers to the ways in which conversation is distributed among two or more participants who take turns at speaking. In many routine conversational interactions two contiguously occurring related utterances are commonly found and are called adjacency pairs. For example, such conversational encounters as, greeting–greeting, question–answer, offer–acceptance/rejection, etc., occur frequently in everyday social interactions and constitute fundamental units of conversational analysis.

3.4 Linguistic and Social Variation

One of the primary objectives of sociolinguistic research has been to investigate linguistic variation as it relates to social variation. While dialectological studies have long focused on linguistic variation, such a focus was primarily on geographical variations in individual phonological and grammatical units within a linguistic community. Sociolinguists have been interested in finding out the relationship between language variation and such biosocial factors as age, sex, race, socioeconomic class, occupation, ethnic identity, whether such relationships are systematic and collective rather than idiosyncratic, and whether they are persistent over time. Another related objective is to discover to what extent the social networks of individual speakers, their notions of correct speech, status and prestige, and their motivations and desire of upward mobility influence their speech. In short, the goal is to discover the structure of variation.

Correlational sociolinguistic studies generally select certain phonological, morphological and/or syntactic variables and discover how their variants are socially distributed, that is, which variants of these variables are used by members of groups with differential class, racial, ethnic, sexual, and age backgrounds. One methodological problem is that some social variables are not amenable to clearcut classification. While it is fairly easy to correlate the occurrences of the variants of a linguistic variable to such factors as sex and age which are easy to categorize, it is difficult to relate linguistic variants to such factors as race and ethnicity which are subjective in nature. This is also the case to some extent with social class membership.

While the objectives of correlational studies have been in keeping with the broad scope of sociolinguistic inquiry, the process of developing methodology for such studies has been slow and difficult, especially since the emphasis has been on a quantitative approach due to the importance given to such criteria as exactness, methodological rigor and, verifiability. Several early studies which looked at differences within a linguistic community and linked them to social status did not necessarily use quantitative methodology. However, they drew attention to the fact that intralanguage variation carries with it certain social status and positive as well as negative attitudes and cultural values.

The identification by Geertz (1960) of three different styles in Javanese and of their association with elite, merchant, and peasant groups, and the identification by Ferguson (1959) of diglossia (see *Diglossia*), that is, stable existence of high and low speech varieties, among Arabic, Greek, and Tamil language communities in which speakers did not generally accord the status of language proper to the low varieties, but only to the high ones, are examples of linguistic variation as related to sociocultural factors.

However, since the mid-1960s innovative thinking and new methodological strategies have been developed and used successfully in several studies which demonstrated systematic correlation between linguistic and social variables in certain types of speech events (Labov 1966, 1972, Wolfram 1969, Trudgill 1974b). Such criteria as education, occupation, and income have been used to set up social class categories by applying various scaling techniques. Labov's methods in his study of New York speakers (1966) included anonymous observation, sociolinguistic interviews, and participant observation of social groups and networks, and such linguistic data as word lists, reading style, and samples of careful and casual speech from the most formal to the most informal.

The linguistic variables that sociolinguists interested in correlational studies chose to investigate have been primarily phonological, but grammatical variables have also been studied. One of the earliest studies (Fischer 1958) in fact investigated the occurrence of the variants [ɪŋ] and [ɪn] of the English suffix 'ing' in the speech of young children in a New England community. The results showed their systematic distribution as linked to social and personality factors, formality of the situation, and specific verbs used in particular topics in conversation.

There now exist several correlational studies of linguistic and social variables conducted (see *Sociolinguistic Variation*): among English-speaking populations in the USA, England, and Ireland (see discussion and references in Guy 1988; among French-speaking populations in Canada (Sankoff and Cedergren 1971); and among Persian speakers in Iran (Jahangiri 1980). While there is no unanimity regarding the usefulness of the results of these studies and of their impact on linguistic theory of language change, they have enabled sociolinguists to gain some insights into the origins and nature of changes that languages undergo. The nature of linguistic variation as it relates to sociocultural factors is now much better understood. Additionally, these studies have contributed significantly to the refinement of existing methodology and to the development of new methodological techniques in sociolinguistic studies.

It is now generally accepted that linguistic variation is neither random nor confined to the idiosyncracies of individual speakers. Correlational studies show that individual speakers are aware of positive and/or negative societal attitudes towards particular linguistic features; that they try, consciously or unconsciously, to change their speech patterns to acquire the prestige variants of linguistic variables which are often part of the standard variety of a language. Overt societal prestige is thus generated from the top down.

It has also been evident, however, that factors such as group membership and group solidarity can be countervailing forces whereby the negatively perceived linguistic variants may be maintained by individuals. According to Labov they are maintained because of their covert prestige, in that speakers reject linguistic markers of socially prestigious speech and prefer to maintain linguistic features which identify them with their own social groups.

3.4.1 Language and Gender

Among all the research endeavors into linguistic variation, the question receiving the most attention is perhaps that of the relationship between language and gender (see *Gender and Language*; *Gay Language*). This has been an offshoot of the feminist movement and consequent emphasis on women's studies. While in the past differences between men's and women's speech had been noted by linguists, especially in non-Indo–European languages, such studies did not go beyond the goal of mere structural and lexical description of sex-related linguistic differences. There was little attempt to link them to social structure, behavioral patterns, and cultural values.

Lakoff's study in 1973 was instrumental in changing this situation, and since then numerous studies focusing on women's language have been published. Some have attempted to further verify Lakoff's subjective and impressionistic observations (Crosby and Nyquist 1977, Dubois and Crouch 1976). Others have investigated the causes behind the differences between men's and women's speech, and their conversational strategies, and at least in the USA there has begun a movement to change the nature of what are considered to be sexist expressions. The extent to which the introduction of gender-neutral usages has been influential is reflected in a recent newsletter of the Linguistic Society of America and in publications of the Modern Language Association of America, both of which include guidelines for avoiding sexist language.

Sociolinguistic studies of gender differences demonstrate that men's and women's language is intimately connected to sociocultural patterns which reflect sexual inequality and male dominance in many societies. Men and women are said to grow up in different cultures whereby they develop different communication styles. Until recently, both men and women had accepted this inequality which is generally based on ideal cultural role models for men and women. It is expected that women be modest, submissive, nurturing, and concensus-seeking, while men be aggressive, forthright, dominant, and individualistic. Language differences and conversational strategies of both sexes seem to reflect these cultural values and commensurate behavioral patterns.

Sociolinguistic investigations of the differences in men's and women's communicative styles in North American society (Kramarae 1981, Lakoff 1973, Tannen 1990) seem to suggest that women emphasize indirectness in their speech, say one thing when they mean another, are not forthright in expressing their views, and seem less keen on forcefully expressing themselves in interpersonal interactions or in social situations involving several participants. In conversational strategies, women seem to depend much more on metamessages than do men. A primary cause of miscommunication between men and women in intimate relationships is the lack of understanding about the differences in the conversational strategies used by the sexes (Tannen 1990).

In many societies, cultural values dictate that women do not explicitly refer to or discuss matters relating to sexual activity. They are often constrained from using abusive and/or obscene language or taboo words, and from participating in ritual insults or verbal duels, because such activities may reflect on their moral and sexual character. Additionally, politeness (see *Politeness*) is seen as a positive aspect of women's linguistic and social behavior (Apte 1985: 74–75). In general, then, it appears that there are differential rules for language usage as pertaining to different sexes and that most of the constraints are on women's linguistic performance, which in turn reflects the overall social and political inequality between men and women.

While much of the literature on the relationship between language and gender focuses on English in the context of North American society (Kramarae 1981, Thorne and Henley 1975), there is a growing interest in looking at sexual differences in language structure and use across cultures (Philips et al. 1987). The implications of such studies are that power relations in society are closely linked to both structure and usage of language (see *Power and Language*; *Critical Sociolinguistics*).

3.4.2 Language and Race

In recent years, the concept of 'race' has come under considerable scrutiny in social science research literature, especially in anthropological writings. The general consensus in anthropology is that racial categories as used in the anthropological publications before 1950 represented a purely descriptive taxonomy. It is now well established that the divisions between people of different races are arbitrary, because the genotypical and phenotypical traits on which they are based cannot be neatly differentiated. Despite this state of affairs in the scientific community, the idea of race is very much alive in the popular mind in most societies. The concept of race is often fused with that of ethnic identity, though other factors such as place of origin, cultural background, religion, and language are also aspects of this. Anthropologists, however, have rejected race as an important factor in defining ethnic groups (Fried 1965, Montagu 1964).

In discussing linguistic variation, sociolinguists have faced a real challenge in refuting popular beliefs concerning the linguistic performance of members of different races, namely, that members of particular races are incapable of learning and speaking a language properly. Earlier anthropologists such as Boas and Sapir made it quite clear that the degree of structural complexity of a language had no relationship with the biological and cultural attributes of its speakers. Yet notions of the existence of primitive languages still persist, as do those of racial inferiority in linguistic competence.

Since the 1960s, the major controversy in the sociolinguistic literature concerning the relationship between language and race has focused on the speech of Americans in the USA. While African-American speech was at one time labeled a corrupt dialectal version of standard American English, and African-Americans were assumed to be incapable of learning the standard variety, considerable research has shown that the African-American speech variety, commonly referred to as Black English (BE), Black English Vernacular (BEV), or African-American Vernacular English (AAVE) in the literature, is a distinct speech variety in its own right. It has even been claimed that BEV cannot be treated as a mere dialect of American English, but, rather, should be recognized as a variety of English comparable to such others as Australian, South African, South Asian, or West-Indian English. Another important result of this research is the awareness that not all African-Americans speak in the same way, and that there are linguistic variations among different segments of the African-American population in the USA.

Equally important is the fact that linguistic features in which African-American English, differs from standard English are systematic and persistent (Dillard 1972). It has been argued that part of the problem faced by African-American children in the school environment is the insistence by teachers that only the standard variety be used in classrooms. While many African-Americans are quite proficient at code-switching between the standard and their own speech variety, the resurgence of pride in African-American identity has strengthened the use of African-American speech. It has also been shown that African-American children, adolescents, and young men and women are quite capable of presenting arguments in a logical and rational way using their own speech patterns (Baugh 1983, 1988, Labov 1972).

Language socialization, and prejudicial or positive attitudes towards language often have a significant effect on speech. The study by Heath (1983) (see *Heath, Shirley Brice*) of school children in two communities of White and Black populations in South Carolina showed quite distinct language socialization patterns in each of these culturally different communities. Black children seemed to have an innovative and creative way with words, and a playful attitude towards language; they did not hesitate in experimenting with it. Once the teachers became aware of the differences between Black and White children concerning language socialization patterns, they were able to devise innovative techniques to introduce Black children to mainstream language. That African-Americans have a playful and creative attitude towards language has been amply demonstrated by several studies of speech play among them. They seem to have an extensive repertoire of different ways of talking (Kochman 1972).

The controversy regarding the relationship between language and race is by no means settled, and the view that lack of 'proper' usage of language reflects genetically inferior intellectual ability (Jensen 1969) still persists to some degree in the public mind. However, there is increasing awareness in the population at large of the influence of negative racial stereotyping and prejudice on popular views. There is also a growing realization that linguistic differences are not necessarily reflective of racial differences, but, rather, of economic, political, and sociocultural factors and of differential upbringing (see *Code, Sociolinguistic*).

4. Directions for Future Research

Sociolinguistics is such a vigorously growing field of inquiry that it is difficult to predict the directions in which it will develop. It is safe to say that the more culture-specific and cross-cultural studies focusing on many issues related to linguistic variation, language use, and language function are made available in the future, the greater the potential for developing universal sociolinguistic theories pertaining to the numerous issues discussed in this essay. Judging by the plethora of publications that have emerged since the 1960s, the future of sociolinguistic research seems bright.

See also: Sapir–Whorf Hypothesis; Ethnography of Speaking; Kinship Terminology; Verbal Duel; Sociolinguistic Variation.

Bibliography

Apte M L 1985 *Humor and Laughter: An Anthropological Approach*. Cornell University Press, Ithaca, NY

Apte M L 1987 Introduction. In: Apte M L (ed.) Language and humor. *International Journal of the Sociology of Language* 65

Austin J L 1962 *How to Do Things with Words*. MIT Press, Cambridge, MA

Basso K, Selby H A (eds.) 1976 *Meaning in Anthropology*. University of New Mexico Press, Albuquerque, NM

Baugh J 1983 *Black Street Speech: Its History, Structure and Survival*. University of Texas Press, Austin, TX

Baugh J 1988 Language and race: Some implications for linguistic science. In: Newmeyer J (ed.) *Linguistics: The Cambridge Survey. Vol. 4: Language: The Socio-cultural Context*. Cambridge University Press, Cambridge, UK

Bauman R, Sherzer J (eds.) 1974 *Explorations in the Ethnography of speaking*. Cambridge University Press, Cambridge, UK

Berlin B, Kay P 1969 *Basic Color Terms*. University of California Press, Berkeley, CA

Black M 1962 *Models and Metaphors*. Cornell University Press, Ithaca, NY

Bloomfield L 1933 *Language*. Allen and Unwin, London

Boas F (ed.) 1911 *Handbook of American Indian Languages*. Smithsonian Institute, Washington, DC

Brown G, Yule G 1983 *Discourse Analysis*. Cambridge University Press, Cambridge, UK

Brown R, Lenneberg E H 1954 A study in language and cognition. *Journal of Abnormal and Social Psychology* **49**: 454–62

Burgess D, Kempton W, MacLaury R E 1983 Tarahumara color modifiers: Category structure presaging evolutionary change. *American Ethnologist* **10**: 133–49

Carroll J B (ed.) 1956 *Language, Thought, and Reality: Selected Writings of Benjamin Lee Whorf*. MIT Press, Cambridge, MA

Chomsky N 1965 *Aspects of the Theory of Syntax*. MIT Press, Cambridge, MA

Conklin H A 1955 Hanunoo color categories. *Southwestern Journal of Anthropology*. **1**: 339–44

Coulthard M 1985 *An Introduction to Discourse Analysis*, 2nd edn. Longman, London

Crosby F, Nyquist L 1977 The female register: An empirical study of Lakoff's hypotheses. *Language In Society* **6**: 313–22

Dijk T van 1977 *Text and Context*. Longman, London

Dillard J L 1972 *Black English: Its History and Usage in the United States*. Random House, New York

Dubois B L, Crouch I 1976 The question of tag questions in women's speech: They don't really use more of them, do they? *Language in Society* **4**: 289–94

Fairclough N 1989 *Language and Power*. Longman, London

Ferguson C A 1959 Diglossia. *Word* **15**: 325–40

Fisher J L 1958 Social influence in a choice of a linguistic variant. *Word* **14**: 47–56

Fried M H 1965 A four-letter word that hurts. *Saturday Review* October 2

Geertz C 1960 *The Religion of Java*. Free Press, Glencoe, IL

Geertz C 1973 *The Interpretation of Cultures*. Basic Books, New York

Gleason H A 1961 *An Introduction to Descriptive Linguistics*. Holt, Rinehart and Winston, New York

Goodwin C 1981 *Conversational Organization: Interaction between Speakers and Listeners*. Academic Press, New York

Grice H P 1975 Logic and conversation. In: Cole P, Morgan J L (eds.) *Syntax and Semantics. Vol 3: Speech Acts*. Academic press, New York

Gumperz J J 1982 *Discourse Strategies*. Cambridge University Press, Cambridge, UK

Gumperz J J, Hymes D 1972 *Directions in Sociolinguistics: The Ethnography of Communication*. Holt, Rinehart and Winston, New York

Guy G R 1988 Language and social class. In: Newmeyer F J (ed.) *Linguistics: The Cambridge Survey. Vol. 4: Language: The Socio-cultural Context*. Cambridge University Press, Cambridge, UK

Heath S B 1983 *Ways With Words*. Cambridge University Press, Cambridge, UK

Hockett C F 1960 The origin of speech. *Scientific American* **203**: 89–96

Hoijer H (ed.) 1954 *Language in Culture*. University of Chicago Press, Chicago, IL

Hymes D H 1964 Introduction: Toward ethnographies of communication. *American Anthropologist* **66**(6:2): 1–34

Hymes D H 1972 Models for the interaction of language and social life. In: Gumperz J J, Hymes D H (eds.) *Directions in Sociolinguistics: The Ethnography of Communication*. Holt, Rinehart and Winston, New York

Hymes D H 1974 *Foundations in Sociolinguistics: An Ethnographic Approach*. University of Pennsylvania Press, Philadelphia, PA

Jahangiri N 1980 A sociolinguistic study of Tehrani Persian (Doctoral dissertation, University of London)

Jefferson G 1978 Sequential aspects of storytelling in conversation. In: Schenkein J (ed.) *Studies in the Organization of Conversational Interaction*. Academic Press, New York

Jensen A 1969 How much can we boost IQ and scholastic achievement? *Harvard Educational Review* **39**: 1–123

Kay P, Kempton W 1984 What is the Sapir–Whorf hypothesis? *American Anthropologist* **86**: 65–79

Keesing R 1974 Theories of culture. *Annual Review of Anthropology* **3**: 73–97

Kochman T (ed.) 1972 *Rappin' and Stylin' Out*. University of Illinois Press, Urbana, IL

Kramarae C 1981 *Women and Men Speaking: Frameworks for Analysis*. Newbury House, Rowley, MA

Kroeber A L, Kluckholm C 1952 *Culture: A Critical Review of Concepts and Definitions*. The Museum, Cambridge, MA

Kuhn T 1970 *The Structure of Scientific Revolutions*. University of Chicago Press, Chicago, IL

Labov W 1966 *The Social Stratification of English in New York*. Center for Applied Linguistics, Washington, DC

Labov W 1972 *Sociolinguistic Patterns*. University of Pennsylvania Press, Philadelphia, PA

Labov W (ed.) 1980 *Locating Language in Time and Place*. Academic Press, New York

Lakoff G, Johnson M 1980 *Metaphors We Live By*. University of Chicago Press, Chicago, IL

Lakoff R 1973 Language and woman's place. *Language in Society* **2**: 45–80

Lavandera B R 1988 The study of language in its sociocultural context. In: Newmeyer J (ed.) *Linguistics: The Cambridge Survey. Vol. 4: Language: The Sociocultural Context*. Cambridge University Press, Cambridge, UK

Leech G 1981 *Semantics*, 2nd edn. Penguin Books, Harmondsworth, UK

Lucy J A, Shweder R A 1979 Whorf and his critics: Linguistic and non-linguistic influences on color memory. *American Anthropologist* **81**: 581–615

Montagu A (ed.) 1964 *The Concept of Race*. Free Press, Glencoe, IL

Mesthrie R, Swann J, Deumert A, Leap W 2000 *Introducing Sociolinguistics*. Edinburgh University Press, Edinburgh, UK

Philipsen G, Carbaugh D 1986 A bibliography of fieldwork studies in the ethnography of communication. *Language in Society* **15**: 387–97

Philips S U, Steele S, Tanz C (eds.) 1987 *Language, Gender, and Sex in Comparative Perspective*. Cambridge University Press, Cambridge, UK

Pride J B, Holmes J (eds.) 1972 *Sociolinguistics: Selected Readings*. Penguin Books, Harmondsworth, UK

Ray V F 1952 Techniques and problems in the study of human color perception. *Southwestern Journal of Anthropology* **8**: 251–9

Rosch E 1976 Classification of real-world objects: origins and representation in cognition. In: Erlich P, Tulving E (eds.) *La Memoire Semantique*. Bulletin de Psychologie, Paris

Sacks H, Schegloff E, Jefferson G 1974 A simplest systematics for the organization of turn-taking in conversation. *Language* **50**: 696–735

Sankoff G, Cedergren H 1971 Some results of a sociolinguistic study of Montreal French. In: Darnell R (ed.) *Linguistic Diversity in Canadian Society*. Linguistic Research, Edmonton, AB

Sapir E 1921 Language: *An Introduction to the Study of Speech*. Harcourt Brace. New York

Schaff A 1973 *Language and Cognition*. McGraw-Hill, New York

Schffrin D 1987 *Discourse Markers*. Cambridge University Press, Cambridge, UK

Schffrin D 1988 Conversation analysis. In: Newmeyer F J (ed.) *Linguistics: The Cambridge Survey. Vol. 4:*

Language: The Socio-cultural Context. Cambridge University Press, Cambridge, UK

Schneider D M 1976 Notes toward a theory of culture. In: Basso K, Selby H A (eds.) *Meaning in Anthropology.* University of New Mexico Press, Albuquerque, NM

Searle J R 1969 *Speech Acts: An Essay in the Philosophy of Language.* Cambridge University Press, Cambridge, UK

Sherzer J 1987 A discourse-centered approach to language and culture. *American Anthropologist* **89**: 295–309

Shweder R, LeVine R (eds.) 1984 *Culture Theory: Essays on Mind, Self and Emotion.* Cambridge University Press, Cambridge, UK

Tannen D 1990 *You Just Don't Understand: Women and Men in Conversation.* William Morrow, New York

Thorne B, Henley N (eds.) 1975 *Language and Sex: Difference and Dominance.* Newbury House, Rowley, MA

Trudgill P 1974a *Sociolinguistics: An Introduction to Language and Society*, rev. edn. Pelican Books, Harmondsworth, UK. (4th edn.: 2001).

Trudgill P 1974b *The Social Differentiation of English in Norwich.* Cambridge University Press, Cambridge, UK

Wolfram W 1969 *A Sociolinguistic Description of Detroit Negro Speech.* Center for Applied Linguistics, Washington, DC

Multiculturalism and Language
J. R. Edwards

Focusing upon linguistic and cultural contact means focusing upon group identity. It is this sense of 'groupness'—ethnic or national—and the recognition which both underpins and reflects it that constitute the core of the discussion on multiculturalism, a discourse that is essentially sociopsychological and usually emotionally charged. This can be true from either side of group boundaries: linguistic and cultural continuity, for example, can be both a rallying point for members of a beleaguered minority and an irritant (or worse) for those fearful of social balkanization or fissiparous movements. Multiculturalism is an icon for some, an illusion for others. And language—particularly in its symbolic roles, as well as in those communicative ones that link past to present, that bear culture across generations—is in many instances the centerpiece of the multicultural thrust. During and after language shift, it is certainly possible to maintain cultural distinctiveness and the sense of border that is the heart of group definition. However, this is not a viewpoint likely to be endorsed by people who feel themselves at risk of assimilation, nor can it be denied that continuity of language use is a powerful cultural buttress.

The politics of identity—the skeleton, that is to say, which is fleshed out by cultural and linguistic differences, details and demands—is of special current salience. Our age is one of transition, and transitions are often difficult and painful. In the territories of the former Soviet Union, in the increasing western European federalism, in the killing fields of Africa—but also in the struggles of indigenous peoples in North and South America, in the debates about multicultural accommodations in new-world 'receiving' societies (Canada, Australia, the USA)—we see contexts in flux, identities up for re-negotiation, languages in contact or conflict, 'small' cultures attempting to resist larger ones, and so on. It is true that, in some cases, the 'ethnic' factor in conflict is something of a red herring. The Hutus and the Tutsis of Rwanda essentially share the same culture, religion, and language and, consequently, ethnic difference was not the real nub of the conflict that led to the massacres in 1994. In Africa, Asia and elsewhere, colonialism planted many delayed-action devices, emphasizing and stiffening cultural difference. But even if ethnic or nationalist roots are not, in themselves, causal phenomena (in situations of group friction), their very existence—the fact that they are *there*, the fact that dormant, or even unreal, traditions can be evoked and played upon, the fact that manipulated or selective history can be made to serve current ends—is of considerable importance. In some other cases, matters of language and culture are not only symbolic markers signaling deeper waters, but are more centrally implicated in inter-group conflict. It is not economic deprivation or lack of effective political representation in federal corridors that primarily fuels the sovereignty movement in Quebec—yet its power has come within a hair's breadth of breaking up the country.

Multiculturalism usually implies multilingualism and, at a *de facto* level, they exist in virtually all countries, in very few of which national and state borders are coterminous (see Connor 1978). At a *de jure* level, languages are more often accommodated than are cultures. Still, despite a large number of languages and a small number of states—about 5,000 and 200, respectively—only about a quarter of the world's polities recognize more than one language (and recognition itself rarely implies or reflects equivalent status; see Edwards 1995).

Legislated attention to cultural diversity is rare, and Canada and Australia are virtually alone in having official multicultural policies. The Canadian approach is generally illustrative. Two years after the establishment of linguistic duality (with the Official Languages Act of 1969), a policy of multiculturalism was announced, and an Act was passed in 1988—the aims were, from the first, to assist cultural groups to develop and to contribute to the larger society, and to help them learn either or both of the two official languages. Further elaboration (as found in the Act) stressed the preservation and enhancement of other languages—but this is supposed to coincide with the strengthening of English and French, too, the national commitment to which is reaffirmed. The Canadian policy demonstrates, then, the generalities employed when cultural maintenance or the continuity of non-official languages is under discussion (the Act talks of enhancing the Canadian 'multicultural heritage'), as opposed to the specificity attaching to the status of legally sanctioned varieties. Unsurprisingly, this package has been seen as rather an empty one; more pointedly, the feasibility of *multi*culturalism within a *bi*lingual framework and the depth, therefore, of real government commitment has been questioned. Of course, reactions to official multiculturalism range very widely, from the mistaken notion that it is a spur to ethnic separatism and an impediment to national unity (perhaps, indeed, to the emergence of some eventual, nonhyphenated *Canadian* identity), to the naïve belief that it enshrines and reflects a general tolerance for diversity— evidence for the moral superiority of the Canadian 'mosaic' over the more southerly 'melting pot.'

But the Canadian policy, for all its generality and its possible interpretations, is more broadly significant as an example of political response to diversity. Liberal democracies are of course obliged by deepest principle to consider multicultural realities—but consideration does not imply uniformity of sensitivity or reaction. In the Canadian approach to multiculturalism, an apparent response at the level of the group, the collectivity, is arguably of such a general nature (and, one should add, is so weakly supported, financially and otherwise) that it represents only a tiny course adjustment to the more traditional liberal stance in which rights are seen to inhere in individuals, a stance broadly descriptive of contemporary western society. So, to the reactions already mentioned, we can add two further interpretations of multicultural policy: it represents only politically opportunistic lip-service to the idea of cultural maintenance (a view which could of course be *endorsed* by the cynical assimilationist); or, it is a genuine response to heterogeneity, but one that is unfortunately flawed in its framing and its application. It need hardly be said that these and other stances are not unique to the Canadian context.

The appropriate democratic response to cultural diversity is of course the underlying issue here. Should there be formal multicultural policies at all and, if so, should they enshrine some level of commitment to group rights? What level? And what groups? The literature on multiculturalism and its ramifications—pluralist accommodation, the negotiation of identity, the rights of minorities, the obligations of the liberal state, and so on—has only recently turned to such matters. The turn, however, has been significant, and there is now a concern for 'identity' that extends from literature, to the social and political sciences, to philosophy.

In his treatment of 'identity politics,' Taylor invokes the idea of 'recognition' and, more specifically, the politics of equal recognition as fundamental. But this can shade easily into a politics of group difference, in which the uniqueness of group identity is emphasized. It is this, of course, which adherents claim is at risk of being ignored or, worse, assimilated to some overarching majority (the 'cardinal sin against the ideal of authenticity': Taylor 1994: 38). So we arrive at an interesting juncture: the principle of universal equality is stressed but within that, as it were, arise demands for the recognition of distinctiveness. The demands of general respect, on the one hand, and of particularity, on the other, lead to difficulties:

> The reproach the first makes to the second is just that it violates the principle of nondiscrimination. The reproach the second makes to the first is that it negates identity by forcing people into a homogeneous mold that is untrue to them (Taylor 1994: 43).

Bearing in mind the traditional liberal sense that society ought to ensure individual equality but remain neutral as to the desired contents of lives, but aware of the concerns of cultural collectivities (especially, of course, those under threat from powerful neighbors), Taylor argues for a more 'hospitable' liberalism that departs somewhat from this traditional neutrality, for the idea that cultures should be given some means of self-defense, for at least an initial presumption of equal worth—for something, that is, between a cruel homogenization and an ethnocentric self-immurement.

Kymlicka (1995) has also addressed the matter, arguing that it is within the bounds of liberal democracy to provide groups with the means to ensure their cultural continuity—and, where these groups are specially disadvantaged, this may in turn require special attention, perhaps special rights. In this connection he defends treatment differentiating between indigenous minorities and immigrant groups. Kymlicka (see also 1998) has concerned himself particularly with the Canadian context, suggesting that the multicultural policy is—or could be—an effective instrument. It is interesting (given what I have noted above) that he repeatedly points out that this policy, now to be understood as a vehicle for the provision of group rights, is, after all, no real threat to the *status quo*. Diversity will be subject to reasonable limits, and existing conceptions of rights, freedoms and human dignity will not be overturned.

It is impossible to analyze here the rich detail of these sorts of arguments (or, indeed, to note the criticism they have elicited). But they are the ones we now need, since they confront the underpinnings of multiculturalism and may thus lead to useful generalities applicable across contexts. A great deal of the literature has, for too long, consisted of special pleading for one group or another, under the guise of a broad concern for pluralist accommodation. A more profound assessment of multiculturalism will necessarily involve its linguistic components, and that is why I have emphasized the former in this brief discussion. It is of course possible to attend to language *per se* without much concern for its cultural foundations. But an instrumental approach omits the essence of the matter here: the interweaving of language as a strand in the larger fabric, as part of a broad concern with identity and belonging.

See also: Anthropological Linguistics; Identity and Language; Heritage Languages; Nationalism and Language.

Bibliography

Connor W 1978 A nation is a nation, is a state, is an ethnic group, is ... *Ethnic and Racial Studies* **1**: 377–400
Edwards J 1995 *Multilingualism*. Penguin, London
Kymlicka W 1995 *Multicultural Citizenship*. Clarendon, Oxford, UK
Kymlicka W 1998 *Finding Our Way*. Oxford University Press, Toronto, ON
Taylor C 1994 *Multiculturalism*. Princeton University Press, Princeton, NJ

Pragmatics and Sociolinguistics
J. L. Mey

1. Introduction
1.1 The Origins of Pragmatics

Among pragmaticians, there seems to be no agreement as to how to do pragmatics, nor as to what pragmatics is, nor how to define it, nor even as to what pragmatics is *not* (see Mey 1989). Pragmatics appears to be the first, historically motivated approach towards a societal relevant practice of linguistics. Naturally, such an approach does not originate *ex nihilo*: at least three (and perhaps four) developments, or developmental tendencies, can be distinguished, which together (in unison or in counterpoint) have made pragmatics into what it was in the early 1990s.

1.1.1 The 'Antisyntactic' Tendency

This tendency can be seen as a reaction to the 'syntacticism' of the Chomskyan School of linguistics, whereby all of linguistic science (including phonology and semantics) was supposed to fit into the syntactic framework. Linguists such as George Lakoff and John Robert ('Haj') Ross were the first to protest against this syntactic straitjacket; of the numerous alternative 'frameworks' proposed in the late 1960s (such as 'Generative Semantics'), none was truly pragmatic in orientation. Furthermore, these alternatives were (naturally as well as geographically) limited to North America; they never caught on in Europe.

1.1.2 The 'Social-Critical' Tendency

This tendency had its origin and heyday in Europe (starting independently in the UK, in Germany, and in Scandinavia, and spreading over most of the continent and later also outside, especially to Australia). Characteristic of this tendency is the need for a socially useful science of language, together with a wish to leave the narrow perspectives of the 'single discipline' behind. Not surprisingly, the effects of language on people's lives, especially in situations of unequal societal power, attracted the interest of these early pragmaticians (such as Basil Bernstein in England, or Dieter Wunderlich in (the then West) Germany). The impact of their work was felt throughout the 1970s and far into the 1980s (for more on this topic, especially Bernstein's work, see Sect. 2.6; also see Wunderlich 1970 and *Critical Sociolinguistics*; *Critical Language Awareness*).

1.1.3 The Philosophical Tradition

Originating in the British critical tradition of language investigation (illustrated by names such as Bertrand Russell, Ludwig Wittgenstein, John L. Austin, Gilbert Ryle, and others of the school of 'ordinary language philosophy,' and many more), this tendency was virtually unknown outside the UK until the late 1960s. It was only after the publication of Austin's student John Searle's landmark work *Speech Acts* (1969; see *Speech Act Theory: Overview*) that the first inroads into what later became known as pragmatic territory were made by Chomsky's rebellious students. To their great surprise, they found the region populated and partly cultivated by people such as those mentioned above (to use Geoffrey Leech's colorful image):

> When linguistic pioneers such as Ross and Lakoff staked claim in pragmatics in the late 1960s, they encountered

there an indigenous breed of philosophers of language who had been quietly cultivating the territory for some time. In fact, the more lasting influences on modern pragmatics have been those of philosophers; notably, in recent years, Austin (1962), Searle (1969), and Grice (1975) (Leech 1983: 2).

1.1.4 The Ethnomethodological Tradition

Finally, mention must be made of a 'Johnny-come-lately' (but a rather influential one): the so-called ethnomethodological tradition. In this tradition, the emphasis had always been on communication rather than on grammar; how people got their messages across was considered more important than the ways in which they constructed their sentences, or whether or not their utterances were syntactically correct or logically consistent.

The ethnomethodologists (see *Ethnomethodology*) were clearly, in this respect as in many others, a different breed from the linguists and the philosophers (including those whose main interests had avowedly been 'ordinary' or 'everyday' language). The notion of language as the object of a scientific investigation that will make possible the description, classification, and definition of language phenomena in an abstract way, with the aid of objective correctness criteria (interpreted as providing univocal answers to questions such as whether an utterance is 'in the language' or not, à la Chomsky), is never taken seriously in ethnomethodology. Conversely, most of the linguists of this early period never took the ethnomethodologists and their results, especially in the domain of conversation analysis (see *Conversation Analysis*), seriously either.

Saying that this research tradition came late in the day, relative to the other tendencies, is of course itself a relative assertion-relative, to be exact, to the point of time at which the linguists first started to recognize the ethnomethodologists, their methods, and their results. While the precise 'moment of truth' cannot be established, it seems safe to say that from the mid-1970s, references to ethnomethodological research start turning up in the linguistic literature. By the early 1980s, the ethnomethodologists are firmly ensconced in pragmatics; thus, Levinson devotes roughly a quarter of the entire text of his book *Pragmatics* (1983) to their ideas and techniques (Chap. 6: 'Conversational Structure'). Names such as Harvey Sacks (see *Sacks, Harvey*), Emanuel Schegloff (see *Schlegoff, Emanuel*), and Gail Jefferson became household words in linguistic circles after the publication of their groundbreaking article in the prestigious linguistics journal *Language* in 1974; their style of investigation (often referred to by the nickname of the 'Santa Barbara School') has also been widely adopted in other research environments.

Still, even in the 1990s, many (mostly pure-theory oriented) linguists deplored this intrusion into their discipline by methods that are not strictly linguistically accountable, inasmuch as they derived their proper object from sciences such as ethnology and anthropology.

2. Societal Pragmatics

2.1 Linguistics and Society

The question of societal pragmatics is intimately connected with the relationship between linguistics as a 'pure' science and the practice of linguistics as applied to what people use their language for, to 'what they do with their words.' Traditionally, in linguistics this split reflects itself in the cleavage of the discipline into two major branches that do not seem to speak to each other: *theoretical* linguistics and *applied* linguistics.

Traditionally, too, the former kind of linguistics has carried all the prestige of a 'real' (some would say 'hard') science, whereas the latter was considered the soft underbelly of linguistics, prone to all sorts of outside and irrelevant, because 'extralinguistic,' kinds of influences.

It has been one of the hallmarks of pragmatics, ever since its inception as an independent field of study within linguistics, to want to do away with this split. Pragmatics admonishes the linguistic 'scientists' that they should take the users of language more seriously, as they, after all, provide the bread and butter of linguistic theorizing, and it tells the practical workers in the 'applied' fields of sociolinguistics, such as language teaching, remedial linguistics, and the like (see *Applied Linguistics and Sociolinguistics*), that they need to integrate their practical endeavors toward a better use of language with a theory of language use. However, despite much goodwill, many efforts, and a generally propitious climate for such endeavors, the 'unification' of linguistics is not something that is easily achieved. Pragmatics will probably, for a long time to come, be considered by many linguists not so much a 'science' in its own right as an aspect (albeit a valuable one) of, and a complement (albeit a necessary one) to, traditional linguistics.

The *user* aspect has from the very beginning been the mainstay of pragmatics. Already in the very first mentions of the term (such as by Charles Morris (1938), following earlier work by Charles S. Peirce), the term 'pragmatics' is closely tied to the user of language; pragmatics is thus clearly distinguished from, even opposed to, both syntax and semantics, as isolated disciplines.

However, the users not only had to be discovered they also had to be positioned where they belonged, in their *societal context*, 'context' to be taken here not only as the developmental basis for their activity as language users but as the main conditioning factor that made that activity possible. The question of how people acquire their language turned out to be more of a social than a developmental problem that could only be discussed in a strictly psychological environment (as had been hypothesized earlier). A societal window on language acquisition and language use was opened, and pragmaticists soon found themselves joining hands with sociologists and educationalists that had been working in these areas for many years.

The question naturally arises as to what distinguishes pragmatics from those neighboring disciplines (among which several others could have been mentioned). The answer is that pragmatics focuses on the user and his or her *conditions* of language use. By this is meant not only that the user is considered as being in possession of certain language facilities (either innate, as some have postulated, or acquired, or a combination of both) which have to be developed through a process of individual growth and evolution, but, more specifically, that there are certain societal factors that influence the development and use of language, both in the acquisition stage and in usage itself (see *Bilingualism and Language Acquisition*; *Language Change and Language Acquisition*).

Whereas earlier (according to mainstream, especially faculty psychology) the use of speech was said to develop only if it was stimulated during the so-called psychologically 'sensitive' period, it has become somewhat of a pragmatic tenet that such stimulation is social more than anything else. This entails that the social conditions for language use are 'built in,' so to say, to the very foundation of language acquisition and use; but also, that such conditions are difficult to detect and determine as to their exact effect. The results of linguistic development in very early life only become evident much later, when young people enter the first stages of their formal education by joining the school system.

It is therefore not surprising that some of the earliest research interests of a truly pragmatic nature concentrated precisely on the problems of school environment versus home environment. A positive correlation could be established between children's school performance and their social status; school achievement is in important respects dependent on the learner's earlier development in the home. White middle-class children, as a whole, could be shown to be significantly better school performers than their peers from lower strata of society, that is, from nonwhite and, in general, non-mainstream environments. (The name of Basil Bernstein is inextricably bound up with this important research, even though later workers came to have a more critical view of his conclusions, see below, Sect. 2.6.)

The case of the young person's school achievement is a good illustration of what pragmatics is really about, because it very clearly demonstrates why the pragmatic pattern of thinking originally met with such resistance, and why the earliest impulses to pragmatic research had to come from the outside, so to speak; from the ranks not of linguists, but of educationalists and sociologists. The core of the matter here is that the pragmatic determiners are nearly always totally hidden: one has to postulate them almost without any regard to initial plausibility. Social theory, at least as it was practiced until the mid-1960s, had no explanation to offer for its own statistical results. It was not until the hidden conditions of societal structure and domination were brought out into the open that certain pragmatic features could be identified as important for language use. One of the most crucial of these turned out to be the question of the 'ownership' of cultural goods, and how this ownership was administered through various patterns of 'hegemony' (a term originally due to the Italian Marxist theoretician and linguist Antonio Gramsci), in cultural as in other respects (see *Hegemony*).

The following subsections deal with some of these hidden assumptions by playing some of the characteristic themes, all orchestrated as variations on the main theme: 'Whose language are we speaking, when we use *"our"* language?' (see Mey 1985).

2.2 Language in Education: A Privileged Matter

'Morals are for the rich,' Bertolt Brecht used to say, echoing an earlier saying by Georg Büchner (Woyzeck 1838). With a slight variation on this dictum, it could be said that education is only for those who can afford it. Here, one must consider not only the prohibitively high costs of education in the so-called free enterprise system (at the beginning of the 1990s, tuition costs for US private universities ranged from $14,000 to over $20,000 a year; source: *Daily Northwesterner*, January 10, 1991), but also the affordances having to do with coming from the right social background. The same classes that have established the institutions of higher education have also been material in structuring that education and organizing their curricula; and here one is faced with a self-perpetuating, co-opting system that favors those who are most similar to itself—*par nobis*, as the expression used to be.

One of the requirements for those who aspire to participate in any college or university program is to pass the appropriate tests. Characteristically, these tests are geared to the values of the white, middle-class, male-dominated segments of society; minority students typically do less well on these tests, as is also the case with foreigners. It is not uncommon to observe a foreign student who performs relatively well on the mathematical parts of the GRE (the

'Graduate Record Examination,' a prerequisite to entering graduate school), but who almost fails the verbal part. This alone should induce a healthy skepticism toward the value of such testing as a whole, and draw attention to the part that language plays in devising and administering the test.

At stake here is, among other things, what many educational researchers have dubbed the 'hidden curriculum.' Schools are not only supposed to mediate a professional subject matter through their teaching; equally important are the attitudes and beliefs that are fostered and reinforced through the educational institutions. If one asks what these attitudes are about, one has to go back once more to the question of societal *power*, raised earlier: the prevalent attitudes reflect the attitudes of the powerful segments of society, and are (implicitly or explicitly) geared toward perpetuating the possession of that power among the ruling classes (see Mey 2000: 291–297; *Power and Language*; *Symbolic Power and Language*).

This means, with respect to language, that those people who are able to decide what language can be deemed acceptable, which uses of language should be furthered and encouraged, and which demoted and discouraged, are in a position of power and hence can control the future of whole segments of the population by controlling their actual language behavior.

The classic case of this linguistic *oppression* (as it is called) is that of 'low' versus 'high' prestige dialects of one and the same language, or that of 'pidgin' versus 'standard' languages, where pidgins are considered to be mere deteriorated variants of some higher entity called 'the' language (see *Pidgins and Creoles: An Overview*; *Diglossia*). Gross cases of oppressive linguistic behavior control include the total or partial criminalization of local or vernacular idioms, as in the case of the 'Basque stick' (a punitive device used in the schools of the Basque lands, by which pupils were forced to carry a stick on their outstretched arms as punishment for having used a Basque word or expression, to be relieved only by the next sinner in line; cf. Mey 1985: 27).

In a more profound sense, the question can be asked 'whose language' is the controlling norm and guideline for people's linguistic behavior. This question boils down to asking whose behavior is to be the standard of language use, and what aims such a use should set for itself. Such questions can be answered by referring back to Brecht, as quoted at the beginning of this section. If morals are indeed for the rich, moral behavior is something that one should be able to afford (but, as a rule cannot). However, by appealing to some universally valid laws of justice and equity (which are strictly valid only under idealized circumstances, in a so-called perfect but nowhere existing society of the Utopian kind), the rich are allowed to get away with corruption and embezzlement, while the sheep thief and the poacher are strung up: 'One man can steal a horse and another cannot look over the fence' (cf. Brecht and Dudov 1932).

What is happening here is not only oppression, as defined above; it might also be called linguistic *repression*, a term covering the subtle but ever so pernicious form of social control through language, as characterized above (see Mey 1985: 26; the distinction between 'oppression' and 'suppression' is originally due to Pateman 1980). The concept of repression plays an important role in defining and describing some pragmatic paradoxes that arise in late twentieth-century pedagogical thinking: either the student is considered to be a completely passive receptacle for the ideas and knowledge to be imparted by the teacher—the 'banking' concept, as Freire has aptly called it (e.g., Freire 1973, Freire and Macedo 1987: xvi)—or the students are supposed to be in the possession of exactly those qualifications, as prerequisites to learning, that the teaching is supposed to imbue them with. In either case, the underprivileged student is doomed to come out a loser: either he/she enters the 'rat race' on the ruling classes' premises (and obtains the privilege of membership in the rat club), or he/she never makes it in society, owing to an underprivileged start in life.

2.3 Other Social Contexts

Even though the educational system is perhaps the most obvious instance of the unequal distribution of social privilege, as it reflects itself in and is perpetuated through language, it is by no means the only one. Among the cases of linguistic repression that have attracted most attention are the language of the media (see *Media Language and Communication*) and the medical interview (see *Doctor–Patient Language*; *Medical Language*). In both these cases, hidden presuppositions of the same kind as the ones characterized above are to be found.

The French sociolinguist Michèle Lacoste has, in a thoughtful study (Lacoste 1981), drawn attention to the fact that the doctor-patient interview, despite its obvious usefulness and even necessity, sins gravely by way of linguistic repression. What the physician allows the patient to tell him or her, is not what the patient wants to tell, or is able to tell, but rather what in the institutionalized 'discourse' of the doctor-patient relationship is *pragmatically* possible. That is to say, the pragmatic presuppositions that govern the use of language in this particular case are those that are defined by the social institution of the interview in which the interaction between doctor and patient takes place.

For the patient, talking in this way has nothing to do with expressing oneself or manifesting one's problems; it is more akin to filling out a form with preset categories of questions and answers, or to submitting oneself to a 'multiple choice' type of examination.

In Lacoste's case, an elderly lady is complaining to her doctor about pains in her spleen. However, the doctor denies this, and instead locates the pains in the lady's stomach. When the patient repeatedly and rather indignantly rejects this suggestion on the grounds that it is *her* body, and that she, if anyone, must be familiar with her own pains, the doctor cuts her off abruptly by saying that she does not even know what a spleen is, even less where it is located in the body.

This example shows two things: for one, the mere knowledge of a linguistic expression in medical terminology (such as 'spleen') and the ability to use it correctly are worth nothing, if the pragmatic preconditions for such a use are not met. The old lady's voice is not heard because she does not possess the necessary societal standing and clout to make her understood.

The other point to be made in this connection is that the linguistic repression, which is taking place, has some very dangerous side effects. The powerlessness of the repressed can easily turn into self-incrimination (by which the powerless attribute their lack of societal value to factors such as fate, God's will, their predestined stance in society ('know your place'), their own lack of capability and potential, and so on). Or else it results in resignation, as happens in the case of the old lady, who ends up saying: 'Whatever you say, doctor'—thereby possibly exposing herself to the risk of a faulty diagnosis, with all its concomitant dangers both to herself (as a patient) and to the physician (as the potential target of a malpractice suit). Clearly, what is needed here is some form of technique or strategy aimed at providing appropriate aid to the societally and linguistically repressed; more on this in Sect. 2.6.

Summing up, then, the case of the medical interview is a clear example of institutionalized discourse in which the value of the individual's linguistic expression is measured strictly by the place that he or she has in the system. Only utterances which meet the criteria of the official discourse are allowed, and indeed registered; others are either rejected or construed as symptoms of (physical or mental) illness, lack of knowledge or even intelligence, and in general of dependent or inferior status. Erving Goffman remarks, much to the point (his observation has primarily to do with mental institutions, but applies to all sorts of institutional discourses; see *Discourse*):

> Mental patients can find themselves in a special bind. To get out of the hospital, or to ease their life within it, they must show acceptance of the place accorded them, and the place accorded them is to support the occupational role of those who appear to force this bargain. (Goffman 1961: 386)

2.4 Language and Manipulation

Goffman's 'special bind' is a particularly clear case of what can be called manipulation, understood as making people behave in a certain way without their knowing why, and perhaps even against their best interests and wishes. Most often, the instrument of manipulation is language—hence the notions of linguistic manipulation and *manipulatory language*. The latter can be defined as the successful hiding (also called 'veiling'; see Mey 1985) of societal oppression by means of language (see *Manipulation*).

A case in point is the professional manipulation in psychiatric environments of schizophrenic patients' speech ('schizophrenese') and its classification as a 'nonlanguage,' that is, a symptom (so-called 'schizophasia') rather than a means of communication. To see this, consider the following two analogical cases.

Suppose that a political prisoner complains to his legal counsel about his letters being opened. Such a complaint makes sense in the context; the prisoner may not be successful in stopping the guards' practice of letter opening, but his utterance 'They are opening my mail' is at least taken seriously.

Not so with the psychiatric patient. The same utterance, in a psychiatric institutional context, is registered as a schizophrenic symptom, proving that the person who utters the sentence is duly and properly a resident of the State Hospital. The patient, by complaining about his or her letters being opened, has furnished conclusive proof of the fact that he or she is not normal, hence has no right to complain. So, ironically, and in accordance with Goffman's observation quoted above, the only correct way of complaining is not to complain; which of course is sheer madness, and proves the point of the patient's being committed.

But it is not necessary to go as far as the psychiatric institutions to find examples of linguistic manipulation. Consider the following. Suppose I am looking for a job. I tell myself that I must make a good impression on my potential future employer; I put on my best suit and tie, and go to the interview in the hope that he will 'give me the job.' Now, I may not be so lucky: the employer may tell me that the job has been 'taken'; somebody else 'got it.' That means they 'have no work' for me, and so on and so forth. In this linguistic universe, employers give, and employees take, viz., jobs. Such is our language.

In real life, however, a totally different picture emerges: it is the employer who takes the employee's labor and converts it to his own profit. The employee gives his or her labor power to the employer, in exchange for a salary offered; but there is one big catch: the wages, although they are called 'fair' and are arrived at in 'free' negotiation, represent a form of societal oppression. The employer knows that he must make the employee accept less than the value of his or her labor, or else there would not be any profits. The wages are not the equivalent of a certain amount of work: rather, they represent a period of time during which the employer is entitled to press all the labor out of the employee that he possibly can. Wages express the market relation between labor power as a commodity, and whatever else is bought and sold in the marketplace; hence the wages can be called 'fair' only in the sense that they reproduce the market laws, and not by their equitable representation of a certain amount of work.

In this case, too, the language that people use hides the real state of affairs: and thus people can be manipulated into doing whatever the powerful in society (such as employers and doctors) tell them to do. This is what the case of the medical/psychiatric consultation and the job interview have in common.

Somebody might object and say that the worker is not *obliged* to take the employment: an employee is a free agent, and can refuse the employer's offer, and also give notice at any time. However, the very expression of this idea is again a case of manipulatory language use: since a linguistic relation exists between the two nouns, *employer* and *employee*, being respectively active and passive, one is led to believe that the relation between the two 'bearers' of those names is equally symmetrical. The employer is at one end of the employment relation, the employee at the other, but basically it is the same relationship, only in inverse directions. The employer employs the employee; the employee is employed by the employer. Even the language shows us that this is a fair, symmetrical deal.

However, what the language does not tell, and this is the catch, is which of the two is the powerful one in the relationship. The employer is the one who has the sole right to employ or not to employ. Conversely, for the employee there is no right to be employed, which shows where the true power in this situation lies, despite the superficial linguistic symmetry of the employment relation and its manipulatory potential (see *Manipulation*).

2.5 Wording the World

Researchers have paid much attention to language as a means of 'seeing' the world. In well-known studies, Lakoff and Johnson (1980) and Lakoff (1987) have investigated the importance of metaphor as one way of realizing this 'wording.'

Metaphorical wording is different from the classical, referential view of language according to which words are thought of as 'labeling' things in the 'real' world. Metaphors express a way of conceptualizing, of seeing and understanding one's surroundings; in other words, metaphors contribute to one's *mental* model of the world. Because the metaphors of a language community remain more or less stable across historical stages and dialectal differences, they are of prime importance in securing the continuity, and continued understanding, of language and culture among people.

While one may disagree with some aspects of this view of metaphor, it is certain that understanding the common, metaphorical use of language is essential for an understanding of how people communicate, despite differences in class, culture, and religion, across geographical distances and even across languages. The study of metaphors may thus be one of the keys to solving problems in foreign language understanding and acquisition.

However, the view of metaphor as the only way to understand human cognitive capability is too restrictive. True, metaphors are ways of wording the world. But this wording, in order to obtain the true pragmatic significance that it is usually assigned, should include and respect its own context (see *Context*), because after all, the contexts of people's lives determine what metaphors are available and what their wordings are going to be. An uncritical understanding of metaphor, especially as manifested in a purely descriptive way of dealing with the issue ('Look and describe, but ask no questions') is not only wrong, but downright dangerous from a pragmatic point of view (Mey 1985: 223). And even if our metaphors cannot provide all the answers, pragmatic questions still have to be asked. As an illustration, consider the following.

Lakoff and Johnson routinely assign the female human person to the metaphorical 'low' position, whereas the corresponding 'high' is taken up by the male; this happens about 10 times in the course of one and a half pages (1980: 15–6). Clearly, some explanation has to be found for this curious phenomenon, and it seems reasonable to assume that the authors' particular wording (that is, their choice of metaphors) has a lot to do with the way in which society is structured: men on top, women at the bottom of the 'power pyramid.'

The point here is not to move directly from one 'universe' to another (viz., from the universe of power to the universe of language), but to understand that the way in which people see the world is dependent on the way in which they metaphorically *structure* the world, and that, vice versa, the way in which people see the world as a coherent, metaphorical structure helps them to deal with the world. Put in another way, metaphors are not only ways of solving problems: they may be, and in a deeper sense, ways of *setting* the problems. As Schön remarks, in an important earlier study,

> When we examine the problem-setting stories told by the analysts and practitioners of social policy, it becomes apparent that the framing of problems often depends upon metaphors underlying the stories, which generate problem setting and set the directions of problem solving. (1979: 255)

There is, in other words, a dialectic movement that goes from word to world and from world to word. Neither movement is prior to the other, logically. Ontologically, both movements arise at the same time in the history of human development. In particular, as regards the individual human's development, the child, in acquiring language, is exposed to 'worlding' at the same time as it begins its wording process; one cannot postulate any general, ontological priority of the world as entailing an epistemological or linguistic priority. As Franck and Treichler remark,

> [it can be] argue[d] that language constructs as well as reflects culture. Language thus no longer serves as the transparent vehicle of content or as the simple reflection of reality but itself participates in how that content and reality are formed, apprehended, expressed, and transformed. (1989: 3)

In order to determine what a particular wording is worth, therefore, one has to investigate the conditions of use that are prevalent in the context of the wording. As for metaphors, the question needs to be asked what kind of 'seeing' a metaphor represents, and in what way this 'seeing' affects one's thinking or determines a particular mind-set (for which it was developed in the first place, in all likelihood).

The consequences of this view of wording are that one cannot understand one's interlocutors unless one has a good grasp of their word-and-world context (which includes, but is not limited to, metaphoring). That is, in order to understand another person's wording, the language user has to participate in his or her contexts, to word the world with him or her. Thus, the pragmatic view of language (and, in general, of all societal activity; cf. the quote from Schön (1979) above) demands a 'sympathetic' understanding, as a practice of 'co-wording', in solidarity with the context. To understand an utterance, the language user would ideally have to be able to say it her/himself, in the context of her/his conversational partners—which, after all, is not more than is generally expected of interlocutors in any good conversation. Language-in-use (and in particular, the use of metaphor) is therefore at the same time a necessary instrument of cognition and the expression of that cognition itself. It is a user's language, a user's pragmatic precondition to understanding their context, and to being understood in and through that context (which includes other language users).

2.6 Pragmatics and the Social Struggle

The growing interest in pragmatics as a user-oriented science of language naturally leads to the question of the sense in which pragmatics is *useful* to the users. In particular, given the fact that a sizable portion of the users of any language are 'underprivileged' in their relation to language, and are so, on a deeper level, because of their underprivileged position in society, it seems only reasonable to assume that an insight into the causes of societal underprivilege could trigger a renewed insight into the role of language in social processes, and that, vice versa, a renewed consciousness of language use as the expression of social inequalities could result in what is often called an 'emancipatory' language use.

The first efforts at establishing 'remedial' programs of language training date back to the 1960s, when the so-called 'Head Start' programs endeavored to give underprivileged children from US urban ghettos a chance to keep up with their white, suburban peers by teaching them the extra skills (in particular, language capabilities) that they needed to follow the regular curriculum. The results of these programs, if there were any, usually did not last, because they concentrated on the pure transfer of skills, without any connection to the contexts in which these skills were going to be used, or to the real reasons for the lack of culture and educational privilege: the societal context of the children in question.

The insights that resulted from Basil Bernstein's (1971–90) work with underprivileged children came to serve as guidelines for much of western (European) sociolinguistic and pragmatically inspired research in the 1970s. The terminology that Bernstein developed (in particular, his distinction between an 'elaborated' and a 'restricted' code; see *Code, Sociolinguistic*) was, for a decade or so, dominant in the discourse of emancipatory linguistics (see *Bernstein, Basil*).

Briefly, according to Bernstein, lower-class children, by virtue of their social origin, do not have access to the 'elaborated' linguistic code that is used in schoolteaching. These children, being native speakers of a 'restricted' code, cannot identify with the school language (which simply is not theirs). Therefore, their school achievements stay significantly below those of the other children, who are dealing with the school's 'elaborated' code as a matter of course, since they have been exposed to that code all their lives.

For all its good intentions, Bernstein's solutions to the problem of selective, deficient school instruction did not yield the desired results. For one thing, he focused exclusively on the formal (morphological, syntactic, etc.) aspects of the 'codes', rather than on matters of content and how that content was transmitted. Also, he did not pay explicit attention to the societal background of his codes, except as descriptive scaffolding and motivational support. But on the whole, and from a general sociolinguistic standpoint, one can safely say that Bernstein's notion of the societal context, especially as this concept is manifested in his theory of social stratification, despite all its weaknesses, was significantly more relevant than the class analyses practiced by the majority of his contemporary American and earlier

European colleagues (such 'analyses' mainly consisted in setting up levels of social standing depending on how much money people made, or how often they went to the theater or concert hall, and so on; see Mey 2000: 293–7, *Social Class*).

The question now is whether, in the face of these failed efforts to apply the findings of linguistics to the problems of society, there can be any hopes of practicing pragmatics in the sense of what is so hopefully called 'emancipatory' linguistics.

The answer to that question, of course, depends to a great extent on what is understood by 'emancipation.' If that concept is understood as the elimination of social injustice, as getting rid of the 'bonds' that are inherent in the very word 'emancipation,' then language is not the tool to use. However, if the focus is placed on the *consciousness* of the bondage that is instrumental in creating and maintaining the divisions in society, between haves and have-nots, between rich and poor, between male and female, young and old, and so on, then there are many opportunities for pragmatic linguists to step into the fray and contribute positively to the outcome of the social struggles. The way to do this is for linguists to stay linguists, while orienting themselves toward the pragmatic aspects of their science that is, focusing on the users. The question is thus simply how a 'raised-consciousness' linguistics can contribute to making the users more aware of the language they are using, and in particular, how it can make the underprivileged users 'transcend' the boundaries of their underprivileged ('restricted') use without having them buy into the myths and fantasies of the privileged classes. And vice versa, how the privileged users' consciousness can be raised, so that they no longer consider the privileges of their position as natural and uncontroversial, societally speaking.

Some of the best illustrations of the potential of this (admittedly modest) approach are the results that have been obtained in the 'linguistic war against sexism' that has been going on since at least the 1960s (see *Gender and Language*). Of course, the mere substitution of a combined pronoun such as *he/she* for the supposedly 'generic' *he* (understood as the assertion of '[t]raditional grammars ... that the word *man* functions ... to encompass human beings of both sexes'; Frank and Treichler 1989: 3) does not, in and by itself, change anything in the conditions of society that underprivilege its female members. But if it is true, as McConnell-Ginet says (1989), that 'earlier feminist research has established that *he*, no matter what its user intends, is not unproblematically interpreted as generic, and the consequent shift in the community's beliefs about how *he* is interpreted has influenced what one can intend the pronoun to convey,' then it is also permissible to use this example as one of the areas in which emancipatory linguistics has actually been successful, albeit to a modest degree, that is, by establishing a whole new code for the use of pronouns in English-pronouns that reflect the growing consciousness of women's presence in society, but that at the same time, and with apparent success, change the ways in which society's members (both female and male) speak, write, and think about women, treat women, and interact with women. As examples, compare the growing number of journals that subscribe to guidelines for 'nonsexist' use of language promulgated and adopted by various scientific societies and journals (such as the American Psychological Association, the Modern Language Association of America, the Linguistic Society of America, and their respective journals).

Language, in McConnell-Ginet's words, 'matters so much precisely because so little matter is attached to it; meanings are not given but must be produced and reproduced, negotiated in situated contexts of communication (1989: 49),' that is, between the users of language themselves in their social and communicative relations, in people's *pragmatic* interaction in and through *linguistic* structures.

Bibliography

Bernstein B 1971–90 *Class. Codes and Control*, 4 Vols. Routledge and Kegan Paul, London

Brecht B, Dudov Z 1932 *Kühle Wampe, oder: Wem gehört die Welt?* Präsensfilm, Berlin

Bühler K 1934 *Sprachtheorie*. Fischer, Jena

Frank F W, Treichler P A (eds.) 1989 *Language, Gender, and Professional Writing: Theoretical Approaches and Guidelines for Nonsexist Usage*. The Modern Language Association of America, Commission on the Status of Women in the Profession, New York

Freire P 1973 *Pedagogy of the Oppressed*. Seabury Press, New York

Freire P, Macedo D 1987 *Literacy: Reading the Word and the World*. Routledge and Kegan Paul, London

Goffman E 1961 *Asylums*. Doubleday, Garden City, NY

Lakoff G 1971a On generative semantics. In: Steinberg D D, Jakobovits L A (eds.) *Semantics: An Interdisciplinary Reader in Philosophy, Linguistics, and Psychology*. Cambridge University Press, Cambridge, UK

Lakoff G 1971b Presupposition and relative well-formedness. In: Steinberg D D, Jakobovits L A (eds.) *Semantics: An Interdisciplinary Reader in Philosophy, Linguistics, and Psychology*. Cambridge University Press, Cambridge, UK

Lakoff G 1987 *Women, Fire, and Dangerous Things: What Categories Reveal about the Mind*. University of Chicago Press, Chicago

Lakoff R 1989 The way we were; or, The real truth about generative semantics: A memoir. *Journal of Pragmatics* **13**(6): 939–88

Lakoff G, Johnson M 1980 *Metaphors We Live By*. University of Chicago Press, Chicago

Leech G N 1983 *Principles of Pragmatics*. Longman, London

Levinson S C 1983 *Pragmatics*. Cambridge University Press, Cambridge, UK

McConnell-Ginet S 1989 The sexual (re)production of meaning: A discourse-based theory. In: Frank F W and

Treichler P A (eds.) *Language, Gender, and Professional Writing: Theoretical Approaches and Guidelines for Nonsexist Usage.* The Modern Language Association of America, Commission on the Status of Women in the Profession, New York

Mey J L 1985 *Whose Language? A Study in Linguistic Pragmatics.* John Benjamins, Amsterdam

Mey J L 1989 The end of the Copper Age, or: Pragmatics $12\frac{1}{2}$ years after. *Journal of Pragmatics* **13**(6): 825–32

Mey J L 2000 *Pragmatics: An Introduction*, 2nd edn. Blackwell [1993] Malden, MA and Oxford, UK

Morris C H 1938 *Foundations of the Theory of Signs* (original monograph). Reprinted 1969 In: Neurath O, Carnap R, Morris C (eds.) *Foundations of the Unity of Science Towards an International Encyclopedia of Unified Science,* University of Chicago Press, Chicago, Vol. 1

Pateman T 1980 *Language, Truth and Politics.* Strond, Lewes, UK

Schön D A 1979 Generative metaphor: A perspective on problem-setting in social policy. In: Ortony A (ed.) *Metaphor and Thought.* Cambridge University Press, Cambridge, UK

Searle J R 1969 *Speech Acts: An Essay in the Philosophy of Language.* Cambridge University Press, London

Wunderlich D 1970 Die Rolle der Pragmatik in der Linguistik. *Der Deutschunterricht* **22**(4): 5–41

Prescriptive and Descriptive Grammar
C. Cullen

Linguistics involves both the writing of grammars and the specification of rules. Therefore it is important to distinguish between the descriptive grammars that linguists are interested in and the prescriptive grammars and grammar rules that people may be more familiar with. Many linguistics courses and elementary textbooks such as Fromkin and Rodman (1997) and Lyons (1981) present the distinction early on so that the nonprescriptive nature of linguistic rules can then be assumed.

Linguists write rules and grammars to provide detailed and accurate descriptions of the knowledge that speakers have of their language. Linguists' rules are statements about what people do in the language, not regulations for what they should do. In this sense, the linguist's use of the word 'rule' is rather like the scientist's use of the word 'law.' The Law of Gravity does not say that objects should/must/ought to fall to the ground, but that objects *do* fall to the ground.

As it happens, much of the time, the linguists' descriptive rules do not conflict with any prescriptive conventions. For instance, when a linguist says that an English Noun Phrase can be made up of a Determiner (such as 'the') followed by an adjective (such as 'red' or 'big') followed by a noun (such as 'bus' or 'book'), the description is both accurate—a good reflection of the knowledge of native speakers of the language—and inoffensive. Even the most opinionated prescriptivist will accept that all of the following phrases are grammatical in English: 'the big bus, the big book, the red bus, the red book.'

But in other situations there may be a difference between descriptive output—rules that show the regular patterns of sentences in a language—and prescriptive conventions. In such cases, it is particularly important to realize that the linguist's interest is in description rather than prescription. For instance, in most dialects of English a normal and grammatical response to the question 'Who's that?' would be 'It's me,' and a 'descriptive' rule could be written by the linguist for the structure of 'It's me.' However, a common 'prescriptive' rule would say that 'It's me' is bad English (or ungrammatical, in a popular sense) and should be disallowed. The rule would further prescribe that the correct way in which to answer the question 'Who's that?' is to say 'It's I.'

Prescriptive rules are sometimes taught to people in school, sometimes passed on by other speakers, and sometimes found in writers' manuals containing recommendations for clear expression or correct usage. The origins of prescriptive rules vary: some are based on misleading analogies between the grammar of, for example, English and the grammar of some other (often Classical) language or languages. The prescriptive rule forbidding the sentence 'It's me,' for instance, could be justified by the prescriptivist saying that copula 'is' should be followed by a nominative form, not by an accusative form such as 'me,' on analogy with a rule of Latin. No such rule seems to be genuinely operational in early twenty-first-century English.

Some prescriptive rules are rationalized on logical grounds. A common prescriptive rule forbids double negation, which linguists recognize as a grammatical structure in many dialects, and gives logic as the grounds for the prohibition. 'I didn't do nothing' would be described by a linguist's rule if it was grammatical in the variety being studied. It would be rejected by the prescriptivist, who would say that 'I didn't do nothing' could only be used to mean 'I did something' because 'two negatives make a positive.' Now, it *is* true that in logic two negatives make a positive, but it is *not* true in most varieties of English that 'I didn't do nothing' has always to mean 'I did something.' A linguistic description of English will be based on speakers' knowledge of their language, not on the knowledge of logicians.

The descriptive rules that linguists produce reveal how language is, not just how—because of logic or analogy—it has been agreed it should be. Because the linguists' rules reflect speakers' knowledge, they will vary from the description of one regional or social variety to another. For instance, there will need to be a rule for some varieties of English that describes sequences of modal verbs, as in the sentence 'My daughter may can do that.' For other varieties, sequences of modals do not occur and the descriptive rule will be different. Similarly, 'ain't' will be the grammatical negative occurring in sentences like 'I ain't going home this week' in some varieties of English, while 'I'm not' will be the grammatical form in other varieties.

Having descriptive rules provides recognition of the linguistic equality of all varieties: their shared regularity, their equivalence in patterning. The investigation of social factors which make some varieties better received or more widespread than others is a separate endeavor.

See also: Standardization; Standard English and Education Policy; Verbal Hygiene.

Bibliography

Fromkin V, Rodman R 1997 *An Introduction to Language*, 6th edn. Holt, Rinehart and Winston, New York

Lyons J 1981 *Language and Linguistics: An Introduction*. Cambridge University Press, Cambridge, UK

Role Theory
R. H. Turner

Role theory is often traced back to William Shakespeare's famous lines in *As You like It*:

All the world's a stage,
And all the men and women merely players;
They have their exits and their entrances;
And one man in his time plays many parts ...

Use of the term rests on two complementary commonsense observations. On the one hand, different people, when they find themselves in similar positions, behave and even think and feel similarly. On the other hand, the same individual, when placed in different positions, behaves, and often thinks and feels, differently. Furthermore, each role includes a cluster of expected behaviors—a *gestalt*—so that it is viewed as odd, inconsistent, or wrong when the physician sweeps up his own office, the parson frequents gambling parlors on his day off, or a child takes charge of family finances.

1. Definitions

A social role can be formally defined as: a comprehensive pattern for behavior and attitude; constituting a strategy for coping with a set of recurrent situations; socially identified, more or less clearly, as an entity; subject to being played recognizably by different individuals; supplying a major basis for identifying and placing people in society; and constituting a framework from which meanings are assigned to people's individual actions.

There are many useful ways to classify roles, but an initial distinction can be made among four types.

First are 'basic' roles such as gender and age roles. These are roles that individuals carry with them and are expected to play in almost every situation. They are partial determinants of eligibility to perform many specific roles and of how those more specific roles are to be played. 'Position' or status roles are more specific and are attached to formally designated positions in groups, organizations, and larger formalized social units. They include family roles, occupational roles, political office roles, and roles associated with participation in particular activities such as golfer, surfer, and stamp collector. 'Functional group' roles are behavior patterns that emerge informally in the course of sustained interaction in any group. For example, someone may play the role of leader without any formal group decision; others may play devil's advocate, mediator, or counselor. 'Value' roles are the roles that develop about strongly positively or negatively valued activity, such as the role of hero, saint, group exemplar, murderer, or thief.

Basic roles are embedded in culture so that thinking and acting in terms of them seem automatic, though aspects of them are often written into law for reinforcement. Position roles in social institutions such as the family are culturally defined, often with legal enforcement, while position roles in organizations are defined through some decision process accepted as legitimate for that organization. By contrast, both functional group roles and value roles are quite informal and based on images conveyed in the culture. In the course of sustained group interaction, individuals may wittingly or unwittingly pattern their behavior so as to play a particular role with some consistency. Furthermore, people tend to categorize each other informally, and to interpret each other's behavior and behave toward each other according to the functional group roles. Once people are labeled in value terms, they are expected to continue to behave consistently with the label, so that heroes must live up to their prior achievements and criminals are constantly suspected of more evil doing.

Among the first social scientists to use the concept was the German sociologist, George Simmel. Brought to America, the concept was prominently embodied in four streams of scholarship. Robert E. Park and George Herbert Mead used it in laying the foundations for symbolic interactionism, a school of thought stressing human flexibility and creativeness, and using social interaction as the starting point for understanding larger social systems. Jacob Moreno used the concepts of role and role playing in his psychodrama and sociodrama as a way of making people aware of their own systems of interpersonal relationships, as an opening stage in psychotherapy. Kurt Lewin used the concept role to extend the insights of *Gestalt* psychology to a social psychology that stressed the structure and interrelationship of the social settings that link actors to one another. The most influential formulation of role was that of the anthropologist, Ralph Linton, who saw it as the key to refining the concept of culture so as to acknowledge that not everyone subjected to a common culture shared the same set of understandings.

2. Structural versus Interactional Role Theory

Linton's conception of roles as the sets of norms attached to particular statuses, culturally transmitted to the incumbents and interactants of given roles, accorded well with the behaviorist orientation of the early twentieth century. However, the overly mechanistic and consensual view of roles was challenged from two quarters. Robert Merton (1957) replaced impersonal cultural norms with 'expectations' conveyed by incumbents in the appropriate 'role set.' Like school superintendents who must accommodate their role enactment to the demands of teachers, students, parents, and school board members, role incumbents must deal with the divergent expectations produced by the diverse interests and points of view of a set of closely related other-roles. Because there are several alternate strategies for reconciling these diversities, there is room for considerable variability and innovation in role behavior.

Scholars in the symbolic interactionist tradition, incorporating the idea of role as a *gestalt*, posed a more fundamental challenge to structural versions of role theory. Interactionists argued that in most situations roles are vague and ill-defined, but individuals act as if they were clear-cut. The implicit assumption that roles are real and that people are enacting roles provides the framework within which individuals attempt to interpret each other's behavior and to shape roles for themselves. Interaction is a highly tentative process, crucially hinging on 'role taking'—imaginatively placing oneself in the position of other interactants so as to infer the roles they are playing and how they are playing them—and 'role making'—improvising a role for oneself that enables one to deal with others.

3. Role Differentiation

Whichever approach is taken, fundamental questions that arise are why and how various behaviors and attitudes become differentiated and grouped into roles, how actors are allocated to particular roles, and how roles are actually enacted. The principle that the division of labor becomes more complex, with tasks assigned to more and increasingly specialized roles, as the size of an organization or society increases and as the nature of the tasks becomes more complex, has been abundantly documented. Much less progress has been made, however, in understanding the principles that govern the way that tasks and attitudes are grouped and separated to form roles. Robert F. Bales demonstrated that artificial groups, meeting for several successive sessions, and assigned formal tasks to accomplish, often tended to develop two complementary leader roles. By concentrating on getting the job done, the task or instrumental leader created tensions in the group and had little time for dealing with members' interpersonal problems. If these tensions were not to disrupt group functioning, there had to be a social–emotional or expressive leader, who worked with members to relieve tensions and resolve interpersonal frictions. At one time this observation was proposed as the explanation for the nearly universal pattern of role differentiation in families, between husband as instrumental leader and wife as expressive leader. However, further research suggested that differentiation between instrumental and expressive leadership roles only evolved when group members lacked sufficient incentive for achieving group goals. On this and other grounds, use of Bales's observation to justify traditional family role patterns is discredited.

It has been proposed that the pattern of role differentiation is shaped by considerations of functionality, tenability, and representationality. Functionality refers to a division of labor that minimizes incompatibility of goals and means and conflicts of interest within roles, and accommodates to the differentiations of ability and disposition in the pools from which role incumbents are recruited. Representational differentiation separates and combines elements so as to accentuate value differences and similarities, and is often an overlay on functional differentiation. A role is tenable when there is a tolerable balance between the rewards and costs of playing the role to the incumbents. What role construction is tenable depends upon the power that incumbents bring to the role and what configuration of behavior and attitude harmonizes with incumbents' self conceptions.

4. Role Allocation and Learning

The obverse of role differentiation is role allocation, the 'assignment' of individuals to particular roles. According to a substitutability principle, discordant or ineffectual role relationships often can be resolved alternatively by redifferentiating the roles or by reallocating individuals or categories of individuals among existing roles. When role theory is approached structurally, an important distinction is made between allocation by ascription or achievement. Ascription means that individuals are required to perform certain roles and not others by accident of birth or life stage, according to cultural or legal mandate. Achieved roles are acquired through the individual's own efforts or conduct, and include most roles except gender and age in modern societies.

The interactional approach sees role allocation as the everchanging product of negotiation in interpersonal and intergroup relationships. An important feature of this negotiation is a process of 'altercasting,' of attempting to manipulate situations so as to cast relevant others into those roles that enable individuals to seize the desired roles for themselves. Altercasting on an institutional scale is illustrated by the way in which blind people are coerced into playing a stereotypic blind role in order to receive services from social agencies and to have harmonious dealings with strangers and acquaintances (Scott 1969).

Whether ascribed or achieved, roles must be learned in order to be enacted. Thornton and Nardi (1975) have proposed that learning involves four stages. First is the anticipatory stage, in which one hears or reads about the role or observes a role model, but without directly experiencing the role. Understanding at this stage is superficial, often idealized and unrealistic. It is followed by a stage of formal learning in which the role is learned through attention to rules and regulations, official declarations, and cultural norms. Transition to this stage begins with entry into trade or professional school, apprenticeship, or directly into the role. It typically characterizes the early experience in the role when the individual is guided by formal rules and values. As one gains experience in a role one begins to learn that the role is not generally enacted strictly according to the formal rules, and one learns the role as it is more informally understood by experienced incumbents. In a final stage, the incumbent becomes sufficiently secure in performing the role to begin to develop unique variations on the standard formal and customary informal role. The role is thus modified so as to fit uniquely the personality of the incumbent. Starting from a structural framework, this outline of stages concludes by stressing individual variability, consistent with an interactional approach.

The interactional approach calls attention to the fact that roles are normally learned in pairs or sets. Since role-playing depends upon role-taking significant other-roles, individuals must learn a good deal about these other-roles in order to master their own roles. While the learning of other-roles is usually limited to the anticipatory and formal stages and tends to be biased by the focal role's role-stand-point, individuals are sometimes able, in an emergency or other unusual situation, to assume and play the other-role when it has been abandoned. This process of 'role appropriation' has been observed when a child unexpectedly fills in for a temporarily incapacitated parent.

5. Role Enactment

Most social roles can only be enacted in interaction with relevant other-roles, and the nature of that interaction supplies the role's meaning. An important contribution of structural role theory has been to think of roles as consisting of rights and duties. The tenability of a role depends in large part on the balance between rights and duties, as it relates to the incumbents' relative power in the situation. A role is thought to be legitimate or fair if duties are balanced with rights. However, as interactionists point out, balance is largely in the eye of the beholder.

Seen interactionally, the balancing of rights and duties also means reciprocity, since one role's rights become another role's duties. At the very minimum, implementation of rights in one role requires that other-roles involve a duty not to prevent the focal role incumbent from exercising those rights. But the reciprocity is often much more active, as when the child's right to food and lodging implies an obligation for parents to provide those benefits, and as the employee's right to be paid for working implies the employer's duty to pay the worker. There is also another kind of reciprocity, in that what the focal role provides for the other should be in reasonable balance with what the other-role provides for the focal role. Thus 'exchange theory' and role theory come together at this point. It is a major proposition of role theory that discontent, inter-role friction, poor role performance, and disruptions of the role system result from incumbents' conviction that relationships are unfair because of an absence of reciprocity or balance in any of these respects. Again, interactio-nists caution that judgments, that contributions are not equivalent and feelings of unfairness are often the consequence rather than the cause of disenchantment in role relationships.

Roles can be enacted with varying degrees of 'role adequacy,' and people tend to be evaluated within an organization and as persons on the basis of the adequacy with which they perform their roles. Besides personal skills and ability and disposition or motivation, role adequacy depends upon opportunity and resources. Role adequacy is also affected by 'intra-role conflict,' the presence of relatively incompatible expectations inherent in the role. Such incompatibility may be a consequence of the role set (as already discussed) or of an incompatible combination of tasks, as in the role of teacher who must be both educator and disciplinarian in a neighborhood of unruly children.

A further obstacle to adequate role performance can be 'inter-role conflict.' Role conflict refers to the experience of incompatible obligations from two or more of a person's roles. An example would be a minister of a church whose religious responsibility is to accept a very modest salary gratefully, but who, as a father, feels obligated to secure the best education for his children that money can buy. Role conflict can be a fairly moderate or quite intense experience, depending upon how deeply and equally committed the individual is to the roles involved and how irrevocable the consequences of a particular decision may be. For example, conflict between a business trip and a meeting of one's monthly bridge group is usually resolved with a minimum of stress by opting for the business trip because commitment to the occupational role is much stronger than commitment to the bridge group, and because consequences of missing the bridge group occasionally are not serious or irrevocable. By contrast, commitment to family roles such as parent, husband or wife, son or daughter, and brother or sister, is usually high. Nevertheless, in daily life, conflicts involving family roles are often resolved without great stress by temporarily setting aside family commitments because the effects are minor and temporary, and there are abundant opportunities to compensate. But when the life, safety, or health of a family member is at stake so that the consequences of failing to carry out one's responsibilities could be severe and irrevocable, the experience of role conflict will be intense unless the conflicting role is easily set aside.

Two quite different kinds of inter-role conflict are 'role value conflict' and 'role overload.' Value conflict is the more serious because it means that the more adequately the individual performs one role, the more he or she is dishonored in terms of the other role. But with the growing multiplicity of roles people play in modern societies, much more research has been devoted to role overload—the simple problem of not having enough time to perform all of one's responsibilities or of being unable to be in two places at the same time.

The term 'role strain' is sometimes used to describe the state of personal stress in the role-conflicted individual (Goode 1960), or the person who is unable to perform an allocated role adequately, according to his or her own standards, for any of the reasons reviewed. The ways in which people try to resolve role strain will be quite different, depending upon whether the cause of role strain is role conflict, inability to perform a task, or some other condition.

There are several ways to deal with role conflict. One way is 'role abandonment,' that is, opting for the responsibilities of one role and neglecting the responsibilities of the other. But abandonment can be permanent or temporary. The executive whose business trips conflict with bridge club meetings may resign from the bridge club, or the volunteer firefighter whose emergency duties too often conflict with family or occupational responsibilities may resign from the volunteer fire brigade. More often role abandonment is attempted as a one-time solution. But such one-time abandonment usually carries penalties or at least requires assurances of more serious commitment to the abandoned role in the future. For example, the father who is absent on his daughter's birthday because of a business trip will be expected to bring home a special gift and treat his daughter to some special entertainment as a 'peace offering' on his return.

When commitment to both roles is high, people often try to resolve role conflict either by contriving to perform both roles in some way, or by performing only part of their responsibilities to each role. For example, one may attempt to attend two conflicting meetings, leaving one early and getting to the other late. Or one might try to perform the responsibility that could be completed in less time first, before taking up the more time-consuming responsibility. Needless to say, this approach is often counterproductive, with the result that both roles are performed poorly, if at all. Still another resolution might be called double role abandonment. Early research showed that workers who were pressured by their employers to hold one opinion (employee role) and by their union officials to hold a different opinion (union member role) often lost interest in the issue entirely. Whatever resolution is chosen, the stress of severe role conflict can affect concentration, motivation, and attitude toward the roles in question.

While the association of role overload with stress in modern societies had long been accepted as proved, Samuel Sieber (1974) challenged the necessary connection between multiple roles and role stress. According to a principle of 'role accumulation,' benefits (rights) often accumulate faster than duties when one assumes additional roles. One can often combine the duties of two or more roles into a single act, or use the benefits gained from one role as resources to help meet obligations of another role. This reasoning also led to questioning the common assumption that women who attempted to combine homemaker and professional roles suffered exceptional role strain. Several studies have now shown that levels of satisfaction are often higher among women who combine these two roles than among women who are involved in either homemaking or career exclusively. Specific outcomes are clearly affected by whether the single or dual role is a matter of personal choice or not and other variables not yet fully explored. Likewise, there is still much to be learned about the conditions that determine whether multiple roles will intensify role strain or lead to a rewarding role accumulation.

6. Organizational Roles

Most position roles are units in the division of labor by which some organization or institution functions. Consequently the content and arrangement of roles reflect the goals of the organization or institution. To insure that this is the case, organizations vest certain roles with the authority of 'legitimate role definers,' whose incumbents can change the organizational role structure and evaluate role performance in the organization. In order to minimize disruptive 'role ambiguities,' intrarole conflicts, and other role related threats to organizational functioning, highly formal descriptions of roles and their interrelationships are typically evolved. However, even in such rigidly formalized organizations as the military and police, incumbents of each organizational role develop their own shared informal role definitions. These informal roles incorporate practices which the role incumbents agree upon (informally) as the appropriate way to enact the role. They provide a role that is either more functional, more tenable, or more acceptable representationally than the formal role. They fill in remaining ambiguities in the formal role; for example, police must not use excessive force in making arrests, and police officers look to their peers to help define what is and is not acceptable force. They indicate which aspects of the role should contribute most to the incumbents' sense of self-fulfillment. They take account of compromises that must be made on pragmatic grounds, but which are unlikely to be admitted publicly in formal role descriptions.

Whether the informal role fosters the goals of the organization or undermines them depends upon the functionaries' degree of enthusiasm for organizational goals and their relationships toward organizational authorities. For example, the common practice of factory employees evolving their own standard of what constitutes a good day's work and informally sanctioning both under- and overachievers may be either a hostile slowdown of production or a means for keeping production at an optimum level consistent with maintaining worker well-being.

While role ambiguities and intrarole conflicts are generally considered to be damaging to organizational functioning, there is evidence to suggest that this is not always the case. For one thing, overly specific role statements may impair needed flexibility to deal with the unforeseen. For another, some ambiguity and intrarole conflict can serve as a challenge, making role performance more interesting to the incumbent and encouraging innovations that may improve organizational functioning.

7. Roles in Society

The role that one plays and the adequacy with which it is played largely determine one's standing in an organization. For most roles there is little carryover of standing from one organization to another. But the implications of one's basic roles and value roles usually transcend any particular organizational setting. In addition, some highly valued position roles, such as one's profession, supply an important basis for standing in the society and not merely in the workplace.

Every society provides for certain situational or temporary roles that serve to exempt incumbents from normal responsibilities in most of their roles. Best known among these is the sick role. Talcott Parsons identified the sick role as a set of balanced rights and duties. When suitably certified as sufficiently ill—normally by a physician in modern societies but in other ways in other societies—role incumbents are temporarily relieved from many responsibilities in their occupational, family, community, and even friend roles and are entitled to be treated compassionately, provided that they are seriously cooperating with their physician and others in an effort to recover from the illness. The concept of how ill one must be and the criteria by which one is certified as ill, along with the kind of ministrations expected from family and friends and the range of responsibilities from which one is relieved vary greatly among different cultures and subcultures. Bereavement is another universally accepted exempting role. Other roles such as the drunken role and the stress role have their culturally specific configurations and are recognized as exempting roles under some circumstances in some cultures.

8. Role and Person

Because each individual plays different roles in different situations and at different life stages, and because people generally know each other by the roles they have an opportunity to see them play, the question for individuals and for those who know them is: who is the real person beneath the various role facades? Often people must play roles with which they would not want to be personally identified, and even more often, they are concerned that the person revealed through a single role will be mistaken for their whole person. Under these circumstances, people often engage in 'role distancing' by feigning detachment from the roles they are playing or making light of their role performance.

For those behavioral scientists who believe there is a 'person' behind the various roles, it has been proposed that each individual's role repertoire is organized into a hierarchy of salience. The individual's self-conception is built around the most salient roles. The hierarchy is partly determined by cultural selection of 'master roles,' such as one's occupation in the USA and one's family roles in more traditional societies. But it also varies uniquely from individual to individual, based on one's personal socialization experience. The most salient roles are those to which the individual is most committed, and which the individual should perform most conscientiously. For the salient roles there is a process of role–person merger, indicated by a tendency to continue playing the role even in situations where it is not called for, to resist giving up the role even in exchange for a more advantageous role, and internalization of attitudes and beliefs appropriate to the role.

Role–person merger is caused in part by how others view one and is governed by an 'appearance' principle, that in the absence of contradictory cues people tend to accept each other as they appear to be; an 'effect' principle, that the greater the effect of one's particular role on others, the more they conceive one as the person revealed in that role; and a 'consistency' principle, that one is identified as a person on the basis of observed behavioral consistencies between situations. In spite of a 'consensus' principle, that we tend to see ourselves as others see us, individuals are also active in shaping their self-conceptions by emphasizing roles they play best and with greatest autonomy, and by identifying most strongly with roles in which they have invested the most effort, creativeness, and personal sacrifice.

Situational compartmentalization is the most important tactic by which people handle the variety of roles they play during a given span of time. However, the life course is characterized by a great many 'role transitions,' when people give up one role to take on another. These transitions, from only child to sibling, from single to married, to parenthood, to empty nest, from dependent child to self-supporting adult, through occupational promotions and demotions, to retirement, and many others, can take place smoothly or with much stress. Transitions to roles with less favorable privileges-to-obligations ratios, such as divorce, widowhood, unemployment, and often retirement are inherently stressful. In most other transitions the stress is attendant on mastering and being accepted in the new role, so the stress level reflects the degree of difference between the old and new role and, inversely, the social support from the role set in the new role. In some instances, the stress is less in acquiring a new role than in divesting oneself of the old role. Helen Ebaugh (1988) has examined the difficult experience of former nuns, formerly married persons, former convicts, and former alcoholics, who continue to be known as exnuns, exconvicts, divorcees, widows, and exalcoholics while attempting to assume new roles for themselves.

9. Role Change

Historic changes in gender roles, age roles, family roles, occupational roles, and others have been extensively documented and analyzed. Roles may divide like an amoeba, or coalesce; new roles may be created or old ones die out. Research, however, has mostly dealt with changes in the content of continuing roles. The impetus for change usually comes from broader cultural change in values connected with the focal role; social structural changes that modify demand for the services provided by the role, the availability of resources, or social support for performance of the role; or the size and personal qualifications of the pool of potential recruits to the role. These changes can work indirectly through modifying the role's supporting network or by inducing change in other-roles that are part of the role set, or directly by creating role–person misfit. If these conditions are not relieved by reallocation or by negotiating idiosyncratic roles for the misfits, they contribute to either dysfunctionality, untenability, or inappropriate representationality in the role.

Whether the impetus for change will lead to negotiated change in the role depends upon the costs of alternatives, structural autonomy of the role, unity and mobilization of role incumbents, mobilized client demand for services that the revised role would render, cultural credibility of the changed role pattern, and institutional support for change. If the role change would encroach on the rights and duties of other roles, active resistance and conflict can be expected, depending upon the costs of the change to the encroached and their unity and mobilization in resisting change, and on the scarcity and monopolizability of skills held by the focal role incumbents and the role's support structure. If enough of these conditions are sufficiently unfavorable for change, the outcome can be resignation. But if the balance is favorable, changes in the focal role and accommodating changes in the role set should follow.

10. Conclusion

Linguistically, social roles are among the most important nouns, naming the categories of persons who participate in language. From the perspective of the sociologists, all kinship terms (see *Kinship Terminology*) such as *mother, father,* or *cousin* name roles. But the lexicon of roles is vast, including for example professional roles (*doctor, judge*), positions in sports (*quarterback, coach*) and nonfamily personal relationships (*leader, lover*). Indeed, to the sociologist any term that identifies a position in a social system can be understood as the name of a role.

One can speak of a grammar of roles, because every role exists in relation to other roles and each particular relationship entails expectations concerning how role incumbents will communicate. A leader is expected to speak authoritatively, while a follower is expected to cheer the leader's words. A judge pronounces judgments. A quarterback calls plays but listens to the advice of the coach. A doctor gives diagnoses and prescriptions. Lovers share intimate words that must not be uttered in public. As researchers pay increasing attention to the linguistic variations that exist within a speech community, they will be well advised to examine the effect of role playing upon language.

As we have seen, most roles can be assigned to one of four categories: basic roles, position or status roles, functional group roles, and value roles. Structuralist analysis emphasizes the consensual character of norms that define roles, while symbolic interactionists describe a more tentative process in which roles are taken and made. Sociologists of both schools have examined how behaviors and attitudes coalesce to form differentiated roles, and they also study how roles are allocated to individuals, learned by them, and enacted reciprocally with other roles. Of special interest to sociolinguistics, organizations vest certain roles with the authority to define and transform other roles. Throughout life, individuals play a variety of roles, more or less adequately, managing role transitions, changes, and communications with others concerning the genuine person who wears all the masks. Language is the medium through which roles are created, and each role in turn shapes the language of the person who plays it.

See also: Social Psychology; Sociology of Language; Register; Ethnography of Speaking.

Bibliography

Allen V L, van de Vliert E 1984 *Role Transitions*. Plenum, New York
Biddle B J 1979 *Role Theory: Expectations, Identities, and Behaviors*. Academic Press, New York
Ebaugh H R F 1988 *Becoming an EX: The Process of Role Exit*. University of Chicago Press, Chicago, IL
Goode W J 1960 A Theory of role strain. *American Sociological Review* **25**: 483–96
Heiss J 1981 Social Roles. In: Rosenberg M, Turner R H (eds.) *Social Psychology: Sociological Perspectives*. Basic, New York
Kahn R L, Wolfe D M, Quinn R P, Snoek J D 1964 *Organizational Stress: Studies in Role Conflict and Ambiguity*. Wiley, New York
Merton R M 1957 The role set. *British Journal of Sociology* **8**: 106–20
Scott R A 1969 *The Making of Blind Men*. Russell Sage Foundation, New York
Sieber S 1974 Toward a theory of role accumulation. *American Sociological Review* **39**: 567–78
Thornton R, Nardi P M 1975 The dynamics of role acquisition. *American Journal of Sociology* **80**(4): 870–85
Turner R H 1990 Role change. *Annual Review of Sociology* **16**: 87–110
Zurcher L A 1983 *Social Roles: Conformity, Conflict, and Creativity*. Sage, Beverly Hills, CA

Sapir–Whorf Hypothesis
O. Werner

1. Statement of the Hypothesis

The relationship between language and culture, or language and world view, has been noted at least since Wilhelm von Humboldt (1836). But discussion remained relatively dormant until the 'Golden Age of Native American Indian Linguistics' in the first half of the twentieth century.

Although everyone calls it the Sapir–Whorf hypothesis, its most persistent proponent was Whorf (Carroll 1956; see also *Whorf, Benjamin Lee*). And yet, perhaps surprisingly, the most popular formulation comes from Sapir (see *Sapir, Edward*).

1.1 Sapir's, or the Lexical, Version

Sapir never sought the interface between language and culture anywhere but in the lexicon. The quote below is used most commonly to characterize the Sapir–Whorf hypothesis:

> Human beings do not live in the objective world alone...but are very much at the mercy of the particular language which has become the medium of expression for their society. The worlds in which different societies live are distinct worlds, not merely the same world with different *labels* attached.
>
> (Sapir in Mandelbaum 1963: 162, emphasis added)

A similar statement stressing the classificatory or categorizing nature of language is expressed in even stronger terms by Whorf (though this quote is seldom used to characterize the hypothesis):

> We dissect nature along lines laid down by our native languages. The categories and types that we isolate from the world of phenomena we do not find there because they stare every observer in the face...
>
> (Whorf in Carroll 1956: 213)

Both quotes emphasize the words or lexical resources of a language. That is, both stress that while nature is continuous human beings cut nature into discrete categories and each culture does this cutting somewhat differently. People make up words or concepts in order to talk about their world or cultural universe.

This version of the Sapir–Whorf hypothesis is one of two alternatives. It is called the lexical version in this article. While one could ascribe the 'anomaly' that the hypothesis is usually characterized by the first, or Sapir's quote to some historical accident, there seem to exist deeper reasons that will soon become apparent.

1.2 Whorf's, or the Grammatical, Version

The view expressed by Whorf in the second quote (above) is relatively unusual. He searched for the interface between language and culture beyond the vocabulary (or the lexicon) and sought to discover the roots of cultural regularities in a language's grammar:

> ...the grammar of Hopi bore a relation to Hopi culture, and the grammar of European tongues to our own 'Western' or 'European' culture.
>
> (Whorf 1939: 73)

(The Hopi Indians live in villages in Arizona and speak a language of the Uto–Aztecan language family), and:

> By 'habitual thought' and 'thought world' I mean more than simply language, i.e., than the language patterns themselves.
>
> (Whorf in Carroll 1956: 147)

(following the usage of the times one can equate 'language patterns' with grammar), and again:

> ...the background linguistic system (in other words the grammar) of each language is not merely a reproducing instrument for voicing ideas but rather is itself the shaper of ideas, the program and guide for the individual's mental activity, for his analysis of impression, for his synthesis of his mental stock in trade.
>
> (Whorf in Carroll 1956: 212)

Finally, in the statements in which Whorf gives the Sapir–Whorf hypothesis its alternate name, he again sees the relationship of language and culture in grammar.

> ...the 'linguistic relativity principle,' which means, in informal terms, that users of markedly different grammars are pointed in different evaluations of externally similar acts of observations, and hence are not equivalent as observers but must arrive at somewhat different views of the world.
>
> (Whorf in Carroll 1956: 221)

These quotes represent the second way of interpreting the Sapir–Whorf hypothesis—the grammatical version.

1.3 Discussion

The two versions of the Sapir–Whorf hypothesis or the 'linguistic relativity principle,' namely, the lexical version, espoused by Edward Sapir, and the grammatical, the predominant view of Benjamin Lee Whorf, have created considerable mischief in the profession. The reasons for the confusion lie in the different definitions of language used by anthropologists and linguists.

To anthropologists it was self-evident that the lexical resources of a language are part of that language. Therefore, the anthropological definition of language, at least implicitly, consists of phonology, grammar (syntax), *and* the lexicon.

The definition of language used by linguists explicitly excludes the lexicon. To this day linguists tend to give the lexicon short shrift. The science of linguistics considers only the structured parts of language amenable to analysis. One can easily detect pattern (i.e., structure) in phonology and in grammar (syntax). The lexicon was perceived as a 'collection of idiosyncratic features' (Gleason 1962), therefore not amenable to scientific analysis, and therefore outside of linguistics proper and, in the end, outside of what linguists considered to be language (perhaps best stated as 'language is what linguists do'). H. A. Gleason summarizes this view: 'lexicography is something that cannot be done but must be done.'

Several conferences about the hypothesis in the 1950s (Hoijer 1954, Hymes 1960, McQuown 1960) remained strangely inconclusive, largely because participating anthropologists and linguists operated with a basic misunderstanding about the nature of language. These conferences demonstrated vividly Kuhn's (1970) notion that discussions between members subscribing to two different scientific paradigms (views of the world) are always inconclusive. The irony of these discussions is that they are about language and world view, though Kuhn (1970) demonstrates that all world view disputes are hampered by the same sounding words used with different senses (e.g., 'language' as used by linguists versus anthropologists).

The Sapirean formulation of the hypothesis gained wide acceptance. The influence of grammar on world view was difficult to demonstrate. Whorf's exotic interpretations of Hopi thought were often attributed to his imaginative native consultant (Carl F. Voegelin, personal communication). (Most of Voegelin's later work, with Florence M. Voegelin, dealt with the Hopi Indian language and culture, e.g., Voegelin and Voegelin 1957.)

Meanwhile the basic linguistic attitude changed from an orientation that 'every language must be described in its own terms' (the structuralist paradigm) to a preoccupation with language universals ushered in by Chomsky's transformational/generative revolution in linguistics. Suddenly all languages looked very similar.

Many more or less serious statements were made to this effect. Robert E. Lees is credited with asserting that 'all languages are dialects of English.' A few years later James McCawley 'corrected' Lee's assertion by declaring that 'all languages are dialects of Japanese.' McCawley's remark was prompted by the surface structure of Japanese which appeared to be very close to a universal, hypothetical deep structure valid for all languages.

The interdependence of a culture and the lexicon that speakers associate with that culture to talk about their experiences seems almost obvious—especially to anthropologists. The validity of the hypothesis was, of course, of much greater interest to anthropologists than to linguists and found, concurrent with the Chomskyan revolution but independent of it, expression in the New Ethnography (Sect. 3).

In 1970 Oswald Werner demonstrated that the contribution of grammar to world view can only take place through grammatical categories. However, grammatical categories are, in the prevailing theories of linguistics, inherently part of the lexicon—specifically of lexical entries. In transformationalist theories of language these lexical entries are in the semantic component of the grammar of specific languages. Each entry of the form (C, P) has a conceptual part C—a representation of the 'meaning'—and a phonological part P—representing directions for pronouncing the entry. Therefore, the 'linguistic relativity principle' becomes an investigation of the relationship between a culture and its associated lexicon—including grammatical categories.

It may be useful to recapitulate briefly Werner's argument. His demonstration starts with the Chomskyan assumption that the parts of a grammar are known and can be represented by the formula (1):

$$G(\#, \frown, \rightarrow, S, V_{nt}, V_t) \qquad (1)$$

where the # symbol represents the boundary conditions of a sentence (or utterance). This is the silence (absence of speech) that precedes and follows every sentence. The $\frown$ symbol stands for the operation of concatenation. The rewrite symbol $\rightarrow$ (right arrow) stands for the rewrite operation that specifies structure, for example, the formula (2):

$$S \rightarrow NP \frown VP \qquad (2)$$

(read: 'rewrite sentence as consisting of a noun phrase followed by a verb phrase') specifies the structure of S, the sentence, that consists of a noun phrase followed by a verb phrase. Thus, S in (1) stands for sentence, V_{nt} for the nonterminal vocabulary of the grammar, such as NP and VP in (2), and V_t for the terminal vocabulary. These lowest level units of a grammar or grammatical categories have no further structure (no rewrite rules can be applied and therefore these symbols never appear on the left side of any rewrite rules). In the process of sentence generation or production, actual lexical entries replace terminal vocabulary items in each language in question. (For details on the rules governing lexical insertion into terminal grammatical categories see the publications of Noam Chomsky.) Typical terminal categories are 'mass noun,' 'count noun,' 'performative verb,' 'manner adverbial,' 'definite article,' etc.

Obviously, #, $\frown$, and $\rightarrow$ are part of the formalism of all grammars, hence language universals, and cannot therefore contribute to meaning and world view.

The high level nonterminal vocabulary V_{nt} are assumed by linguists to be also universal, that is, they occur in every language and cannot therefore influence language specific world views. Languages such as Nootka (one of a large number of languages spoken on the northwest coast of the USA) which consists almost entirely of verbs, and Sierra Miwok (one of a large number of languages spoken in the state of California), which consists almost entirely of nouns, can be made to conform naturally to the structure of noun phrases and verb phrases. In Nootka nouns are formed by nominalizing verbs (English analog: to walk—to take a walk) and in Sierra Miwok verbs are formed by verbalizing nouns (English analog: table—to table, e.g., a motion).

The above argument leaves only the low level nonterminal (V_{nt}) and the terminal (V_t)—the lowest level of grammatical categories of a given language—as potential contributors to language specific aspects of world view.

If M. A. K. Halliday's principle of 'delicacy' is now added, that states that when the limit of linguistic analysis (the ultimate delicacy) is reached, then every lexical item in every language represents its very own unique grammatical category.

The parts of grammar that could contribute to world view are therefore the low level nonterminal and the terminal grammatical categories. But since these are part of the lexicon, in any language, the interaction of language and culture must be seen as firmly rooted in the lexicon.

67

Ultimately, therefore, the Sapirean definitions and the definition of the hypothesis in Whorf's first quote of this article prevail. In the other, the Whorfian formulation, the terms 'grammar,' or 'pattern,' should be consistently read as standing for 'low level grammatical categories,' or 'language specific grammatical categories.'

2. The Contribution of Grammatical and Lexical Categories

Before examining the issue of how these language specific categories contribute to world view, two additional notions require discussion: the strong version of the Sapir–Whorf hypothesis, according to which language *determines* thought, and the weak version, which asserts that language has a tendency to influence thought. Whorf is often viewed as representing the strong version. However, a review of his quotes (for example, in Sect. 1.2) reveals that he always qualifies his assertions.

While Whorf does say that speakers of different languages 'must arrive' at different interpretations of the world, these interpretations are not totally different only 'somewhat different' (Whorf in Carroll 1956: 221). Hopi grammar does not determine Hopi culture only 'bore a relation to [it]' (Whorf 1939: 73). And the 'background linguistic system' is not a determiner of ideas but merely a 'shaper of ideas.' He talks about 'habitual thought' rather than thought fully determined by the language of the speakers. It is thus difficult to find representatives of the strong version of the hypothesis.

All other points of view, including Whorf's, represent relatively stronger or relatively weaker versions of the weak version of the cultural relativity principle. The Sapir–Whorf hypothesis can therefore be paraphrased as follows:

> The categorial system of every language, including lower level grammatical and all lexical categories, points its speakers toward somewhat different evaluations of externally similar observations. Hence speakers of different languages have somewhat different views of the world, somewhat different habitual thought, and consequently their language and cultural knowledge are in a somewhat different relationship to each other. They don't live in the same world with different labels attached but in somewhat different worlds. The more dissimilar two languages are, in their lexicon—that is, in conceptual and grammatical categories—the greater their tendency to embody different world views.

Finally, Whorf's search for traces of world view in grammar, or in grammatical categories, is not without merit considering that different parts of language tend to change at different rates. Thus lexical items referring to objects change fastest as technology and customs change. For example, in Anglo–American culture new words like 'jeep,' 'radar,' 'laser,' 'napalm,' 'frozen yogurt,' 'yuppie,' and many others are quickly adopted into everyday use.

Verbs change more slowly. For example, until 1957 only planets, comets, and meteorites could orbit. Since Sputnik, the Soviet Union's first artificial satellite, an assortment of objects propelled into space are in orbit. A few years ago a telescope could not be thought of as orbiting. However, with the Hubble Deep Space Telescope in orbit, the range of the verb has been extended even to human beings. For example almost everyone understands the sentence *The astronauts are orbiting the earth*. There are other verbs introduced or extended by the rapid changes in Anglo–American culture. For example, *I word processed all morning*; *This program is good at error trapping*, etc. Not too surprisingly, new verbs are harder to think of than new nouns.

Still rarer are examples of changes in low level grammatical categories. These aspects of language change slowest and have therefore a much more lasting influence on 'habitual thought.'

In the following sections the amended definition of the Sapir–Whorf hypothesis (above) is used to explain a number of anomalies in the relationship between language and culture.

2.1 The Role of Different Symbol Systems

This amended definition still contains some mystification, for example, the dilemma of how it is that different categorial systems, that is, different languages, lead to somewhat different world views.

The insight that the choice of a symbol system is crucial to the solution of a mathematical problem is attributed to the Hungarian mathematician George Polya. A solution may be easy, difficult, or impossible depending on how a problem solver symbolizes the problem. Though mathematical problems are hardly identical with human problems for which language may provide a symbolization, mathematical problems display many similarities to such problems. Language provides human beings with categories of thought (see Lucy and Shweder 1979, below); these may or may not facilitate thinking in a given cultural domain.

It is clear from the Ethnoscience movement of the 1960s and 70s that speakers of different languages often do classify things very differently. For example, the Navajo Indians classify the plant world as in Fig. 1.

It is clear from Fig. 1 that Navajos use different criteria for classifying plants than do speakers of English. Strangely, in Navajo—with about 500 named plants—no further subdivisions of even the largest class of flexible plants seem to exist.

However, alternate classifications do exist. One Navajo medicine man classified all plants according to their use. The surprise was a subclass of dangerous

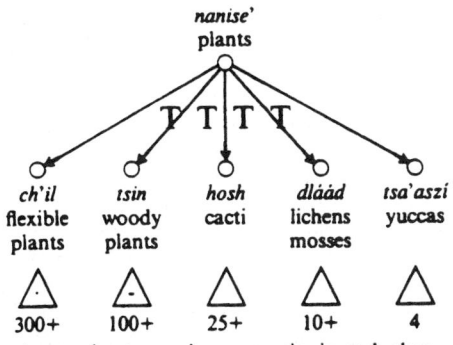

Figure 1. Navajo classification of plants. The T's symbolize the taxonomic relationship, e.g., *hosh nanise' át'é*, or 'A cactus is a (kind of) plant.'

plants that were poisonous. However an even greater surprise was that each dangerous plant has an antidote plant that can undo the effect of the poison.

One more unusual example showing that a language can facilitate talk (and solutions?) on some topics: the Navajo language has a rich vocabulary for describing the 'behavior' of lines. I list half a dozen examples from a growing corpus of about 100:

dzígai	a white line running off into distance (infinity)
adziisgai	a group of parallel white lines running off into distance
hadziisgai	a white line running vertically upward from the bottom to the top of an object
ahééhesgai	more than two white lines form concentric circles
ałch'inidzígai	two white lines coming together to a point
áłnánágah	a white line zigzagging back and forth

The ease with which Navajos talk about the behavior of white and other colored lines is amazing. This facility with 'geometry' is perhaps explainable by Navajo names or descriptions of features of the landscape that rarely utilize similarities to everyday objects (e.g., Hat Rock). Instead Navajos use geometrical description of verticals, horizontals, lines, and points. For example, a rock formation near Tuba City, Arizona, called by Navajos *Tsé Áhé'ii'áhá*, 'two rocks standing vertically parallel in a reciprocal relationship to each other' was named by English speakers 'Elephant's Feet.'

2.2 Language and Culture Do Not Covary

The *perfect* correlation of different cultures speaking different languages was an artifact of the biases of early cultural anthropology. In the formative years of the profession each ethnographer selected his or her own tribe with a distinct language. Nevertheless, anomalies to language/culture homogeneity were soon noted.

Three small tribes in Northern California represent the paradigm case. The Yurok, Karok, and Hupa Indians (the Yurok language is distantly related to the Algonquian, Karok to the Siouxan, and Hupa to the Na-Dene (Athabascan) language family) in the Klamath and Trinity river valleys near the California–Oregon border speak three different languages belonging to three different language families, yet their cultures are almost identical.

The linguistic record is incomplete, but there is evidence that many lexical categories (and possibly grammatical categories) were converging in the three languages. For example, all three use the phrase 'fish eater' for naming the sea otter.

There is growing evidence that extensive language and cultural leveling appears in areas where speakers of very different languages live in close proximity and in intimate contact with each other. For example, on the border of the Indo-European and Dravidian languages of India there are communities where vocabulary and grammar of the two languages (Marathi, Indo-European and Kannada, Dravidian) converge to such a high degree that people do seem to live in an almost identical world with different labels attached (Gumperz 1971).

In other words, very different languages can, over time, under the influence of their converging cultures, level many of their differences, while similar languages may diverge over time if their cultures are developing in different directions.

Examples of the latter case are the Apachean languages of the southwest USA. The Navajo Indian language, in the Apachean group, accommodates a culture that incorporates many Puebloan traits into its world view. None of the Apachean-speaking tribes live in villages. The Puebloan villagers have relatively homogeneous cultures but speak a diversity of languages. The other Apacheans did not assimilate Puebloan elements into their culture. Navajo and the other Apachean languages do remain similar, but the Navajos use extensive specialized vocabularies (and folk theories) appropriate to their world view that is alien to the other Apachens.

2.3 Language Mixing

Bilinguals when in each other's company tend to mix languages. The reasons seem obvious. There are many things that can be said better, more efficiently, in an aesthetically more pleasing manner, in one language than in another. Language purity is usually maintained only in the presence of (especially) high status monolinguals who would consider mixing the discourse with an unknown language offensive.

Language mixing, a universal occurrence when bilinguals converse, provides a good indicator of the utility of the idioms or technical vocabulary of one language over another. That is, different languages offer different (more or less elegant?) solutions to speech about the same or similar 'cultural things.'

2.4 Language Acquisition

Since all definitions of culture stress that culture includes all things '... acquired [learned] by man as a member of society' (Tylor 1958), any language learned by children belongs therefore within culture. This fact underlies the formulation of the relationship as 'language *in* culture.'

However, many scholars became concerned that language is not just 'in culture' or 'part of culture,' but is also the major vehicle for the acquisition of culture. The confusion of culture with its chief vehicle of transmission proved troublesome, particularly since language is held responsible for the cumulativeness of culture. That is, language makes possible not only the transmission of culture, but also the increase of culture from generation to generation. This cumulativeness through language is the major mechanism of cultural evolution.

The solution, while 'obvious' in light of the developments of cognitive anthropology (Ethnoscience and New Ethnography are near synonyms) was nevertheless never clearly formulated (see *Ethnography of Speaking*).

Only one additional assumption need be made: the acquisition of language by a child has a natural history and in the course of this development language changes its function. At first the child learns its native language 'as a member of society' and therefore following the standard definitions of culture, language is part of culture (see *Child Language: An Overview*).

However, there is more to it. Language acquisition specialists agree that language learning is complete by the age of 4–6 years. Formal education, the institutionalized commencement of the acquisition of culture through language, begins after the child fully masters its native language. This happens universally at the age of 5 or 6 years. The child has now completed learning those aspects of culture that do not require language and begins to learn the accumulated wisdom and technology of the social group in which it is growing up, and that is encoded in language. Through language the child learns the verbalizable aspects of his or her culture. The function of language has shifted, now culture is in language, or it is acquired through language.

3. Cognitive Anthropology and the Sapir–Whorf Hypothesis

The New Ethnography or Ethnoscience entered anthropology with two papers published in *Language* by Floyd Lounsbury (1956) and his student Ward Goodenough (1956). The topic was a componential analysis of the Pawnee (which belongs to the Cadoan language family and was spoken in the southern Great Plains) and the Trukese (Austronesian-speaking Micronesians) kinship systems.

The point of componential analysis, in the context of the Sapir–Whorf hypothesis, is that kinship terminology (see *Kinship Terminology*) or the kinship lexicon of every language/culture combination views the same kinship space, but tends to subdivide it differently. The examples of kinship terminologies confirm the 'linguistic relativity principle.' Speakers of languages in different cultures experience the same 'objective reality' but assign different terminology to it. The speakers of different languages lexicalize (set to words) the universal kinship space very differently.

For example, the Yankee kinship system used by English-speaking North Americans merges all cousins: most Americans no longer fully understand the terminology that classifies cousins by degree (first, second,... cousin) based on the distance from a common ancestor (first cousin = two generations, i.e., shared grandparents, etc.) and by generational distance (once, twice,... removed).

For example, Tagalog, the main language of the Philippines, makes no distinction between grandparents and grandparents' brothers and sisters. Crow and Omaha, both Siouxan languages spoken in the Great Plains, merge some of the terms for cousins with certain aunts or uncles. Since the Crow reckon descent through the maternal line (they are matrilineal) and the Omaha through the parental line (they are patrilineal) the two systems are mirror images of each other. Navajo and Hungarian, a Finno–Ugric language of central Europe, on the other hand, make a careful distinction between the relative age of brothers and sisters. The list of culturally prescribed differences in kinship terminologies is virtually endless.

Componential analysis was soon followed by the discovery of folk taxonomies. Folk classifications had been noted before (e.g., Mauss 1964) but this was the first time that anthropologists/ethnographers collected folk taxonomies systematically. The seminal monograph was Conklin's *Hanuno'o Agriculture* (1954; the Hanuno's are Austronesian speakers living on the island of Mindanao in the Philippines). A flurry of activity followed taxonomizing everything from ethno-anatomies to folk zoologies. Werner et al. (1983) even presented the taxonomic aspects of the entire traditional Navajo universe.

In this lively debate the Sapir–Whorf hypothesis was mentioned only rarely and often outside the context of the New Ethnography. The participants in this ferment tacitly assumed that componential analysis and folk taxonomies clearly demonstrate the weak lexical version of the hypothesis.

Out of these developments arose cognitive anthropology that took as its goal the investigation of human cognition, especially cultural knowledge. It soon developed two branches. One is ethnoscience ethnography, which tacitly assumes the validity of the weak lexical form of linguistic relativity but does not elaborate this link to the past. The more pressing task is seen as the perfection and systematization of ethnography.

The second branch moved closer to cognitive psychology and by that route to cognitive science. Berlin and Kay (1969) soon emerged as the leaders in this field with their work on color terminology. That different language/culture groups have different color terminologies was considered in the debates of the 1950s and early 1960s the prime example of the lexical version of the Sapir–Whorf hypothesis. Obviously, the color spectrum is a continuum of colors from red to purple, but human beings in different parts of the world partition this continuum differently.

Berlin and Kay's first important discovery was that the color spectrum is not a good example for the hypothesis. '[C]olor categorization is not random and the foci of basic color terms are similar in all languages' (Berlin and Kay 1969: 10) and '... the eleven (see Fig. 2.) basic color categories are pan-human perceptual universals' (Berlin and Kay 1969: 109).

However, Berlin and Kay (1969: 160 n.2) stress that their work should not be confused with a thorough study of the ethnographic ramifications of color terminology. That is, '... to appreciate the full cultural significance of color words it is necessary to appreciate the full range of meanings, both referential and connotative...' or the lexical/semantic fields in which individual color terms are embedded.

Their second discovery was that color terminology evolves in a very lawful sequence. Although their formula has been 'fine tuned' following new cross-cultural data, it can be represented as shown in Fig. 2. (their original formulation, 1969: 4).

Lucy and Shweder (1979) revived the controversy by showing in several well-designed experiments that color memory is highly sensitive to the lexical resources of a language and culture. They conclude that the universality of color categories is overstated by Berlin and Kay and that the weak Sapir–Whorfian lexical formulation corresponds more closely to the facts.

Willet Kempton extended the methodology of cognitive anthropology to the shapes of objects, thus exploring the boundary between categories. Cecil Brown applied the evolutionary idea in Fig. 2. to other aspects of human vocabularies, especially botanical and zoological terminologies.

Ethnographers soon expanded their view beyond componential analysis after it was shown by a number of anthropologists and linguists that components are also lexical items and hence most often language specific rather than universal. John Lyons's critique of componential analysis as a universal theory for cultural knowledge (and semantics) is devastating. Nevertheless, componential analysis remains a superb tool for understanding exotic kinship terminologies.

In 1970 Casagrande and Hale, who had collected a large number of folk definitions in Papago (an Uto–Aztecan language of southern Arizona) published 13 lexical/semantic relations. They failed to find examples of a postulated 14th, the part/whole relation. A close analysis of their data shows that the part/whole relation did appear in its inverse form: that is, instead of 'A is a part of B' they found and classified as a spatial relation the inverse 'B has an A.'

Casagrande and Hale's work was seminal for a number of researchers (see the summary in Evens et al. 1980). Through these scholars their work was linked to the cognitive sciences. However, this link did not develop into strong ties.

The major insight of field theory can again be framed in terms of the linguistic relativity principle: the weak lexical version is accepted as self-evident. The lexical/semantic fields of the languages used in different cultural contexts look very different. However, there is unity because the lexical/semantic fields are held together by *universal* lexical/semantic relations.

Unfortunately there is no agreement on the basic set of lexical/semantic relations which range from Werner's (Werner and Schoepfle 1987) two to the over 50 lexical relations of Apresyian et al. (1970). Werner's two relations are 'taxonomy' and 'modification' plus several derived complex relations, a relation for sequential phenomena, and logical relations, including modal logic. Apresyian et al.'s relations are derived from practical lexicography or the construction of more systematic dictionaries. For example, their relation EQUIP is the relation in 'ship' EQUIP 'crew' ('A crew operates a ship'). The folk taxonomic model can be applied to whole cultures. Closely related encyclopedic works display the lexical

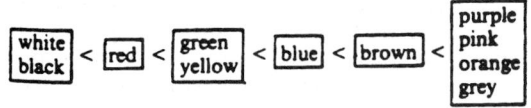

Figure 2. The cultural evolution of color terminology. If a language has the term 'red,' then it also has 'black' and 'white'; if a language has the term 'green' and 'yellow,' then it also has 'red,' 'white,' and 'black,' etc. The more technologically developed a given culture, the more of the 11 basic color terms are in use. (In the third box either order of [green < yellow] or [yellow < green] is possible.)

and cultural knowledge dimensions of a culture. That is, a background document fully exploring the lexical resources of a language represents an important aspect of the culture as a whole.

Ethnography is seen by many scholars as translation *par excellence*. Ethnographic translation fundamentally encourages translator's notes (definitions), which explain cultural ramifications of lexical items (or phrases) in native texts. Therefore, a carefully documented encyclopedic lexicon may represent an extensive set of translator's notes prepared in advance of the analysis of any future ethnographic texts.

An extension of these ideas is the recent focus on cultural schemata (Casson 1983). Schemata, recast into the lexical version of the Sapir–Whorf hypothesis, are folk theories often labeled by words (especially verbs) or phrases that usually require complex (e.g., up to monograph length and beyond) explanations or folk definitions.

4. Summary and Conclusions

The choice of the symbol system (e.g., language) affects the ease or difficulty with which one can talk about particular domains of cultural reality and solve problems in them. Thus the lexicon of language does provide a loosely laced straitjacket for thinking because it limits individuals to customary categories of thought. Only in this sense does it constrain thought.

At the same time language allows the inventive human mind to create alternative categorizations for solving new problems. This history of science and the rich diversity of thousands of human languages and cultures attests to the inventiveness of the human spirit.

True, the combinatorial possibilities in human language are enormous. Thus the very use of language results in a drift of meanings and with it inadvertent changes in world view. This process is analogous to genetic drift. But in addition there are analogues and historical examples of meaning mutations: conceptual revolutions and conversions.

However, these escapes from the mold of one's habitual language patterns are never easy— '... anomaly is recognized only with difficulty' (Kuhn 1970). It usually takes genius to show the rest of humanity how to see the world in a new light, that is in new categories. In such conversion experiences the language is affected 'to the core' (Kuhn 1970)— specifically, most grammatical categories remain the same but geniuses revamp lexical categories in ways that facilitate new thought which the rest of humanity may in time follow.

5. Epilogue

In a volume of edited articles, the editors, Gumperz and Levinson (1996) propose a new approach to linguistic relativity. They and their authors assume that indexicality, a broader concept than deixis, is highly culture specific and use it as their point of departure. Most simply, indexical terms are extra-linguistic references such as 'here,' 'there,' 'this,' etc. that depend on the cultural context of the utterance for their proper interpretation. Interestingly, all of the authors of this volume seem to assume that the notion of 'context' is not problematic nor is it theoretical. With a few exceptions (e.g., Hanks) context is assumed to be somehow intrinsically given and not linked to folk-theoretical knowledge of the physical, spatial, temporal, and ultimately the cultural world of the speaker. Unfortunately, this notion of 'context of situation' as extralinguistic goes back at least to Malinowski (1923) (see *Malinowski, Bronislaw Kaspar*).

Context must be viewed as a theoretical concept that has to be matched by experience when language is applied to that experience. This is not unlike the matching of attributes to events in the 'real' world. For example, the attribute 'green' must match the 'real' world grass when we talk about grass, or the shape and stripes of a tiger have to match a 'real' tiger or a picture of it, if that is what we are talking about. In this sense what we generally designate as context is like a generalized attribute; one that is not attached to individual words, but adheres to parts of or an entire discourse. Context, or contextual attributes, must be viewed as nested: larger ones within more local ones. For example, within scientific discourse, there are many further specifications of subcontext attributes possible.

However, sudden shifts in context, that is, in discourse attributes, are not uncommon in every day speech. Human beings are very good at detecting such shifts almost instantly. These shifts are associated with partitions of a person's cultural knowledge. That is, there does not exist any situation (or context) that requires all of human knowledge to be engaged simultaneously. This accounts for the fact that while language is in general highly ambiguous, humans are rarely aware of the ambiguity of their speech. Recognition of such a set of 'contextual attributes' allows only a very limited set of interpretations; very often it constrains interpretation to just one plausible understanding.

An added advantage of the contextual partition of cultural knowledge is that the 'same' words, phrases, or sentences can be used with different interpretations in such contexts that are analogous to partition of memory. This makes language adaptable to a much wider range of experience than would be possible if meanings were rigidly context (knowledge partition) independent. It is also clear that memory partitions (i.e., contexts) are highly culture specific.

A situation (or a hierarchy of the situation's attributes) either match our previous knowledge and expectations or they do not. Without the theoretical notion of such matches context mistakes would be impossible. Yet context mistakes are common and may be viewed as situations in which the expectations of a speaker do not match the assumptions of his or her potential audience. For example, someone shouting within a library, or a church, or a lecturer speaking about a serious topic becoming unintentionally funny.

If we define culture as cultural knowledge (encompassing everything a member of a culture needs to know to function appropriately), then we can equate cultural situations with what we often call 'context.' Since cultural knowledge accrues to any human group over time, so too does context sensitivity adapt to the expectations of the group. Because all of us as human beings belong to several human groups (perhaps $7+2$ groups based on the limitations of our short term memory), we are all multicultural. Hence as the group-we-are-in changes so does the contexts that determines the framing for indexical expressions. We tend to be very sensitive to these changes. Thus indexicality, by its very nature, is culture bound and indexical expressions tend to be highly culture specific. That is, of course, precisely what the authors in the Gumperz and Levinson (1996) volume advocate while failing to consider the notion of 'context' as problematic and theoretically interesting.

See also: Sapir, Edward; Whorf, Benjamin Lee.

Bibliography

Apresyian Y D, Mel'čuk I A, Žolkovsky A K 1970 Semantics and lexicography: Toward a new type of unilingual dictionary. In: Kiefer F (ed.) *Studies in Syntax and Semantics*. Reidel, Dordrecht, The Netherlands
Berlin B, Kay P 1969 *Basic Color Terms: Their Universality and Evolution*. University of California Press, Berkeley, CA
Carroll J B (ed.) 1956 *Language, Thought, and Reality: Selected Writings of Benjamin Lee Whorf*. MIT, New York
Casagrande J B, Hale K L 1967 Semantic relationships in Papago folk definitions. In: Hymes D H, Bittle W E (eds.) *Studies in Southwestern Ethnolinguistics*. Mouton, The Hague
Casson R 1983 Schemata in cognitive anthropology. *Annual Review of Anthropology*: 429–62
Conklin H C 1954 The relation of Hanuno'o culture to the plant world (Doctoral dissertation, Yale University)
Evens M W, Litowitz B E, Markowitz J A, Smith R N, Werner O 1980 *Lexical/Semantic Relations: A Comparative Survey*. Linguistic Research, Edmonton, AB
Gleason H A 1962 The relation of lexicon and grammar. In: Householder F W, Saporta S (eds.) *Problems in Lexicography*. Indiana Research Center in Anthropology Bloomington, IN
Goodenough W H 1956 Componential analysis and the study of meaning. *Language* **32**: 195–216
Gumperz J J 1971 Dialect difference and social stratification in a North Indian village. In: Gumperz J J, Dill A (eds.) *Language in Social Groups*. Stanford University Press, Stanford, CA
Gumperz J J, Levinson S C (eds.) 1996 *Rethinking Linguistic Relativity*. Cambridge University Press, Cambridge, UK
Hoijer H (ed.) 1954 *Language in Culture*. University of Chicago Press, Chicago, IL
Humboldt W von 1836 (1960) *Über die Verschiedenheit des menschlichen Sprachbaues*. Dürmler, Bonn
Hymes D H 1960 Discussion of the symposium on the translation between language and culture. *Anthropological Linguistics* **2**(2): 81–4
Kuhn T S 1970 *The Structure of Scientific Revolutions*, 2nd edn. University of Chicago Press, Chicago, IL
Lounsbury F G 1956 A semantic analysis of the Pawnee kinship usage. *Language* **32**: 158–94
Lucy A J, Shweder R A 1979 Whorf and his critics: Linguistic and nonlinguistic influences on color memory. *American Anthropologist* **81**: 581–615
Malinowski B 1923 The Problem of meaning in primitive languages. In: Ogden C K, Ranards I A (eds.) *The Meaning of Meaning*. Kegan Paul, London
Mandelbaum D G (ed.) 1963 *Selected Writings of Edward Sapir in Language, Culture and Personality*. University of California Press, Berkeley, CA
Mauss M 1964 On language and primitive forms of classification. In: Hymes E (ed.) *Language in Culture and Society*. Harper Row, New York
McQuown N A 1960 Discussion of the symposium on the translation between language and culture. *Anthropological Linguistics* **2**(2): 79–80
Tylor E B 1958 *Primitive Culture*, new edn. Harper, New York
Voegelin C F, Voegelin F M 1957 Hopi domains: A lexical approach to the problem of selection. *International Journal of American Linguistics* **23**(2)1: Memoir 14
Werner O, Manning A, Begise K Y 1983 A taxonomic view of the traditional Navajouniverse. In: Sturtevant W C, Ortiz A (eds.) *Handbook of North American Indians*. Vol. 10: *Southwest*. Smithsonian Institution, Washington, DC
Werner O, Schoepfle G M 1987 *Systematic Fieldwork, vol. 1: Foundations of Ethnography and Interviewing, vol. 2: Ethnographic Analysis and Data Management*. Sage, London
Whorf B L 1939 The reaction of habitual thought and behavior to language. In: Sapir L (ed.) *Language, Culture, and Personality*. Sapir Memorial Publication Fund, Menasha, WI

Saussurean Tradition and Sociolinguistics
J. E. Joseph

The Swiss linguist Ferdinand de Saussure (1857–1913) established his reputation at an early age, with his 1878 monograph *Mémoire sur le système primitif des voyelles dans les langues indo–européennes* ('the original vowel system of the Indo–European languages'). *The Mémoire* posited the existence of two Proto-Indo–European 'sonant coefficients' which appeared in no attested forms of the daughter languages, but could account for certain vowel developments which had previously appeared irregular. Fifty years later an *H* with exactly the distribution of Saussure's sonant coefficients was discovered in Hittite, confirming his hypothesis. After his 1881 doctoral thesis on the absolute genitive in Sanskrit, Saussure published no more books, only articles on specific topics in historical linguistics.

But in 1907, 1908–1909, and 1910–1911, he gave at the University of Geneva three courses in general linguistics, a topic on which he never published anything. Soon after his death in 1913, his colleagues Charles Bally (1865–1947) and Albert Sechehaye (1870–1946), appreciating the extraordinary nature of the courses Saussure had given, began gathering what manuscript notes they could find, together with the careful and detailed notebooks of students who had taken one or more of the three courses, especially Albert Riedlinger (1883–1978). From these they fashioned the *Cours de linguistique générale*, published at Lausanne and Paris in 1916. It would become one of the most influential books of the twentieth century, not just for linguistics, but for virtually every realm of intellectual endeavor.

In order to trace the Saussurean tradition in twentieth-century linguistics, this article considers nine key elements of Saussure's view of language. For each a summary is given of the condition prior to Saussure, of Saussure's own view, and of how his view has shaped linguistic inquiry in the years since the publication of the *Cours*.

1. The Establishment of Synchronic Linguistics

At the time of Saussure's lectures, the study of language had been dominated for over 30 years by (a) historical work on the language of written texts (work which had only gradually come to be distinguished from 'philology,' inquiry aimed not at the language but at better understanding of the text itself); (b) dialectological work based on field investigation of local dialects; (c) phonetics, which demanded increasingly minute observation in strong adherence to the positivistic spirit; and (d) psychology, the principal domain of a global perspective on language, dominated by the ideas of Wilhelm von Humboldt (1767–1835) and his followers, notably Heymann Steinthal (1823–1899) and Wilhelm Wundt (1832–1920).

A fifth approach existed—the study of language as a general phenomenon independent of historical or psychological considerations—but it had made little progress since the death of its principal exponent, the American scholar William Dwight Whitney (1827–1894). Furthermore, the publication of a major study of language in 1900 by the Leipzig psychologist Wundt appeared to signal that the new century would give the 'general' study of language over fully to that discipline.

Saussure's problem was to delineate a study of language that would be neither historical nor ahistorical, neither psychological nor apsychological; yet more systematic than Whitneyan general linguistics, so as to be at least the equal in intellectual and methodological rigor to the historical, psychological, and phonetic approaches. His solution was to make a strong distinction between the study of language as a static system, which he called 'synchronic' linguistics, and the study of language change, which he called 'diachronic' linguistics (or, until 1908, 'evolutive'). Saussure's rejection of the traditional term 'historical' seems to have been based in part on a disdain for the reliance it suggested upon extralinguistic factors and written texts, and in part on a desire for terminological symmetry with 'synchronic.' Synchronic linguistics would henceforth designate the study of language systems in and of themselves, divorced from external considerations of a historical or psychological sort, or any factor having to do with actual speech production.

This is the single most sweeping of Saussurean traditions for insofar as twentieth-century linguists have focused their efforts neither on simple description of languages, nor on their evolution, nor on their connection to 'national psychology,' they have realized Saussure's program of synchronic linguistics. Furthermore, historical linguistics has largely become the diachronic enterprise envisioned by Saussure (though the term 'historical' continues in general usage), and even the purely 'descriptive' approaches have been profoundly marked by the Saussurean concept of language as a system where *tout se tient* ('everything holds together'), a phrase often associated with Saussure, though there is no record of his using it in his Geneva lectures. It may be that its first use was in a lecture delivered by Antoine Meillet in 1906 (see Meillet 1921: 16).

In establishing synchronic linguistics, Saussure was not engaging in an exercise of scholarly exactitude, but serving notice upon psychologists and others that the general study of language should fall to persons with historically based training in specific languages and language families, rather than to experts in the functioning of the mind. Many of Saussure's statements about language can best be understood in conjunction with this need for establishing the autonomy of linguistic inquiry vis-à-vis adjoining fields.

2. The Primacy of Spoken Language

The idea that speech is the original and primal form of language, and writing a secondary imitation of speech, runs counter to the general popular accordance of greater prestige to writing. Yet the primacy of spoken over written language became embedded in linguistics in the early nineteenth century, doubtless in connection with the Romantic belief that folk traditions embodied the national spirit more deeply than urban practices like writing, which were more subject to external influences. The trend continued over the course of the nineteenth century as linguistics moved away from philology and became increasingly concerned with the gathering of spoken forms from living dialects. By the turn of the twentieth century few linguists would have disputed that the best source for determining the original form of anything in any language was to reconstruct it from its living descendant dialects, and not from written records surviving from intermediate stages.

Saussure formalized the marginalization of written language as well as anyone, and if its survival is often viewed as a Saussurean tradition, it is because he has borne the brunt of the 1967 attack on this marginalization by Jacques Derrida (1930–   ). For Saussure, writing is not language, but a separate entity whose only 'mission' is to represent real (spoken) language. The 'danger' of writing is that it creates the illusion of being more real and more stable than speech, and therefore gains ascendancy over speech in the popular mind. Derrida demonstrated the irrationality and internal inconsistency of this extreme phonocentrism; in his deconstructionist wordplay, all language is a kind of 'writing' (in a sense that is unique to Derrida).

But so deeply ingrained is this tradition in twentieth-century linguistics that few linguists saw the need to respond to Derrida, whose critique was summarily dismissed. Well over 10 years passed before linguists began to admit that the marginalization of writing had been carried to an irrational extreme; and despite some tentative steps toward a linguistics of writing in various quarters, this tradition of privileging spoken language—shared though not founded by Saussure—is in no danger of passing away.

3. The Object of Linguistics: *Langue* versus *Parole*

The role of the human will in language production has constituted a problem for linguistic thought at least since Plato's *Cratylus*: humans are constrained by the conventions of language, yet it is through language that will and individuality are shaped and realized. Since modern science is predicated upon the elimination of the will from any object of inquiry, human desire, action, and creation came to be excluded from the 'scientific' study of language. This has necessitated a considerable abstraction of language away from its role in human affairs, treating it as if it existed independently of speakers and speech acts. But here two problems arose: (a) the metaphor of language as organism (which qua metaphor had been fruitfully employed by early nineteenth-century linguists) became extremely attractive as a way of talking about language independently of speakers, and as Michel Bréal (1832–1915) complained in the introduction to his *Essai de sémantique* (1897), the metaphor was taken literally by many people, giving rise to gross misunderstandings; (b) Wundt's *Völkerpsychologie* ('national psychology') seemed to offer a more sophisticated way of dealing with linguistic phenomena: it eliminated the metaphysical abstraction of 'language,' but replaced it with still less satisfactory explanations that revolved around the 'spirit of peoples,' were untestable, and could not sustain any approach to language that was detailed or systematic.

Saussure's contribution was to dissect the total phenomenon of language (*language*) into (a) actual speech production (*parole*), including the role of the individual will, and (b) the socially shared system of signs (*langue*) that makes production and comprehension possible. Although he spoke of a linguistics of *parole* that would cover the phonetic side of language and the products of individual will, Saussure made it clear that the linguistics of *langue* is the essential, real linguistics. *Langue* is beyond the direct reach of the individual will. Saussure's formulation is both a defense and a refinement of the procedures of traditional grammar and historical linguistics, yet at the same time it stakes out an autonomous realm for general linguistic inquiry.

Despite much debate among scholars as to just what Saussure meant by *language, langue*, and *parole*, the distinction has held firm throughout twentieth-century linguistics. It has been suggested that certain work in stylistics (e.g., by Saussure's disciple Bally) and in discourse pragmatics constitutes an attempt at a linguistics of *parole*, but it is not yet clear how any aspect of language, once it is systematized, fails to enter the sphere of *langue*. The human will remains in exile from linguistics, and *langue* (naturally somewhat evolved from Saussure's original conception of it) continues to be the object of study of virtually every approach to which the name 'linguistics' is accorded (see Sect. 4).

4. *Langue* as a Social Fact

Saussure's insistence upon the social nature of *langue* grew during the years in which he lectured on general linguistics, largely at the expense of psychologically based considerations. Again, this may be tied in part to the need to establish synchronic linguistics independently of the dominant post-Humboldtian psychological establishment. The young science of sociology embodied the spirit of positivism, with which it shared the same recognized founder, Auguste Comte (1798–1857). Positivism was coming to be equated with scientificness in general thought, making classical psychology appear old-fashioned and metaphysical. For the sociologists, Wundt's *Völkerpsychologie*, based on nonempirical generalizations (and more akin to what today would pass as philosophy of mind, not psychology) was already unacceptably passé.

Much ink has been spilled regarding the degree to which Saussure's conception of language was directly influenced by work in sociology, particularly by Emile Durkheim (1858–1917) and Gabriel Tarde (1843–1904). Saussure's former student and lifelong intimate Antoine Meillet (1866–1936; see also) was closely allied with Durkheim and his journal *L'Année sociologique*; and there is often a close correspondence between Saussure's and Durkheim's use of terms like 'social fact' and 'collective consciousness.' But since Saussure never cites Durkheim or Tarde (he was after all teaching a course, not writing a book), support for any claim of direct influence is lacking.

In Saussure's view, *langue* is a 'treasury' or 'collection of impressions' that is 'deposited' in identical form in the brain of each member of a given speech community. He uses the metaphor of a dictionary, of which every individual possesses an identical copy. What the individual does with this socially-shared system falls entirely into the realm of *parole*. This distinction (which was not yet clear to Saussure at the time of his first course in general linguistics of 1907) differentiates Saussure's dichotomy from that between 'competence' and 'performance' established in the 1960s by Noam Chomsky (1928–). Chomsky explicitly related competence with *langue* and performance with *parole*, though in actual fact the analogy was only partial: for Chomsky, competence (derived from innate universal grammar) is mental and individual, and performance the locus of its social actuation. Furthermore the considerable differences between Saussure's orientation toward language as a semiotic system and Chomsky's toward competence as a mental faculty make any such equations difficult.

Saussure's views on the social nature of language have had a great resonance in linguistics and many other fields. By the mid-1930s it was commonplace to equate 'synchronic linguistics' (indeed, 'scientific linguistics') with 'social linguistics,' and to include under this heading the work of Meillet and his many European disciples, including Alf Sommerfelt (1892–1965; and Joseph Vendryès (1875–1960; the American structuralists Leonard Bloomfield (1887–1949; and Edward Sapir (1884–1939; see *Sapir, Edward*); and even the 'social behaviorists' (or 'pragmatists') John Dewey (1859–1952) and George Herbert Mead (1863–1931). Bloomfield in particular exploited the power of the social as an antidote to the psychological (or 'mentalist') approach at the time of his conversion from Wundtian social psychology to empirical behaviorism. Beginning in the 1940s dialect geographers such as Raven McDavid (1911–1984; see also *McDavid, Raven Ioor, Jr*) began to realize the crucial importance of social factors in linguistic production; around the same time, the sociologist Paul Hanly Furfey (1896–1992) began training students jointly in the techniques of social class measurement and descriptive linguistics. By the early 1950s inquiry combining empirical sociological and linguistic techniques was underway, to be refined significantly by William Labov (1927–) (see *Labov, William*) and others in the 1960s.

In terms of Saussurean traditions, sociolinguistics pursues the Saussurean view of the social nature of *langue*, while Chomskyan generative linguistics (to which sociolinguistics has stood in irreconcilable contrast for a generation) pursues the Saussurean view of the mental and abstract nature of *langue*. An eventual reconciliation of this split—to which a deeper understanding of Saussure's thought may provide a clue—would certainly constitute a major breakthrough in the understanding of language.

5. *Langue* as a System of Signs: Semiology

The semiological conception of language as a collection of signs (a sign being understood as the collation of a signifying word and a signified concept) was anticipated in the philosophy of Aristotle (384–322 BCE), elaborated by the Stoics, and reached its summit in the 'speculative grammar' of the twelfth century. But starting in the fourteenth century, the view of language as a sign system began to cede pride of place to that of language as a social institution, an approach more characteristic of Plato (ca 429–347 BCE), the diffusion of whose works defines the new era of humanism that led to the Renaissance. The semiological perspective was never entirely lost, and would resurface notably among the seventeenth-century British empiricists. But the 'conventional' perspective with which it coexisted periodically overshadowed it, and the early nineteenth century was one such period, when abstract systems disembodied from human activity ceased to be of central interest.

As noted in Sect. 3 abstraction and disembodiment would reemerge as part of the 'scientific' spirit of the later nineteenth century; and it is thus no great coincidence that the 'semiotic' perspective on language was reopened independently by Charles Sanders Peirce (1839–1914) in the USA. Pierce's work in this area, like Saussure's, went unpublished during his lifetime, and was not seriously revived by philosophers until the 1930s. Only in the 1950s and 1960s were attempts made at unifying Saussurean 'semiology' (practiced mostly by European linguists) and Peircean 'semiotics' (practiced mostly by American philosophers) into a single paradigm, under the organizational leadership of Thomas A. Sebeok (1921–).

For Saussure, the network of linguistic signs which constitute *langue* is made up of the conjunction of a *significant* ('signifier'), understood as a sound pattern deposited in the mind, and a *signifié* ('signified'), a concept that is also deposited in the mind. Saussure compares them to the front and back of a single sheet of paper. It is important to note that the signifier is wholly distinct from the actual uttered word, as is the signified from the actual physical thing conceived of (if one exists). Although the distinction between concept and object has existed since antiquity, that between sound pattern and actual sound is Saussure's own contribution, of which some have seen a foreshadowing in the hypothetical 'sonant coefficients' of his early *Mémoire*.

Saussure predicted that *sémiologie*—the study of signs both within and outside of language—would have linguistics as its 'pilot science' (a further challenge to psychology, for the semiological domain is precisely where language is most explicitly mental), and indeed this came to pass in the founding of modern semiotics discussed above. But while linguistics has furnished the paradigmatic model for semiotics, the impact of semiotic inquiry upon linguistics has been slow in coming, with a certain acceleration perceptible in the last decade.

The one place where linguistics has been profoundly affected is in the nearly universal acceptance of Saussure's concept of the signifier as an abstract sound pattern. This view became the cornerstone of the concept of the phoneme as elaborated by Jan Baudouin de Courtenay (1846–1929) and Mikolai Kruszewski (1851–1887) in Russia, and subsequently by N. S. Trubetzkoy (1890–1938) in Vienna and Roman Jakobson (1896–1982) in Brno and Prague; Daniel Jones (1891–1967) in the UK; and Kenneth L. Pike (1912–2000) in the USA, to name only the most prominent figures (see *Firth, J. R.*) It resulted in the banishment of experimental phonetics from linguistic inquiry in favor of more abstract phonology, based not upon physical differences of sound, but on the ability to distinguish between concepts (see Sect. 8). The distinction between a physical 'etic' level (from phone*tic*) and an abstract 'emic' level (from phone*mic*) would be extended to every level of linguistic structure, and would become a hallmark in particular of postwar American linguistics.

6. The Arbitrariness of Linguistic Signs

As with the semiological nature of language, the arbitrariness of language—the fact that a signifier like the series of sounds /paj/ has no internal connection with the concept of a 'pie' which it signifies—reflects an ancient doctrine that had never fallen very far from the center of debate about the nature of language up through the end of the eighteenth century. Though not a direct concern for most of the historical linguists of the nineteenth century, the ancient debate between *physis* 'nature' and *nomos* 'convention' in the establishment and operation of language had been revived by Whitney and the Humboldtian psychologists, with Whitney's views of language positioned on the side of *nomos* and the Humboldtians' on the side of *physis*. Saussure, who at age 21 had met Whitney and greatly admired his work, doubtless encountered the debate there.

Saussure's precise formulation of the linguistic sign allows him to situate arbitrariness—which he called the 'first primary concept' of linguistics—precisely at the conjunction of signified and signifier, just as presented in the first sentence of the preceding paragraph. This represented an advance over most earlier formulations of arbitrariness, which (despite Aristotle) focused upon the relationship between the sign as a whole and the real-world objects conceptualized in the signified. Unfortunately, the *Cours* is not consistent in its presentation of arbitrariness, and quickly falls back into the older schema. Another problem with the presentation in the *Cours* is that the arbitrariness doctrine is first encountered in radical form in a very tense, strongly worded, and memorable section; then only later is this tempered with a section on relative arbitrariness that is often ignored, but without which Saussure's conception of language is inaccurately understood. Saussure's point in the later section is that while signifiers are always arbitrary relative to signifieds, they can be motivated relative to other signifiers. Thus, for example, the French numbers *dix-neuf* '19' and *vingt* '20' both show arbitrariness between signifier and signified, yet *dix-neuf* is motivated relative to the numerals *dix* '10' and *neuf* '9' which compose it, hence *dix-neuf* is relatively arbitrary while *vingt* is radically so. (This is connected to Saussure's distinction between syntagmatic and associative relations, discussed in Sect. 8) Cases of onomatopoeia, where there seems to be a motivated relationship between signifier and real-world analog, are dismissed as not really part of linguistic systems.

The fact that the *Cours* presents the radical version of arbitrariness first and most forcefully led to its assuming the status of dogma in twentieth-century linguistics (though undoubtedly it also appealed to something deeper in the Zeitgeist). It is one of the first views of language to which budding linguists are exposed in introductory courses and textbooks, often as one of the design features of language identified in 1958 by Charles Hockett (1916–). Like most dogmata, the radical form of arbitrariness is counterintuitive and requires a certain faith beyond what reason can sustain. Also, it is not always observable in the practice of those who preach it, particularly because of the influence of Jakobson, who beginning in the early 1930s mounted a sustained attack on radical arbitrariness through his work on markedness, child language acquisition, and aphasia, which suggested that linguistic elements differ in naturalness. Jakobson was to have a significant impact upon Chomsky, Joseph Greenberg (1915–), and many others, with the result that language is not treated as exhibiting anything like the radical arbitrariness of the dogma. Besides Jakobson, arbitrariness was problematized by Louis Hjelmslev (1899–1965), Émile Benveniste (1902–1976), and numerous others in a series of attacks on and defenses of the Saussurean view (often poorly represented) appearing from 1939 to about 1947.

7. The Linearity of Signifiers

After arbitrariness, the second primary principle of linguistics for Saussure is that linguistic signifiers are 'linear,' in the sense that, because they have a temporal existence, they represent a dimension that is measurable only as a line. This is one of the more mysterious of Saussure's ideas, in that he never made clear to what he was opposing it (he notes that it is obvious to everyone, but that its implications have not been appreciated). Linearity is part of what distinguishes spoken language as 'real' language, as opposed to writing, a secondary representation that is not necessarily linear (see Sect. 2); and it is what allows us to analyze connected discourse into meaningful units. One also detects a hedging on the inherent psychologism of the semiological view of language as consisting of perfectly juxtaposed signifiers and signifieds: Saussure here insists that signifiers exist in a completely separate dimension.

This principle has given rise to many interpretations. Jakobson formulated his doctrine of distinctive features in phonology—the idea that phonemes are not monoliths, but consist of bundles of features existing simultaneously—as part of a critique of the linearity of the signifier. Others have argued that Saussure's principle is not in disharmony with the concept of constituent features, but rather was intended (a) to deny the accumulation of signifiers, not their decomposition (a distinction which depends upon what one classifies as a signifier), (b) to insist that, however constituted, signifiers cannot be conceived apart from the dimension of time, and (c) to prepare the ground for the introduction of syntagmatic relations (see Sect. 8).

8. Syntagmatic and Paradigmatic Relations: *Langue* as Form, Not Substance

Saussure distinguished between the 'syntagmatic' relations a linguistic element has with the elements preceding and following it in an utterance, and 'associative' (now usually called paradigmatic) relations it has to other elements with which it shares partial identity, but which do not occur in the particular utterance at hand. For example, in the sentence *Crime pays* the element *crime* has a syntagmatic relationship with *pays* that determines, among other things, their order relative to one another and the fact that *pays* has the inflectional -*s*. At the same time, *crime* has paradigmatic relations with countless other elements, including the inflectionally related *crimes*, the derivationally related *criminal*, the conceptually related *misdemeanor* (and the conceptually opposite *legality*), and the phonetically related *grime*. As the last example suggests, each sound of the word *crime* /kraim/ has paradigmatic and syntagmatic relations with at least the sounds around it: /k/ is paradigmatically related to the /g/ that could in principle replace it; and syntagmatically related to the following /r/, since in English the presence of /k/ as the initial element of the word immediately restricts the following sound to /l r w/ or a vowel.

Saussure notes that the two types of relations, which correspond to different types of mental activity, contribute in different ways to the 'value' of the sign. In particular, the paradigmatic relations generate a negative value: the identity of the /r/ in /kraim/ is essentially that it could be, but is not, /l w/ or a vowel. This is important because the actual sound that represents /r/ can differ dramatically from one English dialect to another (being rolled, flapped, retroflex, etc.); but the actual sound content does not matter, so long as /r/ is kept distinct from the other sounds to which it is associatively related. *Langue*, Saussure insisted, is form, not substance.

Before Saussure, the syntagmatic relations of morphemes within a given utterance were certainly recognized as a matter of linguistic concern, though relatively neglected. But there was little or no precedent for the idea suggested by the *Cours* (implicitly if not explicitly) that there exists a syntax not only of words, but of sounds, meanings, and the relations uniting them; or that every time a sound, word, or meaning is chosen, a vast network of related elements is summoned up in absentia. The latter concept in particular set the study of language on a new course of abstraction that did not rely on psychological theorizing, but remained internal to language.

In many ways, the Saussurean notion of paradigmatic and syntagmatic relations would become the hallmark of twentieth-century linguistics: first, because it proposed that a single principle of structure unites all the levels at which language functions—sound, forms, and meaning; secondly because it suggested a way of analyzing language that would not depend on a simple listing of elements with their 'translation' into either another language or some sort of philosophical interpretation. Elements could henceforth be analyzed according to the relations they maintained with other elements, and the language could be understood as the vast system—not of these elements—but of these relations. This was the point of departure for structuralism (see Sect. 9).

To a large extent, the distributional method developed by Bloomfield is a working out of this Saussurean notion, with special emphasis on the paradigmatic relations. With the work of Bloomfield's student Zellig S. Harris (1909–1992) the syntagmatic relations assumed a status of equal importance, and with Harris's student Chomsky, overriding importance. (Regarding word order, Saussure's view is that the syntagmatic relations constitute that part of syntax which is predetermined—like the use of a third person singular verb form after the singular subject *crime*—and so a part of *langue*; while the rest of syntax, being subject to free combination, is relegated to *parole*.)

9. The Systematicity of *Langue*: Structuralism

Certainly the most wide-reaching Saussurean intellectual tradition, both within and outside of linguistics, derived from Saussure's characterization of *langue* as a wholly self-contained network of relationships among elements which as discussed above, have no positive content or value, but only the negative value generated by their differing from one another. Like most of his contemporaries, when Saussure thought of language he thought first of sounds and their combinations, and extrapolated outward from that level. The study of sounds had for several decades been a battleground between those who, later in the twentieth century, would be called the 'phoneticians,' proponents of an extreme form of positivism who believed that the key to understanding language lay in ever more precise measurement of sound waves and vocal apertures; and those who would now be called 'phonologists,' who preferred to operate on a more abstract (and traditional) plane, dealing with classes of sounds rather than the minute differences within classes. But the phoneticians were steadily gaining prestige, since their positivistic approach had the characteristic look of modern science.

As noted in Sect. 4, Saussure was attracted to postivism, but within limits. If psychology represented the Scylla of hyperrationalism, experimental phonetics was the Charybdis of hyperempiricism, equally to be avoided. Perhaps more so: whereas Saussure never attempted a complete divorce of language from the domain of the mind, his characterization of *langue* as a network of pure relations, of form and not substance, succeeded in marginalizing phonetics to the point that within a few decades it would retreat to the position of an auxiliary discipline to linguistics. The term *phonème*, used by Saussure as early as 1878 (five years after its coinage by A. Dufriche-Desgenettes, 1804–1879) to denote an abstract unit representing sound, but never actually defined by him, was taken up by Boudouin de Courtenay and Kruszewski and joined to an essentially Saussurean conception: 'phoneme' became the name for Saussure's abstract mental sound pattern, identifiable as the minimal unit of sound capable of changing the meaning of a signifier in a language. It eventually became the basis for further, related new concepts: the morpheme (coined by Baudouin de Courtenay) or moneme (minimal unit of meaning), tagmeme (minimal meaningful unit of syntax), toneme, and so on.

The full implications of Saussure's view of *langue* were localized in Prague, principally by Trubetzkoy, who elaborated complete phonological schemata for a panoply of languages from all over the world; and Jakobson, who extended the implications of 'functional' phonology to other domains of linguistic (and literary) inquiry. But strikingly similar projects were underway in other quarters: in the USA with Bloomfield, who saw himself as at least partly under the influence of Saussure (in a 1945 letter he described his major work *Language* as showing Saussure's influence 'on every page'); in Denmark, with the overtly Saussurean glossematics of Hjelmslev; in France, where Meillet had transmitted the Saussurean perspective to a whole generation of students, including André Martinet (1908–1999); Gustave Guillaume (1883–1960); and Benveniste. All the lines of affiliation among these 'schools' are not yet clear. But their work came to define the mainstream of linguistics in the twentieth century, and all of it assumes the conception of *langue* set out in the *Cours*.

The idea that language forms a self-contained system justified the autonomy of linguistic study not only vis-à-vis phonetics, but every other discipline as well, including psychology, anthropology, and sociology (the latter, again, was never deemed a threat). The only discipline under whose aegis it hypothetically fell was semiology, but even had semiology existed, the status of linguistics as its pilot science meant that it yielded its autonomy to no other field. Indeed, between the 1940s and the 1960s most fields of human knowledge came under the domination of 'structuralism' (a term first used in linguistics around 1928), understood in this context as the extrapolation out of linguistics of Saussure's concept of *langue* as a self-contained system of syntagmatic and paradigmatic relations among elements of negative content (see Joseph 1994). Its most widely heralded application was in the field of anthropology, by Claude Lévi-Strauss (1908–), who discovered Saussure in 1942 in a course taught by Jakobson. Other areas and their most prominent structuralist practitioners include: biology, Ludwig von Bertalanffy (1901–72) and C. H. Waddington (1905–1975); literary theory, Roland Barthes (1915–1980); Marxist theory, Louis Althusser (1918–1990); mathematics, 'Nicholas Bourbaki' (the pseudonym of a group of French mathematicians); psychoanalysis, Jacques Lacan (1901–1979); and psychology (where the groundwork for it had already been laid by the concept of

Gestalt), Jean Piaget (1896–1980). The rejection of structuralism by such figures as Jacques Derrida and Michel Foucault (1926–1984; see *Foucault, Michel*), which became widespread as part of the French student revolts of 1968, launched the 'poststructuralist' era, whose very name indicates that the Saussurean tradition remains an active force even when shaping the direction of reactions against it.

Within linguistics, the effects of poststructuralist thought are only beginning to be felt; the field in which structuralism began is the last to let it go. Precisely at mid-century the great British linguist J. R. Firth (1890–1960) was able to state that 'Nowadays, professional linguists can almost be classified by using the name of de Saussure. There are various possible groupings: Saussureans, anti-Saussureans, post-Saussureans, or non-Saussureans.' As we approach the twentieth-century's end, the only change one is tempted to make to Firth's statement is to remove 'non-Saussureans,' as it is doubtful that any survive. All work on or against language as an autonomous, self-contained system—and this includes work in generative grammar, universal–typological linguistics, discourse pragmatics, and sociolinguistics—falls squarely within the most important of Saussurean traditions.

See also: Sociolinguistics and Language Change.

Bibliography

Culler J 1986 *Ferdinand de Saussure*, 2nd edn. Cornell University Press, Ithaca, NY
Engler R 1989–90 *Édition critique du Cours de linguistique générale de F. de Saussure*. Harrassowitz, Wiesbaden, Germany
Gadet F 1989 *Saussure and Contemporary Culture*. Hutchinson Radius, London
Harris R 1987 *Reading Saussure*. Duckworth, London
Holdcroft D 1991 *Saussure: Sign, Systems and Arbitrariness*. Cambridge University Press, Cambridge, UK
Joseph J E 1994 Twentieth-century linguistics: Overview of trends. In: Asher R E, Simpson J M Y (eds.) *Encyclopedia of Language and Linguistics*, Pergamon, Oxford, UK, Vol. 9, pp. 4789–99
Joseph J E 1999 Structuralist linguistics: Saussure. In: Glendinning S (ed.) *The Edinburgh Encyclopedia of Continental Philosophy*. Edinburgh University Press, Edinburgh, UK, pp. 515–27
Joseph J E 2001 The exportation of structuralist ideas from linguistics to other fields: An overview. In: Auroux S, Koerner E F K, Niederehe H-J, Versteegh K (eds.), *History of the Language Sciences/Histoire des sciences du language/Geschichte der sprachwissenschaften*. Walter de Gruyter, Berlin
Joseph J E, Love N, Taylor T J 2001 *Landmarks in Linguistic Thought 2: The Western Tradition in the Twentieth Century*. Routledge, London
Koerner E F K 1973 *Ferdinand de Saussure: Origin and Development of his Linguistic Thought in Western Studies of Language*. Vieweg, Braunschweig, Germany
Koerner E F K 1987 *Saussurean Studies/Études saussuriennes*. Slatkine, Geneva, Switzerland
Meillet A 1921 *Linguistique historique et linguistique générale*. Champion, Paris
Saussure F de 1916 *Cours de linguistique générale*. Payot, Paris
Saussure F de 1922 *Recueil de publications scientifiques*. Sonor, Geneva, Switzerland
Saussure F de 1972 *Cours de linguistique générale*. Payot, Paris
Saussure F de 1983 (trans. Harris R) *Course in General Linguistics*. Duckworth, London

Social Psychology
W. S. Bainbridge

Social psychology is an interdisciplinary academic field, lying between psychology and sociology, with less substantial connections to economics and to literature. At many universities, competing social psychology courses are taught in both the psychology and sociology departments, and on rare occasions joint departments in social relations have been founded. The division between psychology and sociology is so extreme that it has become fashionable to speak of 'two social psychologies' rather than one. Despite its fragmentation, social psychology speaks with a strong voice on the importance of language in human relations, and many of its theories and research findings should be of direct concern to linguistics. Several essays in this *Encyclopedia* examine in detail aspects of the social psychology of language, and this essay provides an overview. After sketching the structure of the field, a sampling of major language-related topics will be considered: the social psychology of speech, attitudes, symbolic interactionism, meaning, and microsociology.

1. The Structure of Social Psychology

Stephan and Stephan (1985) say that sociological social psychology concerns social experience stemming from individuals' participation in groups, social interaction, the effects on both of these of the cultural environment, and the emergence of social structure from interaction. In contrast, psychological social psychology focuses on the thoughts, feelings, and behaviors of individuals as influenced by others. In sociology, Stephan and Stephan contend, two distinct schools of thought exist: symbolic interactionism, which holds that reality is socially constructed through the meanings people communicate, and the personality and society perspective, which emphasizes the attitudes and values that individuals derive from their cultures. Psychological social psychology seems even more diverse, including social learning theory, exchange theory, role theory, and attribution theory.

While such a typology can have heuristic functions, no single conceptual division of the field has achieved wide consensus. Not only is it difficult to map social psychology at a given point in time, but as Sahakian's review of the history of the field proves, its contours and divisions have changed over the decades. A. M. McMahon and a number of other authors have argued that social psychology of all varieties experienced a crisis in the late 1970s, when many critics charged that the field had lost sight of fundamental questions, and the knowledge gained by each successive research project seemed to illustrate the law of diminishing returns.

George Homans frequently remarked that human beings must have always known the chief truths concerning social behavior, or else they would not have been able to sustain successful relations with each other. If true, this observation sets sharp limits to the achievements possible for academic social science. Prior to the late 1970s, however, social psychologists had made striking claims for a number of rather counterintuitive theories, and part of the crisis that followed may merely have been their empirical disproof.

McMahon (1984) says that psychological social psychology was dominated by two classes of theorizing: trait theories of individual behavior and field theory. Trait theories assert that social conditions shape individuals, giving them distinct personalities or attitudes that become fixed and thus render behavior consistent across many very different situations. When human behavior was found to be significantly inconsistent, and attitudes refused to stabilize in study after study, trait theories lost ground. Field theory asserts that the proper unit of analysis is the social system, but beyond this its advice has not been clear its influence has faded as its terminology has been replaced by fresher metaphors.

Sociological social psychology, for McMahon, either borrowed its perspectives from psychology, in which case it suffered the same crisis, or drew upon the often compatible sociological schools of thought known as 'symbolic interactionism' and 'structural functionalism.' In textbooks of a generation ago, symbolic interactionism was used to explain individual-level phenomena, while structural functionalism explained phenomena on the societal level. Supposedly, society was a structure of institutions, organized around a coherent set of values and beliefs, that served vital functions for the entire system. Individuals were socialized, greatly through symbols exchanged during social interaction, to play their necessary roles in the institutions. However, in the 1960s structural functionalism crashed, its theories seeming either factually wrong or vacuous, and its relative political conservatism was no longer attractive to the increasingly radical sociologists. Symbolic interactionism has retreated from its partnership with the now bankrupt structural functionalism, and it continues to be a vital school of thought recruiting new scholars and publishing at a great rate. Yet its theories have never been particularly adapted to unambiguous empirical testing, and the increasing quantification and empiricism of the main journals shunted symbolic interactionism over to the sidelines.

2. The Social Psychology of Speech

A few older textbooks on social psychology contain distinct sections on language, notably the excellent texts by Roger Brown (1965) and by Krech et al. (1962) but most textbooks of the late 1980s and early 1990s disperse their material on language across several chapters ostensibly devoted to other topics. For example, studies on interpersonal influence are found throughout these texts, offering many insights that might be applied to linguistic analysis of accommodation (see *Speech Accommodation*), the adjustment of speech to match that of persons with whom one is speaking.

The study of psychopathology has particularly generated theory and research concerning language. Psychotherapy, the talking cure, assumes that emotional problems are sufficiently language-rooted that the insight or catharsis that can come from talking about them is curative. The theory of the double bind, to mention a specific example, asserts that mental problems can arise from contradictory messages imposed on a powerless person by a powerful one. One form of therapy, albeit a deviant one, was explicitly linguistic in nature, the general semantics movement that asserted that all human social and emotional pathologies resulted from misuse of language. Research has also been conducted on deception, the conscious use of language to misinform the listener, including a large body of studies on the socalled Machiavellian personality who habitually lies (Christie and Geis 1970, Hyman 1989).

Social psychologists have learned about language not only by studying it, but also by perfecting research methods that rely heavily upon it. For example, interviewers have been forced to learn how to maximize rapport with their research subjects, thus gaining general insights into how successful communication can be achieved. Richard A. Berk and

Joseph M. Adams (1970) have suggested four principles of establishing rapport with respondents who are apt to be suspicious of the researcher: always be honest, be prepared to inconvenience oneself as a sign of commitment, always keep one's word, and speak in as flattering terms as possible, consistent with plausibility.

Berk and Adams have also listed techniques for establishing respect and acceptance. While it is important for an interviewer dealing with subjects who speak a different language to communicate in their terms, the interviewer should not adopt the slang style of the subjects unless it is very natural for the interviewer. The subjects may appreciate the special effort the interviewer makes to learn their language, but they know the interviewer is not a member of their group and may be offended by a pretense of membership. Other language-related techniques include remaining unshaken even when one hears things that are very shocking to the researcher's personal standards, and occasionally revealing some intimate facts about oneself in recognition that really successful communication requires a reciprocal relationship between the speakers.

Raymond L. Gordon (1969) has identified eight factors that inhibit communication in interviews: competing demands for time made by activities outside the interview, threats to the person's ego that various topics may constitute, etiquette rules that prohibit saying certain kinds of things in public or to certain kinds of people, the pain of recounting past traumatic experiences, simple forgetting, confusion about the chronological order of events, inferential confusion about the meaning of events, and unconscious behavior patterns that set hidden agendas for the conversation. The best antidotes to these inhibitors are eight facilitators: the respondent's desire to fulfill expectations, the recognition he or she seeks from the interviewer, altruistic appeals that stress the ultimate values served by the interview, sympathetic understanding of what the person expresses, the new experience that an interview affords, emotional catharsis, the opportunity to place memories and feelings in a meaningful context with an intelligent listener who asks guiding questions, and extrinsic rewards such as money paid for talk.

3. Attitudes

Perhaps the most widely used concept in psychological social psychology is *attitude*, often defined as the positive or negative evaluation of an object, with anything, tangible or intangible, capable of being the object of an attitude. As the term is generally used, each person is presumed to possess a large number of attitudes that can be expressed almost instantly in words and that are the key determinants of behavior with regard to the object. People who say they favor political party X can be expected to vote for it; people who express positive attitudes toward particular foods are likely to eat them. The standard way of measuring attitudes is through self-report questionnaires or interviews, and the underlying assumption of this research is that attitudes are coded verbally in the brain, thus making them linguistic phenomena.

Linguists have begun systematic research on attitudes towards speech styles (see *Style*), in light of the fact that speakers and dialects are often evaluated harshly if they do not meet some set of standards applied by listeners. Standard psychological experimental methodology has been applied to this topic, through the matched guise technique (MGT), described by Peter Ball and Howard Giles (1988). Respondents are played a set of recordings of voices and asked to judge the speakers' capabilities, personalities, emotional states, and various other social and linguistic characteristics. The challenge in such a method is to control for differences in the speakers' voices that are unrelated to the independent variable in question. In MGT, speakers are chosen to make the recordings who are capable of speaking in two distinctly different ways, for example equally fluently in French or English, thus matching all voice characteristics other than the one under examination.

Perhaps the classic example of social psychological research on attitudes is the work on attitude change that was performed at Yale University around 1950, still relevant and constantly being extended in the 1990s. Two of the experiments done at Yale by Carl I. Hovland and his associates will demonstrate the wide range of language-related phenomena that were studied, one concerning the credibility of communicators, and the other exploring the role of public proclamations in stabilizing attitudes. In an experiment reported by Hovland et al. (1953), a recorded lecture about juvenile delinquency was played to high school students who were asked to judge how fair it was. The first of three experimental groups was told that the speaker was a judge in a juvenile court, someone who was a real expert on the topic, and highly respectable as well. A second group thought the speaker was an ordinary member of a radio program's studio audience, and a third group was told that the speaker was a former juvenile delinquent currently awaiting trial on a charge of drug peddling. The judge was considered fair by 73 percent of the subjects, and 63 thought the ordinary person was fair, but only 29 percent gave a favorable rating to the accused drug pedlar. The vast literature of similar studies that have followed on from the Yale research support and give scientific specificity to the commonsense notion that speech has a variable impact on listeners, depending upon who speaks it.

The second attitude change experiment divided student respondents into two groups who were given a pair of lectures on the issue of the voting age, which was 21 years old at the time of the study. In the first phase of the experiment, the subjects heard a speech giving one side of a debate on voting age. Then the students were asked whether they agreed or disagreed with the following statement: 'The voting age should be reduced from 21 years to the draft age of 18 years.' After that, they all wrote an essay, giving their views on the voting age debate. The second phase consisted of another speech, giving the other side of the voting age debate. Finally, the students were asked again to state their view on whether the voting age should be reduced from 21 to 18.

The experimental manipulation concerned the essay the student wrote at the end of the first phase. Half of the students were told to sign their essays and were informed that they would appear in the next issue of the school newspaper, while the other half of the respondents were left to believe that their essays and opinions were private. The researchers hypothesized that making a public commitment to an opinion reduced the chances that a person would change his or her views subsequently. Indeed, among the group that signed their essays and believed they would be published, only 14 percent changed their opinion to agree with the second speaker, while in the control group, 41 percent did so. Thus, expressing an attitude in public strengthens the individual's commitment to it.

Research on attitudes is conducted at such a high rate in the late twentieth century, that the *Annual Review of Psychology* summarizes it regularly (Cooper and Croyle 1984, Chaiken and Stangor 1987, Tesser and Shaffer 1990). Yet serious questions remain about the efficacy of the concept. In particular, questions continue to be raised about the connection between attitudes and behavior (see *Attitudes and Behavior*), and many studies indicate that what people say and what they do are quite different things. Certainly the concept of attitude asserts a theory about the power of language, and much research on the topic will be of interest to linguists.

4. Symbolic Interactionism

Symbolic interactionism is a distinct school of thought, acknowledging a unified heritage that many say began with George Herbert Mead. Although some symbolic interactionists have accepted the canons of positivist science, others, notably Herbert Blumer, believe that social reality is too multifaceted and fluid to be captured in a few rigid hypotheses. Some of the most influential members of this school, Erving Goffman (see *Goffman, Erving*), for example, offer suggestive interpretations of the meaning of human behavior and symbolic expression, but refuse to subject them to any process of unequivocal evaluation. To that extent, symbolic interactionism is more like poetry or music than it is like the natural sciences.

Some writers distinguish two brands of symbolic interactionism, the Chicago School, which stresses interpretation of humanly constructed meanings to the exclusion of hypothesis testing, and the Iowa School, which allows the possibility of logically framing and empirically testing somewhat general statements about human behavior. But in all its manifestations, symbolic interactionism offers a sharp critique of the currently dominant approach in the central sociology journals, which stresses the computerized analysis of frequently superficial numbers far removed from the richness of human meanings.

Among the early concepts that continue to have great influence is definition of the situation, proposed by Thomas and Znaniecki in 1918. The meaning of something does not immediately announce itself to us, but must be read into every situation, typically on the basis of the culture shared by participants and prior experiences of the individuals. To some extent, such definitions are arbitrary, and there are always alternative definitions that fit a situation equally well. But once a definition has been adopted, it conditions people's actions, feelings, and further perceptions.

Among the most important entities that requires definition is the self. A glance at an English dictionary reveals that *self* appears in literally hundreds of compounds, from *self-abandoned* to *self-worship*, and it primarily serves to indicate reflexivity. As George Herbert Mead analyzed it, this reflexivity is both subject and object, the first person in both nominative and objective cases, the *I* contemplating the *me*. Clearly, there are several ways one might analyze *self* linguistically, and in various usages it is frequently listed as pronoun, adjective, noun, and even verb. As a noun, it is an abstraction referring to the entire person of an individual. Symbolic interactionists have both examined the concept closely and employed it to great effect in their analyses of individual behavior and of society. As Hazel Marcus and Elissa Wurf (1987) noted, social psychologists of several varieties have come to see self-concepts as dynamic, multifaceted, and implicated in social phenomena of all kinds.

Among the ways a self can manifest itself is through the playing of roles, and role theory (see *Role Theory*) has been developed and applied by literally hundreds of symbolic interactionists. Language enshrines many roles, such as 'father,' 'mother,' 'priest,' 'judge,' and 'teacher.' The complete set of roles in a society provides a kind of social grammar, defining how persons (rather than words) are supposed to interact, and they are among the most thoroughly linguistic of social phenomena. Many sociologists argue that social roles are scripted by society and define *role* as 'a set of expectations governing the behavior of persons holding particular positions in society; a set of norms that defines how persons in a particular position should behave' (Stark 1989: 686). Symbolic interactionists have given rather more stress to the capacity of individuals to script their own roles, for example, through constant *impression management* intended to give the most favorable impression of oneself to others, and to the way that the roles in a particular social group are constantly undergoing change. In the extreme, it can be argued that the self is nothing more than the set of roles played by a given person.

The self comes into existence through interaction with others, and the other, as an alternate self, comes into existence reciprocally through the same process. Important in symbolic interactionism is the concept of the *generalized other*, a kind of indefinite second person that represents the shared perspective of all the particular others who interact with the self. By taking that perspective, in the imagination, a person can view himself from outside as it were, thus attaining a clear concept of self. At one level, the generalized other can represent all of humanity minus one, but there also can exist several more limited generalized others, including groups that serve as reference points for the definition of the self.

A reference group is a category of persons, real or imaginary, toward whom the individual orients his behavior and which he uses to define himself. Often, the individual desires the approval of the reference group and tries to become a worthy member of it. A negative reference group, however, is a category of people one wishes to disassociate from, and one method to achieve this it to broadcast the twin message that the traits of the group are abhorrent and that one possesses very different traits. For years, reference group theory has been influential in business marketing research, and advertising is often designed to communicate messages associating a product with groups that are positive reference groups for many consumers.

Early in the twentieth century, symbolic interactionism greatly influenced educational theory in the United States, and in diluted and often unrecognized forms, it continues in the 1990s to shape discourse about the means by which good citizens and responsible adults are created. Many community leaders, social workers, and journalists talk the language of symbolic interaction without necessarily understanding its technical meaning or the relatively distinct philosophy of life embodied in it. In sociology, symbolic interactionism has been important in shaping conceptions of values, and it has contributed to our understanding of the role of symbols in social conflict through labeling theory of deviant behavior and the analysis of social movements as symbolic crusades.

5. Meaning

Not surprisingly, *meaning* is one of the most difficult words to define, especially as it is used in social psychology to refer to humanly constructed frameworks for perception, emotion, and action. A dictionary may say that meaning is what is conveyed by language, but how this 'what' exists apart from the language that conveys it is not clear, and the meaning of *meaning* has been the special focus of ethnomethodology, attribution theory, and branches of semantics that spread into social psychology.

Ethnomethodology (see *Ethnomethodology*) is a school of sociology concerned with how human beings make sense of their everyday lives, and like symbolic interactionism, it stresses the processes by which people achieve definitions of objects, roles, and even the internal states of their own minds. Of particular interest to linguists, ethnomethodology was in great measure the source of the movement known as 'conversation analysis' (see *Conversation Analysis*). Ethnomethodology is distinct from symbolic interactionism both in arising from German philosophical roots rather than American ones, and for giving rather greater emphasis to the internal subjectivity of the individual, and less to the role of the other. Indeed, while symbolic interactionist George Herbert Mead was concerned with how other people participate in the building of an individual's self, ethnomethodological precursor Alfred Schütz wrote about how a person gains insight into other's subjectivity through consideration of his or her own.

Richard Hilbert (1990) has argued that ethnomethodology (including conversation analysis) should not be considered a part of social psychology because it transcends the distinction between microsociology and macrosociology, and yet with its emphasis on the contents of the human mind and its empirical emphasis on the details of interactions between individuals, it seems appropriate to consider it here.

A classic empirical study in the ethnomethodological tradition was Peter McHugh's (1968) experiment that ostensibly studied a new method of counseling. Each research subject sat alone in a room, speaking into a microphone about his personal problems and asking questions answerable by 'yes' or 'no.' After the counselor in another room responded, the research subject was supposed to say aloud what the answer meant to him, then proceed to present more of his problems and ask further yes–no questions. In fact, the yes–no answers were given according to a prearranged pattern, and had nothing to do with the questions asked. The fact that the subjects typically found the answers meaningful was interesting, but the study also allowed close examination of the framework people used to construct the meaning they believed they had found.

Many ethnoemethodological studies have concerned direction-giving of one kind or another. In one design, the researcher telephones various businesses, asking directions for how to come over but continually failing to understand them; this forces the unwitting research subjects on the other end of the phone to struggle to orient the caller in terms of landmarks or abstract principles like compass directions. A less intrusive method is to listen in on the radio messages used to dispatch taxicabs. One researcher merely observed what medical personnel said to patients who were awakening from general anaesthesia, words apparently chosen to reorient the person and prevent them from panicking and thrashing around.

Ethnomethodology is in great measure based on phenomenology, a philosophical tradition associated with Edmund Husserl. For example, a technique of philosophical analysis called 'reduction' can be adapted to the study of the meaning of concepts. In reduction, one contemplates a particular concept, noting all the characteristics that seem associated with it. Then one mentally examines each characteristic in the list, determining whether the concept in question could exist without it, and crossing the characteristic off the list if it could. Eventually, one arrives at an irreducible list of attributes of the concept in question, a pristine definition of it shorn of all nonessentials.

What is a telephone call? The phone rings, someone picks it up, and a person says 'Hello.' That's a phone call. But is the ring essential? No; there could be a flashing light, or other signal. Is some kind of signal necessary? Perhaps; that question needs further study. Is it essential for there to be something to pick up? No. Must there be someone on the other end of the line? Yes. Must that person be aware that there is somebody on this end of the line? Yes. Is the exchange of words necessary? Eventually, after close thought to resolve any ambiguities, reduction would produce the essential definition of *telephone call*. In their empirical research, ethnomethodologists force ordinary people to act out this procedure, or they watch them employing their *ethnomethods* to make sense out of natural problems of definition that present themselves in the world of everyday life.

In psychological social psychology, the 1970s and 1980s saw the emergence of a major approach to meaning called attribution theory. When it first emerged in the 1960s, attribution theory had some similarities to ethnomethodology; both stressed the ways people make sense of their surroundings and both made radical claims about the novelty of their findings. For example, attribution theorists frequently asserted that people do not know their own minds but infer their attitudes on the basis of observing their own behavior or being told by others how they felt.

A host of experimental studies seemed to confirm this diagnosis of human self-ignorance. Subjects given injections of epinephrine felt and behaved quite differently, depending on what they had been told the effects would be or on how the experimenter's confederate behaved. Subjects who had received a series of painful electric shocks could endure more or less further pain depending on whether they were told they had been assisted in tolerating the earlier shocks by a drug. Despite initial appearances, attribution theory turned out not to be one of the faddish excesses of the 1960s, but a solid contribution, and in the 1990s it can now be seen that much work before the 1960s actually laid the basis for the recent developments. Attribution theory focuses most closely on the social and psychological processes by which people define the causes of events, but its ideas are remarkably similar to those of contemporary symbolic interactionism, except supported by a far stronger empirical research program.

Another development in psychological social psychology that focuses on meaning is the research technique known as the 'semantic differential.' It consists of a set of paired opposites, such a good–bad and happy–sad, presented as questionnaire scales. The respondent is required to rate a concept on each of these scales, and statistical analysis then maps the concept along three dimensions: evaluation, potency, and activity. Widely used in a variety of studies conducted in many languages, the semantic differential is believed to measure the connotative meaning of terms. Very recently, as John Digman (1990) reports, the three semantic dimensions have been related to a system of five dimensions of personality that has achieved much consensus among psychologists: extraversion/introversion, friendliness/hostility, conscientiousness, neuroticism, and intellect. Digman further notes that the personality typologies employed both by psychologists and by ordinary people are rooted in language and may be little more than the system human language possesses for classifying human behavior.

6. Small Groups and Other Microstructures

At present, judging from course enrolments and book sales, the psychological brand of social psychology is more popular than the sociological brand, and thus perhaps it is more influential. However, much of the work done in sociology that could be called social psychology is given other names. Rodney Stark (1989: 682–3), among others, calls it 'microsociology,' which he defines as 'the study of small groups and of face-to-face interaction among humans,' to be contrasted with macrosociology, 'the study of large groups and even of whole societies.' Much microsociological research is performed in the field, for example, observational studies of families, religious groups, or deviant subcultures, while psychological social psychology is more wedded to the laboratory and to the experimental method. Some varieties of microsociology eschew psychology altogether, if by 'psychology' is meant the study of the individual psyche, and focus instead on the structure of social relations in small groups and networks.

In both sociology and psychology, small group research (see *Small Group Research*) has been carried out vigorously for many decades. Groups establish norms concerning proper language; the status structure of groups often demands deferential or commanding language, and groups shape the language of members through cohesive social relations and the socialization of values. Among the research techniques developed to study communication patterns in small groups, interaction process analysis is notable not only for its great influence but also for providing a novel theory of the categories of speech.

Microsociologists have become increasingly dissatisfied with the concept of group, however, noting that many of the stable social relationships that affect the individual occur in open structures that might better be called 'networks.' Sociometry (see *Sociometry*) is the technique for studying social networks, and the measurement of linguistic influence across complex social structures has progressed considerably in recent years.

Some scholars, in both psychology and sociology, prefer to begin their analysis with the exchanges that take place between individuals, and exchange theory has become a prime rallying point for social psychologists who emphasize the economic nature of human behavior. Like symbolic interactionism, exchange theory focuses on the give and take that transpires between individuals, but it ignores symbols in favor of rewards, whether tangible or intangible. Thus, exchange theory appears to give a lesser role to language than do the other perspectives described above. In the extreme, as practiced by George Caspar Homans, exchange theory is thoroughly behavioristic, denying the importance of the subtle contents of the human mind, words included.

7. Conclusion

The diversity of social psychology is at once a blessing and a curse. Few practitioners are aware of the potentially great value of uniting social psychology with linguistics, and those few can at best create narrow bridges between their own particular subfields or schools of thought and scholarly linguistics. Thus, a convergence of social psychology and linguistics will be difficult to achieve. However, language plays such a tremendous role in so many branches of social psychology, and a variety of its theories and research traditions have so much insight and information to offer linguists, that a marriage of the disciplines is worth promoting.

See also: Sociology of Language.

Bibliography

Ball P, Giles H 1988 Speech style and employment selection: The Matched Guise Technique. In: Breakwell G M, Foot H, Gilmour R (eds.) *Doing Social Psychology: Laboratory and Field Exercises*. Cambridge University Press, Cambridge, UK

Berk R A, Adams J M 1970 Establishing rapport with deviant groups. *Social Problems* **18**: 102–17

Brown R 1965 *Social Psychology*. Free Press, New York

Chaiken S, Stangor C 1987 Attitudes and attitude change. *Annual Review of Psychology* **38**: 575–630

Christie R, Geis F L 1970 *Studies in Machiavellianism*. Academic Press, New York

Cooper J, Croyle R T 1984 Attitudes and attitude change. *Annual Review of Psychology* **35**: 395–426

Digman J M 1990 Personality structure: Emergence of the five-actor model. *Annual Review of Psychology* **41**: 417–40

Engel J F, Blackwell R D, Kollat D T 1978 *Consumer Behavior*. Dryden Press, Hinsdale, IL

Gordon R L 1969 *Interviewing: Strategy, Techniques, and Tactics*. Dorsey, Homewood, IL

Hilbert R A 1990 Ethnomethodology and the micro–macro order. *American Sociological Review* **55**: 794–808

Hovland C I (ed.) 1957 *The Order of Presentation in Persuasion*. Yale University Press, New Haven, CT

Hovland C I, Janis I L, Kelley H H 1953 *Communication and Persuasion*. Yale University Press, New Haven, CT

Hyman R 1989 The psychology of deception. *Annual Review of Psychology* **40**: 133–54

Krech D, Crutchfield R S, Ballachey E L 1962 *Individual in Society*. McGraw Hill, New York

Marcus H, Wurf E 1987 The dynamic self-concept: A social psychological perspective. *Annual Review of Psychology* **38**: 299–337

McHugh P 1968 *Defining the Situation: The Organization of Meaning in Social Interaction*. Bobbs-Merrill, Indianapolis, IN

McMahon A M 1984 The two social psychologies: Postcrisis directions. *Annual Review of Sociology* **10**: 121–40

Mead G H 1934 *Mind, Self, and Society*. University of Chicago Press, Chicago, IL

Ryan E B, Giles H 1982 *Attitudes Toward Language Variation*. Edward Arnold, London

Sahakian W S 1982 *History and Systems of Social Psychology*. Hemisphere, Washington, DC

Schütz A 1967 *The Phenomenology of the Social World*. North Western University Press, Evanston, IL

Snyder M 1977 Impression management. In: Wrightman L S (ed.) *Social Psychology*. Brooks/Cole, Monterey, CA

Stark R 1989 *Sociology*. Wadsworth, Belmont, CA

Stephan C W, Stephan W G 1985 *Two Social Psychologies*. Dorsey, Homewood, IL

Tesser A, Shaffer D R 1990 Attitudes and attitude change. *Annual Review of Psychology* **41**: 479–523

Socialization
C. B. Cazden

Socialization is the process of internalization through which human beings become members of particular cultures, learning how to speak as well as how to act and think and feel. The term 'language socialization' is used more often for the primary socialization that takes place during childhood within the family (for which Schieffelin and Ochs 1986, is the best short review); but it should also refer to secondary socializations throughout life to specialized forms and uses of language in school, community, and work settings.

Language socialization is a more inclusive term than language acquisition, emphasizing pragmatic as well as syntactic and semantic competence; it is the preferred term in linguistic anthropology, sociolinguistics, and culturally oriented psychology.

1. Relationships Between Language and Socialization

Language relates to socialization in three ways. First, language is the primary medium for socialization into culture; that is, there is socialization by or through language, where language is the means. Second, there is socialization for language, where situation-specific and culture-specific language use is the outcome. Third, there is socialization about language in the form of knowledge about, and attitudes toward, language forms and functions. While these three aspects of socialization occur together in real life, they are often studied separately, and by different research techniques.

2. Socialization Through Language

Language plays an especially important role in socialization because it is such a pervasive and orderly feature of everyday life in every culture (Sapir 1962). Three characteristics of language contribute to this role: its propositional nature makes possible explicit cultural instruction; its reference to the non-here-and-now permits the sharing of memories and knowledge of the past, plans for the future, and imagined worlds; its indexicality means that units of language, such as terms of address or speaking one dialect rather than another, point to culturally interpreted aspects of the nonverbal world. (Ochs 1990 discusses this last, and more subtle, relationship.)

3. Socialization for Language

Learning to speak is never simply a matter of learning a particular language or dialect—i.e., the words, syntactic patterns, and accent spoken in a particular community; it also involves learning multiple registers, i.e., particular ways of using language in particular settings within that community.

When one shifts registers, one also often shifts what one is talking about, and the values and beliefs implicit in those words. For this reason, Gee uses the term 'discourses' for 'forms of life which integrate words, acts, values, beliefs, attitudes, and social identities' (1996: 127; see *Discourse*). He then distinguishes primary and secondary discourses (including literacy in the latter), and also dominant and nondominant discourses according to their social prestige and power.

Even young children exhibit some register variation—for example, by speaking differently to adults or their peers (reviewed in Andersen 1990). For most people, secondary socialization in additional registers continues into adulthood, as they acquire new ways of speaking in new roles. Examples include the nearly universal, but culturally expressed, roles of student (Cazden 2001) or parent (Snow and Ferguson 1977); professions such as doctor or lawyer (Philips 1982); age-specific rhetorical styles such as 'the talk of the elders of bygone days' in Mexicano communities in the southwestern USA (Briggs 1986); and occasional oral tasks like chairing meetings, or conducting sociolinguistically appropriate interviews in a particular speech community (Briggs 1986).

Most research on language socialization is ethnographic. But experimental situations such as role playing can reveal register knowledge for roles never enacted in reality. Andersen (1990) provides both a research review of such knowledge in children, and a report of experimental research in which 4- to 7-year-old children gave a doctor puppet lower pitch and more imperatives and questions when talking to a nurse, and gave the nurse more polite requests to the doctor.

4. Socialization About Language

Socialization about language includes both knowledge and attitudes. One kind of metapragmatic knowledge is evidenced in the way speech is reported in narrative. Whereas 7- and 10-year-old children frame direct speech, usually with 'said,' 4-year-olds often provide no verbal framing but sometimes differentiate voices by pitch (Hickmann 1985).

Other kinds of knowledge become important when children enter school and confront the task of learning to read. Where alphabetic orthographies are used, learners must become aware of the sounds in oral language and their relationship to letters; and even teachers, whose mental representation of language has been influenced by experience with written texts, may have to learn to distinguish the number of phonemes in a word from the number of letters (see *Speech and Writing*).

As with oral language, 'literacy socialization' is a more inclusive term than 'literacy acquisition': while the latter may refer only to learning to encode, decode, and comprehend print; the former points also to uses of reading and writing for different purposes in different settings.

Attitudes toward language can often be inferred from observations of which forms available in an environment are in fact learned, and from spontaneous comments about other people's oral or written language use. More systematic study of language attitudes requires more experimental techniques, often by social psychologists. One widely used technique is the matched guise in which subjects evaluate messages spoken in different languages or dialects but, unknown to the subjects, by a single speaker.

5. Environmental Influences on Language Socialization

There is general agreement that primary socialization occurs through participation, and through interaction between children and more mature speakers, both adults and peers. In fact, family and community settings for the virtually universally successful process of language socialization are often cited as the prototype of effective learning environments. While implicit immersion in language-related activities is certainly crucial, there is also evidence that more explicit tuition also occurs, e.g., in elicited imitation routines found in many cultures in which an adult will direct a child to say a word or phrase (Ochs 1990).

How secondary socializations can be aided in school is less clear, and educational controversies continue over the most effective combination of implicit immersion and explicit instruction. Heath (1983) gives a vivid picture of primary socialization in three communities that differ in race and social class, and an optimistic report of how teachers adapted their teaching for more effective secondary language socialization in school—including getting learners to 'become ethnographers' and study language use themselves.

In the study of language socialization, gender differences in ways of speaking—sometimes referred to as genderlects—are especially interesting because most children are exposed to both men's and women's speech during their primary socialization. Differential socialization cannot, therefore, be explained by differential exposure (Warren-Leubecker and Bohannon 1989).

6. Socialization and Resistance

Many writers on language socialization imply that language socialization is always successful as long as the learning environment is at least minimally adequate. But resistance does occur. Familiar examples are immigrant children resisting speaking the language of their primary socialization at home, if the language of the school is also the language of wider society, or nondominant dialect speakers resisting speaking a standard dialect despite its availability at school and on television.

Writing about the more general field of the socialization of cognition Goodnow (1990: 280) states: 'I seek an account of socialization that goes beyond saying that the individual must be regarded as agent or actor, or that influences are bi-directional... [E]ven if much of one's life is spent in puppet fashion, there remain at least the occasional times when one notices the strings and decides to cut them.'

Of all forms of learning, language is closest to one's social and individual identity; and that identity helps to account for both resistance and learning, and is also their result. In Sapir's words, 'In spite of the fact that language acts as a socializing and uniformizing force, it is at the same time the most potent single known factor for the growth of individuality' (1962: 19).

See also: Home Language and School Language; Ethnography of Speaking.

Bibliography

Andersen E S 1990 *Speaking with Style: The Sociolinguistic Skills of Children*. Routledge, London
Briggs C L 1986 *Learning to Ask: A Sociolinguistic Appraisal of the Role of the Interview in Social Science Research*. Cambridge University Press. Cambridge, UK
Cazden C B 2001 *Classroom Discourse*, 2nd edn. Heinemann, Portsmouth, NH
Gee J P 1996 *Social Linguistics and Literacies: Ideology in Discourses*. Taylor and Francis, London
Goodnow J L 1990 The socialization of cognition. In: Stigler J W, Shweder R A, Herdt G (eds.) *Cultural Psychology: Essays In Comparative Human Development*. Cambridge University Press, Cambridge, UK
Heath S B 1983 *Ways with Words: Language, Life, and Work in Communities and Classrooms*. Cambridge University Press, Cambridge, UK
Hickmann M 1985 Metapragmatics in child language. In: Mertz E, Parmenter (eds.) *Semiotic Mediation. Sociocultural and Psychological Perspectives*. Academic Press, Orlando, FL
Ochs E 1990 Indexicality and socialization. In: Stigler J W, Shweder R A, Herdt G (eds.) *Cultural Psychology: Essays on Comparative Human Development*. Cambridge University Press, Cambridge, UK
Philips S U 1982 The language socialization of lawyers: Acquiring the cant. In: Spindler G (ed.) *Doing the

Ethnography of Schooling. Holt, Rinehart and Winston, New York

Sapir E 1962 In: Mandelbaum D G (ed.) *Culture, Language, and Personality: Selected Essays.* University of California Press, Berkeley, CA

Schieffelin B, Ochs E 1986 Language socialization. *Annual Review of Anthropology* **15**: 163–91

Snow C E, Ferguson C A (eds.) 1977 *Talking to Children: Language Input and Acquisition.* Cambridge University Press, Cambridge, UK

Warren-Leubecker A, Bohannon J N 1989 Pragmatics: Language in social contexts. In: Gleason J B (ed.) *The Development of Language*, 2nd edn. Merrill, Columbus, OH

Sociolinguistics of Sign Language
C. Lucas

Natural sign languages are autonomous linguistic systems, independent of the spoken languages with which they may coexist in a given community. As sign languages are fully fledged autonomous linguistic systems shared by communities of users, the sociolinguistics of sign languages can be described in ways which parallel the description of the sociolinguistics of spoken languages. That is, the sociolinguistics of sign languages concerns the interrelationship of sign language and social structure. As with spoken languages, sign languages are at once used to communicate information and to define the social situation, i.e., to make statements about individual identity, group loyalties, and one's relation to one's interlocutors. The sociolinguistics of sign languages includes the study of regional and social variation, bilingualism and language contact phenomena, language maintenance and choice, language attitudes, language policy and planning, and discourse analysis (Lucas 1995, 1996, 2001). However, it is very important to understand that while each of these areas has relevance for deaf communities, the sociolinguistics of sign is a relatively young discipline and there exist few if any empirical studies in some of these areas.

1. Regional and Social Variation

Regional and social variation in sign languages has been described mainly at the phonological and lexical levels, and to a lesser extent at the morphological and syntactic levels (see *Dialect and Dialectology*). Variation at the phonological level involves variation in the production of the component parts of signs such as handshape, location, palm orientation, nonmanual signals, and segmental structure. For example, the American Sign Language (ASL) signs FUNNY, BLACK, and CUTE might be produced with the thumb extended or with the thumb closed; the ASL signs BORED and DEAF might be produced with the little finger extended or with the little finger closed; the ASL sign WEEK might be produced with the palm of the dominant hand facing upward or the palm facing downward; the ASL sign KNOW might be produced on the forehead or on the cheek. Lexical variation concerns different signs for the same concept. Regional differences have been described in British Sign Language (BSL), for example, between Reading and York for the signs LEARN, SUNDAY, and WHO (Deuchar 1984: 131). Lexical variation in BSL has also been described by Kyle and Woll (1985). Lexical variation has also been looked at in New Zealand Sign Language, Italian Sign Language, Dutch Sign Language, Swiss German Sign Language and Swiss French Sign Language, Brazilian Sign Language, and ASL. Variation in terms of ethnicity has been looked at by Woodward (1976) and Aramburo (1989), i.e., differences between black and white signers in the USA. Gender variation has been looked at in ASL, in Chinese Sign Language, and in Irish Sign Language. One large-scale study of sociolinguistic variation in American Sign Language similar to the ones undertaken for spoken languages (Lucas et al. 2001) demonstrates that variation in sign languages needs to be considered in the light of unique factors such as school language policy and language use in the home.

2. Bilingualism and Language Contact Phenomena

There exist different kinds of bilingualism in deaf communities. For one, most deaf individuals have at least some exposure to the spoken language of the majority community in which they live. This exposure may be primarily exposure to the written form of the majority language, although in many countries a signed code to manually represent the spoken majority language has been devised, with signs invented to represent the bound morphemes of the spoken language. A discussion of bilingualism in deaf communities necessarily requires a re-examination of the term 'bilingual' as it has been used to describe spoken language communities. This is because many deaf people with a firm command of the written version of the majority spoken language choose not to use their voices because they are not able to hear themselves and hence monitor the volume or pitch of their speech. Bilingualism in deaf communities does not necessarily include *speaking* the languages in

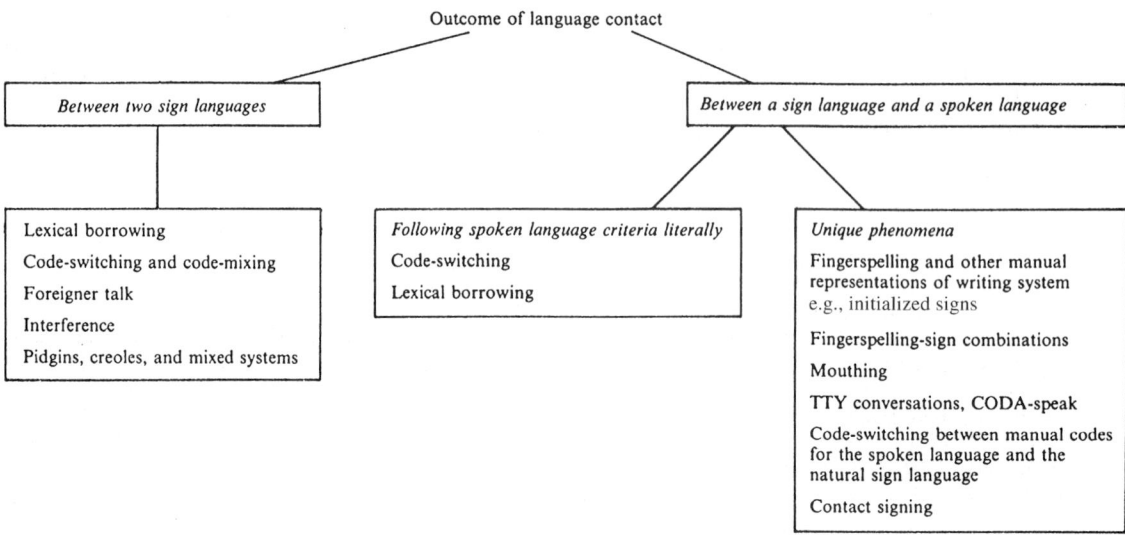

Figure 1. Outcome of language contact.

question, at least not in the way that the term *speaking* is generally understood by linguists.

There are many occasions for language contact in deaf communities. Fig. 1 presents a model of the linguistic outcomes of language contact. A fundamental distinction is made between a situation involving contact between two sign languages and a situation involving contact between a sign language and a spoken language, a distinction necessary because of the difference in modality between sign and spoken languages. Naturally, the situation is not entirely straightforward, as two sign languages may be in contact, both of which may incorporate outcomes of contact with their respective spoken languages, outcomes which may then play a role in the contact between the two sign languages.

As can be seen from Fig. 1, the outcomes of contact between two sign languages parallel the outcomes that have been described for contact between spoken languages, namely lexical borrowing of various kinds, code-switching and code-mixing, foreigner talk, interference, pidgins and creoles, and mixed systems. Again, it should be remembered that while there is much anecdotal evidence for many of these outcomes, there are not many empirical studies of the outcomes of contact between two sign languages. Signers borrow the signs from one language into their own; bilinguals may code-switch and code-mix elements from two sign languages; a signer may alter his signing and simplify it when signing to a nonnative, and signers may show interference from one sign language when using another. Signers have been observed to have 'accents.' As concerns contact between a sign language and a spoken language, a distinction is made between outcomes which reflect literal adherence to the spoken language criteria defined for those outcomes. For example, code-switching would mean ceasing signing and beginning to talk. This is distinct from unique phenomena that occur, such as contact signing, as observed in the American deaf community: the simultaneous production of ASL lexical forms in English word order with mouthing of English words, with the possible inclusion of inflected ASL verbs and ASL nonmanual signals. Some analyses have characterized this as a pidgin but more recent analyses find the features of this kind of signing to be inconsistent with the features of pidgins (Lucas and Valli 1992). Fingerspelling is also a unique phenomenon, because although the forms are part of the natural sign language—i.e., the handshape, the location, orientation, and the segmental structure—it is a representation of the writing system of the majority spoken language. Signers in contact with languages which use the Roman alphabet fingerspell, but signers in contact with Arabic, Russian, Japanese, Vietnamese, and Chinese also represent the writing systems of their respective spoken languages. Other unique phenomena include the English sometimes produced by the children of deaf adults (CODA-speak, Jacobs 1992), and the English of typed telephone conversations that often incorporates features of ASL (Mather 1991).

3. Language Maintenance and Choice

Typically, the use of natural sign languages has been restricted to a very limited set of functions and has been totally excluded from the educational process. Such a sociolinguistic situation has led to the characterization of language use in the deaf community as diglossic, the majority spoken language being the H variety and the natural sign language being the L variety (Stokoe 1969). There is a lot of evidence that some signers clearly see their natural sign language as appropriate only for intimate, informal situations, and the signed version of the majority spoken language as appropriate for public, formal situations, be the interlocutors hearing or deaf. However, as many countries around the world begin to use natural sign languages in deaf education, these sign languages are acquiring functions that they have not had before, and the spoken or signed version of the majority spoken languages may lose functions they once had or be restricted to the functions of reading and writing. Because of the clear need in deaf communities for both a natural sign language and for some form of the majority spoken language, the situation in most deaf communities can be characterized as one of maintained bilingualism. Unlike many minority languages in a majority language situation, it would not appear that natural sign languages are in any danger of disappearing.

4. Language Attitudes

Language attitude studies in deaf communities concern signers' attitudes toward their natural sign language and toward the majority spoken language, attitudes toward users of the sign and spoken language, attitudes of teachers of the deaf and professionals toward natural sign languages, attitudes toward the invention and introduction of new signs, and attitudes toward the outcomes of language contact (Kannapell 1989). Language attitude studies often reveal conflicting attitudes toward the natural sign language and the majority spoken language in a given community, as a result of lack of recognition of the status of the sign language as a viable and autonomous linguistic system. That is, pride with respect to the sign language may co-occur with an attitude that its use reveals a lower educational level or even lower intelligence in the user, while use of a signed version of the majority spoken language may be viewed as evidence of good education and superior intelligence. Pride with respect to the natural sign language may coexist with the misconception that it is not a real language or is a deficient form of the spoken majority language.

5. Language Policy and Planning

Language planning has been defined as deliberate decision making in response to language problems. Deaf communities have very often been perceived as the sites of language *problems*, particularly as concerns the education of deaf children, for the obvious reason that deaf children do not have easy access to the spoken majority language as a medium of instruction (Ramsey 1997). Approaches since the 1970s have involved the invention of manual codes to represent the majority spoken language and may involve the simultaneous production of the spoken language and the sign language, referred to as sign-supported speech (Johnson et al. 1989). However, many deaf communities around the world are beginning to use the natural sign language of the community as the medium of instruction. All of these approaches have implications for language planning, either in the invention of manual codes for educational use, or in the use of the natural sign language for functions it has not previously had. This may entail expanding the lexicon of the natural sign language, an expansion which leads to other language planning issues, such as whether signs should be invented for new concepts or whether new concepts should be represented with fingerspelling. Issues of access and hence of language policy and planning are not limited to deaf education. For example, providing deaf adults with full access to the business of the majority language community—i.e., media, government, the law, medical care—entails decisions as to how linguistic access will be provided: whether closed-captioning is preferable for television news to a sign language interpreter; whether a sign language interpreter, if provided, should use the natural sign language or a signed version of the spoken majority language; what the interpreting policy should be in an international gathering of deaf people—the natural sign language of the location of the gathering or an international variety of both. These are all issues that are the subject of debate in many deaf communities around the world.

6. Discourse Analysis

As with spoken languages, the discourse of natural sign languages is structured and subject to sociolinguistic description (see *Pragmatics and Sociolinguistics*). Signers use natural sign languages and choices between natural sign languages and other kinds of signing make statements about who they are, what their group loyalties are, how they perceive their relationship to their interlocutors, and what kind of speech event they consider themselves to be involved in. Sign languages are used to establish or reinforce social relations and to control the behavior of others. Sign language discourse has internal structure and is governed by norms such as how many people sign at once, how much one person should sign, what can be signed about in public, how a conversation should be entered or left, how turns should be allocated, how repairs should be undertaken, and so forth (Metzger 1999, 2000, Winston 1999). Topic and the world knowledge that individuals bring to the discourse may also structure it (Roy 1989), and sign language discourse can be described in terms of register variation (Lawson 1981, Deuchar 1984, Zimmer 1989). The concept of 'language as skilled work' is applicable to sign languages, as skill is demonstrated both in everyday use of language and in special forms such as storytelling and poetry.

Bibliography

Aramburo A J 1989 Sociolinguistic aspects of the black deaf community. In: Lucas C (ed.) *The Sociolinguistics of the Deaf Community*. Academic Press, San Diego, CA
Battison R 1978 *Lexical Borrowing in American Sign Language*. Linstock Press, Silver Spring, MD
Battison R, Markowicz H, Woodward J 1975 A good rule of thumb: Variable phonology in American Sign Language. In: Shuy R W, Fasold R W (eds.) *New Ways of Analyzing Variation in English*. Georgetown University Press, Washington, DC
Davis J 1989 Distinguishing language contact phenomena in ASL interpretation. In: Lucas C (ed.) *The Sociolinguistics of the Deaf Community*. Academic Press, San Diego, CA
Deuchar M 1984 *British Sign Language*. Routledge and Kegan Paul, London
Hansen B 1980 Research on Danish sign language and its impact on the deaf community. In: Baker C, Battison R (eds.) *Sign Language and the Deaf Community*. NAD, Silver Spring, MD
Jacobs S 1992 Coda talk column. *Coda Connection* **9**(1)
Johnson R, Liddell S, Erting C 1989 *Unlocking the Curriculum*. Gallaudet University Press, Washington, DC
Kannapell B 1989 An examination of deaf college students' attitudes toward ASL and English. In: Lucas C (ed.) *The Sociolinguistics of the Deaf Community*. Academic Press, San Diego, CA
Kyle J G, Woll B (eds.) 1983 *Language in Sign: An International Perspective on Sign Language*. Croom Helm, London
Kyle J G, Woll B (eds.) 1985 *Sign Language: The Study of Deaf People and Their Language*. Cambridge University Press, Cambridge, UK
Lawson L 1981 The role of sign in the structure of the deaf community. In: Woll B, Kyle J, Deuchar M (eds.) *Perspectives on British Sign Language and Deafness*. Croom Helm, London
Llewellyn-Jones P, Kyle J, Woll B 1979 Sign language communication (Unpublished paper presented at the International Conference on Social Psychology and Language, Bristol)
Lucas C (ed.). 1989 *The Sociolinguistics of the Deaf Community*. Academic Press, San Diego, CA
Lucas C (ed.) 1995 *Sociolinguistics in Deaf Communities Vol. 1*. Gallaudet University Press, Washington, DC
Lucas C (ed.) 1996 *Multicultural Aspects of Sociolinguistics in Deaf Communities* (*Sociolinguistics in Deaf Communities, Vol. 2*). Gallaudet University Press, Washington, DC
Lucas C 2001 (ed.) *The Sociolinguistics of Sign Languages*. Cambridge University Press, Cambridge, UK
Lucas C, Bayley R, Valli C 2001 *Sociolinguistic Variation in American Sign Language*. (*Sociolinguistics in Deaf Communities, Vol. 7*). Gallaudet University Press, Washington, DC
Lucas C, Valli C 1992 *Language Contact in the American Deaf Community*. Academic Press, San Diego, CA
Mather S 1991 The discourse marker OH in typed telephone conversations among deaf typists (Doctoral dissertation, Georgetown University)
Metzger M 1999 *Sign Language Interpreting. Deconstructing the Myth of Neutrality*. Gallaudet University Press, Washington, DC
Metzger M (ed.) 2000 *Bilingualism and Identity in Deaf Communities* (*Sociolinguistics in Deaf Communities, Vol. 6*). Gallaudet University Press, Washington, DC
Nowell E 1989 Conversational features and gender in ASL. In: Lucas C (ed.) *The Sociolinguistics of the Deaf Community*. Academic Press, San Diego, CA
Ramsey C 1989 Language planning in deaf education. In: Lucas C (ed.) *The Sociolinguistics of the Deaf Community*. Academic Press, San Diego, CA
Ramsey C 1997 *Deaf Children in Public Schools: Placements, Context, and Consequences*. (*Sociolinguistics in Deaf Communities, Vol. 3*). Gallaudet University Press, Washington, DC
Roy C 1989 Features of discourse in an American Sign Language lecture. In: Lucas C (ed.) *The Sociolinguistics of the Deaf Community*. Academic Press, San Diego, CA
Schermer T 1990 *In Search of a Language: Influences from Spoken Dutch on Sign Language of the Netherlands*. Eburon, Delft, The Netherlands
Stokoe W C 1969–70 Sign language diglossia. *Studies in Linguistics* **21**: 27–41
Stokoe W C (ed.) 1980 *Sign and Culture: A Reader for Students of American Sign Language*. Linstok Press, Silver Spring, MD
Sutton-Spence R, Woll B, Allsop L 1990 Variation and recent change in fingerspelling in British Sign Language. *Language Variation and Change* **2**: 313–30
Winston E (ed.) 1999 *Storytelling and Conversation. Discourse in Deaf Communities* (*Sociolinguistics in Deaf Communities, Vol. 5*). Gallaudet University Press, Washington, DC
Woll B, Kyle J, Deuchar M (eds.) 1981 *Perspectives on British Sign Language and Deafness*. Croom Helm, London
Woodward J C 1976 Black southern signing. *Language in Society* **5**: 211–8
Zimmer J 1989 Toward a description of register variation in American Sign Language. In: Lucas C (ed.) *The Sociolinguistics of the Deaf Community*. Academic Press, San Diego, CA

Sociology of Language
W. S. Bainbridge

Sociology can contribute to linguistics in four main ways. First, a subdiscipline often called the 'sociology of language' applies sociological techniques of research and explanatory theories directly to language topics. Second, language appears as a variable in numerous sociological research studies, and considerable factual material of interest to linguistics can be culled from them. Third, several major theories of society place such great stress upon language that they can justly be called 'linguistic theories.' And, fourth, techniques of sociological research have undergone considerable development in the second half of the twentieth century, and many of them can be transferred to linguistics. In return, linguistics can certainly give sociology a greater awareness of the importance and subtlety of language studies. Indeed, sociologists in several subfields seem largely unaware that their work is essentially linguistic, and they could benefit from the rigor and depth of knowledge that professionals in linguistics achieve. Many articles in this *Encyclopedia* have been written specifically to identify the connections between linguistics and sociology, with the hope that these two related scholarly disciplines will cooperate more fully in future.

1. Sociological Studies of Language

Sociologically oriented linguistics, whether called 'sociolinguistics' or the 'sociology of language,' coalesced in the 1960s, although studies of the relation between society and language go back many decades earlier. Dell Hymes dates its emergence in the years 1964 through 1972, explaining that many different factors combined to produce a new interdisciplinary academic field. Writing from the vantage of 1984, Hymes saw the current period as one of transition and consolidation, but transition to what remains unclear. While many scholars now acknowledge the importance of social factors in shaping language, a specific paradigm identifying key questions and establishing correct methods of research for attacking them has not appeared.

In 1972, Hymes introduced the first issue of the important journal *Language in Society* by suggesting that any general theory of language as part of social life and productive empirical research on the topic needed to start with a definition of the field comparable to the following: sociolinguistics is the study of 'the means of speech in human communities, and their meanings to those who use them.' These means and meanings are the forms of speech and their social functions, respectively. Hymes has repeatedly argued that these important questions have been given far less attention than they deserved, greatly because the dominant paradigm within linguistics is the analysis of the formal structure of language, divorced from its social context, as exemplified by the work of Chomsky.

As Joshua Fishman has noted, the difference between sociology of language and sociolinguistics may be one of mere degree, because both are concerned with the correlation between variations in language usage and variations in other socially patterned behavior. In principle, sociolinguistics takes its agenda from linguistics, and the sociology of language takes its from sociology, the latter stressing the social variables. Fishman (1985: 114) suggests: 'Sociolinguists have continued to be far more often trained in linguistics than in sociology, the latter often being considered useful only for informal exposure and orientation rather than as a substantive and formal body of technical skills and theoretical propositions.'

An important example is the great body of research on social class differences in language. While sociolinguists without number have documented class-related variation in speech, hardly any of them asked themselves what social class was. They treated class as a key independent variable, with variations in speech dependent upon class variations, yet they never considered the meaning of their independent variable. In consequence, they seldom attempted anything like a theory of why class should have an impact, and even more rarely examined their measures of class to see if they were methodologically defensible.

As Michael Macy explains in the essay on social class (see *Social Class*), there is little agreement on the meaning of the term. Sociologists differ on whether society is divided into distinct classes of whether one should speak instead of continuous variation along a number of poorly correlated measures of social influence and status. Competing definitions of class stress ownership of property, control over productive forces, occupational prestige, educational attainment, and many other statuses and resources that confer power and respect upon some members of society. Surely, sociolinguists cannot be expected to solve the difficulties that beset stratification theory in sociology, but before they can employ social class concepts they must become informed about the alternative definitions, explicitly select one that fits their research questions and intellectual leanings, and employ empirical indicators appropriate to their conceptualization. Macy's essay is a good beginning for linguists who want to take this social variable seriously, and every other important sociological concept deserves similarly close study before inclusion in language studies.

Sociology, perhaps more than any other science, emphasizes abstract theory. The central journals are primarily dedicated to empirical studies, but these invariably are attempts to test theories, and purely descriptive research is considered to be of little value. This situation stands in extreme contrast to anthropology, which still believes that documenting the way of life of the peoples of the world is valuable in itself, as well as for whatever light the data can shed on theories. Because much sociolinguistics strikes sociologists as atheoretical, they consider it unimportant, and perhaps for this reason the central sociological journals hardly ever publish articles whose topic is language.

Thus, if sociolinguists are to be taken to task for failing to give sociology its proper respect, sociologists have returned the insult by ignoring linguistics. One reason may be the ignorance of languages by American sociologists, in a time when America dominated sociology worldwide. When students applied for admission to graduate studies in sociology at Harvard in 1970, the regulations demanded proficiency in two languages beyond English, but by 1971 no foreign languages were required at all. Indeed, the climate in most of the major American sociology departments has strongly discouraged students from studying languages, and some of the programs demand so many courses in quantitative methods and substantive fields of sociology that no time is left over for language study, especially with the great financial and social pressures exerted on the students to complete their degrees quickly. Considering the poor quality of writing by many American sociologists, it may be an exaggeration to say that they are monolingual.

Yet language studies have been officially recognized as a subfield within sociology. A section of the standard reference periodical, *Sociological Abstracts*, is devoted to language, and at least two specialty journals can be said to cover the sociology of language: *Language in Society* and *The International Journal of the Sociology of Language*. However, despite its name the latter of these does not look much like a social science journal, and the former is as close to social psychology as it is to sociology.

Several special issues of *The International Journal of the Sociology of Language* have been devoted to particular languages (Welsh, Dutch, Frisian, Jewish languages) and the language situations of several nations (Australia, Ireland, India, Belgium, and the former Yugoslavia). Few sociologists would recognize these essays as sociological, however, because they are almost without exception wholly descriptive, with no hint of explanatory theory. Like the standard sociology journals, *Language in Society* introduces each article with an abstract, while *The International Journal of the Sociology of Language* does not have them. It is difficult to write an abstract for an essay that consists of a collection of descriptive details, while the abstracts in scientific journals can efficiently state the intellectual problem the research sought to solve, give a brief outline of dataset and methodology, and conclude with a sentence or two reporting how the theory fared in its encounter with the data.

2. Ordinary Sociological Research in Which Language Plays a Key Role

Strewn throughout the vast library of published sociological research is a tremendous amount of information about language usage in various communities and subgroups of the population. Unfortunately for the linguist, no catalogs exist explaining where to find particular data, and nothing short of an intensive literature review will reveal the fruitful sources of linguistic data.

2.1 Studies of Subcultures

Within each large society exist numerous subcultures and countercultures, limited groups of people who share a set of perceptions and behaviors, usually communicating with each other by somewhat unique language. In anthropological parlance, the term 'a culture' has the unfortunate effect of implying the existence of a completely distinct and coherent set of beliefs and customs. Yet individuals within any group of people vary, and every society is a bewildering overlay of innumerable, overlapping subcultures. Ideally, 'subsociety' should be distinguished from 'subculture,' the former referring to a somewhat distinct set of people, and the latter to a somewhat coherent set of cultural elements. Often the two correspond, as when a group of Gypsies remains distinct from the surrounding society, both socially and linguistically. But in many cases, individuals participate in several subcultures simultaneously, while not sharing the same set of subcultural memberships as the fellow members of any particular one.

Consider Tom, Dick, and Harry, three participants in the subculture of illegal drug users. Tom is a computer programmer, Dick a politician, and Harry a burglar by profession. The trio may employ subcultural language while discussing drugs, but when the conversation turns to their work, each lacks appreciation of the argot of the others' professional subcultures, and they are forced to use the common language of their society. Because each subculture has special interests, activities, and artifacts, it will develop a somewhat special lexicon. Countercultures are direct challenges to the dominant culture of their society, and thus they often intentionally invent alternatives for ordinary terminology.

Criminologists have occasionally created dictionaries of the subcultures they were studying. Edwin Sutherland's book about a professional thief contains a glossary defining terms from thief argot, such as *booster* 'shoplifter,' *moll-buzzer* 'someone who steals from the pockets of women,' and *glim-dropper* 'a con man who uses an artificial eye as part of his racket.' A dictionary of inmate terminology was included in Rose Giallombardo's study of a women's prison where same-sex marriages were contracted between *studs* 'husbands' and *femmes* 'wives,' while those who refused to participate in this subculture were called *squares*.

The sociology of religion records key terminology of new religious movements, often providing etymologies and sufficient information to understand the social mechanisms that generate terminology of various kinds. The sociology of religion roughly distinguishes two varieties of new religious movements: sects and cults. 'Sects' are schismatic movements that arise within standard religious traditions. Typically populated by persons suffering relative deprivation, such as the poor and members of oppressed groups, sects tend to emphasize the otherworldly and revolutionary aspects of the standard religious tradition of the society, but despite their social radicalism they tend to be culturally conservative. Therefore, they do not generate much new terminology, although they not infrequently assign somewhat new meanings to ordinary words.

In contrast, 'cults' are culturally novel or exotic, either arising through processes of radical cultural innovation or being imported from alien societies. Thus, they tend to be rife with neologisms and words adapted from foreign languages. Whereas many cult groups are founded quite independently of any preexisting religious organization, individual founders of cults almost universally served apprenticeships in other cults. At the moment of its birth, therefore, a new cult tends to be a whirlwind of cultural innovation, but it often draws upon the lexicons of the earlier cults to which the founder had belonged. Like sects, cults are capable of schism, but social rifts in a cult are far more likely to generate new language, because cults are by definition dedicated to cultural innovation.

Literary and artistic schools may also be conceptualized as subcultures, and many have been studied by sociologists. For example, science fiction literature has been produced for more than 60 years by a tight-knit subculture of *fen* 'fans' (*fan/fen* by analogy with *man/men*) and *pros* 'professionals,' with its own extensive lexicon (Bainbridge 1986). H. G. Wells had called his early fiction *science-fantasy*, but when Hugo Gernsback published the first magazine entirely devoted to this kind of literature, he called it *scientifiction* 'scientific fiction.' Gernsback lost financial control of this magazine, founded a rival to it in 1929, and felt forced to coin a new term, coming up with *science-fiction*. The hyphen was gradually dropped by the subculture, to give *science fiction*, which is used in many languages beyond English. The hyphen reappeared in the 1950s when Forrest J. Ackerman coined the slang synonym, *sci-fi*, by analogy with *hi-fi* 'high fidelity sound recordings.' While the literature is often called *sci-fi* by persons outside the subculture, insiders abhor this term, preferring *SF*. While few of the thousands of neologisms invented by science fiction writers have found their way into ordinary parlance, sociology and linguistics can combine in research on how this subculture generates the vast lexicon it does, and a particularly refined minor field is the study of invented languages in literature.

The sociology of slang (see *Slang: Sociology*) has not only documented various brands of substandard speech, but it has identified particular environments that are unusually productive of this level of usage, especially cosmopolitan, urban centers. Indeed, the very term 'slang' may not be capable of definition in strictly linguistic terms, but must be defined sociologically, perhaps as the urban part of popular speech. Among its social functions is the generation of new terminology that may find its way into standard speech. In principle, all subcultural language is a marker not only of social distinctions but of conflict, and slang gives voice to groups and sentiments that currently lack social power.

2.2 Major Social Categories

As mentioned earlier, sociologists have concentrated much effort on understanding social class, and other social divisions have been examined with nearly equal energy, including ethnic groups, professions and occupations, rural and urban populations, and immigrants. The study of sexism and sex differences has been exceedingly fruitful, and sociologists have placed great stress on the role that language may play in sustaining or diminishing power differentials based on gender.

The voluminous sociological research on youth has provided much information on adolescent peer group language (see *Adolescent Peer Group Language*), and young people create and sustain rapidly changing linguistic subcultures that can be studied to understand how new language of potentially any kind is coined and gains acceptance. Youth need special words and symbols to conceal their activities from adults, to provide a sense of group solidarity, and probably to sustain a feeling of leading the vanguard of cultural developments. Youth often seem to feel that they have dreams and experiences previously unknown to the human race, and whether this perception is correct or illusory, it can stimulate the proliferation of neologisms.

Sociology can contribute little to the lexicography of scientific nomenclature and technological nomenclature, simply because scientists and engineers are so active in compiling dictionaries of their own fields. However, many sociologists have investigated both the origins of systems of scientific terminology and the consequences for science of nomenclature that may implicitly assume certain unproven theories are true. Sociological research on technology has often focused on how inventions and terminology spread from one site or application to another, what is generally termed 'diffusion.' Thus, sociology has elucidated the processes through which scientific and technological language emerge and through which they may influence the thought of scientists and engineers.

2.3 Surveys

The vast library of attitude and opinion surveys that can be found in social science computing centers and special repositories, as well as in published reports, contains much largely unappreciated information about language. This is true because many kinds of question ask respondents to say what some stimulus concept means. Often, secondary analysis of archived datasets can extract more information somewhat indirectly by examining the correlations between items; if two concepts are responded to in very much the same way, they must have similar meaning to respondents. Furthermore, surveys have been administered to many different groups of people, and most surveys contain questions that allow the researcher to distinguish subgroups of respondents, thus permitting one to chart variations in meaning across social categories.

The range of linguistically relevant data is immense, so two examples must suffice. In 1924, Bogardus introduced the 'social distance scale,' a question format that asks respondents to say how close they feel to particular kinds of people, such as Germans, Russians, Italians, Caucasians, Asians, Baptists, and Communists. Responses from a number of people allow one to map the concepts and identify groups of them that share substantial overlap in meaning. In the 1950s, Charles Osgood developed a technique, called the 'semantic differential,' that employed statistical analysis of questionnaire items based on antonyms, to chart the affective meaning of concepts. While such techniques can be very useful to linguists planning future surveys, the point worth stressing here is that the data already collected through such methods may now be reexamined profitably from a specifically linguistic perspective.

3. Language-oriented Sociological Theories

At a first approximation, the major theories of society and social interaction may be divided into two classes: idealist and materialist. The latter, including sociobiology, behaviorism, utilitarianism, and Marxism, have little to say about language, with the notable exception of the Marxian concept of false consciousness. However, the idealist theories are based on assumptions about language, give language the dominant role in shaping human behavior, and frequently prompt research with clear implications for linguistics.

3.1 Elements of Social and Cultural Structures

For decades, the most influential sociological theories in the United States were symbolic interactionism and structural functionalism, often combined. The first emphasizes the way language shapes the individual, for example, through development of verbally coded self-symbols called 'personal identity,' 'self,' or 'role.' The second emphasizes the shared concepts of the society, such as institutions, values, norms, and generalized beliefs. In linguistics, there is much talk about the 'deep structure' of language, but sociological concepts like 'role' and 'value' refer to the 'deep content.' In its structuralist guise, structural functionalism analyzed the relationships between elements of the culture (e.g., between roles and institutions), thus placing these elements into a comprehensive conceptual structure where they were mutually dependent.

For decades, practically every introductory sociology textbook has explained to students that every society is based on a coherent set of values which constitute the goals individuals and groups are supposed to strive for and which provide the necessary cultural basis for social stability. Supposedly, societies differ greatly in their value systems, and an historical change of values will have a profound effect on a society. While linguistic in nature and communicated through speech, values are of such a general nature that they dwell implicitly in all messages rather than being stated explicitly in a few words, except in special public occasions such as religious sermons and political speeches.

However, research has generally failed to find very solid support for these sweeping hypotheses about values, and a host of alternative perspectives has arisen since the 1950s that place far less credence in values and portray society as far less coherent and far more conflictual. For instance, exchange theory, exemplified by the antisociological sociology of George Caspar Homans, holds that humans act so as to maximize individual gain, guided by past personal experience more than by abstract values communicated through language.

The distinctively sociological brand of social psychology known as 'symbolic interactionism' continues to give language great importance, especially in creation of potent abstractions such as self and the variety of behavior-orienting concepts associated with role theory. Research on attitudes and behavior has shown that words and deeds often diverge, good reason to doubt that words have the distinctive power to shape human action and social organization that earlier generations of sociologists assumed. But this merely limits the presumed power of values and roles; it does not automatically render them impotent.

Under social conditions that researchers are increasingly able to specify, words can have great power over the individual mind and collective behavior. Most importantly, to the extent that a set of people are united by social bonds into a cohesive group, clearly bounded from other groups and sharing a unique fate, then a coherent set of values, norms, roles, and self-conceptions is likely to arise. Once such a symbolic system exists, supported by social unity and ideological consensus, it possesses all the potency attributed to culture by earlier generations of sociologists. The only question is the extent to which modern societies have such cohesion.

More or less organized forms of thought and culture are expressed through collective representations and constitute conceptual systems. Traditional religion possesses the coherence and absolutism required to sustain a conceptual system and value orientation, as do some modern totalitarian political parties (Stark and Bainbridge 1985). However, secularization and pluralism appear to undercut the authority of religion considerably, and history in the late twentieth century has shown the impossibility of maintaining totalitarianism without savage, brute force. Thus one must anticipate that the present fluid situation will continue, with values and similar language-based abstractions holding sway only in limited social environments, conceptual systems rising and falling in chaotic manner, thus challenging the social scientist to determine when words possess or lack distinctive power in society.

The branch of sociology that has considered these issues most deeply for the longest period of time is the sociology of knowledge. This subdiscipline is concerned with the ways that material and social factors condition people's beliefs, thought, and general culture. Recognizing that human knowledge is historically bounded, writers in this tradition have considered the role of social change and group conflict in strengthening ideological fixity, as well as in weakening it.

3.2 Social Conflict: Language as Battleground
Acknowledging that words often diverge from deeds, when people say one thing and do another, words can also be deeds of a particularly powerful kind. Through words, people may define social conditions in ways favorable to their own interests, gaining influence over the language of discourse as if it were a battleground contested in a war of words. Sociologists have examined in depth how labels may create reality, and if some of the theories have outstripped the truth, the sociological schools of labeling theory and social constructionism offer much of interest to linguistics.

3.2.1 Labeling Theory
The labeling theory of social deviance, often called 'social reaction theory' or 'societal reaction theory,' contends that much if not most deviance is caused by definitions unnecessarily imposed on individuals and actions by capricious society. As Ronald Akers explains, labeling theory is rooted in symbolic interactionism, the influential sociological perspective that considers each person to be the creation of the symbols he or she has received in communication with other people. Thus, society can create a criminal or a madman by taking an otherwise undistinguished person and applying these negative labels to him. Akers's report that scientific evidence tends to refute some of the more striking statements of labeling theorists does not diminish the fact that this is a thoroughly linguistic theory of crime, mental illness, and other forms of deviance.

Among the creators of labeling theory and the societal reaction perspective was Edwin Lemert, who distinguished two categories of norm violation. 'Primary deviation' has many causes, arising out of a variety of social, cultural, psychological, and physiological factors, and Lemert finds it quite uninteresting. 'Secondary deviation' consists of responses to problems created by societal reaction to primary deviation, and thus it is the result to a very great extent of the labels people attach to behavior they dislike. Among the narrowly linguistic studies published by Lemert from this perspective are two that concerned stuttering among the indigenous people of British Columbia, Polynesia, and Japan. He contended that societies which strenuously attempt to correct stuttering, such as Japan, will have more of it than societies which respond less aggressively to minor speech defects, such as Samoa. The primary deviation represented by mild and occasional stuttering produces more or less harsh reaction from listeners, depending upon the norms of the culture, and harsh reactions will cause greater self-consciousness on the part of the stutterer, thus aggravating the condition and producing much secondary speech deviance.

Another linguistic application appears in the analysis of schizophrenia offered by Thomas Scheff. Contemptuous of psychiatry, Scheff summarizes five decades of research and 5000 publications in just five words: 'no progress has been made.' To fill this void, Scheff offers a labeling theory that considers schizophrenia to be a pattern of secondary deviation caused by reaction to a variety of primary deviation he calls 'residual deviance.' In a thought experiment, Scheff asks us to imagine listing all the kinds of norm violations that exist, and to check off those that have explicit labels in the language of the society, words like 'crime, perversion, drunkenness, and bad manners.' He then says, 'After exhausting these categories, however, there is always a residue of the most diverse kinds of violations, for which the culture provides no explicit label.' Psychiatric symptoms, according to Scheff, violate norms that are poorly articulated by the culture, and societal reaction to random violations of this kind can magnify and stabilize them into full-fledged madness. Indeed, being mentally ill is nothing more, for Scheff, than being labeled mad and playing the role of mad person as scripted by the society.

Extreme versions of labeling theory hold that everything is a matter of definition, but it is an objective fact that such definitions often have great importance for public policy. In a study of abortion, homosexuality, and drug addiction, Edwin Schur argued against criminalization of acts which have no victims. He defines victimless crimes as 'the willing exchange, among adults, of strongly demanded but legally proscribed goods or services,' thus implying that no one involved in the exchange has any complaint. A 'victim,' for Schur, is a person who has the legal standing to appear in court and wishes to lodge a complaint. To sustain this definition, he has to argue that an aborted fetus is not a person with legal standing, that society is not harmed by any sexual practices of its members, and that *drug addict* is a misnomer for a person who merely wants to ingest proscribed substances. Schur notes that members of society disagree about all these matters of definition, yet the term 'victimless crime,' widely used by reformers of the 1990s, seeks to define the debates in terms of one particular side to them.

3.2.2 Social Constructionist Perspectives

The phrase, 'social construction of reality,' is extremely popular among sociologists, but is open to very different interpretations. Many take it to mean that reality is socially created, for instance, that the categorization schemes of science are arbitrary choices made entirely on a whim by the social groups who happen to be in charge of scientific institutions. For them, the word *construction* comes from the verb *to construct* and suggests that scientific definitions are built from scratch under purely social influences. Translations of German sociology often render *Aufbau* as *construction* in this sense. An alternative derivation of *construction* is from the verb *to construe*, suggesting that humans merely interpret or explain realities that exist in nature quite apart from the meanings humans attach to them. These can be called the strong and the weak meanings of the social construction of reality.

According to the strong social constructionist view, social problems originate in public opinion and the actions of interest groups, rather than in objective conditions. Armand Mauss (1975) contends that social problems are generated by social movements, and, in a sense, that problems are nothing but movements. A traditional definition of social problem is 'an undesirable social condition,' but this leaves entirely open the question of who has the right to decide what is undesirable. Mauss is able to document the importance of social movements in defining aspects of many conditions as undesirable: crime, juvenile delinquency, drug abuse, alcohol abuse, prostitution, homosexuality, abortion, racism, pollution of the environment, and the population explosion.

An objective condition is not problematic until it is defined as such. Because crime is violation of law, there are no crimes until there are laws, so crime is caused by legislatures and the social movements that agitate them. Many brain-affecting drugs are consumed in great quantities, including alcohol, tobacco, aspirin, and coffee; such behavior does not become *drug abuse* until activists in the medical profession or politicians define free use of a particular substance as bad, a maneuver that generally succeeds only with substances like marijuana that are consumed primarily by politically weak segments of the population. Sexually explicit literature and pictures only become *pornography* when defined as unwholesome by religious or other movements that are seeking some means of promoting themselves with the public.

The mechanism by which social movements typically produce social problems is the launching of 'symbolic crusades.' These can be defined as collective struggles to promote, resist, or repair symbolizations. In other words, they are attempts made by a more-or-less organized group of people to make the culture accept a particular set of definitions.

A classic example is the Temperance Movement, which emerged in the United States early in the nineteenth century, then spread its doctrine of moderation or abstinence in alcohol use to Europe. Joseph Gusfield argued that this movement was not really about drinking but about intergroup conflict over status, power, and wealth: 'Issues of moral reform are one way through which a cultural group acts to preserve, defend, or enhance the dominance and prestige of its own style of living within the total society' (Gusfield 1963: 3). If it can get its particular set of ideal norms officially accepted by the society, then it will gain respect, prestige, and emulation from other groups.

American cultural groups traditionally differed in their attitudes toward alcohol, Catholics accepting drinking more readily than Protestants, for example. Rural, native-born, Protestants valued self-control, industriousness, and impulse renunciation, according to Gusfield, and uninhibited imbibing was contrary to their culture. Many of the new immigrant groups whose members and political strength grew as the years passed had a more favorable attitude toward drinking. The old citizens and new citizens were frequently at odds over economic issues, but because economic conflict takes a muted form in American politics, symbolic issues like alcohol policy came to have an exaggerated importance. As they felt their political power slipping, the older ethnic groups tried to assert the superiority over other citizens through advocating laws to promote their own temperate drinking patterns as the dominant norm. If their customs became law, their declining social status would be symbolically bolstered. This analysis has been expanded by Seymour Martin Lipset and Earl Raab (1970) to include a range of conservative symbolic crusades that apparently arose in response to persistent problems of social status experienced by the same ethnic groups.

Like labeling theory, the theory of symbolic crusades exhibits social definitions on two levels. First, it is a theory of how a social movement promotes particular sets of symbols. Second, the social theorists themselves aggressively apply definitions to the social movement under study, almost invariably beginning from a personal rejection of the definitions possessed by the people they are defining. Simply put, the social theorists are of liberal or left-wing political persuasion, and the movements they analyze are conservative or right-wing. In part, the theory of symbolic crusades arose in the attempt to explain why socialist movements had failed to become prominent in the United States. The left-wing sociologists were convinced it was in the workers' interests to support socialism, and yet the American working class has often seemed attracted to the political right. Some invoked the Marxist concept of false consciousness, arguing in effect that the working class had been tricked into accepting the definitions of the ruling class, and the theory of symbolic crusades similarly asserts that members of a movement are deceived or deceiving about the real meaning of their symbols.

Often a distinction is made between 'interest politics' and 'status politics.' When a class supports political parties and movements that promote its economic interests, then it is practicing interest politics. But when it engages in activity counter to, or irrelevant to, its economic interests, in an apparent attempt to gain status through invoking certain cultural symbols, then it is engaging in status politics. Flag-waving by persons who are not members of the ruling class thus becomes understandable as a grab for status through claiming to embody traditional values of the society.

Despite its origins on one side of political debates, the concept of symbolic crusades can be applied more widely. For example, movements to establish or expand civil rights of a subordinate group often recruit many people who are not members of the oppressed, and their participation may be explained in terms of status politics. Most leaders of the movement to abolish slavery were not themselves slaves. In the early 1960s, a substantial proportion of the activists in the American Civil Rights Movement were Northern Whites who believed themselves to be embodying the best traditions of their nation, and thus they were asserting claims to the highest moral status. Clearly, the theory of symbolic crusades has a tendency to debunk the claims of the crusaders, and thus the attractiveness of the theory depends to some extent upon it being applied only to movements with which one does not personally sympathize.

3.3 Social Construction of Languages

Perhaps the most significant symbolic crusades are the attempts to create a sense of shared national identity. As Greenfeld explains in her article on nationalism and language (see *Nationalism and Language*), the conventional view of the relationship between nations and languages is that nationhood rests on a shared language; for example, that Germany is defined as the nation of people who speak German. But an alternate view holds that nations are fictions created symbolically, and among the most effective methods for achieving this is the creation of a national language (see *National Language/Official Language*).

Nations do not exist in the world of nature any more than races do; while human beings vary along a number of dimensions, including habits of tongue and hues of skin, no substantial population has ever been wholly separate from other populations. Thus, the concept of 'nation' is in many respects a creation of the imagination, and Greenfeld charts the rather complex history of this word, arguing that England invented nationalism in the sixteenth century, and that all other nations have adopted the concept from the English. Every student of linguistics is aware that several lesser modern languages have been codified as instruments of nationalism, among them Afrikaans, Hebrew, and Norwegian. But Greenfeld's examples are far more influential and spoken by far vaster populations: English, French, German, and Russian. Arguing that language is not the foundation of nationalism but its product, she firmly establishes the need of linguistics to become rooted in sociology.

In his discussion of colonialism (see *Power Differentials and Language*), Pierre van den Berghe notes that the concept of 'ethnic group' has some of the properties Greenfeld attributes to 'nation.' In principle, an ethnic group is a set of people defined as descended from common ancestors, but such definitions may be partly fictitious. Often, language is the chief marker of ethnicity, in part because endogamy maintains both ethnic and linguistic boundaries. Ethnic groups, and thus their languages, differ in power, and the world has seen many instances in which a colonial power has sought to impose its language upon conquered ethnic groups, from the Classical world of Greece and Rome to the empires of England, France, and Russia. Imperialism establishes the dominance of one ethnic group over others, and thus it is accompanied by linguistic stratification in which the language of the conquerors is defined as better than those of the conquered. Only in extreme circumstances, such as slavery, are the languages of the oppressed annihilated, however, and the decline of colonial empires is almost inevitably followed by the resurgence of the previously dominated languages.

Within modern societies, certain professional groups have sought cultural dominance over others, notably intellectuals and physicians. Kontopoulos (1994) notes the many competing definitions of this term, but for present purposes the fact can be stressed that intellectuals manipulate ideas, including definitions, in order to impose their often oppositional agendas upon the society. They may do this under the guise of professional expertise, but often it is the sheer mental facility with which they organize thought that compels a measure of acceptance.

In a process called 'medicalization,' physicians and their allies redefine phenomena as medical in nature, thus convincing the public to grant them the sole right to manage the phenomena. For example, heavy alcohol drinking has been seen as a personal choice, a character defect, or a sin requiring religious treatment. By analogy, and without clear scientific evidence, doctors redefined heavy drinking as *alcoholism*, a medical syndrome, and thus they gained social power over it. Another example is *hyperactivity* in children. Modern society demands that girls and boys sit quietly in school chairs for many hours each week. Some children, chiefly boys, fail to comply with this demand. Their physical activity is greater than their teachers wish, and the doctors have come to the teachers' rescue by defining the unruly children's behavior as a medical syndrome. Such a definition discredits the children's behavior and thus prevents them from successfully asserting their rights. The hyperactive children are often given drugs to alter their behavior, and the educational system is defended against any hint that it might be founded upon false principles.

4. Linguistic Research Methodologies

While most sociological research uses language, a few important techniques provide such valuable insights into language and are so solidly based on plausible theories of language that they deserve to be mentioned here. At the same time, methodological insights from all branches of sociology will help sociolinguistics improve the accuracy of their results. Especially important issues of research methods concern questions of reliability, validity, bias, sampling, scaling, and understanding of meaning.

4.1 Problems of Reliability and Validity

'Reliability' and 'validity' are two different aspects of the quality of a method of research or source of information. The reliability of a research technique is the consistency of results that it provides. A reliable questionnaire item tends to get the same response from a respondent if administered twice, so long as the relevant circumstances have not changed. Validity has to do with whether the technique measures what the researcher intends it to. A valid questionnaire item accurately reflects the desired aspect of the respondent's thoughts, behavior, or characteristics. Thus both validity and reliability are problems of measurement, and both need to be achieved to create confidence in the results of research.

An example of invalidity is offered by Calvin Veltman (1986), who severely criticized the two language questions in the Canadian census, one seeking information about what language is used at home and the other asking whether the person can carry on a conversation in one of the two official languages of Canada, French and English. Veltman surveyed hundreds of Greek and Portuguese immigrant households, asking a variety of questions about language use and competence. Answers to the census question about the language used at home revealed that 64 percent of the children of Greek families used Greek exclusively, and 68 percent of the Portuguese children used only Portuguese at home. However, when the same respondents were asked what language they used to speak to family members of different generations, huge discrepancies emerged. When conversing with parents and grandparents, the overwhelming majority spoke the mother tongue, whereas when speaking with siblings and friends, most children spoke French or English. Thus the 'home language' question is an invalid measure of the language habits of young people, and more directly reflects the habits of the older generations.

Veltman is critical of the question about the respondent's capacity to carry on a conversation in an official language, because it is not demanding enough. His own research inquired if respondents speak French or English 'very well' or 'quite well.' This more stringent approach indicates a substantially higher proportion who are effectively monolingual in Greek or Portuguese. Furthermore, Veltman found that the relationships between the questions vary in often unpredictable ways, showing somewhat different patterns among the two groups of immigrants. Whether or not Veltman has found the right way to collect statistics on language usage, his work has cast a dark shadow of suspicion over the validity of the language data from the Canadian census.

4.2 Respondent and Interviewer Bias

An interview is a social interaction, and thus the validity of a respondent's answers may be shaped by the characteristics of the interviewer and of the interview situation itself. A questionnaire is merely an attenuated form of interview, and thus its results also may suffer from biases introduced by the act of collecting the data (Block 1965, Berg 1967).

'Response bias' is the tendency of a respondent to answer questions in a particular way, regardless of what the question specifically is about. A very common bias is 'acquiescence,' the tendency of a respondent to agree with whatever an interviewer or survey says, regardless of its content, or to disagree. A tendency to agree is called *yea-saying*, and a tendency to disagree is called *nay-saying*. The tendency of a respondent to give socially acceptable answers to questions, putting himself in a good light, is called 'social desirability bias.' This form of bias is especially troublesome in linguistic surveys, because the formal setting of the interview may encourage respondents to be more formal than usual in their manner of expression, shifting their speech toward the prestige standard.

These are not new problems. In 1929, Stuart A. Rice discovered 'contagion bias,' the tendency of the data to be infected by the attitudes of the interviewer, either because respondents adjust their answers to fit their impression of what the interviewer wants, or because the interviewer adjusts the answers when writing them down. And in 1942, Daniel Katz examined 'interviewer bias' in a survey of opinions about labor-related and war-related issues, finding significant differences in response depending upon the social class of the interviewer. Similarly, respondents give significantly different patterns of response to interviewers of a different race than to members of their own group. Anderson et al. (1988) found that Black respondents replied differently to questions about race relations, depending on the race of the interviewer. This phenomenon has been discovered independently in linguistics, where it is called 'accommodation,' the tendency of one person to adjust speech style to match that of another (see *Speech Accommodation*).

Howard Schuman, who has vast experience in constructing and administering surveys, prefers to conceptualize these issues in terms of the question–answer process in attitude surveys (see *Attitude Surveys: Question–Answer Process*). Research employing two or more versions of a question has revealed often substantial differences in responses, dependent upon often subtle differences in wording. Apart from alerting linguists to methodological problems that need to be avoided or solved, this body of research has unearthed evidence about language itself. For example, supposed synonyms may get different responses, including synonyms that are the negation of an antonym; for example, 'forbid' turns out to mean something substantially different to respondents than does 'not allow.' Similarly, the effect of the interviewer on responses reminds us that words do not have precise, invariant meanings, but take on meaning depending upon the social situation in which they are uttered.

4.3 Methods of Survey Sampling

While the aim of social research is to arrive at justified conclusions about human populations, there is seldom time or other resources to survey every single member, and resort must be made to sampling. There are many kinds of samples, however, and they differ greatly in their suitability for various kinds of research (Kish 1965). At the extreme, a sample may be so hopelessly biased that it completely ruins research based on it.

A 'convenience sample' is a subset of the population polled simply because they were easy to contact, and highly accessible respondents may often exhibit somewhat different language from less accessible ones; for example, they may be better educated than the average, or belong to particular ethnic groups that are more hospitable to strangers. In a 'snowball sample,' the researcher begins with some individuals who are appropriate informants and then asks them for referrals to other appropriate informants; for example, one might locate Greek speakers in Edinburgh by visiting a Greek restaurant and asking each Greek one meets to give the names and addresses of other Greeks. The danger here is that one may survey one stratum or subgroup in the Greek population, without knowing which one or how the others differ.

A 'purposive sample' consists of a set of cases which the researcher has carefully considered and which in his or her judgment will serve the needs of the research; for instance, school teachers with apparently Greek names could be taken from a list of all school teachers in Edinburgh. A 'quota sample' sets targets for how many people are to be included from each of several categories; one might survey 100 middle-class Greeks and 100 working-class Greeks. This approach allows one to evaluate linguistic differences between the categories, but it has little power to guard against problems caused by divisions in the population other than those explicitly considered by one's quota system.

Perhaps the standard sampling approach is the 'simple random sample,' created using random numbers or other chance-based procedures, selecting individuals from the population at random. Each member of the population has an equal chance of appearing in the sample, and every combination of a given number of individuals also has an equal chance. A 'systematic sample' is a cheap imitation of a random sample, taking perhaps every tenth name from a list; it saves a little time in actually drawing the sample but offers less confidence in the results and has no justification today when computers can quickly draw true random samples. A 'cluster sample' also saves time and money, by drawing a modified random sample in which respondents are clustered together geographically into groups that can be visited more cheaply than if the individuals were strewn across the landscape.

Often, a combination of quota and random sampling can achieve better results than either approach alone. At the outset, the researcher can identify categories of people in the population, just as in quota sampling, and decide how many of each is needed. For example, in doing a survey in Quebec one might want substantial numbers of both French speakers and English speakers in the final dataset. Then, a random sample is drawn for each of the categories separately, and the result is a 'stratified random sample.' A 'proportionate sample' is a sample that sets quotas for the groups of respondents that match their distribution in the population.

One may sample not only persons from a population but linguistic features from a comprehensive style and language fragments from a larger text. When McIntosh and his colleagues worked with such diligence to produce the *Linguistic Atlas of Late Mediaeval English*, they did not record every instance of every variant of every feature in the 1200 manuscripts they studied. Instead, they worked with samples of text, and the principles of sampling developed for use with questionnaire surveys are readily adapted to sampling any other kind of universe. For example, a 'multistage sample' could be drawn from a corpus of texts by first taking a random sample of texts, say 10 percent of the total, then taking a random sample of lines from the selected texts.

4.4 Multivariate Approaches

Many of the statistical techniques used by social scientists in the late twentieth century are designed to work with several variables simultaneously, and such multivariate techniques will undoubtedly be of ever greater prominence in linguistics. Restricting one's scholarly labors to a single variable is like trying to do dialectology by listening to only one word. In the Bible, it proved possible to distinguish Gileadites from Ephramites by attention to how they pronounced the initial sound in *shibboleth*, but modern scholarship would want to combine many pieces of information. Generally, two justifications are given for the multivariate approach. First, a combination of variables is probably more reliable and precise than any single measure, in part because a single variable is apt to contain a considerable amount of random variation or noise. Second, it is possible to measure a general concept by combining data about a number of its aspects; for example, information about wealth, education, and community power may be combined to measure social class.

Roughly speaking, there are two ways to combine many variables into a composite measure, the synthetic and the analytic. In order to measure a general concept with precision, several variables are blended into a new, synthetic variable, called a scale or index. Or, there can be at the outset a large number of variables that presumably measure different concepts, and use techniques of statistical analysis to divide them into groups, each of which reflects a particular concept.

In his article on scaling (see *Scaling*), Earl Babbie notes a variety of ways to combine variables to make a composite scale. Perhaps the simplest is to add together a set of separate variables, giving each one an equal weight. For example, late Middle English manuscripts can be distinguished in terms of whether they were Northern or Southern, and a particular manuscript could be described by counting what percentage of a list of linguistic features were Northern. Often, however, there is good reason to believe that the individual measures are not equal, some being more powerful than others, or some kinds of measures being more numerous than others, and there is a need to weight the variables in some way before combining them. For example, if dialects were to be distinguished both phonetically and lexically, and there was somewhat more information about the written form of words than their pronunciation, then each particular lexical variable might be given less weight, so that in total they equaled the weight of the data on pronunciation.

Factor analysis is one of a number of widely used techniques for arranging a number of variables along a set of dimensions, and once this is done the variables clustered along one dimension can be combined into a reliable scale. An example relevant to language is a study of the ideologies of science fiction literature (Bainbridge 1986). Nearly 600 participants at a world science fiction convention rated their preferences among 73 well-known authors, and a computer calculated the 2628 correlations linking pairs of authors, under the assumption that highly correlated authors in the preference ratings must share important stylistic and ideological qualities. A factor analysis then discovered four dimensions of variation, essentially dividing most of the authors into four groups, purely on the basis of the statistical data from respondents. One group was simply classic writers, such as Jules Verne and H. G. Wells. The other three dimensions were clearly different kinds of modern literature, and it was possible to correlate them with other items in the questionnaire to identify each one in terms of the underlying messages it conveyed.

The statistical analysis revealed that 'Hard-Science' authors based their fiction on the physical sciences and new technology, extrapolating what might be the next steps taken in particular sciences, and their stories were very similar to factual science articles and reports on the space program. Their protagonists were unemotional and intelligent, and the reader could expect a rational explanation for everything that happened. In contrast, 'New Wave' writers wrote avantgarde fiction that experimented with new styles and was based on the social sciences. Their fiction deeply probed personal relationships and feelings, often concerned harmful effects of scientific progress or was critical of society, and included a considerable body of feminist literature. The 'Fantasy Cluster' of authors and styles included several subtypes of literature, including myths, legends, sagas, epics, 'sword-and-sorcery,' ghost stories, and tales of horror. Based on magic rather than science, and having affinities with art and poetry, it concerned alien cultures, strange characters, and protagonists who were brave and aggressive. This study sought high-level, abstract messages communicated by dozens of authors in hundreds of publications, but factor analysis can be applied to analysis of meanings and linguistic forms in many different kinds of data.

William Rau believes that multidimensional scaling will find greater applications in linguistics than factor analysis (see *Statistics in Sociolinguistics*), because it is suited to a wider range of data. The first step in factor analysis is the calculation of a matrix of correlation coefficients, and this requires that the variables meet certain mathematical criteria that may not often be met by language data. In demonstrating how multidimensional scaling can be applied to three different kinds of linguistic data, Rau explains that students of language may want to employ these techniques in a very different way from that typically used by sociologists. Both factor analysis and multidimensional scaling can discover the structure either of the variables or of the cases, depending on how these techniques are applied. Sociologists usually want to learn how the variables relate to each other, while linguists may want to understand relationships among cases. That is, the student of language may want to analyze speech differences across regions of a nation or individual persons within a community, and Rau convincingly demonstrates how this can be done profitably for linguistic scholars.

4.5 Content Analysis

Any systematic approach that seeks to measure the patterns of meaning communicated through existing samples of language can be called 'content analysis.' Many research traditions in sociology and numerous specific studies have developed coding schemes or other techniques for extracting meaning from utterances. A classic example is the Kuhn and McPartland twenty-statements test (Kuhn–McPartland 1954). In the original version, a respondent was asked to write 20 statements beginning with the words 'I am.' The researcher would then assign each statement to one of two main categories, *consensual* and *subconsensual*. The consensual responses 'refer to groups and classes whose limits and conditions of membership are matters of common knowledge.' Examples given included: student, girl, husband, Baptist, from Chicago, premed, daughter, oldest child. In contrast, the subconsensual responses 'require interpretation by the respondent to be precise or to place him relative to other people.' Examples were: happy, bored, pretty good student, too heavy, good wife, interesting.

During the 1980s, researchers have tended to use a slightly different coding scheme in which the first category is social, those responses that identify the person in terms of social roles or membership in social groups. A second category is psychological, responses that describe a mood or mental attitude. It has been suggested that the proportion of responses in each category varies from decade to decade, or from one group of respondents to another, some being more oriented toward other persons, and some more oriented toward the self. Such a coding scheme can readily be applied to naturally occurring speech or written text, as well as to text generated in response to the researcher's instructions.

As Kathleen Carley points out in her article on content analysis, a classic approach, exemplified by the General Inquirer computer system, was to count the number of times each word appeared in a sample of text, with the assumption that the more often something was mentioned the more central it was to the meanings being communicated. In the 1980s and early 1990s, techniques have been developed for examining the connections between words or concepts, indeed for determining the meaning of a term in the ways respondents associate it with other words. Another technique, which has been applied to the problem of determining the authorship of texts, is the analysis of values or other high-level meanings contained in texts (Rokeach et al. 1970). Clearly, coding schemes for categorizing naturally occurring speech are tools of linguistics, even though most of them have been developed by sociologists and psychologists.

4.6 Qualitative Approaches

Although the methodology of quantitative research has progressed rapidly, sociologists have not abandoned qualitative methods, especially those designed to extract meaning from human actions and speech. In particular, the classic work of Max Weber continues to be influential. Weberians argue that one cannot understand the action of an individual unless one appreciates what the elements of the situation mean to that individual, and the process of seeing things from the perspective of the person is given the technical name '*Verstehen*', from the German verb 'to understand.' Weberian analysis is often conducted through the creation of 'ideal types,' abstract formulations that identify categories of meaning to which phenomena may be assigned, yet which preserve their qualitative distinctiveness and the subjective meanings that may be assigned to them. This approach has influenced the development of ethnomethodology (see *Ethnomethodology*), which in turn has encouraged analysis of conversation in linguistics. Ideal-typical analysis has generally been applied to widely shared cultural phenomena, such as Protestantism, but it also dovetails with much work done in social psychology.

5. Disorganization and Reorganization

A union of sociology and linguistics could not lead to the conquest of one by the other, if for no other reason than that sociology is highly fragmented, rife with factional battles and schools of thought that have nothing to say to each other. At various times, attempts were made to unify sociology around one or another set of theoretical or methodological principles, and all were failures. One reason is the great diversity of phenomena that sociologists study; only a fanatic would assert that one theory was capable of explaining family life, crime, urbanism, modernization, religion, industrial relations, and sex roles. Another is the ideological burden that sociology sadly bears; a substantial portion of those recruited to the ranks of sociologists are already committed to one or another reform movement, a fine thing for social progress but an impediment to objective analysis and to development of really scientific social science. Still another reason is the practical and moral difficulty in testing social theories conclusively, which means that practically every idea ever proposed remains plausible to at least some school of thought; the relative merits of opposing positions can seldom be determined objectively, and the intellectual pruning required for progress seldom takes place.

Still, the wealth of ideas, information, and insights possessed by sociology is immense, much of it valuable for language scholars. Sociologists in many fields study language, and many would profit from the realization that they are practicing amateur linguistics and from the professional training that would elevate the level of their work. The resurgence of sociology outside the United States, in nations where knowledge of several languages is the hallmark of an educated person, bodes well for the future of the sociology of language. The extreme disorganization of sociology has set the stage for at least partial reorganization, and the fact that language is the central phenomenon for many subdisciplines and perspectives suggests that a reorientation of sociology toward linguistics could achieve a new paradigm for the study of human social life.

Bibliography

Anderson B A, Silver B D, Abramson P R 1988 The effects of the race of the interviewer on race-related attitudes of black respondents in SRC/CPS national election studies. *Public Opinion Quarterly* **52**: 289–324

Bainbridge W S 1986 *Dimensions of Science Fiction*. Harvard University Press, Cambridge, MA

Bainbridge W S 1992 *Social Research Methods and Statistics*. Wadsworth, Belmont, CA

Berg I A (ed.) 1967 *Response Set in Personality Assessment*. Aldine, Chicago, IL

Block J 1965 *The Challenge of Response Sets*. Appleton-Century-Crofts, New York

Bogardus E S 1924 Measuring social distance. *Journal of Applied Sociology* **9**: 299–308

Fishman J A (ed.) 1968 *Readings in the Sociology of Language*. Mouton, The Hague

Fishman J A (ed.) 1971 *Advances in the Sociology of Language*. Mouton, The Hague

Fishman J A 1985 Macrosociolinguistics and the sociology of language in the early eighties. *Annual Review of Sociology* **11**: 113–27

Giallombardo R 1966 *Society of Women*. Wiley, New York

Gusfield J 1963 *Symbolic Crusade Status Politics and the American Temperance Movement*. University of Illinois Press, Urbana, IL

Hertzler J O 1965 *A Sociology of Language*. Random House, New York

Hymes D 1972 Editorial introduction. *Language in Society* **1**: 1–14

Hymes D 1984 Sociolinguistics: Stability and consolidation. *International Journal of the Sociology of Language* **45**: 39–45

Katz D 1942 Do interviewers bias poll results? *Public Opinion Quarterly* **6**: 248–68

Kish L 1965 *Survey Sampling*. Wiley, New York

Kontupoulos K M 1994 Intellectuals. In: Asher R E, Simpson J M Y (eds.) *Encyclopedia of Language and Linguistics* **4**: 1693 5, Pergamon, Oxford, UK

Kuhn M H, McPartland T S 1954 An empirical investigation of self-attitudes. *American Sociological Review* **19**: 68–76

Lemert E M 1967 *Human Deviance, Social Problems, and Social Control*. Prentice-Hall, Englewood Cliffs, NJ

Lipset S M, Raab E 1970 *The Politics of Unreason*. Harper and Row, New York

Mauss A L 1975 *Social Problems as Social Movements*. Lippincott, Philadelphia, PA

McIntosh A, Samuels M L, Benskin M (eds.) 1986 *A Linguistic Atlas of Late Mediaeval English*. Aberdeen University Press, Aberdeen, UK

Osgood C E, Suci G J, Tannenbaum P H 1957 *The Measurement of Meaning*. University of Illinois Press, Urbana, IL

Pfohl S J 1985 *Images of Deviance and Social Control*. McGraw-Hill, New York

Rice S A 1929 Contagion bias in the interview. *American Journal of Sociology* **35**: 420–3

Rokeach M, Homant R, Penner L 1970 A value analysis of the disputed Federalist Papers. *Journal of Personality and Social Psychology* **16**: 245–50

Scheff T J 1966 *Being Mentally Ill*. Aldine, Chicago, IL

Schur E M 1965 *Crimes Without Victims*. Prentice-Hall, Englewood Cliffs, NJ

Stark R, Bainbridge W S 1985 *The Future of Religion*. University of California Press, Berkeley, CA

Sutherland E H 1937 *The Professional Thief*. University of Chicago Press, Chicago, IL

Turner J H 1986 *The Structure of Sociological Theory*. Dorsey, Chicago, IL

Veltman C 1986 The interpretation of the language questions of the Canadian census. *Canadian Review of Sociology and Anthropology* **23**: 412–22

Speech Community
B. B. Kachru

The terms 'speech community' and 'linguistic community' are widely used by linguists and other social scientists to identify communities on the basis of their languages (e.g., Swahili speech community, English speech community, linguistic communities of India). In linguistic descriptions and analyses, these terms are used to make descriptive and theoretical generalizations. However, speech community, like another often-used term, 'dialect,' cannot be defined rigorously. True, all users of a language seem to know what speech community (or communities) they belong to, or not belong to. This intuitive affiliation with a given speech community is not different from the lay-person's notion of a dialect, and dialect identification.

1. Toward a Definition

The definitions range from Bloomfield's (1933: 42) rather broad conceptualization of 'a group of people who interact by means of speech,' to the very complex characterization by Bolinger (1975: 333):

> There is no limit to the ways in which human beings league themselves together for self-identification, security, gain, amusement, worship, or any of the other purposes that are held in common; consequently there is no limit to the number and variety of speech communities that are to be found in society.

Hymes (1974: 47–51) considers a speech community 'a social rather than linguistic entity.' Such a community shares 'knowledge of rules for the conduct and interpretation of speech' (see *Hymes, Dell Hathaway*).

Firth's (1959: 208) distinction between 'a close *speech fellowship* and a wider *speech community* in what may be called a language community comprising both written and spoken forms of the general language' is very useful (see *Firth, J. R.*). The fellowships are based on the social, caste, religious, geographical, and professional identities one desires to establish. A restricted definition, that members of a speech community usually inhabit the same area and speak the same variety or standard of a language, is misleading.

2. Characteristics of Speech Communities

In characterizing a speech community, one must note several features. First, a speech community crosses political boundaries: for example, English cuts across the political boundaries of Canada, the USA, Australia, and New Zealand. In South Asia, the Bengali speech community is divided between Bangladesh and India, the Tamil-speaking speech community between Sri Lanka and India. In Africa, the Swahili speech community is spread over Kenya, Tanzania, Uganda, and Democratic Republic of Congo. Arabic is used as the first or an additional language in several states in the Arab world and in parts of Africa and Asia.

Second, a speech community does not necessarily represent one religion or culture. Bengali, for example, is spoken by two separate religious groups within two distinct cultural contexts in Bangladesh, and in the state of West Bengal in India.

Third, speech communities comprise idiolects and dialects. An idiolect is the total speech repertoire of a single person, and a dialect marks a person's membership in a particular group (see *Dialect and Dialectology*).

3. Types of Speech Communities

Speech communities are classified into four major types on the basis of their linguistic composition (see Ferguson 1996, Kachru 1997).

3.1 Multilingual

A 'multilingual' community officially recognizes more than two languages. In South Asia, India provides a paradigm example of such a community, recognizing 15 national languages out of the estimated 1652 or more languages and dialects used in the country. In Africa, Nigeria recognizes four official languages: English, Hausa, Igbo, Yoruba. In East Asia, Singapore has four official languages: Chinese, English, Malay, Tamil. In Europe, Switzerland recognizes three official languages: German, French, and Italian. The recognition of linguistic pluralism does not mean that in terms of functional range, and societal depth of use all the recognized languages have identical status and currency. In India, for example, for pan-Indian and international functions, the 'associate' official language, English, has greater currency. Hindi, the 'official' language, has wider uses than the regional languages such as Bengali and Tamil. In Singapore, Tamil has fewer functions than has Chinese, Malay, or English. A country may officially declare itself multilingual, but in reality its constituent states may be essentially monolingual. In Switzerland, for example, in Geneva, Zurich, and Ticino, the majority of the population use only French, German, and Italian, respectively (Kloss 1967).

A multilingual country generally adopts a contact language, often with an official status. During the Austro–Hungarian monarchy, German served this purpose in parts of Austria until 1918. In India, Hindi–Hindustani performs this function, as did Russian in what was until 1991 the USSR.

3.2 Bilingual

A 'bilingual' community has two languages with an official status, In Botswana, Tswana and English are official languages. In Cameroon, French and English have this status. In Canada, English and French have official status. In Finland, Finnish and Swedish, and in Sri Lanka, originally Sinhalese and Tamil were two official languages. When Sinhalese was made the sole official language, the result was years of unrest, violence, and open demands for secession by the Tamil minority.

Among bilingual speech communities, there is a difference between, for example, Belgium and Canada, where two languages are recognized but the two constituent units are essentially monolingual, as opposed to Singapore and India where bilingualism/multilingualism is part of the linguistic behavior and linguistic repertoire of most individuals.

3.3 Diglossia

Originally, 'diglossic' community (*di* 'two,' *glossia* 'languages') was used in the specific sense of two varieties of one language which are functionally complementary. The earliest use of the term, 'diglossie,' was probably by Krumbacher (1902) to show the relationship between the two varieties of Greek, the written and the oral. Ferguson (1959) used the term to refer to:

> ...a relatively stable language situation in which, in addition to the primary dialects of the language (which may include a standard or regional standards), there is a very divergent, highly codified (often grammatically more complex) superposed variety...

In a diglossic situation, there are two varieties of a language, High (H) and Low (L). The H variety is generally used in formal contexts (see *Diglossia*).

There are many diglossic communities. Arabic-speaking communities make a distinction between Classical and colloquial varieties of the language. Among Greek-speaking communities this distinction has been applied to the H variety, termed Katharévousa and the L variety, termed Dhimotiki (Demotic). In this case of Tamil, a Dravidian language spoken primarily in Tamil Nadu state of India and in parts of Sri Lanka, a distinction has traditionally been made between literary and classical varieties. In Telugu, spoken in Andhra Pradesh state of India, two distinct varieties, 'granthikā' (literary; H variety) and 'vyavhārikā' (colloquial; L variety) are used. In Bangladesh and India, Bengali makes a distinction between 'sādhu bhāsā' (cultivated speech; H variety) and čolit bhāsā (colloquial speech; L variety). In Switzerland, the German-speaking parts have a H variety of German ('Hochdeutsch,' the standard) and an L variety termed 'Schwyzertüütsch,' which includes a range of regional dialects of Swiss. In a diglossic context, the L variety is acquired as a child while the H variety is generally acquired later. There has been considerable discussion of diglossic communities and the implications of diglossia for education and allocation of linguistic power. Diglossia has also been used for what actually are bilingual situations: one community using two languages, e.g., the use of Spanish and English by the Puerto Ricans in New York. There has also been an attempt to shift away from the earlier use of this term by Ferguson, particularly in the work of Gumperz (1964), Fishman (1967), and Hymes (1974; see also Hudson 1980).

Among diglossic communities distinction must be made between, for example, the situation of the Arabic-speaking populations and Haiti. Haiti is considered a diglossic community where children first learn Haitian Creole and later, when they enter school, learn French. In Arab countries, the Arabic-speaking children learn the formal variety of Arabic in school.

3.4 Monolingual

A 'monolingual' community essentially recognizes one language, as in Japan, Korea, Malta, and Portugal. However, the term is a misnomer, since monolinguals have a verbal repertoire which includes various dialects, styles, and registers. Switches in styles and registers often entail special efforts in learning and education. In earlier literature, the USA and the UK were perceived as monolingual speech communities but this perception was actually based on an attitude and not on the facts.

4. Speech Community and Linguistic Repertoire

The members of a speech community command a 'linguistic repertoire,' 'code repertoire,' or 'verbal repertoire.' The terms, used more or less interchangeably, refer to the total range of languages, dialects, styles, and registers available to a member of a speech community for interaction with other members. A multilingual country may recognize such a repertoire in the educational system, as India, for example, recognizes the 'Three Language Formula.' The formula, proposed in the 1960s, requires study of three languages in school: English, Hindi, and the regional language. In the Hindi areas (Central India) students are required to study a Dravidian language (Kannada, Malayalam, Tamil, or Telugu) to balance what is termed the 'language load.'

In the case of monolinguals, such a repertoire may entail dialect, style, and register shift. The use of a particular code out of the total repertoire may also mark a hierarchy of contexts or shift in linguistic identities and functions (Kachru 1982).

5. Speech Community, Language Rivalry, and Conflicts

Speech communities are rarely harmonious. They manifest various types of rivalries and conflicts. In postcolonial Africa and Asia the issues primarily relate to language standardization, e.g., the development of terminology to equip languages for modern scientific and technological demands, for administration and education, for developing and stabilizing registers and for providing writing systems or simplification of graphemic systems. The conflict may be motivated by seeking recognition for a language or a dialect not recognized in the language policy, e.g., demands of the Rajasthani, Maithili, and Urdu speakers in India (Kachru and Bhatia 1978). Such conflicts may result from attitudinal readjustment toward a language or its varieties, e.g., the demands for recognition by the minority language speakers in the UK and India, and by the speakers of Black English in the USA. The underlying motivations for such rivalry and conflicts are to establish language identity (Heller 1987).

In multilingual speech communities, interaction in many languages and dialects may result in development of new codes of communication (see *Code-switching: Overview*).

6. Conclusion

In conceptualizing a speech community one may either emphasize the shared linguistic rules, or the societal and functional factors. The institutionalized languages of wider communication used across languages and cultures (e.g., English) have raised many interesting theoretical and descriptive issues concerning terms such as 'speech community' (Kachru 1988, 1996).

Bibliography

Bloomfield L 1933 *Language*. Holt, New York
Bolinger D 1975 *Aspects of Language*, 2nd edn. Harcourt Brace Jovanovich, New York
Britto F 1986 *Diglossia: A Study of the Theory with Applications to Tamil*. Georgetown University Press, Washington, DC
Ferguson C A 1959 Diglossia. *Word* **15**: 325–40
Ferguson C A 1996 *Sociolinguistic Perspectives: Papers on Language in Society 1959–1994*. (Chapters 1–6) Oxford University Press, Oxford, UK
Firth J R 1959 The treatment of language in general linguistics. In: Palmer F R (ed.) 1968 *Selected Papers of J. R. Firth 1952–59*. Longmans, London
Fishman J A 1967 Bilingualism with and without diglossia; diglossia with and without bilingualism. *The Journal of Social Issues* **23**(2): 29–38
Gumperz J J 1964 Linguistic and social interaction in two communities. *The Ethnology of Communication* **284**: 137–53
Heller M 1987 Language and identity. In: Ammon U, Dittmar N, Mattheier K J (eds.) *Sociolingustics: An International Handbook of the Science of Language and Society*. Walter de Gruyter, Berlin
Hudson R 1980 *Sociolinguistics*. Cambridge University Press, Cambridge, UK
Hymes D 1974 *Foundations in Sociolinguistics: An Ethnographic Approach*. University of Pennsylvania Press, Philadelphia, PA
Kachru B B 1982 The bilingual's linguistic repertoire, In: Hartford B, Valdman A, Foster C R (eds.) *Issues in International Bilingual Education: The Role of the Vernacular*. Plenum, New York
Kachru B B 1988 The spread of English and sacred linguistic cows. In: Lowenberg P H (ed.) *Language Spread and Language Policy: Issues, Implications and Case Studies*. Georgetown University Press, Washington, DC
Kachru B B 1996 The paradigms of marginality. *World Englishes*. **15**.3: 241–55
Kachru B B 1997 World Englishes and English-using communities. *Annual Review of Applied Linguistics* **17**: 66–87
Kachru Y, Bhatia T K 1978 The emerging 'dialect' conflict in Hindi: A case of Glottopolitics. *International Journal of the Sociology of Language* **16**: 47–58
Kloss H 1967 Types of multilingual communities: A discussion of ten variables. *International Journal of American Linguistics* **33**(4): 7–17
Krumbacher K 1902 *Das Problem der neugriechischen Schriftsprache*. Akadamie, Munich

SECTION II
Language and Interaction

Antilanguage
P. A. Chilton

'Antilanguage' is a term used by the British linguist M. A. K. Halliday to refer to the variety of a language spoken by an 'antisociety,' that is by such social subcultures as criminals, immigrant and other disadvantaged communities, as well as marginal groups such as students, conscripts, and prisoners. Such subcultures, according to Halliday, stand in a 'metaphorical' relationship to the main society: they are a part of that society, but are peripheral or antagonistic to it. This ambivalent relationship is represented in the 'antilanguage' characteristic of such groups. Examples are the language of the criminal underworld in Elizabethan England ('pelting'), the Bengali underworld variety of twentieth-century Calcutta, and 'grypserka,' the antilanguage found in Polish prisons in the 1970s. The function of antilanguages is in part to maintain secrecy, but also to symbolize the symbiotic relationship between society and antisociety. The linguistic characteristics of antilanguages include metathesis, syllable addition, transposition of syllables (as in 'pig-Latin' and French 'verlan'), and transposition of consonants: e.g., in the Bengali antilanguage of Calcutta, *kodān* ('shop') derives from standard Bengali *dokān*. Many lexical items of the standard language are replaced and multiplied by grammatical expansion and metaphorical or metonymic substitution: e.g., Elizabethan pelting *darkmans* ('night'), *Rome-booze* ('wine'). On the phonological, grammatical, and semantic levels, therefore, antilanguages can be said to create alternative meanings and alternative realities, which are mirror images of the standard language and society.

See also: Halliday, Michael Alexander Kirkwood; Slang: Sociology; Adolescent Peer Group Language.

Bibliography
Halliday M A K 1978 Antilanguage. In: Halliday M A K *Language as Social Semiotic*. Arnold, London
Mallik B 1972 *Language of the Underworld of West Bengal*. Research Series 76, Sanskrit College, Calcutta, India
Salgādo G (ed.) 1972 *Cony-Catchers and Bawdy Baskets: An Anthology of Elizabethan Low Life*. Penguin, Harmondsworth, UK

Audience Design
A. Bell

Audience Design is a theory of language style (see *Style*). Proposed in Bell (1984), who derived the term from Clark (Clark and Carlson, 1982), it has become the most widespread approach to style in sociolinguistics (Eckert and Rickford, 2001). Audience Design proposes that speakers' style choices are primarily a response to their audience.

The framework has been summarized (Bell, 1997) under nine headings:
(a) Style is what an individual speaker does with a language in relation to other people. Style is essentially interactive and social, marking interpersonal and intergroup relations.
(b) Style derives its meaning from the association of linguistic features with particular social groups. The social evaluation of a group is transferred to the linguistic features associated with that group. Styles carry social meanings through their derivation from the language of particular groups.
(c) The core of Audience Design is that speakers design their style primarily for, and in response

to, their audience. Audience Design is generally manifested in a speaker shifting their style to be more like that of the person they are talking to—'convergence' in terms of Speech Accommodation Theory.

(d) Audience Design applies to all codes and levels of a language repertoire, monolingual, and multilingual.

(e) Variation on the style dimension within the speech of a single speaker derives from and echoes the variation, which exists between speakers on the 'social' dimension. This axiom claims that quantitative style differences are normally less than differences between social groups.

(f) Speakers show a fine-grained ability to design their style for a range of different addressees, and to a lessening degree for other audience members such as auditors and overhearers.

(g) Style shifts according to topic or setting derive their meaning and direction of shift from the underlying association of topics or settings with typical audience members.

(h) As well as the 'responsive' dimension of style, there is the 'initiative' dimension where a style shift itself initiates a change in the situation rather than resulting from such a change. Sociolinguists have drawn attention to this distinction at least since Blom and Gumperz's proposal of situational versus metaphorical styles (1972). In responsive style shift, there is a regular association between language and social situation. Initiative style trades on such associations, infusing the flavor of one setting into a different context, in what Bakhtin (see *Bakhtin, Mikhail M.*) has called 'stylization' (1981). Language becomes an independent variable which itself shapes the situation.

(i) Initiative style shifts are in essence 'referee design,' by which the linguistic features associated with a group can be used to express affiliation with that group. They focus on an absent reference group rather than the present audience. This typically occurs in the performance of a language or variety other than one's own (see Rampton's (1995) concept of Crossing; *Ethnicity and the Crossing of Boundaries*).

Audience Design has been contested on a variety of grounds—the priority it gives to social variation over style, disregard of the role of attention to speech, and in particular inadequate attention to the active, constitutive role of language in interaction.

Later developments in Audience Design (e.g., Bell, 2001) have countered by stressing the proactive nature of language style in identity formation and presentation. Responsive and initiative style are treated as different but concurrent dimensions of language usage, manifesting the structure/agency duality familiar in social theory. This accords both with the stress in contemporary social theory on language as constitutive, and with the dialogical theory of Bakhtin (1981). The range of linguistic analysis in Audience Design has also been increasingly extended to include qualitative and co-occurrence analyses as well as quantification.

See also: Dialogism; Speech Accommodation.

Bibliography

Bakhtin M M 1981 *The Dialogic Imagination*. University of Texas Press, Austin, TX

Bell A 1984 Language style as audience design. *Language in Society* **13**: 145–204

Bell A 1997 Style as audience design. In: Coupland N, Jaworski A (eds.) *Sociolinguistics: A Reader and Coursebook*. Macmillan, London, pp. 240–50

Bell A 2001 Back in style: re-working Audience Design. In: Eckert P, Rickford J R (eds.) *Style and Sociolinguistic Variation*. Cambridge University Press, New York, pp. 139–69

Blom J-P, Gumperz J J 1972 Social meaning in linguistic structure: Code–switching in Norway. In: Gumperz J J, Hymes D (eds.) *Directions in Sociolinguistics*. Holt, Rinehart and Winston, New York, pp. 407–34

Clark H H, Carlson T B 1982 Hearers and speech acts. *Language* **58**: 332–73

Eckert P, Rickford J R (eds.) 2001 *Style and Sociolinguistic Variation*. Cambridge University Press, New York

Rampton B 1995 *Crossing: Language and Ethnicity among Adolescents*. Longman, London

Conversation Analysis
P. Drew

Research in conversation analysis (hereafter CA) has paralleled the development within sociolinguistics, pragmatics, discourse analysis, and other fields in linguistics, toward a naturalistic observation-based science of actual verbal behavior. Recordings of naturally occurring conversations are analyzed in order to discover how participants understand and respond to one another in their turns at talk, and how therefore *sequences* of activities are generated. Conversation Analysis is thereby a bridge between linguistic analysis (especially pragmatics) and the sociological investigation of sociality, conversation being a primary medium of interaction in the social world, and the medium through which children are socialized into the linguistic and social conventions of a society. The main objective of CA is to uncover the sociolinguistic competences which underlie the production and interpretation of talk in social interaction. While the principal focus of CA is 'ordinary conversation,' its perspective and methods are also applied to interaction in institutional settings such as classrooms, medical consultations, courts, psychiatric therapy sessions, news interviews, and the workplace.

1. The Origins of Conversation Analysis

The most immediate origin of CA is the period during 1963–64 which Harvey Sacks (see *Sacks, Harvey*) (1935–75) spent at the Center for the Scientific Study of Suicide in Los Angeles. Drawn by his interests both in the ethnomethodological concern with members' methods of practical reasoning and commonsense understandings (arising from his association with Garfinkel), and also in interaction (somewhat stimulated by his having been taught by Goffman (see *Goffman, Erving*) while a graduate student at Berkeley), Sacks began to analyze telephone calls made to the Suicide Prevention Center (see Schegloff 1989; see *Schegloff, Emanuel*). Without any diminished sensitivity to the plight of persons calling the SPC, Sacks investigated how callers' accounts of their troubles were produced in the course of, and were designed to be fitted into, their interactions with the SPC staff member with whom they were talking. This led him to explore the more generic 'machinery' of conversational turn-taking, and of the sequential patterns or structures associated with the management of activities in conversation. Through the collection of a larger corpus of more mundane telephone calls, and through his collaboration with Jefferson and Schegloff, that exploratory work has been considerably refined and developed, so that now there is quite a comprehensive picture of the conversational organization of turn exchange; overlapping talk; repair; topic initiation and closing; sequences initiated by such activities as greetings, questions, invitations, and requests; agreement/disagreement; story telling; discourse markers (such as 'well' and 'oh'); laughter; non- or quasi-lexical response tokens; and of the integration of speech with nonvocal activities. Conversation Analysis research reveals how such technical aspects of talk are the structured, socially organized resources whereby participants perform and coordinate activities through talking together.

2. Data and Transcription

The primary data for CA are recordings of naturally occurring interactions, detailed transcriptions of which enable researchers to search through episodes in many different conversations (with varying content, different participants and different contexts) with the aim of identifying stable systematic phenomena, and collecting multiple instances of those phenomena. The following extract from the recording of a telephone call is representative of the transcribed data used in CA research.

[NB: II: 2: 17–18]
1 Emma: Wanna c'm do:wn 'av a bah:ta lu:nch with me?=
2   = Ah gut s'm beer'n stu:ff,
3   (0.3)
4 Nancy: Wul yer ril sweet hon; uh:m
5   (.)
6 Emma: ⌈ Or d'you 'av sump'n ⌈ else( )
7 Nancy: ⌊ Let- I: hu   ⌊ n:No: I haf to: uh call Roul's
8   mother, h I told'er I: 'd call 'er this morning
9   I ⌈ gotta letter from 'er en .hhhhhh A:nd uhm
10 Emma: ⌊ (Uh huh.)
11   (1.0)
12 Nancy: .tch u-So: she in the letter she said if you ca:n why
13   (.) yihknow call me Saturday morning en I j'st haven't
14   h ⌈ .hhhh
15 Emma: ⌊ Mm hm:=
16 Nancy: =T's like takin a beating. (0.2) kh ⌈ hh hnhh hnh hnh
17 Emma: ⌊ M m:::. No one
18   heard a wo:rd hah.
19 Nancy: Not a word.

A transcript such as this does not replace the original audio/video recording from which it was made: the recording and transcript are analyzed in conjunction with one another. The transcription system employed (developed by Jefferson; see Atkinson and Heritage 1984: ix–xvi) is, like all transcription systems, necessarily selective: it does not, for instance, represent aspects of sound production in as much detail, or as systematically, as might a phonetic transcription. However, it does enable many essential characteristics of speech delivery to be conveyed, including some morphological and phonetic alternations, lexical choice, speech perturbation, and aspects of prosody including stress and sound lengthening. CA transcripts capture especially well those aspects of talk which are believed to be interactionally salient, and which other transcription systems often fail to notice and record. Particular care is taken to represent accurately features associated with the sequential development of talk, notably the transition from one speaker to the next, including the exact placement of overlap onset, and pauses. CA transcripts of recorded conversations display the actual verbal behavior of speakers, in just the way it happened, including the kind of syntactic and other disfluencies which Chomsky regarded as the corrupt details of linguistic performance, and which consequently have been widely ignored in linguistic analyses of hypothetical and idealized versions of 'well-formed' sentences.

Such disfluencies as *self-repair* are evident in the above extract, for instance in line 7 where the speaker cuts off the beginning of her turn, and twice restarts it; and again in line 12, when after 'So: she' the syntax of her utterance is interrupted by inserting the phrase 'in the letter,' before then resuming with 'she said....' Self-repair is quite methodically related to interactional concerns (e.g., speaking in overlap; constructing an account or story), and hence part of speakers' interactional competences (Schegloff, et al. 1977, Goodwin 1981). Aspects of talk such as those captured in the above transcript could not be recovered by making field notes, by precoded schedules, or by recollection. Through the repeated re-examination of data which CA transcripts make possible, analysts are able to investigate and uncover the organization of many aspects of verbal behavior in interaction, including the kind of disfluencies illustrated (self-repairs associated with turn restarts, and insertions) which have previously been dismissed as the nonstandard products of randomizing factors, and therefore not subject to linguistic or social organization. However, CA transcripts are undoubtedly not complete, and other compatible interactional organizations may be revealed by closer transcription of some phonetic detail (Couper-Kuhlen and Selting 1996, Kelly and Local 1989).

CA has typically relied on the analysis of tape-recorded telephone calls, thereby controlling out nonvocal behaviors (e.g., bodily movement, gaze, gestures) which may be related to talk in face-to-face interactions. Nevertheless, its perspective and methodology are perfectly applicable to the investigation of the systematic relationships between verbal and nonvocal conduct (Goodwin 1981, Atkinson and Heritage 1984, Peraklya 1995).

3. The Sequential Context of Turns-at-Talk

The fundamental objective of CA research is to explicate the ways in which, during the turn-by-turn progression of conversation, coparticipants make sense of one another's talk, and how they design their own turns at talk so as to be appropriate next moves. Thus the sequential patterns which analysis uncovers are the emergent products of participants' understsandings of what each other said in a prior turn, and their response to that in their 'next turn.' From a participant's perspective, conversation is a collaborative activity, in which one turn/move progressively leads to a next on the basis of an analysis/understanding (i.e., participant's analysis) of that prior turn. CA aims to capture that progressivity in the production of successive turns at talk, by explicating the procedures whereby (a) the transfer of speakership from one participant to the next is organized, such that speakers take turns, and (b) the analysis/understanding which each makes of the other's prior turn/action is displayed in the design or construction of their next turn.

A central property of conversation appears to be that it is organized into single speaker turns, with regular transitions between speakers. Participants take turns at talk, with one party at a time occupying a turn, then a next, and so on. The transition from one to the next is coordinated so as to achieve minimal gap (i.e., pauses) and minimal overlap. The procedures or techniques for managing smooth transitions from one speaker to a next are general enough to take into account such local contextual variations as the identities and number of speakers, length of turns, content, setting, etc. Sacks et al. (1974) formulated a set of rules for turn-taking which are context free (i.e., allow for such local variations), but which are applicable to the local circumstances of particular turns in particular conversations. These rules, in which either current speaker selects next speaker, or if current speaker has not done so then another may self-select, operate at each point where a turn could be treated as 'meaningfully' and recognizably complete, i.e., at the end of each 'turn construction unit' (TCU), the end of such a unit being a turn transition relevance point.

Participants' orientation to the completion of a construction unit as a point where speaker transition may legitimately occur is evident in some of the detail in the transcript above. For example, at the end of line 1, where a unit of talk (an invitation) is recognizably complete, and therefore at just the point where recipient might begin speaking, Emma 'rushes through' (indicated by the 'equals' symbol) to add an inducement to accepting her invitation:

1 Emma: Wanna c'm do:wn 'av a bah:ta lu:nch w ith me?=
2   = Ah gut s'm beer'n stu:ff.

Hence speaker latches on a next TCU before recipient has the opportunity to self-select and begin speaking on completion of the TCU/invitation in line 1.

An orientation to the completion of a TCU and hence the legitimate relevance of turn transition is manifest in the occurrence of *overlap* (Sacks et al. 1974, Jefferson 1986, Schegloff 2000). In line 6 of the data extract, Emma starts to speak, happening thereby to start simultaneously with Nancy who continues (line 7) her response to Emma's invitation: they thereby talk (briefly) in overlap. Although apparently a violation of the 'one speaker at a time' expectation, the onset of overlap is orderly insofar as Emma begins speaking at a point where Nancy has produced a complete TCU ('Wul yer ril sw<u>ee</u>t hon<u>:</u>'), and which is therefore a transition relevance point. Nancy also orients to the 'one speaker at a time' expectation, by cutting off her turn in line 7 until the end of Emma's turn in line 6 is projected. The onset of overlapping talk is overwhelmingly located at or very close to the completion of a TCU, and hence at the projected end of current speaker's turn (even if it should turn out, as here, that current speaker continues). Thus overlap in conversation is the orderly product of those procedures for managing smooth transfer from one speaker to the next.

When a next speaker takes a turn at talk, he/she displays in the design of that turn an understanding or analysis of the prior speakers' turn. That is, following speaker A's 'initial' turn, speaker B's next turn will be designed to be fitted with or be an appropriate response to speaker A's prior turn: hence B's next turn will exhibit his/her understanding of what A just said/did. So for example, Emma's turn in line 6 of the above extract displays her understanding of Nancy's prior turn in line 4:

```
4   Nancy:   Wul yer ril sweet hon: uh:m
5            (.)
6   Emma:    Or d'you 'av sump'n    else (  )
```

It is evident in line 6 that Emma treats Nancy's prior turn as implying that she has a difficulty accepting Emma's invitation, i.e., that she may have 'something else' to do.

Because participants' analyses of each other's talk are manifest in their responses or next turns, adjacent or 'next turn' is a basic structural position in conversation. To begin with, it is the slot in which, if B discerns something amiss or incorrect in A's prior turn, then B may initiate *repair* in his/her next turn. Furthermore, insofar as the meaning which B attributes to A's prior turn is exhibited in an adjacent next turn, speaker A may inspect B's response to discover whether B properly understood, i.e., to check the adequacy or correctness of B's understanding. If A finds B's understanding to be wanting or in error, then A may in his/her next turn (in effect, the third position in a sequence) initiate repair in order to correct B's misunderstanding. In either respect, next or adjacent turn is the primary position for establishing mutual comprehension and for the initiation of repair in conversation. It is the slot in which adequate understanding is displayed, confirmed, or remedied: it is, therefore, the major location and resource for establishing and continuously updating 'intersubjective understandings' in talk-in-interaction (Schegloff 1992).

A turn's construction, therefore, involves speaker selecting a relevant or appropriate next action in response to the perceived action in a coparticipant's prior turn: in other words, a turn is constructed with respect to its placement in a sequence of actions. However, a further aspect of turn construction or design should be emphasized, that of 'recipient design.' The descriptive terms which speakers select are contextually sensitive: they take into account not only the topic of conversation, but also contextual circumstances relevant to the talk (see *Context*). These circumstances may include relative states of knowledge; for instance, in reference to persons, speakers select between alternative forms of reference, and particularly between those forms premised on recipient knowing the person to whom reference is made, and those which assume recipient does not know that person. An illustration is provided in the data extract, when in lines 7–8 Nancy refers to 'Roul's m<u>o</u>ther....' The selection of a proper name assumes that her recipient, Emma, will recognize that the person so named is her exhusband Roul: but by referring to his 'm<u>o</u>ther' instead of naming her, Nancy orients to any difficulty Emma might have in knowing/recognizing whom she has to telephone that morning were she to refer to her by name. Hence speakers' descriptions of persons—involving the selection between proper names and other identifications (here, a relational term, 'mother')—are so designed as to take into account recipient's relative knowledge about the persons thus described. Thus in the recipient design of her descriptions, speaker orients to relevant features of the *context* of the conversation, and in particular what coparticipants know about one another and their circumstances (evident also in Emma's implied reference in lines 17–18 to what she knows about Nancy's troubled relationship with her exhusband).

4. Adjacency Pair and Preference Organization

The extract above further illustrates one of the central concepts in CA research, that of 'adjacency pair,' which links the apparatus for turn transfer and next speaker selection, with the production of the next turn in an action sequence. When in line 1 Emma asks if Nancy would like to come down and have a bite of lunch, she makes an invitation. In her response in line 4, Nancy embarks on what Emma plainly believes to be the beginning of a possible rejection of that invitation. An invitation, followed by its acceptance/rejection, is one of the class of paired actions known as adjacency pairs.

Many kinds of current turns at talk sequentially implicate a range of possible responses on the part of recipient: e.g., if current speaker announces some form of trouble or bad news (see Nancy's idiomatic reference to 'trouble' in line 16 above), then recipient might be expected to respond by sympathizing, or enquiring further about the speaker's trouble (as Emma does in lines 17–18). But for a certain class of initial actions, such as questions, greetings, invitations, requests, accusations, offers, etc., that expectation applies in a particularly 'strong' and circumscribed fashion. The production of one of these initial actions projects and requires that in his/her adjacent next turn recipient should produce a quite specific second, complementary action. For example, if speaker asks a question, the appropriate response by recipient is expected to be an answer: or if speaker makes an invitation, recipient is expected to respond by accepting or declining it. Similarly accusations are paired with defences, a greeting with a return greeting, requests with grantings/rejections, and offers with acceptances/rejections.

Hence the production of the first part of an adjacency pair, e.g., an invitation, sets up a constraint that the speaker thus selected should follow directly by producing the second part in the relevant pair i.e., an acceptance/refusal. This constraint might appear to be violated in cases where one first pair part is met by next speaker producing another first pair part, as when a request, such as *Can I borrow the car?* gets the response *How long do you need it?* However, in responding that way recipient can be heard to ask a question which is a preliminary to dealing with the request, that is checking out information which recipient may need in order to decide whether or not to grant the request. Thus recipient's question initiates an 'insertion sequence,' on the completion of which (as when first speaker replies *Just until lunchtime*) a response to the request (i.e., a granting/rejection) is still 'conditionally relevant.' The conditional relevance of an appropriate response to the first part of an adjacency pair does not refer to a statistical generalization about the adjacent sequencing of actions: instead it highlights the 'normative' character of the constraint or expectation that next speaker should produce an action which is the second part of a pair initiated by a prior speaker's asking a question, making an invitation, etc. Participants' orientation to the normative character of adjacency pairs is evident, for example, in the accounts which may be provided when a response to a first pair-part is not forthcoming from recipient—accounts which may range from the possibility that recipient did not hear, through to the recognition that recipient disagrees with some premise or position taken in the initial action (so if a speaker has taken a position in a question, and there is no immediate response from recipient, speaker may infer from that that recipient disagrees: speaker may therefore reformulate the question to modify the position to bring it in line with what is now assumed to be recipient's position. (See below on agreement and disagreement.)

Whereas the initial actions in some adjacency pairs relevantly get only one type of response, for instance questions get just answers, some other adjacency pairs listed above allow for alternative actions to be done as responses to the initial actions, e.g., invitations may get either acceptances or rejections, and requests may be granted or rejected. These alternative second pair parts are not equivalent. Broadly speaking, there is a bias towards those next/second actions which promote social solidarity and which avoid conflict (Heritage 1984: 265–80). That is, there is a 'preference organization' associated with the selection of acceptances and rejections (e.g., of invitations), in which acceptances are preferred actions, and rejections are dispreferred actions. 'Preference' here does not refer to any personal psychological or motivational dispositions of individual speakers. It refers instead to the finding in CA research that these alternative actions are routinely performed in systematically distinctive ways. Briefly, preferred actions such as acceptances are normally produced unhesitatingly, without delay, are delivered right at the start of the response turn, are packaged in short turns, and are unmitigated. In contrast, when a dispreferred response such as a rejection is delivered, the turn-start is often delayed (e.g., by a pause), and the dispreferred action itself further delayed by being prefaced by other components, including such brief objects as 'uh,' 'well,' and 'I'm not sure,' and in some cases by 'positive' forms (e.g., token agreements, appreciations). Dispreferred actions are normally produced in variously mitigated or attenuated forms: and they are often accompanied by accounts, explanations, and the like.

Some of these features associated with dispreferred responses help to account for how in line 6 of the above extract Emma anticipates that Nancy may be going to reject her invitation (i.e., these are features which are oriented to by participants in understanding one another). Nancy's response is first delayed by the 0.3 sec. pause in line 3; it is then preceded by 'Well' (line 4), one of those components which both further delays the response, and expresses some reservation. The rest of her response in that line consists of an [appreciation] component,'.... yer ril sw<u>ee</u>t ho<u>n</u>: <u>uh</u>:m,' a 'positive' form which often prefaces and mitigates an upcoming rejection, as in *Well that's awfully sweet of you, I don't think I can make it this morning. hh uhm I'm running an ad in the paper and–and uh I have to stay near the phone* (Atkinson and Drew 1979: 58). This rejection of an invitation is preceded by an [appreciation]; the [rejection] component is mitigated (in 'I don't think I can make it,' rather than 'I can't make it'); and is then accompanied by an [account] for her inability (rather than unwillingness) to come this morning (note that Nancy's account in line 7 is similarly formed as a constraint or inability, 'I <u>haf</u> to: uh ca̱ll...'). Emma treats Nancy's production of the [appreciation] here as premonitoring rejection, and offers on Nancy's behalf an account for not being able to accept, 'or d'you ' <u>a</u>v sump'n <u>el</u>se.' In this way first speaker's activities (here, Emma's) can collaboratively contribute to the avoidance of explicit versions of dispreferred actions, and hence to the maintenance of social solidarity.

The general point is, therefore, that 'preference organization' refers to certain systematic differences in the design of alternative but nonequivalent responses, in terms of their sequential properties (notably delay of dispreferred actions) and the designs of the turns in which preferred and dispreferred actions are produced. This applies also to the organization of 'repair/correction' in conversation (see Schegloff, et al. 1977 on the preference for self-repair over other repair); and most notably to 'agreement' and 'disagreement' in conversation. Research shows that a speaker's agreement with prior speaker is expressed directly and without delay (often just overlapping the turn with which agreement is being expressed), and in an explicit unmitigated form, often by repeating some form used by prior speaker (see Nancy's confirmation of what Emma proposed, lines 17–19 above) or by upgrading the prior speakers' assessment. By contrast, disagreements are often delayed sequentially, by pauses or by a series of prior turns; they are frequently delayed by being prefaced with agreement components; and when they are stated, their expression is often mitigated or 'weakened' (Atkinson and Drew 1979, Heritage 1984, Levinson 1983, Pomerantz 1984). In all these and other respects, there are formal social or institutionalized procedures which work to maximize agreement and other affiliative actions, and minimize disagreement and disaffiliative actions. These formal procedures reside in the details of the sequential management of preferred and dispreferred actions, and in the details of the design of the turns in which they are performed.

5. Topics of CA Research, and Connections with Linguistics

This review of the central importance of 'next position' as the locus for displaying understanding, and some aspects of adjacency pairs and associated preference organization, serves to highlight the interdependence in CA research of the investigation of sequential management of actions in conversation, and the way in which the performance of an action shapes the design of the turns in which they are performed. While CA's concern with turn design is focused principally at the level of lexical choice, together with certain non- or quasi-lexical verbal objects, the organizations or patterns which have been identified at that level are likely to be consistent with other levels of linguistic organization, e.g., phonological variations (Kelly and Local 1989, on phonological aspects of turn holding versus turn transfer). On this and other issues concerning the interactional salience of prosodic features, and studies of how next speakers' responses are systematically related to prosodic variations, see Couper-Kuhlen and Selting 1996. But the distinctive contribution of CA has been to identify and explicate the patterns manifest in the interrelationship between action sequences and turn design: and to have demonstrated that participants themselves, in their contributions to the turn-by-turn development of conversation, orient (though not necessarily consciously) to those very organizations, patterns, or systematic procedures.

The sequential patterns identified through CA research are, in very real ways, bound up with the interactional enterprises which engage participants in conversation. Among such patterns are those associated with presequences (enquiries which are preliminaries to making invitations or requests, designed to check the likely success of such actions); troubles tellings; repair initiation, and particularly the avoidance of explicit correction of one's coparticipant; the elicitation and display of affiliation through laughter; telling stories; the initiation and closing of topics, and the more imperceptible 'stepwise' transitions from one topic to another; performing delicate actions 'off the record' or unofficially; and greetings, complaint, request, and invitation sequences.

Topics such as these are intrinsically relevant to those perspectives in linguistics which are concerned with language use in interaction. But CA research has a further and quite direct contribution to make to a range of areas in linguistics, including the analysis of (indirect) speech acts (CA has shown that speech activities are understood by participants contextually, by reference to the placement of turns within sequences of actions); the pragmatics of description (the relation between lexical selection and sequential environment, recipient design, and self-repair are all relevant); discourse markers (studies have shown that markers such as 'well,' 'anyway,' 'oh,' etc. perform specific sequential and interactional functions); syntax (the relationships between syntactic constructions and the management of turn transfer); prosody and phonetic organization (e.g., again, related to turn transfer); and discourse cohesion (for a review of CA's contribution to understanding the relation between conversational and linguistic structures, see Levinson (1983), and for what CA can contribute to our understanding of grammar 'at work' in interaction, see Ochs et al. 1996).

Finally, it should be noted that although CA has developed through and has its primary focus in ordinary conversation, it is more properly a perspective for analyzing 'talk-in-interaction,' including adult–child interaction, and talk in workplace and institutional environments. Research into the latter, especially those settings in which talk is subject to specialized speech exchange systems and restricted participation rights (especially involving question–answer exchanges), is beginning to identify distinctive sequential patterns associated with the particular interactional purposes and goals which participants have in institutional contexts (Atkinson and Drew 1979, Drew and Heritage 1992, Drew and Sorjonen 1997).

See also: Conversational Maxims; Discourse; Doctor–Patient Language; Ethnomethodology; Language in the Workplace; Institutional Language; Interactional Sociolinguistic Research Methods; Pragmatics and Sociolinguistics.

Bibliography

Atkinson J M, Drew P 1979 *Order in Court: The Organization of Verbal Interaction in Judicial Settings*. Macmillan, London
Atkinson J M, Heritage J 1984 *Structures of Social Action: Studies in Conversation Analysis*. Cambridge University Press, Cambridge, UK
Button G, Lee J R E 1987 *Talk and Social Organization*. Multilingual Matters, Clevedon, UK
Couper-Kuhlen E, Selting M (eds.) 1996 *Prosody in Conversation: Interactional Studies*. Cambridge University Press, Cambridge, UK
Drew P, Heritage J (eds.) 1992 *Talk at Work*. Cambridge University Press, Cambridge, UK
Drew P, Sorjonen M-J 1997 Institutional discourse In: Van Dijk T (ed.) *Discourse Analysis: A Multidisciplinary Introduction*. Sage, London, pp. 92–118.
Goodwin C 1981 *Conversational Organization: Interaction between Speakers and Hearers*. Academic Press, New York
Heritage J 1984 *Garfinkel and Ethnomethodology*. Polity Press, Cambridge, UK
Jefferson G 1986 Notes on 'latency' in overlap onset. *Human Studies* **9**: 153–83
Kelly J, Local J 1989 *Doing Phonology*. Manchester University Press, Manchester, UK
Levinson S 1983 *Pragmatics*. Cambridge University Press, Cambridge, UK
Ochs E, Schegloff E A, Thompson S 1996 *Interaction and Grammar*. Cambridge University Press, Cambridge, UK
Peraklya A 1995 *AIDS Counselling: Institutional Interaction and Clinical Practice*. Cambridge University Press, Cambridge, UK
Pomerantz A 1984 Agreeing and disagreeing with assessments: Some features of preferred/dispreferred turn shapes. In: Atkinson J M, Heritage J (eds.) *Structures of Social Action: Studies in Conversation Analysis*. Cambridge University Press, Cambridge, UK
Sacks H 1992 *Lectures on Conversation*, 2 vols. Blackwell, Oxford, UK
Sacks H, Schegloff E A, Jefferson G 1974 A simplest systematics for the organization of turn-taking for conversation. *Language* **50**: 696–735
Schegloff E A 1992 *Introduction to Harvey Sacks, Lectures on Conversation*, Blackwell, Oxford, UK, Vol. 1
Schegloff E A 2000 Overlapping talk and the organization of turn-taking for conversation. *Language in Society* **29**: 1–63
Schegloff E A 1992 Repair after next turn. *American Journal of Sociology* **97**: 1295–345
Schegloff E A, Jefferson G, Sacks H 1977 The preference for self-correction in the organization of repair in conversation. *Language* **53**: 361–82

Conversational Maxims

J. Thomas

H. P. Grice had worked with the philosopher J. L. Austin at Oxford in the 1940s and 1950s. Grice's work on the cooperative principle (CP) (see *Cooperative Principle*) and its related conversational maxims arises from the same tradition of ordinary language philosophy. In his book *How to Do Things with Words* (1962; 2nd edn. 1976), Austin made the distinction between what speakers say and what they mean. Grice's theory tries to explain how a hearer might get from the level of expressed meaning to the level of implied meaning.

It is perhaps easiest to begin with a concrete example of the type of problem which Grice's theory was designed to handle. On a visit to London, two friends returned to their parked car to find that it had been wheel-clamped by the police. The driver turned to his passenger and said: *Great, that's just what I wanted!* It would doubtless have been clear to the passenger, as it would have been to any competent interactant, that what the driver intended to imply was very different (just the opposite, in fact) from what he actually said. Grice set out to explain the mechanisms by which such implicatures are generated and interpreted.

Grice first outlined his theory in the William James lectures, delivered at Harvard University in 1967 (a version of which was published in 1975 in his paper 'Logic and Conversation'), and expanded upon it in papers published in 1978 and 1981. Grice never fully developed his theory—there are many gaps and several inconsistencies in his writings. Yet it is this work—sketchy, in many ways problematical, and frequently misunderstood—which has proved to be one of the most influential theories in the development of pragmatics (see *Pragmatics and Sociolinguistics*).

1. The Four Conversational Maxims

Grice (1975) proposed the four maxims of 'quantity,' 'quality,' 'relation,' and manner,' which were formulated as follows (1):

Quantity: Make your contribution as informative (1) as is required (for the current purpose of the exchange).
Do not make your contribution more informative than is required.
Quality: Do not say what you believe to be false.
Do not say that for which you lack adequate evidence.
Relation: Be relevant.
Manner: Avoid obscurity of expression.
Avoid ambiguity.
Be Brief (avoid unnecessary prolixity).
Be orderly.

A speaker might observe all the maxims as in the following example (2)

Father: Where are the children? (2)
Mother: They're either in the garden or in the playroom, I'm not sure which.

The mother has answered clearly (manner), truthfully (quality), has given just the right amount of information (quantity), and has directly addressed her husband's goal in asking the question (relation). She has said precisely what she meant, no more and no less, and has generated no implicature (that is, there is no distinction to be made here between what she says and what she means).

Grice was well aware, however, that there are very many occasions when people fail to observe the maxims (this might be because, for example, they are incapable of speaking clearly, or because they deliberately choose to lie). In his writings, he discussed each of these possibilities, but the situations which chiefly interested him were those in which a speaker *blatantly* fails to observe a maxim, not with any intention of deceiving or misleading, but because the speaker wishes to prompt the hearer to look for a meaning which is different from, or in addition to, the expressed meaning. This additional meaning he called 'conversational implicature,' and he termed the process by which it is generated 'flouting a maxim.'

2. Flouting a Maxim

A 'flout' occurs when a speaker *blatantly* fails to observe a maxim at the level of what is said, with the deliberate intention of generating an implicature. There follow examples of flouts of each of the maxims in turn, and also a review of Grice's discussions of the reasons for flouting a maxim.

2.1 Flouts Necessitated by a 'Clash between Maxims'

A speaker flouts the maxim of quantity by blatantly giving either more or less information than the situation demands. For example, imagine someone asked a departmental colleague who was standing next to the clock if he would tell them the time. Imagine he replied: *Well, according to this clock it's a quarter to four*, when he could simply have said: *It's a quarter to four*. According to Grice, such a response would set in motion a process of informal reasoning which would lead one to derive and additional piece of information. This might work in the following way (3):

(a) Your colleague has clearly given you more (3) information than you required. He appears to have breached the maxim of quantity.
(b) However, you have no reason to believe that he is being deliberately uncooperative (i.e., that he is failing to observe the cooperative principle (CP)).
(c) You must conclude that his failure to observe the maxim of quantity is due to his wish to observe the CP in some other way. You must work out why the CP should force your colleague to give more information than you requested.
(d) The failure to observe the maxim of quantity can be explained if you assume that your colleague also wishes to observe the maxim of quality. You conclude that for some reason he is confronted with a clash between these maxims (either he tells the truth or he gives you just the right amount of information).
(e) His reply is a compromise, which leads you to deduce that he is not sure that he has given you the exact time because the clock in the department is often inaccurate.

Thus, Grice's explanation for the nonobservance of the maxim of quality in this instance is that the speaker was faced with a clash of maxims. The speaker found himself unable simultaneously to observe the maxims of quality and quantity, signaled his dilemma by flagrantly failing to give the right amount of information, and prompted his interlocutor to draw an inference. A similar explanation might be offered for the following instance of nonobservance of the maxim of quantity. In this case, the second speaker gives less information than the situation demands (4):

A: Has Chris given up smoking? (4)
B: Well, he's certainly stopped buying his own.

B might simply have replied: 'No.' It would be possible to argue that his failure to do so stems from a clash between the maxims of quantity and quality (B does not know for sure whether Chris has given up smoking, and speaks only on the basis of the evidence he has). But this explanation is rather implausible. It is better explained by what Grice terms 'exploiting' the maxims.

2.2 Flouts which 'Exploit' a Maxim

According to Grice's theory, interlocutors operate on the assumption that, as a rule, the maxims will be observed. When this expectation is confounded and the listener is confronted with the blatant non-observance of a maxim (that is, the listener has discounted the possibility that the speaker may be trying to deceive, or is incapable of speaking more clearly, succinctly, etc.), he or she is again prompted to look for an implicature. Most of Grice's own examples of flouts involve this sort of 'exploitation.'

Flouts which exploit the maxim quality, for example, occur when the speaker says something which is blatantly untrue or for which she or he lacks adequate evidence. In the 'wheel-clamping' example given in the opening section, an implicature is generated by the speaker's saying something which is patently false. Since the speaker does not appear to be trying to deceive the listener in any way, the listener is forced to look for another plausible interpretation. According to Grice, the deductive process might work like this (5):

(a) A has expressed pleasure at finding his car clamped. (5)
(b) No one, not even the most jaded masochist, is likely to be pleased at finding his car clamped.
(c) His passenger has no reason to believe that A is trying to deceive him any way.
(d) Unless A's utterance is entirely pointless, he must be trying to put across to his passenger some other proposition.
(e) This must be some obviously related proposition.
(f) The most obviously related proposition is the exact opposite of the one he has expressed.
(g) A is extremely annoyed at finding his car clamped.

The following example (6) works in much the same way, but this time involves what Grice rather vaguely terms 'generating a conversational implicature by means of something like a figure of speech.' The speaker is the *Peanuts* character, Linus, who comments wearily: *Big sisters are the crab grass in the lawn of life.*

(a) It is patently false that big sisters are crab grass. (6)
(b) Linus does not appear to be trying to make readers believe that big sisters are crab grass.
(c) Unless Linus's utterance is entirely pointless, he must be trying to put across some other proposition.
(d) This must be some obviously related proposition.
(e) The most obviously related proposition is that, like crab grass in lawns, big sisters are a bane.

What Grice's theory (at least as originally formulated) fails to say is why in this example one is expected to seek a comparison between crab grass in lawns and big sisters in life, whereas in the previous example one looked for a proposition which was the exact opposite of the one expressed. Developments in relevance theory (Sperber and Wilson 1986) could help to rescue Grice's theory at this point.

Examples of floutings of the maxim of relation are legion. The one in (7) is typical (it has to be assumed that it is clear in the context that B has heard and understood A's question):

A: Who was that you were with last night? (7)
B: Did you know you were wearing odd socks?

It would be tedious once again to work through all the steps in the informal deductive process—suffice it to say that A is likely to come to the conclusion that B is irritated or embarrassed by the question and wishes to change the subject. Again, Grice's theory fails to address a very important issue, viz. why does B choose to indicate only indirectly that she is irritated or embarrassed? After all, if A were a particularly insensitive person, there is the risk that she might ignore B's hint and pose the question again. B could remove that possibility by saying: *Mind your own business!* In the 1970s and 1980s much effort in the field of pragmatics was put into developing theories of politeness (see, for example, Brown and Levinson (1987) and Leech (1983)) which, proponents argue, 'rescue' Grice's theory by explaining the social constraints governing utterance production and interpretation (see *Politeness*).

The following example (8) illustrates a flout of the maxim of manner. It occurred during a radio interview with an unnamed official from the United States Embassy in Port-au-Prince, Haiti:

Interviewer: Did the United States Government play any part in Duvalier's departure? Did they, for example, actively encourage him to leave? (8)
Official: I would not try to steer you away from that conclusion.

The official could simply have replied: 'Yes.' Her actual response is extremely long-winded and convoluted, and it is obviously no accident nor through an inability to speak clearly, that she has failed to observe the maxim of manner. There is, however, no reason to believe that the official is being deliberately unhelpful (she could, after all, have simply refused to answer at all, or said: *No comment*).

The hearer must therefore look for another explanation, and once again, there is nothing in Grice's theory to help explain the official's flouting of the maxim of manner. In this case, it is not a clash of maxims which has caused her to flout the maxim of manner in this way. Rather, it is occasioned by the desire to claim credit for what she sees as a desirable outcome, while at the same time avoiding putting on record the fact that her government has intervened in the affairs of another country. In fact, this exchange was widely reported and the implicature spelt out in news broadcasts later the same day: *Although they have not admitted it openly, the State Department is letting it be known that the United States was behind Jean-Paul Duvalier, 'Baby Doc's,' decision to quit the island.* Nor can one sensibly ascribe the speaker's use of indirectness to any desire to be 'polite' (at least, in the normal sense of the term)—it appears to be motivated by the fact that she has two goals which are difficult to reconcile. This 'desire to say and not say' something at the same time is lucidly discussed by Dascal (1983), together with other social factors which lead speakers to employ indirectness.

The important thing to note in each of these cases is that it is the very blatancy of the nonobservance which triggers the search for an implicature. The same is true in each of the cases which follow.

3. Common Misrepresentations of Grice's Theory

There are many criticisms which can be made of Grice's work. However, there are four criticisms of his work which are made very frequently (particularly by nonspecialists) and which are totally unfounded. The first is that Grice had a ludicrously optimistic view of human nature: that he saw the world as a place full of people whose one aim in life was to cooperate with others. This is a complete misreading of Grice's work and is discussed in detail in another article (see *Cooperative Principle*).

The second unfounded criticism is that Grice was proposing a set of rules for good (conversational) behavior. This misunderstanding probably stems from the unfortunate fact that Grice formulated his maxims as imperatives. But it is clear from everything else he wrote on the subject that his chief objective was simply to describe linguistic behaviors which, by and large, people do observe in conversation unless they wish to generate an implicature, or are deliberately setting out to mislead, or are prevented for some reason from so doing (e.g., nervousness, an inadequate grasp of the language).

The third misconception represents Grice as believing that his maxims are always and invariably observed. This is simply false—such a claim would make complete nonsense of his theory. Discussing the maxims in his 1978 and 1981 papers, Grice refers to them as being:

> standardly (through not invariably) observed by participants in a talk exchange.

> desiderata that normally would be accepted by any rational discourser, though, of course, they could be infringed and violated.

The fourth misunderstanding is to confuse the different types of nonobservance of the maxim. This seems to come from an incomplete reading of Grice's articles, or a reliance on second-hand accounts (few general linguistics textbooks discuss any categories other than flouting). A typical criticism of this order (this one is from Sampson 1982: 203) runs as follows:

> people often flout his [Grice's] maxims. To anyone who knew, for instance, my old scout at Oxford, or a certain one of the shopkeepers in the village where I live, it would be ludicrous to suggest that as a general principle people's speech is governed by maxims such as 'be relevant'; 'do not say that for which you lack adequate evidence' (!); 'avoid obscurity of expression, ambiguity or unnecessary prolixity' (!). In the case of the particular speakers I am thinking of ... the converse of Grice's maxims might actually have greater predictive power.

What Sampson is discussing is not the flouting of a maxim (that is, the blatant nonobservance for the purpose of generating an implicature). What he is describing is the unmotivated or unintentional nonobservance of a maxim, which Grice calls 'infringing' (see Sect. 4.2).

Grice was well aware that there are many occasions on which speakers fail to observe the maxims, even though they have no desire to generate an implicature, and even though his categories seem to cover all possible instances of nonobservance.

4. Categories of Nonobservance of the Conversational Maxims

In his first paper (1975: 49), Grice listed three ways in which participant in a talk exchange may fail to fulfill a maxim: the speaker may flout a maxim, 'violate' a maxim, or 'opt out' of observing a maxim. He later added a fourth category of nonobservance: 'infringing,' a maxim. Several writers since Grice have argued the need for a fifth category—'suspending' a maxim, and this category is considered along with the others. Having made all these distinctions, it is irritating to note that Grice himself does not always use the terms consistently, and that remarkably few commentators seem to make any attempt to use the terms correctly. The distinctions which Grice originally made are important for a full understanding of his theory. Flouting has already been examined in detail, and each of the others is now considered in turn.

4.1 Violating a Maxim

Many commentators incorrectly use the term 'violate' for all forms of nonobservance of the maxims. But in his first published paper on conversational cooperation (1975), Grice defines 'violation' very specifically as the *unostentatious* nonobservance of a maxim. If a speaker violates a maxim, he or she 'will be liable to mislead' (1975: 49).

Example (9) is an extract from an interaction between a headmaster and a pupil. It has already been established that the addressee, Hannah (a girl aged about 12), and her friend played truant from school. What is at issue now is where they went on the afternoon in question and, in particular, whether they had been to Simon Connolly's house:

Headmaster: You know that I now know where you (9)
went, don't you?
Hannah: We were in the woods.

It is later established that Hannah's assertion that they were in the woods is true, but not the whole truth (she does not volunteer the information that they had first been to Simon Connolly's house 'for a little while'). But there is nothing in the formulation of Hannah's response which would allow the headmaster to deduce that she was withholding information. This unostentatious violation of the maxim of quantity generates the (probably intentionally) misleading implicature that they went to the woods and nowhere else, that is, that they did not go to the boy's house.

Pragmatically misleading (or potentially pragmatically misleading) utterances of this sort are regularly encountered in certain activity types, such as trials, parliamentary speeches, and arguments. So regularly do they occur, in fact, that they could be seen as the norm for this type of interaction, and be interpreted in that light by participants. For more on this point, see Sect. 4.4.

Initially, it might appear that violating a maxim is the exact opposite of flouting a maxim. In the case of the violation by the schoolgirl, the speaker says something which is *true* (as far as it goes) in order to imply an untruth. In the case of a flout (as in the wheel-clamping example), a speaker may blatantly fail to observe the maxim of quality at the level of what is said, but nevertheless imply something which is true. All the examples of flouts which Grice himself gives are of this order. However, there is no principled reason to expect that an implicature will be *true*—a speaker can imply a lie almost as easily as he or she can say one.

4.2 Infringing a Maxim

As has been already noted, a speaker who, with no intention of generating an implicature, and with no intention of deceiving, fails to observe a maxim, is said to infringe the maxim. In other words, the nonobservance stems from imperfect linguistic performance, rather than from any desire on the part of the speakers to generate a conversational implicature (this is the phenomenon which Sampson was describing above). This type of nonobservance could occur because the speaker has an imperfect command of the language, or because the speaker's performance is impaired in some way (nervousness, drunkenness, excitement), or because of some cognitive impairment, or simply because the speaker is constitutionally incapable of speaking clearly, to the point, etc.

4.3 Opting Out of a Maxim

A speaker opts out of observing a maxim by indicating unwillingness to cooperate in the way that the maxim requires. Examples of opting out occur frequently in public life, when the speaker cannot, perhaps for legal or ethical reasons, reply in the way normally expected. Alternatively, the speaker may wish to avoid generating a false implicature or appearing uncooperative. Here is an example from a British MP, who had been asked a question about talks he had had with the Libyan leader Colonel Gadaffi: *Well, honestly, I can't tell you a thing, because what was said to me was told me in confidence.*

When a speaker explicitly opts out of observing a maxim, she or he could be seen to provide privileged access into the way in which speakers normally attend to the maxims, which in turn offers prima facie evidence for Grice's contention that there exists on the part of interactants a strong expectation that, *ceteris paribus* and unless indication is given to the contrary, the CP and the maxims will be observed.

4.4 Suspending a Maxim

Several writers have suggested that there are occasions when there is no need to opt out of observing the maxims because there are certain events in which there is no expectation on the part of any participant that they will be fulfilled (hence the nonfulfillment does not generate any implicatures). This category is necessary to respond to criticisms of the type made by Keenan (1976), who proposed as a counterexample to Grice's theory of conversational implicature the fact that in the Malagasy Republic participants in talk exchanges 'regularly provide less information than is required by their conversational partner, even though they have access to the necessary information' (Keenan 1976: 70). Keenan's examples do not falsify Grice's theory if they are seen as instances where the maxim of quantity is suspended. There is no expectation at all on the part of interactants that speakers will provide precise information about their relatives and friends, in case they draw the attention of evil spirits to them. Although the Malagasy may appear to be underinformative at the level of what is said, the uninformativeness is nevertheless systematic, motivated, and generates implicatures which are readily interpretable by members of that community.

Suspensions of the maxims may be culture-specific (as in Keenan's examples) or specific to particular events. For example, in most cultures, the maxim of quantity appears to be selectively suspended in, for example, courts of law, committees of inquiry, or indeed in any confrontational situation where it is held to be the job of the investigator to elicit the truth from a witness. The witnesses are not required or expected to volunteer information which may incriminate them, and no inference is drawn on the basis of what they do not say (cf. the example of the schoolgirl in Sect. 4.1).

4.5 Distinguishing Between Different Types of Nonobservance

As has been seen, a flout is, by definition, so blatant that the interlocutor knows that an implicature has been generated. One very important point which Grice failed to address is how an interlocutor is supposed to distinguish between a violation, possibly intended to mislead, and an infringement, not intended to generate any implicature.

5. Conclusion

Grice first put forward his ideas concerning the conversational maxims in 1975, and his work continues to serve as the basis for much (probably most) work in pragmatics. Yet, as this article demonstrates, the theory is full of holes. Some of those holes have been or are being plugged, particularly by people working in politeness theory and in relevance theory, but the fact of the matter is that, unsatisfactory as Grice's work is, it has yet to be replaced by anything better.

See also: Cooperative Principle; Politeness; Pragmatics and Sociolinguistics.

Bibliography

Austin J L 1976 *How to Do Things with Words*, 2nd edn. Oxford University Press, London
Brown P, Levinson S C 1987 *Politeness: Some Universals in Language Usage*. Cambridge University Press. Cambridge, UK
Dascal M 1983 *Pragmatics and the Philosophy of Mind I: Thought in Language*. Benjamins, Amsterdam
Grice H P 1975 Logic and conversation. In: Cole P, Morgan J L (eds.) *Syntax and Semantics Vol. 3: Speech Acts*. Academic Press, New York
Grice H P 1978 Further notes on logic and conversation. In: Cole P (ed.) *Syntax and Semantics*, vol. 9. Academic Press, New York
Grice H P 1981 Presupposition and conversational implicature. In: Cole P (ed.) *Radical Pragmatics*, Academic Press, New York
Keenan E O 1976 The universality of conversational postulates. *Langauge in Society* **5**: 67–80
Leech G N 1983 *Principles of Pragmatics*. Longman, London
Levinson S C 1983 *Pragmatics*. Cambridge University Press, Cambridge, UK
Sampson G 1982 The economics of conversation: Comments on Joshi's paper. In: Smith N V (ed.) *Mutual Knowledge*. Academic Press, London
Sperber D, Wilson D 1986 *Relevance Communication and Cognition*. Blackwell, Oxford, UK

Cooperative Principle
J. Thomas

The cooperative principle (CP) was first proposed by H. P. Grice in a series of lectures given in 1967. It runs as follows: 'Make your contribution such as is required, at the stage at which it occurs, by the accepted purpose or direction of the talk exchange in which you are engaged.'

Already there is a problem. The way in which the CP is worded makes it seem as if Grice was telling speakers how they ought to behave. What he was actually doing was suggesting that in conversational interaction people work on the assumption that a certain set of rules is in operation, unless, that is, they receive indications to the contrary. In all spheres of life, assumptions are made all the time. For example, a car driver assumes that other drivers will observe the same set of regulations—the traffic system would grind to a halt if such assumptions were not made. Of course, there are times when a driver has indications that another driver may be liable to disobey the rules (a learner, a drunk, a person whose car is out of control), or that he may be following a different set of rules (a car with foreign number plates), and on these occasions the usual assumptions have to be reexamined or suspended altogether. And, of course, there are times when a driver wrongly assumes that others are operating according to the rules, and then accidents occur. So it is with conversation. When talking, speakers operate according to a set of assumptions, and, on the whole, get by, although inevitably misunderstandings and mistakes occur and sometimes a speaker is deliberately misled.

Grice's work has been, and continues to be, extremely influential. It has also been widely criticized and widely misunderstood. This article discusses various interpretations of his work, and argues in favor of the weaker of the two most common interpretations of the notion of 'conversational cooperation.'

In setting out his cooperative principle, together with its related maxims (see *Conversational Maxims*), Grice was interested in explaining one particular set of regularities—those governing the generation and interpretation of 'conversational implicature.' For example, my brother comes in carrying an ice cream and says: *I didn't bother buying one for you*, to which I reply: *That's uncommonly generous of you!* On the face of it, my reply is untrue. However, the CP would lead him to assume that, in spite of appearances, I was making an appropriate comment on his behavior. He would therefore conclude that I had sacrificed a conversational maxim at one level, in order to uphold it at another. In other words, I had said something false, but implied something that was true. Grice argues that without the assumption that the speaker is operating according to the CP, there is no mechanism to prompt someone to seek another level of interpretation.

1. Different Interpretations of the Notion of Conversational Cooperation

Many critics of Grice's work on conversational implicature (Grice 1975, 1978, 1981) have been arguing at cross-purposes, and one important reason for this is that the very term 'cooperation' is misleading, since what in everyday terms would be seen as 'highly uncooperative' behavior, such as arguing, lying, hurling abuse, may yet be perfectly cooperative according to some interpretations of Grice's (1975) term.

Grice's own definition of the cooperative principle is ambiguous and inconsistent, and this has enabled both those who have adversely criticized his work and those who have adopted his theories to interpret what he has written to suit themselves. The majority of interpretations, it should be said, can be justified in terms of what Grice actually *wrote*, although some appear to be rather perverse interpretations of what he *meant*. What is striking, however, is how few of those who have drawn so heavily on Grice's theories appear to have noticed the many ambiguities which exist in his work, or, if they have noticed, have taken the trouble to define the way in which they themselves have interpreted the concept of conversational cooperation or are using the term 'cooperative.'

Outlined below are the most strikingly divergent interpretations of Grice's theory, followed by discussion of the different shades within each view. Common to all interpretations is the assumption that the speaker (S) and hearer (H) have some shared interest in conforming to certain linguistic and pragmatic norms, and in a *typical* conversation they do so. However, the question is what it means to conform to linguistic and pragmatic norms.

The most extreme view, which is introduced here only in order to dismiss it totally as a complete misinterpretation of what Grice was concerned to do, says that the maxims of quality, quantity, relation, and manner must at all times be observed at the level of what is said. According to this view, the example given in the introductory section (*That's uncommonly generous of you!*) would be seen as an instance of uncooperative behaviour. Now, Grice states unequivocally that the ostentatious nonobservance of a maxim at the level of what is said (that is, what he originally defined as a 'flout'—see *Conversational Maxims*) in no way contravenes the CP. On the contrary, it is the mechanism which is required in order to generate an implicature.

The first view which is worthy of serious consideration (if only because it is so widely held) could be called 'real-world goal-sharing.' According to this interpretation, Grice is arguing that, in a 'normal' conversation, S and H actually have some shared interests which, by means of conversation, they 'jointly conspire to promote.' 'Real-world goal-sharing' refers to situations in which S shares with H some common aim or purpose beyond that of getting H to understand which proposition is being expressed or implied. According to this definition, compliance with the CP is possible only against a background of shared goals or interests, which might include (minimally) such local goals as 'keeping the conversation going,' but would generally involve a greater degree of 'real cooperation,' such as a shared interest in establishing the truth. Kiefer interprets Grice in this way:

> Now the Gricean maxims attempt to describe cooperative communication in which the participants strive after the same goal and are equally interested in achieving this goal, furthermore in which the participants have the same social status and finally in which the only goal of the communication is the transmission of information (in a maximally economical way).
>
> (1979a: 60)

According to a third school of thought, which could be called 'linguistic goal-sharing,' Grice intended the cooperative principle to have a much more limited scope. It applies only to the observance of linguistic conventions and presupposes no shared aim or purpose beyond that of establishing correctly S's illocutionary intent (that is, getting H to understand which proposition is being expressed or implied). In particular, it does not presuppose that the proposition which is expressed, entailed, or implied is necessarily polite, relevant to any of H's real-world (extralinguistic) social goals, or even presuppose (according to some interpretations) that it is truthful. This is the interpretation for which Holdcroft (1979) argues in his excellent discussion paper.

2. Real-world Goal-sharing View of Cooperation

Apostel (1980), Bollobás (1981), Corliss (1981), Kasher (1976, 1977a), Kiefer (1979a), Pratt (1977, 1981), and Sampson (1982) are among the writers who understand Grice to be using the term 'cooperation' in what is called here the 'real-world goal-sharing' sense: that is, they believe that when Grice speaks of cooperation he means that S shares H some common goal or purpose *beyond that of efficient message-communication*. (It should be pointed out that hardly any of these writers actually subscribe to the real-world goal-sharing view themselves—indeed, Apostel, Kasher, Kiefer, Pratt, and Sampson expres-sly dissociate themselves from it—but they do app-arently believe Grice to have been propounding it.)

According to this view, Grice's CP 'rests on the assumption of cooperation and shared purposes' (Kasher 1976: 201–2, 1977a). That Kasher (1977a: 332) is using 'cooperation' in the 'real-world goal-sharing' sense becomes clear when he says that the principles which he himself proposes, unlike Grice's: 'do not presume the existence of mutual ends for talk-exchanges, but merely the existence of an advantage for limited cooperation.' Kasher's counter-examples only serve as such to the goal-sharing view of cooperation. Sampson (1982: 204) likewise interprets cooperation in the very strong real-world goal-sharing sense, and attacks Grice's putative view with some vehemence, criticizing the CP on the grounds that it 'embodies assumptions which ... are very widely shared by students of language, but which imply a profoundly false conception of the nature of social life.'

Kasher, Kiefer, Pratt, and Sampson all believe that Grice's theory rests on a false view of the nature of participants in a conversation. Pratt (1981) caricatures the Gricean speaker as a 'cricketer-cum-boy-scout,' 'an honorable guy who always says the right thing and really means it!' All argue that Grice's explanation works only in the rather limited number of situations in which there is 'full cooperation.' They also consider that Grice's maxims apply only to 'cooperative communication in which participants strive after the same goal' (Kiefer 1979a: 60; see *Communication*), situations which they do not see as representing any sort of conversational norm (Pratt 1981):

> only some speech situations are characterized by shared objectives among participants. Clearly it is at least as common for speakers to have divergent goals and interests in a situation... there is no good reason at all to think of shared goals as representing any kind of natural norm in verbal interaction.

Apostel, Kasher, Kiefer, Pratt, and Sampson are right to reject social goal-sharing as a realistic model of human interaction. Their mistake, however, is in assuming that Grice was proposing it as such, a confusion which presumably stems from Grice's over-reliance in his 1975 paper on the analogy between linguistic behavior and other forms of cooperative endeavor, such as repairing a car. It is perhaps significant that he does not pursue the analogy in either of his subsequent papers on the subject of conversational implicature (Grice 1978, 1981), but concentrates on linguistic behavior alone.

This article dismisses the notion of real-world goal-sharing, both as a realistic model of linguistic interaction and as a reasonable interpretation of what Grice was concerned to do. It argues in favor of the linguistic goal-sharing view.

3. The Linguistic Goal-sharing View of Cooperation

The dispute between the social goal-sharers and the linguistic goal-sharers can be summarized as follows. For the linguistic goal-sharers, 'conversational co-operation' is concerned with the relationship between what is said and what is implied: 'Use language in such a way that your interlocutor can understand what you are saying and implying.' For the social goal-sharers, 'conversational cooperation' means: 'Tell your interlocutor everything s/he wants to know.'

Those linguists who consider that Grice's theory does have some explanatory power have assumed that the CP and its maxims relate to a theory of linguistic interaction alone, rather than to a more general theory of social interaction, and all their examples are concerned with relating utterances to (implied) propositions. This implies a rejection of the real-world goal-sharing interpretation of cooperation in favor of linguistic goal-sharing, though lamentably few state this explicitly. Honorable exceptions to this stricture are Holdcroft (1979) and Weiser. The latter states his position unambiguously:

> The observation that people follow Grice's cooperative principle in conversation doesn't mean that people are cooperating with each other, but that they are conscious of a system of [regularities] which allows others to make 'strong inferences' about them ... If you ought to do something and you don't do it, others are entitled to make some inference about your omission. If you show that you're aware that you're not doing something you ought to, then other strong inferences will be made, depending on how you demonstrate your awareness...

For this group, the CP relates to a theory of linguistic interaction only, and is 'the general assumption on the part of H that S will not violate conversational procedures' (Grice 1981: 185). A further difficulty is introduced, however, when one considers precisely what constitutes for them 'a violation of conversational procedures.' It is clear that flouting, opting out, or unintentionally infringing a maxim do not constitute a 'violation of conversational procedures.'

What is not clear is whether Grice himself and/or the linguistic goal-sharers consider the unostentatious nonobservance of a maxim at the level of what is said to be a 'violation of conversational procedures.' Consider example (1):

A: Do you know where Paul is? (1)
B: Are the pubs open yet?

On the face of it, B has flouted the maxim of relation and has generated the implicature that he does not know for certain where Paul is, but it is very likely that he is at the pub. Now suppose that B actually knows full well where Paul is — he is at this moment breaking into A's toolshed. There is nothing whatever in the way in which B has responded which would indicate to A that B is implying something which is untrue.

The important question for the present discussion is: 'Was B being conversationally cooperative or not?' To answer 'no' would be to adopt the real-world goal-sharing fallacy—one knows that B was understood by A to have implied precisely what he intended to imply (viz. that he did not know exactly where Paul was, but was probably at the pub). The only reason for calling him 'conversationally uncooperative' in these circumstances would be on the grounds that he failed to tell his questioner exactly what his questioner wanted to know.

The linguistic goal-sharers would therefore have to reply 'yes,' arguing that the fact that what B implied was untrue has nothing to do with conversational cooperation or with a theory of implicature. The fact that B has deceived A is of no interest to the linguist (though it might be a suitable question for a social psychologist or a moral philosopher). However, to answer 'yes' in these circumstances makes it very difficult to say what, if anything, is not conversationally cooperative (that is, whether the concept of conversational cooperation is vacuous).

4. Conclusion

If one rejects the social goal-sharing interpretation of Grice's theory, then the concept of conversational cooperation does become trivially true. If, as some commentators maintain, even saying nothing or walking away is interpretable as 'opting out,' then it becomes difficult to find any instances of talk conducted in the presence of another person which do not *count* as cooperative.

Margolis (1979), in common with many others, has attacked Grice on the grounds that he provides only vague, sloppy, and circular notions of rules and discovery procedures. Margolis's criticisms (and similar ones proposed by Holdcroft 1979) that the CP is vacuous and unfalsifiable may be largely justified, but it would be a mistake to underestimate the insights which Grice has given into the process of utterance interpretation. To have pointed out what ordinary interactants take for granted is recognized within ethnomethodology, for example, as a major theoretical contribution. Altieri (1978: 92), commenting on Margolis's strictures, makes the following observation:

> with Grice, charges like Joseph Margolis' claim that his maxims are only principles of common sense may indicate his strength rather than his weakness. A *sensus communis* is not a bad ground on which to base our capacity to understand the pragmatics of meaning.

Grice can claim credit for asking a lot of very exciting questions, which have led linguists to think about language in a completely new way. But in the end, what is left is a set of very informal procedures for calculating conversational implicature, which cannot really withstand close scrutiny. On the other hand, flawed as Grice's work is, no one else, in the view of this writer, has yet come up with anything better with which to replace it.

See also: Pragmatics and Sociolinguistics; Conversation Analysis.

Bibliography

Altieri C 1978 What Grice offers literary theory: A proposal for 'expressive implicature.' *Centrum* 6(2): 90–103
Apostel L 1979 Persuasive communication as metaphorical discourse under the guidance of conversational maxims. *Logique et Analyse* 22: 265–320
Bollobás E 1981 Who's afraid of irony? An analysis of uncooperative behavior in Edward Albee's 'Who's afraid of Virginia Woolf?' *Journal of Pragmatics* 5(3): 323–34
Corliss R L 1972 A theory of contextual implication. *Philosophy and Rhetoric* 5: 215–30
Grice H P 1975 Logic and conversation. In: Cole P, Morgan J L (eds.) *Syntax and Semantics Vol. 3: Speech Acts*. Academic Press, New York
Grice H P 1978 Further notes on logic and conversation. In: Cole P (ed.) *Syntax and Semantics, Vol. 9*. Academic Press, New York
Grice H P 1981 Presupposition and conversational implicature. In: Cole P (ed.) *Radical Pragmatics*. Academic Press, New York
Holdcroft D 1979 Speech acts and conversation I. *Philosophical Quarterly* 29: 125–41
Kasher A 1976 Conversational maxims and rationality. In: Kasher A (ed.) *Language in Focus*. Reidel, Dordrecht, The Netherlands
Kasher A 1977a Foundations of philosophical pragmatics. In: Butts R E, Hintikka J (eds.) *Basic Problems in Methodology and Linguistics*. Reidel, Dordrecht, The Netherlands
Kasher A 1977b What is a theory of use? *Journal of Pragmatics* 1(2): 105–20
Kiefer F 1979a What do the conversational maxims explain? *Linguisticae Investigationes* 3(1): 57–74
Kiefer F 1979b A brief rejoinder. *Linguisticae Investigationes* 3(2): 379–81
Margolis J 1979 Literature and speech acts. *Philosophy of Literature* 3: 39–52
Pratt M-L 1981 The ideology of speech act theory. *Centrum* [New Series]: 5–18
Sampson G 1982 The economics of conversation: Comments on Joshi's paper. In: Smith N V (ed.) *Mutual Knowledge*. Academic Press, London

Deaf Community: Structures and Interaction
J. G. Kyle

Deaf people are members of a social grouping who share a life experience and who have usually been educated in contact with groups of other deaf children. They have made a choice to associate with others from a similar situation. They form a community which differs from other communities in that deaf people do not live together in a community group (though they do intermarry), they do not work together, and they normally use their language in interaction in situations which are social rather than commercial. Interaction in the community is most commonly seen at the deaf club where deaf members gather (most evenings in city clubs, and less frequently in rural clubs). The deaf community can be described as a multipurpose community (embracing all features of personal and social activities), as distinct from the single-purpose societies in which hearing people now find themselves involved (e.g., sports, religious, political associations).

1. Membership

Three conditions are usually necessary for membership: a degree of hearing loss, sign language competence, and positive identification with other deaf people, the last being the most important.

Some people are 'born into' the deaf community as the children of deaf parents. However, only 5 percent of the community will have both parents deaf and a further 5 percent may have one parent deaf. Up to 20 percent will have a deaf sibling but this figure may include some of those in the 10 percent above (Kyle and Allsop 1982). Other deaf members are drawn from (nonsigning) families where there is no deafness and where isolation is a common early experience. When there is some contact with deaf adults, sign language will be acquired and used for effective interaction. For those with no contact with other deaf people in the early years, the communication problems can be immense.

One further factor which affects membership is that 90 percent of children born to deaf parents are hearing and do not usually remain involved in the community in adulthood.

2. Losing One's Membership

One cannot resign by nonattendance at the club, so there has to be a realignment of loyalties. For most deaf people this is unlikely—it would be very difficult to 'switch off' the deaf part and to identify more with hearing people. People living in isolated parts of the country would still be considered as part of the community even if they are very rarely seen by others.

Other circumstances could lessen the ties: in a mixed marriage a deaf partner may feel more drawn to the hearing society of the spouse and may forsake deaf company. Where members break the rules of the community they may be ostracized. One instance of this is divorce. Because of the small numbers of deaf people in any one area, marital breakup, particularly where there is infidelity, is likely to be public knowledge and one party may find it difficult to face the other member of the community.

3. Characteristics

Deaf people, while interwoven with society in everyday life, are only partly integrated into its framework. They achieve less in the education provided, have poorer jobs and wield less power. The commonest observation on employment is that people are 'underemployed rather than unemployed.' Deaf people generally have jobs in the unskilled and semiskilled occupations; very few are found in professional/managerial jobs. Significantly there are differences between White and non-White deaf people in employment with the latter less likely to be employed and likely to earn much less.

Jones and Pullen (1990), in a study of European countries, found evidence of underemployment, thwarted ambition, and even occupational segregation. Interestingly, they found that jobs were usually acquired through personal contacts rather than on the open market or through the rehabilitation or job-finding agencies.

Major studies of national samples in different countries highlight failure in education on a massive scale. Deaf children read poorly (profoundly deaf 16-year olds at an average reading age less than 9 years), speak unintelligibly, have limited lip-reading skills (Conrad 1979). They are less likely to go to college in the USA (Christiansen 1982) though they are more likely to go into further education in the UK (Kyle and Pullen 1985).

Not surprisingly then, deaf people in most countries have been considered in terms of their failures and are the subject of care, rehabilitation, social work, and service provision which is generally supplied without consultation. These supporting services may further weaken the decision-making possibilities and social power of the deaf community.

4. The Deaf Community as a Social Structure

There have developed two different levels of activity in the deaf community. On one level there is official provision and associations. On the other level are deaf people, their interaction, and what was once described as 'their secret language' (see *Sociolinguistics of Sign Language*).

In most countries, there is a network of Deaf Clubs and societies. Most have their origins in the associations initiated by deaf people but organized by hearing people. Some remain as charitable bodies with their own hearing-dominated board of management. Some are still dominated by the religious groups. In the nineteenth century, these associations catered for the moral and spiritual welfare of deaf people as well as providing further education and often providing training for a trade. Many were stifling of initiative being wholly controlled by hearing people who could sign or by partially-hearing people who could function well in the hearing world.

This infrastructure was seldom part of the 'Deaf Way' (Deaf culture). The interaction among deaf people takes place on a different plane (the social club) which only occasionally interfaces with this overt hearing organization. From the social club deaf people organize activities, care for the children and for the elderly, arrange trips, and create interclub events. The larger the membership the wider the range of activities (both sports and social) and the greater the degree of social skill required. In many respects the Deaf social club functions as the 'heart of the village of deaf people.'

5. Hearing People

Deaf people may accept that there is a place for hearing people in the deaf club. The question of whether they belong in the deaf community is rather more difficult to answer. People with a hearing 'attitude' are generally excluded. However, the hearing interface which deaf people need is seldom adequate—all over the world there is a lack of trained interpreters.

6. The Culture of Deaf People

Until recently there was no single sign for 'culture.' Deaf people described the differences in their lifestyle, in terms of the sign for 'possession' linked to the sign for 'deaf'—generally glossed as Deaf Way. Although incomplete, current attempts to describe the culture highlight certain behavioral patterns. These include:

(a) *Attention-getting and Touch*. Deaf people touch each other more than do hearing people. Attention-getting is often done by touch, rather than by the use of vocatives. When a person is out of reach, other devices are used such as waving or even stamping the floor or banging on the table. When the attention of a whole audience is required the lights of the room may be flashed.

(b) *Turn-taking*. The signer during a conversation may look away from the viewer indicating a wish to hold the floor. The viewer may attempt to break into the conversation by waving with a wrist action or touching on the arm.

(c) *Breaking into a Two-person Conversation* is also rule-bound. The third person, who is interrupting, has to apologize to the second signer, not to the person with whom he or she wishes to converse; only then can a message be given to the first person.

(d) *Turning Away* is generally an insult and when attention is called away, the signer has to adopt a convention to ensure that the viewer is not upset. This is often done by signing HOLD-ON or holding the viewer's arm while turning away.

(e) *Privacy and Confidentiality* are more difficult to achieve in the deaf community because of the visibility of conversations. Topics which are personal will not be discussed in the social area of the deaf club unless they are already common knowledge.

Customs exist in weddings, funerals, and in timekeeping (where a myth that deaf people have a different concept of time, can be dispelled). Many traditional stories within the deaf community relate to development in the adversity of oralism or of education. Experiences such as those of deaf children in UK schools in the early twentieth century, where they were referred to by number rather than by name are passing into the folklore of the culture. Frequently deaf people will use humor to exorcise some of the awful experiences. Such stories are 'traditional' among deaf people at gatherings.

Deaf games are also another feature of cultural life. Parties are not characterized by loud music but rather by the gradual unfolding of increasingly complex deaf games.

7. The Status of the Deaf Community

Deaf communities are in different stages of development in different countries. Everywhere there is an increasing awareness and evolving pride in being deaf, but this is still based on an inadequate knowledge base. Such a lack of empowerment should be a thing of the past in view of the rights afforded to deaf people in Sweden, in view of the European Parliament's recent recognition of the sign languages of the member states, or in view of the major events which took place in Washington in March 1988.

There has been no spreading revolution nor any major restatement of the rights of deaf people in any country.

See also: Sociolinguistics of Sign Language.

Bibliography

Christiansen J 1982 The socioeconomic status of the deaf community. In: Christiansen J, Eggleston-Dodd J (eds.)

Working Papers No. 4, Socioeconomic Status of the Deaf Population. Gallaudet College Press, Washington, DC

Conrad R 1979 *The Deaf School Child*. Harper and Row, London

Jones L, Pullen G 1990 *Inside We are All Equal*. European Commission Regional Secretariat of the World Federation of the Deaf, London

Kyle J G, Allsop L 1982 *Deaf People and the Community*. Final Report to Nuffield Foundation. School of Education, Bristol, UK

Kyle J G, Pullen G 1985 *Young Deaf People in Employment*. Final Report to the Medical Research Council. School of Education, Bristol, UK

Dialogism
T. A. Marshall

It was in the early 1980s that the term 'dialogism' started to enter the debates and the changing vocabularies of literary and cultural studies in western Europe and America. It did so via translations of the work of the Russian scholar M. M. Bakhtin. Incomplete as this body of work still remains for the western audience, its rate of assimilation and wide appeal continues to be remarkable. The history of its reception, when it is written, will very likely situate this appeal within the latter end of concerted challenges, in the postwar period, to a dominantly humanistic conception of human culture. It has also been favorably taken up by strands of post-1968 Western Marxism and multiethnic forms of cultural studies. This is all in marked contrast to the immediate reception of Bakhtin's work in Russia in the late 1920s and early 1930s. The dangers of Soviet intellectual life are sometimes thought to have obliged Bakhtin to publish under the names of friends and associates more in favor with the authorities. The works under the names of V. N. Voloshinov (see *Voloshinov, Valentin Nikolavic*) and P. N. Medevedev are now accepted by some as Bakhtin's own (see *Bakhtin, Mikhail M.*).

1. Terms

Besides 'dialogics' as a specific philosophical principle, Bakhtin offers a range of distinct but related terms: 'heteroglossia,' 'monologic,' 'polyphony,' 'reported speech,' 'multi-accentuality,' and 'carnivalization.'

2. Dialogism

Writing against idealist accounts of the relationship between language and consciousness, Bakhtin argues for a reversal of the more usual way of viewing the relationship between the world of signs (or ideology and culture) and consciousness. Within idealist philosophies of culture, signs are viewed as the means through which the inner thoughts and feelings of individuals are expressed. This view makes the sign into the external, objective manifestation of the inner world of consciousness; it puts consciousness prior to language. Such a conception is unacceptable to Bakhtin, for whom exactly the reverse is the case: 'Consciousness can arise and become a viable fact only in the material embodiment of signs.' (Voloshinov 1973.) In other words, not consciousness but language is the logically prior term. It is constitutively intersubjective, therefore social, and precedes subjectivity. To have a subjectivity, to be a person, is to have in the first instance entered via language into dialogue with others. Bakhtin's categorical claim that each of us is constituted dialogically thus strikes at received humanist assumptions that each of us is an autonomous individuality, clearly separable from other selves, authentic in privacy only, free of external influences. The self, for Bakhtin, is social and collective no less, for it is literally made up of what he calls 'languages,' the 'voices' spoken by others, all of which enter in and contend within oneself from birth onwards. In this way also Bakhtin conceives of ideology as inescapable in every movement of thought and speech, of words-laden-with-values. Indeed his list of the sources of ideology is deceptively short and simple: scientific statements, religious symbols and beliefs, works of art (see *Ideology*).

For each person, however, the list will always be longer than this and in principle it will be impossible to conclude or subordinate its items. Even within the same society the diversity might include parents, reading, other persons, nationality, class, color, profession, social circles, generation, epoch, political affiliation, educational biography, family; and each listing could break down ever further. Where, amid this diversity, does one rule out all voices but 'my own'? Short of an artificial pretense, it is impossible to do so, for this diversity is what Bakhtin means by 'polyphony': it constitutes each of us, and can even be taken to mean that each one of us is a variable compound of a 'we' and an 'I.' This same principle of multiplicity holds true for texts as well as persons. Bakhtin distinguishes between a 'heteroglot' text, that is, one composed of many voices, and a 'monoglot' one, one which is singular in its discourse and view of the world (see the essay 'Discourse and the Novel' in Bakhtin 1981). Better known is the identical distinction drawn between the 'dialogical' and 'monological' text, between Dostoyevsky and Tolstoy, in Bakhtin's pioneer work (1984). Comparable to this distinction, and compatible, is Barthes's theory (S/Z 1970) that all narratives are composed of an interweaving of voices that cannot finally be structured into any controlling hierarchy.

3. Heteroglossia

Before an exploration of the literary and linguistic aspects of Bakhtin, and by way of stressing the broad base of his appeal to Western theorists, this definition of 'heteroglossia' by a writer in the field of communication studies is relevant:

> Bakhtin's basic scenario for modelling variety is two actual people talking to each other in a specific dialogue at a particular time and in a particular place. But these persons would not confront each other as sovereign egos capable of sending messages to each other through the kind of uncluttered space envisioned by the artists who illustrate most receiver-sender models of communication. Rather, each of the two persons would be a consciousness at a specific point in the history of defining itself through the choice it has made — out of all the possible existing languages available to it at that moment — of a discourse to transcribe its intention in this specific exchange.
>
> (Newcomb 1984)

Bakhtin is always concerned to set this 'heteroglossia,' in society as well as texts, in a context of power relations. For every social group relates differently to the linguistic community, each in a continuing struggle to draw meanings into their own subculture and re-accent them for their own purposes. The forces with social power in society will always attempt, in their own interests, to extend their control; subordinate interests tend either to resist, or negotiate, or even to evade the dominant power. In Bakhtin's words (1981), heteroglossia is 'that which ensures the primacy of context over text ... all utterances are heteroglot in that they are functions of a matrix of forces practically impossible to recoup, and therefore impossible to resolve. Heteroglossia is as close a conceptualization as is possible of that locus where centripetal and centrifugal forces collide.' 'Centripetal' here means a force working towards a unified language, to which the 'centrifugal' is a counterforce tendency, an undermining of such ambitions and pretensions. Heteroglossia, then, is the representation of social differences textually. Precisely as voices and meanings will be in conflict with each other, the heteroglossia (of a written or television text, for example) enables such texts to engage in dialogic relationships with text users.

4. Langue and Parole

Historically Bakhtin's ideas are situated within the intellectual movements of Formalism and Marxism, but typically in a relationship to both of polemic and critique. Marxist premises, for example, are used to criticize Formalism's assumptions of the autonomy of art and 'literariness'; but contrariwise, the formal characteristics of works of art are also insisted upon by Bakhtin in cautioning Marxism against crude arguments from ideological contexts. The basic disagreement with Formalism, however, and indeed later with Structuralism, emerges in Bakhtin's confrontation with the structural linguistics of Ferdinand de Saussure. In *Marxism and the Philosophy of Language*, Voloshinov objected primarily to Saussure's distinction between *langue*, the system of rules underlying and structuring any utterance, and *parole*, speakers' actual linguistic performances. In terms of how language works this means that Formalists and Structuralists stress the 'system,' the synchronic whole which enables meaning to emerge within individual utterances. Bakhtin did not reject the existence of the system, but he argued that it offers no way of explaining how particular meanings are generated within particular utterances. In his concern to understand language as an abstract system, Saussure ignored the 'diachronic' nature of language in actual use: 'the actual reality of language — speech — is not the abstract system of linguistic norms ... but the social event of verbal interaction implemented in an utterance' (Voloshinov 1973).

As a diachronic event, language in actual use is also a dialogical event, in that the meaning of an utterance is given not by the intention of an individual, but by its context. It is always addressed to another and, likewise, because language precedes each addressee, is already quoting another. Saussure's emphasis on *langue*, according to Voloshinov and Bakhtin, failed to take account of the fact that from the viewpoint of the speaker's consciousness and actual speech in social intercourse, there is no direct access to the abstract system. Thus speech is as much a social process as a rule-governed performance, always taking place within the field of cultural relations. For this reason Bakhtin conceptualized language not as a system producing meaning solely through the relationship of sign to sign, but as a field of possibilities. Traditionalist objections to the structuralist approach, which are not shared by Bakhtin, resist the dispersal of meaning across a field of signifiers precisely by insisting upon meaning residing in the intending subject. This is the humanist approach: it resists what has become called the decentering of the subject, and insists upon meanings residing in words or statements guaranteed by authorial-utterer intentions. In Bakhtin, the speaking subject as the guarantee of essential meanings is indeed decentered. But this occurs within the process of cultural negotiation that determines which possibilities of meaning are actually realized. The sign is a social fact precisely because it responds to differences and balances of power: 'each word... is a little arena for the clash and criss-crossing of differently orientated social accents. A word in the mouth of a particular person is a product of the living interaction of social forces.' Voloshinov (1973). A good example of the sign as an arena is the multiple currency of the word 'patriotism' in the late eighteenth-century English political context. As Hugh Cunningham has shown, at the time both the right and the left ends of the political spectrum—those defending the status quo and those demanding radical reform—sought to present themselves as the truly patriotic voice (Cunningham 1981: 12). But this example aside, the general point is that every sign has the potentiality to carry the inflections of different social groups. Hence for Bakhtin the domain of ideology coincides with the domain of signs.

Bakhtin's critique of abstraction in Saussure may also be extended to other major Western theorists of language. Chomsky is another important point of reference in this respect, for his difference from Bakhtin highlights the latter's characteristically dialogical thrust of cultural polemic. The Chomskyan distinction, for example, between 'competence' and 'performance' assumes a transcendent grammar to which actual speech performance can only be imperfectly compared. This model appears to provide a criterion of linguistic correctness, for Chomsky has stated that: 'Any interesting generative grammar will be dealing, for the most part, with mental processes that are far below the level of actual or even potential consciousness; furthermore, it is quite apparent that a speaker's reports and viewpoints about his behavior and competence may be in error' (Chomsky 1965: 8). Now Bakhtin would not acknowledge any such criteria of correctness, save only in instances of language instruction itself, for to do so is to move to 'correct' matters that must be judged and understood by ideological criteria. The social and political consequences of such an abstract linguistics, in Bakhtin's vocabulary, are centripetal, and need to be perceived against the backdrop of the very heteroglossia they seek to deny. In other words, distinctions between language and speech, and between synchrony and diachrony (which are traced by Bakhtin back to Cartesian rationalism and Leibniz's conception of a universal grammar) are themselves contextualized by Bakhtin—in a shrewd polemical move—and seen to serve the needs of sociopolitical centralization. The social home of Cartesianism is State policy; it services rationales to exclude bi- and multilingual education; it occurs in language requirements attaching to immigration restrictions; it appears in tensions between nonstandard and standard dialects (which themselves are fictions that help to create a transcendent 'standard'). In general, as a form of monologism, it militates against change and linguistic creativity. A relevant point of comparison here is Roland Barthes's early work, his demystification of cultural and historical artefacts that pass themselves off as more or less natural, inevitable phenomena. In *Writing Degree Zero* (1967) Barthes examined the intellectual value, and virtue, attached in France to *la clarté*, or lucidity. Lucidity, he pointed out, is widely supposed to inhere in the French language as a somehow self-evident virtue which all must recognize. In Barthes's analysis, *la clarté* is located as historical phenomenon, specific to court usage in the seventeenth century. It was falsely universalized through agencies such as the Port Royal grammarians, who actually imposed their own idiom as the paradigm of the language as a whole. Barthes dubbed *la clarté* class idiom, and exposed its political and rhetorical value, its connections to power. *La clarté,* in Bakhtin's term, is a centrifugal force.

5. Multi-accentuality

Saussure is famous for his articulation of the arbitrary nature of the sign, by which he meant the arbitrary relationship between the sound–image and concept of the sign, signifier and signified (see *Saussurean Tradition and Sociolinguistics*). In the absence of intrinsic properties, the values that signs carry, Saussure maintained, 'owe their existence solely to usage and general acceptance,' that is, to convention. Bakhtin's acknowledgement of the arbitrariness of the sign is cautious nevertheless, and once again polemical. For he understood Saussure to be claiming that a verbal sign is ultimately a mental construct, that the acoustic image and the concept are both contained in an arbitrary closed system no different in principle from systems of mathematical signs. The idea of the arbitrariness of the sign can, Bakhtin cautions, encourage an insensitivity to the ideological meanings that give signs their content. For crucial to Bakhtin's sense of the social life of the sign is the fact that every sign without exception is capable of signifying different values. In addition to sound–image and concept an 'evaluative accent' comes into play in our use of signs. Signs possess 'an inner dialectic quality,' or 'multi-accentuality':

> Class does not coincide with the sign community, i.e., with the community, which is the totality of users of the same set of signs for ideological communication. Thus various different classes will use one and the same language. As a result, differently oriented accents intersect in every ideological sign. Sign becomes an arena of the class struggle. This social *multiaccentuality* of the ideological sign is a very crucial aspect. By and

large, it is thanks to this intersecting of accents that a sign maintains its vitality and dynamism and the capacity for further development. A sign that has been withdrawn from the pressures of the social struggle— which, so to speak, crosses beyond the pale of the class struggle—inevitably loses force, degenerating into allegory and becoming the object not of live social intelligibility but of philological comprehension... The very same thing that makes the ideological sign vital and mutable is also, however, that which makes it a refracting and distorting medium. The ruling class strives to impart a supraclass, eternal character to the sign, to extinguish or drive inward the struggle between social value judgments which occurs in it, to make the sign uniaccentual. In actual fact, each living ideological sign has two faces, like Janus. Any current curse word can become a word of praise, any current truth must inevitably sound to many other people as the greatest lie. This *inner dialectic quality* of the sign comes out fully in the open only in times of social crises or revolutionary changes.

(Voloshinov 1973: 23)

This amounts to a profound refusal to see language as a closed system of self-identical forms, that is, the one-to-one correspondence of a signifier to a signified. While acknowledging that the sign is not stable or fixed, Voloshinov insists nevertheless that multiplicity of meaning is a function of the sign's multi-accentuality, its openness to different evaluative orientations. The somewhat dated and historically obligatory Marxist orthodoxy of the class struggle should not deter us from realizing the relevance of this model to any analysis of the signs of power. The metaphor of an arena of power applies just as cogently to any conflict of interests carried by signs; it gains appropriateness from the fact that contending social forces always seek to fix the 'meaning-potential' of signs with an evaluative accent according to their interests and objectives. Until recently, for example, a 'norm' of a sort existed—not least in academic and other forms of 'serious' expository prose—to use the pronoun 'he' to denote not a male person but any person, male or female. This is a uni-accented sign that constructs and sustains a norm in which patriarchal interests are affirmed. As with any sign, its value is not simply a linguistic value but an ideological one as well, for it is not always possible to choose to employ alternatives to protocol. Another example of a uni-accented sign (cited by Hartley 1982) is Sir Thomas Elyot (1531) describing democracy as 'a monster with many heads.' It was because democracy was such a political threat to the monarchical society of the day that Elyot's discourse strove to make it appear to be intrinsically endowed with negative attributes. Even as ideological values enter this representation, the uni-accented sign functions to *naturalize* it as an unchangeable fact. As Hartley puts it: '... since signs are necessarily multi-accentual, any discourse which seeks to "close" their potential, and to prefer one evaluative accent over another is ideological: such discourses present evaluative differences as differences of fact' (1982: 124). Any sign can in principle inflect in ways contrary to Saussure's rubric of 'general acceptance,' a formula to Saussure's rubric of 'general acceptance,' a formula that somewhat understates the realities of the power struggle within society: kings in their time have also been seen as monsters.

6. Changing Signs: The Example of Literature

A significant moment in Bakhtin's reception in the West was marked in 1976 with the publication of *Keywords* by the socialist critic Raymond Williams. The volume's subtitle *A Vocabulary of Culture and Society* is an intertextual reference to an earlier work by Williams himself (*Culture and Society 1780–1950, 1958*), in which he undertook to discriminate the historical ideas carried by the sign 'culture' in its general modern uses. *Keywords* continued this inquiry, concentrating on and recovering the changing meanings carried in English by such terms as 'industry,' 'nature,' 'organic,' 'mass,' 'leisure,' and many others. This inquiry, notably, is not subtitled as a dictionary but a vocabulary. It thus accords exactly with Bakhtin's sense that words come not out of dictionaries but out of concrete dialogic situations. For Bakhtin the distinction between dialogic words (or 'utterances') and dictionary words is a distinction between theme and 'meaning.' 'Meaning, in essence, means nothing; it only possesses potentiality—the possibility of having a meaning within a concrete theme' (Voloshinov 1973: 101). Words acquire meaning exactly and only by the way they always recall earlier contexts of usage, whether covertly or overtly. This point bears crucially, for example, on Williams's entry in *Keywords* on the sign 'literature':

> What has then to be traced is the attempted and often successful specialization of 'literature' to certain kinds of writing... Clearly, the major shift, represented by the modern complex of 'literature,' *art, aesthetic, creative,* and *imaginative* is a matter of social and cultural history. 'Literature' itself must be seen as a late medieval and Renaissance isolation of the skills of reading and of the qualities of the book; this was much emphasised by the development of printing... Then 'literature' was specialised towards *imaginative writing*, within the basic assumptions of Romanticism... Significantly in recent years 'literature' and 'literary,' though they still have effective currency in post-C18 senses, have been increasingly challenged, on what is conventionally their own ground, by concepts of *writing* and *communication* which seek to recover the most active and general senses which the extreme specialization had seemed to exclude.
>
> (Williams 1976: 150–4)

Here Williams is discriminating a uni-accented sign under challenge, thus turning multi-accentual. The history he charts has had implications for teaching and pedagogic practice in the humanities. It is not a historical accident that in the twentieth century the institutionally sanctioned study of literature in the West has greatly concentrated upon formal and textual aspects at the expense of the historical and contextual. In a distinctly Bakhtinian move, Williams is countering the latter tendency by recovering the history it excludes: he opens the sign. The elevation, and evaluation, of 'literature' into a pure essence uncontaminated by history, or modernity, is itself a historical fact: it favored and for a long time stabilized the concepts of practical and new criticism.

A brief historical survey of the origins of practical and new criticism is relevant here, for these discourses display, in Bakhtin's sense, centripetal tendencies. Nineteenth-century historical and philological research based itself on European vernacular literature: texts were regarded, on analogy with biblical and Classical texts, as documents in the history of a culture and language and as contributions to a more newly found sense of European national identity. It remains, however, something of a paradox that the upshot of this extensive research was an emergent awareness of patterns of meaning and form that apparently transcended specific cultural or linguistic contexts: patterns, that is, that seemed capable of being described as universal. They were somehow autonomous idioms at once engaging and transcending particular languages and cultures. To later authoritative readers, within this tradition as diverse as Victor Shklovsky, F.R. Leavis, and Cleanth Brooks, something like an intrinsic and codifiable language of literature seemed to exist in these texts. In this broad context 'literariness' accommodated 'defamiliarization' (Shklovsky 1917), 'canonization' (Leavis 1948), and 'paradox' (Brooks 1947). The notion of 'literariness' implies a linguistic domain constituting 'literature' in essence, in opposition to what it constructs as 'ordinary discourse.' In fact, however, the distinction and the value-judgment it carries has proved at once tenacious and, in theoretical terms, difficult to sustain. Within a Bakhtinian scheme, for example, these essentializing tendencies privilege text over context. 'The text itself' is a piece of Formalist critical parlance that leaves scant room for social changes in language practice to play an explanatory role vis-à-vis the text-as-object. (By contrast, a phrase such as 'ordinary discourse itself' sounds merely odd.) The text's mediation via the authoritative subjectivity of the professional critic (another relatively recent historical development in fact), until recently, at least, has played a role in limiting, or marginalizing, the role of the reader. The favorable reception accorded to Bakhtin has had much to do with his encouragement to recontextualize the 'literary' as social discourse, and an agenda to emphasize literary history, readers, social institutions, the academy included. It coincided with a revived post-1968 Marxism committed to historical critique; with emergent feminism; with calls for interdisciplinary work with an ever-present popular culture and the newer visual media.

7. Genre

The question of genre in Bakhtin remains open to considerable interpretation. His concerns here go far beyond Formalist interests in stylistic variations between works or between particular authors. As Clark and Holquist have described it, genre for Bakhtin is 'a crystallization of the concepts particular to a given time and to a given social stratum in a specific society' (1984: 275). So, for example, historically variable time–space configurations, or 'chronotopes,' are indices of cultural diversity. Different historical concepts of time and space play a role in distinguishing narrative genres. In the Greek romance, for example, time involves no clear progression and place remains mere background. In the romance, circumstances may help or impede the hero, but never change him (or her). An example could be Plutarch's *Lives,* in whose chronotope character is a given: Camillus simply lives his destiny out, manifesting unchanging, essential qualities. In the novel's chronotope, by contrast, the social world enters action, thought, and choice, defining and shaping irreversible possibilities. In the novel, unlike the epic, there is always a noncoincidence between hero and environment, a gap between self and social categories. It is this sort of distinction that Bakhtin makes when differentiating genres. In another broad link between social concepts and genre, Bakhtin reads Rabelais's work as articulating a disintegration of inherited religious and institutional dogma which accords hierarchical primacy to transcendent spirit over matter. Rabelais's uncompromisingly material presentation of the human body is read by Bakhtin as disintegrating fixed social configurations and creating new ones, infiltrating matter with new penumbras of meaning.

Bakhtin certainly prefers some forms of literature to others, according to his distinction between centrifugal and centripetal. He is most of all unforthcoming on drama, the one form above others which in the West has often been viewed as the political art par excellence. But despite the superficial polyphony, the dramatist still imposes upon his or her characters what they say and how they say it. The least satisfactory part of the work on genre, however, is perhaps Bakhtin's implicit submission that all poetry assimilates to the lyric and is centripetal in tendency. It is arguable that these are moves by Bakhtin within a larger frame of strategic objectives, not least of which is to contest the centripetal tendencies of literary critics themselves, and by extension the hegemony of poetry as the supposed essence of literary form. It is certainly noteworthy that Bakhtin's reception in the West coincides in time with moves, even within practical criticism, to account for the language of prose fiction with an attention to detail hitherto mainly reserved for poetry (Lodge (1966) was a pioneer work.) The other strategic move is to introduce a study of novelistic discourse which in scope and time extends well beyond what is usually understood by the novel. Bakhtin valorizes 'novelistic discourse' as the form, par excellence, that in its very fabric opens itself to heteroglossia: ideally, it is the most comprehensive denial possible of the absolutism of a single and unitary language. As Bakhtin explains (1984: 47–77), this involves not at all a merely pell-mell simulacrum of people's speech, but a 'representation' of speech. The paradigm of novelistic discourse that he finds in Dostoyevsky incorporates the copresence both of the author's and the character's fully-fledged voices. The speech of the characters is dialogized exactly by the author's inclination and ability to dialogize, and thus relativize, his own relation to their words. As Wayne C. Booth introducing Bakhtin (1984), puts it: '…techniques [are viewed] as performing their highest service by observing the autonomy of the novel's characters…all are treated not as objects serving the author's plans, but as subjects, ends in themselves, defying any temptation the author may have to fit them into his [or her] superior plans' (Bakhtin 1984, Introduction by W. C. Booth: xxiii). The diverse consciousnesses and voices making up the novelist's thought are bound up in a struggle with one another for dominance; no one voice is the bearer of ultimate conceptual authority. (It is typical also that the title of the great study of Dostoyevsky implies a body of unresolved problems, an openness to dialogue.) This is technique that discards any external epistemology of knowing, based on 'objectification.' As subjects rather than objects, Dostoyevsky's characters are never exhaustively known, defined, or finalized, as they would be, were any such authority to have the first and last word. Like the genre itself, personality in the novel is always unfinished and incomplete, as opposed to personality in the epic, where it is finished and complete at the outset.

Accordingly, the techniques that most interested Bakhtin were the resources of narrative in prose to incorporate languages other than the author's or the reader's. The second half of *Marxism and the Philosophy of Language* (1973a) is an investigation, rich in working examples, of 'indirect' and 'quasi-direct' discourse, multileveled speech acts in which more than one voice participates. They are studied not just as grammatical and syntactic categories, but as ways in which one speaker or writer can orientate himself or herself to the words of another. There have been, to date, some sophisticated and detailed studies of multivoicedness in prose, based specifically on the numerous forms of 'free indirect discourse' (often abbreviated to FID), where the vocabulary and prosody of a character's speech are rendered without quotation marks in what is nominally the narrator's voice; James Joyce's short story 'Eveline' in *Dubliners* is a good example (for studies of the variations of FID, see McHale 1978, Banfield 1973, Rimmon-Kenan 1983). A good first introduction to this kind of technical issue is provided by Bakhtin's own essay 'Discourse in the Novel' (1981), which uses Dickens's *Little Dorrit* as exemplary of the novel's ability to represent an interanimation of socio-ideological languages. In this essay Bakhtin makes the important point that the dialogic nature of the novel can be either open or closed: the author can either let heteroglossia speak for itself or can impose a privileged authorial metalanguage. On the premises of the argument the single-voiced monological text exists as a suppression of dialogic activity; the author's superior voice has for a long time served as a critical fiction, closely resembling idealism's inner world of consciousness, and placed historically in Williams's survey of 'literature.' But the promise extended by Bakhtin is that attention to technique and linguistic aspects can enable even 'omniscient' ideological voices in prose to be read and produced by readers as the suppressive and naturalized voices that they are. An (admittedly virtuoso) analysis of just this kind was offered by Barthes (1970), in a reading of 'Sarrasine,' a short story by Balzac, Barthes's insistence on the supremacy of 'writerly,' *scriptible*, literature over 'readerly,' *lisible*, literature has a good deal in common with Bakhtin's preference for polyphony over single-voiced texts. In both cases the latter term is derived and extracted from the former; in both cases value-judgments favoring polyphony are made explicit and defended within a broader cultural polemic. An important part of this polemic, it should be added, is that Bakhtin never treats the monological as a species of merely theoretical error or illusion. For as just stated, it is a form of discourse itself with real, albeit mystifying effects, and a theory of language should offer an account of these. Centrifugalism remains implicitly an ethical imperative, for the monological text is a partial report.

8. Carnivalization

Bakhtin never intends us to understand dialogism as an equilibrium of voices, a common ground of give-and-take, or a pluralism of amicable disagreements. He insists on power inequalities, on fierce and even intractable social struggle. 'Carnivalization,' a term drawn from his study of Rabelais, is his term for dialogic activity of an especially intense, iconoclastic kind. It is a world of head-on confrontations between voices and energies which otherwise only rarely surface within the existing social and ideological arrangements.

The carnival culture that Bakhtin described (1968) in the works of the medieval writer Rabelais is a space of urgently emergent voices outspeaking and overturning official hierarchies, pieties, and prohibitions. The carnival abolishes the seriousness of life; nothing that is permanent or completed survives, the solemnity of all ready-made ideas and truths collapses. In this world-turned-upside-down officialdom's gravitas is mocked and absorbed back into a collective 'grotesque body' of laughter, excess, offensiveness, and degradation. A collision and inversion of languages—the high, validated language of classicism and the low, parodic vernacular—is perhaps the core event of carnival rule-breaking. It is part of the spectacle of differentiated forms of the self—degraded back to a level of sheer materiality on which everyone for once is equal. As a form that never forgets the carnival spirit, the novel for Bakhtin is less a genre than an antigenre. It recognizes, often in parody, the arbitrariness and conventionality of forms and norms; instead of knowing, it asks how we know. In Bakhtin's scheme the carnival-novelistic spirit has old historical foundations, and includes the ancient Menippean satire with its direct roots in the world of saturnalian folklore. Another historical form is the genre of the Socratic dialogue, discourse in which the discovery of truth is conducted as an unfolding exchange of views rather than as an authoritative monologue. Great interest continues to be shown in Bakhtin's provocative study of Rabelais: arguments continue as to whether carnival is a conservative or a revolutionary force, a means of containment and surveillance tolerated (or even sponsored) by officialdom itself, or genuinely unlicensed life. A valuable summary of the present debate is given in recent work by Stallybrass and White (1986).

See also: Genre; Voloshinov, Valentin Nikolavic; Bakhtin, Mikhail M.; Discourse; Marxist Theories of Language.

Bibliography

Bakhtin M M 1968 (transl. Iwolsky H) *Rebelais and His World*. MIT Press, Cambridge, MA
Bakhtin M M 1981 (transl. Emerson C, Holquist M) *The Dialogic Imagination*. (contains 'Discourse and the Novel' essay.) University of Texas Press, Austin, TX
Bakhtin M M 1984 (transl. Emerson C) *Problems of Dostoevsky's Poetics*. Manchester University Press, Manchester, UK
Banfield A 1973 Narrative style and the grammar of direct and indirect speech. *Foundations of Language* **10**: 1–39
Banfield A 1978 The formal coherence of represented speech and thought. *Poetics and Theory of Literature* **3**: 289–314
Barthes R 1970 *S/Z*. Hill and Wang, New York
Brooks C 1947 *The Well Wrought Urn*. Methuen, London
Chomsky N 1965 *Aspects of the Theory of Syntax*. MIT Press, Cambridge, MA
Clark K, Holquist M 1984 *Mikhail Bakhtin*. The Belknap Press of Harvard University, Cambridge, MA
Cunningham H 1981 The language of patriotism. *History Workshop*, No. 12
Hartley J 1982 *Understanding News*. Methuen, London
Leavis F R 1948 *The Great Tradition*. Chatto and Windus, London
Lodge D 1966 *The Language of Fiction*. Routledge and Kegan Paul, London
McHale B 1978 Free indirect discourse: A survey of recent accounts. *Poetics and Theory of Literature* **3**: 249–87
Medvedev P N, Bakhtin M M 1973 (transl. Wehrle A J) *The Formal Method in Literary Scholarship*. Johns Hopkins University Press, Baltimore, MD
Morson G S (ed.) 1986 *Bakhtin*. University of Chicago Press, Chicago, IL
Newcomb H 1984 On the dialogic aspects of mass communication. *Critical Studies in Mass Communication* **II**: 34–50
Rimmon-Kenan S 1983 *Narrative Fiction: Contemporary Poetics*. Methuen New Accents, London
Shklovsky V 1917 Arts as technique. In: Lemon L T, Reis M J (eds.) 1965 *Russian Formalist Criticism: Four Essays*. University of Nebraska Press, Lincoln, NE
Stallybrass P, White A 1986 *The Politics and Poetics of Transgression*. Methuen, London
Todorov T 1984 (transl. Godzich W) *Mikhail Bakhtin. The Dialogical Principle*. Manchester University Press, Manchester, UK
University of Ottawa Quarterly **53** January–March 1983 (special Bakhtin Edition; includes bibliography of criticism)
Voloshinov V N 1973 (transl. Matejka L, Titunik I R) *Marxism and the Philosophy of Language*. Seminar Press, New York
Voloshinov V N 1976 (transl. Titunik I R) *Freudianism: A Marxist Critique*. Academic Press, New York
Williams R 1976 *Keywords: A Vocabulary of Culture and Society*. Fontana, London

Discourse

A. McHoul

'Discourse,' used as a mass noun, means roughly the same as 'language *use*' or 'language-*in-use*.' As a count noun ('a discourse'), it means a relatively discrete subset of a whole language, used for specific social or institutional purposes—as in 'the medical discourses of the middle ages.' Occasionally the 'count' usage becomes 'massified'—as in 'Aristotelian scientific discourse' or (and therefore ambiguously) 'the discourse on childhood.' The second usage carries the implication that discourse is a way of ordering categories of thought and knowledge, echoing the 'ordinary' meaning of 'a discourse' as a kind of text or treatise. In some critical branches of philosophy and semiotics, the term 'discursive' carries with it the sense of 'textually or linguistically produced.' Thus madness, for example, may be referred to as 'discursively constructed,' to show that it does not exist as a 'real fact' in the world but is fabricated within certain forms of knowledge or 'disciplines,' often for particular political purposes.

1. The Term(s)

Already the term 'discourse' is seen to be being used extremely diversely, both within linguistics (and its subdisciplines) and within other areas of the social sciences and humanities, particularly sociology (historical reasons for this are dealt with by Hodge 1984). So while it will always be possible to find the term being used in other ways, a basic definition can be given as follows. 'Discourse,' as a mass noun only, and in its rather strict linguistic sense, refers to *connected* speech or writing occurring at suprasentential levels (at levels greater than the single sentence). Harris (1952) pioneered this approach to discourse, arguing that the methods of formal linguistics could be used to understand how sentences are connected, and not simply the formal structure which exists *within* the sentence itself. While Harris used invented data and attempted to find the formal structural properties of connected speech, this is now atypical—and not essential to Harris's definition of 'discourse.' Most discourse analysts these days (possibly beginning with Mitchell 1957) prefer to work with naturally occurring data (actual talk, actual texts) and to pursue the local–contextual features and social functions of them rather than their purely 'linguistic' (or systemic) properties. In this sense, a focus on discourse entails a shift in linguistics away from competence and the *langue* (the language system) and towards performance and *paroles* (actual speech events) (see *Saussurean Tradition and Sociolinguistics*).

However, the above definition is only an ideal type. There are many variations upon it and some discourse analysts would totally disagree with it (Frawley 1987). In what follows, after a brief look at the history of discourse and its analysis, there is an outline of, arguably, the three main approaches to it in contemporary scholarship: the formal linguistic approach (discourse as text), the empirical sociological approach (discourse as conversation), and the critical approach (discourse*s* as power/knowledge).

Note, then, that it is in the last domain, associated with critical history and sociology, that we find the term '*a* discourse' most commonly used, referring to the nexus between bodies of historically volatile disciplinary knowledge and specific linguistic usages at social-institutional sites (hospitals, prisons, and schools, for example). However, the two terms ('discourse' and 'a discourse') are often used as proxies for one another, especially in the adjectival form 'discursive' which can refer to both domains. In some definitions the two are conflated:

[Discourse] is a domain of language use, structured as a unity by common assumptions. There may be competing discourses, and discourses will change over time. For example, M. Foucault ... describes the existence of discourses of madness ... which have changed over the centuries. He also suggests that there may well be similarities between discourses at any time. The discourse of political economy in the eighteenth and nineteenth centuries, for instance, takes the same *form* as that of natural history.

(Abercrombie et al. 1984: 70)

2. History and Diversity of the Term(s)

As van Dijk (1985a) points out, our modern linguistic conception of discourse (as language use) owes much to the ancient distinction between grammar and rhetoric. Grammarians explored the possibilities a language can offer as a 'calculus' for representing the world, and were concerned with correctness of usage. By contrast, rhetoricians focused upon practical uses of speech and writing as means of social and political persuasion. Grammar was akin to a reductive science, while rhetoric was more of an applied art. Although the ancient Greeks took both disciplines to be 'prescriptive,' modern linguists and sociologists are clearly more 'descriptive' in their approach; though it can still be useful to distinguish between language and discourse in terms of grammar, on the one hand, and rhetoric, on the other, as topics for that description. Continuing with van Dijk's brief history: after revivals of rhetoric in the middle ages and the seventeenth and eighteenth centuries, by the nineteenth and twentieth centuries, and particularly under the influence of Saussure, linguistics proper came to dominate the field of language study. Consequently attention was concentrated on modern versions of grammar: namely, formal properties of the language system.

However, the study of discourse has never been entirely neglected. Such early twentieth-century schools as the Russian Formalists continued alternative ('rhetorical') traditions, focusing on textual discourse (especially folktales (Propp 1958)) rather than on the standard linguistic categories of phonology, morphology, syntax, and semantics for their own sake. In addition, French structuralism and semiotics, in particular the early Barthes (1967), extended Saussure's original conception of the verbal language system to include forms of communication such as the fashion and food systems.

In this sense, the study of discourse (as language use) can be broadly and roughly associated with applied linguistics and particularly with the area of it which is now called 'pragmatics.' Indeed, sometimes the terms 'pragmatics' and 'discourse analysis' are used interchangeably (Levinson 1983)—even though the former term can also have a more technical meaning: the study of how speech acts (Austin 1975) are used in concrete social settings (see *Pragmatics and Sociolinguistics*). However pragmatics, considered broadly *as* discourse analysis, appears to have the following ideal-typical features: (a) it criticizes the idea that whole languages are exclusively formal grammatical sentence systems by proposing to examine actual contexts of language-in-use; (b) it construes language as primarily discourse(s)—as heterogeneous social actions in the first place rather than, say, as an innate property of the human mind which is merely put into social action or 'performed'; (c) it considers language to be produced and analyzable only in terms of the connection between utterances (writing and speech events) rather than in terms of single sentences; (d) it favors (though it does not exclusively use) naturally occurring rather than elicited or invented data. These data are typically transcripts of talk by more than a single speaker made from audio or video recordings; or else texts such as newspaper reports which would have been produced and consumed by social actors even if the analyst had no interest in them.

Not surprisingly, then, disciplines outside linguistics have laid claim to discourse as their proper object. These would include anthropology (Pike 1967), social psychology (Argyle 1969), artificial intelligence studies (Schank 1975), literary criticism and theory (Frow 1986), philosophy (Searle et al. 1980) and, particularly, sociology (Schenkein 1978). However, as yet, no single approach to discourse has emerged as dominant. And despite a number of textbooks and handbooks (van Dijk 1985b, Brown and Yule 1983), critics of very different persuasions seem to be convinced that no interdisciplinary synthesis has yet emerged (Stalpers 1988, Frawley 1987). Indeed, some have argued that a single, integrated and monolithic approach is actually less satisfactory than a piecemeal and multitheoretical approach (McHoul and Luke 1989).

Given the diversity of the field and the contestability of the above ideal-type criteria for discourse and its analysis, we must now examine how discourse has been analyzed and understood in the three major approaches already mentioned: the formal, the empirical, and the critical. Each is, in itself, multidisciplinary. Each has its own tensions, controversies, and contradictions; and each has occasionally been put into contention and/or synthesis with at least one of the other two. But each is sufficiently different from the others to offer a preliminary definitional scaffolding.

3. The Formal Approach

What can be called the 'formal approach' to discourse tends, by and large, to construe discourse as text. It is the most direct descendant of Harris (1952) and Mitchell (1957). Like Harris, it continues to have faith in formal linguistic methods of analysis. Like Mitchell, it moves in the direction of social functions and naturally occurring samples. It thus overlaps the equally diverse domains of sociolinguistics (Giglioli 1982) and the ethnography of communication (Gumperz and Hymes 1972). In the form of text linguistics (including text grammars), it has a precursor in the Russian Formalist school which, in its turn, via French structuralism (Saussure, Lévi-Strauss, and the early Barthes), connects this approach to structuralism in general and, perhaps, to the post-structuralist approach to discourse of Foucault, a principal theorist of the critical school.

However, via the systemic functionalism of Halliday (1973) and, more especially, via the extension of Halliday into social semiotics and critical linguistics by such analysts as Hodge and Kress (1988), the formal approach also connects with empirical sociological approaches to discourse. 'Critical linguistics,' in this sense, is perhaps currently at the forefront of discourse analysis—a major contender for being the dominant paradigm. For although it does not always pick up on the work of the French critical discourse theorists (such as Foucault)—though see Fairclough (1989)—it promises a unique amalgam of a firm linguistic base (Hallidayan systemic functionalism) with an interest in actual rather than invented texts and a attempt to 'read' those texts as socially classed, gendered, and historically located. In some of its more directly political modes, it has begun to contribute to feminist theory and practice (Threadgold 1988) by challenging linguistically naive critiques of, for example, the gendering of pronouns (Spender 1980) and arguing that discourse analysis must look not at how a language in general is gendered but at how gender-differential forms of access to particular discursive registers and genres have become normal and dominant through complex historical processes.

In addition, some other analysts have begun to extend formalist methods to examine how discourses are 'owned' in terms of social class and ethnic identity. Mey (1985), for example, has looked at instructional texts in German for Turkish 'guest'-workers in terms of the subset of that natural language (the particular discourses within it) which the workers are permitted to command such that they can be and become economically efficient without having full access to the cultural and linguistic environment in which their labor occurs and to which it contributes by reproducing materially crucial infrastructures.

However, these critical and political uses of formal linguistic methods are only one side of the coin. At another extreme, the formalist approach is mechanistic—attempting as it does to read off quite general discursive norms from imagined or invented texts, as though discourse were less of a social phenomenon and more of a formal system in its own right, requiring a relatively narrow linguistic description. As with certain kinds of speech act theory, this extreme formalism appears to hold to a vaguely pragmatized notion of competence—as if '*paroles*' (performed utterances) had a discursive system to them which was other than (but formally like) the '*langue*' (the language system).

A classic instance of this is the work of Grice (1975) who is often associated with speech act theory and who attempted to generalize from how he thought conversations operated in order to list a number of 'postulates' for conversational practice. In this sense, he believed he was describing a kind of practical linguistic universal: conversational competence. The postulates (which boil down to 'be polite,' 'be economical' and so on) are by no means universally found in actual conversations. Moreover they seem to give an ideal-rational version of socially pragmatic events so that it seems virtually irrelevant that the objects of the analysis (conversations) are both suprasentential and constitute a form of social action.

A more recent heir to the formalist approach has been text linguistics (TL). The term was first used by Coseriu (1955–56) and taken up by Weinrich (1967). But it was internationally pioneered by van Dijk (1972) and later developed by de Beaugrande (1980, 1984)—though van Dijk has, to some extent, recast TL as discourse analysis, thus departing fundamentally from the original TL project. That project owes much to the subdisciplines of poetics, stylistics, and narratology and is one of the many instances where discourse analysis shows its attachment to and development from formal literary interests. TL's goal is to be able to read off, for example, literary or 'social' effects from the strictly linguistic level of texts. TL analysts have, therefore, attempted to ask (at one extreme) 'what kind of speech act is a poem?' (Levin 1976) and (at the other) how phonological parallelism operates in the advertising of cheap motels (de Beaugrande 1985: 54–61). Thus, in its most formal mode, TL attaches itself to the logical/philosophical tradition of Searle and Austin and, in its most contextualized mode, it joins contemporary literary theory in becoming highly piecemeal in its conception of textual meaning. However, it should be remembered that even in this latter form, TL retains Harris's initial interest in fairly traditional analytic versions of language and can often be no more than formal linguistics applied to noninvented data.

Thus we find attempts to link intonation directly with semantics (Johns-Lewis 1986); analyses which attempt to read off discursive coherence at the morphological level (Dressler 1985); similar attempts to locate discursive cohesion at the lexical level (Petöfi 1985); re-readings of formal semantics in terms of discursive function (van Dijk and Kintsch 1983); and studies which use readers' protocols as the basis for analyzing discourse comprehension (Ericsson and Simon 1984). What is lacking from such studies is, however, a critical theory of discourse as social action. In its place there is a matching procedure between quite separate linguistic and discursive levels, with the linguistic construed in terms of well-tried formal concepts and the discursive in terms of suprasentential concepts such as coherence, cohesion, and function. At best, this work contributes to a micrological ethnography of how some actual texts may operate in specific settings. At worst, it is probably a misnomer to call it 'discourse analysis' at all; Brown and Yule (1983) being a case in point.

In this respect, even more peripheral uses of the term 'discourse' have occurred in other fields. For example, the term is frequently used in cognitive psychological analyses of text processing (Freedle 1977). Such studies are almost uniquely confined to psychological interests, subsuming discourse under a concept of text, and text under a traditional psychological conception of memory. Insofar as they assume doggedly consensus models of social interaction (if they refer to the social at all) and since they are more interested in cognitive processing than material practice, their use of the term 'discourse' is probably marginal to pragmatic conceptions of discourse. Indeed, Coulter (1983) has offered a thorough-going critique here, precisely in terms of psychological naivety about actual speech situations.

A few analysts who have been classed as social psychologists have, it is true, examined how social interaction is managed through discourse (Argyle 1969). But otherwise, because of their insistence on understanding 'discourse' in terms of individuated cognition and 'behavior,' social psychological approaches are as yet marginal to discourse analytic interests. When the central focus of analysis is on, for example, personality rather than social practice, it is probably true to say that one is not actually dealing with anything that most social scientists (including linguists) would recognize as discourse. It may be fascinating to find that personality (measured by standard technical indices) varies according to social contexts; or that social contexts are 'influenced' by the 'personalities' which contribute to them. But the fact that either is a function of the other would seem to promote a technical–correlational mode of analysis, essentially removed from both linguistic and sociopolitical relevances.

Moreover, very little psychological work on discourse has paid attention to the precise detail of actual materials, recorded in the field; rather it has preferred elicited 'responses' or completely contrived data (Edmonson 1981). Elicitation suggests quantification (Allen and Guy 1974) or controlled 'scientific' experimentation; while contriving data suggests that the object of analysis is a unitary single language rather than local domains of discourse. To examine discourse or discourses, as such, would seem to mean avoiding or negating both of these extremes.

4. The Empirical Approach

The 'empirical approach' largely consists of sociological forms of analysis which have taken 'discourse' to mean human conversation. Yet its object has been not merely the formal description of conversational 'texts' but also the commonsense knowledges at the basis of conversational rules and procedures. While several approaches could be dealt with in depth—for example the Birmingham school (Sinclair and Coulthard 1975)—arguably the most fruitful work to date has been accomplished in the area of conversation analysis (CA), pioneered by Sacks and based on the ethnomethodological approach to sociology of Garfinkel (1967) (see *Conversation Analysis*; *Sacks, Harvey*).

Garfinkel offers a critique of American structural functionalism, based as it is in the assumptions of Durkheim. Whereas Durkheim took pre-existing social facts to be sociology's proper object of inquiry, Garfinkel (1974) coined the term 'ethnomethodology' to refer to an interest in how social members (ethnos) rely upon a relatively stable corpus of general methods for the accomplishment of social facts. Although the approach stems from Schutz's (1962) insight—roughly, that social objects are preinterpreted by members and are therefore essentially different from natural objects—Garfinkel disagreed with Schutz as to how social objects are constituted. Schutz favored a phenomenological position, considering social action to be a function of consciousness and locating the bases of action in a set of anthropological constants (such as the assumption of the 'reciprocity of perspectives'); whereas Garfinkel preferred to think of social action as an entirely technical or methodic accomplishment on the part of social members, taking place audially and visually in actual, material circumstances.

On this basis, Sacks asked how conversations (as social objects) are accomplished by their participants via a set of relatively stable techniques. His seminal work, with his colleagues Schegloff and Jefferson (Sacks et al. 1974), on turn-taking and on correction (Schegloff et al. 1977) in conversation are the field's classics. While some commentators (Frawley 1987) have argued that Sacks's main motivation was to find 'deep' or underlying social competences in the form of cognitive rules, it is also possible to argue that, throughout his work, Sacks was devoted to an approach which begins with the analytic object itself. Thus most CA work begins with a corpus of materials, rather than theoreticist arguments about the mind, cognition, or human nature.

CA's typical materials consist of transcriptions of conversations which would have taken place in (and as) actual social settings, regardless of the analyst's interest in them. If, as Garfinkel argues, society is accomplished audio-visually (or 'scenically'), then videotapes and their transcripts will (at least to some degree) provide reliable representations of what goes on in (and as) society. The analytic point is then to find regular ways in which particular conversational phenomena are routinely accomplished—across a variety of occasions—by a meticulous inspection of conversational 'texts.' To this extent, CA may be thought of as a poetics of ordinary talk—one which is empirically rather than theoretically grounded.

At the sociological 'end' of things, CA is less interested in correlating official statistics on, say, suicide with other social variables (race, religion, ethnicity, gender, and so on) than in understanding, in this case, how persons routinely, in actual cases of interaction, represent the condition of, say, 'having no one to turn to' (Sacks 1967). Rather than collect statistics in classical Durkheimian mode, the conversation analyst would collect calls to counsellors and suicide prevention centers and inspect them (as Sacks did) for regular features—for example how callers refer to particular categories of social members (family, friends, professionals, etc.) in terms of the temporal ordering of their availability and candidature as 'someone to turn to,' such that not just any person can be turned to in just any sequence, thereby establishing the eventual category of 'having no one to turn to' as the product of highly organized social affairs. In this way, a sociological understanding of how practical discourses on suicide are accomplished can be built up. So rather than take suicide as a given social-structural phenomenon, CA looks instead at how practical social competences (methods) are able to produce effects (such as 'suicides') which are read, after the fact, by traditional sociology as structural. Yet, insofar as come CA does indeed try to locate general forms of conversational competence (while other CA work is entirely piecemeal and occasion-specific), it can sometimes be mistaken for a strictly formalist inquiry into discourse. Nevertheless, even a brief look at the history and development of the approach lends credence to the view that it is, in fact, empirically rather than formalistically motivated.

In its earliest forms, CA was interested in particular kinds of conversational sequence, and especially in the ways in which conversational utterances are accomplished in pairs such as QUESTION + ANSWER. In an early study of telephone calls, Schegloff (1968) showed how opening turns consist of specific paired slots such that, when a second pair-part is absent, both the caller and the person being called can hear that a structural requirement of phone calls has been breached and may be in need of repair. This interest in pairs led Schegloff and Sacks (1973) to investigate how conversational openings and closings are accomplished through collaborative work on paired turns by each participant. Accordingly, this interest in sequential requirements and options led CA to investigate conversational turn-taking rules generally (Sacks et al. 1974), and to ask how conversational repairs are carried out in terms of a structural preference for self- versus other-correction (Schegloff et al. 1977; for 'preference' see below).

Heritage (1984) gives a comprehensive account of the variety of topics analyzed in CA. He divides the field into six parts, each of which will be dealt with separately below.

Picking up on the work of Schegloff et al. (1977), analyses of 'preference organization' use the term 'preference' not in a psychological sense but in one which stresses the discursive and institutional aspects of certain types of utterance. Some sequences are routine or 'unmarked' (for example, OFFER + ACCEPTANCE); others can require delays, qualifications, or mitigations (for example, OFFER + REJECTION). The first types are referred to as 'preferreds'; the second as 'dispreferreds' (Levinson 1983).

A second development noted by Heritage is the analysis of topic organization. In particular a number of analyses have been made of how topics move across boundaries. Button and Casey (1982) have shown how topic boundaries are worked by participants, in distinct but cooperative ways. They suggest a set of 'boundary procedure types,' each with a different suitability for specific kinds of conversational environment. As Heritage notes, this aspect of CA is still under development but it may yet prove to be an alternative to traditional proposition-based approaches to topic (Brown and Yule 1983: 106–14).

The third development mentioned by Heritage is the analysis of nonlexical items: particularly 'response tokens' ('mm, hm,' 'oh,' and so on) and laughter. The first of these reflects CA's propensity to focus upon sequential aspects of ordinary talk: that is, there are relatively precise slots where response tokens may occur, for example at and around the termination points of turn-constructional units (points where a speaker's turn may come to an end—though speakers can indeed 'speak through' them). To this extent, response tokens are positioned at actual ends of turns, or else at audibly 'end-appropriate' slots within the turn (Schegloff 1982). The analysis of laughter shows how CA treats discourse in its particularity; no topic can be taken off the agenda, *a priori*, simply because it appears unimportant from standard linguistic or sociological points of view. Some psychologists have assumed that 'random laughter is obviously pathological' (Frawley 1987: 382), directly against Jefferson's (1985) CA-informed insistence that it is a sequential and far-from-random discursive event. Indeed, Jefferson's work has begun to show just how surprisingly consistent the sequential positioning of laughter in conversation can be. In this respect, CA can begin to claim that what some disciplines write off, preanalytically, as 'random' or 'pathological' are in fact organized social practices and outcomes, brought off publicly and materially by social members in collaborative ways.

Another move in CA has been towards the analysis of nonvocal aspects of discourse (gesture, gaze, etc.) in terms of their position within conversational organization as a whole. Goodwin (1981), for example, lays particular stress on how gaze operates both during (and as an integral part of) exchanges of speakership and hearership. It appears that requesting and achieving gazes and taking and exchanging turns can be highly related interactional activities.

A further extension of CA—and one which offers some possible connections with critical modes of discourse analysis—has been its move away from 'conversation' as such and towards other modes of discourse that occur within specific institutional settings such as schools (McHoul 1978) and courtrooms (Atkinson and Drew 1979). Unlike conversations, discourse in these locations has a somewhat more 'preallocated' character to its turn-taking procedures so that not all participants have identical rights and obligations to speak or listen. It is a matter of some conjecture as to whether this kind of analysis will stretch sufficiently to dovetail with critical discourse analyses of power. However, it appears to be the case that CA has something to offer more critical work in the sense that it can locate 'disparities' and 'inequities' with some analytic precision, in actual conversations, and without resort to mere theoretical speculation (Clegg 1975). For example: it does not require the assumption that 'power' is simply an inherent property of particular social roles or positions.

Finally, Heritage suggests that some work of the 1980s, such as Jefferson's (1980a, 1980b) on troubles talk, has moved CA away from its interest in specific conversational episodes and slots (turn-transition points, openings and closings, etc.) and towards the analysis of extended episodes of talk. In her analyses, Jefferson shows how the telling of troubles and anxieties is negotiated between participants in six stages: approach, announcement, exposition, 'work-up,' 'close implicature,' and exit. Whether this might lend microprecision to critical analyses of the 'confessional' (Foucault 1979)—a central social institution by which surveillance of the interiority of subjects is accomplished—is an exciting avenue for further research on the boundary between these two approaches to discourse.

In any case, Heritage's location of recent developments in CA suggests that it is becoming a much more extensive approach to discourse than is often assumed from a limited inspection of the classics on turn-taking and Q–A pairs (see above). And in this respect, a development Heritage does not describe is the growing body of CA-inspired analyses of written texts—fiction, newspaper articles, etc. (Chua 1979; Morrison 1981). Relatedly: while CA 'proper' continues to have a largely technical interest in the sequential accomplishment of linguistic–discursive features, quite a number of CA-trained analysts are now moving towards the possibility of using CA's undoubted analytic precision to support (or indeed reject) more speculative but politically committed moves in other branches of institutional discourse analysis.

Emmison (1989), for example, has looked at how CA might shed light upon the authenticity of a 'conversation' which was in doubt during a major trial: where a suspect may (or may not) have been framed by the police on the basis of a taped talk between an officer and an informant. Hartland (1989) has analyzed trial transcripts as discursive events produced by and for pro-state procedures. He speculates on the idea that what traditional sociologists refer to as 'the state' may itself be produced, literally, in and by such discursive events, and that CA may therefore have something to offer critical theories and analyses of the state. McHoul (1986) has applied CA to the analysis of a university lecture as a highly localized contribution to the policing and enforcement of dominant modes of sexual morality and training. In addition, Smith (1987) has used ethnomethodological and CA insights into discursive practices (in conjunction with other sociological approaches) to generate a unique methodology for feminist sociology.

In such ways, CA, while remaining committed to actual rather than invented materials, and while insisting on analytic precision rather than ungrounded theorizations of discourse, is already beginning to extend its boundaries. While it already overlaps formal-linguistic approaches to discourse, it is now coming, albeit slowly, to some preliminary points of contact with critical approaches. It is to the latter that we now turn.

5. The Critical Approach

As noted above, continental discourse theorists such as Foucault, Lyotard, Donzelot, Pêcheux, and De Certeau tend to use the term 'discourse' to refer to relatively well-bounded areas of social knowledge. So, at any given historical conjuncture, it is only possible to write, speak, or think about a given social object (madness, for example) in specific ways and not others. '*A* discourse' would then be whatever constrains—but also enables—writing, speaking, and thinking within such specific historical limits. Thus while a discourse can be thought of as linguistic in one sense, it also has to be treated in terms of the conditions of possibility of knowing a specific social object.

This type of 'discourse theory' may be less well-known in Anglophone linguistics circles than formal and empirical approaches. It originated in continental, largely French, philosophical traditions and has its most cogent application (not in relation to language systems but) in relation to the history of ideas O'Sullivan et al. (1983: 72–3) argue that it originated with the early structuralists' opposition to 'inherited habits of thought and analysis' which assumed that social and cultural 'objects' existed in the 'real world.' The structuralists tried to show that, on the contrary, these objects exist only 'as products, not sources, of ... signification.' But this structuralist and eventually poststructuralist position on discourse does not mean that 'anything goes,' that we can make the world into anything we want simply by speaking, writing, or thinking in a certain way (cf. Macdonell 1986). On the contrary, it is intended as a critique of individualism and idealism. For what an individual, a group, or a society as a whole, can imagine (let alone put into practice) is both permitted and constrained by the discursive possibilities at its disposal.

As Wittgenstein (1968) put it, 'to imagine a language means to imagine a form of life.' Thus 'the world' and our consciousness of it are discursive products; but, at the same time, discourse is a material condition which enables and constrains the socially productive 'imagination.' These conditions can therefore be referred to as 'discourses' or 'discursive conditions of possibility.' Moreover, as Voloshinov (1973) first showed, such discourses can come into contention and struggle. And this would include analytic discourses themselves; leaving them with (not so much a 'methodological' problem as) a problem of intervention and strategy.

Examples of this kind of interventional critical discourse analysis are to be found in the work of the anthropologist Eric Michaels (e.g., 1987) and the coproductions of Australian Aborigines with discourse analysts (e.g., Benterrak et al. 1984) which owe as much to contemporary literary theory as they do to poststructuralist discourse theory. At the same time, such interventions cannot afford to neglect a firm theoretical basis and it is to this that we now turn by looking at how Foucault characterized the 'components' of discourse. The focus here is on Foucault's (see *Foucault, Michel*) own contribution to discourse theory, neglecting the many offshoots and applications of his work in such fields as the history of statistics (Hacking 1981, 1982), the family (Donzelot 1980), legal discourse (Wickham 1987), literary discourse (Williamson 1989), feminism (de Lauretis 1984), photography (Tagg 1988), the body (Turner 1984), and pedagogy (Luke 1989).

Foucault has argued that formal and empirical approaches have tended to work on the side of the enunciation (*énonciation*) of discourse. Such a narrow focus can only include the surface of language use, the ways and means by which concepts and meanings are spoken or written. In place of this emphasis, Foucault (1972) proposes to look at discourse*s* at the level of the enounced (*énoncé*) or, as his translators put it, the 'statement.' Rethinking his own earlier work (Foucault 1970) on the historical emergence of the discourses on life, labor, and language (eventually, biology, economics, and general linguistics), Foucault (1972: 80) considers his failure to specify the terms 'discourse' and 'statement':

> ... instead of gradually reducing the rather fluctuating meaning of the word 'discourse,' I believe that I have in fact added to its meanings: treating it sometimes as the general domain of all statements, sometimes as an individualizable group of statements, and sometimes as a regulated practice that accounts for a certain number of statements; and have I not allowed this same word 'discourse,' which should have served as a boundary around the term 'statement,' to vary as I shifted my analysis or its point of application, as the statement itself faded from view?

In order to clear up the confusion, Foucault asks whether it is possible to think of the statement as a unit of (a) discourse. If so, it is then necessary to ask what kind of unit it is. For example, could it be the same as a proposition, a sentence or a speech act? Let us take these in order.

A statement cannot be identical with a proposition. To cite Foucault's (1972: 81) own example, 'No one heard' and 'It is true that no one heard' have identical propositional contents but may constitute two different statements. If each were to occur as the first line of a novel, he goes on, they would involve different orders of narration. The first might be 'an observation made either by the author, or by a character' while the second 'can only be in a group of statements constituting an interior monologue, a silent discussion with oneself, or a fragment of dialogue, a group of questions or answers' (1972: 81). Thus, Foucault's first criterion for a statement is that it should be responsive to what Pêcheux (1975) calls 'functioning.' Propositional content is, at least traditionally, thought to transcend local specifics of usage. Unlike propositions, statements—as components of discursive formations—have to be thought of primarily as functional units.

A statement cannot be identical with a sentence. This is not simply because truncated 'sentences'—such as 'Absolutely!'—can carry the force of statements. This objection would be trivial since even formalist approaches acknowledge that such truncations can count as sentences. Further: since the sentence itself is so poorly defined, it will never be possible to pronounce decisively on its equivalence or otherwise with the statement. However, it is possible to say that certain word groupings which are clearly not sentences do carry the force of statements. Foucault's (1972: 82) example is the paradigm of the verb *amare*: *amo, amas, amat*.... This is a 'statement of the different personal inflections of the ... verb.' Thus classificatory schema, tables, taxonomies, etc., though rarely expressed in sentential form, can carry the force of statements. And more importantly, perhaps, they show clearly how coherent groupings of statements (discursive formations) act as constraints upon, and enablers of, specific knowledges. Just as the statement is not propositional, neither is it characterized by its grammatical form, for expressions which do not use verbal language may count as statements: 'a graph, a growth curve, an age pyramid, a distribution cloud...' (1972: 82) may all be statements but have no clear grammatical form unless one is to stretch the term 'grammar' into metaphorical domains beyond its normal confines.

A statement cannot be identical with a speech act. This is because some but not all speech acts require more than a single statement in order to be 'felicitous' (Austin 1975). Hence, 'empirical' equivalences between (some) speech acts and (some) statements are merely coincidental. Speech act theorists may see equivalence between the utterance 'I promise' (said as a proposal of marriage within the discourse of medieval romance) and 'I promise' (said by a character in a modern soap opera as an agreement to meet for lunch). But each is a different statement, being located within totally different social 'technologies' and historically formed discursive practices. Each produces individual human subjects or 'actors' in distinct ways. Each (re)creates and maintains different sociopolitical institutions.

Thus a statement is not strictly a unit at all in the sense that the proposition, the sentence, and the speech act are. Instead, it is a 'function that operates vertically in relation to these various units, and which enables one to say of a series of signs whether or not they are present in it' (Foucault 1972: 86). It is 'not itself a unit, but a function that cuts across a domain of structures and possible unities, and which reveals them, with concrete contents, in time and space' (1972: 87). Therefore, statements are best understood in terms of the rules which govern their functioning.

But these rules are no longer susceptible to a general theory of language. Statements and their rules are neither purely linguistic nor purely material but exist in, and as, the nexus between these two domains. In order to analyze or describe rules, one must always turn to specific historical conditions of usage—to the piecemeal, the local, and the contingent. For events, no matter how specific, cannot happen just anyhow. They must happen according to certain constraints, rules, or conditions of possibility; according, that is, to 'power relations' in Foucault's sense.

For Foucault, 'power' is not equivalent to traditional sociopolitical concepts which go by the same name, since it is never devoid of discourse. Discourse is not a mere effect or end-product of a prediscursive 'power.' In this sense, power is not 'owned' by some privileged group and exercised 'simply as an obligation or a prohibition on those who "do not have it"' (Foucault 1977: 27).

> Power is everywhere; not because it embraces everything but because it comes from everywhere.... Power comes from below; that is there is no binary and all-encompassing opposition between ruler and ruled at the root of power relations, and serving as a general matrix—no such duality extending from the top down and reacting on more and more limited groups to the very depths of the social body. One must suppose rather that the manifold relations of force that take shape and come into play in the machinery of production, in families, limited groups and institutions, are the basis for wide-ranging effects of cleavage that run through the social body as a whole.
> (Foucault 1979: 93–4)

Yet, as Eco (1986: 244) has it, this radically diversified conception of power is by no means 'unlinguistic.' Power and discourse not only constitute one another reflexively but also:

> [Foucault's]... image of power closely recalls the idea of the system that linguists call *the given language*. The given language is, true, coercive (it forbids me to say 'I are him,' under pain of being incomprehensible), but its coercion doesn't derive from an individual decision, or from some center that sends out rules in all directions: It is a social product, it originates as a constrictive apparatus precisely through general assent.... I'm not sure we can say that a given language is a device of power... but it is surely a model of power.
> (Italics added)

Thus the linguistic system (the '*langue*') is not the sovereign source of discourses which are its mere effects. On the contrary, the linguistic system is just one instance (or 'model') of power considered as a diverse, piecemeal, local, and pragmatic/discursive set of relations of force. Hence, methodologically speaking, these relations cannot be known in advance from some grand theoretical 'prediction.' Only determinate (archaeological) investigations can specify them. And possibly, as Hunter (1988) has pointed out, even the *Archaeology of Knowledge* may already be too generalist in this respect.

Returning to statements then: they are best approached not as single items but in terms of the systems or 'archives' of which they form a part. Hence what can be said or not said about a specific 'object' is neither absolutely fixed, nor is it open to complete indeterminacy in any actual case. For:

> the archive... determines that all these things said do not accumulate endlessly in an amorphous mass, nor are they inscribed in an unbroken linearity, nor do they disappear at the mercy of chance external accidents; but they are grouped together in distinct figures, composed together in accordance with multiple relations, maintained or blurred in accordance with specific regularities.
> (Foucault 1972: 128)

Effectively then, the statement is a sociohistorical function rather than a strictly linguistic one. Yet (and this is probably Foucault's contribution to the neolinguistic study of discourse) the statement can still be located in talk and texts, thereby allowing us a method of working from 'empirical' statement to 'systemic' archive and thence to a sense of the double uniqueness-and-continuity of social histories of thought, knowledge, and power. In an interview, Foucault (1981) called this method of tracing the systematic (archival) properties of piecemeal and local affairs 'eventalization'—the heuristic of turning either documents or 'grand' historical movements into concrete events. It is no accident, then, that he refers to the archive as 'the very root of the statement-event' (1972: 129).

However, the concept of the discursive archive cannot be a simple replacement for concepts like 'system,' *langue* and so on. Rather, analyses of an archive as a condition of enunciation, or of its stable system of functioning (at specific conjunctures), must be taken hand-in-hand with analyses of its historical flux, of 'the general system of the formation and transformation of statements' (1972: 130). In this sense 'archive' is a much more mobile and fluid term than the relatively fixed concept of 'episteme,' used in the earlier *Order of Things* (1970). The concept 'deprives us of our continuities' (1972: 131) and establishes the fact that human subjects are not firm and discrete (id)entities but are fragmented and changing sites across which the play of difference moves. The archive, more radically, 'establishes that we are difference, that our reason is the difference of discourses, our history the history of difference, ourselves the difference of masks' (1972: 131)—a position which Goffmanians (see *Goffman, Erving*) will readily identify with. The discipline which describes that radical formation of individual and historical subjectivity, Foucault (1972; 131) calls 'archaeology.' As an example of it, we could turn to his and his students' analyses of the case of Pierre Rivière (Foucault 1978).

One way in which Foucauldian discourse analysis is critical is that it describes how social scientific and other disciplinary discourses repress more marginal, less dominant, forms of knowledge. In *I, Pierre Rivière ...* (1978), Foucault and his co-workers reproduce many of the original documents pertaining to the case of a multiple murderer caught in the contradictions between two official discourses on punishment, roughly those of the eighteenth and nineteenth centuries. Thus they are able to analyze a specific conjucture (via its archival trace) in which one system of statements on punishment comes to replace another. The earlier system is corporeal, involving as it does overt and ritualistic public punishment of individual bodies. The later one tries to control populations (rather than bodies). And it does this in a very different way: by putting them under constant watch, under a scientifically justified and controlled gaze. The first involves punishment by spectacle (public hangings, for example); the second involves punishment by surveillance, typified in Jeremy Bentham's panoptic prison designs (see Foucault 1977). Moreover, it should be noted as a methodological point that, in analyzing this particular case, Foucault shows the interrelations between at least two adjacent fields of discourse: the first comprising statements (events of punishment inscribed on bodies), the second comprising official discourses whose statements construct and circulate around acts of justice. These are two 'large groups of statements' (1972: 37) or discursive formations; but, as Foucault has pointed out elsewhere (1971), statements do not overdetermine the discursive formations which they form. Instead, discourses are regulated by 'adjacent fields' and practices. Hence any actual event (such as the Rivière case) requires an analysis in terms of adjacency; and hence the doubling of the discursive field in this case.

Rivière is trapped between the two; between the new public and panoptic discourse on punishment, and the old mode of spectacular retribution. The courts cannot decide whether to 'make an example' of him, after the moral techniques of the eighteenth century or whether to be 'humane' and condemn him to a life of continual surveillance. There was an effective crisis, at the time, over what was to count as the official discourse on punishment. The emergent scientific discourses of medicine and protopsychiatry had the same problems: did the theoretical object called 'monomania' actually exist? And if so, to what extent could its existence 'excuse' a multiple murder by replacing the individual with a 'disease' as the responsible agent? Likewise, as Foucault shows, popular discourses (such as journalism) were equally at odds over the issue, showing how discourses in adjacent fields can coincide to give the effect of collusion or conspiracy where none exists. Insofar as Rivière is caught between these two moments of official (and popular) dispute on the best course of punishment, his own account is continually pressed back into the margins and cannot be heard in the open space of official discourse.

The problem then for the social sciences (for law, medicine, etc.) is to know how to treat, in both senses, Rivière's remarkable personal memoir of the murders. Because scientific discourses seek to 'explain' crime, the criminal's own discourse is reduced (by, for example, criminology) to the same status as the criminal conduct to be explained. It becomes, for example, a confession. And so it is interesting to trace Foucault's own discursive strategies in the Rivière text; because, for Foucault, to repeat a practice uncritically is to support it—and it would therefore seem contradictory were he to side with the disciplinary techniques of law, criminology, pathology, etc. For example, in his debate with the Maoists, recorded in *Power/Knowledge* (1980), Foucault argues that the strategy of setting up a court to try the police for their crimes constitutes merely a repetition of bourgeois forms of justice. The point is that a technique, whatever its 'content' or the class polarity of its content, is a bearer of power in itself. Critique consists in ceasing; in ceasing to repeat the scientific/official technique.

Clearly then, Foucault's treatment of the Rivière texts is not an 'analysis' in any sense that traditional linguistics could recognize. It shows rather than says how the operations of power worked at a particularly contradictory site. For to say those operations, even in the guise of a technical/analytic discourse, would be to continue to repress the alternative and marginal construction(s) of the murder (and the events prior to and after it) provided by Rivière himself. An upshot for critical/interventional discourse analysis might therefore be framed in terms of the following question: how can discourse analysis provide a place for the mad, the imprisoned, the marginalized, the cultural and political 'other' to speak or write without the appropriation of 'their' discourse by translation into the terms of apparently neutral (but in fact highly repressive) scientific/analytic discourses—including the discourses of formal linguistics and sociology?

To take just one case: what is the point of Labov (1982) saying, analytically, how the logic of 'non-standard' black English works—morphologically and syntactically—using the language of the academy, when, all along, the 'non-standard' discourse, by definition, has no clearly sanctioned possibility of being heard or written in the academy as an equal and alternative discourse? If discourse analysis is to be involved in political struggles—that is, in changing rather than simply describing social conditions of possibility—it may have to face the fact that the 'disciplines of discourse,' as van Dijk (1985b) calls them, are, at the beginning of the twenty-first century, no more than discourses of discipline—armatures of dominant modes of social power. (At least, a discourse-theoretical investigation of much contemporary discourse analysis might show that, in a disciplinary sense, discourse analysis *is* official discourse, Burton and Carlen 1979.) A radical rethinking of the distinction between theory and practice, or between commentary and text, would appear to be a major priority in discourse analysis. The first domain (theory/commentary) would have to consider itself in terms other than those of mere analytic accuracy or scientific coherence and validity—thus using its insights into (supposedly) 'actual' discursive processes in order to facilitate discursive spaces for the second domain (practice/text) to be able to speak and write in, and on, its own terms.

See also: Power and Language; Discourse in Cross-linguistic and Cross-cultural Contexts; Ideology.

Bibliography

Abercrombie N, Hill S, Turner B S 1984 *The Penguin Dictionary of Sociology*. Penguin, Harmondsworth, UK
Allen D E, Guy R F 1974 *Conversation Analysis: The Sociology of Talk*. Mouton, The Hague
Anderson D C 1978 Some organizational features in the local production of a plausible text. *Philosophy of the Social Sciences* 8: 113–35
Argyle M 1969 *Social Interaction*. Methuen, London
Atkinson J M, Drew P 1979 *Order in Court: The Organisation of Verbal Interaction in Judicial Settings*. Macmillan, London
Austin J L 1975 *How to do Things with Words*, 2nd edn. Oxford University Press, Oxford, UK
Barthes R 1967 *Elements of Semiology*. Cape, London
Bauman R, Sherzer J (eds.) 1974 *Explorations in the Ethnography of Speaking*. Cambridge University Press, London
Benterrak K, Muecke S, Roe P 1984 *Reading the Country: Introduction to Nomadology*. Fremantle Arts Centre Press, Fremantle, Australia
Brown G, Yule G 1983 *Discourse Analysis*. Cambridge University Press, Cambridge, UK
Burton F, Carlen P 1979 *Official Discourse: On Discourse Analysis, Government Publications, Ideology, and the State*. Routledge and Kegan Paul, London
Button G, Casey N 1982 Topic nomination and topic pursuit (Unpublished manuscript, Plymouth Polytechnic)
Chua B-H 1979 Democracy as textual accomplishment. *Sociological Quarterly* 20: 541–9
Clegg S 1975 *Power Rule and Domination: A Critical and Empirical Understanding of Power in Sociological Theory and Organizational Life*. Routledge and Kegan Paul, London
Coseriu E 1955–56 Determinación y entorno. *Romanisches Jahrbuch* 7: 29–54
Coulter J 1983 *Rethinking Cognitive Theory*. Macmillan, London
de Beaugrande R 1980 *Text, Discourse, and Process*. Longman, London
de Beaugrande R 1984 *Text Production*. Ablex, Norwood, NJ
de Beaugrande R 1985 Text linguistics in discourse studies. In: van Dijk T A (ed.) *Handbook of Discourse Analysis. Vol. 1: Disciplines of Discourse*. Academic Press, London
de Lauretis T 1984 *Alice Doesn't: Feminism, Semiotics, Cinema*. Indiana University Press, Bloomington, IN
Donzelot J 1980 *The Policing of Families*. Hutchinson, London
Dressler W U 1985 Morphology. In: van Dijk T A (ed.) *Handbook of Discourse Analysis. Vol. 2: Dimensions of Discourse*. Academic Press, London
Eco U 1986 *Travels in Hyper-reality: Essays*. Harcourt Brace Jovanovich, San Diego, CA
Edmonson W 1981 *Spoken Discourse: A Model for Analysis*. Longman, London
Emmison M 1989 A conversation on trial?: The case of the Ananda Marga conspiracy tapes. *Journal of Pragmatics* 13: 363–80
Ericsson K A, Simon H A 1984 *Protocol Analysis*. MIT Press, Cambridge, MA
Fairclough N 1989 *Language and Power*. Longman, London
Foucault M 1970 *The Order of Things: An Archaeology of the Human Sciences*. Tavistock, London
Foucault M 1971 Orders of discourse: Inaugural lecture delivered at the Collège de France. *Social Science Information* 10(2): 7–30
Foucault M 1972 *The Archaeology of Knowledge*. Tavistock, London
Foucault M 1977 *Discipline and Punish: The Birth of the Prison*. Allen Lane, London
Foucault M (ed.) 1978 *I, Pierre Rivière Having Slaughtered My Mother, My Sister, and My Brother... A Case of Paricide in the 19th Century*. Peregrine, London
Foucault M 1979 *The History of Sexuality. Vol. 1: An Introduction*. Allen Lane, London
Foucault M 1980 *Power/Knowledge: Selected Interviews and Other Writings 1972–77*. Harvester Press, London
Foucault M 1981 Questions of method: An interview. *Ideology and Consciousness* 8: 3–14
Frawley W 1987 Review article on van Dijk 1985. *Language* 63: 361–97
Freedle R O (ed.) 1977 *Discourse Production and Comprehension*. Ablex, Norwood, NJ
Frow J 1986 *Marxism and Literary History*. Blackwell, Oxford, UK
Garfinkel H 1967 *Studies in Ethnomethodology*. Prentice-Hall, Englewood Cliffs, NJ
Garfinkel H 1974 The origins of the term 'ethnomethodology.' In: Turner R (ed.) *Ethnomethodology: Selected Readings*. Penguin, Harmondsworth, UK
Giglioli P P (ed.) 1982 *Language and Social Context*. Penguin, Harmondsworth, UK
Goodwin C 1981 *Conversational Organization Interaction Between Speakers and Hearers*. Academic Press, New York
Grice H P 1975 Logic and conversation. In: Cole P, Morgan J (eds.) *Syntax and Semantics*. Academic Press, New York, Vol. 3
Gumperz J D, Hymes D (eds.) 1972 *Directions in Sociolinguistics: The Ethnography of Communication*. Holt, Rinehart and Winston, New York
Hacking I 1981 How should we do the history of statistics? *Ideology and Consciousness* 8: 15–26

Hacking I 1982 Bio-power and the avalanche of printed numbers. *Humanities in Society* **5**: 279–95

Halliday M A K 1973 *Explorations in the Functions of Language*. Arnold, London

Harris Z S 1952 Discourse analysis. *Langauge* **28**: 1–30

Hartland N 1989 The power of paper. *Journal of Pragmatics* **13**: 395–405

Heritage J 1984 Recent developments in conversation analysis. *Warwick Working Papers in Sociology* **1**: .1–36

Hodge B 1984 Historical semantics and the meanings of 'discourse.' *Australian Journal of Cultural Studies* **2**(2): 124–30

Hodge B, Kress G 1988 *Social Semiotics*. Polity Press, Cambridge, UK

Hunter I 1988 From discourse to *dispositif*: Foucault and the study of literature (Unpublished manuscript. Griffith University)

Jefferson G 1980a *Final Report to the SSRC on the Analysis of Conversations in which 'Troubles' and 'Anxieties' are Expressed*. Social Science Research Council, London

Jefferson G 1980b On 'trouble-premonitory' response to inquiry. *Sociological Inquiry* **50**: 153–85

Jefferson G 1985 An exercise in the transcription and analysis of laughter. In: van Dijk T A (ed.) *Handbook of Discourse Analysis. Vol. 3: Discourse and Dialogue*. Academic Press, London

Johns-Lewis C (ed.) 1986 *Intonation in Discourse*. Croom Helm, London

Labov W 1982 The logic of nonstandard English. In: Giglioli P P (ed.) *Language and Social Context*. Penguin, Harmondsworth, UK

Levin S R 1976 Concerning what kind of speech act a poem is. In: van Dijk T A (ed.) *Pragmatics of Language and Literature*. North-Holland, Amsterdam

Levinson S C 1983 *Pragmatics*. Cambridge University Press, Cambridge, UK

Luke C 1989 *Pedagogy, Printing and Protestantism: The Discourse on Childhood*. State University of New York Press, Albany, NY

Macdonell D 1986 *Theories of Discourse: An Introduction*. Blackwell, Oxford, UK

McHoul A W 1978 The organisation of turns at formal talk in the classroom. *Language of Society* **7**: 183–213

McHoul A W 1986 The getting of sexuality: Foucault, Garfinkel and the analysis of sexual discourse. *Theory, Culture and Society* **3**: 65–79

McHoul A W, Luke A 1989 Discourse as language and politics: An introduction to the philology of political culture in Australia. *Journal of Pragmatics* **13**: 323–32

Mey J 1985 *Whose Language?: A Study in Linguistic Pragmatics*. Benjamins, Amsterdam

Michaels E 1987 *For a cultural Future: Francis Jupurrurla Makes TV at Yuendumu*. Artspace, Melbourne

Mitchell T F 1957 The language of buying and selling in Cyrenaica. *Hesperis* **44**: 31–71

Morrison K L 1981 Some properties of 'telling-order designs' in didactic inquiry. *Philosophy of the Social Sciences* **11**: 245–62

O'Sullivan T, Hartley J, Saunders D, Fiske J 1983 *Key Concepts in Communication*. Methuen, London

Pêcheux M 1975 Analyse du discours, langue et idéologies. *Languages* **37**: whole issue

Petöfi J S 1985 Lexicon. In: van Dijk T A (ed.) *Handbook of Discourse Analysis. Vol. 2: Dimensions of Discourse*. Academic Press, London

Pike K L 1967 *Language in Relation to a Unified Theory of the Structure of Human Behavior*. Mouton, The Hague

Propp V 1958 *Morphology of the Folktale*. Indiana University Press, Bloomington, IN

Sacks H 1967 The search for help: No one to turn to. In: Shneidman E (ed.) *Essays in Self-destruction*. Science House, New York

Sacks H, Schegloff E A, Jefferson G 1974 A simplest systematics for the organization of turn-taking for conversation. *Langauge* **50**: 696–735

Schank R C 1975 *Fundamental Studies in Computer Science. Vol. 3: Conceptual Information Processing*. North-Holland, Amsterdam

Schegloff E A 1968 Sequencing in conversational openings. *American Anthropologist* **70**: 1075–95

Schegloff E A 1982 Discourse as an interactional achievement: Some uses of 'uh huh' and other things that come between sentences. In: Tannen D (ed.) *Analyzing Discourse: Text and Talk*, Georgetown University Round Table on Languages and Linguistics 1981. Georgetown University Press, Washington, DC

Schegloff E A, Jefferson G, Sacks H 1977 The preference for self-correction in the organization of repair in conversation. *Language* **53**: 361–82

Schegloff E A, Sacks H 1973 Opening up closings. *Semiotica* **7**: 289–327

Schenkein J N 1979 The radio raiders story. In: Psathas G (ed.) *Everyday Language: Studies in Ethnomethodology*. Irvington, New York

Schenkein J N (ed.) 1978 *Studies in the Organization of Conversational Interaction*. Academic Press, New York

Schutz A 1962 *Collected Papers. Vol. 1: The Problem of Social Reality*. Nijhoff, The Hague

Searle J R, Kiefer F, Bierwisch M (eds.) 1980 *Speech Act Theory and Pragmatics*. Reidel, Dordrecht, The Netherlands

Sinclair J, Coulthard M 1975 *Towards an Analysis of Discourse: The English Used by Teachers and Pupils*. Oxford University Press, Oxford, UK

Smith D 1987 *The Everyday World as Problematic: A Feminist Sociology*. Toronto University Press, Toronto, ON

Spender D 1980 *Man-Made Language*. Routledge and Kegan Paul, London

Stalpers J 1988 The maturity of discourse analysis. *Langauge in Society* **17**: 87–97

Tagg J 1988 *The Burden of Representation*. Macmillan, London

Threadgold T 1988 Language and gender. *Australian Feminist Studies* **6**: 41–70

Turner B S 1984 *The Body and Society: Explorations in Social Theory*. Blackwell, Oxford, UK

van Dijk T A 1972 *Some Aspects of Text Grammars*. Mouton, The Hague

van Dijk T A 1985a Introduction: Discourse analysis as a new cross-discipline. In: van Dijk T A (ed.) *Handbook of Discourse Analysis. Vol. 1: Disciplines of Discourse*. Academic Press, London

van Dijk T A (ed.). 1985b *Handbook of Discourse Analysis. Vol. 1: Disciplines of Discourse.* Academic Press, London
van Dijk T A, Kintsch W 1983 *Strategies of Discourse Comprehension.* Academic Press, New York
Voloshinov V N 1973 *Marxism and the Philosophy of Language.* Seminar Press, New York
Weinrich H 1967 Syntax als Dialektik. *Poetica* **1**: 109–26
Wickham G (ed.) 1987 *Social Theory and Legal Politics.* Local Consumption Publications, Sydney
Williamson D 1989 *Authorship and Criticism.* Local Consumption Publications, Sydney
Wittgenstein L 1968 *Philosophical Investigations.* Blackwell, Oxford, UK

Discourse in Cross-linguistic and Cross-cultural Contexts
M. Clyne

This article first differentiates between three types of cross-linguistic and cross-cultural situations. It then concentrates on communication between people with different first languages sharing one language which is their second or later language. The study of such communication is located within the discipline of linguistics. The main issues of research in this area are enumerated and the theoretical and practical value of such research and the methodology employed are discussed. An attempt is made to explore the role of underlying cultural value systems in determining cultural differences in communication patterns.

1. The Field

The term 'discourse' is used here to refer to continuous passages, whether oral or written, which extend beyond the sentence level.

Because of migration patterns, opportunities for travel, international teamwork projects, and greatly improved communication technologies, communication between people of different ethnolinguistic and cultural backgrounds is commonplace. Such communication may be between:

(a) people sharing two or more languages;
(b) people with different first languages sharing one language which is a second or later language for some or all of them;
(c) people not sharing any language or with both (all) having only a limited competence in a shared language.

In case (a), the context may be one such as a migration (or colonial) situation in which one language is replacing another. This situation will usually be characterized by the transference of rules, features, and meanings from L2 (the second language) to the original L1 (first language). For instance, Italian speakers in Australia will transfer the meaning of English 'factory' to similar-sounding *fattoria*, originally meaning 'farm' ('semantic transference'), and integrate English 'farm' into Italian (make it part of the Italian system) as *farma* (phonologically integrated 'lexical transfer'). Some Dutch–English bilinguals in Australia generalize the SVO (subject–verb–object) word order as in English so that:

Maar als wij *praten* in het Hollands, *ze verstaan* drommels goed.
(But when we speak in Dutch, they understand damned well.)
replaces
Maar als wij in het Hollands *praten, verstaan ze* drommels goed
('Syntactic transference')

Communication in bilingual situations will also often be marked by 'code-switching.' A switch from one language to the other will be conditioned by a change of interlocutor or silent participant, a change of venue, a different role relationship with the interlocutor, a shift in domain (e.g., from home to work or school) or a variation in type of interaction (e.g., serious business to joke). It may be due to stylistic considerations, such as the inability to express something in as idiomatically adequate a way in the other language or the switch may become a symbolic part of the message, e.g., it may signal membership of the in-group.

In the bilingual discourse that develops in many immigrant families, where parents use L1 and the children respond in L2, where L2 = the national language of the immigration country, key words from either language will be inserted in discourse in the other language:

Parent: Wenn du allein gehst.
   (if you are going on your own.)
Child: But I'm not going *allein*.

In case (c) above, simplification will occur where both speakers have only a limited proficiency in the target language. This can lead to the use of a pidgin (e.g., Tok Pisin in New Guinea) in contact between speakers of more than two different languages. In contact situations between native and non-native speakers, the former may employ a simplified register known as 'foreigner' talk (see *Foreigner Talk*). Nonverbal means of expression (e.g., gestures) will usually be employed to replace or supplement verbal ones even more than occurs between speakers with full competence in a common language. Like all communication rules, gestures will also vary in meaning and interpretation between cultures.

In case (b), people will generally transfer to their L2 discourse, communicative behavior and expectations from their first language and culture. This situation will provide the main focus of the present article.

The extension of the 'linguistic model' from purely grammatical considerations to include the social setting (e.g., in the works of Labov, Hymes, Gumperz) and to recognize variation as central has made it possible for wider issues of communication to be included in 'mainstream linguistics.' Four linguistic traditions have contributed particularly to the study of intercultural communication—ethnography of communication, linguistic pragmatics, discourse analysis, and conversational analysis. Also, some studies on cross-cultural discourse analysis involving cultures in developing nations have employed the tagmemics framework.

There are a number of ways in which discourse in cross-cultural contexts is examined. One is for speech acts, such as requests, complaints, and apologies, to be taken out of the discourse framework and their realization by mother-tongue speakers of different languages contrasted. An instance of such a project is the Cross-Cultural Speech Act Realization Project contrasting Australian English, Argentinian Spanish, Canadian French, German, and Israeli Hebrew (reported in Blum-Kulka et al. 1989; see also *Pragmatics and Sociolinguistics*). Another approach is to focus on the pragmatic rules of acquirers of a second (or later) language whose interlanguage contains instances of L1 interference, simplification, overcomplexity, hypercorrection, and overgeneralization (see Blum-Kulka and Kasper 1994). These two approaches sometimes overlap. The investigation of culture-specific rhetorical/textual patterns is conducted either in a contrastive framework or as an interlanguage analysis. In the kind of interactive situations which are being discussed in this article, the boundaries between pragmatic and discourse areas are fuzzy.

2. The Issues

People from kindred cultures (but not necessarily with the same L1 or from related L1 backgrounds) are likely to share expectations and patterns of communication. This is partly due to conversational inferences (deductions made about the intended meaning) being influenced by socio-cultural knowledge. The Vietnamese worker who, when asked by her Austrian superordinate at the start of a workplace communication in an Australian factory shortly before Easter: 'You have five days off. What are you going to do?' inferred that she was going to be laid off, was not able to make the right sociocultural connections. Where communicative expectations and patterns are not shared, experience or training can make people conscious of the range of communicative behavior and understand hidden implications. Without this knowledge a mismatch between communicative intention and communicative effect may lead to a communication breakdown. This can take the form of 'noncommunication,' where neither the intended message nor any other message is conveyed, or 'miscommunication,' where an unintended message is conveyed. The latter is more serious insofar as it can pass unnoticed by either party, thereby exacerbating ethnic and racial stereotypes and causing communication conflict in which dignity and trust are threatened. Miscommunication will not only be due to a lack of shared expectations and behavior. An anticipation of culture-specific communicative behavior may be inappropriate where interlocutors have adapted their communication patterns to those of the other group. This expectation of stereotypical patterns can lead to misinterpretation. In some cases, a clash between communicative behaviors can lead to communication conflict and friction between the parties.

Research has, until the early 1990s, been based largely on contrasts between the pragmatic rules (rules for performing speech acts, such as apologies, complaints, compliments, promises, requests) of English (British, American, or Australian) and those of a small number of other languages/cultures—German, Japanese, Polish, Hebrew, Spanish (see, for example, Blum-Kulka et al. 1989, Olesky 1989). A theoretical basis has yet to be firmly established. Some of the discussion is still anecdotal.

The main issues that have been raised are covered in the following sections.

2.1 Intercultural Variation in the Performance of Speech Acts

These are notably requests, complaints, and, to a lesser extent, apologies, promises, and greetings, and opening and closing routines. The following attempt at a typology starts with the seemingly most trivial whose absence or culturally inappropriate use can cause communication conflict as well as communication breakdown because they involve politeness and face. Contrasting formulaic routines include:

(a) The absence or presence of a rule—e.g., 'good appetite' or 'I am eating' said to mark the beginning of a meal. (The failure to observe this routine may be regarded as impolite by continental Europeans, Chinese, and Indonesians.)

(b) Formulas of completely different structures to perform a speech act—English 'excuse me' or Central European 'goodbye' for leave-taking at a restaurant table.
(c) Formulas of opposite structures employed to perform a speech act in different languages—e.g., English 'Is this seat taken?'/continental European 'Is this seat free?' This is even more likely to promote communication breakdown where speakers do not share a common language and their nods and head-shakes are based on different formulas.
(d) Formulas of corresponding structures employed to realize different speech acts—e.g., Australian English 'How are you (going)?' is often misinterpreted by Central Europeans as an inquiry about a person's well-being and the ensuing response considered by the Australian longwinded and unnecessary. 'Have you eaten already?' a greeting used by many Chinese and Southeast Asians when speaking English, can cause either miscommunication or noncommunication. It is not understood by the 'uninitiated' Australian, American, or English person and misinterpreted as an indirect invitation by some Central Europeans. The greeting 'Where are you going?' used in English by Singaporeans is misunderstood to be an inquiry by speakers of British, Australian, or American English.
(e) Formulas of corresponding structures used to realize speech acts with the opposite intention, e.g., 'Thank you' employed by English native speakers to denote the acceptance of an offer and by people from some continental European backgrounds to mean the rejection of the offer.

The distinction is often made between directness and indirectness. This encompasses the following dichotomies:

(a) *Direct* and *indirect* speech acts—e.g., the difference between the direct formulation, 'May I ask you to shut the door?' (or simply 'Shut the door') and the indirect, 'Don't you think it's rather cold in here?' Hinting rather than directly requesting a favor is considered to be polite in Southeast Asian cultures but sometimes devious when similar communication patterns are employed in communication with Britons or Australians or New Zealanders.
(b) The use of *downgraders*, such as 'well,' 'would you mind...?' conditional forms (could, would, should), impersonal constructions and agentless passives (e.g., It could be interpreted as..., This is seen to be), as opposed to *upgraders*, such as 'obviously,' 'absolutely.' 'I insist that...'
(c) *Positive* vs. *negative politeness*—related to the notion of 'face' and developed in Brown and Levinson's (1987) pragmatic model based on degree of relative power, social distance, and the ranking of impositions in a particular culture. Negative politeness avoids conflicts through modesty, formality, and restraint (i.e., not imposing); whereas in positive politeness people draw closer by showing appreciation of one another, for instance, through solidarity strategies such as teasing or through what may be perceived as outspoken frankness. In different cultures, people lose face by apologizing, not apologizing, not apologizing in a particular way, or not successfully soliciting a reassurance (see *Politeness*).

It is surmised by some that communicative styles of certain cultures are more direct (given to 'overstatement'), the styles of others more indirect (given to 'understatement'). For instance, House and Kasper (1981) found that Germans showed a higher level of directness (more upgraders, less downgraders) than English people in the performance of requests and complaints. In the Cross-Cultural Speech Act Realization Project (Blum-Kulka et al. 1989: 62), downgraders in indirect requests were distributed according to the rank ordering—Australian English, Canadian French, Hebrew, and Argentinian Spanish, with the English speakers using twice as many downgraders as Canadian French and Hebrew speakers. The others make up for the lower incidence of downgraders by the increased use of please.

The directness-indirectness dichotomy has been challenged (e.g., by Wierzbicka 1991) on the grounds that these assumptions are based on selected aspects and have *relative* foundations. Anglo–American cultural style is direct when compared to Japanese but indirect when compared to Black American or Jewish–American style. Anglo–American style is direct in some ways, and more indirect in others. Within a particular supranational language there may be divergent tendencies not only in national cultures (American, British, Australian, Indian) but also in religious or ethnic subcultures. Wierzbicka has proposed a system of 'cultural scripts' based on a set of universal semantic principles, i.e., expressed in terms of basic elements such as: *I, you, want, don't, say, think, do, this, like this, good, bad*. She argues that the advantage of this approach is that it avoids arbitrariness in the formulation of absolutes and in the positioning of relatives. A counterargument is that the primitives may not be as universal as she assumes.

2.2 Intercultural Variation in Discourse Organization
This obtains in rules for the structure of telephone conversations, letters, school essays and academic

treatises, the conduct of meetings, consultations with professional people, and business transactions. This encompasses:

(a) turn-taking rules, i.e., who talks when in an interaction, how it is (or is not) possible to take over a turn from someone else, or prevent another person from appropriating your turn, and how long different interlocutors can talk for; and

(b) the various rules in written discourse and formal meetings which influence the degree of linear progression and symmetrical balance between propositions or segments of text or oral discourse.

English academic discourse has been found to be more linear and symmetrical than its German equivalent. This corresponds to variation in the dominant cultural expectations of good academic discourse and corresponding differences in the structure of meetings in English-speaking and German-speaking countries. Discourse in Japanese, Korean, Chinese and, to some extent, in the Indian traditions, tends to keep returning to the baseline. Arabic discourse marks parallels between elaborating or conflicting arguments. These organizational structures are to be found in both L1 and L2 discourse. Such differences can lead to difficulties in participating in democratic structures and problems in getting books, articles, and conference papers accepted or positively evaluated. Here too, ethnic stereotypes can result from discourse patterns that may seem to promote digressiveness or longwindedness when viewed from another culture.

In English, little creativity or special ingenuity is required for a conversation to flow from opening routines. In German, for instance, constraints are placed on the way in which communication can proceed between strangers unless they have established 'common ground.' Intercultural communication conflict may develop where one speaker considers the other to be either offensively forward or arrogantly uncooperative.

2.3 Intercultural Variation in Systems of Address

Some languages/cultures have more complex systems of address than others, involving different pronouns of address, verbal endings and titles according to status, relationship, and sometimes gender. Others (e.g., Australian English) do not mark these distinctions and also tend to prefer the general use of first names. Intercultural communication between people from cultures with different patterns of address may therefore engender problems of face, with interlocutors appearing too forward or too reserved. Speakers accustomed to marking status and special relationships through pronouns and titles will often find it difficult to interact in L1 with people with whom their common work language is English where such relationships are less linguistically marked.

2.4 Intercultural Variation in Channel/Medium Rules

These rules indicate whether the communication situation requires face-to-face interaction, telephone or letter contact, or the completion of a form. For instance, in communication with bureaucracy, the telephone can be employed much more in English-speaking countries than in continental Europe where face-to-face communication (especially in Southern Europe) or form-completion (especially in Germany) is required. The choice of an inappropriate channel can limit access to information and/or success in communication with management or officialdom.

2.5 Linguistic Creativity Rules

These indicate the scope of 'language play'—rhymes, puns, limericks, verbal insults, and verbal irony. Such phenomena may be thought of as a 'luxury' layer, the province of writers, journalists, and cabaret writers and performers. They may simply not be understood in some cultures but they are a part of normal communicative behavior in others. So verbal insults from Turks, Hungarians, or Black Americans may be considered 'just offensive' by people from some other cultures, Central European irony may be completely missed by British or Anglo–Americans, and continental Europeans may simply not understand the punning of English speakers and its significance.

2.6 Small Talk

This obtains in the context of (casual) phatic communication to establish empathy between individuals, and it may be employed and understood quite differently across cultures (see *Phatic Communion*).

2.7 Intercultural Variation in Honorific Patterns

This is found especially in letters. In some cases these introduce an element of creativity into a conventional context. Some examples from the letters of Indian students:

Expressions of deference—I beg to say (to state), I have the honor to intimate.
Vocative of respect (to an 'ordinary person')—Respected Sir, Your Honour.
Adjectival honorific—Your esteemed university, your respected school.

2.8 Some General Principles on the Above

Interaction with all these categories of rules is 'interlocutor-based' and 'domain-based.' *Who* is allowed to say this *to whom*? In what institutional contexts does this apply? The domain division may be stricter or less marked, according to culture, but all cultures have rules on how particular interactions proceed (e.g., political interviews, university seminars), as well as constraints on their content. German conversation has been found to be characterized by a greater degree of directness than English conversation while German written academic discourse (in linguistics and sociology) contains more hedging devices than its English counterpart.

2.9 Intonation Patterns

These can influence not only the perception of the speaker's attitude but also the communicative intent (request or command). Gumperz (1977) gives the example of Indian and Pakistani cafeteria workers in Britian, whose use of falling intonation in the question 'Gravy?' was interpreted as unfriendly by their English customers who in the same situation would employ a rising intonation.

In another example from Indian English conversations, Gumperz et al. (1982) show that the intended meaning of a given utterance is, in fact, the inverse of the most straightforward prepositional interpretation. In the utterance:

> Building societies and the council have got no objection, *doesn't mean* that if a council house, council mortgage, you can still sell it.

The phrase 'doesn't mean' is used in this context, not to relate these clauses so much as to refer to assumptions expressed in the preceding dialogue. (On the surface this would appear to mean that one is not permitted to sell a council house; in fact the intended meaning is that one *is* free to sell it.) This is a further characteristic of Indian English likely to be misunderstood by speakers of other national varieties of English. Roberts et al. (1992) show how such variation can lead to discrimination in job interviews and in workplace communication.

2.10 Negotiation of Meaning and Resolution of Communication Breakdown

Where the interlocutors do not share common expectations of the interaction, the meaning needs to be negotiated, e.g., 'Do you mean you want a reason?' in response to a request for information followed by a long monologue on the part of the interlocutor. Where a communication breakdown has occurred, it needs to be resolved in a similar way. This is often done through slow, loud repetition or paraphrase depending largely on the level of competence of the speakers in the common language and their cultural backgrounds. South Asians are very likely to employ repetition. Even the response to the occurrence of communication breakdown varies across cultures in accordance with specific face-saving practices, for example,

(a) It may be ignored;
(b) It may be admitted according to culture-specific honorific rules;
(c) The other may be blamed for it;
(d) It may be 'laughed away.'

2.11 Some Intercultural Differences in Verbal Interaction

In a study of dyadic (workplace) communication in Australia (Clyne 1994) subject to individual, gender, and status differences, Central Europeans, South Asians, Latin Americans, and Filipinos tend to employ longer turns, to think aloud, and to interrupt one another's flow of speech—this can result in overlapping speech. East and Southeast Asians tend to employ shorter turns and long silences and not to expect small talk at work. Turn maintenance and appropriation tends to be achieved through an increase in speed and volume among people of Southern and Central European background and through a decrease in speed, rising intonation, and repetition among many of Southeast Asian origin. South Asians and some Central Europeans may excel in formal discourse or group discussions but not necessarily in small talk. Central and Southern Europeans will, on the whole, present an argument rather than a simple 'yes' or 'no' response, while comparable Southeast Asians will prefer the simple response which avoids an argument.

Among the effects of such variation in cross-cultural discourse are:

(a) Central Europeans' long apologies causing impatience to Anglo–Australian or Southeast Asian interlocutors with the Central Europeans, in turn, feeling rejected.
(b) In a complaint by a Central European, a surface request made for a reason ('Give me the reason') not accompanied by an opportunity for such a justification, leading to confusion on the part of Southeast Asians (see Sect. 2.10).
(c) Anglo–Australians' and Southern Europeans' rejection of clumsy attempts at small talk by a South Asian who himself takes over meetings through his domineering eloquence.
(d) Southeast Asians' inability to identify small talk in work communication.
(e) Central European women's competence at arguing with a Central European superordinate because they understand the hidden implications in his discourse and Southeast Asian women's inability to argue with him because they do not fathom out these implications.

For some people, silence in group situations is normal; for others it is intolerable as it causes alienation. Finns and Vietnamese immigrants in Australia are a cultural group who tend to observe long silences, especially in communication with strangers, while many Turks would expect to have long turns and not be interrupted. This has caused difficulties, for example, for Finnish business people and Turkish migrant workers in Germany. In some cultures, such as Arabic, close proximity is a marker of friendliness but it causes discomfort to members of other cultures, such as Britons, Scandinavians, and Southeast Asians.

3. Value of This Type of Research

This type of research is of both theoretical and practical value. As has been shown in the papers in Tomić and Shuy (1987), 'real life' data can contribute to advances in theory development. On the basis of evidence form cross-cultural communication, the universality of the conversational assumptions postulated by Grice's (1975) 'cooperative principle,' for example, may be challenged. The maxim of quality 'Be genuine and sincere' contradicts the face/politeness rules required by the principle of harmony in Chinese and Vietnamese cultures, for example (see Young 1994). This culture clash, in fact, contributes to communication breakdown and communication conflict between people of Chinese and Vietnamese background on the one hand, and those of Western European or Anglo–American background on the other. Maxims of quantity such as 'Be brief' and 'Be orderly' are open to cultural variation in discourse rules (see *Conversational Maxims*). Central European cultures emphasize content, and formal organization necessarily becomes a secondary matter. In South Asian and some Central and Eastern European cultures, brevity is not a virtue. The whole notion of 'cooperation' may be seen, in effect, as somewhat culturally biased since in some cultures (e.g., German, Austrian, Swiss, Jewish–American, Israeli), either contrariness or putting forward one's independent viewpoint is considered desirable and more normal than collaborative discourse formation—'text sharing,' as Watts (1989) call it, a characteristic of English discourse (cf. also Wierzbicka 1991). Such variation also promotes communication breakdown and conflict. On the other hand, Neil (1996) shows that a good deal of collaboration takes places between speakers of different minority cultural backgrounds to achieve harmonious and effective communication.

Blum-Kulka et al. (1989: 63–4) do support the theoretical framework for speech act research (e.g., Searle 1969), although the degree and manner of cross-linguistic variation in rules for expressing indirect speech acts suggest to them a need to modify universalistic claims. This applies particularly to various maxims such as the maxim of tact ('Be tactful') introduced by Leech (1983). In practice, indirectness is interpreted as quite impolite and insincere in some cultures, e.g., Israeli.

The practical value of this type of research is in its application in education and training (second language teaching, cultural sensitivization in the workplace, pre-overseas placement programs, medical, legal, social work, and teacher training in multicultural societies). The development of functional–notional approaches to second/foreign language teaching (Wilkins 1976, Van Ek 1980) facilitated the input of such research outcomes into language syllabuses. Also, business people involved in export trade and academics engaged in international networks need to be aware of the implications of this field. While communication breakdown due to grammatical or phonological interference is generally tolerated, intercultural variation in pragmatics and discourse organization is often mistaken for arrogance, deviousness, an absence of logic, or confusion.

4. Methodology

Different methods and instruments can be, and have been applied in this type of research and may be found to complement each other. These include:

(a) The collection of a large corpus of taped spontaneous interactions, representing various institutional domains and culturally heterogeneous and (for comparison) culturally homogeneous groups of interlocutors. As the influence of nonverbal factors cannot be discounted, and because of the possible impact of the interlocutor's total being, it would be useful for at least part of the corpus to be on videotape. Ethical factors and the 'observer's paradox' (the goal of linguistic research—to ascertain how people use language when they are not being systematically observed—being achieved only through systematic observation; see Labov 1972) need to be offset against advantages as sophisticated video equipment becomes smaller and more manageable and more part of the everyday experience of people.

(b) Role-played situations which can form the basis for response tests. This can be done by videoing informants while they are watching videoed role plays, but this method is very time consuming.

(c) Direct questioning and interviews are easy to administer, but it is by no means certain whether people's responses are their spontaneous responses or their statement of the norm, whatever they may declare. Also, such questionnaires present problems for some cultural or subcultural groups. Responses to attitudinal tests on discourse are intrinsically significant in cross-cultural discourse studies but they should not be regarded as satisfactory substitutes for spontaneous data.

(d) Participant observation can provide a valuable starting-point for further investigations, but it is only useful to supply data if it is recorded. Its great advantage is its naturalness and unobtrusiveness. (On the pros and cons of interviewing and participation observation, see Heidelberger Forschungsprojekt 1975: 45–8; see also Milroy 1980.)

Until the early 1990s, most corpuses have been the result of role-play elicitations which have some of the limitations mentioned (but cf. Blum-Kulka et al. 1989). Often this type of data is the only feasible means of obtaining a corpus. For a good review of methods, see Bardovi-Harlig and Hartford (in press).

5. Cultural Value Systems

There are underlying cultural value systems which play a central role in determining intercultural variation in discourse production, processing, and expectations. Features of these include:
(a) more verbal or more literate orientation;
(b) more philosophical (content) or more spatial (formal) orientation and, linked with this, the relative importance of linearity and the relative importance of rhythmic or spatial symmetry;
(c) the relative emphasis on the individual or on the group;
(d) the relative power distance;
(e) the relative importance of harmony and conflict avoidance; and
(f) relative tendency towards concreteness and abstraction.

This influences, among other things:
(a) the extent to which people choose to perform a task in writing or verbally, the length of their turns, and the relative value of writing and speaking effectively;
(b) the organization of their written and spoken discourse, and their expectations of this organization in the discourse of others;
(c) the extent to which they will yield their turn to others;
(d) the extent to which they will explicitly contradict another interlocutor and the way they will develop an argument;
(e) who will say what to whom in what circumstances; and
(f) reader or author responsibility in written texts, i.e., is it the author who needs to take care that the text is comprehensible to the readers or is the onus on the reader to make the effort to understand it?

The analysis of discourse in cross-cultural settings is therefore a key to the understanding of cultural values of different ethnic and national groups as well as establishing communication patterns across cultures.

6. Future Research

There is a need for far more studies of discourse in cross-cultural settings involving different groups, whether culturally more similar or more distant. An increased range of data would facilitate the establishing of parameters, the separation of the relative from the absolute, and the further development of a culturally neutral mode of description. The latter would be aided if research could be jointly conducted by scholars in mirror image situations (e.g., Americans working on Japanese discourse and Japanese working on American discourse) or at least if there were more opportunities for networking in this field. Research in the twenty-first century should draw more on studies of cultural value systems, of which there is a shortage of accessible examples for many cultures.

See also: Pragmatics and Sociolinguistics; Code-mixing; Foreigner Talk; Conversational Maxims.

Bibliography

Bardovi-Harlig K, Hartford B in press Spontaneous conversation, institutional talk, and interlanguage pragmatic research

Blum-Kulka S, House J, Kasper G (ed.) 1989 *Cross-Cultural Pragmatics*. Ablex, Norwood, NJ

Brown P, Levinson S L 1987 *Politeness: Some Universals in Language Usage*. Cambridge University Press, Cambridge, UK

Clyne M 1987 Cultural differences in the organization of academic texts. *Journal of Pragmatics* 11: 211–47

Clyne M 1994 *Inter-Cultural Communication at Work*. Cambridge University Press, Cambridge, UK

Garcia O, Otheguy R (eds.) 1989 *English across Cultures: Cultures across English*. Mouton de Gruyter, Berlin

Grice H P 1975 Logic and conversation. In: Cole P, Morgan J (eds.) *Syntax and Semantics. Vol. 3: Speech Acts*. Academic Press, New York

Gumperz J J 1977 Sociocultural knowledge in conversational inference. In: *Annual Round Table Monograph Series on Language and Linguistics*. Georgetown University, Washington, DC

Gumperz J J 1982 *Discourse Strategies*. Cambridge University Press, Cambridge, UK

Gumperz J J, Aulakh G, Kaltman H (eds.) 1982 Thematic structure and progression in discourse. In: Gumperz J J (ed.) *Language and Social Identity*. Cambridge University Press, Cambridge, UK

Heidelberger Forschungsprojekt Pidgin–Deutsch 1975 *Sprache und Kommunikation ausländischer Arbeiter*. Scriptor, Kronberg

House J, Kasper G 1981 Politeness markers in English and German. In: Coulmas F (ed.) *Conversational Routine*. Mouton de Gruyter, The Hague

Kasper G, Blum-Kulka S (ed.) 1993 *Interlanguage Pragmatics*. Oxford University Press, New York

Labov W 1972 *Sociolinguistic Patterns*. University of Pennsylvania Press, Philadelphia, PA

Leech G 1983 *Principles of Pragmatics*. Longman, London

Milroy L 1980 *Language and Social Networks*. Blackwell, Oxford, UK

Milroy L, Muysken P (eds) 1995 *One Speaker Two Languages*. Cambridge University Press, Cambridge, UK

Neil D 1996 *Collaboration in Inter-Cultural Discourse*. Lang, Frankfurt, Germany

Olesky W 1989 (ed.) *Contrastive Pragmatics.* Benjamins, Amsterdam
Pride J 1985 (ed.) *Cross-Cultural Encounters.* River Seine, Melbourne
Roberts C, Davies E, Jupp T 1992 *Language and Discrimination.* Longman, London
Searle J R 1969 *Speech Acts.* Cambridge University Press, Cambridge, UK
Tomić O M, Shuy R W 1987 (eds.) *The Relation of Theoretical and Applied Linguistics.* Plenum, New York
Van Ek J A 1980 *Threshold Level English* (*in a European Unit/credit System for Modern Language Learning by Adults*). Council of Europe/Pergamon Press, Oxford, UK
Watts R J 1989 Relevance and relational work: Linguistic politeness as politic behaviour. *Multilingua* **8**(2–3): 131–61
Wierzbicka A 1991 *Cross-Cultural Pragmatics.* Mouton de Gruyter, Berlin
Wilkins D A 1976 *Notional Syllabuses.* Oxford University Press, Oxford, UK
Young L 1994 *Crosstalk and Culture in Sino-American Communication.* Cambridge University Press, Cambridge, UK

Doctor–Patient Language
M. Lacoste

Doctor–patient language is among the most frequently studied discourse types in institutional settings. The professional dialogue between physician and patient belongs to a socially crucial and linguistically fascinating situation. After years of purely sociological or psychological approaches to the study of medical interview, the consideration of the language used in such interviews has been recently included in this type of study, thereby palpably transforming and enriching it. Most analyses deal with it from two points of view, linguistic and social, but differ in emphasis and stress one aspect more than the other.

While most of them are based on medical interviews, the analyses differ as to: (a) the models of language used by the researchers; (b) the ways the situation is viewed along the various dimensions of power, activity, and knowledge.

1. Language Models

1.1 Language as Behavior: Quantitative Studies on Verbal Exchange

Basing themselves loosely on information theory, many quantitative studies consider the verbal exchange itself to be a social indicator, and do not take the meaning into account. The variables used are, for example, addresser (speaker), addressee (hearer), duration and frequency of each participant's speech contribution, in order to compare doctor and patient with regard to use of language. Some other studies derive a version of turn-taking from conversation analysis (see *Conversation Analysis*) but simplify it in a quantitative perspective, offering some statistics on phenomena such as pauses or interruptions. What such comparative analysis has shown is that in most cases doctors speak more and interrupt more frequently than patients do, something which confirms the thesis of the asymmetrical and unequal structure of the medical interaction.

1.2 Language as a Sequence of Speech Acts

Pragmatics, and more specifically speech act theory, allows another kind of analysis based on the illocutionary force of verbal utterances. This pragmatic orientation has produced different kinds of analyses.

The simplest type identifies the basic speech acts recurring in medical communication, and then codes and quantifies the obtained data. In most cases speech acts produced by the doctor are studied in greater detail here, since patients respond more often than they initiate. This type of analysis has enabled researchers to compare medical interviews in order to see what forms doctors use most: statements, direct or indirect questions, positive or negative assessments, requests for agreements, etc. However, researchers, also being interested in sequences of speech acts, have attempted to analyze initiative/response pairs and initiative/response/acknowledgment triples. It would seem that discourse in medical interviews is characterized by this kind of triple, just as is the case for classroom discourse: both are institutionalized situations where one participant has a greater right to speak than others (Fisher and Todd 1983; see *Discourse*).

1.3 Language as a Conversational Cooperation

Ethnomethodology (see *Ethnomethodology*) has developed a theoretical perspective in which every action is considered to be coproduced by the participants in the action. Conversation analysis has underpinned this theory with empirical studies of language in everyday and institutional settings. From the outset, doctors' and patients' contributions are seen to be strictly interrelated throughout the course of conversation. Thus, a fairly detailed examination of the occurring language sequences appears to be the only suitable way of analyzing what goes on between the doctor and his or her patient.

This approach has had a heavy impact on the analysis of medical interviews. For instance, the medical interview is no longer considered to be a homogeneous whole; rather, it is considered to be made up of heterogeneous parts, such as initial small talk, the medical exchange on the main topic, and medical exchanges on minor or side topics. Each part provides a specific context for analysis.

Various conversational procedures have been described in great detail. For instance, a fine-grained analysis including nonverbal cues shows that after the delivery of the diagnosis, a short pause is often made by the doctor, but that patients generally do not use it to take the floor and ask questions about the diagnosis. This shows that the asymmetry is not imposed by the doctor only, but is in fact cooperatively constructed (e.g., Heath 1986).

In the same way, many other phenomena such as repair and negotiation devices, disturbances in the dialogue between doctor and patient, silences, interaction openings and closings, etc., appear relevant to what is going on in the interaction.

1.4 Language as an Ideological Discursive Construction

An interest in social and cultural variation, mixed with a certain tradition of discourse analysis (especially Foucault's; see *Foucault, Michel*; *Discourse*; *Ideology*), critical sociology, and reference to Goffman's symbolic interactionism (see *Goffman, Erving*), have led some researchers to investigate the correspondence between social forms of medicine and language forms. Looking into various medical settings, such as general practice versus specific specializations, or private versus public services in the UK, etc., they have produced socio–ideological typologies of medicine. The studies do not refer to any systematic model of language; rather, they stress the importance of various language elements with regard to the context, e.g., the use of pronouns or forms of address as rhetorical devices, something which appears to be characteristic of certain types of medical discourse. By focusing on these matters, these researchers have shown the uniformity of medical discourse to be an illusion. Thereby, some interesting phenomena have been studied, such as the specific kind of discourse that occurs between doctor, parents, and sick children; it reflects the participants' different strategies, coalitions, and power relationships (Strong 1979). Interestingly enough, investigation has shown that the use of medical jargon and technical terms by the doctor is rather uncommon, even if it does sometimes occur for strategic purposes.

Of course not all studies on medical interaction exactly fit into the frame presented here. For instance, Labov and Fanshel (1977) conducted a deep and very specific analysis on the interaction between a therapist and a patient, combining speech act analysis and a kind of discourse analysis (see *Discourse*).

2. The Characteristics of the Medical Situation

2.1 Power, Social Categorization, and Ritual

Many authors see the power of the physician as an instance of social dominance, reflected in the unequal right of interrupting, asking questions, and giving names to symptoms. This dominance appears occasionally as direct and rude, especially when patients are dealt with as if they were children. At other times, it is mitigated by social politeness and plays in more subtle ways on distance and proximity in order to preserve face for the interactants. These factors of variation need further investigation.

Social categorization is at work in medical language too. Sometimes this operates in the medical interview as such (e.g., when classifying people as good versus bad patients), sometimes it reflects larger social categories, mainly male versus female. The dominance of the doctor over the patient seems to be at its strongest whenever the patient is a woman and the doctor a man; by contrast, the least dominance by the doctor occurs when the roles are switched.

2.2 Knowledge and Expertise

The medical situation is basically one of cooperation between an expert and professional, the doctor, and a lay consultant, the patient. This has some immediate consequences in terms of knowledge dominance and discourse control by the doctor. A more careful analysis reveals the presence of subtle distinctions among respective knowledge territories: thus, there is doctor-specific knowledge versus patient-specific knowledge versus shared knowledge, etc. Following cognitive trends in the 1980s, attempts have been made to compare the medical diagnosis in real situations with the functioning of expert systems. But the medical interview in fact comprises different kinds of expertise. The doctor relies not only on 'declarative,' but also on 'procedural' knowledge; this latter is reflected in the language in the form of deictic and other context-bound devices, unlike in expert systems, where declarative knowledge is dominant (Cicourel 1987).

Following this lead, one has come to distinguish between two tasks in medical work: one is the problem-solving activity of the doctor in diagnosis and decision; the other is the management of the interaction with the patient. Language production reflects the interplay of these two tasks.

2.3 Language and Medical Activity

Even if the main focus of interest during the medical interview has been on the dialogue, it behoves us increasingly to consider this dialogue as an element of a more global type of activity which, for the doctor, also includes instrumental actions, physical examination, consulting documents and health forms, and writing reports. Thus, a purely linguistic analysis has to be combined with an analysis of the activity.

Ethnomethodology and cognitive sociology have offered some insights into these matters. For instance, a few studies have stressed the importance of the interactional structure during the physical examination (e.g., Heath 1986).

3. Current Trends

Under the influence of these trends, the topic of doctor–patient language seems to be developing in new directions by working on data that: (a) are richer, broader, and more systematic (The intensive use of videotapes has revealed that the interrelation between verbal and nonverbal dimensions of activity is crucial. Moreover, given the increasing number of studies, data no longer come from a single source, but may be made up of sequence samples extracted from various sources. In this way, phenomena can be compared, and the way is opened towards greater generalization.); (b) include knowledge concerning phenomena that are complementary to the interaction, by means of interviews, ethnographic explorations, and information on the organization (Taking such phenomena into consideration is essential to a more relevant interpretation of discourse production.); (c) arise out of a more systematic study of the cultural, social, and organizational varieties of medical encounters (Until the early 1990s, the focus has been, with few exceptions, on Western medicine, particularly on American, British, and German health systems. Given the origins of the researchers, such a restriction may have been unavoidable, but the studies need to be broadened to encompass other cultures or subcultures.); (d) are procured from more varied medical situations, i.e., not only from interviews or medical visits in the hospital, but also from sophisticated technical examinations and other different types of medical care; (e) extend over a broader sample of participants, i.e., including not only the doctor alone, but also, as is more often the case in modern hospitals, medical teams with nurses, medical technicians, and various specialists (Löning and Rehbein 1993, Grosjean and Lacoste 1998).

See also: Discourse; Power and Language.

Bibliography

Cicourel A 1987 Cognitive and organizational aspects of medical diagnostic reasoning. *Discourse Processes* **10**: 347–67
Fisher S, Todd A D (eds.) 1983 *The Social Organization of Doctor–Patient Communication*. Center for Applied Linguistics, Washington, DC
Grosjean M, Lacoste M 1998 *Communication et intelligence collective: le travail hospitalier*. PUF, Paris
Heath C 1986 *Body Movement and Speech in Medical Interaction*. Cambridge University Press, Cambridge, UK
Labov W, Fanshel D 1977 *Therapeutic Discourse–Psychotherapy as Conversation*. Academic Press, New York
Löning P, Rehbein J (eds.) 1993 *Artz-Patienten–Kommunikation*. De Gruyter, Berlin
Strong P M 1979 *The Ceremonial Order of the Clinic Patients, Doctors, and Medical Bureaucracies*. Routledge and Kegan Paul, London

Ethnography of Speaking
G. Philipsen

Speaking, the use of language in the conduct of social life, is organized in culture-specific ways. The ethnography of speaking is concerned with describing such ways of speaking and with interpreting the meanings they have for those who participate in them. It is concerned further with developing cross-culturally valid concepts and theories for interpreting and explaining the interaction of language and social life.

The term 'ethnography of speaking' was proposed by Dell Hymes (see *Hymes, Dell Hathaway*), whose writings have provided programmatic impetus to the enterprise (Hymes 1962, 1964, 1972, 1974). 'Ethnography' refers to fieldwork which culminates in a written description of the culture or way of life of a particular people, produced in such a way as to permit comparison across diverse cases. Applied to speaking, its concern is with how, in a given community, speaking is conceptualized—what symbols and meanings, premises and rules there are, pertaining to communicative conduct. Attention to native categories goes hand in hand with delineating observed patterns of speaking, with study of a community's indigenous codes and its indigenous speech acts, events, and situations.

'Ethnography of speaking' and 'ethnography of communication' have been used interchangeably by many scholars. 'Speaking' was used initially to draw attention to the diverse, creative, and strategic ways languages are used, in contrast to language as an abstract, idealized system. Where 'speaking' is used it can be taken as a surrogate for all communicative modalities (verbal, kinesic, proxemic, etc.); 'communication' makes explicit this breadth of concern. Both speaking and communication refer to the use of codes in the production and interpretation of messages, with language being the code of primary importance in some situations but not in others. Although the emphasis is on a culture-specific approach to what speaking (or communication) is to be taken as, leaving this to be circumscribed in each case, nonetheless the ethnography of speaking emphasizes the deliberate use of signs and their interpretations, in the conduct of social life. What to call communicative resources and activities, how they are structured, what enters into them, and what their significance is to those who use them—these are left open to discovery in particular cases.

When the ethnography of speaking was proposed in 1962, established approaches to linguistic description took the phonology and grammar of a language as the principal frames of reference, an approach which privileged attention to linguistic signs within a closed linguistic system, to the exclusion of speech. Patterns of speaking had likewise been neglected in anthropological descriptions of cultures, ethnographers assuming that speech—and other modes of communicative activity—could be taken for granted rather than be made an object of investigation. The ethnography of speaking was designed to remedy the neglect of speaking in grammars and in ethnographies. Hymes proposed the ethnographic study, in diverse speech communities, of 'the situations and uses, the patterns and functions, of speaking in its own right' (1962: 16). Such studies, designed to fill the gap in knowledge which was left by established approaches in linguistics and anthropology, were to be ethnographic in basis and communicative in the range and kind of subjects which they would essay.

1. The Structure of Speaking

A fundamental assumption of the ethnography of speaking is that speaking, like language(s), can be described in terms of rule and system. Wherever people speak, they organize their speech in ways over and above those governed by rules of grammar or by physical laws. In any communicative situation, even though it might be grammatically acceptable and physically possible to make any of two or more linguistic choices, such choices are not randomly produced. Choices as to which language to use in a particular situation (for bi- or multilingual speakers), how to address an interlocutor, whether to delete or add sounds to words, whether to speak or remain silent, are not in free variation but are patterned, according to rules which are part of the social knowledge of a particular community. It follows that much of the meaning to interlocutors, of their speech activity, is derived from knowledge of local patterns and expectations.

Speaking, from this perspective, is a complex social as well as a linguistic act. To explain speaking activities—why they occur as they do and what they mean to those who participate in them—requires reference to their social contexts. Thus to characterize what people are doing and saying when they speak, involves reference to the settings, participants, ends, act sequences, topics, and so forth, which comprise the social situation. This goes beyond the rules of language structure to a consideration of rules specifying who may say what to whom, in what language or style, to what ends, and on what occasions.

Speaking is not absolutely determined. It is patterned, but in ways which its participants can circumvent, challenge, and revise. Its rules are violated, new rules and meanings are created. Any given speech community is an organization of diversity. Its spoken life is fashioned from diverse, even discrepant, motives, practices, and preferences, but nonetheless there is, in any particular community, a knowable system in its language use. To acknowledge that the patterns are mutable and that they subsume diverse strands does not negate the fact that there are patterns, the knowledge of which speakers exploit in their speaking activities and in their interpretations of same.

The idea that speaking within a society is governed by rules which speakers can use to associate message forms with social meanings is illustrated in an extensive body of research into personal address (Philipsen and Huspek 1985). When, for example, one interlocutor addresses another with a pronoun of personal address this can involve the selection from among forms which are grammatically and semantically equivalent but whose use has social meaning. For example, although present-day English provides only one form (*you*) for pronominal address, in the seventeenth century speakers of English selected from *thee, thou, ye*, and *you*. Although these forms were equally acceptable grammatically and had the same referential meaning, which of the forms was used was highly predictable and was socially prescribed, given knowledge of the social situation: *thou* and *thee* were prescribed for address in intimate or everyday situations; *ye* and *you*, although plural forms, were prescribed as honorific forms for addressing an individual to whom one wished, or was obligated, to pay respect or deference.

That these pronominal address forms carried social meaning was attested to not only by contemporaneous commentary but also by the usage of the seventeenth century English Quakers, who intentionally flouted the conventions of the dominant speech community. According to the Quakers' reading of the Scriptures, *thou* and *thee* were employed by Christ, and the generalization of the plural *you* to an individual addressee was, they believed, an affectation adopted vainly by popes and emperors. The Quakers prescribed that *thou* and *thee* be addressed to everyone, even to those outside their fellowship who expected *you* and *ye*, at once expressing their own conviction that 'Christ respects no man's person' and undermining what they believed to be an ungodly practice in the society at large (Bauman 1970).

Ethnographers of speaking have shown that a wide range of speaking phenomena is systematically organized in ways which are meaningful to speakers and hearers. This includes community-specific practices with regard to verbal forms, prosodic features, and extralinguistic signs. Attention to the social organization of speaking has also been extended to the structure of speech acts, activities, events, situations, and roles, as well as to the organization of greetings, leave-takings, narratives, genres, and conversations, all of which potentially can be found to have a high degree of patterning in particular contexts.

The principle that speaking is structured has been extended to the patterning of a community's entire range of speech situations and speech events. Sherzer's (1983) study of San Blas Kuna Indians in Panama, which is based on detailed observation and tape-recordings of naturally-occurring speech, articulates the Kuna way of life in terms of the patterning of resources, contexts, and uses of speaking. All major social activities among the Kuna—everyday informal conversations, teaching and learning sessions, public political meetings, and curing and puberty rituals—are defined through showing how every aspect of Kuna speaking—grammar, vocabulary, sound patterns, and gestures—is intimately linked to what is considered intelligible and appropriate conduct within these contexts.

The systematic description and analysis of all major speech situations within the San Blas community provided the basis for delineating its overall sociolinguistic structure. Most of Kuna spoken life is filled with, indeed is defined by, carefully controlled and organized talk; most major social activities involve systematically different uses of the voice and of the community's linguistic resources. But, for this highly voluble people, not every social moment is a speaking moment. Set against the prevailing preoccupation with highly ordered talk are a few contexts in which speaking is proscribed (during certain curing ceremonies in which it is believed that speaking might attract the attention of evil spirits) and in which uncontrolled yelling, arguing and fighting are permitted, even encouraged (during puberty rites and festivities). The meanings, to the Kuna, of their various ways of speaking can only be appreciated by setting each one in the context of the larger pattern. Another way that attention to the full range of speaking situations and events proved instructive in the Kuna case was the discovery that the speaking style primarily associated with particular situations penetrated into other contexts. For example, Kuna speakers incorporated miniature, momentary versions of ritual speech into everyday discourse for two different purposes: to show off (in the case of ritual specialists who could demonstrate their esoteric knowledge) and to parody the ritual context. The meanings of these momentary versions of ritual speech would be uninterpretable without the comprehensive background provided by Sherzer's description.

2. Speaking as Culturally Distinctive

Studies such as those of the Kuna, when placed side by side and comparatively analyzed, reveal that speaking, like other systems of behavior, is not only organized within a society but also organized in each society in culture-specific ways which must be discovered in each case. Societies differ as to what communicative resources are available to their members, in terms of languages, dialects, registers, routines, genre, artistic formulas, etc. They also differ in how these resources are patterned in use, in the functions served in (and serviceable by) speech and other communicative means, and in the evaluation of speaking as an instrument of social action.

Speaking is not everywhere valued equally. It is an object of a high degree of interest, elaboration, and positive evaluation in some societies. Along with the San Blas Kuna of Panama, whom one Kuna described as 'a talking people,' there are speakers on Roti, a small island in Eastern Indonesia, of whom Fox says,

> the pleasure of life is talk—not simply an idle chatter that passes time, but the more formal talking of sides in endless dispute, argument, and repartee or the rivalling of one another in eloquent and balanced phrases on ceremonial occasions... Lack of talk is an indication of distress. Rotinese repeatedly explain that if their 'hearts' are confused or dejected, they keep silent. Contrarily, to be involved with someone requires active verbal encounter.
>
> (Fox 1974: 65)

In other societies, the ideal standard for adult behavior is relative taciturnity. Among the Paliyans, a tribal people in South India, by the time a man reaches 40 years of age he practically stops speaking altogether (Hymes 1962). In a working-class neighborhood in Chicago, local rules proscribe speaking in many contexts of male role enactment, including disciplining children, defending the honor of female relatives, and asserting oneself politically and economically (Philipsen 1975).

Differences in valuation are reflected in the distinctiveness of cultural terminologies for the act of speaking. Although all known languages have a word for 'to say' or 'to speak,' languages differ as to the number of words referring to a linguistic action. In a Mayan community of Tzeltal speakers, 416 variants of the Tzeltal form *k'op* 'speech' were elicited, all of which have the form MODIFIER + *k'op* (Stross 1974). An analogous list in English would include 'sweet talk,' 'back talk,' and a few others but would, according to the linguist who elicited the Tzeltal terms, have fewer than 10 items. Languages differ also as to which aspects of the domain of speaking are linguistically elaborated: a Chamula folk taxonomy contains many terms for ritual speech (Gossen 1974), as does that of the Kuna; St Vincentians have many words for the way of speaking called 'talking nonsense' (Abrahams and Bauman 1971).

Culturally distinctive vocabularies about the act of speaking have been of interest to ethnographers of speaking because they index or reflect attitudes and knowledge of members of the community. A portion of the social reality which attaches to the category 'speaking' (and, by extension, to social life more generally) is expressed in a people's distinctive terministic screen and vocabulary of motives for speaking. Carbaugh has written, 'As speech is identified and labeled through cultural categories, its efficacy as an action—what it is doing, what it should and should not do, what it can and can not do—is displayed' (1989: 124). It follows that as conceptions of speaking, displayed in talk, vary from people to people, so too the way of life, expressed and constituted in talk, varies across speech communities.

The transmission of information is not always or everywhere the exclusive or even primary function of speech. In the working-class neighborhood in Chicago, mentioned above, much speech behavior functions, not primarily to report or to describe, but to link interlocutors in a social relationship, and to affirm and signify the interlocutors' sameness and unity. Speech there is predominantly a means to symbolize one's place in a local social hierarchy defined in terms of ethnicity, gender, age, and place of residence. By contrast, among upper-middle-class Americans, speech about one's experiences serves not only to inform the listeners about those experiences but to give the speaker an opportunity to express his or her personal uniqueness; among these speakers a high value is placed upon 'communication,' glossed as 'close,' 'open,' and 'supportive speech' in which the interlocutors reciprocally disclose personal information and validate the other's images of self. These examples suggest not only that something more than information transmission is being accomplished with speech, but also a difference, across groups, in what is accomplished (Katriel and Philipsen 1981).

3. The Speech Community

If speaking is examined as socially situated human action, which varies across the social fields in which it occurs, it is important to place it within the speech activity of a particular community. Investigators inspired by some version of linguistic determinism (as in the various versions of the Sapir–Whorf hypothesis) make the linguistic code the primary focus of investigation, describing a language and then ascertaining its communicative and cognitive correlates. The ethnography of speaking emphasizes a different approach, identifying a social community and ascertaining the codes, patterns, and functions which can be observed in that context. Hymes states as a working assumption: 'if there exists a set of social relationships, then there will exist communicative (and, by extension, linguistic) features considered specific to the relationship by the participants' (1968: 23).

Taking the social community as the starting point for the study of speech places the emphasis not on a single code but on the diverse variety of language codes and speech styles available to members of a community. This contrasts with defining the speech community as 'all the people who use a given language (or dialect)' (Lyons 1970: 326). It thus allows for the possibility (often realized in fact) that among a group of interacting speakers there will be two or more languages or dialects, and that one thing which is significant to know about their spoken life is how these different codes are deployed and what they mean to those who use them. It contrasts as well with a conception of the speech community as homogeneous and unitary (one language, one society), emphasizing rather that linguistic, political, social, and geographical boundaries are seldom coterminous and must be discovered in each case.

The complexities of linking social and linguistic patterns is suggested in the case of Indians in the Vaupes territory of southeastern Colombia (Jackson 1974). There are over 20 tribes, each of which has its own distinct language. All speakers in the area share rules for speaking and there is a lingua franca, Tukano, which makes communication possible among speakers who speak different primary languages. The men in the tribes are forbidden to marry within their tribe, thus assuring that their wives will have grown up learning another language in the home. The wives come to live in the husband's tribal longhouse, where the husband's language is spoken and where the children learn the father's language. The longhouses, which may house several families, thus are multilingual social groups. To account for the facts of linguistic usage in this language area and within any particular longhouse in the area, requires a conception of social unit which allows for overlapping social and linguistic boundaries.

In order to accommodate such cases, Gumperz has defined a speech community as, 'any human aggregate characterized by regular and frequent interaction by means of a shared body of verbal signs and set off from similar aggregates by significant differences in language use' (Gumperz 1968). This definition, which has been influential in the ethnography of speaking, emphasizes patterns of interaction and communication on the social side of the expression and leaves open the linguistic criteria which constitute a speech community. Hymes defines speech community as 'a community sharing rules for the conduct and interpretation of speech, and rules for the interpretation of at least one linguistic variety' (1972: 54). The emphasis is on a social community as the basis for describing ways of speaking, leaving open the criteria for identifying the social community. Hymes (1972) also includes among the social units which can provide a basis for description such related concepts as 'speech area,' in which speaking rules are shared among speakers of contiguous languages, as where speakers of Czech, Hungarian, and German may be found to share norms as to greetings, acceptable topics, and the organization of conversations; 'speech field,' as the total range of communities within which a person's knowledge of varieties and speaking rules potentially enables him to move communicatively; and the 'speech network,' the specific linkages of persons with whom one actually speaks (1972: 55).

Much of the research in the ethnography of speaking effectively conjoins the emphasis by Gumperz on patterns of interaction and the emphasis by Hymes on shared rules for conduct and interpretation of speech by focusing interest on a particular speech event (or events) and the rules which govern activity within it (them). By identifying locally defined events (or situations or scenes) for speaking, and the rules attending them, an ethnography of speaking focuses on concrete activities which are meaningful contexts for action, contexts in which patterns of interaction and rules for speaking jointly meet.

Speech events, e.g., a conversation at a party, can be viewed, in particular cases, as consisting of particular speech acts, e.g., a joke within the conversation. A speech act may be the whole of a speech event, as when a single prayer constitutes an entire rite; but more often a speech event will consist of several different speech acts. Both speech events and speech acts, from the perspective of the ethnography of speaking, are to be discovered in particular speech communities, rather than to be assumed from a general knowledge. The discovery of such events and acts, which may or may not be named in a given language, is part of the descriptive work of the ethnographer of speaking, who seeks to account for the distinctive patterns and uses of speaking in a particular speech community.

4. A Descriptive Framework for Speaking

The initial formulation of the ethnography of speaking (Hymes 1962) included a framework for describing the particularities of ways of speaking in diverse speech communities. It was designed to provide an acontextual format for discovering, describing, and comparatively analyzing unique cases. It included four major headings: Speech Community, Speech Events, Factors in Speech Events, and Functions in Speech Events.

The speech community is the largest descriptive unit. Within a speech community, from one view constitutive of it, are speech events, locally defined contexts for speaking, each of which has an internal structure which differentiates it from other events in a community. Hymes (1962) extended Jakobson's (1960) model of a speech event by increasing the number of constitutive factors and functions from six to seven. Thus, any speech event is comprised of seven factors, including minimally, a 'sender,' who sends a 'message' to a 'receiver.' The message is sent via a physical 'channel,' implying as well some psychological connection between or among the interlocutors, and is expressed in a 'code' which is at least partially shared by the sender and receiver. The message is about something, i.e., its 'topic.' And the event occurs in a particular time and place, its 'setting.' As the factors which make up any act of verbal communication, these are factors to attend to in describing indigenous speech events and the speech acts which comprise them.

Corresponding to these factors are seven types of functions. The 'expressive' function focuses on the attitude which the 'sender' expresses toward what he is speaking about or toward the situation itself. The 'directive' function, sometimes called the 'conative' or 'persuasive' function, focuses on what the sender is asking the 'receiver' to do, in responding to the verbal message. The 'poetic' function focuses on the form of the 'message,' with particular emphasis on its artistic or aesthetic value to the interlocutors. Whether contact is established, and whether the 'channel' is opened and maintained between or among interlocutors, is the 'phatic' function, with emphasis on verbal contact being established or maintained. Whenever the interlocutors turn their attention to the 'code' itself (or the codes) being used, a 'metalinguistic' function is performed. A focus on 'topic,' the subject of the verbal communication, signals attention to the 'referential' function. The 'setting' may be the focus of emphasis in an act of verbal communication, as when attention turns to the social context or social relationship which forms a backdrop to the speech event, or which becomes the object of the speech event, as when interlocutors use speaking to define or redefine their social relationship; in these cases, a 'contextual' (or situational) function is emphasized. Although all features of a speech event may participate in all the functions, there may be specifiable linkages of factor and function, to be investigated in given cases.

In any act of verbal communication, one or more of these factors and their corresponding functions may be emphasized or foregrounded. For example, the seventeenth-century Quaker use of *thou* and *thee* rather than the conventional *you* and *ye* foreground a focus on the addressee and the directive function in the effort to induce the addressee to abandon his pretension to worldly rank rather than, say, an emphasis on the topic and the referential function. So, too, speech communities can differ in the relative emphasis placed on factors and functions. Among the Kuna, for example, there is considerable community interest in the aesthetic quality of verbal behavior, with an emphasis on message form; among the seventeenth century Quakers, 'plain speech' is preferred, with relatively less attention and valuation given to the artistic dimension of speaking.

Hymes's (1962) framework was proposed tentatively in the hope that it would provide a basis for empirical studies. In the 30 years following its publication there were some 250 studies which used its categories (Philipsen and Carbaugh 1986) and the framework was revised extensively as it was applied and tested through fieldwork. Important extensions include development of the social units of description, with attention given to speech network and speech field; a typology for characterizing societies as to the quantitative and qualitative importance of speaking; formalized procedures for rule-discovery and rule-statement; and expansion of the number of factors in speech events. The factors in speech events were reformulated in the mnemonically coded 'speaking,' thus: Setting or Scene; Participants; Ends; Act Characteristics, including both the form and content of the message; Key or Tone of the event; Instrumentalities, including Channels and Codes; Norms of Interaction and of Interpretation; and Genres.

The framework is intended to provide, not so much a checklist of things to describe, as an initial set of questions and descriptive possibilities in the study of ways of speaking in particular communities. It is intended to provide as well a format for comparison across communities, i.e., a set of categories for the articulation of similarities and differences, where these are found. In both of these regards, the framework is heuristic, set up so that the results of particular studies can be used to expand and develop it.

5. Communicative Competence

Chomsky posited an innate capacity to learn language and made the claim that 'every speaker of a language has mastered and internalized a generative grammar that expresses his knowledge of his language' (1965: 8). 'Knowledge of language' in this view consists of the ability to produce and understand a seemingly infinite number of novel, grammatical sentences in a language.

Against this notion of idealized linguistic competence Hymes has set the term 'communicative competence' (see *Communicative Competence*). Instead of referring exclusively to a speaker's knowledge of linguistic forms, 'communicative competence' refers to an ability to use language appropriately in the social situations of a speech community.

> Within the social matrix in which it acquires a system of grammar a child acquires also a system of its use, regarding persons, places, purposes, other modes of communication, etc.—all the components of communicative events, together with attitudes and beliefs regarding them. There also develop patterns of the sequential use of language in conversation, address, standard routines, and the like. In such acquisition resides the child's socio-linguistic competence (or, more broadly, communicative competence), its ability to participate in its society as not only a speaking, but also a communicating member. What children so acquire, an integrated theory of socio-linguistics must be able to describe.
>
> (Hymes 1974: 75)

Descriptions of the ways of speaking in particular speech communities reveal that as speakers humans are capable of a great deal linguistically—capable, for example, of exploiting the linguistic resources of their communities for all the varied ends of linguistic activity, including the referential, the poetic, the persuasive, etc. And as speakers they not only enact and experience but also undermine, challenge, and negotiate the local meanings which attach to and are expressed in complex arrays of linguistic activity. Thus, from the standpoint of the ethnography of speaking, speakers are seen (or heard) to display a wide range of speaking competencies, a range which the term 'communicative competence' was proposed to encompass.

6. Future Directions

Since its inception in 1962, the ethnography of speaking has developed its basic categories and modes of statement. A large body of fieldwork has been conducted under its auspices, with the aims of providing descriptions of particular ways of speaking, developing a descriptive framework, and

Language and Interaction

developing cross-cultural generalizations about the interaction of language and social life. With the development of the conceptual framework and of a body of fieldwork materials, drawn widely from many languages and many areas of the world, it is possible to begin comparative work in speaking, that is, to search for cross-cultural regularities in communicative conduct and to delineate more sharply than previously possible the dimensions of cross-cultural variation in speech behavior.

See also: Conversation Analysis; Communicative Competence; Discourse in Cross-linguistic and Cross-cultural Contexts.

Bibliography

Abrahams R D, Bauman R 1971 Sense and nonsense in St Vincent: Speech behavior and decorum in a Caribbean community. *American Anthropologist* **73**: 762–72

Bauman R 1970 Aspects of 17th century Quaker rhetoric. *Quarterly Journal of Speech* **56**: 67–74

Carbaugh D C 1989 Fifty terms for talk: A cross-cultural study. *International and Intercultural Communication Annual* **13**: 93–120

Chomsky N 1965 *Aspects of the Theory of Syntax*. MIT Press, Cambridge, MA

Fox J J 1974 'Our ancestors spoke in pairs': Rotinese views of language. In: Bauman R, Sherzer J (eds.) *Explorations in the Ethnography of Speaking*. Cambridge University Press, Cambridge, UK

Gossen G H 1974 To speak with a heated heart: Chamula canons of style and good performance. In: Bauman R, Sherzer J (eds.) *Explorations in the Ethnography of Speaking*. Cambridge University Press. Cambridge, UK

Gumperz J J 1968 The speech community. In: Sills D L (ed.) *International Encyclopedia of the Social Sciences*. Collier-Macmillan, London, pp. 381–6

Hymes D 1962 The ethnography of speaking. In: *Anthropology and Human Behavior*. Anthropological Society of Washington, Washington, DC

Hymes D 1964 Introduction: Toward ethnographies of communication. In: Gumperz J J, Hymes D (eds.) *The Ethnography of Communication. American Anthropologist* **66**(3) (part 2): 1–56

Hymes D 1968 Linguistic problems in defining the concept of 'tribe.' In: Helm J (ed.) *Essays on the Problem of Tribe*. University of Washington Press, Seattle, WA

Hymes D 1972 Models of the interaction of language and social life. In: Gumperz J J, Hymes D (eds.) *Directions in Sociolinguistics: The Ethnography of Communication*. Holt, Rinehart and Winston, New York

Hymes D 1974 *Foundations in Sociolinguistics: An Ethnographic Approach*. University of Pennsylvania Press, Philadelphia, PA

Jackson J 1974 Language identity of the Colombian Vaupes Indians. In: Bauman R, Sherzer J (eds.) *Explorations in the Ethnography of Speaking*. Cambridge University Press, Cambridge, UK

Jakobson R 1960 Concluding statement: Linguistics and poetics. In: Sebeok T A (ed.) *Style in Language*. MIT Press, Cambridge, MA

Katriel T, Philipsen G 1981 'What we need is communication': 'Communication' as a cultural category in some American speech. *Communication Monographs* **48**: 301–17

Lyons J 1970 (ed.) *New Horizons in Linguistics*. Penguin, Harmondsworth, UK

Philipsen G 1975 Speaking 'like a man' in Teamsterville: Culture patterns of role enactment in an urban neighborhood. *Quarterly Journal of Speech* **61**: 13–22

Philipsen G, Carbaugh D 1986 A bibliography of fieldwork in the ethnography of communication. *Language in Society* **15**: 387–97

Philipsen G, Huspek M 1985 A bibliography of sociolinguistic studies of personal address. *Anthropological Linguistics* **27**: 94–101

Sherzer J 1983 *Kuna Ways of Speaking*. University of Texas Press, Austin, TX

Stross B 1974 Speaking of speaking: Tenajapa Tzeltal metalinguistics. In: Bauman R, Sherzer J (eds.) *Explorations in the Ethnography of Speaking*. Cambridge University Press, Cambridge, UK

Ethnomethodology

G. Psathas

Ethnomethodology represents a new dimension in the social sciences which undertakes to study the everyday world as an achieved social reality. Its position is that all human action is irremediably indexical and reflexively related to the occasions and settings within which it occurs. Members are continually engaged in making sense, achieving intelligibility, and providing for themselves and others, interpretations of the self-same actions and utterances which, in turn, constitute the social situation in which they find themselves. Ethnomethodology proposes that the serious study of how members produce, sustain, achieve, and maintain 'the social world' requires close attention to the methods (i.e., members' methods or ethnomethods) of that production, achievement and maintenance, which methods include all manner of practical reasoning and practical actions. The discovery, description and analysis of such methods constitutes ethnomethodology's main tasks.

1. Major Figures

Harold Garfinkel, the founding father of ethnomethodology, (PhD Harvard, 1952) was early concerned with the problem of social order, i.e., how members make sense of the social world. His position can be considered a radical counter position to Talcott Parsons, a major theorist in American mid-twentieth-century sociology and an advocate of positivist, structural functional analysis as set forth in his book, *The Social System* (1950) with its pattern variables and in his general theory of social action.

Garfinkel was early influenced by his readings of the German phenomenologist philosopher Edmund Husserl, the sociologist and phenomenological philosopher, Alfred Schutz, as well as by Aaron Gurwitsch, phenomenologist and psychologist, by the French phenomenological psychologist and philosopher, Merleau-Ponty, and later by the German philosopher Martin Heidegger.

Garfinkel worked most closely over a period of more than 12 years with Harvey Sacks. Their collaboration was extensive and one of mutual influence. Sacks (who died in 1975) went on to develop, with Emanuel Schegloff, what has come to be known as 'Conversation Analysis,' now considered to be one of the important offshoots of ethnomethodology. Researchers in this field include, in addition to Schegloff, Gail Jefferson in the Netherlands and many others.

Centers for ethnomethodological study in the US developed at UCLA (H. Garfinkel, E.A. Schegloff, M. Pollner, J. Heritage, S. Clayman, C. Goodwin, M. Goodwin), the University of California, Santa Barbara (D. Zimmerman, T. Wilson, G. Lerner) and at Boston University (J. Coulter, M. Lynch, G. Psathas, A. Pomerantz, R. Frankel). Ethnomethodology spread to the United Kingdom in part influenced by the visits of Garfinkel and Sacks to Manchester, Cicourel to the University of London and Manchester in the early 1970s and later by Gail Jefferson to Manchester (1979–81) and York (1982–85), and Anita Pomerantz to Oxford (1981–84). Sociologists who have been most active in the UK have included R. J. Anderson, J. M. Atkinson, G. Button, R. Dingwall, P. Drew, D. Francis, C. Heath, S. K. Hester, J. Hughes, W. W. Sharrock, and D. R. Watson. In Canada, A. Blum, P. Eglin, J. Heap, P. McHugh, J. O'Neill, D. Smith, R. Turner, and P. Weeks all have been involved in various ways in ethnomethodological studies; in Germany, J. Bergmann, C. Meier, and H. Knoblauch; in France, B. Conein, A. Coulon, R. Dulong, M. de Fornel, and L. Queré; and in The Netherlands, G. Jefferson, P. ten Have, M. Huisman, M. L. Komter, H. Maizland, and H. Houtkoop-Steenstra.

2. The Name 'Ethnomethodology'

The ethnomethodological approach studies the *methods* actually practiced (used) by *members* of society for accomplishing (doing) whatever it is they are doing (including their ways of talking about whatever it is they are doing). A serious and careful study of the methods used by members for accomplishing practical actions in the world of everyday life would result in descriptions and analyses of *the methodology of everyday life* or of the ethno- (member of a group or the group's) methodology, or members' methods.

When Garfinkel first developed the term he was studying how the members of a jury performed (accomplished) the task of jurying. He believed (1967) that 'Ethno' seemed to refer, somehow or other, to the availability to a member of common-sense knowledge of his or her society as common-sense knowledge of the 'whatever.' But, rather than refer to members' methods for doing jury work as 'ethno-jurying' or 'ethno-law,' which would provide subdivisions of members' methods according to the (substantive) topics with which their activities were concerned, he took a broader perspective.

Perhaps, ethnosociology or 'members' ways of doing sociology' would have been an alternative term. But actually this term would not be consistent with Garfinkel's intended topic of study which is namely, how members accomplish social order, not how members describe or analyze their society. For example, in anthropology there had developed a perspective called 'ethnoscience' which aimed to discover the ways that members of a particular culture name and classify objects and products, e.g., ethno-botany, ethno-musicology, ethno-history, etc.; i.e., the particular classification systems of particular cultures at particular times and places. As Garfinkel stated (1967), his concern was with:

> the *how* it (society) gets put together; the *how* it is getting done; the *how* to do it; the social structures of everyday activities...studying how persons, as parties to ordinary arrangements, use the features of the arrangement to make for members the visibly organized characteristics happen.

Another way of saying this is that he is concerned with 'everyday praxis.'

The 'methodology' part of the term ethnomethodology is to be understood as referring to the 'how,' *the actual situated practices, the methods by which everyday activities are accomplished*. So, ethnomethodology represents the search to discover members' methods of accomplishing the complex tasks of everyday life, including methods of reasoning, methods of interpretation, methods of communicating, methods of interacting, methods of doing conversation, methods of doing *whatever*. And, since many of these practices are repeated and patterned, their methodical character, their orderliness, i.e., their organization, can be discovered. Ethnomethodology is oriented to the discovery and analysis of such orderliness. It is not interested in explanation or the analysis of originary or causal relations.

3. Indexicality and Reflexivity

Two of the major concepts of ethnomethodology are 'indexicality' and 'reflexivity.' Indexicality refers to the fact that, for members, the meaning of what they say and do is dependent on the context in which their doing and saying occurs. Members are able to understand an action or utterance because they also know something about the time and place of occurrence, who the parties were, what had occurred previously, the relationship between the parties, what occurred next, and so forth.

Members are interested in the particularities of actions and utterances and not in standardized or idealized meanings. In achieving understanding, members take notice of and utilize all that is available to them in the context. Such details Garfinkel has called 'indexical particulars.' Indexicality is thus part and parcel of every ordinary situation of action and talk and cannot be remedied by developing standardized or idealized concepts or terms. Members do and must use indexical particulars in making sense of their circumstances; it is an essential property of the way they make interpretations, arrive at sense, decision, action, etc.

Reflexivity refers to the fact that, for members, 'the features of the real society are produced by persons' motivated compliance with these background expectancies,' that is, commonsense knowledge provides members with knowledge of the features of society and these same features are then complied with. There is thus a reflexive relation between the 'facts' about society and the ways that members use practical reasoning and commonsense knowledge to depict society. Accounts are reflexively tied to those matters and circumstances which are being accounted for. Garfinkel (1967: 4) has stated this as:

> members' accounts are reflexively and essentially tied for their rational features to the socially organized occasion of their use, for they are *features* of the socially organized occasions of their use.

Accounts reveal features of the setting, as Leiter (1980: 139) has put it,

> which, in turn, depend on the setting for their specific sense. The features of a setting that are revealed by descriptive accounts and behavior do not just explicate the setting; they, in turn, are explicated by the setting... (B)ecause accounts consist of indexical expressions they depend on the setting for their meaning. At the same time, a feature of any setting is the production of accounts. The setting gives meaning to talk and behavior within it, while at the same time, it exists in and through that very talk and behavior.

4. The Ethnomethodological Attitude

The natural attitude, as Husserl and Schutz have shown, is the attitude of the person living in the world of everyday life. In that attitude persons accept things as they are, as they appear to be, without question. Social reality is regarded as simply there, as a world existing independent of perception. For persons who operate within the natural attitude, these 'facts' are accepted, they are not subjected to further study. That is, how members have achieved this 'sense' or 'interpretation' of what the world is, how members actually experience and describe the social world as 'factual,' how members achieve, for themselves and for others, this sense of the massive, external, 'objective' quality of the social world, is *not* studied. But it is precisely *this* which ethnomethodology wishes to study. Therefore, these methods for achieving a 'sense of the social world' as 'factual' as 'out there' as 'external' must be studied directly.

The ethnomethodologist does not say that the social world *is* this way or that, instead he or she brackets, that is, sets aside, all such ideas and beliefs and does not consider them *true or false*. Instead the focus in on *how* persons make the social world 'factual,' 'observable,' and 'real' for themselves. This would include, of course, how they talk about it. So, rather than taking a position that one version of the world or the other is 'correct' the ethnomethodologist would ask instead, how do members go about deciding matters of 'correctness' (or 'truth'), what interpretations do they engage in, how do they talk about such matters, and how do they achieve what they would recognize as and call 'correct'?

Society is not 'denied' nor does it 'disappear' as some critics have claimed. For members, society is 'always there,' but, for the ethnomethodologist, that which members consider to be 'society' is capable of study only in and through members' practices. These practices include their completed (past) activities as well as their present, still on-going activities, including speaking and acting. Past activities are available for study through recall, written materials, and in whatever ways these are referred to and retrospectively analyzed by members.

5. Ethnomethodology is not Ethnography

Ethnomethodology represents a 'methodography,' i.e., a search for the practices or methods by which the 'substantive features of the setting are made observable' (Zimmerman and Pollner 1970). It is therefore not the same as ethnography. Rather than focusing on what members do, in terms of such substantive headings as, for example in family sociology, marriage, divorce, kinship, property, (which are concerns of conventional ethnography), an ethnomethodological approach would focus on members' methods for making visible, demonstrable and accountable the particular settings' features, e.g., how members recognize, describe, and make accountable, for themselves, the settings' features. The result would be discoveries with regard to a set of members' practices for accounting for such matters as, for example, 'marriage' or 'divorce' or 'kinship,' what and how categorization devices are used, how persons are 'counted' ('traced,' 'located') or not counted; how persons are 'classified' and 'unclassified,' 'collected' and 'separated' for particular purposes, and in what ways matters such as these are 'decided and done' and various types of occasions and for various purposes.

Ethnomethodological studies may discover categorization practices which underlie 'family' or 'kinship' terminological assignments and, as a collection of practices, members' categorization practices (or, as Sacks called them, membership categorization devices or MCDs) may be found to display general (or invariant) features (or structures) which hold across particular occasions, across particular speakers, etc. The discovery and analysis of 'methods of categorization' may lead more deeply into kinship terminologies or away from kinship to everyday practices in other areas, e.g., racial, class, personality, or pronoun references. The phenomenon of 'members' methods of categorization, as a members' method, is not limited by virtue of any prior preconceptions to such conventional topics as kinship (cf. Jayyusi 1984, Hester and Eglin 1997).

Ethnomethodological studies may be said to be, in part, critical of conventional work in the social sciences. The criticism is this: that conventional studies do not seek to study the phenomenon as a members' phenomenon, in all its details, following it wherever it may lead but, instead, try to specify, in advance, even before the research has begun, what the topic is exactly, how the topic is to be studied, and what form the results of the inquiry should take. For example, conventional studies demand that variables must be defined, that measurement is necessary, that statistical or quantitative analysis is essential, that empirical generalizations must be proposed, that interpretation of findings in relation to prevailing general theories (as found in the sociological literature) is necessary, and that, preferably, a casual theory be developed.

It is not difficult to understand why social scientists who accept such a model of research are skeptical and critical of ethnomethodological studies which do not appear in this form at all. Further, ethnography tries to describe the everyday practices of members of society but uses descriptions to make the events and activities observable and understandable.

Such use of description to make events observable and understandable is a way of 'constructing' everyday reality. It is a way of creating a 'sense of social structure.' That is, description would be considered by ethnomethodology to be a set of accounts whose meaning is understood from within the framework of commonsense understandings. Descriptions produce classifications, organization, coherence, relevances, rule in some matters, rule out others, etc. The use of description hides its indexical and reflexive character as a members' practice.

Ethnographers are interested in such matters as beliefs and the content of beliefs, i.e., what beliefs are about. The ethnographer may then describe what persons believe, what they tell each other to believe, what they tell their children, to whom they tell certain beliefs, how they separate their beliefs by categories such as religion, tradition, economics or politics. The emphasis in such research is on systematically collecting and observing such beliefs. In contrast, instead of being concerned with the contents of beliefs, the ethnomethodologist would consider beliefs as *members' ways of accounting to themselves for certain matters.* Beliefs, and their expression, would be studied to see how they are *used*, what *work* they actually do for members, i.e., what they *accomplish*. One discovery may be that 'beliefs' serve to explain action, for example, it may be said of a person that he watered his crops *because of his 'belief'* that water helped crops grow. The use of such words, as 'believe,' may be used, by members, to interpret, make sense of, peoples' actions (Coulter 1979b). Ethnomethodology would study the ways members have of making sense of activities and events. If such ideas as 'belief' or 'motive' are used by them then how these are used and what their use accomplishes would be subjected to study. Such studies would reveal what commonsense knowledge and understandings in their everyday meanings (uses) are for members by making commonsense knowledge and understandings the topic of study.

6. Knowing How and Knowing 'the How'

Ethnomethodology says that members of society cannot be asked how they accomplish their everyday activities and their answers then used as proportional knowledge. The reasons offered are first, that members are, essentially, *not interested* in analyzing how they do things, they are only interested in *doing* them. Second, members are not *aware*, in any explicit sense, of how they do things. Therefore, even if asked to try to explicate, or analyze, what they do, their analyses are inadequate.

For members of society, the effective test of whether they 'know how' to do something is whether they can actually do it, whether it be to have a conversation, draw a map, give directions, diagnose a disease, or give a lecture. Members operate with certain assumptions, take matters for granted, know how to do things without ever analyzing the 'how' of what they know, i.e., without ever having propositional knowledge.

For the ethnomethodologist, the methods which members actually use to accomplish whatever it is they are doing are an 'awesome mystery.' The discovery, description and analysis of these methods is a task for someone with a special interest, whose focus of attention will be on such matters directly. If the social scientist is to analyze commonsense understandings, simply using the same commonsense understandings that members use will not achieve the desired result. Instead, the commonsense understandings must themselves be analyzed and made into topics of study (not simply used as resources for producing the activity itself).

Ethnomethodology proposes to analyze commonsense knowledge, to discover how commonsense knowledge comes to be constituted, what produces, for members, the sense that it is 'knowledge,' and how 'knowledge' is *used*. For Garfinkel knowledge is not 'in the head' but consists of the 'doing,' i.e., knowledge is not a mentalistic phenomenon but 'praxis.' (A knowledge claim is a claim; knowing how to do something is demonstrable only in the doing itself.) However, social scientists cannot escape using commonsense knowledge (understandings) in their own work. After all, they live in the world of everyday life, they talk, write, communicate using the same language and linguistic practices as members do. Their own use of talk (language) can also be examined to discover the methods whereby talk makes 'visible' the matters talked about. Such methods as 'citation of typical cases,' 'referencing behavior to rules,' 'glossing,' 'making arguments as to reasonableness,' etc. may be methods used by members and social scientists alike.

Or, as another example, the social scientist engages in practical actions of collecting, observing, classifying, counting, describing, etc. These may be done in the same ways that 'ordinary' members accomplish these same activities, e.g., the use of categorization devices, deciding on object constancy, seeing another one like the last one, seeing an item as one of a type, etc.

Such methods, because they are used by social scientists, are not somehow transformed into 'better' or 'different' methods, or into 'scientific methods.' Rather, these methods can be subject to ethnomethodological inquiry also. The result is that ethnomethodology produces a view of all activities within the world of everyday life, even those of social scientists, as first and foremost practical activities subject to ethnomethodological analysis. This does not result in ethnomethodology becoming a 'sociology of science' or a 'sociology of sociology.' Rather the methods of sociology and all of the sciences are revealed to be practical accomplishments in their own right (cf. Coulter 1989, Lynch 1993).

Ethnomethodology is an approach or attitude or perspective by which any and all practices for accomplishing whatever, in and of the world of everyday life, are revealed as members' practices. This means that ethnomethodology is a perspective which has relevance for all the social sciences. In political science, history, anthropology, and economics, for example, ethnomethodological studies could be done of practical political, historical, or economic reasoning.

When the social sciences are studied as practical activities, the topic is not the *content* of knowledge developed by the social science but the *methods* used by the social sciences to produce and accomplish such 'knowledge,' i.e., that which is considered to be 'knowledge.' (However, this does not mean that ethnomethodology *must* analyze its own methods of practical reasoning, only that it *can* do so. And, it is not to be inferred that ethnomethodological studies will inevitably be caught in an endless infinite regress of analyzing how 'studies of the studies of the studies' are done.) Ethnomethodology treats social scientists' practices as practical activities deserving of study in themselves. In this sense, ethnomethodology can be considered a reflexive social practice which seeks to analyze the methods of all social practices (including its own). Ethnomethodology is, therefore, a genuine, reflexive social science. As such, it offers to contribute to all studies of the world of everyday life, including studies of the work of the sciences themselves.

See also: Conversation Analysis; Sociology of Language; Sacks, Harvey.

Bibliography

Atkinson P 1988 Ethnomethodology: A critical review. *Annual Review of Sociology* **14**: 441–65

Atkinson J M, Heritage J 1984 *Structures of Social Action*. Cambridge University Press, Cambridge, UK

Benson D, Hughes J A 1983 *The Perspective of Ethnomethodology*. Longman, London

Boden D, Zimmerman D H 1991 *Talk and Social Structure: Studies in Ethnomethodology and Conversation Analysis*. Polity Press, Cambridge, UK

Button G 1991 (ed.) *Ethnomethodology and the Human Sciences*. Cambridge University Press, Cambridge, UK

Cicourel A 1964 *Method and Measurement in Sociology*. Free Press, New York

Coulter J 1979a *The Social Construction of Mind: Studies in Ethnomethodology and Linguistic Philosophy*. Macmillan, London

Coulter J 1979b Beliefs and practical understanding. In: Psathas G (ed.) *Everyday Language*. Irvington, New York

Coulter J 1989 *Mind in Action*. Humanities Press, Atlantic Highlands

Garfinkel H 1967 *Studies in Ethnomethodology*. Prentice-Hall, Englewood Cliffs, NJ

Garfinkel H 1986 (ed.) *Ethnomethodological Studies of Work*. Routledge and Kegan Paul, London

Garfinkel H 1996 Ethnomethodology's program. *Social Psychology Quarterly* **59**(1): 5–21

Garfinkel H, Sacks H 1970 On formal structures of practical actions. In: McKinney J C, Tiryakian E A (eds.) *Theoretical Sociology*. Appleton Century Crofts, New York

Garfinkel H, Wieder D L 1992 Two incommensurable, asymmetrically alternative technologies of social analysis. In: Watson G, Seiler R M (eds.) *Text in Context: Contributions to Ethnomethodology*. Sage, Newbury Park, CA

Heritage J 1984 *Garfinkel and Ethnomethodology*. Polity Press, Cambridge, UK

Hester S, Eglin P 1997 *Culture in Action: Studies in Membership Categorization Analysis*. International Institute for Ethnomethodology and Conversation Analysis and University Press of America, Washington, DC

Hill R K, Crittenden K (eds.) 1968 *Proceedings of the Purdue Conference on Ethnomethodology*. Purdue University, West Lafayette, IN

Jayyusi L 1984 *Categorization and the Moral Order*. Routledge and Kegan Paul, Boston, MA

Leiter K 1980 *A Primer on Ethnomethodology*. Oxford University Press, New York

Livington E 1987 *Making Sense of Ethnomethodology*. Routledge and Kegan Paul, London

Lynch M 1985 *Art and Artifact in Laboratory Science*. Routledge and Kegan Paul, London

Lynch M 1993 *Scientific Practice and Ordinary Action: Ethnomethodology and Social Studies of Science*. Cambridge University Press, Cambridge, UK

Parsons T 1950 *The Social System*. Free Press, Glencoe, IL

Psathas G 1968 Ethnomethods and phenomenology. *Social Research* **35**: 500–20

Psathas G 1980 Approaches to the study of the world of everyday life. *Human Studies* **3**: 3–17

Psathas G 1979 (ed.) *Everyday Language: Studies in Ethnomethodology*. Irvington and Wiley, New York

Psathas G 1995 *Conversation Analysis: The Study of Talk-in-Interaction*. Sage, Thousand Oaks, CA

Rawls A 2000 Harold Garfinkel, In: Ritzer G (ed.) *The Blackwell Companion to Major Social Theorists*. Blackwell, Oxford, pp. 545–76

Sacks H 1972 An initial investigation of the usability of conversational data for doing sociology. In: Sudnow D (ed.) *Studies in Social Interaction*. Free Press, New York

Sacks H 1974 On the analyzability of some stories told by children. In: Turner R (ed.) *Ethnomethodology*. Penguin, Harmondsworth, UK

Sacks H 1989 Lectures 1964–65. *Human Studies* **13**: 3–4

Sacks H 1992 (ed. Jefferson G) *Lectures on Conversation*, 2 vols. Blackwell, Oxford, UK

Schenkein J (ed.) 1978 *Studies in the Organization of Conversational Interaction*. Academic Press, New York

Sharrock W W, Anderson R J 1986 *The Ethnomethodologists*. Tavistock, London

Sudnow D (ed.) 1972 *Studies in Social Interaction*. Free Press, New York

Sudnow D 1978 *Ways of the Hand*. Harvard University Press, Cambridge, MA

Turner R (ed.) 1974 *Ethnomethodology*. Penguin, Harmondsworth, UK

Wieder D L 1974 *Language and Social Reality: The Case of Telling the Convict Code*. Mouton, The Hague

Zimmerman D, Pollner M 1970 The everyday world as a phenomenon. In: Douglas J D 1970 (ed.) *Understanding Everyday Life*. Aldine, Chicago, IL

Identity and Language

R. Mesthrie and A. Tabouret-Keller

Most linguists, following Hockett (1966) would view language as specific to the human species, notwithstanding the great respect they accord to the intricacies of the communicative abilities of dolphins, bees, and chimpanzees. Furthermore following Chomsky (1959) and Pinker (1994) they would also accept language as a biological trait or instinct. The interface between the social and the biological is, however, not much discussed in sociolinguistics. An exception is Chambers (1995) who has a chapter entitled 'Adaptive Significance of Language Variation' in his book *Sociolinguistic Theory*. For Chambers the underlying cause of sociolinguistic differences is the human instinct to establish and maintain social identity. He refers specifically to the profound need for people to show they belong somewhere, and to define themselves, sometimes narrowly and sometimes in more general ways: 'We must mark ourselves as belonging to the territory, and one of the most convincing markers is by speaking like the people who live there' (1995: 250). Differences that exist are to a large extent explainable in terms of status and gender differences in society. Tabouret-Keller (1997) stresses the concrete physiological basis that makes speaking seem a part one's being. As oral behavior language necessarily includes corporeal elements resulting from the physiological channels that the voice has to pass through (upper ends of the digestive and respiratory tracts) which give it its phonetic qualities. Speech and language are thus frequently associated with life itself: speech–breath–spirit–soul. Most discussions of identity within sociolinguistics have however, not surprisingly, focused on group identity. We provide an overview of how different schools of sociolinguistics have contributed to our understanding of the topic, before discussing the model of Le Page and Tabouret-Keller, which ties some of the strands together.

1. Regional Identity

It was well known amongst dialectologists of the nineteenth century that speech carries geographical overtones. Many language varieties and languages have names that tie them to a locality and confer a badge, if not an identity, upon their habitual users. Even where a specific name does not exist and the localized speech form is taken for granted amongst people who live in close networks with little geographical mobility, an occasional visit out of the terrain is enough to jolt a speaker into linking geography with a sense of personal and/or group identity. One of the pioneering studies of modern sociolinguistics, Labov's Martha's Vineyard study (see *Dialect and Dialectology*; *Sociolinguistic Variation*; Labov 1963) is ultimately concerned with the effect a localized island accent has on a sense of identity. Crucial to identity formation was the relationship between local people who relied on the tourist economy to boost income, and the rich tourists who tended to overrun parts of the island in the summer. Labov showed that a particular feature of accent (centralized first elements of diphthongs /aɪ/ and /aʊ/) was sufficient to distinguish the speech of younger Vineyarders from older inhabitants of the island whose own speech norms in this regard had over time been falling in line with those of the surrounding mainland areas. Young people showed a reverse pattern which accentuated the centralized diphthongs. Labov remarked that using a pronunciation like [rəɪt] ('right') is a subconscious affirmation of belonging to the island and being one of its rightful owners. It was, as a later commentator on this study, McMahon (1994: 242) remarked, like wearing a T-shirt that says 'I'm not a tourist, I live here.' This is not only a regional statement however, but a social one too, as the islanders in general belong to a lower socioeconomic category than the rich summer tourists from the mainland, from whom they seek to differentiate themselves linguistically.

2. Social Identity

Indirectly following the lead of intellectuals like Saussure (1857–1913) and Durkheim (1858–1917) most sociolinguists argue that the social group is more important than the individual as far as language use is concerned. An important strand in this line of thinking is Labov's model of social variation (see *Sociolinguistic Variation*; *Sociophonetics*; *Labov, William*). Labov (1966) showed that some variables like postvocalic (r) in New York City (the /r/ after vowels in words like *car* and *park*) show fine or gradient stratification according to social class. The variable is subject to 'shared norms and common evaluation' by the society at large, with higher status groups making proportionally higher use of [r]. Labov showed that with respect to other variables like (th) the same society might display a class division; stratification is sharp rather than fine, with a chasm between the working class and lower working class. This kind of stratification seems even more applicable in parts of the UK (Trudgill 1978) and pre-industrial contexts elsewhere (see Rickford 1986, for Guyana).

Similarly the model of social networks which places central emphasis on the types of links between individuals within a network (see Milroy 1987; *Social Networks*) has a great deal to suggest about identities that are formed by habitual interaction, especially linguistic interaction. Also evident in the social network model is the interaction between region of origin and social class.

3. Ethnic Identity

In some societies, ethnicity may be more salient than class stratification and language may play a key role in reflecting and indeed in maintaining and 'reproducing' an ethnic identity. Ethnicity is notoriously difficult to define and may not be as objective a phenomenon as sometimes assumed. Edwards (1985: 8) quotes Weber (1966) who regards ethnic groups as 'those human groups that entertain a subjective belief in their common descent—it does not matter whether or not an objective blood relationship exists. Ethnic membership differs from the kinship group precisely by being a *presumed* identity.'

Edwards therefore argues against the notion of a 'primordial ethnicity' which one sometimes finds in the literature on language maintenance. Edwards (1985: 163) stresses that group identity can survive language shift. On the other hand it is difficult to imagine a sense of ethnicity that does not entail significant differences in language use (e.g., religious and cultural vocabulary, and nuances of accent are well-attested in ethnic dialects). Postmodern people of the twenty-first century have multiple identities, playing out a number of roles in a single day, each of which may require different language choices.

In some contexts a first language may not be the only, and possibly even the main, bearer of a sense of community identity. In connection with the situation in Cameroon, Wolf (1997) argues that speaking English as a second language gives a sense of unity to 'Anglophone' Cameroonians, rather than their mother tongues, which are ethnically marked. In this context Wolf sees language as a prime shaper of ethnicity, but de-emphasizes the role of the mother tongue. Ethnically diverse groups have redefined their primary ethnic allegiance via a specific type of bilingualism (see *Bilingualism, Societal*). In some situations (though not in the Cameroonian situation described by Wolf) such a redefinition may eventually open up the way for language shift, with possible further implications for readjustments of identity.

4. Gendered Identity

In earlier gender and language research (see Lakoff 1975, *Gender and Language*) the main aim was to demonstrate a broad linguistic split between the sexes. Subsequent research has increasingly become more nuanced. Eckert (1989) stresses the interplay between gender and social class in setting up various overlapping identities. From anthropology and Gay Studies has come the notion that a simple two-way dichotomy is misleading; that there are differing degrees of masculinity and femininity (see *Gay Language*; Johnson and Meinhof 1997, Kulick 2000).

5. National Identity

Many writers see nationalism as a kind of ethnicity writ large (see *Nationalism and Language*), but with geographical borders and formally defined structures. Edwards (1985) writes that nationalism, with or without a linguistic component, is based essentially upon the same sense of groupness, which informs identity. For Anderson (1985) the state is able to exploit the possibilities offered by the print media to form 'imagined communities' within artificial physical boundaries. How the rise of the Internet (see *The Internet and Language*) and its 'virtual' communities affects Anderson's thesis remains to be seen.

Modern nation-states can weigh heavily upon the idealized union of language and identity by commanding many ways by which a language is forced upon their citizens, be it by constitutional definition of an national, official or State language, or by one of many other ways like the control over the language(s) allowed for school education, for law and justice, etc. As a matter of inherent paradox, though not openly expressed, the formation of states rests on discourse (and eventually on law!) justified by mother-tongue ideology, and calls on population territorial identity at the same time that these States in setting their frontiers ignored the language people used and their identity. As a result, frontiers between states seldom coincide with dialect areas.

Multilingual situations illustrate the two aspects of identification by language features or by a language label. Linguistic features deriving from language contact may identify a bilingual speaker. According to the social situation, this gives rise to feelings of devalorization, discrimination, eventually of exclusion from the dominant group, or feelings of familiarity, recognition, complicity among those who have this particular language in common or share the contact situation. Mastery of the dominant language is regarded as witnessing allegiance to the State which imposes it, and integration to a community mistakenly based on a unique linguistic identity. Such sociolinguistic constraints point towards the subjective difficulties which may arise in contact situations.

6. The Projection Model of Le Page and Tabouret-Keller

The work of Le Page (1978) and Le Page and Tabouret-Keller (1985) forms a useful way of tying together the different strands of research on identity. In this model individuals have priority; well defined social groups may or may not exist beforehand. For Le Page and Tabouret-Keller (1985:14) linguistic behavior is 'a series of *acts of identity* in which people reveal both their personal identity and their search for social roles.' In this view identity and language use are potentially fluid. In the highly multilingual and heterogeneous communities they studied in the Caribbean the researchers found it necessary to pay attention to the processes of emergence and disintegration of identities in relation to linguistic processes of focusing and diffusion. The terms 'focusing' and 'diffusion' are based on the metaphor of the cinema with the projection of images. Speech acts are acts of projection: the speaker projects his inner universe via a common language (with its nuances of grammar, vocabulary, and accent) or via a particular choice of language where choices exist (in multilingual settings). The speaker implicitly invites others to share his projection of the world, insofar as they recognize his language as an accurate symbolization of the world, and to share his attitudes towards it (1985: 181). The feedback he receives from those with whom he talks may reinforce him, or may cause him to modify his projections, both in their form and content. To the extent that he is reinforced, his behavior in that context may become more regular, more focused; to the extent that he modifies his behavior to accommodate others it may for a time become more variable, more diffuse. In time, however, the behavior of the group—that is, he and those with whom he is trying to identify—will become focused. The individual thus creates for himself patterns of linguistic behavior so as to resemble those of the group or groups which he wishes to be identified at different times. Le Page stressed four provisos to this hypothesis:
(a) that one can identify the groups;
(b) that one has adequate access to the groups and the ability to analyze their behavioral patterns;
(c) that the motivation for joining the group must be sufficiently powerful and is either reinforced or lessened by feedback from the group;
(d) that one has the ability to modify one's behavior.

Le Page and Tabouret-Keller's model thus teases out the kind of variation evident in a society from its historical moments: is it a society in the making or in flux (diffuse) or is it historically speaking, focused?

7. Critical Sociolinguistics and Identity

Critical sociolinguists and post-structuralists in general (see *Critical Sociolinguistics*) have a different 'take' on issues of identity. Their starting point is not the predefined group; but power relations in societies and the ideologies they engender. Their approach to the subject of identity is therefore not an essentialist one—the individual subject is 'decentered.' Power is considered to be diffused, concealed, or buried by the effects of ideology, and therefore requiring an archaeology of its own. For Foucault (1972) (see *Foucault, Michel*), the most important thinker on the subject, power is everywhere, it is not a commodity that can be acquired but exists in all kinds of relations including the political, economic, and educational arenas. In his early work Foucault pursued 'the constitution of the subject,' a theme Althusser had brought up in connection with the effects of ideology. The individual subject (i.e., human being) was for Foucault not imbued with an individualized consciousness or personality, rather s/he was an 'empty entity,' the intersection point of a number of 'discourses' (see *Discourse*).

Foucault's notion of speaking subjects being 'empty entities' stands in stark contrast to more humanist approaches, which see people as individuals having a full 'command' over language. The implication of Foucault's approach is that to understand the self (or speaking subject) researchers have to study language and discourse. For some critical theorists there is a sense in which language speaks through people! Potter and Wetherell (1987: 109) comment on this position from a perspective within social psychology that has come to be called social constructivism (or the social construction of identity):

> In this tradition people become fixed in position through the range of linguistic practices available to them to make sense. The use of a particular discourse which contains a particular organisation of the self not only allows one to warrant and justify one's actions ... [as an individual being], it also maintains power relations and patterns of domination and subordination. In constructing the self in one way, other constructions are excluded, hence to use a common phrase found in this tradition, the creation of one kind of self or subjectivity in discourse also creates a particular kind of subjection.

Few sociolinguists would go all the way in accepting Foucault's idea of completely decentered human subjects, which amounts to a Whorfian (see *Sapir–Whorf Hypothesis*) view of how language controls consciousness. It is difficult to comprehend, despite Foucault, how discourses originate without some kind of human agency. It is nevertheless easier to accept that once discourses arise, they may 'flourish' via the individual child or adult subject. Research on identity in this tradition is rather abstract and lacks the empirical richness of some of the more conventional studies cited above. But the effort to link ethnicity with forces beyond the level of the group, that is to power relations that predate the birth of any particular individual, is a perspective that is worthy of consideration.

8. Conclusion

The study of identity is something of a by-product of sociolinguists' interest in other topics, e.g., language variation. There are tensions between approaches that take individuals and groups for granted, those that take power relations rather than individuals as central, and those that stress individuals over groups. All research on language and identity starts from the assumption that identities make sense, that they are meaningful. Although some answers have been given in terms of symbolic functions of language and identities as language-embedded elements, the question remains open for the social psychologist and the sociolinguist how exactly these symbolic functions operate. As yet, we do not know enough about the ways in which identities themselves mediate between the various symbolic resources of different groups and also how, under certain conditions, they function as a means of power in normative social systems.

See also: Ethnicity and Language; Ethnicity and the Crossing of Boundaries; Sociolinguistic Variation; Language Maintenance, Shift, and Death; Bilingualism, Societal.

Bibliography

Anderson B 1985 *Imagined Communities—Reflections on the Origins and Spread of Nationalism*. Verso, London

Chambers J K 1995 *Sociolinguistic Theory*. Blackwell, Oxford, UK

Chomsky N 1959 Review of B F Skinner, verbal behavior. *Language* **35**: 26–58

Eckert P 1989 The whole woman: sex and gender differences in variation. *Language Variation and Change* **1**(3): 245–68

Edwards J 1985 *Language, Society, and Identity*. Blackwell, Oxford, UK

Foucault M 1972 *The Archaeology of Knowledge*. Tavistock, London

Hockett C A 1966 The problem of universals in language. In: Greenberg J (ed.) *Universals of Language*. MIT Press, Cambridge, MA

Johnson S, Meinhof U H (eds.) 1997 *Language and Masculinity*. Blackwell, Oxford, UK

Kulick D 2000 Gay and lesbian language. *Annual Review of Anthropology* **29**: 243–85

Labov W 1963 The social motivation of a sound change. *Word* **19**: 273–309

Labov W 1966 *The Social Stratification of English in New York City*. Center for Applied Linguistics, Washington, DC
Lakoff R 1975 *Language and Woman's Place*. Harper and Row, New York
Le Page R B 1978 *Projection, Focussing, Diffusion or Steps Towards A Sociolinguistic Theory of Language, Illustrated from The Sociolinguistic Survey of Multilingual Communities*. Society for Caribbean Linguistics, Trinidad
Le Page R B, Tabouret-Keller A 1985 *Acts of Identity: Creole-based Approaches to Language and Ethnicity*. Cambridge University Press, Cambridge, UK
McMahon A 1994 *Understanding Language Change*. Cambridge University Press, Cambridge, UK
Milroy L 1987 *Language and Social Networks*, 2nd edn. Blackwell, Oxford, UK
Pinker S 1994 *The Language Instinct*. Penguin, London
Potter J, Wetherell M 1987 *Discourse and Social Psychology: Beyond Attitudes and Behavior*. Sage, London
Rickford J 1986 The need for new approaches to social class analysis in sociolinguistics. *Language and Communication* **6**(3): 215–21
Tabouret-Keller A 1997 Language and identity. In: Coulmas F (ed.) *The Handbook of Sociolinguistics*. Blackwell, Oxford, UK
Trudgill P 1978 Sex, covert prestige, and linguistic change in the urban British English of Norwich. *Language in Society* **1**: 179–96
Weber M 1966 *Economy of Society*. Bedminster, New York
Wolf H-G 1997 Transcendence of ethnic boundaries: the case of the Anglophones in Cameroon. *Journal of Sociolinguistics* **1**(3): 419–26

Kinesics
A. Kendon

The term *kinesics* was introduced by Ray L. Birdwhistell in 1952, to refer to the study of the communicative role of body motion in interpersonal interaction. Elaborating on certain ideas in anthropological linguistics then gaining currency, he suggested that bodily carriage, posture, gesture, facial expression, and the like, should be looked upon as communicative modalities that, like language, are culturally patterned. This contrasted with the view, widely held at the time, that such phenomena are merely symptoms of feelings or expressions of character. Birdwhistell also proposed that if body motion functioned as a communicative code analogous to language, it could be analyzed using methods similar to those used in linguistics—specifically, the analytical methods of American structuralism (Hymes and Fought 1981). Although this aspect of Birdwhistell's suggestions has not been followed out in detail, the communicative approach to body motion he articulated has proved very influential.

1. Early Studies

That bodily posture, movement, and facial expression play an important role in human communication has been recognized since antiquity (Schmitt 1984). Thus, Cicero in his *De Oratore* and Quintilian in his *Institutiones Oratoriae* wrote about bodily conduct in public speaking. Quintilian's discussion was an important source for treatises devoted to this topic that appeared from the seventeenth century onwards, for example by Bonifacio (Italy 1616), Cresollius (Paris 1620), and Bulwer (London 1644). Of the later works, one of the most influential is Gilbert Austin's *Chironomia* of 1802, used by writers of textbooks on the art of public speaking for at least a century. In the eighteenth and nineteenth centuries, treatises on the use of the body in acting also appeared, of which the most important include the works of Engel (Germany, 1785–86) and works expounding the system of Delsarte (France, 1811–71).

In the nineteenth century, scientific works in this field began to be published. Facial expressions were studied by anatomists such as Sir Charles Bell and physiologists such as Duchenne, and Darwin discussed them in terms of evolutionary theory in his *On the Expression of the Emotions in Man and Animals* of 1871. A long tradition of investigation followed, especially in psychology, with particular emphasis on the question of the universality of facial expression (Ekman 1973, 1982). Gesture, regarded as being relevant for theories of language origins, was discussed by Edward Tylor in anthropology (1865) and Wilhelm Wundt in psychology (1902). Garrick Mallery dealt with studies of American Indian sign language in a comparative perspective in a publication that appeared in 1880. Both Mallery and Wundt drew upon the earlier work of Andrea De Jorio, whose *La mimica degli antichi investigata nel gestire napoletano* of 1832 is possibly the first truly scientific book in this field (cf. Schmitt 1984, Kendon 1995). In this treatise, gesture and other bodily expressions observed among the Neapolitans are described and, by drawing comparisons with pictorial and sculptural works of antiquity, the author seeks to demonstrate historical continuity between the expressions of ancient and modern inhabitants of Naples. He also discusses links between gesture and spoken language, the importance of context for interpretation, the relationship between gesture, form, and meaning, and other issues still of importance today.

2. Development of the Kinesic Approach

For the first half of the twentieth century, the study of facial expression, posture, and gesture was dominated by the viewpoint of an individualistic psychology, although there were those such as the linguist Edward Sapir (see *Sapir, Edward*) (1927) who pointed out that it could also be looked upon as a culturally patterned communicative code. This view was also held by Sapir's teacher, the anthropologist Franz Boas (see *Boas, Franz*), who provided the theoretical basis of Efron's (1972) study of cultural differences in gesticulation, first published in 1941. However, the view that body motion could be considered as a form of communication did not become widespread until the 1950s (Ruesch and Kees 1956). Two factors were important here. First, mental disorder began to be seen as a disorder of communication rather than as a consequence of heredity or infantile trauma, so that communication in psychotherapy became a focus of research. Second, following the expansion of US activities overseas after World War II, there was an increase in awareness in the USA of cultural differences in interpersonal conduct. Birdwhistell, in laying the foundations of kinesics, worked in association with the linguist G. L. Trager and the anthropologist E. T. Hall at the Foreign Services Institute in Washington, DC, a division of the US State Department charged with foreign language training for diplomats. Both Trager and Hall insisted on the importance of including training in the interactional conventions of the cultures associated with the languages being studied and they together formulated a framework for the study of communicative functions of spacing, time, and body motion as culturally determined and structured in ways that were thought to be analogous to the structure of spoken language (Hall 1959).

Together with the anthropologist Gregory Bateson and the linguists Charles Hockett and Norman McQuown, Birdwhistell also took part in a project known as the 'Natural History of an Interview,' the first attempt to provide a comprehensive and integrated analysis of the linguistic, spoken and kinesic components of interaction. Though never published, this study, begun in 1956, played a central role in advancing the conceptual development of kinesics and is the source of Birdwhistell's most systematic statement of the subject (Leeds-Hurwitz 1987). In addition, the sociologist Erving Goffman (see *Goffman, Erving*), with his early work on 'self-presentation' (Goffman 1959) and his studies of the ways in which people, when in each other's presence, regulate every detail of their conduct in accordance with shared norms (Goffman 1963), provided further concepts important for later developments in kinesics.

3. A Contemporary View

Body movement functions communicatively in interaction in a number of different ways. It serves as a source of information about an individual's background, status, and situational role; it functions in creating and sustaining the context essential for the process of specific encounters, such as conversations; it has an intimate relationship with spoken expression, contributing to the interactional organization of utterances, to the way in which they are structured, and to the expression of content.

3.1 The Communication of Background, Status, and Role

People in one another's presence unavoidably provide each other with information about themselves in terms of which each guides his conduct in respect to others. Body size, carriage, clothing, and hair-style, patterns in the use of facial expressions and manner, and amplitude of gesturing and other bodily movements are, to a greater or lesser degree, culturally patterned, and contribute information about the sex category and age-grade of an individual, as well as providing clues to social class, geographical origin, social status, and situational role (see La Barre 1964, Birdwhistell 1970; see also Ekman and Friesen, and Seaford in Kendon 1981). Further, as Goffman (1959, 1963) has made clear, since, to some extent, these aspects are under the voluntary control of individuals, they can be managed by them to ensure that the kind of information that is conveyed is consistent with their own view of themselves and to ensure that they are perceived by others as fitting a certain part or role within a given situation, whatever this may be.

3.2 The Regulation of Interaction

The activities people are engaged in are also sources of information. For example, pedestrians on a city street, in virtue of how they walk and where, when and at whom they look, provide each other with information about the direction in which they are moving, whether or not they take account of others nearby, whether they are intent on reaching a certain goal or just surveying the environment. All of this is made use of in the process by which collision-free passage is achieved.

Co-present individuals often engage in interaction in which there is a sharing of attention, as in conversation. Participants in such 'focused interaction' (Goffman 1963) tend to arrange themselves spatially in a fashion that distinguishes them as a group, distinct from others who may be about. It is common, for example, for two or a few individuals talking together to arrange themselves so that they can look at each other easily and this often gives rise to an arrangement that is roughly circular. Such arrangements, cooperatively maintained, provide a way in which people can display to one another the part they are currently playing in the event. The shape of the arrangement also provides clues to its organization. For example, if it is the role of one person to talk more than the others, or if it is the role of one person to control the activities of several others, then the person who talks more, or is in control, tends to assume a distinct spatial position, so that the spatial arrangement of the group as a whole is different from the arrangement seen where the roles of all participants are similar.

Especially in seated groups, the sustained bodily postures of the participants show a patterning that is consistent with their manner of participation. Scheflen (1973) showed that conversationalists typically display a restricted range of postures, and that changes in posture and bodily orientation are often coordinated with changes in the kind of interaction that is taking place. For example, in interviews, where the interviewer may alternate between asking questions and listening to the interviewee's replies, consistent changes in posture may be observed which are associated with these shifts in activity. Sustained postures, Scheflen showed, serve as visible brackets for a given phase of activity and shifts in posture can mark changes from one phase of activity to the next. Sustainment of posture and changes in posture, thus, may play an important role in the process by which the shared orientation framing the interaction is achieved.

The question of how participants organize turn-taking in conversation (see *Conversation Analysis*) has been much studied. Included here are issues such as, how participants know when to speak or when to listen, how it is recognized to whom an utterance is directed, how participants show attention or inattention, how they provide responses to what another is saying, how they show they are or are not ready to take a turn at talking, how the difference between finishing a turn at talking and suspending it while searching for what to say next is displayed, and so on. Gaze direction, head and face gestures, posture shifts, and other bodily movements have all been shown to play an important role (Goodwin 1981, Heath 1986). Some studies have shown that there are dialect-like differences in how these aspects of interaction are handled, which, in encounters between people of different cultural backgrounds, can be a source of difficulty (Erickson and Shultz 1982).

3.3 Kinesics, Speech, and Language
Body motion, then, plays an important role in making possible the attentional coordination necessary for focused interaction and in providing cues that are important for the regulation of various aspects of spoken utterance exchange. It also plays a role in conveying information about the phrasal structure of what is being said, as well as about content. Birdwhistell summarized observations on how head, face, and hand movements associated with spoken utterance pattern with stress and intonation and he showed that, in addition to providing visual markers of linguistic stress, differences in the directions of these movements are consistently associated with the different referents of the pronouns and demonstratives they accompany; thus, they also convey semantic information as well. Studies of the hand movements often associated with speech have shown that these are organized in parallel with the phrasal organization of speech, and that the hand-shapes and movement patterns employed may depict shapes and movements that represent actual concrete objects or actions, which either are being referred to directly by the speaker or which serve as metaphors for more abstract concepts. Evidently, visual imagery is drawn upon directly as a source of expression alongside syntactically organized lexical expression (McNeill 1992).

Communicative bodily actions can also become stabilized and established within a community as so-called 'emblematic gestures.' As such they can function like spoken items, either as if they are interjections or as true words. Further, if circumstances prevail in which speech cannot be used, whether because of deafness or for ritual reasons, such lexical usages of bodily movement can become very elaborate, and 'sign languages' may emerge (see *Sociolinguistics of Sign Language*).

See also: Communication; Sociology of Language; Goffman, Erving; Phatic Communion.

Bibliography

Birdwhistell R L 1970 *Kinesics and Context*. University of Pennsylvania Press, Philadelphia, PA
Efron D 1972 *Gesture, Race, and Culture*. Mouton, The Hague
Ekman P (ed.) 1973 *Darwin and Facial Expression: A Century of Research in Review*. Academic Press, New York
Ekman P (ed.) 1982 *Emotion in the Human Face*. Cambridge University Press, Cambridge, UK
Erickson F, Shultz J 1982 *The Counselor as Gatekeeper*. Academic Press, New York
Goffman E 1959 *The Presentation of Self in Everyday Life*. Doubleday, Garden City, NY
Goffman E 1963 *Behavior in Public Places*. Free Press, Glencoe, NY
Goodwin C 1981 *Conversational Organization: Interaction between Speakers and Hearers*. Academic Press, New York

Hall E T 1959 *The Silent Language*. Doubleday, Garden City, NY

Heath C C 1986 *Body Movement and Speech in Medical Interaction*. Cambridge University Press, Cambridge, UK

Hymes D, Fought J 1981 *American Structuralism*. Mouton, The Hague

Kendon A (ed.) 1981 *Nonverbal Communication, Interaction and Gesture*. Mouton, The Hague

Kendon A 1995 Andrea De Jorio—The first ethnographer of gesture? *Visual Anthropology* 7: 371–90

Kendon A, Sigman S J 1996 Ray L. Birdwhistell (1918–1994). Commemorative essay. *Semiotica* 112: 231–61

La Barre W 1964 Paralinguistics, kinesics and cultural anthropology. In: Sebeok T A, Hayes A S, Bateson M C (eds.) *Approaches to Semiotics: Transactions of the Indiana University Conference on Paralinguistics and Kinesics*. Mouton, The Hague

Leeds-Hurwitz W 1987 The social history of 'The Natural History of an Interview': A multidisciplinary investigation of social communication. *Research on Language and Social Interaction* 20: 1–51

McNeill D 1992 *Hand and Mind*. University of Chicago Press, Chicago, IL

Ruesch J, Kees W 1956 *Nonverbal Communication: Notes on the Visual Perception of Human Relations*. University of California Press, Berkeley, CA

Sapir E 1927 The unconscious patterning of behavior in society. In: Dummer E S (ed.) *The Unconscious: A Symposium*. Knopf, New York

Scheflen A E 1973 *Communicational Structure: Analysis of a Psychotherapy Transaction*. Indiana University Press, Bloomington, IN

Scherer K R, Ekman P 1982 *Handbook of Methods in Nonverbal Behavior Research*. Cambridge University Press, Cambridge, UK

Schmitt J-C 1984 Introduction and general bibliography. In: Schmitt J-C (ed.) Gesture. *History and Anthropology* 1: 1–28

Kinship Terminology

E. L. Schusky

Linguists and anthropologists have been studying kinship terminology for more than a century. Linguists have tended to analyze this terminology in terms of how it relates to the rest of language while anthropologists have regarded kinship as a part of society and analyze it for its cultural components. The former view treats kinship terminology strictly as one part or one domain of language; the latter approach assumes kinship terms are a cultural construct that relates people in unique ways.

Both approaches must recognize that kinship terminology exists in all languages, and that all peoples have approximately the same meaning for 'relative.' That is, a domain of kinship is precisely marked off by the idea of 'relative.' Also, almost universally people have terms of address for some relatives that differ from terms of reference; they use a term like 'dad' when speaking to him and a term like 'father' when speaking about him.

Everywhere people have modeled their relations on biological connections, and their terminology shows they make distinctions between relatives of descent and relatives of marriage. Descent ties produce relatives known as 'consanguine'; relatives through marriage are 'affines.' Although exceptions occur, kinship terminology distinguishes consanguine from affine. Students of kinship study what other distinctions among relatives are made on the basis of kinship terminology. When they found that the reasons for distinctions varied widely among peoples and the resulting kin networks were organized quite differently, they searched for factors in the variation. The discovery of variables causing differences in kin organization remains basic in the study of kinship terminology in the 1990s.

If kinship is regarded as only a part of language, then the variables examined are linguistic. Kinship terms are made to fit the rules of the rest of language. When kinship is regarded as part of society and culture, the variables examined are sociocultural ones, or culture is regarded as adaptive and kinship is assumed to be a product of adaptation of the environment.

1. Origins of the Study of Kinship Terminology

In the nineteenth century, Lewis Henry Morgan studied the Seneca of the Iroquois nation and discovered they organized their kin very differently from Europeans. Their mother's sisters' children and father's brothers' children were classified as 'brothers' and 'sisters.' Thus, Seneca had many more siblings than any Indo-European speaker. When Morgan discovered that other Indian tribes classified relatives in the same way, even when speaking a completely different language, he proceeded to send questionnaires all over the world to collect kinship terms. The schedules of terminology showed that some peoples in all continents classified their kin the way Seneca do.

Morgan also discovered various other systems of kinship terminology. Many peoples in the Pacific, for example, regarded all their cousins as brothers and sisters, lacking any kinship term for 'cousin.' For these people, all the siblings of mother and father were classified as 'mother' and 'father.' In parts of Africa, Morgan found that each of the cousins had their own kinship term with a separate term for each of the siblings of the parents.

Like other social evolutionists, Morgan assumed that such cultural differences must represent stages of evolution, and that his own kinship system must represent the highest level of development. Thus, whatever was most different from Indo-European organization would represent 'primitive man.' That system must be the Pacific one which failed to recognize any differences between siblings and cousins or parents and uncles and aunts.

To generalize these differences, Morgan spoke of 'descriptive' systems of kinship terminology versus 'classificatory' systems. A descriptive system had kinship terms for lineal relatives, such as 'father,' 'grandfather,' and 'great-grandfather' that were distinct from 'uncle' and 'great-uncle.' A classificatory system grouped some collateral relatives, such as 'cousin' or 'aunt' with 'sister' or 'mother.' Hawaiian kinship terminology that grouped all collaterals with lineal relatives was an extreme example of a classificatory system; English terminology that separated every lineal from every collateral exemplified a lineal system.

In his major work on kinship terminology, Morgan explained these different systems as arising from marriage practices. He reasoned that 'primitives' first had group marriages so that offspring did not know their true mothers and fathers, that everyone in the family a generation above them must have been seen as mother and father. All the children of the same generation would be brothers and sisters to each other. In contrast, where marriage had evolved to a monogamous state, lineal relatives could be kept separated from collaterals and a descriptive system of kinship terminology would arise. In later work, Morgan saw that kinship systems also correlated with types of property and its ownership. These types were also forced into stages, with Morgan insisting on a 'comparative study' that placed the different systems on an evolutionary continuum.

Edward Tylor, a contemporary of Morgan, took kinship studies in a different direction. He noted that various peoples around the world instituted a practice of mother-in-law avoidance, sometimes suggesting the avoidance through the term for mother-in-law. His focus was upon correlating the practice with other social factors, and he discovered that avoidance commonly occurred where people practiced matrilocal residence, a custom of residing with the bride's original family. This line of research ceased until development of statistical techniques for proving correlations, but it focused attention on the necessity to see kinship behavior within the arena of culture.

2. Kinship Terminology as a Part of Language

Twentieth-century scientists rejected social evolution asserting all cultures were of equal value. Evolution suggested a superiority of European and American peoples, which anthropologists denied. In his rejection of social evolution, A. L. Kroeber misinterpreted Morgan's definition of the term classificatory in order to force kinship terminology totally within the realm of language and make English appear to be highly classificatory.

From this view, Kroeber proceeded to examine how languages of other peoples classify or categorize their relatives. He saw his search as demonstrating the equal validity of all cultures; it was meant to delineate the principles by which peoples of the world formulate systems of kinship terminology. These principles were used in similar ways by everyone.

Kroeber listed eight principles. Most systems distinguish people in the same and different generations; they indicate differences between lineal and collateral relations; they mark differences of age within the same generation (lacking in English); they indicate sex of the relative; they denote the sex of the person through whom a relation exists (lacking in English); they discriminate consanguine from affinal; they denote whether the relative is dead or alive (lacking in English). In sum, the word 'niece' denotes a relative a generation below the speaker, a female, and a collateral.

Viewing kinship terminology as language, Kroeber argued that when the same word is used for male cousin and husband (as it is in some Indian languages), the correspondence is due to both relatives being of the same sex, the same generation, of opposite sex to the speaker, and both collateral. Morgan would have had to argue that the correspondence was due to a marriage practice that directed one to marry a cousin (a practice that was found to be more widespread than Kroeber realized). Kroeber concluded that the identical terms had to be explained as a linguistic phenomenon resting on the same psychological mechanisms that ordered other mental classifications. The ultimate reasons had to be determined by psychology.

While Kroeber searched for general, psychological principles to explain kinship terminologies, W. H. R. Rivers was developing a genealogical method for studying kinship that advanced anthropological fieldwork. Like Morgan, Rivers saw kinship as cultural and recognized it as closely tied to most other cultural aspects. Unlike Morgan, he did not attempt to tie practices to evolutionary stages; rather he sought to show how kinship terminology designated the roles that kin were to play toward each other, fitting their kin groups into the total society. In sum, Rivers' work continued to emphasize how kinship terminology reflected social relations while Kroeber was battling for a psychological and linguistic explanation.

3. Functional Theory and Kinship Terminology

The next generation of anthropologists further developed Rivers's thinking, although they gave Emile Durkheim credit for their inspiration. A. R. Radcliffe Brown led in the study of kinship terminology, believing it basic for the understanding of society or social structure. Following Durkheim's view that society was an organic whole, Radcliffe-Brown posited the parts of social structure to be related to each other as the digestive, respiratory, and nervous systems are related to each other, not causally but functionally. Thus politics, religion, and economics were mutually tied together; for Radcliffe-Brown, kinship would likely have been the skeleton of social structure, providing a framework for the other systems of the organic whole.

To study kinship terminology, Radcliffe-Brown relied on the development of scientific principles that explained why two or more relatives were called by the same term. For example, 'father' and 'father's brother' are often grouped together as are 'mother' and 'mother's sister.' He argued that such classification arose from a principle of 'the equivalence of siblings.' Two men who were brothers were easily merged into one role; likewise with two sisters. The principle was further followed when a person called his mother's sisters' children, 'brother and sister.' They were, after all, children of his 'mother.' The principle sometimes even explained why siblings of opposite sex were virtually merged; in some places father's sister becomes a 'female father.' That is, the kinship term has 'father' as a stem, with a feminine affix. The mother's brother then becomes a 'male mother.'

Another principle of Radcliffe-Brown's was a 'lineage principle.' Members of a descent group could be considered as close to each other as siblings, especially when viewed from the outside. So a member of a matrilineage could merge together all the male members of his father's matrilineage, in effect calling them all 'father' even when some of these 'fathers' were in the same or descending generations. Systems of terminology that classify 'fathers' in such a way are called 'Crow.' In an 'Omaha' system of terminology, women in different generations but in one's mother's patrilineage would all be grouped together.

The two different systems appear to be mirror images of each other in their terminology with Crow descent passing through females while descent is through males in Omaha. Crow–Omaha terminologies remain central in discussions of kinship, and Meyer Fortes has detailed their similarities. Radcliffe-Brown's development of 'principles' to explain such organization of terminology differed little from Kroeber's principles, although Radcliffe-Brown would have insisted his theorems rested on social facts, not psychological ones.

Fred Eggan extended Radcliffe-Brown's work to include ecological variables. In a controlled study of social organization among the western Pueblo Indians, Eggan showed how adaptation to irrigation in the Rio Grande Valley influenced kinship. He also emphasized the importance of Spanish contact and its influence upon social organization, demonstrating the importance of history for understanding kinship.

George Peter Murdock worked along parallel lines but with a different methodology. While Radcliffe-Brown and Eggan examined in depth a small number of societies to develop their principles, Murdock developed a large inventory of different cultures and began to test hypotheses statistically. In effect, he perfected the work that Tylor had begun.

Murdock's major discovery was determining the reasons for the different systems of descent. He concluded that the ecological adaptations leading to rules of residence were basic in evolving kinship terms. Horticulture often meant that females controlled plots of land so daughters remained home at marriage, in matrilocal residence. As daughters, then daughters' daughters, followed by daughters' daughters' daughters stayed in place to form a matrilineage, kinship marked off the importance of matrilineal relatives. Eventually the terminology would be Crow, but it could begin like that of the Seneca.

As Murdock's work progressed he came to realize that kinship terminology resisted change more than other parts of society. A people might leave horticulture, such as practiced by the Mandan and Hidatsa Indians, to become bison hunters once the horse was introduced. The Crow Indians did just this, separating from the Hidatsa. When discovered by anthropologists, the Crow were living much like bilateral peoples, no longer practicing matrilocal residence, but they maintained a Crow system of terminology. Recognition that kinship terminology can be used as an index of culture change meant that it became a subject of interest to ethnohistorians and even archaeologists.

While Murdock built a case that kinship systems arose because of ecological adaptation, Claude Lévi-Strauss revolutionized thinking about kinship by claiming that most of what was structured in culture was because of the way the mind works. Art, mythology, and face painting are structured because the brain processes information by oppositions. The structure of kinship was due to the working of the mind.

Lévi-Strauss argued that kinship began with the origin of marriage. It was a form of alliance that tied relatives by descent to other descent groups. A basic structure or opposition was built into kinship by the contrasting groups of those one could marry and those one could not marry. 'Sister' was an obverse of 'wife' just as 'brother' was an obverse of 'husband.' Within the descent group, relationships were like those between siblings; relationships outside the descent group were ones of affinity. These relatives were 'in-laws.' Kinship terminology often reflects these oppositions, a fact noted by Morgan and expanded upon by Kroeber.

4. The Semantic Analysis of Kinship Terms

In a compromise between the grand theory of Lévi-Strauss and the pragmatism of Kroeber, Floyd Lounsbury proposed a new method for the analysis of kinship terminology which he borrowed from linguistics and logic. He proposed to limit examination of kin terms to a formal analysis. His first step was to identify all the basic kin terms of a language; he then generated all the rules that predicted when a term would be used for a particular relative. The research was to be judged solely on its parsimony and its sufficiency. The set of rules ought to account for all of the relatives called by a single term, and all of the kinship terms ought to be predictable by the rules. The method emphasized necessary and sufficient causes.

Lounsbury realized that most anthropologists would be dissatisfied with parsimonious explanation because it overlooked the many ways in which kinship is functionally related to the rest of culture, but he reasoned that such a concise account was the best means for making cross-cultural comparisons. He hoped that formal accounts would best pinpoint the common features giving rise to the various types of kinship systems.

In his own account of Seneca kinship, Lounsbury pointed up a number of components that distinguish one relative from another in the domain of kinship. These components are much like those of Kroeber; what Lounsbury added was a number of rules that account for terms being applied to relatives such as a half-sibling. He also pointed out to linguists that kinship was not a unique linguistic domain, as sometimes thought. Anthropologists were discovering parallel, circumscribed domains in ethnobotany, color and disease taxonomies, and even cosmologies.

Since such study identified the components comprising a term, it was known as 'componential analysis.' The procedure emphasized a close relation between linguistics and anthropology, recognizing that cultural content is expressed by language. The search focused on domains in language that could be precisely limited; classification within a domain was determined by discovering the components that characterized a class. For example, the components that define 'aunt' for an English speaker are: a relative by blood or marriage who is (a) female; (b) two degrees genealogically distant from the speaker; (c) a collateral; and (d) a generation above the speaker. As in denoting contrasting phonemes, 'aunt' can be contrasted with 'uncle' by changing sex of the relative, or with 'niece' if relative generation is varied.

Ward Goodenough demonstrated the method by analyzing Truk kinship terms. Many of his components resembled those of Kroeber, but he discovered others and demonstrated a method that exhausts the components of all kin terms. He argued that the method can also be applied to other linguistic domains. Even color categories, which are classifications along a continuum, can be analyzed for their components, although Goodenough recognized that the significata of the classes are not as precise as those for kin.

Goodenough also concluded that in the domain of kinship, a category is linguistic, not behavioral. Cultural anthropologists generally assume that a kin term suggests appropriate behavior; he warns that 'suggest' is the most a term does. A cultural meaning for 'father' exists in any society that suggests how a father should behave, but fathers often behave in quite contrary ways. It is the components of the kinship term alone that determine who one calls 'father.' Neither the behavior of that person nor the behavior of the 'daughter' or 'son' decide who is called 'father.'

Anthropologists did not ignore behavior, however, in their study of kinship. In an extensive study of contemporary American kinship David Schneider demonstrated its continued importance, despite it no longer being a part of most economic or political life. Kinship remained important in affective relations, and the usage of kin terms was adapting to contemporary conditions. American kin terminology reflected individualism and allowed a wide range of adaptation to many unique situations. In later work, Schneider concentrated on the symbolic value of kinship terminology and its reflection of American values.

Harold Scheffler urged a reevaluation of Schneider's work from a perspective of componential analysis which he believed would correct a view that saw genealogy as relatively unimportant. Schneider noted how 'father' is extended to priests, or 'mother' to the Cub-Scout 'den mother,' as evidence that genealogical distinctions lack relevance. Scheffler dismissed this evidence, seeing it as only a metaphoric extension of a component based on descent.

This debate over kinship terminology illustrated how a behavioral study of kinship could lead one to conclude that genealogy is unimportant as a factor in American kinship. Schneider did present convincing evidence. Scheffler's componential analysis, however, gave a different perspective, illustrating not only that genealogy is a part of American kinship terminology but also that componential analysis can complement the behavioral study of cultural anthropology.

5. Kinship Terminology in the Postmodern Period

By the 1980s, a reaction to the highly systematic construction of meaning in kinship terms had begun, illustrated most vividly in new forms of observing and writing ethnographies. Anthropologists seemed deliberately to avoid parts of culture which were extensively organized with the result that kinship terminologies were ignored.

What has happened is that ethnographers have often concentrated on a particular individual, and in their descriptions have paid unusual attention to the relationship between their informant, who is now called a 'consultant,' and themselves. In writing of this relation, their aim has been to evoke what the other person feels and thinks, often including the author's own feeling and thinking in the process.

The result has been an ethnography that startles or upsets the reader, much as impressionist painters hoped to evoke feelings with their art. Just as the impressionist's scene was of the mundane but often fleeting moment, the postmodern ethnographers record parts of a life that may not be related to any other lives in the other culture. No longer concerned with how representative a biography may be, the post-modern ethnographer makes no attempt to account for systems throughout a culture such as those found in kinship, with its easily collected index, kinship terminology.

The new view offers, instead, the idea that kinship is paradoxical. While terms may persist over generations, the feelings of what it means to be a 'wife' or a 'son' change with each generation and even within a generation. The new writing often captures how a consultant juggles relationships widely within the confines of a kinship term, with that term imposing few limits on thinking and feeling. In this perspective on kinship, it is seen as something not particularly learned but as experienced and thus dynamic, changing quickly in a variety of contexts.

Kinship terminologies are not recorded as systematic, even if kin terms are sometimes reported, because the postmodernist sees fieldwork as a fragmentary experience and so descriptions of the experience are likewise fragmentary. Economic and ritual systems, just as kinship systems, go unnoted. The new method appears to contradict the whole history of the study of kinship, but it is giving new insights into the dynamics of kinship behavior and the possible rapid changes in that behavior.

6. Summary

Kinship terminology has been the subject of anthropology and linguistics for more than a century. Anthropology has focused on behavior and looked for the causes of kin terms in other parts of culture or in the adaptation peoples make to their environments. Linguists have treated kinship terminology as one domain of language, although at times recognizing it as a special domain. Recognition of kinship terminology as language meant that it was treated as psychological and accepted as a given, without search for causal factors.

Some anthropologists are among those regarding kinship terminology as psychological, as represented by componential analysts and by Kroeber. Some linguists have studied the behavior involved in kinship and looked for its causes. Both approaches have always recognized the systematic nature of kinship, especially as it is recorded in kinship terminology. Postmodernism reflects a major break with this tradition. Concentration is upon fragments of experience with no attempt to record any systems within culture. This work provides no basis for cross-cultural comparisons; indeed, what postmodernists record of kinship within a culture is likely to vary widely among individuals.

The postmodern development contrasts sharply with the century of kinship study that preceded it. The new approach may be a necessary swing of the pendulum against the trend of componential analysis that lost sight of human actors in concentrating only on the language of kinship terminology, but it is hard to see how any scientific endeavor can ignore the system and regularity that is revealed in kinship terminology.

For the future, it appears likely that scientists will return to both the psychological and cultural approaches. Which one will prove superior is unknown, but it is clear that the systematic nature of kinship terminology makes it too attractive to linguists and anthropologists to ignore. The immediate future is likely to see a revived study of kinship terminology as both a domain of language and of culture.

See also: Anthropological Linguistics.

Bibliography

Eggan F 1950 *Social Organization of the Western Pueblos*. University of Chicago Press, Chicago, IL
Fortes M 1953 The structure of unilineal descent groups. *American Anthropologist* **55**: 17–41
Goodenough W H 1956 Componential analysis and the study of meaning. *Language* **32**: 195–216
Kroeber A L 1909 Classificatory systems of relationship. *Journal of the Royal Anthropological Institute of Great Britain and Ireland* **39**: 77–84
Lévi-Strauss C 1969 (transl. Bell J H, van Sturmer J R, Needhan R) *The Elementary Structures of Kinship*. Beacon Press, Boston, MA
Lounsbury F G 1964 A formal account for Crow- and Omaha-type kinship terminologies. In: Goodenough W (ed.) *Explorations in Cultural Anthropology: Essays in*

Honor of George Peter Murdock. McGraw-Hill, New York
Lounsbury F G 1956 A semantic analysis of the Pawnee kinship usage. *Language* **32**: 158–94
Morgan L H 1871 *Systems of Consanguinity and Affinity of the Human Family*. Smithsonian Institution, Washington, DC
Murdock G P 1949 *Social Structure*. Macmillan, New York
Radcliffe-Brown A R 1952 *Structure and Function in Primitive Society: Essays and Addresses by Alfred Reginald Radcliffe-Brown*. Oxford University Press, London
Rivers W H R 1910 The genealogical method of anthropological enquiry. *Sociological Review* **3**: 1–2
Scheffler H W 1976 The 'meaning' of kinship in American culture: Another view. In: Basso K H, Selby H A (eds.) *Meaning in Anthropology*. University of New Mexico Press, Albuquerque, NM
Schneider D M 1968 *American Kinship: A Cultural Account*. Prentice-Hall, Englewood Cliffs, NJ
Tylor E B 1889 On a method of investigating the development of institutions: Applied to laws of marriage and descent. *Journal of the Royal Anthropological Institute of Great Britain and Ireland* **18**: 245–72

Language in the Workplace
B. Holmqvist and P. B. Andersen

Language associated with a workplace is often classified as a specialist jargon or specific terminology belonging to a specific scientific area or craft. But a workplace is as complex as a whole nation. In this article vocabulary research is disregarded, and a less investigated area, namely 'communication' in work is described. For example (1), exchanges like the following:

A: Are you going to keep that one? (1)
B: I don't know, there was a number I changed that I had to look up in the book. Am I supposed to change it on the list?
A: Piss on it.

Most of the communication in a workplace is of this kind, just ordinary casual talk among fellow workers performing daily tasks; a 'work-language' that is necessary in order to render a service or produce a commodity or to reproduce social relations and values in the working group. Language used in this communication is not primarily characterized by its vocabulary, but rather by its context-dependency (see *Context*).

1. The Workplace as an Empirical Basis for Linguistics

Although communication in organizations has been an object of investigation for quite a time, it has yet to be properly integrated into linguistics and sociolinguistics. Although pragmatics (see *Pragmatics and Sociolinguistics*) and discourse analysis (see *Discourse*) emphasize context and language as action and cooperation, the empirical basis is rather specialised, such as, for example, classroom conversations, or therapeutic or juridical contexts.

There are several good reasons for linguistics to broaden its empirical basis with studies of language in the workplace. Most people spend a considerable part of their life in a workplace. They spend this time in specific work situations that manifest constraints not found in leisure time communication or artificial examples. The work situation highlights the contextual aspect of language since work-language is language usage in a concrete situation.

The action aspect of language is highlighted since in a workplace—more than any other place—one uses language to get things done.

The cooperative aspect of communication is highlighted, since in a workplace, one uses language to get things done in cooperation with others.

The associated work-language may provide partial explanations of the properties of the sociolect if its definition includes the speaker's role in production.

Finally, work-language has considerable practical importance in planning and understanding organizational changes, especially in connection with the introduction of new information processing equipment.

2. Sociolinguistics

From a work-language perspective, some studies of sociolects become problematic. Basil Bernstein's, theories suggest that linguistic codes (see *Code, Sociolinguistic*) are inherited within the family, but then how did the family get its communicative habits in the first place?

Different conditions of work and communicative opportunities can often give quite transparent and down-to-earth explanations of sociolinguistic differences. A good reason for managers and administrative staff to use elaborated code, and for blue-collar workers to use restricted code is that the former are paid to describe absent objects or events, or classes of them as the manager in the following example (2):

> One of the purposes of the Optical Character (2)
> Recognition is of course that one can read every-
> thing optically—directly, that is—for example our
> pay-in slips 'C'; because they have complete rows of
> optic codes, so they never have to pass the B25.
> (Holmqvist 1989)

while the latter are paid to produce the objects, not to talk about them. And when talk is necessary, it will tend to concern present, concrete objects as below (3):

> They code a lot of C-slips that have this optic (3)
> area—the machines are able to read it, and so they
> read the slip and we don't have to touch it—when
> we put it into the frame, the machine reads it and
> then we lift the blue box, and then they are ready.
> (Holmqvist 1989)

Work-languages neither coincide with national languages (see *National Language/Official Language*) nor with sociolects. The Volvo plant in Gothenburg provides a good example of this. On the one hand, the Swedish workers in the plant share a lot of morphological, phonological, and lexical forms with other working-class speakers in the city. On the other hand, more than 50 percent of the workers are immigrants who hardly speak Swedish at all; still, they do communicate and make themselves understood in the work situation. In this case, the work-language may comprise several different national languages.

3. Economy and Organization

Economic viewpoints are more relevant in the workplace than elsewhere. The organization can be seen as a network of economic exchanges. Contracts are set up in order to control initiation, execution, and conclusion of these exchanges, and the labor involved in this causes costs. Computerization is seen as one way of reducing communicative transaction costs.

One must ascertain the function of communication before it is changed, in order to avoid unintended difficulties; hence it is important to link work-language with organizational issues. One way to do this is to look at the organizational functions it serves and how it does it: for example, whether language is used to coordinate work, to distribute work, to instruct, or just to keep communication channels intact.

A work-language is dependent upon the type of work organization it is used in. A comparison of a large organization and a small-scale enterprise showed that many of the communicative functions found in the latter were not verbalized at all in the former, and some of them only on rare occasions. This was true of *ordering*, work *coordination*, work *distribution*, i.e., functions concerning the organization of work, and of *control, supervision*, and *reporting*, i.e., control functions. The overall organizational routines took care of this in the form of written schedules and internalized knowledge. But communication types that may seem to be superfluous from an economic point of view (*talk-in-the-work, greetings, comments*), considering only the isolated task, played an important role in reproducing knowledge and social relations in the organization, and were indispensable for its proper functioning.

4. Nonverbalized Meaning

Semantic analysis of work-language must be contextualized, as otherwise one would get a distorted picture of the language.

Classical linguistic analysis bases semantic analysis on some variant of the commutation test. This principle is a sound one, insofar as it prevents setting up meaning units that cannot be empirically justified. However, it presupposes that meanings are verbally expressed, and this presupposition is clearly inadequate in analyzing work-language. If a language is conceived of as a set of latent possibilities that are realized in actual speech, serious methodological difficulties can arise. A work-language researcher will typically be in the situation of understanding only a fraction of the data. Only a thorough knowledge of the work situation enables him or her to interpret it. Noncommunicative acts may substitute for communicative ones: only a part of an utterance is verbalized, the rest being manifested as work; or a work operation may be performed with a secondary communicative purpose, 'telling by showing.' In some coordinative functions, the very structure of the utterances depends upon the work process in which they are embedded. One may say that communicative acts are subordinate to noncommunicative ones as in the following exchange during a car repair (4):

> B: Yes a little further out and up, a little higher up
> towards you—there (4)
> A: Try and hold it
> B: Yes
> A: It's okay
> B: Can I start to screw?
> A: Yes—I think it's there
> (Holmqvist and Andersen 1987)

If one associates linguistic analysis closely to the situation type, and define a work-language as a language used *in* a work situation, one can say that the implicit meanings in the conversations between two skilled workers can be observed explicitly in other situations, where language is used *about* the work situation to an outsider, e.g., a novice, a visitor, a superior, etc. In such situations contextual meanings are verbalized and a comparison between the different situation types makes a catalysis of nonmanifest meanings empirically justifiable.

5. Information Technology

Constructing computer systems implies constructing and communicating an interpretation of the tasks and of the organization in which the system is used. The language users of standardized computer-mediated communication are often distinct from the 'language designers.' This means that the language may cease to be a bearer of the collective experience and identity of the workers.

In the following quotation, two workers are discussing the same system, the topic being the control area of the screen where descriptions of the tasks are displayed (5):

> A: Like, if we say, now it says 'completion' up here, but then, when I finish the pile, then it says 'production,' how come? (5)
> B: Because then you begin a new 'production,' then, when you type, when you have typed the first one and the last one, then it says 'completion.'
> A: Yes.
> B: It always says here exactly what you're doing.
>
> (Holmqvist 1989)

In this case, A has a different idea of 'what she is doing' than the system. On the researchers direct question A reveals a proper knowledge of the system but ends up referring to the work in a non-computer based, but still new term (6):

> R: You say 'complete,' do you? (6)
> A: Well, but we usually say—*anyway, we call this registering*;

Often workers in fact reject systems terms and spontaneously invent words that for some reason fit better to their conception of the task than the one provided by the system.

While the communicative functions of computer systems are often unambiguous and task related, in work-language, communication types serving to reproduce consensus about past and present events are intertwined with types that are more directly related to actual work, as shown in this exchange during a brake repair (7):

> B: No doubt about it, the drums must be stripped, in any case, we need two new front drums (7)
> A: Oh
> B: This is the worst I have ever seen
> E: You can use them as sandpaper
> A: He has driven long enough with these
> B: I have never seen anything like this before
> A: They are much worse on the other side
> E: There are only the rivets left
> B: Have you ever seen anything like it before
> A: No, not that I know of, it looks very bad
> B: Yes it does, doesn't it?
> A: It'll probably be too thin if it is stripped
> B: It certainly will
>
> (Holmqvist and Andersen 1987)

Utterances about the bad condition of the brakes are repeated in variations throughout the text. The speakers try to persuade themselves and their colleagues to agree on a certain interpretation of an ambiguous situation. In this situation, work-language is not only *rational* and to the point. It is also a piece of everyday life art.

Although a systems designer should not design the computer based sign system as a copy of the existing work-language, some knowledge of the latter is a good basis for understanding the part of design that has to do with the users' interpretation of the system.

6. Future Work

The growth of information technology entails an increasing interest in language at the workplace. It is a serious challenge for pragmatics to contribute to the future methodological and theoretical development of this emerging field.

A variety of application areas are presented in Holmqvist et al. (1996).

Bibliography

Andersen P B 1990 *A Theory of Computer Semiotics*. Cambridge University Press, Cambridge, UK
Holmqvist B 1989 Work, language and perspective. *Scandinavian Journal of Information Systems* **1**: 72–96
Holmqvist B, Andersen P B 1987 Work language and information technology. *Journal of Pragmatics* **11**: 327–57
Holmqvist B, Andersen P B, Klein H, Posner R (eds.) 1996 *Signs of Work*. De Gruyter, Berlin
Wynn E 1979 *Office Conversation as an Information Medium*. Department of Anthropology, University of California, Berkeley, CA

Narrative, Natural
M. Toolan

One of the most significant intellectual and disciplinary shifts within applied language studies of all kinds in the 1970s and 1980s could be summarized as an enlargement of basic analytical resources, beyond the sentence, to include the story. The decontextualized constructed sentence perhaps remains the chief research instrument of core linguistic areas (especially syntax), a vehicle for probing linguistic knowledge of various kinds. But increasingly researchers in psycholinguistics, sociolinguistics, second-language acquisition, discourse analysis, and pragmatics also use the situated narrative as a research instrument. Situated narratives may be produced spontaneously or in a relatively natural situation (in the context of Western education, even showing three pictures to a child and later asking him or her to recall the story counts as a relatively natural experience for that child). By comparison with other kinds of linguistic data, such narratives, it is held, furnish a less forced or artificial (and so more sociologically and psychologically real) display of language behavior, mental faculties, and whatever else may be involved in cultural and communicative competence. The following sections chart just some of the influential ways in which natural or situated narratives have been studied and used to advance understanding of topics as diverse as cognitive development and covert discrimination in education.

1. Labov and Narrative Structure

A great deal of exciting work on naturally occurring narrative—particularly the narratives of ordinary people in their everyday lives—stems from just two seminal essays by the American sociolinguist William Labov (Labov and Waletzky 1967, Labov 1972). Labov hypothesized that fundamental narrative structures are to be found in oral versions of personal experience—the ordinary narratives of ordinary speakers. Using basic techniques of structural linguistic analysis, Labov sought to relate linguistic-structural properties to functions, isolating two such functions as essential in situated narrative. The first of these is the referential function: narrative is a means of recapitulating experience in an ordered set of clauses that matches the temporal sequence of the original experience. The second is the evaluative function. Here, narrative is expressive of a teller's—and addressee's—involvement with and reaction to a story: the linguistic reflexes, in the narrative telling, that the story is not simply something to be reported in a detached way, but is and was a part of the teller's lived experience. Part of the evaluative function is the standard requirement that a narrative have a point and be deemed, in the given situation, worth telling.

A foundational claim is that fully narrative clauses, the backbone of narrative as defined by the referential function, are temporally ordered independent clauses that must occur in a fixed presentational sequence. It is the potential mobility of subordinate clauses around the main clause from which they depend (without alteration of the basic event sequence, the story), that excludes them from consideration as fully narrative clauses. The very opposite of a fully narrative clause is typically one describing the circumstances surrounding the fixed sequence of events, moveable to any point in the text, and so known in Labovian terminology as a free clause. Interestingly, mainstream functionalist linguists who do not necessarily subscribe to Labov's proposals are now directing much attention to such questions as what counts, cognitively and linguistically, as an 'event'; how discoursally real are impressions of 'background' and 'foreground,' and what grammatical factors in different languages contribute to backgrounding (e.g., tense, aspect, realization in subordinate clauses); what part in such stagings is played by word-order and, in complex sentences, clause order; and whether there are patterns in the use of discourse anaphora (vs. nonpronominal subsequent mention of an individual in a story), which are sensitive to the discourse-salience of the individual being referred to.

Narrative and free clauses respectively enact the two core functions of narrative: the referential recall of temporally ordered experience, and the evaluative staging of the story so as to convey its point and tellability. Intermediate clause-types, with limited mobility in the text, may be subtle but analyzable and predictable blends of these functions (Labov's names for these include narratively coordinate clauses and restricted clauses).

Labov's scheme really only attracted wider attention when he applied it in the study of a cultural phenomenon of rather more political contention than Propp's Russian fairytales: he used the model to highlight the logic and structure of oral narratives elicited from lower-class young black males in New York City. In Labov 1972 a six-part structure is posited of a 'fully-formed oral narrative':

(a) Abstract: What, in a nutshell, is this story about?
(b) Orientation: Who, when, where, what?
(c) Complicating action: Then what happened?
(d) Evaluation: So what, how is this interesting?
(e) Result or resolution: What finally happened?
(f) Coda: That is the end of the story, the speaker has finished and is 'bridging' back to the present speaker–addressee situation.

Some brief remarks on these numbered elements are in order. Evaluation, while associable with a most expected place in the progression of a narrative (i.e., just prior to the resolution), in practice may well permeate the entire telling, occurring anywhere. Together with the coda, the abstract can be thought of as one of the optional margins of a narrative. Complicating action, on the other hand, the phase in which most of a story's positionally-fixed narrative clauses occur, is the obligatory nucleus. An abstract may serve three distinct ends: it may sketch a narrative in a severely abridged form (while never being an adequate telling of it); it may constitute the request of an extended turn of talk necessary to tell a story; or it may function as advertisement or trailer for a story.

A variant of the normal pattern in which a single teller provides both abstract and following story is that where a coconversationalist supplies an abstract of a story considered worth the telling, in the process of prompting or inviting another participant to tell it. This technique may appear in many settings where at least two of the participants know each other well, but it is particularly noticeable in the behavior of long-established couples at social gatherings. One interesting consequence of the technique is that worries about tellability are no longer, as usually, directed at one's addressees: the prompter has effectively gone on record asserting the tellability of a story, and the prompted teller has the luxury of proceeding or not (politeness permitting), depending on whether he/she thinks the story tellable. The collaborative story-introduction is, however, fraught with uncertainties over, for example, the willingness of the selected teller to take up the task of narrating, and the acceptability to that teller of the story abstract which has been supplied.

As indicated above, orientation specifies the participants and circumstances, especially of place and time, of the narrative, and is equivalent to what is very commonly called 'setting' in literary discussions. While orientation material can be embedded within opening narrative clauses, it more commonly comes in a block of free clauses prior to the development of the narrative action. Or at least one might think of the position between abstract and complicating action as the unmarked and logical position for orientation. In the orientation, verb-forms can be expected other than extensive verbs (i.e., transitive or intransitive verbs involving action) in the simple past tense. Thus here may be found past perfectives and past progressive verb phrases, and intensive verbs (*be, become, seem*, etc.) in relational clauses specifying attributes and identities. But perhaps the most interesting use of orientation is where components of it are strategically delayed, and the audience is told salient facts about the setting late in a narrative. This, like analepsis, may create effects of considerable surprise, even of shock. It may be particularly used where the teller himself, as participant in a sequence of events, has only belatedly learned some salient facts of a situation and wants to put his audience in a similar experiential position.

2. Evaluation

Evaluation consists of all the means used to establish and sustain the point, the contextual significance and tellability or reportability, of a story. It may take very many forms and appear at almost any point in the telling, although it is often particularly clustered around the 'hinge' or climatic point of the action, just before—and in effect delaying—the resolving action or event. It is the preeminent constituent by means of which the narrator's personal involvement in a story is conveyed.

The Labovian subtypes of evaluation are first distinguished according to whether they appear inside or outside the fixed-position clauses of narrative. Evaluations appearing outside the narrative clause are of five subtypes:

(a) wholly external evaluation; here the narrator breaks out of the frame of the story-telling to address the listener directly, expressing a current of still-valid general comment on the distant events;

(b) evaluation embedded as a comment reported as made by the teller-as-participant at the time of the events themselves;

(c) a comment made by the teller-as-participant to another participant;

(d) an evaluative comment reported as made by another participant;

(e) evaluative action; how some participant responded in physical rather than merely verbal terms to the ongoing events.

All the above modes of evaluation involve a temporary suspension of the action, a brief 'time out' from the telling of the story proper. When well-placed, such maneuvers do indeed create suspense, set apart whatever narrative follows (often the concluding resolution), and heighten the listener's interest. But all such more external suspensions can be contrasted with the narrative–clause–internal modes of evaluation.

Narrative–clause–internal evaluation is categorized by Labov into four subtypes.

(a) Intensifiers. Here are included gestures (often accompanied by deictic *that*), expressive phonology, exaggerating quantifiers, repetitions, and ritual utterances.

(b) Comparators. These indirectly evaluate, by drawing attention away from what actually happened by alluding to what might have been, what could be, but what does not happen. The main types of comparators are expressions of negation, modulation, and futurity (all encoded in the auxiliary verbal elements), as well as questions, imperatives, and, most overtly, comparative or superlative phrases. All of the above involve an indirect evaluative departure, in the lexicogrammar, from the simple direct telling of the narrative actions. A more complex departure is the use of simile or metaphor in narrative clauses.

(c) Correlatives. These combine events in a single independent clause, and require complex syntax (and are hence often beyond the control of young narrators): progressives (BE + V-ing), and appended participles (adjacent verbs in nonfinite V-ing form), both of these emphasizing simultaneity of occurrence of actions.

(d) Explicatives. These are appended subordinate clauses which qualify, or give reasons for, the main events reported: thus, clauses introduced by *while, although, since, because*, and so on.

A particular attraction of the sociolinguistic analysis of the oral narrative of personal experience is that it seems to underlie the structuring of many literary narratives too. Chapter 2 of Pratt (1977) presents numerous examples of novels and short stories revealing various forms of abstracts and orientations, though usually on a greatly enlarged scale. All sorts of departures from the unmarked or canonical narrative format, with adequate abstract, orientation, and so on, are to be found in literary narratives. Thus many novel- and story-openings project the reader into the flow of events, with insufficient orientational briefing, which may paradoxically function as an assumption of familiarity, or a radical denial of its possibility.

Pratt articulates the important point that no radical gulf divides literary narratives from everyday ones: the same devices, used for the same purposes, operate in both. She concludes:

> What is important about the fact that literary narratives can be analyzed in the same way as the short anecdotes scattered throughout our conversation? To begin with, it casts grave doubt on the Formalist and structuralist claims that the language of literature is formally and functionally distinctive.... Unless we are foolish enough to claim that people organize their oral anecdotes around patterns they learn from reading literature, we are obliged to draw the more obvious conclusion that the formal similarities between natural narrative and literary narrative derive from the fact that at some level of analysis they are utterances of the same type.
> (Pratt 1977: 67, 69)

One kind of qualification to Labovian analysis, with its seemingly sharp division of narrative doings from evaluative sayings, is influenced by the work of the philosopher J. L. Austin, and his speech-act analysis of language, according to which use of words in interaction is typically a performing of actions and not merely an asserting of true or false (hence evaluative) statements. (Labov's own informants demonstrate this vividly in other interactions he analyzes: their developed skills of dueling, rapping, and sounding demonstrate how speech itself can perform both complicating and resolutory action.) A more suspicious mode of analysis might also focus more on the degree to which a teller may distort and repress actual events in his or her retelling. Culler (1981: 184–5) notes that in the assumption that there is first a sequence of actions (the narrative) which is then decorated so as to enhance their point or tellability (evaluation), the possibility of a reverse order of impulses is being ignored, namely that, guided by the prior awareness of the tellability-requirement, tellers' evaluations shape their plots.

3. Stories in Society

Another approach to the evaluations in stories, and to the point of telling them, less directly attentive to linguistic form than Labov, more interested in community-wide motivations, comes in the work of those who try to relate tellability directly to cultural presuppositions and values. Thus in numerous papers Tannen (e.g., 1979) (see *Tannen, Deborah*) shows in some detail how one's 'structures of expectation' based on past experience influence the particular ways one constructs stories, and interprets those of others. This in turn would predict that the kinds of stories that get told, and are valued, in one cultural milieu may differ quite considerably from those that get told in another. Such seems to be the case, not simply when stories and story-points in two quite different societies are compared, but even when contrasting stories and their evaluation between two communities within the same larger society. This was the finding of Heath (1983), in her comparative study of language use in two small-town working-class communities in the rural southeast of the USA, one black and the other white. These two communities reveal quite different views of stories and storytelling, often with neglected educational and intercommunal consequences and misunderstandings (see *Literacy*).

4. Narrative Performance

Over the past few years a number of sociolinguistic studies have appeared using the folkloristic term 'performance' to describe a certain type of particularly involved and dramatized oral narrative. The term has been adopted and espoused despite resistance from some traditional folklorists, for whom the term standardly denotes the retelling of stories that are part of a tradition, are 'collectively' known, and are non-innovative.

The elaboration of the idea that narratives are often performances seems to have first emerged in the work of the Russian Formalist Eichenbaum (in his celebrated analysis of Gogol's 'The Overcoat'), whose concept of *skaz* (the teller-expressive 'yarn') has been highly influential in poetics. Most recently Hymes (see *Hymes, Dell Hathaway*), and Goffman (see *Goffman, Erving*), have advanced the study of narratives as performances, with the fullest sociolinguistic exposition of the issues coming in Wolfson (1982). To 'perform' a story is to furnish one's addressee with a more vivid and involving experience of that story, while exploiting special performance features as resources for highlighting the story's main point. These performance features include:

(a) direct speech;
(b) asides;
(c) repetition;
(d) expressive sounds;
(e) sound effects;
(f) motions and gestures;
(g) conventional historic present (CHP) (alternating with narrative past tense).

Clearly, many of these are already incorporated in some part of Labov's typology of evaluation devices, and only items (b) and (g) are noticeably new. In an aside a teller exits briefly from the time-reference of the story-dialogue he is recounting in order to add some comment about the content which has continued relevance in the present time of the teller and listeners. Both more innovatory and controversial is the explanation of conversational historic present (henceforth CHP). Wolfson questions the traditional grammarian's view that historic present, in conversation-embedded narratives, is there simply to make a story more vivid and immediate. Historic present, as used in conversation-embedded narration, has a distinct function for Wolfson (hence the emphasis on conversational historic present), and that function relates not directly to the occurrence of CHP itself, but to the patterns of switching between historic past and present tense. The switches or alternations, she says, create three main effects:

(a) an intervention by the teller;
(b) a focusing of attention on certain portions of the narrative; and
(c) a dividing up of the flow of action into distinct events.

These claims have met with some resistance from other theorists. If consistency of tense is proposed as the unmarked option in story-telling, tense-switching clearly becomes marked and noticeable; but other analysts see it as only one of very many mechanisms of teller 'intervention.' Significantly, historic present often appears only in the complicating action of oral narratives—precisely the section of stories where tense does not have to do any special task of temporal orientation (since temporal and presentational order can be assumed to be congruent). The consensus view is that tense-switching is a major potential (but not essential) means of separating out events in narratives, while CHP itself is highly evaluative and addressee-involving.

But a fuller examination of the varying relative weightings of different evaluative devices in narrative is still in progress. Wolfson's work on CHP specifies a number of variable factors which seem to influence a teller's decision to perform or not perform a narrative:

(a) similarity (or not) of sex, age, ethnicity, occupation, status, between teller and addressee;
(b) whether the teller and audience are friends;
(c) the teller's assessment of the audience's similarity of attitudes and background;
(d) whether the speech situation itself is conducive (e.g., the interview situation is not conducive); and
(e) more directly to do with the story itself: whether the story topic is appropriate to the audience, whether the events are recent or not, and whether the story includes physical or verbal interaction or not.

The probing of the influence upon tellers of various performance features taken as a group can evidently be undertaken, in principle, for any other evaluative device or group of devices. But simple trends are not always to be expected—e.g., the greater likelihood of stories to be 'performed' where conversationalists are of the same sex, of similar age, similar status, are similar in attitudes, background, status, and so on. For evaluation undertakes a larger, more crucial task, than that of performance: the task of articulating the point of a story and persuading the audience of its tellability. And where there are few dimensions of similarity between conversationalists, it may transpire that evaluation has a greater role to play, in spelling out the significance of a tale for a teller to a listener who does not share an 'unspoken understanding.' Thus greater rhetorical efforts of displayed evaluation may be involved where interactants are, in fact, remote or unaffiliated in various ways, and lack communicational closeness or mutuality.

5. Diffuse, Embedded, and Group Oral Narratives

There are other types of personal narrative, more subtly interleaved with the ongoing conversation, than those Labov extracted. One variant has been termed the 'diffuse story': here, a portion of a story is followed by an extent of multiparty conversation glossing, clarifying, and amplifying aspects of the story-portion just told. In such a format, story-evaluation can become a collaborative exercise. Diffuse story format shades into practices of embedding where, for example, several short stories are spread out and interrupted by conversational interludes, but can also be treated as the several sections of a single, overarching story.

The group story is in some respects an admirably collaborative and egalitarian storytelling mode, built on a heightened degree of interdependence. The division between tellers and listeners falls away, as does anxiety over tellability, and a spirit of benevolent mutual indulgence may prevail: all are contributing to a story that each already knows. But, in some ways, and with more scope than usual, a competitive rivalry may shape the several contributions to the telling, there may not be full agreement on the point of the story, nor as to who among the teller-participants comes out of the story well, and so on. In some ways, given the general familiarity with the broad story outlines, the exercise may become more oral-literary, with great attention paid to the most effective and entertaining methods of verbal expression. The group story is an arena where greater fictionality may be tolerated; credibility or vraisemblance is not a prime concern, since focus is less on any particular teller than on the tale for the tale's own sake. The retelling may be for purposes of reminiscence and social binding, with the emphasis less on the incidents themselves than on painting a rich picture of the situation. But again one should avoid being overly stipulative. In practice, a group story may become more a series of hypotheses or conjectures about what might have been the case (the true resolution, the proper evaluation) concerning some set of events, particularly where all the group-tellers were detached witnesses of those events, with limited inside knowledge. And the more that a group's talk becomes an unordered set of overlapping conjectures, the more talk returns from narrative mode to that of ordinary conversation or gossip.

6. The Development of Narratives in Children

Considerable psycholinguistic and sociolinguistic attention has been devoted to the emergence of storytelling and story-comprehension skills in children. The kinds of questions this research addresses include: what kind of competence (linguistic or cultural?) is involved in the child's growing narrative sophistication?; are children's stories best seen as simplified versions of adult ones or less directly related?; how attuned are children to the story models adults give them (e.g., in story books)?; can story complexity be nurtured and accelerated, or is it chiefly a matter of cognitive ability and readiness?; and how is the activity of storytelling best harnessed to broader skills-development in the child, such as learning to read, write, and write in ways appropriate to some constrained task?

In the area of emergent literacy, well-established findings are that invaluable preparation for literacy can begin at home, particularly where the child has there an enthusiastic and supportive interactant attuned to the child's 'prewriting' aptitude. Vygotsky's theory of cognitive development and his notion of a zone of proximal development have been highly influential here, for the older caregiver is in effect assisting the child to occupy each new zone of cognitive and interactive difficulty. One form of this assistance is the use of a teacher–scribe in preschools and kindergartens: the child retains responsibility for formulating the story to be dictated, but the scribe subtly assists with focusing, reminders of the structure and narrative line under way, matters of clarity, and so on. Dictation is in effect 'doing writing without (the physically overwhelming work of) doing writing.' It also fosters both a degree of detachment from the events of the kind essential to effective story-orientation and reflexive self-awareness. Reading back a dictated story to a child introduces him or her to the possibilities of second thoughts, self-correction, assisted improvement, and objectified verbal production. All this is further enriched and enlarged when dictated stories are subsequently dramatized, and issues of plausibility, vividness, and coherence are raised.

Besides dictation and dramatization, the activity of 'sharing time' or 'share, show and tell' is perhaps the most productive and revealing vehicle in young children's narrative development. But as noted briefly in Sect. 4 above, sharing stories can be problematic, particularly when teacher and children do not, in fact, share a common set of assumptions about what counts as an effective and tellable story. Additionally, and by contrast with the relative intimacy of dictation, sharing time is more dauntingly public narrative production. Heath (1983) vividly shows how even three geographically adjacent American communities have quite different orientations to literacy in general and to narrative in particular, so that the required adjustments to school and schooling have to be quite different in each case (or should be, so as to achieve the educational success to which each community declaredly aspires). One contrast of storytelling styles seems to be that between a 'topic centered style' in which an overtly grounded topic is pursued with copious lexicogrammatical markings of cohesion and coherence, and a 'topic associating style' in which implicit connections are more relied upon, no single topic serves as a foregrounded subject matter, and coherence and evaluation are carried more by rhythm and intonation than by conjunctions, pronouns, and lexis (there are similarities and differences between these styles and Bernstein's (see *Bernstein, Basil*) elaborated and restricted codes (see *Code, Sociolinguistic*)).

In the field of cognitive studies of children's narratives, Piaget's pioneering work (1926) still commands respect. He found, in the story-recall ability of 8-year-olds by contrast with 6-year-olds, that lapses in attention to matters of order, causality, and orientation were far less frequent. Younger children do not adequately encode either the order of story events or cause-and-effect relations, and their 'egocentric' use of pronouns (with all events oriented to the child's spatiotemporal present) led to confusions in their recall of stories. An invaluable study is that of Peterson and McCabe (1983), analyzing structures and content in a large corpus of informally elicited stories from children ranging in age from 4- to 9-years old. Alongside the increasingly common Labov-style story, with a high point and resolution, a less complex chronological structure was found to persist even in the older children's productions:

stories with temporal sequence but little or no sense of contour, resolution, or evaluative point. Again, subjecting the same corpus to an alternative analytic method, that of story grammars, they found that alongside increasingly complex story episodes there was a persistence of certain merely additive sequences—especially reactive sequences, in which a set of conditions causes changes to occur, but without evident planning or goals on the part of any participant. In addition, countless studies have charted older children's growing attention to means of evaluation, story-decontextualization, -elaboration, and -dramatization, and displayed reception of others' stories. Some have seen in these enlarged competences an increasing mastery of metapragmatic and metalinguistic behavior.

Before leaving children's narratives mention should be made of important research, from those applying and developing systemic–functional grammar, on children's achievements and difficulties in mastering the different genres of writing required of them as they enter middle or secondary school. Here it seems that attention has been paid to developing narrative style and internalizing narrative genre, to the neglect of the argumentative and expository styles so much expected in science and social science classes. Systemic linguists see registers or genres such as narrative as complex combinations of lexicogrammatical choice expressing concomitant choices in field, mode, and tenor of discourse. By charting children's developmental grasp and use of these lexicogrammatical choices (most notably, grasp of the linguistic systems of reference and conjunction), these studies can demonstrate the typical child's acquisition of genres through the school years (the 'prenarrative' nondisplaced activity of observing and commenting is superseded by recount style, then personal narrative, then vicarious narrative, and finally, rather later, thematic narrative).

7. Natural Narratives as Naturally Political

A final contemporary corpus of studies of interest are those which analyze narratives in their political context, on the assumption that the linguistic texture of such stories will itself disclose ideologically motivated emphases and omissions and preconceptions—sometimes of a kind sufficiently backgrounded lexicogrammatically as to escape the conscious attention of the socially situated reader (see especially Fowler et al. 1979, Fowler 1991). Such studies go under various names, including critical linguistic (see *Critical Sociolinguistics*), and critical language studies, and have been directed chiefly at newspaper accounts of contentious issues, media narratives about ethnic minorities, stories embedding forms of class and sex discrimination, the narrativized aspects of legal cases, and stories embedded in medical and other institutionalized and professionalized interviews or examinations. What most if not all of these discourses have in common, albeit covertly and perhaps barely perceptibly, is some process of assigning responsibility to specified social actors, and so facilitating attributions of blame. Put another way, critical linguistic analysis is often predicated on the existence of an underlying ideologically formed narrative, with known actors and predicted eventual outcome; the assumption is then that, for example, a newspaper's local narratives about industrial action will strive—and show the marks of that striving—to be congruent with the covert master narrative.

While various linguistic features have been examined for the way they may mediate ideological affiliations, the systemic–functional linguistic description (of English) has been particularly drawn upon, since that theory takes as axiomatic that a language is the most powerful form of social semiotic, that the grammar offers plentiful choices among ways of encoding a message, and that such encodings are functionally motivated rather than arbitrary. The approach implies the widespread possibility and practice of narrative discoursal transformation (in a wide, nongenerative sense of the term 'transformation'). Among the narrative textual features particularly traced have been: options in clause transitivity (including ascriptions of agency, affectedness, circumstantial marginality, and admission or exclusion of an individual as a process participant); passivization and agentless passives; nominalization; under- and over-lexicalization, and collocational emphasis; modality; theme and rheme patterns, and thematic structure; naming patterns and covertly evaluative descriptions; grammatical metaphor (see Halliday 1985); and linguistic and ideological presupposition.

See also: Sociolinguistic Variation; Literacy; Oracy.

Bibliography

Culler J 1981 *The Pursuit of Signs: Semiotics, Literature, Deconstruction*. Routledge and Kegan Paul, London

Fowler R 1991 *Language in the News: Discourse and Ideology in the British Press*. Routledge, London

Fowler R, Hodge R, Kress G, Trew T 1979 *Language and Control*. Routledge and Kegan Paul, London

Halliday M A K 1985 *An Introduction to Functional Grammar*. Arnold, London

Heath S B 1983 *Ways with Words*. Cambridge University Press, Cambridge, UK

Labov W 1972 *Language in the Inner City: Studies in the Black English Vernacular*. University of Pennsylvania Press, Philadelphia, PA

Labov W, Waletzky J 1967 Narrative analysis: Oral versions of personal experience. In: Helms J (ed.) *Essays on the Verbal and Visual Arts*. University of Washington Press, Seattle, WA

Peterson C, McCabe A 1983 *Developmental Psycholinguistics: Three Ways of Looking at Child's Narrative*. Plenum Press, New York

Piaget J 1959 *The Language and Thought of the Child*, 3rd edn. Routledge and Kegan Paul, London

Pratt M L 1977 *Toward a Speech-Act Theory of Literary Discourse*. Indiana University Press. Bloomington, IN

Tannen D 1979 What's in a frame? In: Freedle R O (ed.) *New Directions in Discourse Processing*. Ablex, Norwood, NJ

Wolfson N 1982 *CHP, The Conversational Historic Present in American English Narrative*. Foris, Dordrecht, The Netherlands

Phatic Communion
D. Abercrombie

Language is not by any means always concerned with the communication of thoughts. The conversations which English people hold about the weather, for example, do not as a rule leave the participants any the wiser; only on rare occasions can information be said to have been exchanged. As far as communicating thought is concerned, they get nowhere. Are they then quite pointless? No; a little reflection will show that this kind of use of language has great social value.

Most peoples have a feeling that a silent man is a dangerous man. Even if there is nothing to say, one must talk, and conversation puts people at their ease and in harmony with one another. This sociable use of language has been given the name 'phatic communion.' The anthropologist Bronislaw Malinowski (1923) (see *Malinowski, Bronislaw Kaspar*) created the term, 'actuated by the demon of terminological invention'; and although he was half in joke, the name has caught on. Malinowski defined it as 'a type of speech in which ties of union are created by a mere exchange of words.' It enters the everyday experience of everybody, from the most highly civilized to the most primitive, and far from being useless, this small talk is essential to human beings getting along together at all.

The actual sense of the words used in phatic communion matters little; it is facial expression and intonation that are probably the important things. It is said that Dorothy Parker, the American humorous writer and satirist, when she was alone and rather bored at a party, was asked 'How are you? What have you been doing?' by a succession of distant acquaintances. To each she replied, 'I've just killed my husband with an axe, and I feel fine.' Her intonation and expression were appropriate to party small talk, and with a smile and a nod, each acquaintance, unastonished, drifted on.

Although the sense matters little, however, certain subjects only are reserved for use in phatic communion, and these chosen subjects differ widely among different peoples. Each of the following questions is, in some part of the world, good form when meeting a person:

How are you?
Where are you from?
How much money do you earn?
What is your name?
What do you know?

Some of them, however, would cause deep offence when used in other parts of the world, though in each case the replies required, and expected, are purely formal.

A knowledge of the spoken form of any language must include knowledge of its conventions of phatic communion. Conversation is impossible unless one is equipped with meaningless phrases for use when there is nothing to say, and the language teacher dealing with advanced students will take care to give them command of the necessary formulas and rules governing their use.

The word *phatic* is derived from a Greek verb meaning 'to speak' and, as originally used by Malinowski, his term meant *communion* (the creation of 'ties of union') which is *phatic*, i.e., by speech, While it has been generally adopted, *phatic* has been wrongly interpreted as 'establishing an atmosphere of sociability rather than communicating ideas.' This misunderstanding has given rise to some curious expressions. It is reasonable to speak, as has one writer, of the phatic sharing of emotional burdens, but—in the light of the original use of *phatic*—it is less reasonable to speak of the phatic function of language, while the widespread 'phatic speech' is, from an etymological point of view, as tautological as 'phobic fear' would be.

See also: Malinowski, Bronislaw Kaspar; Kinesics.

Bibliography

Malinowski B 1923 The problem of meaning in primitive languages. In: Ogden C K, Richards I A (eds.) *The Meaning of Meaning*. Kegan Paul, London

Politeness
G. Kasper

In ordinary language use, 'politeness' refers to proper social conduct and tactful consideration of others. Politeness in this nontechnical sense contrasts with 'rudeness.' What counts as polite in any given context is socioculturally and historically determined. For instance, the lexical element *li* in Chinese *limao* ('polite appearance') underwent important semantic changes which reflect such an historic sensitivity: in Confucius's writings (551–479 BCE), *li* referred to the slavery-based social hierarchy of the Zhou Dynasty, which Confucius advocated to be restored. The modern concept of *li* was first documented in the book *Li Ji* (attributed to Dai Sheng, ca. 200–100 BCE), where *li* was equated with demonstration of self-denigration and respect for the other person, especially in vertical relationships (Gu 1990). In English, 'polite' dates back to the fifteenth century ('polished'); in the seventeenth century, a polite person was 'of refined courteous manners' (*The Oxford Dictionary of English Etymology*). Politeness was thus associated with the norms of social conduct extant in the upper classes, and this sense of the term has survived in collocations such as 'polite society.' The semantic association of 'polite' with behaviors of the upper classes is even more obvious in German '*höflich*,' French '*courtois*,' Spanish '*cortes*,' all of which are adjectival derivatives of nouns for court (German *Hof*, Fre. *cour*, Sp. *corte*).

Even though the etymology of 'polite' sheds light on its historic and current usage, 'politeness' as a technical term in linguistic pragmatics (see *Pragmatics and Sociolinguistics*) refers to a broader, substantially more democratic concept. Since the object of pragmatic inquiry is linguistic action, 'politeness' as a pragmatic notion refers to ways in which linguistic action is carried out—more specifically, ways in which the relational function in linguistic action is expressed. This is about as far as one can go in identifying a common denominator for the variety of politeness concepts which have been proposed in the pragmatics literature.

1. Politeness Concepts

According to Fraser (1990), four views of politeness can be distinguished. The 'social norm view' is the one reflected in ordinary language use as referred to above. What counts as polite behavior at any given time in different cultural contexts has been codified in manuals of etiquette, from Erasmus of Rotterdam's *De civilitate morum puerilium* (1530) to the latest version of *The Amy Vanderbilt Complete Book of Etiquette* (Vanderbilt and Baldridge 1978). Elias's exploration of the 'civilizing process' (1978) documents vividly how transformations of affect structure were expressed in different behavioral norms extant in European aristocracy from the Middle Ages onwards, e.g., in prescriptions for table manners. Socialization practices testify to caretakers' efforts to train children in socially acceptable conduct, speech included (Clancy 1986, Blum-Kulka 1990).

Scientific conceptualizations perceive politeness as a 'conversational maxim' (see *Conversational Maxims*), as 'face-saving' activity (see below), or as 'conversational contract' (Fraser 1990). The 'conversational maxim view' postulates a Politeness Principle as complement to Grice's Cooperative Principle. The Cooperative Principle regulates conversation whose purpose is maximally efficient transmission of information, i.e., a primarily referential orientation. The Politeness Principle addresses relational goals, serving primarily 'to reduce friction in personal interaction' (Lakoff 1989: 64). The most comprehensive proposal of a Politeness Principle was formulated by Leech (1983). The global statement 'Minimize the expression of impolite beliefs' (p. 81) is elaborated into six 'interpersonal maxims,' as follows:

> Tact maxim: minimize cost to other. Maximize benefit to other.
> Generosity maxim: minimize benefit to self. Maximize cost to self.
> Approbation maxim: minimize dispraise of other. Maximize praise of other.
> Modesty maxim: minimize praise of self. Maximize dispraise of self.
> Agreement maxim: minimize disagreement between self and other. Maximize agreement between self and other.
> Sympathy maxim: minimize antipathy between self and other. Maximize sympathy between self and other.
> (Leech 1983: 119ff.)

Less detailed versions of a conversational maxim approach (see *Conversational Maxims*) to politeness have been suggested by Lakoff (1973, 1989), Edmondson (1981), and Kasher (1986).

The 'face-saving view' of politeness, proposed by Brown and Levinson (1987), has been the most influential politeness model to date. Its fundamental assumptions are a Weberian view (see *Social Class*) of communication as purposeful–rational activity, combined with Goffman's concept of 'face' (1967; see *Goffman, Erving*), an individual's publicly manifest self-esteem. Social members are endowed with two kinds of face: 'negative face,' the want of self-determination, and 'positive face,' the want of approval.

Participants are assumed to adopt as a global interactional strategy 'the diplomatic fiction of the virtual offense, or worst possible reading' (Goffman 1971: 138f), i.e., the working hypothesis that face is constantly at risk. Consequently, any kind of linguistic act which has a relational dimension is seen as inherently face-threatening, and needs to be counterbalanced by appropriate doses of politeness. Brown and Levinson distinguish a number of major politeness strategies, ranging from avoiding the face-threatening act (FTA) altogether, to carrying it out in different guises. Off-record FTAs are performed indirectly; due to their inherent ambiguity, they have the greatest potential for negotiation (including denial). On-record performance of FTAs can be achieved without redressive action ('baldly'), or by adopting either or both of two kinds of redress: positive politeness, addressing the hearer's positive face wants, or negative politeness, addressing negative face wants. Positive politeness strategies emphasize closeness between speaker and hearer by confirming or establishing common ground, or by referring to desirable attributes in the hearer (hence the term 'solidarity strategy,' Scollon and Scollon 1983); negative politeness strategies suggest distance by accentuating the hearer's right to territorial claims and freedom from imposition (referred to as 'deference strategy,' Scollon and Scollon 1983).

The conversational maxim approach and the face-saving view of politeness converge in categorizing certain types of linguistic action as inherently impolite, or face-threatening. They agree furthermore in perceiving politeness as a continuous rather than an on-off phenomenon. Hence, speakers who intend to perform an FTA have to determine just how much politeness is appropriate to counterbalance the disruptive effect of an 'impolite' action. In Leech's model, each of the six interpersonal maxims has an associated set of scales which help establish the requisite degree of tact, generosity, etc. Thus for the tact maxim, the following scales obtain:

> Cost-benefit scale: representing the cost or benefit of an act to speaker and hearer.
> Optionality scale: indicating the degree of choice permitted to speaker and/or hearer by a specific linguistic act.
> Indirectness scale: indicating the amount of inferencing required of the hearer in order to establish the intended speaker meaning.
> Authority scale: representing the status relationship between speaker and hearer.
> Social distance scale: indicating the degree of familiarity between speaker and hearer.
>
> (Leech 1983: 123, 126.)

The corresponding mechanism to assess the severity of an FTA in Brown and Levinson's model adds up the values of three independent variables: (a) social distance between speaker and hearer, (b) their relative power, and (c) the degree of imposition associated with the required expenditure of goods or services (1987: 74ff). All three factors are culturally and situationally defined. Just as for Leech's scales, the assumption is that there is a linear relationship between the values assigned to each factor and the severity of the FTA, and hence the kind and amount of redress required to counterbalance face-threat.

The conversational maxim view of politeness emphasizes enhancement of interpersonal relationships through abiding by 'social regulations' (in the sense of uncodified prescriptive norms), which help minimize friction between participants and thus ensure efficient functioning of social aggregates. By contrast, the face-saving view, rather than resorting to (internalized) socially sanctioned behavioral prescripts, conceptualizes politeness as essentially addressing members' 'individual needs' ('wants'). It is through the reciprocal attribution of face wants and their symbolically exchanged appreciation in the form of politeness strategies that cohesive social ties are maintained and indeed reinforced.

The 'conversational contract view,' proposed by Fraser (e.g., 1990) represents the most global perspective on politeness. Rather than being conceived of as additional to cooperation, such as redress in view of face-threat, polite conduct implies acting in accordance with the requirements of the conversational contract at any given moment of an encounter. At the outset, the terms of the conversational contract are determined by participants' rights and obligations; however, these may change during, and as a result of, the interaction itself. What exactly the current terms of the conversational contract are would depend on each participant's assessment of the relevant contextual factors and of the conversational interchange itself. Acting politely, then, is virtually the same as using language appropriately. In order to distinguish politeness in this broad sense from speakers' deliberate expression of respect and appreciation, Fraser follows Goffman (1971) in referring to this aspect of linguistic activity as 'deference.'

A further conceptual distinction, largely originating in a critique of the face-saving view of politeness (see below), has been suggested. On the conversational maxim and the face-saving view, politeness serves to implement speaker's goals when such goals are face-threatening or involve 'impolite beliefs.' This type of politeness has therefore been referred to as 'strategic,' or 'volitional' politeness, and needs to be distinguished from politeness as 'social indexing,' or 'discernment' (Hill et al. 1986). Unlike strategic politeness, discernment operates independently of the speaker's current goals. Rather, it represents interlocutors' ascribed and achieved social properties, as these are linguistically encoded in address terms and other forms of personal reference (see Fasold 1990 for overview), honorifics (see *Honorifics*), and speaker/hearer dependent styles of speaking (e.g., Hori 1986). The study of discernment politeness is thus predominantly a sociolinguistic, rather than a pragmatic concern. Yet insofar as social marking is optional, it lends itself to strategic exploitation (e.g., the choice of more or less formal or intimate terms of address). Unexpected deviation from obligatory social indexing gives rise to 'interactional implicatures' about the speaker's covered attitude to the hearer and the message she is conveying (Matsumoto 1989).

2. Politeness: A Universal in Language Use?

The politeness models by Leech, Brown and Levinson, and Fraser aspire to universal validity (see *Pragmatics and Sociolinguistics*). Least problematic is this contention in Fraser's conversational contract approach, because he offers a structural framework for appropriate communication which needs to be socioculturally implemented: the conversational contract does not exist outside specific speech communities and their members.

The conversational maxim approach is more problematic, because no empirical evidence has yet been provided to support the universality of the proposed maxims. Rather, in an application of the conversational maxim approach to mainland Chinese politeness, Gu (1990) hypothesized two of Leech's maxims (tact and generosity) as underlying Chinese interaction; as it turned out, two further maxims (an address maxim and a generosity maxim) had to be added to account for the major normative orientations of Chinese interlocutors. In analogy with the conversational contract view, the level of abstraction at which the universality claim of the conversational maxim view can be sustained appears to be structural rather than substantive: certainly each speech community has a set of normative orientations in accordance with which members organize their verbal interaction. However, just what these norms are will be at variance across cultures. A methodological problem inherent in the conversational maxim approach is the derivation of the maxims. They are neither induced from qualitatively and quantitatively representative data, nor deduced from some basic theoretical construct by means of a rigorous procedure. Intuitively recognizable as they seem to members of the same or sufficiently similar cultures, their formulation remains nonetheless *ad hoc*. Since there is no theory-inherent criterion to delimit the number of maxims, new maxims may indefinitely be added, which represents a violation of a metatheoretical requirement or parsimony.

Brown and Levinson's face-saving approach is the only one which satisfies the criteria for empirical theories, such as explicitness, parsimony, and predictiveness. However, their strong claim to universality has met increasing theoretical doubt and empirical counterevidence. The most serious theoretical concerns center around the semantics of such fundamental categories as 'politeness,' 'face,' and 'face-threat.' As 'face' is closely related to the concept of self (Arndt and Janney 1992), universally valid conceptualizations of 'face' would presuppose identical notions of self across cultures. A review of psychological and anthropological studies (Markus and Kitayama 1991) provides overwhelming evidence to the contrary. Two distinctly different construals of self are suggested, the independent and the interdependent. The independent construal, endorsed by most Western cultures, builds on 'faith in the inherent separateness of distinct persons' (Markus and Kitayama 1991: 226). The interdependent construal, favored by many non-Western cultures, insists on 'the fundamental connectedness of human beings to each other' (ibid: 227). Hence, emphasis on individuals' autonomy and unique configurations of personal attributes and achievements contrasts with concerns about 'social relativism' (postulated by Lebra 1976, for Japanese culture), embracing both attention to participants' relative social positions and reciprocal assumption of emotional responses. Such differential, culturally mediated representations of self form the backdrop against which notions of face are conceptualized by cultural members. A classic account by Hu (1944), examining the historical and then-current notion of face in Chinese culture, distinguishes two face concepts, one referring to the moral character publicly attributed to an individual (*lien* [lian]), the other relating to an individual's reputation achieved through success and ostentation (*mien-tzu* [mianzi]). Neither of these face concepts is compatible with the notion of negative face. Self-concepts and notions of face will have to be emically reconstructed, in order to avoid misleading cross-cultural generalizations and inaccurate causal attributions to (linguistic) behaviors.

Even more problematic for Brown and Levinson's theory is the link between face and politeness. It is a viable working assumption that all cultures have some notion of face, and some notion of politeness. That face necessarily motivates politeness is a much stronger assumption which does not hold up against cross-cultural evidence (Watts 1989). Gu (1990) argues that it is not so much participants' social needs, but their normative orientations which motivate politeness in (mainland) Chinese society. Ide (1989) and Matsumoto (1988) propose that the overriding interactional imperative in Japanese culture is not to save face but mark place, i.e., to appropriately index social relationships (hence the proposed distinction between discernment and strategic politeness). There are thus fundamental conceptual differences in politeness notions which discourage universalist theories. (See Arndt and Janney 1992 for an historical and systematic critique of universality and relativity in politeness research.)

3. Politeness in Linguistic Action

Brown and Levinson (1987) offer rich evidence for the microstrategies available to implement each of the major strategic choices for carrying out face-threatening acts. Most of the subsequent studies have examined how specific speech acts are realized, within a particular speech community or cross-culturally/cross-linguistically.

For a number of speech acts, finite repertoires of realization strategies, or speech act sets, (see *Speech Act Theory: Overview*) have been identified. For example, for

(a) requests (Ervin-Tripp 1976)
(b) apologies (Olshtain and Cohen 1983)
(c) complaints (House and Kasper 1981)
(d) compliments (Manes 1983)
(e) refusals (Ueda 1974)
(f) disagreement (Sornig 1977)
(g) chastisement (Beebe and Takahashi 1989b)
(h) giving embarrassing information (Beebe and Takahashi 1989a)
(i) corrections (Takahashi and Beebe 1993)
(j) thanking (Eisenstein and Bodman 1986)
(k) suggestions (Banerjee and Carrell 1988)
(l) offers (Fukushima 1990).

Late twentieth-century evidence suggests that the established speech act sets are cross-linguistically robust. Thus for requests, modificatory dimensions include three major levels of directness (direct, conventionally indirect, indirect), measured in terms of distance between locution and illocution; internal modification of the requestive act, by mitigating or aggravating impositive force; and external modification, expressed by 'adjuncts' supporting the request proper. The speech act set of apology consists of an expression of regret, admission of the offense, assumption of responsibility, account, minimizing the offense/responsibility, and offers of compensation (Blum-Kulka et al. 1989). However, cross-cultural and cross-linguistic variation in the performance of linguistic action is manifest in other aspects of politeness investment (see Kasper 1990 for overview).

3.1 The Distribution of Linguistic Action

Some types of linguistic action are carried out more frequently in some cultures than in others. Hearer-beneficial acts such as complimenting and thanking occur more regularly in some Western contexts (e.g., the USA) than in some Asian cultures (e.g., mainland China), reflecting both the strong positive politeness orientation and reluctance to impose on others in mainstream American culture, on the one hand, and the assumption, in China, that participants act according to their social positions and associated roles and obligations, on the other. Also, hearer-costly acts such as refusals are perceived as being more socially offensive by Japanese and Chinese interlocutors and thus tend to be avoided, whereas it seems more consistent with American interlocutors' right to self-determination not to comply with another person's wishes.

3.2 Politeness Values: Different Strategies

The equation 'the more indirect, the more polite,' proposed by both Brown and Levinson (1987) and Leech (1983), was not supported by empirical evidence. For American English and Hebrew, conventional indirectness, rather than nonconventional indirectness, was shown to be the most polite requestive strategy; next in politeness value were direct strategies in the perception of Israeli raters and nonconventional indirectness according to American raters (Blum-Kulka 1987). In interaction with familiars but not intimates, direct strategies (e.g., imperatives, statement of hearer's future action) are far more acceptable in the Slavic languages, Hebrew, and German than in any of the standard varieties of English examined so far. It has been suggested that directness to speakers of these languages connotes sincerity, straightforwardness, and cordiality (Katriel 1986) rather than imposition on their freedom of action. It must be kept in mind, though, that in these languages direct strategies are often combined with mitigating modal particles, diminutives and other linguistic means which do not alter the direct expression of pragmatic intent but soften impositive force: explicit marking for politeness is thus taken care of by different linguistic expressions, rather than dispensed with altogether.

3.3 Linguistic Implementation of Realization Strategies

Languages differ in the conventionalization of pragmatic force and politeness (pragmalinguistic variation, Leech 1983). For instance, structures questioning the hearer's willingness or future action (e.g., 'will/would you do x') serve to express conventional indirectness in the Germanic and Romance languages as well as in Hebrew, Japanese, and Chinese, but not in the Slavic languages (Wierzbicka 1991: 32ff, 204). Repertoires of polite formulae index recurrent social events which are most efficiently handled by language-specific prefabricated routines (see *Formulaic Language*; Coulmas 1981). It is part of the pragmalinguistic knowledge shared by members of a speech community to recognize the contextual distribution of such frozen forms, whereas they do not usually have an awareness of the semantic structure of politeness routines. Since such formulae encapsulate events which require routinely conveyed politeness, they provide pragmaticists with a window to a speech community's value structure and notion of politeness.

3.4 Choices from a Speech Act Set

The strategies composing specific speech act sets, and global modificatory dimensions such as indirectness, minimization, and maximization of pragmatic force (House and Kasper 1981) have been demonstrated to be valid across the languages and communities studied so far. Yet, the selections participants make from such repertoires vary between speech communities, and these variations systematically reflect different cultural orientations. Chinese speakers in the People's Republic not only compliment less, but also on different attributes, compared to English speakers in the USA. Thus, physical attractiveness is not regarded a suitable topic for public praise by most Chinese people (Hsu 1981: 2). Danish interlocutors were found to invest more effort into supporting their requests by justifications than native speakers of English and German (Faerch and Kasper 1989). Ritual refusal of offers and invitations is required in Chinese culture (Gu 1990), but not everywhere else. Americans have a greater proclivity to preface corrections with positive remarks than Japanese speakers (Takahashi and Beebe 1993) and to maximize compliments, both of which reflect a positive politeness orientation. In refusals, Japanese and Chinese speakers use proverbs and philosophical statements more often than speakers in the USA. These generalizations, extracted from databased studies, are, of course, somewhat risky. They represent cultural trends rather than predictions of the politeness investment afforded by individual members of each speech community, and apply only under comparable conditions (see Blum-Kulka et al. 1989). This leads to the final source of cross-cultural variability.

3.5 Contextual Variation in Conveying Politeness

Brown and Levinson (1987) and Leech (1983) proposed a positive correlation between the weight of contextual factors (social distance, power, and imposition) and politeness investment. This hypothesis has not been confirmed by evidence. Wolfson's (1989) analysis of a number of speech acts, performed in a US East Coast middle-class community, demonstrates that intimates use the same politeness patterns as status unequals and strangers. Non-intimates such as status-equal friends, co-workers, and acquaintances invest the most politeness, which is taken to be reflective of the high relationship negotiability extant in such interlocutor constellations. Wolfson referred to this pattern as the 'Bulge Theory' (see Boxer 1992).

The impact of contextual factors on expended politeness varies intra- and interculturally. Each of the proposed factors represents a composite construct which needs to be culturally and contextually elaborated. Social power includes factors such as speakers' and hearers' relative positions in institutional hierarchies (workplace, family), age, sex, as well as acquired and ascribed personal attributes (which have as yet been entirely overlooked in politeness research). Intraculturally, the weight, of each factor might vary contextually, e.g., in many Western contexts, age may be important in personal interaction but not at the workplace, where it may be superseded by seniority. Interculturally, age matters more among most Asian interlocutors than to most Westerners, for instance, among participants in equivalent positional roles. Sex was identified as determining the amount of complimenting and apologies received by New Zealand interlocutors, women receiving consistently more (mostly from other women, see Holmes 1988). Comparing politeness in requests, students in the USA were found not to vary politeness according to sex role relationships, whereas Hispanic students were more polite towards the other sex (Rintell 1981). Different positional roles in institutional hierarchies (university, workplace) alter the politeness investment of American and Japanese interlocutors; however, the Japanese vary their politeness strategies more dramatically, depending on whether speaker or hearer is the superior in status (Beebe and Takahashi 1989a).

The specification of 'imposition' is tied to the linguistic act and the event to which it refers. For apologies, a variety of studies has found that severity of offense is the decisive factor, subsuming obligation to apologize and likelihood of apology acceptance (Bergman and Kasper 1993). For requests, options for different strategies selected by German speakers were hearer's ability and willingness, required urgency, and legitimacy (whether the requestive goal entails compliance with the requester's contractual rights or a favor granted by the requestee (see Hermann 1982)). Of these factors, urgency was *not* found to be operative in Japanese request realization (Morosawa 1990). Asked to evaluate the same requestive contexts, Israelis, Germans, and Argentinians differed in their perceptions of interlocutors' rights and obligations, likelihood of hearer's compliance, and speaker's sociopsychological difficulty in carrying out the request.

Finally, rather than estimating costliness, or facethreat, as the summative effect of contextual variables, it has been proposed that the 'discourse domain' (see *Discourse*) overdetermines what counts as polite, and provides a functional explanation of politeness. In the context of a 'backstage event' such as family dinner conversations, directness functions as enhancement of intimacy and strengthens affective bonds (Blum-Kulka 1990). The public character of legal trials symbolically sets the courtroom apart from ordinary interaction, whereas the solidarity politeness adopted by therapist and client in psychotherapy emphasizes the intimacy required for sanction-free self-disclosure and confrontation (Lakoff 1989). Yet even within a given discourse domain, politeness can vary, even if none of the contextual factors mentioned above alters its value. Studies of different work contexts have shown that politeness may be drastically reduced due to 'real-world exigencies' (Fraser and Nolen 1981), such as problematic flight conditions (Linde 1988), instant surgery (cf. the movie *M.A.S.H.*), or Alpine mountaineering (Moretti 1989).

The complex research program to be addressed by future politeness studies is not only to specify and examine the relationship between contextual variables and discourse domains. Such research will also have to uncover how the ongoing discourse itself constitutes, maintains, and alters participants' rights and obligations, increases and reduces distance, fosters liking and disliking, and so forth. Politeness will therefore have to be studied not only as a dependent variable but as a major force in shaping human relationships.

See also: Conversational Maxims; Sociology of Language; Pragmatics and Sociolinguistics; Phatic Communion; Identity and Language.

Bibliography

Arndt H, Janney R W 1992 Universality and relativity in cross-cultural politeness research: A historical perspective. *Multilingua* **11**
Banerjee J, Carrell P L 1988 Tuck in your shirt, you squid: Suggestions in ESL. *Language Learning* **38**: 313–47
Beebe L M, Takahashi T 1989a Do you have a bag? Social status and patterned variation in second language acquisition. In: Gass S, Madden C, Preston D, Selinker L (eds.) *Variation in Second Language Acquisition: Discourse and Pragmatics*. Multilingual Matters, Clevedon, UK
Beebe L M, Takahashi T 1989b Sociolinguistic variation in face-threatening speech acts. In: Eisenstein M R (ed.) *The Dynamic Interlanguage*. Plenum, New York
Bergman M L, Kasper G 1993 Perception and performance in native/nonnative apology. In: Kasper G, Blum-Kulka S (eds) *Interlanguage Pragmatics*. Oxford University Press, New York
Blum-Kulka S 1987 Indirectness and politeness in requests: Same or different? *Journal of Pragmatics* **11**: 131–46
Blum-Kulka S 1990 You don't touch lettuce with your fingers: Parental politeness in family discourse. *Journal of Pragmatics* **14**: 259–88
Blum-Kulka S, House J, Kasper G (eds) 1989 *Cross-Cultural Pragmatics*. Ablex, Norwood, NJ
Boxer D 1992 Social distance and speech behavior. *Journal of Pragmatics* **17**
Brown P, Levinson S C 1987 *Politeness: Some Universals in Language Usage*. Cambridge University Press, Cambridge, UK
Clancy P M 1986 The acquisition of communicative style in Japanese. In: Schieffelin B, Ochs E (eds.) *Language Socialization across Cultures*. Cambridge University Press, Cambridge, UK
Coulmas F (ed.) 1981 *Conversational Routine*. Mouton, The Hague
Edmondson W J 1981 *Spoken Discourse*. Longman, London
Eisenstein M, Bodman J W 1986 'I very appreciate': Expressions of gratitude by native and nonnative speakers of American English. *Applied Linguistics* **7**: 167–85
Elias N 1978 *The History of Manners. Vol. 1: The Civilizing Process*. Blackwell, Oxford, UK
Ervin-Tripp S 1976 Is Sybil there? The structure of some American English directives. *Language in Society* **5**: 25–66
Faerch C, Kasper G 1989 Internal and external modification in interlanguage request realization. In: Blum-Kulka S, House J, Kasper G (eds.) *Cross-Cultural Pragmatics*. Ablex, Norwood, NJ
Fasold R W 1990 *The Sociolinguistics of Language*. Blackwell, Oxford, UK
Fraser B 1990 Perspectives on politeness. *Journal of Pragmatics* **14**: 219–36
Fraser B, Nolen W 1981 The association of deference with linguistic form. *International Journal of the Sociology of Language* **27**: 93–109
Fukushima S 1990 Offers and requests: Performance by Japanese learners of English. *World Englishes* **9**: 317–25
Goffman E 1967 *Interaction Ritual: Essays on Face-to-Face Behavior*. Doubleday Anchor Books, New York
Goffman E 1971 *Relations in Public*. Allen Lane, London
Gu Y 1990 Politeness phenomena in modern Chinese. *Journal of Pragmatics* **14**: 237–57
Hermann T 1982 Language and situation: The pars pro toto principle. In: Fraser C, Scherer K R (eds.) *Advances in the Social Psychology of Language*. Cambridge University Press, Cambridge, UK
Hill B, Ide S, Ikuta S, Kawasaki A, Ogino T 1986 Universals of linguistic politeness: Quantitative evidence from Japanese and American English. *Journal of Pragmatics* **10**: 347–71
Holmes J 1988 Paying compliments: A sex-preferential positive politeness strategy. *Journal of Pragmatics* **12**: 445–65
Hori M 1986 A sociolinguistic analysis of the Japanese honorifics. *Journal of Pragmatics* **10**: 373–86
House J, Kasper G 1981 Politeness markers in English and German. In: Coulmas F (ed.) *Conversational Routine*. Mouton, The Hague
Hsu F L K 1981 *Americans & Chinese: Passage to Differences*. University of Hawaii Press, Honolulu, HI
Hu H C 1944 The Chinese concepts of 'face.' *American Anthropologist* **46**: 45–64
Ide S 1989 Formal forms and discernment: Two neglected aspects of linguistic politeness. *Multilingua* **8**: 223–48
Kasher A 1986 Politeness and rationality. In: Johansen J D, Sonne H (eds.) *Pragmatics and Linguistics: Festschrift for Jacob Mey*. Odense University Press, Odense, Denmark
Kasper G 1990 Linguistic politeness: Current research issues. *Journal of Pragmatics* **14**: 193–218

Katriel T 1986 *Talking Straight: Dugri Speech in Israeli Sabra Culture*. Cambridge University Press, London
Lakoff R 1973 The logic of politeness, or minding your p's and q's. *Chicago Linguistics Society* **9**: 292–305
Lakoff R 1975 *Language and Woman's Place*. Harper Row, New York
Lakoff R 1989 The limits of politeness: Therapeutic and courtroom discourse. *Multilingua* **8**: 101–29
Lebra T S 1976 *Japanese Patterns of Behavior*. University of Hawaii Press, Honolulu, HI
Leech G 1983 *Principles of Pragmatics*. Longman, London
Linde C 1988 The quantitative study of communicative success: Politeness and accidents in aviation discourse. *Language in Society* **17**: 375–99
Manes J 1983 Compliments: A mirror of cultural values. In: Wolfson N, Judd E (eds.) *Sociolinguistics and Language Acquisition*. Newbury House, Rowley, MA
Markus H R, Kitayama S 1991 Culture and the self: Implications for cognition, emotion, and motivation. *Psychological Review* **98**: 224–53
Matsumoto Y 1988 Reexamination of the universality of face: Politeness phenomena in Japanese. *Journal of Pragmatics* **12**: 403–26
Matsumoto Y 1989 Politeness and conversational universals—observations from Japanese. *Multilingua* **8**: 207–21
Moretti B 1989 *L'interazione comunicativa durante l'arrampicata. Uno studio di pragmatica linguistica*. Lang, Bern, Switzerland
Morosawa A 1990 Intimacy and urgency in request forms of Japanese: A psycholinguistic study. *Sophia Linguistica* **28**: 129–43
Olshtain E, Cohen A 1983 Apology: A speech act set. In: Wolfson N, Judd E (eds.) *Sociolinguistic and Second Language Acquisition*. Newbury House, Rowley, MA
Rintell E 1981 Sociolinguistic variation and pragmatic ability: A look at learners. *International Journal of the Sociology of Language* **27**: 11–34
Scollon R, Scollon S B K 1983 Face in interethnic communication. In: Richards J C, Schmidt R W (eds.) *Language and Communication*. Longman, London
Sornig K 1977 Disagreement and contradiction as communicative acts. *Journal of Pragmatics* **1**: 347–73
Takahashi T, Beebe L 1993 Cross-linguistic influence in the speech act of correction. In: Kasper G, Blum-Kulka S (eds.) *Interlanguage Pragmatics*. Oxford University Press, New York
Ueda K 1974 Sixteen ways to avoid saying 'no' in Japan. In: Condon J C, Saito M (eds.) *Intercultural Encounters with Japan*. Simul Press, Tokyo
Vanderbilt A, Baldridge L 1978 *The Amy Vanderbilt Complete Book of Etiquette: A Guide to Contemporary Living*. Doubleday, Garden City, NY
Watts R J 1989 Relevance and relational work: Linguistic politeness as politic behavior. *Multilingua* **8**: 131–66
Wierzbicka A 1991 *Cross-Cultural Pragmatics: The Semantics of Human Interaction*. Mouton, Berlin
Wolfson N 1983 An empirically based analysis of complimenting in American English. In: Wolfson N, Judd E (eds.) *Sociolinguistics and Language Acquisition*. Newbury House, Rowley, MA
Wolfson N 1989 *Perspectives*. Newbury House, Cambridge, MA

Speech Accommodation
H. Giles

Accommodation is the adjustment of one's speech or other communicative behaviors vis-à-vis the people with whom one is interacting. Communication accommodation theory (CAT) is a framework designed to explore accommodative phenomena and processes, and in its early years was concerned with the antecedents and consequences of shifting one's language variety towards or away from another, called speech convergence and divergence, respectively (for a recent review see Shepard et al. 2001). Whether verbal or nonverbal, some accommodative processes can have profound social implications. For instance, satisfaction with medical encounters and patients' willingness to comply with crucial medical regimes can be influenced by doctors' attempts to accommodate to patients' speech norms (see *Doctor–Patient Language*). Other examples include reactions to defendants in court and hence the nature of the judicial outcome, job satisfaction, and hence group productivity. There are many ways of performing accommodative acts, many reasons for so doing, with some beneficial and others detrimental to one or more participants. Such complexities will be introduced as will more recently developed discoursal elaborations.

1. Convergence

The extent and frequency of interpersonal convergence has been demonstrated across a plethora of linguistic/prosodic/nonverbal features (e.g., speech rate, pausal phenomena, phonological variants, smiling, and gaze) and in many Western and Eastern languages besides English. Indeed, the ubiquity of this phenomenon (which goes under various nomenclatures in different theoretical traditions, e.g., 'listener-adaptedness,' 'synchrony,' 'congruence') is so well-recognized that a number of scholars have considered it to be a universal. Indeed, data suggests that it emerges very early on in a child's social life.

1.1 Convergence Distinctions, Motives, and Evaluations

Descriptively, convergence can be labeled: (albeit value-ladenly) 'upward' or 'downward' depending on the relative sociolinguistic status of the convergee; 'full' or 'partial' (e.g., a shift from one's idiosyncratic speech rate baseline of say 50 words-per-minute to match a target's 100 words exactly versus accelerating to just 75 words-per-minute) or even 'cross-over' (in this case an overshoot to 120 words or hypercorrection beyond a standard user's dialect to more exaggeratedly prestigious forms); and 'symmetrical' or 'asymmetrical' (i.e., whether both speakers are, or only one participant is, converging). Most of the studies of this genre are laboratory-controlled investigations, yet many have emerged in more naturalistic settings. Examples are a demonstration of John Dean's convergence of median word frequencies to his Senate interrogators in the Watergate trials and a British travel agent's convergence of phonological variants to her socioeconomically diverse clients.

CAT proposes that speech convergence reflects a speaker's or a group's need (often nonconscious) for social integration or identification with another. It has been argued, and often found, that increasing behavioral similarity (or put another way, reducing dissimilarities) along communicative dimensions in social interaction is likely to increase speakers' perceived (a) attractiveness; (b) predictability and supportiveness; (c) level of interpersonal involvement; (d) intelligibility and comprehensibility; and (e) speakers' ability to gain their listeners' compliance. A variety of studies have shown speech convergence (over speech maintenance from interpersonal context to context) to have been positively evaluated on certain dimensions, both cognitive and affective as in (d) and (a) above, respectively. The first of these, in Montreal, showed that the more effort in convergence a speaker was perceived by recipients to have made (e.g., in this case the more French was used by English–Canadians when sending a message to French–Canadians), the more favorably that person was evaluated and the more these same listeners would converge back in return. Convergence, therefore, is considered a reflection of an individual's desire for social approval: if people are cognizant of (and/or have experienced in the past) positive outcomes from convergence then this is sufficient grounds to consider that an approval (or perhaps instrumental) motive may often trigger it. Not surprisingly then, the power variable is one that is endemic to accommodation research and has surfaced regularly in ways that support CAT's central predictions. As but one example, a study of code-switching in Taiwan found that salespersons converged their dialects more to customers than viceversa, as customers hold more of the economic reins in these commercial settings.

CAT recognizes however, that convergence is not always evaluated favorably by recipients, or by bystanders, and such occasions would include those when the convergent act is (a) nonetheless a movement away from valued social norms (e.g., converging to a nonstandard interviewer but in a formal job interview); (b) attributed with suspicious intent (e.g., to machiavellianism); (c) attributed by eavesdroppers as a betrayal of ingroup identity when the recipient is an 'outgroup' member (e.g., children in class seen by their peers to adopt the teacher's language style when talking to him or her); and (d) at a magnitude and/or rate beyond which recipients feel are sociolinguistic optima.

1.2 Sociolinguistic Origins and Beyond

The convergence construct was developed originally, in part, as a foil to the then *Zeitgeist* of norms being modeled as the determinants of speech diversity. The first publications in this tradition emerged in 1973 when the present author demonstrated the phenomenon of interpersonal accent convergence and introduced his 'accent mobility' model. Therein he also critiqued some aspects of the original Labovian paradigm. For example, interviewees' casual speech, it was argued, may have been produced not so much because of any informality of the context per se but, perhaps more precisely, because the commanding interviewer (equally prone to sociolinguistic forces) had shifted himself to less standard forms when he introduced certain topics (e.g., being near death) and when the interview was supposedly over (i.e., the tape-recorder was supposedly turned off). In other words, the normative supposition that context-formality determined phonological prestigiousness could be supplanted by an interpretation in terms of a mechanism of interpersonal influence—interviewee convergence to the interviewer. This then was the legacy of CAT. Since then, theoretical refinements have come in profusion and have intermeshed with empirical developments as well, not least of which has been CAT's recognition in the domain of language change (Trudgill 1986). The mechanics of such day-to-day interpersonal convergences in important social networks are the breeding ground for longer-term shifts in individual as well as group-level language usage. Indeed, much of the literature on long- and mid-term language/dialect acculturation can be interpreted in convergence terms (see also Sect. 2 on divergence below) where immigrants often seek the economic and social advantages (as well as costs in some instances) that linguistic assimilation sometimes brings.

2. Divergence

Divergence has received relatively less empirical, albeit not less theoretical, attention and refers to the ways in which speakers increase perceived dissimilarities of speech and nonverbal differences (see Giles and Wadleigh 1999) between themselves and others. Like convergence, it can take on many forms (e.g., upward/downward; full/partial; symmetrical/asymmetrical) and there may be a hierarchy of divergent strategies available to speakers from perhaps the emphasis of a few ingroup stereotyped phonological features and lexical items to abrasive humor, to verbal abuse, to language switches, to interactional dissolution. To the extent that divergent strategies are adopted probably more often in situations where the participants derive from different social backgrounds, the incorporation of ideas from sociopsychological theorizing about intergroup behavior and social change provides an important influx of ideas. From this stance divergence is deemed a tactic of intergroup distinctiveness of individuals in search of a positive social identity. By diverging one's communicative style (e.g., slang, work/sports jargon, grammatical complexity, posture and gait, accent), members of an ingroup can accentuate the differences between themselves and a relevant outgroup on, usually, a highly valued dimension of their group identity. In some cultural contexts like Wales, encounters have to be construed in very 'intergroup' terms for, in this case, bilingual Welsh people even to anticipate diverging away from an English person (by using the Welsh language or even using some Welsh words and a Welsh accent in English). Indeed, for this to happen the latter have to threaten directly core elements of Welsh speakers' cultural identity to which they are strongly committed.

A number of studies of impression formation have shown that the transsituational maintenance of a speech style and divergence are often seen by its recipients as rude and hostile—unless, that is, it can be attributed situationally to extenuating circumstances (e.g., the speaker is known to be extremely fatigued or under stress) and/or the adherence of valued conversational norms (e.g., the speaker moves to a prestige language variety when being very formally interviewed for an executive position by a nonstandard speaker). At the same time, onlookers may react very positively to a member of their ingroup diverging from an outgroup member in a public competitive situation. It is little wonder then that the divergence aspect of CAT has been developed theoretically further into domains of second language learning and language maintenance and death (see Giles and Coupland 1991). Relatedly, increasing accentuation of ethnic speech markers in the recorded Hebrew singing of certain Arab-speaking Jews over a particular historical period covaried with the increasing vitality of that group over the same time. But not all divergences need be intergroup in nature as they can signal personal disdain regarding another's dress, mannerisms, habits, arguments, and so forth. Moreover, and as with convergence, its motivational origins need not always be affective and allied to facework or the maintenance or creation of a social identity. Rather, it may function more cognitively so as to provide a mutually understood basis for communication and to facilitate the coordination of speech patterns. As an example, divergence may be strategically employed to bring another's fast speech rate down to a more acceptable and conversationally comfortable level fostering thereby better comprehensibility.

3. Further Distinctions

Archetypal convergence would occur when the speaker intends to converge linguistically to another, the linguistic movement is measured objectively as indeed having happened that way, and the psychological climate attending it in both speaker's and receiver's eyes is one of interpersonal association. Similarly, classic divergence would be where the speaker wishes to diverge subjectively from another, the linguistic movement is measured as actually having happened as intended, and the psychological climate is perceived by both participants as being dissociative. However, such ideals do not always eventuate as intended and in any case the situation is far more complex and a few complications will be introduced here.

3.1 Converging as Divergence and Diverging as Convergence

First, perceptions of one's own and others' speech can be grossly biased and stereotyped such that one sometimes does not hear people sound the way they actually are. Hence, people may assume they are moving towards where they believe others are, with this often being in complete contrast to where these targets actually reside or alternatively where they think they are located linguistically. For example, Chinese-Thai bilingual children sometimes use Chinese phonological features when talking with an (objectively) standard Thai speaker who looks ethnically Chinese—arguably an instance of miscarried convergence which amounts to actual divergence. Similarly, some native English Australian speakers mismanage their downward convergent attempts toward what they believe (somewhat erroneously) Singaporeans and Aborigines sound like. Misattributions and misunderstandings under these circumstances can of course be potentially rife.

Second, sometimes moving closer to another person psychologically is managed by diverging from them given the social meanings attending the linguistic outcome. This can often occur in role-discrepant situations and has been labeled, 'speech complementarity.' For instance, some young American women sound more 'feminine' (e.g., higher and more variable pitch) when talking to an intimate, as opposed to an unknown, male over the telephone. CAT also provides—in the context of the multiple goals so often embraced in social interaction and even during single speech acts—for the possibility that convergence, divergence, and even complementarity may be encoded simultaneously but with respect of course to differing linguistic and nonverbal features. Indeed, it has been argued that a fine meshing of physician convergence and complementarity is essential for patient satisfaction and compliance to health regimes.

Third, and conversely, sometimes moving away from another psychologically is managed by converging towards where she or he is believed to be located linguistically. For instance an accommodation norm emerged in Catalonia in the early 1980s dictating that 'Catalan should be spoken only between Catalans.' Then, Castilians who accommodated Catalan speakers with their language would more than likely be responded to in Castilian. In an attempt to structure the foregoing and beyond, Thakerar et al. (1982) formulated a three-dimensional model of accommodation wherein a complex range of logical possibilities, including the above-mentioned, exist. This theoretical position is the sociopsychological heartland of CAT as emphasis is placed on what participants believe they are doing accommodatively and how language strategies help situational definitions and redefinitions rather than on what comprises the linguistic constituents of convergence and divergence.

3.2 Attuning, Discourse, and Health Care

More sociolinguistic infusion, however, was soon to be rendered with Coupland et al. (1988) not only broadening the scope of strategies invoked by CAT, but doing so in ways that embraced a discoursal perspective in a gerontological context. Thus far, the focus on recipients, the audience, or addressees has been on speakers' perceptions or expectations of the latter's communicative performance or patterns of production. With this in mind, Coupland et al. termed the foregoing convergent, divergent, and complementary acts as 'approximation strategies' arguing that they were but one subset of 'attuning behaviors,' the complete class of which, together with enriched addressee foci, better represented the spirit of CAT thinking.

Three additional attuning strategies were proposed. First, an alternative addressee focus to recipients' productive performance was their interpretive competences. Sometimes, as sadly with the case of certain older folk, such competences are stereotyped deficiently in terms of a presumed impaired facility to comprehend. Accommodating in this case could lead to 'interpretability strategies' so as to reduce complexity, increase clarity, and within set topic boundaries (e.g., by decreasing lexical diversity, increasing vocal amplitude). Second, another addressee focus was recipients' conversational needs which can lead to a wide range of 'discourse management strategies' aimed at facilitating, to varying degrees, partners' interactive accomplishments (e.g., by offering turns, back-channeling, repairing, maintaining other's face). The final addressee focus in this framework was recipients' social roles which would lead to a set of 'control strategies' wherein, say, status discrepancies can be accommodated and the floor, for example, given over to a new junior faculty member in a committee meeting.

High attuning then, caveats above notwithstanding, can reduce sociolinguistic distance between interactants and bring them psychologically closer and facilitate conversational smoothness. Naturally enough, counterattuning can likewise fulfill the same functions and attract the same consequences as classic divergence; other possibilities such as under- and overaccommodation have been explicated. Empirical work largely derived from this attuning elaboration has led to some important new insights into applied social domains including the medical, organizational, and legal, as manifest in some of the chapters of Giles et al. (1999) and in the Williams et al. (1999) collection. Relatedly, it has been claimed that accommodative discourse may be integral to being socially supported—a process deemed vital to psychological wellbeing and physical health. Indeed, feeling supported can be a function of the extent of attuning one receives—with those known to possess attuning skills being sought out as preferred supporters. That said, attuning may not always covary with offering support or feeling supported. Indeed, high attuning can be *non*-supportive behavior where familial security and empathy encourages overdependence and lack of autonomy. Similarly, there may be occasions when long-term support is engineered through counterattuning where indulgences and habits are denigrated, albeit with socially constructive intent and form. Many exciting challenges for a future empirical research program are held out by CAT being grounded in emotional, health, and social network possibilities.

4. Epilogue

CAT has developed its potential as an interdisciplinary heuristic since its self-appellation of an 'embryonic' framework in the 1970s. It has been robust enough to sustain radically different methodologies, become far less alinguistic, and even begun to examine some of the ideological structures underlying certain of its own attuned acts—a kind of meta-accommodation. Put another way, it has developed theoretically at many levels significantly beyond the concepts and stances which were its precursors and independently derived peers. It is uniquely able to attend to (a) social consequences (attitudinal, attributional, behavioral, and communicative), (b) macrosocietal factors, (c) intergroup as well as interpersonal variables and processes, (d) discursive practices in naturalistic settings, and (e) individual lifespan language shifts and community-wide language change. Doubtless some skeptics claim, divergently, that the theory has been repeatedly 'massaged' to meet the ever-increasing demands of complex, situated, and sequential acts to the extent it is no longer a testable theory—if it ever was one. CAT has, however, been summarized a number of times in propositional format (e.g., Gallois et al. 1995), therein formalizing hypotheses about the antecedents, correlates, and consequences of attuning, and thereby devising a parsimonious and predictive model allowing for falsification. This is not the context to set up defenses but rather to underscore the fact that accommodation theorists have always welcomed and confronted constructive criticism as well as been eager to reach out hands to other related paradigms (see introduction in Giles et al. 1991). Much still needs to be achieved, such as studying the relationships between multiple perceived goals and attuning; the specification of which language and nonverbal features are contextually implicated accommodatively and which are not and why; a more precise analysis of which evaluative and attributional dimensions (and accounting parameters) are associated with what kinds of attuning and when; and programmatic application of relevant aspects of the theory to other communicative modes besides the oral including telecommunications and computer-mediated communications (see Giles and Ogay in press). However, given the level of debate and constructive criticism, innovative research, and more sophisticated theory and applications in crucial social contexts across cultural boundaries so far generated by CAT, it seems likely that it will continue to be a resource for much-needed collaboration between social psychologists and sociolinguists (Meyerhoff 1998).

See also: Audience Design; Code-switching: Socio-pragmatic Models; Communicative Competence; Context; Social Psychology; Style.

Bibliography

Coupland N, Coupland J, Giles H, Henwood K 1988 Accommodating the elderly: Invoking and extending a theory. *Language in Society* **17**: 1–41
Gallois C, Giles H, Jones C, Cargile A, Ota H 1995 Accommodating intercultural encounters: Elaborations and extensions. In: Wiseman R, (ed.) *Theories of Intercultural Communication*. Sage, Thousand Oaks, CA
Giles H, Coupland J, Coupland N (eds.) 1991 *Contexts of Accommodation: Developments in Applied Sociolinguistics*. Cambridge University Press, New York
Giles H, Coupland N 1991 *Language: Contexts and Consequences*. Open University Press, Milton Keynes, UK/Brooks Cole, Pacific Grove, CA
Giles H, Ogay T in press Communication accommodation theory. In: Whalen B, Samter W (eds.) *Explaining Communication: Contemporary Theories and Exemplars*. Erlbaum, Mahwah, NJ
Giles H, Wadleigh P M 1999 Accommodating nonverbally. In: Guerrero L K, DeVito J A, Hecht M L (eds.) *The Nonverbal Communication Reader: Classic and Contemporary Readings*, 2nd edn. Waveland Press, Prospect Heights, IL
Meyerhoff M. 1998 Accommodating your data: The use and misuse of accommodation theory in sociolinguistics. *Language and Communication* **18**: 205–25
Shepard C, Giles H, LePoire B 2001 Accommodation theory. In: Robinson W P, Giles H (eds.) *The New Handbook of Language and Social Psychology*. Wiley, Chichester, UK
Thakerar J N, Giles H, Cheshire J 1982 The psychological and linguistic parameters of speech accommodation theory. In: Fraser C, Scherer K R (eds.) *Advances in the Social Psychology of Language*. Cambridge University Press, Cambridge, UK
Trudgill P 1986 *Dialects in Contact*. Blackwell, Oxford, UK
William A, Gallois C, Pittam J (eds.) 1999 Special section: Communication in intergroup miscommunication and problematic talk. *International Journal of Applied Linguistics* **9**: 149–245

Speech Act Theory: An Overview
K. Allan

1. The Speech Act as an Aspect of Social Interactive Behavior

A speech act is created when speaker/writer S makes an utterance U to hearer/reader H in context C. Speech acts are a part of social interactive behavior and must be interpreted as an aspect of social interaction (cf. Labov and Fanshel 1977: 30). In the words of Habermas (1979: 2), S utters something understandably; gives H something to understand; makes him/herself thereby understandable; and comes to an understanding with another person. Habermas indicates further requirements on S: that S should believe the truth of what is said, so that H can share S's knowledge (cf. Grice's 1975 maxim of quality; see *Cooperative Principle*); S should 'express his/her intentions in such a way that the linguistic expression represents what is intended (so that [H] can trust [S])'—compare Grice's maxims of quantity and manner; S should 'perform the speech act in such a way that it conforms to recognized norms or to accepted self-images (so that [H] can be in accord with [S] in shared value orientations)' (1979: 29). Additionally, S and H 'can reciprocally motivate one another to recognize validity claims because the content of [S's] engagement is determined by a specific reference to a thematically stressed validity claim, whereby [S], in a cognitively testable way, assumes with a truth claim, obligations to provide grounds [,] with a rightness claim, obligations to provide justification, and with a truthfulness claim, obligations to prove trustworthy' (Habermas 1979: 65).

2. J. L. Austin

Interest in speech acts stems directly from the work of J. L. Austin, and in particular from the William James Lectures which he delivered at Harvard in 1955, published posthumously as *How to Do Things with Words* in 1962 (revised 1975). Austin came from the Oxford school of 'ordinary language philosophers,' which also spawned Geach, Ryle, Strawson, Grice, and Searle. It was intellectually engendered by Wittgenstein, who observed (e.g., 1963: Sect. 23) that logicians have had very little or nothing to say about many of the multiplicity of structures and usages in natural language. Austin's concern with speech acts exhibits an informal, often entertaining, philosopher's approach to some uses of ordinary language.

Austin insisted on a distinction between what he called constatives, which have truth values, and performatives which (according to him) do not (cf. Austin 1962, 1963). The distinction between truth-bearing and non-truth-bearing sentences has a long history. Aristotle noted that 'Not all sentences are statements [*apophantikos*]; only such as have in them either truth of falsity. Thus a prayer is a sentence, but neither true nor false [therefore a prayer is not a statement]' (*On Interpretation* 17a, 1). Later, the Stoics distinguished a judgment or proposition (*axiōma*) as either true or false whereas none of an interrogation, inquiry, imperative, adjurative, optative, hypothetical, nor vocative has a truth value (cf. Diogenes Laertius 1925: 65–68). For more than two millennia, logicians and language philosophers concentrated their energies on statements and the valid inferences to be drawn from them to the virtual exclusion of other prepositional types (questions, commands, etc.). Austin was reacting to this tradition (cf. Hare 1971: ch. 6):

The constative utterance, under the name so dear to philosophers, of *statement*, has the property of being true or false. The performative utterance, by contrast, can never be either: it has its own special job, it is used to perform an action. To issue such an utterance *is* to perform the action—an action, perhaps, which one scarcely could perform, at least with so much precision, in any other way. Here are some examples:
I name this ship 'Liberté.'
I apologise.
I welcome you.
I advise you to do it.

(Austin 1963 22)

Austin's point is that in making such utterances under the right conditions, S performs, respectively, an act of naming, an act of apologizing, an act of welcoming, and an act of advising (it has become usual to speak of 'acts' rather than 'actions'). Performatives have 'felicity conditions' (see Sect. 5 below) in place of truth values. Thus according to Austin, (1) has no truth value but is felicitous if there is a cat such that S has the ability and intention to put it out, and infelicitous—but not false—otherwise:

I promise to put the cat out. (1)

This contrasts with (2), which is either true if S has put the cat out, or false if not:

I've put the cat out. (2)

Austin's claim that performatives do not have truth values has been challenged from the start, and he seems to be wrong. Roughly speaking, their truth value is less communicatively significant than what Austin called the 'illocutionary force' of U. He observed that utterances without performative verbs also perform speech acts, for example, (3) can be used to make a promise:

I'll put the cat out. (3)

Austin would say that (1) and (3) have the same illocutionary force of promising; the function of the performative verb in (1) is to name the 'illocutionary act' being performed. In the later lectures of Austin (1962), he identified two other components of a speech act: locution and perlocution. Linguists recognize three acts which Austin conflates into his locutionary act.

3. The Hierarchy Within Speech Acts

Speaking (and writing—which will from now on be properly included under 'speaking' for simplicity of exposition) comprises a hierarchy of acts. To begin with, language only comes into existence if someone performs an 'act of utterance.' People recognize utterance acts on the basis of brute perception: by hearing them spoken, seeing them signed or written, feeling them impressed in braille. Individuals can readily recognize an utterance act in a language that is completely unknown to them, in which they cannot distinguish the words or sentences used. One can utter sounds which have nothing to do with language.

Speech act theory is concerned with utterances where S utters a language expression and thereby performs a 'locutionary act.' Performing a locutionary act, S uses an identifiable expression E from language L (where E is a sentence or sentence fragment) spoken with identifiable prosody Φ (the pattern of pause, pitch level, stress, and tone of voice; its counterpart in the written medium is punctuation and typography). The consituent structure of E and of Φ, together with their proper senses (meanings), are also identifiable to a typical fluent speaker of L. Recognizing the locution means recognizing that E spoken with prosody Φ means ' ...': consequently, a locution is produced and then recognized by someone who has knowledge of the grammar, lexicon, semantics, and phonology of L.

S uses the senses of language-expressions in the locution (E and its constituents) to identify things in the particular world that s/he is speaking of. This constitutes the 'propositional act of referring' or 'denotational act.'

The final act in the hierarchy of speaking is the 'illocutionary act.' S *does* something in uttering U to H in context C, for example, states a fact or an opinion, confirms or denies something, makes a prediction, a promise, a request, offers thanks or an invitation, issues an order or an umpire's decision, gives advice or permission, names a child, swears an oath. Thus U is said to have the 'illocutionary force' or 'illocutionary point' of a statement, a confirmation denial, a prediction, a promise, a request, and so forth. Obviously, under normal conditions of use, S makes an utterance, use a locution, denotes with it, and expresses at least one illocution, all at one and the same moment.

With very few exceptions, the purpose of speaking is to cause an effect on H (Austin described this as 'securing uptake'): speakers want their opinions to be recognized if not adopted, their assertions to be agreed with, their requests to be enacted, questions answered, advice taken, warnings heeded, commands complied with, thanks appreciated, apologies accepted, and so forth. These are called 'perlocutions' or 'perlocutionary effects.' The perlocutionary effect of U is the consequence of H recognizing (what s/he takes to be) the locution and illocutionary point of U—otherwise the effect is *not* perlocutionary. Although extremely significant within a theory of communication, perlocutionary acts/effects fall outside of linguistics because they are not part of language per se but instead responses to the illocutions in utterances. What linguists can properly look at, however, are the intentions of speakers to bring about certain perlocutionary effects; these intentions appear in definitions of speech acts as 'illocutionary intentions' or 'perlocutionary intentions.'

4. The Speaker's Reflexive-intention; Hearers, and Overhearers

In the spoken medium, there is never more than one S per utterance; however, two S's may utter identical U's in unison or S may speak on someone else's behalf. Coauthors generally take joint responsibility for what is written; but, normally, each writes only a part of the text. This all starkly contrasts with the number of H's which any given S may have for an audience.

H is anyone whom, at the time of utterance, S reflexively intends should recognize the illocutionary point of U. There are a couple of explanations to interject here. The simpler one is that the illocutionary point of U is S's message. The second point is that S tailors U to suit H, taking into account what s/he knows or guesses about H's ability to understand the message which S wants to convey. The notion of a reflexive-intention is S's intention to have a person in earshot recognize that S wants him/her to accept the role of H and therefore be the/an intended recipient of S's message and consequently react to it. This, of course, renders the definition of H circular, and so something closer to Grice's (1957, 1968, 1969) original proposal should be considered, adapted to our customary terminology and with some updating from Recanati (1987: chap. 7): S's reflexive intention toward H is the intention to have H recognize that when uttering U in context C, S intends that U have a certain perlocutionary effect on H partly caused by H recognizing that S has the intention to communicate with him/her by means of U. (So, when Joe hears Sue talking in her sleep, he will not assume she has a reflexive-intention toward him, and therefore not expect that she intends her utterance to have any perlocutionary effect on him—though she might unintentionally keep him awake.)

Clark and Carlson (1982) distinguish between H as 'direct addressee' and H as 'ratified participant,' the latter being a member of the audience participating in the speech act (cf. Goffman 1981: 131). The notion of face (Brown and Levinson 1987; see *Politeness*) is useful in distinguishing between two kinds each of H's and overhearers. An 'addressee' is someone who cannot reject the role of H without serious affront to S's face. Direct address is determined contextually— by direction of gaze, pointing a finger, touching an arm, using a name, or on the basis of who spoke last; less commonly, the nature of the message will determine who is the intended addressee. Note the change of addressee in *Joan, Max bought me this beautiful ring for our anniversary, didn't you Max, you sweetie!* and the nonspecific addressee in

Congratulations, whoever came first! A 'ratified participant' can reject the H role more freely than an addressee and with less of an affront to S's face. When S is speaking, all those who can reasonably consider themselves ratified participants are expected, as part of the cooperative endeavor, to keep tabs on what is said, so that if called upon to participate they may do so appropriately.

Any other person hearing U is an overhearer: either a bystander or an eavesdropper. People in earshot are expected to overhear, though not necessarily to listen; only H's are properly expected to listen. As everyone knows, it can happen that U is overheard by someone when there was no original specific intention on S's part that this should happen; to put it more precisely, S has a reflexive-intention towards H but not towards an overhearer. An overhearer may perchance understand the message the same way that H does; but, because s/he is not necessarily party to the appropriate contextual information relevant to the correct interpretation of the utterance, it is possible that s/he may seriously misinterpret it. So, a bystander within earshot was not originally intended as a H and may, depending on circumstances, accept or reject the role of H without loss of face; consider an occasion where X is arguing with Y in earshot of Z:

[X to Y as addressee]	Shut up or I'll lay one on you.
[Y to Z as ratified participant]	You heard him threaten to hit me, didn't you?
[X to Z as bystander]	You mind your own business.
[Z to both X and Y, rejecting the role of H]	I wasn't listening.

An eavesdropper can only admit to listening in at the expense of their own positive face, because it makes her/him look bad, and sometimes also at the expense of S's negative (impositive) face, because S feels affronted by the intrusion.

5. Felicity Conditions

Austin argued for four kinds of felicity conditions: (a) a preparatory condition to establish whether or not the circumstances of the speech act and the participants in it are appropriate to its being performed successfully; (b) an executive condition to determine whether or not the speech act has been properly executed; (c) a sincerity condition—which has a similar function to Grice's (1975) maxim of quality (see *Cooperative Principle*); and (d) a fulfillment condition determined by the perlocutionary effect of the speech act. If all the relevant felicity conditions were satisfied for a given illocutionary act, Austin described it as 'happy' or 'felicitous.' One can immediately dismiss (d) as irrelevant to a linguistic theory of speech acts because it has only a contingent link with the meaning of U. The other three felicity conditions merit brief discussion here.

The statement of preparatory conditions is obligatory in definitions of illocutions. The preparatory conditions identify what ought to be presupposed in a felicitous use of the illocution. For example, the preparatory condition on an assertion such as *France is a republic* ($=p$) is 'S has reason to believe that p.' If S had said *France is not a republic*, S would be condemned for being ignorant, deluded, insane, or maliciously attempting to mislead H. It is notable that presupposition failure (in, say, *In 1990, the King of France died*) gives rise to exactly the same response. In both cases, Austin would say 'the utterance is void.' Condemnation as a response to preparatory condition failure is common to all illocutions. Take the preparatory condition on thanking: 'H, or someone or something in H's charge, has done some deed D with the apparent intention of benefiting S (directly or indirectly)'; if S thanks H for D when H never did D, H will conclude that S is either deluded or is being sarcastic. Finally, take the case of the tennis player in the US Open who claims that his opponent's ball is 'out' when the umpire disagrees: the claim has no standing because the player is not a person sanctioned by the preparatory conditions on this illocutionary act to declare the ball out of play. Again, by violating the preparatory conditions, S risks condemnation. The question arises whether the preparatory conditions on an illocutionary act really are its presuppositions, as Karttunen and Peters (1979: 10) apparently believe. The problem, which cannot be solved here, is that only some illocutionary acts have truth conditions, yet the standard definition of presupposition is based on truth conditions (X is a presupposition of Y if it is true that Y entails X and also true that ¬Y entails X). Some alternative definition of presupposition seems called for, cf. Seuren (1985, 2000), Allan (2001).

Austin requires that the procedure invoked by the illocutionary act 'must be executed by all participants correctly and completely.' He exemplifies this 'executive condition' with *I bet you the race won't be run today* said when more than one race was arranged for that day. But such misexecutions should be dealt with under generally applicable maxims of the cooperative principle. The only executive condition which still seems warranted to linguists is one on declarations which either bring about or express decisions on states of affairs such as marriage, job appointment/termination, or umpiring. Because they rely for their success on S being sanctioned by the community to perform the acts under stipulated conditions, it may be necessary to safeguard society's interest with an executive condition requiring some watchdog other than S to ensure that the sanctions are respected. These sanctions need to be written into the preparatory conditions on the act; they identify the attitude or behavior that must be observed by S when executing the illocutionary act in order for it to be felicitous.

The sincerity condition on a speech act involves S's responsibility for what s/he is saying (asking, etc.). If S is observing the cooperative maxim of quality, then s/he will be sincere; and, normally, H will assume that S is being sincere unless s/he has good reason to believe otherwise. Generally, scholars have assumed that different kinds of illocutionary acts involve different kinds of sincerity conditions: for example, assertions and the like are sincere if S believes in the truth of the proposition asserted; requests are sincere if S believes that H can do A and might be willing to do A; declarations are sincere if S believes that s/he has the proper authority to make the declaration. Obviously, sincerity reflects on whether or not S upholds the preparatory conditions, so only one sincerity condition should be necessary: in uttering U, S knows or believes (or believes s/he knows) that all clauses of the preparatory condition hold. This puts a burden on precise statement of the preparatory conditions; but that seems exactly where it should lie, because preparatory conditions identify the particular circumstances appropriate to performing a given illocutionary act.

To sum up: the only one of Austin's original felicity conditions that remains obligatory in the definitions of all illocutions is the preparatory condition. An executive condition may be valid for declarations. Some scholars still include sincerity conditions within definitions for illocutionary acts, but sincerity can be captured by generally applicable conditions on language use. Finally, linguists rarely attend to fulfillment conditions, nor should they—though these will remain important to scholars in other disciplines concerned with perlocutionary effects of utterances. The burden of felicitous illocution will depend on proper observation of the preparatory conditions on each illocutionary act. These conditions provide the grounds for motivating S to make the utterance and grounds from which H will evaluate the illocutionary act expressed in the utterance.

6. Explicit Performative Clauses

The characteristics of explicit performative clauses are as follows. The clause must contain a verb that names the illocutionary point of the utterance, for example, *admit, advise, apologize, ask, assert, authorize, baptize, bet, charge, claim, command, congratulate, declare, order, pardon, permit, prohibit, promise, refuse, say, suggest, swear, tell, thank, urge*. It must be in the present tense; in English, it is typically in the simple aspect, but may be progressive: thus *I promise/am promising to accompany you* are performative; *I promised/have promised to accompany you* are not.

An explicit performative clause may be negative; it may be emphatic; and it may contain the adverb *hereby*, meaning 'in/by uttering this performative' (but not meaning 'using this,' referring to something in the context). It must be 'realis' and denote the actualization of the illocutionary act; therefore *I must hereby take my leave of you* is a performative, *I might hereby authorize your release* is not. Finally, S must be agent for whoever takes responsibility for enforcing the illocutionary point of U.

7. Classes of Speech Act

There have been two approaches to classifying speech acts: one, following Austin (1962), is principally a lexical classification of so-called illocutionary verbs; the other, following Searle (1975a), is principally a classification of acts. Lexical groupings of semantically similar illocutionary verbs are made on an intuitive basis, perhaps with some reference to the syntactic environment of the verb (as in Vendler's 1972 classes), for example, expositives N_i V *that* p, such as *state, contend, insist, deny, remind, guess* versus, say, commissives N_i V *to* V, such as *promise, guarantee, refuse, decline*; exercitives 'exercising of powers, rights, or influences' (N_i V N_j *to* V), for example, *order, request, beg, dare*; or behabitives N_i V N_j P nom (past (V)), for example, *thank, congratulate, criticize*, or Ballmer and Brennenstuhl's (1981) formula *Someone* VERB ((ADDRESSEE) *by saying*) '...' (ABBREVIATION: nom = nominalization).

Searle (1975a) used four criteria—illocutionary point, direction of fit, S's psychological state, and propositional content—to establish five classes of speech acts. 'Representatives' have a truth value, show words-to-world fit, and express S's belief that *p*. 'Directives' are attempts to get H to do something, therefore they show world-to-words fit, and express S's wish or desire that H do A. 'Commissives' commit S to some future course of action, so they show world-to-words fit, and S expresses the intention that S do A. 'Expressives' express S's attitude to a certain state of affairs specified (if at all) in the propositional content (e.g., the underlined portion of *I apologize for stepping on your toe*). There is no direction of fit; a variety of different psychological states; and propositional content 'must ... be related to S or H' (1975a: 357ff.). 'Declarations' bring about correspondence between the propositional content and the world, thus direction of fit is both words-to-world and world-to-words. Searle recognizes no psychological state for declarations. Searle's classification has been widely adopted.

Using H's evaluations as criteria, it is possible to establish links between classes of illocution and major clause types. 'Statements' (including denials, reports, predictions, promises, and offers) are principally expressions of S's belief about the way the world was, is, or will be, and are most typically formulated with a declarative clause. They can be judged in terms of the question 'Is *p* credible?' 'Invitationals' are a proper subset of Searle's directives, and include requests, exhortations, suggestions, warnings, etc. which principally invite H's participation. Many are formulated in an interrogative clause and prompt the question 'Does S really want A to be done, and if so is H both able and willing to do it?' 'Authoritatives' include the rest of Searle's 'directives' and his 'declarations' (commands, permissions, legal judgments, baptisms, etc.) which have S 'laying down the law.' Many of them are formulated in an imperative clause, the rest in a declarative. For these, H must consider the question 'Does S have the authority to utter U in the given context?' 'Expressives' (greetings, thanks, apologies, congratulations, etc.) have social-interactive-appropriateness values: 'Has something occurred which warrants S expressing such a reaction to it?' These principally express social interaction with H; many are idiomatic, the rest are in the default declarative clause format. All four classes of speech acts can be conveyed using a declarative clause; but interrogatives typically indicate invitationals, imperatives authoritatives, and idioms expressives.

8. Definitions of Illocutions

Definitions of illocutions are an extension of the semantics of the key verb naming the illocution, for example, *assert, deny, boast, suggest, promise, threaten, offer, command, baptize,* etc. Such a verb is just one kind of illocutionary force-indicating device or IFID. Another kind of lexical IFID is *please*: compare the information-seeking question *Are you leaving?* with the request that H leave in *Are you leaving, please?* The hyperbole in *Your bedroom's a pigsty!* implies not only condemnation but also often the command to clear it up. Idioms like *Would you mind ...* minimize an impending imposition. There are morphological IFIDs marking clause-type and politeness levels in Japanese and other oriental languages. There are syntactic IFIDs like word order and clause-type (mood), cf. *You can do A versus Can you do A?* Versus *Would that you could do A.* Last, there is prosody or punctuation; contrast *Out?* with *Out!* In most utterances, the recognition of an illocution requires reference to cooperative conditions and/or the context of utterance (see Sects. 9, 10, 11 below).

Austin cleared the ground and laid the foundations for speech act theory, and to him goes the credit for distinguishing locution, illocution, and perlocution. But it was Searle (1969: chap. 3) who first established criteria for the definitions of illocutions, using promising as his example. (a) 'Normal input and output conditions obtain.' That is, the situation of utterance (including participants) is favorable to successful communication. (b) 'S expresses the proposition that *p* in [U].' (c) 'In expressing that *p*, S predicates a future act A of S.' Conditions (b) and (c) constitute the 'propositional content' referred to in specific definitions of illocutionary acts (in this instance, promising); scholars since Searle have usually extended this component of a definition to a description of utterance content that names the illocution, thereby including the IFID that Searle expressly omits (Vanderveken 1990 is an exception). Rules (d) and (e) identify 'preparatory conditions' on the illocution; (d) being specific to promising, and (e) being 'to the effect that the act must have a point.' Rule (e) should be enshrined within general statements of cooperative conditions on language use because it is normally relevant to all illocutionary acts and does not need to be stated within any particular definition. (f) is a sincerity condition (see Sect. 5 above). (g) 'S intends [U] will place him under an obligation to do A' is to be taken together with (h), which identifies S's reflexive-intention, 'S intends (i-I) to produce in H the knowledge (K) that [U] is to count as placing S under an obligation to do A. S intends to produce K by means of the recognition of i-I, and he intends i-I to be recognized in virtue of (by means of) H's knowledge of the meaning of [U].' Searle calls this 'counts as' condition 'the essential rule.' Others have adopted or adapted it into an 'illocutionary intention.'

A survey of speech act definitions in Searle (1969), Bach and Harnish (1979), Edmondson (1981), Levinson (1983), Allan (1986), and Wierzbicka (1987) reveals great similarity despite the different perspectives of these scholars. The obligatory components of the definitions of illocutions are the preparatory condition and S's illocutionary intention. The propositional or utterance content will be either given or inferable from one or both of these. Finally, it was suggested in Sect. 5 that a single sincerity condition holds for all acts.

9. Being Literal or Nonliteral, Direct or Indirect, On-record or Off-record

An indirect speech act is one in which S performs one illocutionary act (e.g., stating *It's cold in here*), but intends H to infer by way of relying on their mutually shared background information, both linguistic and nonlinguistic, another illocution (e.g., requesting the heating to be turned up); cf. Searle (1975b: 61), Bach and Harnish (1979: 70). Sadock (1974) identified some exotic species of indirect acts: 'whimperatives' indirectly request (the function of the imperative in Sadock's view) by means of S directly asking a question, for example, *Can't you (please) do A?* and *Do A, will you?* (this analysis is criticized in Allan 1986: 216); using a 'queclarative,' S directly questions and indirectly makes an assertion—*Does anyone do A any more?* means 'Nobody does A any more'; 'requestions' are quiz questions to which S knows the answer, for example, *Columbus discovered America in*? Because the clause-type determines the direct or primary illocution (Allan 2001), all speech acts are indirect; so, rather than postulating a binary distinction (direct versus indirect), it is preferable to allow for an open-ended series of illocutions ranged from the primary illocution (determined by clause-type) to the last illocution that can be inferred from a given utterance (which is the illocutionary point).

The study of indirect speech acts has overwhelmingly dealt with requests. Blum-Kulka et al. (1989: 18) identify nine points on an indirectness scale for requests. Their 'direct strategies' are used when S is dominant: (a) imperative *Clean up that mess*; (b) performative *I'm asking you to clean up that mess*; (c) hedged performatives *I would like to ask you to come for a check-up*; (d) obligation statements *You'll have to move that car*; (e) want statements *I want you to stop calling me*. What they call 'conventionally indirect strategies' are H-oriented: (f) suggestory formulas *How about cleaning up?*; (g) query preparatory (Sadock's 'whimperatives') *Could/Will you clear up the kitchen, please?* Finally, their 'nonconventionally indirect strategies' are off-record: (h) strong hints *You've left the kitchen in a dreadful mess*; (i) mild hints *I say, it's a bit chilly in here, isn't it?* (said when the heating is off and the window open).

The contrast between direct and indirect illocution is muddied by the related contrasts between being on-record versus off-record, and being literal or nonliteral. Blum-Kulka et al.'s 'nonconventional indirect' requests could be classified 'off-record'; the 'direct' and 'conventionally indirect' ones 'on-record' because an on-record U spells out the message explicitly. Note that S can be on-record and either direct or indirect; but if S is off-record, s/he is necessarily indirect. For someone who is not very close to S to respond to the invitation *Do you want to come to a movie tonight?* with the bald-on-record refusal *No* is downright offensive. To avoid giving offence, people hedge, apologize, prevaricate, and speak off-record, giving reasons for not accepting the invitation or complying with the request. Thus, to politely refuse the invitation, one says things like *I have to wash my hair* or *I'd love to, but my mother's coming to dinner tonight*. Note that these might be literally meant on-record statements of S's plans, but their illocutionary point is indirect and off-record refusal.

A nonliteral U such as the sarcastic *I'm sure the cat likes you pulling its tail* is an indirect, off-record request for H to desist. What makes it nonliteral is that S does not really mean it as a direct assertion about what the cat likes; in other words, it is the illocution which is nonliteral. However, there is no reason to believe that the literal meaning of *Max is a bastard* is any more direct than an utterance intending the nonliteral meaning of 'bastard'; furthermore, both interpretations are on-record. The psycholinguistic evidence (cf. Gernsbacher 1990: 89) is that all possible senses of a language expression are activated, and context then suppresses the activation of inappropriate meanings; consequently, there is no reason to believe that the nonliteral meaning of a lexically ambiguous term takes longer to process than its literal meaning; and there are therefore no grounds at all for suggesting that it is less 'direct.' What is nonliteral in the last example is the locution, not the illocution. Take another, problematic example: *If it's not Schlitz, it's not beer*. This is a direct, on-record assertion, but it is nonliteral because S does not really mean that a can of Budweiser or Foster's is not beer, though S might literally mean that in S's opinion (but not everybody's) Budweiser and Foster's lack the properties necessary for it to be properly classified as beer. Thus, one concludes that S is indirectly asserting the opinion that Schlitz is the best beer—and literally means this; there will be different views on whether or not this opinion is on the record.

It is not enough to retain the term 'indirect illocution' only for an illocution that is either off-record or nonliteral or both. Suppose S asserts *Ted's BMW is giving him trouble*. This entails the on-record proposition that 'Ted has a BMW' and it is indirect because S does not directly assert it (pace Russell). Presumably S literally means 'Ted has a BMW' because s/he presupposes its truth (i.e., purports to do so). One concludes that illocutions which are on-record and apparently literally meant are 'indirect' if they are entailed or implicated in U; also if they are off-record, or nonliteral, or both. The so-called 'conventionally indirect' illocutions are on-record, not S-dominant but H-oriented: this solves the problem that they do not necessarily translate into other languages (see Sect.12).

10. More Than One Illocution in U

Coordinate, conjoined, and appositive clauses contribute more than one illocutionary point to U. With *I resign from the board and promise not to speak to the press*, S resigns and makes a promise. With *Welcome to the show; now, what do you do for a living?*, S welcomes H and asks a question. With *I met Celia— Did you know she was married, by the way?—at a party last night, and she told me the latest scandal at number 25*, S performs an informative interrupted by a question and conjoins its informative a report.

One serious weakness with speech act theory has been to pretend that each U has only one illocutionary point. As Labov and Fanshel (1977: 29ff.) pointed out, 'most utterances can be seen as performing several speech acts simultaneously....

Conversation is not a chain of utterances, but rather a matrix of utterances and actions bound together by a web of understandings and reactions.... In conversation, participants use language to interpret to each other the significance of the actual and potential events that surround them and to draw the consequences for their past and future actions.' Speech acts must be interpreted with attention to their context and to their function as an integral part of social interactive behavior. Here is a common enough example:

S_1: Would you like another drink?
S_2: Yes, I would, thank you.

S_1 asks a question and concomitantly makes the offer to bring S_2 a drink, if that is what s/he wants. S_2 responds positively both to the question and to the offer, and coordinates with these illocutions a statement of thanks. Some situations allow for quite a large number of illocutionary points to be scored. Consider a public condemnation like that of the woman at a party who cries out *Mrs Trumpington, will you please ask your husband not to touch me up?!* S does several things simultaneously: (a) she makes a literal on-record request to Mrs T that she ask Mr T to stop harassing S; (b) she broadcasts on-record, literally, but indirectly, what Mr T is doing; (c) she makes a literal on-record indirect request that he stop—despite the on-record indirect expression of her belief that he will not stop of his own volition; (d) off-record, S indirectly intends not only that Mrs T condemn her husband for sexual harassment of S, but (e) that everyone in earshot should do so too.

Another weakness of speech act theory is to pretend that S's illocutionary intentions can be precisely pinned down. Suppose that one morning as H is getting ready for work, S volunteers *It's 7.45.* This informs H of the time. One may or may not be overestimating S's intention if one assumes that s/he thereby implies that it is past the time when H should have already left for work, hence warning H that s/he is running late and furthermore counseling H to hurry. U may merely have been intended to draw H's attention to the time, leaving H to draw whatever conclusion s/he wished. H might be grateful for having the matter brought to his/her attention; get angry with S for interfering; respond by hurrying; respond by suing for divorce; there are innumerable possible responses. S discovers only through H's response the perlocutionary effect of U, and thence whether his/her intentions have been realized—always assuming S has any clear idea what these are!

11. The Inferential Analysis of Speech Acts

The inferential theory of speech acts developed out of proposals originally made by Searle (1975b), subsequently refined in the 'speech acts schema' described by Bach and Harnish (1979), and in Allan (1986: chap. 8). When S wishes to communicate with H, s/he will express him/herself in a way that s/he presumes will enable H to comprehend the intended message. The inferential theory of speech acts presents an abstract model of each step necessary in H's reasoning out of S's illocutionary point(s) in uttering U. There is an assumption that both S and H are normal human beings—that is, neither is a genius, a clairvoyant, nor a fool; both know the language L and how to use it; and they have the general knowledge that one can reasonably attribute to such persons in the particular context of utterance.

The stages in H's reasoning are taken to be as follows:

(a) Perception and recognition of U as linguistic.
(b) Recognition of U as an expression *E* of language L spoken with prosody Φ, and of the sense or senses of the locution. This is done on the bases of the cooperative principle (the term is used here to include the reasonableness condition, the communicative presumption, face concerns, and the like), and H's knowledge of lexiconic syntactic, and prosodic contributions to meaning—all of which must be specified within a general theory of meaning, though not within a theory of speech acts.
(c) Recognition of what S is denoting/referring to in the (model of the) world and time spoken of, $M^{w,t}$ (cf. Allan 2001).
(d) Recognition of the primary illocution of U on the basis of the mood of the clause in the locution, and the definitions of the five or so primary illocutionary acts which form part of the theory of speech acts.
(e) S's presumed reason for performing this primary illocution is sought in the light of various assumptions and presumptions of the cooperative principle, knowledge of L, and the use of L (including knowledge of the definitions of illocutionary acts), context, and background information of many kinds. This process may lead to a number of illocutions being inferred, ranged in a sequence from primary illocution to illocutionary point.
(f) The illocutionary point (or points) of U, that is, S's message in U, is recognized when at last no further illocutions can be inferred, and the inference schema shuts down.

An utterance such as (4) trades on the cooperative requirement that H should have a good reason not to comply with such a request:

Why don't you be quiet?

Consider the following inference schema:

In uttering (4), S intends H to reason that:

	Basis:
1. S utters U in C. [Recognition of the utterance act]	Hearing S utter U in C.
2. U = ΦE in English, and ΦE means 'S asks why don't you be quiet?' [Recognition of the locution]	1, cooperative principle, knowledge of English.
3. By 'you,' S means 'H.'	2, theory of reference, context.
4. S is using ΦE to mean 'S asks H to give a reason not be quiet.' [Recognition of reference and denotation]	2, 3, theory of denotation, context.
5. S reflexively-intends U to be taken as asking a reason to be given for H not to be quiet. [Recognition of the primary illocutionary intention]	4, definitions of illocutionary acts.
6. S is asking for a reason to be given for H not to be quiet. [Recognition of the primary illocution]	5, definition of interrogatives.
7. S's reason for asking this is to be informed of the reason for H not to be quiet; that is, S reflexively-intends U to be taken as a reason for H to tell S H's reason not to be quiet. [Recognition of the secondary illocutionary intention]	6, cooperative principle, definitions of illocutionary acts.
8. S is questioning H as to H's reason not to be quiet. [Recognition of the secondary illocution]	7, definition of questions.
9. S's question presupposes that H has been noisy. Noise imposes on others; it seems it has imposed on S. It is impolite to impose on others, therefore the person doing it should desist or else give a reason for not being able to desist. Any other action is uncooperative, and S must know this.	8, semantic theory, ?context, cooperative principle.
10. Therefore S reflexively-intends that U be taken as a reason either for H to be quiet or to inform S of the reason for being unable to be quiet. [Recognition of the tertiary illocutionary intention]	8, 9, definitions of illocutionary acts.
11. S is requesting H either to be quiet, or to tell S the reason for being unable to be quiet. [Recognition of the tertiary illocution]	10, definition of requestives.
12. There is no reason to believe any further illocutionary intention can be inferred, therefore S is either requesting H to be quiet or questioning the reason for being unable to be quiet. [Conclusion as to the illocutionary point of U]	4,11, context, background information.

People are not expected to expressly offer reasons for being cooperative, but they are expected to offer reasons for not being cooperative: which is why there is the disjunctive illocutionary point to (4). Notice how the question illocution is carried down through the schema to become one of the disjuncts of the illocutionary point of the speech act.

Having recognized the utterance act, H must recognize S's locution. To accomplish this, H must recognize that U consists of expression E from language L spoken with prosody Φ. The first step in the process is for H to make the communicative presumption that S intends to communicate with him/her using language as a medium. This presumption is based in part on a categorizing ability to which H must have recourse at various levels in the analysis of utterance meaning. H takes the sense data from constituents of U and categorizes them using his/her linguistic knowledge, so as to perceive them in terms of a linguistic category. Perhaps the initial categorization is to recognize U as made in language L; this might be crudely described as matching H's perception of U and its parts with the languages that s/he knows. In practice, H usually has a clear expectation about which language S is using because of former experience with S or the situation of utterance; where this is not the case, there will be a heuristic interactional process along the following lines: (a) U sounds as though it is made in L_b; (b) constituent e_i of U seems to be a constituent of L_b; (c) if constituent e_j also seems to be a constituent of L_b, then e_k will be another; (d) if there is no counterevidence, then S is speaking L_b (this procedure is speculative and not experimentally confirmed). Having established that U is made in L, H must use his/her knowledge of L when categorizing what s/he perceives in U as particular lexiconic, syntactic, and prosodic constituents of L. For instance, H needs a knowledge of L's lexicon and how to use it, in order to match the appropriate set of lexicon entries with the lexicon items which s/he perceives S to use in U. H must use knowledge of the syntactic properties of lexicon items in establishing their scope relations and the syntactic structures which combine them in U. Once these are recognized, H can determine the meanings of E's constituents, and the meaning of E itself; H will then take into account the effect of the prosody Φ on the meaning of E in order to determine the sense or senses of the locution ΦE.

The next step for H is to recognize what S is denoting in the (model of the) world and time spoken of, $M^{w,t}$. To do this, H will match the sense(s) of E's constituents with entities in $M^{w,t}$, using knowledge of the correlation between sense and denotation/reference. Having determined the denotation/reference of U, H uses knowledge of the definitions of illocutionary acts to determine S's illocutionary intention in U. Once again, it is a matter for H's categorizing ability: this time, H perceives what S is denoting by means of the locution ΦE, and s/he must determine what kind of message S intends to communicate using this proposition. The set of illocutionary intentions is located among the definitions of illocutionary acts which constitute a part of H's linguistic knowledge (and are presumably located along with other information about meaningful properties and meaning relations). Recognition of the illocutionary intention will lead to the identification of the illocutionary act which it helps to define. There are only five primary illocutionary acts, each being determined by the form of the locution. To determine the illocutionary point of U, H invokes the reasonableness condition and seeks some reason for S's primary illocution in the context, C; the conversational maxim of relation (or relevance) will often be invoked too, and so may the other maxims of the cooperative principle—though these are more likely to be called upon at later stages. H will need to keep tabs on the meaningful properties of U and its constituents at this as in all subsequent steps leading to the decision on the illocutionary point of U; s/he must also constantly monitor the semantic relationships of U and its constituents to their textual environment; the semantic properties and relations of U may well be significant to its proper interpretation. In seeking a reason for the primary illocution, H looks to the context C, and will also check background knowledge of many kinds, including knowledge of the kinds of things that people might say in C, and the kinds of reasons that other speakers might have had when employing a similar primary illocution; in other words, H uses knowledge of L and the use of L to infer from the primary locution and the circumstances of utterance what the illocutionary point might be. This may lead through a number of indirect illocutions. The illocutionary point is only recognized when H can infer no further illocutions in U. When H recognizes the illocutionary point, s/he has finally determined the meaning of U.

Although this description offers a rational model for H's understanding of U, it is misleading because it pretends that each step is completed before the next is begun. This cannot be true because, in reality, people interpret parts of utterances as they are presented. The inferential theory of speech acts needs to be reworked to allow for this.

12. Speech Acts and Intercultural Pragmatics

Different cultural conventions and belief systems in different language communities result in different cooperative conventions. For example, there are different linguistic politeness strategies to reflect the culturally validated perceived roles of S and H, and whatever is being spoken of. Social interactive practices such as societal attitudes to the roles of men and women vary greatly across cultures; and, as a result, so do the language conventions which people use. Acts of complimenting and thanking are more frequent, in Anglo communities than in, say, China or Africa. The Japanese and Chinese find refusing more offensive than Americans do, and so refuse off-record by using proverbs and impersonals. Preparatory conditions on illocutionary acts defined for one language cannot be expected to be universal. Intercultural miscommunication arises from the assumption that the language strategies appropriate to the delivery of the intended meaning in L_x can be used with equal efficacy in L_y. For instance, direct translation of the English *Would you like to go the cinema with me?* into Polish *Czy miałabyś ochotę pójść ze mną do kina?* will be interpreted as a direct question and not an invitation; the counterpart Polish invitation *Możebyśmy poszli do kina?* 'Perhaps we would go to the cinema?' will probably misfire in English as an intended invitation, because the off-record implication in Polish—'if I asked you?'—is lost (cf. Wierzbicka 1991: 29).

All major speech act theorists have ignored cultural diversity, leaving it to empirical studies such as the Cross-Cultural Speech Act Realization Project (CCSARP) to investigate (cf. Blum-Kulka et al. 1989) (see *Discourse in Cross-linguistic and Cross-cultural Contexts*). This project investigated and confirmed cultural differences in strategies for requesting and apologizing in German, Hebrew, Danish, Canadian French, Argentinian Spanish, British, American, and Australian English. For instance, both Americans and Israelis generally prefer to use on-record H-oriented requests rather than off-record ones, but the second preferences differ: Hebrews prefer S-dominant direct requests, whereas Americans favor the off-record strategy. Interacting with familiars but not intimates, Slavs, Hebrews, and Germans use direct on-record requests mitigated with, for example, modal particles and diminutives (cf. Wierzbicka 1991); English lacks such devices and therefore uses fewer S-dominant strategies. There is much ongoing research into illocutions which touch on politeness concerns, because it is so very important to avoid inadvertently causing offense in social interaction, especially when H is from another culture. (See *Politeness*; *Ethnography of Speaking*.)

13. Speech Acts and Discourse

Speech act theories have treated illocutionary acts as the product of single utterances based on a single sentence, thus becoming a pragmatic extension to sentence grammars. In real life, people do not use isolated utterances: U functions as part of a larger intention or plan. Attempts to break out of the sentence-grammar mold were made by Labov and Fanshel (1977) and Edmondson (1981), and then increasingly by researchers into cross-cultural spoken discourse (see Blum-Kulka et al. 1989). The field of artificial intelligence has taken up speech acts in the context of modeling S's plans and intentions when uttering U (see Cohen et al. 1990). Consider the following interchange in a pharmacy:

Customer:	Do you have any Actifed? [Implies the intention to buy on condition Actifed are available, seeks to establish preparatory condition or transaction]
Clerk:	Tablets or linctus? [Offers a choice of product, establishes preparatory condition for transaction]
Customer:	Packet of tablets, please. [Requests one of products offered, initiates transaction. Notice that in this context, even without the IFID 'please,' the noun phrase alone will function as a requestive]
Clerk:	That'll be $10. [Directly states the payment required to execute the transaction; thereby indirectly requesting payments to execute it]
Customer proffers money:	OK. [Agrees to contract of sale and fulfills buyer's side of the bargain]
Clerk accepts money, hands over goods:	Have a nice day. [Fulfills seller's side of the bargain and concludes interaction with a conventional farewell]

As in most interactions, the interlocutors each have an agenda; and to carry out the plan, the illocutions within a discourse are ordered with respect to one another. The effect is to create coherent discourse in which S upholds his/her obligations to H. Future work on speech acts needs to account for the contribution of individual speech acts to a discourse or text; and that leads into the realm of conversational or discourse analysis (see *Discourse*; *Conversation Analysis*).

Very little work has been done on the contribution of the illocutions within utterances/sentences to the development of understanding in written texts. Texts, whether spoken or written, display one or more of four perlocutionary functions, according to Brewer and Lichtenstein (1982). Social interaction predominates in what Malinowski (see *Malinowski, Bronislaw Kaspar*) called phatic communion (social chit-chat), informativeness predominates in academic texts, persuasiveness in election speeches, and entertainment in novels. But many texts combine some or all of these functions in varying degrees to achieve their communicative purpose; for instance, although an academic text is primarily informative, it also tries to persuade readers to reach a certain point of view; it needs to be entertaining enough to keep the reader's attention; and most academic texts try to get the reader on their side through social interactive techniques such as use of authorial 'we' to include the reader. The contribution of the illocutions of individual utterances to the understanding of topics and episodes (macrostrucures) within texts is sorely in need of study.

See also: Pragmatics and Sociolinguistics.

Bibliography

Allan K 1986 *Linguistic Meaning*. Routledge and Kegan Paul, London, Vol. 2
Allan K 2001 *Natural Language Semantics*. Blackwell, Oxford, UK
Anderson S R 1971 *On the Linguistic Status of the Performative Constative Distinction*. Indiana University Linguistics Club, Bloomington, IN
Austin J L 1962 *How to Do Things with Words*. Clarendon Press, Oxford, UK
Austin J L 1963 Performative–constative. In: Caton C E (ed.) *Philosophy and Ordinary Language*. University of Illinois Press, Urbana, IL
Bach K, Harnish R M 1979 *Linguistic Communication and Speech Acts*. MIT Press, Cambridge, MA
Ballmer T, Brennenstuhl W 1981 *Speech Act Classification*. Springer-Verlag, Berlin
Blum-Kulka S, House J, Kasper G 1989 Investigating cross-cultural pragmatics: An introductory overview. In: Blum-Kulka S, House J, Kasper G (eds.) *Cross-Cultural Pragmatics: Requests and Apologies*. Ablex, Norwood, NJ
Brewer W, Lichtenstein E H 1982 Stories are to entertain: A structural-affect theory of stories. *Journal of Pragmatics* **6**: 473–86
Brown P, Levinson S 1987 *Politeness: Some Universals in Language Usage*. Cambridge University Press, Cambridge, UK
Clark H H, Carlson T B 1982 Hearers and speech acts. *Language* **58**: 332–73
Cohen P R, Morgan J, Pollack M E (eds.) 1990 *Intentions in Communication*. MIT Press, Cambridge, MA
Diogenes Laertius 1925 (trans. Hicks R D) *Lives of Eminent Philosophers*. Heinemann, London, Vol. 2
Edmondson W 1981 *Spoken Discourse*. Longman, London
Fraser B 1974 An examination of the performative analysis. *Papers in Linguistics* **7**: 1–40
Gernsbacher M A 1990 *Language Comprehension as Structure Building*. Lawrence Erlbaum, Hillsdale, NJ
Goffman E 1981 *Forms of Talk*. University of Pennsylvania Press, Philadelphia, PA

Grice H P 1957 Meaning. *Philosophical Review* **66**: 377–88

Grice H P 1968 Utterer's meaning, sentence meaning, and word-meaning. *Foundations of Language* **4**: 225–42

Grice H P 1969 Utterer's meaning, and intentions. *Philosophical Review* **78**: 147–77

Grice H P 1975 Logic and conversation. In: Cole P, Morgan J (eds.) *Syntax and Semantics. Vol. 3: Speech Acts.* Academic Press, New York

Habermas J 1979 (trans. McCarthy T) *Communication and the Evolution of Society.* Beacon Press, Boston, MA

Hare R M 1971 *Practical Inferences.* Macmillan, London

Harnish R M 1975 The argument from *Lurk. Linguistic Inquiry* **6**: 145–54

Karttunen L, Peters S 1979 Conventional implicature. In: Oh C-K, Dinneen D A (eds.) *Syntax and Semantics. Vol. 11: Presupposition.* Academic Press, New York

Katz J J, Postal P M 1964 *An Integrated Theory of Linguistics Descriptions.* MIT Press Cambridge, MA

Labov W, Fanshel D 1977 *Therapeutic Discourse.* Academic Press, New York

Lakoff G 1972 Linguistics and natural logic. In: Davidson D, Harman G (eds.) *Semantics of Natural Language.* Reidel, Dordrecht, The Netherlands

Lakoff R 1968 *Abstract Syntax and Latin Complementation.* MIT Press, Cambridge MA

Levinson S C 1983 *Pragmatics.* Cambridge University Press. Cambridge, UK

Recanati F 1987 *Meaning and Force: The Pragmatics of Performative Utterances.* Cambridge University Press, Cambridge, UK

Ross J R 1970 On declarative sentences. In: Jacobs R A, Rosenbaum P S (eds.) *Readings in English Transformational Grammar.* Ginn, Waltham, MA

Sadock J M 1974 *Toward a Linguistic Theory of Speech Acts.* Academic Press, New York

Searle J R 1969 *Speech Acts.* Cambridge University Press, Cambridge, UK

Searle J R 1975a A taxonomy of illocutionary acts. In: Gunderson K (ed.) *Language, Mind, and Knowledge.* University of Minnesota Press, Minneapolis, MN

Searle J R 1975b Indirect speech acts. In: Cole P, Morgan J (eds.) *Syntax and Semantics. Vol. 3: Speech Acts.* Academic Press, New York

Searle J R 1979 *Expression and Meaning: Studies in the Theory of Speech Acts.* Cambridge University Press. Cambridge, UK

Seuren P A M 1985 *Discourse Semantics.* Basil Blackwell. Oxford, UK

Seuren P A M 2000 Presupposition, negation and trivalence. *Journal of Linguistics* **36**: 261–97

Vanderveken D 1990 *Meaning and Speech Acts.* Cambridge University Press, Cambridge, UK

Vendler Z 1972 *Res Cogitans.* Cornell University Press, Ithaca, New York

Wierzbicka A 1987 *English Speech Act Verbs: A Semantics Dictionary.* Academic Press, Sydney, NSW

Wierzbicka A 1991 *Cross-Cultrual Pragmatics: The Semantics of Human Interaction.* Mouton de Gruyter, Berlin

Wittgenstein L 1963 *Philosophical Investigations.* Blackwell, Oxford, UK

SECTION III
Language Variation: Style, Situation, Function

Advertising
M. L. Geis

The language of advertising is language that is used in efforts to persuade or otherwise entice people to purchase products or services, vote for particular political candidates, modify their behavior (*Just say 'No'!*), or come to adopt a favorable view of some corporate entity (*We're working to keep your trust*). In the case of commercial advertising, by far the most common type of advertising, an advertisement will normally offer some product or service that is represented as satisfying some consumer need or desire—a tablet which is represented as relieving pain or alleviating the symptoms of a cold, a frozen food that is represented as being easy to prepare, nutritious, and tasty, or a brand of beer that is said to be *less filling* or to *taste great*.

1. The Advertising Register

Much of the language that occurs in commercial advertising is characteristic of what might be called the 'advertising register' (see *Register*), in which certain types of expressions are frequently used, such as elliptical comparatives (25 percent *less tar* (than what?)), complex comparatives (*More car for less money*), imperatives used to make suggestions such as *Try it, you'll like it*, rhetorical questions (*My friends, what is hamburger? Chopped ham?*), adjectivalizations (*meaty taste*), and the use of count nouns as mass nouns (*more car*). As a result, much if not most advertising language is readily identifiable as such by consumers.

Though the language of advertising contains the elements of the language of ordinary life, it is not infrequently used differently from how ordinary speakers use it. For example, in conversational uses of English, an assertion like *I'll wait for up to an hour* would normally be made, not to make a promise to wait, but to set limits on an antecedently made promise to wait, and is therefore more like a warning than a promise. Significantly, though *I'll wait for up to an hour* is logically consistent with the speaker's waiting for less than an hour, when a speaker says this the speaker implies that he or she will wait at least an hour, for were the speaker actually to plan to wait less than an hour, Grice's Maxims of Quantity (see Sect. 3.1 below) would force him or her to say so. In contrast, when advertisers say that a nasal spray *lasts and lasts up to 12 continuous hours*, they are typically using the *up to*-construction not to restrict an antecedently made promise of 12 hours relief but to make the central promise of the commercial. However, consumers can be expected to interpret this *up to*-claim much as they do conversational occurrences of *up to*-claims and draw the inference that they will get twelve hours of relief.

Advertisers often qualify claims with the verb *help*, as in *Such-and-such helps form a seal between your dentures and gums...helps keep food out, dentures in*. Such an advertiser does not mean to imply that a seal will be created or that food will be kept out or that dentures will be kept in as a result of using the product. However, when an ordinary person says, *I'll help you mow your lawn* he means to imply that he will stay with the task till the lawn is mown. And, advertisers very rarely seem to make truthful *More for less claims*, e.g., *More car for less money*. A major American automobile manufacturer (cf. Geis 1982) has, for instance, three times offered more car for less money to consumers, but the comparison class that made *more car* true was in each case different from the comparison class that made *less money* true. Normally, in the case of a comparative claim, one holds the comparison class constant throughout a claim.

2. Language in Media

The role of language in advertising depends significantly on the advertising medium. In radio advertising, all that can be presented is oral language, music, and sound effects, and the efficacy of the advertisement will therefore depend heavily on what is said. In print advertising, both verbal and graphic information is presented, and the language that is used can play a variety of roles ranging from that of attracting attention, to illustrating graphic images, to presenting information. Television advertising combines all three elements—music and sound effects, spoken and written language, and visual images—and shares with radio advertising the fact that it occurs in 'real time.' Though television is usually perceived as a visual medium, the fact is that what is said in a television commercial is often as important, if not more important than what is shown. Exceptions would be for products about which little of real substance can be said—advertisements for beer, soft drinks, perfumes, etc.

Because it is both a visual and verbal medium and occurs in 'real time,' television advertising imposes great perceptual and cognitive demands on viewers and sometimes exploits their limited perceptual capabilities by presenting conflicting written and oral language, e.g., a strong, short, and easily comprehended written claim (*Lasts 12 hours per dose*) competing with a hedged and more difficult to comprehend oral claim (*Such-and-such lasts up to 12 hours per dose*), or by presenting essentially unreadable small-print written disclaimers qualifying the oral text at the same time that the oral text is presented. Both techniques exploit the fact that people cannot simultaneously process oral and written language which is different in substance.

3. The Exploitation of Normal Modes of Consumer Reasoning

Human beings are 'inferencing' creatures, trained to 'read into' what is said as much as is consistent with the literal meaning of what is said and the context in which it is said. Thus, if a parent says *I'll give you five dollars if you'll mow the lawn* to a child, the parent expects the child to draw the inference that the parent will not give the child five dollars if the child does not mow the lawn—an invalid, but nevertheless quite compelling inference. Advertisers routinely exploit our tendency to draw such inferences.

3.1 The Cooperative Principle

Paul Grice observed that people normally conduct themselves in conversation in accord with what he called the 'Cooperative Principle,' (see *Cooperative Principle*) according to which participants in conversation are enjoined to make their contributions such that they further the purposes of the conversation by saying only things they believe to be true and have some evidence for (Quality Maxims), by saying as much as is required, but not more (Strength Maxims), by saying only relevant things (Relation Maxim), and by being orderly, brief, nonobscure, and the like (Manner Maxims). Advertisers routinely exploit these maxims by way of encouraging us to draw inferences they are unable to defend.

When an advertiser says that his product does not contain some particular ingredient, he implies that this ingredient has undesirable properties (otherwise the claim would not be relevant) and, further, that the product itself does not have these properties as a result of containing some other ingredient (otherwise the advertiser will not have said as much about this product as is relevant and is required). Thus, when the advertiser of a cold remedy says that a competing product *Contains aspirin. Can upset your stomach*, but says of their own remedy that it *does not contain aspirin*, they imply that their remedy will not upset consumers' stomachs, an inference that the advertiser very possibly cannot defend. Indeed, this product may contain some other chemical compound that is capable of causing stomach upset in some persons. The attractiveness of implying something rather than asserting it overtly derives from the fact that one does not have to defend unasserted claims and consumers seem not to defend well against them.

3.2 Generic Claims in Advertising

Advertisers also routinely exploit normal modes of interpreting generic claims. Generic claims like *Dogs have four legs*, *A body in motion tends to stay in motion*, or *Force equals mass times acceleration* are normally interpreted as being very strong, even if not always universally true, claims, for they are used to attribute intrinsic properties to things, make law-like statements, and give definitions. Indeed, it was once common for linguists and philosophers to paraphrase an assertion like *Carrots are good for you* as *If something is a carrot, it is good for you* or even *All carrots are good for you*, very strong claims indeed.

Claims like *Such-and-such removes impurities from the air* or *Such-and-such gives temporary relief for hours from hemorrhoidal flareups* abound in advertising. Construed as a simple assertion, *Such-and-such removes impurities from the air* must be said to be true if the product removes as little as 40 or 20 or 10 or even 5 percent or less of the impurities in the air. Thus, surprisingly, the generic claim turns out to be quite weak.

However, an advertisement can be seen as a type of offer (a kind of Speech Act) (see *Speech Act Theory: An Overview*) in which some product or service is offered to satisfy some consumer need. Importantly, offers are subject to a sincerity condition according to which the speaker must believe and have evidence that what is being offered will satisfy the need that gives rise to the offer. In the example at hand, the need in question is for some sort of reasonable air quality, and it can be said that the offer in question is a sincere one only if the product removes sufficient impurities from the air to afford a health benefit. It is because consumers necessarily hear generic claims like this as constituents of offers when they occur within advertisements, not simply as assertions intended only to convey information (as might be the case were they to occur in a scientific report), that they are construed as being strong claims.

4. Conclusion

Consumers can be expected to interpret the language of advertising as they do the language of ordinary life. As a consequence, when advertisers use language in some nonnormal fashion or fail to use it in accord with the Cooperative Principle, or fail to make offers that are sincere, they are able to exploit normal modes of language comprehension without actually saying things that are false. The result is deception and a deception consumers are not in a position to defend against.

See also: Register; Media Language and Communication.

Bibliography

Bhatia T K 2000 *Advertising in Rural India*. Institute for the Study of Languages and Cultures of Asia and Africa, Tokyo
Geis M L 1982 The *Language of Television Advertising*. Academic Press, New York
Grice H P 1975 Logic and conservation. In: Cole P, Morgan J L (eds.) *Syntax and Semantics III. Speech Acts*. Academic Press, New York
Searle J R 1969 *Speech Acts: An Essay in the Philosophy of Language*. Cambridge University Press, Cambridge, UK

Blessings

B. G. Szuchewycz

Blessings are utterances associated primarily with the sphere of religious activity, but they also appear with varying frequency in the politeness formulas and parenthetical expressions of everyday conversation. In both contexts the dominant linguistic feature is the use of formal and/or formulaic language. Blessings, particularly in religious ritual, may also be accompanied by specific nonlinguistic features including gestures (e.g., laying on of hands, the sign of the cross) and the use of special objects (e.g., a crucifix) or substances (e.g., water, oil). Concern with such patterned relationships between linguistic form, on the one hand, and social context and function, on the other, is central to the study of the role of language in social life.

Linguistically, blessings (and their opposite, curses) are marked by the use of a special language which may be either a highly formal or archaic variety of the dominant language (e.g., Classical Arabic) or a different code entirely (e.g., Latin). In addition to their specific content, linguistic features such as repetition, special form (e.g., parallel couplets), special prosody (e.g., chant), and fixity of pattern distinguish blessings from other types of speech and contribute to their formal and formulaic character.

The concept of blessing in Jewish, Christian, and Muslim thought, as in many other traditions, is concerned with the bestowal of divine favor or benediction through the utterance of prescribed words. As such, blessings represent an example of the belief in the magical power of words, other manifestations of which include the use of spells, incantations, and curses.

As an aspect of religious behavior, blessings are associated with essential components of public and private ritual activity. They are performed by religious specialists in situations of communal worship as, for example, in rituals where a general blessing of those present marks the end of the event. Blessings are also used by nonspecialists to solemnize, sacralize, and/or mark the boundaries of social events. In traditional Judaism, for example, *brokhe* 'blessings' include short formulaic expressions used in a wide variety of situations as well as longer texts associated with domestic ceremonies (e.g., a grace after a meal) and specific occasions or rites (e.g., Passover, weddings, funerals). Common to all is a fixity of form and the strict association of specific texts to specific occasions.

In the Bible, the Hebrew root *brk* 'blessing' is associated with a number of meanings. A blessing may be an expression of praise or adoration of God, a divine bestowal of spiritual, material, or social prosperity, or an act of consecration which renders objects holy. The Greek *eulogia* of the New Testament stresses the spiritual benefits which are obtainable through Christ, the gospels, and the institution of the church (e.g., liturgical blessings). Each instance—praise, benediction, and consecration—represents a social and religious act accomplished through the use of a highly conventionalized form of language.

Blessings often function as 'performatives' (see *Speech Act Theory: Overview*). A performative is a speech act which when uttered alters some state of affairs in the world. Under the appropriate conditions, if a minister states, 'I pronounce you man and wife,' then a marriage has been socially established. If someone says, 'I promise,' then a promise has been made. Similarly, blessings function as religious performatives, in that the utterance of the requisite expression precipitates a change in spiritual state.

Mastery of the linguistic formulas, however, is not sufficient for the successful realization of blessings (and other performatives). The existence of an extra-linguistic institution (e.g., family, descent group, religious institution, etc.) with differentiated social roles and statuses for the blessor and blessee(s) is a necessary precondition to an authentic and valid performance of the act. Only certain individuals may pronounce a couple man and wife and create a legally binding marriage. The same is true of blessings.

Catholicism, for example, distinguishes those blessings exchanged between lay persons, the spiritual value of which depends on the personal sanctity of the blessor, from liturgical blessings, which carry the force of the ecclesiastical institution. As the institution itself is hierarchically organized, so too is the right to confer particular blessings. Some may be performed by the pontiff alone, some only by a bishop, others by a parish priest, and yet others by a member of a religious order. Similarly, and in a very different ethnographic context, among the Merina of Madagascar the *tsodrano* is a ritual blessing in which seniors act as intermediaries between ancestors and those being blessed, their juniors. A father bestows fertility and wealth on his son through a ceremonial public blessing which transfers to the son the power of the ancestors in a ritual stressing the continuity and reproduction of the descent group.

Like other performatives, blessings operate properly only within a context of social and cultural norms and institutions, which are necessary for their realization and to legitimate and maintain their force.

Much of human face-to-face interaction is ritualistic in nature, and it has been argued that the use of formalized and prepatterned linguistic and non-linguistic behavior in everyday life is evidence of a link between interpersonal rituals of politeness on the one hand, and ritual behavior in the sacred sphere on the other (Brown and Levinson 1987). Blessings are an example of a specific linguistic routine common to both.

In nonreligious contexts, blessings are evident in the politeness formulas and parenthetical expressions of everyday conversation: for example, the English 'Bless you!' as a conventional response to a sneeze. Similarly, in greetings, thanks, and leave-takings, blessings are exchanged between interlocutors and, although they may literally express a wish for supernatural benefits, their primary communicative function is as highly conventionalized markers of social and/or interactional status. In both their religious and secular uses, blessings thus function as expressions of solidarity, approval, and good will.

When embedded parenthetically within larger sentences or longer texts, blessings may also function as semantically and interactionally significant units. In oral narratives the use of a blessing (or curse) serves to communicate directly the emotional state or attitude of the speaker towards the topic, providing a means of internal evaluation and signaling speaker involvement in the text. Yiddish speakers, for example, make extensive use of a large set of fixed expressions, many of which are blessings, for just such a purpose (Matisoff 1979).

See also: Politeness; Religion and Language.

Bibliography

Brown P, Levinson S C 1987 *Politeness: Some Universals in Language Usage*. Cambridge University Press, Cambridge, UK
Bruder K A 1998 A pragmatics for human relationship with the divine: An examination of the monastic blessing sequence. *Journal of Pragmatics* **29**: 463–91
Matisoff J A 1979 *Blessings, Curses, Hopes and Fears: Psycho-Ostensive Expressions in Yiddish*. Institute for the Study of Human Issues, Philadelphia, PA
Westerman C 1978 *Blessing: In the Bible and the Life of the Church*. Fortress Press, Philadelphia, PA

Business Language

G. Rasmussen

'Business language' is a commonly used expression but it is not always clear what is meant by it. This article deals first with what is captured by the category 'business language.' Why divide language into such subcategories as 'technical,' 'political,' 'legal,' or 'business' language? In other words, why talk about 'business language' rather than just the notion of language? Second, the article examines business language in terms of language use, comparing it with other kinds of language use.

1. The Category 'Business Language'

Business language is one of several categories of language in use. This subcategorization of language addresses the 'contextual sensitivity' of language use; that is, business language is not a language *sui generis* with exclusive morphosyntactical structures. Business language is language used for the specific purpose of doing business; it involves the actions (including speech acts) that are undertaken for that purpose. Business actions are social actions, designed for recipients who interpret and respond to them as such. Business language is thus language used for the specific purpose of carrying out business interactions.

The notion of 'contextual sensitivity' has radical consequences for defining a certain kind of language used as business language. The fact that language users are business people is not sufficient for categorizing the way they use language as business language. Business people have other societal roles: they may be friends, tennis partners, politicians, fathers, mothers, and so forth. These roles do not influence every action they undertake; that is, these identities do not automatically have an influence on any given occasion. To say that the same language users use language for business purposes in contrast to, for instance, political purposes, is to say that they embrace the contextual feature 'business' in the language used. In other words, they make the business context relevant, by creating and affirming it through the linguistic choices they make and by the actions they undertake. In this way they orient themselves towards their roles as business practitioners.

1.1 Language in Business Interactions versus Business Language

Not all actions in business interactions are related to the business setting. Sometimes, for instance, participants in face-to-face business interactions engage in small-talk or make conversations in which the work setting has no consequence for the way they produce their actions and for the way they use language. But, some actions (for instance negotiations over the price of a product) are related to the business setting and it is through these actions that the participants realize that setting. Moreover, a specific business setting is realized (and constructed) through these very actions, and these may refer to particular business settings and the institutions or areas they represent such as, for example, marketing or production. Business language and business actions are thus produced interactively in response to situational constraints, at work in the wider context: the identities of the participants (business people), the section of the institution they represent (marketing or production), and those aspects of the local context, namely the activity that they are about to construct, such as the negotiation of a price. In sum, business language is constituted of actions in which the business setting acts both as a resource and as a framework for interpreting these actions in different ways.

2. What Constitutes Institutional Interactions as Opposed to Ordinary Interactions?

Business language is used in an institutional setting (see *Institutional Language*). The notion of business and institutional interaction invokes at least an implicit comparative dimension. Institutional interactions are task related, bearing in mind the shifts between task-related talk and small-talk in face-to-face-interactions, which are mentioned above. The participants show their orientation to these tasks by the way they conduct their interaction and, more so, by the goals they pursue. The goals differ according to institutional contexts: in a medical setting it may be a diagnosis, in a business setting the selling and buying of a product.

The institutional setting imposes constraints on the contributions the participants make, as it invokes expectations about how they are supposed to act. A news interview, courtroom proceedings, or a face-to-face business negotiation are heard as different from, for instance, conversational talk, because of the ways the participants are expected to act in these settings.

Institutional settings can even have an influence on how inferences are made by the participants. Doctors orient themselves to the institutional character of their medical interactions with patients by withholding expressions of surprise. In turn, a particular patient responds to that same institutional context by not interpreting the doctor's apparent reticence as disaffiliative, something which the patient might well have done in a conversational context (Drew and Heritage 1992).

2.1 What Constitutes Business Interactions as Opposed to Other Institutional Interactions?

Institutional interactions may be subcategorized into formal and non-formal, or less formal, settings. With regard to face-to-face interactions, courtroom proceedings impose many more constraints on the contributions of participants than other kinds of setting. The participants orient themselves to that context by exercising very few choices in terms of lexical choice, 'turn-design' (how to formulate a question), 'sequential organization' (question–answer formulae), and overall structural organization (different phases in courtroom proceedings). By these means, the participants confirm and construct the highly formal character of courtroom settings.

In comparison, business interactants make use of more choices, with the effect that the patterns of business interactions exhibit less uniformity. Face-to-face business interactions are task related but, the turn-taking procedures (Sacks et al. 1974) come close to normal conversational modes (Drew and Heritage 1992). Even business writing, which is widely considered to be formal (as opposed to literary writing and face-to-face business interactions), is less formal than legal indictments and sentencing documents.

Nevertheless, interactants talk and act in a way by which they are heard to do *business* interactions as business people. In order to be heard as—and categorized and analyzed as—business interactions done by business people, activities that they engage in—such as advertising, buying and selling, making telephone calls, and attending business lunches—must necessarily have features that differ from other activities, and that differ from these same activities as they are performed by laypeople. What could these features be?

So far, research has shown that lexical choice is very important, but so too are ways of organizing negotiations by telex, fax, and telephone (Firth 1991) and ways of producing written texts (Pogner 1995). These can be related to the participants' identities as business people. Furthermore, instances of ways of organizing international and intercultural interactions have been related to the business setting in which these interactions were created. Concerning the international arena, business people can show that they represent an international institution and that the international status actually guarantees the reliability of the company they represent. In intercultural settings, business people cope with cultural differences by normalizing these in order to realize their tasks and goals (Firth 1996, Rasmussen 1996).

See also: Advertising; Institutional Language; Language in the Workplace.

Bibliography

Drew P, Heritage J 1992 *Talk at Work: Interaction in Institutional Settings*. Cambridge University Press, Cambridge, UK
Firth A 1991 Discourse at work: Negotiating by telex, fax, and 'phone. (Doctoral dissertation, Aalborg University, Aalborg, Denmark)
Firth A 1996 The discursive accomplishment of normality: On 'lingua franca' English and conversation analysis. *Journal of Pragmatics* **26**: 237–60
Pogner K H 1995 Energiekonzept für Wendenburg: Arbeitsteilige Produktion fremdsprachlicher Texte an einem technischen Arbeitsplatz. (Doctoral dissertation, Odense University, Odense, Denmark)
Rasmussen G 1996 Zur Kulturalität in interkulturellen interlingualen Gesprächen. (Doctoral dissertation, Odense University, Odense, Denmark)
Sacks H, Schegloff E, Jefferson G 1974 A simplest systematics of turn-taking organization. *Language* **50**: 696–735

Code, Sociolinguistic
U. Ammon

'Code' in the sense with which this article deals is often specified as 'linguistic'; it seems, however, more adequate to specify it as 'sociolinguistic.' Otherwise it can be easily confused with other meanings of the highly ambiguous term 'code' which are quite different. Even with this specification it could be mistaken for the concept to which the term 'code-switching' relates, which is also often, or even mostly, used in a sociolinguistic context (see *Code-switching: Overview*). In the term 'code-switching' 'code' means nothing else than 'variety (or dialect) of a language.' Code-switching then is the switching from one variety to another, either of the same language or of different languages, in speech or writing.

This article does not deal with 'code' in this sense of variety of a language, but exclusively in the other sociolinguistic sense which this term takes on when it relates to the so-called 'restricted' or 'elaborated codes.' More specifically, it deals with the following aspects: (a) the definition of the term 'sociolinguistic code'; (b) the social conditions which generate restricted or elaborated codes (see *Socialization*); (c) some empirical evidence for restricted or elaborated codes; (d) the educational implications of the sociolinguistic codes (see *Education and Language: Overview*); and (e) some misinterpretations of the code theory and the critique based on these misinterpretations.

1. Definition of the Term 'Sociolinguistic Code'

The terms 'restricted' and 'elaborated code,' of which the term 'sociolinguistic code' is a hypernym, have only gradually taken on their meaning, as a result of Basil Bernstein, the inventor of the terms, and other researchers developing the theory for which they are constitutive (cf. the collections of articles which mirror this history in Bernstein 1971, 1973, and Bernstein's own presentation of the history of his theory in Bernstein 1987; see *Bernstein, Basil*). The original terms were 'public language' (restricted code) and 'formal language' (elaborated code). Rather than speaking of different languages, it would have been adequate to speak of modes of 'language use' (or styles of speech or writing). This terminology might also have caused less misunderstanding than did the term 'code.' A restricted and an elaborated code are, according to more recent conceptions, an implicit versus an explicit mode of language use. Following this line of thought, a restricted code is readily understandable only to members of the same social group or network to which the speaker him/herself belongs (see *Sociology of Language*; *Social Networks*), while an elaborated code is also readily understandable to nonmembers of the group.

These abstract concepts (theoretical constructs) have been operationalized for empirical research by means of a number of indicators which have not always been specified clearly enough. Some of the indicators of a restricted code are, for instance, the use of pronouns instead of nouns for initial reference; a language use which presupposes that the hearer (reader) has already identified the referent; or by recurrent 'sympathetic circularity'—e.g., tag questions like 'isn't it?' or comments like 'you know'—by which the speaker attempts to confirm the common basis of knowledge and values on which one can usually count in in-group communication. Other indicators suggested for a restricted code were, for instance, a smaller variety of adjectives and verbs, fewer subordinated clauses or less use of the personal pronoun 'I' than in the case of an elaborated code. It seems quite clear that these are indicators of two different, though closely related, aspects of sociolinguistic codes, namely the utterance's implicitness or explicitness and the speaker's heteronomy/autonomy vis-à-vis his/her social group or network.

It also seems plausible enough that restricted and elaborated codes need not only be conceived of as binary (classificatory) concepts but, for more refined purposes, rather as a continuum of more or less restrictedness or elaboratedness, which poses the task of constructing scales for their measurement.

Furthermore, it seems important to make a distinction between an individual's implicitness of verbalization only in particular situations and his/her implicitness of verbalization in all situations. Only in the latter case is the individual's mode of language use a restricted code which, therefore, should be specified as the general habit of implicit language use, or even the inability (or incompetence) of explicit verbalization. An elaborated code is, in contrast, not limited to implicit language use but comprises both possibilities—implicit as well as explicit verbalization.

Finally, it should be stressed that these concepts are of necessity relative to the experience and modes of language use in different societies. It seems, therefore, hardly possible to give a detailed universal definition of restricted or elaborated codes.

2. The Social Conditions Which Generate Restricted or Elaborated Codes

Restricted codes tend to develop in social networks (see *Social Networks*) which are closed, i.e., members have but few outside connections, and multiplex, i.e., pairs of members share several social relationships (e.g., A is B's brother, and A and B are members of the same club, go regularly to the same pub, and the like) (cf. Fasold 1990). In such networks or social groups there is, as a rule, a broad basis of common understanding (experience and values) which does not require explicit verbalization in most situations.

Networks of that type are to be found more frequently in the working class than in the middle class, or, more generally speaking, more frequently in the lower than the higher social classes, at least within industrialized capitalist societies (see *Social Class*; *Class and Language*). The reason is that members of lower social classes are, for want of other resources, more dependent on mutual assistance in everyday life, which also explains why solidarity usually ranks high as a value among them.

Among workers and other lower-class professions there is also less need for explicit verbalization at the workplace, particularly if work is mainly manual and involves few social contacts beyond immediate colleagues (see Ammon 1977: 45–74). Therefore, as a rule, no stimuli for a change of verbal habits can be expected from contacts outside the private networks.

There is also a preference in the working class for a more status-oriented instead of a person-oriented family structure, or of a more imperative instead of an argumentative mode of child-rearing. Status orientation in a family means that roles and tasks are primarily dependent on the individual's position as, for instance, being the father, mother, oldest brother and so forth, and hardly adjustable according to personal preferences or momentary circumstances. This aspect of family structure can be understood to come about or to be stabilized as a consequence of a feedback relation with a restricted code. It provides fewer opportunities for explicit verbalization, i.e., tends to generate or stabilize a restricted code on the one hand, and the restricted code, i.e., the preference for implicit rather than explicit verbalization, makes this family structure less liable to questioning and change on the other hand. Similarly, the imperative mode of child-rearing can be explained in the form of a feedback in relation to a restricted code.

To avoid misunderstanding, it should be pointed out that these traits of social structure should again not be conceived of as binary concepts but rather as rank or interval scales (more or less closed or multiplex social networks, status-oriented family structure, and imperative mode of child-rearing), nor do they necessarily exist in the entire working class or are totally absent in other social classes. They are only statistical, not categorical differences between the social classes. Nevertheless these statistical differences amount to the fact that restricted codes are more common among the working class than among the middle class.

3. Some Empirical Evidence for Restricted and for Elaborated Codes

The study by Schatzman and Strauss (1955), which stimulated Bernstein's conception of the theory and which still seems valid, deserves mention here. The authors interviewed lower- and middle-class witnesses of a tornado in Arkansas. The lower-class witnesses set the scene in a way which was only partially understandable to strangers, since they referred to their personal background and to views of friends whom the interviewers could not know, while middle-class informants constructed events in a generally understandable way which did not presuppose common contextual information. Bernstein himself found discrepancies in lower-class students between verbal and so-called nonverbal IQs, which could not be confirmed for middle-class students. Verbal IQs were considerably lower than nonverbal IQs, which seems to indicate that in lower-class families verbal skills are not trained to the same degree as they are in middle-class families. There is, of course, also the possibility of social class biases of verbal IQ tests. Bernstein also found longer and more frequent pausing in utterances of middle-class students than of lower-class students, which he explained as an effect of more careful verbal planning.

Numerous studies have been done in different countries, mainly in Western Europe and North America, with findings like the following. In comparison to middle-class informants, the utterances of lower-class informants showed a smaller diversity of content words (nouns, verbs, adjectives), fewer subordinated or embedded clauses, particularly multiple embedded clauses, less use of the personal pronoun 'I,' and more sympathetic circularity. It has also been found that the utterances of lower-class informants tend to be fewer and shorter on the whole. The validity of the latter findings has been questioned on grounds of the formality of the test situation which is less familiar to lower-class informants and, therefore, has more of an inhibiting effect on them. One could, however, take this objection as a supportive argument for the code theory. It concedes the lower-class informants' increased difficulty in handling unfamiliar situations, which can be explained as a consequence of their closed social networks and restricted codes.

4. Educational Implications of the Sociolinguistic Codes

The restricted codes have been seen as a major cause, among others, of school failure of lower-class students. The negative effects of a restricted code have been assumed to occur on various levels of school requirements, though valid and reliable empirical corroborations of these assumptions are still missing.

It seems plausible that teachers value explicit verbalization in class, orally as well as in writing, which is comprehensible not only to the 'in group' but also to persons with different experiences and values. School is even, as a rule, supposed to provide students with such verbal skills, since they are part of a general qualification for many professions, particularly middle-class professions, which require the performance of public speeches or the production of generally understandable written texts. Students who already possess these skills to some degree when they enter school, i.e., middle-class students, have some advantage over those who do not, i.e., lower-class students.

The school difficulties of students with a restricted code may be aggravated by the fact that the teacher is not fully aware of their problems and, therefore, does not try to offer adequate remedy; which, as will be seen, would be hard to provide anyway. The teacher may even interpret the students' more implicit verbal behavior as a general lack of intelligence. Such a misjudgment may have far-reaching consequences. It may misguide a teacher's evaluation, his kind of encouragement, or other aspects of behavior towards the student.

There is also the possibility that restricted and elaborated codes affect apparent intelligence or learning motivation more deeply. Someone with a more implicit language use may run into fewer intellectual challenges than someone with a more explicit language use. It is an everyday experience that, only when one tries explicitly to formulate a problem, does one notice that one does not have a full grasp of it and, as a consequence, is sometimes stimulated to achieve a better understanding. It might well be true that this mechanism functions more often in middle-class families or in individuals with an elaborated code, than in lower-class families or in individuals with a restricted code, and that its effects may add up to substantial differences in learning motivation and knowledge or apparent intelligence. It seems hardly necessary to stress that these effects are not related to innate intelligence.

It has also been argued, to some degree by Bernstein himself, that a restricted and an elaborated code might enhance different views of the world, in a similar way as has been assumed for different languages by Wilhelm von Humboldt, Edward Sapir, or Benjamin L. Whorf (see *Sapir–Whorf Hypothesis*). This assumption has, however, been refuted for good reasons by pointing out that codes do not actually differ with respect to semantics, or even vocabulary or syntactic structure, but are only different ways of using the same linguistic system.

The most important educational endeavors that have been stimulated by the code theory, though not exclusively by it, are the various attempts at so-called 'compensatory education.' Since such attempts have, as a rule, been based on more comprehensive assumptions of verbal or intellectual deprivation, their designs have also been more comprehensive than just the training of explicit language use. The children's verbal 'deprivation' in such educational contexts has often rather been seen in regional or social dialects (e.g., Black English in the USA) than in restricted codes, or both concepts have not been carefully kept apart (see *Dialect and Dialectology*). Restricted codes and social or regional dialects (or varieties) are, as pointed out in Sect. 1 quite different and should not be confused conceptually and in theory. It is, however, true that they often co-occur in social reality and that both of them can cause school difficulties, though for quite different reasons.

Theoretical shortcomings of this kind are certainly among the reasons why compensatory education has, on the whole, not lived up to the expectations it has raised. For most of the children who received it, lasting educational success could not be achieved. There are some reasons for these shortcomings which relate to the nature of the sociolinguistic codes. Perhaps the most important of them is that the codes are, as may be assumed, an integrated component of an individual's personal identity. To speak generally implicitly, or to speak explicitly in certain situations is by no means a superficial habit which can be changed rather easily by training. It is rather a deep-seated character trait which is socially highly significant and therefore crucial in educational contexts. Children who change from an implicit to an explicit mode of language use may be estranged from their social surroundings and even from their parents. Even if such a language behavior is limited to some formal situations like school and is not applied in other social contexts, its acquisition puts a lot of psychological strain on the child, apart from the fact that it is hard to retain as a skill if it cannot be applied in everyday life. These and other difficulties, which have caused compensatory education to fail in many cases are, however, no proof that successful compensatory education is generally impossible. It can yet perhaps be modeled in a way that provides educational success to many socially deprived children.

Among the numerous objections against compensatory education, of which some took issue with the whole idea while others only questioned certain of its aspects, the argument has been put forward that too much emphasis has been placed on changing the children and their habits instead of changing the school system or, for that matter, the entire society according to children's needs. This seems to be a valid general objection. If the argument was meant to imply, however, as sometimes has been the case, that—to state it baldly—the school, or even the entire society, should turn to the restricted code or simply accept it as equivalent to the elaborated code, then it seems hardly realistic. The reason is that explicit modes of verbal expression are most likely functional in numerous situations in modern societies, and in particular, in situations which occur frequently in typical middle-class professions.

5. Misinterpretations and Critique of the Code Theory

There is no question that the theory of the sociolinguistic codes, even today, does not really meet rigorous scientific standards. Besides its remaining conceptual fuzziness and theoretical shortcomings, the empirical evidence which has been presented for its support leaves much to be desired in terms of validity and reliability, as Bernstein himself would be the first to admit. There have, however, been some notorious misunderstandings, which have unjustly contributed to the theory's refutation in some quarters of the scientific community and which should be corrected.

One of these misunderstandings is the confusion of the sociolinguistic codes with dialects or varieties of a language, in spite of Bernstein's explicit warnings against this confusion. Attacks on the theory on the grounds that it would evaluate the codes as 'deficits' instead of mere 'differences' of socially determined language behavior, seem to be largely based on this confusion. The deficit objection often refers to Labov's (1970) analysis of Black English in the USA (see *Sociolinguistic Variation*; *Ebonics and African American Vernacular English*). This study convincingly shows that some of the features of Black English which seem to be irregular or the expression of illogical thinking, e.g., double negation—with the meaning of single negation—are in reality perfectly regular and just another way, different from Standard English, of expressing the same logical ideas. Following this sound line of thought, the deficit objection puts forth the well-known postulate, which is widely accepted among linguists, that all linguistic systems are equivalent, though of course different means of expressing human thinking. Even if this statement is accepted unchallenged (though it is, if not specified further, highly questionable in view of findings of societal language development and language modernization), it definitely misses its point, since restricted and elaborated codes are not two different linguistic systems but two different modes of use of the same linguistic system.

In the same article, Labov (1970) contrasts a lower-class and a middle-class person, finding the former's utterances succinct and logical and the latter's redundant and verbose. This evaluation has also been used extensively against the educational objective of teaching the elaborated code to lower-class students. It gives indeed reason to think about class-biased evaluations of the quality of verbal utterances. Labov's findings deserve, however, to be scrutinized with respect to representativity (only single representatives of the social classes) on the one hand, and functionality of communication in various situations on the other hand. It is questionable whether the latter can be judged adequately by a single researcher on a largely intuitive basis as has been done by Labov (1970). Therefore, these and other intuitive judgments are hardly a sufficient basis for dismissing the entire code theory as ill grounded or just a reflection of class prejudices, as has been suggested.

The code theory deserves to be formulated and tested more rigorously than has been done so far. One of the central questions for empirical testing should be whether there really are differences in explicitness of verbalization between the social classes, even in situations when it is clear to the speakers that the addressees are strangers (not members of the 'in group'), and whether the spoken or written texts produced by lower-class people in such situations are really not fully comprehensible to strangers. The empirical research necessary to answer these questions goes well beyond the frame of linguistics, or even sociolinguistics, in any narrower sense, since questions of comprehensibility of verbal utterances are of major importance for them.

See also: Literacy; Oracy; Class and Language; Bernstein, Basil; Diglossia.

Bibliography

Ammon U 1977 *Probleme der Soziolinguistik*. Niemeyer, Tübingen, Germany
Bernstein B 1971 *Class, Codes and Control: Theoretical Studies Towards a Sociology of Language*. Routledge and Kegan Paul, London
Bernstein B 1973 *Class, Codes and Control: Applied Studies Towards a Sociology of Language*. Routledge and Kegan Paul, London
Bernstein B 1987 Social class, codes and communication. In: Ammon U, Dittmar N, Mattheier K J (eds.) *Sociolinguistics/Soziolinguistik*. Walter de Gruyter, Berlin
Edwards J 1987 Elaborated and restricted codes. In: Ammon U, Dittmar N, Mattheier K J (eds.) *Sociolinguistics/Soziolinguistik*. Walter de Gruyter, Berlin
Fasold R 1990 *The Sociolinguistics of Language*. Blackwell, Oxford, UK
Labov W 1970 The logic of nonstandard English. In: Alatis J E (ed.) *Report of the Twentieth Round Table Meeting on Linguistics and Language Studies*. Georgetown University Press, Washington, DC
Schatzman L, Strauss A 1955 Social class and modes of communication. *American Journal of Sociology* **60**: 329–38

Context
U. M. Quasthoff

'Context' is one of those linguistic terms which is constantly used in all kinds of contexts but never explained. In a broad sense, it refers to the relevant elements of the surrounding linguistic or nonlinguistic structures in relation to an uttered expression under consideration. This expression is normally a unit corresponding to a sentence, but can also be a word or a global discourse unit.

In a more particular sense, the concept of context is widely context-dependent: it varies with the context of each particular linguistic approach, terminological system, or analytical unit. The concept also depends on the historical context: it has varied in the course of the history of linguistics in the same way that the role of context has varied in the course of the history of language(s) and ontogenetic linguistic development. What is considered to be context-independent can be proven to be highly context-bound in a different context: in archaic texts found in Mesopotamia, numbers do not represent abstract ideas of quantity, but vary in their quantification with the measured items. Thus, the same number word may mean different 'numbers' relative to what is counted (Damerow 1988).

This article will not be able to deal with all aspects of the linguistic use of the term 'context.' It will mention some, omit others, and focus on one issue which is considered to be among the most important ones for future research. The different roles and meanings of context in the context of linguistic paradigms, analytic levels, and sets of categories will be mentioned. The notion of 'context' as part of modern discourse analysis will be made explicit in some depth.

1. The Theoretical Role of Context

The central role that context plays in linguistic theorizing may be inferred from the fact that one could systematize a history of recent linguistics by describing the role of context in successive theoretical systems. In the substitution of a new paradigm for an old one, and in most of the evolutions within one and the same approach from the 1960s onwards, the global changes generally have been from a very reductive treatment of context towards models which pay more and more attention to conditions of use. (This is not to say that before 1960 there had been no place for the notion of context in linguistic theory. In the 1940s and 1950s, 'context of situation' was a dominant feature in Firthian linguistics and, before Firth, in the work of Malinowski: see *Firth, J. R.*; *Malinowski, Bronislaw Kaspar*.)

Generative–transformational grammar's concept of an autonomous syntax (Chomsky 1965) as *the* 'standard' language theory was challenged first by 'generative semantics,' which moved more and more into contextual issues (e.g., Lakoff and Johnson 1980). Speech act theory (see *Speech Act Theory: An Overview*) subsequently became a popular conceptual alternative in that it considered speaking as acting under contextual conditions (Searle 1969). Furthermore, sociolinguistics defined situational and social variables in terms of 'social context.' Finally, discourse analysis (see *Discourse*) conceptualized structure in general as sequentially ordered units establishing locally and globally, forward and backward operating contextual forces (see Sect. 4 below).

Formal semantics moved from the formal representation of propositions by means of predicate logic to intentional semantics, in which the formal representations included utterance-oriented coordinates such as time and place of utterance, speaker, etc. (Lewis 1972).

As to language acquisition, conceptualizations changed from context-independent grammatical generalizations such as those of pivot grammar (Braine 1963) to the concept of 'rich interpretation' as an analytic approach to the contextual boundedness of children's utterances (Bloom 1973). Finally, early language acquisition was viewed as a process of replacing the nonverbal elements of the child's interactive situation by verbal ones (Greenfield and Smith 1976, Bruner 1974/75). The acquisition of discourse by older children has come to be seen as enabled by contextualized patterns of adult–child interaction which are specific to the child's age (Hausendorf and Quasthoff 1992).

In the course of its movement from a peripheral to a more central position in linguistic theorizing, context itself developed from a somewhat static conception in terms of one or more related utterances towards a more processual notion. Context is viewed as being built up in production as well as in comprehension of text, as changing with every new utterance, as being structured in itself. The establishment of relevant context is seen as a mutual achievement of the participants in verbal interaction, in its effect negotiable to a certain degree (see Sect. 4).

Context is dichotomized in various ways, just as it is used itself to establish other dichotomies: verbal and nonverbal elements of a relevant distribution are differentiated. The term 'context' refers solely to the linguistic environment, whereas context in this juxtaposition refers to linguistic and situational elements. A difference is made between sentence-oriented and utterance-oriented context (Wunderlich 1979), reflecting the dichotomy of language and speech, competence and performance, linguistic structure, and linguistic use. The sequential boundedness of utterances in discourse (see Sect. 4) is grasped in terms of local and global dependencies (see *Discourse*).

Context itself is used as a distinctive criterion for the differentiation of various poles in linguistic description. Spoken versus written language (see *Speech and Writing*), early stages versus late stages of language acquisition, as well as language change, everyday versus standard registers, and language varieties, are distinguished—among other aspects—by the degree of context-dependency. However, context, and consequently context-dependency, have very different readings in accordance with the unit of linguistic analysis under consideration.

2. Context in its Relation to Different Units of Linguistic Analysis

Sentence-oriented syntax acknowledges various aspects of word order as being influenced by contextual relations. The theme–rheme structure of each sentence reflects the known–new structure of the context (Sgall et al. 1973, Bátori 1981) or at least 'interpenetrates' with the given–new structure (Halliday 1985: 40). Topicalization (Sgall et al. 1973), left dislocation (Gülich 1982), left embedding (Kvam 1979), and sometimes passive voice (Quirk et al. 1978: 943) react to contextual elements in that all these factors contribute to coherence as a structural condition of transsentential units. Thus, in spite of the sentence being the unit of analysis, contextual elements have to be taken into account in syntactic description. These contextual elements can be represented in terms of the structure of neighboring sentences or the informational contours of small textual segments.

'Textual grammar' (Halliday and Hasan 1976; see *Halliday, Michael Alexander Kirkwood*) deals with various aspects of the relationship between sentences, such as coherence and cohesion, coreference, ellipsis, and even 'intertextual' relations beyond the individual texts. In other words, if text is the object of description, what is actually being described are different kinds of contextual relations.

Semantic approaches which offer structural descriptions of (elements of) propositions deal with contextually bound phenomena, or use descriptive models which rely on contextual information, or combine these two aspects. One of the most important tissues among the contextually bound phenomena is 'reference.' The semantic conditions with respect to definite or nondefinite descriptions rely on anaphorical relations as well as on world knowledge; both determine the uniqueness of referents relative to a certain text or (part of the) world, respectively. Various types of semantic inference, presuppositions, and entailments, to mention another phenomenon, belong to the logical representation of a proposition. In view of textual chaining, however, they belong to the contextual information, to the knowledge pool associated with a prepositional expression.

Among the contextually bound descriptive formats, intensional semantics (Lewis 1972) and possible world semantics (Montague 1973) have already been mentioned. At issue here are attempts to represent possible use conditions in terms of situational determinants in the formal description of a proposition.

Procedural notions of semantics (Habel 1985b), which operationalize (sentence-)meaning as processing structures, acknowledge the context-dependency of propositional and conceptual meaning to the point where the boundary between knowledge of language and knowledge of the world becomes irrelevant. The acceptance of, for instance, defaults (that is, preliminary assumptions on the basis of world knowledge rather than cogent inferences based on logical relations), in the process of meaning attribution, shows the degree to which this approach has incorporated contextual determinants as a matter of course (Habel 1985a).

Cognitive science and artificial intelligence, as prominent representatives of this paradigm, have consequently suggested frameworks such as 'frames' (Minsky 1975), 'schemata' (Rumelhart 1977), and 'scripts' (Schank and Abelson 1977), which systematize relevant nonlinguistic knowledge elements necessary for the processing of linguistic expressions.

To summarize, in the case of semantic analysis, context can be operationalized in terms of referentially relevant elements of the utterance situation. Furthermore, 'context' can denote systems of knowledge and belief: knowledge which is logically implied but not made explicit in the proposition, or knowledge of the world which is used in terms of expectations to process sentences.

Most of what has been said in connection with propositional semantics also holds for 'lexical semantics.' On the lexical level of analysis, the focus is on the classical case of contextual influence: disambiguation of lexical items—in the cases of polysemy and homonymy—or, in terms of truth-conditional semantics, specification of the context-specific semantic value (sense) of an expression as opposed to its general 'meaning' (Pinkal 1985).

To take an example: according to Palmer, there are at least five homonyms for *mail*: 'armour,' 'post,' 'payment,' 'halfpenny,' and 'spot' (Palmer 1976: 67). Normally, the syntactic and lexical environment within a sentence already provides for the fact that in actual communication, these homonyms are almost never mixed up. Speakers and listeners in everyday situations normally do not even realize that there are other readings to a word besides the one which they have selected.

It is a descriptive task for the truth-value approach to lexical semantics to explain the fact that, for example, the announcement made at a conference (1):

There will be coffee in the lounge at 10:30   (1)

is not normally associated with the interpretation 'there is a bag of coffee on one of the tables in the lounge' or 'there will be some coffee powder spilled on the carpet in the lounge,' although in all these cases some variant of the lexical meaning of *coffee* is instantiated and the sentence thus would be true (Bosch 1985: 251). This task must of course be solved by models of semantic structure which combine sense and meaning in their representation.

'Pragmatic analysis' has some close connections to the semantic phenomena referred to above: while representing situational elements in the semantic description of a proposition—even if only in order to interpret deictic elements (*I, you, here, there, come, go*)—one actually crosses the border into pragmatics in the strict sense of the term. Pragmatics in this sense includes every theory with explicit reference to situational elements. Hence, Lewis's (1972) contextual indices such as time coordinate, place coordinate, speaker coordinate, and audience coordinate actually add pragmatic elements to his semantics (see *Pragmatics and Sociolinguistics*).

A more prototypical variant of pragmatic analysis, however, is speech act theory. It specifies the object of linguistic description as the act of speaking rather than as a structural system. If speaking is a special—symbolic, highly conventionalized—way of acting, then linguistic theory becomes a variant of action theory. Consequently, context comes into play in terms of felicity conditions for actions, that is, situational prerequisites which allow speech acts to be performed in the intended way: one cannot open a door which is already open. In the same way, one cannot promise something which one is expected to do anyway. Or, to quote one of Searle's (1969: 59) well-known conditions for the illocutionary act of promising: *It is not obvious to S [speaker] and H [hearer] that S will do A [future action] in the normal course of events* (see *Speech Act Theory: Overview*).

Situational conditions play an even more decisive role in the case of indirect speech acts (Searle 1975, Gordon and Lakoff 1975), where—roughly speaking—utterance form and illocution do not coincide. *The phone is ringing*, analyzed as an indirect speech act, would not be meant as a statement, but as a request to answer the phone. It would certainly be heard as a request instead of a statement, if the utterance situation were such that the addressee could be assumed to hear the phone him/herself. In this case, the interpretation of the utterance as a statement would not make sense because it would violate one of the basic conversational maxims (Grice 1975), namely *Be relevant* (see *Conversational Maxims*). Since speakers do not assume these maxims to be violated, they infer via 'conversational implicature' (Grice 1975) the indirect interpretation of the illocutionary act. In other words, they use contextual information, in combination with their knowledge about general principles of communicative acting, to determine the kind of speech act in question.

In sum, from the viewpoint of speech act theory, context essentially focuses on the situational conditions for the performance and interpretation of single verbal acts. As a result, what cannot be grasped within this framework is the impact of the contextual relations formed by the rule-governed *sequences* of acts in *global structures* of *actual discourse*. This aspect is taken up by discourse analysis (see Sect. 4).

Finally, 'sociolinguistics' also clearly conceptualizes context in terms of situation (see *Sociolinguistic Variation*). Quantitative sociolinguistic studies often take into account situational factors as independent variables. Situational characteristics such as formal/informal (Labov 1972) are thus treated like other independent variables (e.g., class or ethnic group) and investigated with respect to their impact on phonological or syntactic variables. In contrast, qualitative or microanalytic sociolinguistics does not envisage the speech situation as analytically independent from verbal behavior—which would be a prerequisite for allowing correlations in a statistical sense. Rather, ethnographic and ethnomethodological conceptions (see *Field Methods, Ethnographic*; *Ethnomethodology*) visualize the definition of a situation as one of the achievements of verbal activities. In other words, situational context is not viewed as something that linguistic features have to *adjust* to; instead, a specific situational frame (Goffman 1974; see *Goffman, Erving*) is seen as *created* by means of specific verbal and nonverbal behavior in the *process* of communication.

The pragmatic insight into the action quality of speech and the microsociolinguistic conception of situational context as being achieved by communicative activities have had a strong influence on the development of discourse analysis and its concept of context (see Sect. 4). In relation to what has been said so far, however, one must generally conclude that the notions of context used on different levels of linguistic analysis are very disparate. They can refer to syntactic or semantic aspects of the immediate linguistic surrounding, or to physical elements of the utterance situation, or to mental entities like knowledge structures, or to situational conditions for the performance of acts. What is lacking is some integrated conception of the role of context in the sequentially ordered process of producing and interpreting communicative moves.

Before attempting to outline such a conception, a more precise formulation will be given of the different notions of context in relation to their corresponding theoretical frameworks, while focusing on problems that arise in connection with the various approaches.

3. Problems Associated with the Notions of Context

> Aside from the surrounding deictic coordinates, aside from the immediate linguistic context and accompanying gestural expressions at closer view, the following determinants can influence the attribution of sense; the entire frame of interaction, the individual biographies of the participants, the physical environment, the social embedding, the cultural and historical background, and—in addition to all of these—facts and dates no matter how far removed in dimensions of time and space. Roughly speaking, *'context' can be the whole world in relation to an utterance act.*
> (Pinkal 1985: 36; contributor's italics and translation)

On the object level, this quotation reflects the variability of context presented in Sect. 2 above. The tremendous descriptive problems which follow from the fact that 'the whole world can be context in relation to an utterance act' are evident:

(a) some notion of *relevance* (Sperber and Wilson 1986) with reference to context has to be operationalized;
(b) the context has to be *structured*;
(c) *change* of context in the course of an utterance (Pinkal 1985: 36) must be handled by the descriptive format;
(d) in addition to the speaker's perspective, the *perspective of the listener* has to be taken into account (Pinkal 1985: 37).

In other words, a satisfactory descriptive model of context must be able to answer the following questions:

(a) How do discourse participants decide which elements of physical or verbal surroundings or of episodic or semantic knowledge systems are *relevant* for the planning or interpretation of an utterance; that is, what has become 'context'?
(b) How do participants *organize* the relevant *contextual units*, and how do they convey this organization in interaction?
(c) How are contextual relationships *dynamically* tied into process of the participant's mutually oriented way of producing and comprehending utterances?
(d) In what are the contextual structures *interactively* achieved and mutually displayed by all the participants in a piece of discourse?

There is no theory of context which is able to answer all these questions with sufficient theoretical explicitness. So it is not astonishing that the concepts of context discussed so far fall short in one way or the other.

Semantic notions of context are normally speaker-centered and have difficulties in accounting for the sentence-internal dynamics of context (Pinkal 1985). Text-grammatical descriptions of coherence relations mostly rely on context as being unstructured and operating only locally. They typically have a static concept of contextual relations.

Contextual notions in terms of speech act theory can be formulated as rules for the successful and sincere performance of the relevant acts. In this respect, they can be said to deal with the relevance issue: only the relevant aspects of the situational context of an action are part of the rules. With respect to the claims for an internally structured, dynamic, interactively oriented reconstruction of context, however, classical speech act theory falls short.

The processual conceptions of the information-processing paradigms are oriented towards structurally explicated knowledge systems (e.g., frames or scripts) and the dynamics of contextual conditions. They also operationalize relevance in certain small domains in order to obtain 'running' programs which generate and/or comprehend linguistic expressions. They are knowledge-based. Consequently, their model of interactivity is a cognitive one, which incorporates into the automatic system's planning not only adequate reactions to the moves of the system's partner, but also images and expectations as to his/her likely choice of procedure (Morik 1984).

The fact that artificial intelligence has developed operational solutions to the problems listed above—at least with respect to small domains of dialogic competence—certainly has to do with the fact that automatic simulation of cognitive and communicative processes is a demanding empirical field. Empirics cannot be cheated by reductionism which abstracts from essential elements of the phenomenon, whereas the kind of theory which simulates the use of utterances per introspection is often in danger of doing just that.

In order to see how discourse analysis relates to the four problems listed above, an empirically based model of the contextualized use of discourse units in conversational interaction will be examined.

4. Context and Sequentiality in Discourse

The ways in which the four descriptive problems listed in Sect. 3 were transformed into the corresponding research questions already indicate the basic orientation in the solution of these problems: an ethnomethodological insight is followed which leaves the solution of structural problems and ambiguities to the participants of the interaction. Thus, the analysis has to reconstruct how the communicative partners define, for their mutual understanding, what is relevant context.

The basic idea of the sequential model employed (Hausendorf and Quasthoff 1989, 1992) is a threefold analysis of 'jobs,' 'devices,' and 'forms' in the reconstruction of the interactive process which is constituted by the joint performance of each discourse unit in everyday conversation. Narrative data is used to develop the model; consequently storytelling is the case of discourse units, which will be presented in an exemplary way.

The descriptive level of the jobs represents the global narrative tasks to be fulfilled jointly by both participants. Consequently, this descriptive level does not yet allow the differentiation into narrator and listener activities, respectively.

Jobs are structural in nature and sequentially ordered. They are assumed to be generally applicable and thus context-free. If a narrative was successfully told, the jobs must have been done, no matter how, no matter by whom, and in no matter which situation.

The devices are formulated to be narrator- and listener-specific. They comprise the pragmatic acts of each participant. Devices are divided into local 'moves,' which organize the joint fulfillment of the global jobs, and into text-semantic elements, which constitute the global semantic coherence of the schematic structure. Devices are sequentially ordered on the basis of conditional relevances: if someone realizes move a, then move b or c can be expected on the basis of the predictions of the (inductively developed) model. These sequential dependencies of devices form the interactive patterns which operate in the sense of globally bound adjacency pairs (see *Conversation Analysis*). The typical interactive patterns accomplish the contextualization of the actual discourse activities. In other words, the situational frame of each storytelling in terms of what interactive game is being played (child tells mother about ... , colleagues tell stories at a party ... , instructor gives an example of ...) is a matter of the particular sequences of devices.

The forms are the linguistic surface realizations of the semantic-pragmatic units provided for by the devices. Forms are sentence-bound.

Linguistic analysis in the classical lexico–syntactic sense (forms) is thus systematically bound to the pragmatic level of single linguistic acts (devices), which in turn are tied to the interactive level of the common achievement of global organization (jobs).

The role and the understanding of context in this kind of analytical model needs to be assessed (see Fig. 1). Unlike in other approaches, where a contextual relation between an utterance under consideration and its relevant surroundings has to be defined, this model gives a perspective on threads of discourse such that each utterance is viewed as a focused-on

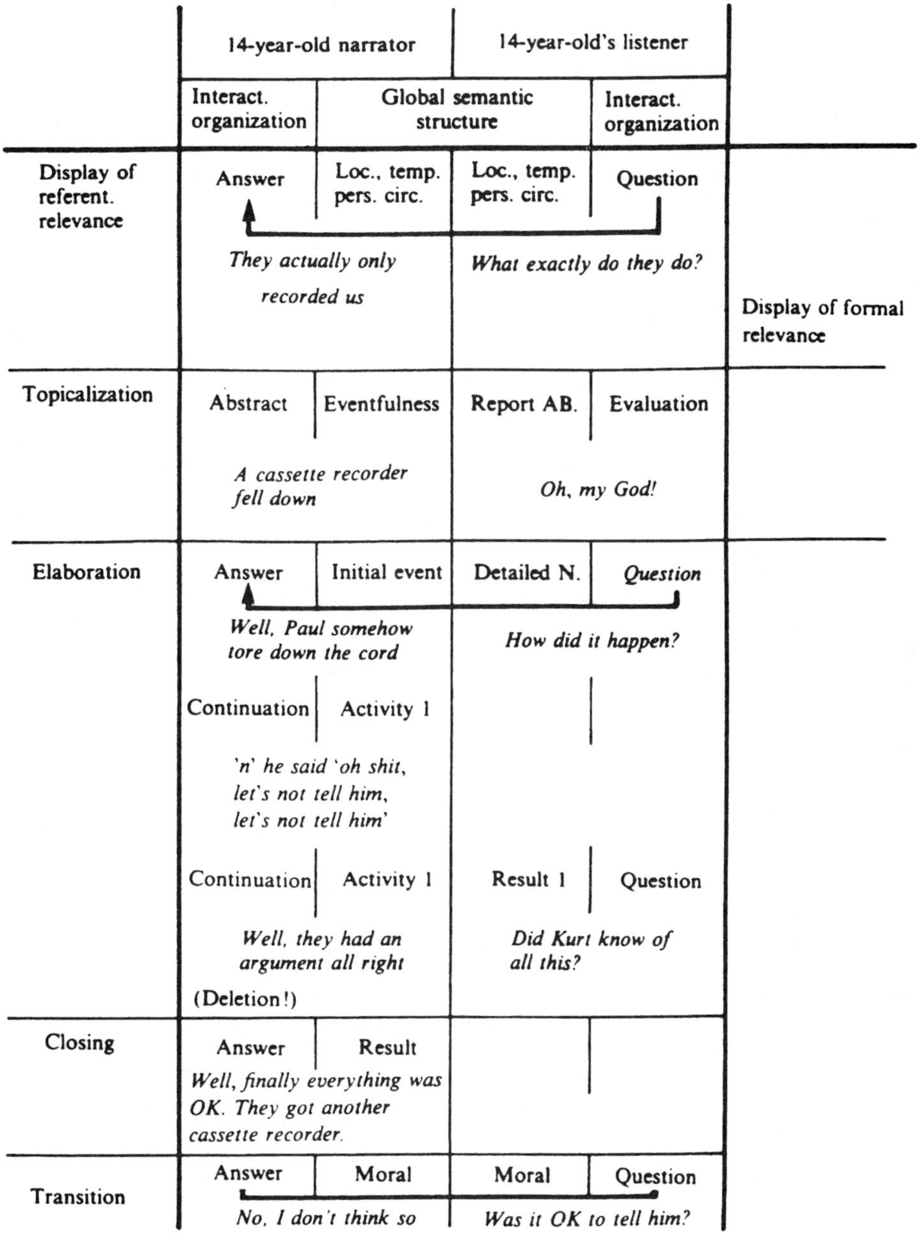

	14-year-old narrator		14-year-old's listener		
	Interact. organization	Global semantic structure		Interact. organization	
Display of referent. relevance	Answer	Loc., temp. pers. circ.	Loc., temp. pers. circ.	Question	Display of formal relevance
	They actually only recorded us		*What exactly do they do?*		
Topicalization	Abstract	Eventfulness	Report AB.	Evaluation	
	A cassette recorder fell down		*Oh, my God!*		
Elaboration	Answer	Initial event	Detailed N.	Question	
	Well, Paul somehow tore down the cord		*How did it happen?*		
	Continuation	Activity 1			
	'n' he said 'oh shit, let's not tell him, let's not tell him'				
	Continuation	Activity 1	Result 1	Question	
	Well, they had an argument all right		*Did Kurt know of all this?*		
	(Deletion!)				
Closing	Answer	Result			
	Well, finally everything was OK. They got another cassette recorder.				
Transition	Answer	Moral	Moral	Question	
	No, I don't think so		*Was it OK to tell him?*		

Figure 1

utterance and as a context at the same time. In other words, each single unit in discourse is considered at the same time as disambiguating and defining the contextual conditions given by preceding utterances in a 'backward' orientation on the one hand, and as providing contextual offers for subsequent units to deal with in a 'forward' orientation on the other.

The basis on which participants and linguistic analysis assign structural meanings in this process of backward and forward oriented patterns of 'conditional relevances' is threefold. It contains:
(a) the rule-governed sequential implicatedness on a global and local basis which is explicated in the sequential orderings of jobs and devices in

the model and which assigns to each form a global and local structural position;
(b) the negotiation among the participants as to the assignment of particular functional roles to an utterance;
(c) the contextualization cues (Gumpez 1982) in the utterance-forms which express the discourse function associated with the utterance (Quasthoff 1992).

To take an example from narrative discourse units: the form *Paul dropped the cassette recorder* positioned in the course of the job 'display of thematic relevance' *can* be assigned the role of a story abstract. Whether it actually acquires this structural role, however, depends on the way in which the following turns treat this utterance. If the same speaker continues with *and Louise bumped her head but nothing else went wrong*, then the contextual potential of a story opening has not been used. If, however, the next speaker continues with *Oh, my God! How did that happen?* then the structural implication for a narrative discourse unit has been established and must be either obeyed or formally discharged by the subsequent moves.

The next utterance in this constructed discourse could very well be *Paul tripped over the cord*. It could also be *Paul was going to walk over there and there was this cord hanging down and he tripped over the cord*. In the case of this last utterance, the fact that Paul's action plan was disrupted by some unforeseen event is expressed in the surface of the utterance. Since the indication of a break of plans is the 'narrative function' of this 'initiating event,' it can be stated that this form offers a contextualization cue for the assignment of its structural role in the process of mutual contextualization (Quasthoff 1992).

The systematicity of the pattern produced by the participants of each actual storytelling event establishes the type of interaction which is being performed by and with these particular narrative activities. In other words, the 'situational context' is built up in the course of generating each utterance in its unambiguous functional value.

It has become possible to sketch preliminary answers to the four questions listed above in connection with the problems that will have to be solved by a satisfactory theory of context.
(a) Relevance is displayed by formal contextualization cues and finally established by the forward and backward oriented sense-making forces of each move. The establishment of these conditional relevances operates on the basis of rule-governed sequential expectations and constraints. Relevance is mutually focused structural attentiveness with respect to 'situational' and 'linguistic' sense-making procedures alike.
(b) Contextual relations are organized 'horizontally' and 'vertically' in terms of the sequential model. In other words, in a horizontal dimension, each realized form is produced and heard locally as an expression of a particular element of thematic coherence and as a particular move in the organization of interactive patterns. Globally, each form is at the same time a particular contribution to the execution of the interactive job being performed.

In the vertical, that is, sequential dimension, there are the global and the local patterns following the conditional relevances of jobs and devices. Within the framework of discourse units, the global pattern is represented by the sequence of jobs. The discourse unit is opened with 'topicalizing' and closed with 'closing.' These two jobs can thus be viewed as the contest for the discourse unit proper.
(c) The dynamic quality of the contextual relations represented by the model is indicated by the fact that the sequential implications of the interactive model can be formulated in terms of a cognitively oriented generation model (Quasthoff 1991). There, the planning procedure of linguistic forms incorporates the described influential factors on an 'on-line' basis.

But context is also viewed as a dynamic concept in that it is not represented as given by a certain utterance or situation. Rather, it is locally constructed move-by-move by the linguistic forms of each semantic–pragmatic device in fulfillment of an interactive job. This implies that context is negotiable, and that displays of relevance can be ignored, rejected, or changed to a certain degree.
(d) The interactive quality of context has already been described in connection with the rebuttal of a static notion of context. The sequential model, however, not only offers a format for the disambiguation of the implicational forces of local moves in terms of the interactive pattern. It also provides for a structural concept which represents *joint* interactive achievements as a unit in itself. The is done by the descriptive level of the jobs.

The interactive quality of discourse structures (and thus of context structures) implies a mutual disambiguation of the structural values of each move as one of the tasks of the sense-making machinery of everyday communication. Joint participation in the achievement of the same structure is only possible if the kind of structure to be achieved jointly is focused on and (made) unambiguous to the contributing participants. This is done in the course of the activities by the activities themselves, using resources such as sequential position, content, discourse markers, and contextualization cues.

In a discourse-analytic perspective, then, context is the ensemble of locally and globally operating conditional relevances in their forward and backward orientation, in the sense that each utterance form in the dynamic flow of discourse is the expression of its functional and structural values.

See also: Register.

Bibliography

Bátori I 1981 *Die Grammatik aus der Sicht kognitiver Prozesse*. Gunter Narr Verlag, Tübingen, Germany
Bloom L 1973 *One Word at a Time: The Use of Single Word Utterances before Syntax*. Mouton, The Hague
Bosch P 1985 Lexical meaning contextualized. In: Hoppenbrouwers G A J, Seuren P A M, Weijters A J M M (eds.) *Meaning and the Lexicon*. Foris Publications, Dordrecht, The Netherlands
Braine M 1963 The ontogeny of English phrase structure: The first phase. *Language* **39**: 1–14
Bruner J 1974/75 From communication to language—A psychological perspective. *Cognition* **3**: 255–87
Chomsky N 1965 *Aspects of a Theory of Syntax*. MIT Press, Cambridge, MA
Damerow P 1988 Individual development and cultural evolution of arithmetical thinking. In: Strauss S (ed.) *Ontogeny, Phylogeny, and Historical Development*. Ablex, Norwood, NJ
Duranti A, Goodwin C 1989 *Rethinking Context*. Cambridge University Press, Cambridge, UK
Goffman E 1974 *Frame Analysis. An Essay on the Organization of Experience*. Harper and Row, New York
Gordon D, Lakoff G 1975 Conversational postulates. In: Cole P, Morgan J L (eds.) *Syntax and Semantics 3: Speech Acts*. Academic Press, New York
Greenfield P M, Smith J H 1976 *The Structure of Communication in Early Language Development*. Academic Press, New York
Grice H P 1975 Logic and conversation. In: Cole P, Morgan J L (eds.) *Syntax and Semantics 3: Speech Acts*. Academic Press, New York
Gülich E 1982 La 'phrase segmentée' en français et en allemand: une technique particulière à la communication orale. In: *Didactique des Langues Etrangères. Français, Allemand. Actes du Coloque tenu à l'Université Lyon II en mars 1981*. Presses Universitaires, Lyons, France
Gumperz J J 1982 Contextualization conventions. In: Gumperz J J (ed.) *Discourse Strategies*. Cambridge University Press, Cambridge, UK.
Habel C 1985a Das Lexikon in der Forschung der Künstlichen Intelligenz. In: Schwarze C, Wunderlich D (eds.) *Handbuch der Lexikologie*. Athenäum Verlag, Königstein, Germany
Habel C 1985b *Prinzipien der Referentialität. Untersuchungen zur propositionalen Repräsentation von Wissen*. Springer-Verlag, Berlin
Halliday M A K 1985 Dimensions of discourse analysis: Grammar. In: Dijk T A van (ed.) *Handbook of Discourse Analysis. Vol. 2: Dimensions of Discourse*. Academic Press, London
Halliday M A K, Hasan R 1976 *Cohesion in English*. Longman, London
Hausendorf H, Quasthoff U M 1989 Ein Modell zur Beschreibung von Erzählerwerb. In: Ehlich K, Wagner K R (eds.) *Erzähl-Erwerb*. Peter Lang, Bern, Switzerland
Hausendorf H, Quasthoff U M 1992 Patterns of adult–child interaction as a mechanism of discourse acquisition. *Journal of Pragmatics* **17**(3): 241–59
Kvam S 1979 Diskontinuierliche Anordnung von eingebetteten Infinitivphrasen im Deutschen. *Deutsche Sprache* **7**: 315–25
Labov W 1972 The isolation of contextual styles. In: Labov W *Sociolinguistic Patterns*. University of Pennsylvania Press, Philadelphia, PA
Lakoff G, Johnson M 1980 *Metaphors We Live By*. University of Chicago Press, Chicago, IL
Lewis D 1972 General semantics. In: Davidson D, Harman G (eds.) *Semantics of Natural Language*. Reidel, Dordrecht, The Netherlands
Minsky M 1975 A framework for representing knowledge. In: Winston P H (ed.) *The Psychology of Computer Vision*. McGraw-Hill, New York
Montague R 1973 The proper treatment of quantification in ordinary English. In: Hintikka J, Moravcsik J, Suppes P (eds.) *Approaches to Natural Language*. Reidel, Dordrecht, The Netherlands
Morik K 1984 Partnermodellierung und Interessenprofile bei Dialogsystemen der Künstlichen Intelligenz. In: Rollinger C-R (ed.) *Probleme des Textverstehens—Ansätze der Künstlichen Intelligenz*. Niemeyer, Tübingen, Germany
Palmer F R 1976 *Semantics: A New Outline*. Cambridge University Press, Cambridge, UK
Pinkal M 1985 Kontextabhängigkeit, Vagheit, Mehrdeutigkeit, In: Schwarze C, Wunderlich D (eds.) *Handbuch der Lexikologie*. Athenäum Verlag, Königstein, Germany
Quirk R, Greenbaum S, Leech G, Svartvik J 1978 *A Grammar of Contemporary English*. Longman, London
Quasthoff U M 1980 *Erzählen in Gesprächen*. Narr, Tübingen, Germany
Quasthoff U M 1991 Towards the generation of discourse units in conversation. In: Denhiere G, Rossi J P (eds.) *Text and Text Processing*. North Holland, Dordrecht, The Netherlands
Quasthoff U M 1992 *Towards the Acquisition of Linguistic Forms in Discourse: Interactive Mechanisms*.
Rumelhart D 1977 Understanding and summarizing brief stories. In: LaBerge D, Samuels J (eds.) *Basic Processes in Reading: Perception and Comprehension*. Erlbaum, Hillsdale, NJ
Schank R, Abelson R 1977 *Scripts, Plans, Goals, and Understanding*. Erlbaum, Hillsdale, NJ
Searle J 1969 *Speech Acts: An Essay in the Philosophy of Language*. Cambridge University Press, Cambridge, UK
Searle J 1975 Indirect speech acts. In: Cole P, Morgan J L (eds.) *Syntax and Semantics 3: Speech Acts*. Academic Press, New York
Sgall P, Hajičová E, Benesová E 1973 *Topic, Focus and Generative Semantics*. Scriptor, Kronberg, Germany
Sperber D, Wilson D 1986 *Relevance: Communication and Cognition*. Basil Blackwell, Oxford, UK
Wunderlich D 1979 Meaning and context-dependence. In: Bäuerle R, Egli U, Stechow A von (eds.) *Semantics from Different Points of View*. De Gruyter, Berlin

Diglossia

A. Hudson

The term 'diglossia,' was introduced into Anglo–American sociolinguistic scholarship in 1959 by Charles A. Ferguson. In Ferguson's formulation, diglossia refers to 'a relatively stable language situation in which, in addition to the primary dialects of the language (which may include a standard or regional standards), there is a very divergent, highly codified (often grammatically more complex) superposed variety, the vehicle of a large and respected body of written literature, either of an earlier period or in another speech community, which is learned largely by formal education and is used for most written and formal spoken purposes but is not used by any sector of the community for ordinary conversation' (1959: 336).

1. Characteristics, Origins, and Evolutionary Course of Diglossia

Ferguson proposed a set of nine features by which diglossia might be identified and distinguished from other sociolinguistic situations:

(a) the superposed variety (H) and the vernacular variety (L) are in strict complementary functional distribution;
(b) H is uniformly held in higher esteem than L by members of the speech community;
(c) H has associated with it a substantial and highly regarded body of written literature;
(d) proficiency in H is typically attained as a result of formal schooling, whereas proficiency in L is attained through the natural process of mother-tongue acquisition;
(e) the pronunciation, grammar, and vocabulary of H are standardized and tolerate only limited variation, whereas there is wide variation in the pronunciation, grammar, and vocabulary of L;
(f) diglossic situations are extremely stable, and typically persist for several centuries at least;
(g) there are always extensive differences between the grammatical structures of H and L;
(h) there exists a series of phonologically unrelated lexical doublets for concepts frequently expressed H and L; and
(i) the sound systems of H and L constitute a single phonological structure of which L is the basic system (Ferguson 1959: 328–36).

Diglossia is distinguishable from the typical instance of a standard with dialects (see *Dialect and Dialectology*) in that 'no segment of the speech community in diglossia regularly uses H as a medium of ordinary conversation' (1959: 336–7). Likewise, diglossia is clearly to be distinguished from 'the analogous situation where two distinct (related or unrelated) languages are used side by side throughout a speech community, each with a clearly defined role' (Ferguson 1959: 325 n.2).

Ferguson rejected the proposition that diglossia occurs 'always and only at a certain point in some kind of evolution' (1959: 326–7), and instead took the position that 'diglossia may develop from various origins and eventuate in different language situations' (1959: 327). Nevertheless, diglossia is particularly likely to evolve (a) when there exists a sizeable body of literature in the language of the community, or in a language closely related to it, which embodies the fundamental values of the community; (b) when literacy in the written variety is limited to a small elite; and (c) when a protracted length of time, on the order of several centuries, has elapsed between the formation of a literary tradition and the democratization of literacy (see *Literacy*; see also Ferguson 1959: 338). Although the diglossic system represents an inherently stable situation once fully matured, its disintegration is frequently accompanied by tendencies toward more widespread literacy, greater communication across social and regional boundaries, and a heightened sense of linguistic nationalism (see *Nationalism and Language*; see also Ferguson 1959: 338). In the aftermath of diglossia, H most typically 'fades away and becomes a learned or liturgical language studied only by scholars or specialists and not used actively in the community,' while some form of L, or a compromise between H and L, replaces H as the standard (Ferguson 1959: 339).

2. Incidence of Diglossia

Diglossia, so Ferguson has claimed, has probably occurred hundreds of times over the course of history, and is realized in dozens of instances in the modern age (1959: 338).

Diglossia has been described as a sociolinguistic areal feature of South Asia, and has been reported for Bengali (Chatterjee 1986) and Sinhala (Gair 1986), as well as for Kannada, Malayalam, Tamil, and Telugu (Bright and Ramanujan 1972: 158, Britto 1986). Whether Sanskrit ever coexisted with any of its Indo–Aryan relatives in a diglossic relationship is a matter of scholarly debate. Sanskrit was still a spoken vernacular in Pāṇini's time (ca. 500 BCE), but had become a superposed, scholarly variety by the first century BCE, the mass of the population then being proficient in Prakrit only (Deshpande 1986: 315, 317).

Diglossia appears to have existed in China since about the first century CE (Norman 1988: 4, 248–9), and in Japan since at least the seventh (Coulmas 1987: 115–6). The centuries-old three-way opposition between classical written Chinese, vernacular written Chinese, and vernacular spoken Chinese represents an instance of diglossia, or even triglossia, par excellence. Classical Chinese remained the predominant medium for official documents and for literary and philosophical writing intended for the consumption of the educated ruling classes until the fall of the Qing dynasty in 1911 (Barnes 1982: 262).

Classical Chinese was also employed as the earliest medium for writing in Japan (Coulmas 1991: 129, Habein 1984: 3). Beginning around the seventh century CE, with the incorporation of Japanese words not translatable into Chinese and of Japanese syntactic patterns, this system was gradually nativized, becoming distinct from the Classical Chinese model while at the same time remaining vastly different from spoken Japanese (Coulmas 1991: 129; Habein 1984: 8–10). This style of writing, known as 'kan-bun,' was to remain the style 'in which every respectable book was expected to be written until the Meiji Restoration' (Coulmas 1987: 125 n. 8). A more indigenous system of writing Japanese, known as 'wabun,' which employed the native Japanese *hiragana* syllabary as well as Japanese vocabulary and syntax, was begun some time in the ninth century and perfected by the eleventh; however, although this style of writing initially reflected the spoken language of the period, its basic grammar remained similar to that of the eleventh century, even up until the end of the nineteenth century (Coulmas 1991: 133, Habein 1984: 3–4, 28). By the end of Meiji era in 1911, however, most literary prose was being written in a style much closer to colloquial Japanese.

While some scholars maintain that diglossia in Arabic emerged with the Islamic conquests of the seventh century CE (Blau 1977: 182, 190), others hold that the language of pre-Islamic poetry was radically different from that of the colloquials, and so trace the roots of Arabic diglossia to a period predating the rise of Islam (Altoma 1969: 4, Rabin 1955: 26). Classical Arabic, however, had ceased to be a spoken variety, and had become a purely literary idiom, by the end of the Umayyad caliphate in 750 CE (Rabin 1955: 20). Classical Arabic is still used for religious purposes, and is formally taught in schools, particularly in preparation for the study of religion or the study of the Arabic language and Arabic literature (Cadora 1985: 74). Modern Standard Arabic, a modernized and somewhat simplified derivative of Classical Arabic, has become the medium for serious writing, broadcasting, and formal public speaking, and one or other variant of colloquial Arabic, substantially different in structure from the latter, is employed in all informal interaction (Cadora 1985: 75–6).

Diglossia is also to be found in several other Semitic languages. In Palestine, from about 1000 BCE, spoken Hebrew differed significantly from the Hebrew used in the composition of the Old Testament (Fellman 1985: 28, Rendsburg 1980). The latter variety was used for prayers and formal literary composition, while all normal discussion and teaching of religious matters took place in the former (Spolsky 1991). In Ethiopia, the Ge'ez language, which died out as a spoken language between the ninth and the thirteenth centuries, remains in active use as the language of worship and sacred literature in the Ethiopian Orthodox Church, although as a language of literature it has now largely been replaced by Amharic (Bender et al. 1976: 99–100).

Although the language and dialects of oral and written literature in Greek have always differed from the vernaculars, the years following the Roman conquest saw the rise of a movement to replace the Hellenistic koiné, by then the normal medium for all prose writing, with the classical Attic Greek of the fourth century BCE (Alexiou 1982: 179–80, Browning 1982: 48–50). Up until the end of Ottoman rule in 1821, colloquial varieties of Greek were employed for literary purposes only in peripheral areas of Greek influence or in works of popular edification, not for serious literature in the core areas of Greek cultural influence (Browning 1982: 52). With the establishment of the new Greek state in 1830, an artificially classicized and 'purified' variety of Greek, known as 'katharévousa,' was adopted as the national language, and as the language of civil government and public education (Browning 1982: 53–4); by contrast, the gradual industrialization of Greece, the birth of a nationalist ideology, and the demands for an effective system of public education in the nineteenth century resulted in popular support for colloquial Greek, known as '*demotiké*' (Browning 1982: 56). Since the fall of the last military junta in July 1974, *demotiké* has been adopted as the official language of the Greek state, and a decisive expansion of the latter into domains formerly regarded as the preserve of *katharévousa* has taken place (Browning 1982: 58).

The seeds of diglossia in Latin may be identified in the second and first centuries BCE with the differentiation of written Classical Latin from the popular spoken variety and the emergence of a Latin literary standard (Hall 1986: 215). From about 100 BCE to 400 CE, Classical Latin was widely understood (Pei 1976: 49, 55), although its mutual intelligibility with popular Latin was decreasing steadily (Hall 1986: 213). Later, the functional complementarity between Classical Latin and the early vernacular Romance varieties, combined with the decline in the rate of popular literacy, set the stage for diglossia (Hall 1978: 102, 109). Latin–Romance diglossia of the ninth century was buttressed for a time by Charlemagne's efforts to reform the pronunciation of Latin among the clergy but, by the thirteenth and fourteenth centuries, the growth of urban commercial activity, the decline in the relative importance of the clerical orders in secular administration, and the development of oral and written poetry in the vernacular had begun to fuel the expansion of the Romance vernaculars into virtually all domains of interaction (Parker 1983: 336, 338–40).

Instances of classical diglossia may be found at various times in Persia, the Slavic lands, and Ottoman Turkey. By the end of the seventh century CE, Middle Persian, or *parsi*, had become markedly different from spoken Persian, or *dari*, and had become the medium of administration, religion, and written literature, while *dari* remained the language of everyday oral communication, (Jeremiás 1984: 273, Lazard 1975: 596, 598–9). In Russia, the introduction of writing along with Christianity in the tenth century CE, gave rise to diglossia between vernacular Old Russian and a partly Russianized version of Old Church Slavic (Comrie 1991: 161, 165–8). Old Church Slavic was the language of the Orthodox liturgy and of the Old Russian chronicles, although the reported speech of the latter, and legal documents of the period, contain almost exclusively vernacular forms (Comrie 1991: 165–6). In the late twentieth century, Russian Church Slavic is the language only of the Russian Orthodox liturgy, although its influence on Modern Standard Russian vocabulary is pervasive, particularly in religious and more learned and abstract domains (Comrie 1991: 169). Finally, in sixteenth-century Ottoman Turkey, the court and literary varieties of Turkish began to diverge from the vernacular, becoming maximally distinct early in the eighteenth century (Karpat 1984: 189, 190–1). By the end of World War I, however, Ottoman Turkish, or *osmanlica*, had become completely moribund and was being replaced by a new standard based largely upon the spoken language of the educated classes of Istanbul and the larger cities (Gallagher 1971: 163).

The best known case of diglossia in Western Europe is that between Swiss German and Standard High German in Switzerland. High German, as the liturgical language of Protestantism, the German literary language, and the language of higher education, became the unquestioned norm in the domain of high culture throughout the German-speaking lands (Schiffman 1991: 178). However, whereas *Hochdeutsch* in time began to displace local dialects of German as a mother tongue in Germany, in Switzerland, antipathy toward nineteenth- and twentieth-century German expansionism has resulted in the relegation of *Hochdeutsch* to written and formal spoken functions only (Barbour and Stevenson 1990: 215, Keller 1982: 87–8). A similar diglossic situation is said to exist in Liechtenstein, where Standard German is the language of administration, parliament, the courts, religious services, and education (Clyne 1984: 18). Yet another instance of diglossia exists in Luxembourg between Standard German and *Letzebuergesch*, with French as an additional high variety (Clyne 1984: 20–1, Barbour and Stevenson 1990: 230–4, Keller 1982: 73).

It seems not to have been recognized that classical diglossia has also existed in Irish and in Welsh. Although a case might well be made for diglossia in the Old Irish period of the eighth and ninth centuries (Ó Murchú 1985: 38), a clearer case is the emergence, around the beginning of the thirteenth century, of a single, tightly controlled, universally accepted, national literary language (Corkery 1968: 41). From the thirteenth to the seventeenth centuries, three main literary styles of Irish could be distinguished, all of them significantly different from the popular vernaculars of the day: an archaizing style used primarily in historical and pseudohistorical writings; a mainstream literary usage known as 'the poets' standard'; and a relatively more casual norm possibly based on the spoken language of the educated classes (Ó Murchú 1985: 42). In Welsh, from the twelfth through the fourteenth centuries, the literary works of the court poets, characterized by deliberate archaism in vocabulary and syntax, became the norm for the Welsh literary language, as did the language of their successors, the poets of the nobility, from the fourteenth century until the sixteenth (Jones 1988: 126–7). With the translation of the New Testament into Welsh in 1567, and subsequently the translation of the entire Bible, yet another literary standard for Welsh was born, one which was again substantially different from the Welsh of casual social interaction, and one which exercises considerable influence on written Welsh even up to the present day (Jones 1988: 128–31).

3. Typology

No single effort to extend, to narrow, or to differentiate Ferguson's definition of diglossia has been as profoundly influential as Joshua Fishman's essay on the relationship between bilingualism and diglossia (1967) and its various revisions over a period of more than 20 years (Fishman 1970, 1980, 1985, 1989). As defined by Fishman, diglossia is '*an enduring societal arrangement*, extending at least beyond a three generation period, such that two "languages" each have their secure, phenomenologically legitimate and widely implemented functions' (1980: 3). The 'languages' in question may be distinct languages or varieties of the same language which are sufficiently different from one another that, without schooling, the elevated variety cannot be understood by speakers of the vernacular (Fishman 1980: 4). Diglossia is the 'stable, societal counterpart to individual bilingualism' (Fishman 1980: 3) in that, while the latter is 'a characterization of *individual* linguistic versatility' (Fishman 1970: 83), the former represents 'a well understood and widely accepted social consensus as to which language is to be used between which interlocutors, for communication concerning what topics or for what purposes' (Fishman 1967: 34).

Fishman's account of diglossia differs from Ferguson's in two significant respects. First, whereas Ferguson restricts the definition of diglossia to situations where the codes in question (see *Code, Sociolinguistic*) are strikingly divergent varieties of the same language, Fishman, although limiting the definition to 'significantly discrepant... varieties,' nonetheless includes within its compass situations where the elevated and vernacular varieties are genetically unrelated (1980: 4). Second, Fishman, unlike Ferguson, recognizes two types of compartmentalization of codes in diglossia: a functional compartmentalization, where different codes are assigned by social consensus to nonoverlapping speech contexts within a single speech community; and a territorial or political compartmentalization, where codes are distributed along population lines within social or political entities comprised of multiple speech communities (Fishman 1967: 33, 1980: 7–8).

Fishman's 1980 account of diglossia differs from Ferguson's in recognizing four major categories of diglossia based upon the linguistic relationships between the elevated and vernacular varieties within the code matrix. Ferguson and Fishman both recognize a classical variety of diglossia exemplified by the Arabic and Greek cases, as well as a category, represented by Swiss–German diglossia, where the elevated code is not a classical variety, but rather a written or formal spoken norm in functional opposition to the 'significantly discrepant' variety of spontaneous discourse (Fishman 1980: 4). However, Fishman departs from Ferguson in distinguishing between those instances of diglossia in which the high variety, whether classical or not, is a structural variant of the vernacular and those cases where it is not. Thus, the case of Hebrew and Yiddish in many Jewish speech communities is advanced as an instance of a classical variety in diglossic partnership with an unrelated informal variety, while the case of Spanish and Guaraní in Paraguay is advanced as an example of a nonclassical, formal, or written norm in a diglossic relationship with a genetically unrelated indigenous vernacular.

Fishman's extension of the term 'diglossia' to include cases where the elevated and vernacular varieties are not genetically related in any immediate sense has led to numerous efforts to develop a typology of diglossic situations. Most commonly, the degree of relatedness between the codes in the speech repertoire has formed the principal axis along which the various types have been differentiated. Thus, Kloss distinguishes between in-diglossia, or *Binnendiglossie,* referring to diglossia between genetically related codes, and out-diglossia, or *Aussendiglossie,* referring to diglossia between genetically unrelated codes (1976: 316). Timm (1981: 363–4) and Pauwels (1986: 15) capture the same distinction with the terms 'intralanguage diglossia' and 'interlanguage diglossia.' Fasold (1984: 52–4) uses the term 'broad diglossia' to subsume the categories of 'superposed bilingualism' in the case of distinct languages, 'classic diglossia' in the case of significantly discrepant varieties of the same language, and 'style shifting' in the case of minimally differentiated stylistic variants. This same tripartite division surfaces again in Britto's terminological distinction between 'superoptimal codes,' 'optimal codes,' and 'suboptimal codes' (1986: 10).

Among the various typologists of diglossia, Britto and Pauwels, in particular, note the importance of the nature and degree of social compartmentalization of codes as an axis of classification orthogonal to that of structural relatedness. For his part, Britto distinguishes between situations where the varieties in question are used by separate speech communities having no direct linguistic contact with each other, situations where the dialect of one particular region or social group is used as the standard variety by speakers of other dialects, and situations where a single community uses two or more distinct codes for within-group communication, each with its own particular range of functions (Britto 1986: 35–40). Britto refers to the first of these categories, where there is no within-group differential functional allocation of codes, as 'pseudodiglossia'; to the second, where the elevated or standard variety is not a superposed variety for all members of the larger community, as 'user-oriented' or 'dialectal diglossia'; and to the last, akin in this respect to the classical diglossia of Ferguson, as 'use-oriented' or 'diatypical diglossia' (1986: 35–40). Pauwels makes a comparable distinction between situations in which virtually all of the members of a speech community learn the elevated variety as a superposed variety, which she refers to as 'general diglossia'; and situations, which she labels 'partial diglossia,' in which only a substantial proportion of the members of a speech community acquire the high variety as a superposed variety (1986: 15). Pauwels also distinguishes between 'rigid diglossia,' in which there is minimal functional overlap between codes, and 'fluid diglossia,' in which some functions, at least, are less rigidly associated with a particular code (1986: 15).

The proliferation of diglossia types, and the many attempts to systematize these types within a general classification, reflects the multiple ambiguity which has crept into the use of the term since it was first employed by Ferguson in 1959. It is this ambiguity that is in large measure to blame for the often conflicting points of view which different scholars in the field hold with regard to the origins, evolutionary course, and social consequences of diglossia. There is little prospect of progress on these issues until such time as a single definition of diglossia is adopted to the exclusion of all others, or, until the various subcategories of broad diglossia are expressly and consistently identified in any theoretical treatment of the phenomenon. There is little agreement on how to proceed. Fasold (1984), Britto (1986), and Pauwels (1986) advocate the use of the term 'diglossia' in a general sense to refer to a situation where a speech community makes use of high and low variety ranges, each with its distinctive functional allocation, and where the high variety, or repertoire of varieties, is customarily acquired later in life, normally through the process of formal schooling. Others, including Hudson (1991: 16), advocate a return to the essence of Ferguson's original definition.

The most comprehensive bibliography on diglossia, containing more than 3,000 entries, is that by Fernández (1993). A shorter bibliography was published by Hudson (1992). A special issue of the *International Journal of the Sociology of Language*, focussing on diglossia, is scheduled to appear in August 2002.

See also: Literacy; Bilingualism, Societal.

Bibliography

Alexiou M 1982 Diglossia in Greece. In: Haas W (ed.) *Standard Languages: Spoken and Written*. Barnes and Noble, Totowa, NJ

Altoma S J 1969 *The Problem of Diglossia in Arabic: A Comparative Study of Classical and Iraqi Arabic*. Center for Middle Eastern Studies, Harvard University, Cambridge, MA

Barbour S, Stevenson P 1990 *Variation in German: A Critical Approach to German Sociolinguistics*. Cambridge University Press. Cambridge, UK

Barnes D 1982 Nationalism and the Mandarin movement: The first half-century. In: Cooper R L (ed) *Language Spread: Studies in Diffusion and Social Change*. Indiana University Press, Bloomington, IN

Bender M L, Hailu F, Cowley R 1976 Two Ethio–Semitic languages. In: Bender M L, Bowen J D, Cooper R L, Ferguson C A (eds.) *Language in Ethiopia*. Oxford University Press, London

Blau J 1977 The beginnings of the Arabic diglossia: A study of the origins of Neoarabic. *Afroasiatic Linguistics* **4**: 175–202

Bright W Ramanujan A K 1972 Sociolinguistic variation and language change. In: Pride J B, Holmes J (eds.) *Sociolinguistics: Selected Readings*. Penguin, Harmondsworth, UK

Britto 1986 *Diglossia: A Study of the Theory with Application to Tamil*. Georgetown University Press, Washington, DC

Browning R 1982 Greek diglossia yesterday and today. *International Journal of the Sociology of Language* **35**: 49–68

Cadora F J 1985 Who are the Arabs?: A sociolinguistic view. In: *Inaugural Lectures 1984–85*. College of Humanities of Ohio State University, Columbus, OH

Chatterjee S 1986 Diglossia in Bengali. In: Krishnamurti Bh, Masica C P, Sinha A K (eds.) *South Asian Languages: Structure Convergences, and Diglossia*. Motilal Banarsidass, Delhi, India

Clyne M G 1984 *Language and Society in the German-speaking countries*. Cambridge University Press, Cambridge, UK

Comrie B 1991 Diglossia in the Old Russian period. *Southwest Journal of Linguistics* **10**: 160–72

Corkery D 1968 *The Fortunes of the Irish Language*. Mercier Press, Cork, Eire

Coulmas F 1987 What writing can do to language: Some preliminary remarks. In: Battestini S P X (ed.) *Developments in Linguistics and Semiotics, Language Teaching and Learning, Communication across Cultures*, Georgetown University Round Table on Languages and Linguistics 1986. Georgetown University Press, Washington, DC

Coulmas F 1991 Does the notion of diglossia apply to Japanese?: Some thoughts and some documentation. *Southwest Journal of Linguistics* **10**: 125–42

Deshpande M M 1986 Sanskrit grammarians on diglossia. In: Krishnamurti Bh, Masica C P, Sinha A K (eds.) *South Asian Languages: Structure, Convergence and Diglossia*. Motilal Banarsidass, Delhi, India

Fasold R 1984 *The Sociolinguistics of Society*. Basil Blackwell, Oxford, UK

Fellman J 1985 A sociolinguistic perspective on the history of Hebrew. In: Fishman J A (ed.) *Readings in the Sociology of Jewish languages*. E J Brill, Leiden, The Netherlands

Ferguson C A 1959 Diglossia. *Word* **15**: 325–40

Fernández M 1993 *Diglossia: A Comprehensive Bibliography with Supplements*. Benjamins, Amsterdam

Fishman J A 1967 Bilingualism with and without diglossia: Diglossia with and without bilingualism. *Journal of Social Issues* **23**(2): 29–38

Fishman J A 1970 *Sociolinguistics: A Brief Introduction*. Newbury House, Rowley, MA

Fishman J A 1980 Bilingualism and biculturism as individual and as societal phenomena. *Journal of Multilingual & Multicultural Development* **1**: 1–15

Fishman J A 1985 Bilingualism and biculturism as individual and as societal phenomena. In: Fishman J A, Gertner M H, Lowy E G, Milán W G (ed.) *The Rise and Fall of the Ethnic Revival*. Mouton, Berlin

Fishman J A 1989 *Language and Ethnicity in Minority Sociolinguistic Perspective*. Multilingual Matters, Clevedon, UK

Gair J W 1986 Sinhala diglossia revisited or diglossia dies hard. In: Krishnamurti Bh, Masica C P, Sinha A K (eds.) *South Asian Languages: Structure, Convergence and Diglossia*. Motilal Banarsidass, Delhi, India

Gallagher C F 1971 Language reform and social modernization in Turkey. In: Rubin J, Jernudd B H (eds.) *Can Language Be Planned? Sociolinguistic Theory and Practice for Developing Nations*. University Press of Hawaii, Honolulu, HI

Habein Y S 1984 *The History of the Japanese Written Language*. University of Tokyo Press, Tokyo

Hall R A Jr 1978 Bi-(multi-)lingualism and diglossia in Latin and Romance. *Forum Linguisticum* **3**: 107–17

Hall R A Jr 1986 From bidialectalism to diglossia in early Romance. In: Elson B F (ed.) *Language in Global Perspective: Papers in Honor of the 50th Anniversary of the Summer Institute of Linguistics 1935–1985*. Summer Institute of Linguistics, Dallas, TX

Hudson A 1991 Toward the systematic study of diglossia. *Southwest Journal of Linguistics* **10**: 1–22

Hudson A 1992 Diglossia: A bibliographic review. *Language in Society* **21**: 611–74

Jeremiás E M 1984 Diglossia in Persian. *Acta Linguistica Academiae Scientarum Hungaricae* **34**: 271–87

Jones D G 1988 Literary Welsh. In: Ball M J (ed.) *The Use of Welsh*. Multilingual Matters, Clevedon, UK

Karpat K H 1984 A language in search of a nation: Turkish in the nation-state. In: Scaglione A (ed.) *The Emergence of National Languages*. Longo, Ravenna, Italy

Keller R E 1982 Diglossia in German-speaking Switzerland. In: Haas W (ed.) *Standard Languages: Spoken and Written*. Barnes and Noble, Totowa, NJ

Kloss H 1976 Über 'Diglossie.' *Deutsche Sprache* **4**: 313–23

Lazard G 1975 The rise of the New Persian language. In: Frye R N (ed.) *The Cambridge History of Iran. Vol. 4: The Period from the Arab Invasion to the Saljuqs*. Cambridge University Press, Cambridge, UK

Norman J 1988 *Chinese*. Cambridge University Press, Cambridge, UK

Ó Murchú M 1985 *The Irish Language*. Government of Ireland, Department of Foreign Affairs and Bord na Gaeilge, Dublin, Eire

Parker I 1983 The rise of the vernaculars in early modern Europe: An essay in the political economy of language. In: Bain B (ed.) *The Sociogenesis of Language and Human Conduct*. Plenum Press, New York

Pauwels A 1986 Diglossia, immigrant dialects and language maintenance in Australia. *Journal of Multilingual & Multicultural Development* **7**: 13–30

Pei M 1976 *The Story of Latin and the Romance Languages*. Harper and Row, New York

Rabin C 1955 The beginnings of Classical Arabic. *Studia Islamica* **4**: 19–37

Rendsburg G A 1980 Evidence for a spoken Hebrew in Biblical times (Doctoral dissertation, New York University)

Schiffman H 1991 Swiss–German diglossia. *Southwest Journal of Linguistics* **10**: 173–88

Spolsky B 1991 Diglossia in Hebrew in the late Second Temple Period. *Southwest Journal of Linguistics* **10**: 85–104

Timm L A 1981 Diglossia old and new: A critique. *Anthropological Linguistics* **23**: 356–67

Discourse Analysis and the Law

D. Eades

1. Introduction

The term 'discourse analysis' is used in a wide range of meanings. In this entry it is used with the traditional meaning of the analysis of language beyond the level of the sentence, namely that level of linguistic analysis that complements phonetics, phonology, morphology, syntax, and semantics. In this sense, the term is sometimes seen to correspond to the broader meaning of the term 'pragmatics' (see *Pragmatics and Sociolinguistics*).

In legal contexts, discourse analysis is generally carried out in order to shed light on questions of sociolegal significance. Most studies to date have analyzed language in courtrooms, where access to data is much easier than in other legal contexts, such as police or lawyer interviews. Most of the literature on this topic written in English deals with the adversarial legal system, found in countries such as the UK, the USA, Australia, and other Anglo countries. The particular methodological approaches used include ethnography, formal linguistic analysis, critical discourse analysis, conversation analysis, and interactional sociolinguistics. (See *Conversation Analysis*; *Critical Sociolinguistics: Overview*; *Ethnography of Speaking*; *Interactional Sociolinguistic Research Methods*.)

2. Courtroom Discourse

One of the earliest studies in this area addressed the influence of language factors on legal decision-making. The linguistic anthropologist W. M. O'Barr and lawyer John Conley headed the Duke University Language and Law Project, focusing on different speech styles used by witnesses in US courtrooms in the late 1970s. They combined an ethnographic study to find out about variations in language forms, with a psycholinguistic experimental study to find out the effects of these variations in form on trial processes. Their ethnographic study found that witnesses tend to use one of two different styles, termed 'powerful' and 'powerless.' The powerless style is characterized by many of the features which had earlier been said to typify women's speech, such as a high frequency of intensifiers (e.g. *very, really*), and the use of hedges (e.g. *sort of, like*). The powerful style, on the other hand, without such linguistic features, sounds much more precise and confident. And the experimental study found that witnesses using the more powerful style were considered by jurors to be more convincing, truthful, competent, intelligent, and trustworthy than those using the powerless style were. So, it is clear that the details of the way in which witnesses present their evidence can be very important to the outcome of a case.

The concern in the Duke study with the relative power (or lack of power) of witnesses has remained central to many of the more recent studies. A number of these have demonstrated the strong power imbalance between a witness on the one hand, and a lawyer and a judge/magistrate on the other, exemplified in such discourse features as these:
  (a) witnesses are typically asked a large number of questions requiring a minimal response;
  (b) witnesses say very little compared to the verbosity of those questioning them;
  (c) the majority of questions put to witnesses contain already completed propositions; and
  (d) witnesses are not in control of telling their own story.
The greatest imbalance occurs in hearings in which the witness is a second language or nonstandard dialect speaker, or a child.

A particular focus of studies of language and power in the courtroom starts with the knowledge, which is common to lawyers and police officers, that some types of questions allow the interviewee more freedom, while others are much more restrictive. Through careful choice of the actual question structure then, lawyers have powerful linguistic means for being conducive, controlling, coercive, or manipulative. By examining the answers logically expected from the structure of the questions, and in some cases, by also looking at the actual answers elicited, a number of linguists have organized question types into courtroom 'hierarchies of control.' These hierarchies show that the most controlling questions are Yes–No questions with a tag (e.g., *You were at the beach that day, weren't you?*), and the least controlling are broad WH questions (*why, what, how*). Thus it is not surprising to find that most cross-examination is dominated by Yes–No questions, many of them with tags, while there are typically more WH questions in examination-in-chief (= direct examination).

But there is more involved in the exercise of power and control in the courtroom than simply question type: for example, depending on intonation, a tag question could be an extremely pressured and harassing act, or it could be one of simple verification. And indeed, in examination-in-chief the so-called most controlling questions can be taken by witnesses to be invitations to explain. In this way, for example, a question with a Yes–No tag structure may *function* as if it is a broad WH question.

In addition to question structure, researchers have found a number of other linguistic strategies used by lawyers to exercise control over witnesses, including:
  (a) interruptions;
  (b) reformulation of witness's descriptions of events or people (e.g., from *my friends* to *a group of louts*);
  (c) manipulation of lawyer silence, for example with the use of strategic pauses;
  (d) nonrecognition of some witnesses' need to use silence as part of the answer, which can be particularly important, for example, for Australian Aboriginal witnesses;
  (e) incorporation of damaging presuppositions in questions (such as *Did you all laugh while the car was being thrashed?*);
  (f) metalinguistic directives given to the witness (such as *You must answer this question*); and
  (g) management of topics in order to convey a particular impression to the jury.
A particular concern which arises from detailed discourse analysis of both rape cases and child sexual assault cases is that the courtroom hearing may be so manipulative of the witness and so traumatic, that the process of giving evidence actually amounts to revictimization of the victim-witness.

2.1 Second Language and Non-standard Dialect Speakers

An important issue in the investigation of power imbalance in the courtroom concerns the situation of witnesses who do not speak the language of the court. In many countries, there is a growing awareness of the need to provide interpreters. Discourse analysis of interpreted proceedings has shed light on the way in which legal interpreters function, which has important implications for the training both of interpreters and of legal professionals who work with them. The most important work in this field contradicts the predominant legal perception of the interpreter as a conduit or 'language machine' through which language is processed. Instead, detailed discourse analysis by Susan Berk-Seligson and others shows that the interpreter is an important courtroom participant, whose job involves much more than translating propositional content. The interpreter must also be finely tuned to the subtleties of pragmatics, distinguishing for example between different types of English tag questions used in cross-examination for different pragmatic purposes.

While second language speakers often have access to interpreter services, the situation of non-standard dialect speakers' access to justice is more complex. Communication difficulties, while not as extreme as with second language speakers, are compounded by the general lack of recognition of nonstandard dialects, combined with frequent prejudice against such dialects and their speakers. Most of the research on speakers of nonstandard dialects in legal contexts has focused on Australian Aborigines, whose imprisonment rate is the highest recorded for any ethnic group in the world. Discourse analysis of Aboriginal English speakers in legal contexts highlights a number of pragmatic features which are largely unrecognized or misinterpreted, and which clearly affect their dealings with the law. For example, in contrast to the Anglo legal system and society generally, where silence in an interview is generally taken to mean that a speaker has nothing to say, many speakers of Aboriginal English (as well as traditional Aboriginal languages) use silence as a positive and productive part of communication. Thus, Aboriginal English silence is often the first part of the answer to a question, and it can signal that the speaker considers the question important enough to warrant serious consideration before speaking.

3. Lawyer–Client Interviews

While interaction between lawyers and their clients forms an important legal context, there is to date little discourse analysis of these interactions. Research has so far investigated the ways in which lawyers make sense of the legal process for their clients, and has found that there are quite different ways of seeing the client's problem. Lawyers tend to be focused on legal rules and the categories both of law and of legal problems. Their clients, on the other hand, tend to be more oriented to telling their story. Interestingly there appears to be little difference between the way that male and female lawyers talk to their clients. However, both male and female clients are more deferential to male lawyers than to female lawyers.

4. Police Interviews

Analysis of police interviews has primarily focused on interviews with suspects and has addressed the important legal issue of the comprehensibility of the police caution (about the rights of a suspect, known in the USA as the Miranda Rights), as well as the questions put to suspects. Researchers have found that the typical wording of the Miranda Rights requires the equivalent reading skills of a tenth grade high school student. In Australia, linguists have presented expert evidence analyzing nonnative speakers' difficulty in understanding both the caution and certain questions in specific police interviews. And further, several linguists have been involved in projects to simplify the wording of the police caution and to translate it into a number of local indigenous languages.

5. Conclusion

Work on discourse analysis in the law has some immediate practical relevance, in examples such as those discussed above. In addition, expert linguistic evidence is increasingly being provided by some scholars in the analysis of language, which is used in evidence in criminal cases. Such use of linguistic analysis as expert evidence is dealt with in the article *Forensic Phonetics and Sociolinguistics*. (Note that this term is also sometimes used more broadly to refer to linguistic studies of language in legal contexts.)

Discourse analysis in legal contexts is a relatively new field of study, and one that involves not just description and analysis of this specialized area of language use. Sociolinguists are increasingly using detailed microanalysis of the way that language is used in the legal process, to help shed light on exactly how it is that the legal system often fails to provide justice.

See also: Conversation Analysis; Forensic Phonetics and Sociolinguistics; Power and Language.

Bibliography

Atkinson J M, Drew P 1979 *Order in Court: The Organisation of Verbal Interaction in Judicial Settings*. Humanities Press, Atlantic Highlands, NJ
Berk-Seligson S 1990 *The Bilingual Courtroom: Court Interpreters in the Judicial Process*. University of Chicago Press, Chicago, IL
Brennan M 1995 The discourse of denial: Cross-examining child victim witnesses. *Journal of Pragmatics* **23**: 71–91
Conley J, O'Barr W 1998 *Just Words: Law, Language, and Power*. University of Chicago Press, Chicago, IL
Eades D 1995 (ed.) *Language in Evidence: Issues Confronting Aboriginal and Multicultural Australia*. University of New South Wales Press, Sydney, NSW
O'Barr W 1982 *Linguistic Evidence: Language, Power, and Strategy in the Courtroom*. Academic Press, New York
Tiersma P 1999 *Legal Language*. University of Chicago Press, Chicago, IL

Formulaic Language
F. Coulmas

'Formulaic language' is a cover term for ready-made constructions which can be used without having to be built up from scratch. Various kinds of formulaic locutions such as proverbs, similes, and other loci communis were traditionally treated in Rhetoric or Stylistics. Jespersen (1924) was the first to make a general distinction between 'formulas' and 'free expressions' which 'pervades all parts of grammar.'

Free expressions are created in each case, whereas formulas are drawn from memory. Formulaicity is considered by some scholars (e.g., Bolinger 1976) to be a basic property of language which makes it unnecessary to fully exploit for every utterance the productivity of grammar and, at the same time, curtails it. Formulaic speech is believed to be a universal phenomenon found in every speech community.

1. Kinds of Formulaic Expressions

The four main types of formulaic expressions are (a) fixed phrases for daily use, (b) ritualistic formulas, (c) routine formulas, and (d) poetic formulas. Each of these encompasses a great variety of subtypes.

Fixed phrases include idioms ('a red herring'), phrasal verbs ('to drive something home'), standard metaphors ('iron curtain'), binominals and other paired items ('part and parcel,' 'alive and kicking,' 'on and off'), collocations ('beyond reproach'), conventional similes ('she is like a rose'), clichés ('the good old days'), slogans ('Ha! Liberté, égalité, fraternité'), curses, familiar quotations (Shakespeare's 'tooth of time').

Ritualistic formulas are characteristic of explicitly prescribed language use, for example in religious exercise including blessings, absolutions, vows; magic incantations; law, as in contract formulas; and government, e.g., oath of office, public announcements, diplomatic invitations.

Routine formulas, also called 'pragmatic idioms,' comprise fixed expressions for highly recurrent communicative tasks such as salutations, introductions, thanks, apologies, excuses, compliments, toasts, epistolary beginnings and closings, as well as conversation management, e.g., claiming, passing or soliciting a turn, interrupting, introducing a topic, requesting repetition or explication, closing a topic or conversation.

Poetic formulas are phrases which are repeated in the same form whenever an idea or person is mentioned in an epic. They include stock epithets ('Achilleus of the swift feet') as well as longer phrases which have been employed as tools of metrical composition.

2. Properties of Formulaic Speech

The formulas of a language are generally known by its speech community and distinguished by their popularity and conventionality. Some can be recognized, even if they are not known as formulas, on the grounds of formal peculiarities. From the point of view of grammar, formulaic speech is conspicuous because of the non-generative nature of many formulaic expressions. Although they exhibit an internal structure, they are not generated by the rules of ordinary syntax. They violate syntactic rules or exemplify obsolete rules which have become unproductive. As a result, their structures are unique or arbitrarily restricted in productivity and distribution. Syntactic patterning and semantic composition are not matched. Many formulas are therefore semantically not transparent since their meanings are not deducible from their structures.

These features of speech formulas—that is, frozen structure, semantic opacity, and syntactic deviance—are graded rather than categorical properties, and hence formulaicity itself is a graded notion.

3. Functions of Formulaic Speech

The psycholinguistic significance of formulas is that they are stored and retrieved whole, hence serving a function in speech production of easing the pressure of simultaneous planning and execution of long stretches of speech. Like other automatisms, pre-patterned formulas drawn from memory as stock items, save time for planning. There is evidence that the ability to produce fluent speech depends partly on a sufficiently large stock of formulas (Pawley and Syder 1983), although not every expression which has formulaic qualities for an individual speaker is necessarily recognized as a formula by the speech community at large. That there is a distinction between individual and social formulas is underscored by observations of language acquisition. It was found that in both first and second language acquisition 'unanalyzed chunks of speech' (Peters 1983) are stored in the memory and accessed as such, some of them formulas of the language, others formulaic items of an idiosyncratic nature. These functions of formulaic speech raise important questions about the units of language to be accounted for in a performance model.

From a sociolinguistic point of view, formulaic speech incorporates sociocultural knowledge. For handling many recurrent communicative tasks characteristic of a society or social group the appropriate expressions are socially recognized formulas (Coulmas 1981). In that they embody accepted ways of responding verbally to a variety of situations, they facilitate social relations and thus have an adaptive value. Since they are indicative of conventions and etiquette, they are a means of social control. Many situations leave very little choice for the 'right word.' Using the expected formulas is a strong indication of belonging, social identity, or acculturation. Their knowledge creates and reinforces social cohesion.

Formulas also fulfill functions on the interaction level, especially for discourse control. As metacommunicative signals formulas are used to define the nature of a conversation, to establish an agenda of topics, to steer the flow of discourse from one stage to another, to distribute speaking rights, and to indicate cognitive attitudes, such as belief, surprise, disagreement.

As regards their poetic functions speech formulas are mnemonic devices used for handing down from one generation to the next, in poetic form, knowledge and beliefs, indicating the traditional conceptualizations of man and the universe (Watkins 1989). Much attention has been paid to formulas in the study of oral literature (Lord 1960, Duggan 1975), because their pervasive occurrence there can explain how lengthy works of poetry could be remembered without written recording.

See also: Oracy; Religion and Language.

Bibliography

Bolinger D 1976 Meaning of memory. *Forum Linguisticum* **1**(1): 1–14
Coulmas F 1981 *Conversational Routine*. Mouton, The Hague
Duggan J J 1975 *Oral Literature*. Scottish Academic Press, Edinburgh, UK
Jespersen O 1924 *The Philosophy of Grammar*. George Allen and Unwin, London
Lord A B 1960 *The Singer of Tales*. Harvard University Press, Cambridge, MA
Pawley A, Syder F 1983 Two puzzles for linguistic theory: Nativelike selection and nativelike fluency. In: Richards J, Schmidt R (eds.) *Communicative Competence*. Longman, London
Peters A 1983 *The Units of Language Acquisition*. Cambridge University Press, Cambridge, UK
Watkins C 1989 New parameters in historical linguistics, philology, and culture history. *Language* **65**(4): 783–99

Genre

T. Threadgold

'Genre' was originally a literary term. Its history in literary and rhetorical studies continues to mark the associations that it has come to have with literature and pedagogies of literacy (the teaching of reading and writing). The literary background is also evident in the extension of genre into anthropology and cultural studies; into ethnography, sociolinguistics, critical discourse analysis, and social semiotics, which have sought to provide explicit linguistic and contextualized accounts of the functions of genres in a wide variety of social practices and sites. It also has strategic uses in feminist and poststructuralist literary and cultural theory where it functions as the locus of textual transgressions designed to restructure the disciplines, and as a means of understanding and attempting to change the sociocultural construction and transmission of patriarchy.

1. Overview of Genre Theories and Classifications

All these enterprises are still marked by the Aristotelian literary origins of the genre concept, along with a metaphysics and an epistemology which derive from Aristotle's natural philosophy, and a link (implicit in Aristotle) between the philosophy of Natural Kinds, genres as kinds of texts, and sociocultural classes of people (Hauptmeier 1987). Biological metaphors, introduced into genre studies by aspects of Aristotelian naturalism which reached its epitome in the taxonomies of Linnaeus, are as significant in the construction of later genre theory as are the Aristotelian metaphysical and social metaphors. Just as the discipline of biology overcame the dualism between naturalism and conventionalism with the development of evolutionary theory, which provided a way of both motivating classifications and freeing fixed essences to historical development, so genre theory, in the work of the Russian Formalists, the Prague School, Bakhtin (see *Dialogism*); the Tel-Aviv School of Poetics, and reception theory, to name only the major influences, turned to theories of evolution and of interaction between texts and environments to explain and motivate systems of 'kinds' (text types and literary systems) and changes in those systems. Questions of literary genre and biological taxonomies are historically connected in Aristotelian thought, and genre and biology, genre and gender, or genre and sexuality, are etymologically connected in the ambiguity of genre in French. This history and the dominance of these metaphors and connections have only begun to be explored: late twentieth-century poststructuralist and feminist work has sought to demonstrate the conventional, socially constructed nature of both genre and biology, and to explore the complex relations between genre and gender, genre and power, genre and institutions, genre and discipline, and genre and the teaching of literacy.

There have always been implicit or explicit social, aesthetic, and even moral values associated with the classification of genres. The earliest classifications of Classical poetics and rhetoric into high, middle, and low kinds are typical: they assume an implicit homology with a sociocultural classification of kinds of people according to the modes and styles of speech or writing which characterized them (Fowler 1982: 240 ff.). These early classifications later become the high/popular culture distinction. Hierarchies of genres and social and moral values, whether part of an explicit or covert pedagogy, are essential to the business of canon formation, and to the institution of literary study and of literacy (which is a technology for social control: see Hunter 1988). The historically constant classification of genres associated with the most powerful social and cultural institutions of government, religion, law, and pedagogy (and thus literature and science) as 'high' has also contributed to the establishment of the distinction between national standard languages and 'nonstandard' languages; to the construction and maintenance of current disciplinary structures in schools and universities; and, many would say, to all kinds of global, national, social, ethnic, racial, and gender inequalities.

Genres, in most analyses, are considered to have specific forms which organize the matter or substance of which the genre is made. The form may impose a subject matter, a manner or mode, and a typical text structure. Forms themselves can be classified. One typical classification of kinds or forms derives from Aristotle's *Poetics*, mediated by Cicero and Quintilian, the normative rhetorics and poetics of the sixteenth centuries, and the neoclassical rhetorics and poetics of the eighteenth and early nineteenth centuries. This survives in the organization and teaching of literary studies, and in rhetorical approaches to the teaching of writing. The classification into lyric, dramatic, and narrative, which is basic to the division of literary texts into the 'kinds' of poetry, the novel, and drama, is at least as old as Plato and Aristotle, and still functional in many places.

In literary and rhetorical uses of such classifications, each kind will be characterized by particular topics (the *topoi* of Classical rhetoric), modes (such as narrative, allegory, satire), forms of argumentation (the deliberative, the epideictic, the forensic, for example, ancestors of the modern expository, descriptive, and legal), and styles—high, middle, low. These are associated with varying distributions and uses of the figures of rhetoric, e.g., metaphor and metonymy, which still serve to separate the literary from the ordinary in style and language; and methods of organization (*dispositio*, what are often called schematic structures). The most typical of all such schemata of textual organization is the Aristotelian one of the text which must have a beginning, a middle, and an end, the prototype of the texts explored in narratology (Coste 1989), a text defined by its internal conflict, climax, and denouement, and by the rational synthesis which produces its closed, complete, and coherent structure.

Fowler (1982) argues that knowledge of genre, for the classically educated, provided the framework for a recognition of 'allusion' and generic patterning in texts, a recognition of the system of values associated with the system of genres, and an explicit pedagogy for, and practice of, literary criticism and writing and reading. Explicit genre-based rhetorics have also always tended to stabilize the relations between production and reception of texts, so that mismatches between the codes used to produce and to receive—formalized by Eco (1976), and alluded to in Fowler's account of the decline of Classical education and its effect on the reading of earlier texts—are minimized and controlled.

Some of the most interesting aspects of literary rhetorical theories of genre are the evolutionary tendencies to be found associated with the terms 'kind' and 'mode,' which Fowler says are both 'generic' terms, or ways of defining genre. He suggests that 'kind' is a nominal term, and 'mode' an adjectival or modulating one, and that the two are used together to characterize combined or mixed genres such as the pastoral elegy or the heroic epic. Mode, however, is always dependent on kind, and modes are derived or evolved from kinds. Thus, kinds such as epic, biography, tragedy, and comedy can be realized as modes—epic, biographical, tragic, comic—within other genres. So the gothic 'kind' can be extended as a 'mode' to modulate the kinds of the crime novel, the short story, the film script, or science fiction. Fowler argues that literary genre theory, still influenced by Romanticism, has been dominated by modes (romance, lyric, narrative, dialogic, dramatic, tragic, comic), not kinds, because the modes are less formally and historically circumscribed than the kinds, which tend to be linked to specific social institutions and practices. There is in this an implicit recognition of the ubiquity of modes like narrative and dialogue in all kinds of other genres and media, and of the difference between narrative, dialogue, and genres (Coste 1989, Jauss 1989, Swales 1990 calls narrative and dialogue 'pre-genres'). The literary theory anticipates later poststructuralist accounts of the crucial cultural and socially constructive importance of both narrative and dialogue, and of the multigenericity of many text types (Bakhtin 1968: 86). This is in sharp contrast to linguistic work on genre, which continues to treat narrative as a genre and has rarely explored or recognized the problem of mixed genres.

In all contexts, classifications and theories of genre function both as descriptive/analytical and as prescriptive/pedagogic devices. The use of the term has always included not only descriptions of the characteristics of actual texts, classes of texts, and systems of classes of texts, but also descriptions of schemata assumed to provide guides for the making or writing of texts, whether these are theorized as being in people's heads—formulated as cognitive schemata, knowledge of the world (Hauptmeier 1987)—or as systemic potential modeled from other texts, formulated as generic structures, generic structure potential (Hasan 1978). Post-structuralism has developed a very different process-based theory of the way in which generic meanings are construed between and across texts in both reading and writing (Kress and Threadgold 1988). The use of genre theory has also extended from models where the understanding of the production and structure of texts was paramount (Marxist, literary critical, and formalist theories) to use in models of text reception and reading: reception theory, semiotics, poststructuralism, and feminism (de Lauretis 1984), where the primary interest is on the interaction between text structures and reading strategies. These may be formulated as reading protocols, codes, or genres of reading, and in the last case involve explicit theories of subjectivity, positioning, embodiment, and discipline (Foucault 1979, Grosz 1989). These theories develop a new rhetoric of intertextuality which, in striking distinction to the old, does not work through the liberal humanist subject as conscious agent, but attempts to describe the way in which practices of reading and writing and of text-making produce that subject and the social world that s/he inhabits. It therefore frames the categories of intertextuality, discourse, genre, and narrative in explicitly political and strategic ways.

Such a theory of genre is a long way from the earlier rhetorical literary theories, but it also shares a good deal with them. In both cases, the theory and the rhetoric of genre has been applied to other semiotic media, visual, architectural, musical, theatrical, and multimedial (Fowler 1982, Coste 1989); in both cases there is a recognition that categories like narrative and dialogism (and probably exposition) are larger, less institutionally and historically constrained than genres; in both there is a narrative of institutional forms constraining and structuring modes and contents; and in both there is a homology between social and generic hierarchy which is potentially disrupted by generic change and transformation.

2. Linguistic Accounts of Genre, and Future Directions

Concepts of genre used in explicitly linguistic (usually sociolinguistic or ethnographic) settings are borrowed fairly narrowly from literary and rhetorical, or structuralist-functionalist sources. The work of Labov (1972) on narratives of personal experience offered a thoroughly Aristotelian schema for the episodic structure of conventional narrative: abstract + orientation + complicating action + evaluation + result or resolution + coda. This was theorized as a regular sequencing of optional and obligatory elements which constituted the 'generic structure of the text' (see *Narrative, Natural*). Similar schemas are elaborated in the tagmemic work on genre (Longacre 1974); and by Hymes on the rhetorical structure of native American folktales (1981: 106–7). The systemic functional work on genre, primarily in Australia, repeats these schemata for narrative with surprisingly little variation (Martin 1985), and, even when the genre involved is supposedly a different one, such as exposition, the pattern remains very similar. For example, Martin's schema for exposition: Introduction + Body (a series of arguments supporting a thesis) + Conclusion (restates thesis, sums up arguments) (1985: 86) still has the basic Aristotelian pattern of beginning, middle, and end, with the middle involving conflict of some kind that is resolved in the conclusion.

Also rhetorically derived are categories like description, procedure, adhortation, report, explanation (Longacre 1974, Martin 1985). In most cases, the narrative and other labels and schemata are produced *as if* they were motivated by linguistic analysis; but in fact there is a tendency simply to impose a preconceived schema, derived from traditional rhetoric and narratology, on to the linguistic analyses. In other cases, where the schematic elements are apparently motivated by the linguistic analysis, as for example in Hasan's structuralist–functionalist account of the buying and selling genre, there is an equally ad hoc 'naming' of parts which does not tell one very much more than any native speaker could have: that is, the 'names' for the parts of the genre have a folk-linguistic character and are little more than native informant glosses on content.

Such generic schemata seem to represent both the system potential for the making of genres and the classifications of actual text types. The linguistic detail which accompanies such analyses (Wignell et al. 1990), is derived and motivated in its approach, as Swales (1990) points out, from register theory (see *Register*) and often shares its limitations. His criticism of the latter is that its tendency to focus on patterns of language (and on content) as characteristic of 'scientific' or 'legal' or 'media' English, or in the Wignell et al. (1990) case, 'the discourse of Geography,' has had a homogenizing tendency which has inhibited the taking up of issues (the range and variety of genres that actually constitute the institution of the law or science, for example) that have been more readily explored in rhetorically based research on genre. This is why Swales turns to rhetorical theories of genre, derived from literary models, and with a much more complex sense of the relations between texts and their contexts (cf. Bazerman 1988), to complement the linguistic theories in his work on the genres of academic English.

Van Leeuwen's account of 'Generic strategies in press journalism' (1987) offers the kind of combination that Swales envisages, and includes a level of metatheoretical analysis derived from poststructuralism which theorizes the everyday practices that it investigates. It begins with detailed lexicogrammatical analysis, using Halliday's functional grammar, and motivates the description of the genre of the news story on that basis. The labels which van Leeuwen uses for the 'stages' of his text are carefully derived from and related to the institutional and social contexts and purposes of such texts. They are not derived from preconceived generic schemata or from the linguist's intuitions about 'what is going on' in this text. The interest is in the way in which, in the 'news story,' 'many different, partly contradictory, partly overt and partly covert social purposes are translated into generic structures' (1987: 199). Van Leeuwen identifies the news story as involving subgenres such as 'short reports,' 'features,' and 'editorials,' and including phases of narration, description, exposition, procedure, and adhortation. He is able to bring together native informant type analyses/labelings of genres and modes with explicit linguistic accounts of the ways in which these are realized in parts of an actual text, to describe the way that the text develops in stages according to an institutional and local set of purposes, and to demonstrate that the labeling of the text as 'news story' does not in any way relate to or substantiate its construction as a monologic narrative genre with a typical or single narrative generic schema. In fact, the folk-linguistic label 'story' has to do with the institutional purpose of constructing the news story as primarily factual narrative description and report, in order to disguise the controlling function of the media (its expository, interpretative, and adhortatory purpose). Van Leeuwen argues that there is no evidence for a single generic schema of obligatory or even obligatory and optional stages which could explain the genre of the texts. He sees the structure and production of the texts as better explained in terms of a network of generic choices, which are available within the media as context-specific strategies for realizing the social purposes of journalism in textual form.

The difference between van Leeuwen's work and that of the linguists discussed above is in the degree and depth of contextualization that is involved. His work is not just about language or about narrowly defined text structures derived from folk-linguistic labels. It is a critique and an analysis of those labels, and it is about social structure, cultural realities, socially produced and disciplined agents of social institutions and practices (journalists and the media), and about the very complex relations between what the linguist Halliday called the 'text' and the 'higher order social semiotic' (1978). Halliday's own (1988) work on the contemporary functions and historical evolution of lexical density in science texts, while still within the register tradition of analysis, demonstrates a similar concern with contextualization and the metatheoretical level of critique. Such work in fact involves the same kind of intertextual labour of mapping meanings from text to text which has become the interpretative critical practice of poststructuralist and social semiotic reading practices.

The social semioticians who have also been using systemic linguistics to work on genre, like van Leeuwen, would argue that the three approaches—the functional linguistic, the rhetorical concern with textual histories and families, and the politics and metatheory of intertextuality—are complementary (Kress and Threadgold 1988, Threadgold 1989). All indications are that future work on genre in interdisciplinary and postdisciplinary settings will bring these different but complementary trends together.

See also: Literary Language; Register; Narrative, Natural.

Bibliography

Aristotle 1983 Poetics. In: Russell D A, Winterbottom M (eds.) *Ancient Literary Criticism: The Principle Texts in New Translations*. Clarendon Press, Oxford, UK
Bakhtin M M 1968 *Rabelais and His World*. MIT Press, Cambridge, MA
Bazerman C 1988 *Shaping Written Knowledge: The Genre and Activity of the Experimental Article in Science*. University of Wisconsin Press, Madison, WI
Coste D 1989 *Narrative as Communication*. University of Minnesota Press, Minneapolis, MN
Eco U 1976 *Theory of Semiotics*. Indiana University Press, Bloomington, IN
Foucault M 1979 *Discipline and Punish: The Birth of the Prison*. Random House, New York
Fowler A 1982 *Kinds of Literature: An Introduction to the Theory of Genres and Modes*. Clarendon Press, Oxford, UK
Grosz E 1989 *Sexual Subversions: Three French Feminists*. Allen and Unwin, Sydney, NSW
Halliday M A K 1978 *Language as Social Semiotic*. Edward Arnold, London
Halliday M A K 1988 On the language of physical science. In: Ghadessy M (ed.) *Registers of Written English: Situational Factors and Linguistic Features*. Pinter, London
Hasan R 1978 Text in the systemic–functional model. In: Dressler W (ed.) *Current Trends in Textlinguistics*. Walter de Gruyter, Berlin
Hauptmeier H 1987 Sketches of theories of genre. *Poetics* **16**: 397–430
Hunter I 1988 *Culture and Government: The Emergence of Literary Education*. Macmillan, London
Hymes D 1981 *'In Vain I Tried to Tell You': Essay in Native American Ethnopoetics*. University of Pennsylvania Press, Philadelphia, PA
Jauss H R 1989 *Question and Answer: Forms of Dialogic Understanding*. University of Minnesota Press, Minneapolis, MN
Kress G, Threadgold T 1988 Toward a social theory of genre. *Southern Review* **21**: 215–43

Labov W 1972 *Language in the Inner City*. University of Philadelphia Press, Philadelphia, PA
Lauretis T de 1984 *Alice Doesn't: Feminism, Semiotics, Cinema*. Indiana University Press, Bloomington, IN
Leeuwen T van 1987 Generic strategies in press journalism. *Australian Review of Applied Linguistics* 10(2): 199–220
Longacre R E 1974 Narrative versus other genre. In: Brend R M (ed.) *Advances in Tagmemics*. North-Holland, Amsterdam
Martin J R 1985 *Factual Writing: Exploring and Challenging Social Reality*. Deakin University Press, Geelong, VIC
Swales R 1990 *Genre Analysis: English in Academic Settings*. Cambridge University Press, Cambridge, UK
Threadgold T 1989 Talking about genre: Ideologies and incompatible discourses. *Cultural Studies* 3(1): 101–27
Wignell P, Martin J R, Eggins S 1990 The discourse of geography: Ordering and explaining the experiential world. *Linguistics in Education* 1(4): 359–92

Institutional Language

S. Sarangi

'Institutional language' is an umbrella term to refer to our everyday experience of officialese, small print, news-speak, etc., as we fill in official forms, read standard circulars from government and public agencies, and consult legal and medical records. An official memo, for instance, has a recognizable format containing standard abbreviations, forms of address, and even disclaimers such as *Please ignore this request if you have already written to us*. Likewise, a medical case note has a set of identifiable features which distinguish it not only from other institutional documents, such as an affidavit or a bank statement, but also from our acquaintance with written language in the personal sphere (e.g., letters from friends and relatives). We can extend these differences to spoken language use across institutional settings and between institutional and everyday settings.

1. Institutional Language: Problem of Definition and Scope

Based on a principle of dualism, a definition of institutional language can be rendered in negative terms: it is unlike everyday, ordinary language. As Agar (1985) puts it, institutional discourse is 'non-natural non-conversation.' This characterization highlights the fixed, patterned and rule-governed behavior in institutional settings, as opposed to the levity and fluid nature of everyday conversational exchanges. A major problem with a binary opposition between the institutional and the everyday or ordinary is that we are assumed to have a clear understanding of what ordinary language or conversation is (Wilson 1989).

We can examine institutional language from two interrelated perspectives: (a) to what extent it is situation- and setting-specific; and (b) to what extent it is style-specific (both linguistically and interactionally). A number of scholars in sociolinguistics and pragmatics have addressed these issues in their study of the role of language in a wide range of institutional and professional domains (e.g., Alatis and Tucker 1979, Atkinson and Heritage 1984, Atkinson and Drew 1979, Boden and Zimmerman 1991, Coleman 1984, 1985, di Pietro 1982, Drew and Heritage 1992, Fisher and Todd 1983, 1986, Gunnarsson et al. 1997, Labov and Fanshel 1977, O'Barr 1982, Sarangi and Roberts 1999, Sarangi and Slembrouck 1996, Wheeler 1969).

A common interest in the study of institutional language, following Douglas (1986), rests on the assumption that because institutions are primarily organizers of information, a study of patterned institutional routines can tell us something about how institutions work. This is the case if we turn to institutional practices in record-keeping and to the routine nature of information exchange in, say, emergency helpline calls, courtroom cross-examinations, medical consultations where accurate and precise information is sought in a sequential manner, in order to aid institutional and professional action.

2. Situational Aspects of Institutional Language

Among others, Labov and Fanshel (1977: 6) suggest that institutional language is 'specialised by its situation.' Drew and Heritage (1992), on the other hand, argue that setting or situation is not a definitional criterion of institutional interaction. Rather than equate institutional language with institutional settings, they claim that 'interaction is institutional insofar as participants' institutional or professional identities are somehow made relevant to the work activities in which they are engaged.' Following Levinson's notion of activity type, this includes: (a) orientations to institutional tasks and functions; (b) restrictions on the kinds of contributions to the talk that are, or can be, made; and (c) distinctive features of interactional inferences (Drew and Heritage 1992: 25). It is, however, arguable that in professional–client encounters, participants do not necessarily display explicit orientation to the institutional agenda, thus making it difficult for analysts to locate setting-specific or style-specific features.

3. Linguistic and Stylistic Features of Institutional Language

Traditionally, using genre analysis (Swales 1990, Bhatia 1993), institutional language has been examined as text-types with identifiable linguistic and stylistic features. According to Redish (1983), institutional language, mainly in its written form, has a *nominal style* consisting of: (a) overuse of nouns (rather than substituting pronouns); (b) nominalization (verbs transformed into nouns as in *Failure to follow these directions will result in disqualification of the applicant*); (c) preference for passive constructions; and (d) use of noun strings (e.g., *healthcare maintenance organization*; *host area crisis shelter production planning workbook*). At the sentence level, institutional language is characterized by parallel syntactic structures, and these are particularly salient in the repetitive and tautological expressions in legal texts. The occurrence of complex syntactic structures can be partially explained by the written bias in institutional discourse.

Jargon or special vocabulary (including abbreviations) is another distinct feature of institutional language (Hudson 1978). Various professional groups, such as doctors, social workers, psychotherapists, use terms like 'muscular dystrophy,' 'deficient parenthood,' 'dysfunctional relationship,' without every time explaining the meaning of these terms. The use of technical terminologies is, as far as the 'insiders' are concerned, justified in terms of precision and indexing of expert knowledge. In different professional and institutional settings, everyday words can also acquire technical meanings. This observation underscores the analytical difficulty in divorcing style from setting in any discussion of institutional discourse.

4. Clash of Frames and Recontextualization Processes in Institutional Discourse

The discursive practices that professional groups draw on can be summarized as follows (Goodwin 1994: 606): (a) coding, which transforms phenomena observed in a specific setting into the objects of knowledge that animate the discourse of a profession; (b) highlighting, which makes specific phenomena in a complex perceptual field salient by marking them in some fashion; and (c) producing and articulating material representations.

Generally speaking, these practices are rooted in a notion of context which emphasizes the figure–ground relation (Duranti and Goodwin 1992). At another level, the categorization and representation associated with institutional discourse are also a reflection of differences in knowledge structure between professionals and clients (Collins 1987). For Agar (1985), there are not only two distinctly different interpretative systems—'institutional frames' and 'clients' frames'—but there is also a lack of fit between these frames. On the occasion of competing definitions of the situation, it is the institutional definition which often prevails. In the healthcare setting, for example, the difference between what Mishler (1984) calls the 'voice of medicine' and the 'voice of lifeworld' becomes marked and it is the 'voice of medicine' which is consequential. Central to this asymmetry of knowledge is the notion of recontextualization. As Cicourel (1983: 236–7) observes, patients often code information within a particular semantic domain using a 'content-based abstraction strategy' (and in a narrative style which includes feelings and emotions). Professionals and institutions, on the other hand, tend to map clients' information into a different symbol system which 'employs formal language abstraction.' Lifeworld conditions are thus transformed into abstract categories and, by extension, legitimated.

A further aspect of recontextualization involves the transformation of spoken interaction to written records in various professional settings. Note that institutions rely heavily on written language, in particular, medical consultation, social work, police interrogation, courtroom trial, psychiatry, etc. In the police interrogation setting, Jönsson and Linell (1991) point out that the written report is marked by a clearly elaborated narrative structure and a legally relevant language. Recontextualization here involves changes from vagueness to precision; from relative incoherence to coherence and a clear chronology; from emotionality to an objectively identified sequence of events and actions. As Garfinkel (1967) asserts, in professional settings records serve specific functions and are targeted at specific readers: there are 'good organizational reasons for "bad" clinical records.'

5. Asymmetrical Interactional Routines in Institutional Settings

Beyond the threshold of linguistic and stylistic features, and the differential distribution and recontextualization of knowledge among clients and professionals, information exchange in institutional settings is characterized by an asymmetry which is realized through interactional dominance: forms of address, amount of talk, and distribution of conversational rights (turn-taking, question–answer sequences, patterns of interruption).

If we take the systematic organization of turn-taking in conversation (see *Conversation Analysis*) as the norm (Sacks et al. 1974), then turn-taking patterns in the courtroom (Atkinson and Drew

1979), in the classroom (Sinclair and Coulthard 1975), and in news interviews (Heritage and Greatbatch 1991) are distinctively different: 'It is notable that these settings all involve the production of "talk for an overhearing audience"' (Heritage and Greatbatch 1991: 96). In sum, audience participation is controlled through turn design.

Turns constituted in question–answer sequences have been identified as a distinct parameter of institutional discourse. It may be possible to rank different institutional settings by type or question–answer sequence. For instance, the question–answer sequence is at its extreme in any kind of interrogation situation (courtroom, police, customs, immigration, etc.). Cross-examinations in courtroom settings operate with a prespecified speech-exchange system where each turn is either a question or an answer (Atkinson and Drew 1979). Questions are formulated in order to constrain and influence what the witness can or cannot say in reply, and by analyzing such exchanges it can be shown that in most cases the witness is positioned or encouraged simply to confirm statements. In medical-consultation settings, doctors typically ask a string of questions prefaced by *and* in a procedural manner to seek information from patients in order to arrive at a diagnosis. West (1984) reports that in doctor–patient communication, 91 percent of questions are initiated by doctors and only 9 percent by patients (see *Doctor–Patient Language*). In news interviews, interviewers start with a prefatory statement which establishes the context for a subsequent question. Interviewees withhold their response until a question is posed.

Prevalence of question–answer sequences in certain distributive patterns is not the only form of interactional asymmetry in institutional discourse. The right to interrupt (followed by topic shifts) is another mode of control. Other interactional features which constitute institutionality and which index the asymmetrical nature of the interaction include the absence, for example in talk used in meetings, of response tokens and backchannel cues, such as *mm hm, yes, oh, really, did you* (Boden 1994).

6. Discourse Strategies and Sociopragmatic Parameters of Institutional Discourse

If we adopt a view of language as action, the felicity and sincerity conditions associated with speech acts can be linked to the fact that institutional members are invested with authority and legitimacy. As Bourdieu (1991) (see *Bourdieu, Pierre*; *Symbolic Power and Language*) rightly points out, to think about speech acts in purely linguistic terms is to undermine the authority bestowed upon language by factors external to it. In this respect, the stylistic (linguistic and interactional) features are tied up with discourse strategies both at the levels of situated encounters and broader sociopolitical structures.

With regard to situated unequal encounters, Thomas (1985) suggests that certain pragmatic features (see *Pragmatics and Sociolinguistics*) are characteristic of the speech of dominant participants, while they are systematically absent from that of the subordinate participants. She calls these strategies 'metapragmatic acts' (illocutionary force indicating devices [IFIDs]; metapragmatic comments; upshots and reformulations), which dominant participants use to make explicit reference to the intended pragmatic force of their own or their subordinates' utterances. Metapragmatic acts, in explicating the communicative intent, can potentially remove the possibility of negotiating interactional outcomes. In conversational (equal) discourse, within Brown and Levinson's (1987) model of face-work and politeness (see *Politeness*), IFIDs occur in what they call 'costly-to-Speaker situations.' By contrast, in unequal discourse IFIDs occur in 'costly-to-Addressee situations.' The subordinate participant (that is the witness or defendant in court-room settings) is often forced to make on-record statements (which may be costly to himself/herself) through a carefully designed question–answer sequence.

In situations of potential conflict, the dominant speaker counters the challenge by demonstrating the necessary felicity conditions (appeal to official position, institutional procedure; rights and authority attached to position of speaking, etc.). This links with roles, modes of speaking, and face-management in institutional contexts (cf. Goffman's (see *Goffman, Erving*) notion of 'footing' and 'participant structure' in relation to information exchange; Goffman 1981). Participants in institutional settings occupy different role categories and they signal movement between available role categories linguistically using 'contextualization cues' (Gumperz 1982).

As with Brown and Levinson's principles of politeness, the Gricean maxims of cooperation also apply differentially in institutional settings. For instance, the maxim of manner is often violated in institutional discourse (jargons, complex syntax, etc.). Maxims of quantity, quality, and relevance are generally contested to a point at which distorted communication and noncooperation can be said to be characteristic features of institutional discourse (Habermas 1984, Harris 1995, Sarangi and Slembrouck 1992, 1996).

7. Language, Ideology and the Institutional Order

The surface-level realizations of institutional discourse (both stylistic and interactional) need to be accounted for with reference to social constructionism (Berger and Luckmann 1967, Herzfeld 1992) and, more generally, in the context of social theoretical accounts of institutional order (Foucault 1971, 1979, Weber 1930, 1947). Weber, for instance, outlines the following principles underlying institutional activities; habitualization; depersonalization; economic rationality; norms; rules and procedures; neutrality. This suggests a kind of rigor about institutional discourse; however, from a critical perspective, discourses are to be seen as social practices which are subject to change over time. Foucault's historical accounts of institutionalization of health and illness, normality and deviance, etc., make the point about the reconfiguration of institutional orders of discourse; see also the thesis about 'the colonization of the lifeworld' put forward by Habermas (1989), which raises the issue about the private–public distinction with regard to language use (Sarangi 1995).

At another level, institutional discourse is increasingly being conversationalized (in terms of simulation of equality and informality) as a means for maintaining strategically the power differential between social groups (Fairclough 1992). Using critical discourse analytic methods, we can detect how local discursive changes are mapped onto broader sociopolitical events and vice versa. Here Giddens' (1984) model of duality of 'structure' and 'structuration,' which goes beyond the juxtaposition of the micro and the macro, is extremely useful.

In sum, as we have seen, institutional language is not an object which can be readily categorized using linguistic and interactional markers. Even informal, conversational diversions become embedded in institutional discourse and go on to confirm the predominance of the institutional way of thinking and doing, despite the choice of code and style. One is tempted to ask the question: does the Plain English Campaign, with its call for simplifying institutional language, actually amount to less bureaucracy with less bureaucratic language? Or, does it act as a further strategy to make the bureaucratic machinery less transparent (despite intentions that are opposite to this)? While paying attention to discursive shifts within and across institutional and professional settings over a period of time, it is also important to aim to consolidate recent findings about the institutional dimension of discourse in general. There are three possible directions for future research. First, there is a need for an analytic distinction between institutional and professional modes of talk, which would complement the growing number of studies devoted to institutions/professions versus clients (Sarangi and Roberts 1999). Second, a reassessment of various methodological frameworks (genre analysis, conversation analysis, [critical] discourse analysis, and corpus analysis) is necessary in light of our understanding of what constitutes institutional discourse. Third, and more specifically in the context of research in pragmatics, the pragmatic theories of face, politeness, cooperation, and relevance need to move beyond the speaker-oriented dyadic models of interaction, and at the same time become grounded in broader sociocultural parameters (e.g., power, inequality) which impinge on the study of institutional discourse.

See also: Doctor–Patient Language; Medical Language; Language in the Workplace; Discourse in Cross-linguistic and Cross-cultural Contexts.

Bibliography

Agar M 1985 Institutional discourse. *Text* **5**(3): 147–68
Alatis J, Tucker G (eds.) 1979 *Language in Public Life*. Georgetown University Press, Washington, DC
Atkinson J M, Drew P 1979 *Order in Court: The Organization of Verbal Interaction in Judicial Settings*. Macmillan, London
Atkinson J M, Heritage J (eds.) 1984 *Structures of Social Action: Studies in Conversation Analysis*. Cambridge University Press, Cambridge, UK
Berger P, Luckmann T 1967 *The Social Construction of Reality: A Treaty in the Sociology of Knowledge*. Penguin, Harmondsworth, UK
Bhatia V 1993 *Analysing Genre: Language Use in Professional Settings*. Longman, London
Boden D 1994 *The Business of Talk: Organizations in Action*. Polity Press, Cambridge, UK
Boden D, Zimmerman D (eds.) 1991 *Talk and Social Structure*. Polity Press, Cambridge, UK
Bourdieu P 1991 *Language and Symbolic Power*, edited with an introduction by Thompson J B, trans. Raymond G, Adamson M. Polity Press, Cambridge, UK
Brown P, Levinson S 1987 *Politeness: Some Universals in Language Usage*, 1st edn. 1978. Cambridge University Press, Cambridge, UK
Cicourel A 1983 Hearing is not believing: Language and the structure of belief in medical communication. In: Fisher S, Todd A D (eds.) *Discourse and Institutional Authority: Medicine, Education and Law*. Ablex, Norwood, NJ, pp. 221–39
Coleman H (ed.) 1984 Language and work 1: Law, industry, education. Special issue *International Journal of the Sociology of Language* **49**
Coleman H (ed.) 1985 Language and work 2: The health professions. Special issue *International Journal of the Sociology of Language* **51**
Collins J 1987 Conversation and knowledge in bureaucratic settings. *Discourse Processes* **10**: 303–19
di Pietro R J (ed.) 1982 *Linguistics and the Professions*. Ablex, Norwood, NJ
Douglas M 1986 *How Institutions Think*. Syracuse University Press, New York
Drew P, Heritage J (eds.) 1992 *Talk at Work: Interaction in Institutional Settings*. Cambridge University Press, Cambridge, UK
Duranti A, Goodwin C (eds.) 1992 *Rethinking Context: Language as an Interactive Phenomenon*. Cambridge University Press, Cambridge, UK
Fairclough N 1992 *Discourse and Social Change*. Polity Press, Cambridge, UK
Fisher S, Todd A D (eds.) 1983 *The Social Organization of Doctor–Patient Communication*. Center for Applied Linguistics, Washington, DC
Fisher S, Todd A D (eds.) 1986 *Discourse and Institutional Authority: Medicine, Education and Law*. Ablex, Norwood, NJ

Foucault M 1971 *L'ordre du discours*. Gallimard, Paris
Foucault M 1979 *Discipline and Punish: The Birth of the Prison*, trans. Sheridan A. Vintage, New York
Garfinkel H 1967 *Studies in Ethnomethodology*. Polity Press, Cambridge, UK
Giddens A 1984 *The Constitution of Society: Outline of the Theory of Structuration*. Polity Press, Cambridge, UK
Goffman E 1981 *Forms of Talk*. Blackwell, Oxford, UK
Goodwin C 1994 Professional vision. *American Anthropologist* **96**(3): 606–33
Grice H P 1975 Logic and conversation. In: Cole P, Morgan J L (eds.), *Syntax and Semantics Vol. 3: Speech Acts*. Academic Press, New York, pp. 41–58
Gumperz J 1982 *Discourse Strategies*. Cambridge University Press, Cambridge, UK
Gunnarsson B-L, Linell P, Nordberg B (eds.) 1997 *The Construction of Professional Discourse*. Longman, London
Habermas J 1984 *Theory of Communicative Action, Vol. 1: Reason and the Rationalization of Society*, trans. McCarthy T. Beacon Press, Boston, MA
Habermas J 1989 *The Structural Transformation of the Public Sphere: An Inquiry into a Category of Bourgeois Society*, 1st published 1962, trans. Burger T with Lawrence F. Polity Press, Cambridge, UK
Harris S 1995 Pragmatics and power. *Journal of Pragmatics* **23**(2): 117–35
Heritage J, Greatbatch D 1991 On the institutional character of institutional talk: The case of news interviews. In: Boden D, Zimmerman D (eds.) *Talk and Social Structure*. Polity Press, Cambridge, UK, pp. 93–137
Herzfeld M 1992 *The Social Production of Indifference: Exploring the Symbolic Roots of Western Bureaucracy*. University of Chicago Press, Chicago, IL
Hudson K 1978 *The Jargon of the Professions*. Macmillan, London
Jönsson L, Linell P 1991 Story generations: From dialogical interview to written reports in police interrogations. *Text* **11**: 419–40
Mishler E 1984 *The Discourse of Medicine: Dialectics of Medical Interviews*. Ablex, Norwood, NJ
O'Barr W 1982 *Linguistic Evidence: Language, Power and Strategy in the Courtroom*. Academic Press, New York
Redish J C 1983 The language of bureaucracy. In: Bailey R E, Fosheim R M (eds.) *Literacy for Life: The Demand for Reading and Writing*. The Modern Language Association of America, New York, pp. 151–74
Sacks H, Schegloff E A, Jefferson G 1974 A simplest systematics for the organization of turn-taking in conversation. *Language* **50**(4): 696–735
Sarangi S 1995 Public discourse. In: Verschueren J, Östman J-O, Blommaert J, Bulcaen C (eds.) *Handbook of Pragmatics*. Benjamins, Amsterdam, pp. 1–21
Sarangi S, Roberts C (eds.) 1999 *Talk, Work and Institutional Order: Discourse in Medical, Mediation and Management Settings*. Mouton de Gruyter, Berlin
Sarangi S, Slembrouck S 1992 Non-cooperation in communication: A reassessment of Gricean pragmatics. *Journal of Pragmatics* **17**: 117–54
Sarangi S, Slembrouck S 1996 *Language, Bureaucracy and Social Control*. Longman, London
Sinclair J, Coulthard M 1975 *Towards an Analysis of Discourse: The English Used by Teachers and Pupils*. Oxford University Press, Oxford, UK
Swales J 1990 *Genre Analysis*. Cambridge University Press, Cambridge, UK
Thomas J A 1985 The language of power: Towards a dynamic pragmatics. *Journal of Pragmatics* **9**: 765–83
Weber M 1930 *The Protestant Ethic and the Spirit of Capitalism*, trans. Parsons T, foreword Tawney R H. George Allen and Unwin, London
Weber M 1947 *The Theory of Social and Economic Organization*, trans Henderson A M, Parsons T, introduction Parsons T. Free Press, Glencoe, IL
West C 1984 *Routine Complications: Troubles in Talk between Doctors and Patients*. Indiana University Press, Bloomington, IN
Wheeler S 1969 *On Record: Files and Records in American Life*. Russell Sage, New York.
Wilson J 1989 *On the Boundaries of Conversation*, Pergamon, Oxford, UK

Literary Language

R. Carter

One of the most defining characteristics of literary language is the impossibility of defining it in any simple way. Accounts of literary language are closely bound up with definitions of the term literature itself; and literature is a term which has been and continues to be subject to constant semantic change and redefinition.

Williams (1976) in *Keywords* points to how before the nineteenth century the term literature was used in an inclusive sense to mean 'writing' in the broader definition of written texts such as diaries, essays, letters, or travelogues. (In fact, such meanings continue to the present time when we refer to the literature on dog breeding, or the literature of an academic subject, or travel literature.) Since the nineteenth century, literature (and with it literary language) has acquired a less inclusive, more specialized sense and has come to be associated with imaginative or fictional writing in the main genres of prose, poetry, and drama. Such a definition still has institutional authority insofar as it is sanctioned by universities, school examining boards, and the media establishment. It also carries a distinctly qualitative association with writers and literacy texts being canonized as either major or minor. Within such a definition it is clearly problematic to say that literary language is the language found in literature.

1. Intrinsic and Extrinsic Definitions

Definitions of literary language have tended to be intrinsic rather than extrinsic definitions; that is, there has been a focus on the language itself rather than on the source of the definition or on the institutional or ideological context in which the definition is made. Intrinsic definitions have concentrated on the perceived distinctiveness of literary language.

2. Formalism: Foregrounding and De-automatization

The Russian and Czech formalists were among the first in this century to explore the distinctiveness of literary language stressing above all some of the ways in which literary language can be said to draw attention to itself. One of the formalists' main theories is that of 'de-automatization' or estrangement which accounts for the ways in which literary language is marked when set against the 'norms' of ordinary language use. The notion is explained by the Czech formalist Havránek who uses the term 'foregrounding' to cover the ways in which literary style deviates from a background of normal or automatized language:

> By *automatization* we thus mean such a use of the devices of language, in isolation or in combination with each other, as is useful for a certain expressive purpose, that is, such a use that the expression itself does not attract any attention: ... By *foregrounding*, on the other hand, we mean the use of the devices of the language in such a way that this use itself attracts attention and is perceived as uncommon, as deprived of automatization, as deautomatized ...
>
> (Havránek 1964)

In his classic paper, Mukařovský (1964) argues that poetic language aims at 'the maximum of foregrounding,' that is, 'the aesthetically intentional distortion of linguistic components.'

For Mukařovský, 'The distortion of the norm of the standard is ... of the very essence of poetry.'

Furthermore, Mukařovský extends Havránek's inference that foregrounded usages attract attention to themselves by arguing that this special, 'poetic' language does not communicate in a way which is comparable with the normative, standard language. In fact, its main function is to be self-referring and primarily to communicate about itself:

> In poetic language foregrounding achieves maximum intensity to the extent of pushing communication into the background as the objective of expression, and of being used for its own sake; it is not used in the services of communication, but in order to place in the foreground the act of expression, the act of speech itself.
>
> (Mukařovský 1964)

3. Deviation and Parallelism

According to the formalists two main instances of foregrounding are 'deviation' and 'parallelism.' Deviation occurs when particular rules of grammar or of semantics are broken, as in this example from a poem by Gerard Manley Hopkins:

> There lives the dearest freshness deep down things; And though the last lights off the black West went Oh morning, at the brown brink eastwards, springs—
>
> (*God's Grandeur*)

Good examples of 'parallelism' would include anything which involved repetition. This can range from lexical parallelism as in the following example:

> What is this life, if full of care,
> We have no time to stand and stare.
> No time to stand beneath the boughs
> And stare as long as sheep and cows.
>
> (W. H. Davies *Leisure*)

to a more complete parallelism in which whole structural units are marked by being placed in a relationship of congruent repetition. A striking example of this structural parallelism is found in the first and last stanzas of William Blake's *Tyger* (in which one key word is replaced):

> Tyger, Tyger, burning bright
> In the forests of the night;
> What immortal hand or eye,
> Could frame thy fearful symmetry?

> Tyger, Tyger, burning bright
> In the forests of the night;
> What immortal hand or eye
> Dare frame thy fearful symmetry?

4. Contexts of Reading

There are a number of problems with formalist definitions of literary language. First, norms are difficult to define which in turn makes deviation difficult to measure. Second, to equate deviation with literariness is to suggest that literary language cannot result from adherence to norms, which in certain literary periods was a prerequisite for the creation of patterns of literary language. It is to equate literariness in language only with maximally deviant forms. Third, a context of reading is displaced. What is defamiliarizing stylistically in 1922 may not have the same effects 30 years later when readers have acquired a different set of expectations. Fourth, the opposition of literary and 'normal' or 'ordinary' language or of 'poetic' and 'practical,' everyday language can be deconstructed by pointing out that deviation routinely occurs in discourses such as advertizing, jokes, and newspaper headlines which are not institutionally connected with 'literature.' The main problem with this kind of definition is its focus on the text-immanent, self-referential properties of literary language which are not located within a broader context. H. G. Widdowson points to a possible direction for a more inclusive, extrinsically related definition:

> It was observed in the preceding chapter that although it is quite common to find deviant sentences in literary writing, deviance of this linguistic kind is not a defining feature of literature. What does seem crucial to the character of literature is that the language of a literary work should be fashioned into patterns over and above those required by the actual language system. Whether the components of these patterns are deviant or non-deviant or both is of secondary importance. What I want to suggest now is that the effect of this patterning is to create acts of communication which are self-contained units, independent of a social context and expressive of a reality other than that which is sanctioned by convention. In other words, I want to suggest that although literature need not be deviant as text it must of its nature be deviant as discourse.
>
> (H. G. Widdowson 1975: 47)

5. Speech Act Theories

Accounts of literary language which attempt more boldly to underscore the role of the reader interacting in a sociolinguistic context with the sender of a verbal message are generally termed 'speech act theories' of literary discourse. Speech acts are uses of language which, either directly or indirectly, commit the user or recipient to a particular 'action.'

A basic proposition is that in literature the kinds of conditions which normally attach to speech acts such as insulting, questioning and promising do not obtain. Instead we have quasi- or mimetic speech acts. Ohmann (1971) puts it:

> A literary work is a discourse whose sentences lack the illocutionary forces that would normally attach to them ... specifically, a literary work purportedly imitates (or reports) a series of speech acts, which in fact have no other existence ... Since the quasi-speech acts of literature are not carrying on the world's business—describing, urging, contracting, etc., the reader may well attend to them in a non-pragmatic way and thus allow them to realize their emotive potential ...

Thus, the literary speech act is typically a different kind of speech act—one which involves (on the part of the reader) a suspension of the normal pragmatic functions words may have in order for them to be regarded as in some way representing or displaying the actions they would normally perform. That is, a promise or warning or threat by a character in a novel or by a person in a poem cannot be taken as a literal speech act. No one expects it to have any real-world effect. The statement 'come live with me and be my love' is the first line of a poem, not an invitation to the reader.

The notion of a displayed, nonpragmatic, fictional speech act certainly goes some way towards explaining why we do not read Blake's *Tyger* for information about a species of animal or Wordsworth's *Daffodils* because we are contemplating a career in horticulture. Or why we cannot be guilty of breach of promise when that promise is in a love poem rather than a love letter (see Widdowson 1975, 1992).

However, speech-act or contextualist theories of literary discourse suffer from an essentialist opposition between literary and nonliterary which careful consideration does not really bear out. Pratt (1977), for example, has convincingly demonstrated that nonfictional, nonpragmatic, mimetic, disinterested, playful speech acts routinely occur outside what is called literature. Hypothesizing, telling white lies, pretending, playing devil's advocate, imagining, fantasizing, relating jokes or anecdotes, even using illustrations to underscore a point in scholarly argument, are then, by Ohmann's definition, literary.

6. Literariness in Language

There are thus basic problems in attempting to define literary language in essentialist terms or in terms which presuppose literary and non-literary polarities. As a result some stylisticians (e.g., Carter and Nash 1990, Carter 1999) have preferred to talk of literariness *in* language rather than of literary language, seeing a phenomenon of literary language as a cline or continuum rather than as an exclusive yes/no category. Within such a notion of literariness in language, texts are seen as displaying different degrees of literariness according to a *range* of 'tests' such as: the density of polysemic effects; the displaced character of the interaction between author and reader; the extent of independence of the text from other media (such as pictures, diagrams); the kinds of re-registrations of words and phrases from one context to another; and the density of iconic or representational uses of language. The tests are applied to a variety of texts ranging from car instructional manuals (nonliterary) to a novel by Anthony Burgess (literary) but with several 'intermediate' categories such as advertizing copy, jokes, and travel writing. Carter (1999) relates these notions to creativity in spoken discourse.

It must be recognized, however, that notions of literariness in language are as much in the reader as notions of literary language. They are not therefore objectively verifiable or attestable because they depend for their recognition on the readers who read them. Readers are socially situated and will read according to different ideological positions. Much will also depend on how they have been taught to read for literary language, in as much as literature is what gets taught as such—is the product of a certain kind of reading. In more than one sense therefore literary language is an institutional category and extrinsic definitions serve as validly as intrinsic or essentialist definitions. Literary language may therefore best be seen as a socially and historically variable term with differently positioned readers framing different answers to questions concerning an appropriate definition. A very clear summary of this position is in Fowler (1981).

> To treat literature as discourse is to see the text as mediating relationships between language-users; not only relationships of speech, but also of consciousness, ideology, role and class. The text ceases to be an object and becomes an action or process. This anti-formalist approach is pretty much at odds with received opinion in conventional literary aesthetics. Among my heresies, from this point of view, are a willingness for literary works to be kinetic; denial of their alleged formal autonomy; acceptance of the relevance of truth-values to literature. It is not my purpose in this paper to argue a collision of linguistics and aesthetics, however—as I said, my immediate object is methodological. Furthermore, I shall assert, without offering any formal justification, one other assumption implicit in my position—that is, that no plausible essentialist or intrinsic definition of literature has been or is likely to be devised. For my purpose, no such theory is necessary. What literature is can be stated empirically within the realm of sociolinguistic fact. It is an open set of texts, of great formal diversity, recognized by a culture as possessing certain institutional values and performing certain functions.
>
> (1981: 80–1)

Intrinsic analysis helps to point up these values and functions but will always be a necessary but insufficient condition for a definition of literary language. As stated earlier, literary language is not in any simple sense the language of literature.

See also: Register; Genre; Style.

Bibliography

Carter R A 1999 Common language: corpus, creativity and cognition *Language and Literature* **8**(3): 1–21
Carter R A, Nash W 1990 *Seeing Through Language: An Introduction to Styles of English Writing*. Blackwell, Oxford, UK
Fowler R 1981 *Literature as Social Discourse*. Batsford, London
Havránek B 1964 The functional differentiation of the standard language. In: Garvin P (ed.) 1964 *A Prague School Reader on Esthetics, Literary Structure and Style*. Georgetown University Press, Washington, DC
Mukařovský J 1964 Standard language and poetic language. In: Garvin P (ed.) 1964 *A Prague School Reader on Esthetics, Literary Structure and Style*. Georgetown University Press, Washington, DC
Ohmann R 1971 Speech, action and style. In: Chatman S (ed.) *Literary Style: A Symposium*. Oxford University Press, Oxford, UK
Pratt M L 1977 *Toward a Speech Act Theory of Literary Discourse*. Indiana University Press, Bloomington, IN
Widdowson H G 1975 *Stylistics and the Teaching of Literature*. Longman, London
Widdowson H G 1992 *Practical Stylistics*. Oxford University Press, Oxford, UK
Williams R 1976 *Keywords: A Vocabulary of Culture and Society*. Fontana, London

Media Language and Communication
K. C. Schrøder

The study of media language has not always taken seriously the fact that media language is part of a communicative process. But although many analysts have tended to treat media texts as relatively isolated objects of analysis, they have not (particularly in the areas of news and advertising language) refrained from making strong claims both about the possible motives of the senders in media institutions, and about the potential (ideological) impact of media language upon audiences. More often than not, when media language has been related to its production circumstances in media organizations, or to the audiences to which it is addressed, the focus has been on such behavioral–sociological aspects as journalistic work routines and gate-keeping processes, or on the commercial or ideological effectiveness, rather than on the detailed verbal and visual signifying processes that characterize media messages at all stages from sender to receiver. The 1990s have witnessed a development towards a more holistic perspective on media language, especially with respect to the crucial role of audience reception processes for the potential social influence of the media in contemporary society.

This article deals first, with mass communication as a sociocultural phenomenon, conceptualizing a general framework within which media language can be meaningfully explored. Second, some of the most important approaches to the analysis of media language will be presented: critical linguistics and the analysis of news; semiotic approaches to advertising; discourse analysis and the broadcast media; and sociolinguistic perspectives on media voices. Finally, a concluding section will briefly outline developments towards an empirical pragmatics of media language.

1. The Mass Media as a Process of Communication

Mass communication can be briefly characterized as an institutionalized process encompassing the production, dissemination, reception, and interpretation of public sociocultural discourse (see *Discourse*). Historically, the modern media originate in the parallel emergence of the commercial and industrial bourgeoisie in the economic realm, and of the public sphere in the political realm. The dual role of the early printed press as a vehicle of both commercial and political interests has continued as social and technological development has made possible new types of media in the field of broadcasting. In recent years the emergence of a range of new electronic media and information technologies is heralding a partial convergence of mass-mediated and interpersonal forms of communication, as the mass media become more dialogic (or 'conversationalized' as Fairclough (1995) puts it) and new fora of interpersonal communication emerge on the Internet (Reardon and Rogers 1988, Slevin 2000; see *The Internet and Language*).

Since the 1980s the commercial and political aspects of the media have become increasingly intertwined, as all media are functioning under the necessity of capturing an audience. Consequently, even those (broadcasting) media whose 'public service' status might be thought to exempt them from commercial pressure have had commercialization forced upon them as they have to legitimate their existence by competing for listeners and viewers with commercial media organizations. Increasingly, therefore, the major media institutions address their audiences as both citizens and consumers, establishing a cultural and political forum constituted by a continuum of informative and entertaining genres.

It is only possible to understand the complex opportunities and constraints resulting from these communicative processes if one adopts a holistic perspective on media products. And since the media are above all disseminators of various types of sociocultural signs, it is necessary to approach them from a theoretical perspective that can explain mass communication as a signifying process. Such a broadly semiotic perspective is available in the so-called 'encoding/decoding' model of mass communication (Hall 1980) (see Fig. 1). What this model

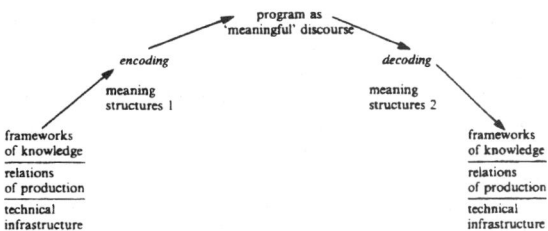

Figure 1. (Reproduced with permission from Hall 1980).

implies is not that any study of a media genre or media coverage of real-world events must research, in addition to the textual aspects, the production and reception stages to which the text belongs. The model should serve to constantly remind analysts that in analyzing a text they are dealing not with a fixed structure of meaning, but with a volatile phenomenon resulting from the codes at the disposal of both the producers and the recipients of the text (see *Code, Sociolinguistic*). And crucially, these codes need not be identical; indeed, since the codes at the disposal of any individual consist of a unique assemblage of the meanings assimilated during that person's life history, the codes of producers and receivers are in principle nonidentical. In fact, some instances when analyses of news discourse accuse the news reports of 'distorting' reality may be explained by a difference between the codes of the analyst and the codes underlying the construction of the news text.

On the other hand, the occurrence of aberrant meanings that do not conform with the intended (so-called 'dominant') meanings should not be exaggerated; after all, people do belong to interpretive communities (constituted by such factors as class, race, gender, age, profession, location, etc.), in which meanings are shared to a large extent (see Schrøder 1994). Therefore, a purely textual analysis can still be justified in generalizing about the meaning structures found, as long as these generalizations are either offered cautiously as potential meanings, or made on behalf of a specific interpretive community whose sign universe makes these meanings plausible.

It has long been conventional wisdom within linguistics that the social context of a type of discourse heavily affects the specific features of that discourse, so as to enable linguists to characterize different variants of use, or registers. 'Media language' is much too diverse in terms of genres to make such a characterization possible, and the same holds for the language of individual media. One should not expect this article to deliver sweeping generalizations about 'the language of television,' or 'newspaper language,' although a skeletal characterization of advertising and some news genres will be attempted.

247

However, some researchers have attempted to generalize about the communicative mode of a medium, though not on the basis of its specific linguistic features. Thus Fiske and Hartley (1978: chap. 6) have defined national television as a 'bardic' medium with the communicative features usually associated with the bards of early European history: oral, dramatic, ephemeral, and communal, as opposed to the literate, linear, permanent, individual mode of print media. Arguing that these modes may correspond to Bernstein's restricted and elaborated codes (of working-class and middle-class language, respectively), they propose that television, with its broader appeal, is inherently more popular and democratic than print media.

2. Approaches to the Study of Media Language

2.1 Critical Linguistics and the Analysis of News

One of the most influential traditions in media language research since the late 1970s is that associated with the work of Roger Fowler, Bob Hodge, Gunther Kress, and Tony Trew (Fowler et al. 1979). Previous studies of the language of newspaper reporting (Crystal and Davy 1969: chap. 7) had analyzed the graphic, syntactic and morphological dimensions of news reports from a purely descriptive surface-structure perspective, leaving out any consideration of semantic and ideological aspects. The work of 'critical linguistics' faced head-on the issue of ideological transmission of social reality through the specific linguistic choices encountered in news reports (Fowler 1991).

The fundamental question which critical linguists are concerned with is the representation of social reality through language. As there can be no knowledge of social reality except through language, the way in which language represents the world to newspaper readers not only reflects, but effectively constructs the categories, frameworks, and values that people use to interpret their social environment. This is basically a Whorfian framework (see *Whorf, Benjamin Lee*) according to which the categories of language impose a mental/ideological grid on speakers' perception of reality. Moreover, since social reality in Western parliamentary democracies is penetrated by class conflict between dominant and dominated social groups, there will be a power dimension in all portrayals of that reality (see *Power and Language*).

Language and ideology are thus inseparable, and given the present relations of ownership and control of the press, newspapers are likely to present a version of social conflict that is ideologically biased in favor of the existing socioeconomic order and its concomitant relations of power and privilege. However, to conceive of news reports as ideological also implies that their partisan accounts of events appear as natural, unquestionable truth, 'the way things are.' It is the task of critical linguistic analysis to unmask the seemingly objective news accounts, to demystify the obscurations and distortions that would pass unnoticed without such analysis. The underlying epistemological project of critical linguistics is thus concerned with the political enlightenment of citizens whose confidence in the truthfulness of the news makes them accept a version of social reality that is not in their best interest. The underlying assumption, though never stated bluntly, is that if informed truthfully about social reality, people will take action in order to create a social order based on a more genuine freedom and equality.

The analytical toolbox which critical linguistics brings to the task of demystifying textual ideology is conceptualized within the framework of Halliday's functional grammar, and operates almost exclusively on the syntactic and lexical levels of textual organization. It is usually presented in the form of a checklist, describing a range of linguistic dimensions in which the choice of one form rather than another has ideological consequences:

(a) *transitivity features*, which belong to the ideational dimension and realize events, states, and processes by combing different types of participants (agent, affected, beneficiary, etc.) with different types of action signified by verbs. (As Fowler (1985) points out, the theoretical foundation of this analytical tool is akin to Fillmore's case grammar);

(b) *modality features*, which point to the interpersonal dimension of language, e.g., through naming conventions, personal pronouns, modal verbs, and adverbials;

(c) *transformations* like nominalization and passivization which, by condensing more complex structures, may obscure the real-world social processes they seemingly portray;

(d) *classification/lexicalization*, i.e., the way in which lexical choice orders reality in a specific manner, for instance, by activating powerful metaphorical meanings;

(e) *coherence,* which deals with the correspondence, or the lack of it, between surface cohesion and semantic, or logical, coherence.

In the following one of the classic analytical examples of critical linguistics will be presented in order to demonstrate how this tradition literally reads off the ideological significance from the linguistic choices and processes in a text (Trew 1979):

> Before Zimbabwean independence a violent clash in then Southern Rhodesia between black demonstrators and

white police was reported in the following manner by the English newspaper *The Times:*

RIOTING BLACKS SHOT DEAD BY POLICE AS ANC LEADERS MEET.
Eleven Africans were shot dead and 15 wounded when Rhodesian Police opened fire on a rioting crowd of about 2000.

In the first part of an extensive analysis of the entire news report Trew notes how the choice of the passive form in the headline puts the syntactic agents of the killing, *police*, in a less focal position. In the next sentence the transformation process is carried one step further as the syntactic agent is deleted, or identified only weakly by implication through the temporal adverbial phrase *when police...*, etc. Second, looking at vocabulary, Trew notes how the choice of the word *riot* establishes a framework which legitimizes police action, because riot is by definition civil disorder requiring police action. Other analyses in this tradition emphasize the significance of metaphorical patterns established by lexical choice, as in a report which couches an antiapartheid demonstration in military terms (Kress 1985).

This type of analysis can be extremely rewarding as it scrutinizes the smallest detail of linguistic expression for its possible ideological implications. However, both in the analytical practice of its inventors and in that of their numerous followers, one finds exaggerated claims about the fatal consequences of agent deletion, passivization, nominalization, etc. First, although analysts often proffer assurance that a single linguistic transformation, like passive-deletion, does not have a one-to-one relationship to a specific ideological position, nevertheless in much analytical practice such individual instances of transformations are treated as if they did have direct ideological effects. Second, the analyses are generally based on erroneous assumptions about the 'non-recoverability' of transformed or deleted linguistic items; surely, on the basis of their overall knowledge of power in the world, their familiarity with yesterday's news reports, and their communicative competence, the average newsreaders will usually have no difficulty reconstructing who did what to whom. And, finally, the fact itself that war metaphors are used in the description of social conflict in no way predetermines whose side you are on. Interestingly, an empirical study of readers' understandings of newspaper articles previously analyzed by Trew found that the ideology of the articles did not determine the readers' view of the event reported, which depended on their life histories as much as on an ideological effect attributable to the news language (Sigman and Fry 1985).

By way of conclusion, then, 'critical linguistic' analyses of a news text are usually based on an *a priori* oppositional ideological position to that from which the report is written, and the linguistic insights are used as weapons in an ongoing ideological struggle. In this sense, the analyst himself appears to speak from a position beyond ideology, for instance as he concludes that a news text just analyzed:

is so far from the truth that only a powerful grip on the press and information and the diligence of the media in resolving the flood of anomalies which they report are adequate to preserve the pretence that the press is truthful.

(Trew 1979: 106)

In some ways Fairclough's (1995, 2000) 'Critical Discourse Analysis' may be seen as a less dogmatic inheritor to the 'critical linguistics' approach, as it tries to cross-fertilize linguistic and sociological insights for the analysis of media discourse.

2.2 Semiotic Approaches to Advertising

The linguistic study of advertising has been motivated by concerns similar to those of critical linguistics described in the preceding section. Accordingly, the critical arsenal of advertising analysis has been shared with critical linguistics as far as the analysis of the verbal elements of advertising is concerned. However, because of its reliance on a combination of verbal and visual components, advertising has posed a particular challenge for textual analysis, which could clearly not afford to ignore the crucial visual/photographic dimension of advertisements. This challenge has been met by adopting the analytical framework developed in general semiotics.

Advertising serves a social function which is intimately connected to the foundation of the capitalist socioeconomic order: its job is to assist manufacturers in recovering profitably and as quickly as possible the capital outlay invested in production. It addresses people in their capacity as consumers, trying to catch their attention in order to motivate them to buy the commodities produced by the manufacturer. This function can be fulfilled in several ways, for instance, by providing factual information to consumers about the merits of a given product. However, for decades manufacturers have had to compete in a market characterized by the near-identity of products within product groups (detergents, cigarettes). It has therefore been necessary to develop advertising strategies which add to the material use-value of a product—or substitute for the material use-value—a symbolic or social use-value which is presented as the main attraction to consumers.

It is these 'suggestive' or 'persuasive' (as opposed to informative) strategies that have been the main target of advertising analysis, as they try to seduce consumers into irrational social behavior. It has thus been demonstrated how advertisements exploit rhetorical strategies in order to present social prestige, sexual success, or family happiness as their unique selling proposition, deluding consumers into attempting to solve the problems emanating from social or psychological tensions by the acquisition of symbol-laden products. Such irrational consumer behavior lies at the heart of a major social malady: 'consumerism,' and it has been the purpose of hundreds of books about advertising to cure this widespread disease by unmasking the pleasant and fascinating verbal and visual surface of advertisements in order to penetrate into the underlying ideological manipulation. The dual aim of these studies has been to protect consumers by (a) provoking legislative intervention that could purify advertising of its manipulative devices and transform advertising into sober information, and (b) educating consumers about the pernicious strategies employed by advertising, so as to equip them with an immunity shield with which to resist the barrage of persuasive messages.

The principal concepts developed to handle the visual aspects of advertisements come from two sources: Roland Barthes's operationalization of the concepts of denotation and connotation for the analysis of photographs (Barthes 1964), and the adoption by many analysts of Peirce's concepts of iconic, indexical, and symbolic signs (Fiske 1990: chap. 3, Vestergaard and Schrøder 1985: chap 2).

Barthes finds it necessary to distinguish between two orders of meaning in a photograph: the 'denotative' level, which carries the innocent, factual meanings available to any observer irrespective of cultural or social background, and the 'connotative' level which carries the visual meanings that a specific culture assigns to the denotative message. Thus Barthes's original example presents an advertisement which denotatively pictures a string shopping bag with a number of items: onions, a green pepper, a can of tomato sauce, and two packets of pasta; the colors are yellow and green on a red background. In a French context this visual message acquires the cultural meaning (connotation) of 'Italianicity,' and as a selling proposition the advertisement offers not just a number of unrelated products, but the whole atmosphere associated with Italian cuisine. In similar fashion other advertisements may offer connotations like sexuality, family happiness, etc. in addition to the material use-value of the product. However, the fact that these connotations are grafted on to the underlying denotations, because carried by the same visual forms, may make them appear as equally naturally given and thus conceal from the consumer the fact that they are really ideological constructs. Consequently, message senders may use connotation to convey taken-for-granted meanings that are shared within a culture, without making these meanings explicitly available for critical scrutiny.

Before leaving the concepts of denotation and connotation it should be mentioned that although the distinction is extremely useful for analytical purposes its theoretical status within semiotics is highly questionable (Eco 1968).

The analytical terms borrowed from Peircean semiotics have to do with the relation between signs and their real-world referents: an 'icon' is a sign that is related to its referent through similarity (a photograph is an iconic sign of the phenomenon it represents, as is also a map); an 'index' is a sign which signifies by existential or physical connection with its object (smoke is an index of fire); and a 'symbol' is a sign whose connection with its object is purely a matter of convention (words and numbers are thus symbols).

All advertisements which have a pictorial element rely on the iconic relationship to real-world objects. This means that such advertisements lead themselves to analysis according to the denotation/connotation dimensions just described. In an extended sense, it is also an iconic relationship that is at work when advertisements employ visual metaphors: it is thus the visual similarity between a lipstick and the male sexual organ that leads some analysts to suggest that the lipstick may act as a phallic metaphor which may allegedly have subconscious effects on the female consumer. Similarly, verbal metaphors, in replacing one word by another which resembles it in meaning, rely on an iconic relationship between meanings; the classic advertising slogan *Put a tiger in your tank* exploits the iconic relationship by equating the (strength of the) tiger with (that of) ESSO gasoline.

In advertisements the indexical relationship appears in the way the product advertised is made visually contiguous to something else (for instance, a lifestyle) which is generally considered to carry favorable connotations. If the advertisement is successful, these connotations will then rub off on the product, although the juxtaposition may be quite arbitrary. The indexical relation may also occur in the form of a metonymic sign, in which a part is made to stand for the whole. For example, in a series of Rothmans cigarette advertisements a whole type of man was metonymically represented by a hairy, tanned hand in an aeroplane cockpit, signifying a masculinity associated with wealth, power, and control.

As is the case with connotations, indexes and metonyms may carry powerful ideological implications because they may seem to be naturally connected to that for which they stand. Their arbitrariness is easily ignored, so that they receive the status of unquestionable truths. This can also be misleading in news reports where the necessarily partial account of real-world events directs one's perception of the whole of those events in specific directions. Thus a metonymic photograph of a single violent incident may convey a wrong impression of a demonstration that was otherwise peaceful and orderly. As this last example indicates, the semiotic framework may also be usefully employed in the analysis of news (Fiske and Hartley 1978: chaps. 6, 8, Hartley 1982).

So far, no mention has been made of the different types of implicit meaning: entailment, presupposition, and expectation. Although their occurrence is by no means restricted to advertising, their frequency of occurrence in this genre makes them into particularly useful analytical categories here. What they have in common is that something more is implied than is actually said. Where they differ is with respect to the origin of their implied meaning: with entailment and presupposition the implicit meaning is textually located, 'between the lines' so to speak. With expectation the implicit assumption arises from the situational context in which the utterance occurs. Advertisements will often use implicit meanings as a device to bring out of focus controversial meanings likely to enhance the advertisement's appeal to the consumer.

Entailment is what one can logically conclude from a statement. Thus when an advertisement promises that after a Pears Foam Bath *the world will seem a nicer place*, it is entailed that the world is usually not such a nice place—something the advertisement would never wish to declare straightforwardly.

Presupposition is what necessarily has to be the case for an utterance to be meaningful at all. Thus, when an ad. headline asks *Which of these continental quilt patterns will suit your bedroom best?* it presupposes both that *all these continental quilt patterns will suit your bedroom* and that *one of these continental quilt patterns will suit your bedroom better than the others*—so it is definitely worth the consumer's while to take a closer look at those quilts!

Expectation builds on the good-reason principle. Whenever something is said, it is assumed that there must have been some reason for saying it. The reason can be that what is said is not always the case, that the addressee would not have been aware of certain facts unless they were pointed out to him/her, and so on. One type of expectation consists of a sentence containing a negative word and an adjective in the comparative: *Beauty wise, value wise, you can't buy better than Rimmel* expects *Rimmel is the best you can buy*, although it actually asserts only *Rimmel is as good as anything else you can buy*. Whenever a negation is used to claim that the product is free of some undesirable characteristic, such a claim makes sense only because the rules of expectation permit us to deduce that competing products do have these characteristics—otherwise why bother to say it at all? Thus to say of a moisturizing cream that *it's not greasy or sticky* raises the expectation that *Other moisturizing creams are greasy and sticky*. While this type of expectation may be relatively harmless to the experienced consumer, others may be more pernicious in their ideological implication. Thus when an advertisement for two new types of canned Chinese food assures prospective buyers that *Here are two orientals you'll want to invite to dinner again and again*, it carries the expectation that, normally, Orientals are not welcome at your table and, by treating this prejudiced attitude as the most natural thing, the advertisement helps to legitimate it.

As the examples show expectation is an inferential process which may be theoretically accounted for in terms of Grice's Cooperative Principle (see *Cooperative Principle*) and Conversational Maxims (see *Conversational Maxims*).

Any observer will testify to the fact that advertisements vary immensely in form. However, they all have to accomplish certain communicative tasks for the advertisers; this makes it possible to suggest that in spite of their formal heterogeneity, ads generally follow the so-called 'AIDA' structure: an advertisement must (a) attract *Attention*, (b) arouse *Interest*, (c) stimulate *Desire*, and (d) get *Action*. In order to accomplish these tasks, advertisements tend to use specific communicative and linguistic strategies. Thus, in order to attract attention and interest, they will typically present visually fascinating material accompanied by speech acts of the *claim* or *promise* types, supported by such rhetorical devices as puns, metaphors, parallelisms, rhyme, alliteration, etc. The stimulation of desire will often be done through informational language in the main text (the so-called '*body copy*'), sometimes supported by celebrity and/or expert statements, appeals to science, and so on. Finally, in order to get action advertisements will usually refrain from flat imperatives urging the consumer to *buy*; they tend instead to rely on a range of indirect invitations to *try, ask for*, or *discover* the product (for a more detailed account for such linguistic strategies, see Vestergaard and Schrøder 1985: chap. 3).

In recent years, more and more scholars have adopted an increasingly skeptical attitude to the supposed effectivity of advertising's rhetorical tricks. It has long been recognized that people distrust the overt claims made by advertising. Possibly, after years of exposure to print and TV advertisements, people are far beyond merely distrusting exaggerated claims. As reception studies have shown, they may well have developed from gullible victims into resourceful skeptics, with an awareness that ads belong to the realm of illusion and should be approached with a mixture of caution and playfulness (O'Donohoe 1997, Schrøder 1997). Aesthetic and rhetorical changes in the advertisements themselves since the 1980s, especially the meta- and intertextual dimensions in advertisements addressing the young generation, may be interpreted as indicators of a communicative change in progress taking advertising beyond the role of the dreaded hidden persuader (Nava and Nava 1990, Cook 1993, Myers 1994).

2.3 Discourse Analysis and the Broadcast Media

Discourse analysis (see *Discourse*) is here used in a wide sense, which includes all approaches to media language that focus on the textual levels above the sentence. The 'applied' perspective on theoretical positions adopted in this article makes it unnecessary to distinguish between the slightly different emphases of the two main traditions that have contributed significantly to the analysis of the larger units of media discourse: on the one hand, coming out of linguistics, discourse analysis proper, which is concerned with the extension of the structural models of linguistic description to the levels beyond the sentence; on the other hand, conversation analysis, coming out of microsociological ethnomethodology, which focuses on speakers' routine accomplishment of everyday verbal interaction (see *Conversation Analysis*).

Both approaches build on a pragmatic speech act perspective (see *Pragmatics and Sociolinguistics*) that makes it natural for them to address the complex interrelation of textual and contextual factors, and not to overemphasize linguistic structure itself. The analysis of news reports within this perspective thus tries to take into consideration the organized conventional knowledge (called 'frames' or 'scripts') (see *Artificial Languages*) which news readers/listeners/viewers bring to the interpretation of the news message. Such frames are held, for instance, to enable recipients to disambiguate headlines, and to interpret temporal adverbial clauses as causal indicators (e.g., ...*when police opened fire* ...). While acknowledging the analytical potency of the categories used by 'critical linguistics' (see Sect. 2.1), discourse analysts tend not to jump to conclusions about ideological impact. In this sense discourse analysis is descriptive rather than evaluative, and the question of audience response is referred to empirical investigation (van Dijk 1983).

One thing that discourse analysts have explored is the possibility of developing a narrative grammar for different textual genres. Van Dijk (1983) proposed the model of the macrostructure of news discourse shown in Fig. 2. These categories are said to be 'prototypical' of news discourse, i.e., they need not all be present in all news reports. It will be seen that this structural model has been extended by analogy from the well-known constituent models of structural–descriptive sentence grammar and transformational

1. Summary/introduction
 1.1 Headlines (with super-, main-, and sub-headlines, and captions)
 1.2 Lead

2. Episode(s)
 2.1 Events
  2.1.1 Previous information
  2.1.2 Antecedents
  2.1.3 Actual events
  2.1.4 Explanation
   2.1.4.1 Context
   2.1.4.2 Background
 2.2 Consequences/reactions
  2.2.1 Events
  2.2.2 Speech acts

3. Comments
 3.1 Expectations
 3.2 Evaluation

Figure 2. The macrostructure of news discourse.

grammar. It may even be represented in a hierarchical tree diagram, and the various categories may be subjected to transformations before they appear in actual news performance in a different order, or with empty slots after the deletion of optional elements. On their passage from underlying structure to actual news text, the narrative categories must be embedded within a 'presentational structure,' consisting of layout features, photographs, and illustrations, etc.

In order for such models to be applicable to broadcast news they have to be supplemented by a consideration of the presentational variables specific to these media, taking into account two communicative axes: that between the various participants in the newsroom (anchorman, co-anchors, interviewer and interviewee, on-location reporters, news footage voice-over, etc.), and that between the aggregate news broadcast and the audience.

As regards the latter, the fact that broadcast news is a type of simulated interaction makes necessary the constant insertion into the news text proper of a range of meta-discursive devices which guide the audience from one element to another (*Our next story deals with* ...) or which identify the status of whoever happens to be speaking (the tags under interviewees' faces; presentations like *We have an eyewitness report from*...). Television news obviously requires a detailed semiotic attention to the visual aspects and their relation to the verbal report (Hartley 1982).

Not surprisingly, discourse analysts have devoted a great deal of interest to the most interactive genre of broadcast news: the news interview (Heritage 1985, Greatbatch 1988). In such studies one looks in vain for an analysis of the possible ideological meanings of utterances; all attention is focused on the interactive dynamics of the interview exchanges as their turntaking patterns are explored through a comparison with those of ordinary everyday conversation in order to illuminate the specific constraints and options that govern the production of such interviews.

Noting that news interviews deviate systematically from ordinary conversation in replacing the latter's question–answer–receipt pattern (*A: How's yer foot?—B: Oh it's healing beautifully—A: Good*) with a question–answer–question sequence, Heritage (1985) explains this difference by the fact that news interviews are produced primarily for an overhearing audience: by avoiding the evaluation inherent in the third-turn 'receipt response' characteristic of normal conversation, the interviewer declines the role of answer recipient while maintaining the role of answer elicitor. The importance of the overhearing audience also manifests itself in the frequent occurrence of so-called 'formulating' utterances (*Interviewer: So you're suggesting that ...*) in which an interviewer may sum up an interviewee's answer, or make explicit potentially controversial implications of the answer. These 'formulations,' performed on behalf of the viewers, serve to maintain the news audience (rather than the interviewer) as primary recipients. In addition, formulations may serve an important function within the institutional framework of public-service broadcasting, which requires its employees to maintain impartiality and balance in the coverage of controversial matters: with a formulation an interviewer can bring attention to a sensitive aspect while ostensibly merely rephrasing what the interviewee has already said.

A completely different type of TV interaction for an overhearing audience is analyzed by Crow (1986), who explores the conversational pragmatics of *Good Sex*, a New York-based phone-in advisory program, a genre which falls between private interpersonal talk and talk explicitly designed for an overhearing audience. The hierarchical structure shown in Fig. 3 (based on Crow 1986) is proposed for this type of program. As with news interview studies, the sole emphasis here is on the conversational dynamics and structural pattern of the televised telephone talk, on the 'rules' which make this type of conversation work and the strategies for handling possible 'breakdowns,' and any interest in the program content as such or the appropriateness of the advice is expressly disclaimed.

Attempts have also been made within discourse analysis to analyze broadcast monologue. Montgomery (1986) takes up the challenge of analyzing disc jockey (DJ) talk, a type of extempore monologue between records whose lack of turntaking sequences makes it hard to isolate the structural units of which it consists. Whereas the monologue of radio news is a third-person genre, DJ talk operates along the axis between first and second person, foregrounding the relationship to the audience. Thus, the DJ of Montogomery's study summons his unknown, invisible listeners by name, region, occupation, star sign, etc. He thereby establishes a direct interpersonal relation to one individual or segment of the audience, for the moment relegating the rest of the audience to the status of overhearing audience, only to shift the boundary between addressee and overhearers with his next summons. He thus potentially involves the entire audience in the I–you relationship. Also, as he simulates a dialogue with his listeners the DJ employs the first utterance of an adjacency pair (see *Conversation Analysis*) such as greetings and question–answer pairs, without any sign of awkwardness that the second is never forthcoming. By thus constantly making his listeners aware of other (invisible) members of the audience and their own potential participation, the DJ seeks to implicate each listener in an imagined community constructed from colloquial monologue. Scannel (1991) presents a diverse range of studies on different types of linguistic interaction encountered in the broadcast media. For recent examples of media discourse analysis based on discursive psychology, see Billig 1995, Potter 1996.

2.4 Sociolinguistic Perspectives on Media Voices

One of the ways in which speech and writing differ from each other lies in the signifier's capacity to function as a social indicator: the material form of speech inevitably acts as a signifier for such categories as gender, class, ethnicity, age, etc., while written language, and in particular print language, is more or less neutral with respect to these social categories of the speaker.

For this reason, print media have historically been more inclined to grant equal access to individuals

Episode		Call			
Sections	Opening	Problem Formulation	Advice	Closing	
Sequences (consisting of 'acts')	Greetings Identification (Compliment)	Pre-question Question	Answer Formulation	Pre-closing Thanking Update request Terminal exchange	

Figure 3. Structure of phone-in TV dialogue (based on Crow 1986).

who did not belong to the 'right' class, gender, race, etc. It has been shown how the selection of the 'right' accent for BBC radio speakers has been related to the wider social and sociolinguistic context in the UK since the 1920s, resulting in the exclusive recruitment until the 1960s of speakers of Received Pronunciation (RP), a nonregional prestige accent. Leitner (1983) thus finds that it was the unspoken assumption for decades, although never proven empirically, that RP was better understood in the UK than any other accent, and that it was the only appropriate accent for radio. This language policy was in line with the paternalist educational aim of public-service broadcasting in the UK, as well as in many other European countries, where the broadcasting intelligentsia felt a need to establish daily in the minds of the public what correct speech should be. From the 1960s, modified versions of RP and some regional accents gradually became acceptable, as social developments towards greater equality and less formality called for a more symmetrical relationship between broadcasters and audiences. The emergence of nonstandard accents in broadcasting news is also related to the increased division of labor in the newsroom and to the competition between channels which have put a premium on immediacy and authenticity, promoting a more popular idiom in pronunciation as well as in vocabulary and syntax (Leitner 1983).

Research on gender and media has looked specifically at the way the female voice has been stigmatized in media discourse: the low social prestige and authority possessed by women has been transferred to the properties of their voice, which has consequently been deemed unsuitable for broadcasting at least until around 1980. Thus a BBC Announcer's Handbook in 1959 stated that 'women's delivery is lacking the authority needed for a convincing newscast' (quoted in Key 1975: 72); in the USA, a TV network president declared in the early 1970s that 'audiences are less prepared to accept news from a woman's voice than from a man's' (quoted in Eakins and Eakins 1978: 106). Similarly, female voices have been used quite rarely for the authoritative-expert voice-overs in TV commercials (Marecek et al. 1975: 160). However, as increasing numbers of women reach the upper echelons of the social hierarchy, the social value attached to their speech (and hence their visibility/audibility in broadcasting) is increasing proportionately.

3. Future Perspectives: Towards a Pragmatics of Media Language

Since the mid-1980s, growing numbers of scholars have begun to question with increasing intensity the validity of the claims made on the basis of textual analysis alone about the ideological impact of media messages on recipients. How valid, for instance, is the insight gained from an elaborate analysis of the metaphorical meaning of a reference in a *Dynasty* episode to 'The Boston Tea Party,' if this soap opera's massive non-American audience decodes this expression as a reference to a hypothetical tea party in the immediate serial past (Schrøder 1988)? Or how could one have anticipated through textual analysis that in Madonna's rock video 'Papa don't preach' the teenage protagonist's decision that I'm keepin' my baby' is taken by white audiences to refer to her facing the prospect of teenage pregnancy, while black audiences take the word 'baby' to refer to the boyfriend her father wants her to give up (Brown and Schulze 1990)?

Such problems cannot just be done away with as if they merely arose from 'misunderstandings' of individual words. It has to be realized that linguistic meanings are not univalent units in an abstract language system as supposed in Saussurean theory, but polyvalent, as held by theorists like Peirce and Voloshinov. It is thus no coincidence that a change of theoretical perspective is emerging where the Peircean definition of the sign is perceived to be more adequate for a science of the life of signs in society, because it accords a crucial role of those who use the signs: 'A sign (...) is something which stands *to somebody* for something in some respect or capacity. It *addresses somebody*, that is, creates in the mind of that person an equivalent sign (...)' (Peirce 1985: 5, emphasis added).

In other words, a Peircean perspective conceptualizes the analysis of media language not within a general, abstract linguistic system where meanings are fixed, and assumed to be mechanically transferred to recipients' minds, but in a communicative context where meanings are only potential until actualized by socially situated human beings (Jensen 1995).

What is being developed is a comprehensive social semiotic where verbal language is conceived in relation to all other socially constituted sign systems, treated as social practices (Halliday 1978). However, analysts differ in their assessment of the theoretical and methodological implications of such a revised perspective. Pateman, for instance, argues that textual analyses of connotations often have an extremely 'hazardous character, inviting the question "How do you know?"' (1983: 187). But as Pateman calls for a revised, more pragmatic perspective which takes into account the 'active comprehension of texts and images,' he nevertheless declines to add an empirical dimension to connotation analysis, fearing that this will 'place the locus of interpretation solely in the receiver, which is just as much an error as to place it wholly in the text' (1983: 200). Others, however, think that the empirical inclusion of senders and receivers is imperative for the analytical credibility of media language research (Deacon et al. 1999, Gavin 1998).

One consequence of the adoption of a holistic social-semiotic perspective on media language will be that in addition to focusing the analytical spotlight on media language itself the analyst must also explore the discursive practices through which media texts are encoded and decoded. This requires the analyst to supplement traditional forms of critical analysis of the media text with ethnography-inspired fieldwork, which then produces new textual objects of analysis in the shape of transcripts of qualitative interviews with media producers and audience members about the meaning processes they engage in (Lindlof 1995). Clearly this new research agenda is no less imbued with theoretical and methodological hazards than that of traditional media language analysis, which may explain the reluctance of media discourse analysts to for instance embark on the kind of audience fieldwork whose necessity they readily acknowledge (Fairclough 1995).

Whether one is interpreting the language of a media text or audience discourse about such a text, it should be remembered that any code or language has embedded within it a vast number of separate codes or languages that are molded by race, class, region, gender, etc.:

> At any given moment of its historical existence language is heteroglot from top to bottom: it represents the coexistence of socio-ideological contradictions between the present and the past, between different epochs of the past, between different socio-ideological groups in the present, between tendencies, schools, circles and so forth, all given a bodily form. These 'languages' of heteroglossia intersect each other in a variety of ways, forming new socially typifying 'languages.'
> (Bakhtin 1981: 291, quoted in Newcomb 1984: 39)

In other words, in a heteroglot society meaning is multiply variable, and any understanding of a text produced by another human being, or social institution, is a translation from that speaker's idiolect into one's own. No textual analysis is exempt from the fact that every decoding is always another encoding.

See also: Advertising; Register; Critical Sociolinguistics.

Bibliography

Bakhtin M 1981 *The Dialogic Imagination*. University of Texas Press, Austin, TX

Barthes R 1964 Rhétorique de l'image. *Communications* **4**: 40–51. English transl. in Barthes R 1977 *Image Music Text*. Fontana/Collins, London

Billig M 1995 *Banal Nationalism*. Sage, London

Brown J D, Schulze L 1990 The effects of race, gender, and fandom on audience interpretations of Madonna music videos. *Journal of Communication* **40**: 88–102

Cook G 1993 *The Discourse of Advertising*. Routledge, London

Crow B K 1986 Conversational pragmatics in television talk: The discourse of 'Good Sex.' *Media, Culture and Society* **8**: 457–84

Crystal D, Davy D 1969 *Investigating English Style*. Longman, London

Deacon D, Fenton N, Bryman A 1999 From inception to reception: The natural history of a news item. *Media, Culture and Society* **21**: 5–31

Dijk T A Van 1983 Discourse analysis: Its development and application to the structure of news. *Journal of Communication* **33**: 20–43

Eakins B, Eakins R G 1978 *Sex Differences in Human Communication*. Houghton Mifflin, Boston, MA

Eco U 1968 *La Struttura Assente*. Valentino Bonipani, Milan, Italy

Fairclough N 1995 *Media Discourse*. Edward Arnold, London

Fairclough N 2000 *New Labour, New Language*. Routledge, London

Fiske J 1990 *Introduction to Communication Studies*. Routledge, London

Fiske J, Hartley J 1978 *Reading Television*. Methuen, London

Fowler R 1985 Power. In: Dijk T Van (ed.) *Handbook of Discourse Analysis*, Vol. 4. Academic Press, London

Fowler R 1991 *Language in the News Discourse and Ideology in the Press*. Routledge, London

Fowler R, Hodge B, Kress G, Trew T 1979 *Language and Control*. Routledge and Kegan Paul, London

Gavin N T 1998 *The Economy, Media and Public Knowledge*. Leicester University Press, London

Greatbatch D 1988 A turn-taking system for British news interviews. *Language in Society* **17**: 401–30

Hall S 1980 Encoding/decoding. In: Hall S, Hobson D, Lowe A, Willis P (eds.) *Culture, Media, Language*. Hutchinson, London

Halliday M A K 1978 *Language as Social Semiotic*. Edward Arnold, London

Hartley J 1982 *Understanding News*. Methuen, London

Heritage J 1985 Analyzing news interviews: Aspects of the production of talk for an overhearing audience. In: Dijk T Van (ed.) *Handbook of Discourse Analysis, Vol. 3*. Academic Press, London

Jensen K B 1995 *The Social Semiotics of Mass Communication*. Sage, London

Key M R 1975 *Male/Female Language*. Scarecrow Press, Metuchen, NJ

Kress G 1985 Ideological structures in discourse. In: Dijk T Van (ed.) *Handbook of Discourse Analysis, Vol. 4*. Academic Press, London

Leitner G 1983 The social background of the language of radio. In: Davis H, Walton P (eds.) *Language, Image, Media*. Blackwell, Oxford, UK

Lindlof T R 1995 *Qualitative Communication Research Methods*. Sage, London

Marecek J, Piliavan J A, Fitzsimm E, Krogh E C, Leader E, Trudell B 1975 Women as TV experts: The voice of authority? *Journal of Communication* **28**: 1

Montgomery M 1986 DJ talk. *Media, Culture & Society* **8**: 421–40

Myers G 1994 *Words in Ads*. Edward Arnold, London

Nava M, Blake A, MacRury I, Richards B (eds.) 1997 *Buy This Book: Studies in Advertising and Consumption*. Routledge, London

Nava M, Nava O 1990 Discriminating or duped? Young people as consumers of advertising/art. *Magazine of Cultural Studies* **1**: 15–21

Newcomb H 1984 On the dialogic aspects of mass communication. *Critical Studies in Mass Communication* **1**: 34–50

O'Donohoe S 1997 Leaky boundaries: Intertextuality and young adult experiences of advertising. In: Nava M, Blake A, MacRury I, Richards B (eds.) *Buy This Book: Studies in Advertising and Consumption*. Routledge, London

Pateman T 1983 How is understanding an advertisement possible? In: Davis H, Walton P (eds.) *Language, Image, Media*. Blackwell, Oxford, UK

Peirce C S 1985 Logic as semiotic: The theory of signs. In: Innis R I (ed.) *Semiotics. An Introductory Anthology*. Hutchinson, London

Potter J 1996 *Representing Reality: Discourse, Rhetoric and Social Construction*. Sage, London

Reardon K, Rogers M E 1988 Interpersonal versus mass media communication. A false dichotomy. *Human Communication Research* **15**

Scannell P (ed.) 1991 *Broadcast Talk*. Sage, London

Schrøder K C 1988 The pleasure of 'Dynasty.' In: Drummond P, Paterson R (eds.) *Television and its Audience*. British Film Institute, London

Schrøder K C 1994 Audience semiotics, interpretive communities and the 'ethnographic turn' in media research. *Media, Culture and Society* **16**: 337–47

Schrøder K C 1997 Cynicism and ambiguity: British corporate responsibility advertisements and their readers in the 1990s. In: Nava M, Blake A, MacRury I, Richards B (eds.) *Buy This Book: Studies in Advertising and Consumption*. Routledge, London

Sigman S J, Fry D L 1985 Differential ideology and language use: Reader's reconstructions and descriptions of news events. *Critical Studies in Mass Communication* **2**: 307–22

Slevin J 2000 *The Internet and Society*. Polity Press, Cambridge, UK

Trew T 1979 Theory and ideology at work. In: Flower R, Hodge B, Kress G, Trew T (eds.) *Language and Control*. Routledge and Kegan Paul, London

Vestergaard T, Schrøder K 1985 *The Language of Advertising*. Blackwell, Oxford, UK

Medical Language

J. Maclean and J. C. Maher

By 'medical language' the lay person usually means the technical terms of medicine. In linguistics, the term medical language is used in a wider sense to refer to the variety of language used by medical personnel in communication with each other and with patients. It therefore includes not only the register of medical terminology, but also the preferred choices of lexis and syntax, typical discourse structures (case histories, operation notes, research articles, etc.), and any other features which are distinctive conventions of the language used in medical contexts.

1. Medical Terminology

Medical terminology is primarily a nomenclature of labeling and description. In this respect it differs from, say, law, where the function of the terminology is to construct through definition a system of concepts. Anatomical parts, physiological processes, symptoms and signs of disease, etc. once identified are given names, which often are descriptive labels. For example, the 'stapes' (Latin *stapes* 'stirrup') is a stirrup-shaped bone in the ear; the 'sublingual nerve' (Latin *sub* 'under,' *lingua* 'tongue') is the nerve under the tongue; 'hematuria' (Greek *hemat-*'blood,' *ur-* 'urine') is blood in the urine. The great majority of medical terms are nouns.

Registers of medical terminology are developed as new terms are introduced for new findings and concepts. This process is most evident when one culture encounters and absorbs the science of another culture so quickly that terms have to be borrowed from the other language. Thus Latin incorporated much terminology from Greek, borrowed at the time of the Roman conquest of Greece, where the Romans found a science of medicine far in advance of their own. Likewise, Japanese borrowed most of its terms for the internal organs from Chinese in the sixth century. More recently, Navajo (*Navajo*), which has a detailed vocabulary for the skeletal system but almost none for the circulatory and nervous systems, has had to borrow medical terminology extensively from English.

From the fifth to the seventeenth century, Latin was the European lingua franca for medicine as for other fields of knowledge. To the Greek-derived terms already predominant in early medical Latin (e.g., *asthma*) the anatomists added terms from lay Latin (e.g., *pollux*). As the science developed, new terms were created in all fields of medicine, either making direct use of Latin and Greek words (e.g., Latin *scapula humeri*; Greek *anorexia*) or creating new words from Latin and Greek roots (e.g., 'cardiopulmonary').

In the second half of the twentieth century English emerged as the predominant lingua franca in medicine. As was the case in medical Latin, in English the register of medical terms contains lay terms (e.g., the nouns 'heart,' 'liver,' 'nerve'). These exist alongside terms of Latin and Greek origin (e.g., the adjectives 'cardiac,' 'hepatic,' and 'renal'). English is used for some new terms, particularly for the naming of syndromes (e.g., 'acquired immunodeficiency syndrome'), but Latin and Greek roots continue to be used for new terms in the biological sciences and even in clinical medicine (e.g., *status anginosus*). Terms formed from Latin and Greek words or roots predominate in most European languages (e.g., English 'hepaticotomy'; German *Hepatikotomie*; Spanish *epaticotomia*). Etymological studies indicate that words derived from Greek or Latin account for as much as 90 percent of the medical terminology in international use today.

1.1 Morphology of English Terms Derived from Latin and Greek

Words taken directly from Latin and Greek generally retain their Latin and Greek plural forms: e.g., 'conjuctiva, PL conjuctivae'; 'bacillus, PL bacilli'; 'metastasis, PL metastases'; 'arthritis, PL arthritides'; 'dendron, PL dendra.'

Many Latin and Greek derived medical terms consist of two roots joined with the so-called combining -*o*-, often with an affix. Combinations are made with two noun roots (e.g., 'musculoskeletal') or with an adjective and a noun root (e.g., 'microcephaly').

Prefixes can be Greek and Latin prefixes (e.g., 'anemia, exophthalmos, diverticulitis') or Greek and Latin prepositions (e.g., 'hypokalemia,' 'hypertension', 'diarrhea,' 'epigastric,' 'pericardium,' 'transurethral'). Suffixes include: '-itis' = inflammation (e.g., 'appendicitis'); '-osis' = abnormal condition, often an excessive quantity (e.g., 'erythrocytosis'); '-algia' = painful condition (e.g., 'neuralgia'); '-oma' = tumor (e.g., 'melanoma'); '-tomy' = cutting (e.g., 'tonsill-ectomy').

The last syllable of the original Latin or Greek root is sometimes dropped from the first of two combining forms (e.g., 'tenosynovitis' instead of 'tenontosynovitis'; 'hemochromatosis' instead of 'hematochromatosis'; 'volumetric' instead of 'volumometric'; 'pulmotor' instead of 'pulmonomotor'; 'contra-ception' instead of 'contraconception'; and even 'urinalysis' instead of 'urine analysis').

The formation of adjectives from nouns ending in '-ology' is different in American and British English. For example, American English has 'biologic,' 'pathologic,' and 'pharmacologic' compared with British English 'biological,' 'pathological,' and 'pharmacological.'

1.2 British English Spelling of Terms Derived from Latin and Greek

British English retains the spelling *ae* ('anaemia, aetiology,' etc.) and *oe* ('oedema, diarrhoea,' etc.), whereas American English has replaced both *ae* and *oe* with *e* ('anemia,' 'etiology,' 'edema,' 'diarrhea'). The anomalous form foetus (Latin *fetus*) found in many British English texts and dictionaries presumably results from overgeneralization of the British–American spelling contrast.

1.3 Eponyms

A characteristic feature of many compound medical terms is the inclusion of the name of the physician, surgeon, or medical scientist who first recognized, discovered, proposed, or invented the entity named by the term. Thus we have: 'Bell's palsy,' 'a Colles' fracture,' 'Coombs' test,' 'the Epstein-Barr virus,' 'Golgi cells,' 'Kaposi's sarcoma,' 'Koplik's spots,' 'Kussmaul breathing,' 'the Laurence-Moon-Beidl syndrome,' 'McBurney's point,' 'Parkinson's disease,' 'Romberg's sign,' 'Wernicke's encephalopathy,' 'Willett forceps,' and many more.

In a related set of terms, a condition typical of a person or a group retains that name whatever the context. Examples are: 'tennis elbow'; 'housemaid's knee'; 'farmer's lung'; 'Legionnaires' disease.'

Eponymic terms cause difficulties in alphabetical indices, partly because attribution may be made to different physicians, or variously to one worker or co-workers (as in 'Dorothy Reed cells,' also called 'Sternberg–Reed cells'). Terms including both names of one person (as in 'Dorothy Reed cells') are also a problem to place alphabetically. There is inconsistency in the use of '*s*: e.g., both 'the Babinski response' and 'Babinski's response' are found. Attempts are being made by some editorial bodies to replace some eponymic terms and to standardize others. In particular, some recommend dropping the '*s* in all eponymic terms.

1.4 Noun Compounding

Noun compounding is a common feature of medical terminology in some languages, the English equivalent being the use of nouns to modify a head noun. Examples are the Japanese *ketseki-gyoko-inshi*, equivalent to the English 'blood clotting factor,' and German *Antigen-Antikörper-Reaktion* and *Blutkörperchensenkungsgeschwindigkeit*, equivalent to the English 'antigen antibody reaction' and 'erythrocyte sedimentation rate.'

1.5 Metaphor in Medical Terminology

Medical terminology, being descriptive, makes much use of metaphor. Examples from food are: 'orange-peel skin,' 'café-au-lait spots,' 'a strawberry nevus,' 'a chocolate cyst'; from architecture: *lumen* (Latin 'threshold'), 'the abdominal wall,' 'the aortic arch'; and from clothing: *tunica intima* (Latin 'inner garment'), *sinus* (Latin 'fold containing a cavity'), 'glove-and-stocking sensory loss.' A 'capillary vessel' is a container like a hair (Latin *capillus* 'hair'). The shapes of the following lesions are clear from their names: 'stellar angioma,' 'spider nevus,' 'butterfly rash,' and 'splinter hemorrhage.'

2. International Medical Communication

English is now widely employed as a medium of instruction in medical schools in countries where it is a second or foreign language. It is the main medium for medical textbooks, journals, and abstracting indexes, and is by far the most used language in international medical meetings (Maher 1986).

The English used in medical education and research shares many characteristics with the English used in any academic scientific field. The lexis, apart from medical terminology, is typically 'subtechnical academic': it has been pointed out, for example, that physiological processes do not 'happen'; they 'occur.' Studies of the genre of the English language research report (Swales 1990) indicate the typical discourse moves and their linguistic exponents; the distribution and frequency of the passive voice; linguistic evidence of strategies of politeness and hedging in discussion; and the functions of verb tense choice in expressing authorial attitude when citing other work. Complex noun phrases have been noted in several studies to be a particularly striking feature of medical writing, especially complex premodification (e.g., 'the *in situ* saphenous vein bypass'; 'carbohydrate-stimulated high oxidative shunt enzyme tissue levels').

Medical writing is distinguished from other academic writing in the degree of control exercised by eminent medical editors and writers (Council of Biology Editors 1983, Huth 1987). The so-called Vancouver style format is now the recognized standard information structure for medical research reports. Authoritative lists or nomenclatures exist to encourage international consistency in the use of medical terminology. Standardized units of measurement are advocated. Advice is also given, perhaps with less success, on 'good medical style': i.e., avoiding pomposity, slang, cumbersome noun phrases like those quoted above, dangling participles, and overuse of the passive.

3. Medical Language in Hospitals

Communication networks and other procedural aspects of communication in hospitals have been much studied, but there are comparatively few studies of the language used in the communication of medical information.

Communication about patient care is standardized in the hospital record system in reports, forms, and charts, all with well-defined information structures.

Pathology reports and operation notes have been analyzed with respect to syntactic and grammatical features, but little has been written about the case report, which is the central report in hospital medicine. A case report is divided into sections on the presenting complaint, past history, investigations, diagnosis, management, and outcome, each section having typical linguistic exponents. For example, in the presenting complaint section there typically occur complex time and tense expressions, listing of symptoms, and standardized collocations (e.g., 'presented with,' 'complained of,' was admitted with'). The examination and investigation sections are typically in past time, in simple or coordinate sentences, presenting both negative and positive findings, and utilizing a different restricted set of collocations (e.g., 'on examination,' 'no abnormality was found,' 'microscopy revealed').

The medical language used in hospitals reflects the working environment with semitechnical words like 'trolley,' 'syringe,' and 'ward round'; verbs and verbal collocations denoting clinical actions, e.g., 'to pass a tube,' 'to insert a drain,' 'to withdraw a catheter,' 'to set up a line,' 'to scrub up'; certain prepositional collocations, e.g., 'on admission,' 'on discharge,' 'on auscultation,' 'on palpation'; 'at laparotomy,' 'at delivery,' 'at autopsy.' Abbreviations are common: e.g., 'A & E,' 'OPD,' and 'CCU' are the Accident and Emergency Department, the Outpatient Department, and the Coronary Care Unit. Abbreviations are extremely common in case notes, for symptoms (e.g., 'D & V' for diarrhea and vomiting), signs (e.g., 'JVP' for jugular venous pressure), investigations (e.g., 'LFTs' for liver function tests), diagnoses (e.g., 'ca. Br.' for bronchial carcinoma) and so on. Report forms of all kinds further encourage the use of abbreviations, which are transferred to speech: e.g., 'we had a DOA night' (i.e., dead-on-arrival); 'it might be an MI' (i.e., a myocardial infarction); 'her Alk. Phos. is raised' (i.e., alkaline phosphatase level); 'have you done the tprs yet, nurse?' (i.e., the temperature, pulse, and respiration rates). Form-filling is also the source of such expressions as 'she's got query appendicitis' and 'urine three plusses.'

Medical writers have commented, usually with disapproval, on the creation of verbs from nouns: e.g., 'laparotomize' from 'laparotomy,' 'diurese' from 'diuresis,' 'hemoptysize' from 'hemoptysis,' 'endoscope' from 'endoscopy.' They have also noted the 'sloppy' use of medical terminology in expressions like 'the diabetic leg' and 'a severe pathology.'

Nonstandard language is frequent. It is ephemeral, jocular, and sometimes macabre (e.g., *gorked out* 'comatose'; *GOK* 'God only knows'; *a crumbly* 'an old person'). It has been suggested that medical slang may relieve feelings of distress in the face of sickness and pain, and, together with the technical jargon, may serve to reinforce the bonding of the members of the group.

4. Doctor–Patient Language

In hospitals in many parts of the world, notably Africa, the Middle East and the Indian subcontinent, different languages are used for speaking with patients and speaking with colleagues: the local language when speaking to patients and the official hospital lingua franca (usually English) for communicating with medical staff and for medical records.

However, even in an English-speaking environment, doctors use different varieties of English with patients and with colleagues. Medical terminology represents shared expert knowledge, and is not normally appropriate for communicating with patients. Thus, doctors speaking to patients are likely to say: e.g., 'thighbone' rather than 'femur'; 'whooping cough' rather than 'pertussis'; 'navel' rather than 'umbilicus'; 'bend' and 'straighten' rather than 'flex' and 'extend.' A few terms are specific to this variety of English (e.g., 'front passage' instead of 'vagina'; 'waterworks' instead of 'urinary system'; and 'motions' instead of 'feces'). These refer to body parts and functions for which other terms are either inappropriately medical or inappropriately vulgar. The difference between expert and lay knowledge leads to different meanings for some words: e.g., 'anxiety' and 'shock' have more stable and specific meanings in medical terminology than in the patient's language.

See also: Doctor–Patient Language; Register.

Bibliography

Council of Biology Editors 1983 *CBE Style Manual. A Guide for Authors, Editors and Publishers in the Biological Sciences*, 5th edn. American Institute of Biological Sciences, Washington, DC
Dirckx J H 1976 *The Language of Medicine: Evolution, Structure and Dynamics*. Harper and Row, New York
Huth E 1987 *Medical Style and Format*. ISI Press, Philadelphia, PA
Maher J C 1986 The role of English as an international language of medicine. *Applied Linguistics* 7: 41–52
Swales J M 1990 *Genre Analysis. English in Academic and Research Settings*. Cambridge University Press, Cambridge, UK

Register
W. Downes

'Register' describes variation in language according to use. It captures the intuition that there are functionally distinct varieties of language in such contexts of situation as sport, science, or advertising. Such variation contrasts with variation by user, or dialectal variation. Literary texts are often characterized by an allusiveness to nonliterary registers. This makes relevant the social meanings of the language alluded to, deploying its context into the text. Such 'reregistration' (Carter and Nash 1983: 129) is arguably central both to intertextuality (the interdependence of a text on all those that have gone before it) and the literariness of literary texts. The question remains open whether literature itself defines a register.

1. Register as Meaning Potential

Although register is sometimes used loosely in sociolinguistics, stylistics, and applied linguistics to label a 'way of speaking,' the term itself is particularly associated with the systemic–functional school of linguistics and with the functionalist stylistics associated with that school (for references see Birch 1989: 25–9, 139–45, Birch and O'Toole 1988: vi–ix, 1–11). Thus, the notion finds its place within the linguistics of M. A. K. Halliday (see *Halliday, Michael Alexander Kirkwood*) and his associates and has undergone considerable development as a technical term. In its early use a situation type was claimed to determine uniquely frequencies of linguistic forms, producing, appropriately to the situation, a characteristic textual pattern of superficial lexical and grammatical items (see Halliday et al. 1964: 87–98). It is worth noting at the outset that register has always been a probabilistic entity and therefore is, like 'dialect,' vague in the absence of quantifiable situational parameters. It nevertheless remains an intuitively valuable analytic tool (see *Dialect and Dialectology*).

In *Language as Social Semiotic* (Halliday 1978) the concept of register has a role in a much more comprehensive sociological linguistics. The strength of this theory is that it connects text to the social system and the context of culture. A text is an interactive semantic process. It is interpreted as an instantiation of meanings, semantic choices from the totality of potential contrasts of meaning encoded in grammar but which originate in social life. An analyst can interpret these social meanings and their historical–ideological context of culture in any text. Literary and nonliterary texts are the same in this respect.

We begin with the social system, since it is here meanings are made. The multidimensional sources of human significance are interactively created and exchanged in semiotic systems. This 'making of meaning' occurs in social institutions and their recurring social contexts or situation types. Such situations are themselves semiotic constructs—we can recognize them and what they 'mean' within our culture. Each type has three dimensions relevant to potential meanings (1):

> field = social activity performed
> tenor = social roles enacted
> mode = the role of language in the situation. (1)

'Mode' includes both channel (written, spoken, etc.) and genre (literary, 'narrative,' 'lyric,' etc., and nonliterary, 'interview,' 'casual conversation,' 'argument,' etc.) (see also *Genre*). The genres, or rhetorical norms, available in a culture precode language to perform the social activities and roles of each situation type and thus enable language to play the constitutive part which the social system demands of it as regards 'field' and 'tenor.'

The language system functions in these contexts of situation and, Halliday argues, it has been shaped to do so. 'What can be meant' falls into three functional domains which serve the three aspects of situations. Language functions (2):

> ideationally = to represent experience
> interpersonally = to enact social relationships
> textually = to create text relevant to situations. (2)

Each function interprets the 'meaning potential'— 'what can be meant'—in a given situation type. Out of the whole range of potential semantic contrasts, speakers statistically enact only *some* in a situation. This situationally constrained set of options is a register; 'the necessary mediating concept that enables us to establish the continuity between a text and its sociosemiotic environment' (Halliday 1978: 145). By analyzing these meaningful choices, as realized in the grammar and lexis instanced in a text, we can interpret its register and thus how the text is functioning to both enact and create a social situation.

2. The Interpretation of Text

The above theory provides a framework for the statement of ideational, interpersonal, and textual meanings. It is the task of linguistic analysis to analyze such patterns of encoded choice. But a reader's interpretation also involves contextualization of textual patterning at a higher level. This process is relative to the reader's social positioning, critical practices, and ideological interest within the context of culture. Some 'higher level semiotics' of the culture (see Sect. 1 above) become relevant. A literary text, produced and consumed in situations within the social institution of 'literature,' also makes relevant a 'literary universe of discourse' and 'literary norms and assumptions' including the body of other literary and literary critical texts. It is the job of the linguist to describe this process of interpretation— how a text might be understood. And although subjective relativity and hence indeterminacy of readings is normal, it is also assumed that there is some community of the plausible which is replicable across readers based on common linguistic and cultural resources (Halliday 1971, Birch 1989).

There is no mechanical procedure for interpreting, merely various heuristic practices. However, some textual patterns are prominent. If this prominence figures in interpretation in terms of higher level semiotics, then it is seen as 'motivated prominence' or 'foregrounding' (Halliday 1971; see also *Style*).

The analyst approaches foregrounded patterns first of all in terms of the choices they exhibit according to the functions of language. How is a world represented (see *Representation*)? How does the speaker reveal him or her self and manipulate the addressee? How does the 'texture' of the patterning relate it relevantly to itself, its cohesion, and to its contexts of situation and culture, its coherence in terms of higher level semiotics? The analyst intertwines description with higher level interpretation, each guiding the other.

Most analyses concentrate on the 'representativeness' of a text world in terms of the semantics of processes and participants (see *Representation*). Halliday (1971) studies Golding's *The Inheritors* in this way and contrasts the represented world of a Neanderthal community with that of early man. In an influential article, Burton (in Carter 1982: 194–214) subjects a passage from Plath's *The Bell Jar* to a similar analysis and pointedly interprets the foregrounded representation in terms of the higher level semiotic of feminism. Two articles which survey this approach are Kennedy (in Carter 1982: 83–99) who analyzes Conrad's *The Secret Agent* and Joyce's *Two Gallants*, and Simpson (1988) where the opening of Le Carré's *The Little Drummer Girl* is treated. Much of this analytic work has a usefully pedagogic orientation (see Carter 1982, especially the Introduction: also Brumfit and Carter 1986, Carter and Simpson 1988). In the work of Fowler (1981, 1986) we find emphasis on all three functional domains but increasingly on the interpersonal dimension of literary texts, an orientation he explicitly connects to the dialogism of Bakhtin (see *Dialogism*, see also as regards the interpersonal, Weber in Carter and Simpson 1988: 95–111, Toolan in Birch and O'Toole 1988).

3. Sovereignty and Reregistration

The functional patterning of a text is also interpreted in terms of the field, tenor, and mode of its context of situation. The situations enacted provide another route upwards to higher level meanings.

In literary texts such contextualization is on two levels (Halliday 1978: 146). On the first level, the text is related to the social situation of its *own* production and consumption. One can talk of the 'field' of verbal art, the 'tenor' of the authorial presence (the 'implied' author and reader) and the genre, the conventions of which preshape and enable these. This is the context of literary theory and the sociology of literature. Halliday (1978: 145–50) provides such a context for a Thurber fable. The second level is produced by a general feature of the first level. In literary texts, the immediate social environment does not determine the form, except via its genre. Compare this with a practical situation like buying a bus ticket where the language actually achieves the buying and this determines what is meant. By contrast, the literary text 'creates its own immediate context of situation'; the text is 'self-sufficient' (Halliday 1978: 140–6). By deploying a pattern from *anywhere* in the language, the author recreates that situation and its higher level meanings and thus a virtual reality, the text world, through language. For example, deployment in written mode of the register of casual speech 'creates' a virtual situation in which inferable 'personae' spontaneously speak.

Carter and Nash (1983) label this feature of literary texts 'sovereignty.' They write, 'this denotes the self-supporting capacity of the text, its power to generate and develop a pattern of meaning, without reference to externals and without requiring of its readers any prior knowledge other than the common stock of experience' (Carter and Nash 1983: 130). This generic displacement from the exigencies of immediate demands permits a literary text to utilize any register and paradoxically, through its very self-sufficiency, to integrate the social meanings made outside the literary universe of discourse into the literary text. This process is termed 'reregistration' (Carter and Nash 1983: 129). The imported meanings both add an extra layer of contextual meaning to the text (a form of equivalence not noted by Jakobson 1960) and the allusive register items take on new meanings or interpretative potential in the new text. Reregistration is an important contributor to the characteristic polysemy or semantic density of literary texts (Carter and Nash 1983: 120, 140). This register identification across texts is one important dimension of intertextuality.

Carter (in Steele and Threadgold 1987: 442) illustrates reregistration by demonstrating the language of the travel brochure or geography book in a work of fiction and cites the use of journalistic and historical forms in Rushdie's *Midnight's Children* and *Shame*. Auden's employment of 'officialese' in *The Unknown Citizen* is cited by Carter and Simpson (1988: 22; see also Fowler 1981: 29–32 for an analysis of the registers of bureaucracy). O'Toole (in Birch and O'Toole 1988: 12–30) demonstrates the interaction of two registers in Reed's *Naming of Parts*. Carter and Nash (1983: 129) point out how even a single technical expression like 'double indemnity' from the register of insurance when deployed as the title of a crime novel takes on a new relevance and generates an extra layer of meaning in that literary context. Simpson (1988: 12ff.) investigates reader responses to the Le Carré passage mentioned above (Sect. 2). He finds that 'the basic novelistic format has been overlaid by elements of a tourist–travelogue register' and his informants recognize this as well as the text genre as 'thriller–spy novel' (see Simpson 1988 for further references to examples of reregistration).

4. Issues and Outlooks

Is literature itself a register? This is the issue of literariness (see *Literary Language*). We ask whether the functioning of language in literary situations itself generates characteristic patterns of choice. Some sources talk as if this was the case (see Halliday 1983: xi). Others adamantly deny it (Halliday in the foreword to Birch and O'Toole 1988: vii, Simpson 1988).

Reregistration suggests that literary situations do not constrain authorial options because linguistic patterns from any situation can be deployed. If register is a probabilistic 'linguistic' pattern of semantic options, then all patterns are unpredictably equiprobable in a literary text. However, it has recently been claimed that such deployments, producing 'register mix,' are a characteristic of many texts. O'Toole writes '... texts are not simply 'instances' of register but institutionally determined, multiregisterial discourses ...' (Birch and O'Toole 1988: 111–25). Hudson (1980: 49) sees register as the output of a speaker's internalized norms. In this respect, a speaker's utterance would convey, like a dialect or accent, that particular mix of social meanings he or she opted for out of a multiplicity of norms, perhaps in a situation of normative conflict or lack of focus. The statistical realization of this register mix would precisely convey that mix of meaning.

In spite of sovereignty and reregistration, it is clear that literary texts do function in first-level social situations, those in which they are produced and consumed, and these must somehow relate to their linguistic patterns. The normative nonlanguage factor that relates situation to text patterns is not register but genre. It is there that we find the normative dimension of literariness (see *Genre*).

It is also through genre, as a contingent historical part of situations, that the language itself is related upwards to the social institutions (education, publishing, literary criticism, etc.) and social practices (methods of reading, generic conventions, etc.) that construct literariness with respect to its function in societies (see Fowler 1981, Kress, in Birch and O'Toole 1988: 126–41). Pointing downwards to language choice, the genre specifies those sociohistorical clusters of text pattern that are recognizably 'literary,' for example, Simpson's 'basic novelistic format' above. Such a text will mix and interweave reregistered items and generic texture in a rich brew which exhibits literariness, no feature of which is found only in literature. This 'pattern of patterns' functions to enable the inferential methods of reading which have evolved in literary institutions, which in turn function ideologically in some historical context of culture. It is a matter of terminology, but the first level generic features of literary texts might be seen as registerial, although paradoxically the whole 'mix' cannot, because of reregistration.

The main recent research in social semiotics integrates it with other contemporary trends. Some relates register to broader discursive practices and links functionalist stylistics to poststructuralist thought, Foucault in particular (see Halliday in Birch and O'Toole 1988: 31–44, Halliday 1987), Threadgold in Steele and Threadgold 1987: 549–97, Threadgold in Birch and O'Toole 1988: 169–204; (see also *Foucault, Michel*). Another trend is towards the critical analysis of language, ideology, and power (see Kress in Birch and O'Toole 1988: 126–41; see also *Ideology*). Social semiotic approaches to literature can also be closely related to discourse and pragmatic approaches in that all equally approach literary texts as a use of language in context.

See also: Genre; Style.

Bibliography

Birch D 1989 *Language, Literature and Critical Practice*. Routledge, London
Birch D, O'Toole M (eds.) 1988 *Functions of Style*. Pinter, London
Brumfit C, Carter R (eds.) 1986 *Literature and Language Teaching*. Oxford University Press, Oxford, UK
Carter R (ed.) 1982 *Language and Literature: An Introductory Reader in Stylistics*. Allen and Unwin, London
Carter R, Nash W 1983 Language and literariness. *Prose Studies* **6**(2): 123–41
Carter R, Simpson P (eds.) 1988 *Language, Discourse and Literature*. Unwin Hyman, London
Fowler R 1981 *Literature as Social Discourse*. Batsford Academic, London
Fowler R 1986 *Linguistic Criticism*. Oxford University Press, Oxford, UK
Halliday M 1971 Linguistic function and literary style: An inquiry into the language of William Golding's *The Inheritors*. In: Chatman S (ed.) *Literary Style: A Symposium*. Oxford University Press, New York
Halliday M 1978 *Language as Social Semiotic*. Arnold, London
Halliday M 1983 Foreword. In: Cummings M, Simmons R *The Language of Literature: A Stylistic Introduction to the Study of Literature*. Pergamon Press, Oxford, UK
Halliday M 1987 Language and the order of nature. In: Fabb N, Attridge D, Durant A, MacCabe C (eds.) *The Linguistics of Writing*. Manchester University Press, Manchester, UK
Halliday M, McIntosh A, Strevens P 1964 *The Linguistic Sciences and Language Teaching*. Longmans, London
Hudson R 1980 *Sociolinguistics*. Cambridge University Press, Cambridge, UK
Jakobson R 1960 Concluding statement: Linguistics and poetics. In: Sebeok T (ed.) *Style in Language*. MIT Press, Cambridge, MA
Simpson P 1988 Access through application. *Parlance: The Journal of the Poetics and Linguistics Association* **1**(2): 5–28
Steele R, Threadgold T (eds.) 1987 *Language Topics: Essays in Honour of Michael Halliday, Vol. II*. Benjamins, Amsterdam

Religion and Language

J. F. A. Sawyer

Religion has always played a role, often a very significant and even crucial one, in the history of language and linguistics.

1. Sacred Texts

Sacred texts have a central role to play in most religious traditions and the language in which they are written and read is often crucial. Sacred scripts or 'hieroglyphics' were sometimes invented with a special religious function, and exquisite calligraphy evolved as in Islamic art and the great monastic manuscript traditions of medieval Europe.

In Islamic doctrine, the Qur'ān represents the actual words of the deity delivered directly, in Arabic, to Muhammad in the early seventh century CE, and must only be read in Arabic. Thus for the majority of ordinary Muslims throughout the world, who have no knowledge of Arabic, translation into the vernacular is officially discouraged and the Qur'ān is recited in the original language with amazing devotion and accuracy, but minimal understanding. Similar conservatism applies to the reading of Sanskrit texts in modern Hindu temples, Avestan texts in Zoroastrian worship, and Biblical texts in Hebrew, even in the more liberal Jewish synagogues. In some cases it is the language of a widely used translation that assumes this role as in some varieties of Christianity where Greek, Latin, Slavonic, Syriac, Ge'ez, and other versions, not to mention the King James Authorized Version, have been treated with the same awe as if they were the original text. The same applies to some versions of the Buddhist canon which are in most contexts preferred to the original Pali.

2. Special Languages

In addition to the languages of their sacred texts, many religious communities employ special languages or language varieties for other purposes. Glossolalia or 'speaking in tongues' is a conspicuous example where utterances in a language unknown to virtually everybody present has an important prophetic function. Untranslateable or 'nonsense' languages are a feature of religious rites among the Australian aborigines of northern Arnhem land, while some American Indian medicine men use an incomprehensible language when talking to each other or to supernatural powers. Probably as much for social and political reasons as for spiritual ones, Rastafarians have evolved a distinctive mode of speech among themselves, unintelligible to the outsider. The same applies to the cargo cults and several other new religious movements. Monastic sign language is another example of a special language evolved within a purely religious context.

There are many examples of the belief that everyday language is not sacred enough for religious purposes. They include the use of Sumerian in ancient Near Eastern rituals long after it had ceased to be a living language, of Sanskrit in Hindu worship, and of Ge'ez in Ethiopian Christianity, Syriac in Eastern Christianity (in Kerala in South India, for example, to this day), Hebrew in Judaism, and, until the twentieth century, Latin in the Roman Catholic Church all over the world.

The notion that no human language at all, ancient or modern, natural or artificial, is adequate, appears both in the well-known Quaker predilection for silent worship and in the 'language-transcendent' meditation techniques of some varieties of Buddhism and Christianity.

Within the context of a religious community meeting regularly for worship, special varieties of language are often used for public prayer, hymn-singing, and preaching, partly to heighten people's awareness of the sacredness of the moment, and partly to highlight the continuity of what they are doing with the worship of other communities elsewhere. Thus, for example, Jews all over the world using precisely the same Hebrew words as their ancestors have used for generations, as they celebrate Passover or Yom Kippur ('the Day of Atonement'), experience a sense of solidarity as 'God's people' which would not be possible if any other language was used.

The same applied until the twentieth century to the use of Church Latin in the Catholic Mass, and to the distinctive English of the 1661 Book of Common Prayer in the Church of England. The introduction of the vernacular into worship places the emphasis more on communication and the fuller participation of the people, although the precise wording of the modern Catholic 'Missal' and of the Anglican 'Alternative Service Books' is still controlled by the ecclesiastical authorities. Conservative opposition to using the vernacular in worship is common as in the case of the Anglican 'Prayerbook Society,' dedicated to preserving the use of the 1661 Book of Common Prayer.

The dynamics of prayer in which human individuals believe they are engaged in dialogue with a deity or saint, also determines the variety of language adopted. In the language of hymns, too, metrical constraints, the popularity of traditional melodies, and other factors lead to the survival of bizarre archaisms which would rarely be heard outside that special context. Frequently, tension between a desire to uphold an ancient religious tradition, by preserving Latin or Hebrew or Sanskrit, for example, and a move towards making public worship more generally intelligible, has produced interesting compromises. The need to train preachers in the use of a language variety designed to elicit the appropriate response, has produced elaborate homiletical strategies down the ages, particularly in Christian tradition.

3. Beliefs about Language

Belief in the power of language to influence reality is expressed in many ways all over the world. In European tradition this implies a Platonic view of language in which there is a direct connection between the world of names and the world of things. The Chinese doctrine of the 'rectification of names' was similarly based on the belief that there is (or ought to be) a formal correspondence, between names and functions, titles and duties, especially in politics. In Hindu philosophy the sacred sound *om* was understood to be the consummation of the Vedas and as such to denote their ultimate referent Brahman, source of all intelligibility and being.

Personal names are believed to have special powers, and great care is taken by many communities to protect their children by naming them according to a set of carefully controlled rules. Some African tribes give their children unattractive names to make them uninviting to evil spirits. In some American Indian and Australian Aboriginal communities, the name of a recently deceased person is taboo, and even words that resemble it are meticulously avoided. Jews at one time changed the names of their children to deceive the angel of death, and the name of their God was believed to be surrounded by such a powerful aura of sacredness that it was never to be pronounced except by the High Priest in a very special ritual context. Some Christians apply a similar taboo to the name 'Jesus' in the late twentieth century.

Written language has a special role to play in this respect as beliefs about the Hebrew alphabet and the Tetragrammaton in Jewish tradition illustrate. Egyptian hieroglyphics, Nordic runes, and Chinese characters also have a long and fascinating history of magical uses and beliefs.

Several religious traditions believe in the creative power of the divine word or command: in Ancient Egyptian tradition the god Ptah created heaven and earth by his word. The same creative power is attributed to the word of the god Prajapati in Hinduism, and to the creator god of Jews, Christians, and Muslims. In Hindu iconography, the god Siva Nataraja ('Lord of the Dance') is represented as producing the sound which creates, sustains, and destroys the world. Highly complex mythological and doctrinal elaborations of this concept appear in Hinduism, Christianity, and elsewhere.

Primary myths about the origin of language, on the other hand, are surprisingly rare. The biblical stories of Ham, Shem, and Japheth, the three sons of Noah, and of the Tower of Babel, an elaborate West African example from the Dogon of Mali, and a passing reference in Greek mythology seem to be exceptions. Maybe the focus on language as a key to understanding human nature and society is a modern one.

In striking contrast to this situation are the many modern 'secondary myths,' clearly motivated by political and social factors, including sixteenth-century claims that Adam and Eve spoke a Teutonic language and that the Mayan script was of Semitic origin, and more recently, quite blatant attempts to prove the superiority of the Aryan race—or the Semites or the Africans—by the use of linguistic evidence.

4. Influence of Religion on Linguistics

The belief that, to be effective, ritual utterances, frequently in a language or language variety other than that of the priests performing them, have to be recited with absolute accuracy, has had profound effects on the history of language and linguistics. In the first place, it means that religious authorities insist on a very large part of their educational programs being devoted to language teaching. Thus the training of Catholic priests, Jewish rabbis, Muslim imams, and Hindu brahmins had to include the study of the ancient language in which their scriptures and their liturgy were written—Latin, Hebrew, Arabic, Sanskrit, respectively—whatever their mother tongue was, and whatever the language of the people they would be working among. At the same time, religious schools are set up in which children are taught at least the rudiments of the appropriate language to enable them to recite texts correctly from an early age. Muslim Qur'ān schools are a good example. In many cases religious institutions exert, or are bound by, legal authority to preserve and protect the sacred language. This applies as much to the vernacular wording of the modern Catholic Mass and the English of the Church of England liturgy, as to the sacred languages of Judaism, Islam, and Hinduism. The effect on the survival or spread of such languages and language varieties, as also on perceptions of their superiority above indigenous or colloquial languages and dialects, can readily be appreciated (see *Linguistic Imperialism*).

Second, elaborate scribal and grammatical techniques were worked out to ensure that the sacred text was accurately transmitted. Thus ancient languages which might have been totally forgotten have been preserved in the context of religious institutions of many types. A very large proportion of the linguistic material that has survived from the ancient world is of a religious nature, preserved in temple libraries and the like. Scribes engaged in copying a sacred text, the Jewish masoretes, for example, worked under the strictest rules governing every aspect of their craft. They also devised elaborate systems of 'pointing' to preserve correctly every minute phonological detail, including cantillation marks, after Hebrew had ceased to be their first language. This and other developments, especially contact with Arabic grammarians, led eventually to the emergence of Hebrew linguistics.

In early Hindu tradition, by contrast, the primary form of language was speech, not writing. The Vedas are regarded as *śruti* 'hearing,' to be transmitted word-perfect from generation to generation. Here too the linguistic precision required led not only to some astonishing feats of memory, but also to the appearance of some remarkable pioneers in the history of linguistics, of whom Pāṇini is certainly the most celebrated.

Finally, the communication, interpretation, and translation of sacred texts have influenced language and linguistics in a number of significant ways. The history of Bible translation is by far the best documented example of this. In many languages, such as Gothic and Old Church Slavonic, as well as countless modern spoken languages in Africa and

Asia, the Bible was the first text to be written down. In many cases new writing systems had to be devised, while others like the Korean Han'gŭl system, came to be more widely used as a result of the efforts of Bible translators, so that they were no longer the possession of an intellectual elite. It is probably true to say that, because of European colonial and postcolonial educational policies, there is still very little published in most of the African languages except for church purposes.

Important contributions to all branches of linguistics have been made as a result of the activities of Christian scholars and missionaries, from the early pioneering work of men like the Jesuit Matteo Ricci (1552–1610) in China and the eighteenth-century English Baptist William Carey in India, not to mention St Jerome and Martin Luther, to the more recent and more technical research associated with the Protestant Bible Societies, the Vatican (where incidentally there is still a thriving Latin Department), and the Summer Institute of Linguistics (see *Missionaries and Language*). As a result of their work, many languages and dialects were recorded for the first time, and the first grammars and dictionaries produced. Theological controversies, like the 'term question' in nineteenth-century China, focused for the first time on important semantic issues, and some recent advances in comparative semitic linguistics are due to the activities of a new generation of biblical scholars.

The effect of Buddhist missionary activities, especially in Central and Eastern Asia, has been considerable too, but less well-documented. It appears that Buddhist teachings were from the beginning translated into regional languages and dialects. The early history of translation into Chinese, for example, can be traced for 1000 years, from the earliest attempts by polyglot monks in the second century BCE, to the establishment of official translation bureaus. It was for the purpose of translating the Buddhist canon into Tibetan that the Tibetan script was created in the seventh century CE, and this in turn was used as a model for the Mongolian writing system, created under the patronage of Kublai Khan in the thirteenth century.

See also: Missionaries and Language; Blessings.

Bibliography

Gill S D 1981 *Sacred Words: A Study of Navajo Religion and Prayer*. Greenwood Press, Westport, CT
Gomez L O 1987 Buddhist views of language. In: Eliade M (ed.) *Encyclopedia of Religion, Vol. 8*. Macmillan, New York, pp. 446–51.
Samarin W (ed.) 1976 *Language in Religious Practice*. Newbury House, Rowley, MA
Tambiah S J 1968 The magical power of words. *Man* NS **3**: 175–208
Wheelock W T 1987 Language. In: Eliade M (ed.) *Encyclopedia of Religion, Vol. 8*. Macmillan, New York, pp. 438–46.

Slang: Sociology
I. L. Allen

Slang is more a sociological than a purely linguistic idea and is best understood in the theory of modern society and culture. Dictionaries usually define slang with at least two senses. First, slang is the special, restricted speech of subgroups or subcultures in society and, second, it is a highly informal, unconventional vocabulary of more general use. This article is concerned with both senses, but especially with why and how restricted subgroup speech becomes general slang. Slang in use is a marker of social differences and, as such, is a vocabulary that has become used and understood with social purpose beyond the boundaries of the subgroup that originated the lexical items or their special meanings.

1. Origins

Slang first emerged in abundance where diverse peoples met at the cultural crossroads of the ancient market city; it flourished in the more diverse and occupationally interdependent medieval city. For the same but more complex reasons in the nineteenth century, slang became part of the life of modern cities, or more validly today, of modern society in general. By its very nature slang emerges from the organization of diverse society and in small ways serves both to maintain and to change social structures, or the power relationships among social groups. Slang is a necessary and inevitable cultural product of a plural, complex, dynamic, and highly interdependent modern society.

The word 'slang,' of uncertain origin, has been dated to about 1750 and was soon thereafter defined at least once as 'street language.' Slang originally denoted cant, or the restricted speech of the low, often criminal classes of society. However, the idea of slang gradually evolved to denote other subcultural speech, both high and low, as well as more general but unconventional vocabulary. By 1890 slang had taken on its present sense of a level of language below standard and of a body of lexemes derived from yet lower and more restricted levels of speech. The more general idea of popular speech, which includes slang, is today coming into a newer and wider use by language scholars. Popular speech encompasses older forms of folk speech, which are associated with rural society and with the oral tradition, and newer forms of folk speech, often slang, which are associated with cities and modern society and with the mass media. Popular speech includes both spontaneous folk expressions and popular locutions prompted by the mass media. Sociologically speaking, slang is the urban part of popular speech and has historically found many of its incentives and referents in the socially diverse urban setting.

2. The Late Twentieth-century Idea of Slang

Slang is not a class of lexemes that can be described and then circumscribed and does not differ from standard or other levels of speech in any purely linguistic characteristic. Every effort to define slang as a kind of vocabulary has failed to cast a net wide and fine enough to catch all that looks, feels, sounds, and works like slang. The indefinite class of words labeled slang in general dictionaries or included in any dictionary of slang will testify to this problem. Nonetheless, dictionaries usually characterize slang by describing its informality, unconventionality, ephemerality, ellipsis, bizarre metaphors, playfulness, and the like. People of a Whitmanesque bent have said that slang is the poetry of everyday life and the free and natural speech of the common people. While slang expression is acute, the metaphors occasionally brilliant, and it sometimes alliterates and rhymes, slang is more a level or register of speech than a poetic form of the folk (see *Literary Language*).

For practical lexicographers, slang is a 'place,' a way station and a proving ground for cheeky new words and phrases. The label of 'slang' is a necessary one for lexicographers who are obliged to indicate levels of usage to guide dictionary users. The most neutral and unassailable definition of slang is simply that of a level of usage (Flexner 1974). Slang is 'below' standard and 'correct' informal usages and socially is less acceptable in formal discourse. On the other hand, slang is more widely used or at least more widely understood than restricted subgroup speech, such as regional and social dialects, argot, cant, or jargon. In this sense, slang is 'above' subcultural speech, where so much slang began its upward and outward-bound career into general usage.

Viewed as a level of usage, slang is vocabulary in limbo. Slang is, so to speak, applicant language that is awaiting acceptance or rejection by standard usage, or endlessly awaiting neither—and perhaps quiet withdrawal. Slang has at least four resolutions (Maurer and High 1980). If an item of slang proves durable and virtuous in the usage of the general public and, to a lesser extent, in the eyes of arbiters of elite usage, it may enter standard usage, as much slang has and does all the time (e.g., *movies*). Or it may remain slang for years, decades (e.g., *cool* 'very good'), or even centuries (e.g., *to snitch* 'to inform'). Or it may be tried out, found wanting, redundant, or boring, and returned to the worldly regions of its subcultural origins, or perhaps just assigned the stigma of datedness (e.g., *to dig* 'to understand'). Much slang just disappears, not to be heard from again (*wizard* or *some pumpkins!* 'superb!'), unless resuscitated in later years (*pig*, 'a policeman' in the 1840s, was revived over a century later in the 1960s). All this is only the beginning of the story. Slang is too vital an idea to rest easily under the umbrella of popular speech or upon a rung on the social ladder of usage.

3. The Interactional Uses of Slang

The view of slang as a level of usage, or as a marker of social position in systems of difference, often of vertical stratification, however, opens the way to see the distinctive uses of slang in social interaction and foreshadows its larger sociology. The difference between standard, proper, or elite speech, on the one hand, and low, unconventional slang, on the other, provides the tension that enables slang to serve as a language of social opposition. The role of slang in subcultural confrontation has long been known but perhaps not generally appreciated. Slang is a class of language used, among other social and psychological uses, to deny allegiance to genteel, elite, and proper society and to its standard linguistic forms. Slang is thus used to assert social opposition, ranging from the most vicious and hostile verbal aggression to the gentlest, teasing contrariness and playful disruptiveness. The utterance of subcultural words and phrases is also a way to seek bonds with sympathetic others and, as a new group, to oppose or just to break with the dominant tone of discourse. Slang in any case is used earnestly or playfully in order to lower, or to shift laterally, the register of discourse.

Dumas and Lighter have articulated this view and call for the retention of the concept of slang in linguistics to denote a functional category of lexemes that 'are identifiable primarily by the intent (or perceived intent) of the speaker or writer to break with established linguistic convention.' They also note another basic distinction of most slang: 'Slang characterizes a referent; jargon and standard English only indicate it' (Dumas and Lighter 1978: 13). The social utility of slang, then, lies in the disruptive rhetoric it produces and using the speech of stigmatized subcultures is one way to lower the register (see *Register*) of discourse (Lighter 1994).

Slang also facilitates a variety of distinctive interactions in modern society, insofar as it retains widely recognizable subgroup origins and meanings. Slang is used to manage the multiple, overlapping, and shifting identities of modern life—a world of 'masks and mirrors.' A skill of city living, for those who adventure into its diversity, is knowing the subcultural talk of other groups. This knowledge is a way to attribute meaning to the seeming jumble and noise of modern life. The anonymity and public life of the large city, especially, offer many opportunities for interactional games, deceptions, identity switches, and opportunities for impression management for either fun or profit, and slang with subcultural associations facilitates these manipulations. Slang, for example, may be used to signal that the speaker is conversant with, or maybe even belongs to, a subculture of titillating or prestigeful reputation. The use of subcultural speech becoming slang, then, is often a tame adventure in verbal slumming, or in social climbing.

4. The Essential Urbanness of Slang

Modern slang is a distinct level or register of language that arose during the Great Transformation from homogeneous rural to heterogeneous urban society. While in principle, general slang can arise in any situation of social difference, the modern industrial city in the nineteenth century intensified every material condition that creates slang: the aggregation of large and variegated social groupings, their proximity and high visibility to one another, the complexity of their economic interdependencies, and the necessity and desirability of contact and exchanges of every sort. Heavy migration and settlement in ethnic enclaves of the great cities influenced slang throughout the nineteenth century and are influencing it again at the beginning of the twenty-first century. To this potent mix was added the intensifying ingredient of common knowledge of the city through the mass media, especially the newspapers and the comics and, in another medium, the popular cultures of minstrelsy and vaudeville.

The lexicographer Stuart Berg Flexner developed the idea of slang in diverse society (Flexner 1974). General slang and other nonstandard varieties of language can arise only in the presence of third parties or subgroups in society—the primitive urban situation. Flexner suggested a simple sociology of number, in both the grammatical and numerical senses, that is reminiscent of the triadic theory of the German sociologist Georg Simmel (Wolff 1950: 135–6). Slang develops when the conversation between the first and second persons, who have agreed upon a common language, begins to include the speech of third parties or subgroups and thus to allude to other, external meanings and realities. General slang is, thus, an epiphenomenon of diverse urban society and, by sociological definition, can exist only in plural societies of multiple, interacting social worlds.

Historically, cities have been generators of cultural and technological innovation, new forms of social organization, new social varieties, new forms of inequality and, thus, of lexical innovation to express these new thoughts and new social objects. American slang, however, is often traced to the period after the War of 1812 when the old frontier set the emerging tone of American speech with, in H. L. Mencken's words, 'its disdain of all scholastic rules and precedents, its tendency toward bold and often bizarre tropes, its rough humors, its not infrequent flights of what might be called poetic fancy, its love of neologisms for their own sake.' Yet 'to the immigrants who poured in after 1850, even the slums of the great Eastern cities presented essentially frontier conditions' (Mencken 1963: 148).

Language scholars of a social bent have long associated slang with cities and urban society. John Camden Hotten, the London publisher and lexicographer of slang, in 1859 wrote in the preface to his early compilation that the most favorable conditions for the appearance of slang are those of 'crowding and excitement, and artificial life' (Hotten 1859: 35). Or, to elaborate this observation for the end of the twentieth century, slang grows from the density, intensifications, and social releases of urban life, in contrast to life in traditional, homogeneous, or rural communities. The philologist George Philip Krapp wrote that, in general, slang 'is found in the speech of persons whose social relations are extensive, varied, and animated. It is the product of the city rather than the country, of sophisticated rather than naive society' (Krapp 1925: 317). Eric Partridge, noting the presence of slang in Ancient Greek and Latin, wrote that 'knowing the characteristics of urban life, we may assume that slang dates from the massing of populations in cities' (Partridge 1963: 37).

Yet general slang can arise in markedly nonurban places, as Partridge and others so abundantly found in the military, where slang served as a freemasonry of speech among persons of diverse backgrounds. Slang can arise in any place that simulates the social diversity of the cities and where diverse peoples meet, even at rural crossroads, or in any situation where people of different social ranks meet and, at least initially, culturally oppose one another. In principle, general slang can arise from the most rudimentary differences of social role, in any situation where third-group locutions can be introduced.

Large metropolitan centers have been the most fertile producers of slang about all things. Anglo–American commentators on slang throughout the nineteenth century regularly associated slang with big cities, especially New York and London. Early lexicographers collected the distinctive vocabularies of various urban groups; they noted the role of the printed mass media in the diffusion of slang; they contrasted stable rural dialect with the bizarre fleeting talk of the big cities; they noted the origins and use of slang in high society as well as in low; they understood its uses in social opposition; and they glimpsed the principles of diffusion. Population density and crowd psychology in the streets did the job of circulating slang that mass communication does in the late twentieth century. In 1852 Charles Mackay, in his essay 'The popular follies of great cities,' marveled at how the catch phrases, such as *quoz, Oh, what a shocking bad hat!*, and *flare up*, seized the lower orders of London. 'London is particularly fertile in this sort of phrase,' Mackay wrote, 'which springs up suddenly, no one knows in exactly what spot, and pervades the whole population in a few hours, no one knows how' (Mackay 1980: 620).

Throughout the modern period down to, say, 1950 one may well be struck by the number of words and phrases in slang that denote the essences of city life. Segmental, impersonal, and often exploitative social relations were expressed in the idea of the city as a *jungle*, an employment agency as a *slave market*, or in the irony of *my uncle* 'a pawnbroker.' An awareness of class and ethnic differences were expressed in hundreds of well-known ethnic slurs and similar class derogations. Personal appearances and styles of dress as seen in city streets are recorded in terms such as *plug ugly, jelly bean, dude*, and *gussied up*. A variety of urban social locations and roles were expressed in *lounge lizard, ritzy, rubbernecker, skid row, coontown, black-and-tan dive, the 'burbs*, and in other slang denotations of urban class and status. Unconventional styles of life and bizarre occupational specializations were denoted in *panhandler, mushroom faker, taxi dancer*, and *sandwich man*. The importance of money is apparent in the many slang synonyms for money, often ill-gotten, and the lavish spending of it (*big spender* and *butter-and-egg man*). Sexual and other social relations that are casual, segmental, impersonal, commercial, and exploitative are implicit in *sugar daddy, gold digger, hooker, pimp, bouncer, puller-in*, or *steerer*. New experiences of every kind in the industrial city, including its machines, were amply denoted in slang: *bus, taxi, el, rattler* 'a streetcar,' *skyscraper*, or *an Ameche* (passingly, 'a telephone' about 1940 and an allusion to the actor Don Ameche who played the inventor Alexander Graham Bell in a popular movie).

Moreover, the semantics of slang, especially its names for kinds of people (ethnic, class, and other social types), display a pervasive structure of vertical stratification and binary opposition, frequently expressed in invidious distinctions between 'Us' and 'Them.' Slang is greatly about the new and different and, in the social realm, often expresses stressful social relations and a dislike for the unlike.

5. The Urban Sociology of Slang

Slang derives from the multiple subcultures of urban, that is to say modern, society. For the most part it denotes vocabulary that has diffused through and perked up into wider use from myriad intersecting social circles. The neoclassical or subcultural theory of urbanism explains how cities create a variety of subgroups and subcultures that vary in number directly with population size (Fischer 1975). Large cities attract as migrants large numbers of different kinds of people, who then join and enlarge the diversity of groups already in the city. The greater numbers of people with specialized interests in cities provide the sufficient numbers or 'critical masses' that enable subcultures to sustain and intensify. Eventually, nascent subgroups within larger subgroups reach the numbers necessary and sufficient for even more specialized interest groups to break away and form yet other subcultures.

The many direct and indirect contacts and communications among most subgroups in the dense, compact, intensely interactive market city, as people learn more and more about one another, cause some subcultures to become more alike, in some cases even to assimilate or merge into one. Other groups recoil from the culture clash they experience and, as a result, entrench, reaffirm their original identities, and become even more different than before. The city, precisely because of its large size, density, and social variety, creates a continual process of sustaining, reinforcing, and creating ethnic groups, social classes, styles of life, and every imaginable kind of subculture, including many so-called deviant ones. As a necessary part of this process, many meanings are exchanged, which results in the learning and diffusion of borrowed subcultural words and phrases. The creation of subcultural speech, intergroup contact, and the diffusion of these words through intersecting social networks into wider usage, or into general slang, recapitulate and illustrate Fischer's modified theory of urbanism and may be taken as a special application of it.

Most general slang comes from the restricted, special vocabularies of these many subgroups in modern society and becomes slang as it diffuses through the word-of-mouth networks and between the intersecting social circles that lace together much of the whole society. The diffusion of lexical innovation follows the same principles that govern the diffusion of any cultural innovation: it spreads in direct proportion to population density, intensity of communication and—above all—perceived usefulness in social interaction. In this way, restricted subcultural usages pass into general or at least into wider usage, often with the augmentation and amplification of the mass media.

In the process of diffusion, the subcultural expression becoming general slang often changes meaning to some degree, usually widening in denotation and connotation, and so becoming useful in more social situations. If the word or phrase proves useful or amusing in its new social setting, it may pass further into more and more circles until it reaches a wide enough audience, who at least understand its meaning, to say that it is in general slang and part of the general culture. If such slang stays in wide use for decades, it may lose its subcultural associations and seem just to be there in the language, its subgroup origins remote or forgotten.

More than half of historical American slang, it has been estimated, came from the chiefly male subcultural speech of lumberjacks, railroaders, musicians, hoboes, sportsmen, show business, teenagers, college students, ethnic minorities, the military, and various deviant subcultures, such as criminals and drug users (Flexner 1960). Subcultures, as the prefix of the term implies, were once thought of as little social worlds that were 'below' the general culture or ones that were marginal to society or isolated within it. The idea of subcultures more validly embraces all subgroups of society, including social classes, genders, variant sexual interests, all majority and minority ethnic groups, regional groups, age groups, and a host of occupational, life-style, and consumer cultures, as well as all the groups more traditionally described as subcultures. A subgroup is any set of people generally linked in communication and bound by a common interest. These groups vary greatly in their level of organization and degree of self-consciousness. Ultimately, almost any distinguishing set of common experience and meaning can be described as a subculture of a subgroup. Everyone, it follows, belongs to multiple, overlapping subgroups and subcultures, the number depending on the variety and breadth of their interests and social engagements. The general culture of a society is the meanings and values that most of its subcultures have in common, and this includes its language and general slang.

Many subcultures, some of which may be called speech communities, have their own dialects or varieties of English in degrees of distinction from standard speech. Each variety, and most are merely nascent, may include distinctive pronunciations, special words or special meanings of ordinary words, or even grammatical differences. These special words, or as often ordinary words with special meanings, sometimes escape their little social circles or leak into one or more intersecting or tangential circles, where they are provisionally adopted. The subcultures of male homosexuals, drug users, and lower-class blacks are examples of leaky subcultures whose special words and phrases diffused into the general culture and its slang in the 1960s and 1970s (Maurer and High 1980). Previously, these subcultures were structurally tighter, or more isolated, and their words leaked out slowly and were transmitted largely by word-of mouth. The diffusion, or at least knowledge, of their norms was accompanied by the diffusion of their language, especially through the mass media. At the beginning of the twenty-first century such stigmatized subcultures are much less isolated and more subgroups of all kinds are leaking lexical expressions of their cultures—and leaking them faster—especially through television and the movies. Adopting slang, heard either in interpersonal or in mass communications, is a traditional way young people flirt with forbidden and other attractive subcultures.

The mass media can bring almost instant lexical diffusion. Mass-communicated slang and neologisms initially leapfrog communities and are introduced at once into many thousands of local social circles. If they catch on in many of these circles, they have a big headstart in the diffusion process and spread even further by word-of-mouth, now able to go like multiple brushfires through the verbal culture of a society. Slang-like advertising slogans, for example, are repeatedly reimplanted in local networks, from which they are sometimes spread from person to person. In modern societies laced together by the mass media, folk lexical culture (categories invented by people) blends with mass lexical culture (categories invented by media writers for people). This is how almost all new words now spread, slang or not.

6. Slang at the Beginning of the Twenty-first Century

In the past slang has been used more by men than by women and more by younger than by older people. In this sense, general slang itself was a semirestricted vocabulary of youthful male subculture and reflected its distinctive social construction of reality. But this is changing as gender and age subcultures merge a little in their social experiences. Much historical slang came from stressful male social worlds of the barroom and brothel, the life of tramps and hoboes, rough occupations, the military, sports, and deviant subcultures. Sociolinguists report that, until the 1970s at least, women used less slang than men and, even if they knew its meaning, used it in fewer social situations. Proper English signaled proper behavior, and the avoidance of slang reflected the greater pressures on women toward conventional behavior, at least in mixed company.

These subcultural walls are breaking down as women move into male preserves and so into situations of greater cultural variety and clash, which prompted male slang in the first place. Even low-register sexual and scatological expressions used as slang hardly raise an eyebrow in gatherings of sophisticated young men and women. Such vulgar and taboo expressions were formerly the restricted speech of male subculture, which is today losing its exclusiveness and isolation. Yet slang remains to some extent the province of the young—of socially engaged young men and women. The cultural boundaries of yet other social categories—ethnic, class, style of life—are weakening as well.

In the more self-conscious atmosphere of cultural and linguistic relativism, slang is more acceptable in many situations, is no longer so shocking, and in a functional sense is ceasing to be slang—in a kind of postmodernist collapse of old social categories. At one time all slang, echoing rebellion and disrespect, might have raised eyebrows in the most formal contexts. But today some of the norms and useful parts of the language of deviant subgroups have been absorbed by straight society. The former, critical distinction of these different registers is diminishing. Slang depends on social differences, often tense hierarchies. If the norms and language of low-status outgroups were ever totally absorbed by elite ingroups, 'slang and gentility would die together' (Sledd 1965: 699). But new social differences and hierarchies are continually arising. Slang will certainly retain a role in the inevitable cultural conflict among them.

See also: Gender and Language; Sociology of Language; Subcultures and Countercultures; Urban and Rural Forms of Language.

Bibliography

Dumas B K, Lighter J 1978 Is *slang* a word for linguists? *American Speech* **53**: 5–17
Fisher C S 1975 Toward a subcultural theory of urbanism. *American Journal of Sociology* **80**: 1319–41
Flexner S B 1960 Preface. In: Wentworth H, Flexner S B (eds.) *Dictionary of American Slang*. Crowell, New York
Flexner S B 1974 Slang. *Encyclopaedia Brittanica, Vol. 16.*
Hotten J C 1859 *The Slang Dictionary*. Chatto and Windus, London
Krapp G P 1925 *The English Language in America, Vol. 1.* Century, New York
Lighter J E (ed.) 1994 Introduction. In: *Historical Dictionary of American Slang, Vol. I.* In: Random House, New York
Mackay C 1980 *Memoirs of Extraordinary Popular Delusions and The Madness of Crowds*. Bonanza, New York
Maurer D W, High E C 1980 New words—Where do they come from and where do they go? *American Speech* **55**: 184–94
Mencken H L 1963 *The American Language*, 4th edn. Knopf, New York
Partridge E 1963 *Slang To-Day and Yesterday*, 3rd edn. Bonanza, New York
Sledd J 1965 On not teaching English usage. *English Journal* **54**: 698–703
Wolff K H (ed.) 1950 *The Sociology of Georg Simmel*. Free Press, New York

Speech and Writing
J. E. Miller

The contrast between spoken and written language is crucial for the study of human societies and language, affecting categorization, reasoning, the storage of knowledge, the running of societies, and the very concept of text (Goody 1977, Ong 1982). It relates to literacy and education, the social consequences of literacy and illiteracy, and the dissemination and control of information. Adopting a micro-approach, this article focuses on the grammatical, lexical, and textual differences between spoken and written language, indicating their implications for first language acquisition (including written language), language typology, and syntactic analysis.

1. Priority of Spoken Language

The priority of spoken language over written language is attested by various facts: no community has a written language only, though many have a spoken language only, and children learn spoken language first and most easily; every normal child learns the spoken language of its community, but some children fail to become literate. Nonetheless, it is essential to take account of the immense prestige of written language, its central role in literate societies, and the large divergences between the spoken and written varieties of what counts as the same language. Written language has a life of its own (Stubbs 1980).

The serious and publicly verifiable study of spoken language only became possible with the invention of the tape recorder, and only became widespread with the advent of the cassette recorder. The discussion below is based on various bodies of spoken language collected since the early 1960s: the Glasgow Map Task Corpus collected by Anderson and Garrod—here abbreviated to AG; the Human Communication Research Centre Corpus collected by Anderson et al. 1991—here A; the corpus of spontaneous conversation collected by Brown and Miller (1980)—BM; Kapanadze and Zemskaja (1979)—KZ; Höhne-Leska (1975)—HL; Macaulay (1991)—M; and Wackernagel-Jolles (1971)—WJ.

2. Spoken Language

The most obvious difference between spoken and written language, the medium of communication (vibrations in the air as opposed to marks on paper) is superficial compared with the deep, pervasive differences, not just in grammar and vocabulary, but also in the general organization of discourse or text (cf. Ong (1982) on the psychodynamics of sight versus hearing, and see Sect. 3 below). Not every text that is spoken counts as genuine spoken language. The most interesting examples, because furthest from written language, are informal, spontaneous conversation and dialog produced during the performance of a task. These are what children are first exposed to, and represent typical adult linguistic activity. Other examples of spoken language are formal conversation, say on television, and (semi-) planned discourses such as lectures, sermons, and political speeches, which are closer to written language. Depending on circumstances, spoken narratives may be close to spontaneous conversation or written language or equidistant from the two.

These differences are important too because they have engendered different views among investigators on the nature of spoken language. The essential influence is experience of written language. The longer and more intense that experience, the greater its influence on an individual's speech. The data here, from speakers with no higher education and therefore with limited practice in written language, yield an analysis compatible with results from work on other languages but different from accounts such as those of Kroll (1977) and Halliday (1989), based on, respectively, the recorded discourse of undergraduates and observations of speech in academic communities.

3. Properties of Spoken Language in Contrast with Written Language

Spoken language is not degenerate written language but a different system designed for a different task. Language is discussed publicly only by literate speakers for whom writing plays a large role and who therefore see written language as basic and central and spoken language as an imitation (often unsuccessful) of written language. The historical facts are precisely the opposite. Written language is a later and specially elaborated variety developed over a long time by a small set of users. The major properties distinguishing spoken from written language are as follows.

First, informal spoken language is produced in real time, impromptu, with no opportunity to edit. Only the most skillful speakers can produce complex language in these conditions. Writing allows pauses for thought and editing, which enables writers to produce more complex syntax and to choose a wider range of vocabulary.

Second, spontaneous speech is subject to the limitations of short-term memory, which reinforces the no-editing effect.

Third, speaking is much faster than writing, and reading is much faster (and more effective) than listening. That is, listeners must process instantly a rapidly produced and evanescent stream of speech, a task facilitated by simple syntax and simple vocabulary. Readers, dealing with permanent text which can be quickly scanned and reread, can process complex syntax and esoteric vocabulary, resorting to a dictionary if necessary.

Fourth, spontaneous speech is typically produced by people talking face-to-face in a particular context. It is accompanied by gestures, eye-gaze, facial expressions, and body-postures, all of which signal information. Gestures may signal attitudinal meaning, imitate the rhythm of speakers' utterances, and reinforce information encoded verbally, for example, a swift downward movement of the arm by a speaker describing a climber slipping down a slope.

Fifth, and finally, spoken language, especially informal spoken language, possesses resources of pitch, amplitude, rhythm, and voice quality which speakers exploit to the full. These resources are used to express emotion, to frighten, soothe, and cajole. They are widely used to convey reported speech; avoiding the special indirect-speech constructions of written language and phrases such as *so she exclaimed...*, *so she said...*, speakers signal reported speech only by a change of pitch, with appropriate voice-quality (see Brown and Miller 1980, Kitajgorodskaja 1988).

4. Grammatical Differences Between Spoken and Written Language

4.1 Sentences and Clauses

Written language is analyzed in terms of sentences, clauses, and phrases, and writers following the conventions of writing mark clearly the boundaries of units. (Of course, different societies have different conventions.) Spoken language, especially conversation with interrupted and overlapping turns, is hard to analyze, but phrases and clauses can typically be recognized unequivocally. The sentence is problematic. Clauses that could be written as one sentence occur quite independently, separated by long pauses and each with its own pitch contour. They may occur in different turns, either of the same speaker or of different speakers. Different listeners produce very different sentence-renderings of one and the same spoken text, as do speakers listening on different occasions to one and the same recording of their own speech (see Wackernagel-Jolles 1971). It is more appropriate to analyze speech as collections of clauses and phrases, the relations between the clauses being handled by discourse analysis, not sentence grammar.

These points are illustrated in (1) below, from dialog produced by one person instructing another how to draw a route on a map with certain landmarks, and in (2), from spontaneous conversation.

In (1), *taking a gentle curve south-west* in A's second turn relates to *you go down to the bridge*. The former modifies the latter, but one is led to wonder what criteria could be invoked to justify treating A's two turns as containing a split sentence. The sequence of turns is orderly, and it cannot be argued that A intended to produce a sentence with a main clause and a participial phrase, since A only produces the second turn in response to B's question. In (2), *where I capsized* is a relative clause modifying *canoeing*, the head and its modifier being in contributions from different speakers. The listener's task is to recognize *where I capsized* as a relative clause, and to find the constituent that it modifies. Just as anaphorical relations stretch across sentence boundaries in written language and must be handled by techniques of discourse analysis, so must clause relations in spoken language. The relevant technical term—'clause-complex'—has been provided by Halliday (1989), who argues that the sentence is a unit of writing which has grown out of the clause-complex:

A: *you go down to the bridge* (1)
B: *uhuh—to the left of the swamp?*
A: *to the left of the swamp—taking a gentle curve southwest*

A: *the first day we went canoeing* (2)
B: *where I capsized*

4.2 Main and Subordinate Clauses

The distinction between main and subordinate clauses remains relevant to spoken language. In English and many other languages, the distinction is signaled by a complementizer or special word order, but the subordinate clause may be quite separate from any main clause. Subordinate clauses, being semantically incomplete, typically cannot function as the sole initial clause in a piece of discourse. (Note that all the clauses treated here as subordinate contain finite verbs; infinitive and gerund phrases were excluded.)

There has been controversy as to whether the proportion of subordinate clauses to main clauses in informal spoken language is less than in formal written language. The essential condition is long exposure to and use of written language, which is ensured by higher education. Having higher education is not of course a necessary precondition for the ability to use complex spoken language. Macaulay (1991) presents the proportions of subordinate clauses in narratives from working- and middle-class speakers in Ayr, Scotland. The percentage of subordinate clauses in the contributions of the working-class speakers ranges from 15.7 percent to 24.3 percent, with one score of 35.5 percent and a mean of 25 percent. The percentage for the middle-class speakers ranges from 22.7 percent to 32.5 percent, with one score of 45 percent from the best-educated person in that subset of informants and a mean of 30.4 percent. If the single abnormal score in each group is removed, the mean drops to 20.3 percent for the working-class and 28.18 percent for the middle-class speakers.

The corpus described in Brown and Miller (1980) contains, inter alia, conversations between two 18-year-old girls from East Lothian, Scotland, containing discussion, jokes, and narrative. One (LS) had been accepted for study at university, and the other (AB) was hoping to collect enough qualifications to go to university too. For LS, the percentage of subordinate clauses is 26 percent; for AB, 25 percent. LS is middle-class and AB is working-class, but they both had six years of secondary education and their scores fall midway in the range of normal scores in Macaulay's study.

Macaulay (1991) further remarks that the social-class groups in his data differ in more than quantity. The middle-class speakers used more complement clauses, indirect questions, conditional clauses, and adverbial clauses of reason and concession, whereas the lower-class speakers used more adverbial clauses of place, time, and comparison. The data in Brown and Miller (1980) show a preponderance of complement and relative clauses, hardly any indirect questions (see Sect. 4.3) or indirect speech constructions, and a small number of adverbial clauses of place, time, reason, and condition. As mentioned in Sect. 4.1, many adverbial clauses, and some instances of relative clauses, were produced in different terms from the main clauses to which they related, and even by different speakers. Some types of adverbial clause were absent (see Sect. 4.5).

For comparison, consider the proportion of subordinate clauses in samples of different written texts: Penelope Lively *Judgment Day* (serious novel), sample 1–20 percent; James Herbert *Lair* (light novel)—24.7 percent; letters to *The Times*—29.7 percent; Bernard Levin centrepage article in *The Times*—30.9 percent; Penelope Lively *Judgment Day*, sample 2–31.6 percent; leaders in *The Times*—40.4 percent; article in *Geographical Magazine*—44 percent; Sperber and Wilson *Relevance* (monograph)—46 percent. The mean is 33.4 percent, not far from either middle-class mean in Macaulay's study but much farther from the working-class mean. Only one written sample is as low as the working-class mean, and the academic texts are more than 20 percentage points ahead of it, a difference that is relevant to the discussion of literacy and education in Sect. 5.

The proportion of subordinate to main clauses for different groups of speakers of English is paralleled in speakers of other languages. Höhne-Leska (1975) claims that 65.23 percent of all sentences in the spoken language (German) are simple, that is, consist of a main clause only. The tables of data in Wackernagel-Jolles suggest a figure of 41 percent for the proportion of subordinate to main clauses in spoken German, but that figure makes no distinction between speakers with and without higher education, and an inspection of the texts reveals large differences between the language of manual workers and the language of university professors and ministers of religion.

In the transcriptions of spoken Russian in Kapanadze and Zemskaja (1979), the mean proportion of subordinate to main clauses is approximately 24 percent. The texts are all produced by people with higher education, and the figures range from 30 percent in reminiscences by a senior university professor to 8 percent in an account of a camping expedition by a young scientist.

It is commonly supposed that the statement of, for example, conditions and concessions requires the appropriate type of subordinate clause. The supposition is wrong because speakers and hearers remember previous statements and draw on their knowledge of the topics under discussion and on their general background knowledge, both cultural and technical. Typically, speakers assume that hearers who cannot make sense of the communication will ask questions. Consider the example in (3).

ok we install the extractor there's no guarantee it's going to keep working (3)

Example (3) occurred in a discussion about installing a new extractor fan in a computer room. The question arose as to whether the old fan should be repaired or replaced. The first clause in (3) could be replaced by a concessive-conditional clause *even if we install the extractor*, but was in any case correctly interpreted by the hearer. Installing a new extractor was only a possible event, and the clauses *there's no guarantee it's going to work*, in spite of the present tense, only made sense if they described the situation following installation of a new fan. Using this information, the hearer correctly interpreted the speaker as conceding a point, establishing a condition, and making a statement about the situation contingent on that condition.

Important too is the extent to which speakers (and writers) use fixed expressions, that is, expressions with a relatively fixed syntax and stock of lexical items. Examples are: *Some people are hard to please*; *There's no pleasing some people*; *It's none of your business*; *Once you've done that, the rest is easy*; *I'll believe it when I see it*; *I thought you'd never ask*. Such fixed expressions or clichés are frequent and have a role to play in the first and second language learning. Of course, speakers of a given language produce and recognize combinations of syntactic units and lexical items that they have not heard or used before; but, given the exigencies of spoken language listed in Sect. 3 and the fact that speaking is often combined with other tasks, both manual and cognitive, the existence and use of fixed expressions can be seen as providing a solution to large cognitive burdens.

4.3 Constructions Typical of Written English but Rare in Spoken English

A significant number of constructions occur in (formal) written English but are rare in informal spoken English.

First, there are subordinate clauses introduced by *although, since, as*. The 100 hours of conversation described in BM contain no subordinate clauses of concession. Speakers do concede points in the course of the discussion but avoid the written construction, as in *Although she knows nothing about maths, she's a pretty good programmer*, preferring a main clause ending in *though*, as in *She's a pretty good programmer—knows nothing about maths though*. Subordinate clauses of reason introduced by *because* are relatively frequent, but there are no clauses of reason introduced by *as* or *since*. There are no subordinate clauses of purpose or result. M's corpus contains three purpose clauses, 16 result clauses, and 23 concession clauses from the working-class speakers, compared with 158 conditional clauses, 436 time clauses, and 72 place clauses. For the middle-class speakers, the numbers are, respectively, three, 28, 31, 164, 247, and 38. That is, subordinate clauses of concession, result, and purpose are infrequent even in the mature adults recorded by M and are absent from the 16-, 17-, and 18-year-olds recorded by BM.

Typical constructions in formal prose are gapping, a construction in which two clauses are combined by means of ellipsis, as in *Celia likes van Gogh, and Bill—Rembrandt*, and right-node-raising, as in *Sue likes, and Bill hates, cross-words*. Neither construction is reported by BM or M.

There are short gerunds, as in *washing dishes*, and long gerunds, as in *his washing the dishes*. Long gerunds are completely absent from AG, B and M, and short gerunds occur as complements—as in *I hate washing dishes* and *It's no bother picking you up at the station*, but never as subjects. M reports the occurrence of gerunds but does not specify their function. Infinitives are likewise very common as the complements of verbs—*He refused to work*, *She persuaded him to tell his parents*—but not as subjects. Examples such as *To do nothing to help strikes me as stupid* are typical of written English but are not to be found in informal spoken language.

The structure accusative+infinitive, as in *I considered her to be the best candidate*, does not occur in AG, A, or BM and is not mentioned by M.

Participial phrases do occur in noun phrases, but not in subject noun phrases, as in *It's got animals drinking at it*, or *We noticed the man sitting at the window*. Another structure, the free participial construction that modifies a clause, as in *Sitting at the window, I noticed a car at the bank* and *Covered in confusion, he apologized*, is very rare in spoken English. It is completely absent from AG and BM, and M reports an occurrence of 2.5 per 1000 words.

It does occur in A (cf. example (1) in Sect. 4.1), but it is important to note that the A corpus was provided by first-year university undergraduates, that is, by people who had reached higher education and had a good command of written English.

Certain conditional constructions occur: the usual subordinate conditional clause introduced by *if* is quite typical in spoken English (cf. subordinate clauses introduced by *although*, etc., discussed above). Completely absent from the data is the construction exemplified in *Were you to write to her, she would forgive you* and *Should you meet him, pass on my best wishes.*

The typical construction of indirect questions in written English consists of a complement clause dependent on a verb or preposition, the complement containing the indirect question. The complement has a WH word but declarative word order: compare *We asked what she had written*; *This is not just a case of whether the two words can combine*; *She raised the question of who we could persuade to take on the task.* In spoken English, the typical construction consists of a verb or preposition followed by a clause with the syntax and word order of main interrogative clauses: compare *We asked what had she written*; *This is not just a case of can the two words combine*; *She raised the question who could we persuade to take on the task.*

4.4 Relative Clauses in Spoken English

Relative clauses occur in spoken English, but their structure differs from the structure of relative clauses in written English. In the BM, AG, and A databases, they are typically introduced by *that*—as in *the student **that** phoned*, and definitely not *the student who phoned*. *Whom* and *whose* are completely absent, though *where* and *when* are found, as in *the place where the bridge is*. Shadow pronouns (in bold) are found, as in *the girl that **her** eighteenth birthday was on that day was stoned, couldnae stand up*; *the spikes that you stick in the ground and throw rings over **them***; *an address which I hadn't stayed **there** for several years*. Prepositions are always at the end of relative clauses (*the shop I bought it in*) but are regularly omitted (omissions marked by the bold brackets)— *there's a rope that you can pull the seat back up [ ]*; *I haven't been to a party yet that I haven't got home [ ] the same night*. *That* is omitted in existential constructions—*we had this French girl [ ] came to stay*; *there's a man in our street [ ] has a Jaguar*. There are no WH infinitival relatives such as *a house in which to stay*: compare *I've got a place to start* (versus *I've got a place from which to start*).

4.5 Discourse Devices in Spoken English

Speakers combine clauses into discourses. Spoken English has a range of devices for catching the hearer's attention, putting items into prominence, or focusing sharply upon them. The devices are different from those of the standard written language: different because they belong to speech and not writing and facilitate the interpretation of evanescent utterances for the standard human listener with limited short-term memory and limited impromptu processing capacity. The devices, however, are no less subtle or consistent than the devices of standard written English.

Speakers spread information over small chunks of syntax. The spoken English in the corpus is organized in small phrases or clauses juxtaposed—that is, not integrated. Compare (4), which is an utterance produced by a participant in the Map Task describing part of the route on his map. Note that in B's utterance, the information about how to reach the waterhole is expressed by a conditional clause *if you go down...* and that the description of the waterhole is spread over four clauses (separate clauses are shown on separate lines). The paraphrase in (5) is a typical edited piece of dense written syntax packed into a single clause:

B: right if you go from the front giraffe's foot about
hold on let me see— (4)
if you go down about—straight down about 6 cm
you find the waterhole
and it's a big hole with reeds round the side of it and
animals drinking out of it
and it's about—it's a an oval hole
it's about 2 cm wide north to south
and from the side to side it's about—3 cm wide...
It's a big oval waterhole about 2 cm wide north to south and about 3 cm wide from side to side, surrounded by reeds and with animals drinking out of it. (5)

Speakers often announce a new topic by means of a noun phrase followed by a complete clause containing a pronoun referring back to the noun phrase. This construction, exemplified in (6), is not just a device for avoiding syntactic tangles, since it occurs frequently with simple noun phrases and with no hesitations. The noun phrase may be introduced by *there's*, as in (6d).

it's not bad— ma Dad he doesn't say a lot (6a)

—the driver he's really friendly—you get a (6b)
good laugh
with him

—well another maths teacher that I dinnae (6c)
get he must've
corrected my papers

—and there's one girl she's a real extrovert (6d)

Written English possesses what are called the IT cleft and WH cleft constructions. The former, as in *It was Bill who left*, occur regularly but no frequently in informal spoken language. However, WH clefts such as *What I want is a large cup of coffee* are much rarer. Another WH cleft, as in *What he does is to interrupt at every turn*, focuses on a verb and its modifiers and through them on an event. This construction is very rare in spoken language, but the same effect is achieved by a relatively common construction in which the *what X does* part is followed by a whole clause, as in *so what you had to do was you got a partner and you got a match*... or *but what you did in the evening you carried a sandwich or two*. The latter example does not even have *was/is*. The essential difference is that the spoken construction has two separate complete clauses—*what you had to do + was + you got a partner*, whereas the written construction has the second clause reduced and integrated with the first—*what you had to do + was + get a partner*. In contrast, WH clefts are quite frequent in questions, as in *where is it he works again?* and *who is it that's been murdered?*.

Various focusing devices give prominence to items (or propositions) that the speaker wishes to introduce into the discourse. Entities deemed new to the hearer are introduced by expressions such as *can you see an X?*; *do you have an X?*; *have you got an X?*; *do you see an X? can you see a fast-flowing river?*; *do you see a lions' den?*; *have you got an abandoned cottage?*; *do you have a golf course?*. Entities deemed known to the hearer are introduced by *Can you/do you see*... but also by *you know X*, or just *know X?*, and by *You see X* (or just *see X?* in some nonstandard varieties of English): *Can you see the castle?*; *Know the bridge across the fast-flowing river?*; *(You) see the crashed plane?* (examples from the AG and A databases.)

The word 'see' can have its basic perception sense, as in *(you) see those old houses*... *this area was all houses like that right round*, but the connection grows more tenuous in (7), where *see* introduces a proposition. Note also the imperative use of *see* as in *see here! I've had enough of this nonsense!*

A: there's a car park (7)
B: aye—see—I hate going in there

(You) see introduces and highlights subordinate clauses, as in *see if you go straight down—but not go straight to the aeroplane—right? see where the—see where the pilot would go—that wee bit*.

Propositions and properties are introduced by *the thing is* and *thing is*, as in *but the thing is—at our age what is there what sort of facilities can you provide* and *thing is—he's watching the man he's not watching the ball*. A prepositional phrase can be added, as in *the thing about school is that you can get them to relax*, or an adjective phrase, as in *that's the bad thing—there's always someone knocking on your door*.

New propositions or entities can be introduced and highlighted by a question uttered and answered by the speaker: *Do you know what he's just done? He's invited his sister to come and stay*, or *And who's coming to stay with us? His sister!*

Another highlighting item is *like*. It is dismissed by some analysts as a pause-filler, but has specific functions and occurs frequently where there are no pauses or hesitations. It typically highlights an item explaining a preceding piece of discourse or leading to an explanation. In interrogatives, it concentrates a request for information on a particular point.

so like you were left with three teachers
there? (8)
[the speaker is checking on information that has already been given by the addressee]

A: we get lectures there as well I've been on a (9)
    chemistry one
B: I've been on a chemistry one as well—that was a right
    bore the sex life of insects
C: really in chemistry? I thought that would be in like
    biology
[emphasizes contrast between biology and chemistry]
B: no it was chemistry they kept giving us all the silly
    formulas

A: ...sometimes I go there with my family you (10)
    know— it's really tremendous cause—there's
    wee kiddies' pool you know where my wee girl
    can swim you know—she has her wings
    like—she jumps right in ...
[explaining that A's daughter is not really precocious, merely that she does not need to keep herself afloat]

5. Linguistics and Spoken and Written Language

Ong (1982) presents evidence that 'nonliterate folk' (his term) reason, communicate, and remember information differently from 'literate folk.' The work reported above demonstrates the distance between spoken and written English, and differences between standard and nonstandard further complicate matters. For spoken and written Russian, for example, the problems are even greater, basic constituent structure being affected along with the arrangement of clauses, types of referring expressions, and the case system, quite apart from the organization of discourse.

A number of fundamental research questions arise. Spoken language being acquired naturally, but written language being taught in schools, and the move from nonliteracy to literacy entailing large cognitive changes as argued by Ong (1982) and Goody (1977), the adequacy of theories of first language acquisition and those of language typologies is called into question. English is not classified as a language with double negation and the relative clause structure of general complementizer and shadow pronoun, yet these constructions are typical of much nonstandard-spoken and general-spoken English, respectively. One is also led to question the adequacy for spoken language of theories of constituent structure, based on edited, integrated, manipulable, written texts rather different from loosely structured, informal, spoken texts. The problem has been noticed with respect to, for example, certain Australian aboriginal languages, which seem to lack complex constituent structure, but it has not even been addressed with respect to the spoken varieties of the major written languages. Spoken and written language is an immense topic. Its importance has gone largely unrecognized in linguistics (the Prague School are honorable exceptions) but its theoretical day approaches.

See also: Literacy; Oracy; Register.

Bibliography

Brown E K, Miller J 1980 *Syntax of Scottish English*. End of Grant Report to the Social Science Research Council
Goody J 1977 *The Domestication of the Savage Mind*. Cambridge University Press, Cambridge, UK
Halliday M A K 1989 *Spoken and Written Language*. Oxford University Press, Oxford, UK
Höhne-Leska C 1975 *Statistische Untersuchungen zur Syntax gesprochener und geschriebener deutscher Gegenwartssprache*. Akademie-Verlag, Berlin
Kapanadze L A, Zemskaja E A 1979 *Teksty*. Nauka, Moscow
Kitajgorodskaja M V 1988 Nabljudenija nad postroeniem ustnogo prostorechnogo teksta. In: *Raznovidnosti Gorodskoj Ustnoj Rechi*. Nauka, Moscow
Kroll B 1977 Combining ideas in spoken and written English. In Keenan E O, Bennet T L (eds.) Discourse *across Time and Space. Southern California Occasional Papers in Linguistics* **5**: 69–108
Macaulay R K S 1991 *Locating Dialect in Discourse*. Oxford University Press, New York
Ong W J 1982 *Orality and Literacy*. Methuen, London
Stubbs M 1980 *Language and Literacy*. Routledge and Kegan Paul, London
Wackernagel-Jolles B 1971 *Untersuchungen zur gesprochenen Sprache: Beobachtungen zur Verknüpfung spontanen Sprechens*. Alfred Kümmerle, Göppingen, Germany

Speech Play

M. L. Apte

Since both language and play are panhuman activities, it is not surprising to find language as manifested in speech to be the object of play in most societies. Not until the nineteenth century, however, did scholars begin to regard speech play as a worthwhile topic of research. This was in keeping with the neglect of the topic of 'play' itself. Although play is one of the most common and fundamental activities not only of humans but also of many animals, it was not given serious attention by scholars.

The situation has changed, however, during the second half of the twentieth century. It has become increasingly clear to linguists, anthropologists, folklorists, historians, antiquarians, and scholars from related disciplines that play in general, and speech play in particular, is a major activity in its own right in most cultures of the world. The form, function, and sociocultural context of both structured and unstructured play have been and continue to be extensively analyzed.

1. The Concept of Play Defined

The single most influential work in the domain of play is that of Huizinga (1955). Since then, others have studied the phenomenon of play extensively, and several theories have been presented concerning the form and function of play. In 1974, scholars from various disciplines in the humanities and the social and natural sciences in the USA, who were interested in researching play, established The Association for the Study of Play (TASP). Since its inception, the association has held annual meetings, and several volumes of papers presented at these meetings have been published. The association also publishes a journal, *Play and Culture*.

In general, play is considered an activity that is carried out within the boundaries of space and time, is voluntary in nature, and is distinct by its lack of seriousness and purpose except that which arises from within its arbitrarily defined context. It is also marked by manipulation of objects, movements, and sheer creativity. The function of these activities is solely the pleasure derived from them. There is no outside reference or aim toward which it is directed. Play is most often carried out in an 'as if' reality, a second reality which is distinct from the sociocultural reality.

2. Speech Play

Speech play is a type of play in which language is the principal focus of attention. Language is manipulated in various ways as a part of the social interaction within the play frame. The purpose of engaging in such activity is entertainment, amusement, and aesthetic pleasure. Both adults and children engage in speech play. Speech play can be unstructured or structured. If the latter, it constitutes the category of games within the broad conceptual domain of play.

The remainder of this section indicates the scope of research carried out up to the time of writing, and more is likely to be undertaken in the future. The disciplinary and theoretical orientations of the scholars often determine which aspects of play are emphasized.

The first objective has been the identification, analysis, and description of different types of speech play in individual cultures. The main purpose is to establish some kind of typology of verbal games and unstructured speech play. In addition, the underlying patterns, conventions, formulaic rules, etc. which characterize each type of speech play are described in detail. Established types are often referred to as speech genres, and indigenous folk labels for them are identified. Research conducted during the second half of the twentieth century has resulted in the establishment of several types of speech play, such as puns, nursery rhymes, counting-out rhymes, nonsense words, limericks, riddles, ritual insults, verbal contests, mnemonic devices, and jokes, to name just a few. The broad structural characteristics of each have been identified. Such a typology is useful as an initial descriptive framework for an investigator just beginning research on speech play in a specific culture until s/he can establish the culture-specific categories.

The second objective is the description of the sociocultural contexts in which various types of speech play take place. Although speech play is generally a leisure-time activity, existing ethnographic evidence suggests that well-established genres of speech play in some cultures take place in very specific nonleisure environments. For instance, they are used in competition for selecting the most versatile, articulate, and creative individual, who thereby acquires social prestige. Occasionally, speech play is a part of religious rituals.

The third objective is the examination of the putative or actual functions served by verbal games. It is important to note that although children are thought to be the most active participants in speech play, it is not unusual in many cultures for adults also to engage in speech play.

Cross-cultural comparison of speech play is the fourth objective, in order to discover which types have a wide distribution reflecting panhuman patterns and universal human tendencies. For example, it can be assumed that punning occurs in all cultures. Similarities and differences in form and content of various types of speech play need to be investigated, and cross-cultural variations need to be explained. For example, the riddle may be a universal category, but the structure, rules, and sociocultural contexts of riddles may differ across cultures.

The final objective has been to evaluate the relevance and effectiveness of theories for explaining the universal and culture-specific nature of speech play and its place in the sociocultural system as a whole. New theories need to be developed if the existing ones appear unsatisfactory for explaining the forms and functions of speech play within a universal framework or for accounting for cross-cultural variation.

There is extensive ethnographic literature describing and analyzing speech play in many cultures. Many ethnographic studies have focused on specific types of speech play. For instance, there is extensive literature on puns, riddles, tongue-twisters, nonsense words, secret languages, counting games, ritual insults, jokes, and verbal duels (see the bibliography in Kirshenblatt-Gimblett 1976). Whether or not these genres are to be considered universal categories is a moot issue.

3. Linguistic Characteristics of Speech Play

Since speech play involves the use of language in innovative ways for amusement, there is no limit to the kinds of games that can be invented. It appears that all structural elements and domains of language can be and are involved in speech play. For example, the label 'tongue-twisters' is used to describe speech play that is typically based on the difficulties of articulation when a sentence having several similar speech sounds is uttered rapidly. For example, the English sentence *She sits and shells, she shells and sits* is a tongue-twister, since it contains the consonants [s] and [ʃ], which are similar and which appear in close proximity in succession. The virtuoso performance involves repeating such a sentence rapidly and correctly. If mistakes in such a performance result in the sentence becoming obscene and/or scatological, it is considered even more amusing. Anyone trying to utter the above example rapidly can quickly find out what happens.

Another type of speech play involves inventing utterances that sound the same when recited forward and backward. The Marathi-speaking children in India show off by reciting such utterances as [cimā kāy kāmācī] 'What use is Chima [proper name of a female] for work?' and [to gajānana jāgto] 'That Gajanan [proper name of a male] stays awake' in which the sequences of syllables sound the same forward and backward. Such structural play is based on language-specific phonotactic constraints, and the existing permissible phonological sequences are exploited for novel creations.

Secret and/or play languages are created by changing the phonological structure of words in utterances. The most commonly employed mechanisms for developing such languages are addition, subtraction, reversal, and substitution. Pig Latin is probably the best-known secret language among English-speaking children. The utterances in it are created by phonological transformation of the first phoneme of each word to the end of it and then tacking on the vowel glide /ey/. Thus an English sentence *He does not know it* becomes *ehay oesday otnay owknay itay*.

Such secret and/or play languages have been described from many cultures. Among the Cuna Indian children of Panama, there exist several play languages which have been analyzed by Sherzer (1976), who has also presented French and Javanese play languages. One interesting aspect of the play languages which Sherzer described was that they were all derived from extremely colloquial speech varieties among the respective linguistic communities. The novel creations resulting from the various mechanisms mentioned above do not always have to be meaningful for sheer aural pleasure. Very young children often string together sounds of their language in an arbitrary way, creating nonsense words, and can actually converse with other children until they all end up giggling.

Speech play is also based on morphology. Children often create new words using various affixes. They also enjoy combining words in unusual ways. Creating the longest words or creating utterances which are alliterative are some of the common games that children engage in.

Semantics is the basis of much speech play. Puns are based on exploiting the relationship between form and meaning. A word or a phrase is used in discourse in such a way that the primary or literal meaning gives way to metaphorical and/or secondary meaning. Many children's riddles are based on such punning. For example, note the following riddle:

Question: Who crosses the river twice and is still not clean?
Answer: A dirty double-crosser.

Puns occur not only in the speech of children but also in that of adults. Some adults seem particularly prone to punning, which has been both highly praised and strongly criticized. For some, punning reflects an intellectual skill, while for others it is the lowest type of humor. Redfern (1984) takes the view that the pun has been given a bad name without justification. There is extensive literature on the nature and function of puns, including interlingual puns.

Whether mistakes committed in linguistic performance can be considered speech play or not is debatable. The intention of the speaker is a crucial criterion in such determination. For example, the most commonly found types of inadequate linguistic performance are spoonerisms and malapropisms. In a spoonerism, transposition of linguistic units such as phonemes, syllables, morphemes, words, or phrases occurs in an utterance, thereby resulting in a different one often unintended by the speaker. William Spooner, the dean and warden of New College in Oxford, from whose name the label is supposed to have been derived, was well known for such utterances. For example, among the popular spoonerisms associated with him are *noble tons of soil*, *You have hissed all my mystery lectures*, and *You have tasted the whole worm*. It is doubtful that Spooner was deliberately engaging in speech play when he uttered these sentences.

Similarly, a malapropism is defined as 'ridiculous misuse of a word in place of one it resembles in sound, especially when the speaker is seeking a more elevated or technical style than is his wont and the blunder destroys the intended effect' (Hockett 1967: 927). The term is derived from the fictional character Mrs Malaprop, to whom is attributed the following utterance: *If I reprehend anything in this world, it is the use of my oracular tongue, and a nice derangement of epitaphs* (Nash 1985: 149). In the occurrence of malapropisms, the speaker is not even aware of the fact that s/he has committed an error. Thus, while from the listener's viewpoint such errors may be mirth-evoking, they cannot be described as speech play since such may not be the intention of the speaker.

4. Speech Play and Performance

Since verbal interaction is an inevitable aspect of social interaction, it is not surprising that speech play is a social phenomenon. As such, those who are skillful at displaying their virtuosity are often in demand and achieve prestige and status by their display. In many cultures, such performance becomes part of a competitive interaction. The most stylized forms of speech play involving such competition are ritual insults and verbal duels, which occur in many societies. For example, they are popular among African-American boys and girls, Turkish boys, Samoan children, and children and adults among the Chamula Indians in Mexico, and they have been analyzed (see also *Verbal Duel*).

While the use of language in everyday social interaction is rarely labeled as performance in common parlance, there are well-established conventions for performances of music, dance, and drama. In theater, comedies use speech play extensively, and spectators who watch them have a full expectation of deriving pleasure from such a display by various characters. The performative aspect of speech play becomes important in the proper execution of conventions established for different genres of speech play.

Although during the early period of language acquisition children go through several stages of spontaneous, unstructured speech play, they increasingly learn various types of structured speech play which often take the forms of linguistic games. Children also learn and memorize from their peers many ready-made examples of such genres of speech play as rhymes, jokes, taunts, insults, and riddles.

Linguistic games have established rules which the children learn from their older siblings and more experienced peers, since knowledge of the rules is a prerequisite for participation in these games. Some children even become very adept at exploiting the existing rules for their personal benefit (Goldstein 1971). Some are also better at playing these games than others. What is important is that all participants know the rules of whatever games are being played, so that nonconformity is not tolerated. Therefore, structured speech play assists in the process of socialization.

5. Speech Play and Verbal Art

The views in the existing literature concerning the difference between these two concepts are not clearcut. Sanches and Kirshenblatt-Gimblett (1976) claim that in speech play there is more emphasis on the process itself, in contrast to verbal art, which focuses on the form rather than the content. They also claim that the concept of verbal art is more appropriate to adult activity involving speech performance, since children are not aware of the notion of art, and that children are engaged in speech play activity as an end in itself. Despite these and other attempts to separate speech play and verbal art, the fact remains that they overlap considerably, and only contextual factors can determine whether or not a given occurrence of verbal performance can be labeled as speech play or verbal art.

6. Speech Play and Humor

The nature of the relationship between humor and speech play is complex and multifaceted. Since both frequently lead to a mirthful state of mind, and since both focus extensively on language, there is much overlap. Another similarity is that both are culturally conditioned. Many humor genres can also be considered as types of speech play (Esar 1952). For example, riddle and pun are humor genres as well as types of speech play. Both are based on performance, innovative ability, and creativity, and have fixed structures.

Only linguistic games which involve competition can be said to be devoid of humor. This is true only for the contestants, however. The spectators of verbal duels and/or ritual insults and other types of competitive speech play are not concerned with who wins but are keen on enjoying the entertainment and amusement provided by them. It is, therefore, almost impossible to list criteria that can be uniformly applied to separate humor from speech play. Whether a particular verbal performance is an example of speech play or of humor or of both can only be contextually determined. For the most part, its allocation to one or the other category may be somewhat arbitrary.

7. Speech Play and Cognitive, Linguistic, and Sociocultural Development Among Children

Children in all societies and cultures learn language as an essential part of their enculturation and socialization process. One significant way in which children learn to master the language of their community is speech play. Many types of speech play, such as riddles, jokes, play languages, and counting-out rhymes, facilitate children's cognitive development. They also contribute to children's social development by enabling them to gain experience of how to plan strategies, how to put on public performances, and how to deal with interrogation, ambiguity, and humiliation. Speech play is thus important in children's understanding of the nature of social relationships and their place in them. Children engage not only in manipulating the structure of the language in their speech play, but also in mimicking the speech of adults by pretending to act out various social roles in their play activities. Thus, speech play assists considerably in children's mastery of both the structure of language and its culturally appropriate use.

See also: Verbal Duel; Slang: Sociology.

Bibliography

Abrahams R D 1964 *Deep Down in the Jungle*. Folklore Associates, Philadelphia, PA
Apte M L 1985 *Humor and Laughter: An Anthropological Approach*. Cornell University Press, Ithaca, NY
Bryant M 1983 *Riddles: Ancient and Modern*. Hutchinson, London
Dundes A, Leach J W, Ozkok B 1970 The strategy of Turkish boys' verbal dueling rhymes. *Journal of American Folklore* **83**: 325–49
Esar E 1952 *The Humor of Humor*. Bramhall House, New York
Farb P 1974 *Word Play*. Alfred A Knopf, New York
Goldstein K 1971 Strategy in counting out: An ethnographic field study. In: Avoden E, Sutton-Smith B (eds.) *The Study of Games*. Wiley, New York
Hockett C F 1967 Where the tongue slips, there slip I. In: To honor Roman Jakobson. *Janua Linguarum, Series Maier* **32**: 910–36
Huizinga J 1955 *Homo Ludens*. Beacon Press, Boston, MA
Jorgenson M 1983 Anti-school parodies as speech play and social protest. In: Manning F E (ed.) *The World of Play*. Leisure Press, West Point, NY
Kirshenblatt-Gimblett B 1976 *Speech Play*. University of Pennsylvania Press, Philadelphia, PA
Kochman T (ed.) 1972 *Rappin' and Stylin' Out*. University of Illinois Press, Urbana, IL
McDowell J 1979 *Children's Riddling*. Indiana University Press, Bloomington, IN
Mitchell-Kernan C, Kernan K T 1975 Children's insult: America and Samoa. In: Sanches M, Blount B G (eds.)

Sociocultural Dimensions of Language Use. Academic Press, New York
Nash W 1985 *The Language of Humour.* Longman, New York
Opie I, Opie P 1959 *The Lore and Language of School Children.* Oxford University Press, Oxford, UK
Pepicello W J, Green T A 1984 *The Language of Riddles: New Perspectives.* Ohio State University Press, Columbus, OH
Redfern W 1984 *Puns.* Basil Blackwell, Oxford, UK
Sanches M, Kirshenblatt-Gimblett B 1976 Children's traditional speech play and child language. In: Kirshenblatt-Gimblett B (ed.) *Speech Play.* University of Pennsylvania Press, Philadelphia, PA
Schieffelin B B 1982 Talking like birds: Sound plays in a cultural perspective. In: Loy J (ed.) *The Paradoxes of Play.* Leisure Press, West Point, NY
Sherzer J 1976 Play languages: Implications for (socio)-linguistics. In: Kirshenblatt-Gimblett B (ed.) *Speech Play.* University of Pennsylvania Press, Philadelphia, PA
Stewart S 1979 *Nonsense: Aspects of Intertextuality in Folklore and Literature.* Johns Hopkins University Press, Baltimore, MD

Style
M. Short

The most commonsensical understanding of the meaning of the word 'style' is that it relates to the typical way(s) in which one or more people do a particular thing. Thus, eating one's food slowly, chewing each mouthful 50 times with one's mouth closed constitutes a different style of eating when compared with someone who eats quickly, hardly chewing the food at all. As Ohmann (1964) puts it, style is a *way* of doing *it*. Style in language behavior thus becomes alternative ways of expressing the same content. This commonsense starting point will be used for this discussion of style.

1. Style as Linguistic Choice

It should be clear that style in the sense outlined above can only exist if there is more than one way of saying or doing the same thing. Hence, substituting a *b* for a *p* before *-in* does *not* constitute a phonetic *style* choice because the two different results, *bin* and *pin*, have different contents. Saying *bin* in a gravelly voice on the one hand, or a squeaky voice on the other, could be a style marker. The equivalent of this kind of distinction at a lexical level can be seen when comparing (a) *He mounted his horse* with (b) *He mounted his bicycle* and (c) *He mounted his steed.* The change of noun from *horse* to *bicycle* involves reference to a different entity in the word, and so (a) and (b) are not two ways of saying the same thing, but descriptions of two different actions. On the other hand, replacing *horse* with *steed* or *nag* (see (a) and (c) above) can be said to constitute a style choice because the resulting sentences can be seen as alternative ways of describing the same action. It is from this kind of observation that it has been noted that style can be construed as linguistic choice (cf. Enkvist 1964, 1986, Halliday 1971), although, given the above discussion of *bin* and *pin*, and *horse* and *bicycle*, it would be more accurate to say that linguistic choice is a necessary but not a sufficient condition for the existence of style in language. As linguistic choice can occur at any linguistic level, it will be clear that particular styles may result from choices made at any linguistic level or combination of levels.

In particular linguistic contexts, however, choices apparently made possible by the language system will not necessarily be available, as Fowler (1972) makes clear. Consider the two sentence *She called him* and *He was called by her.* The active sentence and its passive reformulation would appear to be two equivalent syntactic ways of expressing the same content. But, with different preceding linguistic contexts, the apparently free choice disappears. The first of the above two sentences appears more or less obligatory when preceded by *And then you'll never believe what the rat did next ...* , while the second is demanded by a preceding sentence like *And that wasn't all that happened to her.* In essence, what happens here is that other, more important considerations make an apparently free choice obligatory. In this case, given/new relations in the information structure of the sentences are paramount. But a whole range of considerations are almost certainly involved, for example, the avoidance of ambiguity or inelegance. So, *He looked the book up* has *He looked up the book* as an alternative. But if the beginning of the sentence in which the clause appears is *He looked up the stairs and then ...* , the second of the above two choices is unlikely because it predisposes the hearer/reader toward an interpretation where the subject of the sentence peers along the book's cover, from top to bottom, rather than consulting a library catalog. On the other hand, *He looked up the book upstairs* is much more likely than *He looked the book up upstairs*, at least in written English, because it avoids inelegant immediate repetition of *up*. Hence, what constitutes linguistic choice is not always as straightforward a matter as it might at first seem.

In looking thus at possibilities of style choice within the boundaries of the system of rules which constitutes the English language, it is clear that an understanding of style must involve comparisons between what actually occurs and what might have occurred. But it is also worth noting that writers can make *deviant* choices, that is, choices which fall outside the normal bounds of English. Such choices may affect style and/or meaning (Enkvist 1964, 1973: 98–108, 1986). If a modern writer wants to give his writing a highly 'poetic' style, for example, he might well choose archaic words (e.g., *haycock*) and structures (e.g., adjective after, instead of before, the noun—*haycocks dry*). A novelist might choose a much more informal language for his narrations than is conventional (e.g., Mark Twain, J. D. Salinger, Alan Sillitoe), thus giving his writing a characteristic style by deviating from the assumed norms for the novel. Some writers (e.g., the poet E. E. Cummings) have created characteristic writing styles by deviating from the grammatical, semantic, and orthographical norms of English in very dramatic ways.

It will be clear from the foregoing that a consideration of style must in some sense be comparative. At a microlevel, one compares what occurs with other choices which might have been made within or outside the language system to express roughly the same content. This comparative aspect does not, however, have to be conducted in such a restricted way. For example, it is possible for someone to talk about Conrad's style as opposed to that of James or Lawrence, in spite of the fact that the contents expressed are unlikely to be equivalent. Indeed, to find two writers producing different versions of the same content is comparatively rare (but compare parodies and rewritings, for example, Twain's rewriting of a piece by James Fenimore Cooper, see Hendricks 1976: 183–210). For styles to be established irrespective of content, regularity of choice with respect to particular style features becomes paramount.

2. Style and Iterativity

For a style to exist, the same sort of linguistic choice must be repeated on a reasonably consistent, iterative basis. One of the style features commonly thought to be characteristic of the language of science, for example, is the regular use of passive constructions with deleted agents (e.g., 'the copper sulfate was placed in the test-tube'). This does not mean that other kinds of writers do not use this construction, or indeed that scientists always use passives with agent-deletion in preference to active constructions or passives without agent-deletion. Instead, a statistical assumption is being made to the effect that, all other things being equal, scientific writing will display a significantly higher use of this construction than, say, romantic fiction. This statistical basis for style is made clear in Leech and Short (1981: 42–73). But the issues concerning what is to be counted, how big differences between two writers have to be in order to be significant, and so on, are both complex and technical (see, for example, Doležel and Bailey 1969, Morton 1978), and many analysts and students of language and literature have shied away from taking the study of style to its ultimate, quantified conclusion because they feel either that the work needed does not justify the effort expended, or that such a 'mathematical' approach is unsuited to the humanist discussion of literature. A further issue, which is by no means fully understood, is the way in which linguistic structure, including structural iteration, interacts with context and with expectations on the part of the reader or hearer. Because people expect to find passives in scientific writing, or abstract nouns in the prose of Henry James, they are likely to respond more to such entities when coming across them in these contexts than in other texts, even if those other texts contain a higher proportion of the features concerned. At the end of the day, however, style must have some quantitative basis.

3. 'Style = Content' versus 'Style = Meaning'

This discussion of style began with the familiar notion that a style is a particular *way* of doing *it*. This way of looking at style, what is left after content is removed, is a longstanding one, going back at least to Aristotle's *Poetics*, and having many elegant proponents, including Pope (in *Essay on Criticism*):

> True wit is nature to advantage dressed,
> What oft was thought but ne'er so well expressed.

The most prominent view of style in the twentieth century, however, has appeared to contradict the traditional, commonsense account, by suggesting an equivalence between style and meaning. This view notes that there are no complete synonyms in language, that *horse, steed*, and *nag*, for example, do not mean exactly the same thing, and that the same can be said of the use of alternative grammatical constructions, like active and passive, which, at the very least, change given/new relations and the weighting of words in sentences. It has also been claimed that changing even apparently minor aspects of a text's linguistic structure may change its meaning. This is particularly true of short texts, like lyric poems.

This apparent bind, where style at the same time is and is not a bearer of meaning, is not easily escaped. The clue is in the exact words that the proponents of the different accounts use. On the one hand, style is separable from 'content.' On the other hand, it is not separable from 'meaning.' 'Meaning' is a much wider concept than 'content,' including content and other things besides, like connotation and significance. Leech and Short (1981: 19) argue that writers have choices both at the level of content (what to represent) and in terms of how that content is expressed, that is, style. But style choices can themselves still be meaningful in the widest sense of the term.

Since the 1960s, there has been a tendency to equate particular views of style with particular models of grammar and their proponents, as the title to Hendricks (1976), *Grammars of Style and Styles of Grammar*, makes manifest. So, Richard Ohmann (1964), working within an early version of the transformational–generative paradigm, has used the deep structure/surface structure distinction to articulate the content/form distinction, whereas Halliday (1971), using his systemic grammar, which admits no such binary distinctions as deep and surface structure, has been a proponent of the 'style = meaning' school. But it should be clear that although the structures of these two different systems of grammatical description tend to lead their proponents toward different characterizations of style, there is no *necessary* relationship between a particular grammatical account of language and a particular view of style. For example, the idea that different transformational derivational histories had no effect whatever on meaning has been clearly abandoned by transformational grammarians.

4. The Domain of Style

Style is most often discussed in the context of literary studies. This is not surprising, as western culture has tended to study literary writing more than any other form of language. But it should be clear that any person's reasonably consistent linguistic behavior could be said to constitute a style, whether it is spoken or written, or whether the language producer is deemed to be a literary figure or not. Different weather forecasters on the television have characteristically different ways of expressing the same information, different politicians typically give their speeches with different styles, and newspaper columnists also have different styles.

Although style is most often discussed with respect to some individual writer, the domain of style does not have to be that of an individual. There can also be what Hendricks (1976: 101–72) calls group styles. Hence, a group of writers with the same outlook, or coming from the same period of time, might well share a group style. Thus, one can talk of a gothic style or even an eighteenth-century style within discussion of the novel. For discussions of nonliterary group styles, see Crystal and Davy (1969), Huddleston (1971), and Todd and O'Donnell (1980). Within literary studies, most detailed discussions of style tend to concentrate on the domain of the individual writer.

5. Authorial Style and Text Style

If one examines the apparently simple notion of authorial style characterized by Buffon's famous phrase '*style, c'est l'homme même*' (see Ullmann 1973: 64–92), it can be seen that even in this domain there are at least two notions of style being used. The first amounts to the writing equivalent of an author's fingerprints, and is seen almost exclusively in studies trying to resolve authorship. There has been a long-running dispute over the authorship of some works traditionally attributed to Shakespeare, and there are similar debates over the authorship of some of the *Spectator* papers, and, in the USA, the *Federalist* papers. Representative examples of authorship studies are Francis (1966) and Morton (1978). In this sort of study, the items counted tend to be extremely frequent and as devoid of meaning as any linguistic items can be, for example, average word and sentence length, or the repetition rate per 1000 words for so-called grammatical words like 'and' or 'of,' because such differences among writers are least likely to be affected by changes in the topic or viewpoint.

The second version of authorial style is more recognizable to students of literature. This is when they characterize someone's writing as loose, copious, tight, abstract, baroque, and so on. In this case, statements about general characteristic beliefs of the writer concerned and his view of the world are often allied to the observed style characterizations. For this kind of authorial style, the items counted typically have rather more content, for example, abstract versus concrete nouns, or dynamic versus stative verbs. Typical examples of works of this kind of style study are Milic (1966, 1971) and Ohmann (1964). This understanding of style is coterminous with the notion of 'mind-style' related to authors, and of course it can also be associated with narrators and characters. It should be clear that what has been said about authorial style above applies equally to group styles.

Finally, many scholars try to characterize what might be called text style. In this case, the items examined are likely to be even more integrally connected with meaning. Examples would be Nash (1982) and Carter (1982). Leech and Short (1981: chap. 3) combine a comparative study of the second kind of authorial style with text style analysis. The fact that this is possible indicates that text style and the two kinds of authorial style outlined in this section are best seen not as mutually exclusive, but as different, partially overlapping sections of a continuum from finger-printing at one end to text style at the other. It also helps to explain some of the confusion surrounding the term 'stylistics,' which at first sight looks as if it should be used to denote the study of authorial and group style, in spite of the fact that most proponents of stylistics concentrate on the relationship between linguistic structure and textual meaning.

It should also be stressed that a text does not need to keep consistently to one style. Indeed, style variation within some text is invariably perceived by readers as significant and hence meaningful, as a consequence of the process of internal deviation. Adamson (1989) and Trengove (1989) discuss style variation within literary texts, and Fairclough (1988) examines such variation in a Barclaycard advertisement.

Discussion of style variation within literary texts has in a sense reintroduced the issue of the domain of style. In order for styles and changes of style to be significant within literary texts, they must be correlatable with style choices made in the language as a whole. A switch from travelog-like description to legal language in a novel by Dickens can only be understood if the reader can recognize such styles, or 'languages,' outside the novel. What is true of style features related to subject matter and domain is also true of features like formality. The traditional literary discussion of high, middle, and low styles presupposed the existence (which continues) of formality-related styles which speakers of a language switch among, independent of subject matter, either to conform to particular social norms (coffee-bar talk is more informal than debates in the House of Commons), or to produce unexpected and meaningful effects by departing from those norms in an obvious way.

See also: Literary Language; Register.

Bibliography

Adamson S 1989 With double tongue: Diglossia, stylistics and the teaching of English. In: Short M (ed.) *Reading, Analysing and Teaching Literature*. Longman, London
Carter R 1982 Style and interpretation in Hemingway's *Cat in the Rain*. In: Carter R (ed.) *Language and Literature: An Introductory Reader in Stylistics*. Allen and Unwin, London
Crystal D, Davy D 1969 *Investigating English Style*. Longman, London
Doležel L, Bailey R 1969 *Statistics and Style*. Elsevier, New York
Enkvist N E 1964 On defining style. In: Spencer J (ed.) *Linguistics and Style*. Oxford University Press, London
Enkvist N E 1973 *Linguistic Stylistics*. Mouton, The Hague
Enkvist N E 1986 Style as parameters in text strategy. In: Peer W van (ed.) *The Taming of the Text*. Routledge, London
Fairclough N 1988 Register, power and socio-semantic change. In: Birch D, O'Toole M (eds.) *Functions of Style*. Pinter, London
Fowler R 1972 Style and the concept of deep structure. *Journal of Literary Semantics* 1: 5–24
Francis I S 1966 An exposition of a statistical approach to the Federalist dispute. In: Leed J (ed.) *The Computer and Literary Style*. Kent State University Press, Kent, OH
Halliday M A K 1971 Linguistic function and literary style. In: Chatman S (ed.) *Literary Style: A Symposium*. Oxford University Press, Oxford, UK
Hendricks W O 1976 *Grammars of Style and Styles of Grammar*. North-Holland, Amsterdam
Huddleston R 1971 *The Sentence in Written English: A Syntactic Study Based on an Analysis of Scientific Texts*. Cambridge University Press, Cambridge, UK
Leech G N, Short M H 1981 *Style in Fiction*. Longman, London
Milic L T 1966 Unconscious ordering in the prose of Swift. In: Leed J (ed.) *The Computer and Literary Style*. Kent State University Press, Kent, OH
Milic L T 1971 Rhetorical choice and stylistic option: The conscious and unconscious poles. In: Chatman S (ed.) *Literary Style: A Symposium*. Oxford University Press, Oxford, UK
Morton A Q 1978 *Literary Detection: How to Prove Authorship and Fraud in Literature*. Bowker, London
Nash W 1982 On a passage from Lawrence's *Odour of Chrysanthemums*. In: Carter R (ed.) *Language and Literature: An Introductory Reader in Stylistics*. Allen and Unwin, London
Ohmann R 1964 Generative grammars and the concept of literary style. *Word* **20**: 424–39
Todd L, O'Donnell W R 1980 *Variety in Contemporary English*. Allen and Unwin, London
Trengove G 1989 'Vers de Société': Towards some society. In: Short M (ed.) *Reading, Analysing and Teaching Literature*. Longman, London
Ullmann S 1973 *Meaning and Style*. Blackwell, Oxford, UK

Taboo Words

M. L. Apte

The word 'taboo' (also spelled 'tabu') was introduced into English from Polynesian cultures where it played a significant part in the religious belief systems. The concept of taboo has been discussed in the writings of the anthropologists Frazer, Van Gennep, Wundt, Radcliffe-Brown, and Mead. Freud has also discussed it extensively in his book *Totem and Taboo*. Steiner (1967) provides the full history of the origin of the word, its various cognates and their meanings in Polynesian languages, its significance and functions in the religious belief systems of Polynesian cultures, and its relevance to anthropological and psychoanalytic theories. Under the entry 'Tabu' in the *Encyclopedia of Social Sciences*, Margaret Mead

(1937: 502–5) defined the concept as 'a negative sanction whose infringement results in an automatic penalty without human or superhuman mediation.' According to her, one of the several meanings of the Polynesian concept of taboo is 'any prohibitions which carry no penalties beyond the anxiety and embarrassment arising from a breach of strongly entrenched custom' (quoted in Steiner 1967: 143).

1. Taboo Words Defined

The primary semantic attribute of the concept of taboo in English seems to be the same as the meaning by Mead quoted above. Prohibition or avoidance is socially determined and its breach results in anxiety, embarrassment, and public shame. This seems to be the primary aspect of the notion of linguistic taboo. Taboo words are those that are to be avoided because they are deemed unfit for normal linguistic usage and by community consensus are banned in everyday language in the public domain. In Webster's *Ninth New Collegiate Dictionary* (1990) the second meaning of taboo as an adjective is 'banned on grounds of morality or taste.' As a noun its secondary meaning is 'a prohibition imposed by social custom or as a protective measure' and as a verb 'to avoid or ban as taboo.'

Much of the discussion of taboo words in popular and scholarly literature has been based on the assumption that certain words are offending, dangerous, or sacred. Thus, underlying the avoidance of taboo words are cultural values and belief systems according to which attitudes are formed and judgments are made regarding the offending, dangerous, or sacred nature of certain words. Since there are cross-cultural variations in attitudes and belief systems, there are also differences concerning the semantic range and topical nature of taboo words. Despite such differences, it appears that in many societies words pertaining to objects, actions, and phenomena within the following domains are considered taboo.

In general, words referring to processes and states of human biological existence appear to be taboo because of their association with danger and their anxiety-provoking nature. Words referring to birth, death, pregnancy, various illnesses and diseases, menstruation, sexual and excretary activities, feces, urine, blood, and semen are considered taboo in many societies. Another taboo domain is that of deceased persons, animals considered to have special powers, ancestors, and benevolent and malevolent supernatural beings and their activities. In many cultures, referring to dead persons, sacred objects, and animals and deities is considered taboo except when done by those endowed with special powers in situations of ritual significance.

One underlying belief regarding taboo words is the magical power of the spoken word. It is as if uttering a taboo word may bring about the occurrence of the object, action, or phenomenon it refers to. Words that refer to supernatural beings are also taboo because they, too, can invoke dangerous phenomena beyond the control of human beings. Taboo words are to be avoided because they are powerful and cause unforeseen consequences. It needs to be noted that there are degrees of tabooness and some words are much more strongly tabooed than others.

Whatever the taboo words, all societies have ways of obliquely expressing their meanings using paraphrases, synonyms, euphemisms, and code words. These linguistic processes are universal. In English, for example, many speakers will use the expression 'to pass away' instead of 'to die,' or instead of saying that a woman is pregnant an expression such as 'she is carrying' is used. Use of code words is quite common. Some are phonetically similar to the taboo words, e.g., 'shoot' for 'shit' or 'fudge' for 'fuck' or they are phonetically similar nonsense syllables, e.g., 'frig' for 'fuck,' 'heck' for 'hell.' Occasionally, abbreviations are also used, e.g., 's.o.b.' for 'son of a bitch' (Saporta 1988–9: 164–5). In English language cartoons in the USA, the established convention to indicate a character's use of taboo words is to use punctuation and diacritical marks as well as other symbols commonly found on typewriter keys, e.g., '!?#%@.'

2. Other Related Concepts and Words

Terms such as 'swear words,' 'curse words,' 'obscene words,' 'four-letter words,' and 'dirty words' are often used interchangeably with the expression 'taboo words' in popular and scholarly writings. Although avoidance or prohibition is the semantic attribute shared by all of them, the range of each is slightly different. Swear and/or curse words are those which invoke damnation, misfortune or degradation of the targeted person or object. Swearing and/or cursing reflect a speaker's wrath or frustration towards a person or an object. In English 'hell,' 'damn,' 'Jesus,' and 'Christ' are commonly used curse words and 'damn it,' 'God damn it,' 'damn you,' and 'go to hell' are frequently used swearing/cursing expressions. Swearing and cursing are thus ways of venting a strong emotion.

Defining the semantic range of obscene words is difficult because notions of obscenity vary across cultures, over a period of time within a culture, and from one person to another. It appears that words that refer to sexual organs and acts are obscene. Words referring to the same organs and activity in physicians' usage and in scientific writings, however, are not considered obscene. Words that refer to the various body elimination processes and excretary substances—'shit' is the most commonly used word—are also considered by many to be obscene though they are generally labeled 'scatological' in scholarly writing. The use of obscene and scatological words evokes disgust or repugnance in many listeners. In this respect obscenity is determined by the hearer of a linguistic utterance, in contrast to tabooness which is determined by the speaker. It is the hearer who is affected by obscene words while it is the speaker who decides which words are to be avoided because s/he considers them taboo. Not all taboo words are obscene from a speaker's point of view. Obscene words and phrases are also used for swearing and thus can belong to the category of swearing/cursing expressions. In English, a common swearing expression, for example, is 'fuck you.'

The expression 'four-letter words' is restricted because it is language specific. It is valid only for English in which many so-called obscene words, e.g., 'cock,' 'cunt,' 'fuck,' 'ball,' and 'shit' have only four letters in their spelling. It is quite possible that comparable words in other languages may also be spelled or written with four characters. No systematic comparative linguistic studies focusing on this issue exist.

The label 'dirty words' indicates a very personal and subjective attitude. For many individuals dirty words are those that refer to sexual organs and acts, body elimination processes such as defecation and urination, and excretary substances. In cultures where such acts are considered defiling and where an attitude of repugnance towards them exists, the mere use of such words arouses a strong reaction of disgust.

Whether or not a word used in speech belongs to any of the above categories depends on the sociocultural context. Generally, the use of taboo, obscene, swear/curse, four-letter, and dirty words is determined on the basis of whether the situation falls in the public or the private domain and whether the linguistic discourse is formal or informal. Words designated by any of the above labels are usually avoided in formal language in the public domain. The greater the aura of respectability in any social situation, the stricter the ban on using words that may be viewed as even mildly taboo. On the other hand, taboo words are likely to be used in social interactions among friends in a private domain where an informal speech style prevails. The use of slang among members of a close-knit group encourages the use of taboo words. According to popular belief persons in certain occupations such as the army, the navy, or construction work tend to use taboo words frequently. Their speech is considered 'colorful' by some (see also *Verbal Duel*; *Slang: Sociology*).

3. Cross-cultural Differences in Attitudes Towards Taboo Words

The domain of taboo words varies cross-culturally. The inclusion of vocabulary items for particular phenomena, acts, objects, etc., in the taboo word category depends on sociocultural values and attitudes. It can be hypothesized that in societies where sexual and excretary acts are generally accepted as necessary and natural, and attitudes towards them are casual and/or relaxed, there is less likelihood that words referring to sexual and excretory organs and acts will be treated as taboo. On the other hand, in societies with attitudes of disgust or repugnance towards sexual and excretary organs and acts, there is greater likelihood that words referring to them will be considered taboo.

Even in individual cultures attitudes towards sexual and excretary acts are likely to change over a period of time so that words once considered taboo may be used in speech. In nineteenth-century England and America, the puritanical ethics of communities and society at large resulted in an almost total ban on using words that referred to sexual and excretary organs, acts, and bodily excretions. Until the 1960s, these words were not used in print in the USA. In their place only the first letter, an empty space, or dashes were used. Even with liberalized attitudes, in the USA and other English-speaking communities from the mid-1960s onward, sexual and scatological words do not routinely occur in newspapers and magazines though they are now used in fictional writing. In a mass medium such as television, taboo, obscene, and swear/curse words are still not used. If they occur in real-life interview situations, they are beeped out. In the published transcripts of the taped conversations between US president Richard Nixon and his White House associates, which were full of taboo and obscene words, the expression 'expletives deleted' was used rather than the verbatim conversations.

To a large extent the sociocultural context of speech and the backgrounds of the participants in social interaction determine the use of taboo words. Such factors as enculturation and socialization, age, gender, social status, degree of religiocity, and educational level influence the use of taboo words in speech. Children and adults in agricultural rural communities have many opportunities of observing animal sexual behavior. Children growing up in poor families who lack privacy because of limited living space have many occasions to observe adult sexual activities. In such an environment references to sexual and excretory organs and activities may be common and casual. No sense of disgust or repugnance may be associated with the use of taboo or obscene words. On the other hand, a rural community may be strongly religious and hence is likely to avoid using blasphemous and swear/curse words. Much depends upon the socialization and enculturation processes which determine an individual's attitude regarding the taboo quality of words. An individual brought up in a religious and orthodox household with puritanical values is likely to consider many more words taboo than one brought up in a nonreligious atmosphere which may treat body-waste elimination processes and sexual and procreation acts as natural, not shameful or repugnant. Therefore, even within a specific culture, words that may be shocking to one individual and/or a particular group of people may not necessarily be so to others of a different background.

In general it appears that women, old persons, educated individuals, urbanities, and elites are less likely to use taboo, obscene, and swear words in public domains than men, young people, uneducated persons, rural folk, and the proletariat. Cultural notions of modesty and politeness often constrain individuals, especially women, from using taboo words in the public domain. In many societies such language is not permitted in social settings where both men and women are present.

Although women generally abstain from using taboo words in the public domain, in some cultures old women beyond menopause are known to compete with men in freely using such words (Apte 1985: 79–80). Even those who normally avoid taboo words in their routine use of language are given to using them on special occasions such as specific festivals and rituals. There is ethnographic evidence which indicates that in many societies saturnalian celebrations create an atmosphere where the use of taboo words and lewd and lascivious behavior on the part of participants is quite common. Such occasions have been labeled 'Rites of Reversal' (Apte 1985: 152–3).

4. Functions of and Responses to Taboo Words
The use of taboo words is generally associated with strong emotions. Therefore, speakers use them to express strong feelings and listeners respond with equally strong feelings and reactions. Speakers who are aware of the potential of taboo words to arouse strong reactions may deliberately use them to shock their listeners. The use of taboo words gives an individual a feeling of momentary freedom from social conventions and constraints. Individuals may also use taboo words as a protest against what they consider antiquated values regarding speech because using these words will make their listeners uncomfortable. The use of taboo words in such a context can also be considered a form of verbal aggression since those who believe in avoiding such words in their speech will be forced to hear them. In a way, then, one function of taboo words is to degrade listeners, especially women who are much less likely to use them because of the ideas of modesty that dominate women's actions and speech in many cultures (Apte 1985: 74–5). For the same reason the use of taboo words is common in ethnic slurs since such words reflect the strong aggressive and hostile feelings a speaker may have towards certain ethnic groups. Their use is meant to insult and offend the targeted group.

In some contexts the use of taboo and obscene words may serve an opposite function, namely to show affection. Verbal encounters among close friends may be full of taboo and obscene words as terms of endearment (Bloomfield 1933: 155, 401, Cameron 1969: 101) and occasionally may even be accompanied by insults and horseplay, all of which is seen as joking. This usually results in loud laughter (Apte 1985: 259).

Individuals may use taboo words to express pent-up emotions such as anger or frustration. Persons who have occupations that are stressful also tend to use taboo words since using them relieves tension. Anthropologist W. W. Pilcher (1972) who studied a community of longshoremen in the city of Portland, Oregon, USA, observed that there was a high degree of taboo word use among these men when they were working on board the ship since such work was quite hazardous and stressful. Once they were off the ship and engaged in leisure activities, the use of taboo words declined significantly. The longshoremen were also very careful in totally avoiding swearing, obscenities, and the use of taboo words in family surroundings.

The repeated use of taboo words diminishes their tabooness since the prohibition on their use is the crucial attribute of such a designation. Individuals who use taboo words excessively in their speech may become insensitive to both the socially determined taboo nature of these words and the fact that such words are offensive to listeners. Individuals known for their excessive use of taboo words may be avoided by others who do not wish to be offended.

5. Taboo Words and Linguistic Differentiation and Change
Linguistic research has shown that in many societies the speech of men and women differs and that the degree of such difference can vary from one society to another. One explanation put forward for this is that the phenomenon of taboo causes these gender speech-differences since men in many linguistic communities use words in several contexts that woman never use. However, linguistic differences attributed to gender differences occur not only with regard to vocabulary, but also with regard to phonology, morphology, and syntax (Trudgill 1983: 78–99). The extensive research done on the topic of language and gender (see references in McConnell-Ginet 1988) since the mid-1970s reflects the complexity of the problem.

To what extent language change is due to the existence of taboo words has not been systematically investigated. It is common for speakers of a language to avoid not only taboo words but other phonetically similar words which consequently may fall out of use and become extinct. An explanation for the replacement of the old word 'coney' (pronounced [kʌni]) by the word 'rabbit' is that the former sounds very similar to a taboo word (Trudgill 1983: 31). No quantitative studies exist, however, to test such a hypothesis.

See also: Slang: Sociology; Anthropological Linguistics.

Bibliography

Apte M L 1985 *Humor and Laughter: An Anthropological Approach.* Cornell University Press, Ithaca, NY
Baudhuin E S 1973 Obscene language and evaluative response. *Psychological Reports* **32**: 399–402
Bloomfield L 1933 *Language.* George Allen and Unwin, London
Cameron P 1969 Frequency and kinds of words in various social settings or what the hell's going on? *Pacific Sociological Review* **12**(2): 101–4
Eckler A R 1986–87 A taxonomy for taboo-word studies. *Maledicta* **9**: 201–3
Fleming M 1977 Analysis of a four-letter word. *Maledicta* **1, 2**: 173–84
Hartogs R, Fantel H 1976 *Four-letter Word Games: The Psychology of Obscenity.* M Evans and Co. Delacorte Press, New York
Jay T B 1977 Doing research with dirty words. *Maledicta* **1, 2**: 234–56
McConnel-Ginet S 1988 Language and gender. In: Newmeyer F J (ed.) *Linguistics: The Cambridge Survey IV, Language: The Socio-cultural Context.* Cambridge University Press, Cambridge, UK
Mead M 1937 Tabu. In: Seligman E R A (ed.) *Encyclopaedia of Social Sciences, Vol. 14.* Macmillan, New York
Montagu A 1967 *The Anatomy of Swearing.* Macmillan, New York
Partridge E 1947 *Usage and Abusage: A Guide to Good English.* Hamish Hamilton, London
Pilcher W W 1972 *The Portland Longshoremen: A Dispersed Urban Community.* Holt, Rinehart and Winston, New York
Sagarin E 1962 *The Anatomy of Dirty Words.* Lyle Stuart, New York
Saporta S 1988–9 Linguistic taboos, code-words and women's use of sexist language. *Maledicta* **10**: 163–6
Steiner F 1967 *Taboo.* Penguin Books, Harmondsworth, UK
Trudgill P 1983 *Sociolinguistics: An Introduction to Language and Society.* Penguin Books, Harmondsworth, UK
Wentworth H, Flexner S B 1967 *Dictionary of American Slang.* Crowell, New York

The Internet and Language
C. Thurlow

Weblish, netlingo, e-talk, tech-speak, wired-style, geek-speak, netspeak, and so on are all terms used popularly to describe the sort of language and communication in the different channels (or 'niches') of the internet (or net): emails, chatrooms, bulletin boards, newsgroups, websites, and 'virtual worlds.' As a subfield of Computer-Mediated Communication (CMC), what interests sociolinguists most about language on the internet are the particular forms and functions of *netlingo* or *netspeak*, and whether they are sufficiently different from other varieties of language to justify such distinctive labels.

1. Mapping the Potential Field

In spite of increasingly widespread usage, there is still only a modest literature on the sociolinguistics of the internet; nevertheless, interest in language and the internet may be divided loosely into five interrelated themes:
(a) *multilingualism* (e.g., the prevalence and status of different languages on the internet);
(b) *language change* (e.g., lexical, syntactic, grammatical, stylistic, and other linguistic changes over time);
(c) *conversation/discourse* (e.g., changing patterns of social interaction and communicative practice);
(d) *stylistic diffusion* (e.g., the spread of internet jargon and linguistic forms into general usage);
(e) *metalanguage and folklinguistics* (e.g., the way these linguistic forms and changes are labeled and discussed).

2. The Contexts of Computer-mediated Communication (CMC)

There is no homogenous speech community on the internet; equally there is no single language of the internet. New ways of communicating on the internet are evolving and emerging all the time in response to technological and social changes. As research shows, any evaluation of language and communication on

the internet therefore needs to take certain contextual factors into account, for example:
- (a) the format and type of channel (e.g., email or webpages);
- (b) the participants (e.g., male or female, young or old);
- (c) the length and nature of their relationship (e.g., long-term or fleeting, personal or business);
- (d) the topic and purpose of the exchange (e.g., medical advice or romantic date);
- (e) the general attitude of participants towards communication on the internet (e.g., enthusiastic or skeptical); and,
- (f) whether interaction is asynchronous (i.e., not in real-time) or synchronous (i.e., in real-time).

3. Multilingualism: The Languages of the Internet

The tendency when speaking of netlingo has been to assume—rightly or wrongly—that it is necessarily a variety of English. While the proportion of English used on the internet remains considerably high, figures supplied by organizations such as *Cyberatlas* confirm the diminishing influence of English. (English-speaking internet users: 1996—80 percent, 2000—50 percent, 2005—30 percent.) The dominance of English as the language of the net will inevitably be diminished by the rise of other languages (especially Chinese), not least in the face of increasing commercialization which demands an attention to niche markets.

4. Language Change: Writing That Looks Like Speech?

Influenced by the physical constraints of the technology itself (e.g., typed text) and shifting socialeconomic priorities (e.g., globalization), *netlingo* emerges from the coinages, jargon, and communicative practices of those specialist groups (e.g., computer *geeks* and *hackers*) driving the development of communication technologies.

The emphasis in *netlingo* is on a mixture of speed, efficiency, informality, and creative typography whereby many of the traditional rules of grammar and style are subverted. To this end, *netlingo* relies principally on expression which is QWERTY-driven (i.e., whatever is possible with the computer keyboard) and economic (i.e., saving a keystroke wherever possible). Some of the most commonly recognized patterns of language change are:
- (a) lexical compounds and blends: e.g., *weblish, shareware, netiquette, e-* and *cyber-* anything;
- (b) abbreviations and acronyms: e.g., *THX* 'thanks,' *IRL* 'in real life,' *F2F* 'face-to-face,' *some1* 'someone';
- (c) minimal to no use of capitalization, punctuation, and hyphenation: e.g., *cooperate* and, of course, *email* and *internet*;
- (d) generally less regard for accurate spelling and/ or typing errors;
- (e) less or no use of traditional openings and closures: e.g., *Dear...* (sometimes *Hi* or *Hello* instead) or *Yours sincerely*.

Based on a sample of nine bulletin boards, Collot and Belmore (in Herring 1996) have compared a 200,000-word *Electronic Language Corpus* with traditional genres of written and spoken English. Noting the relative frequency and configuration of different linguistic features, they have found that the language is more 'involved' than 'informational,' less narrative (e.g., fewer makers of reported speech), and uses fewer overt expressions of persuasion. As such, the *netlingo* of this particular niche most closely resembles that of public interviews and letters (personal and professional).

Similarly, Baron (1998) has drawn a complex, linguistic profile of emails, concluding that they are a 'creolizing linguistic modality'—a hybrid of speech and writing in terms of format, grammar, and style. Again, the tendency is to break the traditional, rule-bound conventions of written language in favor of the more sociable-interactive orientation of speech.

5. Conversation/Discourse: Speech That Looks Like Writing?

The communicative/conversational style of internet language is best observed in the channels of synchronous CMC (or *netspeak*) with its imaginative attempts to overcome technological restraints (e.g., transmission time lags) and to reinstate social cues often absent from written text. Such channels are the open-ended, text-based exchanges of online chatrooms; the elaborate, text-based role-playing games of MUDs (Multi-User Domains); or, more recently, the graphical chat environments of Virtual Worlds.

Communication in these niches is highly interactive, with added demands for speed, spontaneity and, often, brevity; it is also more likely to involve multiple participants. As such, *netspeak* is invariably more dynamic, unpredictable, spontaneous, and public, and some of the most common strategies are those used in pursuit of brevity, paralinguistic restitution, relationship, and play:
- (a) letter homophones (e.g., *RU* 'are you,' *OIC* 'oh I see'), acronyms (e.g., *LOL* 'laugh out loud,' *WG* 'wicked grin'), and a mixture of both (e.g., *CYL8R* 'see you all later');
- (b) creative use of punctuation (e.g., multiple periods..., exclamation marks !!!!);
- (c) capitalization or other symbols for *EMPHASIS* and *stress*;
- (d) onomatopoeic and/or stylized spelling (e.g., *coooool, hahahaha, vewy intewestin* 'very interesting');

(e) keyboard-generated *emoticons* or *smilies* (e.g., :--) 'smiling face,' ,-) 'winking face,' @>--;-- 'a rose');
(f) direct requests (e.g., *A/S/L* 'age, sex, location?' and GOS 'gay or straight?');
(g) interactional indicators (e.g., *BBL* 'be back later,' *IGGP* 'I gotta go pee,' *WDYT* 'what do you think?'); and
(h) with more elaborate programming, colored text, *emotes* (e.g., *{Sender} eyes you up and down*, *{Sender} cries on your shoulder*) and other graphic symbols (e.g., images of gifts and accessories in Virtual Worlds).

In reviewing the distinctive communicative style of online chat in two IRC channels, Werry (in Herring 1996) has characterized it as 'interactive written discourse.' In particular, he notes the complex organization of sequences and exchange structures, evidenced in, for example, the juxtaposition of conversational strands, short turns (usually only about six words), high degrees of 'addressivity' (i.e., the use of *nicks* (nicknames) to avoid ambiguity with multiple participants), and minimal backchannelling from listeners (e.g., *uh huh, mm hm*).

6. Stylistic Diffusion: The Spread of Netlingo

A popular claim made about *netlingo* is its proliferation beyond the immediate context of CMC. Coupled with the diffusion (and indeed codification into dictionaries and other official usage) of technical, computer-related terminology, and concepts (e.g., *multitasking, windows, hacking*), common examples of lexical diffusions from *netlingo* are *spamming* (i.e. sending electronic junk mail), *cyberspace, cyberculture, shareware, hypertext, snail mail,* and *flame* (a hostile interaction).

Also of interest is the impact of *netlingo* on other languages, as well as official and/or isolated moves towards reclamation and resistance such as reports of *CyberSpanglish* (e.g., *surfeando el Web* and *estoy emailando*) and the preference of *La Francophonie* for terms like *bavardage* (rather than *chat*) and *un pirate informatique* (rather than *hacker*).

7. Metalanguage and Folklinguistics

Finally, as already indicated, the metalanguage of the internet is itself a potential site of sociolinguistic curiosity. In addition to labeling such as *weblish* or *netlingo*, other changes-within-changes are occurring all the time; for example, regarding the hyphenation and capitalization of netlinguistic terms (e.g., *E-mail > e-mail > email*, or *internet > Net > net*, or *Web > web*). There is also an intense public discourse about the perceived (negative) impact of *netlingo*, blamed for the 'death' of the apostrophe, the loss of capitalization, and the informality of communicative exchanges more generally.

8. Looking to the Future

As technologies of communication continue to develop and change, so too will associated linguistic forms and communicative practices. Some of the very latest technologies of communication which will inevitably impact on CMC are mobile phone text-messaging (SMS), Virtual Worlds (adding a visual dimension to chat), as well as voice-recognition and video technology. And so, where the demand for typographical speed and economy is heightened in one context of CMC, in others the ease and richness of face-to-face communication is being approximated ever more closely.

Bibliography

Baron N S 1998 Letters by phone or speech by other means: The linguistics of email. *Language and Communication* **18**: 133–70
Cherny L 1999 *Conversation and Community: Chat in a Virtual World.* CSLI Publications, Stanford, CA
Cyberatlas. Available at http://cyberatlas.internet.com/
Hale C (ed.) 1996 *Wired Style: Principles of English Usage in the Digital Age.* HardWired, San Francisco, CA
Herring S C (ed.) 1996 *Computer-mediated Communication: Linguistic, Social and Cross-cultural Perspectives.* Benjamins, Philadelphia, PA

Verbal Duel
R. Ackerman

The term 'verbal duel' may refer to a contest, fight or to a friendly competition between two individuals carried out through language. Verbal duels adhere to strict implicit rules stipulating the ages, gender and social status of the contenders and their listeners as well as the range of topics suitable for dueling. The interpretation of the duel—either as an aggressive game or as an act of real aggression—varies culturally, depending on the history of the relationship between the contenders, the setting in which the duel takes place and the code that is chosen. Some cultures treat verbal duels as aggressive games while others value them as real aggression. Even in cultures which treat them as aggressive games, the meaning of the interaction may change according to the relative position of the participants and the history of their relationship. In every situation, the winner of a verbal duel normally leaves his opponent without retort.

1. A Basic Difficulty of Classification

The seriousness of a speech act (see *Speech Act Theory: An Overview*) in which two individuals exchange insults cannot be properly assessed without understanding the cultural background in which it takes place. The relationship between the individuals and the intentions behind their aggression will usually provide the audience with a clue as to its significance. The same utterance may be variously interpreted in different contexts. In some instances, the mutual verbal aggression is part of a long-standing relationship, and the phrases exchanged are quite conventional and formulaic. They are not meant to be taken seriously, least of all personally, and retaliation is frowned upon. They are rather an aggressive game or play, a 'joking relationship.' However, in another context within the same societies, the same utterance could carry a heavy semantic load if its message were to be taken seriously. The individuals insulting each other are also trying to destroy each other through words, lower each other's self-esteem as well as show superior verbal wit. In both kinds of duel—aggressive play and real aggression—strict adherence to sociolinguistic rules is crucial.

Among Quechua speakers, in agricultural activities, two teams compete against each other in physical and verbal feats. A man, or several, in one team insults a member of the other by hinting at his physical incapacity and sexual impotence. The topics chosen for these occasions are highly standardized. It would be unacceptable, for instance, to insult members of that man's family. The insulted party may win the duel by reversing the situation through his verbal prowess. This kind of verbal duel is highly public and no offense is socially permissible. In contrast, insults exchanged in private are referred to by the same term used for rape. They are far more personal, less standardized and more offensive. The winner of these private duels is the one who does not repeat himself or herself, and who can come up with the most creative metaphors.

2. Verbal Duels and Their Relationship to Social Norms

Often verbal duels select topics that are otherwise taboo in the culture and that stand in inverse relationship to what is considered proper social norms. They allude to inappropriate behavior. The topics vary a great deal since generally the aim of the duels is to lower and profane the opponent's self-esteem within the values provided by the culture. They may involve matters of personal and family honor. Verbal abuse against members of the contenders' immediate family is common. A common pattern takes the form of direct accusations of improper sexual conduct, especially in relation to members of the addressee's family breaking sexual taboos. Additionally, the same result may be achieved through the use of sexual themes that are excluded from proper etiquette in reference to members of the addressee's family.

Research on North American Black youths describes that their insults make a great deal of allusion to the person of the mother, in all her physical, social, and sexual behavior. They are also implicitly subversive of White cultural values, by infringing upon as many taboo concepts as possible. Likewise, verbal duels among Turkish adolescents center, among others, on themes of passive homosexuality, bestiality, and improper behavior of female relatives. The attackers, on the other hand, all claim excess of masculinity and strength.

A researcher of Chamula (Maya Indian) verbal behavior provides an excellent example which illustrates the relationship between verbal abuse and social norms. 'The improper behavior implied in the duel is precisely the opposite of the behavior which accords rank and status to adult men in real life. The exchange begins with homosexual nuances and suggestions of incestuous or promiscuous sexual behavior on the part of the other's female siblings, continues with insults to the other's family, sexuality, and sexual apparatus, and concludes with a long exchange of directions between two sexual partners. Rapid sexual role reversal between the two players appears throughout' (see Gossen 1976: 138).

3. Duels and the Socialization Process: Rites of Passage

Verbal duels begin to take place during an intense period of socialization among children and adolescents who are learning and trying out the social world of adults. Even though verbal dueling is not limited to children and adolescents, it is often found among these age groups. Duels in these situations become the experimental ground on which the values of the adult world are dramatized. The insults of children and adolescents are often a mimicry of the more poignant adult ones. Among children, it is a matter of semantic oversimplification which reflects their incomplete acquisition of the sociolinguistic rules of their culture. Children transpose an insult which appeared to them to be effective in one setting into another. Adolescents are more adept at duels, though the sophistication of their duels is usually below that of their adult counterparts. Adolescent duels are usually stylistically and thematically simpler than those of adults, adhering more closely to formal rules.

While in some instances it is the case that adults have readier access to physical force, youths do not simply replace physical force by an alternative mode of violence. Rather, they choose an outlet in which the values of the adult world are dramatized. Youths are often excluded from the adult world or are not yet full participants in it. This is particularly true in terms of their exclusion from two areas of social life which are the focus of public attention: sex and prestige. And it is precisely these aspects of the adult world which become the acceptable focus of duels among adolescents. Duels then become the socialization arena in which the youths will get their training in the values that will be taken seriously later on in life.

4. Indirection

Verbal dueling is always done by means of indirectness. What is said does not literally express the meaning. The listener must engage in some form of nonliteral interpretation to understand the intended meaning. The message and the metamessage are not the same. Messages are carefully clothed in a veneer of verbal wit. To interpret them one must go beyond the literal meaning into the metaphorical one, as well as take into account relevant paralinguistic features. For these interpretations to be successful, one needs to be familiar with the particular dueling tradition.

The following account, given by a researcher of Black American English, illustrates indirectness in a verbal duel. 'A man coming from the bathroom forgot to zip his pants. An unescorted party of women kept watching him and laughing among themselves. The man's friends hip (inform) him to what's going on. He approaches one woman—"Hey, baby, did you see that big Cadillac with the full tires, ready to roll in action just for you?" She answers, "No, mother-fucker, but I saw a little gray Volkswagen with two flat tires"' (Kochman 1969: 27).

To the initiated, as well as to most people vaguely familiar with North American Black culture, it is clear that what the speakers are discussing has much more to do with sex, cross-sexual tensions, and insecurity than it has to do with automobiles. The metaphor used by the man emphasizes power and class. The woman retorts by building on the metaphor used by the man and reversing the implicit message. This building up of the response upon the original metaphor is called 'signifying' among the speakers of North American Black English vernacular. The woman here is clearly the winner. Her reply effectively reverses the claims of the original speaker without leaving the metaphorical realm chosen by the initiator of the exchange (see Mitchell-Kernan 1972: 174).

5. The Winner of a Verbal Duel

The aim of duels is often to destroy one's opponent with words. The winner must show superiority in a number of areas. Above all, winning at verbal duels requires the ability to manipulate language. The winner is the one who shows superior verbal skill in producing the most effective insults and who can respond to the challenge with an even more devastating statement. In addition, the winner must demonstrate his or her mastery of the duel rules. The permissible themes, codes and demeanor must be followed. Successful participants in a verbal duel adhere to the stylistic rules and demeanor. They avoid the two capital sins of verbal dueling: having recourse to everyday prose and having recourse to direct physical violence.

An example that brings together the qualities of a winner was provided by a researcher of Puerto Rican verbal duels. 'One cannot become embarrassed... or become angry and curse, or even resort to the ultimate sanction of violence. In such a contest the self maintained in the interaction is attacked on two levels: its positive qualities are assailed; in addition, one is treated by the rest of the participants, not as a participant, a full social person, but as a mere focus of attention' (see Lauria 1964: 61).

6. Duels and Verbal Art

Insults employ unique stylistic techniques—rhyme, meter, or metaphoric language—while at the same time emphasizing creativity. These characteristics draw them closer to poetry, albeit an execrative one. A Black American verbal duel could begin with a persuasive speech event called 'rap' and then, after destroying an opponent, move on to the more indirect 'signifying.'

The following excerpt, aimed at rescuing someone already destroyed through words, reflects the free verse style of modern American poetry. Note in particular the author's use of parallelism at the syntactic level to emphasize the oxymora at the semantic level.

'Man, I can't win for losing.
If it wasn't for bad luck, I wouldn't have no luck at all.
I been having buzzard luck.
Can't kill nothing and won't nothing die.
I'm living on the welfare and things is stormy.
They borrowing their shit from the Salvation Army.
But things bound to get better 'cause they can't get no worse.
I'm just like the blind man, standing by a broken window.
I don't feel no pain ...'

(Brown 1972)

See also: Speech Play.

Bibliography

Brown H R 1972 Street talk. In: Kochman T (ed.) *Rappin' and Stylin' Out*. University of Illinois Press, Urbana, IL

Dundes A, Leach J W, Özkök B 1970 The strategy of Turkish boy's verbal dueling rhymes. *Journal of American Folklore* **83**: 325–49

Gossen G H 1976 Verbal duel in Chamla. In: Kirshenblatt-Gimblett B (ed.) *Speech Play*. University of Pennsylvania Press, Philadelphia, PA

Kochman T 1969 'Rapping' in the black ghetto. *Trans-Action* **6**(4): 6

Lauria A 1964 'Respeto,' 'Relajo' and inter-personal relations in Puerto Rico. *Anthropological Quarterly* **37**: 53–67

Labov W 1972 Rules for ritual insults. In: Kochman T (ed.) *Rappin' and Stylin' Out*. University of Illinois Press, Urbana, IL

Mitchell-Kernan C 1972 Signifying and marking: Two Afro–American speech acts. In: Gumperz J J, Hymes D (eds.) *Directions in Sociolinguistics: The Ethnography of Communication*. Holt, Rinehart and Winston, New York

Mitchell-Kernan C, Kernan K T 1975 Children's insults: America and Samoa. In: Sanches M, Blount B G (eds.) *Sociocultural Dimensions of Language Use*. Academic Press, New York

SECTION IV

Language Variation and Change: Dialects and Social Groups

Accent

J. M. Y. Simpson

A spoken variety of language is realized in speech-sounds: any one system of such sounds and their combinatorial possibilities constitutes an 'accent' of that variety of language. Just as a written language may be realized visually in different styles of print or handwriting (or in some cases in totally different writing systems), so a spoken language may be realized in more than one accent, even though it may be standardized to a greater or lesser extent in grammar and vocabulary. For example, Standard English is fairly homogeneous in grammar and vocabulary, but Standard English spoken by an American 'sounds' different from Standard English spoken by someone from Australia or Ireland.

Such differences of accent arouse interest from several points of view. The phonetician-phonologist studies the ways in which accents differ and how these differences can be described technically. The sociolinguist investigates correlations between accents and regional and/or social groups of speakers and also examines attitudes towards accent, that is, how a hearer makes judgments about speakers on the basis of their accents. Finally, in second-language teaching the problem arises as to *which* accent of the language being taught should be chosen as the model for learners. In this article these points are addressed by taking examples from Standard English, but the principles apply to any variety of language.

1. Differences between Accents

The point should be made first of all that, since accents of English vary phonetically and phonologically, it is impossible to describe the phonetics and phonology of English without specifying the accent(s) under discussion, for no one accent is 'the' accent of English.

If a phonemic framework is adopted for the description of an accent, one component of the description would be an inventory of the phonemes; another would be the allophonic realizations of these phonemes in various environments. Both of these may vary from accent to accent.

The number of phonemes available may differ. For example, most Scottish speakers of English will use different diphthongs in *tied* and *tide* while English speakers of English will pronounce these words as homophones. Thus at that point in the system the Scottish accent has one more phoneme than the English. On the other hand, most speakers of RP (Received Pronunciation, an accent of English, see below) will have six different vowel phonemes in the words *bad, balm, cot, caught, pull, pool*; most Scots will have identical vowels respectively in *bad* and *balm*, in *cot* and *caught*, and in *pull* and *pool*. At this point in the system, the Scottish accent has three vowels as against six in RP. Some American accents (for example, General American, see below) will have the same vowel in *balm* and *not*, so where English English has six vowel phonemes, some American accents have five (see Fig. 1). (Notice that what is under discussion in this article is not the language variety known as Scots but Standard *English* as pronounced by educated Lowland Scots.)

	General American	Scottish English	RP
bad	a	a	a
balm	ɑ		ɑ
cot		ɔ	ɒ
caught	ɔ		ɔ
pull	ʊ	u	ʊ
pool	u		u

Figure 1. Phonemes in General American English, Scottish English and RP.

Similarly allophonic realizations differ. For example, the same vocalic phoneme is used in a word such as *rope* by American, English, and Scottish speakers of Standard English; however, while a typical Scottish speaker will realize this as a rounded half-close back monophthong [o], the majority of speakers from England and the USA will realize it as a closing diphthong, the particular quality of which may range from [oʊ] to [ɜɤ].

A third difference concerns permissible sequences of phonemes in connected speech, the realm of phonological structure. For example, in General American an /r/ phoneme can appear postvocalically before a consonant and before a pause: thus *car* and *card* are phonemically /kar/ and /kard/; such an accent is termed 'rhotic.' Other rhotic accents of English are Canadian, Scottish, Irish, English West Country, some Indian, and some Welsh. But in RP an /r/ phoneme cannot appear in these positions, so that *car* and *card* are phonemically /ka/ and /kad/ respectively; such an accent is 'nonrhotic.' Other nonrhotic accents are Australian, English Midland, London, most New Zealand, most Northern English, South African, West African, and West Indian. Both rhotic and nonrhotic accents will, of course, permit an /r/ prevocalically, as in *red* /red/.

A fourth area of difference concerns the characteristic selection of comparable phonemes to realize particular words. Thus *buoy*, *lever*, and *tomato* are respectively /'bui/, /'lɛvr̩/, and /tə'meɪtoʊ/ in General American but, with a different selection of vowel in the stressed syllable, /bɔɪ/, /'livə/, and /tə'matoʊ/ in RP.

Various phenomena observable in word-sequences may differ. Some 50 words in RP have different phonemes according to whether the words are stressed ('strong forms') or unstressed ('weak forms'). Thus *from* in *Where's he from?* is normally stressed and realized as /frɒm/; in *He's from London* it is normally unstressed and realized as /frəm/. Such an alternation is unknown in most Scottish accents. Similarly, a sandhi-form appears in some types of RP when a word ending in one of certain vowels is followed by a word beginning with a vowel, a 'linking-r' /r/ is inserted, thus *law and order* /'lɔr ən 'ɔdə/. This phenomenon is unknown in General American.

Finally, dynamic (or suprasegmental) features vary. Voice quality differs from accent to accent, such differences being described by the layman in impressionistic terms: to an RP-speaker a typical General American voice may sound 'strident,' while the typical RP-speaker's voice may sound 'effete' or 'languid' to an American. English worldwide has several regional sets of intonation tunes, differing in the number of tunes available and in their contours. The stress-patterns of individual words may differ: thus *magazine* is variously stressed on the first or last syllable. Syllabification may vary: in Scottish English consonants can 'jump' across word boundaries to release syllables (e.g., *post office* /'pos'tɔfɪs/) but not normally in other accents. And rhythmic organization varies: *meter* will have syllable lengths (not vowel lengths) of 'long-short' in some American and Yorkshire, 'short-long' in Scottish English, and 'equal-equal' in RP (see Simpson 1979: 79–83).

Differences of this kind raise the important question of whether it is possible to posit one underlying phonology of the English language from which every accent can be derived. This seems impossible. The situation is rather that of a number of individual speakers who can understand each other, in spite of differences of accent. Indeed differences between speakers involve not only accent but vocabulary, grammar, idioms, and style. This consideration emphasises the fact that the idea of *a language* is merely a convenient fiction which facilitates the description of one aspect of human behavior (see *Language*).

2. Groupings of Speakers and Accents

In the particular case of English, the majority of accents are regional, belonging to geographical areas of various sizes. There exist, for example, identifiable Australian, Canadian, Indian, Irish, New Zealand, South African, and Scottish accents of English. Within such accents, it may be possible to make further distinctions. Thus the accents of the USA are grouped into three main types: Eastern (Maine, New Hampshire, and the eastern parts of Vermont, Massachusetts, and Connecticut); Southern (the Southern states); and General American (the rest of the Union). And within these it is in many cases possible to recognize finer differences of accent characterizing increasingly smaller areas. (Indeed the concept and the term 'General American' are rejected by some scholars precisely because of such differences within the accent in question.)

But differences of accent may correlate with factors other than regional: with social, religious, educational, or even political groupings, for instance, though it may not be possible to exemplify all of these factors from English. One unusual example is found within England (but not the other countries of the British Isles) in Received Pronunciation (RP). This grew up in the 'public' (i.e., exclusive boarding) schools of England, which, until the advent of broadcasting, remained virtually the only source of its propagation. It cannot, of course, be held to be the 'educated' accent of England: many highly educated Englishmen use other accents. Speakers of RP thus constitute a social, self-recognizing, accent-group. RP is therefore a nonregional accent within England itself, though outside England it is regional in the sense of marking a speaker as coming from that country. Again, it must be pointed out that RP is by no means a homogeneous accent and that it is undergoing changes.

The investigator of how speaker-groupings correlate with accent is faced with problems of various kinds. Determining the accent itself may not be easy. For example, a speaker's pronunciation may not be consistent in successive utterances of the same words (see Labov 1966). This raises the issue whether it is possible to regard one of these competing pronunciations as 'the' pronunciation of the speaker and what conclusions can be drawn from such inconsistency. Moreover, how does one determine the relevant grouping? While it may be comparatively easy to assign membership of a religion or of a geographical area, in other cases the delimitation of the group itself is not obvious. For example, in determining social class, a variety of factors may be relevant—income, occupation, education, area of residence, leisure activities—and their relative importance also needs to be determined. Even when the principles of assigning groupings have been settled, the problems arise of deciding *how* typical of the group a given speaker may be and hence of generalizing from the accent of one speaker to that of a group. Such problems are not peculiar to the investigator of accent, of course: they confront the investigator of any sociolinguistic variable.

3. Attitudes to Accents

It follows from the definition of accent above that, contrary to popular usage, it is impossible to 'speak without an accent.' Every speaker has an accent. From a linguist's point of view, all accents are objects of interest and all are of equal value: an accent as such cannot itself be 'good,' or 'bad,' or 'educated,' or 'vulgar.' Equally it is impossible to set up some esthetic scale by which one may judge the euphony of an accent.

Nevertheless, judgments about accents *are* widely made. In everyday life, some accents are indeed regarded as socially preferable to others, or variously as beautiful, ugly, educated, vulgar, comic, bucolic, snobbish, and so on. Such judgments can be the result of sheer prejudice (for or against) or of transferring a judgment about a speaker to his speech; though irrational (or perhaps because of that), they can be very strongly held (see *Sociophonetics*).

Probably no generalizations are possible about which linguistic features will account for particular judgments (or prejudices). For example, within England a nonrhotic accent of English is socially preferable, but in the General American area it is a rhotic accent that is socially preferable. In British urban accents, the use of a glottal stop as a replacement (or realization) of intervocalic /t/ in such words as *water* is stigmatized but in RP a comparable realization of preconsonantal /t/ in a phrase such as *that man* goes unremarked. It is therefore impossible to predict how a given accent will be judged except by taking into account particular hearers or groups of hearers. Support for this view is given by the finding that hearers who are asked to evaluate the accents of a language they do not understand are unable to make any judgments (Giles and Powesland 1975).

However, hearers who understand what is being said and who are part of the sociolinguistic fabric of the language variety in question will very quickly make judgments about accents, both in everyday life and in controlled sociolinguistic experiments. Where a number of accents are found which realize the same variety of language in a particular area, these may well be assigned a place on a cline of high-to-low prestige. Demonstrably on occasion, such judgments (or prejudices) are obviously about accents, and not about other characteristics of the speakers involved, since in the relevant experiments speakers are heard but not seen. Accents act as cues which arouse social expectations, and judgments about the speakers' personalities are made on the basis of these cues.

In such experiments, which employ the Matched Guise Technique, subjects hear tapes which include recordings of the same passage read by the same speaker but in different accents. The subjects are then asked to evaluate what they imagine to be different speakers in terms of such characteristics as intelligence, ambitiousness, friendliness, honesty, and so on. It is striking that the same individual can be ranked differently on such scales depending on the accent used. Indeed the actual content of a text, for example the quality of the speaker's argument, may be differently assessed according to the accent (see *Attitude Surveys: Question–Answer Process*).

All accents can fulfill the function of demonstrating the bonding or solidarity that holds within a group of some kind; an accent is a marker of group identity. There is evidence that speakers who belong to the core of the same social network will share an accent that is similar in the finest phonetic detail. One therefore assumes that these speakers want to conform to the accent of their peers. Other things being equal, one would further assume that a speaker would evaluate his or her own accent most highly. But other things are not always equal and in some cases a speaker will rank accents *other* than his own as being superior on some particular scale of values. Presumably in such cases there are two conflicting pressures, that of retaining one's accent in order to conform to the peer group and that of changing one's accent so that it resembles one perceived to be superior. Individuals will vary according to which pressure is felt to be more important, for the obverse of an accent's role as marker of group identity is its role as marker of an individual's identity, and this includes group membership, both actual and desired. On occasion, speakers will temporarily change their accent in conversation with the intention either of emphasizing membership of the same group as their hearers or underlining their membership of a different group (see *Speech Accommodation*).

4. Model Accents for Language Learners

Second-language learners inevitably face the problem of learning the pronunciation of their new language. In the case of English (and many other languages) this should ideally involve choosing a model accent by taking account of certain factors outlined below. However, a genuine choice is not available to many learners for two reasons. It has to be admitted that after the 1940s the importance attached in the first decades of the twentieth century to pronunciation in language-learning and -teaching was largely forgotten, so that many native-English-speaking teachers lack not only awareness of the issues outlined in Sect. 1 but also the technical expertise to teach pronunciation adequately. In the second place, certain languages are vigorously promoted by governments and official agencies. Inevitably, the agencies of any one country will assume that an accent of that country should be the model for foreign learners; any ensuing difficulties or the possibility of alternative models are ignored.

It is, of course, crucial that the learner should acquire the essential articulatory skills. Given this, if the learner is living in an area where the new language is spoken, then he will presumably aim at the accent spoken by that group to which he would wish to belong, if of course he is aware of the relevant groupings and accents. But when the learner is in a country where the new language is not generally spoken and where there is a possibility of choosing from alternative accents, various considerations are relevant to deciding among them.

(a) From a phonetic-phonological point of view, the ideal model accent would be that which approximates in the greatest number of respects to the sound-system of the learner's own language. If such an accent does not exist, then the next-best model accent would be that which is simplest in terms of phonemic inventory, phonological structure, and dynamic features.

(b) If the learner is going to encounter only speakers with a particular accent, for example, by going to live in an area where it is spoken, then it is only reasonable to learn that accent. Otherwise, if the learner is going to meet speakers with a variety of accents, it is advisable to avoid adopting an accent intelligible in only a restricted area.

(c) If possible, an accent should be selected which is expounded in a sufficient range of teaching materials.

(d) Consideration should be given to the accent of any available native-speaking teachers.

(e) A model accent should not be perceived negatively, because of either social or political reasons, among the users of the language (whether native speakers or not) with whom the learner will come in contact.

Unfortunately, these considerations may conflict. For example, RP was brilliantly investigated by Daniel Jones and was expounded by him as a model for foreign learners. Although Jones maintained that learners should be free to choose whichever accent they find appropriate, RP is virtually the only accent employed in the plethora of English as a Foreign Language (EFL) teaching-materials emanating from the British Isles. However, the number of speakers of genuine RP is extremely small. This means that the number of RP-speaking teachers is low and also that the learner's chances of meeting RP-speakers in the British Isles is low. Moreover, the phonology of RP is complex: it has a larger vowel system, with many diphthongs, than most accents of English and displays the intricacies of such things as weak versus strong forms and linking-r. More importantly, though RP has prestige in some places, principally England, it is negatively perceived in others and may even arouse hostility, being associated (whether rightly or wrongly) with colonialism and similar pretensions. Nevertheless, RP is still regarded, rather curiously, as 'the' accent of English by certain European educational authorities (see Abercrombie 1990a).

Another possible model is General American, the accent used in EFL materials produced in the USA and other countries coming under the influence of the USA. It is from a practical point of view preferable to RP: it has a simpler vowel system and is rhotic, so that an ⟨r⟩ which appears in spelling is pronounced. Apart from that, it is readily understood in a very large part of the English-speaking world. But it too is disliked in certain quarters (for example, by some from Portuguese- and Spanish-speaking American countries who may nevertheless have adopted it as a model) as having colonialist overtones, while by certain Europeans it is unreasonably regarded as being in some vague way undesirable.

It has been suggested that a Scottish accent of English would be an excellent model on the undeniable grounds that it has a simple vowel system (the qualities of which conform very closely to what could be called 'Standard Average European' vowels), it is rhotic, and it is highly intelligible internationally. Furthermore, it is widely admired and free from the political associations of RP and General American (see Abercrombie 1975, 1990a). However, there is a total lack of teaching materials using this accent as a model and the number of teachers who speak with this accent is strictly limited. There is in any case no tradition of a Scottish accent being used as a model.

The question can properly be asked whether it is necessary that a model accent should be a *native* accent of English at all. Admittedly it is the case that some foreign accents of English can be negatively perceived, either because they are difficult to understand or because they inadvertently signal inappropriate apparent attitudes, such as arrogance, through the use of dynamic features, for example, voice quality or intonation, that are neutral or even convey friendliness in the learner's language, but send very powerful negative messages in English. Nevertheless other nonnative accents that are immediately intelligible, are devoid of unfortunate overtones, whether political or attitudinal, and can be regarded as being on a par with native accents. For example, the accent used by many fluent English-speakers whose native language is Arabic is for these reasons perfectly acceptable (indeed in many respects, though not in voice quality, it is very like a Scottish accent) and there would seem to be no reason for suggesting that such speakers should adopt a native accent. Indeed it has even been suggested (see Abercrombie 1990a) that French should be the basis for the accent of French learners of English.

On the other hand, certain accents of even native speakers from the 'Outer Circle' of the New Englishes (countries in the Caribbean, the Indian sub-continent, and West Africa) are at present internationally not widely intelligible (perhaps because of their syllable-timing) and thus would not be the best accents to take as models (see *New Englishes*). This situation will change, of course, if these accents become widely known outside their home areas. It should be emphasized that no accent is objectively more comprehensible than any other; familiarity with an accent is the key to its comprehensibility.

Finally, it may be observed that because an accent is so strong a marker of individual personality, speakers may be totally averse to adopting one different from that which they habitually employ. This reluctance may characterize certain learners of English, who do not wish to be seen to belong to any English-speaking group at all, and also some native speakers of English who have moved from their original home: the latter may sometimes argue explicitly that their accent is a native, hence 'correct,' one and in no way inferior to any other. Both groups may underestimate the apparently negative attitudes they convey or even the very real problems of intelligibility they present to their hearers.

Bibliography

Abercrombie D 1975 The accents of Standard English in Scotland. In: Abercrombie D 1990b *Fifty Years in Phonetics*. Edinburgh University Press, Edinburgh, UK
Abercrombie D 1990a RP today: Its position and prospects. In: Abercrombie D 1990b *Fifty Years in Phonetics*. Edinburgh University Press, Edinburgh, UK
Abercrombie D 1990b *Fifty Years in Phonetics*. Edinburgh University Press, Edinburgh, UK
Giles H, Powesland P 1975 *Speech Style and Social Evaluation*, Academic Press, London
Labov W 1966 *The Social Stratification of English in New York City*. Center for Applied Linguistics, Washington, DC
Simpson J M Y 1979 *A First Course in Linguistics*. Edinburgh University Press, Edinburgh, UK
Wells J 1982 *Accents of English*, 3 vols. Cambridge University Press, Cambridge, UK

Adolescent Peer Group Language
R. L. Taylor

Much of the reality and significance of adolescent social life is concealed from adult society by linguistic devices contrived by youths for this purpose. However, the distinctive terminology or language of adolescents is more than an instrument of concealment or obfuscation, for it reflects their perceptions and assessments of their status in society, their values, interests, beliefs and world view, and serves as an index of solidarity and alienation. As a group phenomenon, adolescent language crystallizes, objectifies, and communicates the collective experiences of youth as these experiences are shaped by such factors as age, gender, class, race, and other differences among adolescent subgroups in a society. This article focuses first on the social conditions that give rise to the language of adolescents and its role in promoting group definition and distinctiveness; particular attention is then given to the lexis of Black adolescents as an illustration of some of the important differences in the sociolinguistic patterns of adolescent subgroups.

1. Families and Peers in Adolescence

Adolescence, the period of transition from childhood to adult status, is widely recognized as a crucial stage in human development. It is characterized by changes at all levels of integration: social, psychological, and physiological. As a social phenomenon, adolescence in modern, industrial societies is marked by the experience of status discontinuity in which adolescents find themselves in an ill-defined marginal position: they have lost their former childhood status but have not yet acquired the status of the adult, and they are confronted with few norms and clearly defined role expectations to guide their behavior. As a psychological phenomenon, adolescence is a period in which the adolescent is expected to replace an ascriptive identity, based on place in family, by a more mature and socially recognized identity based on universalistic criteria (Eisenstadt 1956). Insofar as adolescents are segregated during this period, they are forced to look to each other to develop their own standards and codes of behavior as a means of acquiring a temporary identity in the flux of adolescence.

The emergence of adolescent society and culture, embodied in distinctive norms, values, and a language intelligible to members of this age-grade, can be traced to the problems of socialization associated with advanced industrialized societies, where a highly specialized division of labor, requiring a prolonged period of education and training in preparation for the assumption of adult roles and responsibilities, prevails (Schwartz and Merten 1967). Such extensive preparation forestalls the age at which self-support and independence begins, and when an identity based on mature roles can be consolidated. Hence, adolescent subcultures attempt to solve problems arising from the interim position of adolescents, providing a sense of security and belonging during a period of status discontinuity.

Through age segregation, secondary schools provide the major locus of contact among the various segments of local adolescent populations, and are the typical settings within which adolescent societies emerge (Coleman 1961). In the adolescent subculture of the school, peer group interactions are guided by distinctive evaluative standards and status terminology which form the basis of the peer group's prestige hierarchy, and determine the kinds and amount of respect the occupant of a status category can claim in the adolescent social system. While the status system that evolves in schools is influenced to some degree by criteria borrowed from adult society, the multiplicity of discrete norms which regulate relations between peers are integrated into a relatively coherent system by distinctively adolescent conceptions of personal worth. Such peer group norms enforce a degree of conformity upon its members that is considerably tighter than that found among adults, and they pattern their preferences, sentiment, and behavior in matters of appearance, dress, speech, and other expressive activities in ways that are highly predictable. Motivation to comply with such norms is inspired as much by the adolescent's need for acceptance and fear of rejection, as by the desire to alleviate the frustration and confusion associated with an interim status.

Various media of mass communication (i.e., radio, newspapers, television, etc.) play a major role in linking youth together from different localities, in nationalizing their interests and concerns, and in strengthening their values and norms. Yet many aspects of adolescent culture remain hidden behind a veil of secrecy erected to escape the scrutiny and control of adults. The language of adolescents becomes an effective means of concealing their interests, sentiments and experiences from adults, while sharing them with members of their peer group. To be sure, not all adolescents in a society speak the same language nor share in the same subculture. There are in fact important differences in the sociolinguistic patterns of adolescent subgroups which derive from a diversity of experiences associated with class, ethnicity, race, and gender. Therefore, adolescents may be expected to exhibit different subcultural patterns of behavior depending upon whether they are characterized by one or more of such variables.

2. The Language of Adolescents

The growth in influence of peer groups on the evolving perceptions, attitudes, and linguistic behaviors of youth during adolescence continues a process begun much earlier in the life cycle. Opie and Opie (1959) describe how children's games and activities bring them together in age-graded groupings where large amounts of lore and language are shared and contribute to the creation of a separate childhood culture. However, the language of adolescents is distinguished from the language of children by its intended purposes, functions, and consequences for behavior and experience (Gusdorf 1965). For children, language is the medium through which the world is discovered and the means by which society and people are increasingly understood. Its functions are integrative and inclusive. The linguistic forms of adolescents have their function as markers of social identities and group exclusiveness, and are sometimes used as weapons to oppose, confuse, or offend (Romaine 1984, Rose and Ross 1994).

2.1 The Functions of Adolescent Language

Few features of the lives of adolescents during this transitional period so clearly reveal their movement away from the family and their integration into a peer-defined social world as the special language they adopt for use in communicating with each other. The acquisition of such a language makes the adolescent a member of two linguistic communities, one essential for communicating with adults at home and in school, the other necessary for conversing with peers (Lewis 1963). The reason why such a special language evolves and is so tenaciously maintained must be sought in its functions. At least three major functions can be discerned.

Basic to the emergence of adolescent language is the drive for autonomy or independence from parental authority and the need for bonding with members of one's peer group. The use of slang, taboo words and alliteration, the style of articulation, and other kinds of verbal play, proclaim for the adolescent membership in, and allegiance to, a particular group, and serve as forms of resistance to adult control. Hence, the special language of adolescents arises from the need for differentiation and social distance from adult society, and functions as an instrument of in-group solidarity and distinctiveness. In order to maintain its function as a marker of group distinctiveness and solidarity, and to minimize the potential encroachments of adults, adolescent terminology constantly changes: old terms replaced by new ones to refer to roughly the same phenomena, thereby preserving the secret codes by which in-group members identify and communicate with one another (see *Slang: Sociology*).

In addition to its role in promoting group identity and cohesiveness, the language of adolescents is a means of expressing the values and experiences of group members. The use of a special language, whether employed by adults (e.g., medical students, academics, gamblers, etc.) or by adolescents, has much the same function for both groups, namely, to facilitate communication among individuals who share common interests and concerns, and who need a common vocabulary for talking about such matters.

A good part of the interests and concerns of adolescents revolve around such forbidden topics as sexual activities, drinking, drugs, and lawbreaking, for which a special vocabulary unintelligible to adults is required. Slang and elliptical utterances, vague in reference, are shorthand devices to save time and effort by summing up complex and recurrent phenomena and experiences. Although intended for a different purpose, Bernstein's (1973) distinction between 'elaborated' and 'restricted' language codes which are associated with different systems of social relationships, could well be used to illustrate the differences between adolescents and adults in the way they use language (see *Bernstein, Basil*; *Code, Sociolinguistic*). By 'elaborated code' Bernstein refers to a relatively abstract speech style which orients the user to universalistic meanings, where principles and operations are made linguistically explicit. It allows for subtle differences in meaning by utilizing qualifications, and does not assume a high degree of shared contextual experience between speaker and listener. Such codes employ a widely varied vocabulary and complex syntax, as evidenced by a high proportion of subordinate clauses, conjunctions, uncommon adverbs, passive verbs, and adjectives. In contrast, the restricted code is a concrete and egocentric speech style which assumes a high degree of shared contextual experience between speaker and listener, is oriented to particularistic meanings, and is emotionally expressive. Restricted codes are characterized by fairly simple syntax, make use of a high proportion of pronouns, especially 'you' and 'they,' and tag phrases (e.g., 'stuff like that'). The tendency of adolescents to employ a restricted language code is related both to the 'egocentric' form of consciousness typical of this age group (i.e., the failure to distinguish between what they and others think about), and the desire to communicate with peers in a style of discourse that reflects their common experiences and assumptions (Britton 1970).

The restricted speech code employed by adolescents might more appropriately be referred to as their 'pubilect' or dialect of puberty, following terminological practices in linguistics. As Danesi (1989) has shown, three basic psychosocial categories of speech programming characterize pubilect in its various manifestations: emotive, connotative, and socially coded language programming. The tendency of adolescents to externalize strongly felt emotional impulses, accompanied by such bodily reactions as rapid increases in rate of speech, expressive voice modulations, simplified clause structure, and the like, are all manifestations of emotive language programming. As the most dominant aspect of the adolescent's structuring of speech acts, emotive language programming inspires an overabundance of exclamations, interjections, and grunts in their discourse which serve to call attention to their feelings, attitudes, and opinions. Connotative language programming refers to the tendency to invent new terms and idioms, or modify the meaning of existing ones, in ways that evoke vivid images or sum up complex phenomena in one or several words. While adolescents may experience some difficulty in giving precise definitions of such terms as *awesome, cool, nerd, geek*, or other terms which may be in current use among peers, the connotations of such terms are clearly understood and prompt them toward expected emotions and actions. Socially coded language programming refers largely to the manner in which adolescent discourse is structured to promote intragroup bonding. Much like adolescent norms regarding correct appearance (i.e., clothing, grooming, makeup, etc.), socially coded language programming reflects adherence to peer group norms regarding style of verbal discourse, and highlights the fact that youths are highly conscious of how they 'come across' linguistically in the company of their peers.

Establishing status and associational patterns within the adolescent social system are other important functions of the special language of youths (Labov 1982). Adolescent society provides a status system and terminology which enable youths to engage in predictable and consistent interactions with their peers, and to acquire a sense of personal worth based on subcultural standards rather than the norms of adult society. The status terminology employed is affectively coded such that a youth's status in the local prestige hierarchy is partly a function of the meanings associated with the terms peers use to connote his or her character and group affiliations (Schwartz and Merten 1967). These terms have laudatory or pejorative connotations and are in part related to the adolescent's interpersonal skills and accomplishments, as measured by the norms, standards, and values of the peer group.

In the school-based social structure of adolescents, social differentiation typically takes place along two dimensions: one relating to lifestyles (i.e., modes of dress, speech, demeanor) which give rise to horizontal social strata; the other relating to highly esteemed interpersonal accomplishments and talents which constitute the vertical dimension, according to which the adolescent's rank and popularity within one of the horizontal social strata is established. While the status terms used to assign peers to one or another status category within the system are likely to reflect to some degree the socioeconomic characteristics of the local community, adherence to differentially evaluated adolescent life styles and associated values are more precise determinants of assignment to prestige categories (Eckert 1988). Various terms are used to refer to high and low status category affiliations within the social structure of the school. At different times and in different places, these categories may have different names and styles. Such terms as *collegiates, socies* (for socialites), *jocks,* and *Preppies,* have sometimes been used as status terms for adolescents affiliated with elite groups within the school system, while terms like *greasers, hoods, scraggs,* and *freaks,* have been applied to those of low standing. Such terms define the polar extremes between which the majority of adolescents, sometimes referred to as *normals, out-of-its,* or *in-betweens,* form a heterogeneous category.

3. Gender-specific Uses of Adolescent Language

Beyond the general functions of adolescent language noted above are gender-specific uses of peer group language. Differential patterns of socialization and extensive interaction in single-sex peer groups account for some of the gender-specific uses of language found among adolescents, and for differences in social structure between peer groups (Romaine 1984). It is a common observation that boys and girls learn different ways of speaking and different rules for interacting with their peers (Meditch 1975), and that such differences appear at a fairly early age (Haas 1979). Observed differences in speech and behavior patterns involve much more than the simple imitation or assimilation of adult 'genderlects' and rules by school-age children, but are learned from peers at a time when boys and girls interact socially primarily with members of their own sex (Brooks-Gunn and Matthews 1979; see *Gender and Language*). Groups of girls and groups of boys engage in different types of activities (e.g., skip rope vs. football) which entail different patterns of interaction and involvement. Such differences in social organization and associated patterns of interaction contribute to gender-specific patterns of language use among adolescents (Maltz and Borker 1982).

Since boys and girls typically interact in homogeneous groups and in different social contexts, they tend to develop different genres of speech and different skills for doing things with words. The peer-group networks of adolescent females are typically smaller, and games or other recreational activities are generally cooperative and noncompetitive. Differentiation between girls is a function of closeness rather than power, and groups tend to be nonhierarchical. Friendship involves intimacy, mutual commitment, and loyalty. The idea of 'best friend' is central for girls. When disputes or conflicts arise, the group breaks up. Because of the inherent contradiction in the structure of girls' social relationships created by adherence to an ideology of equality and cooperation in interactions on the one hand, and the reality of difference and conflict on the other, girls learn to deal with the conflicting pressures through the use of language in several ways: (a) to create and maintain relationships of closeness and equality; (b) to criticize others in acceptable ways; and (c) to interpret accurately the speech of other girls (Maltz and Borker 1982). Through talk, girls learn to give support, to use inclusive language such as *let's, we could, we're gonna,* in enlisting the cooperation of others, and to direct others in task-oriented activities without appearing bossy. Since closeness is manifested by sharing secrets and other information that could be used against one another, girls learn to read the intent and loyalty of others, given shifting relationships and indirect expressions of conflict (Goodwin 1980).

By contrast, boys' groups are typically larger and more hierarchically structured than girls' groups. Relative status in the hierarchy is paramount and is the one thing that boys learn to manipulate in their interactions with one another. Though members of a group may often deny the existence of a leader and insist upon an ethic of equality, certain linguistic practices and patterns of behavior clearly reveal the hierarchical and power-oriented nature of such groups (Labov 1982). Posturing and counterposturing is a prominent feature of the male adolescent social world, where patterns of speech are designed to accomplish at least three objectives: (a) to assert one's position of dominance; (b) to attract and maintain an audience; and (c) to assert oneself when other speakers have the floor (Maltz and Borker 1982).

Perhaps the best-documented sociolinguistic aspect of boys' peer groups is the use of speech for the expression of dominance (Savin-Williams 1976). As Maltz and Borker (1982) have shown, social success among boys is based on knowing how and when to use words to express power. Verbal dueling, storytelling, joke-telling, and other narrative performance events are highly valued and cultivated in boys' peer groups (see *Narrative, Natural*; *Verbal Duel*; *Speech Play*). An important sociolinguistic skill a boy is expected to learn is how to get the floor to perform, maintain his audience in the midst of a series of challenges, and successfully complete his performance. Boys learn to assert their identity and opinions in such contexts by side comments, put-downs, and challenges. Although some of the most extensive research on the verbal skills of male adolescents has been conducted in Black communities in the USA (Kochman 1972, Labov 1972), research conducted in other countries (e.g., Turkey) and on other populations (e.g., rural youths) reveals similarities in the speech patterns and functions of language across adolescent peer groups.

These patterns of adolescent speech and strategies for management of social interaction show marked continuities with adult sex-specific patterns of speech and behavior. Storytelling, arguing, and verbal posturing are common features of the speech style of men and boys. Verbal aggression, in the form of practical jokes, put-downs, and insults are considered normal among friends (LeMasters 1975). Women, on the other hand, employ a mode of speech that is more interactional, with more frequent use of personal and inclusive pronouns such as 'you' and 'we.' They send out and look for signs of agreement and engagement, and seek to create continuity in conversation. While elements of conflict, competition, and criticism occur in the conversations of women, such elements are more often disguised or conveyed in an idiom of support that give them a distinctive tone (Kalčik 1975). These and other observed differences between male and female conversational styles suggest that patterns of interaction and socialization in sex-specific peer groups lead to particular styles of discourse which prevail in adulthood. To a considerable degree, adult patterns of friendly interaction involve learning to overcome some of the gender-specific styles of discourse typical of adolescents (Maltz and Borker 1982).

4. The Language of Black Youth

As noted above, a considerable body of sociolinguistic work exists on the idiomatic usage and verbal skills of Black (African American) adolescents in the USA. Speech features of Black teenage idiom, once thought to be deficient or unintelligible, were discovered to have the properties of a conceptual and rule-governed system which, though related to mainstream usage, incorporates aspects of experience that are culturally specific (Smitherman 1977, Labov 1972). A number of terms have been used to refer to the language of Black youth: 'Afro–American slang,' 'Black English,' 'soul-talk,' 'jive-talk,' 'Black argot,' African–American street speech, and the like. In her fine-grained sociolinguistic analysis of Black teen language, Folb (1980) uses the phrase 'Black English vernacular vocabulary' to refer to the mixture of general slang, argot, Africanisms and culture-bound idioms that make up the pool of Black vernacular expressions. Black youth invent and utilize a terminology which serves the referential functions of providing labels for concepts and experiences that are particular to their subculture and that provide an emotional and critical outlet for group feelings (Goodwin 1990, Mitchell-Kernan 1980).

Other social functions are also apparent in shaping the vernacular expressions of Black youths (and adult usage as well). Among subgroups of Black teenagers and adults, Black vernacular serves not only as an instrument of group definition and solidarity but as a marker of the separateness of Black Americans as a distinct ethnic group. Such vernacular expressions as *blood, bleed, soul brother, soul sister*, among others, are terms used to refer to a kind of kinship that unites Black people on the level of group identity, while maintaining social distance between the Black community and other speech communities (see *Ebonics and African American Vernacular English*).

For many Black adolescents, introduction to the vernacular lexicon comes early in life—even before some have reached the stage of real comprehension. They mimic older siblings, parents, relatives, and friends of the family. Along with the vernacular, children learn the paralanguage and body language appropriate to its use (see *Kinesics*). The period during which youngsters become the most ardent users of vernacular vocabulary is between 10 and 13, while the period between 16 and 19 is a time for expanding and consolidating knowledge of the vocabulary (Lerman 1967). Although gender does affect access to vernacular vocabulary, as well as the scope, depth, sureness of knowledge, and usage, vernacular vocabulary usage is not exclusively a male phenomenon (Mitchell-Kernan 1972). Vernacular vocabularies relating to such common activities as partying, dancing, male–female interactions, sexual preferences and habits, and drug-related activities are widely shared among males and females, as are certain expressive and manipulative aspects of verbal behavior such as *signifying, sounding*, or *playing the dozen*, all of which refer to well-organized speech events which occur with great frequency in the verbal interactions of Black adolescents (see *Verbal Duel*; *Speech Play*). Nonetheless, females use less vernacular vocabulary in their conversations than do males, in part because the latter are involved in a wider range of activities that generate such vernacular expressions, and in part because of the greater family and community constraints to which females are subjected. Though much of the vernacular vocabulary of Black youths is known and shared across socioeconomic and geographic boundaries, there are, nonetheless, disparities between middle-class adolescents and their inner-city counterparts based on differences in degree and kind of exposure to certain environment-bound life experiences, and the type of terminology that gets generated and used (Folb 1980).

As the preceding implies, Black vernacular vocabulary is learned in context, i.e., in the context of shared experiences that come from common life conditions which provide a frame of reference enabling Black youths to decipher the meanings for a variety of vernacular terms that many have heard since childhood. Hence, the meanings of many vernacular terms are difficult to grasp or interpret outside of this shared perspective, and apart from the paralinguistic and kinetic elements which accompany their use. Indeed, the kinetic element, both as it relates to body movements, gestures, and facial expressions, and a preference for terms or phrases that possess the quality of rapid and unrestricted movement (e.g., *dig, stepping, groovy, hustling*), is a prominent feature of Black vernacular expressive forms, and distinguishes the speech events of Black adolescents from those of their White counterparts (Kochman 1972, Labov 1972).

See also: Slang: Sociology; Sociology of Language; Code, Sociolinguistic; Labov, William; Ebonics and African American Vernacular English; Black English in Education: UK.

Bibliography

Bernstein B 1971–1975 *Class, Codes and Control, Vol. 2*. Routledge and Kegan Paul, London
Britton J N 1970 *Language and Learning*. University of Miami Press, Coral Gables, FL
Brooks-Gunn J, Matthews W S 1979 *He and She: How Children Develop Their Sex-Role Identity*. Prentice-Hall, Englewood Cliffs, NJ
Coleman J S 1961 *Adolescent Society*. Free Press, Glencoe, IL
Danesi M 1989 Adolescent language as affectively coded behavior: Findings of an observational research project. *Adolescence* **24**: 311–9
Eckert P 1988 Adolescent social structure and the spread of linguistic change. *Language and Society* **17**: 183–207
Eisenstadt S N 1956 *From Generation to Generation*. Free Press, Glencoe, IL
Folb E A 1980 *Runnin' Down Some Lines: The Language and Culture of Black Teenagers*. Harvard University Press, Cambridge, MA
Goodwin M 1980 Directive-response speech sequences in girls' and boys' task activities. In: McConnell-Ginet S, Borker R, Furman N (eds.) *Women and Language in Literature and Society*. Praeger, New York
Goodwin M 1990 *He-Said-She-Said: Talk as Social Organization Among Black Children*. Indiana University Press, Bloomington, IN
Gusdorf G 1965 *Speaking* (*La parole*). Northwestern University Press, Evanston, IL
Haas A 1979 The acquisition of genderlect. In: Orasnu J, Slater N, Adler L (eds.) Language, sex and gender. *Annals of the New York Academy of Sciences* **327**: 101–13
Kalčik S 1975 Like Ann's gynecologist, or the time I was almost raped: Personal narratives in women's rape groups. In: Farrar C R (ed.) *Women and Folklore, Journal of American Folklore* **88**(347): 3–11
Kochman T 1972 The kinetic element in Black idiom. In: Kochman T (ed.) *Rappin' and Stylin' Out*. University of Illinois Press, Urbana, IL
Labov T 1982 Social structure and peer terminology in a Black adolescent gang. *Language in Society* **11**: 391–411
Labov W 1972 *Language in the Inner City*. University of Pennsylvania Press, Philadelphia, PA
Lerman P 1967 Argot, symbolic deviance and subcultural delinquency. *American Sociological Review* **32**: 209–24
LeMasters E E 1975 *Blue Collar Aristocrats: Life-Styles at a Working-Class Tavern*. University of Wisconsin Press, Madison, WI
Lewis M M 1963 *Language, Thought and Personality in Infancy and Childhood*. Basic Books, New York
Maltz D N, Borker R A 1982 A cultural approach to male–female miscommunication. In: Gumperz J J (ed.) *Language and Social Identity*. Cambridge University Press, Cambridge, UK
Meditch A 1975 The development of sex-specific speech patterns in young children. *Anthropological Linguistics* **17**(9): 421–33
Mitchell-Kernan C 1972 Signifying, loud-talking, and marking. In: Kochman R (ed.) *Rappin' and Stylin' Out*. University of Illinois Press, Urbana, IL
Mitchell-Kernan C 1980 Foreword. In: Folb E A (ed.) *Runnin' Down Some Lines: The Language and Culture of Black Teenagers*. Harvard University Press, Cambridge, MA
MuFwene S, Rickford J, Baugh J, Bailey G 1998 *African American Vernacular English: History, Structure, Use*. Routledge, London
Opie I, Opie P 1959 *The Lore and Language of School Children*. Oxford University Press, London
Romaine S 1984 *The Language of Children and Adolescents*. Basil Blackwell, Oxford, UK

Rose T, Ross A 1994 *Microphone Fiends: Youth Music and Youth Culture*. Routledge, New York

Savin-Williams R C 1976 The ethological study of dominance formation and maintenance in a group of human adolescents. *Child Development* **47**: 972–9

Schwartz G, Merten D 1967 The language of adolescence: An anthropological approach to the youth culture. *American Journal of Sociology* **72**: 453–68

Smitherman G 1977 *Talkin' and Testifyin': The Language of Black America*. Houghton Mifflin, Boston, MA

Chain Shifts
G. J. Docherty and D. J. L. Watt

1. Chain Shift: Definition

Chain shift refers to a type of sound change whereby changes in a vowel's phonetic quality trigger changes in one or more of the other vowels in the system, without affecting the number of phonetic contrasts the system expresses. The simplest subtype is the minimal chain shift (Labov 1994: 118–9). A vowel /B/ changes over time in quality, vacating the region of vowel space it previously occupied; a vowel /A/ then comes to occupy that part of the space. Contrast between /A/ and /B/ is thus preserved, although the actual phonetic nature of the contrast will have altered. This process can be represented thus:

$$/A/ \rightarrow /B/ \rightarrow$$

The second basic subtype is the extended chain shift (Labov 1994: 119). This involves coordination of minimal chain shifts, such that as /A/ moves to occupy /B/'s vacated space, /B/ moves into the space left by a third vowel /C/, and so on.

$$/A/ \rightarrow /B/ \rightarrow /C/ \rightarrow /D/ \rightarrow \ldots$$

Chain shifts, then, perpetuate the system of oppositions expressed by the vowel system, and should therefore be distinguished from merger. Merger occurs when /A/ moves into the space occupied by /B/, but /B/ does not move away to compensate for /A/'s encroachment. Two formerly contrastive elements collapse together, becoming homophonous, and thereby reducing the number of contrasts by one. Since such a loss is argued to reduce the system's capacity to express lexical distinctions, chain shift acts as a means by which vowel systems can optimize communicative potential by regulating their internal structures.

2. Labov's Principles of Chain Shift

In modern (historical) sociolinguistics chain shifts are most closely associated with the work of William Labov (see *Labov, William*; *Sociolinguistic Variation*). One of the fundamental contributions of the Labovian paradigm to the field has been the elaboration of the principles appearing to underpin chain shift, as evidenced by historical and synchronic observations. Labov's principles build on the work of earlier analysts such as Sweet (1988), Haudricourt and Juilland (1949) and Martinet (1955), but are also generalized to take account of synchronic developments in the vowel systems of a range of languages. Stated in a basic form that applies to completed chain shifts (rather than ongoing synchronic ones), the three principles are:

> PRINCIPLE I: In chain shifts, long vowels rise.
> PRINCIPLE II: In chain shifts, short vowels fall.
> PRINCIPLE IIA: In chain shifts, the nuclei of upgliding diphthongs fall.
> PRINCIPLE III: In chain shifts, back vowels move to the front.
> (Labov 1994: 116)

3. The Great Vowel Shift

One such reconstructed historical chain shift—and indubitably the best-known, most thoroughly researched of all chain shifts—is the series of changes affecting fifteenth-century southern Middle English (ME) known as the Great (English) Vowel Shift (GVS). First analyzed as a unitary phenomenon by Luick (1896) and later Jespersen (1909), it exemplifies best Principle I, in that the ME long vowels /aː/, /ɛː/, /eː/, /ɔː/ and /oː/ all raised by one height. The close vowels /iː/ and /uː/, unable to raise any further, 'sidestepped' the rising /eː/ and /oː/ by diphthongizing, their nuclei dropping one height to [ei] and [ou], respectively. Subsequently, these fell further (Principle IIA), giving the modern /aɪ/ and /aʊ/ diphthongs. This sequence (with later developments in parentheses) can be summarized as follows:

ME		ModE			Example
iː	→	ei	→	(aɪ)	*five*
eː	→	iː	→	iː	*geese*
ɛː	→	eː	→	iː	*clean*
aː	→	ɛː	→	(eɪ)	*name*
uː	→	ou	→	(aʊ)	*house*
oː	→	uː	→	(uː)	*goose*
ɔː	→	oː	→	(əʊ)	*goat*

The GVS is generally agreed to have been completed by the late sixteenth or early seventeenth centuries, the final stage being the raising to /iː/ of the merged

ME /ɛː/ (e.g., *meat*) and /eː/ (e.g., *meet*). (Note that there are a small number of exceptions, such as *steak, break, great, broad*, etc.)

Debate continues over how the shift started (Lass 1999, Stockwell and Minkova 1999). Of the two main camps, the first follows Jespersen (1909) in believing that the GVS was triggered by diphthongization of /iː/ and /uː/, a change which stimulated /eː/ and /oː/ to rise into the resulting gaps. This position exemplifies the pull or drag chain model, whereby vowels vacating their former positions 'pull' others along behind them. The second camp adheres to Luick's (1896) account which reverses this order of events: as they raised, /eː/ and /oː/ shunted /iː/ and /uː/ aside (the push chain model). Luick's account incorporates aspects of a drag chain, since as /eː/ and /oː/ ousted /iː/ and /uː/, so /ɛː/ and /ɔː/ rose behind them. An element common to both approaches is the notion of systemic symmetry: what applies to back vowels will apply to front vowels at equivalent heights, and vice versa.

4. Ongoing Chain Shifts

The framework within which historical phonologists developed the chain shift model persists in modern sociolinguistics, with Labov's work, in particular, seeking to unite generalizations emerging from post hoc reconstructions of historical sound changes with research motivated by the axiom that synchronic sound change (see *Sound Change*) can be observed as it happens. Findings emerging from large-scale instrumental studies of vowel variation in North American English (Labov et al. 1972, in press, Labov 1991, 1994) underlie a broad typology postulating two major patterns of chain shift. The first—exemplified by the so-called Northern Cities Shift (NCS)—is characterized by a 'clockwise' rotation of the short vowels /i/, /e/, /ʌ/, and /o/ plus the long vowel /oh/, that is triggered by the raising of /æ/ to the position occupied by /iə/ (we conform above to Labov's phonemic notation system, which differs somewhat from IPA notation). The NCS exhibits elements of both push and drag chains, and is schematized in Fig. 1; the numbers represent each step of the sequence.

The NCS affects the English of the industrial inland northern USA but is most advanced in the region's largest cities (Syracuse, Rochester, Buffalo, Cleveland, Toledo, Detroit, Flint, Gary, Chicago, Rockford) (see *The Atlas of North American English: Methods and Findings*). NCS-type changes are also reported to be underway in other US varieties and parts of Canada.

All three of Labov's principles are argued to govern the NCS, though an additional factor—peripherality—is invoked to explain why in chain shifts falling vowels do not clash with vowels rising towards them. Peripherality is not an absolute measure but is defined relative to the vowel system as a whole, and is modeled in terms of two parallel 'tracks.' The peripheral track runs around the perimeter of the vowel space, while the nonperipheral track sits within the peripheral track. Vowels raise and front along the peripheral track, but switch to the nonperipheral track when falling or retracting (Labov 1994: 177).

Principles II and III are less well exemplified in the historical record, with Principle II appearing to be of greater relevance to synchronic variation (see below). Principle III, however, is invoked to account for substantial historical evidence of back-vowel fronting in a wide variety of languages at many periods. With respect to the GVS, Principle III could have governed the fronting of ME /oː/ to

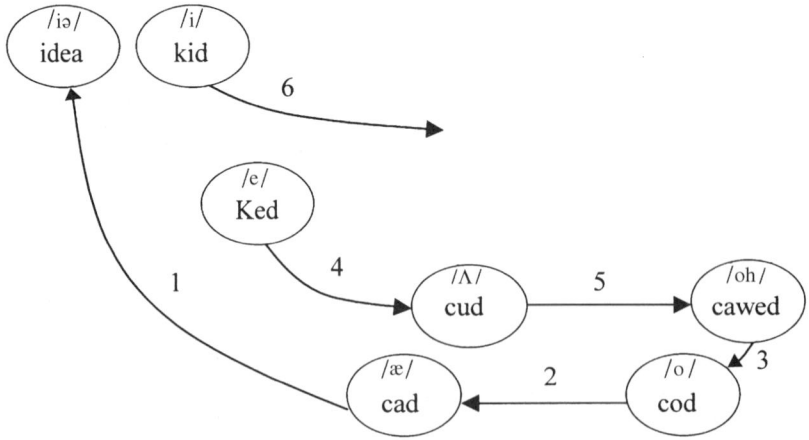

Figure 1. The Northern Cities Shift (after Labov 1998. Reproduced with permission).

[øː] in northern British English dialects, a development, which—owing to the consequent lack of pressure on /uː/ from below—did not necessitate diphthongization of ME /uː/ in these varieties (preserving forms like [huːs] 'house' and [duːn] 'down' which persist in Northumberland and Scotland. [oː], presumably in accordance with Principle I, then raised to [yː] and later unrounded to [iː], as in *boot, moon, do*, etc.; see Lass 1999).

The addition of the peripherality factor allows Labov to collapse the three principles to a single statement ('In chain shifts, peripheral vowels become less open and nonperipheral vowels become more open'). He claims this applies to the fronting of back vowels as well as raising/lowering in the height dimension, and it is clearly relevant in the description of the second major chain shift underway in contemporary American English. The 'Southern Shift,' affecting the dialects of the southern, south Middle Atlantic and south-midland states, involves laxing and centralization of long close and mid-vowels (Labov 1991, 1994, Labov et al. in press). Contrary to the NCS, its rotation is 'counterclockwise,' though the sequence appears to be less consistent than is the case for the NCS. Labov generalizes the Southern Shift to govern the vowel systems of dialects in southern England, Australia, New Zealand, and South Africa. Its operation in these varieties consequently becomes difficult to explain in terms of contact and resultant diffusion of innovations between northern and southern hemisphere Englishes. We must therefore consider system-internal explanations of the raising of nonclose vowels and the fronting of back vowels (see especially Trudgill et al. 2000). These processes are argued by some scholars to result from properties of vowel systems which arise from the mismatch between the communicative needs of speakers/listeners and the limitations imposed on them by vocal tract morphology and the auditory system. Some of the arguments proposed in support of this position are discussed in the following section.

The first two of the three main approaches to the explanation of why chain shifts are triggered in the first place are based on aspects of speech production and perception that are claimed to be universal (it ought, therefore, to be possible for chain shifts to occur in any spoken language, at any time). The first emphasizes the trade-off between articulatory constraints and discriminability of vowel sounds, and the perpetual instability of vowel systems resulting from the tension between the two. Vowels raise and front, it is hypothesized, because the lower back area of the vowel space is overcrowded: although vowel systems tend toward phonological symmetry, the articulatory space available for vowel production is inherently asymmetrical (Haudricourt and Juilland 1949, Martinet 1955, Samuels 1972). Such overcrowding will obviously be more acute in languages featuring three or four distinctive vowel heights (such as Germanic and Romance languages; note that most of the languages for which Labov reports completed or ongoing chain shifts are members of these groups). Lindblom (1986) argues cogently for this position, stating that (a) the articulators have more mobility at the front of the mouth; (b) there is a richer supply of structures for sensory control at anterior vocal tract locations; (c) acoustic-perceptual effects are greater at the front than at the back. The logical product of these factors, however, would be systems composed exclusively of merged or minimally distinct close front vowels; clearly, some force must counteract this trend. Samuels (1972) suggests that a drive to maximize sonority keeps the system's elements in circulation. Close vowels, being relatively low in sonority, tend to fall in order to boost their sonority/contrastiveness, but rise again, as merger with existing open vowels becomes a threat.

The second explanation abstracts away from articulatory issues to focus more narrowly on perceptual and communicative factors. Vowel systems are in this view self-organizing, homeostatic, closed systems in which the preservation of auditory distinctiveness and communicative potential are paramount. A vowel system's geometry emerges from the interplay of several antagonistic pressures: (a) the need to maintain sufficient contrasts for successful communication to take place; (b) a requirement that these contrasts be perceptible to listeners (and crucially learners); and (c) the necessity for a system to maximize the acoustic/perceptual distance between each term in the system, regardless of how many terms the system contains (see e.g., de Boer 2001). Chain shifts (at least those involving push chains) arise from this interaction: if instability is introduced anywhere in the system such that merger is threatened, the system will compensate by moving the vowel that is being encroached upon out of harm's way. Equilibrium is restored when the threat of merger diminishes. The system also seeks to maximize contrast in other ways, e.g., by exaggerating the distance between nucleus and glide in diphthongal reflexes of close vowels, as Stockwell and Minkova (1999) argue for the GVS (see also Labov 1994).

A third approach, which derives most heavily from the neogrammarian and structuralist traditions, stresses systemic configuration, in particular the role of front-back symmetry. Neither articulatory nor perceptual factors are given much consideration here: rather than the communicative needs of speakers and listeners, the system's own requirements instead govern the behavior of its individual constituent elements. In this strongly internalist model, chain shifts are seen as unitary phenomena which, like the GVS, may take centuries to complete, and which to modern (socio)linguists may appear rather too teleological to be plausible (see *Sociolinguistics and Language Change*). The system is indeed seen as functionally independent of the speakers who use it, the latter being seen as conduits through which changes diffuse when the system seeks to reorganize itself (see Samuels 1972: 42). The speaker-system relationship is always problematic in accounts of sound change, and is clearly a central issue when establishing the validity of any chain shift model. Some associated problems are discussed briefly in the final section.

5. Further Questions

Recent methodological developments have meant that chain shifts can be studied much more objectively than was previously possible. Initial observations were made from fragmentary historical evidence based on orthographic clues, and by comparing the vowel systems of closely related languages and dialects. However, since we usually have no means of verifying data drawn from older written sources, their validity cannot be beyond question. Comparison of languages and dialects is also problematic, in that reconstruction of stages intervening between two varieties and a common ancestor usually necessitates interpolation made in the absence of documentary evidence.

More recent analyses derive from detailed auditory transcriptions of vowel variation in synchronic varieties, and since the groundbreaking work of Labov et al. (1972), have been augmented via instrumental phonetic methods aimed at capturing important acoustic properties of vowel sounds. Vowel quality in such studies is represented by cross-plotting the frequencies in Hertz (or some transform thereof) of the lowest two formants (F1 and F2) of vowel tokens against one another. Chain shifts in progress can be detected by comparing the differences between formant values in samples for multiple speakers, and/or for the same speaker(s) at different times. If the differences between samples affect several vowel categories at once, and do so in some coherent way, the differences may be interpreted as the kind of coordinated change expected when chain shift is taking place.

Much idealization is, however, necessitated by the mapping of continuous, highly variable acoustic data onto the discrete categories they are theorized to express. This is true, for example, of Labov's classification of vowels as [±peripheral], a feature he argues is based on tongue position rather than acoustic criteria, but which is probably at least as difficult to define articulatorily as it is acoustically. Indeed, the emphasis on articulatory and acoustic properties of vowels underpinning much work on chain shifts may be misplaced, in that listeners only have access to auditory representations of the sounds in question. Warping of acoustic space by the auditory system may mean that purely acoustic representations of vowels cannot unambiguously determine their perceptual values, so it may be rather too simplistic to say that increases or decreases in formant frequency values relative to some putative 'target' or 'prototype' will be perceived as, say, fronting or raising, especially in view of the fact that the auditory system has been demonstrated to utilize a broad range of cues in vowel perception (duration, F0, formant transitions into and out of adjacent consonants, etc.), rather than solely the frequencies of F1 and F2 at the vowel's midpoint. Furthermore, present accounts take a solidly 'bottom-up' (purely signal-based) approach to speech perception, and have little to say about the roles of lexical factors or listener experience in the process by which listeners recognize spoken words (Lindblom 1990, McClelland and Elman 1986).

Despite these and other problems that attend any formulation of a theory of chain shift, the contributions of Labov and his coworkers are absolutely central to our understanding of the phenomenon. Although most research carried out in the area has, understandably, focused upon (North American) English, there is clearly great scope to test the validity and predictive power of Labov's principles on data from other languages. Ultimately, principles of chain shifting would need to be part of a superordinate theory of sound change which accounts for the apparently contradictory processes of both chain shift *and* merger; while system functionality looks to be important from a chain shift point of view, mergers, which are essentially dysfunctional, are—as Labov himself acknowledges—actually more common. At present, we have a powerful set of principles to account for chain shift, but there remain many questions to be answered—not just those concerning the details of how chain shifts operate, but also in terms of the fundamental assumptions upon which much of the current research in the area is built.

See also: Labov, William; Language Change and Language Acquisition; The Atlas of North American English: Methods and Findings; Sociophonetics; Sound Change.

Bibliography

de Boer B 2001 *The Origins of Vowel Systems*. Oxford University Press, Oxford, UK

Haudricourt A G, Juilland A G 1949 *Essai pour une histoire structurale du phonétisme français*. C. Klincksieck, Paris

Jespersen O 1909 *A Modern English Grammar on Historical Principles, Part I: Sounds and Spellings*. George Allen and Unwin, London

Labov W 1991 The three dialects of English. In: Eckert P (ed.) *New Ways of Analyzing Sound Change*. Academic Press, Orlando, FL, pp. 1–44

Labov W 1994 *Principles of Linguistic Change, Vol. I: Internal Factors*. Blackwell, Oxford, UK

Labov W 1998 *The Organization of Dialect Diversity in North America*. URL: ⟨http://www.ling.upenn.edu/phono_atlas/ICSLP4.html⟩

Labov W, Ash S, Boberg C in press *Atlas of North American English*. Mouton de Gruyter, Berlin

Labov W, Yaeger M, Steiner R 1972 *A Quantitative Study of Sound Change in Progress*. US Regional Survey, Philadelphia, PA

Lass R 1999 Phonology and morphology. In: Lass R (ed.) *The Cambridge History of the English Language, Vol. III: 1476–1776*. Cambridge University Press, Cambridge, UK, pp. 56–186

Lindblom B 1986 Phonetic universals in vowel systems. In: Ohala J J, Jaeger, J J (eds.) *Experimental Phonology*. Academic Press, Orlando, FL, pp. 13–44

Lindblom B 1990 Explaining phonetic variation: A sketch of the H&H theory. In: Hardcastle W J, Marchal A (eds.) *Speech Production and Speech Modelling*. Kluwer, Dordrecht, The Netherlands, pp. 403–39

Luick K 1896 *Historische Grammatik der Englischen Sprache*, 1964 reprint. Blackwell, Oxford, UK

Martinet A 1955 *Economie des Changements Phonétiques*. Franck, Bern, Switzerland

McClelland J L, Elman J L 1986 The TRACE model of speech perception. *Cognitive Psychology* **18**(1): 1–86

Samuels M L 1972 *Linguistic Evolution, with Special Reference to English*. Cambridge University Press, Cambridge, UK

Stockwell R P, Minkova D 1999 Explanations of sound change: Contradictions between dialect data and theories of chain shifting. In: Upton C, Wales K (eds.) *Dialectal Variation in English: Proceedings of the Harold Orton Centenary Conference, 1998*. University of Leeds, Leeds, UK, pp. 83–102

Sweet H 1988 *A History of English Sounds*. Clarendon Press, Oxford, UK

Trudgill P, Gordon E, Lewis G, Maclagan M 2000 The role of drift in the formation of native-speaker southern hemisphere Englishes: Some New Zealand evidence. *Diachronica* **17**(1): 111–38

Class and Language
F. Gregersen

Class is a sociological concept originating with Marx (see *Marxist Theories of Language*). As such, it implies a conflict-view of society, a view that taken to its linguistic conclusion seems to imply that a continuous linguistic class struggle is characteristic of capitalist society. The concept of linguistic class struggle, however, has hardly played a role in linguistic research; the prevalent use of the concept of class has, rather, been that of a speaker variable within sociolinguistics (see *Sociolinguistics and Language Change*; *Sociology of Language*; *Social Class*).

Two kinds of sociolinguistics, viz. theoretical and empirical sociolinguistics, may be distinguished.

1. Class in Theoretical Sociolinguistics

In theoretical sociolinguistics, the relevant questions pertaining to class language are:

(a) Is there any logical connection between the sociological concept of a class, defined with respect to the conditions of production, power relations (see *Power and Language*), or political consciousness on the one hand and the various levels of language on the other? If so, what are the mediating factors?

(b) How can the effect of class be detected in an individual member's everyday language use?

An attempt to answer such questions may be found in a somewhat difficult book by the Soviet researcher Voloshinov (1973). (Some researchers have tried to identify V. N. Voloshinov (see *Voloshinov, Valentin Nikolavic*) with the literary theoretician M. M. Bakhtin (see *Bakhtin, Mikhail M.*; *Dialogism*) Voloshinov's book *Marxism and the Philosophy of Language* (originally published 1929) is in a sense a classic, but it has not led to the establishment of a research tradition. The book did influence literary stylistics and the study of discourse phenomena such as indirect speech (see *Discourse*; *Representation*), but it has not been much discussed by sociolinguists. The comprehensive reviews of the field, Fasold (1984, 1989) and Chambers (1995), do not even mention Voloshinov; though Mesthrie et al. (2000) attempt to correct this imbalance.

1.1 Theoretical Sociolinguistics: The Relationship between Class and Language

The specific relationship that Voloshinov sketches takes material existence to be basic and consciousness to be its—though not direct—reflection. The individual's continuous coming to grips with his or her material existence produces a 'world view.' This world view is ideology, and ideology is of central concern for a Marxist theory of language and thus for its recent offsprings, such as critical discourse analysis, as well (see *Marxist Theories of Language*; *Critical Language Awareness*). Since class is based on differential relationships to the forces of production, the members of a given class share material conditions of existence, and thus to a large extent will produce similar world views. In this theory, the relationship between class and language is that class, as a convenient shorthand for material conditions, determines language, in that the semantics underlying any particular utterance will be found to vary along class lines. The argument is not easy to follow, but it is suggestive and, what is more important, in the early 2000s it is still the only worthwhile effort to forge a theoretical link between objective social existence and its subjective perception as this results in language use. The mediation between class and language use takes two paths. On the one hand, the class specific culture subsumes certain class specific speech events and in turn specific genres, registers, speech acts, and thus finally specific meanings. On the other, certain common speech events are typically carried out in class specific ways; this too goes for the linguistic hierarchy, thus, for example, creating class specific narratives as well as class specific ways of narrating. Whether this perception is, in fact, too abstract to be related to everyday language use depends on the place assigned to semantics in one's theory of language. If what people (may) mean determines what they (may) say, chances are that semantics determines language use. The functional systemic theory of Michael Halliday (see *Halliday, Michael Alexander Kirkwood*) is based on a view of language which facilitates this line of thinking (cf. below on semantic variables).

2. Empirical Sociolinguistics: Studies of Class Language

Much more frequent and well-known are empirical studies of the relationship between specific linguistic variables and class as a speaker variable.

2.1 Problems with Class as a Speaker Variable

It is not that simple to decide which persons belong to which class. First of all, the abstract Marxist concept has to be operationalized.

'Operationalizations' are helpful only insofar as they point to easily detectable features of a person's social background. There is thus a very real danger that operationalization may take the place of analysis. In a penetrating study of the class concept used by sociolinguists, Glyn Williams (see *Williams, Glyn*) argues convincingly that the structural functionalist theory of Talcott Parsons has been taken as the more or less conscious point of departure for any operationalization. The normal operationalizations of class revolve around power, education, income, and type of work. For instance, William Labov (see *Labov, William*), in his ground-breaking study of the New York Lower East Side speech community (Labov 1966), used the last three latter factors in order to produce a composite index. This index was scalable, and thus the number of social strata could be arbitrarily defined. In fact, Labov used both a six-strata and a nine-strata measure of social background. Obviously, class in this tradition is no longer a Marxist concept, since the difference between classes is reduced to being quantitative instead of qualitative.

Class as a measure of social background should be used with caution. First, it is not valid in nonindustrialized societies, and, to say the least, it is also very hard to apply in nonindustrialized sectors of otherwise industrialized societies. This is the reason why different measures of social position have been brought into play within social dialectology and the sociolinguistics of the Third World (see *Dialect and Dialectology*; *Linguistic Imperialism*).

Second, class tends to be a synchronic measure, unless one differentiates, for example, between newcomers to a class and those born into it, or one takes into account the position of the family through generations.

Third, class as a concept does not work well with women, children, and youngsters who have not yet found a permanent position. Since this excludes quite a significant proportion of a given population from the analysis, various other measures of social background have been introduced. Most importantly, there is a growing uneasiness about purely quantitative measures of social background. Comparable trends are found within the rest of the social sciences, as witness the success of network analysis, anthropological analyses of social structure, and life-history approaches.

2.2 Class and Field Methods

All of this amounts to an enormous challenge to sociolinguistics.

Sociolinguistics is concerned with the relationship between society and the social characteristics of individuals on the one hand and language and language use on the other. This field can only be studied empirically if it is possible to find linguistic data produced by persons whose own social background is known. Since Labov's early studies, the universally used method of collecting such linguistic data has been the sociolinguistic interview (see *Sociolinguistic Variation*; *Field Methods in Modern Dialect and Variation Studies*).

A sociolinguistic interview consists of a semistructured conversation between a fieldworker and an informant. The job of the interviewer is to lead the informant to produce speech of various kinds, speech belonging to two or more different styles. The interview is a useful way of collecting linguistic data, but it must be remembered that this is not a way of getting to know the total cultural background and everyday practice of informants.

Obviously, one cannot interview 'the' working class or 'the' middle class; one must limit oneself to interviewing individual members of those classes. Since interviewing is not a 'natural' speech event for anyone, this calls for an analysis of what is for any given class the most obvious equivalent of the sociolinguistic interview. This, however, can only be done if one has recourse to data concerning the total repertoire of speech events. It is very likely that such repertoires will manifest significant differences, when analyzed precisely from the point of view of class. Class is supposedly a cultural concept in addition to being a sociological one, or rather, the sociological fact of class has definite cultural consequences.

2.3 Which Classes?

There is an interesting difference between sociological models that allow any member of a given society to be classified and models which take certain characteristics to be decisive for the allocation of an individual to a specific class, thus allowing for unclassified persons. The Marxist conception of two opposing classes, one defined as having power over the forces of production (the capitalists), and the other as being exploited by the first mentioned class, has never been taken as a relevant starting point for empirical studies. The two classes opposed have universally been (some variant of) the middle class (MC) and (some variant of) the working class (WC). Since these two classes are not defined according to strictly Marxist criteria, at least in the classical sense, there is a choice as to whether they are seen as differing from each other quantitatively or qualitatively. In most industrialized countries, the middle-class member has an academic education and holds higher-level jobs. The income is at least above the average. The typical WC member, on the other hand, has less education, less power in his job, and earns less than the typical MC member. (Obviously, these are only statistically valid characteristics; any one member of the MC or the WC may deviate in one or more respects.)

Originating with Labov, a further distinction may be made within the MC, viz. between the lower middle class and the 'real' middle class. When doing quantitative studies, this distinction may be important, since there is much evidence to confirm that these two sections of the MC differ linguistically (see Sect. 2.6).

2.4 Quantitative Studies of Class and Language

Quantitative studies feature a collection of individuals distributed on a number of background characteristics so as to make up various mini-populations, for example, the working class versus the middle class, or the lower working class versus the working class proper and the higher working class, etc.

The linguistic features to be studied here are known as 'sociolinguistic variables.' The definition of a sociolinguistic variable has been a matter of discussion. Previously, the state of the art dictated that sociolinguistic variables were almost all phonetic ones, whereas in the 1990s the continuation of the work of Bernstein (see *Bernstein, Basil*) by R. Hasan has been influential in shifting the focus to semantic variables (see Hasan 1989). Phonetic variables have, however, been by far the best-studied (see *Sociophonetics*; *Sociolinguistic Variation*).

The results of these studies have been summarized by Fasold (1989: 223ff.) and Chambers (1995: 34ff.) and may be found in any manual of sociolinguistics. A prominent feature of a number of studies is that linguistic stratification can be shown to parallel exactly social stratification. Thus, a result which is found repeatedly is that certain sociolinguistic variables seem to ape social structure. If an individual belongs to a specific class, that individual's use of the variable is statistically predictable.

This has led to speculations why this is so. On the one hand, the result is somewhat tedious; one does not obtain any new information, since the social stratification was known from the start. On the other hand, the very tedious repetition of the result at least demonstrates that language use is patterned sociologically. This is news to the public at large, since it makes discussions of the correct pronunciation or the right way of spelling rather more complex. If pronunciations vary statistically with class, there cannot be any one correct pronunciation that is neutral as to class membership.

2.5 Class Language and Norms

Most European countries have a long tradition of language planning (Joseph 1987). The ideal which most planning agencies have striven towards realizing has never been defined in class terms. It is evident, however, that the ideal norm has been modeled on the speech of the leading classes in society. Since the leading classes have a way of promoting their own culture or their own ideas as natural, it should not come as a surprise that the linguistic norm has been thought to be natural as well. Sociolinguistic results have at least had the beneficial effect of revealing the true class character of any norm based on authentic speech.

2.6 Class and Style: Hypercorrection

It is the purpose of the sociolinguistic interview to provoke different speech styles. This is done by manipulating the conversation in various ways (see *Manipulation*; *Conversation Analysis*); the crucial fact is, however, that style variation in itself can only be explained in terms of a conflict between the norms of the various subgroups within a speech community. Taken universally, the result of sociolinguistic studies is that individuals from all conceivable strata vary individually in important ways. This intraindividual variation is called 'style variation.' The relationship between class-determined variation and style variation is normally that speakers converge more, the more formal the style. There seems to be general agreement on the part of the speakers about what is most appropriate in formal styles, just as there seems to be a general tendency to differ more, the more casual the style. This has been taken to mean that a defining characteristic of a speech community is the agreement on what should be counted as worth imitating; as a definition, this is hardly valid. A competing explanation is that the more formal situations are regulated by the norm either directly (schools, public service, (state) television, etc.) or by association with people representing the norm. And the norm is—naturally—more akin to (if not identical with) the speech of the higher social classes.

The perception of the speech of the higher social classes as socially attractive is brought out very nicely in the phenomenon of hypercorrection. In Labov's studies, the lower middle class had a curious 'cross-over' pattern in the more formal speech styles, that is, they produced more higher-class forms than the 'real' MC members did themselves. This phenomenon is called 'hypercorrection.' The lower middle class correctly perceives that the real MC members differ from the rest in that they produce more (or less) of certain (mostly phonetic) sociolinguistic variables; consequently, the lower middle class members produce as many (or as few) as possible of these sociophonetic variables in the situations that call for prestige forms. In this, they succeed too well, only to succeed in revealing their belonging to the lower middle class (see *Sociolinguistic Variation*).

The importance of the phenomenon of hypercorrection for the study of class language is that it shows convincingly that the link between class and sociophonetic variables is much more indirect than might be suspected, if one just looks at parallel stratification patterns.

See also: Language in Society: Overview; Power and Language; Social Class.

Bibliography

Chambers J K 1995 *Sociolinguistic Theory*. Blackwell, London
Fasold R 1984 *The Sociolinguistics of Society*. Blackwell, Oxford, UK
Fasold R 1989 *The Sociolinguistics of Language*. Blackwell, Oxford, UK
Joseph J E 1987 *Eloquence and Power*. Frances Pinter, London
Hasan R 1989 Semantic variation and sociolinguistics, *Australian Journal of Linguistics* **9**: 221–75
Labov W 1966 *The Social Stratification of English in New York City*. Center for Applied Linguistics, Washington, DC
Labov W 1984 Field methods of the project on linguistic change and variation. In: Baugh J, Sherzer J (eds.) *Language in Use*. Prentice-Hall, Englewood Cliffs, NJ
Mesthrie R, Swann J, Deumert A, Leap W 2000 *Introducing Sociolinguistics*. Edinburgh University Press, Edinburgh, UK
Voloshinov V N 1973 *Marxism and the Philosophy of Language*. Seminar Press, New York
Williams G 1992 *Sociolinguistics. A Sociological Critique*. Routledge, London

Dialect and Dialectology

S. Romaine

Dialectology is a long-established branch of linguistics: the existence of geographical diversity was among the first observations made by the Greeks. Dialectology determined to a great extent the nature of scientific research into language in the nineteenth century. The investigation of local dialects was seen as a way to recapture linguistic history and to provide the missing links for comparative historical reconstruction, the primary enterprise of linguistics at that time. It was believed that dialects preserved older speech patterns in pure form. Research into dialects was also spurred on by the Romantic movement, which fostered a more general interest in folklore. Robert Burns and many other poets chose to write in their dialects rather than in the standard literary language.

1. The Term 'Dialect'

In both its traditional and modern sense dialectology has to do with the origins and distribution of dialects. The term 'dialect' has generally been used to refer to a subordinate variety of a language, such as English, which has many dialects. A regional dialect is a language variety associated with a place, such as the Yorkshire dialect in England or the Bavarian dialect in Germany. Dialects of a language tend to differ more from one another the more remote they are from one another geographically. In this respect dialectology has to do with boundaries, which often coincide with geographical features such as rivers and mountains. Boundaries are, however, often of a social nature, e.g., between different social class groups, 'social dialects' (see *Language in Society: Overview*).

The term dialect also has historical connotations. Historical linguists, for instance, speak of the Germanic dialects, by which they mean the ancestors of language varieties now recognized as modern Germanic languages, such as English, Dutch, and German. The entities labeled 'English language' or 'Flemish dialect' are not, however, discrete. Any variety is part of a continuum in social and geographical space and time. The discontinuities that do occur, however, often reflect geographical and social boundaries and weaknesses in communication networks (see *Language*).

Some classic cases of related dialects are the West Romance and Germanic dialect continua. The West Romance dialect continuum stretches through rural communities from the Atlantic coast of France through Italy, Spain, and Portugal. Mutual intelligibility exists between adjacent villages, although speakers of the standard varieties of French, Italian, Spanish, and Portuguese find one another mutually unintelligible to varying degrees. Similarly, the Germanic dialect continuum connects a series of historically related varieties that differ from one another with respect to one or more features.

2. The Term 'A Language'

The dividing line between the languages called Dutch and German is linguistically arbitrary but politically and culturally relevant. Max Weinreich's often quoted dictum, 'a language is a dialect with an army and a navy,' attests the importance of political power and the sovereignty of a nation-state in the recognition of a variety as a language rather than a dialect. Situations in which there is widespread agreement as to what constitutes a language arise through the interaction of social, political, psychological, and historical factors, and not any inherent properties of the varieties concerned.

Certain varieties of the West Germanic dialect continuum are considered to be dialects of Dutch and others, dialects of German because of the relationship these varieties have to their respective standard languages. The process of standardization is connected with a number of sociohistorical factors such as literacy, nationalism, and cultural and ethnic identity. It results in the selection and fixing of a uniform norm of usage, which is promoted in dictionaries, grammars, and teaching. A standard language is a variety that has been deliberately codified so that it varies minimally in linguistic form but is maximally elaborated in function.

Chambers and Trudgill (1998) distinguish between autonomous and heteronomous speech varieties as alternative labels to language and dialect. The Dutch dialects are dependent on or heteronomous with respect to standard Dutch, German dialects with standard German. This means that speakers of German are taught German in school. They look to standard German as a reference point. The term 'language' is employed for a variety that is autonomous together with all those varieties with which it is heteronomous.

Because heteronomy and autonomy reflect political and cultural rather than purely linguistic factors, they can change. Often through political developments formerly heteronomous varieties can achieve autonomy, as in the case of Afrikaans in South Africa, which was standardized in the 1920s and recognized as a language and not a dialect of Dutch. Conversely, autonomous varieties may lose their autonomy, as Scots did when it ceased to function as the language of the Scottish court after the Union of Crowns in 1603.

3. Differences between Dialects

Some linguists make a further distinction between accent and dialect. An accent consists of a way of pronouncing a variety (see *Accent*). A dialect, however, varies from other dialects of the same language simultaneously on at least three levels of organization: pronunciation, grammar or syntax, and vocabulary. Thus, educated speakers of American English and British English can be regarded as using dialects of the same language because differences of these three kinds exist between them. In practice, however, speakers of the two varieties share a common grammar and differ from each other more in terms of vocabulary and pronunciation. Some examples of these differences are illustrated in Table 1.

4. Dialect Geography

The beginnings of traditional dialect geography are found in the work of Georg Wenker who prepared 40 sentences designed to yield information on dialect differences in German, e.g., *Im Winter fliegen die trocknen Blätter herum* 'In the winter the

Table 1. Some differences between American and British English

	American	British
Pronunciation	ate /eit/ (rhymes with *mate*)	/ɛt/ (RP; see *Accent*) (rhymes with *met*)
Grammar/Syntax	Jane had gotten used to it.	Jane had got used to it. (pp of *get*)
Vocabulary	Sam took the elevator rather than the stairs.	Sam took the lift rather than the stairs.

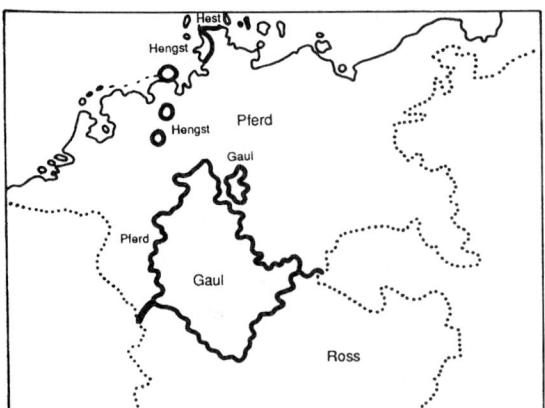

Figure 1. Dialect map for the names given to 'horse' in Germany.

dry leaves fly around' (see *Wenker, Georg*). From 1876 onwards he sent these out to schoolteachers in numerous localities. The teachers were asked to transcribe the sentences using the speech characteristics of the area. The material was then mapped and the characteristic features of dialects were plotted by the geographic location of their occurrence. The linguistic boundaries between varieties are called 'isoglosses.'

Major dialect boundaries are often characterized by a bundle of isoglosses. Figure 1 shows one of the maps produced by this type of investigation. It displays the names given to 'horse' in Germany. The main terms used are *Pferd* (which has become standard High German), *Gaul*, and *Ross*. *Hengst* is also used in the northwest and *Hest*, in the north. Most dialect investigations presented their results in linguistic atlases which provided a geographical representation of linguistic facts. Because such maps were difficult and expensive to produce, many of the results of dialect investigations took decades to publish, and some such as Wenker's never appeared in published form.

Wenker's methods had some other disadvantages, a major one being the idiosyncrasies in the transcribing procedures used by the schoolteachers. His sentences were also designed to elicit mainly phonological (and lexical) rather than syntactic or morphological variation. The Germans, however, remain a major influence on dialectology, especially in the English-speaking world. Much of the early work on Scottish dialects was done by Germans and most surveys owe much to the methodology of the Germans.

In France, Jules Gilliéron (see *Gilliéron, Jules*) drew on the work of Wenker and trained one fieldworker, Edmont, to collect the material for the French linguistic atlas which was published in entirety in 1910. Edmont cycled to 639 locations in France, where he personally gathered material by direct questioning.

The next major dialectological investigation took place in the United States, where the methods of Wenker, Gilliéron, and Jaberg and Jud (1928–40) were adapted (see *Jaberg, Karl*). Hans Kurath (see *Kurath, Hans*) attempted to overcome some of the shortcomings in earlier European work by paying more attention to the selection and training of fieldworkers, as well as the selection of informants and localities, and the preparation of a questionnaire.

The first large-scale dialect study in the United States produced the *Linguistic Atlas of New England* (referred to by the acronym LANE), a survey of 213 rural and urban communities. Subsequent atlases such as PEAS (*Pronunciation of English in the Atlantic States*), LAGS (*Linguistic Atlas of the Gulf States*), LAUM (*Linguistic Atlas of the Upper Midwest*) dealt with other regions such as the Atlantic States. Large-scale dialect geography began in England slightly later with Orton's survey of 300 small villages in England and the Isle of Man.

5. Dialect Patterns

The availability of the American and English atlases allowed dialect patterns in the United States and Britain to be compared. American isoglosses rarely terminate abruptly, which indicates a basic difference between the structure of dialect differentiation in the two countries. The American population has always been more mobile both socially and geographically so that the conditions for the development and maintenance of local dialects were never met to the same extent in the United States as they were in Europe.

Nevertheless, the findings of American dialectology dispelled the myth that there was a general American speech. Instead there were a number of speech areas, each of which was divided into a number of smaller subareas. Each major region constituted a unity and had its own regional standard of pronunciation. In England, however, the most local dialects were associated with the groups at the lower end of the social hierarchy, while those at the top spoke RP (Received Pronunciation), which showed no trace of regionalisms. In the eastern United States three major dialects were identified: North (including New England and the Hudson Valley); Midland (Pennsylvania and the Alleghenies); and South (Chesapeake Bay, Virginia Piedmont, and the Carolinas). Each major area is enclosed by a large number of isoglosses representing differences in lexis, grammar and phonology (see Fig. 2).

It also became possible to trace the transference of patterns from Britain to the United States. Before Kurath's work, the prevailing opinion was that American English was essentially Southern Standard English of the seventeenth and eighteenth centuries

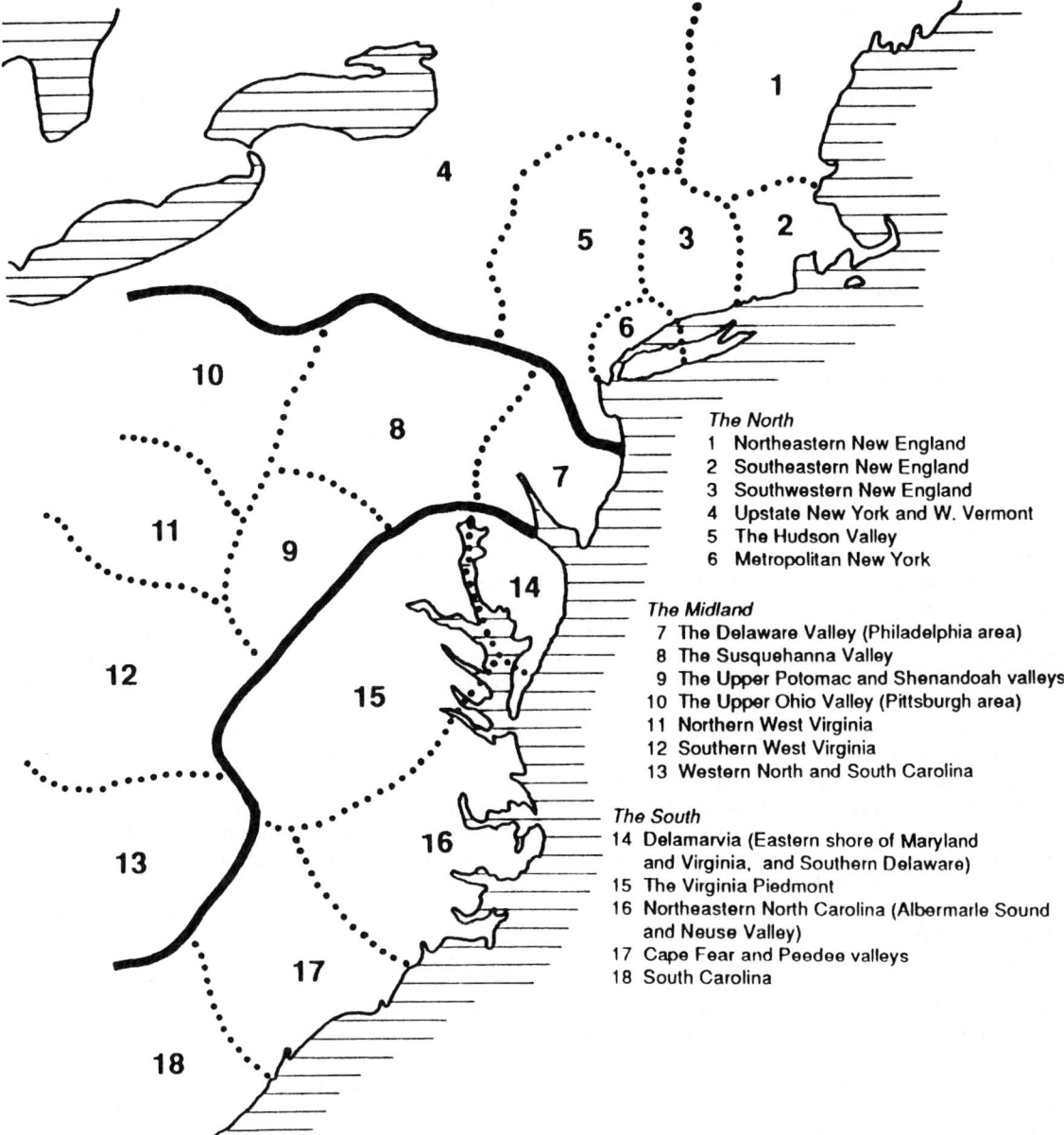

Figure 2. Speech areas of the Atlantic states (Kurath and McDavid 1961: map 2).

as modified locally. Kurath, however, demonstrated that most of the dialect differences in the United States have their basis partly in regional varieties of British English which earlier settlers brought with them. In Britain, for instance, the words *brook, burn*, and *beck* show broad regional distribution. *Brook* is dominant throughout the Midlands and into the south; *beck* is found in the area of former Danish settlement, and *burn* (from Scots) extends from Scotland into the border counties of northern England. *Brook* was transported across the ocean and, although it had strong regional ties in England, it was the form accepted as standard. Its rival regional variants were left behind and two new regional forms developed in the United States, *run* (found in the Midland dialect) and *branch* (Southern). The form *brook* is northern. Thus, an item showing a broad regional pattern in England became narrowly local in the United States.

There is linguistic evidence for a historical connection between American speech of the north and west and that of northern England, and to some extent that of the American south and the pronunciation of southern England. These linguistic similarities are well supported by the history of American colonization, patterns of westward movement, and later immigration. This is illustrated in the distribution for postvocalic /r/, as in *cart, barn*, etc.

In Britain the distribution of postvocalic /r/ based on Orton's (1962) *Survey of English Dialects* shows that nonrhotic dialects were the result of an historical innovation which began somewhere in the east or center of England before spreading northwards. Before Irish immigration to the United States, the population of eastern New England came from the southeastern counties of England, where varieties closest to RP are spoken. RP lacks postvocalic /r/. Western New England, on the other hand, had a large number of Scots–Irish immigrants, whose dialects had postvocalic /r/. The Virginia tidewater region and the coastal south were also settled largely by the Scots–Irish. Thus, nonrhotic speech (i.e., without postvocalic /r/) was typical of coastal areas and rhotic speech of inland areas. Hence there are clusters of nonrhotic speech around the major ports of Boston, New York, and Charlestown. This was true not only for reasons of settlement pattern, but for cultural reasons. The coastal areas which had nonrhotic speech kept it because they were in touch with English prestige patterns of speaking. The population of the Mid-Atlantic states was mixed. Philadelphia was an exception to the port pattern of nonrhotic speech because of Quaker settlement. The Quakers attracted immigrants from all parts of Britain and the rest of Europe. They maintained less trade with Britain and sent fewer children back to English universities. Since World War II, rhotic speech has become more prestigious in the United States.

6. Dialects and Sound Change

Since its beginnings in the nineteenth century dialectology has contributed both theory and methods to linguistics. The early work done in Germany and France provided a basis for interpreting the linguistic significance of the patterning of isoglosses. Most importantly, however, it seriously challenged prevailing views of sound change. Ironically, early studies of dialects had set out to support the neogrammarian hypothesis that sound change took place according to sound laws that admitted no exceptions. In the case of the second Germanic sound shift, an important test case, neogrammarian principles would predict that all late Proto–Germanic instances of /k/ would become /x/ all over the High German territory.

It was Georg Wenker, who showed that the second Germanic sound shift had exceptions. This can be seen in the set of isoglosses in Fig. 3, which separates Low from High German. The isoglosses run from east to west across Germany (slightly north of Berlin) and the Netherlands. The features comprising the isoglosses include the pronunciation of final consonants such as /p/, /t/, and /k/ in words such as *dorp/dorf* ('village'), *dat/das* ('that,' 'the'), and *ik/ich* ('I'). The first member of each of these pairs is the Low German variant, as found in modern standard Dutch; the second is the High German variant, as found in modern standard German. The isoglosses for *machen* cross the Rhein near Benrath, slightly south of the point where the isogloss for *ich* crosses the Rhein at Urdingen. This is one of the most important dialect boundaries in German, the Benrath–Urdingen line, which divides Low from High German. As one moves eastward, the isoglosses for the two words and also for *dat/das, dorp/dorf*, etc., are the same. The point at which the isoglosses meet the Rhine is marked by a fanning out of the isoglosses. For this reason the isogloss has been called the Rhenish fan. In villages along this area speakers may have some Low German features and some High German features, for example, both *dat* and *dorf*.

In practice, most changes are not completely regular because all innovations diffuse through time and space at different rates. In fact, many inconsistencies such as these were found, which illustrated the complexity of dialect differentiation and the need to invoke explanations from external historical factors.

The explanation for the pattern of variation found in the Rhenish fan comes from cultural history. The Benrath line corresponds to the extent of influence of the city of Cologne from the thirteenth century, and the Urdingen line to its influence from the sixteenth century. The forms for *machen* were fixed at an earlier date than those for *ich*. The differences in the isoglosses can be accounted for by assuming that a sound change had taken place in southern Germany and spread northward. The extent of spread of this innovation was determined by both geographical and social factors. Among the latter was the social prestige of the urban speakers who used the new forms.

Such areas of prestige form focal points which transmit innovations into the surrounding hinterland. At the limits or peripheries of such centers of diffusion we find transition areas which typically show characteristics of two neighboring

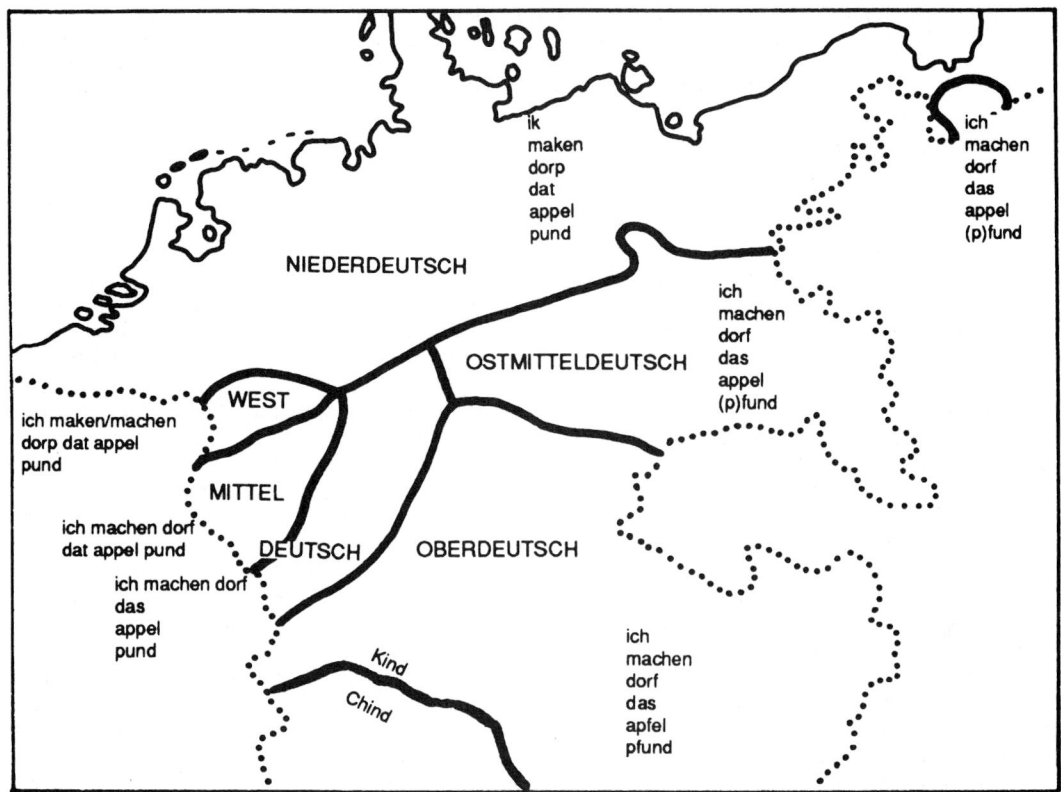

Figure 3. Distribution of isoglosses in Germany and the Netherlands.

focal areas. Beyond these are relic areas which are removed from the effect of expanding isoglosses. Relic areas are generally found in places that are not so easily accessible. Prestige innovations and settlement patterns can often be traced by examining isoglosses and place names. Linguistic innovations often hop from one urban center to another (compare the American port cities pattern of rhotic speech) and only later spread out to rural areas in between.

The Rhenish fan is an important isogloss not just in dialectology, but also for the questions it raised about change for historical linguistics more generally. Table 2, which is a schematized description of the isogloss bundle, shows a step-like patterning of the isoglosses between north and south German in geographical space. This model suggests that the new pronunciations gained in frequency while both shifted and unshifted forms coexisted. The numbers 1 to 7 can be thought of as different dialects. Stage 1 represents a dialect which has undergone no change and stage 7 shows the completed change. Dialects 2 through 6 show intermediate stages in the shift. For all practical purposes, the beginning and end stages show that the net effect of the change is as if it had applied uniformly and simultaneously to all dialects.

Table 2 gives a picture of the transition phase and the line drawn through it indicates the trajectory of the change as it spreads from dialect to dialect and from one lexical item to another. In the 1970s theoretical discussions of this pattern of change referred to it as 'lexical diffusion' (see Chen and Wang 1975). On the basis of evidence from patterns such as these, Gilliéron proposed, instead of regular sound change that *chaque mot a son histoire* ('Each word has its own history').

Late twentieth-century work on dialect variation has attempted to formalize this view of change which assumes that innovations spread in waves. Models proposed by Bailey (1973) and others predict that a change moves through the grammar (in the case of the Germanic sound shift, a rule which changes /p/ to /f/, etc.), affecting one environment in one (iso)lect at a time. Bailey has backformed the term 'lect' from 'dialect' as a more neutral term for a clustering of

Table 2. Implicational scale of isoglosses between Low and High German consonant shift /p t k/ → /(p)f s x/.

Dialects	Lexical items	ich	machen	dorf	das	apfel	pfund
Low	1.	ik	maken	dorp	dat	appel	pund
	2.	ich	maken	dorp	dat	appel	pund
German	3.	ich	machen	dorp	dat	appel	pund
Middle	4.	ich	machen	dorf	dat	appel	pund
German	5.	ich	machen	dorf	das	appel	pund
	6.	ich	machen	dorf	das	apfel	pund
High German	7.	ich	machen	dorf	das	apfel	pfund

Table 3. Implicational scale of isoglosses between Low and High German consonant shift /p t k/ → /(p)f s x/. (+) = environments with a rule; (−) = environments without a rule.

Dialects	Lexical items	ich	machen	dorf	Das	apfel	pfund
Low	1.	−	−	−	−	−	−
	2.	+	−	−	−	−	−
German	3.	+	+	−	−	−	−
Middle	4.	+	+	+	−	−	−
German	5.	+	+	+	+	−	−
	6.	+	+	+	+	+	−
High German	7.	+	+	+	+	+	+

linguistic features. Many linguists now prefer the term 'variety' or 'lect' to avoid the sometimes pejorative connotations of the term 'dialect'.

Table 3 shows an implicational scale for the sound shift in which lects and lexical items are implicationally ordered. Environments either have a rule (+) or they don't (−), while others are variable, i.e., in the process of transition from plus to minus. Since isolects are located in both space and time in such a model, they participate either earlier or later in an incipient rule change at any given point in the spatiotemporal continuum. It is possible to incorporate many lects into a polylectal or panlectal grammar, which would consist of all possible sets of rules for an arbitrarily limited area in space and time. Bailey and others maintain that such models are also psychologically real because speakers have polylectal competence rather than just competence in their own lect.

Linguists have also made predictions about the direction and rate of rule spread based on considerations such as markedness. Bailey claims that the farther a rule travels from its origin, the fewer will be the environments above it on an implicational scale. Change begins in the most heavily weighted environment and works its way through the grammar by spreading through successively less heavily weighted environments. This pattern of spread has the consequence that rules generalize in time, but seem to become less general in space because the temporally earlier changes move farther than the later ones. Only linguistic factors count in the Baileyan model towards an explanation of variation. Bailey claims that, since grammars are ongoing entities in time, time alone accounts not only for spatial patterns of variation, but for age, social class, and stylistic patterns of variation.

7. Theoretical Underpinnings

A dialect continuum can be social rather than geographical. Implicational scales and polylectal grammars have also been used to model post-Creole continua. A good example is found in Jamaica, where at one time those at the top of the social scale, the British, spoke English, while those at the bottom spoke Jamaican Creole. Over time the gap between the two has been filled by a range of varieties that are either more like the Creole or more like English. Most speakers use several varieties that span a range on this post-Creole continuum and shift among them according to context or addressee. Any division of the Jamaican social dialect continuum into English versus Jamaican Creole would be linguistically as arbitrary as dividing the Germanic dialect continuum into Dutch and German. There is no social, political, or geographical reason for saying that English begins at one particular point and Jamaican Creole at another.

Other attempts to provide dialectology with theoretical underpinnings can be found in Weinreich (1968), who proposed a structuralist dialectology (see *Weinreich, Uriel*). Most of the differences studied by dialectologists are lexical, and concern the different names people in different areas have for things. Thus, in the north of England the term *stee* refers to the same item which *ladder* refers to in the south of England. Such cases are dealing with the mapping of different names onto the same referent. The item itself serves as a reference point. The maps produced from such studies are known as 'onomasiological' maps. American dialect geography has dealt exclusively with onomasiology. The Survey of English dialects is also largely concerned with differences in naming practices. However, the words collected from such an investigation will not necessarily be etymologically connected, e.g., *spade, shovel* and *spit*, or *stee* and *ladder*.

It is possible to start from names and to look at how their meanings vary. In this case the point of reference is the word itself which may have more than one meaning. Thus, in Texas *hydrant* refers to an outdoor 'faucet' or 'tap,' while *fire plug* refers to what in most other areas of the United States is known as a (*fire*) *hydrant*. Maps showing distributions of meanings are called semasiological. Figure 4 is a semasiological map depicting the meaning of *shtul* in East European Yiddish. There are two major dialect areas, A, where *shtul* means 'chair' and B, where it means 'easychair.' Each semasiological map then gives rise to as many onomasiological maps as the number of dialect areas it contains and vice versa, i.e., one has to chart the terms for 'easychair' in dialect A and for 'chair' in dialect B. This can be seen in Fig. 5. In dialect A *benkl* is the term used to refer to a 'little bench,' while in dialect B it means a plain 'seat.' In dialect A the borrowed term *fotel* is used to mean 'easychair.'

It is not sufficient to say that *shtul* in dialect A of Yiddish is the same as in dialect B, if in A it is part of a three-way opposition in meaning but only a two-way one in B—similarly for phonology. As in Bailey's polylectal grammar, this approach gave dialectology a basis for the study of dialects with reference to internal linguistic patterning. A diasystem was constructed without consideration of geographical, or cultural factors. It was primarily a linguistic method of analysis.

An example can be taken from the Linguistic Survey of Scotland, which was one of the first dialect investigations to be influenced by Weinreich's ideas about structural dialectology. It also drew on the

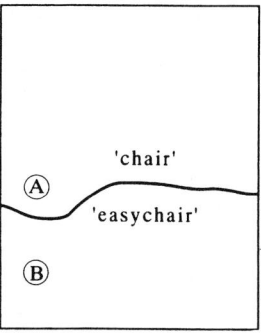

Figure 4. A semasiological map of the meaning of *shtul* in East European Yiddish (Weinreich 1968: 318).

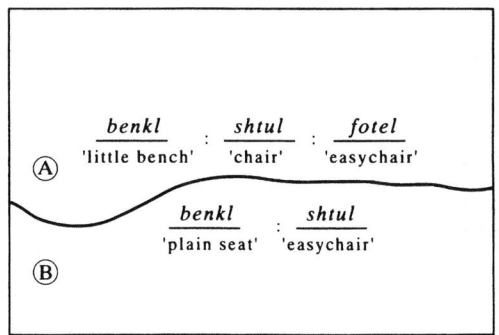

Figure 5. An onomasiological map of the terms in Fig. 4 (Weinreich 1968: 318).

polysystemic approach of Firth (see *Firth, J. R.*), which viewed language or parts of language as systems. The Linguistic Survey of Scotland examined the distribution of vowel contrasts in eleven different environments or subsystems based primarily on place of articulation, e.g., before /r/, before /t/, etc. Researchers identified a basic vowel diasystem consisting of eight units whose phonetic realization and distribution in lexical items varied from dialect to dialect. Figure 6 shows this system, where E, Y, and A refer to additions which may occur at the points indicated. The unit E may contrast with the front series in terms of length or quality or both, while Y may contrast with /i/ and the front vowels in rounding. Two modifications may take place in the low, back area: A_1 represents a vowel which may contrast with /a/ by being further back or rounded or both; A_2 refers to a rounded vowel between A and /o/. Systems are classified in two ways, in terms of number of units, i.e., inventory; and in terms of the internal arrangement of contrast in the system.

The advantage of this approach is that it reveals phonological similarity between dialects which might be otherwise overlooked since comparison at the phonetic level tends to emphasize differences. This method can also be used to generate testable hypotheses about the types of systems likely to be found. The basic system plus various additions yields 12 theoretical possibilities, two of which have not been discovered in investigations so far, i.e., the basic system plus E and the basic system plus E and Y.

Figure 7 shows how the various vowel systems are distributed geographically. The maximal 12-vowel system occurs in three widely separated areas: Shetland; south Kincardineshire, north Angus, east Perthshire; and the extreme southwest. This similarity may reflect the historical fact that many of the Scots who settled Shetland came from the metropolitan area of Fife and the Lothians. Although the 12-vowel system is no longer found in the latter area, it still occurs along the northern periphery. This suggests that the 12-vowel system is a survival, and that sixteenth-century Scots may have had such a system. Its occurrence in Galloway also supports this hypothesis since Gaelic was replaced there at around the same time as Norn (a variety of Norwegian) was in Shetland.

The structuralist model provided a basis for a generative interpretation of dialect variation (see, for example, Newton 1972). If a diaphonemic inventory is a composite of all the individual inventories of dialects which comprise a language, then it is possible to relate all dialects directly to a single underlying diaphonemic system on the basis of which dialects may be compared as to the number, scope, order, and form of rules needed to derive their distinctive characteristics.

8. Envoi

Some linguists have been critical of dialectology because it is biased towards rural speech of elderly informants and thus does not provide any knowledge of how the majority of people residing in urban areas speak. Dialect surveys have also for the most part relied on individuals, generally men, as the source of data for a particular area (see, however, Kurath

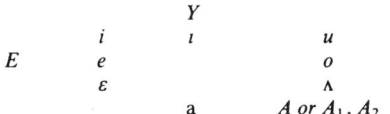

Figure 6. Basic Scots dialect vowel system (from Catford 1958: 111–12).

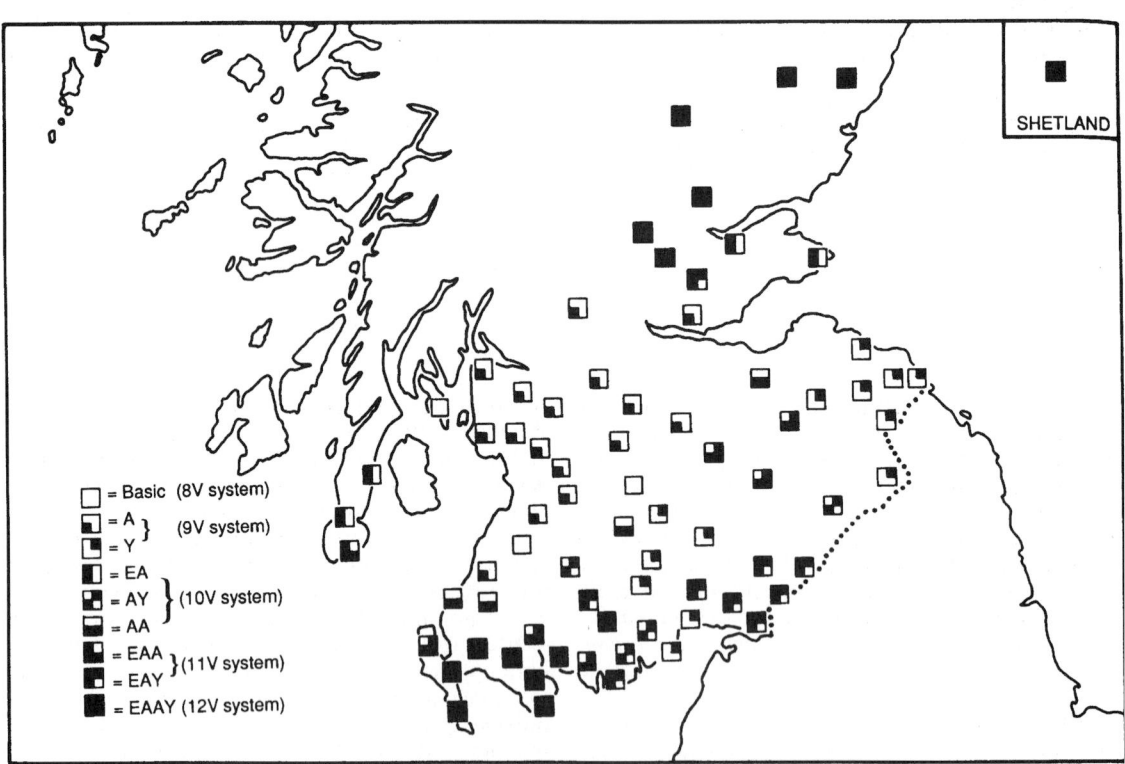

Figure 7. Some Scots dialect vowel systems, classified in terms of the internal arrangement of the system.

1939). Traditional dialectology was often seen as a rescue operation to record traditional forms of speech before they died out. Dialects are not in principle always more archaic nor is there any evidence to suggest that dialect speakers are progressively adopting more standard forms of speech. Although dialects do often preserve forms which were standard at a previous stage and have since been superseded, in some cases they innovate in different directions from the standard. Dialect surveys have been started in new areas such as Australia (Bryant 1991) and the more general study of language varieties has taken a central place in modern linguistics. The high point of twentieth-century dialectology is the Atlas of North American English, combining computer generated maps with modern field methods (Labov, Ash, and Bober, in press; see *The Atlas of North American English: Methods and Findings*).

See also: Language; Maps: Dialect and Language; Areal Linguistics; The Atlas of North American English: Methods and Findings.

Bibliography

Allen H B 1973–76 *The Linguistic Atlas of the Upper Midwest*, 3 Vols. University of Minnesota Press, Minneapolis, MN
Bach A 1950 *Deutsche Mundartforschung*. Carl Winter Universitätsverlag, Heidelberg, Germany
Bailey C-J 1973 *Variation and Linguistic Theory*. Center for Applied Linguistics, Washington, DC
Bryant P 1991 A survey of regional usage in the lexicon of Australian English. In: Romaine S (ed.) *Language in Australia*. Cambridge University Press, Cambridge, UK
Catford J C 1958 Vowel systems of Scots. *Transactions of the Philological Society*: 107–17
Chambers J K, Trudgill P 1998 *Dialectology*, 2nd edn. Cambridge University Press, Cambridge, UK
Chen M, Wang W 1975 Sound change: Actuation and implementation. *Language* **51**: 255–81
Davis L M 1983 *English Dialectology: An Introduction*. University of Alabama Press, Alabama, AL
Francis W N 1983 *Dialectology*. Longman, London
Gilliéron J, Edmont E 1902–10 *Atlas Linguistique de la France*. Paris
Jaberg K, Jud J 1928–40 *Sprach-und Sachatlas Italiens und der Südschweiz*. Ringler, Sofingen, Switzerland
Kurath H 1939 *Linguistic Atlas of New England*. Providence, RI
Kurath H, McDavid R 1961 *The Pronunciation of English in the Atlantic States*. University of Michigan Press, Ann Arbor, MI
Labov W, Ash S, Boberg C in press *Atlas of North American English: Phonetics, Phonology and Sound Change*. Mouton de Gruyter, Berlin
Mather J Y, Speitel H H 1975–77 *The Linguistic Atlas of Scotland, Vols. 1 and 2*. Croom Helm, London
McIntosh A 1952 *An Introduction to a Survey of Scottish Dialects*. Thomas Nelson, Edinburgh, UK
Mitzka W 1952 *Handbuch zum deutschen Sprachatlas*. Marburg, Germany
Newton B 1972 *The Generative Interpretation of Dialect*. Cambridge University Press, Cambridge, UK
Orton H 1962 *Introduction to the Survey of English Dialects. Vol. 1: Basic Material* (and subsequent vols 1962–71). University of Leeds Press, Leeds, UK
Weinreich U 1968 Is a structural dialectology possible? In: Fishman J A (ed.) *Readings in the Sociology of Language*. Mouton, The Hague

Dialect Humor

M. L. Apte

The basis of dialect humor is speech variation in a community. Wherever such variation exists there is a potential for dialect humor, a phenomenon in which one or more specific speech varieties become the target of fun and/or ridicule. Jokes, dialect stories, and the exaggerated imitation of the phonological and grammatical characteristics of the speech of a specific geographical community or of a certain social class of people constitute dialect humor. Language and speech, in short, becomes the topic of this type of humor.

1. What Constitutes a Dialect?

The term 'dialect' (see *Dialect and Dialectology*) has generally been used in linguistics to refer to varieties of speech based on geographical location and/or social background. It is used in contrast to the term 'language.' If a language is spoken over a large territory and by a substantial number of people, there exist phonological, grammatical, and lexical differences among its speakers. The reason for this is that frequent communication between each and every one of the speakers, which would considerably reduce any structural differences, is not feasible. Rather, there are concentrated networks of communication in villages, towns, subregions, and cities, as well as among people with similar subcultural backgrounds, occupations, or socioeconomic conditions. It is important to note however, that speech differences do not always hinder communication across geographical or social groups within a linguistic community.

While linguists, since the late 1970s, have used the term 'speech variety' instead of the term 'dialect' to describe the diverse patterns of structure and usage that may occur in a society, lay persons often still describe such speech varieties as 'dialects.' The term carries a pejorative connotation because of the assumption that people who speak a dialect have not been exposed to the influence of the cultural center of a society and its prestigious speech patterns. They are not upwardly mobile and continue to maintain their subregional or low class identity. Linguists use the 'speech variety' primarily to avoid the negative connotations and value judgements associated with the term 'dialect.'

Linguists have also found that in large linguistic territories, especially if they are nation-states, there generally exists a cultural and/or political center—almost always a region or a city—and the speech of its inhabitants is usually considered the most prestigious. This speech variety is used for administrative functions, as the medium of instruction, and also in mass media. Generally, such a speech variety is identified as the 'standard' and for foreigners, as well as many people outside the political center, it is equated with the language of the region.

2. Attitudes towards Dialect Speakers

People who speak the standard (see *Standardization*) variety of a language often find the speech patterns of people from faraway regions or at the lowest stratum of society 'strange,' and these patterns may become the topic of humor. Those who make fun of such speech generally find one or more characteristics of it inherently amusing. It could be, for instance, an unusual pronunciation, the use of unfamiliar words, nasalized speech, peculiar phrases, or the overall slowness of speech. These and other such linguistic features are then mockingly imitated in an exaggerated manner in order to generate humor. It is this kind of humor that is generally labeled 'dialect humor.' In those linguistic communities where the speech variation is considerable, there is much more likelihood of one or two dialects being made fun of because of their perceived low prestige.

However, any analysis of dialect humor will inevitably lead to this question: Is mere speech difference, no matter how extreme it may be, sufficient to make certain groups of people become the butt of humor or do other factors also play a role? It appears that underlying dialect humor are certain attitudes on the part of those who practice it. The joke-tellers generally look down upon those whose speech they make fun of.

The attitude of those who engage in dialect humor is one of disdain towards their target. The speech being made fun of is considered 'inferior,' 'crude,' or 'primitive' and its characteristics are often attributed to backwardness, stupidity, and other negative qualities. If the speech to be made fun of is marked by slowness of tempo, long drawn out vowels, or slurred consonants, it is assumed that this is due to the overall slow-wittedness of its speakers. Once created, such stereotypes are difficult to get rid of even if the gross generalizations on which they are based are false and the associations made between speech and mental ability are invalid, which they are.

Dialect humor becomes 'accent humor' (see *Accent*) when the target speech variety is caricatured through exaggerated imitation, especially of easily noticeable features such as tone, inflection, or choice of words. It should be noted that the objects of accent humor are not always speakers from a region remote from the cultural and political center or of the lowest socioeconomic class. They could very well be the elites who speak the standard variety. The target of accent humor can also be a foreign language. Therefore, dialect humor can be considered one type of accent humor though frequently the targets of accent humor are dialects.

3. Universality of Dialect Humor

Dialect humor appears to be universal. Davies (1990: 52–3) provides a list of countries in which specific dialects and languages are the object of jokes and those who speak these are perceived to be stupid, ignorant, or inept. The following are some speech varieties which have been the target of dialect humor.

In the USA, the Southern dialect and the Brooklyn and the Boston speech varieties have been the targets of dialect humor. The Southern speech variety has been a particularly popular target as evidenced by the existence of many books purportedly teaching non-Southerners how to speak the Southern dialect (Dwyer 1971, Mitchell 1976, Wilder 1977). In England, the Cockney dialect of London has been the target of dialect humor. In Italy, southern Italian dialects such as Neopolitan or Sicilian are the objects of such humor. In North India the Hindi spoken by Panjabi speakers in New Delhi has been similarly mocked. In the Marathi-speaking region of Western India a coastal dialect known as 'Malvani' has been the object of dialect humor. Entire comedies have been written in this dialect by several playwrights and they have been enormously successful. From the same coastal region, the excessively nasalized speech of the Brahmans, traditionally the highest caste in the social hierarchy, has been made fun of.

Because a particular speech variety or language is associated with a specific group, dialect and/or language can be part of ethnic, religious, regional, political, or social identity. Therefore, dialect humor should be considered as a subcategory of ethnic humor (see *Ethnicity and Language*). Any time a particular group is identified by its language or speech variety, such an association leads to the development of its linguistic stereotype.

Although much dialect and accent humor is verbal, it has been represented in print, resulting in the publication of dialect-joke-and-story collections of which many copies have been sold. In English and in many other languages, techniques have been developed for transcribing dialect humor and conventions have been established to represent the speech peculiarities. These conventions taken together can be called 'eye dialect' (Falk 1978: 295), a term used to designate a technique in which spelling differences represent the target speech variety. For example, the inability of some dialect speakers of American and British English to pronounce the dental fricative consonants and their substitution by the dental stops is indicated by the substitution of 't' and 'd' for 'th' and 'dh' in conventional spelling of such speech so that words such as 'this' and 'that' are written as 'dis' and 'dat' respectively. The final 'g' consonant of words that end in 'ing' is often dropped in uneducated speech. This is indicated in the written version by doing the same so that words such as 'interesting' are spelled as 'interestin.' The combination 'is not' is often represented as 'ain't.'

So long as there is intralanguage variation, there will always be one or more speech varieties in every linguistic community that are the targets of dialect humor. It is also likely that negative stereotypes exist of the speakers of such varieties and that they are likely to be perceived as backward, slow-witted or even stupid. Hence those who engage in dialect humor will almost always feel superior to their targets.

See also: Stereotype and Social Attitudes.

Bibliography

Blair W, McDavid R I Jr 1983 *The Mirth of a Nation: America's Great Dialect Humor*. University of Minnesota Press, Minneapolis, MN
Davies C 1990 *Ethnic Humor Around the World*. Indiana University Press, Bloomington, IN
Dwyer B 1971 *Dictionary for Yankees and Other Uneducated People*. Merry Mountaineers, Highland, NC
Falk J S 1978 *Linguistics and Language*. Wiley, New York
Mitchell S 1976 *How to Speak Southern*. Bantam, New York
Wilder R Jr 1977 *You All Spoken Here*. Gourd Hollow Press, Raleigh, NC

Ethnicity and the Crossing of Boundaries
B. Rampton

Sociolinguistics has long been interested in the relationship between language and ethnicity, but it has tended to assume that speakers are relatively settled in their own ethnic identities. More recently, however, research has started to document a range of ways in which people use different speech varieties to renegotiate their ethnic affiliations, and this presents something of a challenge to the traditional sociolinguistic view of language and community.

1. Language and Stable Ethnicities

Two views of ethnicity have hitherto been dominant in sociolinguistics. In the first perspective, ethnicity is seen as a tacit cultural and communicative inheritance, acquired through interaction in the early years at home and in local community networks. Socialization within different ethnic groups is held to produce distinctive patterns of language use, and since the 1960s, sociolinguistics has sought to document these differences, together with the ways in which mainstream institutions in general, and schools in particular, neglect or misinterpret the distinctive linguistic resources introduced by ethnically diverse populations (e.g., Labov 1969, Philips 1972). Even so, the idea of ethnicity as an ingrained disposition faces a serious problem. It is certainly true that deep-seated language habits often make it hard for people to adapt to the standard language practices demanded in modernist institutions, but what are the reasons for assuming that these differences are best understood as being rooted in ethnicity rather than, say, class, gender, neighborhood, family etc? The language practices in question seldom exist in perfect overlap with ethnic category membership, and so on its own, independent of a host of other social variables, ethnicity is inadequate as a basis for understanding the origins and distribution of these differences.

The second perspective on ethnicity overcomes this problem by emphasizing the interpretations that people make in the situations and moments when particular forms are actually being used (and discussed). Rather than being a symbolic meaning inscribed in the linguistic objects there-and-then during the period when they were first acquired, 'ethnicity' is seen as one of the discursive and cultural frameworks that participants use to make sense of distinctive language practices in the here-and-now. In this view, language use is 'ethnic' where participants construe it as such, and it entails the symbolic *assertion* (or attribution) of an inherited identity, strategically activated in different ways in different settings. Social backgrounds certainly do endow people with distinctive communicative styles, but rather than being this linguistic and cultural inheritance itself, ethnicity is viewed as a contrastive construct or image, which people use to notice, create, express, and interpret a variety of social and political differences, tensions and solidarities (e.g., McDermott and Gospodinoff 1979, Gumperz 1982). Indeed, seen as a framework that is used to make sense of intergroup relationships, ethnicity is not only an identity that people claim for themselves—it also figures in the identification and description of outgroups, and there are significant bodies of research which show how language is used in the characterization of foreigners (Ferguson 1975), how ethnic stereotypes are linked to language attitudes (e.g., Ryan and Giles 1982), and how racist representations are managed in talk and media discourse (Wetherell and Potter 1992, Blommaert and Verschueren 1998).

These two views of ethnicity have underpinned major research contributions to our understanding of the relationships between language and interaction on the one hand, and culture, ideology and politics on the other. Much of this research has assumed, however, that for the individual, ethnic identity is relatively fixed (though Le Page and Tabouret-Keller 1985 are an important exception). This is obvious in the essentialism of the first perspective, where ethnicity equates with where you were born and grew up, but even in the second, the possibilities for individuals look limited. Where research focuses on ingroup identity, ethnicity has been cast as something that people can only 'turn up' or 'down,' so to speak, either embracing and cultivating the ethnolinguistic legacy passed on by older generations, or alternatively, dropping it as a category that is personally relevant to them. Similarly, in the research on racist representations and outgroup stereotypes, it is generally assumed that speakers know which ingroup they belong to, and that the ethnic categories they are referring to are definitely 'other.'

What happens, though, in situations of intensive interethnic contact, where communities of interest often cut across the boundaries of ethnic descent (so that in the 1991 UK census, for example, 40 percent of Black-Caribbean men aged 16–34 and 20 percent of Black-Caribbean women aged 16–34 were living with a white partner (Berrington 1996: 199)? Equally, what happens when ethnicity is commodified, and ethnic forms, products, and symbols are marketized and widely disseminated as desirable commodities, lifestyle options and aesthetic objects? Both conditions can make people reluctant to confine themselves only to those ethnic identities that (hitherto) dominant ideologies have placed them in, and recent research makes it very clear that 'language maintenance' and/or the 'linguistic assimilation' of minorities are not the only significant ethnolinguistic processes involved in contemporary urban settings. People with majority ethnic backgrounds sometimes shift towards minority ethnicities, and minority languages can play an important role in this process.

2. Ethnicity and 'Language Crossing'

The use of minority ethnic languages by members of ethnic outgroups (both majority and other minority) has now been quite widely documented, and recent studies investigate, for example, the use in the UK of Caribbean Creole by young Anglos and Asians and of Panjabi by Anglos and African Caribbeans (Hewitt 1986, Rampton 1995), the use of Turkish by young people from Iran, Bosnia or Afghanistan in Germany (Auer and Dirim in press), the use of African American Vernacular English by white adolescents in the US (Bucholtz 1999, Cutler 1999), as well as white uses of Spanish in American popular media (Hill 1999). There is considerable diversity in these practices, but racism and social stratification are often powerful circumambient influences, and these can make 'language crossing' (as this process has been called) a sensitive and ambiguous practice.

Whenever speakers make clear but unexpected use of a speech variety that is not normally associated with them, they are likely to draw attention and/or commentary from their audience, and if there is a sense that they are moving across ethnic boundaries that are sharply felt, the legitimacy of their action may well be challenged. In line with this, crossing often occurs in moments and events where the routine flow of everyday social order is uncertain or relaxed, and switches into a conspicuously outgroup language can be found in activities and genres like greetings, self-talk, jocular abuse, games and musical performance—activities and genres where other people are less likely to think that the speaker truly believes in the identity he or she is projecting. Even so, crossing is a practice that is open to very different kinds of meaning and interpretation. In some occurrences, crossing is fairly obviously intended as parodic mockery and derogation, though the racist force of this is often partially masked in humor. Elsewhere, with crossing into an ethnic variety that has popular cultural prestige and is associated with urban 'cool,' there is a risk of looking pretentious, or being accused of expropriating a valuable resource that rightfully belongs to other people. There are other circumstances, however, where shared experience, friendship and co-memberships of class, generation, gender, neighborhood, etc. outweigh ethnic difference, creating a space where it is relatively safe to explore or experiment with the ethnically specific linguistic and cultural resources that 'belong' to your interlocutor(s). In fact, here crossing can play an important symbolic role, as illustrated by British youngsters of Pakistani descent who take their white friends' knowledge of Panjabi words as a sign that they are 'in our sort of community' and 'one of us.' Admittedly, for some, this kind of cross-ethnic engagement belongs to a phase of relatively intensive interethnic sociability that eventually proves ephemeral, but for others, the affiliation can be enduring. In one way or another, though, crossing can play a significant role in 'the construction of...a new conception of ethnicity: a new cultural politics which engages rather than suppresses *difference* and which depends, in part, on the cultural construction of new ethnic identities' (Hall 1988: 29 original emphasis).

3. 'Language Crossing' in Sociolinguistics

The language practices sketched above can be socially consequential, and defining it as the use of a language variety that somehow feels anomalously 'other' and that is not readily acknowledged as an uncontroversial part of the speaker's habitual repertoire, 'language crossing' is convenient as a general term to identify them. But how does 'crossing' as a concept relate to sociolinguistics more generally?

Although 'crossing' can play a significant role in the enunciation of new ethnicities, other linguistic processes are obviously also involved. Minority ethnic language forms often become integrated into multiethnic local vernaculars in more routine ways, and if 'crossing' was emphasized to the exclusion of these less noticeable developments, it would run the risk of reifying interethnic processes, implying a movement from one well-defined ethnic category to another when in fact these categories were changing, blurring and/or merging. Indeed, even when speakers in ethnicity-salient situations switch fairly conspicuously into a variety outside their normal repertoire, the boundaries they are crossing are not necessarily interethnic—the voice or language they are putting on can, for example, be some relic from an ingroup inheritance that is attributed to them but that generally, they are keen to leave behind, as when people with family links to another country do versions of the 'foreigner' varieties either spoken by the generation that migrated, or as caricatured in dominant media. In sum, the 'others' evoked by this kind of code-switching can exist in a range of complex and intimate relationships with the speaker's habitual self, and these other voices and personae can also be related to, for example, generation, gender, region, even specific individuals (Hall 1995, Johnstone 1999). In fact, along with all these other kinds of symbolic evocation, the crossing practices described in Section 2 can be usefully subsumed within Mikhail Bakhtin's (see *Bakhtin, Mikhail M.*) much more encompassing notions of stylization and 'double-voicing' (Bakhtin 1984, Rampton 1999).

Even so, as a contemporary illustration of Bakhtinian processes in operation, research on ethnic language crossing presents a particularly vivid challenge to two assumptions that have been fundamental to sociolinguistics, at least in the 1970s and 1980s: (a) the idea that language study is centrally concerned with systematicness in grammar and coherence in discourse, and (b) the belief that these properties come from community membership, that people learn to talk grammatically and coherently from extensive early experience of living in fairly stable local social networks (Pratt 1987). Sociolinguists certainly have fought hard against the view that language and society were homogenous and they have championed ethnolinguistic heterogeneity, but on encountering diversity and variation, their strongest instinct has been to dig out what they imagine to be the orderliness and uniformity beneath the surface, an orderliness laid down during early socialization. In contrast, language crossing presents us with a salient and sometimes socially productive interactional practice that contests preconceived ideas about family rootedness, and it also often makes extensive use of (non-family) material from public and popular media. In crossing, ethnolinguistic resources are drawn into the spotlight for reflexive evaluation and critique among the participants (Bauman and Briggs 1990, Kroskrity et al. 1992), and the central role it gives to improvization, rupture and the denaturalization of convention makes structural regularity and tacit systematicness in language highly problematic as governing research preoccupations.

At another level, research on crossing draws sociolinguistics alongside relatively recent developments in the humanities and social sciences, where instead of trying to define the core features of any social group or institution, there is major interest in fragmentation, hybridity, indeterminacy and ambivalence, in boundaries of inclusion and exclusion, and in the flows of people, knowledge, texts, images, and objects across social and geographical space. There is a widespread feeling in sociology, for example, that the image of society as a 'compact, sealed [and systematic] totality' is rather uncomfortably based on an idealization of the nation state (Bauman 1992: 57), and that 'the reality to be modelled is...much more fluid, heterogeneous and "under-patterned" than anything that sociologists tried to grasp intellectually in the past' (Bauman 1992: 65). Racism and ethnicity continue to be powerful forces in both politics and history, but sociolinguistics needs to ensure that essentialist assumptions about language and community do not inadvertently obstruct our efforts to understand these processes. The study of ethnic language crossing can help us to avoid this.

See also: Sociology of Language; Socialization; Identity and Language.

Bibliography

Auer P, Dirim Ý in press Socio-cultural orientation, urban youth styles and the spontaneous acquisition of Turkish by non-Turkish adolescents in Germany. In: Androutsopoulos J, Georgakopoulou A (eds.) *Discourse Constructions of Youth Identities*. Mouton, Berlin
Bakhtin M 1984 Discourse in Dostoevsky. In: *Problems of Dostoevsky's Poetics*. University of Minnesota Press, Minneapolis, MN, pp. 181–269
Bauman R, Briggs C 1990 Poetics and performance as critical perspectives on language and social life. *Annual Review of Anthropology* **19**: 59–88
Bauman Z 1992 *Intimations of Postmodernity*. Routledge, London
Berrington S 1996 Marriage patterns and inter-ethnic unions. In: Coleman D, Salt J (eds.) *Ethnicity in the 1991 Census: Volume I*. Office for Population Censuses and Surveys, London
Blommaert J, Verschueren J 1998 *Debating Diversity*. Routledge, London
Bucholtz M 1999 You da man: Narrating the racial other in the production of white masculinity. *Journal of Sociolinguistics* **3**(4): 443–60
Cutler C 1999 Yorkville crossing: White teens, hip hop, and African American English. *Journal of Sociolinguistics* **3**(4): 428–42
Gumperz J 1982 *Discourse Strategies*. Cambridge University Press, Cambridge, UK
Ferguson C 1975 Towards a characterisation of English foreigner talk. *Anthropological Linguistics* **17**: 1–14
Hall S 1988 New ethnicities. *ICA Documents* **7**: 27–31
Hall K 1995 Lip service on the fantasy lines. In: Hall K, Bucholtz M (eds.) *Gender Articulated*. Routledge, London, pp. 183–216
Hewitt R 1986 *White Talk Black Talk*. Cambridge University Press, Cambridge, UK
Hill J 1999 Language, race, and white public space. *American Anthropologist* **100**(3): 680–9
Johnstone B 1999 Uses of Southern-sounding speech by contemporary Texas women. *Journal of Sociolinguistics* **3**(4): 505–22
Kroskrity P, Schieffelin B, Woolard K (eds.) 1992 Language ideologies. *Pragmatics* **2**(3): 235–453
Labov W 1969 The logic of non-standard English. *Georgetown Monographs on Language and Linguistics* **22**: 1–22, 26–31
Le Page R, Tabouret-Keller A 1985 *Acts of Identity*. Cambridge University Press, Cambridge, UK
McDermott R, Gospodinoff K 1979 Social contexts for ethnic borders and school failure. In: Trueba H, Guthrie G, Au K (eds.) *Culture and the Bilingual Classroom*. Newbury House, Rowley, pp. 212–30
Philips S 1972 Participant structures and communicative competence: Warm Spring children in community and classroom. In: Cazden C, John V, Hymes D (eds.) *Functions of Language in the Classroom*. Teachers College Press, New York, pp. 370–94
Pratt M L 1987 Linguistic utopias. In: Fabb N, Attridge D, Durant A, McCabe C (eds.) *The Linguistics of Writing*. Manchester University Press, Manchester, UK, pp. 48–66
Rampton B 1995 *Crossing: Language and Ethnicity among Adolescents*. Longman, London
Rampton B (ed.) 1999 Styling the 'Other'. Special issue of *Journal of Sociolinguistics* **3**(4)
Ryan E B, Giles H (eds.) 1982 *Attitudes Towards Language Variation*. Arnold, London
Wetherell M, Potter J 1992 *Mapping the Language of Racism*. Harvester Wheatsheaf, Hemel Hempstead, UK

Ethnicity and Language
E. F. Kotzé

The relation between language and ethnicity can best be understood within an ecological framework, i.e., as an interactional relation between the societal environment and the speakers of a language (or language variety) who are structurally integrated into this environment (Haugen 1972: 325). This means that the relation between language and ethnicity is an indirect one, only observable through the ways in which speakers use language to signal ethnic identity. Like many frequently used terms, 'ethnicity' has several connotations, some of which are stigmatized (see Sect.4) and some not. This article will deal with both types in order to reflect as closely as possible the full spectrum of interpretations. Likewise, the meaning of the term 'language' can vary considerably, depending on the context. It can, for instance, be used to refer to a particular language, like French, to usage (as in 'Watch your language!'), to literary style (as in 'the language of Shakespeare'), to a particular variety (such as the language of the Gypsies), and so forth. Because ethnicity is primarily concerned with group identity, in this article 'language' refers to either the comprehensive label attached to all the varieties subsumed under a language name, such as English, or to a single variety, which will be specified with reference to the group of speakers associated with that variety (e.g., African American Vernacular English).

Most authors do not distinguish between ethnicity and ethnic identity (cf. Hoffmann 1991: 194), and Edward's definition (1979: 10) of ethnic identity thus equally applies to ethnicity:

> Ethnic identity is allegiance to a group—large or small, socially dominant or subordinate—with which one has

ancestral links. There is no necessity for a continuation, over generations, of the same socialization or cultural patterns, but some sense of a group boundary must persist. This can be sustained by shared objective characteristics (language, religion, etc.) or by more subjective contributions to the sense of 'groupness,' or by some combination of both.

An objective characteristic which Edwards introduces later, namely race (Edwards 1979: 254), has contributed a great deal to the controversy surrounding the use of the term 'ethnic,' and whenever it is implied as a factor in determining ethnicity, a racialist bias is assumed (see also Sect. 4).

Ethnic communities are similarly defined by reference to both subjective and objective aspects. Smith (1982: 147) proposes a definition of an ethnic community as

... a group of people who possess a myth of common ancestry, a shared history, one or more elements of common culture and a sense of solidarity.

In the wider context of society, ethnic groups interact because of environmental factors influencing their members. This is a corollary of the ecological approach to the study of language and ethnicity. In this framework, external and internal ecological factors can bring about integration or separation of ethnic groups. For instance, the isolation of such a group may be due to the fact that it is geographically separated from other groups. This is an external ecological factor. On the other hand, the members of a group may be averse to contact with another group, in which case the isolation is an internal ecological factor (Haarman 1986: 1). Because interethnic relations are primarily conducted by means of language, a thorough understanding of the function and place of ethnicity in society cannot be achieved if the linguistic effects (and causes) of such interaction are ignored.

1. Language as Marker of Ethnicity

Language is not only used as a tool for communication and individual expression—the use of a particular language or language variety often serves as an indication of the speaker's group identity. Furthermore, the way in which such a language is used, through pronunciation, syntactic construction and the inclusion of vocabulary items, is not only indicative of the speaker's membership of an ethnic group, but expresses relevant cultural items (types of clothing, aspects of wedding rituals, etc.), and it is often thought that such cultural lexical items are untranslatable (Fishman 1977: 25).

1.1 The Role of Ethnicity in Mother Tongue Varieties

Although ethnicity is often linked to national identity (see Sect.3.2), and language can be regarded as the most central symbol of emerging nationhood, political entities that comprise a homogeneous, monolingual national group are rare (Crystal 1987: 34). In fact, a study by Connor revealed that only 9.09 percent of all existing states in 1971 were true nation-states, in that for all practical purposes only one ethnic group constituted the total population. The multiplicity of language groups in multilingual states (which often correlate with ethnic groups) is further complicated by the fact that various ethnic groups may share the 'same' mother tongue, albeit different varieties, or ethnolects, of that language. A case in point is the variety of English in the USA now known as 'African American Vernacular English' (AAVE), which is spoken by lower-class African-Americans in urban communities. In spite of the existence of strong emotions regarding the sociolinguistic classification of this variety and the color prejudice which has promoted the (linguistically invalid) view that 'black' English is necessarily inferior to 'white' English, AAVE and standard American English are both widely regarded as the same language, and its speakers as having the same mother tongue. However, there was a strong counter-argument central to the Ebonics controversy of the 1990s (see *Ebonics and African American Vernacular English*) that AAVE was structurally, historically, and culturally independent of the mainstream. A comparable situation is that of the language spoken by the Cape Muslim, or Malay community of Cape Town, whose variety of Afrikaans is characterized by a large component of Islamic vocabulary (Arabic or Malay loanwords), as well as a rapidly expanding percentage of English loanwords, a fully deflected auxiliary verb system and advanced phonological assimilation.

In some cases, notably among Native Americans, ethnic sentiment is reinforced when individuals give up by force of circumstances their own minority ethnic language in favor of a common (English) lingua franca, which may itself become a new marker of ethnicity (Ross 1979). A comparable change in ethnic association occurs among West Indians in the UK (documented by LePage and Tabouret-Keller 1982), where, because of the attitudes of white Britons, island labels and island identities were replaced by a general West Indian (British) identity. These examples illustrate the fact that ethnic identity is not dependent on language loyalty to the ancestral mother tongue. The subjective forces of a sense of solidarity here and now can surpass the objective reality of a shared history and a myth of common ancestry in which a particular language served as a symbol of identity.

1.2 Ethnicity in Cross-cultural Communication

On the interface between culture, ethnicity, and language lies the ritualization of communication patterns. Pragmatic rules exist in every ethnic group which determine the sequencing of questions and replies in starting a conversation. Among the Nguni and Sotho in Southern Africa, for instance, an interlocutor is obliged to enquire about his addressee's well-being before coming to the point. In an exchange of greetings, it is expected that a socially superior (older) person will speak first. In some Western cultures, however, a socially subordinate (or younger) person is required to show respect by greeting first. It is clear that bilinguals (or monolinguals being addressed in their mother tongue by a bilingual person from another culture) who are not informed about the pragmatic rules governing successful communication in the 'other' culture could unintentionally cause misunderstanding, which might in turn lead to negative stereotyping and even conflict.

Sociocultural relations (such as family structure and status differences) are often reflected in the lexicon of particular ethnic groups. Terms of address vary according to the particular setting, age difference, and relative social position of asymmetric dyads (or peers) involved in conversation. A number of researchers, starting with Brown and Gilman (1960), have studied address systems in different cultures, based on the choice between the formal and informal second person pronouns and verbs (cf. French *tu parles*, German *du sprichst*, informal mode, with French *vous parlez*, German *Sie sprechen*, formal mode) in a number of European languages, to express a relation of power or solidarity with the addressee. Here again, if a bilingual speaker, when addressing native users of another language, applies the same set of pragmatic rules governing address forms in her/his mother tongue, (s)he may appear to be rude, arrogant, strange, or ignorant, because (s)he does not observe the concordance of linguistic items and cultural conventions.

1.3 The Role of Ethnic Attitudes in Language Maintenance

Although it has been shown (see Sect.1.1) that the use of a particular language need not be an integral part of ethnic identity, it can be indicated that where language does have such a symbolic value, there is a very close link between a person's identification with an ethnic group and the (continued) use by that person of the language which is a component of the group's ethnic identity. The language preference of a group of bilingual Gujarati- and English-speaking students in Leicester, UK was studied by Mercer et al. (1979), who found that the degree of identification with being Indian rather than British correlated positively with the use and maintenance of Gujarati. In another study (Lowley et al. 1983), representatives of three American ethnolinguistic groups, French, Spanish, and Yiddish, were interviewed, and the conclusion was that all three groups wished to maintain their specific ethnic identity alongside their American identity. Their ethnic mother tongue was considered to be its most vital and visible expression (see Appel and Muysken 1990: 14).

It is also possible that language shift can take place, i.e., that a group can lose its original language and, for whatever reason, adopt another one, but that the 'lost' language still retains a particular symbolic value for the group, thus contributing to the maintenance of ethnic boundaries (cf. Irish Gaelic in the Republic of Ireland). This situation obtains especially among immigrant communities who have been assimilated linguistically into their adopted country, but retain their ancestral language for religious or cultural purposes (eg., Hebrew among American Jews; Tamil, Hindi, Urdu, Gujarati and Telugu among South African Indians, etc.).

2. Ethnicity in Language (and Human) Rights

The subject of the constitutional accommodation of the language rights of ethnic minorities is often a bone of contention. Whereas human rights are based on the freedom of the individual, language rights involve, of necessity, the prerogative of ethnic groups to use their mother tongue in multilingual situations, something which has the potential of causing conflict. Such conflict can only be resolved by means of language planning, and more specifically status planning. The title of a book by Tollefson (1991) touches on the essence of the problem: *Planning Language, Planning Inequality*. In an unpublished manuscript, Neustupny (reported in Bartsch 1987: 241) says: 'It is obvious that any act of language planning seriously affects language rights of the community concerned.' If a particular language is either selected as official language, or otherwise chosen as a medium of instruction by a majority of speakers in the community, members of an ethnic minority with a different mother tongue have to acquire a sufficient command of the chosen medium to be able to benefit from the education system. Individual levels of proficiency will further determine the degree of academic (and possibly professional) success of such speakers. The inference is that the functions of ethnic minority languages can be severely curtailed, be it through legislation or convention, to the disadvantage of individual members of the group.

3. The Resolution of Ethnolinguistic Problems

Problems resulting from the interaction of ethnic groups in a multilingual environment can range from minor to severe, depending on (a) the importance of the mother tongue for the specific group, and (b) the degree to which restrictions are imposed upon members of the group because of their dependence on the mother tongue for self-fulfillment. The resolution of such problems is to be found either in the field of politics (where the granting of language rights is determined) or in the field of education (where the status quo is accepted and addressed, and an attempt is made to facilitate the process of acculturation).

3.1 Problems in the Field of Education

The phenomenon of ethnic groups (minority or majority) who are dependent on the use of another language for their educational needs is a worldwide one, and occurs in practically every country in Africa, where the erstwhile colonial languages have continued to serve as medium of instruction. It is not to be denied that this situation can cause enormous problems. Skutnabb-Kangas (1984), for instance, attests that unless the educational system takes proper account of minority (read also 'majority,' in the African context) children's special language needs in both languages, they will not become fully functional in either of the codes (see *Semilingualism*). Unfortunately, this viewpoint has not been followed generally by educational authorities in either Africa or Western Europe, where the system reflects the one-state one-language principle (see *Multilingual States*) applied for a long time in many countries (Hoffmann 1991: 43). No provision is made for the special linguistic needs of pupils whose home language differs from the medium of instruction. Indeed, repressive methods have been employed in places such as Gaelic-speaking Scotland, Wales, Brittany, Catalonia, and Galicia (in northwest Spain), so that children were forced to acquire the language of the majority under difficult circumstances (see *Linguicide*). In some countries, however, there exists nowadays a more lenient approach to the plight of ethnic minorities at school. Special classes have been instituted to assist children in learning the second language before they are assimilated into the educational mainstream (e.g., English as a Second Language (ESL) provision, in the UK, and '*Deutsch als Zweitsprache*' for migrants' children in some German states). Voluntary private schemes to teach minority-language children who already form part of the mainstream system are also in evidence in France, the UK, Germany, and Scandinavian countries, but their success is dependent on individual participation, motivation, and resources.

An approach which is widely followed in Africa is to select as the medium of instruction a language which is ethnically neutral (invariably also an official language) because of the fear of 'tribal dominance' (Schmied 1991: 27). In most cases, the former colonial language was an automatic choice: it served as a symbol of erudition and provided access to well-developed resources. However, in the case of Namibia, a politically motivated preference was exercised against the selection of Afrikaans (which had been the colonial language), because a large percentage of citizens use it as mother tongue, and the continued use of the language as the medium of instruction would have benefited that group (cf. Schmied's reference to fear of 'tribal dominance' above). The solution is then what can be termed the 'equal distribution of disadvantage,' in that English, the selected medium of instruction is a second (or foreign) language to the vast majority of inhabitants, and all ethnic groups are therefore on an equal footing with regard to the task of having to master another language in order to benefit from the teaching.

3.2 Problems of Language Politics as a Result of Ethnic Attitudes

Because a language very often is linked to the identity of an ethnic or social group, this relation finds its expression in the attitudes of the individuals towards such a language and its speakers. Appel and Muysken's (1990: 16) illustration of the resulting chain reaction is shown in Fig. 1. Negative attitudes towards a particular language and its speakers mostly originate in the fear that the target group, and therefore its speakers and its language would pose a threat to the continued well-being of one's own group, its culture, and language. When there is enough solidarity among the threatened group, collective action and insistence on the accommodation of language rights for that group might follow. Many examples of such actions have been recorded, among others the campaign for French in Quebec, Canada, for Flemish in Belgium, for Welsh in Wales, and for Catalan in Catalonia, Spain. An ethnic majority in a particular region speaking the language as mother tongue can achieve some success in this respect, as it is evident from the position in the early 1990s of Catalan, which was used on an equal footing with Spanish at the 1992 Olympic Games in Barcelona. In Wales, however, less than five percent of the population speak Welsh, and the basis for wider recognition of the language is weakened by this fact.

Language as a symbol of ethnicity may contribute also to shape and maintain feelings of national identity and solidarity. The so-called 'ethnic revival' which is especially apparent in Eastern Europe, has led to secessionist struggles and the creation of new political entities based on cultural (and particularly

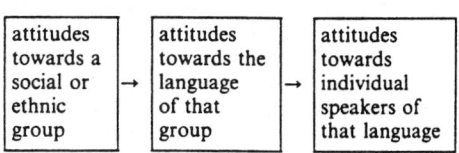

Figure 1.

language) identity. Events in the former Yugoslavia and the (peaceful) resolution of the ethnic conflict in Czechoslovakia are indicative of the strong link between language, nationalist sentiments, and ethnicity.

4. Changing Views on Ethnicity

The first connotations given to the terms 'ethnic' and 'ethnicity' reflected a patronizing attitude among British and French lexicographers towards non-European peoples. In the third edition of *Chamber's Twentieth Century Dictionary*, for instance, the noun 'ethnic' is glossed as 'a heathen,' 'ethnicism' as 'heathenism,' and 'ethnography' as 'the scientific description of the races (sic) of the earth.' In *Petit Larousse Illustré* (1973) the lemma 'ethnolinguistique' is defined as the study of the speech of illiterate peoples. The 1990 edition of the *Concise Oxford Dictionary of Current English* provides for a wider variety of possible meanings of 'ethnic' (adj), inter alia '(of a social group) having a common national or cultural tradition,' '(of clothes) resembling those of a non-European exotic people,' 'denoting origin by birth or descent rather than nationality (*ethnic Turks*),' 'relating to race or culture (*ethnic group*; *ethnic origins*),' '(archaic) pagan, heathen.' The expression 'ethnic minority' is defined as 'a (usu. identifiable) group differentiated from the main population of a community by racial origin or cultural background.' In scientific literature, especially in linguistics (including socio- and ethnolinguistics), the reference to racial origin has become irrelevant, because of the much finer distinctions required when comparing groups on a worldwide scale. However, in countries where ethnicity and color are burning political issues (e.g., South Africa and the USA), the terms 'ethnicity' and 'ethnic' have come to be regarded as synonymous with 'race' and 'racial' in common parlance, and thus are treated with some suspicion.

However, the phenomenon of ethnicity itself is being reevaluated because of the collapse of socialism in Eastern Europe and the realization that individual and group rights can be attained in a more democratic environment. This is leading to a reawakening also of interest in ethnic minority languages and identification with the languages of the group as a symbol of group identity.

5. Ethnicity: Cause or Result of Language Change?

There can be no doubt that the adoption of a language other than the ancestral one by an ethnic group will lead to the genesis of a new variety of the adopted language (see Sect. 1.1). This variety will be influenced, not only by structural elements of transfer from the ethnic group's original mother tongue, such as pronunciation and syntax, but indeed also by lexical items expressing ethnic characteristics of the group. Reference has already been made to such characteristics in Malay Afrikaans, but immigrant varieties of English in the USA, such as the Italian and Yiddish ethnolects, contain typical items of vocabulary from the relevant cultures, in addition to elements of language transfer. Such influence is known as a substratum effect (see *Language Transfer and Substrates*). However, the development of such a new ethnic variety need not always be in the direction of the substratum language. Sometimes immigrants attempt to overcorrect what they feel to be a faulty accent, resulting in a change away from the substratum language, to such an extent that their variety of the adopted language develops new characteristics (Aitchison 1984: 117). Labov has indicated, for instance, that second-generation Italian–Americans, instead of using the native Italian low vowel [a], as their parents do, in words such as *cap, fat, tack*, tend to raise the vowel to [e] as a corrective for the influence of Italian (Labov 1978: 298). This form of 'hypercorrection' is a typical characteristic of ethnic minorities reacting to the environment of a different culture.

As language is one of many indices of ethnic identity (and not even an essential one), the effect of language change cannot have a determining effect on the underlying ethnicity of a group. So, even if a group adopts a new language, the basic patterns of ethnic behavior remain undisturbed by it, and can only be altered by a more encompassing process of acculturation.

6. Conclusion

After considering the different ways in which language and ethnicity interrelate, it can be concluded that there exists no necessary relation between ethnicity and a particular language. In his study of the language of ethnic groups in Canada, Lieberson (1970) noted that there are many instances of such groups with distinct languages, but also groups sharing a common language. A particular language, therefore, may or may not be included in the group's cultural bag (Appel and Muysken 1990: 15). However, it is also evident that the language, or variety of a shared language used by an ethnic group, becomes characterized by elements of that group's ethnic identity and reflects the interaction between man and its cultural environment in a very distinct way.

See also: Language in Society: Overview; Ethnicity and the Crossing of Boundaries; Discourse in Crosslinguistic and Cross-cultural Contexts.

Bibliography

Aitchison J 1984 *Language Change: Progress or Decay?* Fontana, London

Appel R, Muysken P 1990 *Language Contact and Bilingualism*. Edward Arnold, London

Bartsch R 1987 *Norms of Language*. Longman, London
Baugh J 1988 Language and race: Some implications for linguistic science. In: Newmeyer F J (ed.) *Linguistics: The Cambridge Survey, Vol. IV (Language: The Sociocultural Context)*. Cambridge University Press, Cambridge, UK
Baugh J 1999 *Out of the Mouths of Slaves: African American Language and Educational Malpractice*. University of Texas Press, Austin, TX
Brown R W, Gilman A 1960 The pronouns of power and solidarity. In: Sebeok T (ed.) *Style in Language*. MIT Press, Cambridge, MA
Crystal D 1987 Ethnic and national identity. In: *The Cambridge Encyclopedia of Language*. Cambridge University Press, Cambridge, UK
Edwards A D 1979 *Language in Cultural and Class*. Heinemann, London
Fishman J A 1977 Language and ethnicity. In: Giles H (ed.) *Language, Ethnicity and Intergroup Relations*. Academic Press, London
Haarman H 1986 *Language in Ethnicity: A View of Basic Ecological Relations*. De Gruyter, Berlin
Haugen E I 1972 *The Ecology of Language*. Stanford University Press, Stanford, CA
Hoffmann C 1991 *An Introduction to Bilingualism*. Longman, London
Labov W 1978 *Sociolinguistic Patterns*. Blackwell, Oxford, UK
Laponce J A 1987 *Languages and Their Territories*. University of Toronto Press, Toronto
LePage R, Tabouret-Keller A 1982 Models and stereotypes of ethnicity and language. *Journal of Language Policy and Implementation*
Lieberson S 1970 *Language and Ethnic Relations in Canada*. Longman, New York
Lowley E G et al 1983 Ethnic activists view the ethnic revival and its language consequences: An interview study of three American Ethnolinguistic minorities. *Journal of Multilingual and Multicultural Development* 4
Mercer N et al 1979 Linguistic and cultural affiliation amongst young Asian people in Leicester. In: Giles H, Saint-Jacques B (eds.) *Language and Ethnic Relations*. Oxford University Press, Oxford, UK
Ross J A 1979 Language and the mobilization of ethnic identity. In: Giles H, Saint-Jacques B (eds.) *Language and Ethnic Relations*. Oxford University Press, Oxford, UK
Schmied J 1991 *English in Africa: An Introduction*. Longman, New York
Skutnabb-Kangas T 1984 *Bilingualism or Not*. Multilingual Matters, Clevedon, UK
Smith A 1982 Nationalism, ethnic separation and the intelligentsia. In: Williams C (ed.) *National Separatism*. University of Wales Press, Cardiff, UK
Tollefson J W 1991 *Planning Language, Planning Inequality: Language Policy in the Community*. Longman, New York
Trudgill P 2001 *Sociolinguistics: An Introduction*, 4th edn. Penguin, Harmondsworth, UK
Whorf B L 1956 Science and linguistics. In: Carroll J B (ed.) *Language, Thought and Reality*. MIT Press, Cambridge, MA

Forensic Phonetics and Sociolinguistics

P. Foulkes and J. P. French

Forensic analysis of speech and language is a relatively young discipline. A specialist academic and professional journal for the field—*Forensic Linguistics: the International Journal of Speech, Language and the Law*—was only established as recently as 1994. Appropriate strategies for applying phonetic and sociolinguistic knowledge and methodologies to legal problems are in the process of being refined, expanded, and their reliability tested.

The International Association for Forensic Phonetics (IAFP) was established in 1991 in order to regulate and assist the practice of speech analysis for legal purposes. It aims to ensure practitioners are suitably qualified, to fix ethical and practical guidelines for analysis, and to promote research in the area (see www.iafp.net). Another important role played by the IAFP is to raise awareness among members of the legal profession and other interested parties of both the values and also the limitations of forensic phonetic analysis.

Applications in the legal context of techniques developed in phonetics and sociolinguistics fall into four main categories: (a) deciphering the content of 'difficult' recordings; (b) speaker profiling; (c) speaker identification; and (d) constructing voice 'line-ups' in order to evaluate ear-witness testimony. These activities are discussed in turn below. More extensive introductions can be found in French (1994), Hollien (1990), Künzel (1987) and Nolan (1991, 1997).

1. Deciphering the Content of Difficult Recordings

Tape recordings, which may contain information relevant to court hearings, can be problematic or difficult to decipher for a variety of reasons. For instance, they may be contaminated by extraneous noise, which obscures the conversation of interest, or the speakers may have pathological or otherwise nonstandard—perhaps foreign—patterns of pronunciation.

In relation to noisy recordings, the sound filtering and signal processing techniques developed by audio engineers can be of help in improving speech to noise ratios and thereby rendering the speech signal more audible/intelligible. However, phonetic and sociolinguistic analysis may also be crucial in arriving at a final determination of what was said.

Hirson and Howard (1994), for example, analyzed the content of the 'black box' flight recorder recovered from the wreck of a South African Airways aircraft which had been lost in mid-flight in 1987, with the loss of 159 lives. The black box records the last 30 minutes of activity in the aircraft's cockpit, via a microphone housed in the ceiling. It was hoped that the spoken material would offer vital clues as to the cause of the accident. However, the recording proved to be problematic in various respects: the tape was highly degraded after having spent over a year under water; it contained only 81 seconds of speech after the first indication that there was a serious problem (a fire alarm); and the aircraft crew were multilingual, speaking English and Afrikaans. The poor signal-to-noise ratio of the recording meant that even deciphering which language was being spoken was far from straightforward. Ultimately, phonetic (auditory and acoustic) analysis enabled the majority of the spoken material to be transcribed, and revealed no evidence of a bomb, or of human error on the part of any of the crew. This case also resulted in recommendations to the Federal Aviation Administration for improving the structure and positioning of flight recorders.

In certain instances the problem of interpreting the content of a recording may be extremely 'localized,' with only a closely circumscribed section of speech being at issue. Such cases have been referred to as ones involving 'disputed utterances' (French 1990). The latter study reports a case concerning a Greek-born doctor working in the UK, who had been accused of illegally prescribing drugs for profit. An investigative journalist, posing as an addict, managed to obtain a prescription for a controlled drug and secretly recorded the encounter. The dispute, at a subsequent Medical Council tribunal, concerned whether the doctor had told the journalist 'you *can* inject those things,' or whether he had warned 'you *can't* inject those things.' The disputed word was pronounced [kan]. While such a pronunciation would clearly indicate *can* in Standard British English, it is ambiguous in other varieties, including the Greek-accented one spoken by the doctor. In order to assess which word was intended, acoustic analysis was undertaken to compare the disputed word with undisputed examples of *can* and *can't* from the doctor's speech. Although they were auditorily very similar, analysis of the vowel formant frequencies revealed that the disputed word more closely matched the doctor's formant patterns for *can't*.

2. Speaker Profiling

A combination of phonetic and sociolinguistic analysis of a voice can aid in establishing information about the speaker's background. Speaker profiling is regularly requested in the early stages of kidnappings, where a recording of the kidnapper's voice may be the only clue to his or her identity. Information can be gleaned about the speaker's sex, age, regional and social background, and idiosyncrasies such as speech disorders. The strength of conclusions varies and is highly dependent on the length and quality of material, the degree of any disguise involved, and the extent of descriptive dialectological and sociolinguistic information available. Establishing a speaker profile helps in defining a 'target' population and thereby narrowing the search for the culprit.

One of the best known examples of speaker profiling was undertaken in the case of the serial murderer known as the 'Yorkshire Ripper' (Ellis 1994). During the investigation the police received tapes from a man claiming to be the killer. Profiling by Ellis established that the man most likely came from, or had lived for a substantial period of time in, the Sunderland area of northeastern England. However, time proved that the real killer in fact came from Yorkshire, a county to the South of the area identified. The sender of the tapes, who was evidently a hoaxer, remains at large.

Detailed phonetic analysis may also serve to indicate the likelihood that a speaker is intoxicated, although the precise effects of alcohol on speech are not clearly understood or consistent across individuals (Künzel et al. 1992). The recorded speech of the captain of the Exxon Valdez oil tanker, which ran aground in Alaska in 1989, was investigated to assess whether he was intoxicated at the time of the accident (Hollien 1993).

More recently, sociophonetic analysis has been used as evidence to pinpoint the origins of asylum seekers in some European countries, in order to verify the legitimacy of their asylum claims (Simo Bobda et al. 1999).

3. Speaker Identification (SID)

Perhaps somewhere between 70 percent and 80 percent of all forensic cases involve SID: that is, identifying, by means of comparative phonetic testing, a person heard speaking in a criminal recording. A 'criminal recording' in this context may be anything from a hoax bomb warning recorded over an emergency telephone line, to a death threat left on a tape posted through the victim's letterbox, or a surveillance recording made secretly by the police within the home of someone planning a robbery.

The commonest scenario is for a forensic phonetician to compare the questioned voice in the criminal recording with a speech sample from the suspect, in order to assess the likelihood of their being the same person. Labov (1988), for example, reports the case of a New Yorker accused of making threatening calls to Pan Am airlines. Detailed phonetic transcripts and instrumental evidence comparing the caller with the accused suggested beyond reasonable doubt that the caller was in fact from Boston, resulting in the acquittal of the accused. Many other example cases are detailed by Baldwin and French (1990), and in the journal *Forensic Linguistics*.

It is now widely accepted that there is no indelible feature of an individual's voice. That is, there is no vocal equivalent of a fingerprint or a DNA profile, which can offer irrefutable proof of speaker identity. Research in sociolinguistics and phonetics has shown that an individual's speech may vary as a result of many factors, including the dimensions of the vocal tract, and features acquired as a result of the speaker's social and regional background. Speech features may also vary markedly from situation to situation: for example, as a result of stress, conscious disguise, or the effect of speaking on a telephone. Different voices may also be affected in different ways. For instance, most people, but not all, speak more loudly when using a telephone, which results in a rise in average fundamental frequency (Hirson et al. 1994).

In casework, various segmental and suprasegmental features may be analyzed, as well as lexis and grammar. Nowadays SID usually includes both auditory and acoustic phonetic analysis, although debate on the relative merits of the two approaches can be found in the earlier literature (Kersta 1962, Baldwin and French 1990, Nolan 1990, French 1994). Much research focuses on determining which phonetic parameters of a voice are the most useful in identifying an individual speaker, and also the degree of variability individuals display along various phonetic and sociolinguistic dimensions. In all cases the strength of conclusion that can be drawn is dependent on reference information, including—where available—population statistics, from fields such as phonetics, phonology, dialectology, sociolinguistics, and speech pathology. For the majority of forensic phoneticians, and all IAFP members, the outcome of an SID analysis is an expression of opinion ranged on a scale of confidence, rather than a categorical statement that the suspect is or is not the culprit. And although either the prosecution or the defence initially engages an analyst, the IAFP promotes the view that a neutral comparison of samples should always be undertaken. Analysts therefore do not set out to try and win the case for the side which engages them.

4. Speaker Identification by Lay Witnesses

While the bulk of forensic cases involve speaker identification by linguists using tape-recorded materials, in certain cases there is no permanent record of the voice involved in the crime. Instead, the perpetrator may simply have been heard by a 'lay' (i.e., phonetically-naïve) witness. Examples include the receipt of obscene phone calls, or witnessing a crime committed in the dark or by a masked robber.

It is now generally acknowledged that a witness must be able to demonstrate recall of a voice in a formal test, although this has not always been the case. Milroy (1984) reports a blackmail case from Northern Ireland in which a family received telephone threats following an incident where a masked intruder had entered their home. A suspect was arrested and subsequently given a ten-year prison sentence after his voice was overheard in a police station by the family members. No formal testing established their ability to identify the suspect as the man who had made the phone calls. Milroy's analysis of the sociolinguistic features of the suspect and the phone caller later revealed significant accent differences between them.

The most likely means of testing a witness's recall of a voice is by identifying the perpetrator of the crime in a *voice parade* or *line-up*. This consists of a set of recorded voices, including that of the suspect. In such cases forensic phoneticians may be called upon either to construct the parade itself, or to analyze the contents of the parade to ensure that no samples stand out unfairly in relation to the others, for example through a markedly different accent, voice quality, or recording fidelity. A detailed description of the construction of a voice parade for use in a rape case is provided by Nolan and Grabe (1996), while Butcher (1996) exemplifies the assessment of samples in a voice parade used to identify an armed robber.

There is at present, however, no incontrovertible method of constructing or administering a voice parade (see Broeders 1996, Hollien 1996). However, the most carefully argued and rigorously constructed set of guidelines may be found in the seminal article by Broeders and Rietveld (1995).

Testing recall of voices is complicated by research showing that witnesses' performance in recall tasks varies markedly as a result of numerous factors. These include hearing ability, the degree of familiarity with the voice, and whether exposure to the voice was active or passive (Künzel 1994).

It is widely assumed that recall of familiar voices is straightforward or even automatic. However, while it is generally true that recall of familiar voices is better than that of unfamiliar ones, even close friends and family members can show a significant degree of inaccuracy or inability to recognize voices that are well known to them (Foulkes and Barron 2000). It has also been demonstrated that memory of a voice tends to decay over time, so that it is imperative to begin constructing a line-up test as soon as possible after the witnessing of the event

(Hollien 1996). In practice, though, there may be long delays as a result of failure to apprehend a suspect quickly.

5. Conclusion

There remain many controversial issues in the practice of forensic phonetics. As far as speaker identification is concerned, it is unlikely that any speaker-specific invariant parameter will ever be discovered, such that statements of speaker identity might come to emulate the strength of those derived from DNA testing or fingerprinting. That said, it is encouraging that research in relevant areas is undergoing continued growth.

See also: Discourse Analysis and the Law.

Bibliography

Baldwin J, French J P 1990 *Forensic Phonetics*. Pinter, London
Broeders A P A 1996 Earwitness identification: Common ground, disputed territory, and uncharted areas. *Forensic Linguistics* 3: 1–13
Broeders A P A, Rietveld A C M 1995 Speaker identification by earwitnesses. In: Braun A, Köster J-P (eds.) *Studies in Forensic Phonetics*. Wissenschaftlicher Verlag, Trier, Germany
Butcher A 1996 Getting the voice lineup right: Analysis of a multiple auditory confrontation. *Proceedings of the 6th Australian International Conference on Speech Science and Technology*. Flinders University, Adelaide, SA
Ellis S 1994 The Yorkshire Ripper enquiry: Part 1. *Forensic Linguistics* 1: 197–206
Foulkes P, Barron A 2000 Telephone speaker recognition amongst members of close social network. *Forensic Linguistics* 7: 180–98
French J P 1990 Analytic procedures for the determination of disputed utterances. In: Kniffka H (ed.) *Texte zu Theorie und Praxis Forensischer Linguistik*. Max Niemeyer, Tübingen, Germany
French J P 1994 An overview of forensic phonetics with particular reference to speaker identification. *Forensic Linguistics* 1: 169–81
Hirson A, French J P, Howard D M 1994 Speech fundamental frequency over the telephone and face-to-face: Some implications for forensic phonetics. In: Windsor Lewis J (ed.), *Studies in General and English Phonetics*. Routledge, London
Hirson A, Howard D M 1994 Spectrographic analysis of a cockpit voice recorder tape. *Forensic Linguistics* 1: 59–69
Hollien H 1990 *The Acoustics of Crime*. Plenum, New York
Hollien H 1993 An oilspill, alcohol and the Captain: A possible misapplication of forensic science. *Forensic Sciences International* 60: 97–105
Hollien H 1996 Consideration of guidelines for earwitness lineups. *Forensic Linguistics* 3: 14–23
Kersta L G 1962 Voiceprint identification. *Nature* 196: 1253–7
Künzel H 1987 *Sprechererkennung: Grundzüge Forensischer Sprachverarbeitung*. Kriminalistik-Verlag, Heidelberg, Germany
Künzel H J 1994 On the problem of speaker identification by victims and witnesses. *Forensic Linguistics* 1: 45–58
Künzel H J, Braun A, Eysholdt U 1992 *Einfluß von Alkohol auf Sprache und Stimme*. Kriminalistik-Verlag, Heidelberg, Germany
Labov W 1988 The judicial testing of linguistic theory. In: Tannen D (ed.) *Linguistics in Context*. Ablex, Norwood, NJ
Milroy J 1984 Sociolinguistic methodology and the identification of speakers' voices in legal proceedings. In: Trudgill P (ed.) *Applied Sociolinguistics*. Academic Press, London
Nolan F J 1990 The limitations of auditory-phonetic speaker identification. In Kniffka H (ed.) *Texte zu Theorie und Praxis Forensischer Linguistik*. Max Niemeyer, Tübingen, Germany
Nolan F J 1991 Forensic phonetics. *Journal of Linguistics* 27: 483–93
Nolan F J 1997 Speaker recognition and forensic phonetics. In: Hardcastle W J, Laver J (eds.) *Handbook of Phonetic Sciences*. Blackwell, Oxford, UK
Nolan F J, Grabe E 1996 Preparing a voice line-up. *Forensic Linguistics* 3: 74–94
Simo Bobda A, Wolf H G, Peter L 1999 Identifying regional and national origin of English-speaking Africans seeking asylum in Germany. *Forensic Linguistics* 6: 300–19

Gay Language

W. L. Leap

Gay language is a relatively new area of interest in sociolinguistics. The recent emergence of this topic reflects, in part: the general growth of lesbian, gay, bisexual, transgender, and queer studies within many academic disciplines; efforts in feminist theory to move beyond binary-based discussions of female/male differences and to examine gender dynamics in historically situated, socially constructed terms; as well as a maturing of the interests in language, gender, and sexuality which have been addressed through sociolinguistic research for some time.

1. Defining Gay Language

The subject matter of gay language research continues to be a matter for discussion. Earlier work assumed somewhat unquestioningly that gay men and lesbians use language in distinctive ways, and called for studies designed to explore the details of this linguistic distinctiveness. The results of these studies included collections of words relevant to gay or lesbian experience, and descriptions of language use in situations where the gay or lesbian focus of the speech event was already marked, e.g., humorous conversations in gay bars (Goodwin 1989), silence during anonymous sexual encounters (Delph 1978), verbal dueling at all-gay dinner parties (Murray 1979), and linguistic risk-taking in conversations in department stores, airplanes, and other public locations (Leap 1993).

In most cases, these studies take for granted the speakers' lesbian, gay or other same-sex identities, and leave unexplored how text-making contributes to and frequently confirms the speakers' understandings of sexual sameness. What results is a seemingly circular relationship between language and identity, where use of gay language is confirmed by the (homo)sexuality of the speaker, while at the same time speaker sexuality is confirmed by those self-same linguistic practices (Kulick 2000).

Understandably, more recent research has begun to look more closely at these particular relationships which link language use, (homo)sexuality, and speaker subjectivity. Some of these studies examine the linguistic practices through which same-sex identified women and men construct or conceal claims to sexual identity within speech events (Leap 1996: 49–73). Other studies show how a speaker's use of certain linguistic practices prompt interlocutors to *assume* gay/lesbian presence within the speech event, whatever the speaker's claims to sexual identity (Cameron 1977). And others explore how a speaker's use of particular linguistic practices bring messages about sexual sameness into the foreground of an otherwise heterosexually focused text-making, or otherwise transform (or 'queer') the linguistic moment (Gaudio 1997).

These examples remind us that same-sex desires and experiences are constructed within the social moment and must be studied within linguistic and social context. Marginality is also a part of that context, and so are the heterosexism and homophobia which often surround public expressions of same-sex identities, practices and desires. In some ways, these politics are similar to those surrounding linguistic practices of *any* group of speakers located at a distance from domains of power and privilege. Accordingly, there is some interest in broadening the focus on *gay* language study within sociolinguistics to a more inclusive focus on language and desire (Kulick 2000). At the same time, broadening the focus diverts attention from a close analysis of particular linguistic practices and their connections to other features within the social context. Understandably, another emerging line of inquiry proposes exploring connections between language, sexual identity, and same-sex desire within the context-centered structures of political economy (Leap in press).

2. Characteristic Features, Uniqueness vs. Significance

Whether there are characteristic features of gay language, or whether the 'gayness' of these codes lies outside of textual detail, also remains a matter of ongoing debate. There is some agreement that specialized vocabulary (including words and phrases with unmarked, ingroup meanings), along with phonological features like distinctive intonation patterns and extended vowel length, are some of the features commonly associated with identifiable gay *English* linguistic practice, and some indication that similar features may be attested in other languages. Some researchers would also include in this listing *camping* and *queering* and other forms of transgressive verbal performance, as well as *masquerade, language of the closet*, and other practices of linguistic concealment.

There is less consensus regarding the existence of gay/lesbian-related conversational structures and narrative styles. In some cases, what at first appears to be a specifically gay or lesbian focused language use is found to be a reflection of a gay or lesbian topic under discussion, or the linguistic practices which any speaker might employ under similar circumstances, whatever the sexual identity. But even when the linguistic structures reflect gay-centered topics or have parallels in the language use within other speech settings, gay language speakers are still using language to encode gay/lesbian content, speaker identity, or other same-sex related presence strategically within the social moment. Gay-related linguistic practices do not need to be unique to have a significant effect on text-making—and therefore to be of interest to sociolinguistic description.

3. Language Socialization and Language Diversity

3.1 Gay Language Socialization

While language often appears to be a widely accessible cultural resource, gay-related linguistic practices are not always in the foreground of local communication so identifying sources of information, and gaining access to those sources, figure prominently in the coming out process and in subsequent events in the speaker's gay/lesbian career (Leap 1999). The workings of gay language socialization become an even more complex enterprise for would-be speakers now that gay languages are emerging in parts of the world where same-sex desire has not previously been publicly articulated (see Sect. 5.1).

3.2 Gay Language Diversity

Moreover, not everyone learns the gay language of the speech community in entirely the same ways, and not everyone has access to these resources. These variations in gay language/(homo)sexual socialization anticipate the other forms of diversity that structure language use by gay men and lesbians.

3.2.1 Diversities Based on Gender

Building on claims from French language/gender studies, some theorists argue that because language is closely associated with the everyday experiences of men, including gay-identified men, lesbians, because they are women, will always find gay language to be in some way inaccessible (Irigaray 1985, Penelope 1990). This argument endorses a literal reading of the term *gay language*—that is, *gay men's language*—as the focus for inquiry, since lesbian language is an internally contradictory, if not impossible construction, under these conditions. The absence of terminology for women-identified women, compared to the richness of terms for same-sex identified men, is a widely attested reference pattern outside of North Atlantic domains, and is often cited to show how the contradictions surrounding lesbian language can be resolved through public silence. Whether such silence creates opportunities for women-centered discourses to emerge privately, or is another erasure of lesbian/female voices in another form, has to be examined in site-specific terms (Kendall 1999, Thadani 1999).

3.2.2 Diversities Based on Race, Ethnicity, and Class

Gay language is rarely the exclusive property of the affluent, the comedian, the activist, or the academic. Conversations framed in terms of gay linguistic practices, and lesbian linguistic practices where attested, have been reported in all domains of everyday life and among speakers occupying various social and economic statuses. And even though some speakers may appear to be especially proficient in these ways of speaking, gay language is not the parochial domain of any single individual, but is socially constructed and is closely associated with particular 'communities of practice' (Wong and Zhang in press).

While distributed widely, these practices are never distributed evenly across the social terrain. Much as is often found to be the case in sociolinguistic inquiry, divisions of race and class provide important sites of variation in that regard. In the USA, for example, the Gay Men's English, which is stereotyped in films and other forms of popular culture and is widely attested in urban gay venues and other public locales, is closely associated with *whiteness* and with 'passing for white' by same-sex identified men of African American, Hispanic, and Asian/Pacific Islander backgrounds. Members of these groups have their own ways of expressing same-sex identities and perspectives within their linguistic text-making. This includes an African American gayspeak whose linguistic details draw heavily on kinship terms, discussions of domestic practices and other African American female-associated centered referencing; the *swardspeak* of the Filipino-American *bakla*; the 'talking *kush*' popular among South Asian gay men; or the distinctive Spanish text-making of the Latin American *maricon*.

In the case of swardspeak, the language has strong associations with the Filipino homeland and varieties of swardspeak are attested among same-sex identified men in Manila and in other urban and rural settings. Accordingly, even *gay* identified Filipino-American men, who would never claim *bakla* identity (in public settings, at least) master swardspeak at some level and integrate it into everyday conversations with Filipino same-sex identified friends. That some speakers of swardspeak, whether *bakla* or gay-identified, are also speakers of the white-oriented Gay Men's English is another indication of the complex ties between language, sexuality, and political economy which underlie and help to structure diasporic experience (Manalansan in press).

4. Worldwide Emergence and Globalization

4.1 Worldwide Emergence

Swardspeak is one example of a gay language emerging in one area of the world (the Philippines) and spreading to other areas under conditions of displacement, relocation and other forms of diaspora. Gay languages have equally complex histories in other parts of the world, and are also connected to globalization, diaspora, and other conditions of late modernity in complex ways.

Polari, a gay language spoken by some British gay men during the first half of the twentieth century, had its origins in the antilanguages (see *Antilanguage*) of British criminals, prostitutes, and theater people, and shows influences of Italian and other continental languages, as well. Polari makes use of familiar English vocabulary, but reworks meanings and sentence forms so that speakers can produce statements which are completely unclear to those not familiar with the code (Baker in press). *Gayle*, a gay language spoken in South Africa, also applies coded meanings to a distinct a set of lexical items, many of which are women's names, so that speakers can shield conversations from the surveillance of outsiders (Kleinbooi 1995). Speakers of Polari and Gayle also insist that speaking these languages can be a superb form of recreation.

In North American Indian contexts, traditional gay languages draw more heavily on conventions of sentence structure and meaning found in ordinary discourse. Alterations in such features as pronoun structures, verb endings and speaker–audience cross-reference markers allow the speakers to code their sexual marginality in formats which audiences will be able to recognize, whether or not they can reproduce them (Thomas 1977).

4.2 Globalizations of North Atlantic-based Lesbian/Gay Languages

'Lesbian' and 'gay' are often used by researchers as markers for same-sex identities worldwide and as indicators of linguistic practices associated with those identities. However, the meanings suggested by 'lesbian' and 'gay' are closely aligned with the emergence of particular forms of same-sex identity under nineteenth and twentieth century North Atlantic capitalism (D'Emilio 1983). As a result, same-sex identified women and men imply connections with North Atlantic-based meanings of same-sex desire when they describe themselves as lesbian or gay or when those labels are applied to them by others. But the circulation of lesbian and gay is not always locally totalizing. With 'lesbian' and 'gay' expressing international meanings, site-specific understandings of same-sex experience are underscored, e.g., by invoking terminology from local languages, by means of paraphrase, by reworking local meanings of 'woman' and 'man,' and/or by silence. Under such arrangements, referring to 'local' languages of same-sex desire as 'gay' language may imply a consistency of same-sex experiences worldwide which is not attested by the historical record or by local life story narratives.

Distinguishing between 'local' and 'North Atlantic'-based languages of same-sex desire is especially important, given that other components of North Atlantic (homo)sexual cultures have joined the transnational flow of lesbian/gay based identity categories and linguistic practices. Primary agents of the circulation include: ever-expanding accessibility of electronic communication; international circulation of films, videos, recorded music, and other popular media; sexual tourism and other travel/tourist practices, voluntary and enforced displacement and diaspora, as well as new understandings of citizenship which sanction *flexible* instead of singular claims to political and cultural identities.

It is a serious misreading of these data to argue that a single 'gay culture'—and with it, a single 'gay language'—is now emerging worldwide. Global circulation of North Atlantic sexual languages and cultures engages local constructions of language, culture, and sexuality in complex ways, sometimes providing helpful alternatives to indigenous understandings and practices, and in other instances prompting an enhancement of details of sexual culture as already locally conceived. The use of English as a language of public lesbian/gay experience in Israel, after years of struggling to adapt modern-day Hebrew for this purpose, is one example of such an outcome (Moriel 1998). The Thai distributions of sexual identities (and with that, associated text-making practices) across English vs. Thai linguistic options is another example: that is, English *gay* is the accepted term for same-sex identified men, while an English based, Thai-like linguistic hybrid *tom dee* (*tom* from the first syllable of *tom-boy, dee* from the last syllable of *lady*), provides the marker for same-sex identified females, and traditional Thai reference for male-to-female gender crossing, *cath*, provides the discursive focus for traditional (cross-dressing) as well as modernized (e.g., surgically enhanced) transgendered identification (Jackson and Sullivan 1999).

See also: Gender and Language.

Bibliography

Baker P in press Nanti polari, heartface: The decline of the UK's secret gay language. In: Leap W (ed.) *Gay Language Without Gay English?* University of Illinois Press, Urbana, IL

Cameron D 1977 Performing gender identity: Young men's talk and the construction of heterosexual masculinity. In: Johnson S, Meinhof U H (eds.) *Language and Masculinity*. Blackwell, Oxford, UK, pp. 47–64

D'Emilio J 1983 Capitalism and gay identity. In: Sintow A, Stansell C, Thompson S (eds.) *Powers of Desire: The Politics of Sexuality*. Monthly Review Press, New York, pp. 100–15

Delph E W 1978 *The Silent Community: Public Homosexual Encounters*. Sage, Beverly Hills, CA

Gaudio R 1997 Not talking straight in Hausa. In: Livia A, Hall K (eds.) *Queerly Phrased*. Oxford University Press, New York, pp. 416–29

Goodwin J P 1989 *More Man than You'll Ever Be: Gay Folklore and Acculturation in Middle America*. University of Indiana Press, Bloomington, IN

Irigaray L 1985 *This Sex Which is Not One*. Cornell University Press, Ithaca, NY

Jackson P, Sullivan, G 1999 A panoplay of roles: Sexual and gender diversity in contemporary Thailand. In: Jackson P, Sullivan G (eds.) *Male and Female Homosexuality in Contemporary Thailand*. Harrington Park Press, Binghamton, NY, pp. 1–28

Kendall K 1999 Women in Lesotho and the (western) construction of homophobia. In: Blackwood E, Wieringa S (eds.) *Same-sex Relations and Female Desires: Transgender Practices Across Cultures*. Columbia University Press, New York, pp. 157–80

Kleinbooi H 1995 A Zelda on my doorstep. *Bua* 9(4): 26–9

Kulick D 2000 Lesbian and gay language. *Annual Review of Anthropology* **29**: 243–85

Leap W L 1993 Gay men's English: Cooperative discourse in a language of risk. *New York Folklore* 19(1–2): 45–70

Leap W L 1996 *Word's Out: Gay Men's English*. University of Minnesota Press, Minneapolis, MN

Leap W L 1999 Language, socialization and silence in gay adolescence. In: Bucholtz M, Liang A C, Sutton, L (eds.)

Reinventing Identities: The Gendered Self in Discourse. Oxford University Press, New York

Leap W L in press Language and gendered modernity. In: Holmes J, Meyerhoff M (eds.) *Handbook of Language and Gender*. Blackwell, London

Manalansan M in press *Remapping Frontiers: The Lives of Filipino Gay Men in New York.* Duke University Press, Durham, NC

Moriel L 1998 Diva in the promised land: A blue-print for newspeak. *World Englishes* **17**(2): 225–38

Murray S O 1979 The art of gay insulting. *Anthropological Linguistics* **21**: 211–23

Penelope J 1990 *Speaking Freely: Unlearning the Lies of the Fathers' Tongues.* Teachers College Press, New York

Thadani G 1999 The politics of identities and languages: Lesbian desire in ancient and modern India. In: Blackwood E, Wieringa S (eds.) *Same-sex Relations and Female Desires: Transgender Practices Across Cultures.* Columbia University Press, New York, pp. 67–91

Thomas W 1977 Navajo cultural constructions of gender and sexuality. In: Jacobs S-E, Thomas W, Lang S (eds.) *Two Spirit People: North American Gender Identity, Sexuality and Spirituality.* University of Illinois Press, Urbana, IL

Wong A, Zhang Q in press The linguistic construction of the Tongzhi community. *Journal of Linguistic Anthropology* **10**

Note: http://www.msu.edu/greenm14/outil/gaybib.html is a regularly updated bibliography of sources relevant to gay language research.

Gender and Language
K. M. McCormick

As a field of research, language and gender studies is interdisciplinary and relatively new. Until the late 1990s, most sociolingiuistic studies of language and gender focused on language as the phenomenon to be explained, and did not recognize the complexity of gender (Cameron 1996).

A wave of intense debate and empirical research was prompted by Robin Lakoff's book *Language and Woman's Place*, published in 1975. This is not, however, to suggest that there was no interest in matters relating to it before that date. Academic papers by linguists, historians, and anthropologists had dealt with some aspects, and written records of various kinds provide evidence that for centuries and in many countries people have had strong beliefs and attitudes about the way women and men speak or should speak, and about acceptable ways of describing males and females. This article describes those beliefs and research into them.

As used here, the term 'gender' does not refer to 'grammatical gender' (the system to be found in some languages of organizing certain word classes into contrasting categories of 'masculine,' 'feminine,' 'neuter'). Here gender refers to social categories based on sex but encompassing behavior, roles, and images that, although not biologically determined, are regarded by a society as appropriate to its male or female members. What is seen as appropriate to each gender thus differs in different societies and eras. Gender is distinguished from 'sex' in that sex is taken to refer to biological characteristics of male and female whereas gender encompasses what is socially learned and acquired. Gender is also distinguished from 'sexuality' and 'sexual orientation' though much research on the latter does not make the distinction clear (see Kulick 2000; *Gay Language*).

Several popularly accepted pronouncements on men, women, and language have been based on the assumption that the different characteristics of male and female language use are a direct result of biological differences between the sexes. Better explanations for almost all observed male/female language differences are to be found less in the biological constitution of the human body and more in the social and psychological formation of the human subject.

A historical perspective on prescriptive and descriptive views of the relationship between language and its male and female users can be gained from an examination of texts written by people with a professional interest in language: lexicographers, grammarians, dialectologists, editors, and, of course, writers of plays and novels. Other sources of information are to be found in a variety of texts produced by people concerned not primarily with language, but with prescribing proper ways of behaving, since one aspect of this is the recognition of the speech community's rules about who may speak and how they may speak in public and private spheres. In most societies these rules indicate differences in what is regarded as appropriate use of language about and by women and men, girls and boys.

In the twentieth century, research in anthropology, sociology, psychology, sociolinguistics, and discourse analysis provided a wealth of interesting material about how various contemporary societies give verbal expression to their perceptions of boys and girls, men and women, about how they regard the language use of their male and female members, and about the factors that impinge upon these attitudes. Some of this work concentrated on describing ways in which aspects of linguistic form vary depending on sex of speaker or addressee. Other research sought to explain causes and effects of observed covariation and also of patterns in the ways women and men are described.

In the late twentieth century, work on language use was drawn into a broader framework which examined silence and silencing as the other side of the coin of speech and writing. This framework is predicated upon the belief that societal power relationships manifest themselves in the granting or withholding of 'speaking rights' in the broadest sense. In the humanities and social sciences there is an interest in discerning whose voice is heard and taken to be representative or truthful, and whose voice goes unheard in various contexts. A striking example of this is the critical study of colonial history and its rewriting, the narration refocused by the use of different source material. But the privileging of some voices over others does not happen only where two (or more) different societies interact. In all societies some individuals and groups have greater speaking rights than others, especially in the public domain, and the meanings that are encoded in publicly available texts are predominantly those of the society's powerful groups. As men are more powerful than women in most societies, it is their perceptions that are publicly articulated more often than women's and then uncritically taken to be those of the society as a whole. The effect on the socialization of women of this privileging of male perceptions constitutes a focus of research in disciplines such as psychology, sociology, political studies, and critical literary studies (see *Socialization*).

There is a considerable interest in the central role of language in the construction both of the individual subject and of group identity, and as the medium for the expression, maintenance, and questioning of competing ideologies. Of particular note in regard to language and the gendered subject is the work of theorists working in France in semiology, psychology, and philosophy. An understanding of their radical critique of patriarchy and the role of language in sustaining it depends on grasping the ways in which they have engaged with psychoanalytic theory particularly in its Lacanian form. In an article of this length it is not possible to supply the theoretical context that would have to preface an adequate summary of their arguments. For this reason subsequent references to them will provide little more than pointers to some issues on which they focus (see *Identity and Language*; *Ideology*).

Work arising from all of the approaches mentioned above will be touched on in this overview of what is believed, what is known, and what is being investigated about the relationship between language and gender. An examination of gender-distinctive use of linguistic variables will be followed by an account of findings about male and female participation in extended discourse. Socialization processes accounting for male and female differences in language use will be discussed. Finally there is a brief discussion of how gender attitudes are manifested in language as a system. Much of the illustrative material throughout is from Western, industrialized societies because it is there that most research on language and gender has taken place. Where possible, however, perspectives from other societies are included.

1. Gender-distinctive Use of Language

It seems that in all societies gender has a bearing on the distribution of roles and the ascription or achievement of status which then affect access to domains of economic and social activity and to the education that prepares for them (see *Role Theory*). All of these factors, in turn, affect language use. It is therefore not surprising that all societies investigated for the existence of gender-related differences in language use have manifested them. The forms that they take vary from one society to another. They may manifest themselves in preferences for or competence in different languages or dialects; vocabulary; pronunciation; participation in extended discourse(s).

In Koasati, a native American language, a few syntactic structures have different forms for the use of male and female speakers. Less common, but also possible, is that sex of addressee affects choice of form. In Kurukh, a Dravidian language, inflectional morphology is determined by sex of both speaker and addressee. These are two instances of sex determining linguistic form. Rarely is it the only determinant. What usually happens is that it interacts with other factors in shaping what are perceived as gender differences in language use.

Rochefort's seventeenth-century study of a community in the lesser Antilles seemed to indicate that these differences might go as far as male and female members of a speech community speaking different languages. In the community he described the women were Arawaks whose male ancestors had been killed by invading Caribs. The invaders then married the Arawak women. Rochefort claimed that the women preserved their language and taught it to their daughters while their sons, who understood the women's language, preferred to speak the language of their fathers, the result being that the two sexes spoke different languages. However, a re-examination of the data showed this interpretation to be unsound: only 10 percent of the recorded vocabulary on which Rochefort had based his claim was not shared by men and women. In other words, some vocabulary, rather than a whole language, was gender-specific.

There can, however, be differences in degrees of bilingualism between boys and girls, or men and women within a community (see *Bilingualism, Societal*). These tend to be a result of differing educational or economic opportunities for males and females. For example, if the women have to travel to sell wares in a market town while the men are locally employed then the women are more likely to learn a language of wider use than are the men.

Command of the language of wider access may be a factor in a cycle of other changes as was found to be the case in a bilingual community in Austria where Hungarian is associated with peasant life and German with urban opportunities. Moving out of the peasant economy requires, among other things, fluency in German. Those who wish to take this route are using every opportunity to develop their command of this language and it would seem that women feel a greater urgency to do so then men do. Women are choosing to use far more German and less Hungarian than men are. This is prompted by their disinclination to take on the arduous double burden of agricultural and domestic work which is the lot of peasant wives, and by their preference for urban life and work with its labor saving devices and more regular hours. 'Peasant men can't get wives...,' announces the title of an article on language shift in the community (Gal 1978). The outcome of changing marriage patterns will probably be the further withering of Hungarian and a shift toward German (see *Language Maintenance, Shift, and Death*).

The seventeenth-century Antillean community was not unique in having gender-specific lexical pools. Verbal taboo systems can create quite striking differences in the vocabulary available to women and men (see *Taboo Words*). Societies in places as far apart as Mongolia and South Africa have speech communities whose married women are forbidden to use the names of their husband and his male relatives. To use those names would be intolerably disrespectful. The taboo is not limited to the names of male in-laws: it is extended to cover all other words that sound like the taboo names—women have to avoid these and choose synonyms that sound different. For women in these societies, getting married entails a reorientation toward the lexicon of their home language. There are no reports of societies placing comparable restrictions exclusively on men's speech though there is a speech community in Australia which places a taboo on the use of one of its languages by a newly wed couple in the presence of a mother-in-law and some other relatives.

Linguistic taboos of a less far-reaching kind are common. In many societies obscenities are supposedly taboo but in fact it may be acceptable for men but not for women to use them among themselves. In some cases there is an assumption that 'decent women' should not even know these words. That the taboos do not have the effects they are supposed to emerges from empirical studies of men and women swearing. It is not uncommon for there to be covert tolerance of women using obscenities in single-sex groups, and in some social groups men and women may use them in mixed-sex groups without incurring censure. Age can make a difference as it does in cases where the young women of a community conform to the norms of demureness or silence expected of them, while the older women indulge in raucous and sexually explicit joking.

There is a widespread belief that women's use of language is and should be more refined than men's, while not being expected to match theirs for adventurousness and rigor. The contrasting qualities are often felt to be biologically based, extensions of women's supposedly greater softness and delicacy, and of the greater toughness and energy ascribed to men. To discover whether there is empirical evidence to underpin the belief that women's speech is more refined than men's, the rather subjective notion of 'refinement' has to be tied to observable features of language use—vocabulary, pronunciation, syntax —which the speech community regards as indices (see *Speech Community*).

Vocabulary range in certain fields is sometimes regarded as an index of refinement: for example, a wide vocabulary for color terms and a narrow range of obscenities could be taken to be signs of refinement. There are serious methodological limitations on what vocabulary studies can reliably show about differences between the sexes in this respect. First, sound sampling of men and women as two groups for any kind of language study is impossible unless one controls adequately for other factors because neither group is homogeneous: educational, class, ethnic, religious, and economic factors interact with gender to create significant differences among men and among women. Second, situations or tests designed to elicit vocabulary range are problematic because the person being tested may well censor his or her responses in the face of particular kinds of interviewers or elicitation procedures. At best what an empirical study can tap is differences between men's and women's observed usage in populations and situations that are in other respects comparable.

Research conducted in the United States, Canada, and the UK on pronunciation differences between women and men has shown that, except in casual speech, women tend to use more prestigious variants than men do. (There are speech communities where this is not the case.) Early quantitative studies selected variants that were known to be prestigious and to have a stigmatized counterpart. The relative frequency of usage of each of the pair of variants was measured among subjects from particular regions, grouped by social class and sex of speaker.

In his well-known study of social class stratification in New York speech, Labov (1972) measured the relative frequency of the presence or absence of postvocalic (r)—its absence is stigmatized—and of the prestigious fricative (th) and its stigmatized affricate and stop counterparts. There was variation by social class and age as well as gender but one clear finding was that, in careful speech, women used fewer low-prestige forms than men did in all social classes (see *Sociolinguistic Variation*).

Trudgill's findings were similar regarding gender and class stratification in Norwich speech. He elicited data with four different levels of formality, from joke telling at one end of the spectrum to the reading of minimal pairs of words at the other and found that in all social classes women had a lower percentage of stigmatized forms in all styles than men (Trudgill 1974).

Having obtained recordings of his subjects' speech, Trudgill went on to investigate their perceptions of their speech. He played tape recordings of words pronounced in both a prestigious and a stigmatized way and asked each subject to say which his or her own pronunciation most resembled. Subjects' responses were then checked against the recordings of their speech. There were inaccuracies in self-report among both men and women, but the nature of the inaccuracy varied: more men than women 'underreported,' identifying their pronunciation with the version more stigmatized than their own, whereas women did the reverse and identified with the form more prestigious than the one they used.

Trudgill and Labov offer similar explanations for the class- and sex-related differences in accents. They argue that groups which see themselves as almost within reach of higher social status will use prestigious speech as a means of gaining acceptance to or signaling actual membership of a higher status group. (Those already in high status groups can afford to be more relaxed about their speech.) They think that women may use 'better' speech as a means of gaining entry into a social group of higher status because it is less easy for them to do so on the basis of their own education, work, and earnings, their status usually being ascribed to them on the basis of the education, work, or earnings of their fathers or husbands (see *Social Class*). Moreover, as primary care-givers for the society's children, women are expected to provide good models for children's speech.

But what accounts for the greater identification with low-prestige speech by men? Trudgill explains the apparent anomaly as a product of the operation of two different kinds of prestige, overt and covert. Society as a whole openly recognizes some accents as better than others. In Britain, Received Pronunciation is associated with qualities such as competence and intelligence. At the same time, however, working-class speech is often associated with some highly valued personal qualities such as humor and sincerity. Trudgill believes that it is also associated with the toughness and masculinity believed to be characteristic of the men of that class. Where toughness is thought to be an aspect of 'real masculinity,' desirable in all men, working-class speech patterns confer covert prestige in that respect. Hence some men of other social classes imitate working-class speech and also perceive their own speech to be more working-class than it is. Clearly, in the study of pronunciation differences, more is at issue than degrees of refinement.

The assumptions and the methodology underlying these and other related studies have been criticized and the value of the findings reassessed. Labov and Trudgill used the common practice of defining a woman's social class by the criterion of the social class of the man on whom she is presumed to be dependent: father or husband. Coates and Cameron (1988) find this anomalous in an age of high male unemployment and single-parent families where women are the only breadwinners. They also challenge the assumption underlying the 'covert prestige' explanation of men's tendency to associate themselves with vernacular culture, namely that this culture is masculine. This assumption has the effect of placing women outside the working class, and of ignoring the specific realities of working-class women in social and labor structures. They claim, moreover, that the studies have obscured the fact that, even within each social class, neither men nor women form a homogeneous group—subgroups arise as a result of differing educational, economic, and social opportunities. They argue that it may well be that it is these which shape pronunciation preferences, rather than broad stereotypical male and female images and roles (see *Stereotype and Social Attitudes*).

It is now felt to be essential to examine the aspirations, opportunities, and experiences of men and women when attempting to explain gender-related linguistic patterns. This kind of analysis allows for the foregrounding of different aspects of an individual's identity and concomitant features of language use in different circumstances. Face-to-face interaction among small groups of people who share work or leisure activities creates solidarity and this affects the way group members speak, particularly in one another's presence. Research methodology based on social network theory focuses on effects of this kind (see *Social Networks*).

Lesley Milroy's study of language and social networks in three working-class areas of Belfast showed that while there was gender-related variation in speech in each area, there were differences among the three male groups and among the three female groups (Milroy 1980). It is clear from her multidimensional analysis of the data that the interaction of age, gender-division of labor, economic and leisure opportunities, and types of social networks is very complex, and that explanation of linguistic variation between and within small groups of people has to take this complexity into account. No single variable has an overriding explanatory or predictive value. Milroy found that while in all areas males and females use the vernacular as a symbol of their loyalty to the local community, they did not always use the same variables to express this function. A study of working-class adolescents in Reading reveals the same thing: both girls and boys used vernacular features but different clusters of them (Cheshire 1982) (see *Adolescent Peer Group Language*).

Gender-related ability and willingness to use the standard dialect is also quite widely attested. Sometimes a community's expectation that it is proper for one sex to have a command of the standard is strong enough to bring that about before external factors (such as employment) make direct demands on individuals. In other cases the explanatory factor is that the jobs available to one sex require proficiency in the standard dialect, whereas those for the other sex do not. That both explanations may be valid in one community can be seen in Waccamaw Neck, South Carolina, where the language continuum ranges from Gullah (a creole), through Black English to a regional standard English. From the age of 10 onward, girls use more standard English features than boys from the same neighborhood and even from the same family. Ten is the age at which girls begin to be regarded as young ladies and are expected to spend less time playing with their peers (of both sexes) and more time on domestic responsibilities. Employment opportunities and rewards differ for young adult men and women: the best-paying jobs for women are in teaching, nursing, and sales—all of which require standard English, but they pay women less than men can earn in blue-collar jobs, where standard English is not necessary. The combination of social expectations and economic realities thus results in greater use of standard English by females than males between the ages of 10 and 60. In the oldest generation, however, it is the women whose speech is furthest from standard English. In their earlier years these women were illiterate and confined to their immediate community, while the men were economically more mobile and had more contact with standard English (Nichols 1983).

2. Gender-distinctive Conversational Style

Popular notions, often encapsulated in proverbs, express strong beliefs about differences in the quantity, quality, topics, and patterns of men's and women's speech. Coates (1993) provides a rich and varied sample from which the examples below are drawn. A common belief is that women are constitutionally verbose:

> Ou femme y a, silence n'y a. (France)
> The North Sea will sooner be found wanting in water than a woman at a loss for a word. (Jutland)
> Many women, many words; many geese, many turds. (England)

The belief that women talk far too much is closely linked with a belief that what they say is of little importance, if not actually unpleasant or tiresome. This is exemplified in the last proverb quoted above and is captured in many cartoons depicting chattering women and their exhausted spouses. The implication is that, ideally, women should be silent or quietly spoken, and that they should be good listeners, not only in the sense of hearing but also of complying.

That men and women differ in the topics of conversation they choose and are competent to discuss is another commonly held belief. Women are thought to prefer personal topics; men, public issues. Linked to notions about preferred topics are strong beliefs about differences in the ways in which women and men conduct conversations. Men are believed to be better than women at sustaining logical and dispassionate arguments involving complex issues. In dealing with ideas men are held to be clearer and more forceful, and women more confused and hesitant. Women are thought to be able to articulate feelings and intuitions better than men, being more willing and able to find verbal images for the nonrational. The putative differences are often assumed to be a direct result not of socialization and restriction of opportunity, but of innate differences between male and female. Reasons for the belief in (and the results of) differences in language use have been explored both in contemporary psychoanalytic theory (see Sellers 1991) and in empirical research.

Observation of conversations and detailed examination of transcripts have shown differences between men's and women's single-sex conversations, and have also provided evidence of gender-related patterns of behavior in mixed-sex conversation. These are discussed below. It should, however, be noted that the social and economic factors which create differences between and within each sex group affect discourse patterns just as they affect the use of particular linguistic variables. Thus, wide generalizations should not be drawn on the basis of studies of particular male and female conversations. Relatively few of the empirical studies of conversational style were designed to be comparative across age and cultural groups.

In the single-sex conversations that have been analyzed women do indeed describe and discuss their feelings more than men, who prefer impersonal topics such as sport and current affairs. When feelings are expressed men are likely to respond by giving advice, rather than by self-disclosure, which is a common female response. In an article which was based on analysis of real and literary dialogs, Sattel (1983) suggests that by withholding expression of their feelings, males are concealing their limitations and the resulting image helps them to exercise power. This suggests that the notion of strategy, conscious or unconscious, would not be out of place in an analysis of conversational patterns. The broad gender-related differences in conversational style revealed by empirical studies will now be examined (for more detail see Coates 1993).

Competitive style is more likely to be used by males than by females, whereas the converse is true of cooperative style. The discourse features giving rise to these characterizations are, chiefly, aspects of conversation management. The 'one-to-many' pattern—one person wanting or competing for the attention of all participants—is quite common in all-male groups, whereas in all-female groups there will often be several smaller conversations going on, not competing for center-stage.

Women are more likely than men to do the work of ensuring that conversation is maintained. To do so they use responses such as 'yeah,' 'mhm' to signal attention to what the speaker is saying. They also ask questions or, by means of gesture or glance, invite others to participate, thus easing the movement from speaker to speaker and topic to topic. Men, on the other hand, are typically more preoccupied by the subject matter under discussion and do not give much attention to smoothing the transition from one topic or speaker to the next. Verbal aggressiveness is more common among male than female speakers. One linguistic manifestation of it is the tendency to interrupt. In same-sex groups the level of interruption is relatively low and is similar for males and females. (The level of resistance to interruption is similar for males and females—both tend to concede the speaking turn to the interrupter.) In mixed-sex groups there is a striking gender difference in interruptions. Zimmerman and West found that, whether or not speakers knew one another, and regardless of setting—natural or laboratory—the rate of men interrupting women was far higher than the reverse. In their data the ratio of male to female interruption in a conversation ranged from 63 percent : 37 percent to 100 percent : 0 percent. They argue that interruptions are gestures of power and that taken singly they may be minor, but because they occur constantly they help to constitute women's subordinate status (Zimmerman and West 1975).

Mixed-sex conversations provide evidence regarding the belief that women talk more than men do: the opposite seems to be true. Males 'have more say' than females: in mixed groups, whether of children or adults, it is usually the males' topics that are taken up and developed, males who change topics of conversation, and males who talk more often and for longer stretches than females. It might be imagined that women would take the dominant role in a conversation if they were of a higher social class than the male participants or if they rated higher on some other important criterion, such as expertise. However, male speaking rights prove to be strongly entrenched. A study designed to see whether a high level of expertise in a valued field would confer on women and men the same right to uninterrupted speech showed that it did not: female medical practitioners were interrupted by their male patients far more frequently than were male doctors (West 1984).

If in mixed-sex conversations female speakers are subject to more interruption than males, and if new points that they introduce into conversations are seldom taken up by other speakers, it is hardly surprising that people believe that women cannot sustain or develop arguments as well as men can! And they have not found it any easier to be read than to be heard. A brief but well-documented account of the difficulties faced by women wanting to get their work published is provided by Joanna Russ (1983) in a book entitled *How to Suppress Women's Writing*. She gives a description of subtle and less subtle attempts to silence women with respect to certain topics, literary forms, types of publication, and types of readership. Her ironic, condensed version of the processes makes them seem ridiculous, but her analysis of attitudes underlying them, and the examples taken from reviews, diaries, and letters by writers and publishers are combined in a serious and sobering account of centuries of prejudice and waste.

Many French feminists argue that languages have developed to meet the requirements of men, and do not easily carry women's meanings. They argue that it is primarily through writing that women must seek to break the linguistic bonds that have silenced or distorted their experience. Some feel that ultimately what should be sought is a new language, while others feel that it would suffice to disrupt current syntactic norms and to create new words and new rhythms which give expression to women's bodily experiences and to their ways of relating to other people (see Sellers 1991).

Unfortunately some sociolinguistic research on language and gender is not informed by adequate gender theory or theory of identity construction. In such cases both research design and interpretation of findings are flawed in one or both of the following ways: over-simplification of gender variation (on the assumption that there are universally only two categories—masculine and feminine—which exist in binary opposition to each other); failure to recognize that because gender always intersects with other socially salient factors it is unlikely to be the only factor accounting for observed features of male or female language use.

3. Development of Gender-related Differences in Language Use

The only differences that seem to have a primarily biological base are that first-language acquisition is often more rapid among girls than boys; that boys are more subject to stuttering and dyslexia than girls; and that men have deeper voices than women. Empirical research suggests that the other differences are socially learned (Phillips et al. 1987).

Late-twentieth-century developments in psychoanalytic theory in France locate the beginning of differentiation between male and female relations to language in their differing early psychosexual development. Regarded as crucial by some theorists are the processes of separation from the mother and of identification with the same-sex parent, processes vital to insertion into the symbolic order, which includes language.

How do communities transmit to children their gender-specific norms of appropriate language use? In the opening section of this article mention was made of overt teaching or publication of normative codes, but much of the learning happens more diffusely. Modeling on adults' verbal behavior, noting differences in adults' responses to the speech of boys and girls, participating in peer subcultures —all of these are part of acquiring communicative competence as a boy or girl.

Embryonic versions of characteristic adult male and female discourse patterns can be observed among children, for example adversarial and cooperative styles of organizing themselves in play situations. Some research has focused on how children learn these and other aspects of linguistic behavior. Another approach has been to do a longitudinal ethnographic study of the whole process of learning what it means to speak appropriately as boys or girls in a particular society, uncovering the interaction of a variety of linguistic and nonlinguistic factors that impinge on young children.

Shirley Brice Heath's account of a Carolina speech community suggests that the sex of the child affects verbal behavior toward him or her from very early on and shows young children responding to models of male and female language use in their family and in the community. For example, women are supposed to be able to 'fuss' (which means to bring family and community members' behavior into line) and very young girls are allowed to practice this on adults. Girls are also supposed to know and be able to elaborate a repertoire of intricate skipping and clapping rhymes which they perform as a group. Men and boys need to be able to engage in audacious and amusing verbal repartee, and to have an answer for challenges and reprimands from women or other men. The domain for fussing is domestic. For rhymes it is somewhat more public but it is an all-girls sphere, whereas male speech skills are for public display. Little boys learn to meet teasing and challenges with sharp verbal responses in the most public area in the neighborhood, namely the 'plaza' at the end of a cul-de-sac. Girls acquire their skills in more private places watched almost exclusively by girls, or as individuals on their own in front of a mirror—a striking manifestation of the contrast in domains considered proper for male and female speech (Heath 1983).

In many societies women have not been entitled to speak in the society's most prestigious public domains. (This is changing in some places but it is still relatively rare to find women preaching, participating equally in political decision-making forums, or being appointed judges.) Schools tend to extend the family and community's expectation that males will and should speak more in public and semipublic spheres. Observation of classroom interaction has identified factors which reflect and encourage this expectation, even when teachers are consciously trying not to give more speaking space to boys: teachers' gazes are more frequently directed toward boys, and boys are more successful than girls in catching teachers' attention by raising their hands faster or calling out. In class discussion groups girls often play the facilitative role in keeping conversation going while boys dominate topic development, patterns that continue into adult life. It is important to note that gender socialization is not over and done with by the end of adolsecence. As people's circumstances change or as they enter a new socially recognized age group they have to learn linguistic and other behavior that is regarded by their communities as gender-appropriate. (They may, of course, choose to disregard the norms in practice.) (See also *Discourse*; *Socialization*.)

4. The Encoding of Gender Differences in Language

The preceding discussions deal with gender differences in the use of language. But what of language as a system? What of the lexicon available to the speakers of a language to describe members of the two sexes—does it embody significant nonbiological differences in the encoding of 'masculine,' 'feminine,' and related terms? And if it does, is there any evidence that this has consequences for the way people are categorized and regarded in practice by themselves and by others? How deterministic is language?

Enormous heat has been generated in English-speaking speech communities by challenges to traditional terms of address for women and to the convention of using the masculine pronoun when referring to persons whose sex is unknown, or to a category including both sexes. In fact, a very common perception of language and gender research among those outside the field is that these are its central questions, if not its entire scope. This perception is inaccurate, of course, but, as gender-related terms of address and pronouns are so much in the public eye, they will be considered in some detail here.

Many societies use titles which indicate the sex of the person being referred to or addressed. A title may also encode age and, in the case of women, marital status. Surnames and titles are at issue in societies where the terms of address used for females conventionally indicate whether or not the woman has ever married whereas the term for men does not. This lack of parity has raised objections. There was a suggestion in the early twentieth century that another title be created for men so that references to them would also indicate marital status. It seems not to have found many supporters. There are practical problems with marriage-related titles: in spoken and written transactions in business and civil service where the female addressee's marital status is unknown, the possibility of using an inappropriate title is high. Style manuals published in the 1950s for use in the commercial world suggested the use of *Ms* as a title to be used for women irrespective of their marital status. In the 1970s and thereafter, the use of the title was supported by feminists who have a principled objection to women's marital status but not men's automatically being indicated, even in encounters where it is not relevant. They see the convention as one aspect of an ideology that always places women in terms of their relationship to men.

The patrilineal transmission of surname is another. It is common for a woman to lose the surname she had before marriage (usually her father's family name) and to take on that of her husband. The change in the formal term of address for a woman when she marries can be quite thorough: in some English-speaking speech communities it has been proper in formal circumstances to address or refer to a married woman as *Mrs* followed by husband's first name and his surname. For example, *Miss Anne Smith* would, after her marriage, be referred to as *Mrs Reginald Brown*. Some other societies have the convention that the woman keeps her surname and adds her husband's, while the surname of their children is a combination of one surname from each parent. However, the section of the surname that is transmitted from parent to child is the one that came from the father of each of the parents. Strong objections to these patrilineal traditions are made on the grounds that they contribute to processes in and beyond language which mark women as appendages to men, or which render them invisible. Such objections have led women to challenge naming conventions by taking their mothers' names or choosing surnames that come from neither family.

In many languages male forms are used for common gender. The word for 'man' is used in generalizations about human beings: 'the ascent of man,' 'man is the only creature with language.' The use of the masculine pronoun as the common one in languages which have masculine and feminine pronouns extends this practice. This produces sentences such as 'The medical advances made by man suggest that he will be able to extend average life expectancy for mankind even further' which are supposed to cover females as well as males. But do they? The pervasive habits of thought and speech which they embody have been said to create false and damaging impressions of the relative importance of men compared with women. Nonetheless they persist, supported by the argument that, as 'man' and 'he' are generic as well as sex-specific terms, when they are used in generalizations they include women. A second defense is that stylistic awkwardness results from attempts to be more inclusive in the use of pronouns when generalizing. One argument in favor of abandoning the use of masculine forms as generic is that they are no longer truly generic. The status of 'man' as a generic has been gradually eroded. Baron (1986) shows that from the eleventh to the thirteenth century 'man' could be used in contexts in which it would sound odd now. For example, Aelfric could write, in 1000 AD, 'His mother was a Christian named Elen, a very full-of-faith man, and extremely pious.' But by 1752 Hume does not assume that the reader would automatically take 'man' to include women, so, when he intends it to, he indicates this, writing: 'All men, male and female ....' By the 1990s the function of 'man' as a male referent interferes with its ability to serve as a generic—the following sentences sound contradictory: 'As a mammal, man gives birth live and suckles his young'; 'Anne Grey was the first man to row the full length of the Exwy River.' The substitution of 'person,' 'people,' 'human beings,' or 'humankind' for 'man' and 'mankind' is fairly easy to effect, but attempts to create new single-sex pronouns (e.g., 'thon') to replace the masculine as generic have not been successful. The most common practice is to use both, indicating in some way that they are alternatives, for example 'he or she,' 's/he.' The use of 'they' as a third person singular pronoun in cases of general reference is quite common in speech and is starting to be used in writing.

The lexicon of a language provides interesting evidence of gender perceptions. Historical studies have examined lexical entries for the same items over several centuries to show changes in meaning. Attention has also been given to whose meanings were represented, and who the lexicographers were—women or men. Men overwhelmingly outnumber women in this field. There are feminists who claim that men control language but there are also feminists who contest this (see Cameron 1985). A long line of women writers have spoken of their sense that the languages in which they were producing poetry or fiction did not have words to express what they regarded as experiences peculiar to women. Various contemporary French feminists also claim that there are lexical gaps which result in the silencing or distortion of women's meanings. They link the existence of these gaps to fundamental differences in the construction of male and female sexuality.

Miller and Swift's *Words and Women*, and Baron's *Grammar and Gender* give detailed historical accounts of the encoding of gender perceptions in English. Centuries of linguistic evidence that male and female are not simply perceived as different but equal prompts Baron to say, in the introduction to his text, that his compilation of opinions about women and language 'presents what can be viewed as a depressing litany of insults' (1986: 9).

A history of changes in the meanings and forms of words relating to women and men can show something of changing societal realities and perceptions. Agent nouns are a particularly interesting set. In Old English suffixes indicated the sex of the referent: 'er(e)' was the male suffix and 'ster(e)' the female suffix. Words referring to those who baked, spun, and sewed were *baxter, spinster*, and *seamster* as this work was done by women. When men moved into these occupations the word did not always change its form to indicate this: *seamster* could be used for anyone who sewed, male or female. If, however, men became dominant in a formerly female occupation they often took over the job's common designation and new terms were coined to refer to women still in these occupations, e.g., *seamstress*.

Miller and Swift claim that this pattern is one manifestation of the prevailing tendency to regard the referent as male unless indicated otherwise. ('Marking' is the technical term for 'indicating otherwise'—showing that one member of an oppositional pair is restricted in ways that the other is not.) In English, terms that can refer to both sexes are almost always the terms that are used to refer to males, for example *actor, author*. In contrast, terms that are morphologically marked as referring to females (such as *actress, authoress*) are never applied to males. There are a few exceptions to the male-as-norm rule. For example, *nurse* is taken to be female unless indicated otherwise by the use of the prefix 'male-,' giving *male-nurse*. As more men move into the nursing profession this prefix may well drop away.

Markedness is of interest to people concerned with the role of language in maintaining dominant societal perceptions, for several reasons. They argue that, as long as words referring to women and not to men have to be marked for gender, the belief will persist that it is exceptional for women to be in these positions. As long as it is male terms that are also the common gender terms, women's presence will tend to be obscured, as it is by the use of 'man' and 'he' as generics.

Where there are gender-distinct terms, there is not necessarily parity between them. An examination of some word pairs with a common stem and a gender suffix shows that there is a tendency for the word carrying the female suffix to be not only different from but also unequal to its male counterpart, the female form carrying a connotation of relative triviality. For this reason a woman at the head of a bank or a state would not use the form *manageress* or *governess* to refer to herself—the fields of control associated with the female terms are less significant than those associated with the terms *manager* and *governor*. A more explicit reductiveness is manifest in terms that are simultaneously marked by their suffix as female and diminutive, for example, *majorette*.

Comparisons of word pairs reveal not only an association between diminished importance and femaleness, but also what Miller and Swift refer to as 'semantic polarization' and the pejoration of words referring to women. Paired words that might be assumed to contrast with each other only in sex of referent in fact contrast in other ways too, ways that are derogatory to women. The fields of meaning become polarized so that there is little common semantic ground left in the sense in which they are frequently used. For example, the element of control originally implied in the terms *master* and *mistress* is no longer central to both. Nowadays the domain of control associated with *mistress* would probably not extend beyond the activities of her dog (unless she were a *sportsmistress* or a *headmistress* in which case she would have charge of children). In contrast, *master* has retained its association with control in a range of important fields.

As has happened with *mistress*, pejoration of the female term occurs largely through frequent linkages with implications of sexual promiscuity. As examples, consider the pairs *master/mistress, knight/dame, sir/madam*—none of the male terms but all of the female counterparts have connotations of illicit sexual activity for financial gain. In themselves these examples might seem simply to be interesting, but it is argued that they indicate a problematic general tendency to see women but not men primarily as objects of sexual attention, a tendency that makes it difficult for other aspects of women's being to emerge. Studies of insults in several languages provide further evidence of this association: by far the most common form of insult, whether directed at males or females, is a derogatory reference to female sexual promiscuity.

5. Conclusion

The material presented above has shown that there are gender-related differences in the use of language by, to, and about males and females. In shaping them, gender may be neither the only nor the overriding factor. Where males and females are treated differently in language, it is seldom a case of separate but equal: the inequality is an extension of the prevailing power-relations between them in nonlinguistic fields. There is evidence, barely touched on here, of the psychological, social, and material consequences of gender discrimination through language, consequences which can be serious, even if each particular instance of discrimination seems minor. Of course, language can be and has been used to identify and challenge harmful discrimination and the linguistic forms in which it is manifested, and to suggest alternative dispensations and forms. Whether such changes of form are desirable is debatable: they could serve to mask underlying and enduring sexism. On the other hand, by going against the grain, the alternative forms could alert people to unconscious habits of mind and behavior which, once identified and understood, might be willingly rejected.

See also: Gay Language; Gender, Education and Language.

Bibliography

Baron D 1986 *Grammar and Gender*. Yale University Press, New Haven, CT
Cameron D 1985 *Feminism and Linguistic Theory*. Macmillan, London
Cameron D 1996 The language-gender interface: Challenging co-optation. In: Bergvall V L, Bing J M, Freed A F (eds.) *Rethinking Language and Gender Research: Theory and Practice*. Longman, London
Cheshire J 1982 *Variation in an English Dialect*. Cambridge University Press, Cambridge, UK
Coates J 1993 *Women, Men and Language*, 2nd edn. Longman, London
Coates J, Cameron D (eds.) 1988 *Women in their Speech Communities*. Longman, London
Gal S 1978 'Peasant men can't get wives': Language change and sex roles in a bilingual community. *Language in Society* 7: 1–16
Graddol D, Swann J 1989 *Gender Voices*. Basil Blackwell, Oxford, UK
Heath S B 1983 *Ways with Words: Language, Life and Work in Communities and Classrooms*. Cambridge University Press, Cambridge, UK
Johnson S, Meinhof U H (eds.) 1997 *Language and Masculinity*, Blackwell, Oxford, UK
Kulick D 2000 Gay and lesbian language. *Annual Review of Anthropology* 29: 243–85
Labov W 1972 The study of language in its social context. In: Giglioli P P (ed.) *Language and Social Context*. Penguin, Harmondsworth, UK
Lakoff R 1975 *Language and Woman's Place*. Harper and Row, New York
Miller C, Swift K 1976 *Words and Women: Language and the Sexes*. Penguin, Harmondsworth, UK
Milroy L 1980 *Language and Social Networks*. Basil Blackwell, Oxford, UK
Nichols P C 1983 Linguistic options and choices for black women in the rural south. In: Thorne B et al. (eds.) *Language, Gender and Society*. Newbury House, Rowley, MA
Philips S U, Steele S, Tanz C (eds.) 1987 *Language, Gender and Sex in Comparative Perspective*. Cambridge University Press, Cambridge, UK
Romaine S 1999 *Communicating Gender*. Erlbaum, Mahwah, NJ
Russ J 1983 *How to Suppress Women's Writing*. Women's Press, London
Sattel J W 1983 Men, inexpressiveness and power. In: Thorne B et al. (eds.) *Language, Gender and Society*. Newbury House, Rowley, MA
Sellers S 1991 *Language and Sexual Difference: Feminist Writing in France*. Macmillan, London
Steedman C, Urwin C, Walkerdine V (eds.) 1983 *Language, Gender and Childhood*. Routledge and Kegan Paul, London
Thorne B, Kramarae C, Henley N (eds.) 1983 *Language, Gender and Society*. Newbury House, Rowley, MA
Trudgill P 1974 *The Social Differentiation of Speech in Norwich*. Cambridge University Press, Cambridge, UK
Vetterling-Braggin M 1981 *Sexist Language: A Modern Philosophical Analysis*. Littlefield, Adams and Co., Lanham, MD
West C 1984 When the doctor is a 'lady': Power, status and gender in physician–patient encounters. *Symbolic Interaction* 7: 87–106
Zimmerman D, West C 1975 Sex roles, interruptions and silences in conversation. In: Thorne B et al. (eds.) *Language, Gender and Society*. Newbury House, Rowley, MA

Language Change and Language Acquisition
E. L. Bavin

Historical linguistics has been concerned mainly with changes that have occurred within languages and language families in the course of their development. However, in order to understand why and how languages change, there is a need to examine the motivation for change as well as the paths of development. For this reason, child language acquisition (see *Child Language: An Overview*), social variation (see *Sociolinguistic Variation*), and the development of pidgins and creoles (see *Pidgins and Creoles: An Overview*) are related topics. They all examine aspects of variation and change. Language acquisition deals with change in the developing grammar of the individual, while the other two topics examine change within the language system. While there are parallels between changes observed in the history of languages and innovations that a child produces in the course of acquiring a language, the exact relationship between the changes for the individual learner and for the system as a whole is not yet clearly understood.

1. The Child as the Source of Change

Both nineteenth-century and present-day linguists have viewed the child as the major source of change. For example, at the beginning of the twentieth century Grammont pointed out that features of child language reflected the types of historical changes found in languages of the world. Later, particularly in the field of generative phonology, scholars suggested that imperfect learning results as the child acquires the language and constructs a grammar. Halle argued that the child constructs a grammar by induction, and thus may not arrive at a grammar which is identical to the adult's, while Kiparsky discussed sound change as the result of simplification and imperfect learning by the child. Thus one view of language change is that the source is to be found in the process of language acquisition.

Some changes as the result of imperfect learning are plausible. Marked structures in the input language (that is, the language to which the child is exposed) may lead to reanalysis by the child. While the grammar that the child acquires may differ from the model provided, the differences may be minor so that mutual comprehensibility is maintained. However, while observable differences might be assumed to be minor, they may represent larger differences in the abstract grammar of the child. That is, the child may have reanalyzed the linguistic input and thus internalized a grammar that differs from that of the adult. It can be assumed that the language input to the child must provide some impetus for reanalysis by the child. If the reanalysis involves a word order change, the input language would need to have some constructions with a marked word order, that is, a word order that is different from the basic order. Children acquiring the language will extend the contexts for the marked word order from generation to generation, and thus the change is gradually effected, with observable differences between the adult and child productions being minor at each stage. The marked order would gradually become the basic order.

2. Language Change: Stampe's View of Natural Rules

Stampe's view of the acquisition of a sound system is that there are certain phonetic processes which reflect innate properties of the human speech tract. When a child acquires a language there must be suppression of some of these 'natural' processes, those to be suppressed depending on the specific language. Stampe argues that sound changes will occur in a language if the child fails to suppress a relevant process for the language being acquired. While some features of sound change are also features of child language, notably the devoicing of word final consonants and the simplification of consonant clusters, it is not possible to draw parallels between all phonological processes in child language and language change. For example, a young child will often produce a stop in a fricative context (e.g., [tu] for 'shoe'), but in time the child will suppress this substitution. In the history of languages, the substitution of a stop for a fricative (consonant strengthening) is far less common as a process of change than consonant weakening, the replacement of a stop by a fricative (see *Sound Change*).

Other changes cannot be attributed to children failing to suppress natural rules. For example, while many languages lose word final syllables over time, even though this may result in the loss of grammatical information as with the loss of inflections in the history of English, young children often drop the initial syllables of words in their early attempts to pronounce the words of their language. Syllable reduction in child speech is often related to stress. Since an unstressed syllable is perceptually less salient than a stressed syllable, a child will often produce the part of the word that is stressed, leaving out the unstressed syllables. For example, English-speaking children may produce *nana* for 'banana' and *puter* for 'computer.' A Greek child may produce *ate* for *elate* 'come Plural.' Pye reports that young children acquiring K'iche' Maya first produce the final syllable of a word, that is, the stressed syllable. For example, the form *loh* is produced for the adult expression *kawiloh* 'I like it' with *loh* a stressed syllable consisting of the final morpheme (an inflection) and the final consonant of the preceding one. Although Czech has word stress on initial syllables, these syllables are often dropped in young children's speech. What is perceptually salient to a child, then, is the end of the word or utterance or a stressed syllable.

Another example of the problems raised in trying to match children's forms with diachronic change relates to vowel and consonant harmony, both of which should be natural processes following Stampe. Both are found in children's speech in languages, which do not regularly utilize vowel or consonant harmony. For example, the form *tity* may be heard for 'kitty' from an English-speaking child, and *esese* for *epese* 'it fell' from a Greek child. Warlpiri children regularly use *Lalala* for the name *Nangala*; the language uses vowel harmony but not consonant harmony. The assimilation processes may be reflected in only a few words for each child. In those languages which do utilize vowel harmony processes (e.g., Turkish, Hungarian, and Warlpiri), children seem to have no problem with acquiring the rules. This supports the view that vowel harmony is a 'natural' process, but since there are few reported examples of vowel or consonant harmony developing in a language over time, these child language modifications do not parallel diachronic changes in language. There is likely to be dissimilation diachronically, not assimilation or harmony.

A feature of child language is reduction in consonant clusters. For example, a Greek child may produce *vato* for *val' to* 'put it' and *klito* for *klis' to* 'close it' while an English-speaking child may produce *poon* 'spoon' and a Warlpiri child *naka* for *nyangka* 'look.' Consonant clusters may develop in languages (e.g., homorganic oral–nasal clusters), but there are also examples of clusters being broken up with epenthetic vowels, and of nasals being lost from clusters (e.g., Gurrinji). Such examples do suggest similarities between child language and language change. Overall, however, there is no clear correlation between processes in language change and the suggested 'natural' phonological processes noted in the early stages of language acquisition.

3. Innovations in Child Language

3.1 Lexical and Syntactic Innovations

Children create and produce new forms in the stages of acquiring a language; these forms may be lexical, syntactic, or morphological. They may be the result of missegmentations, as when an English-speaking child treats *behave* as two words on analogy with *be good*, or a French-speaking child treats *l'avion* as two words (*la vion*). Such missegmentations are evident in the history of languages. Children produce novel items to fill lexical gaps, when they do not know a word for a concept they wish to express. These lexical innovations are not arbitrary; rather they are formed following principles of word formation that are available in the language being acquired (Clark and Clark 1979, Clark 1982). For example, the innovation *to broom* for 'to sweep' follows the principle that verbs can be derived from nouns in English (cf. 'to shelve something'). A similar denominalization is noted in a German child's use of *leitern* for 'to ladder' when talking about using a ladder for climbing (Clark 1982: 404). In Warlpiri *ngapa-kurlangu* 'water-belonging' was used by one child to refer to a fish, and this follows a productive means for creating new words in the language. Such child innovations are generally preempted by the conventional words when the child perceives a mismatch between the innovation and the forms used by others. It is clear that adults also coin new words and functions for words as the need arises, and these innovations follow the same principles used by the children; that is, they follow the word formation patterns that exist in the language. While the creations may be short-lived, some may be adopted into the language.

Children's language also reveals syntactic innovations. For example, structures with double tense marking are sometimes heard from young English-speaking children, with both auxiliary and main verb marked. Bowerman, in particular, has illustrated overgeneralizations with dative alternation, as in *Push me the box* (cf. 'Give me the box') and with noncausative verbs, as with *Don't fall me down* (cf. 'Don't push me down').

These innovations indicate that the child is making hypotheses about the language system being acquired; they also reflect a lack of knowledge on the part of the child about the established norms. The assumptions made by the child when segmenting a string of words into meaningful units, or when determining form–meaning correspondences, or when generalizing about a particular structure do not necessarily lead to the right conclusions, and thus there is a mismatch between the adult and child forms. If the innovations persist, there has been 'imperfect learning' of the system. However, many of the innovations *are* short-lived and get dropped from the child's grammar as it gradually approximates more closely that of the adult. Thus there is a serious problem in suggesting that change originates in child forms.

3.2 Morphological Leveling

There are many examples of morphophonemic alternations in paradigms being leveled diachronically, with a semantically unmarked form being used as the basis for the new forms. For example, Bybee (1985) illustrates that in Romance languages the third person stem has often been generalized to other persons. The semantically unmarked forms in a paradigm are generally the least marked morphologically, and for some languages these are the forms that children acquire first. They are also frequently the forms used by children as the basis for innovations. In the process of acquiring a verb paradigm a child will analyze an unmarked stem as the formal expression of a basic semantic notion, and will then add to the stem to show additional semantic components, for example, tense or number or person. The form of the addition will be selected from what is available in the input data. Patterns that apply over a range of items are reinforced and so will be more readily applied to new items; that is, they will be more productive if more frequent.

An example of paradigm regularization is noted in the Warlpiri child's construction of the pronominal clitics which mark the person and number of the subject and object arguments. The established form first person singular subject is *-rna*. The dual form is *-rlijarra* and the plural *-rnalu*. A creation by the children is the use of *rnapala* for dual. The form *rna* has been selected as the person form throughout, with an added morpheme to mark number; *lu* is the third person plural subject marker, and *pala* is the third person dual subject marker. The second person forms *npa, npapala* and *npalu* reinforce the choice in the first person of one morpheme for person (*rna*) and one for dual (*pala*).

The process of leveling irregularities in a paradigm indicates a general preference for one form–one meaning, that is, semantic transparency. When several forms seem to be available for marking a similar semantic notion, the child may select one of the allomorphs and overgeneralize by applying it to all instances. For example, a Russian child overgeneralizes the feminine gender marker to other genders, and a Warlpiri child overgeneralizes the form of the ergative case used by adults on two syllable words to longer words. The examples all indicate that the child may attribute a meaning (function) to a form that is not identical to the adult's.

4. Similarities Between Child and Adult Innovations

An area in which overgeneralizations are noted in English child language is in the use of the regular past tense form for irregular verbs. Thus the form *bended* might be used for 'bent' and *thinked* for 'thought.' Bybee and Slobin (1982) studied documented historical changes in the past forms of English verbs and compared these with the innovations made by *both* children and adults when producing past tense forms of irregular verbs. They identified three common areas, one being that the verbs most frequently regularized were the least frequent ones. This supports other findings that infrequent items are the most susceptible to change by analogical leveling, while frequent irregular items are more resistant to change. Infrequent items are less familiar, and thus the established norms are less likely to be well known.

Bybee and Slobin also found that the verbs which were regularized most frequently by the children and adults were those which end in /d/ and form their past by changing the final consonant to /t/. For example, instead of *bent* the form **bended* would be produced. It is of interest that a number of verbs which end in /d/ have already regularized in English. For example, the past form of *blend*, is now *blended*, not **blent*. A third finding was that some speakers used innovations for the past tense forms of those verbs which show vowel alternation, verbs such as *ring, sing*, and *swim*. About half of the adult innovations were in the choice of the vowel for the past tense for verbs in this class. For example, *shrunk* (the past participle) was used as the past form of *shrink*. This type of innovation accounted for most of the innovations from the children. This suggests that the leveling of the distinction between the past participle and past forms for verbs in the class is increasing. Historically, the distinction has already been lost for some verbs. Thus a historical trend is continuing, with young children propagating the changes. A few of the innovations used in the study parallel the historical trend of adding new verbs to the vowel-change class (e.g., **brung* as the past for *brought*). The verbs *ring, dig, sing*, and *fling* are some of those that have been added to this class since the Old English period. These verbs now all form their past by a vowel change.

That children are not the only instigators and perpetrators of morphophonemic change is clear from the fact that the older children and adults were more likely to add a regular past suffix to verbs ending in /t/ that do not change to form the past tense than were the youngest children tested (e.g., **hitted* for 'hit'). Being aware that the form already contains phonetic material of the past affix, the youngest children avoided 'double' marking. This is a strategy found in applying plural marking as well; young children at first avoid adding the plural affix to nouns that already end in /s/ or /z/, although they add the appropriate affix for nouns ending in other consonants. However, the older subjects showed a preference for marking the past tense category rather than using zero marking, another example of a preference for semantic transparency.

5. The Propagators of Change

There are some similarities between the innovations made by a child in the course of language acquisition and historical changes in languages, but as indicated above, this does not imply that the change originates in the process of language acquisition. In order for a language to change, the innovations must be maintained and adopted into the system. Adults may also innovate, as they revise and adapt the system they have acquired as children.

A major problem with attributing the cause of change to the innovations made by the child is the need to explain why only certain innovations are retained, and why they are adopted in a certain period in the history of a language and not some other. Another problem is that children over-generalize on frequent words, but infrequent words are the most susceptible to change diachronically. For example, for infrequent English words which end in /f/, the regular plural /s/ is now used as in *safes*, and *reefs*, but frequent words retain the old plural /v/ + /z/, as in *wives* and *handkerchieves*. Irregular items must be rote learned, but for an infrequent irregular item, which is likely to be a late acquisition anyway, there is more likelihood that an adult will not remember the exceptional form. This accounts for the tendency for adults to regularize, as noted in the regularized forms produced by the adults in the

Bybee and Slobin study. So change may be motivated by frequency, with older children and adults being the propagators of change.

The 'imperfect learning' view assumes that the child is receiving traditional or standard forms and structures in the input, and that there is no variation, so the child is modifying the system. However, the child may be exposed to forms that already show some variation from the assumed norms. That is, both psycholinguistic and sociolinguistic factors must be considered in studies of language change. Labov has argued that the locus for change is later than early childhood; the peer group is the medium through which change is perpetuated (see *Sociolinguistics and Language Change*; *Sociolinguistic Variation*). Young adults adopt forms used by their peers following social pressure to conform. The view suggests that the source of change must be in the language already as a variable form, and the young child is exposed to the variations in the course of acquisition.

Age-graded studies on variation of forms show a pyramid structure; that is, the oldest people use the most traditional forms, some variation is noted in the middle age groups, and more variation in the youngest. As early as 1905, Gauchat, investigating phonological variables in a Swiss village, documented such a pattern. The implication is that one age group provides the main input for the next, so that variations at one age level will become more widespread with the next. While such patterns indicate a change in progress in the language, one needs to be sure that the young speakers will not adopt the forms used by the older people as they themselves grow older, through formal education or other social pressure.

6. Conclusion

There is some relationship between the acquisition process and language change. For example, it is clear that forms that are acquired late are the most susceptible to loss or change (e.g., the relative clause in Turkish). Rules will be susceptible to loss if they are inconsistent with typological features of the language. In addition, as a language is passed from generation to generation, there may be perceptual reinterpretations by the child as well as articulatory substitutions, both vehicles for change.

Semantic change may also be related to the acquisition process. For example, there are many examples from young children's speech to suggest that the form–meaning (or function) mapping for the child is not the same as for the adult. A word may be used with a wider meaning than for the adult (overextension), or narrower (underextension). Diachronically, word meanings change in both directions. If the early meanings attributed to a form by the child are perpetuated, change will result. However, semantic reanalysis is gradual. As the late-twentieth-century research on grammaticalization reveals, lexical items change gradually in both meaning and form to develop into grammatical morphemes.

Frequently there are differences between the young child and adult meaning for a grammatical morpheme. Many cross-linguistic reports indicate that when a child first uses tense morphology the meaning for the forms is aspectual not temporal, since the forms encode information about the nature of the event (e.g., whether completed or ongoing) rather than information about the temporal location of the event (Slobin 1985). The saliency of aspect over tense for the young child as parallels in language history in that aspect markers frequently develop into tense markers. However, this developmental change only parallels diachronic change; it does not motivate it.

The preference for one form–one function in child language is illustrated in analogical leveling and in the use of periphrastic causatives over lexical causatives; for these features of child language there are historical parallels, but this does not imply a causal link. Innovations must be perpetuated for change to take place. The preference for overt forms for semantic functions is reflected in a child's preference to use pronouns in a pro-drop language where they are not required in the adult system, as in Italian. But there is no evidence that the use of overt pronouns by the child is indicative of a change in the language.

Overall, there are problems with the view that all children's 'errors' (or innovations) survive as diachronic changes. Children's leveling of irregularities in morphological paradigms may survive, as many subtle differences in the interpretations of words and grammatical morphemes, and extensions in the contexts for variable structures. Thus some change may be viewed as a consequence of the acquisition process.

However, adults are also innovators. The motivation for innovations from adults is not necessarily the same as for children. While the child is hampered by memory limitations and lack of muscular control (Aitchison 1991), the adult is influenced by the demands of the communicative situation. Slobin (1977) has argued that the needs for the speaker to be quick yet expressive constrain the direction of change. A consequence of being quick leads to phonological attrition which may affect the morphemes in a language, with a resulting reduction in the functional load of a morpheme; another part of the grammar picks up the function to fulfill the need to be expressive. Whether changes are initiated in the acquisition process or by the adult, they may be slowed down or stopped; changes must be tolerated by the speech community if they are to persist. Since changes must be institutionalized if they are to affect a language's history, it must be assumed that the changes are not the result of idiosyncratic learning by a child, but reflect some general processing and communicative principles that influence many speakers in the language community.

See also: Syntactic Change; Sociolinguistics and Language Change; Sound Change.

Bibliography

Aitchison J 1991 *Language Change: Progress or Decay?*, 2nd edn. Cambridge University Press, Cambridge, UK
Baron N S 1977 *Language Acquisition and Historical Change*. North Holland, Amsterdam
Bybee Hooper J 1979 Child morphology and morphophonemic change. *Linguistics* **17**: 21–50
Bybee J L 1985 *Morphology: A Study of the Relation Between Form and Meaning*. Benjamins, Amsterdam
Bybee J L, Slobin D I 1982 Rules and schema in the development and use of the English past tense. *Language* **58**: 265–89
Clark E V 1982 The young word maker. In: Wanner E, Gleitman L (eds.) *Language Acquisition: The State of the Art*. Cambridge University Press, Cambridge, UK
Clark E V, Clark H H 1979 When nouns surface as verbs. *Language* **55**: 767–811
Drachman G 1978 Child language and language change: A conjecture and some refutations. In: Fisiak J (ed.) *Recent Developments in Historical Phonology*. Mouton, The Hague
Romaine S 1989 The role of children in linguistic change. In: Breivik L E, Jahr E H (eds.) *Language Change: Contributions to the Study of its Causes*. Mouton de Gruyter, Berlin
Slobin D I 1977 Language change in childhood and history. In: Macnamara J (ed.) *Language Learning and Thought*. Academic Press, New York
Slobin D I 1985 *The Crosslinguistic Study of Language Acquisition*. Erlbaum, Hillsdale, NJ

Maps: Dialect and Language
J. M. Kirk

1. Introduction

Three broad classes of geographically and demographically distributed information and interpretations are represented by linguistic maps:
(a) *languages* (often in contrast, or in contact, with other languages);
(b) *dialects* (with some externally-conditioned expectation about geographical distribution or borders, which may be known or fixed at the outset);
(c) *geolects* (i.e., linguistic or spatial variation, without any externally conditioned geographical expectation or borders, which may be variable, mapping what the data reveal).

Maps used to represent folk or popular perceptions about dialect areal distribution as in Preston (1989) are not dealt with here.

As the new millennium begins, linguistic maps are undergoing a silent revolution. Over traditional paper copy bound in atlases, the web resources of the Internet medium provide unprecedented opportunities for display, for multimedia interaction, for interpretation, as well as for distribution. Any browser search on key terms such as 'linguistic geography,' 'linguistic atlas,' or 'linguistic map' or their equivalent in international languages of scholarship such as German (*'Sprachgeographie', 'Sprachatlas,'* or *'Sprachkarte'*) or French (*'geographie linguistique', 'atlas linguistique'* or *'carte linguistique'*) already yields hundreds of responses. Maps in full color, databases, and sound files—some compiled in response to the new medium, others digitized from earlier resources—may be downloaded in an instant, regardless of language or dialect, or of place of origin or processing, and are available to end-users conveniently and inexpensively like never before, removing the need for costly publications or for visits to archives or libraries. Wenker's *Deutscher Sprachatlas* is now available at *www.uni-marburg.de/dsa/*; Maurmann's *Karte der Deutschen Mundarten*, reproduced in its original colors, is to be found at *www.heimatvest.de/sprachkarte.htm*. The benefits of color are well demonstrated in Comrie et al. (1996), Goebl (2000), (Graddol (1981)), König (1982), Kunze (1998), Viereck, Viereck and Ramisch (in press).

2. Languages

Maps are an inextricable part of the presentation of information about the number of languages in the world (Crystal 1997, Moseley and Asher 1993). Wurm (1996) and the ethnologue website (*http://www.sil.org/ethnologue/*) show the location of languages which are dying. Maps in Bailey and Görlach 1982 and Crystal 1995 deal with the global spread of certain languages and the increasing globalization of English, especially in countries where it is an official, second-official, or semi-official language, or where its foreign language status is rapidly changing to second language status (Graddol 1997, Hartmann 1996). Such language maps can also indicate types and degrees of societal bilingualism and multilingualism, as in Ryckeboer (2000) on the use of French and

Dutch on the French-Belgian border. Language maps are based on a combination of knowledge of a particular area and fieldwork, as in Breton (1997), Masica (1976), and Wurm et al. (1996) for South-East Asia, or Hock (1986) for Africa, Europe, and Asia. Many such regional language maps are now on the Internet: 'Linguistic Map of Timor Island' at *rspas.anu.edu/linguistics/UabMeto/map.html*, 'Linguistic Map of India' at *www.askasia.org/image/maps/india4.htm*, or linguistic maps of East Africa at *www.urich.edu/~kkasongo/LinguisticMap.htm*. Ethnolinguistic maps of post-war Europe are at *www.multimedia.calpoly. edu/libarts/mriedlsp/History 315/map3.html*, or of the Caucasus Region at *www. geocities. com/Athens/Parthenon/9860/etnokau.jpg*.

3. History of Dialect Maps

Although an awareness of geographically-conditioned linguistic variation within a language has existed for centuries, maps with a linguistic content have existed only since the early nineteenth century (the first appear to be by J. A. Schmeller and date from 1821; the first map of English appears to be by Prince L. L. Bonaparte in 1876). Such early maps dealt primarily with sounds or words and, until recently, linguistic maps have continued to adopt an individual, item-centered approach, usually showing the reflexes of an older phoneme or the responses to a questionnaire item. They are typified in the *Deutscher Wortatlas*, the *Sprachatlas der deutschen Schweiz*, the *Atlas linguistique de la France*, the *Linguistic Atlas of England*, and the *Linguistic Atlas of New England*. From the outset, there was always an implicit belief that the mapping of sounds or words would assist with an identification of dialect areas, where there would be some correlation between geography and language. There have still been few attempts to do this systematically, or to consider the individual items in groups, or to interpret or to explain or to criticize existing work. Davis (2000) summarizes recent critical work on American English. Geolinguistic maps, which simply map what the data reveal, without regard to physical, geographical, or social factors, are only emerging; in the future, newspaper corpora or, on a larger scale, the national components of the International Corpus of English may also be used. The earliest nineteenth-century maps primarily reveal a concern that the fieldwork upon which they were based was presented with authenticity and faithfulness (hence the popularity of 'documentary maps'). These early maps challenged the prevailing philological doctrine held by the neogrammarians that sound laws knew no exceptions by demonstrating that a study of geographical variation within a language could help to explain historical development for (as expressed by Gilliéson) 'each word has its own story.' The purpose of such maps was the expression of a two-dimensional statement about linguistic variation which fused, item-by-item, geography with history, and space with time, as shown in Kirk (1985).

Since the 1960s, and increasingly in line with parallel developments in cognate subjects, linguistic maps have been subjected to numerous innovations in cartographical style. Dissatisfaction with traditional methods has led for some time to the grouping together of items on a single map in a much stronger effort to use qualitative data for the establishment of dialect areas, as in the Collective Maps of the *Atlas of English Sounds*. The flourishing of structural linguistics subsequently led to the demonstration that linguistic maps could also be concerned with the mapping of geographically-differentiated linguistic systems and structures, as in Anderson (1987) and Moulton (1960). Recent maps at *www.upenn.edu/phono_atlas/maps/* show the relationship between production and perception as between distinct or merged minimal pairs, such as *Dawn/Don* or *Mary/merry* in American English. The impact of sociolinguistics has led to a reflection of social dimensions in survey maps as in the *Linguistic Atlas of the Gulf States*, on which see also Montgomery and Nunnally 1998.

At the same time, maps began to present quantitative analyses and interpretations of the invariably copious data made available by national and regional linguistic surveys. Quantitative approaches have developed in two ways: Davis (1990) and Kretzschmar (1997) apply statistical tests to dialect data; and Goebl (1993, 2000), and Schiltz (1996, 1997) developed dialect-specific tests (generally known as 'dialectometrical tests') including several different measures of 'distance.' These two approaches have culminated in the application of dual and multi-dimensional scaling (see below). Moreover, Bailey et al. (1993), Kretzschmar and Schneider (1996), Trudgill (1983), and Wikle (1997) show how patterns of sociolinguistic variation can be explained by invoking techniques of cultural geography such as diffusion studies and spatial ratios.

All of these approaches have benefited from two concurrent developments during the 1990s:

(a) The resources and capacities of desktop microcomputers now capable of massive data storage, complicated analysis, sophisticated and innovatory graphic displays, and scope for active and instantaneous interfacing.
(b) The world-wide-web for remote accessibility, interactivity, and distribution.

Constant upgrades in bandwidth and networking and huge increases in capacity and speed in desktop processing have led in turn to innovations in, and the sophistication of cartographical techniques.

Nevertheless, publication in book/paper format is likely to continue in the meantime; especially as long-running projects reach fruition. *The Computer*

Developed Linguistic Atlas of England was published in two large volumes in 1991 and 1997; the *Survey of the Gaelic Dialects of Scotland* was published in four volumes in 1994 and 1997; the *Atlas Linguarum Europae* (website at *www.uni-bamberg.de/~ba4es1/ ale-d.html*) published fascicle 5 in 1997; the *Atlant linguitisch dl ladin dolomitich y di dialec vejins* was published in four volumes of maps and three volumes of indices in 1998. Although computer-generating techniques were used in each of these cases and in probably all cases in the future, computer-generated means have created their own paradigm on CD and CD-ROM, led by Bauer et al. (1999–2000), *ALD I-CD: 98 Tonproben zum ALD I/CD-ALD I: 98 campioni fonici per l'ALD I.*, Klemola (in press) for the *Survey of English Dialects*, and Labov et al. in press, developed from their webmaps at *www.ling. upenn.edu/phono_atlas/atlas_chapters/* (see *The Atlas of North American English: Methods and Findings*).

The future of map publication rests beyond any doubt with the Internet, as shown by the Internet maps of the Telsur [Telephone Survey] Project on American English at *www.ling.upenn.edu/phono_atlas/ maps/* (as exemplified in Map 1) and the Linguistic Atlas of Dolomitic Ladinian and Neighboring Dialects (ALD) at *www.sbg.ac.at/rom/people/proj/ald/*, where users are able to interact live and on-line with a database and, with the aid of appropriate retrieval and mapping software, produce their own maps dynamically, upon request, in seconds. Soundfiles of regional or local accents are increasing on the web: see *www.uni-marburg.de/dsa/* for German, or *us.*
english.uga.edu for American English. Haimerl (1997, 1998) discuss his new program for sound digitization and web display; Pennisi (1995) discusses the possibility of web-based audio-*visual* maps.

Dialectologists have traditionally sought to present survey data as clearly, authentically, and as uninterpreted as possible. There are notable exceptions such the *Linguistic Atlas of England*, idiosyncratically interpreted by Orton, or the *Linguistic Atlas of Scotland* (Vol. 3), in which it is not possible to reconstruct either the actual realizations or the incidence of particular phonemes but only the incidence of polyphonemes, but see Johnston (2000) for guidance. From language or dialect 'atlas maps,' the end product of fieldwork-based survey investigations, maps may be 'derived' by phonologists, syntacticians (cf. Gerritsen 1991), lexicographers, or others, for their own specialist purposes.

In these ways, the role and function of linguistic maps has plainly shifted from the original demonstration of the distribution of individual linguistic items (what is specifically known as *linguistic geography*, more specifically *word geography*, and more widely *dialectology*) to the use of geography to explain inherent linguistic variation (what is specifically known as *geographical linguistics* or *geolinguistics*). The qualitative approach of historically-oriented, paradigm-based, item-centered, 'traditional' *dialectology* has now become complemented, 100 years later, with the quantitative approach of sociolinguistics, variation theory, and now *geolinguistics*. Geolinguistics seeks to relate linguistic

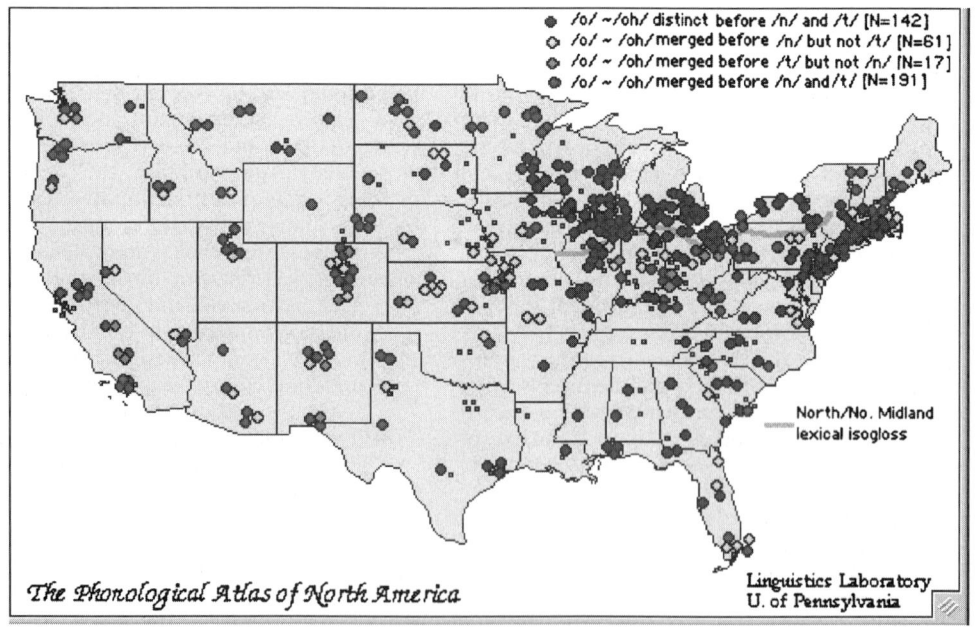

Map 1. /o/~/oh/ merger in North American English.

variables and their underlying systems not only with the implicit social characteristics of the speaker's identity (the approach of sociolinguistics) but also with any geographical factors (in the widest possible sense of 'geographical') which might contribute to that distribution and correlation of identity. While more complex than internally-focused historical or comparative philology, the geolinguistic approach is also more realistic, for it correlates qualitative and quantitative analyses of data with qualitative and quantitative analyses of external conditioning factors. The journal *Language Variation and Change* encourages geolinguistic approaches to dialect data (as in the two dialect surveys of Oklahoma and Texas by Bailey et al. (1991, 1993) or in a study of diffusion along the US-Canada border by Boberg 2000). This growing distinction has been made permanent in the name of the subject's international society: *The International Society for Dialectology and Geolinguistics*, launched in 1989, and its journal *Dialectologica et Geolinguistica* which contains many relevant articles, on the dialects of many different languages (*www.uni-bamberg.de/~ba4es1/sidg.html*).

4. Sources of Map Information

Linguistic maps, whether of languages or dialects, usually derive from the material gathered from large-scale international, national, or regional surveys. Durrell (1990) and Schneider (in press) provide alternative overviews, Veith (1989) a full bibliography, and an Internet bibliography is at *staff-www.uni-marburg.de/~naeser/geo.htm*. Further references, including some of the history of linguistic cartography, are to be found in the article on 'Linguistic Maps' in Goebl et al. (1997).

Dialect surveys make use of different methods of data collection. Interviews conducted directly with informants involve the spontaneous oral elicitation of responses to questionnaires or of responses to exchanges in an ongoing discourse usually involving the fieldworker as one of the participants. Ideally, naturally occurring speech is recorded, without the participation of the fieldworker. Montgomery (1993) provides a possible elicitive questionnaire. Several recent phonological surveys are based on telephone interviews, as described by Bailey and Bernstein (1989) and Bailey et al. (1991, 1993) and at *www.ling.upenn.edu/phono_atlas/maps/*. The circumstances of elicitation are usually described in terms of a speaker identity profile and in terms of the elicited speech's speech-act function and of its 'style.'

Data are also gathered by a so-called 'indirect' method, which involves written responses to written questionnaires. The use of written data (especially the elicitation of 'funny spellings' to suggest a local pronunciation) as well as different practices for transcribing spoken data orthographically have not won universal approval and are usually regarded as less reliable, as discussed by Francis (1983, 1993).

Dialect maps are thus derived from the information gathered in their data sources: transcriptions made by the fieldworker in location and any accompanying notes; or edited versions of such transcriptions; or there may be tape-recordings as well as transcriptions; or there may be solely written records. Some maps have been produced from published versions of basic material or from previous maps.

5. Properties of Linguistic Maps

Linguistic maps usually have certain characteristic properties:

(a) They use an *areal base map* which includes some combination of physical and/or administrative details, internal boundaries, or the location and names of major urban centers, or the inclusion of rivers and mountain ranges, all of which are excluded from multi-dimensional scaling techniques of analysis (see below).

(b) They use *graphic coding devices* for the representation of the particular data in respect of places and/or areas predicted by the map or inferred by the reader.

(c) They use specifically chosen *localities* for which information is presented so as to predict some underlying reality for the linguistic structure of the area as a whole.

By these characteristics, linguistic maps are inherently two-dimensional constructions in which the graphic coding superimposed on the base map enables the prediction or inferring of a relationship between language and geography.

'Atlas maps' (i.e., graphically coded base maps in respect of all the localities) have several further characteristics:

(a) They are *diatopic* because they represent recognizable spatial (or areal) distributions to the exclusion of other primary forms of organization. Linguistic maps usually come to foreground a region or area in revelation of a hitherto unknown distributional pattern showing or predicting relationships of propinquity not just between localities and other localities, but between each individual locality and the area as a whole.

(b) They are *synchronic* because the data represents one period of time (usually the present day or a delimited period in the past, as in the period atlases of English: the *Linguistic Atlas of Late Medieval English*, the *Linguistic Atlas of Early Medieval English*; the *Linguistic Atlas of Older Scots*, as discussed in Williamson (1992–3), Laing and Williamson (1994) and Smith (1992), or in the papers on historical dialects by Fisiak). Depending on the coding and its intended relationship to the data, maps can offer historical interpretations to present-day data from which the source and direction of internal linguistic development within the area can be inferred. A good diachronic map of the linguistic-historical as well as geographical development of European words for 'cucumber' appears in Hildebrandt (1993).

(c) They are usually *monosocial* because the data usually represents only one social group or indiscriminately social because no attempt is made to discriminate between the data's inherent social values and because of difficulties of multivariate cartography. Expanded locality slots present social variables alongside linguistic variables in the *Linguistic Atlas of the Gulf States* (Vols. 6–7).

6. Base maps

Base maps show only the geographical position of the localities, which have been surveyed. In the case of the *Linguistic Atlas of Scotland*, for instance, the user must realize that the Lowland Scots-speaking area did not extend to the mountain regions of the Highlands and beyond, or to the Gaelic-speaking islands and West Coast; or that in the *Atlas Linguistique de l'Est du Canada* and *Atlas Linguistique du Vocabulaire Maritime Acadien* (cf. Cichocki et al. 1997) all the localities are maritime. Location identification is usually carried out within an administrative and/or physical context, although the *Linguistic Atlas of the Gulf States* and the *Linguistic Atlas of the Middle and South Atlantic States* (as in Kretzschmar and Schneider 1996) create their own areal subdivisions as 'zones' and 'sectors' to facilitate quantitative analyses (e.g., same numbers of informants or population in each zone). The base map of the *Dictionary of American Regional English*, or Bailey and Görlach's (1982) map of English as a World Language (see *New Englishes*) are 'distorted' to reflect demographic factors whereby the size of each state or English-speaking country is presented respectively in proportion to its population. Demographic shifts of English/Creole speakers in the seventeenth century and since 1700 are mapped in Holm (1984).

In the representation of localities, there are several current practices:

(a) *reference numbers* set on a background with considerable topographical detail (usually colored), the numbers remaining visible after the insertion of data, as in the *Linguistic Atlas of the Pacific Area* or the *Südwestdeutscher Sprachatlas*. In future, because of the enhanced capabilities of computer graphics and web resources, there is likely to be greater use of ordinance survey brown-and-green contour maps as base maps.

(b) *pin-point size dots*, usually where there are a great many localities ('dot maps'), the dots becoming substituted by the insertion of data, as in the *Atlas linguistique de la France*, or the *Sprach- und Sachatlas Italiens und der Südschweiz*.

(c) *individual character slots* on the screen of a computer monitor where the lines and columns of the screen are used as a grid ('plotter grid maps') with the slots (like the dots) displaying a symbolic (usually character letter) representation of the data, and the constellation of slots mnemonically configuring the whole (or part) of the survey area, as in the *Linguistic Atlas of the Gulf States*.

(d) *schematic configurations of lines and columns* ('matrix maps') which can accommodate any part of the whole area, ranging from one of four zones (which run in an east to west direction), to individual states, or to the much smaller county-based sectors within states and which can also organize the data automatically. These charts inevitably depend on the full-scale map for recognition of their abstracted configuration. There is also the 'expanded matrix map' where each locality slot becomes expanded into its own multiple slot grid to accommodate a range of responses (such as synonymic responses to the same item), as in the *Linguistic Atlas of the Gulf States*.

(e) *open circles* (often disproportionately enlarged) which are then 'filled' by color or hatching and function as variants on the 'dot' and 'matrix' methods, as shown in Kirk et al. (1994).

Because of their compatibility with a conventional physical base map, circle maps are probably more realistic than matrix maps.

7. Map Data

Several types of data have qualified as objects of study for representation of linguistic maps:

(a) Different regional varieties within a group of languages, which maps the areal distribution of a country's numerous indigenous languages, as in the *Linguistic Atlas of Kenya* or in *The Atlas of Languages* (Comrie et al. 1996).

(b) Different regional varieties within a single country (not necessarily identical with the entire area where the language is spoken), as with the areal distribution of German's numerous dialects as in Wiesinger 1982–3 or of the traditional and modern dialects of England as in Trudgill 1990.

(c) Individual *features* especially sounds, words ('lexemes'), synonyms (i.e., different responses for the same onomasiological concept), meanings (including distributions of different senses of the same word), word forms or other morphological variants, syntactic variants, and in the case of historical dictionaries, spellings.

(d) Responses to questionnaire-elicited attitudes towards language within an area, as in the *Hessischer Dialektzensus* (Dingeldein 1989).

8. Qualitative Mapping Techniques

Linguistic maps make use of different types of cartography depending on the data, the analysis desired, and the kind of semiotic statement intended. Two types of qualitative linguistic maps are conventionally distinguished:

(a) so-called 'basic,' 'direct,' 'raw-data,' 'locality,' 'uninterpreted,' 'display,' or 'documentary' maps, which focus primarily on the presentation of the data ('the French method');

(b) 'areal,' 'analyzed,' 'interpreted,' 'predicting,' or 'interpretive' maps, which focus on making explicit the regional distribution of the data ('the German method'). A subtype of 'interpretive' map is the 'derived' or 'explanatory' map, which focuses on explaining why the data and the distribution are coinciding where they do.

8.1. Documentary Maps

Documentary maps are a traditional type of map in linguistic geography. Based on the identification of individual localities, they are sometimes referred to as 'locality maps.' They make use of two styles of cartography: the *text map* and the *symbol map*. The function of such maps is to display the occurrence of data at the appropriate localities without further interference by the map maker and without interpretation, leaving readers to draw their own inferences about the geographical distribution of any 'historical,' 'systematic' or 'structural' relationships which might exist in the data.

8.1.1 Locality Text Maps

In a *locality text map*, genuine 'text' (words or phonetic transcriptions) is superimposed 'directly' at each locality. This technique is regarded as being highly objective for it represents the data in question directly and 'honestly' because it is uninterpreted; it is sometimes called the 'raw data' or the 'French' method (because of its widespread practice with linguistic maps of French, as in the *Atlas linguistique de l'Alsace* (Coseriu 1979, Geisler 1993). A recent example for England is Britain 1999 where different parts of the country are labeled with the outcomes of a merger. The disadvantage of text maps is that it is hard to infer the data's regional distribution. Although the desire for interpretation and explanation has led to more complex maps, this method of presentation occurs with several computer applications, as shown by Davis et al. 1989. This long-serving technique has found a new context in the maps derived from multidimensional scaling techniques.

8.1.2 Locality Symbol Maps

In *locality symbol maps*, 'symbols' are superimposed beside, within, or in substitution of, the locality dot or marker. These symbols represent the actual data via a legend of correspondences and usually comprise geometric shapes, sometimes in different colors. This technique is regarded as objective; although it appears merely to substitute the data, the selection of symbols requires preparation and pre-interpretation; it also allows for some submerging. The great advantage of the symbol style is its clear overview both of the symbols themselves and their distribution. This method is sometimes referred to as the 'German' method (because of its widespread use in maps of German as in the *Sprachatlas Bayerisch-Schwaben* or *Wortatlas der kontinentalgermanischen Winzerterminologie* or in other German-inspired atlases such as the *Dialect Atlas of Carpathia* as described in Siatkowski (1991) or the *Linguistic Atlas of Eastern Nepal* as described in Winter (1993)) and also occurs with several computer applications, as presented by Kelle (1997) for the *Südwestdeutscher Sprachatlas* or by Kretzschmar (1996) and at hyde.uga.edu/atlas for the point plotter for the *Linguistic Atlas of the Middle and South Atlantic States*.

8.2. Interpretive Maps

Interpretive maps are also a traditional type of map in linguistic geography. They are concerned with the identification of areas on the basis of contiguous localities, which share identical linguistic forms; they are sometimes referred to as 'area maps.' The function of interpretive maps is to display explicitly the distribution of areas, which share the same response data. Like documentary maps, they also make use of the text and symbol cartographical styles but, in the coding of the areas, interpretive maps make use of two further graphic devices: lines and hatchures. In the interpretation of areas, this method involves some interpretive interference by the map maker, sometimes leaving the map user with quite decided distributions, as in the *Linguistic Atlas of England,* but criticized by Graddol (1981: Map 24 and overlays).

8.2.1 Area Text Maps

In *area text maps,* localities with identical responses are regarded as forming contiguous areas, into which genuine 'text' is superimposed to represent the data. The areas so formed are established by circumference lines and may be left blank (except for the 'text') or filled in with hatching (and related to the data via a legend). This method is used in Upton and Widdowson (1996) and in Parry (1999).

8.2.2 Area Symbol Maps

In *area symbol maps,* localities with identical responses are regarded as forming contiguous areas, into which symbols are superimposed to represent the data. The areas so formed are established by circumference lines and may be left blank (except for the symbol) or filled in with hatching (and related to the data via a legend), as in the *Linguistic Atlas of Scotland* (Vols. 1 and 2). This method is particularly useful for the use of complex symbols depicting systems or structures or some other aspect of complex internal variability, for use of multiple symbols showing different variables for each locality as well as different realizations for each variable, as shown by Kallen (2000) for Ireland and Ryckebeer (2000) for Dutch-speaking France. Because of its tolerance of overlap, hatching is often used to represent co-occurrence, but the superimposition of four or more hatchures has the danger of illegibility.

Text and symbol styles are sometimes combined to form a continuum between more or less abstraction—which style is chosen depending on the quality and quantity of the data, as shown in Glauser 1974, 2000.

8.2.3 Area (or Regional) Pattern Map

In the 'area (or region) pattern map' in a speciality of the *Linguistic Atlas of the Gulf States* where the entire area is subdivided into six land regions: Highlands, Piedmont, Coastal, Plains, Piney Woods and Delta, as well as numerous subregions, one of which is always the focus of the regional pattern map. In addition, each map combines four separate items, which occur predominantly in the chosen area and are thus highly characteristic features of it. 'Regional pattern' maps invert conventional mapping processes: usually items are first mapped individually, and the consequent distribution is presented; here, a region is first selected and four of the prominent features of the region are mapped for it and all other regions, thus showing the distribution of those regionally characteristic features. According to Kretzschmar (1998), 'area (or regional) pattern maps' show 'chosen' or 'attributive' or 'locality' dialects. The choice of items in LAGS is evidently subjective, in that only the editors could inspect the individual distributions before making a choice. Although the map has been constructed around the project's individual localities, it is able to link together contiguous areas of distribution and join them up using different hatching styles.

8.2.4 Qualitative Line Maps

If lines are used to delimit identical responses in a single and seemingly contiguous area, such interpretive maps are sometimes referred to as 'line maps.' 'Line maps' are intended to display discrete areas which do not overlap. If the areas do overlap, the lines inevitably intersect. As far as the interpretation of lines is concerned, there are several contrasting possibilities:

(a) the line is viewed as a perimeter boundary; because it encompasses 'identical language,' it is sometimes called an *isoglosses;*

(b) the line is a midway point between two responses; because it contrasts 'different language,' it is sometimes called a *heterogloss.* Occasionally, these terms have been interchanged.

A third definition is of the line as 'the midpoint of a transition zone' is given in Chambers and Trudgill 1998.

The actual location of lines has been shown to be problematical. The function of lines drawn on maps is to make the distribution of the mapped data explicit in terms of the whole area. Almost none of the existing studies conceptualize the line as a fixed point, preferring to interpret the line as indicative of a sizeable area where the change from one linguistic form to another is assumed to be gradual. Good demonstrations of the issue include the various narrow and wide distributions for 'frightened' presented in Graddol (1981: Map 24 and overlays), the alternative isoglossic and algorithmic mappings of *piggin* (as a synonym of *pail* and *bucket*) in Kretzschmar (1992), and the interrelationship between lines and symbols in Glauser (1974), revisited in (2000). Further analyses are presented in Davis et al. (1997). Occasionally, lines can be given a directional interpretation, i.e., that such-and-such a line represents the northern or the southern limits of a particular item. As a perimeter, however, the line further suggests that the area on its far side does not have the particular form.

Whether the outer limits of variants are to be interpreted as 'perimeters' or 'boundaries,' different lines may represent the dynamics of change within a speech area (insofar as the progressive development of change can thereby be reconstructed). By identifying the outer limits of progressive stages of development, lines can be interpreted as charting the course of diffusion of linguistic innovations from 'active' areas (where innovations have arisen) into 'passive' areas (where they are received).

Because unrelated items can have the same regional distribution, lines for different data can occur in the same place, i.e., 'in bundles.' An accumulation of similarly located lines is usually taken as evidence of a dialect boundary, although it is far from clear exactly how many isoglosses are required for a bundle—occurrences of single features seem hardly sufficient. The concept of 'line bundles' has led to different suggestions for counting and weighing them, thus establishing different degrees of line strength: the more lines, it seems, the stronger the boundary. This 'heteroglossic' method is used to establish dialect boundaries in the *Linguistic Atlas of Java*, or in Goeman et al. (1993) and other studies of Dutch dialects, or with the selections of *Survey of English Dialects* phonological, lexical, and morphological materials in Viereck (1985a, 1985b) or in Elmer and Rudin (1997) and Elmer (1999). There still remains, however, no explicit or well-justified criterion for grading isoglosses or heteroglosses or for their reliability.

8.3 System Maps

Not all atlas-oriented dialectologists see the construction of 'systems' as their task or goal, so that it is rare to find 'system' maps (typically 'derived maps' or 'process maps') in atlases.

For the 'specialist,' it is considered no longer sufficient or adequate to produce documentary or interpretive atlas maps of individual items. Rather, the identification of different dialect areas depends on maps displaying entire systems, together with their internal structure, because it would be on the basis, not of items, but of differences of exponence within systems, and of the consequent differences in the structure of equivalent systems, that dialects would be seen to vary and therefore to be distinguished and distinctive one from another. Such maps as have been produced from the *Survey of English Dialects* data are published in Glauser (1985a, 1985b, 1986) and Anderson (1987).

In future, there are likely to be only more maps offering 'systematic' or 'structural' interpretations.

9. Quantitative Mapping Techniques

9.1. Quantitative Text and Symbol Maps

Quantitative analysis has hitherto taken two overall approaches: the application to dialect data of general statistical tests and the application to dialect data of new tests specifically devised for the purpose of identifying structural patterns within the corpus of data gathered for a particular area as a whole. Quantitative maps differ from qualitative maps in that they use documentary and interpretive styles to present numerical information. There is almost no uniformity of practice. A useful critical overview appears in Schneider (in press).

There are several documentary approaches:
(a) The *choroplethic* approach, which inserts numerical information into the fullest space available contiguous to the locality, as shown by Goebl (1993) and in Map 2.
(b) The *circles* approach, where the circles are colored or hatched whereby numerical information is inserted into locality circles and displayed by hatching, as in Kirk (1994).
(c) The *pie-chart* approach, as in the *Atlas linguistique de l'Est du Canada*.
(d) The *binary* approach, whereby the circles express a binary numerical choice (1 or 0) to express the presence or absence of a feature, as in the *Linguistic Atlas of Scotland*, Vol. 3.
(e) The *plotter grid* and *matrix map* approaches, where the locality slot on the screen is used to display numerical information, as in the *Linguistic Atlas of the Gulf States*.

Sometimes the representation of distance has been done 'directly' by insertion of numerical values on the map or the combination of insertion with hatching within locality circles. Other approaches, based on cluster analysis, use tree diagrams or dendograms to display the distribution of localities, as in the *Linguistic Atlas of the Gulf States*.

9.2 Quantitative Line Maps

Since the mid-1980s, lines have been quantified and given a numerical value, leading to the new concept of *isopleth*, where each line has a value, and for each value a line is drawn (rather like contour lines on a physical map), as shown by North (1985) and Thomas (1993).

Between two isopleths, there are constant values, but neither the distance between the isopleths need be regular, or the area uniform. Because isopleths represent numbers, their interpretation points to the source and direction of the linguistic development. The nonlinear, nonwave shape of the isopleths is further interpreted as a good instance of sound change in progress, reinforcing the observation that sound changes in progress jump from one urban center to another and miss out intervening areas. Using phonological material from Dutch, Wattel (1990) and Goeman et al. (1993) propose mathematical models which draw isopleths at different proportional intervals. The resulting maps show the rate of adoption of numerous innovations from an active area into a passive area so that, over a longer timescale, the lines might be thought of as forming a succession of steps over a very broad area.

9.3 Dual-dimensional and Multidimensional Scaling Maps

Cichocki (1988, 1989) creates a fresh paradigm for linguistic maps known as 'dual and multidimensional

Language Variation and Change: Dialects and Social Groups

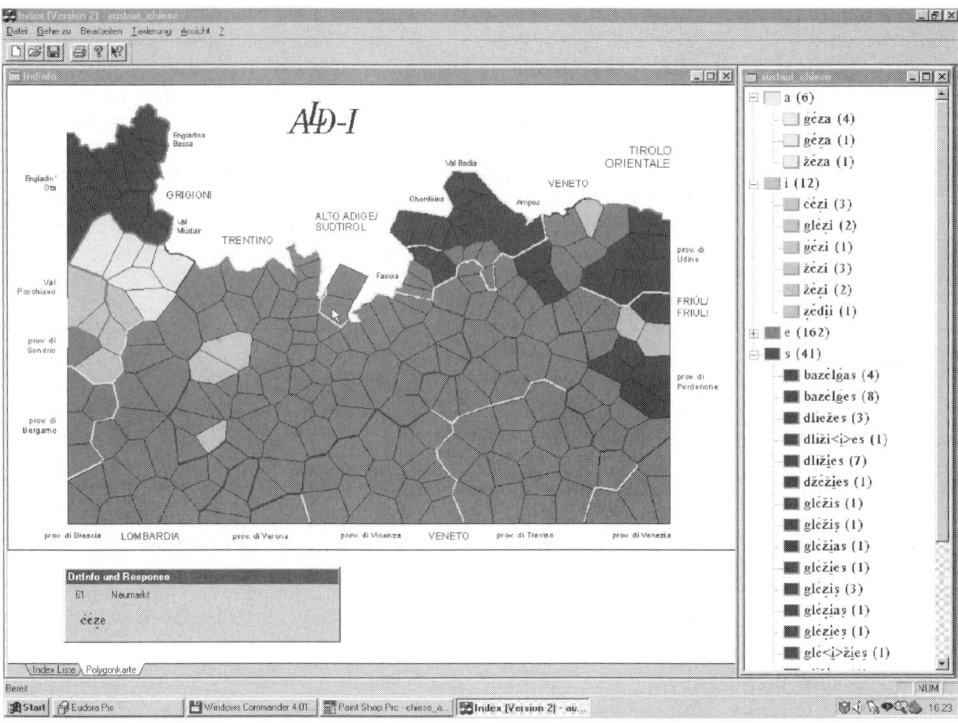

Map 2. Plural endings of *Chiese* ('churches') in the *Atlant linguistic dl ladin dolomitich y di dialec vejins I*. © Roland Bauer 1999 http://www.sbg.ac.at/rom/people/proj/ald/ald-home.htm (reproduced with permission).

scaling.' Scaling techniques are used to plot locality references on a graph, and are thus quite different from conventional 'physical' maps. The relationship between the locality references is a linguistic and not a physical one (i.e., if locality references cluster together, they reflect places with the closest linguistic similarity). The user has to decipher the references to discover the geographical position of the localities. In a study of material from the Survey of English Dialects, Labov (1992, repeated in 1994) uses multi-scaling both to chart the diffusion and direction of sound change through the lexicon. By using multiscaling techniques, Labov is able to show that sound laws work through the lexicon at different rates so that, eventually, all environments will be affected and changed, thus vindicating, on the grounds of lexical diffusion rates and time, the sound-exceptionless laws of the neogrammarians. Ainsaar and Ross (1993) present another approach. A critical overview of multidimensional scaling is provided by Chambers (1997).

10. Dialect Areas

While dialect areas have traditionally been inferred or predicted on maps, on the presence or absence of a small number of selected key features, speakers have always constructed their own subjective dialect boundaries and formed mental maps about language and linguistic distance. It has, however, never been established scientifically *which* features are the key features, or *how many* such features are necessary. In the identification of one area from another, some boundary lines are more important than others, usually for nonlinguistic reasons. Despite a century's intensive research, there is general agreement that dialectologists are still a long way from establishing objective procedures for the measurement of linguistic difference, divergence and distance, as discussed by Hinskens et al. (2000).

The identification of dialect areas has been considered as the goal of dialect research, in an attempt to substantiate the judgments about their existence made by speakers. There is, however, no agreement about either the nature or the number of features necessary to establish a dialect area in its own right, and it seems dubious that this can be done by dialectometrical techniques as currently developed. At best, dialect areas can be established on the basis of the sufficiency of a selection of features, so that the concept of a 'dialect area' is a convenient fiction. The best dialect maps are not therefore maps of dialect areas but of dialect features, for it does not appear possible to do better.

Some refinements to the idea of absolutism of 'dialect area' have led to the discrimination on maps by cartographical techniques of 'focal areas' with 'transitional areas.' Even these, however, are arbitrary and have never been identified systematically. There is no reason why one set of features should count for more than another.

11. Explanatory Factors

Dialect areas are justified in terms of external geographical, historical, political, administrative, social, or cultural criteria with which they are associated and thus established. As the internal discrimination and criterial foregrounding between features for dialect identification are arbitrary, explanations for the particular location of isoglosses are inevitably external.

Physical geographical features are relevant only insofar as they influence developments by impeding or promoting social intercourse, or by coinciding with other borders; few important linguistic boundaries fall precisely with them. Rivers and mountain ranges as well as dense forests and marshlands have recurrently coincided with dialect boundaries. An effective demonstration of this relationship between language and physical geography has been made by the use of topographical overlays for mountains regions, plains, coastal areas, and the Mississippi delta area in several volumes of the *Linguistic Atlas of the Gulf States*.

If linguistic diversity has been caused by the differential diffusion of linguistic innovations, linguistic borders may be the result of historical movements or settlements into, or between, which innovations have not spread. Many linguistic divisions reflect historical settlement patterns and population movements. But total identification of modern dialect regions with historical settlement areas is clearly impossible and developments cut across them. Dialect areas in Germany are considered to reflect settlement patterns of Germanic tribes, just as dialect areas in England can be shown to reflect the Scandinavian settlement. Those in the US are also considered to reflect later immigration and settlement history there, and indeed formed the basis of much of Kurath's research in the eastern US. Postmedieval political boundaries have also influenced the identification of linguistic boundaries. The Scottish-English political border ranks as a very strong linguistic boundary, whereas other boundaries, as between Germany and Denmark or between Germany and The Netherlands, tend to reflect an unbroken dialect continuum. By contrast, geolinguistic maps are arbitrary with regard to the above criteria (but cf. Goebl 1996).

Explanatory maps might make greater use of base maps, which include the details of external influencing factors. Although geographical and historical boundaries have all influenced the diffusion of linguistic innovations and the formations of areas of relative linguistic homogeneity insofar as these are crucial to the establishment of geographical sociocultural groupings, it is just as likely that linguistic diversity has emerged through the desire to be identified, through linguistic behavior, as belonging to one sociocultural group and not to another. For this view, present-day isogloss patterns result from various historical stages of such processes. It is impossible to disentangle social factors in the description and explanation of linguistic variation. This recognition led to their incorporation in the *Linguistic Atlas of the Gulf States*.

The strongest case for the depiction on maps of explanations of regional linguistic variation possibly rests with an accumulation of these criteria, including innovating social tendencies and the growing urban influence on the surrounding rural hinterland or on the adjacent urban areas but excluding the hinterland in between, the one correlating and reinforcing the other. There is no doubt that a multiplicity of factors underlying linguistic diversity, but as these are difficult to establish, the boundaries are sometimes fluid.

As this article repeatedly shows, although not using the social geographer's terminology, many objections to traditional dialectology have been met by the *Linguistic Atlas of the Gulf States*. There are answers to the challenges about the percentage of speakers using particular forms; and how often they use them; there is automatically retrievable, mapped, information about the age (people over or below the age of 65), sex, ethnicity, and level of education (up to tenth grade or beyond it) of the speakers; there is information about synonymic or allophonic variation in relation to all these social variables; and so on. It is unlikely that anybody would seriously commence a large-scale survey these days without explicitly taking situational and stylistic factors into account, or without studying the dialectological as well as the sociolinguistic and geolinguistic methodology of the *Linguistic Atlas of the Gulf States*—Vol. 7 maps the predominant social variables and their correlations with particular lexical, morphological, and phonological features and seeks to show how certain combinations of these sets of variables predominate in particular parts of the LAGS territory.

12. Conclusion

No atlas is complete in itself, and derived studies will always be needed. As Trudgill (1983) argues:

> Dialectologists should not be content simply to describe the geographical distribution of linguistic features. They should also be concerned to *explain*—perhaps, more accurately, to adduce reasons for—this distribution. Only in this way will we be able to arrive at an

understanding of the sociolinguistic mechanism that lie behind the geographical distribution of linguistic phenomena, the location of isoglosses, and the diffusion of linguistic innovations. [my italics]

Dialectologists, who typically investigate map features, can only be encouraged to produce more *explanations* of the distributions of their investigated features in the future.

Four characteristics of linguistic mapping stand out at present:
(a) dialectologists map features rather than structures or systems;
(b) the computer is now prominent and is rapidly becoming exclusive as a graphical and especially cartographical tool;
(c) the Internet is a convenient means of distribution and accessibility;
(d) traditionally-trained dialect geographers are showing a willingness to extend and revise their techniques by incorporating helpful insights from sociolinguistics, social and cultural geography, and other neighboring disciplines.

Better-drawn maps are now being produced, and explanatory maps are emerging. Linguistic maps remain a central resource in linguistic geography, for they enable their users to access, present, analyze, interpret, and explain their data. A map's usefulness as well as its purpose and value are repeatedly reiterated and vigorously defended. With these reaffirmations and the widespread use of microcomputers, map users may expect the linguistic map to remain center-stage for a long time to come as a productive and indispensable research resource and tool in dialectology offering ever new understandings about the nature of regional linguistic variation or about the distribution of languages.

See also: Dialect and Dialectology; Urban and Rural Forms of Language; Sound Change; Sociolinguistic Variation; The Atlas of North American English: Methods and Findings.

Bibliography

Ainsaar S, Ross J 1993 Nonmetric multidimensional scaling in dialectology: Estonian experience. In: Viereck W (ed.) *Verhandlungen des Internationalen Dialektologen-kongresses Bamberg 1990*, Vol 1. Franz Steiner Verlag Beihefte der ZDL, Stuttgart, Germany, pp. 304–13

Anderson J M 1987 *A Structural Atlas of the English Dialects*. Croom Helm, London

Bailey G, Bernstein C 1989 Methodology of a phonological survey of Texas. *Journal of English Linguistics* **22**: 6–16

Bailey G, Wikle T, Tillery J, Sand L 1991 The apparent time constraint. *Language Variation and Change* **3**: 241–64

Bailey G, Wikle T, Tillery J, Sand L 1993 Some patterns of linguistic diffusion. *Language Variation and Change* **5**: 359–90

Bailey R, Görlach M (eds.) 1982 *English as a World Language*. University of Michigan Press, Ann Arbor, MI

Bauer R, Goebl H, Haimerl E 1999–2000 *ALD-I CD-Rom*, Vols. 1–3, Institut für Romanistik, Salzburg, Austria

Boberg C 2000 Geolinguistic diffusion and the US-Canada border. *Language Variation and Change* **12**: 1–24

Breton R J-L 1997 *Atlas of the Languages and Ethnic Communities of South Asia*. Sage, London

Britain D 1999 Locating the baseline of linguistic innovations. *Cuadernos de Filología Inglesa* **8**: 177–92

Chambers J K 1997 Mapping transitions. In: Thomas, pp. 284–93

Chambers J K, Trudgill P 1998 *Dialectology*, 2nd edn. Cambridge University Press, Cambridge, UK

Cichocki W 1988 Uses of dual scaling in social dialectology: Multidimensional analysis of vowel variation. In: Thomas A (ed.) *Methods in Dialectology*. Multilingual Matters, Clevedon, UK

Cichocki W 1989 An application of dual scaling in dialectometry. *Journal of English Linguistics* **22**: 91–6

Cichocki W, Péronnet L, Banich M 1997 *Atlas Linguistique du Vocabulaire Maritime Acadien Final Progress Report*. In: Thomas, pp. 109–19

Comrie B, Matthews S, Polinsky M (eds.) 1996 *The Atlas of Languages: The Origin and Development of Languages Throughout the World*. Bloomsbury, London

Coseriu E 1979 *Die Sprachgeographie*. Gunter Narr, Tübingen, Germany

Crystal D 1995 *Cambridge Encyclopedia of the English Language*. Cambridge University Press, Cambridge, UK

Crystal D 1997 Part X: Language in the world. In: *Cambridge Encyclopedia of Language*, 2nd edn. Cambridge University Press, Cambridge, UK

Davis L M 1990 *Statistics for Dialectologists*. University of Alabama Press, Tuscaloosa, AL

Davis L M 2000 The reliability of dialect boundaries. *American Speech* **75**: 257–9

Davis L M, Houck C M, Kelly B B 1989 Easily manipulable databases for linguistic atlases: Using Intergraph. *Journal of English Linguistics* **22**

Davis L M, Houck C M, Upton C 1997 The question of dialect boundaries: The SED and the American atlas. In: Thomas, pp. 271–83

Dingeldein H J (1989) *Hessicher Dialektzensus*. (Hessische Sprachatlanten Kleine Reihe 3.) Niemeyer, Tübingen, Germany

Durrell M 1990 Language as geography. In: Collinge N E (ed.) *An Encyclopedia of Language*. Routledge, London

Elmer W 1999 The Phonetic Database Project (PDP)—a new tool for the dialectologist. *Leeds Studies in English* **30**: 31–58

Elmer W, Rudin E 1997 The survey of English dialects as an electronic database for research in areal and variationist linguistics. In: Thomas, pp. 234–46

Francis W N 1983 *Dialectology*. Longman, London

Francis W N 1993 The historical and cultural interpretation of dialect. In: Preston D R (ed.) *American Dialect Research*. Benjamins, Amsterdam

Geisler H 1993 Dialect data processing with personal computers. In Viereck W (ed.) *Verhandlungen des Internationalen Dialektologenkongresses Bamberg 1990 Vol 1*. Franz Steiner Verlag, Stuttgart, Germany

Gerritsen M 1991 *Atlas van de Nederlandse Dialectsyntaxis*. P J Meertens-Instituut, Amsterdam

Glauser B 1974 *The Scottish-English Linguistic Border.* Francke Verlag Cooper Monographs Vol. 16, Bern, Switzerland

Glauser B 1985a Linguistic atlases and generative phonology. In: Kirk J M, Sanderson S, Widdowson J D A (eds.) *Studies in Linguistic Geography.* Croom Helm, London

Glauser B 1985b BOYS and GIRLS, SONS and DAUGHTERS: The evidence of the survey of English dialects. *English World-Wide* **6**: 37–58

Glauser B 1986 This, that and tothers. In: Fischer A (ed.) *The History and the Dialects of English* Carl Winter, Heidelberg, Germany, pp. 253–77

Glauser B 2000 The Scottish/English border in hindsight. *International Journal of the Sociology of Language* **145**: 65–78

Goebl H 1993 Dialectometry: A short overview of the principles and practice of quantitive classification of linguistic atlas data. In: Köhler R, Rieger B B (eds.) *Contributions to Quantitative Linguistics.* Foris, Dordrecht, The Netherlands

Goeble H 1996 La convergence entre les fragmentations geolinguistique et géo-génétique de l'Italie du nord. *Revue de Linguistique Romane* **60**: 25–49

Goebl H 2000. La dialectométrisation de l'ALF: présentation des premiers résultats. *Linguistica* **49**: 209–36

Goebl H, Nelde P H, Starý Z, Wölck W (eds.) 1997 *Kontaktlinguistik*, 2 Vols. Walter de Gruyter, Berlin

Goeman A C M, van Reenan P Th, Wattel E 1993 The diphthongisation of West Germanic *i* and its relation to West Germanic *u* in modern Dutch dialects: A quantitative approach. In: Viereck W (ed.) *Verhandlungen des Internationalen Dialektologenkongresses Bamberg 1990*, Vol 2. Franz Steiner Verlag, Stuttgart, Germany, pp. 76–97

Graddol D 1981 *Linguistic Variation and Diversity.* Open University Course E263 Language in Use Course Book Block 1. Open University Press, Milton Keynes, UK

Graddol D 1997 *The Future of English?* The British Council, London

Haimerl E 1997 *ALD 1*—A linguistic atlas published on multiple media. In: Thomas, pp. 200–10

Haimerl E 1998 A database application for the generation of phonetic atlas maps. In: Nerbonne J (ed.) *Linguistic Databases.* CSLI, Stanford (See also *wwwsbgacat/rom/people/proj/ald/card/englischhtm*)

Hartmann R (ed.) 1996 *The English Language in Europe.* Intellect, Exeter, UK

Hildebrandt R 1993 Atlas Linguarum Europae (ALE): Europäische Wortgeschichte am Beispiel 'concombre/cucumber/Gurke'. In: Viereck W (ed.) *Verhandlungen des Internationalen Dialektologenkongresses Bamberg 1990*, Vol. 2. Franz Steiner Verlag, Stuttgart, Germany

Hinskens F, Kallen J L, Taeldeman J (eds.) 2000 Dialect convergence and divergence across European boundaries. *International Journal for the Sociology of Language* **145**: 1–28

Hock H-H 1986 *Principles of Historical Linguistics.* Mouton de Gruyter, Berlin

Holm J 1984 English in the Caribbean. In Burchfield R (ed.) *The Cambridge History of the English Language Vol 5: English in Britain and Overseas: Origins and Development.* Cambridge University Press, Cambridge, UK

Johnston P 2000 Taming volume III of the linguistic atlas of Scotland. *Scottish Language* **19**: 45–65

Kallen J L 2000 Two languages, two borders, one island: Some linguistic and political borders in Ireland. *International Journal of the Sociology of Language* **145**: 29–63

Kelle B 1997 The computation of maps in word geography. In: Thomas, pp. 211–23

Kirk J M 1985 Linguistic atlases and grammar: The investigation and description of regional variation in English Syntax. In: Kirk J M, Sanderson S, Widdowson J D A (eds.) *Studies in Linguistic Geography: The Dialects of English in Britain and Ireland.* Croom Helm, London

Kirk J M 1994 East Central Scots: A computerised mapping package. In: Fenton A S, MacDonald D A (eds.) *Studies in Gaelic and Scots.* Canongate, Edinburgh, UK

Kirk J M, Munroe G, O'Kane D J M 1994 Elecronic word maps. In: Hockey S, Ide N (eds.) *Research in Humanities Computing.* Oxford University Press, Oxford, UK

Klemola J in press *The Survey of English Dialects on CD-ROM: The Spoken Corpus Recorded in England 1948–1961.* Routledge, London

König W 1982 *Dtv-Atlas zur deutschen Sprache.* Deutscher Taschenbuch Verlag, Munich, Germany

Kretzschmar W A 1992 Isoglosses and predictive modeling. *American Speech* **67**: 227–49

Kretzschmar W A 1996 Quantitative areal analysis of dialect features. *Language Variation and Change* **8**: 13–39

Kretzschmar W A 1997 Generating linguistic feature maps with statistics. In: Bernstein C, Nunnally T, Sabino R (eds.) *Language Variety in the South Revisited.* University of Alabama Press, Tuscaloosa, AL

Kretzschmar W A 1998 Analytical procedure and three technical types of dialect. In: Montgomery M B, Nunnally T E (eds.) *From the Gulf States and Beyond: the Legacy of Lee Pederson.* University of Alabama Press, Tuscaloosa, AL

Kretzschmar W A, Schneider E 1996 *Introduction to Quantitative Analysis of Linguistic Survey Data: An Atlas by the Numbers.* Sage, Thousand Oaks, CA

Kunze K 1998 *Dtv-Atlas Namenkunde.* Deutscher Taschenbuch Verlag, Munich, Germany

Labov W 1992 Evidence for regular sound change in English dialect geography. In: Rissanen M et al. (eds.) *History of Englishes: New Methods and Interpretations in Historical Linguistics.* Mouton de Gruyter, Berlin

Labov W 1994 *Principles of Linguistic Change*, Vol. 1. Blackwell, Oxford, UK

Labov W, Ash S, Boberg C in press *The Atlas of North American English.* Mouton de Gruyter, Berlin

Laing M, Williamson K (eds.) 1994 *Speaking in Our Own Tongues: Papers from the Edinburgh Colloquium on Historical Dialectology.* Boydell and Brewer, Woodbridge, UK

Masica C P 1976 *Defining a Linguistic Area.* University of Chicago Press, Chicago, IL

Montgomery M 1993 Questionnaire for the study of South Carolina English. In: Glowka A W, Lance D M (eds.) *Language Variation in North American English: Research and Teaching.* The Modern Language Association of America, New York

Montgomery M B, Nunnally T E (eds.) 1998 *From the Gulf States and Beyond: The Legacy of Lee Pederson and LAGS.* University of Alabama Press, Tuscaloosa, AL

Moseley C, Asher R E 1993 *Atlas of the World's Languages*. Routledge, London

Moulton W G 1960 The short vowel systems on northern Switzerland: A study in structural dialectology. *Word* **16**: 155–83

North D 1985 Spatial aspects of linguistic change in Surrey, Kent and Sussex. In: Viereck W (ed.) *Focus On: England and Wales*. Benjamins, Amsterdam

Parry D 1999 *A Grammar and Glossary of the Conservative Anglo-Welsh Dialects of Rural Wales*. The National Centre for English Cultural Tradition, Sheffield, UK

Pennisi A 1995 Modelli artificialisti per la rappresentazione della variabilità linguistica nell'OLS e nell'ALS. *Dialectologia et Geolinguistica* **3**: 59–95

Preston D 1989 *Perceptual Dialectology: Nonlinguists' Views of Areal Linguistics*. Foris, Dordrecht, The Netherlands

Ryckeboer H 2000 The role of political borders in the millennial retreat of Dutch Flemish in the north of France. *International Journal of the Sociology of Language* **145**: 79–108

Schiltz G 1996 *Der dialektometrische Atlas von Südwest—Baden*, 4 Vols. Elwert, Marburg, Germany

Schiltz G 1997 A dialectometrical analysis of the dialects in the Grand-Duchy of Luxemburg. In: Thomas, pp. 94–108

Schneider E in press Quantitative techniques in the analysis of linguistic atlases. In: Kastovsky D (ed.) *Anglistentag 2001 Wien*. Wissenschaftlicher Verlag, Trier, Germany

Siatkowski J 1991 Der Atlas der Karpatischen Mundarten. *Zeitschrift für Dialektologie und Linguistik* **58**: 257–66

Smith J J 1992 A linguistic atlas of early middle English: Tradition and typology. In: Rissanan M et al. (eds.) *History of Englishes: New Methods and Interpretations in Historical Linguistics*. Mouton de Gruyter, Berlin

Thomas A R 1997 *Issues and Methods in Dialectology*. University of Wales, Bangor, UK

Thomas E R 1993 Plotting vowel changes in linguistic atlas data by means of contour intervals. In: Viereck W (ed.) *Verhandlungen des Internationalen Dialektologenkongresses Bamberg 1990*, Vol. 2. Franz Steiner Verlag, Stuttgart, Germany

Trudgill P 1983 Linguistic change and diffusion: Description and explanation in geolinguistics. In: Trudgill P *On Dialect*. Blackwell, Oxford, UK

Trudgill P 1999 *The Dialects of England*, 2nd edn. Blackwell, Oxford, UK

Upton C, Widdowson J D A 1996 *An Atlas of English Dialects*. Oxford University Press, Oxford, UK

Veith W 1989 Sprachatlanten weltweit: Eine Auswahlbibliographie zu abgeschlossenen und fortgeschrittenen Projekten. In: Veith W, Putschke W (eds.) *Sprachatlanten des Deutschen: Laufende Projekte*. Studien zum kleinen Deutschen Sprachatlas Vol. 2. Niemeyer, Tübingen, Germany

Viereck W 1985a Dialectal speech in England: Orton's lexical evidence. In: Kastovsky D, Szwedek A (eds.) *Linguistics Across Histoical and Geographical Boundaries: In Honour of Jacek Fisiak*, 2 Vols. de Gruyter, Berlin

Viereck W 1985b Dialectal speech in England: Orton's phonetic and grammatical evidence. *Journal of English Linguistics* **19**: 240–57

Viereck W, Viereck K, Ramisch H (forthcoming) *Dtv-Atlas zur englischen Sprache*. Deutscher Taschenbuch Verlag, Munich, Germany

Wattel E 1990 A mathematical model to describe the boundary of a vowel shift in the past on the basis of data from contemporary Dutch dialects. Vrije Universiteit Amsterdam Faculteit Wiskunde en Informatica Ropport no. WS - 359

Wiesinger P 1982–83 Die Einteilung der deutschen Dialekte. In: Besch W, Knoop U, Putschke W, Wiegand H E (eds.) *Dialektologie: ein Handbuch zur deutschen und allgemeinen Dialektforschung*, 2 Vols. Walter de Gruyter, Berlin

Wikle T 1997 Quantitative mapping techniques for displaying language variation and change. In: Bernstein C, Nunnally T, Sabino R (eds.) *Language Variation in the South Revisited*. University of Alabama Press, Tuscaloosa, AL

Williamson K 1992–93 A computer-aided method for making a linguistic atlas of older Scots. *Scottish Language* **11/12**: 138–73

Winter W 1993 Abstract mapping. In: Viereck W (ed.) *Verhandlungen des Internationalen Dialektologenkongresses Bamberg 1990*, Vol. 2. Franz Steiner Verlag, Stuttgart, Germany

Wurm S A (ed.) 1996 *Atlas of the World's Languages in Danger of Disappearing*. UNESCO and Pacific Linguistics, Paris

Wurm S A Mühlhäusler P, Tryon D T (eds.) 1996 *Atlas of Languages of Intercultural Communication in the Pacific Asia and the Americas*. Mouton de Gruyter, Berlin

Social Class

M. W. Macy

Although social class is one of the key sociological concepts in language studies, there is little agreement or clarity about the meaning of the term. Linguists frequently research class differences in speech, syntax, and grammar without their criteria for classification, leaving unspecified the underlying social causes of the variations they report. For Marxists, class refers to ownership or control of the means of production (factories, land, tools, etc.), with the fundamental cleavage dividing the owners and managers of large corporations from the class of proletarian wage earners. Other theorists use class to refer to unequal bargaining positions in markets for labor and capital, with the population stratified along multiple and cross-cutting dimensions of inequality rather than sharply divided into polarized groups. The causal order is also generally unclear; do distinct class voices reflect material divisions that correspond to class inequalities, or do material circumstances reflect differences in the possession of language skills and styles required for upward mobility? Finally, is the distinctive language of the lower classes indicative of cultural deficit and deprivation, or do such claims reflect the class bias of the scholars who advance them? These controversies have been particularly sharp surrounding the eminent work of Basil Bernstein, perhaps the foremost theorist of the language of class (see *Code, Sociolinguistic*; *Bernstein, Basil*).

1. From Static Taxonomy to Historical Change

References can be found in both the scholarly and popular literatures not only to blue-collar workers but also students, the aged, the handicapped, ethnic groups, women, welfare recipients, and renters as subordinate classes. At a minimum, the term class implies only that certain people share a distinctive attribute of interest to the observer, hence the diverse assortment of people who find themselves 'classified.' While Marxists emphasize property relations as the defining attribute, others include knowledge and skill, authority, and more recently, power and cultural capital. Some see class inequality as evidence of injustice, the monopolization of valued resources by a privileged minority. Others see class differentiation as a natural and highly functional expression of individual differences in taste and talent.

These diverse usages should not tempt us to search for an inflexible formula or authoritative definition that might give the term greater coherence. Models of the class structure are not descriptive typologies or taxonomic schemas but rather theories of social and political contestation and historical change. A social class is more than a category; each grouping implies a corresponding theory about the importance and unequal distribution of the defining attribute. Hence, there is a need to examine the origins of fundamental inequalities in the social division of labor and the processes that perpetuate them. The reader can then use and interpret the term more effectively, particularly in sociolinguistic applications. Special emphasis will thus be placed on the role played by language—how these inequalities are manifested in distinctive voices and how these in turn promote, attenuate, or alter the reproduction of class inequalities over time.

2. Class According to Marx and Weber

Marx devoted a lifetime of intellectual labor to unraveling what he saw as the central paradox of human history: humans must work in order to live, yet the more they labor, the stronger become the forces that compel them to work. The problem centers on the alienation of propertyless producers from the means of production they create and on which they depend for survival. The products of their labor belong not to them but to those who own the land, factories, equipment, tools, and materials, all of which are themselves products of labor but now confront their makers as something hostile and alien. In Marx's Hegelian language, the creative process is turned upside down in an inversion of subject and predicate such that 'man's own deed becomes an alien power opposed to him which enslaves him instead of being controlled by him' (1978: 160). In capitalist production, the dependence of the propertyless proletarian on the means of production owned by capital also leaves the worker unable to command remuneration for a day's labor commensurate with what the capitalist could obtain in selling what the worker produced in a day. Reduced to homogeneous raw material, the producers are themselves consumed by the very productive forces they have created. In brief, the workers forge their own chains.

Indeed, the producers are dominated not only by the means of production but by all that they have produced, including politics and religion. The creators of God are thus banished from the real world to the garden of Eden: the more of himself man attributes to God, Marx writes, 'the less he retains in himself. The worker puts his life into the object, but now his life no longer belongs to him but to the object' (1978: 72). Similarly, the dependence of the producers on the propertied class for survival causes the economic interests of that class to take on the appearance of the universal interests of society, the interests that are in turn sanctioned by the state, even when it is democratically controlled. As the embodiment of this universal interest, 'the executive of the modern State is but a committee for managing the common affairs of the whole bourgeoisie' (1978: 475). Contrary to what is often crudely portrayed by his critics, no conspiracy by a prescient ruling class is implied by Marx's famous dictum. Nor are the masses brainwashed by the bourgeoisie. While 'the ideas of the ruling class are in every epoch the ruling ideas,' their dominion is always subject to contestation. The antagonism of interest between the propertied class and the producers creates the material basis for often bloody class struggle, with the potential to transform the property relations that are the root of the conflict.

Marxists in the late twentieth century, faced with the embarrassment of classifying salaried managers and professionals as wage-earning proletarians, broadened the meaning of relationship to the means of production to include both ownership and control (Wright 1979). This elaboration of the classical doctrine resonates with Marx's early emphasis on the domination of the producers by the products of their own labor and also has important ramifications for the socialist agenda; it is not enough for the workers to own collectively the means of production, they must also control it, which implies not only a democratic state but also a democratic enterprise. The failure of that vision to survive the test of practical politics in the twentieth century, in both East and West, has motivated continuing efforts to rethink Marxist class theory. Nevertheless, the political systems of most of the industrial democracies are closely tied to class-specific constituencies, and Marx's seminal contribution remains the single most important intellectual influence on contemporary applications.

The neo-Marxist distinction between ownership and control owes extensively to a prominent non-Marxist, Ralf Dahrendorf, who argued that property is merely a special case of a more fundamental class relation based on authority. Dahrendorf's command class may be found not only in the process of production but in all 'imperatively coordinated associations,' including schools and churches. While this seems to imply an even broader and more radical agenda for the class struggle, Dahrendorf draws the opposite conclusion. The ubiquity of the command class means that opportunities exist for subordinates in one sphere of social life to serve as bosses in another. These cross-cutting cleavages suggest not class polarization but rather a pluralist model of highly stable industrial democracies.

The German sociologist Max Weber, whose stature in class theory rivals that of Marx, also challenged the assumption that class societies tend towards polarization and irreconcilable conflict. Weber countered that property relations need not correspond to other dimensions of social stratification, namely political power and social prestige; that is, the correspondence between class, status, and power is empirically and historically variable.

Marxists from the second half of the twentieth century generally agree, but insist that there are structural, economic limits on the political power of the working class, even where labor parties have enjoyed decades of uninterrupted political rule, as in social democratic Sweden. Efforts to redistribute profit and protect workers from the threat of the sack ultimately confront the inexorable logic of the competitive market, a conclusion that conservative economists readily affirm.

Weber also broadened the Marxist notion of property. Like Marx, Weber believed that '"Property" and "lack of property" are ... the basic categories of all class situations' (1978: 927). By this Weber means specifically a market situation, that is, a bargaining position in markets for labor, capital, or credit. Like Marx, Weber saw the propertyless as powerless in the bargaining encounter, but he differs in that his notion of property is more nuanced. For Weber, Marx's proletariat is not one but two classes, those who possess a marketable skill and those with only their raw labor power to sell. The bargaining power of the unskilled laborer is vastly inferior to that of the expert machinist. Weber thus introduces the idea that knowledge, educational credentials, and skill can be marketable assets comparable to physical means of production and therefore relevant to the differentiation of classes. This has become one of the primary interests of contemporary class theorists, with important implications for the role of language, to be addressed momentarily.

As Weber seems to have recognized, his theory of market situation suggests gradational stratification rather than classification. The market capacities associated with the level of skill or the value of accumulated assets form a continuum with no intrinsically meaningful categories. In what sense then can Weberian classes be understood as qualitatively distinct? The solution proposed by Weber is the concept of *social* class based on the probability of movement from one position to another. Social classes can then be differentiated within a continuum of market capacities by mobility patterns: 'the totality of those class situations within which individual and generational mobility is easy and typical' (1978: 302). Social classes are thus characterized by common socioeconomic backgrounds as these open/restrict access to a given set of market positions. While inherited wealth may be the most obviously important, what has fascinated class theorists of the late 1980s and early 1990s is the inheritance and accumulation of cultural capital: educational credentials, knowledge and skill in the symbolic manipulation of language and figures, verbal style and proficiency, cultural taste, and knowledge of how to play the educational game.

3. Classes of Persons and Classes of Positions

Weber's distinction between economic classes defined by market situation and social classes bounded by mobility barriers introduces a dimension of class analysis that is largely missing from Marxist accounts: the social and cultural backgrounds of the incumbents of class positions. For Marxists, it is the inequality of positions within the social division of labor, and not the inequality of persons in access to those positions, that motors history. Hence 'individuals are dealt with only in so far as they are the personifications of economic categories, embodiments of particular class-relations and class-interests' (Marx 1978: 297).

This approach has informed numerous empirical studies that demonstrate pronounced differences in political and ideological alignment that reflect the interests inscribed in what structuralists call the empty places of the division of labor, empty in that it matters not who fills them. Simply put, the job makes the man, independently of the social and cultural orientations that incumbents may bring with them to their positions. Put the children of workers in executive positions and they will think and act not like their parents but like their golf partners. Hence, social closure and class inheritance are not necessary to reproduce the class structure.

Writers working in the Weberian tradition, on the other hand, are more likely to think in terms of classes of persons defined by their access to valued resources, not classes of positions defined by locations in the social division of labor. Persons, as the units of class analysis, provide the nodal points at which the vocational dimensions of class intersect with inequalities outside the workplace, like differential access to marriage partners, private clubs, residential neighborhoods, and social networks. From Hollingshead's Elmtown to Warner and Lunt's Yankee City, these classic studies aggregate classes from the similarities of personal attributes affecting individual life-chances and social standing, in which family and education, as well as wealth and occupation, are what usually matter.

In broad strokes, this theoretical perspective places the social and cultural composition of classes at the center of class analysis and draws particular attention to problems of social mobility and status attainment. Incumbents do more than vivify their parts in a structural *deus ex machina*. Classes differ in their ideology, life-style, and voice because they systematically recruit incumbents with distinctive social and cultural backgrounds. Social closure is therefore essential to the reproduction of class. While acknowledging the Marxist canon that classes 'share a common function in the broad social division of labor,' the Ehrenreichs reject what they see as a 'vocational approach to class,' because it 'leaves out everything else which shapes a person's political consciousness and loyalties—their ... social and cultural existence' (Ehrenreich and Ehrenreich 1979). Social closure based on exclusionary practices also entails intentional collective action, such that consciousness is a constitutive element of social class and not an epiphenomenon as assumed by structural Marxism, an approach that the eminent British sociologists Anthony Giddens and Frank Parkin claim vitiates class as a tool of empirical analysis. It is not incumbency of position in a formally defined structure but rather the organized effort to monopolize and usurp access that usually corresponds to political alignment and behavior.

Personal attributes that typify locations may also produce an association between persons and positions such that members acquire the class outlook of the positions typified by their background—the positions where they 'belong' as signified by their cultural marker. Members of an ethnic or other cultural collectivity historically associated with particular places in the division of labor may identify with the position signified not by where they are but by who they are, that is to say, not by their own class-structural location but by the location of those persons with whom they associate and typically interact. For example, one widely cited study suggests that middle-class blacks are more likely than whites in comparable class locations to identify with the working or lower class. Studies of overeducation have also found that college-educated respondents are more likely to identify as middle or upper class than others in similar blue-collar occupations, suggesting that membership in the middle class is based on the possession of credentials and not actual location in the social division of labor.

4. Knowledge Workers on the Road to Class Power

The rise of the new middle class is clearly one of the most important changes in the class structure of the advanced industrial societies, both East and West. The class is new in that its members derive their power, prestige, and overall life chances not from the sale of material commodities, as did the old petty bourgeoisie of family owned and operated businesses, but as salaried knowledge workers.

The term 'new class' was first proposed by Djilas in his pioneering work on the former state elites in Eastern Europe. The term was imported to the West by theorists of postindustrialism who broadened the concept to refer to structural changes in the social division of labor in both the public and private sectors: the separation of ownership and control, the growth of the public and nonprofit sectors, and the increasing centrality of highly specialized knowledge. The rapid ascension of these new administrative and professional positions has aroused the hopes and fears of left and right as they hazard the prospects of a robust and liberal counterweight to the political influence of business. Prominent neoconservatives like Peter Berger and Irving Kristol predict a political inversion in which these purveyors of symbolic knowledge supplant the proletariat as the major antagonists of capitalism. Others, including some neo-Marxists, claim only that large sections may be a potentially vital (if unstable) ally of the working class in countering the power of propertied interests (Wright 1979).

New-class opposition to corporate prerogatives, market logic, and entrepreneurial values has been attributed to the material interests of credentialed knowledge workers who find their road to power and privilege blocked by the propertied class, much as the bourgeoisie once confronted an older aristocracy. Those 'with an interest in having privilege based on educational credentials,' Berger hypothesizes, tend toward 'a general antagonism ... against the capitalist market system that, in principle, is open to anyone regardless of education' (1986: 69–70). Moreover, 'like all rising classes, the knowledge class rhetorically identifies its own class interests ... with the down–trodden (just as the early bourgeoisie did in its conflict with the *ancien régime*).' This opposition is reflected in and reinforced by what Alvin Gouldner (1979) has called a 'culture of critical discourse' that questions tradition, deference to authority, inherited privilege, and the voice of money rather than reason.

Neoconservative writers have also emphasized the role of the state as the Trojan horse of the intellectuals on the road to class power. As Berger argues, the growth of the state and nonprofit sectors provides the structural basis for the emergence of a counterelite that opposes propertied interests and supports state intervention on behalf of those perceived as victims of market inequity. Those whose work and advancement is not governed by the logic of commodity production may be less likely to accept the necessity or desirability of profit-centered activity and more disposed toward criticism of entrepreneurial values. However, critics such as Daniel Bell and C. Wright Mills have sharply questioned the independence of managers and highly paid professionals from the propertied interests that support them and with whom they socialize and marry.

These controversies have animated a plethora of empirical studies by leading researchers, including Samuel Stouffer and Seymour Martin Lipset. Evidence abounds of widespread support among college-graduate professionals for left-of-center positions on social issues: personal freedom, racial and cultural tolerance, rights of women and minorities, environmental and consumer protection, and antimilitarism. However, there is little evidence to suggest that either higher education or professional position promote antipathy toward business or free enterprise or support for greater economic equality.

Framed by Gouldner's theory of a culture of critical discourse, consistent cross-national evidence of the subjective salience of occupational self-direction suggests a plausible interpretation of new-class dissent on social issues. Melvin Kohn, who pioneered these studies, has accumulated, over three decades and in a variety of countries in the East and West, a vast archive of evidence pointing to the psychological impact of the experience of self-directed work (Kohn 1977). His extensive research reveals striking class differences in the exercise of critical discourse: tolerance, intellectual skepticism, moral flexibility, openness to social change, and a critical orientation towards tradition and authority. Classes differ ideologically not only because incumbents have different material interests, but also because they experience systematically different social relationships, from which they draw different generalizations about the world and their relationship to it, minimizing the dissonance between the values inscribed in their occupational roles and those in the world outside. Hence those required to submit in the workplace are uncomfortable with self-directed inquiry, situationist ethics, and scientific uncertainty, while those in jobs that entail the exercise of discretionary responsibility find moral majorities equally bothersome.

Although Kohn and his associates do not test the implications of their model for class differences on social issues, other studies find strong support for the effects of occupational self-direction in promoting greater openness to social change. However, there is no evidence that this extends to an antibusiness animus. The weight of the evidence so far leans heavily to the conclusion that the rising middle class provides a powerful constituency for social reform but is unlikely to challenge the power and privilege of the propertied class.

Others have suggested reversing the causal order in Kohn's model. The personality traits associated with occupational self-direction may instead be acquired long before entering the workplace, through processes of socialization in the home and school. In their influential critique of the educational system, Bowles and Gintis contend that middle-class families tend to have children in student-centered, inquiry-oriented classrooms that model the employee-centered social relations of the office. In contrast, working-class children are more likely to find themselves in teacher-centered schools oriented toward discipline and compliance, corresponding to the more authoritarian social relations of the shop floor. As a result, despite class similarities in native intelligence, schools reinforce psychic and cultural differences that limit both the aspirations and opportunities of the less privileged. This view of the educational system, not as the great equalizer but as the axial mechanism for class inheritance, has provided the point of departure for important sociolinguistic studies of class attainment.

5. The Theory of Discursive Capital

The rise of a new middle class, endowed with cultural rather than material assets, has altered the process by which class inequalities are reproduced over time. Although cultural stocks like educational credentials, knowledge, and manners are highly marketable, they differ from material assets in that they cannot be readily probated. As a result, family socialization and education have attracted considerable scholarly attention as vehicles of class inheritance. It is in this context that theories of linguistic class differences assume special prominence. Basil Bernstein's work on the accumulation of what he calls 'discursive resources' represents one of the leading contributions, as well as one of the most controversial (see *Code, Sociolinguistic*; *Bernstein, Basil*).

Following Emile Durkheim, the influential French sociologist of the late nineteenth century, Bernstein argues that a more complex and fully differentiated division of labor entails changes in family interactions and corresponding linguistic codes. The simpler the social division of labor, Bernstein writes, the more restricted the coding orientation. The more complex the social division of labor, the more elaborated the coding orientation. These distinct semiotic grammars in turn facilitate or restrict access to locations in the division of labor, thereby reproducing and legitimating class inequalities across the generations (1981: 327–32).

The theory begins with a Weberian concept of a positively privileged class whose position is based on the possession of marketable knowledge, skills, and credentials, with access largely controlled by the educational system. Bernstein argues that the family relationships in this class differ fundamentally from the interpersonal relationships in working-class families. The latter are characterized by closed, position-oriented family relations in which interactions are determined by ascribed status as parent–child and male–female. The closed, position-oriented working-class relationships foster communalized roles outside the family that require consensus among the interactants, shared cultural history, similarity of experiences, and common assumptions that family members do not need or want to articulate, a pattern Durkheim called 'mechanical solidarity.'

According to Durkheim, mechanical solidarity derives from similarities in roles and functions, in which common experiences and shared identities bind members to the collectivity, as exemplified by tribal systems. This contrasts with what he called 'organic solidarity,' which derives from highly differentiated, interdependent roles, with bonds based on mutual need rather than identity of position. Mechanical solidarity is centered on the group, within which members are interchangeable parts. Organic solidarity is centered instead on the indispensability of specialized roles, leading to what Durkheim called the cult of the individual.

This cult of the individual, Bernstein argues, is more likely to typify middle-class families. They tend to exhibit open, person-oriented interactions, in which decisions are open to discussion and criticism, with less deference to the position of the speaker. Roles are more flexible and status within the family is negotiated rather than ascribed. Hence children can shape their role in the family so as to reflect their individual social and cognitive attributes and unique experiences. The open, person-oriented middle-class relationships carry over into what Bernstein characterizes as individualized roles outside the family that permit and encourage differences among interactants in backgrounds, cultural assumptions, and points of view (see *Role Theory*).

Bernstein also follows Durkheim in the emphasis he places on the social structuring of meanings and on their diverse but related contextual linguistic realizations. Bernstein's approach is thus diametrically opposed to the Whorfian school which sees language as primary to the structuring of social relationships, determining the conceptualization and ordering of experience. Here it is the other way around. Distinctive patterns of interpersonal relationships provide different opportunities for the use of language. The interpersonal relationships in which working-class children communicate involve 'restricted codes' in which the speakers rely on shared understandings, with implicit meanings that speakers find difficult to articulate directly. 'The most general condition for the emergence of this code is a social relationship based upon a common, extensive set of closely shared identifications, and expectations self-consciously held by the members ... The meanings are likely to be concrete, descriptive, or narrative rather than analytical or abstract ... there will be a low level of vocabulary and syntactic selection; and *the unique meaning of the individual is likely to be verbally implicit*' (Bernstein 1966: 256–7).

Conversely, the individualized roles of the middle-class family, where the intent of the other person cannot be taken for granted, are conducive to *elaborated codes*, with a more complex grammatical sentence structure and more subordinate clauses, adverbs, and adjectives. Communication among highly differentiated roles requires speakers to be more explicit about meanings, with fewer assumptions about the common base of knowledge and experience on which speakers might rely.

These elaborated codes in turn reinforce a self-directed relationship with others. 'The user of an elaborated code comes to perceive language as a set of theoretical possibilities available for the transmission of unique experience,' Bernstein continues. 'The concept of self, unlike the self-concept of a speaker limited to a restricted code, will be verbally differentiated, so that it becomes, in itself, the object of specialized perceptual activity.'

The argument has striking implications for theories of the new middle class. Gouldner, for example, cites Bernstein's concept of elaborated codes as key to the critical discourse of the intellectuals. The model also addresses Kohn's research on occupational self-direction, suggesting that linguistic elaboration may account for the widely observed correspondence between self-directed work and ideational flexibility, openness to change, tolerance of diversity, and intellectual skepticism. What appear to be the psychological consequences of occupation may turn out to be latent cultural attributes, embedded in speech patterns, that incumbents bring with them to the job.

However, the major application of the model has been as an explanation for class differences in educational success. Elaborated codes facilitate expression of complex and abstract ideas valued by the school, while the grammatical structure of the restricted code inhibits logical reasoning, promotes inconsistency, and limits interest in generalization, thereby precluding discursive inquiry and compromising the probability of academic achievement. 'If a child is to succeed as he progresses through school,' Bernstein concludes, 'it becomes critical for him to possess, or at least to be oriented towards, an elaborated code' (1966: 259).

Bernstein's novel and provocative explanation for the meritocratic reproduction of class inequality has motivated a new cottage industry of empirical studies. Bernstein's own investigations report that British upper-class children are significantly more likely to use elaborated codes, passive voice, and first-person pronouns, even when nonverbal IQ is controlled. Another five-year British study found that compared to working-class mothers, middle-class mothers favor abstract and implicit definitions over explicit and concrete definitions, and favor open-ended, heuristic answers to children's questions. An Australian study of 96 high-schoolers showed distinct social class differences in verbal linguistic coding.

Nevertheless, many others have found that Bernstein's model fits the data rather poorly and have had difficulty replicating his results, especially outside the UK. One study of the speech of 39 British 11-year-olds found no rigidity in the lower working-class children's speech, nor persistence of any restricted and elaborated codes. Similar findings have been reported from Australia. An American study of written language usage of 100 high school freshmen found no relationship between parental socioeconomic status and word usage or sentence structure. Several other US studies have also failed to show any direct relationship between social class and children's verbal communicative styles. Neither social control strategies nor school achievement scores were differently related to elaborated and restricted variants. An Israeli study of formal and informal speech situations for 72 male 12-year olds found no support for the claim that lower class children have less access to an elaborated code.

Thorlindsson's (1987) study of 338 Icelandic 15-year olds represents one of the most thorough and exhaustive attempts to fully test Bernstein's model. Thorlindsson found that linguistic elaboration does not play its predicted role, with no significant association with either social class, family interaction patterns, or scholastic achievement.

These inconsistent results may indicate substantial measurement error in key variables like linguistic elaboration and child-centered family interactions. Investigators disagree over the need to test spoken versus written language, the use of formal and informal contexts, and whether young children or parents should provide data on parental roles in the family. Thorlindsson also suspects that Bernstein's findings among British children reflect peculiarities of British upperclass values as these are reflected in the schools.

6. The Deficit Controversy

The empirical problems have been overshadowed by the other major criticism of Bernstein's work. His theory has invited interpretation and sharp controversy as a deficit theory of academic failure among working-class youth. Deficit theories, critics charge, blame the victims for conditions that are imposed on them and over which they exercise no real control. Class inequalities may then be rationalized as natural expressions of innate differences rather than outcomes of a competitive struggle.

Critics such as Gecas complain that restricted codes imply that the user could be expected to have lower cognitive abilities of abstract reasoning and analytic thinking. Bernstein is thus regarded as lending support to controversial theories of cultural inferiority such as those of Bereiter and Engelmann who hold that the dialect of blacks in the USA is not merely an underdeveloped version of standard English, but basically a nonlogical mode of expressive behavior.

Although Bernstein has been roundly criticized for advocating a deficit interpretation, it is clear even in his early writings that this is a serious distortion of his intent. Bernstein never contends that working-class children are cognitively deficient but only that they lack the opportunities for language use that middle-class children experience. To begin with, restricted codes are used at some time by all members of society, Bernstein emphasizes, including the middle class. 'Children socialized within middle class and associated strata can be expected to possess both an elaborated and a restricted code; while children socialized within some sections of the working class strata, particularly the lower working class, can be expected to be limited to a restricted code' (1966: 259).

This limitation is not a matter of ability. Working-class children are fully capable of using elaborated codes but lack opportunities to do so. Those thrust into highly differentiated roles have no choice but to respond to the needs for specialized communication inscribed therein. 'The orientation towards these codes, both elaborated and restricted, may be independent of the psychology of the child, independent of his native ability,' Bernstein continues, 'governed entirely by the form of the social relation, or more generally by the quality of the social structure.' The problem is not innate ability but rather unequal access to different speech systems based on status position in a given social structure, such that children may adopt quite different social and intellectual procedures, despite a common potential. Thus Bernstein concludes that:

> The relative backwardness of lower working class and rural children may well be a form of culturally induced backwardness which is transmitted to the child through the linguistic process. The code the child brings to the school symbolizes his social identity. It relates him to his kin and to his local social relations. The code progressively orients the child towards a pattern of relationships which constitute for him his psychological reality, and this reality is reinforced every time he speaks.

In his later work, Bernstein underscores the point that the differences are based on power, not cognitive function. Using less neutral terminology, Bernstein argues that class relations 'generate, distribute, reproduce, and legitimate distinctive forms of communication, which transmit dominating and dominated codes...[that function as] culturally determined positioning devices' (Bernstein 1981: 327).

For example, Labov's (1972) study of language use among black gang members suggests that the experimental setting can generate the linguistic deficit that the investigator is seeking to measure. Labov found that when an inner-city black child is interviewed by an educated white person using elaborated codes, the child defends himself against what is perceived as an unsympathetic and probably hostile person by resorting to monosyllabic expression and minimal response. Labov then replaced the interviewer with an unthreatening black person who allows the child's best friend to come along and who sits on the floor with the children and shares a snack. The child then becomes verbally enterprising and shows no cognitive deficiency. Labov concludes that the social situation is the principal determinant of verbal behavior. Once this is taken into account, street dialect appears to be structurally equivalent to standard English, the speech patterns merely alternative expressions of the same latent linguistic construction (see *Ebonics and African American Vernacular English*; *Sociolinguistic Variation*).

Other studies also call into question the assumption that working-class children are victims of class-based socialization patterns. In his compelling ethnography of a white working-class gang in a British factory town, Willis (1977) shows how the gang members construct what he calls a counterschool culture in active defiance of dominant patterns that threaten their gendered self-esteem. The boys do not passively adopt coding orientations that handicap them in the schools; they not only know how to use elaborated codes, they delight in exaggerated mimicry of the ineffectual ambience projected by 'proper' expression. From this perspective, the concreteness of their discourse expresses their potency, while the official language of the school provides an endless source of ridicule that delights the boys and ritually affirms their masculine prowess. The paradox is that the boys are condemned to follow their parents into stultifying and low-paying jobs not because the school fails to appreciate their obvious ability and creativity, but because they reject the school as a scam designed for fools and a threat to their authenticity as concrete actors. To return to Marx, it would seem that the inversion of subject and predicate in the world of work leaves the boys with no choice but to speak in their own voice, a voice that mocks the ineffectual white-collar world and celebrates the robust efficacy of manual labor, echoing the sturdy proletarians depicted in the murals of socialist realism. But the celebration is cut short when the boys soon discover that life does not imitate art.

See also: Ideology; Critical Sociolinguistics; Social Networks; Class and Language.

Bibliography

Berger P 1986 *The Capitalist Revolution*. Basic Books, New York
Bernstein B 1966 Elaborated and restricted codes: An outline. *Social Inquiry* **36**(2): 126–33
Bernstein B 1981 Codes, modalities, and the process of cultural reproduction: A model. *Language in Society* **10**(3): 327–63
Dahrendorf R 1959 *Class and Class Conflict in Industrial Society*. Stanford University Press, Stanford, LA
Ehrenreich B, Ehrenreich J 1979 In: Walker P (ed.) *Between Labor and Capital*. South End Press, Boston, MA
Gouldner A 1979 *The Future of Intellectuals and the Rise of the New Class*. Seabury Press, New York
Kohn M L 1977 *Class and Conformity: A Study in Values, with a Reassessment*, 2nd edn. University of Chicago Press, Chicago, IL
Labov W 1972 The logic of nonstandard English. In: Giglioli P P (ed.) *Language and Social Context*. Penguin, Harmondsworth, UK
Marx K 1978 Manifesto of the Communist Party. In: Tucker R C (ed.) *The Marx–Engels Reader*, 2nd edn. Norton, New York
Thorlindsson T 1987 Bernstein's sociolinguistics: An empirical test in Iceland. *Social Forces* **65**(3): 695–718
Weber M 1978 (transl. Fischoff E et al.) *Economy and Society: An Outline of Interpretative Sociology*. University of California Press, Berkeley, CA
Willis P E 1977 *Learning to Labor*. Columbia University Press, New York
Wright E O 1979 *Class Structure and Income Determination*. Academic Press, New York

Language Variation and Change: Dialects and Social Groups

Social Networks
A. L. Milroy

Dialectological and historical linguistic research has consistently revealed the persistence, often over centuries, of low status and nonlegitimized dialects and languages in rural and urban communities, despite pressure from powerful standard languages like English and French. In contemporary western society where nonstandard dialects are publicly and generally stigmatized, such pressure is exerted in many ways—for example, through the educational system, through social and economic penalties springing from public use of nonstandard dialects, and through the language used and attitudes expressed in the broadcast and printed media. An individual's social network is quite simply the sum of relationships which he or she has contracted with others, and social network analysis examines the differing structure and properties of social networks. Such analysis has been applied in dialectology to explicate the day by day social mechanisms which allow speakers to maintain their nonstandard dialects, despite pressure from national standard languages. Conversely, change in the operation of these social mechanisms has been used to elucidate the phenomenon of linguistic change.

1. The Concept of Social Network

Social network analysis of the kind which is particularly relevant to dialectology originates in anthropological research, mainly during the 1960s and 1970s (see Li 1996). Scholars from many different disciplines employed the concept for a range of theoretical and practical reasons; Johnson's (1994) survey alludes to a wide range of approaches within anthropology, which hardly overlap with the largely quantitative modes of analysis described by Cochran et al. (1990). Procedures for analyzing the social networks of individuals were developed as a result of dissatisfaction with what some anthropologists saw as an overreliance on highly abstract social concepts (such as that of social class) in accounting for differences in everyday social behavior. Personal networks were generally seen as contextualized within this broader social framework, which constantly constrained behavior. However, it was 'bracketed off' to allow attention to be concentrated on developing less abstract modes of analysis which could account more immediately for the variable behavior of individuals. A fundamental postulate of network analysis is that individuals create personal communities which provide them with a meaningful framework for solving the problems of their day to day existence (Mitchell 1986: 74), and this kind of focus makes it very suitable for studying small and relatively well-defined urban and rural communities.

A social network may be seen as a boundless web of ties which reaches out through a whole society, linking people to one another, however remotely. But for practical reasons social networks are generally 'anchored' to individuals, and interest focuses on relatively 'strong' first-order network ties—i.e., those persons with whom an individual directly interacts. Second-order ties are those to whom the link is indirect (see Fig. 1). This principle of 'anchorage' effectively limits the field of network studies, generally to something between 20 and 50 individuals. Thus, for example, if the objective was to look comparatively at the network structures of 40 speakers of a nonstandard urban dialect, one way to proceed would be to discover the 20 individuals whom each saw as his or her most significant daily contacts. Then the contrasts between these various 'networks' of 20 could be examined with respect to linguistically relevant characteristics such as whether they were dialect speakers or not, kin or not, had contacts with each other or not, and so on. In fact this is parallel to the procedure adopted by the social anthropologist Clyde Mitchell in a 1980s study of homeless women in Manchester, UK. His interest is in the effects of their personal network structures upon the length of time they are homeless. A different way of examining network structure is described in Sect. 2.

1.1 Multiplexity and Density as Properties of Networks

The two concepts of 'multiplexity' and 'density' are of critical importance in a comparative analysis of social networks. In a maximally dense and multiplex network, everyone would know everyone

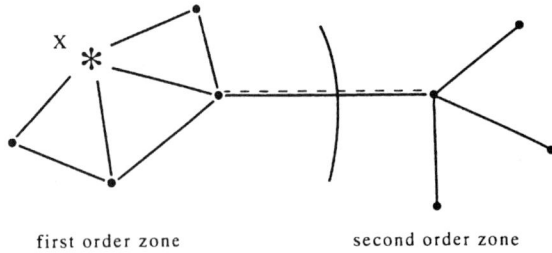

Figure 1. High-density personal network structure, showing first and second order zones. X is the focal point of the network.

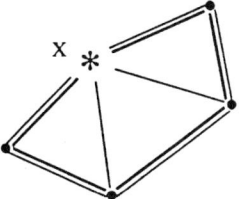

Figure 2.1 High-density, high-multiplexity personal network structure: X is the focal point of the network.

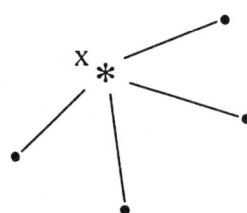

Figure 2.2 Low-density, uniplex personal network structure: X is the focal point of the network.

else (density), and the actors would know one another in a range of capacities (multiplexity). Social anthropologists now generally agree that a social network of a dense, multiplex type, which in effect constitutes a bounded group, has the capacity to impose general normative consensus upon its members. The idealized maximally dense and multiplex network is shown in Fig. 2.1 in contrast with a loose-knit, uniplex type of network (Fig. 2.2). Close-knit networks, which will of course vary in the extent to which they approximate to such a representation, have the capacity to maintain and even enforce local conventions and norms—of dress, religion, and general behavior, for example—and linguistic norms are no exception to this generalization. Close-knit networks are very common worldwide in low-status communities, both rural and urban, and they flourish in the absence of social and geographical mobility. It has been argued that close-knit networks with their characteristic reciprocity and solidarity ethic constitute a basic survival and support mechanism in poor communities in the absence of material resources. It will be shown in Sect. 2 how the characteristics of such networks are important in encouraging the long-term survival of socially disfavored dialects.

2. Social Networks and Language Variation

In this section some applications of the network concept in dialectology will be described, with particular reference to small-scale close-knit communities. Particular attention will be given to a study carried out in the mid-1970s of the urban dialect of Belfast, Northern Ireland (see Milroy and Milroy 1978, Milroy 1987). This research is in the quantitative tradition developed by William Labov (see *Sociolinguistic Variation*; *Labov, William*). Using the concept of the sociolinguistic variable, the language patterns of 46 speakers from three inner-city communities were examined. Eight phonological variables (seven vowel variables and one consonant variable) were selected for analysis in relation to the network structure of individual speakers; all were quite characteristic of the dialect. Speakers varied, however, in the extent to which they used the vernacular realization of these variables; they were not isolated individuals, but had contracted long-standing social ties with each other within their neighborhoods. All three communities, Ballymacarrett, Clonard, and Hammer, were poor working-class communities where the informal social structure corresponded to the dense, multiplex, often kin-based patterns, described by many investigators as characteristic of long-established working-class communities (see, for example, Young and Wilmott 1962). The communicative pattern which recurs in these accounts is one of persons interacting mostly within a clearly-defined territory, tending to know each others' social contacts (i.e., having relatively dense social networks) and tending to be linked to each other by multiplex ties.

Although this dense, multiplex network structure was evident in all three communities (in very sharp contrast to middle-class neighborhoods) the extent to which individuals were linked to local networks varied considerably. Some people, for example, worked outside the area and had no local kin and no local ties of friendship, while others were linked to local networks in all these capacities. These differences in personal network structure, which appeared to spring from many complex social and psychological factors, were related to a number of other variables, such as the age and sex of the speaker and the type of locality. For example, young men seemed on the whole to contract denser and more multiplex network ties than young women, and urban redevelopment programs which relocated communities in outer urban areas seemed to have the effect of disrupting long-term network ties. Social network structure is also class-related in that middle-class networks are more frequently loose-knit. This point is returned to below.

2.1 Measuring Social Network Structure

Although when considered in terms of their social class they formed a very homogeneous group, the Belfast working-class speakers varied in their use of the linguistic variables, some sounding very much more vernacular than others. The device used to examine the relationship between this linguistic variation and variation in network structure was a six-point network strength scale which measured speakers' network characteristics on various indicators of multiplexity and density. Two examples of these indicators are kin orientation and territorially based friendship ties (see Milroy 1987: 141 for full details). Since this network strength scale quantified the extent to which speakers interacted with others in the community and the strength of the ties contracted there, it could be interpreted as a measure of the pressure exerted by the close-knit network upon its members. A series of statistical tests revealed a strong correlation between personal network structure and patterns of language use, even allowing for the interaction of other social variables such as the age and the sex of the speaker; the strongest dialect speakers were those whose informal social ties were the strongest. Figure 3 illustrates their relationship in Ballymacarrett, in showing a tendency for speakers who are plotted high on the vertical axis also to be plotted towards the right of the graph. The linguistic behavior at issue is the presence versus absence of the consonant [ð] intervocalically in such words as *mother, brother*. Deletion scores for each speaker, whose age group and sex are also specified, are plotted as percentages against his or her network strength score. It is on the basis of such language/network relationships that the close-knit network may be viewed as an important social mechanism of dialect maintenance, encouraging the long-term survival of nonstandard and socially disfavored language varieties.

2.2 Applications of the Network Concept in Small-scale Communities

Apart from its potential for explaining why nonstandard dialects persist, a network approach has been found methodologically useful for investigations of subgroups in the population in situations where a social class model such as that provided by William Labov (1972) in his study of the urban dialect of New York City is less practical. This happens when the class distribution of the speakers to be studied is uneven, as is the case with most nonstandard dialect speakers. A network analysis has several rather obvious methodological advantages in such situations, which can be stated quite briefly. First, it provides a useful means of studying relatively small, self-contained groups in more detail than is possible within a large-scale survey framework such as Labov's. Second, it provides a means of approaching an analysis where the concept of social class is difficult to apply; this is a problem commonly encountered by researchers studying minority ethnic groups, migrants, rural populations, or populations in nonindustrialized societies (see, for example, Horvath 1985). Finally, network analysis offers a procedure for dealing with variation between speakers at the level of the individual rather than the group. These points are all relevant to the studies by Edwards (1986) of the language of British black adolescents and by Bortoni-Ricardo (1985) of changes in the language of rural migrants to a Brazilian city. A brief review of these studies follows.

One of the limitations on choice of method encountered by Edwards was that since there is no enumerated list of British black persons (even assuming that this is a well-defined category), a sample frame could not be constructed to allow speakers from the British black community to be systematically sampled from a range of social classes. Even if the use of social class as a speaker variable were feasible in this rather fundamental practical sense, it would in any case be unlikely to yield much insight into the interplay between social and linguistic differentiation. This is for the rather obvious reason that a social class index cannot distinguish in an illuminating way between members of a group who are mostly unemployed or concentrated in low-status occupations. But since it seems to be possible to analyze the black community as a whole as consisting of overlapping sets of relatively close-knit groups, the network variable is, as Edwards found, rather more helpful in describing the relationship between linguistic variability and the social characteristics of speakers.

The crucial variable from a dialectologist's point of view underlying any measure of personal network structure is degree of integration into a close-knit group. However, the same indicators (see the description in Sect. 2.1 of two of those used in Belfast) are not necessarily relevant to different groups. Even if attention is confined to the UK, membership of groups associated with religious institutions might well be irrelevant in a contemporary northern English coal-mining community, but highly relevant in a Midlands' black community such as the one Edwards studied. In fact the indicators used by Edwards were chosen for their capacity to distinguish between individuals who associated themselves to varying degrees with the norms and values of the black community; of particular importance is the distinction between black and nonblack ethnicity. For this reason, Edwards' indicators were designed to measure in various ways the extent to which speakers had contact with black

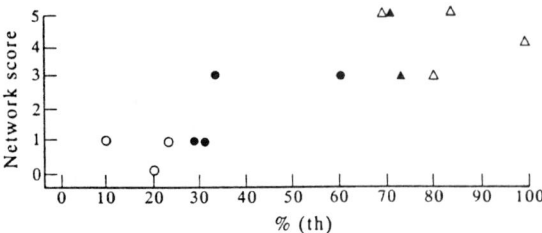

Figure 3. Ballymacarrett—individual scores on network strength scale.

friends and neighbors and participated in black social activities. Whether or not the speakers were employed at all was also taken into account, since employment will almost always involve fairly extended interaction with nonblack individuals. In fact, the index of integration into the black community which was constructed using these indicators correlated well with the extent to which the individual speakers used the 'patois' characteristic of that community.

Bortoni-Ricardo's account of the sociolinguistic adjustment of rural migrants to Brazlandia, a satellite city of Brasilia, is a particularly interesting and innovative application of the network concept. A survey based on a social class analysis is not appropriate or feasible for a sociolinguistic study carried out in Brazil; the chief objections are that the notion of a continuum is neither congruent with the sharp distinction between rich and poor, nor does it adequately discriminate between the individuals studied, all of whom were relatively poor. Bortoni-Ricardo did not posit a linguistic movement by the migrants in the direction of an urban standardized norm (of Portuguese) of the kind familiar in studies using the social class variable; taking the group's own linguistic norms as a starting point, she examined the extent to which speakers had moved away from their stigmatized Caipira dialect.

Bortoni-Ricardo's main hypothesis about change in social structure associated with the change from rural to urban life is that it involves a move from an 'insulated' network consisting largely of kinsfolk and neighbors to an 'integrated' urban network where the links will be less multiplex and associated with a wider range of social contexts. The linguistic counterpart of this process is analyzed as one of dialect diffuseness—a movement away from the norms of the Caipira dialect. Two separate network indices are used to measure the changing patterns of the migrants' social relationships; the first is the integration index and the second the urbanization index. The integration index expresses numerically certain relevant characteristics of the three persons with whom each migrant most frequently interacts—for example, whether or not they are kinsfolk, or whether the ties have been contracted in the premigration period. The score assigned to each migrant is intended to characterize progress in the transition from an insulated to an integrated type of network, and as such is a tool capable of investigating loose-knit types of personal network structure (see further below). As Bortoni-Ricardo shows, integration scores correlate with a linguistic movement away from the norms of the Caipira dialect.

The urbanization index is designed to supplement this structural measure, representing the extent to which the members of each migrant's personal network are integrated into urban life. A number of indicators are used to compute this index, two of which are educational level and occupational mobility; the indicators are selected for their capacity to measure the extent to which the persons with whom a migrant customarily interacts is integrated into (i.e., participates in) urban life.

From both a methodological and a theoretical point of view, Bortoni-Ricardo's work is particularly interesting. In developing two types of index it extends the application of the network variable beyond an analysis of small, close-knit groups of the kind described so far to consider the extent to which individuals have detached themselves from such groups. The theoretical significance of this advance is explored below. Section 3 will concentrate on the theoretical implications of the link between a close-knit network structure and language maintenance and its obvious corollary; that a loosening of close-knit ties is likely to be associated with linguistic change.

3. Strong and Weak Network Ties: Theories of Language Maintenance and Language Change

A general methodological problem associated with the use of the network variable is that although it can be readily operationalized as described above to study speakers whose networks are of a relatively close-knit type, it cannot easily handle socially and geographically mobile speakers whose personal network ties are not predominantly dense or multiplex. However, such persons make up a substantial proportion of the population in a postindustrial society, particularly in cities. Loose-knit networks are hard to deal with chiefly because social network analysis involves comparing speakers who differ from each other in certain respects—for example, in respect of the multiplexity of the ties which they have contracted at the workplace—but are still similar enough in other related ways to make such a comparison meaningful. For example, it is evident that relative to someone who has changed employment and place of residence several times, the networks of the Belfast inner-city speakers described in Sect. 2.1 are all close-knit. While one might make this general point and follow through its implications in a comparison of, for example, these speakers with residents of lower middle-class areas of the city, it is much less easy to see how the relatively loose-knit network structures of individual lower middle-class speakers might meaningfully be compared with each other. This problem was encountered in an attempt to apply social network analysis in the prosperous Berlin suburb of Zehlendorf (Dittmar and Schlobinski 1988).

In Belfast, language variation in two lower middle-class areas, Braniel and Andersonstown, was analyzed to supplement the inner-city studies described in Sect. 2.1. Many of the Braniel and Andersonstown speakers owned cars and telephones, which they used as a means of maintaining important personal ties over long distances, but the capacity of these 'distance' ties to influence their behavior (linguistic or otherwise) is not clear. Some speakers seemed to be relatively exposed to standardizing mainstream influences, in that they had contracted few personal ties which were likely to exert normative pressure on their behavior; but in any case the geographical spread of the ties contracted by most Braniel and Andersonstown speakers made them difficult to investigate. In general, however, these individuals seemed less likely than the inner-city speakers to be subject to the pressures of their personal networks and more likely to be subject to a less localized outside influence, which in turn exposes them to external pressure from a linguistic standard.

3.1 The Importance of Weak Ties in Elucidating Linguistic Change

Loose-knit networks are likely to play an important part in the construction of a theory of linguistic diffusion and change, at the level of theory, although they are difficult to analyze empirically (but see the discussion above of Bortoni-Ricardo's study of rural immigrants to a Brazilian city). Following Granovetter's work (1973) Milroy and Milroy (1985) have argued that 'weak' and apparently insignificant interpersonal ties (of 'acquaintance' as opposed to 'friend,' for example) are important channels through which innovation and influence flow from one close-knit group to another, linking such groups to the wider society. To support this argument, a detailed quantitative analysis of the history and present-day distribution of three Belfast phonological variables is presented. The spread of one of them apparently across sectarian lines of demarcation to penetrate the dialect of young speakers is difficult to explain except in such terms. The change involved is a realization of a limited set of lexical items such as *pull, put, foot* with an unrounded rather than a rounded vowel. This weak-tie model of change and diffusion is also applied to account for the tendency of some languages to be more resistant to change than others (Icelandic versus English, for example), the general argument being that a type of social organization which is based on overlapping close-knit networks will inhibit change, while one based on mobility (for whatever reason), with a concomitant weakening of network ties, will facilitate it. Weak intergroup ties are argued to be critical in transmitting innovations from one group to another, despite the rather general commonsense assumption in sociolinguistic and dialectological work that strong ties fulfill this role. For example, in suggesting that the network concept is important for a theory of linguistic diffusion, Downes (1998: 155) assumes that it is strong ties which will be relevant, and Labov (1980: 261) presents a model of diffusion and change where the innovator is seen as an individual with strong ties both inside and outside a local group.

Although the idea that innovations are transmitted through weak network links may at first sight seem counterintuitive, a little thought suggests that it is plausible. First of all, it is likely (in the networks of mobile individuals at least) that weak ties are more numerous than strong ties. Second, many more individuals can be reached through weak ties than through strong ties; consider, for example, the links set up by participants at academic or business conferences, which link cohesive groups associated with each institution and through which new ideas and information pass. Conversely, information relayed through strong ties tends not to be innovatory, since those linked by strong ties tend to share contacts (that is to belong to overlapping networks). Thus, mobile individuals who have contracted many weak ties, but as a consequence of their mobility occupy a position marginal to any given cohesive group, are in a favourable position to diffuse innovation. Interestingly, this conclusion is in line with the traditional assumption of historians of language that the emergent, mobile merchant class were largely responsible for the appearance of Northern (and other) dialectal innovations in Early Modern (Standard) English (see, for example, Baugh and Cable 1978: 194).

The norm-enforcing capacities of groups built up mainly of strong ties partly explains why innovators are likely to be persons weakly linked to the group; indeed, using a measure of network strength, the Belfast community studies described in Sect. 2.1 showed that susceptibility to outside influence increased in inverse proportion to strength of tie with the group. Where groups are loose-knit—that is linked internally mainly by weak ties—they are therefore likely to be generally more susceptible to innovation. This conclusion is consistent with Labov's principle that innovating groups are located centrally in the social hierarchy, in his terms upper-working or lower-middle class (Labov 1980: 254). For it is likely that in British (and probably also North American) society close-knit networks are located primarily at the highest and lowest strata, with a majority of socially and geographically mobile speakers falling between these two points.

3.2 An Apparent Problem: The Weak Tie Model of Diffusion and Change

One apparent difficulty with a theory which argues that innovators are only marginally linked to the group is in explaining how they can successfully diffuse innovations to more central members; two related points are relevant here. First, since resistance to innovation is likely to be strong in a norm-conforming group, a large number of persons will have to be exposed to it and adopt it in the early stages for it to spread successfully. Now in a mobile postindustrial society, weak ties are likely to be very much more numerous than strong ties. Thus, an innovation like the Cockney merger between /v/:/ð/ and /f/:/θ/ reported in Norwich teenage speech (Trudgill 1986: 54ff.) which appears to 'jump' over a considerable distance is likely to be transmitted through a great many weak links between Londoners and Norwich speakers. Trudgill's suggestion of tourists and football supporters as individuals who might contract such links and transmit the change is quite consistent with the model outlined in this section. Second, persons central to a close-knit, norm-enforcing group are likely to find innovation a risky business; but adopting an innovation which is already widespread on the fringes of the group is very much less risky. Thus, instead of asking how central members of a group are induced to accept an innovation from marginal members, this can be viewed as a prudent strategy on their part. For it is likely that a necessary (but not sufficient) condition for the ultimate adoption of a candidate innovation is that it is positively evaluated, either overtly or covertly. Thus, Norwich speakers, whether they are central or marginal to their local groups, in some sense view vernacular London speech as desirable—more desirable than the speech of other cities. Central members of a group diminish the risk of potentially deviant activity by adopting an innovation from persons who are already linked to the group, rather than by direct importation.

This weak tie model of linguistic change remains to be developed further. However, it seems to be capable of illuminating some puzzling patterns of variation and change which are difficult to explain in terms of the usual unqualified assumption that linguistic change is encouraged by frequency of contact and relatively open channels of communication, and discouraged by boundaries of one sort or another, or weakness in lines of communication.

4. Social Network, Social Class, and the 'Quantitative Paradigm'

An extension of network analysis which focuses on the properties of weak ties provides a crucial link with the variable of social class, which is used extensively in social dialectology to account for variation in urban dialects. Social anthropologists have linked the variables of class and network by arguing that class differences in small communities begin to emerge over time as the proportion of multiplex relationships declines. Such observations suggest a route for constructing a two-level sociolinguistic theory, linking small-scale structures such as networks in which individuals are embedded and act purposively in their daily lives with larger scale social structures (classes) which determine relationships of power at the institutional level. Such a dual level of analysis is needed in order to understand the frequently reported tendency of speakers of urban vernaculars to downgrade their dialects (describing them as 'sloppy,' 'vulgar,' and the like) while nevertheless continuing to speak them in the face of intense standardizing pressure. Recall that while strong ties give rise to a local cohesion of the kind described in inner-city Belfast, they lead paradoxically to overall fragmentation. It is this potential for explaining both patterns—local stability and cohesion versus overall fragmentation and conflict—which allows network analysis to be related to macrolevel social structure.

Some comments made about network models assume that they cannot easily be linked with class-based analyses of language variation because they are concerned only with strong ties in close-knit communities. Network is frequently seen as a microsociological concept, while class is macro-sociological. While this is a reasonable point if network analysis is applied only to close-knit communities, an analysis of loose ties provides a link between the two levels. Furthermore, an initial concentration on network, which emphasizes the extent of local fragmentation in socially stratified societies, suggests that a social class model based on conflict is more appropriate for urban dialectological work than one based on consensus. A number of researchers have been critical of the currently widely accepted consensus model which underlies the work of Labov.

It was pointed out in Sect. 3 that an analysis which makes use of the weak-tie concept agrees with a Labovian class-based analysis in locating linguistic innovators centrally in the class structure. For in British and North American society at least close-knit networks are located primarily in the highest (most powerful) and lowest (least powerful) classes; with regard to the former, consider Mills' (1956) description of the USA power elite. The majority of socially and geographically mobile speakers falls between these two points. Thus, if a network analysis is extended to include an examination of loose-knit network types, which are susceptible to outside (frequently standardizing) influences, it is plain that network-based and class-based analyses are not contradictory as is sometimes suggested; rather they complement each other. This suggests the possibility of an integrated analysis of the relationship between language variation and social structure, combining the variables of social class and social network. Such an analysis would present particular social groups as both internally structured and connected to each other with varying proportions of strong and weak ties.

4.1 Class-related Types of Social Network

The characteristic network structure of distinguishable social groups is certainly related to social class (see *Social Class*) variation (and indeed to other intersecting social variables such as gender and ethnicity) and is likely to have a powerful effect on the kind of dialect spoken both by individuals and by the group as a whole. For example, ethnic subgroups in the UK such as the black speakers studied by Edwards have a predominantly strong-tie internal structure, but seem to be linked with relatively few weak ties to white working-class groups. These white groups in turn might have a similar internal network structure but have more weak-tie links with other white working-class groups. Vertical links to middle-class groups are likely to be fewer (this seemed to be the case in Belfast) and moreover to be frequently institutional in content (to such persons as doctors, lawyers, teachers, welfare personnel, and the like). Middle-class groups for their part—professional, neighborhood, and friendship groups—are characterized by a higher proportion of weak ties internally than working-class groups; hence the problems of studying them systematically in network terms in Zehlendorf, Berlin, and in outer-city Belfast.

However, the controversial concept of social class is interpreted and however close-knit networks are investigated and described, Granovetter's concept of the weak tie can be used to link close-knit community level groupings to more abstract institutional structures. A network perspective on social dialects attributes the behavior of speakers to the constraining effects of the network, or the diminution of those effects which enables standardizing linguistic influences to permeate communities. This avoids a direct appeal to the notion of prestige as defined by the perceived attributes of speakers who are seen to *belong* to different status groups. Social class is viewed as a structural concept rather than a set of labels which might be attached to particular individuals. Thus, local and individual social and linguistic behavior is not seen as directly related to class but as mediated through smaller scale network structures.

Network analysis has recently been used by historical linguists to examine the social trajectories of earlier changes (Tieken-Boon van Ostade et al. 2000), and has been employed for a range of analytic purposes in many different kinds of contemporary monolingual and bilingual communities (see Milroy 2001 for a recent review).

See also: Sociology of Language; Sociolinguistic Variation; Urban and Rural Forms of Language.

Bibliography

Baugh A C, Cable T 1978 *History of the English Language*, 3rd edn. Routledge and Kegan Paul, London
Bortoni-Ricardo S M 1985 *The Urbanisation of Rural Dialect Speakers: A Sociolinguistic Study in Brazil*. Cambridge University Press, Cambridge, UK
Cochran M, Larner M, Riley D, Gunnarsson L, Henderson C R Jr 1990 *Extending Families: The Social Networks of Parents and Their Children*. Cambridge University Press, Cambridge, UK
Dittmar N, Schlobinski P 1988 *The Sociolinguistics of Urban Vernaculars*. de Gruyter, Berlin
Downes W 1998 *Language and Society*, 2nd edn. Cambridge University Press, Cambridge, UK
Edwards V 1986 *Language in a Black Community*. Multilingual Matters, Clevedon, UK
Granovetter M 1973 The strength of weak ties. *American Journal of Sociology* **78**: 1360–80
Horvath B 1985 *Variation in Australian English*. Cambridge University Press, Cambridge, UK
Johnson J C 1994 Anthropological contributions to the study of social networks: A review. In: Wasserman S, Galaskiewicz J (eds.) *Advances in Social Network Analysis: Research in the Social and Behavioral Sciences*. Sage publications, Thousand Oaks, CA, pp. 113–51
Labov W 1972 *Sociolinguistic Patterns*. Pennsylvania University Press, Philadelphia, PA
Labov W (ed.) 1980 *Locating Language in Time and Space*. Academic Press, New York
Li Wei 1996 Network analysis. In: Goebl H, Nelde P, Zdenek S, Woelck W (eds.) *Contact Linguistics: A Handbook of Contemporary Research*. de Gruyter, Berlin, pp. 805–12
Mills C W 1956 *The Power Elite*. Oxford University Press, Oxford, UK
Milroy J, Milroy L 1978 Belfast: Change and variation in an urban vernacular. In: Trudgill P (ed.) *Sociolinguistic Patterns in British English*. Arnold, London
Milroy J, Milroy L 1985 Linguistic change, social network and speaker innovation. *Journal of Linguistics* **21**: 339–84
Milroy L 1987 *Language and Social Networks*, 2nd edn. Blackwell, Oxford, UK
Milroy L 2001 Social networks. In: Chambers J, Trudgill P, Schilling-Estes N (eds.) *Handbook of Variation and Change*. Blackwell, Oxford, UK
Mitchell J C 1986 Network procedures. In: *The Quality of Urban Life*. de Gruyter, Berlin
Rickford J 1986 The need for new approaches to social class analysis in linguistics. *Language and Communication* **6**(3): 215–21
Tieken-Boon van Ostade I, Nevalainen T, Caon L (eds.) 2000 Social network analysis and the history of English. *European Journal of English Studies* **4**(3) (special issue)
Trudgill P 1986 *Dialects in Contact*. Blackwell, Oxford, UK
Young M, Wilmott P 1962 *Family and Kinship in East London*. Penguin, Harmondsworth, UK

Sociolinguistic Variation
R. Mesthrie

Sociolinguistic Variation

This article surveys the approach to linguistic variation taken by William Labov and the school of sociolinguistics that has stemmed from his influence. The work of this school is known by several other names, which give some indications of its main preoccupations: the quantitative paradigm, sociolinguistics proper, variationist studies and urban dialectology.

1. The Goals of Sociolinguistics

Prior to Labov's work in the early 1960s, dialectology had scored its main successes in studies of regional differentiation. Researchers had certainly been aware of linguistic distinctions of a social nature within a region, but had not developed systematic ways of describing them. Earlier explanations of nonregional variation fell into one of two categories: dialect mixture and free variation. 'Dialect mixture' implies the coexistence in one locality of two or more dialects, which enables a speaker to draw on one dialect at one time, and on the other dialect(s) on other occasions. 'Free variation' refers to the random use of alternate forms within a particular dialect (e.g., two pronunciations of *often* [with or without the /t/ sounded]). Both views relegate variation to an extralinguistic domain, and mistakenly identify structuredness with homogeneity. Labov argued, instead, that language involved structured heterogeneity. While he was not the first to point to the interplay between social and linguistic determinants of certain linguistic alternations (e.g., Fischer had discussed the social implications of the use of *-in* versus *-ing* in a New England setting in 1958), Labov was the initiator of an elaborate body of work which broke new ground in understanding language in its social context, accounting for linguistic change, and broadening the goals of linguistic theory. An important motivation in his early work was to understand one of the unsolved problems of historical linguistics—how sound changes like [p] > [f] are effected. He also wondered how, if a language has to be structured in order to function efficiently, people continue to talk while the language changes. The problem was shown to be less intractable once one invoked the idea of systematic variation among different groups of speakers within a speech community (see *Sociolinguistics and Language Change*). Labov's study of English on Martha's Vineyard provided strong evidence for the claim that native-like command of a language includes the control of heterogeneous structures.

2. An Early Study—Martha's Vineyard

The island of Martha's Vineyard off the New England coast was the setting of Labov's study (1963) of the significance of social patterns in understanding language variation and change. The island is inhabited by a small number of indigenous Indians, larger numbers of descendants of old families of English stock, and people of Portuguese descent. Furthermore, it is overwhelmed by tourist summer residents from the mainland. Among a range of phonetic characteristics of English on the island, Labov chose to study variations in the diphthongs /ay/ and /aw/, as in *white* and *out* respectively. Instead of the neighboring New England [aɪ] and [aʊ], these frequently have centralized elements ([ɐɪ] and [ɐʊ], or even [əɪ] and [əʊ]) on Martha's Vineyard. The variables (ay) and (aw) fulfill three criteria that make them focal elements in the study of language in its social setting: (a) they are frequent enough in ordinary conversation to appear unsolicited in brief interviews; (b) they are structurally linked to other elements in the linguistic system—that is, to the system of diphthongs in the dialect; (c) they exhibit a complex and subtle pattern of stratification by social groupings.

Labov undertook 69 interviews with native Vineyarders. These are relatively formal—involving a lexical questionnaire, a reading passage, and questions exploring the social orientation of the respondent, especially designed to elicit the (ay) and (aw) variables. Observations of casual speech in public settings served only as a supplementary check on the tape-recorded speech. The interviews thus did not involve the techniques that were to become synonymous with the Labovian paradigm.

There did not appear to be much style shifting in the interviews, perhaps because of the methodology (although Labov suggests that these were essentially single-style speakers). Variation was apparent along a number of dimensions including ethnicity, occupation, and geographical location. There was also a linguistic dimension to the variation in that centralization was favored in certain environments. If voiceless alveolar and labial elements (/t/, /s/, /p/, /f/) followed, centralization was most favored; if liquids or nasals (/l/, /r/, /n/, /m/) followed, centralization was least favored.

This article will concentrate on the most salient factor that shows covariation with centralization: age. In his analysis, Labov used a scoring system of 0 for [a], 1 for [a⫟] and [ɐ⫠], 2 for [ɐ] and [ɐ⫟], and 3 for [ə] (see Fig. 1). Averaging the values of all the tokens per age group, and expressing them as a

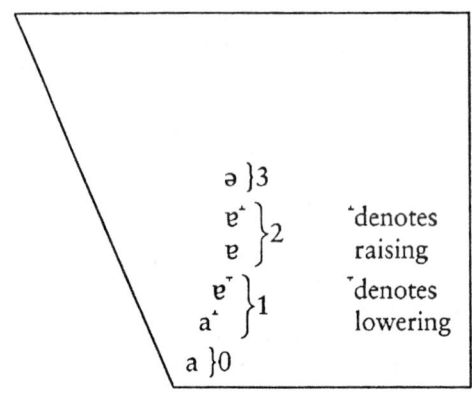

Figure 1. Variants of the first element /a/ in the diphthong in WHITE, RIGHT, KIND in Martha's Vineyard, and values assigned to them.

Table 1. Centralization index for Martha's Vineyard.

Age	(ay)	(aw)
75–	25	22
61–75	35	37
46–60	62	44
31–45	81	88
14–30	37	46

percentage of the total occurrence of each variable per age group yields the centralization index given in Table 1. Scores may thus range from 0 to 300: the higher the score, the greater the use of island variants rather than the general New England [a].

Table 1 shows an increase in island variants with a decrease in age, with the exception of the youngest group. A comparison with earlier records of the *Linguistic Atlas of New England* (LANE) undertaken by Kurath et al. in 1941, reveals that this is not a self-repeating age-graded pattern (as the use of slang might be, for example). The rest of this section will concentrate on the simpler case of the (ay) variable. The centralized form of /ay/ was once the more usual, going back to seventeenth-century England, and still recorded in moderate numbers in New England and Martha's Vineyard in the LANE records. Comparing LANE records with those of late twentieth-century Martha's Vineyard, it is evident that there had been an intervening drop in centralization. That is, Martha's Vineyard was once in line with the rest of New England in showing a decline in centralization; but the trend has been reversed, with younger people accentuating a pronunciation that was becoming less common in the speech of their elders. In answering the question of why younger people of Martha's Vineyard seemed to be turning their backs on the history of English phonology, Labov appealed to social relationships between the inhabitants of the island (poor by American standards) and the rich summer residents. A high degree of centralization of (ay) and (aw) is closely linked with strong resistance to the incursions of the summer people, which have to be tolerated for economic reasons. It is especially since around World War II that the social and economic pressures have brought on this resistance among younger groups. Using a pronunciation like [rɐɪt] 'right' or [hɐʊs] 'house' is a subconscious affirmation of belonging to the island and being one of its rightful owners.

Although the oldest groups show reduced levels of centralization, the one resistant group was a group of fishermen from a part of the island called Chilmark. Labov argues that the ways of these Chilmark fishermen—independent and stubborn defenders of the old way of living—served as a reference point for those of the younger generation throughout the island who might be seeking an identity opposed to that of the tourists. Finally, in answering the question of why the 14- to 30-year-old group does not exhibit the revived island-centralization pattern, considerations regarding attitude and identity are again crucial. According to Labov's argument, these speakers do not feel the full stress experienced by the 30+ age groups, who have grown up in a declining economy, and who have made a more or less deliberate choice to remain on the island, or, having sought work in the mainland, have elected to return to Martha's Vineyard. The youngest group, which included many high-school pupils, either harbored hopes of going to the mainland or had not yet made their choice. This indecision is unconsciously reflected in their indices for the two sociolinguistic variables.

The Martha's Vineyard study shows that the Chomskyan characterization of linguistic competence with reference to an idealized speaker-hearer in a homogeneous setting is far too narrow. The rules of a language (and perhaps language in general) cannot be fully accounted for without examining their patterning over social space. Native-like command of heterogeneous structures is not necessarily a matter of multidialectism or 'performance,' but part of a unified linguistic competence. In the case of a language used in a complex society, it may well be that it is the absence of structured heterogeneity which would count as dysfunctional. In addition to expanding the goals of a Chomsky-dominated linguistics, Labov argued against the introspective methods of the generative school, where a researcher often used his or her idiolect as the only source of data. He stressed, instead, the importance of studying the vernacular speech of individuals in its community setting.

By 'vernacular' is meant the style of speech that one uses in the least self-conscious mode in informal settings, as when laughing and chatting with friends. It is the basic style of speech learnt in pre-adolescent years, which may be modified later on by other styles encountered at school and at work. Labov believed that the vernacular provided the most systematic data for linguistic analysis. This does not mean that it is devoid of variation: it may involve 'inherent variation'—that is, alternate forms belonging to the same system acquired simultaneously, or nearly so, at an early age. The rules governing variation in the vernacular appear to be more regular than those operating in formal, superposed styles acquired in postadolescence. Each speaker has a vernacular style in at least one language; this may be the prestige dialect (as in the case of standard English) or, more usually, a nonstandard variety.

Labov developed an empirical approach to the study of the vernacular that involved careful sampling of populations to ensure representativeness, fieldwork methods designed to elicit a range of styles from the least to the most formal, and analytic techniques based on the concept of the linguistic variable. The linguistic variable is an item which has identifiable variants: for example, one may consider the participial ending -*ing* to be a linguistic variable—written within rounded brackets as (-*ing*)—which has the variants [-ing] and [-in] in many dialects. Whereas the alternation between variants may sometimes depend purely on a linguistic context, the ones of greatest interest to sociolinguists are those which show social conditioning as well.

The Martha's Vineyard study was a clear and relatively simple illustration of the interplay between linguistic and social factors. In subsequent studies, Labov worked on more complex situations—large urban centers, and large populations with several ethnic groups, multiple-style speakers, and with rapid change and upward mobility.

3. Postvocalic (r) in New York City

This is Labov's most influential study, showing essentially that if any two subgroups of New York City speakers are ranked in a scale of social stratification, they will be ranked in the same order by their differential use of certain linguistic variables, most notably in their use of (r) after vowels in words such as *park* in casual speech styles. However, the influence of the study goes beyond mere correlation of variables—it contributed decisively to the development of a sociolinguistic methodology, fieldwork techniques, and the study of language change in progress.

The study used, for the first time in linguistic fieldwork involving extensive interviews, a proper sampling procedure. It drew on an earlier sociological survey of the Lower East Side of New York City conducted by a sociological research group. The original survey used a random sample of 988 adult subjects representing a population of 100,000. Originally aiming to interview 195 of those respondents who had not moved house in the previous 2 years, Labov managed to reach 81 percent of these. Interviews were conducted on an individual basis (see Sect. 4) and involved four types of activity: (a) the main part consisted of continuous speech in response to the interviewer's questions; (b) reading of a short passage; (c) reading lists of words containing instances of pertinent variables; and (d) minimal pairs involving variables (e.g., the vowels in *god* and *guard*, which both have the vowel /ɑ:/ in New York City English). Moving from (a) to (d) clearly corresponds to increasing formality and focus on language itself. At the stage of analysis, sections of the continuous speech were assigned to the subcategories 'formal' and 'casual,' depending on the interviewee's responses.

In grouping his speakers, Labov used a 10-point socioeconomic scale, devised earlier by the sociological research group. It was based on three equally weighted indicators of status: occupation of breadwinner, education of respondent, and family income. On the 10-point scale, 0–1 was taken as lower class; 2–4 as working class; 5–8 as lower middle-class; and 9 as upper middle-class. Of the many variables examined by Labov, postvocalic (r) will be concentrated on here. For contrast, however, the use of (th) will be examined first.

The main variants of the (th) variable—that is, the initial consonant in words like *thing*—are the general American interdental fricative [θ] and less prestigious variants: the affricate [t̪θ] and dental stop [t̪]. These are scored as 0, 1, and 2, respectively. Figure 2 shows the stratification of this variable according to class

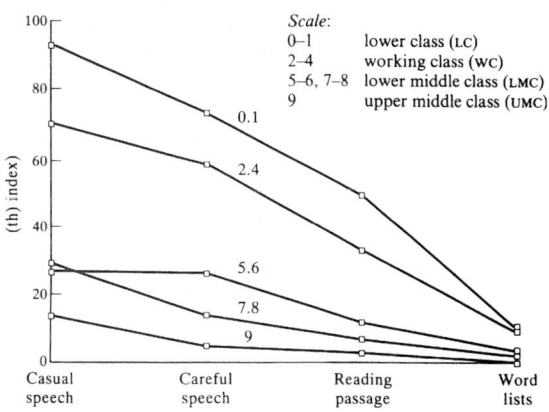

Figure 2. Social stratification of the (th) variable in New York City (after Labov 1972a).

and style for 81 speakers. The vertical axis is a scale of average (th) index scores per socioeconomic group; while the horizontal axis represents the four contextual styles. The scores range from a possible 0 (for fricatives only) to a possible maximum of 200 (for stops only).

The graphs show that the greatest occurrence of nonfricative forms is in casual speech for all groups, with decreasing frequency when moving through the more formal styles. There is a stable pattern insofar as the graphs for each class are roughly parallel (apart from the equal LMC and UMC scores for casual speech). Defining the (th) index in the way that Labov did yields a monotonic-decreasing relationship between social class and the (th) variable. That is, an increase in social class or status groups is accompanied by decreasing index scores for (th). The variable may be characterized as sharply stratified, since there is a relatively large divide between the LC and WC groups as against the MC groups.

Turning to postvocalic (r) as used by the same speakers, with a scoring system of 1 for use of [r] and 0 for its absence, and an additional style drawing on minimal-pair lists, Labov arrived at the patterns shown in Fig. 3.

The patterning of (r) shows the following tendencies:

(a) There is fine rather than sharp stratification of the variable—that is, the divisions between the social classes are not as great as for (th). New Yorkers ranked on a hierarchical scale by nonlinguistic criteria follow the same scale in (r) usage.

(b) The differences between the groups are not categorical; that is, no group is characterized by the complete presence or absence of postvocalic /r/.

(c) Nevertheless, at the level of casual speech, only the UMC shows a significant degree of r-pronunciation. The other groups range between 1 and 10 percent on this variable. It can be said that in everyday life, the pronunciation of postvocalic [r] functions as a marker of the highest-ranking status group.

(d) All groups show an increase when moving from informal to more formal styles.

(e) As one follows the progression toward more formal styles, the LMC shows a greater increase in the use of [r], until in word-list and minimal-pair styles they overtake the UMC averages.

Labov termed this last phenomenon 'hypercorrection.' The LMC overshoots the mark and goes beyond the highest status group in its tendency to use the pronunciation considered correct and appropriate for formal styles. In this sense, hypercorrection is not the sporadic or irregular treatment of a word class as is the case in second-language or dialect acquisition; rather, it denotes the movement of an entire word class or phonological sequence beyond the target set by the prestige model. This crossover pattern differentiates the (r) variable from the stable (th) variable; Labov advances the hypothesis that this crossover pattern, coupled with differential scores in the various age groups, is an indication of sound change in progress (see *Sociolinguistics and Language Change*).

Labov demonstrated the claim that LMC speakers have the greatest linguistic insecurity by using subjective-reaction tests. In one of his experiments, subjects were asked to rate a number of short excerpts on a scale of occupational suitability (that is, whether the speaker would be acceptable as a secretary, television personality, factory worker, etc.). The tape contained 22 sentences from five women readers in random order. As these were taken from the reading passage, subjects were already familiar with the material. All subjects between 18 and 39 agreed in their subconscious positive evaluation of [r] usage, irrespective of their own level of use of the variable. This was arrived at by rating as 'r-positive' a reaction which assigned to a speaker a higher occupational position for a sentence containing postvocalic [r], than (unknowingly) for the *same* speaker on a sentence where postvocalic [r] was absent. The percentage of r-positive responses of subjects between the ages of 18 and 39 years was 100. Subjects over 40 showed a mixed reaction in their social evaluation; but the LMC speakers showed higher r-positive responses than the UMC. Generally, members of the highest and lowest status groups tend not to change their pronunciation after it becomes fixed in adolescence; members of middle-status groups may do so, because of their social aspirations. The great linguistic insecurity of the

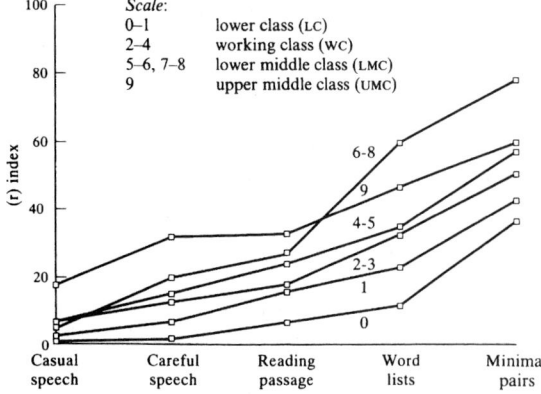

Figure 3. Social stratification of the (r) variable in New York City (after Labov 1972a).

LMC leads to especial fluctuation in formal speech contexts: hence Labov's claims about the consistency of vernacular speech over other styles.

The New York study showed two aspects of sociolinguistic stratification: linguistic differentiation and social evaluation. Labov remarks upon the uniform evaluation of linguistic features such as (r) by New Yorkers as a single speech community, despite the increasing stratification in speech performance.

It is necessary to distinguish between linguistic variables of several types, since not all of them show the stratification and style-shifting characteristic of (r). 'Markers' are those variables like (r), which show stratification that defines the speech community, which all members react to in a more or less uniform manner, and which is subject to style-shifting. Markers contrast with 'indicators,' which show differentiation by age or social group without being subject to style-shifting, and which have little evaluative force in subjective reaction tests. Only a linguistically trained observer is aware of indicators. Examples are the merger of the *hock* and *hawk* vowels in New York, and the use of positive *anymore* in Midland USA (e.g., *That's the way it is with planes anymore*). 'Stereotypes' are forms that are socially marked—that is, they are prominent in the metalinguisic awareness of speech communities, as in the case of 'h-dropping' in Cockney and other English dialects, or the stigmatization of the *toidy-toid street* 'thirty-third street' pronunciation of New York speech (based on an older vowel [əˈ]). Judgments that bring about stereotypes are not necessarily phonetically accurate, and stereotypes may live on in folk linguistics long after the stigmatized forms have changed. The stigmatized New York vowel [əˈ], for example, is not the same as [ɔɪ]: *bird* and *Boyd* are not homophones, except to outsiders.

The issue of prestige is generally an important—and complicated—one in sociolinguistics. Labov distinguished between 'overt' and 'covert' prestige. The former refers to positive or negative assessments of variants (or of a speech variety) in accordance with the dominant norms of the public media, educational institutions, and middle-class speech. In the New York City studies, interviewees who used the highest degree of a stigmatized feature in their own natural speech showed the greatest tendency to stigmatize others for their use of the same form. On the other hand, the stability of working-class speech norms calls for other explanations, since these speakers did not, in fact, readily adopt middle-class norms. 'Covert prestige' refers to this set of opposing values implicit in lower- and working-class lifestyles, which do not appear in conventional subjective-reaction tests. (It will be seen that the New York City pattern has not always been replicated, and that the notion of prestige is more complex than allowed for in this early formulation.)

Generally, the New York study showed that socioeconomic differentiation cannot be ignored in studies of language structure. Change originates in specific subgroups of a speech community (in this case, the highest-ranking subgroup). The behavior of each class in different styles does not involve random switching. The character of (r) as a prestige feature within the linguistic system can only be gauged within the network of stylistic and social inequalities.

4. Fieldwork Methods

The variationist school stresses the importance of the collection and analysis of a corpus that adequately represents the speech of members of the community under study. Labov was perhaps the first to exploit fully the invention of the tape recorder for sociolinguistic purposes. Labov's attempts to ensure representative sampling of the New York community under study have already been discussed. In practice, sociolinguistic surveys are based on anything from 40 to 150 speakers. Samples going beyond 150 individuals tend to increase data-handling problems without a significant gain in analytic insights. Stressing the need to study the vernacular in its social context gives rise to what Labov termed 'the observer's paradox': the vernacular, which the linguist wishes to observe closely, is the very style which speakers use when they are not being observed. This is akin to the experimenter effect of other disciplines, and the need to ensure that the data which one collects are unaffected by the process of investigation. Labov has used a variety of techniques to get around the problem, the most favored being the sociolinguistic interview. This involves a tape-recorded, personal interview lasting about an hour per person. The session is designed to be as informal as possible in an attempt to defuse the relative status of participants (usually middle-class researcher versus the other). Identification of the interviewer with the teaching profession would invariably typecast him or her as the one from whom information flows, rather than the other way around. The counterstrategy of the sociolinguistic interview is to emphasize the position of the interviewer as learner (about local ways and attitudes), and hence in a lower position of authority than the person to whom the interviewer is speaking. Interviewees are encouraged to talk about everyday topics of personal interest, and thus to take the lead during some parts of the interview. Successful topics often center around childhood games, accusations of blame for things one may not have done, family, religion, dating, and the opposite sex. The most famous one has come to be known as the 'danger of death' question. Interviewees are asked to talk informally about their most frightening moment, when 'you thought you were in serious danger of being killed—where you thought to yourself, "This is it."' Speakers embarking on such a narration often become so involved in it as to be temporarily diverted from the act of being interviewed. Their speech consequently shows a marked shift away from formal style to the vernacular.

Labov stressed that interview speech should not be mistaken for intimate vernacular style. However, by using an empathetic approach and the right techniques, it brought one as close to the vernacular as was possible, while still obtaining large quantities of comparable and clear data. Among the 'channel cues' that signify a relatively successful interview are modulations of voice production, including changes in tempo, pitch, and volume, alternations in rate of breathing, and occasional laughter. Regarding fieldwork ethics, surreptitious recordings are generally considered undesirable. Gains in gathering natural speech via a concealed tape recorder are usually offset by the accompanying poor sound quality. Furthermore, such deceit may negate good relations necessary for long-term contact with a community.

The individual interview is not the only technique advocated by Labov, who has used a variety of other methods for other purposes.

First, participant observation of adolescent gangs in Harlem, together with other fieldworkers, formed an important database for the study of Black English vernacular. The significance of adolescent gangs lies in the naturalness of these self-selected groups and the checks (conscious and subconscious) by members on any individual who produces nonvernacular forms solely for the benefit of the tape recorder. Some sessions resembled a party rather than a discussion with outsiders. By using separate-track recordings in several group sessions, the researchers obtained clear, varied, and voluminous data which informed their study of sociophonetic variables, syntax, narrative, and adolescent street culture.

This approach was refined by Milroy in the Belfast studies (see *Social Networks*), and by Labov in the long-term neighborhood studies in Philadelphia. The neighborhood studies were designed to obtain a large amount of linguistic and social data on the major social networks of different neighborhoods. Participant observation in Philadelphia has allowed unlimited access to the linguistic competence of the central figures in individual networks, and group recordings which elicit close to vernacular styles. Included in the neighborhood studies are systematic sociolinguistic interviews developed along the earlier New York City models. These remain the best source for comparable data on all members of a social network. Labov's later work thus moves away from an emphasis on a random sampling of a large community to judgment-sample selection of neighborhoods for intensive study.

The second method involves rapid and anonymous surveys. In certain strategic locations such surveys enable the study of a large number of people in a short space of time, provided that the social identity of the subjects is well defined by the situation. Labov's pilot study of (r) in New York department stores (which preceded the full-scale study discussed in Sect. 3) is a paradigm example. Employees of three large department stores were asked for directions for an item that was predetermined to be on the fourth floor. The reply would therefore contain two tokens of the (r) variable, in two linguistic contexts (before a consonant and at the end of a word). By pretending not to hear the reply the first time, Labov obtained another two tokens in deliberate style. The variable of class/status was built into the study on the hypothesis that departmental assistants tended to approximate (or accommodate to) the speech associated with their customers—the three stores were sharply stratified in respect of their clientele. This simple (and amusing) study showed significant variation in rhoticity (pronunciation of postvocalic /r/) according to linguistic context, speech style, and social class associated with each store. The results were even more finely grained—for example, on the quieter and more expensive upper floors of the highest-ranking store, the percentage of [r] was much higher than amid the hustle and bustle of the ground floor.

The third method involves telephone surveys: in later work, Labov complemented the intensive but nonrandom neighborhood studies by broader (and shallower) representation using a telephone survey. Subjects chosen by a random sample participated in a 15-minute telephone interview, which included some spontaneous conversation, wordlists, and minimal pairs. The emphasis was on communication in Philadelphia, with reference mainly to telephone speech, and special words and pronunciations in the Philadelphia dialect that might be sources of misunderstanding.

Finally, Labov has used a variety of field experiments to tackle specific problems. The subjective evaluation test cited above is but one instance of these.

5. Syntactic Studies

Although the most salient sociolinguistic variables are usually phonological in nature, there are a number of studies of dialect syntax informed by variation theory. Labov's work on Black English syntax was an important contribution to the difference–deficit debate of the 1960s in American education. Working on the assumption that the English dialect of black pupils entering schools contained numerous linguistic deficiencies, compensatory education programs attempted to eradicate nonstandard forms in favor of the standard equivalents. Labov's contribution was to point to the shaky linguistic underpinnings of the deficit hypothesis. In a careful examination of certain aspects of Black English vernacular (BEV) syntax from a sociosystemic perspective, he demonstrated that what was taken to be a deficit (e.g., double or multiple negation, or nonuse of the third singular verb ending -*s*) was in fact a systematic difference between dialects, subject to internally governed rules. He emphasized that the BEV system was not completely different from that of other English dialects: in fact, it shared a great majority of rules with them. Within that overall similarity, however, were subsets of rules which might not be easily integrated into other English grammars. These may even be located at strategic points, close to the grammatical core of the dialect.

This section will first examine Labov's approach to the syntax of double and multiple negation in BEV and other dialects. Prescriptivists took the view that the dialect-speaking child who produces *She don't know nothing* is trying to say *She knows nothing*, but has unwittingly used an extra negative and so conveys the opposite meaning. Labov stressed that this was a false interpretation: a BEV speaker, like standard American English speakers, is capable of distinguishing between ordinary negation and emphatic negation. The means of doing so are different in each dialect. (In emphatic negation, where two negatives result in a positive, BEV uses stress on both negatives. Such stress is lacking in ordinary negation where two or more negatives yield a negative.) The two dialects differ thus:

	White dialect	BEV
Positive:	He knows something	He know something
Negative:	He doesn't know anything	He don't know nothing
Double neg:	He doesn't know *nothing*	He *don't* know *nothing*.

The main rules for negation can be summarized as follows:

(a) In all dialects, the negative is attracted to a lone indefinite before the verb (e.g., *Nobody knows anything*, rather than **Anybody doesn't know anything*).
(b) In some white dialects, the negative may also combine with other indefinites (e.g., *Nobody knows nothing*; *He never took none of them*).
(c) In other white dialects, the negative combines with all indefinites and occurs in preverbal position in the same clause (e.g., *Nobody doesn't know nothing*).
(d) In BEV, negative concord is obligatory in all indefinites within the clause, and may even occur in preverbal position in following clauses (e.g., *It ain't no cat can't get into no coop*, equivalent to standard English 'There isn't any cat that can get into any coop').

From the point of view of language variation and logic, two important generalizations can be made. First, all dialects share a categorical rule which attracts the negative to an indefinite subject. Second, dialects differ mainly in the extent to which the negative particle is also distributed to other indefinites and to preverbal position in the main and subordinate clauses. Some important parallels arise between this study and those of phonetic variables: (a) the syntax of negation shows the effect of linguistic conditioning—certain environments enhance it, others do not; (b) negation is subject to variation according to social group (in this case, at least with respect to ethnicity); and (c) style is a factor which should enter into consideration—for example, in the choice between single versus double negation in certain dialects, or negation across clauses in BEV.

Another example within BEV syntax which might easily be misconstrued as logically inferior to the standard pattern concerns the deletion of the copula (essentially the verb *be* before an adjective, preposition, or noun phrase; for example, *He is tall*, although some researchers, including Labov, include auxiliary *be* as in *She is playing* in their analyses). This area of syntax will be discussed in some detail, not so much to iterate Labov's position in the difference–deficit debate, but to show the interplay between phonology and syntax and the development of the concept of variable rules.

BEV frequently shows the absence of *be* in a range of syntactic environments (another construction showing the presence of invariant, habitual *be* in BEV and other dialects, will not be examined):

NP:	She ɸ the first one started us off.
Predicate adj:	He ɸ fast in everything he do.
Locative:	You ɸ out the tape.
Negative:	But everybody ɸ not black.
Participle:	He just feel like he ɸ getting cripple up from arthritis.

In attempting to establish whether this phenomenon is rule-governed, it is important to check whether there are any contexts in which copula deletion is *not* permissible. Among these is the past tense, which always requires *was*. Other environments which frequently, if not mandatorily, require some form of the copula are the first person form *I'm*; the form *ain't*; interrogative questions (*Is he dead?*, not **He dead?*); tag questions (*Is that a shock or is it not?*); and infinitives (*You got to be good*, not **You got to good*). *Is* ([z̲]) and *are* ([ə] or [ər]) are deleted, but not *am* ([m]). Since there are general phonological processes deleting certain sounds in unstressed syllables (notably [r], [ə], and [z]—but not [m]), Labov sought to account for copula

383

deletion in BEV in terms of an interplay between these processes and syntactic environments, rather than as a purely syntactic process. The most inspired part of the analysis was a careful comparison between contexts in which standard American English (SAE) frequently contracted the copula, and in contexts in which it did not. Labov pointed out that wherever SAE permits contraction, BEV permits deletion:

SAE	BEV
She's the first	She ϕ the first
He's fast	He ϕ fast
You're out of the tape	You ϕ out the tape

More significantly, the contexts in which SAE disallows contraction are precisely those in which deletion is ruled out in BEV (zero denotes a deleted copula):

	SAE	BEV
(a)	*Sentence-final position*	
	*He's as nice as he says he's.	*He's as nice as he says he ϕ.
	*How beautiful you're!	*How beautiful you ϕ!
	Are you going? *Yes I'm.	Are you going? *Yes I ϕ.
(b)	*An unstressed following word*	
	*Who's it?	*Who ϕ it?
	*What's it?	*What ϕ it?
(c)	*Ellipsed elements*	
	Is he running? *He's—now.	Is he running? *He ϕ—now.

The isomorphism between the two dialects with respect to the contexts of contraction and deletion suggests that they are governed by the same logic. From a detailed examination of general phonological rules like glide deletion, [r] deletion, and consonant-cluster reduction, Labov concluded that the correct analysis of the copula was one which posited a general contraction rule on a common underlying form for both dialects, followed by a deletion rule in BEV. He did so using the techniques of (early) generative grammar and quantitative analysis of variation. At the same time, he claimed to have widened the concept of 'rule of grammar.'

6. Variable Rules

Variable rules were first introduced in Labov's analysis of the BEV copula in 1969. They are based on the model of rules in generative phonology, but are adapted to account for variation. Rules in generative phonology are either optional or obligatory. A simplified version of a generative rule for the deletion of [t] or [d] at the end of words in English could be written:

$$t, d \rightarrow \phi/[+ \text{cons}] - \#\#[-\text{syll}] \quad \text{(optional)}$$

Informally, this says that a word-final [t] or [d] is deleted after a consonant if the following word does not begin with a vowel, and that the rule is an optional one (key: → = 'becomes'; ϕ = 'zero'; / = 'in the following environment'; [+cons]— = 'after a consonant'; —## = 'before a word boundary'; [–syll] = 'nonsyllabic element').

Labov noted that, in a large corpus, the frequency of application of an optional rule might depend to a large extent on particular aspects of the linguistic context. Two or more contexts which satisfy the structural description of such a rule might not have the same effect—one may favor application 90 percent of the time, the other 15 percent of the time. Variable rules are an attempt to incorporate such tendencies into the formal statement of a rule. They differ from the rules of generative phonology in two respects: they include social factors as a possible constraining environment; and they specify the likelihood of a rule applying in a particular environment on the basis of social and linguistic constraints. The following variable rule version of t/d deletion contains the further specification that [t] and [d] are more likely to be deleted when they are not part of the past-tense morpheme:

$$t, d \rightarrow \langle \phi \rangle / [+ \text{cons}]^\beta \langle -\# \rangle - \#\#^\alpha \langle -\text{syll} \rangle$$

The angled brackets are used to signify variability: [t] and [d] are variably deleted; and $\langle -\# \rangle$ (i.e., the lack of a morpheme boundary) and $\langle -\text{syll} \rangle$ are variable constraints. The absence of angled brackets around [+cons] and ## implies that these are obligatory environments for the rule. The Greek letters suggest a weighting of the optional constraints: α is a more significant constraint than β, and so on. That is, the phonological constraint of a following consonant is weighted more heavily than the grammatical constraint of t/d not being part of the past-tense ending. The rule thus informally states that word-final [t] or [d] is variably deleted after a consonant, more often if it is not a separate grammatical morpheme, and even more often if it is not followed by a vowel.

It is also possible to add social factors to create a combined sociolinguistic environment. Thus, features like [+ middle class], [+ female], etc. might be considered to have a constraining effect parallel to that of the linguistic environment. In the original variable-rule proposal, social factors were placed outside the system of variable linguistic constraints to predict relative frequencies of occurrence.

The variable rule was further developed in the work of Cedergren and Sankoff (1974), who devised a system of assigning probabilities (weightings) to each of the constraints by a procedure known as 'maximum likelihood.' The analysis is performed using as input the data on rule applications in various environments. The method of calculation assumes that the constraints are independent of each other for their effects. The computer program that they developed for the analysis, called VARBRUL, has since been considerably revised and updated by Sankoff and Rousseau (see *Statistics in Sociolinguistics*). In VARBRUL analysis, the constraints (or 'factors') are arranged into factor groups. For the t/d deletion rule, the factor groups would include [+ #], [− #] (i.e., whether t/d belonged to a grammatical morpheme or not); [+ syll], [− syll], and φ (i.e., whether t/d was followed by a word with an initial consonant or vowel, or was sentence-final); plus the various social groups judged to be relevant to the analysis (e.g., [UMC], [LMC], [WC], etc.; [+ female], [− female]). The elements in a factor group are in complementary distribution: they exhaust the group without overlapping with each other. VARBRUL generates two important analyses for the sociolinguist. One is a probability or weighting associated with each of the factors, ranging from 0 to 1. A factor that receives a weighting greater than 0.5 favors the rule; a value less than 0.5 disfavors it. A factor value of 1.0 does not imply 100 percent application when that factor is present in the rule environment—rather, it signifies that the factor favors application more than any other in its group. The second analysis generated by VARBRUL is an input weighting (or input probability) which reflects the propensity of the rule to apply on its own, apart from the influence of the environment.

Labov insisted that he was not merely writing up statistical statements or approximations to some ideal grammar, but that he was setting up a set of quantitative relations which are the form of the grammar itself. This has been the subject of much criticism, notably on the grounds that variable rules conflict too much in intent with the rules of generative phonology to be accommodated in the latter system. Variable rules are located in language use, and—in Chomsky's terms—form part of performance, rather than the competence characteristic of the initial language state. (On the other hand, Chomsky's ideal grammar is unable to deal adequately with language change and, especially, variation.) The real issue, then, is the psychological status of the variable rule: whether human languages are structured around variable rules which include probability statements regarding application, or whether these are convenient descriptions of language use. The criticism has been raised that children cannot have access to information regarding large and varied samples summarized in variable rules.

In a study concerning the acquisition of rules governing the alternation between /-ing/ and /-in/ and the deletion of /t/ and /d/ at the end of words, Labov (1989) argued that the child is in some ways a perfect historian of a language. The acquisition of centuries-old variable rules like these by children between the ages of four and nine precedes the acquisition of many other features of grammar.

Children first show social and stylistic constraints on variation, and later the language-specific grammatical and articulatory constraints. (Social and stylistic constraints in this case concern narrative versus other styles and peer-group versus parents' speech; grammatical constraints on t/d concern whether or not they are part of a morpheme like the past-tense ending or the negative *n't*; and articulatory constraints involve the presence of consonant clusters.) Labov concludes that there is little evidence to support the notion of a language-learning faculty isolated from social and historical development. Children appear to focus on the pattern of social and stylistic variation and to reproduce the historically variable patterns.

Nevertheless, the variable rule is no longer widely used in sociolinguistic descriptions. For one thing, the rules of phonology that variable rules were designed to be hooked onto are not as prominent as they were in the early days of generative grammar. VARBRUL continues to be used as a valuable statistical means of analyzing large bodies of data; and it is usual for scholars to list input probabilities and factor weightings for salient sociolinguistic processes, without attempting to write a formal variable rule.

7. The Syntactic Variable

The linguistic variables studied in sociolinguistics are often phonological ones. Such items are favored because they are of high frequency, are relatively immune from conscious suppression in an interview, and can be easily quantified. But these are not the only units subject to social variation and evaluation. The quantitative study of larger units has been successful mainly at the morphological level (e.g., studies of the choice between the complementizer *que* or a zero morph in Montréal French). Attempts to analyze syntactic choices within the same framework have been less successful. Weiner and Labov's (1983) study of the English passive in sociolinguistic perspective involved treating the active and passive variants of a sentence as truth-conditionally equivalent and as referring to the same state of affairs—that is, as potential variants of a variable. As many critics have pointed out, this analysis is far removed from the earlier phonological studies, since the potential syntactic variables can hardly be said to be semantically neutral or functionally equivalent in the way that phonological variants are. Differences between the active and passive sentences stem from the way in which information is presented in a stretch of discourse.

Another problem in attempting a sociolinguistic syntax concerns what Labov termed 'closing the set of variants'—or noting not only each instance of a particular variant, but also the number of instances when it might have occurred but did not. In the case of relative clauses, for example, it is not possible to contrast occurrences with nonoccurrences, for there are no means of establishing conclusively within a stretch of discourse all the alternate ways of presenting information specifiable by relative clause structures. Although quantitative studies of syntax are on the increase, they generally do not take the linguistic-variable route (see *Syntactic Change*).

8. Refinements, Criticisms, and Pseudocriticisms

The Labovian framework has been successfully adapted by other scholars to the study of language variation in diverse settings. Some refinements of the generalizations based on North American studies have been inevitable. In terms of methodology, individual researchers have had to tailor aspects of the interview format to suit their particular situation. Residents of Norwich, England, lead less stressful lives than New Yorkers and have little to say about personal brushes with death. On the other hand, Belfasters tend to underplay the topic, since it is a fact of daily life. In some communities, women may not be allowed to speak to strange male interviewers. The tests of style-shifting based on reading passages and minimal pairs presume a literate community, and may be unduly stressful to interviewees in a barely literate one. (One way of getting around this problem might be to focus on the recitation of rituals and prayers in eliciting formal styles.)

It has been suggested that it is confusing to the interviewee's expectations *not* to be put in a subordinate position as the one facing the questions in the interview. This criticism misses the point that the good interviewer *does* come with a carefully planned list of questions, but does not let any opportunity slip for digressions and discussions initiated by the interviewee. Most interviews in the variationist tradition have rightly approximated a social visit with chit-chat, rather than an interrogation session.

More significantly, notions like prestige, gender roles in language change, and style-shifting have been modified by closer scrutiny since Labov's early discussions. A striking finding concerning prestige comes from Trudgill's (1983) study of vowel variants in Norwich, in the lexical sets NOSE, ROAD, MOAN (ranging from [ʋu] through [u:] to [ʊ]) and GATE, FACE, NAME (ranging from [eɪ] to [æɪ]). As part of the interview, he used a self-evaluation test in which informants were asked how they usually pronounced words like these. In the prototype test in New York, people showed a distinct tendency to claim higher use of the prestige form than was evident in their interview speech. Norwich informants were far more prone to underreport their use of prestige forms in favor of working-class norms. In particular, male informants were much more likely to underreport, female informants to overreport. Although Labov had pointed to the existence of covert prestige in his New York study, he was unable to tap into it in evaluation tests. Trudgill conjectures that the difference in attitudes reflects differences in class-consciousness in the two countries—especially a lack of corporate or militant class-consciousness in the USA and the relative lack of embourgeoisement of the British working class. However, the most compelling factor relating to covert prestige was gender, not social class. Many middle-class males (in contrast to middle-class females) appear to share with working-class males the characteristic that they have not so completely absorbed the dominant mainstream values of their American counterparts.

Trudgill used these insights to explain a seemingly contradictory type of change in progress in Norwich, from [ɑ] or [a] to [ɒ] in the lexical set TOP, DOG, HOT. At first sight, these appear to involve a change from a regional to a prestigious RP variant. The contradiction lay in the fact that WC women had higher scores of the nonprestige [ɑ] or [a] than WC men. (For the MC, women had lower scores than men on the nonprestige variant, as expected.) Trudgill shows it to be a two-pronged change in progress: one from above the level of social consciousness, introduced by MC women who have access to RP in a way that WC women do not; the other from below the level of social consciousness, this time by men, who are introducing the low-prestige variant ([ɒ]) from the neighboring counties. Middle-class males follow the lead of working-class males. Thus, it is the working-class women who to any great extent have preserved the unrounded vowel.

It is generally true in all English-speaking communities, Western Europe, and Latin America that for stable sociolinguistic variables women use more prestige variants and fewer stigmatized variants than men. Studies in certain localities in non-Western countries like Kenya, Iran, Jordan, and India suggest the opposite. The reversal of the patterning of prestige variants (as compared to Western findings) seems to appear in all social classes, including those educated women who play a major role in public life. More rural studies from non-Western countries are needed to complete the picture concerning gender-based responses to prestige in language.

Sociolinguists at the beginning of the twenty-first century accept a more general conception of style-shifting than implicit in Labov's early work, based on Bell's (1984) notion of 'audience design' (see *Audience Design*). Bell stressed that stylistic variation was governed not so much by monitoring of one's speech habits (or attention paid to speech), as by a speaker's perception of his or her interlocutor's characteristics. Style is thus a special (and subconscious) 'tailoring' of language to fit the requirements of various types of listener. Although monitoring may be inherent in the reading style studied by Labov, a more general explanation would link it to the enactment of a role played out in front of a reading audience—that is, to a teacher in a classroom situation. This notion of style fits in with the accommodation theory of language-use stressed by social psychologists (see *Speech Accommodation*). However, it is not easy to operationalize within the constraints of the sociolinguistic interview.

Labov's initial analyses of BEV stressed its overwhelming similarities with other American English dialects, motivated in part by the counterclaims of the deficit school of thought. Much more attention has since been paid to the ongoing divergence between black and white speech (Labov and Harris 1986), as witnessed in innovations like the use of *-s* as the marker of the past in narratives. Even the celebrated analysis of the copula has been modified in ways that stress the difference between BEV and mainstream American English (Baugh 1980). Baugh used an extension of Labov's original database (utilizing the data from the Harlem adolescent groups in full) and an update of the Cedergren and Sankoff (1974) program in his re-examination of the copula in BEV. With the resulting extra tokens, he was able to separate two environments that Labov had conflated out of procedural necessity (the original number of tokens for locative and adjective environments being too small for reliable statistical analysis). Baugh showed that these two environments had a different effect: for locatives, contraction was favored over deletion; for adjectives, the reverse held. Baugh concluded that the phonological and grammatical conditions on the copula contraction/deletion rule operate independently, yet simultaneously. It was more feasible to posit a zero copula in adjectival environments than a contraction rule followed by deletion. The re-analysis thus illuminates a fundamental similarity with Caribbean Creole English varieties, and a significant difference from other American English dialects. While calling into question Labov's synchronic analysis of the BEV copula, Baugh's study validates the broad quantitative framework. (Labov's observation on the relationship between the two dialects can be modified to state that where SAE permits contraction, BEV permits deletion, or—in the case of the locative—a zero copula.)

Appraisals of Labov's approach to social class (see *Social Class*) are widely divergent, even contradictory. One view holds that his work does not deal with social class at all: what he calls social class is actually status, since this is what a socioeconomic index measures. Class is seen as a fundamental cleavage over the means of production and the extraction of surplus profit from labor. This aspect of the class struggle is not consonant with Labov's stress on shared norms and common evaluation in a stratified model. In fairness to Labov, it must be said that he does show awareness of the class/status distinction in much of his work (see, for example, Labov 1972a: 44–5). Implicit in much of the research on BEV is the idea of dialect conflict, as well as the interplay between class and ethnicity. His later work stresses divergence rather than a common body of shared norms. Critics who advocate the conflict approach to social class have themselves found it an extremely difficult concept to use in variationist analysis. The socioeconomic scales are a practical means of reflecting stratification patterns in a society and its members' subjective perceptions, whatever the deeper causes of such phenomena. Certainly, variationists need to take greater care in motivating some of the categories posited on their socioeconomic scales. Characterizations like 'middle working-class' and 'middle middle-class' need to be clarified in terms of what their typical members in specific communities are, and how they differ from members of adjacent categories.

Another school of thought criticizes Labov for overuse of social class/status, and would prefer to see a focus on individual behavior. An early criticism was that a group analysis might mask the significant behavior of certain individuals—average scores hide the extreme cases. Horvath (1985) has argued against an approach that first puts individuals into social classes and then examines the linguistic behavior of the preconstructed group. In her study of English in Sydney, Horvath first examined the clustering of linguistic variants using a statistical technique known as 'principal components analysis,' and then examined how the intrinsic internal structure corresponded with combinations of social factors. She argues that this procedure reveals certain patterns that are hidden by *a priori* determination of the relevant social groups. In particular, individual speakers are never 'lost,' since individuals are plotted on graphic displays. The claim that individuals are lost in the traditional Labovian analysis seems unwarranted, if one recollects his detailed discussion of the degree of membership in core and outer groups in the Harlem studies. The characterization of 'lames'—people on the fringe of BEV usage, showing some features of the dialect, but generally peripheral to the core group socially and linguistically—is an early forerunner to the kind of approach that Horvath calls for. However, both approaches to the analysis of linguistic behavior have to face the problem of defining social groupings and deciding which individuals fall into which group: cluster analysis of the sort proposed by Horvath seems to postpone it to a later stage. In the same vein, a major objection of the neo-Labovian school spearheaded by Romaine (1982) is that the cities which it has studied fail to show the monotonically increasing patterns of variation found in New York City.

Romaine advocates a breakaway from what she describes as the exclusively status-based theory and straightforward correlational methodology of the Labovian paradigm. The most important work in this vein is that of Milroy (1980) on social networks, and LePage and Tabouret-Keller (1985) on focusing and diffusion. However, the criticism of Labov's work as largely correlational does scant justice to the breadth and subtlety of the work in Martha's Vineyard and New York, on BEV, and the work on Philadelphia vowel systems. The patterning of sociolinguistic variants in New York City does not look nearly so monotonic when Labov's work on gender and ethnicity are taken into account. Any proposal that class structure has nothing to do with linguistic variation and change does not seem very promising.

Macaulay (1988), working within the variationist paradigm, criticizes it for concentrating too much on what is easily quantifiable (e.g., phonological variants) and thereby failing to exhaust the richness of the carefully collected materials (e.g., in discourse strategies and syntactic choices). This criticism cannot be levelled at Labov, who has worked variously at the structure of narratives, ritual insults, broad syntactic structures, pedagogical implications of dialect use, and applications and testing of sociolinguistic theory within the judicial system. More generally, the criticism has been raised that the variationist school stresses statistics and quantification to the detriment of an overarching sociolinguistic theory. It is perhaps true that Labov's sociolinguistic focus seems to be increasingly narrower (as in the fine-grained studies of vowel-shifting in northern US cities) (Labov 1994, 2001, Labov et al. forthcoming). However, scholars with other perspectives (e.g., gender, the political economy of language, and social psychology) are increasingly using variationist findings in their attempts at constructing theories of social behavior.

As Fasold (1985: 552) writes, there is no substitute for human insight to be found in statistical analysis, or in other predetermined organization of raw data. Yet there is little reason to accept the validity claimed by a researcher based only on flashes of insight. Validity in sociolinguistics should be established on the common grounds of objective analysis. If that analysis can be supported by appropriate quantitative techniques, so much the better.

9. Conclusion

A whole school of sociolinguistics has arisen out of Labov's early studies, not entirely in ways that he envisaged. In particular, linguistics and sociolinguistics have not converged in the way that Labov hoped, and sociolinguistic rules describing variation have not been incorporated into nonsociolinguistic theory. With the benefit of hindsight, this state of affairs is not to be lamented. The strengths of sociolinguistic analyses lie not so much in their contributions to a Chomskyan conception of linguistic theory, but more in addressing their own internally generated problems concerning the relatively structured use of variable resources of a language for certain social purposes, as well as their implications for language change.

See also: Social Class; Social Networks; Dialect and Dialectology; The Atlas of North American English: Methods and Findings; Labov, William; Sound Change.

Bibliography

Baugh J 1980 A re-examination of the Black English copula. In: Labov W (ed.) 1980 *Locating Language in Time and Space: Quantitative Analyses of Linguistic Structure, Vol. 1*. Academic Press, New York

Bell A T 1984 Language style as audience design. *Language in Society* **13**: 145–204

Cedergren H, Sankoff D 1974 Variable rules: Performance as a statistical reflection of competence. *Language* **50**: 333–55

Fasold R 1985 Perspectives on sociolinguistic variation. *Language in Society* **14**: 515–25

Fasold R 1989 *The Sociolinguistics of Language*. Basil Blackwell, Oxford, UK

Fischer J L 1958 Social influence in the choice of a linguistic variant. *Word* **14**: 47–56

Horvath B 1985 *Variation in Australian English: The Sociolects of Sydney*. Cambridge University Press, Cambridge, UK

Kurath H, Hanley M, Bloch B, Lourman GS 1941 *Linguistic Atlas of New England*. Brown University Press, Providence, RI

Labov W 1963 The social motivation of a sound change. *Word* **19**: 273–309

Labov W 1972a *Sociolinguistic Patterns*. University of Pennsylvania Press, Philadelphia, PA

Labov W 1972b *Language in the Inner City: Studies in the Black English Vernacular*. University of Pennsylvania Press, Philadelphia, PA

Labov W (ed.) 1980 *Locating Language in Time and Space: Quantitative Analyses of Linguistic Structure, Vol. 1*. Academic Press, New York

Labov W 1989 The child as linguistic historian. *Language Variation and Change* **1**: 85–97

Labov W 1994 *Principles of Linguistic Change Vol. 1. Internal Factors*. Blackwell, Oxford, UK

Labov W 2001 *Principles of Linguistic Change Vol. 2. Social Factors*. Blackwell, Oxford, UK

Labov W, Ash S, Boberg C in press *Atlas of North American English*. Mouton de Gruyter, Berlin

Labov W, Harris W A 1986 De facto segregation of black and white vernaculars. In: Sankoff D (ed.) *Diversity and Diachrony*. Current Issues in Linguistic Theory 53. Benjamins, Amsterdam

LePage R, Tabouret-Keller A 1985 *Acts of Identity*. Cambridge University Press, Cambridge, UK

Macaulay R 1988 What happened to sociolinguistics? *English World Wide* **9**: 153–69

Milroy L 1980 *Language and Social Networks*. Blackwell, Oxford, UK

Romaine S (ed.) 1982 *Sociolinguistic Variation in Speech Communities*. Edward Arnold, London

Trudgill P 1983 *On Dialect: Social and Geographical Perspectives*. Blackwell, Oxford, UK

Weiner J E, Labov W 1983 Constraints on the agentless passive. *Journal of Linguistics* 19: 29–58

Sociolinguistics and Language Change
J. Milroy

It may seem surprising to the lay person that orthodox historical linguistics has not taken very much account of social factors in attempting to explain linguistic change. Some experts insist that social factors are of little relevance, and that the causes of change are to be found in phenomena that are more central to language structure, for example, 'natural' phonetic processes (see *Language Change and Language Acquisition*). However, there is one important difficulty, which applies especially to the explanation of *sound* change. This is that if one does not take social factors into account, there appears to be little reason why sound change (and some other kinds of change) should take place at all. If, at some place and time, the sound [a] should change to [o] in all relevant words, the language has not gained anything by the change, as one tiny segment of sound cannot be 'better' or more efficient than another. Indeed, it can be argued that change is dysfunctional, since, when a change is introduced by some section of a speech community, it is in principle possible that the new form will not be immediately understood. However, change is continuously in progress, and its operation has greatly altered the sound systems and structural characteristics of languages in the course of history: Old and Middle English, for example, were clearly very different in pronunciation and grammar from twentieth-century English, and language change can be very rapid.

It seems that the causes of change are not to be found in the structure of languages as such, but in the behavior of speakers. As speakers in social groups manifestly attach great social importance to quite small differences in pronunciation, which are arbitrary in linguistic terms (i.e., one sound is just as good as another), sociolinguists argue that collecting and analyzing the language of live speakers in social groupings can be used to advance the understanding of the causes of linguistic change. The basic problem to be solved is known as the 'actuation problem,' and it can be stated thus:

> Why do changes in a structural feature take place in a particular language at a given time, but not in other languages with the same feature, or in the same language at other times?

Thus, one might ask why the French language has lost many final consonants in the course of history, while Spanish and Italian have preserved them, and (at the dialectal level) why some dialects of English have lost final and preconsonantal [r] in words such as *car, card*, while others (for example, Scottish and North American English) have retained it. Although the actuation problem cannot be completely solved, sociolinguists attempt to come closer to understanding it.

Most changes in language, as far as is known, take place without self-conscious attempts being made by speakers to implement them; yet, paradoxically, they must in some way be implemented through speaker activity, as the new forms are accepted and used by new generations of speakers. Self-conscious institutional intervention in language is generally known as 'language planning.' Another phenomenon that may be brought about by institutional intervention is language standardization; from a sociolinguistic point of view, standardization can be seen as an attempt to impose uniformity on a phenomenon which is by nature variable (language), and part of its purpose is to prevent linguistic change. Sociolinguists have up until the time of writing been mainly interested in change that comes about 'naturally,' without conscious intervention.

Three main approaches can be distinguished. The first is associated with the work of anthropological linguists, and focuses on 'language shift'—the replacement of one language by another, perhaps with discernible effects on one or both languages (see *Language Transfer and Substrates*). Work in this tradition traces the replacement patterns as they progress through bilingual populations. It is typically found that some social groups (e.g., females as against males, or a particular social class) lead in the shift, and that the recessive language is replaced by the incoming language in different social situations at different rates: for example, the recessive language normally persists in domestic environments after it has been replaced in most other functions. The study of recessive languages in these situations is referred to as the study of 'language death.' Typically, these languages undergo a great deal of internal change during the process.

The second approach to language change focuses on monolingual situations in much greater linguistic detail, and is associated with the name of William Labov. It can be called quantitative social dialectology (see *Sociolinguistic Variation*), as it makes use of quantification to reveal patterns of variation in terms of the social characteristics of the speakers studied—age, sex, and social class, for example. By this means, linguistic changes in progress can be detected and traced in fine detail as they diffuse in an orderly way through populations of speakers. These studies usually focus on quite small communities of speakers, and they have shown that, in order to understand linguistic changes, one must first think of changes as coming about in the speech community rather than in the national language as a whole. That is, changes originate not in 'English,' but in some localized variety of English. From localized situations, they may diffuse much more widely, and these wider patterns of diffusion are also studied.

The third relevant approach concerns Pidgin and Creole languages (see *Pidgins and Creoles: Models*). Like the first approach, this involves contact between languages, except that the replacement of one language (an established native language) is abrupt—it is brought about by upheaval of populations who are then thrown together with strangers in situations where there is no common language. Creoles are normally based on colonial languages such as English or Portuguese, with much reduced syntax. Pidgin and Creole studies have greatly advanced the understanding of universals of language change, particularly syntactic universals.

So far, theoretical advances in traditional historical linguistic concerns have come mainly from work in the second approach above. They have been chiefly concerned with sound change and have borne in mind the traditional neogrammarian axioms, which propose that sound change is phonetically gradual and lexically abrupt. In this view, change is believed to proceed by imperceptible degrees affecting all members of a word-class at the same time (e.g., all words with the vowel [a], as in *bat, bad, hand*, etc.). Many sociolinguistic patterns, however, have proved to be different from this: they are lexically gradual and phonetically abrupt, and sound change is often observed to spread gradually through the relevant lexicon, affecting some words before others. Similarly, phonetic differences are not necessarily imperceptible, but may be quite marked. The relevance of these traditional concerns is a matter of debate; what is certainly clear is that sound change is *socially* gradual. It spreads gradually through populations of speakers.

Influenced by Labov, many attempted accounts of language change have used social class as a background to their arguments (see *Social Class*). Change has been seen as spreading upward and downward from some central point in the social-class hierarchy, and social-class differentiation seems to have been thought of as a cause of change. Sex differentiation in language has also been cited as an equally important variable in linguistic change, as males and females are always found to differ in speech, usually with females using more 'careful' or less 'vernacular' speech than males.

Argumentation based on the idea of varying solidarity within and between communities and operationalized in terms of social network has been used to propose a theory that can account for different language situations—encompassing those studied by the three approaches enumerated above. This suggests that, as close and solidary personal ties in communities result in dialect maintenance and resistance to change, linguistic change is facilitated by the development of large numbers of weak ties (see *Social Networks*). If this model is used in interpretation, it appears to account in a coherent way for situations of different orders of magnitude. It is proposed that:

> Linguistic change is slow to the extent that the relevant populations are well established and bound by strong ties, whereas it is rapid to the extent that weak ties exist in populations.

Although traditional historical linguistics neglected speakers (partly because it did not have access to tape recorders), languages that have no speakers do not change. A theory of change must therefore have a place for speakers, and it has been proposed that a distinction should be drawn between innovations and changes in language. An innovation is an act of the speaker, which may or may not lead to a *change*, which is something that is embedded in the language system. In order to make progress here, one must attempt to understand the way in which some innovations in some circumstances can become changes, whereas others fall away without trace. Although the actuation problem is still a very long way from being solved, it is to be hoped that the typical sociolinguistic focus on speaker behavior will make further contributions to linguists' understanding of the nature of linguistic change.

See also: Sociolinguistic Variation; Language Change and Language Acquisition; Sound Change; Social Networks.

Bibliography

Aitchison J 1991 *Language Change: Progress or Decay?*, 2nd edn. Cambridge University Press, Cambridge, UK

Labov W 1972 *Sociolinguistic Patterns*. University of Pennsylvania Press, Philadelphia, PA

Labov W 1994 *Principles of Linguistic Change. Vol. 1: Internal Factors*. Blackwell, Oxford, UK

Milroy J 1992 *Linguistic Variation and Change*. Blackwell, Oxford, UK

Trudgill P 1986 *Dialects in Contact*. Blackwell, Oxford, UK

Sociophonetics

S. Wright. Revised by C. M. Sangster

Sociophonetics involves the study of speech in its social context, combing the techniques of sociolinguistics and experimental phonetics, particularly acoustic and/or articulatory analysis. The aim of this approach is to discover the influences of social, situational, and phonetic factors on the articulatory processes which, taken together, amount to 'pronunciation.' Although the term has generally been used to refer only to sociolinguistic research using instrumentally acquired or acoustically analysed data, it can also refer to quantitative phonetic work based solely on auditory analysis. Sociophonetics is the work of phoneticians in the field of variationist or quantitative sociolinguistics (Foulkes and Docherty 1999 propose the term 'accent studies' as an alternative). This article will sketch the field's background in sociolinguistics, describe the nature of the linguistic variables examined, introduce some techniques from experimental phonetics, and then report some results of recent sociophonetics research (see *Sociolinguistic Variation*; *Dialect and Dialectology*).

1. Background in Sociolinguistics

The principal methodological antecedents of sociophonetics lie in large-scale sociolinguistic investigations of urban societies in the USA (Labov 1966, 1972) and Britain (Trudgill 1974). Projects investigating the social motivation of sound change (see *Sound Change*) in Philadelphia, USA, made extensive use of instrumental phonetic techniques and analysis using acoustic as well as auditory methods. Labov employed instrumental techniques, analyzing spectrographic recordings of the speech of his informants in order to measure vowel quality differences. The acoustic specification of vowel quality for each informant was matched with his or her social profile. This social profile included information about the following social variables: age, sex, social class, social mobility, ethnicity, neighborhood, communication patterns, and knowledge of other languages. The resulting equations enabled researchers to gain a picture of the range of variation in pronunciation likely to exist in any one section of the speech community, and to indicate the nature of the differences between sections of the community. The analysis of the resulting categories pairing vowel measurement and social groups yielded the basis for an interpretation of changes in vowel pronunciation in the Philadelphia speech community. Labov concluded that the social factors most salient for the variation and changes in progress in the Philadelphia speech community included ethnic diversity and neighborhood or locality, while socioeconomic class (see *Social Class*) was not a significant factor.

In this research, instrumental phonetic techniques, such as the spectrographic analysis of vowel sounds, were used as supplementary, interpretative aids in the examination of linguistic variation and change in its social context. Other early explorations of the combination of sociolinguistic and phonetic techniques are represented by the work of Dressler and Wodak (1982) and Kerswill (1987). It should be noted, however, that although such analysis of vowel differences using F1-F2 plots became quite widespread in sociophonetic work, they have been criticised for not revealing information about lip-rounding, duration or the third formant, and for problems normalising the data; and they are by no means the only acoustic analysis possible. For example, Docherty and Foulkes (1999) and Sangster (2001) report acoustic analyses of variation in closure and friction in the consonant /t/ in two British urban accents, while Yaeger-Dror (1997) and Grabe et al (2000) have used fundamental frequency analysis to explore variation in pitch and intonation.

2. Techniques

Standard techniques in laboratory phonetics include experiments with a relatively small number of speakers and multiple repetitions, but the value of combining the rigour of quantifiable experimental techniques with the use of sociolinguistically structured groups of subjects is increasingly being recognised (Scobbie et al 2000). Experimental phonetic techniques generally control more closely for variability owing to phonotatic effects and speech rate than sociolinguistic interviews intended only for auditory analysis. Recording quality has to be particularly 'clean' if acoustic analysis is to be carried out on interview recordings.

2.1 Sociolinguistic Interviews

In a sociolinguistic interview, there may be recordings of the reading of a constructed narrative passage in 'formal' and 'colloquial' styles; of wordlists, and of natural speech, for example, open-ended conversation with a researcher or a co-interviewee (see *Field Methods in Modern Dialect and Variation Studies*). If interviews are not conducted one-to-one but with pairs or groups of informants, collaborative talk about tasks such as amp tasks may also be recorded. A range of recordings from several speakers provides a large corpus of speech suitable for auditory and acoustic analysis of selected variables and allows an expanded analysis of particular variables.

2.2 Acoustic Analysis

Recordings of informants' speech are transferred to a computer for spectrographic analysis, where amplitude and frequency of the signal are plotted along a timeline. Durations of periods of closure or friction can be measured, or analysis of formant frequencies for vowels and sonorants can be carried out. Line spectra for single instances can be generated, and other elements of the acoustic signal, such as voicing and fundamental frequency, can also be analysed (Johnson 1997).

2.3 Instrumental Analysis

Various pieces of laboratory equipment are used to gain an insight into some particular aspect of the speech process, usually simultaneously with an audio recording. These approaches can include the following: imaging techniques such as ultrasound or fMRI to examine the motion of the tongue and other organs of speech; airflow measurement with a face mask or plethysmograph; electromagnetic midsagittal articulometry (EMMA) to track the motions of the articulators in relation to one another; or the use of low electrical currents to measure rapid changes in the state of the vocal folds (electroglottography), in the muscles involved in speech (electromyography) or contact of the tongue on the palate (electropalatography). See below for more details on electropalatography, the technique used in the experiments discussed in Sect. 3 below; otherwise see, e.g., Stone 1996 for more details about these speech physiology instrumental techniques.

2.3.1 Electropalatography

Parallel audio and electropalatographic recordings provide a limited visual analog of (palatal) articulatory gestures for each speaker in the sociolinguistic sample. These data allow the detailed articulatory analysis of variables that may be noted in conversational recordings, and provides a basis for the development and selection of materials for use in controlled listening experiments. The technique is used to obtain data on the exact location and timing of tongue contacts with the palate during continuous speech (Hardcastle et al. 1989). A subject wears a moulded acrylic artificial palate which is embedded with electrodes. When the tongue touches one of these, an electrical circuit is completed, and the resulting signal from that electrode is recorded and stored on a computer. The data are subsequently formatted in diagrams modeling the arrangement of electrodes on the palate, with a dot indicating no-tongue contact, and a circle indicating contact for at least a minimal period of that particular scan. A specimen is illustrated in Fig. 1.

2.4 Phonetic Experiments

2.4.1 Production Experiments

These allow the researcher to carry out detailed analysis of selected variables. Experiments involve audio recording, under controlled conditions, of speakers reading texts designed to focus on particular targeted variables. Either the audio recording will be used for acoustic as well as auditory analysis, or an instrumental recording such as an eletropalatographic recording is made simultaneously. Unlike sociolinguistic interviews, the text is precisely controlled, and often repeated several times. Stimuli presentation tools and carrier sentences are commonly used.

2.4.2 Perception Experiments

These are aimed to assess whether listeners are sensitive to particular sociophonetic variables, and if so, whether they consistently use them in making judgments of a sociolinguistic kind. There are different methods for eliciting listener judgments:

(a) The selection of example of different values of a variable from the corpus of sociolinguistic recording to elicit listener judgments. The problem with this method can be the lack of control over listener-sensitive variables such as

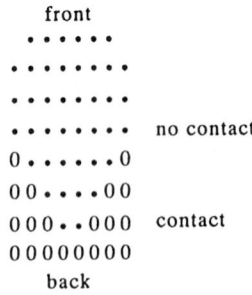

Figure 1. Schematic patatographic printout of a velar closure.

voice quality, speaking rate, and nonidentity of tokens which are different from those targeted.
(b) The use of recordings of constructed parallel texts produced by a single speaker in the sociolinguistic sample (Labov 1972: 146). The problem with this method is the difficulty of controlling the subject's own variation in the articulation of a number of variables in the text.
(c) The matched guise technique, developed by Lambert et al (1960). In this, a speaker able to control more than one accent or register reads a text using different varieties. Using one speaker ensures that listener evaluations are not affected by aspects of personal voice quality. The problem with this technique is that the performer may share and subconsciously encode other cues to the sociolinguistic prejudices being tested.
(d) Informant training. Using listening techniques, and electropalatography as a practical teaching aid to train a subject in the sociolinguistic sample to produce and distinguish different variants of targeted variables as preparation for a sociolinguistic perception experiment. This strategy is an advance on using a trained phonetician in the construction of materials for use in listener experiments.

3. Case-study Illustrating Sociophonetic Methods

One area amenable to study with an explicitly sociophonetic approach involves a set of local, context-sensitive phonetic phenomena called 'connected speech processes' (CSPS), which occur in the stream of everyday speech as a result of a reduction of articulatory effort (Kerswill and Nolan 1989). These natural speech processes may be phonetically motivated (for example, by local phonetic context and speaking rate) but they may also be dialect-specific and socially motivated. Kerswill et al. (1991) conducted a project investigating the social motivation of connected speech processes in the English of Cambridge. Several CSPS which may convey social information about local Cambridge speakers were identified through the auditory analysis of a sociolinguistic survey of Cambridge speech and results of experiments using electropalatography. The socially sensitive features were identified as the processes of /l/- vocalization (where the word *bill* sounds like *biw*), glottalization (where /t/ is realized with a glottal or glottalized stop [ʔ] or [ʔt]), and palatalization (or yod-coalescence, Trudgill 1974) reflected in the representation of the phrase *bet you* as *betcha*. These features carry social information about people and the society to which they belong. Other processes, such as assimilation of adjacent consonants, did not appear to be sensitive to social factors. It was concluded that sociolinguistic CSPS are not influenced by situational features such as style and rates of speaking in the same way that phonetically-conditioned CSPS are.

Kerswill et al. (1991) also investigated the diffusion of sociophonetic features. The diffusion model has been central to the study of linguistic change, from the spread of regional dialect features (Chambers and Trudgill 1988: 182ff), through the postcreole continuum, to language death. According to this model, phonological processes spread through language via linguistic environments and speaking styles. At first, a process is variable and optional in a given environment and style, then it becomes categorical. Finally, the process becomes phonologized. Well-known examples of phonologization are the fronting of velars in Italian and many other languages, and the coalescence of [z] and [j] in English, resulting in the new phoneme /ʒ/. These studies investigate the diffusion of two features in the speech of local Cambridge speakers: /l/-vocalization and yod-coalescence. The focus of the study was the role of social factors such as age, and style of speaking in influencing spread.

3.1 /l/-vocalization

/l/-vocalization is a London dialect feature known to be spreading across south-east England. The spread of vocalization across phonological environments was considered, examining conversational data for older and younger speakers of a particular speech community in South East: local Cambridge English.

Four phonological environments were considered:

1. V–C e.g., *called,*
2. V– #C e.g., *call Susan,*
3. V–V e.g., *believe, calling*
4. V–V e.g., *call Andy*

Southern British English and RP speakers would be expected to produce 'dark /l/' (a velarized or vocalized /l/) in the first two environments. The third was included to facilitate the monitoring of the possible use of nonclear variants (only clear /l/ is expected in this environment), at the same time as serving as a control. The fourth environment was included following informal observation of vocalization in a manner suggesting the spread of the CSP to new environments. The auditory transcription of the data produced a simplified set of auditory categories: 'clear,' 'dark,' and 'vocalized.'

Fig. 2 shows the percentage of the realizations which are vocalized.

Overall, younger speakers did not appear to vocalize more frequently than other age groups. Although the proportions are roughly similar for each group in the two preconsonantal environments, it is significant that older speakers vocalized word-internally more frequently than before a word

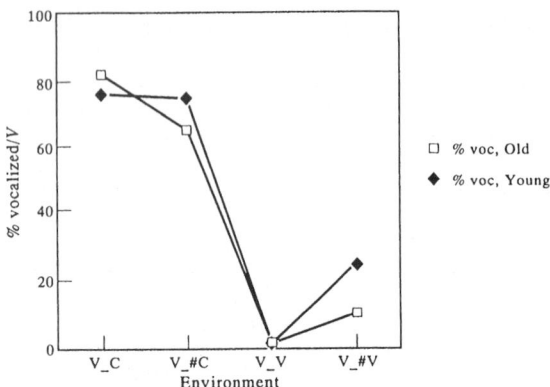

Figure 2. Percentage of vocalization in four environments—conversational data.

demonstrating the essentially sociolinguistic process by which a CSP expands its domain. Kerswill et al. explain the synchronic presence of variation as follows. Although these speakers usually vocalize, their systems coexist in the community with systems without vocalization (fluctuation being expected in any transition stage). Normative pressures against vocalization from prestigious varieties, from norms of correct speech and from spelling, pose difficult choices for these speakers. In the interview situation, the speakers may have been affected by overt social pressures, and may have attempted to avoid the stigmatized vocalized /l/. Since many of them have no dark /l/ in their repertoire, the only alternative is to produce a clear /l/, even in preconsonantal environments.

3.2 Yod-coalescence

Yod-coalescence in English is considered to be neither socially stigmatized nor spreading. But this was not always so. It dates back to well before the eighteenth century, when /s/ + /j/ and /z/ + /j/ coalesced as /ʃ/ and the new phoneme /ʒ/ in words such as *nation* and *measure*, respectively (Gimson 1980). In these examples, the CSP was phonologized. By contrast, it has probably never been phonologized across word boundaries, because the coalesced pronunciations of *did you, miss you*, etc., can always be 'unpacked.' Kerswill et al. analyzed three cross-boundary environments: /d/ + /j/, /s/ + /j/ (including /z/ + /j/), and /t/ + /j/. The last environment included a glottal variant, [ʔ]. Fig. 3, below, shows the percentage coalescence for d + j, s/z + j and t + j.

Fig. 3 shows the incidence of l-vocalization and yod-coalescence, and for comparison, the incidence of glottaling. There are two striking features: (a) young speakers have a much higher incidence of coalescence for both d + j and s/z + j than older speakers; (b) they have a much lower incidence for

boundary. This group's behavior suggested that they differentiate between the environments, whereas younger speakers do not.

Two other results suggest a change in progress. First, while the overall rate of vocalization in canonically 'dark' (i.e., preconsonantal) environments was around 75 percent, some subjects produced clear /l/ in this environment. Kerswill et al. considered whether this behavior represents a change in the phonological representation of the words for these speakers, since these subjects were all high vocalizers. The change would be from structure with a lateral consonant in the syllable coda to one with a syllable-nuclear diphthong. Their data supported this interpretation. All speakers categorically used clear /l/ in the V–V environment, but occasionally there was some use of nonclear variants in the V–#V environment. While the older speakers produced 13 percent (3 percent velarized + 10 percent vocalized), younger speakers' use of nonclear variants was much higher, at 31 percent (7 percent verlarized + 24 percent vocalized). The difference between the two age groups was highly significant. It was observed that for some young speakers, words of the relevant structure ended in a diphthong, effectively making it impossible to resyllabify (and 'clarify') a final /l/ before a vowel. They suggest that the presence of a fairly high proportion of dark l's in this context should be interpreted as a sandhi feature, not unlike 'intrusive' /r/ in nonrhotic accents. They concluded that the younger speakers could be beginning to phonologize the l-vocalization CSP.

Second, the fact that the younger speakers did not seem to distinguish between the two preconsonantal environments might indicate that they had generalized the process. By contrast, the older speakers continued to differentiate between the preconsonantal environments to a significant degree. The speech of the young speakers may therefore be construed as

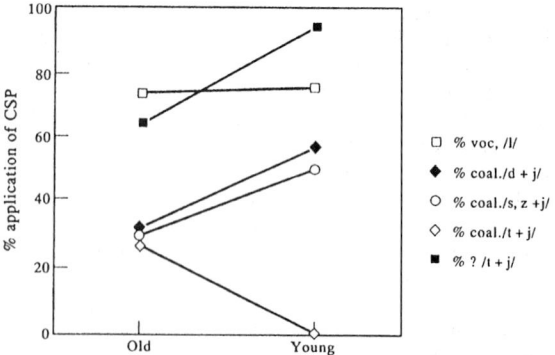

Figure 3. Percentage of scores for yod-coalescence, t-glottaling and l-vocalization, old and young speakers.

t+j, which seems to be mirrored by a much higher incidence of glottaling. The apparent time increase in yod-coalescence does not, it is argued, indicate linguistic change (the phonologization of yod-coalescence across word boundaries) because there was no evidence that young speakers apply this CSP in a categorical manner. But they did observe that yod-coalescence was phonetically gradual and subject to speaking rate and level of formality.

This observation prompted them to consider the role of style in accounting for the dramatic apparent-time increase in yod-coalescence, since the variable of speaking style may intervene between the linguistic environment affecting a CSP and the CSPS realization.

Thus, they argued that a CSP may be subject to sociolinguistic style, despite the tendency for it to apply more readily at fast speaking rates. They adopted Bell's (1984) concept of sociolinguistic style as 'audience design' (see *Audience Design*): the speaker's total response to the audience—immediate interlocutors, overhearers, and 'referees,' an absent reference group which the speaker wishes to identify with. The possible stylistic influences on the application of yod-coalescence are as follows.

First, the influence of the interview situation itself: young and older speakers could have been reacting differently to the interview situation as a consequence of systematic differences in the relationship between the interviewer and each subject due to the variation in the age difference. Second, social change (e.g., the likelihood that less overtly formal relationships between strangers are becoming the norm) may account for the fact that young speakers treated the interview situation as more informal than did older speakers. Third, older speakers may have a wider range of speech styles at their disposal—or are simply more willing to use them.

The second notable feature of Fig. 3 is the marked apparent-time reduction in yod-coalescence of /t+j/ and the equally marked increase in t-glottaling/ deletion. The results reflect a complementary pattern in the application of these processes. One process 'bleeds' the other; in phonetic terms, if /t/ has been deleted, it can no longer coalesce with the following palatal glide. The converse is not true: there is no reason why /t/ should not be glottalized/deleted after yod-coalescence. The quantitative patterns in their data confirm this view. They argue that if yod-coalescence is assumed to be a unitary process, the coalescence of /t+j/ would be expected to show the same increase as the other two environments. And they suggest that the reason that /t+j/ does not show the same increase is related to the steep apparent increase in glottaling, which prevents coalescence. They conclude that the reason for the apparent-time increase in glottaling is most likely stylistic; specifically, it is a sign of an informal style.

3.3 Comparison of /l/-vocalization and Yod-coalescence

Kerswill et al. discuss the apparent-time increase of l-vocalization and yod-coalescence as the possible outcome of phonetically, phonologically, and sociolinguistically similar factors, and consider whether they reflect different, complex interactions of factors. They observe that l-vocalization is nearing completion in preconsonantal environments, and is spreading prevocalically where there is an intervening word boundary. They also infer that it is heavily implicated in phonological restructuring because of its occurrence prevocalically (outside the traditional domain of 'dark' /l/) and by the sporadic unexpected occurrence of clear /l/ preconsonantally. Finally, it is socially stratified, but not overtly stigmatized. They conclude that the small apparent-time differences do not obviously result from style differences. The younger speakers' greater use of vocalized and dark /l/ before a vowel is the opposite of what might be expected from their more casual speech style. Preconsonantally, there is little difference between older and younger speakers.

Kerswill et al. note that yod-coalescence is the exact converse of l-vocalization in its patterning. They conclude that while it is neither subject to social stratification, nor to change in its linguistic status, it is sensitive to style changes. However, it is sensitive to a combination of interacting stylistic features. Yod-coalescence is directly affected by speaking rate and attention to articulatory clarity in addition to formality of speech situation. It is not a Labovian marker, that is, a variable showing stylistic variation that exactly parallels its stratification, with 'correct' forms occurring in formal styles and in the speech of higher social classes. However, as part of Labov's concept of formality, speaking rate and attention to articulatory clarity do co-vary with it. The likelihood that higher social classes use yod-coalescence less than classes lower in the stratification would imply that the former speak more carefully (a reasonable assumption based on the level of education and concomitant beliefs about 'correct' and 'good' speech). Kerswill et al. argue that its patterning might resemble that of a Labovian marker though for different reasons. For while the relationship between Labov's variables and the social values they encode is essentially arbitrary (for instance, there is nothing about a vowel's height that directly symbolizes 'class'), there is a nonarbitrary relationship for yod-coalescence, since its application is directly relatable to articulatory economy.

4. Future Work

Future work in sociophonetics will focus increasingly on investigating the relationship between sociolinguistic variation and sound change within a speech community. Acoustic analysis can grant further insight into many areas of sociolinguistic investigation and experimentation, and there are further dimensions of observation offered by instrumental articulatory analysis. The advance of the field will continue to depend on increasingly sophisticated and accessible instrumentation for analyzing natural speech in its social context. As the technology improves, and as sociolinguists realise the value of precisely-controlled phonetic experimentation while phoneticians recognise the significance of sociolinguistic factors, the field of sociophonetics will continue to grow.

See also: The Atlas of North American English: Methods and Findings; Dialect and Dialectology; Forensic Phonetics and Sociolinguistics.

Bibliography

Bell A 1984 Style as audience design. *Language in Society* **13**: 145–204
Chambers J C, Trudgill P 1988 *Dialectology*. Cambridge University Press, Cambridge, UK
Docherty G J, Foulkes P 1999 Derby and Newcastle: Instrumental phonetics and variationist studies. In: Foulkes P, Docherty G J (eds) *Urban Voices*. Arnold, London
Dressler W U, Wodak R 1982 Sociophonological methods in the study of sociolinguistic variation in Viennese German. *Language in Society* **11**: 339–70
Foulkes P, Docherty G J 1999 *Urban Voices*. Arnold, London
Gimson A C 1980 *An Introduction to the Pronunciation of English*, 3rd edn. Arnold, London
Grabe E, Post B, Nolan F, Farrar K 2000 Pitch accent realisation in four varieties of British English. *Journal of Phonetics* **28**: 161–85.
Hardcastle W J, Jones W, Knight C, Trudgeon A, Calder G 1989 New developments in electropalatography: State-of-the-art report. *Clinical Linguistics and Phonetics* **3**: 1–38
Johnson K 1997 *Acoustic and Auditory Phonetics*. Blackwell, Oxford, UK
Kerswill P E 1987 Levels of linguistic variation in Durham. *Journal of Linguistics* **23**: 25–49
Kerswill P E, Nolan F J 1989 The description of connected speech processes. In: Ramsaran S (ed.) *Essays in Honour of A. C. Gimson*. Routledge, London
Kerswill P E, Nolan F J, Wright S M 1991 *The Interaction of Sociophonetic Features and Connected Speech Processes*, Report of Award Ref R00023 1056. Economic and Social Research Council Report, London
Labov W 1966 *The Social Stratification of English in New York City*. Center for Applied Linguistics, Washington, DC
Labov W 1972 *Sociolinguistic Patterns*. University of Pennsylvania Press, Philadelphia, PA
Lambert W E, Hodgson R, Gardner R C, Fillenbaum S 1960 Evaluational reactions to spoken languages. *Journal of Abnormal and Social Psychology* **60**: 44–51
Sangster C M 2001 Lenition of alveolar stops in Liverpool English. *Journal of Sociolinguistics* **5**: 3
Scobbie J M, Timmins C, Stuart-Smith J, Tweedie F, Hewlett N, Turk A E 2000 Fieldwork in the urban jungle: An empirical phonological study of Glasgow English. *7th International Conference on Laboratory Phonology* (LabPhon 7), Nijmegen, The Netherlands
Stone M 1996 Instrumentation for the study of speech physiology. In: Lass N (ed.) *Principles of Experimental Phonetics*. Mosby, St. Louis, MO, pp. 495–524
Trudgill P 1974 *The Social Differentiation of English in Norwich*. Cambridge University Press, Cambridge, UK
Yaeger-Dror M 1997 Contraction of negatives as evidence of variance in register-specific interactive rules. *Language Variation and Change* **9**: 1–36

Sound Change
J. J. Ohala

Sound change refers to changes in pronunciation of words or morphemes over time when these changes seem to be attributable to phonetic and phonological causes, not morphological, semantic, or cultural. Pronunciation changes due to the latter factors have other designations, for example, analogical leveling, expressive change due to sound symbolism, spelling pronunciation, and so on.

Introduction

Sound change manifests itself in many ways. When reading older literature one becomes aware that certain words are used in rhymes which do not rhyme in twentieth-century pronunciation, as, for example, in the following lines from Chaucer's *Knight's Tale*:

But mercy, lady bright, that knowest weel [= 'well']
My thought, and seest what harmes that I feel.

The vowels in these words 'well' and 'feel,' which are [ɛ] and [i], were both [e:] in Chaucer's speech.

Regional dialectal differences must be due to sound change if it is allowed that the same word must have had a uniform pronunciation at some point in the past, for example, presence versus absence of postvocalic *r*s in American versus British English: 'beer' is [biɹ] in the USA but [biə] in British Received Pronunciation; similarly, [tʃɛɹ] and [tʃeːə], respectively (see *Dialect and Dialectology*).

On a much broader scale of 'dialect' differences, an examination of the pronunciation of cognate words in related languages also suggests the action of sound change:

English	Italian	(1)
foot [fʊt]	piede [pieɖe]	
fish [fɪʃ]	pesce [peʃ:e]	
flat [flæt]	piatto [pjat:o]	

Within a given language, morphemes that have a different pronunciation in different morphological contexts (e.g., due to the addition of affixes) give evidence of sound change that occurred in one morphological environment and not another, for example,:

extreme [ɪkˈstɹiːm]	extremity [ɪkˈstɹɛmɪti]	(2)
repose [ɹɪˈpʰouz]	repository [ɹɪˈpʰazɪtɔɹi]	
act [ækt]	actual [ˈækʃuəl]	

Such changes are said to exhibit 'morphophonemic alternations.'

Finally, some cases of contextually determined variation in the phonetic form of a given phoneme may be a manifestation of sound change, for example, the phoneme /t/ may be realized as [tʰ] or as [ʔ] in some American dialects:

Trenton/ˈtɹɛntən/
[tʰɹɛ̃tʰn̩]~[tʰɹɛ̃ʔn̩] (3)

1. The Importance of Sound Change

A systematic analysis of such evidence of sound change and other forms of language stimulated the development of linguistic science at the beginning of the nineteenth century and led to the development of the comparative method which permitted the reconstruction of languages past. On the assumption that sound change must be happening in the twentieth century as it has in the past, researchers in language acquisition have been motivated to examine the errors of first and second language learners in order to discern possible parallels between variation that is diachronic (across time) and synchronic (at one point in time) (see *Language Change and Language Acquisition*).

Physiologists often gain valuable insights into the workings of the healthy body by studying the diseased body. Parallel to this strategy, many researchers regard sound change as a failure of speech communication, that is, a failure to convey a pronunciation norm, and examine it for hints on how speech production and perception—both their physiological and the cognitive aspects—work normally and successfully.

2. The Literature on Sound Change

The documentation of sound change is enormous and represents one of the great scientific treasures of linguistics. From comparative grammars of language families as well as the vast literature giving descriptions of the phonemic and morphophonemic systems of single languages it is possible to extract much valuable information on sound change. Unfortunately the digging is hard in this quarry because there is no standardization of terminology or phonological symbols and the methods of presenting the data vary widely. A few of the more common forms of sound change are reviewed here with examples of each.

2.1 Assimilation

This is a change of a speech sound so that it becomes more similar or identical to another adjacent sound:

'contend' is derived from the original Latin morphemes (4a)
com + tendere 'with' + 'stretch, strain'; the final *m* of *com* became *n* by assimilating to the place of the following *t*.
Italian *notte* comes from the Latin stem *noct-* 'night'; here (4b)
the *c* (= k) assimilated completely to the following *t*.

The overwhelming majority of sound changes are assimilations.

2.2 Dissimilation

This is a change of a speech sound so that it becomes less like another sound in its vicinity or even disappears entirely, for example, 'pilgrim' comes ultimately from the Latin *peregrīnus* 'foreign' (from which the English 'peregrination' is derived). At some time in its history one of the two original *r*'s dissimilated and became *l*. A similar dissimilation relates 'colonel' to original *colonnello* 'column (of soldiers)'; though still spelled with two *l*s, it is pronounced with only one still intact.

2.3 Loss of a Sound

This may occur by 'syncope,' 'apocope,' and so on, depending on where in the word the loss occurs; for example, English 'every' is often pronounced as [ˈɛvɹi], without the medial vowel.

2.4 Epenthesis

Epenthesis is the insertion of a sound in the middle of a word, for example, 'arithmetic' is occasionally pronounced with the medial [-θm-] cluster broken up by an inserted schwa [ə]. Some commonly cited cases of epenthesis, for example, the introduced [p] in 'warmth' [wɔ̃ɹmpθ], are best considered cases of assimilation: the [p] is the result of the latter portion of the [m] assimilating to the voicelessness and the elevated velum of the following [θ].

2.5 Haplology

This is the loss of one of two successive sounds or sound sequences that are the same or identical, for example, Latin *nutrix* 'nurse' derives from the stem *nutri-* plus the feminine agentive suffix *-trix*, that is, *nutri + trix*. One of the two successive identical syllables *tri* was lost. In English the term 'mineralogy' from 'mineral' + *ology* shows haplology with respect to two original successive syllables that were similar but not identical.

2.6 Metathesis

This is the transposition of two adjacent sounds. In Old English the source of the word 'wasp' had two varying forms, *wæsp* and *wæps* (as did its Indo-European source *wopsā* and *wospā*). Similarly, Old English showed variant forms *āscian* and *ācsian* for 'ask.' In some nonstandard dialects of American English this word may be pronounced [æks].

3. The Process of Sound Change

Among those who study sound change some of the greatest controversies arise over how and why sound change takes place. In fact these disputes have been raging for well over a century since approximately the neogrammarian revolution in the mid 1870s. No discernible consensus has been reached yet. This short article attempts to convey some of the origins of these disputes and their parameters.

Although speculation about sound change can be found as early as Plato's *Cratylus* and was very common throughout the eighteenth century, it was not until the pioneering work of philologists such as Samuel Gyarmathi, Rasmus Rask, and Jakob Grimm, that a rigorous, systematic study of sound correspondences between cognate words of different languages was undertaken. What has come to be known as Grimm's Law (Grimm 1822), but was first proposed by Rasmus Rask in 1818; documented a fairly regular (but not exceptionless) correspondence between Greek voiceless stops and Germanic voiceless fricatives: Greek p, t, k = Germanic f, þ(= [θ]), h (= [x]); Greek voiceless aspirates and Germanic voiced stops, ph, th, kh = b, d, g; Greek voiced stops and Germanic voiceless stops, b, d, g = p, t, k. Some examples are given in Table 1.

Two fundamental assumptions about sound change started the controversy. The first is the fairly commonplace observation that sound change seems not to happen all of a sudden. There has never been a report in history that, 'Today on November 23, 1753, we all ceased pronouncing nasal consonants after vowels and instead made the vowel distinctively nasal.' This leads to the belief that sound change occurs so gradually as to be virtually undetectable.

The second belief arose when Hermann Grassmann and Karl Verner discovered in the 1860s and 1870s rules for two major classes of exceptions to Grimm's Law. The impact of this achievement on the philological community of the time cannot be overestimated: for more than four decades philology had accepted, with Grimm, that sound change, whatever its causes, showed the same messiness in application as other aspects of human behavior: there were generalizations to be made but there were inevitably exceptions to these general statements. When Grassmann and Verner showed that even the exceptions (at least a major part of them) could be accounted for by a general rule, they came to believe that sound change operated mechanically and without exception (unless dialect borrowing and analogy interfered with the regular pattern).

As a consequence of sound change applying mechanically and without exception—that is, that all eligible words were affected by it—it was supposed that sound change must progress in a phonetically gradual way. In opposition to the neogrammarians and their view that sound change applied mechanically and without exception were the traditional philologists who insisted that 'each word has its own history' (and thus defies a rule-based account).

The neogrammarians were aware of certain exceptions to the sound changes they discovered but usually attributed them to psychological and cultural factors (analogy and borrowing from other dialects) which they acknowledged could override the forces that propelled these phonological changes.

In the twentieth century, many linguists, the intellectual descendants of the neogrammarians, acknowledge that sound change does not apply without exception, but they still adhere to the notion that it is phonetically gradual and suppose that, for example, the change of the original Indo–European voiceless stops (preserved in classical Greek) changed to the Germanic voiceless fricatives through a process of gradual weakening of the stop closure. (Even if adherence to the doctrine of the exceptionless of sound change has lessened, virtually everyone agrees that the concept was useful heuristically and had a profound effect on the development of linguistics as a rigorous discipline.) On the other hand there is a renewed acceptance of the traditional philological notion that some or all of the gradualness of sound change—which makes it imperceptible—comes about because a given sound change moves gradually through the lexicon affecting first a few words, then more, and then, possibly, most or all eligible words. This is known as 'lexical diffusion' (Wang 1977). Furthermore, a sound change can create

Table 1. Examples of sound correspondences between Greek and the ancient Germanic languages as covered by Grimm's Law (relevant correspondences are highlighted in bold).

Greek	Germanic	English
poûs, **p**odós	**f**ôtus (Gothic)	foot
grá**ph**ein	**gr**a**b**an (Gothic)	dig, cut (engrave)
to	**þ**at (Gothic)	that
o**d**oús, o**d**óntos	tun**þ**us (Gothic)	tooth
thugátēr	**d**aúhtar (Gothic)	daughter
kánnabis	**h**enpr (Old Norse)	hemp, cannabis
génus	**k**inn (Old Norse)	beget, family, kin
kholé	**g**all (Old Norse)	bile, gall

pronunciation variants which connote social class membership, such that two or more alternate pronunciations are available to a speaker, for example, 'floor' as [flɔ] or [flɔɹ]. Speakers might then fluctuate between one form and another depending on what sort of social impression they would like to convey. A change in social valence of one variant could allow it to spread gradually at the expense of the other (Labov 1972). In a pivotal work, Weinreich et al (1968) advocated, among other things, that a strict distinction be made between how a new pronunciation norm starts vs. how it spreads (from word to word, from speaker to speaker, from one socially marked style of speech to another). Some of the imperceptible gradualness, then, could be in the latter domain. (See also *Weinreich, Uriel*; *Labov, William*.)

4. The Occurrence of Sound Change

4.1 Teleology

There have been many theories regarding why sound change takes place. Among the many early speculations on the matter, now discredited, were that the speech organs evolved to necessitate the change, that migrations to different climates (colder regions, windy regions) caused a change in speaking habits. Among the theories still current in the early 1990s, some important divisions remain. One of these is between those that characterize sound change as teleological or purposeful and those that do not. Another is whether or not it is thought that sound change improves a language in some way. Many purposes have been posited behind phonological change, most of them operating unconsciously. Speakers change their pronunciation, it is claimed, to make the act of speaking easier (i.e., to reduce energy expenditure), to make speech clearer for the hearer, to optimize the structure of the language (the grammar) in a variety of ways, and therefore to make it easier to learn, to process, and to remember.

There is no doubt that speakers do vary the amount of energy they put into speaking; the speech of someone who is tired or ill is often poorly articulated and thus harder to understand. It is also a common observation that speakers may change aspects of their pronunciation in anticipation of the needs of the hearer, for example, hearing-impaired or nonnative listeners, or when the environment or the channel utilized, for example, a telephone line, is noisy. However, it is not clear in such cases whether speakers are introducing a new pronunciation norm as opposed to trying to convey the community norm to the best of their ability. Sound change proper should be limited to cases where there is a change in pronunciation norm.

Among the hundreds of ways that speakers are claimed to change the structure of their language in order to optimize it are the following:

(a) To make the segment inventory more symmetrical, for example, although Old English had voiced and voiceless stops, it had only voiceless fricatives; Middle English added voiced fricatives thus making the voiced/voiceless contrast symmetrical among the obstruents.

(b) On the assumption that there is something unusual or difficult in making syllables terminating in consonants and especially consonant clusters, any simplification of syllable endings is viewed as a move toward optimization, for example, in North American English 'can't' is often pronounced [kʰæ̃t]. Many languages spoken in southeast Asia are known to have undergone remarkable simplifications of the syllable structure such that by the twentieth century some allow only open syllables (those not terminated by a consonant).

(c) Languages are said to eliminate phonological contrasts which serve little communicative function, that is, where they are redundant. Thus it has been observed that of the four nasal vowels of Modern French /ɛ̃ œ̃ ɑ̃ ɔ̃/, /œ̃/ serves to differentiate so few words that it is merging with /ɛ̃/.

(d) To simplify the phonological rules governing morphophonemic alternation, for example, around the ninth century French had a rule distinctively nasalizing just the low vowels before a following nasal in the same syllable; by approximately the thirteenth century this rule had been generalized and thus simplified so that all vowels were nasalized in such an environment.

The problem with analyses such as these and with hundreds of similar ones is that there are so many possible structural features of a language—and occasionally its cultural or political environment—which can be invoked after the fact to 'explain' a given change, that it is often difficult to discern any rigor or discipline in such explanations. It would help if there were statistical studies showing that in an unbiased sample of languages those with a given structural feature underwent a certain type of change at a rate greater than chance—change in a direction judged to represent an optimization.

Structural linguistics introduced a new element into speculations about sound change, namely, the underlying structure of a language, which is often posited to be quite distinct from the patterns and elements directly observable. This underlying structure has been viewed as the relations between phonological elements by the Prague School, where this type of theorizing about language change started around the 1930s, or as rules of grammar by generative phonology, and its descendants. In fact, so different are the proposals that different generations of structural linguists have made about a language's underlying structure, that there has never been a sufficiently stable and long-lived theoretical base on which to launch extensive and wide-ranging research on sound change.

4.2 Sound Change and Language Improvement

The claim that sound change brings about an improvement to the language in which it occurs is independent of the claim that there is teleology. As with the evolution of species, many might believe that individuals who survive at the expense of others in the face of environmental pressures are in some way better adapted, but they would still not suggest that there was any teleology, any ultimate goal, in determining the direction of evolution. Invoking principles similar to evolution, Lindblom proposes that there are universal 'environmental' pressures helping to shape the sound systems of language and has presented one of the few rigorous statistical studies in support of this: Lindblom and Maddieson (1988) demonstrated that languages utilized simple segment types (e.g., [p, l, j, a]) before utilizing complex segment types (e.g., [t^w, p' k͡p, ã]). Most languages use exclusively simple segment types.

Some have suggested that there is an inherent teleological element in sound change without t here being any net benefit from such change: language users implementing change for the sake of change—similar to their change in fashions of clothes and automobiles from one year to the next (Postal 1968).

Whatever good does come to a language from sound change it must be localized in time and to a particular domain of language structure because the evidence suggests that there seems to be no net drift of all human languages toward a common sound pattern. The fate of consonant clusters between Sanskrit and Modern Hindi illustrate this. Sanskrit had a fairly rich set of medial consonant clusters; according to some these are relatively complex phonological structures and liable to change. Prakrit which developed from Sanskrit, simplified virtually all of these clusters and changed them to geminates (5):

Sanskrit	*Prakrit*	*English*	(5)
ʃuṣka	suk^h:a	dry	
karpūra	kap:ūra	camphor	

However, in Modern Hindi, a descendant of Sanskrit through Prakrit, there are some very common morphological processes which involves deletion of an interconsonantal schwa [ə] thus giving rise to complex clusters again. In some cases the form with a cluster came from concatenated morphemes that twentieth-century speakers are no longer aware of:

Stem	*Suffixed form*	*English*	(6)
nəmək	nəmkin	salt, salty	
k^{h}əp + ək + i	k^h·əpti	crazy	

While it is certainly not the norm that phonological processes are eventually undone, there seems to be nothing except chance that would prevent it.

5. Phonetics and Sound Change

Phonetic studies of speech have been applied to issues of sound change for well over a century. Some of the first instrumental phonetic studies were motivated by a desire to explain sound change (e.g., Rousselot's 1891 dissertation). One important finding is common to all these studies: there is a remarkable similarity to the variability found in details of pronunciation—that is, in speech production—by twentieth-century speakers and sound changes that took place in centuries past. Some ventured the opinion that the variation found was ongoing sound change, sound change 'on the hoof,' as it were (see Labov 1981). Some studies have again emphasized the isomorphism between diachronic and synchronic phonetic variation but have taken a different path after that (Ohala 1993).

A great deal of variation is found in speech production, it is noted, but this by itself does not constitute sound change, that is, a change in pronunciation norms, because there is evidence from speech perception studies that listeners are usually able to normalize such variant forms and deduce the norm intended by the speaker. For example, the fricative [s] when produced before a rounded vowel like [u] (as in the name 'Sue' is 'colored' a bit to sound less like [s] in other vocalic environments and more like [ʃ]). This change in [s] is caused inadvertently by the assimilation of the lip shape to that of the following vowel [u]. Nevertheless, listeners have no trouble identifying this variant as the phoneme /s/ as long as they detect the /u/ and can 'blame' it for the distortion. Such perceptual normalization must be similar to those operating in perceptions based on other sensory modalities, for example, vision, where viewers successfully normalize for variations in the size, color, and shape of objects viewed from different distances, different ambient lighting, and different angles. However such phonetically caused perturbations of speech sounds makes speech potentially ambiguous to the listener who has to 'parse' the contextual distortion with the context and not with the given speech segment. Although usually successful in doing this, listeners occasionally fail. In these cases of parsing errors, listeners perceive the contextually changed segment as it is heard, that is, changed, and this becomes the basis for their subsequent changed pronunciations. Further elaborations of this account of sound change as listeners' parsing errors suggest an explanation for dissimilation.

In contrast to most prior accounts of sound change this one attributes the change to the *listener*, not the speaker. The speaker causes the variation which gives rise to potential ambiguity in the acoustic–auditory signal but this variation only leads to sound change due to the misapprehension by the listener. The error of the listener is unmotivated, probabilistic, and nonteleological, just like inadvertent errors by medieval scribes or modern typists copying manuscripts or students taking lecture notes. The change is phonetically abrupt although its subsequent spread, mediated by nonphonetic factors (psychological mechanisms such as analogy and social mechanisms, as discussed above), could be gradual. A further advantage of this account is that it has demonstrated how certain sound changes can be simulated in the laboratory.

6. Trends in Research on Sound Change

Nineteenth-century linguistics *was* historical linguistics. Synchronic studies existed but were usually not at the center of the linguistic community's attention. In the first quarter of the twentieth century, structural linguistics changed this and synchronic studies dominated. In the 1990s it may be said that, with attention being given to sound change by sociolinguistics, by those in language acquisition, by the phonetic sciences, and in the theoretical domain by generative phonology and its heirs, it is again one of the most active and hotly debated research areas in linguistics.

See also: Chain Shifts; Dialect and Dialectology; Sociolinguistic Variation; Sociolinguistics and Language Change.

Bibliography

Grimm J 1822 *Deutsche Grammatik, Vol 1*, 2nd edn. Dieterich, Göttingen, Germany
Hock H H 1986 *Principles of Historical Linguistics.* Mouton, The Hague
Labov W 1972 *Sociolinguistic Patterns.* University of Pennsylvania Press, Philadelphia, PA
Labov W 1981 Resolving the neogrammarian controversy. *Language* **57**: 267–308
Lindblom B, Maddieson I 1988 Phonetic universals in consonant systems. In: Hyman L M, Li C (eds.) *Language, Speech and Mind. Studies in Honour of Victoria A. Fromkin.* Routledge, London
Ohala J J 1993 The phonetics of sound change. In: Jones C (ed.), *Historical Linguistics: Problems and Perspectives.* Longman, London, pp. 237–78
Postal P M 1968 *Aspects of Phonological Theory.* Harper and Row, New York
Rousselot P-J 1891 *Les modifications phonétiques du langage, étudiées dans le patois d'une famille de Cellefrouin (Charente).* H. Welter, Paris
Wang W S-Y (ed.) 1977 *The Lexicon in Phonological Change.* Mouton, The Hague
Weinreich U, Labov W, Herzog M I 1968 Empirical foundations for a theory of language change. In: Lehmann W P, Malkiel Y (eds.) *Directions for Historical Linguistics.* University of Texas Press, Austin, TX

Subcultures and Countercultures
R. L. Taylor

The terms 'subculture' and 'counterculture' are widely used in sociological research and writing to delineate not only the boundaries around presumed systems of values and norms (i.e., rules and expectations regarding social conduct) that differ from a larger normative system of which they are a part, but to emphasize the diversity of norms and values to be found in heterogeneous societies. These terms are not synonymous, however, but differ in their etiology, in the specificity of their boundaries, and in their relationship to the surrounding or dominant culture. This article deals with the analytical distinction between these constructs (though their empirical manifestations may be mixed), their referents and boundaries, and the processes involved in their genesis, maintenance, and change over time.

1. Subcultures

Although originally employed in the study of juvenile delinquency and criminality, the concept subculture has found much broader application in sociological research—from the study of ethnic, religious, and adolescent peer groups, to the analysis of class and regional differences between population segments within a society (Yinger 1960). In its most common usage, subculture refers to the distinctive norms, values, beliefs, and lifestyles of a group which set it apart from other groups and from the larger cultural and normative system of which it is a part. Though linked to the larger society and culture through a network of social institutions and shared values, a subculture is characterized by a set of 'focal concerns' and a range of components—from the ideational to the physical or material—which differentiate it from the broader culture (Fine and Kleinman 1979). Thus, at one extreme are subcultures sharing few elements of the national culture (e.g., Gypsies), and at the other extreme are subcultures having few truly distinctive elements, but only variant patterns (e.g., regional or class subcultures). Between these extremes are to be found a variety of other subcultures whose members exhibit varying degrees of attachment to the larger society.

Social differentiation in a society encourages the formation of subcultures. The more complex the culture and the more heterogeneous its population, the greater is the number of subcultures. Age, gender, ethnicity, class, religion, place of residence, and region often combine to create a diversity of subcultures in modern, industrialized, and complex societies, all with somewhat differing norms and expectations of conduct. Thus, subcultures tend to overlap one another and the national culture, and individuals may participate in several subcultures simultaneously and to different degrees.

1.1 Subcultural Boundaries

The variety of referents for the term subculture identified above implies that the sharpness of the boundaries dividing one subculture from another is likely to vary, depending upon the focal concerns of the subculture and the degree to which it serves as a major source of identity for its members. Some subcultures are tightly bounded, with well-established interests or concerns which command persistent attention and a high degree of emotional involvement on the part of their members. Others are more loosely focused, with no clearly articulated structure or coherent identity, and only limited agreement on subcultural norms. The boundaries of ethnic subcultures are usually reinforced and sustained through customs, language, and a network of organizations and informal relationships which serve as a source of group identity and solidarity. The boundaries of youth subcultures, on the other hand, are less sharply drawn, though youth in general share certain age-specific focal concerns, ideologies, and styles of behavior that set them apart from children and adults (Hall and Jefferson 1976). For some groups, the boundaries of the subculture may come into focus only on certain occasions, as when their interests or identity are directly threatened. The stigmatizing reactions of the larger society may also serve to sharpen the boundaries of a subculture and set it off against that of the dominant culture. Since the degree of involvement in and attachment to the subculture vary, not all participants are likely to draw its boundaries in the same way.

Although there is no widely accepted procedure for defining the parameters of a subculture, an important part of the process involves a determination of which aspects of the social life of participants in the subculture are not affected by its norms and values, that is, those domains where the culture rules of the larger normative system prevail, and the extent to which membership in the subculture constitutes a major component of identity (Clark 1974). Thus one can have, at one extreme, membership in an established church or social club requiring a nominal investment of time and affect, and at the other extreme, membership in a religious sect, such as the Amish subsociety in the USA, where norms of behavior as well as economic and social activities are rigidly prescribed.

1.2 Genesis of Subcultures

Several explanations or hypotheses are advanced for the emergence of subcultures. One explanation emphasizes the role of exogenous factors (e.g., immigration) in generating subcultures in societies. Thus contact between groups of different cultural backgrounds brought together in the same society, but prevented through formal or informal means from full assimilation into the national culture, give rise to subcultures based on ethnicity (Yinger 1960). In the USA, for instance, Thernstrom (1980) has identified more than 125 ethnic subcultures derived from the diversity of nationalities that immigrated to that country over the past 200 years, and some 1200 religious subcultures have been identified by Melton (1988). Although members of these ethnic subcultures share many of the cultural elements and norms of the national culture, such values and norms are often blended or refracted through the prism of their particularistic traditions (Gordon 1964).

Subcultures are also seen to arise from differential patterns of interaction or association between individuals who share similar statuses in a society. Segments of the population sharing similar structural positions (e.g., age, gender, class, occupation, etc.) tend to interact more frequently with each other than with individuals belonging to other segments, owing to common problems associated with their status and their relative isolation from individuals occupying different positions. In time, a system of norms, values, and beliefs, i.e., a subculture, emerges, and through interpersonal communication, mass media, and other communication interlocks, may be diffused throughout the social network of individuals who, though widely distributed spatially in society, share a common identification with it (Arnold 1970).

A third hypothesis views subcultures as emerging in response to problems of adjustment, deprivation, or status frustration, created by normative or cultural contradictions in the larger society. This hypothesis, developed as an explanation for juvenile delinquency and other forms of deviant behavior, has been expanded to encompass the study of a wide variety of groups that are marginal to society in one way or another, and whose lifestyles clash with that of the wider culture. The classic and most influential example of this view remains A. K. Cohen's *Delinquent Boys* (1955), wherein a general theory of subcultures is presented which incorporates the theory of anomie, as developed in the work of R. Merton (1938), in its explanation of the rise and persistence of subcultures. Merton argued that a condition of anomie (i.e., norm conflict) occurs when there are discrepancies or discontinuities between culturally prescribed goals (e.g., higher material achievement) and institutionalized, legitimate means available for achieving them. This situation creates a strain between aspirations and achievement for individuals in certain positions in society whose access to established means are severely limited or denied. In consequence, adherence to prescribed means is weakened or rejected, and various forms of deviance follow. Building on Merton's theory, but adding a psychological dimension to it, Cohen explains the rise of delinquent subcultures among working-class youth as a function of the 'status-frustration' these youths experience in their pursuit of middle-class values and goals, owing to blocked opportunities for success or because of their social inadequacies. The solution to this problem is the delinquent gang or subculture which enables working-class youths not only to strike back at a system that stigmatizes them, but to acquire status on the basis of criteria they can more easily attain. Although some writers object to various aspects of Cohen's conceptualization, most accept his basic argument that subcultures arise in response to persistent structural problems encountered by a sufficient number of individuals who are in effective interaction with each other.

A specifically Marxist interpretation of the rise of subcultures has been advanced by P. Cohen (1972), who emphasizes the relationship between the changing dynamics of class conflict and the emergence of working-class subcultures, together with the symbolic and resistant functions they serve. More specifically, Cohen links the rise of various youth subcultures in England (e.g., the Mods, Teddy Boys, and Skinheads) to changes in the material and social conditions of life in working-class communities, and to historical and economic forces which highlighted certain structural contradictions in the wider society. The tension between the working-class and parent cultures finds symbolic expression in subcultural style, that is, in the argot, dress, music, and rituals of working-class youth which contradict the myth of social cohesion and consensus (see *Social Class*).

Despite differences in theoretical position and/or emphasis, most writers agree that subcultures are likely to arise in societies characterized by social differentiation based on such factors as age, gender, ethnicity, class, or other structural variables, coupled with social, political, and/or economic marginality, which promote differential patterns of interaction and collective identity.

1.3 Subcultural Maintenance and Change

The conditions or circumstances that give rise to a subculture are not necessarily the same as those which sustain or transform it. Structural conditions may change, or the focal concerns of the adherents to a subculture may be redefined or transformed under the weight of new realities, or discovery of alternative solutions to their problems. Much depends on the nature of the subculture and its relationship to the larger society. Its values and norms may inspire a range of community reactions, from bemused indifference, to public anxiety or hysteria, with important consequences for the dynamics of subcultural development and change. A strongly negative community response, involving the media and other agencies of social control, may serve as a catalyst for more intensive subcultural identification and activate a diffusion of its values and norms to a larger segment of the population—a process termed 'deviance amplification' (Wilkins 1965). For example, the negative portrayal of the Punks and Mods in the British press and on television gave instant notoriety to these groups which, in turn, attracted the interest and participation of other youths in these subcultures. On the other hand, the severity of negative public reactions to a subculture may threaten or undermine its continued existence by making it difficult or costly for adherents to participate actively and openly in the group, or by forcing them to seek alternative solutions to their problems. One alternative is to minimize contacts between members of the subculture and the larger society, thereby avoiding public scrutiny and sanctions. Examples include religious and sectarian communes and drug subcultures. In short, negative public reactions may contribute to a sharpening of subcultural definitions and ideology, enlarge the scope of its influence, and promote greater normative isolation and solidarity.

Where community reactions are generally more positive or sympathetic, adherents to a subculture may be allowed considerable freedom to pursue their peculiar values and beliefs without fear of punitive sanctions so long as they do not disturb allegiance to the core values of the larger culture. Indeed, some of the stylistic innovations of a subculture (e.g., dress, music, argot) may be selectively appropriated by some segments of the population, or packaged by entrepreneurs for wider diffusion into mainstream society, and in the process lose much of their distinctive and subversive quality. The conversion of some elements of youth subcultural styles into commodities for mass production (e.g., clothing boutiques, small-scale record shops, etc.) illustrates the process of subcultural assimilation, as does the incorporation of selected aspects of ethnic traditions into the mainstream of American life.

In sum, the fate of a subculture is much influenced by the nature of public reactions, by the strength of formal and informal sanctions, and by the centrality of subcultural identification for its adherents. Where a subculture is violently repressed by social control agents, it is likely to be driven underground, to develop and refine an ideology of resistance, and to draw its boundaries with greater specificity. Conversely, lacking the means to escape the intrusion of mainstream values or its sanctions, the subculture may be abandoned or driven to extinction. Here, of course, much depends on the centrality of the subculture as a source of personal and collective identity, and the availability of alternative models. Where subcultures are granted some measure of legitimacy or tolerance, they are also subject to change, either because of increasing interaction between those who share the subcultural tradition and those that do not, or because of the assimilating influence inherent in participation in mainstream institutions.

Since each subculture represents a response to a specific set of circumstances, problems, or contradictions, it is ultimately changes in these structural conditions, often impelled by subcultural movements themselves, that induce changes or major transformations in subcultures.

2. Countercultures

Subcultures are only one of several different responses that individuals and groups can make to specific structural conditions or problems they encounter in modern complex societies. The formation of countercultures is another. Following Yinger (1960), who first proposed the term, a counterculture refers to those values and norms of a group that are in sharp conflict with the values and norms of the larger society (see *Antilanguage*). Although countercultures share many of the characteristics of subcultures, they are distinguished from the latter by their inversion of dominant values, and by certain characterological predispositions of their members, including their nonconformist or deviant behavior.

Whereas subcultures seek a 'negotiated version' of the dominant values and institutions in order to preserve the uniqueness of their members' ethnic, religious, occupational, class, or other lines of group identification (Parkin 1971), countercultures attempt to provide alternative values (or to place an exaggerated emphasis on existing ones), around which new identities and norms can be constructed. And whereas subcultures are typically lodged in traditional subcommunities (i.e., ethnic, religious, etc.) of the larger society and evolve slowly over time in response to specific historical and structural circumstances, countercultures are emergent phenomena, arising from frustrations and conflict-laden situations of more recent origin. Countercultures, like subcultures, are not independent cultures but are characterized by a dialectical relationship to the larger society and cannot be fully understood apart from it.

2.1 Sources of Countercultures

Countercultures are both symptoms of, and solutions to, social dislocations, cultural crisis, and deeply experienced personal frustrations in a society. Although it is possible to distinguish, analytically, between the structural, cultural, and individual sources of countercultures, these sources are highly interdependent and often mixed in their empirical manifestations.

On the structural or macro level, the rise of countercultures is associated with major economic and demographic changes in society which undermine traditional social bonds and statuses and nourish the potential for normative innovations. Rapid economic development, accompanied by affluence, expanding opportunities, and population growth, were all associated with the emergence of countercultures during the neolithic revolution, the eleventh-century industrial revolution, the commercial revolution of the sixteenth century, and the industrial revolution of the nineteenth century (Musgrove 1974). Similar conditions inspired the rise and spread of countercultures among youth in the USA during the 1960s and 1970s. Hence unprecedented economic expansion and related developments are the basic generating forces behind the rise of countercultures in societies, with cultural traditions and historically specific circumstances acting as more precise determinants.

Major economic changes produce social dislocations which upset the balance between norms and values in a society and make the appearance of countercultures more likely. In a rapidly changing and uncertain environment, traditional values become increasingly inadequate as guidelines for behavior and many of the rituals, myths, and symbols of the culture may lose their emotional appeal or meaning. The perceived inadequacies of the prevailing cultural configuration encourage the search for new values and interactional norms, or the inversion of existing ones, as designs for living. This is where countercultures come in. Some seek to reconstruct the social order through radical protest activities or other nonconformist behavior, while others advocate withdrawal from society into separate countercommunities or sectarian groups where new values and norms can be cultivated as paradigms for a new society. Rather than attack the social order to withdraw from it, some countercultures seek simply to facilitate individual ecstasy and self-enlightenment through transcendental experiences (often with the aid of drugs) as a means of discovery of new values and a new way of life.

Certain characterological features or tendencies of individuals also play an important role in the emergence of countercultures. Early experiences of parental rejection, emotional isolation, or other experiences that assault self-confidence and esteem, may predispose some individuals to various forms of negativism, including the adoption of inverted values and oppositional lifestyles, and thus mark them as likely candidates for recruitment to countercultural movements (Yinger 1982). For many such individuals, countercultures offer creative ways of dealing with feelings of personal inadequacy, loneliness, or alienation, while experimenting with alternative values and lifestyles. Positive impulses may also incline some individuals to embrace oppositional values or inverted standards. Individuals whose socialization experiences have enabled them to achieve a high level of moral development whereby self-chosen moral principles guide their behavior, are more likely to be represented among active participants in countercultures than those whose standards of morality are less well developed (Haan et al. 1968). The growth in social inequality, greed, and various forms of human suffering and perversity that follow in the wake of economic development and social change may violate individual standards of morality and increase the probability that oppositional norms and values will be adopted.

A variety of communication interlocks (i.e., multiple group memberships, media diffusion, etc.) serve to link the social, cultural, and individual sources of countercultures together, and create a common universe of discourse which facilitates the invention, propagation, or acceptance of countercultural values (see *Social Networks*).

2.2 Varieties of Countercultures

Countercultures are often distinguished by the values they embrace (or reject), as well as by the methods they employ to promote their values. Although there is an enormous range of inverted values to which counterculturalists may be seen to subscribe, the areas in which opposition to dominant values are most vigorous relate to matters of truth, ethics, and aesthetics (Musgrove 1974, Yinger 1982). That is, the prevailing beliefs and practices of society may be regarded by some countercultural groups as foolish or absurd, evil and immoral, or vulgar and ugly. In response, they may attack the established order and promote alternative values through direct political action or symbolic inversions in the form of art, rituals, or writings.

Some countercultures emphasize the value of transcendental knowledge over knowledge derived from science and rationalism, viewing self-enlightenment and mystical insights as the only roads to true knowledge and beneficial social change. Intuitive ways of knowing the world can come from within, through meditation, chants, mystical exercises, or 'consciousness expanding' drugs; or from without, through contact with the hidden forces in nature via the occult, the astrological, or the magical (Zicklin 1983). Such practices are designed to dissolve established conceptions of how elements of organic and inorganic life are assumed to relate through time and space, and to call into question the empirical and logical processes of science. The realization of such values requires psychological and/or physical retreat from a world dominated by science and rational calculation, to a place where self-enlightenment and ecstasy can be achieved. Countercultures based on a mystical experiential approach to truth and well-being are epitomized in religious sects of many different periods, and proliferated in the USA during the 1960s and 1970s in the form of such movements as Hare Krishna, Meher Baba, and Maharaj Ji's Divine Light Mission.

Other countercultures may emerge around opposition to hierarchy and privilege, power, and authority, or other perceived obstacles to personal fulfillment and the attainment of the good life. Such opposition may include attacks on technology and bureaucratic controls, on the family and the work ethic, and distinctions based on class, race, gender, and creed. Objections to the quality and direction of social life may come from both the political Left and the Right; the former concerned with institutional reconstruction and the satisfaction of human needs, the latter threatened by the erosion or destruction of old standards and the possibility of status reversals. Each seeks to promote or preserve its vision of the good life through political action, ranging from nonconformist or illegal acts designed to affirm new standards of behavior, to acts of violence or terrorism undertaken to challenge the right of the state to monopolize coercive power. Examples include student activists and Hippies of the 1960s and 1970s (including such extremist or revolutionary groups as the Weathermen and Symbionese Liberation Army in the USA) on the Left, and John Birch Society, Ku Klux Klan, and neo-Nazi groups on the Right.

Some of the more noxious features of advanced technological development which assault personalistic-expressive values or aesthetic norms may galvanize individuals into oppositional groups for the purpose of restoring the balance between sensuality and cold rationality, or creating new standards by which the meaning and beauty of life can be judged. Along with affluence, advanced industrial development is seen to bring in its wake increases in violence, rapacity, and ugliness which pollute the natural and social landscape and impoverish the human spirit.

Opposition to such trends finds expression in the aesthetic countercultures of writers and artists of every variety, whose writings, paintings, music, or other creative productions are used to expose the inauthenticity, weaknesses, and absurdities of prevailing values, and to promote alternatives they regard as more aesthetically enriching. The Romantics of the nineteenth century exemplify the countercultural responses of artists to the destructive aspects of technology and change during that period, as does the Dadaist movement in literature and art which emerged in Switzerland, France, and the USA during World War I. Expressions of countercultural themes during the twentieth century can be found in a variety of artistic forms: Surrealism in painting, 'acid' and 'punk' rock in music, and the century-long influence of existentialism on literary works (Yinger 1982).

The preceding does not exhaust the variety of countercultural groups that emerge in opposition to dominant values and practices in a society. Countercultural tendencies are also found among disadvantaged groups, among some individuals engaged in criminal activities, and among those who subscribe to inverted family and sexual practices.

Countercultures are rarely static systems but are usually in a state of flux. Over time, the focal concerns of a group may shift from an emphasis on one set of inverted values to another, or it may attempt to combine different modes of opposition to, and criticism of, the established social order. Such shifts in concerns and approaches often engender internal division and dilemmas which eventually lead to the transformation, incorporation, or demise of the group, or its succession by another.

2.3 Countercultures and Social Change

Although sometimes dismissed as social aberrations or epiphenomena associated with socially and historically specific circumstances, countercultures should be recognized as important sources of social and political change in society. They highlight, dramatize, and communicate the existence of major societal problems, anxieties, and dilemmas (or impending disorders), and give expression to the emergence of new collective sentiments antithetical to the prevailing ethos (Slater 1970). As such, they are vital aspects of the process of social change. To be sure, not all countercultures carry the same implications of social or cultural transformations. Some are relatively isolated, sectarian movements, with little impact on the established order; others may subscribe to inverted values too extreme or dangerous to attract widespread support. But many of the effects of countercultures on social institutions and values are indirect and unintended rather than planned or anticipated. The dissenting tradition created by oppositional movements of mid-seventeenth-century England survived to influence the political history of that country and USA long after the demise of these movements. Likewise, the Hippies of the 1960s and 1970s, whose aberrant behavior and lifestyles were largely rejected during their heyday, have had a significant influence on mainstream American attitudes toward authority, interpersonal relationships, and sexuality. Moreover, many of their innovations in language, music, dress, and art have become accepted styles within the larger society.

Given their profoundly important role in the process of social change, countercultures require the most intensive investigation, both for their creative and destructive influences on society.

3. Conclusion

Every subculture has a distinctive language. This fact is obvious for ethnic subcultures, which at least in part speak the language of their native land as well as that of the surrounding dominant culture. Subcultures that arise from differentiated patterns of social interaction diverge into somewhat separate speech communities, differing both because of language drift and because of distinctive focal concerns. Particularly interesting are subcultures that emerge out of contradictions in the larger society. Linguistic differences are accentuated by the conflict that brings them into existence, and they can develop into full-blown countercultures. Their inversion of dominant values requires them to violate language standards and assert their own vocabulary and even grammar in direct opposition to those of the larger culture that surrounds them. Sometimes they achieve partial success, changing the language of the society, adding their distinctive terms to its vocabulary, and even shifting the values and attitudes that shape social life.

See also: Adolescent Peer Group Language; Small Group Research; Sociology of Language; Slang: Sociology; Antilanguage.

Bibliography

Arnold D O 1970 *Subcultures*. Glendessary Press, Berkeley, CA
Clark M 1974 On the concept of 'sub-culture.' *British Journal of Sociology* 25: 428–41
Cohen A K 1955 *Delinquent Boys: The Culture of the Gang*. Free Press, New York
Cohen P 1972 Subcultural conflict and working class community. *Working Papers in Cultural Studies*, no. 2. University of Birmingham, Birmingham, UK
Fine A G, Kleinman S 1979 Rethinking subculture: An interactionist analysis. *American Journal of Sociology* 85(1): 1–20
Gordon M 1964 *Assimilation in American Life*. Oxford University Press, New York

Haan N, Smith M, Block J 1968 Moral reasoning of young adults: Political-social behavior, family background, and personality correlates. *Journal of Personality and Social Psychology* **10**(3): 183–201
Hall S, Jefferson T 1976 *Resistance through Rituals: Youth Subcultures in Post-war Britain.* Hutchinson, London
Melton J G 1988 *The Encyclopedia of American Religions*, 2nd edn. Gale Research Company, Detroit, MI
Merton R 1938 Social structure and anomie. *American Sociological Review* **3**: 672–82
Musgrove F 1974 *Ecstasy and Holiness: Counterculture and the Open Society.* Indiana University Press, Bloomington, IN
Parkin F 1971 *Class Inequality and Political Order.* MacGibbon and Kee, London
Slater P E 1970 *The Pursuit of Loneliness.* Beacon Press, Boston, MA
Thernstrom S 1980 *Harvard Encyclopedia of American Ethnic Groups.* Belknap Press of Harvard University, Cambridge, MA
Wilkins L T 1965 *Social Deviance: Social Policy, Action, and Research.* Prentice-Hall, Englewood Cliffs, NJ
Yinger J M 1960 Contraculture and subculture. *American Sociological Review* **25**: 625–35
Yinger J M 1982 *Countercultures.* Free Press, New York
Zicklin G 1983 *Countercultural Communes.* Greenwood Press, Westport, CT

Syntactic Change

N. Vincent

One of the most striking facts about languages is that, given time, they change. The different subsystems of language seem to change in different ways and at different speeds. Thus, neologisms may arise and become current very rapidly, especially with modern methods of mass communication. Conversely, expressions may disappear from usage virtually overnight. Sound changes take longer, spreading gradually through the speakers of a language and through the vocabulary over decades and even centuries. Some changes seem to involve an imperceptible transition from one stage to the next, as when a stop becomes a fricative, e.g., [k>x>h] or [k>c>tʃ>ʃ]; in other instances there is an apparently abrupt shift, as when *holpen* is replaced by *helped* as the past particle of *help*. The patterns involved and the principles required to explain the patterns have been a focus of attention in linguistic inquiry ever since the end of the eighteenth century. Nineteenth-century linguistics in particular saw the development of carefully worked out theories of phonetic and morphological change.

Something of a stepchild in this heyday of the historical approach to language was syntax, for two not entirely independent reasons. First, there were no well worked out theories of syntax, and second syntactic systems are least susceptible to the piecemeal, atomistic treatment that nineteenth-century scholars accorded to linguistic phenomena in general (see *Saussurean Tradition and Sociolinguistics*). This does not mean that earlier scholars had not formulated some profound insights into the workings of change in syntax, as the writings of Georg von der Gabelentz (1891) or Antoine Meillet (1912) will attest. Nor that some of the great compendia of that century's scholarship, such as Meyer-Lübke (1890–6) or Brugmann and Delbrück (1897–1916), did not contain much pertinent data (see *Sociolinguistics and Language Change*). However, two important twentieth-century developments were required before the fundamental questions underlying change in syntax could be posed and headway then made on answering them. Ironically, this has in turn sometimes led to a revival of the ideas of earlier scholars, Meillet being a notable example in this connection. These key developments are first the Saussurean recognition of the importance of system and structure in understanding the nature of linguistic units. This brought with it the valuable, though in the event overly rigid, dichotomy between synchrony and diachrony. Second was Chomsky's insistence on the rule-governed nature of syntax and later, his formulation of the principles that govern both universal structure and cross-linguistic diversity in this domain. A third development in the twentieth century which has had a notable effect on studies of language change in the field of phonetics, namely Labov's discovery of the principled nature of linguistic variation (see *Sociolinguistic Variation*), has been rather slower to make its impact on syntactic change, but it too is now contributing major new insights into the workings of change in the syntactic component (Kroch 1989).

1. Syntactic Change: The Problem

The central problem of syntactic change can be seen by comparing the Latin and French sentences in (1) and (2) below:

Paulus dixit regem venisse
Paul.NOM say.3SG.PERF king.ACC come.INF.PERF (1)
'Paul said that the king had come'

Paul a   dit   que le   roi était venu
Paul has said.PP that the.MSG king was come.PP (2)
'Paul said that the king had come'

As the English translations make clear, these two sentences have very similar semantic content, but grammatically they are structured entirely differently. The nouns in Latin bear case endings to indicate their syntactic roles; past time in Latin is referred to here by a single finite verb form—the so-called perfective, where French has an auxiliary *avoir* 'have' plus a past participle; the tense in the embedded clause in Latin is indicated again by a perfective verb form, but this time the infinitive, while French again has the combination of finite auxiliary plus particle, only this time the auxiliary is *être* 'be.' Other notable points are that the subject of the Latin infinitive is in the accusative case, French has an overt marker of subordination in the complementizer *que*, the order of words in French is fixed as that which appears in (2), while the Latin words in (1) could be rearranged into almost any one of the logically possible orders and the sentence would remain grammatical and would have, matters of emphasis apart, the same meaning.

If two genetically unrelated languages, say English and Georgian, were being compared, and a similar catalogue of differences was noted, this would occasion no surprise. The difficulty here lies in the fact that French evolved out of Latin and therefore there must be sequences of change which connect the structures evidenced in (2), for which analogs can be found in all the Romance languages, with those in (1). Moreover, and here is a further puzzle, all the parts of French sentence structure that do not find immediate correspondents in Latin, namely articles, auxiliaries, and complementizers, nonetheless derive from Latin etyma (*le* < Latin, *illum*, *était* < Latin *stabat*, *que* < Latin *quod*). The structural properties which characterize the syntax of Latin are clearly different, therefore, from those operative in French, but at the same time the items of French are for the most part reflexes of Latin items.

There is then a paradox of continuity and discontinuity. On the one hand, grammatical systems have an internal structure (rules, paradigms, etc) in terms of which individual items are held in place and, in Saussure's term, motivated. When there are shifts, therefore, these must necessarily be discontinuous as the language moves from one state to another. At the same time there is clearly continuity at some level since communities exist and communication is achieved more or less successfully across generations. The two principal approaches to the phenomenon of syntactic change have taken complementary—though in the long run not necessarily incompatible—views, generativists preferring to give weight to the discontinuity and the abruptness of change while theorists of grammaticalization have sought rather to emphasize the factors leading to gradual and continuous evolution along language independent, semantically determined paths of change.

2. The Generative Model of Syntactic Change

Although diachronic questions had occasionally been addressed in earlier work, the foundations of a generative account of syntactic change were laid by Lightfoot (1979). Lightfoot (1988) is an updated summary of this position and Lightfoot (1991) represents a reformulation of his ideas in the light of the development of the so-called parametric approach to syntax. A key article in this latter connection is Roberts (1985). The 1980s has seen a considerable burgeoning of generative research into syntactic change, much of it summarized and the theoretical position advanced in Roberts (1993).

The starting point of the generative account is the standard Chomskyan view that languages are epiphenomena which can only properly be understood by investigating the constraints on, and the acquisition of, the grammars that generate them. In particular, there is no sensible notion of the diachronic continuity of disembodied languages, despite the apparent implication to the contrary in traditional formulas such as Proto Indo European *p, t, k> Germanic f, θ, h. Equally there is no continuity at the level of grammars, which die with the speakers who have internalized them. Rather, there is a set of unchanging background conditions, namely the principles of universal grammar (UG) which are hypothesized to be innate and therefore to be available afresh and without prior tutoring to each new generation. Against this background, each learner acquires a grammar on the basis of exposure to the data available in the speech community. The fundamental mode of reasoning here is abductive (cf Andersen 1973): forms must be associated with rules and principles and in the process mismatches and reanalyses may occur. Socially or phonetically induced changes may occur in the data, in virtue of which new associations with rules or principles may arise. Once a speaker has internalized a grammar which incorporates such new associations, new patterns will be observable in the linguistic behavior (performance) which is based on that grammar (competence), and there will thus be constituted a subtly altered pattern of data for succeeding generations, in turn providing the seeds for future abductive shifts. Apart from the limiting conditions of UG, what keeps the process in check is the need to preserve communication between members of the speech community. The effects of overly drastic abductive reorganization will therefore be edited out and a semblance of continuity will be preserved.

The key mechanism of change on the generative view is thus reanalysis: at a particular moment in its history a given structure is capable of two interpretations and a 'jump' occurs as speakers opt for one rather than the other. A favorite example is the history of English modals, which etymologically are clearly members of the larger class of verbs, and with which they share properties such as full inflectional paradigms, the possibility of taking direct objects and of combining with each other. At a certain point, argued in Lightfoot (1979) to be around the beginning of the sixteenth century, a series of exceptional properties build up to such an extent that a new category of modals comes into existence, which then has a history of its own, and does not participate in subsequent changes such as the rise of the periphrasis with *do* in negative and interrogative contexts. Lightfoot's earlier interpretation of this change as involving a somewhat mystical 'transparency principle' was quickly replaced by a more securely grounded analysis in terms of the notion of parameter resetting (cf Roberts 1985). In Old and Middle English morphological inflection had the power to govern verbs and permit them to express their associated arguments. Phonetic changes caused morphological government to be lost, so that only syntactic government was possible; only those items that do not have arguments to express, namely modal verbs, can then occupy the old inflection position, which they proceed to do, thereby changing their superficial syntactic behavior. The option of morphological government vs syntactic government is a parameter which is set differently at different stages of the language. Roberts (1993) documents a number of other such cases, drawing on a wide database of change in word order, morphological marking, distribution of pronouns, etc in English and the Romance languages.

Lightfoot (1991) develops the conceptual underpinning of the parameter resetting model at greater length and takes the opportunity to reply to his critics, particularly those who have sought to argue that change should be seen as continuous and gradual rather than abrupt, and to challenge those such as Allen (1986), who have developed a formal account of change using a lexically-based model of language. The book also contains a valuable discussion of an unduly neglected concept in historical linguistic work, that of obsolescence. Lightfoot argues (1991: chap. 6) that, while new items may arise in languages as a result of spontaneous pressures such as the need for greater expressivity or the effects of borrowing and language contact, old items will only disappear as a result of changes in the system which render them unlearnable to new generations. Obsolescence then is a side effect of parameter resetting and as such a valuable indication of the working out of a change (cf Vincent 1989 for a brief discussion of this notion).

3. Grammaticalization Theory

Sharply contrasting with the generative approach to the understanding of syntactic change has been that of a number of scholars who have rallied around the concept of grammaticalization (cf Heine et al. 1991, Traugott and Heine 1991, Hopper and Traugott 1993). It is important, however, to distinguish grammaticalization as a mechanism whereby new function words may be generated, which is empirically undeniable and needs to be recognized by any theoretical approach, from the wider philosophy of grammar which links most of those who have taken up the cause of grammaticalization and which is indeed in conflict with many of the fundamentals of the Chomskyan metaphysic which unites scholars such at Lightfoot and Roberts.

The mechanism of grammaticalization is still best captured in the classic definition of Meillet (1912: 133): '*l'attribution du caractère grammatical à un mot jadis autonome*' and examples are legion. Indeed, probably the vast majority of so-called function words in languages—articles, auxiliaries, complementizers, intensifiers, particles of mood, polarity, etc.—are the outcome of such a process of change. Within these changes there are recurrent and cross-linguistically valid directions of development. Thus, English has two periphrases that express futurity: *will* + V and *be going to* + V, and both of these have numerous parallels in other languages. Thus, a future auxiliary deriving from a verb of volition is attested in many of the Balkan languages (Rumanian, Serbo-Croat, Albanian, Greek), and also in Swahili (Heine et al. 1991: 170ff); and from a verb of motion in French, Norwegian, Ewe, Acholi, and Tamil, to name but a few. Other common patterns are complementizers derived from verbs of saying and definite markers derived from distal deictics.

On the basis of evidence of this kind, a number of theoretical conclusions have been drawn. In the first place, grammaticalization is argued to be gradual (Lichtenberk 1991) and therefore not easily compatible with the scenario of abrupt reanalyses required by the generative view. Second, the mechanism at work here is also found in semantic change, where it is traditionally known as generalization. More generally, the categories of metaphor and metonymy used to classify semantic change may also be seen to underly and motivate grammaticalization (Heine et al. 1991: chap. 3). Semantic categories are in turn relatable to pragmatic ones and grammaticalization is often seen at work in the emergence of markers of discourse structure, textual cohesion and speaker's attitude (Traugott 1982). The fundamental motivation for linguistic categories is thence argued to be found in their function in discourse, and grammar is seen as being determined not by the innate properties of a genetically present UG but by the everyday needs of human communication. On this view categories are fuzzy rather than clearcut, there are only tendencies and not absolute universals, and indeed even the sharp distinction between synchrony and diachrony is called into question. The most extreme proponent of this approach is Hopper, who argues that grammatical categories are secondary and depend on discourse structure for their existence. They are always developing and being replaced so that there is never grammar but only grammaticalization. Once we have reached this point, we have moved a long way from the ontology of grammar which inspires the generative program, and grammaticalization has become a label for an alternative linguistic paradigm rather than simply a type of change (Hopper and Traugott 1993: chap. 1).

4. Relations between Syntactic and Morphological Change

Many of the issues that arise in the domain of syntactic change are also to be found in the area of morphology, a fact which is hardly surprising since it is well known that it is hard to establish a clearcut boundary between the two. Indeed, a large part of the reason for their inseparability is diachronic. Items that at one stage of history have a clearly syntactic function may with the passage of time become morphologized. Thus, the future inflections of the French verb, *chanterai, -as, -a*, etc. are a residue of what in Late Latin was an independent auxiliary which took the infinitive as a complement: *cantare + habeo*, etc. Developments of this kind are clearly a continuation of the process described as grammaticalization above. Givón has argued that the process may go further and that morphology becomes phonology; in other words that what is synchronically no more than a part of the phonemic structure of an item may in fact be an independent meaningful item if one goes back far enough. For example, the *hui* in the French work *aujourd'hui* 'today' is in fact the Latin word *hodie* 'today,' which in turn contains within it the Latin word *die* 'day.' Ultimately even the phonology disappears by processes of phonological attrition and the item goes off the historical stage once and for all.

Meillet (1912) pointed out that grammaticalization also has an important complementary relation to the kind of morphological change known as analogy. The effect of the latter is to be seen if the imperfect forms of Spanish and Italian are compared, both of which have descended from Latin: *amabam, -as, -at* > Sp *amaba, -as, -a* and > Italian *amavo, -i, -a*. The Spanish endings simply continue the Latin ones with due allowance being made for the effects of sound change. In Italian, by contrast, the endings *-o, -i* have been analogically extended from other parts of the verbal paradigm. As Meillet notes, in one sense analogical changes are never productive of new patterns in a language but simply alter the distribution of existing ones. It is only grammaticalization, which can bring into the syntactic system and thence into the morphology new patterns of linguistic exponence. Analogical changes may however contribute to new patterns of form–meaning parallelism, an instance of iconicity at work in linguistic change.

It is to be noted in contrast that analogy as a force in linguistic change does not figure within the generative approach. This is principally because analogy as a pattern of direct connection between form and meaning runs counter to the generative view that any patterns of linguistic structure are mediated by the covert conditions of UG. The generative expectation, therefore, is that the immediate surface distribution of linguistic items will be at best only a partial and indirect reflection of the factors at work in determining that distribution. Some of the effects of what is traditionally labeled analogy do emerge, however, in the generative concept of reanalysis. By the same token, generative grammarians have been less impressed by the wider role of form-meaning iconicity as a factor in understanding language structure and change.

5. The Typological Approach

Theorists of grammaticalization have also been closely involved in or associated with work on syntactic typology which has burgeoned in recent years (see manuals such as Comrie 1989: chap. 10, Croft 1990: chap. 8 for discussion of the diachronic implications of typology). Once again, however, it is necessary to separate the general philosophy of grammar espoused by many of those who call themselves typologists (the term is often expanded to functional typologists—e.g., Givón, Hopper, Li, Thompson, etc.) from the facts of linguistic typology itself, which are neutral as between theoretical approaches and indeed have done much to inform debate in generative grammar in its 'Principles and Parameters' phase. For instance, the original Greenberg correlations about word order properties in natural languages have inspired a considerable literature from scholars seeking to utilize them to explain patterns of syntactic change. These same correlations can equally be reformulated in parametric terms: languages may be 'head first' or 'head last.' Such a parameter shift is intrinsic to the account given by Lightfoot (1979) of the history of *like* in English and to his argument in Lightfoot (1991: chap. 3) concerning the differential development of word order in main and subordinate clauses.

6. The Explanation of Syntactic Change

In the late twentieth century, historical linguists have been greatly exercised by the problem of how to explain linguistic change, and more broadly, with the philosophical status of explanation in historical linguistics. (See Lass 1980 for an attractive if polemical discussion and Koopman et al. 1987 for a collection of individual studies. Keller 1990 seeks to import into linguistics the so-called 'invisible hand' model of explanation more familiar in the study of the history of economic systems and social institutions.) Theoretical linguists, whether of a structuralist or a generativist persuasion, have tended to prefer the law-based or deductive–nomological model of prediction and explanation found in the natural sciences. The problem here is that there are very few, if any, convincing historical cases of such a model at work. A much more common situation is one in which the linguist can, after the event, offer a plausible scenario of the mechanisms involved in the change while still knowing that it was not a matter of causal necessity that the change took place. Analogical changes provide a very simple instance: it may make good intuitive sense that the irregular past particle *holpen* has been replaced by the regular one *helped*, but it could not have been predicted in advance that the change was bound to happen. Similarly, many changes can be seen afterwards as bringing one aspect of a language's structure into harmony with its other properties, along lines indicated by typological correlations (cf. Hawkins 1983 for extensive documentation and application of this methodology), yet there can be no advance guarantee that such changes will take place. Many languages continue for many hundreds of years in states of typological inconsistency. Similarly, both typological and analogical explanations often run the risk of invoking illegitimate teleological modes of explanation: a given change is argued to have happened *in order to* achieve consistency or eliminate irregularity, without it being clear how either the speaker or the language itself could have influenced change in this way.

One type of explanation that has found a good deal of favor is that based on the presumption of a drive towards motivation or transparency in linguistic structure. This too seems to risk a charge of unjustified teleology, but that has not deterred scholars such as Haiman (1985) or many of the proponents of grammaticalization in the 1990s (for an interesting reflection on iconicity in language from the perspective of generative grammar, see Newmeyer 1992).

Within the field of sound change, great progress has been made in the study of sociolinguistic variation and this has provided a convincing model for the explanation of change in terms of language independent factors such as sex, race, class, regional identity, and so on. Until recently this model had not worked so well when it came to the study of syntax because it could not be guaranteed that variations in form were not motivated by semantic or other structural considerations. It did not therefore seem possible to construct sociolinguistic variables and investigate their correlation with nonlinguistic factors in a simple and straightforward way. However, Kroch (1989) has proposed a way in which this may be done, essentially by considering the unit for the purposes of correlation to be not the individual linguistic form but a grammatical subsystem. In this way, the twin power of formal grammatical theories and sociolinguistic variable analysis may be combined.

See also: Sound Change; Sociolinguistics and Language Change.

Bibliography

Allen C 1986 Reconsidering the history of *like*. *Journal of Linguistics* **22**: 375–409
Andersen H 1973 Abductive and deductive change. *Language* **49**: 765–93
Brugmann K, Delbrück B 1897–1916 *Grundriss der vergleichenden Grammatik der indogermanischen Sprachen*, 2 Vols. Trübner, Strassburg, Germany
Comrie B 1989 *Language Universals and Linguistic Typology*, 2nd edn. Blackwell, Oxford, UK
Croft W 1990 *Typology and Universals*. Cambridge University Press, Cambridge, UK
Gabelentz Georg von der 1891 *Die Sprachwissenschaft: Ihre Aufgaben, Methoden und bisherigen Ergebnisse*. Weigel Nachf, Leipzig, Germany
Haiman J 1985 *Natural Syntax*. Cambridge University Press, Cambridge, UK
Hawkins J A 1983 *Word Order Universals*. Academic Press, New York
Heine B, Claudi U, Hünnemeyer F 1991 *Grammaticalization; a Conceptual Framework*. University of Chicago Press, Chicago, IL
Hopper P 1991 On some principles of grammaticization. In: Traugott E C, Heine B (eds.) *Approaches to Grammaticalization*, 2 Vols. Benjamins, Amsterdam
Hopper P, Traugott E C 1993 *Grammaticalization*. Cambridge University Press, Cambridge, UK
Keller R 1990 *Sprachwandel*. Francke Verlag, Tübingen, Germany
Koopman W, van der Leek F, Fischer O, Eaton R (eds.) 1987 *Explanation and Linguistic Change*. Benjamins, Amsterdam
Kroch A 1989 Reflexes of grammar in patterns of language change. *Language Variation and Change* **1**: 199–243
Lass R 1980 *On Explaining Language Change*. Cambridge University Press, Cambridge, UK
Lichtenberk F 1991 On the gradualness of Grammaticalization. In: Traugott E C, Heine B (eds.) *Approaches to Grammaticalization*, 2 Vols. Benjamins, Amsterdam
Lightfoot D 1979 *Principles of Diachronic Syntax*. Cambridge University Press, Cambridge, UK
Lightfoot D 1988 Syntactic change. In: Newmeyer F (ed.) *Linguistics: The Cambridge Survey. Vol I: Linguistic Theory: Foundations*. Cambridge University Press, Cambridge, UK

Lightfoot D 1991 *How to Set Parameters: Arguments From Language Change*. MIT Press, Cambridge, MA

Meillet A 1912 L'evolution des formes grammaticales. In: Meillet A *Linguistique historique et linguistique générale*. Champion, Paris

Meyer-Lübke W 1890–96 *Grammaire des langues romanes*, 4 Vols. Paris

Newmeyer F J 1992. Iconicity and generative grammar. *Language* **68**: 756–96

Roberts I 1985 Agreement parameters and the development of English modal auxiliaries. *Natural Language and Linguistic Theory* **3**: 21–57

Roberts I 1993 *Verbs and Diachronic Syntax*. Kluwer, Dordrecht, The Netherlands

Traugott E C 1982 From propositional to textual and expressive meanings: Some semantic–pragmatic aspects of grammaticalization. In: Lehmann W P, Malkiel Y (eds.) *Perspectives on Historical Linguistics*, Benjamins, Amsterdam

Traugott E C, Heine B (eds.) 1991 *Approaches to Grammaticalization*, 2 Vols. Benjamins, Amsterdam

Vincent N 1989 Observing obsolescence. *Behavioral and Brain Sciences* **12**: 360–1

The Atlas of North American English: Methods and Findings
S. Ash

1. Introduction

The Atlas of North American English (Labov et al. in press) grew from a pilot project covering six states to a survey of the phonetics, phonology, and processes of sound change in all of North America. From its inception, it has rested crucially on the method of interviewing by telephone in order to sample the largest possible number of speakers over the largest possible geographical area given practical constraints on time and funds. The Linguistic Atlas of the USA and Canada, ambitiously conceived in 1929 and carefully executed under the direction of Hans Kurath for many years, has yielded tremendously rich data (see *Dialect and Dialectology*). However, in the 60 years that have elapsed since the first published reports, when new materials are still being published, dramatic changes have continued to take place in the language. Lamentably, support for the various Linguistic Atlas projects was not enough to provide full coverage of the country. The intent of the Atlas of North American English is to capture a synchronic view of the state of North American English at a particular moment in time. The fieldwork for the Atlas of North American English, comprising about 800 interviews, was accomplished in half a decade, beginning in 1993.

The Atlas of North American English thus presents the first maps of phonetic and phonological variables of North American English as a whole. It must be stipulated that the variety of English under consideration is that of white North Americans. A sample of African-American speakers was interviewed in 1997 and 1998, but those interviews are not included in the Atlas. The African-American community in the USA is linguistically separate from the Euro-American community, and indeed, its vernacular is continuing to diverge from local white vernaculars. Furthermore, African-American Vernacular English (AAVE) (see *Ebonics and African American Vernacular English*) is remarkably uniform across the northern USA, in the vast territory to which African-Americans migrated in large numbers in the course of the massive population movements that began following World War I and were renewed after World War II. This variety of English has been examined in many studies of individual speech communities, but no one has as yet undertaken a survey of the dialect as a whole. The same applies to Southern dialects of African-American English, which are distinct from the Northern dialect and are more differentiated from each other. This needed research is not yet part of the Atlas project.

Given the limitation to white vernaculars of North American English, the Atlas project aims first to define the sound changes in progress that affect large groups of the speakers of North American English. It is not possible to pin down every sound change that is occurring in every community of any size. However, it was known from the outset that dramatic changes were in progress in the phonological systems of large regions, such as the Inland North and the South (Labov 1991), where chain shifts (see *Chain Shifts*) are moving sets of vowels in opposite directions. The goal has been to define the major dialects of North American English in terms of the structure of the phonological system, which entails a focus on the vowel system. The consonantal linguistic variables are comparatively few and do not serve to distinguish regional varieties.

A second goal of the Atlas is to determine the extent of geographic dispersion of the changes in progress that have been described by the many sociolinguistic studies of major cities carried out since the mid-1960s (see *Sociolinguistics and Language Change*; *Sound Change*). This is the second part of the riddle of linguistic change: once a sound change is underway, how and where does it spread? Since not all speakers who exhibit a given variant of a linguistic variable use that variant with the same frequency, it follows that sound change spreads from a point of origin, but the manner in which it spreads may be complex. For example, within the state of Oklahoma, Bailey et al. (1993) identified patterns of diffusion along both hierarchical and contrahierarchical lines, as well as contagious diffusion and patterns exhibiting elements of more than one model of diffusion.

Thus the Atlas of North American English is a project for testing theories of language change as well as for describing the state of North American English. It strives to present its object of description at a particular moment in time and to use that object to examine the diffusion of linguistic patterns across a continent.

2. Sampling

The sampling strategy for the Atlas was designed with the goal of representing the largest possible population and focusing on those speakers who were expected to be the most advanced in processes of linguistic change. It has been well established that most sound changes are initiated in urban centers, and since the bulk of the population lives in urban centers, these are the places that are most representative of the population in any case. Accordingly, the USA was divided into areas defined by 145 'Central Cities' to serve as centers of 'Zones of Influence.' The Central Cities are, in most cases, urbanized areas with a population over 200,000, but in order to gain satisfactory geographical coverage, about a third of the Central Cities have smaller populations. The basic plan was to interview two speakers in each of the Central Cities, except that in the 33 urbanized areas with a population over one million, four speakers were to be interviewed. In every city, at least one speaker was to be a woman between the ages of 20 and 40, since these are the speakers who are typically found to be at the forefront of sound change. For a variety of reasons, many additional speakers were interviewed; this adds greatly to the depth and richness of the data and provides further confirmation of the validity of the methods employed through the consistency of the findings that they yield.

3. Selection and Recruitment of Speakers

The most important criterion of an Atlas speaker is that s/he be linguistically a native of the speech community that is being represented. To qualify, a person must have lived in that place at least from the age of four until the end of high school. Preferably, at least one parent is also from the area. For each place which was selected for interviewing, the census records were consulted to determine the most prominent national ancestral groups. Then telephone listings were scanned for listings with surnames marked for the desired national ancestry. When a call was made, the initial interchange with a person who answered the telephone was the identification of the interviewer by name, giving the affiliation with the University of Pennsylvania. This was followed by the explanation that a study of communication among people from different parts of the country was being conducted and the question of whether the speaker had grown up in the town where s/he was located. If the answer was affirmative and the speaker was willing to be interviewed, permission to record the interview was requested.

Locating speakers in some places was difficult because speakers with the desired credentials were comparatively few. In Queens County, New York, for instance, 28 percent of the residents are not native-born Americans, according to the 1990 census. In addition, 22 percent are African-American and 20 percent are Hispanic.

Another problem is social class. Most sound changes come about below the level of conscious awareness, and such innovations typically arise in the lower middle and upper working classes. We can rely on finding a shared structure of the phonological system throughout a speech community, but to be confident of having representation of the newest changes in progress, it is necessary to collect data from those speakers who are most likely to be the leaders of linguistic change in the community. Therefore, it is essential that the Atlas sample include speakers from the interior social classes (i.e., the upper working class and the lower middle class).

A complicating factor is that the incidence of unlisted telephone numbers increases rapidly with decreasing social class, which presents an obstacle to obtaining adequate representation of the social classes below the middle on the social scale. (For working class people, a telephone listing makes an individual available to bill collectors, sales people, survey takers, and other undesirable outsiders. The attributes of a telephone listing that are seen as advantages by the upper middle class do not apply.) Nonetheless, the Atlas speakers do provide good representation of all social classes. A modest deficit in the number of upper working class speakers as compared to the general population is compensated for by a relative surfeit in the number of middle middle class speakers. These middle middle class speakers may not be on the cutting edge of linguistic change in progress, but they can still be expected to be solid representatives of both the entrenched and innovative forms of the speech community.

Still, for some variables social class is critical. For example, in New York City the status of postconsonantal /r/ is a crucial issue. /r/-vocalization is waning fast among upper middle class speakers, so its status had to be determined in the working and lower middle classes, where vocalization historically has been very high.

The problem of locating the ideal speaker—an upper working or lower middle class white person who is native to the place of interest—out of millions of phone listings is handled by further consultation of the census reports. The Census Bureau provides data by census tract on a variety of social variables, including nativity, ethnicity, and educational attainment, the last of which is directly correlated with social class. Census tracts are small, with an average population of about 4000, and so restricting telephone calls to a census tract with the desired demographic characteristics produces a high rate of success in the effort to contact the ideal speaker.

4. The Atlas Interview

Following the introduction, in which the interviewer identifies her/himself, obtains permission to record, and establishes that the respondent is a native of the community where s/he lives, the interview is divided into six sections.

(a) It begins with a section on demographic information that records the native and local status of the respondent: place of birth, complete residence history, father's and mother's places of birth, and languages spoken.

(b) The largest portion of spontaneous speech is obtained from a discussion of recent developments in the city, the state of the downtown area, and travel outside the city. If a topic of special interest to the speaker is raised, it is pursued to the fullest extent possible. Speakers often talk about their jobs, hobbies, or other interests in this portion of the interview.

(c) The respondent then provides word lists that do not require reading: counting, days of the week, articles of clothing, and others.

(d) The next portion of the interview is devoted to specific linguistic variables. The most formal parts use minimal pairs in the form of judgments on rhyming (*sock* vs. *talk*) or same versus different (*pin* vs. *pen*). In each case, the respondent is asked to say the desired word without its being pronounced by the interviewer and then to make a judgment on the contrast or identity of sounds.

Spontaneous pronunciations of crucial lexical items are obtained through the use of the semantic differential technique (Labov 1984), which uses questions about differences in meaning between two words, such as *cot* vs. *bunk* and *pond* vs. *pool*. Such questions often produce a considerable volume of speech, including several highly stressed tokens of each word without attention to the pronunciation. Previous research shows that the use of the variables in the semantic differential approaches the values of spontaneous speech quite closely (Labov 1989).

(e) When the elicitation of linguistic variables is complete, more detailed information on the demographic background of the subject is gathered, including occupation, education, and national ancestry.

(f) The final section is the request for the respondent to continue participation in the research by reading a word list, which is to be mailed to the speaker. This requires that the speaker provide his or her name and address. A small number of speakers decline to give this information or refuse to participate in this second part of the interview, and some ask for additional reassurance that they will not be subject to solicitations from salespeople or other unwanted callers. Most speakers readily agree to the follow-up interview and greet the interviewer as a familiar acquaintance when s/he calls again. The duration of the first interview averages about 30 to 45 minutes, ranging from 20 minutes to well over an hour.

5. The Follow-up Interview

The second interview is designed to obtain more specific information on lexical distribution through the reading of a word list and more detailed information on contacts outside the community. It begins with the speaker reading the full-page list of words which had been sent to them in the mail (or occasionally by email) after the first interview. The word list covers the areas of variable contrast and variable lexical distribution in the speaker's region, as well as a fairly complete inventory of the phonological system as a whole. The second interview also goes more deeply into the patterns of travel, friendship, kinship, and communication that relate the respondent to other cities in the region.

6. Impressionistic Coding

The first stage of analysis is the transcription of all demographic data, recording of lexical choices and judgments of syntactic constructions, and the coding of the speaker's pronunciation of diagnostic words in the formal part of the interview. For the phonological variables, the analyst records both the speaker's and the coder's judgments of 'same' and 'different' and then enters a narrow phonetic transcription of the speaker's pronunciation.

7. Acoustical Analysis

Instrumental analysis of the entire vowel system has been carried out for more than half the speakers who have been recorded, using the CSL hardware and software package from Kay Elemetrics. The recordings are digitized in sections, and words bearing full sentence stress are segmented and saved.

Spectrograms are produced for each saved word, formant trajectories are calculated by linear predictive coding, and one point in time is selected to represent the stressed vowel. The corresponding F1 and F2 measurements are written to a log file with a record of the point that was selected, a code for the classification of the vowel, and comments where appropriate. The formant values are normalized using the log mean normalization procedure (Nearey 1977) on a speaker population of 345, and the vowel system is charted using the Plotnik program (Labov 1997). (See Boberg forthcoming, for a full description of these procedures.) The total volume of speech obtained proved to be more than was expected from the earlier telephone survey of Hindle (1980). Ninety percent of the speakers are charted with at least 200 vowels, and half have provided 300 or more.

8. Findings

What, then, are the dialect areas of North American English? Figure 1 maps the areas established by the Atlas. As will be seen, a fairly limited number of phonological features determine these dialect areas. A full discussion of these features, the configurations they create, and the rationale on which the divisions rest is the subject of the Atlas itself and will not be attempted here. The following is rather an inventory of the features as they determine the major dialects of North American English. Many of these features apply in discontinuous regions, in a distribution that depends heavily on settlement history and subsequent population movements. The feature that perhaps makes the greatest cut in North American English (in terms of area and number of speakers) is the presence or absence of the unconditioned merger of /o/ and /oh/, as in *cot* and *caught*, *Don* and *dawn*, *hock* and *hawk*, *collar* and *caller*. Not only does this merger have the structural consequence of reducing the number of entities in the phonemic system, but it also produces a large number of homonyms, as is implied by the list of examples given. Plausibly, this merger has come about as a result of crowding in the low back corner of the vowel space.

A second feature that plays a prominent role in distinguishing the major dialects of North American English is the position, on the front-to-back dimension, of the nuclei of the back upglides, /uw, ow, aw/, as in *boot*, *boat*, and *bout*. The initial position for these vowels is taken to be at the back of the articulatory space; many dialects depart from this pattern in significantly fronting one or more of these vowels. The fronting frequently does not apply to allophones of the vowel preceding liquids, which form a special class in many cases of sound change. /uw/ is being fronted generally, although it is most advanced in the South and the Midland and seems to be just getting underway in the North. /aw/ distinguishes the North from other regions, as the North is characterized by /aw/ being further back than /ay/. Of this set of vowels, /ow/ does the most to differentiate the dialects of North American English. The status of the /o/-/oh/ merger and the fronting of /ow/ with respect to the major dialects is as follows:

/o/-/oh/ merged	fronting of /ow/
Canada	no
Eastern New England (except Providence, Rhode Island, where there is no merger of /o/ and /oh/, but r-vocalization prevails)	no
North Central region	no
The West	advances gradually from north to south
Western Pennsylvania	yes

/o/-/oh/ distinct	fronting of /ow/
Western New England	no
Inland North	no
Central Midland	yes
Mid-Atlantic region	yes
The South	yes

The characterization of dialects by these two features covers much ground, but the sum is a patchwork which is incomplete. The following paragraphs will review the four major dialects by region—North, Southeast, Midland, and West—and distinguish the subregions included in each. The North consists of the subregions of Canada, Eastern New England, Western New England, the Inland North, the North Central region, and interstitial areas, south to and including New York City.

Canada is distinguished from the USA by the Canadian Shift, first described by Clarke et al. (1995). This chain shift, the lowering and backing of /i/ and /e/ and the backing of /æ/, is found throughout English-speaking Canada, except for the Atlantic Provinces (New Brunswick, Nova Scotia, Prince Edward Island, and Newfoundland). So-called 'Canadian raising,' the centralization of the nuclei of /ay/ and /aw/ before voiceless obstruents (Joos 1942, Chambers 1973), is also found throughout Canada, including in the Atlantic Provinces. The centralization of /ay/ before voiceless segments is characteristic of much of the North of the USA as well, though centralization of /aw/ is not.

Two noncontiguous regions, Eastern New England and the North Central region, share the merger of *cot* and *caught*, along with the retention of back /ow/, which is characteristic of the North generally. These two subregions are differentiated from each other by preconsonantal /r/-vocalization, which is found in Eastern New England (as well as in New York City) but not further west.

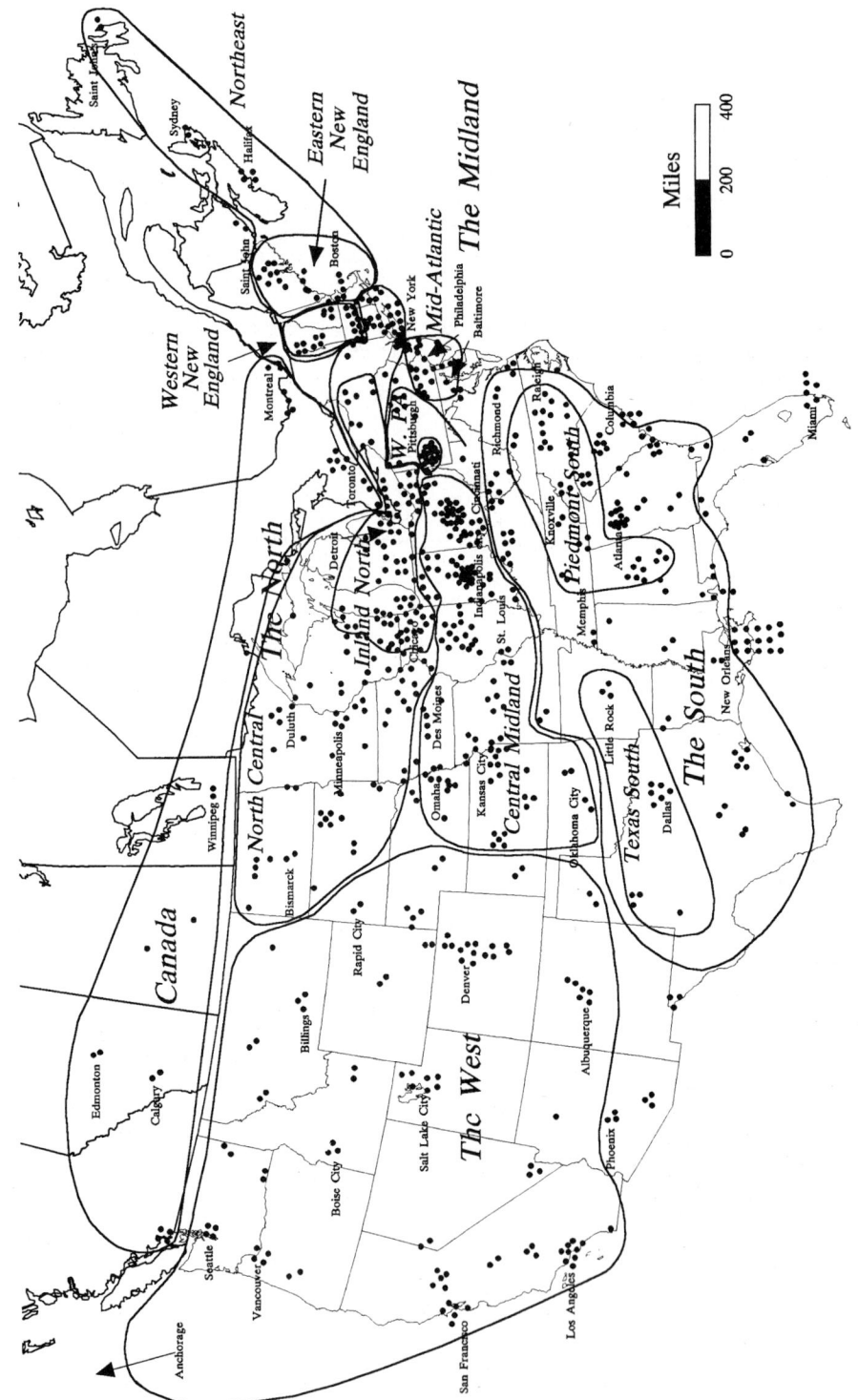

Figure 1. Dialect areas of North American English. (Each dot represents one Atlas speaker).

The remaining regions of the North are areas in which /o/ is distinct from /oh/. The Inland North, the industrial region stretching along the Great Lakes from western New York State to southern Wisconsin, is distinguished by the Northern Cities Shift. This is a dramatic rotation of six vowels, without restructuring of the phonemic system by merger or split. In this chain shift, /æ/ is tensed and raised as a whole (*tack* becomes a high, ingliding vowel, moving in the direction of *tech*), short /e/ is either backed or lowered (*tech* goes to either *tuck* or *tack*), /ʌ/ is backed and rounded (*tuck* goes to *talk*), long open /oh/ is lowered and fronted (*talk* goes to *tock*), and short /o/ is fronted (*tock* goes to *tack*). Like the Inland North, Western New England is a conservative area with respect to the back upglides. It also shows some evidence of the Northern Cities Shift in the relative positions of short /e/, which is backed, and short /o/, which is fronted.

The vast Midland area, stretching from the East Coast to the Great Plains, is unified by the fronting of /ow/, which is not found in the North, and the near-absence of /ay/-monophthongization, which characterizes the South. (/ay/-monophthongization occurs in the Midland sporadically in the most favored environments, before liquids and nasals, e.g., in *mile* and *time*.) Otherwise, within this region there is diversity, in which each big city seems to have its own cluster of special characteristics. The easternmost cities—Philadelphia, Wilmington, and Baltimore, which comprise the Mid-Atlantic region—show a phonemic split of /æ/ into tense and lax classes, /æh/ and /æ/. (This split, with a superset of tensing environments, is shared by New York City, as is mentioned above, but New York is nonetheless part of the North, based on other lexical and phonological criteria.)

Western Pennsylvania is a subregion of the Midland centered on Pittsburgh. This is the one Midland city in which /o/ and /oh/ are fully merged, and it is unique in that /aw/ is fronted and monophthongized to /ah/.

West of Pennsylvania is the Central Midland. Cincinnati is distinguished by a short *a* system that is unique in the Midland. Short *a* is a single phoneme, but the distribution of allophones echoes that of New York City: words with following alveolar fricatives (*cash*, *hash*) and with following voiced stops (*sad*, *bad*, *mad*) have short *a* in the highest and frontest portion of the distribution.

St. Louis is another special case. It is losing its characteristic merger of *card* and *cord* and re-aligning itself with the North; as a result it shares many features with Chicago. Other features are generally shared by the Midland cities. While the Midland is considered to be a region in which /o/ and /oh/ are distinct (except for Pittsburgh), there is in fact a weakening of the distinction for many speakers.

Throughout the Midland, and to a greater extent than anywhere else, there is also a weakening of distinctions among back vowels preceding /l/, as in the pairs *full-fool, bull-bowl, gull-goal*, and *skull-full*. Every Midland city except Philadelphia and St. Louis exhibits this feature to some extent.

The most general definition of the South is that it is the outer limit of the area in which /ay/ is monophthongized finally and before voiced obstruents. This definition excludes Florida; however, a broader definition of a Southeast region as the area in which /ow/ is at least moderately fronted and the distinction of /o/ and /oh/ is maintained in perception includes this highly populous state.

Within the South, two core areas are defined, the Inland South of the Piedmont and the Texas South. These are regions where the monophthongization of /ay/ has advanced to the environment preceding voiceless obstruents and the Southern Shift has advanced to the point of a reversal of the relative positions of /i/ and /iy/ as well as of /e/ and /ey/.

The West is set apart from other dialects that have the merger of /o/ and /oh/ by exhibiting strong fronting of /uw/ but not /ow/. However, this must be qualified. In roughly the northernmost third of the region, /ow/ is fully back. In the middle third of the region, /ow/ is slightly fronted, and in the southernmost part, /ow/ moves still further in the direction of the South. Nowhere in the West, however, do speakers attain the degree of /ow/-fronting that is found in the South and the Midland.

The Atlas of North American English thus provides a sense of the structure and pattern of North American dialects and of the richness and vigor of ongoing sound changes in North American English today.

See also: Dialect and Dialectology; Sociolinguistic Variation.

Bibliography

Bailey G, Wikle T, Tillery J, Sand L 1993 Some patterns of linguistic diffusion. *Language Variation and Change* **5**: 359–90

Boberg C (forthcoming) The acoustic measurement of English vowels. In: Preston D, Bayley R (eds.), *Quantitative Approaches to Language Data*. Benjamins, Amsterdam

Chambers J K 1973 Canadian raising. *Canadian Journal of Linguistics* **18**(2): 113–35

Clarke S, Elms F, Youssef A 1995 The third dialect of English: Some Canadian evidence. *Language Variation and Change* **7**: 209–28

Hindle D 1980 *The Social and Structural Conditioning of Phonetic Variation*. Ph.D. dissertation, University of Pennsylvania

Joos M 1942 A phonological dilemma in Canadian English. *Language* **18**: 141–4

Labov W 1984 Field methods of the project on linguistic change and variation. In: Baugh J, Sherzer J (eds.)

Language in Use. Prentice Hall, Englewood Cliffs, NJ, pp. 28–53
Labov W 1989 The exact description of the speech community: Short *a* in Philadelphia. In: Fasold R, Schiffrin D (eds.), *Language Change and Variation.* Georgetown University Press, Washington, DC, pp. 1–57
Labov W 1991 The three dialects of English. In: Eckert P (ed.), *New Ways of Analyzing Sound Change.* Academic Press, New York, pp. 1–44
Labov W 1997 *Plotnik 04.* Program available from US Regional Survey, 3550 Market St., 2nd floor, Philadelphia PA 19104
Labov W 2001 *Principles of Linguistic Change, Vol. 2, Social Factors.* Blackwell, Oxford, UK
Labov W, Ash S, Boberg C in press *Atlas of North American English: Phonetics, Phonology, and Sound Change.* Mouton de Gruyter, Berlin
Nearey T 1977 *Phonetic Feature System for Vowels.* Dissertation, University of Connecticut

Urban and Rural Forms of Language
A. M. Hamilton

Dialect geographers use the terms *urban* and *rural* to classify communities, and by extension, the speakers who live in those communities. There are no language features that can be associated with either an urban or a rural environment regardless of region, but there certainly are scholarly assumptions regarding what constitutes urban and rural forms of language. Modern evidence has led to a reexamination of the traditional assumptions that a rural community, by virtue of low population density and insularity, will tend to preserve archaic speech features, while an urban community, by virtue of high population density and the continual influx of outsiders, will fail to preserve archaic and regionally marked speech features.

1. Assignment of Urban and Rural Classifications

Dialect corpora differ with respect to the assignment of *rural* and *urban* to targeted communities, but generally base their definitions on population density. For example *The Dictionary of American Regional English* (1985) distributed its data collection among five types of communities, ranging on a scale from urban to rural, the extremes of which are: (1) *Urban*: a specific section within a metropolitan area, with a population usually in the thousands within a total of a million or more; and (5) *Rural*: an area with unconcentrated population—farm dwellings, small crossroads settlements—and a population in the hundreds (Cassidy 1985: xiii). The definition of urban and rural community types for the *Linguistic Atlas of the Middle and South Atlantic States* (LAMSAS), on the other hand, is based directly on 1940 US Census specifications: any city or town with more than 2500 inhabitants was classified *urban* (Kretzschmar and Schneider 1996: 68).

2. The Traditional Preference for Rural Informants

While the labels *rural* and *urban* were assigned to a speaker on the basis of community type, the labels also suggest the value of the speaker for early dialect researchers. The preference for rural folk speakers in dialect research began with the European survey methods of Gilliéron and Edmont's French Atlas (1902–10) and Jaburg and Jud's Italian/Swiss Atlas (1928–40) (see *Gilliéron, Jules*; *Jaberg, Karl*). European villages were known to preserve older forms of language and maintain features that distinguish them from even nearby villages. While dialect features vary more gradually across the USA than across Europe, there is still a tendency for rural areas of the USA to preserve regionally marked speech features, so dialect geographers of the USA adopted the preference of European researchers for rural speakers during the early twentieth century (see *Kurath, Hans*).

An ideal *rural* speaker is one who has resided in a sparsely populated locale all his life—usually a region with a farm based economy—and is therefore expected to speak with features representative of his geographic location. *Urban* speakers were less valuable in early dialect studies because they were expected to have associated with a great variety of regional groups, and were therefore assumed to be less representative of their locale linguistically.

3. The Evolution of Assumptions

The growth of cities in the USA during the twentieth century has challenged early assumptions about dialect preservation in urban communities. While generally there is a tendency for regional dialect features to be erased in an urban environment for the educated middle class, there may be a covert prestige force motivating the working class to differentiate itself from the upper classes by maintaining the local vernacular. In this sense, the urban area is as likely as the rural area to preserve local speech features for members of certain socioeconomic classes (see *Sociolinguistic Variation*).

At the same time, assumptions that rural communities preserve regional identity have not been revised in light of new data. Johnson's (1996) comparison of dialect survey data in the Carolinas and Georgia from 1930 and 1990 demonstrates that urban/rural community type accounts for the same amount of variation in each survey. So rural/urban community type remains an explanatory factor for language variation.

4. Some Observed Differences Between Urban and Rural Speech

Generally, we expect rural speakers to use more precise lexical forms that refer to ranching, farming, and animal husbandry, while urban speakers ill show relative ignorance about such terminology. We also expect rural speakers to preserve older forms of speech based on the assumption that language changes occur at a relatively slower rate in areas of lower population density relative to areas of high population density. The three major types of linguistic features that can be more or less closely correlated with a rural or an urban identity are lexical, phonological, and syntactic features.

Lexical features reflect cultural and occupational differences between rural and urban communities. Johnson's (1996) analysis of rural and urban lexical differences in the Carolinas and Georgia revealed more older forms associated with rural identity. A prime example is the older rural form *polecat* for the newer *skunk*. The lexical form *living room*, on the other hand, is a newer variant significantly associated with urban affiliation (Johnson 1996: 67).

Phonological differences between urban and rural speakers are also based primarily on degree of insularity and cultural identity. For instance, farmers and ranchers in the El Paso, Texas region preserve more East Texas and Southern phonetic features than their urban counterparts, due to their relative isolation from city life. One example is the monophthongization of /ay/, in words like *line*, which is correlated only with rural El Paso native speech (Hamilton in press). This observation of the association between rural identity and an archaic phonological feature supports the notion that rural communities preserve archaic speech features.

Syntactic differences between rural and urban groups are less tangible, though the assumption persists that rural speakers can be expected to use a nonstandard system of grammar in a conversational setting. Just as they have been demonstrated to preserve archaic lexical forms and phonological features, rural speakers may also preserve archaic syntactic features.

A familiar example is a-prefixing on *-ing* participles in the Appalachian and Ozark regions, where a speaker might say, 'We was *a-huntin'* all day' (see Christian et al. 1988: 51–84). The mountainous geographic features of the Appalachian and Ozark regions have discouraged urban development and have thus maintained isolation of speech commun-ities, thereby encouraging preservation of a-prefixing.

The emphasis of urban schools on prescriptive grammar serves to discourage nonstandard syntactic features in the educated urban middleclass. However, nonstandard syntactic features in an urban setting can be observed in neighborhoods that limit socioeconomic and ethnic variety.

While urban and rural linguistic differences are observable on a local level, nothing suggests that individual features are associated with either a rural or an urban identity, regardless of region. This is not unexpected, since rural and urban classifications are not linked to homogenous groups of speakers in any sense other than farming and ranching occupations for a limited number of rural speakers.

5. Future Work

Research in language variation is likely to continue exploration of the extent to which dialect leveling or preservation occurs in both rural and urban communities. Of particular interest is the perception and possible reality of a standard register developing in urban communities among educated participants in mobile urban culture, those who move from city to city for professional advancement.

See also: Dialect and Dialectology.

Bibliography

Cassidy F G, Hall J (eds.) 1985 *Dictionary of American Regional English*. Belknap Press, Cambridge, MA

Christian D, Wolfram W, Dube N 1988 Variation and change in geographically isolated communities: Appalachian English and Ozark English. *Publication of the American Dialect Society* **74**

Gilliéron J, Edmont E 1902–10 *Atlas Linguistique de la France*. Champion, Paris

Hamilton A M in press *A Foundational Comparison of Urban and Rural English in El Paso, Texas*. Ph.D. dissertation, University of Georgia

Jaburg K, Jud J 1928–40 *Sprach- und Sachatlas Italiens und der Sudschweiz*. Ringier, Zofingen, Switzerland

Johnson E 1996 *Lexical Change and Variation in the Southeastern United States, 1930–1990*. University of Alabama Press, Tuscaloosa, AL

Kretzschmar W A, Schneider E 1996 *Introduction to Quantitative Analysis of Linguistic Survey Data: An Atlas by the Numbers*. Sage Publications, Thousand Oaks, CA

Vernacular
R. Macaulay

The term vernacular is used in two distinct ways. One is to refer to a separate language as in the 1953 UNESCO definition of a vernacular: 'A language which is the mother tongue of a group which is socially or politically dominated by another group speaking a different language' (UNESCO 1953: 46). This use is relatively uncontroversial.

The second use is with reference to a form of language (usually speech) that is held to differ in significant ways from the socially approved prestige or standard language. It is this latter use that has concerned many sociolinguists, although no clear definition has been established.

1. Vernacular as Non-standard Dialect

A recent collection of articles on nonstandard syntax states:

> ...we will mainly use the term *vernacular syntax* to refer to those features that are uncontroversially not part of the established standard...we mean by *vernacular* those features that are situated at some distance from the formal written pole, and more towards the vernacular spoken pole. We will also use the terms *nonstandardized syntax* and *spoken syntax* without attempting to distinguish between them. (Cheshire and Stein 1997: 2)

In this definition there are the oppositions standard/nonstandard and written/spoken and it is not clear which is primary. A further problem is that the terms standard and nonstandard are themselves ambiguous (Macaulay 1973).

2. Vernacular as Unwritten Language

Sociolinguists who are studying the social uses of language are usually interested in differences in the spoken language that may not be represented in the written standard. There has been uncertainty about the labels to apply to varieties of the spoken language that differ significantly from the standard form. The words dialect, basilect, low variety, and vernacular have been used in different situations. The term dialect is most frequently used with reference to regional varieties, usually those with a long history (see *Dialect and Dialectology*). The term basilect is generally restricted to creole situations in which there is a continuum ranging from the acrolect with the highest prestige to basilect at the bottom (see *Pidgins and Creoles: An Overview*). The term low variety is used in diglossic situations where there is a distinct contrast between a high variety and a low variety (see *Diglossia*).

3. Vernacular as Non-official Language

The traditional use of the term vernacular was to refer to an independent language that had not been accepted as the language for official transactions or intellectual endeavors (Macaulay 1988). In this sense, English and French were vernaculars when Latin was used as the medium for serious written communication. Until recently, languages such as Breton, Occitan, and Corsican could similarly be considered vernaculars. In present-day Africa most tribal languages are vernaculars in this sense.

4. Vernacular as Colloquial Speech

In sociolinguistics the term vernacular was popularized by Labov, who used it to avoid the negative connotations of early labels such as Nonstandard Negro English, which he had used previously. Unfortunately, Labov extended his use of the term vernacular to other situations which are less clearly defined. The most problematic of these is given in Labov (1970: 46) where the vernacular is defined as 'the style in which the minimum attention is given to the monitoring of speech.' This is similar to the term casual speech used in Labov (1966: 100): 'By casual speech, in a narrow sense, we mean the everyday speech used in informal situations, where no attention is directed to language.'

Labov also claims that 'the most consistent vernacular is spoken by those between the ages of 9 and 18' (1973: 83) and defines the vernacular as 'that mode of speech that is acquired in preadolescent years' (1981: 3). This led him to a potentially confusing claim:

> There are communities where the basic vernacular is a prestige dialect, which is preserved without radical changes, as the adolescent becomes an adult. The class dialect used in British public schools [i.e. private boarding schools] had that well-formed character, and presumably a British linguist raised as a speaker of Received Pronunciation can serve as an accurate informant on it. (Labov 1973: 112)

All RP speakers are presumed to speak Standard English, though not all speakers of Standard English have an RP accent. Labov's claim would imply that there could be vernacular speakers of the standard language.

5. Conclusion: Vernacular: a Polysemic Term

The use of the term vernacular will probably remain confusing until there is a clear distinction between a language and a dialect, a situation that is unlikely to be resolved soon (Macaulay 1997b). In the meantime, it is likely that vernacular will be used in multilingual situations to refer to those languages that are not widely approved for use in education, official communications, and the media. In monolingual situations the term vernacular will probably continue to be used with reference to a spoken variety that is deemed by some criterion to differ from the standard variety and that is not endorsed by the educational system, though its definition may remain fuzzy. This situation will trouble only those who seek clarity and precision in this murky area of linguistic terminology.

See also: Language; Dialect and Dialectology; Power and Language.

Bibliography

Cheshire J, Stein D 1997 'The syntax of spoken language.' In: Cheshire J, Stein D (eds.) *Taming the Vernacular: From Dialect to Written Standard Language*. Longman, London, pp. 1–12

Labov W 1966 *The Social Stratification of English in New York City*. Center for Applied Linguistics, Washington, DC

Labov W 1970 The study of language in its social context. *Studium Generale* **23**: 30–87

Labov W 1973 The linguistic consequences of being a lame. *Language in Society* **2**: 81–115

Labov W 1981 Field methods of the project on linguistic change and variation. Sociolinguistic Working Paper, No. 81. Southwest Educational Development Laboratory, Austin, TX

Macaulay R 1973 Double standards. *American Anthropologist* **75**: 1324–37 (Revised version in Macaulay 1997a, pp. 21–31)

Macaulay R 1988 The rise and fall of the vernacular. In: Duncan-Rose C, Venneman T (eds.) *On Language: Rhetorica, Phonologica, Syntactica: Festschrift for Robert P. Stockwell*. Routledge, London, pp. 106–13 (Revised version in Macaulay 1997a, pp. 7–19)

Macaulay R 1997a *Standards and Variation in Urban Speech: Examples from Lowland Scots, 1997*. Benjamins, Amsterdam

Macaulay R 1997b Dialect. In: Verschueren J, Olastman J, Blommaert J, Bulcaen C (eds.) *Handbook of Pragmatics*. Benjamins, Amsterdam, pp. 1–14

UNESCO (United Nations Educational, Scientific, and Cultural Organization) 1953 *The Use of Vernacular Languages in Education*. Paris

SECTION V
Language Contact

Areal Linguistics
J. M. Y. Simpson

Geographical areas can be identified in which the languages spoken are not necessarily genetically related but are nevertheless characterized by features in common not found in languages outside the area. The identification of such areas and the consideration of the processes by which they come about are the concerns of 'areal linguistics.' This concentrates on similarities between languages and on language convergence and is particularly concerned with languages that are not genetically related. In this respect it is complementary to historical linguistics which is primarily interested in the ways in which genetically related language varieties grow apart with the passage of time, that is, it concentrates on language divergence. The concerns of areal linguistics overlap with those of dialect geography and of sociolinguistics and are illuminated by the findings of these related studies.

This article deals in turn with possible types of similarities, with the ways in which similarities spread and suggested reasons for this, with the nature of such geographical areas, and finally with some problems within areal linguistics. (Areal phenomena affecting genetically related languages are not avoided.)

1. Genesis of Areas of Similarity

Concerning such areas of similarity, it may sometimes be inferred that the features in common were originally present in only one of the varieties and subsequently spread to the others. The necessary condition for this situation is that at least one person must have had some knowledge, however minimal, of more than one variety of language. These varieties may be extremely close genetically or quite disparate.

1.1 Lexical Borrowing

Speakers may indulge in 'code-switching'; that is, they may use more than one variety of language in the course of conversation. The reasons for such code-switching may be the nature of the topic under discussion or the different linguistic abilities of speaker and hearer (see *Code-switching: Overview*).

The duration of stretches in different varieties can vary considerably, but it is possible that a speaker of variety A may introduce only one word X in a different variety B before reverting to A; this can take place, for example, because there is no name in A for the object to which X refers. (It is in fact perfectly possible that the speaker's active knowledge of B is limited to this one word X.) Thereafter the speaker and an increasing number of other users of A will employ X as a normal word in A. This process accounts for the phenomenon of *borrowing* by which a variety of language is said to acquire items of vocabulary from another language; thus English has acquired—among thousands of borrowings from other languages over the centuries—*spaghetti* from Italian, *nuance* from French, *kayak* from Inuit and *kangaroo* from one of the Australian languages (see *Borrowing*).

Where such borrowings concern entities or concepts previously unknown to speakers of the receptor language (as in the above examples), they may be informally termed examples of 'exotic borrowing.' These may be from any other language in the world and therefore will not necessarily have any implications for areal linguistics.

However, while much borrowing is understandably of the 'exotic' type, sometimes existing native words, even those from what could be termed the 'inner core' of the vocabulary, are ousted by borrowings. (By the 'inner core' is meant numerals, pronouns, minor parts of speech such as particles and prepositions, words for parts of the body, for blood relatives, for natural entities such as sun, moon, stars, water, sky and so on.) Indeed there seems to be no limit on what core words can be borrowed: Russian borrowed its numeral for '40' from Greek; English took the pronouns *they* and *them* from Norse; *plus* and *via* from Latin are used in English as conjunction and preposition respectively; *stomach* came via French from Greek; *aunt* and *uncle* came via French from Latin, as did *river*. This phenomenon could be informally termed 'core borrowing'; it implies a much greater active knowledge of the donor language on the part of the original borrowers and can have implications for areal linguistics. Thus the presence of *stomach* and *river* in English (contrasted with their absence in German) would allow us, in these particular respects, to contrast English and German (Germanic languages) and group English with French (a Romance language).

1.2 Grammatical Borrowing

Speakers may also transfer grammatical features from one variety into another. This can be termed 'grammatical borrowing' and could be regarded as a kind of imperfect code-switching since the change of variety is not complete, one aspect—the grammatical—being, so to say, 'left behind.' For example, the Scottish Gaelic and Irish equivalent of the English *I have just said that* is 'I'm after saying that,' involving a preposition and a verbal noun. Speakers of nonstandard English from the West of Scotland and Ireland may produce utterances such as *I'm after saying that*, even though ignorant of Scottish Gaelic or Irish. The assumption is that on some occasions in the past Gaelic-speakers with a less than perfect command of English produced an example of imperfect code-switching in the form of a literal translation of what they would have said in their native tongue; this new syntactic construction was then imitated by other speakers, including in time those who knew only English. The result is that the variety of English in which this construction is found is in this respect grouped with geographically contiguous Irish and Scottish Gaelic (Goidelic languages) in contrast to other varieties of English.

To take two further examples: speakers of the Semitic languages of Ethiopia have adopted the SOV word-order and various other syntactic devices of neighboring Cushitic languages; Osmanli Turkish introduced certain Arabic and Persian conjunctions and with them subordinate clause constructions containing finite verbs, thus displacing native Turkic verbal noun and participial constructions (see *Language Transfer and Substrates*).

Morphological devices and grammatical categories, too, may be borrowed for the same reason. Thus speakers of Spanish in Paraguay may borrow a nominal tense-marker from Guaraní (e.g., *mi novia-kue*, my girl-friend-PAST'='my ex-girl-friend'). Such devices may be imitated in a different phonological form: Romanian *om, omul* (the latter from Latin *homo ille*) is paralleled by Albanian *burr, burri* and Bulgarian /tʃovek/, /tʃovekət/—each pair is respectively 'man,' 'the man.'

An example of a feature disappearing is seen in the geographically contiguous group of Armenian, Persian, and Turkish; these are distinguished by a lack of grammatical gender. Since many other Indo-European relatives of Armenian and Persian do show gender, it is possible that the latter have lost it under the influence of Turkish.

All these are examples of how contiguous languages can in some grammatical respect become similar and hence different from their genetic relatives. For instance, the Albanian, Bulgarian, and Romanian definite articles mark off a geographical Balkan group in contrast to the genetic relatives of Romanian (the other Romance languages have a preposed definite article) and of Bulgarian (other Slavic languages have no definite article).

1.3 Phonetic and Phonological Features

It can be the case that the phonology of the receptor language is expanded to accommodate possibilities offered by the borrowed word: for example, native Welsh words do not begin with /tʃ/ but the volume of potential borrowings from English (such as *chips*) with this initial cluster together with the bilingualism of Welsh speakers have ensured that this is now the initial cluster normally pronounced in such borrowings into Welsh. Changes in phonology of this kind are again relevant to areal linguistics, for in this respect Welsh is grouped with English in contrast to its genetic Celtic relative Breton.

When individual speakers of one variety of language acquire another they may retain features of pronunciation of the first variety and use them in the new one; they will have, in everyday words, a 'foreign accent.' When a group of speakers with the same native language acquire a new variety the situation is no different. It is claimed that when Gaulish speakers acquired Latin, they could not pronounce the rounded close back vowel [u] (roughly the vowel in English *boot*) found in Latin *murus* 'wall' but substituted instead a rounded close front vowel [y], the sound still heard in French *mur* 'wall.'

In this particular case of language-contact, Latin can be regarded as the *superstratum* ('the language of a conquering or dominant group') because of military and cultural factors. Nevertheless it is Gaulish, the subservient language or *substratum* ('the language of a conquered or subordinate group'), that exerted an influence on the new language of the population. In this particular respect French is marked off from Standard Italian and Spanish, its Romance genetic relatives and neighbors, for they do not possess the sound [y]. (See *Language Transfer and Substrates*.)

New sounds may develop in a language as a result of internal development, as in the appearance of retroflex consonants in the Indo-Aryan languages. The borrowing of words containing these sounds from the neighboring Dravidian languages resulted in the status of retroflex consonants being strengthened in that they were used more frequently and in new phonetic environments. A noncompeting neighboring language which has effects of this kind can be

Table 1. The geographical limits of certain German sound changes.

	k->kx- 'child'	p->pf- 'pound'	-t>-s 'that'	Vp>Vf 'on'	-rp>-rf 'village'	VkV>VxV 'make'	-k>-x 'I'
Zürich	Kchind	Pfund	das	auf	Dorf	mache	ich
Freiburg	Kind	Pfund	das	auf	Dorf	mache	ich
Heidelberg	Kind	Pund	das	auf	Dorf	mache	ich
Trier	Kind	Pund	dat	auf	Dorf	mache	ich
Luxembourg	Kind	Pund	dat	op	Dorf	mache	ich
Aachen	Kind	Pund	dat	op	Dorp	mache	ich
Düsseldorf	Kind	Pund	dat	op	Dorp	make	ich
Kaldenhausen	Kind	Pund	dat	op	Dorp	make	ik

referred to as an *adstratum*. It may be that a language borrows totally new sounds from an adstratum; this seems to be the case in Xhosa and Zulu (Bantu languages) which use clicks, frequent in neighboring Khoisan languages but absent in other Bantu languages.

2. Wave Theory

Emphasis on the spatial spread of language changes was laid by Johannes Schmidt in the nineteenth century in his *wave theory* (*Wellentheorie, Ausbreitungstheorie*), though the point was also made by Hugo Schuchardt (see *Schuchardt, Hugo*). This visualizes a language change as operating from a geographical point and spreading outwards, like ripples resulting from a stone being thrown into water. It is assumed that, consciously or unconsciously, individual speakers will have successively imitated or acquired some desirable linguistic feature. But eventually the expansion ceases, leaving an area of change surrounded by an area where the change has not occurred. For example, about the sixth century CE several sound-shifts in German spread northwards from the area of present-day Switzerland. Each halted on a different line. Seven of them and their end-points are indicated in Table 1. The test words are quoted in modern German orthography (⟨ch⟩ = [x]) (see *Dialect and Dialectology*).

These sound-changes, though involving similar phonetic processes and operating in the same geographical direction are independent: in fact at the western end /VkV>VxV/ halted before /-k>-x/ giving in Düsseldorf *ich make*, but further east /-k>-x/ halted before /VkV>VxV/ giving in Berlin *ik mache*. The dialect picture resulting from these and associated changes is complex, and it is made even more fragmented by over a dozen other changes which spread out from different points in the middle of the area (Keller 1961: xii–xiii).

In that instance, the varieties of language are related and geographically close ones will be mutually intelligible. However, in wave changes the varieties involved need *not* be mutually intelligible. In other words, wave-expansions affect not only what are regarded as dialects of the same language, but also quite different languages.

For instance, one particular phonological feature is found in Finnish, Saami, dialects of Norwegian and Swedish, and Icelandic. This is a sequence of voiceless vowel (an h-sound) followed by a voiceless plosive, as in Finnish *lehti* 'leaf'; it is known as pre-aspiration. These languages are not mutually intelligible, indeed Finnish and Saami belong to one family, the Uralic, while the others belong to another, the Indo-European. Since they are spoken in geographically contiguous areas it is tempting to regard this pre-aspiration as the result of a wave change which passed from one language to another through one or more learner or bilingual speaker; this speaker made an imperfect code-switch and was imitated by monoglot speakers of the receptor language.

But strikingly this particular wave did not stop there. Pre-aspiration is also found in the Scottish Gaelic of the Outer Isles (as in *cat* 'cat' /k^{h}a^{h}t/), presumably under the influence of Norse-speaking invaders in the Middle Ages. Yet pre-aspiration is not found in the Scottish Gaelic the Scottish mainland. However, pre-aspiration is a feature of the English of the Outer Isles (e.g., *white* /ʍ∧i^{h}t/ *white*), even among monoglot English-speakers.

The conclusion is that the wave expansion of pre-aspiration has led to the convergence, in this respect, of mutually unintelligible languages in part of Northern Europe. Where the advance has halted, it has separated accents of speakers of Scottish Gaelic and accents of speakers of English. A wave expansion therefore leads both to convergence and divergence.

A similar wave is the spread of a uvular approximant or fricative in place of an earlier alveolar sound (trill, tap, or fricative). This began in Paris in the seventeenth or eighteenth century and subsequently spread through most of France. However, it also crossed language barriers and is now found among speakers of Dutch, German, Danish, Swedish, Norwegian, and even Italian and Icelandic. Interestingly, it came to characterize speakers in the Newcastle area, a part of the mainland of England

Language Contact

that faces the 'uvular' European mainland (though this pronunciation is now dying out as stigmatized).

An example of a grammatical wave-expansion is the loss of the Latin comparative form of the adjective in -*ior* (*altus* 'high,' *altior* 'higher'). This was at first replaced with a phrase consisting of the adverb *magis* 'more' followed by the adjective, e.g., *magis altus*; subsequently, in the center of the Romance area a change to a similar construction with *plus* 'more' spread out, e.g., *plus altus*. The result is that Italian and French have *più alto* and *plus haut*, respectively, while on the periphery one finds Portuguese *mais alto*, Spanish *más alto*, and Romanian *mai înalt*.

3. Indo-European Areal Features

The phenomenon of wave-expansion can, it is claimed, shed light on certain problems in historical linguistics. For example, wave-expansion suggests an explanation of similarities between different branches of the Indo-European (I-E) family which are or were in geographical proximity. In this case the varieties, though genetically related, are (in their latest attested forms) not mutually intelligible (see Bloomfield 1933: 314–6).

(a) Somewhere to the east of the center of the I-E family a change occurred by which a velar [k] or palatal [c] plosive became fronted to an alveolar [s] or palato-alveolar fricative [ʃ]. The languages affected are the Indo-Iranian and Balto-Slavic groups, Albanian and Armenian. These are known as the *satem* languages (from Avestan/ satəm/ 'hundred'). Languages which retained the velar (or subsequently changed it to [h]) are known as the *centum* languages (Latin *centum*/kentum/'hundred'). These are the Italic and Germanic groups, Greek, Hittite, and Tocharian, situated to the west of the area and on the southern and eastern periphery.

(b) In Greek, Armenian, and Indo-Iranian certain past tenses are formed with a vocalic prefix (an 'augment').

(c) In Celtic, Latin, Hittite, and Tocharian, a passive is formed with a suffix including the letter *r* (the 'passive in -*r*') as in Latin *necatur* 'he is being killed'). These languages are on the periphery, and this fact, together with a related form in -*r* in Indo-Iranian (though not with a passive meaning), leads us to conjecture that the center of the I-E area introduced alternative means of expressing the passive voice.

(d) Germanic and Balto-Slavic languages have certain case-endings not found in other I-E languages.

(e) Italic languages and Greek show the idiosyncratic feature that certain feminine nouns have masculine endings.

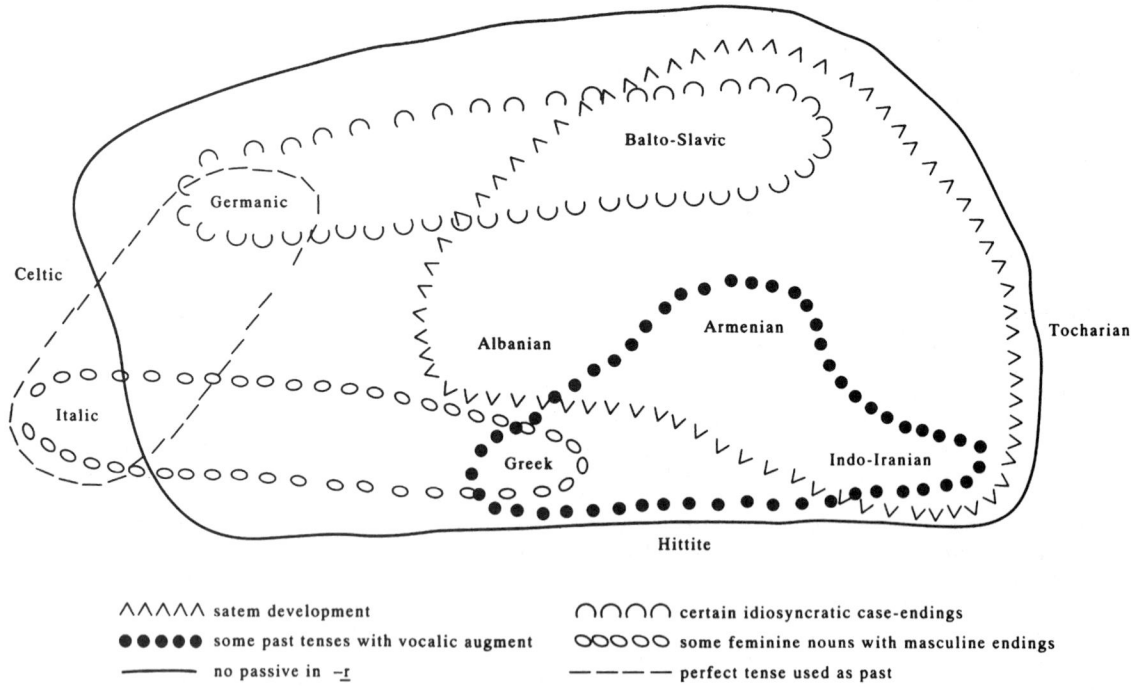

Figure 1. Some areal features of the Indo-European family (adapted from Bloomfield 1933: 316).

(f) Italic and Germanic began to use a perfect tense as a nonperfect past (though the modern Romance and Germanic languages subsequently developed a periphrastic perfect).

Figure 1 shows how these various wave-expansions intersected. This model allows one to plot similarities and differences that cannot be captured in a family-tree analogy.

4. Explanation of Wave-changes

Wave-expansions are characterized by the spread of an innovation and, in some cases, by the cessation of the spread. These phenomena are in reality the result of the behavior of individual speakers and such behavior is, to some extent, explicable. Explanations may be sought from sociolinguistic observations and from social history.

Where a change moves from one variety of language to a mutually unintelligible one, it is as the result of imperfect code-switching on the part of one or more speakers. The question then arises why this innovation is copied.

In the first place, the individuals in a community sharing a language will be liable to make the same transfers, via imperfect code-switching, from this language to a new language. The result will be a mutual reinforcement of such transfers. These transfers may in fact become markers of group solidarity (see *Speech Accommodation*). This would explain the appearance of pre-aspiration in bilingual speakers of English (see Sect. 2 above), thus continuing the southern expansion of this cross-language phenomenon. It can even be the case that a community gradually loses a language; successive generations will show increasingly less proficiency in the old language (the substratum) and increasingly greater in the new prestige one (see *Language Maintenance, Shift, and Death*). In a final stage, children learn only the new language from bilingual parents and so as monoglots acquire substratum features.

Where the substratum shows regional variation, this will be reflected in the acquired language. For this reason, English as spoken by bilingual and monoglot speakers in the Gaelic-speaking area of the Scottish mainland does not have pre-aspiration. The result is a geographical division characterizing both Scottish Gaelic and English, mutually unintelligible languages.

But wave-expansions also occur in an area where there was previously a more or less homogeneous language variety. In such cases, an innovation (however it comes about) may be imitated because the original innovator was regarded as a desirable model. The imitation is then copied as something fashionable or a marker of group-solidarity. Since before the advent of mass literacy and of radio, communication was necessarily in face-to-face interaction, such imitation inevitably spread geographically.

A wave movement may stop because of geographical factors—rivers or mountains—which inhibit communication. There may also be political boundaries. Bloomfield (1933: 343–44) gives five instances of obsolete political boundaries which coincide with isoglosses of northern German dialects. There may be other, less obvious reasons. Labov (1972; Chap. 1) gives an account of a very localized sound-change in American English: his suggested explanation is that this is in order to accentuate the difference between natives of an area (Martha's Vineyard), marked by the innovatory sound, and visitors or incomers (see *Sociolinguistic Variation*).

5. Irregular Advance of Wave-movements

However, the word *wave* as applied to linguistic phenomena is a metaphor and, as often happens, the metaphor itself may mislead. The impression gained, and reinforced by simple maps, is that wave-expansions advance in a continuous line. But since the phenomena described as wave-expansions are aspects of speech behavior on the part of individuals, the spread may occur in rather more complex ways. Social factors play a part. Changes may 'leap' from town to town, ignoring intervening rural areas, not unexpectedly given such things as trade-routes and patterns of travel. Age too may play a part, younger speakers may be more likely to adopt new ways.

For example, it was stated in Sect. 2 above that the uvular realization of /r/ was found among speakers of German. This does not mean that all speakers of German use this sound and a map which attempted to show the actual situation would be impossible to draw. Three tendencies seem to be in play: the uvular realization is used more by young speakers, by urban speakers, and by speakers from the north of the German-speaking area; the alveolar realization is used more by older, rural speakers from the south.

The social connotations of individual words may even play a role in disrupting the continuity of a wave-movement. In most Dutch dialects the words for *house* and *mouse* have the same vowel (which may be one of four qualities); but in three areas *house* is /hy:s/ (an innovative vowel) but *mouse* is /mu:s/ (an earlier one). Since the Hollandish prestige vowel was /y:/ and since the word *house* would occur much oftener than *mouse* in official speech, the word *house* with the prestige vowel spread into districts which preserved the earlier vowel in *mouse*. (Bloomfield 1933: 330.) Here again a wave-change has proceeded erratically.

6. Sprachbund and Linguistic Area

The term *Sprachbund* (plural *Sprachbünde*) (literally 'language federation') was introduced by Trubetzkoy and the term *linguistic area* by Emeneau (see *Emeneau, Murray Barnson*) to refer to a group of adjacent languages showing similarities of any of the types illustrated above and in consequence differences from their genetic relatives.

The Sprachbund known as the Balkan languages was perhaps the first to be recognized (by Schleicher). The principal languages in question are Albanian (A), Bulgarian (B) Greek (G), and Romanian (R). Though all Indo–European, they belong to different branches of that family.

(a) They are characterized by many loanwords from Turkish (T), some originally from Arabic or Persian. (For centuries, the Balkans were ruled by the Ottoman Empire and not surprisingly there is a strong Turkish influence on these languages.)

(b) In A and B, and to some extent in R, there are verbal forms which distinguish reports of attested actions (those witnessed by the speaker) from unattested ones, those that the speaker has heard about at second hand; this is a characteristic feature of T grammar.

(c) Morphologically, the genitive and dative cases are identical in A, B, G, and R.

(d) A future tense on a relic of a verb 'want' is found in Tosk (Southern) A, B, G, and R.

(e) A postpositioned definite article is found in A, B, and R (see above).

(f) The infinitive has been replaced by a finite clause, ('I want that I go' instead of 'I want to go') in B and G; this occurs to a lesser extent in A and R.

(g) The comparative of adjectives is formed analytically ('more short' rather than 'shorter') in A, B, G, and R, as it is in T.

(h) Noun phrases used as direct or indirect objects can or must be preceded by particles (originally preposition or pronoun) in A, B, G, and R. This, together with morphological indication of accusative, allows identification of the O in the frequent sentence order OVS.

Other Sprachbünde have been recognized in Amazonia, on the Baltic coast, in Ethiopia, in Central America, on the Northwest Coast of America, and in South Asia (see Masica 1976).

7. Problems in Areal Linguistics

It should be pointed out that, in the absence of documentary evidence, inferences of mutual influence in areal linguistics are drawn on the basis of probabilities. As more evidence, or other probabilities, are taken into account, then inferences may change. Above all, coincidence cannot be discounted.

7.1 The Validity of Assumed Wave-expansions

The assumption of wave-expansions must not be made lightly. Eastern Armenian contains a series of ejective consonants, not found in Western Armenian or other Indo-European languages. It was assumed that these had spread from the geographically contiguous Caucasian languages which are rich in such sounds. If, however, the plausibility of the 'glottalic' theory of Indo-European is accepted, then it is possible that Eastern Armenian has, alone among Indo-European languages, retained an archaic feature.

Similarly, it cannot be ruled out that some similarities are due to coincidence, perhaps on the basis of a universal human tendency. For example, many of the Romance languages show a satem-like development, in that certain Latin velar plosives have been fronted, resulting in dental, alveolar or palato-alveolar fricatives, or palato-alveolar affricates (Latin *centum*/kentum/, Spanish *cién*/θjen/, Portuguese *cem* /sẽĩ/, French *cent*/sã/, Italian *cento*/'tʃento/. Indeed this process has gone further in French than in the others (Latin *campus* 'field,' Portuguese *campo* /'kãpo/, Italian *campo*/'kampo/, French *champs* /ʃã/). But central dialects of Sardinian do not show this development. This change in the Romance languages could be regarded either as a wave-movement (beginning in French and encircling Sardinian) or as the result of a universal tendency, for a similar process is observable in many other languages, among them Old English, accents of modern Greek, Scandinavian languages, and Turkish. The latter is more plausible, for the precise details of the fronting in Romance vary: even within the French area we find medieval Picard /kaʃe/against (modern) Standard French /ʃase/*chasser* 'to hunt.' The possibility can therefore be entertained that in I-E there were various independent satem-developments and that Fig. 1 gives a false impression in this respect.

It could be suspected that phonological similarities may be more likely than grammatical ones to be due to coincidence. However, grammatical developments may also occur independently. While it may be the case that the Celtic languages aided the introduction of the progressive tenses (e.g., *I am going*) in English and that this can therefore be regarded as an areal feature characterizing a group of languages of the British Isles, the same device is found in modern Italian, Spanish and Portuguese (though not in French). This feature is presumably independent of the British Isles one. Since developments can occur independently in geographically separate areas, there is no reason why they may not occur independently in adjacent areas.

The use of a perfect tense as a nonperfect past, which was regarded in Sect. 3 as a wave-movement characterizing Italic and Germanic, is in fact typical of modern spoken French, northern Italian and some kinds of German. While this modern development itself may well be due to a wave-movement, the fact remains that a development has repeated itself, in other words, occurred independently. That being so, it may be the case that the historical developments in Italic and Germanic were independent.

7.2 The Nature of Sprachbünde

It cannot be taken for granted that where a Sprachbund or linguistic area is recognized, the similarities are due to the spread of features in common from only one of the varieties, unless there is evidence for this. It may be the case that there are overlapping wave moments originating at different points.

Linguists have addressed the problem of whether or not the languages in such geographically similar groups should be genetically related or not. Trubetzkoy drew a distinction between 'language families' (*Sprachfamilien*) whose most important characteristic is regular correspondences between sounds and 'language federations' (*Sprachbünde*) which do not have regular sound correspondences, but which have been in geographical contact and show similarities in syntax and semantics. In a similar vein Emeneau defines a 'linguistic area' as 'an area which includes languages belonging to more than one family but showing traits in common which are found not to belong to the other members of (at least) one of the families.' Both definitions appear to exclude groupings of genetically related languages and hence would make it impossible to recognize a Balkan Sprachbund, since the languages in question are all I-E.

However, the essential point is that the similarities in question are not inherited but have spread geographically. Seen from this point of view, the process by which features spread within mutually intelligible varieties (the concern of dialect geography) is no different from that by which they cross from one variety to a mutually unintelligible one (the concern of areal linguistics). This condition is met by the Balkan group.

Sprachbünde are not discretely delimited any more than are dialects or languages (see *Language*). There may be more or less typical members of a given Sprachbund. Thus Serbo-Croat may be regarded as a fringe member of the Balkan group since it shows a Balkan type future tense; indeed nonstandard dialects of Serbo-Croat show a postpositioned definite article and other Balkan features. On the other hand, although Armenian has lost the distinction between genitive and dative it is not generally reckoned to be a member of the Balkan Sprachbund.

There are many instances of areal similarities where no Sprachbund is generally recognized. Examples were given in Sect. 1.2 above of similarities between English and contiguous languages. Hungarian (but not other Uralic languages) and German have verbs with separable prefixes. Hungarian, Slovak, and Czech (but not other Slavic languages) have the palatal consonants [c] and [ɟ], long versus short vowels, and initial word stress. In all such instances influence of one language on the other(s) may be suspected but confirmatory evidence is essential.

It may be that there is a problem of delimiting the relevant geographical areas. It is said that there is an area running diagonally over northern Europe in which rounded front vowels (e.g., French *pur, peur,* German *Hüte, Söhne*) are found; the languages in question are Breton, French, Dutch, German, Danish, Norwegian, Swedish, and Finnish. These vowels are also found in adjacent northeast Italian dialects, e.g., that of Milan, but are absent from some southern German dialects. The resulting area is geographically continuous. Two problems arise. The first is that this alleged grouping is suspect for there are in fact two separated areas of southern German dialect (centered on Zürich and Vienna respectively) which do have rounded front vowels as well as one in the central German dialect area. Moreover, similar vowels are found in geographically adjacent Hungarian and in at least one dialect of Scots, spoken in a location (North Angus) which happens to face the northern European rounded front vowel area across the North Sea. How much of this should be regarded as a potential linguistic area? The second problem is the familiar one of the possibility of coincidence. The processes by which the French and German rounded front vowels have developed are intelligible without reference to each other or to any other language. Only if some geographical spread can be proved can coincidence be ruled out.

8. Envoi

In spite of problems in areal linguistics (and historical linguistics is not without its own problems), consideration of the effects of languages being spoken in adjacent territories is indispensable both in studying the histories of individual language varieties and in forming a general conception of how languages may change. In this connection, it should be remarked that once a feature acquired by language contact is established in a language, that feature is as liable to historical change as any other. It may therefore be the case that where adjacent language varieties show similarities, it may be virtually impossible to decide whether these are due to genetic relationship or cross-language borrowing. This can raise immense problems in language classification and lead to consequent differences of opinion between scholars.

See also: Sociolinguistic Area; Emeneau, Murray Barnson; Borrowing.

Bibliography

Bloomfield L 1933 *Language*. British edn. 1935. Allen and Unwin, London
Emeneau M B 1980 *Language and Linguistic Area*. Stanford University Press, Stanford, CA
Keller R E 1961 *German Dialects: Phonology and Morphology*. Manchester University Press, Manchester, UK
Labov W 1972 *Sociolinguistic Patterns*. University of Philadelphia Press, Philadelphia, PA
Masica C P 1976 *Defining a Linguistic Area: South Asia*. University of Chicago Press, Chicago, IL
Trubetzkoy N S 1928 Proposition 16. In: *Acts of the First International Congress of Linguists*, Leiden: 17–8

Bilingualism and Language Acquisition
C. Letts

The issue of language development in the global majority of individuals who will grow up to be bi- or multilingual is often ignored in discussions of child language acquisition. This is especially so where mechanisms of acquisition and explanatory models are the focus of study. The justification for this would seem to be that bilingualism adds unwanted complexity to consideration of the data, and that bilingualism can only be addressed when a satisfactory model of monolingual acquisition has been developed. Studies of bilingual language acquisition have then tended to be descriptive in nature, and to have focused on issues such as sequence of development, separation of the language involved, and use and choice of languages.

Related issues include language use within the individual's wider community, and in particular within education. Political and cultural factors influence the perceived status of the child's languages, and the desirability of maintaining these languages. In addition, there has been considerable debate concerning the effect of bilingual language development on the child's cognitive and academic abilities.

1. Types of Bilingualism

Individuals commonly held to be bilingual (see *Bilingualism, Individual*) may vary considerably in their skills and use of their languages. This variation results from wide differences in particular linguistic situations, and also in the way in which bilingualism is acquired. Individuals become bilingual for a wide range of reasons; they may have parents who speak different native languages, they may live in a community where two languages have long been in use as a result of political and historical factors (e.g., Wales in the UK), they may live in diglossic societies, where language is selected according to social convention, or they (or their forebears) may have migrated from one linguistic community to another.

Within each of these situations, individuals will vary as to the time at which they are first exposed to each language, and the degree of exposure at any one stage of development.

While it can be argued that each bilingual individual is different, traditionally there has been a rather crude division into 'simultaneous' and 'sequential' bilingualism. These terms relate to the way in which bilingualism is acquired. With simultaneous acquisition the child is assumed to have more or less equal exposure to two languages from birth. Where acquisition is sequential, exposure to one language begins some time after the child has begun to acquire the other language (for convenience, these will be referred to as L2 and L1, respectively). For the sequential bilingual, L2 acquisition, generally assumed to occur naturalistically, may overlap with 'learning,' if the child experiences some formal teaching to help with his or her L2.

Bilingual individuals may also be grouped according to the degree of bilingualism they display in different sociolinguistic situations. Complete equal and native control of two languages is probably rather rarer than the skilled use of each language for particular situations, resulting in an individual who has appropriate linguistic skills for all social situations encountered (for example, students generally find it easiest to discuss a topic in the language that was used when they were first exposed to the subject area). At the other extreme, there are bilinguals who may use one of their languages only in very restricted circumstances, for example in the home and with older family members, and who may have no knowledge of its written form.

2. Bilingual Language Acquisition
2.1 Simultaneous Acquisition

The most usual situation in which two languages are acquired simultaneously, is where the parents each have different native languages which they use with the child. There have been many diary-style studies of such children (for example, the study reported by Leopold 1939–49 was so careful and detailed that it became a seminal work on child language acquisition in general), so it has been possible to describe some overall stages in the acquisition process. One of the clearest accounts is given by Volterra and Taeschner (1978), who collected data from two sisters, acquiring Italian and German simultaneously. They describe three principal stages. At stage one, corresponding rather to the single-word stage in monolingual children, the child appears to be operating with only one lexical system (see *Child Language: An Overview*). Vocabulary is drawn from both languages, but only one word expresses one meaning; the child does not have a choice of lexical items for the same entity. At stage two, she appears to be operating with two lexical systems. She is now producing multiword utterances, but words in any one utterance tend to be selected from the same language. There is more confusion as regards syntax, however, the child tending to simplify and combine rules from both languages (the problem of the negative particle for example, which comes before the verb in Italian, but after the verb in German, was solved by one of the sisters by always placing it at the end of the sentence). More recent accounts, however, have suggested separate development of syntactic systems from the beginning (for example, De Houwer 1990).

The final stage is characterized by growing separation of the two languages, at both lexical and syntactic levels. A common feature of this stage is that the child rigidly associates particular languages with particular people, and may become distressed if adults do not conform to this. It is hypothesized that this rigid association helps the child to keep the two linguistic systems apart, at a time when they are rapidly developing in complexity. Awareness that there are two languages also develops around this time; before this stage is reached, the child will find requests to translate incomprehensible.

2.2 Sequential Acquisition

There are fewer studies of sequential bilingualism available, but generally it is thought that young children acquiring an L2 go through similar developmental stages to the monolingual child acquiring that same language. With older children, the developmental sequence may be influenced by formal second language teaching. There is growing evidence that L2 acquisition may be influenced by the child's personality, general approach to the problem, and particular language-learning strategies, just as it is in language-learning adults. Bates et al. (1988) provide a particularly striking example of a child who uses very different strategies to acquire a second language (admittedly on the basis of very limited exposure), than she previously used to acquire her first language.

There has been much interest in the importance of age in determining a child's success in acquiring a second language. It is often thought that the young child acquires languages especially easily, with this ability declining as he or she approaches the end of the critical period (though when exactly this is, is controversial). However, there is some evidence that, while younger children are particularly adept at acquiring L2 phonology (segmental and nonsegmental), older teenaged children may be better at acquiring grammatical patterns.

2.3 Language Dominance and Attrition

Bilingual language acquisition does not occur in a vacuum, and it is unlikely that the bilingual child will have equal input from both languages at any one time. For any individual at a given point in time, one of his or her languages will be dominant, used in more situations than the other one, and used more skillfully. Any form of testing or assessment in the nondominant language will lead to a false picture of the child's overall language development.

It is also well documented that if input ceases for a language, knowledge of that language will quickly be lost by the child. This is known as language 'attrition.'

2.4 Transfer

A common source of interest regarding the bilingual child is the extent to which there is transfer from one language to the other. Transfer (once called 'interference') consists of elements of one language influencing an utterance that is mainly in the other language. Parents and educators may become alarmed when this happens, as they may feel it is an indication of confusion between the two languages (although this will be perfectly normal in the early stages of simultaneous acquisiton—see Sect. 2.1 above). However, transfer is common and well-tolerated in many bilingual communities, where speakers may switch rapidly with little awareness that they are doing so. Also common in bilingual communities is code-switching (see *Code-switching: Overview*), in which there is alternation between languages over longer stretches of discourse.

Anecdotal evidence suggests that, providing the two languages are kept separate in input (i.e., if speakers are consistent in which language they use with the child, and do not code-switch or show features of transfer themselves), the child is unlikely to show much evidence of transfer once the initial stages of language acquisition are passed. Fantini (1985) in his study of his Spanish–English bilingual son Mario, notes limited transfer at a number of linguistic levels. As regards phonology, Mario lacked control over some allophonic variants of English, tending to deploy phonemes according to Spanish phonological rules. As regards syntax and morphology, transfer of morphemes and grammatical relations from one language to the other was noted and some effects on word-order. Loanwords were sometimes transferred from one to the other, and given appropriate morphological endings. Lexical borrowing tended to occur when he did not have an equivalent word (expressing the same meaning) in the other language. Fantini also notes some confusion of cultural norms of behavior (e.g., shaking hands or kissing), and some interference affecting conversational and discourse convention.

3. Effects of Bilingualism on Cognitive and Academic Development

In the past, being bilingual was felt by many monolinguals to be profoundly detrimental to a child's psychological, social, and cognitive development. Hence in Wales in the UK, for example, strenuous efforts were at one time made to stamp out the use of the nondominant language, Welsh, in schools. Such attitudes have long been discredited. Early experimental work that claimed to show the detrimental effects of bilingualism has been shown to have a number of serious methodological weaknesses, including testing in the child's less dominant language, ignorance of cultural differences that would influence the child's response to testing, and prejudice on the part of experimenters. More recent research suggests that bilingual children may have some cognitive advantages over their monolingual peers, developing metalinguistic awareness earlier, and displaying more flexibility in cognitive tasks. Baker (1988) presents an excellent discussion of these issues.

Continuing concern has been expressed, however, for the plight of some sequential bilinguals who are required to acquire an L2 rapidly upon commencing education, or following migration to a new country. Results of studies have been misleading. While some children cope well and have an enhanced quality of life and experience as a result of their bilingualism, other groups fail consistently to do well in school. The research centers around the work of Cummins (see *Cummins, Jim*) and colleagues in Canada who set up and evaluated the highly successful 'immersion' programs for English-speaking school entrants acquiring French (see, for example, Cummins and Swain 1986). These children, who were taught by bilingual teachers entirely through the medium of French for the first two years, did well. The conclusion was that this success resulted from careful planning, teachers who understood and accepted English from the child, and the fact that French was a new language for all the children.

Less fortunate children who have to acquire an L2 rapidly in a sink-or-swim context may give the appearance of competence in L2 in day-to-day conversation. However, it is suggested that they may fail to acquire more academic (and less contextualized) language in the early days of formal education when this may be crucial for later academic development. They are still at this stage inexpert in the L2, and do not have opportunities to develop this style of language use in L1, since it is not used in school. These findings remain controversial, but the implications are that carefully planned introduction of the L2, and/or mothertongue programs so that use of the L1 can be maintained and extended into new areas, are desirable. Good bilingual education can then become a positive asset.

See also: Bilingualism, Individual; Bilingualism, Societal; Code-switching: Overview; Language Transfer and Substrates.

Bibliography

Baker C 1988 *Key Issues in Bilingualism and Bilingual Education*. Multilingual Matters, Clevedon, UK
Bates B E, Bretherton I, Snyder L 1988 *From First Words to Grammar*. Cambridge University Press, Cambridge, UK
Cummins J, Swain M 1986 *Bilingualism in Education*. Longman, New York
De Houwer A 1990 *The Acquisition of Two Languages from Birth: A Case Study*. Cambridge University Press, Cambridge, UK
Fantini A 1985 *Language Acquisition of a Bilingual Child: A Sociolinguistic Perspective*. College Hill Press, San Diego, CA
Leopold W 1939–49 *Speech Development of a Bilingual Child: A Linguist's Record, Vols. 1–4*. Northwestern University Press, Evanston, IL
Volterra V, Taeschner T 1978 The acquisition and development of language by bilingual children. *Journal of Child Language* **5**: 311–26

Borrowing
J. Heath

A 'borrowing' is a form that has spread from one linguistic variety (the 'source') into another variety (the 'target' or 'replica'). In this sense it is nearly synonymous with 'loanword,' but a borrowing is often really a stem (smaller than a word), and may be a phrase (larger than a word). Borrowing is also the term for the act of incorporation itself, so there is a certain semantic ambiguity between process and result in the usage of the term. Although the focus here is on language-to-language transfer (see *Language Transfer and Substrates*), the concept may also be used when discussing the spread of a form among mutually intelligible dialects of a single language, or even among registers or idiolects (see *Register*).

The close analysis of borrowings involves many aspects of linguistic structure—particularly phonetics/phonology, morphology, and lexical semantics. The study of borrowings is of interest to general linguistics because the borrowing language may have several possible ways of incorporating the foreign form into its own phonological, morphological, and semantic systems, and the options implemented may reveal something about deep-seated developmental tendencies of the language that are not otherwise clearly evident. But the study of borrowings cannot rely entirely on considerations of pure linguistic structure, however 'deep.' Rather, borrowing patterns also reflect the social and historical context in which the language contact takes place. For this reason, borrowings play an important role in historical linguistics and sociolinguistics.

1. Basic Concepts and Terminology

1.1 Borrowing versus Code-switching

The term 'borrowing' is semantically misleading from the start, since it implies that the source language relinquishes a form in lending it temporarily to the target language, which is expected to return the form later (with or without interest). It is a historical quirk that the term 'borrowing' is used instead of spreading, imitation, proliferation, cloning, or mitosis. However, there is a more substantive terminological difficulty due to the sometimes fuzzy boundaries between borrowing and code-switching.

In extreme cases, the difference between borrowing and code-switching (see *Code-switching: Overview*) is clear. The word 'money' is a thirteenth-century borrowing from French, but few modern speakers of English would be aware of its foreign origin. At the other extreme, a pair of bilingual speakers might converse for a while in pure English, then shift abruptly into French for a ten-minute stretch—because French seems more appropriate to a new topic, because they do not want an eavesdropping English monolingual to overhear them, or for some other reason. In other words, a borrowing is (ideally) a historically transferred form, usually a word (or lexical stem), that has settled comfortably into the target language, while code-switching is (ideally) a spontaneous, clearly bounded switch from sentences of one language to sentences of another, affecting all levels of linguistic structure simultaneously.

However, if actual speech patterns in bilingual environments are observed, one finds that borrowing and code-switching are not always so clearly distinct.

For one thing, many borrowings are only partially nativized into the target language, and even monolingual speakers may be conscious of their foreign status. Second, widely used (hence presumably borrowed) forms may have a degree of internal phrase structure that speakers are (to varying degrees) aware of, as when French *femme fatale* or Latin *quid pro quo* is used in English. Coming from the other direction, spontaneous mixing of material from two languages most often takes the form of incorporating phrases or words from a foreign language into slots in a clearly primary base language, rather than abrupt shifts from entire sentences of one language to those of another. In other words, borrowings may resemble code-switches in retaining a foreign status and/or a discernible internal structure, while code-switches often resemble borrowings in brevity (words, short phrases) and in being fitted into another language's syntax.

To deal with such problems, some scholars have expanded the terminology by adding a third term such as 'code-mixing' to cover certain intermediate cases such as phrasal code-switching. Still further terms are needed for special cases, such as 'loanblend' for combinations of a borrowed and native element, like the German *altfäschen* 'old-fashioned' (containing German *alt* 'old'). However, the basic difficulty is not the lack of labels—which could easily be multiplied further—but the intrinsically gradient and fuzzy nature of the continuum, and it is perhaps best to keep the terminology simple while remaining aware of its limitations.

An additional problem in using degree of nativization to distinguish borrowings from code-switches is that nativization may be more advanced on one linguistic level than another. For example, the phonological segments of the foreign form may be closely adhered to, as when an English speaker carefully replicates the voiceless u of the Japanese borrowing *sukiyaki*, but the prosody (stress, intonation, etc.) may be entirely native. In a case like *formulae* [formjəli ~ formjəlay], some English speakers make a point of retaining the Latin (nominative) plural suffix, even if occasionally mispronounced, but the phonology of the stem is adapted to English, as seen especially in the intrusive [j] before original *$\bar{u}$. On the other hand, there are cases like (plural) *femmes fatales* [fam fatal-z], where an English speaker can pronounce the final *s* [z] as the (English) plural marker, while carefully retaining the segmental pronunciation and even prosody of the French noun phrase. In general, a form may behave like a nativized borrowing on one level, and like a spontaneous code-switch on another. Even on a single level, the extent of nativization of various segments may be inconsistent. In some cases, moreover, whether nativization has occurred is moot, as when a string of segments in a foreign form happens to require no phonetic adjustment in the target language, or when (say) a plural ending happens to be shared by the two languages.

1.2 Borrowing versus Transfer

'Borrowing' requires an actual copying of forms (stems, morphemes, words, phrases). 'Transfer' (also called 'interference') is a more subtle result of language contact, whereby inherited forms already in the target language are adjusted in some way under the influence of one or more source languages. If the source language producing the interference is spoken by a dominated group within the speech community, it is called a 'substratum' language (frequently a substratum dies out after a few generations, leaving its imprint on the surviving language); if the source is a neighboring language it is called an 'adstratum.' Mutual interference may be called 'convergence,' and regions containing three or more languages that have converged extensively over a long period of time are called *Sprachbünde* (singular *Sprachbund*), using a German word meaning 'language-association.' Typological convergence among dozens or hundreds of languages in a major region (USA, Southern Asia) is the focus of 'areal linguistics' (see *Areal Linguistics*), which provides tantalizing maps of trait distribution (without usually being able to trace the myriad of individual historical shifts that produced it).

The most obvious kind of transfer is what is popularly referred to as a 'foreign accent,' consisting of several segmental and prosodic features carried over from the source (substratum) into the target language. Under favorable sociohistorical conditions, an initially foreign accent may become established over time as the norm for the speech community. Language families that result from sudden expansion due to rapid military conquests tend to be highly divergent phonetically (and phonologically) because at least the outlying languages strongly reflect pronunciation patterns of various foreign languages (perhaps subsequently lost). This is a major reason why French (with Celtic and Germanic substrata) and Romanian (in a *Sprachbund* with an important South Slavic element) seem so different from each other and from Latin, while Italian (particularly as spoken in Tuscany and Rome) retains much of Latin phonetics and prosody. Going back further in time, the rapid expansion of ancient Indo–European languages from their original homeland into western and southern Europe, the Indian subcontinent, and other distant areas is reflected in the radically different phonologies of languages like Old Irish, Old Norse, Latin, Greek, Albanian, Sanskrit, and Tocharian, which makes recognition of cognates difficult. Another major case of rapid expansion was the Arab conquest of (Berber and Coptic) North Africa, Persia, and the Aramaic-speaking Levant.

Transfer is also important in morphology and syntax. While some actual borrowing of affixes can take place (see Sect. 2.5), the more common pattern in a *Sprachbund* or stable bilingual zone is some borrowing of mutual convergence in the semantics and pragmatics of grammatical categories, with little or on actual borrowing of affixes. For example, Basque (a non-Indo–European isolate) has now cohabited with the Romance languages Spanish and French for nearly two millennia, and it is no accident that Basque has a system of grammatical categories (including perfective/imperfective aspect, a subjunctive mood, and an infinitive) that resembles those of its neighbors. However, the actual affixes are native Basque forms (with one or two interesting exceptions), and there is little sign of convergence in such formal details as the order of stems and morphemes within the verb or noun.

Morphosyntactic interference is usually gradual, involving many slight rearrangements of native structures, and for this reason it is particularly difficult to distinguish ordinary, language-internal historical change from change due to external interference. In fact, to the extent that each language is a well-integrated grammatical system (a point emphasized by many typologists and functionalists), a sharp distinction between internal and external causation is impossible to make. For one thing, the target language is inevitably selective in undergoing only a subset of the theoretically possible morphosyntactic pattern transfers favored by contact with the source language. For another, any significant change in one component of the target language (e.g., due to external interference) is likely to have an immediate ripple effect, by which other components are adjusted formally or functionally to jibe with or to compensate for the initial change. In actual historical linguistic practice, successful analyses of morphosyntactic change generally consider complexes of external and internal factors simultaneously.

Long-term bilingualism also favors significant semantic convergence in the lexicon, in addition to actual borrowings. John Gumperz and Robert Wilson have claimed that the three languages spoken in Kupwar, a town in India, have converged to the point of virtually complete grammatical and lexical interanslatability. One form of lexical convergence is the 'calque': the recreation, using native material, of a compound or phrase from another language. English 'skyscraper' is copied by German *Wolkenkratzer* ('cloud-scraper'), French *gratte-ciel* ('scrape-sky'), and other European equivalents. English speakers learning another modern European language may fumble a few lexical distinctions, but thanks to an accumulation of calques and other lexical convergences they can count on finding translation equivalents for such words as *yes* and *thank you*, and in general do not have to enter a new thought world. They are not so lucky when learning Navajo or Warlpiri, and even Latin poses problems ('yes' is a diffused innovation absent in ancient Indo–European languages, as Antoine Meillet pointed out in 1925).

2. Borrowing Mechanics

In some cases, borrowing a stem presents no special phonetic, phonological, or morphological difficulties. If the stem is the source language happens to consist of segments, syllabic combinations, and a prosodic (e.g., stress) pattern that are already quite normal within the target language, no phonetic adjustment is necessary. This presumably facilitates borrowing between closely related languages, not to mention dialects of the same language. If, in addition, the relevant word class in both languages has a high-frequency form (e.g., the nominative singular of nouns) that lacks affixes, the stem can readily be borrowed in this morphologically bare form, and can then be fed into the regular derivational and inflectional system of the target language in order to create whatever morphologically marked forms (plural, dative, etc.) are needed.

However, in almost all cases of borrowing across language boundaries, at least some of the borrowings require phonological adjustment. Moreover, the target and/or source languages may have inflectional systems that make it impossible to transfer stems in unaffixed form. Insofar as the pronunciation and/or morphology of the source form are clearly nonnative to the target language, choices among several alternatives have to be made.

2.1 Phonological Adaptation of Stems

The first variable is whether the aberrant source form is adjusted to fit the new phonological system, or retains much of its original pronunciation even as it becomes common in the target language. The French borrowing *déjà vu* occurs in a variety of pronunciations in English, ranging from [deʒɑ vy] through [deʒɑ vuw] to [deʒɑ vjuw]. Here the second variant changes the aberrant front rounded vowel [y] to a more native English vowel (long or tense /u/, realized as [uw]); the third form proceeds to insert [j] between a consonant and this vowel, as in many other English words, so that *vu* is pronounced like *view*. Clearly the extent of the speaker's (and the community's) bilingualism, and various situational factors, play a role in such variation.

In addition to the degree of nativization, choices must be made among two or more possible ways to nativize the source forms. A foreign phoneme (i.e., a cluster of phonological features) that has no exact equivalent in the target language is likely to be equidistant from two or more target phonemes each differing from it in one feature. For example, French high front rounded [y] in *vu* is nativized into English as high back rounded [uw], but there is no obvious reason why it could not have been borrowed with a high front unrounded vowel as *[vij], both changes involving adjustment of one phonological feature.

It is also necessary to consider suprasegmental aspects of nativization into a target language. Not only does each language have characteristic prosodic patterns (stress alternations, pitch-accent, tone contours, or whatever), but these prosodies often interact closely with segmental phonology. The most significant recent revisions of phonological theory have involved the recognition of previously unsuspected syllabic and rhythmical bases for many phonological phenomena. Thus, English stems borrowed into Japanese must be supplied with a pitch-accent pattern, while multisyllabic Japanese stems entering English must be adapted to the target language's system of alternating stressed and unstressed syllables, as in *sukiyaki* pronounced [ˈsukiˌyaki] or [ˈsuwkiˌyæki].

Somewhat similar problems arise when the target (but not source) language is characterized by vowel-harmony patterns (as in Turkish, borrowing from Arabic, Persian, or English), or by rigid canonical-shape restrictions on stems (Arabic, borrowing from European languages). Interesting problems also arise when the source or target language is rich in consonantal but weak in vocalic distinctions, while the opposite prevails in the other language.

2.2 Spelling Pronunciations

Because literacy, including multilingual literacy, is now so pervasive, it is almost impossible to understand the phonology of recent borrowing in some regions (notably Europe) without recognizing the mediating role of spelling. Of course, this can hardly be avoided in borrowings from defunct languages, such as newly coined Latinisms, but the issue is also important in connection with living languages. The most obvious demonstration of orthographic interference is the frequent pronunciation of 'silent' letters in borrowed forms, corresponding to zero in the actual source form. Thus, standard dialects of Spanish (both continental and Latin) long ago ceased to pronounce initial *h*, but it is often revived in borrowings into English such as *hacienda*.

However, there are probably many other cases where a phonological adaptation, though of a type not incompatible with oral transmission, may have been influenced by orthography. In the case of (*déjà*) *vu* discussed above (Sect. 2.1), the consistent avoidance of front unrounded *[iy] in favor of back rounded [uw] in nativized pronunciations may have been subtly favored by the orthography (as well as by other factors including the pre-existing English stem *view*).

Even when the source and target languages have entirely different scripts, the transcription of source forms in the written form of the target language may result in pronunciation differing from what one would expect from oral transmission. For example, the transcription of *sukiyaki* in restaurant menus may well have played a role in pointing toward English pronunciations like [ˈsuwki͵yæki]. Had the transmission been entirely oral, the voiceless *u* would very likely have been missed by English speakers, resulting in a pronunciation beginning with *[ski...]. Of course, to the extent that orthographies (which often omit prosodic information) mediate borrowing, the earlier comment about the relevance of source-language prosody must be reconsidered.

Orthographic complications are substantially absent in borrowings that take place in many intertribal, colonial, immigrant, and native-minority contexts, where literacy in the target and/or source languages is low. There are also some contexts where literacy in both languages is fairly high, but where sharp differences in scripts, or puristic avoidance of loanwords in written language, effectively eliminate literacy as a factor in borrowings. One example is European (French, Spanish, Italian, English) borrowings into North African Arabic, which are rarely mediated by written languages. Here, for example, the French high front rounded [y] is often converted into *i* rather than *u*; French *bureau* [byʁo] is borrowed as [biru].

2.3 Relexification and Hybrid Borrowings

'Relexification' occurs when vocabulary from one source language is largely replaced by vocabulary from a successor source language. This happens in pidgins and creoles (see *Pidgins and Creoles: An Overview*), but can also apply to borrowed lexicon in less traumatic circumstances. Examples are Third World countries that have been under the successive political and cultural influence of different European powers. In Morocco, Spanish was the first dominant European influence (on the coasts), to be followed by a more thorough domination by French, while English has increased in popularity. In the Philippines, Spanish was the long-term colonial language, but English has completely replaced it under American influence. Former German, Portuguese, Italian, and Dutch colonies or zones of influence (e.g., Tanzania, Angola, Somalia, Indonesia) are in various stages of transition, usually toward English as a sort of neocolonial language.

Because the successor source language has many cognates with the previous source language, 'hybrid borrowings' result. For example, Moroccan Arabic initially borrowed Spanish *interés* as *intiris* '(bank) interest,' but most Moroccans know the word in the form *antiris*. The first syllable has been changed under the influence of French *intérêt*, the middle syllable is neutral, and the final syllable unmistakably continues the original Spanish borrowing. (For a different type of multiple-source contamination, see Sect. 3.2.)

In many other cases, there is no such residue of the earlier borrowing, which has simply been replaced by a new borrowing from the successor source language. However, when the earlier and later borrowings are similar in form (as when they come from cognates in the two European languages), one may suspect that the historical process was not so much a second borrowing as a kind of updating of the old borrowing, like the partial updating seen in the hybrids.

2.4 Morphological Adaptation of Borrowings

It is true that some borrowed forms are strikingly impervious to visible morphological embellishment in target languages. Thus, a number of borrowings from Berber or other languages into Moroccan Arabic refuse to take the normal definite prefix *l-*, hence *bəllarž* 'stork(s)' or 'the stork(s),' *atay* 'tea' or 'the tea'; contrast native *kəlb* 'dog,' *l-kəlb* 'the dog.' Similarly, some English speakers are uncomfortable with adding the English plural [−z] to weakly assimilated French borrowings like *bête noire, éminence grise*, or *femme fatale* (while other speakers have no such compunctions).

In extreme cases, a borrowing may be sufficiently inert or unstable morphologically in the target language to make its word-class status indeterminate. In Moroccan Arabic, the borrowing *himri* 'hungry, hunger' (a fairly old loan from Andalusian Spanish *hambre* 'hunger,' but secondarily associated with English *hungry*) is used indiscriminately as a noun or adjective in a manner not characteristic of native lexical items. A related situation is exemplified by German *Gesundheit* 'health,' which occurs in English only as an exclamation after someone else sneezes. Such examples might be said to constitute a minor, pidgin-like lexical stratum in the target language.

However, in most cases a borrowed noun or verb stem eventually acquires the normal set of inflectional and derivational possibilities of its word class. When both languages are highly inflected, as is often the case at least for verbal morphology, it is no simple task to decide how a stem from one language is to be transferred to the other. Indeed, target languages often resort to stratagems that evade the problem, for example, by borrowing verbs in an infinitive or other relatively simple form and adding a native verb like 'be' or 'do' in auxiliary function, or adding a 'thematizing' derivational affix between the borrowed root and regular target-language affixes.

The auxiliary structure is typical of borrowings from Arabic into Turkish. For example, instead of attempting to find an inflected form of the Literary Arabic verb 'to thank' (perfective stem *šakar-* with pronominal suffix, or imperfective *-škur-* with pronominal prefix and suffix) that could be directly borrowed, Turkish took an Arabic verbal noun *tašakkur* 'thanking,' combined it with the native Turkish verb *etmek* 'do' (used here as an auxiliary), and produced the verb phrase *teşekkür etmek* 'to thank.'

An example of a thematizing affix is German *-ieren*, which is used heavily in verb borrowings, particularly from Latin and French: *finanzieren*, *diktieren*, etc. Similarly, Mexicano (Nahuatl) has thematizers such as *-oa* for borrowing Spanish verbs: *costar-oa* 'to cost' (Spanish infinitive *costar*).

2.5 Borrowing of Grammatical Morphemes

Linguists have sometimes argued that while lexical stems are readily borrowed, the morphosyntactic systems of each language are so tightly structured, and so far below the level of consciousness, that they do not permit direct borrowing of affixes and other bound forms from other languages except in peripheral cases. However, it is known that borrowing of bound morphemes is less rare than previously thought.

To begin with, it turns out that subordinating or conjoining particles ('because ... ,' '(so) that ... ,' etc.) are rather easily borrowed in some contexts, including colonial or postcolonial zones where native languages have borrowed heavily from an overlain European language. Such particles are mechanically rather easy to integrate into the target language, since they typically occur at the beginning or end of the clause and can therefore be appended to the periphery of what is otherwise an intact clause in the target language. For example, younger speakers of many languages spoken in Francophone West Africa (Senegal, Mali, Burkina Faso, etc.) routinely use French *mais* 'but,' *parce que* 'because' (locally pronounced [paskə]), *pour que* 'so that,' *à moins que* 'unless,' and similar clause-introducers, so that their complex grammar is at least superficially quite different from that of their grandparents. Hill and Hill (1986) report that many Spanish connectives and other particles like *pero* 'but,' *para* 'in order to,' and *porque* 'because' are common in modern Mexicano (Nahuatl).

However, the introduction of a foreign affix into target-language word morphology is more problematic. Sometimes a source-language plural (or definite) affix acquires a precarious foothold in the target language when unaffixed/affixed pairs are borrowed, as in English *formula*, plural *formulae* from Latin, or Moroccan Arabic *pisin*, definite *lapisin* '(the) swimming pool' from French (*la*) *piscine*. When such affixes occur also with nonborrowed stems, the question arises whether the affix was directly borrowed as such, or whether it was secondarily isolated by target-language speakers after digesting a number of such paired borrowings. For example, the minor English suffix *-ette* (from French) is used with non-French stems, not always in the original diminutive sense (*kitchenette*, *majorette*). However, it is difficult to describe the formative process in question as direct affix borrowing. Rather, English may simply have had a sufficient stock of double borrowings from French, like *cigar* and *cigarette*, to permit monolingual English speakers to recognize *-ette* as a derivational ending and to extend it (sporadically) to new combinations. When the source language has many lexical doublets involving a high-visibility derivational ending such as *-ette*, by the time the target language has absorbed a few hundred borrowed stems its native speakers are likely to segment the affix and may then expand its usage.

More difficult to borrow are true inflectional affixes, such as pronominal-agreement or tense/aspect/mood affixes on verbs, and case affixes on nouns, but a number of cases have been known for some time and many others have been reported. In one Romanian dialect, certain pronominal endings on verbs have been altered under Bulgarian influence: *aflu 'I find' became *aflum*, and *afli 'you find' became *afliš* (the local Bulgarian endings are *-am*, *-iš*). In 1953, Uriel Weinreich explained this in terms of the sheer productivity of the relevant Bulgarian paradigm, which helped it 'overflow' into Romanian, but also in terms of the pre-existing 'congruence in structure' of verbal paradigms in the two languages. Later theory tends to emphasize two points: (a) the initial phonological similarity between Romanian *-i* and Bulgarian *-iš* as a kind of phonological catalyst, and (b) the increased phonological distinctiveness of the resulting paradigmatic endings. While factor (a) helps make the crosslinguistic morpheme association possible, (b) is more teleological, suggesting 'formal renewal' of a categorial distinction (threatened with neutralization due to phonetic erosion) as a therapeutic or functional basis for this type of borrowing.

One may conjecture that borrowings like this Romanian one take place in communities with heavy long-term bilingualism, resulting in frequent sentence-internal code-switching whereby Bulgarian words and phrases are inserted into Romanian sentence frames, leading to a certain blurring of the boundary between code-switches and borrowings.

3. Borrowing Routines

3.1 Historical Development of Routines

Studies of twentieth-century borrowing patterns, particularly in (ex-)colonies with a dominant European language, suggest that relatively streamlined 'routines' for instant borrowing of foreign stems (including verbs) are developed over decades or centuries, after an early period of more sporadic and uneven borrowing. Because some early-period borrowings become stable lexical items in the target language, at later stages it is possible to recognize them as an archaic 'borrowing stratum,' distinct in type from the wave of later and incoming borrowings (including on-the-spot adaptations) that obey the existing productive routines.

As noted in Sect. 2.4 the principal routine for nativizing European verbs into Moroccan Arabic is to borrow the Spanish infinitive form in -*ar* (-*er*, -*ir*) as the Moroccan stem, and to borrow a composite of French forms (differing from one French conjugation to another) characterized by a final front vowel as the Moroccan imperfective stem. However, examination of early colonial borrowings that have survived, and the direct testimony of colonial-period publications, show that these routines were not automatic in the earlier periods. Some early borrowings appear to have been based on shorter source forms (vowel-final forms in -*a* or -*e* for Spanish, and consonant-final unsuffixed forms for French). Thus French *déserter* 'to desert (from army),' a familiar military term in the colonial period, is recorded in Moroccan as *zrti* or *zrt*, showing reduction of French vowels to fit typical Moroccan verb shapes, and fluctuation between vowel- and consonant-final form; if it were to be (re-)borrowed using existing borrowing routines, it would take the form **dizirt*, retaining the original syllabic structure and ending obligatorily in *i*.

Routines develop when a particular pattern of source/target phonological and morphological correspondences—not necessarily dominant in the earliest borrowing stratum—succeeds in becoming the productive method for incorporating new borrowings. A fully streamlined routine, which may emerge only after decades of community bilingualism, permits instant borrowing (e.g., application of target-language affixes) of any source-language form of the appropriate word- or conjugation-class. Routines permit Moroccans who know French to toss off forms like *ma ta-y-t-ʔytilizi-w-š* 'it is not used,' where the very un-Arabic-looking French verb *utiliser* 'use' is flanked by strings of Moroccan Arabic affixes and particles to create a sentence nucleus.

3.2 Relexification and False Routines

In Sect. 2.3, it was pointed out that a borrowed stem may be a hybrid, by which an early borrowing from one source language was later partially (e.g., in its first syllable) reshaped under the influence of a cognate from a new source language. However, there is also another type of hybridization found in these contexts in which routines play an important role.

When one European language gives place to another as the source of new borrowings for a native language in this situation, old borrowings from the first source language are secondarily associated with cognate forms in the successor source language. A Filipino, speaking Cebuano and English (but not Spanish), will notice many apparent English–Cebuano verb correspondences such as *cultivate/kultibar* and *complicate/kumplikar*. Of course, the Cebuano forms are historically from Spanish -*ar* infinitives *cultivar* and *complicar* but, with the near-disappearance of Spanish as a second language in the Philippines, English/Cebuano bilinguals conceptualize the correspondences as a routine 'add -*ar* to the English verb.' This results in occasional pseudo-Spanish forms like Cebuano *kumplinar* 'complain' which can only be based on English (cf. the unrelated Spanish synonym *quejarse* 'complain'). In Morocco too, -*ar* (modeled on early Spanish borrowings) is recorded in a few French borrowings like *siñar* 'to sign' (the Spanish synonym is *firmar*), and stem-final -*i* (typical of true French borrowings) is to be found in the first verb borrowings from English such as (slang) *spiki* 'speak (English).'

Some of these 'false routines' produce only a handful of forms and then sputter out, giving way to emerging routines better adapted to the new source language. The Moroccan form *siñar* has been largely replaced by (or update as) *siñi, sini*, or *sni*.

4. Borrowing in Social and Historical Context
4.1 Official Languages

In the modern world, much borrowing into standard languages is mediated by multilingual literacy and may be literally controlled or monitored by official organizations or committees. Scientific and other academic terminology, for example, typically takes the form of *neologisms* coined from Latin or Greek compounds. These terms pass easily from English to French to Spanish, or vice versa in any direction—the suffixes are adjusted to the local language by well-oiled routines, the orthography of the stem is otherwise largely retained, and local spelling pronunciations emerge. It is debatable whether these international words can even be called borrowings—the original compounds may never have existed in Classical Latin or Greek, and it is often unclear whether one modern language X has borrowed the terms from a particular other modern language or has simultaneously (re-)created the classical neologism using its own Latin-to-X routines.

The role of advertising and (other) propaganda also deserves a mention. At the time of writing, the world had been bombarded with *perestroika* and *glasnost*, Russian terms that have become synonymous with administrative reforms in the former Soviet Union. Television audiences in the USA have likewise been saturated with commercials from Volkswagen emphasizing the word *Fahrvergnügen* 'pleasure of driving (or traveling).' By virtue of their novelty and foreignness, such terms combine a (theoretically translatable) general meaning with a precise, almost proprietary association to a particular government or corporation.

For a very different aspect of the role of official institutions in borrowing, see Sect. 4.7, Purism.

4.2 Colonial (and Postcolonial) Contexts

For the purposes of this article, the label 'colonial' is applied to any system in which the large majority of natives are politically, economically, and/or culturally subordinated to one of the world's hegemonic powers. This applies to some so-called 'protectorates' (e.g., Morocco), 'administered territories' (e.g., Puerto Rico), 'zones of influence' (e.g., Palestine), and annexed lands treated as provinces (e.g., Algeria), as well as to nominal 'colonies.' Moreover, most independent former colonies are included, as they have usually become more dependent culturally on the former colonial power than during the colonial period itself because of the huge postcolonial expansion of formal education, literacy, and broadcast media.

The extent of borrowing from colonial to native languages depends, to begin with, on the length of time involved and on the extent of actual colonial penetration. Some coastal regions were of interest to the colonial power essentially because of a port or to protect a sea lane; other colonies were valued as buffers against other hegemonic powers. Still others, like India and Algeria, were intensively colonized—settlers were brought from the home country to exploit local agricultural or other resources, modern European quarters arose beside native towns, natives worked for Europeans as laborers and domestics, and at least a small native elite was educated in European-type schools. With mass education, usually after independence, the colonial language took on a new importance, and the former power usually took pains to maintain its cultural (and hence political and economic) influence by sending teachers and textbooks, and by bringing native students and other visitors to the European country. In many parts of the Third World, the former colonial language is now an important vehicle for intertribal and regional communication (e.g., French and English in Africa).

If there is a consistent colonial language throughout this political sequence, one can expect a fairly standard 'life cycle' of borrowing patterns. At first, few natives speak more than a pidgin-like approximation to the colonial language, and colonial words are absorbed only painstakingly into the native (target) language, with significant phonetic distortion, morphological fusion or missegmentation, and speaker-to-speaker variation. Over several decades, at least partial bilingualism becomes widespread, a few hundred borrowings with recognizable connections to the colonial source form have become established (so that models are available to establish source-to-target equivalences), and new borrowings more closely adhere to the pronunciation and exact sense of the source form. Sentence-internal code-switching has become common in the fluently bilingual segment of the native population, and the distinction between code-switching and borrowing begins to break down. Routines have been developed to borrow verbs as well as nouns, so that lexical stems can be spontaneously borrowed (i.e., inserted seamlessly into a native-language frame). Patterns of borrowing and code-switching diffuse to some extent throughout the native community, but there is always a sociolinguistically significant asymmetry between young and old, urban and rural, privileged and underclass.

The whole system is, of course, disrupted by a sudden replacement of one colonial language by another, as when German or Italian colonies and zones of influence were reallocated after World War II. In the second half of the twentieth century, there has been a more gradual worldwide shift in favor of English, which is fast becoming an important and popular second foreign language even in the most strongly entrenched, defiantly non-English region of the Third World (Francophone West Africa). Some linguistic phenomena associated with relexification of borrowed vocabulary in such contexts were touched on in Sects. 2.3 and 3.2.

4.3 Diglossia

'Diglossia,' a term introduced by Charles Ferguson (See *Ferguson, Charles A*; *Diglossia*), is the co-occurrence in a community of sharply different H and L ('high' and 'low,' i.e., official versus vernacular) varieties of the same language. The somewhat provocative labels high and low generally reflect the attitudes of native speakers, not of the sociolinguists who study the systems. To some extent, any language that is spoken on the streets, is written, and is used in schools and other formal contexts is characterized by some high/low variation, but the term 'diglossia' is most often applied in cases like Arabic and (Modern) Greek, where the language of writing (and of lectures and news broadcasts) is quite distinct from the modern vernacular. Standard Literary Arabic, for example, is close to the language of the Qu'rān and does not vary from one Arab country to another, while dozens of mutually unintelligible vernaculars have developed, from Timbuktu to Central Asia, in the intervening 1300 years. Until the Romance languages became widely used in writing during the Renaissance, one could describe their relationship to Latin as diglossic, though for the illiterate masses the matter was mostly irrelevant to daily life.

Diglossic borrowing (from the H variety into the spoken L form) is rather similar to borrowing from a colonial language. Again a local vernacular is up against a dominant international or at least suprar-egional variety used in schools, writing, and broadcast media, in a world with ever increasing literacy and exposure to media. Accordingly, the type of vocabulary that is borrowed from the H to the L variety tends to be of the same semantic types as in colonial contexts. In Morocco, where the local Arabic dialects borrow both from French and from Literary Arabic, these latter compete as suppliers of new borrowings, and although there is a partial division of labor (Literary Arabic for Islamic subjects, French for sports), this division is not sharp and is being undermined by shifts in official language usage (the gradual Arabization of the educational system and the bureaucracy). Because the diglossic H form is not considered foreign, there is no puristic weeding out of diglossic borrowings (as there often is with foreign ones).

Mechanically, diglossic borrowing is much more straightforward than borrowing from unrelated or distantly related foreign languages. Since the vernacular already shares many true cognates with the H variety, phonological and morphological correspondences are usually obvious, and new borrowings can simply follow these correspondences. Some diglossic borrowings may form an identifiable lexical stratum by virtue of containing a sound or other feature not characteristic of the L variety, like Moroccan suʔal 'question' (glottal stops occur in Literary but, except for such borrowings, not in vernacular Moroccan). However, large numbers of diglossic borrowings blend imperceptibly into the L variety.

Subordinating particles and connectives noted above (Sect. 2.5) for bilingual borrowing are also important in diglossic borrowing. For example, younger Moroccans regularly use such Literary Arabic clause-introducers as bi-ʔanna 'that' (quotative) and li-ʔanna 'because' instead of older dialect forms, a change with important syntactic ramifications.

4.4 Native Minority Communities
In the colonial cases discussed in Sect. 4.2 the politically dominant group is less numerous than the native population. However, there are also cases, notably in the Americas and Australia, where the native ethnic groups have been overwhelmed numerically by the intruders and have come to function permanently as ethnic minorities. A considerable variety of linguistic scenarios can develop in the situation, depending on such factors as the size, degree of intactness, and isolation of the minority groups, as well as less easily measurable cultural phenomena. Thus, in the Americas, the number of speakers of Nahuatl and Quechua, or even Navajo, has assured the vernacular viability of the languages despite extensive bilingualism with English or Spanish; some much smaller groups in the pueblos or canyons of Arizona and New Mexico have remained relatively intact due to conscious resistance to cultural domination. On the other hand, many Native American and Australian languages have already disappeared and others are dying off.

As long as the minority language (see *Minority Languages*) remains viable as a vernacular, the type of borrowing observed is similar to that found in ordinary colonial situations like Morocco, the Philippines, and Indonesia. However, as minority languages lose their viability and head toward eventual extinction, more extreme phenomena connected with 'language death' (see *Language Maintenance, Shift, and Death*) are observed. The native language, whose grammar is subject to simplification and instability among marginal speakers (e.g., when addressing monolingual grandparents), ceases to be the unquestioned base language for code-switching and the target language for borrowing. Instead, some form of the dominant majority language comes be to used among younger members of the minority group. At a certain point, the native language, along with other forms of traditional behavior associated with aged persons, comes to be viewed by the newer generation as a quaint anachronism or a symbol of low status, and as their elders die off the native language vanishes with them.

In this drastically altered landscape, one might still be able to speak of a 'minority dialect' (e.g., Native American English) of the majority language spoken among members of the minority. In some cases, a pidgin or creole may have developed among the natives, the lexicon coming mostly from the majority language (see *Pidgins and Creoles: An Overview*); later on this will slowly decreolize, producing a narrower continuum with the standard form of the majority language (an example is Australian Aboriginal English). In less extreme cases, the most consistent marker of the native dialect may simply be a noticeable accent. However, even as the minority dialect shows signs of merging completely with the standard majority language, a small number of highly visible and symbolically important borrowings from the original native language are maintained or even resurrected as expressions of ethnic identity. It is debatable whether such forms should be considered as borrowings into the majority language, or as the residue that has survived a continuous piecemeal replacement of minority by majority language material.

4.5 Immigrant Communities
Until the early-twentieth century, immigrants to the Americas could, if they wished, obtain unoccupied farmland and recreate in the New World the towns they had left behind. Since then, immigrants have

formed ethnic neighborhoods or small kin-based networks, usually in large cities.

A wide variety of attitudes and behaviors toward language are observed within immigrant families, whether the children came with the parents or were born in the host country. Sometimes the parents attempt to maximize the use of the ethnic language (and ethnic culture in general), an approach that may reflect the hope of returning to the motherland, but may also be associated with strong parental control of children's behavior. Alternatively, some parents make explicit decisions to shift to the new majority language, an approach that may be consciously intended to improve the children's educational and career prospects.

In any event, sociolinguistic forces within immigrant neighborhoods or even simple families are extraordinarily complex, as the choice of spoken language becomes a critically important and easily manipulable symbol of identity. Moreover, in such communities there is considerable asymmetry in degrees of mastery of the respective languages, not only across generations but also, say, between elder and junior siblings within a family. Unless the ethnic community is regularly replenished by new waves of immigrants, linguistic assimilation is usually complete no later than the third generation (the second born in the new country). However, even at this stage, if ethnic identity has retained any significance in the host country, interesting ethnic varieties ('ethnolects') of the majority language may persist, consisting of a slight accent along with a repertoire of lexical items borrowed (or retained) from the ethnic language. Some of these lexical items are not understood by nonmembers, so the variety can function as a litmus test for ethnicity and as a barrier. A third-generation immigrant who smiles at the quaintness of his/her grandparents and has no strong identification with the old country may nonetheless find considerable satisfaction in using the ethnolect with peers, since it effectively expresses a special, intermediate identity.

Under very particular conditions, ethnic languages and dialects can endure over centuries. This happens when minority ethnic or religious groups coexist with majority populations over many generations but remain residentially and socially segregated. Jews in Europe and in Arab countries, particularly before the Nazi genocide (1939–45) and the mass immigration to Israel (after 1951), furnish many examples. The boundaries between Jews and Gentiles in some regions were sufficiently sharp to permit long-term coexistence of mutually unintelligible languages (Yiddish and Ukrainian; Judeo–Spanish and Bulgarian; Judeo–Arabic and Berber). In other cases, local populations of Jews and Gentiles spoke structurally quite distinct dialects of the same language (Yiddish and German, Judeo-Arabic and Muslim Arabic).

Under late-twentieth-century conditions in Europe and the USA, some but by no means all Jews can still be readily identified by accent (especially in New York City and Philadelphia, where there are large Jewish concentrations). Some speakers can switch into an in-group, Jewish English ethnolect (often known as 'Yinglish') involving a variable amount of Hebrew and Yiddish vocabulary in an English base.

4.6 Decreolization

A pidgin is a relatively unstable variety developed in marketplaces, plantations, and similar environments for limited communication among native speakers of different languages; a creole is a pidgin that has become a native language for a new generation and has stabilized its grammar accordingly. Most pidgins and creoles (see *Pidgins and Creoles: An Overview*) are lexically derived from a European language (English, French, Portuguese, etc.). Of interest here is the fact that creoles tend to undergo extensive grammatical and lexical change subsequent to their emergence.

In many cases, the creole continues to be in a diglossic relationship to its original lexifier language—creole and standard English in Jamaica, creole and standard French in Haiti, creole and standard Portuguese in the Cape Verde Islands. In this case, the diglossic borrowing patterns described in Sect. 4.3 are applicable. The resulting convergence of the creole with the lexifier language is called 'decreolization.' In such contexts, there is a continuum of varieties ranging from the 'acrolect' (the standard European language) through the intermediate 'mesolect' to the 'basilect' (closest to the original creole), with the long-term tendency generally a contraction of the continuum around the acrolectal pole.

However, the vicissitudes of politics may result in the superimposition of a distinct European language on the creole. Tok Pisin (spoken in Papua New Guinea) is usually classified as an English-based creole, but it originated as a German-based creole (or pidgin) and was relexified when German power ended in the region. A major topic in creolistics is the difficult philological unraveling of similar replacements of lexifier languages in the early development of other pidgins and creoles, such as Papiamentu (Guianas) and Hawaiian Pidgin. In any event, relexification is basically the same process whether the target language is a creole or an ordinary language with a large stratum of borrowings (cf. Sect. 2.3) (see also: *Pidgins and Creoles: Morphology*; *Pidgins and Creoles: Models*).

4.7 Purism—The Target Language Fights Back

Even in unofficial contexts, borrowing (and code-switching) has powerful symbolic connotations. In many cases, borrowings are highly conspicuous, perhaps because of some telltale phonological or orthographic feature or just because most people know they are foreign. Borrowings are therefore a prime target of linguistic nationalists and (other) purists, who find them an insult to their language.

The formative period of Modern Turkish is an instructive example. Under the influence of a charismatic political leader, Attatürk, Turkey emerged as an independent country after World War I, and promptly set about refashioning its cultural and political allegiances, shifting away from the Arabo–Persian sphere into the European one. The Arabic script that had been used in Turkish under the Ottoman Empire was thrown out in favor of the Latin orthography still in use. Official committees sifted through the lexicon, throwing out hundreds of well-entrenched Arabic and Persian borrowings, and incorporating many new borrowings from European languages. In case this latter development was interpreted as a challenge to Turkish sovereignty, the 'sun language' theory was propounded, claiming that Turkish was the original human language, so that borrowings from European languages were long-lost brethren being belatedly reintegrated into the fold.

Every modern standard language has passed through periods of intense lexical development, and in each case an elite group had to decide how to produce new vocabulary. The Romance languages, and to a large extent English (with its significant component of French borrowings dating to the Norman period), mined Latin and to some extent Greek for much of this vocabulary. The development of standard German took a mixed approach, accepting some of this Latinate vocabulary (along with many French borrowings), but self-consciously balancing them with internally generated German compounds—often transparent calques like *Fernsehen* modeled on television ('distant-seeing'). When literary Arabic was developed in the early Caliphate, Greek academic vocabulary was the semantic model, but new vocabulary was generated from Arabic roots using various derivational mechanisms, rather than by direct borrowing from Greek, and written Arabic continues to avoid European borrowings. Scholars engaged in the development of other standard languages (Basque, Swahili, Tok Pisin) continue to agonize over this perennial issue. In the case of standard French, the elite is less concerned with expanding an already impressive vocabulary than with stemming an unseemly flood of English borrowings.

4.8 Borrowing and Special Registers

While the conspicuousness of borrowings makes them anathema to patriotic purists, it may also make them attractive in various special contexts. A sprinkling of foreign words gives sociolinguistic content to an ethnolect (Sect. 4.5), and a *je ne sais quoi* of erudition to a highbrow conversationalist. Urban street slang is a fertile ground for borrowings, at least in bilingual areas. Moroccan slang (from Fes) provides such examples as *kambu* 'country bumpkin, hick' (old borrowing < Spanish *campo* 'field'), *xwadri* 'pal, brother' (playful mixture of Moroccan *xu-* 'brother' and the Spanish kin-term type seen in *madre* and *padre*, with the canonical shape *CCaCCi* influenced by a Moroccan derivational formation of this template), the diglossic slang expression *l-ʕadama* 'terrific!' (< Literary Arabic 'magnificence' or 'majesty'), and the English loan *tt-sṭuna* 'get stoned (on drugs, etc.).'

See also: Language Transfer and Substrates; Contact Languages; Koinés; Intertwined Languages; Code-switching: Overview.

Bibliography

Hill J, Hill K 1986 *Speaking Mexicano*. University of Arizona Press, Tucson, AZ
Mallory J P 1989 *In Search of the Indo–Europeans*. Thames and Hudson, London
Myers-Scotton C 1993a *Social Motivations for Switching: Evidence from Africa*. Clarendon Press, Oxford, UK
Myers-Scotton C 1993b *Duelling Languages*. Clarendon Press, Oxford, UK
Odlin T 1989 *Language Transfer*. Cambridge University Press, Cambridge, UK
Thomason S G, Kaufman T 1988 *Language Contact, Creolization, and Genetic Linguistics*. University of California Press, Berkeley, CA
Weinreich U 1968 *Languages in Contact: Findings and Problems*. Mouton, The Hague

Code-mixing
R. Mesthrie

The term 'code-mixing' is a fluid one that overlaps with 'code-switching' and 'mixed code' (see *Code-switching: Overview; Intertwined Languages*), but can be distinguished from them in some ways. However, the terms are sometimes used interchangeably and not all contact linguists (including the influential Myers-Scotton, see *Myers-Scotton, Carol*) would agree that the terms are distinguishable. Milroy and Muysken (1995: 12) describe the failure of prominent researchers working on a European

Science Foundation project to come to agreement on terminology:

> ... the field of code-switching research is replete with a confusing range of terms descriptive of various aspects of the phenomenon. Sometimes the referential scope of a set of these terms overlaps and sometimes particular terms are used in different ways by different writers. When we started working together in the Research Network, one of our first endeavours was to standardise this terminology, with a view to imposing some order on a heterogeneous field of enquiry and ultimately producing rather more reader-friendly publications. This soon turned out to be an impossible task, and as a consequence no clear set of defined terms uniformly used by all authors can be found in this book.

Insofar as a distinction can be made we might say that prototypically code-switching is relatively 'clean' while mixing is relatively 'ragged.' That is, the breaks between the two codes being switched are more or less discernible (e.g., formally, across clauses or sentences; or functionally, to include a newcomer who knows only one of the codes). For code-mixing the breaks between the codes are somewhat blurred, constant switching back and forth within clauses would prototypically count as mixing. Thus code-switching leans towards the transactional, the situational, or the pragmatic—as when people switch codes according to topic or interlocutor appropriacy, say in switching from a local language like Luhya to another language of wider communication like Swahili at a marketplace in Kenya. On the other hand, code-mixing leans more towards the metaphorical function or solidarity functions as when speaker and listener are both familiar with more than code and may interchange them for special effect. The very act of mixing codes signals allegiance to a particular relationship, or local set of values. That is, the code interchange is not functional in a pragmatic sense, but rather symbolizes a lifestyle and attitude to language (hence metaphorical). Such codes may even have names that are often derogatory: e.g., Tex-Mex for code-mixing between English and Spanish in Texas.

Sometimes frequent mixing may become the norm; Myers-Scotton (1993) calls this an unmarked variety. In such a case a mixed code may well stabilize. This seems to be happening increasingly in many urban centers. However, not all code-mixing leads to a mixed code. That is, code-mixing may remain a strategy exhibited by some speakers, rather than a stable, (covertly) socially sanctioned code. Bakker and Muysken (1995) prefer the term 'intertwined languages' (see *Intertwined Languages*) in cases where the grammars of the two codes are woven together in clearly predictable ways. Thus, Michif, a North American contact language (see *Contact Languages*) has its verb phrases from Cree and its noun phrases from French (Bakker and Muysken 1995). Not all mixed codes are as predictable as this however; and it makes sense to differentiate intertwined languages as a special class of mixed codes.

Finally mixing can involve borrowing (see *Borrowing*) but is theoretically (if not always in practice) distinguishable from it. The term 'nonce borrowing' is sometimes used to show up the similarity between code-mixing and borrowings that are not established or not permanent (alternating with a word from the other language). Essentially, borrowing does not presuppose mastery of the code being borrowed from—one can use the word *perestroika* without knowing Russian. Prototypically, code-mixing does presuppose the mastery of the codes being mixed. This can be shown when in certain domains speakers might 'unmix' them; e.g., a person may speak in a mixed code *A–B* to a friend, but only use *A* with parents and only *B* with a schoolmaster. For a mixed code to be identified there ought to be a generation (or a particular social group) for whom such 'unmixing' is not possible for at least one of the two codes *A* and *B*.

See also: Code-switching: Overview; Code-switching: Discourse Models; Code-switching: Structural Models; Contact Languages; Intertwined Languages; Borrowing.

Bibliography

Bakker P, Muysken P 1995 Mixed languages and language intertwining. In: Arends J, Muysken P, Smith, N (eds.) *Pidgins and Creoles—An Introduction*. Benjamins, Amsterdam

Gumperz J J 1982 Conversational code switching. In: Gumperz J J (ed.) *Discourse Strategies*. Cambridge University Press, Cambridge, UK

Milroy L, Muysken P 1995 *One Speaker, Two Languages: Cross-Disciplinary Perspectives on Code-Switching*. Cambridge University Press, Cambridge, UK

Myers-Scotton C 1993 *Social Motivations for Code Switching: Evidence from Africa*. Clarendon, Oxford, UK

Code-switching: Discourse Models
P. Auer

One way of looking at bilingualism is to take the perspective of the bilingual conversationalist. For him or her, being bilingual means first of all being able to use two or more languages in conversation.

Although this ability to code-switch may not always be appreciated in the bilingual communities themselves, it provides specific resources not available to monolingual speakers for the constitution of socially meaningful verbal activities.

1. Conversational Code-switching

It is useful to start the discussion with two somewhat extreme positions on the meaning of conversational code-switching. The first one assumes that certain conversational activities prompt the usage of one language or the other qua activity type. A particular activity type is seen as being linked to language B such that in the environment of language A, code-alternation occurs as soon as conversationalists initiate this activity type. Code-switching occurs quasi accidentally as a consequence of alternating between activity types (cf. e.g., Fishman 1965, 1971). Blom and Gumperz (1972) speak of 'situational switching' (a notion taken up in Myers–Scotton's 'code-switching as the unmarked choice,' 1993), and believe that the situation determines language choice. The weakness of this approach becomes apparent as soon as language choice is investigated empirically. In modern bilingual societies, the relationship between languages and speech activities is by no means unambiguous. Many speech activities are not tied to one particular language, and even among those which have a tendency to be realized more often in one language than in another, the correlation is never strong enough to predict language choice in a more than probabilistic way.

The opposite view would hold that the conversational meaning of code-switching results from the mere juxtaposition of two codes which has a signaling value of its own, independent of the direction of code-alternation. No association between languages and speech activities needs to be presupposed. Rather, the language chosen for one utterance must be seen against the background of language choice in the preceding utterance. From this perspective, the question is not what verbal activities are associated with one language or the other, but instead: during which activities do bilinguals tend to switch from one language into the other. In answering this question, researchers on code-alternation have developed elaborate typologies of code-switching. They seem to converge across bilingual communities on certain conversational loci in which switching is particularly frequent (cf. Gumperz 1982), such as: (a) reported speech; (b) change of participant constellation, particularly addressee selection (this includes the use of code-switching in order to include/exclude/ marginalize co-participants or by-standers); (c) parentheses or side-comments; (d) reiterations, i.e., quasi-translations into the other language, for example for the purpose of putting emphasis e.g., on demands or requests (cf. Auer 1984b) or for purposes of clarification, or for attracting attention, e.g., in the regulation of turn-taking (e) change of activity type, also called mode shift or role shift; (f) topic shift; (g) puns, language play, shift of key from serious to playful or the other way round; and (h) topicalization, topic/comment structure.

Although lists such as this one are useful because they demonstrate that some conversational loci are particularly susceptible to code-alternation, the mere listing of such loci is problematic, for it can tell us nothing about why code-alternation may have a conversational meaning or function. The list itself will hardly ever be a closed one, which shows that code-alternation is used in a creative fashion, and that it can have conversational meaning even if used in a particular conversational environment only once. Also, the listing of conversational loci for code-alternation implies that code-alternation should have the same conversational status in both directions, i.e., from language A into B or vice versa. However, although the conversational loci for alternation listed above may in fact be used for switching in both directions in one and the same speech community, the exact conversational meaning of these cases of alternation is often not identical (cf., e.g., Auer 1984a, 1984b, Gal 1979: 112ff, Sebba and Wootton 1998, and particularly Alfonzetti 1998 for a careful discussion).

2. Conversational Patterns of Switching

In the typical bilingual speech community, the correlation between language and activity is not strong enough to make code-alternation predictable, but the direction of switching is nevertheless important for reconstructing its conversational meaning in most communities. How can this situation be accounted for? A number of studies have attempted to answer this question by applying conversation analytic methodology to code-switching, and by subjecting this phenomenon to a strictly sequential analysis (Auer 1984a, Li Wei 1994, 2002, Shin and Milroy 2000). This conversational approach has partly been complemented by looking at the meaning of code-switching as a contextualization cue, i.e., a means by which participants can contextualize the conversation locally (Gumperz 1982). Paying close attention to the details of the conversational level does not imply that 'macro' dimensions are irrelevant for the interpretation of code-switching for these researchers. Quite the contrary, the indexicality of patterns such as the ones proposed in Auer (1984a) and schematized in Auer (1995: 125ff.) provides a built-in sensibility for these dimensions: conversational regularities are both context-independent and context-sensitive. Investigation of a particular instance of switching will therefore consist of a sequential analysis of its occurrence, as well as an analysis of how the switching indexes values and stereotypical experiences attached to the two languages in the community (if any).

The most important conversational patterns of switching may be described as follows:

2.1 Discourse-related Alternational Code-switching

This refers to the alternation between a stretch of talk in one language and a stretch of talk in the other with the aim of structuring and organizing the conversation; schematically:

> *Pattern Ia:* ... A1 A2 // B1 B2 B1 ... or
> *Pattern Ib:* ... A1 // B1 B2 B1 B2 ...

(Where letters stand for languages, and numbers for speakers.) For instance, a stretch of talk in language A addresses one co-participant, and the subsequent stretch of talk by the same speaker in language B addresses another coparticipant.

2.2 Discourse-related Insertional Code-switching (Ad Hoc Borrowing)

This is the insertion of language B materials into surrounding talk in language A, again with the effect of structuring the conversation or contextualizing the meaning of the utterance in which it occurs. For instance, a lexical insertion may evoke some particular effect such as turning the utterance into a humorous one:

> *Pattern II:* ... A1[B1]A1...

The same (i.e., insertional) pattern also occurs without a discourse-related interpretation, as a consequence/indication of a speaker's or recipient's lack of competence in language A (competence-related insertional code-switching).

2.3 Preference-related Alternational Code-switching

This involves the following pattern:

> *Pattern IIIa:* ... A1 B2 A1 B2 A1 B2 A1 B2 ...
> (sustained divergence of language choices between two participants) or
> *Pattern IIIb:* ... A1 B2 A1 B2 A1// A2 A1 A2 A1 ...
> (language negotiation sequence: convergence of language choices; cf. Auer 2000).

3. Analyzing the Patterns

In contrast with discourse-related switching, where the new language prototypically evokes a new 'frame' or 'footing' for the interaction which is then shared by all participants, preference-related switching results in more or less persistent phases of divergent language choices. This is a marked state of affairs for many bilingual speech communities, though certainly not for all, which is often accounted for by reference to certain attributes of the individual who performs this switching, or his or her coparticipants (hence the notion of participant-related switching in Auer 1984a). The exact nature of this ascription is dependent on the wider social, political, and cultural context of the interaction at hand (cf. Rampton 1998).

Discourse- and preference-related switching are not strictly separated. In pattern IIIb, for instance, the transition from divergent to convergent language choices (i.e., the moment where one common language-of-interaction is found) may take on discourse-related meanings. The same holds for the beginning of a sequence of divergent language choices, unless it coincides with the beginning of the episode as a whole.

The focal case of most research on code-switching has been Pattern I so far. In Auer 1999, I have portrayed the prototypical case of this discourse-related, alternational code-switching as follows: (a) It occurs in a sociolinguistic context in which speakers orient themselves towards a preference for one language at a time; i.e., it is usually possible to identify the language-of-interaction which is valid at a given moment, and until code-switching occurs; (b) through its departure from this established language-of-interaction, code-switching signals 'otherness' of the forthcoming contextual frame and thereby achieves a change of 'footing.' The precise interpretation of this new footing needs to be 'filled in' in each individual case, although previous episodes may also be brought to bear on the interpretation of the case at hand; (c) it seems possible to describe the mechanisms by which code-switching relates to the two codes and to the context in which it occurs in very general ways. Contexts are theoretically innumerable, of course, as are the interactional meanings of code-switching; however the ways in which these meanings are construed remain constant from one community to the next; (d) code-switching may be called a personal or group style. As a group style, its use may be subject to normative constraints valid within a speech community; however, it certainly is not a variety in its own right; (e) most code-switches occur at major syntactic and prosodic boundaries (at clause or sentence level). Since switching serves to contextualize certain linguistic activities, the utterance units affected by the switch must be large enough to constitute such an activity. For this reason, code-switching (in this restricted sense) does not provide much interesting data for syntactic research; (f) although code-switching bilinguals may be highly proficient in both languages, balanced proficiency is by no means a prerequisite. Indeed, code-switching is possible with a very limited knowledge of the 'other' language.

In order to ascertain that we are dealing with code-switching in a particular case of the juxtaposition of two co-occurring sets of structural parameters, it is essential to show that speakers orient themselves towards this juxtaposition. Therefore the question of what counts as a code must refer to participants', not to linguists' notions of 'code A' and 'code B.' An 'objective' statement (i.e., one exclusively informed by the 'linguistic facts,' such as (the absence of) phonological or morphological integration, or frequency) that a given arrangement of signs constitutes a combination of elements of two systems is not only very difficult to make at times, it is also irrelevant. There may be cases in which the two codes juxtaposed are 'objectively speaking' very similar, yet regarded by the members of a bilingual community as completely separate (as in some cases of some dialect/standard switching; cf. Alfonzetti 1998 for Sicily), just as there may be codes which are 'objectively speaking' very distinct but nevertheless are seen as nondistinct by the speakers. Also, it needs to be remembered that the languages involved in code-switching in a bilingual community may be considerably different from their monolingual relatives due to convergence as a consequence of long-standing language contact (cf. Clyne 1987, Gumperz 1982: 84ff.). A methodology to prove participants' orientation towards the juxtaposition is precisely to show that it is used as a contextualization cue (i.e., that it is 'functional' cf. Alvarez-Cáccamo 1998). Further evidence is provided by self- and other-corrections of language choice (cf. Gafaranga 2000).

Keeping this restricted and strict notion of (discourse-related) code-switching in mind, it goes without saying that there are many phenomena of bilingual speech, which do not conform to it. Those, in which the boundaries between one language and the other are less clear, in which the notion of what is language A and what is language B is open to dispute, in which the preference for one language at a time does not hold and in which the use of more than one language may not carry any or only highly ambivalent meanings (cf. Woolard 1999). The large field of these 'other' phenomena of bilingual speech is subsumed under various headings, such as 'mixing' (Auer 1999, Meeuwis and Blommaert 1998), 'frequent code-switching,' or 'code-switching as the unmarked choice' (Myers-Scotton 1993). The question of how in these forms of talk an analysis can be made from a discourse perspective is still largely open.

Bibliography

Alfonzetti G 1998 The conversational dimension in code-switching between Italian and dialect in Sicily. In: Auer P (ed.) *Code-switching in Conversation*. Routledge, London

Alvarez-Cáccamo C 1998 From 'switching code' to 'code-switching': Towards a reconceptualisation of communicative codes. In: Auer P (ed.) *Code-switching in Conversation*. Routledge, London

Auer P 1984a *Bilingual Conversation*. Benjamins, Amsterdam

Auer P 1984b On the meaning of conversational code-switching. In: Auer P, Di Luzio A (eds.) *Interpretive Sociolinguistics*. Narr, Tübingen, Germany

Auer P 1995 The pragmatics of code-switching: A sequential approach. In: Milroy L, Muysken P (eds.) *One Speaker, Two Languages*. Cambridge University Press, Cambridge, UK

Auer P 1999 From code-switching via mixing toward fused varieties: Steps toward a dynamic typology of bilingual speech. *International Journal of Bilingualism* **3**: 309–32

Auer P 2000 Why should we and how can we determine the 'base language' of a bilingual conversation? *Estudios de Sociolingüística* **1**: 129–44

Blom J P, Gumperz J J 1972 Social meaning in linguistic structures: Code-switching in Norway. In: Gumperz J, Hymes D (eds.) *Directions in Sociolinguistics*. Holt, Rinehart and Winston, New York

Clyne M 1987 Constraints on code-switching: How universal are they? *Linguistics* **25**: 739–64

Fishman J A 1965 Who speaks what language to who and when? *La Linguistique* **2**: 67–88

Fishman J A 1971 *Sociolinguistics*. Newbury, Rowley, MA

Gafaranga J 2000 Medium repair versus other-language repair: Telling the medium of a bilingual conversation. *International Journal of Bilingualism* **4**: 327–50

Gal S 1979 *Language Shift*. Academic Press, New York

Gumperz J 1982 *Discourse Strategies*. Cambridge University Press, Cambridge, UK

Li Wei 1994 *Three Generations, Two Languages, One Family*. Multilingual Matters, Clevedon, UK

Li Wei 2002 What do you want me to say? On the conversation analysis approach to bilingual interaction. *Language and Society* **31**(2)

Meeuwis M, Blommaert J 1998 A monolectal view of code-switching: Layered code-switching among Zairians in Belgium. In: Auer P (ed.) *Code-switching in Conversation*. Routledge, London

Myers-Scotton C 1993 *Social Motivations of Code-switching*. Clarendon Press, Oxford, UK

Rampton B 1998 Language crossing and the redefinition of reality. In: Auer P (ed.) *Code-switching in Conversation*. Routledge, London

Sebba M, Wootton A 1998 We, they and identity: Sequential versus identity-related explanation in code-switching. In: Auer P (ed.) *Code-switching in Conversation*. Routledge, London

Shin S J, Milroy L 2000 Conversational codeswitching among Korean-English bilingual children. *International Journal of Bilingualism* **4**: 351–84

Woolard K A 1999 Simultaneity and bivalency as strategies in bilingualism. *Journal of Linguistic Anthropology* **8**: 3–29

Code-switching: Overview
K. M. McCormick

Taken broadly, the term 'code-switching' refers to the juxtaposition of elements from two (or more) languages or dialects. There is, however, little agreement among scholars on either the semantic scope of the term as they use it, or the nature of distinctions to be drawn between it and other, related terms such as diglossia, code shifting, code mixing, style shifting, borrowing. Despite several papers addressing the problems of terminological confusion, there is still no consensus.

Disagreement arises on classificatory criteria such as length of the juxtaposed utterances (whole discourses at one end of the spectrum, to single words containing morphemes from two languages, at the other); density of switches in a given spoken or written text; whether the switch in question is an individual and unusual one or an instance of a type that is common in the speech community; the presence or absence of social significance in the switch and, where the switch is significant, the nature of that significance; consciousness on the part of the speaker that elements from two codes are being used. Figure 1 is a schematic representation of what the terms have, variously, been used to signify with regard to relative length of juxtaposed elements and density of switching. It is no more than a rough guide to indicate areas of overlap or synonymy.

Terms	Length of juxtaposed utterances	Density of switching
diglossia	whole discourse types	low
situational code-switching	whole conversations, in one context	low
metaphoric code-switching	whole conversations, each within one role relationship	low
conversational code-switching; style shifting; code mixing	whole conversational turns/chunks within a turn: whole sentences or clauses/whole clause constituents	high
single-word code-switching; borrowing	words	low/high
integrated loanwords	morphemes	low/high

Figure 1. Schematic representation of scope of terms used to designate types of code juxtaposition.

Code-switching of all kinds is of interest to sociolinguists, while particular types are of interest to other disciplines. Switches involving longer elements such as whole discourses indicate something about societal patterns and are thus of interest to sociologists and anthropologists. Conversation analysts examine switches of all types that occur within a conversation since they are often ways of realizing various conversational strategies. Of interest to psycholinguists are questions of how the brain stores, distinguishes between, and selects various codes for use in particular instances. A rich field for syntacticians is the area of intrasentential switching between languages, especially in cases where the rules for the formation of particular structures are different in the two languages. For linguists in general, code-switching raises metatheoretical challenges. These include how to conceptualize boundaries between languages; how to develop criteria for classifying loanwords; how to use the scope of analytic models using binary opposition and those using the idea of a spectrum; and how to exploit the heuristic value of system-based and speaker-based perspectives on data (see *Language in Society: Overview*; *Sociology of Language*; *Code, Sociolinguistic*).

This article deals with topics and developments within the field of code-switching research in the order in which they arose, which is roughly as follows. Early work (in the 1950s and 1960s) focused on the functional distribution of codes in speech communities. Arising out of this work was research which looked at the factors that facilitated or prevented the acquisition of particular codes by some social groups but not others, and at the relevant societal power-relationships between the groups. Complementary to this concern with broad societal dynamics was the narrower focus—particularly by conversation analysts—on how individuals deployed their repertoire of codes, for example switching from one to another in order to shift the balance of power during a conversation, or to achieve a particular stylistic effect. By the mid-1970s syntacticians were examining the structures of intrasentential code-switches to see what kinds of rules governed them. During the course of this work questions arose about the relative merits of different explanatory models and different kinds of grammar. This, in turn, has led to a radical questioning of assumptions on which earlier work was based, for example the assumption that dialects are sufficiently distinguishable from one another linguistically to make possible the identification of points at which there is a switch from one to another. In the 1990s an important research focus was the relationship between the associations that a language variety as a whole had in a community, and the significance of a switch to that language variety in a particular conversational turn. It was found that there is not necessarily a transfer of associations from the macro to the micro level. Much contemporary work on code-switching is metatheoretical, seeking to construct theoretical models which take into account the social, grammatical and cognitive aspects of code-switching. (See for example Tabouret-Keller 1995.) For a sense of recent directions and findings in code-switching research, see the papers in Milroy and Muysken (1995) and Auer (1998).

1. Code-switching Governed by Societal Norms

In diglossic speech communities (see *Diglossia*) the functional distribution of codes is publicly acknowledged and institutionally supported. As the term 'diglossia' suggests, there are two codes that feature prominently in the community. One is used on high status occasions (and has come to be referred to in studies of diglossia as the 'H code'), and the other is used for more mundane, low status functions (and is known as the 'L code'). In such communities there is very little overlap in the codes' functions. Typically, the H variety is learned at school, not at home, and is reserved for very formal discourse such as public prayer, secular ceremonies, legal transactions, news broadcasts. The other code is used for less formal discourse, for example for discussing a lecture given in the H variety. The H may be a classical form of the language (as in the case of literary Tamil and classical Arabic) as distinct from the local contemporary dialects of those languages which are used for L functions. The H may also be the contemporary standard dialect (for example standard German in Switzerland) as distinct from a regional dialect (like Swiss German). The term 'diglossia' has been extended to cover situations where the H and L codes are different languages, one of which has greater prestige than the other. All members of a diglossic speech community would know that they ought to switch to the H variety in particular circumstances but in those communities where the H variety is learned only through formal education, people whose formal education was limited would not be able to code-switch with ease: they would be unable to use the H code in any but the most ritualized exchanges for which appropriate responses could have been learned by rote.

In many bidialectal, bilingual, or multilingual speech communities distinctions among occasions and codes are not primarily hierarchical: the codes may be perceived as different but be equally valued, and similarly the situations may be differentiated on grounds other than prestige. This 'looser' kind of code-switching for different occasions is commonly referred to as 'situational code-switching.' Although the term foregrounds the situation, other factors which are relevant in determining code choice are; what the topic of conversation is and who the speakers are—this includes a consideration of their roles and of their personal relationship. An account of situational switching which gives both broad patterns and cameos of interpersonal interaction is to be found in Denison's (1972) study of a speech community in northern Italy (see also *Speech Community*; *Role Theory*).

At the time when the study was done, everyone in the district of Sauris spoke dialects of Friulian and German and the national language, Italian. There were clear norms of appropriateness governing code choice: German was for use between spouses in the home; Friulian with neighbors in informal settings such as the market and the tavern; and Italian for more formal interactions centered on church, school and the workplace and also for use in the presence of strangers. There was a developing tendency for parents to try to use Italian at home with their children in order to promote their skill in the language of the school.

In communities like this one where the domains requiring different codes are those of everyday life, it would be normal for adult members of the speech community to have a good command of all codes because they would use all of them fairly frequently. Competence in switching appropriately would not be the preserve of those with formal education, as is the case in many diglossic communities. Inappropriate language choice would be recognized as a breach of convention with particular social significance, as is seen in Denison's account of an incident in a Saurian tavern.

An argument took place between husband and wife in the tavern, a public but informal setting where the normal code choice would be Friulian. The husband was in the tavern talking to his friends when his wife entered, clearly angry. She addressed him in German, the language of the home, thus defining the situation as a domestic one. He replied in Friulian, attempting to redefine it as a public social occasion where domestic strife should not appear. After just one phrase in Friulian she resisted the switch, persisted in German, and he eventually capitulated, in German. What seems to be at issue is the definition of the social space as public or private: if public, Friulian would be spoken and a domestic row would be out of place; if private, German would be used and domestic strife would be accommodated. The speakers' initial resistance to each other's code choices was part of the contest for power.

An uncontested change of code during an interaction between two people can mark the foregrounding of a different facet of the relationship between them. Scotton (1979: 85) provides an example of such a switch which has the effect of limiting the scope of one set of rights and obligations and bringing another set into play. The encounter took place in a shop in Kenya.

> A brother who runs a wholesale shop greets his sister, who has come to buy a few grams of salt. Both are Babukusu (a subgroup of the Baluyia). The brother greets the sister in their own first language, Lubukusu. But he soon switches to Swahili, the locally recognized language of trade. 'This codeswitching reminds the sister that the shop is run as a business geared to profit-making,' reported our correspondent about this incident. 'By continuing to speak some Lubukusu, he lets his sister know that he remembers their relationship, but by speaking some Swahili, he reminds her that he is a businessman and that she cannot ask for more free salt.'

It is possible that all participants in conversation quite unconsciously use a code which they consciously regard as inappropriate for a particular circumstance. This was observed in a village in northern Norway when students, home on vacation from a university further south, were engaged in arguments among themselves in which their intellectual status was at issue. On these occasions they switched to the standard language, Bokmål, from the local dialect, Ranamål, towards which they had very positive feelings and which is the only dialect regarded as appropriate for informal conversation among friends. Blom and Gumperz (1972) report that the students were shocked to find that they had switched in this way and undertook to refrain from doing so in future, their use of Bokmål having transgressed norms that they respected. In spite of their determination, further transgressions occurred. Instances such as these suggest that code-switching is not always a matter of conscious choice and control.

In sum, if there is a change in any one of the factors associated with situational switching—context, topic, participants—or if there is a change in perceptions of that factor, it may trigger a switch to another code (see also *Bilingualism, Societal*).

2. Conversational Code-switching

Conversational code-switching differs from situational switching in that its occurrence is not dependent on a change of interlocutors, topic or situation. It is to be found within conversations and not necessarily only between turns—a switch may take place within one speaker's turn as it does in the following sentence (Gumperz and Hernandez-Chavez 1972: 87):

> *Te digo que este dedo* has been bothering me so much [I tell you that this finger ...]

The factors governing conversational switching appear to be more subtle than those involved in situational switching. Consequently, they may be harder to identify with certainty. In some cases—like the switch quoted above—they are practically impossible to account for. At times speakers are conscious of switching while at other times they are not. Switching by fluent bilinguals serves a range of stylistic purposes and may also signal minor fluctuations in the interlocutors' feeling towards each other during the course of the conversation in which the broad roles remain the same.

Research into conversational code-switching has three main foci: the social factors underlying switching, the stylistic and other pragmatic effects achieved by it, and the linguistic features of discourse containing frequent code-switches. The first two are dealt with in this section and the third in Sect. 3.

Whether or not, and how a speaker switches languages or dialects during a conversation may convey social information. It may, for example, indicate the recognition of a bond between interlocutors arising from shared background or interests. This purpose can be served by switches of different lengths and density.

If dense code-switching is a preferred mode of discourse in a group it may come to be, itself, a code that is to be distinguished from monolingual codes in the wider community. Where this has been documented, the mixed code serves to identify its users as people who, for various reasons, do not feel part of the communities most strongly associated with either of contributing languages. The mixed code can serve as an indicator of group identity. It has done so for many Chicanos in the Southwestern USA who feel that they are a group distinct from non-Hispanic English speakers and also from Spanish-speaking Mexicans. One way of indicating their group identity as Chicanos is to draw freely on both languages. This practice results in a code which speakers use when the context demands a contrast with the standard dialects of the two contributing languages and what they symbolize. A working-class speech community in South Africa, classified 'colored' and marginalized through the application of a series of apartheid laws, reveals its dissociation from white English and Afrikaans speakers and from the middle class, linguistically. It is unacceptable to speak the standard dialects of either language to one's neighbors. The vernacular, characterized by dense code-switching, is at once the medium of communication and a powerful symbol of belonging to the local community. In response to the question about what would happen if a neighbor addressed one in standard English or Afrikaans, the following was a typical response:

> For one thing I think the person himself will feel quite awkward. People would look at him strange, you know. They'd straight away identify there's something wrong with the person's speech and he will automatically try to rectify it and try to join in. I think that is why people mix their language also, you know.
>
> (McCormick 1990: 91)

An aspect of a speaker's identity can also be signaled by a brief excursion into a second code: by dropping a word or phrase from another language or dialect into a conversation, a speaker can make evoke a reference group that would be recognized by other participants. For example, using a Yiddish exclamation such as 'Oi gewalt!' in an English conversation gives a glancing acknowledgment of Jewish background. Such switches often serve as much a symbolic function as a referential one. They mark the speaker as an insider in the domain or reference group in which the term has currency. Speakers who switch in this way may or may not wish to suggest that the interlocutors are also insiders. They do not always indicate that the speakers are proficient in the language or dialect from which the phrase was taken—often they are not. Limón (1982: 320) discusses the conscious political and strategic use of code-switching made by members of a Chicano student society. One of the means by which they try to gain credibility is to switch of folk Spanish, as is indicated by an interviewee (see also *Ethnicity and Language*):

> Yeah, with these guys you have to do that [use Spanish] otherwise nobody listens to you ... it's really funny ... even though the members don't speak that much Spanish ... if you don't use some ... they'll think you're *agringado* ... these guys are good at it *y te chingon* [they'll screw you].

Switching back and forth between two languages or dialects can be a strategy to indicate a speaker's neutrality with respect to contending parties or ideas if these are associated with different codes (Scotton 1979).

Among speakers who share a command of the same code repertoire, switching can be a means of achieving a range of stylistic effects within a conversation. Sometimes a speaker will switch to another code while making a remark that is not part of the main narrative. The switches into and out of a new code mark the boundaries of the parenthetic remark. According to Sebba and Wootton (1984: 4), this is what happens with the switch from London Jamaican into London Black English in the following extract of a conversation where the speaker interrupts her main narrative to try to recall when the event took place:

> man Leonie 'ave party when ... don' remember when it was *bot shi did tel aal o dem no fi (t) se notin kaaz shi no waan tu moch Catford gyal di de*
> [man Leonie had a party ... but she did tell all of them not to say anything because she didn't want too many Catford girls there]

Material may also be foregrounded by a change of code. This often happens when someone quotes what was said on another occasion: the quoted words are given in a code other than the one being used in the current conversation to distinguish them from it. The examples below show a switch from Judeo-Spanish to Hebrew (Berk-Seligson 1986: 323–4):

> Le díši *'ma aní asé?'*
> [I said to her 'What am I to do?']
>
> 'Ma yeš?' le digo. *'Šš, givéret, ma at tsoéket!'*
> ['What's the matter?' I say to him. 'Sh. madam, what are you shouting about!']

It should be noted that this changing of code for direct quotation is not always mimetic; it does not always capture the code actually used by the original speaker.

Apparently simple repetition may gain added force from a change of code as in the extract below, where the London Jamaican version suggests that the speaker 'won't ever' go outside for air:

> I don't wanna go outside for fresh air, right, *mi na a go outsaid fa no fresh ier*
>
> (Sebba and Wootton 1984: 7)

Semantic contrast and balance in syntactic structure may be highlighted by having two focal sections of an utterance in different codes:

> *No vay ronto como iba pero* I still believe in it you know [I don't go as much as I used but ...]
>
> (Pfaff 1979: 312)

The choice of code for each section may not be random, though it may be unconscious. It has been found, for example, that matters particularly associated with ethnic identity are often described or referred to in the code most strongly associated with that identity. Bentahila (1983: 235) describes the typical switch from French to Arabic when bilingual Moroccans mention matters to do with religion, and gives the following example:

> c'est une femme de marque qui est *f ši škl tmši tzur SSalḥi:n*
> [she is a special woman who is the sort who goes to visit saints' tombs]

A switch from one language variety to another may index a particular socially significant factor, but it may not. Not all switches are linked to macro factors. Some simply serve as contextualisation cues, alerting the listener to a slight change in conversational activity, for example from narrating to commenting.

Humor can be achieved (or heightened) by a shift to another language or dialect if this triggers particular associations in the minds of the listeners. Sarcastic or ironic comment may also be delivered in a contrasting code. Like several other writers whose readers are bilingual, Dangor takes advantage of the possibility of switching languages to heighten contrast in register. In the following extract from a short story, a character's bitter response to news that his lover is to be respectably married finds expression in the juxtaposition of a high register word in English with an obscenity in Afrikaans:

> And tomorrow you marry, medora on your head, your face veiled and hidden. Cossetted like a virgin, offered as noble sacrifice. And the willing smile on your face. Destiny Destiny!
> Destiny *sc moer* [Literally, 'Destiny's womb']
> (Dangor 1981: 2)

Some kinds of code-switches seem to have more to do with linguistic factors than with stylistic effect of social context. They arise as a result of either a lexical gap in the language itself or in a speaker's vocabulary. It has been suggested that single loanwords may trigger a switch into a different language even when the rest of the utterance would have been equally possible in the first language, as in the following example of a switch from Arabic to French:

> ana maʕrftš fuqaš jži raši:d qalk l *weekend je ne sais pas quand est-ce que le weekend d'après lui*
> [I don't know when Rachid is coming: he said at the weekend. I don't know when the weekend is according to him.]
> (Bentahila 1983: 236)

With 'weekend' having become established in the French lexicon, and Arabic having no equivalent, this speaker inserts 'weekend' into an Arabic sentence and then continues in French. The first French phrase is clearly not an instance of filling a lexical gap as it is the equivalent of the opening Arabic phrase.

There are times when a switch may help cope with gaps that exist not in the language but in the speaker's vocabulary. Sometimes these are temporary gaps, resulting from an inability to recall a word in the language being used at the time, but able to recall it in another one. In such cases it is not uncommon to find that the speaker stays in the second code longer than is necessary to fill the lexical gap, as the following example shows: the repetition and voiced hesitation suggest a lexical gap in English for 'children'—a temporary gap, as a later stage of the conversation showed (McCormick 1990: 104) (see also *Bilingualism, Societal*; *Borrowing*):

> that is the day really a day of giving too because the the uh *kinders kom en hulle wil ook 'n stukkie eet nou*
> [...children come and they also want to eat a bit now...]

3. Grammatical Analyses of Intrasentential Code-switching and the Theoretical Issues it Raises

Analysis of dense intrasentential code-switching is very challenging, particularly as there is often some phonological and syntactic convergence as well as lexical borrowing. This makes code boundaries difficult to identify. The example below is part of an adolescent boy's account of a wedding. He was a Panjabi speaker born and brought up in Leeds. (The text is given in phonetic script with the word by word translation immediately below each line.)

> saːre ɟəne otthe / ɔlukən siːɪz rɛd / gɛɔ aɔ /
> all people there / all you can see is red / get a
>
> wumən wɛərin rɛd suːts / mus bi feːvrɪt kulə / ʌnd
> women wearing red suits / must be favorite color / and
>
> ɟʌnɟ bunɖi otthe kotʃ ɟaːnɖa: / waef nu lɛke / t̪ə
> marriage takes place there coach goes / wife having taken / and
>
> ɟelo pagz paidijã: / t̪e otthe drunk hunɖa: feːz /ʌn ðə we /
> yellow turbans wear / and there drunk gets then / on the way /
>
> sʌmtaim faʌɔs: /maːr piːpəl drink tuː mʌtʃ /ɪɔgaɔs ɪn yuʌ had /
> sometimes fights /hit people drink too much /it gets in yours head /
>
> dʒʌs haːpi ða de / ðaɔsɪɔðn /nɛks de brin ðə waif hɪe /
> just happy that day / that's it 'then / next day bring the wife here /
>
> avunɖə paːɔi ən wi ɔl go hoːm /
> have another party and we all go home /
> (Agnihotri 1987: 129)

Intrasentential code-switching involving two (or more) languages is particularly interesting to syntacticians because it entails the interplay of grammatical rules from different systems and the rules for the formation of some structures may be incompatible. For example, the Spanish and English rules for the placement of adjectives in a noun phrase are diammetrically opposed: the Spanish rule places almost all adjectives after the noun whereas the English rule places them before the noun. How do fluent Spanish–English code-switchers construct a noun phrase that contains an adjective? Do they avoid switching within the NP or do they make a choice which violates the rule of one of the languages? Although lay people often judge code-switching to be both a product and a sign of linguistic incompetence, early analyses of fluent conversational code-switching data yielded little evidence of ungrammaticality. This led linguists to believe that there might be grammatical constraints on where switches could take place—the operation of these constraints would prevent the formation of ungrammatical strings. Later analysts, who detected nonstandard but regularly occurring structures composed of elements from two languages, argued that fluent, dense code-switching might affect the grammar of either or both dialects, causing them to converge.

Research on the grammatical aspect of code-switching can be seen as falling into four broad types, depending on the researcher's prime concern (though in most projects there are traces of one or more of the other types). They examine: language-specific constraints; the possible existence of universal constraints; the requirements of a model of grammar that would best capture the rules of code-switching; the validity of the assumptions underlying research into grammatical constraints on code-switching.

Much of the work done in the 1970s was directed towards finding evidence of nonrandomness in morphosyntactic aspects of code-switching. Studies tried to identify the rules which disallowed switching at particular junctures. Reports of the findings often included lists of several rules governing particular structures. The data for these early studies usually came from particular bilingual situations—the studies were not comparative. The constraints identified were thus language-specific though sometimes the wording suggested that they were general.

In 1980, Poplack (see *Poplack, Shana*) suggested that two constraints might be universal. They were the 'free morpheme constraint' and the 'equivalence constraint,' which she defined as follows:

The free morpheme constraint. Codes may be switched after any constituent in discourse provided that constituent is not a bound morpheme. This constraint holds true for all linguistic levels but the phonological (p. 587).
The equivalence constraint. Code-switches will tend to occur at points in discourse where juxtaposition of L1 and L2 elements does not violate a syntactic rule of either language, i.e., at points around which the surface structures of the two languages map onto each other p. 586).

These hypothesized universals were regarded with great interest and in the early 1980s their applicability to various sets of data was tested. Studies of other Spanish–English data seemed to validate the constraints, but the universality of the equivalence constraint was found not to hold in cases of switching between languages less similar to each other than English and Spanish, for example Arabic/French and Spanish/Hebrew. The free morpheme constraint, on the other hand, did hold.

Closely related to the work on grammatical constraints were attempts to find a model for a grammar which would be able to account for rule-governed code-switching. The necessity of positing a 'third grammar,' a grammar of switching was considered, as was the possibility that rule-governed switching could be adequately accounted for on the basis of the rules of the two contributing languages. Pfaff (1979) thought there was no need to argue for a third grammar, whereas Poplack, a year later, suggested that code-switching might emanate from 'a single code-switching grammar composed of the overlapping sectors of the grammars of L1 and L2' (1980: 615). Sankoff and Poplack (1981) developed that idea by suggesting that a 'third grammar' could subsume the two monolingual grammars, thus providing a single framework within which discourse characterized by dense code-switching could be analyzed. Romaine argued that a third grammar might not simply draw two monolingual grammars into one framework, but might have to be what she called a 'convergent grammar' because it was possible that 'the internal structure of the mixed constituent need not conform to the constituent structure rules required for monolingual grammars of either language' (Ms n.d.: 27).

An alternative to positing the existence of a third grammar, was the suggestion that rule-governed switching could be accounted for by the modification of existing frameworks (see *Code-switching: Structural Models*). Models of grammar that had been developed to account for monolingual structures were explored and compared for their capacity to be extended to cover bilingual structures. For example, Di Sciullo et al. (1986: 23) claim that:

the general restrictions on code-mixing need not be stated anywhere, but arise from general conventions of language indexing.

Analysis of the grammaticality of utterances containing a code-switch depends on identifying the switch point in an utterance, and, where there has been convergence between the two codes, this identification is not a simple matter. It generates a series of questions that have important implications for other fields of linguistics. Work on dense code-switching has brought to the fore problems about the often *ad hoc* way in which, in practice, words are categorized as belonging to one language or another. From what might be called a 'systems perspective' (based on knowledge of the set of structures and the lexicon said to constitute a particular language), a word might seem to belong to Language A and be a foreign import in Language B, because the historical roots of the word are known to the analyst doing the categorizing. But what of the speaker's perspective? What if the speaker does not know that a particular word is a loanword, should it necessarily be regarded as one? If the word in question is at the juncture between phrases in two codes, to which should it be said to belong? If one takes a long historical perspective, a large part of the vocabulary of many languages could be said to consist of loanwords. All languages change. What should the criteria be for categorizing what was once a loanword as an established item in the receiving language's lexicon? Length of time over which it has appeared in the receiving language? Frequency of use, and if so, use by whom—formally educated speakers? Speakers' awareness of the word's origin, and if so, which speakers? Coexistence with or replacement of equivalent item in the receiving language? Morphological or phonological adaptation to the system of the receiving language?

If it is difficult to give clearcut answers to these questions when two languages are involved, it is even more difficult to answer them when dealing with switches between two dialects or styles. In the case of dialect or style switching there is a far larger proportion of the vocabulary and other linguistic features common to both codes, and systematic descriptions of both codes are seldom available for use as points of reference. In such cases analysts have to rely more heavily on their (or their subjects') intuitions about what constitutes each of the codes juxtaposed in the switch. But if code-switching between languages and between dialects serves similar stylistic and social purposes, should the analysis not deal with them in the same way, giving equal weight to systems or to speakers? It has recently been argued (Auer 1998: 13) that the speaker's perspective should carry more weight than the linguist's in determining what constitutes a code or an instance of code-switching. This approach makes it possible to conceive of a bilingual code. It allows for dense switching between two language varieties to be regarded as one code in cases where such switching functions as one code for its users (see *Code-switching: Discourse Models*). In much early research the term 'code' was assumed to be synonymous with 'language variety' and it was thus assumed that alternation of language varieties constituted code-switching. The assumed synonymy has recently been questioned. Different perspectives generate different analytic models and tools which illuminate different aspects of the data. In doing lexical and syntactic analyses of dense code-switching linguists might benefit from the example of physicists who find it productive to analyze light as both waves and particles, although these two models might appear to be irreconcilable. Some contemporary work explores the productiveness of using both speaker's and linguist's perspectives on what constitutes a code and a code-switch in a particular speech community's repertoire.

4. Code-switching: Deficit or Skill?

When code-switching is discussed the question of speakers' competence is frequently raised: are code-switching and linguistic competence mutually exclusive? Because it is popularly believed that switching is a result of incompetence rather than of a fine sense of the unique effects that it can achieve, switching is often stigmatized. People say that those who switch 'can't speak properly' or 'make a mess' of the languages they use.

On closer examination it appears that two types of switching are differently regarded. Whereas diglossic and situational code-switching are often regarded as necessary manifestations of bilingualism, and are valued as part of a speaker's communicative competence, conversational switching is often overtly stigmatized. Covertly it may be valued for its rhetorical possibilities and as a group-marker. The crucial linguistic difference between the two types of switching that probably accounts for this difference in attitude is that situational switching involves the production and comprehension of long strings in each language, so fluency is apparent, whereas in conversational code-switching the switch is frequently intrasentential, allowing for an impression that speakers are insufficiently proficient in either language to be able to finish what they want to say, in one language.

A common assumption is that people switch languages because of gaps in their personal vocabulary. As is shown in examples cited above, this is true in some cases but not in others. The study of a large corpus of data from a member of a bilingual, code-switching community will often show the speaker using the words for a concept from both languages. Witty, quick, elegant shifts between codes are often appreciated in the speech community. Proficient bilinguals or bidialectals who switch codes consciously or unconsciously achieve particular social, political, or rhetorical effects. They are able to draw on a bigger linguistic pool than they would be if they and their interlocutors were monodialectal or monolingual.

> Code switching is a communicative skill, which speakers use as a verbal strategy in much the same way that skillful writers switch styles in a short story.
> (Gumperz and Hernandez-Chavez 1972: 98)

See also: Code-mixing; Code-switching: Sociopragmatic Models.

Bibliography

Agnihotri R K 1987 *Crisis of Identity: A Sociolinguistic Study of Sikh Children in Leeds*. Bahri Publications, Delhi, India

Amastae J, Elias-Olivares L (eds.) 1982 *Spanish in the United States: Sociolinguistic Aspects*. Cambridge University Press, Cambridge, UK

Auer P (ed.) 1998 *Code-switching in Conversation: Language, Interaction, and Identity*. Routledge, London

Bentahila A 1983 Motivations for code-switching among Arabic–French bilinguals in Morocco. *Language and Communication* 3(3): 233–43

Berk-Seligson S 1986 Linguistic constraints on intrasentential code-switching: A study of Spanish/Hebrew bilingualism. *Language in Society* 15: 313–48

Blom J P, Gumperz J J 1972 Social meaning in linguistic structures: Code-switching in Norway. In: Gumperz J J, Hymes D (eds.) *Directions in Sociolinguistics: The Ethnography of Communication*. Holt, Rinehart and Winston, New York

Clyne M 1987 Constraints on code switching: How universal are they? *Linguistics* **25**: 739–64
Dangor A 1981 *Waiting for Leila*. Ravan Press, Johannesburg, South Africa
Denison N 1972 Some observations on language variety and plurilingualism. In: Pride J B, Holmes J (eds.) *Sociolinguistics*. Penguin, Harmondsworth, UK
Di Sciullo A M, Muysken P, Singh R 1986 Government and code-mixing. *Journal of Linguistics* **22**: 1–24
Gumperz J J, Hernandez-Chavez E 1972 Bilingualism, bidialectalism and classroom interaction. In: Cazden C, John V P, Hymes D (eds.) *Functions of Language in the Classroom*. Columbia Teachers College Press, New York
Limón J 1982 El meeting: History, folk Spanish, and ethnic nationalism in a Chicago student community. In: Amastae J, Elias-Olivares L (eds.) *Spanish in the United States: Sociolinguistic Aspects*. Cambridge University Press, Cambridge, UK
McCormick K 1990 The vernacular of District Six. In: Jeppe S, Soudien C (eds.) *The Struggle for District Six: Past and Present*. Buchu Books, Cape Town, South Africa
Milroy L, Muysken P (eds.) 1995 *One Speaker, Two Languages: Cross Disciplinary Perspectives on Code-switching*. Cambridge University Press, Cambridge, UK
Pfaff C W 1979 Constraints on language mixing: Intrasentential code-switching and borrowing in Spanish/English. *Language* **55**(2): 291–318
Poplack S 1980 Sometimes I'll start a sentence in English Y TERMINO EN ESPAÑOL: Toward a typology of code-switching. *Linguistics* **18**: 581–618
Romaine S (Ms n.d.) The notion of government as a constraint on language mixing: some evidence from the code-mixed compound verb in Panjabi.
Sankoff D, Poplack S 1981 A formal grammar for code-switching. *Papers in Linguistics* **14**: 3–46
Scotton C M 1979 Code-switching as a 'safe choice' in choosing in lingua franca. In: McCormack W C, Wurm S (eds.) *Language and Society: Anthropological Issues*. Mouton, The Hague
Sebba M, Wootton T 1984 Conversational code-switching in London Jamaican. Paper presented at Sociolinguistics Symposium, University of Liverpool, Liverpool, UK

Code-switching: Sociopragmatic Models
S. Gross

In many bi- and multilingual communities around the world, speakers need to choose, often at an unconscious level, which language to use in their interactions with other members of the community. One of the choices that bilingual speakers often make is to code-switch; that is, speakers switch back and forth between languages, even within the same utterance. The research question that sociolinguists have been seeking an answer for is why speakers choose to engage in code switching.

1. The Advent of Code-switching Research

Perhaps the earliest attempt to address the question of why speakers code switch was Blom and Gumperz's (1972) study of language use in Hemnesberget, a small village in northern Norway. In Hemnesberget, two varieties of Norwegian are used: Ranamål, a local dialect, and Bokmål, the standard variety (see *Dialect and Dialectology*). However, the speakers' decisions regarding which variety to use is in no sense arbitrary or haphazard. Blom and Gumperz report that the villagers use these two varieties on different occasions largely because of the different social meanings they fulfill. Ranamål is used for locally based activities and relationships reflecting shared identities with the local culture. In contrast, Bokmål is used in official activities, such as school, church, and mass media, communicating an individual's dissociation from the local group.

Blom and Gumperz observed that in the villagers' conversations, switching from one variety to the other might occur in response to a number of factors. For example, when an outsider joins a group of locals engaged in a conversation, the locals will often shift from Ranamål to Bokmål. This type of shift, occasioned by a change in participants, is referred to as 'situational' code-switching. A more complex type of code-switching that occurs in response to a change in topic is termed 'metaphorical' code-switching. The classic example of metaphorical code-switching is of a conversation at the local community administration office, where two villagers switch from the standard variety of Norwegian, in which they have been discussing official business, to the local variety to discuss family and other private affairs.

Blom and Gumperz's study is important because it illustrated that code-switching is a complex, skilled linguistic strategy used by bilinguals to convey important social messages above and beyond the referential content of an utterance. In addition, this study sparked an interest in studying code-switching data in terms of a dynamic, interactional model that focuses on individual choices rather than static factors related to an individual's social status (see *Social Class*).

2. The Audience Centered Approach to Code-switching

Howard Giles and his associates have developed a model of interpersonal communication that considers how speakers change the way they speak according to their audience. Giles refers to this type of strategy as accommodation (see *Audience Design*; *Speech Accommodation*). Within Giles' speech accommodation theory, speakers are motivated by their desire for approval vis-à-vis their desire to dissociate themselves from the hearer. These concerns are cognitively salient and are realized by speech convergence (similar styles of speaking) or divergence (different styles of speaking). Thus, convergence and divergence are linguistic strategies to either decrease or increase communicative distance.

Although the premises behind speech accommodation theory have not been tested using code-switching data in any comprehensive way, it is not difficult to see how the model could be used to explain the motivations for code-switching. For example, in an experiment testing the divergence aspect of speech accommodation theory, Bourhis et al. (1979) tried to get at the social meaning behind the code-switching behavior among Flemish–French bilinguals in their interactions with French speakers in Belgium. The researchers found that the Flemish-speaking participants in the experiment viewed a switch to Flemish as a strategy for expressing disagreement with French speakers.

Speech accommodation theory has been successfully applied mainly in contexts of dialect or style switching. However, the theory and its predictions still await further testing on code-switching in bilingual settings.

3. The Markedness Model: A Speaker Centered Approach to Code-switching

One of the most highly developed models designed to explain the sociopragmatic motivation for code-switching is Carol Myers-Scotton's markedness model, which developed out of her field research in East Africa. The central premise of the markedness model is that speakers are rational actors who make code selections in such a way as to minimize costs and maximize rewards; that is, speakers are concerned with optimizing the outcomes of an interaction in their own favor.

This notion of the speaker as a rational actor is also evident in speech accommodation theory as well as Gumperz's interactional approach to code-switching. However, unlike these other models, which consign the primary motivation for code-switching to the addressee or to some other factor external to the speaker (e.g., topic or social setting), the markedness model is primarily a speaker-centered approach to communication.

4. Markedness and Communicative Competence

Within the markedness model, all code choices fall along a continuum as more or less 'marked' or 'unmarked.' The unmarked choice simply refers to the linguistic variety that is expected, given the societal norms for that interaction. In contrast, marked choices fall at the other end of this continuum; that is, they are in some sense unusual or unexpected for the particular social interaction.

Furthermore, all speakers possess what Myers-Scotton calls a markedness evaluator, or the capacity to evaluate linguistic choices in terms of markedness, as part of their innate communicative competence (see *Communicative Competence*). While the capacity to assign markedness readings to linguistic choices is innate, the markedness continuum is established through exposure to the different options used in the community.

5. Explaining Speakers' Choices

All code choices can ultimately be explained in terms of speakers' motivations to optimize the outcomes of the interaction for themselves. Most choices that speakers make affirm the norms that are in place for a particular exchange. These are unmarked choices, and they are usually the safest choices to make. The particular code used by the speaker is important only insofar as the participants view its status as marked or unmarked for that type of interaction. Thus, in a multilingual setting such as Nairobi, Kenya, the unmarked choice for most business transactions between strangers is Swahili. For example, if the participants discover during the course of their interaction that they are members of the Luyia ethnic group they will often switch into Luyia to continue the conversation. Luyia, then, becomes the unmarked choice. However, code-switching between Swahili and English within the same turn, within the same sentence, and even within words is typically the unmarked choice for informal social gatherings between educated, middle class peers. Hence, the markedness of linguistic choices must be evaluated in terms of the norms for a particular exchange; the unmarked setting may even change within the same conversation.

In contrast to the safety of unmarked choices, marked choices carry with them some element of risk for someone who wishes to defy the norms. Importantly, the interpretation that a marked choice receives derives from its contrast with the unmarked choice for that particular interaction. That is, the unexpectedness, the 'otherness' of a marked choice carries significant social meaning. Marked choices are typically used to redefine the relationship between the speaker and addressee, often as an expression of the speaker's authority or power, to indicate anger, or to assert one's ethnic identity (see *Identity and*

455

Language; *Power and Language*). All these strategies can be subsumed under a single general principle: speakers make marked choices to negotiate a change in the expected social distance between the participants, either increasing or decreasing it.

6. The Significance of the Markedness Model

Since its formalization, the markedness model has been successfully used to explain code-switching between languages, between dialects and registers, and even between stylistic choices in literary contexts. The strength of the markedness model is its ability to explain not only unmarked choices, which most other models do as well, but also its ability to explain marked choices. Furthermore, the markedness model addresses the universal aspects of communicative competence in terms of cognitive abilities to use readings of markedness to assess speakers' intentions. For these reasons, the markedness model is a powerful tool not only for code-switching research, but also for any examination of the ways in which speakers use language to achieve their interactional goals.

See also: Code, Sociolinguistic; Code-switching: Discourse Models; Code-switching: Overview.

Bibliography

Blom J P, Gumperz J J 1972 Social meaning in structure: code switching in Norway. In: Gumperz J J, Hymes D (eds.) *Directions in Sociolinguistics*. Holt, Rinehart, Winston, New York, pp. 409–34

Bourhis R G, Giles H H, Leyens J P, Tajfel H 1979 Psycholinguistic distinctiveness: language divergence in Belgium. In: Giles H H, St. Clair R (eds.) *Language and Social Psychology*. Blackwell, Oxford, UK, pp. 158–85

Jacobson R (ed.) 1990 *Code-switching as a Worldwide Phenomenon*. Peter Lang, New York

Milroy L, Muysken P (eds.) 1995 *One Speaker, Two Languages: Cross Disciplinary Perspectives on Code-Switching*. Cambridge University Press, Cambridge, UK

Myers-Scotton C 1993 *Social Motivations for Code Switching: Evidence from Africa*. Clarendon Press, Oxford, UK

Myers-Scotton C 1998 A theoretical introduction to the markedness model. In: Myers-Scotton C (ed.) *Codes and Consequences*. Oxford University Press, New York, pp. 18–38

Code-switching: Structural Models
R. M. Bhatt

1. Introduction

One of the most pervasive phenomena of bilingual behavior is code-switching, the ability of bilinguals to switch back and forth between the languages they control, exemplified most strikingly in the title of Poplack's (1980) paper, 'Sometimes I'll start a sentence in Spanish y termino en español.' The assumption guiding much of the research in code-switching is that different languages in the bilingual's verbal repertoire are not kept hermetically in sealed boxes; their mutual spillover and influence provide useful clues to our understanding of bilinguals' language use, acquisition, and change (see Bhatia and Ritchie 1996, Muysken 2000). This entry focuses on research that deals with the structural design of code-switching, the knowledge and ability underlying bilinguals' use of two languages within a sentence. This ability known variously as 'code-mixing' (see *Code-mixing*), or 'intra-sentential code-switching' is illustrated in the Hindi-English code-switching examples below. As in the case of modern syntax, it is important to consider unacceptable switches (marked with a *) as much as actually occurring and acceptable switches.

(1a) aapkii *sister*   aajkal   kyaa   paRhaatii   hai
      your   these days   what   teaches   is
      'What does your sister teach these days?'

(1b) **your* behan   aajkal   kyaa   paRhaatii   hai
            sister   these days   what   teaches   is
      'What does your sister teach these days?'

(2a) Suresh bought flowers apnii behan   ke liye
                             his   sister   for
      'Suresh bought flowers for his sister.'

(2b) *Suresh bought flowers for   apnii behan
                                   his   sister
      'Suresh bought flowers for his sister.'

The research output in the 1980s in the area of structural constraints on code-switching has challenged the claim in the earlier sociolinguistic literature that code-switching is random (e.g., Labov 1971: 457, Lance 1975: 143), and instead put forward the view that code-switching is systematic and rule-governed. As such, these studies introduced, inductively, several structural (syntactic) constraints to account for cross-linguistic generalizations of code-switching. Relatively recently, however, attempts have been made to ground the syntactic constraints in formal linguistic theories to account for what Ferguson (1978) called the 'bilingual's grammar.' Inquiries into the structure of the bilingual grammar has been rationalized by the fact that code-switching is automatic, and the fact that fluent bilinguals have fairly consistent judgments on the well-formedness of code-switched sentences (cf. Singh 1985).

2. Bilingual's Grammar: Earlier Proposals

Some of the earliest attempts toward structuring code-switching resulted in descriptive generalizations, encoded as language-specific constraints. Kachru (1978), for instance, proposed the following surface syntactic constraints in Hindi-English code-switching: (a) the 'Determiner Constraint,' banning switching of the determiner (see, e.g., examples (1) and (2) in Sect. 1); (b) the 'Conjunction Constraint,' requiring the conjunction to belong to the same language as the second conjunct, correctly predicting the ill-formedness of expressions like *John aayaa ('came') nahiiN ('not') lekin ('but') I must wait for him 'John hasn't come but I must wait for him'; and (c) the 'Complementizer Constraint,' requiring the complementizer to belong to the language of the matrix clause, correctly predicting the illformedness of expressions like *mujhe lagtaa hai that John will come tomorrow 'I think that John will come tomorrow.' The bulk of research on structural constraints on code-switching in the 1980s was, however, done on Spanish-English, two languages that share several surface structural properties. Poplack (1980), following Lipski (1977) and Pfaff (1979), proposed two constraints that seemed at once general enough and restrictive enough to be able to account for all-and-only instances of Spanish-English code-switching. The first constraint is the 'Free Morpheme Constraint,' which bans switching of bound morphemes, as shown by the ungrammaticality of (3) below.

(3) *Estoy   *eat*-iendo
    am   eat-ING
    'I am eating.'

The second constraint, the 'Equivalence Constraint,' which has received the most attention in the code-switching literature (see also Muysken 2000), permits code-switching only at points where the surface structure of the two languages map onto each other. This constraint correctly predicts the grammaticality contrast in (4) below: (4a) is acceptable (Lipski 1977) because the grammars of English and Spanish coincide, but (4b) is unacceptable because the two grammars differ with respect to the placement of the object pronoun (Spanish requiring an object pronoun before the verb, unlike English).

(4a) Tonces salio eso que   *she wanted to take mechanics*
     'It turned out that she wanted to take mechanics.'

(4b) *I   saw   *lo*
                  it
     'I saw it.'

Sridhar and Sridhar (1980) extended the empirical scope of the Equivalence Constraint by proposing the 'Dual Structure Principle' to account for Kannada-English code-switching of the type given in (5) below, where the switched constituent of the 'guest' language, English, does not violate the linear precedence rules of the 'host' language, Kannada.

(5) nanna abhipraayadalli *his visiting her at home* sariyalla
    my   opinion-in   proper-not
    'In my opinion, his visiting her at home is not proper.'

Sridhar and Sridhar thus introduced a conceptualization of code-switching where the participating languages were assumed to have asymmetric roles: the host language provides the constituent structure of the entire code-switched utterance and the guest language provides elements into the host language. Later works on code-switching took this asymmetric relationship between participating languages as axiomatic.

Another important contribution to the literature on structural constraints in code-switching came from the work of Aravind Joshi (1985). He observed that closed class items, e.g., determiners, quantifiers, prepositions, possessive, Aux, Tense, helping verbs, etc., were most recalcitrant to switching. His 'Closed Class Constraint' formalizes his observation. Later works of Myers-Scotton (1993) and Belazi et al. (1994) make extensive use of his insight.

3. Code-switching in Generative Grammar

Although most of the constraints proposed were able to capture the descriptive generalizations of code-switching for specific language pairs, they invariably failed to generalize, because of their structural design, beyond the data-sets for which they were proposed (see Bokamba 1989, Clyne 1987). The real challenge then was to couch the proposals in generative grammatical theory so that theoretical models of code-switching could be developed, ones that made claims about the bilingual's language competence. The methodologically plausible goal of such an enterprise was to spell out, in some detail, the elaborate and abstract computations, the formal principles, that make possible the creative aspect of bilingual's language use, code-switching.

One significant beginning, after Woolford's (1983) and Bentahila and Davies' (1983) initial attempts, was the 'Government Constraint' proposed by Di Sciullo et al. (1986), elaborated later by Halmari (1997) and Muysken (2000). This constraint bans code-switching at a structural position, which is governed (by a head like a verb or a preposition). The grammaticality contrast in (6) below illustrates how their constraint works. (6a) is the grammatical option because the V(erb), with language index E(nglish), governs, and therefore requires, the specifier (*your*) of the object NP to carry the same language index, which it does. (6b), on the other hand, is the ungrammatical option because the specifier (*tumhaarii*) of the object NP does not carry the language index of the verb, resulting in the violation of the Government Constraint.

(6a) I heard your *burii khabar* today
                  bad news

'I heard your bad news today.'

(6b) *I heard *tumhaarii burii khabar* today
              your   bad news

'I heard your bad news today.'

Although this constraint correctly predicts the contrasts noted above in (1), (2), (4), and (6), several counterexamples of it are reported in the literature (see Belazi et al. 1994, Bhatia 1989).

In the 1990s, the use of grammatical theory to account for code-switching became the received methodology. Mahootian (1993), for example, uses a computationally-based formalism, the Tree Adjoining Grammar, to account for Farsi-English code-switching. Her analysis, essentially following Pandit's (1990) insight, is based on the assumption that in code-switching the language of the head determines the syntactic properties of its complement. Her analysis is unable to account for the ungrammaticality of (2b) and (6b) in Sect. 1: neither the switched complement of the prepositional phrase in (2b) violates the properties of the head (preposition) nor the switched complement of the verb phrase in (6b) violates the properties of the head (verb). In her theory, therefore, both (2b) and (6b) are incorrectly predicted to be grammatical code-switches (see also Bhatt 1997a).

Myers-Scotton (1993) uses a combination of production mechanisms and aspects of grammatical theory to propose her Matrix Language Frame (MLF) Model of code-switching. The model is built on two central hierarchies: the matrix language (ML) vs. embedded language (EL) distinction and the content vs. system morpheme distinction. These oppositions yield the Morpheme Order Principle and the System Morpheme Principle, which, taken together, state that morpheme order and all syntactically-relevant system morphemes in mixed (ML + EL) constituents will come from the ML. This model has several theoretical, methodological, and empirical problems, as pointed out, among others, by Bentahila (1995).

The MLF model is now augmented with two sub-models: the 4-M model and the Abstract Level model. The major innovation in the new version is that now there are four, not two, different types of morphemes (content morphemes vs. three types of ['early,' 'bridge' and 'late'] system morphemes) available at different levels of grammatical organization and activated and combined by different mechanisms in production (for details see Myers-Scotton and Jake 2000).

Two other proposals advanced recently— Belazi et al. (1994) and MacSwan (1999)—use the 'Minimalist' (Chomsky 1995) technology to account for bilingual code-switching. These accounts presuppose familiarity with the most recent version of Chomskyan syntax and is not easy to summarize in the space available. Essentially, Belazi et al. proposed the 'Functional Head Constraint,' stated as: 'The language feature of the complement f-selected by a functional head, like all other relevant features, must match the corresponding feature of the functional head.' This constraint is thus designed to ban switching between functional heads (e.g., C(omplementizers), Infl(ection), D(eterminers)) and their corresponding complements (e.g., IP = (S), VP, NP). Thus, in their theory, they extend the feature 'checking domain' (à la Chomsky 1995) of functional heads to include 'internal domains.' The idea is simple, yet attractive—that functional heads engage in checking not only the properties of their specifiers, but also the properties of their complements. Assuming, especially in bilingual language use, 'language' to belong to the set of morphological features that needs to be checked off for licit derivation, it follows that code-switching will be disallowed only in those instances where there is a mismatch between a functional head and its complement in the language feature, which yields an illicit derivation. Although theoretically attractive, their proposal makes false predictions (see Bhatt 1997b, Mahootian and Santorini 1996). [Abbreviations: NP—noun phrase; IP—inflection phrase; S—sentence; VP—verb phrase.]

MacSwan (1999) carefully accounts for Nahuatl-Spanish code-switching purely on Minimalist assumptions (Chomsky 1995). A Minimalist account, however, does not block the derivations of (1b) and (2b), since neither the structure-building operations (Merge, Move) nor any Checking (Case, EPP), Computational (Last Resort, Minimal Link Condition), or Economy (Full Interpretation, Procrastinate, Shortest Derivation Condition) principles are violated by the switched items in these examples. The data in (1b), for example, is both LF and PF convergent. There are no special lexical requirements of the Hindi subject DP that would lead the derivation to crash: the nominative (phonologically null) Case of the (Hindi) Subject DP, sitting in Spec-TP, is checked by T. In other words, an account of variation in code-switching remains problematic under strict Minimalist interpretation of generative grammatical theory. [Abbreviations: DP—determiner phrase; LF—logical form; T—tense; TP—tense phrase; PF—phonetic form.]

4. Code-switching, Language Variation, and Optimal Grammars

In order to account for language variation in code-switching, Bhatt (1997a) proposes an optimality-theoretic (OT) account of the phenomena. In OT (Prince and Smolensky 1993), Universal Grammar is conceptualized as a set of potentially conflicting constraints holding in all languages, with cross-linguistic variation arising from the fact that different languages resolve the conflicts among these constraints differently. This framework thus holds promise for a theory of code-switching by recruiting structural constraints proposed for different pairs of languages and allowing them all to interact to account for cross-linguistic generalization.

Bhatt (1997a, 2001) argues that the constraints offered in the past to express distributional generalizations of code-switching were categorical: their violations lead to illicit structures. Instead of using categorical constraints, a slight adjustment in the theory—from inviolable to 'violable' (soft) constraints—yields the relevant generalizations. These soft constraints are violable in just those contexts in which they conflict with a higher ranked constraint. The claim, then, is that a code-switched constituent that violates a particular constraint has its well-formedness 'reduced' by a certain amount (cf. also Singh 1985).

Bhatt (1997a) begins with the observation that languages involved in code-switching have 'preferences' for what counts as 'well-formed.' This cross-linguistic observation affords the plausible assumption that the syntax of code-switched constructions strives toward well-formedness, i.e., when the guest (embedded) constituents are mixed into the host (matrix) language, the syntax operates to optimize well-formedness. In other words, when the guest items are introduced to the host language, certain adjustments follow, naturally, since items (words, phrases) from one language with one set of well-formedness conditions move to a language with another set of well-formedness conditions.

The constraints recruited in Bhatt (1997a, 2001) are universal; they have appeared in the literature in different guises and under different names, either in the form of concrete proposals or in the form of background assumptions. Thus, the 'Head Syntax Constraint'—the grammatical properties of the language of the head are respected within its 'minimal domain'—is a synthesis of Mahootian (1993), Pandit (1990), and Sridhar and Sridhar (1980). Similarly, the 'Linear Precedence Constraint'—the order of the arguments of the verb must follow the requirements of the language of Infl—is a reformulation of Myers-Scotton's (1993) Matrix Language Hypothesis. The 'EQUI Constraint'—maximizing harmony in code-switching when the well-formedness conditions of the switched items are met—is a reformulation of Pfaff (1979), Poplack (1980), and Sridhar and Sridhar (1980). The Specifier Constraint—the Specifier of an XP must be of the same language as the head which assigns Case to that XP—is discussed in Joshi (1985), Kachru (1978), and Singh (1985). Finally, the Complaisance Constraint—if Spec-XP switches then head X switches too—is a fidelity constraint, discussed by Backus (1992). Although these constraints are, consistent with the logic of Optimality Theory, universal, the effect of the presence or nonpresence of a constraint in code-switching is more a matter of its ranking relative to other constraints in a particular bilingual grammar. The cross-linguistic variation in code-switching arises from different constraint-ranking configurations opted for by different bilingual grammars. [Abbreviations: Infl—inflection; Spec—specifier.]

Although it is not possible here to present a detailed exposition of the optimality account of code-switching, it suffices to say that even subtle contrasts, noted in English-Hindi (7) and Spanish-English (8) code-switching, that do not compartmentalize neatly into grammatical-ungrammatical distinctions are also easily explained as a result of constraint interaction and satisfaction, as outlined in Optimality Theory. In both examples (7) and (8), the (a) options are the best code-switches, followed by (b) which appears slightly degraded compared to (a). The (c) options (marked*) are absolutely unacceptable.

(7a) √Ramesh bought an expensive watch *apne bhaaii ke liye*
                                                      his brother for

'Ramesh bought an expensive watch for his brother.'

(7b) ?Ramesh bought an expensive watch *apne* brother *ke liye*
                                                    his   for

(7c) *Ramesh bought an expensive watch his brother *ke liye*
                                                           for

(8a) √I saw *la casa*
         the house

(8b) ?I saw the *casa*
               house

(8c) *I saw *la* house
         the

These subtle contrasts are captured straightforwardly by the interaction and satisfaction of two constraints, *SPEC and COMP: the grammar of English-Hindi code-switching yields the contrast by ranking *SPEC over COMP and the grammar of Spanish-English code-switching yields the contrast by ranking COMP over *SPEC (see Bhatt 2001, for details).

The claim, then, is that the patterns of code-switching, as in (1)–(8) above, emerge from the interactions of structural constraints—the optimal adjustment between items of the two languages yielding the grammatical option. Given an OT perspective, the grammatical differences between different code-switching grammars are reduced to the different constraint rankings each grammar chooses.

5. Conclusions

Studies on structural constraints on code-switching have, over the years, attempted to systematize the linguistically significant generalizations of bilinguals' language use. Although these accounts have become increasingly theoretically sophisticated, insofar as they present optimism for speculations on the bilingual mind design, they are, unfortunately, based on the methodological premise that constraints are infallible. This leads to the familiar predicament that the predictions are not borne out when tested across different pairs of code-switching languages. Further progress in our understanding of bilinguals' grammar can perhaps be made with a slight conceptual shift—that generative grammar defines a set of violable constraints, prioritized in language-specific ways. The observed syntactic differences among languages involved in code-switching will then turn out to be different constraint-ranking configurations opted for by different bilingual grammars.

See also: Code-mixing; Code-switching: Discourse Models; Code-switching: Overview; Code-switching: Sociopragmatic Models.

Bibliography

Backus A 1992 *Patterns of Language Mixing: A Study in Turkish-Dutch Bilingualism*. Otto Harrassowitz, Weisbaden, Germany
Belazi H, Rubin E, Toribio A J 1994 Codeswitching and X-bar theory: The functional head constraint. *Linguistic Inquiry* 24: 221–37
Bentahila A 1995 Review of duelling languages. *Language* 71: 135–40
Bentahila A, Davies E E 1983 The syntax of Arabic-French code-switching. *Lingua* 59: 301–30
Bhatia T K 1989 Bilingual's linguistic creativity and syntactic theory: Evidence for emerging grammar. *World Englishes* 8: 265–76
Bhatia T K, Ritchie W C 1996 Bilingual language mixing, universal grammar, and second language acquisition. In: Ritchie W C, Bhatia T K (eds.) *Handbook of Second Language Acquisition*. Academic Press, New York
Bhatt R M 1997a Code-switching, constraints, and optimal grammars. *Lingua* 102: 223–51
Bhatt R M 1997b Code-mixing and the Functional Head Constraint. *World Englishes* 16: 171–6
Bhatt R M 2001 Argument licensing in optimal switches. In: MacSwan J (ed.) *Grammatical Theory and Bilingual Code-switching*. MIT Press, Cambridge, MA
Bokamba E G 1989 Are there syntactic constraints on code-mixing? *World Englishes* 8: 277–92
Chomsky N 1995 *The Minimalist Program*. MIT Press, Cambridge, MA
Clyne M 1987 Constraints on code-switching: How universal are they? *Linguistics* 25: 739–64
Di Sciullo A, Muysken P, Singh R 1986 Government and code-mixing. *Journal of Linguistics* 22: 1–24
Ferguson C 1978 Multilingualism as object of linguistic description. In: Kachru B B (ed.) Linguistics in the seventies: Directions and prospects. *Special issue of Studies in the Linguistic Sciences* 8: 97–105. Department of Linguistics, University of Illinois, Urbana, IL
Halmari H 1997 *Government and Code-switching: Explaining American Finnish*. John Benjamins, New York
Joshi A K 1985. Processing of sentences with intrasentential code switching. In: Dowty D R, Karttunen L, Zwicky A M (eds.) *Natural Language Parsing: Psychological, Computational, and Theoretical Perspectives*. Cambridge University Press, Cambridge, UK
Kachru B B 1978 Toward structuring code-mixing: An Indian perspective. *International Journal of the Sociology of Language* 16: 28–46
Labov W 1971 The notion of 'system' in Creole languages. In: Hymes D (ed.) *Pidginization and Creolization of Languages*. Cambridge University Press, Cambridge, UK
Lance D 1975 Spanish–English code-switching. In: Hernández-Chavez E, Cohen A D, Beltramo A F (eds.) *El lenguaje de los Chicanos: Regional and social characteristics used by Mexican Americans*. Center for Applied Linguistics, Arlington, VA
Lipski J 1977 Code-switching and the problem of bilingual competence. In: Paradis M (ed.) *Aspects of Bilingualism*. Hornbeam Press, Columbia, SC
MacSwan J 1999 *A Minimalist Approach to Intrasentential Code-switching*. Garland, New York
Mahootian S 1993 *A Null Theory of Codeswitching*. Northwestern University dissertation, Evanston, IL
Mahootian S, Santorini B 1996 Codeswitching and the complement/adjunct distinction. *Linguistic Inquiry* 27: 464–79
Muysken P 2000 *Bilingual Speech: A Typology of Code-mixing*. Cambridge University Press, Cambridge, UK
Myers-Scotton C 1993 *Duelling Languages: Grammatical Structure in Codeswitching*. Oxford University Press, Oxford, UK
Myers-Scotton C, Jake J L 2000 Explaining aspects of codeswitching and their implications. In: Nicol J (ed.) *One Mind, Two Languages: Bilingual Language Processing*. Blackwell, Oxford, UK
Pandit I 1990 Grammaticality in codeswitching. In: Jacobson R (ed.) *Codeswitching as a Worldwide Phenomenon*. Peter Lang, New York

Pfaff C 1979 Constraints on language mixing. *Language* **55**: 291–319
Poplack S 1980 Sometimes I start a sentence in English y termino en Español: Toward a typology of code-switching. *Linguistics* **18**: 581–618
Prince A, Smolensky P 1993 *Optimality Theory: Constraint Interaction in Generative Grammar.* University of Colorado and Rutgers University, Colorado, MS
Singh R 1985 Grammatical constraints on code-mixing: Evidence from Hindi-English. *Canadian Journal of Linguistics* **30**: 33–45
Sridhar S N, Sridhar K K 1980 The syntax and psycholinguistics of bilingual code-mixing. *Canadian Journal of Psychology* **34**: 407–16
Woolford E 1983 Bilingual code-switching and syntactic theory. *Linguistic Inquiry* **14**: 520–35

Contact Languages
S. G. Thomason

Three types of new language arise from contact: pidgins, creoles, and bilingual mixed languages. Each of these types emerges under social conditions that are relatively unusual. Pidgins are the most common type by far, followed by creoles and then, a distant third, bilingual mixed languages. Structural and historical generalizations about pidgins and creoles are drawn primarily from the results of intensive research over the past four decades. In spite of the large and growing body of data on these contact languages, however, virtually every theoretical proposal about the nature and origin of pidgins and creoles is controversial. The situation is different with stable bilingual mixed languages: so few of them have been sufficiently well documented and systematically investigated that generalizing about them is probably premature. Below is a sketch of each type, together with brief indications of a few of the major controversies surrounding them.

The typical pidgin (see *Pidgins and Creoles: An Overview*) is created in a new contact situation involving two or more (almost always more) languages when a medium of communication is needed for use in limited social contexts, for instance trade. The groups in contact retain their respective native languages, and they do not learn the other groups' languages. A certain amount of time is obviously required, at least a few years—the exact amount of time is unknown, because the process has never been observed—before the emerging contact medium *crystallizes* into a pidgin language, with its own lexicon and grammar that must be learned by new speakers. Some scholars refer to the formative stage(s) of pidgin genesis as *pre-pidgin* or *jargon* (see *Jargons*) stage(s). The lexicon comes primarily (up to ca. 90 percent) from one of the languages in the contact situation, the *lexifier language*. The grammar, however, comes neither from that language nor from any other single language. Its sources are a matter of controversy; the two major contenders are cross-language compromise and simplification by all speakers of their native languages until they end up with a set of maximally simple structures. A third view, which used to be more popular than it is now, is that pidgin structures are derived from simplification of the lexifier language alone, by its own speakers and also by others who are creating the contact language. The main reason this view is no longer widely held is that a great many pidgins have structures that demonstrably cannot be derived, by simplification or any other means, from the lexifier language—such as the inflectional categories of dual and trial number and inclusive vs. exclusive 'we' in the pronominal system of Tok Pisin, an English-lexifier pidgin that is now one of the official languages of Papua New Guinea.

Thanks, apparently, to the limited functions fulfilled by a typical new pidgin, its linguistic systems are also limited. The lexicon is small relative to the lexicon of other natural languages, stylistic registers are limited or nonexistent, there are relatively few complex sentence structures, and there is relatively little morphology or, in many cases, none at all. Typical examples of trade pidgins include Chinook Jargon, once spoken from northern California to Alaska in the US and Canada, and Chinese Pidgin Russian, once spoken along the Russo-Chinese border. In some pidgin genesis contexts, speakers of the lexifier language deliberately withhold their full language so that outsiders (e.g., trading partners or slaves) cannot learn it; instead, they use a simplified version of their native language, which then becomes the lexifier of the new pidgin. An example is Hiri Motu, one of the three official languages of Papua New Guinea, which crystallized after it was designated as the language of the ethnically diverse police force that was established by British colonial authorities late in the nineteenth century.

One theory of pidgin structure, mentioned above, is that pidgins are maximally simple—that their structures reflect, and perhaps even provide evidence for, universally unmarked structural features. There are several weaknesses in this view. In particular, pidgins are by no means all alike; many pidgins have at least a few universally marked features (for instance the Tok Pisin pronominal categories or the elaborate, consistent, and highly marked consonant inventory of Chinook Jargon); and some pidgins have morphological structures that are by no means candidates for unmarked status. Most other controversies about pidgins parallel some of the creole controversies (see *Pidgins and Creoles: Models*), which tend to be more heated (and often, in fact, to provide more heat than light).

Like pidgins, creoles develop in contact situations where two or more (almost always more) languages are spoken by groups whose members do not learn each other's languages. Also like pidgins, creoles are mixed languages in the strong historical linguist's sense: their lexicon and structure do not come primarily from the same source language. As with pidgins, the lexicon comes primarily (up to ca. 90 percent) from one language, but the grammar comes from no single language. Unlike the typical pidgin, the typical creole serves as the (or a) main language of a speech community. Neither its social functions nor its structures are limited in any way.

Creoles seem to have arisen in at least three different ways. First, some pidgins have turned into creoles, through functional and structural expansion and eventual *nativization* (so that they are learned as first languages by the community's children). Tok Pisin is a prime example: it apparently began—somewhere in the Pacific, though perhaps not in New Guinea itself—as a trade pidgin; its uses in New Guinea expanded beyond trade into a wide and increasing variety of social functions, and its lexicon and grammatical resources expanded along with its functions, until eventually it became a creole.

Second, some creoles apparently emerged abruptly, without going through a stable pidgin stage. This would happen in a new contact situation where, for some reason, the various groups of speakers cannot continue to use their respective native languages. The adults' initial mode of communication in such a case would perhaps be a pre-pidgin, but not a fully crystallized pidgin language, because the new contact medium would be required for all social interaction, they and their children—the relative amounts of input from adults and children is disputed—would create an *abrupt creole*. It was once thought that this scenario fit most or all creoles that arose as a result of the Atlantic slave trade, on the assumption that newly enslaved Africans could not, or would not, learn the slavemasters' languages and could not retain their native languages (see e.g., Alleyne 1971). This scenario is no longer attractive, in part because we now know that in many Caribbean colonies people did continue using their native languages (so that a crystallized pidgin stage was both possible and likely). But there are still a few plausible candidates for abrupt creole genesis, for instance Hawaiian Creole English (see e.g., Bickerton 1999: 51ff.) and Pitcairnese, the creole that developed after 1790 when the nine *Bounty* mutineers settled on Pitcairn Island with their mostly Tahitian companions. According to Bickerton's Language Bioprogram Hypothesis, children born into a new multilingual community develop specific proposed structures that are argued to be universal in abrupt creoles, to account for the creation of an abrupt creole. His view continues to be controversial and is currently more popular among specialists in language acquisition and formal syntactic theory than among creolists. A rival current theory of abrupt creole genesis is that the structures of abrupt creoles, like those of new pidgins, derive from cross-language compromise among the languages of their creators, through a process that has been called 'negotiation' (Thomason 2001: 180–2, Thomason and Kaufman 1988: chaps. 6–7). On this view, the genesis of both pidgins and abrupt creoles can be usefully compared to shift-induced interference—that is, to imperfect second language acquisition—although the analogy is far from complete. The general approach is traditionally referred to in the literature as the *substrate theory* (see e.g., Boretzky 1983, Holm 1988–1989; see *Language Transfer and Substrates*), and in current theories it is usually integrated with markedness-based universalist considerations (see e.g., Thomason and Kaufman 1988: chaps. 6–7).

The third route to creole genesis is not merely comparable to shift-induced interference, but is actually shift-induced interference. On this view, proposed most prominently by Chaudenson (e.g., 1992) for French-lexifier creoles, creoles emerge through a gradual process of repeated instances of group second-language acquisition, with shift-induced interference at each stage accumulating until the result is a creole language, too distant linguistically to be considered a dialect of the lexifier language that provided the original target for language learning. The social circumstances under which the process began involved small farms with roughly equal numbers of French speakers and African slaves who learned French; the farms were eventually succeeded by large plantations, with each wave of newly imported slaves learning the plantation's lingua franca from earlier slaves. Reunionese, the French-lexifier creole of Reunion, has been proposed as a prime example of a language that arose in this way, and it is possible that some Caribbean creoles also followed this route—although it has also been argued, e.g., in Singler (1996), that the change from small farm to large plantation was too abrupt in certain Caribbean colonies to accommodate a steady gradual process involving successive influxes of large new groups of slaves.

Most specialists do not believe that creoles can be characterized by a 'laundry list' of linguistic features, in spite of the fact that most of them share with most pidgins (sometimes, of course, because they have arisen through nativization of a pidgin) an analytic structure with relatively little morphology, and also a relatively simple phonological system. Earlier investigators believed in a laundry-list approach to identifying creoles ('if the language has this set of features, it must be a creole'), but the view fell out of favor when the most-studied creoles, those spoken in the Caribbean, turned out to vary considerably among themselves in general and to lack some of the proposed pan-creole features in particular. In addition, some languages that are not believed by anyone to be creoles have the entire proposed set of 'creole' features. The laundry-list approach has been revived recently (see McWhorter 1998), but it has not convinced skeptics to reconsider their rejection of the idea. Another proposal, which has not been discussed as much, is that creoles can only be identified from an historical perspective, i.e., as languages which cannot be shown to have descended as entire languages, lexicon as well as all grammatical subsystems, from a single parent language (see e.g., Thomason 1997b, Thomason and Kaufman 1988).

The above sketch of pidgin and creole structure and genesis necessarily omits mention of some lively areas of debate within the field. One more of these must be mentioned briefly: how do we draw the line between a pidgin and a creole? The traditional view has been that pidgins are languages without native speakers, while creoles have a population of native speakers. This distinction was once believed to correlate with levels of linguistic elaboration: the common-sense assumption was that a trade pidgin, with no native speakers and with functions restricted to typical second- (or third-, etc.) language uses would of course have limited linguistic resources, while a creole, serving as the main language of a speech community, would have all the elaboration in lexicon and structure that any other native language has. Unfortunately, this tidy correlation breaks down when one considers pidgins that have expanded their functions dramatically without acquiring native speakers. Tok Pisin, although it eventually did acquire a native-speaker population, was such a language during part of its history: its functions expanded until they covered many or most aspects of daily life, and were limited only in the (presumable) lack of baby-talk and perhaps a few other aspects of home life. There is now no clear, simple, generally accepted way of distinguishing pidgins from creoles, though scholars continue to debate the issue. My own view (which is not shared by all specialists) is that any definition based on spheres of usage and their correlation with linguistic resources will inevitably have to allow for a very fuzzy boundary between pidgin status and creole status. How many functions are required for creole status? How much structure and lexicon are required for creole status? And if a population of first-language speakers is considered necessary after all, how many children constitute a population? It is hardly surprising, given the fact that pidgins can turn into creoles (by whatever set of criteria one adopts), that no sharp line can be drawn between the two categories; but the issues continues to be a matter for lively debate.

Bilingual mixed languages, the third type of contact language, differ sharply from pidgins and creoles, both linguistically and socially. What all three types have in common socially is their origin in some extreme form of contact—pidgins and creoles because they are needed for interethnic communication, bilingual mixed languages because they are needed (or at least wanted) as a symbol of ethnic identity. Pidgins and creoles always develop in the absence of full multilingualism, where there is no shared medium of communication; bilingual mixed languages always develop among bilinguals, who share not just one but two (and possibly more) languages. Bilingual mixed languages are not, therefore, needed for purposes of interethnic communication; on the contrary, they are in-group languages.

As the name suggests bilinguals create bilingual mixed languages. Although it's hard to be sure, given the paucity of well-understood cases, these languages seem to fall into two categories: most arise (relatively) abruptly as symbols of new ethnic or subethnic identities, but others arise gradually as symbols of ethnic identity among persistent ethnic groups—groups that had their own language originally but have come under so much cultural pressure from another speech community that their group identity is threatened. Michif, the language of mixed-blood French and (primarily) Cree speakers in south-central Canada, is one example of an abruptly created bilingual mixed language; Mednyj Aleut, the language of mixed-blood Russian and Aleut speakers on Mednyj (Copper) Island off the east coast of Russia, is another. In both cases, the mixed-blood population was viewed by its members and by the larger community as a separate group, with different economic and social and sometimes even legal status from pureblood members of the two component groups. A well-documented bilingual mixed language that apparently arose gradually is Ma'a, a Tanzanian language of (by hypothesis) a Cushitic speech community that became partially integrated with two different Bantu-speaking communities. Ma'a is a case of unusually stubborn resistance, perhaps over several centuries, to total assimilation by two culturally dominant Bantu-speaking groups.

Structurally, the languages in the two groups differ significantly, though this assertion must be taken with a large grain of salt in view of the small number of examples. In the abrupt type there is a sharp split between the linguistic components taken from the two languages: Michif has French noun phrases (lexicon, phonology, and morphosyntax) and Cree verb phrases (lexicon, phonology, morphosyntax); Mednyj Aleut has mainly Aleut lexicon and structure (albeit with numerous Russian borrowings) except in the finite verb morphology, which has been imported virtually intact from Russian, replacing the entire elaborate Aleut system of finite verb inflection (see *Intertwined Languages*). A third example, Media Lengua of Ecuador, has an entirely Spanish lexicon and an entirely Quechua structure (phonology and morphosyntax). In sharp contrast, in the gradually developing type of bilingual mixed language, e.g., Ma'a, all parts of the structure and lexicon of the threatened language are influenced by the dominant group's language. In its earliest documented form, Ma'a had a few non-Bantu structural features in different grammatical subsystems; present-day Ma'a has almost entirely Bantu structure, and its non-Bantu material is confined to a large but not numerically dominant proportion of the lexicon, including much or most of the basic vocabulary. Describing Ma'a as a gradually-developed mixed language is still a controversial stance (for a discussion of the controversy and arguments for gradual development, see Thomason 1997a), at least to some extent, but the scenario for absolutely abrupt creation is also controversial (see e.g., Mous 1994 for arguments in favor of abrupt creation).

It has been claimed that bilingual mixed languages consist of the lexicon of one language and the grammar of another (Bakker 1997, Bakker and Muysken 1995). But this scenario doesn't fit several of the few languages that have so far been systematically described in any depth—Media Lengua fits the picture, but Michif, Mednyj Aleut, and Ma'a do not—so that it does not seem at present to be a very promising theory. It is safe to predict that other theoretical controversies will arise as more bilingual mixed languages are discovered and analyzed.

See also: Pidgins and Creoles: An Overview; Pidgins and Creoles: Models; Intertwined Languages; Code-switching: Overview; Bilingualism, Societal.

Bibliography

Alleyne M C 1971 Acculturation and the cultural matrix of creolization. In: Hymes D (ed.) *Pidginization and Creolization of Languages*. Cambridge University Press, Cambridge, UK

Arends J, Muysken P, Smith N (eds.) 1995. *Pidgins and Creoles: An Introduction*. Benjamins, Amsterdam

Bakker P 1997 *A Language of our Own: The Genesis of Michif, the Mixed Cree-French Language of the Canadian Me'tis*. Oxford University Press, Oxford, UK

Bakker P, Mous M (eds.) 1994. *Mixed Languages: 15 Case Studies in Language Intertwining*. Institute for Functional Research into Language and Language Use (IFOTT), Amsterdam

Bakker P, Muysken P 1995 Mixed languages and language intertwining. In: Arends J, Muysken P, Smith N (eds.) 1995. *Pidgins and Creoles: An Introduction*. Benjamins, Amsterdam

Bickerton D 1999 How to acquire language without positive evidence: what acquisitionists can learn from creoles. In: DeGraff M (ed.) *Language Creation and Language Change: Creolization, Diachrony, and Development*. MIT Press, Cambridge, MA

Boretzky N 1983 *Kreolsprachen, Substrate und Sprachwandel*. Otto Harrassowitz, Wiesbaden, Germany

Chaudenson R 1992 *Des îles, des hommes, des langues*. Harmattan, Paris

Holm J 1988–1989 *Pidgins and Creoles, Vol. 1: Theory and Structure*, 1988; *Vol. 2: Reference Survey*, 1989. Cambridge University Press, Cambridge, UK

McWhorter J H 1998 Identifying the creole prototype: Vindicating a typological class. *Language* **74**: 788–818

Mous M 1994 Ma'a or Mbugu. In: Bakker P, Mous M (eds.) *Mixed Languages: 15 Case Studies in Language Intertwining*. Institute for Functional Research into Language and Language Use (IFOTT), Amsterdam

Muysken P 1997 Media Lengua. In: Thomason S G (ed.) *Contact Languages: A Wider Perspective*. Benjamins, Amsterdam

Singler J V 1996 Theories of creole genesis, sociohistorical considerations, and the evaluation of evidence: The case of Haitian Creole and the Relexification Hypothesis. *Journal of Pidgin and Creole Languages* **11**: 185–230

Thomason S G 1997a Ma'a (Mbugu). In: Thomason S G (ed.) *Contact Languages: A Wider Perspective*. Benjamins, Amsterdam

Thomason S G 1997b A typology of contact languages. In: Spears A K, Winford D (eds.) *Pidgins and Creoles: Structure and Status*. Benjamins, Amsterdam

Thomason S G 2001 *Language Contact: An Introduction*. Edinburgh University Press, Edinburgh, UK

Thomason S G, Kaufman T 1988 *Language Contact, Creolization, and Genetic Linguistics*. University of California Press, Berkeley, CA

Endangered Languages
L. A. Grenoble and L. J. Whaley

A language is classified as endangered if there is an imminent risk of it no longer being spoken. While the risk to the vitality of a language may arise from any number of factors, often acting in combination, two basic types of language endangerment situations exist. First, many languages are endangered because there has been a measurable decline in the percentage of children who learn to speak them over the course of two or more generations. The trajectory of the decline in the number of people learning these languages is such that at some point intergenerational transmission will cease. At that point, the language is considered moribund and has little to no chance for survival. The second type of endangered language is one that has a small number of speakers overall. Though many such languages are thriving under the social conditions that currently hold, their limited speaker base renders them susceptible to rapid language loss should conditions change.

Within these two broad categories of endangered languages there is a high degree of variation in how close to extinction particular languages are. For example, Orok, an indigenous language of Russia and Japan, has fewer than 100 fluent speakers, none of them children. In contrast, Nenets, another minority language of Russia, has 27,000 speakers, including a sizable number of children, and live in relatively isolated conditions, with limited contact with other languages. Still, there is an obvious trend towards children learning Russian rather than Nenets. While both these languages are endangered, it is all but certain that Orok will cease to exist as a living language within the next 50 years, whereas the prospects for the long-term survival of Nenets, though still not good, are better.

In order to capture the difference between the different types of endangered languages and the relative degrees of vitality among them, several different classifications have been proposed. Though differing somewhat in the details and terminology, all these classifications make at least a four-way distinction. First, 'threatened languages' are those languages for which long-term survival is a possibility, but which are vulnerable to rapid language loss. The vulnerability may stem from a number of factors, e.g., a small population of speakers or social transformations that decrease the necessity for using the language in daily activities. Second, 'declining languages' are those languages that are evincing a steady erosion to their speaker base, primarily due to the fact that fewer and fewer children learn the language in their homes. Third, 'moribund languages' are those languages that are no longer being learned by children as first languages. Short of extraordinary measures to revitalize such languages, they will cease to be spoken fluently by anyone within the span of a generation. Finally, 'extinct' languages are those languages that have no speakers left.

With regard to the fourth category, it is important to identify a crucial difference between the notion of an 'extinct language' and a 'dead language' such as Latin or Sanskrit. While the former describes a language whose loss is brought about by a disruption in intergenerational transmission, the latter is a language that represents a prior historical stage of a living language. For instance, though Latin is no longer spoken as it was in the fourth century, in a very real sense it is still being spoken, though in forms that are now called by different names such as French, Italian, and Spanish. Language change is a natural and constant process; spoken languages are continually evolving. In contrast, moribund and extinct languages generally arise at the point when they are no longer evolving because speakers have shifted to using a different language. Therefore, while extinct languages and dead languages share the property of having no fluent speakers in the contemporary world, the reasons for this are dramatically different (see *Language Maintenance, Shift, and Death*).

1. Statistics on Endangered Languages

Accurate statistics on the number of languages that are endangered, declining, or moribund do not exist. Part of the reason for this fact lies in the differing conceptions of what constitutes a language versus a dialect (see *Language*), thereby making it difficult to establish how many languages there are in the first place. Moreover, inadequate linguistic surveys have been undertaken for some regions of the world, which contributes to the problem of establishing how many languages are spoken. Even so, most experts place the number somewhere between 6000–7000. More significant than the indeterminacy in the overall number of languages, is the paucity of knowledge about how widely they are used and by whom. The single best source of information of this type is found in the *Ethnologue* (Grimes 2000), yet even this source contains only limited data on language vitality.

While precise calculations on the number of endangered languages are not available, good estimates have been made about the current situation. Perhaps the most widely cited figures are those of Michael Krauss (in Hale et al. 1992). Krauss calculates that there are 600 languages in the world that can be considered 'safe,' i.e., not endangered, declining, or moribund. He defines this class as containing those languages with a speaker population of over 100,000 people or with official state support. Assuming there to be 6000 languages in the world, Krauss thus establishes that only 10 percent of languages are safe. He further estimates that of the 90 percent of languages that are not safe, well over half are moribund, though this number is primarily impressionistic.

Statistics such as these must be treated with some care since they are cast in summary fashion and do not take regionally specific variables into consideration. While the claim that 90 percent of the world's languages are endangered, declining, or moribund has been widely accepted, there is some disagreement over what number of these languages is likely to become extinct in the present century. This apparent discrepancy arises because facts about numbers of speakers and language use are ultimately meaningless unless they are interpreted within the context of the regions where the languages are spoken. For example, in the People's Republic of China, a language spoken by most members of an ethnic group numbering in the tens of thousands must be considered in a precarious state since the number of monolingual Chinese speakers living in the same region is proportionately much higher and because China has an educational policy that aggressively promotes Mandarin Chinese over minority languages. However, a language in a speech community of the same size in Papua New Guinea, where there are hundreds of small language groups, would represent one of the larger languages in the country. In this sort of context, one might predict the continued use of the language into the indefinite future.

2. Causes of Language Endangerment

Regardless of whether one puts the number of languages that are likely to disappear from the earth in the next 100 years at 50 percent or 90 percent of the current total, the statistic is alarming. The conditions necessary to bring about this extreme rate of language extinction have their roots in the period of colonization and in the rise of industrialization and the modern nation-state (see Nettle and Romaine 2000 for a good overview). Colonization meant, in many instances, the decimation of indigenous populations around the world due to the spread of disease and conquest. It further entailed the displacement of many indigenous groups from traditional lands. With the onset of industrialization and the formation of nations came governments that implemented educational systems and language policies designed to unify their populations. Either explicitly or implicitly, such efforts included the drive to assimilate indigenous groups. Many of the languages of the world are known to have become moribund as a direct result of these efforts.

Recognizing the effect of such historical trends provides some understanding as to why declining and moribund languages are not evenly distributed throughout the world. In regions of the world where a colonizing group successfully conquered indigenous people and descendants of the colonizing groups now represent the majority culture of a country, an extremely high percentage of languages are moribund or near moribund. Such regions include most parts of the Americas, Russia, Australia, and China, among others. In regions where colonization did not occur, or did not occur in the same way, such as many parts of South East Asia and Africa, the percentage of moribund language is much lower.

The sociopolitical composition of the modern world, and perhaps more importantly its economic systems, do not provide a favorable environment for endangered languages. In many countries, educational policy promotes monolingualism in a nationally or regionally dominant language. This is reinforced by telecommunications technology such as radio, television, and the Internet, that relies on widely spoken languages. The exploitation of natural resources increasingly leads to the displacement of minority populations that speak endangered languages. The ensuing disruption to their cultural patterns often leads to language decline. Civil wars have a similar effect. In many communities where endangered languages are spoken, there are changing attitudes towards material prosperity and subsistence that lead to increasing numbers of young people leaving the community. The majority of the world's population speaks an ever decreasing number of languages. Mandarin Chinese, Spanish, English, Bengali, Arabic, and Hindi are among the most rapidly growing languages, acquiring speakers at the expense of a large array of languages with a smaller speaker base.

The rate of language decline and extinction is far greater now than it has ever been in history. The linguistic diversity of the world will almost certainly be cut in half in the next 100 years, and the modern situation does not paint an optimistic picture for the vitality of countless other languages. For this reason, an increasing amount of interest and research has been generated on the topic of endangered languages in the last several decades. There has been a groundswell of interest by communities that speak endangered and declining languages to revitalize or maintain this aspect of their heritage. As a result, language programs have sprung up around the world. It remains to be seen whether such efforts can be successful for the long term.

See also: Endangered Languages Projects (An Inventory), Reversing Language Shift; Language Maintenance, Shift, and Death.

Bibliography

Crystal D 2000 *Language Death*. Cambridge University Press, Cambridge, UK
Dorian N C (ed.) 1989 *Investigating Obsolescence: Studies in Language Contraction and Death*. Cambridge University Press, Cambridge, UK
Grenoble L A, Whaley L J (eds.) 1998 *Endangered Languages: Current Issues and Future Prospects*. Cambridge University Press, Cambridge, UK
Grimes B F (ed.) 2000 *Ethnologue*, 14th edn. SIL International, Dallas, TX
Hale K, Krauss M, Watahomigie L J, Yamamoto A, Craig C, La Verne Masayesva J, England N 1992 Endangered languages. *Language* **68**: 1–42
Matsumura K (ed.) 1998 *Studies in Endangered Languages*. Hituzi Syobo, Tokyo
Nettle D, Romaine S 2000 *Vanishing Voices: The Extinction of the World's Languages*. Oxford University Press, Oxford, UK
Robins R H, Uhlenbeck E M (eds.) 1991 *Endangered Languages*. Berg, Oxford, UK

English as a Foreign Language
G. Abbott

The term 'English as a Foreign Language' (EFL) implies the use of English in a community where it is not the usual means of communication, 'English as a Second Language' (ESL) being used where the language has important social functions in the community—as a medium of education or jurisdiction, for example. The terms EAP and ESP refer to contexts in which the adult learner has an academic or other specific purpose. In educational contexts the label EAL (English as an Additional Language) is also used so as to emphasis the value of the learner's first language. The American term TESOL (Teaching English to Speakers of Other Languages) is ousting its British equivalent, ELT (English Language Teaching). All these terms contrast with 'English as Mother Tongue' (EMT) or 'English as First Language' (EL1). Though this article will concentrate on EFL, the other aspects cannot be entirely excluded. It will first review the major reasons for the phenomenal increase in the use of English worldwide and illustrate current uses of EFL as an international language. Some developments in the Teaching of English as a Foreign Language profession (henceforth TEFL) and its associated industries are then described. The final sections deal with three issues likely to be of continuing concern: issues of education, culture, and intercomprehensibility.

1. The Diffusion of English

The first extant textbook for foreign learners of English was written for French Huguenot immigrants by Jacques Bellot, himself a Huguenot. It was published in London in 1580 at a time when English, according to Bellot's contemporary John Florio, was 'worth nothing past Dover' and even within Britain was not understood everywhere. Since then the use of English has spread throughout the world until at conservative estimates, in the late twentieth century, there are 300 million mother tongue speakers, a similar number of ESL users and a further 100 million fluent EFL speakers. The development of TEFL since Florio's time is chronicled in Howatt (1984). The sheer quantity and distribution of English speakers (see Crystal 1987: 358–9) are directly attributable to the rise of two successive world powers, Britain and the USA.

The administration of the British Empire's largely multilingual territories necessitated the use of a common language, and in most cases English was the only feasible choice. Although the use of the vernacular (see *Vernacular*) was encouraged in the first years of primary schooling, the selective secondary schools usually drew multilingual groups from much wider catchment areas. English was therefore inevitably chosen as the medium of instruction.

By the time the British Empire had been dismantled the foundations of the 'English Empire' had been laid. The British Council and the BBC continued the diffusion of English and the USA, by the mid-twentieth century a formidable world power, had her own reasons for encouraging the world to learn English—reasons which were largely ideological. A decision to teach exotic languages to armed forces personnel during World War II had given an impetus to foreign language teaching approaches which were then applied to English, Fries (1945) being especially influential. The ensuring Cold War prompted the US State Department's Foreign Service

Language Contact

Institute to employ applied linguists to produce courses in languages of strategic importance, and the success of the first Sputniks further stimulated this activity. The Center for Applied Linguistics was established and the export of English was supported by the Ford Foundation, the Fulbright Program, the Peace Corps, and the Voice of America radio transmissions.

The growing international status of English was not simply the result of a quest for Empire and a crusade against totalitarianism. Immigration into America, the UK, Australia, and Canada also acted as a spur to domestic ESL provision, which in turn influenced TEFL methodology. However, the emergence of English as an international language probably owes more to a phenomenon observed long before in Bengal.

2. English as an International Language

West (1926: 107) had noted that in the publication of books on technical subjects not only was the combined production of Britain and the USA almost 50 times larger than the local output, but also the continuing expansion of technical knowledge published in English would outpace any attempt to translate it into Bengali. For countries not technologically developed, English was already an invaluable means of access to new scientific, medical, and technical information. By 1980 more than two-thirds of the world's scientists were writing in English and of all the world's electronically stored information, 80 percent was in English (Crystal 1987: 358). Since the First World/Third World development gap appears to be widening, this function of English will probably continue to grow.

Improvements in the technology of travel brought commerce and tourism to a point where a single common language was needed, and the world chose English. Advances in electronics produced global networks for sound and vision providing instant access to the world's news: in repressed societies British, American, and Australian news in English was relied upon for its accuracy. Politically, English became the international language of protest and economic development.

2.1 Restricted Englishes

Restricted forms of English were established for international operational purposes. The speed, volume, and geographical range of modern transport systems had necessitated internationally agreed ways of ensuring that traffic flows were as efficient and hazard-free as possible. In international civil aviation a common language was needed for air crews and ground control staff to exchange messages, and English was the obvious choice. However, natural languages contain potential ambiguities which in certain circumstances could lead to fatal misunderstandings. The instruction 'Go ahead,' intended to mean 'Proceed with your message,' had on one occasion been interpreted by a pilot as 'Continue your present course,' and his aircraft had crashed. It is therefore a carefully restricted English called 'Airspeak' which, by international agreement through the United Nations, is used by today's world airlines (see Robertson 1987).

Controlling heavy traffic in sea lanes and responding rapidly to mariners' calls for help present fewer problems now that there is an internationally agreed language of ship-to-ship and ship-to-shore radio communication, a disambiguated English called 'Seaspeak' (see Weeks et al. 1988). With the linking of the UK to Europe by means of the Channel Tunnel, another restricted English was needed for the police forces at each end to use when communicating by telephone. This operational English is called 'Policespeak.'

3. TEFL as a Profession and as an Industry

The increasing international dependence upon English as a working language enhanced not only the size but also the status of the TEFL profession in those countries where it is the mother tongue. Here the world's growing need for well-trained teachers was catered for by the establishment of specialist TEFL postgraduate courses, up to doctorate level, both for nationals of the various countries seeking such assistance and for mother-tongue speakers of English wishing to teach EFL/ESL overseas. This in turn necessitated the recruitment of suitably experienced and qualified academic staff.

The incessant demand for tuition in EFL led to a massive growth of provision in the private sector, a development encouraged by US/UK economic policies from the 1980s onwards. In the UK, quality-control systems were set up to award recognition only to establishments found to be of satisfactory standard; participation in such schemes is voluntary, however. Some recognized private institutions undertake teacher education and other high-level training activities both at home and abroad, as well as direct language teaching.

3.1 Publishing

On both sides of the Atlantic, publishers hastened to add TEFL to their repertoires or to expand their existing lists. They now produce a plethora of textbooks, books for teachers, workbooks, visual aids, sound and video cassettes, and computer software. The publication of such materials is in itself a multimillion dollar international industry in which some textbook-writers have become millionaires.

3.2 Testing

The higher education systems of these countries also began to cater for a growing number of applicants from overseas, especially from the Third World, who had to pursue their various fields of study through the medium of English. There was consequently a need not only to provide training in the use of English for academic purposes but also to develop reliable methods of assessment which would determine for each applicant the amount and nature of the tuition needed. The best known of these standardized tests are the TOEFL (Test of English as a Foreign Language) used in America and the IELTS (International English Language Testing Service) developed by the British Council. Another highly profitable industry arose from a demand for certificates of proficiency that would help the holders to obtain employment or promotion, or even to become EFL teachers themselves. In the UK, so many examining boards established their own tests at various levels of proficiency that, in order to help learner, teacher, and employer alike, the English Speaking Union commissioned a framework (Carroll and West 1989) to facilitate comparison of the tests in terms of level, content, and coverage.

3.3 Anglocentrism

A perhaps inevitable consequence of the activity mentioned above was 'anglocentrism,' a tendency to assume that what was suitable for the privileged circumstances of a school in Los Angeles or London was suitable for use in Venezuela or Vietnam. The modern communicative movement in language teaching (see *Communicative Competence*) was developed in circumstances in which well-trained and well-paid teachers taught highly motivated students in smallish groups able to move about in spacious well-equipped classrooms, and usually had access to reprographic facilities and secure storage space. It was sometimes forgotten that, in a worldwide perspective, these were unusually privileged circumstances and that communicative methods had to be modified, sometimes severely, in less favored conditions. Though there has been a resurgence of interest in the issue of large classes, there has been no breakthrough in the problem of how to deal satisfactorily with classes of, say, 200 students—a quite normal feature of TEFL in Pakistan, Burma, and elsewhere.

A welcome development which may counteract anglocentrism was the establishment of professional organizations far from the 'anglocenter.' Teachers' associations such as the USA-based TESOL, TESL Canada, and the UK-based IATEFL were at one time balanced only by RELC (SEAMEO Regional Language Centre) in Singapore, and CIEFL (Central Institute of English and Foreign Languages) in Hyderabad, and even these were not run by teachers. The 1970s and 1980s witnessed the setting up of EFL teachers' associations in various parts of the world. Examples include MELTA (Malaysian English Language Teachers' Association) in Kuala Lumpur and SPELT (Society of Pakistan English Language Teachers) in Karachi. Enthusiasm and commitment are often such that the groups produce their own journals and organize national and even international conferences.

4. EFL as Education

Although state school TEFL in many parts of the world benefited indirectly from the lively professional activity outlined above, research and development tended to focus on postschool rather than in-school needs—in contrast to the ESL context, in which a great deal of useful school work was done (see *Education and Language: Overview*). In 1971 the Council of Europe asked a term of applied linguists to devise specifications for the teaching of languages in the EC member states; the objective was to provide, for those whose employment involved crossing European linguistic borders, syllabus components that were comparable whatever the language being learnt. The outcome was an inventory based upon the predictable workaday language needs of such citizens. This inventory, complied with working adults in mind, was merely copied when a subsequent specification for schools was produced.

While TEFL has seen great advances in the identification and use of the particular language forms and functions needed in a given higher education of course or occupation, no comparable energy has been devoted to the development of a rationale for EFL as a school subject. Where adults have current language needs that are analyzable and imminent needs that are predictable, the EFL learner in school usually has neither; the younger the learner the more TEFL becomes TENOR (the child having 'No Obvious Reason' for studying English) and the more important are one's educational aims in teaching the language. Stern (1984: 10) rightly pointed to 'a lack of contact among applied linguists with curriculum theory in general educational studies.'

The uneducative content of many an EFL textbook was often cited as a case in point. Too often the books contained inconsequential passages, frequently about pseudotypical characters (e.g., 'The Smith Family'), followed by mindless exercises comprising lists of sentences, unrelated except for the grammar point they illustrated. Suggestions for a more educative content were put forward and some have begun to materialize in school teaching materials. They include: teaching another subject through English, as in ESL contexts; imparting facts that are considered important as general knowledge; using the nature of language and communication as a subject of study; and using the pupils' own preoccupations as lesson material. Last, but by no means least in a world of increasing multiculturalism and widening interdependence, such educational objectives as 'awareness of world problems' and 'tolerance of cultural difference' may well prove at least as important as merely linguistic aims. If so, EFL programs in the world's schools will be required to play their part; but for that to happen TEFL needs to be incorporated into a sound framework of educational theory in which it is the needs of the child as a developing person, rather than the demands of the state and the employer, that are paramount.

5. EFL and Culture

To the applied linguist as to the anthropologist, a 'culture' is the sum of learnt systems shared by and defining a social group; it is not limited to the fine arts that the West associates with Culture, an abstraction with a capital C, but embraces all the group's methods of ordering and expressing its way of life, including its use of language, facial expression, and gesture. One normal consequence of teaching any natural language, therefore, is the imparting of elements of the culture that the language reflects. Kramsch (1998) provides a recent overview of the relationship between language and culture which is of relevance to TEFL practitioners. Given the scale of EFL teaching and use, it is not surprising that in many areas of the world uneasiness has been expressed concerning the transmission of Western culture.

Cultural transmission may take place in at least three ways in the language classroom: as lesson content it may be intentional, incidental, or inherent.

5.1 Intentional Transmission

If the passages, dialogues, and illustrations in an EFL program have an EMT setting, e.g., 'An American Family' or 'The British Queue,' it may be assumed that the material is an intentional cultural component of the learning program. (If on the other hand the textbook material were to depict local children in local settings conversing in faultless English, the lack of authenticity would elicit ridicule. Finding appropriate settings can be a problem.) Intentional content may either be left to speak for itself or discussed, through the MT if need be, in contrast to a corresponding component of the learner's culture (e.g., 'Boarding a Bus in London and Lahore'). Texts representing 'high culture' may also be used. EFL programs in the former USSR, for instance, included study of certain poems by Robert Burns and selected passages for Dickens, Jack London, and Hemingway, at which point English Literature was deemed to stop—a reminder that 'culture' includes 'ideology.'

5.2 Incidental Transmission

The expatriate teacher, as a native speaker of English, has a worldview laden with cultural values different from those of his students. These include preconceptions about morality, education, and classroom behavior which color everything that happens in a class, however unaware the teacher may be that this is happening. Educational authorities may prefer local staff to such guest teachers for this reason.

Also included here, though some might prefer to view it as intentional cultural transmission, is the linguistic and nonlinguistic behavior demanded of even local teachers by syllabuses aiming at communicative competence (see *Discourse in Cross-linguistic and Cross-cultural Contexts*). For example, to ask a young woman student or teacher to express strong emotion and to accompany her utterances with body language typical of an EMT community will be seen in Southeast Asian societies as a very embarrassing cultural imposition. On the other hand, learning what to expect in the foreign culture, and learning what to avoid doing, are seen as helpful. People of certain Asian cultures about to depart for the UK will be happy to learn not only how to form grammatically correct questions in English but also that certain questions (*How old are you? How much do you earn?*) are not used on first acquaintance. Comparisons of the MT rules for communicative competence and the English equivalents are improving EFL programs in this respect.

5.3 Inherent Transmission

It has long been accepted that one cannot learn a language without imbibing some of the cultural information it embodies. It was for this reason that regimes diametrically opposed to EMT cultural values used language teaching texts that were merely party ideology translated into English, simple words such as *correct* being made to take on new meanings, and *democracy* meaning opposite things in the two camps. In Eastern Europe, where it was often necessary in public to use a Stalinist dialect which contradicted everyday realities—a situation that has been labeled 'political diglossia'—effects similar to schizophrenia were reported.

Applied linguists agree to differ on how far one's mother tongue influences the structure of one's thinking processes (see *Sapir–Whorf Hypothesis*), but few would deny any causal connection. It seems unlikely that learning to use EFL would greatly influence the mentality of the learner unless English came to replace the mother tongue.

5.4 Cultural Imperialism

Any of these aspects of cultural content in EFL lessons may be seen as neoimperialism, depending on the particular circumstances—the real or perceived intentions of the teacher, the wishes of the students, the views of their parents, the ideological stance of the education authorities, and so on. There is certainly a danger that some communicative activities might be seen as assimilationist ('You should behave more like us'); common sense and cultural sensitivity are needed on the part of both materials writer and teacher. It has further been suggested by Abbott (1992) that Third World perceptions of the benefits accompanying a command of English may, by undermining indigenous cultures, inhibit the development process. Certainly, an uneasy feeling persists in many quarters that the promotion of TEFL is a form of cultural imperialism (see *Linguistic Imperialism*).

6. Intercomprehensibility

The need to avoid cross-cultural incomprehension or misunderstanding gave rise to the restricted Englishes mentioned above (Sect. 2.1) and to a proposed general-purpose code called 'Nuclear English' (Quirk 1981) which would be culture-free and therefore not perceived as neo-imperialist; but Quirk's proposals were not developed into a usable code. The need worldwide is to ensure comprehensibility among natural Englishes.

6.1. Natural Englishes

Quite apart from the varieties that constitute 'English' in the minds of its native speakers and which Kachru (1985) labels 'the inner circle,' there are also what he calls 'the outer circle' and 'the expanding circle' of Englishes. The outer circle comprises all those forms of English such as Indian English or Nigerian English which, though not indigenous and not the users' mother tongues, have become 'institutionalized' (i.e., part of the nation's working life) and 'nativized' (i.e., modified by the local cultures and thus more comfortable and efficient as vehicles for international messages). Kachru's 'expanding circle' consists of truly foreign Englishes such as Japanese English and Iranian English. Given that nonnative speakers of English already outnumber its native speakers and that the quantity of international communication in English within and between the outer and expanding circles is increasing, there is a continuing need to ensure intercomprehensibility (see *New Englishes*).

6.2 The Learning-model Question

In the expanding circle, the need to have an inner circle standard form of English as a learning-model has not seriously been questioned, Europe traditionally opting for British English and 'received pronunciation' (see *Accent*). In outer circle countries, however, it has been proposed that the standard form of each nativized English should serve as the national model. Nigerians, for example, who rightly regard English as their own (it is their national language), might well find this policy attractive for reasons of national identity and pride. It has been objected that since all nonnative Englishes whether nativized or foreign are subject to mother-tongue interference (see *Language Transfer and Substrates*) they would, in the absence of a shared model, be pulled in different directions, thereby threatening intercomprehensibility.

Where international intelligibility is the aim, there may have to be a high degree of commonality among the models used, and at present only the mother-tongue standard Englishes of the inner circle can satisfy this requirement. The image of non-mother-tongue Englishes held in orbit by the gravitational force of mother-tongue standard Englishes may at first seem neoimperialist; but this maintenance of an optimum distance from the center may be justifiable not primarily because proximity to the center is important but because the greater the radius, the greater the distance between the nonnative Englishes. Increasingly, these Englishes are likely to differ considerably in their vocabularies and vary somewhat in their grammars; but if intercomprehensibility is to be assured, each variety may need to maintain a similar number of systematic phonemic contrasts. Another advantage of such a policy would be the maintenance of a reasonably close relationship between the spoken Englishes and the orthography of English, which allows very little variation in spelling. However, such a vast field may not lend itself to applied linguistic activity at all, and Crystal (1997) believes that a common global dialect, 'World Standard Spoken English' is likely to arise naturally. McArthur (2001) gives an up-to-date overview of the global condition of English.

Though education, culture, and intercomprehensibility have been addressed separately above, they are of course not discrete phenomena in the practice of TEFL. Since attitudinal factors are a significant influence in language learning, the successful education of English-users, whether native or non-native speakers of the language, will include the promotion of positive intercultural attitudes which in turn will facilitate mutual understanding across linguistic boundaries

See also: Language Spread; New Englishes; Linguistic Imperialism.

Bibliography
Abbott, G 1992 Development, education and English language teaching. *English Language Teaching Journal* **46**: 172–9
Bellot J 1580 *Le Maistre d'escole anglois: The English Scholemaister*. Henry Dizlie, London (facsimile reprint 1967, Scolar Press, Menston)

Carroll B J, West R 1989 *ESU Framework: Performance Scales for English Language Examinations*. Longman, Harlow, UK

Crystal D 1987 *The Cambridge Encyclopedia of Language*. Cambridge University Press, Cambridge, UK

Crystal D 1997 *English as a Global Language*. Cambridge University Press, Cambridge, UK

Fries C C 1945 *Teaching and Learning English as a Foreign Language*. University of Michigan Press, Ann Arbor, MI

Howatt A P R 1984 *A History of English Language Teaching*. Oxford University Press, Oxford, UK

Kachru B B 1985 Standards, codification and sociolinguistic realism: The English language in the outer circle. In: Quirk R, Widdowson H G (eds.) *English in the World: Teaching and Learning the Language and Literatures*. Cambridge University Press, Cambridge, UK

Kramsch C 1998 *Language and Culture*. Oxford University Press, Oxford, UK

McArthur T 2001 World English and world Englishes: Trends, tensions, varieties and standards. *Language Teaching* **34**: 1–20

Quirk R 1981 International communication and the concept of Nuclear English. In: Smith L E (ed.) *English for Cross-Cultural Communication*. Macmillan, Hong Kong

Robertson F 1987. *Airspeak: Radiotelephony Communication for Pilots*. Prentice-Hall, London

Stern H H 1984 Review and discussion. In: Brumfit C J (ed.) *General English Syllabus Design*. Pergamon Press, Oxford, UK

Weeks F, et al. 1988 *Seaspeak Training Manual*. Pergamon Press, Oxford, UK

West M 1926 *Bilingualism (with Special Reference to Bengal)*. Government of India, Central Publication Branch, Calcutta, India

Ethnolinguistic Vitality

H. Giles

Communication between groups depends not only on the nature of the immediate context in which it occurs, but also on the sociostructural background in which the social categories are historically embedded. In order to explore the latter in (originally) the interethnic sphere as well as relate it to sociolinguistic usage, Giles et al. (1977) introduced the concept of 'ethnolinguistic vitality.' This articulated the main sociostructural features defining a group's relative position to others in society vis-à-vis three principal components. Derived, in large part, from factors found predictive of language maintenance, these were *status* (e.g., economic, historical), *demography* (e.g., numbers, birthrates), and *institutional support* (e.g., representation of the group and its language in the media and education).

Subsequently, scholars have fruitfully analyzed groups' 'objective vitalities,' such as the number of TV programs and newspapers in an in-group's language, and contrasted these with other out-groups' capital. The real challenge of the vitality framework was, however, to provide a *subjective* assessment of how members of ethnic collectivities judged the societal conditions impinging on their own and relevant out-groups. To this end, Bourhis et al. (1981) devised a 22-item instrument (the SVQ) to tap individuals' vitality *perceptions*—and this scale has subsequently been accorded high internal reliability.

SVQ research has underscored the notion that the supposedly same societal conditions can be viewed in different ways by interested parties involved. For instance, Anglo-Australian students in Melbourne polarized vitality differences between their own group and Greek-Australians who, in turn, attenuated them (see Harwood et al. 1994 for a typology of different intergroup vitality profiles). In Hong Kong, a more differentiated intergroup vitality profile emerged where Western and Cantonese students each favored their own in-group on items relating to language status, yet considered their respective out-groups to have significantly more control and power on other scales. Furthermore, and comparing Hong Kong bilinguals' ratings before, with those immediately after, the signing of the Sino-British Treaty (1983), Chinese vitality was perceived to have increased whereas Western vitality diminished. Arguably, little (if any) objective changes accrued during this 18-month period.

Vitality is not then static given but, rather, a malleable social construction depending on social group memberships and fluctuating sociopolitical circumstances. Also, vitality perceptions are a function of which target groups are in the evaluative frame, whether the context is the very local neighborhood community or a larger provincial entity, and so forth. Allard and Landry (e.g., 1986) have extended our conceptions of *general* in out-group vitalities to encompass other related belief systems (e.g., how groups feel the relative positions should be as well as what they could be in the future—their normative and goal vitalities, respectively), and related these to individuals' linguistic networks. The empirical pursuit of which belief system is more predictive of language behaviors than others has engaged comparative research yet, doubtless, future work will indicate each is potent in different sociolinguistic terrains.

Sociopsychological theorizing about language (e.g., ethnolinguistic identity theory) has accorded vitality an important mediating role in the sense that cognitive representations about it influence sociolinguistic behaviors. It has been argued that the more vitality in-group members believe they possess the more psychological resources they have available to bolster, as well as invest in, a strong sense of ethnic identification. Given that unique linguistic (and other communicative) criteria can be core elements of a valued in-group identity, such feelings could engender linguistic differentiation from out-group members (e.g., dialect divergence) in social interaction. Indeed, high-perceived vitality is proposed to be necessary to preserve a whole range of language maintenance and survival strategies.

Hence, the more vitality another group is seen to possess, the more motivated people are to acquire their modes of communication (see, for example, Cenoz and Valencia 1993). One soldier in Barkhuizen and de Klerk's (2000) study of a South African army camp commented: 'Yes, but I'm a Sotho, because of the majority of the peoples here they are Xhosa speakers, you see. So that is why most of the time I try to learn Xhosa. The Sothos and Venda they try to learn Xhosa' (p. 108). Nonetheless, and as the intergroup model of second language learning suggests, the desire to assimilate towards a highly vital language can be stymied when speaking it threatens learners' sense of group belonging (see Harwood et al. 1994 for related propositions and their schematic 'vitality theory'). Relatedly, perceiving and reading about the ever-increasing vitality of minority out-groups in terms of increased numbers (with political influence) can foster language ideologies among Anglo-Americans, such as the English-only Movement (Barker et al. 2001). Such sentiments can become acute when an out-group's language becomes more and more visible in the 'linguistic landscape' via public and commercial signs.

While such empirical relationships have not always emerged, and *low* perceived in-group vitality can even *mobilize* intergroup linguistic differentiation among very ethnically-identified individuals, work continues to blossom cross-disciplinarily and cross-culturally concerning the descriptive and explanatory roles of vitality (e.g., Atkinson 2000, Ellinger 2000). Indeed, it has been found (among Vietnamese-Australians) that perceived high in-group vitality is an important predictor of non-language outcomes, such as satisfaction with home life, educational achievements, and occupational aspirations.

Although the vitality construct has at times attracted controversy and been subjected to healthy scrutiny (e.g., McCann 2000), its utility extends beyond interethnic encounters into theoretical discussions of between-gender, heterosexual–homosexual, and intergenerational communication. Clearly, the psychological weight afforded the different vitality constituents (and doubtless others to be located) will depend on the particular intergroup context studied—and this is a compelling prospect for future research. Furthermore, what Harwood et al. (1994) refer to as the volume, tone, and focus of 'vitality talk' in their discursive analyses of small group discussions and the newspaper media open up exciting new directions (ethnographic and other) for understanding the critical roles of this construct in diverse sociolinguistic domains.

See also: Attitudes and Behavior; Bilingualism and Language Acquisition; Bilingualism, Societal; Ecology of Language; Language Maintenance, Shift, and Death; Politics and Language; Social Psychology; Sociology of Language.

Bibliography

Allard R, Landry R 1986 Subjective ethnolinguistic vitality viewed as a belief system. *Journal of Multilingual and Multicultural Development* **7**: 1–12

Atkinson D 2000 Minoritisation, identity and ethnolinguistic vitality in Catalonia. *Journal of Multilingual and Multicultural Development* **21**: 185–97

Barkhuizen G, de Klerk V 2000 Language contact and ethnolinguistic identity in an Eastern Cape army camp. *International Journal of the Sociology of Language* **144**: 95–118

Barker V, Giles H, Noels K, Duck J, Hecht M, Clément R 2001 The English-Only Movement: A communication perspective. *Journal of Communication* **51**: 3–37

Bourhis R, Giles H, Rosenthal D 1981 Notes on the construction of a subjective vitality questionnaire for ethnolinguistic groups. *Journal of Multilingual and Multicultural Development* **2**: 145–66

Cenoz J, Valencia J F 1993 Ethnolinguistic vitality, social networks and motivation in second language acquisition: Some data from the Basque Country. *Language, Culture, and Curriculum* **6**: 113–27

Ellinger B 2000 The relationship between ethnolinguistic identity and English language achievement for native Russian speakers and native Hebrew speakers in Israel. *Journal of Multilingual and Multicultural Development* **21**: 292–307

Giles H, Bourhis R Y, Taylor D M 1977 Toward a theory of language in ethnic group relations. In: Giles, H (ed.) *Language, Ethnicity, and Intergroup Relations*. Academic Press, London

Harwood J, Giles H, Bourhis R Y 1994 The genesis of vitality theory: Historical patterns and discoursal dimensions. *International Journal of the Sociology of Language* **108**: 167–206

McCann C C 2000 Reviewing ethnolinguistic vitality: The case of Anglo-Nigerian Pidgin. *Journal of Sociolinguistics* **4**: 458–74

Foreigner Talk
M. Clyne

Foreigner talk (also known as xenolect) is a variety of a language employed to a person identified as a foreigner, usually in order to ease communication. Like baby talk (motherese), it generally involves a reduction or simplification. The term was devised by Ferguson (1971). Descriptions of foreigner talk in a number of languages are available (including Dutch, English, Finnish, French, German, Russian, and Turkish). Sometimes, foreigner talk may reflect a condescending attitude towards foreigners or frustration with their language proficiency.

1. Linguistic Indices

Foreigner talk is subject to considerable variation between speakers and to variation within one speaker's speech according to the interlocutor and the nature and function of the discourse segment. Explanations and narratives are most susceptible to simplification. Roche (1989) has postulated four levels of German utterances in communication with foreigners: (a) native-type, (b) gravitation towards the standard language, (c) slight grammatical reductions and lexical simplifications, and (d) gross grammatical reductions and lexical simplifications. It is the last level that has been described most frequently.

The major linguistic indices are:

> elliptic sentences, e.g., *soon ready*;
> deletion of grammatical endings, e.g., *she never come*;
> the non-realization of function words such as the copula (*be*), articles, auxiliaries, prepositions and/or pronouns, e.g., *he busy*; *no start*; *he nearly finish*; *how long time take you?*;
> and the simplification of the lexicon, e.g., German *nix gut* ('no (nothing) good' for *schlecht* 'bad'), *mehr schwer* ('more heavy' for *schwerer* 'heavier').
> In some languages, the infinitive form is overgeneralized.

With the absence of inflexions, which provide vital information for comprehension, some word-classes are ambiguous. For instance, the second word in 'No finish' could be interpreted as either a noun or a verb. In German and Dutch, the Subject–Object–Verb (SOV) word order is frequently overgeneralized, e.g., *Heute nix arbeiten?* (Standard German *Heute arbeiten Sie nicht?*).

Apart from being syntactically marked, foreigner talk can be phonologically marked, where the native speaker will attempt to produce more 'foreign' sounds. Some speakers of Australian English will replace English diphthongs by monophthongs, for example, [e:] instead of [ɛɪ] and [o:] instead of [ou]. They will also articulate a trilled [r]. Foreigner talk is also louder and slower than normal native speech, with longer pauses between the crucial items.

The level chosen at the beginning of an interaction is determined by assumptions of foreignness which may sometimes be influenced by extralinguistic factors (racial features, dress). The level is adjusted according to the interlocutor's command and the type of discourse (Roche 1989).

2. Contexts of Foreigner Talk

Foreigner talk is, and has been, used in colonial plantation situations. It is very prevalent today on the factory floor and in service encounters in countries that attract many immigrants, migrant laborers, and tourists. It is also employed in family situations by some children of immigrants to their (grand)parents. Here it usually replaces an ethnic language which the children have not maintained. In such cases it may form the beginning of an ethnolect such as Greek Australian English or Jewish Australian English.

3. Users

Foreigner talk has been described between indigenous children and foreign adults, between indigenous adults and foreign adults, between children of immigrants and their parents and other older members of their ethnic group, and between foreign adults and indigenous adults of a different race (e.g., Tok Masta spoken by expatriate Australians in New Guinea, Mühlhäusler 1981).

4. Relation Between Pidgin and Foreigner Talk

Foreigner talk tends to be used in convergence toward the speech of those with limited competence in the target language and using a pidginized learner variety of it. The question of whether such a variety is promoted and/or reinforced by foreigner talk is controversial (see, e.g., Meisel 1975 and *IJSL* 1981). Such a causal relationship seems to have existed in the early stages of Tok Pisin (Mühlhäusler 1981). In industrial settings, the linguistic markers of foreigner talk and early phases of learner varieties are much the same but represented in different proportions (Clyne 1977). Also, non-native speakers of a language with a native-like competence in it may be reverting to an early stage in their second language development when they use foreigner talk.

5. Methods of Studying Foreigner Talk

Foreigner talk has been investigated mainly through the taping of spontaneous conversations, occasionally with the same native speaker interacting with several foreigners or the same foreigner interacting with different native speakers. Sometimes foreigner talk versions of 'native' sentences are elicited from native speakers. This is supplemented by examples from literature.

6. Use of Foreigner Talk in Literature

A stylized version of foreigner talk, whose function is to characterize foreignness, is to be found in literature, including *Robinson Crusoe,* the German adventure novels of Karl May, *Watership Down,* and the French comic book series *Les aventures de Tintin.* Literary foreigner talk shares some linguistic indices with actual foreigner talk but they diverge in some ways. For instance, the use of the infinitive of auxiliaries and the ungrammatical inflections of verbs and adjectives prevalent in Karl May do not occur in actual German foreigner talk.

7. Future Directions

More empirical studies are needed in as many languages as possible so that universals of foreigner talk can be established. The use of videotape in research would improve understanding of how nonverbal phenomena such as gestures can supplement foreigner talk.

See also: Register; Pidgins and Creoles: An Overview.

Bibliography

Clyne M 1977 Multilingualism and pidginisation in Australian industry. *Ethnic Studies* **1**(2): 40–55
Ferguson C A 1971 Absence of copula and the notion of simplicity. In: Hymes D (ed.) *Pidginization and Creolization of Languages.* Cambridge University Press, Cambridge, UK
Hinnenkamp V 1982 *Foreigner Talk und Tarzanisch.* Buske, Hamburg, Germany
International Journal of the Sociology of Language (IJSL) 1981 **28**
Meisel J 1975 Ausländerdeutsch und Deutsch ausländischer Arbeiter. *Zeitschrift für Literaturwissenschaft und Linguistik* **5**(18): 9–53
Mühlhäusler P 1981 Foreigner talk: Tok Masta in New Guinea. *International Journal of the Sociology of Language* **28**: 93–113
Mühlhäusler P 1984 Tracing the roots of Pidgin German. *Language and Communication* **4**(1): 27–57
Roche J 1989 *Xenolekte.* de Gruyter, Berlin
Werkgroep Taal Buitenlandse Werknemers 1978 *Nederlands tegen Buitenlanders.* Instituut voor Algemene Taalkunde, Amsterdam

Interlanguage
E. Tarone

The notion of 'interlanguage' has been central to the development of the field of research on second-language acquisition (SLA), and continues to exert a strong influence on both the development of SLA theory and the nature of the central issues in that field.

The term interlanguage (IL) was introduced by the American linguist Selinker to refer to the linguistic system evidenced when an adult second-language learner attempts to express meanings in the language being learned. The interlanguage is viewed as a separate linguistic system, clearly different from both the learner's 'native language' (NL) and the 'target language' (TL) being learned, but linked to both NL and TL by interlingual identifications in the perception of the learner. A central characteristic of any interlanguage is that it fossilizes—that is, ceases to develop at some point short of full identity with the target language. Thus, the adult second-language learner never achieves a level of facility in the use of the target comparable to that achievable by any child acquiring the target as a native language. There is thus a crucial and central psycholinguistic difference between child NL acquisition and adult second-language (L2) acquisition: children always succeed in completely acquiring their native language, but adults only very rarely succeed in completely acquiring a second-language. The central object of interlanguage research is to explain this difference—essentially, to describe and explain the development of interlanguages, and also to explain the ultimate failure of interlanguages to reach a state of identity with the target language. Thus, some central research questions are: What are the psycholinguistic processes which shape and constrain the development of inter-languages? How are these different from those processes which shape and constrain the development of native languages? How might these differences account for the phenomenon of fossilization?

475

1. The Interlanguage Hypothesis

1.1 Origins of the Concept of Interlanguage

The notion that the language of second-language learners is in some sense autonomous and crucially distinct from both NL and TL was developed independently at about the same time in the work of several different researchers (see Selinker 1992 for a detailed account of the historical development of this notion). Slightly different conceptualizations of learner language were referred to as 'approximative system' by Nemser and as 'transitional competence' by Corder. However, the notion of interlanguage seemed to be the one which caught on, and which is used in the literature on second-language acquisition in the 1990s.

Prior to the development of the idea of interlanguage, contrastive analysts had asserted that the second-language learner's language was shaped solely by transfer from the native language. Because this was assumed to be so, a good contrastive analysis of the NL and the TL could accurately predict all the difficulties which that learner would encounter in trying to learn the TL. These claims were made on logical grounds and almost always supported only by reference to anecdotal evidence. It is important to note that these claims were not supported by reference to data obtained from the systematic study of learner language itself, but usually only to utterances which analysts happened to have noticed and remembered. Unfortunately, it is all too likely that analysts tend to notice data their theories predict, and not to notice data which do not fit their theories. Learner utterances which were clear evidence of transfer were noticed and quoted, but learner utterances which did not provide evidence of transfer apparently went unnoticed or were classified as 'residue.' Thus, in the late 1950s and the 1960s, there were virtually no systematic attempts to observe learner language and to document scientifically the way in which learner language developed, or to independently and objectively verify the strong claims of the contrastive analysis hypothesis that language transfer was the sole process shaping learner language.

Lado (1957: 72), in an influential statement, explicitly characterized the predictions of contrastive analysts as statements which should be viewed as hypothetical until they could be validated by reference to 'the actual speech of students.'

Error analysis was an enterprise born of the attempt to validate the predictions of contrastive analysis by systematically gathering and analyzing the speech and writing of second-language learners. For perhaps the first time in history, the focus moved from teaching materials and hypotheses about second-language learning problems, to the systematic observation of learner language. The focus was what scientific study could reveal about the real problems of second-language learners. Preliminary evidence from early studies began to come in, the results of which showed an increasingly large 'residue' of errors which did not in fact seem to be caused by transfer as contrastive analysts had predicted. These errors became an increasingly major source of difficulty for the contrastive analysis hypothesis, a hypothesis which had posed the interesting question of what shapes learner language, but which, increasingly clearly, could not answer that question satisfactorily.

Corder (1967, 1981) was the first and most persuasive scholar to develop an alternative framework: the idea that second-language learners do not begin with their native language, but rather with a universal 'built-in syllabus' which guides them in the systematic development of their own linguistic system, or 'transitional competence.' Thus, the second-language learner's transitional competence is different from either the NL or the TL or even some combination of the two, since it begins with an essential, simple, probably universal grammar. Corder also pointed out that the native language often serves as a positive resource for second-language acquisition, facilitating the learning of TL features which resemble features of the NL. Corder argued that second-language learners' errors were evidence of the idiosyncratic linguistic system which they were building, and so were valuable data for research into the nature of the 'built-in syllabus.' Corder called for research involving the analysis of learner errors gathered longitudinally, proposed a framework for eliciting and analyzing those errors, and posed the goal as one of characterizing the built-in syllabus and the transitional competence of second-language learners. His students and colleagues set about pursuing that enterprise.

The term 'interlanguage' was most persuasively introduced and developed into a set of testable hypotheses by Selinker (1972), after long conversations with Corder and other scholars in the field. The interlanguage hypothesis was intended to, and did, stimulate systematic research into the development of the language produced by adult second-language learners, with a view to objectively identifying psycholinguistic processes (transfer included) which shaped learner language, explaining how learners set up interlingual identifications across linguistic systems, and accounting for the troubling tendency of adult learners to stop learning, or to fossilize.

1.2 Defining Interlanguage

The term interlanguage was defined by Selinker (1972) as the separate linguistic system evidenced when adult second-language learners attempt to express meaning in a language they are in the process of learning. This linguistic system encompasses not just phonology, morphology, and syntax, but also the lexical, pragmatic, and discourse levels of the interlanguage. The interlanguage system is clearly not simply the native language morphological and syntactic system relexified with target language vocabulary; that is, it is not the morphological and syntactic system which would have been evidenced had the learner tried to express those meanings in his/her native language. Just as clearly, it is not the target language system which would have been evidenced had native speakers of the target language tried to express those same meanings. Rather, the interlanguage differs systematically from both the native language and the target language.

Interlanguage is usually thought of as characteristic only of adult second-language learners (but see Sect. 2.1)—that is, learners who have passed puberty and thus cannot be expected to be able to employ the language acquisition device (LAD)—that innate language learning structure which was instrumental in their acquisition of their native language. Children acquiring second languages are thought to have the ability to reengage the LAD and thus to avoid the error pattern and ultimate fossilization which characterize the interlanguages of adult second-language learners.

Central to the notion of interlanguage is the phenomenon of fossilization—that process in which the learner's interlanguage stops developing, apparently permanently. Second-language learners who begin their study of the second-language after puberty do not succeed in developing a linguistic system which approaches that developed by children acquiring that language natively. This observation led Selinker to hypothesize that adults use a latent psychological structure (instead of a LAD) to acquire second languages.

The five psycholinguistic processes of this latent psychological structure which shape interlanguage were hypothesized (Selinker 1972) to be (a) native language transfer, (b) overgeneralization of target language rules, (c) transfer of training, (d) strategies of communication, and (e) strategies of learning. Native language transfer, the process which contrastive analysts had proposed as the *sole* shaper of learner language, still has a major role to play in the interlanguage hypothesis; while it is not the *only* process involved, there is ample research evidence that it does play an important role in shaping learners' interlanguage systems. Selinker (1972, 1992, following Weinreich 1968: 7) suggests that the way in which this happens is that learners make 'interlingual identifications' in approaching the task of learning a second language: they perceive certain units as *the same* in their NL, IL, and TL. So, for example, they may perceive NL 'table' as exactly the same as TL *mesa*, and develop an interlanguage in which *mesa* can (erroneously in terms of the TL) be used in expressions like 'table of contents,' 'table the motion,' and so on. Selinker follows Weinreich in pointing out an interesting paradox in second-language acquisition: in traditional structural linguistics, units are defined in relation to the linguistic system in which they occur, and have no meaning outside that system. However, in making interlingual identifications, second-language learners typically 'stretch' linguistic units by perceiving them as the same in meaning across three systems. An interesting research issue is how they do this; and what sorts of units are used in this way; for example, they could be linguistic units like the taxonomic phoneme or the allophone, or syllables. Selinker raises questions about the ability of traditional linguistics frameworks, based as they are on assumptions of monolingualism, to handle interlanguage data in which transfer across three linguistic systems plays a central role.

A second psycholinguistic process is that of over-generalization of target language rules. This is a process which is also widely observed in child language acquisition: the learner shows evidence of having mastered a general rule, but does not yet know all the exceptions to that rule. So, for example, the learner may use the past tense marker *-ed* for all verbs, regular and irregular alike: *walked, wanted, hugged, laughed, *drinked, *hitted, *goed*. The overgeneralization error shows clear evidence of progress, in that it shows that the learner has mastered a target language rule, but it also shows what the learner has yet to learn. To the extent that second-language learners make overgeneralization errors, one might argue that they are using the same process as that employed by first language learners.

Transfer of training occurs when the second-language learner applies rules learned from instructors or textbooks. Sometimes this learning is successful; that is, the resulting interlanguage rule is indistinguishable from the target language rule. But sometimes errors result. For example, a lesson plan or textbook which describes the past perfect tense as the 'past past' can lead the learner to erroneously use the past perfect for the absolute distant past—for all events which occurred long ago, whether or not the speaker is relating these to any more recent or foregrounded event, as in the isolated statement, *'My relatives had come from Italy in the 1700s.' These have also been called 'induced errors.'

Strategies of communication are used by the learner to resolve communication problems when the interlanguage system seems unequal to the task. When, in the attempt to communicate meaning, the learner feels that the linguistic item needed is not available to him, he can resort to a variety of strategies of communication in getting that meaning across. So, for example, if the learner wants to refer to an electrical cord in English and does not know the exact lexical item to use in referring to it, he can call it 'a tube,' 'a kind of corder that you use for electric thing I don't exactly the name,' or 'a wire with eh two plugs in each side.' The linguistic forms and patterns used in such attempts may become more or less permanent parts of the learner's interlanguage.

Strategies of learning are used by the learner in a conscious attempt to master the target language. One such strategy of learning is learners' conscious comparison of what they produce in IL with the NL and a perceived target, setting up interlingual identifications (see the example given above for transfer). Other examples of learning strategies are the use of mnemonics to remember target vocabulary, the memorizing of verb declensions or textbook dialogs, the use of flash cards, and so on. Clearly, such strategies are often successful, but they can also result in error. Memorized lists can get confused with one another, for example, or the mnemonic mediator word may become confused with the TL word. An example of the latter might be that an English-speaking learner of Spanish might use a mediator word *pot* in order to remember that the Spanish word for *duck* is *pato*—but might end up using *pot* in interlanguage references to a duck.

Research evidence was provided to show that all five of these psycholinguistic processes could affect the construction of interlanguages, and a call for more research went out. Many research projects were undertaken in response to this call to investigate each of these hypothesized processes, and the result was a flurry of papers, conferences, and publications, and ultimately something which was referred to as a field of research on second-language acquisition.

1.3 The Relevant Data for the Study of Interlanguage
In his 1972 paper, Selinker stated clearly that the relevant data to be used in the study of interlanguage consisted of utterances produced by second-language learners when they were trying to communicate meaning in the target language. The relevant data were clearly *not* learner utterances produced in response to classroom drills and exercises where the learner was focusing attention on grammar rules or target language form. Just as clearly, the relevant data were *not* the learner's introspections and intuitions about what was grammatical in the target language; such data, according to Selinker, would not provide information about the interlanguage system, but only about the learner's perception of the target language system—and these were different things.

It is important to note that although Selinker was clear about what *he* thought the relevant data of interlanguage study were, there was disagreement on this point from the beginning. Corder, for example, argued early on and strongly that researchers ought to draw upon a whole range of data sources in exploring learners' language, and learner intuitions of grammaticality were clearly a valuable data source. Others, particularly those investigating the role of universal grammar in SLA, have shared Corder's perspective.

A serious question, however, is this: when one uses different data elicitation techniques in the study of interlanguage, do all those data pools provide information about the same linguistic system? There are, after all, three linguistic systems involved: NL, IL, and TL. If one asks a second-language learner whether a given sentence is grammatical, one cannot be sure whether that learner's response is based upon the NL norm, the IL norm, or the learner's perception of the TL norm; all of these may differ strikingly from the IL norm revealed when one analyzes that same learner's utterances produced in the attempt to communicate meaning. In essence, the most basic research design question involved in the study of interlanguages—what data shall one use to study interlanguage?—raises very complex issues concerning the relationship between intuitions of grammaticality, language production, and language perception, very similar to issues raised by Labov (1970; see *Labov, William*) in sociolinguistic work (see *Applied Linguistics and Sociolinguistics*). This issue is unresolved in SLA research, and in fact is complicated by evidence that interlanguage seems to vary by discourse domain (see Sect. 2.1).

2. Development of the Interlanguage Hypothesis to the 1990s

Soon after Selinker set out the Interlanguage Hypothesis, Krashen proposed the Monitor Model. The Monitor Model initially relied heavily upon the work of a group of researchers (the creative constructionists) who claimed that there was *no* evidence at all of native language transfer in the morpheme accuracy rates of child second-language learners; thus, the contrastive analysts had got it all wrong, at least as far as children were concerned. Where the Interlanguage Hypothesis accords a central role to native language transfer, the Monitor Model does not. The Monitor Model suggests that when second-language learners, adult or children, acquire a second language unconsciously, there will be no evidence of native language transfer; it is only when they consciously learn a second language that transfer effects appear. The study of the role of universal grammar in the process of second-language acquisition, similarly, has tended to downplay the role of native language transfer in that process. One of the contributions of the Interlanguage Hypothesis to the field of second-language acquisition in the 1990s is, thus, a historically-rooted, research-based, and theoretically-motivated framework for the study of second-language acquisition which can easily account for both the role of native-language transfer and of universal grammar in shaping interlanguage.

2.1 The Revised Interlanguage Hypothesis

By the late 1990s the central claims of the Interlanguage Hypothesis remain essentially unchanged, and the intervening years have provided substantial support for them. However, there have been some modifications and expansions since its first detailed proposal in print in 1972. Some of these have been hinted at, and will be expanded upon below.

The original interlanguage hypothesis was restricted to apply only to adults acquiring second languages. However, evidence emerged subsequently that children in language immersion programs, such as the French immersion programs in Canada, also produce interlanguages, in that they evidence apparently fossilized linguistic systems with substantial influence from native language transfer. There appear to be sociolinguistic reasons for this phenomenon; the children receive native-speaker input only from their teacher, and give each other substantial non-native input. They have not usually been given enough opportunity and incentive to produce what Swain calls 'comprehensible output'—attempts to use the interlanguage to communicate meaningfully with significant others. To the extent that these children produce interlanguages in these contexts, there is some question whether they are using their LADs to internalize the target language, or whether they are using those psycholinguistic processes described as more characteristic of adults learning second languages. A great deal more research is needed with this population in order to find out how, if at all, they differ from adult learners.

A second expansion of the IL hypothesis has occurred in response to the growing interest in the influence of universal grammar upon the development of interlanguage. The crucial question here, early on, was this: universal grammar is assumed to be central to the development of natural languages; but is interlanguage a natural language? There have been two positions taken in response to this question. Selinker's initial hypothesis takes the first position: that it is not, at least as the notion 'natural language' has been defined in linguistics. This early position argues: (a) natural languages are produced by language acquisition devices (LADs); (b) language universals exist in human languages by virtue of the way in which the language acquisition device is structured; (c) but interlanguages, unlike native languages, fossilize and evidence native language transfer; (d) interlanguages therefore are a product of latent psychological structures, not LADs; and (e) so interlanguages do not have to obey language universals. Adjémian (1976), and following him others, took the opposing position that interlanguages *are* natural languages (although, unlike other natural languages, IL rule systems are 'permeable'). As natural languages, interlanguages do have to obey language universals; central to this position is the view that interlanguages are products of the same language acquisition device which produces native languages. In this view, interlanguages fossilize because of complex changes in cases where parameters have already been set for one language, and a second language must be learned. Debate on this issue is certainly ongoing and lively.

A third modification has been a growing emphasis upon something barely hinted at in 1972: the way in which interlanguage development seems to vary in different social contexts, or discourse domains. Increasing research evidence seems to show that learners can produce a significantly more fluent, grammatical, and transfer-free interlanguage in some social contexts than in others. International teaching assistants, for example, may be more fluent and grammatical in lecturing on their academic field than when talking about an everyday topic like favorite foods or bicycling. Key processes such as fossilization may be more prominent for a given learner in one context than in another. This variation in interlanguage production, documented in dozens of studies reviewed in Tarone (1988), is probably related to the problem of data elicitation discussed in Sect. 1.3 above, and certainly has profound implications for data elicitation in research. As suggested above, SLA researchers have argued for the use of a range of elicitation devices in investigating interlanguage. However, if learners do vary at a single point in time in the fluency and grammaticality of the language they produce, depending on variables such as topic, focus on form, interlocutor, and so on, then how are researchers to handle the data they elicit when they do use a variety of tasks? Minimally, when researchers interpret their data, they need to keep the data from each elicitation technique separate, and to keep track of the contextual variables which were in play in each elicitation. Conceptually, this chameleon-like character of ILs raises serious questions about whether and how traditional linguistic notions developed to account only for monolinguals can apply to interlanguages. This is a complex problem for SLA researchers to resolve.

A fourth issue which has occasioned substantial discussion in the literature centers upon the phenomenon of fossilization itself and whether it is inevitable. Selinker argues, essentially, that no adult learner can hope to ever speak a second language in such a way that they are indistinguishable from native speakers of that language. There are inevitable forces which lead to the cessation of learning. In Selinker's view, there are neurolinguistic reasons for this inevitability. Scovel proposed the Joseph Conrad Phenomenon, in order to draw attention to the very common case where an adult learner's phonological system may fossilize, but the morphology, syntax, and lexicon may not, continuing to develop until reaching full identity with the target language. Scovel (1988), like Selinker, argues that the causes of phonological fossilization are neurolinguistic in nature, and related to the process of cerebral lateralization, which is completed at puberty. But there is certainly disagreement among interlanguage researchers as to both the inevitability of fossilization, and (relatedly) the causes of fossilization. Typically, those who argue that fossilization is caused by sociolinguistic forces (such as the NL group pressure to conform, or one's need to identify with the NL social group rather than the TL social group) also argue that fossilization is not an inevitable process. Such researchers suggest that if learners can identify with the TL social group, or if their need is great enough, they will be able to continue learning the second language until their production/perception is indistinguishable from that of native speakers. This issue also is far from settled, since it relates to matters of human potential rather than humans' actual behavior.

There has been some change in the way in which some of the psycholinguistic processes shaping interlanguage are viewed. For example, native language transfer is viewed as operating selectively; some things transfer from the NL to influence IL, and some things do not. Some crucial questions, therefore, remain: what gets transferred? can we predict in advance what NL characteristics will influence an IL and which ones will not? One promising notion is that of multiple effects: when NL transfer combines with other influences, such as markedness factors, learning strategies, or transfer of training, then there will be greater likelihood of fossilization. So, for example, an early stage of verbal negation common among all second-language learners involves putting a negator (like *no*) before the verb. Learners whose native languages (like Spanish) do negate verbs this way (as in 'Juan no habla' for 'John doesn't talk') will be more likely to fossilize at this stage (producing 'John no talk'). Thus, negative NL transfer has the effect of amplifying the possibilities for fossilization when it interacts with other negative influences. Another psycholinguistic process shaping interlanguage is the learning strategy. A great deal of research has been done (e.g., Cohen 1990), using elicitation techniques such as verbal reports, in order to gain insight into the ways in which learners may consciously set about trying to internationalize aspects of the target language. Some interlanguage researchers have drawn heavily upon the work of cognitive psychologists who have studied the influence of the use of mnemonics on memory. The result of this research has lent itself easily to educational applications, such as the establishment of workshops and even centers to train students in the use of language-learning strategies.

Finally, research of interlanguage has expanded far beyond its original focus on phonology, morphology, syntax, and lexis, to include the sociolinguistic component of communicative competence. Research on interlanguage includes comparative work on the way in which learners execute speech acts across three linguistic systems; Cohen and Olshtain (1981), for example, have studied the way learners attempt to apologize, using their interlanguage, in target language social contexts, and compared this to the way native speakers of both the NL and the TL apologize in the same contexts. Learners' politeness strategies in NL, IL, and TL have been examined on a number of levels by researchers such as Beebe, who have explored miscommunications which have arisen when learners have transferred NL politeness strategies into IL–TL communications.

The Interlanguage Hypothesis provided the initial spark which ignited a field of research on second-language acquisition/learning, and it continues to provide what some feel to be the most productive framework for research. The research questions it originally raised continue to be among the most central and interesting research questions in the field.

See also: New Englishes; Applied Linguistics and Sociolinguistics; Bilingualism and Language Acquisition; Language Transfer and Substrates.

Bibliography

Adjémian C 1976 On the nature of interlanguage systems. *Language Learning* **26**(2): 297–320
Cook V 1996 *Second Language Learning and Language Teaching*. Edward Arnold, London
Cohen A 1990 *Language Learning*. Newbury House, New York
Cohen A, Olshtain E 1981 Developing a measure of sociocultural competence: The case of apology. *Language Learning* **31**(1): 113–34
Corder S P 1967 The significance of learners' errors. *International Review of Applied Linguistics* **5**(4): 161–70
Corder S P 1981 *Error Analysis and Interlanguage*. Oxford University Press, Oxford, UK
Krashen S 1981 *Second Language Acquisition and Second Language Learning*. Pergamon Press, Oxford, UK
Labov W 1970 The study of language in its social context. *Studium Generale* **23**: 30–87
Lado R 1957 *Linguistics Across Cultures*. University of Michigan Press, Ann Arbor, MI
Nemser W 1971 Approximative systems of foreign language learners. *International Review of Applied Linguistics* **9**: 115–23
Scovel T 1988 *A Time To Speak*. Newbury House, New York

Selinker L 1972 Interlanguage. *International Review of Applied Linguistics* **10**: 209–31

Selinker L 1992 *Rediscovering Interlanguage*. Longman, London

Tarone E 1988 *Variation in Interlanguage*. Edward Arnold, London

Weinreich U 1968 *Languages in Contact*. Mouton, The Hague

Intertwined Languages
P. Muysken

Intertwined languages for a long time have been the subject of heated debate, and in more recent times, as data gathering techniques improved, they have become the object of serious study. The term intertwined was first suggested by Norval Smith, and much work has been done on the subject by Peter Bakker. There is now no doubt that there are intertwined languages, whichever definition is adopted. Three kinds of issues come to the fore in studying them: (a) issues of demarcation and definition; (b) issues of formal properties and structural constraints; and (c) issues of function and genesis.

1. Demarcation and Definition

The question of definition will be approached here in a roundabout manner. In current years there has been an explosion of work in the area of language contact (e.g., Arends et al. 1995, Muysken 2000, Myers-Scotton 1993, Romaine 1995, Sebba 1997, Thomason 1996, 1997). Much of this has been concerned with code-mixing (see *Code-mixing*; *Code-switching: Overview*), the use, within bilingual speech, of two languages in one utterance. Some code-mixed utterances very much look like they belong to an intertwined language, as in examples (1) and (2). Here the italicized inserted elements, glossed bold, are in Dutch, in otherwise Sranan and Moluccan Malay sentences, respectively.

(1) wan heri *gedeelte* de ondro *beheer* fug *ewapende machten*
 'One whole **part** is under **control** of armed forces.'
 Sranan/Dutch code-mixing
 (Bolle 1994: 75)

(2) aku *nog steeds vinden* akan *raar* [kata koe *bellen* aku 1s **still find** it **strange** that 2s **call** 1s *twee keer* [*zonder* dapat *gehoor*]]
 two time without get **hearing**
 'I still find it strange that you called me twice without finding anyone home.'
 Moluccan Malay/Dutch code-mixing
 (Huwaë 1992)

Intertwined languages differ from code-mixed bilingual speech, however, in at least two ways. In intertwined languages, the mixing is obligatory rather than optional. Furthermore, in code-mixing, the number of elements from a second language is rarely as large as in (1) and (2).

Intertwined languages should also be distinguished from languages with extensive borrowing. Compare utterance (3a) in Media Lengua, an intertwined language with a Quechua morphosyntax and phonology and Spanish root shapes, with utterance (4) in Cochabamba (Bolivia) Quechua, a heavily hispanicized variety of Quechua (a key to abbreviations used occurs at the end of this article):

(3) (a) *uwixa*-buk *yirba nuwabi*-shka
 guinea.pig-for grass there.is.not-SD
 'There turns out to be no grass for the sheep.'
 (b) llama-buk k'iwa illa-shka   (Quechua)
 (c) No hay hierba para las ovejas (Spanish)
 Media Lengua
 (Muysken 1996a)

(4) Chay-manta-qa *niña ni* ima mikhu-na ka-jti-n,
 that-AB-TO girl NEG what eat-NOM be-SD-3,

 ni ropa ni ka-jte-n-qa *sastre*-mán tukuy ima-ta
 NEG clothes NEG be-SD-3-TO, tailor-AB all what-AC

 sua-rqa-mu-sqa.
 steal-INT-CIS-SD.

 'Then when there was nothing to eat, and neither were there any clothes, the girl went to steal everything from the tailor.' Bolivian Quechua.
 (Urioste 1964)

Even though in (4) all nouns and the negator *ni* are from Spanish, there are quite a few roots from Quechua as well, including the verbs and the function words. In contrast, in (3b) all roots are from Spanish. There is a quantitative leap from 45 percent Spanish roots in heavy borrowing settings to 97 percent Spanish roots in the intertwined language. There is also a qualitative leap from many content words and a few function words (the case of borrowing) to all content and function words that are roots (the intertwined language). In addition, in intertwined

481

languages like Media Lengua the phonetic shapes of the roots are Spanish, while their semantic properties are Quechua. Thus, a new Spanish verb *nuwabi-* is used in (3a), modeled on the Quechua negative existential verb *illa-*. This process is called relexification.

Finally, we should distinguish intertwined languages from spontaneous cases of language mixing, as in the mixed Japanese/English jargon of American Mormon missionaries in Japan, who are practicing their Japanese vocabulary while speaking English:

(5) Hey *dode*, have you *benkyo*ed your *seiten*s for our
    companion   study   scriptures
sukay today yet?
meeting
'Hey companion, have you studied your scriptures for our meeting today yet?'
Japanese/English

(Smout 1988)

In contrast to the three language contact phenomena cited so far, the elements from a second language in intertwined languages are (a) systematic; (b) highly frequent; and (c) obligatory. The notion of an intertwined language necessarily then is a diachronic one; the original contributing languages need not be present in the speech community any more in a pure form.

2. Formal Properties and Structural Constraints

If the presence of elements from two languages is systematic, this means that not just individual items from one language are systematically present in another one, but preferably also classes of items. Thus in the Media Lengua example (3a) and in (6), a historically documented example, the roots are from one language, the affixes from another one. (Abbreviations are explained at the end of this article.)

(6) Heeltemaal-se natuur-a-xu bedorven-he   (Basters)
totally-ADV nature-CAS-P rotten-PASS
'totally rotten in nature'
Hoaraga-se = ûb-a-xu gau-he (Nama/Khoikhoin)
Van nature helemaal bedorven. (Dutch)
Basters Hottentot

(den Besten 1987: 23)

However, in Michif, still spoken in parts of western Canada and the neighboring US states, the noun phrases are from French, and the verb phrases are from Cree:

(7) kî-nipi-yiwa *son frère* aspin kâ-*la-petite-fille*-iwi-t
PST-die-OBV.SU 3s.POSS.m brother COMP-the-little-girl-be-3s
'Her brother died when she was a young girl.'
Michif

(Bakker 1997)

In yet other cases, the function words may be from one language, the content words from another,

similar to the code-mixing cases in (1) and (2). What all these cases have in common is a certain asymmetry, analyzed by Myers-Scotton (1993) (see *Code-switching: Structural Models*; *Myers-Scotton, Carol*) in terms of the matrix language/embedded language contrast. The affixes in Media Lengua and Basters Hottentot, as well as the verbal morphology in Michif, may be construed as constituting a functional skeleton for the clausal structure. Thus we can propose the following tentative generalization:

(8) Intertwined languages typically show a matrix/embedded language asymmetry.

There may well be counterexamples to this, along the lines of Silverstein's (1972) analysis of Chinook Jargon as a multilevel generative system, but they are not frequent. There may be a second possible generalization, which so far has been implicitly in the background; namely that all cases of intertwined languages at least involve systematic lexical mixing. At least lexical elements from different sources are combined, and in addition possibly, but not necessarily, morphological, phonological, and syntactic elements. Thus:

(9) Intertwined languages at least have lexical elements from different sources.

Again, counterexamples are conceivable, perhaps along the lines of the systems drawn attention to by Gumperz and Wilson (1971), where lexicons are distinct but grammatical rules have converged (see *Areal Linguistics*). However, this type of setting generally also involves lexical borrowing.

3. Function and Genesis

Intertwined languages may well have one of three basic functions: they may function as group (mixed) identity markers, as secret languages, and as ritual languages. Group identity languages are e.g., Media Lengua, Michif, and Basters Hottentot. Here the presence of elements from two languages marks the resulting language as reflecting a double identity. Cases of secret languages are the forms of Para-Romani documented by Bakker and Cortiade (1991); here the systematic presence of alien vocabulary made the language incomprehensible to outsiders. Cases of ritual intertwined languages are Ma'a (Mous, in prep.) and Callahuaya (Muysken 1996b). Here the systematic presence of alien vocabulary marks the ritual language as special or sacred. Ritual and secret intertwined languages necessarily are symbiotic (Smith 1995), i.e., spoken in addition to other languages.

As to the genesis of intertwined languages, the psycholinguistic processes involved in their birth are various. On the one hand, these may involve phonetic shapes of lexical items, as in the relexification of Media Lengua. On the other, there may be cases where processes of code-mixing are frozen and lead to an intertwined language, as in the case of Michif. Whatever process was involved, its outcome was adopted as a fixed code.

Abbreviations in the glosses: AB = ablative; AC = accusative; ADV = adverbial; CAS = case marker; CIS = cislocative (toward the speaker); COMP = complementizer; INT = intensifier; m = masculine; NEG = negator; NOM = nomin-alizer; OBV.-SU = obviative subject; P = postposition; PASS = passive; POSS = possessive; PST = past tense; SD = sudden discovery and narrative tense; TO = topic; 3s = third person singular.

See also: Borrowing; Code-mixing; Code-switching: Overview.

Bibliography

Arends J, Muysken P, Smith N (eds.) 1995 *Pidgins and Creoles. An Introduction*. Benjamins, Amsterdam
Bakker P 1997 *A Language of our Own. The Genesis of Michif, the Mixed Cree-French Language of the Canadian Métis*. Oxford University Press, Oxford, UK
Bakker P, Cortiade M (eds.) 1991 *In the Margin of Romani: Gypsy Languages in Contact*. Publications of the Institute for General Linguistics, University of Amsterdam, Nr. 58
Besten H den 1987 Die Niederlandischen Pidgins der alten Kapkolonie. In: Boretzky N et al. (eds.) *Beiträge zum 3. Essener Kolloquium über Sprachwandel und seine bestimmenden Faktoren, vom 30.9–2.10 1987 [sic: 1986] and der Universitat Essen*. Studienverlag Dr. N. Brockmeyer, Bochum, Germany
Bolle J 1994 *Sranan Tongo—Nederlands. Code-wisseling en ontlening*. MA thesis in linguistics, University of Amsterdam, Amsterdam
Gumperz J, Wilson R 1971 Convergence and creolization: a case from the Indo-Aryan-Dravidian order. In: Hymes D (ed.) *The Pidginization and Creolization of Languages*. Cambridge University Press, Cambridge, UK
Huwaë R 1992 *Tweetaligheid in Wierden: het taalgebruik van jongeren uit een Molukse gemeenschap*. MA thesis, University of Amsterdam, Amsterdam
Mous M (in prep.) *Adlexification in Inner Mbugu*. Benjamins, Amsterdam
Muysken P 1996a Media Lengua. In: Thomason S G (ed.) *Contact Languages: A Wider Perspective*. Benjamins, Amsterdam
Muysken P 1996b Callahuaya. In: Thomason S G (ed.) *Contact Languages: A Wider Perspective*. Benjamins, Amsterdam
Muysken P 2000 *Bilingual Speech: a Typology of Code-mixing*. Cambridge University Press, Cambridge, UK
Myers-Scotton C 1993 *Duelling Languages. Grammatical Structure in Codeswitching*. Clarendon Press, Oxford, UK
Romaine S 1995 *Bilingualism*. Blackwell, Oxford, UK
Sebba M 1997 *Contact Languages—Pidgins and Creoles*. Macmillan, London
Silverstein M 1972a,b Multilevel generative systems: The case of Chinook Jargon, I and II. *Language* **48**: 137–85, 243–97
Smith N 1995 A list of pidgins, creoles, and mixed languages. In: Arends J, Muysken P, Smith N (eds.) *Pidgins and Creoles. An Introduction*. Benjamins, Amsterdam
Smout K D 1988 A missionary English from Japan. *American Speech* **63**: 137–49
Thomason S G (ed.) 1996 *Contact Languages: A Wider Perspective*. Benjamins, Amsterdam
Thomason S G (ed.) 1997 A typology of contact languages. In: Spears A K, Winford D (eds.) *The Structure and Status of Pidgins and Creoles*. Benjamins, Amsterdam
Urioste J L 1964 *Transcripciones Quechuas*. Instituto de Cultura Indígena, Cochabamba, Bolivia

Jargons
P. Mühlhäusler

Whereas in everyday language the term jargon is applied to a wide range of different phenomena, including the specialist register of professionals such as lawyers or sailors, sociolinguists employ terms such as sublanguage, register, or sociolect to most phenomena called everyday jargon. The main technical use of the term jargon is found in pidgin and creole linguistics where it refers to an unstable minimal contact language. Such a variety is unstable both linguistically and socially, showing no consistent pattern of transmission and a tendency to construct the language as the situation requires. Jargons can be located on the idealized continuum of creole development which ranges from jargon to stabilized pidgin, extended pidgin to creole. It is difficult to make nonarbitrary cuts and the boundary between a jargon and a stable pidgin remains ill defined. It seems clear however, that creolization does not require prior stabilization.

Schuchardt introduced the term jargon in a technical sense in 1883. He observed that Philippines Spanish varied from user to user in the extent that Malay influenced Spanish in contrast with the stable situation of Portuguese creole in Macau (Macanese) and Malacca (Kristang). Linguistic instability is a necessary but insufficient attribute for the characterization of jargons. A second one is linguistic impoverishment, i.e., a small lexicon and heavy dependency on contextual information and paralinguistic means of communication such as gestures (cf. Mühlhäusler 1997: 128ff.).

Alternative labels for jargons include 'secondary hybrids,' 'makeshift language,' 'multilingual idiolect,' 'multilevel generative systems,' and the ubiquitous 'broken language.'

Silverstein (1972) emphasizes the macaronic character of jargons, their having multiple grammars, each user group apparently generating sentences from their own grammatical base. Communication is possible because each party strips the complexities of their own grammar and a kind of common core denominator emerges—a strategy that can lead to misunderstanding and communication breakdown.

It has been noted by Ferguson (1971) that the similarities of reduced systems such as foreigner talk or baby talk are much greater than similarities between human languages and it might be that strategies of regression to earlier stages of development is adhered to in communication across language boundaries (see *Foreigner Talk*; *Pidgins and Creoles: An Overview*).

The strategies used when speakers of different languages have to establish verbal communication can vary widely from speaker to speaker with universal transfer and cultural practices such as baby talk playing varying roles. The majority of jargons remain ephemeral, unrecorded, unnamed, and poorly studied. Exceptions are a few longer lasting contact situations, mainly associated with European expansion, which have resulted in jargons such as the Chinook Jargon, Pichingli of the Canary Islands, Tarçanca used by Germans and Turks in tourism, Butler English of servants in British India and Thai Boi of the corresponding group in French Indo-China as well as jargon varieties of Dutch, Swedish, and many others (documented in Arends et al. 1995) that have not developed greater stability in spite of extended use.

Jargons can remain undeveloped or be the first stage of an interlanguage continuum (targeted language learning) or a prepidgin continuum during initial contacts.

The relevance of jargons to sociolinguistics would seem to lie primarily in the complex way in which structural and situational information combines. Records of nonstructural aspects of jargons are rare but with modern recording technology there should be no problems in obtaining observationally adequate data.

Another area deserving sociolinguists' attention is cultural differences in use and tolerance of jargons. Instability, one of their defining features reflects individual solutions to the problems of intercultural communication whereas the emerging stability of pidgins has in part to do with people creating new identities. Mobilian Jargon was unstable only when used between Europeans and Amerindians whilst among different groups of the latter it was a stable Pidgin signaling regional identity.

Impoverishment, again has both an individual aspect—individual learners are in the early stages of L2 learning, but also has a social reason: the topics on which members of different groups are permitted to communicate may be restricted by mutual agreement (in the case of the Hiri Trade language of Papua one was not supposed to discuss women) or by acts of power on the part of one group—foreigners typically are given limited access to esoteric languages. The learning of Danish by non-Europeans appears to have been discouraged by the Danes and no stable pidgin Danish developed in Kristianborg, Gold Coast, or Tranquebar.

The study of jargons raises a number of wider issues including:

(a) The question of the 'locus' of language in individuals or society.
(b) The question of variants and dialects. Are jargons such as Chinook Jargon variants of Chinook or English? This question is particularly important in the case of 50/50 jargons encountered in the early stages of Aboriginal-English contact in Australia (e.g., 'pidgin' Kaurna of Adelaide,) or in the case of Macaronic mixtures.
(c) The question of accommodation and cooperation in conversation—and the extent to which verbal means of communication are involved in successful outcomes.
(d) The question of continuity—in what sense are jargons' earlier stages of later pidgins and creoles and the related matter of?
(e) Reinvention versus diffusion over time and space.
(f) The extent to which jargons reflect innate or natural communication strategies as against culture-specific conventions.

The notion that people communicate because they share a code has come under considerable scrutiny in recent years (Love 1985) and may well turn out to be a much less useful construct than linguists originally assumed. The same can be said for the notion that languages are rule governed, something, which many cognitive scientists no longer subscribe to. Jargons thus may turn out to be at the extreme end not just of the Pidgin and Creole continuum, but extreme examples of the more general human condition that one always has to communicate with others whose knowledge, experience, and ability to express these differs from one's own.

As yet disappointingly little has been done in the area of jargon studies. Instead of further marginalizing them one should see them as a challenge to much current thinking in linguistics and sociolinguistics.

See also: Contact Languages; Foreigner Talk; Pidgins and Creoles: An Overview.

Bibliography

Arends J, Muysken P, Smith N 1995 *Pidgins and Creoles. An Introduction*. Benjamins, Amsterdam

Ferguson C F 1971 Absence of copula and the notion of simplicity. In: Hymes D (ed.) *Pidginization and Creolization of Languages*. Cambridge University Press, Cambridge, UK, pp. 141–50

Love N 1985 The fixed-code theory. *Language and Communication* 5: 1–18

Mühlhäusler P 1997 *Pidgin and Creole Linguistics*. University of Westminster Press, London

Silverstein M 1972 Chinook Jargon: Language contact and the problem of multi-level generative systems. *Language* 48: 378–406, 596–625

Koinés

R. Mesthrie

The term 'koiné' refers to a language variety that has arisen from contact between dialects of the same language. It originates from koiné, the Greek word for 'common' (in both senses of 'general' versus 'particular,' and 'vulgar' versus 'cultivated'). The term was used in connection with the type of Greek arising in the era of Hellenic unity and the spread of Hellenism (between ca. 450 BCE and ca. 200 BCE).

1. The Greek Koiné

Classical Greek (used up to ca. 300 BCE) had a number of dialects, the main ones being Attic–Ionic, Arcado–Cyprian, Aeolic, Doric, and North-West Greek. Literary dialects took shape from these varieties. (The oldest of these, the Epic or Homeric dialect which goes back to ca. 800 BCE, was an artificial style based primarily on Aeolic, Arcado–Cyprian, and Ionic.) With the spread of Greek influence throughout the Mediterranean region, there arose a tendency toward unification of the dialects. Attic became the form favored by educated Greeks for public discourse.

Thomson (1972) traces the origins of the Koiné to the seaport of Athens, Piraeus, where people from all parts of the Mediterranean mingled. A mixed dialect arose, which was the forerunner of the Hellenistic Koiné (or 'the Koiné') based mainly on Attic, but including elements from Ionic and other dialects.

After Alexander's conquest of Persia (334 BCE), the Koiné became the official language of the Macedonian Empire, which extended as far as the borders of India. Initially it was a second dialect or second language for a majority of its speakers, coexisting in Greece with the other city-state dialects, but no doubt gaining some prestige on account of its association with government and administration. That it was something of an international medium can be seen from its use as the original language of the New Testament, although its composers were largely Aramaic-speaking. Palmer (1980) remarks that the adoption of this Attic-based Koiné by non-Attic as well as non-Greek speakers over a wide area did not lead to profound linguistic change, apart from lexis. The Koiné eventually became a first language, and formed the basis for the modern Greek colloquial dialects.

2. Modern Use of the Term *Koiné*

There is much ambiguity in the modern use of the term, stemming in part from the many properties of the Greek prototype. Each of the following aspects of the original Koiné has been taken as criterial by one or another modern writer:

(a) its development as a new, common variety based on existing dialects of the language (common is taken in the sense of 'shared');
(b) its use as a common (or 'vulgar') medium of communication between speakers with different first languages or speakers from different dialect areas;
(c) its use as the standard/official language of a politically unified region;
(d) changes in its structure on account of its wide use as both first and second language (involving a synthesis of these at some stage).

The Greek Koiné thus embodied formal (a and d) as well as functional properties (b and c). Modern writers show little agreement about which are more basic. One stream of thinking assumes the formal criteria to be primary, leaving the circumstances of origin open; the other takes the use of the language in official or trade domains as primary, and the linguistic characteristics as secondary. The major objection to (b), (c), or (d) alone as a defining criterion is that on its own each defines a language variety or linguistic process that has a well-established label: (b) is synonymous with lingua franca (and the process of language spread); (c) is better described as 'standardization'; and (d) describes the phenomenon of substrate influence in second-language acquisition or in language shift.

For the term koiné to have any significance apart from these three concepts it is necessary to insist on the property of dialect mixing in a contact situation, leading to the development of a new variety. The process of dialect mixing has come to be called 'koinéization,' and the end product of the mixing, a koiné. The importance of criterion (a) over (b) and (c) can be seen in the fact that a speech variety can become a standard language or a lingua franca without necessarily involving koinéization.

Criterion (d) is more problematic. It is not the case that all stable second-language varieties are koinés, nor that koinéization and substrate influences in language shift are synonymous. However, if a number of L2 varieties develop under certain conditions, remain in contact with the superstrate variety, and give rise to a compromise form, then the result may be termed a koiné. Hence some writers have labeled Vulgar Latin a koiné, since it is a synthesis between L1 Latin and related L2 versions. Labeling Vulgar Latin a koiné might appear to contradict the strict definition already offered. This can be easily resolved by allowing the notion of 'related dialects' to include, in special circumstances, L2-influenced varieties arising from language shift.

Given the fuzzy boundary between the terms 'language' and 'dialect,' some flexibility in interpreting the phrase 'related dialects of the same language' is needed. The varieties involved in koinéization should be mutually intelligible for the most part, irrespective of whether they are generally considered different languages or not.

The most salient of the sociohistorical conditions giving rise to koinés (in the narrow sense of (a)) is the convergence of speakers of different dialects (and possibly of some non-native speakers) of a language. Where this takes place in proximity to the original dialects one may speak of a 'regional koiné,' as in the first stages of the Greek Koiné at Piraeus. The opening up of new urban centers may also result in koinéization. In recent world history, however, it is the 'immigrant koiné' which has proliferated, with the movement of speakers of related dialects from one geographical territory to another, often across continents. One might further distinguish between the movements of people associated with colonial powers—administrators, soldiers, missionaries, and settlers—as against subordinate groups moving to fill servile positions in other territories. This forms the basis for a division between a 'superordinate' and a 'subordinate' immigrant koiné.

While the processes involved in koinéization are of considerable interest to the linguist, once a koiné has formed there may be nothing to distinguish it from older dialects of the language. (However, subordinate immigrant koinés do often show a significant reduction in inflections.) Generally, the designation koiné might be appropriate at a particular stage in the history of a language, but loses significance once the variety becomes established as the first language of a new generation. Like any other natural language a koiné may in time develop new regional subdialects, as shown by the history of Greek.

3. Some Examples of Koinés

3.1 A Superordinate Immigrant Koiné—Australian English

The defining feature of this koiné is, as argued above, not that it is the official language of the country or the common language shared by all people of the territory, but that the English developed in Australia shows the effects of contact between various dialects of the UK and Ireland, while not resembling any one in exact detail. Furthermore, the learning of this dialect of English by others in the country (indigenous peoples as well as later immigrants from outside the UK and Ireland) is not a defining characteristic of the koiné since these speakers have not been influential in the koinéizing stage. Australian English is typologically a 'South of England' variety, though the lexical influence of other varieties like Hiberno–English can also be seen. Trudgill (1986) believes its vowel system, probably its most salient characteristic, to be closest to systems characteristic of the vernacular in London and the southeast of England in the eighteenth and nineteenth centuries (for example, the very close Australian vowel in *bid*; [e] in *bed*; [ɛ] in *bad*; and [aː] ~ [æː] in *path*). Mixing of the features of these dialects probably occurred in Australia, rather than in England itself. This process of koinéization resulted in a new dialect, whose early uniformity has been much remarked upon.

3.2 A Suboridinate Immigrant Koiné—Bhojpuri and Hindi in Former European Colonies

In the nineteenth and early twentieth centuries European colonial powers shipped hundreds of thousands of Indian peasants on indentured contracts to (British) Guyana, Mauritius, Trinidad, Natal, Dutch Guyana (now Suriname), and Fiji. Among people of North Indian descent were speakers of a variety of Indic languages and dialects stretching from the Bay of Bengal well into the interior of northern and central India. The majority of people spoke Bhojpuri (or related varieties) or Awadhi (and related varieties); but there were also speakers of other mutually intelligible forms of eastern or western Hindi, as well as small numbers

Table 1. The past singular of transitive verbs in colonial varieties of Bhojpuri and Hindi, and their sources.

Variety	1st person	2nd person	3rd person
Mauritius	-lī/-nī	-le	-lak
Guyana	-lī	-le	-le
Trinidad	-lī	-le	-al
South Africa	-lī/-ā	-le/-ā	-lak/-las/-is
Suriname	-lī	-le	-is
Fiji	-ā	-ā	-ā/-is

Sources:
 1st person: -lī Bhojpuri and other Bihari dialects
  -nī some Bhojpuri dialects
  -ā standard Hindi and Awadhi
 2nd person: -le Bhojpuri and other Bihari dialects
  -ā standard Hindi and Awadhi
 3rd person: -lak Magahi, Maithili, some Bhojpuri dialects
  -las most Bhojpuri dialects
  -al some Bhojpuri dialects
  -is Awadhi and other eastern Hindi dialects
  -ā standard Hindi

of speakers of distinct languages like Bengali, Rajasthani, Panjabi, etc. In each colony a uniform speech variety developed within a generation, showing the influence of many of the input dialects. In Mauritius, Guyana, Trinidad, and Natal the resultant varieties were closer to Indian Bhojpuri than any other dialect, though they clearly show a blend of features from other sources. In Fiji and Suriname the speech form shows greater resemblance to the interior dialects of Eastern Hindi, especially Awadhi, but the blending of input features is even more clear. In matters of morphological detail, especially, each colonial variety is different from the other and from the parent dialects of rural India. The process of selection can be seen in Table 1, which illustrates the paradigms for the singular of the past tense of transitive verbs in each new koiné, and their sources in Indic dialects:

3.3 A Revived Koiné—Hebrew in Israel

After centuries of use in literary and religious contexts, as no one's first language, Hebrew was proposed for adoption as a vernacular in the 1880s in Palestine. The success of the revival extends to its use as the official language of the state of Israel and as colloquial language of around a million people. Although one particular form of the classical language was aimed at (the Oriental or Sephardic form), general Israeli Hebrew shows influences from the East European (Ashkenazic) and other traditions of pronunciation. The resulting variety, derived from interaction between idiolectal approximations of a classical tongue, has been labeled a koiné (Blanc 1968). Its defining feature is, again, contact between related versions of the same language (Hebrew), rather than direct interaction between the different languages of the Jewish diaspora. What makes this a very special case, however, is that the contributory dialects were all second-language varieties artificially adapted for use in colloquial domains.

4. Processes of Koinéization

The only necessary process in koinéization (in the strict sense) is that of the incorporation of features from several regional varieties of a single language. In the early stages one can expect a certain amount of phonetic heterogeneity, and possibly differences in phonemic systems, morphology, and syntax. Unification between previously distinct groups (along regional or social lines) results in speech accommodation. The process of accommodation between adult speakers will result in a neutralization of the social meaning attached to linguistic variants. That is, the variation in the early stages of koiné formation will no longer correlate clearly with nonlinguistic factors like region, function, social status, etc. More salient variants will be retained, while minority features will be 'accommodated out.' Forms which are more regular, and therefore more easily learnt (by adults), stand a better chance of being retained. Where several alternatives occur, frequency of a particular form must assume some importance: the more dialects a form occurs in, the greater its chances of survival in the koiné. Accommodation probably does not occur in a haphazard manner: in determining who accommodates to whom, and what forms win out, demographic factors involving proportions of different dialect speakers and relative prestige of groups will clearly play an important role.

In time, as the new town, colony, or region inhabited by new groups begins to assume a new identity, and with the rise of a generation of child language-learners, focusing takes place. Essentially, this results in a reduction of the possible variants of linguistic forms and the stabilization of norms. While accommodation is a characteristically adult process, selection of accommodated forms, and stabilization, are more likely to be associated with child acquirers of the koiné.

These processes are evident in the Bhojpuri diaspora; the illustrations are from the South African variety (Mesthrie 1992):
 (a) Variation in the early stages of the koiné can be reconstructed from the speech of isolated rural individuals, whose speech contains morphological markers from some Indian dialects, which are not used in the mainstream of South Africa, Bhojpuri: e.g., a past tense transitive marker *-lis*.
 (b) Blending of regionalisms: Whereas Indian Bhojpuri can be broadly subdivided into western and eastern varieties, the distinction

cannot be found in the South African koiné, which is a blend of eastern and western features: e.g., its 3rd person past transitive verb endings follow the easterly pattern, while the 1st person endings follow the more westerly dialects.
(c) 'Accommodating out' of marked, dialect-specific features: e.g., the synthetic negative copula, *naikhī̃*, characteristic of easterly Indian Bhojpuri dialects does not occur in South Africa.
(d) Stabilization and focusing of choices: With few exceptions, regional variants of the parent variety have been leveled out in South Africa. For example, whereas some of the parent dialects have present copula *hai*; others have a form like *bā, baṭi* or *bānī*; and still others have both *hai* and one of *bā/bāṭi/bānī*; the South African koiné has only *hai*.
(e) Restructuring of social variation: Gradations in rural dialect pronominal forms and in certain verb paradigms for the purposes of signaling 'respect' have generally been lost in the South African koiné.
(f) Demography: On the whole, the koiné in South Africa has a less westerly character than the one in Fiji, and a less easterly character than the one in Mauritius. This accords well with the patterns of migration, since recruitment of workers to Mauritius occurred first from the northeast regions of India, and then proceeded further into the interior for colonies like Natal (South Africa) and furthest in for Fiji.

Other processes frequently found in, but not diagnostic of, koinéization are simplification, reduction, and stylistic reallocation. 'Simplification' refers to an increase in regularity of structure via-à-vis some other dialects of the language. 'Reduction' denotes the loss of grammatical categories or the development of lexical means of expressing them. These two processes are found in subordinate immigrant koinés, but less so in superordinate ones. Thus, simplification and reduction are uncharacteristic of Australian English, but are present in diaspora Bhojpuri (e.g., simplification in pronoun systems; and reduction in verb paradigms with the nonuse of plural verb forms). 'Stylistic reallocation' refers to the occasional retention of purely regional alternants, with a realignment of functions, one serving as formal, the other as colloquial variant. Thus the *dance* vowel is [a] in northern British English, [æː] in some Midland dialects, and [ɑː], [aː], or [æː] in the south. The last two forms occur in Australian English, and in the eastern states have social rather than regional significance. That is, [æː] is the more general form, but [aː] occurs in higher sociolects and formal styles.

5. Koinéization in Relation to Other Linguistic Processes

Koinés form a continuum with other types of contact phenomena, some of which they have been erroneously identified with. A brief consideration of the following outcomes of language contact will clarify the essential characteristics of koinéization: dialect convergence; intimate borrowing and code-switching; substrate influences in language shift; convergence; pidginization; creolization.

Dialect convergence denotes a situation in which two or more dialects of a language occur in stable contact along regional or social borders. Mutual influence may occur, without the development of a new variety. Thus, there is no question of koinéization.

In intimate borrowing and code-switching we see the extensive lexical influence of one language upon another. Modern urban vernaculars showing the (primarily lexical) effects of contact between an indigenous language and a world language of prestige (e.g., urban varieties of educated Hindi in India; Town Bemba in the Zambian Copper Belt) have sometimes been labeled koinés. Until genuinely mixed languages of this sort stabilize, there is little need for a new term. In any case, the designation koiné is not appropriate; 'process' terms like intimate borrowing and code-switching will probably suffice.

Substrate influence in language shift: The term koiné has sometimes been used in the context of the acquisition by a community of a second-language associated with a world or regional power, or with trade. The regional language often takes on new characteristics in different regions on account of differential influences from first languages. Thus the Swahili spoken in some parts of Africa (e.g., the central and southeastern parts of the Democratic Republic of Congo) is said to be a koiné. However, the designation koiné is not appropriate for purely second-language varieties. If, in the process of becoming a first language, an L2 retains some features of the former language(s), it is appropriate to speak of substrate influence. It is possible to conceive of a special case where one or more of such substrate-influenced L1's remain in contact with the superstrate variety, giving rise to a new dialect. This has occurred several times in the history of Vulgar Latin, but has to be demonstrated for other putative substrate-influenced koinés.

Convergence of languages which have been in long periods of contact involving widespread bilingualism can lead to mixing at the structural level, while keeping lexicons separate—the paradigm example being Gumperz and Wilson's (1971) study of Urdu–Marathi–Kannada trilingualism in the village of Kupwar in India. One or two writers have considered this kind of convergence to be akin to koinéization, with the criterion for 'related dialects' generalized to 'typologically similar languages.' However, language convergence of this sort is easily distinguishable from koinéization by the nonappearance of a new variety involving mixing. In Kupwar, for example, the languages have not merged; they continue as three systems, clearly distinguishable at the lexical level.

Pidginization: All writers agree that pidginization involves a far greater degree of simplification and reduction, so that while koinés are structurally continuous with the language varieties they arise from, pidgins are not. The oft-cited condition that a pidgin develops in situations involving more than two distinct languages (i.e., mutually unintelligible or minimally intelligible varieties) is clearly responsible for this state of affairs.

Creolization: Apart from those who link convergence and creolization, few linguists would be tempted to claim similarities between creoles and koinés. The degree of expansion and elaboration that a pidgin undergoes in creolization is not matched in koinéization, since koinéization involves a large proportion of native speakers of the same language from the outset.

6. Conclusion

Although definitions and criteria abound, only the strict sense of koinés being new varieties which develop from mutually intelligible varieties ('related dialects of the same language') is warranted in linguistics. (These dialects may, in special cases, include L2 varieties.) However, other uses of the term persist, which may be better served by labels like 'standard language,' 'lingua franca,' 'official language,' and—less commonly—'language convergence,' 'intimate borrowing,' and 'substrate influence.'

See also: Contact Languages.

Bibliography

Blanc H 1968 The Israeli Koiné as an emergent national standard. In: Fishman J A, Ferguson C A, Das Gupta J (eds.) *Language Problems in Developing Nations*. John Wiley and Sons, New York

Ferguson C A 1959 The Arabic Koiné. *Language* **35**: 616–30

Greenberg J 1986 Were there Egyptian Koinés? In: Fishman J A, Tabouret-Keller A, Clyne M, Krishnamurti B, Abdulaziz M (eds.) *The Fergusonian Impact, Vol. 1*. Mouton, Amsterdam

Gumperz J J, Wilson R 1971 Convergence and creolization: A case from the Indo–Aryan/Dravidian border in India. In: Hymes D (ed.) 1971 *Pidginization and Creolization of Languages*. Cambridge University Press, Cambridge, UK

Hancock I in press The emergence of Romani as a Koiné outside of India. In: Acton T (ed.) *Scholarship and the Gypsy Struggle. Commitment in Romani Studies*. University of Hertfordshire Press, Hertford, UK

Kahane H, Kahane R 1988 Language spread and language policy: The prototype of Latin and Greek. In: Lowenberg P H (ed.) *Language Spread and Language Policy: Issues, Implications, and Case Studies*. Georgetown University Round Table on Languages and Linguistics 1987. Georgetown University Press, Washington, DC

Mesthrie R 1992 *Language in Indenture: A Sociolinguistic History of Bhojpuri-Hindi in South Africa*. Routledge, London, UK

Palmer L R 1980 *The Greek Language*. Faber, London, UK

Siegel J 1985 Koinés and Koinéization. *Language in Society* **14**: 357–78

Thomson G 1972 *The Greek Language*. Heffer, Cambridge, UK

Trudgill P 1986 *Dialects in Contact*. Blackwell, Oxford, UK

Language Enclaves
K. Mattheier

A language enclave or speech island (German *Sprachinsel*) is a special type of a linguistic minority. As in the case of other linguistic minorities, language enclaves are characterized by the fact that speakers (or groups of speakers) of a dominant language (i.e., the majority language), and speakers of a minority language live together within an administrative and/or sociohistorical unit.

1. Types of Linguistic Minorities

Linguistic minorities can be understood in different ways (see *Minority Languages*). Statistical minorities exist in those cases where there are a certain percentage of speakers of a second (non-dominant) language within a speech community. More important however, is the concept of a sociocultural linguistic minority. This refers to a specific sociolinguistic constellation, which is characterized by the fact that speakers of a different language form a relatively homogenous settlement and a linguistic community within a certain geographical area or territory, and usually show an awareness of their linguistic, cultural, and ethnic identity. Within this constellation one can distinguish two societal types of linguistic minorities. On the one hand, there are those groups, which are linguistic minorities in the strict sense of the term. These are isolated, small (or very small) linguistic communities, which are situated within the territory of a dominant speech community. Examples are, the settlement area of the Westslavic Sorbian speech community in the southeast of Germany, and the Breton speaking community in the west of France. In these cases there exists no additional political or geographical region where the minority language is spoken (possibly even as a dominant language), outside of the particular settlement area. If however there exists in addition to the minority settlement something like a 'language homeland,' then we use the term 'language enclave' or 'speech island.' Examples of such language enclaves are the Bhojpuri/Hindi speech communities in Mauritius and Fiji, the Venetian/Italian-speaking communities in Mexico, the 'Hunsrückisch' (a Middle German dialect) and 'Plautdietsch' (Mennonite Low German) speaking groups in the south of Brazil and in Russia, and the Pennsylvania Dutch (i.e., German) speaking groups all over North America.

2. General Characteristics of Language Enclaves

The concept of language enclaves or speech islands is particularly common in German linguistics and dialectology, where it has a research tradition of more than 100 years (cf. for example, the investigation of the German-speaking communities in Russia and Siebenbürgen, Romania). The study of the linguistic and historical connections between language enclave and 'language homeland' initially focused largely on questions of ethnic origin. However, more theoretical implications relating to sociolinguistic variation can be detected from as early as Viktor M. Schirmunski's seminal work on the German dialects in Russia during the 1920s. Outside of Germany the relationship between the languages of homeland and the isolated external settlements has typically been considered from the perspective of linguistic minority research. However, there are a number of factors which suggest that it is useful to consider language enclaves as specific types of linguistic minorities. On the one hand, there exist deep historical and social relations between the language enclave and the homeland. Occasionally such relations have been reinstated after decades or even centuries, when—as, for example, in many parts of the US—folkloristic traditions of the homeland are again cultivated. Moreover, there can exist, over long periods of time, on-going immigration from the native country to the language enclave. There are also cases in which the native country fulfills more or less extensive governmental/administrative responsibilities. These can include educational provisions and the supply of teachers for mothertongue instruction, cultural support, and even the legal protection of minority rights. In Germany, these responsibilities are extended to include the right of return for descendants of the original settlers (many of whom had left Germany during the eighteenth century).

Finally, language islands are often characterized by a national or ethnic sense of belonging to the native country. This sense of ethnic belonging can inhibit identification with the new surrounding society (see *Ethnicity and Language*). With regard to the German-speaking minorities in Hungary this has been described as a 'floating identity.'

All these factors are absent in the case of a linguistic minority in the strict sense of the term. Language enclaves and linguistic minorities therefore exhibit different developmental tendencies. However, there also exist situations in which a language enclave largely breaks off contact with the native country after its foundation. In such historical constellations the status of a 'speech island' is conceptually problematic, as in the case of the Pennsylvania Dutch language enclaves which had no contact with their area of origin (the Palatinate in Germany) in 1775.

The origin and development of language enclaves depend on a specific sociohistorical and sociolinguistic constellation, which has so far attracted little comparative research. Such a constellation was given in different areas at certain times during history, such as the large-scale migrations caused by religious conflicts, which took place after 1550 in Europe, or the colonial expansion of European nations in the seventeenth and eighteenth centuries. In all these cases a prerequisite of the process is a motivation of members of a community to leave the social structures of their regional or national homeland as a group. Such motivations can be found in the conditions of the natural environment (e.g., great natural catastrophes) and in the ethnic-political context of the dominant society; moreover they can be of a religious kind or simply economic. The migrations themselves are often based on settlement plans and organized voyages, which significantly shape the settlement structures in the 'new homeland' and which support the formation of ethnic or religious solidarity in a clearly specified territory. The latter constitutes a prerequisite for the development of an independent identity in opposition to the new majority society. Moreover, in the process of establishing the new society one often observes activities of divergence and dissociation by members of the speech enclave as well as by members of the majority society.

Such constellations have been common and are still common in many regions. Examples are the language enclaves of Turkish migrants in Germany or Sweden, and those of South Asian (Indian, Pakistani, Bangladeshi, and Sri Lankan) or Caribbean groups in England. In most of these cases, the language enclave only survives for a limited time and the development usually concludes with the abandonment of the heritage culture. For example, most of the many Middle-Low German language enclaves which had emerged since the fourteenth century due to the activities of the *Hanse* (an important trade organization) around the North Sea and the Baltic Sea, had already disappeared in the eighteenth century.

3. Definition and Research Perspectives

Taking into account the considerations outlined in the previous section regarding the general socio-historical and sociolinguistic conditions of the phenomenon 'language enclave,' the following definition can be formulated:

> A language enclave (or speech island) is a communication community which is separated geographically from its 'language homeland,' and exists as a linguistic minority within a linguistically/ethnically different contact society, whose language dominates within the territory (German *Überdachung*). The language enclave keeps itself apart from the contact society (and is kept apart by the contact society) because of a number of objective characteristics or factors which define the special status of its members. This supports the emergence of a special sociopsychological disposition or mentality of the language enclave, which can explain the prevention or retardation of full linguistic-cultural assimilation to the contact society.

Within the language enclave we thus find a number of objective factors (circumstances and influences) which work together in creating what one might term a 'language enclave mentality' or a 'language enclave identity' among the members of the community. The existence of a 'language enclave consciousness' is the reason why the normal process of intergenerational assimilation to the foreign language of the new environment is interrupted or retarded. Outside of language enclave constellations, this process of linguistic-cultural assimilation and acculturation usually takes place within three or four generations (see *Language Maintenance, Shift, and Death*).

The comparative study of language enclaves—also in contrast to linguistic minorities in the strict sense of the term—should focus on exactly this relationship, that is, on the combination of a number of objective (i.e., economic, demographic, administrative, and general social) factors and the developing ideas of an identity within a language enclave, which make possible the separation from the outside world. Furthermore, research should study the reactions of the contact society towards these developments. For example, in many of the economically motivated, rural, dialect-dominant, German language enclaves in the US and Canada, the use of three varieties (a German dialect as well as the German standard language and—within limits—English) had consolidated by the late nineteenth century. There were hardly any signs of language shift and several indications of the development of a local German-American language mentality. The spread of industrialization into the rural areas and especially the outbreak of World War I shattered this identity; the process of linguistic assimilation towards American English started with increasing force, and came to an end in most language enclaves three generations later.

The selection of the range of objective factors, which are crucial for the formation, and development of a language enclave has been debated time and again in the literature (cf. Clyne 1985, 1994, Kloss 1966). In these discussions several language maintenance factors have been emphasized. Of central importance is the field of demography, in particular in connection with the language and variety profile within the language enclave and its environment. It is not entirely clear in this context how small language enclaves can be with regard to their demographic structure. One also needs to pay attention to the regional expansion of language enclaves, especially their degree of compactness. Pennsylvania Dutch-speaking groups in the central counties of Pennsylvania never constitute a group of more than 18 percent of the total population. Thus one cannot speak of a compact settlement. Other formative influences can be found in the economic structure, the legal-administrative structure, the social structure (such as the degree of endogamy), and the sociolinguistic structure of language and variety use. First comparative analyses of these factors and their effect on language maintenance and language loss show that, for example, in the German-based language enclaves language maintenance is indicated reliably by only one factor: the religious orientation of Anabaptist groups. Only within the conservative groups of the Old Order Amish, the Mennonites, and the Old Colony Mennonites, which live in isolation from 'the world,' is the local dialect (Pennsylvania Dutch and Plautdietsch, respectively) not endangered. Language maintenance factors other than those linked to the field of religion are of little relevance when assessing the development of these language enclaves. On the other hand, it is methodologically difficult to adequately understand phenomena such as language enclave identity or mentality. Here comparative analyses of diverse language enclaves with different heritage languages and contact or target languages can help to refine our theoretical ideas and to differentiate between different language enclave constellations.

See also: Language Maintenance, Shift, and Death; Ethnolinguistic Vitality; Migrants and Migration; Minority Languages; Heritage Languages; Ethnicity and Language.

Bibliography

Clyne M G 1985 Language maintenance and language shift: Some data from Australia. In: Wolfson N, Manes J (eds.) *The Language of Inequality*. De Gruyter, Berlin

Clyne M G 1994 What can we learn from Sprachinseln? Some observations on 'Australian German.' In: Berend N, Mattheier K J (eds.) *Sprachinselforschung*. Peter Lang, Frankfurt, Germany

Kloss H 1966 German-American language maintenance efforts. In: Fishman J A (ed.), *Language Loyalty in the United States*. Mouton, The Hague

Mattheier K J 1994 Theorie der Sprachinsel. Voraussetzungen und Strukturierungen. In: Berend N, Mattheier K J (eds.) *Sprachinselforschung*. Peter Lang, Frankfurt, Germany

Language Loyalty
R. Mesthrie

Language loyalty is a term one occasionally encounters in the literature on language maintenance and shift. That it is intended in a non-technical, self-evident sense is evidenced by the lack of a definition in books and articles carrying the term in their titles. The term was first used by Fishman, a pioneer in the field of language maintenance and shift (see *Fishman, Joshua*; *Language Maintenance, Shift, and Death*). His book *Language Loyalty in the United States* deals with 'the maintenance and perpetuation of non-English mother tongues by American ethnic and religious groups' (to quote its sub-title). Fishman (1966: 15) does not define the term 'language loyalty,' but styles the book as 'a study of the self-maintenance efforts, rationales, and accomplishments of non-English speaking immigrants on American shores.'

As such the term loyalty may be taken to be the impulse behind language maintenance (or its opposite, shift). Indeed Fishman (1966: 21) writes that 'language maintenance, prompted by one or another variety of language loyalty has frequently been a component—and, at times, a catalyst' in the efforts of ethnic minorities to maintain themselves. Fishman's own work and that of his successors makes it clear that the equation 'loyalty = maintenance; disloyalty = shift' would be simplistic and incorrect. The reason for this is that the term loyalty itself covers conscious, practical manifestations (e.g., recognizing the danger of shift and setting up counter-measures like special language classes outside mainstream schooling) as well as more vague and unconscious attitudes which underlie language choices (see *Attitudes and Behavior*).

In many communities undergoing shift loyalty to the ancestral language is frequently avowed overtly; yet unconscious (or covert) language choices made by community members often favor the incoming dominant language. The terms 'overt' and 'covert' are here borrowed from the better known dichotomy set up by Labov (1972) between overt and covert prestige to explain why, despite openly articulated professions of the superiority of a standard or dominant variety, speakers of a (stable) vernacular (see *Vernacular*) nevertheless are happy to persist with their lower status speech within their own social networks. In her study of language shift from Gaelic to English in East Sutherland, Scotland, Dorian (1981: 104) noted that such a conflict between attitudes and behaviors:

> It is *not* acceptable to behave as though one did not know Gaelic oneself, but it *is* acceptable to do nothing to see that one's children know it.

It would probably be a case of blaming the victim to style such behavior as disloyalty: rather it seems a mix of 'symbolic loyalty' (to the ancestral language) with pragmatic allegiance (to the dominant language). In language shift we thus have a reversal of the roles of 'overt' and 'covert' prestige, with overtly stated allegiance to a (lower status) ancestral language accompanied by covertly sanctioned use of the dominant language (the new vernacular). The variety that once had covert prestige now has attachments of 'symbolic loyalty' (or overt professions of worth and prestige).

This is perhaps an oversimplification of the complex and frequently poignant dynamics of language shift (see *Language Maintenance, Shift, and Death*), but it is necessary to unpack the implications of the term 'language loyalty' which turns out to be more complex than the lay sense after all. Language loyalties may underpin maintenance efforts but are in some circumstances also outcomes of the maintenance-shift dialectic. Speakers readjust loyalties according to changing power dynamics of the linguistic market (see *The Linguistic Marketplace*). Loyalty therefore seems destined, like its counterpart 'prestige' in sociolinguistics (to which it is closely tied) to remain a useful but undertheorized term.

See also: Language Maintenance, Shift, and Death; Vernacular; Reversing Language Shift; Sociolinguistic Variation.

Bibliography

Dorian N 1981 *Language Death—The Life Cycle of a Scottish Gaelic Dialect*. University of Pennsylvania Press, Philadelphia, PA

Fishman J 1966 *Language Loyalty in the United States*. Mouton, The Hague

Labov W 1972 *Sociolinguistic Patterns*. University of Pennsylvania Press, Philadelphia, PA

Language Maintenance, Shift, and Death
R. Mesthrie

Language shift and death are overlapping terms used to describe situations in which a language ceases to be used by a speech community. *Language shift* occurs when a new language is acquired by a community with the concomitant loss of its erstwhile primary language. If that community is the last (or only) one to use the obsolescent language it is possible to speak, in addition, of language death. *Language death* may also describe a situation in which a language is lost without a new one replacing it. This is occasioned by the destruction of the speech community itself. *Language maintenance* denotes the continuing use of a language in the face of competition from a regionally and socially more powerful or numerically stronger language.

1. History

The extinction of Cornish in England in the eighteenth century is an example of language death as well as shift (to English). The demise of an immigrant language like Norwegian in the USA exemplifies shift without death, since the language survives in its original setting in Norway. (Some commentators might, however, speak of the death of this immigrant dialect of Norwegian.) Language death without shift is exemplified by the fate of Tasmanian, whose speakers were almost entirely wiped out just 73 years after the first contacts with British settlers in 1803. The last speaker of Tasmanian is said to have died with her own language intact, and with no knowledge of English, save for a few loanwords (Swadesh 1948).

Although, in popular parlance, languages like Latin, Ancient Greek, and Sanskrit are referred to as dead languages, this use of the term is inapplicable within the framework of this article. Languages like these gradually evolved by continuous intergeneration transmission into dialects which gave rise to autonomous and eventually standardized speech forms. At no stage was there a sharp break from one colloquial speech system to another. On the other hand, it is accurate to speak of the death of ancient languages like Pictish, Etruscan, and Gothic.

Hebrew provides the unusual example of a language which did die as the medium of everyday conversation, but was revived with considerable effort in the late nineteenth and early twentieth century.

It is estimated that in the period 1490–1990 about half of the world's languages disappeared. However, one scholar (Brenzinger 1992) is of the opinion that for East Africa, at least, language shift and death are not necessarily more frequent today than before—they have been side effects of migrations and expansions of ethnic groups over the last 5000 years.

In the last twentieth century, Aboriginal languages of Australia were greatly in decline. It is estimated that of the 200 languages of precontact Australia, fewer than 50 have viable communities in which children are able to speak the language. In the USA the fate of Amerindian languages is not much better, although at least one language—Navajo—is thought to have had as many speakers at the close of the twentieth century as it had at any stage of its history. (However, allowing for population growth and the fact that not all children from the community are acquiring Navajo, there seems little room for complacency.) In Europe the Celtic languages struggle to survive against English and French. In Southern Africa languages of the Khoi and San families have been the victims of shift and death. Generally, minority languages on the African continent have given way to other more prestigious African languages rather than languages of European colonialism.

2. Causes of Shift

For a large number of cases involving indigenous languages in Australia and the Americas the causes of shift and death are clear. Once viable and autonomous speech communities were either destroyed or deprived of their traditional land and resettled with other groups who did not always share the same language. Eventual reorientation to a new westernized society further attenuated the viability of traditional forms of the surviving languages among the young (see *Endangered Languages*).

It is one of the few points of agreement in studies of minority and immigrant languages that there is no single set of factors that can be used to predict the outcome of language maintenance efforts. Causes of shift are generally multiple and interrelated. Kloss (1966) has pointed out that many of the factors may even cut both ways. Thus, no uniform or predictable consequences for language maintenance or shift are derivable from (a) absence or presence of higher education in the dominated language, (b) relatively large or relatively small numbers of speakers of the dominated language, (c) greater similarity or greater dissimilarity between groups speaking the dominant and dominated languages respectively, and (d) positive or hostile attitudes of the dominant group to the minority.

The factors that are most often discussed in individual cases of shift can be grouped as follows: economic changes; status; demography; and institutional support.

2.1 Economic Factors

Economic changes are by far the most salient of the factors leading to shift, though the relation is neither necessary nor sufficient. The juxtaposition of different speech communities is frequently brought about by invasion, seeking of refuge, immigration of workers, or trade. All of these (except, perhaps, for refuge) have an underlying economic motive. In many countries modernization, industrialization, and urbanization often lead to bilingualism in a vernacular language and a more widespread regional language associated with the economy. In conjunction with other factors (discussed below) these may lead to shift.

Jones (1981) traces the beginnings of language shift in Wales to the creation of an upper ruling class from the Tudor period onwards, which became increasingly Anglicized as it grew more and more drawn to the social, economic and cultural sphere of London. The second phase in the decline of Welsh involved immigration of English speakers into the coalfields of south-east Wales in the second half of the eighteenth century. With respect to Scots Gaelic, Thomson (Haugen et al. 1990) argues that the exodus of people from the Scottish Highlands in search of work in English-speaking areas in the nineteenth century was a key factor in its eventual decline. Economic factors thus counteracted the efforts of the Gaelic Schools Society to foster stable Gaelic–English bilingualism.

Less commonly, economic changes can positively affect a threatened language. Paulsen (1981) describes the case of the Ferring dialect of Frisian spoken in the North Sea islands of Föhr and Amrun. After the decline of traditional herring fishing a school was founded in the sixteenth century to teach navigation skills to boys, who subsequently found employment in the new Dutch overseas shipping companies. Speaking Ferring was an advantage and immigrants had to learn it if they wished to become members of this closed seafaring community. This was one of the main factors enhancing maintenance of a previously threatened language.

2.2 Demographic Factors

Numbers of speakers do have a bearing on successful language maintenance: it might seem obvious that the smaller the size of a community, the stronger the threat of language shift and death. However, it is not possible to specify a 'critical mass' of speakers necessary for the survival of a language. Brenzinger et al. (1991) cite the case of Bayso, an Eastern Cushitic language of southern Ethiopia, which has resisted language replacement for over 1000 years although the number of its speakers has always been small (in 1990 in the region of 500).

Apart from absolute numbers, or proportions of speakers of dominated language to dominating language, the distribution of speakers is of some significance. Enforced or *de facto* segregation of immigrant communities would appear to offer better chances of language maintenance, all other things being equal. Li (1982) found that third-generation Chinese Americans residing in Chinese-dominant neighborhoods ('Chinatowns') were less likely to have adopted English as their mother tongue than their agemates outside the Chinatowns. Endogamy within an immigrant group will also improve chances of a family language being transmitted to offspring. Brenzinger cites intermarriage between the Yaaku and Maasai of north central Kenya as one of the main factors leading to a shift in economic practices among the former (from hunter-gatherers to pastoralism), and to an eventual shift in language.

2.3 Institutional Support

The use of a minority language in education, religion, the media, or administration may assist attempts to bolster its position. But for minorities, this can only be done at great cost. There are limits to the extent to which a nondominant immigrant language (or, more usually, languages) can be used in schools. A majority asymmetry exists between use of a minority language in educational settings (associated with formal and standard norms of a language) and the hypercolloquial and localized use characteristic of a language in its dying stages. The role of German in the religious sphere among the Old Order Amish and Mennonites is considered to be a primary cause of maintenance of Pennsylvania German, though other factors are also implicated (endogamy, resistance to economic and social change, etc.). For many communities religious activities demand an archaic form of their language or a register far removed from colloquial speech.

2.4 Status

Some writers consider a group's self-esteem and the status of their language (oral or written, vehicle for scared texts, major regional language elsewhere in the world, etc.) to play a role in maintenance or shift. These are not entirely separate from economic and class factors, however. Thus, Arabic is a high-status language in the Middle East, but not in Europe, where it is mainly connected with immigrant working-class speakers.

In his review of the field, Fishman (1972) emphasizes the ambivalence of generalizations that might seen to have obvious validity. Thus, language maintenance is not necessarily a function of intactness of group membership, particularly of such ideologized expressions of group loyalty as nationalism. Urban dwellers are not necessarily more prone to language shift than rural dwellers. It is not always the case that the more prestigious language displaces the less prestigious one. Women may be in the rearguard of shift in some instances, men in others.

3. The Course of Shift

It is obvious that a shift from one language to another cannot be effected without an intervening period of bilingualism. In the initial phases of the relationship the languages may show characteristic distribution patterns over specific domains. More formal domains may, by force of circumstances, be allotted to the dominant societal language; more informal domains like the home to the minority language. Language shift involves the progressive redistribution of the languages over these domains—the home, religion, folk songs and tales usually being the last bastions of survival for the dominated language.

Many shifts involve more than one minority language, whose positions are weakened not only by the dominant language but by each other. Immigrant communities from different areas of origin may develop close associations in the workplace and neighborhood, which demand the use of a lingua franca. The most expedient or neutral choice is often the dominant societal language. A similar ethos among different Amerindian groups in the USA, and Aboriginal groups in Australia forced into reservations, has accelerated the pace at which English developed as a lingua franca, often to the detriment of the indigenous languages.

The process of shift is often gradual, involuntary, and unconscious. While the circumstances of the shift may be centuries in the making (as with Welsh, Irish, Scots Gaelic, etc.), there are instances of languages which have been demographically stable for several centuries experiencing a relatively rapid shift. Dorian (1981: 51) (see *Dorian, Nancy*) characterizes this as a sudden 'tip,' after which the demographic tide flows strongly in favor of some other language. Two examples recently cited include the tip from Nubian to Arabic in Egypt, and from Scots Gaelic to English in Cape Breton, Nova Scotia in the 1930s and 1940s.

Leap (1981) believes that there have been no instances, historical or contemporary, where an Amerindian community has intentionally allowed ancestral language fluency to disappear. Although this would appear to be the general norm worldwide, there have been a few instances of shift which have been deliberately hastened by members of the speech community. Eidheim (1969) discusses the case of the Saami fjord community which aspires to full participation in the public network, as it is defined by Norwegians. Many families have taken the drastic decision of preventing their children from learning Saami. Brenzinger et al. (1991) describe the conscious decision made by the Yaaku of East Africa in the 1930s to give up their language in the face of social, economic, and linguistic pressure from the dominant Maasai. After adopting the value system of the pastoralists, the Yaaku considered the Maasai lifestyle and their language to be superior and to have higher prestige than their own 'hunter-gatherer' language. They discouraged the use of the old language even within their own community, insisting that the Yaaku language with its semantic emphasis on hunting was unfit for a cattle-breeding society.

The shrinkage of domains in the course of shift is paralleled by receding generational competence in the outgoing language. In its last stages speakers may exhibit an age-graded range of competence from full command to zero. In between these are the competences of young fluent speakers, semispeakers and passive bilinguals (Dorian 1981). *Young fluent speakers* are those who have native command of the ancestral language, but who show subtle deviations from the fluent older speakers' norms. *Passive bilinguals* have full receptive skills in the ancestral language, but are unable to use the language in productive speech. *Semispeakers* are those who have had insufficient exposure to the ancestral language, but continue using it in an imperfect way some of the time, out of a high degree of language loyalty. Dorian characterizes the semispeakers of Gaelic in East Sutherland, Scotland, as having relatively halting delivery, speaking in short bursts and exhibiting linguistic deviations of which older speakers are mostly aware. On the other hand, they are able to build sentences and alter them productively, a trait which distinguishes them from the passive bilinguals.

Other scholars draw finer distinctions between reasonably fluent semispeakers (who are still able to interact with older speakers despite lack of full proficiency) and weak semispeakers or terminal speakers (whose interaction arises mainly out of necessity of clarifying things for older monolingual speakers, rather than out of language loyalty). A finer distinction can also be made between passive bilinguals and 'rememberers.' The latter exist in the last stages of shift, when a group of older fluent speakers no longer exists with whom to exercise their receptive and productive skills. That is, passive bilinguals interact within the community of ancestral language users, rememberers cannot.

Some language death situations give no evidence of the semispeaker phenomenon. Swadesh (1948) reports on the extinction of the Yahi language of northern California, whose last speaker's competence he characterizes as 'flawless.' This man, Ishi, learnt English only in his last years, after being taken to the University of California in 1911. The Californian languages, Luiseño and Cupeño, whose obsolescence involves shift and death, apparently have no semispeakers. People either speak fairly well or not at all (Dorian 1981: 115). The emergence of semispeakers might seem to hinge on the rapidity of death or shift: protracted shift allows for semispeaker competence (and a command of the new language): rapid shift (or 'tip') and death do not. However, this generalization, like much else in the field, admits of many exceptions—Luiseño and Cupeño are cases in point (languages with a relatively protracted period of shift, but no semispeakers).

Dorian attributes the existence of semispeakers (rather than young fluent speakers or passive bilinguals) in East Sutherland to the following factors.

(a) Late birth order in a large, relatively language-loyal family. In such a family the eldest might emerge as a fluent speaker, whereas the last two or three children may emerge as semi-speakers. Although their parents might continue addressing the last two or three children in Gaelic, the influence of elder siblings who bring back English from the school and play ground is stronger.

(b) A second factor is strong attachment to one or more grandparents (most often a grandmother), who usually use far more Gaelic than one's parents. Less commonly, it is the influence of aunts and parents that encourages the semispeaker phenomenon.

(c) Temporary absence from the community often fosters a reawakening of loyalty to the dominated language, which may be first achieved as semispeech if there are fellow exiles who share those feelings.

(d) An inquisitive and gregarious personality might also lead some young people to participate in conversations with elders in Gaelic. Presumably, such outgoing individuals actively wish to conduct conversations in the preferred language of the other party, irrespective of the possible stigma of their own errors.

4. The Linguistics of Obsolescence

Where the actual effects of incomplete acquisition histories on linguistic performance are concerned, equal diversity is found in case studies. An early hypothesis was that dying languages might undergo many processes reminiscent of pidginization. In dying languages and pidgins, for example, vocabulary is relatively restricted, inflections are simplified or generalized, and movement rules lost. A preference for more analytic syntax (compared to the base languages) is another common feature of pidgins and dying languages. Pidginization often involves a degree of language mixing that was thought to hold for semispeaker speech as well. A second hypothesis saw semispeech as a kind of creolization in reverse, since pidgins become creolized by entering into the primary socialization of children, whereas dying languages case to be used for primary socialization (see *Pidgins and Creoles: Models*).

The pidginization hypothesis has not stood up to close scrutiny. Unlike pidgins, dying languages do not show a tendency to uniformity in word order. Nor are there any reports of the kind of wholesale breakdown of morphology in dying languages that one finds in pidgins. In connection with dying East Sutherland Gaelic, Dorian maintains that allomorphic variety does not undergo substantial change (see below), that word order is unchanged, embedding handled with ease, and certain categories which have marginal or indirect semantic significance persist. None of these is suggestive of processes of pidginization.

Dressler (1972) suggests that languages die on account of rule loss, rule simplification, and the like. Denison (1977) rejects this line of reasoning, claiming that languages become obsolete when speakers no longer deem it worthwhile to communicate with children in a particular variety, and children are no longer motivated to acquire an active competence in that language. In the same vein, Mohan and Zador (1986) place a question mark over exactly when a language may be said to be dead, claiming that the language of semispeakers is not the prelude to death, but the visible signs of an event that has already come to pass. They suggest that the biological metaphor of death is apt in implying a state, not an ongoing process and that languages die intact and earlier than suggested by other writers.

Part of the controversy, and other inconsistencies in pinpointing the characteristics of semispeech, can be resolved by taking into account the amount of exposure that the semispeaker has had to the ancestral language as a child, and of opportunities for its use early on. As Menn (1989) emphasizes, a learner who has encountered the language in question through heavy exposure to ritual language will display rote or formulaic language, but rarely preconventional speech involving overgeneralization of words, morphemes, and constructions. A learner who has had good exposure to the ancestral language till school-going age, and little further opportunity, will lack a formal register in that language. Such speech can be expected to lack embedding and other constructions that are rare in care-taker speech. On the other hand, overgeneralization of morphemes by analogy is to be expected.

Some characteristic features of individual dying languages will now be considered. These must be taken as examples of individual out-comes, rather than of a grand design. One of the problems facing researchers is that the kinds of changes that dying languages undergo are not qualitatively different from ordinary, contact-induced change in 'healthy' languages, and even from language-internal developments, in noncontact situations. It is the quantity of such changes in a relatively short timespan in dying languages that is the distinguishing factor.

Breatnach (1964), describing obsolescent dialects of Irish, claims that the effects of disuse are evident at all stages mainly in the vocabulary, and secondarily in morphological, phonological, and syntactic patterns. The purely phonetic character of the language resists influence to the end.

Dorian's (1978) characterization of the morphology of East Sutherland Gaelic will be taken as a more detailed exemplification of the linguistics of language obsolescence. Among the ways of forming the plural of nouns in the traditional dialect of the area are the following:

(a) Suffixation of the ending *-en* to some nouns
(b) Final mutation (e.g., $t^h \rightarrow \tilde{c}^h$)
(c) Suppletion (e.g., $t^h\varepsilon$ 'house' (sg) versus $t^hro:r$ 'houses')
(d) vowel alternation (e.g., mak^h 'son' (sg) versus mik^h 'sons')

There are still other ways of forming the plural of specific nouns, involving combinations of the above processes (e.g., final mutation plus suffixation; vowel alternation plus final mutation plus suffixation, etc.).

In semispeaker performance some degree of simplification is present. There is the notable rise of suffixation (especially the use of a 'favored' suffix by individuals), which leads to grammar simplification. However, a great deal of the original complexity remains. Final mutation, vowel alternation suppletion, quantity change, subtraction, and zero formation are still in use among semispeakers, though to a lesser extent than among fluent speakers. Dorian (1978: 608) concludes that 'East Sutherland Gaelic may be said to be dying, at least with regard to noun plurals and gerunds, with its morphological boots on.'

Mithun (1989) outlines the characteristics of an obsolescing polysynthetic language—Cayuga (an Iroquoian language) of Oklahoma. There is a shrinkage of the lexicon, with specific terms being lost before more general ones. Words for objects no longer observed have been forgotten (e.g., animal terms like 'moose,' 'beaver,' 'mink,' 'weasel'). Other changes that do exist in obsolescent Cayuga are quite subtle. Although the inventory of affixes is unchanged, speakers rarely combine several affixes within a word. The reluctance to combine morphemes within single words extends to noun incorporation. In terms of phonology and syntax there are no major changes, leading Mithun to remark upon the nearly complete retention of an amazingly complex morphological and phonological system under limited opportunities to use it.

5. Conclusion

Studies in language maintenance and shift are clearly of great importance, for their potential to contribute to language planning on a societal level as well as for theoretical linguistics. The experience of sociolinguists in this area can be used to help beleaguered language communities to stabilize their languages in the face of the encroachment of major regional and world languages (see *Salvage Work (Endangered Languages)*). From the internal viewpoint of linguistics, the study of dying languages has insights for the historical linguist concerned with substrate influences in language change. Furthermore, the study of semispeech has the same potential to contribute to linguistic theory as other instances of marginal language use—aphasic speech and pidgins. This potential has yet to be fully realized.

See also: Sociology of Language; Endangered Languages; Salvage Work (Endangered Languages); Ethnolinguistic Vitality.

Bibliography

Blanc H 1968 The Israeli koiné as an emergent national standard. In: Fishman J A, Ferguson C A, Das Gupta J (eds.) *Language Problems in Developing Nations*. Wiley, New York

Breatnach R B 1964 Characteristics of Irish dialects in process of extinction. In: *Communications et rapports du premier congrès international de dialectologie générale*. Centre International de Dialectologie Générale, Louvain, Belgium

Brenzinger M 1992 Patterns of language shift in East Africa. In: Herbert R K (ed.) *Language and Society in Africa: The Theory and Practice of Sociolinguistics*. Witwatersrand University Press, Johannesburg, South Africa

Brenzinger M, Heine B, Sommer G 1991 Language death in Africa. In: Robins R H, Uhlenbeck E M (eds.) *Endangered Languages*. Berg, Oxford, UK

Crystal D 2000 *Language Death*. Cambridge University Press, Cambridge, UK

Denison N 1977 Language death or language suicide? *International Journal of the Sociology of Language* **12**: 13–22

Dorian N C 1978 The fate of morphological complexity in language death. *Language* **54**: 590–609

Dorian N C 1981 *Language Death—The Life Cycle of a Scottish Gaelic Dialect*. University of Pennsylvania Press, Philadelphia, PA

Dorian N C (ed.) 1989 *Investigating Obsolescence—Studies in Language Contraction and Death*. Cambridge University Press, Cambridge, UK

Dressler W U 1972 On the phonology of language death. In: Peranteau P M, Levi J N, Phares G C (eds.) *Papers from the Eighth Regional Meeting of the Chicago Linguistic Society*. Chicago Linguistic Society, Chicago, IL

Eidheim H 1969 When ethnic identity is a social stigma. In: Barth F (ed.) *Ethnic Groups and Boundaries*. George Allen and Unwin, London

Fishman J 1972 Language maintenance and shift as a field of enquiry (revisited). In: *Language in Sociocultural Change. Essays by J. A. Fishman, Selected and*

Introduced by A. S. Dil. Stanford University Press, Stanford, CA

Gal S 1979 *Language Shift—Social Determinants of Linguistic Change in Bilingual Austria*. Academic Press, New York

Grenoble L A, Whaley L J (eds.) 1998 *Endangered Languages: Current Issues & Future Prospects*. Cambridge University Press, Cambridge, UK

Haugen E, McClure J D, Thomson D S (eds.) 1990 *Minority Languages Today*. Edinburgh University Press, Edinburgh, UK

Jones B L 1981 Welsh: Linguistic conservatism and shifting bilingualism. In: Haugen E, McClure J D, Thomson D S (eds.) 1990 *Minority Languages Today*. Edinburgh University Press, Edinburgh, UK

Kloss H 1966 German–American language maintenance efforts. In: Fishman J *Language Loyalty in the United States*. Mouton, The Hague

Leap W L 1981 American Indian languages. In: Ferguson C A, Heath S B *Language in the USA*. Cambridge University Press, Cambridge, UK

Li W L 1982 The language of Chinese-Americans *International Journal of Sociology of Language* **38**: 109–24

Menn L 1989 Some people who don't talk right: Universal and particular in child language, aphasia and language obsolescence. In: Dorian N C (ed.) *Investigating Obsolescence—Studies in Language Contraction and Death*. Cambridge University Press, Cambridge, UK

Mithun M 1989 The incipient obsolescence of polysynthesis: Cayuga in Ontario and Oklahoma. In: Dorian N C (ed.) *Investigating Obsolescence—Studies in Language Contraction and Death*. Cambridge University Press, Cambridge, UK

Mohan P, Zador P 1986 Discontinuity in a life cycle: The death of Trinidad Bhojpuri. *Language* **62**: 291–319

Nettle D, Romaine S 2000 *Vanishing Voices: The Extinction of the World's Languages*. Oxford University Press, Oxford, UK

Paulsen F 1981 The recent situation of the Ferring language, the North-Frisian language of the islands Föhr & Amrun. In: Haugen E, McClure J D, Thomson D S (eds.) 1990 *Minority Languages Today*. Edinburgh University Press, Edinburgh, UK

Schmidt A 1985 *Young People's Dyirbal—An Example of Language Death from Australia*. Cambridge University Press, Cambridge, UK

Swadesh M 1948 Sociologic notes on obsolescent languages. *International Journal of American Linguistics* **14**: 226–35

Language Spread
R. Mesthrie

The term *language spread* was used by Cooper (1982: vii) (see *Cooper, Robert Leon*) to denote a process whereby the 'uses or the users of a language increase.' More formally he defines it as 'an increase, over time, in the proportion of a communication network that adopts a given language variety for a given communication function' (1982: 6). In modern times this phenomenon applies to languages like English, French, Spanish, Swahili, Russian, Amharic, Hindi, and many more. Such languages are known as 'Languages of Wider Communication' (or LWCs for short). In eras gone by language spread applied to Sanskrit, Greek, Latin, Arabic, and so forth. 'Language spread' is a rather apolitical way of describing what is often the result of language imposition by a greater power, creating new linguistic relations in particular territories (Phillipson in press). It is also somewhat metaphorical insofar as languages cannot spread without human agency and a degree of acceptance (or tolerance) by human subjects. However, since not all cases involve political force or coercion but may involve relatively peaceful diffusion (as with the increase of uses and users of Tok Pisin in Papua New Guinea) the term is perhaps a useful one.

Wardhaugh (1987: 6) stresses that a necessary (but not sufficient) condition for a language to spread is that there be the geographical opportunity for one language to spread into the traditional area of another language or languages. These opportunities may be provided by rivers, seas, or traditional trade routes and in the modern era by air travel. Tourism for example may afford niches for some dominant languages, even if there hadn't been colonial domination previously. The Ancient Greeks spread their language via colonization of the Mediterranean area (see *Koinés*), which typically in colonization came to represent authority and administration, but also culture and religion. Wardhaugh (1987: 6) discusses the case of Amharic as follows:

> In the nineteenth and twentieth century speakers of Amharic spread themselves through Ethiopia largely as a result of military conquest but it was the availability of road systems and towns on those systems that enabled them to spread their language and consolidate the position in the newly acquired domains.

Once imposed by colonization or military conquest a language may remain in an area well beyond the term of conquest. Post-independent African states find it useful to retain a European colonial language like French, Portuguese, or English for certain functions. The field of language spread is clearly an important one for sociolinguistics and political sociology. It is also of some significance in historical linguistics (see *Borrowing*; *Language Transfer and Substrates*). Cooper had hoped to found a coherent theoretical area within sociolinguistics that would examine what individual cases of spread have in common:

> What are the psychological, social, and linguistic phenomena which, in interaction, account for language spread? Do languages spread in the same way as single items of vocabulary, pronunciation, or grammar? Do languages spread according to the same laws of innovation more generally? (1982: 5).

Such questions remain largely unanswered. One reason for this is that the questions may be too broad and ambitious. Sociolinguists have thus concentrated on more specific aspects of the field, as the discussion of the following topics in this encyclopedia will show: *Linguistic Imperialism*; *Language Conflict*; *Linguicide*; *New Englishes*; *Language Diffusion Policy*; *Contact Languages*; *Pidgins and Creoles: An Overview*.

See also: International Languages; Language Planning: Models; Statistics: Principal Languages of the World (UNESCO); Power Differentials and Language.

Bibliography

Cooper R L (ed.) 1982 *Language Spread*. Indiana University Press, Bloomington, IN
Fishman J A, Cooper R L, Conrad A W (eds.) 1977 *The Spread of English*. Newbury House, Rowley, MA
Lowenberg P H 1988 *Language Spread and Language Policy: Issues Implications and Case Studies*. Georgetown University Press, Washington, DC
Phillipson R in press Language spread. In: Ammon U Mattheier K, Nelde P, Trudgill P *Sociolinguistics: An International Handbook of the Science of Language and Society*. De Gruyter, Berlin
Wardhaugh R 1987 *Languages in Competition*. Blackwell, Oxford, UK

Language Transfer and Substrates
T. Odlin

1. Introduction

Terms such as *language transfer* and *cross-linguistic influence* often denote myriad factors at work when either the native language or some other previously (and perhaps imperfectly) learned language affects the acquisition of a new language. (The use of *native language* henceforth should be understood as shorthand for any previously acquired language.) Other recently used terms denoting more or less the same phenomenon include *mother-tongue influence* and *substrate influence*, with the latter especially common in discussions of cross-linguistic influence in historical studies of language contact, as seen below. Whatever the descriptor employed, the phenomenon designated is distinct from other types of cross-linguistic influence including cases where a second language affects knowledge and/or use of one's native language (sometimes called *borrowing transfer*) and cases of code switching among bilinguals highly proficient in two different languages. Still two other terms sometimes used to characterize the phenomenon of language transfer are *language mixing* and *interference*, but both have serious drawbacks. Although the effects of one's native language on the acquisition of a second can indeed be seen as mixing, so can borrowing transfer and code switching. The notion of interference likewise seems applicable in undesired cases of borrowing transfer as well as in undesired influence from the native language. A further problem with the term *interference* is that it implies a psychological construct distinct from what sociolinguists sometimes call *convergent influences*, as when, for example, English learners of French note the lexical similarity between *difficult* and French *difficile*. In second language research, such convergences are often called *positive transfer*, as opposed to *negative transfer*. Even though the latter two terms have their liabilities, they correctly suggest that the underlying psychological factors involved in the two kinds of transfer have something in common.

The use of *positive transfer, negative transfer*, and simply *transfer* has sometimes led linguists to conclude that such notions are necessarily linked to some form of behaviorist psychology. However, the use of *transfer* as a term and a concept independent of behaviorism goes back to the nineteenth century and continues to the present. Apart from the behaviorist controversy, work on language contact and second language acquisition has had no shortage of people skeptical about the reality or the

importance of cross-linguistic influence. When controversies about such influence do arise, three arguments are often made either implicitly or explicitly:
  (a) Psycholinguistic argument: transfer is (sometimes) impossible.
  (b) Sociolinguistic argument: (individual) transfer will not alter the language of a speech community.
  (c) Methodological argument: transfer is (sometimes) impossible to determine.

As Odlin (1992) notes, the strong form of each of these arguments—the versions when the parenthetical qualifiers are dropped—is not at all credible. At various points to follow, evidence refuting the strong forms of the first two arguments will appear, and the next section will take up the issue of methodology. On the other hand, the weaker form of each argument can be true in particular language contact situations, and the plausibility of the 'weak' arguments in these situations show many of the difficulties inherent in developing a thoroughly satisfactory account of substrate influence.

2. Methodology

A good understanding of the neurological basis for cross-linguistic influence seems a long way off, but facts about the performance of second language learners leave no doubt about the reality of such influence—or about the existence of a sound methodology to determine such influence. The acquisition of English in Finland has offered a convenient, though not unique, opportunity to employ convincing methods. One book-length study of the Finnish situation (Ringbom 1987) compares the performance of two groups having highly different native languages: Finnish and Swedish. The vast majority of Finnish citizens (some 93 percent) speak the former as their mother tongue although a minority of about 6 percent speaks Swedish. While speakers of both languages often learn some (often a great deal) of the language of the other community, the native language difference shows up clearly in how well students in the two communities acquire English. The 'Swedes' (to use Ringbom's term) tend to do better on global measures of proficiency even though both groups have highly comparable socioeconomic and educational backgrounds and even though some 'Finns' are highly successful. The difference in performances is consonant with the fact that Swedish, a Germanic language rather similar to English, allows many more opportunities for positive transfer than does Finnish, a non-Indo-European language. Other research points to a similar advantage for the Swedes (e.g., Sjöholm 1995), and Jarvis (2000) has extended the methodology by looking at the performance of Swedes and Finns in their native languages in a film narration task: specific differences in their use of Swedish or Finnish show up in the English patterns of the two groups.

Not all language contact situations allow for the systematic comparisons seen in the Finnish research, but sometimes researchers can use the implications of such methods to make convincing arguments about cross-linguistic influence. The use of so-called *after* perfects in Ireland and Scotland offers one such example. Speakers of English in some parts of both regions often use *after* to mark temporal meanings involving 'hot news' and other notions: e.g., *I'm after forgetting all that lot now* (= *I have forgotten all that now*) (Sabban 1982: 155). Close translation equivalents can be found in both Irish and Scottish Gaelic, and the likelihood of transfer is all the greater because *after* perfects rarely if ever appear in learner varieties of English in places outside the Celtic lands. One can argue whether it was positive—as opposed to negative—transfer that led to the spread of *after* perfects in the days when English was still new in many parts of Ireland and Scotland (especially in the eighteenth and nineteenth centuries). In either case, however, the pattern illustrates a likely instance of cross-linguistic influence. It is not only in cases of explicit comparisons such as the difference between the English of Finns and of Swedes that allow for good inferences about transfer. Instances such as the *after* perfect constitute comparisons no less sound between contact in the Celtic lands and contact elsewhere, cases which may be called *implicit comparisons*.

3. Transferability

As the discussion in Sect. 2 indicates, the strong version of the methodological argument against substrate influence ('Transfer is impossible to determine') is not credible. The other two arguments in their strong form likewise fail empirically, though at the same time it must be said that researchers have not always found cross-linguistic influence in every case where it is imaginable. For instance, it is conceivable that Chinese learners of English might try to create a system of lexical tone in their interlanguage since their native language employs such a system. Such attempts, however, are either very rare or completely nonexistent in a fairly copious research literature about the difficulties encountered by Chinese learners. In such cases, it seems reasonable to posit constraints on language transfer. Yet although such constraints appear plausible in many cases, empirical work shows that learners actually ignore some supposed constraints and draw on their native language to try to make sense out of the target language.

One supposed constraint that has had longstanding appeal involves bound morphology. In its strongest form this constraint would have it that learners never rely on either the inflectional or derivational system of their native language in acquiring grammatical categories in the target language. Somewhat weaker versions have focused on putative constraints involving inflectional systems. However, Jarvis and Odlin (2000) have discussed empirical work that refutes any strong claim about the nontransferability of inflectional morphemes. One study (Orr 1987) indicates a very different level of success of speakers of an Indo-European language (Gujarati) and speakers of a Bantu language (Ngoni) in learning the complex inflectional system of noun prefixation in Chichewa, another Bantu language—not too surprisingly, the speakers of Ngoni generally had an easier time with the target language prefixes in comparison with the speakers of Gujarati, a suffixing language. While the Orr study shows clear evidence of positive transfer, Jarvis and Odlin have identified unambiguous cases of negative transfer involving prepositional choices by Finnish learners of English, choices that show influences from the inflectional system of the Finns' native language. For example, in recounting events in a film several Finns described a scene where two people sit on a lawn with the predicate *sit to the grass*, which reflects an allative case suffix in Finnish. The likelihood of this interpretation is very high since a comparable group of learners whose native language was Swedish never used the predicate *sit to the grass*, and instead chose prepositional constructions compatible with those in Swedish. Moreover, a number of Finns writing in their native language used the allative case to describe the same referent in the same discourse context (i.e., *nurmikolle*, 'to the grass'). The studies by Orr and by Jarvis and Odlin thus indicate that either positive or negative transfer can occur in some situations even though there may be some rather specific constraints on the transferability of bound morphology.

Some work on the acquisition of syntax likewise shows strong evidence of native language influence. The domain of relativization has attracted several transfer researchers, and their investigations suggest that the variation in relative clause patterns of the first language can result in highly different interlanguage patterns of relativization. Work on the acquisition of English and of Swedish discussed by Odlin (1989) makes clear that pronoun retention is one possible outcome as when, for example, speakers of Persian might say in English, *I know the woman that John gave the potato to her*, which reflects the argument structure of Persian. A study by Mesthrie (1992) shows still other relativization strategies affecting interlanguage patterns. One involves word order reflecting the prenominal modification strategy favored in Dravidian languages as in the sentence *People* (*who got working-here-for-them*) *sons, like, for them nice they can stay* ('It is nice for people who have sons (who are) working for the company, since they are allowed to stay on in the barracks'). In the case of some speakers of Indic languages, however, Mesthrie found a different relativization strategy involving correlated elements as in *But now, which-one principal came here, she's just cheeky like the other one.* ('The principal who arrived recently is just as stern as the previous one.') Yet another relativization strategy that can lead to varying interlanguage patterns is seen in the specific choice of a pronoun. In a recent study Odlin and Jarvis (2000) found that speakers of Finnish chose *what* in relative clauses normally calling for *who, whom,* or *that* as in *But same lady what he meet come to police car too*. A comparable group of native speakers of Swedish did not employ *what* in such cases. The evidence reviewed in this paragraph thus suggests that transferable relativization strategies include pronoun retention, constituent order, correlation, and pronoun choice. Not only do relative clauses appear to be highly transferable; each of these particular strategies seems a likely candidate for transfer in structural patterns not involving relativization. For example, Filppula (1999) has seen evidence for Irish influence in pronoun retention in the English vernacular of Ireland called Hiberno-English in structures other than relative clauses, and Keesing (1988) has shown likely transfer patterns of personal pronoun distinctions from Oceanic languages into Melanesian Pidgin.

4. Social Diffusion of Transfer Patterns

The cases of transfer involving bound morphology and relativization constitute an important part of the evidence refuting any strong claim about the psycholinguistic impossibility of transfer even in the controversial domains of morphology and syntax. However, not all the research cited so far has focused on cases where cross-linguistic influence has led to widespread social diffusion. Thus in the case of Finland, for example, the differences between Swedes and Finns in using English as a second (or third) language do not seem to have much of an effect on English more generally. Although English is indeed used as a lingua franca between Finns and Russians, for instance, there seems to be only a minimal impact of Swedish and Finnish on the structure of English as used in Europe (much less the rest of the world). If all cases of transfer had the limited social scope seen in the Finnish context, the strong sociolinguistic argument cited above ('Transfer will not alter the language of a speech community') might seem viable. However, evidence from contemporary and historical cases of language contact suggests that cross-linguistic influence can sometimes have a lasting impact on the diachrony of a language, the impact often being termed a *substrate*.

The clearest cases of substrate influence arise in situations where there are still bilinguals more proficient in one language than in another (see

Bilingualism and Language Acquisition). For example, Sabban (1982) found that older Gaelic/English bilinguals in the Scottish Hebrides showed more frequent retention of tense, modality, and aspect patterns influenced by Gaelic in comparison with younger bilinguals. Filppula (1999) similarly found differences in the frequency of cleft and absolute constructions parallel with ones in Irish, with these structures being especially common in regions of Ireland where bilingualism was until recently very widespread. Although some types of cleft and absolute constructions appear in most varieties of English, some occur almost exclusively in the Celtic lands, and as these structures have counterparts in Irish and Scottish Gaelic, they provide further support for Filppula's substrate analysis. For example, Odlin (1997) notes the co-occurrence of a reflexive pronoun and a cleft construction as in *It was himself that told me that up in a pub*, with such cases reflecting the common use of reflexive pronouns in cleft structures in Irish and Scottish Gaelic. One methodological problem that arises in the Celtic regions has also complicated the study of language contact elsewhere; a pattern said to be unique to a region can sometimes have its source in a nonstandard superstrate (target language) variety. However, the studies cited in this paragraph have taken such possible effects into account. As long as accurate information about nonstandard superstrates is available, it will sometimes be possible to determine the relative contribution of substrate and superstrate influence (cf. Odlin 1991).

Studies of pidgins and creoles have frequently invoked substrate influence as an explanation for the development of particular structures. Although such explanations have often proved highly controversial, some cases leave little doubt that there have arisen language transfer patterns in historical cases of language contact. For instance, the pronoun systems of many Oceanic languages have frequently grammaticalized dual and trial number as well as inclusive/exclusive distinctions. With the development of Pacific pidgins (see *Pidgins and Creoles: An Overview*) using mainly English vocabulary, pronoun systems quite different from the superstrate have emerged in various places such as the Solomon Islands (Keesing 1988), where duels are part of the pronoun system (e.g., the dual *iutufala*, literally you-two—fellows, 'you two,' in contrast to the plural *iufala*, literally you fellows, 'you'). This development is certainly not characteristic of all pidgins and creoles worldwide, nor is it characteristic of second language acquisition in other settings (even though one might imagine learners engaging in some kind of creative construction of new pronoun categories). This example from language contact in the Pacific conforms, then, to the methodological point made before of where researchers can sometimes use an implicit comparison as strong evidence of cross-linguistic influence.

The cases of language contact in the Celtic lands and in the Pacific discussed in this section come from recent history. Not surprisingly, the farther back in time one goes the greater the uncertainties. For instance, the use of the auxiliary *do* in English may reflect an early Celtic substrate, one that presumably developed the wake of the conquest of much of Celtic Britain by the Anglo-Saxons. Poussa (1990) has made interesting arguments for just such a scenario, but inevitable problems make it unclear whether historians of Old and Middle English will concur on the substrate explanation in this case. Such difficulties arise from a lack of any bilingual speech samples from the time, as well as from uncertainties about just what shape the substrate pattern in Welsh and Cornish took, not to mention uncertainties in interpreting existing written evidence relevant to the problem.

In the case of the Old English period, there is at least some certainty about what languages were spoken in a contact situation, which no doubt existed. The linguistic evidence gets thinner in some cases where researchers in other fields seem reasonably sure about identifying distinct populations that would have been users of substrate and superstrate languages. For example, the archeologist J. P. Mallory (1999) argues that the simplification of the more highly inflected Ogam Irish to Old Irish reflects a language contact situation in Ireland existing some time between 2000 to 3000 years ago. In this interpretation, the superstrate language is a known variable, but not the substrate. Still more ambitious are the distinctions that some DNA researchers see between older and newer populations. Looking at the distribution of a Y-chromosome in Western Europe and the Middle East, a team of geneticists has argued that inhabitants in the West of Ireland share the chromosome most clearly with inhabitants of the Basque region of Spain, a commonality that may reflect a settlement pattern stretching back 4000 years (Hill et al. 2000). Although it is tempting to deem Basque the substrate language, there is no certainty on that point (or, of course, on what Basque might have been like four millennia ago). In the absence of linguistic methods hard to conceive of now, it will remain a hazardous venture to make strong claims about the language contact situations of prehistory.

5. Conclusion

This article has considered the strong form of arguments against the possibility of language transfer (a.k.a. substrate influence) and found all three of them (the methodological, the psycholinguistic, and the sociolinguistic) to be empirically unsound. Yet while the strong form of each argument is insupportable, it would be wrong to conclude that transfer operates in every conceivable situation. Much empirical work remains to be done before researchers can specify the precise conditions under which transfer does or does not operate (see further Odlin 2002).

See also: Borrowing; Contact Languages; Interlanguage.

Bibliography

Filppula M 1999 *The Grammar of Irish English*. Routledge, London
Hill E, Jobling M, Bradley D 2000 Y-chromosome variation and Irish origins. *Nature* **404**: 351–2
Jarvis S 2000 Methodological rigor in the study of transfer: Identifying L1 influence in the interlanguage lexicon. *Language Learning* **50**: 245–309
Jarvis S, Odlin T 2000 Morphological type, spatial reference, and language transfer. *Studies in Second Language Acquisition* **22**: 535–6
Keesing R 1988 *Melanesian Pidgin and the Oceanic Substrate*. Stanford University Press, Stanford, CA
Mallory J P 1999 Language in prehistoric Ireland. *Ulster Folklife* **45**: 3–16
Mesthrie R 1992 *English in Language Shift: The History, Structure, and Sociolinguistics of South African Indian English*. Cambridge University Press, Cambridge, UK
Odlin T 1989 *Language Transfer*. Cambridge University Press, Cambridge, UK
Odlin T 1991 Irish English idioms and language transfer. *English World-Wide* **12**: 175–93
Odlin T 1992 Transferability and linguistic substrates. *Second Language Research* **8**: 171–202
Odlin T 1997 Bilingualism and substrate influence: A look at clefts and reflexives. In Kallen J (ed.) *Focus on Ireland*, 35–50. Benjamins, Amsterdam
Odlin T 2002 Cross-linguistic influence. In: Doughty C, Long, M (eds.) *Handbook of Second Language Acquisition*. Blackwell, Oxford, UK
Odlin T, Jarvis S 2000 *Cognate Vocabulary, Language Proficiency, and Syntactic Transfer*. Paper presented at the annual meeting of American Association for Applied Linguistics, Vancouver
Orr G 1987 *Aspects of the Second Language Acquisition of Chichewa Noun Class Morphology*. Unpublished PhD dissertation. University of California, Los Angeles, CA
Poussa P 1990 A contact-universals origin for periphrastic *do*, with special consideration for OE-Celtic contact. In: Adamson S, Law V, Vincent N, Wright S (eds.) *Papers from the 5th International Conference on English Historical Linguistics*. Benjamins, Amsterdam, pp. 407–34
Ringbom H 1987 *The Role of the First Language in Foreign Language Learning*. Multilingual Matters, Clevedon, UK
Sabban A 1982 *Gälisch-Englischer Sprachkontakt*. Julius Groos, Heidelberg, Germany
Sjöholm K 1995 *The Influence of Crosslinguistic, Semantic, and Input Factors on the Acquisition of English Phrasal Verbs*. Abo Akademi University Press, Turku, Finland

Lingua Franca
M. Barotchi

The term *lingua franca* (plural *lingue franche* or *lingua francas*) is used to refer to any form of language serving as a means of communication among speakers of different languages, for example, Swahili in East and Central Africa or English worldwide. The terms 'common language' and 'auxiliary language' are also used to refer to such a language.

1. Origin of the Term

The Italian term *lingua franca*, means literally 'French' or 'Frankish language,' apparently an adaptation of the Arabic phrase *lisan alfiranj*, 'language of Western/Latin-speaking Europeans,' (Zago 2000). It originally referred to a vernacular Romance tongue spoken along the Mediterranean coast between Marseils and Genoa, an early relative of modern Italian and Provençal. This was adopted as an auxiliary language among the Crusaders—who spoke different languages—and became mixed with Arabic, Greek, Spanish, and other elements. In time this Crusader language became extinct but the name *lingua franca* survived as a general term of any comparable language. *Sabir* and *Petit Mauresque* are nineteenth-century versions of Lingua Franca used during the French colonization of Algeria and North Africa (Corré 2000).

2. Definition and Application

In the 1953 UNESCO Conference on Vernacular Languages, *lingua franca* was defined as 'a language which is used habitually by people whose mother tongues are different in order to facilitate communication between them' (UNESCO 1953). This definition applies also to pidgins and creoles, perhaps more to Creoles because of the requirement of habitualness (see *Pidgins and Creoles: An Overview*). Samarin 1968 points out that while all pidgins are lingua francas, not all lingua francas are pidgins. The term covers not only pidgins and creoles but other

503

natural languages and specially devised artificial auxiliary languages (see *Artificial Languages*).

3. Types of Lingua Franca
Samarin 1968 recognizes three types of lingua franca: 'natural,' 'pidginized,' and 'planned.' The 'Koiné' or Common Greek is one of the earliest known natural language lingua francas, spread as a result of the conquests of Alexander the Great, Greek colonization, and the dissemination of the Eastern (Orthodox) Christianity (see *Koinés*). Latin was another early lingua franca, associated with the rise of the Roman Empire and, for long after the fall of this Empire, with the Roman Catholic Church.

It could be argued that the 1953 UNESCO definition of a lingua franca quoted above makes it difficult to include pidgins as lingua francas in that pidgins are used only for restricted purposes and hence, it could be contended, are not used habitually. Since pidgins are quite clearly auxiliary languages used to facilitate communication between speakers of different languages, one might suggest that the word 'habitually' could be removed from the UNESCO definition.

The third type of lingua franca is artificial in the sense of being planned; languages such as Esperanto, Frater, and Interlingua fall into this category, being devised respectively by Ludovik Zamenhof, Pham Xuan Thai, and a team of scholars belonging to the International Auxiliary Language Association. Though they are comparable to pidgins in possessing a mixed lexicon and a simplified syntax, they differ from them in being deliberately designed, sometimes indeed for specific uses, as is the case with Loglan, devised for use among certain scientists for restricted purposes.

See also: Koinés; Pidgins and Creoles: An Overview.

Bibliography
Corré A D (ed.) 2000 *A Glossary of Lingua Franca*, 3rd edn. http://www.uwm.edu/People/corre/franca/go.3.html
Fishman J A (ed.) 1968 *Readings in the Sociology of Language*. Mouton, The Hague
Rossetti R 2000 An introduction to Lingua Franca. In: Corré A D (ed.) *A Glossary of Lingua Franca*, 3rd edn. http://www.uwm.edu/People/corre/franca/go.3.html
Samarin W J 1968 Lingua Francas of the world. In: Fishman J A (ed.) *Readings in the Sociology of Language*. Mouton, The Hague
Todd L 1984 *Modern Englishes: Pidgins and Creoles*. Blackwell, Oxford, UK
UNESCO 1953 The use of vernacular languages in Education. In: Fishman J A (ed.) 1968 *Readings in the Sociology of Language*. Mouton, The Hague
Zago R 2000 A dissertation on Lingua Franca. In Corré A D (ed.) *A Glossary of Lingua Franca*, 3rd edn. http://www.uwm.edu/People/corre/franca/go.3.html

Migrants and Migration
A. M. Pavlinić

1. The Origin of the 'Problem'
The Europe of the second half of the twentieth century has been characterized by multinational, plurilingual states, and cultural heterogeneity, with the exception of the linguistically homogeneous and monolingual Iceland and Portugal. The fusion of nations, cultures, and languages has been greatly accelerated by the migration of people coming from the underdeveloped and rural regions of Greece, Italy, Turkey, Spain, Portugal, the former Yugoslavia, North Africa, South and Southeast Asia, etc. in search of more lucrative employment or a better life in highly developed industrial and urban areas.

The migration situation during the economic boom of the early 1970s, before the oil crisis, could best be understood by applying the *Gastarbeiter* model of rotating migrant workers. It implied a temporary employment in the host country, and a return to the home country as soon as the migrants' services were no longer necessary or when their material interests were satisfied. Castles, an expert in the political economy of migration, was among the first to use the 'subclass' denomination to describe the position of migrant workers being reduced to their working role. With their settlement on a more permanent basis, the ensuing process of so-called family reunification and of migrant family reproduction in the recession period, their developing new communities in most major European cities and industrial centers, and their gradual insertion in social and societal processes which do not stem solely from labor, it became more appropriate to refer to their position as 'ethnic minorities' (generally meaning newer minorities resulting from migration, as opposed to traditional ones). Suddenly, faced with the growing problems of migrants and their families, the countries of immigration became aware of the fact that, to paraphrase

Max Frisch, 'labor was invited, but there came people.' Consequently, immigrants' adaptation and integration (assimilation) became crucial issues in the richer communities of Europe in the 1970s, and have remained important, especially where 'second-' and 'third-generation' migrants are concerned, and in view of the global integration of Europe, which officially started in 1992.

It is well-known that a profound sense of attachment to their homeland is preserved by most migrant workers, sometimes also serving as some kind of protection in their new environment. However, they also develop strategies of integration with their adoptive setting in capitalist industrial society. But there is a social distance, very difficult to overcome, between the indigenous population and immigrant groups, even between foreign workers and native ones. A crisis such as an economic one (growing scarcity of primary goods available, particularly employment and housing, loss of purchasing power, reduced social welfare and funds for special purposes, including mother-tongue tuition) has an impact on relations between various sociocultural groups (in the form of growing nationalism, rising xenophobia, and the shutting in of immigrant and native communities on themselves). Class relations are underlined through social and economic segregation: internal and interclass conflicts are further deepened. The indigenous working class generally adheres to the country's sociopolitical system and immigration policies, which keep its members assured that the system of discrimination is necessary so that their own interests, seemingly threatened by the presence of foreign workers, can be protected. The political integration of foreigners is not even at issue, unlike their sociocultural integration, because no such sociocultural–political order has been created in which they would have a say. By 1990 only three European host countries had granted immigrants the right to participate in (municipal only) elections: Belgium, Sweden, and the Netherlands.

1.1 How to Define a Migrant?

The term 'migrant,' pregnant with connotations, changes according to whether it is viewed from a legal, economic, sociological, anthropological, psychological, pragmatic, or political point of view, especially if the term is used to refer to the children of migrants (or former migrants). A most comprehensive and acceptable definition can be found in the Council of Europe's *Project No. 7* (1986):

— when defined BY HIS PAST, a migrant is *someone uprooted from his homeland*, from his community and his 'rural society,' through 'economic violence' (lack of means of livelihood) or 'political violence' (refugees): this context has a profound effect on his present and his plans for the future, and it is one with which he maintains a relationship; as *someone with a given nationality*, he is perceived as different by the society of the country of residence (which is associated with historical, economic, political, cultural factors); the differential treatment and perception of identity strengthen his tendency to identify with his ethnic group (ethnic cohesion); as a *carrier of linguistic and cultural codes*, his daily behavior is governed by this fact; coding may relate to time, space, cooking, clothes, religious practices, etc., revealing a number of cultural factors that are 'universal';

— when defined BY HIS PRESENT, he is a *settler* ('resettler'), who has resided in a given country, sharing the problems and interests of the local community; he has civic communication needs and social communication needs (system of predominantly accepted norms and values); as a *worker*, he has a specific role to play within the national production system and within the framework of the international distribution of labor; he lives on new class loyalties shared with indigenous workers; as a *non-citizen*, he has no political rights and a precarious residence status; he is, sometimes, a *member of a minority* (where his group often has negative connotations in relation to the society of residence); 'immigrant minorities' are to be distinguished from all other minorities on account of their origin, history and present positon; as a *deprived person*, he lacks means of communication, particularly linguistic means, he belongs to a disadvantaged social category (lack of schooling and vocational training), and is liable to social discrimination;

— if defined BY HIS FUTURE, he is a 'mutant' or *cultural traveler* caught in a 'transit' situation (being forced to change his 'cultural spectacles' on account of his new social itinerary); as an *agent of social and cultural change*, he is engaged in a process of reaction to a new setting which is itself influenced by his presence; the 'transplanted' immigrant changes in and with settings which themselves change; as a *progenitor*, he is a producer of new generations marked by his economic, social and cultural experience; he tries to pass on his language of origin, his models of behavior and values; he projects on his offspring his own aspirations, but he also transfers his own frustrations to them; as a *child of immigration*, not only does he undergo the socialization and cultural influence of his family, but he is increasingly marked by the new socializing and educational influences outside the family (school, district, recreations, media, peer groups, etc.), refusing to confine himself to the cultural profile of his parents. This is how migrant workers' offspring, especially 'second-generation' (most often, but not invariably defined as those who were born in the country of emigration and came to the receiving country to join their parents, complete their education, and eventually find employment there themselves), even 'third-generation' migrants (those who were born in the country of immigration) are most frequently referred to: as *carriers of bipolarity*, their sociocultural integration in the host community being limited by influences and feelings pertaining to the country of origin, and, vice versa, their acceptance of sociocultural patterns, structures and values pertaining to the adoptive country meaning their 'sacrificing' their indigenous characteristics, originality and self-reliance.

It is clear who is the controller, and who the controlled in the world of immigration.

2. Factors Affecting the Integration of Migrant Workers' Children

According to some estimates, there were probably 20 million migrant workers in the world at the beginning of the 1980s. It has also been estimated that in the year 2000, one-third of the population under the age of 35 in highly developed Europe is of immigrant background. The young foreign population can therefore be considered as the new Europeans, carrying the variety of different cultural expressions emerging from their own national or regional cultures. It is a tremendous challenge for those in control of cultural and educational policies to recognize this potential, and provide the opportunity whereby they can be made an asset for European unity, understanding, and progress.

While migrant parents have been the target of selective integration (the able-bodied, skilled, very healthy, communicative, and ambitious are favored), their children lend themselves more easily to full integration (assimilation, 'cultural homogenization'), for both objective and subjective reasons, especially if the process started at the earliest age, from birth.

Migrant children permanently undergo and deal, more or less successfully, with the conflicting impact of factors related to their education, personality development, and culture: the home and family on the one hand, and the school as a purveyor of knowledge, cultural heritage, achievements, value orientations, norms of behavior, relating to the majority society on the other. It is probable that 'third-generation' migrants will find it easier to cope; 'second-generation' migrants are in a specially vulnerable position, because they were first socialized in a different sociocultural milieu, by means of a different language, and the switch may have left permanent scars on their psychosocial life.

The school success of young foreigners is, naturally, crucial to their sociocultural integration and for their future standing in the labor market (economic integration). Their majority language (L2) competence is the most important instrument for achieving a good school career as well as a key opening the door to a successful integration. In an early article on migrant children's language problems, Trim remarked:

> A language course which aims at a generalised competence and has no social context is likely to prove ineffective....
> We should in our teaching try to analyse a hierarchy of social problems, and then look for the language which will *enable the young migrant to assert his social rights within the problem areas*, developing his ability to do so in an order of priority which results from the magnitude of the problem, taking into account both long and short term aims.
>
> (Trim 1977: 217–8)

The earliest objective of keeping the language (L1) and culture of origin alive in the host countries was encouraged by the hope of the (re)integration of migrant children in the school should they return to their home country. Although an important conclusion has been reached in recent years, namely, that a pupil's knowledge of his origin enhances his (her) ability to integrate in either of the two (or more) societies, a top-down focus of the host country's power structures and majority language teachers has remained on L2 acquisition, often combined with a rather negative attitude toward maintaining L1. Indeed, stress is sometimes put on preserving (ethnic) culture rather than the language, as if one could exist free from the other. There is a matching bottom-up focus of dominated groups (including minority language teachers) and of the countries of their origin on mother tongue and ethnic culture maintenance, for the purposes of bridging a gap between the parents and the children, building and preserving ethnic identity, and acquiring L2 more successfully (see Sect. 3). A consensus of opinion about the weight of the two languages in the school curriculum has not been reached yet despite a long debate and despite contrary claims on the policy level.

In addition to the migrant home and the host country's school as the two crucial sources of the children's culture, there are also other influences to be taken into account in view of their integration in the dominant society. An important factor is the institutions (including migrant associations, mass media) that encourage the cultures of the country of origin or of the adoptive country. (There is usually a lack of such institutions, or a lack of 'official support for cultural and language maintenance,' as it is generally called.) The importance of the peer group also deserves to be stressed in this context, especially when socialization in childhood, as well as in adolescence, is concerned. Last but not least, one internal factor should not be overlooked: *Selbst-Aktivität* (to use the German term meaning 'self-activity') is known to have performed miracles in individual instances. It may be defined as a person's strategies to make the best of his (her) heredity- and society-related dispositions, although either or both can be adverse, in direct or in indirect consequence of migration.

2.1 The Political Lever in Operation

It has been argued so far that migrant children's problems should be viewed as a consequence of migration-related phenomena (in addition to their possibly being, as far as some aspects are concerned, children's universal problems), that their causes should be sought in the community of origin and/or the receiving community, and that the linguistic aspects of their school achievement problems cannot be separated from the economic, cultural, and political aspects of their situation. This last factor deserves to be dealt with by itself, because it is unavoidable in the past, present, and future of migrants' lives.

It may be called the *political lever*, a concept which includes immigration and emigration policies alike, educational and language policies, and language planning. Examples of the political lever in operation are numerous. Compared with other European policies, the UK was early in adopting a new terminology, substituting the word 'minorities' for 'migrants' in the early 1970s. Among other things, such a change enables the host society to distinguish itself in a new way from the new cultural and linguistic groups; also, it makes a reception and integration policy possible which does not depend on the assumption of a return home or departure, as is often the case elsewhere in Europe; it also gives the white population a particular identity enabling it to call itself the 'majority' (Bottani 1989: 39). The European Community ensures for its members greater mobility within and between its more developed countries, better employment conditions, more flexible school conditions for the pupils, etc., which leaves the non-EC members outside, void of comparable provision. The Elementary Education Act in the Netherlands (1985) has reduced the number of classes per week spent on language and culture of origin instruction (in Dutch, OETC or 'onderwijs eigen taal en culture'), and made such tuition obligatory for pupils only at the request of their parents. Churchill (1987: 67) has made an interesting general remark concerning what he calls 'strong political interventions': that the response of the educational system to problems presented by the education of linguistic and cultural minorities is always confined within the bounds of what is tolerable for dominant (majority) opinion; stepping beyond these limits usually results in strong political interventions that can override what educational policy makers have done. Churchill also reports (1987: 80), however, a positive development in the OECD countries: most of their jurisdictions have eliminated negative stereotyping of different cultures and ethnic groups from their school textbooks and their official educational culture; also,

the right or need of the minority to learn about its own history and customs is recognized, so the teaching of 'culturally relevant' topics such as social studies, history and geography, may occur in the minority language.

One of the very few books dealing with the question of power in language and the language of power is J. Mey's *Whose Language? A Study in Linguistic Pragmatics* (1985). This very question is implied in its title: 'whose language' do people speak, the language of the colonizer, or that of the colonized? The author's point of departure is his acute awareness of the fact that the powerful in society, as well as the less powerful and the powerless, all depend on the socioeconomic conditions in that society. Consequently, he believes that for a socially oriented theory of language use a detailed analysis of such conditions is absolutely necessary. The book is also an answer to the question that has been the author's preoccupation for a long time concerning the role of science in society and, more specifically, the role of linguists and linguistics. It is both a political statement and a contribution to science. (Some politicized issues pertaining to migrants' mother tongues can also be found in Dabène et al. 1983.)

3. A Brief Overview of Minority-related Linguistic Issues and Some Selected Literature

With immigrants and their families establishing themselves in the receiving societies came the realization that the speech communities had acquired a new repertoire of *varieties*, whether registers, dialects, diatypes, or languages (see *Language; Dialect and Dialectology; Register*). Labov defined a speech community as a group of speakers who share a set of social attitudes towards language. It has been supported by sociolinguistic theory and successfully proven by the same author that some of the elements that set off variation, i.e., the choice of alternative linguistic forms and switching (see *Code-switching: Overview*) between varieties in general, come from conditions external to the speaker and others from internal states (for studies of this nature see also articles in Pride and Holmes 1972). 'Communicative competence' is an important step on an abstract, theoretical level, in the development of sociolinguistics as a science, and on a concrete level, as a contribution to the study of the language problems of disadvantaged children (see Hymes in Pride and Holmes 1972). It indicates some major dimensions: the capacities of persons, the organization of verbal means for socially defined purposes, and the sensitivity of rules to situations. (See *Language in Society: Overview*.)

The concept of 'diglossia' has been taken to refer to any two languages in contact as well as to cases where two or more varieties of the same language are used in different social settings (see Grosjean 1982: 131–2). As diglossia concerns the social allocation of functions to different languages or varieties, it can be applied to immigrants' communication, with a distribution of functions between their mother tongue/diaspora language (See also *Minority Languages*; Grosjean 1982: 179 ff.).

In the diaspora context, the acquisition and use of the dominant language (L2) is in the focus of interest of migrants; if theirs is a minimalistic approach, they want to maintain their mother tongue at least to keep up language-links with the country of origin. Psycho- and sociolinguistic research on ethnic minority groups is also oriented towards the second language. Far less attention is given (for various reasons) to the dominant language (L1), although it is recognized at least as the expression of a person's primary identity and the language through which initial concept formation takes places (cf. Pattanayak 1986: 7). With various issues in the debate on inter- and multicultural education being increasingly accompanied by contradictions, hesitation, uncertainty, and backtracking (cf. Bottani 1989), and within a more global minority language revival trend in Europe, the 'mother tongue' concept has been receiving growing attention (see Denison et al. 1986, Ringbom 1987).

Bilingualism (see *Bilingualism, Individual*) is a characterization of individual and societal linguistic versatility; a bilingual person has skills (within the range from minimal to maximal) in two languages. Bilingualism in the context of migrants in present-day Europe is the subject of an edited collection by Extra and Verhoeven (1999). Skutnabb-Kangas (1984) (with a comprehensive bibliography) is an important work, especially on bilingualism relating to the education of minority children; for minority education issues see Skutnabb-Kangas and Cummins 1988 (See also *Cummins, Jim*).

If active, balanced bilingualism, that is (at least theoretically) as 'complete' a bilingualism as possible, can be discerned at one end of the continuum, (double) semilingualism—insufficient competence in both languages—might be seen at the other end (see Skutnabb-Kangas and Toukomaa 1976, Wande et al. 1987; see also *Semilingualism*).

The three most important linguistic contributions to the (gradual) establishment and promotion of bilingual education in multicultural, plurilingual settings seem to be:
  (a) the claim that all languages are the same in value;
  (b) research findings about the positive (cognitive) effects of bilingualism (see e.g., Baker 1988);
  (c) Skutnabb-Kangas's research findings (1976 onward), together with Cummins's interdependence hypothesis.

At the core of the hypothesis is a distinction between CALP (cognitive/academic language proficiency) and BICS (basic interpersonal communicative skills); Cummins claims that both L1 CALP (L1 competence and performance) and L2 CALP are manifestations of the same underlying dimension. Both Skutnabb-Kangas and Cummins are keen proponents of mother tongue medium maintenance education for minorities (L1 as the main medium of education, at least during the first six years of schooling, if not longer, with the major language as a second language).

4. The Definition of Language in Migrant Situations

When all considerations concerning the situation of migrant workers and their children are taken into account, a definition of language may be proposed:
  (a) from the majority perspective;
  (b) from the minority perspective; first, as the tool for controlling society in a field of tension between 'me/us' and 'you/them' is language; second, as the tool for becoming adapted to the controlling society in a field of tension between 'me/us' and 'you/them' and for making the best of the adoptive world is language.

5. Efficient Multicultural Education Program: A Desirable and (In)accessible Goal?

Mackey (see Grosjean 1982) was among the pioneers to propose a complex typology of educational programs, ranging from monolingual education in the majority language through bilingual education in both languages to monolingual education in the majority language (for programs that lead to linguistic and cultural assimilation and those that lead to linguistic and cultural diversification see Grosjean 1982: 208–22). Despite later work by other scholars, really efficient multicultural education programs and policies have not yet been drawn up. There is the mass of evidence pertaining to inter-/multicultural (education) experience, but on the implementation level, still much to be desired. The main obstacle to more efficient bilingual education programs seems to be the notion of 'one language–one culture' still imbedded in the educational systems of former nation states in Europe.

Research in some Scandinavian countries and elsewhere has been directed at language transfer, interlanguage syntax, and similar issues (cf. Færch 1983, Færch and Kasper 1987, Hyltenstam 1987, Ringbom 1987).

An approach with more pragmatic goals, in that it is aimed at improving minority students' school careers, is that of Cummins (1990); his point of departure is that minority students are educationally disempowered in very much the same way that their communities are disempowered by interactions with societal institutions. In other words, minority students are 'empowered' or 'disabled' as a direct result of their interactions with educators in the schools, and the 'problem' cannot be located within themselves. These interactions are mediated by the implicit or explicit role definitions that educators assume in relation to four institutional characteristics of schools. These characteristics reflect the extent to which: (a) minority students' language and culture are incorporated into the school program; (b) minority community participation is encouraged as an integral component of children's education; (c) the pedagogy promotes intrinsic motivation on the part of students to use language actively in order to generate their own knowledge; and (d) professionals involved in assessment become advocates for minority students by focusing primarily on the ways in which student's academic difficulty is a function of interactions within the school context. Each dimension can be analyzed along a continuum: one end reflects an intercultural orientation (role definition); the other reflects the traditional dominant-group-superiority orientation (cf. Cummins 1990: 165). The former serves the purpose of empowering students; the latter contributes to disabling them.

See also: Bilingualism, Societal; Linguistic Imperialism; Linguicide.

Bibiliography

Baker C 1988 *Key Issues in Bilingualism and Bilingual Education*. Multilingual Matters, Clevedon, UK
Bottani N 1989 *One School, Many Cultures*. OECD, Paris
CERI 1987 *Multicultural Education*. OECD, Paris
Churchill S 1987 Policy development for education in multicultural societies: Trends and processes in the OECD countries. In: *Multicultural Education*. OECD/CERI, Paris
Council of Europe 1986 *Project No. 7 Final Report* (Document DECS/EGT(86)6 Final). Council of Europe, Strasbourg, France
Cummins J 1990 Multilingual/multicultural education: Evaluation of underlying theoretical constructs and consequences for curriculum development. In: Vedder P (ed.) *Fundamental Studies in Educational Research*. Swets and Zeitlinger, Amsterdam
Dabène L, Flasaquier M, Lyons J (eds.) 1983 *Status of Migrants' Mother Tongues*. European Science Foundation, Strasbourg, France
Denison N et al. (eds.) 1986 *Grazer Linguistische Studien* No. 27, *Muttersprache (n)*. Institut für Sprachwissenschaft der Universität Graz, Graz, Austria
Extra G, Verhoeven L (eds.) 1999 *Bilingualism and Migration: Studies on Language Acquisition*. Mouton de Gruyter, Berlin
Færch C (ed.) 1983 *Strategies in Interlanguage Communication*. Longman, London
Færch C, Kasper G 1987 Perspectives on language transfer. *Applied Linguistics* **8**(2): 111–36
Grosjean J 1982 *Life with Two Languages (An Introduction to Bilingualism)*. Harvard University Press, Cambridge, MA
Hyltenstam K 1987 A framework for the study of interlanguage continua. In: *Working Papers No. 16*. Phonetics Laboratory, Department of General Linguistics, Lund University, Lund, Sweden
Mey J L 1985 *Whose Language? A Study in Linguistic Pragmatics*. Benjamins, Amsterdam
Pattanayak D P 1986 Educational use of the mother tongue. In: Spolsky B (ed.) *Language and Education in Multilingual Settings*. Multilingual Matters, Clevedon, UK
Pride J B, Holmes J 1972 *Sociolinguistics: Selected Readings*. Penguin, Harmondsworth, UK
Ringbom H 1987 *The Role of the First Language in Foreign Language Learning*. Multilingual Matters, Clevedon, UK
Skutnabb-Kangas T 1984 *Bilingualism or Not: The Education of Minorities*. Multilingual Matters, Clevedon, UK
Skutnabb-Kangas T, Cummins J (eds.) 1988 *Minority Education: From Shame to Struggle*. Multilingual Matters, Clevedon, UK
Skutnabb-Kangas T, Toukomaa P 1976 *Teaching Migrant Children Their Mother Tongue and Learning the Language of the Host Country in the Context of the Sociocultural Situation of the Migrant Family*. Tutkimuksia Research Reports 15. University of Tampere, Tampere, Finland
Trim J L M 1977 Helping migrant children to communicate: Some implications of the Council of Europe work in language systems construction. In: de Grève M, Rosseel E (eds.) *Problèmes linguistiques des enfants de travailleurs migrants*. AIMAV, Didier, Brussels, Belgium
Wande E, Anward J, Norberg B, Steensland L, Thelander M (eds.) 1987 Aspects of multilingualism. *Proceedings from the Fourth Nordic Symposium on Bilingualism 1984*. Acta Universitatis Upsaliensis, Studia Multiethnica Upsaliensia 2, Uppsala, Sweden

Missionaries and Language
P. Lewis

Missionaries of all religions have long had a strategic interest in language. As pioneer communicators of the message of their faith, missionaries have inevitably confronted linguistic barriers and have sought ways to deal with them. Missionaries have a very practical motivation to engage in the study of language: linguistics, language acquisition, applied linguistics (translation, literacy), and sociolinguistics, and they have been at the forefront of linguistic data gathering, analysis, and application. Missionaries have also contributed to the development of linguistic theory, primarily as a foundation for achieving their practical ends.

1. Religious Ideology and Approaches to Language

Although missionaries are universally concerned with language and with the communication of their message, not all religions have approached language from the same perspective. Differing theological perspectives on the nature of deity and the relationship of that deity to the world result in different communicative strategies and religious language policies.

Judaism is nonproselytizing in nature and is closely associated with a biological and ethnic membership in the group. Converts to Judaism are generally expected to learn some Hebrew, the language of the Bible and of worship, but translations of the Hebrew writings are freely available and readily used.

In contrast, Islam holds that the only valid linguistic medium for divine revelation is the Koran in the original Classical Arabic. Translation of the Koran is therefore not a high priority. Instead, the general approach of Islamic missionizing has been through mass conversion and the arabicization of entire populations, at least in the religious domains of language use.

Hinduism, while not overtly proselytizing ideologically, has had at least segments of its practitioners who have undertaken the translation of the Hindu sacred writings and other religious materials for the purpose of making the teachings of Hinduism more widely accessible. As a prime, and perhaps extreme, example of this missionary spirit is Swami Vivekananda (1863–1902), a disciple of Ramakrishna, founded in India the Ramakrishna Mission or Vedanta Society. It was devoted particularly to philanthropic activities but also to the idea of a worldwide religion founded on a *Vedanta* adapted to the needs of modern societies. Vivekananda traveled extensively in the West expounding his views and has been called the 'St. Paul of the movement' (Pitt 1955: 46–7). Another Hindu missionary movement, the Arya Samaj, had as its slogan 'back to the *Vedas*' and linked Indian identity closely to adherence to Hinduism, resulting in a program aimed at converting Muslims and Christians in India to Hinduism. The linguistic consequences of such missionizing have been the propagation of Hindu sacred writings in the vernacular languages, while at the same time maintaining the Sanskritic tradition among the more educated.

Consideration of missionary activity is most often focused on Christianity, with its large corps of missionary personnel (over 400,000 worldwide by some estimates). The Christian theology of mission is founded firmly on the 'Great Commission' spoken by Jesus which commands Christians to 'go into all the world and make disciples.' It is also rooted in an ideology that the Christian Scriptures (the Bible) are the basis for faith and godliness and therefore must be adequately and accurately understood.

From its earliest days Christianity has been characterized by a drive to translate the Bible as a means of providing a basis for the preservation of orthodoxy and an accurate recounting of the life and teachings of Jesus. In practice, Christian missionaries generally see the need to lay the groundwork for the reception and use of the translated Scriptures as well. Thus, a range of applied linguistics activities frequently accompanies Bible translation. In cases where a language is unwritten, missionaries would consider it appropriate to develop an adequate orthography (e.g., Cyril, Methodius, Stefan of Perm). Where there are no readers, missionaries would consider it important to facilitate access to the Bible through literacy instruction and the production of other reading materials. Often missionary linguists also provide phonological, morphological, syntactic, and semantic descriptions of languages, and may also produce pedagogical grammars, dictionaries, and other linguistic materials. Linguists and scholars have benefited greatly from the linguistic, anthropological, and sociolinguistic data that missionaries have collected in thousands of languages in all parts of the world.

2. Missionaries and Language Identification

Because of the Christian mandate to go into all the world, Christian missionary linguists are preoccupied with the identification of the world's languages. Scholars, missionary and non-missionary alike, have made attempts to begin inventories of the languages of the world and to track the progress of Bible translation. The *Ethnologue* (Grimes 2000) is one of the most comprehensive catalogs of the languages of the world and relies heavily on field research done by missionary linguists and others.

The work done by missionaries in identifying the languages of the world has contributed to the development of the notions of language and dialect, inherent intelligibility, the role of language attitudes in intelligibility and language identification, and ethnolinguistic vitality (see *Ethnolinguistic Vitality*). In addition, missionary linguists have been pioneers in the development of techniques for the investigation of dialect intelligibility, language proficiency assessment (particularly in the less commonly used languages), and the investigation of language attitudes and use. Current work in language identification includes research in pidgins and creoles, signed languages, and other nonstandard varieties used widely alongside national or regional standard languages.

3. Missionaries and Bible Translation

The list of Bible translators is long and colorful. As Christianity spread across, and then outside of the Roman empire, the Bible was translated into more and more languages. The earliest translations were the Aramaic and Syriac versions. The Vulgate translated (into Latin) by St. Jerome (340–420) was commissioned by Pope Saint Damasas I and completed in 405 CE. Ulfilas (311–382) devised an alphabet and translated the Bible into the Gothic language. He omitted the Old Testament books of the Kings, however, feeling that they were 'too bellicose to be edifying for a people already extremely fierce and warlike' (Shelley 1982: 173–4).

One notable example of a missionary as a linguist from the eighteenth and nineteenth century is William Carey (1761–1834), who set sail from England for India in 1793 and, though untutored, became a specialist in Oriental languages, particularly Sanskrit, Marathi, and Bengali. By the time of his death he had, with assistance from his colleagues, translated the Bible into 44 languages of South Asia and also had produced dictionaries and grammars in many of those languages.

At the forefront of modern Bible translators are two large interdenominational organizations, the United Bible Societies (a consortium of national Bible distribution and promotion agencies) and Wycliffe Bible Translators International (comprised of national and regional organizations around the world). They are joined by a number of smaller organizations, which are generally associated with a specific church body or denomination. Wycliffe Bible Translators works closely with SIL International, a Christian language development organization, which engages in linguistic research, literacy work, and translation.

Missionaries have contributed significantly not only to the production of Bible translations in numerous languages of the world, but also to the development of translation theory and practice. Nida (1947) (see *Nida, Eugene Albert*), Beekman and Callow (1974), Larson (1984), and others have developed practical translation methodology based on linguistic and sociolinguistic models of language and communication.

4. Missionaries and Applied Linguistics

Missionaries are motivated to engage in applied linguistics as a means of facilitating access to the Bible and other religious materials. They have been contributors to both theory and practice in applied areas such as language learning, orthography design, literacy instruction and instructional materials, writer training, translation theory, bilingual education, and language development in general.

5. Missionaries and Sociolinguistics

Missionaries have had a small but important role in the development of sociolinguistics as a separate area of academic specialization. Early on, missionaries were aware of the important role that nonlinguistic factors played in the communicative process and recognized that language is very much situated in, and part of, culture. They have had a healthy respect for the importance of ethnographic aspects of language, although anthropologists and ethnographers have not always reciprocated that respect towards missionary anthropologists and linguists.

Kenneth L. Pike (1912–2000), early in his training as a linguist, recognized the importance of an holistic approach to language and culture and developed tagmemics, a theoretical model for linguistics, based on the recognition of three universal structural features: contrast, variation, and distribution. As Pike attempted to apply this approach to larger and larger units (first phonological and grammatical units, then entire languages) he realized that 'The English language was distributed into culture and was a part of culture' (Pike 1997: 211). This work led to his *Language in Relation to a Unified Theory of the Structure of Human Behavior* (Pike 1954) which is a summation of how language and society relate to and affect each other. A decade before sociolinguistics as such, was formally constituted – 1964 is the year of the birth of sociolinguistics in the United States according to most sources, (cf. Paulston and Tucker 1997)—Pike was struggling with variation and recognizing that the conditioning environment for much of the variation that linguists noted had to be social rather than linguistic. That concept would not be widely accepted and written about for another decade.

Eugene A. Nida of the United Bible Societies also wrote extensively on the sociolinguistic aspects of translation and the role that social structures play in communication.

The majority of missionary investigators who are writing in sociolinguistics are producing sociolinguistic descriptions of language communities, which include in-depth analyses from the perspectives of the sociology of language and linguistic anthropology. So far, missionaries have not done much work in microsociolinguistics, particularly in the area of variation analysis.

Several missionary sociolinguists are making substantial contributions to the development and application of Relevance Theory (Blass 1990, Gutt 1991). Semantics, pragmatics, discourse analysis (cf. Longacre 1983) and social network theory (see *Social Networks*) are also of considerable interest to the missionary community, since they have direct application to translation.

6. Missionaries and Endangered Languages

Perhaps the most controversial topic regarding missionaries in the last several decades has been language endangerment and the role that missionaries have had in regard to the status of endangered language groups. Critics accuse Christian missionaries of fomenting language and culture loss through their introduction of a message, which is culture changing and often associated with Western values and worldview.

Many missionaries, on the other hand, see themselves as champions of the use of the vernacular languages and argue that their interventions in communities where the language and culture is already endangered because of increasing contacts with outsiders often slows the pace of language shift, promotes a sense of self-esteem, and in some few cases has even preserved the use of a dying language. They argue that the introduction of literacy equips preliterate peoples to defend themselves in the encroaching literate world. In addition, missionary linguists, working with the last few elderly speakers of a language have preserved knowledge of those now-extinct languages. That knowledge is valuable both to the academic world and to the descendants of those speakers.

See also: Nida, Eugene Albert; Endangered Languages; Religion and Language; Orthography.

Bibliography

Beekman J, Callow J 1974 *Translating the Word of God with Scripture and Topical Indexes*. Zondervan Publishing House, Grand Rapids, M1

Blass R 1990 *Relevance Relations in Discourse: A Study with Special Reference to Sissala. Cambridge Studies in Linguistics*, 55. Cambridge University Press, Cambridge, UK

Grimes B F (ed.) 2000 *Ethnologue: Languages of the World*. SIL International, Dallas, TX

Gudschinsky S C 1973 *A Manual of Literacy for Preliterate Peoples*. Summer Institute of Linguistics, Ukarumpa, Papua New Guinea

Gudschinsky S C 1974 Fragmentos de ofaié: A descrição de uma língua extinta. *Série Lingüística* 3: 177–249

Gutt E A 1991 *Translation and Relevance: Cognition and Context*. Blackwell, Oxford, UK

Headland T N 1996 Missionaries and social justice: Are they part of the problem or part of the solution? *Missiology* 24: 167–78

Kindell G E, Lewis M P (eds.) 2000 *Assessing Ethnolinguistic Vitality: Theory and Practice*. SIL Publications in Sociolinguistics. SIL International, Dallas, TX

Larson M L 1984 *Meaning-based Translation: A Guide to Cross-language Equivalence*. University Press of America, Lanham, MD

Longacre R E 1983 *The Grammar of Discourse*. Plenum Press, New York

Nida E A 1947 *Bible Translating: An Analysis of Principles and Procedures, with Special Reference to Aboriginal Languages*. American Bible Society, New York

Nida E A 1977 Translating means communicating: A sociolinguistic theory of translation. In: Saville-Troike M (ed.) *Georgetown University Roundtable on Languages and Linguistics*. Georgetown University Press, Washington, DC

Nida E A 1986 Sociolinguistics and translating. In: Fishman J A, Tabouret-Keller A, Clyne M, Krishnamurti B, Abdulaziz M (eds.) *The Fergusonian Impact*. Mouton de Gruyter, New York

Nida E A 1987 Intelligibility and acceptability in verbal communication. In: Lowenberg P H (ed.) *Georgetown University Round Table on Languages and Linguistics*. Georgetown University Press, Washington, DC

Parker S G 1989 The sonority grid in Chamicuro phonology. *Linguistic Analysis* 19: 3–58

Paulston C B, Tucker G R (eds.) 1997 *The Early Days of Sociolinguistics. Memories and Reflections*. SIL Publications in Sociolinguistics, Summer Institute of Linguistics, Dallas, TX

Pike K L 1954 *Language in Relation to a Unified Theory of the Structure of Human Behavior*. Summer Institute of Linguistics, Glendale, CA

Pike K L 1987 The relation of language to the world. *International Journal of Dravidian Linguistics* 16: 77–98

Pike K L 1997 A note on holism. In: Paulston C B, Tucker G R (eds.) *The Early Days of Sociolinguistics. Memories and Reflections*. Summer Institute of Linguistics, Dallas, TX

Pitt M 1955 *Introducing Hinduism*. Friendship Press, New York

Wendell M M 1982 *Bootstrap Literature: Preliterate Societies Do It Themselves*. International Reading Association, Newark, DE

Shelley B L 1982 *Church History in Plain Language*. Word Books, Waco, TX

Native Speaker
A. Davies

1. The Native Speaker: Myth or Fact

The native speaker, like Lewis Carroll's snark, is a useful and enduring linguistic myth; again, like the snark, itself a product of the debate over idealism in philosophy, it must be taken with a large pinch of salt. Linguists may have given a special place to the native speaker as 'the only true and reliable source of languages data' (Ferguson 1983: vii), but there is little detailed discussion of the concept, which is often appealed to but difficult to track down. Full-length treatments of the topic (Coulmas 1981, Davies 1991, Paikeday 1985) have yet to attract much comment. Ferguson's argument has to do with language use rather than with language knowledge:

> much of world's verbal communication takes place by means of languages which are not the users' mother tongue but their second, third or nth language, acquired one way or another and used when appropriate. This kind of languages use merits the attention of linguists as much as do the more traditional objects of their research.
>
> (Ferguson 1983: vii)

It is possible to agree with Ferguson's desire that linguistics pay more attention to language use without agreeing with his dismissal of the native speaker: 'In fact the whole mystique of native speaker and mother tongue should preferably be quietly dropped from the linguist's set of professional myths about language.'

2. Theoretical Issues

Theoretically, the 'native speaker' concept is rich in ambiguity. It raises, quite centrally, the issue of the relation between the particular and the universal. Chomsky, as a protagonist of the universalist position, conveys to Paikeday's questioning approach about the status of the native speaker (Paikeday 1985) the strongest possible sense of the genetic determinants of speech acquisition, which, as he sees it, means that to be human is to be a native speaker.

Chomsky equates language development with other normal development, finding no interest in questions about developmental states or stages, which he regards as contingent. In the same vein, Chomsky finds distinctions between synchronic states of language or languages and dialects uninteresting: 'the question of what are the "languages" or "dialects" attained and what is the difference between "native" and "non-native" is just pointless' (Chomsky quoted in Paikeday 1985: 57). Chomsky's whole argument depends on a rationalist opposition to 'incorrect metaphysical assumptions, in particular the assumption that among the things in the world there are languages or dialects, and the individuals come to acquire them' (Paikeday 1985: 49). And so Chomsky must conclude that 'everyone is a native speaker of the particular language states that the person has "grown" in his/her mind/brain. In the real world, that is all there is to say' (1985: 58). This is a major thread in the range of views on the native speaker, and will recur later. Chomsky's view is uninfluenced by any social factor or contextual constraint. Variety and context, he seems to argue, are trivial. This is a thoroughgoing 'unitary competence' view of language in which language use is contingent and the native speaker is only a realization of that competence at linguistic and not at language level. For Chomsky, like many theoretical linguists, is not interested in languages: what he studies is language.

3. Educational Issues

Halliday (see *Halliday, Michael Alexander Kirkwood*) appears not to use the term 'native speaker'; however, what he says about the mother tongue is very relevant. He comments:

> Opinions differ regarding the uniqueness of the mother tongue ... for very many people ... no language ever completely replaces the mother tongue. Certain kinds of ability seem to be particularly difficult to acquire in a second language. Among these, the following are perhaps most important in an educational context:
> (a) saying the same thing in different ways,
> (b) hesitating, and saying nothing very much...
> (c) predicting what the other person is going to say...
> (d) adding new verbal skills (learning new words and new meanings) when talking and listening.
> It is not being suggested that we can never learn to do these things in a second language ... Nevertheless, there are vast numbers of children being educated through the medium of a second language, and of teachers trying to teach them, who have not mastered these essential abilities.
>
> (Halliday 1978: 199–200)

To what extent educational disadvantage can be attributed to not being a native speaker is debatable, especially since a similar argument of lacking adequate language resources is made for certain groups of native speakers who, it has been claimed (Bereiter and Engelmann 1966), suffer from a language deficit (see *Code, Sociolinguistic*). The basic question here is which code (whether language or dialect) one is supposed to be a native speaker of.

A contrary view to Halliday's is given by the American linguist, Leonard Bloomfield, author of *Language* (1933) and student of Native American languages in the anthropological tradition of early twentieth-century American linguistics. Like Halliday, Bloomfield does not use the term 'native speaker' but writes instead of 'the native language':

> The child growing up in the province, say, in some mountain village, learns to speak in the local dialect. In time, to be sure, this local dialect will take in more and more forms from the standard languages ... The child, then, does not speak the standard language as his native

tongue. It is only after he reaches school, long after his speech-habits are formed, that he is taught the standard language. No language is like the native language that one learned at one's mother's knee; no-one is ever perfectly sure in a language afterwards acquired. 'Mistakes' in language are simply dialect forms carried into the standard language.

(Bloomfield 1970: 151)

In another context, Bloomfield does refer to the native speaker: 'The first language a human being learns to speak is his native language; he is a native speaker of this language' (1933: 43). Bloomfield makes the obvious point that children learn to speak as they learn to do everything else, by observation, participation, and interaction with the people around them.

4. Psycholinguistic Issues

Katz and Fodor, more concerned with the relation between language and the mind, argue that 'The goal of a theory of a particular language must be the explication of the abilities and skills involved in the linguistic performance of a fluent native speaker' (1962: 218). In this way, the native speaker becomes central to the interests and concerns of linguistics, with the native speaker being the relevant example of natural phenomena for scientific study. Chomsky refers to the native speaker as being both the arbiter of a grammar and (when idealized) the model for the grammar: 'A grammar,' he says, 'is ... descriptively adequate to the extent that it correctly describes the intrinsic competence of the idealized native speaker' (1965: 24).

Chomsky thereby neatly compounds one of the central ambiguities of the 'native speaker' idea, using it to refer to both a person and an ideal. Or, as Coulmas says, 'The native speaker leads a double life in Chomsky's work, (a) as a creature of flesh and blood, that is the linguist himself, (b) an idealization' (Coulmas 1981: 10). Richards et al. in their *Dictionary of Applied Linguistics* (1985) and Crystal in his *First Dictionary of Linguistics and Phonetics* (1980) emphasize the importance of intuition in defining the native speaker, Crystal helpfully pointing to the need to take account of bilinguals who are native speakers of more than one language.

5. The New Englishes

Tay's contribution to the discussion is original in that she comments on the status of the native speaker in relation to the so-called New Englishes (see *New Englishes*), that is, the English of Singapore, India, and so on. She refers to the lack of clarity of most definitions, and notes that the two factors usually appealed to are priority of learning and an unbroken oral tradition. She comments that both are unsafe criteria; the first because of bilingualism, the second because an adult may have shifted dominance from one first language to another or because a second learned language may have had as much influence on a first learned as the other way around. Tay therefore proposes that a native speaker of English who is not from one of the traditionally native-speaking countries (e.g., the USA or the UK) is:

one who learns English in childhood and continues to use it as his dominant language and has reached a certain level of fluency. All three conditions are important. If a person learns English late in life, he is unlikely to attain native fluency in it; if he learns it as a child, but does not use it as his dominant language in adult life, his native fluency in the language is also questionable; if he is fluent in the language, he is more likely one who has learned it as a child (not necessarily before the age of formal education but soon after that) and has continued to use it as his dominant language.

(Tay 1982: 67–8)

These views indicate the accuracy of Coulmas's statement that a tension exists between the flesh and blood and the idealization definitions.

6. Practical Issues

The practical importance of the term is emphasized by Paikeday (1985), pointing to the employment discrimination against those who lack the 'ideal' native speaker attributes: 'native speakership should not be used as a criterion for excluding certain categories of people from language teaching, dictionary editing, and similar functions' (1985: 88).

Paikeday's own solution seems to be to separate the ideal and the operative meanings of native speaker, making proficiency the criterion for employment, and personal history the criterion for ideal membership. Such a rigid distinction is difficult to maintain when it comes to judgments of grammaticality which Paikeday wants to associate with the 'proficient user' meaning of 'native speaker' rather than with the 'ideal member' use: 'the people we refer to as arbiters of grammaticality are not really so because true arbiters of grammaticality are proficient users of languages, not just native speakers' (1985: 53).

The challenge which Paikeday sets is essentially which native speaker to choose, and lurking behind all such choices is undoubtedly his dilemma of whether a new model (which can be supported by acknowledged proficiency) outweighs a distant 'historically authentic' model; for example, Indian-English models or Nigerian-English models versus British or American models. However, this dilemma is just one example of the more general case. There is a dispute between the British and American models just as there is among other metropolitan models, and just also as there is between any Standard and other dialects. The important choice of a model therefore raises issues of acceptability, of currency, and of intelligibility. It is in part for this reason, that Paikeday's distinction between the 'ideal' native speaker definition and the 'operative' one is not finally tenable.

Nevertheless, the distinction is of practical importance in the institutionalized activities of publishing and examining, in the written language, and of selecting radio and television newsreaders in the spoken. There has generally been consensus in favor of a model type being used. It is also usual for a particular type of native speaker (or native-speaker-like non-native speaker) to be chosen—the prestige model. However, the prestige model has been rejected by some influential groups. In 1991, the large, international organization, Teachers of English to Speakers of Other Languages (TESOL), issued a statement (Forhan 1992) condemning any action which 'supports the exclusion of individuals who are nonnative speakers of English from employment opportunities within the profession.'

The term 'native speaker' is used in two distinct (but related) senses in relation to the prevailing consensus. The first is that in some way the native speaker is taken to represent an idealized model. The second is that an individual native speaker is him/herself used as an exemplar of such a model.

In academic settings, requests for native speakers to come forward (to take tests, to act as informants) may cause offense. First, what is not stated is that what is typically being referred to (in the UK or USA) is being a native speaker of English; second, it is ignored that everyone is a native speaker of some code; and third, it is denied that a highly proficient nonnative speaker may also have acquired both linguistic and communicative competence and be, therefore, in terms of what is required in formal higher education, indistinguishable from a native speaker.

7. Racism

What is also ignored is the racism of such remarks; what is so often meant by native speaker in the above context is the deliberate exclusion of those who are in with a chance. A Singaporean, a Nigerian, or an Indian might see him/her as a native speaker of English but feel a lack of confidence in his/her 'native speakerness.' The counterargument is that, in all such cases, it is really up to the individual to identify him/herself; no one else can do it. Where there is doubt, people define themselves as native speakers or as nonnative speakers of particular languages. As far as English is concerned, the problem is peculiarly one for those who belong to the postcolonial communities, such as Singapore, Nigeria, or India, where the New Englishes are in use. Membership as native speakers is largely a matter of self-ascription, not of something being given; it is in this sense that members decide for themselves. However, those who claim native-speaker status do have responsibilities in terms of confidence and identity. They must be confident as native speakers and identify with other native speakers. That is precisely what is required in acquiring any new ethnicity.

8. Related Terms

To be the native speaker of a language means, in a definition cited in Sect. 3, to speak it 'from your mother's knee' (Bloomfield 1970) as your mother tongue or first language (L1). Such a definition is not straightforward and is difficult to uphold. It is not wholly clear, for example, what is meant by mother tongue and by first language. Other terms used to indicate a claim to a language by an individual are 'dominant language' and 'home language' (Stern 1983, Davies 1991).

8.1 Mother Tongue

The 'mother tongue' is literally just that, the language of the mother, and is based on the reasonable view that a child's first 'significant other' is the mother. However, it is not always straightforward: the role of 'mother' may be taken by some other adult; similarly, the mother, biological or not, may provide bilingual or multilingual input for the child, either because the 'mother' is herself bilingual or because the role of mother is shared by several adults who use more than one language in speaking to the child. To what extent the child's own developing idiolect is identified as that of the mother rather than that of the child's own peer group is a matter for empirical investigation (Ochs 1982).

8.2 First Language

'First language' refers to the language which was first learned. Again, this seems straightforward. One's first language is the language ('tongue') learned from one's mother, biological or not. However, many people live in multilingual societies, and everyone lives in multidialectal society. In such cases, the mother tongue and the first language may be different: it may be that the mother tongue is influenced by peers as well as by parents, or it is more than one language and then it is not easy to decide which one is first; it may be that what is the first language changes over time. For example, a young child for whom Welsh is the mother tongue, and the first language in the sense of time of learning, may gradually come to use English more and more and relegate Welsh to a childhood experience: it may not be completely forgotten but is in some sense no longer as useful, no longer generative or creative, and therefore no longer *first*. For the large number of people in this category, the mother tongue is no longer the first or dominant language. Alternatively, such people may claim to have more than one first language. In the case of the bilingual or multilingual or dialectal mother, if it is accepted that one's mother tongue is the code of the individual mother and is not isomorphic with any one or more language, then it may be surmized that what mothers speak is either an interlanguage (see *Interlanguage*) (Selinker 1992) or a set of semilingual (see *Semilingualism*) codes (Martin-Jones and Romaine 1986).

8.3 Dominant Language

The term 'dominant language' is linked because of the underlying assumption that what was one's first language can change over time and another code take its place as one's first language. This must be the case of the child speaking a localized language who moves through education or some other major life-change into a situation in which they use English, French, or some other language of wider communication for most if not all purposes. In such cases, it is English or French which is dominant outside the home while the mother tongue is still dominant at home. In other words, the child has more than one dominant language, each language being dominant in certain areas of life (see Singh 1998).

8.4 Home Language

The 'home language' is the language of the home (and may, as with mother tongue, in reality be a mixed language or a set of languages/dialects) (see *Code-switching: Overview*; *Intertwined Languages*). Home language is defined negatively in terms of what it is not, since it is perhaps easier to define the public code, which often is a recognized (and described) standard English, French, and so on. The home language then is—for many children—what is left after the public, standard code has been removed. At the same time, for some children, the standard code is also the home language. Thus, in the case of middle-class native English speakers, the home language may well be largely identical with official Standard English, which is used as the medium in schools and is taught to foreigners (this applies equally in the UK, the USA, Australia, and other metropolitan, native English-speaking countries).

All these terms can be defined in relation to what they are not: first language in relation to a second language; dominant language in relation to the language it has superseded; home language in relation to the official code; and mother tongue in relation to what one's peers are speaking. The term native speaker tends to be used in each of these ways, for having language X as one's mother tongue, as one's first language, as one's dominant language, or as one's home language.

8.5 Linguistic Competence

Other terms invoked as being relevant to the native speaker are 'competence,' both linguistic and communicative, and '*langue*,' an older term. Saussure's use of *langue* (Saussure 1966) was an attempt to define not the native speaker but what it is that is shared by a language community.

The related notion of competence was introduced by Chomsky (1965) both to specify the knowledge of an indiviual which enables language acquisition to take place and also to signify the goal of linguistic theory. The notion of linguistic competence moves the argument one stage onwards, in that it seeks to answer the question of whether competence needs to assume a community langue.

There are two answers to this question. The first is that competence is about idealized speakers; indeed, Chomsky's definition of linguistics as being about the idealized native speaker in a homogeneous speech community is of obvious relevance. Such an approach is not a social one; it takes no account of situation, purpose, domain, or variety. It is psycholinguistic or cognitive–scientific and linked to the computer analog for the brain. However, even so extreme and rigorous a view must take some account of limited social aspects, since any eliciting of data, and even the concept of the idealized native speaker, must mean that there is some account being taken of the speaking world. Otherwise, it would be possible for someone who does not know the language or whose speech is full of performance errors of a severe kind or who is aphasic to be used for elicitation, and clearly that is not what happens. So, even here, there is a tacit assumption that the world is made up of speech communities of more than one person. Or, to use Coulmas's image, the double life of the native speaker does come together on occasion; the idealization can put on flesh and blood (Coulmas 1981: 10).

The second answer to the question of whether competence needs to assume langue is that it does because language itself needs an explanation as to how it is that (native) speakers understand one another. In other words, what competence sets out to do is indeed to provide a description of langue.

8.6 Communicative Competence

Chomsky's insistence on examining competence without social factors has been challenged by such anthropologically minded linguists as Halliday (1978) and Hymes (1970, 1989). Hymes proposed the term 'communicative competence' (see *Hymes, Dell Hathaway*; *Communicative Competence*) in order to point to the learned knowledge of cultural norms which is crucial to language use. The position taken up by communicative competence is that knowing what to say is never enough; it is also necessary to know how to say it. By 'how' here is not meant the performing of the speech, that is, getting the words out, but rather, the using of the appropriate register, variety, code, script, formula, tone, and formality. Once again, the issue for consideration is to what extent such cultural knowledge can be acquired late, and to what extent getting it right, that is, using the appropriate forms, privileges native speakers.

8.7 Second and Foreign Language

The discussion above, of defining the mother tongue and the first and dominant language in opposition to, for example, the 'second language,' suggests that one might hope to define in separate and perhaps rigorous ways the second language and the foreign language. However, a second language is in fact defined in terms of a language which is learned after the first language (Stern 1983). Thus, it remains impossible to define the first language except in terms of what is earliest acquired.

A distinction is perhaps useful between the language acquired by a bilingual (or multilingual) child in the home, or in an environment where more than one input is available, and that of the child who acquires a nonhome or nonintimate language in a more public setting (Romaine 1995, Hamers and Blanc 2000). Such a setting is often education, and the term second language is sometimes used to define a situation in which the child is being educated in a language medium which is not the home language. Not that the second language has to be the language of education—it may be the lingua franca of the public environment in which the child begins to grow up (e. g., English in Nepal). What seems to underline the use of the term second language is that it indicates a command which is less than that of the first language, but stronger than that of the foreign language.

Foreign languages, then, seem to be acquired in order to interact with foreigners, that is, groups outside one's native environment. That also seems to imply that a foreign language does not carry with it the kind of automatic grasp of its systems that are appealed to in terms of the first language and are suggested in some areas of the second language. A foreign language has not been, it can be surmized, internalized in the same way that a first (and perhaps a second) language has. A foreign-language speaker cannot be appealed to for authoritative pronouncements about the language's rules and its use. First-language speakers, of course, can be, and this is the problematic and very interesting issue about second languages: whether control of a second language can become as internalized as the first; whether being a native speaker and being a first-language speaker (or a mother-tongue speaker) are synonymous; and whether a second-language speaker can be a native speaker of that second language.

9. Defining the Native Speaker

To attempt a definition, the native speaker may be characterized in six ways. The native speaker:

(a) acquires the L1 of which they are a native speaker in childhood;
(b) has intuitions (in terms of acceptability and productiveness) about their idiolectal grammar;
(c) has intuitions about those features of the standard language grammar which are distinct from their idiolectal grammar;
(d) has a unique capacity to produce fluent spontaneous discourse, which exhibits pauses mainly at clause boundaries (the 'one clause at a time' facility), which is facilitated by a huge memory stock of complete lexical items (Pawley and Syder 1983); and in both production and comprehension the native speaker exhibits a wide range of communicative competence;
(e) has a unique capacity to write creatively (and this includes, of course, literature at all levels from jokes to epics, metaphor to novels);
(f) has a unique capacity to interpret and translate into the L1 of which they are a native speaker. Disagreements about an individual's capacity are likely to stem from a dispute about the standard language.

In considering the extent to which the L2 learner can become a target-language native speaker, one can again consider the six criteria.

(a) *Childhood acquistion*. The second-language learner, by this definition, does not acquire the target language in early childhood. If they do, then they are a native speaker of both L1 and the target language (TL).
(b) *Intuitions about idiolectal grammar*. It must be possible, with sufficient contact and practice, for the second-language learner to gain access to intuitions about their own idiolectal grammar of the target language.
(c) *Intuitions about group language grammar*. Again with sufficient contact and practice, the second-language learner can gain access to the standard grammar of the target language. Indeed, in many formal learning situations, it is exactly through exposure to a TL standard grammar that the TL idiolectal grammar emerges, the reverse of the L1 development.
(d) *Discourse in the language classroom and pragmatic control*. This may indeed be a descriptive difference between a native speaker and a nonnative speaker, but it is not in any way explanatory—that is to say, it in no way argues that a second-language learner cannot become a native speaker.
(e) *Creative performance*. With practice it must be possible for a second-language learner to

become an accepted creative writer in the TL. There are, of course, well-known examples of such cases, for example, Conrad, Beckett, Senghor; but there is also the interesting problem of the acceptability to the L1 community of the second-language learner's creative writing. This is an attitudinal question, but so too is the question of the acceptability to the same community of a creative writer writing in an alternative standard language (e.g., Scots).

(f) *Interpreting and translating*. This must be possible even though international organizations generally require that interpreters should interpret into their L1.

All except (a) are contingent issues. In that way, the question of whether a second-language learner can become a native speaker of a target language reduces to whether it is necessary to acquire a code in early childhood in order to be a native speaker of that code. To answer that question is to ask a further question, about what it is that the child acquires in acquiring his/her L1. However, that question has already been answered in criteria (b)–(f) above, and so the question again becomes a contingent one.

No doubt there is a need to ensure in addition a cultural dimension, that is, (b) and (c) above, since the child L1 acquirer does have access to the resources of the culture attached to the language and particularly to those learnt and encoded or even imprinted early. Still, there are always subcultural differences, for example, between the Scots and the English; different cultures with the same standard language (e.g., the German-speaking European nations); and different cultures with different standard languages (e.g., the British and the American). There is also International English, and isolated L1s in multilingual settings, for example, Indian English. Given such interlingual differences and the lack of agreement and norms that certainly occur among such groups, it does appear that the second-language learner has a difficult but not impossible task to become a native speaker of a target language.

10. Coppieters's Results

Such a conclusion is probably more sociological than linguistic or psychological. For, in addition to the tension referred to between the ideal and the flesh-and-blood approaches to the native speaker, there is a further opposition between the sociological and the psychological views; they are not easily reconcilable. Coppieters points out the lack of fit in his account of a grammatical judgment experiment (Coppieters 1987). He took a group of 27 non-native adult speakers of French who had 'so thoroughly mastered French that it was no longer clearly possible to distinguish them from native speakers by mistakes which they made, or by the restricted nature of their choice of words and constructions' (1987: 544). For baseline data, he took 20 native speakers of French, matched with the experimental group as far as possible. He used 107 sentences illustrating various aspects of French and asked his subjects individually for acceptability judgments. His results indicated that the two groups belonged to two different populations, with no overlap between, even at extremes. Even so, he accepted an argument in favor of identity theory (Tajfel 1981): 'A speaker of French is someone who is accepted as such by the community referred to as that of French speakers, not someone who is endowed with a specific formal underlying linguistic system.'

However, for Coppieters, such an argument is strongly sociological, and, in his view, competence must include a psychological dimension. He continues: 'it is also clear that the variation between native speakers and non-native speakers cannot simply be subsumed as a special case of the variation among native speakers: that is non-native speakers have been found to lie outside the boundaries of native speaker variation' (1987: 545). Native speakers, reports Coppieters, 'did not need the help of an explicit context. No matter how skilful non-native speakers might be at deriving the appropriate interpretation of a sentence in context, their inability to do so in the absence of an explicit context indicates a fundamental difference between their knowledge of the language and that of native speakers' (1987: 566–7).

Given the idiolectal and dialectal differences among native speakers themselves, Coppieters's claim is a strong one: his argument for cognitive rather than formal dissonance between native and non-native speakers concerns the grammar of the standard or common language learned before the critical period (Lenneberg 1967). His view is widely shared among psycholinguists and second-language researchers (Gass and Varonis 1985).

11. The Native-speaker Myth

Coppieters represents the uncompromising psychological view. According to that, the native speaker is defined by early acquired knowledge. Bartsch (1988) takes the more sociological view, allowing for the importance of attitude and identity. Although both views concern control of the standard language, they are probably not reconcilable. Nevertheless, the concept of native speaker is used entirely appropriately in these quite different ways. It is probable that what is most enduring about the concept has nothing to do with truth and reality, whether or not individuals are native speakers; what matters most is the enduring native speaker myth combining both knowledge and identity: in that myth, the two views have an equal role.

But there are those who disagree; Birdsong (1992) disputes the claim that the learner's 'ultimate attainment' can never be equal to native speaker competence, concluding from his partial replication of Coppieters' study that 'ultimate attainment by nonnatives can coincide with that of natives' (1987: 739). Such non-natives are, of course, exceptional learners, but the fact of their success indicates that the native speaker is as much a sociolinguistic construct as a developmental one. Birdsong's conclusion is supported by Bialystok (1997) who queries the role of maturational factors in second language acquisition.

See also: New Englishes; Bilingualism, Societal.

Bibliography

Bartsch R 1988 *Norms of Language*. Longman, London
Bereiter C, Engelmann S 1966 *Teaching Disadvantaged Children in the Preschool*. Prentice-Hall, Englewood Cliffs, NJ
Bialystok E 1997 The structure of age: in search of barriers to second language acquisition. *Second Language Research* **13**: 116–37
Birdsong D 1992 Ultimate attainment in second language acquisition. *Language* **68**: 706–55
Bloomfield L 1933 *Language*. Holt, Rinehart and Winston, New York
Bloomfield L 1970 Literate and illiterate speech. *American Speech* **2**: 432–9
Chomsky N 1965 *Aspects of the Theory of Syntax*. MIT Press, Cambridge, MA
Coppieters R 1987 Competence differences between native and near-native speakers. *Language* **63**: 544–73
Coulmas F (ed.) 1981 *A Festschrift for the Native Speaker*. Mouton, The Hague
Crystal D 1980 *A First Dictionary of Linguistics and Phonetics*. Andre Deutsch, London
Davies A 1991 *The Native Speaker in Applied Linguistics*. Edinburgh University Press, Edinburgh, UK
Ferguson C 1983 Language planning and language change. In: Cobarrubias J, Fishman J (eds.) *Progress in Language Planning*. Mouton, Berlin
Forhan L E 1992 Nonnative speakers of English and hiring practices. *TESOL Matters* **2/4**: 23
Gass S M, Varonis E M 1985 Variation in native speaker speech modification to non-native speakers. *Studies in Second Language Acquisition* **7**: 37–57
Halliday M A K 1975 *Learning How to Mean: Explorations in the Development of Language*. Edward Arnold, London
Halliday M A K 1978 *Language as Social Semiotic*. Edward Arnold, London
Hamers J F, Blanc M H A 2000 *Bilinguality and Bilingualism*, 2nd edn. Cambridge University Press, Cambridge, UK
Hymes D H 1970 On communicative competence. In: Gumperz J J, Hymes D H (eds.) *Directions in Sociolinguistics*. Holt, Rinehart and Winston, New York
Hymes D H 1989 Postscript. *Applied Linguistics* (special issue: 'Communicative competence revisited') **10**(2): 244–50
Katz J J, Fodor J A 1962 The structure of a semantic theory. *Language* **39**: 170–210
Le Page R B, Tabouret-Keller A 1985 *Acts of Identity*. Cambridge University Press, Cambridge, UK
Lenneberg E 1967 *Biological Foundations of Language*. John Wiley, New York
Martin-Jones M, Romaine S 1986 Semilingualism: A half-baked theory of communicative competence. *Applied Linguistics* **7**(1): 26–38
Ochs E 1982 Talking to children in Western Samoa. *Language in Society* **11**: 77–104
Paikeday T M 1985 *The Native Speaker is Dead!* Paikeday, Toronto, ON
Pawley A, Syder F H 1983 Two puzzles for linguistic theory: Naturelike selection and nativelike fluency. In: Richards J C, Schmidt R (eds.) *Language and Communication*. Longman, Harlow, UK
Richards J C, Platt J, Weber H 1985 *Longman Dictionary of Applied Linguistics*. Longman, Harlow, UK
Romaine S 1995 *Bilingualism*, 2nd edn. Blackwell, Oxford, UK
Saussure F de 1966 (transl. Baskin W) *Course in General Linguistics*. McGraw-Hill, New York
Selinker L 1992 *Rediscovering Interlanguage*. Longman, Harlow, UK
Singh R 1998 *The Native Speaker—Multilingual Perspectives*. Sage, New Delhi, India
Stern H H 1983 *Fundamental Concepts of Language Teaching*. Oxford University Press, Oxford, UK
Tajfel H 1981 *Human Groups and Social Categories*. Cambridge University Press, Cambridge, UK
Tay M 1982 The uses, users and features of English in Singapore In: Pride J (ed.) *New Englishes*. Newbury House, Rowley, MA

New Englishes
B. B. Kachru

The 'New Englishes' are the result of the global spread of English during the Colonial period. It was during this period that English gained the status of an international language and left other competing natural and artificial languages behind (e.g., French and Esperanto). There are now considerably more non-native users of English than native users, and it is the non-natives who have become the instruments for the continued spread of the language.

1. The Diffusion of English and Its Concentric Circles

The diffusion of English is best captured in terms of three concentric circles: the Inner Circle, the Outer Circle, and the Expanding Circle. The Inner Circle

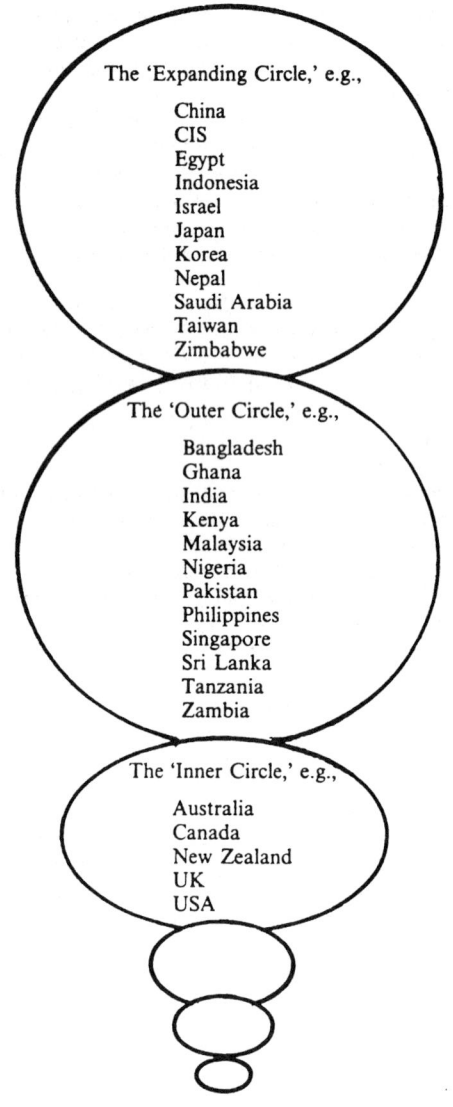

Figure 1.

represents the traditional historical and sociolinguistic bases of English in the regions where it is used as a native or first language. The Outer Circle represents the regions of the world formerly colonized by Britain and the USA; in those regions English was the language of empire building. The Expanding Circle includes the areas in which English is primarily a foreign language (see Fig. 1).

2. Terminology

The term 'New Englishes' is primarily used for the varieties of English which have developed in the Outer Circle. All such varieties—which exist in practically every continent—are transplanted and have therefore also been labeled 'diaspora' varieties (Kachru 1992a). The use of the term 'new' is a misnomer; in a historical and linguistic sense these varieties are not new. In South Asia, English was institutionalized in 1835 with the Minute of Thomas B. Macauley (1800–59). English also has a long his-tory in parts of Africa and Southeast Asia. The 'new-ness' of these varieties lies in the recent recognition of their linguistic and literary institutionalization.

From the 1960s these varieties attracted the serious attention of scholars working in the fields of linguistics, sociolinguistics, lexicography, language acquisition, and literature. The New Englishes have a long history of acculturation in geographical, cultural, and linguistic contexts, quite different from the developments of English in the Inner Circle.

The term 'World Englishes' is a synonym for 'New Englishes,' one which I now prefer. It symbolizes formal and functional variation, diverse sociolinguistic and pragmatic contexts, and canons and canonicities that the English language embodies in its global multilingual and multicultural contexts. The emphasis is on pluralism, not on the dichotomy between 'us and them,' 'native and non-native.' This perspective demands re-evaluation of traditional theoretical, methodological, literary, and ideological conceptualizations of the study of the English language. The term is not to be confused with World English, used earlier by Tom MacArthur among others. World Englishes implies 'the democratization of attitudes to English everywhere in the globe, in the process questioning the received model of the English as Native Language, English as Second Language, and English as Foreign Language nations...This is a more dynamic model than the standard version... [which] suggests mobility and flux and implies that a new history is in the making' (MacArthur 1993: 334).

3. Users and Functions of New Englishes

An estimated 130 million speakers in the Outer Circle use English with one or more other languages. This conservative figure considers only 10 percent of the total population in this circle as English-knowing. The term 'English-knowing' is rather tricky, since there is a cline of competence in the use of English. One end of the cline includes users of educated English; at the other end are those whose English has been characterized as 'broken.'

All the countries in the Outer Circle, for example, India, Nigeria, Singapore, Zambia, and the Philippines, are multilingual and multicultural, and English has official status in their national language policies as a language of wider communication across ethnic and linguistic groups. The Indian Constitution recognizes English as an 'associate' official language; in Nigeria and Zambia, English is one of the state languages; and in Singapore and the Philippines, English continues to be a major language of education, the legal system, and administration. In all these regions English, in various forms, plays an important role in interpersonal interaction and in literary creativity.

The New Englishes have thus penetrated deep into the societies of the Outer Circle. This societal penetration has resulted in the development of several subvarieties, ranging from educated to pidginized, e.g., Nigerian pidgin in West Africa, basilectal or colloquial English in Singapore, Hong Kong, and Malaysia, and Babu English and Butler English in India and Pakistan. In these countries English also plays a vital *intra*national communicative function as a link language; the *inter*national role, though important, is secondary.

The New Englishes continue to have an instrumental function in higher education, particularly in science and technology, and as a pan-regional language. They have a regulative function in national and intranational trade and commerce, in the network of national administrative and military service, and in the higher legal system. English is an important language for the media and for sociopolitical discourse.

4. The New Englishes as 'Contact' and 'Interference' Varieties

In the literature, two other terms are used to refer to the New Englishes: 'contact' varieties and 'interference,' varieties (see *Language Transfer and Substrates*). The term 'contact' highlights the multicultural and multilingual contexts in which these Englishes are used, and the impact of local sociolinguistic contexts on these varieties. The impact—or to use a more precise term 'transfer'—manifests itself in pronunciation, lexis, grammar, discourse, speech acts, and stylistic strategies. The new Englishes have thus acquired distinct linguistic and cultural identities. This has resulted in the expansion of the literary and sociocultural canon of English. These distinct canons of the New Englishes are not identical to the Judeo-Christian canon, traditionally associated with English literature and language (Kachru 1992a).

The degree of localization of English determines the depth of impact at various linguistic levels in each variety of English. The resultant linguistic processes have been termed, for example, the 'Africanization' and the 'Indianization' of the English language. The major contact varieties of English include South Asian English, West African English, Singapore English, and Philippine English (see Bailey and Görlach 1982, Kachru 1986).

The term 'interference' varieties is another way of describing the phenomenon of language contact: it refers to the linguistic readjustments in the bilinguals' use of English. The bilinguals' readjustment shows in the transfer of features of a dominant language on pronunciation, grammar, vocabulary, and discoursal features. Quirk et al. (1985: 27–8) consider interference varieties of English '... so widespread in a community and of such long standing that they may be thought stable and adequate enough to be institutionalized and hence to be regarded as varieties of English in their own right rather than stages on the way to more native-like English.' Each variety thus has stable identificational features.

4.1 Identificational Features

The identificational features of the New Englishes are of two types: those which entail transfer from a local language into English, and result in distinct phonetic, grammatical, or discoursal characteristics, and those which are essentially lexical and result in lexical transfer. The earlier research on transfer was primarily restricted to pronunciation and vocabulary. However, in recent research, the concentration has been on syntax, discourse, and interactional contexts (Smith 1987), the aim being to investigate variety-specific nativization (e.g., Nigerian English) and area-specific characteristics (e.g., African English, South Asian English). In certain ways all the New Englishes share several productive processes (Platt et al. 1984). The following characteristics are illustrative.

4.1.1 Pronunciation

The native varieties of English generally use stress-timed rhythm, i.e., stressed syllables occur after identical intervals. On the other hand, the New Englishes in South Asia (e.g., India, Pakistan, Sri Lanka), Southeast Asia (e.g., Singapore, Malaysia, Hong Kong), and West Africa (e.g., Nigeria, Ghana) generally use syllable-timed rhythm, i.e., an arrangement of equal numbers of syllables per unit of time. This difference is one of the factors which causes problems in intelligibility.

4.1.2 Grammar

A number of grammatical features are typical of a variety and of a region. In South Asian English there is a tendency to form interrogative questions without changing the position of the subject and auxiliary items (e.g., *What you would like to eat? When you would like to go?*). In South Asian and African English *isn't it?* is used as a universal tag (e.g., *He isn't coming, isn't it? You are not going tomorrow, isn't it?*). The use of articles and complementation also shows several differences in the new varieties (see Bailey and Görlach 1982, Cheshire 1991, Kachru 1992a, 1992b).

4.1.3 Lexis

The lexical features are of two types. The first type includes those items which are borrowed (see *Borrowing*) from the local languages. A small number of such lexical items are shared with British and/or American English (e.g., *pundit, nirvana, guru*). In local varieties of English, however, such items are used extensively (e.g., in South Asian English *jantā* 'people,' *gāḍī* 'train'; in South African English *kloof* 'ravine, valley,' *skorokoro* 'jalopy'; and in Singaporean/Malaysian English *makan* 'food,' *kampong* 'a small settlement'). The new Englishes make frequent use of such items in conversation, newspapers, and in creative writing. The second type includes hybridized items, in which local language items are mixed with English to create new words (e.g., *lathi charge* 'charge with baton,' *tiffin carrier* (*tiffin* 'snack,' 'light meal') in South Asian English *dunno drums* 'a type of drum,' *kraal family* 'family sharing the same enclosure' in South African English).

4.1.4 Collocations

These include translations of contextually appropriate local words into English. This type of lexical innovation marks the functional acculturation of the New Englishes in local—that is African and Asian—sociocultural contexts. For example, the use of *twice-born* 'one who has been initiated as a Brahmin,' *co-brother-in-law* 'wife's sister's husband,' *cow-worship* 'worship of cows' in South Asian English; and *cry die* 'wake, funeral rites,' *head tie* 'head scarf,' *throw water* 'offer a bribe,' and *co-wife* 'the second of two wives' in African English.

4.1.5 Idioms

A vast number of idioms and comparative constructions are translated from local languages, e.g., *to whisper together* 'to talk privately,' and *to have no shadow* 'to have no courage,' in African English; and *as honest as an elephant* and *as good as kitchen ashes* in Indian English.

4.1.6 Discourse and Style

This refers to the use of localized speech acts, and discoursal and stylistic strategies. The innovation of such culture-bound discourse strategies in interaction and in literary creativity has given a distinct identity to the New Englishes (Kachru 1986: 159–73, Smith 1987) (see *Discourse in Cross-linguistic and Cross-cultural Contexts*).

4.1.7 'Mixing' and 'Switching'

The processes of code-mixing and code-switching (see *Code-switching: Overview*) are distinctive markers of the multilinguals' creativity in New Englishes. Mixing entails hybridization by using words or larger units from local languages in the stream of discourse in English (e.g., English–Hindi mixing in *der ho rahī hai, let us lagāo khānā* 'It is getting late, let's set out the food'). Code-switching involves changing from one language to another (e.g., English to Swahili). The motivations for mixing and switching are varied, e.g., marking identity, function, participants, settings.

4.2 Varieties within a Variety

The varieties of New Englishes are not homogeneous. Institutionalization over an extended period and various societal functions of the variety have resulted in a cline of varieties. The institutionalized New Englishes have an educated variety, and several other subvarieties. The subvarieties are based on proficiency (e.g., Butler English or Bazaar English in South Asia, Nigerian Pidgin in West Africa); societal level (e.g., basilect or colloquial English in Singapore and Malaysia); ethnic identity (e.g., Anglo–Indian English in India, Igbo English in Nigeria, Burger English in Sri Lanka); geographical area (e.g., Bengali English); and schooling (e.g., Convent English in South Asia).

5. Norms and Models for New Englishes

The question of norms and models has become a major concern with the universalization and consequent diversification of English. The issue has several dimensions: pedagogical, attitudinal, pragmatic, social, and linguistic (Kachru 1992b).

There are three types of speech fellowships of English: the norm-providing (the Inner Circle); the norm-developing (the Outer Circle); and the norm-dependent (the Expanding Circle).

In the Outer Circle, endocentric norms have well-recognized linguistic, literary, and cultural identities. The controversy, however, has not completely abated. In this Circle there is an ongoing debate between the appropriateness and pragmatics of local and external norms—a conflict between language behavior and attitude. In the Expanding Circle, the pedagogical models (norms) continue to be external, the choice being primarily between the general American and the educated British varieties.

6. Literary Creativity in New Englishes

The New Englishes have vibrant and fast-developing literary dimensions (King 1980). This literary tradition has developed in all the countries in the Outer Circle. The nativized literary traditions are now considered part of the local literary tradition and national literatures. This body of literature includes various genres: novel, short story, poetry, essay, and journalism. The localized identity of these literatures is reflected in modifiers such as Nigerian English literature, Indian English literature, and Singaporean English literature. In such creativity, various types of linguistic and stylistic experiments and innovations are made. These literatures are primarily the result of linguistic and sociocultural contact of two or more languages and cultures, and are thus appropriately considered as products of bilinguals' creativity (Kachru 1986). In designing such texts the linguistic resources of two or more, related or unrelated, languages are used. This is often done consciously as in Chinua Achebe, Salman Rushdie, and Raja Rao.

There are two ways in which the institutionalized contact literatures in English reveal their distinctiveness: 'nativization' and 'acculturation.' Nativization refers to the formal textual features of such creativity, and acculturation to the thematic or contextual localization of such writing. Nativization contributes to linguistic processes which are localized and provide an identity to the text. Indian philospher–novelist Raja Rao's *The Serpent and the Rope* is an example of the Indianized text; and Gabriel Okara's *The Voice* is an example of an Africanized text. On the other hand, acculturation of texts is a matter of cultural identity which English acquires by its Africanization or Indianization. The two processes together mark the New English literatures as being distinct and give them identities separate from the canons associated with British and American literatures. It is in this sense that the New Englishes have expanded the literary and cultural cannons of English. These literatures have received international recognition: Wole Soyinka of Nigeria received the Nobel Prize in literature (1986) as did Derek Alton Walcott of the West Indies (1992), and Raja Rao of India received the Neustadt International Prize (1988).

Contact literatures in English have been studied within three paradigms: linguistic, literary, and padagogical. In linguistic studies, though belated, the shift is from an 'interference-oriented' model to a model based on comparative (contrastive) discourse. Creativity is seen as innovation within non-Judeo–Christian, non-Western contexts (Smith 1987). The emphasis is on the underlying contextual reasons for style shifts, change in lects, and strategies for nativized speech acts and discourse. These stylistic experiments invariably involve transfer from the style repertoire—literary or oral—of local languages. Such creativity in English is now recognized as such by the national literary academies (e.g., in India, Pakistan, Singapore) as an extension of local literary traditions. Padagogical uses of such writing are discussed in courses on stylistics, and in cross-cultural uses of English.

7. Ideology and Methodology

The development of New Englishes, and their distinct identities raises a string of ideological, theoretical, and methodological questions (Kachru 1988). These questions have come into the forefront for two reasons: the use of sociolinguistic models for the study and understanding of New Englishes and attempts to relate innovations to their social meaning; and the study of the New English literatures as extensions of the local literary traditions. There is a trend toward breaking away from the Eurocentric approaches, and new creativity is essentially considered in local and particular contexts. Achebe (1975: 11) argues, 'I should like to see the word *universal* banned altogether from discussions of African literature until such a time as people cease to use it as a synonym for the narrow, self-serving parochialism of Europe.'

What is the relationship between the medium and the ideological message? Do the New Englishes represent the Western or local cultural ethos? Can the medium be localized and molded to have new cultural and ideological identities and develop new canons? In other words, what are the processes used for the 'decolonization' of English (Thumboo 1988)? These questions continue to be debated. In methodological terms, one asks: how insightful are the research methodologies used for monolingual societies and their creativity for understanding the innovations and creativity of linguistically and culturally pluralistic societies?

All these questions are invariably related to a wider question of the power and politics of English and various manifestations of such strategies for power (Kachru 1986, Phillipson 1992, Tollefson 1991) (see *Linguistic Imperialism*).

8. Current Issues

The major issues concerning the New Englishes relate to four aspects. First, the implications of 'pluricentricity' and 'diversification' of English on international and intranational intelligibility and its implications for the English language and literature. Second, strategies for codification and its consequences. Third, attitudes toward the diversification and 'multi-identities' of Englishes. Fourth, the implication of new literary and linguistic canons and their impact on mutual intelligibility.

9. Resources

The period following the 1980s has been the most active period for research and debate on World Englishes in general and the New Englishes in particular. An overview of such research is provided in compilations (Cheshire 1991, Kachru 1992b, Viereck et al. 1984); and in state-of-the-art surveys (e.g., Kachru 1992a).

See also: Bilingualism, Societal; Areal Linguistics; Native Speaker; Language Transfer and Substrates.

Bibliography

Achebe C 1975 *Morning Yet in Creation Day*. Heinemann Educational, London
Bailey R W, Görlach M (eds.) 1982 *English as a World Language*. University of Michigan Press, Ann Arbor, MI

Baumardner R J (ed.) 1996 *South Asian English: Structure, Use & Users*. University of Illinois Press, Urbana, IL

Bhatia T K, Ritchie W (eds.) 1989 Code-mixing: English across languages. *World Englishes* **8**(3)

Cheshire J (ed.) 1991 *English Around the World: Sociolinguistic Perspectives*. Cambridge University Press, Cambridge, UK

Görlach M 1991 *Englishes*. Benjamins, Amsterdam

Kachru B B 1986 *The Alchemy of English: The Spread, Functions, and Models of Non-native Englishes*. Pergamon Press, Oxford, UK

Kachru B B 1988 The spread of English and sacred linguistic cows. In: Lowenberg P H (ed.) 1988 *Language Spread and Language Policy: Issues, Implications, and Case Studies*. Georgetown University Press, Washington, DC

Kachru B B 1992a World Englishes: Approaches, issues, and resources. In: *Language Teaching*. Cambridge University Press, Cambridge, UK

Kachru B B (ed.) 1992b *The Other Tongue: English Across Cultures*, 2nd edn. University of Illinois Press, Urbana, IL

King B 1980 *The New English Literatures: Cultural Nationalism in the Changing World*. Macmillan, London

Lowenberg P H (ed.) 1988 *Language Spread and Language Policy: Issues, Implications, and Case Studies*. Georgetown University Press, Washington, DC

MacArthur T 1993 The English language or the English languages? In: Bolton W F, Crystal D (eds.) *The English Language, Vol. 10. Penguin History of Literature*. Penguin Books, London

MacArthur T 1998 *The English Languages*. Cambridge University Press, Cambridge, UK

Machan T W, Scott C T (eds.) 1992 *English in its Social Contexts: Essays in Historical Sociolinguistics*. Oxford University Press, New York

Phillipson R 1992 *Linguistic Imperialism*. Oxford University Press, Oxford, UK

Platt J, Weber H K, Ho M L 1984 *The New Englishes*. Routledge, London

Quirk R, Greenbaum S, Leech G, Svartnik J 1985 *A Comprehensive Grammar of the English Language*. Longman, London

Smith L E (ed.) 1987 *Discourse Across Cultures: Strategies in World Englishes*. Prentice-Hall, London

Thumboo E 1988 The literary dimension of the spread of English: Creativity in a second tongue. In: Lowenberg P H (ed.) *Language Spread and Language Policy: Issues, Implications, and Case Studies*. Georgetown University Press, Washington, DC

Tollefson J W 1991 *Planning Language, Planning Inequality: Language Policy in the Community*. Longman, London

Viereck W, Bald W (eds.) 1986 *English in Contact with Other Languages*. Akademiai Kiado, Budapest, Hungary

Viereck W, Schneider E W, Görlach M 1984 *A Bibliography of Writings on Varieties of English, 1965–1983*. Benjamins, Amsterdam

Pidgins and Creoles: An Overview

L. Todd

In 1953, the pidgin English of Papua New Guinea was described as 'inferiority made half articulate' and its grammar was criticized as 'crude and incredibly tortuous' (French 1953). In the last decade of the century, the same language is called Tok Pisin (Talk Pidgin): it is the chosen language of debate in Port Moresby's parliament; it is employed for news and entertainment on the media; it is officially recognized in the constitution as one of the country's national languages; it is used in official speeches by visiting dignitaries; and it is spoken as a mother tongue by over 20,000 Papua New Guineans and as a lingua franca by an estimated 1.5 million people. The change in the status of Tok Pisin resembles the change in attitude towards pidgin and creole languages generally. In the period between 1950 and 1975, these languages stopped being described and dismissed as 'marginal languages' and 'bastardized jargons,' and became central to linguistic discussion on acquisition of language linguistic universals, and language change.

1. Definitions

It seems likely that 'pidginization,' a process of simplification and hybridization, is as old as contacts involving speakers of different languages or dialects. Many contemporary pidgins and creoles can, however, be traced back to European 'discoveries' in the sixteenth and seventeenth centuries, a period of linguistic procreation, when new languages came into being, languages which are lexically related to Dutch, English, French, Portuguese, and Spanish, and which are spoken in the late twentieth century, in some form, by perhaps 100 million people. (It is not easy to estimate the number of speakers of pidgins and creoles, but this figure may be seen as conservative when it is pointed out that Afrikaans, a semi-creolized Dutch, is spoken by over 5 million, Cape Verde Crioulo by over 3 million, Haitian Créole by over 5 million, Nigerian pidgin English by over 20 million, and Tok Pisin by 1.5 million.)

The origins of the word 'pidgin' are still debated. It is possible that it derives from *Pidian* (South American Indian), from a Chinese pronunciation of

English *business* or Portuguese *ocupaçao* (business), from Hebrew *pidjom* (barter), from Portuguese *pequeno* (little, and suggesting baby talk), or from a combination of any of these, reinforced by English *pigeon*. The term is applied to a lingua franca which develops as a simple means of communication between people speaking different languages. 'Creole' derives ultimately from Latin *creare* (to beget) and more immediately from Portuguese *crioulo*, Spanish *criollo* and French *créole*. The term 'creole' was applied to Europeans who were born in the New World, then to Africans born there, to both, to people of mixed race, to the forms of language spoken by people in the Americas, and eventually, to any pidgin which has become a mother tongue for a community.

2. Social Attitudes

Pidgins and creoles used to be stigmatized. There are three main reasons for this. First, their speakers were usually non-Caucasian, slaves or servants, and their low prestige was transferred to the languages they spoke. (The metaphors used to describe the languages provide insights into the asymmetry of the human relationships. Individual languages were described and dismissed as a 'barbarous dissonance,' a 'bastardized language,' and a 'mongrel lingo.') Second, they tended to be spoken only, and therefore lacked the status of languages with long literary traditions. Third, many were recognizable as varieties of European languages, and were presented as simplified or corrupted versions of these. The technique of using modified European orthographies for pidgins and creoles reinforced the notion that they were imperfect versions of metropolitan languages:

> Littee Jack Horner
> Makee sit inside corner,
> Chow-chow he Clismas pie;
> He put inside t'um,
> Hab catchee one plum,
> 'Hai yah! what one good chilo my!'
>
> (Leland 1876: 75.)

3. Widespread Nature of Pidgins and Creoles

As has been shown, many pidgins and creoles can be traced to the period of European exploration and colonization, but others evolved outside such contacts. Pidgins and creoles have developed in multilingual societies in every continent. In Papua New Guinea, for example, Hiri Motu came into being prior to European contacts to facilitate trade between speakers of Motu and other Papuan languages; in Indonesia and Malaysia, the so-called 'Bazaar Malay' has had widespread currency among travelers and traders for at least four centuries; in India, in the State of Assam, which recognizes 13 distinct languages, Naga Pidgin, a form of Assamese, continues to have value in interlingual contacts; in the Central African Republic, Sango arose from contacts between speakers of mutually unintelligible African languages; in England, Anglo-Romani, a creolized form of Romani, has evolved; and in America, there is evidence of pidginization of Amerindian languages. It seems likely that a form of Chinook Jargon (see *Jargons*) existed as a link language between speakers of Chinook and Nootka before it was used as a lingua franca by speakers of French and English. Pidginization is widely found in all contacts involving speakers of different languages; marginal pidgins develop when simple communications across linguistic barriers are regular but superficial; elaborated pidgins come into being to facilitate long-term but non-intimate communications between people; creoles arise when pidgins become mother tongues.

4. Characteristics of Pidgins

Pidgins and creoles are found throughout the world and are lexically related to languages from virtually all the world's language families. They are classified together because of sociological and linguistic criteria. Stable pidgins share the following characteristics:

(a) Phonologically, they are simpler than any of the languages involved in their evolution. Often, they have a five- or seven-vowel system, as shown below.

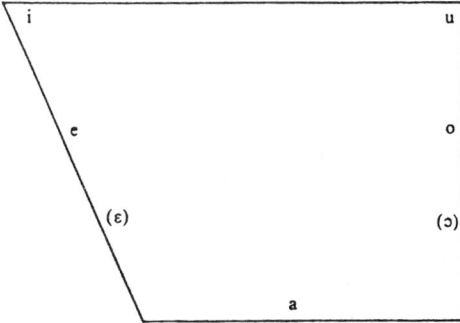

Nasalized and rounded front vowels are avoided, as are dental and lateral fricatives and clicks, even if they occur in one or more of the donor languages.

(b) They have a small vocabulary, drawn mainly from the language of the socially dominant group. English-based pidgins, for example, derive as much as 90 percent of their lexicon from English:

English	Kamtok (Cameroon)	Tok Pisin
arm, hand	*han*	*han*
back, return	*bak*	*bak(im)*

become pregnant	gɛt bɛlɛ	gatim bel
blood	blɔd	blut
stomach, seat of emotions	bɛlɛ	bel
come	kam	kam
give	gif	gifim
go	go	go

(c) Most words are polysemous. Kamtok's *hia* (<hear), for example, means 'hear,' 'sense,' 'understand.'

(d) Most words are multifunctional. Kamtok's *bad* (<bad) can function as an adjective:

tu bad pikin (two bad children)

as a noun:

Wi no laik dis kain bad. (We do not like this kind of badness.)

as an adverb, modifying a verb:

A laikam bad. (I like it very much.)

as an adverb, modifying an adjective-verb:

I gud bad. (He's very good.)

as an adjective-verb:

Di pikin bad. (The child is bad.)

(e) Emphasis is often indicated by reduplication:

Kamtok	*big* (big)	*big big* (enormous)
	luk (see)	*luk luk* (stare at)
Petit Nègre	*gran* (big)	*gran gran* (enormous)
	vwa (see)	*vwa vwa* (stare at)

(f) They often have a small number of prepositions, sometimes as few as two, one to indicate location, another to indicate possession. In Tok Pisin, for example, the two most frequently used are *long* (<along) and *bilong* (<belong):

Mi stei long Mosbi. (I live in Port Moresby.)
haus bilong mi (my house)
haus bilong wanpela meri (a woman's house).

(g) Abstractions are often indicated by compounds. In Kamtok, for example, one finds:

big ai (<big+eye)=greed, greedy
drai ai (<dry+eye)=brave, bravery (in a man), brazen, brazenness (in a woman)

and in Tok Pisin, there is:

big maus (<big+mouth)=conceit, conceited
drai bun (<dry+bone)=tough, toughness.

(h) Word order is rigid. In many pidgins, including Kamtok, it follows the pattern of:

(Adjunct) + Subject + Predicate + (Object) + (Adjunct)
Las nait   wi   bin si   wi papa   fɔ haus

Last night we saw (visited) our father in his house.
Wɛti   yu   di fain   jɔsnau?

What are you looking for now?
Wuna   go   kwik kwik.
Go immediately.

(i) Inflection is nonexistent or minimal:

Kamtok	Tok Pisin	English
wan man	*wanpela man*	one man
tu man	*tupela man*	two men
a go	*mi go*	I go
i go	*em i go*	he/she/it goes
wi go	*mipela go*	we go
yu bin go	*yu go pinis*	you (sg) went
wuna go go	*bai yupela go*	you (pl) will go
a go go?	*bai mi go?*	Shall I go?

(j) Temporal and aspectual distinctions are indicated by context, by an adjunct, or by a set of auxiliaries which occur in a fixed order:

ɛni dei ɛni dei, a mek chɔp. (Every single day, I cook.)
Las nait, a mek chɔp. (Last night, I cooked.)
Wɛti a bin du? A bin mek chɔp. (What did I do? I cooked.)
A bin di soso mek chɔp. (I was invariably cooking.)
Smɔl taim a go mek chɔp. (In a little while, I'll cook.)

(k) Negation is usually indicated by placing a negator before the verb:

Kamtok	Tok Pisin	English
Kam	*Kam*	Come
No kam	*No kam*	Don't come
I no kam	*Em i no kam*	He isn't coming/hasn't come

Multiple negation is common as a form of emphasis.

No man no laik mi no smɔl. (Nobody likes me at all.)

When a pidgin is creolized, its simple structure is often carried over, but a mother tongue must be able to fulfill all its speakers' linguistic needs and so the vocabulary expanded, polysemy reduced, additional prepositions introduced, and the syntax made less dependent on context.

5. The Origin of Pidgins

Each pidgin and creole derives most of its vocabulary from a single language. Those that share their core vocabulary with English are called 'English-based' or are said to have English as their 'superstrate' or their 'lexical source language.' If one looks at phonological or syntactic data, however, the classification is much less easy. French is the lexical source language for Haitian Créole, for example, but if one compares some of its structures with those of Kamtok, one sees that they share similarities not shared by French and English:

Li bel.=Il/elle est beau/belle. (lit. 3rd person pronoun (pers pron)+lovely)
I fain.=He/she/it is handsome/pretty. (lit. 3rd pers pron+lovely)

Li bel? = Est-il/elle beau/belle? (lit. 3rd pers pron + lovely + rising intonation)

I fain? = Is he/she handsome/pretty? (lit. 3rd pers pron + lovely + rising intonation)

Li te kone... = Il/elle connaissait... (lit. 3rd pers pron + past time marker + base form of verb)

I bin sabi... = He/she knew (lit. 3rd pers pron + past time marker + base form of verb)

Li pa te kone... = Il/elle ne connaissait pas... (lit. 3rd pers pron + negator + past time marker + base form of verb)

I no bin sabi. = He/she didn't know (lit. 3rd pers pron + negator + past time marker + base form of verb)

Li gro pas u. = Il/elle est plus gros que vous (lit 3rd pers pron + big + pass + you)

I big pas yu. = He/she is bigger than you (lit. 3rd pers pron + big + pass + you).

In addition, some of the pidgins which are lexically unrelated to European languages share structural features with English-based pidgins and creoles:

Ewondo Populaire	Krio	English
Me bo	A du	I do
Me ke bo	A nɔ du	I don't do
Me nga bo	A bin du	I did
Me ke nga bo	A nɔ bin du	I didn't do.

The classification of pidgins and creoles causes three main problems. First, the vocabulary points unequivocally to one parent language, whereas the syntax does not. Second, the process of pidginization of European languages has resulted in the wholesale discarding of concord, inflection, and morphology, and these are the very features that are used in showing linguistic relationships. Third, the sound changes which words have undergone in being adopted into pidgins imply a greater passage of time than is actually the case. This point suggests that one must be careful in the rigid application of the findings of glottochronology to language change in the past.

Many theories have been advanced to explain the origin of pidgins, but the three most comprehensive are monogenesis, polygenesis, and linguistic universality.

Monogeneticists suggest that all pidgins related to European languages derive ultimately from *one* Mediterranean trade language, which may have been a form of *Lingua Franca* or *Sabir* (see *Lingua Franca*), the medieval link language between Muslims and Christian Crusaders. This language is referred to many times in books of exploration dating from the seventeenth century. It may have formed the basis of a maritime 'Sailors' Jargon,' which would have been used on board ship and in the ports where many of the pidgins first developed. The structural similarities of pidgins and creoles related to Dutch, English, French, Portuguese, and Spanish would support this theory, as would the facts that all of these languages have nautical elements (for example, Krio's *gali* = kitchen, and Haitian Créole's *mare* = to tie) and share lexical items such as *pikin/pikinini* = child and *sabi* = know. According to this theory, speakers of a Portuguese pidgin in an African port would have relexified the language towards Dutch, French, or English, depending on the strength of contact with the individual colonial power. Against this theory is the fact that pidgins such as Ewondo Populaire (Cameroon) and Hiri Motu (Papua New Guinea) also share many of the same structural features although they do not derive from European languages.

Polygeneticists suggest that all pidgins and creoles followed independent but parallel developments. The early pidgins related to European languages evolved in conditions of slavery or extreme social deprivation. The European 'masters' would have simplified their language and the 'slaves' would have learned an imperfect version of the target language. Since the differences in social status did not allow for the close linguistic contact that would have enabled the 'slaves' to move beyond their baby-talk version, the simple lingua franca was retained and passed on to subsequent generations. Supporters of this theory account for the structural similarities in two ways. First, they point out that the superstrate languages are all Indo-European and so share deep-rooted similarities. Second, they suggest that all Atlantic pidgins and creoles share a common West African substrate and many of the Pacific varieties share a similar Pacific substrate. It is probably true that many Europeans adopted a condescending linguistic attitude to the peoples of Africa, Asia, Australia, and Polynesia; it is also likely that learners of pidgins used baby-talk strategies in their acquisition of the languages; and it is undoubtedly true that pidgin speakers were influenced by their mother tongues. African pidgins and creoles reveal idioms, metaphors, and proverbs calqued from West African languages:

dei klin (day clean) = dawn
nak han (known hand) = lament, mourn
Wan han no fit tai bɔndul (one hand no fit tie bundle) = People must cooperate.

Equally, pidgin speakers from Papua New Guinea calqued from their vernaculars:

gras bilong ai (grass belong eye) = eyebrow
tu bel (two belly) = doubting
tingting long bel (think think long belly) = reflect.

The difficulty inherent in accepting polygenetic theories of origin is that, while many of the claims are correct or reasonable, they cannot explain the structural similarities found in pidgins which have arisen in different parts of the world, where such pidgins have had little or no connection with European languages.

In an attempt to overcome the difficulties inherent in both monogenetic and polygenetic theories, some creolists argue that the solution is to be found in a universalist approach. They suggest three main reasons for the structural similarity of pidgins and creoles. First, the social conditions in which pidgins arose are similar. People who did not share a language, and who were often in an asymmetrical relationship, needed to communicate simply and quickly, usually about trade. Second, learning strategies are similar. The baby-talk and 'foreigner talk' of English are structurally similar to those of Arabic and Igbo. Third, human languages are similar and any child can learn any language. The children who learned pidgins as a first language and who lacked an adult mother-tongue model created creoles using their inherent linguistic skills. The comprehensiveness of this theory is its most attractive quality. Africans, Americans, Asians, Europeans, and Polynesians would have used their innate linguistic abilities to create simple communication systems which could be elaborated by having recourse to their mother tongues or to the linguistic common denominators which are thought to underlie all human languages. This theory has thus far been impossible to prove. It is likely that children are genetically programmed with particular attributes to acquire languages. It is also likely that speakers, in contact situations, simplify their languages in particular ways. However, it is impossible to be precise about the character and nature of innate linguistic abilities.

6. The Development of Pidgins

Each pidgin and creole is unique in terms of its origin, uses, and linguistic characteristics, and even closely related varieties, such as Sierra Leone's Krio and Gambia's Aku, differ in pronunciation and lexis. It is possible, however, to distinguish four phases in their development, although it must be stressed that they often overlap. The phases may be described as 'Marginal Contact,' 'Nativization Period,' 'Influence from Dominant Language,' and 'Continuum Phase.'

In the Marginal Contact phase, a makeshift pidgin evolves. It uses a limited vocabulary and short utterances, and communication is facilitated by gesture, mime, frequent repetition, and by speaking loudly and slowly. In this phase all speakers tend to use the phonologies of their mother tongues, although all syllables are likely to be stressed. This type of pidgin can be heard in ports and market places where a language is not shared but where people wish to carry out simple transactions. Several pidgin Englishes of this type have also arisen in times of war, for example in Japan, Korea, and Vietnam in the course of the twentieth century. Makeshift pidgins either die out when they no longer serve a purpose or they become more useful by being stabilized and expanded. They most frequently die out in bilingual contacts and are most frequently elaborated in multilingual communities.

In the Nativization Phase, the pidgin becomes increasingly valuable as a lingua franca in a multilingual environment between local people who do not share a language. Its vocabulary is expanded so that it can be used for purposes other than trade and, the more it is used, the more flexible and stable it becomes. The phonology tends to be that of one's mother tongue, although uncommon sounds are avoided. The vocabulary is expanded by means of borrowing from indigenous languages:

akara (bean cake, from West Africa)
kaikai (eat, food, from Polynesia)

calquing:

chɔpdai = wake for an old person [eat + die]
kraidai = wake for a young person [cry + die]

compounding core vocabulary to create abstractions:

man han (man + hand) = right
wuman han (women + hand) = left
tai han (tie + hand) = mean, meanness

and reduplication:

krai = cry
kraikrai = cry continuously.

The word order becomes relatively fixed and temporal distinctions are often made. Such distinctions can be illustrated by referring to Fanakalo, formerly called 'Mine Kaffir':

hamba = walk, go
mina hamba = I walk, go
yena hamba = he/she/it walks, goes
tina hambile = we walked, went (ile = past)
wena yazi hamba = you (sg) shall walk, go
nina zo hamba = you (pl) shall walk, go
yenazonke funa hamba = they want to walk, go.

When a pidgin reaches this stage of elaboration, it is capable of being used as a mother tongue. Some pidgins become mother tongues from necessity; others from usefulness. In the past, many of the pidgin speakers on the multilingual plantations in Africa, Australia, and the New World had no option but to use their pidgin as a home language; more recently, urban settlers in both Africa and Papua New Guinea have begun to use the local pidgin as one of the languages of the home, with the result that their children often use the language as one of their mother tongues.

The third phase occurs when the pidgin or creole coexists for a considerable time with a language which is used in government and education. Usually, as in the case of Haitian Créole or Nigerian Pidgin, this is the lexical donor language. In this case, the pidgin or creole is influenced at all levels by the socially dominant language. One can illustrate such influences by means of Nigerian Pidgin, where different periods of borrowing can be seen:

Early	Late Twentieth Century	English
maʃ		smash
	smail	smile
sukuru		screw
	skram	scram
tori		story
	stia	stair
man pikin	boi	boy
smɔl	yɔŋ	young
tik/stik	tri	tree
dei	bi	existential BE
fɔ haus	at hom	at home
wi papa	aua fada	our father

When the dominant language is not the lexical source language, then it too influences the pidgin or creole, causing a certain amount of relexification. Examples of this can be provided by the three creoles in Surinam. Djuka and Sranan were originally English-based, and Saramaccan seems to have been Portuguese-based. All three creoles show some influence from the country's official language, Dutch. Speakers make use of a voiced palatal fricative in the pronunciation of 'gulle' (guilder). The vocabulary is changing:

Djuka	Sranan	Saramaccan	English	Dutch	Portuguese
ala	ala	ala/tuu	all	alle	todo
beligi	bergi	kukuna	hill	berg	colina
bɔmiki	brɔmki	fɔlɔ	flower	blommetje	flor
dɔti	mɔrsu	dɔti	dirt(y)	mors(ig)	sujo
kaabu	krabu	kaabu	scratch	krab(ben)	arranhao
sikiifi	skifi	sikifi	write	schrijven	escrever

and some overt marking of plurality occurs in nouns.

The Continuum phase is found in all communities where an elaborated pidgin or a creole coexists with its superstrate, especially when this superstrate has national and international status. In such circumstances, an unbroken continuum of forms links the pidgin or creole (known as the 'basilect') to the standard, official language (the 'acrolect') through a series of intermediate forms (the 'mesolect'). In Nigeria, for example, the following is found:

A bin kam, kariam go.
A kɔm, kariam go.
A kɔm, kariam awe.
A kem an kari it awe.
I came and carried it away.

It is possible that a pidgin or creole in an advanced stage of decreolization would become virtually indistinguishable from the lexical source language. Many scholars, for example, believe that American Black English was originally a creole which has been decreolized towards Standard American English (see *Ebonics and African American Vernacular English*).

7. The Early Twenty-first Century Position of Pidgins and Creoles

Pidgins and creoles continue to be spoken by millions of people throughout the world, and so it is only possible to offer broad generalizations. Throughout society, the media, and particularly television, are affecting all nonstandard varieties, causing many to become recessive. Numerous pidgins and creoles, like dialects, are growing closer to the metropolitan norm in pronunciation, lexis, and syntax. This process can be detected in Barbados, Cameroon, India, Nigeria, Papua New Guinea, Sierra Leone, and Queensland, and may be regarded as a speeded-up form of phases three and four.

In an ideal world, where all people had equal access to education and a comfortable standard of living, it could be predicted that pidgins and creoles would gradually merge with the standard form of their lexical source language, perhaps extending that language's cultural and idiomatic repertoire. For some speakers of pidgins and creoles, this is undoubtedly happening, but not for all. There is evidence from urban communities especially in the Caribbean, England, and the United States, that for some speakers the expected decreolization has stopped, and a certain amount of recreolization has occurred. The recreolization is found mostly in the speech of young people who are disaffected or feel neglected by society. In some families in London, for example, it is possible to find grandparents, of Caribbean origin, whose English has fewer creole features than that of their teenage grandsons. Some of these young black people use a variety, referred to by many names including 'Patwa' (<Patois), 'Soul Talk,' and 'Rasta Talk,' as a badge of their cultural identity and values. The variety has much in common with the Creole English of Jamaica, but is not identical with it. Nor is it a direct development of it. Such recreolization may fade or grow stronger depending on social conditions.

It is always difficult to predict future linguistic developments, but perhaps four generalizations can be made. First, pidginization will continue to occur, as it has done throughout recorded history. It will be found in ports, holiday resorts, and youth hostels, where people who do not speak each other's language come into contact. It will also be a feature of contact between local people and a non-local army. Such pidginization may result in a makeshift pidgin if the contact is prolonged. Second, the social upheavals which accompanied slavery and blackbirding, and which were a perfect breeding ground for pidginization and creolization, are unlikely to recur. ('Blackbirding' is the name given to a system of indentured labor practiced mainly in the nineteenth century. Laborers from many Polynesian islands were taken to plantations, mainly in Queensland. They were on the multilingual plantations for two or three years before being paid and, theoretically, returned to their home island.) It is thus improbable that such widespread development and spread of pidgins and creoles as occurred between the sixteenth and nineteenth centuries will happen again. Third, most speakers of creoles and elaborated pidgins will also control the standard language and will have an extended linguistic repertoire. And fourth, as scholars learn more and more about, and from, pidgins and creoles, these languages will be seen not as linguistic sports, but as keys to the understanding of how languages can develop, evolve, and die. They have already shed light on how Latin was transformed into a family of Romance languages, and how contacts in England caused highly inflected Germanic dialects to develop the creole features that characterize modern English.

See also: Pidgins and Creoles: Models; Pidgins and Creoles: Morphology; Jargons; Contact Languages.

Bibliography

Arends J Muysken P, Smith N (eds.) 1995 *Pidgins and Creoles: An Introduction*. Benjamins, Amsterdam

French A 1953 Pidgin English in New Guinea. *Australian Quarterly* **23**(4): 57–60

Holm J 1988–89 *Pidgins and Creoles*, 2 vols. Cambridge University Press, Cambridge, UK

Leland C G 1876 *Pidgin English Sing-Song*. Trubner, London

Romaine S 1988 *Pidgin and Creole Languages*. Longman, London

Sebba M 1997 *Contact Languages: Pidgins and Creoles*. Macmillan, London

Todd L 1984 *Modern Englishes: Pidgins and Creoles*. Blackwell, Oxford, UK

Todd L 1990 *Pidgins and Creoles*, 2nd edn. Routledge, London

Pidgins and Creoles: Models

J. Aitchison

The formation of pidgins, and the way they develop into creoles has attracted a massive amount of interest over the past 20 or so years. Interest was particularly stimulated in the 1980s by the controversial claims of Derek Bickerton (see *Bickerton, Derek*) of the University of Hawaii that creoles reveal the workings of an inbuilt linguistic 'bioprogram,' with which all humans are genetically endowed (Bickerton 1981, 1984). Others argue that pidgins and creoles embody normal processes of change, speeded up by the circumstances of their formation (Aitchison 2001, Arends 1993, Arends and Bruyn 1995). This view presumes that pidgins and creoles primarily represent a sociolinguistic 'mixed language' phenomenon, in which features of a substrate language are combined with those of a superstrate language, with the superstrate's lexicon playing a major role. Below, the 'bioprogram' model will be compared with the newer 'mixed language' model—though both models assume that pidgins and creoles reflect crucial features of the human language 'instinct.'

1. Definitions

A pidgin is a subsidiary language system used for communication by people with no common language. Within this broad definition, most people agree that pidgins have independent rules of their own which cannot be invented by nonspeakers. But a minority assumes that pidgins are a hotchpotch with no real rules, in line with popular ideas that a pidgin is a general name for any type of broken language. Some of the confusion arises because a pidgin is likely to pass through various stages in the course of development: a jargon, prepidgin or minimal pidgin, is likely to become a stable pidgin, which in turn may become an extended pidgin—even though such stages have blurred edges, and merge into one another.

A creole is a pidgin which has become someone's first language, according to its most widely accepted definition, though a minority still use the term to refer to mixed 'full' languages, such as the Spanish-English mix sometimes spoken on the Mexican-USA border. The nature of a creole varies widely depending on the maturity of the pidgin from which it has developed, and some researchers have attempted (controversially) to distinguish 'true creoles' from others (e.g., Bickerton 1981).

Because of the fluid and constantly changing nature of pidgins and creoles, many researchers prefer to talk about processes rather than systems. That is, discussions are carried on under the headings of pidginization (how a pidgin develops), creolization (how a creole develops), and decreolization (how a creole gets reabsorbed into its (superstrate) base), and the tricky question of structural characteristics is therefore avoided.

2 Points at Issue

Before the question of models can be settled, other major issues need to be explored. Two repeatedly surface in discussions of pidgins and creoles: the 'universals question' and the 'pidgin vs. creole question.'

2.1 The Universals Question

Most pidgins are overtly adapted from a so-called 'base' or 'superstrate' language, which is different from the language(s) of its speakers, the 'substrate' language(s). For example, Tok Pisin, spoken in Papua New Guinea, is overtly based on English, as in *Yu mas klinim tit bilong yu* 'You must clean your teeth' (from a toothpaste advertisement), although its speakers are mostly native speakers of a local language. A few pidgins and creoles are formed from the mutual adaptation of two equal languages, as possibly in Chinook Jargon, a pidgin of the Pacific Northwest of the USA and Canada, which arose among Indians out of mutual trading needs, as did Russenorsk in North Norway, spoken between Norwegian and Russian fishermen and traders. But whatever their linguistic origin, a wide variety of pidgins and creoles show striking similarities. There is consequently a lively controversy as to how much of any pidgin or creole is derived from the source language(s), and how much is due to independent universal principles.

2.2 Pidgin vs. Creole Question

A crucial question is whether pidgins are fundamentally different in nature from creoles. By definition, pidgins are nobody's first language, while creoles must be someone's first language. Consequently, pidginization is often likened to the reduction and impoverishment which characterizes foreign language learning, and creolization is compared with the apparent naturalness and creativeness of first language acquisition.

The theoretical divide between pidgins and creoles is supported by the 'critical period hypothesis,' the claim that a person's innate language faculty functions only during a limited timespan, and that major language changes are impossible after adolescence. This is being increasingly challenged. There seems to be evidence for a 'sensitive period,' a time when it is particularly advantageous to be exposed to language, especially the sounds. But there is no reason for language learning and language change to come to a shuddering halt (Aitchison 1999). On the contrary, teenagers are particularly prone to altering the language, at least temporarily, and many language changes are now thought to be initiated by adults. This therefore calls into question the assumption that second language speakers are incapable of elaborating a pidgin, and that creoles are fundamentally different in nature from pidgins.

3 Pidginization: Early Stages

Until relatively recently, little attention was paid to superficially 'broken' language, namely, foreigner talk (speech addressed to non-native speakers; see *Foreigner Talk*), learners' interlanguage (the intermediate forms created by learners en route to a full grasp of a language; see *Interlanguage*), and various jargons (for example, the nautical jargon supposedly once used widely around the world by sailors). But these are likely to form the basis of a pidgin. They turn out to be surprisingly complex phenomena.

The lexicon is of prime importance in incipient pidgins. Morphology is erratic, and often absent. Word order is inconsistent. A possible example of a pre-pidgin is found in the various types of English spoken in India to and by servants at the time when India was part of the British empire, known by names such as 'Butler English,' and 'Kitchen English,' linguistically first reported by the German linguist Hugo Schuchardt (see *Schuchardt, Hugo*), who quoted (for example) a brief Butler English account of a servant who systematically stole quantities of his master's milk:

> Butler's yevery day taking one ollock for own-self, and giving servants all half half ollock; when I am telling that shame for him, he is telling, Master's strictly order all servants for the little milk give it—what can I say, mam, I poor ayah woman.
>
> (Schuchardt 1980: 47)

Studies of the Butler English of a number of Indian domestics, some old, some young, have shown their speech to be fairly inconsistent, but to contain features of pidginization which may be universal (Hosali 2000, Hosali and Aitchison 1985). 'Reduction' was particularly prominent, with numerous 'little words' (auxiliaries, articles, prepositions) and inflectional endings missing, as in: *I poor boy* 'I'm a poor boy,' *I no go Jesus* 'I won't go to heaven.' 'Simplification' (regularization) was also evident, as in a tendency to use *is* for all forms of the verb *be*: *There is so many people no madam?* 'There are so many people aren't there, madam?' There were also examples of 'overgeneralization,' especially the overuse of 'markers,' features which were felt by speakers to characterize this variety of English, such as *-ing* as an all-purpose verb ending, as in *After I traveling India* 'Afterwards I traveled around India,' as well as a preference for starting a sentence with *is*: *Is only one father and one brother* 'I have only one father and one brother.' There were also some signs of potential 'reanalysis,' the reinterpretation of an existing linguistic form or structure in a new way, such as the occasional use of *been* as a past tense marker: *I* been working lots of memsahib 'I worked for lots of European ladies'; and *all* as a plural pronoun or pluralizer: *All is take a nail* 'They (all) took a nail.' None of these processes was applied reliably, and lack of consistency is a recurring finding in studies of foreigner talk and learners' attempts. But they provide the basis on which a pidgin could have been formed.

The universal processes of reduction, simplification, overgeneralization, and reanalysis are directed down particular channels by the nature of the languages involved. For example, in the Butler English studies mentioned above, utterance initial *is* was possibly in origin a conflation of English *he's, I's, it's*, and *if*, perhaps due to the difficulty which speakers of Dravidian languages have in distinguishing these forms. English *been* is a relatively salient form, and *bin/ben* marking pastness or anteriority has emerged independently in several English-based pidgins, for example, *ben* in Jamaican Creole, *bin* in Guyanese Creole and also in Tok Pisin (e.g., Tok Pisin *mi bin go* 'I went'). Similarly, *ol* from *all* is a fairly natural development, and is found both as a pronoun meaning 'they' and a plural prefix in Tok Pisin (e.g., Tok Pisin *ol man* 'the men'). Pastness and plural are two of several common linguistic categories, which tend to emerge early in any language system. Their widespread use may be due to an inbuilt language program, but is more likely to stem from a widespread need in human life everywhere to distinguish between past (or anterior) and non-past (Bybee et al. 1994), and between one and more than one.

Prepidgin phases typically involve 'vertical' influence, the foreigner talk of masters to servants and back (Mühlhäusler 1997). A stable pidgin develops when there is regular 'horizontal' use of the jargon among equals, and when in addition; these users have become removed from the original language model. However, a vertical phase is not essential, since pidgins can arise out of mutual accommodation to one another's speech, as in the case of Chinook Jargon and Russenorsk.

The early pidginization phase indicates that nothing arises out of nothing. The processes of change outlined above—reduction, simplification, overgeneralization, and reanalysis—are ordinary ones, and their effect can be seen in stable pidgins. In Russenorsk, for example, many nouns end in *-a*, as in *silka* 'herring,' *fiska* 'fish,' and many verbs in *-om*, as in *drikkom* 'drink,' *kopom* 'buy,' *slipom* 'sleep.' When two languages are involved, common elements are likely to be retained, and idiosyncratic ones dropped: Russenorsk lost sounds which occur in only one of its languages, so Norwegian *hav* 'sea' became Russenorsk *gav*, and Russian *orech* 'nut' (ending in [x] which is not found in Norwegian) became Russenorsk *oreka*. Russenorsk also retained the subject-word-object word order common to Russian and Norwegian, as in: *moja kopom fiska* 'I buy fish,' *tvoya vegom silka* 'You weigh herring.' Perhaps the main difference between early pidginization changes and 'normal' change is that the processes of change differ in the proportions in which they occur. In early pidgins, reduction, simplification and overgeneralization are likely to be widespread, while reanalysis may be less in evidence.

4. Pidginization: Later Stages

Pidginization tends to be regarded as a special case of foreign language learning. For this reason, many consider pidgins to be of limited interest, and relatively little attention has been paid to their stabilization and extension, due to the unfounded assumption that all major changes must have occurred at the creole stage.

Yet pidgins may develop some quite sophisticated linguistic features. Tok Pisin, spoken in Papua New Guinea, is a well-documented example of a stabilized and extended pidgin. Over the course of around a century, it has become structurally elaborated, with a firm distinction between intransitive and transitive verbs, marked by an ending *-im* (e.g., *masket i pairap* 'the gun went off' versus *man i pairapim masket* 'the man fired the gun'). It also has incipient auxiliary verbs (e.g., *yu mas go* 'you must go,' *yu save smok?* 'Are you accustomed to smoke, do you smoke?'), and markers are available for pastness, futurity and plurality, though these are not obligatory (e.g., *mi bin go* 'I went,' *bai mi go* 'I shall go,' *ol meri* 'the women'). There are even simple relative clause structures (e.g., *Dispela man i slip, em i papa bilong mi* 'The man who is asleep is my father,' *Dok yu paitim asde i gat sik* 'The dog you hit yesterday is ill'), and also simple complement structures (e.g., *Mi kam long helpim pren bilong mi* 'I came to help my friend').

But Tok Pisin is not such an exceptional case as is sometimes claimed. There is increasing evidence that numerous other pidgins were more stable and extended than previously thought. Indeed, it has been claimed that 'many New World creoles were predominantly nonnative languages throughout the entire slave-trade period' (Goodman 1985: 119). In short, pidgins may become stable, relatively homogeneous and fairly elaborate, at a time when they are spoken only by people using them as a second language, without the aid of native speakers.

The elaborated constructions found in extended pidgins arise largely out of the processes, which have already been mentioned. Reanalysis may be particularly important, a process in which an existing form or sequence is reinterpreted. Re-analyses typically involve the demotion or 'grammaticalization' of a full, content word to one of subsidiary status. The demotion of English *belong* to the status of a preposition *bilong* 'of,' as in *mama bilong mi* 'my mother' happened early in the history of Tok Pisin. Another long established re-analysis involved Tok Pisin *save* 'know' which developed an additional meaning, 'be accustomed to,' and came to be regarded as an incipient auxiliary verb. The reinterpretation probably occurred in ambiguous contexts, such as *mi save kukim kaukau*, in which 'I know how to cook sweet potatoes' came to be 'I am skilled at cooking sweet potatoes' and finally 'I am accustomed to cook sweet potatoes.'

The role of the substrate language is also important. Prominent features in the substrate may be directly translated by a near equivalent in the superstrate. For example, the so-called Tok Pisin 'predicate marker,' a meaningless *i* inserted before the verb, as in *man i am* 'the man came' is possibly due to the identification of English *he* with a 'subject-referencing pronoun' which is obligatory in the Oceanic substrate languages (Keesing 1988).

Increasingly, convergence or 'developmental conspiracies' (Mühlhäusler 1997) are recognized to be an important factor. This is when an element in the superstrate language happens to coincide with one in the substrate (as in the example above), especially when these elements appear to fulfill a communicational need. To take another example, the suffix *him* or *um* was possibly sporadically and unsystematically attached to verbs by Europeans in their 'foreigner talk,' as in some examples of nineteenth century Australian 'jargon' quoted by Hugo Schuchardt (1980: 19): *me like him grog* 'I like wine,' *me no look him* 'I didn't see him,' *him fight him my finger* 'it (pin) pricked my finger.' This *him*, found also in early samples of Melanesian pidgin, was interpreted by speakers of Oceanic languages as equivalent to their own transitive suffix, and *-im* became firmly established in Tok Pisin as a transitive suffix. Similar convergence allowed Tok Pisin to develop primitive relative clauses (examples above), even though embedding is not usually found in pidgins: arguably, surface similarities between English relative clauses and Oceanic ones caused their creation, even though at a deeper level the languages are profoundly dissimilar (Keesing 1988). In short, when there is apparent agreement between structural features of substrate languages and an intermittently occurring feature in the superstrate, this is likely to be assigned a firm function, especially if it seems to be needed in human interaction.

Sometimes, constructions emerge which are in the substrate languages but not in the superstrate. For example, Tok Pisin has a distinction between *we* inclusive (*yumi*, as in *yumi mas painim pik* 'You who are here and I must look for the pig') and *we* exclusive (*mipela*, as in *mipela mas painim pik* 'I and others not here must look for the pig'). This distinction is widely found in the native languages of the region, but is foreign to English. Examples such as these have suggested to some people that pidgins are relexified substrate languages, that is, that they consist of the grammar of a substrate language translated into the lexical items of the base. However, this extreme view does not take into consideration the surprising similarities, which exist between different pidgins—even though the influence of the substrate varies from pidgin to pidgin, and may be more extensive in some cases than in others.

There are possibly two reasons why existing pidgins are so similar. First, a restricted system must by its nature depend on word order to express major syntactic relations (such as those between subject, object, and verb). Consequently, there are only a limited number of options available, and a limited number of permutations of these. The chance that several pidgins will choose the same route is not only highly likely, it is probably inevitable. Each choice will entail further consequences, which will heighten the similarities. For example, topicalization, the fronting of an important topic, might make the consistent marking of transitive verbs more probable, in order to make subjects and objects easier to identify. A preference for topicalization is also likely to affect question words, which will probably be brought to the front, and so on. A second reason why pidgins are similar is that human life the world over is likely to find certain concepts useful in language, such as the distinction between a repeated action and a single one. Such distinctions will tend to emerge independently in different pidgins, especially if they are already marked in the substrate or superstrate.

In conclusion, pidgins can, and often do, become stable and elaborated. Consequently, the move from a pidgin to a creole may be less abrupt and less traumatic than is sometimes suggested. Non-native speakers supplement an early pidgin, and provide a firm base on which creole speakers continue to build.

5. Creolization

A common assumption is that a creole represents a dramatic event, the sudden creation of a language from a rudimentary jargon. Yet such a happening may be a rare phenomenon. (It has been found among deaf signers in Nicaragua (Kegl 1997)). An infant may acquire the creole as a first language from parents who have no common language, but in most cases this infant learns the language of one or both his/her parents alongside, or soon after the creole. Only occasionally will the unfortunate child be a linguistic orphan faced with a minimal system which must immediately be emended—and even then, the emendation cannot take place until s/he is part of a stable peer group.

According to Bickerton in his widely discussed book *Roots of Language* (1981), a first generation creole speaker is inevitably faced with a primitive hotchpotch. At this point, the infant brings a linguistic 'bioprogram' into play, in which certain distinctions are bound to surface, such as a primitive tense-mood-aspect system involving anteriority versus nonanteriority (*she was ill/she is ill*), punctual versus nonpunctual (*he fought/he was fighting*), irrealis versus realis (*they will go/they are going*) (Bickerton 1981, 1984). Bickerton argues that these distinctions also emerge early in normal child language acquisition, which provides further evidence for the existence of a 'bioprogram.' However, the Bickertonian scenario does not seem to be supported by the evidence, though he deserves considerable credit for the large amount of valuable research, which has been stimulated by his ideas.

There are three major problems with Bickerton's bioprogram approach, over and above the fact that his narrow definition of a creole excludes a wide range of material. First, many features identified as part of the bioprogram were possibly already in existence in any preceding pidgin, as discussed above. Second, the parallels between child language and creoles are largely unsupported (Aitchison 1983). The bioprogram notion supposes that the same distinctions automatically surface in both. However, findings which superficially supported some of Bickerton's claims turned out to be a mirage: the clear-cut distinctions reported by some early workers on child language may have been an artifact of poor experimental methods, and in reality the situation is far from straightforward.

A third problem with the bioprogram hypothesis is that there is a lack of uniformity among creoles, in that several fail to fit in with the predicted bioprogram. Bickerton has suggested that such exceptions may be due to their relative nearness to the superstrate language, unlike radical creoles, which are furthest from the superstrate, and nearest to the bioprogram. But degree of radicalness turns out to be impossible to assess.

In short, Bickerton's bioprogram is more a measure of statistical probability than absolute necessity. The bioprogram hypothesis is not sustainable, but it nevertheless encapsulates probable similarities between creoles.

Some of the reasons for the similarities have already mean mentioned under pidginization. One is the limited potentiality of a pidgin. There are relatively few routes along which it can develop, so similar phenomena are bound to emerge. Another is the recurring need of humans to express certain distinctions, such as one versus more than one. A third, less obvious factor is typological consistency. Languages seem to have a need for internal consistency—though the governing factors underlying it are controversial. For example, any VO system (one in which objects follow verbs as in *chase the pig*) is likely in the long run to develop prepositions, and auxiliaries which precede verbs. Universal implicational principles of this type are probably of more importance than any simple contrast (e.g., punctuality versus nonpunctuality) which might emerge. Although the notion that creole speakers suddenly invent a new language seems not to be borne out in most cases, there are differences between pidgin speakers and creole speakers, which have profound repercussions on the language, even though the effects may not be as immediate as is sometimes supposed.

First, creole speakers talk much faster than pidgin speakers do. Consequently, frequently occurring items get reduced phonologically. Tok Pisin creole speakers reduce *save* 'be accustomed to' to *sa, long* 'to' to *lo, bilong* 'of' to *blo*, and the 'predicate marker' *i* is not always audible, particularly after high vowels. This speed and phonological reduction can have a significant effect on the grammar. For example, in some contexts the predicate marker *i* has disappeared, in some others it is regarded as part of a following lexical item.

Second, the lexical resources of the language are increased, both by new word formations, and by borrowing. Concepts, which in the pidgin had to be expressed by periphrases, are lexicalized. In Tok Pisin, a phrase such as *man bilong pait* 'an aggressive man, a man given to fighting' becomes *paitman*, and *bun bilong baksait* 'backbone' becomes *bakbun*. The vocabulary has been supplemented by numerous borrowings from English, such as *football, sandwiches*.

Third, there is a tendency for optional elements to be used redundantly, and then to become categorical, or near categorical. In pidgin Tok Pisin *bin* is an optional past tense marker, used primarily when pastness is not clear from the context. In the first generation of creole speakers it is used frequently and seemingly unnecessarily (e.g., *mi bin sik, mi no bin go lo skul* 'I was ill, I didn't go to school'). However, total regularization is unlikely to happen within a generation.

Fourth, there is elimination of unnecessary variety. Pidgins tend to have a number of incipient methods of expressing common functions, which may overlap e.g., pidgin Tok Pisin has a preverbal habituality marker *save* (*pikinini i save krai* 'The child habitually cries'), alongside a postverbal durativity marker (*pikinini i krai i go* 'The child keeps on crying'). Among some creole speakers, the postverbal markers are rarely used, and the distinction between habituality and durativity is disappearing, with preverbal *sa* (from *save*) used for both.

Fifth, simple sentences tend to be conflated and amalgamated, resulting in the continuing development of complex sentence structures. In pidgin Tok Pisin, the word *olsem* 'thus' is used to introduce direct speech (e.g., *Meri i tok olsem: 'Yumi mas kisim pis'* 'The woman said: "We must get the fish"'). In the creole, *olsem* is clearly equivalent to the English complementizer *that: Yu no save olsem em i sik?* 'Don't you know that he is ill?'

Gradually, the resources of the language become greater, though a creole does not overnight become a perfectly neat system: the tidying up might last over several generations, and can even be partially counteracted by a profusion of new formations, and the effects of phonological reduction. But overall, creolization makes a language-system richer, more efficient, and more streamlined. After several generations, it will possibly be indistinguishable from any other 'full' language.

6. Decreolization

When a creole is spoken in the same geographical area as its original base, there is a tendency for it to be replaced by this more prestigious superstrate, a phenomenon known as 'decreolization.' This is a messy process, involving a range of speakers whose dialect could be a fairly extreme creole, known as the 'basilect,' a middle variety, the 'mesolect,' or the 'acrolects,' a variety of the creole fairly like its (superstratal) base. There is also some overlap between creolization and decreolization, so that it is sometimes unclear which process is under way. For example, superstrate lexical items tend to replace the creole forms in decreolization, yet this also happens in creolization, where intensive borrowing increases the vocabulary stock. Pidgin Tok Pisin has a phrase *bilong wanem* 'because,' which in the creole is often replaced by *bikos*, though this might be interpreted by some as decreolization. However, genuine decreolization can be identified when creole speakers forget the function of creole forms, as when one creole Tok Pisin speaker appeared to have forgotten the meaning of *sa* 'be accustomed to,' because in addition to its normal use to mark habitual actions, she also used it for once-only events in the past (e.g., *Ol sa karim mi lo haus sik* 'They carried me to the hospital'). Increasingly, distinctions found in the creole, but not the base, disappear, and more and more forms found in the superstrate get imported into the creole. For example, decreolized speakers of Tok Pisin use far more examples of English plural *-s* than do genuine creole speakers, for whom it is limited to a small subset of lexical items.

From the point of view of change, the situation is no different from any other type of language contact situation in which extensive borrowing occurs.

7. Conclusion

Structurally, pidgins cannot be neatly separated from creoles, and pidginization, creolization, and decreolization all overlap. They utilize processes found in ordinary language change, especially reduction, simplification, overgeneralization, and reanalysis. They differ mainly in the proportions in which the processes are applied, with more reduction in pidginization, and more reanalysis in creolization.

As in ordinary change, language proceeds by sprouting out multiple options—though these are all possibilities inherent in the system or the surrounding languages. Nothing develops out of nothing. These options are in competition. Eventually one is likely to win out, and the others gradually fade away.

Convergence is often the key to understanding change, both in pidgins and creoles, and in 'full' languages. When substrate and superstrate superficially agree, a firm construction is likely to emerge, especially if this ties in with human communicational needs. In addition, languages need to be internally consistent, in that certain constructions tend to be reinforced within a particular language type, whereas inconsistent ones gradually fade away.

In short, phenomena due to language contact and inbuilt principles are intertwined in an inextricable mix, as in all language change. But pidgins and creoles provide an especially valuable workshop for the study of change because of the relatively increased speed and greater number of alterations, or in the words of the nineteenth century scholar Addison van Name (see *Van Name, Addison*), they exhibit 'greater violence of the forces' (van Name 1869–70: 123).

See also: Pidgins and Creoles: Morphology; Pidgins and Creoles: An Overview; Pidgins, Creoles and Minority Dialects in Education; Contact Languages.

Bibliography

Aitchison J 1983 On roots of language. *Language and Communication* 3: 83–97
Aitchison J 1996 *The Seeds of Speech: Language Origin and Evolution*. Cambridge University Press, Cambridge, UK
Aitchison J 1999 *The Articulate Mammal: An Introduction to Psycholinguistics*, 4th edn. Routledge, London
Aitchison J 2001 *Language Change: Progress or Decay?* Cambridge University Press, Cambridge, UK
Arends J 1993 Towards a gradualist model of creolization. In Byrne F, Holm J (eds.) *Atlantic Meets Pacific*. Benjamins, Amsterdam
Arends J, Bruyn A 1995 Gradualist and developmental hypotheses. In Arends J, Muysken P, Smith N (eds.) *Pidgins and Creoles: An Introduction*. Benjamins, Amsterdam
Arends J, Muysken P, Smith N (eds.) 1995 *Pidgins and Creoles: An Introduction*. Benjamins, Amsterdam
Bickerton D 1981 *Roots of Language*. Karoma, Ann Arbor, MI
Bickerton D 1984 The language bioprogram hypothesis. *The Behavioral and Brain Sciences* 7: 173–221

Bybee J, Perkins R, Pagliuca W 1994 *The Evolution of Grammar: Tense, Aspect, and Modality in the Languages of the World*. University of Chicago Press, Chicago, IL.

DeGraff M (ed.) 1999 *Language Creation and Language Change: Creolization, Diachrony and Development*. MIT Press, Cambridge, MA

Goodman M 1985 Review of Bickerton (1981). *International Journal of American Linguistics* **51**: 109–37

Holm J 2000 *An Introduction to Pidgins and Creoles*. Cambridge University Press, Cambridge, UK

Hosali P 2000 *Butler English: Form and Function*. DR Publishing, Delhi, India

Hosali P, Aitchison J 1985 Butler English: A minimal pidgin? *Journal of Pidgin and Creole Languages* **1**: 51–79

Keesing R M 1988 *Melanesian Pidgin and the Oceanic Substrate*. Stanford University Press, Stanford, CA

Kegl J, Senghas A, Coppola M 1999 Creation through contact: Sign language emergence and sign language change in Nicaragua. In De Graff M (ed.) *Language Creation and Language Change: Creolization, Diachrony and Development*. MIT Press, Cambridge, MA

Mühlhäusler P 1997 *Pidgin and Creole Linguistics*. University of Westminster Press, London

Schuchardt H 1891/1980 *Pidgin and Creole Languages*, edited and translated by Gilbert G G. Cambridge University Press, Cambridge, UK

van Name A 1869–70 Contributions to creole grammar. *Transactions of the American Philological Association* **1**: 123–67

Pidgins and Creoles: Morphology

F. C. V. Jones

Pidgins and creoles are essentially analytic languages in which the structure of words is morphologically simple. This is because inflectional and derivational affixes from the parent languages are the first casualties of the pidginization process and the last to redevelop. Syntactic features like tense, aspect, and plurality, for example, which are expressed by affixes in many languages, are signaled by separate morphemes in these languages. The morphological formatives which do develop are usually suffixal, or, in a few cases, prefixal additions to the root, and do not involve suppletion (irregular morphological forms like *go-went*) or vowel mutation of the *foot > feet* type.

The growth of morphology in pidgins and creoles is consistent with the phases of development of these languages. These phases are: the jargon or prepidgin, the stabilization, the expanded or extended pidgin, the creolization, and the postpidgin or postcreole.

Most of the information on the growth of morphology during the earlier phases especially comes from accounts of Pacific pidgins, which have been particularly well-studied from their earliest phases of development.

1. The Jargon Phase

During this phase (see *Jargons*), when a pidgin is being born, morphological formatives in words from the parent languages are generally dropped. The few that remain are forms in which the root and its affix have been fossilized or frozen, with morpheme boundaries disappearing, making the word monomorphemic. They are usually adoptions of frequently heard (plural or past tense) forms from the source languages. In some French-related pidgins (and creoles), for example, the final sound of the plural definite article (pronounced /lez/ before a noun beginning with a vowel, but /le/ elsewhere) is attached to the pidgin noun to form a single morpheme that can be either singular or plural in denotation; for example, *zie* 'eye' from the French plural *les yeux* /lezyø/ instead of the singular *oeil*. English-related pidgins (and creoles) have items like *sus* < 'shoes,' meaning 'one or more shoes.' The main reasons for the dropping of affixes is that morphological formatives are a marked or complex category, and their presence would militate against the learning of the emergent, fledgling languages.

In the absence of morphology, there is very little established grammar (time references, for example, are expressed by the use of time adverbials), and there is the widespread use of word-class multifunctionality, with one form being used, for example, as a noun, a verb, an adjective, and an adverb.

2. The Stabilization Phase

It is during this phase that some morphology can begin to emerge, as the pidgin is now developmentally ready for it. However, since the pidgin is still at an early stage of development, very little morphology does occur, while word-order conventions tend to become firmly established. Unmarked or less marked (i.e., more commonly occurring or simpler) features begin to emerge before marked or more marked (rarer or more complex) features, and the universal principle that derivational morphology precedes inflectional morphology also applies. Developments are internally motivated, showing reanalysis in the grammatical development of the pidgin as it progresses toward the achievement of autonomy as a system.

Morphology can develop to mark word (sub)classes, after considerable variation over time and space, and in sentence position. This seems to be a distinguishing feature of many Pacific pidgins. For example, *-pela* (derived from English 'fellow') is suffixed to monosyllabic adjectives when they are used attributively. Also, transitive verbs are marked by the suffixing of *-(a/i/u)m* or *-it*. In pidgins in general, gender and diminutive distinctions in nouns, though not in pronouns, may begin to develop. A word meaning 'man,' 'woman,' or 'child' is preposed (or in a few cases postponed) to the noun. Also universal during this phase is the use of the word *man* (which in this case is semantically bleached or may simply be regarded as meaning 'human') or its reflex as an agentive suffix to a verb or adjective; for example, (English-related) Tok Pisin: *kamman* (come man) 'new arrival.'

Multifunctionality is even more widespread during this phase, and indeed persists throughout the lifespan of a pidgin/creole. It also characterizes word-formation devices like compounding and reduplication, which begin to develop (see Sect. 3). Another universal feature in pidgins is the fact that equivalents of wh- question words are bimorphemic compounds expressing units of meaning, rather than monomorphemic words, as is usual in their lexifier languages. Examples are: Kenya Pidgin Swahili, *titu gani?* (thing which?) 'what?'; Cameroon Pidgin English, *wusai?* (which side?) 'where?'

3. The Expanded Pidgin and Creolization Phases

Morphology continues to develop as the autonomy of the language becomes even more firmly established. However, even when it has creolized, the language remains essentially analytic. Morphological (like other linguistic) developments continue to be largely internally motivated, following a clear developmental and markedness hieararchy.

Two universally distinguishing word-formation features which can be particularly clearly seen in English-related pidgins and creoles—compounding and reduplication—assume marked sigificance. Word-level compounds (for example, Tok Pisin *skinwara* [skin water] 'sweat') develop from phrase-level compounds (*wara bilong skin*), which may have originated from lengthier circumlocutions. Such compounds are typically transparent, productive, endocentric types that may have started their existence as fixed collocations. Many are, however, metaphorical innovations that are used deliberately to increase the lexicon, in response to the growing communicative needs of the growing language. An example is Guinea Bissau (Portuguese related) Creole *piis-kabalu* 'hippopotamus,' from Portuguese *peixe* 'fish' and *cavalo* 'horse.' More abstract patterns, in exocentric compounds, including calques (word-for-word or morpheme-by-morpheme loan translations from substrate languages—the first languages of the pidgin speakers) may also develop. For example, many English-related Atlantic Creoles have *bigeye/bigyai* < 'big eye,' calqued from a West African substratum language, Igbo: *anya uku* (literally 'big eyes') 'covetous (ness).' Some compounds are tautologies designed to reduce the number of homophones in the language, comprising words from the same or from different languages; for example, English-related Trinidadian Creole *go:tkidi* 'kid' (which may have been formed to avoid homophony with *kid* 'child').

Reduplication—the partial or complete doubling (and, in a few cases, triplication) of a word to give a new lexical item—is also mainly an internal development, but is usually accelerated by substrate influence, including straight borrowings. In many pidgins and creoles, in the absence of, or in conjunction with, grammatical words, clitics, and formatives, notions of plurality, accumulation or collectiveness, distribution, and iteration—among others—are frequently expressed by reduplication, which may or may not be a productive process. Examples of reduplication are Nigerian Pidgin English *benben* 'crooked' (from English *bend*); Spanish-related Papiamentu *potopoto* 'muddy' (from substratum language sources).

Some derivational morphology may be borrowed from local vernaculars. Very little inflectional morphology is found in Atlantic pidgins and creoles that are not in their postpidgin or postcreole phase. One example is the use of the suffix *-du* by the Portuguese-related creoles of West Africa (reflecting a conflation of superstrate—lexifier language—and substrate influence) to mark the past participle or to give a verb a passive meaning. In expanded pidgins of the Pacific, inflections have developed from free forms; for example, sentential adverb *baimbai* ('by and by') moving from sentence initial to preverbal or prefix-on-verb position is replaced by *bai*, which functions as the future tense marker *bai*. Morphological causatives have also been achieved, for example, in Tok Pisin, by the suffixation of *im*, first to stative intransitive verbs, next to adjectives, then to non-stative (dynamic) verbs, and finally to transitive verbs.

The application of recursiveness in the development or adoption of affixes, which was severely restricted in earlier stages of the languages (a word could not contain more than one affix) begins to take place.

These changes continue with creolization and become generalized. Restrictions continue to be relaxed. Creole languages generally evince a hotchpotch of diverse word-formation processes and devices, including many lexicalizations, semiproductive processes, and borrowings, mainly from the superstrate.

4. Postpidgin/Postcreole Phase

This phase is particularly characterized by the borrowing (and possible reinterpretation) of some inflectional and derivational affixes from the (current) superstrate (for example, the English -s plural in English-related post-pidgins/creoles). These affixes may be used to express a marked increase in the nonreferrential (i.e., stylistic) use of the language; for example, the suffix -ed in the Krio word ɛdyuketɛd 'educated' gives the word a superlative connotation. Words may even be spontaneously created, based on superstrate models, as in the case of English-related Bahamian Creole *spokadacious* 'very attractive (of women).'

The proliferation of the borrowing of these formatives helps to increase the complexity of the (post)pidgin/creole, and can even facilitate its depidginization or decreolization. However, the continued borrowing or creation of derivational affixes may eventually lead to a significant decline in multifunctionality and establish a clear morphological patterning that will contribute to promoting the overall naturalness of the language.

See also: Pidgins and Creoles: An Overview; Pidgins and Creoles: Models; Pidgins, Creoles and Minority Dialects in Education.

Bibliography

Holm J A 1988 *Pidgins and Creoles*, Vols. 1 and 2. Cambridge University Press, Cambridge, UK

Mühlhäusler P 1997 *Pidgin and Creole Linguistics*, 2nd edn. University of Westminister Press, London

Sociolinguistic Area
J. D'Souza

A sociolinguistic area is an area in which languages belonging to several different families converge as a result of their daily interaction and because they are called upon to express certain shared social and cultural experiences and adhere to sociocultural norms accepted by members of the society at large. Such an area is marked by widespread bilingualism or multilingualism and by the fact that common social, cultural, and linguistic factors have influenced the languages of the area. A sociolinguistic area, therefore, is characterized by diverse social groups and diverse language families, both of which in the course of time begin to share a grammar of language and a 'grammar of culture.'

The concept of a sociolinguistic area fulfils a critical need as it puts emphasis equally on society and on language, highlighting the significance of each in understanding the other. It provides a new and interesting approach to the study of multilingual areas and sets up new criteria for the study of convergence. The term owes its origins to Emeneau's (see *Emeneau, Murray Barnson*) idea of a linguistic area (1980). His example was of the Indian subcontinent in which languages could be shown to belong to one of four distinct language families. Yet coexistence for over 2000 years had led to a great deal of structural similarity between the languages (see *Areal Linguistics*). The term 'sociolinguistic area' introduced by Pandit (1972) is meant to indicate that convergence can take place not just structurally, but in terms of sociolinguistic phenomena too.

Sociolinguistic areas are also 'culture areas.' Not all culture areas, however, are sociolinguistic areas. A culture area may be a monolingual area while a sociolinguistic area, by definition, is a bi- or multilingual area in which the shared culture is in part responsible for linguistic convergence. A shared grammar of culture is an important feature of a sociolinguistic area as it provides social motivation for language change and affects linguistic diffusion. The grammar of culture decides the acceptable possibilities of behavior within a given culture area. Included among these are certain uses of language such as expressions of gratitude, terms of address and reference, greetings, farewells, and, in a multilingual society, even the choice of language. As all languages in a sociolinguistic area are affected by a common grammar of culture the possibilities for convergence are increased.

Several areas of the world may be seen as potential sociolinguistic areas primarily on the basis that they are multilingual. To claim that they are indeed sociolinguistic areas one would have to show that the languages of the area have been exposed to common social, cultural, and linguistic forces, have begun to converge, and share a common grammar of culture which acts in consonance with the various languages. One would, therefore, also need to differentiate between convergence phenomena, familial traits, and language universals.

South Asia is a prime example of a sociolinguistic area. Four language families coexist in the region: Austro-Asiatic, Dravidian, Indo-Aryan, and Tibeto-Burman, and bilingualism/multilingualism is widespread. Convergence is a striking characteristic of the area. Despite linguistic and cultural variation the people of the region share a grammar of culture.

Evidence comes from the study of phenomena like diglossia, echo words, explicator compound verbs, onomatopoeics, modernisation, politeness phenomena, and onomastics.

See also: Areal Linguistics; Borrowing; Emeneau, Murray Barnson.

Bibliography

D'Souza J 1987 *South Asia as a Sociolinguistic Area*. PhD dissertation, University of Illinois at Urbana-Champaign, IL

D'Souza J 1994 Characterising a 'sociolinguistic area.' *Orbis* **37**: 148–61

Emeneau M B 1980 *Language and Linguistic Area*. Stanford University Press, Stanford, CA

Pandit P B 1972 *India as a Sociolinguistic Area*. University of Poona, Poona, India

SECTION VI
Language, Power, and Inequality

Critical Language Awareness
J. L. Mey

In pragmatics, the origin of the term 'critical' goes back to an early article which the present author wrote under the title of 'Towards a critical theory of language' (Mey 1979). At about the same time, a group of researchers in England (Roger Fowler and his colleagues at the University of East Anglia; Fowler et al. 1979) developed the notion 'critical linguistics,' in which they put great emphasis on the relationship between social power and language use; they intended to show how the ruling classes of society also determine the ruling language.

In a book I wrote some years later (Mey 1985), I applied my own 'critical' thinking to the problems of social language use, in particular the language of labor disputes and their reflections in the media, and the language used in (or imposed on) second language training for (adult) immigrants. The recurrent themes of that book can be condensed in one brief rule-of-thumb: to find out what language is used for, you have to find the user, and determine what makes him or her speak. The capitalist speaks in a different fashion than does the worker, and this is not so much a matter of the various dialects they use, but of the different ways in which they 'word the world,' as I call it (Mey 1985: 166).

In the late 1980s and early 1990s, with the growing impact of pragmatics on the linguistics and language scene, several further movements arose, professing a critical approach to matters of language use. Institutional discourse, in particular, became a focus of attention not only of people such as Teun van Dijk (in a number of articles and through his influential journal *Discourse and Society*, published since 1990), but also, and mainly, of the so-called Lancaster School of 'critical language awareness' (CLA), centered around Norman Fairclough and his co-workers (1989, 1992, 1995; see *Fairclough, Norman*).

For Fairclough, too, 'critical' has to do with examining the fundamental relations that assign power to various groups in our society; however, he also insists on having language, the 'text,' along, the latter being one particularly important instrument of exercising that power. In Fairclough's work, the language people speak and write looms large, as it does in the writings of his collaborators and (former) students (Clark, Talbot, Wallace, just to name a few; see the collection edited by Fairclough in 1992). The other aspect, that of power, is emphasized as that which one seizes through discourse; power *is* discourse in a power-oriented society (Fairclough 1992: 50). This means that we read a text in different ways, depending on whether we as readers construe it in a powerful or in a powerless situation.

Even though in the eye of the naive beholder, *power* and its executors may seem the most obvious element of oppression (the SS guard cracking the whip over a line of camp inmates), what characterizes power as a social factor is not its brute force as such but rather, its being accepted as a *natural* thing. 'You can't fight City Hall' is the philosophically resigning expression of such a naturalized relation to the powers that be.

Naturalization is said to happen whenever what should be critically examined and resisted is taken as a 'natural' thing, the self-evidence of the common-sensical world which 'goes without saying because it comes without saying,' to borrow Bourdieu's immortal quip (1977: 167, see *Bourdieu, Pierre*). It is natural for the police to question a prospective detainee, and even if the law tells us that the only information we need to give out are our names and addresses (and perhaps, in certain countries, our social security numbers or equivalents), it is 'natural' for somebody who is pulled over to answer police questions even if they sometimes go far beyond the limits of the morally and legally permissible.

In the following extract (from Fairclough 1995), the legitimacy of the policemen's interventions is never questioned by the detainee, even though they must under every aspect proper to 'normal conversation' (turn-taking, cooperation, and so on) be characterized as 'out of order.'

(*A young woman is brought into a police station in England, having accused three men with rape. A is the woman, B and C are police officers.*)

541

C:...so we can confirm...that you've had sex with three men...if it does confirm it...then I would go so far as to say...that you went to that house willingly...there's no struggle...

C:...so what's to stop you...shouting and screaming in the street...when you think you're going to get raped...you're not frightened at all...you walk in there quite blasé you're not frightened at all...

A: I was frightened

C: you weren't...you're showing no signs of emotion

B: you're female and you've probably got a hell of a temper...if you were to go...

A: I haven't got a temper

B: I think if things were up against a wall...I think you'd fight and fight very hard... (1995: 29–30)

The point of this 'conversation' is for the officers to categorize the complainant as a person who has no right to complain about being raped: first, she probably was asking for it; second, if she had been attacked, she would have put up a struggle; and third, since she has a violent temper, she would have been able to fight off her aggressors quite easily. All this is expressed both in innuendoes and direct statements, and no matter what the woman says or tries to deny, the policemen do not budge an inch from their preconceived notions about what has happened; they are not going to take this case seriously.

The naturalness of this interview in terms of police officer behavior and client response is attested by the fact that at no point during the interrogation is the legitimacy of the police's interventions questioned, not even when they flatly accuse the woman of lying, of being hysterical, of making things up, and so on. Again, it is a case of 'You can't fight City Hall' or, for that matter, the Precinct: the harder we try, the more entrapped we get in our own submission and the more vicious the authorities' retributions for what they consider to be impertinent behavior.

It is the task of a CLA to examine the conditions that underlie such naturalized behaviors (which are frequent also in other societal settings; for a medical parallel, cf. Nijhof 1998). As Fairclough remarks, 'naturalization gives to particular ideological representations the status of *common sense*, and thereby makes them...no longer visible as ideologies' (1995: 42; my italics; the expression 'common sense' is borrowed from the work of Gramsci; see *Gramsci, Antonio*). The ideology of the police as powerful friends of the population ('your friendly local police') masks the reality of police oppression by naturalizing and 'familiarizing' it. When asking for the conditions implicitly determining this situation, we must resort to an analysis of the political power that drives the ideology.

The social aspects of pragmatics are many, but they all have this in common: they deal with the question of 'whose language' we are speaking, and on whose authority we can form our words and utter our sentences. What is important in CLA is to understand the social functioning of our language, not as a matter of linguistic variation, to be described in purely theoretical terms, not as a sociological variable denoting class or other societal parameters. The main impact of pragmatics as a 'social science' is in the way it can help us recognise and fight social discrimination, using instruments such as CLA.

See also: Hegemony; Pragmatics; Power and Language; Critical Sociolinguistics.

Bibliography

Bourdieu P 1977 *Outline of a Theory of Practice*. Cambridge University Press, Cambridge, UK (Original title: *Esquisse d'uses théorie de la pratique*. 1972.)

Fairclough N 1989 *Language and Power*. Longman, London

Fairclough N (ed.) 1992 *Critical Language Awareness*. Longman, London

Fairclough N 1995 *Critical Discourse Analysis*. Longman, London

Fowler R, Hodge R, Kress G, Trew T 1979 *Language and Control*. Routledge and Kegan Paul, London

Mey J L 1979 'Zur kritischen Sprachtheorie'. In: Mey J L (ed.) *Pragmalinguistics: Theory and Practice*. Mouton, The Hague, vol. 1, pp. 411–34

Mey J L 1985 *Whose Language? A Study in Linguistic Pragmatics*. Benjamins, Philadelphia

Nijhof G 1998 Naming as naturalization in the medical encounters. *Journal of Pragmatics* **30**(6): 735–53

Critical Sociolinguistics

G. Kress

Sociolinguistics is an enterprise developed as a response to certain problems of mainstream linguistics, by and large the nagging worry that language is too obviously imbedded and involved in social practices to sustain the fiction of language as an autonomous object, and of the possibility of linguistics as an autonomous discipline. Any attempt, however, to situate particular linguistic forms or practices in a social context immediately has critical potential. Taking some criterial examples in the early history of sociolinguistics will show this clearly. Asking a question about code switching (Blom and Gumperz 1972) (see *Code-switching: Overview*) implies questions about a social structure marked by differences of access and by differences of power. To ask questions about the differential uses of micro-level phonetic features (Labov 1972) is to point not only to a class-segmented society, but also to the different social histories of speakers, and to their consequent differential standing in a 'language community' (see *Class and Language*). Included here should be socially important work on language use in courtrooms in professional–client interactions (see *Doctor–Patient Language*), in classrooms (see *Spoken Language in the Classroom*), and other work of a similar kind.

Generally speaking, while this enterprise created opportunities for quite fundamental critiques of society, such critiques were not developed. Linguistic inequality is described, but no particular socially critical point is developed; or, to be more precise, the public ideology (see *Ideology*) of the social equality of a democratic society means that such situations are treated as malfunctions, as 'noise' in an otherwise sound system: a technical problem with a technical solution. Hence any 'problem' in a doctor–patient interaction can be fixed by giving the doctor a course in interpersonal management skills. A similar situation exists with regard to other forms of sociolinguistics with an inherently critical potential, for instance, conversation analysis (CA; see *Conversation Analysis*), and pragmatics. Conversational analysis focuses on microanalyses, with interactants quite deliberately described outside of any social context (see *Pragmatics and Sociolinguistics*). A certain type of pragmatics deals with the problems of use exported to it from syntactic theories (see *Context*), and deals with these not in terms of specifically socially located questions, but in terms of universalizing rules of use.

Feminist analysis of 'women's language,' so-called, is the striking exception (see *Gender and Language*). While it is generally located in the sociolinguistic paradigm (see *Language in Society: Overview*), it provides explicitly political, critical descriptions of particular forms of language, or of language use (Kramarae et al. 1984, Seidel 1988). In this, it has been able to draw on the political and critical project of feminism, a project aimed at interrupting present structurings of power and at a redistribution of power (see *Power and Language*). As well as description, therefore, feminist analysis and theorizing of language have had as one of their major aims a project of 'reconstruction': to imagine and theorize possible new forms of language which would correspond to (or possibly even assist in producing) new forms of social practice.

A second broad movement of critical sociolinguistics (CSL) has from the outset had quite explicit political and socially critical aims (see *Politics and Language*). Its various strands are broadly complementary but have different origins and methodologies. All aim to reveal social inequalities produced or supported by particular linguistic forms, processes, and practices. One distinguishing factor which may be helpful in thinking about two emphases of this movement is that one tends to take particular social issues as its focus: racism, sexism, militarization, ethnic discrimination (see *Migrants and Migration*), the portrayal of social/geographic regions in the western media ('the Third World,' 'Africa,' etc.), the nuclear arms issue, and so on (see *Linguistic Imperialism*). Studies in this mode describe the manner in which texts construct particular issues from the point of view of those who have power—whether they are groups within one society, or 'north versus south'—focusing on larger-scale textual structures, characteristic and systematic uses of words, syntax, textual forms, etc. (Chilton 1985, van Dijk 1987, 1991, Mey 1985, Wodak et al. 1990) (see *Representation*). The label for this work commonly used by its practitioners is 'critical discourse analysis' (CDA). Theoretically, linguists in this strand tend to draw on existing work in pragmatics, CA, discourse analysis, and text linguistics, but importantly also on work in the social psychology of text production and reception, and on work in cognition generally.

The other body of work is more interested in the linguistic–ideological constitution of discourse (see *Discourse*), in the ideological characteristics and effects of grammatical forms and syntactic structures and processes. In other words, it focuses on the materiality of language itself as politically, socially, culturally, and therefore ideologically constituted (see *Ideology*). It treats all of language as the product of social processes, so that its critical movement is to attempt to reveal the ideological, social constructedness of all linguistic form in order to show and thus open to critique the operations of power in and through language (see *Power and Language*). It too takes texts as the relevant units of analysis. Its practitioners commonly use the labels 'critical linguistics' or 'critical discourse analysis' (where CDA is taken to be a development of, and to include, work in critical linguistics) to describe their work (see Fowler 1991, Fowler et al. 1979, Fairclough 1989, 1992, Hodge and Kress 1979, Kress 1989, 1991, Kress and Hodge 1989).

Theoretically, the antecedents of critical linguistics are both from linguistics—systemic linguistics predominantly (Halliday 1978, 1985); with certain uses of realist interpretations of an *Aspects*-type transformational grammar (Chomsky 1965); as well as the important influence of the work of Basil Bernstein on codes (Bernstein 1968, 1990, see *Code, Sociolinguistic*); and from sociological, political, and philosophical theories, and the work of Freud and Marx (see *Marxist Theories of Language*).

One significant difference between the latter and the former kinds of CDA lies in the fact that critical linguistics had always seen it as one part of its projects to reform and reconstitute mainstream linguistics, to make it more responsive to social considerations, and to shift it from its definition as an autonomous discipline to a definition which saw linguistics as a socially responsible and responsive discipline. This aim may be considered to have been a failure; nevertheless, there are significant signs of change. One is the sheer number of linguists working in a framework of overtly critical sociolinguistics, of whatever kind. Another is the growing strength of CDA, and of the practitioners happy to work (together) under that label.

Critical discourse analysis (as a cover term for all of this kind of CSL) is positively multi- and interdisciplinary: this reflects the fact that CDA sees the domain of its application as other than that of linguistics; and certainly not autonomous in any sense. It is in the process of defining its domain; and this implies necessarily, that it is in the process of defining its theoretical constitution. Previously, all of CSL had been willing to take categories and (descriptive) methodologies from existing linguistic theories. This is in the longer run an unsatisfactory situation, as theoretical categories cannot simply be transported from one theoretical framework to an entirely different—perhaps even ideologically hostile—one. The problems of mainstream linguistics, from the point of view of CSL and particularly of CDA, are numerous, and these will need to be addressed in a new theory of language. There follows a list of these problems from the point of view of CSL/CDA.

(a) Mainstream linguistics (ML) is ahistorical; CSL needs a theory which is fully historical, at a micro- and macro-level. Without history, linguistic theory cannot account for linguistic change, and in particular it cannot account for changes in particular directions which correspond to the arrangement of forces in society. CSL needs a theory which is equally attentive to the micro-level histories of conversations, interviews, writings, and readings of written texts, and can connect these with each other and to the macro-histories of cultural groups and of society as a whole.

(b) ML is autonomous; CSL, as its name declares, needs a theory which is fully social. The move from an autonomous conception will allow social categories to become the categories which are productive (generative) of linguistic form, at all levels, from morpheme to textual structures.

(c) ML has no theory of the individual language user as a socially and historically formed subject, with particular social histories, and operating in specific social positions, hence always in structurings of power. In a recast theory, the individual language user will be seen as active and agentive, as the bearer of social structures and therefore of differential power in relation to the production of texts, and, consequently in relation to linguistic change. It is through the actions of socially formed language users that the contradictory forces of linguistic convergence and difference can be explained in the production of a hegemonic structure socially and linguistically (see *Hegemony*).

(d) ML is a gendered discipline, as a consequence of (a), (b), and (c); it is also blind to its formation in relation to class (see *Class and Language*), and to very many other fundamental social categories (see *Social Class*). In a socially founded theory, gender along with other fundamental social categories will form one of the set of productive (generative) categories, and will therefore enter from the beginning into analyses and descriptions.

(e) ML is a sentence- or clause-based discipline; CSL and CDA are text-based. Text is a crucial unit in that, as the site of realization and production of meaning, it is the site of contestation of the meaning systems of the producers of the text, in a field of power difference which bears on the outcome, that is, on the text that is produced.

(f) ML is a formalistic discipline. To use Saussurean notions, it is a discipline which has focused on the signifier (form) to the exclusion of the signified (meaning). CLS and CDA need a notion of the sign, not as an arbitrary conjunct of signifier and signified (see *Saussurean Tradition and Sociolinguistics*), but as a socially, ideologically motivated structure. The motivation itself derives from the 'interest' if the producer(s) of the sign, that is, their social histories and present social locations.

(g) ML is a monologic, producer-based theory. CSL needs a heteroglossic account, and a communicative one, that is based equally on hearer/readers and speaker/writers. The facts of contemporary multicultural societies make heteroglossic accounts essential, although all societies are likely to be heteroglossic due to significant differences based on class, profession, and region, for instance.

It is clear that CSL is at a crucial stage in its development. It cannot continue to draw eclectically on sets of categories from theories which were constructed for entirely different purposes, and with quite different political motivations. For one thing, to do so actually not only imports theoretical/ideological problems into CSL, but it also reinforces existing theories by leaving them unchallenged, as both appropriate for and accurate in *their* domain. The initial project of CSL is in a real sense accomplished; the new project is quite clearly a much more far-reaching one, namely to construct the theory implied by and necessary for the ongoing range of activities. This theory, a new conceptualization of language, can then as a theory of language act as a challenge to those social structures being dealt with in the early 2000s by an essentially inappropriate analytic and descriptive methodology.

In its new form, it will of course cease to be CSL, the dichotomy of linguistics and sociolinguistics, critical and uncritical theories having been superseded. The new linguistic theory will need to reflect on its own place, on the place of language in the total assembly of modes of communication, and become reflexive and critical of its own position.

See also: Language in the Workplace; Language as a Social Reality; Critical Discourse Analysis; Representation.

Bibliography

Bernstein B 1968 Some sociological determinants of perception: An inquiry into sub-cultural differences. In: Fishman J A (ed.) *Readings in the Sociology of Language*. Mouton, The Hague
Bernstein B 1990 The *Structuring of Pedagogic Discourse*. Routledge, London
Blom J P, Gumperz J J 1972 Social meaning in linguistic structures: Code switching in Norway. In: Gumperz J J, Hymes D H (eds.) 1972 *Directions in Sociolinguistics: The Ethnography of Communication*. Holt, Rinehart and Winston, New York
Chilton P (ed.) 1985 *Language and the Nuclear Arms Debate: Nukespeak Today*. Frances Pinter, London.
Chomsky N 1965 *Aspects of the Theory of Syntax*. MIT Press, Cambridge, MA
Chouliaraki L, Fairclough N 1999 *Discourse in Late Modernity*. Edinburgh University Press, Edinburgh, UK
Dijk T A van 1987 *Communicating Racism: Ethnic Prejudice in Thought and Talk*. Benjamins, Amsterdam
Dijk T A van 1991 *Racism and the Press*. Routledge, London
Fairclough N 1989 *Language and Power*. Longman, London
Fairclough N 1992 *Discourse and Social Change*. Polity Press, Cambridge, UK
Fishman J A (ed.) 1968 *Readings in the Sociology of Language*. Mouton, The Hague
Fowler R 1991 *Language in the News*. Routledge, London
Fowler R, Hodge R, Kress G, Trew T 1979 *Language and Control*. Routledge and Kegan Paul, London
Gumperz J J, Hymes D H (eds.) 1972 *Directions in Sociolinguistics: The Ethnography of Communication*. Holt, Rinehart and Winston, New York
Halliday M A K 1978 *Language as a Social Semiotic*. Edward Arnold, London
Halliday M A K 1985 *An Introduction to Functional Grammar*. Edward Arnold, London
Hodge R, Kress G 1989 *Social Semiotics*. Polity Press, Cambridge, UK
Hymes D H 1964 *Language in Culture and Society*. Harper and Row, New York
Hymes D H 1968 The ethnography of speaking. In: Fishman J A (ed.) *Readings in the Sociology of Language*. Mouton, The Hague
Kramarae C, Schulz M, O'Barr W (eds.) 1984 *Language and Power*. Sage, New York
Kress G 1989 *Linguistic Processes in Sociocultural Practice*. Oxford University Press, Oxford, UK
Kress G 1991 Critical discourse analysis. In: Grabe W (ed.) *Annual Review of Applied Linguistics*, vol. II. Cambridge University Press, New York
Kress G, Hodge R 1979 *Language as Ideology*. Routledge and Kegan Paul, London
Labov W 1972 On the mechanism of linguistic change. In: Gumperz, J J, Hymes D H (eds.) *Directions in Sociolinguistics: The Ethnography of Communication*. Holt, Rinehart and Winston, New York
Mey J 1985 *Whose Language? A Study in Linguistic Pragmatics*. Benjamins, Amsterdam
Seidel G (ed.) 1988 *The Nature of the Right: A Feminist Analysis of Order Patterns*. Benjamins, Amsterdam
Wodak R et al. 1990 *Wir sind unschuldige Täter. Studien zum antisemitischen Diskurs im Nachkriegsösterreich*. Suhrkamp, Frankfurt

Discrimination and Minority Languages
T. Skutnabb-Kangas and R. Phillipson

People can be discriminated against on the grounds of their gender, class, race, or language. The reality of such discrimination, and the urge to combat the injustice of it, has inspired many human rights covenants and some national legislation.

Language can itself also be discriminatory in several ways, or it can be used in discriminatory ways. The 'form' of the language itself, its vocabulary (or lack of vocabulary in areas of importance to dominated groups) and connotations, can be racist ('nigger') or ethnocentric ('developing' country), sexist (see *Gender and Language*), classist, ageist, militaristic, nationalistic, etc. Words can make some groups of people or their characteristics invisible (the rights of 'Man'), or appendices to others ('lady doctor,' 'male nurse'), or stereotype them negatively ('Third' World). Language can also be *used* in discriminatory ways, so that some groups become invisible ('the anglophone countries of Africa' ignores the fact that the vast majority of the population in such countries have no command of, or do not habitually use, English). Several professional associations and publishing houses have issued codes of linguistic conduct, which instruct authors how to avoid such discriminatory language.

Individuals and groups can also be discriminated against on the basis of language: how they speak (class background, gender, geographic origin, etc.) or which language(s) they speak (or do not speak). Judgments of class background or mother tongue or gender made on purportedly linguistic evidence lead to attributions of competence and moral qualities as well as to the creation of esthetic norms and feelings of solidarity, as social psychological studies have shown. The class bias of the 'standard' language that schools inculcate has a major influence on school achievement and discriminates against many children. The present article concentrates on the kinds of discrimination that speakers of dominated/minority languages, indigenous, national, regional, or immigrant, encounter because of their mother tongue(s) (see also *Minority Languages*).

1. Linguistic Rights and Human Rights

Many minority groups were granted specific protection in the treaties signed at the end of the First World War. Since 1946, the United Nations has had a Sub-Commission on Prevention of Discrimination and Protection of Minorities; interestingly, it has recently been renamed and is now called Sub-Commission on the Promotion and Protection of Human Rights. Within the UN framework, a series of human rights covenants have been devised, signed, and ratified. These attempt to provide minorities with at least some of those human rights (hereafter HRs) that majority/dominant populations often take for granted, including linguistic human rights (hereafter LHRs). Article 27 of the International Covenant on Civil and Political Rights (1966) still contains the most far-reaching binding protection for LHRs for minority languages. It declares:

In those States in which ethnic, religious, or linguistic minorities exist, persons belonging to such minorities shall not be denied the right, in community with the other members of their group, to enjoy their own culture, to profess and practice their own religion, or to use their own language.

A major survey was conducted for the UN (Capotorti 1979) to analyze juridical and conceptual aspects of protection against discrimination and to solicit information from governments worldwide so as to assess how minorities are treated *de jure* and *de facto*. Immigrant minorities were explicitly excluded from consideration, 'because of their voluntary assimilation' (Capotorti 1979: 10), or because they were not to be encouraged to 'form within that State separate communities which might impair its national unity or its security': they 'could not be regarded as minorities as this would endanger the national integrity of the receiving States' (Capotorti 1979: 33). These fears reflect a monolingual norm (see below). They are still one of the main reasons why states are so reluctant to guarantee proper protection to minority languages and their speakers. Still, the fears seem to be largely unfounded (see Joshua Fishman's comparative study of correlations between number of languages in a country, economic prosperity, social strife, and many other variables; Fishman 1989, see also Eide 1995.) Often it is precisely the lack of LHRs that causes conflicts that can then be labeled 'ethnic.' The Capotorti report concluded that most minorities, not least linguistic ones, were in need of much more substantial protection. It stressed the key role of education through the medium of the mother tongue for linguistic and cultural maintenance and vitality. It also interpreted article 27 as imposing an obligation on states to actively promote minority languages. This presupposes that states provide adequate financial support for these languages. The UN Human Rights Committee interpreted in a General Comment (6 April 1994) Art. 27 as protecting all individuals on the state's territory or under its jurisdiction (i.e., also immigrants and refugees), irrespective of whether they belong to the minorities specified in the article or not. The General Comment also stated that the existence of a minority does not depend on a decision by the state but requires to be established by objective criteria. It recognized the existence of a 'right,' and imposed positive obligations on the states.

There is however abundant evidence of groups and an individual being deprived of their LHRs. Often language shift occurs as a result (see *Linguicide*). Many international covenants beginning with the UN Charter, declare that discrimination should be outlawed but do not in their binding articles oblige states to promote minority languages. Many states in fact expect their indigenous and immigrant minorities to assimilate to the dominant culture and language.

2. Action Against Linguistic Discrimination

Using the HRs system might be one way forward in protecting diversities in a globalized 'free market' world. Instead of granting market forces free range,

HRs, especially economic and social rights are, according to human rights lawyer Katarina Tomaševski (1996: 104), to act as correctives to the free market. The first international HRs treaty abolished slavery. Prohibiting slavery implied that people were not supposed to be treated as market commodities. ILO (The International Labour Organisation) has added that labor should not be treated as a commodity. But price tags are to be removed from other areas too. Tomaševski states (1996: 104) that 'the purpose of international HRs law is... to overrule the law of supply and demand and remove price-tags from people and from necessities for their survival.' These necessities for survival include not only basic food and housing (which would come under economic and social rights), but also basics for the sustenance of a dignified life, including basic civil, political and cultural rights, including LHRs.

The international HRs regime started to develop in a prominent way directly after the Second World War under the auspices of the United Nations. Most of the initial rights were individual rights. This resulted in non-development for most of those rights, which during the League of Nations had included some language rights, namely, minority rights (which are necessarily collective). One of the arguments was that if every individual had certain rights, people were protected as individuals, and collective rights were not needed. Today, certain collective rights are increasingly being included in the HRs regime.

Awareness of linguistic discrimination has led, inter alia, to the Council of Europe elaborating a 'European Charter for Regional or Minority Languages' and a 'Framework Convention for the Protection of National Minorities' (both in force since 1999). But international and regional (African, American, and European) binding Covenants, Conventions, and Charters give very little support to LHRs in education, and language is given a much poorer treatment than other central human characteristics. Often language is present in the lofty non-duty-inducing phrases in the preambles of the HRs instruments, but disappears completely in educational parts. When it is there, the Articles dealing with education, especially the right to mother tongue medium education, are more vague and/or contain many more opt-outs and modifications than any other Articles, as has been shown in many books and articles (see the bibliography). At the most, languages have negative rights (non-discrimination prescriptions) rather than positive rights where the clauses or articles about them would create obligations and contain demanding formulations and where the states would be firm dutyholders and be obliged to ('shall') act in order to ensure the specified rights. A couple of illustrations of each type follow the ones where language disappears, and the ones with vague formulations, modifications and opt-outs (see Chapter 7 in Skutnabb-Kangas 2000 for a fuller treatment).

Language disappears completely in the *Universal Declaration of Human Rights* (1948) where the paragraph on education (26) does not refer to language at all. Similarly, the *International Covenant on Economic, Social and Cultural Rights* (adopted in 1966 and in force since 1976), having mentioned language on a par with race, color, sex, religion, etc. in its general Article (2.2), does explicitly refer to 'racial, ethnic, or religious groups' in its educational Article (13). However, it omits reference to language or linguistic groups.

In the *UN Declaration on the Rights of Persons Belonging to National or Ethnic, Religious and Linguistic Minorities*, adopted by the General Assembly in December 1992, most of the Articles use the obligating formulation 'shall' and have few let-out modifications or alternatives—except where linguistic rights in education are concerned. Compare the unconditional formulation in Articles 1.1 and 1.2 about identity with the education Article 4.3 (emphases added, '*obligating*' in italics, '**opt-outs**' in bold):

1.1. States *shall protect* the existence and the national or ethnic, cultural, religious and linguistic identity of minorities within their respective territories, and *shall encourage* conditions for the *promotion* of that identity.

1.2. States *shall* adopt **appropriate** legislative *and other measures to achieve those ends*.

4.3. States **should** take **appropriate** measures so that, **wherever possible**, persons belonging to minorities have **adequate** opportunities to learn their mother tongue **or** to have instruction in their mother tongue.

The questions one can ask are what constitutes 'appropriate measures,' or 'adequate opportunities,' and who is to decide what is 'possible'? Does 'instruction in their mother tongue' mean through the medium of the mother tongue or does it only mean instruction in the mother tongue as a subject? The opt-outs and alternatives permit a reluctant state to meet the requirements in a minimalist way, which it can legitimate by claiming that a provision was not 'possible' or 'appropriate,' or that numbers were not 'sufficient' or did not 'justify' a provision, or that it 'allowed' the minority to organize teaching of their language as a subject, at their own cost.

The Council of Europe *Framework Convention for the Protection of National Minorities* Article covering medium of education is so heavily qualified that the minority is completely at the mercy of the state:

> In areas inhabited by persons belonging to national minorities traditionally or in **substantial** numbers, **if**

there is **sufficient demand**, the parties shall **endeavour** to ensure, **as far as possible** and **within the framework of their education systems**, that persons belonging to those minorities have **adequate** opportunities for being taught in the minority language **or** for receiving instruction in this language (emphases added).

The conclusion is that we are still to see the right to education through the medium of the mother tongue become a human right. There are some examples of what we consider positive recent developments, at least on paper: HRs instruments, draft instruments, recommendations, declarations, or comments. They might give some cautious reason for hope. The impact of the recent positive developments in counteracting linguistic genocide in education and the killing of linguistic diversity has yet to be seen.

Implementation needs to follow. Without implementation, monitoring and proper complaint procedures, much of the potential in the new or emerging instruments will be lost.

A draft *Universal Declaration of Linguistic Rights* was presented to UNESCO in 1996 as a first step towards further elaboration and adoption, but it is unlikely that it will be adopted, even in a revised form. It was, however, the first major international attempt to specify universal linguistic rights. Even in this Declaration, it was clear that educational language rights, in contrast to cultural rights, were not seen as inalienable.

Court action can be a significant way of challenging linguistic discrimination. In the USA, a number of cases have been brought for this purpose. Significant is the case of *Lau vs. Nichols*, in which students of Chinese ancestry claimed that the San Francisco Unified School District failed in its obligation to provide adequate education for them. The US Supreme Court ruled that 'Under these state-imposed standards there is no equality of treatment merely by providing students with the same facilities, textbooks, teachers, and curriculum; for students who do not understand English are effectively foreclosed from any meaningful education' (quoted in Center for Applied Linguistics 1977: 7). Many court cases in the USA have challenged discrimination on the basis of language or dialect in education, hiring practices, and promotion.

A case of central relevance to minority education was brought against the Norwegian State. A Saami (called 'Lapp' in colonial language), Johan Gávppi, who knew no Norwegian when he went to school and whose teachers knew no Saami, got little benefit from school and was illiterate until his own children taught him to read and write. He sued the Norwegian State for damages for failing to give him the basic education he was entitled to under Norwegian law. All Norwegian courts and the European Commission on Human Rights deemed the case obsolete but other cases may follow. This case has wide symbolic significance. If the principle is established that a minority child is entitled to financial compensation for inappropriate education, then one can envisage indigenous and immigrant minorities worldwide following suit.

The relevant academic arguments were already assembled back in 1953 in an authoritative UNESCO report which considers it 'axiomatic that the best medium for teaching is the mother tongue of the pupil' and that this should be 'extended to as late a stage in education as possible.' This has been confirmed in educational guidelines issued for the OSCE High Commissioner on National Minorities, Max van der Stoel, *The Hague Recommendations Regarding the Education Rights of National Minorities & Explanatory Note* (October 1996). The Hague Recommendations are one of the recent positive developments. In the section on 'Minority education at primary and secondary levels,' mainly mother tongue medium education is recommended at all levels, including bilingual teachers in the dominant language as a second language (Articles 11–13). The Recommendations are an authoritative interpretation of international human rights law (see the special issue on them, *International Journal on Minority and Group Rights. Special Issue on the Education Rights of National Minorities* 4:2, 1996/1997). The education of minorities is still a controversial issue. What also needs stressing is that relatively little research has been conducted by minority group researchers themselves. The structure of the academic world (research financing, careers, dominant paradigms, etc.) militates against minority voices being heard (but see Skutnabb-Kangas 1988).

3. From Sticks to Carrots and Ideas; From Biologically-based Racism to Ethnicism and Linguicism

The means of control over all dominated groups (not just minorities) are progressively shifting from 'sticks' (physical violence) to 'carrots' (negotiation) and 'ideas' (psychological violence). Resisting the power-holders used to lead to physical punishment (an external negative sanction) and later on to shame, a guilty conscience, or a feeling of having chosen wrongly (an internal negative sanction). Submitting leads now to rewards (internal positive sanctions). Rewarding those who submit and making them feel they have made the right choice (by glorifying the dominant language, stigmatizing dominated languages, and making the choice to drop these in favor of the dominant language seem rational), is a less expensive and more efficient way of upholding control than the use of physical violence (armies, police, etc.). Making those who do *not* submit and achieve rewards believe that their own characteristics, deficiencies, and handicaps are to blame, ensures hegemony in a less risky way than the use of physical force.

An important criterion worldwide for determining which groups obtained less than their fair share of power and resources used to be their so-called 'race.' 'Race' has, for several reasons, become an untenable criterion. It is no longer claimed that certain 'races' are more fit to rule than others are. Biologically based racism as an important ideology of hierarchization has been progressively replaced by ethnicism (Mullard 1988) and linguicism (see *Linguistic Imperialism,* Skutnabb-Kangas 1988), which relate to cultural (rather than biological) characteristics ascribed to various ethnic groups and languages. Instead of superior races, certain ethnic groups (or cultures) and languages are now seen as fitter to rule and expand; others are to adopt their cultures and learn their languages. The characteristics attributed to these cultures and languages relate to modernization, technology, efficiency, development, Western capitalist middle-class market-oriented values, and so on.

Since global market connections and the colonization of the mind of the less powerful require the use of a common language, the smaller languages are marginalized and underdeveloped. Internationally there is a hierarchy with functional differentiation between local languages and a 'world' or 'international' language (and its concomitant culture). Internally in countries which do not boast a 'world' language, local languages are increasingly confined as the traditional languages of the home and hearth, whereas the major languages are used for international instrumental roles in business, administration and politics, and also increasingly in domestic contexts (for instance, as the in-house language in transnational corporations, in higher education, in the media, etc.). These processes underlie the dramatic rise of English as an 'international' language in recent decades (Phillipson 1992, see also *Linguistic Imperialism*).

Discrimination by means of language can be analyzed as a reflection of linguicism. Linguicism is defined as:

> Ideologies, structures and practices which are used to legitimate, effectuate and reproduce an unequal division of power and resources (both material and non-material) between groups which are defined on the basis of language
>
> (Skutnabb-Kangas 1988: 45)

Language is thus in several ways increasingly important as the instrument through which groups with less access to power and resources are controlled.

Proficiency in the colonists' language was vital for social mobility in the colonial period, and this position has generally not changed since independence. For immigrant groups, the dominant group regards proficiency in the official or national language(s) of the country of residence as the vital goal of education. This is so, even when there is plenty of research evidence that educating minority children through the mother tongue would be advantageous for their overall educational, cognitive, psychological, and social development and can lead to high proficiency in the dominant language (Cummins 1996, Skutnabb-Kangas 2000). Linguicism ensures that most resources, in teacher education, curriculum development, and teaching schedules are allocated to the dominant language. An ideology of maximum support for the dominant language and marginalization of other languages accompany these structural measures. The latter tend to be regarded as educational handicaps rather than as resources. Education is inspired, misguidedly, by a monolingual norm. This norm implies at a societal level a belief that 'one state, one nation, one language' is a desirable and inevitable state of affairs, necessary for national unity, modernization, and progress, and that multilingualism leads to national disintegration, backwardness, inefficiency, and poverty. At an individual level monolingualism is seen as normal and healthy, and bi- or multilingualism as a temporary, negative phase on the path from monolingualism in one language (e.g., minority mother tongue) to monolingualism in another language (the majority language). The monolingual norm also implies 'either–or' thinking: either you maintain your minority mother tongue, and that means that you do not learn the majority language properly, or you want to learn the majority language, and therefore you cannot maintain your mother tongue (Skutnabb-Kangas 1996). Education inspired by this monolingual norm is organized subtractively (see Lambert 1975) for minority language speakers: they learn a major language instead of or at the cost of their own, not in addition to it (see *Bilingualism, Societal*). By contrast the foreign language learning of the dominant group is additive, they add more languages to their existing linguistic repertoire, at no cost to their mother tongue. It is subtractive learning of dominant languages that turns these languages into killer languages and threatens the world's linguistic diversity. What is needed for linguistic diversity to be maintained on earth and for discrimination to stop is proper protection of the LHRs of minorities, especially an unconditional right to mother tongue medium education, and additive learning of other languages.

See also: Linguistic Imperialism; Linguicide; Minority Languages; Semilingualism; Bilingualism, Societal; Diglossia; Endangered Languages; Reversing Language Shift.

Bibliography

Capotorti F 1979 *Study on the Rights of Persons Belonging to Ethnic, Religious and Linguistic Minorities*. United Nations, New York

Center for Applied Linguistics 1977 *Bilingual Education Current Perspectives. Vol. 3. Law*. Center for Applied Linguistics, Arlington, VA

Cummins J 1996 *Negotiating Identities. Education for Empowerment in a Diverse Society*. California Association for Bilingual Education, Ontario, CA

Eide A 1995 Economic, social and cultural rights as human rights. In: Eide A, Krause C, Rosas A (eds.) *Economic, Social and Cultural Rights. A Textbook*. Martinus Nijhoff, Dordrecht, The Netherlands

Fishman J 1989 *Language and Ethnicity in Minority Sociolinguistic Perspective*. Multilingual Matters, Clevedon, UK

The Hague Recommendations Regarding the Education Rights of National Minorities & Explanatory Note 1996 (October) [for the use of the OSCE High Commissioner on National Minorities, Max van der Stoel], The Hague, The Netherlands

Lambert W 1975 Culture and language as factors in learning and education. In: Wolfgang A (ed.) *Education of Immigrant Students*. Ontario Institute for Studies in Education, Toronto, ON

Mullard C 1988 Racism, ethnicism and etharcy or not? The principles of progressive control and transformative change. In: Skutnabb-Kangas T, Cummins J (eds.) *Minority Education from Shame to Struggle*. Multilingual Matters, Clevedon, UK

Phillipson R 1992 *Linguistic Imperialism*. Oxford University Press, Oxford, UK

Skutnabb-Kangas T 1988 Multilingualism and the education of minority children. In: Skutnabb-Kangas T, Cummins J (eds.) *Minority Education from Shame to Struggle*. Multilingual Matters, Clevedon, UK

Skutnabb-Kangas T 1996 Educational language choice—multilingual diversity or monolingual reductionism? In: Hellinger M, Ammon U (eds.) *Contrastive Sociolinguistics*. Mouton de Gruyter, Berlin, Germany

Skutnabb-Kangas T 2000 *Linguistic Genocide in Education—or Worldwide Diversity and Human Rights?* Lawrence Erlbaum Associates, Mahwah, NJ

Tomaševski K 1996 International prospects for the future of the welfare state. In: *Reconceptualizing the Welfare State*. The Danish Centre for Human Rights, Copenhagen, Denmark

van der Stoel M 1997 Introduction to the seminar. *International Journal on Minority and Group Rights. Special Issue on the Education Rights of National Minorities* **4**(2): 153–55

UNESCO 1953 *The Use of Vernacular Languages in Education*. UNESCO, Paris

Hegemony

G. Mininni

'Hegemony' (from Greek *hegéomai* 'I lead') is the key word summarizing Antonio Gramsci's (see *Gramsci, Antonio*) original contribution to the working out of a Marxist theory of society. Gramsci's hegemony theory is also an exemplary meeting of Marxism and linguistics, as it emphasizes the close connection between the language question and social organization, a connection marked by the ideological clash and temporary consents to systems of values or hegemonic meanings. The social dialectic between 'consent' and 'dissent' is regulated by the hegemonic function of human groups and of their own ideas. Social uses and the nature of a language itself provide an evident model of this dialectic, as every discursive event is regulated by the synchronous activation of the principles of dialogicity and opposition, cooperation and competition.

1. Hegemony as an 'Apparatus of Spiritual Government'

Forced to wonder about the reasons for the labor movement's defeat in the 1920s—a defeat he personally experienced in the cells of a fascist jail—the leader of the working class in Italy dedicated his life to investigating a subject that Marxism had neglected: the 'spiritual' conditions needed for the socialist revolution to succeed. His early meditations about the Party, which 'works through millions and millions of spiritual connections' as 'an irradiation of prestige,' are generalized in the concept of hegemony; this gradually loses its Leninist connotation of 'proletarian dictatorship' and acquires new nuances which turn out to be more and more connected to an 'ideal,' 'cultural,' 'moral,' and 'linguistic' supremacy. In short, hegemony indicates an 'apparatus of spiritual government' as it points out the ability of a group to lead the whole community to accept them freely as the ruling group. Such an ability belongs to the 'civil society' that wins the spontaneous consent of the masses of a nation to the legitimately expressed power.

2. A Passage from Society to the State

Gramsci inserted the complex dynamics between 'civil society' and 'political society' (or 'state') into the traditional Marxist scheme of dialectic relations between the economic basis and ideological superstructures, thus refining the historical materialist explanation of social control devices. The dominant class within a society takes possession of the state and the practice of this power is to be seen both as an intellectual as well as a moral management of the kindred groups and as a coercion of the opposing groups. If a class dominates over the whole community through forms of government which are based on coercion mechanisms only, this means that it has lost its hegemonic function. Whenever a detachment between the civil and political societies occurs, the dominant class is no longer ruling. This means that 'a new problem of hegemony has arisen; in other words, the historical basis of the State has shifted.' The notion of hegemony is consistent not only with the tactic of the 'historical block' between workers and peasants to carry out a social revolution in Italy, but also with Gramsci's interpretation of the 'Modern Prince': an authority interiorized in the collective conscience, a freely accepted need, a 'categorical imperative' which directs social behaviors. Hegemony highlights the social superego activation processes. Due to this complex dynamic, the concept of hegemony magnetizes the rather static notions of 'culture' and 'ideology' (Williams 1977), thus showing how the social reproduction of a group is given in the historical reality of uneven relationships, asymmetries in resources, and gaps in competences; a reality that always revises the organic picture of the fight for power. The task of the subordinate class, which is interested in a fairer and freer social order, is to secure the necessary instruments for hegemony in order to realize 'modern democracy,' through its own system of alliances and mediations. These instruments are in the hands of the intellectuals.

3. Hegemony as a Praxis for Intellectuals

As the hegemonic dimension of a class is expressed in its ability to organize the world's experience and to give life a sense, its implementation is mainly attributed to a group (which is often closed into a caste) of persons who are able to plan the whole sphere of the social psyche. The intellectuals can derive a 'spontaneous consent' to the orientation the chief, dominant group gives to social life from the trust and prestige they historically command on the part of large masses of population. The intellectuals' ruling function originates from the 'political' direction they give to their special knowledge and from the 'pedagogic relationship' they set up with the other social forces. The intellectuals decide the hegemonization processes of a class both when they spare no efforts to renovate higher culture (arts, science, philosophy) and when they devote themselves to school organization or to a specific use of mass-communication instruments. It is understood that the intellectual acts as a pole of attraction or as a 'permanent persuader,' mainly thanks to the privileged relationship he is able to epitomize with the group's language.

4. The Linguistic Matrix of Hegemony

Gramsci's conception of hegemony has an evident linguistic matrix (Lo Piparo 1979). It is two-edged: from a historical point of view, the concept of 'linguistic prestige'—derived from his early glottology studies at the school of the neolinguist Matteo Bartoli—acts as a first organizing basis for the idea of hegemony; from an illustrative point of view, this finds evidence of its validity in the nature and function of language. The premises of a Marxist language sociology (the priority of the sociocommunicative function and of the cultural restraints which are historically imposed on its use) are revised by Gramsci's notion of hegemony in such a way that both the communicative needs of a historical community and the dynamics within the systematic organization of a language are safeguarded (Rosiello 1959). As a result, evoking what Vico said, changes in language are connected with the metaphorization process concerning the sense, but this specifically linguistic resource is activated by the tension to hegemony pervading the cultural formation of a group. Not only is the formation of national languages explained as a result of hegemonic relations between dialects and of a larger intellectual and social hegemony, but the social awareness of linguistic problems—from the educational aspects concerning the normativeness of 'immanent grammar' in the system to the social diffusion of poetic styles—reveals the conflicting interests existing within hegemony processes.

> Every time the question of the language appears, in some way or other, this means that some other problems are arising: the formation and growth of the ruling class, the need for establishing closer and safer relationships between ruling groups and the popular, national mass; that is, the need for reorganizing cultural hegemony.
> (Gramsci 1971)

The notion of hegemony enables Gramsci to penetrate the dialectic which sees the language both as an expression and a component of the social and political process in a human community.

See also: Marxist Theories of Language; Nationalism and Language; Class and Language.

Bibliography

Gramsci A 1971 *Prison Notebooks*. Lawrence and Wishart, London
Lo Piparo F 1979 *Lingua intellettuali egemonia in Gramsci*. Laterza, Bari, Italy
Rosiello L 1959 La componente linguistica dello storicismo gramsciano. In: Caracciolo A, Scalia G (eds.) *La citta futura. Saggi sulla figura e il pensiero di Antonio Gramsci*. Feltrinelli, Milan, Italy
Williams R 1977 *Marxism and Literature*. Oxford University Press, Oxford, UK

Honorifics
M. Shibatani

The term 'honorifics' refers to special linguistic forms that are used as signs of deference toward the nominal referents or the addressee. The system of honorifics constitutes an integral component of the politeness dimension of language use, but whereas every language appears to have ways of expressing politeness, only certain languages have well-developed honorifics. Generally speaking, the languages with highly developed honorifics systems are concentrated in Asia—Japanese, Korean, Tibetan, Javanese, and Thai being among the best-known languages of this group. A thorough study of honorifics requires a two-pronged approach. The description of honorifics as grammatical forms is one thing and is relatively easy to arrive at, whereas the description of their actual use requires wider pragmatic as well as sociolinguistic perspectives that take into consideration elements of a conversational situation, such as the relationship between the speaker and the addressee, and the functional role that honorifics play in communicative interaction. While the pragmatic aspects of honorifics usage are gaining increasing attention in the field, the available descriptions are, by and large, purely grammatical with little information on usage. This article endeavors to correct this imbalance by devoting one half to the grammatical aspects of honorifics, and the other half to the pragmatic and sociolinguistic issues, where aspects of Japanese honorifics usage are examined in some detail.

1. Referent Honorifics

'Referent honorifics' are those forms that are used to show deference toward the nominal referents. This type of honorifics is most widespread and the historical development of the honorifics system, as available in the case of Japanese, indicates that this is the most basic form of the honorifics (see *Politeness*).

1.1 Titles

The commonest forms of referent honorifics are honorary titles used together with the name. Many languages have honorary titles similar to the English form *Mr* and the German form *Herr* that derive from the nouns designating higher social roles or divine beings. Also common are titles deriving from the names of occupations or ranks in specific social groups, e.g., a military unit, a business group, and kin-terms that are considered high in social standing; e.g., *doctor, professor, general, uncle, aunt*.

Something similar to the honorary titles are honorific endings observed in Korean, Japanese, and others. The Korean suffix *-s'i* attaches either to the full name of a respected person or just to the family name of a person engaged in a menial labor, whereas the higher-level ending *-nim* attaches to the combination of a family name and a professional title; e.g., *Kim kyoswu-nim* (Kim professor-SUFFIX) 'Professor Kim.' The Japanese ending *-san* and its higher-level counterpart *-sama* attach to family names as well as given names yielding honorified forms; e.g., *Yamada-sama* 'Mr Yamada,' *Masao-san* 'Masao (honorified first name).' These are, in fact, part of the general amelioratory system of reference, which includes other endings such as *-kun* (used for the names of male equals or inferiors) and the diminutive *-tyan* (used typically for children's first names).

1.2 Pronouns

Pronominal forms, especially those referring to the addressee, namely the second-person pronouns, are often the target of honorific elaboration. The best-known example of this case is the use of the plural pronouns, such as the forms for *you* (PL), *they* and *we*, in reference to a singular addressee (or a third-person referent) as a sign of respect; e.g., French *vous*, German *Sie*, Russian *vy*, Tagalog *kayo* 'you.PL,' *sila* 'they,' Turkish *siz* 'you.PL,' Ainu *aoko* 'we.INCL.' Javanese presents one of the most complex prominal systems elaborated along the honorific dimension (see Table 1).

One notable honorific aspect having to do with the second-person pronominal forms is that many languages of Asia, e.g., Japanese, Korean, Dzongkha (Bhutan), simply avoid using the second-person pronominals to a superior out of deference (see Sects. 3 and 5). In these languages, the second-person reference, if the need arises, is made by the use of a professional title, e.g., Japanese *sensei* 'teacher,' Korean *sacangnim* 'company president,' or of kin-terms, e.g., Korean *emeni* 'mother,' or of a combination of a kin term and an honorific ending, e.g., Japanese *ozi-san* 'uncle.'

1.3 Nouns

The honorified nouns express deference either directly toward the referent or indirectly toward the owner, the creator, or the recipient of the referred object. As opposed to the first two categories of the referent honorifics, the number of languages with this system declines sharply.

Both suppletive and regular morphological processes as well as combinations of both are observable. Korean nominal honorific forms *cinji, yonse, songham* supplete *pap* 'meal,' *nai* 'age,' *irum* 'name,'

Table 1. Javanese personal pronominal forms (adapted from Sakiyama 1989).

	Ordinary	Middle	Honorific	Super-honorific
1st person	aku tak-, dak- -ku	kulå	kulå	kawulå abdidalem
2nd person	kowé ko(k)-, -mu	(an) dikå	sampéyan	panjenengan nandalem sampéyan dalem slirå
3rd person	dhéwék(n)é dhék(n)é di- -(n)é	piyambaké kiyambaké	piyambakipun kiyambakipun dipun- -ipun	panjenenganipun -ipun

respectively. Often suppletive honorific forms are loanwords borrowed from superior cultures. For example, the honorific forms *bida* 'father' and *manda* 'mother' for the native Thai words *po* and *me*, respectively, are from Pali. Likewise, many honorific forms in Javanese are loanwords from Sanskrit and Arabic; e.g., *arta* 'money' (Sanskrit), *kuwatir* 'to fear' (Arabic).

Kin terms in Japanese are made honorific by the suffixation of honorific endings *-sama* or *-san*. Between *o-kaa-sama* 'mother,' and *kaa-san* 'mother,' for example, the first form with the honorific prefix *o-* (see below) and the *-sama* ending is the more elevated form.

Nominal honorific forms typically refer to objects possessed or created by respected persons. The favorite nominal honorific derivation in Japanese is by means of the prefix *o-* or *go-*; e.g., *o-kaban* 'bag,' *go-hon* 'book,' *o-hanasi* 'talk,' *go-koogi* 'lecture.' A combination of suppletion and prefixation is observed in the Japanese form *o-mesimono* for *kimino* 'Japanese-style clothes' or *huku* 'Western-style clothes.'

The all-purpose Japanese nominal honorific prefixes *o-* (for native words) and *go-* (for Sino–Japanese loanwords) have their etymologies in words with meaning associated with greatness (for the native *o-*) and ruling (for the Chinese *go-*). Tibetan nominal honorific prefixes, on the other hand, have a classificatory scheme as their basis (Kitamura 1974). Thus, the honorific form *bdu* for *mgo* 'head' functions as an honorific prefix for objects having to do with the head, upper part, or superior; e.g., *skra* 'hair' → *bdu-skra*, *zhwa-mo* 'hat' → *bdu-zhwa*. Likewise, the honorific form *gsol* for *bzas* 'eat' and *btung* 'drink' goes with those objects having to do with foods and eating; e.g., *ito* 'food' → *gsol-chas*, *thab-tshang* 'kitchen' → *gsol-thab*.

1.4 Subject Honorifics

Just as the possession can be the target of honorification, one's being or action can be honorified as a way of showing deference toward the referent of the subject nominal, namely the actor. Of course, a subject nominal itself can be honorified by, for example, the choice of the second- or third-person pronominals (see above), but the case under consideration involves alternations in verbal form. A case can be clarified by comparing the plain Japanese sentence (a) *Tanaka ga ki-ta* (Tanaka NOM come-PAST), 'Tanaka came' and the honorific counterparts, (b) *Tanaka-kyoozyu ga ki-ta* (Tanaka-professor NOM come-PAST), and (c) *Tanaka-kyoozyu ga ko-rare-ta* (Tanaka-professor NOM come-HON-PAST 'Professor Tanaka came.' Sentence (b) with a professional title for the subject nominal expresses a certain degree of deference toward the teacher. But a more appropriate form would be sentence (c), in which the verb also changes its form in accordance with the speaker's deference toward the referent of the subject.

Japanese, Korean, and Tibetan have a highly developed system of subject honorification. As shown in the above example, Japanese uses the passive/potential/spontaneous suffix *-(ra)re* attached to a verbal stem and derives the subject honorific verbal form: *ik-u* (go-PRES) 'go' → *ika-re-ru* (go-HON-PRES). Korean has the subject honorific suffix *-si* that attaches to a verbal stem: *o-ta* (come-IND) 'come' → *o-si-ta* (come-HON-IND). Tibetan uses the honorific form *gnang* for the verbs of giving and receiving as a productive subject honorific verbal suffix; *thugs* 'meet' → *thugs-gnang* (meet-HON), *bzos* 'make' → *bzos-gnang* (make-HON).

Besides these productive honorific forms, a fair number of suppletive subject honorific forms are also seen in all of these languages. The Japanese form *irassyaru* suppletes *iru* 'be,' *iku* 'go,' and *kuru* 'come.' *Khesi-ta* is the Korean subject honorific form of *iss-ta* 'be.' The Tibetan form *gnang* seen above suppletes *ster* 'give,' *btang* 'send,' and *sprad* 'hand over.'

In addition to these, Japanese has a circumlocution subject honorific form. This involves the following processes: (a) the conversion of the verbal complex into a nominalized form, (b) the attachment of the honorific prefix *o-/go-* to the nominalized form of the verbal complex, and (c) the predication of the subject by the verb *naru* 'become' together with the adverbial complement form of the nominalized verbal complex. This converts the sentence *Tanaka-kyoozyu ga aruk-u* (Tanaka-professor NOM walk-PRES) 'Professor Tanaka walks' into *Tanaka-kyoozyu ga o-aruk-i ni naru* (Tanaka-professor NOM HON-walk-NOMINALIZER DAT become), where the *o-aruk-ini* (HON-walk DAT) portion is the adverbial complement form of the nominalized verbal complex. Notice that this type of circumlocution is fully grammaticized in the sense that it is associated only with the honorific value, with no literal reading available. In fact, this grammaticization aspect is a basic defining characteristic of honorifics that distinguishes them from ordinary polite expressions such as English *Will you open the door for me?* and *Do you mind opening the door for me?*, which are still associated with literal meanings.

The Japanese honorific prefixes *o-/go-* also attach to adjectival predicates, yielding the third type of subject honorific form in the language; e.g., *Hanako wa utukusii* (Hanako TOP beautiful) 'Hanako is beautiful' → *Hanako-san wa o-utukusii* (Hanako-HON TOP HON-beautiful).

(Abbreviations in this section and below: NOM—*nominative*; ACC—*accusative*; HON—*honorific*; TOP—*topic*; PRES—*present*; IND—*indicative*; DAT—*dative*; HUM—*humbling*; GEN—*genitive*).

1.5 Humbling Forms

One may show deference toward a superior by humbling oneself or one's speech directed toward a superior. A fair number of languages have humbling first-person pronominals.

The ordinary Thai first-person pronoun *chan* is replaced by *phom* or by the even more humbling form *kha* '(lit.) servant' or *kha cau* '(lit.) master's servant.' Korean *na* 'I' can be replaced by the humbling form *co*. In letter writing, a Japanese male may humble himself by referring to himself by the Chinese derivative *syoo-sei* '(lit.) small person.' In fact, the Japanese epistolary style contains a whole series of honorific/humbling noun pairs adopted from Chinese; e.g., *rei-situ* '(your) honorable wife': *gu-sai* '(my) stupid wife,' *gyoku-koo* '(your) splendid article': *sek-koo* '(my) humble article.'

Less common are humbling verbal forms, which are sometimes called 'object honorifics,' because they express deference toward the referents of nonsubject nominals by humbling the actor's action directed toward them. The Japanese humbling forms include both suppletive verbal forms, e.g., *sasiageru* and *o-me ni kakaru* for *yaru* 'give' and *au* 'meet,' respectively, and a circumlocution, the latter being quite pervasive. The humbling circumlocution involves (a) the prefixation of the nominalized verbal form by the prefix *o-*, and (b) the verb *suru* 'do.' This converts the plain form *Watasi wa Tanaka-kyoozyu o tazune-ta* (I TOP Tanaka-professor ACC visit-PAST) 'I visited Professor Tanaka' into *Watasi wa Tanaka-kyoozyu o o-tazune si-ta*.

Tibetan also has a number of suppletive humbling forms of verbs; e.g., *thugs* 'meet' → *mjal*, *ster* 'give' → *phul*. *Nga pa-pha dang thugs byung* (I father.PLAIN with meet PAST) 'I met (my) father (plain)' → *Nga pa-lags dang mjal byung* (I father.HON with meet.HUM PAST) 'I met (my) father (humbling).'

Subject honorification and the humbling processes are controlled by the referents of different nominals—the former by the subject nominal and the latter by the nonsubject nominal—and thus they can be in theory combined. Indeed, such a combination appears possible in Tibetan (Kitamura 1974). As in the above example, the word *mjal* 'meet' is the humbling form expressing the speaker's deference toward the person to be met. As discussed in Sect. 1.4, *gnang* is the productive subject honorific form. The combination of the two, *mjal gnang*, thus expresses the speaker's deference to both the person who is meeting someone and the one who is met; e.g., *Pa-lags sku-mdun dang mjal gnang song* (father.HON Dalai Lama with meet.HUM HON PAST) '(My) father met Dalai Lama (humbling-subject honorific).' In the case of Modern Japanese, however, such a combination of a subject honorific form and a humbling form is generally avoided, and, when the occasion arises, simply a subject honorific form alone is used; e.g., *Tanaka-kyoozyo ga gakubu-tyoo ni o-ai ni natta* (Tanaka-professor NOM dean DAT HON-meet DAT became) 'Professor Tanaka met the dean (subject honorific).'

2. Addressee Honorifics

Addressee honorifics are those forms that show the speaker's deference toward the addressee. In the case of honorific second-person pronouns, the reference honorific function and the addressee honorific function converge, but certain languages have special addressee-oriented honorific forms.

Perhaps the most familiar is the use of *sir, ma'am,* etc. in English as in, *Yes, sir* or *Thank you, ma'am.* Many languages mark addressee honorifics by the use of particles; e.g., Tagalog *po*, Thai *kha* (female), *khrap* (male), Tamil *nka, lii.*

More elaborate systems are found in Korean and Japanese, both of which have special verbal endings. Korean attaches the suffix *-sumni* and Japanese *-mas*.

Notice that subject honorifics and addressee honorifics are again two independently parameterized systems, and therefore that one can, in principle, occur independently of the other. Thus, the Japanese subject honorific form *Tanaka-kyoozyu ga ika-re-ru* (Tanaka-professor NOM go-S.HON-PRES) 'Professor Tanaka goes' can be used by itself between two students. One can then combine the subject honorific ending *-(ra)re* (S.HON) with the addressee honorific ending -*mas* (A.HON), when the same sentence is uttered toward a respected person; *Tanaka-kyoozyu ga ika-re-mas-u* (Tanaka-professor NOM go-S.HON-A.HON-PRES). When the subject referent is not appropriate for showing the speaker's respect, only the addressee honorific form can occur as in: *Watasi ga iki-mas-u* (I NOM go-A.HON-PRES) 'I go.'

In Japanese, even further respect toward the addressee can be shown by the use of humbling verbal forms. The last sentence above can be made even politer by suppleting the verb *iku* 'go' by the humbling equivalent *mairu* as, *Watasi ga mairi-mas-u*.

3. Avoidance Languages

The use of honorific forms may be conditioned by those who are in the vicinity, especially when a respected person being talked about is within earshot. Thus, a Japanese student who normally utters a plain form such as *Sensei ga ki-ta* (teacher NOM come-PAST) 'The teacher came' might use the subject honorific form *Sensei ga ko-rare-ta* when he notices the presence of the teacher in question.

Much more regulated forms of bystander honorifics are seen among the Australian aboriginal languages. The variation of language, known as the 'mother-in-law' or 'brother-in-law' language, is used specifically in the presence of certain 'taboo' kins.

In the case of the 'mother-in-law' language of Dyirbal, a speaker must switch from the 'everyday' language, Guwal, to the 'mother-in-law' language, Dyalnguy, when a taboo relative, e.g., a parent-in-law of the opposite sex, appears within earshot. Dyalnguy is in fact part of the avoidance behavior between certain taboo relatives that was once strictly observed in Australian aboriginal societies. A son-in-law avoids speaking directly to his mother-in-law, while the mother-in-law must use Dyalnguy in speaking to her son-in-law (Dixon 1972).

In Guugu Yimidhirr society, a male ego and his mother-in-law cannot speak to each other directly, and, accordingly, the avoidance language is more like a 'brother-in-law' language, for it is used typically when one speaks to his brother-in-law or father-in-law (Haviland 1979).

The avoidance language has an honorific function as well. In Guugu Yimidhirr, the brother-in-law language is a language to be used with certain kins that must be treated with respect. It is spoken slowly in a subdued voice accompanied by a behavioral pattern of avoidance of facing the addressee directly, e.g., by sitting sideways with some distance maintained. The Guugu Yimidhirr brother-in-law language also has linguistic features of honorific languages. For example, the everyday second-person plural pronoun *yurra* is employed as a second-person singular pronoun, as in the case of Russian *vy* and French *vous*. Honorifics often neutralize semantic distinctions made in ordinary words, and so does the Guugu Yimidhirr brother-in-law language. The polite second-person pronoun *yarra* 'you' neutralizes the distinctions among the singular, the dual, and the plural forms. With various suppletive forms, certain brother-in-law expressions show a marked difference from the everyday language: e.g., *Nyundu buurraay waami?* (you water found) 'Did you find water?' (everyday) → *Yurra wabirr yudurrin* (you water found) 'Did you find water?' (brother-in-law).

Speech behavior involving avoidance languages is akin to that of honorifics languages like Javanese and Japanese in three other respects. Voice modulation is also seen in Javanese honorific speech, where 'the higher the [honorific] level one is using, the more slowly and softly one speaks' (Geertz 1968: 289). In the feudal society of Japan, inferiors were not permitted to speak to their superiors of the highest rank in close proximity to them. Emperors received courtiers behind a bamboo screen, and warlords were addressed by vassals of lower rank from some distance away. Avoidance of superiors is also manifested in the use of second-person pronouns and names. In languages like Japanese, Korean, and Dzonkha the use of second-person pronouns is avoided in addressing superiors. Japanese, for example, has a polite second-person pronominal form *anata* or even more honorified form *anata-sama*, but these can never be used in addressing a superior; the latter is marginally usable in a highly impersonal situation. Likewise, in Japanese and many other societies (e.g., traditional China, Igbo), the given names of certain superiors cannot be used in addressing by inferiors.

One of the parameters that determines the use of honorifics is the social and psychological distance between the interlocutors (see Sect. 5). The avoidance languages of Australia and similar speech behaviors in honorifics languages point out clearly this correlation, which is often reinforced by physical distance.

4. Beautification

Japanese has extended the honorific prefixes *o-/go-* to other uses where no respect for the referent, e.g., the possessor of the designated object, or for the addressee is intended. Thus, one may attach the prefixes to the nouns designating what belongs to the speaker or to no particular person; e.g., *watakusi no o-heya* (I GEN HON-room) 'my room,' *o-biiru* 'beer,' *o-nabe* 'cooking-pot.' This particular use of honorific prefixes is simply motivated by the speaker's demeanor (see Sect. 5.1) and is called *bika-go* 'beautification language' in Japanese. The form is typically used by women, and accordingly those nouns that take beautification prefixes typically designate domestic matters such as household good and foods.

Though beautification prefixes are not strictly honorifics because they beautify even those nouns designating objects belonging to the speaker, their honorific origins are not entirely obliterated. One cannot use the prefixes to those nouns designating highly personal objects belonging to oneself such as body parts. Even those who are prone to use beautification prefixes excessively would not use words such as *o-yubi* 'finger' or *o-asi* 'leg' in reference to their own fingers or legs, while they are perfectly appropriate as honorific forms used in reference to a respected professor.

5. Use of Honorifics

A more challenging aspect of the study of honorifics perhaps is the description of the actual use of honorifics in speech situations; e.g., who uses them, whom they are used in reference to, and what their functions are in communicative interaction. Since addressing these issues requires knowledge of actual speech situations in some detail, the focus here is on a single language, namely Japanese. But preliminary remarks on some general concepts are in order.

In the case of the avoidance languages of Australia (Sect. 3), their use seems to be controlled rigidly according to the tribal membership and genealogical relationships that determine for each speaker which kinsmen (e.g., mother-in-law, brother-in-law) are taboo and which are to be avoided and treated deferentially. Notice again that the notions of avoidance and of deference converge in the use of a special language. Indeed, the use of honorific speech in general is controlled by the social and psychological distance among the interactants.

5.1 Power and Solidarity

Brown and Gilman (1960), in a seminal work in this area, have identified two factors of 'power' and 'solidarity' that determine social and psychological distance relevant to the use of honorific speech. Power, as determined in each culture according to social class, age, sex, profession, etc., establishes the superior–inferior relationship that characterizes a vertical social distance—the greater the power difference is, the greater the social distance is. Solidarity, on the other hand, determines a horizontal psychological distance. Those having the same or similar attributes (e.g., power equals, members of the same family, profession, or political persuasion) are solidaristic or intimate and short in psychological distance, whereas those that do not share attributes (e.g., power unequals, strangers) are distant. Brown and Gilman have shown that these two differently defined parameters of distance are correlated with the use of pronouns in European languages (e.g., French *tu* vs. *vous*, German *du* vs. *Sie*). Since Brown and Gilman (1960), the former, plain forms are customarily referred to as 'T-forms' and the latter, honorific forms as 'V-forms' in the literature.

Power-based honorifics and solidarity-based honorifics show difference in the reciprocity of the forms used between the interactants. As in the case of German *du* used among intimates and *Sie* used between strangers, the solidarity-based honorifics are formally symmetric or reciprocal, whereas a strictly power-based system is nonsymmetric or nonreciprocal in that the inferior is obliged to use the honorific forms (the V-forms) toward the superior, who returns the plain forms (the T-forms). Brown and Gilman show that in the case of T/V variation in Europe, it was largely controlled by the power relationship until the middle of the nineteenth century, while in the twentieth century solidarity had become a dominant factor.

5.2 Power-based Honorific Pattern

Japanese honorific speech shows both power-based and solidarity-based aspects. Where superiority is fairly rigidly determined as in a business organization, where the rank and age difference are major determinants of superiority, the power-based, non-reciprocal pattern is observed; an inferior consistently uses honorifics toward a superior. A superior might thus invite his subordinate for a drink by using plain form, (a) *Konban nomi ni ikoo ka* (tonight drink to go Q) 'Shall we go drink tonight?' The subordinate must reply in the addressee honorific form as (b) *Ee, iki-masyoo* (yes go-A.HON) 'Yes, let's go,' and never reply in the plain expression (c) *Un, ikoo* 'Yeah, let's go,' which is appropriate to his inferior or equal. When the subordinate asks his superior out, the reverse pattern obtains; the subordinate cannot use (a) and must use its addressee honorific version, (d) *Konban nomi ni iki-masyoo ka* 'Shall we go drink tonight?' and his superior is most likely to reply with the plain form (c).

As far as the inferior is concerned, this pattern of exchange must be maintained even if he and his superior are quite intimate and can converse quite informally. The mutual use of plain speech between non-equals is permitted only in an unusual circumstance like during the late hours of a drinking party, when all the formalities might be done away with.

5.3 Solidarity-based Honorific Pattern

Whether or not a superior uses honorifics toward an inferior depends on a number of factors. Among them, a major factor is psychological distance or degree of intimacy. Though one occasionally witnesses the use of plain or rough speech motivated by power on the part of the superior, it is becoming increasingly rare in contemporary Japanese society to see the power-based use of plain form—a major exception being a scene of conflict or dispute between power-unequals, e.g., between an angry customer and a sales clerk. This trend is due to several factors.

Thus, when a superior uses plain forms towards his intimate subordinate, it is a mark of intimacy, whereas his use of honorific speech creates a distance and is a sign of formality. In other words, a superior's use of honorifics is solidarity-based (but see Sect. 5.4); honorifics are used (as in sentence (d) above) when a superior and his subordinate are not very intimate, while plain speech (e.g., sentence (a)) is directed toward the subordinate as a sign of solidarity, whereby the sense of camaraderie is engendered. Notice, however, that between power-unequals, only a superior has the option of using plain forms—inferiors must always use honorifics—unlike the mutual T-form exchanges in Europe. (Even in Europe, it is power superiors who can initiate the reciprocal T.)

Between power-equals, the plain/honorific variation is by and large controlled by the solidarity factor; plain forms are used among intimates to confirm camaraderie, while honorifics are used between less familiar persons and strangers as a means of keeping psychological distance, by way of which the addressee's personal integrity is honored (but see Sect. 5.4).

In the majority of contemporary Japanese households, the solidarity factor has primacy over the power factor, and thus parents and children and elder siblings and younger ones also exchange plain forms, much like the use of *du* within the contemporary German family. This is one linguistic manifestation of the Western egalitarian ideology, which was introduced to Japan in the middle of the nineteenth century and which spread throughout the country after World War II.

China has witnessed perhaps the most dramatic effect of the egalitarian ideology on honorifics. The socialist revolution in 1949 and the cultural revolution of the 1960s wiped out the traditional social classes, and with the demise of the aristocratic and the elite classes, once-flourishing honorifics too were all but obliterated.

The other manifestation of the egalitarian ideology is the use of honorifics on the part of power superiors, as described above. Even Emperor Akihito of Japan uses honorifics when he addresses an ordinary citizen. Thus, the egalitarian ideology has facilitated the growth of reciprocal solidarity-based use of honorifics in Japanese as well.

But the reciprocal speech pattern can in principle go in either direction; toward the symmetrical honorific pattern or toward the symmetrical non-honorific, plain pattern. As noted above, Chinese has taken the path to the latter. Besides the solidarity factor discussed above, there seems to be another prevailing factor at work in those languages that display the reciprocal honorific speech pattern.

5.4 Demeanor

In some Japanese families, especially between husband and wife and/or between parents and adult children, daughters in particular, nonreciprocal plain/honorific exchanges can be observed. But the motivation for such an exchange seems hardly to be power-based. Instead what underlies speech patterns observed in those families is the idea of proper language usage, which prescribes that superiors be treated deferentially through honorific speech. After all, honorifics are consciously taught and learned by the Japanese with this kind of prescriptive idea. This conscious teaching and learning of honorifics and their historical connection to the nobility has produced a situation in which appropriate honorific usage is regarded as a mark of good breeding.

The use and nonuse of honorifics as indications of class membership has the effect of making the use of honorifics part of the speaker's self-presentation effort, an aspect of what sociologist Goffman (1956, see *Goffman, Erving*) calls 'demeanor.' That is, while correct honorifics usage has the effect of paying respect to the addressee, it is at the same time a way of presenting the speaker himself as a cultivated person of good demeanor.

The demeanor aspect of honorifics usage also has the effect of producing the reciprocal honorific speech pattern, for speakers who have the prerogative of using either plain or honorific speech, as in the case of the Emperor, or power superiors in the business world, or professors in academic life, may constantly use honorifics as a way of self-presentation. An extreme manifestation of this in Japanese is the excessive use of the beautification prefixes *o-/go-* by women (Sect. 4), whereby the level of politeness is consciously elevated to an absurd level at times.

5.5 Formality

Though this article has tried to isolate and delineate those factors that determine the use and non-use of honorifics, they do not in reality occur in isolation. In an actual speech situation all these factors that control speech form are typically compounded. Take the notions of solidarity and of demeanor discussed above. When a woman shops in an elegant boutique in Ginza in downtown Tokyo, she is likely to use honorifics, as in *Motto ookii no o-ari ka sira?* (more large one HON-have Q wonder) '(I) wonder if (you) have a larger one? (honorific),' as opposed to a plain form such as *Motto ookii no aru?* (more large one have Q) '(Do you) have a larger one? (plain),' which might be used when she is shopping in a neighborhood grocery shop. Here, it is likely that both solidarity and demeanor factors are at work. In addition, the formality factor involved in the former situation cannot be ignored.

Formality overrides all the considerations discussed above and requires the use of honorifics on the part of all the concerned parties. Thus, power-equal colleagues, who normally exchange plain forms, would exchange honorifics in a formal meeting or on ceremonial occasions. Other factors contributing to the formality of the speech setting include the nature of the topic of conversation and the turns of conversation that occasion formality such as opening and closing of a new topic.

One clear instance where the formality factor alone dictates the use of honorifics is letter writing. Letter writing is a formal activity, being associated with a long history of a variety of epistolary styles, and it triggers the use of honorifics even if the letter is addressed to an intimate person. For example, a son, who usually uses plain forms to his mother, would write to his mother in the honorific style: On the telephone, he would say to his mother *Raisyuu kaeru yo* (next week return PART) '(I'll) come home next week, all right? (plain),' but he would write, *Raisyuu kaeri-masu* in the addressee honorific style.

5.6 Relativity of Social Distance

One final characteristic of Japanese honorific usage to be discussed here has to do with the relativity of the social distance of a nominal referent. The use of both subject honorifics and humbling forms is essentially determined by the social and psychological distance between the speaker and the nominal referent as described above. One would use a subject-honorific form when the subject referent is a superior or a humbling form when one's action is directed toward a superior. When this kind of pattern is absolutely maintained, regardless of the nature of the addressee, as in the case of the Korean honorific system, then a so-called absolute honorifics system exists. The Japanese honorific system differs from this in that the group identity of the addressee enters into the picture of proper honorific usage.

Japanese society makes a rather clear division between those who belong to one's social group and those who are outside. With respect to outsiders, insiders are treated as an extension of oneself. One consequence of this in regard to honorifics usage is that, with respect to outsiders, status differences among the members of a given social group are obliterated and members are identified with the status of the speaker. Accordingly, when speaking to an outsider, one would not use honorifics with respect to a member of one's social group, e.g., family members, colleagues in a business firm; humbling forms would be used instead even with respect to the superior's action. For example, a secretary would normally use honorifics with respect to her boss when she speaks to her colleagues, as (a) *Syatyoo wa soo ossyatte imasu* (company-president TOP so say.S.HON be.A.HON) 'The company president says so (subject honorofic, addressee honorific).' But when she is speaking to someone from outside her own company, she would treat her boss as if he were herself and would use humbling forms, as (b) *Syatyoo wa soo moosite orimasu* (company-president TOP so say.HUM be.HUM.A.HON) 'The company president says so (humbling, addressee honorific).'

Thus, in Japanese, with its relative honorifics system, the interpretation of honorific value is not as straightforward as in absolute honorifics languages like Korean and Tibetan, in which the (a)-type honorific form is consistently used regardless of the addressee. That is, in Japanese, the interpretation of the honorific index (see Sect. 6) must take into account not only the usual relationships among the speaker, the nominal referent, and the addressee, but also whether the addressee is an insider or outsider with respect to the speaker's social group.

6. Conclusion

Human interaction is facilitated by minimizing conflict between interactants. One of the ways in which conflict arises is by mistreating people such that they feel their personal integrity is threatened, that the expected camaraderie is not confirmed, or that the deference their social standing has earned them has not been paid. Potential conflict is therefore removed when clarification of the relationships of the involved parties is made, and when they are maintained and reinforced with attendant protocols throughout an interaction.

Human behavior, verbal or otherwise, is polite to the extent that it satisfies these requirements for facile interaction. Honorifics permit the speaker to express his relationship to the addressee and the nominal referents in a highly codified manner. They indicate a speaker's recognition of the power and personal integrity of the person spoken to or talked about, and conversely they indicate a speaker's social and psychological position in relation to the involved parties. Thus honorifics remove potential conflict and facilitate communication. It is precisely because of this function of honorifics for smooth communicative interaction that they instantiate a prototypical case of politeness phenomena of language use, and this in turn inspires a study of honorifics within the framework of general theories of linguistic politeness, a field gaining increasing attention thanks to work such as Lakoff (1975) and Brown and Levinson (1987).

Apparently all languages, regardless of the degree of elaboration in the honorifics system, have ways of making speech behavior polite. An interesting issue therefore is what difference, if any, possession of a highly elaborate honorifics system entails in the communicative function of languages. The relevant research, such as Hill et al. (1986), indicates that languages with honorifics are more strongly indexical than those languages like English that lack an elaborate honorifics system. That is, different honorific forms are used according to different types of addressee, and thus honorific forms indicate the types of interactants. Hill et al. (1986) show that American students use the same expression of *May I borrow your pen?* to fairly diversified categories of people, such as professors, strangers, physicians, and store clerks. On the other hand, Japanese students would use the super-polite form *Pen o okarisitemo yorosii desyoo ka* '(lit.) Is it all right if I humbly borrowed your pen?' specifically to their professors, while using the middle-level polite form *Pen o kasite itadake masu ka* '(lit.) Is it possible that you give me the favor of lending me your pen?' for a class or people including strangers, physicians, store clerks, etc. Clearly the Japanese students' speech form sets their professors apart from other categories of people they interact with, reflecting the distinct status that the Japanese students, unlike their American peers, accord to their professors. In other words, the most elaborate honorific expression indexes the occasion in which the most relevant power superior is involved.

This kind of indexing function of honorifics is much more clearly seen in those languages in which speech levels are more rigidly determined in relation to speech situations. A given speech level, called 'register' precisely for the reason being discussed here, in such a language indicates clearly what sort of interaction is involved. For example, Javanese has as many as ten speech levels, and each register indicates the nature of interactants (Sakiyama 1989). For example, the low, ordinary style (*Ngoko lugu*) is used when elders address younger ones or between intimate friends. The middle style (*Madyå ngoko*) is used among female itinerant merchants, among country folk, and when the nobility address their subordinates. The highest form (*Kråmå inggil*), on the other hand, is used when a superior is to be treated with special deference (see also Geertz 1968).

Honorifics, in sum, convey the social meaning as opposed to referential meaning a sentence is normally understood to express. They indicate, among other things, the social categories of the people with whom the speaker is interacting. This in turn has the effect of making the speakers of an honorifics language more attentive to those factors (e.g., age, wealth, occupation, family background) that determine the categories of people. The speaker must ascertain quickly what kind of people he is dealing with so as to choose honorific forms appropriate to his interactants. Thus the presence or absence of an elaborate honorifics system may have a rather profound effect upon how people perceive their environments and how they structure their communicative strategies.

See also: Politeness; Ethnography of Speaking.

Bibliography

Brown R, Gilman A 1960 The pronouns of power and solidarity. In: Sebeok T A (ed.) *Style in Language*. MIT Press, Cambridge, MA
Brown P, Levinson S 1987 *Politeness: Some Universals in Language Usage*. Cambridge University Press, Cambridge, UK
Comrie B 1975 Polite plurals and predicate agreement. *Language* **51**: 406–18
Dixon R M W 1972 *The Dyirbal Language of North Queensland*. Cambridge University Press, Cambridge, UK
Geertz C 1968 Linguistic etiquette. In: Fishman J (ed.) *Readings in the Sociology of Language*. Mouton, The Hague
Goffman E 1956 The nature of deference and demeanor. *American Anthropologist* **58**: 473–502
Haviland J 1979 How to talk to your brother-in-law in Guugu Yimidhirr. In: Shopen T (ed.) *Languages and Their Speakers*. Winthrop Publications, Cambridge, MA
Hill B, Ide S, Ikuta S, Kawasaki A, Ogino T 1986 Universals of linguistic politeness: Quantitative evidence from Japanese and American English. *Journal of Pragmatics* **10**: 347–71
Kitamura H 1974 Tibetto-go no keigo. In: Hayashi S, Minami F (eds.) *Sekai no keigo*. Meiji Shoin, Tokyo
Lakoff R T 1975 *Language and Woman's Place*. Harper and Row, New York
Sakiyama O 1989 Zyawa-go (Javanese). In: Kamei T, Kono R, Chino E (eds.) *The Sanseido Encyclopedia of Linguistics. Part 2: Languages of the World*. Sanseido, Tokyo

Ideology

A. Luke

The term 'ideology' refers to systems of ideas, beliefs, practices, and representations which operate in the interests of an identifiable social class or cultural group (see *Representation*; *Social Class*; *Class and Language*). Common usages generally fall into two categories: a critical definition allied with Marxist theory and a relativist definition used in liberal social theory and popular Neo-Liberal discourse (see *Marxist Theories of Language*; *Discourse*). In Marxist and Neo-Marxist social analysis, the term specifies distorted ideational and linguistic representations of economic reality and social relations that have their sources in, and disguise, political and economic functions of class domination. In liberal social sciences and in the Western popular press, the term marks out configurations of ideas, beliefs, and values ascribed to particular populaces, political formations, and subcultures. These should be taken as provisional definitions only; across the social sciences, debates are going on over what ideology is, how ideology works in the modern and postmodern state, and its connections with language and discourse. Historical and contending definitions retain currency in contemporary social theory. Yet, an examination of the complex relationship between ideology and language, tied to differing understandings of social structure and the human subject, has eluded much contemporary linguistic theory and research. The unresolved problems in such work point to the need for a rethinking of ideology in light of continuing developments in critical linguistics and discourse theory (see *Critical Sociolinguistics*; *Discourse*).

1. Ideology in Critical Social Theory

Following its initial use to describe the claims of 'ideologues' in the aftermath of the French Revolution, Marx and Engels (1970) redefined ideology as a systematic distortion in perception of social and economic relations. This definition remains central for explaining 'false consciousness,' a misrecognition of one's class position and an embrace of a particular system of ideas and understandings which serve dominant interests. It is based on the possibility of nonideological perceptions and understandings, of an emancipatory class-consciousness developed in concert with a science of historical materialism. For Marx and Engels, language is 'practical consciousness,' arising from the functional necessity of concrete social, and economic relations. This formulation of the relationships of ideology, consciousness, and language became a central feature of Marxist doctrines of language through the work of Stalin; Marr, and others.

In their critique of Formalism and nineteenth-century European linguistics, Bakhtin and Voloshinov (see *Voloshinov, Valentin Nikolavic*; *Bakhtin, Mikhail M.*) moved beyond doctrinal explanations. They too maintained that language and semiosis are imbedded in 'concrete social reality' which in turn consists of an 'ideological environment ... [of] realized, materialized, externally expressed social consciousness' (Bakhtin and Medvedev 1985: 16–17). The word is the 'ideological phenomenon par excellence' because it stands, unlike other forms of semiosis, 'wholly absorbed in its function of being a sign' (Voloshinov 1973: 13–14). Yet ideology is not a possession of mind, a corpus of illusions and abstract ideas residing in consciousness; it has a material social existence in language, text, and discourse. Accordingly, language use is not explicable by reference to a creative, autonomous speaker/writer.

Rather the subject is constrained and shaped by the available stock of situations and signs, texts and genres. These constitute cultures', communities' and individuals' discourse resources. Nor can ideology be explained in terms of a dominant, inescapable set of meanings. Because lived and experienced 'behavioral ideology' is less formally framed and constraining than institutionally 'established' ideologies, the subject retains an agency for the 'partial or radical restructuring of ideological systems' (Voloshinov 1973: 93). Within this milieu, particular texts are not univocal expressions of dominant ideologies. All texts are 'heteroglossic' expressions of other voices and texts, genres, and social contexts (Bakhtin 1981). Nonetheless, this does not prevent 'the ruling class ... [trying] to impart a supraclass, eternal character to the ideological sign' (Voloshinov 1973: 23), closing down its 'polyphonic' semantic possibilities and making it 'uniaccentual.'

Language and semiotics, seen as a complex politics of representation, thus ideologically position the language-using subject. Yet despite a recognition that 'there is no such thing as experience outside of embodiment in signs' (Voloshinov 1973: 85), for Voloshinov ideology remains contingent on a material reality outside itself. Language becomes the terrain on which 'class based struggle' for the representation of the real is waged. Language change is therefore the extension of 'differently oriented social interests within ... the same sign-community' (Voloshinov 1973: 23).

The nexus of ideology and language remains central in the social science debate over the degrees of power (see *Power and Language*) that can be assigned to social structure and human agency (Therborn 1980, Thompson 1984). In many respects, Bakhtin and Voloshinov set the terms for current work: the challenge of a comprehensive social and linguistic theory that explains how ideology constructs and positions the human subject through language, and how that subject uses language as a material means for entering into history and engaging the social world. This role of textually coded ideology in positioning and enabling the subject is taken up in structuralist semiotics. A primary ideological effect of text semiotics is to make social and historical configurations appear natural and inevitable (Barthes 1972). Textual ideologies hide themselves and their artifice, insulating themselves from recognition and critique. The key to this reconceptualization is a rigorous skepticism towards referential theories of language. Ideologies thus cannot be construed as independent ideas with freestanding referents, but indeed are constituted by the play of differences between and within systems of signification and representation. This play of different signs can effect closure of possible meanings and understandings (Eco 1976), making the text and its readings 'uniaccentual.' It is thus difficult to establish whether an utterance or text is ideological solely by reference to extant economic conditions or social relations outside of itself. Nor can a discourse-free perception of social and material reality or, for that matter, consciousness or concepts with a life of their own outside of language, texts and intertextuality be claimed.

This perspective signals a major shift in ideology critique from analysis of social structure (see *Social Class*) to text structure and discourse configuration. Yet while ideology may not be a simple reflection of a material base, it remains an articulation of the unspoken values of dominant classes (Althusser 1971). The ritual practices of ideology are lodged within what Althusser termed 'ideological apparatuses': schooling, media, church, and so forth. These institutions are the cultural sites where ideologies are transmitted to and internalized by the subject as valid knowledge, beliefs, and explanations. Although it is an expression of dominant class interests and leads to misrecognition of one's relations to the means of production, ideology is not a direct consequence of economic relations. It takes on a material existence of its own in the cultural domain. Yet, for Althusser, it remains an over-arching, controlling entity operating through institutional 'interpellation': ideology 'hails' and 'recruits' individuals into categorical status as subjects.

This model of ideological interpellation has been criticized for its downplaying of human agency and the possibilities for resistance. Hence, much Neo-Marxist theorizing has turned to broader conceptions of cultural hegemony drawn from Gramsci (1971) (see *Hegemony*; *Gramsci, Antonio*) which stress the human subject's active participation in rule by consent' through immersion in forms of cultural signification. A similar construct is found in Voloshinov's (1973: 94) specification of a 'behavioral ideology,' a 'whole aggregate of life experiences and the outward expressions directly connected with it.' This alternative position is critical of notions of ideology as a unitary, all-encompassing consciousness from which there is no escape, and it stresses the role of language in both positioning the subject and enabling contestation.

Ideological interpellation can only occur through a field of meanings. Pêcheux (1982: 187) observes: 'a meaning-effect does not pre-exist the discursive formation in which it is constituted. The production of meaning is an integral part of the interpellation of the individual as subject.' Semantics can be seen as tied to ideological configurations; ideologies have a material deployment only in institutionally located discourse. For Pêcheux, class struggle is manifest in discourses that traverse particular speech situations and texts, ordering words and meanings. Discourses in institutional sites of ideological apparatuses constrain 'what can and should be said' (Pêcheux 1982: 111), and thereby produce the subject as the object of *discourse*. Yet neither discourses nor ideologies are unitary and all-encompassing: meanings are constituted and indexed by 'interdiscourse' and thereby become the very sites of struggle between a multiplicity of contending ideologies. Nevertheless, language, discourse and thought retain in the first instance a basis in 'a given moment in the development of class struggle' (1982: 184).

Social and semiotic theory, then, has moved from the analysis of ideologies as dominant and distorting systems of ideas to a definition of ideologies as material discourse practices both shaped by and shaping of the social and economic domains. But a gap remains between macrosocial theories and microlinguistic analyses. The task of integrating concepts of ideology into linguistic theories and of developing analytic techniques for studying ideologies in everyday speech and texts has proven more elusive.

2. Ideology in Linguistic Theory and Analysis

Descriptive linguistics, various branches of sociolinguistics and the ethnography of communication have stopped short of theorizing ideology, the state, and power. Descriptive linguistics takes language as a synchronic object of study, uncontaminated by the social and political. While some significant attempts at articulating a political linguistics have been undertaken (Mey 1986), work in the sociology of language has stopped short of engaging with the foregoing concerns raised in social theory and the philosophy of language.

This limitation has its basis in theories of the sociolinguistic subject. In most models, the subject is seen as the source of speech, discourse, and text. Although situated in and influenced by social context (see *Context*), utterances and texts remain explicable in terms of individual intents and goals, which in turn are seen to reflect social norms, functions, and procedures. The absence of a normative social and political analysis precludes examination of the ideological role of discourse in the formation of the speaking subject. This location of ideology within the subject also characterizes cognitive and psycholinguistic models of text processing. Where it is taken up at all, ideology is explained in terms of cognitively organized clusters of attitudes and knowledge developed in close relation to individual and group interests. As in other contemporary information theory, text macrostructures, and mental schemata are seen as neutral ideational formations, akin to Kuhn's paradigms, that exist within social organizations without political economies.

By contrast, Halliday's theorization of language as social semiotic begins from a recognition of the relationship of social structure and language, stressing that language development and use is not subjective and psychological: 'it is not only the text (what people mean) but also the semantic system (what they can mean) that embodies the ambiguity, antagonism, imperfection, inequality and change that characterize the social system and the social structure' (Halliday 1978: 114). The insight that social function precedes linguistic form foregrounds the social, potentially ideological bases of semantics and lexicogrammatical structures. In this way, systemic linguistics offers frameworks for establishing the ideology/discourse/language relationship theorized by Pêcheux. Further, Halliday develops a dialectical model of semiotic representation and reality, an undertaking that 'social reality is shaped, constrained and modified' by social semiotics (1978: 126). But while systemic linguistics locates language codes in ideological configurations, drawing on Vygotsky (1987) to stress the sociogenesis of meaning its theory of society remains structural–functionalist, and its stress on social hierarchies, roles (see *Role Theory*), norms, and status stops short of a full theorization of state, class conflict and power.

Beginning from Halliday's critique of generative grammars, critical linguistics sets out to theorize and explicate asymmetries of power between class and gender interests in conversation and written texts (see *Power and Language*; *Gender and Language*). Kress (1989) and Fairclough (1989) take the position that all discourse is mediated by institutions which, in turn, position readers and writers, speakers and listeners in differential positions of power and knowledge. The task of critical linguistics thus becomes the unmasking of the role of ideology in everyday social and textual relations, and the analysis of the linguistic transformation of ideological positions and values into a natural and transparent common sense. Kress and Hodge (1979), for example, examine how syntax constructs conflicting versions of agency and action in social structure, focusing on the lexicogrammar of differing accounts of a strike. Particular generic and literary conventions, syntactic choices can act as ideological devices, 'positioning' readings and controlling interpretations (Kress 1989).

In critical linguistic studies, analyses of classroom and interview transcripts, for instance, are used to trace asymmetrical speech acts and situations (see also Habermas 1984) and the unequal educational distribution of linguistic competence as cultural capital (see also Bourdieu and Passeron 1977) (see *Symbolic Power and Language*).

Fairclough (1989) recognizes that ideology is constituted through discourse and, moreover, that discourse is dialogical, produced by and producing the social relations of addressers and addressees. However, in many critical linguistic analyses, ideology remains conceptualized as a set of ideas which serve class interests (see *Class and Language*; *Power and Language*). For example, Kress and Hodge's (1979) analysis of strike reportage presupposes a systematic distortion of a social reality outside text and discourse *per se* (i.e., there is an authentic, reportable version of the forces and power at work in the strike). Hence, while critical linguistics takes up Foucault's notions of discourse as technology for moral and political regulation (Chouliaraki and Fairclough 1999), its claim that some discourses and texts can be nonideological, nonsexist, and indeed emancipatory, again suggests an ideology/discourse/social reality differentiation. Yet the normative and linguistic grounds for distinguishing ideological from emancipatory texts and conversational exchanges remain unexplicated.

3. Ideology, Discourse, Power

The relationships between ideology, language, and discourse are being explored as key areas of social theory and linguistic inquiry. A central problem facing social theory and analysis is the impossibility of pursuing ideology as an entity in and of itself, independent of and preceding the sites and formations of discourse (Foucault 1980). For its part, linguistic analysis requires an expanded theorization of social structure and conflict, and unequal power and knowledge relationships. The task of connecting ideology with language, of joining macrosocial theory with close textual analysis of spoken and written texts may require new hybrids of linguistics, critical sociology, feminist, and discourse theory. But such efforts should be tempered with Voloshinov's and Pêcheux's insight that linguistic theorizing itself is not outside ideology. It too constitutes a discourse which may represent and work in the service of particular dominant interests.

A further consideration for the study of ideology and language is the emergence of globalized service and information-based economies which rely extensively on language, discourse, and information as commodities for exchange. This move from industrial modes of production to multinational 'modes of information' (Poster 1990) underlines the difficulties facing Marxist analyses that proceed from a separation of economic base and cultural superstructure (Williams 1977), with language and discourse seen to reside in the latter (see *Marxist Theories of Language*). A social and linguistic theory of ideology is incomplete without attention to changing economic and political control over the actual media of textual representation. One recourse is to reconceptualize language as labor, subject to economic and cultural orders governing its production (Rossi-Landi 1975), and to focus on language and discourse as 'cultural capital,' with a constitutive role in the cross-generational reproduction of power and status, class and gender (Bourdieu and Passeron 1977). Future work can begin from the redefinition of ideologies as plural practices which are effects both of discourse and of extradiscursive material conditions. Current work focuses on how language as a principal form and cultural capital is made to count. Such a theorization is also helpful within political theory for analyzing the efficacy of discourses as forms of political critique and strategy, and within feminist theory for analyzing the role of ideology in patriarchal discourse.

If indeed ideology is always constituted within and deployed through discourse, then the strategic power and knowledge relationships between institutions, social movements and collectivities, and among discourse-based ideologies bear further scrutiny by critical linguistics. In large part, the task has remained unchanged since Bakhtin and Voloshinov's work: the development of discourse analysis as a form of ideology critique which attends to larger matters of social structure and retains explanatory power in the analysis of everyday texts and utterances.

See also: Discourse; Hegemony; Sociology of Language; Critical Sociolinguistics; Marxist Theories of Language; Context; Symbolic Power and Language.

Bibliography

Althusser L 1971 *Lenin and Philosophy and Other Essays*. Brewster B (transl.). New Left Books, London
Bakhtin M M 1981 *The Dialogic Imagination*. Emerson C. Holquist M (transl.). University of Texas Press, Austin, TX
Bakhtin M M, Medvedev P N 1985 *The Formal Method in Literary Scholarship*. Wehrle A J (transl.). Harvard University Press, Cambridge, MA
Barthes R 1972 *Mythologies*. Lavers A (transl.). Jonathan Cape, London
Bourdieu P, Passeron J C 1977 *Reproduction in Education, Society and Culture*. Nice R (transl.) Sage, London
Chouliaraki L, Fairclough N 1999 *Discourse in Late Modernity*. Edinburgh University Press, Edinburgh, UK
Eco U 1976 *A Theory of Semiotics*. Indiana University Press, Bloomington, IN
Fairclough N 1989 *Language and Power*. Longman, London
Foucault M 1980 *Power/Knowledge*. Gordon C (ed.) Pantheon, New York
Gramsci A 1971 *Selections from the Prison Notebooks*. Hoare Q, Nowell-Smith G (transl.). Lawrence and Wishart, London
Habermas J 1984 *Theory of Communicative Action*. McCarthy T (transl.). Heinemann, London
Halliday M A K 1978 *Language as Social Semiotic*. Edward Arnold, London
Kress G 1989 *Linguistic Processes in Sociocultural Practice*. Oxford University Press, Oxford, UK
Kress G, Hodge R 1979 *Language as Ideology*. Routledge and Kegan Paul, London
Marx K, Engels F 1970 *The German Ideology*. Lawrence and Wishart, London
Mey J L 1986 *Whose Language?* Benjamins, Amsterdam
Pêcheux M 1982 *Language, Semantics and Ideology*. Nagpal H (transl.). Macmillan, London
Poster M 1990 *The Mode of Information: Poststructuralism and Social Context*. Polity Press, Cambridge, UK
Rossi-Landi F 1975 *Linguistics and Economics*. Mouton, The Hague
Therborn G 1980 *The Ideology of Power and the Power of Ideology*. New Left Books, London
Thompson J B 1984 *Studies in the Theory of Ideology*. Polity Press, Cambridge, UK
Voloshinov V I 1973 *Marxism and the Philosophy of Language*. Matejka L, Titunik I R (transl.). Seminar Press, New York
Vygotsky L 1987 *Thinking and Speech*. Plenum, New York
Williams R 1977 *Marxism and Literature*. Oxford University Press, Oxford, UK

Language Conflict

D. P. Pattanayak

Language conflict is as much a feature of dominant monolingual countries as of multilingual countries and is related to language use. Choice of a dialect, a language, medium of instruction, medium of communication, medium of administration may be so manipulated as to result in conflict. From another perspective conflict may arise because of linking and delinking of identities, ethnicities, attitudes and use, disuse, and misuse of language in different domains.

1. Language Conviviality versus Language Conflict

Language signals conviviality as well as conflict. It is the seam where human communities communicate and cooperate; it is where they separate and differentiate. It is the basis of family cohesiveness, society formation, as well as of national integration. When, in order to escape from insoluble conflict or irreconcilable contradictions, people abandon the meaning structure of their culture, new group formation results. A nation may disintegrate if competing loci of standard try to establish exclusive identities.

Language provides identity to a group. Maintenance of border is one of the mainstays of linguistic identities. However, language borders are often fuzzy. In a multilingual situation the languages merge their identities and subsume the smaller identities under a macro label without losing the smaller ones. Thus, Attic, Doric, and Ionic which were at one time in complementary use were known as Greek; in India Bhojpuri, Maithili, Magahi, Braj, Avadhi, Rajasthani, Pahari, etc., are known as Hindi. Languages sometimes split, accepting new identities and rejecting overarching identities in a process of differentiation. Venetian trying to establish its identity distinct from Italian, Konkani rejecting the overarching suzerainty of Marathi and forming a new State in the Indian Union are examples of these.

2. Conflict in Socialization

Socialization processes differ in different cultures, but the academic tendency to generalize often results in tension. Murray, after generalizing the Western experience, contends that the nuclear family provides greater coping ability for children to meet the contingencies of modern life. In Asia, Africa, and Latin America, the results of socialization in extended family structures are completely ignored by the above statement. In a monolingual country, in the process of enculturation, conflict in family roles caused by defective or distorted communication may result in permanent deformation of the personality of the child. Socialization in the home dialects as well as the standard are possibilities. In a multilingual environment a child may grow up with as many as six mother tongues. An Oriya man married to a Tamil woman speaking English at home, living in the Bengali environment of Calcutta and the children growing up with an Hindustani ayah and a Nepali security man has the initial socialization in six languages. As in monolingual situations dialects are used for complementary purposes, in a multilingual situation different languages are used in different domains and situations. In such situations languages are not adversaries, though because of later attitudinal developments conflicts may ensue.

3. Language Conflict

Language conflict results from the assertion of one variety of a language or of one language among many. Variation is the nature of living organisms. Language is no exception to this. Many varieties of a language in a dominant monolingual situation and many languages in a multilingual situation coexist where varieties are used in defined domains and for specific purposes. When one of them aspires to be the sole medium of expression or the sole conduit for attainment of rank, status, and wealth in society, conflict may result.

While the instrumental role of language and social mobility may cause conflict, the integrative role may also result in conflict. Conflict resolution mechanisms in different parts of the world give better insight into language conflicts. The melting-pot theory in the USA predicted that different identities would be melted and fused to form an American identity. After 200 years of experimentation, it was found that the pot was melted, not the identities. A new theory, the salad-bowl theory, was then suggested. As in a salad bowl different entities retain their individual identity, similarly within a nation state different languages retain their identities. However, the metaphor of an edible dish speaks eloquently of the approach towards different languages. Joining the mainstream is the euphemism that the majority languages use for assimilation. They expect that all minor and minority languages would lose their identity and be assimilated to the majority language. That after 200 years English is declared as the official language of the USA under the Hayakawa Amendment makes explicit the majority expectations.

In Paraguay, Spanish, spoken by 5 percent or fewer of the population, was inflicted on the remaining 95 percent Guaraní speakers. A similar situation exists in the Jammu and Kashmir State of India where the minority language Urdu is the State language though the majority speak Kashmiri. Where majority languages are suppressed and minority languages act as colonial languages, there is bound to be conflict. English with its colonial heritage in the non–english speaking world comes into conflict with majority languages as it seeks to usurp their function.

3.1 Conflict of Dialects

A good example of conflict of dialects is that between Black and White dialects of English. White American English is so much publicized as the standard that universities in the Middle East which have arrangements with American universities for educational cooperation refuse to accept American Black or Brown speakers of English as teachers. In the UK, there is a three-way conflict between the Jamaican Creole, the late-twentieth-century Black variety of English, and Standard English. In India, Hindi was known by different names in different periods of history. In the late twentieth century speech varieties like Bhojpuri, Maithili, Rajasthani, and Pahari are staking their claim as different languages in a spirit of identity assertion. Language loyalty made speakers of different varieties choose a single literary idiom for reading and public interaction. The same language loyalty when politicized to mobilize groups for ensuring closer political participation for the minorities results in language conflict. The socioeconomic competition among these groups spurs them into developing newer standards. Though Serbian and Croatian in the former Yugoslavia, and Hindi and Urdu in India, are two styles of one and the same language, they are perceived in each case as two different languages and conflict between the two communities has, in the case of the former Yugoslavia, resulted in war and political instability.

3.2 Conflict of Scripts

Writing dates back to about 5000 years in human history. With variations in writing systems and greater variation in spoken words there is no wonder that there would be conflict as to which writing system should receive primacy over others. Thus it has remained a moot point as to whether new scripts should be invented for unwritten languages or they should be written using one of the existing writing systems. In India, the Sanskrit language continued to act as the cultural standard as it was permitted to be written in different scripts of the land. Sometimes the independent status of languages depends on the separation of scripts. Panjabi written in the Gurumukhi script and Urdu written using the Perso-Arabic script owe their identity to these scripts. Were they written in Devanagari, the fear is that they would lose their identity.

One of the extreme forms of script reform is the replacement of one script by another. The replacement of the Arabic script of Turkish by Roman was at one time considered as a great act of social reform. The romanization of Chinese does not have the same credibility. Chinese script is the unifying force among the different Chinese dialects. In the romanized form it is bound to lose the cohesive force which binds different dialects together and consequently it would be the first step towards conflict among the contending varieties. The revival of Hebrew with the Talmudic script is one of the newest wonders of the world. In a rare act of expression of identity a dead language as well as a dead script has been revived.

In India, there is evidence of one language being written using different scripts and at the same time there is evidence of one script being used for writing many languages. While in the case of Hindi and Marathi, Nagari script is the medium and is so accepted without serious political objections, in the case of Bengali, Assamese, and Manipuri using the Bengali script, there is a good deal of political objection against the Bengali script. Although the scripts employed for writing Kannada and Telugu differ only in diacritical marks on a few letters and this constitute a single script, they are treated as two scripts as are the Bengali and Assamese scripts which, too, differ only in a few letters.

In India, the two important conflicts regarding scripts are the Bodo and the Santhali scripts. The Bodo language in Assam, which was earlier written in the Assamese script, rejected the script in favor of the Roman alphabet as a mark of distinct identity. Confronted with the drawbacks of Roman alphabet, the Bodo speakers finally chose the Nagari script for their language. Santhali, spread over many linguistic states, was written using Oriya, Bengali, Nagari, and Roman scripts. One of the Santhali elites devised a script, Ol Chikki, which became the fifth contending script and began displacing all the others. Both the script movements are connected with political movements for separate statehoods, in one case Bodoland and on the other Jharkhand. Script movements in both cases are symptoms of a deeper malady of socio-economic exploitation of the concerned groups.

3.3 Conflict of Styles

Choice of a style sometimes leads to conflict. In the controversy whether Hindi should have a Sanskritized or Persianized style, Gandhi had suggested a mixed style, Hindustani, which was not acceptable to the Hindi elite. As a result, Hindi and Urdu remained in a permanent state of confrontation. While the use of a high Sanskritized style makes Hindi accessible to the regional educated elite, it results in a growing chasm between the elite and the masses. In Telugu until the late 1980s books were written in Granthika style which was nobody's spoken language. Due to social pressure it has to be replaced by Sista Vyavaharika style.

3.4 Conflict in Standardization

Whether it is corpus planning or status planning, language standardization is prone to conflict. The quantum and sources of borrowing, creation of neologisms, the manner and nature of enrichment, all of these may lead to controversies. Which language variety or style should be given prominence in the production of reading material, which dialect should be accepted as the basis for the standard are issues which spark controversies. Shifting standard can be seen between the non-acceptance and acceptance of the split infinitive by the BBC as well as shift from Poona Marathi to Bombay Marathi. There is divergence between the spoken and written standards of a language. Effecting cohesion and coherence between the two sometimes may appear insurmountable. The difference between spoken and written Arabic is as much as between two different languages. However, as one is used for scriptural purposes and purposes of writing documents and the other in other domains, they are complementary and not conflicting. Status planning of languages generates conflict because of conflicting goals, ideologies and evaluative criteria. Standardization lends status to a language. Therefore controversy and conflict generated by standardization assume greater proportions in the study of planning for languages.

4. Conflict of Attitudes

There are approximately 3000–5000 languages in the world. Whether it is for diplomacy or exploration, for commerce or for exploitation, friendship and interdependence, people speaking all these languages must communicate to collaborate. In this process of communication, however, different attitudes color perceptions. With the development of dominant monolingualism as the point of departure in the West, multilingualism was associated with under development, poverty, malnutrition, and diseases. With the development of nation states around unitary symbols in the West many mother tongues were seen as a threat to the nation state. Western elitism had reached such heights that in thirteenth-century England, the English language was forbidden in the schools where French, the language of the normal elite, and Latin, the classical language, reigned supreme. Elitism had assumed such proportions that mother tongue, community language, ethnic language, and even dialect assumed pejorative import and became labels for minor and minority languages.

The attitudes of loyalty and the attitude of pride may cause conflict. Loyalty can be instrumental in bringing about cohesion as well as disaffection and disintegration. Similarly, the recognition of pride of others might result in respect for the different, or the assertion of the superiority of pride might condemn the different as deficient.

In a stratified pluralist society diverse attitudes to a single phenomenon are to be seen at any one time. In a situation where language distance is measured, the attitude of the dominant language speakers to the speakers of languages having subordinate status is one of indifference, avoidance and disparagement. In situations where interdependencies are charted the attitude is one of conviviality. The attitude of indifference can be studied in five parameters:
 (a) condescension—the minority language speakers are treated as children;
 (b) foreign talk—the distance and superiority of speakers is sunk in others through slow and loud talk;
 (c) terminologies—deficient and non-ambitious use mark the relative lowliness of the other language;
 (d) distinct accents—carefully cultivated distinct accents mark the superiority of the dominant language speakers;
 (e) pretense of identification—occasional use of lexical or suprasegmental features of the minority language heightens the distance.

The attitude of avoidance similarly can be studied under five parameters:
 (a) the direct characteristics are emphasized to distinguish oneself;
 (b) specific phonological characteristics are deleted or added;
 (c) high powered abstractions, professional jargon and technical terminology are added;
 (d) 'you people' as distinguished from 'I/we' is used;
 (e) pretence of non-understanding, signal avoidance.

The attitude of disparagement can also be studied in terms of five parameters:
 (a) use of derogatory terms and epithets towards 'other' languages;
 (b) use of ethnic jokes and humor while referring to 'other' languages;
 (c) use of hyberbolic descriptions and even four-letter rhetoric about 'other' languages;
 (d) use of one's own language with complete disregard to its impact on the situation;
 (e) imitation (parody) of the 'other' language to signal disparagement.

All the above three attitudes reflect the intent of the speaker, who is convinced of the richness and superiority of his or her language over others. They also reflect his or her uneasiness with many languages.

5. Conflict of Language(s) of Wider Communication with the Local as well as National Languages

The conflict between the language of wider communication and national language on the one hand, and local languages on the other, has been viewed variously by scholars. According to Fishman, language of wider communication leads to the development of nationism whereas a national language leads to the development of nationalism. Whether the language of wider communication (LWC) is perceived as neutral and equally inconvenient to all the encompassing languages or a unifying force which stops competition among contending languages to be dominant, the fact remains that there are elements inherent in the context of its use which could be manipulated to generate conflict. Whether it is Kiswahili in Africa or Nagamese and Sadri in India being LWCs among mutually unintelligible divergent languages, they by and large serve the interest of the elites. Local elites created in the process come into conflict with the masses of the population speaking different languages as well as with those who use dominant national languages. The absorption of the LWC in the national language depends on the density of communication between the two and the assumption of LWC functions by the national language.

5.1 Conflict Arising from Use, Disuse and Misuse of Languages in Different Domains

Sindhi is one of the Indian languages for the maintenance of which there is considerable political demand, but in reality Sindhi parents prefer Hindi-medium education for their children. Use and disuse of language can thus be a major source of conflict. In Wales, the Welsh identity assertion movement is a protest against Anglicization. In Quebec, the French–English controversy is well known for its acrimony. The misuse of a language by way of its imposition over another is the cause of conflict. In Karnataka in India, where 64 percent of the population speak Kannada as a mother tongue, Kannada was declared the first language of every child in the State. Thanks to the resistance of the minority, this declaration has been stayed. The conflict is the result of the misuse of the majority right of the Kannada language.

6. Conclusion

Language is a symbol as well as an instrument. It is a repository of power. An expression of identity as well as associate of ethnicity it is a source of conflict. Language differences reflect social tensions. When these tensions are socially or politically manipulated, conflict ensues. Intra-group convergences and inter-group distances give rise to conflicting situations. Integration can be through structural incorporation of differences rather than through assimilation. Conflicting situations can be resolved by compromise.

See also: Power Differentials and Language; Minority Languages.

Bibliography

Ammon U (ed.) 1989 *Status and Function of Languages and Language Varieties*. Mouton de Gruyter, Berlin
Das Gupta J 1970 *Language Conflict and National Development*. University of California Press, Berkeley, CA
Dua H R 1985 *Language Planning in India*. Harnam Publications, New Delhi, India
Fishman J A 1968 Nationality–nationalism and nation–nationism. In: Fishman J A, Ferguson A, Das Gupta J (eds.) *Language Problems of Developing Nations*. Wiley, New York
Fishman J 1969 National languages and languages of wider communication. *Anthropological Linguistics* **11**: 111–35
Gumperz J J 1971 Language in social groups. In: Dil A S (ed.) *Essays by John J Gumperz*. Stanford University Press, Stanford, CA
Inglehart R, Woodward M 1967 Language conflicts and the political community. In: Giglioli P P (ed.) *Language and Social Context*. Penguin, Harmondsworth, UK
Kachru B B 1986 The power and politics of English. *World Englishes* **5**(2/3): 121–40
Kelman R C 1971 Language as an aid and barrier to involvement in the national system. In: Rubin J, Jernudd B H (eds.) *Can Language be Planned?* East–West Center, University Press of Hawaii, Honolulu, HI
Laitin D D 1987 Linguistic conflict in Catalonia. *Language Problems and Language Planning* **11**(2): 129–47
Lidz T 1964 *The Family and Human Adaptation*. Hogarth, London
Neustupny J 1968 Some general aspects of 'language' problems and 'language' policy in developing countries. In: Fishman J A, Ferguson C A, Das Gupta J (eds.) *Language Problems of Developing Nations*. Wiley, New York
Pandit P B 1978 Language and identity: The Panjabi language in Delhi. *International Journal of the Sociology of Language* **16**: 93–108
Pattanayak D P 1981 *Multilingualism and Mother Tongue Education*. Oxford University Press, Delhi, India
Pattanayak D P 1985 Writing: Some reflections. *CALTIS*
Pattanayak D P 1986 On being and becoming bilingual in India. In: Fishman J A, et al. (eds.) *The Fergusonian Impact*, vol. 2. Mouton de Gruyter, Berlin
Pattanayak D P 1990 Language and ethnic issues. Paper presented at IPRA Seminar, Chandigarh, India
Pool J 1972 National development and language diversity. In: Fishman J A (ed.) *Advances in the Sociology of Language*, vol. 2. Mouton, The Hague
Skutnabb-Kangas T 1986 Who wants to change what and why?—Conflicting paradigms in minority education research. In: Spolsky B (ed.) *Language and Education in Multilingual Settings*. Multilingual Matters, Clevedon, UK
Skutnabb-Kangas T, Phillipson R 1986 The legitimacy of the arguments for the spread of English. Paper presented at Post Congress Session on Ethnocentrism in Sociolinguistics, CIIL, Mysore, India
Sonntag S, Pool J 1987 Linguistic denial and linguistic self denial: American ideologies of language. *Language Problems and Language Planning* **11**(1): 46–65
Weinreich U 1963 *Languages in Contact*, 2nd edn. Mouton, The Hague
Weinstein B 1986 Language planning and interests. In: *Proceedings of the International Colloquium on Language Planning*. Les Presses de L'Université Laval, Quebec, PQ

Linguicide

T. Skutnabb-Kangas and R. Phillipson

1. Definition

A taxonomy of policies, which a state can adopt towards minority languages (Cobarrubias 1983: 71) distinguishes between the following:
 (a) attempting to obliterate a language;
 (b) letting a language die;
 (c) unsupported coexistence;
 (d) partial support of specific language functions;
 (e) adoption as an official language.

The first policy is overtly linguicidal, the second and third may be covertly linguicidal. Linguicidal policies have at times been overt, for instance US policy in

Pacific islands such as Guam in the early twentieth century (Kloss 1977). Calvet (1974) describes French colonial overtly linguicidal policy as *glottophagie* ('linguistic cannibalism'), dominant languages replacing and extinguishing dominated languages and as *la guerre des langues*, ('linguistic warfare') in 1987. The latter title seems less a metaphor and more the reality of the politics of language and relations between languages (see Mateene 1985, Phillipson 1992, for further analyses).

Linguicide or linguistic genocide is the extermination of languages, an analogous concept to physical genocide, whereas language death is the withering away of languages, by analogy with natural death (see *Language Maintenance, Shift, and Death*). Linguicide, by contrast, implies that there is an agent involved in causing the death of languages. The agent can be active ('attempting to obliterate a language') or passive ('letting a language die,' or 'unsupported coexistence'), also often leading to the death of minority languages. In liberal ideology, only an active agent with the intention to kill languages would cause linguicide, whereas the other two would fall within the domain of language death. Linguicide is the extreme end result of linguicism (linguistically argued racism) at group level. Seen from the perspective of a conflict paradigm, the causes of linguicide and linguicism (see *Linguistic Imperialism*; *Discrimination and Minority Languages*) have to be analyzed from both structural and ideological angles, covering the struggle for structural power and material resources, and the legitimization, effectuation, and reproduction of the unequal division of power and resources between groups based on language. The agents of linguicide/linguicism can also be structural (a state, e.g., Turkey vis-à-vis Kurds; an institution, e.g., schools; laws and regulations—e.g., those covering linguistic rights or the position of different languages on time-tables in schools; budgets—e.g., for teacher training or materials in certain languages) or ideological (norms and values ascribed to different languages and their speakers). There is thus nothing 'natural' in language death. Languages cannot be treated in an anthropomorphic way, as organisms with a natural life span. Language death has causes, which can be identified and analyzed.

When the United Nations did preparatory work for what was to become the *International Convention for the Prevention and Punishment of the Crime of Genocide* (E 793, 1948), linguistic and cultural genocide were discussed alongside physical genocide, and were seen as serious crimes against humanity. When the Convention was accepted, Article 3, which covered linguistic and cultural genocide, was voted down and is thus not included in the final Convention of 1948 (see Capotorti 1979: 37). What remains, however, is a definition of linguistic genocide (in Art. 3, 1) as: prohibiting the use of the language of the group in daily intercourse or in schools, or the printing and circulation of publications in the language of the group.

But the present Convention has two definitions of genocide which describe most indigenous and minority education in the world:

Article II(e), 'forcibly transferring children of the group to another group'; and

Article II(b), 'causing serious bodily *or mental* harm to members of the group' (emphasis added).

2. Language Loss

First language attrition and loss have been described fairly extensively in research literature and fiction. Kouritzin (1999) describes many cases in Canada where immigrant minority children have lost a language within one generation so that they as adults, for instance, are no longer able to speak to their parents in that language. Wong Fillmore (1991) has described the consequences for families in the USA. Mühlhäusler (1996) discusses results of linguistic imperialism in the Pacific. Janulf (1998) shows in her longitudinal study that of those Finnish immigrant minority members in Sweden who had Swedish-medium education, not one spoke any Finnish to their own children. Even if they themselves might not have forgotten their Finnish completely, their children were certainly forcibly transferred to the majority group, at least linguistically. This happens to millions of speakers of threatened languages all over the world. For hearing minority students, education through the medium of a dominant majority language often leads to the students using the dominant language with their own children later on. Over a generation or two the children are linguistically and often also culturally assimilated, forcibly transferred to a dominant group. Since there are no alternatives in formal education (i.e., schools or classes that teach mainly through the medium of the threatened indigenous or minority languages), the transfer happens by force. For it to be voluntary, alternatives should exist, and parents would need to have enough reliable information about the long-term consequences of the various choices. None of these conditions are usually fulfilled for indigenous or minority parents and children, i.e., the situations where children lose their first language, can often be characterized as genocide.

Since most deaf children are born to hearing parents, parents and children do not have the same mother tongue by origin, and many of the deaf children will in their turn have hearing children. Deaf children of hearing parents are in many countries still taught through oral methods, i.e., taught lip-reading and speaking in a dominant majority language, to the exclusion of a sign language. They are not learning their 'own' language, a sign language, which is for all deaf children the only type of language through which they can express themselves fully, i.e., it is their mother tongue by competence. Thus both hearing indigenous and minority children and deaf children, taught predominantly through the medium of a dominant oral majority language, are undergoing linguistic genocide: both groups of children are forcibly transferred from their 'own' language group to dominant majority language group (see *Sociolinguistics of Sign Language*).

Some countries commit linguistic genocide openly and brutally, and Turkey is the most blatant example in the contemporary world (see Skutnabb-Kangas and Bucak 1994): imprisonment, torture, and killing of thousands of people, in addition to threats, hefty fines and confiscation of Kurdish books, journals, and property. But linguistic genocide is today mostly committed in more covert and sophisticated ways, e.g., in educational systems. Here the use of a minority language is prohibited more indirectly, by ideological and structural means. The use of a minority language is in fact prohibited 'in daily intercourse or in schools' every time there are minority children in daycare centers and schools, but no bilingual caretakers and teachers who are authorized to use the languages of the minority children as the main languages of teaching and learning in child care, and at least primary education. This is the situation for most immigrant and refugee minority children in all Western European countries and in the US, Canada, and Australia. Immigrant minority education in these countries is thus the main cause of linguistic genocide, as defined by the UN. So is the education offered to most indigenous first nations, and to numerically large but politically dominated groups in most African and many Asian countries (see Skutnabb-Kangas 2000 and Brock-Utne 1999 for Africa). Dominant or majority languages expand at the expense of dominated (or minorized) languages when minority language speakers are forced to learn dominant languages in a *subtractive* way (instead/at the cost of their own languages), where it would be perfectly possible to learn them in an *additive* way, adding competence in dominant languages to maintenance and further development of their own languages (see *Bilingualism, Societal*).

Linguists estimate that up to 90 percent of today's oral languages (and most sign languages) may not exist in the year 2100 (Krauss 1992). Binding linguistic human rights are urgently needed to prevent linguicide. The UN, UNESCO, ILO (International Labor Organization), OSCE (Organisation for Security and Cooperation in Europe), OAU, Council of Europe, etc. have been concerned about the 'endangered languages' of indigenous peoples and linguistic minorities, but existing international, regional and national protection and support are clearly completely inadequate. Several book-length presentations of language rights have appeared in tandem with the increasing salience of language issues and ethnicity in many post-communist and post-colonial trouble spots. (Only a few are cited here: e.g., Benson et al. 1998, Guillorel and Koubi 1999, Kibbee 1998, Kontra et al. 1999, Phillipson 2000, Skutnabb-Kangas 2000). Subtractive learning of dominant languages turns these into killer languages, whereas additive learning would support the maintenance of linguistic diversity. Widespread linguicide and language death are fatal for linguistic diversity and, through that, also to biodiversity on earth (Harmon in press, Maffi 2001, Maffi et al. 1999). Through linguicide, we are also in the long run seriously undermining the prerequisites for life on the planet.

See also: Endangered Languages; Teaching Endangered Languages; Linguistic Imperialism.

Bibliography

Benson P, Grundy P, Skutnabb-Kangas T (eds.) 1998 Language rights. Special issue, *Language Sciences* **20**: 1
Brock-Utne B 1999 *Whose Education for All? Recolonizing the African Mind?* Garland, New York
Calvet L-J 1974 *Linguistique et colonialisme: petit trait de glottophagie*. Payot, Paris
Calvet L-J 1987 *La guerre des languages et les politiques linguistiques*. Payot, Paris
Capotorti F 1979 *Study of the Rights of Persons Belonging to Ethnic, Religious and Linguistic Minorities*. United Nations, New York
Cobarrubias J 1983 Ethical issues in status planning. In: Cobarrubias J, Fishman J (eds.) *Progress in Language Planning: International Perspectives*. Mouton, Berlin
Guillorel H, Koubi G (eds.) 1999 *Langues et Droits. Langues du Droit, Droit des Langues*. Bruylant, Brussels
Harmon D in press *In Light of Our Differences: How Diversity in Nature and Culture Makes Us Human*
Janulf, P 1998 *Kommer finskan i Sverige att fortleva? En studie av språkkunskaper och språkanvändning hos andragenerationens sverifinnar i Botkyrka och hos finlandssvenskar i Åbo,* (Will Finnish survive in Sweden? A study of language skills and language use among second generation Sweden Finns in Botkyrka, Sweden, and Finland Swedes in Turku, Finland). *Acta Universitatis Stockholmiensis, Studia Fennica Stockholmiensia 7*, Almqvist and Wiksell, Stockholm
Kibbee D A (ed.) 1998 *Language Legislation and Linguistic Rights*. Benjamins, Amsterdam
Kloss H 1977 *The American Bilingual Tradition*. Newbury House, Rowley
Kontra M, Phillipson R, Skutnabb-Kangas T, Várady T (eds.) 1999 *Language: A Right and a Resource. Approaching Linguistic Human Rights*. Central European University Press, Budapest
Kouritzin S 1999 *Face[t]s of First Language Loss*. Lawrence Erlbaum, Mahwah, NJ
Krauss M 1992 The world's languages in crisis. *Language* **68**: 4–10

Maffi L, Skutnabb-Kangas T, Andrianarivo J 1999 Language diversity. In: Posey D (ed.) *Cultural and Spiritual Values of Biodiversity. A Complementary Contribution to the Global Biodiversity Assessment.* Intermediate Technology Publications, London

Maffi L (ed.) 2001 *On Biocultural Diversity. Linking Language, Knowledge and the Environment.* The Smithsonian Institute, Washington, DC

Mateene K 1985 Colonial languages as compulsory means of domination, and indigenous languages, as necessary factors of national liberation and development. In: Mateene K, Kalema J, Chomba B (eds.) *Linguistic Liberation and Unity of Africa.* OAU Inter-African Bureau of Languages, Kampala, Uganda

Mühlhäusler P 1996 *Linguistic Ecology. Language Change and Linguistic Imperialism in the Pacific Region.* Routledge, London

Phillipson R 1992 *Linguistic Imperialism.* Oxford University Press, Oxford, UK

Phillipson R (ed.) 2000 *Rights to Language. Equity, Power and Education.* Lawrence Erlbaum, Mahwah, NJ

Skutnabb-Kangas T 2000 *Linguistic Genocide in Education—or Worldwide Diversity and Human Rights?* Lawrence Erlbaum, Mahwah, NJ

Skutnabb-Kangas T, Bucak S 1994 Killing a mother tongue—how the Kurds are deprived of linguistic human rights. In: Skutnabb-Kangas T, Phillipson R (eds.), in collaboration with Rannut M *Linguistic Human Rights. Inequality or Justice in Language Policy.* Contributions to the Sociology of Language 67. Mouton de Gruyter, Berlin

Wong Fillmore L 1991 When learning a second language means losing the first. *Early Childhood Research Quarterly* **6**: 323–46

Linguistic Imperialism

R. Phillipson and T. Skutnabb-Kangas

The study of linguistic imperialism focuses on how and why certain languages dominate internationally (become 'world languages'), and attempts to account for such dominance in an explicit, theoretically founded way. The same type of processes can also be at work internally in a country, making some languages dominate over others.

In recent centuries the languages of European settlers and colonists have been taken to all continents, and many of them have remained there. Language is one of the most durable legacies of the age of imperial expansion. Thus in Africa the languages of the colonizing powers (France, UK, The Netherlands, and Portugal) were more firmly entrenched in the late twentieth century than they were in the colonial period; on the Indian subcontinent, English is still the language of power. Spanish and Portuguese are the dominant languages of Latin America.

Such facts about the contemporary world raise many questions that the study of linguistic imperialism can help clarify. Has the winning of political independence led to a linguistic liberation in Third World, underdeveloped (Rodney 1972) countries, and if not, why not? Are the former colonial languages a useful bond with the international community and necessary for state formation and national unity internally? Or are they a bridgehead for Western interests, permitting the continuation of a global system of marginalization and exploitation? What is the relationship between linguistic dependence (continued use of a European language in a former colony) and economic dependence (the export of raw materials and import of technology, know-how, etc.)?

1. The Nature of Linguistic Imperialism

Imperialism theory has traditionally (Hobson 1902, Lenin 1973) been primarily concerned with economic and political aspects of dominance. More recent theorists have been concerned with the whole range of activities, structures, and ideologies which link powerful countries, the 'Center,' with powerless countries, the 'Periphery.' As a result such dimensions as military, social, communication, and cultural imperialism have been added to economic and political imperialism (e.g., Galtung 1980). All the constituents are seen as contributing to the maintenance of a structure of exploitation from which rich countries benefit, and poor countries suffer. Resources are also distributed unequally internally within each country, which has its own Center and Periphery.

Each type of imperialism interlocks with the others in mutually reinforcing ways. Linguistic imperialism therefore presupposes an overarching structure of asymmetrical, unequal exchange, where language dominance dovetails with economic, political, and other types of dominance.

Linguistic imperialism can be regarded as a subcategory of cultural imperialism. Other subcategories are media imperialism (e.g., news agencies, the world information order), educational imperialism (e.g., the export of Western institutional norms, educational systems, teacher training, textbooks, etc.), scientific imperialism (e.g., dissemination of paradigms and methodologies from the Center, which controls knowledge about the Periphery). Linguistic imperialism may closely dovetail with media, educational, or scientific imperialism. It is almost certainly the language of the dominant power which is used as the medium of communication in each of these domains of cultural imperialism, just as it is in other areas, e.g., political, economic, etc., not only in international relations but also internally. This gives the dominant language and the learning of it as a second or foreign language a crucial role in the mediation and in the reproduction of an asymmetrical relationship.

Imperialism theories attempt to link the various types of imperialism in a principled way, so as to account for the connections between one factor, for instance language, and others operating in conjunction with it, for instance military conquest (which almost invariably accompanies colonial occupation) or religion—consider the spread of Spanish and Catholicism; or analogies and contrasts between this and the spread of Arabic and Islam; or the role of missionaries in alphabetizing indigenous languages in Africa, Asia, and Latin America, e.g., the work of the Summer Institute of Linguistics (see *Missionaries and Language*).

2. Creation of Beliefs and Structures to Sustain Linguistic Dominance

Language is frequently involved in the maintenance of relations of dominance. The maintenance of a hierarchical relationship usually involves a pattern of stigmatization of dominated languages, glorification of the dominant language, and rationalization of the relationship between the languages, always to the benefit of the dominant one. Thus the Greeks stigmatized non-Greek speakers as 'barbarians' (speakers of mumbo-jumbo, a non-language). The 'Welsh' were foreigners, people who spoke a 'strange language' that 'one does not understand' (cited in the Oxford English Dictionary, 1648). The languages of colonized people were categorized as 'primitive,' mere 'patois.' 'Local languages' in France are characterized by an 'incapacity to serve beyond their limited frameworks' and their speakers have 'difficulties in adapting them to the development of ideas and techniques' (a French Government assessment, quoted in Capotorti 1979: 13) (see *Dialect and Dialectology*).

One's own language, on the other hand, was glorified as the language of God (Arabic, Dutch, Sanskrit), the language of reason, logic, and human rights (French in recent centuries), the language of the superior ethno–national group (German in Nazi ideology), the language of modernity, technological progress, and national unity (English in much postcolonial discourse), etc. The speakers of stigmatized languages can therefore only benefit from using the 'superior' languages. Such beliefs serve to legitimize the linguistic and social hierarchy (see *Power and Language*).

But linguistic imperialism is not just a question of labels, attitudes, and beliefs. It presupposes a structure regulating social and institutional power. In an imperialist structure one society or collectivity exploits another, e.g., Europeans taking their languages worldwide, to the detriment of the cultures and languages of native peoples in the Americas, Australasia, etc. 'Internal' colonization of this kind can also be regarded as imperialist. Second, structural dominance is asserted through the allocation of more material resources to one language rather than another, and via regulations and practices that stipulate that one language rather than another should be used. This structure explains why, for instance, English has thrived while the other languages of the UK have been marginalized. In France this hierarchical and linguicidal model has been official policy since the sixteenth century (see *Linguicide*). The edicts of the French Revolution were initially disseminated in the many languages spoken in France, but from the early 1790s the message of 'freedom, fraternity and equality' was propagated through the exclusive medium of French. The monolingual ideal associated with the 'modern' state has been exported worldwide.

One difference between French and British colonial policy was that the indigenous languages were seldom used in education in the French empire, whereas they were widely used in the British empire in the initial years of schooling. However, local languages invariably had low status, and it was the colonizers' language which provided access to power and resources. The linguistic hierarchy was thus comparable in each empire. This is also borne out by what has happened since the 'independence' of countries from each empire: the former colonial languages remain as the dominant languages, to the advantage of those who can use them, while indigenous languages remain, with few exceptions, marginalized. Gilbert Ansre, the Ghanaian sociolinguist, describes linguistic imperialism as:

> the phenomenon in which the minds and lives of the speakers of a language are dominated by another language to the point where they believe that they can and should use only that foreign language when it comes to transactions dealing with the more advanced aspects of life such as education, philosophy, literature, governments, the administration of justice, etc. ... Linguistic imperialism has a subtle way of warping the minds, attitudes and aspirations of even the most noble in a society and of preventing him from appreciating and realising the full potentialities of the indigenous languages (1979: 12).

As a result of linguistic imperialism, the vast majority of languages in former colonies have not gone through the processes of development which most European languages have experienced in recent centuries. Their growth and expansion has been kept in check by the presence of the former colonial languages, and the vested interests, national and international, associated with these (on African languages, see Mateene 1985, Ngũgĩ 1986; on India, Pattanayak 1986, on the Pacific region, Mühlhäusler 1996). 'Aid' in the language and education field has contributed to impeding the elaboration of local solutions to meet local problems. When the former colonial languages have been used as the medium of education in schooling, the gulf between the ruling class and ordinary people has been widened. However, there is an increasing awareness that such aid was culturally and educationally flawed: for a Ford Foundation analysis describing the failings of their projects, see Fox 1975; on the inappropriateness of Western training in linguistics for Third World language management purposes, see Jernudd 1981; on ethnocentric, unscientific tenets in applied linguistics and English language teaching, see Phillipson 1992.

As many scholars from the 'underdeveloped' world have pointed out, the arguments used to justify the continued use of European languages in such contexts are quite false and neglect the educational, cultural, and linguistic realities and needs of all except the elites (who are the ones with strong links with Center countries, having often been educated there or through the medium of the Center language). Just as the economies of countries in the Periphery have been underdeveloped through their subordination to the economies of the Center countries, their languages have also been underdeveloped. Linguistic underdevelopment occurs whenever these languages are not used for the full range of societal functions that Ansre lists, with these functions being reserved for a supposedly 'superior,' Western language. This situation even still holds in countries which have made substantial efforts to promote a local language. In Tanzania there is a triglossic (see *Diglossia*) situation, English being 'high' vis-à-vis Swahili, and Swahili 'high' vis-à-vis the other indigenous languages.

3. Promotion of Dominant Languages

Language plays a vital role in international contexts. This role has become ever more important as brute physical force (conquest, occupation) has given way to subtler types of control. Language not only mediates links (in the media, business, military, etc.); it is itself an object of cultural dissemination. The 'Alliance Française' has been promoting knowledge of the French language outside France for over a century. Many other Western European nations run similar, state-supported operations, as does Japan. Saudi Arabia provides substantial financial aid for the teaching of Arabic in underdeveloped countries. The rise of English as the international language par excellence of the postwar period has not been left to chance. It has been declared government policy on both sides of the Atlantic to promote English worldwide, and simultaneously to curb the extension of possible competitor languages, whether the Cold War enemy's language, Russian, other Western European languages, or the languages of newly independent countries, Arabic, Hindi, etc. In the words of a director of the Center for Applied Linguistics in Washington DC:

> From a minor language in 1600, English has in less than four centuries come to be the leading language of international communication in the world today. This remarkable development is ultimately the result of seventeenth, eighteenth, and nineteenth century British successes in conquest, colonization, and trade, but it was enormously accelerated by the emergence of the USA as the major military world power and technological leader in the aftermath of World War II. The process was also greatly abetted by the expenditure of large amounts of government and private foundation funds in the period 1950–70, perhaps the most ever spent in history in support of the propagation of a language. (Troike 1977: 2)

The expenditure has gone toward the establishment of professional infrastructure (specialist university departments, institution building, teacher training, curriculum and textbook development, etc.) in the Center and the Periphery. There have been close links between the academic world, government (or paragovernmental agencies such as the British Council), and publishing houses. The role of American 'philanthropic' foundations in promoting worldwide cultural links has been well analyzed (see Arnove 1982). The Center for Applied Linguistics in Washington DC, was established with Ford Foundation funds. Ford had language and education projects in over 30 countries in the 1960s and 1970s, a decisive period in the transition from colonialism to the contemporary, neocolonial phase. The British Council has a substantial number of language experts scattered over the world, many of them in advisory or catalyst, 'multiplier' roles rather than as classroom teachers. Such government-financed language activities are designed to create dependence on the dominant language in order to further its use for those purposes which the language otherwise serves, generally in a structure of linguistic imperialism.

4. Approaches to Linguistic Dominance

There are many academic specializations with concerns which are close to those of linguistic imperialism: language planning, the sociology of language, sociolinguistics, and applied linguistics. However, these disciplines have tended to shy away from directly confronting the issue of the power of languages internationally. Even from a country-internal perspective, little work has been done to develop a unifying theory of linguistic inequality, despite the extensive documentation of pervasive linguistic inequality worldwide (for instance studies of language attrition and death, of language revival, of postcolonial education policy). Work in the field of 'language spread' (see Phillipson in press) is often strong on identifying and quantifying factors involved in language spread, but tends to be relatively weak in analyzing causal, structural factors.

Slavery and colonization were imposed by physical violence and legitimated with reference to primitive biologically-based racism. In the contemporary world the physical violence of the stick, associated with crude racism, has given way to psychological violence. To capture this phenomenon and account for the way language is used as a means of hierarchizing, in similar ways to racism and sexism, the concept 'linguicism' has been coined (Skutnabb-Kangas 1988). Linguicism is defined as 'ideologies, structures, and practices which are used to legitimate, effectuate and reproduce an unequal division of power and resources (both material and non-material) between groups which are defined on the basis of language.' The concept has been used in the study of minority education (ibid.), and in a study of the spread of English as a 'world' language and the specific contribution of applied linguists and English language teaching 'experts' in facilitating this spread (Phillipson 1992).

Linguicism facilitates the control of dominated groups by means of carrots rather than sticks, ideas rather than threats. When benefits accrue only to those who learn and use a dominant language, and when shame and guilt are inculcated in those who use a stigmatized, dominated language, the oppressive structure and linguicist ideology are likely to be internalized. It then appears to be in the interest of speakers of dominated languages to shift language. This has been the reality of most indigenous and immigrant minorities in Europe and Europeanized countries.

The expansion of English in colonial and postcolonial periods has also been analyzed in terms of the discourses of cultural politics (Pennycook 1994). Analysis of contemporary English in a wide range of countries in British and American spheres of influence leads Fishman et al. to see the need for English to be 'reconceptualized, from being an imperialist tool to being a multinational tool ... English ... being post-imperial (as the title of our book implies, that is in the sense of not directly serving purely Anglo-American territorial, economic, or cultural expansion) without being post-capitalist in any way' (1996: 8). Fishman et al. regard the continued strength of English as being determined locally and voluntarily in such countries, but this underestimates the way a western-dominated globalization agenda is being implemented by the transnational corporations, the World Bank, the IMF, and the World Trade Organization. English is being strengthened through regional trading alliances, such as the North American Free Trade Agreement and the European Union. English is increasingly used in EU institutions and member states, despite a great deal of EU rhetoric proclaiming the wish to maintain linguistic diversity. It is arguable that new forms of linguistic imperialism worldwide (in the media, military, political, scientific and educational worlds, youth culture, etc.) mean that English represents a threat to all other languages, though the analysis of the interlocking of English with processes of globalization and localization is still in its infancy (Phillipson 2000).

See also: Power and Language; Pragmatics and Sociolinguistics; Minority Languages; International Languages; Linguicide; Language Planning: Models.

Bibliography

Ansre G 1979 Four rationalisations for maintaining European languages in education in Africa. *African Languages* **5**(2): 10–17

Arnove R F (ed.) 1982 *Philanthropy and Cultural Imperialism: The Foundations at Home and Abroad*. Indiana University Press, Bloomington, IN

Capotorti F 1979 *Study on the Rights of Persons Belonging to Ethnic, Religious, and Linguistic Minorities*. United Nations, New York

Fishman J A, Conrad A W, Rubal-Lopez A (eds.) 1996 *Post-imperial English. Status Change in Former British and American Colonies, 1940–1990*. Mouton de Gruyter, Berlin

Fox M J 1975 *Language and Development: A Retrospective Survey of Ford Foundation Language Projects, 1952–74*. Ford Foundation, New York

Galtung J 1980 *The True Worlds: A Transnational Perspective*. Free Press, New York

Hobson J A 1902 *Imperialism: A Study*. Allen and Unwin, London

Jernudd B H 1981 Planning language treatment: Linguistics for the Third World. *Language in Society* **10**: 43–52

Lenin V I 1973 (1st edn. 1916) *On Imperialism and Imperialists*. Progress Publishers, Moscow

Mateene K 1985 Colonial languages as compulsory means of domination, and indigenous languages, as necessary factors of liberation and development. In: Mateene K, Kalema J, Chomba B (eds.) *Linguistic Unity and Liberation of Africa*. OAU Bureau of Languages, Kampala, Uganda

Mühlhäusler P 1996 *Linguistic Ecology. Language Change and Linguistic Imperialism in the Pacific Region*. Routledge, London

Ngũgĩ wa Thiong'o 1986 *Decolonising the Mind: The Politics of Language in African Literature*. James Currey, London

Pattanayak D P 1986 Language, politics, region formation, and regional planning. In: Annamalai E, Jernudd B, Rubin J (eds.) *Language Planning: Proceedings of an Institute*. Central Institute of Indian Languages, Mysore, India

Pennycook A 1994 *The Cultural Politics of English as an International Language*. Longman, Harlow, UK

Phillipson R 1992 *Linguistic Imperialism*. Oxford University Press, Oxford

Phillipson R 2000 English in the new world order: Variations on a theme of linguistic imperialism and 'world' English. In: Ricento T (ed.) *Ideology, Politics, and Language Policies. Focus on English*. Benjamins, Amsterdam

Phillipson R in press Language spread. In: Ammon U et al (eds.) *Sociolinguistics. A Handbook of the Science of Language and Society*, 2nd edn. de Gruyter, Berlin and New York

Rodney W 1972 *How Europe Underdeveloped Africa*. Bogle l'Ouverture, London

Skutnabb-Kangas T 1988 Multilingualism and the education of minority children. In: Skutnabb-Kangas T, Cummins J (eds.) *Minority Education: From Shame to Struggle*. Multilingual Matters, Clevedon, UK

Troike R 1977 The future of English (editorial). *The Linguistic Reporter* 19(8): 2

Manipulation
N. Fairclough

The strategies that people use to get others to do what they want them to do are partly linguistic, involving manipulative uses of language. 'Linguistic manipulation' is the conscious use of language in a devious way to control others (see *Power and Language*), where 'using language in a devious way' means using it in a way which hides one's strategies and objectives. This happens quite commonly in conversation; for example, saying how busy or how tired one is can be a devious way of getting out of a responsibility or commitment. In such cases, linguistic manipulation involves the use of 'indirect speech acts' (see *Speech Act Theory: Overview*) which are oriented more to the 'perlocutionary' effects of what is said (what it allows the speaker to achieve) than to the apparent 'illocutionary' acts that are performed (claiming to be busy, expressing tiredness) (see *Pragmatics and Socio-linguistics*). Of course, attempts at linguistic manipulation are not always successful; people become adept to a greater or lesser degree at 'seeing through' what is said.

There are various institutional domains in which manipulative discourse (see *Discourse*) is systematically used and indeed expected, such as police interrogations of suspects, or cross-examination of witnesses in a court of law. In the latter case, for example, cross-examining counsel may try to linguistically manipulate both the witness and the jury. The manipulation of witnesses involves counsel exploiting their control over the interaction by strategically constructing sequences of questions designed to gradually build up evidence and lead to accusations. The manipulation of juries includes various devices for suggesting that a witness's testimony is not to be trusted, such as forcefully repeating a question after the witness has answered it, or showing disbelief through a combination of intonation and facial expression.

Linguistic manipulation is also a feature of political rhetoric (see *Politics and Language*). Political discourse is in the business of persuasion, be it persuading people to take political action or persuading people to support a party or individual, and recourse to devious means is not uncommon. In modern societies, politics is largely conducted through the mass media (see *Media Language and Communication*), and this leads to new forms of linguistic manipulation; political organizations put a great deal of effort into press conference and press statements, and into constructing slogans and catch phrases in ways that make them likely to be adopted by the media. One aspect of manipulation in political discourse that has received extensive attention is the exploitation of the connotative meanings of words. For example, in attempts by the most powerful countries of 'the West' to exercise political hegemony over smaller countries, a widely used device in the late twentieth century has been accusing governments and other groups of supporting or being 'soft on' terrorism. Political discourse also makes extensive use of the persuasive potential of repetition and grammatical parallelism (e.g., *We don't want the poll tax to be reviewed, we don't want the poll tax to be reduced, we want the poll tax to be abolished!*). Rhetoric is of course not exclusively used in political discourse; some research has shown, for example, how articles in scientific journals use rhetorical devices to convince readers.

Advertising (see *Advertising*) uses a combination of language and visual imagery to get people to buy particular products or, increasingly, to give people a positive image of an individual, organization, or service. Although the motives of advertisers are clear to most people, linguistic manipulation on a grand scale is used to achieve them. Words and images are used to jointly construct imaginary or heavily idealized worlds or 'lifestyles' which people can imagine themselves a part of. This often gives the manipulatory language of advertising a pseudopoetic quality (e.g., from an advertisement for sanitary towels, *I came back. I came back to softness and comfort. I came back to Dr White's.*).

A feature of the late twentieth-century sociolinguistic order in Britain and various other countries is a process of 'technologization of discourse,' wherein discourse practices are systematically subjected to research and redesign, the results of which are incorporated in the training of various types of institutional personnel. Consider interviewing as an example. A great deal of research has been carried out on interviewing practices in institutional contexts (different types of research interview, job interview, disciplinary interview, etc.), which has led to recommendations for redesigning interviews to make them more effective in one way or another, and to the training of institutional personnel in interview techniques. Experts in relevant branches of social scientific research (especially in psychology) are being brought into organizations to carry out such work on a systematic basis. The same sort of expertise is being seen as relevant to widely divergent institutional contexts, and techniques like interviews are coming to be defined in universal and context-free ways, as transferable skills which are in principle useable anywhere. This implies the colonization of institutional orders of discourse by culturally salient practices, and a standardization of practices across institutions. Technologization of discourse is rather different from the forms of linguistic manipulation discussed above. But it can be regarded as an indirect, mediated form of linguistic manipulation: in so far as it succeeds in reshaping discourse practices, it can surreptitiously bring the behavior of whole groups of people under control.

However, those who use practices such as interviewing which have been redesigned in this way are not necessarily or even usually using them manipulatively. Members of professional groups such as doctors, teachers, or personnel officers acquire interviewing techniques as part of their professional training, and may normally use them as a matter of common sense without any manipulative intent. Such techniques do contribute to controlling people, but they do so because of the ways in which they are ideologically invested (see *Power and Language*) rather than necessarily with manipulative intent, and they control all those who use them (interviewers as well as interviewees in this example).

See also: Media Language and Communication; Linguistic Imperialism; Representation.

Bibliography

Atkinson J M, Drew P 1979 *Order in Court: The Organisation of Verbal Interaction in Judicial Settings*. Macmillan, London

Mey J L 1985 *Whose Language? A Study in Linguistic Pragmatics*. Benjamins, Amsterdam

Marxist Theories of Language
G. Mininni

The hinges of a Marxist consideration concern the links binding the language to the structure of society, to models of material praxis, and to forms of ideology. An evaluation of relationship between Marxism and the sciences of language coincides with the overall judgment expressed by many scholars on the historical experience of the so-called 'real socialism': the questions on the agenda are relevant and unavoidable, but the answers given are, on the whole, misleading or disappointing. The questions posed by Marxism as an interpretive methodology of social relationships may be worded as follows: which linguistic arguments prove that 'man is the sum of social relationships?' How are the different systems of beliefs, socially shared knowledge, cultural values, and rules of a human community continuously rebuilt in his language? How do the ideal–typical needs for mutual understanding and the real contingencies of differentiation and social struggle weave together in the language? These queries question all the symbolic articulations connected with the difference between manual labor and intellectual work.

1. Looking for a 'True' Marxism in Linguistics

What is the meaning of 'being a Marxist in linguistics?' First of all, it must be stressed that from a methodological point of view, it is not a question of applying Marxism to linguistics (Ponzio 1989), as such an approach carries the idea of a 'will of power' which is not acceptable for cultural practices guided by the paradigm of the search for a historical, consensual truth. Any attempt at a mere external application legitimates a defense mechanism aiming at protecting the autonomy of language science against the obtrusiveness of ideological knowledge. To adhere to a Marxist theory of the language does not mean to draw the proposals of a linguistic explanation from the dogmas of social philosophy, but to identify a route of interpenetration between the problems posed by linguistic practice (or meditation) and the possibilities of an unbiased analysis of the same at a social level, just like the one Marx carried out to explain how the capitalist economy of his time worked.

1.1. Classics' Indications

The hypothesis of a direct accessibility between Marxism and language sciences may seem surprising when one considers that the assertions concerning language are poor and fragmentary in the classical literature of Marxism. Some passages from *The German Ideology* are extremely enlightening, especially those where Marx and Engels (1970) explain that language originated from the need for relationships with others, and is the matter that from the beginning 'contaminates' the spirituality of a 'real, practical conscience' which is typical of man. Other noteworthy references can be found in the section about *Nature's Dialectic*; here Engels develops Darwin's theme of the ape's humanization processes and suggests the existence of a strict connection between language and work. Of course, from an early date (Lafargue 1936), scholars' attention was attracted by the possibility of identifying a class-prejudiced characterization both in the use of language and in the process of its historical evolution. This assumption does not justify in the least the absurd contraposition of a 'socialist' or 'revolutionary linguistics' to a 'capitalist' or 'reactionary one,' which would necessarily occur if Marxist theoretical and ideological principles were schematically applied in a scientific investigation of linguistic problems.

1.2 Scylla and Charybdis in Marxist Linguistics

A subtle plot of historical and political conditions led Joseph V. Stalin to denounce the fact that Nikolai J. Marr (the recognized spokesman of Marxist theory in linguistics until then) had incurred such an aberration in his doctrine, as he had reconciled his own monogenetic (or Japhetic) hypothesis of language with assertions about its superstructural and class prejudiced nature. The great normalizer of the Soviet State often intervened in the linguists' debate published in *Pravda* (summer 1950), and—as an expert on Marxism, not on glottology—he presumed to outline the correct picture of a Marxist interpretation for linguistic questions. Stalin's position—which seems to be supported by common sense and is consistent with the scientific programs of Saussure's structuralism and Durkheim's sociology—turns out to be fundamentally incorrect both in its method and in substance, although it is absolutely justified by virtue of a certain sociolinguistic policy. As a matter of fact, on the one hand, the pretension to solve a scientific debate by a substantial appeal to authority appears unacceptable; on the other hand, the rebuttal of Marr's thesis is carried out with the help of trivializing arguments. However, from the point of view of the history of thought, Stalin's intervention is an affirmation and, at the same time, a denial of a Marxist theory on language. It is an affirmation because it demonstrates *de facto* that any theoretical language elaboration is bound by reasons of social and political practice. Language sciences, too, obey precise constraints deriving from the development of human relationships and draw inspiration from the ideological climate in which a society lives. Actually Stalin's concern to preserve languages conceals the 'sovietization' process imposed on the different nationalities gathered in the former USSR, and aims at defusing social conflicts. But Stalin's position patently clashes with that dimension of Marxist theory, so it necessarily adheres to a 'critical linguistics,' that is to say, a linguistics which tries to unveil the dominant mechanisms operating in communicative practices. For a number of reasons, Stalin could not adopt such a view, and in order to avoid the problems that Marr had reasonably posed but incorrectly solved (Borbé 1974), he takes refuge in an attitude of denial: as a language system has its own autonomous organization and is an instrument of national identification, language is not a superstructure, and does not have a class character; so Marrism is not the equivalent of Marxism in linguistics. Stalin's position is not only mistaken, as he commits the 'minimalist error' (Mey 1978) of considering language as a mere by-product of the cultural life of a nation, but it is also responsible for putting an end to the debate on the potential of Marxism in linguistics, through its own mystification (Marcellesi and Gardin 1974).

2. Language Sciences and Critique of Ideologies

If we escape both monsters of Marrism and Stalinism, are there other implemented models of interpenetration or mutual control between the social theory of Marxism and linguistic questions?

2.1 'Bakhtin's Circle'

In fact, an authentically Marxist position in the language sciences is worked out in the post-revolution decade in Russia by the so called 'Leningrad School.' Mikhail M. Bakhtin (see *Bakhtin, Mikhail M.*), Valentin N. Voloshinov (see *Voloshinov, Valentin Nikolavic*) and Pavel N. Medvedev try to develop a semiotic theory of culture based on Marxist principles. Their conceptual pattern sets three interpretative routes: decoding psychic processes both historically and socially; exploring the polyphonic dialogics (see *Dialogism*) intrinsic in a language; identifying the sociological constraints of a literary text. The Marxist relevance criterion of such an approach is the criticism of the forms of ideology and the way ideology works. In Voloshinov's opinion (1973), a Marxist conception of the problems posed by language philosophy is warranted by the need to explore the sign nature of ideological phenomena. As a result, the study of the ideologies embodied in the ethical, religious, juridical political, and literary institutions of a society must be based on an explanation of the principles regulating their constitutive elements: i.e., signs. The identification of the ideological sphere with semiotics enables us to explain the formation of an individual conscience as a socio-ideological phenomenon; one must therefore imagine an unseizable dialectic interaction between the mind's working and the activation of sign-ideological systems. The specifically psychological aspects of such an explanatory route were developed by Lev S. Vygotsky; his theory advocates that superior psychic processes (memory, language, will, etc.) are interiorizations of social interactions mediated by signs. To explain the connection between language and ideology, Voloshinov resorts to a metaprocedural strategy: he shows which ideologies are carried by linguists. Two macrotrends are therefore identified in the study of language, which appear as epistemological constants and are still in force: individualist subjectivism (from Humboldt to Croce and Vossler) and abstract objectivism (which was exemplarily represented by Saussure). Voloshinov demonstrates that the Marxist point of view calls for an analysis of the socio-ideological material 'molded' by verbal interaction in order to rebut both the unsubstantiality of individual creativity in linguistic expression and the narrow-mindedness of a superindividual system of rules escaping the manifold pressures of language usage.

2.2. Social Cognition and Linguistic Praxis

The debate interrupted by Stalin and the programs started by the 'Leningrad School' were reconsidered in the 1960s both by Soviet scholars who were interested in giving a historical and materialist direction to semiotic structuralism (Reznikov 1964), and by other scholars working in the field of social criticism in the capitalist West (Cornforth 1965). An interesting bridge between these two perspectives had been anticipated in Italy by Antonio Gramsci's brilliant intuitions (see *Hegemony*), and was later consolidated by Adam Schaff (1967). The need for 'Marxist linguistics' was set by the Polish philosopher in the sphere of a knowledge theory beyond the opposite extremes of mechanistic materialism and subjective idealism. According to Schaff, a Marxist theory emphasizes the role of mediating procedure that language plays between what is subjective and objective, mental and social, biological and cultural. This theory acts as a central support for a conception of man as the being who is responsible for the creation of his own cognitive and relational models. Even if some differences can be found from the point of view of inner logic as well as on the level of philogenetic and ontogenetic acquisition, the process of 'thinking–speaking' is substantially unitary, as cognition is an effect of social praxis and communicative relations are full of cognitive contents. This dialectic unity enables us to reject both the reflex theory suggested by a naïve materialism and the theory of significant systems autonomy, proposed by some updated versions of idealism. Furthermore, Schaff's Marxist language theory aims at being immediately employed in the practical questions weighing on the decision-making ability of a human person as an actor and a maker of his/her social world. On this subject, Schaff also considers a social categorization process which emphasizes the connection between ideology and language, that is 'thinking–speaking by stereotypes.' The resort to stereotype and to prejudices gives emphasis to the fact that as the relationship between the individual mind and reality is mediated by the sphere of meanings, the workings of the mind itself are influenced by historical and social conditionings. Stereotypes reveal the real control that social groups have over the contents and processes of individual thought. Schaff's pragmatic point of view allowed him to give stereotypes of that socio-integrative and defense function which makes them compatible with the political structure of society. Similar conclusions are drawn by all those currents of sociolinguistics and pragmalinguistics that wonder about the connections between the conscience of sociality carried by the language and the limits of what the historical conditions of praxis allow human subjects to mean when they are diversified by factors such as age, sex, culture, class, degree of social control, etc. Some theories within 'social linguistics' are marked by an implicit adhesion to a Marxian inspiration, such as 'praxematics,' coming from Lafont's school or Mey's pragmatic approach. Lafont (1978) works out a linguistics focused on the 'praxeme': this is an instrument for the production of sense in speech and, at the same time, a unit of analysis in the relation between the language user and the practical social conditions which make it possible for the uses of linguistic varieties to clash. In outlining the basic question 'Whose language?,' Mey (1985) makes a constant, critical comparison between the categories obtainable from analysis of industrial society (such as production, oppression, and manipulation) and the instruments of linguistic analysis. According to Mey, the Marxian inspiration in sociolinguistics lies in the need for a theory which can explain the intricate relationship between language as a sociocultural product and the forms of the overall reproduction of a society. The solution he proposes entrusts pragmatics, as the theory of linguistic use, with the task of explaining the various 'wording' possibilities connected with the clashing nature of groups, with different approaches to knowledge and with different power distributions.

2.3 Sign Systems and Social Reproduction

The principles of historical–dialectical materialism imply that language is interpreted by abstractions which are in turn determined by the sum of practices regulating man's 'organic exchange' with nature, bearing in mind the often distorted representations imposed by the historical limits within which man is obliged to live his social relationships (Erckenbrecht 1973). The Marxist idea of language aims at specifying the features of the production of sense carried out by man in the present circumstances of his history and, therefore, at identifying the role of sign systems within the process of 'social reproduction' as a whole. This category indicates the totality of techniques and procedures through which human groups perpetuate their presence in the world. In this perspective, Ferruccio Rossi-Landi's (1983) tentatively investigated connection between language and work is justified. At first sight, Rossi-Landi seems to exaggerate when he applies the Marxian labor theory of value to the field of language and to other nonverbal forms of human communication. Indeed, the most important thing is the epistemological and methodological indication of the need for passing from the surface level of exchange and/or the sign market to the underlying level of social labor which is implicit in cultural signification and communication processes. This change of focus makes it possible to criticize the dichotomy traditionally accepted by linguists (out of common sense) between the 'system' and 'use' of the language, both in its classical version of Saussure's opposition between 'langue' and 'parole,' and in its neoclassical version of Chomsky's opposition between 'competence' and 'performance.' The adherence to these two categories enables linguists to secure the fetish of an explanatory autonomy, by confining the pertinence of Marxism to the illustration of the social function of a language. On the contrary, in Rossi-Landi's view, those abstractions are useful only if they are rooted in the ground of 'common speaking,' which defines historically the linguistic a priori of the human being. The philosophical methodology of 'common speaking,' which was later generalized in a semiotic methodology of 'common semiosis' by Rossi-Landi, achieves the Marxist theory target of unveiling the ideological consistency of the 'logosphere' and clarifies the mediating role that sign systems play between the economic basis and the superstructures of society.

3. What Shall We Do?

The Marxist perspective, however narrow it may appear, binds those who study linguistic problems to historical–dialectical materialism and obliges them to consider the connections between linguistic theory and the theory of praxis as being relevant. This double bond results in the priority need to explore the linguistic signs' ideological texture. But for the linguist, the adherence to such an explanatory route entails the commitment to carry out his own language investigations according to an emancipatory project concerning the potentials of human beings. To be a Marxist in linguistics means to adopt an intrinsically debunking perspective of the relationships of social control that are formed and/or expressed in the language. Of course, it is not necessary to be a Marxist to work out a critical and emancipatory linguistics, but the opposite is true: it is necessary to take a critical attitude to be authentically Marxist in linguistics. Marxism aims at putting a sort of 'metasemiotics,' meant as a critical theory of ideologies, at the basis of the language sciences. This perspective is shared by those who try to use Marxian categories (class, commodity, labor, surplus value, alienation) in the analysis of the relations of linguistic reproduction in society, and by those who take only a critical stance from Marxism, thinking that this is enough to perfect the technical solutions provided by linguistic knowledge. Both 'revolutionaries' and 'reformers' share the same desire to look for a small red petal in the white cup of meditation on language.

See also: Ideology; Dialogism

Bibliography

Borbé T 1974 *Kritik der marxistischen Sprachtheorie N. J. Marrs*. Scriptor Verlag, Kronberg, Germany
Cornforth M C 1965 *Marxism and the Linguistic Philosophy*. Lawrence and Wishart, London
Erckenbrecht U 1973 *Marx' Materialistische Sprachtheorie*. Scriptor, Kronberg, Germany
Lafargue P 1936 (1894) La langue française avant et après la Révolution. *Critiques littéraires* 35–85
Lafont R 1978 *Le travail et la langue*. Flammarion, Paris
Marcellesi J-B, Gardin B 1974 *Introduction à la sociolinguistique. La linguistique sociale*. Librairie Larousse, Paris
Marx K, Engels F 1970 *The German Ideology*. Lawrence and Wishart, London
Mey J L 1978 Marxism and linguistics: Facts and fancies. *Journal of Pragmatics* 2: 81–93
Mey J L 1985 *Whose Language? A Study in Linguistic Pragmatics*. Benjamins, Amsterdam
Ponzio A 1989 Semiotics and Marxism. In: Sebeok T A, Umiker-Sebeok J, Young E P (eds.) *The Semiotic Web 1988*. Mouton de Gruyter, Berlin
Reznikov L O 1964 *Gnoseologiceskie voprosy semiotiki* (The gnosiological problems of semiotics). University Press, Leningrad
Rossi-Landi F 1983 *Language as Work and Trade*. Bergin & Garvey, South Hadley, MA
Schaff A 1967 *Szkice z filozofii języka* (Essays on Philosophy of Language). Wiedza, Warsaw, Poland
Voloshinov V N 1973 Matejka L, Titunik I R (transl.) *Marxism and the Philosophy of Language*. Seminar Press, New York

Minority Languages
J. M. Y. Simpson

Various international conferences have been held on the subject of minority languages. For example, the First International Conference on Minority Languages held at Glasgow in 1980 had as its theme 'the present-day problems of minority languages, particularly those of the British Isles, The Netherlands, and Scandinavia.' The questions arise: what is a minority language and what kinds of problems does such a language face? The term presents certain difficulties of definition but it seems safe to say that a minority language will exhibit some at least of the features listed below. The problem can be summed up as the danger of the language becoming extinct.

(a) A minority language lives in the shadow of a culturally dominant language, dominant usually because of political factors, which puts the minority language at risk. Thus Irish, Welsh, and Scottish Gaelic live in the shadow of English; Breton lives in the shadow of French; Frisian in that of Dutch; and Sorbian in that of German. In many cases the absolute number of speakers of the minority language is declining.

(b) As a corollary to the above, a minority language is not the language of all areas of activity indulged in by its speakers. It may, for example, be excluded from formal spheres such as administration, education, or the mass media and may be confined to the home, religious life, or literature. Scottish Gaelic, for example, is (within the Gaelic-speaking area) widely used in church services but only marginally employed in other forms of public gathering, e.g., sports fixtures, political meetings, parent–teacher meetings, etc. It has no part in national government and virtually none in administrative paperwork. It is only modestly represented in the press (yet Scottish Gaelic literature flourishes).

(c) Bilingualism is a characteristic of its speakers. Thus, apart from the very young, there are virtually no monoglot speakers of Irish, Scots Gaelic, or Welsh.

(d) In the case of many minority languages, the speakers may be said to form a network rather than a community. For example, there are no urban centers that could be described as Breton-speaking, Irish-speaking, or Scots Gaelic-speaking.

(e) Because the dominant language is used for discussing certain topics, the minority language may lack areas of vocabulary found in other languages that share the same general culture. Indeed its vocabulary may be influenced by that of the dominant language to the extent of accepting borrowings where native terms exist.

(f) There may be no standardized form of a minority language. There is, for example, no agreed standard for Scots. Similarly, conventions for such things as writing letters may be lacking.

(g) The minority language may be at risk from opponents actively dedicated to its extirpation. An early example of this is the 1616 Education Act passed by the Scottish parliament. This established schools in the every parish with the object of imparting the English vernacular so that Scottish Gaelic, described as the source of all barbarity, should be 'abolisheit and remouvit.' Since knowledge of the dominant language is usually necessary for economic advancement, it may be the case that native speakers will not pass on the minority language to their children.

(h) Because the language may lack areas of vocabulary, or because there is no standard, or because speakers are completely bilingual, there may be reluctance on the part of native speakers to speak the language to learners or even to other native speakers from different dialect areas, on the grounds that differences of dialect present insurmountable barriers to mutual comprehension. Thus the minority language becomes the marker of increasingly small in-groups.

(i) Opponents of the language seize upon gaps in the vocabulary, the absence of a recognized norm, and the reluctance to speak the language to outsiders in order to demonstrate that the language is in some sense 'inferior.'

(j) The cause of a minority language may be taken up by proponents (groups or individuals) dedicated to its preservation or revival. *Cymdeithas yr Iaith Gymraeg* ('Welsh Language Society'), founded in 1962, and the Scots Language Society, founded in 1972 as the Lallans Society, are two examples.

(k) Efforts to promote minority languages may include language planning or language purification in order to fill the gaps mentioned in (e) above. Thus there are lists of technical vocabulary compiled and published for both Irish and Welsh.

(l) Problems arise in education and official policy varies from country to country: the language may be banned in school; it may be taught as a subject; or it may even be the medium of instruction.

(m) Historical factors may be relevant. The language may not always have been a minority one and it may therefore have possessed at least written norms that it now lacks. Hence a modern writer may incorporate usages from an earlier written language that are no longer found in any spoken variety.

A curious claim sometimes made by proponents of individual minority languages is that they are 'old.' If such a description has any meaning, either it is that the language in question was established in its present location at an early date, or first written down at a relatively early date, or that it represents an alleged earlier state of historical development. It is not clear what any of these interpretations has to do with the value of a language; unfortunately, 'oldness' continually crops up as a kind of guarantee of respectability.

It should be noted that what is a minority language in one country may well be the dominant language in another. Thus various dialects of German constitute a minority language in France, but Standard German is the official language of (among others) the Federal Republic of Germany. In such a situation the users of the minority language will have a standard to relate to, if they wish to avail themselves of it.

See also: Discrimination and Minority Languages; Endangered Languages; Language Conflict; Language Maintenance, Shift, and Death; Linguicide; Lingusitic Imperialism; Teaching Endangered Languages.

Bibliography

Durkacz V E 1983 *The Decline of the Celtic Languages*. John Donald, Edinburgh, UK
Oftedal M 1969 What are minorities? In: Holmestad E, Lade A J (eds.) *Lingual Minorities in Europe*. Det Norske Samlaget, Oslo, Norway
Price G 1969 *The Present Position of Minority Languages in Western Europe: A Selective Bibliography*. University of Wales Press, Cardiff, UK
Simpson J M Y 1981 The challenge of minority languages. In: Haugen E, McClure J D, Thomson D S (eds.) *Minority Languages Today*. Edinburgh University Press, Edinburgh, UK
Wardhaugh R 1987 *Languages in Competition*. Blackwell, Oxford, UK

Politicized Language
A. Davies

This article is divided into three parts. In the first part, the classificatory surface of language and the issue of 'avoidance' are considered; in the second part, the correlation model in sociolinguistics and its call for 'consciousness raising' are looked at; in the third part, language as a manipulator is considered and the issue of 'deliberate change' in language is examined.

A primary distinction is assumed between the language of politics and the politics of language. By the language of politics is meant the terminology and rhetoric of political activities and of politicians acting in their professional capacity, which is comparable to the discourses of other occupations such as the law, medicine, and religion. A further distinction is made between the politics of language and political (or politicized) language. The politics of language concerns policies and decisions about official and standard languages, language planning, language academies, and educational language policies. Politicized language is neither the preserve of a profession nor the office of the state; it is a resource open to all, allowing (or inviting) one to consider and to use language for suasion and control (including lying and deceit). This article focuses on politicized language and touches only fleetingly on the politics of language, but there is inevitable overlap between the two concerns, if only because politics is necessarily concerned with control, with advertising, with propaganda, and with ideology. It is in this overlap that politicized language and the politics of language meet.

Underpinning the approach taken in this article is a longstanding opposition in philosophy. The epistemological concept of realism assumes that universals exist, implying that scientific truth is attainable and unitary. The opposing doctrine of nominalism makes no such assumption, claiming rather that what is known is always relative, relative to space and to time. Householder (1952) has teasingly suggested that when transferred to linguistics realism may be regarded as the 'God's truth' approach, while nominalism is the 'hocus-pocus' approach. A nominalist position can be argued on the grounds that a realist view denies a critical capacity of flexibility to the language user, imprisoning him/her within the castle of his/her own language. Such an extreme Whorfian position (Whorf 1940) can be challenged on the grounds that it makes no allowance for a separation between language and thought.

1. Language Classification

The concern with the politicizing of language through its classificatory systems emerges more in the discussions of sociologists than of linguists. Edelman (1977) points to the way in which differing connotations for the word 'poverty' may lead to quite contradictory philosophies and political actions (the poor as fraudulent and lazy; the poor as victims of exploitation). Edelman refers also to the social creation of social problems through the conventional mode to naming and classifying. Terms like 'mental illness,' 'criminal,' and 'drug abuse' focus attention on the alleged weakness and pathology of the individual, while diverting attention from their pathological, social and economic environments. 'Conventional names for social problems evoke... dubious beliefs and perceptions. The "welfare" label connotes to many that the problem lies in a public dole, which encourages laziness' (Edelman 1977: 27). Arguments of this sort relate back to the views of earlier sociologists such as C. Wright Mills: 'The languages of situations as given must be considered a valuable portion of the data to be interpreted and related to their condition' (Mills 1940: 911).

Strong (1984) reminds us of Nietzsche's argument about idols which arise out of the anarchy fundamental to human creativity. In the case of language, Nietzsche maintained, 'we suffer from the malady of words and have no trust in any feeling not stamped with its special word' (Strong 1984: 101). According to this view, language, the classificatory tool, comes to dominate the way one sees the world.

In his discussion of sexism, Bolinger (1980), commenting on the words used for women, remarks that 'As with other relatively powerless classes, there is a heavy representation of epithets and similar unfavorable terms, more than for men' (1980: 91). Outside the language and gender issue, similar critiques are made of the ways in which vocabulary can be used to denigrate minorities generally, leading perhaps to the logical dilemma pointed out by D'Souza (1991): 'At Michigan, architecture professor James Chaffers delivered a lecture in which he called the term minority "insulting... minority is the late twentieth-century term for nigger." This fact surely would come as news to most students and faculty at Michigan. No one seems able to keep track of the changing vocabulary, and a white student who used the term "minority" would hardly be giving proof of racist sentiment, conscious or otherwise' (1991: 156). What is underlined here is the dilemma of ever being completely 'politically correct,' that elusive and probably fugitive attempt by 'right-wing writers to isolate and demonise a growing movement among radical students and teachers, minority rights advocates, literary theorists, environmentalists, and others who were concerned to eradicate various forms of prejudice' (McArthur 1992). The Oxford Modern English Dictionary (1992) defines political correctness as '(esp. in the US) avoidance of forms of expression and action that exclude or marginalize racial and cultural minorities; explicit multiculturalism.' The merest suspicion of racism and sexism in words is therefore the cutting edge of politically correct movements. D'Souza quotes Alexander Aleinikoff, a Michigan law professor, on the need for avoidance in the protection of minorities: 'There is some speech that contributes nothing to the dialogue. To me, racial epithets are not speech. They are bullets. They can be outlawed in the same way that bank robbery can be outlawed' (1991: 152). Aleinikoff's confidence is surely excessive. It may be possible to outlaw such epithets, but such action does not remove the problem, which in essence has nothing to do with epithets, however bullet-like they may be. The problem remains, and replacement epithets become in their turn replacement bullets; or they may be replaced by an uncomfortable silence, which, however racially charged, cannot be outlawed anywhere.

Such views on classification (similar to those in the language and gender area with regard to the non-inclusive pronominal and reference systems: *man* for both male and female; *he* for he and she) misinterpret the nature of language and exaggerate the importance of language. If language variety is accepted as basic to the nature of language, then derogatory and negative language cannot be removed by fiat any more than swearing and vulgarity can. There is something naive about the claim that by acting upon the language society and social attitudes are thereby being changed. If only it were that easy! True, there is the argument for consciousness raising.

2. Consciousness Raising

A main motivation for movements such as the inclusive language movement (Doody 1990) is to bring about change in language use. Such movements or campaigns are said to be concerned with 'verbal hygiene.' Cameron (1990) brackets the campaign against sexism in language with the Plain English and Artificial Language movements as well as with language standardization activity. Although in her view these are all examples of metalinguistic activity, clearly they are all intended to affect language use. And where they do not, the aim is that they should raise the level of public consciousness about what language means or can be interpreted as meaning, thereby helping forward a change in attitudes towards minorities.

But there is another area in which consciousness raising has been important in language considerations. This concerns those practices in sociolinguistics reflecting the proposition that 'language reflects society.' Cameron takes proponents of such a proposition to task, directing her major criticism against the work of Labov and his followers working in the 'variationist' or 'quantitative' paradigm. Such an approach, Cameron insists, based on a correlational methodology, matching patterns of linguistic variation with social or demographic features, is inadequate.

> Two things about this kind of account are particularly problematic. The first problem is its dependence on a naive and simplistic social theory. Concepts like 'norm,' 'identity' and so on, and sociological models of structures/divisions like class, ethnicity and gender, are used as a 'bottom line' though they stand in need of explication themselves. Second there is the problem of how to *relate* the social to the linguistic (however we conceive the social). The 'language reflects society' account implies that social structures somehow exist before language, which simply 'reflects' or 'expresses' the more fundamental categories of the social. Arguably however we need a far more complex model that treats language as *part of* the social, interacting with other models of behavior and just as important as any of them.
> (Cameron 1990: 81–2)

Concentration on the classificatory role of language, particularly with lexical labeling, allows the politicizing of language change, often of a quite simplistic kind. Indeed, those active in studies of language and gender have now turned away from such concerns to a more considered interest in uses of gendered discourse. A similar turning-away was observed a generation ago with the rejection of the early Bernstein (1965) contrast of the surface features of restricted and elaborated codes in favor of a discourse/genre model.

Linguistic or sociolinguistic attention on the reflection of society in language, validated in terms of the Labov variationist or quantitative model and using a crudely correlational methodology, appears to have as its concern the description of language in social terms. It is important to note that in spite of her objection to the underlying assumption of such an approach, Cameron does not reject the intention. She regards the Labov paradigm as inadequate rather than false or wrong-headed. Such an account offers further description of language and probably a wider understanding of social categories. Indeed, despite Labov's desire to bring society into linguistics it is probable that his efforts have succeeded in incorporating some aspects of language within the social domain. As a result, whatever consciousness raising is brought about by quantitative approaches, it is likely that those who benefit most are students of sociology rather than of linguistics; they are even less likely to be members of the general public. It is noticeable that while Cameron's objection is on the grounds that the quantitative approach is basically politicized (taking for granted such questionable concepts as norm and identity) she herself does not escape from the need to politicize, in as much as she sees language as purely social to the exclusion of the individual.

3. Deliberate Change

Language as a manipulator and the issue of (deliberate) change in language are examined here. The genre debate in education is considered as liberating or confining discussion and learning. Finally, the issue of free speech is raised.

Fairclough (1989) addresses the issue of control directly. For him 'language has become perhaps the primary medium of social control and power' (1989: 3). In order to bring about political and social change—and Fairclough is quite open about his own political views and about his desire for such change—he recommends once more a form of consciousness raising, through what he and his colleagues term 'critical language study.' This technique 'analyses social interactions in a way which focuses upon their linguistic elements, and which sets out to show up their generally hidden determinants in the system of social relationships, as well as hidden effects they may have upon that system' (1989: 5). Fairclough's examples of ways in which the powerful manipulate language to their own ends draw on their control over discourse types and orders of discourse. He cites the examples of job interviews and of medical examinations, and claims that where such encounters are crosscultural 'white middle-class gatekeepers are likely to constrain the discourse types which can be drawn upon to those of the dominant cultural grouping' (1989: 47). Fairclough appears to assume a fairly strong deterministic position about the use of politicized language. Ikle (1973), on the other hand, while equally clear as to the manipulation of language for political ends (in terms of, for example, bargaining, negotiating, propaganda), assumes that the manipulator actively manipulates: 'as seen by the opponents in a bargaining situation, communication ordinarily serves to convey some truthful information as well as to give false information (or at least to conceal the truth)' (1973: 837). Economizing with the truth is obviously not the preserve of an ambassador, defined by Sir Henry Wotton (1568–1639) as 'an honest man sent to lie abroad for the good of his country.'

Controlling genres or 'discourse types' (Fairclough's preferred term) offers a more solid view of language manipulation. Wallace maintains that 'one of the goals of critical reading is the reconstruction of the discourses within the text. This means looking at the "obvious" and the "taken for granted" in critical ways' (see *Ethnomethodology*) 'so that, for instance, ways of talking about women, blacks, and foreigners, which are so commonplace as to be seen as obvious by most readers, are placed under scrutiny' (Wallace 1992: 68). However, the attempts by genre theorists (Kress and Hodge 1979) to promote the teaching of genre as the major activity in the language classroom may be equally manipulative in that the pedagogy may allow for no alternative ways of constructing genres. Such a pedagogy stems from a deterministic and enclosed view of language. In all concerns with politicization it does seem important to retain a sense of alternative ways of behaving, of alternative language encodings. An issue which resonates through the entire field of politicization is that of free speech. Its consideration is at the heart of the detailed exposure of political correctness (PC) by D'Souza (1991), and one's decision on what position to take up on free speech—as with obscenity and censorship—may reflect a deeper philosophical choice between realism and nominalism.

Fairclough maintains that free speech is a myth because of general social constraints of appropriateness: his view is the genre one that in discourse types there are firm conventions about who has rights and who has access. Harris (1990), however, appears to take up the extreme absolutist position that free speech is an inalienable right: 'freedom of speech is basically the right to participate in those communicational activities available in virtue of one's membership of a linguistic community' (1990: 159). In some measure, as D'Souza's discussion makes clear, these two views are not really in conflict because they are concerned with different aspects. Harris would accept that, in terms of acceptability, some things are not said (in church, in public, in formal settings, etc.); while the freedom he supports is to express one's views, beliefs, and so on. Of course, the freedom even to break the conventions of what is said and not said may not be appropriate, but nevertheless it should not be prevented.

Fairclough's 'myth' is only a myth if his deterministic view is accepted; what Harris shows is that in spite of conventions and constraints people do have freedom of alternative speech. Language does not reflect society, as Cameron argues; language is properly independent of society and while it may be politicized it does not have to be.

Informing the discussion, not always benignly, has been B. L. Whorf and the linguistic relativity hypothesis associated with him and his teacher Edward Sapir. The extreme Whorfian position (which has been aligned with realism) can be challenged on the grounds that it makes no allowance for a separation between language and thought. It has been argued that language and thought, while obviously connected, are distinct. While thought does make use of language as a medium of expression and also as a vehicle for its own activity, it can operate without the use of language and it can also act creatively and plastically on the language with which it is garbed.

Interestingly, it is to a creative writer that one can turn for an understanding of the subtle relationship between language and thought. George Orwell in his essays and novels recognized the nature of politicized language: 'In our time, political speech and writing are largely the defence of the indefensible.... Thus political language has to consist largely of euphemism, question-begging and sheer cloudy vagueness.' At the same time, what the code 'Newspeak' (in his novel *1984*) shows is that his animus was directed against invented and artificial languages such as Basic English. Control may be exercised through such devices, but the individual remains the arbiter of his/her own natural language. After all, in *1984* it is thinking not language which is the object of control.

See also: Manipulation; Critical Sociolinguistics.

Bibliography

Bernstein B 1965 A socio-linguistic approach to social learning. In: Gould J (ed.) *Penguin Survey of the Social Sciences*. Penguin, Harmondsworth, UK

Bernstein B (ed.) 1971 *Class, Codes and Control*, vol. 1. Routledge and Kegan Paul, London

Bloch M (ed.) 1975 *Political Language and Oratory in Traditional Society*. Academic Press, London

Bolinger D 1980 *Language The Loaded Weapon: The Use and Abuse of Language Today*. Longman, London

Cameron D 1990 Demythologizing sociolinguistics: Why language does not reflect society. In: Joseph J E, Taylor T J (eds.) *Ideologies of Language*. Routledge, London

De Sola Pool I, Schramm W (eds.) 1973 *Handbook of Communication*. Rand McNally, Chicago, IL

Doody M A 1990 Changing what we sing. In: Ricks C, Michaels L (eds.) 1990 *The State of the Language*. Faber & Faber, London

D'Souza D 1991 *Illiberal Education: The Politics of Race and Sex on Campus*. Free Press, New York

Edelman M 1977 *Political Language (Words that Succeed and Policies that Fail)*. Academic Press, New York

Fairclough N 1989 *Language and Power*. Longman, London

Fairclough N (ed.) 1992 *Critical Language Awareness*. Longman, London

Fowler R, Hodge R, Kress G, Trew A 1979 *Language and Control*. Routledge & Kegan Paul, London

Harris R 1990 On freedom of speech. In: Joseph J E, Taylor T J (eds.) *Ideologies of Language*. Routledge, London

Householder F W 1952 Review of Z. S. Harris 'Methods in Structural Linguistics'. *International Journal of American Linguistics* **18**: 260–8

Ikle F C 1973 Bargaining and communication. In: De Sola Pool I, Schramm W (eds.) *Handbook of Communication*. Rand McNally, Chicago, IL

Joseph J E, Taylor T J (eds.) 1990 *Ideologies of Language*. Routledge, London

Kress G, Hodge R 1979 *Language as Ideology*. Routledge & Kegan Paul, London

Lee D 1992 *Competing Discourses: Perspectives and Ideology in Language*. Longman, London

McArthur T 1992 Enter the era of caring words. *The Independent on Sunday*, August 23

Mills C W 1940 Situated actions and vocabularies of motive. *American Sociological Review* **5**: 904–13

Ricks C, Michaels L (eds.) 1990 *The State of the Language*. Faber & Faber, London

Shapiro M (ed.) 1984 *Language and Politics*. Blackwell, Oxford, UK

Smith O 1984 *The Politics of Language 1791–1819*. Clarendon Press, Oxford, UK

Stephens J 1992 *Language and Ideology in Children's Fiction*. Longman, London

Strong T B 1984 Language and Nihilism: Nietzsche's critique of epistemology. In: Shapiro M (ed.) *Language and Politics*, Blackwell, Oxford, UK

Wallace C 1992 Critical literacy awareness in the EFL classroom. In: Fairclough N (ed.) *Critical Language Awareness*. Longman, London

Whorf B L 1940 Science and linguistics. *Technology Review* **42**: 229–31, 247–8

Whorf B L 1956 *Language, Thought and Reality: Selected Writings of Benjamin Lee Whorf*. MIT Press, Cambridge, MA

Politics and Language

P. A. Chilton

When politicians are challenged over their use of 'language,' they often reply that the questioner is merely 'playing with semantics,' or confusing 'style' and 'content.' Nonetheless, politicians rely on using language in order to communicate with their electorates or subjects: they make speeches, employ public relations experts, and write in newspapers. Political life, whether totalitarian or democratic, depends in varying degrees on physical sanctions and coercions. However, whether democratic or totalitarian, regimes must communicate in order to inform, issue commands, legislate, persuade, and so forth. This article outlines some of the ways in which 'language' and politics are related.

1. Language, Discourse, and Power

In order to study the relationship between language and politics, it is necessary to make certain terminological distinctions and assumptions. The term 'language' itself appears to have various meanings in the everyday contexts in which it is associated with politics. For instance, when one speaks of 'the language of politics' one seems to imply that it is different in some way from other linguistic behavior; when one speaks of politicians 'misusing or abusing language,' the assumption is made that language is normally and naturally innocent. Other instances—for example, 'the English language'—seem to be entirely apolitical. Yet is this really so?

It is useful to distinguish 'language,' in the sense of the universal capacity of humans in all societies to acquire and to use language, from two other concepts: 'a language' (see *Language*) and 'discourse' (see *Discourse*).

As for the term 'politics' itself, from the point of view of linguistic study, there have been two guiding assumptions. First, one might adopt the classical definition of politics as the art of governance. This leads either to the linguist attempting to describe objectively the properties of the uses of language in various situations and institutions conventionally recognized as political; or to the linguist, rhetorician, or professional communication specialist providing technical advice and training to those who govern. Second, politics can be thought of as being about power, conflict, and cooperation. This leads to the view that politics is not confined to governments, parties, elections, and so forth, but pervades interpersonal interaction in everyday life, a view which has produced studies whose purpose is not merely to describe, but also to expose and criticize the relationship between language and the wielding of power.

Although there is no clear dividing line between descriptive and critical approaches (since critical approaches themselves necessarily depend on description), it is convenient nonetheless to make the distinction. Consequently, Sect. 2 considers the first of these two perspectives, the predominantly descriptive perspective. Sect. 3 considers the second perspective, critical linguistics or discourse analysis.

2. Descriptive Approaches

For many centuries in the West the study of the practical use of language in public life was moulded by the canons of Classical rhetoric. Political life and rhetorical theory are interconnected. The theory and practice of public oratory in legal and political situations appears to predate the first codifications of rhetorical techniques. According to Cicero, rhetoric was first codified in the Greek community of fifth-century Sicily, in order to promote legal proceedings against recently expelled tyrants. These methods are said to have been subsequently introduced to the Greeks in 427 BCE by the Sicilian envoy to Athens, Gorgias, who was himself a famous rhetor.

Over the following centuries codification developed alongside a philosophical debate which centered on the question of whether the rhetor's role was a purely technical one, without moral responsibility for the ideas expressed, or whether the very distinction assumed in this question—that is, the distinction between ideas and expression—was invalid. In the latter case, since ideas and expression could not be separated, the rhetorician and the orator had to bear moral responsibility for their words. For some thinkers—for example, Socrates as represented in Plato's dialogues—the art of persuasive speaking was necessarily deceptive. For others—for example, Isocrates (436–338 BCE) and Cicero (106–43 BCE)—the inseparability of words and ideas demanded a moral commitment on the part of speakers.

2.1 Rhetorical Description

Rhetoric manuals were developed throughout the Classical Greek, Roman, and Medieval periods in the form of highly structured lists, purporting both to describe and prescribe effective techniques for influencing an audience's thoughts and emotions. This is true of the best known and most influential Classical rhetoric manuals—Aristotle's *Art of Rhetoric*, Cicero's *On the Public Speaker*, Quintilian's *Training for Public Speakers*, and the anonymous *Rhetoric for Gaius Herennius*.

All the applications of rhetorical theory and practice were conceived as part of the political life of the community. Three principal applications were recognized: judicial rhetoric for presenting cases in the courts, 'deliberative' rhetoric for promoting policy in political assemblies, and 'demonstrative' rhetoric for ritual use on state occasions. Broadly speaking, the manuals offered speakers the following five-part methodology, adaptable to each of these types of public occasion.

(a) Psychological techniques of memorizing speeches were elaborately devised. It was recognized that maximum effect on the audience could be achieved if a speech were made to seem unpremeditated. The modern equivalent is the politician's use of the 'auto-cue'—a transparent screen, invisible to the audience, onto which is projected the text of the speech.

(b) Under the rubric 'Delivery,' techniques of voice control, gesture, and facial expression (see *Kinesics*) were described and recommended for different persuasive purposes. Twentieth-century politicians have in some significant cases been trained by actors. United States ex-president Ronald Reagan actually was a former actor.

(c) What was termed 'Invention' were in effect recommendations for finding arguments, proofs, and convincing turns of phrase. The latter might be quasi-logical proofs or plausible aphorisms.

(d) Devices of this kind had, of course, to be sequentially presented during the course of a speech, and the 'Disposition' or arrangement part of the manuals specified types of section (like the 'exordium' or rousing introduction, the statement of facts, the proofs themselves, and the 'peroration' or summing up), and ways of ordering them.

(e) The 'Style' section produced an elaborate and lengthy repertory of verbal ornaments. Under the subheadings 'figures of thought' and 'figures of speech' politicians and other public orators were introduced to a range of verbal techniques. Examples of these included questions—'rhetorical questions' (supposedly having an obvious answer), self-answered questions, strings of questions, and the exasperated question addressed to an individual. Furthermore, recommendations were made for verbal arrangements within and between sentences. Examples would be: repetitions of words ('How, how can they do it?'); antithesis ('We propose to raise living standards, the party opposite to degrade them'); sentence pairs of equal length; and alliterative effects. A third technique, felt to be particularly powerful, was the use of metaphor and related devices of analogy and resemblance, such as allegory, irony, and even onomatopoeia.

These techniques were recognized and practiced well into the early modern period. They were undoubtedly of importance to orators in the major Western political developments of the seventeenth to the nineteenth centuries. In the latter half of the twentieth century, the growing importance of all forms of electronic media in the life of almost all political systems also brought with it increased importance of the techniques of verbal presentation. Although Classical rhetorics had long since dropped out of even elite education, many of the techniques apparently continued to be employed. The reasons for this could be transmission in Western verbal culture; alternatively, rhetorical skills could be universal skills spontaneously produced by experienced speakers.

2.2 Modern Descriptive Approaches

Modern linguistics has made available methods of analysis and observation which have been applied to the verbal behavior of politicians.

2.2.1 Redescribing Rhetorical Devices

In line with the Socratic strand in the rhetorical tradition, some analysts have focused on the persuasive, deceptive, and manipulative aspects of politicians' language (see *Manipulation*). Modern linguistic categories of analysis are used to catalogue 'devices' or 'strategies.' The traditional rhetorical way of classifying is thus recast in terms of phonological, syntactic, lexical, semantic, pragmatic, and textual levels of description.

For example, on the phonological level can be placed devices of alliteration, assonance, and rhythm (e.g., 'I like Ike' as a slogan in the Eisenhower election campaign). On the syntactic level, one might list the use of agentless passives: e.g., 'Decisions were taken' fails to mention the identity of the decision-maker. On the lexical level, descriptive approaches will note 'jargon' words, that is words characteristic of some closed group of speakers, neologisms, acronyms, and word formation ('quangos' for 'quasi-autonomous nongovernmental organizations'). On the semantic level, there has been interest in semantic restriction and shifts arising from, for example, paraphrasing and euphemism. On the textual and pragmatic level, linguist commentators have noted modes of argumentation: for example, the use of quoted authorities.

2.2.2 Verbal Behavior of Politicians

Some descriptive analyses do not concern themselves with the problem of rhetorical deception, but seek to provide empirically valid, evaluation-free accounts of politicians' verbal behavior. The descriptive categories used here are the linguistic ones just referred to. In such studies, the analyst is concerned with the verbal characteristics of politicians speaking in speech settings such as parliaments or other assemblies in parliamentary democracies. Here too the customary levels of linguistic description provide a framework.

For example, it has been found that in the Austrian parliament politicians systematically switch between dialect and standard forms (see Moosmüller 1989). Dialect forms and standard forms of a language are subject to socio-political evaluation in all national states: they may be variously associated with sociability, aggressiveness, lack of intelligence, trustworthiness, etc. Politicians who rely on votes tend to exploit dialect switching. In the Austrian parliament, if dialect variants are used, this is only in part because of the social origin of the speaker. Moosmüller (1989) argues that the use of dialect switches also interacts with pragmatic structure in the following way. Although speeches themselves are usually prepared, transitional introductions and interruptions have to be managed more or less spontaneously, and it is at these junctures that dialect switches are used. The reason for their use appears to have less to do with the relatively spontaneous, and therefore less controlled, mode of speaking, than with the social evaluation of dialect forms. Because the dialect forms are negatively evaluated, they can be used to treat interventions and so forth as not-serious and to devalue opposition. Interestingly, this does not occur when speakers (either male or female) are responding to women parliamentarians, presumably because of gender-based expectations of politeness.

Some empirical studies go further than description, and, like the Classical oratory experts, seek to provide rhetorical prescriptions for professional politicians. Videorecording techniques have made it possible to analyze minutely both the verbal and the nonverbal components of the skilled oratorical performance. Gestures, voice quality, wording, phrasing, and speech structure can all be correlated with audience response in order to identify effective techniques.

One major study (Atkinson 1984) has used this methodology for identifying the techniques used by successful politicians to produce 'clap-traps'—those points during the delivery of a speech at which an audience receives a verbal or gestural signal from the speaker that applause is appropriate, or at which television production staff, by the same signal, switch camera focus. At these junctures it is possible to observe simultaneous cues that use gesture, intonation, specific verbal patterns, and pauses. Two important kinds of verbal pattern used in this way are the 'list of three,' and contrastive pairs (or antithesis). Here is an example of the former.

George Wallace, in his inaugural speech as governor of Alabama in 1963, elicited applause for his particular political message with the following list of three:

... and I say segregation *now*, (1)
segregation *tomorrow*, (2)
and segregation for *ever*. (3)

The first two italicized words were accompanied by rising intonation and followed by brief pauses; the third italicized word was accompanied by falling intonation and was immediately followed by applause.

2.2.3 The Mind of Politicians

Whereas such studies concentrate on delivery and phrasing techniques, some analysts, particularly in the discipline of political science, have analyzed the 'content' of political speeches. The purpose of this type of analysis has been to discover the mental predispositions of individual political decision makers, or groups of decision makers. The data are usually the transcripts of political speeches, or translations of transcripts. In the latter case no account is usually taken of cross-language differences.

The content analyst will be interested in the relative frequency of occurrence of particular vocabulary items, such as 'peace,' 'freedom,' 'democracy.' Linguistic 'indicators' of particular political proclivities may be looked for, such as words indicating hostility, aggressiveness, or cooperativeness. In many studies of this type the texts are 'coded,' i.e., the linguistic expressions at issue are tagged in some way by a team of readers. Variants of 'content analysis' are 'operational coding' and 'cognitive mapping.' The term 'operational code' arose in the study of

Bolshevist ideology: the policymakers of the Stalinist period were assumed to behave according to a certain belief system and a certain set of practical policy rules, in short, according to an 'operational code.' In this method, documents and speeches were analyzed by a team of analysts in order to reconstruct this code, in the belief that the future actions of those using it could be predicted. The term 'cognitive map' refers to a technique of analyzing documents and speeches in which the aim is to specify, in the form of a mathematically describable graph or 'map,' the network of causal links that individual policymakers claim or assume between events, actions, and entities in the national or international domain. However, none of these methods of analysis rests on a detailed linguistic theory or linguistic description.

2.2.4 Ideology

The study of the linguistic or textual characteristics of ideologies has had numerous practitioners. In addition to the study of Soviet Communist ideology, which was a concern for some American analysts during the Cold War period, European analysts, in the aftermath of the Second World War, produced studies of fascist ideology. Marxist scholars, however, had for a long time used the notion of ideology in relation to capitalist society, proceeding on the hypothesis that ideology and language were interrelated (cf. Althusser 1971). Many approaches have been applied, but the following aspects of languages and their use in social and political life are relevant (see *Ideology*).

The means of controlling the languages used, the media of public information, and the content of public media are under *direct* political control in totalitarian states. Propaganda and censorship depend on control of the press, radio, and television. Less well-known is control through language planning, in particular the planning of language teaching curricula in schools. In Mussolini's Italy, for example, the teaching of Italian through an increased emphasis on Latin grammar was introduced, the teaching of German was given priority, and Arabic was promoted (for communication and control in the African colonies).

The effect of National Socialist ideology on the language system itself is most obvious on the lexical level. On the lexical level the changes in vocabulary, both in terms of its structure and in terms of denotative and connotative meaning, which came about as a result of national socialism in Germany and as a result of the fascist party in Italy have become widely known. In German, for example, words like *Volk* ('folk' or 'people') and its derived adjective *völkisch* became conventionally associated with National Socialist beliefs concerning race, and after 1945 became unusable in German political discourse. Other well-known terms are *Führer*, *Anschluss* ('joining on' the term used for Hitler's annexation of Austria), *Selbstgleichschaltung* ('voluntary falling into line').

At the level of the use of language in particular situations, descriptions of totalitarian language use have successfully examined characteristic narrative. It is within the narratives—the histories, accounts, stories, explanations—circulated through the controlled media, including education, in a totalitarian society that the individual lexical items mentioned above acquired and retained new conventional meanings.

One of the main problems in approaching language and politics by means of the concept of ideology is the fact that the latter term is often taken to imply a distinction between a false representation of reality and an objectively true one. Yet there is no guarantee that the analyst of ideology occupies a completely neutral position.

3. Critical Approaches

The descriptive strand of study that has been so far discussed tends to take an epistemological position that is close to positivism. That is to say, it tends to treat the political language phenomena it is submitting to scrutiny as neutral independent facts, and to treat the observing analyst as a neutral independent scientist. Questions of value, and questions of the analyst's own standpoint, tend to be excluded or occluded. This is not to say that questions of value do not arise from time to time—as in the Classical tradition in rhetoric. Nor is it to say that a precise description of political language phenomena is not essential for what is described below as the 'critical' strand in the analysis of politics and language.

This approach is distinctive because it assumes a different conception of politics—a conception which emphasizes the importance of power from the point of view of the subject citizen, and assumes connections between the 'macro' structures of state institutions and the 'micro' structures of everyday, person-to-person relationships and interactions. This approach is more characteristic of European than of North American scholarship, although some impact on American social science became visible from the early 1980s (e.g., Shapiro 1984).

Among the European social theorists who have been influential, in different and—some scholars would argue—opposed ways, are Jürgen Habermas and Michel Foucault. Habermas is associated with Frankfurt School 'critical theory' and views the analysis of social practices, including linguistic ones, as a rational enterprise whose purpose is emancipation. 'Distorted communication' derives, in the Habermasian view, from unequal access to the communication process, which itself is a function of the exercise of power. Foucault is associated with a concept of discourse which is examined more closely below (see *Discourse*).

Because of the ambiguities of the term 'language' discussed in Sect. 1, many writers have come to prefer the term 'discourse.' Linguists (as also philosophers, psychologists, information scientists) use the term to refer to language-in-use, as distinct from the language system conceived as grammatical rules, patterns, or properties. In studying discourse they focus on written text, on spoken utterance, and on the processes whereby individuals process texts and utterances (see *Speech and Writing*).

In the 1970s and 1980s, on the other hand, social scientists (including political scientists), were influenced by the way the term 'discourse' was used in European literary and social criticism by writers such as the French philosopher Michel Foucault. Such studies are sometimes referred to as 'postmodernist' or 'deconstructionist.' Some linguists concerned with the critical analysis of language use in relation to politics have also adopted these ideas (e.g., Fairclough 1989).

Among the prominent notions emphasized in this line of thinking are the following.
(a) The relationship between language and power (see *Power and Language*): control and dominance, it is claimed, are exercised increasingly in the modern period by linguistic means.
(b) The pervasiveness of power: control and dominance are everyday phenomena found in encounters of many kinds, e.g., in the classroom, in doctor–patient relations, in the relations between men and women.
(c) The relationship between linguistic and nonlinguistic practices: while the use of language is increasingly crucial in political life, other nonlinguistic forms of action are associated with language, e.g., architectural arrangements.
(d) Orders of discourse: types of talking and writing (e.g., interview, conversation, letters) play different parts in different institutions of a society (e.g., in education, policing, journalism, commerce). In addition, an entire society or polity can be thought of as constituted from several interconnected 'orders of discourse' (e.g., education, political institutions, religion, law, medicine, and so forth), and this overall structuring of a social and political entity, viewed from the point of view of discourse, has also been termed 'an order of discourse.'

3.1 National Language

It can be argued that the concept of 'a language' is itself a political concept. A language, it has been said, is a dialect with an army and a navy. The point of the joke is that what is commonly called 'a language' is not a homogeneous system, but a collection of dialects and varieties. These dialects and varieties may be distinguished in terms of their geographical distribution, but also in terms of their social distribution (see *Language*; *Dialect and Dialectology*). In addition, individuals will command, in different degrees, depending on their socioeconomic provenance and/or their skill, a variety of linguistic resources relating to different functions, situations, and institutions in the culture.

At the level of both intrastate and interstate politics, dialect is significant in the following sense. Dialect boundaries are naturally fuzzy: they do not coincide with political boundaries (see *National Language/Official Language*). However, nation-states have usually selected, codified, and elaborated the dialect of a politically dominant group as the standard. The term 'dialect' includes phonological, lexical, and syntactic variations.

For example, modern standard British English derives from the East Midlands dialect spoken by the merchant class at the end of the medieval period. This dialect subsequently extended the range of functions and situations in which it was employed as growing numbers of people adopted it, and the dialect was increasingly spoken or written in institutions of political power, such as government, administration, law, and religion. In the course of the political centralization of the UK this dialect ousted, for an increasingly wide range of functions, not only Latin and French, but also the Celtic languages, as well as other dialects of English.

In colonial settings, the use of the colonial power's national language (English, Spanish, French, Russian, for example) at the expense of local languages has the most obvious political significance (see *Linguistic Imperialism*). Even in the postcolonial period, states seeking global influence institutionalize overseas language training: the USA and the UK invest to varying degrees in language export, and France likewise seeks to maintain 'la francophonie.' Domestically, governments have more or less explicit policies with regard to standard and majority languages. In many instances the selected standard has been imposed by law and not infrequently enforced by physical sanctions (see *Linguicide*).

It is in this sense that the successful elites of emergent nation-states have typically selected a dialect and developed and imposed a national language. The political effect is both international and domestic. On the one hand, the 'national language' externally defines and differentiates nation-states in the international system; on the other hand, the 'national language' internally defines and differentiates, to the extent that this standard is not equally distributed throughout a population at a given period of time, elites and non-elites, the powerful and the less powerful. It follows that the concept 'a language' has an inherently political basis.

3.2 Critical Discourse Analysis

The term 'critical linguistics,' originally indicated techniques of descriptive linguistics to expose uses of language which were claimed to manipulate addressees, deceive them, or hide material from them. The early emphasis on lexis and syntax had the disadvantage of giving the impression that manipulative, deceptive, or dissimulating procedures, and hence ideology, were attributable to the language system *as such*, and that they had a deterministic quality. Later work has emphasized the receiver's end of the communicative process, however. Feminist linguists and discourse analysts in particular have clarified the importance of this subjective dimension (see *Ideology*; *Manipulation*; *Discourse*).

The linguistic discipline of pragmatics has drawn attention to the fact that language-in-use is a form of social action (see *Pragmatics and Sociolinguistics*). The predominant Anglo-American approach, however, emphasizes individual action and has neglected the dependency between individual acts, including speech acts, and power (see *Speech Act Theory: An Overview*; *Power and Language*). A speech act is an utterance which is identical to some social act, which may be an institutionalized one. For example, promising, requesting, warning, are generalized speech acts, and baptizing, sentencing, declaring war are highly institutionalized ones. Both, however, can be seen as dependent on structures of power.

In the latter examples this is self-evident: only certain appointed individuals, operating according to established procedure, can issue such speech acts. Not everyone can declare a war or sentence someone to prison. The former examples also depend on power. Speech acts have been said to depend on 'felicity conditions.' That is to say, they do not work unless certain conditions obtain: for example, a request only makes sense if, among other things, the speaker wants the hearer to perform some action, and believes the hearer is capable of performing this action. This formulation, however, omits the fact that in certain situations only speakers occupying a certain status with respect to the hearer are entitled to issue a request. Thus many of such examples clearly depend on the *legitimacy* of the speaker and the act. In other words, they depend on a characteristically political concept.

Another aspect of issuing speech acts is what have been termed 'politeness phenomena' (see *Politeness*). Among the generalized or noninstitutionalized speech acts many can be issued in various ways, depending upon circumstances. A request can be made directly or indirectly, with or without overt politeness words: for example, 'Move along there, please,' 'Get out of the way,' 'It's a little crowded in here.' Indirect politeness formulas avoid direct verbal reference to the speaker, hearer, object, or event. In addition, politeness may be achieved by creating common ground between the speaker and the hearer, for instance, by saying 'we,' mentioning common experiences, or using phrases common to the interlocutors.

In most accounts in the literature of pragmatics such phenomena are treated as individual strategies. However, such strategies are clearly useful in the political context. Indeed, the avoidance strategy can be used, precisely because it is conventionalized in politeness practices, to misrepresent, underinform, and evade responsibility. The common ground strategy likewise is a natural procedure for political speakers seeking to establish legitimacy, credibility, and popularity. There is not of course any direct and necessary correspondence between such procedures and a particular type of political action. A critical analysis arises from the critical position of the analyst.

Conversation analysis (CA) has been successful in identifying and describing the sophisticated resources of speakers in the management of talk in various kinds of settings. The taking of turns, for example, is handled according to regular principles, with ends and beginnings of turns being signaled in subtle linguistic ways (see *Conversation Analysis*). The disadvantage of this approach is that it neglects the connection between the 'micro' setting and 'macro' institutions, including the distribution of power (see *Power and Language*). For example, building upon the techniques of CA, analysts have noted the skewed distribution of power in male–female encounters in certain social settings, which is reflected in turn-taking rights, interruption rights, and in speaking time allotted. In general, a high-status interlocutor may interrupt more readily than a low-status interlocutor, and in such instances the motive may be to exercise control.

Conversation analysis can be extended in another politically relevant sense, if the micro-analyses of conversation turn-taking are seen as a metaphor for the macro-communicative processes of the polity as a whole. Such a metaphor points not merely to political questions of censorship, freedom of information, and access to public media, but also to the fundamental question of freedom of speech—in short, to how 'turns' are allocated to individuals and groups in the global 'conversation' of public communication. Placing conversation analysis in the context of political discourse analysis necessarily takes this question beyond simple legal entitlement, and leads to investigation of non-obvious restrictions on access to media and on rights to adopt particular communicative roles.

Some of these implications have been given formulation by using the notion of 'subject position.' The term 'subject' in this notion is deliberately understood in two senses: the political sense in which a person is a passive 'subject' in a political jurisdiction, and the quasi-grammatical sense in which a 'subject' is (at least in many sentences) the active 'doer.' On this basis the critical discourse analyst proceeds to show how a 'subject' is both determined by the discourses available, but is also thereby constituted as a social actor. This is not a determinist model, for 'subjects' have scope for creative maneuver as well as for stereotypical behavior.

An example of this type of analysis would be the discourse of a social institution such as a school or college. Such institutions are structured in terms of the discourse types that are viewed as legitimate for the various functions of the institution: lectures, teacher–pupil talk, staff meetings, examinations, for example. Within each discourse type, certain 'subject positions' are quite rigidly prescribed, in terms of what each can say and when, for the roles of teacher, lecturer, pupil, examiner, chairperson, and so forth. From the point of view of critical discourse analysis such distinctions are not merely a matter of organizational efficiency, but a means of maintaining and reproducing social control, and are thus a part of a political analysis.

A second example would be the analysis of the discourse of political parties. All political parties need to have the support of electors. These electors therefore need to be addressed (media broadcasts and the like) as if they were all members of a homogeneous entity. This may not of course be the case, where a political party needs support from electors of diverse social origins. Another way of stating this problem for the political party is to say that it needs, in its public discourse, to construct a 'subject position' that can be 'occupied' by diverse hearers.

The linguistic means for such constructions can be detailed through analysis of texts and transcripts, and they are of course highly variable and dependent on the analyst's own viewpoint. However, in particular instances, syntactic and other features can be indicated as involved in the projection of subject positions. In the following extract from a radio interview (December 17, 1985) with the then UK Prime Minister, Margaret Thatcher, the use of lists with syntactic coordination can be related to the need to specify a notion of 'the people' which will be assented to by different social sectors:

> and I was always brought up with the idea 'Look, Britain is a country whose people think for themselves, act for themselves, can act on their own initiative, they don't have to be told, don't like to be pushed around, are self-reliant and then over and above that they're always responsible for their families.'

As Fairclough has argued, the syntax of coordination appears here to serve the function of listing attributes with the implication that they are connected in a composite whole. It would also be relevant, in the critical discourse perspective, to note that the speaker assumes the authority to speak truthfully to the people about themselves, and that she does so by reproducing stereotypes that constitute common ground. The speaker thus assumes a particular subject position, a position aided by privileged access to an authoritative medium, and verbalizes a subject position for hearers of the interview.

There are two closely interrelated ways of looking at meaning in relation to political discourse. First, words can be considered in so far as they are part of a resource potentially available to anyone who can be said to know a particular language. Second, meaning can be considered in relation to the words and sentences of a text or utterance produced in particular discourse types.

Of the many theories of semantics, those approaches that have proved fruitful in the analysis of political discourse are those developed in cognitive science and in cognitive theories of comprehension. Texts and utterances are produced and comprehended at least in part by accessing mental representations of objects and processes. These representations include 'image schemata' (basic experiences like moving from one location to another), 'frame' (recurrent static objects like houses), and 'scripts' (repeated events like election procedures). Discourse types are partly characterized by their frames and scripts. They enable people to define what is 'real,' recognize situations, objects, and events, and to draw relevant inferences from allusions to them. Moreover, they provide the source for metaphor, where metaphor is understood as a major cognitive process not merely in persuasive rhetoric, but in conceptualization of complex or remote phenomena such as politics and international relations.

The politically important notion of racial, gender, and enemy 'stereotypes' can be understood in cognitive terms. The stereotype of the Jew, the German, the Communist, for instance, is a set of relatively stable mental representations linking attributes as well as attributed motives and goals. These attributes are negatively valued, and are repeatedly accessed in comprehension and perception. Stereotypes seem to arise when some, often peripheral, subset of a category is taken as the prototypical representative of the entire category. From a cognitive and a semantic point of view this process is metonymic—that is, the process whereby one thing is taken to stand for another thing with which it is associated. But the metonymy itself comes about as a result of some form of social or political promotion, usually by a socially and politically dominant group. The role of Western enemy image stereotypes was apparently recognized in Soviet foreign policy in the 1980s when efforts were made, often explicitly, to modify Western perceptions of the Soviet leadership.

The part played by metaphor in conceptualizing political realities is considerable. Metaphor is used by both theorists and practitioners, although in some political systems the distinction may be blurred. The most well-established metaphor for the state is the 'body politic.' In international relations theory, the state is often conceptualized as a person or as a container. Metaphors have implied meanings that can influence subsequent discourse in its conceptual aspect.

Thus, if a state is a body, it may also be sick, have a cancer within it, need a purge, and so forth. If it is a container-like entity, it will have internal and external affairs, and rigid separation of domestic and international politics might be a consistent part of the discourse's conceptualizations. Stalin's concept of politics and the state seems to have utilized a machine metaphor, entailing 'transmission belts,' 'levers of power,' etc.

Many other key political concepts show conceptual consistency of this type. The notion of 'policy' itself is often expressed in terms of movement along a path: a step-by-step approach, not deviating from the party line, dual track, etc. Crises are often seen as 'cross-roads' or 'turning points' of history. Such concepts might be linked to some larger system of political beliefs in which history is itself viewed as a path through time with an inevitable destination, or in which one's country has been sent on some 'mission.'

Particular metaphors may serve an important role in the conduct of political debate on problematic issues, both by providing a conceptual tool and by providing a means of referring to taboo topics indirectly. But in international, intercultural communication, including diplomacy, there can be distorting effects. An example, is the 'common European house' metaphor, used by the then Soviet president Gorbachev from around 1985, where the word 'house' translates the Russian 'dom.' The cognitive frame for 'dom,' however differs markedly from the stereotypical Anglo-American house, in so far as it typically represents a block containing separate apartments. The political implications of the metaphorical 'dom' and the metaphorical 'house' were divergent.

Although the systematicity and the productiveness of metaphors like these are clear, the implications are less so. It is possible that a well-established metaphor may in some discourse type tend to limit alternative conceptualizations. In persuasive political rhetoric, metaphors of this type may, because they appear natural, contribute to a speaker's legitimacy and credibility.

See also: Power and Language; Manipulation; Hegemony; Discourse; Media Language and Communication; National Language/Official Language.

Bibliography

Althusser L 1971 (transl. Brewster B) Ideology and state apparatuses. In: *Lenin and Philosophy*. New Left Books, London
Atkinson M 1984 *Our Masters' Voices. The Language and Body Language of Politics*. Methuen, London
Dixon P 1971 *Rhetoric*. Methuen, London
Fairclough N 1989 *Language and Power*. Longman, London
Foucault M 1971 *L'Ordre du discours*. Gallimard, Paris
Fowler R, Hodge B, Kress G, Trew T 1979 *Language and Control*. Routledge and Kegan Paul, London
Kress G 1985 *Linguistic Processes in Socio-cultural Practice*. Deakin University Press, Melbourne
Leith R 1983 *A Social History of English*. Routledge and Kegan Paul, London
Moosmüller S 1989 Phonological variation in parliamentary discussions. In: Wodak R (ed.) *Language, Power, and Ideology*. Benjamin, Amsterdam, UK
Shapiro M L (ed.) 1984 *Language and Politics*. Blackwell, Oxford, UK
Wodak R (ed.) 1989 *Language, Power, and Ideology*. Benjamin, Amsterdam

Power and Language
N. Fairclough

For the most part, questions of power have either been ignored in language studies, or dealt with at a rather superficial level. The richest insights into the relationship between language and power have come from increasing attention to language in social theory (its so-called 'linguistic turn'), in the work of Louis Althusser, Pierre Bourdieu (see *Bourdieu, Pierre*), Michel Foucault (see *Foucault, Michel*), Jurgen Habermas, and others. But in the 1980s and early 1990s, there have been attempts to operationalize these insights in language analysis, within 'critical linguistics,' and within more critical work in discourse analysis and pragmatics (see *Discourse*; *Pragmatics and Sociolinguistics*). A major problem for such work is that there are many divergent theories of power, which can lead to different approaches to language. There are also different levels at which the language–power relationship can be investigated: one could focus upon how power relations are enacted in discourse; or alternatively upon power asymmetries associated with unequal access to certain languages or language varieties (including questions of language politics and language planning). This article concentrates mainly upon the former. It discusses, first, meanings of 'power.' It then moves from a rather static view of domination in discourse (see *Linguistic Imperialism*) to a more dynamic view of discourse as embedded within power struggles, discussing in turn power in discourse, power 'behind' discourse, and power struggle in and over discourse.

1. The Concept of 'Power'

Theories of power differ on fundamental issues; for example, whether power belongs to individuals or collectivities or systems, whether it necessarily involves conflict, whether it presupposes resistance, whether it is just repressive and negative (a matter of domination) or also enabling and positive. Within the bewildering divergences, it is possible to differentiate two major contrasting conceptions of power. The first and more general sense is power as transformative capacity, the capacity of agents to affect the course of events. Power in this sense may be enabling and positive as well as repressive, and it is a capacity possessed in some degree by any actor, dominant or dominated. Power in the second sense is a relational concept, 'power over,' and is linked to domination by individuals or collectivities. In critical language studies as in other spheres, there has tended to be a one-sided emphasis upon the latter, giving an overly pessimistic view of the sociolinguistic and discourse practices of a society (see *Language in Society: Overview*; *Discourse*) as simply an apparatus of domination. This article begins with domination and 'power over,' looking first in the section 'power in discourse' at the power of one participant over another in particular interactions, and then in the section 'power behind discourse' at the power of certain collectivities over others arising from their control over the sociolinguistic practices of a community. But in the section 'power struggle in and over discourse,' the more general sense of power is brought in, in the process of arguing that power in language is not simply domination.

2. Power in Discourse

Perhaps the most obvious instances of 'power over' and domination are cases where using language is a way of directly policing or mobilizing people. One example is the orders, threats, or diatribes parents sometimes use to control their children; a more institutionally regulated example is the discourse of military command (e.g., *Attention! From the left, quick march!*).

Domination takes a more indirect form in what are sometimes called 'unequal encounters'—types of discourse such as job interviews or medical consultations or lessons, where participants have unequal institutional status and authority. In such cases, higher-status participants (such as doctors or teachers) may control the development of the discourse, and the contributions of other participants to it, in various ways. For example, a medical consultation may consist largely of questions from the doctor, with the patient being limited to providing answers. This gives the doctor control over the content of the discourse (what topics are raised and how they are dealt with), as well as positioning the patient as a particular sort of medical subject (a passive participant in medical practice, a body worked upon by the doctor), in a particular sort of relationship (subordination and dependency) to the doctor. Generalizing from this example, one can say that power in discourse is exercised over content, relations between participants, and the identities of participants as social subjects.

Higher-status participants may also control the contributions of others by treating them as performances to be evaluated. In classroom discourse, for example, teachers systematically evaluate what learners say (e.g., Teacher: *What's the capital of France?* Pupil: *Paris, Miss.* Teacher: *Yes, Paris*). And there are various other ways of controlling contributions: by interrupting and curtailing them when they are judged to be irrelevant, by providing authoritative summaries or 'formulations' which impose particular interpretations upon them, by asking for them to be reformulated in different words which may force participants to be more explicit than they would wish to be, and so forth.

Power asymmetries between participants of different status may be evident in their orientation to what some pragmaticists call the 'face' of coparticipants (see *Politeness*). Participants may differ in how polite they are to each other, or in how directly or indirectly they say or write things which may be intrusive or offensive or threatening (compare, for example, two ways of asking a question which might be asked in a medical consultation: *How's your sex life?* versus *Are there any aspects of your personal life that might have a bearing on these problems?*). Participants may also differ in the extent to which they try to be accommodating to other participants, for example, by modifying their own usual linguistic practices toward those of others.

But it is not just differences in the institutional status of participants that give rise to discoursal inequality and domination; so too do differences in age, gender, cultural identity, and so forth. One aspect of unequal gender relations is that men sometimes dominate in female–male interactions. A study of the discourse of married couples in the USA, for example, (by Pamela Fishman, reported in Graddol and Swann 1989) showed that men gave women much less supportive feedback when they were talking than vice versa, and that topics introduced by men were much more likely to be taken up than those introduced by women. Such inequalities are aggravated in institutional interactions, where the higher-status participants are men, or members of cultural majorities, and the lower-status participants are women, or members of cultural minorities (see *Minority Languages*). Some research has suggested that, in such situations, higher-status participants systematically misinterpret cultural differences in discourse practices (e.g., between the majority white community in the UK or the USA and black or Asian minority groups), as evidence of lack of cooperation, incompetence, etc., on the part of lower-status participants (Gumperz 1982).

So far 'face-to-face' discourse has been considered where participants are interacting at a particular time and place, and conjointly producing the discourse (though with different degrees of influence on it, as indicated above). But in the case of written discourse, and the discourse of the mass media (radio, television, film) (see *Media Language and Communication*), there is a separation between participants who produce the discourse and those who constitute its audience (be they readers, listeners, or viewers). Producers have power over audience in that they can determine what is included or excluded, and how people, objects, and events are represented. And since mass audiences are so potentially diverse, producers have to build into their discourse 'ideal' readers or listeners or viewers, which may significantly contribute to the social shaping of real readers, listeners, or viewers. Of course, audiences sometimes have means of counteracting the power of producers: they may stop reading or turn the television off, or be hostile audiences that contest producers' discourse in some way or other.

One section of the mass media whose power has been widely debated is the news media, and there is much controversy over the extent to which, and ways in which, news discourse shapes the beliefs and actions of audiences, but broad agreement that it has some significant effect. The central issue is what might be called 'signifying power': if it is assumed that there is no neutral or objective way of representing events, then all reports signify them in particular ways, perhaps according to the strategies (economic, political) and ideologies (see *Ideology*; and Sect. 3.1 below) of the reporter. For example, the headline *Police shoot 100 in riot* is quite explicit about the agency of, and responsibility for, the violence reported, whereas the headline *100 die in riot* is quite inexplicit, and there may be good strategic or ideological motivations for one rather than the other. What is not entirely obvious is who exercises signifying power in the media: behind the journalists and editors are the powerful sections of society (government, industry, the professions, etc.) that constitute the major sources of news, and it is arguable that events are often signified in ways which accord with their interests, strategies, and ideologies. Their power is a hidden power, which might be related to a 'hidden agenda' for the media: to mediate between those who hold power and the mass of the population. Signifying power in the media may be used to consciously manipulate audiences and readerships (see *Manipulation*). A more general and perhaps more insidious effect of signifying power is that particular signifying practices with particular ideological investments become naturalized for media professionals.

3. Power Behind Discourse

'Power in discourse' draws attention to discourse as one site where domination takes place and power relations are enacted; whereas 'power behind discourse' identifies discourse itself as a target for domination and hegemony. Societies and their constituent institutions (e.g., education, health care, law) have 'orders of discourse'—sets of codes, conventions, and norms which are structured in relation to each other in particular ways, and which are open to restructuring. Orders of discourse can be regarded as one domain of cultural hegemony (see *Hegemony*): dominant groups in societies and institutions seek to win consent for particular structurings of orders of discourse, as part of their attempt to achieve hegemony in the sphere of culture (complementing economic and political hegemony).

One dimension of a society's order of discourse is the structuring of relationships between different languages, and different varieties (social dialects—see *Dialect and Dialectology*) of one language. Certain languages or varieties are typically attributed high prestige and designated as appropriate for prestigious functions in law, government, education, and so forth, whereas other languages or varieties may be marginalized by being designated as appropriate only for functions in the private and domestic spheres, or indeed may be excluded through bans or ideological offensives (see *Linguicide*).

'Language standardization' is the process through which one variety of a language becomes the 'standard language' of a society, or even a broader international community—'Standard English' is an example. Standard English developed from the East Midland dialect of the late medieval period, which became the language of the merchant class of London, the class which was to achieve dominance in the transition from feudalism to capitalism. This link between the standard and social class is still there, although its form has changed: it is upper-class and middle-class children who learn Standard English as their mother tongue in the home, and for whom it constitutes the most efficacious 'cultural capital'—a passport to positions of influence and power. The claims of Standard English to be a national language are, it is true, recognized by all sections of British or American society, but it tends to be a forced and superficial recognition on the part of working-class people and cultural minorities, who still adhere strongly in practice to their own varieties and languages (see *Class and Language*). Standard English is universally taught in the school system, yet a substantial proportion of children fail to achieve high levels of competence in it. The process of language standardization does not merely elevate one variety, it simultaneously demotes others, and imposes upon the societal order of discourse which marginalizes 'nonstandard' varieties and other languages (see *Linguistic Imperialism*). Standardization belongs to the era of the modern nation-state with its centralization of national economies, political systems, and cultures. As this era comes to an end, nation-states are simultaneously under pressure from larger international entities and smaller local entities, and so too is the position of standard languages within orders of discourse.

As the last paragraph suggests, power behind discourse is not only a question of securing hegemonic structuring of orders of discourse, it is also a question of controlling access to languages, varieties, and codes which are ascribed prestige within orders of discourse. The educational system is of considerable importance in controlling access, being as Foucault put it 'a political way of maintaining or modifying the appropriation of discourses, along with the knowledges and powers which they carry' (1984: 123). Whatever the political rhetoric of education, the effect of the schools in Britain, for example, has been to consolidate class differences in 'linguistic capital' established in the family, rather than ironing them out. Access to prestigious functional varieties or 'registers' such as varieties of writing (literary, scientific), professional varieties such as legal English, or genres such as interview or public speaking, is similarly filtered by the education system. This is not to say that working-class or cultural-minority children do not acquire them, but that the development of high degrees of competence in them is disproportionately weighted toward upper-class and middle-class children.

Another important aspect of power over orders of discourse is the shaping, imposition, and naturalization of particular variants of the functional varieties just referred to. For example, there are various ways in which medical consultations might be and indeed are conducted, but there has tended to be an approved way of conducting them which has been institutionally 'policed' through inducements, pressures, and sanctions. A particular way of conducting a medical consultation will involve a given distribution of discourse 'rights' and 'obligations' between doctor and patient, such as rights and obligations to take turns at talking (see *Conversation Analysis*), respond to the other's turns in particular ways, develop and change topic, probe into aspects of the other's private life through direct or more tentative questioning, provide summaries of what has been said, give accounts of illnesses and problems, and so forth. What participants are allowed or required to do, and inequalities between participants in this regard, point to implicit assumptions—ideologies—about the nature of medicine, what it means to be a doctor or a patient, what relationship there ought to be between doctor and patient, and so on.

One may say that particular practices of medical consultation, classroom teaching, or interaction between managers and workers, carry particular ideological investments (see *Ideology*). That is, they embody sets of assumptions which correspond to the interests and points of view of particular social groups, but are made to look like mere common sense. This is why the imposition of particular practices is an objective for power holders: they can progressively naturalize ideological assumptions which help reproduce existing social relations and structures. Ideology is one modality of power, which uses control of meaning and definition of common sense as a means of producing and reproducing domination, positioning people as 'social subjects' of various sorts, and underpinning the interpretation of language texts as 'coherent' (see Sect. 3.1). The other major modality of power is the use of force, which may have more immediate effects than ideology, but is less effective in the longer term in maintaining relations of domination. Modern societies, in which domination takes the form of hegemony (i.e., rule through the generation of consent—see *Hegemony*), have become increasingly reliant upon the modality of ideology. They have therefore become increasingly reliant upon discourse, because it is in discourse that ideological processes mainly take place.

3.1 Ideology

Ideology, like power, is a complex and contested concept. It is a central element of Marxism, where ideologies have traditionally been seen as misrepresentations of reality through which the ruling class dominates other classes. Outside Marxism, more general definitions have emerged which see different ideologies as merely different perspectives or points of view. But the power of ideology as a concept is the connection it makes between domination and points of view, meanings, and representations. This link between ideology and domination has been maintained and developed in more recent Marxist theory (see *Marxist Theories of Language*). One influential tradition, based upon the theories of Antonio Gramsci (see *Gramsci, Antonio*) and Louis Althusser, sees ideologies as: (a) generally implicit or 'common-sense' assumptions about the nature of the world, social relationships, and social identities, which (b) invest and shape social practices, including discourse practices, that constitute their material form, and which (c) contribute to reproducing or restructuring relations of domination ('power over'). Most studies of language and ideology have adopted a view of ideology along these lines.

Language texts, written or spoken, may be ideologically 'invested' in various ways and at various levels—that is, choices of vocabulary, grammar, organization of turn-taking, and so forth, may come to be ideologically significant. Words and their meanings have received most attention, on the assumption that contrasting ways of 'wording' (see *Pragmatics and Sociolinguistics*) a particular domain of experience may embody different ideologies. An example would be the contrast between more traditional wordings of educational practices, and current 'commodified' wordings (e.g., *we can offer our customers a range of purpose-built packages to choose between*). But aspects of grammar may also be ideologically invested—compare, for example, the sentences *Thousands are out of work* and *Company directors have sacked thousands of workers* as different ways of reporting the same event (e.g., redundancies in the car industry). The former is an intransitive sentence without an agent which represents a state, the latter is a transitive sentence with an agent which represents an action. Systematic selection among such alternative sentence types may be connected with representations of unemployment as a condition which nobody is responsible for, or alternatively as caused by the actions of specific agents. On a different level of analysis, the turn-taking system operative in a classroom, or the politeness conventions (see *Politeness*) operating in interaction between managers and workers, may be invested with particular ideologies of education and work. Other features of texts are also ideologically important, including the sorts of metaphor that are used, and the sorts of presupposition that are made.

To understand fully the ideological effects of discourse, however, it is necessary to consider the processes of producing and interpreting texts as well as the texts themselves. In this connection, Althusser's emphasis on the relationship between ideology and the constitution of social subjects is important. He claims that ideologies 'interpellate' individuals as subjects of particular sorts, placing them in particular subject 'positions.' Discourse plays a major part in such processes of interpellation. For example, one effect of a set of conventions for medical consultations or classroom teaching is to cumulatively construct definite identities and 'positions' for doctors, patients, teachers, and pupils. If such a set of conventions comes to be dominant and naturalized (a matter of common sense), individuals who wish to become doctors or teachers have to compliantly occupy the positions provided. When a doctor addresses a patient drawing upon such conventions, (s)he implicitly positions the patient through the way (s)he speaks, and the same is true vice versa. Those so positioned may resist these positionings, but it is often extremely difficult to do so. Compliance does not however entail acceptance: people may 'go through the motions' of adhering to conventions, while at the same time privately distancing themselves from them. In favorable circumstances, they may challenge and try to restructure them (see Sect. 4).

At the end of Sect. 3, a connection between ideology and the production of coherent interpretations for texts was referred to. 'Coherence' has been a major concern of discourse analysts, because a central question about discourse is how interpreters can make sense of written or spoken texts which on the surface are highly disjointed and incoherent. However, from the perspective of ideology and the subject, the production of coherent interpretations can be seen as a key moment in the positioning of subjects. In order to establish coherence, interpreters need to draw upon the sort of implicit assumptions and knowledge structures which cognitive psychologists and specialists in artificial intelligence have called 'scripts,' 'frames.' and 'schemata.' Suppose, for instance, that a text contains this sequence of sentences: *She's giving up her job next week. She's pregnant.* To link the sentences coherently, an interpreter needs a 'bridging' assumption, that women who are about to have children stop working. It is an ideological assumption, tied to particular (now contentious) views of gender relations in the family. The point is that in achieving a coherent reading of the text, the interpreter is simultaneously being positioned, or repositioned, within a particular ideology of gender relations which (s)he needs to take for granted in making the next coherent. Similar comments apply to text producers: producing a text is an achievement which rests upon the mobilization of ideological assumptions and knowledge structures, thus ideologically positioning the producer.

4. Power Struggle In and Over Discourse

The view of power in and over discourse which has been presented so far is too static, and overemphasizes the imposition of domination from above. It neglects ways in which power may be contested. This section will adopt a more dynamic conception of power in and over discourse, centered around the concept of power struggle.

4.1 Struggle in Discourse

The exercise of power in discourse frequently meets with resistance, though only under particular subjective and social conditions. In terms of the former, resistance presupposes participants who have the motivation, resources, and confidence to resist. These subjective conditions are often discussed in terms of the 'empowerment' of members of dominated social groups (be it workers, women, or members of cultural minorities). Empowerment can be thought of as educative action to equip people to make use of the power they have—using 'power' now in the more general sense of transformative capacity—to resist in circumstances of domination. But empowerment can be effective only under favourable social conditions: resistance in discourse is more likely to occur, and more likely to take active forms, in institutional locations where the domination of one group over others is partial, precarious, or contested.

Struggle and resistance in discourse take a variety of forms, some of which are more active than others. It was suggested earlier that compliance with dominant discourse practices may amount to no more than 'going through the motions.' A form of passive resistance which may be as much as is possible in certain circumstances. Participants may also resist by fully exploiting the rights made available to then within dominant discourse practices, rather than challenging those practices (e.g., the right of interviewees to question interviewers, which is often offered to them at the end of an interview in the expectation that they will make at most token use of it). Or participants may overtly question the practices themselves; I could, for example, under certain circumstances tell my doctor that he might learn more about my problems if he sat back and listened to me for a while, rather than submitting me to a battery of diagnostic questions. A more covert and more pervasive form of resistance is not conforming with the rights and obligations imposed by dominant discourse practices, and drawing instead upon other practices. For example, provided (s)he has the resources to bring it off and provided the social conditions are favorable, a lower-status participant may be able to prevent a higher-status participant from conducting an interaction as a formal interview by talking (and more generally acting) as if it were a friendly chat.

4.2 Struggle over Discourse

Such forms of struggle in discourse may be manifestations of longer-term processes of contestation between social groups in which the structuring of societal and institutional orders of discourse is at stake. In Sect. 3 the imposition of hegemonies from above was referred to, but hegemonies are also open to challenge from below, and must constantly be reproduced and redefined under conditions of struggle. An example of the challenging of hegemonies from below is the attack by feminists upon what are seen as sexist and male-dominated discourse practices across a range of institutional orders of discourse—in the family, politics, trade unions, the media, education, social services, and so forth. One focus of this attack has been the forms of female–male interaction referred to in Sect. 2, which constitute modes of male domination: forms of conversation, for example, in which women are kept in the marginal and passive roles of listener and respondent, where their contributions are interrupted, where they are expected to talk on men's topics without being able to introduce their own, and so forth. The feminist challenge has made hitherto hegemonic practices problematical for many men as well as women, and led to some restructuring of practices.

Another example is the widespread tendency for institutional discourse (e.g., interviews of various kinds) to become more informal and conversational, less directive and judgmental and more empathetic, sometimes drawing upon the discourse of counseling as a model. This tendency is associated with struggle against traditional authoritarianism and bureaucratic impersonality in relationships between professionals and their clients or publics, and the late twentieth-century ascendancy of values of individualism and consumerism. But this tendency illustrates how challenges from below may be contained and appropriated from above: these new forms of institutional discourse are now widely cultivated by professionals and managers as strategies for attracting clients and consumers, or in personnel contexts for increasing the commitment of employees to the firms they work for, and making a greater range of their skills and talents available for exploitation by the firm. This can be seen as a shift in ideological investment (see Sect. 3.1): the concept of ideological investment implies that a given set of discourse practices or linguistic features does not have one inherent and permanent ideological value, but may come to be differently invested in different contexts, in the course of ideological struggle.

This example points to a basic feature of power struggle over orders of discourse in late twentieth-century society. On the one hand, there are centrifugal tendencies. Modern industrial society has been associated with the imposition of homogeneous and unitary dominant practices for such types of institutional interaction as medical consultations, job interviews, teacher–pupil interactions, or the discourse of managers and workers. There is now a shift away from this, associated with what some see as a 'postmodern' fragmentation of the modern structuring of society into discrete institutional and professional domains. Discourse practices are becoming more heterogeneous, partly because there are more opportunities for challenges from below to have effects. So the practices of medical consultation or classroom teaching are now highly variable, allow-ing the preferences and dispositions of doctors and teachers, patients and learners, to find some expression.

On the other hand, however, there are centripetal tendencies. These may be partly in response to the above centrifugal tendencies, but they also give them fresh impetus. Thus centripetal and centrifugal tendencies are tied into a single dialectic. Late twentieth-century centripetal tendencies involve a process of 'technologization' of discourse: the subjection of discourse practices (e.g., various types of interview) to systematic and institutionalized processes of research, redesign, and training. The technologization of discourse is a form of linguistic manipulation (see *Manipulation*). But as suggested above, these impositions from above may generate resistance and moves toward further diversity (see also *Linguistic Imperialism*; *Discourse*).

5. Conclusion

Absence of serious attention to the relationship between language and power is a major weakness of linguistic theory in the late twentieth century, including much of the work that has been done in sociolinguistics. In the 1960s, a distinction was often drawn between two branches of language study which link language and the rest of society in different ways: sociolinguistics, which places the focus upon language; and 'sociology of language,' which starts from society and social theory. This distinction has dropped out of fashion, and sociology of language has not really developed. The time has come for 'mainstream' linguistics to take note of recent critical work on language and power, perhaps in the form of resurrecting the sociology of language. But work on language and power may have a deeper significance for mainstream linguistics in the longer term: it may lead to new, more socially realistic theories of language which displace currently dominant asocial theories in the center of the discipline.

See also: Hegemony; Ideology; Critical Language Awareness; Symbolic Power and Language.

Bibliography

Bourdieu P 1991 (ed. Thomson J B) *Language and Symbolic Power*. Polity Press, Cambridge, UK
Dijk T A van 1987 *News as Discourse*. Erlbaum, Hillsdale, NJ
Fairclough N 1989 *Language and Power*. Longman, London
Fairclough N 2000 *New Labour, New Language?* Routledge, London
Foucault M 1984 The order of discourse. In: Shapiro M J (ed.) *Language and Politics*. Blackwell, Oxford, UK
Fowler R, Hodge B, Kress G, Trew T 1979 *Language and Control*. Routledge and Kegan Paul, London
Graddol D, Swann J 1989 *Gender Voices*. Blackwell, Oxford, UK
Gumperz J J 1982 *Discourse Strategies*. Cambridge University Press, Cambridge, UK
Hodge B, Kress G 1988 *Social Semiotics*. Polity Press, Cambridge, UK
Mey J L 1985 *Whose Language? A Study in Linguistic Pragmatics*. Benjamins. Amsterdam
Mishler E G 1984 *The Discourse of Medicine Dialectics of Medical Interviews*. Ablex, Norwood, NJ
Thompson J B 1984 *Studies in the Theory of Ideology*. Polity Press, Cambridge, UK

Power Differentials and Language

P. L. van den Berghe

Nearly all human relationships have a power dimension, and are, of course, expressed, to a large extent, through language. It follows that language frequently reflects, maintains, and enforces power differentials (Laponce 1984, Pool 1987). Of the major types of unequal relationships, those involving people of different 'race' or ethnicity, including the special case thereof known as 'colonialism,' have vied with age, sex, and social class in importance (Banton 1983, Horowitz 1985, van den Berghe 1981). This article is an attempt to sketch some of the main sociolinguistic features of ethnic interactions, with the main analytical focus on power and inequality.

1. Linguistic Differentiation

Speech communities, by definition, emerge from sustained, iterated linguistic interaction. Conversely, barriers of any kind to interaction inevitably translate into language barriers. Uninhibited, spontaneous, free and easy speech is only possible to the extent that barriers are absent. The most obvious barriers are those of physical distance. While they are partially breached in recent decades by the telephone, the radio, and television, it continues to be true that language is shaped primarily by people interacting face to face with high frequency, that is, by people in spatial propinquity to one another. Regionalism is, thus, a salient source of linguistic differentiation.

However, while spatial propinquity is a necessary condition for the formulation and maintenance of a speech community, it is not a sufficient condition. Barriers of social status frequently interfere with interaction as well. Age and gender are ubiquitous barriers of social status which lead to linguistic differences. Both sex and age differences are deeply ingrained in the lexicon and even syntax of many languages, leading, for example, to asymmetrical forms of speech between juniors and seniors. Beyond these asymmetries in common speech, when barriers to interaction between age groups and men and women are rigid, linguistic differences between these groups may even emerge. This is particularly pronounced between generations. As language continuously evolves, children often use a different lexicon and even syntax than their parents. Furthermore, children will frequently use different language varieties to their age mates than to their elders.

Social class is another prominent dimension of linguistic differentiation. To the extent that people of different class origins are prevented from having free and open relations with one another, they develop different forms and styles of language use. The more rigid a country's class structure, the more evident linguistic differences become. If class status (including, notably, occupation and access to various types of schooling) is largely ascribed and inherited, class groups readily become socially isolated and quickly turn into speech communities. Even without sharp class barriers in the conventional sense, occupational segregation readily produces that effect: lawyers speak differently from army officers, physicians, sailors, or musicians.

2. Language and Ethnicity

The link between language use and ethnicity is especially close. In the last analysis, an ethnic group (or ethny) is a group that defines itself and is defined by others as descended from common ancestors (van den Berghe 1981). Common biological descent, however, is often difficult to prove; indeed, it may be partly fictitious. Common ethnicity is frequently operationalized in terms of language. One is a Dane if one speaks Danish, at least if one speaks it well enough to pass as a native. The reason why language is such a good criterion of ethnic membership is that our biological programs for language learning lose enough flexibility early enough in life to make it difficult for an adult to learn to mimic the phonetics of a second language. Historically, if one spoke a language others thought to be flawless and accentless, the odds were quite high that one was a native member of the language group. Massive long-distance migration in recent centuries, and consequential intermarriage, have considerably muddied ethnic and linguistic boundaries, and the picture has been further blurred by 'racial' barriers, but, by and large, ethnic and linguistic communities still coincide frequently enough for language use to remain the main marker of ethnicity.

It is true, of course, as Eastman (1983) points out, that there can be a dissociation between language use and even language competence on the one hand, and ethnic identity on the other hand. Learning to become a relatively competent user of a second language does not mean shedding one's ethnic identity and assuming a new one. Language can be, and frequently is, learned, used, and manipulated to instrumental ends more quickly than ethnic identities change. At the limit, one can even totally cease to use one's native language and one's children may never learn it, without the family losing, even for generations, a sense of ethnic identity with the ancestral group. A measure of dissociation between ethnicity and language is most characteristic of countries like Canada, Australia, Argentina, Brazil, and the USA, that have experienced a massive and recent influx of immigrants from many ethnic origins. Thus, in the USA, people may call themselves Japanese, Italians, or Mexicans even though they are no longer fluent in their respective 'home' languages. These cases are rather exceptional, however. In most of human history, and still in the early twenty-first century in most of Europe, Asia, and Africa, ethnicity and language overlap closely.

Ultimately, it is the degree of endogamy which maintains both ethnic and linguistic boundaries. As has been seen, ethnicity is self-defined in terms of common descent. Therefore, mixed ethnic descent, by definition, creates marginal categories of individuals who straddle ethnic groups. Unilineal descent societies, i.e., those that are clearly patrilineal or matrilineal, sometimes resolve that problem by ascribing the offspring to the group of the socially relevant parent (the father or the mother), but such assimilation only 'works' if it is accompanied by complete linguistic absorption. In practice, ethnic intermarriage rates in excess of 25 percent give rise to great fluidity and mixing of ethnic and linguistic boundaries.

3. Language and Power in Ethnic Relations

So far, language and ethnicity have been discussed without reference to power differentials existing between linguistic and ethnic groups. In fact, power differentials are almost always present between ethnic and speech communities. To a large extent, it is the nature and source of power differentials between groups which determines their interrelations and their linguistic behavior. Therefore, power is central to any sociolinguistic analysis. A language has been defined as a dialect with battleships (see *Language*; *Dialect and Dialectology*).

There are several dimensions to power differentials between ethnic and linguistic communities.

(a) Absolute size of the group worldwide. Holding everything else constant, the larger a language group is, the better are its prospects for long-term survival, and the better its position relative to other groups. This is true even if the group in question has few speakers locally.

Thus, for instance, the future of English in India is better than that of Dutch in Indonesia, even though both languages were spoken by small dominant minorities in these respective countries. Both languages were introduced by a dominant colonial power, which lost political control simultaneously. Yet, English is still an important medium of communication in India, while Dutch has virtually ceased to be used in Indonesia. The incentive for a member of the Indian elite to learn English remains much greater than for his or her Indonesian counterpart to learn Dutch. English is spoken by some 360 million native speakers, accounts for some 65 percent of the scientific literature in chemistry and 73 percent in medicine, controls 34 percent of world GNP, and 32 percent of the world's military budget. Dutch, by contrast, is spoken by 20 million people, produces 0.1 and 0.3 percent of the scientific output in chemistry and medicine respectively, accounts for 1.3 percent of world GNP, and 0.9 percent of the world's military budgets (Laponce 1984; chap. 3).

(b) Geographical distribution of speakers. Other things being equal, the more geographically scattered a group is, the better are the chances of diffusion and survival of its language. Thus, despite its enormous number of native speakers, and the appreciable military power of the People's Republic of China, Mandarin is a much less vital international language than English, or even French and Spanish. Similarly, Japanese has more native speakers than French, and Japan is the world's number two economic power, but hardly anyone outside Japan speaks the language. Internationally, even Portuguese or Dutch will get one farther than Japanese.

(c) Relative size of the language group in the population of a state or territory. Barring differences in power or wealth between groups, the larger a language group is in relation to other groups, the more useful its language is to others and the more it is likely to be used, and to spread. A French- or Italian-speaking Swiss citizen, for example, has most incentive to learn German as a second language, and least to learn Romansch. Language learning is always costly to the learner; therefore, the amount of learning of any language is proportional to the benefits the learning confers. The simplest model predicting language learning is utilitarian: people, even young children, pursue a conscious or unconscious cost–benefit calculus in their language behavior, as indeed they tend to do in all their behavior. An occasional individual learns languages for the sheer intellectual fun of it, but that behavior is rare enough to be inconsequential in the aggregate.

(d) Control of a linguistic or ethnic group over scarce resources. The most important of these resources are political power and wealth, one being frequently convertible into the other. Languages along with other cultural products such as religion, diffuse overwhelmingly through conquest and trade. The incentive for the poor and the powerless to learn the language of the rich and the powerful is much greater than vice versa. Indeed, the incentive can be so overwhelming where disparities of power and wealth are great (as under colonialism), that the language of a small dominant minority of 1 or 2 percent can quickly displace majority languages. The spread of Spanish in the wake of the conquest of the Western Hemisphere is a good case in point. Within half a century of the *Conquista*, the language of a few thousand Spaniards was well on its way to becoming that of half a continent.

(e) In addition to power differentials, one additional factor affects whether languages spread, stagnate, or decline, namely: degree of contact between linguistic and ethnic groups. Highly isolated communities, however small, poor, and powerless, can indefinitely maintain their language provided that their isolation persists. Thus, for instance, scores of very small Amazon and Orinoco basin groups held their own for several centuries beyond the frontier of Spanish and Portuguese settlement so long as they remained inaccessible. Conversely, the language of large, powerful, and wealthy groups can fail to spread if states pursue isolationist policies. The cases of Japan and China until the late nineteenth century are good examples.

In sum, a few key factors, in combination, provide good predictors of linguistic behavior. They do so because they are all readily reducible to a simple utilitarian and individualistic model of human behavior. We know that the human brain is extraordinarily adept at acquiring one complex language very early in life. We also know that language learning ability declines with age (though not equally for everyone), and that the cost–benefit ratio of learning additional languages tends to rise steeply with age in most circumstances. Multilingualism is not a normal state of affairs because it is quite costly. Most people only learn second or third languages if the benefits of doing so outweigh the costs. Conditions that affect the cost–benefit ratios of language learning are relatively simple and straightforward. Basically, they have to do with disparities of numbers, and of control over scarce resources, mediated by probability of contact. The latter, in turn, is partly a function of spatial distribution and isolation.

Sociolinguistic situations prevailing in different types of ethnic contact will now be discussed.

4. Slavery

A common feature of slavery is that slaves are strangers to their masters. They are generally acquired from neighboring groups, through warfare or purchase. Often, they come from a multiplicity of ethnies, and thus, are a linguistically fragmented group compared to the rest of their 'host' society. Despite great differences in status, wealth, and power between masters and slaves, the two groups often live in 'distant intimacy,' i.e., they are socially distant but spatially (and often emotionally) close. All these conditions of linguistic fragmentation, powerlessness, and spatial proximity insure that the slave will quickly assimilate to the master's language and culture. Learning the master's language is advantageous both to the master and to the slave. For the master, it makes the slave more useful. For the slave, it helps him make the best of a bad situation, by ingratiating himself to his master or manipulating him. Almost invariably, the burden of learning a new language is on the subordinate. Since masters will not make the effort to learn the language of their slaves, it is almost always the slaves who acculturate to their masters' language and customs.

In the case of domestic slavery, where slaves live in the household of their masters, and, in the case of women, frequently bear their masters' children, slavery is, in fact, frequently a transitory condition. The institution of slavery persists, but individuals move out of slavery in one or two generations through acculturation and interbreeding. Slaves become serfs or freedmen.

In the rarer situation of chattel slavery, which prevailed in the USA, Brazil, the Caribbean, and Spanish America, slave status was racialized (i.e., associated exclusively with black African descent), and was accompanied by an exceptionally harsh and rigid social order. Furthermore, field hands on large plantations did not have close day-to-day relations with their masters. Only an elite of house slaves did. Yet, even in the Western Hemisphere, African slaves had to learn English, Spanish, Portuguese, French, or Dutch, as the case might be. They had little option as their masters' language was the only lingua franca not only to communicate with their masters, but also to talk to one another. Coming from scores of different African societies, they had no common language.

However, conditions of chattel slavery not only forced linguistic acculturation on slaves, they also interfered with the slaves' ability to acquire a full version of their masters' language and culture. Harsh physical conditions, the disruption of families, high mortality and turnover, social barriers, racial segregation, and enforced illiteracy all made it difficult for the slave to acquire the master's language. The result was frequently, for the initial period of contact, the emergence of pidgins, which, after one or two generations, evolved into creoles. The French-based creoles of Haiti, Martinique, and Guadeloupe are good examples of this process (Stewart 1962).

Scholarly and political arguments have long raged as to whether Afro-Americans (and by extension, Afro-Caribbeans. Afro-Brazilians, and Afro-Hispanics) speak distinct languages from their compatriots of European descent. The issue of 'survival' of African languages and cultures in the Western Hemisphere is complex, and there is a lot of local variation. Two areas stand out in terms of a large African contribution to contemporary language, cuisine, religion, and other aspects of culture, namely Haitic, where the Dahomean component is clear, and north eastern Brazil (especially Bahia), where Yoruba influence is obvious.

In the USA, evidence for African survivals is much more tenuous, except in the cultural isolate of the islands off the South Carolina coast, where some linguists have claimed that Gullah is a creole (Hancock 1971). There is also much controversy concerning the classificatory status of African American Vernacular English (AAVE), but most linguists agree that it is a form of English rather than a creole. It has a regional (Southern) and class component, as well as a specifically 'racial' one. Furthermore, many American do not speak AAVE, and most of those who do exhibit large degrees of diglossia. They can switch with relative ease between their dialect and Standard American English, perhaps even more readily than many white speakers of nonstandard dialects, e.g., from rural Kentucky or Maine.

5. Language and Race

The real issue about AAVE, however, is not the extent to which it is spoken by African Americans, nor the degree to which it varies from Standard American English (if, indeed, there is such a thing), but the stigmatization attached to the speech behavior of the black lower class (Sonntag and Pool 1987). AAVE is doubly stigmatized on the basis of class and race, and that stigmatization is a powerful component of racial discrimination in contemporary American society (in such matters as educational and occupational opportunities). African Americans are routinely expected to master Standard American English in order to have access to formal education and to all but the most menial forms of employment. Language use associated with blacks is much more powerfully stigmatized than equally variant forms spoken mostly by whites. These linguistic prejudices thus reinforce racial discrimination and vice versa.

The case of AAVE is but one of the many instances where differences in language use overlap with racial distinctions in a given society. Another case of a postslavery situation is Haiti. During slavery, a sharp distinction evolved between a 'mulatto' class of freed slaves who, through close contact with the white slaveowning elite, came to speak a Haitian variety of standard French and later to rule the country after the revolution of 1791, and the mass of black slaves who developed a French-based creole. The sharp class and linguistic distinction persists in the early twenty-first century, even though there is extensive diglossia in the upper and middle classes. The official language is standard French, which is the passport of admission to the ruling class, but the native language of 80 to 90 percent of the population is a distinct creole, derogatorily referred to by the mulatto elite as a mere patois.

Unlike AAVE, which is clearly a variety of English, Haitian creole is sufficiently distinct from French in both lexicon and syntax to qualify as a separate language. Haitian creole, for instance, is more clearly distinct from French than Afrikaans is from Dutch. Afrikaans, however, was, until 1994, the language of the powerful white ruling class of South Africa, and was an official state language with an extensive literature, while Haitian creole is spoken by impoverished peasants and is seldom written (except in folkloric novels and anthropology monographs). Afrikaans, in short, had an army behind it, and was universally recognized as a separate language. Since the advent of non-racial democracy in 1994, however, the status of Afrikaans though still official has been greatly reduced relative to English. Haitian creole is the language of the oppressed and lacks even a distinct name.

'Racial' groups only exist insofar as physical phenotypes (such as skin pigmentation, hair texture, facial features, and the like) are attributed social significance in a particular society. Where such is the case, racial groups may or may not be culturally and linguistically distinct as well. Racially stratified societies are overwhelmingly the product of large-scale long distance migration across wide phenotypic gradients (van den Berghe 1981). This may happen through conquest as in much of Africa, Asia, and America, or through labor migration (in the form of slavery, indenture, or free labor).

Sometimes, these socially defined groups are also ethnic groups. More frequently, racial groups are made up of many ethnies. Not uncommonly, after centuries of close contact, members of different racial groups may, in fact, share the same language and culture, as is true, for instance, of white and black Anglophone North Americans, and of white and 'colored' Afrikaans-speaking South Africans. Even when different racial groups share a common language and culture, however, the stigma of race itself perpetuates sufficient discrimination and social segregation to maintain great inequalities of status, power, and wealth, and, thus, to create subcultural and dialectal differences between racial groups. These secondary linguistic and cultural distinctions are no different in principle from those that arise between social classes, except for the peculiarly invidious stigma of race itself. Once the stigma of race is entrenched in a society, then any differentiation, however objectively trivial, between racial groups becomes itself stigmatized. It is this element of seemingly intrinsic stigmatization which distinguishes racial from mere ethnic distinctions. Ethnic distinctions are not intrinsically demeaning in the way that racial distinctions inevitably seem to be in those societies that make them (see *Ethnicity and Language*).

6. Imperialism

If imperialism is defined simply as the conquest and rule of one ethny over others, then it follows that imperialism is inevitably accompanied by linguistic stratification. The language of the ruling class has prestige, and spreads at the expense of the other languages because fluency in it confers obvious economic and political advantages. However, linguistic hegemony, especially when it is forcibly imposed by discriminatory practices, frequently arouses opposition in the form of nationalist movements. In short, imperialism is almost invariably accompanied by conflicts which have an important linguistic dimension. Perhaps the most common case is one where one ethny uses its own language as the official language of the state it controls, to the greater or lesser exclusion of all other languages. Classical examples are the use of Russian in the Czarist Empire, of Osmanli Turkish in the Ottoman Empire, of German in the Hapsburg Empire, and of Amharic in Ethiopia.

6.1 Definitions and Distinctions

The linguistic hegemony of the *Staatsvolk* (as the Germans call the ethny that dominates the state) can range from a situation of official tolerance of other languages to active suppression. At one extreme, for instance, all nondominant languages may be excluded from all formal education, from law and administration, and even from public discourse outside the home, and they may be denied access to the printed word and to all public media. Conversely, the dominant language is actively pushed through the schools, the press, the mass media, the courts, the military, and all other organs controlled by the state. Such extreme cases of forced assimilation frequently provoke countervailing nationalist movements. Most imperial ruling classes have, therefore, pursued somewhat more flexible linguistic policies of tolerating the use of other languages, but of simply withholding state-controlled resources from them. Access to the elite, for instance, can only be achieved through mastery of the dominant language. Such relatively 'tolerant' policies have frequently had a double benefit for the *Staatsvolk*: its language spread rapidly because of the benefits mastery of the dominant language conferred, but linguistic policies of laissez-faire and benign neglect prevented the growth of militant nationalisms.

Colonialism is really a special and extreme case of imperialism. Although both definitions and situations of colonialism have varied, the term has generally meant the political and economic hegemony of one state over distant territories inhabited by culturally and 'racially' distinct populations, often much poorer groups with a less developed technology. Such situations made not only for maximum cultural and social distance between conquerors and conquered, but also for sharp inequalities in wealth and power. Indeed, these inequalities in access to scarce resources have often been so large as to enable ethnic minorities of 1 percent or less of the total population to dominate the rest. A few thousand British civil servants, army officers, railway engineers, etc., ruled 300 million Indians, for instance. The same was true of the Dutch in Indonesia, the Belgians in the Congo, the French in West Africa, and so on.

A distinction is frequently made between 'colonies of settlement' like North America, Australia, and New Zealand, and 'colonies of exploitation' like most of tropical Africa, Asia, and Latin America. Colonies of settlement were largely nontropical lands suitable for European settlement, where native populations were so sparse as to make their virtual extermination a likely prospect. Where the native population was dense and had achieved a complex level of social organization, colonies of exploitation resulted, especially in tropical areas unsuited to the biological reproduction of European populations. Would-be colonies of settlement with large native populations (like Algeria, South Africa, Rhodesia (now Zimbabwe), or Angola) had very mixed success in terms of permanent European colonization.

Linguistically, the colonial expansion of Europe covers a wide gamut of situations. Most of the successful English colonies of settlement—Australia, New Zealand, and what became the USA—became effectively monolingual in English, thereby assuring the pre-eminent position of English as an international language since the nineteenth century. The English monolingualism of these countries was the result of massive displacement and reduction of native populations through epidemics, habitat destruction, land expropriation, and military conquest, and of fairly rapid linguistic assimilation of millions of non-English speakers from Europe, Asia, Africa, and Latin America, first under slavery, later under voluntary immigration. Canada's linguistic evolution is somewhat similar, except for its sequential colonization by the French and the British, and, thus, for its stable bilingualism in the respective areas of French and English settlement.

6.2 Latin America

Latin America is also an area where the respective colonial powers—Spain and Portugal—were remarkably successful in imposing their language. In the 'Southern Cone' (Argentina, Chile, and Uruguay), this is not surprising, because the native population was sparse and largely decimated, as indeed was also the case in much of the Amazon and Orinoco basins and the Caribbean. In Mexico, Central America, and the Andean countries, however, the indigenous population was dense, and, although it was also decimated by conquest and epidemics, large concentrations of 'Indians' survive to this day. In tropical American countries, Europeans always remained small minorities, but they interbred extensively with aborigines and African slaves to produce Spanish- or Portuguese-speaking populations of mixed ancestry, a process known in Spanish America as '*mestizaje*.'

In contemporary Mexico, barely one tenth of the nation's citizens still speak indigenous languages (and most of them are bilingual in Spanish), even though something like 85 to 90 percent of Mexicans are of at least partly indigenous descent. In North America, only Guatemala still has a large number (some 3 million) of monolingual speakers of native languages (specifically, 22 Maya languages). There is also a large pocket of some 12 million Quechua and Aymara speakers in the high Andes of Ecuador, Peru, and Bolivia. In addition, large areas of lowland jungle in Brazil, Venezuela, Peru, Ecuador, and Bolivia are sparsely settled by a multiplicity of tiny language groups of *selváticos*, 'forest Indians.'

Paraguay is a special and unique case in Latin America, in that it is officially bilingual in Spanish and Guaraní. Many Paraguayans at all class levels are effectively bilingual, a situation which also prevails in some Andean areas of Peru (with Quechua and Spanish). In both of these areas, in fact, the upper classes tend to be more bilingual than the lower classes. This is an extremely uncommon situation created by Catholic (especially Jesuit) evangelization in a standardized form of Guaraní and Quechua, respectively. These indigenous languages were thus actually spread by the agents of the colonial power, and acquired by many members of the ruling class. The end result was an Indian peasantry monolingual in the native language, and bilingual, urban middle- and upper-class mestizos.

With the exceptions noted above, however, Spanish and Portuguese in their respective areas nearly totally displaced indigenous languages. Given the diversity of cultural origins of the Latin American population and the enormous geographical area it covers, the degree of linguistic uniformity it has achieved is highly unusual. A brutal conquest, followed by devastating epidemics, slavery, and peonage explains the linguistic dominance of the conquerors during the colonial period. The independent republics which followed were dominated by the Spanish- and Portuguese-speaking upper classes which established centralized governments that used exclusively Spanish and Portuguese as languages of administration, education, justice, finance, commerce, and industry, and thus condemned the indigenous languages to growing marginality and disuse.

6.3 Africa and Asia

In contrast to the extensive penetration of the European languages in the Western Hemisphere, European colonialism made little linguistic headway in Africa (except in South Africa), and even less in Asia (except for Israel). The linguistic situation of Israel is quite unique. Jewish settlers from a score or more of European, African, and Asian countries revived a moribund religious language and transformed it into the mother-tongue of nearly all Sabra (Israel-born Jews) in a generation or less. There have been other state-supported attempts to revive 'national' languages, as with Irish in Ireland, but Israel is the only clear-cut success story.

In South Africa, until 1994, the 15 percent white minority imposed the use of their two languages, English and Afrikaans (a Dutch creole), on the rest of the population. Perhaps another 10 to 15 percent (mostly 'coloreds,' or people of mixed descent) became monolingual or bilingual in these two official languages, and millions of black South Africans use one or both of them in addition to their first language. Indeed, South Africa probably exhibits one of the highest degrees of effective multilingualism of any country on earth. It is not uncommon for urban black Africans to speak, in addition to their native Bantu language, both of the European languages with some fluency, and one or two of the closely related Bantu languages besides their own. As is true in most colonial situations, bi- or multilingualism is much more extensive in the formerly subordinate groups than among members of the former ruling oligarchy.

In the rest of Africa, the language of the colonial power—French, Portuguese, Italian, Spanish, German, and English, depending on the area—made only limited inroads in the native population. Everywhere, it remained an elite language acquired by a small minority of generally well under 10 percent of the total, who reached secondary- or university-level education. Primary schooling was frequently in the child's mother tongue, as was much grass-roots evangelization by the Christian missionaries. Outside of North Africa and the northern Sudan, Arabic expanded with Islam, but it failed to become a lingua franca and remained almost exclusively a limited-purpose sacred language among non-Arab Muslims. Even the fact that knowledge of a European language became a near-prerequisite for the acquisition of power and wealth in postcolonial Africa does not seem to contribute to a rapid spread of French, English, or Portuguese in Africa.

In North Africa, both French and Berber yield ground to Arabic, which is becoming the overwhelmingly dominant language from Casablanca to Cairo. Much of the French-speaking population left for France or Israel at independence. As to the Berbers, they are becoming increasingly Arabized, although many remain situationally bilingual. Most tropical African countries (except for a few small ones like Somalia, Swaziland, and Lesotho) are divided into a multiplicity of first language groups, and thus, their elites find it convenient to continue using French, Portuguese, or English as the language of administration. Indeed, elite monopoly over these former colonial languages serves to consolidate the political control of these Europeanized black mandarins. To speak of African countries as Francophone, Anglophone, or Lusophone is a hyperbole. Only a small urban elite—typically under 10 percent, often under 5 percent of the population—speaks these languages with any fluency, and that group is not expanding due to limited educational facilities. Indigenous languages hold their own quite well, since they continue to be used extensively even by the elites who are generally bilingual, and some African languages have even extended their spread well beyond their native speakers to become linguae francae. This is, for instance, the case with Hausa, Wolof, Mandingo, and Fula in West Africa, Lingala in the Zaire basin, and Swahili in East Africa, especially in Tanzania where it has become the unifying 'national' language of an ethnically very diverse country (Polomé and Hill 1980).

The decline of European colonial languages in Asia is even more rapid than in Africa. Where the colonized country had a unified language as in Vietnam, or was successful in imposing one as in Indonesia, the colonial language receded quickly after independence. The main exception is India, and even there, Hindi is slowly supplanting English as the lingua franca of northern India. Only resistance of south Indians to Hindi as a 'national' language maintains English as the lingua franca of the south Indian elite. Even in the few enclaves of Asia which remained European colonies until the late 1990s, such as Macao and Hong Kong, the native language thrives and the European ones are receding.

See also: Nationalism and Language; Sociology of Language; Pidgins and Creoles: An Overview; Power and Language.

Bibliography

Banton M 1983 *Racial and Ethnic Competition*. Cambridge University Press, Cambridge, UK
Berghe P L van den 1981 *The Ethnic Phenomenon*. Elsevier, New York
Eastman C 1983 *Language Planning: An Introduction*. Chandler and Sharp, San Francisco, CA
Edwards J R (ed.) 1984 *Linguistic Minorities: Policies and Pluralism*. Academic Press, London
Fishman J A (ed.) 1978 *Advances in the Study of Societal Multilingualism*. Mouton, The Hague
Fishman J A, Ferguson C A, Das Gupta J (eds.) 1968 *Language Problems of Developing Nations*. Wiley, New York
Giles H (ed.) 1977 *Language, Ethnicity and Intergroup Relations*. Academic Press, London
Giles H, Saint-Jacques B (eds.) 1979 *Language and Ethnic Relations*. Pergamon Press, Oxford, UK
Hancock I F 1971 A survey of the pidgins and creoles of the world. In: Hymes D (ed.) *Pidginization and Creolization of Languages*. Cambridge University Press, Cambridge, UK
Horowitz D L 1985 *Ethnic Groups in Conflict*. University of California Press, Berkeley, CA
Laponce J A 1984 *Langu et Territoire*. Presses de L'Université Laval, Québec, PQ
Polomé E C, Hill C P 1980 *Language in Tanzania*. Oxford University Press, Oxford, UK
Pool J 1987 Thinking about linguistic discrimination. *Language Problems and Language Planning* **11**: 3–20
Romaine S 1988 *Pidgin and Creole Languages*. Longman, London
Sonntag S K, Pool J 1987 Linguistic denial and linguistic self-denial: American ideologies of language. *Language Problems and Language Planning* **11**: 46–65
Spencer J 1963 *Language in Africa*. Cambridge University Press, Cambridge, UK
Stewart W 1962 The functional distribution of Creole and French Haitian. *Language and Linguistics*: 149–59

Representation
R. Fowler

Certain intellectual and cultural trends, and technological developments, originating in the nineteenth century, have formed a set of commonsense beliefs about the relationship between the communicative media and 'reality': the philosophy of utilitarianism; the rise of sociology; realism and naturalism in nineteenth-century fiction; the rise of newspapers (and all the 'information-gathering' services that support them) and their claim of objectivity; the development of still and moving photography, sound recording, and now ever more advanced audiovisual technologies. It is in the nature of these trends to insist that an objectively existing reality can be represented faithfully in language or images (or statistics, etc.).

This naive realism, product of a dominant empiricist and authoritarian climate, has been in this century repeatedly challenged by artistic avant-gardes: cubism, trans-sense poetry, the *nouveau roman*, etc. It has also been subjected to academic critique in different domains, including art history and the sociology of knowledge. Until recently, realism of representation has not been much questioned in linguistics, partly because of an uncritical acceptance of the communication or channel model in which language is a conduit for conveying ideas unaltered from one brain to another; partly because of the problematic nature of one area of theory, the Sapir–Whorf hypothesis (see *Sapir–Whorf Hypothesis*).

An alternative conception of representation in language is basic to critical sociolinguistics (see *Critical Sociolinguistics*). Representation is regarded as a process of construction, not as a modeling. Informally, the proposal is that, whatever 'natural' structure the world might have, our experience of it is shaped to a large degree by the social (cultural, political, etc.) and ideological relationships within which we are positioned. Language has a reciprocal, dialectical, relationship with this constructed reality. On the one hand, conceding the plausibility of 'natural kinds' such as color, shape, directionality, etc., it may be proposed that much of the semantics of a language answers to the life of its speakers: this is easy enough to demonstrate as far as lexical inventory and structure are concerned, anyway. Reciprocally, as the structure of language encodes the categories of thought by which a society manages its reality, it crystallizes them, aiding the simplification of the perceived world and facilitating the transmission of received values.

1. Interdisciplinary Sources

Berger and Luckmann's central thesis is indicated in the title of their book, *The Social Construction of Reality* (1976). Reality as we perceive it and conceive of it is relative to specific cultures, specific kinds of social organizations. It is a product of social interactions among individuals, and of institutional structures and relationships. The structure of the socially constructed world we experience is affirmed when we communicate with one another, and Berger and Luckmann point out that 'conversation' has a particularly significant role in reality maintenance.

Because conversation is casual and uncritical, the ordinary terms which represent our commonsense beliefs can be mentioned without emphasis or enquiry—contrast the language of the classroom or of the law.

A parallel set of ideas, which have been most influential in linguists' formulation of the theory of representation, is found in the work of Michel Foucault (see *Foucault, Michel*). Central to Foucault's contribution is the idea of 'discourse' (see *Discourse*) a system of prohibitions and conventions, culturally originating, about what can be spoken about and how (cf. register as 'range of semantic potential' in Halliday 1978; for a detailed exposition, see *Register*).

In E. H. Gombrich's treatise *Art and Illusion* (1960), representation in the visual arts is not a rendering of a subject but the construction of a way of seeing: an illusion in his striking term. Analyzing many familiar examples, he demonstrates how the deployment of the technical properties of the medium manages the illusion. That most apparently 'natural' of properties of visual representation, perspective, was a historical development. Techniques based on converging lines with attendant differences in size in representations of objects known in world-knowledge to be equivalent in size, guided viewers to sense an illusion of depth and three-dimensionality in their experience of a flat painting.

Gombrich's approach is based on an exemplary union of historical circumstances, variety and change of technical procedures, and the contribution of the viewer's internalized knowledge. The latter dimension of his theory accords well with 'schematic' approaches to language comprehension in psycholinguistics: people understand language in terms of schematized knowledge that they project on to texts (see de Beaugrande and Dressler 1981: chap. 5, Garnham 1985: chap. 7, Johnson-Laird 1983).

The Sapir–Whorf hypothesis contains two claims (see also *Sapir–Whorf Hypothesis*; *Sapir, Edward*; *Whorf, Benjamin Lee*). 'Linguistic relativity' argues (contrasting native American and European languages) that the structures of languages differ in fundamental ways, particularly as the semantics and syntax represent spatial and temporal aspects of experience, and material processes. 'Linguistic determinism' suggests that speakers are constrained to perceive and think along the lines afforded by the structure of their language. As far as relativity is concerned, 'difference of structure' needs defining very carefully. 'Determinism' in the form implied by Whorf is untestable. However, there is some psycholinguistic research to the effect that the simplicity with which a concept is coded has an influence on the accessibility and the memorability of that concept (Carroll 1964, Clark and Clark 1977); coding varies from language to language, even for the so-called 'natural categories.'

The cross-linguistic comparisons which Whorf makes are not central to the linguistic theory of representation, and rather serve to muddy the water; more important is that an individual language provides alternative ways of coding a concept or an event. Alternative wordings or phrasings segment or package experience in ideologically distinct ways.

2. Representation in Functional–systemic Linguistics

Halliday's *Introduction to Functional Grammar* (1994) has a section 'Clause as Representation' which begins in a Whorfian manner. He asks the reader to imagine a natural scene, birds flying overhead: 'perceptually the phenomenon is all of a piece; but when we talk about it we analyze it as a semantic configuration'; and there are different ways of analysis—'birds are flying in the sky' or 'it's winging' (1994: 108). The implication is that alternative linguistic expressions encode differently structured experiences. Halliday locates representational alternativity within what he calls the 'ideational' function of language: 'it is through this function that the speaker or writer embodies in language his experience of the phenomena of the real world' (1971: 332). This representational function is served by systems of linguistic options of which the most important are lexis and transitivity. Lexis (vocabulary) is taxonomically organized: systems of words categorize the objects, qualities, and events recognized by the culture into sets of hierarchical relations, providing an organized mapping of experience; the structure is value-laden—'girl' is opposed to both 'boy' and 'man'; alternatives are richly available which signify different orientations—'money,' 'capital,' 'investment,' 'loot,' 'bread,' etc. In Halliday's terms, transitivity refers to the semantic structure of the clause: who does what to whom, who experiences what, and so on (1994: chap. 5); choices made in the transitivity system are fundamental to the way in which a text offers a perspective on an event.

Halliday's most memorable demonstration (1971) of the construction of a mode of experiencing through linguistic structure concerns a fictional text—William Golding's *The Inheritors*. This is a classic study of the way in which a fictional world is constructed, with consistent and foregrounded transitivity choices defamiliarizing experience for the reader by staging an illusion of the causally restricted cognitive world of 'Neanderthal Man.' This study makes it clear how fundamentally important the linguistic theory of representation is for our understanding of the way in which language is structured to create fictional worlds and 'mind-styles,' but here we are talking about the deliberate textual strategies of a professional novelist.

The crucial point about representation is that the linguistic construction of reality is not limited to deliberate fictional technique: the principle pervades language. Recall Berger and Luckmann on conversation, the casual way in which we share and maintain our society's categorization of experience by uncritically mentioning the terms in which it is divided up and sorted. The same ideological working is found in familiar modes of public discourse: the news media (Fowler 1991), rules and regulations, official documents, interviews, etc., have all been shown to encode commitments to specific systems of values, ways of representing the world (Fowler et al. 1979). These values, which are conveyed in recognizably distinct genres or registers of language (advertisement for women, right-wing newspaper editorial, letter from bank, etc.), are institutionally grounded: they are representations of the world in terms appropriate to the social and economic needs of the organizations that utter them. Representation, which is always from some specific point of view, can be seen not just as an innocent process but a social practice, conscious or not.

See also: Politicized Language; Manipulation; Halliday, Michael Alexander Kirkwood.

Bibliography

Beaugrande R A de, Dressler W 1981 *Introduction to Text Linguistics*. Longman, London
Berger P L, Luckmann T 1979 *The Social Construction of Reality*. Penguin, Harmondsworth, UK
Carroll J B 1964 *Language and Thought*. Prentice-Hall, Englewood Cliffs, NJ
Clark H H, Clark E V 1977 *Psychology and Language: An Introduction to Psycholinguistics*. Harcourt Brace Jovanovich, New York
Fowler R 1991 *Language in the News: Discourse and Ideology in the Press*. Routledge, London
Fowler R, Hodge R, Kress G, Trew A 1979 *Language and Control*. Routledge and Kegan Paul, London
Garnham A 1985 *Psycholinguistics Central Topics*. Methuen, London
Gombrich E H 1960 *Art and Illusion*. Phaidon, London
Halliday M A K 1971 Linguistic function and literary style. In: Chatman S (ed.) *Literary Style: A Symposium*. Oxford University Press, London
Halliday M A K 1978 *Language as Social Semiotic*. Arnold, London
Halliday M A K 1994 *An Introduction to Functional Grammar*, 2nd edn. Arnold, London
Johnson-Laird P 1983 *Mental Models*. Cambridge University Press, Cambridge, UK

Semilingualism

J. Cummins

Considerable debate has focused on the question of whether some students from linguistic minority backgrounds can be characterized as 'semilingual' (sometimes termed 'doubly semilingual'), a condition that implies inadequate development of both first and second languages (L1 and L2). A related question concerns the extent to which such linguistic and/or cognitive deficits may be regarded as causal factors in explaining the poor academic performance of some minority students (Cummins and Swain 1983, Edelsky et al. 1983, Hansegard 1972, Kalantzis et al. 1989, Martin-Jones and Romaine 1986, Paulston 1982, Skutnabb-Kangas 1984, Stroud 1978). In many respects the controversy parallels the issue of whether working-class children are characterized by language deficits that contribute to their difficulties in schools (Bernstein 1971, Labov 1970).

Hansegard (1972) has provided the most elaborate description of the construct of 'double semilingualism' based on his observations among Finnish and Saami communities in Northern Sweden. Six characteristics are outlined by Hansegard:

(a) size of the repertoire of words, phrases, etc., understood or actively available in speech;
(b) correctness with respect to syntactic, phonemic, and discoursal aspects of language use;
(c) degree of automatism in use of the language;
(d) ability to create or neologize in the language;
(e) mastery of the cognitive, emotive, and volitional function of language;
(f) degree of richness in the semantic networks available to the individual through the language.

Edelsky et al. (1983) characterize this description of the construct as 'a confused grab-bag of prescriptive and descriptive components' and argue that to attribute minority students' academic difficulties to 'semilingualism' even as one link in a causal chain constitutes a deficit theory that 'blames the victim.' Paulston (1982) similarly argues that there is no empirical evidence for the construct and deplores its use (primarily by Skutnabb-Kangas) in the Swedish debate as an argument for Finnish home-language classes. Martin-Jones and Romaine (1986) also dispute the existence of 'semilingualism.' They attribute apparent inadequacies of linguistic competence among bilinguals to the normal processes of language contact and language shift.

Skutnabb-Kangas (1984), in response to criticism, makes the point that most of the studies that claim not to have found evidence for inadequate command of two languages have focused on *syntax*, whereas many of those that support the construct have focused on range of vocabulary. She furthermore argues that semilingualism cannot be regarded as a deficiency inherent in the individual but should be treated as one result of the societal and educational discrimination to which minority groups are subjected. In other words, it is a political as much as an educational construct. Semilingualism can be avoided when minority children receive intensive L1 instruction through 'language shelter' (i.e., L1 immersion) programs.

Several authors have adopted an intermediate position with respect to this debate. McLaughlin for example, suggests that:

> Semilingualism may be a useful way of describing those cases where, through extreme social deprivation, bilingual children do not learn to function well in either language. At issue here, however, is whether it is a useful concept when talking about bilingual children in general. If the concept of semilingualism is defined as meaning that bilingual children do not perform as well as native speakers in either language, then there is some agreement that in fact this may be the case at certain points in the development of their languages.
>
> (McLaughlin 1985: 33)

Kalantzis et al. similarly point to the situation 'in which the home language is not continued with growing sophistication past entry to formal schooling either at home or at school, and in which the initial experience of formal schooling does not adequately prepare students for proficiency in their second language' (1989: 30). They suggest that the consequence of this situation can be what they have termed a 'cognitive void' (or what Hansegard has termed 'semilingualism') in which 'children's ability to express themselves and manipulate the world around them through language is hampered' (1989: 31).

Appel and Muysken (1986) make the point that the bilingual's verbal repertoire can be viewed as different and not deficient, even though at some point in their development they may know less of each of their languages than monolingual children. For example, bilinguals' code-switching abilities give them the opportunity to convey messages in subtle and sophisticated ways not available to monolinguals. Appel and Muysken also point out that comparisons with monolinguals may not be justified since bilinguals use their two languages in different domains and for different purposes. In other words, from a sociolinguistic perspective, the two languages of the bilingual can be viewed as one linguistic repertoire that is adequate in a wide variety of situations.

The issues in this debate appear to be less complex than might be indicated by the heated controversy that surrounds the use of the term. In the first place, virtually all theorists on both sides of this issue agree that the major causal factors in minority students' underachievement are sociopolitical in nature; specifically, the pattern of dominant–subordinated group relations in the wider society and the interactional manifestations of these relations in the school context. Second, if one admits that variations in language and literacy abilities exist among monolingual populations, then there is no reason to deny the existence of such variations among bilingual populations in their two languages. It is clear that there are major individual differences in literacy skills and in certain aspects of oral language skills among the general population in their L1s (or first languages). Not everybody is capable of reading and writing at the same level nor does everybody have identical oral repertoires (e.g., oratorical skills). In the same way, bilingual children and adults vary in their degree of mastery of different aspects of their two languages. Even Edelsky et al., admit that 'semilingualism might mean something more substantial (e.g., an inability to use language in its ideational or representational function...)' (1983: 11).

If it is allowed that variation exists, then it appears that certain bilinguals will have relatively low levels of literacy in both their L1 and L2 (or second language), while others will have relatively high levels of literacy in both languages. Certainly some minority children born in the host country who do not receive sufficient L1 instruction at school develop L1 oral and literacy skills only to a very limited extent (Wong Fillmore 1990). These children will also vary in the degree of formal L2 academic skills that they develop at school. The extent of mastery of these formal language skills is directly linked to future educational and economic opportunities. As Kalantzis et al. (1989: 31) point out, 'in the modern world, formal language skills of speaking, reading and writing are the means to certain sorts of futures and power.' They suggest that all children should have the opportunity to develop mastery of these formal language skills and academic researchers 'who have mastered the pinnacle of mainstream language' should not view as unproblematic the fact that a disproportionate number of minority students fail to realize the full range of options in their two languages.

In short, the issue does not seem to revolve around the existence of variation in language and literacy skills among bilingual (and monolingual) populations. The issue is rather whether it is appropriate or theoretically useful to label some of these bilingual children 'semilingual' or 'doubly semilingual' or 'deficient' as a means of characterizing their relatively limited repertoires in certain aspects of their two languages.

There appear to be compelling scientific and sociopolitical reasons to avoid using such labels. First, as the debate clearly shows, there has been no precise linguistic or cognitive operationalization of the term 'semilingualism.' In other words, there is no scientific rationale for choosing one arbitrary cut-off point over another as the level below which it is appropriate to label an individual 'semilingual.' Thus, the term has no explanatory or predictive value but is rather a restatement of the vague notion of 'limited proficiency in two languages.' At a sociopolitical level the term has assumed pejorative connotations and may be misinterpreted as suggesting that linguistic deficits are a primary cause of minority students' academic difficulties, despite denials to the contrary. Furthermore, the futile debates to which use of the term has given rise, suggest that its continued use is counter-productive.

There appears to be little justification for continued use of the term 'semilingualism' in that it has no theoretical value and confuses rather than clarifies the issues. However, those who claim that 'semilingualism does not exist,' appear to be endorsing the untenable positions that (a) variation in educationally-relevant aspects of language does not exist, and that (b) there are no bilinguals whose formal language skills are developed only to a relatively limited level in both L1 and L2. Just as there are monolinguals whose formal language skills are developed only to a limited degree, so too there are bilinguals whose formal language skills are developed only to a limited degree.

See also: Educational Failure; Code, Sociolinguistic; Bilingualism, Societal; Linguicide.

Bibliography
Appel R, Muysken P 1987 *Language Contact and Bilingualism*. Edward Arnold, London
Bernstein B (ed.) 1971 *Class, Codes, and Control*, vol. 1. Routledge and Kegan Paul, London
Cummins J, Swain M 1983 Analysis-by-rhetoric: Reading the text or the reader's own projections? A reply to Edelsky et al. *Applied Linguistics* **4**: 23–41
Edelsky C, Altwerger F, Barkin B, Flores S, Hudelson S, Jilbert K 1983 Semilingualism and language deficit. *Applied Linguistics* **4**: 1–22
Hansegard N E 1972 *Tvavspravkighet eller Halvspravkighet?* Aldus Bonnier, Stockholm
Kalantzis M, Cope B, Slade D 1989 *Minority Languages and Dominant Culture: Issues of Education, Assessment and Social Equity*. Falmer Press, London
Labov W 1970 *The Study of Non-Standard English*. National Council of Teachers of English, Champaign, IL
Martin-Jones M, Romaine S 1986 Semilingualism: A half-baked theory of communicative competence. *Applied Linguistics* **7**: 26–38
McLaughlin B 1985 *Second-language Acquisition in Childhood. Vol. 2: School-age Children*, 2nd edn. Erlbaum, Hillsdale, NJ
Paulston C B 1982 *Swedish Research and Debate about Bilingualism*. National Swedish Board of Education, Stockholm
Skutnabb-Kangas T 1984 *Bilingualism or Not: The Education of Minorities*. Multilingual Matters, Clevedon, UK
Stroud C 1978 The concept of semilingualism. *Lund University Working Papers* **16**: 153–72
Wong Fillmore L 1990 Now or later? Issues related to the early education of minority group children. In: Harris C (ed.) *Children at Risk*. Harcourt Brace Jovanovich, New York

Stereotype and Social Attitudes
M. L. Apte

'Stereotype' is an important concept in the discussion of the social reality of any culturally bound aggregate of human population. The concept was given a definitive formulation by the American journalist Walter Lippmann in 1922. It has been controversial however, and has been much discussed in the social science literature primarily in the context of contact and interaction by various ethnic groups within and across modern nation-states. It is also significant in the exploration, discussion, and analysis of ethnic humor, especially ethnic jokes.

1. Conceptual Formulation of Stereotype
Lippmann (1922) defined stereotype as a mental picture formulated by human beings to describe the world beyond their reach. In his view, stereotypes are at least partially culturally determined. He emphasized however, that their contents are factually incorrect and that they are the products of a faulty reasoning process. He felt that stereotypes are difficult to get rid of, and they persist even when a group is exposed to education and has first-hand experience concerning the phenomenon or human groups about whom stereotypes are held.

A stereotype is now considered to be an overgeneralization and an uninformed one. It is also intertwined with strong positive or negative attitudes. It is inevitable that cultural knowledge includes not only information about one's own actions and behavior, institutions, traditions, customs, and artifacts, but also about other human groups and the environment. The concept of stereotype primarily focuses on the knowledge of other sociocultural groups, especially factual or putative racial and ethnic characteristics and their behavior. In order for one group to hold a stereotype of another, the former does not have to be in direct contact with the latter.

In the 1930s many studies were conducted by psychologists to test the validity of stereotypes. The most well-known among these is that of Katz and Braly (1933). It was based on the experiment conducted at Princeton university in which 100 students were asked to list the traits they considered characteristic of 10 ethnic groups. They were to select the traits from a predetermined list given to them. Many similar studies were conducted during the 1950s and the 1960s. Yet none of them was conclusive regarding the correlation between stereotypes and empirical reality.

To what extent, if at all, prejudice and other negative attitudes are associated with stereotypes is a controversial issue that has been much discussed. Allport (1958) is of the opinion that prejudice is generally an essential aspect of stereotypes, especially negative ones. It has also been argued that ethnocentrism, the natural tendency of each and every sociocultural group to hold its own culture to be superior to all the others is a major cause for developing negative stereotypes. Behavior, customs of dressing, eating habits, speech patterns, sexual practices, and other aspects of culture that substantially differ from those of one's own are perceived as 'primitive' and 'repugnant.' Such conclusions and generalizations do not have to develop from firsthand information, but rather from hearsay evidence or from superficial observation of even a single member of another group.

Although stereotypes are generally considered uninformed opinions it has been argued that they are not totally false, but that there is some degree of truth in them. This has been known as the 'kernel of truth' hypothesis in the literature on stereotypes (Brown 1965: 172). However, one study (La Pierre 1936), much quoted in the literature, showed that stereotypes persist in spite of their contradiction or falsehood in the face of 'objective reality' or 'empirical truth.'

Stereotypes of groups based on such factors as occupation, sex, age, social, or economic status also exist in addition to those based on ethnic and/or national identity. In the culture of the USA, as in many others, women are stereotyped as bad drivers, excessively talkative, and easily given to emotional display. In many societies lawyers are stereotyped as unscrupulous, politicians as corrupt, and villagers as stupid and ignorant. As for the national stereotypes, the Scots are perceived as miserly, the Germans as excessively rigid, the English as stiff, the French as expert in love-making and cooking, the Jews as shrewd and good in business, and American Indians as inscrutable.

Folklore in most societies abounds with oral narratives based on stereotypes of other societies and nation-states. These images in folklore are due to what Jansen (1959) has called the esoteric–exoteric factor in folklore. He describes it thus: 'The esoteric applies to what one group thinks of itself and what it supposes others think of it. The exoteric is what one group thinks of another and what it thinks that other group thinks it thinks' (Jansen 1959: 206). Popular jokes based on national and other stereotypes constitute a major genre of such folklore (Davies 1990, Dundes 1971, 1975, 1987).

2. Stereotypes and Intergroup Interaction

In multi-ethnic nation-states, diverse cultural and linguistic groups and their members come in contact with each other and are forced to interact, even if on a limited basis. Stereotypes hinder such interaction and social discourse because they create misunderstanding. Dominant and/or majority groups tend to use stereotypes to justify their unjust treatment of powerless and/or minority groups. Interestingly, some dominated and/or minority group tend to accept their stereotypic image as created by others, but with a positive rather than a negative attitude. Sociocultural change and major historical events may affect the existing stereotypes in a society.

See also: Class and Language; Ethnicity and Language; Attitudes and Behavior.

Bibliography

Allport G W 1958 *The Nature of Prejudice*. Addison-Wesley, Cambridge, MA
Brigham J C 1971 Ethnic stereotypes. *Psychological Bulletin* **76**: 15–38
Brown R W 1965 *Social Psychology*. Free Press, New York
Davies C 1990 *Ethnic Humor Around the World*. Indiana University Press, Bloomington, IN
Dundes A 1971 A study of ethnic slurs: the Jew and the Polack in the United States. *Journal of American Folklore* **84**: 186–203
Dundes A 1975 Slurs international: Folk comparisons of ethnicity and national character. *Southern Folklore Quarterly* **39**: 15–38
Dundes A 1987 *Cracking Jokes: Studies of Sick Humor Cycles and Stereotypes*. Ten Speed Press, Berkeley, CA
Jansen W H 1959 The esoteric–exoteric factor in folklore. *Fabula* **2**: 205–11
Katz D, Braly K 1933 Racial stereotypes of one hundred college students. *Journal of Abnormal and Social Psychology* **28**: 280–90
La Pierre R T 1936 Type-rationalization of group anti-play. *Social Forces* **15**: 232–7
Lippmann W 1922 *Public Opinion*. Harcourt Brace, New York
Samuels F 1973 *Group Images: Racial, Ethnic, and Religious Stereotyping*. College and University Press, New Haven, CT

Symbolic Power and Language
C. B. Vigouroux

Just as the military strategist Clausewitz saw war as an extended form of politics, Pierre Bourdieu sees language not only as a self-contained system, but also as the political instrument of power struggles, a kind of 'battlefield.' By identifying language as an area in which power relations are created and exercised, Bourdieu (1977: xx) shows that the act of speaking does not merely involve exchanging information: 'language is not only an instrument of communication or knowledge but an instrument of power.' An important aspect of the Bourdieusian approach is the linking of Marxist and Weberian thought. Whereas Marxist society is based on the dominant/dominated dichotomy, Weber sees social reality as a combination of relations of meaning which give place to a symbolic dimension: power can also be administered symbolically.

Language for Bourdieu is considered within a wider attempt to deconstruct the mechanisms of domination, which form the basis of social relations. Language is everywhere, embracing all levels of society, and for Bourdieu it is an ideal means of getting to the bottom of this domination: while a physicist will talk about physics, a football fan about football, a computer programmer about computers, the common factor between them all is the use of language. Just as the psychoanalyst uses language to listen to that which his/her patient suppresses, Bourdieu the sociologist uses language to listen to that which society conceals.

1. The Economics of Linguistic Exchanges

Bourdieu seeks to construct a 'general theory of the economy of practice.' In the same way as we have a monetary economy, we also have a linguistic economy: language is exchanged as a product, which, within an *economy of linguistic exchanges*, is given a *price* and a certain *value*. Thus Bourdieu talks of linguistic, cultural, or political capital, etc. Linguistic capital acquires its value within *linguistic markets*, which include, for example, the education system, the labor market, the arts, government, etc. These act as authorities, which legitimize language, use and govern *price formation*. For Bourdieu communication does not only involve the giving and receiving of messages, but it also implies economic or symbolic value. While speaking like a politician will be appreciated within the appropriate settings, at the same time it may be devalued within other settings (e.g., among certain younger age groups) where it will be considered 'wrong currency.' While a word like *fuck*, for example, is not permitted in school, it may be taken up elsewhere by certain groups of people and used as an identity marker. The linguistic market therefore exists because language, like any other product, can be subject to transactions.

Language does not convey an individual's experiences. Rather, it is the individual's experience itself in that he/she is a historical individual, evolving within a particular social environment. Bourdieu's approach, rather than treating language as a closed system, takes the speaker along with the conditions of communication as the central aspect: 'a scientific approach to speech must take into account the conditions in which communication takes place since the expected reception conditions are bound up within the production conditions' (1977: 21). By doing this Bourdieu disputes the validity of a structuralist (i.e., Saussurean, see *Saussurean Tradition and Sociolinguistics*) approach to linguistics which attempts to explain linguistic features in terms of internal patterned organization or structure. Although Bourdieu does not deny language's autonomous nature as a *structured structure* (means of communication, language, or culture vs. discourse behavior), he goes on to add, however, that it is also a *structuring structure* (instruments for knowing and constructing the objective world) and can, therefore, become an *instrument of domination*.

2. Ideology and Legitimation

With the idea that the individual is born into a language—i.e., into an already existing system, with its phonological, syntactical, lexical, and morphological features—comes the idea of being born into a certain ideology relative to the language in question. Language is, above all, a means of apprehending the world: learning Mandarin for a European, for example, means not only learning the language system, but also learning to organize and categorize the world differently. If we take the example of a writer, writing in his/her first language, his/her particular style will reflect a certain vision of the world (see *Sapir–Whorf Hypothesis*).

An individual or an object cannot exist without a name: by giving people or things names we admit their existence. The naming of a newborn baby amounts to giving him/her a social baptism. The English philosopher Austin (1962) shows how 'saying is doing' with the speech-act example of the ship which is named by pronouncing the words 'I name this ship the *Queen Elizabeth*.' However, Bourdieu would argue that by actually naming the ship, the person demonstrates his/her legitimate right to do so; 'doing is saying.' So, while speaking implies saying something to somebody, it also amounts to telling somebody who we are and what we stand for. Stylistic variation can be linked to the speaker's motivated communication strategy vis-à-vis his/her audience: for example, a pensioner who refers to someone as 'well cool,' not only manifests an appreciation of the person in question, but also adopts a particular stance (identifying with the young or trendy) in choosing this register. More importantly than, for example, morphology or syntax, it is the way in which the language is actually put to use which interests Bourdieu: the *mise en scène* of language gives us an insight into society's hidden structures.

Words are actualized within a given context of communication; they take on specific meanings according to the speakers involved. This implies complicity and the establishing of a tacit contract between speaker–formulator and listener–decoder alike. For Bourdieu, society can not only be split into dominant/dominated groups but it can also be divided up into 'fields' (*champs*). These consist of small spheres, which dispose of their own value systems. Within a given field, a previously dominated subject can become the dominant one. The speech of a given individual will be more or less 'legitimate' according to the particular field in which it occurs. For example, if a book reviewer who is not a literary specialist writes in a newspaper that a book is 'interesting,' his/her judgments will have a particular value. However, within another field, such as that of the university, these may be played down.

3. Symbolic Power

Power is rarely exercised overtly as a physical force for any length of time. Rather, it takes on a symbolic form. In order for *symbolic power* to be exercised it must first of all be *interiorized*, i.e., acknowledged as something natural, which goes without saying by those who are subjected to it. In the case of language prescription, where the norm or 'approved correctness' in speech is prescribed by the education system, for example, this process does not only involve the simple imposition of a given linguistic variety, but it also implies speakers' interiorization of the idea that their variety is of low prestige. And, while those concerned may get the impression that this takes place at a purely linguistic level, it is in actual fact another kind of domination. So, it is not only by *recognizing* the means of domination, but also by '*misrecognizing*' its ends, that symbolic power is transformed into *symbolic violence*. The nature of *symbolic violence* for Bourdieu is, then, twofold, being based on the recognition–misrecognition pair. This is part of a key concept in Bourdieusian sociology, i.e., *habitus*, which concerns the ways in which social structures are impressed upon our minds and bodies (*corporal hexis*) becoming *durable* and *transposable dispositions* (*Le sens pratique*, 1984). A further example can be seen in the process of colonization by European countries. This not only concerned the colonization of space, but also extended to the colonization of the mind. The language of the colonizer, with all it conveys (imposition of the dominant science, history, technology, and ideology), contributed to the colonized subject's interiorization of the master as a master to the extent that the former came to discredit his/her own language(s), history, science, and technology.

Given that language not only forms part of our environment, but also serves to construct our environment, totalitarian regimes have always sought to control language in order to subdue society or to control society in order to subdue language. The French Revolution provides us with an example of the reworking of time via the implementation of new ways of naming things with the setting up of a calendar with new names for the months of the year (*vendémiaire, brumaire, pluviôse*). The many different forms of domination operate most discretely and also most violently in language. As Baudelaire points out, all the devil's trickery lies in making us believe that he does not exist. Thus language, of all forms of power, is the one which can have the greatest effect. It is the fact that language is a symbolic form of power that an individual, group, or institution can use it as a weapon to exercise symbolic violence.

See also: Hegemony; Power and Language; Linguistic Habitus; The Linguistic Marketplace.

Bibliography

Austin J L 1962 *How to do Things with Words*. Clarendon Press, Oxford, UK

Bourdieu P 1972 *Esquisse d'une théorie de la pratique, précédé de trois études d'ethnologie kabyle*. Droz, Geneva [English transl., *Outline of a Theory of Practice*. Cambridge University Press, Cambridge, UK, 1977]

Bourdieu P 1977 Economie des échanges linguistiques. *Langue française* **34**

Bourdieu P 1979 *La distinction. Critique sociale du jugement*. Ed. de Minuit, Paris [English transl., *Distinction: A Social Critique of the Judgment of Taste*. Harvard University Press, Cambridge, MA, 1984]

Bourdieu P 1982 *Ce que parler veut dire*. Fayard, Paris [English transl., Thompson, J B (ed.) *Language and Symbolic power*. Harvard University Press, Cambridge, MA, 1991]

Bourdieu P 1984 *Le sens pratique*. Ed. de Minuit, Paris [English transl., *The Logic of Practice*. Polity Press, Cambridge, UK, 1990]

Bourdieu P 1984 *Homo academicus*. Ed. de Minuit, Paris [English transl., *Homo academicus*. Polity Press, Cambridge, UK, 1988]

Bourdieu P 1989 *La noblesse d'État. Grandes écoles et esprit de corps*. Ed. de Minuit, Paris [English transl., *The State Nobility: Elite Schools in the Field of Power*. Polity Press, Cambridge, UK, 1996]

Bourdieu P 1993 *La misère du monde*. Ed. du Seuil, Paris [English transl., *The Weight of the World: Social Suffering in Contemporary Society*. Stanford University Press, Stanford, CA, 1999]

Bourdieu P, Passeron J C 1964 *Les héritiers, les étudiants et la culture*. Ed. de Minuit, Paris [English transl., *The Inheritors, French Students and their Relation to Culture*. University of Chicago Press, Chicago, IL, 1979]

Bourdieu P, Passeron J C 1970 *La reproduction: Eléments pour une théorie du système d'enseignement*. Ed. de Minuit, Paris [English transl. *Reproduction in Education, Society and Culture*. Sage Publications, London, 1977]

The Linguistic Marketplace
I. Gogolin

The idea of the existence and functioning of a linguistic marketplace was originally created by the French sociologist Pierre Bourdieu; it is described in detail in Bourdieu's 1991 work *Language and Symbolic Power*.

Throughout his works, Bourdieu examines the question of how power relations in a society emerge and stay relatively stable, and how they are traditionalized although certain changes take place. A key concept for the explanation of these processes is that of *habitus* (see *Linguistic Habitus*). According to Bourdieu, a habitus is the set of dispositions, which incline the manner of action and reaction of the individual. A habitus generates durable practices and attitudes in people; it pilots their perception of normality. As a habitus is acquired under certain social conditions of an individual's existence, members of a social class and people of similar backgrounds tend to relatively homogeneous habitus.

The concept of habitus allows the principles which underlie the practices and perceptions of the individual to be described. Complementary to these, Bourdieu offers the concept of *field* or—as a largely synonymous metaphor—*market* for a description of the social contexts within which individuals act. Though these terms are borrowed from economics, the analysis based on these terms goes far beyond the assumption of simple economic transaction in human action.

A field or market may be seen as a structured space of positions, which are determined and interrelated by the distribution of different kinds of *capitals*. These are special resources, which an individual is equipped with—namely by heritage, but possibly also by one's own achievements. Bourdieu proposes that there are different forms of capitals: *economic capital* (money, stocks, shares, property, etc.), *cultural capital* (skills and knowledge, cultural acquisitions, and other qualifications, etc.), *social capital* (human relations, contacts, and connections, etc.). When these capitals are officially accepted as the worth of an individual, they function as *symbolic capital*: the accumulated honor of a person (see Bourdieu 1998). The capitals can be converted into the other; for example, social capital as well as cultural capital can be exchanged for reputable jobs.

The actors in a field or market usually have a tendency to either preserve their position or struggle for a better one, depending on where they are located. In these struggles—Bourdieu also refers to them as *games*—all participants share a common set of rules or unquestioned beliefs, to which belong the interpretations of the values and operation of capitals. But participation in the struggle or game is not to be understood as the mere result of constant conscious calculation. Individual practices are more likely a result of habitus: predisposed ways of action, deep-seated, unconscious beliefs and presuppositions. Apart from strategic activities, the ways of accumulation of capital and of investing capital are clearly influenced by habitus.

Linguistic utterances are forms of practice, which can be understood as the product of the relation between linguistic habitus and linguistic market (Thompson 1991: 17). The linguistic habitus of a person—as part of the habitus as such—governs his or her ways of language behavior as well as the judgment about the values of languages, forms of speech, or linguistic expressions. Articulatory styles differ according to class and region, and can also differ according to sex. The different styles are endowed with different values, which are related to the distribution of other forms of capital. The symbolic value, which is connected with a language or an articulatory style, is handed down historically. In many societies, especially the classical European nation states, the best recognized language variations, i.e., those which receive unquestioned respect by everybody, at any given time and which are connected to the highest amount of symbolic power, are the official national languages in their standard form. Nevertheless, the values of different articulatory styles differ in particular contexts or markets. For example, in a youth group, a conversation in standard language will probably not be adequate, and in a rural area the local dialect may be the appropriate medium for an address at an official celebration.

Linguistic competence in this approach does not refer to a uniform notion of formal correctness or to the technical command of a language, but refers to the ability of using language or language variants in a manner that secures a 'profit of distinction.' The social and symbolic power of languages or language use does not derive from language as such, but from the settings—the particular contexts or markets—in which communication takes place. The reproduction of symbolic power related to languages or to language use functions by virtue of every speaker's assessment of market conditions. Speakers modify their language use according to their anticipation of its reception and acknowledgment. If they struggle for a better position in a society, they will probably try to reproduce the expressions and styles, which they know as valued more highly than others. This is why people from lower classes tend to give up their modes of expression when they aspire to a better position in society. On the other hand, people from upper class backgrounds usually respond with relative ease to the demands of different language situations. Their linguistic habitus enables them to handle diversity, and this may include the use of a regional dialect or social variant in specific situations. The socially constructed dispositions of the linguistic habitus imply a certain propensity to express oneself in an appropriate manner and a capacity to speak. This capacity involves the linguistic capacity to generate an infinite number of discourses as the social capacity to use this competency adequately in specific situations. The structures of the linguistic market impose a system of specific sanctions and censorships on speakers (Bourdieu 1991: 37).

The concept of a linguistic market was developed from a (Western) European perspective and describes the part of language in the process of social distinction in capitalistic societies. But it can also be useful as a frame of reference for the study of power relations in other areas of the world, namely colonial and post-colonial countries (cf. Goke-Pariola 1993).

See also: Linguistic Habitus; Symbolic Power and Language; Bourdieu, Pierre.

Bibliography

Bourdieu P 1991 *Language and Symbolic Power*, 1st edn. Polity Press, Cambridge, UK

Bourdieu P 1998 *Practical Reason: On the Theory of Action*. Stanford University Press, Stanford, CA

Bourdieu's works: comprehensive, contextual, and referential bibliography of: www.iwp.uni-linz.ac.at/lxe/sektktf/bb/hyperbourdieu.html

Goke-Pariola A 1993 Language and symbolic power: Bourdieu and the legacy of Euro-American colonialism in an African society. *Language and Communication* **13**(3): 219–34

Thompson J B 1991 Editor's introduction. In: Bourdieu P (ed.) *Language and Symbolic Power*, 1st edn. Polity Press, Cambridge, UK

SECTION VII
Language Planning, Policy, Practice

Academies: Dictionaries and Standards
L. C. Mugglestone

National academies, influential and often authoritarian bodies devoted to the maintenance and regulation of individual languages, first appeared in Europe in the sixteenth century, though the Hebrew Language Academy was, for example, founded as late as 1953. The production of a dictionary was often given as a major objective in the foundation of such institutions, particularly since a dictionary was seen as one of the main ways by which the issues of language maintenance could be realized. As a result, academy dictionaries frequently reflect the ideals of conscious linguistic standardization which came to prevail in the Renaissance as well as afterwards.

1. The Accademia della Crusca and the First Academy Dictionary

The Italian Accademia della Crusca was, in 1584, the first such academy to be established, its guiding principles being based in the intended regulation of the language, and the production of a dictionary being given as one of its main aims. Like the Académie Française which was to follow in 1635, or the attempts to found a similar body in England around the end of the seventeenth century, the Crusca was in many ways explicitly preoccupied by the notion of linguistic authority, and by the need for a national standard of linguistic usage. Its dictionary, the *Vocabulario degli accademici della Crusca*, published in Venice in 1612, naturally embodies these aims; the words it records are those supported by the written authority of great works, rather than by current usage, and lexical innovation is tolerated only where felt to be unavoidable.

Such principles of lexical selection were employed under the joint banners of patriotism and purism; the intention was to remedy the perceived 'degeneration' since the linguistic 'Golden Age' of the fourteenth century, and also to reflect a new concept of the vernacular, as a language in its own right, rather than as a debased form of Latin. The linguistic concerns are therefore normative and conservative, and the *Vocabulario* was felt to be the preserve only of the best usage, and more specifically, the best literary usage.

2. The French Academy

The role of academy dictionary as linguistic exemplar was also adopted within the methodological principles of the Académie Française, one of its founding tenets being 'to labor with all possible diligence to give definite rules to our language, and to render it pure.' Its own dictionary, published in 1640, is shaped by these issues of linguistic propriety; recording only those usages felt to be redolent of 'le bel usage,' it is above all, like the *Vocabulario*, a dictionary of the written language, literary authority sanctioning the introduction of words where current usage could not, with the result that archaic words are often admitted to the exclusion of newer ones. As the Preface to the seventh edition of 1877 records, 'A word is not dead because we no longer employ it, if it lives on in the works of a Molière.' Many of the original authoritarian principles were maintained in successive editions; the Preface to the second edition of 1718, for example, makes explicit its decision to exclude words such as *fichu, ratafia, bizarre,* and *sabler*, whilst that of 1877 notes that words which seemed ill-composed, or contrary to 'the genius of the language' have likewise not been admitted. The academy dictionary in this way becomes not a dictionary of the language in itself, but instead a dictionary of the words felt to merit existence in that language.

3. Proposals for an English Academy

Such standardizing ideals within the preserve of lexicography in turn exerted their influence upon England. Daniel Defoe in his *Essay upon Projects* (1697) urged the creation of a legislative body in linguistic matters which would 'polish and refine the English tongue, and advance the so much neglected faculty of correct language...to purge it from all the irregular additions that ignorance and affectation have produced.' Such a plan, however, never came to fruition, and Dr Johnson's own dictionary (1755), praised, for example, by David Garrick as the English equivalent of the *Dictionnaire* of the Académie Française, is tempered by a sense that the dicta of academies cannot control lexical change, nor fix its norms of propriety. As he notes in his own Preface in 1755

> With this hope, however, academies have been instituted, to guard the avenues of their language, to retain fugitives, and to repulse intruders; but their vigilance and activity have hitherto been in vain;... to enchain syllables, and to lash the wind, are equally the undertakings of pride, unwilling to measure its desires by its strength.

4. The Twentieth-century Context

Though academies attempted therefore to prescribe lexical norms, and to codify the patterns of the best usage in terms of literary authority, the principles of lexical exclusion and selectivity which they advocated were not followed in the actual language itself, where usage is the only guide to lexical existence, rather than the arbitrary norms of official institutions. Recent lexicographical developments, even within the sphere of academy dictionaries, have in a number of ways come to recognize this fact, though the dicta of the Académie Française can still be marked by a certain lexical xenophobia, as well as by a qualitative bias in the words it records: the Preface to the *Dictionnaire* of 1935, for example, noted that new words have indeed been listed, but only those which have been judged of sufficient dignity to merit admittance.

See also: Prescription in Dictionaries; Verbal Hygiene.

Bibliography

Bolton W F 1966 *The English Language. Vol. I: Essays by English and American Men of Letters 1490–1839*. Cambridge University Press, London

Chiappelli F (ed.) 1985 *The Fairest Flower. The Emergence of Linguistic National Consciousness in Renaissance Europe*. International Conference of the Center for Medieval and Renaissance Studies, University of California, Firenze Presso l'Accademia, Florence, Italy

Collison R L 1955 *Dictionaries of Foreign Languages*. The Hafner Publishing Company, London

Artificial Languages
A. Large

An artificial language has a vocabulary and a syntax, a writing system, and normally also a phonology. It is used to communicate between human beings although some artificial languages such as programming and command languages are used by humans to issue instructions to machines. Unlike a natural language, however, it has one or more creators who were responsible for its design. Artificial languages are related to other kinds of linguistic creations such as cryptographs and shorthand systems. Although some speakers have learned an artificial language from their parents at the hearth, in most cases such languages are learned through study. It is worth adding that many users of artificial languages do not themselves care for this terminology. They believe that artificial implies such negative characteristics as lifeless, second-rate, or unnatural, and prefer the terms 'constructed language' or 'planned language.'

At a conservative estimate some 500 artificial languages have been created since the seventeenth century and new ones regularly appear. Few have attained wide-spread use, however. Esperanto, now more than a century old, must be acknowledged the most successful when measured by numbers of active users, geographical distribution, and publications. Precise and reliable figures for artificial language users are difficult to come by. This is partly because a clear definition of user is difficult to formulate for languages which are normally learned as a foreign language rather than as a mother tongue. Users can range from those who are fluent (itself by no means unambiguous) in speech and writing to mere purchasers of language primers. Quantification is also problematical in a partizan field where statistics have a propaganda value and estimates vary dramatically between supporters and detractors of any particular language.

1. Categorization

Artificial languages can be categorized as *a priori* or *a posteriori*. An *a priori* language is composed entirely of invented elements not found in any natural language, and is usually based on a logical classification of ideas. Relationships between things in the real world can be expressed taxonomically by the language itself, the object being to remove ambiguity and create, as Leibniz put it, an 'instrument of reason.' In practice, however, this tends to make the language more difficult to learn and use. Ro is an example of an early twentieth-century *a priori* language. Knowledge is divided into 25 main classes, each with further levels of subdivision. Related concepts are indicated by alphabetically similar words so that *bod* is universe with subclass related terms such as *bodam, bodas*, and *bodar* for moon, sun, and star, respectively.

An *a posteriori* language is based on elements of grammar, vocabulary, and syntax drawn from one or more natural languages. This more pragmatic approach is usually motivated by a desire to design a workable auxiliary language which can be easily learned and used by everyone. Natural languages, however, are replete with irregularities and inconsistencies. An *a posteriori* language like Occidental attempts to remain close in form to its natural language parents (chiefly the Romance languages) and is therefore relatively easy to read, at least, for the educated elite of western Europe. Unfortunately this naturalistic element can only be purchased at the expense of numerous irregularities in Occidental. *A posteriori* languages like Esperanto and its offshoot, Ido, are much more regular but thereby less closely identifiable with the European languages on which they were based.

Modified natural languages are closely related to naturalistic *a posteriori* languages, having many similarities in approach and objective. In practice the distinction between a naturalistic artificial language like *Latino sine flexione* and a modified natural language such as Basic English is relatively minor. The objective here is to simplify acquisition and use of a natural language by eliminating its most awkward features—usually irregularities of grammar, spelling, and pronunciation—coupled with a reduction in vocabulary. Basic English, for example, functions with a vocabulary pared down to fewer than 1000 words, achieved by eliminating synonyms and by building complex terms from their simple components. The drastically-reduced vocabulary certainly facilitates reading but requires considerable linguistic ingenuity and skill on the part of the writer.

2. History

Although interest in language creation goes back much further, it was in seventeenth-century Europe that the idea of constructing languages first became a serious proposition. Many different motives have attracted people to this task. An intrinsic interest in language itself is essential but rarely sufficient of itself, and few language constructors have been professional linguists. The early schemes of the seventeenth century were prompted by philosophical, religious, scientific, and commercial considerations. The decline of Latin as an international language prompted a quest for a new vehicle to communicate the growing output of scientific publications, while traders and missionaries needed a language which could be taught to the natives of the Far East and Americas so as better to trade goods and save souls. Of even more importance, however, was the desire to construct rational, philosophical languages which would avoid the confusion and discord created by ambiguous, ill-structured natural languages. It was this goal which attracted the likes of Descartes, Leibniz, and Wilkins to their linguistic endeavor.

Of the many universal language projects contemplated or actually constructed at that time, the clergyman John Wilkins's *An Essay Towards a Real Character and a Philosophical Language* (1668) is the most impressive and most fully developed. Relying largely upon the Aristotelian distinction between genus and difference Wilkins attempted to allocate 'all things and notions' to 40 classes so as to group related concepts in some kind of meaningful order. He then provided grammatical rules by which simple concepts could be assembled into complex ideas. This *a priori* language played a role in the standardization of scientific nomenclature and inspired Roget during the compilation of his *Thesaurus*, but Wilkins did not succeed in establishing a universal language.

The construction of philosophical languages held less attraction in the eighteenth century and enthusiasm for universal language projects flagged without quite disappearing. Its reappearance in the second half of the nineteenth century was prompted not by the desire to create a philosophical language but by the perceived need for a practical, ethnically neutral language for international communication. Growing cross-border contacts at the personal, institutional, and governmental levels highlighted the barrier caused by language diversity and emphasized the advantages to be gained from the adoption of an international auxiliary language. Such practical considerations were further buttressed by idealistic motivations. For example, the German priest, Schleyer, envisaged his language, Volapük, as contributing towards universal peace, while the Jewish oculist and creator of Esperanto, Zamenhof, was haunted by the memory of ethnic conflicts in his native Poland to which he believed linguistic differences had contributed. More recently the authors of another language wrote that 'Glosa is not an end in itself, but a means of helping to rid the world of poverty and ignorance.'

This more practical concern with the growing need for an international auxiliary language has reduced the numbers of a priori schemes although they do still appear from time to time. Attention has been increasingly devoted to *a posteriori* languages, an early example of which was sketched by a Frenchman, Faiguet, in 1765. Volapük, which drew its vocabulary from the heavily modified roots of various European languages, was the first artificial language to win widespread popular support. First published in 1880, Volapük initially registered considerable successes but dissension among its supporters soon tore the movement apart. The language soon to be called Esperanto (after the pseudonym of its creator, Doktoro Esperanto—'one who hopes') was published in a Russian edition a few years later in 1887. Despite setbacks and schisms Esperanto has experienced greater success, surviving as an active and organized movement for more than a century.

3. Characteristics

Although artificial languages are linguistically diverse, a number of general characteristics have assumed prominence. Ease of acquisition is a major criterion for any language which is to seek mass support. *A posteriori* languages attempt to facilitate learning by incorporating syntactic and morphological features found in natural languages. *A priori* languages normally look much less familiar and their difficulty to acquisition is a major argument directed against them. Yet even here their creators frequently claim that mastery can be assured with little effort. John Wilkins, for example, claimed that more of his Real Character could be learned in one month than in 40 months' study of Latin.

Precision is a second sought characteristic. In this case the language is intended to provide an unambiguous and logical medium of communication in contrast to natural languages which, it is asserted, lack clarity and consistency. *A priori* seventeenth-century schemes in particular pursued this goal. Their classifications of concepts, however, mirrored their creators' perception of knowledge and have proven neither universal nor eternal. Wilkins's Real Character, for example, is based upon seventeenth-century reality, leading him to decisions such as the classification of the whale as a fish rather than a mammal.

In most cases artificial languages have been intended for all kinds of communication and must therefore cope with the syntactic and lexical demands of numerous specialized subject domains as well as the everyday needs of their speakers. Furthermore, they must accommodate new words and constructions if they are to evolve in the way of natural languages. The supporters of Esperanto, for example, stress its receptivity to new words.

How successfully have artificial languages met these goals? The philosophical *a priori* languages have too often been difficult to memorize and use, inhospitable to new concepts and rational only to those who agree with their designer's identification and classification of concepts. *A posteriori* languages may be easier to learn, but such ease is dependent upon the learner's familiarity with the natural language or languages on which they are based. The internationalism of artificial languages primarily based upon languages in the Indo-European group, for example, might be questioned. Linguistic evolution tends to be more problematic for artificial than natural languages. The fact that the language is designed according to a blueprint can lend force to conservatism; at the same time linguistic stability can be threatened by proposals for reform which are seldom in short supply in movements whose *raison d'etre* is language. Disputes over the use of circumflexed letters in Esperanto orthography, for example, have been frequent and bitter. The history of the artificial language movement all too often has been one of acrimonious dispute, sectarianism, and fission: creators and supporters of artificial languages are ill-equipped to compromise on such matters as grammar or lexicography.

4. The Future

Artificial languages may not be so rational, expressive, neutral, and easy to learn as their supporters sometimes assert, but nevertheless they can function very effectively as a medium for written and spoken discourse. A language like Esperanto is spoken in all parts of the world, as well as possessing the linguistic richness to accept in translation the greatest literary works from a wide variety of natural languages and, indeed, to convey a sizeable body of original prose and poetry. The major problem which has always faced artificial language creators, however, is to persuade enough people to use them. An international language, to be effective, must be spoken by most if not all the world's population. Yet the total number of artificial language speakers from the seventeenth century to the present represents a mere fraction of late twentieth-century English speakers. How can people be persuaded to devote the time and energy necessary to learn even the most regular, natural, and straightforward artificial language and then to use it as a medium of communication with people who do not share their own natural language? This is the fundamental problem facing any artificial language and it is political rather than linguistic in nature.

There are two ways in which an artificial language might be adopted as a vehicle for international communication. A *de jure* decision might be taken by an international body such as the United Nations to select a language for this role. In the twentieth century a Delegation for the Adoption of an International Language was created which appointed a committee to examine scientifically the merits of a number of schemes with a view to recommending universal adoption; it only succeeded in generating a deep rift in the Esperantist movement. Once a language has been selected by the international organization it would then be necessary to ensure its acquisition by as many people as possible as quickly as possible, a task requiring international collaboration on a scale so far sadly absent from world councils.

Alternatively, an artificial language might become *de facto* the international language through sheer weight of numbers. No language movement is remotely big enough to suggest this is probable. Although a number of international organizations have toyed with the idea of adopting an artificial language (usually Esperanto) for at least some of their activities, natural languages have not been dislodged from their stranglehold even in this most fertile ground for constructed languages. The task of winning worldwide support is formidable for an artificial language which depends for its promotion on a dispersed social group and lacks the political, economic, and cultural pressure which states can afford their natural languages.

See also: Language; Language Development; International Languages.

Bibliography

Couturat L, Leau L 1903 *Histoire de la Langue Universelle*. Librairie Hachette, Paris

Kennaway R 2001 *Some Internet Resources Relating to Constructed Languages*. http://www.sys.uea.ac.uk/~jrk/conlang.html

Large A 1985 *The Artificial Language Movement*. Blackwell, Oxford

Large J A 1984 'Of one language, and of one speech': Artificial languages and international communication. *Multilingua* **3**: 11–7

Pei M 1958 *One Language for the World*. Devin-Adair, New York

Heritage Languages
J. Cummins

In a general sense the term *heritage languages* refers to languages other than the official or majority languages of a country. The apparent simplicity of this general definition, however, is misleading in an area as highly contested as the status of different languages in society and the social and educational rights that accrue to speakers of different languages. These struggles around status, identity, and rights are reflected in the variety of terms that have been used in Canada and other countries to refer to heritage languages. The terms *ancestral, ethnic, immigrant, international, minority, non-official, third* (after English and French), and *world* have all been used at different times and in different contexts. The term used in Quebec is *langues d'origine* (languages of origin). In other countries the term *community languages* has been used (e.g., Australia, New Zealand, the United Kingdom) and the term *mother tongue teaching* is also common.

In the Canadian context, the federal policy of support for multiculturalism within the framework of two official languages, announced in 1971, legitimated demands among ethnocultural communities that federal and provincial governments support maintenance and development of heritage languages. Advocates argued that a policy of multiculturalism was vacuous if it claimed only to support 'culture' in the absence of concern for the languages in which those cultures were embedded.

The term came into widespread use in 1977 with the establishment of the Heritage Languages Program in the province of Ontario. Funded by the provincial government for the past 25 years, this program provides support for the teaching of heritage languages for up to two-and-a-half hours per week outside of the regular five-hour school day. The term *heritage languages* was intended to acknowledge that these languages constitute important aspects of the heritage of individual children and communities and are worthy of financial support and recognition by the wider society.

In the early 1990s, the term *heritage languages* was changed to *international languages* by the provincial government, reflecting misgivings among ethnocultural communities that the notion of 'heritage' entailed connotations of learning about past traditions rather than acquiring language skills that have significance for children's overall educational and personal development. The term *international languages* was intended to communicate that, in an era of globalization, these languages were highly relevant to business and cultural exchanges and had economic as well as 'heritage' value.

Indigenous communities have resisted attempts to include their languages within the categories of 'heritage' or 'community' languages on the grounds that as 'First Nations,' the status of their languages is very different than the status of immigrant languages. Deaf communities have also grappled with the status of sign languages vis-à-vis heritage languages. For example, in Ontario, the Deaf community in the early 1990s resisted having American Sign Language (ASL) taught as just another heritage language and argued successfully for the institution of ASL as a language of instruction within a bilingual/bicultural program in the provincial schools for the Deaf. Thus, definitions of *heritage languages* remain dynamic rather than static, reflecting the contested cultural and political terrain to which the term refers.

See also: Sociolinguistics of Sign Language; Minority Languages; Reversing Language Shift; Salvage Work (Endangered Languages).

Bibliography

Cummins J, Danesi M 1990 *Heritage Languages: The Development and Denial of Canada's Linguistic Resources.* Our Schools/Ourselves, Toronto, ON

Krashen S, Tse L, McQuillan J 1998 *Heritage Language Development.* Language Education Associates, Culver City, CA

International Languages
U. Ammon

In modern times international communication has become increasingly important. As a consequence, international languages (ILs) gain more and more practical significance. Though international communication does not necessarily depend on ILs (it can also take place via translation from one language into another), in many situations using an IL is much more convenient than translating.

The meaning of the term 'International Language' may appear clear enough at first view. A closer look, however, shows that some clarification may be useful, especially since there is no significant research tradition within which a widely accepted concept could have been established. An attempt at conceptual clarification will also open up perspectives for future research.

1. The Concept 'International Language'

'International language' is not usually found as a lemma in dictionaries of linguistic terminology. An exception is Pei (1966: 132, 128) who defines it as a language 'created or suggested for adoption for purposes of international communication.' While this definition fits a language that is *intended* as international, a more adequate way to specify the meaning of IL would be 'a language *used* for international communication.'

By definition, international communication occurs between nations, or rather, individuals belonging to different nations. The problem is that the concept of 'nation' itself is interpreted in various ways, namely at least the following two: (a) country or autonomous state; (b) nationality, defined by a common language, culture, history, and an idea of belonging together.

If possible, the definition of an IL should take into account these interpretations. A communicative act (see *Communication*) may be called 'international' if it occurs between different countries, i.e., between inhabitants or citizens of different countries, or between different nationalities, i.e., roughly speaking, between (native) speakers of different languages. If only one of the two conditions is fulfilled, the respective communicative act could be called international *only in a wider sense*. Examples would be a communicative act either between a speaker of German and a speaker of Hungarian, both of whom are citizens of Hungary, or between a citizen of Germany and a citizen of Hungary, both of whom are speakers of German. If, however, both conditions coincide in a communicative act, it seems adequate to consider it *international in the narrower sense*, i.e., if the communicative act occurs on the one hand among (native) speakers of different languages (e.g., a speaker of German and a speaker of Hungarian) who on the other hand are citizens or inhabitants of different countries (e.g., Germany and Hungary). The more a language is used in international communication, either in the wider sense only, or also in the narrower sense, the more likely it is to be seen as international.

From the above, one sees that it would be wrong simply to separate languages into ILs vs. non-ILs (which is the approach taken by Braga 1979). Instead, the conceptual framework offered above asks for a ranking of languages, or even a measuring by intervals according to degree of internationality (Ammon 1990a: 135–8). Empirical research is necessary to determine to which extent the various languages are actually used in international communication. Only on the basis of such empirical findings will it then be justified to delimit a certain set of languages as *the most important ILs*.

2. The Most Important ILs

Trivially, the importance of a language as an IL varies with the course of time. Therefore, any characterization of a language as an IL should be specified as to the period of time for which such a characterization holds true. Thus, ancient Greek was an important IL in classical antiquity; in the late twentieth century neither classical nor modern Greek are. For reasons of space, the following considerations will be limited to ILs in the twentieth century, with only occasional glimpses back into history. For the same reason, ILs which are limited to religious functions, such as Latin for Roman Catholic Christians or Pali for Buddhists, will not be dealt with; Arabic, which is the religious language for

Muslims, is another matter, since it does not only serve religious functions.

Since it is impossible to observe all international communicative acts, empirical investigations into ILs have to rely on relatively limited samples, or even on mere indicators of international communication. The value of these indicators can often only be judged intuitively, for the same reason.

It seems clear that the number of (native) speakers of a language is of some limited significance as an indicator of its importance as an IL; however, it certainly is not too reliable a measure. Chinese has, for instance, more speakers than English, and Bengali has more than French or German; it is, however, quite obvious that English is a more important IL than Chinese, and that French or German are more important ILs than Bengali. More significant with respect to its importance as an IL is a language's *economic strength*, understood as the economic strength of its language community (i.e., the community of all its native speakers). Superior economic strength is thus one of the factors responsible for the eminent international importance of English as compared to Chinese, or of the greater international importance of French or German as compared to Bengali. Likewise, the expansion of Japanese as a foreign language can in part be explained by the considerable economic strength of its language community. A language community's economic strength makes the study of its language appear more rewarding, because that language community appears as a more promising market—to mention just one of the reasons why economic strength enhances the international importance of a language. According to one calculation (Ammon 1991: chap. 3, 4) the strength of the six economically strongest language communities around 1985 was (in terms of their GNP in billions of $US):

1. English	4271
2. Japanese	1277
3. German	1090
4. Russian	801
5. Spanish	738
6. French	669

Another significant indicator of the international importance of a language is the number of countries in which it is used, either as the native language of a considerable portion of the population, or as an official language of the country. If the number of 'its' countries is greater, the chances of a language to serve for international communication naturally increases. Around 1985, the following six languages ranked highest with respect to the number of countries in which they were official, either on a national or on a regional level (source: Banks et al. 1987):

1. English	63
2. French	34
3. Spanish	23
4. Arabic	22
5. German	8
6. Portuguese	7

The extent to which languages are studied as foreign languages could serve as another indicator of their importance as ILs; as a rule, it may be assumed that the more a language is used for international communication (in the narrower sense), the more it is studied as a foreign language. Unfortunately, worldwide comparisons of various languages as to the degree to which they are studied as foreign languages are not readily available. The only figures which are readily accessible are those of foreign students studying in the mother tongue countries of the following six languages (according to Conrad and Fishman (1977) for the older figures of some of the languages; according to the writer's findings from the same source (*UNESCO Yearbook*) for the other languages and for newer figures):

	1967	1986
English	156,403	409,920
French	44,078	142,480
German	39,178	96,172
Spanish	25,161	10,821
Italian	16,957	34,720
Russian	16,100	?

The data are not complete, since the number of foreign students (per country of provenance) is not always given for every mother tongue country of each language. In particular, the figures are incomplete for Spanish, which is underrepresented here; figures are entirely missing for Russian for 1986. Nevertheless, the overall tendency may be assumed to be correct. The figures presumably also correspond roughly to the overall degree to which the respective languages are studied as foreign languages worldwide—with the exception of Spanish, which is probably studied to a similar extent as is German and even clearly exceeding it in certain regions, particularly in North America. The foreign students represent those learners of the respective language who, as a rule, acquire solid skills in it and therefore are, at the same time, most likely to actually continue using it for communication afterwards.

A closer look at certain domains provides some insight into the actual use of various languages for international communication. Most revealing are, of course, the typically 'international domains,' i.e., those with high proportions of international communication. Of these, some data relevant to this study are available for the domains of economy, diplomacy, and science.

In which languages do international business contacts mainly take place? An answer, admittedly preliminary, is provided by the German Chambers of Commerce (Ammon 1991: chap. 7.3), which on the basis of their extensive experience regularly issue recommendations for German companies as to which languages to choose for business contacts with other countries. This is particularly important for sales purposes: here, the choice of a language is a much more sensitive issue than in the case of buying. Even allowing for this sensitivity, one may find the recommendations somewhat biased towards German (which is natural, given the geographical location of the authors). For the year 1989, the six languages below are recommended for the following number of countries (for some countries, several languages are given):

1. English   122 (sole language in 64 countries)
2. French   57 (sole language in 24 countries)
3. Spanish   26 (sole language in 17 countries)
4. German   36 (sole language in 1 country)
5. Arabic   12 (sole language in 0 country)
6. Portuguese   8 (sole language in 0 country)

These figures should be weighed against the economic strength of the languages, as given above: just listing the number of countries can be misleading, especially with respect to a language's importance for international business communication. If the economic strength of the languages were taken into consideration, Japanese would probably have to be moved up, and French somewhat down as regards their importance for international business.

In the area of diplomacy, a language's status in the UN is of considerable importance, since this has some impact on its status in other international political organizations and conferences, as well as on the language training of diplomats in a number of countries. The following six languages are 'official,' and at the same time 'working' languages of the UN (the distinction between official and working languages has been largely blurred in the late twentieth century): English, French, Spanish, Russian, Chinese, and Arabic (Ostrower 1965: 405–31). German has the lower status of a 'documentary' language, i.e., one into which more important documents are translated (Tabory 1980: 9). The privileged status of official languages in the UN is due to one or several of the following attributes: being an official language in a great number of member countries (English, French, Spanish, Arabic); having a great number of speakers (Chinese); representing a mother country with significant political and military strength (Russian).

Another indicator of a language's importance in diplomacy is its use in the texts of treaties between countries. Particularly revealing with respect to international communication is the asymmetrical use of a language or its use as a lingua franca in treaty tests. A language is used asymmetrically if it is the national, official language of one of the countries involved and is used for (an authoritative version of) the treaty, to the exclusion of other national, official languages of any of the involved countries. A language functions as a lingua franca if it is used without being the national, official language of any of the countries involved. During the period 1900–63, the following six languages were most frequently used asymmetrically or as lingua franca in treaty texts. (In the table, the first number indicates the entire period 1900–63, the number in parentheses indicates the period from 1950–63. Source: Rönnefarth and Euler 1963.)

Asymmetrical use		Lingua franca	
1. English	56 (24)	1. French	49 (16)
2. French	53 (21)	2. English	26 (18)
3. Portuguese	11 (4)	3. Russian,	
4. German	9 (3)	Spanish	1 (1)
5. Chinese	6 (5)	4. Swedish	1 (0)
6. Italian	5 (2)		

The most spectacular change occurring in the period is perhaps the demotion of French in favor of English as a lingua franca. This may be connected with a general change in rank order between the two languages as to their importance in diplomacy.

In science, international communication has always played an important role. In particular, a sizeable number of printed publications in one language have always also been studied by speakers of other languages. The number of scientific publications in a language may, therefore, serve as a rough indicator of the amount of international communication which takes place in it. Figure 1 shows the share of the five most important languages of scientific publication in the time period 1880–1980. (Source: Tsunoda 1983. The figures were calculated as the arithmetic means, first of the five sciences, and second of all the national bibliographies included by Tsunoda.)

Figure 1 shows that whereas English, German, and French were somewhat on a par as languages of scientific publication at the beginning of the century, English has since clearly outstripped the other two. It seems, in fact, likely from other observations that international scientific communication largely happens in English, while the use of other languages is more and more restricted to the own language

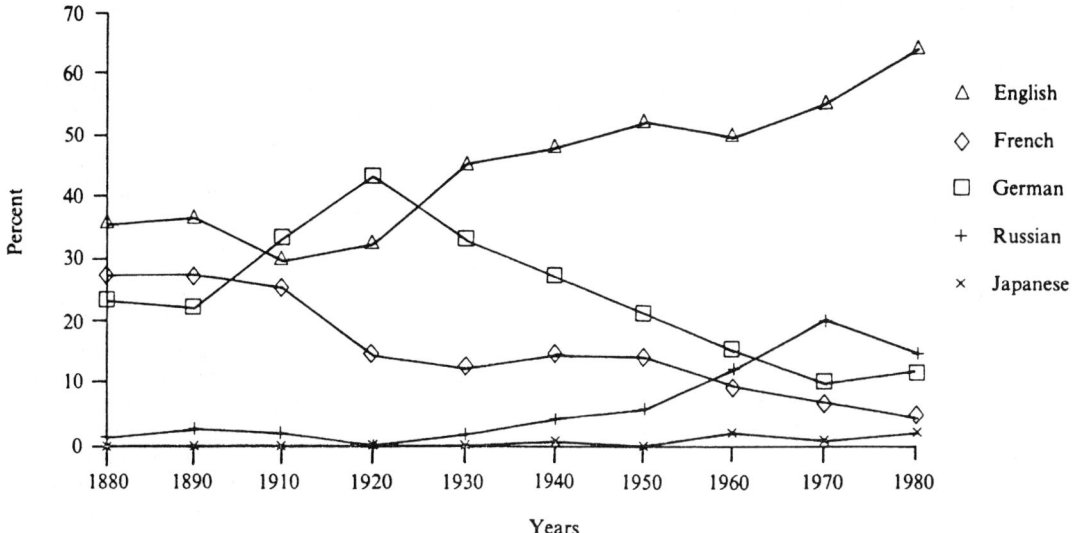

Figure 1. Percentage of publications in different languages in the natural sciences.

communities. Similarly, new languages of scientific publication, such as Japanese, hardly serve for communication beyond their national market.

These data reveal some overall tendencies. English clearly is, in the late twentieth century, *the* IL in all important respects. It has outdone former competitors, even in their specific domains such as diplomacy (French) and science (German). This process has taken place in the course of the twentieth century. Nevertheless, some other languages still play a limited role in international communication (even taken in the narrower sense), particularly French, Spanish, German, Russian, Portuguese, Arabic, Italian, Japanese, and Chinese. In particular, this can be observed in these languages' asymmetric use in bilateral contacts with speakers of even less widely used international languages. Thus, French will still often be used between a French person and, e.g., a Portuguese; German between a German and, e.g., a Czech; and so on. The choice of language in such bilateral (or multilateral) contacts has, however, not been studied systematically on a larger scale; neither has the choice of a lingua franca been studied comprehensively. By and large however, the tendency seems to be for English to be the most frequent choice by far in the late-twentieth-century world. English is in a certain sense the contemporary 'world language.'

3. Factors of Relevance for the Rise and Stabilization of an IL

How does a particular language become and/or stay an IL? The task of finding convincing explanations for the facts presented above and of identifying and evaluating the reasons behind them is no less difficult than specifying macro-sociological factors in general. Such factors cannot be studied experimentally, because the circumstances cannot be manipulated (as would be necessary for such studies), and because the possibilities of doing statistical analyses are very limited for want of a sufficiently large number of cases. Nevertheless, some preliminary insights can be extracted from the available empirical and theoretical findings.

The question why a language becomes an IL should not be confused with that of a language's spread, even though the two issues certainly are related. In particular, the question why certain languages which were imposed by conquest (as in the case of colonization) became firmly established in their new area, while others did not, is of relevance in this context. A number of factors have been identified here: first of all, a colonial rule of long duration (e.g., the long-lasting British versus the short-lived German colonial rule); a high degree of multilingualism in the colonized territory (the imposed language thus becoming indispensable as a lingua franca); and, after decolonization, the continued existence of tight economic ties with the former colonial power (Fishman et al. 1977). The imposed language became, of course, firmly established particularly in cases where colonialism was accompanied by massive immigration from the colonial power (and later on also from other countries), such that the indigenous populations were virtually eliminated together with their languages, as was the case in the Americas and Australia.

The factors which establish a language as an IL have varied a great deal in the course of history. Thus, victories in major wars seem to have been a factor of some importance in modern times. For instance, English was established as an official language of the League of Nations after World War I, because, among other things, the US President insisted on English along with French being the official languages of the Versailles Treaty (the treaty which included the covenant of the League of Nations); German and Russian, being the languages of the defeated war parties, were not considered. Similarly after World War II, none of the languages of the defeated countries became an official language of the UN, whereas Russian, this time the language of one of the victorious powers, did. In contrast, French was not challenged in the nineteenth century as the (sole) language of peace treaties, even after the defeats of 1815 and 1871.

Military victories alone, however, have never been sufficient to establish a language as an IL. Extreme cases are the military successes of the Huns or the Mongols in medieval Europe, which in no way sufficed to make their languages international. Even a long-lasting political control over a defeated country does not necessarily establish the language of the victorious power as an IL. This is illustrated by the case of the Turks, whose language receded to their own country when their reign of hundreds of years, in some places even a thousand years, over the countries of the Middle East and of Southeast Europe came to an end. Economic strength, often accompanied by scientific and cultural prominence, seem to be the most important factors in establishing and maintaining an IL. Weakness in these respects seems to be the main reason why Russian presently is losing its status as an IL in Eastern Europe with the Soviet Union's military and political control over this region coming to an end. Contrariwise, the success of English as an IL in this region may be due to its economic and cultural or scientific strength compared to German, despite the latter language's long tradition there as an IL and as the language of a geographical neighbor.

One other factor of considerable importance deserves to be mentioned: an established IL stabilizes, even strengthens, itself in this function (Lieberson 1982), as it appears most attractive for being studied as a foreign language, and therefore is the 'normal' choice in contacts between speakers of different languages. For an established IL to be substituted by another language in this function requires a clear superiority of the latter in relevant areas such as economic strength of its language community, etc.

4. Native IL-Speakers: Privileged or Not?

It has often been suggested that people who do not speak an IL natively should be envied for being forced to study foreign languages with all the advantages which such a study implies, such as mind-training, insights into different cultures, awareness of linguistic relativity (see *Sapir–Whorf Hypothesis*). In contrast to these somewhat abstract blessings, the privileges of native speakers of an IL are more immediately evident, particularly if their language is the major IL, the 'world-language,' i.e., in the 1990s English. First of all, such native speakers are not forced to study any foreign languages in order to communicate internationally, but can spend their precious time on other, perhaps more rewarding endeavors. (This does not, of course, prevent them from studying foreign languages with all the said blessings involved.) Thus, they have a real choice, in contrast to the members of other language communities. Second, they are, as a rule, linguistically superior in the IL to non-native speakers of the IL, i.e., they can express their ideas more precisely, more correctly as to grammar, more elegantly, and more fluently; their discourse will therefore often be more convincing. Such advantages may not be relevant in all situations; in some, however, they certainly are, as, for instance, in diplomatic or business negotiations, or in discussions between scholars or scientists, especially when they take place in front of an audience.

However, one person's privilege is another's disprivilege, as is felt quite acutely by many communicators. Thus, among German scientists, a considerable number clearly feels disprivileged vis-à-vis English as the dominant language of science (Ammon 1990b). Many of them (25 percent) professed difficulties even in reading English, over a third (38 percent) in understanding the spoken language, and more than half (54 percent) in writing it. Even those who did not explicitly mention the latter difficulties were often handicapped in their written communication, since their secretaries usually were unable to handle English (88 percent of them). No wonder then that more than half (58 percent) of this sample of German scientists claimed that producing a text in English caused additional expenses (for translators, for corrections by native speakers, and/or for typing). Consequently, a considerable number of the scientists confessed to not being willing (at least on some occasions) to participate in scientific conferences (19 percent) or publication projects (33 percent) if English was the required language; similarly, they would abstain from other contacts with colleagues if such contacts had to be in English (25 percent). Similar difficulties may be expected in other groups for whom it is essential to communicate internationally. These difficulties are probably less serious in language communities with a longer tradition of having to use another language for international communication, as such communities have more or less adjusted themselves to the situation; however, certain difficulties probably remain even for them in one way or another.

Still other advantages (or, as the case may be, disadvantages) arise from the fact that an IL, particularly if it serves for various functions, tends to be brought up to date constantly. Here, members of the IL-community have better access to the current terminology than do members of other language communities. Modern terminology, in particular technical terminology, is often taken over in its original, untranslated form by the non-IL, thus—among other things—increasing the gap between experts and lay people in the non-IL-communities.

For all these reasons, it is by no means astonishing that all larger language communities try to spread their language internationally, to the best of their abilities; that is, they try to increase their languages' degree of 'internationality' (Ammon and Kleineidam 1992). Even the major countries of the English language community are heavily engaged in such endeavors, in spite of the international dominance which their language has already gained (Phillipson 1991: chaps. 5, 6). If successful, such endeavors are also economically rewarding, since a more prominent IL will, as a rule, also be studied more intensively as a foreign language—to the advantage of the language teaching industry, as well as of the language teachers and linguists of the respective countries.

5. Artificial ILs: A Utopia?

The problems of ILs have often been closely associated with those of artificial languages proposed as ILs (e.g., Burney 1966, Pei 1966: 128, 131, see *Artificial Languages*). Such proposals have a long tradition, materializing in Europe as early as the seventeenth century. But it was not until the nineteenth century that projects were launched which, for at least some time, seemed to have real chances of success. The most successful of these is Lazarus L. Zamenhof's *Esperanto*, the first version of which was published in 1887 (*Linguo internacia*); a more refined version (1905, *Fundamento de Esperanto*) is in principle valid even in the early 1990s.

There is no question that Esperanto actually has become an IL and functions as such in the late twentieth century. However, it has fallen far short of the hopes that its creator and the members of the Esperanto Movement held out for it, namely to be *the* IL of the entire world, the means of communication between all human beings, no matter what their native languages, and an additional language for everyone. Esperanto was constructed in such a way that it would be particularly easy to learn (Roman script and regular orthography, an 'easy' phonology, simply morphology, etc.), no matter what actual language served as the learner's starting point. Thus, it also contains a fair share of the vocabularies of a number of different (European) languages. This endeavor for 'fairness' was complemented by the idea that no language community should be at a disadvantage in international communication, since the speakers of the strongest of them would communicate in a foreign language just the same as would the speakers of the weakest language community.

That the project of Esperanto has thus far failed, is often ascribed to a number of more or less subtle reasons: e.g., structural insufficiencies (these could have been amended), its 'artificial' character, and so on. Rather, such reasons have served as arguments for those who rejected the entire project anyway. The real objections came from all those language communities or their representatives who hoped finally to realize their own native language as *the* IL of the world. Thus, Hitler and Stalin were among the most fervent adversaries of Esperanto. Some of the internationally dominant, or would-be-dominant, language communities did not fight the idea openly, but simply lent it no support whatsoever and instead promoted their own language as an IL; here, the major English-speaking countries are examples (see *Linguistic Imperialism*).

The Esperanto project has certainly been a utopia in that it presupposed that the powerful language communities would give up their linguistic advantages in favor of weaker language communities, allowing for a 'fair' solution to the problems of international communication. What those powerful language communities actually did in order to guard their vested linguistic interests seems to be in accordance with no less than a sociolinguistic 'law,' whose existence the 'Artificial IL Movements' have failed to recognize. It is, however, an open question whether such a sociolinguistic law (as sketched above) is a human universal, that is, whether it will determine all future development. If that were indeed the case, it would imply that a 'fair' solution to the problem of international communication, whether or not it was realized using an artificial language, would never have a chance.

See also: Artificial Languages; Linguistic Imperialism; Linguicide; Language Spread.

Bibliography

Ammon U 1990a German as an international language. *International Journal of the Sociology of Language* **83**: 135–70

Ammon U 1990b German or English? The problems of language choice experienced by German-speaking scientists. In: Nelde P H (ed.) *Language Conflict and Minorities/Sprachkonflikte und Minderheiten*. Dümmler, Bonn

Ammon U 1991 *Die internationale Stellung der deutschen Sprache*. de Gruyter, Berlin

Ammon U, Kleineidam H (eds.) 1992 Language spread policy. Vol. I: Languages of former colonial powers. *International Journal of the Sociology of Language* **95**

Banks A, et al. (eds.) 1987 *Political Handbook of the World: 1987: Governments and Intergovernmental Organizations as of March 15, 1987*. CSA Publications, Binghamton, NY

Braga G 1979 International languages: Concept and problems. *International Journal of the Sociology of Language* 22: 27–49

Burney P 1966 *Les langues internationales*, ('*Que sais-je?*' No. 968), 2nd edn. Presses Universitaires de France, Paris

Conrad A W, Fishman J A 1977 English as a world language. The evidence. In: Fishman J A, Cooper R L, Conrad A W (eds.) *The Spread of English*. Newbury House, Rowley, MA

Fishman J A, Cooper R L, Rosenbaum Y 1977 English around the world. In: Fishman J A, Cooper R L, Conrad A W (eds.) *The Spread of English*. Newbury House, Rowley, MA

Lieberson S 1982 Forces affecting language spread: Some basic propositions. In: Cooper R L (ed.) *Language Spread*. Indiana University Press, Bloomington, IN

Ostrower A 1965 *Language, Law and Diplomacy*, 2 vols. University of Pennsylvania Press, Philadelphia, PA

Pei M 1966 *Glossary of Linguistic Terminology*. Anchor, Garden City, NY

Phillipson R 1991 *English Language Teaching and Imperialism*. Blackwell, Oxford, UK

Rönnefarth H K G, Euler H 1963 *Konferenzen und Verträge: Vertrages-Ploetz, Teil II*. Ploetz, Würzburg, Germany

Tabory M 1980 *Multilingualism in International Law and Institutions*. Sijthoff & Noordhoff, Alphen aan den Rijn, The Netherlands

Tsunoda M 1983 *Les langues internationales dans les publications scientifiques et techniques*. Sophia Linguistica, Tokyo

Language Adaptation and Modernization
S. Bowerman

1. Introduction

'Language adaptation' refers to linguistic change, whether deliberate or spontaneous, whose goal is to adapt a language to the changed or changing needs of its speech community. The term is nearly synonymous with 'language modernization,' as the needs of a speech community are often a function of the times. Coulmas (1989: 1) argues that the term 'modernization' is less suitable, as it is often taken to refer to the present day. Language adaptation is a relatively new term in sociolinguistics, but the phenomenon affects all languages at all times.

The field of language adaptation and modernization largely intersects with that of language planning (see *Language Planning: Models*), in that a language is sometimes deliberately adapted to fulfill new roles. Natural language adaptation is spontaneous, and is unconsciously undertaken by its own speech community. Intervention is only necessary when a language, previously excluded for some reason from certain domains of use, suddenly needs to be used for those functions. It is therefore desirable to distinguish between linguistic change that comes about naturally, and that which is forced.

2. Factors Influencing (Deliberate) Language Adaptation

2.1 Dominance and Domain Exclusion

Many of the world's language communities are dominated in some way by another language community that is politically, economically, or numerically more powerful (cf. Tollefson 1991: 14). The dominant community's language becomes the medium for the higher domains of language use (see *Linguistic Imperialism*; *Power and Language*) such as government, media, education, technology, and commerce, to the exclusion of the dominated language. Because the dominated languages are excluded from these higher domains, their lexicons, for example, do not keep up with the development of the dominant language as new terms are coined to describe new phenomena and experiences. The need for language adaptation is often recognized when there is a change, or a push for change, in the social structures that keep the dominance relationship between language communities intact. When this happens, and the (previously) dominated language is required as a medium for the higher domains, it is often found to be inadequate in terms of technology, modes of expression, etc.

Domain exclusion also impacts upon a language's speech community on a social level. A language that is excluded from the higher domains of language use is reserved for the lower or more basic domains: i.e., the home and community environment. This means that they will not be perceived as tools for economic advancement, and will consequently suffer from low status and prestige (see *Language Planning: Models*; *Linguistic Imperialism*). The language becomes stigmatized, even in its own community, and members of the language community who seek economic advancement will seek to acquire the dominant language. If the status of a language in such a position is not improved, it may well face obsolescence.

The post-colonial experience of many African and Asian nations in the mid-to-late twentieth century was a proving ground for the dominated indigenous languages. The colonial languages had almost invariably been used as media for the higher domains, to the exclusion of the indigenous languages (Phillipson 1993: 112, chap. 5). The demise of colonialism meant that many countries were faced with a dilemma: whether to retain the colonial language as a high-domain medium, or replace it with one or more indigenous languages. Retaining the colonial language carried unpleasant connotations; but it was already developed enough to cope as the medium of a modern industrial state, and was entrenched in that role (Schmied 1991: 19). The indigenous languages, on the other hand, had been excluded from the higher domains and had neither the status nor corpus (see *Language Planning: Models*) to cope with their new roles. Although the indigenous languages were often instituted as symbolic official languages, the colonial language was retained for higher domain use in most cases (Schmied 1991: 20). Although the dominance of colonial languages, particularly those that offer global access, is all but assured (Laitin 1992: 181), there is a concerted effort for the functional expansion of indigenous languages.

2.2 The Transition From Oracy to Literacy

The move from oracy (see *Oracy*) to literacy (see *Literacy*) also creates a need for language adaptation. Indeed, the need for a written language where there was none before reflects a drastic change in the social structure of a community. There are (at least) two ways of fulfilling this need: the adoption of an already written language for these purposes, or the adaptation of the oral language to writing. Most societies have had to face this transition at some point in their history, whether this developed naturally or was thrust upon them from outside. Thus, the written language may differ completely from that which is spoken—which, as Coulmas (1989: 13) points out, is to be expected as speech and writing serve different communicative functions. Moreover, writing in the initial stages of the transition from oracy to literacy is usually the domain of an elite few. However, the adaptation of an oral language to writing reflects a change in the communicative function of that language, which in modern times has spread to the rest of the society. Whereas the 'undiscovered' world coped for millennia without writing, illiteracy in present times is viewed as a scourge.

Coulmas (1989: 12) notes that literacy does not necessarily stimulate language adaptation *per se*; but it serves as a tool for carrying out the process. A written language can easily be codified into a set of rules to be transmitted through education. This in turn affects the acquisition and use (particularly in the higher domains) of a language.

2.3 Attitudes and Language Maintenance

As with any language planning measure, it is the attitude of the people for whom language adaptation is to be undertaken that will determine whether or not it is successful. One crucial factor in forming a community's attitude is the degree to which the language will be useful, i.e., the domains to which a particular language gives access (Phillipson 1993: 79, 80, Cooper 1989: 100, chap. 5). Loyalty to a language and culture is another factor affecting the maintenance of a language. Although the revival of Irish in Ireland has turned out to be little more than symbolic, it is the loyalty of the Irish to their language that led to its extensive adaptation, even though English serves all the language needs of the majority. Languages that are neutral i.e., do not carry ethnic connotations, are more likely than others to be used as languages of wider communication. The neutrality of Swahili in east Africa led to its being extensively adopted as a national language in Kenya and an official language in Tanzania, and therefore to the extensive expansion of its functional range (Cooper 1989: 102).

3. The Process of Language Adaptation

3.1 Two Aspects of Adaptation

The process of equipping a language to deal with the realities of its speech community involves two aspects: one external to the language (involving the speech community) and one internal to the language (involving the structure of the language itself). In order for a language to be successfully adapted, that language must be widely used by its speech community in the domains concerned. This requires not only the elaboration of its lexicon, but also the boosting of its status. Adaptation and modernization through language planning is at an early stage: it is the implementation of language planning measures by a speech community that tells us whether the language has been successfully adapted or not.

3.2 Adaptation Through Status Planning

A common way of boosting the status of a language, and facilitating its adaptation and modernization, is through functional reallocation. Thus, a language previously excluded from the higher domains is allocated to those domains (Cooper 1989: 99, 118). These measures take time to be implemented: before a language can be properly used in a domain from which it was previously excluded, it has to be developed as a medium for that domain.

After their independence from colonial rule in 1962 and 1963, respectively, Tanzania and Kenya wished to establish a national African language in the place of the colonial one (Laitin 1992: 91). Swahili was the natural choice, having few 'tribalist' associations and a long history with the liberation movements (Laitin

Table 1. Terminology development in South African languages.

Method	Example
Calquing: direct translation, especially of compounds	English *cellphone* > Afrikaans *selfoon*
Loan words: borrowing a word, or the sound of a word, by another language	English *cellphone* > Sotho *selula founo*, Zulu *iselula*
Transliteration: use of the Classic stem to coin an equivalent	English *computer* > Xhosa *ikompiyuta*, Zulu *ikhomputha* English *silver* > Xhosa *isilivere*, Zulu *isiliva*
Extension of meaning: use of existing words, but broadening the meaning to include more modern concepts	Zulu *bafana bafana* (reduplication) = 'the boys'; extension of meaning to the soccer team, i.e., young male competitors on the international soccer scene
Neologism: new words created from within the target language	English *unleaded petrol* Afrikaans *ongelode petrol* (Creation of the verb *lood* 'lead,' past participle *gelode* 'leaded' from Afrikaans noun *lood* 'lead.')

1992: 91–2). In Tanzania (then called Tanganyika), Swahili was proclaimed as the language of state and public functions, and shortly thereafter became the 'major language of Parliament,' and was introduced as 'medium of instruction in all public primary schools' (Massamba 1989: 63). Although Swahili still faces serious competition from English, its adaptation and modernization have been widely accepted.

3.3 Corpus Adaptation and Modernization

3.3.1 Terminology Development

In order to fulfill its role as a high-domain medium, a language's corpus (lexicon and grammar) must be sufficiently developed. In cases where a language has been excluded from a domain it now wishes to occupy, its terminology and perhaps modes of expression need to be adapted to its new roles. There are various ways of adapting terminology, taking the target language system into account. It can be achieved through neologism, calquing, transliteration, and meaning extension (Alberts 1998: 233). Alberts (1998) provides some examples of these four methods of terminology development from South African languages, adapted here in Table 1.

As can be seen from some of the examples in Table 1, terminology development must take the target language into account: and we see how calquing and borrowing adapt from the sound system of one language to the other. Grammar is also an important device in language adaptation, and, particularly, terminology development. Table 2 shows how new coinages in Irish were applied to existing grammatical structures. O'Baoill (1988: 116) gives the example of the creation of an Irish term for 'lithograph,' and some of its derivatives. The new lexeme is a Hibernized borrowing from English, to which productive derivational morphemes are applied:

Languages also reflect their adaptation to a new or changed social order by getting rid of certain elements that tie them to the past. The reform of

Table 2. An example of terminology development in Irish.

English term	English derivational morphemes	Standardized Irish borrowing	Irish derivational morphemes
lithograph		liteagraf	
	-er		-ái
	-y		-áiocht

Turkish under Attatürk in the 1920s saw all Persian and Arabic loan-words expelled from the standard Turkish lexicon (Cooper 1989: 154, citing Heyd 1954). Similarly, some sectors of the French government have tried to block the number of loan words entering into French usage (Appel and Muysken 1993: 164).

3.3.2 Grammatical Development

The development of a grammar to suit modern or high domain purposes often results in a simplification of grammatical forms that are considered unwieldy, anachronistic, and unsuited to scientific and commercial discourse. Grammatical development may mean bringing the grammar of a language more into line with that of a dominant language. For example, there have been some attempts to bring the grammar of Irish more into line with that of English (Greene 1972: 15). Developing a standard grammar for Modern Hebrew from Biblical Hebrew processes, as well as innovation, in Israel spurred the creation of a multitude of new word forms. Grammar can be an especial problem in situations where there are a number of varieties of a language. In order for the language to be adapted to modern roles, it requires codification, and therefore standardization (see *Standardization*). Thus, where more than one form is found across varieties, one must be chosen as the standard. This applies to all aspects of the corpus.

3.3.3 Orthography and Spelling

These are two more aspects of the corpus, which are taken into account when conscious adaptation and modernization takes place. Orthography refers to the script that is used to represent the spoken language, and spelling refers (roughly) to the way it is used.

When a language is selected for adaptation and modernization, an orthography needs to be selected for it. If the language has never been written before, an orthography must be created—a process known as graphization. If, however, an orthography already exists, a decision must be made as to whether this system should be retained, or a new system found. This process is known as regraphization (Cooper 1989: 125, 154). Christian missionaries graphized most of the oral languages of southern Africa in the nineteenth and twentieth centuries. Generally, a Roman script was imposed and the spelling system of the missionaries' nationalities informed the orthography and spelling. While graphization is one aspect of language adaptation, regraphization is also important. The change in orthography reflects a change in society. An early example of this was the development of the Cyrillic alphabet, so that biblical and ecclesiastical texts could be translated into Slavic languages. More recently, Turkish adopted a Roman script in place of the Persian orthography it had used before (Haugen 1972: 170, citing Heyd 1954). Orthography can have powerful symbolic value for a speech community (see *Orthography*). In the 1930s, the Soviet government imposed the Cyrillic script on non-Russian languages within the USSR (Mesthrie et al. 2000: 391). Since the disintegration of the USSR, however, a number of these languages have had the non-Cyrillic script reinstated. Mesthrie et al. (2000: 391) cite the case of Moldavia: in August 1990, the Moldavians held a 'Language Festival,' celebrating the reintroduction of the Latin script. A developing adaptation process is also evident in Chinese and Japanese, which are adapting to changing functions by *adding* a Roman orthography, to facilitate the learning of these languages phonetically (Crystal 1995: 313, Sugito 1989: 117).

3.3.4 Standardization and Harmonization

These two terms apply in different ways to the same phenomenon: one language, which has many distinctive varieties in the same area. In some cases, like that of Irish (O'Baoill 1988: 111) or Swahili (Massamba 1989: 61), the varieties are widely recognized by academics and speakers as being varieties of one language. In order for the language to be adapted to a function, it needs to be stabilized and codified, and therefore standardized, and an orthographical/terminological/grammatical form is chosen from one of the dialects and held up as the norm. Otherwise, one dialect will be chosen as the standard, and all its forms held up as the norm by society as well as language planners (Cooper 1989: 134).

Harmonization is a form of standardization, but operates across varieties that are regarded as closely related, but distinct, languages. In essence, harmonization is an attempt to build one standard language from a variety of closely related languages (and all of their respective varieties). The harmonization (also 'unification') question in South Africa was revisited in 1989 by Neville Alexander (1989: 64), who proposed the harmonization of the seven major indigenous languages into two standards:

(a) Standard Nguni, comprising Xhosa, Zulu, Ndebele and Swati.
(b) Standard Sotho, comprising South Sotho, Pedi and Tswana.

Harmonizing the indigenous languages of South Africa would eliminate the need to adapt and modernize every one of the 7 languages that make up Sotho and Nguni. The harmonization of these languages could begin with new terminology, which can be coined as illustrated above. Table 3 illustrates similarities and differences between the Nguni languages:

Table 3. Equivalent terms in Xhosa, English and Zulu (Adapted from *The South African Multi-Language Dictionary*).

Xhosa	Zulu	English
ifoni	ithelefoni	telephone
imoto	imoto	motor car
umbane	ugesi	electricity
ilayibri	ilabhulali	library
ikompiyuta	ikomputha	computer

The similarity between these two languages is striking, and shows the close relation of the languages to each other. Differences in vocabulary and pronunciation appear minor, but are significant to their speech communities that may be concerned that linguistic assimilation means political assimilation (Msimang 1998: 167). Those involved in language harmonization will have to liase extensively across languages to avoid being perceived to value one variety or language group above another.

4. Conclusion

Language adaptation and modernization is essential to the evolution and indeed, survival of any language. The linguistic change brought about through adaptation reflects the dynamics of the society in which it is used. The fact that intervention is sometimes necessary links the field with that of language maintenance: the adaptation of a language to fulfil modern functions is surely a mechanism for language maintenance. It ensures that a language remains valued by its own community and others.

See also: Language Planning: Models; Language Development.

Bibliography

Alberts M 1998 The harmonisation of Nguni and Sotho. In: Prah K K (ed.) *Between Distinction and Extinction: The Harmonisation and Standardisation of African languages.* Witwatersrand University Press, Johannesburg, South Africa
Alexander N 1989 *Language Policy and National Unity in South Africa, Azania.* Buchu Books, Cape Town, South Africa
Appel R, Muysken P 1993 *Language Contact and Bilingualism.* Arnold, London
Cooper R 1989 *Language and Social Change.* Cambridge University Press, Cambridge, UK
Coulmas F 1989 Language adaptation. In: Coulmas F (ed.) *Language Adaptation.* Cambridge University Press, Cambridge, UK
Crystal D 1995 *The Cambridge Encyclopedia of Language.* Cambridge University Press, Cambridge, UK
Greene D 1972 *The Irish Language.* Cultural Relations Committee of Ireland, Cork, Eire
Haugen E 1972 *The Ecology of Language.* Stanford University Press, Stanford, CA
Heyd U 1954 *Language Reform in Modern Turkey.* Israel Oriental Society, Jerusalem
Laitin D 1992 *Language Repertoires and State Construction in Africa.* Cambridge University Press, Cambridge, UK
Massamba D 1989 An assessment of the development and modernization of the Kiswhahili language in Tanzania. In: Coulmas F (ed.) *Language Adaptation.* Cambridge University Press, Cambridge, UK
Mesthrie R, Swann J, Deumert A, Leap W 2000 *Introducing Sociolinguistics.* Edinburgh University Press, Edinburgh, UK
Msimang T 1998 The nature and history of harmonisation of South African languages. In: Prah K K (ed.) *Between Distinction and Extinction: the Harmonization and Standardization of African Languages.* Witwatersrand University Press, Johannesburg, South Africa
O'Baoill D 1988 Language planning in Ireland: the standardization of Irish. *International Journal of the Sociology of Language* **70**: 29–52
Phillipson R 1993 *Linguistic Imperialism.* Oxford University Press, Oxford, UK
Reader's Digest 1985 *South African Multi-Language Dictionary.* Reader's Digest, Cape Town, South Africa
Schmied J 1991 *English in Africa: an Introduction.* Longman Linguistics Library, London
Sugito S 1989 Lexical modernization of Japanese. In: Coulmas F (ed.) *Language Adaptation.* Cambridge University Press, Cambridge, UK, pp. 116–26
Tollefson J 1991 *Planning Language, Planning Inequality: Language Policy in the Community.* Longman, Essex, UK

Language Development

H. R. Dua

The concept of 'development' has been extensively employed in social sciences to an increasingly large number of entities and embraces a wide range of meanings. Its application to language by linguists and language planners is a recent phenomenon. The notion of language development has assumed a great importance because of the role of language in the development of nationalism and nationality formation, the expansion of education and mass media, and the growth of culture, science, and technology. This article first clarifies the conceptual dimension of language development and then characterizes the nature of language features relevant to it. Following this it argues against the unidirectionality and universality of language development models. Finally, it discusses some theoretical and methodological issues involved in measurement of language development. The concluding remarks highlight the future work and prospects in the study of language development.

1. Conceptual Dimension

Perhaps the first explicit formulation of the notion of language development was attempted by Ferguson (1968). Ferguson maintained that judgments of backwardness or limited development of a language could not be made on the basis of linguistic structure. However, he identified three dimensions relevant for characterizing the nature and degree of language development: graphization, standardization, and modernization. In elaborating these dimensions he did not consider how they can be measured, weighted, and summed up to arrive at the degree of language development. Moreover, he interpreted narrowly the notion of language structure and ignored several other issues crucial to language development.

Since Ferguson, no considerable achievement has been made regarding the conceptualization of language development and its measurement. However, the notions of standardization and modernization have been differently interpreted in the context of language planning and related to language planning processes. Fishman (1974) represents an integration of Ferguson's dimensions of language development with language planning processes of selection/implementation, codification, elaboration, and cultivation. He considers the dimensions as possible resultants existing along a continuum of the repeated application of the processes. However, he does not specify, apart from giving certain instances, what points can be established along the continuum, how the language planning processes relate to these points, and how language development can be measured in terms of the dimensions.

Two crucial issues need to be considered to make the concept of language development more comprehensive and to render it more useful in language planning theory and practice. First, what the linguistic features relevant from the point of view of development are and whether the dimensions mentioned by Ferguson adequately represent them. It is obvious that two important features have been ignored, though perhaps implicitly recognized in connection with modernization. The first is the quantum of material production in a specific language which includes not only the specific output of codification and elaboration efforts but also the creative, scientific, technical, and other forms of literature. The second is the number of domains in which a language is used or is intended to be used. The domains of use not only reflect the functional status of a language, but also its level of development. While the various linguistic features amenable to development may be considered independently for analytical purposes, they are intimately related and mutually reinforce each other making measurement of language development an extremely complex task, if not an impossible one. This is evident from the theoretical and methodological issues involved in language measurement.

Second, it is necessary to distinguish between the process and the product of language development. The process of development of a particular linguistic feature involves implementation, evaluation, codification, elaboration, etc., and is spread over a period. The product of language development on the other hand needs to be specified both in quantitative and qualitative terms. It is essential not only to evaluate the total output in the form of specific material, explicit norms or varieties of registers, styles and genres but also to consider how far the output is relevant, useful, and wide in range. The congruence between the process and the product of development indicates the success of language planning and ensures systematic and comprehensive language development.

2. Language Features and Development

For an adequate explication of the concept of language development, the language features can be distinguished in relation to language structure, language use, and language material (Dua 1985, 1989). Broadly interpreted, the language structure can be considered in terms of speech, writing, vocabulary, syntax, and forms of discourse. The nature and scope of these features can be characterized only briefly. Speech involves the development of the formal, semi-formal, and informal styles of speaking, the rules of pronunciation, and the norms of correctness. The development of writing implies not only the creation or adaptation of a writing system but also changes or modification in it in relation to its use for different purposes such as typewriting, printing, computer technology, etc. It also includes the development of orthographic and spelling conventions and formulation of rules for simplification, unification, or systematization of spelling and orthographic subsystems. The development of vocabulary may be considered with respect to the different types of vocabulary, basic, technical, and scientific, the range of abstract and generic terms for different disciplines, the degree of precision, consistency and flexibility in meaning, and the output of words through borrowing, coinage, and derivation. The nature and scope of syntactic development is less clear than vocabulary. It may be tentatively considered in terms of the property of intellectualization in grammar which manifests itself in syntactic devices that allow for 'the constructions of elaborate, yet tightly knit, compound sentences, as well as the tendency to eliminate elliptic modes of expression by requiring complete constructions' (Garvin 1973: 27). It may also involve development of new constructions, rules for foregrounding, coherence, and text organization. Finally, the development at the discourse level may be characterized with regard to the functional differentiation and specialization as related to registers, styles, and genres suitable for scientific, technical, literary, journalistic, and other types of functional prose, and the creation of models of reviewing, abstracting, reporting, drafting, and other such forms of specialized writing.

The level of language development related to language use can be characterized on the basis of the number of domains in which a language is used, and the description of the clustering, ordering, or ranking of the domains of use. It further depends on the oral and written modes of communication and the frequency and pervasiveness with which a language is used in different domains.

The production of different types of creative, original, and translated materials can provide a more concrete basis for the characterization of language development. It would, therefore, be extremely useful to develop a scheme of different types of materials. The following types are suggestive only: reference materials, including dictionaries, thesauri, glossaries, nomenclatures, manuals, grammars; creative literature belonging to different genres; scientific and technical literature; literature in social sciences and humanities; journalistic literature; and textbooks for different levels of education.

The developmental status of the linguistic features discussed above can be specified on the basis of the developmental indices which include standardization (see *Standardization*), codification, elaboration, and cultivation. Standardization implies whether a linguistic feature has attained uniformity, whether uniformity is explicitly or implicitly recognized, whether there are different models or centers of standard, and whether norms of standard are rigid or flexible. Codification of a linguistic feature indicates whether its development has been recorded or not, and if recorded, in what form and to what extent, and whether the codified information is easily available. Elaboration implies whether the development of a linguistic feature shows more than one standard form used for different purposes. For instance, there might be different kinds of fonts used in printing or different types of dictionaries for specific users or purposes. Cultivation involves norms of correctness, efficiency, purity, and esthetics that are invoked in the development of a linguistic feature. The nature and scope of the developmental indices as characterized above were not, in the late twentieth century, fully understood, and their characterization and transformation into scalar values for measurement of language development can be considered still an open question. Furthermore, the development of all the linguistic features may not be equally evaluated with respect to these indices.

The characterization of developmental indices for evaluation of the developmental status of a linguistic feature can be made more useful in terms of what Neustupny (1974) refers to as the characteristics of language treatment patterns. He has suggested four characteristics for studying the treatment patterns: systematicity, theoretical elaborateness, depth, and rationality. For instance, it might be asked how far the standardization of a linguistic feature as elaborated above is systematic, based on theory, and is deep and rational. Thus the characterization of linguistic features and developmental indices along with their characteristics provide a sound framework for considering the nature and degree of language development.

3. Models of Development

Though language development cannot be dissociated from nonlinguistic development, the relationship between the two is far from clear. Another significant issue concerns whether the so-called 'developing languages' pass through similar or different stages of development than what is attested in the case of already developed languages.

As regards the relationship between linguistic and nonlinguistic development, Neustupny (1974) takes an extreme position. He has distinguished between three socioeconomic stages of development which he maintains have a one-to-one correspondence with language treatment patterns and models of language teaching. He distinguishes primarily between policy and cultivation varieties of language treatment patterns. He maintains that not only do the stages of socioeconomic development correspond to specific language treatment patterns but also that the less developed societies are characterized by a high degree of arbitrary social and linguistic heterogeneity and therefore show a predominance of policy approach, whereas the developed nations are linguistically homogeneous and focus on cultivation of code.

Neustupny's thesis has been questioned by several scholars on the basis of data from different situations. Jernudd (1977: 43–8) points out that the policy and cultivation approaches to language development need not necessarily be mutually exclusive. The tradition of language treatment in India, according to him, is characterized by the coexistence of policy and cultivation approaches which 'cyclically share the limelight' (1977: 44). Even Sweden is not found to present a very 'clean' case for assigning it to a 'cultivation' or a 'policy' approach. A 'developed' speech community could be found in any nation, developed ('modernized') or not. Jernudd (1977: 48) concludes, therefore, 'that there is no simple link between the development of a nation and the degree of development of its constituent speech communities.'

Since there is no simple and direct link between the linguistic and the nonlinguistic development, the developing nations need not necessarily pass through the same 'stages' of language development and reach some similar modern outcome. This is further supported by an ecological perspective on development which implies that 'development' depends on language situation, social system, economic processes, and other environment features considered as 'input' at a particular time yielding a specific 'output' given a certain degree of planning. This raises two significant issues from the standpoint of language development and language planning. First, it might be asked what kind of language planning and language development can coexist with what kind of societal conditions. Second, it might be considered whether language diversity is incompatible with national development, modernization, and language development.

The issues discussed above have been further clarified by Fishman (1974: 84) who compares the linguistic and nonlinguistic development on the one hand, and the experience of the Western and the non-Western societies on the other. He points out that 'the basic sociohistorical orientation in both fields points a complex constellation of continua with respect to the outcome of development and the processes of planning.' He finds a great deal of difference between the Western and non-Western societies with respect to the primary and secondary development which, according to him, 'is increasingly calling into question any simplistic notions to the possibility of universal and panchronic unidirectionality with respect to development and developmental planning.' He points out that the process of language development in the developing societies not only encapsulates centuries but also shows a discrepancy between expectations and rate of improvement not known in former centuries. He claims that language development may not only be instructively different as a whole today in comparison with former times, but it may also be variable with respect to certain domains and processes. Hence Fishman concludes that the developing nations must develop their own models of language planning and language development compatible with their language situations.

4. Measurement of Language Development

Even though the measurement of language development is essential for evaluating the vitality of language and the success of language planning, the issues involved in it have not been explored systematically. This is primarily because of inadequate understanding of the theoretical and methodical problems involved in measurement of language development. First, it is essential to understand the relative value of various linguistic features and their contribution to language development as a whole. This issue is complicated for several reasons. The nature and scope of linguistic features may differ from one language to another under different sociolinguistic situations. A particular feature may take some time before it manifests its impact on or contribution to language development. The effect of the feature may appear sooner or later than expected or there may be a different outcome altogether. Thus the weighting of linguistic features for their contribution to language development as a whole is complicated partly because of a differential salience of features and partly because of time and/or effect lag in their development.

Second, the summation of the value of all the linguistic features is no less complicated since it is not clear as to how far a particular linguistic feature is independent of the other. Without understanding the nature of interaction or independence between the linguistic features it is difficult to assess adequately the contribution of a linguistic feature to development. For instance, the development of a writing system has far-reaching implications for development of literary tradition and production of language materials. The latter is intimately related to the role of language in education and the degree of bilingualism in it. This is clear from the Indian linguistic situation. While Hindi shows a clear lead in quantitative terms over English in the production of periodicals during the decade 1971–81, English retains the top position in qualitative terms with respect to the periodicals of science, engineering, and technology. Notwithstanding the growth of periodicals in Hindi, both English and Hindi show a stable complementary relationship due to their role in education and the degree of bilingualism in them. Thus the interaction between the linguistic features on the one hand, and their interaction with sociolinguistic phenomena on the other make it extremely difficult to arrive at an independent developmental score of linguistic features for the purpose of summation.

Finally, the consideration of intertranslatability between developed and developing languages as a measure of language modernization (Ferguson 1968) has confused the issue of measurement of language development. In the first place, intertranslatability as a measure of language modernization implies that in spite of the different 'input' conditions of developing languages due to various sociolinguistic parameters they are assumed to pass through the same 'stages' and end up with some similar modern 'outcome' (Dua 1987). However, even the similarity of 'outcome' between developed and developing languages based on scientific discourse or technical terminology cannot be taken for granted. It has become sufficiently clear that accuracy, efficiency, and exactness of technical terms cannot be achieved in isolation from the general vocabulary, that the specific theory of terminology is language sensitive and that there is a dynamic interaction between special and general language usage which shows creativity, specificity, and uniqueness in language development (Cluver 1980).

In the second place, the degree of intertranslatability cannot be properly determined due to certain methodological considerations. There does not seem to be any valid single comprehensive theory of translation which can provide criteria for different modes of translation, the nature and scope of equivalence of translation in different modes, the selection of topics and forms of discourse for translation, and the relative value of both the form and content of texts of translation (Dua 1987, Fishman 1974, Newmark 1981).

It appears, therefore, that not only have the problematics of measurement of language development not been adequately formulated but also that it has been led into unwarranted directions and problems on both the theoretical and methodological grounds by considering it in terms of intertranslatability.

5. Future Work

Language development is crucial to national development and modernization of linguistically heterogeneous developing societies on the one hand, and success of language planning theory and practice on the other. The utility and relevance of the notion depends upon a deep and explicit understanding of the conceptual dimensions of language development along with a systematic characterization of language features. It further depends upon the theoretical and methodological developments in the measurement of language development rigorously on the basis of developmental indices and their characteristics. This requires a great deal of empirical research in different sociolinguistic situations and language planning contexts. Both the theoretical and methodological research on language development should be able to provide answers to the following questions. How is a particular language underdeveloped or inadequately developed? What is its degree of development? Regarding what characteristics and in relation to what functions is it developed or underdeveloped? What kind of language planning and sociolinguistic conditions are conductive to language development? How does the process of language development interact with socioeconomic conditions and developmental processes on the one hand, and the product of language development on the other? How are the modalities of time, rate, resources, and strategies of implementation related to the nature and degree of development? There could be many more questions. The point is that the notion of language development is potentially rich and vast and at the same time highly demanding from the points of view of theory, methodology, and research. The high expectations raised by the notion can be fulfilled depending upon the future developments in the theory of language development in particular and of language planning in general with respect to the issues discussed here as well as the others that might be raised on the subject.

See also: Language Planning: Models; Language Adaptation and Modernization.

Bibliography

Cluver A D De V 1980 The development of a terminological theory in South Africa. *International Journal of the Sociology of Language* **23**: 51–64
Cooper R L 1989 *Language Planning and Social Change.* Cambridge University Press, Cambridge, UK
Dua H R 1985 *Language Planning in India.* Harnam Publications, New Delhi, India
Dua H R 1987 Intertranslatability as a measure for language modernization: Some theoretical and methodological issues. *International Journal of Dravidian Linguistics* **16**(2): 192–200
Dua H R 1989 Functional types of language in India. In: Ammon U (ed.) *Status and Function of Languages and Language Varieties.* Walter de Gruyter, Berlin
Ferguson C A 1968 Language development. In: Fishman J A, Ferguson C A, Das Gupta J (eds.) *Language Problems of Developing Nations.* Wiley, New York
Fishman J A 1974 Language modernization and planning in comparison with other types of national modernization and planning. In: Fishman J A (ed.) *Advances in Language Planning.* Mouton, The Hague
Garvin P 1973 Some comments on language planning. In: Rubin J, Shuy R (eds.) *Language Planning: Current Issues and Research.* Georgetown University Press, Washington, DC
Jernudd B H 1977 Prerequisites for a model of language treatment. In: Rubin J, et al. (eds.) *Language Planning Processes.* Mouton, The Hague
Neustupny J V 1974 Basic types of treatment of language problems. In: Fishman J (ed.) *Advances in Language Planning.* Mouton, The Hague
Newmark P 1981 *Approaches to Translation.* Pergamon Press, Oxford, UK
Ray P S 1963 *Language Standardization.* Mouton, The Hague

Language Diffusion Policy
C. G. MacLean

The promotion of a language by a government outside the government's territory may be achieved in a number of ways. The evidence of history is various and often paradoxical. Military advances have usually resulted in the spread of the victor's language—or at least parts of it—but the effect has sometimes been only temporary. Missionary activity, not necessarily funded by government, has helped to spread some languages, but in many contexts missionaries (see *Missionaries and Language*) have aimed to make contact in the language of those they wish to convert. Policies of either persuading another to speak one's own language or of learning to speak another's language can be equally imperialistic in politics or religion or commerce.

Propaganda, religious or political, is generally more likely to be effective if it is in the language of the target audience. Likewise, many commercial activities are seen to require the use of the language of the target market: in even the strongest countries, lack of language ability restricts companies from trading abroad.

Tourism is noteworthy: in 1992 France was reported to be the most popular tourist resort in the world. Though the French government is eager to preserve and promote the use of French outside France, it would be unwise to do this in the literature promoting France as a tourist resort, and perhaps it should expect the strength of tourism in France, even with a copious provision of phrase books, to have no more than a marginal effect on the learning of French in schools abroad.

Radio and television have brought their own challenges and techniques. Radio sidesteps some problems of literacy and language learning: one recorded voice can be heard by millions, many of whom may be illiterate, and the one voice may offer instruction in a new language. Television language may be dubbed or subtitled, essential processes if the television programs are to be sold to the target viewers.

While the above factors have all been related historically to language promotion, none may be simply correlated to the proportions of the world population now speaking certain languages. Neither is there a discernible correlation between the numerical supremacy of the major languages (see Table 1) and efforts, as seen in the examples that follow, by governments to promote languages. The promotion of a language is at best a slow and unpredictable process. And the promotion may be significantly and suddenly reversed: compare the learning of Russian in Europe and beyond in the early 1980s and the early 1990s.

This article provides some examples of language promotion by governments in the late twentieth century: the languages are German, French, Hebrew, and English—the last promoted by several governments. All cases reflect, though in different ways, an acceptance of an obvious reality, i.e., that people outside a government's territory have need to or can readily be persuaded to learn the language or languages spoken in the country of that government. Also, all the cases here cited reflect, in various degrees, a combination of self-assurance and self-assertion.

Clearly there is a strong commercial element in most language promotion, but governments tend to give priority in their reports, program proposals, and promotional literature, to loftier aims, with claims that knowledge of the language will allow closer international links to be established. Also, more specifically, offer is made of access to and appreciation of a culture—literary, artistic, social, historical, etc. More precisely, cooperation is made available in fields of scholarship and professional expertise, not least science and technology.

Such activity is at times competitive: 'We have learned to market Britain's strengths against fierce international competition,' said Sir David Orr, retiring chairman of the British Council, in his introduction to the Council's annual report for 1990–91. And: 'How to resist the Anglo-American Steamroller? It is so powerful ... ': see Sect. 2.2.

The information about Canada (Sect. 2.3) differs from what is provided about other countries in that it relates to the entire Canadian aid program. Noteworthy in the context of this article is the fact that Canada has two official languages, English and French. Canada's internal commitment determines in some measure the way it views its aid program: this program divides Africa into Anglophone and Francophone Africa. Any country, in providing aid, may well be influenced by its language, by history, or by geography, all of these probably being related. But the Canadian situation by itself highlights the interlocking of these three and might be used to assess, comparatively, the way in which the language interests of a country providing aid (of any kind) tend to confirm and promote the use of a language or languages in recipient countries or regions.

An appreciable number of governments provide large sums of money and resources in aid of many kinds to other countries or to citizens of those countries. The cultural, educational, and arts elements of such aid vary greatly in proportion to the total sums. The proportion attributed to language promotion cannot be precisely stated or estimated, even when a specific sum is described as allocated under this heading, for there is inevitably some degree of language promotion in most contacts between donor and recipient.

One sector of aid to developing countries (as of all aid between countries with different national languages) which may be expected to promote language is that of scholarships and study grants enabling people to spend time in the donor country. This form of provision may have long-term benefits for the donor country but may be counterproductive long-term as aid to a developing country, compared, for instance, with aid which encourages the developing country to build up its own resources of secondary and higher education—in institutions which are, however, less likely to give priority to the language of the donor country.

Looking to the late 1990s and beyond, so far as culture in its widest sense is concerned, attitudes to the promoting of a nation's language may perhaps come to be affected by internal tensions about the nature of the nation's culture. Immigrants and indigenous groups may assert their right to preserve their own culture, so may eventually argue that their numbers in the nation qualify their culture to be seen as part of a national amalgam, or what a former mayor of New York, David Dinkins, called a 'gorgeous mosaic' (*The Independent* June 22, 1992). They may then argue that they should not be required to speak the official language of the nation: at which point it may be politically inconvenient for the national government to be promoting any one language. For instance, the 'melting pot' policy in the USA, as propounded by President Franklin D. Roosevelt, and envisaging the use of English by all groups in the USA, was resisted in the 1980s. Resistance of this kind is not confined to the USA. The Australian policy of assimilation was discontinued in the 1970s. It remains to be seen whether such resistance affects national policy on aid by any donor government. Certainly by the end of the 1990s policies of and pressures towards multiculturalism and multilingualism had advanced in a number of countries.

The culture argument becomes sensitive, too, if the suggestion is made that the culture brings with it a 'civilizing influence.' There have been times when one language more than another has been seen by some to be associated with civilized values. Below there are examples of unargued claims about 'democratic values.' However, the willing absorption of one foreign country's culture or values through the learning of its language, the reading of its books, and the appreciation of its arts may well in one person be accompanied by the determination to purchase a car or hi-fi equipment from another country, whose civilized values are not considered to be of material importance.

One other cultural issue arises in the context of language promotion. For example, in the information given below, three countries—the UK, the USA, and Australia—all actively promote the learning of the English language. It is to be expected that those who learn from teachers provided by these three countries will bear traces of the countries' distinctive accents and vocabulary. Here the cultural question is twofold: does the donor country attempt to suggest that one of its accents or dialects is superior and preferable? Then does the receiving country eventually develop its own form of the language learned—as of course the USA and Australia have done with English over the years?

The following examples show several ways in which countries perceive, and try to meet, the need for knowledge of their own language outside their own boundaries. They show, too, some of the ways in which such information is provided by government bodies in different countries. No two are easily compared, even within the English-language group. To some extent Germany and Australia may be compared, each in the context of influence on one region of the world. French and English may be compared in the context of historical, imperial influence. The UK and the USA merit consideration as two styles of promoting the same language worldwide. Canada is distinctive in its dual commitment. Israel is perhaps unique in representing a situation with no obvious comparison past or present.

All differ appreciably in output, areas of operation, level and style of funding, arguments deployed, and aims expressed. Together they raise a number of arresting questions about motivation and effectiveness, and not least (against the background of the languages known to be spoken by many and those spoken by but a few) about the likely, possible, and desirable ways in which the popularity of languages here considered, or of any other, will rise or fall.

In this context, three sets of statistics merit thought.

First, UNESCO figures for 1989 (see *Statistics: Principal Languages of the World* (*UNESCO*)) show that the total number of English, French, German, Spanish, and Portuguese speakers, though all numerically in the top 12, represent only 24.8 percent of the entire world population.

Second, of the total number of English speakers, in the UNESCO figures, 23.2 percent are classified as 'potential' (i.e., principally learners rather than mother-tongue speakers), and this number of 'potential' speakers is 48.4 percent of the total number of 'potential' speakers of all languages in the top 12.

Third, such figures may also inform reflection on the fact that (according to *The Independent* of January 8, 1992) in 1992 Radio Finland transmitted a weekly five-minute news bulletin, '*Nuntii Latini*,' in Latin across the globe—perhaps the most minuscule promotion of any language anywhere, in this case not the language of the broadcasting country. Latin was at one time more forcefully promoted, and to some effect. *Sic transit gloria mundi.* Thomas a Kempis's saying is described in Brewer's *Dictionary of Phrase and Fable* as 'a classic statement on the transitory nature of human vanities.' The Latin phrase is intoned at the coronation ceremony of the Pope. On Vatican City State Radio, Latin features in daily broadcasts of the Mass. The words '*Laudetur Jesus Christus*' precede all transmissions and are then repeated in the language of the broadcast; '*Christus Vincit*' is the station's interval signal (*World Radio TV Handbook*). For the rest, Vatican Radio is listed as broadcasting in over 30 languages, even including the international (artificial) language Esperanto (see *Artificial Languages*).

1. National Promotion

1.1 Germany

For the German government, cultural contacts are those not seen as political or economic. Most German organizations devoted to cultural and scientific exchange with other countries have their origins prior to the German economic crisis of 1930 and the Nazi dictatorship of 1933–45. From 1949 exchanges were resumed.

Academic relations are nurtured by the *Deutscher Akademischer Austauschdienst* (DAAD), the German academic exchange service, established in 1925, which promotes relations with other countries, particularly through the exchange of students and academics in all disciplines, including language. DAAD is publicly funded (in 1989 the Federal government and parliament contributed DM220 million), and also receives funds from the European Community and several national and international foundations and institutions.

DAAD projects include the DAAD *Lektoren*, teachers and lecturers who, for the most part, teach German at foreign institutions of higher education for a period of two to five years.

From its origins in the 1920s, the *Carl Duisberg Gesellschaft* (CDG) became an international exchange agency in the field of vocational further training. The developing countries became the organization's favored partners: some 7000 places were provided annually. In the 40 years after 1949 more than 100,000 persons from all parts of the world participated in the organization's programs. More than 60 associations of former scholarship holders were established in 50 countries. In Germany the CDG runs seven language centers with board and lodging facilities for around 700 participants. CDG funds are provided by the German government and the *Bundesländer* (constituent states), and German industry provides trainee places.

In the 1980s the German Foreign Office in Bonn commissioned from the Mannheim-based Institute of the German Language a survey on where German is spoken in the world: the report was entitled 'German-speaking Minorities.' Inevitably classification of varying groups was found difficult. The 1.6 million persons 'speaking German at home' in the USA top the list of the 27 countries; 112,545 speak German at home in Canada. Only about 100,000 of the 635,000 of German origin in Australia speak German at home: the decline is attributed to the Australian policy of assimilation (which was discontinued in the mid-1970s). Barthold Witte, head of the Directorate-General for Cultural Relations at the German Foreign Office, stated:

> Reliable information on the spread and usage of the German language in non-German-speaking countries constitutes an important planning basis for the intended expansion of language promotion for German native speakers and the descendants of German immigrants whose knowledge of German is still incomplete or no longer existent.
>
> (Inter Nationes, Bonn 1992)

UNESCO figures for 'total speakers' of the major languages show German as the twelfth: the figures for 'real speakers' show German as ninth. German is, however, the native tongue of more Europeans than any other. Figures from the Goethe Institute show German as the mother tongue of 110 million people. An article in 1989 says:

> The question of the position German will assume as a foreign language, the opportunities which will accompany the German language into the twenty-first century, will be decided primarily in Europe, in the European Community and in the countries of eastern Central Europe and Eastern Europe which are now beginning to open up.

The end of the Soviet Union and of its dominance over Eastern Europe made thousands of teachers of compulsory Russian redundant: to fill the language-teaching vacuum, German and English have been the main contenders. The Hungarian government decided in 1989 that, of 2000 Russian-language teachers, 1000 should become German-language teachers. For this the Goethe Institute provided teacher-training staff and materials and the German government provided financial assistance for courses in the Federal Republic. Also the German Industrial and Trade Association (DIHT) invited hundreds of functionaries from industry and commerce in the former Soviet Union to Germany: for these meetings the guests required knowledge of German, for which purpose the Goethe Institute provided intensive courses in the Soviet Union.

The Goethe Institute 'for the Cultivation of the German Language Abroad and the Promotion of International Cultural Cooperation' had a budget in 1989 of DM230 million from public funds, it had 149 branch offices in 69 countries. It provides over 1000 courses annually in German within Germany for 25,000 persons (1989 figure). In the early 1990s the Institute established new offices in Warsaw, Cracow, Sofia, Bratislava, Prague, Budapest, and Moscow. The Institute's libraries around the world have developed from purely lending libraries to information centers providing books, magazines, and audio-visual media. Video cassettes are provided for learning German.

The Goethe Institute administers a broad range of examinations in the German language. Looking towards the removal of European trade barriers in the 1990s, courses in German business terminology were provided in European countries. In the late 1980s an examination in Business German was devised jointly by the Goethe Institute, the DIHT, and the CDG. The Institute's promotional literature, accepting that German was already a second language in the Eastern bloc and the former Soviet Union, points out that 'more surprisingly' it is a second language in South America too, and the third language in Canada. Justifying the learning of German, the Institute argues that one-sixth of all Americans are of German descent, that Germans have been the largest ethnic group among American immigrants, that every tenth book published in the world is in German; and that some important journals and papers, especially at research level, are not translated into English. Accepting that most young Germans have learnt English in school, the Institute says that German-speaking countries expect native speakers of English to learn German in order to establish trade—for others who seek to establish trade take that trouble.

The Institute sets out to counter claims that German is either a difficult or a harsh and ugly language (as suggested, say, by films made in the UK and the USA in the years following World War II). Knowledge of German, the Institute says, helps towards an understanding of several other European languages; it helps the tourist in Europe appreciate the part played by German-speaking countries in much that is significant in European history and culture; not least important, the German language is one of the common features between East and West Europe, so it may provide a link that can draw the two sides closer.

Deutsche Welle, the external broadcasting service of Germany, offers its listeners in Europe not only German-language programs but also 14 foreign-language programs. Since July 1990 the service has been broadcast via satellite as well as shortwave. Some other parts of the world are reached by satellite, all parts by shortwave—in a total of 34 languages.

1.2 France

> It is impossible to escape the question in everyone's mind: how to resist the Anglo-American steamroller? It is so powerful, in technology, business, and the audio-visual media. Ignorance of English is coming to be considered a sign of illiteracy. If Europe does not want to lose its soul, impoverish its culture, forget its history, it must take its pluri-lingualism on board.

The plea came from Alain Decaux, France's Minister for Francophonie (*The Independent on Sunday* October 21, 1990). He was speaking at a point when the French government had been reviewing the standing of the French language not only in Europe but around the world. It was a time, too, when there was turmoil in Eastern Europe, where those concerned with the teaching of the French language had to face a challenge as much from the German language as from the English.

The situation at world level was different as shown in Table 1. French government figures assembled about the same time as the UNESCO figures, show that around the world there were 253 schools, colleges, or lycées with French curricula aimed at serving 115,000 students, of whom 3700 were French. Some of the schools operate under local French embassy direction, some in cooperation with a range

Table 1. Number of speakers of the world's major languages (UNESCO 1989; in 1000s).

	Potential speakers	Real speakers	Total speakers
English	137,591.7	456,328.3	593,920.1
French	42,759.1	88,658.3	131,417.4
German	88.8	88,997.6	89,086.4

of local or worldwide bodies, the latter including the French Alliance. The French government decided to fund a reinforcement of teacher supply to these schools, partly to enable an improved flow of students from the schools to foreign universities, also of able students to French universities. The *Conseil pour l'enseignement français à l'étranger* (Council for the Teaching of French Abroad—CEFE) contributes to the integration of relations with all those bodies and people working in partnership with the schools abroad.

The French Ministry for Foreign Affairs works abroad along with institutes and centers, and with committees and affiliates of the French Alliance. There are 120 institutes and centers in 50 countries, all given the status of outside services to the Ministry, and all responsible for arranging conferences, exhibitions, concerts, films, etc. They provide language courses for around 180,000 students every year and they cooperate in a variety of ways with foreign universities. From 1990 onwards the language teaching function was given new impetus, with extended publicity, intensive short courses (some giving special attention to scientific and business French), and to improved libraries.

Every year 7000 French music discs are sent to nearly 500 foreign radio stations in 72 countries. French films are widely distributed by means of videocassettes. International coproduction of films and of TV series is encouraged. France offers, too, training courses in film production and in journalism.

Assuming that around 100 million people outside Francophone areas have learned French as a foreign language, the Secretary of State for Foreign Cultural Relations works to enhance cooperation in all teaching of the French language. Embassies and consulates are required to serve and to stimulate local services engaged in the teaching of French. Special support is given in both developed and underdeveloped countries to university courses in French and to bringing students of French to study in France.

The French Alliance has more than 1000 committees worldwide and serves more than 1600 localities. The network is particularly strong in Latin America. In the 1980s it expanded in Asia and in non-French speaking parts of Africa and it began to serve new areas in Japan, Fiji, Liberia, Morocco, Egypt, Korea, New Zealand, the Philippines, Sudan, and China.

The French Association for Promoting the Arts (AFAA), funded by both government and private enterprise, ensures support for the presentation of French arts and artists abroad, also it welcomes such ventures from abroad to France. The French government gives renewed emphasis to the promotion abroad of French literature and publishing (in 1989, 45 million francs were allocated to this). Five thousand copies are distributed of a monthly bulletin reviewing French books; the English version of this, *New French Books*, has a circulation of 2500. The bi-monthly *Rendez-vous en France* (40,000 copies) is aimed at the educated, French-speaking foreign audience and covers many aspects of French life. Translation of French books, ranging from the humanities to science, is promoted in South America, India, and North Africa. In 1989 new resources were provided for ensuring an increase in translation of French books into foreign languages. New funds were devoted to a joint venture with Quebec to provide scientific works in French.

During the 1980s, looking beyond the academics, the better-educated, the literate, and the artistic in other countries, the French government accepted that in order to make contact with a truly international and sizeable world audience, France must establish a presence in radio (short, medium, and long-wave) and both large and small screen. The Ministry of Foreign Affairs was charged with the responsibility of coordinating efforts to set up a network of image and sound that would eventually cover most of the globe. Radio France International greatly enlarged its sphere of coverage—in Asia, by agreements with China and Japan on frequency allocation; in Europe and the Middle East by collaborating in radio services that provided some programs in local languages and some in French. Also private enterprise was encouraged to provide French cultural programs to be relayed by stations around the world.

A French initiative was launched in 1989 to strengthen and coordinate television services in Europe, and to ensure an open European market for programs. A Francophone channel was established, bringing together French, Belgian, Swiss, and Canadian companies, to reach more than 12 million people in Europe and, by cable, 1.3 million in Canada. Reception of French TV programs was extended to a large part of Italy and to Tunisia.

News programs, mostly originating in French national channels, are distributed by satellite and by cassettes to Francophone Africa, the Near East, Asia, and Latin America: they are received by 71 countries and used by 200 national and regional stations. The French agency AITV was reported in 1990 to rate fourth worldwide as a film/TV agency. Canal France International provides four hours daily a 'bank' for satellite broadcasts to North Africa, the Middle East, and Eastern Europe. France accepted the opportunity to use Olympus, the satellite for direct TV broadcasting, covering western Europe and offering program time to educational and cultural institutes.

The French Secretary of State for International Cultural Relations, along with the Ministry of Education, initiated the development of audiovisual programs for cultural broadcasting, distance teaching, and support for the French language.

1.3 Canada

In her introduction to *Sharing Our Future* (1987), a statement of the Canadian government's strategy for Canadian International Development Assistance (CIDA), the Honorable Monique Landry, Minister for External Relations and Industrial Development, stated that a country's foreign policy must be an expression of the mission of its citizens, of the country's character as a nation; that the message of Canada's strategy for development cooperation was, Canadians care; that the right Canadian resources should reach those most in need, when they need the help most; and that Canadians wished to create new partnerships, both domestically and internationally, in order to build a better world. *Sharing Our Future* reported the establishment in Canada of the International Francophone Center for Distance Learning.

The report, like annual reports of CIDA, was printed within one volume in English and French, with French text on inverted pages so that each language had a front cover and text running from page 1.

The statistics provided in the annual CIDA reports give information about a wide range of government support to many developing countries. Information about the support for Africa reflects the bilingual situation within Canada itself, in that Africa is referred to in terms of Anglophone Africa (Fig. 1) and Francophone Africa (Fig. 2), and CIDA reports use maps presenting CIDA's oversimplified view of the division. Many languages other than English and French are, of course, spoken in Africa.

The flow and exchange of personnel, in numerous professions other than those concerned with education and language, are inevitably language-conscious and require specific language competence. For those developing countries, not only in Africa, where levels of literacy are low, the promise of aid from abroad poses challenging questions related to priorities in language learning and competence, especially at secondary and higher levels, not only in those sectors of the community required to know an official language which has been bequeathed by past imperial rule.

In the year 1989, students and trainees supported by CIDA were categorized in 32 subject groups (from Accountancy to Transportation) and totaled 11,021. Within that total, 272 were listed under Languages

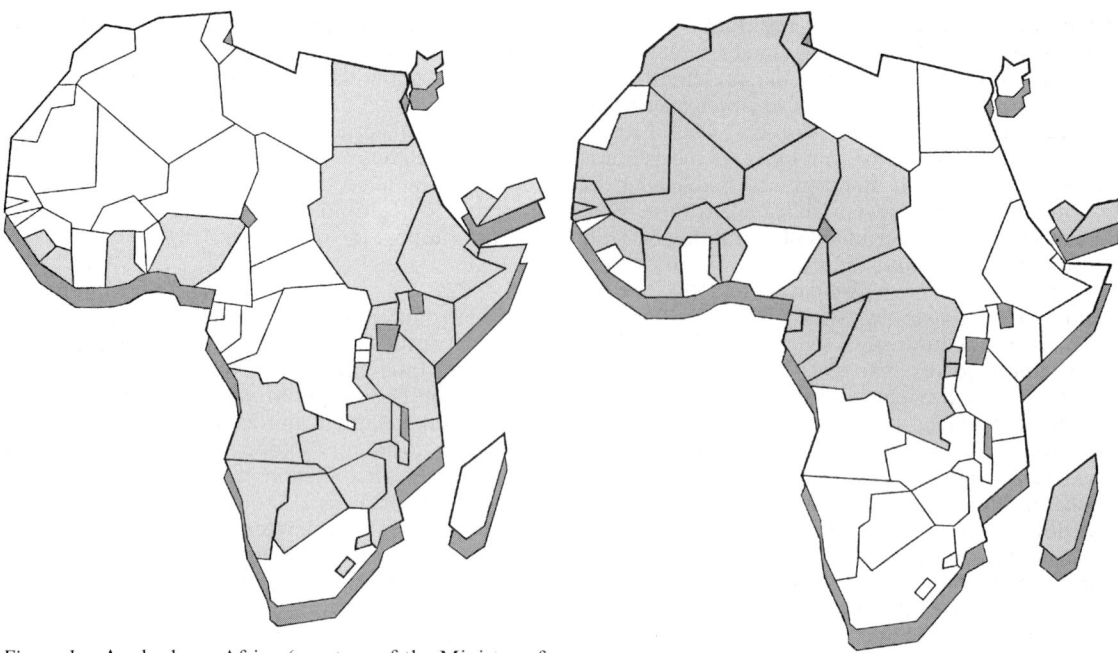

Figure 1. Anglophone Africa (courtesy of the Ministry of Supply and Services, from CIDA Annual Report 1989–90).

Figure 2. Francophone Africa (courtesy of the Ministry of Supply and Services, from the CIDA Annual Report 1989–90).

and Linguistics, 655 under Education, and 105 under Arts and Humanities. The three largest categories were Management and Administration 2175; Engineering and Technology 1339; and Computer Sciences 1182.

CIDA works with Canada World Youth and Canada Crossroads International to involve young Canadians in international development. Each year these organizations arrange over 500 exchanges between young Canadians and young people from developing countries.

Radio Canada International in 1991 relayed programs from the English and French networks of its parent company, the Canadian Broadcasting Corporation. It provided newscasts in English to Asia and Europe, and in French to Africa and Latin America. It broadcast full programs to the Middle East in Arabic, to the former Soviet Union in Russian and Ukrainian, to China in Standard Chinese, and to Latin America in Spanish.

1.4 USA

The United States Information Agency (USIA), known abroad as the United States Information Service (USIS), operates as an independent foreign affairs agency within the executive branch of the US government. Its mandate is: 'to present abroad a true picture of the United States, to promote mutual understanding between America and other countries, and to counter attempts to distort US policies and objectives.' USIA programs have always been directed to overseas audiences.

The US government's first large-scale entry into information activities abroad began during World War I, then dwindled to almost nothing until 1938 when steps were taken to counter German and Italian propaganda aimed at Latin America. In 1942 the Voice of America (VOA) was created to counter adverse foreign propaganda, and the Office of War Information was established. In the immediate postwar years the need was seen to replace arms with words ('This is a struggle, above all else, for the minds of men': President Harry Truman in a speech known as the Campaign of Truth). In 1953 President Dwight Eisenhower created the USIA, the name restored by President Ronald Reagan in 1982 for an organization by then incorporating overseas information programs, educational and cultural exchange programs, the Voice of America, and Television (Worldnet) and Film Services.

> You have informed us truthfully of events around the world and in our country as well, and in this way you helped us to bring about the peaceful revolution, which has at long last taken place ... You will have to inform us about how to create democracy, because we are now beginning to build it, to renew it after long decades, and we have a lot to learn.
> (President Vaclav Havel, of Czechoslovakia speaking to Voice of America February 20, 1990)

Of the US$1093 million appropriated for all USIA activities in 1992, educational and cultural exchange programs received 22.1 percent: these programs included performing and fine arts presentations, book and library programs, and English teaching. Library programs are funded in 111 binational centers (BNCs) in more than 20 countries. Binational centers are independent institutions dedicated to promoting mutual understanding between the host country and the USA: English teaching is often a major component of the binational center's cultural, educational, and information activities.

USIA supports the development of English teaching curricula, textbooks, and training programs. This activity is intended to stimulate and reinforce academic exchange programs between the USA and other countries and to explain American life to audiences abroad. USIA promotes English language instruction at cultural and binational centers in 100 countries. More than 400,000 foreign citizens attend English language classes at these facilities. USIA English teaching officers provide professional guidance on teaching methodologies and materials.

The Agency publishes a professional quarterly for English teachers, *English Teaching Forum*, which is available in the US and abroad: over 120,000 copies of each issue are distributed in 133 countries. The Agency also publishes or supports 14 magazines in 21 languages. The quarterly journal *Dialogue*, first published in 1968 and distributed worldwide, contains articles selected from US magazines, the articles covering American society, politics, and the arts. *Dialogue* appears in 13 languages including English. The quarterly magazine *Topic*, distributed in over 40 countries in Sub-Saharan Africa is intended for young elites in the region and highlights USA commitment to African democracy and economic and social development. It is published in French and English.

USIA exchange programs include International Visitor, Citizen, and Youth Exchanges, as well as an extensive range of academic fellowships. Many academics from most countries in the world go to study in the USA every year.

USIA maintains links with or assists approximately 200 cultural centers and language institutes, approximately half of them binational centers, in nearly 100 countries. These centers conduct English classes, seminars on aspects of life in the USA, and arts and exhibition programs. Some centers are fully funded by USIA, while binational centers, autonomous institutions answerable to their own local boards of directors (local citizens and resident Americans), sometimes receive grants from USIA and may have staff supplied by USIA. Their English teaching programs are open to the public and generally attract large numbers of secondary school students. The direct English teaching programs are more targeted and cater to government and education officials, journalists, and USA Aid grantees but do allow others to enroll as space permits.

In 1989, of 90 binational centers, 78 were in Central and South America and the Caribbean, three were in Indonesia, two in Pakistan, one in Thailand, and six in Europe. There were no binational centers in Africa but USIA supported 15 English language programs in the region.

The Agency's English Language Programs Division has 17 English Teaching Officers and support staff in Washington, and 15 officers serving overseas as Country or Regional English Teaching Officers. Washington and field-based officers rotate regularly. All have advanced degrees in applied linguistics and/or TEFL (Teaching English as a Foreign Language), combined with experience as EFL (English as a Foreign Language) teachers, teacher training, or academic administration. The English Teaching Fellows Program recruits recent MAs in TEFL to increase the American presence and to help improve academic standards at overseas institutions, including binational centers.

In 1992, in an Eastern-European EFL Fellow Program, USIA was seeking applicants for posts as EFL teacher-trainers and ESP (English for Special Purposes)/EFL specialists to work with local EFL teachers in Poland, Hungary, Czechoslovakia, Romania, Yugoslavia, Bulgaria, Albania, Lithuania, Latvia, and Estonia.

USIA and the Voice of America cooperate in promoting English Language Teaching by Broadcast, a multimedia product developed by a US publisher and USIA.

1.5 United Kingdom

In the British Council annual report and accounts for 1990–91 the Director-General's review of the year reports that 'Demand for English teaching programmes and expertise, as a tool for communication, training, and the transfer of technology, remained buoyant—and, in Eastern and Central Europe, insatiable.' The report quotes Professor Svetlana Ter Minasova, of Moscow State University, addressing a conference organized by the Council, the BBC, and the English Speaking Union: 'Teachers of English have never been so important and so wanted and so unable to satisfy the cry for help. For very many people, English is the standard-bearer of democracy.'

Twenty-four English language projects for Eastern and Central Europe were prepared by the British Council in the first few months of 1991 (up to March 31). The biggest of these projects were for Poland, Hungary, and Czechoslovakia, with smaller ones promised for Romania, Bulgaria, Yugoslavia, and the former Soviet Union. Many of the projects involved the development of English language teaching within national education systems 'reflecting the demand for English both as a vehicle for democratic values and as the point of access to expertise vital to the development of the region.' The projects concentrate on the key areas of teacher training and retraining, English for banking, government, finance, and tertiary education; British cultural studies; and resources and self-access centers for students and teachers of English. Almost 100 teaching posts and 30 resource centers were to be created using new funding from the UK Foreign and Commonwealth Office (FCO).

Other innovations reported included a joint venture with the British Tourist Authority and Lille Chamber of Commerce to promote British schools of English and British ELT publishers and examination boards; a project jointly funded with the UK Overseas Development Administration (ODA) and the Mexican government for an English teaching program involving eight universities in central Mexico; arranging high-level training for 25 teachers in Japan, paid for by Monbusho, the Japanese Ministry of Education; a program of ELT support in Turkey; an ELT resource center in Hong Kong for the higher-education sector, while 70 primary school teachers of English were trained at language schools in Britain and 300 at the British Council English Language Centre in Hong Kong.

Looking to the future the Council's annual report (1990–91) said: 'We have urgent priorities to extend our work in Eastern and Central Europe, the Middle East, Hong Kong and Southern Africa.' In seven years the Council's budget grew from £204 million to a projected £395 million for 1991–92 and the Council's overseas presence extended from 133 towns and cities in 81 countries to 162 in 90 countries.

The Council works in close collaboration with the UK FCO and UK ODA. In 1990–91 the Council's expenditure by regions in percentages was: Africa 28; Western Europe 19; Eastern and Central Europe 6; Asia Pacific 17; South Asia 14; Middle East and North Africa 8; Americas 8. In the same year the Council's expenditure by activity in percentages was: interchange of people 57; libraries, books and information 13; English language and literature 13; science and education 12; arts 5.

The Council's total receipts for the year (1990–91) were £362 million. Its sources of funding in percentages were: government grants 35; ODA agency 35; FCO agency 6; other agency 7; revenue 17. Council work for the arts was supported in large part by sponsorship from a range of business companies.

Teaching of English by broadcasts from the UK is the responsibility of the BBC World Service, but the British Council works along with the BBC in language promotion and teaching.

1.6 Australia

The International Development Program of Australian Universities and Colleges (IDP) has Australian Education Centers in Bangkok, Hong Kong, Jakarta, Kuala Lumpur, Manila, Seoul, Singapore, Suva, and Taipei. The centers offer guidance on Australian education, with information, counseling, and application processing to overseas students as well as promotion and recruitment activities of Australian educational institutions.

IDP is joint sponsor with the Indonesian Directorate General of Higher Education in sponsoring the Basic Science Bridging Program (BSBP) for staff from Indonesian universities. The program upgrades and refreshes the scientific knowledge and skills of science teachers.

Since many participants hope to undertake postgraduate work in Australia or other English-speaking countries, the study of the English language is an important part of BSBP. 'English is necessary for anyone seeking to become more qualified in science (even for those with no wish to travel or study overseas) since it is the most widely used language for scientific communication, and most scientific textbooks and journals are written in English.' Under IDP, staff of four universities in Java intending to apply for overseas study programs, may enrol in preparatory English courses conducted by Australian ELT advisors. The courses are provided in the Language Training Centers of the universities.

The Indonesia–Australia Language Foundation (IALF) is a self-funding body subject to Indonesian laws, and operates throughout Indonesia. Created by the governments of Indonesia and Australia in 1988, it aims to contribute to economic, social, and cultural development in Indonesia, and 'to promote mutual respect and understanding, particularly through the medium of high-quality English language teaching and training services.' Its information on education, disseminated in the English language, lays emphasis on 'creating a bridge between two cultures' and on the learning of the English language. IALF clients are Indonesian government departments, non-government Indonesian organizations, universities and other educational institutions, staffs of banks, hotels, etc, and private individuals. The Foundation is funded from Australian government grants; through charges to Indonesian organizations, governmental and otherwise; and through a range of contracts and fees paid by individuals.

IALF services include courses in English for students preparing to study in Australia, New Zealand, the USA, Canada, the UK, and other English-speaking countries. English courses offer preparation for the workplace, academic bridging programs, specialized writing, travel, and 'working in committees—Western style.' The Foundation provides consultancies, technical services, and testing on

English as a foreign language. IALF courses on Indonesian language and culture are offered to people new to Indonesia.

The English Language Center of Australia (ELCA), an affiliation between IDP and the University of the Thai Chamber of Commerce (UTCC) is located at UTCC Bangkok and serves those intending to study in Australia and other countries as well as those wishing to improve their English for business or personal reasons.

Radio Australia, the international broadcasting service of the Australian Broadcasting Corporation, broadcasts in eight languages to an estimated 50 million listeners in Asia and the Pacific. Its English service is broadcast 24 hours a day. (Other language services, broadcast regularly throughout the day seven days a week are in Indonesian, Standard Chinese and Cantonese, French, Tok Pisin, Thai, and Vietnamese.) The English language training programs are broadcast as part of the regular shortwave services to Indonesia, Thailand, China, and Vietnam. The lessons, developed in collaboration with specialist educational institutions in Australia, concentrate on aural comprehension and are supported by reading material which aims to ensure understanding of spelling and grammar.

In 1991 an initial series of 26 half-hour lessons was produced following a request from the Vietnamese government and the broadcasting organization Voice of Vietnam to provide support to their English language broadcasting efforts. Radio Australia's English lessons to China are supported by booklets and cassettes produced for distribution across China: these were launched in China in 1992 and sold in 18 branches of the foreign language bookstore in Beijing, the hope being that the service would be rebroadcast on domestic radio stations. In 1991 Radio Australia began a new series of programs, 'Study in Australia,' aimed at raising awareness in north and southeast Asia of educational opportunities in Australia. The series is available on cassette.

1.7 Israel

> The State of Israel and Jewish society in Israel espouse the Zionist position according to which every Jew, anywhere in the world, is entitled, invited, and called upon, constantly and unceasingly, to immigrate to and live in Israel.
>
> (Israel Government Year Book 1990)

The literature of the Academy of the Hebrew Language asserts that Hebrew is a cornerstone in the national and political rebirth of the Jewish people 'not only as citizens of a proud young state, but as members of a Jewish people with a long history and heritage'; that Hebrew is the expression of 'the Jewish cultural revival'; that it plays an essential role in fusing Jewish exiles from 102 lands into one nation with one common language; that the Academy 'is the supreme authority in the most audacious linguistic experiment ever attempted: the adaptation to the computer age of a tongue unspoken for 1700 years.' Since the mid-1960s the Academy has supervized the Hebrew, including word use and pronunciation, used by Israel's Broadcasting Authority.

For some years after the creation of the state of Israel in 1948 the promotion of Hebrew was seen by some Jews to be in competition with a revival of interest in Yiddish. David Ben-Gurion, Israel's first prime minister, is reported to have said Yiddish sounded repugnant. While a more tolerant attitude has developed in Israel towards Yiddish Israeli resources of language teaching, both within Israel and in the diaspora, are concentrated on Hebrew.

If a professional person, say in Russia or the UK, wishes to work in Israel, the Israeli government, assuming that the family will settle in Israel, pays for six months' support within Israel of both parents and family. This and a variety of other forms of support to immigrants have continued since the 1940s. The teaching of Hebrew has been a strong element in the process of initiation.

> As knowledge of the language of the country is essential to help integrate the many people constantly arriving from all over the world, the *ulpan* method was developed to aid the rapid learning of Hebrew. It consists of an intense course, usually of five months' duration, in which most newcomers acquire adequate proficiency for everyday communication.
>
> (*Facts About Israel: Education.* Israel Information Center 1991)

The term '*ulpan*' (from Old Hebrew 'a place to learn') is used in reference to a wide range of the teaching and learning of Hebrew outside Israel. In *A Short History of the Hebrew Language* (Jewish Agency Publishing Department, Jerusalem 1973) Chaim Rubin claimed that at the beginning of the 1970s there were signs of a tendency to equal a knowledge of modern 'living' Hebrew with personal commitment to the movement of Jewish awakening. This, he said, found its expression in the marked increase of the proportion of Hebrew speakers among young people, not only in the USA and Canada, but also in South America and Western Europe. It found expression, too, in the growing interest of academic youth in Hebrew studies, and in pressure for the development of Hebrew studies in universities. It took its most dramatic form, he believed, in the awakening of the 'Silent Jewry' in the former Soviet Union, among Jews who, at grave personal risk, set up private *ulpanim* for learning Hebrew. Such enthusiasm has helped to ensure that necessary resources are found. At times the Israeli government has made funding, resources, and personnel available for the teaching of Hebrew in the diaspora. The Jewish Agency, the World Zionist Organization, in the UK the Zionist Federation Educational Trust (ZFET), and the Israeli government have all done much to promote the study of Hebrew throughout the world. Specially trained teachers have been sent out from Israel for periods from two to five years. Young people from abroad have gone to Israel to be trained as teachers of Hebrew. Hebrew language workshops have been formed, and crash courses provided for Jews wishing to visit Israel.

A major difficulty has lain in securing a supply of qualified language teachers, this because of the growing demand for the teaching of Hebrew within Israel itself, where immigrants have outnumbered the native population. But the teaching of modern Hebrew is ensured in many parts of many countries.

See also: Multilingual States; National Language/Official Language; English as a Foreign Language; Nationalism and Language.

Language Planning: Models
A. Deumert

Language planning refers to deliberate, conscious, and future-oriented activities aimed at influencing the linguistic repertoire and behavior of speech communities, typically at the state level. Other terms which occur in the literature and which are partially synonymous with language planning are: language engineering; language management; language standardization (see *Standardization*); language determination; and language development (see *Language Development*). Language planning can be distinguished from language policy. Language policy describes the underlying political and sociolinguistic goals that are implied in the activities and measures of language planners.

1. Historical Background

The American linguist Einar Haugen (see *Haugen, Einar*) introduced the term language planning to the literature in 1959. Language planning is a long-standing practice and examples can be found in language history, e.g., the foundation of language academies from the sixteenth century which promoted the European vernacular languages against the dominance of Latin (see *Academies: Dictionaries and Standards*). However, only after World War II, when the newly independent and multilingual nations in Africa and Asia faced the question of selecting national languages for administrative and educational purposes, did language planning emerge as a separate area of sociolinguistic research, and began to develop its own descriptive taxonomies and explanatory models. Language standardization, national language selection as well as the support of linguistic diversity and the maintenance of minority languages have been prominent issues of language planning research during the past decades.

2. The Process of Language Planning

Based on his study of the dual standardization of Norwegian (i.e., the emergence of the two Norwegian standard languages *Bokmål* and *Nynorsk*), Haugen developed a fourfold model, which describes the kind of activities in which language planners typically engage. The model consists of four stages, which need not be sequential.

(a) Selection of norm: the process of selecting a regional and/or social language variety to fulfill certain functions in a given society or nation. The Norwegian standard of *Nynorsk* is a composite of the rural dialects, while the *Bokmål* standard is based on the Danish-influenced speech of the educated urban classes. In Kenya English has been selected as the sole official language; its neighbor Tanzania selected Swahili, the local lingua franca (and limited the use of English to certain legal contexts and post-primary education).

(b) Codification of form: the selection of a writing system and the establishment of linguistic norms through grammars, spelling rules, style manuals and dictionaries. The latter not only decide on the appropriate vocabulary, but also contribute to the standardization of spelling and sometimes pronunciation, e.g., Samuel Johnson's *Dictionary of the English Language* (1755) and Noah Webster's *The American Spelling Book* (1790) established the different spelling traditions of British and American English. In Yugoslavia Vuk Stefanovic Karadzic's grammar of 1814 and his dictionary of 1818 became the foundation of a common South Slavic literary language (Serbo-Croatian).

(c) Implementation: the gradual diffusion and acceptance of the new norm within the language community or territory (see *Language Diffusion Policy*). The process of implementation can involve overt marketing techniques to promote the use of the selected norm (including billboards, radio, and television skits) as well as legal enforcement.

(d) Elaboration of function: the process of extending the functions of the selected norm (legal language, scientific language, etc.). This includes terminological modernization and stylistic development (see *Language Adaptation and Modernization*). In Israel the Academy of the Hebrew Language has established committees to work on the development of Hebrew scientific terminology. Similar bodies have been instituted in other parts of the world, for example, in India (Hindi), Indonesia (Bahasa Indonesia) or Sweden, where the Center for Technical Terminology develops standard terminology for spoken and written Swedish. Elaboration is an ongoing process in every language, as there is a never-ending need to develop new terms for new ideas, innovations, and technologies. This ensures the use of a language in a variety of domains.

3. Status, Corpus, Prestige, and Acquisition Planning

An alternative descriptive model was suggested by Heinz Kloss (1969), a German linguist, based on the observation that language planners focus their attention either on linguistic aspects of the selected language or language variety (corpus planning; i.e., the production of grammars, dictionaries and spelling rules), or on the language's social status, that is, its functions in society (status planning; e.g., official language, provincial language, language of wider communication, medium of instruction, etc.). This binary distinction emphasizes the dual nature of language: language is a system of linguistic elements (the *corpus* or body of language), as well as a social institution and a communicative tool. Codification and elaboration are usually considered aspects of corpus planning. Selection and implementation belong to the domain of status planning.

Although Kloss separates corpus and status planning conceptually, the two dimensions closely interact with one another: the allocation of new language functions often requires changes in the linguistic system such as the development of new styles, discursive devices, and lexical items. Thus, the adoption of Tok Pisin, an English-based pidgin language, as one of the official languages of Papua New Guinea (status planning) required the elaboration of its vocabulary to provide terms for concepts related to the sphere of politics and legislation (corpus planning), e.g., lexical innovations such as *nesional baset* ('national budget'), *minista bilong edukesan* ('minister of education') (see *Pidgins, Creoles, and Minority Dialects in Education*).

Kloss's two-dimensional model has been extended more recently by R. L. Cooper (1989) and H. Haarmann (1990), who introduced the notions of acquisition and prestige planning. Cooper described those activities, which are aimed at promoting the learning of a language as acquisition planning. Unlike status planning which is directed at increasing a language's functions, acquisition planning is directed at increasing the number of users of a given language or language variety. Just as corpus and status planning are intertwined so are status and acquisition planning: new areas of use might attract new users and an increase in the number of users might support the allocation of new language functions (education, administration, technology, etc.). Corpus planning also interacts with acquisition planning. The publication of grammars and dictionaries is important for the development of teaching material and the implementation in the educational system. Haarmann has introduced the dimension of prestige planning to describe those aspects of language planning that are directed towards creating a favorable attitudinal background for corpus, status, and acquisition planning. This is particularly relevant in the case of low-prestige minority languages which often exist in a diglossic relationship with the area's dominant language and whose use has been limited to low-culture functions (see *Diglossia*). In order to make status changes of minority languages acceptable to the speech community, it is often necessary to first improve the (overt) prestige of the respective language or variety.

Both Haugen's and Kloss' taxonomical models are useful heuristics for the systematic description and categorization of the language planning activities carried out by individuals or institutions (such as academies, language societies, governments). However, they do not provide explanations for the success and failure of individual language planning endeavors, nor do they propose general principles on which to base future language planning.

4. Language Planning as the Rational Choice of Linguistic Alternatives?

Early models (e.g., Ray 1963, cf. also some of the papers in Rubin and Jernudd 1971) have approached language planning as an orderly and systematic process of decision-making, and have adopted a positivist and technical attitude to the solution of language issues in society. The decision procedure which underlies language planning efforts has been summarized as follows: once a linguistic problem has been recognized, language planners will specify the long-term and short-term goals of their actions, produce possible solutions, and carefully assess the costs and benefits involved in each of these solutions (cost–benefit analysis, Thorborn 1971). The most rational (economically, socially, and politically viable) solution to the problem will be selected and implemented. Finally, predicted and actual outcomes will be compared, and modifications are introduced if necessary. Lack of a uniform national language, the absence of adequate scientific terminology, and the existence of widespread societal multilingualism have often been identified as problems by language planners.

The description of language planning as a process of rational decision making is based on several assumptions, most centrally the existence of a clearly defined decision-making unit (such as a government ministry or a language academy), which identifies a single set of goals, carefully assesses a range of alternatives, and ultimately selects that solution which maximizes benefits and minimizes costs. It is further assumed that the language-planning unit has the willingness and the ability to collect the information necessary for evaluating the alternative proposals, and that the infrastructure is adequate for the implementation of the solution. The following critiques have been formulated against these assumptions:

(a) In many cases language planners have only limited knowledge of the sociolinguistic facts of the country or area in question. Language surveys, which list, for example, speaker numbers, degree of bilingualism, patterns of language choice, and linguistic attitudes, are frequently incomplete and outdated. This is particularly true of many multilingual countries. The sociolinguistic structure of linguistic diversity is still poorly understood, and many languages and dialects still lack linguistic descriptions.

(b) Decision-making is always shaped by the socio-political context, and the assessment of costs and benefits is open to diverse interpretations which are socially and historically contingent. For example, to introduce Hindi (which is widely spoken as a second language in India), as the exclusive language of the government might be considered economically beneficial, as it would reduce the costs of administrative multilingualism. However such as policy would be felt unfair by speakers of other languages (high social/political costs). India has thus opted for a multilingual language policy (15 official languages, with Hindi as the *primus inter pares* and English as an associate official language). In other contexts, however, language planners have evaluated multilingual policies negatively as too costly and politically and socially divisive. Many African countries, for example, have selected only one official language, usually that of the former colonial power. A single national language was believed to support national unity as well as economic integration with the industrialized Western states. Monolingual policies, however, carry considerable social and educational costs as the former colonial language is usually only spoken by a minority of the population. Many citizens are thus excluded from political participation and post-primary education.

(c) Language issues are not necessarily the only concern of planners, and language planning has been employed to solve linguistic as well non-linguistic problems. In Quebec, for example, the Charter of the French Language (Bill 101), which demands the use of French in all areas of public life, also led to a change in the structure of the labor market which was previously dominated by English-speaking Canadians. In other cases, language planning has been applied to achieve national integration, liberation and equality, or to foster the power of the elite. To account for the diverse (and often unstated and intertwined) linguistic and socio-political interests in terms of an orderly decision-making model and systematic cost–benefit analysis is seldom possible.

(d) Language planning is not necessarily conducted by a central authority, which oversees the process of decision-making and implementation. It is often initiated and supported by informal networks or individuals, as in the case of feminist language planning. Not only is the feminist movement organizationally fragmented and thus lacking a clearly defined decision-making unit, but also its linguistic goals and language planning efforts have been rather diverse. Some initiatives have focused on disrupting the conventional structures of language and creatively feminized lexical items (such as the reanalysis of 'history' as 'his+story' and the use of the feminized form 'herstory'). Others have argued for the need to create a more women-centered language capable of expressing a female perspective (see *Gender and Language*). Most efforts have, however, been directed at neutralizing linguistic usage (e.g., 'chair' or 'chairperson' instead of 'chairman,' 'he/she' or 'they' instead of generic 'he'). Despite the decentralized nature of the feminist movement and the existence of various goals and linguistic strategies, its efforts towards linguistic equality were surprisingly successful. The use of masculine generic forms has declined considerably in most Western nations since the early 1970s and strategies of gender neutralization are today widely accepted.

A characterization of language planning as rationally organized by clearly specified planning bodies or institutions must be understood as an ideal case, which individual societies approach to varying degrees. More often than not language planning is 'a messy affair, ad hoc, haphazard, and emotionally driven' (Cooper 1989: 41).

5. Historical and Ethnographic Analyses: Explanation through Description

Language planning theorists in the 1980s and especially the 1990s have emphasized the ideological dimensions of language planning, which is always a political exercise and cannot be reduced to the application of specialized (socio) linguistic knowledge to perceived language problems. Cobarrubias (1983) has distinguished four main types of language ideologies: pluralism (i.e., supporting the co-existence of different language groups within a state or society); assimilation (i.e., asserting the dominant language as the medium of communication and marginalizing other languages); vernacularization (i.e., the selection and restoration of the local indigenous languages and their use in official functions); and internationalization (i.e., the selection of a non-indigenous language for national communication). Researchers such as James Tollefson (1991) have shown in case studies how language planning reflects and reinforces past and current relationships of economic, social and political dominance, and inequality. Others, such as Harold Schiffman (1996) have drawn attention to the role played by a community's linguistic culture, i.e., the behaviors, beliefs and values, historical experiences, religious or mythological traditions associated with a particular language (e.g., what do people think about their language?; what do they think about other languages?; how do they assess multilingualism?; monolingualism?; is there a strong bond between culture and language?, etc.). The community's linguistic culture is believed to function as an interpretative filter, thus influencing the formulation of language political goals, the specification of language planning measures and the responses of the community. For example, the decision whether to borrow linguistic items from other languages or whether to rely on language-internal word formation rules is often motivated by non-linguistic, cultural preferences, rather than the more technical principles of linguistic efficiency (easy to learn and use), clarity and regularity. In those speech communities where language constitutes a core value of the community and marks regional or national identity, vocabulary extension is typically characterized by puristic tendencies (e.g., France). Historical and ethnographic approaches to language planning, which relate the patterns of actual language use and choice to the historical structures of social and political domination and to the cultural beliefs speakers express about language, have contributed to a more in-depth understanding of the decisions made by language planners and the reasons why some proposals succeed while others fail.

As in the other social sciences, explanatory adequacy in language planning research is largely observational. Understanding is achieved through the careful description of the speech community's linguistic behavior, the discursive penetration of cultural belief systems, the sociopolitical conditions of language use, and the linguistic and non-linguistic interests of the different groups that are engaged in the language planning process. Since language planning cannot be understood in isolation from the complex sociohistorical context in which it is enacted, trans-historical generalizations and law-like predictions are rarely possible.

See also: Academies: Dictionaries and Standards; Language Development; Standardization; Multilingual States.

Bibliography

Cobarrubias J 1983 Ethical issues in status planning. In: Cobarrubias J, Fishman J A (eds.) *Progress in Language Planning*. Mouton, Berlin

Cobarrubias J, Fishman J A (eds.) 1983 *Progress in Language Planning*. Mouton, Berlin

Cooper R L 1989 *Language Planning and Social Change*. Cambridge University Press, Cambridge, UK

Eastman C M 1983 *Language Planning: An Introduction*. Chandler and Sharp, San Francisco, CA

Fishman J A (ed.) 1974 *Advances in Language Planning*. Mouton, The Hague

Fishman J A, Ferguson C A, Gupta J D (eds.) 1968 *Language Problems of Developing Nations*. Wiley, New York

Fodor I, Hagége C (eds.) 1983–1989 *Language Reform: History and Future*. 5 vols. Buske Verlag, Hamburg

Haarman H 1990 Language planning in the light of a general theory of language: a methodological framework. *International Journal of the Sociology of Language* **86**: 103–26

Haugen E 1959 Planning for a standard language in modern Norway. *Anthropological Linguistics* **1**: 8–21

Haugen E 1966 Linguistics and language planning. In: Bright W (ed.) *Sociolinguistics: Proceedings of the UCLA Sociolinguistics Conference, 1964*. Mouton, The Hague

Kaplan R B, Baldauf R B 1997 *Language Planning from Practice to Theory*. Multilingual Matters, Clevedon, UK

Kloss H 1969 *Research Possibilities on Group Bilingualism: A Report*. International Center for Research on Bilingualism, Quebec, PQ

Ray P S 1963 *Language Standardization*. Mouton, The Hague

Rubin J, Jernudd B H (ed.) 1971 *Can Language Be Planned? Sociolinguistic Theory and Practice for Developing Nations*. University Press of Hawaii, Honolulu, HI

Schiffman H 1996 *Linguistic Culture and Language Policy*. Routledge, London

Thorborn T 1971 Cost-benefit analysis in language planning. In: Rubin J, Jernudd B H (eds.) *Can Language Be Planned? Sociolinguistic Theory and Practice for Developing Nations*. University Press of Hawaii, Honolulu, HI

Tollefson J 1991 *Planning Language, Planning Inequality: Language Policy in the Community*. Longman, London

Linguistic Census
L. M. Khubchandani

Language information in the census provides a useful tool for the study of sociology of communication in general. Many countries, when conducting periodic enumeration of their populations' socioeconomic characteristics, collect information on languages in use in the society: language(s) spoken in the household, language(s) in various public domains, knowledge of languages other than one's mother tongue, and so on. The techniques applied in the census are primarily of elicitation, and are not based on participation or observation at length. Demography as such is primarily concerned with the behavior of the 'aggregate,' and not with the behavior of individuals.

The Indian census has a record of presenting a fairly systematic account of mother tongues of the subcontinent since 1881, and of bilingualism since 1931, shedding light on the ethnic and linguistic composition of populations of the vast South Asian region (now comprising India, Pakistan, Bangladesh, and Burma). It is regarded as one of the most thorough-going inquiries into social structure ever to be conducted in any part of the world. Many European censuses highlight the extent of the spread of national and minority languages in different regions (Kirk 1946, Verdoodt 1990). The Canadian census has been eliciting language information since 1901. South Africa has enumerated languages of European populations since 1918.

1. Interpreting Language Claims

Language claims in the census deal with a somewhat abstract sociolinguistic reality. The mother-tongue assertions of different groups in multilingual societies could be merely 'tips of icebergs': much more remains hidden under the surface than is revealed through an individual's declarations. A language census accounts for information on one or more aspects of speech behavior:

(a) population aggregates portraying a picture of language *usage* in a particular region or society;
(b) head counts graded on the basis of language *competence* in a variety of skills (speaking, writing, etc.) in a particular language;
(c) populations signifying unconscious attitudes and pressures of language identity, i.e., the data based on language *image*: 'what they *think* of their speech variety';
(d) populations asserting conscious alignments characterizing the signals of language *posture*: 'what they *prefer* to be aligned with' in the circumstances in a region or society.

The data implicitly reveal the scope of manipulation through language returns.

It is estimated that some 5000 languages are spoken around the globe. Because of the bias in favor of clear-cut categorization, language information in many demographic accounts is often mistakenly handled like physical data (birth, death, sex) without evaluating subjective factors. There have been two basically different approaches among social scientists with regard to utilizing the language census as a tool for social planning. First, universalists show concern for soliciting statistical information on language in standardized categories to enhance human understanding; (a) framing of language questions for eliciting precise and unambiguous responses, (b) orienting the population to provide 'objective' responses, and (c) interpreting responses (Kloss and McConnell 1974). Second, pluralists lay emphasis on the *relevance* of questions specific to a context. Responses and interpretations are regarded as conditioned by ecological and historical perspectives of different sections of society.

Statistical data on language are often interpreted differently by the authorities and by the pressure groups in many countries. Many political agencies interpret language census rigidly, i.e., evaluating language information arithmetically (such as, numerical 'majority' versus 'minority') and incorporating compulsory changes in the administrative or educational structure based on the given information; for case studies on Belgium, see Levy (1960), on Canada, Lieberson (1967), and on India, Khubchandani (1976, 1983), Mahapatra et al. (1989).

Decadal language returns of the Indian census could be taken as a useful indicator of some of the attitudes to language underlying the speakers' assertions, and reveal evasion as well as fluidity which are not always apparent on the surface. Records of the Indian census during the post-independence period show two opposing streams that suggest the following.

(a) There is anxiety to attain prestige by identifying oneself with a major language and not necessarily with one's native speech 'the first speech acquired in infancy through which a child gets socialized. It claims some bearing on 'intuitive' competence, and potentially it can be individually identifiable' (Khubchandani 1983: 45). An amazing example of this characteristic is the claim of 233 million speakers in the 1991 Census that 'Hindi' (proper) is their 'mother tongue' out of the total population of 337 million 'classified' under Hindi language (i.e., 69 percent); the remaining 31 percent speak

markedly different varieties of related languages (such as Pahari, Rajasthani, Maithili, Bhojpuri) for primary communication.
(b) There is inverted pride in 'exclusiveness,' that is, the tendency to assert one's own social identity as being distinct from that of others. Many tribal groups show this tendency because of their feeling of superiority to, or hostility towards neighboring groups.

One cannot justifiably claim to possess a standard measuring index of identifying one's mother tongue or the knowledge of other languages. The seemingly innocent questions asked in the census, 'What is your mother tongue?' could be projected as:
(a) language *first* learned or used (which favors the reporting of minority language maintenance);
(b) language *usually* used in everyday life (which favors reporting assimilation trends towards the dominant language); or
(c) *all* languages which the individual knows (which maximizes the number of speakers of the dominant language (Kirk 1946)).

Knowledge of the criteria employed is a great help in making critical evaluations of language.

Similarly, there is no clear-cut operational definition with which to quantify the knowledge of a particular language. Such knowledge largely depends on an individual's degree of awareness, subjectively interpreted on the basis of: (a) fluency, that is, spontaneity in expression; (b) intensity of use, that is, varieties of communication tasks being performed; (c) proficiency, that is, grasp of the standard variety; (d) knowledge of the script associated with that language; and so on. A perfectionist may hesitate to claim knowledge of a language in spite of having a fairly advanced grasp of that language but with which he is 'not satisfied,' whereas a trader may claim to know a number of languages merely on the basis of knowing a few phrases in those languages.

2. Politicization of Language Data

As language is primarily a time-and-space institutional reality, often political considerations such as the adjustment of district, state, or national boundaries on the basis of language tend to politicize pressure groups around language and influence the language returns of a region. Many censuses apply varying (inclusive and exclusive) criteria to boost the 'majority' claims or to minimize the importance of 'minority' groups.

Hence the tabulations of sociocultural data in a census attain only the appearance of precision. the Austrian census classified Yiddish as a variety of German (even though culturally it carries a distinct Jewish identity); since 1971, the Indian census classifies Bihari, Rajasthani, Pahari, and Chatisgarhi as Hindi. In Australia, 'Carinthian' is distinguished from the Slovenian language of Yugoslavia; Hungary treats Serbian and Croatian as separate languages, whereas the Yugoslav census treated them as one language (with bi-modal standards), Serbo-Croatian (or Croato-Serbian) until the 1980s, before the federation was split into five separate nations: Yugoslavia (confined only to the Serbian-speaking territory), Croatia, Bosnia, Macedonia and Slovenia); Russians treat Moldavian spoken on the Romanian border as distinct from the Romanian language.

Utilizing the inherent ambiguity in the terms 'language' and 'dialect,' various governments make intentional distortions in taking the censuses of their populations, such as applying varying criteria in the grouping of mother tongues into umbrella-like 'languages' or isolating them as distinct entities, as *perceived* by dominant agencies or pressure groups in a region. A normal pattern in these censuses emerges as: (a) maximization of the apparent proportion attributed to the dominant national language; and (b) corresponding minimization of the size of linguistic minorities. The British census tabulates language data in the framework of English speakers and non-English speakers, and thus the 1931 England and Wales census reported only 98,000 non-English speakers (i.e., monolingual Welsh speakers), though at the same time there were 909,000 Welsh-speaking people in the region. The 1931 Scottish census listed only 7000 non-English speakers in Scotland, though the population included 136,000 Gaelic speakers.

Fluctuations in language returns of the North-Central region in India, known as the 'fluid zone,' present an interesting case study of grouping over 330 'mother tongue' labels under a few generic umbrella labels, such as Hindustani, Hindi, Western Hindi, Eastern Hindi, Bihari, Rajasthani, Panjabi, Western Panjabi, Pahari, etc. One finds that language-*identity* patterns and language-*usage* patterns among different communities in the region are not necessarily congruent, resulting in many vacillating trends in the census declarations of mother tongues.

Shifts in declarations of mother tongue from one language to another in successive censuses, depending on the social and political climate, seem to be a frequent feature among 'fluid' speech groups in India. For example, bilingual Muslims oscillate between regional and religious identities when claiming their mother tongue. Urdu growth rates during the decade 1951–61 reveal the dramatic process of consolidation throughout the country—a 69 percent increase of Urdu speakers in India against the country's total population growth of 24.4 percent. Astounding increases in the claims of Urdu mother-tongue speakers in almost all states can be regarded as an assertion of cultural solidarity by bilingual Muslims through Urdu and the relegation of respective regional languages to subsidiary language status in their subjective evaluation of competence, in reaction to the postindependence language politics in the country. What has happened in the case of Urdu is also true of Hindi, Panjabi, Maithili, Kui, Banjari, Nepali, Bodo, and many other Indian languages. This phenomenon demonstrates the magnitude of functional heterogeneity in linguistic communication characteristic of organically plural societies.

Bilingualism claims in the Indian census, by and large, reveal the extent of pressures developed among different speech groups for intragroup and intergroup communication. In a situation of multiple choice, different factors such as heterogeneity, demands made by dominant speech groups, contiguity of language borders, levels of education, occupational specialization, urbanity, and prestige contribute to the claims of regional languages, Hindi, and/or English as contact languages in a state. Communicative pressures exerted by prominent languages in each region of India, if they can be quantified in some ways, should be very useful to evaluate the individual and collective bilingual experiences (Hindi and regional languages based on the subsidiary language claims in the 1961 Census, Khubchandani 1983). These, then, can be correlated to educational and development programs in the process of language planning.

3. As a Tool of Social Planning

Correlational studies comparing the language factor with other relevant variables can help in understanding the speech phenomenon of human behavior in more transparent terms. The language census, as a tool for scientific inquiry, can provide useful insights into the scope of linguistic and sociolinguistic studies, and in relating to the sociocultural aspects of population dynamics such as: language and dialect relationship; standardizing the units for counting speech variation in a community; conceptual fluidity regarding mother tongue in plural societies; language claims reflecting change and stability in population; language as instrument as well as product of 'cohesion' and 'distance'; attitudes regarding one's 'own' and 'contact' languages in multilingual populations; diagnosis of communication environments in different regions.

See also: Statistics: Principal Languages of the World (UNESCO); International Languages.

Bibliography

Khubchandani L M 1976 Language factor in census. In: Verdoodt A, Kjolseth R (eds.) *Language in Sociology*. Institute de Linguistique de Louvain, Louvain, Belgium

Khubchandani L M 1983 *Plural Languages, Plural Cultures: Communication, Identity, and Sociopolitical Change in Contemporary India*. East–West Center Book. University of Hawaii Press, Honolulu, HI

Khubchandani L M 1995 Linguistic censuses around the world. In: *Actes del Simposi de Demolinguistica*. Department de Cultura, Generalitat de Catalunya, Barcelona, Spain

Kirk D 1946 *Europe's Population in the Inter-War Years*. League of Nations, Geneva, Switzerland

Kloss H 1974 *The Linguistic Composition of the Nations of the World*, Vol. 1. Presses de l'Université Laval, Quebec

Levy M G 1960 *La Querelle du Recensement*. Belgian Institute of Political Science, Brussels, Belgium

Lieberson S 1967 Language questions in censuses. In: Lieberson S (ed.) *Explorations in Sociolinguistics*. Mouton, The Hague

Mahapatra B P, McConnell G D, Padmanabha P, Verma V S 1989 *The Written Languages of the World: A Survey of the Degree and Modes of Use. Vol. 2: India*. Kloss H, McConnell G D (gen. eds.). Office of the Registrar General India and International Center for Research on Bilingualism, Laval University, Quebec, PQ

Verdoodt A 1990 *The Written Languages of the World: A Survey of the Degree and Modes of Use. Vol. 3:* Western Europe. Kloss H, McConnell G D (gen. eds.) International Center for Research on Bilingualism, Laval University, Quebec, PQ

Linguistic Habitus
I. Gogolin

Pierre Bourdieu's (1981) concept of habitus denotes a modality, which enables the individual to act routinely as well as creatively and innovatively. Central to Bourdieu's theory is the attempt to describe the dynamic relationships between the structural conditions of an individual existence, the individual's activities as a product of socialization under these conditions and the open-ended yet strictly limited capacity of the individual for action. In the process of socialization (see *Socialization*), a system of permanent dispositions is created in the individual, including sensitivity as one prerequisite for personal development. This system of dispositions and sensitivity is a necessary precondition for successful social activity.

Bourdieu emphasizes a circularity between *structure, habitus*, and *practice*. Habitus functions as an awareness-matrix, an action-matrix, and a thought-matrix for the individual; however, it does not alone determine behavior. A habitus is acquired under a certain set of social conditions, which Bourdieu calls 'objective structures.' To these belong the existential requirements, which characterize and define a social class. A habitus therefore is generated and regenerated by the specific objective structures of a class, and at the same time define and redefine, generate and regenerate the lifestyle and practice of its members. Bourdieu describes this circularity as follows: habitus function as 'structured structures, which are suitable to function and work as structuring structures' (Bourdieu 1979: 167). Implicit in a habitus is a tendency toward self-stabilization—despite the fact that socialization is not completed until death. New experiences are integrated in a habitus which leads to its constantly changing form whilst remaining relatively stable.

The term linguistic habitus thus refers to the set of dispositions in the field of language: to a person's notion of linguistic 'normality' and of 'good' language, to a society's notion of 'proper' ways of language behavior, of 'legitimate' language variations and practice. The term does not describe language as a means of communication in a narrow sense, but refers primarily to the symbolic relations and signs by which language becomes a medium of power (see *The Linguistic Marketplace*). Gogolin (1994) defines the monolingual habitus, which is common to the classical European nation states as an example of a linguistic habitus. In the process of their foundation in the eighteenth and nineteenth century, the basic and deep-seated belief was created that monolingualism is the universal norm for an individual and for a society (cf. Hobsbawm 1990). This idea was disseminated and traditionalized by institutions of the nation-state: jurisprudence, military forces, political, and administrative bodies. Probably most influential for the creation and dissemination of these fundamental elements of the concept of nation state were the modern state school systems, which were established simultaneously to the foundation of the nation state as such. Linguistic homogenization was the main motive for the development of public education systems. The establishment of one national language and of a monolingual national society was (and often still is) seen as essential for the success of the nation state, especially at the economic level.

In reality, hardly any nation in the world ever had a monolingual population. In most countries—especially in the Australasian, Asian, and African world, but also in Europe—people speak more than one, often many languages (see *Bilingualism, Societal*). Despite this reality, the deep-seated belief in monolingualism as natural in a society governs individual and public opinions towards language and language practice. In the cases of European nation states, this becomes obvious in connection with immigration. Roughly one third of the people under the age of 35 years in the member states of the European Unity are migrants, speaking other languages than the national language(s) of the respective state (see *Migrants and Migration*). For example, in the year 2000, more than 350 languages were spoken by children in London schools. Nevertheless, the European state school systems act as if they had monolingual populations. The teaching is centered on the 'legitimate' language of the state or the area, that is to say the national language or the official language of the region. The other languages are rarely taught at schools; children stay illiterate in their second or third language they live in. Consequently, they are unable to develop their other languages towards the most elaborated state (see *Bilingual Education*). By these mechanisms, the hierarchy and power relations between languages become stabilized. Those who have no or less access to the legitimate language are at risk of being excluded from participation and equal success in a society.

The linguistic habitus is the governing mechanism of these processes. The notion of linguistic normality was traditionalized in history, despite multilingualism. There is no collective remembrance of these historical events; the fact that this notion once was created and implemented explicitly has disappeared from collective memory. According to Bourdieu's theory, a habitus functions the better, the less conscious its owner is about it.

A variation of the monolingual habitus seems to be at work in multilingual nation states as well, due to the fact that there is usually one selected language of power. This may not be a national language. In colonial or post-colonial situations especially, the language of power very often is not a national language, which by constitution has legitimate status. Instead, it is the language, which guarantees survival and success in the linguistic market—mainly the language of the former colonists. Whereas in Europe, the standard national languages are usually considered the legitimate variant, in colonial situations symbolic power is linked to the languages of the former oppressors (cf. Goke-Pariola 1993). The linguistic habitus ensures the relative stability of these situations, and thus contributes to the durability of societies of marked disparities in power between different social groups.

Bibliography

Bourdieu P 1979 *Entwurf einer Theorie der Praxis*. Suhrkamp, Frankfurt am Main, Germany

Bourdieu P 1981 Structures, strategies, and habitus. In: Lemert C C (ed.) *French Sociology. Rupture and Renewal Since 1968.* Columbia University Press, New York

Crystal D 1987 *The Cambridge Encyclopaedia of Language.* Cambridge University Press, Cambridge, UK

Gogolin I 1994 *Der monolinguale Habitus der multilingualen Schule.* Waxmann, Muenster, Germany

Goke-Pariola A 1993 Language and symbolic power: Bourdieu and the legacy of Euro-American Colonialism in an African Society. *Language and Communication* 13(3): 219–34

Hobsbawm E J 1990 *Nations and Nationalism since 1780. Programme, Myth, Reality.* Cambridge University Press, Cambridge, UK

Multilingual States

D. D. Laitin

A 'state' is a territorially bounded organization in the permanent business of rule. All states, at least in their early periods of development, have encompassed populations in which there are many speech communities, and therefore were in their origins multilingual states. (A multilingual individual is a person who is competent in more than one language; a multilingual state is a political entity in which there is more than one speech community.) For many states an important component in the business of rule has been to effect language change in the population within their boundaries so that all official communication can be transacted in the language preferred by the rulers. It is possible, through individual multilingualism, to have a single official language in a multilingual state. But, historically, the imposition of a single official language has fashioned monolingual societies, which provided a cultural foundation for a 'nation-state.'

A nation is a modern, socially differentiated society, in which most of the people imagine themselves to be members of a 'community.' Since uniformity of language creates an aura that all inhabitants of the state form a natural community, the homogenization of language helps to create, but is not a necessary condition for, a nation-state. Not all states become nation-states; many remain multinational, with each national community within the state relying on its own language. Societal multilingualism may persist because leaders do not seek to create language uniformity or because substantial numbers of people refuse to learn the language favored by the ruler. Why some states construct language uniformity within their boundaries and others do not remains an important research question in political science. Political scientists also seek to discern the consequences of different language outcomes in the process of state-building, especially for economic growth and democracy.

1. State Rationalization

The nineteenth-century German sociologist Max Weber used the term 'rationalization' to refer to the process of efficient and orderly rule. The development of a professional civil service, with a well-specified division of labor, was for Weber the essence of rationalization in the modern state. The establishment of sharp territorial boundaries, the standardization of the calendar, of weights and measures, and the issuance of a common currency are important examples of state rationalization.

A common language is a crucial element of a rationalization program. Legal uniformity is easier to assure when court decisions are delivered and recorded in a common language. Tax can be collected more efficiently and monitored more effectively if merchants all keep their books in the same language. State regulations can more efficiently be disseminated if translations are not necessary for compliance to take place. And territorial boundaries are easier to patrol if the population at the boundary speaks the language of its political center, one that is distinct from the language of the population on the other side of the boundary. Given these considerations, it is not surprising that rulers of states have sought to transform their multilingual societies into nation-states through policies that can be called 'language rationalization.'

Language rationalization policies usually entail the specification of a domain of language use (e.g., appeals court cases, or church sermons) and a requirement that the language of rule be employed within that domain. When rulers have established power over a territorially based speech community, they are easily able to induce some of its members to become bilingual, so as to translate documents from the language of the speech community to the language of the ruler. To the extent that political rule is stable, more and more members of the population will find it useful to learn the language of the ruling elites. Language rationalization is successful when there is a sufficient number of bilinguals among the speech communities with languages different from the official one so that the business of rule can be transacted in a single language.

In many cases of successful state building, language change is greater than rationalization would demand. On the individual level, rationalization requires only 'unassimilated bilingualism,' that is to say, that individuals use the language of the ruling elites only for specified domains. But individuals can move to 'assimilated bilingualism' where they use the language of the central elites for most domains, and use the language of their speech community only for family affairs. Finally, in some populations, 'assimilation' takes place, where virtually all members of the speech community become monolingual in the language of the political center. When this occurs, a 'nation' that is commensurate with state boundaries can most easily be imagined.

In the real world, there are no examples of the complete elimination of societal multilingualism. Certain minority groups retain their languages despite changes in the rest of the society; immigrant groups often retain the languages of their home area for some generations; and language shifts take place within a single language, yielding *de facto* multilingualism even when members of the various speech communities claim to speak the same language (e.g., African American English). Of even greater political importance, groups that had assimilated into the language of the political center may find themselves parties to a 'language revival' movement that challenges basic assumptions as to whether the country involved really is a national state. These sorts of questions persist in politics because there are no clear divisions between unilingual and multilingual societies, or between multinational state and nation-states. Ambiguity feeds political struggle.

Despite the ubiquity of minority speech communities, many states have successfully pursued language rationalization policies. Here we shall outline the processes of rationalization in France, Spain, and Japan, and discuss the anomalous multilingualism in Switzerland, which is clearly a nation-state.

1.1 Language Rationalization in France

In 1539 King Francis I issued the Edict of Villers-Cotterêts which established Francien as the only official language of the realm. At that time many related dialects, such as Norman and Picard, had more literary prestige, but the Francien dialect was spoken in the capital and the surrounding *Ile-de-France*, so it was politically more attractive. There were in the King's realm a number of German, Flemish, Catalan, and Basque speech communities as well. The many languages of the southern region, collectively called '*langue d'Oc*,' had long literary histories, and were not mutually intelligible with Francien. But the purpose of Francis's edict was not to change the language repertoires of his ordinary subjects from different speech communities; rather it was to give support to a national vernacular as opposed to Latin, which was the prestige language of education and law. The language of the court immediately changed to Francien. It was not until 1762, however, when the Jesuits were expelled from France, that Francien could replace Latin in higher education. Rationalization, then, was a long but successful process.

France nonetheless remained a multilingual state until the final third of the nineteenth century. As late as 1863, by official estimates, about a quarter of France's population spoke no French. The rigid centralization of administration organized by Napoleon, the rapid increase in enrollments in public education which supplanted the Catholic Church in providing basic literacy, and military conscription all worked to create in France a nation-state where virtually all citizens, in large part through sharing French as a mother tongue, imagine themselves as members of a common nation. The nation was not natural, however; it was created through policies of rationalization.

1.2 Language Rationalization on Spain

Spain was multilingual when the Catholic monarchs, Ferdinand and Isabella, presided over the final reconquest of the peninsula from Muslim rule. Castilian, Catalan, Basque, and Galician were the major languages of Spain. The Habsburg kings, following the treaties of Ferdinand and Isabella, respected regional differences in language and in law. Spain's wealth from overseas conquest, however, attracted artists and writers from all over Europe, and Castilian became a language of prestige throughout the peninsula. The literary florescence of the Golden Century (mid-sixteenth through mid-seventeenth century) induced well-to-do-families throughout the country to educate their children in Castilian.

It was not until 1716 and the Decree of the Nueva Planta, under Spain's first Bourbon King, Philip V, that Castilian became Spain's language for official business. A series of decrees in 1768–71 required all primary and secondary education to be in Castilian, and in 1772, all commercial establishments were required to keep their accounts in Castilian. Despite these laws, as is shown in the section on language revivals, multilingualism persists. Spain's status as a nation-state was never fully realized.

1.3 Language Rationalization in Japan

Japan, because it is an island and had insulated itself so long from foreign influence, is often described as the quintessential nation-state. Yet even in Japan, regional dialects (*hogen*) were quite distinct. The four major *hogen* groups are those of Eastern Japan (known as *Kanto*), Western Japan, Kyushu, and Ryukyu, each with subdialects. The Japanese Alps, dividing Japan east to west, helped form the most politically significant dialect divisions. There is a considerable folklore about the deficiencies and lack of intelligibility of the eastern dialect in the west, and vice versa. Over the course of Japanese history, there were many forces which sustained language differences. The seventh-century borrowing of Chinese orthography created a division between written and spoken language which lasted over a millennium. In the Tokugawa period, the establishment of the provinces, or *han*, each with its own lord who blocked open communication with rival *han*, helped to sustain regional differences. On the other hand, the *samurai*, who served as the military officers for the lords, were educated through manuals that emphasized the dialect of the capital city. It was not until the Meiji period (1867) that the notion of a Japanese standard (*hyojungo*) emerged. The Meiji rulers, through national education programs, promoted this standard, based mainly on one of the Tokyo dialects (*Yamanote*) that was heavily influenced by the eastern dialect. This composite is known as *Kyotsugo*. Even with a century of standardization, and with extensive radio and television, Japanese linguists report that people who speak some *hogen*, while they can understand *Kyotsugo*, cannot themselves speak it. Their dialect is hardly comprehensible to *Yamanote* speakers. The political organization of the Japanese state created conditions so that young students from the regions would want to use *Kyotsugo* and deemphasize their reliance on their *hogen*. Japan's nation-state was therefore, at least in part, created politically; the idea that Japan enjoyed a natural condition of linguistic homogeneity is historically suspect.

1.4 Switzerland as a Multilingual State

Language rationalization did not occur in Switzerland, which remains a multilingual state. Four languages—German, French, Italian, and Romansch—all have official status in the Swiss confederation. The key to understanding Swiss language politics is that rationalization occurred not at the political center but at the cantonal level.

Swiss national identity developed over centuries, and did so without need for a common language. From the origins of the Swiss confederation in the late-thirteenth century through the end of the eighteenth century, German was Switerzland's sole official language. In the sixteenth century, the confederation expanded into French- and Italian-speaking areas. The collapse of the confederation during the French Revolution and the installation by the French of the Helvetic Republic, led to the formal recognition of French and Italian. With the fall of Napoleon, however, German again became Switzerland's sole official language. Civil war erupted in the early 1820s, only to yield peace in 1848, in which German, French, and Italian were all accepted as national languages. In 1938, a constitutional amendment declared Romansch as the fourth national language, but it did not receive the same full rights as the other three Swiss languages. Despite societal multilingualism and a history of some language conflict, the imagined community of Switzerland developed without homogenization of the mother tongues.

Yet notions of a common Swiss culture are built upon clear notions of cantonal autonomy. Each canton is permitted to set its own language policies, and the cantons have been strong rationalizers. In 1970, 96 percent of the German Swiss lived in the German region; 92 percent of the French Swiss in the French region; and 79 percent of the Italian Swiss in the Italian region. It is extremely difficult for Swiss citizens living outside their language region to get an accredited education (public or private) through the medium of their mother tongues. Therefore migration of people across language zones has been minimal for centuries.

The rationalization of language at the cantonal level is so important to Swiss national consciousness that language is one of the few areas in which the central government supports welfare redistributions. Because the Italian and Romansch areas do not have the resources to invest in higher education and television in their languages, annual subsidies have been sent to these cantons to help authorities defend their languages.

The case of Switzerland demonstrates that rationalization of language is not a necessary condition for the creation of a nation-state; but it demonstrates as well how important language rationalization is to rulers, even in a country that has accepted its own language diversity.

2. Immigration and Language Rationalization

Nationalism, the ideology behind movements to build nations out the diverse populations within states or to create states to coincide with nations, has often been suspicious of mass immigration (see *Migrants and Migration*), which might threaten the cultural uniformity of the imagined community. Yet massive immigration has, with very few exceptions, led to intergenerational assimilation into the national language. This is so because immigrants leave their home areas—often escaping from poverty or persecution—in order to make a better life for themselves and their families than they could do in their own communities. Except in rare instances when an entire community uproots itself seeking to preserve its lifestyle in another country (for example, the Amish in the USA), each immigrant family finds itself in its new society seeking scarce jobs and limited opportunities. While each immigrant may want to preserve the language and culture of his/her home area, it would be better for him/her if some other immigrant family organized special schools and organized a supply of sufficient reading material to support the language. If every family is better off relying on someone else to help preserve the language, a 'collective action' problem ensues. The likelihood that the preservational activity will be organized is therefore low. Immigration, then, is rarely a threat to the national unity of the host country.

Research on immigrants to the USA, European states, India, and Japan all shows that the degree of love any group has or its own language can only marginally affect the timing of intergenerational shift from monolingualism in the language of origin to monolingualism in the language of the new home. In some cases, where the immigrant group fears it might be deported (southern Indians in North India), or where the immigrant group speaks the language of the political center but not of the region of migration (Andalusians in Catalonia; Russians in Estonia), evidence shows language assimilation to be much less likely. Since the 1960s, there have been political movements in immigrant communities to use the power of the state to help immigrant communities retain their mother tongues. These movements are most often led not by the immigrants themselves but by second- and third-generation citizens who seek to solidify a political bond with their own people by generating support for a popular issue. These efforts will help support 'assimilated bilingualism,' where the descendants of immigrants retain competence, albeit limited, in their language of ethnic origin, but they will not stem the general tide of language assimilation.

3. Language Revivals

Rationalization from the political center is sometimes countered by revival movements from the periphery. These movements are extremely easy to get going, in large part because language is such an emotional issue. Yet they are difficult to sustain, because while people may vote for the revival of a language in desuetude, they may not like the idea of having their own children educated in it. It is a safer investment most of the time to educate one's children in the language of opportunity rather than in a language that is considered by the descendants of its core speech community to be one of folklore but not science.

In modern European states strong revival movements have occurred in those regions where there was more economic growth in the region than in the political center. Under these conditions, an alliance could form between cultural elites who always wanted to preserve the language and the regional bourgeoisie that was interested more in international business contacts than national ones.

Successful revival movements in regions of contemporary states include Catalan in Spain, Flemish in Belgium, Kannada in India, Estonian in the former Soviet Union, and French in Canada. Successful revival movements in countries that overcame colonial rule to become independent countries include Somali in Somalia, Hebrew in Israel, and Finnish in Finland. Unsuccessful revival movements include the Celtic languages in the UK, Alsatian and the d'Oc languages in France, Maithili in India, and the indigenous languages in most newly independent African countries. A particularly long and involved revival movement supporting Landsmål in Norway had mixed results.

The successful revival movements teach us that apparently stable nation-states need not remain officially monolingual. Like Switzerland, countries can develop bases other than language to imagine themselves a community. Yet these revival movements also show us that when rationalization weakens at the center, the pressure for uniformity becomes even stronger in the region. Proposed language laws in Quebec, Catalonia, and Karnataka (where Kannada is the official language) have been far harsher in demanding uniformity than were usually the case in the states from which these regions sought autonomy.

4. Late Development and Stable Multilingualism

In states whose boundaries were settled before the nineteenth century, language rationalization was the norm. Here France, the UK, Spain, Sweden, Japan, and China are the principal examples. In Germany and Italy, following the successful nation-state models of their neighbors, nationalism meant political unification to make the language-based nation and the state commensurate. The ideology of the nation-state was so powerful that the breakup of the Austro-Hungarian empire was organized largely along linguistic lines. Nearly all states in Europe after World War I (except for Switzerland and Russia/Soviet Union) were, at least until language revival movements arose, officially monolingual.

4.1 The Former Soviet Union as a Multilingual State

European Russia might have broken up into monolingual states like Austro-Hungarian empire if it too had lost the war. But the Soviet government was able, until 1991, to retain control over a state with over 100 languages. Like France and Spain, the former Soviet Union achieved a remarkable degree of rationalization, with high percentages of the population of all regions having become competent Russian speakers. The business of central rule could take place entirely through the medium of Russian. But like Switzerland, there were 14 Union Republics outside of the Russian Republic, each with its own official language. The 'titular' nationals who are the majority population in these republics have instituted language rationalization programs. Among the citizens who speak former Union Republics languages, there was considerable resistance to the learning of

655

Russian. Whether there exists an imagined community among these now-independent republics that can override language differences remains to be seen.

4.2 Rationalization in Settler Colonies

In the settler colonies of Australia, New Zealand, and North and South America, the language of the settlers dominated the language of the autochthonous populations, who were excluded from political representation in the period of state formation. Only in the case of Paraguay has an autochthonous language (Guaraní) taken on an important official role. There have been language revival movements elsewhere, but none with any important success. The settler colonies followed the pattern of early developers.

4.3 The Postcolonial Multilingual State

Countries that achieved political independence after World War II have established a new norm, that of the multilingual state. Two factors account for the establishment of the norm of multilingualism for the postcolonial states. First, by the twentieth century, an essential part of the business of rule was to provide public education to all citizens. Heads of state were no longer just interested in efficient extraction of taxes or in the basic provision of infrastructure (e.g., roads and irrigation systems). A highly literate population became associated with economic growth and political power. Ministers of education in multilingual societies recognized the near impossibility of providing literacy in a single language, and they pressed for the state recognition of language diversity.

A second factor which helped sustain multilingualism in these late-developing states has to do with the colonial experience. Countries in Africa and Asia had, under colonial rule, modern bureaucracies before they had political independence. These bureaucracies operated in the colonial language. Students from the colony who were able to learn the colonial language got positions of power and prestige in large part due to their language competence. Once these countries received independence, these bureaucrats were essential to implement the policies of the new nationalist leaders. Yet they had an interest in maintaining the colonial language as the language of administration and higher education. Leading bureaucrats overemphasize the difficulties and political inequalities that would result from the choice of an indigenous language as the sole official language of government. This bureaucratic pressure has made the choice of a single official language quite difficult. A standard compromise has been to rely on the colonial language as *official*, but to elevate one or more indigenous languages as *national*, and to have them play a symbolic role in political life.

4.4 India and the 3 ± 1 Language Outcome

India is a postcolonial multilingual state that is not moving toward rationalization or to linguistic uniformity. During its independence struggle, the Congress Party leaders assumed that upon achieving independence, some form of Hindi should be India's official language. But the Indian Administrative Service and other bureaucratic agencies operated entirely in English, the language of colonial rule. Officials in these agencies had a strong interest in preserving English as the language of administration. Although the Indian constitution called for the imposition of Hindi as the All-Union language 15 years after independence, opposition from bureaucrats and from citizens in non-Hindi-speaking areas indefinitely delayed the change. Consequently, there are now two All-Union languages, each of which can be used for official dealings within the Indian state.

Meanwhile, during the 1950s, citizen pressures at the regional levels compelled the government to redraw federal boundaries consistent with language zones. Each state has an official language today, and most of them are zealously pursuing language rationalization policies within their states. By one official measure, as of 1980, only 2.7 percent of the Indian population has as its primary language a language different from the official language of their state. The Indian constitution, however, assures all minorities the right to an education in their own language.

India thus has a multilingual state in which citizens who wish to have a broad range of mobility opportunities must learn 3 ± 1 languages. English and Hindi are necessary languages for a communicating with the central state. It is necessary as well to speak the language of the state in which you live. This makes for a 3 language outcome. A citizen of Tamil Nadu must learn English, Hindi, and Tamil to be able to operate in a wide range of activities within India.

Those citizens who live in states where Hindi or English is the official language need learn only $3-1$ or 2 languages. Citizens who are language minorities in some states (e.g., Marathi speakers in Karnataka) must learn $3+1$ languages: Hindi, English, Marathi, and Kannada. Thus, there is a range from 2 to 4 (i.e., 3 ± 1) languages that citizens must know. The result has become accepted by most groups in India, and therefore it is probable that India will remain a multilingual state.

4.5 Other Postcolonial States

Many other postcolonial countries, including Nigeria, Kenya, and the Philippines, may follow India's track, with a colonial and an indigenous language sharing central stage in the business of rule. In others, such as Algeria and Zimbabwe, the colonial language will remain as a lingua franca, but not at the expense of the continued official reliance on indigenous languages, at least on the regional level. Some post-colonial states, such as Indonesia, Cambodia, Malaysia, Tanzania, and Somalia, are on the road toward rationalization. The situation in these countries remains fluid and merits continued observation.

5. Political Implications of State Multilingualism

Throughout this discussion state multilingualism was considered as an outcome of social, economic, and political processes. Political scientists and sociologists have also studied multilingualism as a causal factor explaining political and economic outcomes. This research is not fully developed, and clear patterns have not been specified.

5.1 Multilingual States and Economic Growth

Simple correlational studies have shown that multilingual states are less advanced economically than linguistically unified states. However, these correlations are spurious, because so many early developers have become linguistically unified and so many late developers are multilingual. The causal variable here seems to be timing of development rather than level of multilingualism. It is known that multilingualism is not a barrier to economic dynamism, as can be seen in from Switzerland. But the precise role of language diversity for economic dynamism remains to be specified.

5.2 Multilingual States and Democracy

Political science approaches to democratic theory originally emphasized the importance of language uniformity for democratic stability. It was thought that because democracy requires public participation in open debate this would be difficult to sustain when citizens are unable to communicate effectively with each other. More recent models of democracy, sometimes termed *consociational*, suggest that decentralized systems, in which each language community has considerable autonomy, are a viable form of democracy. Belgium and Switzerland are used as models for decentralized democracies. Since the 1970s, with the Catalan and Basque languages in post-Franco Spain, and with French in Quebec, it can be seen that while multilingual states may suffer considerable tensions in managing democracies, multilingualism itself does not preclude democratic stability.

While rationalization of language may have some association with democracy, the process of rationalization necessarily entails the curtailment of minority rights. The suppression of Welsh in Britain, of Catalan in Spain, and of Alsatian in France was not done in a democratic spirit. Leaders prompting similar decrees seeking to rationalize Amharic in Ethiopia and Malay in Malaysia have been accused of contravening basic democratic rights of minorities. In twentieth-century state-building, democrats will be compelled to adjust to multilingualism; they will not, in most cases, be able to rationalize language in their states through democratic procedures.

See also: Language Planning: Models; Language Development; National Language/Official Language.

Bibliography

Anderson B 1983 *Imagined Communities.* Verso, London
Deutsch K W 1953 *Nationalism and Social Communication.* MIT Press, Cambridge, MA
Haugen E I 1966 *Language Conflict and Language Planning: The Case of Modern Norwegian.* Harvard University Press, Cambridge, MA
Kirkland M (ed.) 1990 *Language Planning in the Soviet Union.* St. Martin's Press, New York
Laitin D 1977 *Politics, Language, and Thought: The Somali Experience.* University of Chicago Press, Chicago. IL
Laitin D 1988 Language games. *Comparative Politics* **20**: 289–302
Laitin D 1989a Linguistic revival: Politics and culture in Catalonia. *Comparative Studies in Society and History* **31**: 297–317
Laitin D 1989b Languages policy and political strategy in India. *Policy Sciences* **22**: 415–36
Laitin D 1992 *Language Repertoires and State Construction in Africa.* Cambridge University Press, Cambridge, UK
Lieberson S 1981 *Languages Diversity and Language Contact.* Stanford University Press, Standford, CA
McRae K 1983 *Conflict and Compromise in Multilingual Societies : Switzerland.* Wilfred Laurier University Press, Waterloo, ON
McRae K 1986 *Conflict and Compromise in Multilingual Societies. Belgium.* Wilfred Laurier University Press, Waterloo, ON
Pool J 1986 Optimal strategies in linguistic games. In: Fishman J A et al. (eds.) *The Fergusonian Impact*, vol. 2. Mouton de Gruyter, Berlin
Weinstein B 1983 *The Civic Tongue.* Longmann, New York

National Language/Official Language
C. M. Eastman

The term 'national language' refers to a language which serves the entire area of a nation rather than a regional or ethnic subdivision. As the language of a political, social, and cultural entity, a national language also functions as a national symbol (Garvin 1973: 71), recognized as the nation's own. The term may be used to refer to a language indigenous to an area as distinct from one 'brought in from outside' (Ferguson and Heath 1981: 531). The term is also often synonymous with 'standard language.' An 'official language' is a language used for the business of government, a language 'legally prescribed as the language of governmental operations of a given nation' (Ferguson and Heath 1981: 531). The terms 'national language' and 'official language' were included along with others in a 1951 UNESCO publication entitled *The Use of Vernacular Languages in Education* which outlined 10 language situations in the world which planners need to be aware of when making choices as to which languages might be most appropriate for specific purposes such as building nations, doing government business, conducting trade, teaching school, and the like.

Generally, 'standardization' is involved when a language achieves national or official status (see *Standardization*). Standardization is a process 'whereby a particular social dialect comes to be elevated into what is often called a standard or even "national" language' (Fairclough 1989: 56). Standardization is part of the process of unification undertaken by a nationalizing political, cultural, economic entity. A dialect is chosen to be standardized and then it is 'codified' by being written down in a grammar, provided with a dictionary, and accompanied by rules of pronunciation and 'correct' usage so that there will be as little variation as possible in its form. Standard English, so codified in the late 1700s, was read mostly by industrialists and their families, leading one scholar to observe that 'There is an element of schizophrenia about standard English in the sense that it aspires to be (and is certainly portrayed as) a *national language* belonging to all classes and sections of the society, and yet remains in many respects a *class dialect*' (Fairclough 1989: 56). Standard English is a class dialect in that its dominance is associated with class interests and also because 'it is the dominant bloc that makes most use of it, and gains most from it as an asset— as a form of "cultural capital" analogous to capital in the economic sense' (Fairclough 1989: 58).

Throughout the world, various legislative approaches have been taken with regard to making decisions about national and official languages. National languages are important as an aspect of ethnicity as well as of nationality. Issues having to do with media of instruction are inextricably mixed up with what languages function nationally and officially.

1. National/Official Languages and Media of Instruction

For the most part languages designated as 'media of instruction' tend to be those which have been designated as 'official.' It is less common for 'national languages' to also be used in education unless they are also 'languages of wider communication.' Generally, this is a matter of expedience since such languages have more than likely been 'standardized' and there are likely to be teaching materials available in them. Swahili and English are official languages in Kenya and Swahili is the sole national language there. Secondary and tertiary education is available so far only in English. All primary education in state schools is in the process of moving toward Swahili though there continues to be some very early level primary education in other regional languages.

In increasing areas throughout the world English, as a language of wider communication, is gradually being 'nativized.' That is, a number of different world Englishes are developing which function both sentimentally and instrumentally and may well be the future 'national' and 'official' languages of the world. In essence these Englishes, despite curricular and grammatical prescriptions to the country, are the languages of postprimary education in a number of nations. Such 'nonnative' varieties of English occur, for example, in South Asia, Southeast Asia, Africa, the Philippines, and the West Indies (Kachru 1983: 31).

2. People and National and Official Languages

In 1968, Joshua Fishman introduced a distinction between 'nationism' and 'nationalism.' Nationalism is the 'organization of the beliefs, values and behaviors of a nationality with regard to its own self-awareness' (Fasold 1988: 180). It is a matter of group pride regardless of whether the group has political power or territorial strength. Nationism, on the other hand, recognizes that '[L]egislative bodies have to formulate and record laws in some language or languages, children need to be educated through the medium of one or more languages, military and police organizations must function in one or another language' in order for a nation to operate (Fasold 1988: 181). Here political and territorial integrity is paramount. Where this is the case, nationism is best served by an official language or official languages. The interests of nationalism on the other hand are best served by a national language.

> To overstate the case a bit, a national language can be compared to the national flag. A country's flag functions almost entirely as a symbol. An official language is more like the trackage and rolling stock of a national railroad. Its purpose is more pragmatic than symbolic.
> (Fasold 1988: 181)

Essentially national languages are associated with sentimental attachments to a nation or a state while official languages make reference to instrumental attachments. That is, national languages are those which make people feel good about their country or their group while official languages are those which enable people to get things done, to do a job, to earn money, and achieve social status (Kelman 1971: 24–5). Sentimental attachment is seen by some to be more properly a matter of primordial feelings referring to the attachments 'derived from place of birth, kinship relationships, religion, language and social practices' which are natural for them, are spiritual in character, and allow them to feel an affinity with those with whom they share a common background.

People are sentimentally or primordially attached to a political entity when they see it as representative of themselves, they are instrumentally attached to it when they see it as a way to achieve what they want. A national language represents sentimental attachments by blending a need for unity with a need for having a unique language and culture, a national language is a language *of the people*. As the term is used in a nation-building context, it is 'often contrasted with the language of the former colonial overload' (Garvin 1973: 26). In Indonesia, Bahasa Indonesia is a national language while Dutch is a colonial language. The term 'national language' is also used to distinguish a language serving the entire territory encompassed by a nation as distinct from a regional or ethnic subdivision (Garvin 1973: 25). In Latin America this sense is conveyed by the term '*lengua nacional*' while '*lengua indigena*' refers to languages used within the nation in certain regions or by various ethnic groups. In Mexico, Spanish is the *lengua nacional* while Nahuatl is a *lengua indigena*. An official language represents instrumental attachments by providing a way for people to achieve socioeconomic power, an official language is a language *for the people*. Garvin (1973: 25) points out that one defining feature of an official language is that it receives official recognition by a government authority. Further, a national language tends to be also an official language while the converse is not as often the case. In Kenya, for example, Swahili is the national language and an official language while English is another official language.

When choices are made about what will be the national language in a particular nation, considerations regarding the 'need to satisfy these primordial/sentimental needs of unity and spiritual affinity' (Eastman 1983: 34) are paramount. Where there is a common language extending throughout a political entity sentimental and instrumental attachments may be to a single language. Where this is the case that language is usually a standard language.

> The real spread of a standard variety through a population and across domains of use is one aspect of standardization; rhetorical claims made on behalf of the standard variety—that it is the language of the whole people, that everyone uses it, that everyone holds it in high esteem, and so forth—are another. What these claims amount to is the transmutation of standard languages into mythical *national languages*. A political requirement for creating and sustaining a nation state is that its unifying institutions should have legitimacy among the mass of the people, and winning legitimacy often calls for such rhetoric.
>
> (Fairclough 1982: 22)

However where this is not the case language conflict may arise.

In 1988, what is known as the Recife Declaration was put forward. In consideration of the Universal Declaration of Human Rights, it focuses on the linguistic rights of groups and individuals and urges the United Nations 'to adopt and implement a Universal Declaration of Linguistic Rights, which would require a reformulation of national and international language policies.' Such a declaration asserts the need to promote the dignity and equity of all languages and an awareness of the need for 'legislation to eliminate linguistic prejudice and discrimination and all forms of linguistic domination, injustice and oppression, in such contexts as services to the public, the place of work, the educational system, the courtroom and the mass media.'

3. Language Legislation

At the same time that linguistic rights have become an issue, there are countervailing forces at work as well such as the adoption of English-only policies in various parts of the United States. Decisions resulting in naming specific languages as national or official have ramifications for such issues.

What is known as the 'Muhlenberg legend' has perpetuated the idea that German almost became the national language of the United States in 1794 losing out by just one vote in the house of Representatives. What took place was that Germans from the state of Virginia asked for some laws to be issued in German as well as English. When it came to a vote this request was defeated 42–41 and it is thought that perhaps one Frederick August Muhlenberg cast the deciding negative ballot (Heath 1981: 9).

The United States has long rejected choosing a national language yet Americans believe that they should be able to read and write a 'correct' form of American English (Heath 1981: 6). It comes as a surprise to many people to learn that the United States does not have a national language in any legal sense of the term and that there are a number of languages which may be used officially in different places. For example both French and English are official in Louisiana and have been for a long time and Hawaian is an official language in Hawaii. Only in recent years have states made laws about restricting official language use to English-only in an effort many see to be to stop the spread of Spanish. These people, such as the noted semanticist and former Senator from California, the late S. I. Hayakawa, feel that the motivation for working state-by-state toward making English eventually the national and only official language in the US is to ensure that the United States does not become another Canada. This is in reference to the bilingualism there which has a long and involved history of conflict associated with its having achieved legal status. Indeed, the very linguistic diversity that was a characteristic of the early days of the US and the bilingual tradition in schools, churches, banks, and newspapers through the nineteenth century only gave way to a tradition espousing monolingualism in English in the early twentieth century. The current push to revitalize bilingualism along with a simultaneous call for English-only seems 'to tug the future of English in the United States in different directions' (Heath 1981: 7).

Various political entities have statutes specifying a national language and official language(s). Again, in the USA, there are a number of distinct enclaves where Spanish is the main language (Little Havana in Miami, Spanish Harlem in New York City, and barrios in East Los Angeles). Even though these areas are relatively small, 'such limited territoriality can be and has been used to obtain official bilingual status for an ethnic tongue' (Mackey 1983: 183). In 1973, Spanish became official in Miami. In some parts of the world, percentages of population define 'official minority' status with accompanying language rights. In Finland, if a group comprises 6 percent of the population its language may be accorded 'official status.' In the US constitution, all children of US citizens are granted the right to equal opportunity for public education—including those whose home language is other than English. This amounts to what is known as 'individual official bilingualism' in contrast to the Canadian situation of 'institutional and territorial official bilingualism' (Mackey 1983: 184).

It is rather ironic that '[W]ithout either constitutional or subsequent legal declaration or requirement that English is the *Official* (let alone the *National*) *Language*, a complex web of customs, institutions, and programs has long fostered well-nigh exclusive reliance upon English in public life' (Heath 1981: 517) and a concomitant loss of ethnic languages by members of many groups.

In India, a number of Articles of the constitution (Articles 120, 343, and 344) have to do with official language matters. Articles 120, 343, and 344 'deal with the use of Hindi as the official language of the Union in the parliament and for other official purpose' (Dua 1985: 200). These articles provide for a progressive increase in the use of Hindi and a restriction on English such that Hindi will replace English in 15 years as the sole language of the Union (i.e., as the 'national language' of India). Other constitutional provisions provide for a number of regional languages (including Hindi in its region) having official status in state legislatures. There is a provision whereby the President of India may recognize any language as an additional *official* language for specific purposes or in specific areas (Dua 1985: 201). Such recognition is not frequent given that all but 2.7 percent of the country's people have the language of their state as their primary language (Laitin 1989: 420). In the meantime, English is an associate official language according to the Indian constitution (Kachru 1981: 23). It has become apparent that the constitutional efforts to replace English with Hindi may well run into difficulties due to the practical necessity of the Indian High Court having sanctioned regional state policies. In India there is likely to continue to be many national and many official languages.

If it were to happen that another language became official in the USA, such status would entail citizens' rights to use that language and to expect officials to use it in return in interaction with them. As Mackey observed, 'With more than a quarter-million faceless federal bureaucrats answering the public, someone's language rights are bound to be infringed upon sooner or later' (Mackey 1983: 202). In Canada, precisely to safeguard citizens versus the bureaucracy in exactly this situation, the Official Languages Act provides for a Commissioner of Official Languages who answers 'directly to the people through their representatives in Parliament' (Mackey 1983: 202). Part of this commissioner's ombudsman role is to issue annually a report of failures to enforce Canada's official bilingualism. Constitutionally, the USA has the power to create ethnic states which could have their own national as well as official languages so that there might be, for example, a Spanish state or a French state (Mackey 1983: 203). So far states have only opted for making these languages official—including states which have recently passed English-only legislation.

4. The Struggle for Language Rights

Just as the distinction between national and official language may be seen to parallel a distinction between symbolic and functional language attachments, and between nationist and nationalist goals, a parallel may also be seen when it comes to the use of language. The requirements of a national and an official language differ. The best choice of an official language is often that of the former colonial rulers which most likely set up the polity's system of government in that language. Such a colonial linguistic legacy as a new nation is being forged from a colonial past allows for nationist tasks to be 'carried out with the least disruption' (Fasold 1988: 182). This same language, however, 'is an absolutely atrocious choice as a national language' for '... Nothing could be a worse symbol of a new nation's self-awareness than the language of a country from which it has just achieved independence' (Fasold 1988: 182). However, if the national language of a newly independent nationality is the same language as that of the former colonialists, that language (newly nativized) would work well as both the national and official language of the new nation.

The functional versus symbolic distinction between national and official languages may also be seen clearly when it comes to *bi*- and *multi*-lingualism. Functional bilingualism is served in the USA, for example, by having safety signs on airplanes in both Spanish and English—that is, they 'might actually save lives' (Mackey 1983: 193). Symbolic bilingualism, on the other hand, is served, for example, by having all signs in both Spanish and English even where it makes little difference as on street signs or in monolingual areas. Functional bilingualism is a matter of official language use, while symbolic bilingualism is a matter of national language use.

5. National 'National' Languages

Above, it was noted that national languages are often official as well while official languages are less often national languages. However, there is one sense of the term 'national' language that complicates matters. For some the term applies to what is often thought of as a 'vernacular' language. A vernacular is the first language of a group which has been socially or politically dominated by a group with a different language. For example, in Kenya a very well known author, Ngugi wa Thiong'o, has urged 'that the label *national language* be applied to the languages usually called *vernacular* to maintain the idea that ethnic groups in Kenya are all equal as political, social, and cultural entities and are not dominated by any one group with a different language' (Eastman 1983: 6). This usage is in keeping with the definition of 'national language' mentioned in the introduction above as being indigenous rather than imported. Similarly this usage of the term is in conformity with situation in India where the Union has a national language (Hindi) and two official languages (English and Hindi) and the various states in India each have their own national (regional, indigenous, ethnic) language and various official languages.

In fact in Kenya, opinions have long been expressed that the country needs its own national language based upon the Kimvita dialect of Swahili as spoken in Mombasa, Kenya, rather than adopt the standard form of Swahili based upon the Kiunguja dialect of Zanzibar in Tanzania. Some feel that the relative lack of success Swahili has achieved in Kenya as its national language compared to Tanzania is a matter of Kenyans feeling 'indisposed towards having to give continued preference to forms that are not their own' (Harries 1983: 128). However, instead it might be that the ideology associated with a national language disfavors indigenous languages in favor of developing localized, nativized, and nationalized versions of colonial official languages in recognition of the need to get the nation built as well as to develop nationalistic feelings.

As should be clear from much of what has been said here, there are practical advantages to choosing former colonial languages to be used for official purposes including the fact that they are commonly languages of wider communication which have developed into international languages as well. In their postcolonial territories they often begin to express the new nationalities that have emerged by nativizing in that new setting. In such a manner:

> Indian English, Jamaican English, Philippine English, Singapore English, Nigerian English etc., have become firmly established on the linguistic map of the world; and like American English they are moving in the direction of becoming a powerful symbol of national identity, which in multilingual and multicultural countries such as India or the countries of Black Africa none of the native languages could ever be.
>
> (Coulmas 1988: 18)

Indeed in sub-Saharan Africa, the official language of most nations is the international language in which the nations were formerly governed; French in French and Belgian colonies; English in British territories, Portuguese in Mozambique and Angola. Yet in the nations where these international languages are official relatively few people outside of urban areas know the languages. Choice of an outside language as official has much to do with its neutrality with regard to internal conflicts and everyone, at least theoretically, has an even chance of access to it. However, it is more often the case that certain ethnic groups in an emerging nation will have had more training by missionaries or the military or even by governing officials prior to independence, and members of the traditional elite, as well, may have had a headstart. Indeed to some extent one may define 'elite' in such a context as 'the select speakers of the official language' (Myers-Scotton 1989: 9). This situation allows such people to maintain their status as members of the elite in opposition to others who may have a different power base and who may well argue for the development of national 'national' languages rather than localized, nativized, or nationalized forms of the international official language.

> As a symbol of their own legitimacy, these proto-elites do not seek to acquire the attributes of the elite, including their language use patterns. Thus, disparities in linguistic repertoire across groups can be seen as an indication of contemporary class conflict. An obvious

place for conflict is between an education-based elite which controls the infra-structure of the public sector and those proto-elite with an economic base.

(Myers-Scotton 1990: 11)

See also: Nationalism and Language; Language Planning: Models.

Bibliography

Coulmas F 1988 What is a national language good for? In: Coulmas F (ed.) *With Forked Tongues*. Karoma Publishers, Singapore

Dua 1985 *Language Planning in India*. Harnam Publications, New Delhi, India

Eastman C M 1983 *Language Planning*. Chandler and Sharp, Novato, CA

Fairclough N 1989 *Language and Power*. Longman, London

Fasold R 1988 What national languages are good for. In: Coulmas F (ed.) *With Forked Tongues*. Karoma Publishers, Singapore

Ferguson C A, Heath S B (eds.) 1981 Glossary. In: Ferguson C A, Heath S B (eds.) *Language in the USA*. Cambridge University Press, Cambridge, UK

Fishmann J 1968 Nationality-nationalism and nationnationism. In: Fishman J, Ferguson C A, Das Gupta J (eds.) *Language Problems of Developing Nations*. Wiley, New York

Garvin P L 1973 Some comments on language planning. In: Rubin J, Shuy R (eds.) *Language Planning: Current Issues and Research*. Georgetown University Press, Washington, DC

Harries L 1983 The nationalisation of Swahili in Kenya. In: Kennedy C (ed.) *Language Planning and Language Education*. Allen and Unwin, Winchester, MA

Heath S B 1981 English in our language heritage. In: Ferguson C A, Heath S B (eds.) *Language in the USA*. Cambridge University Press, Cambridge, UK

Kachru B 1981 American English and other Englishes. In: Ferguson CA, Heath SB (eds.) *Language in the USA*. Cambridge University Press, Cambridge, UK

Kachru B 1983 Models for non-native Englishes. In: Kachru B B (ed.) *The Other Tongue*. Pergamon Press, Oxford, UK

Kelman H C 1971 Language as an aid and barrier to involvement in the national system. In: Rubin, Jernudd (eds.) *Can Language Be Planned?* University Press of Hawaii, Honolulu, HI

Laitin D D 1989 Language policy and political strategy in India. *Policy Sciences* 22: 415–36

Laitin D D 1992 *Language Repertoires and State Construction in Africa*. Cambridge University Press, Cambridge, UK

Le Page R B 1964 *The National Language Question: Problems of Newly Independent States*. Oxford University Press, London

Mackey W F 1983 U.S. Language status policy and the Canadian experience. In: Cobarrubias J, Fishmann J A (eds.) *Progress in Language Planning*. Walter de Gruyter, Berlin

Myers-Scotton C 1989 Elite closure as a powerful language strategy: The African case. In: *Paper presented at the Colloquium on the Comparative Study of Ethnicity and Nationality, April 19*. University of Washington, DC

Schiffman H 1996 *Linguistic Culture and Language Policy*. Routledge, London

UNESCO 1951 The use of vernacular languages in education: The report of the UNESCO meeting of specialists, 1951. In: Fishman J A (ed.) 1968 *Readings in the Sociology of Language*. Mouton, The Hague

Nationalism and Language
L. Greenfeld

The understanding of the relationship between nationalism and language hinges upon a clear definition and grasp of the nature of nationalism itself. Though the body of literature dealing with this important phenomenon is vast, so far it has not been properly understood, and as a result the connection between it and other phenomena with which it is commonly associated often appears more problematic than it actually is. This article first presents the conventional view of nationalism and its relationship with language, in which language is seen as a determinant of nationality; then proposes an alternative position; describes the context in which the conventional view emerged; and, finally, provides some important examples of the development of national languages and the influence of nationalism on language.

1. The Conventional View of the Relationship

Of all the institutions which mark a common nationality, language is the one of which a people is most conscious and to which it is most fanatically attached. It is the one conspicuous banner of nationality, to be defended against encroachment, as it is the first object of attack on the part of a power aiming to crust out a distinction of nationality among its subject peoples.... With few exceptions the European nationalities are essentially language groups; and [for some of them] language is the admitted criterion of nationality.

(Buck 1916)

This view, expressed in an article published in the *American Political Science Review* during World War I (Buck 1916), remains dominant in regard to the relationship between nationalism and language (see Anderson 1983, Gellner 1983, Smith 1986 for some contemporary expressions). At the root of this view lies the assumption that the world is naturally divided into separate and self-contained nations and that national identity and consciousness emanate irresistibly and without any assistance from objective national endowments—endowments that are necessarily unique to the given nation—which fall into two categories: either 'ethnic' or geopolitical. This assumption, in turn, derives from a misguided definition of nationalism as a modern form of a generic identity, identity as such, a psychological rather than cultural (or symbolic) phenomenon: 'a high degree of psychological coherence,' or 'group unity which has developed in a given aggregate of people,' on the basis of 'objective or substantive conditions,' the 'very real factors of nationality which make for the separateness and identity of various nations, such as 'the sharing of a common language, the occupation of a territorial area which constitutes a natural unit,' common religion, common mores, and common interests (Potter 1975).

The 'ethnic' attributes which are believed to 'generate nationality include physical type, religious and secular traditions, and language (see *Ethnicity and Language*). Of these, language is most regularly referred to. Excessive concentration on physical type is avoided first of all because of its biological—and therefore, potentially racist—connotations, but also because of its empirical ambiguity. Secular traditions are almost as intangible and hard to use as an explanatory variable, while, on the other hand, with five major religions shared by hundreds of officially recognized and aspiring nationalities, religious traditions which can be defined with precision are also entirely unhelpful in explaining national diversity. Language appears not to have such disadvantages and for this reason is frequently regarded as the ethnic determinant of nationality, one's nationality being, as in the quotation above, considered coterminous with one's linguistic group.

Yet there is no one-to-one correspondence between language and nationality, which should necessarily exist if language is the determinant of nationality. Obvious counterexamples are, on the one hand, Switzerland, in which several linguistic groups—French, German, Italian, and Romansch—emphatically claim the same national identity, and on the other hand, the nation of the USA, which shares its language with the UK, from which it dissociated itself in a most dramatic and unambiguous manner. Indeed, so glaring is the contradiction between the experience of the American nation, which happens to be the nation of a great many contemporary students of nationalism, and the prevailing view of the nature of national phenomena, that many are dubious as to the very existence of American nationality. Those who believe in it feel obliged to defend their position in elaborate disquisitions, often apologetic in tone.

To assert that the American nation is a nation like all other nations is an act of intellectual audacity.

Some abandon the futile attempts to fit cases conspicuously inconsistent with the theory into its framework, and see nationality as determined by geopolitical factors rather than by 'ethnicity.' This, however, does not solve the problem: the relationship between state-formation, centralization, and even territory, on the one hand, and national identity, on the other, is as inconsistent as that between nationality and language, and there is as little evidence to support an emanationist theory of the geopolitical variety, as that of the ethnic or specifically linguistic sort.

2. The Nature of Nationalism

Nationalism is a cultural, not psychological, phenomenon. Like many other stimuli, it arouses psychological responses, and therefore has psychological manifestations. But its specificity (what makes it what it is and distinct from other forms of identity) lies not in the specificity of responses aroused—which, in fact, are not specific to it—but in the specificity of the symbolic stimulus. A nation is not 'a body of people who feel themselves to be one,' it is a collectivity defined and seen (a collectivity the very essence of which consists in the way it is defined and seen) by its articulate members as one in which every member is fundamentally equal to any other. In fact, there are no objective foundations for nationality. Empirical study reveals that all nations—as nations—are artificial constructions. Nationality is not natural. Every social group has an identity, but nationality is not any identity, national identity is an identity of a particular kind and its development in any given society is not socially, biologically, or otherwise imperative. Instead it is in every case a product of an historically distinctive situation. The only foundation of nationalism as such is an idea, it is a particular perspective, or a style of thought. The specificity of national—as opposed to other—identities consists in that these identities derive from membership in a 'people,' a mass of somehow bounded population, whose boundaries and nature are defined in various ways, but which is always perceived as larger than any concrete community, and as fundamentally homogeneous and only superficially divided by status, class, or locality.

It is significant that the word *people* came into its modern use with the emergence of national identities. As a synonym of the 'nation,' it acquired the meaning of the supreme object of loyalty, the bearer of sovereignty, and the basis of political solidarity—and lost its previously common meaning of 'rabble.' The meaning of the word *nation* when this happened was that of 'an elite of representatives.' This, a result of a long history of semantic permutations, was the legacy of medieval church councils where representatives of various ecclesiastical and secular potentates were referred to as 'nations' (Zernatto 1944). In this meaning of 'an elite' the word *nation* was applied, in England, in the sixteenth century to the population of the country. The equation of the two concepts ('people' and 'nation') in fact signified the symbolic elevation of the populace to the position of an elite, and reflected a tremendous change of attitude; it meant that, for some reason, members of all orders, including the highest, wished to identify with a group from which earlier they in no uncertain terms strived to dissociate themselves. The word *nationalism*, which was first used at the end of the eighteenth century, when several societies were simultaneously in the process of conversion to national identity, is an umbrella term for this new attitude. It refers to the novel political and cultural discourse which asserts this principle (of identification with the 'people') as the basis of national identity.

The birth of nationalism was the breakthrough to democracy, and cannot be understood apart from this political meaning. As nationalism spread, the original equivalence between it and what came to be called 'values of the democratic society' was lost, but it still connotes the new, fundamentally leveling, populist, or demotic, attitude. This derivation of identity from membership in a large and essentially uniform population, is common to all nationalisms that have been emerging since the process first started. Apart from this perception of the source of identity, as the vast literature on the subject attests, different nationalisms share little. The national populations—variously titled *peoples*, *nations*, and *nationalities*—are defined in many ways, and the criteria of membership in them vary. This variation is the source of the protean nature of nationalism and the difficulty, even the impossibility to define nationalism by reference to any of the attributes frequently associated with it. Only the subscription to the same principle of identity justifies treating all these varieties as instances of the same general phenomenon. At the same time, derivation of identity from membership in a people distinguishes nationality from other types of identities. In this national identity differs from religious identity, for the latter derives from the transcendental beliefs of the individual, of which membership in a religious community is, essentially, a result. And since the notion of 'people' cuts across divisions of class and locality, and is, however stratified in fact, perceived as fundamentally homogeneous, and the divisions are perceived as having secondary importance, national identity also differs from class, estate, and local identities which emphasize these divisions as essential.

The only generalization possible regarding the emergence of nationalism in different societies is that the incentive for its creation or adoption is invariably provided by the structural condition of 'anomie'—the lack of correspondence between the traditional definition of the social order and the involved agents' place in it, on the one hand, and the changing reality, on the other. This anomie may, but need not, affect the society at large; it does, however, affect the relevant agents (the architects of the national consciousness) directly. These agents are different in different cases, and the anomie is expressed and experienced differently, but frequently it takes the form of a crisis of identity and/or acute status-inconsistency.

Nationalism as a new way of relating to the world emerged in medieval Europe. In all other cases the basic idea was adopted, not created anew. Because of the dominance first of Europe, and then the West as a whole, this style of thought soon became the canon. As the sphere of influence of the West expanded, societies entering it had in fact no choice but to become nations. At the same time every specific nationalism is an indigenous development. It is never imported wholesale, but is modified in accordance with the character and situations faced by every importing group. Every specific nationalism is the end result of these modifications. That is why, while nationalism everywhere has a certain equalizing influence on social life, and changes at least the form of the political discourse and procedure in the direction of democratization, different nationalisms affect the respective societies harboring them in fundamentally different ways.

National, as any other, identity frequently utilized the available primordial or 'ethnic' characteristics of a population, such as language, which contributed to its sense of uniqueness. Yet it should be realized that such characteristics in themselves do not constitute an identity, but represent elements which can be organized and rendered meaningful in various ways, thus becoming parts of any number of identities. The possession of an identity and a sense of uniqueness, however formed, in turn in no way necessitate the emergence of a national identity. As much as language, these are universal attributes of human groupings; in distinction, national identity is an historically circumscribed, modern phenomenon, and cannot be explained by its association with such universal attributes. Any one ethnic element serves as the raw material for the national identity only if interpreted as an element of nationality, namely when the principle of nationalism is applied to and bestows on it a new significance.

3. The Origin of the View of Language as the Determinant of Nationality

The idea of language as the determinant of nationality, then, is a myth, and as any myth it reveals more about what its creators sought to see in reality than about what there was to see. In general, the notion of nationality as a sense or a fact of objective identity, based on objective attributes of a people, whether ethnic or geopolitical, is not a result of empirical study, but of an uncritical acceptance of the European, specifically German, view of nationality, developed by early nationalists and perpetuated in historical scholarship and theories of various social sciences, deeply influenced by German academic traditions. The idea of language as the expression of a people's uniqueness and the basis of national consciousness and identity has its roots in Pietism, a religious tradition which represented a profound formative influence on German nationalism and a movement with a wide appeal and numerous converts within every class of society (see Pinson 1934). Pietism was a variant of religious mysticism which became a widespread phenomenon in Germany after the Thirty Years War and was a response to the misery caused by it. Under its proper name the movement emerged in 1675. An outgrowth of the Protestant Reformation, it was opposed to the established orthodoxy, and represented the adaptation of the dogma to the aspirations, situations, and constraints of the population that adopted it. As mysticism in general, Pietism was a by-product of the attempt to use the official religion (in this case Lutheranism) as a practical philosophy: the means of rendering the existing order of things, in which suffering was the main element, both meaningful and livable. It was a religious ideology of a static society, whose members were unacquainted with worldly success, but intimate with hardship and disaster, which in the form of disease or poverty seemed always to wait around the corner, and which thus fostered a fatalistic outlook. Powerless to change their condition, Pietists interpreted it as a sign of grace. Their misery itself, the 'humility and abnegation' which most of them could not escape if they tried, became a proof of '*certitudo salutis*,' and was freely chosen.

The immediate knowledge of salvation manifest in misery not only led to passive acquiescence with fate, but was actively sought. Election could be proven by active piety and by emotional experience of unity with Christ. Emotionalism was the central characteristic of Pietism, and its counterpart was scorn for doctrine and theological learning, for these did not contain the certainty of salvation. A logical consequence of the de-emphasis of dogma and the view of religion as a personal unity with God was broad tolerance of the forms of Christian worship. Theoretically at least, all forms were legitimate, so long as the faith was sincere, idiosyncrasy being in fact a sign of naturalness, sincerity of faith. The counterpart of this position on a collective level was a new respect for the forms of worship characteristic of ethnic communities (of Christians), and a novel, mystical idea of native language, the vernacular which, in Protestantism, replaced Latin as the medium of worship. Ethnic communities were unique, peculiar expressions of God's love and wisdom. Therefore, it was a matter of Christian piety to preserve one's uniqueness. The mother tongue, in particular, acquired the dignity of the channel through which God manifested himself to a people, the peculiar, individualized link between the deity and a specific community. It was thus sanctioned and acquired value beyond instrumental utility. This mystical idea of language as a peculiar bond with God first appeared in the thought of Jacob Boehme.

The central notions of Pietism were appropriated and secularized by Romanticism, which was thus able to perpetuate them in the age which was becoming increasingly indifferent to religion. The architects of German nationalism were Romantics, and it was through Romanticism that Pietism exercised its most potent influence on German national consciousness. For the nationalists 'of Pietist formation,' who no longer believed in God, uniqueness retained its ultimate value. The innermost unique character of a nation—its individuality—was faithfully reflected in its language, and the German tongue, it was claimed, differed from the rest in that it was not contaminated by borrowings from other languages, but remained pure. In Fichte's words, it was the *Ursprache*, the original language. In the early nineteenth century German language became an object of worship. It was a favorite theme of patriotic poetry. Arndt's *Des Deutschen Vaterland*, one of the most popular examples of such poetry, defined Germany as the realm of the German language. 'Turnvater' Jahn, whose zeal for the perfectly German body did not blind him to the importance of its spirit, but whose obsession with the necessity to combat foreignisms in the German language cast doubt on the much advertized purity of the latter, proclaimed in *Das Deutsche Volkstum*: 'A people is first made into a nation by its mother-tongue,' and called on the State to use the knowledge of German as a qualification for citizenship. In the mind of the creators of the German national consciousness, however, the language, deeply revered as it was, was but an epiphenomenon, a reflection of race, 'the indisputable testimony of common descent.'

German was not the only language to be praised for its purity. Already in the fifteenth century, at least three centuries before the advent of national consciousness in France, but when the sense of a uniquely French (not national) identity was already developed in certain circles, French was similarly belauded. An admirer, Jean de Montreuil, though writing in Latin, extolled its merits as superior to other European languages of note, specifically German and English. The reason for such superiority, thought Montreuil, was the purity and originality of French, in the sense that it remained true to its origins and was impervious to foreign influences which corrupted the other two tongues (see Beaune 1985). Quite apart from the fact that the purity of French, as that of German, was presumed irrespective of evidence, in the French case, clearly, the notion of the purity of the native language in no way contributed to the development of a national sentiment. It did have this effect in the case of German nationalism, because its creators were intellectuals for whom the language was the working tool and whose area of influence extended throughout its domain. It was in their interest to downplay the importance of political boundaries which divided this domain into a multitude of independent principalities, and to define the nation as a linguistic unity. The alleged characteristics of the language in this case became the characteristics of the nation.

4. The Construction of an 'Ancestral' Language

The history of the ascendancy of French deserves consideration, for it provides a particularly telling example of the historically contingent nature of the 'national' language. The French language was not originally the language of France. It was 'the French of Paris,' where indeed it was spoken. Its origin was '*francien*,' the dialect of '*Francie*,' the territory between Somme and Loire, which is the tenth and eleventh centuries constituted the domain of the Counts of Paris, the progenitors of Capetian kings. It was neither spoken nor, apparently, for a long time written in the other parts of France. The literary production in the vernacular was predominantly Anglo-Norman in the eleventh and twelfth centuries, and Picard, Champenois, Bourguignon in the thirteenth to fifteenth centuries, depending on the province and native dialect of the authors (Citron 1987).

The linguistic policy of the Crown was not forceful. While Philip the Fair made French the language of royal edicts in the northern parts of France, in the south the administration still used Latin. Two hundred and fifty years later the Edict of Villers-Cotterets of 1539, under Francis I, extended the use of French to all official deeds. But yet another century had to pass before a Bourbon, Louis XIII, decreed in Code Michaud of 1629 its compulsory use in the registration of baptisms, marriages, and burials.

Throughout the Middle Ages the population of France was divided into at least five linguistic groups (the speakers of *langue d'oil, langue d'oc*, Basque, Breton, and Flamand, some of which were further subdivided into important dialects). This evident lack of linguistic unity, namely the conspicuous absence of the French language, was, paradoxically, a matter of pride rather than mortification for linguistic patriots; it was believed to be a reflection of the imposing size of the kingdom, which compared so favorably to that, for example, of the pitifully small England that could boast but one native tongue. The situation, moreover, in no way prevented the presentation and laudation of the French of Paris as the French language which, beginning with the fourteenth century, and in the atmosphere of the growing appreciation for 'mother' tongues in general, became an object of ardent love among scholars and men of letters—the creators of symbols of collective identity—and as a result, a central symbol of the French identity, and eventually an objective characteristic of the French ethnicity. In many parts of France, however, it was not spoken as late as the second half of the nineteenth century (Weber 1976).

The example of France, one of the paradigmatic early nations, underscores the weakness of the theory which views national identity as a reflection of an objective unity and separateness based on primordial, 'ancestral' ethnic characteristics, and specifically on language. For instance, it is clear that there is no more reason to consider French an ancestral, or native language of the French people, than to regard English as the ancestral language of Americans of non-English origins. A national language is not an inherent attribute of a given nation, rather it is claimed and interpreted as such.

5. The Influence of Nationalism on the Development of Language

While language cannot be considered as a cause of the emergence of nationalism, nationalism in many cases stimulated and directed the development of language. The influence of nationalism on language is evident, first, in the changes in vocabulary, which reflected the replacement of whatever identity the collectivity in question had previously by national identity, and the transformation of the referent of collective loyalty.

For example, the emergence of nationalism in sixteenth century England (the first crucial case of nationalism), was accompanied by the change in political discourse, clearly discernible in Parliamentary papers, and recorded in the dictionaries of the period. Between 1500 and 1650 several crucial concepts altered their meaning and came into general use. Among these concepts were 'country,' 'commonwealth,' 'empire,' and 'nation.' Somewhat later to these was added the concept of the 'state.' Previously defined as 'an elite of representatives,' the word *nation* was now applied to the people of England. The word *country*, the original meaning of which was 'county,' a locality and an administrative unit, already by the 1530s acquired the sense of 'patria,' and became increasingly used as a synonym of the word *nation*. Both *country* and *nation*, therefore, became synonymous with the word *people*, which changed its meaning accordingly. In a 1499 dictionary it could still be found only in conjunction with *common*, and *common people* meant 'plebs.' The concept *empire*, which in medieval political thought referred to the attribute of kingship and denoted supreme authority in temporal matters, lost its medieval connotations and already in the first half of the sixteenth century, due to no small extent to the separation from Rome, was increasingly understood to mean a 'sovereign polity.' It is in this sense that England was referred to at the time as an empire. The word *commonwealth*, the exact English rendition of '*res publica*,' gradually exchanged its meaning of the 'public good' or 'common well-being'—the sense in which it was commonly employed at the very beginning of the sixteenth century—for that of a 'society' and also became interchangeable with *country* and *nation*. The term *state*, was a slightly later addition to the vocabulary and, like *empire*, remained less evocative than the other new concepts. Its initial meaning was that of an 'estate' or 'domain' (specifically, the royal estate). Towards the end of the sixteenth century it acquired the meaning similar to that of *country, commonwealth*, and *nation*.

Similar changes can be observed in other emergent nations (namely, in societies in the process of substituting a national identity for the forms that preceded it). For France, where nationalism emerged in the course of the eighteenth century, some quantitative indicators of this change of sentiment and vocabulary are available. According to a limited but representative sample of the University of Chicago ARTFL database of French literature, between 1710 and 1720, and then again between 1750 and 1760 there occurred a significant increase in the employment of the related concepts *nation, peuple, patrie, and état*, which signified the transfer of loyalty to the community (from the person of the king) and nationalization of discourse. Between 1700 and 1710, the word *nation* was used in the literature only 45 times in 7 volumes out of the corpus of 20. In the next decade it was employed 106 times, in 12 volumes out of 25. Its use steadily increased, going up sharply between 1751 and 1760, when it appeared in 990 instances in 43 out of 95 volumes, and thereafter remaining on this high level. The word *peuple*, which was used 376 times between 1701 and 1710 in 12 volumes, in the next decade appeared 1782 times in 19 texts, and after 1760 became even more frequent. The word *patrie* jumped from the low of 34 instances (used sparsely in 12 texts) per decade (1701–10) to 279 in 14 texts between 1711–20; between 1751–60 it appeared 462 times, being employed in 48 volumes; there were 658 instances (in 61 texts) between 1761–70, and 806 (in 40 volumes) between 1781–90. A similar increase can be observed in the use of the word *état*, although in this case, due to the multiple meanings of the word, plain numbers are less helpful. The meanings of these core concepts changed accordingly. For example, in the dictionaries of the beginning of the century, the word *peuple* was ascribed two meanings, the general one—the sum of individuals inhabiting one country—and the particular meaning defined by opposition to the nobility, the wealthy, and the educated, that is 'plebs.' In the academic dictionary of 1777, the emphasis had changed dramatically: the general, previously neutral, meaning of the word became unmistakably positive, while the particular, derogatory sense, which was stressed in earlier dictionaries, all but disappeared. Both the explicit definition and the examples offered made the 'people' an eminently respectable entity, constituted by laws more than by anything else and the source of truth.

More important than the generation of political vocabulary was the stimulation of the development of general potentialities and expressive capacities of the language provided by nationalism. The burgeoning and triumphant English nationalism of the Elizabethan period, for instance, is chiefly responsible for the remarkable efflorescence of the English language and secular vernacular literature which laid the foundations of modern English culture. Those who contributed to this surge of cultural creativity were fully aware that it was unprecedented and sudden, and that before their time there was little to speak of in the field of English letters. Indeed, the early English authors on whom lavish praise was showered were only three—sic!—in number: Chaucer, Gower, and Lydgate. The rules of English grammar were not yet fixed, and spelling itself, as the sources amply demonstrate, was inconsistent and shifting. The Elizabethan nationalist writers saw themselves as founders of the national culture. 'We Beginners,' wrote Gabriel Harvey to Spenser:

> haue the start and aduantage of our Followers, who are to frame and conforme both their Examples and Precepts, according to that President which they haue of vs: as no doubt Homer or some other in Greek, and Ennius or I know not who else in Latine, did preiudice, and ouer-rule those, that followed them....

Yet, the unformed English tongue was an object of passionate devotion. It was loved as 'our mother tongue,' and cultivated for what it could contribute to the nation's standing—as its 'best glory.' The consummate expression of English linguistic patriotism of the period was Richard Carew's *Epistle on the Excellency of the English Tongue* (1595–96), which he wrote with an intention to prove the equality of English to the more developed languages of the time, 'seekinge out with what Commendations I may attire our english language, as Stephanus hath done for the French and diuers others for theirs.'

Rather than being sparked by language, nationalism led the patriots to focus attention on it, stimulating its systematization and development. It was patriotism, rather than the actual merits of English at the time, which led Samuel Daniel to muse in the 'Musophilus' about the great role it was destined to play:

> And who, in time, knows whither we may vent
> The treasure of our tongue, to what strange shores
> This gaine of our best glory shall be sent
> T'inrich vnknown Nationes with our stores?
> What words in th'yet vnformed Occident
> May come refined with th'accents that are ours?

But this wishful thinking eventually made English great and established it as the foremost language in the world.

Another celebrated language, the one in which some of the finest literature of all ages was written, Russian, was virtually created by nationalism. Russian national consciousness—and Russia as a nation—was born during the reign of Peter the Great (1682–1725) and to a large extent its creation was due to the aspirations and policies of this extraordinary ruler. In the beginning of his reign at the close of the seventeenth century Russia had two languages: the written Church Slavonic, remote from everyday life and intelligible only to a chosen few, and the chiefly spoken language of the mundane—Russian. Both were inadequate for the expression of the new political and social reality; so much so that at some point Peter wanted to make Dutch the official language of his state. Having, apparently, to give up this idea, the great tzar, in 1700, introduced a new, secular type (*grazhdanskaia azbuka*) and thus laid the foundations for modern literary Russian. His decrees and the writings of his close collaborators offer a glimpse into the process of forced, active formation of the new vocabulary: these documents are interspersed with foreign words with Russian endings, and their explanations in parentheses or on the margins.

For at least half a century the infant language, devoid of any agreed-upon orthography and limited in vocabulary, lingered waiting for proper direction. But toward the 1750s it became the focus of attention and devotion of non-noble intellectuals—the first group of Russian men of letters—for whom its successful development was a matter of personal honor. This group was also the first one in Russia which could be characterized as nationalist. The precocious nationalism of the non-noble intelligentsia, which manifested itself in the middle decades of the eighteenth century (1730s–1760s) was all the more remarkable because of the singular ethnic profile of this group. It is possible that as much as 50 percent of this first mass of Russian nationalists were Ukrainians. This fact merits mentioning in the context of the 1990s and adds more than a touch of irony to it, especially since these were also the creators of the Russian language.

The non-noble intellectuals were placed in a structurally imbalanced situation. Like so many other elements of modern Russian society, this intelligentsia was created by Peter the Great from scratch, for before his time there were no secular schools in the country, and all its educational needs had to be satisfied by theological seminaries. The intellectuals represented a new stratum and none of the existing definitions fit them. They needed a new perspective, a new identity, that would confirm the sense of personal worth they acquired with their education, justify their aspirations, and condemn the arrangements which left them unfulfilled. The demotic idea of the nation could answer their needs, and they turned patriots. The intellectual pursuits of this group were motivated by the desire to aggrandize Russian culture and make it comparable to the cultures of Western Europe. The efforts to develop the Russian language attested to this preoccupation most tellingly.

The ultimate expression of eighteenth-century Russian linguistic nationalism is found in the 1755 *Russian Grammar*, written by the greatest luminary of the period—Russia's first grammarian, who was also its first chemist, physicist, historian, and significant poet—'this Pindar, Cicero, and Virgil, glory of Russians,' Lomonosov. In Russian, he wrote, was found:

> the majesty of Spanish, the vivacity of French, the firmness of German, the delicacy of Italian, and the richness and concise imagery of Greek and Latin …. And if something should be found incapable of expression, the fault is not that of the language, but of our own capacity.

At the time when he wrote this, it must be emphasized, the Russian language practically did not exist. The lesser members of the intelligentsia, however, spared no effort to make Russian conform to this exalted image. A Ukrainian Samoilovich urged the creation of a Russian medical vocabulary, 'terms which are not even known in Russian'; at the same time, rather inconsistently with the recognition of the paucity of the language which this implied, he stressed the beauty and richness of Russian and quoted Lomonosov. Another Ukrainian, also a doctor, Maximovich-Ambodic 'like a bee' collected Russian words which could be used in medicine. A 'native Russian' K. I. Schepin, the first Russian professor of medicine, resolutely lectured in Russian, though, as he confessed, 'to deliver ten lectures in Latin is easier than one in Russian.' Still another Ukrainian, Poletika, compiled a comparative dictionary in six languages, juxtaposing Russian with the tongues 'considered most famous and necessary for the sciences.' The intellectuals' awareness of the pioneering nature of their efforts and the newness of the language they tried to develop went hand in hand with an immense pride in it and an unshakable belief in its colossal potential. In 1773, Svetov, the author of *Study in the New Russian Orthography*, called the language he and his associates were forging 'the new-Russian [*novorossiiski*] language' and dated it back only to the 1750s and 1760s. However, at the same time another member of the group, Popovskii, confidently asserted:

> the age of philosophy did not end with Rome: it will not refuse to talk to all nations of the following ages in their languages .... As to the abundance of the Russian language, in this Romans have nothing to boast of in front of us. There is not a thought which could not be expressed in Russian.

In the middle of the eighteenth century this was wishful thinking which had even less foundation in fact than similar paeans to the sixteenth-century English. But due to the efforts of nationalist intellectuals in just a few decades a rich language did emerge; it was to become equal to any and surpassed by none in beauty and power of expression. In the case of Russia, too, and perhaps even more clearly than in other cases, language was not a foundation of nationalism, but its product.

See also: Multilingual States, National Language/Official Language.

Bibliography

Anderson B 1983 *Imagined Communities: Reflections on the Origins and Spread of Nationalism*. Verso, London
Beaune C 1985 *Naissance de la nation France*. Gallimard, Paris
Buck C D 1916 Language and the sentiment of nationality. *American Political Science Review* **10**: 44–69
Citron S 1987 *Le mythe national: L'histoire de France en question*. Les Éditions Ouvrières, Paris
Gellner E 1983 *Nations and Nationalism*. Basil Blackwell, Oxford, UK
Greenfeld L 1992 *Nationalism: Five Rods to Modernity*. Harvard University Press, Cambridge, MA
Laitin D D 1992 *Language Repertoires and State Construction in Africa*. Cambridge University Press, Cambridge, UK
Pinson K S 1934 *Pietism as a Factor in the Rise of German Nationalism*. Columbia University Press, New York
Potter D M 1975 The historian's use of nationalism and vice versa. In: Fehrenbacher D E (ed.) *History and American Society: Essays of David M Potter*. Oxford University Press, New York
Smith A D 1986 *The Ethnic Origins of Nations*. Basil Blackwell, Oxford, UK
Weber E 1976 *Peasants into Frenchmen? The Modernization of Rural France 1870–1914*. Stanford University Press, Stanford, CA
Zernatto G 1944 Nation: The history of a word. *Review of Politics* **6**: 351–66

Orthography
M. Sebba

1. Introduction

Orthography is taken here to mean a system of characters or symbols used for writing a language, together with the conventions associated with its use. Orthography is often treated within linguistics as though it were a socially neutral technology for writing, drawing its theory mainly from phonology. However, social and cultural issues are pervasive in orthography, so that it is reasonable to speak of a 'sociolinguistics of orthography' although there is as yet not a well-developed body of theory in this area. Orthographies—an integral part of *literacies*—often become bound up with the cultural identities of their users, whether they be sub-groups (e.g., adolescent peer groups) or entire language communities; as such they can become powerful markers of group identity. In addition, orthographies have been used to establish boundaries between languages, to set distance between what might otherwise be considered varieties of 'the same' language, and to control what literature speakers of a language may have access to.

2. Two Levels of Symbolism

In writing systems, characters (for example, the letters of the Roman alphabet) are used to represent elements of the language system. For example, in an alphabetically written language like English, there is an association between the letter ⟨z⟩ and the phoneme /z/, though it is fairly easy to find exceptions, like ⟨pizza⟩ ([pi:tsa])—in this case, a consequence of language contact (see *Borrowing*). This is one level of symbolism—a correspondence, sometimes more perceived than actual, between sounds and symbols, or between words and symbols in a language with a logographic writing system.

A second level of symbolism derives from the way that writing is *used*—from the fact that it is a necessary part of a set of social and cultural *practices* surrounding and involving literacy. Writing systems become part of the social and cultural history of the communities which use them, and both the writing system as a whole, and the individual characters of which it is made up, may acquire strong symbolic associations.

For example, in the aftermath of the break-up of the Soviet Union, there have been several cases of language communities replacing Cyrillic-based writing systems introduced during the Soviet period, with older, traditional writing systems. Cyrillic itself had been introduced to some of these languages only after a period of Romanization, as the negative associations of Cyrillic from the Russian imperial era had been too strong to allow its direct introduction.

Equally strong symbolism may attach to individual letters or characters, especially in cases where group identity or boundaries are at stake. For example, in lengthy, heated debates over the best orthography for Haitian Creole, the disputed letters ⟨c⟩ and ⟨k⟩ took on symbolic significance. ⟨c⟩ was seen variously as a symbol of French colonial dominance, or, more positively, of membership in *la Francophonie*, the wider French-speaking community of nations. Meanwhile ⟨k⟩ represented cultural (and by extension, economic) independence from France, but was also associated with non-Catholic missionaries, with English, and by association, with regional domination by the United States (Schieffelin and Doucet 1994).

The processes of standardization (see *Standardization*) and prescription add a further dimension of symbolism. Where a particular standard has been prescribed, a cultural meaning can be produced by flouting it. This is well illustrated by the unconventional spellings associated with advertising, adolescent magazines, and graffiti (see below).

3. Orthographies as Sociolinguistic Problems

Sociolinguistic research has tended to address orthographic issues in two areas only: *language planning* and *education*. Fishman (1977) is an important collection on the former; Augst (1986) deals largely, but not exclusively, with the latter. The language planning literature tends to focus on how to find the 'best' orthography for a language, taking into account both linguistic and (sometimes) sociocultural factors. For most of the last century, the conventional view has been that a phonemic orthography is always preferable to a non-phonemic one. However, this leaves undecided the issue of whether the orthographic conventions should follow those of another widely used language—for example the dominant official or colonial language in the region—or should diverge as much as is prudent from that language. In the first case, literacy using the orthography would be seen as *transitional*, leading to literacy in the dominant language. The second possibility might be favored by a language community anxious to establish (or maintain) cultural independence. By making their language *look different* on the page from other, competing languages, they can assert its distinctiveness. Choice of an orthography can thus have profound social consequences in terms of future development of a language community. Educational concerns usually center around ease of learning of orthographic conventions. Teachers who find their pupils struggling with a conventional orthography are often advocates of reform; but teachers are also often opponents of reform, unwilling to act as conduits for a new set of conventions which they may see as confusing. Since the evidence about which conventions may be learnt most easily or effectively is often not very decisive, educational arguments in debates about orthographic reform tend to be overshadowed by more emotive issues relating to national and cultural identity.

4. Orthographies as Symbols of Group Identities

Particular orthographic choices may be motivated by a desire to keep languages separate, or to create symbolic distance between two similar languages or varieties. Often there is a deeper political or religious motivation for this, as in the case of Polish, which developed a tradition of using digraphs for sounds which, at the same time, were starting to be written using diacritics in Czech. The cultural and—especially—the religious divide, which separated the Poles and Czechs, meant that diacritics were unacceptable to the Poles (Rothstein 1977).

Even a single character may take on significance as a symbol of group identity. Bird (2001) describes how Bamileke speakers who are literate in Bamileke 'strongly identify' with the barred-u symbol ⟨ʉ⟩, which 'iconifies the strong cultural unity of the group with respect to the languages outside the group.' Neighboring languages have the same vowel sound, but it is written differently. Thus ⟨ʉ⟩ has come to symbolize a cultural boundary, between Bamilekes and 'others.' There are parallels here with the way that specific pronunciations of a phoneme can become iconic of a whole group (e.g., speakers from a particular class or region).

Orthographic controversies such as those in Galicia (over whether Galician should look closer to Spanish or to Portuguese: Alvarez-Caccamo and Herrero Valeiro 1996) and German (over a relatively minor spelling reform) often reflect underlying political and ideological debates and insecurities. For example, one view of the German orthographic disputes of the late 1990s is that they were about the German language itself 'as a signifier of cultural and national identity.' (Johnson 2000: 120)

5. Orthographies as Gatekeepers

A common objection to spelling reform is that it will deprive future generations of their heritage by making earlier writings inaccessible or accessible only on a selective basis. Although traditionalists may exaggerate the extent to which this will happen (for example, the opponents of the recent German spelling reform claim it will lead to a 'culture break,' although it will alter only 0.05 percent of all words in running text), orthographies have historically often been used to control what speakers of a language may (conveniently) read. Across-the-board replacement of one writing system for another (for example, replacing Arabic script with Roman for writing Turkish) will ensure that within one generation, older literature can be accessed only selectively by speakers of the language. Spelling reform is less likely to have such a dramatic effect, but can nevertheless lead to older texts being marked out as 'archaic.'

The treatment of loan words is often an issue in spelling reform. For example, most words of French origin, which are spelt in French with ⟨c⟩ may in Dutch be spelt with ⟨c⟩ or ⟨k⟩. The variants with ⟨k⟩ are often preferred by Flemish writers because they differentiate Dutch from French—an issue in the cultural politics of Belgium. The variants with ⟨c⟩, on the other hand, were favored at one time (at least in The Netherlands) because they appeared more 'cultured' than those with ⟨k⟩ did; and ⟨k⟩ may be unpopular with some Dutch writers because it is associated with German. When the Malay language was written using Arabic script, Arabic words could be incorporated easily, and their influence was pervasive. The adoption of the Roman alphabet for Malay opened the way for non-Arabic loans, and made it necessary to adapt Arabic words to the new writing system; this could be (and was) seen either as the removal of a cultural barrier, or as a threat to the traditional language and culture.

6. Orthography as Resistance

Before complete standardization is achieved, many languages go through a period where considerable variation in spelling is normal. English spelling, for example, was standardized first in printed texts—through the practices of printers and typesetters—but variation in personal, non-printed writing was the norm until a much later date. Typically, however, orthographic variation is seen as inappropriate in a standardized language (Norwegian is an exception). Difficulty for learners is often cited as a reason why variant spellings should be forbidden. The result is that few spaces exist where users of the language can legitimately use non-standardized spellings. Where these do appear, they are often the subjects of attacks by prescriptivists who use them as evidence of falling standards of 'literacy.'

In spite of the relative inflexibility of spelling conventions in languages like English, there is some scope for variation in norms. The British/American spelling divide is well known. A similar split exists between Portuguese in Portugal and in Brazil, despite an accord (1990) which was intended to prevent this.

Individuals may also use spellings which vary from the local norm. Personal names are one area where some scope exists for 'creative' spelling. Advertising is another. Non-legitimated types of writing such as graffiti are often the site of intentionally oppositional non-standard spellings. In England, adolescent graffiti often uses deliberate misspellings such as ⟨woz ere⟩ for ⟨was here⟩. In Germany, Androutsopoulos (1999) has noted that unconventional spellings correlate well with the strength of anti-establishment attitudes in small-circulation magazines read mainly by adolescents; the more oppositional the discourse, the more likely are 'deviant' spellings. In Spain, spellings which use ⟨k⟩ where the standard Castilian orthography requires ⟨c⟩ or ⟨qu⟩ (for example, *ke* for *que*) are widely used among anarchists and members of anti-establishment subgroups.

7. 'Postcolonial' Orthography

The fact that certain characters, diacritics, or digraphs may become so closely associated with a language and its users means that those symbols become candidates for removal when political changes take place. For example, Euskara (Basque) now differentiates itself from Spanish conventions by using ⟨k⟩ rather than ⟨c⟩, ⟨ni⟩ for Spanish ⟨ñ⟩, and the digraphs ⟨tz⟩, ⟨ts⟩ and ⟨tx⟩ to represent affricates.

The Dutch digraph ⟨oe⟩ for /u/—which is not shared with any other European language—was replaced in the official orthography of Indonesia shortly after independence (ca. 1947) and in the official orthography of Surinam, also in the post-independence era (1986).

However, at the same time as establishing symbolic independence from the former colonizer's language, these orthographic changes have brought the languages more in line with international practice and, arguably, with English, the internationally dominant language.

8. Conclusion

The embeddedness of orthography within the literacy practices of a culture means that specific signs, especially those which are not shared with other written languages, carry a symbolic load over and above their function as phonological or logographic symbols. One result of this is that orthography planning is as much a matter of culture (and cultural politics) as of linguistics. Another is that orthographies tend to be resistant to change, especially rapid or enforced change, like other long-standing aspects of a community's culture.

See also: Language Adaptation and Modernization; Language Planning: Models; Literacy; Oracy.

Bibliography

Alvarez-Caccamo C, Herrero Valeiro M J 1996 O continuum das normas escritas na Galiza: do espanhol ao português. *Agália* 143–56

Androutsopoulos J 1999 Displays of subcultural identity in mediated (printed) discourse. *Language and Ideology: Selected Papers from the 6th International Pragmatics Conference, Vol. I*, pp. 25–42

Augst G (ed.) 1986 *New Trends in Graphemics and Orthography*. Mouton De Gruyter, Berlin

Bird S 2001 *Orthography and Identity in Cameroon. Written Language and Literacy* 4(2): 131–62

Fishman J A (ed.) 1977 *Advances in the Creation and Revision of Writing Systems*. Mouton, The Hague

Johnson S 2000 The cultural politics of the 1998 reform of German orthography. *German Life and Letters* 53(1): 106–25

Rothstein R A 1977 Spelling and society: The Polish orthographic controversy of the 1930s. In: Stolz B A (ed.) *Papers in Slavic Philology I*, 225–36

Schieffelin B B, Doucet R C 1994 The 'real' Haitian Creole: Ideology, metalingusitics and orthographic choice. *American Ethnologist* 21: 176–200

Prescription in Dictionaries
L. C. Mugglestone

Modern dictionaries, in line with the approaches of twentieth-century linguistic study, attempt to describe rather than to prescribe lexical usage. However, many earlier dictionaries, and particularly those produced before the mid- to late-nineteenth century, were concerned rather to lay down rules of correctness for the use of individual words and meanings, and to proscribe other usages as 'incorrect.'

The desire to erect a standard language, often highlighted by the workings of Academies, such as the Académie Française in France, or the Accademia della Crusca in Italy (see *Academies: Dictionaries and Standards*) often led in these early dictionaries to a strong normative bias in accordance with prevailing attitudes of linguistic purism and codification. In terms of lexicographical practice, this is often evident in the principles of lexical selection adopted, as well as in the employment of restrictive usage labels and value judgments. Dr Johnson's preface to his *Dictionary of the English Language* (1755) can be seen to exemplify some of the notions of linguistic control behind prescriptive methods in lexicography, as in his conception that 'it is the duty of the lexicographer to correct or proscribe' the 'improprieties and absurdities' present in every language. A similar prescriptive bias underlies his decision to exclude the 'casual and mutable' diction of the merchant classes from his dictionary on the grounds that it is merely 'fugitive cant, which is always in a state of increase or decay … and therefore must be suffered to perish with other things unworthy of preservation.' Though Dr Johnson does acknowledge the futility of trying to embalm the language by means of a dictionary, the prescriptive mode nevertheless influences a number of his lexicographical practices, as in the usage labels such as 'barbarous,' 'low,' and 'ludicrous' which he adopts for those lexical usages which, though current, he disapproves of.

1. Usage Labels

Usage labeling, though not necessarily prescriptive, can often take on these implications, so that the word *lesser*, for example, is, in Dr Johnson's *Dictionary* of 1755, condemned as 'a barbarous corruption of less' in spite of its use in English since 1459. Though prescription may be less explicit in these areas in modern dictionaries, it may still operate. *The Oxford English Dictionary*, for example, appends the paragraph sign ¶, by which it designates 'catachrestic and erroneous' usage, to the word *refute* used in the sense 'deny' in spite of both the increasing currency of such a usage in the late twentieth century, as well as the accompanying use of illustrative citations from authoritative publications such as *The Observer*. Users of dictionaries, however, seem to regard the provision of usage labels as essential, and their absence in Webster's *Third New International Dictionary* of 1961 was seen as an abdication of that lexical responsibility and linguistic control popularly (if erroneously) attributed to the preserve of the dictionary. It remains paradoxical that whereas lexicographers on the whole attempt to describe usage without imposing value judgments, the users of such dictionaries tend to see them as encoding linguistic standards, with the result that the inclusion of new words is seen as a legitimization of their existence, and the necessary delay in recording new meanings of older words as proof that such changes have not occurred or are 'incorrect.'

See also: Prescriptive and Descriptive Grammar; Speech and Writing; Verbal Hygiene.

Bibliography

Landau S I 1984 *Dictionaries: The Art and Craft of Lexicography*. Scribner, New York

Reversing Language Shift
J. A. Fishman

Before the advent of sociologically better-informed sociolinguistic theory it was not uncommon to attempt to explain the waning of languages via recourse to such intuitively popular factors as 'proximity to more powerful language' (often referred to cryptically as 'geography'); 'conviction that the language be retained' (often referred to as 'positive language attitudes' or 'motivation'); and absolute number of speakers (often referred to as 'speech-community size'). The problem with such theoretically innocent explanatory attempts is that they do not spell out or relate to societal processes, whether of intra-group interaction or inter-group interaction, that is, they are basically neither sociological (and, therefore, not sociolinguistic) nor are they related to any body of disciplined inquiry or application. 'Geography,' 'attitudes,' and 'size' are all folk concepts that need to be sociologically reinterpreted and operationalized into their manipulable societal counterparts. Reversing language shift efforts are particularly in need of both conceptually integrated social theory and a structured set of priorities for application that derives from such theory. What follows is an effort along such lines.

1. What is 'Reversing Language Shift (RLS)'?

RLS constitutes that corner of the total field of status planning that is devoted to improving the sociolinguistic circumstances of languages that suffer from a prolonged negative balance of users and uses. It is not necessarily entirely an applied field of endeavor, since any hope for successful application—here as well as elsewhere—depends on the prior development of conceptually integrated diagnostic and corrective theory. The initial aim of the field of 'language maintenance and language shift' (Fishman 1964), was that the referents on both sides of the conjunction receive equal attention. Unfortunately, that has not proven to be the case and the negative process has received far more attention than has the positive one. Perhaps that is the result of a general bias, common both to modern humanistic and social science scholarship and to various ideologies of the left, center, and right alike, to assume (and, at times, even to prefer) the uniformation and massification of culture, based upon the massification and unification of the market and of modern technology across cultural boundaries. This bias focuses upon and prefers social class to ethnic stratification as the major societal accompaniment to globalization.

As a result, 'the other side (or the plus side) of the ethnolinguistic ledger' has tended to be neglected, if not ideologically stigmatized. The study of RLS represents an attempt to redress the perspective balance and to direct attention to the fact that not only are millions upon millions of speakers of small languages on all continents convinced of the creative and continuative contributions of their languages (usually their mother tongues but sometimes their historically associated religious languages) to their personal and collective lives, but that many millions are also engaged in individual and collective efforts to assist their threatened mother tongues to reverse the language shift processes that threaten or that have engulfed them (see *Endangered Languages*).

Language shift (see *Language Maintenance, Shift, and Death*) can impinge on various societal communicative functions and, accordingly, the study of RLS must be concerned with the entire sociofunctional profile of language use in any particular community under study. However, sociofunctional features of language use are neither universals nor fixed and they must, in all honesty, be established anew empirically whenever a hitherto unstudied (or not recently studied) ethnolinguistic collectivity is (re)examined. Nevertheless, due to the worldwide encroachment of western-derived modernization, it is possible to make heuristic use of a parsimonious subset of functions that tend to be rather generally encountered (except where undislocated non-western cultures still hold sway, Fishman 2001). In our discussion, below, these sociofunctions will be discussed from the point of view of RLS efforts for the purpose of attaining and augmenting intergenerational mother-tongue transmission. The intergenerational transmission of regional languages (lingua francas), of languages of wider econotechnical communication, or of religious classicals (in general, the intergenerational transmission of additional languages for special purposes) has been discussed elsewhere (Fishman 1991: chap. 12), although it should be stressed that the theoretical underpinnings of that discussion are the same as those which follows here.

2. A Conceptually Parsimonious Approach to Describing and Prescribing: The Graded Intergenerational Dislocation Scale (GIDS)

It would be conceptually parsimonious to adopt an approach to analyzing RLS situations such that it would simultaneously (a) lend itself to comparative (that is, to between-language) description or analysis; and also (b) indicate the nature (location) and intensity (seriousness) of the sociofunctional disarray impacting any particular cases under discussion.

Table 1. Toward a theory of reversing language shift.

STAGES OF REVERSING LANGUAGE SHIFT AND SEVERITY OF INTERGENERATIONAL DISLOCATION
(read from the bottom up)

1. Educational, worksphere, mass media, and (quasi-)governmental operations in Xish at the highest (nationwide) levels
2. Local/regional mass-media and (quasi-) governmental services in Xish
3. The local/regional (i.e., supra-neighborhood) worksphere, both among Xmen and among Ymen
4b. Public schools for Xish children, offering some instruction via Xish, but substantially under Yish curricular and staffing control
4a. Schools in lieu of compulsory education and substantially under Xish curricular and staffing control

II. *RLS-efforts to transcend diglossia, subsequent to its attainment*

5. Schools for Xish literacy acquisition, for the old and/or for the young, and not in lieu of compulsory education
6. The organization of intergenerational and demographically concentrated home–family–neighborhood efforts: the basis of Xish mother tongue transmission
7. Cultural interaction in Xish primarily involving the community-based older generation (beyond the age of giving birth).
8. Reconstructing Xish and adult acquisition of XSL

I. *RLS to attain diglossia (assuming prior ideological clarification)*

Simply put, RLS is in need of an approach to sociofunctional analysis which will both describe the situation and prescribe the necessary ameliorative steps, at one and the same time, in so far as the needs of threatened languages are concerned after an intergenerational period of Western-impacted dislocation. Table 1 represents an effort along those very lines.

Table 1 must be read from the bottom up, to appreciate the fact that the RLS-circumstances and efforts toward the bottom of the table represent more fundamental stages of sociofunctional dislocation. Stage 8 indicates the greatest dislocation of all (from the point of view of achieving intergenerational mother tongue continuity), namely, a language which has lapsed into general disuse sufficiently long ago that it is now in need of reconstruction from shreds of evidence that can be provided by its last speakers and other incomplete and even vestigial sources. In order to shorten the number of steps in the table (the number can be greatly increased if finer functional distinctions are desired), stage 8 also includes those languages for which ample written evidence is available but which have lost their native speakers to such a degree that these languages must first be learned as second languages before further sociofunctional repertoire expansion can be envisioned for them (see *Salvage Work* (*Endangered Languages*)). All in all, stage 8 represents maximal dislocation precisely because it constitutes Xish language use outside of natural society, that is, outside of daily effortless societal interaction among individuals actually implementing Xish ('ex-ish,' the abbreviation for any particular language undergoing shift) in their normal, ongoing, community-based ethnocultural lives.

Note, however, that no evolutionary or implicational (required) progression is implied. Even the attainment (or implementation) of vernacular cultural interaction on a community basis is insufficient for intergenerational mother tongue continuity if the community of speakers consists of individuals who are primarily past childbearing age (stage 7). Indeed, it is precisely the fashioning (attainment or retention) of Xish-implementing intergenerational and demographically concentrated home–family–community life, and the diglossic sheltering of such life from the inroads upon Xish intimacy that can stem from Yish ('why-ish,' the abbreviation for the competitively stronger language surrounding Xish), that is the *sine qua non* of mother-tongue transmission (stage 6). All efforts that come later may (and that should optimally be so regulated that they do) help shelter stage, cannot substitute for it, nor, as we will see, can they directly help stage 6 insofar as its creation or attainment are concerned. In addition certain stages (e.g., stage 5) may be totally unnecessary given certain contextual circumstances. Other characteristics of Table 1, and the underlying theory that it represents, will become clear from the ensuing discussion below, of ambivalences that often enfeeble RLS efforts on behalf of intergenerational mother tongue continuity.

In general terms, stage 6 may be viewed as the dynamic fulcrum of a field of forces. If stage 6 is not attained and vigorously retained, the less contributory to the intergenerational continuity of Xish will be the RLS efforts concentrated at other stages. Efforts closer to stage 6 are more nearly under Xish community control and, therefore, do not depend crucially on Yish support, funding, cooperation, or permission. Although the approach sketched here assumes that something can always be done on behalf of threatened languages (even for those at stage 8), it clearly implies that not everything that is done will contribute with equal ease and directness to intergenerational mother-tongue continuity. This conclusion (often a contra-intuitive one for RLS workers) will be spelled out in the three sections that follow.

3. Some Ambivalences

3.1 Ambivalence 1: The Premature Attraction and Distraction of Pursuing High Status/Power Functions

The striving toward Xish implementation in, and control of, econotechnical modernity, a striving which is so typical of the modern situation which we have assumed generally to be part of the total language shift process impinging upon Xish, leads to an overly early concentration on stages 4 through 1 among those working on behalf of RLS. Such premature efforts to cross the continental divide between *attaining diglossic L protection for Xish* and *dismantling diglossic L status for Xish in favor of diglossic H status* (or even monolingual Xish self-sufficiency) is evidenced by rushing into efforts on behalf of Xish schooling-in-lieu-of-compulsory-education and even by a stress on Xish use in the non-neighborhood worksphere, media and governmental operations. RLS efforts, which pursue such goals prematurely, are inevitably faced by several problems. On the one hand, these goals engender intergroup conflict precisely with respect to functions in which Xmen are weakest relative to Ymen and where they will most often initially require the greatest amount of Yish support and cooperation, even if only a nominal Xish presence is to be approved and funded.

Unfortunately, any nominal Xish presence in upper status and power functions will more often than not be completely overshadowed (if not totally eclipsed) by the vastly more frequent and often far superior Yish presence in those very same functions. The unequal struggle for 'recognition' in these high status and power functions frequently renders RLS efforts completely hopeless, disillusioned, and innocent of concrete results. What is worse, the overly-early concentration on high status and power goals not only does not feed back directly to stage 6 but often postpones the tackling of stage 6 until it is too late from the point of view of capitalizing on still available Xish demographic concentrations and on Xish speakers who are still of childbearing age. Trickle down theories that claim that power functions imply and guarantee intimate mother tongue acquisition and use are seriously mistaken, unless the former are specifically controlled and oriented via feed-back systems so as to constantly keep the latter at the forefront of attention and concern. It is ever thus for non-dominant Xs, where social dynamics flow effortlessly from Y to displace X but never in the reverse direction.

While the attainment of type 4a schools (primarily Xish staffed and regulated) or even 4b schools (primarily Yish staffed and regulated but intended for Xish children) certainly constitute worthwhile RLS goals, nevertheless, many Yish-dominated years must pass before the graduates of such schools can found new Xish speaking families of their own. Of course, such schools can serve to further motivate and protect stage 6, but stage 6 must be alive and well for such motivation and protection to transpire. Finally, and specifically in relation to schools, various postmodernization processes have served to render the school–home continuity relationship more tenuous than ever before (Fishman 1991: chap. 13), even for Yish, thereby rendering schools above the optional type 5 quite questionable investments of time and effort for RLS movements that are still weak and without stage 6 foundations securely under their control. Successful and constant feedback from stage 4 to stage 6 requires ongoing out-of-school and after-school involvement of school staff in most home, neighborhood, and community efforts from the earliest toddler years onward. The Maori Kohanga-Reo nursery schools did just that, with some success for Maori revernacularization.

The Irish RLS case was long a prime example of the inadvisability of disproportionate concentration on stage 4 relative to stage 6, and of the resulting institutionalization of Irish as an occasional, formal second language among the school-focused middle class. Each successive generation in Ireland has nevertheless started, and generally still starts out (even after three-quarters of a century of governmentally sponsored RLS efforts), totally without Irish when it arrives in school, rather than as a mother tongue and informal medium among members of Irish society more generally. The current case of battle fatigue among Irish RLSers, and the substantial peripheralization of their struggle vis-à-vis the interests of society more generally, can be attributed to their precipitous over-concentration on advanced GIDS stages. The latter do not spontaneously feedback to intergenerational mother tongue continuity and require substantial ingenuity (as is always the case for water to flow uphill) if they are to do so even when linkages for that purpose are kept prominently in mind.

3.2 Ambivalence 2: First Attaining and Then Overcoming Diglossia, and Doing Each at an Appropriate Time

If the headlong rush into highly improbable (if not totally impossible) serious competition with Yish represents a distinct danger for the success of RLS efforts on behalf of intergenerational mother tongue continuity, then the insufficient pursuit of substantially self-regulated modern status and power functions, even when such can be erected upon a strong stage 6 base, constitutes an equally great (although far less common) danger to such efforts. A disproportional stress on traditionalism, revivalism, or other expressions of 'anthropological revitalization' exposes RLS efforts to the risk of being rejected by Xmen who seek a path marked by both modernity and Xishness. In the absence of sufficient RLS interest in rationally defining the priorities to be followed in forging such a path, RLS may come to be viewed as anachronistic or backward looking. More symbiotic alternatives to it (combining Xishness and Yish in some fashion) may come into being (e.g., movements on behalf of 'Xmen-via-Yish' as rivals and competitors with the RLS movement per se among Xmen). Some of the ultra-Orthodox Yiddish speaking communities in New York are exposed to this very dilemma today as young people protest against their community's overly slow progression from stage 4 to stage 3. The insufficient availability of stage 3 functions under ultra-Orthodox sponsorship is leading more and more young people into the Yish controlled worksphere (and into social mobility via that worksphere), with evident effect on their own intragroup use of Yiddish. Community leaders, however, are concerned about youngfolks entering stage 3 wholeheartedly, because of its manifold links with the Yish world. The dilemma here needs to be recognized because of its 'damned if you do, damned if you don't' potential. It is a very resource-demanding stage and one that few minority communities can really control and link back to stage 6.

Given that both the premature abandonment of the diglossic (see *Diglossia*) protection of stage 6 and the overly prolonged inability to transcend the encapsulation of stage 6 are clearly problematic vis-à-vis RLS success, it is, nevertheless, clear that the attainment of diglossic protection for Xish by weak RLS movements lacking in stage 6 is infinitely more common and difficult (and less glamorous) than is its subsequent gradual transcendence by an RLS movement with a secure basis in everyday intergenerational life. RLS movements are ethnicity linked and they must build upon the putative kinship claim of all ethnicity movements in order to counteract the blandishments of greater (and often even purportedly unlimited) individual social mobility via Yish and through Yish institutions. Such blandishments render Xmen less ideologically disposed toward the behavioral and motivational prerequisites of RLS movements on behalf of the 'Xmen-via-Xish' model. The Irish and Frisian movements are good examples of the difficulties encountered in this very diglossia attaining connection. Stage 6 never having been reconstituted on a sufficiently ample base (a base which many ultra-Orthodox Yiddish speakers *have* secured), there is no widely available safe harbor in daily life against the influences of the upper Yish-controlled stages.

Furthermore, the transcendence of diglossic bilingualism into a virtually monolingual Xish *de facto* control of everyday public and intergroup life, is often considered by Ymen to be unattainable without civil strife. However, the actual incidence of civil strife is more genuinely related to the removal of authoritarian control after periods of both long term and short term deprivation (Fishman and Solano 1990) than to RLS processes or other ethnolinguistic processes themselves. The Franco-Canadian and the Catalan RLS cases are both examples of relatively successful negotiations of this difficult passage, the latter being almost entirely without serious intergroup recriminations between indigenous Catalans and immigrant Caitlin speakers thus far. Note, however, that without successfully attaining and maintaining stage 6, no sustained transcendence of that stage is possible. There is a dilemma here of no mean proportions.

3.3 Ambivalence 3: The Difficulty of Planning Spontaneity and Intimacy

The basic problem of weak RLS movements is whether the attainment and maintenance of stage 6 is at all susceptible to planning. Given that intergenerational mother tongue transmission is a function of the childhood intimacy and spontaneity that characterizes home–family–neighborhood life, this problem boils down to whether this complex of culturally infused interpersonal processes can only be informally cultivated *in vivo*, so to speak, or whether it can be fostered by rational planning. The evidence supporting the latter alternative is, quite frankly, sparse indeed. The major RLS success cases of the twentieth century generally entered the fray while their stage 6 processes were still (or already) rather intact at least in some language islands (see *Language Enclaves*). Attempts to build stage 6 directly (e.g., the community and housing schemes of Irish RLS efforts in the mid- to late-1980s) have demonstrated how elusive the informal interaction processes really are and how difficult it is to really plan them or to do so without smothering them. Yet the revernacularization of Hebrew in Palestine on the part of secular (indeed, anti-clerical) Zionists was accomplished precisely along the lines of giving priority to self-regulatory home–family–community building for the attainment of intergenerational mother tongue transmission. The movement reached its goal during the immediate pre- and post-World War I decades, much before any power and status functions (beyond the settlements and their community-controlled fields, chicken-coops, nursery–kindergartens, and elementary schools) were seriously entertained on a broader societal base. Years of child-rearing by specially trained care givers transpired in a quite separate children's home, with only very occasional visits on the part of the children to their parents, until the children taught the parents the revived vernacular. Such back-linkages between higher stages and stage 6 require careful and constant attention, so that neither insufficiency nor smothering transpires.

Obviously there is also considerable need for ideological clarification (more about this below) and for neighborhood organization expertise and organization-theory expertise in general (on the latter, see Hart 2001) within the total RLS enterprise. Nevertheless, the dilemma, which underlies this third area of ambivalence, must be recognized as such. Intergenerational mother tongue transmission depends on processes which have too long remained overlooked by RLS movements but, to make matters worse, even when squarely acknowledged, these processes are difficult to plan because they require the establishment and fostering of interactional contexts and relationships which are inherently difficult to plan and to cultivate. Doubly so as long as Xish-imbeddedness in Yish-dominated everyday sociocultural processes remains uninterrupted. It was the very ability of the new Zionist settlements to break away from their dependence on all other Jewish and non-Jewish norms and associations, both in the diaspora and in Palestine itself, that made it possible for them to create home–family–neighborhood (=settlement) contexts in which their preferred Xish was protected and could finally attain intergenerational roots. It was only thereafter that efforts to hebraize others and higher sociocultural processes were successfully focused upon. On the other hand, Eliezer ben Yehuda, who had focused upon such higher order processes from the very outset (ca. 1890) was distinctly unsuccessful in vernacularizing Hebrew, regardless of the subsequent symbolic mythologization of ben Yehuda in that very connection.

4. A Glance at a Few Selected Cases

Table 2 presents data on the standing of a baker's dozen of RLS cases with respect to their present GIDS status. These cases are drawn from three continents (North America, Europe and Asia/Pacific; for Latin American and African cases see Fishman 2001) and include both indigenous and immigrant groups. Both the right and the left margins of Part A of the table consist primarily of the GIDS stages that were presented in Table 1, above, and that have provided the basis of most of the foregoing discussion. The only addition to the table proper is the notation IC (ideological clarification) which has been scored on a three point scale ($+$, $+-$, $-$) reflecting the availability of positive ideological consensuality within the 13 studied RLS circles today. The total GIDS score (referred to as Ts) for each case consists of the grand total of all of the numbers representing stages at which major RLS efforts are concentrated today on behalf of that case. Higher total scores indicate efforts that are still focused on societally more basic dislocated stages. The highest (most dislocated) scores are obtained for Maori, Irish, and Yiddish in secularist circles in New York City and selected Australian Aboriginal 'outstation' cases. The lowest (least dislocated) scores are obtained for Hebrew in Israel, French in Quebec, Catalan in the Autonomous Catalan Community, and Yiddish in ultra-Orthodox circles in New York. Another way of estimating the current relative positions of these 13 communities is by examining their mean GIDS scores. The correlation between the Total GIDS score and the Mean GIDS score is 0.79, confirming that the Ts is not merely an artifact of the number and variety of efforts involved.

It is quite clear from Part A of Table 2 that there are some cases significantly involved in efforts above the 'continental divide' that are, nevertheless, still in a poor state of health with respect to their overall RLS status (e.g., Irish and Basque). There are also (and even more obviously) a few cases where there is little if any ideological focus (IC) on RLS which are doing relatively well with respect to their overall RLS standing (e.g., Navaho [selected reservation] and ultra-Orthodox Yiddish in New York). Part B of Table 2 reveals that the consideration that really seems to distinguish between cases doing well and cases doing less well or poorly, as far as RLS is concerned, is whether stage 6 (home–neighborhood–community) is substantially under self-regulatory RLS auspices.

The average total GIDS score for the four cases in which this is so is 3.75, whereas the average total GIDS score for the nine cases in which it is not so is 15.75. The difference in total GIDS scores between cases with and without positive ideological consensuality is less impressive (10.20 vs. 14.13), although it too is clearly in the right direction (detailed information concerning all 13 cases in the early 1990s can be found in Fishman 1991 and, once again, for the early 2000s in Fishman 2001). Current ambivalence regarding the importance of Hebrew in Israel (particularly in comparison with the unanimity as to the importance of the 'Xmen-via-Xish' position among Francophones in Quebec and among Catalans in the Autonomous Catalan Community) is attributable to a growing philosophical pluralism on

Table 2. Graded Integrational Dislocation Stages (GIDS) in 13 monitored RLS settings.

AA=Australian Aborigines (selected cases); AIR=Australian Immigrant (post-World War II); B=Basque; C=Catalan; FQ=Francophone Quebec; F=Frisian; H=Hebrew; I=Irish; M=Maori; NR=Navaho (selected reservation community); S=Spanish: New York Barrio Puerto Ricans; YO=Yiddish Ultra-Orthodox (NYC); YS=Yiddish Secular (NYC); IC=Ideological clarification; Numbers=GIDS stages (X=stage[s] currently receiving most attention in RLS efforts); Ts=Total dislocation score.

	AA	AIR	B	C	FQ	F	H	I	M	NR	S	YO	YS	
1			x	x	x		x							1
2		x	x	x		x		x						2
3		x	x									x		3
4b						x			x		x			4b
4a	x	x	x					x		x		x		4a
5									x					5
6*	±	−	−	+	+	−	+	−	−	±	±	+	−	6*
7	x	x						x	x	x	x		x	7
8	x		x					x	x				x	8
IC*	±	+	+	+	+	+	±	±	±	±	±	±	±	IC*
Ts**	19	13	18	6	1	13	1	21	24	11	11	7	20	Ts**
	AA	AIR	B	C	FQ	F	H	I	M	NR	S	YO	YS	
Mean	6.3	5.3	5.6	2	1	5.3	1	5.2	6	5.4	5.2	3.5	6.7	Mean

* Average Ts for − or ± at stage 6: 15.75; at IC: 14.13
  Average Ts for +   at stage 6: 3.75; at IC: 10.20

** Languages ranked by sum of their GIDS scores (Ts):

```
              + on 6     + on IC
1=FQ, H         x           x          x
6=C             x           x
7=YO (NYC)      x
10=S (NYCPR)
11=NR
13=AIR, F                   x           x
18=B                        x
19=AA
20=YS (NYC)
21=I
24=M
```

this issue. This pluralism can be attributed to the post-struggle phase, which Xish has now achieved there. The IC analysis clearly implies that even an RLS-engineered ideological consensus (by no means the same as spontaneous 'positive attitudes' or 'positive motivation' relative to Xish) is of clearly lesser RLS importance than establishing Xish supremacy vis-à-vis the societal processes of everyday home–family–community life.

Obviously, Table 2 does not try to show the historical development that has occurred with respect to the RLS statuses of the speech communities involved. Clearly, it deals only with the reasonably current situations in each case. A series of such tables, decade by decade from the beginning of the twentieth century, would unambiguously reveal which cases have advanced, which have regressed, and which have remained stationary with respect to their respective RLS statuses. For relevant information for one such analysis in a less compressed non-tabular, narrative form see Fishman (1991).

5. Some Concluding and Summary Observations

Our discussion has tried to help clarify why 'geographic' considerations, 'absolute size' considerations and attitudinal/motivational considerations cannot be considered either conceptually/analytically fruitful or, indeed, manipulably rewarding dimensions in connection with understanding RLS differentials. Letzeburgisch, the vernacular of Luxembourg, is 'next door' (indeed, surrounded by) two world languages, French and German, both of which are even part of the very Xish identity-and-behavior pattern that Letzeburgisch itself serves to clinch. Furthermore, Letzeburgisch mother tongue speakers constitute a rather small speech community and one which gives its mother tongue rather little explicit ideological attention. Rather than fixating on the former non-manipulable intra-group considerations this article has emphasized intergroup processes and a search for manipulable 'planning' considerations. Nevertheless, a number of ambiguities and dilemmas must be recognized as plaguing or rendering extremely difficult the pursuit of RLS. Even ameliorative efforts that are well understood, correctly sequenced, and interrelated are not thereby necessarily successful, but the pursuit of folk notions, the lack of strong linkages to the crucial stage 6 and the childish belief that 'doing anything (or a little bit of everything in random order) is necessarily better for RLS than doing nothing' are all definitely contraindicated. They only serve to squander time, resources, and trust, commodities that are in short supply and that need to be wisely used and husbanded.

Intergenerational RLS may safely focus on the school, on the church, or on the workplace if specific non-mother tongue functions are being aimed at. However, if intergenerational mother-tongue transmission is being aimed at, there is no parsimonious substitute for focusing on the home–family–neighborhood–community processes which bind together adults and children (most frequently, but not only, grandparents and grandchildren and parents and children) in early bonds of intergenerational and spontaneous affect, intimacy, identity, and loyalty. This is not to say that this arena is itself sufficient to guarantee that mother tongue-focused RLS efforts focused upon it will succeed, but it is to say that RLS control of this arena is necessary, a *sine qua non* for such success. Subsequent stages can provide it with additional latitude and instrumental feedback reinforcement. Much before diglossic arrangements are fully transcended there are types of schooling (particularly type 5 and 4a) that can support this arena materially and with only meager dependence on Yish regulation, approval, or support. Thereafter, Xish with a firm, demographically concentrated community base can increasingly pursue economic and even political co-regulatory power. The increasing attainment of such power leads to cultural autonomy arrangements and to realistic possibilities of further political autonomy arrangements as well.

See also: Endangered Languages; Language Loyalty; Language Maintenance, Shift, and Death; Salvage Work (Endangered Languages).

Bibliography

Fishman J A 1964 Language maintenance and language shift as a field of inquiry. *Linguistics* **9**: 32–70
Fishman J A 1990 What is Reversing Language Shift and how can it succeed? *Journal of Multilingual and Multicultural Development* **11**: 5–36
Fishman J A 1991 *Reversing Language Shift: Theory and Practice of Assistance to Threatened languages*. Multilingual Matters, Clevedon, UK
Fishman J A (ed.) 2001 *Can Threatened Languages Be Saved?* Multilingual Matters, Clevedon, UK
Fishman J A, Solano F R 1990 Civil strife and linguistic heterogeneity/homogeneity: An empirical examination. *Canadian Review of Studies in Nationalism* **17**: 131–46
Hart S 2001 *Cultural Dilemmas of Progressive Politics: Styles of Engagement among Grassroots Activists*. University of Chicago Press, Chicago, IL

School Language Policies
D. J. Corson

School language policies are viewed by many in education as an integral and necessary part of the administration and the curriculum practice of modern schools. A language policy is a document compiled by the staff of a school, often assisted by other members of the school community, to which the staff give their assent and commitment. It identifies areas in the school's scope of operations and program where language problems exist that need the commonly agreed approach that is offered by a policy. A policy sets out what the school intends to do about these areas of concern; it is an action statement.

1. Origin and Early Developments

In 1966 members of the London Association for the Teaching of English began to develop and extend their interest in the concept of 'language across the curriculum' by preparing a discussion document entitled 'Towards a language policy across the curriculum' (Rosen in Barnes et al. 1971). This discussion document provided the catalyst for action that its authors had intended. Schools in various places within Britain, in other countries of the British Commonwealth, and in the United States began to develop their own language policies, using the original document as a reference point. In 1975 the point and value of language policies for British schools received official endorsement in *A Language for Life* (The Bullock Report): Each school should have an organized policy for language across the curriculum, establishing every teacher's involvement in language and reading development throughout the years of schooling.

Subsequently several influential texts (e.g., Torbe 1980) addressed the need for a whole-school language policy, especially at secondary level, and discussed the implementation of such a policy. As the idea of having school language policies spread, practitioners and theorists began to see potential in them for small-scale but important educational reform: for example Knott (1985) presents novel ideas for researching pupil language use and discovering the attitudes of secondary school staff to language issues; and Maybin (1985) provides practical approaches for working towards a primary school policy for implementation in a culturally pluralist school setting.

2. Language Planning, National Language Policies, and School Language Policies

'Language planning' (see *Language Planning: Models*) is another name for the evaluative approach to the sociology of language (see *Sociology of Language*). Broadly conceived, language planning is concerned with any problem area in which language plays some role: it is the organized pursuit of solutions to language problems. Following in the language planning tradition as they do, national language policies are comprehensive and coherent documents that enable national decision makers to make choices about language issues in a rational and balanced way. Australia's 'National Policy on Languages' released in 1987 is an example of a policy of this kind.

In spite of great advances in language planning, researchers in the area have paid very little attention to the school as the basic context for language change. Even those rare texts that have linked language planning with education (Kennedy 1984) tend to address education as a macro phenomenon. However official documents have begun to suggest the need for formal school-level planning. In 1985 *Education for All* (The Swann Report) responded to the growing pluralism in British schools by warning that 'unless there is a school language and learning policy across the curriculum there will be a wastage of effort and often confusion' (see *Black English in Education: UK*). The micro setting of the school as a site for language planning in now receiving more attention, beginning with research studies in New Zealand and Canada that address the role of the school as the key agency in language planning. These studies borrow the model of 'language policies across the curriculum' developed for London schools and extend its original focus on mother-tongue concerns to include second language, bilingual, foreign language, and social justice issues (Corson 1999). The studies argue that the social institutions needed to translate the visions of national policies into strategies capable of enhancing individual lives already exist throughout pluralist societies in the form of their schools. It seems a very reasonable thing to ask schools to be responsible for much of the working end of language planning and of national policies that deal with language issues.

3. Administration, Policy Studies, and Research in Education

The design and implementation of a school language policy are ultimately the responsibility of the school's administration, acting through a policy-making group, departmental subcommittees or possibly through the participation of the whole school's staff and community. As a result the applied value of the ideas in school language policies will depend on how well the concept is integrated into the training and professional development of school administrators and curriculum planners. Moreover many types of small-scale and large-scale research will be necessary in schools if policies are to provide adequate and implementable solutions to local language problems. The training of teachers in basic language research methods will need to become more common. A beginning has been made in all these areas (Corson 1998, 2000).

The rise in interest in school language policies coincides with moves in Canada, the UK, the United States, Australia and New Zealand to devolve most educational decision making away from central bureaucracies and down to school level. A groundswell of interest in school policy making of all kinds has resulted. Perhaps much of the impetus for further development will come from the growing need in modern societies to improve the quality of the solutions offered to the problems of large-scale cultural pluralism. Increasing tolerance worldwide in the treatment of linguistic minorities should hasten this development (see May 1997).

See also: Bilingual Education; Home Language and School Language.

Bibliography

Barnes D, Britton J, Rosen H 1971 *Language, the Learner and the School*. Penguin, Harmondsworth, UK
Corson D 1998 *Changing Education for Diversity*. Open University Press, Milton Keynes, UK
Corson D 1999 *Language Policy in Schools*. Erlbaum, Mahwah, NJ
Corson D 2000 *Language Diversity and Education*. Erlbaum, Mahwah, NJ
Kennedy C (ed.) 1984 *Language Planning and Language Education*. Allen and Unwin, London
Knott R 1985 *The English Department in a Changing World*. Open University Press, Milton Keynes, UK
May S 1997 School language policies. *Encyclopedia of Language and Education* Vol. 1. Kluwer, Boston, MA
Maybin J 1985 *Every Child's Language: An In-Service Pack for Primary Teachers*. Open University Press/Multilingual Matters, Clevedon, UK
Torbe M (ed.) 1980 *Language Policies in Action: Language Across the Curriculum in Some Secondary Schools*. Ward Lock, London

Standardization

E. Haugen

Any vernacular (language or dialect) may be 'standardized' by being given a uniform and consistent norm of writing that is widely accepted by its speakers. It may then be referred to as a 'standard' language.

The requirements posed in this definition involve (a) an explicit norm and (b) speaker acceptance. The first is fulfilled by an individual (or a competent group) who selects the forms of one or more dialects and decides on a suitable transcription for the standard. The second is fulfilled by the wide acceptance of the standard as a desirable mode of writing the vernacular. In its initial phase the users of a standard are usually a tightly knit group of elite members (a coterie, a church, an academy) and are only gradually extended to include a whole people or a nation. Throughout the world, language standards are the product of either military conquest, immigration, or commercial contact.

1. History of Standardization

The idea of standard languages arose during the Renaissance in Europe, and it may be questioned whether there were any standardized languages prior to the invention of printing in the fifteenth century. Most standards were preceded by a profusion of scribal varieties, which reflected either the scribe's local dialect or some personal idiosyncrasy.

An example is Sanskrit, which was based on a dialect spoken by Hindus living in northeast India from ca. 1500 BCE. While the spoken dialects kept changing, Sanskrit was codified in the fourth century BCE by the linguist Pāini. After that it became the sacred medium of Hinduism and was preserved in a ritualized form which resembled the modern standards. But it remained the possession of a small coterie of specialists.

Greek has been known since the fourteenth century BCE but its literature was written in several dialects until the Hellenistic period, i.e., the fourth century BCE. It then achieved a fairly unified form known as the koiné, or common language, based on Attic Greek. Modern Greek is ultimately based on the koiné, but is widely different. When Adamantios Korais (1748–1833) in the early years of the nineteenth century conceived the idea of a new standard language for Greece, he adopted a highly literary form, partly based on the koiné, which came to be known as the Katharevousa, or 'pure' language. Modern writers have in part deviated by adopting elements from spoken Greek, the Demotike, or 'popular' language.

Latin began as just another Indo-European dialect in Italy, spoken from the fourth century BCE. But Rome's conquest of the peninsula in 338 BCE laid the foundation for the replacement of the dialects of Latium by the Latin of Rome. Early writers like Plautus and Terence have been credited with writing the first forms of Latin. In the development of Latin, Greek played a large role. The Latin language was then spread by the conquest of what became the Roman Empire. This was for centuries the learned language of European nations, while the spoken vernacular developed into the modern Romance languages. It was roughly codified by Latin grammarians in the early centuries of our era. Even though it was spread widely, the lack of printing kept it from counting as a true standard language.

2. Institutional Efforts at Standardization

The idea of the Language Academy (see *Academies: Dictionaries and Standards*) as an instrument for creating a standard language was launched in Italy by Count Cosimo I of Florence. He founded the Accademia della Crusca in 1582. A generation later Cardinal Richelieu followed suit by founding the Académie Française in 1635. Richelieu gave its 40 'Immortals' the power to encourage all that was 'noble, polished, and reasonable' in the French language, but as has been pointed out, there was hardly one of the members who was trained in linguistics or lexicography. They were really social arbiters whose function it was to decide on criteria of good taste in language. However, they did produce both a grammar and a dictionary of French.

A similar institution was founded in Spain by King Philip V, the Real Academia Español in 1713, designated to 'clarify, purify, and glorify' the Spanish language. Here the first codification had already been made by Antonio de Nebrija, who presented a grammar of Spanish to Queen Isabella in 1492. In its wake other academies were founded in the countries of the Spanish New World. In Germany *Sprachgesellschaften* sprang up with the idea of 'purifying' the German language. In Sweden an academy was established by King Gustav III in 1786. In Hungary one was established in 1830. Arabic academies grew up in Syria, Iraq, and Egypt. A Russian Academy produced a dictionary (1789–94) and a grammar (1802).

Conspicuous here is the absence of any English institution of similar import. There was active agitation for the creation of one in the eighteenth century by persons as eminent as Daniel Defoe and Jonathan Swift. But in typical Anglo-Saxon manner, private enterprise took over. In 1720 the indefatigable Samuel Johnson produced his English dictionary, which fulfilled the needs of the English. The example was followed in the United States by the work of Noah Webster.

After the Reformation the Scandinavian languages were standardized by the translators of the Bible, working in close contact with the royal chanceries. A Danish version of the New Testament came in 1529 by Christienn Pedersen, who also published a Latin–Danish dictionary (1510). The official Danish Bible appeared in 1550. A Swedish New Testament was translated in 1526 and the complete Bible in 1541 under the guidance of the reformers Olaus and Laurentius Petri. An Icelandic New Testament by Oddur Gottskalkson came in 1540. Norway as a dependency of Denmark did not receive a translation of its own, and consequently no standard language.

Two initiatives to create a Norwegian standard were launched in the mid-nineteenth century, after Norway was detached from Denmark in 1814 and got autonomy in a union with Sweden. In 1853 the dialectologist Ivar Aasen devised a norm of Norwegian based on the rural dialects, especially the western ones which retained most of the Old Norwegian quality. He was opposed by the schoolman Knud Knudsen, who in 1856 proposed a Dano-Norwegian norm that took account of the cultivated speech in the cities, especially in Eastern Norway. Aasen's standard was known as *Landsmål* 'Country Language' (now *Nynorsk* 'New Norwegian'), Knudsen's as *Dansknorsk* or *Riksmål* 'Language of the Kingdom' (now known as *Bokmål* 'Book Language'). These two standards have contended ever since for supremacy; in modern times the Nynorsk has captured only one-sixth of the school districts, none of them urban.

In the twentieth century the Scandinavian languages have emphasized the principle of 'language cultivation' (Swedish *språkvård*, Norwegian *språkrøkt*, Danish *sprogrøgt*). Beginning with the Swedish *Nämnden för svensk språkvård* ('The Committee for Swedish Language Cultivation') in 1944, a whole series of such committees were established in the Scandinavian countries: Swedish Finland, Denmark, Norway, Iceland, and the Faroes. Each of these countries also has Centers of Technical Terminology, with the special task of unifying the specialized terminologies of their languages. After intense controversy the Norwegian Language Committee was reorganized in 1972 as the Norwegian Language Council (*Norsk Språkråd*) with new guidelines. In 1978 a joint Scandinavian Committee was established with offices in Oslo.

3. Means and Effects of Standardization

As will be seen, the creation and propagation of a standard involves on the one hand the creation of instruments for standardization in the form of grammars and dictionaries, and on the other the presence of a population that finds the standard useful in its communicative efforts. Standardization in effect creates a new language, since it can never capture the entire language nor remain entirely static. Beginning as a reading language, it may in time lead to a new standard spoken language, which may in part be imposed on a population, either by coercion or voluntarily. It usually has a greater prestige than the vernaculars on which it is based and serves to unify the population ruled by a central government.

An example is the switch of Turkish from an Arabic to a Roman script, decreed in 1928 by Atatürk. While this in itself did not change the language, it was accompanied by an increased activity in purifying it from Arabic and Persian elements.

The 'revival' of Hebrew in Israel after its settlement by Jewish groups in the 1900s is a striking example of the adoption of a traditional language as a written standard, resulting in a new spoken vernacular, following the initial agitation of Eliezer Ben Yehuda (see *Reversing Language Shift*). However, the modern vernacular is far from identical with biblical Hebrew. It is said to be influenced by the thoroughly Western substratum of its predominantly Yiddish origins (Yiddish being a dialect of German).

Chinese is not a single language, but several mutually unintelligible ones, often called 'dialects.' They are joined by a common writing system, which goes back to a classical script known as 'Wen-yen.' This script has no common pronunciation, but is read by each speaker in his or her particular dialect. The most prestigious variety of Chinese is the Mandarin, spoken in the north; this is known as 'Modern Standard Chinese,' and is based on the Peking (Beijing) dialect. There are two major systems of romanization: the Wade–Giles devised in 1859 by Sir Thomas Francis Wade; the present-day official Chinese romanization is known as 'Pin-yin' and was adopted in 1958. But the traditional characters persist.

Japanese is spoken in various dialects, but the Japanese adopted the characters of Chinese as their writing system in the early centuries CE. The characters are known as '*kanji*' and are still used, though restricted in number. Because of the entirely different structure of Japanese, an additional, more phonetic, system was devised, known as '*kana*.' This comes in two versions, the '*hiragana*' or 'common kana' used for grammatical particles, and '*katakana*' 'one-sided kana,' used for foreign loanwords. This cumbersome system has resisted all attempts at reform, though some changes have been made in a colloquial direction since 1880.

Korean was also first written in Chinese characters, but a native script was introduced in 1446. This

28-letter alphabet was devised by a group of scholars working at the behest of a reigning king, but did not win the recognition of the literati until the beginning of the twentieth century. Korean can be written in two ways in the late twentieth century, one which is purely alphabetic and one which is a 'mixed' script, including some Chinese characters. The former is used in North Korea, the latter in South Korea.

Arabic is a language whose classical form was established by the religion that bore it to triumph through North Africa and the Near and Middle East in the seventh and eighth centuries CE. It was used by Muslims through the Middle Ages and is still the language of the school and administration in all Arabic countries. There is a considerable gap between the often mutually unintelligible vernaculars that are derived from classical Arabic. Except in Malta, which has adopted Roman writing of the language, it is everywhere written in the Arabic alphabet. Both Arabic and Hebrew writing are descended from an alphabetic Phoenician script.

The major Indo-Aryan languages of North India are written in the Devanagari script or varieties of it, developed in the seventh to ninth centuries. It has remained essentially unaltered to the present. Varieties of it spread with Buddhism from India into other south Asiatic countries as far east as Malaya, Indonesia, and the Philippines. The languages have been standardized at various times.

4. Colonial and Missionary Efforts at Standardization

In Africa a number of lingua francas have developed to bridge the tremendous number of native vernaculars of the continent. Of these, Swahili is official in Tanzania and Kenya, and is used widely in East Africa. Others are Lingala, Fanakalo, and Sango. Hausa is used in Nigeria; Amharic is official in Ethiopia, Wolof in Senegal and Gambia, and Kongo near the Congo River. There are also countries where non-African languages are in common use, including Arabic, English, and French. The Island of Madagascar has a Malayo-Polynesian language.

Although the first grammar of an African language (Kongo) goes back to 1659, extensive study was not begun until the nineteenth century. Yoruba boasts the earliest dictionary written by a native speaker (1843). There has been intensive missionary activity, resulting in many local grammars, but there are few languages that can be described as standardized. In South Africa the formerly Dutch population uses Afrikaans, the English a variety of standard English.

American Indian languages are also numerous, with many local grammars and dictionaries, but little if any standardization. As in Africa, most such initiatives were taken by linguists. An interesting exception is the Cherokee syllabary, devised in 1821 by a half-Cherokee native named Sequoyah and widely used for a time. In Greenland the first book in the native Greenlandic was published by the Dano-Norwegian missionary Hans Egede in 1742. A systematic orthography in Roman letters was devised by the German missionary Samuel Kleinschmidt in 1851. But as a self-governing overseas administrative division of Denmark it has Danish as one of its official languages (along with Greenlandic).

As this brief survey of selected languages shows, standard languages are usually artifacts of religious or military penetration and the needs of a central government, abetted by an ever-expanding literate population.

See also: Language Planning: Models; Language Adaptation and Modernization.

Bibliography

Edwards J 1985 *Language, Society and Identity*. Blackwell, Oxford, UK
Haugen E 1972 *The Ecology of Language*. Stanford University Press, Stanford, CA
Haugen E 1976 *The Scandinavian Languages*. Faber, London
Palmer L R 1961 *The Latin Language*. Faber, London
Priebsch R, Collinson W E 1962 *The German Language*. Faber, London
Sebeok T A 1963–1976 *Current Trends in Linguistics*, 14 vols. Mouton, The Hague
Språk i Norden 1961–1989. Cappelen, Oslo, Norway

Statistics: Principal Languages of the World (UNESCO)

J. M. Y. Simpson

In 1989 the Division of Statistics of the United Nations Educational, Scientific, and Cultural Organization (UNESCO) undertook research—actually carried out on its behalf by the 'Groupe d'études de démographie appliquée' (GEDA)—into the numbers of speakers of the principal languages of the world, 'principal languages' being defined as those spoken by at least 100 million people or declared the official language in at least three countries. Relevant to this gathering of statistics is the status of each language in the countries in which it is used; consideration of this factor led to a typology of countries according to the status enjoyed in them by the relevant principal language(s). This article is based on the publication of the results in 1992.

1. Speakers of the Languages

The question immediately arises of what degree of mastery of a language is required before a person can be said to qualify as a 'speaker' of that language. A distinction is drawn between 'real speakers' and 'potential speakers.' 'Real speakers' are defined as those who have a 'perfect command' of the language; this perfect command is acquired either because the language has been learned from childhood as a mother tongue or because it has been used as a medium of instruction during 'a number' (undefined) of years of compulsory schooling in that language. 'Potential speakers' are those who have experienced the language as a medium of instruction for 'fewer' years than real speakers or who have learned it as a taught subject in school or who have learned to use it as a lingua franca (see *Lingua Franca*). It is assumed that real speakers will be able both to speak and write the language, as will potential speakers who have experienced it as a medium of instruction or have learned it as a school subject.

Given the lack of statistics and the complexity of the task of compiling estimates of the above various types of speakers, the study did not take into account potential speakers who had learned to use the language as a lingua franca.

2. Status of the Languages

Three different statuses of language are recognized: official language, national language, and language of instruction.

2.1 Official Language

The official language is that which is 'used in the business of government—legislative, executive, and judicial.' In some countries the official language is specified in the constitution, the constitution itself being normally written in that language. With regard to official languages, countries can be grouped according to whether (a) they have escaped linguistic imperialism and exposure to imported languages or (b) whether at some time in their history a nonindigenous language was in use.

In the case of (a), i.e., countries that have 'naturally' officialized indigenous languages, the latter are the mother tongues of the great majority of their populations. Such countries may be officially monolingual or multilingual.

In the case of (b), i.e., countries where a foreign language has been present, three situations are recognized. First, one or more of the dominant indigenous languages may have been officialized; in this case again, the majority of the population will speak an official language as a mother tongue. Second, the country may be officially bilingual, one official language being indigenous, the other nonindigenous and European. The nonindigenous language may be the mother tongue of a large sector of the population or it may be learned through the medium of education or 'in a specific linguistic context.' Third, a multilingual country may have officialized one or more foreign languages which is/are learned at school and used as medium(s) of instruction.

2.2 National Language

A national language is defined as 'the language of a political, social, and cultural entity'; all the languages of a country spoken as mother tongues have this status. The definition applies above all to officially multilingual states 'seeking to ensure equality for all nationalities through legal and constitutional provision enabling them to use their own language in contacts with the authorities.' 'In most countries without a colonial past, the national language(s) is/are the official language(s).' In countries with a colonial past which have officialized a foreign language, the indigenous languages may have the status of national languages. Sometimes national languages are defined as such in the constitution.

2.3 Language of Instruction

A language of instruction is a medium of primary, secondary, or higher education. It must of necessity be a written language. Its status as a language of instruction is normally set out in the legislation of the relevant Ministry of Education and sometimes also in the constitution. A language of instruction may be an official language as well as the mother tongue of all or part of the population. It may be indigenous or nonindigenous.

3. Scope of the Study

Given the above definition of 'principal language,' 12 languages qualify for investigation in the study: Arabic, Bengali, Chinese, English, French, German, Hindustani, Japanese, Malay–Indonesian, Portuguese, Russian, and Spanish. ('Bahasa Indonesia' and 'Bahasa Malaysia' are subsumed under the heading 'Malay–Indonesian' as being one language. Similarly 'Hindustani' is used as a cover term for Hindi, Urdu, and Panjabi. Arabic and Chinese are each treated as a single language.)

Calculations are made for the number of speakers of each language only in the countries in which they are in use as official languages, national languages, and languages of instruction. A relevant factor in clarifying the distinction between real and potential speakers is the status of the principal languages in the countries concerned. Real speakers are counted as being (a) those who speak the language as a mother tongue in countries where it is an official language or a national language defined as such in the constitution; (b) those who have learned it (to the defined degree) through the education system in countries where it is an official language and/or a language of instruction; and (c) those who have learned it (to the defined degree) through the education system of officially multilingual countries where it is a compulsory subject. Potential speakers are counted as being (a) those who have learned the language (to the defined degree) through the education system in countries where it is the official language and/or the language of instruction and (b) those who have learned it (to the defined degree) in officially multilingual countries where it is a compulsory subject.

Not included in the statistics are (a) those who speak the language in question as a mother tongue in countries where it is neither an official language, nor a national language, nor a language of instruction; (b) those who have learned it as an optional taught subject; (c) those who have learned the rudiments of it 'in a favorable linguistic context.'

4. Country Typologies

The data required as an input are of both a qualitative and a quantitative nature. Qualitative information concerns (a) the status of the language(s) spoken in each country and (b) the organization of the education system. The latter is necessary for countries where the language of instruction is nonindigenous in order to determine at what level or grade the language actually does become the medium of instruction. This information permits the computation for each country of the number of real and potential speakers. The quantitative information concerns (a) the number of mother tongue speakers and the population distribution by level of educational attainment and (b) the total school-going population and the number of repeaters by grade.

The requirements for calculating the number of real and potential speakers vary from country to country. They are determined by (a) the number of official and national languages; (b) whether an official language is indigenous or nonindigenous; and (c) the means by which a language is learned. On the basis of these criteria seven country typologies are established.

(1) Countries in which a single language is the official language: it may be indigenous or nonindigenous and is spoken as the mother tongue by at least 90 percent of the population. In all countries of this group except Pakistan, it is also the sole language of instruction (see Table 1).

(2) Countries in which several languages are official languages: they are indigenous and are learned either as a mother tongue or as a compulsorily taught subject. In such countries part of the population may be monolingual (see Table 2).

(3) Countries in which a single language is the official language: this language is nonindigenous and

Table 1. Countries in which a single indigenous or nonindigenous language is the official language and is spoken as the mother tongue by at least 90 percent of the population.

Arabic	Bengali	Chinese	English	French	German	Hindustani	Malay–Indonesian	Portuguese	Spanish
Algeria	Bangladesh	China	Antigua and Barbuda	France (in. DOM–TOM except Réunion)	Austria	Pakistan		Brazil	Andorra
Bahrain*			Australia		Germany			Portugal	Argentina
Egypt			Bermuda		Liechtenstein				Bolivia
Iraq			Jamaica						Chile
Jordan			Montserrat						Colombia
Kuwait*			New Zealand	Luxembourg					Costa Rica
Lebanon			St Kitts and Nevis	Monaco					Cuba
Libyan Arab Jamahiriya			St Vincent and the Grenadines						Dominican Republic
Morocco			United Kingdom						Ecuador
Oman*			United States						El Salvador
Qatar*									Honduras
Saudi Arabia									Mexico
Sudan									Nicaragua
Syrian Arab Republic									Panama
Tunisia									Puerto Rico
United Arab Emirates*									Spain
Yemen									Uruguay
									Venezuela

* Country with a high percentage of non-Arabic-speaking immigrant workers.

is spoken by less than 90 percent of the population. It is learned through the education system where it is a language of instruction (except in Guatemala where Spanish, the nonindigenous official language, is the mother tongue of part of the population; see Table 3).

(4) Countries in which the official languages are either non-indigenous or nonindigenous and indigenous. Consequently these are learned either as a mother tongue or through the education systems, for example Spanish in Paraguay and Peru, Hindustani in India, English in South Africa, Arabic in Chad and Mauritania, Chinese in Singapore, etc. (see Table 4).

(5) Countries with one indigenous language as the official language but with at the same time other widely spoken national languages. This is the case with Brunei, Indonesia, and Malaysia where the official language is the mother tongue of only part of the population while another part has to learn it through the education system (see Table 5).

(6) Countries in which one of the 12 languages under consideration is (a) either specified in the constitution as a national language or (b) is spoken by a large portion of the population as a mother tongue, though it is not recognized as an official or national language. To the first group belong Urdu in Pakistan, Bengali in India, and German in Belgium; to the second belong Chinese in Hong Kong, Macau, and Malaysia, and Spanish in Belize. Mauritius is a particular case where French, although widely spoken, is not an official language and is the mother tongue of only a small portion of the population (see Table 6).

Table 2. Countries with several indigenous languages as official languages.

Arabic	Bengali	Chinese	English	French	German	Hindustani	Malay–Indonesian	Portuguese	Spanish
(a) *Countries with two official languages*									
Israel			Canada	Canada					
			Ireland						
			Malta						
(b) *Countries with three official languages*									
				Belgium	Belgium				
				Switzerland	Switzerland				

Table 3. Countries with one nonindigenous language as the official language.

Arabic	Bengali	Chinese	English	French	German	Hindustani	Malay–Indonesian	Portuguese	Spanish
			Barbados	Benin				Angola	Equatorial
			Belize	Burkina Faso				Cape Verde	Guinea
			Cook Islands	Central				Guinea-	Guatemala*
			Dominica	African				Bissau	
			Gambia	Republic				Macau	
			Ghana	Comoros				Mozambique	
			Grenada	Congo				São Tomé and	
			Guyana	Côte				Principe	
			Hong Kong	d'Ivoire					
			Liberia	Djibouti					
			Malawi	Gabon					
			Mauritius	Guinea					
			Nigeria	Haiti					
			Pakistan	Mali					
			St Lucia	Niger					
			Sierra Leone	Réunion					
			Trinidad and	Senegal					
			Tobago	Togo					
			Uganda	Zaire					
			Western						
			Samoa						
			Zambia						
			Zimbabwe						

* The estimates for this country are also based on mother tongue data.

Table 4. Countries in which nonindigenous and indigenous or only nonindigenous languages are official languages.

Arabic	Bengali	Chinese	English	French	German	Hindustani	Malay–Indonesian	Portuguese	Spanish
(a) *Countries with two official languages, only one of which is nonindigenous*									
			Botswana						
				Burundi					
			Fiji						
			India			India			
			Kenya						
			Lesotho						
				Madagascar					
			Papua New Guinea						
									Paraguay
									Peru
			Philippines						
				Rwanda					
Somalia*									
			Swaziland						
			Tonga						
			Tuvalu						
			United Republic of Tanzania						
(b) *Countries with two nonindigenous official languages*									
			Cameroon	Cameroon					
Chad†				Chad					
Mauritania†				Mauritania					
			Namibia						
			Seychelles	Seychelles					
		Singapore‡	Singapore‡				Singapore‡		
			South Africa						
			Vanuatu						

* Arabic as an official language is taught only as a second language; thus Arabic speakers in this country cannot be estimated owing to the lack of data.
† Estimates based on mother tongue only.
‡ As well as the three official languages covered by this paper, there is Tamil as a fourth one.

Table 5. Countries with one indigenous official language and, at the same time, strongly represented national languages.

Arabic	Bengali	Chinese	English	French	German	Hindustani	Malay–Indonesian	Portuguese	Spanish
							Brunei		
							Indonesia		
							Malaysia		

Table 6. Countries in which some of the 12 languages are either clearly specified in the constitution as national languages or are the mother tongue of a large proportion of the population.

Arabic	Bengali	Chinese	English	French	German	Hindustani	Malay–Indonesian	Portuguese	Spanish
	India	Hong Kong†		Mauritius‡		Pakistan*			Belize†
		Macau†							
		Malaysia†							

* Countries in which the language is a national language.
† Countries in which the language is the mother tongue of a large part of the population.
‡ For Mauritius see Sect. 4, Country Type 6 above.

Table 7. Countries in which a nonofficial, nonindigenous language is a language of instruction only.

Arabic	Bengali	Chinese	English	French	German	Hindustani	Malay–Indonesian	Portuguese	Spanish
		Brunei	Bangladesh	Algeria					
			Brunei						
			Ethiopia						
			Kiribati						
			Macau	Morocco					
				Tunisia					

Table 8. Speakers of the major languages in 1989.

Languages	Potential speakers	Real speakers	Total speakers	As percent of world population	Total pop. of countries concerned
Arabic	*	206,380,300	206,380,300	4.0	218,419,500
Bengali	*	177,609,100	177,609,100	3.4	948,429,800
Chinese	*	1,077,548,100	1,077,548,100	20.9	1,165,974,500
English	137,591,700	456,328,300	593,920,000	11.5	1,818,816,800
French	42,759,100	88,658,300	131,417,400	2.5	308,110,100
German	88,800	88,997,600	89,086,400	1.7	101,547,000
Hindustani	48,386,800	363,927,300	412,314,100	8.0	954,167,200
Japanese	*	122,846,200	122,846,200	2.4	122,846,200
Malay–Indonesian	49,441,700	63,852,200	113,293,900	2.2	197,612,000
Portuguese	2,629,500	158,447,900	161,076,200	3.1	184,517,200
Russian	*	285,077,900	285,077,900	5.5	285,077,900
Spanish	3,309,500	308,075,300	311,385,300	6.0	317,685,800

* All speakers of these languages are real speakers.

(7) Countries in which a nonofficial, nonindigenous language is used solely as a language of instruction and thus learned through the education system (see Table 7).

Tables 1–7 list according to the above typology all the countries in which are spoken one or more of the 12 languages investigated. Neither Japan nor the USSR (which existed as such at the time of the study) appear in the tables since they constitute yet a further category in that their official language is not widely disseminated in other countries as either an official language or a language of instruction. The information on which the typology was based was gained from various sources, such as the texts of constitutions, philologists, members of Embassies and Permanent Delegations to UNESCO, etc. Table 8 gives the numbers of potential speakers and real speakers of each of the 12 languages.

See also: Language; Linguistic Census.

Bibliography

UNESCO July 1992 *Number of Speakers of the World's Principal Languages in* 1989. (Summary prepared by the Section of Statistics on Culture and Communication, Division of Statistics)

Verbal Hygiene
D. Cameron

It is a truism that linguistics is 'descriptive not prescriptive'—concerned to describe the structure and use of natural languages, and not to make value-judgements on them. *Verbal Hygiene* was the title of a book that prompted debate among sociolinguists, by challenging the view that value judgements are of no relevance for linguistics (Cameron 1995). It argued that competent language users routinely make value judgements on language; ideas about what is 'good' and 'bad' in language are central to their understanding of it, and ought therefore to be of interest to linguists who study language use as a form of social behavior.

1. What is Verbal Hygiene?

The importance language users accord to value judgements is seen with particular clarity in practices of 'verbal hygiene,' i.e., active attempts to improve or 'clean up' language. These practices are many and varied. Examples include not only efforts to impose a standard dialect, pronunciation, or spelling, but also cases like plain-language movements or feminist campaigns to eliminate sexist language, language planning, and 'fringe' movements advocating wholesale spelling reform, the abolition of copular verbs, or the adoption of artificial languages. What these instances have in common is not any single view of what is desirable in language use—the traditional grammarian and the feminist, for instance, will disagree on many points of detail. But they do share the more fundamental assumption that one way of using language may reasonably be preferred to another.

2. Verbal Hygiene and Prescriptivism

That assumption also underlies what linguists have traditionally called 'prescriptivism': how does 'verbal hygiene' differ? Cameron (1995: 3–11) sees the two concepts as overlapping but not coextensive. Her main reasons for wanting an alternative to 'prescriptivism' have to do with the meanings that term has acquired in linguists' usage. First, 'prescriptivism' is most closely identified with a particular subset of normative metalinguistic practices, those that focus on the value of *correctness* and equate 'correct' usage with adherence to the codified norms of a standard language variety. The term 'verbal hygiene' seeks to foreground the existence of normative metalinguistic practices, which intervene in language use in different ways and for different reasons, though they are equally animated by value judgements. Secondly, 'prescriptivism' in linguistics has acquired strong negative connotations: it is associated with ignorance, intolerance, and prejudice, and is usually represented as something extraneous to normal language use. Verbal hygiene, by contrast, is presented as part of a more general metalinguistic function, which is integral to the workings of verbal communication:

> Because language-using is paradigmatically a social, public act, [it] must be carried on with reference to norms, which may themselves become the subject of overt comment and debate. In our everyday interactions we take this for granted...without recourse to such ordinary metalinguistic practices as correcting slips of the tongue, asking what someone meant by something or disputing their usage of particular words, the enterprise of communication would be even more fraught with difficulty than it already is (Cameron 1995: 2).

From this point of view, it makes no sense to condemn linguistic normativity as such. Further, when one considers the full range of normative practices language users are engaged in, it becomes difficult to argue that they all exemplify ignorance (cf. language planning, a 'scientific' enterprise) and/or prejudice (cf. campaigns against sexist and racist language, which embody *resistance* to certain forms of prejudice). While verbal hygiene practices are never value-free, 'correctness' is not the only value that informs them. Others include esthetics (as in discussions of why one local accent is preferable to another); utility (as in arguments for official documents to be written in plain language rather than obfuscatory jargon); and morality (as in debates on sexism and racism in language).

3. The Social/Symbolic Functions of Verbal Hygiene

Although verbal hygiene arises from a metalinguistic capacity which is indispensable for communication, in practice that capacity is used in ways that go well beyond immediate communicative needs—clearly we do not 'need' new spelling systems or arguments about how best to translate the Bible into Klingon (the invented language of a fictional alien species). Many verbal hygiene practices are better understood in terms of the social and symbolic purposes they serve for those engaged in them.

In some cases these purposes are broadly political: verbal hygiene is used to affirm a particular view of the ideal social order. This motivation is evident in conservative defences of standard languages, in feminist arguments for nonsexist language and the counterarguments of their opponents, in purist movements to purge languages of 'foreign' elements and in attempts to preserve or revive minority languages as symbols of ethnic or national identity. Professional and commercial interests (e.g., the interest of publishers in maintaining certain norms of written style) may also motivate verbal hygiene. And it can also be a form of 'language play' (Cook 2000)—this is probably its main function for Klingon enthusiasts, for instance.

4. Debates on Verbal Hygiene

Some linguists (e.g., Kalogjera 2000) have criticized verbal hygiene as a 'revisionist' concept that rehabilitates reactionary forms of prescriptivism, undermines the objectivity of scholarship, and encourages sociolinguists to politicize discussions of language attitudes and linguistic change. In *Verbal Hygiene* (Cameron 1995: xi) it is noted that linguists can study normative practices without necessarily endorsing them. However, the book does challenge claims that linguistics itself is value free (the axiom 'all varieties are linguistically equal,' for instance, is not just a statement of what linguists believe to be true, but implicitly also a value judgement). If we accept that evaluation and verbal hygiene are integral parts of language-using, sociolinguists must engage in critical debates about the *grounds* for particular evaluations rather than denying the legitimacy of evaluation itself.

See also: Attitudes and Behavior; Ideology; Prescriptive and Descriptive Grammar; Standardization.

Bibliography

Cameron D 1995 *Verbal Hygiene*. Routledge, London

Cook G 2000 *Language Play*. Oxford University Press, Oxford, UK

Kalogjera D 2000 A sketch for a chronicle of (anti-) prescriptivism. In: Tomić O M, Radovanovič M (eds.) *History and Perspectives of Language Study*. Benjamins, Philadelphia, PA

SECTION VIII
Language and Education

Applied Linguistics and Sociolinguistics
D. R. Preston

The relevance of sociolinguistics to second language acquisition (SLA) is twofold: First, it is concerned with the variation of language itself—the product, process, storage, and acquisition of such variation, including the variation learners acquire in a target language. That concern is surveyed in Sect. 1—Quantitative Microsociolinguistics. Second, it concerns itself with sociocultural and social psychological aspects of language, again including those involved in the acquisition and use of other languages. That concern is surveyed in Sect. 2.

1. Quantitative Microsociolinguistics
1.1 The Labovian Paradigm
A central claim of this approach is that the alternative forms of variable linguistic elements do not occur randomly. The frequency of their occurrences is predicted (a) by the shape and identity of the element itself and its linguistic context; (b) by the stylistic level of the interaction; and (c) by the social identities a relationships of the interlocutors.

The first attempt to apply this style of analysis to SLA data was very likely Dickerson (1974). Figure 1 shows the sensitivity of Japanese learners' pronunciations of English /r/ to the phonological environment. Before low vowels (_V_{lo}), the pronunciation is fairly accurate (around 75 percent); before mid vowel (_V_{mid}), however, it drops to around 45 percent accuracy, and before high vowels (_V_{hi}), it is categorically wrong. The shape of variable /r/ in the Japanese learner's English is dramatically predicted by the phonological environment.

The predictability of the different realizations of a linguistic variable is often expressed in terms of a variable rule (see *Sociolinguistic Variation*), one aspect of which allows the degree of influence of each determining factor to be expressed as an independent probability. This style of analysis is used by Bayley (1990) to show the influence linguistic, stylistic, and social factors on Chinese learner's deletion of final t/d (in such clusters as *mist, left,* and *walked*). These probability scores are to be read as follows: those above 0.50 have a promoting effect on the rule; those below 0.50 have an inhibiting effect. (Here the rule is of t/d deletion; it could have as well been one of t/d retention, reversing the probabilities.) Like Dickerson's work, Bayley's shows that the following phonological environment is significant: vowels and pauses inhibit t/d deletion; consonants, liquids, and glides promote it.

The stylistic dimension is also important in quantitative sociolinguistic work. The less monitored a performance, the more natural and governed by early-learned rules it will be. Labov (see *Labov, William*) refers to this stylistic level as the vernacular, and to the difficulties inherent in eliciting it in such potentially inhibiting settings as tape-recorded interviews as the 'observer's paradox' (see *Observer's Paradox*). Nonvernacular styles usually reveal not only a greater density of speech community prestige forms but also later-learned and less systematically applied rules (Labov 1972: 208–9).

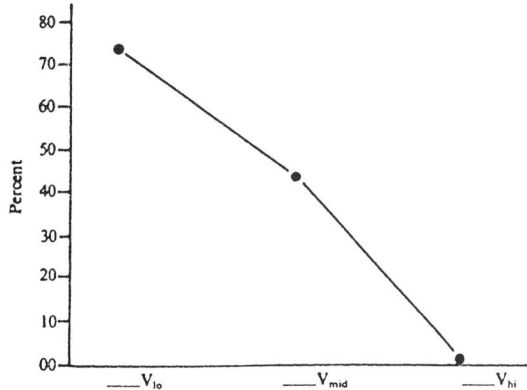

Figure 1. Percentage of acceptable pronunciations of English /r/ in three environments by a Japanese learner (Fasold 1984: 250; adapted from Dickerson and Dickerson 1977: 20).

To tease out stylistic variety, sociolinguists have employed minimal pairs, word lists, reading passages, and techniques which promote various degrees of attention to speech in spontaneous talk. Table 1 shows Bayley's elicitation of the stylistic continuum at three points; his respondents read a set passage, recited a narrative (the story line of which was familiar to them), and engaged in spontaneous conversation. The least-monitored form of the language learners' performance ought to reveal the interlanguage vernacular, and, indeed, these respondents increase t/d deletion in their least-monitored style (0.67) and decrease it in their most heavily-monitored one (0.30).

The stylistic continuum is represented in several SLA accounts of learner variation. Krashen's monitor model, for example, Krashen 1987, turns the continuum into a two-way distinction, suggesting that a few, easily-represented rules are the result of conscious activity (learning) but that most rules, difficult to describe, are the result of nonconscious activity (acquisition). In performance, Krashen claims, learners do not have sufficient time to monitor the learned rules, and their systems fail. Native speaker studies, however, have been little concerned with the monitoring of overtly learned rules. Even the most carefully-monitored (or 'formal') end of the stylistic continuum results from the application of rules of which native speakers lack metalinguistic awareness. From this perspective, monitoring refers to general attention to speech, not to attempts to retrieve consciously formulated rules.

It is true, however, that native speakers, particularly in unfamiliar and/or status-ridden settings, may attempt to monitor ancient secondary school prescriptions or other shibboleths (e.g., *who* versus *whom*), and a relatively small number of such often socially damaging stereotypes exist in every speech community. Krashen may believe that an even greater number of rules have just such a status for the language learner. Since it is only dichotomous, however, the monitor theory provides no explicit account of variation within both learned and acquired sets of rules, nor does it appear to allow learned items to permeate the area reserved for acquired ones.

In contrast, the continuous competence SLA model, for example, Tarone (1982), suggests that the stylistic continuum of the language acquirer operates much like that of the native speaker. The more attention the learner pays to speech, the more prestige forms are likely to occur (where prestige forms are construed to be target language forms or learners' understandings of what those forms are).

Tarone's characterization of what style is, however, borrows heavily from the operational devices used to elicit this dimension rather than from its underlying causes (e.g., degree of formality). Stylistic fluctuation, in her account, is due to the degree of monitoring or attention to form, and varying degrees of attention to form are by-products of the amount of time which various language tasks allow the language user for monitoring (e.g., writing perhaps the most, spontaneous conversation the least). This variation, however, all takes place for the language acquirer within only one envelope of performance or register; language learners, at least those in the early stages, are monoregistral. Only more advanced learners acquire different registers which entail such matters as genre and other complex norms of interaction and use which, in turn, contribute to the positioning of a task on the stylistic continuum.

Perhaps just some such distinction is at work in the data reported by Bayley in Table 1. The operational realization of the stylistic dimension is satisfactorily explained by the notion that greater monitoring leads to more target-like performance (presumably the retention of /t/d/ in final clusters). Oddly, however, the respondents whose network associations show greater contact with native speakers also show an increase of t/d deletion (0.61). This apparent contradiction may be explained in the following way: the respondents with low network associations with native speakers have a single register of performance, something which might be called the learner register. In it, absolute t/d realization is the target norm, and t/d deletion is the learner vernacular. (The sources of the latter may include Chinese syllable structure, universal preferences for syllable structure, stage of learning, and other matters.) For them, the stylistic continuum is operationalized as tasks and is straightforwardly represented in their scores as those tasks allow them more or less monitoring time.

In contrast, the respondents with greater native speaker network contacts may have begun to acquire some of the complex registral factors which lie behind the continuum. In those registers which promote informality (where, presumably, less monitoring goes on), native speakers also delete t/d in final clusters. Superficially, all the respondents appear to be observing a rule that states that the more they monitor, the more they delete. The different network

Table 1. Word-final t/d deletion probabilities (in consonant clusters) in Chinese learner English (adapted from Bayley 1990: 8).

Following segment:	Vowel	0.40
	Pause	0.45
	Glide	0.55
	Consonant or liquid	0.60
Style:	Reading	0.30
	Elicited narrative	0.53
	Conversation	0.67
Social network:	Chinese	0.39
	Chinese and American	0.61

relations, however, suggest that different factors lie behind this performance. For the low network relations group, the stylistic continuum is driven only by the amount of time made available for monitoring by the linguistic task set. For the high network relations group, the continuum is indeed defined by the amount of attention given to a task but as determined both by the purely linguistic shape of the task and by the native-speaker-like registral considerations which contribute to the determination of a task's position on the continuum.

An apparent fly in the ointment of the stylistic continuum, however, emerges in such sets of data as those shown in Table 2. The third person singular indicative marker (3rs) follows the predictions made earlier—the more attention paid to form (obviously here the grammar test), the greater likelihood of native-like performance; but the article shows exactly the reverse trend—the greater attention paid to form, the less target-like the performance.

Preston (1989) suggests that this apparent contradiction may be explained by incorporating something of the monitoring distinction into the continuous competence model. The 3rs in English is clearly marked—it (and only it) of the present indicatives has phonological substance, and it is, except perhaps for its morphophonological adjustment, simple, controlled by the purely local concern of agreement. The article, on the other hand, is multifunctional, has alternative forms (including even null), and is driven by such non-local factors as presupposition, given-new information, and so on.

The 3rs, therefore, is the sort of form which monitoring will provide the right answer for, even if learners have come up with theories of their own rather than being explicitly taught. Rumination on what form (if any) of the article to use, however, is apparently more likely to lead to disaster than success. Its rules are complex and not guided by an immediate, simple context. Preston (1989) concludes that, in general, marked forms will make more rapid progress in the interlanguage development of more highly-monitored styles, and unmarked forms will more quickly develop in the unmonitored ones.

Native-speaker studies of variability were done at least in part to show how variation was central to linguistic change, and studies of respondents of different age groups (studies in apparent time) rather than longitudinal ones have predominated. Only a few SLA studies have followed this lead; Young (1990), for example, shows that for Chinese learners of English the factor of low proficiency retards plural marking on nouns with a probability of 0.32 while the factor of high proficiency promotes plural marking with a probability of 0.60. SLA studies may, therefore, use quantitative methods to indicate the degree to which level of proficiency contributes to the predictability of target-like performance for a given feature.

1.2 The Dynamic Paradigm

The most noteworthy of the competing models in quantitative microsociolinguistics is associated with the work of Bailey, Bickerton (see *Bickerton, Derek*) and DeCamp (see *DeCamp, David*), particularly in its application to creole languages. Their work makes use of an implicational scale, which is sensitive to relations among variables in the entire system rather than to the set of determining influences on one variable.

The first application of such techniques to SLA is very likely Gatbonton (1978). Table 3 shows an implicational array of the voiced interdental (/ð/) for Canadian French learners of English. The controlling environments (here the preceding sound) are arranged on a scale of heaviest to lightest, but these weights are not only related to probabilistic influences of the various environments on the feature in question. The weight is an expression of the relation between one environment and all the others and the lect which that unique relationship defines. Lect 1, for example, is the grammar of learners who have not even begun to vary between non-native and target-like performances of /ð/ in the most likely phonological environment for target-like performance (i.e., after vowels). What is implicational about this arrangement is that every lighter environment also has, predictably, categorial non-target-like performance. Conversely, speakers of lect 11 who have invariant target-like performances in the lightest environment (i.e., the one least likely to promote such performance, here a preceding voiceless stop) predictably have it in every heavier environment. Such implicational arrays are apparently not arbitrary, for of the 28 respondents sampled in Gatbonton's study, only six did not fit one of the predicted lect patterns.

The dynamic paradigm approach is perhaps even more appropriate to semanto–syntactic and morphosyntactic variation, for the emerging lects are seen as ones which reveal redefined form–function units increasingly in line with target language norms. Huebner (1983), for example, in a year-long longitudinal analysis of an adult Hmong acquirer of English, shows, among other things, how *is(a)*

Table 2. VARBRUL probabilities for target-like realization of third singular indicative markers (3rs) and articles in English by Japanese and Arabic learners (Tarone 1985).

	3rs	Article
Japanese	0.63	0.42
Arabic	0.37	0.58
Grammar test	0.63	0.23
Interview	0.48	0.56
Narrative	0.39	0.72

Table 3. Implicational ordering of the acquisition of English /ð/ in five different environments by French Canadians (Preston 1989: 32, adapted from Gatbonton 1978).

			Linguistic environments			
	Heaviest				Lightest	Number of
Lect	V___	VCT___	VS___	VLCT___	VLS___	subjects N
1	1	1	1	1	1	3
2	1, 2	1	1	1	1	7
3	1, 2	1, 2	1	1	1	3
4	1, 2	1, 2	1, 2	1	1	0
5	1, 2	1, 2	1, 2	1, 2	1	2
6	1, 2	1, 2	1, 2	1, 2	1, 2	2
7	2	1, 2	1, 2	1, 2	1, 2	3
8	2	2	1, 2	1, 2	1, 2	1
9	2	2	2	1, 2	1, 2	1
10	2	2	2	2	1, 2	0
11	2	2	2	2	2	0

V___ = preceding vowel
VCT___ = preceding voiced continuant
VS___ = preceding voiced stop
VLCT___ = preceding voiceless continuant
VLS___ = preceding voiceless stop.
1 = categorical presence of nonnative substitute for English
2 = categorical presence of native or native-like English
1, 2 = variation of 1 and 2.

moves, in different environments, from marking asserted (or comment as opposed to topic) information to the range of functions which *is* has in the target language.

At first, there may appear to be only trivial differences between the Labovian and dynamic paradigms. The first studies the exact degree of influence of each factor; the second specifies the categorial states before and after variability and ignores the precise contribution of each controlling factor during variability, although the weight of each shows its relative effect. The psycholinguistic corollaries of the two modes are, however, quite distinct. The system which encloses the variety of probabilistic influences within the Labovian paradigm is a unified one. That is, variability, although clearly related to change, may also be relatively stable within the single competence of a monodialectal speaker. In short, variability is inherent. In the dynamic paradigm, any inherent variability is short-lived, lasting only during the brief transition between categorial presence and absence of form–function change (in a given environment). The greater variability which appears to be present is, in fact, simply the shifting back and forth from one lect to another. In short, most variability is apparent. The psycholinguistic ramifications of these two differing views have not been worked out in either native speaker or SLA contexts.

2. Language in its Social Context

The second group of general research trends surveyed here is represented by a variety of schools, the first three of which in particular are only briefly summarized.

2.1 The Ethnography of Communication

Closely associated with the American anthropological linguists Hymes (see *Hymes, Dell*) and Gumperz (see *Gumperz, John*), this style of sociolinguistic inquiry examines an array of contextual concerns in language performance, status, intent, reception, and the like. The targets of investigation typically include larger forms (e.g., genres, speech acts and events) as well as those investigated in quantitative styles, and the manner of investigation is more often qualitative. The results of such studies characterize the elements necessary to the communicative competence underlying appropriate speech behavior. Generally speaking, the influence of this area of sociolinguistic inquiry on SLA has been on the description of native-speaker behavior as a target model for speech acts (particularly in such culturally variable speech activities as warning, complimenting, requesting, and the like).

2.2 Ethnomethodology and Discourse Analysis

Discourse studies are associated with sociolinguistics, at least in part, due to the important contribution of such sociolingists as Garfinkel, Goffman (see *Goffman, Erving*), and Sacks (see *Sacks, Harvey*). In general, such studies hope to find a grammar of larger units, particularly the grammar that is created in the give-and-take of conversation. Like the ethnography of communication, discourse studies of native-speaker interaction have been held up as models in SLA, although an important additional trend has been that of the study of classroom interaction, and those and other studies have focused on the conversational details of native–non-native and non-native–non-native interactions (see *Discourse*; *Spoken Language in the Classroom*).

2.3 The Sociology of Language

SLA studies have also been sensitive to the larger concerns of societal and individual bi- and multilingualism and to the concerns of language planning, minority languages, area linguistics, and emerging standards and varieties (see *Bilingualism, Individual*; *Bilingualism, Societal*).

2.4 The Social Psychology of Language

Language attitude studies have been related to SLA concerns from their beginnings, although early work in such studies by Lambert (see *Lambert, Wallace E.*) and Fishman (see *Fishman, Joshua*) focused on the affective domain in bilingual settings. Consideration of attitudinal factors (both towards and of acquirers) has been a component of many approaches to SLA. Krashen's monitor theory, for example, includes an affective filter which may impede or promote acquisition. Schumann's acculturation model (e.g., Schumann 1978) suggests that maximum or attenuated social distance between learners and members of the speech community they wish to join may result in a frozen, pidginized variety of the target (a dramatic form of fossilization). Gardner (1985) reviews SLA theories which contain strong social psychological elements or are themselves by-products of investigations into the social psychology of language.

Studies in this framework are generally quantitative, often experimental studies of affective responses to language samples. Some studies, however, focus on linguistic details and others on social factors. Such studies as Schumann's, for example, detail the pidginized forms of an unsuccessful language learner and suggest that the learner's rejection by and of the new language environment is a major factor. On the other hand, studies carried out in the tradition of Giles and his associates, following on earlier work by Lambert and Fishman, detail the attitudes toward native and target languages and their speakers by learners and hosts, and reason that language learning success or failure is related to positive or negative valuations, respectively, on both sides (see *Social Psychology*).

3. Trends and Prospects

The Labovian and dynamic paradigms are being brought together in such quantitative work as Bayley's and Young's, for probabilities are being assigned to underlying semanto-syntactic categories as they emerge in new varieties of a developing interlanguage. Perhaps such focus will provide insights into the important psycholinguistic differences between the two models of research.

For ethnographic and attitudinal studies, Preston (1989) has suggested that the development of an interlanguage (see *Interlanguage*) is best thought of as a process which will produce a competent bilingual, not one which will clone a native speaker. That understanding should allow even more careful investigation of the developing rule systems of an interlanguage, perhaps even singling out those subtle rule differences which effectively symbolize the non-native but successful speech community member. Speech communities are made up of speakers who share norms of communication, not necessarily of those who share the same native language. As interlanguages develop, it is logical to assume that learners are putting together a competent but distinctive system (open to quantitative analysis), which gives them a place in the speech community (or communities) where they intend to interact, such interaction being open to the various means available for the study of language in its social context. Both approaches will surely engage the interest of those who care to look at sociolinguistics in SLA settings.

See also: Language in Society: Overview; Pidgins, Creoles and Minority Dialects in Education.

Bibliography

Bayley R 1990 Modeling interlanguage variation: -t, d deletion in Chinese English. (A paper presented to NWAVE-XIX (New Ways of Analyzing Variation in English), University of Pennsylvania, Philadelphia, PA, October, 1990)

Dickerson L J H 1974 *Internal and External Patterning of Phonological Variability in the Speech of Japanese Learners of English: Toward a Theory of Second-language Acquisition*. Unpublished PhD dissertation, University of Illinois, Chicago, IL

Dickerson L, Dickerson W 1977 Interlanguage phonology: Current research and future directions. In: Corder S P, Roulet E (eds.) *The Notions of Simplification, Interlanguages and Pidgins and their Relation to Second Language Pedagogy* (Actes du 5ème Colloque de Linguistique Appliquée de Neuchâtel, May 20–22, 1976). Libraire Droz, Geneva

Fasold R W 1984 Variation theory and language learning. In: Trudgill P (ed.) *Applied Sociolinguistics*. Academic Press, London

Gardner R C 1985 *Social Psychology and Second Language Learning*. Arnold, London

Huebner T 1983 Linguistic systems and linguistic change in an interlanguage. *Studies in Second Language Acquisition* 6: 33–53

Krashen S D 1987 *Principles and Practice in Second Language Acquisition*. Prentice-Hall, Englewood Cliffs, NJ

Labov W 1972 *Sociolinguistic Patterns*. University of Pennsylvania Press, Philadelphia, PA

Preston D R 1989 *Sociolinguistic and Second Language Acquisition*. Blackwell, Oxford, UK

Schumann J H 1978 The acculturation model for second language acquisition. In: Gingras R G (ed.) *Second Language Acquisition and Foreign Language Teaching*. Center for Applied Linguistics, Arlington, VA

Tarone E E 1982 Systematicity and attention in interlanguage. *Language Learning* **32**: 69–84

Tarone E E 1985 Variability in interlanguage use: A study of style-shifting in morphology and syntax. *Language Learning* **35**: 373–403

Young R 1990 *Variation in Interlanguage Morphology*. Peter Lang, New York

Bilingual Education
M. E. Brisk

Bilingual education, using two or more languages as a medium of instruction, dates from 3000 BCE when scribes in the Mesopotamia were taught in both Sumerian and Akkadian. Most countries in the world offer bilingual programs in government funded and/or private schools. One of the languages is usually the national or official language (see *National Language/Official Language*) while the other language of instruction can be indigenous (Quechua in Perú), another official language (Arabic in Israel), regional (French in Canada), the language of immigrants (Finnish in Sweden), the language of guest workers (Moroccan in The Netherlands), an international language (English in Argentina), or the language of sojourners (Japanese in the United States).

The scope of bilingual education varies throughout the world. In a few countries bilingual education is universal in all schools. In Brunei, education takes place for all in both Standard Malay and in English. In most countries, however, bilingual education serves only a limited number of students. Such programs are the result of efforts of individual or experimental schools. The Foyer project administers five Dutch schools in Brussels serving immigrant children from Morocco, Italy, and Turkey. Students receive instruction in their native language and in Dutch. The use of Dutch increases as they move up the grades. They also take French which is compulsory for all students in Dutch schools.

Some bilingual programs address needs of multilingual student populations. In the United States, national and local legislation support bilingual education for diverse linguistic populations. Such programs serve only about a quarter of the students with limited proficiency in English and are designed to serve students for only a limited number of years.

Changes in the political history of a country are reflected in education policies. As a crown colony, Hong Kong traditionally had dual-system schools, English schools and Chinese schools where Chinese and English were taught as subjects respectively. Since 1997 all schools use Chinese as a medium of instruction in the elementary grades with English taught as a subject. English is the medium of instruction in high schools while Chinese language and history are subjects taught in Chinese.

When a language does not have a written form, bilingual education requires development of a writing system and materials in that language. In Africa, communities and linguists have teamed to promote experimental bilingual programs for the elementary grades using the community language. An alternative is the monoliterate approach to bilingual education in which students are taught orally in the home language while they acquire literacy in the other language.

1. Goals

The five major purposes of bilingual education are enrichment, maintenance, educational assistance, language revival, and serving transient populations. The acquisition of a second language is considered an educational asset. Bilingual education is designed to achieve second language fluency. Students in the Kato Gakuen elementary school in Japan receive instruction in English and Japanese beginning in kindergarten. Each language is employed equally through grade six.

Bilingual schooling is instrumental in language preservation. In a school in northern Arizona, Hualapai children are instructed in English and Hualapai throughout their elementary schooling. At the secondary level most of the instruction is in English with certain subjects taught in Hualapai.

Throughout the world children are socialized in languages other than the major language of education of the country. Bilingual education programs instruct students in their home language while they acquire the major or official language of the country. Eventually, students are integrated into the educational system in the national language. In Guatemala, the *Programa Nacional de Educación Bilingüe* (PRONEBI) provides bilingual education to

Mayan populations in their home language and in Spanish.

Bilingual education also is employed to revive languages. Such is the case of Basque in Spain. Since the 1970s the promotion of Basque through education has helped not only strengthen Basque among Basque people but has made Spanish speakers living in the Basque region conversant in Basque. Parents in this area of Spain may opt to send children to Spanish, Basque, or bilingual Spanish/Basque schools.

Since families of government or multinational employees move frequently, bilingual schools are created to facilitate their language needs and provide some continuity in the education. The central schools in India for families employed by the central government who move around the country offer instruction in the sciences in English and in the humanities in Hindi. Students' mother tongues are taught as a subject. There are a number of European schools created to serve civil servants working with the European Union organizations. Where there is space, local or immigrant students are also included. These schools have subsections for several of the languages of the member states where instruction takes place in the native language of the subgroup of students and another of the member state languages. Third or fourth languages are commonly taught as subjects.

2. Program Models

There are four major types of bilingual programs: dual language; language switch; Canadian Immersion; and transitional bilingual education. Dual language programs use two languages throughout schooling. In language-switch models instruction takes place in one language for some grades, while a different language is used for the remainder of the grades. Canadian Immersion programs start schooling in the children's second language, introducing the home language gradually although instruction continues in the second language. Transitional programs use the native language of the students for a short period as a bridge to learn the second language.

Programs differ greatly depending on their language outcomes, target population, and use of the two languages. Unplanned variation results from teachers', beliefs and level of language proficiency. Although a model may call for the use of one language, some teachers instruct mostly in the other because they believe it is more important or because they are more fluent and comfortable in it.

In dual-language models, which aim at additive bilingualism, (see *Bilingualism, Societal*) students develop two languages. Dual-language programs vary depending on the type of population they serve. Usually students begin school knowing at least one of the languages of instruction. Occasionally a small percentage of students are native speakers of a different language. Private schools catering to elites often feature a bilingual curriculum as in Argentina where the Spanish curriculum meets requirements of the Ministry of Education while instruction in English, French, or German conforms to standard curricula of those countries. An increasing number of programs in the United States attract English speakers as well as speakers of other languages. Two-way programs, as they are called, instruct students in both English and in the other language. The presence of native speakers of both languages is considered an asset for second language development.

Language maintenance (see *Language Maintenance, Shift, and Death*) is another type of dual-language program where language minority populations are schooled in their home and national languages. Navajo students in selected reservation schools in the United States receive instruction in Navajo and English throughout their elementary school. At the secondary level, subjects related to the Navajo culture are taught in that language. Some ethnic schools, initiated by ethnic communities or religious organizations, feature bilingual curricula. Such schools fulfill educational requirements of the country as well as the community's need to maintain their language and culture.

The distribution of the two languages in the curriculum of the various types of dual-language programs varies. Languages may be equally balanced by teaching half a day in each language or alternating days or weeks in each language. In some schools languages are used for specific subjects. In bilingual schools for the deaf both languages are used all the time since the sign language serves face-to-face communication and another is used for reading and writing.

Some countries promote bilingualism by switching the language of instruction after a few grades. To prepare students for the switch, the language is first taught as a subject. In Luxembourg the language is switched not once but twice. Most children arrive in school monolingual in Luxemburger, the language of initial schooling. Instruction gradually changes to German with French taught as a subject and by high school it gradually changes to French.

French immersion programs were developed in Canada to promote bilingualism among English speakers. In the early immersion version of the model, students are introduced to schooling in French, their second language. French remains the only language of instruction for about three years. English, the home language, is then slowly introduced until it occupies 70 percent of instruction time by the secondary grades. Late immersion models start students in English with French taught as a subject. Towards the end of elementary school, French becomes the only language of instruction for two years. English is gradually reintroduced. The early immersion model has been adopted by other countries using other languages for immersion, always aiming at the dominant language population.

Transitional programs prevail where bilingual education aims at assisting students who do not speak the official or national language in which most schooling occurs. The language outcome is subtractive bilingualism because students learn a second language but lose or do not develop their home language. Students are instructed in their home language for a limited time while they develop proficiency in the official language. In England, programs for Punjabi students last one year, Turkish and Moroccan students can attend transitional programs in The Netherlands for two years, while Sweden offers four-year programs. These programs are directed to some of the students who are in special classes until they are ready to join students whose entire instruction is in the official or national language. Some schools attempt to integrate students. In Norway, bilingual instruction directed to Turkish, Urdu, and Vietnamese speakers takes place in classrooms that include Norwegian speaking students. A team-teaching approach is used where one teacher instructs both groups in Norwegian and the other teacher helps immigrant students in the content areas using their native language.

3. Other Education Models for Language Development

Programs that seek to develop fluency in two languages, a second language, or the students' home language are often labeled bilingual education. They are not strictly speaking bilingual since instruction takes place in one language while the other is taught as a subject. In other cases instruction takes place in students' second language. The students become bilingual but the program is monolingual. Yet other programs offer special classes in the mother tongue of language minority students. Communities seek to maintain their children's bilingualism by creating ethnic schools or programs that run on weekends or after school where the home language is taught. Local governments, religious institutions, or foreign governments support these programs. The attendance is voluntary for as long as parents wish to send their children to these programs.

Language programs emanate from a desire for bilingualism, the need to recognize various linguistic groups, educational assistance, language revival, and service to transient populations. Bilingualism is a necessity in Brussels where Dutch schools require French classes for Flemish students and French schools have compulsory Dutch classes. Several linguistic groups may overlap in one country. While each group uses its language for instruction in the school, the language of the other group is offered as a compulsory or elective subject. In Finland parents may choose to send their children to schools that instruct either in Finnish with Swedish taught as a subject or schools that instruct in Swedish with Finnish as a subject. Many countries offer special second language classes to assist students who do not speak the school language. Throughout the United States, school districts offer English as a Second Language to large numbers of immigrant and other home language students. Rather than bilingual schools, some movements to revitalize languages (see *Endangered Languages*; *Reversing Language Shift*) have called for total immersion in the language. Such is the case of Catalan immersion schools in Spain where instruction takes place in Catalan and Spanish is taught as a subject. The same approach is followed in the Gaelscoils in Ireland where instruction takes place in Irish with English taught as a subject.

In international schools which serve transient populations, English is usually the language of instruction while the language of the country as well as other languages are taught as subjects. In the Vienna International School, German is a compulsory subject and a third language is optional. Mother-tongue instruction is encouraged but the parents must pay for it.

4. Debate Over Language Use in Education

The paradox of bilingual education is that when it is employed in private schools for the children of elites it is accepted as educationally valid, but when it becomes a matter of public policy, bilingual education stirs controversy. This debate over choice of language for instruction is the result of universal education. In the past, education was the perquisite of a few. Knowledge of several languages was an important component of education. With the advent of education for all, language use in schools became associated with rights of native speakers of those languages. The use of languages in education became an issue connected with political, economic, and social agendas far removed from the simple notion that bilingualism is the mark of an educated individual.

The need to consider language in education emerges from the presence of indigenous groups that speak diverse languages, the influx of people of other languages and cultures who enter a country as immigrants, guest workers, or refugees, and/or the changes in political boundaries. African countries that adopted European languages after independence as their official language confronted a dilemma: how to educate a population that speaks a variety of languages which often do not include the official language. Similar concerns are present in Australia, the United States, and certain countries in Latin America, such as Mexico and Perú, toward their indigenous populations. Many European countries, Australia, and the United States are destinations of immigrant, guest workers, or refugee populations. These countries have crafted educational policies to address the presence of a multilingual population in their schools.

Changes in the language of education have followed historical events such as the dissolution of the Soviet Union and the retreat of colonial powers in Asia. The rise in power of local groups has created drastic changes in language choice for schooling. Upon the formation of the federation of Malaysia in 1957, the educational policy allowed for Malay, Tamil, Chinese, and English medium schools for the elementary level and Malay and English for the secondary level. The increase in power of local people has translated into education being principally in Malay with some concessions for other languages.

A pioneering study conducted by the United Nations Educational, Scientific, and Cultural Organization (UNESCO) in 1953 revealed that children educated in their second language experienced difficulties in school. The report of experts from around the world, sponsored by UNESCO, declares that the home language is the best initial medium of instruction because it relates to the child's culture, facilitates literacy development and learning of different subjects, and promotes understanding between the home and the school. The report also underscores the importance of teaching language minority students their national language as a second language by gradually introducing it in elementary schools to prepare students for further education.

Many educators and linguists today echo UNESCO's recommendations. Yet others still adamantly oppose instruction through the native languages and believe that intense instruction in the national or official language is the best route to educational success. Emotional and pragmatic reasons abound in these debates on choice of language for education. Arguments often ignore educational principles due to political, economic, social, cultural, linguistic, and psychological pressures. Support for specific languages for instruction derives from notions of national identity and recognition of ethnic groups. The cost of implementing such programs and the practicality of teaching certain languages concern many politicians and administrators while the economic advantages of knowing certain languages persuades others. The social status of languages influences the desirability of including them in schooling. Cultural and linguistic diversity appeals to some and concerns others. The formation of identity and the development of positive attitudes toward languages and their speakers are considered essential by some, while others do not believe it is the task of schools but the duty of families and community organizations.

Many nations have developed educational plans to address the role of languages in education. The scope of these policies varies. Australia's 1987 National Policy on Languages strives for language maintenance of immigrant and aboriginal languages. In contrast, Danish official guidelines for teaching language minorities (*Undervisningsministeriet* 1984) focus on providing for rapid adjustment to instruction in Danish. Regardless of how progressive or limited the policies are, governments have been slow in implementing such plans. In order to succeed, measures that require use of minority languages in education must include support for materials development and teacher preparation. The government of Nepal, pressured by minority language groups and linguistic human rights activists, retreated from its Nepali-only educational policy to allow language minority communities to establish native language primary schools. There has been no visible effort from the government to implement such measures. In Nepal, as in many other nations with other pressing concerns, the preservation or utilization of minority languages in education is not a high priority.

Much of the rhetoric about use of languages in education eludes the principal goal of schools which is to develop knowledgable, thoughtful, and well adjusted individuals. Use of the home language and culture of children has a role in such development. In the present world, knowledge of more than one language is also an educational asset. To achieve such goals it is more important to focus on the quality of schools and instruction than to protect particular languages. Bilingual education research illustrates the features of schools, curricula, instruction, and assessment instrumental in successful education. Knowledge of this research supported by the will to implement its recommendations is a promising formula for quality bilingual schooling.

See also: Minority Languages; School Language Polices; Bilingualism, Societal.

Bibliography

Brisk M E 1998 *Bilingual Education: From Compensatory to Quality Schooling*. Lawrence Erlbaum, Mahwah, NJ

Durgunoglu A Y, Verhoeven L (eds.) 1998 *Literacy Development in a Multilingual Context: Cross-cultural Perspectives*. Lawrence Erlbaum, Mahwah, NJ

European Language Council Homepage. http//www.fu-berlin.de/elc/

Faltis C J, Hudelson S J 1998 *Bilingual Education in Elementary and Secondary School Communities*. Allyn and Bacon, Boston, MA

Fardon R, Furniss G (eds.) 1994 *Aftrican Languages, Development and the State*. Routledge, New York

Glenn C L, de Jong E J 1996 *Educating Immigrant Children*. Garland Publishing, New York

Johnson R K, Swain M (eds.) 1997 *Immersion Education: International Perspectives*. Cambridge University Press, Cambridge, UK

Jones G M, Ozóg A C K (eds.) 1993 Bilingualism and national development, Special Issue. *Journal of Multilingual and Multicultural Development*

Krashen S 1999 *Condemned Without a Trial: Bogus Arguments Against Bilingual Education.* Heinemann Publishing, Portsmouth, NH

Lewis E G 1977 Bilingualism and bilingual education: The ancient world to the Renaissance. In: Spolsky B, Cooper R L (eds.) *Frontiers of Bilingual Education.* Newbury House, Rowley, MA

Mahshie S N 1995 *Educating Deaf Students Bilingually: With Insights and Applications from Sweden and Denmark.* Gallaudet University Pre-College Programs, Washington, DC McCarty T L, Zepeda O (eds.) 1995 *Indigenous Language Education and Literacy. Special Issue. Bilingual Research Journal.* National Association for Bilingual Education, Washington, DC

New Language Planning Newsletter. Central Institute of Indian Languages, Mysore, India

Skutnabb-Kangas T (ed.) 1995 *Multilingualism for All: European Studies on Multilingualism.* Swets and Zeitlinger, The Netherlands

The World Bank Group 1995 *Costs and Benefits of Bilingual Education in Guatemala.* http://www.worldbank.org/html/extdr/educ/edu_econ/biling_g.htm

United Nations Educational, Scientific, and Cultural Organization 1953 *The Use of Vernacular Languages in Education.* UNESCO, Paris

Black English in Education: UK

M. Dalphinis

Although Black English has a longer history as a language of trade and initial contact between Africans and speakers of English on the West African coast from at least 1600, Black English in the UK is the result of the linguistic change from Creole (see *Pidgins and Creoles: An Overview*) languages spoken by older Afro–Caribbean immigrants into the UK which, under the impact of English as the dominant language in the UK have become a more English-like means of communication for the UK-born descendants of these former immigrants.

1. Linguistic Changes

Creole languages in the UK have undergone a process of linguistic change to become Black English: this is similar to the way in which Creoles have changed to Black American speech, in the USA (see *Ebonics and African American Vernacular English*).

These changes have a number of phonological, grammatical, and syntactic features. Phonologically, Creoles are being replaced by largely white working-class English linguistic features, as the latter are the group the Creole speakers have had most sustained contacts with in the UK. For example, the use of ʔ, in *ju wo me?* ('You what mate'), in Black English, represents a clear Cockney influence. Similarly, Jamaican Creole *kyã* ('can't') is pronounced *kã*, under the influence of English 'can't,' by speakers of Black English.

Creole grammatical features in Black English have been retained at a mainly unconscious level of linguistic control, for example, in saying 'John go to market,' when the speaker wants to say (at a conscious level) 'John goes to the market'; this reflects the Creole uninflected verb, *John go makit*. Similarly the phrase *migwann mi ducks* ('I'm on my way, ducks'), reflects a continuation of Creole grammatical structures but with the use of the working-class English loan word 'ducks' (meaning 'dear').

Other grammatical features include the use of Adjectival Verbs, for example, *red* in *it red* instead of English 'It is red.' A major grammatical feature of Black English is the mixed use of both English and Creole grammatical features, for example, *di walls dem*—'the walls' in which both the English plural and Black English plural forms are included.

At the semantic level, Creole concepts have entered into English, for example, English 'wicked' has been extended to include the Creole meaning of 'very good.' The general trend is from Creole to Black English to English. However, Creoles of French vocabulary have not interfaced with English, and instead are involved in the general shift to Jamaican Creole by Black youth irrespective of island origin.

2. Creole Features and Black English

To clarify the differences between Black English and Creole both in the Caribbean and in the UK there is the general recognition by linguists of a basilect (see *Pidgins and Creoles: Models*) of core Creole sentences which contrast with an acrolect/mesolect of Black

English sentences. In this acrolect the majority of the speaker's repertoire consists of English sentences, with an admixture of Creole core sentences.

Some writers also point to degrees of fluency of the speakers in Creole/Black English as another distinguishing factor. Implicit in this factor is the view that Black English is a transitional position between Creole and English. Consequently, its speakers use Creole grammatical features, usually at an unconscious level, while at a conscious level, they use phonetic and semantic features of English, with Creole interjections for particular social effects.

3. Education

The UK context has been one of initially deeply held racist views about Creole speakers and the type and amount of education needed by them. Within this social context, the following main historical trends can be identified in relation to Creole and Black English in UK education.

(a) Eradicate Creole/Black English in the classroom.
(b) Assimilate Creole/Black English in the classroom.
(c) Tolerate Creole/Black English in the classroom.
(d) Accept linguistic pluralism within the overall uniformity of the UK National Curriculum.

These changes are often related to varying emphases in political thinking, as well as changes in the ideologies about teaching and learning. For example, teacher motivation to 'eradicate' Creole in the 1960s was tied up with the then popular learning theory based on the behaviorist stimulus/response ideas of Skinner. This view saw the Creoles as part of 'bad' linguistic behavior which had to be corrected or changed in order that English or 'good' linguistic behavior could emerge.

This corrective view was also linked with many Afro–Caribbeans being put into schools for the educationally subnormal, because their linguistic performance was seen as an aspect of linguistic and cognitive inferiority. The eradication view was followed by assimilationist educational perspectives in the 1980s which were characterized by a wish to ensure that a great deal of English culture was 'soaked up' by the children of Afro–Caribbean immigrants. This, indeed, led to one or two local authorities bussing their Afro–Caribbean pupils around the Local Education Authority so that they did not become too 'contaminated' by their own culture and languages. Later educational perspectives in the 1990s, when ideas of linguistic varieties and repertoires were popular, encouraged a greater tolerance of Creole and Black English, which were used in some London schools as part of linguistic and literacy studies.

Within the National Curriculum documents, Creoles are mainly discussed under the English recommendations from the following perspectives, which would apply inter alia to Black English:

(a) providing information on the spread of English internationally;
(b) information about linguistic change;
(c) information about comparing languages;
(d) information about Creoles;
(e) the use of Creole/Black English as part of class exemplification;
(f) as part of a generally assimilationist process, from Creole to Black English to English.

The Kingman Committee Report on English, indeed, highlights Creole as a language which, amongst others, has enriched English. It highlights similarities between English, Black English and English Creole vocabulary while downplaying syntactic differences.

Black parents have seen standard English, rightly, as the key to access to education in an English-speaking society and have, generally, had expectations of high educational achievement for their children. These expectations were well supported in the Caribbean by both the educational outcomes and the high expectations of Caribbean teachers with regards to their pupils. However, in the UK this traditional Caribbean expectation has been questioned by both the lower educational achievements of pupils of Caribbean origins and in the expectations of UK teachers, for example, as described by Stone (1981) and Coard (1971).

4. Accommodation in the National Curriculum Perspective

In order to accommodate demands by Black parents in addressing the cultural needs of their children, a number of educational texts by Black authors have become part of the National Curriculum, for example, stories by P. Breinberg in the book list for the National Curriculum reading profile component.

The general theme of accommodation is one in which many aspects of Black English culture and language(s) can easily be investigated to fulfill a number of National Curriculum requirements in English, particularly in the area of speaking and listening. However, these are highly dependent upon the skill, interest, and cultural repertoires of the teacher.

Similarly, with standardized assessments in relation to mathematics and science, there is no ruling against the use of mother tongues, including Black English, in the presentation of the mathematical and scientific skills of the pupils.

However, in the same way that the Community Languages which can form part of the schedule of 'foreign' languages taught in the National Curriculum are prescribed (these include Greek and Chinese, but exclude Turkish), so too are the narrow terms within which Creole and Black English are considered in the UK National Curriculum.

While it could be claimed that the National Curriculum implies that Creole/Black English is part of the general bilingual heritage of Afro–Caribbean pupils, it is clear that Creole is described as a 'dialect of English,' although with an 'apology':

> ... The term 'dialect of English' which we have just used is itself problematic. Whether Creole varieties are termed 'dialects of' English or regarded as languages in their own right is a political and ideological question, which concerns the social identity of groups of speakers in UK society. It is not a matter which has a simple linguistic definition.
>
> (Department of Education and Science 1989 4.9)

The issue is how to assimilate an ex-slave population within the wider 'English' family while forgetting that some Caribbean Creoles are derived from French vocabulary. Indeed while accepting linguistic variety, both the Kingman and the Cox Reports focus upon the centrality of English (as was their remit) and see Black English/Creole only as a means of illustrating the international dimensions of English within an overall assimilationist process.

5. Culture and Identity

Issues of identity and of attitudes towards Creole and Black English, remain the areas that lack the attention of educational researchers in the UK. Historical factors have had important influences on these issues. The identity of Creole speakers in the UK, for example, is tied up with UK nationalist attitudes, which do not foster the educational development of an Afro–Caribbean identity, but which suggest that convergence towards a single 'UK' culture is desirable. Black English speakers, therefore, often relate to Creole/Black English as a symbol of identity in the face of monolithic 'UK' racism, irrespective of any high degree of fluency in Creole by the speakers concerned.

Attitudes to Black English by Black English speakers themselves have often been negative, particularly as far as older Creole speakers are concerned. The latter often saw Creole as a barrier to the economic advancement of their children. This has meant that discussing anything to do with Creole in the UK educational system has always begun on the difficult ground of negative parental attitudes towards any such discussion by teachers, who the parents thought were using another strategy to educationally oppress their children, as had been done in relation to issues of educational subnormality previously. Speakers of Black English, therefore, often have the ambivalent background of a negative stereotype of their parents, while wanting to preserve Black English as one of the few manifestations of their differences from a White UK society which they perceive as racist. Black English, therefore, becomes a retreat for Black English pupils who want to restrict contacts with a White society which has proved to be hostile.

Oral literature in Creole remains a productive aspect of Black English and Creole culture, as many Afro–Caribbean poets in the UK use it as a medium, for example, L. K. Johnson and M. Collins. Closely related to the medium of such literary works is the strong African musical tradition which, in Reggae and other Afro–Caribbean music, uses Black English/Creole as an essential cornerstone of its communication. Dub poetry and disc jockey verbal communication in more recent times are also a dimension of African oral art which, although it may not use Creole in its surface structure, is very reliant on Black American speech, which like Black English, is itself on a continuum from a previous Black American Creole.

The question which needs to be asked is what is to be the destiny of Black English in the UK, in the light of previous Black American Creole experiences. Given the much smaller size of the Afro–Caribbean population in the UK than in the USA, the trend of linguistic assimilation into native British varieties may be more profound.

Racial difference will remain accentuated. Africans have, however, always changed the cultures they found themselves in, in order to express their own consciously and unconsciously held beliefs. That trend seems likely also to continue, not least in the area of language.

6. Conclusion

The English National Curriculum accommodates the possibility of Creole usage but politically implies that the usage must be in an assimilationist cause, by relating the Black English/Creole mother tongue to UK English. The culture of young Afro–Caribbeans however, caught in the contradictions of racism, the search for sheer survival and maintenance of a sense of identity, is giving rise to other dimensions of Black English/Creole linguistic development in the UK.

See also: Standard English and Educational Policy; Ebonics and African American Vernacular English; Pidgins and Creoles: An Overview.

Bibliography

Department of Education and Science 1989 *English for Ages 5 to 16*. HMSO, London

Coard B 1971 *How the West Indian Child is Made Educationally Sub-Normal in the British School System*. New Beacon Books, London

Stone M 1981 *The Education of the Black Child in Britain*. Fontana, Glasgow, UK

Child Language: An Overview
S. Strömqvist

The study of child language is first and foremost a window on the developmental process by which individual children acquire a language—whether spoken, signed, or written—in interaction with their environment. Children's language acquisition is situated in a cognitive and a sociocultural context, and the structure of development is shaped by biologically given information-processing capacities and constraints in interaction with the structure of the particular input to the child. All normally developing children are known to follow a similar overall structure of development with lexical and grammatical spurts typically occurring between roughly one-and-a-half and three years of age. At the same time, children's sensitivity to their linguistic environment leads to certain language-particular marks on their developmental profile from very early on.

Some aspects of language, such as pronunciation skills or a basic grammar, are to a large extent already acquired at a relatively early stage of development. Other aspects of what you know when you know a language continue to develop beyond childhood. For example, there is a continuing growth of lexical knowledge and of rhetorical (e.g., narrative, expository, etc.) abilities in adolescent and adult language users. Indeed, language acquisition is an open-ended process and there is neither any perfectly steady state nor any stage of completeness in the linguistic career of a normal human being.

1. Towards a Theory of Child Language Development

The definition of language acquisition as the process by which learners develop a language in interaction with their environment yields five broad concepts or theoretical terms: 'learner,' 'environment,' 'interaction,' 'language,' and 'development.' A comprehensive theory of child language development should integrate and provide a deeper understanding of these terms. To put this somewhat differently, a theory of child language development presupposes theories of what a learner is, the nature of the interaction between the learner and his or her environment, what it takes for something to be a 'language' or constitute knowledge of language, and how the structure of knowledge and skills acquired—as well as the acquisition process itself—change over time (development).

Although there is consensus in the scientific community that a number of factors associated with the above five concepts interact to shape language development in the child, there is no consensus about the exact nature or the relative weight of these factors. Some researchers assume that syntax is the most central aspect of language and that the learner is biologically endowed with crosslinguistically valid knowledge of language ('universal grammar'). According to this theoretical position, the child's input plays a passive role, in that it merely triggers the assumedly innate brain program to work out the central syntactic constraints of the linguistic environment. Indeed, the input to the child is seen as containing a lot of noise, possibly distracting the child from discovering the underlying constraints and regularities of language. Because of this 'poverty of the stimulus,' the argument goes, the child has to be genetically endowed with sufficient knowledge of language in order to be able to acquire language all the same. Further, a consequence of this position is that those aspects of language which are considered to be most important can be said to be fully acquired well before the end of the preschool period—see, for example, Pinker (1996).

Other researchers hold that the central thing about language is the communication of meaning, a position which foregrounds semantic and pragmatic aspects of language, and that language acquisition is not merely the felicitous acquisition of lexical and syntactic forms, but the mapping of these forms onto meanings and communicative functions. According to this view, important parts of language development can be modeled in terms of reorganizations of the mental representations in the learner or, more precisely, reorganizations of the relation between linguistic forms and functions/content. These reorganizational processes are driven both by principles of human information processing (such as principles of clarity, economy, etc.) and by external factors (the input and the learner's adaptation to language usage in new sociocultural contexts), and they characterize the language user not only in childhood but also in adolescence and adulthood. See, for example, Ninio and Snow (1996), Berman and Slobin (1994).

Further, the nature of the biologically given propensity for language learning need not be in the form of inborn knowledge or information. According to the so-called connectionist view, the information-processing capacities emerging from the neural architecture of the brain provide the prime explanation for children's ability to build language on the basis of linguistic input—see, for example, Elman et al. (1997). The interaction between learners and their environment is at the core of this approach, as it is in approaches focusing on pragmatic aspects of language. The input is assumed to play an active, formatting role, in children's acquisition of language.

The variablity and contextual distribution of bits and pieces of language in the input tend to be seen not as noise but as a rich source of information which children can use to discover what these bits and pieces are and how they are used for communication.

A particularly elucidating approach to the role of the input is the crosslinguistic study of language acquisition—see, for example, Slobin (1985–97). Comparisons of child language development across languages which display similarities and differences have helped articulate ways in which diversity of input can effect diversity of acquisition structure. The rapidly growing use of computer technologies in the international research community for sharing and analyzing child language data has greatly facilitated crosslinguistic comparisons (see MacWhinney 1991).

2. The Beginnings of Language in Infancy

Perception experiments using so-called habituation techniques (e.g., the head turning paradigm) show that at around six months of age infants have begun to tune in to their ambient linguistic soundscape. For example, they perform better at discrimination tasks involving sound contrasts that occur frequently in their ambient language; or, they prefer familiar sounds to unfamiliar ones in preferential tasks. The differences between the sounds used in the experiments can be subtle. For example, infants growing up with American English prefer to listen to a [y] typical of American English as distinct from a [y] typical of Swedish. The emerging representations of speech sounds in the infant at this early stage are nothing like proper linguistic representations in the sense that they would be used for contrasting one word form from another. They are, however, an important first step, which, under normal circumstances, will clearly influence the further course of development. A few months later, towards the end of their first year, infants begin to display phonetic qualities of their ambient language in their own babbling. For example, Swedish infants have been shown to babble with a more dental articulation than American English infants, who are distinguished by a more alveolar babbling.

Around the beginning of the second half of their first year, infants typically begin to show signs of having formed mental representations of objects, that is, representations they can to some extent retrieve at will. For example, contingent upon having dropped an object so that it is temporarily out of sight, they can start searching for it. This landmark of cognitive development, known as 'object permanence,' is a precondition to the learning of words. Words typically begin to emerge in children's communicative development around one year of age, at roughly the same time as most children start to walk. Object permanence is also a precondition to 'peek-a-boo' (suddenly hiding, for example, a hand puppet and then suddenly making it reappear), a game which is played with small children across many different cultures of the world.

The learning of words and other meaningful units involves ferreting out units of the input speechstream (the 'segmentation task') and mapping these units/forms onto concepts/functions (the 'mapping task'). The child's job of solving these tasks is determined by a number of different, interacting factors.

In spoken language certain parts of an utterance tend to be prosodically foregrounded (by means of stress, pitch, and/or duration), and others tend to be backgrounded. In child-directed adult speech, these differentiations are often exaggerated as compared to adult-directed adult speech. The exaggerated contour increases the perceptual salience of the foregrounded items even more and thereby serves as a spotlight guiding a child to direct his or her attentional resources to selected parts of the speech stream. This kind of spotlight hits first and foremost content words, to a limited extent function words, and to no or almost no extent affixes. A segmentation strategy based on prosodic spotlight would thus yield a predominance of content words in the child's earliest vocabulary, a prediction which turns out to be correct.

The child's early encounters with language take place in face-to-face interaction, a setting which provides the interactants with a shared perceptual space and the possibility of online feedback and mutual adaptation. In this kind of setting, content words (*car, teddy, fall* (*down*), etc.) and deictic words (*there, that one, this,* etc.) are relatively easy to grasp for the early word learner not only because of their perceptual salience but also because their meaning can be demonstrated or exemplified by reference to objects, relations, and events in the shared perceptual space. Gestures (importantly pointing) and gaze accompanying speech further tend to facilitate the child's mapping task in that they help in securing joint attention to the object or event referred to or commented upon.

In their so-called 'sensorimotor' development, prelinguistic infants manipulate objects in the physical environment, making something fall, putting an object into or taking it out of a container, using force to remove something which is stuck, etc. In this way children are gathering experiences from manipulative motion scenarios in which they themselves are often the causal agent. Children thereby come to shape concepts of various types of objects, or spatial relations (e.g., containment, support, tightness of fit, or direction up, down, in, or out), of causality, and of different types of motion events. Since many of these concepts are precocious in the sense that they develop before children start to acquire words, they might facilitate children's mapping task insofar as they present themselves as candidates for concepts that can be encoded into a linguistic form.

Precocious interactional activities may provide a frame of understanding for novel words and constructions. For example, extending the peek-a-boo game with speech acts (such as *Where did he go?*, *Where is he?*, *There he is again!*), make these speech acts easier for the child to understand than if they were encountered in an equally novel activity type.

For further details, see Clark and Clark (1977), Morgan and Demuth (1996).

3. Vocabulary Development and Grammar in Early Childhood

3.1 The Vocabulary Spurt, Analysis, and Inflectional Morphemes

A child's build-up of the first 25–50 words proceeds slowly, but then there is typically a steep increase in lexical growth rate, the so-called 'vocabulary spurt.' On average, the vocabulary spurt starts towards the end of a child's second year of life. Exceptionally early word learners start their spurt at the beginning of their second year, and slow ones towards the end of their third year.

As to their sound shape, the early word forms in children's language development can have many different relations to the adult target forms. Occasionally, children can hit the target in strikingly accurate fashion, something that might suggest a holistic imitation strategy on the part of the child. Often, however, children's productions are simplified in comparison to the adult targets, suggesting that they have performed some sort of analysis of their input. For example, given the target word *crocodile*, some children would focus on and expend their effort of analysis on its multisyllabic quality, whereas others would focus on the stressed syllable only. The former focus of analysis would typically be at the expense of the details internal to the syllables, resulting in, for example, a form of pronunciation like [kokoko]. The latter focus would typically allow for a greater resolution of segmental details, resulting in, for example, [dajl].

The study of phases of analysis and reorganizational processes is at the core of child language research. Already diary studies contain ample evidence and exemplification of this phenomenon. Consider the following four developmental sequences for the sake of illustration.

The first sequence is indicative of reorganizational processes in the child's phonological representations of the word *pretty*: (a) [prətɪ] → (b) [bɪdɪ] → (c) [prətɪ]. Because of the initial (a) and final (c) similarity with the target form and the medial (b) dip (phase of deviance), this developmental pattern is often described as 'U-shaped.' The dip is revealing of some kind of generalization and top-down processing, resulting in an observable linguistic product which deviates from the target standard. And the developmental move from (b) (deviation) to (c) (target form) represents a reanalysis or adjustment to conform with the adult target. In the developmental sequence just quoted children can be hypothesized to have first learned the form [prətɪ] as an unanalyzed whole ('rote-learning'), whereas in the second phase they have reorganized their representation of the word in terms of its internal segmental structure. If the task was to learn in total, say, only 100 words, it might not be economical to expend cognitive efforts on analysis; rote-learning would suffice. Conversely, the rapidly growing number of words following the start of the vocabulary spurt pushes children to reorganize the principles for encoding, storing, and retrieving word forms.

The second and third illustrations concern children's development of inflectional morphology. The second developmental sequence describes a U-shape with respect to past tense formation of the verb *go*: (a) *went* → (b) *go-ed* → (c) *went*. The third sequence is taken from the development of the formation of the plural of the noun *bok* 'book' in a Swedish child (the adult target plural is *böck-er* with both change of stem vowel *o* → *ö* and the addition of an inflectional suffix-*er*). This sequence is more complex: (a) *bok* 'book' versus *bok-ar* 'book-PLUR' → (b) *bok* versus *böck-er* 'book-PLUR' → (c) *bok, böck* versus *böck-er* → (d) *bok* versus *böck-er*. The developmental sequence includes several phases of analysis. The child first erroneously generalizes -*ar*, the perhaps most productive plural suffix on nouns in Swedish, to the unmodified stem *bok*. And in the third phase, he or she reanalyzes the stem as *böck*, a form which is found in the target plural *böck-er* only (more precisely, in the third phase there is a variation between *bok* and *böck* as the unmarked form).

The fourth illustration concerns the naming of parts of a mushroom and it provides an example of U-shaped semantic development: (a) *stem, cap* → (b) *body, head* → (c) *stem, cap*. In this case the reorganization in phase (b) suggests that the child has become consciously aware of the metaphorical nature of the mushroom terms, rejecting the less transparent pair of metaphors *stem, cap* in favor of a more transparent pair of his or her own choice: *body, head*. The story of U-shaped development ends with an important moral: the child has not necessarily completed the acquisition process simply because an adult-like linguistic behavior has been attained.

For children growing up with languages with inflectional suffixes, there follows close on the heels of the vocabulary spurt a grammatical spurt involving a rapidly increasing use of the first inflectional morphemes. Investigations employing different methodologies (parental reports, longitudinal case studies, connectionistic modeling experiments) converge on the finding that the vocabulary spurt is a precondition for (or, at least, greatly facilitates) the analysis of the internal morphological structure of words and the acquisition of inflectional morphemes. Through the vocabulary spurt the child acquires more and more words, and many of these words share the same inflectional paradigm. Through similarity abstraction (different stems, but same ending) the child can now arrive at a representation of the internal morphological structure of word forms into stems and endings. Provided that this kind of analysis has taken place, an inflectional morpheme can then be generalized in the sense that it can be applied to novel stems. Mostly, these generalizations result in correct target forms, but sometimes they result in deviant forms like *go-ed*.

For further details, see Elman et al. (1997), Bates et al. (1988).

3.2 Early Utterance Structure

Towards the end of their second year, children typically start to combine words within a single utterance, beginning mostly with two words. During this so-called two-word stage, the majority of the utterances produced by the child still consist of just one word. The words entering the child's one or two-word utterances at this early stage are typically non-inflected. They are drawn from children's budding vocabulary of mostly nouns (*daddy, ball* etc.), but also verbs (*fall, eat, etc.*), some deictic words (*that, there*), adverbs (*no, more, up*), adjectives (*wet, pretty*), and feedback words (*yeah, no*).

Crosslinguistically attested semantic roles and relations (indicated by small capitals) between the terms found in children's early two-word utterances include LOCATION of an ENTITY, ACTION, or EVENT as in *there book* or *play garden*; the relation between any two of an AGENT, PATIENT, or ACTION as in *Eve play* or *eat food*; the relation between POSSESSOR and POSSESSED as in *mama dress* ('mama's dress') or *my shoe*, the predication or attribution of a PROPERTY to an ENTITY as in *John sad* or *pretty dress*; and 'quantification' (including negation) as in *no wet, allgone milk*, or *more milk*. At the two-word stage, children typically also use one or two question words to construct questions such as *where ball?*

Children's one- or two-word utterances are situated in a larger span of connected discourse and there is often more structure between utterances than within utterances at this early stage. For example, before children can put together a two-word utterance such as *there book*, they can often produce *there* and *book* as two consecutive one-word utterances; the first, an act of reference to a given object, and the second, a predication or naming of the object just referred to. Typically, children at this stage are also in command of a couple of feedback words (like *no* and *yeah* or *mm*), words which contribute to the cohesion of the communicative interaction in that they signal contact (between the communicating parties), perception (of what the conversational partner just said or is saying) and some sort of attitudinal reaction (e.g., protest or agreement).

Further, adults typically respond to children's one- or two-word utterances (e.g., *more milk* or *where ball*) by expanding their structure, for example *do you want more milk?* or *yes, where is the ball?*, etc. These expansions serve as important models for children to expand their own utterance structures, not the least in terms of providing the required grammatical morphemes (*is, the*, etc.).

For more details, see Brown (1973), Snow and Ferguson (1977).

3.3. Terms for Spatial Relations

The cognitive development during the sensorimotor stage provides a precocious conceptual basis for the acquisition of words and morphemes encoding spatial relations. The languages of the world, however, differ not only with respect to how they encode spatial relational concepts (by lexical means, or by grammatical means such as prepositions, case endings, verb particles) but also with respect to which spatial distinctions are placed more at the center and which ones more at the periphery of the language system. In effect, the same spatial distinction (e.g., IN versus ON) can be more easily available for linguistic usage in one language than in another. The first few spatial terms that emerge in children's early language reflect this diversity of their input. Thus, children growing up with a Germanic language (e.g., English, German, or Swedish) will experience a frequent usage of the morphemes *in* versus *on* across many different situations, where the common denominator between the two spatially related objects is CONTAINMENT for *in* versus SUPPORT for *on*. And already towards the end of their second year these children tend to use *in* versus *on* in linguistic communication to classify the spatial relation between two objects. In contrast, children growing up with Korean will experience a language where the distinction between IN and ON receive much less attention in linguistic communication. Instead, the primary distinction is between TIGHT FIT and LOOSE FIT between two spatially related objects, and this is the distinction Korean children begin to render a linguistic expression towards the end of their second year of life.

The availability of the spatial morphemes to children learning language is also determined by the prosodic prominence and the input frequency of the morphemes. Many languages of the world, including the Germanic languages, frequently distribute information about spatial relations on 'satellites' to the verb, for example, *down, from, off, in*, or *up* in *fall down, from*, or *off*, or *go in, up*, or *down*. In contrast, other languages, including those of the Romance family, tend to encode this kind of information directly into the verb, cf. Spanish *bajar* 'go down,' *subir* 'go up,' etc. As satellites, morphemes like *in,* etc. often receive stress, something which adds to their salience in the input to the child. And, typically, children growing up with satellite-framed languages often produce a small set of these spatial morphemes already at the one-word stage.

Through early language learning children thus come to upgrade certain conceptual distinctions (in that they are supported with frequently used linguistic means), and to downgrade others which are encoded more marginally.

For more details, see Slobin (1985–97), Berman and Slobin (1994), Bowerman and Levinson (1998).

3.4 Personal Pronouns

Another linguistic domain which emerges very early in children's language development are terms for reference to person.

The face-to-face setting of communication provides the domain of referents onto which children can map proper names, common nouns, and personal pronouns. The first, minimal system of contrasting personal terms to emerge in children's development is typically that between a name referring to the individual child and a name referring to the other (e.g., *mama*). When the first usages of personal pronouns emerge (first and second singular *I* and *you*), they typically take over the functions of reference to SELF and OTHER respectively, illustrating the developmental scenario that new forms often first appear in old functions. Following a developmental course of 'decentration,' children later pick up third person pronouns (*he, she, they*) as they extend their sphere of attention to talk about persons beyond the face-to-face setting and the here and now.

A developmental course of decentration can also be seen in the acquisition of nouns for reference to person. Typically, a form like *mama* is first used by children to refer to their mother in a way that resembles a proper name rather than a common noun (*mama* only applies to a child's own mother). Later, children come to generalize the term to other mothers (so that it becomes a common noun), realizing that other children also have mothers and that mothers, in their turn, have mothers whose children they are, etc.

Some children initially fail to realize that the pronoun *you* is deictically shifted (*you* refers either to the child or the other depending on who is speaking) and for a period of time they are stuck with having mapped the form *you* directly onto themselves (the child is referring to himself or herself as *you* on a par with his or her proper name). For example, wanting to claim an object from the adult, the child might say *You!*, whereupon the adult answers *Do you want it? Here you are!* The example further illustrates that adult speech directed to the child need not always help the child get the mapping relation right. In this particular case, the adult response only serves to reinforce the child's idea that *you* applies to the child only. In order to get the mapping relation right, children need to attend to communicative exchanges where *you* is used to refer to someone else than the particular child using the term. Or they need to experience responses to their erroneous usage of *you* which are incompatible with their own usage. For example, an older sibling, competing with a child for the possession of toys, would be more likely to respond to the child's *you* by claiming the object for himself or herself than to say *Do you want it? Here you are!* Indeed, the erroneous mapping of *you* has been found to be much more common in first-born children than in children growing up as a younger sibling. The child's construction of language is indeed deeply interwoven with social interaction.

For further details, see Bruner and Garton (1978), Bowerman and Levinson (1998), Broeder and Murre (1998).

4. Discourse Skills and Development Beyond Childhood

Around three years of age most children have acquired a basic vocabulary and a basic grammar. On a discourse level, the three-year-old has acquired basic skills for engaging in conversations, including initiating topics, making comments, giving feedback, asking and responding to questions, and making and complying with requests. Many genres or linguistic activity types, such as narrative and argumentative discourse, are, however, still to develop considerably before they can be said to have reached a more mature level. Some genres, such as a letter or a composition, are associated with the written medium and typically enter the agenda for language learning only after the preschool years.

Similarly, the function of language to reflect and construct social identity and social roles (child versus adolescent versus adult, boy versus girl, etc.) is a dimension which is largely discovered and explored beyond early childhood. For example, 'discourse markers' such as *well* and *uh* participate in effecting a social-role profile of the speaker (in the case of *well*, a more adult and formal character). Studies based on English-speaking children's role-play speech indicate that by four or five years of age there is a nascent understanding of how such forms can both reflect and manipulate the relative social status of a speaker—see further Andersen (1990).

At the two-word stage, children can already describe simple, conspicuous events, for example, by saying *block fall* to describe a falling block. In picture story tasks, a much practiced technique in investigations of narrative development, children around three to four years of age can produce rich descriptions of individual pictures or scenes. These descriptions, however, tend to be largely driven by details which the child finds interesting, and there is so far little or no global discourse cohesion or narrative structure. For example, in relation to the first two pictures of a picture story a three-year-old might say: (a) *The rabbit is riding a bicycle*, (b) *The cats are playing tennis*. In contrast, children between five and seven apply top-down control processes in the story telling task to effect a strong cohesion, typically at the expense of describing details in the individual pictures, for example: *There's a rabbit on a bicycle. And then he sees two cats*. Here, the rabbit is constructed as the theme of the story through an act of introduction (*there's a rabbit*) and subsequent pronominalization (*he*). Further, the child puts the rabbit into subject position (the 'thematic subject' strategy) and marks the temporal sequencing of the component events by *and then*.

And the sentences the child produces all describe events which move the story line forward. All these linguistic strategies interact to effect a salient story line and a main theme/character, that is, who is doing things and to whom things happen. Still later in development, children typically manage to combine a clear story line with the description of details and events which are off the story line in the sense that they do not contribute to moving the story forward. An example of a narrative sequence by a child in the age range 8–10 years is: *There's a rabbit going for a ride on a bicycle. And then he sees two cats, who are playing tennis*. Here, the off-story-line character of the scene with the cats is linguistically reflected by its placement in a relative clause, whereas events moving the story forward are placed in main clauses.

The presence of the relative clause in the last example is not, per se, an indication of an advanced stage of language acquisition. Relative clauses tend to be part of the basic grammar children have acquired by three years of age. In order to assess the advanced character of the stage of acquisition illustrated in the example, it is crucial to take into consideration the discourse function of the relative clause (to encode an off-story-line scene). As children begin gradually to conquer new genres in the course of their language acquisition career, old constructions are put to partly new uses.

See Karmiloff-Smith (1979), Deutsch (1981), Slobin (1985–97), Berman and Slobin (1994).

See also: Socialization.

Bibliography

Andersen E 1990 *Speaking with Style: The Sociolinguistic Skills of Children*. Routledge and Kegan Paul, London
Bates E, Bretherton I, Snyder L 1998 *From First Words to Grammar: Individual Differences and Dissociable Mechanisms*. Cambridge University Press, Cambridge, UK
Berman R A, Slobin D I 1994 *Relating Events in Narrative: A Crosslinguistic Development Study*. Erlbaum, Hillsdale, NJ
Bowerman M, Levinson S (eds.) 1998 *Language Acquisition and Conceptual Development*. Cambridge University Press, Cambridge, UK
Broeder P, Murre J (eds.) 1998 *Language Development*. Gunter Narr Verlag, Tübingen, Germany
Brown R 1973 *A First Language: The Early Stage*. Allen and Unwin, London
Bruner J, Garton A (eds.) 1978 *Human Growth and Development: Wolfson College Lectures 1976*. Oxford University Press, Oxford, UK
Clark H, Clark E 1977 *Psychology and Language*. Harcourt Brace Jovanovich, New York
Deutsch W (ed.) 1981 *The Child's Construction of Language*. Academic Press, London
Elman J, Bates E, Karmiloff-Smith A, Parisi D, Plunkett K 1997 *Rethinking Innateness*. MIT Press, Cambridge, MA
Karmiloff-Smith A 1979 *A Functional Approach to Child Language: A Study of Determiners and Reference*. Cambridge University Press, Cambridge, UK
MacWhinney B 1991 *The CHILDES Project: Tools for Analyzing Talk*, Erlbaum, Hillsdale, NJ
Morgan J L, Demuth K (eds.) 1996 *From Signal to Syntax: Bootstrapping from Speech to Grammar in Early Acquisition*. Erlbaum, Hillsdale, NJ
Ninio A, Snow C 1996 *Pragmatic Development*. Westview Press, New York
Pinker S 1996 *The Language Instinct*. Penguin, New York
Slobin D I (ed.) 1985–97 *The Crosslinguistic Study of Language Acquisition*, Vols. 1–5. Erlbaum. Hillsdale, NJ
Snow C, Ferguson C (eds.) 1977 *Talking to Children: Language Input and Acquisition*. Cambridge University Press, Cambridge, UK

Ebonics and African American Vernacular English
J. Baugh

The term 'Ebonics' was first introduced in 1973 at a conference devoted to the psychological development of African American children. Professor Robert Williams is the African American psychologist who first combined *Ebony* with *phonics*, thus coining *Ebonics*. The international orientation of Ebonics was immediately evident in his definition of Ebonics as 'the linguistic and paralinguistic features which on a concentric continuum represent the communicative competence of the West African, Caribbean, and United States slave descendant of African origin' (Williams 1975: v).

Williams and other African American social scientists who attended the conference were seeking a term other than 'Black English' or 'Black English Vernacular' (BEV) to describe the linguistic consequences of the African slave trade, and therein lies the promise and the peril of Ebonics. Ebonics resulted from the export of African slaves during European colonization of North and South America. As a result, speakers of Ebonics made contact with different European languages upon capture. Typically Ebonics speakers are African slave descendants who reside in former slave trading colonies that now use English, Portuguese, or Spanish as their sovereign national language. Williams' original definition should therefore be viewed as an international construct.

By comparison, the first documented attestations of the term 'African American English' or 'African American Vernacular English' (AAVE) did not appear until the late 1980s (see Baugh 1991, Smitherman 1991). Moreover, AAVE was introduced in direct relationship to the linguistic legacy of slavery in the United States. The fundamental question can be simply stated: 'Is Ebonics synonymous with AAVE or not?' As might be expected, the most accurate answer is that they are not truly dichotomous. Most scholars who use the terms AAVE or BEV, do so based on Labov's (1972: xx) emphatic claim that 'to suggest that BEV is not English is absurd.' Proponents of Ebonics provide mixed accounts regarding the relationship between AAVE, BEV, and Ebonics. For example, Asanti (1979: 363) observed that 'information about Black English has proliferated, creating a misunderstanding of the scope and function of the language. Ebonics as a designation for the language, usually referred to as Black English, attempts to remove some of the ambiguity created by connecting black with English.' However, four years before Oakland had adopted their controversial Ebonics resolution, Smith rejected the equation of Ebonics with BEV. He argued that 'Ebonics is not "genetically" related to English, therefore, the term Ebonics is not a mere synonym for the more commonly used term "Black English." If anything the term is, in fact, an antonym for Black English' (Smith 1992: 41).

These diametrically opposed interpretations of Ebonics, as the synonym or antonym of 'Black English' (or AAVE) were not fully evident until December 18, 1996. It was on that day that the Oakland, California School Board passed their resolution declaring Ebonics to be the official language of 28,000 African American school children who are enrolled in Oakland's public schools (see Baugh 2000, Rickford and Rickford 2000 Smitherman 2000).

Professional linguists were ill prepared for the glaring public and political scrutiny that pursued Ebonics after its Oakland debut. As linguists pondered their reaction to the statement that 'Ebonics is not genetically related to English,' US Secretary of Education Richard Riley did not hesitate to reject Oakland's non-English assertion. He released a formal statement indicating that bilingual education funds could not be used for speakers of 'Black English.' Secretary Riley's use of 'Black English' rather than 'Ebonics' undercut the linguistic assertion that African Americans speak a language other than English.

It is also noteworthy that former US Secretary of Education's remarks followed swiftly upon Oakland's controversial resolution in less than one week. Again, Mr. Riley's statement stands in striking contrast to Smith's declaration that 'Ebonics is the antonym of Black English' (see Smith 1992).

By remarkable coincidence, the 1997 annual meeting of the Linguistic Society of America (LSA) was held in January, shortly after Ebonics captured global headlines. The Society adopted a formal resolution that differs substantially from Smith's non-English interpretation: 'The variety known as "Ebonics," "African American Vernacular English" (AAVE), and "Vernacular Black English" and by other names is systematic and rule-governed like all natural speech varieties' (1997 LSA Resolution of the Oakland 'Ebonics' Issue).

At the same time that the LSA was seeking to lend support to Oakland's linguistic claims about African American students, politicians were penning anti-Ebonics legislation in states throughout the nation, including California, Texas, and several others (see Baugh 2000). Although many of these legislative efforts died once public attention shifted away from Ebonics, they stand as statutory witness to the hostile reception that Ebonics received from many Americans from every walk of life.

In the immediate aftermath of these events the Oakland School Board revised their resolution, bringing it in line with the LSA resolution, '... these studies have also demonstrated that African Language Systems have origins in West [sic] and Niger–Congo languages and are not merely dialects of English.' (Revised Oakland Ebonics Resolution, January, 1997).

Despite the fact that the definitions in the original and revised resolutions from Oakland are diametrically opposed, the general public—indeed the global public—has come to regard 'Ebonics' as synonymous with AAVE or BEV as exemplified in the LSA resolution.

Another noteworthy interpretation of Ebonics is that put forth by Blackshire-Belay, who draws upon linguistic interpretations that span throughout the African Diaspora, 'I extend the term Ebonics to include all languages of African people on the continent and in the Diaspora that have created new languages based on their environmental circumstances' (Blackshire-Belay 1996: 20).

Once the Ebonics media frenzy subsided, informed scholars turned their attention to the consequences of this event, including Baugh (2000), Perry and Delpit (1997), Rickford and Rickford (2000), and Smitherman (2000). Each author provides a detailed account of Ebonics as it was influenced by events in Oakland and subsequently by governmental policies. Perry and Delpit (1997) edited the first distillation of the Ebonics episode, which included insightful contributions by scholars and educators who are familiar with the plight of African American students and the needs of their teachers. Lippi-Green (1997) refers to mainstream US English in contrast to 'Standard English.' She also considers the Ebonics controversy within the broader context of other stigmatized English dialects.

Faced with public rebuke and global ridicule for their efforts, the Oakland School Board eventually abandoned the term Ebonics in favor of pursuing educational goals that could help increase Standard English proficiency among their entire student population. This includes African American students, but it also includes students other than African Americans who lack adequate proficiency in Standard English to excel academically.

Whereas Ebonics has become highly politicized, many linguists continue to use the term AAVE or African American Language (AAL) (see Baugh 1999). Smitherman (2000) has provided a helpful alternative, introducing the concept of *US Ebonics*. Smitherman's modification allows one to maintain the original international orientation contained in William's (1975) primordial definition of Ebonics, while maintaining its focus on the United States.

Due to the political and racial circumstances that have surrounded the concept of Ebonics since its original inception, its scientific utility has been greatly compromised. This will continue to be the case until scholars come to some common empirical foundations upon which to describe the linguistic consequences of the colonial African slave trade.

See also: Code, Sociolinguistic; Dialect and Dialectology.

Bibliography

Asanti M 1979 Editor's statement: Ebonics (Black English): implications for education. *Journal of Black Studies* **9**(4): 363

Baugh J 1991 Changing terms of self-reference among American slave descendants. *American Speech* **66**(3): 133–46

Baugh J 1999 *Out of the Mouths of Slaves: African American Language and Educational Malpractice*. University of Texas Press, Austin, TX

Baugh J 2000 *Beyond Ebonics: Linguistic Pride and Racial Prejudice*. Oxford University Press, New York

Blackshire-Belay CA 1996 The location of Ebonics with the framework of the Africological paradigm. *Journal of Black Studies* **27**(2): 5–23

Labov W 1972 *The Logic of Nonstandard English. Language in the Inner-City: Studies in the Black English Vernacular*. University of Pennsylvania Press, Philadelphia, PA

Linguistic Society of America 1997 *Resolution Regarding Ebonics*. Linguistic Society of America, Washington, DC

Lippi-Green R 1997 *English with an Accent: Language, Ideology, and Discrimination in the United States*. Routledge, London

Oakland Unified School District 1997 Revised Ebonics resolution. In: Baugh J (ed.) *Beyond Ebonics: Linguistic Pride and Racial Prejudice*. Oxford University Press, New York

Perry T, Delpit L 1997 *The Real Ebonics Debate: Power, Language, and the Education of African American Children*. Beacon Press, Boston, MA

Rickford J R 2000 *African American Vernacular English*. Blackwell, Oxford, UK

Rickford J R, Rickford R 2000 *Spoken Soul: The Story of Black English*. Wiley, New York

Smith E 1992 African American language behavior: a world of difference. In: Dreywer P H (ed.) *Reading the World Multmedia and Multicultural Learning in Today's Classroom*. 56th Yearbook of the Claremont Reading Conference, Claremont Reading Conference, Claremont, CA

Smitherman G 2000 *Talkin' That Talk: Language, Culture, and Education in African America*. Routledge, London

Williams R 1975 *Ebonics: The True Language of Black Folks*. Robert Louis and Associates, St. Louis, MO

Education and Language: Overview

K. Perera

Language is a tool of thought, the medium through which school subjects are taught and a subject of study in its own right. The many and intricate relationships between language and education constitute the rapid developing discipline of educational linguistics (see Alatis 1994, Stubbs 1986).

1. Categories of Language Teaching

The following categories of language teaching can be identified:

(a) Language as a mother tongue—which may be either where the mother tongue is the official language of the country, e.g., English in England, USA, Australia, New Zealand (see *National Language/Official Language*); or where the mother tongue is an indigenous language of the country but not the language associated with political power in the nation as a whole, for example, Welsh in Wales, Maori in New Zealand, Zulu in South Africa; or where the mother tongue is the language of a recent immigrant group (sometimes called a 'community language' or a 'heritage language'), for example, Arabic in Sweden, Italian in Canada, Panjabi in Britain).

(b) Second language teaching, where the language is not the mother tongue but is one of the official languages of the country, for example, English in parts of Wales, Irish in the Republic of Ireland, French in parts of Canada, Hindi in parts of India.

(c) Modern foreign language teaching, where a language is taught that is neither an official language nor a community language, for example, French in Britain, Japanese in Australia.

(d) Classical language teaching, where a language is taught that has an ancient and extensive literature but no native speakers, for example Latin, Ancient Greek, Sanskrit.

The main focus of this article is on mother-tongue teaching.

2. Language Policy and Planning in Education

Given the range of types of language teaching, and the linguistic complexity of many societies, policy decisions have to be made about the role and status of different languages within the education system, and about the provision that is to be made for them (see *Bilingualism, Societal*). In some countries these decisions are made at government level, in some at state (or province) level and in some at local or even school level. Because of the inescapable relationships between language and power, the formulation of school language policies cannot be considered as a purely educational matter, since they reflect and, in due course, contribute to the prevailing political climate (see *School Language Policies*).

2.1 Indigenous Languages in Education

At the end of the twentieth century, there was a fairly widespread acceptance of the importance of the use of the mother tongue as a medium of instruction, at least for pupils who speak a language indigenous to the country. It is recognized that learning through their own language is a key way in which children develop a sense of their own cultural identity and share in their cultural heritage. (It is also clear that it is the only way to prevent the extinction of many of the world's threatened languages.) This represents a major change from the beginning of the twentieth century when Welsh children in Wales and Maori children in New Zealand, for example, were punished if they spoke their mother tongue on school premises, and young Indian and Inuit children in Canada were forced to go to residential schools where the use of their mother tongues was forbidden.

However, this principle is not universally accepted—for example, in Tanzania, English is the medium of instruction in almost all secondary schools even though it is not the mother tongue of either the pupils or the overwhelming majority of teachers (Rubagumya 1990). Nor is the principle completely straightforward. There are practical problems—as in India, for instance, where, according to the 1981 Census, there are 89 languages that are not included in the list of 15 major languages recognized by the Constitution and yet that are spoken by more than 10,000 people; it is hardly feasible for teaching materials to be available in all of these languages. Even speakers of one of the major languages may pay to have their children educated privately in an English-medium school in order to improve their employment prospects.

There are political problems too. Whereas the indigenous peoples of North America, Australia, and New Zealand have fought for the right to be educated in their mother tongue the imposition of mother-tongue primary education on the indigenous population in South Africa by the white minority government during the apartheid regime was seen as an act of repression, since it contributed to the exceptional difficulty black pupils faced in proceeding to secondary and higher education, which was in English and Afrikaans only (Janks and Paton 1990).

2.2 Community (or Heritage) Languages in Education

As far as immigrant groups are concerned, the provision of mother-tongue education varies widely. In Australia, for example, some states encourage the use of the main community languages (e.g., Italian, German) as a medium of instruction in the primary school; and many languages are available as curriculum subjects at both primary and secondary level: there are 17 in addition to English taught in primary schools in Victoria and South Australia (see *Heritage Languages*).

Although Canada has some immersion programs in heritage languages (e.g., Ukrainian and Hebrew), on the whole, the languages are taught as subjects, either as part of the school timetable or after school hours: there are classes in roughly 60 languages in Ontario, for instance.

Sweden also provides primary education through the medium of some of its 126 community languages but there, too, it is more common for the languages to be taught as separate subjects. Children have the right to 2 hours instruction per week in their parents' language; because there are so many different languages dispersed through a relatively small population, this is often provided by peripatetic teachers (see Paulston 1994).

In sharp contrast, in the UK, where there are something like 200 community languages, of which about 20 are spoken by more than 1000 school pupils—there are no exact figures (Department of Education and Science 1990: 83)—the state makes no provision for their use as a medium of instruction and rather little for their teaching as a subject. The Swann Report (Department of Education and Science 1985), which was influential in policy-making with regard to language in education, concluded, 'we cannot support the arguments put forward for the introduction of programmes of bilingual education in maintained schools in this country...we would regard mother-tongue maintenance...as best achieved within the ethnic minority communities themselves' (cited in Alladina and Edwards 1991: 23–4). The survey of 11 speech communities conducted by the Linguistic Minorities Project (Khan 1985), and the accounts of 33 different speech communities reported in Alladina and Edwards (1991) reveal vigorous community-based language-teaching programs but rather few opportunities for the children of immigrants to learn their mother tongue in a state school, especially at primary level. At secondary level, the National Curriculum in Modern Foreign Languages (Department of Education and Science 1990) requires schools to offer teaching in one or more of the eight languages that, with the addition of English, comprise the working languages of the European Community (Danish, Dutch, French, German, Modern Greek, Italian, Portuguese, and Spanish). They may, if they choose, also offer any of the following languages: Arabic, Bengali, Cantonese, Gujarati, Modern Hebrew, Hindi, Japanese, Mandarin, Punjabi, Russian, Turkish, and Urdu. In practice, the number of pupils studying these languages is rather small, partly because there is a shortage of qualified teachers and suitable teaching materials, but also because many of the non-European languages are perceived as having lower status within the British education system.

In the USA, while in some states there is a limited amount of teaching in Spanish, there is an increasing trend towards assimilationist policies, with large bilingual education budgets being spent on English language teaching for pupils who start school speaking a community language (Fishman 1989; see also *Bilingual Education*).

2.3 Standard and Nonstandard Language in Education
Where English is an official language and the main medium of instruction, there is generally a strong expectation, either implicit or explicit, that the standard form of the language will be used (see *Standard English and Education Policy*). The UK English National Curriculum (Department for Education 1995: 2), for example, states:

> In order to be able to participate confidently in public, cultural and working life, pupils need to be able to speak, write and read standard English fluently and accurately.

Although it is clear that pupils need to have access to the standard form if they are not to be at a disadvantage in the formal settings of adult life, such as job interviews and appearances in a court of law, it is nevertheless the case that those who arrive at school speaking a variety of English that is markedly different from the standard may experience considerable difficulty both in becoming bidialectal and in acquiring literacy (see *Educational Failure*).

Within education (though not necessarily in society at large) there is widespread support for the view that pupils should not be expected to relinquish their nonstandard dialect but should be encouraged to expand their linguistic repertoire by the addition of the standard variety. For example, the Cox Report, which formed the original basis for the UK National Curriculum in English, said this:

> To be effective in their teaching of Standard English, schools should teach it in ways which do not denigrate the non-standard dialects spoken by many pupils. It should not be introduced at too early a stage; teaching pupils a new dialect may be confusing when they are learning many other aspects of language use. The profound implications for pupils' relationships with their families and communities should be recognized. ... This is consistent with a general policy of widening the linguistic repertoire of pupils.
>
> (Cox 1991: 30–1)

Such a policy is easier to formulate than to implement (see *School Language Policies*). Closely associated with bidialectalism is the need for pupils to develop an understanding of the concept of linguistic appropriateness in relation to situation, audience, topic, and language mode.

The nature of the relationship between standard and non-standard varieties becomes particularly contentious where Afro–Caribbean varieties are concerned. Here the situation is made complex by the existence of a continuum from acrolectal varieties, which may be very similar to Standard

English, to basilectal varieties which differ from the standard form so substantially in their phonology, lexis, and grammar that they are completely unintelligible to English speakers who do not belong to those speech communities; further, there are creoles spoken in the USA and the UK which are based on French rather than English (Dalphinis 1991, Nwenmely 1991). Where white teachers believe that their black pupils are speaking a nonstandard—or even an impoverished or corrupt—form of English, but the pupils, and their families, see their language as an integral part of their culture and community, it is clear that there is the potential for misunderstanding, alienation, and even conflict (see *Ebonics and African American Vernacular English*).

3. Language and Learning

As language is the medium through which children learn all their academic subjects, the nature of language in the classroom is an important aspect of educational linguistic research. Focusing on spoken language, sociolinguists, ethnographers of communication, and discourse analysts have all sought to identify and describe typical patterns of interaction between teachers and pupils, and among pupils themselves. They have studied how the right to speak is allocated; how questions are asked and answered; how language is used to establish and maintain control; how the specialist terminology of subject disciplines is transmitted, and so on (e.g., Edwards and Westgate 1987, Heath 1983, Sinclair and Coulthard 1975; see also *Observing and Analyzing Classroom Talk*).

Since the 1960s, researchers have looked for possible linguistic differences that relate to social class differences and that might affect children's ability to profit from their schooling. At first these studies concentrated on features of language form, such as pronunciation, vocabulary selection, and—particularly—grammar (e.g., Hawkins 1977). In the 1980s, there was a greater focus on typical conversational styles, and on the range of functions that language serves, such as establishing relationships, describing, and recalling—with special emphasis on those that are thought to be crucial for academic success, such as predicting, imagining, and hypothesizing (see *Educational Failure*).

The 1990s have seen a growing interest in relationships between language and gender and language and ethnicity in the classroom, as evidence accumulates that certain styles of speech and conversational interaction may be disadvantageous as far as educational assessment is concerned.

In addition to the social, 'managerial,' and pedagogic aspects of classroom talk, there are the cognitive aspects. If pupils are given purposeful tasks in structured and supportive settings, they can use talk cooperatively to make what they have learnt their own; to work out solutions to problems; and to formulate and test hypotheses (see *Oracy*).

4. Literacy Learning

Probably the single most important role of the school is to teach children to read and write. Literacy is not just a useful tool for life in the adult world—important though that is. It is the means by which we gain access to the accumulated knowledge of previous generations; the key to both the enjoyment and the creation of literature; and a necessary adjunct to the critical analysis of culture and society (see *Literacy*).

Before they can become literate, children need to have acquired in speech (or in sign language) the words and grammatical structures that they will meet in their reading (see *Home Language and School Language*). Further, they need some awareness of the nature and purposes of print; for example, that it is the black marks on the printed page rather than the pictures that convey the story. Perhaps less obviously, at an early stage in their development as readers—and even more as writers and spellers—they need to have sufficient phonological awareness to be able to identify the individual phonemes in the speech stream, if they are acquiring literacy in English or any other language with an alphabetic writing system.

Whether children learn to read through an approach that has a strong phonic orientation, or through one that emphasizes whole word recognition, or through an informed and principled blend of these strategies (Adams 1990), they will learn most effectively if they read meaningful, coherent texts written in language that is familiar from stories they have heard read aloud. Once they have become skillful readers they can progress to books in which the differences between the structures of speech and writing are more apparent. In this way, their linguistic repertoire is extended, with literacy itself serving as an agent in the continuing process of language development.

From the late 1970s, a small but influential number of people have propounded the view that learning to read is as natural and as easy as learning to speak (e.g., Smith 1978). This position is undermined, however, both by the extensive differences between speech and writing systems with regard to their place and role in the history of the human race as a whole, and by the exceptional difficulty in learning to read that is evidenced by a significant minority of the population. Where such difficulty affects children with normal perceptual abilities, at least average intelligence, and an absence of emotional problems, the term 'dyslexia' is sometimes used, although it is a contentious label.

For many children, a particular source of reading difficulty is the language of their subject textbooks. A number of methods are used to assess the overall level of difficulty of reading material, including cloze procedure and various readability formulae, but the study of the complex interactions between a reader's psycholinguistic processes and particular semantic, syntactic, and discoursal structures in written language is still in its infancy. If children are to succeed in the education system, they need not only to be able to understand the language of academic disciplines but also to produce it. For this reason a vigorous area of educational linguistic research in the 1990s is the description and classification of genres of writing (see *Register*; *Genre*).

5. Learning About Language

Although education necessarily entails the use of language, the extent to which different education systems expect their pupils to acquire explicit knowledge about the nature and structure of the mother tongue varies widely. In Scotland and the USA, for example, language study is an accepted part of the English curriculum, whereas in England and Wales there has been a marked reluctance since the 1960s to engage in any systematic, objective study of language (see *English Grammar in British Schools*). The National Curriculum in English (Department for Education 1995); makes a modest amount of such study obligatory under the heading 'Standard English and Language Study,' as does the National Literacy Strategy (Department for Education and Employment 1998), under the heading 'Grammatical Awareness.' It is important that language is studied not in the expectation that this will enhance linguistic skill, since the evidence available does not support this, but primarily because, as the foundation of human society and civilization, it is interesting and worthy of study in its own right.

See also: Bilingual Education; English Grammar in British Schools; Literacy.

Bibliography

Adams M J 1990 *Beginning to Read*. MIT Press, Cambridge, MA
Alatis J E (ed.) 1994 *Georgetown University Round Table on Languages and Linguistics: Educational Linguistics, Cross-Cultural Communication and Global Interdependence*. Georgetown University Press, Georgetown, DC
Alladina S, Edwards V 1991 *Multilingualism in the British Isles*, vols. 1 and 2. Longman, London
Cox B 1991 *Cox on Cox*. Hodder and Stoughton, London
Dalphinis M 1991 The Afro-English creole speech community. In: Alladina S, Edwards V (eds.) *Multilingualism in the British Isles*, vol. 2. Longman, London, pp. 42–56
Department of Education 1995 *English in the National Curriculum*. HMSO, London
Department of Education and Employment 1998 *The National Literacy Strategy*. DfEE, London
Department of Education and Science 1985 *Education for All* ('The Swann Report'). HMSO, London
Department of Education and Science 1989 *English for Ages 5 to 16*. HMSO, London
Department of Education and Science 1990 *Modern Foreign Languages for Ages 11 to 16*. HMSO, London
Edwards A D, Westgate D P G 1987 *Investigating Classroom Talk*. Falmer Press, Lewes, UK
Fishman J 1989 *Language and Ethnicity in Minority Sociolinguistic Perspective*. Multilingual Matters, Clevedon, UK
Hawkins P 1977 *Social Class, the Nominal Group and Verbal Strategies*. Routledge and Kegan Paul, London
Heath S B 1983 *Ways with Words: Language, Life and Work in Communities and Classrooms*. Cambridge University Press, Cambridge, UK
James C, Garrett P 1991 *Language Awareness in the Classroom*. Longman, London
Janks H, Paton J 1990 English and the teaching of English literature in South Africa. In: Britton J, Shafer R E, Watson K (eds.) *Teaching and Learning English Worldwide*. Multilingual Matters, Clevedon, UK
Khan V (ed.) 1985 *The Other Languages of England*. Routledge and Kegan Paul, London
Nwenmely H 1991 The Kweyol speech community. In: Alladina S, Edwards V (eds.) *Multilingualism in the British Isles*, vol. 2. Longman, London, pp. 57–68
Paulston C B 1994 *Linguistic Minorities in Multilingual Settings: Implications for Language Policies*. Benjamins, Amsterdam
Rubagumya C M 1990 *Language in Education in Africa: A Tanzanian Perspective*. Multilingual Matters, Clevedon, UK
Sinclair J C, Coulthard M 1975 *Towards an Analysis of Discourse: The Language of Teachers and Pupils*. Oxford University Press, Oxford
Smith F 1978 *Reading*. Cambridge University Press, Cambridge, UK
Stubbs M 1986 *Educational Linguistics*. Blackwell, Oxford, UK

Educational Failure

J. R. Edwards

It is a commonplace in education that some pupils fare more poorly than others. Why should this be?

Why do some children seem to be at a disadvantage from first-school entry and why should they continue to achieve less than others, in some cases falling further and further behind and dropping out of school at the earliest opportunity? There are, of course, any number of reasons for individual underachievement, but group disadvantage is, perhaps, a different matter. Certain varieties of class, race, and ethnicity which differ from majority or mainstream society (of which the school is generally representative) seem, unfortunately, to be associated with a broad area of failure. In other words, group disadvantage seems to reside, most basically, in social difference. The important issues here relate to the nature of that difference and its ramifications, and it is no overstatement to suggest that the school, as a point of contact between groups, is an arena of the greatest social and academic importance.

While educational disadvantage should not simply be equated with material poverty, there is clearly a connection and, some quarters, 'disadvantage' has often been a euphemism characterizing the poor. In 1970, Rainwater outlined the most important historical and contemporary perspectives on poverty, all of which continue in various guises. A 'moralizing' view depicts the poor as strong but lacking in virtue, somehow deserving of their deprived state and requiring control.

However, where the poor are seen as weak, a 'medical' assessment may be made—what was once sin is now sickness and social remediation is at least theoretically possible. Poverty viewed as a combination of virtue and weakness forms the basis of a 'normalizing' theory; the poor are morally similar to others, but lack the resources to cope effectively. Suggested solutions to poverty would then involve providing opportunities for self-betterment. Another perspective, reminiscent of Jean-Jacques Rousseau's 'noble savage,' holds that the poor are both strong and virtuous. In this 'apotheosizing' picture, the poor are the basic, uncorrupted, and 'natural' inheritors of the earth. Rainwater (1970) also supplies a different view, one which goes beyond descriptive value judgment and aims to explain poverty in objective ways: this 'naturalizing' view stresses either some version of biological determinism or cultural differences which set the poor apart and explain their lifestyle and values. Unsurprisingly, it is within this last perspective that most social scientific attempts to come to grips with poverty and disadvantage are found.

1. The Nature of Group Difference

Biological determinism has historically been the most pervasive of 'scientific' accounts for group disadvantage, and the 'benign totalitarianism' (to cite Rainwater 1970) often associated with it has had racist and eugenic aims (although it may be anachronistic simply to style Victorian scientists like Galton as racist in the modern sense of the term).

Strong connections were established between the widespread view that some groups were inherently less capable than others and the intelligence-testing movement begun in the last century by Binet, Terman, and others. Assessment of ability in ways that are now seen as clearly ethnocentric and biased in favor of social mainstreams had unfortunate implications in eugenic practice and theory, in the passage of sterilization laws, and in immigration control—the last two being particularly important in America. It surely comes as no surprise to learn that assessment procedures found mental deficiency especially prevalent among the Black population, nor that many Italian, Polish, and Jewish immigrants were classified as feeble-minded compared with their British and northern European counterparts.

The ultimate excesses of the biological view were, of course, evident during World War II. The argument for innate genetic deficiency then languished until Arthur Jensen, beginning in 1969, proposed that American Blacks were indeed below the intelligence levels of normal Whites. While there was a simple and predictable charge of racism leveled against Jensen, his articles did prompt close analysis within the scientific community. Of greatest significance was the relationship between measured IQ and intelligence. Some tests are clearly biased towards particular groups. An instrument designed to measure knowledge associated with culture A would clearly be inappropriate for culture B, where intelligent behavior might take very different forms; nevertheless, tests have been used in this inappropriate way, with predictable results. Aware of this, Jensen restricted himself to so-called culture '-fair' or '-free' tests, supposedly tapping more general ability. However, all tests, however abstract or nonverbal their form, are devised by someone at some time to measure something. A culture-free assessment is impossible. Some cultures are much more 'test-wise' than others and this factor, along with elements of the context within which a test is administered, clearly influences outcomes. There is a practical point to be made here. Jensen found, on average, a 10–15 IQ point difference between Black and White samples, and psychologists and educators have been virtually unanimous in saying that this is insufficient to warrant altered educational provision (Jensen himself had recommended different curricula for children with 'Level I' and 'Level II' ability).

Nonetheless, intelligence testing and its presumed implications for pronouncements about group heritability continued to surface. The studies of identical twins, which began in the nineteenth century (and which are virtually all flawed), were of great interest to Jensen. The now discredited work of Burt was apparently formative and continues to figure in discussions by Eysenck, Kamin, and others (see Edwards 1989). The net result is that while inheritance clearly is a factor in human life, the heritability of intelligence has not been shown to be significant for crossgroup comparison nor can it be so shown until that utopian day when differences attributable to environment and social prejudice have diminished. However, while wishing to discredit the genetic deficiency argument, one has to warn that it is not a dead letter, either in the popular imagination or in academic circles. A Canadian in the Jensen mold emerged in the 1980s, for example, in the person of Rushton, a psychologist who claimed Blacks to be inferior to Whites who, in turn, were inferior to Orientals.

Environmental deficiency has also been seen as the cause of group disadvantage. Children are seen to do poorly at school because early physical, social, and psychological backgrounds are inadequate and stunting. The patterns of socialization found among some groups are believed to result in substantive deficit, hindering both inschool and afterschool success. Thus, low socioeconomic status, large family size, absence of books in the home, disdain for the life of the mind, and, particularly, poor communication between parents and children are all seen to contribute to disadvantage. The products of such homes are themselves said to be characterized by poor language skills, poorly developed 'conscience' and academic motivation, and inability to see intellectually beyond the here-and-now and the concrete.

There are, again, real difficulties with this position. For example, the contexts which generated these observed 'deficits' are suspect and, in any event, the latter are usually discussed in facile and overly general ways. Not enough is known about the links between early environment and these supposedly disadvantageous characteristics, nor about those between characteristics and schools success or failure. How could the environmental-deficiency argument account, for example, for those many pupils who succeed despite having such 'bad' backgrounds?

The chief difficulty with the environmental position is that it is suffused with a middle-class bias. Many of the 'deficits,' for example, associated with disadvantaged children could be seen as strengths in the light of a sensitive awareness of their social situation; a poor 'conscience' might be a sensible adaptation to dangerous and unpredictable surroundings; similarly, an 'inability' to postpone rewards—as demonstrated in experiments in which lower-class children were much more likely than middle-class ones to take one bag of sweets now rather than accept the offer of three bags in a week's time—makes good sense if previous experience suggests that promises are not always fulfilled. No one would deny that backgrounds and lifestyles differ; what is at issue here is whether or not it makes sense to translate difference into deficit.

If the environmental-deficit argument is weak, then it follows that educational innovation based upon it is flawed. This will include many varieties of compensatory education, head-start programs and other well-meaning interventions (including proposals completely to 'resocialize' children whose families are deemed inadequate). However, both inside and outside education, environmental deficiency continues to be seen as a strong argument to explain disadvantage. Recent studies have shown that teachers—to cite one obviously important group—are still very prone to accept it (again, see Edwards 1989 for a comprehensive review here).

If disadvantaged groups' difficulties do not spring from innate inferiorities or intellectually stunting environments, to what can be ascribed their very real educational problems? Logic and the process of elimination lead to the position that disadvantage resides in group differences, rather than in basic cognitive deficiency. Because of social comparison, and because it is clear which groups are relatively powerful and which subordinate, differences essentially become deficits. These are real enough but it is important to realize that they are essentially social deficiencies. while the problems of the disadvantaged remain, their solution can now be seen to lie in the eradication of prejudice and ill-judged assessment. In some ways, this makes disadvantage even more disabling, since history suggests that problems whose existence rests upon social norms and values are among the most intractable. Even wide-ranging social revolutions and redistributions of power are unlikely to eliminate disadvantage. In the aftermath of such movements new players may adopt new roles and the characteristics of disadvantage may alter, but the phenomenon itself seems endemic in stratified societies. This is not to say, however, that nothing can be done.

2. The Language Dimension

Language has a central and obvious position in social interaction and comparison. It is to be expected that 'different' language more accurately characterizes the disadvantaged than does 'deficient' language, and examining the linguistic dimension will flesh out the preceding generalities.

Sociologists and educators who studied class dialects in the early part of the twentieth century generally held that lower-class speakers were both insufficiently exact and grammatically deficient, their speech being less complex in terms, for example, of phrase and clause usage. It is necessary to point out, however, that usage levels, or performance, need not relate to underlying competence (habitual performance is, of course, of some interest in its own right).

The work of the British sociologist, Bernstein (1959, 1960, 1971–75; see *Bernstein, Basil*) is significant in lower-class language analysis. In the 1950s he introduced the terms 'public' and 'formal' language. The former, emphasizing 'emotion' rather than 'logic,' is the lower-class variant, while the latter, rich in sentence complexity, is that of the middle class (which also, however, has access to 'public' forms). Public language is, above all, characterized by concrete and nonsymbolic expression in which syntactic and lexical usage is restricted. Formal language, by contrast, has great symbolic and abstract expressivity. In later writings Bernstein (1971–75) referred to these varieties as 'restricted' and 'elaborated' codes (see *Codes, Sociolinguistic*).

While some of Bernstein's statements about the codes have a decidedly 'deficit' ring to them (e.g., 'the normal linguistic environment of the working class is one of relative deprivation'; Bernstein 1960: 276), he noted some strengths associated with public language ('simplicity and directness of expression, emotionally virile [sic], pithy and powerful'; Bernstein 1959: 322). In the 1970s, Bernstein attempted to distance himself from any 'deficit' interpretation and any group comparison at the level of competence, and he specifically rejected the prevailing sentiments behind compensatory education programs for the disadvantaged. Indeed, despite some of his own rather ambiguous statements, Bernstein should probably be placed within the 'difference' camp. This does not alter the fact, however, that, whether correctly or wrongly interpreted, his work fueled the environmental deficit argument on the linguistic contribution to educational underachievement.

The results of Bernstein's experimental studies certainly showed differences of habitual usage between groups (e.g., groups of working-class messenger boys compared with senior public-school pupils). The question, of course, is what to make of them. Many deficit theorists have had no difficulty here. The intrafamily communication work done by Bernstein and his colleagues in the UK, work which reinforced the view that public language restrictions develop from inadequate mother–child patterns, was taken up in the USA. Lower-class interactions were said to of an 'imperative–normative' kind, with direct and concrete language being used to maintain parental authority and control. Communication between middle-class mothers and children, however, was considered to be of a more rational and explanatory nature, setting the stage for such useful cognitive operations as generalization, logic, and planning. Indeed, in an elegant but vacuous phrase, one American research team noted that 'the meaning of deprivation [is] deprivation of meaning' (Hess and Shipman 1968: 103). All of this work is suspect: the effects of being interviewed and providing language data generally may themselves differentiate social groups; it is difficult to generalize from such data to real home interactions; untested assumptions are made about links between variations in maternal behavior and children's developing cognitive abilities; and so on. Also, there is again in this work a strong sense of the correctness of middle-class standards and practices.

Verbal 'deprivation' was also, unsurprisingly, a powerful element in those programs of compensation underpinned by social deficit theory. One of the most notable here began from the assumption that the lower-class (Black) child was generally retarded. Specifically, his or her language was 'immature' and 'rudimentary,' and, because of this, language was seen as 'dispensable': thus, 'language for the disadvantaged child...is not of vital importance' (Bereiter and Engelmann 1966: 42). On this preposterous basis the authors—who had apparently never observed children from the orally-rich Black culture at play—outlined a program to compensate youngsters for things they were not lacking in the first place.

None of these debatable observations about language was made by linguists, of whom virtually all have rejected the deficit philosophy from which they emerged. The famous anthropological linguist, Sapir, said many years ago that, 'when it comes to linguistic form, Plato walks with the Macedonian swineherd, Confucius with the head-hunting savage of Assam' (Guy 1988: 64) and, although we might not put things quite like that today, Sapir's thesis has proved convincing. Other linguists have rejected the idea of 'primitive' languages and, while languages are not necessarily equivalent in all forms of expression, and while some may be more useful in some contexts, such terms as 'better' or 'worse,' 'superior' or 'inferior,' are not applicable. More specifically, the same can be said for dialects and varieties within a language. All forms are adequate for the needs of speakers within their own speech communities; issues of 'correctness' need to be considered with reference to each variety's own grammar; and problems generally arise only when different varieties come into contact.

In the 1960s and 1970s this matter was thoroughly dealt with by Labov (1973) (see *Labov, William*) and his associates. He was an American linguist who chose as his test case Black English (BE)—a very good test case, since BE was widely perceived as a deficient and 'illogical' approximation to 'proper' English (see *Ebonics and African American Vernacular English*). The work had four important strands.

First, it was shown that the contexts in which 'verbal deprivation' was diagnosed were generally threatening and hence inappropriate. A small Black child questioned by a large White adult typically produced what Labov called 'defensive, monosyllabic behavior (Labov 1973: 27). By simply relaxing somewhat the formalities associated with speech elicitation, the child's performance increased dramatically, coming more to resemble that linguistic richness reflected and valued in the Black speech community.

Second, it proved possible to demonstrate that the 'restricted' speech of the lower class might well, if linguistic prejudices could be set aside, be viewed as more forceful and direct, and less redundant and verbose, than the 'elaborated' forms of the middle class.

Concrete and highly-charged language usage (showing, indeed, that 'pithy' noted by Bernstein) contrasts favorably with a more educated verbosity which hedges basic ideas with a welter of qualification and hesitation. It can be argued that qualification and caution have a place, particularly in contexts in which difficult or abstract issues are under discussion; consequently, this second strand may be the weakest or the least completely developed. Nonetheless, it usefully challenges the received wisdom about the appropriateness of middle-class usage.

The third point of importance touched upon the competence—performance distinction. Black children were found to repeat 'standard' English sentences in Black form. Given that the latter is a valid and rule-governed dialect (see below), and given that these repetitions exactly captured the original meaning, Labov (1973) argued that there was no evidence here at all for any inadequacy in pronunciation, grammar, or, indeed, basic cognitive ability. Children comprehend the meaning of what they hear, then (unsurprisingly) reproduce it in the form most familiar to them. The point was further reinforced by studies showing that White children repeating sentences phrased in BE typically employed standard forms.

The final, and most important, element in the overall argument dealt with specific aspects of BE grammar. The central and necessary point to be established here was that BE forms, though different (if not vastly different, incidentally) from standard ones, were adhered to as regularly as those of other varieties. Just two examples suffice here. One of the obvious features of BE is the deletion of the copula verb (in phrases like *He goin' to the store* or *We on tape*—where standard usage would produce *He is going to the store* and *We are on tape*). The copula verb *does* appear, however, in the past tense (*I was small then*). The regularity here is that in contexts where standard English permits contraction (*He is going* can become *He's going*), BE allows deletion (notice, by the way, that there is no loss in meaning, no ambiguity, in either case). Where standard usage prohibits contraction (for example, *He's as nice as he says he is* cannot become **He's as nice as he says he's*), so BE rules ban deletion. A final point here: the copula deletion traditionally condemned as inaccurate usage does, in fact, exist in approved form in (informal) standard English too: *That your car?*, a strolling policeman might say to an illegally parked motorist.

A second example concerns such constructions as *She be standin' around* or *He be always fooling about*—again, typically seen by White teachers and others as incorrect. Here, the *be* indicates habitual behavior and, were it absent, the BE speaker would be referring to a present action only.

These and other demonstrations convincingly make the case that BE (and, by extension, other English dialects) is a system within which grammatical rules are obeyed, not a haphazard assortment of utterances, Indeed, given what is known of human cognitive development, the 'rule-governed' hypothesis intrinsically makes much more sense than the 'haphazard' one, regardless of specific empirical observation (i.e., what group, wherever and however it lived, could maintain itself adequately with a basically flawed communication system?). Even so, a deficit conception of language continues in many quarters, and popular prejudices still exist towards disadvantaged forms, which are often seen as indicators of innate or acquired intellectual handicap. More worrying is that allegiance to a deficit philosophy is still evident in some academic circles.

One line of argument in such circles is that, while interventions based upon language-deficit models have been of only limited success, the models themselves are not without value. Another related point is that deficit and difference theorists attended to different aspects of language, with the former being mainly concerned with semantics, the latter with grammar. In either case, the linguistically overwhelming evidence against a deficit philosophy is downplayed.

Honey (1983), a British professor of education, succeeded in muddying the waters with a monograph in which linguistic arguments supporting a different viewpoint are rejected. Honey disagrees with the central thesis that all varieties are valid systems, claiming that this undermines attempts to reintroduce 'standards' at school and pushes disadvantaged speakers into a 'language trap.' What these persons really need, according to Honey, is assistance with standard English but he complains that the contemporary linguistic stance, with its respect for all varieties, undercuts this and, in some cases, encourages the school to promote nonstandard forms. Detailed review of Honey's work is impossible here (though it has been undertaken by several prominent linguists, some of who were attacked by name in the monograph), but the main points are easily summarized. First, the author has fallen prey to a confusion between concepts and the words to describe them: thus, so-called 'primitive' groups may lack words or terms current in more 'advanced' societies, but this tells us about their physical and psychological lifestyle, not about the validity of their language (the question of why different groups develop in different ways is, of course, an interesting one, but it need have no relationship to matters of linguistic relativity). Second, in important ways Honey misinterprets the sort of evidence adduced by Labov (1973) which bears upon the linguistic validity of BE. Third, there is a failure to understand that language differences become deficits through the medium of popular convention and prejudice. Finally, Honey mistakenly imagines that a school policy which tolerates and does not stigmatize the use of nonstandard varieties must necessarily lead to an active fostering of these varieties (and a concomitant de-emphasis on standard forms) (see *Standard English and Education Policy*; *School Language Policies*).

Notwithstanding linguistic and other insights into the nature of language variation, it is important to remain vigilant and not imagine that older and less informed views will simply vanish. For a long time social psychology has shown that the more mental energy has been invested in a particular set of perceptions, the more unwilling people are to change them, even when faced with apparently unanswerable contradictions, preferring instead to engage in various forms of denial, distortion, and self-deception.

3. Language Attitudes

It is important to understand the evidence supporting a difference interpretation of language variety. However, it may change little in a practical sense; it would be naive indeed to imagine that widespread diffusion of linguistic findings (assuming that were possible) would speedily eradicate incorrect perceptions. It is therefore necessary to consider in further detail those attitudes which translate language difference into language deficiency.

These are matters with a long history; whether it is language, dialect, or accent that is discussed, preferences and prejudices tend to come to the fore. The sixteenth-century poet, Carew, felt that the Italian language was 'pleasant, but without sinews,' French 'delicate,' Spanish 'majestical but fulsome,' and Dutch 'manlike, but withal very harsh.'

Dialect attitudes are most pertinent here, of course. While social comparison and unequal power is stratified societies lead to one dialect becoming standard (see *Standardization),* others are not substandard either linguistically or cognitively (although, if it can maintain nonpejorative status, 'nonstandard' seems acceptable for these)—a matter of *primus inter pares*, perhaps. However, works of reference have often unfortunately reinforced a 'substandard' interpretation. The *Oxford English Dictionary* (OED), for instance, has referred to dialect as a 'subordinate' form arising from 'local peculiarities'—a definition implicitly held by those for whom 'dialect' means some rustic or regional variety. Similarly, on accent, the OED notes 'peculiar' alterations of pitch, 'mispronunciation,' 'misplacing of stress,' and 'misinflection.' Little wonder, then, that it is still easy to find people who claim they have neither a dialect nor an accent, or to discover others eager to shed unwanted and socially stigmatized forms.

If dialects cannot distinguished linguistically as 'better' or worse,' could it be that some are aesthetically more pleasing than others? This has certainly been a feature of much popular prejudice and in his 1934 monograph, *The Best English,* Wyld claimed that any unbiased listener would find RP ('received pronunciation') the most pleasant, the most educated, and the variety best suited for formal purposes. He touched upon the heart of the matter with the word 'unbiased'—how does one obtain such a listener? Work by Giles and his colleagues attempted to illuminate this. They began by noting two basic possibilities: either some forms *were* intrinsically more pleasing than others (the 'inherent value' hypothesis), or aesthetic judgments proceeded from assessments of the social standing of the speakers. To test this, judges, unfamiliar with language varieties were asked to evaluate them on aesthetic grounds. In one study, Welsh adults with no knowledge of French were unable to differentiate European French, educated Canadian French, and working-class Canadian French on this basis (even though different levels of pleasantness were found by judges drawn within the French speech community). In a second experiment, English speakers knowing no Greek were asked to rate Athenian and Cretan varieties which, in the Greek context itself, are clearly marked as high and low status, respectively. Again, no inherent aesthetic superiority was detected. This leaves what Giles termed an 'imposed norm' explanation, one which rests upon the power of social convention and belief. The comic effect of having a stage duchess with Cockney speech reflects ingrained and widely shared speech-community standards.

A further demonstration of the purely arbitrary nature of status judgments is provided by Trudgill. In England, speakers of the high-status RP do not pronounce the postvocalic *r* (in words like *cart* and *mar*), while in new York exactly the reverse holds— the higher a speaker's social standing, the more likely he or she is to sound the *r*.

More fine-grained analysis of language attitudes followed upon the introduction of the 'matched-guise' technique by the Canadian psychologist, Lambert (see *Lambert, Wallace E.*). Here, judges evaluate recorded speakers' personality traits after hearing them read the same passage in each of two or more 'guises.' Any rating differences can then be ascribed to language factors, since paralinguistic variables (pitch, tone of voice, etc.) are of course constant across samples. Two points are important here: first judges must not realize they are rating the same person using different dialects or accents (and typically they do not); second, the reasonable assumption is made that attitudes towards speech are, in fact, attitudes towards speakers—the speech acts as a trigger for a social stereotype, from which flow specific judgments, preferences, and prejudices.

Widespread use of this method in many different contexts revealed that dialect evaluation generally involved three personality dimensions. Some dimensions of evaluation (including traits like 'intelligence' and 'industriousness') reflect a speaker's perceived competence; some ('helpfulness,' 'trustworthiness') reflect personal integrity; and some ('friendliness,' 'sense of humor') underlie social attractiveness. While, as might be expected, high-status dialects generally evoke high ratings of speaker competence, they do not elicit strong perceptions of integrity and attractiveness: on the contrary, these last two (sometimes collectively seen as representing a larger, group solidarity, dimension) are more associated with lower-class and lower-status varieties. Experimental results are, in fact, more involved than this summary suggests, but a reasonably fair gloss might note that higher-status speech forms are popularly associated (by both middle-class and lower-class judges, incidentally) with speaker intelligence, ambition, and drive, while the dialects of disadvantage connote trust, linking, and a general down-to-earth quality. The findings are not, then, entirely negative for the disadvantaged population by any means, but the great importance of personal competence (or the perception of it by others) remains central in educational and other settings.

Teachers' attitudes are of particular significance here since there is no reason to assume that they will diverge greatly from those of society at large, and because their perceptions may be especially salient in the definition and maintenance of disadvantage. There is a large literature on teacher expectations and the effects they have upon pupils' self-regard and scholastic progress; specifically, it has been shown that the formation of expectations rests upon existing knowledge (and ignorance) and early assessment of children's characteristics. A child whose speech is perceived as substandard, and whose cognitive capabilities are questioned in turn, will be categorized and stereotyped in specific ways. There is, of course, nothing inherently wrong or unnatural with teachers' expectations; they proceed from a universal tendency to simplify and understand a complex world which, without classification, threatens to overwhelm. But the familiar dangers of stereotyping and prejudice involve inaccurate, irrational, or incomplete categorization, often with harmful effects. Educational misperceptions based upon incorrect language assessment may create difficulties where none need exist. There is, perhaps, a special element of tragedy here inasmuch as the disadvantaged children likely to be inadequately understood in this way exactly those children whose lives are already burdened with more tangible and inescapable weights. Experience suggests that the phenomenon of the 'nonverbal' child (to give but one example) may often be one created by teachers insensitive to crosscultural (or cross-subcultural) differences in the domains of competition, response to authority figures, customary reaction to threat, and so on.

It is perhaps unnecessary to state that teachers are not simply and generally being accused of malice, racism, or 'classism' (although these qualities exist among them, as in the general population). Teachers are more concerned than most with the promotion of tolerance and increased social mobility. However, once installed in the classroom, there is evidence that teachers are quickly socialized into the traditional ways of the school. In this way disadvantage is perpetuated. Studies in the 1980s in North America and Europe have confirmed this, and also confirmed that contemporary teachers, more tolerant of language variation than previously, still adhere in the main to a deficit view and still consider one of their major tasks to be the elimination of 'incorrect' speech patterns and the inculcation of 'proper' ones.

For example, in a study of primary and secondary teachers in Nova Scotia, Edwards and McKinnon (1987) found that disadvantage-as-deficit maintained its appeal; while teachers stressed the importance of home background characteristics as contributors to disadvantage, they clearly viewed some environments as substantively deficient. With specific regard to language, teachers believed that disadvantaged children were incapable of properly articulating their thoughts, and generally placed little value no receptive and expressive skills (see Bereiter and Engelmann 1996, Hess and Shipman 1968). Minority-group children (in this study, Blacks and Acadians) were particularly singled out, with Black pupils seen to have a 'slang language all their own.' A European review by Hagen (1987) indicates that some countries, like France, retain a centralist view of standard language, while others (The Netherlands, for example) have more liberal legislative perspectives on dialect variation—even if not always matched by school practice. Citing Dutch and Italian work, Hagen notes that non-standard-speaking children's favorable attitudes to their own speech often decline dramatically as they grow up.

4. Educational Responses to Disadvantage

Language varieties associated with relatively subordinate groups are not inherently deficient, but they do possess negative connotations because of social stratification and comparisons which lead to denigration. Thus, social differences become deficits and nonstandard speech becomes substandard. While still waiting for an end to the unfair and inaccurate language perceptions which contribute to educational disadvantage and failure, it is not unreasonable to consider what schools might be doing.

First, of course, schools and teachers must become more aware of the relevant psychological and linguistic evidence bearing upon disadvantage. The wider society is generally ignorant of this, so there is, then, a real limitation on schools. On the one hand, schools tend to reflect mainstream society more than they lead it; on the other, even were schools to become centers of linguistic enlightenment, their students would still emerge into somewhat darker settings. Given these limitations, it is still quite possible for schools and teachers to be linguistically educated; the essentials of the difference-deficit argument, for example, are not difficult to grasp and do not require lengthy exposition or sophisticated prior knowledge.

Second, given the practicalities of living in a society, it should be assumed that a standard language variety will continue to be important and particularly valued, and that increased mobility will be positively affected by facility with it. The recommendations made by some linguists that schools should actively encourage (in writing, as well as in speaking) nonstandard usage may seem somewhat naive. Indeed, a common accepted standard can be a levelling device rather than an exclusionary one, and a great asset in personal and group communicative efficiency. It would be a cruel irony if a rather innocent regard for all varieties resulted in a social babel where, it may be assumed, certain groups would again end up at the bottom of the heap.

Does this not bring us back to the rejected position associated with Honey (in Sect. 2 above)? The difference is this: while it would be inappropriate and unjust for schools to neglect the standard (and while, incidentally, this would arouse great resentment on the part of disadvantaged groups themselves), a linguistically enlightened policy demands tolerance at school for all forms. Furthermore, the best available evidence indicates that this tolerance should accompany very clear messages that mother-tongue varieties of every kind are both valid and valuable. The aim should be language repertoire *addition*, not *replacement*: a policy of bidialectalism. Again, the evidence suggests that this is not at all an insuperable task to require of children (consider the bilingual facility), nor need it be solely a school-based imposition. When discussing disadvantage, groups existing in the same large society are being treated; in terms of language, this means that disadvantaged groups typically have a considerable, if somewhat passive, exposure to standard forms, forms which are clearly associated with desired social contexts and rewards. Findings concerning sentence repetition indicate this latent standard facility; other evidence supports the fact that disadvantaged children, from an early age, can comprehend standard forms and, indeed, will use them themselves if they judge this appropriate. Schools, then, should activate this knowledge and make it clear to children that a broadening of their performance skills makes sense.

This is a matter of some delicacy, however, for children are being asked to accept two social facts which could easily be seen as contradictory. On the one hand, the message is that the mother-tongue variety is perfectly adequate within the home speech community, both for communicative purposes and as a vehicle of group solidarity. On the other, the child is to be made aware that a life beyond that community may require repertoire expansion. Transmission of these two messages requires tact and sensitivity based upon adequate knowledge of children's language and culture but it will be assisted in many cases by a desire for mobility which is unsurprisingly strong in most disadvantaged communities. Indeed, one might note that the low regard for education supposedly characteristic of the lower class (in the deficit perspective) is much less common than a sometimes overoptimistic hope for mobility through education.

Experience, including that derived from deficit-inspired compensatory programs, suggests that formalized and drill-like language curricula make little sense. They run the risk, above all, of instilling a 'replacement' perspective which is both uncalled-for linguistically and potentially damaging psychologically. A more *laissez-faire* policy seems appropriate, in which teachers act as standard-speaking models (in other words, naturally) and in which children's own good sense will lead to the desired expansion. Anything more formal will be counterproductive and will, at the least, contribute to an unnecessary rift between the child's school life and his or her unselfconscious participation in the community. Moreover, it should be noted again that this apparently *laissez-faire* policy is not simply some default option, but a reasoned and aware reflection of all the evidence and insight presented here.

Developments in fine-grained analysis of classroom communication hold out the hopes of refining awareness and improving practices. For example, the traditional assertions that disadvantaged children's 'restricted' usage leads to difficulties with the 'elaborated' language of school are undercut by real classroom patterns, which are very often delimited exercises in control—both particularistic and concrete. Indeed, the view of schools as middle-class institutions has itself been challenged on these grounds. In fact, this challenge cannot be sustained—schools are middle-class in the attitudes, skills, and values stressed there—but there is clearly more work to be done in ascertaining classroom dynamics (see *Spoken Language in the Classroom*; *Observing and Analyzing Classroom Talk*).

Ethnographic analysis of classroom language are now paying greater attention to such factors as the psychological context in which teacher–pupil interactions occur, a context in which postural configurations, direct and indirect verbal strategies, conversational rhythms, and prosody are important; these and other aspects clarify how impoverished traditional deficit-based and disembodied speech analysis are. Also central here is the interpretation of tacit school rules based upon teachers' needs for order. There is a more subtle treatment of the classroom as speech domain, where a whole cultural 'code' must be mastered for success. The implication is that disadvantage may be partly understood as an incomplete grasping of this code, which combines both knowledge and its 'appropriate' display (see Mehan 1984).

If traditional school practices required pupil adaptation in a sink-or-swim approach, while compensatory intervention programs were heavy-handed with insensitive alterations built upon insecure foundations, new approaches founded on subtle observation may help with both the school adaptation to classroom heterogeneity and a desired repertoire expansion on the part of children. Mehan's (1984) study demonstrated that detailed assessment of language styles between teachers and disadvantaged children allowed practical advice to be given to teachers about how best to adapt. This had the effect of lessening the passivity and 'nonverbality' of the pupils and, once greater participation was established, children were gradually and subtly introduced to 'school styles.'

To reduce educational failure associated with group disadvantage, a combination of practical innovations and the transfer of existing psychological and linguistic information is needed. Ethnographic analysis of classroom discourse promises useful insights which can quickly be turned to the benefit of the disadvantaged (and their instructors). It is equally important, however, to provide teachers and others, such as speech therapists, with a much more detailed knowledge of language variation and its ramifications. While the mechanisms of disadvantage are outside the reach of school alone, there is no reason for classroom experiences to add unnecessarily to children's problems. A failure to try to ease these burdens is, in fact, a repudiation of the essence of education in a civilized society.

5. Developments in the 1990s

Things have not changed greatly in the 1990s; the basic issues underlying educational failure, in the sense discussed here, remain. Thus, the informed, academic support for the different-but-not-deficient interpretation of scholastic and linguistic disadvantage must still contend with broader and more popular views which either perceive disadvantage as substantive deficit (in more or less direct fashion), or else effectively translate difference into deficiency (through the operation of language attitudes and stereotypes, for example). The calls made (in Sect. 4 above) for greater general awareness of the nature of disadvantage, and for more sensitive treatment of language at school, in particular, must unfortunately be reiterated. Controversies surrounding *Ebonics*—as African American venacular English has recently been styled in some quarters—provide a good example of the continuation of those heady intertwinings of knowledge and ignorance, prejudice and innocence, which we have so often seen before.

One or two of the major players mentioned above have re-entered the fray; the general impact, however, has been more to reinforce original positions than to advance understanding. Bernstein (1997: 47) discusses the context within which his code theory was formulated and presented, and—rather disingenuously, perhaps—observes that the difference/deficit debate was 'of little theoretical significance' and 'obscured more than it revealed.' He also offers here an analysis of Labov's 1973 paper, but pays no attention to the grammatical aspects which were characterized (in Sect. 2, above) as 'the most important element in the overall argument.' An interesting defense of Bernstein and his work has also been mounted by Robinson (1998), who correctly points out that many of the views for which Bernstein was most vilified were not, in fact, his views at all. Robinson also maintains that academic criticism of Bernstein was essentially non-constructive, not 'Popperian-based,' and often personalized; while such criticism certainly arose in some quarters, it would be a mistake to imagine that more measured treatments were absent (see Edwards 1989). In a book published in 1997, Honey has re-emphasized his views (initially expressed in 1983) of standard and nonstandard language, views which have attracted considerable criticism for reasons already discussed here (see Sect. 2, above). More recently, Honey (1998) has suggested that academic criticism of his thesis is marred by false argument and innuendo.

In general, then, it is fair to say that the social conditions and the social prejudices which produce and maintain the educational failure associated with group disadvantage are still very much with us. It is also fair to say that much of the discussion of the issue—within and without the academic cloister—continues to generate more heat than light. Consequently, while the sentiments expressed in the final paragraph of the preceding section are still valid, it must be admitted that the 1990s do not suggest much ground for optimism.

See also: Black English in Education: UK; Ebonics and African American Vernacular English; School Language Policies; Code, Sociolinguistic.

Bibliography

Bereiter C, Engelmann S 1966 *Teaching Disadvantaged Children in the Pre-school.* Prentice-Hall, Englewood Cliffs, NJ
Bernstein B 1959 A public language. *British Journal of Sociology* **10**: 311–26
Bernstein B 1960 Language and social class. *British Journal of Sociology* **11**: 271–6
Bernstein B 1971–75 *Class, Codes, and Control,* vols. 1–3. Routledge and Kegan Paul, London
Bernstein B 1997 Sociolinguistics: A personal view. In: Paulston C B, Tucker G R (eds.) *The Early Days of Sociolinguistics: Memories and Reflections.* Summer Institute of Linguistics, Dallas, TX
Edwards J 1983 Review of *The Language Trap* (Honey). *Journal of Language and Social Psychology* **2**: 67–76
Edwards J 1985 *Language, Society, and Identity.* Blackwell/Deutsch, Oxford, UK
Edwards J 1989 *Language and Disadvantage,* 2nd edn. Cole and Whurr, London
Edwards J, McKinnon M 1987 The continuing appeal of disadvantage as deficit. *Canadian Journal of Education* **12**: 330–49
Giles H, Powesland P F 1975 *Speech Style and Social Evaluation.* Academic Press, London
Guy G R 1988 Language and social class. In: Newmeyer F J (ed.) *Linguistics: The Cambridge Survey,* vol. 4. Cambridge University Press, Cambridge, UK, pp. 37–63
Hagen A 1987 Dialect speaking and school education in western Europe. *Sociolinguistica* **1**: 61–79
Hess R, Shipman V 1968 Maternal influences upon early learning. In: Hess R, Bear R (eds.) *Early Education.* Aldine, Chicago, IL
Honey J 1983 *The Language Trap.* National Council for Educational Standards, Kenton
Honey J 1997 *Language is Power: The Story of Standard English and its Enemies.* Faber and Faber, London
Honey J 1998 The straw hippopotamus. *English Today* **14**(3): 41–4
Jensen A 1969 How much can we boost IQ and scholastic achievement? *Harvard Educational Review* **39**: 1–123
Labov W 1973 The logic of nonstandard English. In: Keddie N (ed.) *Tinker, Tailor... The Myth of Cultural Deprivation.* Penguin, Harmondsworth, UK
Mehan H 1984 Language and schooling. *Sociology of Education* **57**: 174–83
Rainwater L 1970 Neutralizing the disinherited: Some psychological aspects of understanding the poor. In: Allen V L (ed.) *Psychological Factors in Poverty.* Markham, Chicago, IL
Robinson W P 1998 Language and social psychology: An intersection of opportunities and significance. *Journal of Language and Social Psychology* **17**: 276–301
Trudgill P 1975 *Accent, Dialect, and the School.* Edward Arnold, London

English Grammar in British Schools

A. M. Philp

Everyone seems to have a view on grammar teaching. In late twentieth century Britain it was a subject of public debate which even involved the Prince of Wales. It is useful, therefore, to trace the development of this controversial topic from the early 1960s, when the established pattern of English teaching in British schools began to change. This development can be viewed in terms of a swing from one extreme to another; from (a) the Traditional Grammar Approach, which regards explicit traditional grammar teaching as central to maintaining linguistic standards, to (b) the Creative Writing Approach, which emphasizes pupils' *use* of English, particularly in imaginative writing, as central to their linguistic and personal development. This second approach rejects explicit discussion of language features in relation to pupils' use of English. However, for many teachers, there was movement to a third, intermediate view, which may be termed Language-Study-Based Approach. This is influenced by a range of academic language studies, and emphasizes talking with pupils about how specific language features create meaning in texts, spoken or written, produced by pupils or by others. It can also involve pupil investigation of aspects of how language varies, how it is acquired, how it changes, etc. Two strands of this third approach can be distinguished, differing as to whether or not teachers should adopt explicit language terminology when discussing language with their pupils.

1. The Traditional Grammar Approach

At the end of the 1950s, pupils were drilled in grammatical analysis of sentences and parsing of 'parts of speech' from upper primary until the final stages of compulsory schooling, and this grammatical prowess was tested in British public examinations at ages 16 or 17. The Bullock Report said of the GCE O-level examination papers established in the early 1920s:

> Forty years later, in the early sixties, they had changed little. There was a precis, letter writing, paraphrase, analysis and other grammatical exercises, the correction of incorrect sentences, the punctuation of depunctuated

passages, and, of course, an essay. [For an example of a typical paper, see Keith 1990.]
(Department of Education and Science 1975: 177)

Such a catalog of activities obviously goes well beyond grammatical analysis, broadly defined by Bullock as: 'an analytical study of those formal arrangements of items in a language by which utterances have meaning' (Department of Education and Science 1975: 169). Yet the emphasis on the eradication of grammatical solecism, and on the practice of punctuation, is what is often popularly meant by 'grammar' teaching.

The thinking behind traditional school grammar was essentially prescriptive, in the tradition of eighteenth-century prescriptive grammarians, such as Robert Lowth, and Lindley Murray, who attempted to 'fix' the language by prescribing exactly what constituted correct usage. The traditional school grammars held sway for at least 200 years. They were based on prescriptive attitudes, on forms and rules derived from Latin, and on exercises on the correction of sentences. There were two central assumptions: (a) that there is a correct standard form of the language normally only found in writing; (b) that pupils' development in written linguistic skill depends upon their being taught this grammar explicitly and being trained in its use (see *Prescriptive and Descriptive Grammars*).

Despite the pressure of the other approaches from 1960 to 1990, the traditional grammar alternative still survived in many schools. The Bullock Report's survey (Department of Education and Science 1975) found that 82 percent of all 9-year-olds surveyed spent at least half-an-hour per week on grammar and punctuation exercises.

Twenty years later, in a survey of 10 local education authorities carried out by the Schools Curriculum and Assessment Authority (SCAA) from 1995 to 1997, it was found that 'explicit planning was patchy and that much coverage was implicit.' Yet the survey did show that, in relation to phrase, clause, and sentence structure, about one-third of schools at Key Stage 2 (ages 8–11) and about one-quarter at Key Stage 3 (ages 11–14) included all the aspects set out for the English Order of the National Curriculum (SCAA 1995). In relation to the grammatical functions of words, about one-third of Key Stage 2 reported covering these and in Key Stage 3 less than half the schools referred to all the categories of words in their schemes of work. Although this situation was hardly satisfactory in the light of the requirements of the English Order, it does suggest that the reaction against traditional grammar which apparently held sway throughout the 1970s and 1980s in England and Wales, did not mean, by the 1990s, the wholesale disappearance of traditional grammar teaching from schools.

2. Reactions Against the Traditional Grammar Approach

In the early 1960s in Britain the dominance of traditional grammar in English mother-tongue teaching was weakened by several pressures, central among which was teachers' dissatisfaction with activities which were seen as boring for pupils and unrelated to the development of skill in writing. This stance was supported by the findings of a number of research projects which questioned the assumption that formal grammar instruction leads to a development of written language skills (e.g., Macaulay 1947). Later the work of Elley and his associates in New Zealand, on a longitudinal study involving traditional grammar, transformational grammar, and a control group, showed that 'English Grammar, whether traditional or transformational, has virtually no influence on the language growth of typical secondary school students'.

Another major factor leading to the reaction against traditional grammar in England and Wales was the growth of interest in the 'creative writing' approach, whereby the child's potential for creativity was to be fostered through a series of motivating experiences involving widespread exposure to talking, reading, and writing. 'Fluency' was to be encouraged; consequently, teachers were careful to avoid attempts to 'correct' or 'improve' the child's creation, either during or after the act of writing. This doctrine fueled the extreme reaction against the traditional approach which was outlined above, although it did survive within O-level examinations.

3. Operational and Explicit Knowledge of Language

The assumption that direct teaching of grammar as an end in itself will lead to improvement in writing is contradicted by the view stated in a bulletin of the Scottish Central Committee on English (1972), *The Teaching of English Language*:

> ... The sorts of language work described here will be facilitated by the use of suitable grammatical vocabulary, some of which will have been acquired earlier by means of 'mention' ... The vital point is that grammatical terminology should be produced only in response to *need*. The grammar to be taught should be limited only to what pupil and teacher require.
> Scottish Central Committee on English (1972: 22)

Grammatical concepts and terminology may be drawn upon by teachers as they discuss with pupils what meaning is being created in written texts, and how it is being created, but this is not the same as teaching grammar on the assumption that the pupil has to be taught the forms in order to be able to use them.

This latter point implies a key distinction between 'operational' (implicit) and 'explicit' knowledge of language. As the Scottish Bulletin explains, 'the knowledge of his language which the schoolchild possesses is an operational one ... His knowledge of language allows him to use it but not to describe how he uses it.' Herein lies the confusion in popular claims that children must be 'taught the rules of grammar' if they are to 'improve' their use of English. In fact, they potentially 'know' most of the grammar already; what they have to be taught is how to utilize this knowledge appropriately. In such teaching it may be beneficial for teachers to draw upon grammatical terminology, if they consider it appropriate. This alternative view of the role of grammar became a central feature of one strand of the language-study-based approach.

4. 'Linguistic' Approaches to Grammar Teaching

By the early 1960s, the reaction within academic linguistics in the USA against the 'unscientific' and 'notional' basis of traditional grammars, coupled with the growth of Structural Linguistics, led to an upsurge of structuralist-based grammar teaching in American and Scottish schools. This 'cut-and-dried,' 'scientific' grammar had an appeal for school teachers, despite its lack of subtlety in relation to meaning. Similarly, there was Scottish interest in Hallidayan Scale and Category grammar, which supplied teachers with a new 'linguistic' grammar to replace the traditional one in classroom teaching.

In the USA, in the later 1960s Transformational Generative Grammar began to replace structural grammar as the preferred model in American schools. Nevertheless, this development in the USA did not lead to the establishment of transformational grammar in British schools at all, perhaps because of the complex demands it made upon both teachers and pupils.

It is worth noting, first, that all these developments still rested firmly on the assumption that grammatical structures should be *taught* in classrooms; and second, that these ideas, while popular in the USA and Scotland, did not become prominent in England and Wales. Throughout the 1960s, in fact, there was a considerable gulf between the broad approach of progressive teachers in England and Wales and those in the USA and Scotland. In England, 'creative writing' approaches and 'Leavisite' views of the central importance of literature as a moral and linguistic developmental force held sway, coupled with an extreme antipathy to anything remotely connected with grammar teaching.

5. Approaches Based on Language Studies

Two other approaches to language teaching which developed in the 1960s became prominent during the 1970s and 1980s. They were two strands of the language-study-based approach, with one taking an implicit, and the other an explicit, approach to discussing language with pupils. The 'implicit' approach, associated with the work of Douglas Barnes, James Britton, John Dixon, and Harold Rosen, saw the development of the child, as language user and mature human being, as being rooted in 'exploratory talk' and 'expressive writing,' as the child strove to find his individual 'voice' and in the process developed as a person. Its proponents saw literature and language study as equally important in this process but they took a stance against the explicit and systematic use of terminology from linguistics. They concentrated on developing their own eclectic approaches to how meanings are made in talk and writing. This view can be summarized as:

> Discussion of the audience's needs and whether they are being fulfilled is often valuable, but this is discussion in terms of content or style. Such discussion, though it necessarily refers to particular features in texts, need not demand that pupils first master an extensive generalised system for describing those features.
> Barnes (1988: 37–38)

The 'explicit' strand of the language-study-based approach had its genesis in the Programme in Linguistics and English Teaching, directed by Halliday at University College London, from 1964 to 1969. This developed an approach which drew directly upon the insights of linguistics and considered their implications for mother-tongue teaching. The *Language in Use* materials which emerged from this program set out a variety of activities which involve pupils in investigations into a wide range of aspects of language as it is used in society: the relations between spoken and written language; language in social situations; patterning in language; etc. (Doughty et al. 1971). The focus is not upon 'teaching grammar' but creating knowledge for pupils about language as they meet it in daily life, and upon their using a range of registers as they investigate these concerns.

The Bullock Report (Department of Education and Science 1975) broadly supported both these strands, although it is fair to say that its basic philosophy was closer to the Barnes–Britton alternative. Nevertheless, the Bullock Committee took a broadly similar stance to the Scottish Central Committee on English (1972) on 'explicit rules and facts about language,' saying that these have direct practical value to pupils when they solve particular problems on the tasks they are engaged on, or when pupils are able to reconstruct for themselves the analysis that led to the rule. The views of the Bullock Committee were summed up thus:

> What we are suggesting then, is that children should learn about language by experiencing it and experimenting with its use. There will be occasions when the whole class might receive specific instruction in some aspect of

language. More frequently however, the teacher will operate on the child's language competence at the point of need by individual or small group discussion. As a background to all this activity, he should have in his own mind a clear picture of how far and in what directions this competence should be extended.

(Department of Education and Science 1975: 173–74)

6. The Role of the Teacher

The question of the teacher's knowledge introduces two key, related, questions: (a) how far teachers, as opposed to pupils, can benefit from an explicit knowledge based on the insights of language study; (b) how far and in what circumstances they should make that knowledge explicit to pupils. The debate which developed in the 1970s between the *Language in Use* team and the linguist Crystal (1976) centred on the issue of how far teachers would have to be trained in linguistics in order to work with *Language in Use* successfully. Certainly, the Kingman Report, published in 1988, saw the issue of training teachers in knowledge about language as a main priority and the LINC (Language in the National Curriculum) in service training project in England and Wales was a direct response to this need. The LINC team questioned the making of a clear distinction between 'implicit' and 'explicit' approaches. The project's director, Carter summed up their position: 'It would be wrong to assume that conscious knowledge operates independently of unconscious knowledge; there is a constant interplay and interaction between different modes of knowing and explicit, analytical attention to language can and should serve to deepen intuitions' (Carter 1990: 18). Carter and his associates, in fact, believe in the coming together of the two strands of the language-study-based approach in the development of the overall language awareness of the pupil.

Certainly, it is important that the teacher should have a clear awareness of how grammatical features serve to create meaning in a text: say, how strings of premodifiers in a noun phrase can create a sense of density and impressive technicality in a car advertisement (as in 'the BMW Motronic digital engine management computer'). The teacher can then decide how far he or she wishes to draw upon such awareness explicitly in discussion with pupils, but it *is* important that the teacher can clearly see how such grammatical features serve to create relevant meaning in texts.

Hasan proposes three levels of literacy: 'recognition literacy,' 'action literacy,' and 'reflection literacy.' These are, in effect, three types of learning outcome, which can drive the approaches of teachers of language. Recognition literacy is the focus upon the recognition of language forms and the labeling of them as ends in themselves—upon isolated sound-symbol correspondences in early reading, upon parsing of parts of speech, and analysis of clauses in traditional grammar. Hasan points out that this kind of language activity 'is a conception of language far removed from social semiotic practice, that is, from the making of meanings which serve our social purposes in life' (Hasan 1996: 388). The latter is largely what she means by 'action literacy.' Yet this is not seen as a denial of the relevance of explicit knowledge of language. As she says,

> It is important to note ... that in order to achieve the goals of action literacy, pupils will need to have internalised the sorts of information that form the content of recognition literacy: they will need to be able to recognise the relations between the written shape and the spoken words, and they will need to know about the lexicogrammar. But there is a crucial difference. In action literacy, all this learning will be harnessed to some act of meaning (Hasan 1996: 401).

Hasan also questions recognition literacy on the grounds that it creates a passive, unreflecting view of literacy:

> Logically, the ideals of recognition literacy demand pupils who are not likely to ask questions, who are willing to follow wherever authority in the guise of the teacher leads them; they have to be pupils who do not expect their educational knowledge of language to have any direct relevance to what they do with language in the living of their life (Hasan 1996: 391).

This leads us to Hasan's third level of literacy, 'reflection literacy,' which advocates that we need to enable pupils to produce, rather than to reproduce knowledge, by developing in them 'the ability to reflect, to enquire, to analyse and to challenge' (Hasan 1996: 411). At first sight this seems very similar to the stance of the Bullock report, but Hasan advocates an *explicit* approach to the ways in which language operates to create meaning in texts. She explains it thus:

> To put a question to a text—to ask why the said is being said, what it implies, and on what grounds—calls for a much deeper understanding of language as a resource for meaning. So teachers will need to sensitise pupils to not simply the overall structure of the text ..., they would also be concerned to show what alternative ways there are of saying the 'same thing.' The point is that one can never say exactly the same thing using a different wording, so in fact the teachers will need to make pupils aware of the sorts of difference in meaning that may arise from putting it one way as opposed to another ... It is from this kind of deeper understanding of what the text means that we can move to explanation questions.

For example, in the discussion of the noun phrase from the car advertisement above, the teacher could encourage enquiry into ways in which the same component could have been described in different ways in other contexts; the implications of this type of writing for the exploitation of potential consumers; the nature of jargon as opposed to technical language; the role of advertising in our society, etc. (see *Critical Language Awareness*).

The approach to teaching outlined here, however, assumes considerable knowledge on the part of teachers, and we must now consider the level of teachers' grammatical knowledge in Britain at the end of the twentieth century.

During the 1990s a number of surveys investigated the extent of teachers' and student teachers' knowledge of grammar in England and Wales. For instance, a detailed study of student teacher attitudes by Williamson and Hardman (1995) concluded that 'while the questionnaire only looked at grammar at the sentence level, which should constitute only one part of a wider framework of language study, it does reveal significant gaps in the student teachers' knowledge, although it is not as low as some critics might have us believe. It also reveals misconceptions and the lack of a metalanguage for talking about and analysing language use' (Williamson and Hardman 1995: 129).

The SCAA survey (1995–97), which investigated teachers' confidence in planning for and teaching aspects of grammar, showed fairly similar results. 'The teachers acknowledged the limitations of not having a technical language to explain grammar, although such terms as noun, verb, adjective, adverb, conjunction and tense were widely used' (QCA 1998: 26). The QCA paper on the survey comments that 'although teachers at both key stages felt confident teaching at whole text level, this confidence did not extend to phrase, clause and sentence structure, either related to reading or in pupils' own writing. Sentence structure was found to be the least systematically covered in planning at both key stages,' and 'the levels of confidence recorded for their knowledge of, and ability to teach, sentence structure were considerably lower than for any other aspect of the survey, except identifying modal verbs' (QCA 1998: 27). Clearly, teachers, at pre-service and in-service stages, needed considerable input in relation to both grammatical descriptions and teaching methodology. On the latter point, the QCA paper reported that 'many (schools) commented on the difficulty of finding effective strategies for teaching sentence structure and grammatical terminology in the context of pupils' reading and writing' (QCA 1998a: 34). The in-service materials for the National Literacy Strategy (DfEE 1998b, DfEE 2000) and the QCA booklet 'Not whether but how: teaching grammar in English at Key Stages 3 and 4' (QCA 1999) were specific attempts at the end of the twentieth century to provide such strategies and information.

7. Developments Since the Bullock Report

The years since the publication of the Bullock Report have seen a range of developments relating to the place of grammar in English teaching, and these can be summarized in relation to the outline in the Cox Report of the kind of grammatical description which is now considered relevant:

It should be:

(1) a form of grammar which can describe language in use;
(2) relevant to all levels from the syntax of sentences through to the organization of substantial texts;
(3) able to describe the considerable differences between spoken and written English;
(4) part of a wider 'syllabus of language study'.
(Department of Education and Science 1989: 4.28)

The first point refers to the need for grammatical descriptions which are functional or communicative, in that they are oriented to describing how meanings are created within various contexts of language use (for a survey of such grammars see Mittins 1988; for exemplars see Department of Education and Science 1989). Such grammars are useful for the teacher insofar as they show how meaning is created within specific texts in particular registers. Perhaps the most useful is Halliday's Systemic–Functional model, which underpins much Australian work aimed at the development and assessment of children's writing within specific genres in primary schools (see Christie 1986; Martin and Rothery 1986).

The second point builds upon the development since the early 1970s of studies in discourse analysis, or how sentences are related to each other in whole texts. This approach has taken grammar beyond the confines of the sentence to provide a more informed basis for teachers helping pupils to improve both the structure of their writing and the cohesive linkage of their sentences.

The third point highlights the growing importance of spoken English, which has led to the examining of talking and listening in both GCSE English in England and Wales and Standard Grade English in Scotland. Also in Scotland, from 1999 onwards, the new national examination framework, 'Higher Still,' included assessment of speaking and listening within English at all levels throughout the upper stages of secondary (see Sect. 9). This interest in the spoken word has led to a great deal more analysis in schools of spoken English grammar and its comparison with written English, sometimes through transcripts collected by pupils or students themselves (see *Oracy*).

On the nature of spoken language and its relationship with written language, Halliday has reminded us of the richness of unselfconscious spoken language. '...it is only in the most spontaneous, un-self-monitored kinds of discourse that a speaker stretches his semantic resources to the utmost...it is in unconscious spoken language that we typically find the truly complex sentences' (Halliday 1988: 38). The educational implication therefore is that teachers ought to enable pupils to develop this potential richness of language use and to take part in investigating it. In another important paper, Halliday also identifies the changing nature of the relationship between spoken and written language in the modern world of word processing and instant playbacks. Yet, as he says, 'it is not ... a question of neutralising the difference between written language and spoken. What the technology is doing is creating the material conditions for interaction between the two, from which some new forms of discourse will emerge' (Halliday 1996: 356). Therefore, the enhanced position of spoken language in schools must take full account of these factors.

The fourth point focuses attention on various initiatives aimed at developing investigative language studies of various kinds, under the aegis of the Joint Matriculation Board version of A-level English Language (for an example of a paper, and an account of developments in this area, see Keith 1990). Among other activities, this work involved the comparative study of dialect variety. Similar investigations were encouraged in work within multilingual schools by Richmond (1982), Houlton (1985), and others. The growth of interest in comparative and investigative approaches to language was also fostered in the 1980s by the Language Awareness' movement, which, as the name implies, aimed to increase pupils' awareness of language throughout the secondary curriculum (Hawkins 1984).

8. The Situation in the 1990s and Beyond: The Return of Traditional Grammar

At the end of the 1980s, despite a political climate which favored a return to the traditional grammar approach, two official reports which focused on this topic for England and Wales, and the equivalent official publication for Scotland (Scottish Office Education Department 1991), put forward a view which was closer to the 'explicit' strand of the language-study-based approach. They advocated that teachers should have a broadly based and accurate knowledge of language, and gave explicit guidance as to which concepts and terms should be introduced at which stages. There is in fact a surprising degree of unanimity among all the official reports on the value of what the Scottish bulletin called 'a grammar of mention,' although Bullock (Department of Education and Science 1975) adopted a rather more 'implicit' stance.

After the LINC materials were produced, the British government of the time refused to publish or support them, presumably because they were not sufficiently traditional in language model or methodology. From that point onward, government policy in this area was aimed at ensuring that all primary teachers and all secondary English specialists in England and Wales would teach traditional grammar, directed at developing competence in standard English, on a regular and systematic basis. Williamson and Hardman (1995: 118) say of the revisions in the National Curriculum Revised Orders that 'they place more emphasis on the need to teach standard spoken and written English and the rules of English grammar to all pupils.' They go on to add that the revisions 'also include more explicit grammatical terminology as part of a 'parts of speech' approach than was the case in the original Cox curriculum.' After several proposals and revisions, then, the final text of the English Order was published in January 1995, in a form which related the development of language to the study and use of texts in context (including pupils' own texts) but which also specified the grammatical terms and concepts which would be taught.

Part of the Order for Writing at Key Stage 2 and Writing at Key Stages 3 and 4 (ages 11–16) is included here, to give an impression of the approach to grammar which is being proposed (QCA 1998: 22, 24). In the full Order much more is included about vocabulary and about the varieties and historical development of English.

Writing (Key Stage 2) (as in the Order)
(a) Pupils should be given opportunities to reflect on their use of language, beginning to differentiate between spoken and written forms. They should be given opportunities to consider how written standard English varies in degrees of formality.
(b) Pupils should be given opportunities to develop their understanding of the grammar of complex sentences, including clauses and phrases. They should be taught how to use paragraphs, linking sentences together coherently. They should be taught to use the standard written forms of nouns, pronouns, verbs, adjectives, adverbs, prepositions, conjunctions, and verb tenses.

Writing (Key Stages 3 and 4)
(a) Pupils should be encouraged to be confident in the use of formal and informal written and standard English, except the grammatical, lexical, and orthographic features of standard English, except where nonstandard forms are required for the effect or technical reasons. They should be taught about the variation in the written forms and how these differ from spoken forms and dialects.
(b) Pupils should be encouraged to broaden their understanding of the principles of sentence grammar and be taught to organize whole

texts effectively. Pupils should be given opportunities to analyze their own writing, reflecting on the meaning and clarity of individual sentences, using appropriate terminology, and so be given opportunities to learn about:

> *discourse structure*—the structure of whole texts; paragraph structure; how different types of paragraph are formed, openings and closings in different kinds of writing;
> *phrase, clause, and sentence structure*—the use of complex grammatical structures and the linking of structures through appropriate connectives; the use of main and subordinate clauses and phrases;
> *words*—components including stem, prefix, suffix, inflection; grammatical functions of nouns, verbs, adjectives, adverbs, pronouns, prepositions, conjunctions, and demonstratives;
> *punctuation*—the use of the full range of punctuation marks.

Perhaps surprisingly, the change of government in Britain in May 1997 did not lead to any appreciable change in the above policy; in fact, the move towards a situation in which all teachers in England and Wales taught grammar was probably accelerated, and certainly made more effective. One key feature of the new government's approach was the National Literacy Strategy, initiated in August 1997. The central component of this strategy was the setting up of the National Literacy Hour, wherein all primary schools—apart from those which could demonstrate an equally worthwhile alternative strategy—would set aside one hour per day in each class for specified language development activities embracing reading, writing, and involving whole-class teaching, together with group and individual work. Within this structured daily hour there was to be, at Key Stage 2, approximately 15 minutes of whole class teaching devoted to a balance over the term of focused word work or sentence work, and 15 minutes on shared text work (reading and writing). There would also be 20 minutes devoted to individual and group work on texts or word and sentence work and 10 minutes whole-class work on review of points covered. Each term's work is set out in a series of closely linked objectives for a particular range of reading and writing, organised in three 'strands' for word level; sentence level and text level. 'Sentence Level' involves 'grammatical awareness and sentence construction and punctuation' (DfEE 1998).

Several other government-inspired initiatives were developed by various official agencies from 1995, with the aim of developing teachers' language awareness, particularly in relation to grammar. The first of these involved the survey of teachers' confidence and awareness of language in relation to teaching, carried out by the School Curriculum and Assessment Authority from 1995 to 1997 (QCA 1998). Secondly, the Teacher Training Agency (TTA) produced a series of papers aimed at enabling teachers to assess their own level of awareness and competence in language teaching (TTA 1998). Thirdly, the Qualifications and Curriculum Authority (QCA) produced a booklet on grammar for teachers, 'The grammar papers,' and these papers have frequently been referred to in this article (QCA 1998). The central principles for their approach, as described in a later QCA booklet (QCA 1999) were that:

> (a) explicit grammar teaching should be integrated into the overall English curriculum;
> (b) grammar teaching should have a well-defined focus;
> (c) systematic planning should ensure progression and development over time;
> (d) grammatical features of texts should be related to function, effect and meaning.

The second QCA publication referred to above, 'Not whether but how' (QCA 1999), 'explores the implications of the principles set out in 'The grammar papers' and gives examples of how the principles can be put into practice. It offers further guidance on the teaching of grammar at Key Stages 3 and 4 but does not attempt to provide complete answers in an area where much remains to be developed.' Part 1, 'Developing pupils' explicit grammatical knowledge,' provides 'help to teachers in implementing the practical implications of the principles outlined above.... Each of the contributors consider whether there is a core grammar or set of grammatical terms and relationships that all pupils need to know.' Part 2, 'Approaches to planning and teaching grammar,' shows 'how English departments can review their existing curriculum plans to ensure the systematic coverage of the grammar requirements,' providing practical advice on schemes of work and on individual units, as well as on the needs of less confident writers, pupils for whom English is an additional language, and on the analysis of children's writing.

With reference to Key Stages 1 and 2, as mentioned in 7 above, the National Literacy Strategy in primary schools was supported by a national programme of in-service training, which was based on a series of published training materials of which the most relevant here is Module 3, 'Sentence Level Work' (DfEE 1998b). The NLS training sessions were followed by the production in 2000 of a website for teachers, the 'Standards Site: Literacy,' as part of the 'Raising Standards' initiative. The online training course on this site which is relevant to this article is 'Grammatical Knowledge for teachers', which provides self-study materials to enable teachers to increase their grammatical awareness (DfEE 2000).

The second initiative aimed at raising teachers' language awareness was the Initial Teacher Training National Curriculum for primary English. This is set out in three sections:

> Section A: what trainee teachers must be taught during their training courses in order to understand how to develop children's abilities to use English effectively.
> Section B: the teaching and assessment methods which trainee teachers must be taught and be able to use.
> Section C: the knowledge and understanding of English which trainee teachers need to underpin their teaching of primary English.

9. The Situation in the 1990s and Beyond: Developments in Scotland

The Scottish guidelines for English Language (SOEID 1991) advocated a staged introduction to grammatical terms, identified within the Knowledge about Language strand of the Writing outcome. Pupils would be expected to be familiar with the main parts of speech by Level D (years 4–6) and with 'subject', 'predicate,' and 'clause' by Level E (years 6–9). Terms for aspects of textual organization, namely, 'paragraph,' 'topic sentence,' 'evidence,' were also required by Level E. The guidelines state that 'the terms included in this strand will enable pupils to understand aspects of the activities in the (other) strands (of Writing). They should be taught within the contexts of such activities and reinforced through regular use' (SOEID 1991: 48). Thus, the approach as set out in the guidelines is broadly similar to that of the English Order for England and Wales, but without the in depth prescription of the details and phasing of KAL which is seen in the National Literacy Strategy objectives (DfEE 1998).

Moreover, in 1998, in the teaching approaches suggested for the new upper secondary National Qualifications examination framework for English (originally known as 'Higher Still'), a broadly similar approach to that set out in the National Curriculum English Order was proposed. For example, with reference to the Intermediate Level 2 (Pre higher) and Higher assessments, the teaching approaches for Literacy Study suggest that:

> In order to respond with maturity to the language use of others, the student should be familiar with:
> (a) language varieties (for example, register, dialect, standard and nonstandard forms, Scots language forms, changing forms of language);
> (b) classification of language (for example, noun, verb, adjective, adverb, preposition, conjunction, article, sentence, clause, phrase/group);
> (c) conventions of written language;
> (d) critical terminology.

The proposals go on much in the tradition of the grammar of mention: 'Whilst appropriate contexts for developing knowledge may occur as a result of unit/course activities, some direct teaching such as modelling or explanation of concepts may be required. The emphasis should then shift to students demonstrating increasing independence in applying methods taught and knowledge acquired to the texts being studied (Scottish CCC, 1998).

Consultation with HM Inspectors for Schools in Scotland suggested that, in the late 1990s and thereafter, the focus for staff development was to continue along the same lines. For instance, Inspectorate comments on secondary English teaching (SOEID, 1999) advocated that 'the study of literature at all stages [should include] much more discussion of language use and the writer's craft as part of exploring the impact and meaning of texts.'

Moreover, in an initiative reminiscent of the Language Awareness movement, joint staff development resources for Modern Language and English Language, for both primary and secondary sectors, known as the Language into Languages Teaching (LILT) resources, were produced in 2001 (SEED 2001). These would set out common aims for these two modes of language teaching and indicate for the two modes the parallel activities through which these common aims could best be achieved. This approach would, it was hoped, encourage cooperation between teachers with an interest in both mother-tongue and second-language teaching (including both foreign languages and ethnic minority languages). The two sides of the approach would, it was hoped, be complementary in that, for modern language teachers, it would emphasize the importance of language in meaningful contexts and, for mother-tongue teachers, it would emphasize both the identification of specific language forms and their appropriate use in texts, as well as an approach to language learning based on investigations and language games. All these aspects, particularly investigations and games, feature in the modern strategies which will be outlined in Sect. 10. This worthwhile Scottish staff development initiative may well lead to the widespread use of a similar investigative approach within English teaching in Scotland.

The LILT resources also include a CD Rom containing a searchable database which defines some 300 language terms in relation to both English and Modern Languages. Teachers can search this database for accurate information on specific aspects of language patterning, together with related strategies relevant to the stage at which they teach. This Scottish resource parallels the self-study training materials for teachers in England and Wales found on the 'Standards: Literacy' website, entitled 'Grammatical Knowledge for Teachers' (DfEE 2000).

10. Early Twenty-First Century Developments: A Commentary

This commentary will consider some of the issues raised by the approaches to school grammar teaching advocated in Britain at the end of the twentieth century, and then outline various specific strategies utilized at that time for raising the level of grammatical awareness in school students.

10.1 The Relevance of Explicit Awareness of Grammar

The QCA paper commenting upon the requirements of the English Order (QCA 1998), in common with most of the other official pronouncements mentioned in this article, makes a clear distinction between 'implicit knowledge' and 'explicit knowledge' of language. It goes on to trace the process by which pupils are enabled through *analysis* of the *functions* and *effects* of linguistic features in texts, to develop *explicit knowledge*.

Unfortunately, this central distinction between implicit and explicit knowledge does not always feature clearly in the actual language of the English Order, at least for Key Stage 2. Yet it is a crucial issue for teaching of grammar, as the Scottish bulletin clearly explains. It is reasonable for Carter to view the growth of explicit knowledge as a process which interacts and overlaps with implicit knowledge, but it is unhelpful to blur the distinction or ignore it, as such a stance probably leads to the folk-linguistic myth that we cannot really expect competence in grammar unless we 'know the grammar.'

10.2 Conscious and Unconscious Use of Language

This aspect raises another pertinent issue: that if explicit knowledge of language is to influence use of language, that use of language must be, or become, conscious, at least for a time. Yet Halliday (1988) reminds us that the complex, dynamic, creative language that we use unconsciously in spontaneous speech depends upon our unconscious grasp of grammar; whereas the typical language of writing or prepared speech depends upon lexis and a dense but usually less complex grammar, and is usually more of a conscious process. Halliday sums up his view thus: 'Our ability to use language depends critically on our not being conscious of doing so—which is the truth that every language learner has to discover, and the contradiction from which every language teacher has to escape' (Halliday 1988: 38).

Certainly, the production of effective writing may become a largely unconscious process for us, but in order to achieve this, we need to have internalized all the language features which would make that writing appropriate. Thus, features of written language can be identified consciously (with or without labeling) and then become internalized through practice within meaningful contexts, so that their use becomes unconscious within the writing process. Yet the central aim of teaching grammar in relation to writing is to extend pupils' writing skills by the use of certain grammatical features which are appropriate or effective within writing contexts—and to achieve that we may teach pupils to label those features so as to facilitate discussion of their use; the aim is *not* to teach the labeling of those features as an end in itself. At times in the National Literacy Strategy objectives, however, the aim *does* seem to be the acquisition of terminology for features which most pupils can already use unconsciously in speech or writing; for example, the teaching of adverbs (Year 4 Term 1, DfEE 1998: 38) and the focus on word-endings, coupled with the point 'that these are important clues for identifying word classes' (Year 4 Term 2, DfEE 1998: 42).

10.3 The Place of Terminology

The emphasis placed by the English Order and the QCA papers on the need for pupils to use grammatical terminology correctly seems misplaced for various reasons.

(a) The central argument for explicit knowledge about language by pupils is that they should acquire awareness of the nature and functions of the concept or class being focused upon, and not that they should be able to label it with the 'correct' term. It is awareness of the class and its functions that matters, and not that we use an official or traditional label.

An approach which focuses clearly on developing awareness of grammatical concepts and classes, while introducing terminology as and when it makes sense is that outlined by Crinson, describing his work with Year 3 pupils (Crinson 1977–99)

(b) Another difficulty with the approach of the Order to terminology is that different terms may be used by linguists for the 'same' class of units, or they may be subdivided in various ways. For example, the terms 'conjunct,' 'conjunctive,' 'connective,' 'link word,' 'sentence adjunct,' and 'sentence adverbial' can all be found being used to refer to items like 'however,' 'nevertheless,' and 'therefore.'

(c) A related difficulty with the approach to terminology of the Order is that linguists, struggling with the meaningful categorization of the richness of language patterning, often use terminology in a fairly cavalier fashion. Hudson (1992) for instance, presenting grammar to teachers for use in the National Curriculum, makes remarks such as 'This isn't a standard name, but it will do for the time being, and it illustrates the need to invent new terminology at times.' The investigative, creative approach to grammar operated by linguists—so different from the 'tablets of stone' approach to grammar of school grammar syllabuses—means that terms may refer to aspects of grammar which are, in some important grammatical models, done very differently.

(d) Most pertinent to this discussion, however, is the absence in the proposed terminology of a 'group' or 'phrase' level of structure, having its own distinctive structure and operating in certain ways within the clause.

Crinson's approach, described above, focuses pupils' attention on the structure of noun and verb phrases with their headwords and modifiers operating in various ways. This is one key weakness of the National Literacy Strategy approach: the phrase or group level is not seen as the fulcrum of the patterning of clauses, and phrase structures mainly appear only as incidental extensions of nouns, verbs, adjectives, etc. For all the apparent theoretical neutrality, then, this is a fairly serious theoretical flaw in the National Literacy Strategy approach to grammatical awareness.

(e) In an important article, Halliday raises an even more fundamental objection to the traditional approach to grammatical categories as seen in the National Literacy Strategy, namely that defining formal categories is an essentially limiting and superficial activity which does not allow us access to the lexicogrammatical and semantic richness of the English language.

Obviously we cannot expect pupils to engage in systemic functional linguistics as such, but Halliday's approach suggests that the richness of the grammar cannot be opened up to pupils' awareness by identifying parts of speech but rather by an engagement with how grammatical structures work *within whole texts*, creating certain kinds of meaning appropriate to those texts. Thus it is particularly unfortunate that the textual possibilities which are opened up within the Text Level Strand of the National Literacy Strategy objectives are not supported by a functional or communicative grammar which at least to some extent would allow these possibilities to be explored by pupils in explicit terms. Moreover, the model advocated in the National Literacy Strategy makes no real concessions to the grammar of spoken English, as was advocated in the Cox Report. These deficiencies are not, however, in evidence in the approach for Key Stages 3 and 4 outlined in the QCA booklet (QCA 1999) which will be commented in Sect. 10.5 below.

10.4 Grammar and Texts

The NATE Position Paper on grammar (NATE 1997) emphasizes that the grammar pupils learn about should relate to their own texts: 'Pupils need to develop a vocabulary with which to talk about language, but it is important that it should arise from reflection on their own speaking, reading and writing and not simply be taught out of context' (NATE 1997: 2).

In fact, the National Curriculum and the National Literacy Strategy do take this stance, to some extent. Moreover, the National Literacy Strategy objectives do make links between the development of grammatical awareness and how grammar is utilized in texts, linking with pupil work in reading and writing at text level; for example, Year 4 Term 1, Sentence-level work: 'e.g. narrative in past tense, explanations in present tense, e.g., "when the circuit is ..."' DfEE 1998: 38).

Yet the Sentence-level and the Text-level strands are not helpfully or consistently linked, with the result that the impression is frequently given that the grammar of parts of speech is being taught for its own sake. For instance, adjectives are to be examined and their use encouraged in the writing of descriptive texts as a central feature, whereas it would be preferable to make the central perspective that of the language features which create meaning in descriptive texts rather than, apparently, the other way around, starting with adjectives. Thus, as an alternative approach, the genre of descriptions, including reports, could be regarded as using attributive clauses with linking verbs and adjectives ('my friend is tall') but only as one typical feature of such texts. Certainly, in Year 6 Term 3 of the National Literacy Strategy objectives there is to be revision of 'the language conventions and grammatical features of the different types of text' (DfEE 1998: 54), but nevertheless this linkage, together with the primacy of text, could be more prominently and regularly emphasized, and, as was indicated above, more textual awareness could be created by the use of a more textually-oriented grammar. Yet perhaps the key issue is that identified by Keith in his paper in the QCA (1999) booklet:

> The approach to teaching grammar illustrated here is a combination of functional grammar and traditional concept and terminology. Functional grammar asks what words or groups of words are doing: how are they being used in a particular text and context? Above all it encourages investigation and provides a good starting point for learning concepts for which traditional terminology continues to be sufficient.

10.5 Ways of Teaching Grammar

One of the obvious issues in this area is how we actually teach grammar in terms of strategies and organization. The essential problem is clearly stated in QCA Paper 1:

> How can grammar teaching be systematic and progressive if it is only taught when it arises ... in the context of pupils' own work. At the same time, how can a systematic grammar avoid being a study of form, divorced from the living language it is meant to represent? QCA 1998: 16).

One answer to the problem is provided by Keith in the following terms:

> What is needed for today's students is a semi-contextualised approach in which their explorations can move in and out of contexts in the manner of good scientific learning or learning a second language
> (Keith 1994: 69).

Keith's answer to the problem posed by QCA was later exemplified in the papers of the QCA booklet for Key Stages 3 and 4 (QCA 1999). In these papers a wide range of practical examples was provided of how choice of grammatical features such as pronouns, tense, or conjunctions can be focused on in Key Stages 3 and 4 classrooms so as to enable pupils to appreciate aspects of the meaning of texts. Such regular discussion of the function of grammatical concepts leads to familiarization with the relevant terms. These terms can be taught explicitly and systematically, and exemplified in texts in context; they can be taught explicitly as the need for them arises when discussing texts, e.g., grouped together for comparison or as examples of a genre, literary or otherwise; or they can be reinforced as teacher and pupils notice their relevance when discussing texts.

As was indicated in Sect. 8 above, the practical examples in the QCA booklet are accompanied by suggestions for a core of grammatical terms. As the QCA booklet points out:

> The most important thing about these suggested cores is that they are not ends in themselves nor simply inert models or lists of terms and labels. They are shown to be some basic tools with which to investigate patterns, relationships, and meanings in language.

In relation to the systematic planning of grammar teaching, the QCA booklet also provides examples based on the review of schemes of work by various secondary English departments so as to include word and sentence level grammar, including several examples of the revision of individual units.

This kind of semi-contextualized approach was also encouraged in a wide range of grammar courses for schools which appeared after 1990 (Keith 1994, Bain and Bain 1996, Bishop 1996, Bain and Bridgewood 1998). As Keith says, this approach, where issues are introduced and then arise in texts (or vice versa), is normal practice in much Modern Language and EFL teaching (Keith 1994). This kind of two-way approach is demonstrated in the National Literacy Strategy in-service materials and is implied but not made explicit in the National Literacy Strategy objectives.

10.6 Discovery and Problem-solving Approaches

Several linguists writing about the teaching of grammar have objected to the dogmatic and simplistic approach they see in most school grammars and have advocated approaches based on investigating grammar, discovering patterns, or solving problems. Hudson, for instance, suggests that pupils discover for themselves general language patterns in material presented by the teacher. He gives an example of starting to teach word-classes by presenting only the words 'dung,' 'clung,' and 'hung' and having the pupils create as many sentences as possible from these words. From the two possible grammatical combinations the pupils should discover that English words are of at least two different kinds, and thus, as Hudson says 'we have started to discover some word classes' (Hudson 1992: 8–9).

Cameron (1997) and Hudson (1992) show the value of discovering language patterns for oneself and also the problem that the complexity of language at times outstrips the grammatical apparatus that we normally supply to pupils for dealing with it. Yet the fact remains that most teachers will not feel confident in dealing with problematical areas in grammar and thus, despite the strength of these arguments, an approach which focuses on grammatical problems as such is not likely to be embraced by many teachers.

10.7 Focus on Ways of Expressing Meanings

One approach to grammar which is currently much under-used in school grammar courses for mother-tongue teaching is described by Halliday thus:

> A language is interpreted as a system of meanings, accompanied by forms through which meanings can be realised. The question is rather: "how are these meanings to be expressed?" This puts the forms of language in a different perspective: as a means to an end rather than as an end in themselves (Halliday 1994: xiv).

In the 1990s, this kind of approach was more common in second language teaching, where students often consider various ways of expressing the same thing and the different implications that these entail. Yet, in mother-tongue teaching too, this approach would be worthwhile, not least because it would focus on language choice in writing at the point at which that choice is probably most conscious.

10.8 Strategies

In the 1990s, the renewed interest in creating worthwhile grammar activities led to a range of innovative course materials aimed at involving pupils meaningfully. The range of strategies adopted can perhaps be adequately reflected through the list of strategies (slightly adapted and expanded here) provided in Bain and Bridgewood (1998).

Playing detectives. e.g., spotting parts of speech in pupils' own reading and writing.
Making lists, e.g., brainstorming lists of specific parts of speech used in particular contexts, or in

Crinson's approach: listing forms of verb tenses used in three different types of text.

Finding patterns and rules from a selected list of words or phrases, e.g., Crinson encouraged pupils to collect verb phrases from two different texts and to try to categorize the types of verb phrase in some way.

Predicting and investigating uses of language for types of text, e.g., uses of types of sentences in different types of texts.

Exploring unexpected uses of language, e.g., exploring the ways in which advertisements and newspaper headlines break patterns and use ambiguity to achieve effect and to attract the reader's attention.

Comparing and contrasting texts, e.g., looking at groups of texts, on the same subject or in different genres, or for different audiences and for different purposes, and considering in each the similarities or differences in vocabulary, sentence structure, and organization.

Messing about with texts, e.g., selecting, changing, adding, and deleting parts of speech in a given text or in pupils' own writing, or reconstructing cut-up texts to determine organizational strategies.

Constructing texts, e.g., following organizational patterns determined through previous investigation of texts, using 'story-boarding' (pictures in sequence) to develop understanding about sentence, paragraph, and narrative structure.

Playing games. There are many activities described in the course materials referred to above which will involve children, through game-playing contexts, in exploring and becoming more aware of aspects of grammatical patterning.

At the end of the twentieth century in England and Wales, then, there was a major initiative centred around the National Curriculum Order for English and the National Literacy Strategy for primary schools. Its purpose was to deliver a language curriculum in which grammatical awareness in relation to texts would be widespread and the fine detail of what was to be taught would be stipulated. While the focus upon text-level work was clearly worthwhile, the grammatical approach which was advocated, with its emphasis upon the identification and labeling of word-classes and its lack of focus on phrase and clause structure, and on the richness of spoken and written language, did not adequately equip pupils to engage with the process of meaning-making in texts. Moreover, since the initiative was to be centralized and developed in a 'top-down' fashion, rather than developing from the involvement of coordinators with area groups of teachers, as had been the LINC Project model, its eventual success was hardly guaranteed.

On the other hand, at the millennium, the initiative for Key Stages 3 and 4, with its text-based approach to grammar teaching and its use of materials from class-room-based research and development by large groups of teachers, seemed to offer a more promising way forward. That way forward was effectively outlined by Carter in his paper in the QCA (1999) booklet:

> Greater classroom attention to grammatical forms can generate a pedagogic climate in which grammar is not a list of terms to be learned but is seen and used as a range of choices and strategies for communication. But, in several senses, a number of boundaries in both theory and in practice have still to be crossed. Properly supported and theorised classroom-based research into the many varied relationships between knowing *about* and knowing *how to use* grammar in reading and writing texts would enable a first major boundary to be crossed.

Bibliography

Bain E, Bain R 1996 *The Grammar Book: Finding Patterns—Making Sense*. National Association for the Teaching of English, Sheffield, UK

Bain R, Bridgewood M 1998 *The Primary Grammar Book*. NATE, Sheffield, UK

Barnes D 1988 Studying communication or studying language? In: Jones M, West A (eds.) *Learning Me Your Language*. Mary Glasgow, London

Bishop J (ed.) 1996 *Grammar (Mother Tongue) and Language Study at Key Stage One*. Scholastic, Leamington Spa, UK

Cameron D 1997 A vote of no confidence in SCAA's grammar test. *The English and Media Magazine* **36**: 4–7

Carter R 1990 The new grammar teaching. In: Carter R (ed.) *Knowledge About Language and the Curriculum: The LINC Reader*. Hodder and Stoughton, London

Christie F 1986 Writing in schools: Generic structures as ways of meaning. In: Couture B (ed.) *Functional Approaches to Writing*. Frances Pinter, London

Crinson J 1997–99 Step-by-step grammar: Noun phrases, verb phrases, prepositional phrases, prepositions. *The Primary Magazine* **2**: 4, 5; **3**: 1–4; **4**: 1, 2

Crystal D 1976 *Child Language, Learning, and Linguistics*. Edward Arnold, London

Department for Education and Employment 1998a *The National Literacy Strategy: Framework for Teaching*. DfEE Publications, Sudbury, UK

Department for Education and Employment 1998b *The National Literacy Strategy: In-Service Training Module 3: Sentence Level Work* (Teacher's Notes) DfEE, London

Department for Education and Employment 2000 *The Standards Site Literacy: 'Grammatical Knowledge for Teachers'*, http://www.standards.dfee.gov.uk/literacy prof_dev/?pd=ssm

Department of Education and Science 1975 *A Language for Life* ('The Bullock Report'). HMSO, London

Department of Education and Science 1989 *English for Ages 5 to 16* ('The Cox Report'). HMSO, London

Doughty P S, Pearce J, Thornton G 1971 *Language in Use*. Edward Arnold for the Schools Council, London

Halliday M A K 1988 On the ineffability of grammatical categories. In: Benson J, Cummings M J, Greaves W S (eds.) *Linguistics in a Systemic Perspective*. Benjamins, Amsterdam

Halliday M A K 1994 *Introduction to Functional Grammar*. Edward Arnold, London

Halliday M A K 1996 Literacy and linguistics: A functional perspective. In: Hasan R, Williams G (eds.) *Literacy in Society*, Addison-Wesley Longman, London

Hasan R 1996 Literacy, everyday talk and society. In: Hasan R, Williams G (eds.) *Literacy in Society*. Addison-Wesley Longman, London

Hawkins E W 1984 *Awareness of Language—An Introduction*. Cambridge University Press, Cambridge, UK

Houlton D 1985 *All our Languages: A Handbook for the Multilingual Classroom*. Edward Arnold, London

Hudson R 1992 *Teaching Grammar: A Guide for the National Curriculum*. Blackwell, London

Keith G 1990 Language study at Key Stage 3. In: Carter R (ed.) *Knowledge about Language and the Curriculum: The LINC Reader*. Hodder and Stoughton, London

Keith G 1994 *Get the Grammar*. BBC Education, London

Macaulay W J 1947 The difficulty of grammar. *British Journal of Educational Psychology* **17**: 153–62

Martin J R, Rothery J 1986 What a functional approach to the writing task can tell teachers about 'good writing.' In: Couture B (ed.) *Functional Approaches to Writing*. Frances Pinter, London

Mittins W 1988 *English: Not the Naming of Parts*. National Association for the Teaching of English, Sheffield, UK

National Association for the Teaching of English 1997 *Position Paper: Grammar*. NATE, Sheffield, UK

Qualifications and Curriculum Authority 1998 *The Grammar Papers: Perspectives on the Teaching of Grammar in the National Curriculum*. QCA Publications, Hayes, Middlesex, UK

Qualifications and Curriculum Authority 1999 *Not Whether but How: Teaching Grammar in English at Key Stages 3 and 4*. QCA Publications, Sudbury, Suffolk, UK

Richmond J 1982 *The Resources of Classroom Language*. Edward Arnold, London

School Curriculum and Assessment Authority 1995 *The National Curriculum Orders: English*. SCAA, London

Scottish Central Committee on English 1972 *The Teaching of English Language (Bulletin No. 5)*. HMSO, Edinburgh, UK

Scottish Consultative Curriculum Council 1998 *Higher Still: Arrangements for English and Communication*. SCCC, Edinburgh, UK

Scottish Executive Education Department 2001 *Language into Languages Teaching: A Staff Development Resource for Scottish Primary and Secondary Schools*. University of Glasgow, Glasgow, UK

Scottish Office Education Department 1991 *National Guidelines on English Language 5–14*. HMSO, Edinburgh, UK

Scottish Office Education and Industry Department 1999 *Standards and Quality: English in Secondary Schools*. HMSO, Edinburgh, UK

Teacher Training Agency 1998 *Assessing your Needs in Literacy: Needs Assessment Materials for Key Stage 2 Teachers*. TTA, London

Williamson J, Hardman F 1995 Time for refilling the bath?: A study of primary student teachers' grammatical knowledge. *Language and Education* **9**: 117–34

Gender, Education, and Language

J. Swann

From around the 1970s there has been an increasing interest, in several countries, in gender and language use in educational settings. Such research explores issues of theoretical significance but also has practical relevance for teaching and learning, and for the development of educational policy. This article considers two related issues: gender and classroom language, and boys' and girls' achievements in spoken and written language. It draws particularly on research carried out at school level in English-speaking contexts.

1. Gender and Classroom Language

Early research in the 1970s and 1980s documented patterns of difference and disadvantage in relation to girls' and boys' language behavior in the classroom. Boys were generally observed to have a more competitive speaking style, and girls were more cooperative. Within the classroom, this allowed boys to dominate mixed-gender talk. Boys' interactional dominance was supported by teachers, who often made unnecessary distinctions between girls and boys; accepted certain behavior (such as calling out) from boys but not from girls; and tended not to perceive disparities between contributions from girls and boys. Girls and boys also made different reading choices and wrote in different ways and about different topics. Books and other resources contained more male than female characters and examples, and these characters/examples were also often stereotypically gendered.

Male characters in stories had less restricted roles than female characters; information books often neglected girls' and women's experiences and contributions to society. Even in literacy, an area in which girls tended to do well, it was suggested that girls' achievements in school did not enable them to succeed in later life. Such observations gave rise to a range of equal opportunities initiatives designed, in particular, to provide a more congenial educational environment, and greater educational opportunities, for girls.

More recent research on language and gender, in education as in other settings, has tended to reject a strict 'binary' distinction between female and male language users, emphasizing instead different forms of femininity/masculinity and the intersection between these and other factors—'race,' class, etc. Such research also emphasizes performativity: femininity/masculinity as contextualized practices, rather than fixed attributes. Language, like gender, is seen as inherently context-dependent: there is a greater focus on uncertainty and ambiguity in language use—in the meanings of what language users say and do. Such a model seems incompatible with generalized claims about (educational) gender differences and inequalities, leading to a focus, instead, on the localized 'working out' of certain forms of femininity/masculinity and other aspects of identity.

Some research has also focused on the educational impact of new technology and the alternative textual forms and practices with which this has been associated. At issue here, in relation to gender, is the extent to which electronic communication affords new learning opportunities, and opportunities for new forms of interpersonal relations, and the extent to which it may reinforce traditional gender inequalities. Further research is needed in this area.

2. Girls' and Boys' Educational Achievements

Research carried out over many years on girls' and boys' achievements in English/language-related activities suggests that girls perform better than boys, on average, in tests of verbal ability; in school, they learn to read earlier; and there are fewer girls than boys in remedial reading programs. Surveys of older children have also found that girls perform better than do boys on many language-related tasks. In terms of educational outcomes, girls have traditionally done well in language-related subjects in public examinations and, in many countries, their performance in these areas has increased relative to boys. Interpreting such findings has not been without problems. While general patterns have been identified there are also differences between tests, and changes to test items may produce different results. Tests measure a variety of aspects of language; it is by no means clear that these can be bundled together into a single coherent category such as 'verbal ability.' General patterns also mask the fact that there are substantial differences in performance between boys and between girls, and educational performance is not necessarily consistent with post-school achievements (in employment, for instance, the 'glass ceiling' is still in evidence in many contexts).

Whilst there have always been concerns about boys' performance in English and in language generally, this surfaced as a major issue during the 1990s and into the 2000s as part of a broader concern about boys' educational 'underachievement.' According to some commentators, this has attained the status of a 'globalized moral panic': it has sometimes been related to a widespread 'crisis of masculinity.' Such concerns have given rise to a number of measures designed to increase boys' motivation and enable them to do better in school. The focus on boys' educational 'underachievement' tends to prioritize boys' interests over girls' and this has led to fears that girls' interests will be marginalized. Some measures designed to increase boys' motivation and achievement bear more than a passing resemblance to educational practices during the 1970s and 1980s that were found to disadvantage girls. It has not been clear how language and gender researchers should respond to this. While some researchers have tried to engage with 'underachievement' on their own terms (e.g., drawing on contemporary research to produce materials that will encourage boys to explore and critique different forms of masculinity), others have maintained a more oppositional stance (e.g., attempting to challenge the whole notion of 'underachievement' and its ideological underpinnings).

Bibliography

Bergvall V L, Bing J M, Freed A F (eds.) 1996 *Rethinking Language and Gender Research*. Longman, Harlow, UK

Bucholtz M, Liang A C, Sutton L A (eds.) 1999 *Reinventing Identities: The Gendered Self in Discourse*. Oxford University Press, New York

Coates J 1998 *Language and Gender: A Reader*. Blackwell, Oxford, UK

Epstein D, Elwood J, Hey V, Maw J (eds.) 1998 *Failing Boys? Issues in Gender and Achievement*. Open University Press, Buckingham, UK

Epstein D, Maw J, Elwood J, Hey V (eds.) 1998 *International Journal of Inclusive Education: Special Issue on Boys' Underachievement* **2**

Hall K, Bucholtz M (eds.) 1995 *Gender Articulated: Language and the Socially-Constructed Self*. Routledge, New York

Johnson S, Meinhof U H (eds.) 1997 *Language and Masculinity*. Blackwell, Oxford, UK

Jones A 1993 Becoming a girl: Post-structuralist suggestions for educational research. *Gender and Education* **5**: 157–66

Moss G 1989 *Un/Popular Fictions*. Virago, London

Myers K (ed.) 2000 *Whatever Happened to Equal Opportunities in Schools? Gender Equality Initiatives in Education*. Open University Press, Buckingham, UK

Spender D 1995 *Nattering on the Net: Women, Power, and Cyberspace*. Spinifex Press, North Melbourne

Swann J 1992 *Girls, Boys, and Language*. Blackwell, Oxford, UK

Swann J in press Schooled language: Language and gender in educational settings. In Holmes J, Meyerhoff M (eds.) *Handbook on Language and Gender*. Blackwell, Oxford, UK

Thorne B 1993 *Gender Play: Girls and Boys in School*. Open University Press, Buckingham, UK

Wodak R (ed.) 1997 *Gender and Discourse*. Sage Publications, London

Home Language and School Language
M. MacLure

When children start school they are already experienced communicators. They are also experienced learners. These two accomplishments are not unconnected: in the preschool years, children learn through language in their interactions with other people. They learn by asking and answering questions, exploring ideas, playing with language through jokes and rhymes, testing out hunches, recalling the past and anticipating the future, sharing feelings and interests through stories, comparing qualities and attributes. Children bring knowledge and expertise to school with them, therefore; and most importantly, they know how to get more. Yet some continue to thrive as learners in school, and some do not. This has led researchers to ask whether children's experience of language at home might contribute to their success or failure at school.

1. 'Mismatch' Explanations of Educational Failure

The basic assumption has been that of a 'mismatch,' for some children, between the language they have become accustomed to at home, and the communicative norms of the classroom. Some children, it is argued, start school poorly equipped to cope with the language of the classroom, and consequently, poorly equipped to learn. There are two rather different versions of that assumption, which have been called 'deficit' and 'difference' approaches. 'Deficit' theories locate the 'problem' in the home, suggesting that some children receive an impoverished range of communicative experiences, which leaves them at a disadvantage in school. 'Difference' theories speak of difference rather than deficit. Without making value judgments, they suggest that there is nonetheless a wider gap between home and school language for some children than for others (see *Educational Failure*).

There may seem to be little difference between these two explanations, since both are based on the notion of a mismatch between children's existing experience of language and the unfamiliar practices of the school. But they tend to be associated with different practical outcomes. Deficit theories often inspire remedial programs designed to 'enrich' the experiences of those children who are felt to be 'linguistically deprived' at home. Difference theories tend to focus strategically on the language of the school, and to propose strategies for broadening its communicative norms so that they are accessible to a wider range of children.

2. What's the Problem? Dimensions of Difference Between Home and School Language

Almost every conceivable aspect of language has been the focus, at one time or another, of research into home and school language. Early studies (now considered of limited interest), tended to concentrate on syntax, and to suggest that the language of some children (usually lower- or working-class children: see below) was syntactically less complex than that of others. More recent work has tended to focus either upon the meanings that children are able to convey, or their understanding of the special rules that govern classroom interaction (see *Spoken Language in the Classroom*).

2.1 Abstractness and 'Higher-order' Thinking

One recurring concern has been children's ability to use language which is not tied to the immediate physical context. When children first learn to communicate, they talk mainly about familiar people, objects, and events. Gradually, they begin to use language in a more 'abstract' and decontextualized way: to reflect on the past, to anticipate the future, to contemplate the world from the viewpoint of other people, and to speculate about possible as well as actual worlds. These latter activities are highly valued in Western education systems, as are the reasoning skills that they involve, such as hypothesizing, interpreting, and evaluating. These are often referred to as 'higher-order' skills, and they are generally held to underpin learning. It has been suggested that some children do not experience much 'abstract' language of this kind at home, and that they therefore start from behind when they get to school.

Some of the assumptions behind such suggestions have been challenged. It has been argued that classroom language is no less 'context bound' than any other kind of language, and that teachers and pupils have to work together, just as parents and their children do, to establish a shared context for their talk. Moreover, some would argue, the so-called 'higher-order' intellectual skills that are valued in school are also present—but often overlooked—in much of the 'informal' talk that goes on in most homes.

2.2 Classroom Discourse and Cultural Diversity

Another strand of work takes a cultural perspective, looking at classroom language as a special kind of discourse, with its own rules about who talks to whom, about how communication should be organized, and about what counts as valid knowledge. Children are required to know, for instance, how (and when) to answer teachers' questions, what will count as a 'relevant' contribution to discussions, how to take part in story-telling sessions, etc. Failure, on this reading, stems from an inability (or unwillingness) to observe the norms of classroom talk. Cultural explanations often focus on the school, rather than the home, as the locus of failure: children fail because their cultural practices and values are not recognized by the monocultural, White, middle-class orientation of schools.

3. Social Dimensions of Success and Failure at School: Class, Ethnicity, and Gender

Educational underachievement tends, in Western cultures, to be linked with sociological factors such as class, race, or gender. It is not surprising, therefore, that such factors have also been prominent in the language-related research. 'Social class' has received by far the most attention. Bernstein (see *Educational Failure*) claimed that the language of working-class (English) families differs at all levels (phonological, syntactic, semantic, and pragmatic) from that of the middle classes, because of their different culture, and hence the different values, beliefs, and purposes that each class encodes in its communicative practices. Bernstein claimed to be making no value judgments in describing working- and middle-class language in terms of two idealized 'codes'—'restricted' and 'elaborated', respectively. However, his work, which has been very influential amongst educationalists, has often been interpreted as a deficit theory of working-class language, and his two codes have entered the language of teacher education. Tough's functional analysis (1973) is another example of a class-based deficit account. Heath (1983), on the other hand, offers a cultural, rather than a deficit, analysis of why working-class and Black children in the USA may be failing in school.

Ethnicity has also been a focus for research. Here, the predominant trend has been towards cultural explanations which hold schools to account for their failure to value the linguistic practices of children from ethnic minority cultures (see *Ebonics and African American Vernacular English*).

Gender, too, has been studied from a cultural perspective. Girls, it has been argued, face obstacles as learners because boys are allowed to dominate classroom interaction. If learning takes place through active participation in classroom talk, girls must be losing out, because they tend to get a smaller share of the interactional 'cake.' Some would go even further, and argue that the value attached to 'abstract' argument and 'impartial' judgment in the education system endorses a masculine orientation which devalues the more person-centered, affective tendencies of girls and women.

4. Reversing the Polarities: Should School be More Like Home?

Parents of young children have been accorded a good deal of the blame—by deficit theorists at least—for failing to 'equip' their children for the demands of school-based learning. There is an alternative view, however, which holds that teachers could learn a good deal from parents, and that children learn most successfully under conditions which resemble those of the home. Parents, according to Bruner (1983), are expert providers of 'scaffolds' for their children's learning: they are able to tune in to their children's interests, willing to let their children take the lead in conversations, yet ready to provide support and guidance at critical moments. If teachers could be more like parents in this respect, it is suggested, learning through language might be more effortless for all children.

5. Future Work

There is no general agreement on the relationship between language and educational success or failure. The most urgent need is for more empirical studies both of home and school language.

See also: School Language Policies; Educational Failure; Spoken Language in the Classroom; Vernacular.

Bibliography

Bernstein B 1974 *Class, Codes and Control*, vol. 1, 2nd edn. Routledge and Kegan Paul, London
Bruner J 1983 *Child's Talk: Learning to Use Language*. Oxford University Press, Oxford, UK
Heath S B 1983 *Ways with Words: Language, Life and Work in Communities and Classrooms*. Cambridge University Press, Cambridge, UK
Tough J 1973 *Focus on Meaning*. Allen and Unwin, London
Wells G 1986 *The Meaning Makers: Children Learning Language and Using Language to Learn*. Hodder and Stoughton Educational, London

Literacy
C. J. Daswani

The term 'literacy' has acquired connotations that go beyond its dictionary meaning of 'the state or condition of being literate'; the word 'literate' being used for a person who is able to read and write. In a very general sense this basic connotation of reading and writing remains, but in the contemporary context the additional connotations of the term derive from the changing demands made on literacy both in the industrialized and the developing world.

In the industrialized countries more and more literate individuals are finding their literacy insufficient for the demands made on it both in the place of work and in civic life. In the developing countries, on the other hand, literacy derives its added connotation in the context of widespread illiteracy which continues to deprive a large number of people of the advantages that accrue through formal education. Furthermore, the more recent specialized uses of literacy have led to newer coinages such as 'computer literacy' and 'legal literacy.'

Imparting of literacy is no longer limited to the school and college curriculum. It is a concern in which the politician, the planner, the development economist, the social activist, and the social scientist all have a part to play.

1. No Single Definition

The multiple connotations of literacy make it difficult, if not impossible, to find an acceptable definition of the term. Even the basic connotation of reading and writing does not help because there is no agreement on what abilities and knowledge would count as literacy. In other words, there is no agreement on the level(s) of literacy that need be achieved for a person to qualify as literate. This is because each society or culture determines specific levels of literacy competence which should be achieved by its members.

To accommodate different cultural contexts and demands, the notion of 'functional literacy' has been introduced. A person is considered to be functionally literate if s/he is able to carry out activities where a certain level of literacy is assumed to be necessary within the culture. However, the notion does not help in the measurement of literacy. No society requires uniform levels of literacy from all its members. Hence functional levels differ from one subgroup to another within the same culture, making it difficult for setting up norms of achievement. It is difficult enough to measure levels of literacy or functional literacy within one cultural context, it is impossible to establish norms that will provide comparative assessment across cultures.

A part of the difficulty of definition comes from the fact that some scholars view literacy in the sociocultural perspective, while others view it as a measurable phenomenon in terms of specific skills and abilities. Although no single acceptable definition of literacy is available at present, there is clearly a need for a broad consensus on what literacy is. Only a clearer definition of the concept will ensure worldwide agreement and action.

2. Levels of Literacy

There is very little empirical research on levels of literacy. In the area of adult literacy, in fact, there is no reliable study to indicate the levels of literacy that adults can or should achieve. There is, however, some theoretical literature, supported by limited research, in the area of reading levels achieved within the formal educational system in the school and college. It must be pointed out that even these studies relate to specific cultural contexts.

Generally six reading levels or stages are identified which a child masters through the school and college, beginning with the prereading stage and ending with the mature and expert reading stage. Normally the formal school learner takes 12 years at school and several years at college to cover the entire range of reading abilities.

The first three stages of reading coincide roughly with the first three grades in school. In these stages the learner progresses from prereading to decoding through to fluency. At this level the reader is able to read what s/he already knows in terms of both language and knowledge. At the fourth stage of reading, which corresponds with school grades 4 to 8, the reader is able to use his reading ability to acquire new knowledge. Through this stage the reader is able to gradually cope with texts that are complicated and carry new information. During reading stage five, corresponding to high school grades 9 to 12, the reader acquires the ability to read a range of complex materials critically. In the final stage which begins at college and goes beyond, the reader becomes a mature reader, able to read for a variety of purposes—professional, personal, and civic.

3. Childhood and Adult Literacy

Children normally require 12 years (of grade school) to master reading at a level where they are able to comprehend complex texts and to make inferences. The progression from prereading to grade 12 reading is slow. Children take up to 3 years to acquire reading abilities to read texts that are within their own vocabulary range. To be able to read texts using new words and knowledge takes much longer.

In the early stages the child reader is able to read words that are common, familiar, concrete, and short. The sentences are simple and the ideas and concepts in the text are common and concrete. As the reader progresses to higher reading stages, the vocabulary becomes more difficult, unfamiliar, and abstract. The sentences become longer and complex, and the ideas and concepts more abstract. The beginning reader has limited world knowledge. As they progress through the reading stages they acquire newer knowledge which facilitates higher reading abilities.

Does the adult reader progress through the same reading stages as a child does? There is no clear answer to this question. Some experts believe that the progression for the child and the adult reader is essentially the same. It is true that an adult reader has a larger vocabulary and more world knowledge. Yet the adult goes through the same stages of reading ability as the child. It has been argued that adults may achieve the initial reading stages of prereading, decoding, and fluency faster than children, but reading with critical comprehension takes much longer despite the knowledge base of the adult reader. Other experts believe that adults (and children) have to be imparted new knowledge and concepts before they can become fluent readers.

One of the major problems arises from the fact that all adults who need to acquire reading (or literacy) skills do not begin at the same level. Some adults (in some cultures) may have acquired basic literacy skills which they have forgotten or which are no longer functional in their contexts. In other situations, the adult learners may have had no prior literacy training. It is therefore difficult to assess the direction and rate of progression in the case of adult readers.

Another problem arises from the paucity of tests for measuring adult reading success. While many measurement tools exist for measuring school and college level reading abilities, scientifically devised tests for measuring adult reading achievements are almost nonexistent. Part of the reason for the lack of tests for adults stems from the reluctance to subject adult learners to formal achievement tests of any kind. However, there is general agreement that for durable reading abilities, adult learners need to achieve reading levels equivalent to grade 12 of the school reading grades. An adult reader who achieves reading abilities of grade 8 is perhaps functional but not a mature reader.

4. Reading and Writing

Although skills of reading and writing must be seen as equally significant in acquisition of literacy, most studies on literacy focus mainly on reading. Consequently, while a considerable amount of data is available on the acquisition of reading both by children and adults, not enough is known about the acquisition of writing skills. It is nevertheless the case that a large number of studies on reading provide some insights in the graphological aspects of writing systems. Such studies relate to the measurement of difficulties faced by beginning readers in recognition of written symbols. For instance, children's memorization of letters and their combinations in words is influenced by the shapes of letters. Such problems are relatable to the kind of script or writing system employed by a particular language.

However, the problems of recognition of letters or characters are significantly different from those of reproduction when a beginning learner has to write the shapes of letters or characters. It is generally believed that children find it easier to recognize letters and characters but find it difficult to write them. Most researchers on acquisition of writing skills concentrate on the problems faced by children. There is very little information on how adults acquire writing skills.

Some researchers working in this area have studied the compositional and rhetorical aspects of writing rather than the purely motor aspects of reproduction of letters or characters. There is some evidence that in addition to the motor act of producing a written test, a learner has to acquire a set of conventions and norms for discourse production; norms which are culturally determined and differ from one cultural group to another. Even these studies deal with writing skills of children and adolescents.

In several adult literacy programs measurable goals of reading and writing are specified and an adult illiterate is declared to have become literate only when he demonstrates his ability to read and write according to the specified norms. However, there is no systematic research on the problems an adult encounters in requiring these skills.

5. Literacy and Language

It is generally agreed that literacy levels are linked to language competence. At the same time there is some evidence to show that literacy practice leads to better language control and critical thinking. Most literacy programs begin with what the learner knows of their language. A child is said to know about 5000 words in its mother tongue before beginning to learn how to read. On becoming literate, they learn to recognize known words in print. Gradually, with the help of known words, they learn new and unknown words while reading at higher levels. In the process s/he also learns to comprehend more complex language structure used in higher level texts. It has been demonstrated that vocabulary range and reading abilities are interlinked.

The adult learner may have the initial advantage, over the young learner, of a larger vocabulary and more complex grammatical structure. But the mutual advancement of literacy and language control operates equally in the case of the adult. Critical reasoning is enhanced with higher reading abilities.

It is universally accepted that literacy is best imparted in the mother tongue. This is not difficult to appreciate because when literacy is in the mother tongue, the learner is merely acquiring the new skills of reading and writing without having to master new language structure and vocabulary. However, in many situations literacy is imparted in a language other than the mother tongue of the learner. This is especially so in the case of adults who have to acquire literacy skills in a language not their own, as in the case of immigrants.

In many multilingual countries children often have to learn to read and write in a language that is not their mother tongue. In such cases the rate of literacy learning is impeded since the learners do not control the language of literacy. Similar problems may also arise in situations where children speak a nonstandard dialect at home and are taught to read and write in the school through the standard language.

In Third World countries where large populations of adult illiterates have to be taught literacy, the choice of the language of literacy becomes very important. In most cases the adult illiterates may be speakers of unwritten languages and dialects which are used for limited in-group oral communication. The goal of literacy in such situations is to enable the adults to function effectively in the larger contexts of work and development. The language in such contexts is invariably the regional or national standard language which may not even be related to the mother tongue of the learner. The willingness to become literate in a second or foreign language correlates with the attitudes of the learner and the community. It is known that in some contexts the learners demand literacy in a second or foreign language for its prestige in the total communication network.

6. Literacy and Oracy

The relationship between the oral and literate modes of language is not easy to understand. Cognitively as well as pedagogically the oral mode is said to depend on the skills of listening and speaking, and the literate mode on the skills of reading and writing. But the skill correlation is not all. There are other complex relationships between the oral mode or oracy and the literate mode or literacy.

It has been argued by some that development of oracy and literacy both follow universal laws of learning as well as universal principles of language learning. In such a view oracy and literacy are seen as varieties of language behavior and, hence, both are believed to share many patterns which should be evident in the processes in which oracy and literacy are acquired. The argument, that there are many speech communities without a written mode of communication, is not considered valid, for it is claimed that if they were to become literate the acquisition of literacy in such communities would follow the same path as in other literate cultures.

There is also the opposite opinion that literacy is not a universal of human life. According to this view literacy is not governed by cognitive universals which develop naturally without any special environment. Even in literate communities, many individuals remain illiterate, which would point to literacy not being parallel to oracy (see *Oracy*). It is also noted that human beings acquire oracy during the initial stages of biological and cognitive development while literacy requires a special environment. However, it may also be mentioned that there are instances when children who have become removed from human language during their infancy have failed to acquire oracy.

There is also a viewpoint that every language community determines the domains in which oracy and literacy may operate, either separately or in conjunction with each other. In fact, both oracy and literacy in themselves reflect a great deal of variety much like different language styles. In other words, in any given communication situation an individual not only has the choice between the oral or literate mode, but within each has several choices which are governed by the total communication setting.

If oracy and literacy are interlinked, it is worth noting that as literacy has gained during the twentieth century, oracy has declined. Many cultures that had vibrant oral traditions have become marginalized in the face of the increased value given to literacy. In fact, limited oracy has never attracted as much attention as limited literacy has since World War II.

Linguists have, unfortunately, not paid as much attention to literacy as they might have. For the linguist, speech or oracy has remained the main focus. Psycholinguists, and in some measure sociolinguists, have addressed the problem of literacy more than the linguist has.

7. Literacy and Illiteracy

Many countries in the Third World have chosen to link economic development to literacy. Following the example of the industrialized countries many of these developing countries have opted for universal literacy as a goal in their effort to evolve egalitarian and industrialized societies. Many of these countries have traditional cultures where literacy has limited and specific functions, and literacy has been the domain of a small number of individuals in the community. To attain the goal of universal literacy in such cultures is not easy. Illiterate adults in such societies do not readily perceive the benefits of literacy.

Nevertheless, the models of development adopted by these countries require some level of literacy. While many of these societies are slowly moving in the direction of increased childhood literacy, the adult population continues to make up the bulk of the illiterates. Unfortunately, in the absence of universal elementary and high school education, the number of illiterate adults has continually grown.

In many of these countries the educated and political elites have sought to bring about a change in the literacy situation through what are known as literacy campaigns. Many of these countries perceive illiteracy as a disease which must be eradicated. Such campaigns are launched with a great deal of fervor and commitment. However, it is not clear how such campaigns can actually end illiteracy. Often the methodologies employed are more to engender motivation for literacy rather than ensure literacy skills amongst the illiterate learners. Also, functional literacy, rather than higher literacy, is the goal of such campaigns.

There is very little research data to make any claims on behalf of such campaigns. It is not known how far such campaigns succeed, and more importantly, whether the newly literate adults are able to utilize their skills. Often, there is relapse into illiteracy since either the new literate does not find his skills of use in his cultural context, or the skills acquired have not been of the order where automaticity has been achieved. As with other kinds of skill learning, stable literacy is achieved only when the learners achieve levels beyond the basic levels.

8. World Literacy

Literacy is a global issue. The Appendix to this article provides basic statistical information about world literacy, reproduced, with permission, from the UNESCO Statistical Yearbook 1991.

The industrialized countries are concerned about their citizens who do not have enough literacy to cope with the increasing demands made on literacy by technology. The number of people who cannot advance in their careers for want of functional literacy is on the increase.

In the developing countries, however, the literacy figures are far below those in the industrialized world. The concern in these countries is with universal elementary education. The illiteracy figures in some of these countries are above 50 percent. While the school literacy figures are slowly mounting in these countries, on account of rapid population growth the absolute number of illiterate adults is ever growing. According to estimates the total number of adult illiterates will touch the one billion mark by the end of the twentieth century. Most of these illiterates will be in the developing countries in Asia, the Middle East, Africa, and Latin America.

The paradox the world faces is that while in the highly literate societies in the industrialized world the levels of literacy are not high enough, in the developing world not enough people have acquired even basic literacy levels. Identifiable sections of the society in these countries have traditionally been outside the pale of literacy and continue to be so. In many developing countries women do not receive formal education because their roles in society are not literacy-dependent.

Developing countries have set themselves the goal of achieving universal literacy in their struggle for economic self-dependence. Yet, there is no evidence that literacy alone is a critical determinant in economic development. In the global context literacy should be seen as one of the factors in achieving a world order which ensures human rights to all. Literacy is a component in the movement of education for all. Most countries in the world are committed to ensuring that all children and adults should have access to education for better and effective participation in their chosen fields of activity in their cultures.

9. Future of Literacy

While both the industrialized and the developing countries strive for world literacy, the future of literacy continues to be full of paradoxes and contradictions. In the industrialized world the present concern is with coping with the high literacy demands of a technologically oriented society. At the same time, technology itself is likely to take on some of the demands on literacy, making it possible for people to function at lower levels of literacy. In the developing countries the goal of universal literacy entails increased outlays on education. At the same time the developing societies have not changed enough to accommodate the concomitant sociocultural impact of universal literacy.

The question that arises is: will a fully literate world be without stratification? The chances are

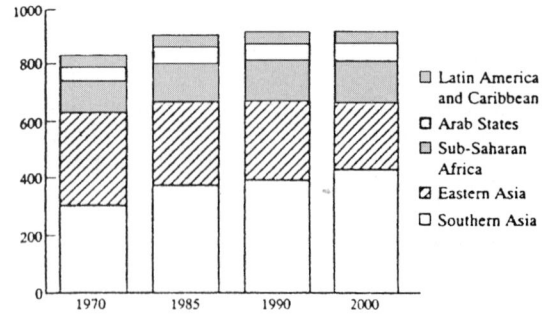

Figure 1. Developing countries, illiterate population aged 15 years and over (in millions).

that even if all human beings are made literate, there will always be markers of individual and group differences. Language has always played a major role in the creation and maintenance of such distinctions.

The impact of literacy in the near future can be very significant. The role of the educator, the social scientist and the policy maker will become more crucial for finding common and acceptable solutions to problems of literacy. For the linguist literacy studies may provide meaningful insights into the structure of the human mind, language universals, and the relationship between oracy and literacy.

APPENDIX (reproduced with kind permission from *The UNESCO Statistical Yearbook 1991*. UNESCO, Paris)
Literacy: Trends and Prospects at the World and Regional Level
1. Significant Facts
- Of the 4294 million inhabitants aged 15 and over living on our planet in 2000, almost 1 billion, or 21.8 percent will know neither how to read nor to write.
- Between 1970 and 1985 the number of illiterates grew by approximately 59 million. Since 1985, the number has remained stable, and there should only be a slight decrease by 2000.
- Relatively speaking, compared to the adult population, this stability in the number of illiterates means a decrease in the rate of illiteracy: 38.5 percent in 1970, 26.5 percent in 1990 and 21.8 percent in 2000.
- Almost all the illiterate population is found, indeed, will continue to be found, in the developing countries: 917 million in 1990 or 34.9 percent of the adult population in these countries.
- At least according to its simplest definition (the inability to read and write a simple text), the amount of illiteracy in developed countries can be considered as negligible: less than 5 percent of the adult population. It is therefore preferable, and more appropriate, in terms of numerical importance, to concentrate the analysis of illiteracy on developing countries.

2. The Developing Countries
- In 1990 in the developing countries taken as a whole, 35 of every 100 adults are illiterate; this proportion which was above 50 percent in 1970 could decrease to 28 percent in 2000.
- Taking the least developed countries on their own, the size of the illiteracy rate will not decrease very quickly and in 2000 one of every two adults will still be illiterate in these countries.
- The numerical predominance of Eastern Asian and Southern Asian developing countries is evident: 677 million illiterates in 1990, that is, 71 percent of the world's total, a relative figure which should last until the year 2000. If these two subregions are considered separately, Eastern Asian countries will experience a drop in the number of illiterates and in the rate of illiteracy, to 23.8 percent in 1990 and 17.2 percent by the year 2000. Of course, this evolution is mainly attributable to demographic trends and the development of schooling in China which,

Table 1. Total and illiterate population aged 15 years and over (in millions).

	Total population aged 15 years and over				Illiterates			
	1970	1985	1990	2000	1970	1985	1990	2000
World	2311.5	3226.2	3580.7	4293.6	890.1	949.5	948.1	935.4
Developing countries	1540.7	2307.6	2626.1	3272.7	842.3	907.2	916.6	919.7
Sub-Saharan Africa	148.6	226.1	263.4	364.4	115.0	133.9	138.8	146.8
Arab States	67.6	107.5	125.4	172.7	49.7	58.6	61.1	65.6
Latin America/Caribbean	164.0	252.1	286.9	362.7	43.0	44.6	43.9	41.7
Eastern Asia	692.5	1036.3	1171.3	1375.1	324.1	295.3	278.8	236.5
Southern Asia	440.0	648.4	738.6	952.2	302.3	374.3	398.1	437.1
Least developed countries	135.2	212.3	245.4	333.4	104.8	138.4	143.2	170.1
Developed countries	770.8	918.6	954.6	1020.9	47.8	42.3	31.5	15.7
Classification by continents								
Africa	200.3	305.2	354.3	485.5	152.6	171.8	177.5	186.4
America	326.0	459.4	503.6	598.1	52.8	54.7	50.4	42.5
Asia	1253.9	1846.8	2088.7	2538.3	652.0	694.4	699.7	695.5
Europe and USSR	518.1	597.0	614.6	649.3	31.1	26.9	19.1	9.7
Oceania	13.1	17.8	19.4	22.3	1.5	1.7	1.4	1.2

because of its size, is predominant in this subregion.
- In Southern Asia, where demographically important countries are also to be found, one adult out of two is illiterate; despite a significant decrease between 1985 and the year 2000, the illiteracy rate (45.9 percent) will still be higher than in all other regions.
- Sub-Saharan Africa in 1990 will have 139 million illiterate inhabitants, representing more than 14 percent of the world's total. Concerning the adult population, here as in Southern Asia, one adult out of two is illiterate. However, if the trends revealed by this assessment are confirmed, this region's illiteracy rate will experience the largest decrease: 40.3 percent in the year 2000 as opposed to 59.2 percent in 1985.
- Although the 61 million illiterates in the Arab States account for only 6 percent of the world total, they represent nearly 50 percent of the adult population of this group of countries. As in the case of Sub-Saharan Africa, this rate should drop sharply to 38 percent by the year 2000.
- Lastly of the developing countries, the region of Latin America and the Caribbean has the smallest number of illiterates and the lowest illiteracy rate, that is, only 11.5 percent by the year 2000.
- In terms of perspectives for the year 2000, these figures indicate that although the illiteracy rates will drop to a relatively low level in Latin America and the Caribbean, and in Eastern Asia, the magnitude of the problem will persist in other regions (Southern Asia, Sub-Saharan Africa and the Arab States).

3. Illiteracy by Sex

- Invariably women represent the largest share of the illiterate population and will continue to do so. As shown in Table 2, in 1990 for the developing countries taken as a whole, the female illiteracy rate is 45 percent compared with 25.1 percent for males. The disparities vary however, between the different groups of countries.

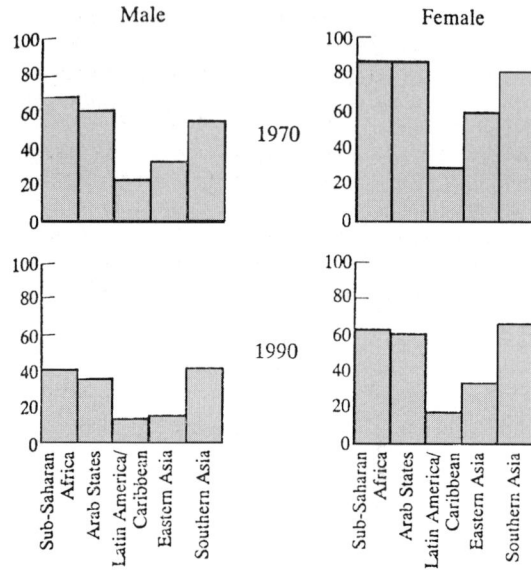

Figure 2. Developing countries' illiteracy rates by sex (%).

Table 2. Illiteracy rates by sex (percent).

	Both sexes				Male				Female			
	1970	1985	1990	2000	1970	1985	1990	2000	1970	1985	1990	2000
World	38.5	29.4	26.5	21.8	30.4	21.9	19.4	15.4	46.5	36.9	33.6	28.2
Developing countries	54.7	39.3	34.9	28.1	42.2	28.9	25.1	19.7	67.4	50.1	45.0	36.8
Sub-Saharan Africa	77.4	59.2	52.7	40.3	67.5	47.4	41.0	29.8	86.8	70.5	63.9	50.4
Arab States	73.5	54.5	48.7	38.0	60.5	40.8	35.7	26.9	86.3	68.5	62.0	49.4
Latin America/Caribbean	26.2	17.7	15.3	11.5	22.5	15.7	13.6	10.3	29.9	19.7	17.0	12.7
Eastern Asia	46.3	28.5	23.8	17.2	32.7	18.0	14.3	10.0	61.3	39.3	33.6	24.6
Southern Asia	68.7	57.8	53.9	45.9	55.2	44.4	40.9	33.8	83.1	72.1	67.8	58.8
Least developed countries	77.5	65.2	60.4	51.0	68.1	53.7	48.6	39.2	87.0	76.6	72.1	62.7
Developed countries	6.2	4.6	3.3	1.5	5.0	3.4	2.6	1.0	7.3	5.7	3.9	2.0
Classification by continents												
Africa	76.2	56.3	50.1	38.4	65.3	44.2	38.3	28.1	86.6	68.0	61.5	48.4
America	16.2	11.9	10.0	7.1	14.0	10.8	9.2	6.5	18.3	13.0	10.8	7.7
Asia	52.0	37.6	33.5	27.4	39.2	26.8	23.4	18.7	65.3	48.9	44.0	36.5
Europe and USSR	6.0	4.5	3.1	1.5	4.3	3.4	2.3	1.0	7.5	5.5	3.8	2.0
Oceania	11.6	9.6	7.5	5.5	11.2	8.2	6.1	4.0	12.0	11.0	8.9	7.0

- The smallest disparity occurs in Latin America and the Caribbean where the rate for females is gradually catching up with that for males.
- Although the illiteracy rates in Eastern Asia are generally smaller than in the other regions the disparity between the sexes is higher than in any other region apart from Latin America and the Caribbean: the rate for females (33.6 percent) is more than twice that for males (14.3 percent).
- In Sub-Saharan Africa, the Arab States and Southern Asia the female illiteracy rates are presently above 60 percent while the rate for males varies between 35 percent and 41 percent. If current trends continue, in 2000 one female adult out of two will still be illiterate in these three regions. In Southern Asia the projected female illiteracy rate for 2000 will still be higher than that observed for males 30 years earlier in 1970.

4. Illiteracy by Age

The amount of illiteracy varies a great deal between the different generations. Table 3 attempts to illustrate this phenomenon by presenting illiteracy rates by age group in developing countries. The base data have been divided into four age groups of different sizes: 15 to 19 years, 20 to 24 years, 25 to 44 years, 45 years and over.

- Of course the older generations have the highest illiteracy rates as they have not profited from the possibilities of schooling given only recently to the younger generations. Unless present trends are altered by an intensive effort to educate adults, the illiteracy rate of persons aged 45 and over risks to stay at a high level until 2000, particularly in Sub-Saharan Africa, the Arab States and Southern Asia: women in this age group will be particularly affected by this situation with an illiteracy rate of around 80 percent in 2000.
- There have been important reductions (in some cases substantial) in the illiteracy rates for the age groups 15–19 years and 20–24 years over the last 20 years and this should continue until 2000. This is the result of the great efforts made since 1960 in most of the developing countries to enroll children in primary school.
- Figure 3 clearly shows both the expected decrease in the illiteracy rates for the youngsters aged 15–19 years and the decrease in the

Table 3. Adult illiteracy rates by age group in developing countries (percent).

	Age group	Total			Male			Female		
		1970	1990	2000	1970	1990	2000	1970	1990	2000
Developing countries	15–19	33.9	19.1	16.1	23.7	13.9	11.8	44.5	24.7	20.6
	20–24	39.8	21.5	17.8	28.2	15.3	13.0	52.1	28.0	22.8
	25–44	52.9	30.9	23.2	39.3	21.6	16.4	67.2	40.6	30.2
	45+	74.4	57.0	45.9	62.2	42.6	32.3	86.4	71.3	59.2
Sub-Saharan Africa	15–19	61.8	35.9	26.4	49.9	28.5	20.9	73.5	43.3	31.9
	20–24	68.3	40.3	31.6	56.2	31.3	25.0	80.3	49.2	38.1
	25–44	79.8	55.5	42.4	69.0	43.2	32.7	90.1	67.2	51.8
	45+	92.6	82.0	72.5	86.6	71.6	59.9	97.8	91.5	83.7
Arab States	15–19	54.6	27.7	20.6	39.3	19.8	14.9	70.5	36.0	26.6
	20–24	61.8	32.9	23.7	45.1	23.3	17.0	78.5	43.1	30.7
	25–44	73.9	48.5	35.2	58.5	34.3	24.7	88.8	63.3	46.2
	45+	85.3	76.3	66.4	74.1	61.1	49.6	96.1	90.3	82.1
Latin America/Caribbean	15–19	14.6	6.2	4.1	13.3	6.1	4.2	16.0	6.3	4.0
	20–24	17.6	7.6	5.1	15.8	7.3	5.1	19.4	8.0	5.0
	25–44	24.9	12.7	8.5	21.4	11.6	8.0	28.3	13.7	8.9
	45+	37.3	27.5	21.4	31.0	23.1	18.2	43.3	31.5	24.3
Eastern Asia	15–19	19.5	6.3	3.6	10.3	4.0	2.5	29.2	8.8	4.8
	20–24	25.5	8.5	4.7	14.0	5.3	3.1	37.9	12.2	6.4
	25–44	43.8	16.8	9.8	27.9	9.0	5.5	61.0	25.0	14.2
	45+	78.0	51.8	36.2	63.5	34.1	20.9	91.6	69.4	51.3
Southern Asia	15–19	56.7	37.7	29.4	42.7	26.8	20.7	72.0	49.5	38.6
	20–24	61.1	42.3	33.4	46.7	30.4	23.7	76.2	55.3	44.0
	25–44	69.2	53.1	44.1	55.4	39.7	32.0	83.9	67.7	57.2
	45+	79.1	71.1	64.7	67.0	57.0	50.0	92.4	85.5	79.7

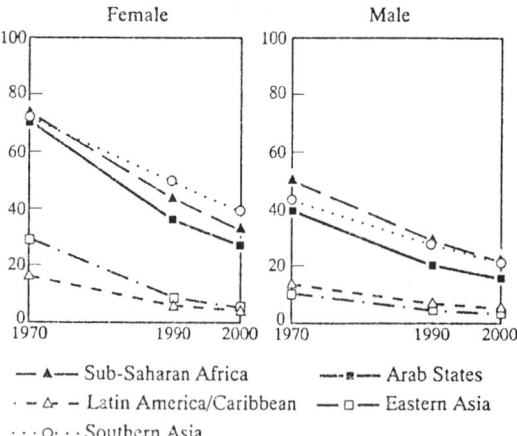

Figure 3. Illiteracy rates in the age group 15 to 19 years in the developing countries (%).

disparity between the male and the female rates. The decreases are most important in the three regions which had very high illiteracy rates (especially for females) in 1970. For example, the illiteracy rate for females aged 15–19 years in the Arab States decreased by half between 1970 (70.5 percent) and 1990 (36.0 percent) and could decrease even further to 26.6 percent in 2000.

- The female illiteracy rate for the age group 15–19 years in Eastern Asia (a region which still has large disparities between the sexes in the global rate aged 15+) has rapidly decreased and by 2000 should be at about the same level as Latin America and the Caribbean. As for males, the illiteracy rate for the age group 15–19 years has always been lower in Eastern Asia than in the other regions.
- In some regions (sub-Saharan Africa, Arab States, Southern Asia), the illiteracy rate for the age group 15–19 years projected for 2000 seems to be still very high and disturbing (over 20 percent). There is always the possibility that such trends could be changed following educational plans and policies decided as part of the program concerning education for all.

See also: Oracy; Orthography; Literacy Research and Methods.

Bibliography

Bhola H S 1984 *Campaigning for Literacy: Eight National Experiences of the Twentieth Century, with a memorandum to decision makers.* UNESCO, Paris
Gray W S 1956 *The Teaching of Reading and Writing.* UNESCO, Paris
UNESCO 1985 *The Current Literacy Situation in the World.* UNESCO, Paris
UNESCO 1991 *The UNESCO Statistical Yearbook 1991.* UNESCO, Paris
Wagner D 1987 *The Future of Literacy in a Changing World.* Pergamon, Oxford, UK

Oracy
A. M. Wilkinson

'Oracy' is a term for talking and listening, by analogy with 'literacy' for reading and writing. It was coined by Wilkinson (1965) in an English and Welsh Schools Council Project at Birmingham University. At that time literacy dominated the school curriculum as a means of learning. A term was needed to give equivalent status to oral/aural activities. Implications of the term were explored in this and a later project (Wilkinson et al. 1974).

Oracy was characterized as 'a condition of learning in all subjects'; as being not merely a skill but the 'essential instrument in the humanizing of the species'; as being a fit subject of educational 'awareness'; as being essentially interrelated with literacy: and as being susceptible of evaluation.

Against the then preoccupation with 'speech training,' it was emphasized that oracy arose in response to the needs of the situation rather than from direct teaching. None of these propositions was part of accepted wisdom in education at that period.

The tenacity of these ideas is indicated by their general currency today in curriculum movements in, for instance, Australia, Canada, and New Zealand, as well as in the UK, where in the early 1990s the National Oracy Project involved over three-quarters of the English and Welsh Local Education Authorities. The continuing influence of the ideas may be seen in the Kingman Report (DES 1988), which focuses on language awareness, and the Cox Report (DES 1989), where evaluation is a central concern, and which quotes the original research on the need to 'create circumstances to which both speaking and listening are the natural responses.' The UK National Curriculum, compulsory in all state schools, prescribes speaking and listening as one of the three Profile Components in English.

The original research team perceived oracy as having more than linguistic implications. The Crowther Report (HMSO 1959) has set out 'numeracy' and 'literacy' as marks of the educated person. With graceful self-restraint the team described this focus as 'academic.' Numeracy, literacy, *and* oracy they argued were the modern equivalent of the nineteenth century's 'three Rs,' that is, basic educational requirements. Thirty years later these three concepts were described by the English and Welsh National Curriculum Council as 'forming the basis of a proper and liberal education to the highest standards parents expect.'

The term was first published in Wilkinson (1965); key passages are reprinted in Wilkinson et al. (1990), which presents aspects of recent thinking on the topic, as does MacLure et al. (1988).

Bibliography

MacLure M, Phillips T, Wilkinson A M 1988 *Oracy Matters*. Open University Press, Milton Keynes, UK

United Kingdom Department of Education and Science 1988 *The Teaching of English Language* ('The Kingman Report'). HMSO, London

United Kingdom Department of Education and Science 1989 *English for Ages 5 to 16* ('The Cox Report'). HMSO, London

Wilkinson A M 1965 *Spoken English*. Educational Review, Birmingham University, Birmingham, UK

Wilkinson A M, Stratta L, Dudley P 1974 *The Quality of Listening*. Macmillan, London

Wilkinson A, Davies A, Berrill D 1990 *Spoken English Illuminated*. Open University Press, Milton Keynes, UK

Pidgins, Creoles, and Minority Dialects in Education
J. Siegel

Pidgins, creoles, and 'nonstandard' or minority dialects (such as African American Vernacular English (AAVE) or Ebonics) are generally stigmatized in formal education. While they may be used informally in the classroom, they generally have no official role and are seen as something to avoid in order to learn the standard language of education.

1. Reasons for Lack of Official Use

The main reason for pidgins, creoles, and minority dialects not being used in formal education is that most people, including educators, still believe that these language varieties are deviant forms of the standard to which they are related. Even when these varieties are recognized as legitimate forms of language, some educators, administrators, and linguists still argue that using them in education would be both impractical and detrimental to students. One argument concerns the lack of autonomy and standardization. Especially in situations where there is a continuum of usage from nonstandard to standard, it is difficult to select a norm to be standardized for use in education. Another 'impractical' argument is that even if a pidgin, creole, or minority dialect could be standardized, the cost of developing written materials would be a disadvantage. Thus, some linguists advocate only the oral use of such varieties in the classroom to facilitate communication in the early years, but not the written use.

However, even oral use is discouraged because of various 'detrimental' arguments. The first of these is that since the goal of the education system is the acquisition of the standard language of education, using a stigmatized variety in the classroom is seen as a waste of time—time that would be better spent learning the standard. Closely related is the 'ghettoization' argument which asserts that using a nonstandard variety of speech in the classroom deprives children of the instruction they need to get the economic benefits that speakers of standard varieties have, and condemns them to permanent underclass status. Third is the 'interference' argument which claims that using a pidgin, creole, or minority dialect in education will make it difficult for students to learn the standard because of negative transfer (see *Language Transfer and Substrates*) or confusion between the two closely related varieties.

2. Arguments for Use

Nevertheless, over the years there have been many calls for legitimizing the use of pidgins, creoles, and minority dialects in education. Some arguments have been mainly socio-political, pointing out the relationship between linguistic and political subjugation and emphasizing the rights of the speakers to express their own linguistic identity and to be educated in their own languages. Other arguments for using pidgins, creoles, or minority dialects have been educational, focusing on one or more of the following obstacles faced by students:

(a) negative attitudes and ignorance of teachers;
(b) negative attitudes and self-image of the students themselves because of denigration of their speech and culture;
(c) repression of self-expression because of the need to use an unfamiliar form of language; and
(d) difficulty in acquiring literacy in a second language or dialect.

In recent years there have been some initiatives to deal with these obstacles. These are of two types: development of resources for teachers, and establishment of educational programs actually using pidgins, creoles, or minority dialects in the classroom.

3. Resources for Teachers

Important references giving background information about creoles have been developed for teachers of Caribbean immigrants in the USA, Canada and the UK. In Australia, public awareness about creoles and minority dialects has been promoted through professional development courses, publications, and information packages aimed at non-linguists, especially teachers and students.

4. Actual Use in Education

There are three types of programs in which pidgins, creoles, and minority dialects are actually used in education: instrumental, accommodation, and awareness. The goals of all three types are usually the same: additive bilingualism or bidialectalism—helping students to acquire the standard language while maintaining their own way of speaking and thus their linguistic self-respect (see *Bilingualism, Societal*). The differences are in the way the students' home varieties are used in the classroom.

In an instrumental program, the home variety is used as the medium of instruction. It is the vehicle for acquiring initial literacy and learning the content of other subjects such as mathematics and health. For primary school children, the standard language is introduced at a later stage, and it eventually becomes the medium of instruction for at least some subjects. National instrumental programs using creoles exist using Seselwa in the Seychelles, Haitian Creole in Haiti, and Papiamento in the Netherlands Antilles. There are also some individual primary programs using Tok Pisin in Papua New Guinea, Kriol and Torres Strait Creole in Australia, Krio in Sierra Leone, Guadaloupean Creole in Guadaloupe, San Andres Creole in Colombia, and nonstandard dialects in Norway and Sweden. In the USA, bilingual programs exist for immigrants speaking Haitian Creole and Capeverdean. Pidgins and creoles are also used in nonformal adult educational programs in Dominica, St. Lucia, Mauritius, Solomon Islands, Vanuatu, and the UK.

In an accommodation program, the home variety is accepted in the classroom, but it is not a medium of instruction or subject of study. In the early years of school, students may use their home varieties of language for speaking and sometimes writing; or teachers may utilize their students' own interactional patterns and stories for teaching the standard. Accommodation programs of this type are reported in the literature for speakers of Hawaii Creole English (HCE) and AAVE. At higher levels, literature and creative writing in a creole may be accommodated into the curriculum, as has been done in Trinidad and Tobago and other parts of the Caribbean.

An awareness program goes a step further by making the students' home language a topic of study. These varieties are put into context by teaching some basic sociolinguistics about language variation, standardization, attitudes, etc. In 'contrastive' awareness programs, the grammatical rules and pragmatics of the pidgin, creole, or minority dialect are explicitly contrasted with those of the standard variety. An additional objective here is separation: helping students acquire the standard by focusing on how its structure and use are different from their own varieties. Awareness programs (or programs with awareness components) have existed for speakers of HCE in Hawaii; for Caribbean Creole English speaking immigrants in the UK, USA, and Canada; for speakers of nonstandard dialects in the Netherlands; for speakers of Aboriginal English and Kriol in Australia; and for speakers of AAVE in the USA. The program proposed by the Oakland School Board that sparked off the Ebonics debate in the 1997–98 was actually an awareness program (see *Ebonics and African American Vernacular English*).

5. Research

Research on instrumental programs in Australia and the Seychelles has shown that students educated bilingually in their creole mother tongue and the standard outperformed students educated in only the standard language—not only in general subjects such as mathematics but also in the standard language itself. Studies in Papua New Guinea, the Caribbean, and Scandinavia have shown that learning literacy in a pidgin, creole, or nonstandard dialect leads to increased reading proficiency in the standard dialect, thus refuting the interference argument. However, with regard to AAVE, opinion is divided about the effectiveness of using 'dialect readers' in teaching reading. Some linguists believe that differences between AAVE and the written standard may not be sufficient to cause problems with reading acquisition if children are allowed to read as they speak.

Research into accommodation programs in Hawaii has shown increased reading achievement and development of spoken standard English as a result of classroom use of patterns of interaction found in HCE. With regard to AAVE, a few studies of the effects of accommodation in the classroom demonstrate greater self-esteem among students, increased participation, higher reading scores, and more use of standard English.

Students who went through programs with awareness components in Hawaii showed improvements in tests of standard English use and oral language skills. Awareness programs in The Netherlands increased the rate of participation of dialect-speaking children as well as the mean length of their utterances. One awareness program for Caribbean English Creole speaking high school students in the USA led to much improved academic performance for most of the participants. Several awareness programs for AAVE-speaking students using contrastive analysis have been beneficial in terms of reduced dropout rates and significant improvements in performance in standard English.

6. Accounting for the Research Results

In summary, the studies and reports evaluating programs of all three types describe various positive results from using pidgins, creoles, and minority dialects in education. There seem to be several obvious reasons for these results. First, for the instrumental programs, students find it easier to acquire literacy skills in a familiar variety of language and then transfer these skills to the standard. Second, in all three types of programs, students can express themselves better in a familiar language (without fear of correction) leading to better cognitive development. Third, teachers have more positive attitudes because of the nature of the programs, which make them aware of the legitimacy and complex rule-governed nature of their students' languages; therefore, they have higher expectations. Fourth, students have more positive attitudes towards their language and themselves, leading to greater interest and increased motivation.

Another reason, however, may be related to aspects of psycholinguistics and second language acquisition. Students who speak a pidgin, creole, or minority dialect often have trouble separating it from the standard variety to which it is related. Because of the many similarities between the home and school varieties, students are often not aware of the differences. But when students look at features of their own varieties in the classroom, they have a greater chance of noticing features of the standard, which are different. This helps them to build the separate mental representation of the standard, which is necessary for language acquisition.

See also: Code, Sociolinguistic; Dialect and Dialectology; Educational Failure; Pidgins and Creoles: An Overview; Spoken Language in the Classroom.

Bibliography

Berry R, Hudson J 1997 *Making the Jump: A Resource Book for Teachers of Aboriginal Students*. Catholic Education Office, Broome, WA
Craig D 1988 Creole English and education in Jamaica. In: Paulston C B (ed.) *International Handbook of Bilingualism and Bilingual Education*. Greenwood, New York
Rickford J R, Rickford R J 2000 *Spoken Soul: The Story of Black English*. Wiley, New York
Siegel J 1999 Stigmatized and standardized varieties in the classroom: Interference or separation? *TESOL Quarterly* **33**: 701–28
Wolfram W, Christian D, Adger C 1999 *Dialects in Schools and Communities*. Erlbaum, Mahwah, NJ

Spoken Language in the Classroom
N. Mercer

The term 'classroom language' is usually taken to mean the language used by teachers and children doing educational activities in schools. It is rarely used with reference to adult education. It is also more usually used to refer to the spoken language of the classroom rather than to what is read or written (though of course written language has a very significant role in school education), and so it is spoken language which is considered here (see *Oracy*).

1. Functions of Spoken Language in the Classroom

Starting with the language of the teacher, its most obvious function is to inform or instruct. Teachers may tell children what they are to do, how they are to do it, when to start, and when to stop. They also assess children's learning through talk, and use talk as a way of providing children with certain kinds of educational experiences which would be hard to provide by any other means (e.g., telling stories, reading poetry, describing objects). One very important function of talk for teachers is to control the behavior of children; indeed, with the demise of corporal punishment in many countries, talk is the main tool of control in the classroom.

Schoolchildren might be expected to use talk primarily to request information and guidance from teachers. However, observational research in classrooms has shown that, as they progress though their school careers, the frequency at which children make spontaneous requests for information from teachers decreases. In secondary schools, most of children's talk in class is in the form of responses to teachers' questions, while requests for information they lack are more often covertly addressed to their peers (see *Observing and Analyzing Classroom Talk*).

In schools in many parts of the English-speaking world (notably the UK and Australia), teaching methods have increasingly come to favor the organization of children into pairs and groups for some learning activities, and this may increase the proportion of both 'on-task' and 'off-task' talk between children. The level of talk in a classroom is, of course, a contentious educational issue. Traditional educational values associate a low level of talk with effective classroom control (success at 'keeping 'em quiet' is a traditional measure of a teacher's effectiveness), but modern methods often place strong emphasis on activities which encourage children to share knowledge with their peers and to develop their oral communication skills (see *School Language Policies*).

The functions of 'off-task' talk have been given little attention by researchers, but for children such talk may on some occasions in school represent the most significant communications which take place. Talk between children working together which seems superficially off-task may be important for developing the working relationship of a pair or group. And, less welcome from a teacher's point of view, children can effectively employ off-task talk to subvert the official social order.

A more general and important function of talk in the classroom, whether between a teacher and one or more pupils or between pupils working together, is as a means for developing shared understanding. Through joint action and talk, participants in the process of teaching and learning build a body of common knowledge which provides a contextual basis for further educational activity. The extent to which educational knowledge is made common through classroom discourse is one measure of the effectiveness of the educational process.

2. The Structure of Classroom Language

The spoken language of the classroom has some interesting and distinctive discourse features (see *Discourse*). (They can be called 'discourse features' because they are aspects of the continuous linguistic text created by the interchanges between teachers and pupils, rather than of discrete utterances.) Consider, for example, the following piece of classroom talk (1):

Teacher: Where is Argentina? (1)
Pupil: In America.
Teacher: Well, yes, in South America.

What happens here is that the teacher 'initiates' an exchange with a pupil the pupil 'responds' and the teacher then provides 'evaluative feedback' on that response. This three-part sequence of 'Initiation–Response–Feedback' (usually summarized by researchers as IRF or IRE) can be described as a minimal episode of teaching-and-learning. It is the frequency of such sequences (called 'exchanges' in the terminology of discourse analysis—see Sect. 2.1) which gives classroom talk its distinctive structure.

2.1 Analysis of Classroom Discourse

The structural analysis of talk can be extended to include larger and smaller units than exchanges. Sinclair and Coulthard (1975) were the first to offer a hierarchical scheme for analyzing classroom talk, shown diagrammatically in Fig. 1. A lesson is first divided into a series of topically coherent units, called 'transactions.' These are then further broken down into 'exchanges,' which in turn can be subdivided into 'moves.' Thus the teaching exchange described consists of three moves, an 'Initiation' (I), a 'Response' (R), and an 'Evaluation' or 'Feedback' (F). Finally, moves are themselves broken down into basic functional units called 'acts.'

Sinclair and Coulthard identified four main types of exchanges initiated by teachers: 'directives,' 'checks,' 'informatives,' and 'elicitations.' They also identified 22 acts, which they claimed were sufficient to describe all classroom discourse. The following is

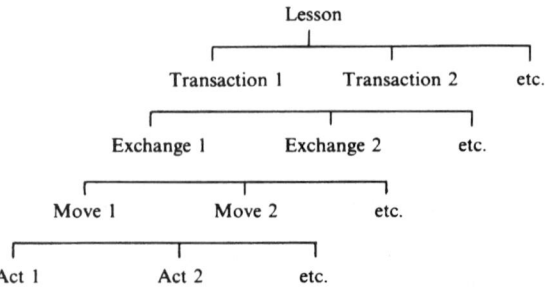

Figure 1. The hierarchical organization of classroom talk (from Sinclair and Coulthard 1975).

an example of a transaction analyzed into exchanges and moves:

```
                                       Moves  Exchanges (2)
Teacher:  What do you notice there—  I       elicitation 1
          what's special about that
          particular section of tape—
          what's that child doing—
          Anybody
Pupil:    Trying to say something    R
Teacher:  Er, right Rosita—what's he F
          actually trying to say     I
Pupil:    Trying to get a word out of R      elicitation 2
          his mouth
Teacher:  And what's the word he's   (F)I    elicitation 3
          trying to get out
Pupil:    Mm daddy                   R
```
(adapted from Graddol et al. 1987: 197)

The first of the three exchanges above begins with the teacher producing a string of acts which make up one move (an initiation). The second exchange can be considered to have no feedback move, or the initiation for the third exchange can be considered to be functioning simultaneously as feedback (indicated by the coding (F)I).

One valuable application of this kind of analysis of classroom talk is to indicate ways in which teachers control the agenda of lessons through discourse. It also shows how being a *pupil* requires children to talk in certain ways which are complementary to those of the teacher. Research suggests that, on entry to school, most children very quickly learn to take on this aspect of the pupil role (see *Home Language and School Language*). Some educationalists see such rapid adaptation to the rules of classroom discourse as a necessary and valuable beginning to children's academic career, while others believe that it demonstrates how schools impose unnecessarily rigid constraints on young children's opportunities for talk and learning (e.g. Willes 1983).

3. Teacher-talk

Observational research in the USA (Flanders 1970) revealed a characteristic of classroom talk which subsequently proved to be a common feature across a wide range of teachers, classrooms, and even countries. It is known as the 'two-thirds rule,' because it has been observed that:
  (a) for about two-thirds of the time someone is talking;
  (b) about two-thirds of this talk is the teacher's;
  (c) about two-thirds of the teacher's talk consists of lecturing or asking questions.

Some teachers and educational theorists have used this discovery as an indictment of teachers' excessive dominance over classroom life and children's opportunities for self-expression and exploration through talk: but such judgments can only safely be made if based on a proper understanding of what teachers are trying to achieve through talking to children in class (cf. Mercer 1995: chap. 3, Wood 1992).

3.1 Teachers' Questions

Teachers are sometimes not only accused of asking too many questions, they are also seen as behaving oddly because it is clear that for the great majority of questions they ask they already know the answers. This seems, on first consideration, to be a rather peculiar kind of language behavior. (There are even jokes about it: *Teacher*: 'How many millimeters in a centimeter?' *Pupil*: 'If you don't know you should be in a different job!') But asking questions of this kind only seems odd if teachers' behavior is judged against some general and abstract standard of language use, whereby the only acceptable function of a question is to provide information requested by the ignorant enquirer. Such standards cannot be appropriately applied, because—as with all situational varieties of language—the nature and function of teacher-talk needs to be considered in context. To understand teachers' unusual use of questions, one needs to know why they ask them.

In order to plan and evaluate their teaching and to assess the learning of their pupils, teachers need constantly to monitor children's knowledge and understanding. Most of the questions they ask are meant to serve this purpose, and on the whole probably do so quite effectively. Teachers and pupils are usually perfectly familiar with this convention (the humor of the joke above depends on the hearer being so), and so few misunderstandings are likely to arise about why they are being asked. However, misunderstandings do sometimes arise because teachers may not choose to ask the most direct, explicit questions. They may want to avoid *putting words into children's mouths* because that would not test children's real understanding, or they may feel that children should be required to put some *mental effort* into making connections between the work they have done and what they are being asked. Consider the following sequence from a science lesson in a UK secondary school classroom, in which the pupils have been doing a series of practical activities about air pressure (3):

```
Teacher:   Well we blew into it and what    (3)
           happened?
Pupil F:   All the water came out of the
           straw.
Pupil P:   The water came out of the s—top.
Teacher:   All came out! Now why? Come
           on! This one's easy.
Pupil F:   'Cos when you were blowing
           bubbles in, all the ... air came up
           the straw ... and the water with it.
Teacher:   Ooh no! I don't think that's quite
           right. When we blew air through
           here ... where did it go?
```

Pupils (*together*):	Into the bottle.
Teacher:	Into the bottle! So was there more air in here or less air?
Pupils (*together*):	More.
Teacher:	More air, wasn't there? There was a lot more air in here. Now this air... wanted to do what?
Pupils (*clash of voices*):	Get out. Push water... push water outside to get room for itself.
Teacher:	Yes, ah. That's a very good answer.

(Barnes 1976: 73–4)

In this extract the teacher uses questions in a kind of guessing game to draw out from the children some key ideas of the lesson. The questions thus are not merely assessment, but are part of the teaching.

3.2 Teachers' Control over Knowledge Content

Teachers use talk not only to control children's behavior and to monitor their understanding, but also to guide children's learning. Through talk, teachers mark some knowledge and experience as significant. They also attempt to create continuities between past, present, and future events in children's classroom experience. Knowledge and experience which is not considered educationally significant or valuable by a teacher will normally be marked as such in their talk, either by simply ignoring it or by dismissing it more explicitly.

One of the most obvious ways in which teachers mark knowledge as significant or otherwise is in their evaluative feedback to children's responses to questions in the IRF exchanges described above. For example, *wrong* answers to a teacher's question are commonly followed by one of the following events: (a) the teacher says the answer is wrong, or (b) the teacher ignores the wrong answer. The teacher is likely then to ask the question again, either in the same words or in a paraphrased form.

Teachers also mark the significance of elements of knowledge and experience in other, more subtle ways. Three features of teachers' discourse which illustrate this are 'cued elicitations,' 'joint knowledge markers,' and 'reconstructive recaps.'

3.2.1 Cued Elicitations

These are IRF exchanges in which the teacher asks questions while simultaneously providing heavy clues to the information required. Cued elicitation may be achieved merely by the wording of the question, but it is often accomplished by some other communicative means such as intonation, pausing, gestures, or physical demonstrations. The extract below, from a primary school lesson, provides a good example of this (nonverbal features of the discourse are shown in italics, and emphatic speech is in bold type). The teacher is talking to the children about Galileo's studies of pendulums:

Teacher:	Now he didn't have a watch but he **had** on **him** something that was a very good timekeeper that he could use to hand straight away	(4)
		Teacher snaps fingers on 'straight away,' and looks directly at pupils as if inviting a response.
	You've got it. **I**'ve got it. What is it? What could we use to count beats? What have **you** got?	*Teacher points on 'You've' and 'I've,' then beats her hand slowly on the table, looking around at the pupils who smile and shrug.*
	You can feel it **here**	*She put her fingers on her wrist pulse.*
Pupils:	Pulse	*Speaking in near unison.*
Teacher:	A pulse. Everybody see if you can find it.	*All copy the teacher, feeling for wrist pulses.*

(adapted from Edwards and Mercer 1989: 142)

3.2.2 Joint Knowledge Markers

These are statements in which a teacher indicates that some shared experience is important and, often, that it is particularly relevant to the present task. One common way of doing so is to use *we* in recalling an event, as in 'Last week, we saw that French nouns can be either masculine or feminine. So what I want you to do now is....' Another way is to point out emphatically to the class that one of them has given a 'very good answer' to a question.

3.2.3 Reconstructive Recaps

These are accounts by teachers of past activities or events shared with the children, in which what went on is selectively reported to highlight aspects seen by the teacher as being educationally significant (and, concomitantly, to play down aspects seen as irrelevant or confusing). For example, in summarizing discussions in class, teachers typically leave out all the 'red herrings' which were raised. To give a more extreme, but real, example: although a series of mishaps had thwarted all but one of many attempts to create a vacuum in a bell-jar, the teacher of the secondary class involved subsequently referred to this occasion as simply 'the lesson in which you made a vacuum.'

4. Technical Language in the Classroom

One of the aims of education is to give children access to important parts of the cultural heritage of their society. A further aim is to enable them to become active participants in the continuing development of that cultural heritage. The pursuit of both of these aims entails children becoming familiar with the technical language of the subjects they study. Used effectively, the technical vocabularies of science, mathematics, art, or any other subject provide clear and economical ways of describing and discussing complex and abstract issues. A shared understanding of musical terminology, for instance—terms like *octave, bar, key,* and so on—makes it possible for two people to discuss, in the abstract, phenomena which otherwise would have to be concretely demonstrated. The discourse of educated people talking about their specialism is explicit only to the initiated. Becoming familiar with the language of a subject is thus an important requirement for entering the intellectual community of scientists, mathematicians, artists, or whatever.

Some technical words which are used rarely in the wider world may be familiar and well-understood by young children because they represent concepts commonly and easily demonstrated in the classroom. (A good example is 'alliteration.') However, the use of technical language in the classroom often causes much confusion and misunderstanding. One reason is that classroom discussions may leave children unsure about what words really mean: teachers may often assume that the meaning of a word is obvious, while children are reluctant to ask questions which reveal their ignorance. Moreover, even the best teacher will find it hard to relate the meaning of some terms to children's concrete experience (concepts like *atomic weight* and *feudalism* can only be read about or discussed, not demonstrated, in class). A consequence may be that many technical words become for children mere jargon, and as such represent an obstacle to their developing understanding. (Educational research has provided many bizarre and salutory examples of how technical terms may be misunderstood, and most teachers will have their own collections. Two such examples are of a twelve-year old who thought that *quandary* meant a four-sided figure, and a school leaver who, after professing no knowledge of *subtractions,* demonstrated that he could nevertheless do *take-aways.*)

5. Conclusion

The analysis of the spoken language of classrooms has made a practical contribution to education by clarifying some of the ways that teachers and children use talk in the pursuit of learning. With a clearer picture of what is said and done, it is more possible to evaluate the processes of teaching and learning in school, and so perhaps plan for more effective communication in the schools of the future. By identifying some typical and distinctive features of language use in one kind of social setting (the classroom), the research which provided this analysis has also made a very significant contribution to the study of language in society, and to language as text, in general.

See also: Observing and Analyzing Classroom Talk.

Bibliography

Barnes D 1976 *From Communication to Curriculum.* Penguin, Harmondsworth, UK
Edwards A D, Westgate D P G 1994 *Investigating Classroom Talk,* 2nd edn. Falmer Press, London
Edwards D, Mercer N 1989 *Common Knowledge: The Development of Understanding in the Classroom,* 2nd edn. Routledge, London
Flanders N A 1970 *Analyzing Teaching Behavior.* Addison–Wesley, Reading, MA
Graddol D, Cheshire J, Swann J 1987 *Describing Language.* Open University Press, Milton Keynes, UK
Hull R 1985 *The Language Gap,* Methuen, London
Mehan H 1979 *Learning Lessons: Social Organization in the Classroom.* Harvard University Press, Cambridge, MA
Mercer N 1995 *The Guided Construction of Knowledge: Talk amongst Teachers and Learners.* Multilingual Matters, Clevedon, UK
Sinclair J, Coulthard M 1975 *Towards an Analysis of Discourse: The English of Teachers and Pupils.* Oxford University Press, London
Stubbs M 1983 *Language, Schools, and Classrooms,* 2nd edn. Methuen, London
Willes M J 1983 *Children into Pupils.* Routledge and Kegan Paul, London
Wood D 1992 Teaching talk. In: Norman K (ed.) *Thinking Voices: The Work at the National Oracy Project.* Hodder and Stoughton, London

Standard English and Educational Policy
M. Farr and A. Ball

The term 'standard English' generally refers to the variety of English used by the formally-educated people who are socially, economically, and politically dominant in English-speaking countries. Although the term is widely used, it is difficult to define precisely because of the variation that exists within what is considered 'standard,' even within one country. Standard English is that variant which is generally taught in schools and is regarded as the 'prestigious' dialect in many English-speaking societies. Non-standard English, in contrast, is spoken by groups of people who have been isolated from the standard dialect, who have not had the opportunity to acquire the dialect of the social elites, or who see value in preserving their own group dialect. The term non-standard English refers to any variety of English which does not conform in pronunciation, grammatical structure, idiomatic usage, or choice of words to the variety that is generally characteristic of formally educated native speakers of English. A distinction can be made between oral and written standard English, the latter varying less within countries, yet still varying somewhat from one English-speaking country to another. We can see that as the English language spreads to different societies in its oral form, it changes through contact with different cultures, so that there are different Englishes (see *New Englishes*) in different parts of the world (e.g., Indian English, Singapore English, Scots English, etc.). Written varieties of English, in contrast, tend to be more standardized, although even these vary from region to region. Even without a fully specified definition of standard English, however, a primary characteristic of any written standard English is the absence of socially stigmatized features (e.g., multiple negation) which are associated with nonstandard English dialects.

1. Standard English in Multicultural Contexts

Demographic changes worldwide have illuminated the multicultural nature of many English-speaking societies. Although the recognition of this multiculturalism has become particularly salient in recent decades, the reality of such pluralism no doubt has existed throughout human history. The identification of individuals with particular population groups (e.g., those based on socioeconomic class, gender, age, ethnic origin, or region of a country) is reflected in their use of particular linguistic items (e.g., a particular pronunciation or lexical item) in their speech and, sometimes, in their writing. Such variation, of course, has significant implications for educational policy (Farr and Daniels 1986).

A few definitions will illuminate the following discussion. The term 'mainstream' is used to refer to those people in societies around the world who are characterized as literate, school-oriented, aspiring to upward social mobility through success in formal institutions, and looking beyond the primary networks of family and community for behavioral models and value orientations (Heath 1983). In English-speaking countries, these are the people who are associated with 'standard' English. 'Nonmainstream,' then, refers to those groups which do not conform to the above characteristics, and whose members speak dialects or non-prestige varieties of English that are considered 'nonstandard.' A dialect (see *Dialect and Dialectology*) is either a regional or a social variety of a language; it is distinguished by specific phonological, syntactic, semantic, and pragmatic features. The latter area, pragmatics, involves the culturally embedded uses of language that characterize a particular group, whether that group is mainstream or nonmainstream. Culture is defined here primarily as a system of knowledge shared by a group of people which both gives rise to behavior and is used to interpret experience. Thus both dialect and culture involve cognition, i.e., both linguistic and cultural competence, or what Hymes (1974) has termed 'communicative competence.'

2. Differences in Communicative Competence

All normal human beings, having been enculturated into one group or another, have communicative competence, i.e., the knowledge to speak the language of their group in ways considered appropriate to that group. Communicative competence, however, can differ from group to group, and problems may arise in intergroup communication (Gumperz 1982, Kochman 1981, Tannen 1986). School, of course, is a primary institutional setting for such intergroup communication. Even if students in a particular school are primarily from one population group, schooling itself, in Western English-speaking societies, is part of mainstream culture, and the communicative competence expected in schools closely resembles that of mainstream, middle class groups. Students from nonmainstream groups enter school with a set of linguistic and cultural resources which may differ from—even conflict with—those of the mainstream school culture (Farr 1993). It is important to understand that such differences in communicative competence are simply differences, not deficits in either a linguistic or cognitive sense, since teacher expectations and attitudes can influence significantly the achievement of their students (see *Educational Failure*).

A substantial body of sociolinguistic research has documented the linguistic characteristics (phonological, syntactic, and semantic) of a variety of nonmainstream English dialects in the USA, UK, and Australia (Farr 1986). A primary finding of all this work is that such dialects are as complex and as regularly patterned as other varieties of English, which are considered more standard. That is, contrary to the common belief among many mainstream groups, speakers of nonstandard dialects do not thereby have linguistic deficits; rather, they often have linguistic rules in their grammars which simply differ from those of standard Englishes.

Other sociolinguistic research has described the culturally embedded aspects of language use, rather than grammatical characteristics, among nonmainstream groups. Such studies, carried out within Hymes's framework for the ethnography of communication, have focused primarily on the contrast between language use at school and in home/community contexts (see *Home Language and School*

Language). These studies have noted that norms for language use, quite apart from the linguistic characteristics of the dialects involved, can differ considerably from one cultural group to another. For example, silence may be considered appropriate in certain contexts for one group, while speaking is the norm in those contexts for another group. Moreover, norms for particular styles of speaking, e.g., with differing levels of directness or indirectness (often indicating degrees of politeness), can vary dramatically from group to group, even when those concerned are speaking the 'same' language (see *Politeness*). In addition, research on the uses of written language among various groups has shown that different cognitive styles underlie different uses of literacy. Thus there is considerable opportunity for miscommunication between speakers (and readers and writers) from different groups, based on differences in language structure, language use, and literary practices.

Schools, of course, as well as other formal institutional settings in modern societies, are a focal point for such cross-cultural communication, especially with regard to the use of literacy. The standard written language, whether in textbooks or on institutional forms (e.g., from banks or government agencies), often reflects the ways of speaking, writing, and thinking of the dominant institutions and groups of the society. Regarding the learning of literacy, many students from nonmainstream cultural groups are faced with a conflict between their own cultural and linguistic systems (and their identity as members of their 'home' groups) and those of the standard written language. The difficulties inherent in resolving such conflicts provide one explanation for low literacy levels among these populations (see *Educational Failure*). Other explanations trace the low literacy levels to lack of access to instruction which emphasizes 'higher order' thinking processes, as opposed to 'lower order' literacy skills. The focus of instruction, either on critical 'literate' thinking or on alphabetic skills, is, of course, guided by attitudes toward and expectations for students on the part of educators and policy makers.

3. Educational Policy

Recognizing the differences that exist between the sociolinguistic resources of students from nonmainstream groups and those that currently are needed for success in formal schooling leads to the need for educational policy regarding what kind of oral and written language should be taught to multicultural student populations (see *School Language Policies*). Three positions can be assumed in this situation: eradication, biloquialism, and appreciation of dialect differences (Fasold and Shuy 1970).

Eradication, the traditional policy in the English teaching profession, assumes the undesirability of language patterns associated with nonmainstream groups and attempts to replace these patterns with more desirable mainstream ones. This, in fact, describes the current, although tacit, policy in most schools, a policy which, many would argue, has not succeeded.

Biloquialism, often termed bidialectalism or biculturalism (as parallels to bilingualism or multilingualism), encourages the learning of mainstream language patterns without eliminating or denigrating nonmainstream ones. The goal of this kind of instruction is to enable students to switch from one linguistic style (or dialect or language) to another according to norms of appropriateness to the context in which the language is used. Since all speakers shift among more or less formal styles depending on context, this position is a natural one, and has, moreover, the advantage of providing a compromise position between the other two.

Appreciation of dialect differences is the logical opposite of eradication. This position maintains that, since research clearly has shown all dialects to be linguistic and cognitive equals, it is unjust to insist on replacing nonstandard dialects with standard ones. Moreover, many have argued (Sledd 1988) that the time and effort spent on eradication (with remarkably unsuccessful results) would be better spent enlightening mainstream groups about the naturalness of variation in language and eliminating prejudices against nonmainstream groups.

Although each of these positions has its advocates, the most pragmatic position seems to be that of biloquialism, which advocates the teaching of mainstream patterns as an expansion of students' linguistic repertoires, not as a replacement for their original ways of speaking. Since bilingualism and bidialectalism exist in societies around the world, such a policy clearly seems to be natural and attainable. Why, then, have nonmainstream students in English-speaking countries not become biloqual in the natural course of events? Research (Ogbu 1990) has shown that some nonmainstream groups maintain their indigenous language patterns as symbols supporting an oppositional identity which resists the mainstream forces which denigrate their vernacular culture. This argument, however, lacks explanatory power for those vernacular speaking minorities in modern urban industrial societies with strong, supportive, and collective ethnic identities who excel academically and who have no difficulty crossing cultural/language boundaries. Other research (Erickson 1984) locates the problem in the micropolitical communicative processes between individuals from different groups. The implication here is that the micropolitical processes reflect more macro ones from the larger society; sociolinguistic differences can either be used to escalate conflict between differing individuals or be put aside in the effort to communicate. For biloquialism to be an effective policy, then, it will have to be supported by a larger social context which respects rather than denigrates linguistic and cultural differences. Changing the *status quo* to one of tolerance toward such differences requires social change beyond the scope of language arts teaching, but education can contribute to such social change by teaching both teachers and students that such differences are not deficits. Rather than using differences as resources for conflict, they can be used as a basis for improving instruction in standard language and literacy to multicultural student populations.

4. Instructional Approaches

Ethnographic studies of community uses of language and literacy have been used to improve instruction in two ways: by modifying instruction to be congruent with local ways of using language, and by involving students themselves in doing, and writing up the results of, ethnographic research in their own communities (Au 1980, Au and Jordon 1981, Heath 1983, Moll and Diaz 1987).

Classroom studies have provided an understanding of principles underlying effective language arts instruction to nonmainstream students (Ball et al. 1997, Heath and Branscombe 1985, Lee 1993, Staton et al. 1988). The most important principle of effective instruction for such students is ethnosensitivity, rather than ethnocentrism, on the part of teachers and educational administrators. That is, because communication between student and teacher is central to learning, it is crucial for educators to understand the extent to which they are interpreting nonmainstream students' behavior according to their own cultural and linguistic patterns, which they see as more 'natural' and 'logical' than those that are alien to them.

A second principle involves providing all current and future teachers with information that presents the results of sociolinguistic research on the differences in communicative competence among culturally and linguistically diverse groups in order to explode the myths of cultural and linguistic deficits and to provide a clearer understanding of the resources that diverse students bring into the classroom.

A third principle involves structuring instructional activities that comprise functional and interactive communication; language that is intended as authentic communication, rather than as an artificial exercise, is more likely to call forth the full range of students' linguistic capabilities and to stimulate them to acquire new ones.

A fourth principle concerns the provision of abundant experience with and exposure to standard oral and written English. Such experience provides multiple examples of the linguistic patterns and the cultural assumptions of academic culture; it also provides opportunities for learning other ways of reasoning, those presumed to be necessary not only for schooling, but also for participating fully in modern societies.

See also: Ebonics and African American Vernacular English; Black English in Education: UK; Home Language and School Language.

Bibliography

Amastae J, Elias-Olivares L 1982 *Spanish in the United States: Sociolinguistic Aspects*. Cambridge University Press, Cambridge, UK

Au K 1980 Participation structures in a reading lesson with Hawaiian children. *Anthropology and Education Quarterly* **11**: 91–115

Au K H-P, Jordon C 1981 Teaching reading to Hawaiian children: Finding a culturally appropriate solution. In: Trueba H, Guthrie G, Au K H-P (eds.) *Culture and the Bilingual Classroom*. Newbury House, Rowley, MA

Ball A F 1998 Evaluating the writing of culturally and linguistically diverse students: The case of the African American English speaker In: Cooper C R, Odell L (eds.) *Evaluating Writing: The Role of Teachers' Knowledge About Text, Learning, and Culture*, pp. 225–248. National Council of Teachers of English Press, Urbana, IL

Ball A F, Williams J, Cooks J 1997 An Ebonics-based curriculum: The educational value. Thought and Action. *The NEA Higher Education Journal* **13**: 39–50

Erickson F 1984 School literacy, reasoning, and civility: An anthropologist's perspective. *Review of Educational Research* **54**: 525–46

Farr M 1993 Essayist literacy and other verbal performances. *Written Communication* **10**: 1, 4–38

Farr M 1986 Language, culture, and writing: Sociolinguistic foundations of research on writing. In: Rothkopf E (ed.) *Review of Research in Education 13*. American Educational Research Association, Washington, DC

Farr M, Daniels H 1986 *Language Diversity and Writing Instruction*. NCTE, Urbana, IL

Fasold R, Shuy R (eds.) 1970 Preface. *Teaching Standard English in the Inner City*. Center for Applied Linguistics, Washington, DC

Ferguson C, Heath, S B 1981 *Language in the USA*. Cambridge University Press, Cambridge, UK

Gumperz J J (ed.) 1982 *Language and Social Identity*. Cambridge University Press, Cambridge, UK

Heath S B 1983 *Ways with Words: Language, Life and Work in Communities and Classrooms*. Cambridge University Press, Cambridge, UK

Heath S B, Branscombe A 1985 'Intelligent writing' in an audience community: Teacher, students, and researcher. In: Freedman S W (ed.) *The Acquisition of Written Language: Response and Revision*. Ablex, Norwood, NJ

Hymes D 1974 *Foundations in Sociolinguistics*. University of Pennsylvania Press, Philadelphia, PA

Kochman T 1981 *Black and White Styles in Conflict*. University of Chicago Press, Chicago, IL
Labov W 1972 *Language in the Inner City: Studies in the Black English Vernacular*. University of Pennsylvania Press, Philadelphia, PA
Labov W 1980 *Locating Language in Time and Space*. Academic Press, New York
Lee C 1993 Signifying as a scaffold for literary interpretation: The pedagogical implications of an African American discourse genre. National Council of Teachers of English Press, Urbana, IL
Moll L, Diaz R 1987 Teaching writing as communication: The use of ethnographic findings in classroom practice. In: Bloome D (ed.) *Literacy, Language and Schooling*. Ablex, Norwood, NJ
Ogbu J 1990 Minority status and literacy in comparative perspective. *Daedalus* **119**(2): 141–68
Sledd J 1988 Product in process: From ambiguities of Standard English to issues that divide us. *College English* **50**(2): 168–76
Staton J, Shuy R, Kreeft-Payton J, Reed L 1988 *Dialogue Journal Communication: Classroom, Linguistic, Social, and Cognitive Views*. Ablex, Norwood, NJ
Tannen D 1986 *That's Not What I Meant!: How Conversational Style Makes or Breaks Your Relations with Others*. Morrow, New York
Tannen D 1990 *You Just Don't Understand: Women and Men in Conversation*. Morrow, New York
Zentella A C 1997 *Growing up Bilingual: Puerto Rican Children in New York*. Blackwell, Oxford, UK

Teaching Endangered Languages
L. Hinton

There are presently more than 6000 languages in the world, but almost half of the human population are native speakers of the top 10 of these languages (Grimes 1996). What this means is that the majority of human languages are spoken by very small numbers of people. We are in the midst of worldwide social change where economic and political forces combined with a revolution in communications are working against the continued existence of these small languages. Language shift (see *Language Maintenance, Shift, and Death*) to the world languages is so rapid and so extensive that we can well expect that over half of the languages on earth will disappear in the coming century (Krauss 1992). We call these languages 'endangered,' especially, as is the case with so many now, they are no longer being learnt at home by children, but are known only to adults or even just to a few elderly speakers.

The decline of linguistic diversity in the world is linked to the world political economy which invades and takes over the territories of indigenous peoples, threatens the ecosystems in which they live, and wipes out their traditional means of livelihood. Because of these links, the right to maintain minority languages has become a human rights issue, supported by such international organizations as UNESCO. A worldwide movement for the rights of indigenous peoples is resulting in the development of language revitalization efforts in thousands of speech communities. The revitalization of Hebrew, which had not been spoken as a native language for 2000 years, was an exceptional early case of the revival of an actually extinct language. A more typical case, however, involves revitalization of a language that still has some (perhaps only a few) speakers. Current strong revitalization programs are underway in such locations as New Zealand (Maori), Hawaii (Hawaiian), Spain (Catalan), Wales (Welsh), and Ireland (Gaelic). The multitude of indigenous languages of the Americas are especially threatened, and in recent years literally hundreds of maintenance and revitalization programs have developed all over the hemisphere.

1. The Role of Schools in Language Revitalization

The core of a language revitalization movement necessarily involves second language teaching, since by definition endangered languages are not spoken by a large portion of the population to which that language belongs. Most revitalization efforts are centered in schools. This has an ironic twist to it, because schools themselves have been one of the parties most responsible for language decline. In North America, for example, the first half of the twentieth century saw a purposeful policy of language eradication toward indigenous peoples through the establishment of boarding schools where children were removed from their families and cultures, and punished whenever they were 'caught' speaking their language anywhere on the school grounds. Even when schools do not purposefully set out to destroy languages, their influence on language development and social development is so strong that the children of minority groups may abandon their language of heritage early in life. The end result is that in one generation or another the language ceases to be spoken at home, at which point it becomes moribund.

Despite the fact that schools have played such a major role in language shift, they are also capable of being the major players in reversing language shift. When the families find their ancestral language silenced at home, their only hope for reversing language shift is in second language learning, and communities look to schools as the place where second language learning can most effectively take place.

2. Differences Between Teaching Endangered Languages and World Languages

The teaching of endangered languages is very different from the teaching of world languages, in terms of the following factors:

2.1 Resources Available for Language Teaching

Resources may be slim for teaching an endangered language. Funding is rarely stable, pedagogical materials may be nonexistent (at least initially), and finding teachers who are also speakers may be difficult or impossible. Expertise may be lacking in state-of-the-art language teaching methods. Thus, any language revitalization program must have a strong training program and must spend a good deal of energy on the development of materials and curriculum, or else on developing a teaching methodology that is not strongly dependent on materials and fixed curriculum.

2.2 Goals

In a typical foreign language classroom, goals are usually simply to learn the language in order to communicate with native speakers of the language or read literature in that language. For an endangered language, the goals are much larger and the stakes much higher. The language has ceased being the language of communication, so not only must people learn to speak it, but communicative functions of the language must be recreated in order for it to be used again. If the classroom is the site of learning, for a language to be revitalized it must also leave the classroom, and be brought back as the language of communication within the community. The goal, then, is Reversing Language Shift (RLS), as termed by Fishman (1991) (see *Reversing Language Shift*). Furthermore, language revitalization must be seen only as part of a more general cultural revitalization, usually accompanied by the reaffirmation of traditional activities and values and possibly efforts toward ecological restoration as well. All of this means that any language program in the school must be part of a community-wide program, and cannot simply be something the school itself designs and implements without strong community involvement. In fact, very frequently revitalization programs involve the setting up of separate schools, rather than the establishment of a program within an existing school.

2.3 The Consequences of Language Teaching

In the case of successful RLS, the second language learners of today will become the main carriers and teachers of the language tomorrow. This means that any incomplete learning (accent, grammatical, or lexical deficiencies, etc.) will become part of the future of the language itself.

The only way for a learner to become fluent is to create an intensive immersion program. In schools, this generally means a program where the language becomes the language of instruction in the school. Endangered languages, which are not presently used as the language of communication, lack much of the vocabulary needed to talk in today's world and today's classroom. Generally connected with intensive second language teaching for endangered languages must be a way to generate new vocabulary, and some authority structure to oversee the development.

All in all, then, one of the consequences of teaching an endangered language is that the language will undergo intensive change.

The social and political changes that accompany RLS are also often very profound, both in the speech community and in the surrounding 'mainstream' community, as we will see in the Hawaiian example below.

3. Hawaii

One of the most successful programs so far in achieving RLS through second language teaching is the Hawaiian program, run by the 'Aha Punana Leo Foundation. It now has nine preschools and two highschools (one public, one private) with Hawaiian as the main language of instruction, and 14 elementary schools with Hawaiian-language tracks. A recently opened Masters Program in Hawaiian Studies at the University of Hawaii at Hilo means students may go all the way to a master's degree with Hawaiian as the main language of instruction. Children enter preschool knowing English only, but through structured immersion principles, they are usually using Hawaiian exclusively in school within 6 months. Since few people of professional age know Hawaiian fluently, people planning on becoming teachers in the program learn the language at the University of Hawaii. As the 'lead group' of students progressed through school, the University of Hawaii at Hilo kept a year ahead of them in producing materials and books, having to develop the curriculum and write or translate books for all school subjects. This also demanded the development of a massive new vocabulary, so a 'Lexicon Committee' was founded which meets regularly to determine what the new words shall be. For the computer, important programs such as Claris Works now have a Hawaiian language version. Since people of parenting age do not know Hawaiian, unless they have learnt it in college, parents of the children in the immersion schools are encouraged to do volunteer service in the classroom, and go to once-a-week night classes to learn basic classroom Hawaiian. Parents sending their children to this program often have a strong commitment to the language, and there are a dozen or so families who have committed to making Hawaiian the language of their homes. In order for this program to succeed it needed legislative support, for up to then, it was illegal to use anything but English in the classroom. After a great deal of hard work, Hawaiian and English were made the co-official languages of the state, and it was made legal for schools to teach in either language. Through the enormous efforts of many dedicated and talented people, this program has resulted in the growth of several thousand new fluent speakers.

4. Other Programs

New Zealand served as a model for the Hawaiian program and, like Hawaii, is experiencing a great resurgence of the Maori language. Some other programs around the world, such as Irish, also teach the language in schools nationwide, but do not have such a strong emphasis on immersion and use of the language as the primary language of instruction (although there are enclaves where such schools exist). Smaller groups, such as the Blackfeet and the Mohawk, have developed immersion programs on a smaller scale. Bilingual education has been the focus elsewhere, such as among the Navajo, and the Quechua in the Andes. In some communities, the schools have not been the primary focus of language education. Some of the Pueblos (e.g., Cochiti) have summer immersion programs and after-school classes. In California, where 50 languages are still spoken, but only by a dozen or less elderly speakers each, a unique intertribal program has developed, called the 'Master–Apprentice Language Program,' where adult learners pair up with elderly speakers and are given training that allows them to interact informally together for up to 20 hours per week using only their ancestral language. Some 60 teams, for over 20 languages, have gone through this program over the last 7 years. The goal is for the young apprentice to gain fluency in the language and then to be able to teach children in whatever setting is available (Hinton 1997b).

5. Documentation

An important part of any revitalization program should also be documentation. In their zeal to get new speakers, sometimes communities forget that while the elders are there to help now, they will not be there in the future and they have much knowledge that will probably not be adequately transmitted during their lifetimes. Audiotapes and videotapes of the elders are of tremendous value long after their death, and often form the basis of excellent CDs, storybooks, and other pedagogical materials.

6. Role of the Linguist

In all of these programs, linguists have played a central role in design, development, training, and implementation. The most important functions of the linguist are to bring analytical knowledge of the language into the program where needed, good knowledge of documentation, and effective theory and methodology of language teaching into whatever kind of program is developed. Immersion, communicative competence, and links to cultural revitalization are stressed in all the most successful programs; the role of writing may also be important (e.g., with Hawaiian and Gaelic), or it may be insignificant (as with the California master–apprentice program, where most of the languages have no official writing system or literary tradition, or with the Cochiti, who have officially decided not to write their language at all). Each community has unique needs, and the linguist and the community must work closely together to develop the right program.

See also: Endangered Languages; Reversing Language Shift; Bilingual Education.

Bibliography

Fishman J A 1991 *Reversing Language Shift: Theoretical and Empirical Foundations of Assistance to Threatened Languages*. Multilingual Matters, Clevedon, UK

Grenoble A, Whaley L J (eds.) 1998 *Endangered Languages*. Cambridge University Press, Cambridge, UK

Grimes F (ed.) 1996 *Ethnologue: Languages of the World*, 13th edn. Summer Institute of Linguistics, Dallas, TX

Hinton L 1997a Hawaiian language schools. *News from Native California* **10**(4): 15–22

Hinton L 1997b Survival of endangered languages: The California Master Apprentice Program. *International Journal of the Sociology of Language* **123**: 177–91

Krauss M 1992 The world's languages in crisis. *Language* **68**: 4–10

Reyhner J (ed.) 1996 *Stabilizing Indigenous Languages*. Center for Excellence in Education, Northern Arizona University, Flagstaff, AZ

Reyhner J (ed.) 1997 *Teaching Indigenous Languages*. Center for Excellence in Education, Northern Arizona University, Flagstaff, AZ

SECTION IX
Methods in Sociolinguistics

Attitude Surveys: Question–Answer Process
H. Schuman

The recent development of the interview or questionnaire survey has been due in good part to advances in probability sampling, statistical analysis, and computing. Yet language lies at the heart of all surveys, for fundamentally they consist of questions and answers. Social scientists who carry out surveys recognize that the responses constituting their data are shaped by the form, wording, and context of the questions, and also by the behavior and characteristics of those who do the interviewing.

The main method used to study the effects due to questions or interviewers is the 'split-ballot' experiment. In it, a sample of respondents is divided into two or more parts on a random basis, and then question types or interviewer characteristics are varied across the parts. Sometimes only a single word in one question differs between two halves of a sample; at other times the changes involve complex factorial designs, with both question and interviewer characteristics varied simultaneously. Supplementing the more usual split-ballot or between-subjects experiment are within-subjects and other designs. Thus, although surveys themselves are rightly regarded as nonexperimetal approaches to studying human behavior, most research *on* surveys is experimental. Of course, if probability methods have been used to draw the total survey sample from a larger population (for example, the adult population of the USA), conclusions from the experiment can be generalized to that population on a rigorous basis.

Each type of question variation—wording, form, and context—as well as variations due to interviewers, will be discussed in this article.

1. Wording of Questions

Often what is thought to be the 'same' question can be worded in two or more ways. A classic example was first reported by Rugg (1941) and replicated more than three decades later by Schuman and Presser (1981). In each case, half of a large national sample was asked one version of the question, and half the other version, as shown in Table 1. Although the words 'forbid' and '[not] allow' have different connotations, in this particular pair of questions their practical meaning is identical: to forbid a speech has the same consequence as not allowing it, and vice versa. The experiment shows that a seemingly innocuous change in question wording can have a quite large effect on answers, shifting the percentage willing to restrict 'speeches against democracy' by 21 percent in 1940 and by 26 percent in 1976.

The results in Table 1 illustrate two important points. First, seemingly minor changes in wording can have an importance influence on the distribution of responses to a single question. (Such single-variable distributions are usually referred to in survey research as 'marginals.') Second, each version of the question in Table 1 shows much the same change over time in willingness to tolerate 'speeches against

Table 1. The forbid–allow experiments.*

	Do you think the United States should forbid public speeches against democracy?		Do you think the United States should allow public speeches against democracy?	
	1940	1976		1940	1976
Yes (forbid)	54%	21%	No (not allow)	75%	48%
No (not forbid)	$\frac{46}{100}$	$\frac{79}{100}$	Yes (allow)	$\frac{25}{100}$	$\frac{52}{100}$
Number of cases	(1300)	(1475)		(1300)	(1375)

*Adapted from Schuman and Presser (1981: 277)

democracy' (33 percent for the 'forbid' version and 27 percent for the 'allow' version), and thus the variation in wording does not affect the conclusion about temporal change, provided that wording is held constant when the time points are compared. More generally, it is often (though not always) true, as will be illustrated further below, that effects due to minor variations in wording occur for marginals but not for relationships (e.g., the relation of response to time). This leads survey researchers to treat relationships as more robust than marginals.

The forbid/allow example is one of the largest question wording effects ever discovered. Furthermore, it has been generalized to some other issues besides 'speeches against democracy,' though for reasons not well understood little or no effect occurs on certain issues (e.g., forbidding versus allowing 'cigarette advertisements on television'). Finally, the effect has been reproduced in German, where terms equivalent to 'allow' and 'forbid' are available.

However, the importance of the effect should not be overstated. First, not every type of wording change affects even marginals, and this includes some changes that seem likely to do so. For example, Schuman and Presser (1981) substituted the words 'end pregnancy' for 'abortion' in one experimental manipulation, expecting it to reduce the negative impact of the latter term, yet discovered no glimmer of an effect. Second, in some cases it is difficult to say whether a change in wording is nonsubstantive, as is argued in the forbid/allow case, or substantive in the sense of changing the issue itself. Thus Mueller (1973) suggested, and Schuman and Presser (1981) confirmed, that adding a phrase about preventing a 'Communist take-over' to a question about possible American intervention abroad would increase support in a national sample by about 15 percent. However, it is not clear whether the added phrase serves mainly as rhetoric to rally support emotionally (a nonsubstantive explanation), or mainly as a useful specification that defines the situation more fully (a substantive explanation).

In addition, the type of effect reflected in the forbid/allow experiment is often cited to show the impact of 'small' changes in question wording, but in a sense such a conclusion is circular, since what is large and what is small are not defined independently. The distinction between the articles 'a' and 'the' may seem trivial to some, yet in certain contexts they have profoundly different implications. Introducing an individual as 'the wife' of the ambassador has a different implication than introducing the same individual as 'a wife' of the ambassador.

2. The Form of Questions

The question variations noted so far are limited to particular types of questions. However, it is possible to vary formal features of questions in a way that applies to virtually any inquiry in a survey. Thus, to almost any question, it is possible for a respondent to say 'don't know' in order to indicate lack of relevant attitude or belief. Standard survey questions usually discourage such responses by not offering that alternative explicitly, or even rejecting it when it is given spontaneously and, instead, urging the respondent to think further. Schuman and Presser (1981) carried out a series of split-ballot experiments where one form of the questions (called the 'filtered' form) offered 'don't know' alternatives and the other form did not, though in the latter cases 'don't know' was accepted if given spontaneously by a respondent. Over a large number of experiments, offering a 'don't know' alternative always raised significantly the proportion of people saying 'don't know,' with the mean increase being 22 percent. Particularly striking was the finding that approximately the same increase occurred regardless of the difficulty of the question—the difficulty being measured by the percentage of 'don't know' responses on the unfiltered form.

Other findings from these experiments were also important. Despite the large variation in the proportion choosing the 'don't know' response, the ratio of the other responses to one another (e.g., of 'yes' versus 'no' answers to the question) was seldom affected by the experimental manipulation. Nor was the relation of these other alternatives to different variables (e.g., education) usually affected. Thus, responses to the 'don't know' alternative itself were greatly influenced by the form of the question, but other results involving the question and its relation to other items were not affected. Subsequent research has produced some exceptions to these empirical generalizations, but by and large they remain valid.

Another and more obvious formal feature of questions is whether they are open or closed. Open questions do not present alternatives for respondents, but instead answers are recorded verbatim and then coded (categorized) at a later point, whereas closed questions present two or more alternatives to respondents and ask for a choice among them. Open questions are relatively infrequent in contemporary surveys because they are more time-consuming both to ask and to code, and therefore more expensive to use. They are also usually assumed to be less reliable because of the difficulty of obtaining clear responses and of later coding vague or ambiguous answers. Schuman and his colleagues have carried out a number of experiments comparing open and closed questions, with several fairly clear results.

First, as Table 2a shows, closed questions can constrain responses considerably: answers given spontaneously to an open question about the most important problem facing the USA are mentioned much less often when they are not among the list of alternatives provided to a closed form of the question, even though the latter allows respondents

Table 2a. Offering rare responses.
The open question was 'What do you think is the most important problem facing this country today?'
The closed question was, 'Which of the following do you think is the most important problem facing this country today—the energy shortage, the quality of public schools, legalized abortion, or pollution—or if your prefer, you may name a different problem as most important.'

Category	Response (%)	
	Open question	Closed question
The energy shortage	0.0 ⎫	5.6 ⎫
The quality of public schools	1.2 ⎬ 2.4	32.0 ⎬ 60.0
Legalized abortion	0.0	8.4
Pollution	1.2 ⎭	14.0 ⎭
All other responses	93.0	39.3
Don't know	4.7	0.6
Total	100 ($n = 171$)	100 ($n = 178$)

Table 2b. Omitting possible responses.
The open question was, 'There have been a lot of national and world events and changes over the past 50 years—say from 1930 right up until today. Would you mention one or two such events or changes that seem to you to have been especially important. There aren't any right or wrong answers to the question—just whatever national or world event or change over the past 50 years that comes to mind as important to you.'
The closed question was, 'There have been a lot of national and world events and changes over the past 50 years—say from about 1930 right up until today. Would you choose from the list I read the event or change that seems to you to have been the most important, or if you wish you can name an event or change different from the ones I mention. There aren't any right or wrong answers to the question—just whatever national or world event or change over the past 50 years that seems most important to you. Here is the list: World War II, the exploration of space, the assassination of John F. Kennedy, the invention of the computer, or the Vietnam War?'

Category	Response (%)	
	Open question	Closed question
World War II	14.1 ⎫	22.9 ⎫
Exploration of space	6.9	15.8
Assassination of John F. Kennedy	4.6 ⎬ 37.1	11.6 ⎬ 94.3
Invention of the computer	1.4	29.9
The Vietnam War	10.1 ⎭	14.1 ⎭
All other responses	52.2	5.4
Don't know	10.6	0.3
Total	100 ($n = 347$)	100 ($n = 354$)

Adapted from Schuman and Scott (1987)

to bypass the proffered list and that list is made up entirely of answers rarely mentioned spontaneously.

This finding suggests that only responses given spontaneously to an open question should be considered to represent the 'real' views of respondents. Such a conclusion is too simple, however, as indicated by the data presented in Table 2b. In this case all but one of the responses to a question about the most important events and changes over the past half century were given frequently both spontaneously to an open question and as choices to a parallel closed question. However, the one exception—'the invention of the computer'—was seldom given to the open question but turned out to be the most frequently chosen of all responses to the closed question. What is evidently happening is that 'the invention of the computer' is a possible answer that does not usually occur to respondents, perhaps because it lacks the dramatic character of events like wars and assassinations, yet when offered explicitly it seems appropriate to many respondents as an answer. The two experiments taken together show that there is no straightforward solution to which form of a question, open or closed, is preferable, and that here, as in many other areas of science, simple rules for application are probably not possible. Other experiments on open and closed questions complicate the picture somewhat further, and there is a good deal still to learn about the difference between open and closed questions—a difference as fundamental as any in the question–answer process.

3. Context Effects on Questions

The experiments described thus far have all involved some change in questions themselves. However, even when question form and wording are held constant, answers can be affected by the location of a question in relation to other questions. For example, Bishop (1987) has shown that respondents' self-reported degree of interest in politics is affected by previous political questions in the survey. If the earlier questions are about attitudes toward a number of political issues, self-reported general interest in politics tends to increase. But if the earlier questions call for answers demonstrating knowledge about politics, self-reported interest tends to decrease. The exact mechanism accounting for these changes is uncertain, for example, whether it involves mainly learning about oneself, as Bem (1972) might argue, or is mainly a matter of self-presentation to interviewers, as Goffman's (1959) writing would suggest. What is clear is that answers to survey questions are not simply reports of preexisting mental states, but are partly a result of generating responses that make sense in the immediate situation of the survey.

A second example of context effect indicates that conclusions about trends over time—which are one of the most important contributions that surveys make—can be affected by question order. As Fig. 1 shows, a question in 1948 on whether journalists from Communist countries should be allowed to report from the USA was greatly influenced by whether it appeared before or after a question about whether American journalists should be allowed to report from a Communist country. When the Communist reporter question appeared second, the opposition to Communist reporters was much lower, no doubt because a norm of reciprocity was made salient, which called for the same treatment on both sides.

When the experiment was repeated in 1980, the same basic effect occurred, but was reduced in size because opposition to Communist journalists had decreased in the context where that question came first. As a result, conclusions about change over time are different for the two contexts. Where the Communist reporter item appears first, there is a significant increase in tolerance for such reporting. Where the Communist reporter item comes second, there is no change over time, presumably because the force of the norm of reciprocity had itself not changed over the 32-year period. Therefore, this experiment shows that a substantive finding about trends over time in attitudes can be importantly influenced by question context. Moreover, it is important to realize that responses in both contexts can be treated as valid, even though they yield different conclusions about attitude change over time.

'Communist reporter' item	Do you think the United States should let Communist reporters from other countries come in here and send back to their papers the news as they see it?
'American reporter' item	Do you think a Communist country like Russia should let American newspaper reporters come in and send back to their papers the news as they see it?

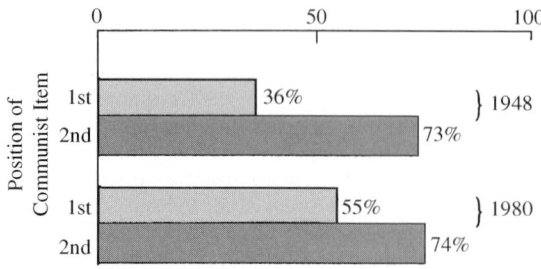

Figure 1. Context effect on reporters' questions.

A final set of findings on context effects is useful to mention, because it shows the value of bringing to bear on the survey theory from both cognitive psychology and the philosophy of language. Several split-ballot experiments have been carried out on the ordering of two questions about self-reported happiness: one dealing specifically with happiness in one's marriage and the other with happiness in general. When the general question is asked second in the sequence, some experimenters have found that self-reported general happiness increases, but other experimenters have found that it decreases. Drawing on the psychological concepts of assimilation and contrast and on Grice's (1975) discussion of conversational norms (see *Conversational Maxims*), Schwarz et al. (1991) hypothesized that when the general question is interpreted by the respondent as a summary of a series of specific questions, general and specific happiness will be correlated and will point in the same direction (e.g., those reporting a happy marriage will report happiness in general). Where format or introductory sentences make it seem as though the general question is intended to be treated apart from, and not redundant with, the specific question or questions, other results can occur. A series of experiments, which cannot be summarized fully here, confirmed this complex set of hypotheses, and indicate the value of more general psychological and psycholinguistic principles in understanding questionnaire-context effects.

4. Interviewer Effects

Although most large response effects in surveys are the result of variations in question form, wording, or context, interviewers can also sometimes influence answers in a systematic way. There is little evidence that this is due to conscious ideological bias, no doubt because interviewers are trained to be neutral and nondirective in their questioning behavior. Bias due to interviewers believing that they can interpret unclear responses without probing for explanation is somewhat more likely, as shown in a classic experiment by Hyman (1954).

Still more serious is the tendency of respondents to try to give answers that they think interviewers would like to hear. At the most general level, this creates 'social desirability' bias, with respondents avoiding answers of an embarrassing or incriminating nature, for example, with regard to use of illicit drugs. Bradburn et al. (1979) describe a set of procedures to try to minimize such bias. Large response effects can also occur for more specific reasons, the best studied being differences between the perceived race of the interviewer and the race of the respondent. Black respondents indicate less hostility towards whites when the interviewer is white rather than black, and white respondents indicate more support for full racial integration when the interviewer is black rather than white. In both these cases, it is easy to assume that cross-racial interviewing creates less valid responses, but this should not be taken for granted. It is possible that same-race interviewing is also biasing, or, from another standpoint, that it is better not to think of such attitudes as having an internal truth and an external presentation that is invalid. Instead, some attitudes might be seen as fundamentally ambivalent and therefore as genuinely varying depending on the situation.

5. Implications of Research on the Question–Answer Process

The many effects due to the question–answer process in survey research do not mean that surveys cannot yield useful knowledge. For one thing, the purpose of this article has been to highlight such effects, and therefore it inevitably exaggerates their frequency and the difficulties they pose. For another, the real lesson from recognition of such effects is the need to analyze survey data with great care, and indeed to build experiments into a questionnaire *before* analysis in order to assess possible response effects. As with any type of scientific data, a set of survey data should not be regarded naively as 'facts that speak for themselves.'

Furthermore, since questions and answers are a basic form of ordinary linguistic interaction, there is potential value in interchange between survey methodologists and linguists, especially those with an interest in pragmatics. The question–answer process in surveys can provide a valuable laboratory for linguistics, and one that, as has been shown, readily allows randomized experiments on probability samples from natural populations. Likewise, survey methodologists should be able to learn a great deal from the theories and methods of linguistics.

See also: Attitudes and Behavior.

Bibliography
Bem D J 1972 Self perception theory. In: *Advances in Experimental Social Psychology,* vol 6. Academic Press, New York
Bishop G 1987 Context effects on self-perception of interest in government and public affairs. In: Hippler H J, Schwarz N, Sudman, S (eds.) *Social Information Processing and Survey Methodology*. Springer-Verlag, New York
Bradburn N M, Seymour S, and Associates 1979 *Improving Interview Method and Questionnaire Design*. Jossey-Bass, San Francisco, CA
Goffman E 1959 *The Presentation of Self in Everyday Life*. Doubleday, Garden City, NY
Grice H P 1975 Logic and conversation. In: Cole P, Morgan J L (eds.) *Syntax and Semantics*, vol. 3: *Speech Acts*. Academic Press, New York
Hyman H H 1954 *Interviewing in Social Research*. University of Chicago Press, Chicago, IL
Mueller J E 1973 *War, Presidents, and Public Opinion*. Wiley, New York
Rugg D 1941 Experiments in wording questions: II. *Public Opinion Quarterly* **5**: 91–2
Schuman H, Presser S 1981 *Questions and Answers in Attitude Surveys: Experiments on Question Form, Wording, and Context*. Academic Press, New York
Schuman H, Scott J 1987 Problems in the use of survey questions to measure public opinion. *Science* **236**: 957–9
Schwarz N, Strack F, Mai H 1991 Assimilation and contrast effects in part–whole question sequences: a conversational logic analysis. *Public Opinion Quarterly* **55**: 3–23

Corpus Linguistics and Sociolinguistics
M. Sebba and S. D. Fligelstone. Revised by W. A. Kretzschmar Jr.

A corpus (pl corpora) is a body of language material assembled with a view to extracting linguistic information from it. It may consist of data specially elicited for this purpose (for example, by interviewing a native speaker informant) or of material originally produced for some other purpose (for example, naturally occurring conversations or published texts of novels or newspaper articles). Historically, corpora were often of the elicited type and used as a basis for a phonological or syntactic description of a language. The modern field of corpus linguistics tends to use material produced with a primary aim other than linguistic study, and concerns itself more with lexical and syntactic description and issues of natural language processing than with phonological description.

1. Historical Background

The American Structuralists, who dominated North American linguistics until around 1960, based their work heavily on corpora, which often consisted wholly of elicited data. There was general agreement that the concise description of the material in a corpus representative of the language under investigation was the first aim of the linguist. The structuralist linguists proceeded mainly inductively on the basis of their corpora, and avoided as far as possible the complications of geographical and social variation by limiting their corpora to 'one dialect' of a language. As their work was largely limited to phonology, quite small corpora were often adequate.

New notions of the goals of linguistic theory introduced by Noam Chomsky (ca. 1957) brought about a sudden change in the status of corpus linguistics. Chomsky emphasized the importance of native speaker intuitions in determining the competence of an idealized speaker–hearer with perfect knowledge of the language, making the collection of a corpus of actual utterances seem irrelevant. A corpus, the Chomskyans argued, was inadequate anyway, since it would inevitably contain an infinitely small fraction of the possible sentences of a language, and would be skewed. The inductive methods of the structuralist corpus linguists quickly came to be seen as ponderous and misguided by the Chomskyans. Corpus linguistics in this period became the pursuit of a minority of linguists and was seen as marginal to mainstream linguistics in most countries. A notable nonconformist at this time was the British linguist R. Quirk, who, in 1959, set out to create the seminal 'Survey of English Usage' (see also *Quirk, Professor Sir (Charles) Randolph*).

With the increasing availability of computers, corpus linguistics began to attract new attention and new research in the 1960s and 1970s. The capability of computers to store very large bodies of data and to provide retrieval facilities made it feasible to assemble corpora of a substantial size and to do statistical analyses of their contents. A number of projects in the USA and northern Europe were devoted to collecting corpora of printed texts intended to be representative of the contemporary state of a language. One of the first of these was N. Francis and H. Kucera's Brown University Corpus of one million words of running English text, taken from different text types, all published in the USA in 1961. The Lancaster/Oslo–Bergen (LOB) Corpus was assembled in such a way as to match exactly the Brown Corpus in size and text types, but was based entirely on texts published in the UK in 1961. In a later development, Jan Svartvik embarked on the encoding of the part of the (originally noncomputerized) Survey of English Usage, which consists of transcribed speech. This project gave rise to the London–Lund Corpus of Spoken English. These corpora are very small by current standards, but are still widely used in research owing to the perceived usefulness of their planned, 'representative' structure, a feature which contrasts sharply with some of the larger-scale collections which have begun to emerge. Due to the difficulty and expense of creating large databases of transcribed speech, most existing corpora consist only or mainly of texts, which originated in written form. The half-million word London–Lund Corpus stands out as a notable early exception to this as it consists of transcribed speech including prosodic and discoursal features.

By the early 1990s several significant projects had commenced. In the USA, the Association of Computational Linguists Data Collection Initiative (ACL/DCI) was assembling a collection of several hundred million words of text and transcribed speech to be 'captured' in a variety of ways. The ACL/DCI produced a CD-ROM, and stimulated the creation of the Linguistic Data Consortium (LDC). The LDC began in 1992 with grant funding at the University of Pennsylvania, and currently supplies numerous text and speech corpora, including some of very large scale. In the UK, work began on the creation of a more structured 100-million word part-of-speech tagged 'British National Corpus' (BNC), and also on a comparably large 'Bank of English,' a dynamic or 'monitor' corpus to be constantly updated so as to contain recent texts drawn from a fixed time span. The BNC was completed in 1994, with the aid of both commercial and public funding. As of October 2000 the Bank of English contained 415 million words. Work was also under way in several countries on the creation of an 'International Corpus of English' (ICE)—an array of parallel one million word corpora representing national and regional varieties. Currently, only the British component of ICE (ICE-GB) is readily available. Most of these projects planned to undertake linguistic annotation of at least part of the material, and to implement the guidelines of the text encoding initiative (TEI), whose aim is to ensure a standard means of encoding machine-readable texts. The TEI Consortium now manages the maintenance of the standard.

The new range of corpus applications has gone together with a new style of corpus linguistics which does not reject the role of intuition in corpus analysis, and which also allows for quantitative methods. Thus has come about a synthesis of the inductive, corpus-based methods of the American Structuralists and the intuition-based methods of the Chomskyans. The creation of large corpora has allowed for the development of statistical approaches to language, which rival the rule-based methods of the Chomskyans.

2. Some Problems of Corpus Linguistics

The memory capacity and processing capabilities of computers make storage and retrieval of texts and transcriptions relatively unproblematic. However, problems of format, ownership, and copyright have to be dealt with in the course of assembling a corpus, while there is a continuing need for new software to meet the requirements of corpus linguists. These two factors impose practical limits on the pace of progress of corpus linguistics. There are also some significant theoretical problems.

2.1 The Problem of Size

To be useful for lexicographical purposes, corpora are required which are very much larger than the one million word Brown and LOB corpora. The Birmingham Collection of English Texts, which formed the basis of the Collins COBUILD dictionary (1987), comprised around 20 million words and several dictionary publishers are now involved in projects to compile much larger corpora (see Sect. 3.1 and Sect. 4). However, no matter how large the corpus, the nature of natural language gives rise to a particular problem: that in any corpus, some 50 percent of the word types are *hapax legomena*, i.e., occur only once. In addition, there are very many words that will occur only a few times, and few words with very high frequencies of occurrence. Increased corpus size does not change this distribution. Thus, increasing the size of a corpus increases the number of *hapax legomena*, increases the number of words that occur only a few times, and increases the number of tokens for frequently occurring words.

This fact has two significant consequences. First, it is not possible to ensure that a corpus always has suitably many examples of each word; there will always be a large number of words represented by just one token or by a few tokens. Second, it is impossible to determine the true frequency of these types with low frequency of occurrence, since their relative frequency within the corpus is generally an overestimation of their true relative frequency in the corpus language. In other words, many of these words are so rare that they should not appear in the corpus at all, and they do so by chance, which exaggerates their true frequency. This last fact is not so much a problem for lexicographers as for those who need word-frequency statistics to drive parsers, taggers, or other types of natural-language processors, which are discussed below, because it may impair the efficiency of such systems.

2.2 The Representativeness Problem

For the corpus linguist to be able to make valid inferences about the language or sublanguage of the corpus, the corpus used must in principle be representative of that language. Perfect representativeness is in theory impossible, since it would involve an infinitely large corpus; corpus linguists must therefore try to maximize the representativeness of their corpora by selecting both a large enough and diverse enough sample. Where the corpus represents what is taken to be a single text type, e.g., newspaper reports or parliamentary proceedings, this may not be problematic. However, corpora which are intended to represent the language in general (e.g., nontechnical written English) are usually composed of weighted proportions of different genres, the proportions being in line with the researchers' notions of the true relative frequency of such text types in the language as a whole. This necessarily involves some fairly arbitrary decisions about what genres merit inclusion and with what weighting. Furthermore, research into text types suggests that in terms of their linguistic characteristics, they do not cluster into groups, which correlate with the hitherto accepted notions of genre. Thus, using the traditional genre types as a basis for assembling a corpus may not be an effective way of making a corpus representative of the language as a whole. It nonetheless seems likely that 'external' criteria such as genre will continue to be used as a means of classifying the contents of text corpora in the first instance.

2.3 The Historical Problem

Another problem which corpus linguists have to address is that of static vs. dynamic corpora. Some of the older corpora such as the Brown and LOB corpora are already over 30-years-old, and thus cannot represent the state of English as it is in the early 1990s, even if they represent English as it was in 1961 (itself doubtful). The need for up-to-date information is especially clear in the case of lexicography, but also applies to other uses of corpora. The task of planning corpora, which are dynamic and subject to constant update, now lies before corpus linguists.

3. Some Applications of Language Corpora

3.1 Lexicography

The value of computerized corpora for dictionary making was clear to lexicographers and a number of widely used dictionaries have been based on large corpora of English text; for example, the American Heritage dictionary (based on reading matter for secondary schools), and the Collins COBUILD English dictionary. This trend has continued, as dictionary publishers have made use of both public (e.g., BNC) and private corpora, and some publishers (such as Oxford University Press in the *New Oxford Dictionary of English*) have even adapted the style of dictionary entries to reflect experience with corpora.

3.2 Linguistic Research

The opportunities which corpora offer for extracting and statistically validating information about the language under study have led to their use by syntacticians, discourse, and conversation analysts, and (for spoken language corpora) phoneticians.

Much of the pioneering corpus-based English language research of recent years has been documented under the auspices of ICAME (International Computer Archive of Modern English), which continues to promote the exchange of information and resources in the area of corpus research and corpus creation.

The use of corpora as a data resource of 'real language' is also becoming widespread in the field of course planning for language instruction and even in language teaching itself.

A primary tool in all of these pursuits is a search-device usually called a 'concordancer/browser,' which facilitates interaction between the analyst and the corpus material. Such a device allows the user to examine or extract from the corpus items which conform to a specified pattern, e.g., a word, a word ending, a part-of-speech marker, or various combinations of these.

3.3 Applications in Computational Linguistics

Corpora are also being exploited in the development of language-processing tools, which are of primary interest to computational linguists and computer scientists. These efforts have strong commercial implications in speech recognition and speech synthesis for computer interfaces.

3.3.1 Tagging and Parsing

The task of applying a single part-of-speech tag to each word in a body of running text serves to illustrate the potential value of corpus processing. Here, probabilistic methodology has had notable success. Using hidden Markov model techniques it is possible, given a string of words and some rules for assigning a set of possible tags to each of those words, to estimate to a high degree of accuracy the most likely sequence of tags for that string on the basis of 'bigram' probabilities for tag sequences, i.e., the probability of a given pair of tags occurring in succession. For a set of, say, 100 part-of-speech tags, a 'probability matrix' is required with estimates of the likelihood of each of the 10,000 possible sequences of two tags. Such a matrix can be derived empirically given a previously analyzed corpus of sufficient size. Thus it was that the tagged Brown Corpus (tagged using a variety of heuristics and subsequent manual correction) was used to derive a probability matrix for the tagging of the LOB Corpus using a probabilistic tagger 'CLAWS' with an accuracy level of about 96 percent, Trigram (i.e., tag-tag-tag) probabilities are in principle a better data source with which to drive a tagging device, and are still computationally tractable, but the derivation of such probabilities from observed frequencies would require a corpus of massive proportions.

Accurate parsing of sentences using corpus-derived probability matrices has proved to be a much more difficult problem. Some approaches involve a phrase structure analysis of sentences, whilst others merely simulate such an analysis by treating grammatical structures as a series of tags, where a tag may be either a part-of-speech marker as described above, or the beginning or end marker of a grammatical constituent. Whichever approach is used, the rarity of many grammatical structures makes parsing difficult to automate due to the lack of reliable frequency data (cf. *hapax legomena*, above).

3.3.2 Machine Translation

Monolingual corpora may be used indirectly in machine translation as sources of lexicographical or other information, which is incorporated into some component of the machine translation system, or to test the effectiveness of the system on an unseen text. Corpora may also be used in a more direct way, where parallel bilingual corpora (i.e., corpora consisting of texts and their translations) already exist. Where new material to be translated is substantially similar to that already in the bilingual corpus (e.g., in the case of technical manuals, which are constantly updated but remain largely the same), translation of a new sentence may be reduced to finding a similar sentence in the corpus and so finding directly its translation in the parallel corpus of translations. Accurate machine translation is hampered by the same distributional facts, which impede automatic tagging and parsing, and in addition must manage the problem of sense disambiguation (selection among various possible meanings for words). It must be considered still to be in an experimental stage.

3.3.3 Speech Recognition and Speech Synthesis

A prosodically and grammatically annotated corpus of spoken language may be used for the derivation of statistically weighted rules to be applied in the production of authentic sounding speech from written text. Recognition of ordinary speech by computers has improved steadily over the years, but remains inadequate for most tasks in daily life. However, for words separated by short pauses, probabilistic approaches closely related to those used for tagging (see above) have proved effective in enabling computers to disambiguate speech signals, i.e., to decide what for a given signal, is the most likely corresponding lexical item, even when a very large vocabulary is used. A calculation of the probability of various sequences of two or three words enables the computer to update its hypotheses as more signals are processed.

The application of corpora to various kinds of natural language processing tasks seems to be a growing trend in a field where logic-driven procedures have tended to be favored over the probabilistic approaches to which machine-readable corpora readily lend themselves (see articles in Lawler and Aristar Dry 1998). There are few these days who are not at least willing to acknowledge that language corpora (as opposed to 'laboratory sentences') represent a useful test bed against which natural language processing (NLP) systems may be evaluated.

4. Corpora Present and Future

The two broad types of corpus exploitation distinguished in this article (the computer-driven statistical or other processing vs. the researcher-driven interactive) are very much related. On a practical level the point is worth elucidating given that one goal pursued by the computational linguist is to develop a grammatical tagger, so success in this task enables the creation of a tagged corpus. This tagged corpus in turn places a new resource at the disposal of the interactive user. In fact, analyzed corpora are proving to be very popular among researchers. The creation of corpora tagged for part of speech is largely a solved problem, but progress in creating parsed and semantically analyzed corpora is much slower and recourse to semimanual methodology is still preeminent. In spite of the unresolved theoretical questions, and the shortcomings of many resources currently available, corpora have demonstrated their usefulness to researchers and are here to stay. Widespread recognition of this has given rise to a concentration of effort on the creation of suitably structured and formatted computer corpora of sufficient size to be of value to the research community as a whole.

Even given its status as an international language, the predominance of English-language corpora over all others is striking. In countries where English is not a first or second language (for example, Norway), research may be concentrated on English-language corpora rather than local-language corpora. While the strong interest in English-language corpora is likely to remain, the increasing availability of suitable hardware and software is likely to lead to more corpora of other languages, and even multilingual corpora for research purposes.

Bibliography

Bank of English http://titania.cobuild.collins.co.uk/boe_info.html
Biber D, Conrad S, Reppen R 1998 *Corpus Linguistics: Investigating Language Structure and Use*. Cambridge University Press, Cambridge, UK
British National Corpus (BNC) http://info.ox.ac.uk/bnc/
Francis W N, Kucera H 1979 *Manual of Information to Accompany a Standard Sample of Present-day, Edited American English, for Use with Digital Computers*, 3rd edn. Brown University, Providence, RI
Hockey S 2000 *Electronic Texts in the Humanities*. Oxford University Press, Oxford, UK
ICAME Journal (formerly *International Computer Archive of Modern English News*) 1987 Norwegian Computing Center for the Humanities, Bergen, Norway
International Corpus of English http://www.ucl.ac.uk/english-usage/ice/
Kennedy G 1998 *An Introduction to Corpus Linguistics*. Longman, London
Lawler J, Aristar Dry H (eds.) 1998 *Using Computers in Linguistics: A Practical Guide*. Routledge, London
Linguistic Data Consortium (LDC) http://morph.ldc.upenn.edu/
Oakes M P 1998 *Statistics for Corpus Linguistics*. Edinburgh University Press, Edinburgh, UK
TEI Consortium http://www.tei-c.org/

Data Collection in Linguistics
J. E. Miller and R. Cann

Accurate descriptions and adequate theories require reliable data. Equally, purposeful and fruitful data collection requires a theoretical framework. Data and theories interact: data searches are guided by theory but theories are modified or abandoned in the light of data. This article focuses on the collecting of data, in which success depends on assembling an adequate sample of texts and/or informants and on obtaining reliable data from the informants.

1. Basic Problems of Data Collection

Analysts must not rely on their intuitions unless with respect to simple constructions in their native language, as is often done in the early stages of formal models. Experience has shown that when the examples become more complex, intuitions become less clear, and there is the unavoidable difficulty of unconscious bias towards an attractive hypothesis. Data must be collected from other sources; of course, this has always been essential for investigators working on languages other than their own or working on nonstandard varieties.

The collection of data in any language will be vitiated unless attention is paid to variation (see *Sociolinguistic Variation*). Is a given construction typical of (possibly excluded from) informal conversation or academic writing? Is a given word typical of informal conversation or poetry? Is a given word only to be used by women? A database for an account of word order in written English will be misleading if a large proportion of the data is from the metrical Psalms.

The study of spoken language requires attention to such factors as the speaker's age, sex, and social class, the audience's age, sex, and social class, the speaker's provenance, the relative authority of speaker and audience, the topic under discussion, the setting and degree of formality of the interaction, the nature of the interaction (conversation, debate, lecture, etc.). Some of these factors are relevant to written texts too, but they are of crucial importance for spoken language.

2. Sampling Texts and Informants

Ideally, distinctions such as those mentioned in Sect. 1 are reflected in data collection. Investigators of written language must classify different types of written text, e.g., detective novels, serious literary novels, school textbooks (but this is a complex task; see Biber 1988) and ensure that equal amounts of data are collected from each type.

For spoken language the factors listed in the last paragraph in Sect. 1 should be taken into account and informants collected to represent the sets defined by possible combinations of variables; e.g., middle-class Scottish women between 50 and 60 with higher education as opposed to women of the same class, age, and provenance but without higher education. In towns and cities with well-established populations sets of potential informants can be established on the basis of areas defined by social and demographic information in census reports, with the actual informants being chosen via personal approaches by the investigators. When the factors involved are more subtle—such as children born in a particular town as opposed to children who are incomers, the informants can be found through organizations such as churches, youth groups, schools, sports clubs, etc.

Apart from the practical difficulty that appropriate informants are not always available, or at least not in sufficient number, the notion of social class is controversial. How does the occupation-related notion of class connect with status, which need not relate to occupation? How are the class and status of women best determined? With respect to language, is it fruitful to regard individual speakers as representing a particular large social class or as belonging to a much smaller social network, as described in Milroy (1987) (see *Social Networks*)? These questions cannot be answered here but they show that sampling a population of speakers is a delicate and complex matter.

3. Collecting Reliable Data

For both written and spoken language there are two basic sources of data; a corpus of texts and elicitation tests. Only a corpus of texts will give an idea of the typical features of particular types of language, whether of academic textbooks or informal conversation, but individual syntactic constructions or lexical items can only be fully investigated by means of elicitation tests. For certain types of data a corpus combined with tests gives the best results. In the investigation of the phonetics and phonology of groups of speakers, for instance, the standard technique is to extract the pronunciation of key lexical items by tests—asking informants to read a list of words and a passage of connected prose—and to obtain data relating to conversational speech by encouraging informants to talk spontaneously. Spontaneous speech is encouraged either by asking informants about exciting and dangerous experiences they may have had or by recording informants in informal surroundings talking to close friends. Obtaining the latter type of data requires trust between informant and interviewer, overt recording with the participants' knowledge and permission, and confidentiality—the deletion from the tape of confidential or private information provided accidentally.

3.1 Working with a Corpus of Texts

Gathering a corpus of texts has four major advantages: analysts cannot influence existing written texts and can easily avoid influencing spoken texts that they are recording by allowing the informants to talk for themselves. A representative sample of the relevant genre can be gathered. A large enough corpus will present unexpected constructions that might not occur to the analyst relying on intuition—this is regularly and frequently experienced by researchers testing and extending speech technology. A given corpus is typically useful for more than its original purpose—no body of data gathered by researchers in the last 20 years has been exhausted and many still await thorough exploitation (see *Corpus Linguistics and Sociolinguistics*).

There are disadvantages; collecting a corpus is time-consuming, in particular a spoken corpus. The informants must be recorded and the recordings transcribed, one hour of conversation requiring approximately 9 hours of transcribing in order to produce a basic transcription in terms of words. Transcribing even the cleanest recording of speech is laborious, but dialogues always involve interruptions, overlapping speech, repetitions, and drops in pitch which greatly complicate the task. The transcription must be coded for the relevant properties such as general type of construction, e.g., WH, TH, or contact relative clause; grammatical properties, e.g., past tense, gerund, animate noun, textual position. Transcriptions (indeed, any text) can be coded for any property. It is important that the analyst have a clear idea beforehand about what properties are relevant so as to avoid repeated revisions of the coding. However, once the coded transcription is stored on computer this labor reaps a large reward in the ease and accuracy with which concordance programs locate all the examples of any word or coded construction and store not only the relevant examples but fragments of the context in which they occur. With the latter information the analyst can quickly pick out the most interesting examples and discard the less interesting. The final but unavoidable drawback, especially for syntactic research, is that even a very large corpus may contain few or no examples of a given construction. The solution lies in elicitation tests, as described in Sect. 3.2.

3.2 Elicitation Tests

The native speakers of a language have intuitions about what is acceptable in their language but tapping these intuitions is not straightforward. The intuitions of any given native speaker are limited in extent and reliability and the limitations vary across speakers. Even inside these limitations intuitions vary from one speaker to another, say with respect to whether a given combination of words is syntactically acceptable or with respect to the exact interpretation of a phrase or sentence.

A different problem is that native speakers' acceptability judgments may not match their practice. Most native speakers of a language are unaware of the syntax they use in speech and in informal writing such as personal letters, and their acceptability judgments may draw on their knowledge of good writing practice. That is, the acceptability judgments of a given native speaker may not correspond with the syntax produced by that speaker.

A final problem arises from the nature of elicitation tests. Suppose informants are asked to judge whether 20 sentences are acceptable. The order in which the sentences are presented may influence the answers, and the influence may be quite unpredictable.

All these problems can be circumvented. That different informants have different intuitions obliges the investigator to use enough informants—a minimum of 30—so that the major and minor patterns become clear. Possible effects of order can be trapped by arranging the examples in four different random orders (using tables of random numbers) and assigning each order to a quarter of the informants. Analysis of the results will reveal whether a particular answer to a given question is associated with a particular order.

The use of different types of elicitation tests reveals mismatches between speakers' acceptability judgments and what they actually say and write. Informants can be asked to provide data in various ways:

(a) by being given a sentence conveying a certain meaning followed by a paraphrase with a gap which has to be filled, e.g., *Do you want me to phone the doctor?* with the paraphrase ____ *I phone the doctor?* where the gap can be filled by *shall, will,* or *should*;

(b) by providing a continuation for a sentence, e.g., *I must go to Glasgow because* ____ , *I've got to go to Glasgow because* ____ , *I have to go to Glasgow because* ____ . The object of these examples was to find out whether the informants' continuations indicated an awareness of the differences in meaning between *must, have to* and *have got to* as described in grammars of English;

(c) by making a forced choice, e.g., insert either *have to* or *must* in *I* ____ *go to Glasgow because I want to see the Cathedral* and *I* ____ *go to Glasgow because I'm appearing in Court*;

(d) by describing a picture or scene. This is appropriate, e.g., for eliciting the use of prepositions. Computer graphics make it possible to elicit descriptions of movement and to adjust details of a scene in order to discover the limits on the use of a particular preposition.

Reliable judgments of acceptability likewise require subtlety of method. To prevent informants falling into a routine or guessing what is at stake, the important examples should be interspersed with distractors, examples unconnected with the key ones. Examples can be presented in lists or they can be incorporated into a piece of text which the informants are asked to judge. Investigators of nonstandard language should avoid asking informants if they find the examples acceptable, as this question triggers prejudices and fears. Rather, they should be asked if they have heard or seen the examples.

For all elicitation tests it is important that the informants be prevented from comparing the answers to the various questions and from thinking about the 'best' answer to each question. Both these problems can be solved if the informants are taken through a given test at a speed which forces them to answer quickly and gives no time for reflection on previous answers. The appropriate length of time per question depends on the type of question and the complexity of the examples but can be determined by means of a pilot test. Although the tests described here are written, they can yield (and have yielded) reliable information about nonstandard spoken varieties of a given language.

When data has been collected by some or all of the methods outlined above, analysis will show whether the acceptability judgments by given informants match the informants' own performance. Central and peripheral patterns of usage can be recognized and statistical tests can be applied to discover which results are statistically significant.

See also: Corpus Linguistics and Sociolinguistics; Field Methods in Modern Dialect and Variation Studies; Field Methods: Ethnographic.

Bibliography

Biber D 1988 *Variation across Speech and Writing.* Cambridge University Press, Cambridge, UK

Milroy L 1987 *Observing and Analysing Natural Language.* Blackwell, Oxford, UK

Field Methods: Ethnographic
M. L. Apte

The fundamental division in sociocultural anthropology is between ethnology and ethnography. Ethnology subsumes the development of conceptual categories and frameworks, methodology, cross-cultural/comparative studies for creating broad typologies, formation and testing of interpretive and explanatory hypotheses, and general theory building. The principal aim of ethnology is to analyze and explain the diverse and multifaceted nature of human existence and the underlying common biological and psychological foundations. In these endeavors ethnology is dependent on ethnography: the study, analysis, and description of individual sociocultural systems all over the world. Ethnography (see *Ethnography of Speaking*), in turn, uses ethnological frameworks and analytical tools for data-gathering and descriptive studies.

1. Nature and Objective of Ethnography

Ethnographic studies entail the collection and analytical description of relevant data concerning individual societies and cultures, i.e., geographical location, climate, flora and fauna, techniques of adaptation to natural environment, technology, food production and food habits, the institution of marriage, family and kinship, child-raising and socialization practices, social roles, religion and rituals, economic transactions, patterns of language structure and use, interactional strategies in social relationships, the political system, folklore, and artifacts; in short, all the major aspects of a sociocultural system. Ethnographic studies also record and analyze the ideology, worldview, and cultural values of the people being studied. Such data are crucial for an understanding of how the individual sociocultural systems are structurally, functionally, and ideologically integrated.

It is an established tradition in sociocultural anthropology that researchers actually live among the members of a culture being studied. This enables them to collect the kind of ethnographic data necessary for their analysis. Anthropological literature is full of both brief and extensive accounts of hundreds of societies and cultures. Ethnographic research and data-gathering is known as fieldwork, and an anthropologist doing fieldwork is called an ethnographer. The techniques generally employed by an ethnographer in collecting data constitute the ethnographic methods.

2. General Nature of Ethnographic Research

Ethnographic research by its very nature is explorative and open-ended. The ethnographer needs time to get adjusted to the field situation and also to establish rapport with the people whose culture s/he wants to study since their acceptance of the investigator is crucial for the success of the enterprise. A major reason for the explorative nature of ethnographic research is the very unstructured nature of the field situation. The researcher has no clear-cut idea of how s/he will be received, what kinds of opportunities will exist to conduct research, what aspects of individual life and community activities will prove easily accessible or difficult to study, and whether or not important information will be made available. No matter how conversant the ethnographer may be with the existing anthropological literature on the community s/he wants to study, s/he will be in for the surprises, joys, and perhaps sorrows of the fieldwork experience. There are also differences of opinion regarding the value of existing literature to the ethnographer about to engage in fieldwork, and familiarity mixed with a questioning attitude towards the published sources is the best solution. Initially, ethnographic research may remain rather unfocused except for the broad and somewhat vague objectives the ethnographer has in mind.

The reception accorded to the ethnographer, her/his judgment of what is and is not accessible, the personal relationships established over a brief period of time with certain members of the community, the estimated duration of stay in the field, and the ethnographer's own research preferences will help dictate the overall nature of her/his research. Unlike pre-1960 fieldwork, which generally studied whole sociocultural systems, contemporary anthropologists generally go to the field with a focus on investigating specific sociocultural aspects. Even then, it is necessary to have a rudimentary knowledge of the other related characteristics of a culture. This is known as the 'holistic' approach, which emphasizes that any single aspect of a sociocultural system cannot be fully understood and analyzed without taking into consideration its relationship to the structural and functional whole of the system.

3. Major Ethnographic Field Methods

The primary ethnographic methods for fieldwork are participant observation, extensive interviewing, systematic note taking and record keeping, recording folklore and other such materials, taking photographs and/or making films, and collecting artifacts. While mechanical and electronic equipment and tools such as tape recorders, cameras, and video recorders are often used in fieldwork, they cannot be used as substitutes for participant observation which is inductive in the sense that after observing a few instances the ethnographer forms tentative generalizations regarding the existing behavioral patterns, and the nature of events, phenomena, causes, relationships, etc. Thus specific observations and interviews constitute the basis of many generalizations.

Although the standardization of ethnographic methods is desirable, it has not been possible in the past. The reasons are many. Traditionally, anthropologists have depended heavily on a qualitative and personal approach to ethnographic fieldwork, and have not systematically formulated the kinds of methods that could be used in the field. Before the 1970s anthropologists believed that 'immersing' oneself in the field situation and establishing good rapport with the people to be studied would lead to a successful gathering of data. They also believed that fieldwork was a unique experience and much depended on the personality, temperament, perseverance, and imagination of the individual ethnographer. Therefore, it was believed that the systematic formalization of ethnographic methods was not possible.

This view gave way during the 1980s and there now exists much literature on research methodology in sociocultural anthropology. A major part of it is devoted to the systematic elaboration of ethnographic methods and their advantages and disadvantages. The development of new conceptual frameworks for the purpose of devising systematic anthropological research methods has also reduced the mystery of anthropological fieldwork.

3.1 Participant Observation

This is the primary method of ethnographic research and involves both direct participation and/or observation of as many of the activities of the community under study as possible. Living in the community enables the ethnographer to utilize this method on a daily basis. The wider and more varied the range of the ethnographer's observation and participation, the better will be his or her ability to understand the sociocultural nature of the activities and their relationships. The ethnographer needs to observe the routine activities of different types of individuals: men and women, children, young and old people, political leaders, religious authorities, tool makers, traders, etc. It is equally important to observe special events which often signify important ritual periods in the life cycle of the individuals and the community. The ethnographer may not get a second chance to observe such special events if they are annual in nature. It is at such occasions that the ethnographer has the opportunity to observe and make sense of the behavior of the specialists in the community.

A major problem in using the participant observation method is that the ethnographer cannot be in all places at all times and thus misses observing many activities. Much depends on the nature of the community itself. If the ethnographer is studying a small village community where the daily activities take place in the presence of many people, then a stroll through the village at different times of the day will help the ethnographer to know what people do at specific times. If, on the other hand, the ethnographer is studying an urban population, it is impossible for him or her to know what is going on everywhere. One way of overcoming this problem is to vary systematically the kinds of social interactions to be observed and the situations in which they occur. The ethnographer may not have access to all such situations, however, and depending on her/his age, sex, social status, and foreignness s/he may or may not be able to participate in or observe certain types of social interaction.

Once the ethnographer has become familiar with the workings of the society, s/he needs to be selective in choosing those social situations that are likely to provide greater insights into the workings of the culture. S/he needs to use her/his observations to develop specific questions to be asked. In other words, observation and participation, whenever possible, should be systematic and not haphazard. There should be a genuine effort to make certain that such observation and participation will help the ethnographer gain a greater understanding of sociocultural patterns.

Participation in the activities of the community occurs in varying degrees. Full participation is not always possible, primarily because the ethnographer is not always cognizant of the appropriate behavior necessary for participating in an event. This is usually the case with special events, in which participation is possible only because of knowledge acquired over many years. Not even all the indigenous members of a community are able to participate in such events.

3.2 Field Notes and Record Keeping

Participant observation by the ethnographer must be followed by extensive and detailed notes of all the events that the ethnographer has witnessed. Without such notes no systematic data collection and analysis is possible. Reliance on memory would be a grave fault for any ethnographer. The more extensive and detailed the field notes, the higher the degree of accuracy and the greater the opportunities for checking and confirming ethnographic facts. It is also crucial to date the field notes so that the ethnographer can check the changing nature of the data collection as s/he becomes familiar with the people and is accepted by them.

Field notes should include not only observed facts but also explanations and interpretations presented by members of the community regarding both daily and special events. Without such explanations the ethnographer cannot gain an understanding of the emic viewpoint which is crucial for acquiring insight into the ideologies and values of the community.

Despite the necessity of making detailed field notes, it is not always possible for the ethnographer to be ready with notebook and pencil to write down every detail of an event being witnessed or participated in. Such an attempt may be seen as an intrusion. Making notes may also distract the ethnographer from actually observing the event. Note taking is a judicious process at which the ethnographer may become more proficient the longer the time spent in fieldwork. Another technique that may be employed is the jotting down of key concepts or words regarding the numerous sequential happenings in an event. These serve to remind the ethnographer of the details later.

If note taking is not possible at the actual time an event occurs, it is generally a good practise to put aside a certain part of the day to write down observed events. Evenings are usually better suited for such a purpose. It is important, however, that daily records be kept. An alternative is to speak into a tape recorder as the event unfolds. Such recorded data should always be transcribed later so that it is not lost through technical errors or accidents.

3.3 Interviewing

Mere observations of sociocultural events in a community do not always make sense and are rarely enough for the ethnographer to gain sufficient knowledge of the community. Events alone cannot make sense without an understanding of the cultural explanations behind them. Therefore, it is necessary for the ethnographer to conduct systematic interviews with members of the community. Such interviews can be informal or formal. Informal interviews are primarily those where the ethnographer asks for and receives information, explanations, etc., while observing events. As the ethnographer gathers additional factual data, she or he begins to formulate specific questions. Eventually, she or he may have many questions concerning the diverse aspects of the society and culture. In particular, she or he may be seeking answers to things that do not make sense to her or him, but seem perfectly sensible to members of the community. The ethnographer also needs to verify facts already gathered. Interviews need to be conducted with individuals such as community leaders, well-known storytellers, religious specialists, craftsmen, and others to gather community lore, myths, stories, songs, proverbs, and other materials that throw light on the cultural values, ideologies, and worldview of the community.

It is crucial that formal interviewing be conducted systematically and that these interviews be structured. It is helpful for the ethnographer to maintain a regular systematic interview schedule. If possible, all formal interviews should be recorded so that opinions, information, and explanations can be recalled for checking and confirmation. If this is not possible, interviews should be written down verbatim as far as possible. Much depends upon the proficiency of the ethnographer in the indigenous language. Without a mastery of the local language, the ethnographer often has to depend on individuals who are bilingual and can translate both the questions and the answers. Much can be lost, however, in such a translation, depending on the ability of the bilingual translator and his or her judgment as to what should or should not be translated. One of the first tasks that most ethnographers undertake, immediately upon arrival in the field or, if possible, before going to the field, is to learn the language of the community they want to investigate. Once in the field, language proficiency can rapidly increase because of the constant exposure and the need to use it. Collection of extensive linguistic texts of diverse types is often a major objective of the ethnographer. The ethnographer may even work exclusively on the indigenous language with a representative native speaker.

Along with structured, formal interviews, it is useful to find opportunities for unstructured, open ones, especially on occasions when people gather together just to talk. An innocent question at the right time can get people talking, and the more discussion that takes place among those present, the better the nature of the information gathered, since differences of opinions and the accuracy of factual information can be checked. In many instances it is preferable for the ethnographer to be a silent listener after prompting a discussion on a particular topic.

3.4 Filming and Photography

Along with detailed field notes, photographs of the numerous diverse activities of the people in the community are useful both for visual impact of special events and also as mnemonic devices. Photographs supplement and strengthen verbal descriptions of events. In recent years, more and more ethnographers have engaged in making ethnographic films as such equipment as video cameras, tape recorders, and movie cameras have become sophisticated enough to be readily operated on batteries, circumventing the need for local electricity. Since the mid-1960s, hundreds of ethnographic films have been made depicting the lives of communities around the world. It is important to emphasize, again, that photographs and films are supplementary materials and cannot replace the meticulous field notes and records kept by the ethnographer.

3.5 Collection and/or Description of Material Objects

In all cultures the results of technology are evident in the equipment, tools, and variety of objects used by the people. Such things as types of houses, household goods, cooking utensils, bedding, toys for children, clothing, agricultural and/or hunting and fishing tools, art, ritual objects (such as masks, sculptures, drawings), and modes of transportation are examples of the kinds of material objects about which it is useful to collect detailed information (such as their structure, the materials used in making them, and their functions).

4. Selection of Informants

Since, in almost all field situations, ethnographers depend heavily upon the assistance of individuals from the culture being studied, it is usually necessary for them to select a few individuals who can act as their assistants. Such individuals, called 'informants' in ethnographic literature, are often primary sources for data that are not readily accessible to the ethnographer. They are also the ones who provide indigenous viewpoints, explanations, and interpretations of acts, events, and things. Thus they are crucial for achieving the ethnographer's principal objective. Selecting an informant can often be very tricky. Generally, the main qualities that are necessary in an informant are an ability to articulate ideas and views and the possession of a large amount of cultural information about the people being studied. An informant should also be of good standing in the community. A person of marginal status is not always privy to all relevant information.

Ethnographers generally do not depend on a single informant, but use several individuals as temporary informants as and when the need arises. It is generally preferable to have informants of different backgrounds, ages, and sexes, so that diverse viewpoints are available and individual bias can be reduced. Several informants are also necessary for checking information given by any single individual. Despite the need for an ideal informant, preferably a bilingual who is proficient in the language of the ethnographer, the field situation often dictates that the ethnographer has as an informant the individual whom s/he gets to know well or who cultivates the acquaintance of the ethnographer. It is possible that in some communities many individuals may vie for the position of being the ethnographer's informant because it may be seen as a financially advantageous and prestigious position. In such a situation, the ethnographer may have a hard time making the selection.

5. Nature of Ethnographic Data

In the past, ethnographic data have tended to be qualitative. However, ethnographers have increasingly undertaken surveys and thus gathered quantifiable data. These data can be grouped under particular headings, for example, number of households, members in each household, acreage under cultivation, kinship networks, and so on. Other kinds of data are also important. Not all data are primary, that is, based on the actual observations or actually collected by the ethnographer. Much is often secondary, that is, consisting of information provided by several informants. Data can also be interpretational, textual, linguistic, and so on. What is crucial in all instances is the reliability of the data. The ethnographer must constantly check and validate it.

6. Future Directions

Because of the importance of explicit methodology as recognized in sociocultural anthropology during the early 1990s, many treatises on ethnographic methods have been published. While an attempt has been made to standardize field methods, the very nature of ethnographic research is such that this is a nearly impossible task. However, the refinement of ethnographic field methods will continue as anthropologists increasingly recognize the importance of both qualitative and quantitative data, and become increasingly proficient at judiciously mixing the two.

See also: Fieldwork and Field Methods; Ethnography of Speaking; Fieldwork Ethics and Community Responsibility.

Bibliography

Agar M H 1980 *The Professional Stranger*. Academic Press, New York

Edgerton R B, Langness L L 1974 *Methods and Styles in the Study of Culture*. Chandler and Sharp, Corte Madera, CA

Jackson B 1987 *Fieldwork*. University of Illinois Press, Urbana, IL

McCall G J, Simmons J L (eds.) 1969 *Issues in Participant Observation*. Addison-Wesley, Reading, MA

Naroll R, Cohen R (eds.) 1970 *A Handbook of Method in Cultural Anthropology*. Natural History Press, Garden City, NY

Pelto P J, Pelto G H 1978 *Anthropological Research: The Structure of Inquiry*. Cambridge University Press, Cambridge, UK

Spradley J P 1980 *Participant Observation*. Holt, Rinehart and Winston, New York

Werner O, Schoepfie G M, et al. 1987 *Systematic Fieldwork. Vol. 1: Foundations of Ethnology and Interviewing, Vol. 2: Ethnographic Analysis and Data Management*. Sage, Newbury Park, CA

Field Methods in Modern Dialect and Variation Studies
K. Hazen

Field methods in modern variation studies can be divided into two major stages: planning and doing. Although this may seem simplistic, investigators must realize that planning is theory in practice and should be given appropriate time allotment in the project. A clear, principled, and written methodology should guide both stages. Although a clear methodology does greatly facilitate replication of the study for future scholars, more importantly it allows for the most efficient data collection possible.

The choice of methodology impacts on the type of data collected and the quality of the access to the speakers: studying a language variety from a discourse analysis perspective should yield different data than that of lexically based dialectology. Methodology depends on the objectives of the study, and field methods should be strictly guided by these objectives. These field methods in turn determine the recording approach (e.g., written survey, audio recorded, or video recorded), the potential subjects contacted, and the questions fieldworkers may ask (Milroy 1987).

1. Goals

In line with the awareness of the general project's methodology, several questions need to be asked to focus the study: is there a linguistic goal, a sociological goal, or a sociolinguistic goal (e.g., impetus for language change)? Will there need to be quantitative assessment, or only qualitative? What kind of language data are the goal (Wolfram 1993)? One point to keep in mind when establishing the kind of data desired is that the vernacular, in the sense of least self-monitored speech, is not the holy grail of sociolinguistic research it once was. Within any human's language production, a variety of styles are produced, and all of these styles can tell researchers about the language variation of both the speaker and the community. In addition, the shifting between more and less standard features in an interview can be an important indication of identity connections (Hazen 2000a, Wolfram et al. 1999).

Several different kinds of studies can be made of any community, and before researchers approach the task of gathering language data, research into the community on several different levels should be made, including social composition, socio-geographic boundaries, and economic issues. Depending on the site of the research, information may be drawn from census tables, city directories, graveyards, local leaders, or visitors bureaus.

What data to gather is an important methodological question, and one that is of course determined by the goals of the research. However, some hierarchies of data collection are more logical than others. Recorded interviews generally precede a matched-guise test. A written survey of potential lexical items or vowel mergers (e.g., *Do ⟨pin⟩ and ⟨pen⟩ rhyme?*) or participant observation can be undertaken at any point during a research project. A reading passage and word list most often follow an interview since such tasks will draw attention to the subject's language and normally cause a shift in style. However, if a style shift of this type is the object of study, researchers may want to open a series of interviews with such a task in order to assess at what point in an interview a speaker shifts to a different style.

2. Communities and Individuals

An overarching question to any variationist project is whether the researchers are investigating the community or individual speakers. Fieldwork can yield a more sociological study or an identity study (Eckert 2000). Variationists investigate how nonlinguistic factors possibly affect linguistic variation in both speech communities and individual speakers. Of course speech communities are composed of individual speakers, but the goal of many variationist studies has been to describe and explain the variation of the speech community as an entity (i.e., the grammar of the speech community). In their argument against the homogeneous idiolect being the only theoretically viable entity for linguistic study, Weinreich et al. (1968) present the study of synchronic and diachronic variation as a study of the grammar of the speech community (see *Sociolinguistic Variation*).

For these two variationist approaches, that of the speech community and that of the individual, the nonlinguistic factors influencing language variation are cast in different ways. Drawing from sociology, the speech-community approach investigates social factors which divide a speech community: age, sex, ethnicity, and social class have become the standard social factors correlated with dependent linguistic variables. By this model, a person is an intersection of social groups: a certain subject would be seen as female, Native-American, older, heterosexual, and middle class. In contrast, drawing partly from Goffman's study of 'self,' the work of anthropological communication studies, and social psychology, the individual approach encapsulates nonlinguistic factors in a person's identity (see *Goffman, Erving*).

Investigating identity allows inclusion of speakers' attitudes and beliefs in the explanation of language variation, which can enhance traditional speech community studies. The overarching identity of a speaker usually comprises subidentities of age, gender, ethnicity, social class, sexual orientation, and communities of practice (Holmes and Meyerhoff 1999).

3. The Sociolinguistic Interview

After clarifying the theoretical underpinnings of the methodology, the researchers should craft the most predominant form of data collection in variationist studies, the sociolinguistic interview. Any sociolinguistic interview should be seen as a type of community interaction.

Before approaching the community, the researchers need to ask several questions: how does the community feel about the study of their language? Is this project initiated from outside the community and would community involvement make a difference in the collection of data? Potential interview subjects may be contacted in numerous ways, but essentially the least effective manner is to approach potential subjects as a stranger, while the most effective manner is to approach them through another member of the community (see *Social Networks*). If an insider can introduce the research team to the community, then many social hurdles can be avoided altogether. The most plausible first contact for many communities might be with members of the community who have moved outside the area but still keep up good relations back in the home community: those who have traveled to school outside the area, or those who have moved for employment reasons. People who can live outside of their home community may be more open to the kinds of research variationists' conduct and might be able to introduce the researchers to members of the home community. The danger in the 'friend of a friend' approach is that original contacts in a community may be harmful to the researchers' later efforts; initial contacts may be disliked by the remainder of the community and the researchers' association may damage the project. As with other matters, the research team's knowledge of the community, including major social networks, will save time and effort when a full-scale interview effort is made.

Perhaps Wolfram's Principle of Linguistic Gratuity would be useful in some communities for collecting data: investigators who have obtained linguistic data from members of a speech community should actively pursue positive ways in which they can return linguistic favors to the community (see *Fieldwork Ethics and Community Responsibility*). If the researchers approach the community with the honest and open intent of helping the community with the data gathered (e.g., the rights of a linguistic minority community, or an educational program for local schools), the community may respond more enthusiastically to the collection of data.

Researchers should also be aware of topics that are taboo for certain social groups. It may be that with certain ethnic, religious, or socioeconomic groups, certain topics are not appropriate for questions and conversation. A breech of local protocol may render an otherwise promising interview useless. For this reason, no one question fits every community. For example, Labov's danger of death question never worked in the research on the Outer Banks of North Carolina and has been found to be 'a really bad idea' with gang member interviews in California (Mendoza-Denton 1997, Wolfram et al. 1999).

One important tool in the interview is crafted long before recording begins: the sociolinguistic module. A sociolinguistic module should focus on matters of importance for the subjects and have a series of language questions, including specific questions about language variation patterns of the area. For this reason, preliminary inquiries about the language variety, if not preliminary interviews, should be made in order to craft the language questions, reading passages, and word lists.

Before an interview begins, researchers should explain themselves. One often helpful and truthful approach to fieldwork is one of ignorance; researchers can present themselves as ignorant but having a desire to learn about the community. Often researchers are outsiders who can quite honestly don the cloak of ignorance. This is but one approach for the researchers to present themselves, but others also include some reflection of the research goals (e.g., working to improve the education of the local community or the education of a wider audience about the community). Researchers must keep in mind, however, that the background assumptions of the community will have the biggest effects on the access and quality of the data.

In any kind of interview, researchers will want to establish situations where the subjects can talk about themselves and the social groups they belong to. Researchers may want to provide a situation where the self-interest of the speakers motivates them to talk about the things that interest them most. To establish this situation, the interview subject must trust the researchers. To establish trust, the researchers should clearly identify who they are, their motivations, and their desires. Most researchers start an interview with the formal questions and then progress to questions about the community. In this rhetorical context the researchers are listeners interested in the community, but interview subjects respond to this situation with different degrees of enthusiasm. If people feel themselves engaged comfortably in a real conversation, they are much more open to tell their stories. Overall, the goal of engaging a community for sociolinguistic research is to observe language variation, from the most restricted phonological alternations to the most widely held social language norms. The constraints on quality and the quantity of the observation are what the researchers hope to maximize.

How long should a recorded interview be? The vague but truthful answer is as long as is needed for the type of research being conducted. For most variationist studies, an interview needs to be as long as needed to get a high enough count of a feature to provide for quantitative analysis. For example, if the research is of word final stops (released, unreleased, glottalized), a half hour of conversation will normally yield a sufficient number of tokens for analysis; but if the research is on past tense *be*, then at least an hour of interview time needs to be taken and the interviewers should guide the subject to tell stories from the past.

4. Participant Observation

It is best to keep in mind that an interview is not just contact with a person; it is contact with a community. For sociolinguistic research, participant observation may or may not help the researchers reach their objectives (see *Field Methods: Ethnographic*). Although it is generally true that the more researchers observe a community, the better the social evaluation, whether or not the researchers need to conduct themselves as participant observers depends on the goal of the study. If the research team wants to know how stigmatized language features are used in a community, the more observation the better the study; however, if the research team is focused on phonetic variation of word-final voiceless stops, then a series of audio recordings will suffice.

How long should researchers spend in an area for effective participant observation? Most likely, there is an inverse relationship between how different the community under study is from what the researchers know and how long they should stay. A native research team from the United States would have to spend longer in a rural community in South Africa than a rural community in West Virginia in order to describe the relevant sociolinguistic details. Some good sociolinguistic studies have been conducted with little participant observation (several weeks) while others have involved over a year of participant observation. Part of the goal of participant observation is to integrate oneself into the community; the other part is to make better (or more) observations than possible with only short visits to the community. Participant observation may also help considerably in improving researcher's identity with the community.

Researcher identity plays an important role in the type of data collected and in access to the data; however, the researcher's identity is not something to be altered like an actor changing costumes. Rather than manipulating their identity, researchers should comprehend how their identities affect the data. In other words, they should not avoid the effects but understand the impact of their presence and role in the setting being studied. In addition, the community views the researchers in terms of what it has experienced. Thus, if it has had bad experiences with universities or simply with people of the researchers' 'type,' then the researchers' position is compromised before ever making contact. The perception of the researchers is a two-input process. Researchers offer up who they are through formal presentations but also through many other factors such as how they dress and their own language variety; the researched community will categorize the researchers according to their own norms. Knowing the community's norms is an important preliminary step, but the researchers are limited to working within the boundaries of those norms. This approach is summed up in the principle of socio-rhetorical field methodology: to produce the most efficient fieldwork, researchers must understand the community's view of them, the varied perceptions of the language under study, and the community's differing self-perceptions (Hazen 2000b).

As practical advice, researchers can at best understand how the community perceives itself, the research, the researchers, and the institutions they represent. Honesty with subjects is of course important, and researchers must be willing to address with the community any area that may cause distrust. Although some communities may eventually be unapproachable, a clear perception of how the community will react to invasive sociolinguistic research will at least eliminate surprises, which is perhaps the best researchers can hope for.

See also: Fieldwork Ethics and Community Responsibility; Field Methods: Ethnographic; Observer's Paradox.

Bibliography

Eckert P 2000 *Linguistic Variation as Social Practice*. Blackwell, Cambridge, MA

Hazen K 2000a *Identity and Ethnicity in the Rural South: A Sociolinguistic View Through Past and Present*. Publications of the American Dialect Society 83. Duke University Press, Durham, NC

Hazen K 2000b The role of researcher identity in conducting sociolinguistic research: A reflective case study. *Southern Journal of Linguistics* **24**: 103–20

Holmes J, Meyerhoff M 1999 The community of practice: Theories and methodologies in language and gender research. *Language in Society* **28**: 173–84

Mendoza-Denton N 1997 Chicana/Menicana identity and linguistic variation: An ethnographic and sociolinguistic study of gang affiliation in an urban high school. Ph.D. dissertation, Stanford University, Stanford, CA

Milroy L 1987 *Observing and Analyzing Natural Language*. Blackwell, Cambridge, MA

Weinreich U, Labov W, Herzog M 1968 *Empirical Foundations for a Theory of Sound Change. Directions for Historical Linguistics*. In: Lehman W, Malkiel Y (eds.) University of Texas Press, Austin, TX, pp. 95–188

Wolfram W 1993 Identifying and interpreting variables. In: Preston D R (ed.) *American Dialect Research*. John Benjamins, Philadelphia, PA

Wolfram W, Hazen K, Schilling-Estes N 1999 *Dialect Change and Maintenance on the Outer Banks*. Publications of the American Dialect Society 81. University of Alabama Press, Tuscaloosa, AL

Fieldwork and Field Methods
U. Canger

The term 'linguistic fieldwork' will make most people think of a linguist in the bush studying some Native American language, or some native language in Africa, Asia, or Australia (see *Field Methods: Ethnographic*). However, the term may just as well refer to the work of a dialectologist mapping out the geographical dialects in the UK (see *Dialect and Dialectology*), or of a sociolinguist investigating spoken variations of sociolects in the country's capital (see *Sociolinguistic Variation*). Doing fieldwork simply means collecting linguistic data where language is spoken.

1. What is Specific to Linguistic Fieldwork?

Specific to linguistic fieldwork is—first of all—that it takes place in the field rather than at a desk; and the 'field' here refers to nothing but the natural environments of spoken language, i.e., wherever people meet and interact. What constitutes the specific field of a given study is defined by the linguist.

Another feature which is crucial for linguistic fieldwork is that the fieldworker—knowingly or not—performs a very first analysis in merely collecting the language data (see *Data Collection in Linguistics*). Whether he records speech on tape, or directly writes down what he hears, he selects and limits his data, and he cuts off material; in transcribing, i.e., writing down the data—directly or from recordings, he will make a great number of decisions, often inadvertently, and those decisions form part of any later more conscious analysis.

Linguists who study written language, on the contrary, base their study on material which has already been through this very first analysis, performed by writers, and the inventors and revisers of the given writing system, the alphabet. This very first analysis, in both these cases, is thus the privilege as well as the burden of the linguistic fieldworker.

2. A Brief History of the Fieldwork Tradition

The traditions for linguistic fieldwork come from the USA; here linguistics has its roots in the work of anthropologists who early in the twentieth century were faced with the task of analyzing a very large number of Native American languages.

The linguist, Franz Boas (see *Boas, Franz*) started the tradition of linguistic fieldwork. He saw it as a goal to have recorded as many of the Native American languages as possible before the advancing American frontier made this recording impossible.

Franz Boas explains how the study of language serves a practical purpose, 'the service which language lends us is first of all a practical one—a means to a clearer understanding of ethnological phenomena which in themselves have nothing to do with linguistic problems.' But he considers the study that focuses on the actual languages no less important than the practical knowledge of them, 'because the fundamental concepts of human language are not distinct in kind from ethnological phenomena; and because, furthermore, the peculiar characteristics of languages are clearly reflected in the views and customs of the peoples of the world.'

His students, Edward Sapir (see *Sapir, Edward*; *Sapir–Whorf Hypothesis*) and Leonard Bloomfield introduced a third purpose for working with the Native American languages: in the study of different language families they both wanted to test—on unwritten languages—the 'comparative method' which had been successfully applied in the historical study of Indo-European languages (see *Sound Change*).

Finally, with a developing interest in the autonomous structure of language, linguists began to collect language data for synchronic analyses, wanting to use them in this theoretical study of language.

In Europe, linguistic fieldwork was practiced by dialectologists who looked for the details of language change in the minute variation found in dialects (see *Dialect and Dialectology*); they traced the variation and history of individual sounds and words. The term 'fieldwork' was not used to characterize their work, but they too collected language data in the field, and the methods they used were closely related to those applied by linguists in the USA. A major difference between the two traditions stems from the fact that European dialectologists were already familiar with the language(s) from which they collected data.

In the 1950s, an interest in language as a social phenomenon, to be studied in a wider context (see *Language as a Social Reality*), returned and steadily increased; the area of linguistic fieldwork expanded to be included in sociolinguistics and ethnolinguistics (see *Ethnography of Speaking*; *Ethnicity and Language*). Above all, the American linguist William Labov (see *Labov, William*) has discussed, developed, and refined the methods used in the collection of linguistic data.

The development of the tape recorder and more recently of the video recorder has opened the way for entirely new methods, and has also influenced the amount of data collected. The balance between collecting the material and transcribing and analyzing it shifted: before the tape recorder, all texts were dictated and simultaneously subjected to a basic analysis, whereas in the early 1990s the linguist will tape-record much material in the field which he will transcribe and analyze only after he has returned to his desk.

These technical innovations have also drastically changed the scope of questions to which the linguist can hope to find answers. The minutest physical detail of spoken language can now be scrutinized. These new possibilities have led to new approaches and to a refinement of the methods. Stylistic and other variation in the language of the individual speaker and between groups is studied.

3. Field Methods

The methods employed in linguistic fieldwork depend entirely on the situation of the language to be studied and on the goals of the study. In working with a language which has no bilingual or multilingual speakers, the linguist must use the monolingual method: by pointing at objects he will hope to have the speakers say something about them or optimally tell him what they are called, and thus begin to collect the names of things. By listening to the speakers and by trying to imitate what he hears, he will approach the phonology. Gradually, some interaction between the speakers and the linguist will emerge; the linguist will pick out longer expressions, and be able to identify them and test his understanding by substituting one word for another. This is a slow and demanding process.

In most cases, however, the linguist is able to locate some speaker who knows at least scraps of a second language and if the linguist also knows this second language, he will work through that. Otherwise, he must use an interpreter who will get him from his own language to the target language, the one to be studied. The optimal situation is to begin the work with a speaker who—in addition to his own language—knows that of the linguist.

The type of research program which the linguist has set up for himself and the prevailing concept of what language is, is even more decisive in dictating approach and method than the kinds of speakers available. Linguists who want to collect a restricted and well-defined body of data, such as lists of words to be used in a dialect survey or in comparative studies of a language family will not plan to spend much time in each locality, and will often be satisfied with working with only one informant. Terrence Kaufman, who has amassed material for an etymological dictionary of the Mayan languages for over twenty-five years, devised a method for collecting—in a short period of time—as exhaustive a corpus of words as possible for each language:

> Mayan languages all share the characteristic that the majority of root morphemes are monosyllabic. Since the number of phonemes is not large, it is a feasible project to systematically generate all possible rootshapes and then verify their existence or non-existence with an informant, at the same time establishing appropriate glosses for the existing root, and establishing the class of each root. The possible root-forms are generated by permuting all possible consonant and vowel combinations, according to the canonical patterns of root morphemes for the particular language.
>
> (Kaufman 1968:1)

During the structuralist period, when language was studied as an autonomous object independent of speakers and context, linguists would work with a limited number of informants, sometimes only one, and would often ignore the surroundings; in some cases they even preferred to move the informant out of his natural setting and take him to a location which was more convenient to the linguist.

3.1 A Full Grammar—Few Informants

In working with a hitherto undescribed language with the purpose of making a grammatical description of it, the linguist will begin by asking for simple words and write them down with all the phonetic detail he is able to distinguish; subsequently, he will attempt to analyze these fine phonetic transcriptions, and by asking the informant to repeat words that seem similar or that may sound identical to him, the linguist will try to identify the *phonemes* and to arrive at a crude and first description of the phonological system; he will decide on a less detailed, but systematic way of transcribing the language, a writing system which notes all the sounds that carry a meaning distinction. While he continues to check and test his hypotheses about the phonology, the fieldworker will go on to collect more vocabulary and data for his description of the morphology. Soon, he will attempt to obtain short texts: these will give rise to innumerable questions to the informant concerning both morphology and syntax. He will go on refining his understanding of the phonology, add on to the vocabulary and to his knowledge about the morphology and syntax.

To keep track of the progress of the analyses and the order in which the data are collected it is a general practice to carefully date everything written down and to enter all the information in notebooks; the vocabulary is copied on to filing slips and kept in alphabetical order so that words can be easily located. Many fieldworkers have taught one or several of their informants to write in their own language and have had them write texts and transcribe tape-recorded stories.

3.2 Narrow Focus—Many Speakers

In this traditional type of fieldwork, the objective is to collect as much vocabulary and as much data about the phonological and grammatical structure of the language as possible. In sociolinguistics, which focuses on variation (see *Sociolinguistic Variation*) and the use of language in relation to the speakers and their interaction in the community, the phenomenon studied may be restricted, but encompassing a great number of speakers. An example of this kind of fieldwork is the now famous department store experiment carried out by William Labov, who in this study focused on the pronunciation of *r* among New Yorkers, often called the 'fourth floor method.' He describes it in this way:

> The application of the study of casual and anonymous speech events to the department-store situation was relatively simple. The interviewer approached the informant in the role of a customer asking for directions to a particular department. The department was one which was located on the fourth floor. When the interviewer asked, 'Excuse me, where are the women's shoes?' the answer would normally be, 'Fourth floor.'
> The interviewer then leaned forward and said, 'Excuse me?' He would usually obtain another utterance, '*Fourth floor*,' spoken in careful style under emphatic stress.
> The interviewer would then move along the aisle of the store to a point immediately beyond the informant's view, and make a written note of the data.
> (Labov 1972: 49)

3.3 Problems

In studies where all the data are collected in fieldwork situations and are based on the speech of informants, the choice of informants and the relationship between the linguist and the informants is important and a potential source of all kinds of problems, both purely practical and psychological but also of methodological consequence (see *Native Speaker*).

If the purpose of the study is to collect a vocabulary or to deliver a structural description of the grammar, then the informant must be able to understand the questions and the basic ideas of the linguist; through the work he will learn and gradually become a better informant. But if the purpose is to study the minute stylistic and other variations, then the speakers should be as unaware of the linguist as possible. This problem is expressed in what William Labov has called

> the *Observer's Paradox*: the aim of linguistic research in the community must be to find out how people talk when they are not being systematically observed; yet we can only obtain these data by systematic observation.
> (Labov 1972: 209)

See also: Field Methods: Ethnographic; Field Methods in Modern Dialect and Variation Studies.

Bibliography

Craig C G 1979 Jacaltec: Fieldwork in Guatemala. In: Shopen T (ed.) *Languages and Their Speakers*. Winthrop Publishers, Cambridge, MA
Dixon R M W 1989 (1983) *Searching for Aboriginal Languages. Memoirs of a Field Worker*. University of Chicago Press, Chicago, IL
Kaufman T 1968 Making monosyllable dictionaries of Mayan languages. *Anthropological Linguistics* **9**: 1–4
Labov W 1972 *Sociolinguistic Patterns*. Blackwell, Oxford, UK
Milroy L 1987 *Observing and Analysing Natural Language*. Blackwell, Oxford, UK
Samarin W 1967 *Field Linguistics: A Guide to Linguistic Field Work*. Rinehart and Winston, New York
Scollon R, Scollon S B K 1979 *Linguistic Convergence: An Ethnography of Speaking at Fort Chipewyan, Alberta*. Academic Press, New York

Fieldwork Ethics and Community Responsibility
B. Johnstone

By inclination and as a matter of necessity, sociolinguists have always been sensitive to the ethical dimensions of fieldwork and thoughtful about their responsibilities to the communities they study. However, definitions of ethical fieldwork and community responsibility have changed somewhat with the times. We are now aware, in a way we have not always been, of how choices about research methods are grounded in assumptions about knowledge, authority, language, and humanity, and we now consider more carefully what such assumptions imply about the best ways to work.

Some sociolinguists still think of themselves as objective observers, whose job is to examine the people and the linguistic facts they study in as detached a way as possible. They can then return to their scientific communities, once fieldwork is over, with new knowledge about the causes of patterns of linguistic behavior. Others, however, ask questions like these: What is knowledge? Are there social and linguistic facts in the world which any disciplined scientist could observe, or are facts, sociolinguistic and otherwise, partly a consequence of often unspoken traditions about what to pay attention to and how to describe things? If so, who establishes such traditions of thinking and seeing, how are they perpetuated, how are they challenged and changed? What is the relationship between the kinds of knowledge scholars develop and circulate and kinds of knowledge developed and circulated by the people we study? If researchers and the people they study are all experts in one way or another, what is the researcher's role vis-à-vis that of the people we have sometimes called 'subjects'?

1. Traditional Fieldwork Ethics: Protecting And Serving

According to the ideas about science and scholarship that prevailed in the 1960s and 1970s, the role of a social scientist was to observe and interpret the behavior displayed by the community under study. Early sociolinguists followed this model, for the most part. They took care to adhere to the basic ethical imperative not to cause harm to those they studied, as sociolinguists continue to do, typically using pseudonyms to protect their privacy, for example.

In early sociolinguistic work, as in the field research in dialectology and descriptive linguistics that preceded it, members of the community under study were sometimes involved in the process of data-collection as assistants, who might help interview others or record or organize data, or as 'informants'—native speakers of the local language or variety who were hired to answer researchers' questions about linguistic structure or meaning. Other people in the community might be involved only as objects of scrutiny or manipulation: as interviewees, as subjects participating in controlled studies or otherwise observed and/or recorded. Although procedures for insuring informed consent are more stringent now than they once were, most sociolinguists have always explained to the people they studied, in one way or another, what they were doing and how the research would proceed, and they have often gone back to the community later on to report to them what they found.

From the beginning, however, sociolinguists have also tried to use what they learned for the benefit of the people they studied. William Labov, who studied the speech of African American youth in a poor New York neighborhood, entered US educational debate to speak out about African American linguistic structure and traditions of language use (Labov 1982). Other variationists have also designed and carried out educational programs meant to make students and teachers aware of the systematicity and value of stigmatized ways of talking (Wolfram et al. 1999). John J. Gumperz (1982) tried to improve workplaces for immigrants to the UK by sensitizing employers and co-workers to sociolinguistic difference. Dell Hymes' (1981) interest in Native American discourse was partly motivated by his wish to preserve important linguistic traditions and texts. Many sociolinguists have taken their results to the public in speaking and writing about issues such as prescriptivism, miscommunication, and linguistic discrimination, in interviews, films, books and articles meant for general audiences.

People continue to be drawn to sociolinguistic work not only for intellectual reasons but also by the desire to understand and help right things that seem wrong. It continues to be important to find ways of systematically incorporating 'service in return' (Rickford 1997) into the design of sociolinguistic research. Newer debates about the sources of truth and the nature of scholarly authority have highlighted the range of possible ways of conceiving of the relationship between sociolinguists and the people they study, the people with whom they work, and the people for whom the products of their work are intended.

2. 'Communities' and Individuals

The research of sociolinguists' typically focuses on groups of people who are thought likely to have something in common in a linguistic sense: speakers of a particular language or variety or a particular combination of languages or varieties; people who all live or work in the same 'speech community,' 'discourse community' or 'community of practice'; and people engaged in the same linguistic activity. It is important to bear in mind, however, that any decision to study a group of people has the effect of creating a group of people. Humans are not born into groups to which they then always and invariably 'belong'; human identity and social organization are flexible, so that a particular individual orients to different identities, different sets of ideas, and different social activities at different times. Even relatively immutable facts about people such as their physical appearance or age can be relevant at some moments and irrelevant at others. The labels sociolinguists typically use in grouping people for study—labels such as 'Spanish speaker,' 'East Asian,' 'lower middle class,' and 'female'—can make social and linguistic categories seem more fixed and permanent than they are, and such labels may fail to correspond to any of the ways the people in question actually group themselves, when they do.

Failure to think carefully about which social and linguistic categories are relevant, and under what circumstances, to the individual people in whom we are interested, can make sociolinguists liable to misunderstand what is happening. It can also cause confusion and hostility, as people find themselves mislabeled and treated as if their behavior were entirely predictable. Like all other scholars, sociolinguists need to come to conclusions that are potentially generalizable across sets of people or situations, but doing this inevitably means describing people as cogs in a sociolinguistic machine. This deprives them of free will, an aspect of their humanity that many people especially value. Because of this, an important aspect of 'community responsibility' is to bear in mind that 'community' is always an abstraction, and that the object of study is ultimately a set of particular individuals with particular motivations and behaviors.

3. Community Members as Co-Workers

Because of the general shift in sociolinguistics from more social-scientific ways of explaining things to more ethnographic ones, it has become increasingly important for sociolinguists to find ways of eliciting the beliefs and perceptions of the people they study in addition to eliciting their behavior. This means that community members are acting as co-researchers in more ways.

Since 'insiders' who study their community thereby partly reposition themselves as outsiders and 'outsiders' acquire roles inside the community by virtue of studying it, the distinction between outsiders and insiders is never completely clear. It may be that in some cases the ideal researchers are themselves members of the community, since insiders have access to 'local knowledge' (Geertz 1973) and local resources in a way outsiders do not. An effective research team may, in other cases, include insiders and outsiders, with complementary orientations and skills.

In many cases, sociolinguists involve the people they study by using them as sources of validation, consulting with them via procedures sometimes called 'member checking.' In sociolinguistic work, this sometimes involves 'playback' or 'feedback' procedures in which tapes are played for the people who were recorded, or similar people, and they are asked what they think was happening and why. Sometimes the people being studied have even more authoritative roles. Although research participants in sociolinguistic work are rarely (if ever) treated as the sole experts—we do not simply transcribe and publish their explanations of things—folk linguistic expertise is often explicitly drawn on, because sociolinguists have come to see that local ideas about language and local ways of attributing social meaning to linguistic phenomena cannot be predicted on the basis of larger social or linguistic patterns, and that access to local knowledge of this sort is crucial for understanding sociolinguistic processes. Sociolinguists have explored numerous ways of drawing out local knowledge; many borrowed from the participant observation techniques of sociocultural anthropology. They include, for example, paying increased attention to local talk about talk and other representations of speech, as in 'stylings,' parodies, and performances of various other kinds.

4. Uses of Research Findings

It was once thought that the purpose of scholarly research was to uncover the truth, in order to add to humanity's store of knowledge. Now that many sociolinguists are no longer convinced that there are absolute truths or that knowledge is a single ever-expanding inventory of scientific facts, new and challenging questions have arisen about the uses of research.

For one thing, we need to think in new ways about the nature and the distribution of expertise. It seems more and more important to many researchers to find systematic ways of incorporating community expertise into the process of scholarly inquiry. Researchers in some fields have adopted 'participatory' research practices that include ways of insuring that all participants in the research—researcher and community members alike—take part not just in data collection and analysis but also in theory-building. Such practices are not widely used in sociolinguistic work, in part because non-linguists' ideas about language—the idea that speakers of stigmatized dialects are stupid, for example, or the idea that there is a single correct way of talking—often strike linguists as not only wrong but potentially harmful. We have often been tempted to dismiss local expertise telling non-linguists, in effect, that their ideas are understandable but ours are correct.

This has repeatedly failed to work. For example, the controversy of the 1990s over 'Ebonics,' or African American Vernacular English (see *Ebonics and African American Vernacular English*), showed that Americans had exactly the same misconceptions about language and ethnicity as they had 25 years previously, despite sociolinguists' repeated educational efforts over those years. An ongoing challenge for sociolinguistics, then, is to find more effective ways of building bridges between community and scholarly expertise.

Another new question about knowledge has to do with the role of social and political critique in the research process. Skeptical that value-free, disinterested, 'pure' description is possible, some sociolinguists suggest the need for greater explicitness about our social and political beliefs, preferences, and goals. Some 'critical sociolinguists' (see *Critical Sociolinguistics*) argue that social and political change should be our expressed goal. The community's wishes are not always the same as the researcher's—community members may want stigmatized varieties to disappear, for example, while sociolinguists are interested in preserving linguistic diversity—and this poses another continuing challenge.

See also: Speech Community; Ethnography of Speaking; Field Methods: Ethnographic; Ideology; Identity and Language.

Bibliography

Cameron D, Frazer E, Harvey P, Rampton M B H, Richardson K 1992 *Researching Language: Issues of Power and Method*. Routledge, London
Cohen A P 1994 *Self-Consciousness: An Alternative Anthropology of Identity*. Routledge, London
Geertz C 1973 *The Interpretation Of Cultures*. Basic Books, New York
Gumperz J J 1982 *Discourse Strategies*. Cambridge University Press, Cambridge, UK
Hymes D 1981. *In Vain I Tried To Tell You: Essays in Native American Ethnopoetics*. University of Pennsylvania Press, Philadelphia, PA
Johnstone B 2000 *Qualitative Methods in Sociolinguistics*. Oxford University Press, New York
Labov W 1982 Objectivity and commitment in linguistic science: The case of the Black English trial in Ann Arbor. *Language in Society* **11**: 165–201
Rickford J R 1997 Unequal partnership: Sociolinguistics and the African American speech community. *Language in Society* **26**: 161–97
Wolfram W, Christian D, Adger C 1999 *Dialects in Schools and Communities*. Lawrence Erlbaum, Mahwah, NJ

Interactional Sociolinguistic Research Methods
N. Berenz

Research methods in interactional sociolinguistics (IS) involve several stages: a preliminary period of ethnography; the main processes of data collection, transcription and analysis; and a final effort of confirming the findings as consonant with current knowledge. These methods have been developed and applied by John Gumperz, his collaborators and students primarily, although not exclusively, in cross-cultural encounters in institutional settings to yield important insights into the role of implicit cultural presuppositions in human interpretative processes (see *Ethnography of Speaking*; *Discourse in Cross-linguistic and Cross-cultural Contexts*).

Because the research objective of IS is the explication of human communicative practices and interpretative processes, it is important for the researcher to be familiar with the cultural presuppositions held by the subjects whose conversational exchanges will be analyzed. This background information is gathered through reading previous studies and literature, where possible, and—crucially—participant observation within the relevant social groups.

1. Interactional Sociolinguistics and Conversation Analysis

In including background information IS differs from conversation analysis (CA), its better-known intellectual 'first cousin.' We believe that the deeper and broader the analyst's understanding of the background against which an interaction takes place, the more accurately the present encounter can be interpreted. An anecdote from a presentation of scholarly work in the CA tradition illustrates this point. The researcher played an audio recording of a particularly acrimonious exchange between a man and a woman that supported a hypothesis about the gendered nature of conversation. Only during the question-and-answer period that followed the presentation did it emerge that an element of conflict was typically part of the different professions of the two participants and further that these participants had a number of encounters previous to the one analyzed in which the level of conflict had escalated by degrees to the acrimonious heights recorded. This background information did not alter the facts of the interaction with respect to interruptions, for example. Rather than supporting a hypothesis that men interrupt women more than they are interrupted by them, a more nuanced analysis of the interaction viewed against the background information would be that a man may enact his irritation towards a woman differently than he would towards another man (see *Conversation Analysis*; *Gender and Language*).

2. Institutions and Settings

We acknowledge, of course, that the concept *social group* is itself problematic, given the ever-increasing complexity of social interaction in a world where modern modes of transportation and communication have blurred traditional ethnic, gender, and social class boundaries. Nevertheless, we can predict with considerable confidence which aspects of participants' social personae may be relevant in particular types of encounters. For example, a Korean and a German, both members of the international business community, may share some presuppositions about business that will facilitate understanding during business negotiations; communicative difficulties are likely to arise instead from differences in presuppositions generally held by people of Korean or German cultural background. On the other hand, either businessperson may encounter communicative difficulties in conversation with their rural kinfolk, which arise from different presuppositions held by traditional or cosmopolitan populations.

When analysis is carried out in an institutional setting, such as a school, corporation or hospital, that institution will have its own particular 'culture' and 'community.' The researcher develops a basic understanding of the institution during an initial period of interviewing and participant observation by gathering information on the institution's history, social characteristics, everyday practices, and goals. From this information, in tandem with information on participants' backgrounds, we isolate encounter types and generate working hypotheses.

For example, in the school setting, we would expect to find classroom lessons, parent–teacher conferences, chatting among students in the lunchroom or playground, peer evaluations of teachers, and so on. We might hypothesize, drawing on pre-existing knowledge, that a power differential between the teacher and the student will be relevant, such that the teacher can be expected to play a bigger role than the students in classroom conversational management, including topic choice and turn allocation. We may find such an expected power balance to be upset, however, in situations where other social characteristics of participants challenge the 'institutional order.' In a classroom in a prestigious private South African school serving a largely affluent, white population, a black teacher may not be readily accorded the same status by the students as his or her white counterpart. In this situation, the teacher's typical rights and responsibilities for conversational management may be subverted by cultural presuppositions based on perceived extra-institutional social group membership, with the result that an unusually heavy classroom discipline burden falls to the teacher. A performance evaluation of the teacher's classroom management skills may fault the teacher as an individual, when in fact the problem is more general.

3. Gathering Data

The initial phase of determining encounter types and generating working hypotheses is followed by the collection of audio or video recordings of social interaction within the particular setting. Here the researcher must attempt to minimize the effect of the intrusion of recording equipment on the naturalness of the interaction, while at the same time fully informing the participants about the presence of recording equipment and securing their informed consent (see *Fieldwork Ethics and Community Responsibility*). Once consent has been given and equipment is in place, experience has shown that participants soon become used to it and the recorded interaction proceeds quite naturally. Despite the complications inherent in collecting audio- or video-recordings, the careful turn-by-turn analysis required by IS is only possible with such data. Ethnographic fieldnotes detailing aspects of the physical and social setting are important, but they never substitute for the interactive details of an encounter captured on tape. These recordings, ranging from a few minutes to several hours, are the major input to the analytic process.

The recordings are the raw data that are categorized into encounter types whose labels such as *job interview, medical consultation, parent–teacher conference* invoke associated folk knowledge about the nature of the interaction and the relationships likely to hold between participants. Folk knowledge is never identical to the implicit schematic knowledge that participants rely on to inform their own conversational moves and to interpret each other's. A job interview may not be solely a cataloguing of the applicant's job-related skills, but may briefly veer off into areas of interest or experience shared by interviewer and interviewee, such as a mention of a mutual acquaintance or an expression of enthusiasm about a preferred leisure activity. Although these 'digressions' may not be part of folk knowledge about the process of job interviewing, they may have significant impact for the development of rapport between the participants that will influence their later assessment of the success of the encounter (Erickson and Shultz 1982). The lack of isomorphy between labels and interpretive practices necessitates the caution that there is never a one-to-one relationship between a signal and a meaning. The interpretation of a particular conversational move is based on knowledge of what has gone before and is supported by information that follows.

4. Transcription and Analysis

The next step after labeling the encounter is to segment it into thematically coherent and empirically boundable events that have beginnings, middles, and ends. The ends are of particular importance because they provide information on what participants might have inferred and how such inferences were cued. Oftentimes, segmentation can only be accomplished after listening or viewing the tape several times. Gradually we discover such passages through turn-by-turn scanning of the content and rhythmic organization of the encounter as a whole. Some events will be more clearly bounded than others, and it is these clearly bounded events that are the focus of analysis.

The basic unit of sequential analysis is the speaking turn: that string of utterances produced by a single speaker and bounded by other speakers' turns. Within the speaking turn we find the informational phrase: a rhythmically bounded, prosodically defined chunk, a lexical string that falls under a single intonational contour. An informational phrase will, in the clearest cases, be a syntactic unit that carries meaning and is bounded on either side by a pause. In the many less than clear cases found in everyday conversation, rhythmic and thematic organization serves to determine phrase boundaries.

With the analytic construct of informational phrase in mind, we now turn to the labor-intensive activity of transcription. The first step is to isolate and mark informational phrase boundaries throughout an event or portion thereof, followed by another pass (or several more) through the recording to mark interactively salient features of the talk. A detailed explanation of the system and example transcripts can be found in Gumperz and Berenz (1993).

The purpose of the transcription system is to capture those perceptual cues that research has shown participants to rely on in their on-line processing of the speech stream. We do not seek to be exhaustive in our representation of the characteristics of talk, but rather to capture the interactionally meaningful features. With respect to pausing, for example, we listen to the encounter to become familiar with the general rhythm of the talk, and then we mark pauses as deviations from expectation. A Native American job applicant with an Athabaskan background, being interviewed by a General American English speaker, may seem to be slow to respond to the interviewer's questions. Either participant's normal rhythm could be taken as the default and the other's rhythm marked as deviations from that norm. For clarity and to allay as much as possible the bias introduced by the act of selection, the assignment of default value should be made explicit in an introductory note to the transcript. We recognize that transcription is not a theory-free endeavor (Ochs 1979), and we maintain that no transcription is final. The best record of what transpired in an encounter will always be the recording. With recent technological advances, it becomes more possible to distribute actual segments of the recording to readers whose interest in the data and analysis exceeds the limits inherent in transcription.

As noted at the outset, IS differs from CA in its inclusion of background information. The two also differ in the importance attributed to prosody and paralinguistic signaling. Focusing on cross-cultural encounters, IS practitioners find that culturally-based prosodic and paralinguistic variation contributes significantly to communicative breakdown. CA practitioners, on the other hand, have tended to examine interactions between participants who may be assumed to share significant socio-cultural background, where signaling conventions are likely to be less variable. A third difference between the two traditions is what I might call *check-back*. By this I mean that, with a preliminary analysis in hand, we solicit further information from an assistant or consultant who shares social group membership with a participant in the interaction, particularly if that participant's behavior remains inexplicable. By way of example, consider a case reported by Gumperz (1982: 30). A black graduate student, in the company of several other black and white graduate students, approached him after an informal seminar, asking, 'Can I talk to you for a minute? I'm going to apply for a fellowship and I was wondering if I could get a letter of recommendation.' Gumperz replied, 'Come along to the office and tell me what you want to do.' The student's next turn, 'Ahma git me a gig,' (roughly equivalent to 'I'm going to get myself some support') seemed to Gumperz a puzzling switch to African American Vernacular English, until he discussed the incident with other graduate students familiar with African American interpretative traditions. From the further information provided, Gumperz interpreted the code switch as signaling a shift in the audience to whom the student was addressing himself. To those who shared the tradition, he was letting it be known that his request could be understood as a typical one for a minority student trying to get support to carry on with his studies.

We see then that IS research methods anchor the findings of the detailed analysis of everyday conversation in the matrix of socio-cultural understandings, participants rely on in their on-line interpretative efforts.

See also: Observing and Analyzing Classroom Talk; Conversation Analysis; Discourse in Cross-linguistic and Cross-cultural Contexts.

Bibliography

Erickson F, Shultz J J 1982 *The Counselor as Gate-keeper*. Academic Press, New York

Gumperz J J 1982 *Discourse Strategies*. Cambridge University Press, Cambridge, UK

Gumperz J J 1999 On interactional sociolinguistic method. In: Sarangi S, Roberts C (eds.) *Talk, Work, and Institutional Order*. De Gruyter, New York

Gumperz J J, Berenz N 1993 Transcribing conversational exchanges. In: Edwards J A, Lampert M D (eds.) *Talking Data: Transcription and Coding of Discourse Research*. Erlbaum, Hillsdale, NJ

Ochs E 1979 Transcription as theory. In: Ochs E, Schieffelin B B (eds.) *Developmental Pragmatics*. Academic Press, New York, pp. 43–72

Literacy: Research, Measurement, and Innovation
D. Wagner

Research on the causes and consequences of literacy and illiteracy has grown dramatically since the 1980s, yet much more needs to be known. Since there exists a great variety of literacy programs for an even larger number of sociocultural contexts, it should come as no surprise that the effectiveness of literacy programs has come under question, not only among policymakers and specialists, but also among the larger public. How effective are literacy campaigns? What is the importance of political and ideological commitment? Should writing and reading be taught together or separately? Should literacy programs include numeracy as well? Is literacy retained following a limited number of years of primary schooling or short-term campaigns? How important are literacy skills for the workplace? Is it important to teach literacy in the individual's mother tongue? These and similar questions—so central to the core of literacy work around the world—remain without definitive answers, in spite of the occasionally strong rhetoric in support of one position or another. Basic and applied research, along with effective program evaluation, are capable of providing critical information that will not only lead to greater efficiency in particular literacy programs, but will also lead to greater public support of literacy programs.

Research on literacy can reveal key policy areas which need to be addressed, as well as methodologies for assessment and monitoring which will be crucial in the coming years. This entry summarizes some of the major areas of literacy research and measurement, and offers some critical areas for future innovation.

1. Literacy Research in Global Perspective

There are three general domains in literacy work that are likely to be the subject of greater attention and will determine to a large extent whether attempts at improving global literacy will be successful. Each of these is reviewed below.

1.1 Defining Literacy: Operationalization for Measurement

With the multitude of experts and published books on the topic, one would suppose that there would be a fair amount of agreement as to how to define the term 'literacy.' On the one hand, most specialists would agree that the term connotes aspects of reading and writing; on the other hand, major debates continue to revolve around such issues as what specific abilities or knowledge count as literacy, and what 'levels' can and should be defined for measurement. The term 'functional literacy' has often been employed, as originally defined by Gray (1956: 19): 'A person is functionally literate when he has acquired the knowledge and skills in reading and writing which enable him to engage effectively in all those activities in which literacy is normally assumed in his culture or group.'

While functional literacy has a great deal of appeal because of its implied adaptability to a given cultural context, the term can be very awkward for research purposes. For example, it is unclear in an industrialized nation like the UK what level of literacy should be required of all citizens. Does a coal miner have different needs than a barrister? Similarly, in a Third World country, does an illiterate woman need to learn to read and write in order to take her prescribed medicine correctly, or is it more functional (and cost effective) to have her school-going child read the instructions to her? The use of the term 'functional,' based on norms of a given society, is inadequate precisely because adequate norms are so difficult to establish.

An adequate, yet more fluid, definition of literacy is '...a characteristic acquired by individuals in varying degrees from just above none to an indeterminate upper level. Some individuals are more or less literate than others, but it is really not possible to speak of literate and illiterate persons as two distinct categories' (UNESCO 1957). Since there exist dozens of orthographies for hundreds of languages in which innumerable context-specific styles are in use every day, it would seem ill advised to select a universal operational definition. Attempts to use newspaper reading skills as a baseline (as in certain national surveys) may seriously underestimate literacy if the emphasis is on comprehension of text (especially if the text is a national language not well understood by the individual). Such tests may overestimate literacy if the individual is asked simply to read aloud the passage, with little or no attempt at the measurement of comprehension. Surprisingly, there have been relatively few attempts to design a battery of tests from low literacy ability to high ability which would be applicable across the complete range of possible languages and literacies in any society, such that a continuum of measurement possibilities might be achieved. UNESCO, which provides world-wide statistical comparisons of literacy, relies almost entirely on data provided by its member countries, even though the measures are often unreliable indicators of literacy ability. However, there were new attempts in the 1990s to undertake literacy surveys in a comparative and international framework in some industrialized nations (OECD/Statistics Canada 1995).

At least part of the controversy over the definition of literacy lies in how people have attempted to study literacy. The methodologies chosen, which span the social sciences, usually reflect the disciplinary training of the investigator. Anthropologists provide in-depth ethnographic accounts of single communities, while trying to understand how literacy is woven into the fabric of community cultural life. By contrast, psychologists and educators have typically chosen to study measurable literacy abilities using tests and questionnaires, usually ignoring contextual and linguistic factors. Both these approaches (as well as history, linguistics, sociology, and computer science) have value in achieving an understanding of literacy. There is no easy resolution to this problem, but it is clear that a broad-based conception of literacy is required not only for a valid understanding of the term, but also for developing appropriate policy actions (Venezky et al. 1990).

Because literacy is a cultural phenomenon—adequately defined and understood only within each culture in which it exists—it is not surprising that definitions of literacy may never be permanently fixed. Whether literacy includes computer skills, mental arithmetic, or civic responsibility will depend on how public and political leaders of each society define the term and its use. Researchers can help in this effort by trying to be clear about which definition or definitions they choose to employ in their work. For overviews of literacy in international context, see Wagner and Puchner (1992), Wagner (1992), Wagner et al. (1999).

1.2 Acquisition of Literacy

The study of literacy acquisition has been greatly influenced by research undertaken in the industrialized world. Much of this research might be better termed the acquisition of reading and writing skills, with an emphasis on the relationship between cognitive skills, such as perception and memory, and reading skills, such as decoding and comprehension. Further, most of this work has been carried out with school-aged children, rather than with adolescents or adults. Surprisingly little research on literacy acquisition has been undertaken in the Third World, where researchers have focused primarily on adult acquisition rather than on children's learning to read. This latter phenomenon appears to be a result of the emphasis to promote adult literacy in the developing world, while usually ignoring such problems, until quite recently, in industrialized societies.

Despite these gaps in the research literature, certain general statements are relatively well established as to how literacy is acquired across different societies. In 1973 Downing published *Comparative Reading*, which surveyed the acquisition of reading skills across different languages and orthographies. He found that mastery of the spoken language is a typical prerequisite for fluent reading comprehension in that language, although there exist many exceptions. Another finding is that in many alphabets children first learn to read by sounding out words with a memorized set of letter–sound correspondences. It is now known that there are many exceptions to this generalization. There are, of course, languages which are not written in alphabets (e.g., Chinese and Japanese). There also appear to be large individual differences in learning styles within literacy communities. Finally, many individuals can read and write languages which they may not speak fluently.

Some specialists have stressed the importance of class structure and ethnicity/race as explications of differential achievement among literacy learners. Ogbu (1978), for example, claimed that many minority children in the United States are simply unmotivated to learn to read and write in the cultural structure of the school. This approach to understanding social and cultural differences in literacy learning has received increased attention in that it avoids blaming the individual for specific cognitive deficits (as still happens), while focusing intervention strategies more on changes in the social and political structure of schooling or the society.

Finally, it has been assumed that learning to read in one's 'mother tongue' or first language is always the best educational policy for literacy provision, whether for children or adults. Based on some important research studies undertaken in the 1960s, it has generally been taken for granted that individuals who have had to learn to read in a second language are at a disadvantage relative to others who learn in their mother tongue. While this generalization may still be true in many of the world's multilingual societies, more recent research has shown that there may be important exceptions. In one such study, it was found that Berber-speaking children who had to learn to read in Standard Arabic in Moroccan schools were able to read in fifth grade just as well as children who were native speakers of Arabic (Wagner 1993). Adequate research on nonliterate adults who learn to read in a second versus a first language has yet to be undertaken.

In sum, considerable progress has been made in understanding the acquisition of literacy in children and adults, but primarily in industrialized societies. Far less is known about literacy acquisition in a truly global perspective, and in multilingual societies. Since the majority of nonliterate people live in these areas of the world, much more needs to be known if literacy provision is to be improved in the coming decades.

1.3 Retention of Literacy

The term 'educational wastage' is common in the literature on international and comparative education, particularly with respect to the Third World. This term typically refers to the loss, usually by dropping out, of children who do not finish what is thought to be the minimum educational curriculum of a given country (often 5 to 8 years of primary schooling). Most specialists who work within this area gather data on the number of children who enter school each year, the number who progress on to the next grade, those who repeat a given year (quite common in many Third World countries), and those who quit school altogether. The concept of wastage, then, refers to those children for whom an economic investment in educational resources has already been made, but who do not complete the appropriate level of studies.

The issue of literacy retention is crucial here, for it is not actually the number of school leavers or graduates that really matters for a society, but rather what they learn and retain from their school years, such as literacy skills. When students drop out of an educational program, a society is wasting its resources because those individuals (children or adults) will not reach some presumed threshold of minimum learning without losing what has been acquired. Thus, retention of learning (or literacy, in particular) is a key goal of educational planners around the world. There are as yet only a small number of research studies published on this question, and their results are highly contradictory. Some show that there is a 'relapse' into illiteracy for those who have not received sufficient instruction, while other demonstrate no serious loss (Wagner 1998a).

2. Literacy Measurement

2.1 Areas of Debate in Literacy Assessment

In order to provide worldwide statistical comparisons, UNESCO (UNESCO 1996, Wagner 1998b) has relied almost entirely on data provided by its member countries. These countries, in turn, typically rely on national census information, which most often determines literacy ability by self-assessment questionnaires and/or by the proxy variable of years of primary schooling. Many specialists now agree that such measures are likely to be unreliable indicators of literacy ability. Nonetheless, through the 1990s, change in literacy measurement has been slow in coming, even though some initiatives have been undertaken.

There is considerable diversity of opinion as to the usefulness of classifying individuals in the traditional manner of 'literate' versus 'illiterate.' Several decades ago, when developing countries began to enter the United Nations, it was common to find that the vast majority of the adult populations of these countries had never gone to school nor learned to read and write. It was relatively easy in those contexts to simply define all such individuals as 'illiterate.' The situation in the late 1990s is much more complex, as some contact with primary schooling, nonformal education programs, and the mass media is now made by the vast majority of families in the Third World. Thus, even though parents may be illiterate, it is not unusual for one or more of their children to be able to read and write to some degree. For this reason, it would seem that simple dichotomies—still in use by some international agencies and most national governments—ought to be avoided, since they tend to misrepresent the range or continuum of literacy abilities that are common to most contemporary societies.

As noted earlier, work on adult literacy has frequently derived its methodologies from the study of reading development in children. This is true of assessment as well, where the diagnosis of individual reading difficulties has held sway for many years, in both children and adults. This diagnostic model of assessment assumes that individuals who do not read well have some type of cognitive deficit which can (often) be remediated if properly diagnosed by a skilled professional. There is little doubt that this model does apply to many adults who have not learned to read, but who have attended school. However, the majority of the world's population of low literates and illiterates (located primarily in developing countries) have received little or no schooling, making the diagnostic method far less relevant. For this latter population, detailed diagnostic measures are unimportant relative to the need for better understanding of who goes to school, what is learned, and which particular social groups are most in need of basic skills. In such cases, as discussed below, low-cost household surveys may be a better assessment technique than diagnostic instruments.

Most countries have formulated an explicit language policy which states which language or languages have official status. Often, the decision on national or official language(s) is based on such factors as major linguistic groups, colonial or postcolonial history, and the importance of a given language to the concerns of economic development. Official languages are also those commonly used in primary school, though there may be differences between languages used in beginning schooling and those used later on. The use of mother tongue instruction in both primary and adult education remains a topic of continuing debate (Dutcher 1982, Hornberger 1999). While there is usually general agreement that official language(s) ought to be assessed in a literacy survey, there may be disagreement over the assessment of literacy in nonofficial languages (where these have a recognized and functional orthography). In many countries, there exists numerous local languages which have varying status with respect to the official language; how these languages and literacies are included in such surveys is a matter of debate. For example, in certain predominantly Muslim countries in sub-Saharan Africa (e.g., Senegal or Ghana), the official language of literacy might be French or English, while Arabic—which is taught in Islamic schools and used by a sizable population for certain everyday and religious tasks—is usually excluded from official literacy censuses. Many specialists now agree that most (if not all) literacies should be surveyed; to ignore such abilities is to underestimate national human resources.

Comparability of data—across time and countries—is a major concern for planning agencies. If definitions, categories, and classifications vary, it becomes difficult if not impossible to compare data collected from different surveys. On the other hand, if comparability is the primary goal, with little attention to the validity of the definitions, categories, and classifications for the sample population, then the data become virtually meaningless. International and national needs, definitions, and research strategies may or may not come into conflict over the issue of comparability, depending on the particular problem addressed. For example, international agencies continue to utilize literacy rates that are measured in terms of the number of 'literates' and 'illiterates.' For most countries, this type of classification presents few problems at the level of census information, and it provides international agencies with a cross-national framework for considering literacy by geographic or economic regions of the world. On the other hand, national planners may want to know the effects of completion of certain grades of primary or secondary school, or of a literacy campaign, on levels of literacy attainment, so that a simple dichotomy would be insufficient. Household literacy surveys, because more time may be devoted to in-depth questioning, offer the opportunity to provide a much more detailed picture of literacy and its demographic correlates than has been previously available.

2.2 Household Literacy Surveys

Assessment surveys have employed varying approaches to defining literacy skill levels in different countries. For example, some assessment surveys have focused on 'ability to read aloud' from a newspaper in the national language; some have included basic arithmetic (numeracy) skills; while still others have focused on being able to write one's name or read a bus schedule. Two main types of literacy survey methods—self-assessment and direct measurement—have been utilized within widely differing contexts.

Most national literacy data collections in the world have utilized self-assessment techniques, which are operationalized by simply asking the individual one or more questions of the sort: 'Can you read and write?' Occasionally, census takers collect information on which language or languages pertain to the above question, but rarely have time or resources been invested beyond this point. Analysis of the relationship between self-assessment and direct measurement of literacy abilities has rarely been sought, so that the reliability of self-assessment methods is very problematic (Lavy et al. 1995).

Direct measurement of literacy typically involves tests which are constructed with the aim of obtaining performance or behavioral criteria for determining literacy and/or numeracy abilities in the individual. The large number and variety of literacy and numeracy assessment instruments precludes a complete discussion in this brief review. Objective measures rely primarily on test items to elicit valid and reliable data from the individual, with rather strict controls on the context and structure of the test. An example would be a multiple choice test where the individual is presented with a short paragraph of text and is asked to choose, among four items, the item which best describes some particular piece of information mentioned in the paragraph. These measures are usually quite reliable in school settings and for silent reading, where test–retest correlations and cross-test correlations may be highly significant. Their use in nonschool settings and with low-literate adults is less well known, since these tests assume a certain equivalence in 'test-taking skill' across individuals tested. Such objective tests are particularly useful in settings where the interviewer has little prior experience in literacy assessment, since relatively little subjective interpretation of test performance is required.

The direct measurement of literacy skills using assessment instruments provides information on more refined categories than available in self-assessment, which usually provides merely a dichotomous categorization. In industrialized countries, there have been a number of important household literacy surveys. The first two were completed in North America: the Young Adult Literacy Assessment (Kirsch and Jungeblut 1986) in the US, and the

Canadian Literacy Survey (Statistics Canada 1988) in Canada. More recently, a major international survey was conducted in about a dozen OECD countries (OECD/Statistics Canada), using a methodology that overlapped rather substantially with the North American surveys, providing in depth individual assessments of reading, writing, and math skills in both abstract and functional contexts (Tuijnman et al. 1997). While the advantage of such in-depth information may be justifiable in the context of industrialized countries, these surveys clearly represent the 'high end' of both detailed analysis and cost in terms of household surveys.

For contexts such as in developing countries or in low-literate ethnic communities in industrialized countries, it may be useful to choose a categorical breakdown which would provide just enough information for use by policymakers, and which could be more easily and simply constructed. This 'low-end' method of assessment is best exemplified in the model developed under the auspices of the United Nations National Household Survey Capability Program, and which has been undertaken in several countries, including Zimbabwe and Morocco (United Nations 1989, Wagner 1990). In this model, there are four main skill classifications which are proposed: (a) *non-literate* for a person who cannot read a text with understanding and write a short text in a significant national language, and who cannot recognize words on signs and documents in everyday contexts, and cannot perform such specific tasks as signing their name or recognizing the meaning of public signs; (b) *low-literate* for a person who cannot read a text with understanding and write a short text in a significant national language, but who can recognize words on signs and documents in everyday contexts, and can perform such specific tasks as signing their name or recognizing the meaning of public signs; (c) *moderate-literate* for a person who can, with some difficulty (i.e., makes numerous errors), read a text with understanding and write a short text in a significant national language; and (d) *high-literate* for a person who can, with little difficulty (i.e., makes few errors), read a text with understanding and write a short text in a significant national language. When these four categories are utilized in conjunction with other variables in the survey, it becomes possible to arrive at answers to questions often posed by policymakers, such as: How does literacy vary by age, grade, geographical region, language group, and so forth?

2.3 Measuring Literacy Levels

Beyond the broad category labels of literacy levels, there is little agreement on how actually to assign such labels to individuals. Does scoring above 50 percent on a test of paragraph comprehension qualify an individual as literate, nonliterate, or in-between? To a great extent, such labeling has been and continues to be arbitrary. In addition, while most assessment instruments utilize school-based and curriculum-based materials, there is increasing awareness among specialists of the importance of measuring 'everyday' or practical literacy abilities. One method for dealing with literacy assessment is to determine the intersection of both literacy *skills* and *domains* of literacy practice (Tuijnman et al. 1997).

There are a great many types of literacy tests, and a great number of skills which specialists have thought were important not only for the measurement of actual literacy ability, but also in terms of the underlying processes involved in being a competent reader or writer. Drawing on recent survey work, as described above, it is useful to think of literacy ability as involving at least four basic types of skills: decoding, comprehension, locating information, and writing.

Individuals who use literacy may perform literate functions on a wide array of materials; in addition, certain individuals may specialize in specific types of literate domains (e.g., lawyers, doctors, agricultural agents). Even individuals with low general levels of literacy skill may be able to cope successfully with written materials in a domain in which they have a great deal of practice (e.g., farm workers who often deal with insecticides). Since governments are generally interested in providing literacy for many categories of people, an assessment should sample across the material domains where literate functions are typically found, such as, single words, short phrases, tables and forms, and texts.

The estimation of literacy skills by text domains involves the use of a matrix of the intersection of literacy skills with the text domains in which literacy skills can be applied. This provides a breakdown of types of component skills in literacy. It should be understood that there is rarely consensus on which specific skills to test in literacy, and that any such matrix is necessarily arbitrary. Nonetheless, a matrix of literacy skills by domain can provide a useful method for collecting the appropriate ('low-end') amount of information needed for policy decisions, and it can be considerably less expensive than some of the comprehensive methods employed in the North American surveys.

3. Literacy Research and Innovation

Based on the growing concern about literacy levels across the globe, it seems clear that new domains of research will begin to open up, such as the topics described below.

3.1 Technology

There are new and exciting ideas about the utility of technology for literacy provision to children and adults. Much of this work is still in the early development stages, such as efforts to utilize synthetic speech to teach reading, or the use of multimedia displays (interactive video, audio tapes, and computer displays) to provide more sophisticated instruction than has been heretofore available. Technological solutions to instruction—known as computer-based education (CBE) or computer-assisted instruction (CAI)—have been used, primarily in industrialized nations, since the early 1980s, and the presence of microcomputers in the classrooms of schools has continued to grow at a phenomenal rate, especially with the advent of the Internet (Anderson 1999, OECD 2000, Wagner and Hopey 1999).

Until the 1990s, the cost of educational technology was too high even for most industrial countries, and therefore far beyond the means of the developing countries. But the price-to-power ratio (the relative cost, for example, of a unit of computer memory or the speed of processing) continues to drop at an astounding rate. While the cost of the average microcomputer has remained constant or declined slightly for about a decade, the power of the year 2000 computer is 10–100 times greater than that produced in 1990. If present trends continue, the capabilities for CAI and CBE literacy instruction are likely, by the year 2010, to go far beyond the elementary approaches of the 1990s.

3.2 Multisectoral Approaches

Literacy skills are utilized in many life contexts outside of academic settings. To date, most research and development has focused primarily on school-based settings. A major challenge rests in determining the ways that literacy can be fostered and utilized in everyday family and work settings. From a policy perspective, more needs to be known about how literacy education can be infused into the significant development work of other sectors, such as agriculture and health. In these two sectors, literacy is a major vehicle for innovation and knowledge dissemination, yet few studies have explored what levels of literacy determine the effectiveness of such dissemination.

3.3 Design of Materials

In developing countries, increased textbook provision has been viewed by donors and ministries of education as a key strategy for the improvement of school instruction (Heyneman and Jamison 1980). However, very little is known about how the design of instructional materials influences comprehension and learning. There are also enormous subject matter and national variations in conventions of text design. Some important work on the relationship between characteristics of textbook discourse and comprehension is being carried out that has implications for improving school textbooks, as well as materials for other sectors. For example, there is a special need to improve instructions for pharmaceutical and agricultural chemicals, whose safe and effective use requires performing complex cognitive tasks with procedural information that is often difficult to comprehend (Eisemon 1988, Wright 1999).

3.4 Mother-tongue and Second-language Issues

As previously discussed many learners enrolled in adult education programs are being taught literacy in a second language. In developing countries, a significant proportion of these students are either illiterate in their mother tongue or receive only a few years of mother-tongue instruction before a second, usually foreign, language is introduced as a medium of instruction. Poor second-language literacy proficiency is a cause of high repetition and wastage rates, and of low achievement in academic subjects in primary and secondary schools with profound consequences for employment and other externalities of schooling.

Because of the significant debate on first- and second-language/literacy policy (often related to national issues of ethnicity and power), most government agencies worldwide have been reluctant to review such policies. However, there are a number of important areas of work which need to be addressed beyond the confines of this debate, such as: (a) Under what conditions should mother tongue literacy be a precondition for the introduction of second-language literacy in school-based and non-formal settings? (b) How does the implementation of language-of-instruction policies affect literacy after schooling? (c) What are the effects of using second-language literacy in school on wastage and grade repetition? (d) What are the implications of using the second-language literacy for academic subjects like mathematics, science, health, nutrition, and agriculture? (e) What roles do orthographic similarity and dissimilarity play in transfer between mother tongue and second literacy? These and similar questions will need to be addressed before major progress can be made in improving literacy levels in national and international contexts.

4. Conclusion

The importance of research, measurement, and innovation in literacy is that they can provide new paths to greater efficiency in literacy provision around the world. While no social program (including research) is without economic costs, such expenditures must be understood in the light of costs involved in not knowing how to carry out literacy programs practically and efficiently. Those who have argued that the literacy crisis is so great that the support of research is somehow wasteful are likely to be proven wrong. To invest resources in implementation without developing the means to learn from such programs is to call into question any purported gains in literacy work.

The year 2000 was a critical moment to reinforce literacy efforts, as global economic changes are requiring significant changes in worker skills and the heightened role of information exchange. In spite of the clear need for cultural sensitivities and specificities, there may be important economies of scale as more is learned about literacy. Methodologies for pilot programs, assessment and evaluation, and computerized textbook preparation, as examples, may be transferable with local adaptations to varying cultural contexts. The need for literacy and other basic skills has never been greater, and the gap between literate and nonliterate lifestyles is becoming ever larger, with parallel growth in income disparities. Literacy and learning are a part of the culture of every society. To produce major changes in literacy requires both a realistic understanding of the kinds of change which people and nations desire, and sustained support to provide appropriate instructional services.

See also: Literacy; Oracy.

Bibliography

Anderson J 1999 Information technologies and literacy. In: Wagner D A, Venezky R L, Street B V (eds.) *Literacy: An International Handbook*. Westview Press, Boulder, CO
Downing J 1973 *Comparative Reading*. Macmillan, New York
Dutcher N 1982 *The Use of First and Second Languages in Primary Education:* Selected Case Studies. World Bank Staff Working Paper, No. 504. World Bank, Washington, DC
Eisemon T E 1988 *Benefiting from Basic Education, School Quality, and Functional Literacy in Kenya*. Pergamon, New York
Gray W S 1956 *The Teaching of Reading and Writing: An International Survey*. UNESCO, Paris
Heyneman S P, Jamison D T 1980 Student learning in Uganda: Textbook availability and other factors. *Comparative Education Review* 24(2): 206–20
Hornberger N 1999 Language and literacy planning. In: Wagner D A, Venezky R L, Street B V (eds.) *Literacy: An International Handbook*. Westview Press, Boulder, CO
Kirsch I, Jungeblut A 1986 *Literacy: Profiles of America's Young Adults*. Final report of the National Assessment of Educational Progress. ETS, Princeton, NJ
Lavy V, Spratt J, Leboucher N 1995 *Changing patterns of illiteracy in Morocco: Assessment methods compared*. LSMS Paper 115. The World Bank, Washington, DC
OECD/Statistics Canada 1995 *Literacy, Economy, and Society*. OECD, Paris
OECD 2000 *Learning to Bridge the Digital Divide*. OECD, Paris
Ogbu J 1978 *Minority Education and Caste: The American System in Cross-cultural Perspective*. Academic Press, New York
Statistics Canada 1988 *A National Literacy Skill Assessment Planning Report*. Statistics Canada, Ottawa, ON
Tuijnman A, Kirsch I, Wagner D A (eds.) 1997 *Adult Basic Skills: Innovations in Measurement and Policy Analysis*. Hampton Press, Cresskill, NJ
UNESCO 1957 *World Illiteracy at Mid-century: A Statistical Study*. UNESCO, Paris
UNESCO 1996 *Education For All: Mid-decade Report*. UNESCO, Paris
United Nations 1989 *Measuring Literacy through Household Surveys: A Technical Study on Literacy Assessment and Related Topics through Household Surveys*. National Household Survey Capability Programme. United Nations, New York
Venezky R L, Osin L 1991 *The Intelligent Design of Computer-assisted Instruction*. Longman, New York
Venezky R, Wagner D A, Ciliberti B (eds.) 1990 *Towards Defining Literacy*. International Reading Association, Newark, DE
Wagner D A 1990 Literacy assessment in the Third World: An overview and proposed scheme for survey use. *Comparative Education Review* 34(1): 112–38
Wagner D A 1992 *Literacy: Developing the Future*. International Yearbook of Education, Vol. 43. UNESCO/International Bureau of Education, Geneva
Wagner D A 1993 *Literacy, Culture, and Development: Becoming literate in Morocco*. Cambridge University Press, New York
Wagner D A 1998a Literacy retention: Comparisons across age, time, and culture. In: Wellman H, Scoot G, Paris (eds.) *Global Prospects for Education: Development, Culture, and Schooling*. American Psychological Association, Washington, DC: pp. 229–51
Wagner D A 1998b *Literacy Assessment for Out-of-School Youth and Adults Concepts, Methods, and New Directions*. ILI/UNESCO Technical Report. International Literacy Institute, University of Pennsylvania, Philadelphia, PA
Wagner D A 2000 *Literacy and Adult Education*. World Education Forum, Dakar, Senegal
Wagner D A, Hopey C 1999 Adult literacy and the Internet: Problems and prospects. In: Wagner D A, Venezky R L, Street B V (eds.) *Literacy: An International Handbook*. Westview Press, Boulder, CO
Wagner D A, Puchner L (eds.) 1992 *World Literacy in the Year 2000:* Research and Policy Dimensions. Annals of the American Academy of Political and Social Science, Newbury Park, CA
Wagner D A, Venezky R L, Street B V (eds.) 1999 *Literacy: An International Handbook*. Westview Press, Boulder, CO
Wright P 1999 Comprehension of printed instructions. In: Wagner D A, Venezky R L, Street B V (eds.) *Literacy: An International Handbook*. Westview Press, Boulder, CO

Multidimensional Scaling
W. C. Rau

Graphic models have a long history in the study of language; the century-old, frequent use of tree diagrams to represent syntax and grammar stands as an eloquent testimony to the need for classificatory tools in language studies (Stewart 1976). Linguists seem much more reluctant, however, to use conventional statistics in their investigations, and texts on statistical applications in linguistics (e.g., Butler 1985) seem rather elementary from the perspective of the social sciences. There are exceptions, of course, with the work of Labov (1980) and Osgood (1975) coming immediately to mind. Nonetheless, one looks long and hard through mainstream journals, such as *Language*, to find the kind of empirical and statistical analysis that a social scientist would recognize. Data do not appear very often, but when they do, they may be presented without further statistical analysis or interpretation (e.g., Lipski 1986, Lehrer 1985). This is unfortunate, because many new statistical tools exist that can profitably analyze a broad range of linguistic phenomena. One such technique is multi-dimensional scaling (or MDS). Linguists will be relieved to see that it presents their data in sheer attire, accentuating rather than concealing what is already there.

1. Basic Procedures

As a preparatory step for analysis, social scientists gather information into a data matrix where observations are placed in the rows, and variables are placed in the columns. For example, Cavalli-Sforza and Wang (1986) analyzed linguistic data from Micronesia that filled a data matrix containing fully 9,136 pieces of information. Imagine their matrix drawn on a very wide sheet of paper. There are 16 rows of data, one for each island's linguistic data. Each of the 571 columns represents a particular gloss or word. Each of the 9,136 cells of this vast table contains the morpheme employed by the particular society (row of the table) for the particular word (column of the table). For example, a full stomach is described as *mat* on the island of Tobi, *math* on Falalop and Mogmog, and *màt* on Woleai, Ifaluk and Satawal. Societies with the same morphemes have cell entries of 1; those with different morphemes receive a zero.

This array of information is referred to as raw data. The point of statistical analysis is to 'boil down' or 'reduce' these raw data to a set of summary indices or dimensions which can then be used to highlight major patterns in the data. One of the more common first steps in this process of reduction is for the analyst to calculate some measure of association among either the variables or observations in the matrix. Pearson's or Spearman's correlation coefficients, one of the numerous matching coefficients, or a distance measure, such as Euclidean distances, represent some of the choices. These measures are then reduced further through use of factor analysis, multidimensional scaling, or regression analysis. When well done, the end result is a parsimonious rendering of the major patterns of association among variables or observations in the original data matrix.

The first step in this process leaves one with a triangular matrix, such as the upper-right triangle in Fig. 1. This table is a small excerpt of the one published by Cavalli-Sforza and Wang, and shows relationships linking only 6 of the 16 islands. Each element in the matrix shows the extent to which one observation (or variable) is similar to or different from another observation (or variable). In Fig. 1 Woleai and Mogmog show the highest correlation, 0.728, and Satawan and Tobi the lowest, 0.446. In the full data matrix, the highest coefficient found, 0.987, is for Falalop and Mogmog, and shows these islands to have nearly all of the 571 linguistic characteristics in common. Tobi and Murilo, however, have the lowest coefficient, 0.406, with less than half the characteristics in common.

Reducing a data matrix to a set of similarity measures is straightforward; any of a number of computer statistical packages will reduce even the largest data matrix in a matter of seconds. The real issue is whether to reduce the data matrix across either the variables or the observations. For example, one can reduce the 16 × 571 Micronesian data matrix to a 571 × 571 matrix of correlations among variables (words) or a 16 × 16 matrix of correlations among observations (islands). Which way does the linguist want to go?

Here, conventional practices in the social sciences are not helpful. Most social scientists are interested in testing hypotheses which, with nearly universal regularity, are couched in the language of variables. Proverbial Variable X is hypothesized to affect Variable Y, so the analyst uses correlation analysis, regression analysis, etc., to determine how changes in

		Miles/Matching coefficient				
	Tobi	Mogmog	Woleai	Satawal	Puluwat	Satawan
Tobi	—	0.643	0.588	0.507	0.466	0.446
Mogmog	667	—	0.728	0.604	0.543	0.507
Woleai	809	298	—	0.716	0.601	0.526
Satawal	987	464	186	—	0.692	0.562
Puluwat	1,112	585	314	129	—	0.657
Satawan	1,360	880	597	417	296	—

Figure 1. Geographical distances and matching coefficients among six Caroline Islands and languages.

Variable X or a set of X Variables is associated with change in Variable Y. In short, social scientists almost always work across the columns in the data matrix.

Linguists would appear to be more interested in patterns among observations. Linguistic analysis is more holistic or relational than most quantitative analysis in the social sciences (cf. Rau and Roncek 1987, Rau and Leonard 1990). If true, then linguists should reduce data across the rows of the data matrix and not across the columns. This crucial difference may be one reason why linguists have been reluctant to borrow statistical tools employed by social scientists. The latter, with their excessive fixation on conventional approaches to hypothesis testing, use statistical tools almost exclusively to analyze variables. Hence, the manner in which some of these tools can be adapted to the analysis of linguistic data has not been clearly demonstrated. It will now be shown below how MDS can assist in holistic analyses of data by reducing measures of association among observations.

2. An Application of the Method

One cannot imagine a better or more parsimonious theory for demonstrating this use of MDS than that provided by Cavalli-Sforza and Wang (1986) in their study of lexical replacement in the Carolines, a chain of islands and atolls in Micronesia. Directly north of New Guinea and the Solomons, to the east of the Philippines, and to the west of the Marshall Islands, the 16 islands and atolls in their study stretch in a ragged but compact band for some 1,400 miles. The Carolines represent an ideal natural laboratory for testing their 'stepping-stone' theory of language change.

In a simplified version of the wave theory of language change, they argue that linguistic diffusion will be a negative exponential function of the distance separating a linear array of discrete language communities. Linguistic diffusion in traditional wave theory is complicated by the multidirectionality of sources of linguistic innovation. Since change can emanate from a number of different directions, a complex network of isoglosses can result. Choice of the Carolines minimizes the problem of multidirectionality since, as noted, the islands are somewhat isolated and spread out in a fairly straight and narrow band. Given these fortuitous geographic circumstances, one can expect linguistic differences among the islands to be a function of their respective geographic distances.

2.1 Creating a Map of the Carolines

The measures published by Cavalli-Sforza and Wang (and excerpted in Fig. 1) can be used to explain the principles in MDS and then to provide a new test of stepping stone theory. First, the miles between pairs of islands are scaled, as given in the lower left triangle in Fig. 1. MDS can scale distances as well as correlations or matching coefficients. Several classic demonstrations of MDS principles produce maps from a matrix of distances among cities (see Kruskal and Wish 1978: 7–10, Borg and Lingoes 1987: 1–5). MDS can produce an accurate map if it is given the miles or kilometers between any number of locations, be they cities or atolls. A map of the Carolines is seen in Fig. 2, with the names of the atolls placed as close as possible to their point locations. It was generated with ALSCAL (Alternating Least Squares Algorithm for Scaling), an MDS algorithm developed by Forrest Young and others (Young 1987, Young and Lewyckyj 1979) and carried by such popular computer statistical packages as SPSS and SAS.

Notice one interesting feature of the plot. When any of the MDS algorithms produces a configuration, the 'compass points' or termini of the resulting coordinates are arbitrary. In the present case, the configuration in Fig. 1 represents a mirror inversion of how the Carolines are presented in a geographic atlas. What is most important in multidimensional scaling is the structure or pattern of relationships among objects in the configuration. Whether the objects come out upside down is completely irrelevant. The researcher can always stand on his head—or simply give the configuration a spin so that it conforms to the conventional, and arbitrary, Eurocentric geographical coordinates. Australians, for example, might find the present configuration entirely sensible!

2.2 The MDS Algorithms

Before getting into substantive issues, it will be useful to explore briefly how MDS algorithms produce configurations. For purposes of illustration the

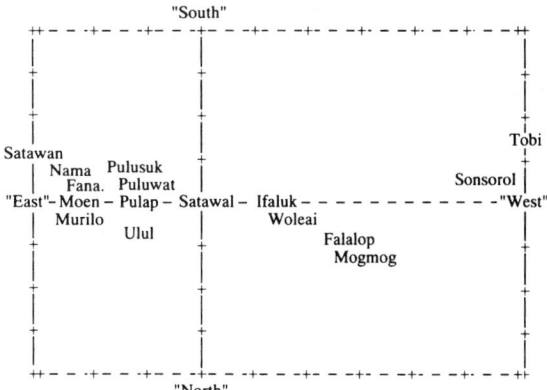

Figure 2. ALSCAL plot of the Carolina configuration.

strategy behind Smallest Space Analysis will be demonstrated. This is an MDS algorithm developed by Louis Guttman (1968) and James Lingoes (1973). Smallest Space Analysis is a close cousin to ALSCAL, and its principles are easier to illustrate.

The lower left triangle of the first matrix in Fig. 3 contains the miles separating six islands, simply copied from Fig. 1. MDS starts with comparisons among each pair of islands, 15 island-pairs in this case. It begins by assigning a ranking number of each pair; the islands separated by the smallest distance are assigned as 1, the pair with the next smallest distance a 2, and so on until 15 numbers are assigned. The D Matrix in Fig. 2 gives the resulting integers for the island-pairs; it gives the rank order structure of distances among the six islands. It shows which islands are closest and furthest away from each other in space. Puluwat and Satawal, separated by a distance of only 129 miles, are ranked at 1; Tobi and Satawan, with 1,284 miles between them, get the rank of 15.

MDS will now produce a configuration of points which tries to reproduce the D Matrix ranking integers within the space or dimensionality specified by the researcher. Since stepping-stone theory assumes a one-dimensional array of language communities, that constraint is applied even though locations in geographic space usually require two or three dimensions for a completely accurate mapping. In the present instance, MDS has the added advantage of testing whether the Carolines approximate the unidimensional ordering assumed in stepping-stone theory. If distances among these islands are in fact sequences in an order approximating a line of stepping-stones, then MDS will be able to fit them onto a one-dimensional line.

Smallest space analysis begins with a principal components solution. Each island gets a numeric value giving its location as a point on the principal components dimension. These values are then used to calculate interpoint distances across each pair of islands. Next, these distances are transformed into 'rank images' and stored in a D* Matrix. Corresponding ranks in the two matrices are compared, and then points in the configuration are shifted about until the rank images in the D* Matrix correspond as closely as possible to the ranking of integers in the D Matrix. This iterative process is guided by a 'badness of fit' measure, called the 'coefficient of alienation' in Smallest Space Analysis (and 'stress' in ALSCAL), which optimizes the fit between the rank images and ranking integers. When and if the coefficient of alienation equals 0, then the rank images and ranking integers correspond perfectly. In the present instance, this would mean that the six islands can be sequenced into a one-dimensional array with no loss of the rank ordering of the mileage in the original distance matrix.

In Smallest Space Analysis, the loss function or coefficient of alienation is given by

$$u = \Sigma d_{ij} d_{ij}^* / \Sigma d_{ij}^2 \quad (1)$$

$$K = (1 - u)^{1/2} \quad (2)$$

The term d_{ij} is the rank ordering of the distance between the ith and jth islands in the D Matrix, and d_{ij}^* is the rank image for the same island-pair. K is the value of the loss function or the coefficient of alienation. On the basis of a hand-estimated point plot of a smallest space configuration in Fig. 3, $K = 0.06$, which means that the six islands can be sequenced in a one-space with almost no loss of the information in the original distance matrix.

Computers do it better, and in this case ALSCAL can fit the 16 islands and 120 island-pairs in one dimension with a stress value of 0.024, thus accounting for over 99 percent of the rank order information in the original distance matrix. While stress in two dimensions is zero, the islands are pretty much in a straight line, thus permitting only one dimension to be used. In short, the Carolines do present an ideal natural laboratory for Cavalli-Sforza and Wang.

Equally comforting is the fit of the matching coefficients presented in the matrix for all 16 islands. As noted, MDS algorithms can also fit similarity coefficients which transform binary data into measures ranging from 0 to 1.00. Since many kinds of linguistic data can be represented in binary form (+, −; yes, no; present, absent), transformation of this information into a matrix of matching coefficients prepares them for MDS analysis. For these matching coefficients, the stress value in one dimension is 0.065; hence 98.7 percent of the information in the coefficient matrix is preserved in a one-dimensional array of the islands.

2.3 Testing Stepping-stone Theory

The stepping-stone theory can now be tested in a simple and direct fashion. The MDS configurations allow the islands to be sequenced into geographical and lexical arrays. If the theory is correct, the position of the 16 islands in the two arrays should be the same, or at least very close. This is in fact the case. From one end, the geographic array begins: Tobi, Sonsorol, Mogwog, Falalop, and Woleai. The lexical array is almost identical, beginning: Tobi, Sonsorol, Falalop, Mogwog, and Woleai. Ten of the 16 islands have exactly the same rank order linguistically as they do geographically, and the rest average only about two ranking steps different in the two arrays. The correlation between the ordering of the linguistic and geographic arrays is 0.926, which is very nice indeed.

One always expects data to depart to some degree from the pure pattern predicted by a theory. In this

			Miles\Rank order				
Island	Tobi	Mogmog	Woleai	Satawal	Puluwat	Satawan	
Tobi	—	5	9	12	14	15	
Mogmog	667	—	4	7	11	13	
Woleai	809	298	—	3	8	10	D Matrix
Satawal	987	464	186	—	1	6	
Puluwat	1,019	466	480	129	—	2	
Satawan	1,284	880	597	417	170	—	

			Spatial distances\Rank images				
Tobi	—	5	9	13	14	15	
Mogmog	40	—	4	8	11	12	
Woleai	70	30	—	3	7	10	D* Matrix
Satawal	90	50	20	—	1	6	
Puluwat	100	60	30	10	—	2	
Satawan	115	75	45	25	15	—	

Hand-estimated point plot

1———————2———————3———————4———5———6
   (40)   (30)   (20)   (10) (15)

Calculation of loss function

d_{ij}	d_{ij}^*	$d_{ij} \times d_{ij}^*$	d_{ij}^2	$u = \Sigma d_{ij} d_{ij}^* / \Sigma d_{ij}^2$
5	5	25	25	
9	9	81	81	= 1,238/1,240
12	13	156	144	
14	14	196	196	= 0.998
15	15	225	225	
4	4	16	16	$K = (1-u^2)^{1/2}$
7	8	56	49	
11	11	121	121	= $(1-0.997)^{1/2}$
13	12	156	169	
3	3	9	9	= 0.057
8	7	56	64	
10	10	100	100	
1	1	1	1	
6	6	36	36	
2	2	4	4	
		1,238	1,240	

Figure 3. An illustration of the MDS fitting process.

case, islands that are but a stone's throw away from each other may have reversed orders, such as Mogwog and Falalop. In addition, Fig. 2 shows islands in the Truk District (The Eastern Carolines) to have as much longitudinal displacement as latitudinal displacement. And the positions of Murilo and Satawan differ five and four steps, respectively, in the linguistic and geographic rankings. Such deviations should come as no surprise. Among the great maritime navigators in premodern times, Micronesians could transverse the distances among islands in the Truk District (Gladwin 1970, Lewis 1972). Different population sizes and rates of trading and exchange could account for these minor deviations.

3. Pronunciation in Dialects of Spanish

Another area for which MDS is suited concerns the study of dialects. This area already has lent itself to imaginative map making. Maps such as those made by Dennis Preston (1986) require a rather direct correspondence between geographic regions and systems of pronunciation, however, and the distribution of dialects does not always prove so convenient. Spanish is a case in point. Moreover, the nature and distribution of Spanish dialects is a major educational issue as well. In the USA, Anglo students are taught in the dialect of Mexican Spanish, and they assume that since it is taught in the schools it must therefore be the 'standard' or 'correct' pronunciation. When students have difficulty understanding Cubans or Puerto Ricans, for example, they often assume 'that Puerto Rican and Cuban pronunciation is somehow sub-standard or inferior, and therefore the lack of comprehension is the fault of the native speakers themselves and not the students or the school system' (Terrell 1977: 35).

How then does Mexican or so-called 'standard Latin–American pronunciation' compare with other dialects? MDS can show this by plotting a *figurative* map giving the similarities and differences among any number of dialects. One of the raw data matrices mentioned earlier will illustrate this, a compilation of the field work of John Lipski and others (Lipski 1986). The original data matrix presents different ways of pronouncing the phoneme /s/ in seven cities or areas in Spain and another 21 cities or countries in Central and South America. It appears that in most of these studies 10 respondents with a high school education (typically from capital or major cities) were interviewed for one half hour in an informal or conversational style. Tape recordings were then analyzed for the frequency of occurrence of different ways of pronouncing /s/ in five different spoken contexts, such as immediately after another consonant or after a word break and a stressed vowel. Three different pronunciations of /s/ were noted: simple sibilant, aspiration, or deletion.

3.1 Analyzing the Spanish Data

Considering just /s/ after a consonant, three cities can be compared to note the kinds of differences present in the dataset. In Barcelona, Spain, 99 percent of the time a simple sibilant was spoken, and 1 percent of the time an aspiration was given instead. The percentages were very similar in Madrid, 94 and 6 percent. But in Granada, a sibilant was never spoken, while 82 percent of the time there was an aspiration, and in the remaining 18 percent the sound was deleted altogether. Clearly, Barcelona and Madrid are similar, while Granada is quite different from both of them. It is easy to quantify this difference. To determine the linguistic 'distance' between two cities, the Euclidean distance formula will be used to total the differences between the percentage figures for all the language characteristics in the data set.

These data have been transformed into a matrix of Euclidean distances among the pairs of countries or cities. Two cities with the same patterns of pronunciation would have a distance of 0. They would have the same frequency or percentage of occurrence for the 15 variables represented as columns in the data matrix. As distances between pairs increase, they become less and less similar. MDS can reveal both the range and variety of differences contained in a matrix. Put differently, it can reveal both quantitative and 'qualitative' differences. But first the number of dimensions needed for an accurate point configuration must be determined.

The ALSCAL stress values for three through one dimensional solutions are as follows. A three-dimensional solution has a stress of 0.042, a very small departure from a perfect fit, while a two-dimensional solution does almost as well, with a stress of 0.068. A one-dimensional solution is markedly worse, at

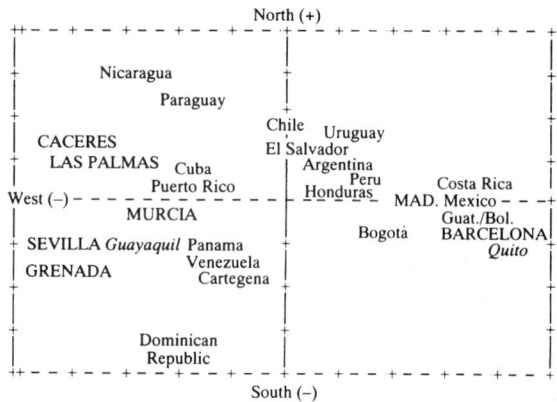

Figure 4. ALSCAL configuration for Spanish dialects.

0.206. Another way to evaluate the solutions is in terms of R^2, the 'variance explained,' a measure of how well the solution captures the information in the data matrix. R^2 for three dimensions is 0.991, almost the theoretical maximum of 1. But a two-dimensional solution is not far behind, with an R^2 of 0.980, while one dimension explains considerably less of the variance, with 0.871. Clearly, a two-dimensional solution is nearly as good as a three-dimensional one, and far better than a one-dimensional solution, almost completely reproducing the information in the original matrix. And two dimensions are easier to visualize than three. Therefore, two dimensions can provide our figurative map of similarities and differences among Spanish pronunciations.

Figure 4 is the resulting map. Compare the locations of Mexico, Cuba, and Puerto Rico. Their distance apart brings out the difference in their phonological systems. Mexican pronunciation is most similar to the Spanish spoken in the six to seven countries directly adjacent to it at the center east end of the plot. By the same token, Mexican Spanish is hardly the hub of Lipski's sample of dialects. If, for the moment, the seven dialects clustered around Mexico are ignored, then Cuba and Puerto Rico, along with Murcia become the hub or center for the remaining 17 dialects.

Note also, as in the case of Spain, the diversity of pronunciations that can occur within a country. The Spanish spoken in Madrid (MAD in the plot) is most similar to that spoken in Mexico and very similar to that of Barcelona, but it is clearly not representative of the other areas in Spain. Those areas, which are capitalized in Fig. 4, form a sideways V at the west end of the plot. Although Madrid and Mexican Spanish and highly similar, Murcian Spanish is more similar to the other dialects in Spain. With regard to the phoneme /s/, someone from Murcia would pronounce words very much like a Cuban or Puerto Rican, and not at all like someone from Madrid or

Barcelona. To the extent that the first coordinate (the east–west axis) is more important than the second (the north–south axis), then there is more dialect diversity within Spain proper than in the Latin American areas featured in Lipski's sample. Sampling of a number of sites within each of the other countries might increase the overall diversity, however. As a case in point note the difference between Guayaquil and Quito in Ecuador—and to a lesser extent, the differences between Bogotá and Cartagena in Colombia.

3.2 Interpretation of an MDS Map
This brings up the issue of interpreting the properties of dialect clusters or regions in Fig. 4. Two interrelated strategies can help to determine why one group of observations locate in one region of the configuration, and other groups of observations locate elsewhere. More generally, these strategies identify the properties of each of the dimensions framing a configuration. Figure 4 has two dimensions. What aspects of the data, then, are responsible for observations locating at either the east or west end of dimension 1, or the north or south end of dimension 2? Clearly, this is not a simple case of diffusion like that illustrated by the Micronesian data considered above, because there is little correspondence between the linguistic map in Fig. 4 and the geographic positions of the observations. The configuration must be understood in some other way.

One simple and direct approach is to choose a set of observations which extend across one dimension while varying little on the other dimensions. The analyst then inspects the data matrix and finds those variables which change in the most consistent and dramatic fashion as one moves along the dimension. For example, as one scans along dimension 1 from Barcelona through Bogotá, Panama, and Guayaquil to Sevilla, the data reveal a great decrease in the use of sibilants. But picking a route through the observations is a bit subjective. Also, especially when the data set contains a great variety of variables, it can be difficult to decide which variables are most responsible for the configuration.

A second approach is to use regression analysis (Kruskal and Wish 1978) to establish the relationship between the variables in the raw data matrix and numerical scores for the dimensions in the MDS solution. For Lipski's data, the 28 observations have numerical scores on each of the 15 variables in the raw data matrix plus another score on each of the dimensions or coordinates in the MDS configuration. Each of the 15 variables can simply be regressed onto the values for the two dimensions. Variables with the largest regression weights for a particular dimension are the ones that will change in the most consistent and dramatic fashion for observations located at different points along the projection of that dimension. Thus, these two strategies are complementary.

The results for the regression strategy are in Fig. 5. The decimal values under each dimension are standardized regression weights or betas. The betas for each row establish the relative contribution that scores for each dimension make to the variance explained for a variable. The R^2 value gives the total variance explained by both dimensions. For example, the two dimensions account for 87 percent of the total variance in the first variable (sibilated consonants), and dimension 1, with a beta of $+0.93$, is responsible for nearly all of this variance. As a matter of convention, ALSCAL assigns positive numeric values to dimension scores to the east and north of the center of a configuration; dimension scores to the west and south are negative. Thus, the positive sign for this beta means that the percentage of sibilated consonants increases as one moves from west to east on the first dimension. More generally, the beta weights are roughly analogous to factor loadings in factor analysis (for a discussion of factor analysis see Rummel 1970). They tell us which variables are associated with which dimensions.

The results in Fig. 5 present the kind of distinctive statistical attire that reveals that stately beauty of human language. The clarity and strength of the patterns are striking and are reminiscent of Einstein's famous adage: if God does not play dice with the universe, then the Spanish certainly do not play dice with their dialects. In this table Lipski's variables have been rearranged to bring out the numerical expression of the rules of pronunciation contained in his data. If /s/ is rendered as a sibilant after a

	Variable	Dimension 1	Dimension 2	R^2
Simple Sibilant [s]				
1	Consonant	0.93	−0.06	0.87
4	WB Consonant	0.90	−0.13	0.82
7	Before Pause	0.91	0.18	0.87
10	WB Stressed Vowel	0.84	−0.02	0.71
13	WB Unstressed Vowel	0.93	0.08	0.88
Aspiration [h]				
2	Consonant	−0.82	0.40	0.83
5	WB Consonant	−0.74	−0.55	0.85
8	Before Pause	−0.32	0.53	0.39
11	WB Stressed Vowel	−0.60	0.54	0.66
14	WB Unstressed Vowel	−0.82	0.32	0.78
Deleted [0]				
3	Consonant	−0.44	−0.65	0.62
6	WB Consonant	−0.43	−0.61	0.56
9	Before Pause	−0.81	−0.38	0.79
13	WB Stressed Vowel	−0.58	−0.54	0.64
15	WB Unstressed Vowel	−0.69	−0.65	0.89

Symbol: WB = Word Break

Figure 5. Standardized regression coefficients of ALSCAL dimensions for each phonetic variable.

consonant, then it is also rendered as a sibilant after stressed or unstressed vowels and pauses or word boundaries. To a lesser but still striking degree, the same rule holds for aspiration or deletion.

Next, the results in Fig. 5 can be used to help identify the phonological differences responsible for the dispersion of the 28 dialects into different regions and clusters in the two-dimensional configuration. The regression weights for dimension 1 show that speakers at the east end of the configuration pronounce /s/ as a sibilant; those at the west end resort to either aspiration or deletion. We can distinguish further aspiration from deletion by means of dimension 2. Those at the north end of coordinate 2 rely on aspiration, those at the south end, on deletion.

4. Scaling Individual Speakers

One more example may prove useful. Thus far, aggregated data, i.e., islands and cities have been analyzed. MDS can be just as useful in analyzing patterns among individuals, although loss functions may run higher. For purposes of illustration, the individual-level data provided by Mohan and Zador (1986) are examined.

These researchers were interested in the process of 'language death' (see *Endangered Languages*) which they characterize as the point at which an ethnic community loses the ability to speak in its native language. A major question is whether language death is a slow, gradual process akin to Darwinian evolutionary change, or whether it is marked by sharp discontinuities among groups of speakers who possess qualitatively different degrees of fluency in the ethnic language. Mohan and Zador chose the (South Asian) Indian community in rural Trinidad, West Indies, for study of this issue. Beginning in the mid-nineteenth century, the area received migrants from Uttar Pradesh and western Bihar who worked as indentured laborers on sugar plantations. Once the common language of the Indian community, Trinidad Bhojpuri is now only spoken frequently by older, rural inhabitants of the island. Creole and Standard English have become the languages of choice among Indians born in Trinidad.

To determine the nature of language change in this community, Mohan and Zador tested the language competence of 40 speakers of Trinidad Bhojpuri who were grouped into four age categories. Speakers' ages ranged from 26 to 96, but the key group consisted of speakers under age 35. While the older subjects were representative of their age groups, Mohan and Zador were hard pressed to find younger subjects who were capable of speaking Trinidad Bhojpuri for any length of time. Subjects number 31 through 40, all under age 35, were thus chosen on an *ad hoc* basis. Eight of these respondents consisted of sibling pairs who were close in age.

Mohan and Zador then tape recorded half-hour segments of speech in Trinidad Bhojpuri and calculated the average speed of speech, five different kinds of errors, and ten incidence counts of features of Trinidad Bhojpuri that a fluent native speaker would possess. Taken as a whole, their 16 measures were designed to elicit the kind of speech—fast, correct, and articulate—that competent speakers of any language will possess. If the loss of a native language is a gradual process, then a gradual loss of speed and grammatical complexity and a gradual increase in errors would be expected. On the other hand, if there is a relatively discontinuous loss of language, a qualitative break in performance across these measures could be expected.

The MDS analysis of the structure of relations among observations is ideally suited to test issues of this sort. If major discontinuities exist, an MDS configuration will show large gaps resulting in noncontinuous groups of subjects. The 40×16 matrix was transformed to a matrix of Euclidean distances among the 40 subjects, and then analyzed with ALSCAL A one-dimensional solution had a stress of 0.205 and R^2 of 0.898, not terribly impressive. Solutions with two, three, and four dimensions had stresses of 0.132, 0.098, and 0.071, respectively. There is no hard and fast rule for determining an acceptable stress value, but as a general rule analysts like to get stress below 0.10, although this is not always possible or necessary. In this case, a three-dimensional solution achieves this criterion. Inspection of the plots for both two-dimensional and three-dimensional solutions leads to the same outcome.

Figure 6 uses the first and second dimensions of a three-dimensional solution, and it reveals the gap expected by advocates of theories of discontinuous language change. Six of the under age 35 group locate at the far east end of the configuration. Only two isolates (speakers 37 and 39), also under age 35, occupy a large empty region before one encounters a much larger cluster of competent Trinidad Bhojpuri

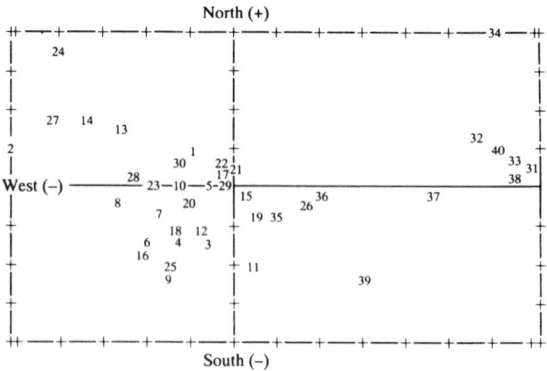

Figure 6. Plot of dimensions 1 and 2 for Trinidad Bhojpuri configuration.

speakers in the center west region of the configuration. Only two speakers under age 35 (numbers 35 and 36) are adjacent to this cluster, so the configuration establishes a large, decisive break in the linguistic competence of the older and younger respondents.

The techniques of MDS permit further refinements in this analysis. For one thing, the solution suggests either that some of the variables employed by the researchers measure something other than competence, or that competence itself is not unidimensional. Regression analysis can help us interpret the dimensions. The east–west dimension, not surprisingly, is strongly associated with rapidity of speech, with the slow speakers in the east, and the fast ones in the west. This dimension has some claim on the label of 'general competence,' because most of the 10 features of Trinidad Bhojpuri are associated with the fast-speaking west end of the configuration, and most of the five errors are associated with the east end. However, some of the features are far more strongly associated (conjunctive markers, compound verbs, and noun definitizers) than are others (relative clauses and numerical classifiers). The second dimension is greatly defined by lack of relative clauses, use of numerical classifiers and noun definitizers, and omission of copulas.

A fresh analysis could further differentiate the large cluster of speakers in the center west of Fig. 6, and there is the small group in the northwest to consider as well. Interpretation of the groupings—and definitive interpretation of the dimensions—would require a scholar with the understanding of Trinidad Bhojpuri possessed by Mohan and Zador. The important point is that Fig. 6 identifies some noticeable differences among fluent speakers of Trinidad Bhojpuri, as well as charting the distribution of degrees of competence in this dying language. In short, MDS offers linguists a powerful tool for systematically identifying both large and subtle differences in linguistic competence.

5. Conclusion

Several ways have been shown in which multi-dimensional scaling of observations can assist linguists in their study of the structure of language. Whether one is concerned with individuals or communities, one period of time or several, MDS can assist in the identification and interpretation of patterns in data. A few linguists, such as Cavalli-Sforza and Wang or Mohan and Zador, already use conventional statistical tools to good effect. The MDS strategy employed here provides additional confirmation for their theories while demonstrating the advantages of complementing conventional statistical tests with results from MDS. Additionally the technique could be of value to linguists who have never used statistical tools, conventional or otherwise.

See also: Sociology of Language; Scaling; Statistics in Sociolinguistics.

Bibliography

Borg I, Lingoes J 1987 *Multidimensional Similarity Structure Analysis*. Springer, New York

Butler C 1985 *Statistics in Linguistics*. Blackwell, Oxford, UK

Cavalli-Sforza L L, Wang W S-Y 1986 Spatial distance and lexical replacement. *Language* **62**: 38–55.

Gladwin T 1970 *East is a Big Bird: Navigation and Logic on Puluwat Atoll*. Harvard University Press, Cambridge, MA

Guttman L 1968 A general nonmetric technique for finding the smallest coordinate space for a configuration of points. *Psychometrika* **33**(4): 469–506

Kruskal J B, Wish M 1978 *Multidimensional Scaling*. Sage, Beverly Hills, CA

Labov W (ed.) 1980 *Locating Language in Time and Space*. Academic Press, New York

Lehrer A 1985 Markedness and antonymy. *Journal of Linguistics* **21**: 397–429

Lewis D 1972 *We, the Navigators: The Ancient Art of Landfinding in the Pacific*. University Press of Hawaii, Honolulu, HI

Lingoes J C 1973 *The Guttman–Lingoes Nonmetric Program Series*. Mathesis Press, Ann Arbor, MI

Lingoes J C, Borg I 1978 A direct approach to individual differences scaling using increasingly complex transformations. *Psychometrika* **43**(4): 491–519

Lipski J M 1986 Reduction of Spanish word-final /s/ and /n/. *Canadian Journal of Linguistics* **31**: 139–56

Mohan P, Zador P 1986 Discontinuity in a life cycle: The death of Trinidad Bhojpuri. *Language* **62**: 291–319

Osgood C E, May W H, Miron M S 1975 *Cross-cultural Universals of Affective Meaning*. University of Illinois Press, Urbana, IL

Preston D R 1986 Five visions of America. *Language in Society* **15**: 221–40

Rau W, Leonard W 1990 The evaluation of Ph.D. programs in sociology: Theoretical, methodological, and empirical considerations. *The American Sociologist* **21**: 232–56

Rau W, Roncek D 1987 Industrialization and world inequality: The transformation of the division of labor in 59 nations, 1960–81. *American Sociological Review* **52**: 359–69

Rummel R J 1967 Understanding factor analysis. *The Journal of Conflict Resolution* **11**: 444–80

Rummel R J 1970 *Applied Factor Analysis*. Northwestern University Press, Evanston, IL

Shye S 1985 *Multiple Scaling: The Theory and Application of Partial Order Scalogram Analysis*. North-Holland, New York

Stewart A H 1976 *Graphic Representation of Models in Linguistic Theory*. Indiana University Press, Bloomington, IN

Terrell T D 1977 Constraints on the aspiration and deletion of final /s/ in Cuba and Puerto Rico. *Bilingual Review* **4**: 35–51

Young F W 1987 *Multidimensional Scaling: History, Theory, and Applications*. Erlbaum, Hillsdale, NJ

Young F W, Lewyckyj R 1979 *ALSCAL User's Guide*. L. L. Thurstone Psychometric Lab, Chapel Hill, NC

Observer's Paradox
A. Davies

The term 'observer's paradox' refers to the well-known methodological problem in linguistic research: how to collect samples of authentic casual speech. Labov (1972, see *Labov, William*) presents it thus:

> the aim of linguistic research in the community must be to find out how people talk when they are not being systematically observed; yet we can only obtain these data by systematic observation. The problem is of course not insoluble: we must either find ways of supplementing the formal interviews with other data, or change the structure of the interview situation by one means or another.
>
> (1972: 209)

The term 'observer's paradox' is appropriate because it suggests that the data of speech which the observer wishes to elicit are (or may be—there is no way of knowing) contaminated by the presence of the observer. The methodological problem, therefore, is how to observe without observing. This is of particular relevance to sociolinguistic research, given the importance accorded by Labov to the most casual speech (which he terms 'the vernacular') in determining the direction of language change.

As Preston points out, 'the more aware respondents are that speech is being observed, the less natural their performances will be. The underlying assumption is that self-monitored speech is less casual and that less casual speech is less systematic, and thus less revealing of the ... vernacular' (Preston 1989: 7). Labov's concern with the methodological imperatives of his search places him in the anthropological tradition of participant observation. In that tradition, the anthropologist attempts to share the daily routines of the society s/he is studying as a means of gaining a better understanding and heightening rapport with the people s/he is studying. In private, normally inaccessible, settings, there are well-known techniques, using 'poses' or 'disguises,' for gaining access which might otherwise be denied. Such techniques include posing as a patient in a mental hospital, a prison inmate, or a newspaper reporter.

Labov offers a number of techniques for gaining access to these private speech situations which are normally inaccessible: 'various devices which divert attention away from speech and allow the vernacular to emerge' (1972: 209). The subject, says Labov, may be involved in questions and topics 'which recreate strong emotions he has felt in the past or involve him in other contexts.' The best-known of such questions in the Labov methodology is the 'Danger of Death' question: 'Have you ever been in a situation where you were in danger of being killed? Narratives given in answer to this question almost always show a shift of style away from careful speech towards the vernacular' (Labov 1972: 209–10).

Labov seems uninterested in the ethical questions posed by such techniques, questions which exercise many social science researchers. In addition to the doubtful ethicality of poses and disguises, there is the question of their effect on research validity. Whether or not such techniques as a pose or a disguise, or a misinforming of the subject by pretending to ask about some incident while really being interested in his/her speech, or again a surreptitious recording machine, are ethical, the fundamental philosophical problem of perception remains. This is an enduring problem of philosophy, associated with Bishop Berkeley's '*esse est percipi*' (to be is to be perceived) and with the tradition of phenomenalism, according to which the reality of an external physical object is based on its being perceived by someone.

To such a powerful view there is no logical answer, as Boswell drily comments in his account of Dr Johnson's famous commonsense 'refutation' of Berkeley 'I shall never forget,' writes Boswell, 'the alacrity with which Johnson answered, striking his foot with mighty force against a large stone, till he rebounded from it, "I refute it thus"' (1922: 162).

Labov is indeed correct in referring to the problem as a paradox. In sociolinguistic research, one can never be sure that the observer, however disguised, however familiar, has no influence, and that 'good' vernacular data have been elicited. After all, the only valid vernacular data that can be observed are the observer's own, and phenomenalism's flip side of solipsism ensures that we can never be sure that other people are like us when we are not observing them. Labov's confidence that his techniques do indeed bring about a shift of style towards the vernacular may therefore seem to be too certain. No methodology can completely remove the ethical and the philosophical constraints, although one may choose, like Dr Johnson, to suspend disbelief and assume that it does.

See also: Fieldwork Ethics and Community Responsibility; Sociolinguistic Variation; Vernacular.

Bibliography

Boswell J 1922 *Boswell's Life of Johnson*. Macmillan, London
Labov W 1972 *Sociolinguistic Patterns*. University of Pennsylvania Press, Philadelphia, PA
Preston D R 1989 *Sociolinguistics and Second Language Acquisition*. Basil Blackwell, Oxford, UK

Observing and Analyzing Classroom Talk
A. D. Edwards and D. P. G. Westgate

Although talk constitutes such a large part of what goes on in classrooms, its live recording and detailed analysis have only developed since the late 1960s. This article illustrates the wide range of research approaches which are now clustered under the heading of classroom talk. Although the boundaries between them should not be marked too rigidly, there are substantial differences in the comprehensiveness and detail of what is recorded and transcribed. These differences are not a matter of pure versus applied research. They reflect the extent to which the primary interest is in what the patterning of communication reveals about the relationship of teacher and students and the communication of classroom knowledge, and whether and how far the analysis is informed by linguistic theory and shaped by a predominant interest in linguistic structure.

1. Research Traditions

Toward one end of that research continuum, studies using what Stubbs (1983) calls 'insightful observation' seek to heighten practitioners' awareness of the scope and quality of their exchanges with students without engaging in any linguistically sophisticated analysis. However valuable as a stimulus to reflective practice, such studies raise difficult questions about how immediately and directly open to interpretation those exchanges are. If spoken language is not treated as a transparent medium, something to be looked through rather than looked at, then how far is it possible to apply methods of 'looking' without extensive knowledge of the specialized academic areas from which they derive? From a linguistic perspective, it is argued that researchers can only scratch the surface of classroom language if they merely select as evidence whatever features appear to be pedagogically interesting; 'principled' analysis of linguistic forms is a necessary condition for revealing their functions. It may also be argued that, with notable exceptions (e.g., Bernstein 1996, Cazden 1988), sociolinguists have tended to neglect classroom talk as a setting for fundamental research.

Different ways of investigating classroom talk will now be outlined to emphasize how the researcher's purposes shape the methods which are used and reflect certain assumptions about the phenomena being observed (see also Edwards and Westgate 1994).

1.1 Systematic Classroom Observation

Practitioners of this approach certainly 'look through' the language being exchanged. The decision is made to code what is said by teacher and students using a schedule which preselects those features of their interaction which are judged to be relevant to the inquiry. This practice of 'systematically' coding classroom events as they happen, depends on a certain positivist confidence in their 'transparency.' Most obviously, it assumes that the words being exchanged can be treated as conventional tokens of a shared situational understanding and their functions appropriately categorized (see Galton et al. 1999). This makes it possible to gather evidence from a large number of classrooms in a fairly short time: an hour's observation yields an hour's data immediately available for analysis.

1.2 Ethnographic Approaches

Those who make audio or audiovisual recordings of classroom talk perceive teacher and students as developing and revising their meanings as the talk proceeds, drawing as they do so on background knowledge of which the observer may be unaware. Transcription of the talk makes it possible to examine these subtleties retrospectively. There are large differences in how this is done, notably in how the 'context' of the talk is understood and used in the analysis, how comprehensively the talk is recorded and transcribed, and how much information (for example, about pausing or intonation) is contained in the transcript.

1.3 Insightful Observation

The approach described as 'insightful' observation' might also be termed unsystematic ethnography. For while it usually requires that the researcher spends enough time in that classroom to gain an understanding of its culture, it rarely involves detailed structural analysis of the discourse. The focus is usually on what 'the patterning of communication' (Barnes and Todd 1995: 1) reveals about the simultaneous managing of relationships and meanings in conditions where it is usual for the boundaries between the teacher's knowledge and the students' ignorance to be regularly and sharply marked. This approach has been widely used to identify styles of teaching and learning or, more specifically, to describe the verbal 'scaffolding' through which the teacher enables students to extend their understanding (Edwards and Mercer 1987). Apparently limited demands on the researcher's linguistic expertise partly explain why this approach has been widely used by teachers investigating the opportunities provided in their own classrooms for students to develop skills in talking and listening. It is a form of action research encouraged by recognition of the centrality of those skills in the learning process (see *Oracy*; *Spoken Language in the Classroom*).

1.4 Linguistic Ethnography

Teachers' control over classroom knowledge is especially evident in the frequency of their questions, and in the frequency with which the consequent exchanges make it evident that the answers are already known to the questioner. Although both the counting of questions and the assessment of their cognitive difficulty (or level) have been commonplace in classroom research, Dillon (1994) has drawn attention to alternative and possibly more effective ways of eliciting student contributions and promoting discussion.

There are also methodological objections to taking questions out of context. In what has variously been called 'linguistic' or 'constitutive' ethnography, the whole structure of classroom discourse is systematically described. Although questioning is still treated as giving rise to 'the essential teaching exchange' of teacher-initiation, student-response, and teacher-evaluation, such regularly occurring sequences are embedded in a comprehensive analysis covering every item of turn-taking and all those methods by which teacher and students secure cohesive and coherent discourse (see Mehan 1979, Cazden 1988). By seeking to derive from the participants' ordering of that discourse the rules from which their situationally appropriate participation is generated, such analysis has drawn attention to possibilities of serious misunderstanding, even of more or less overt cultural conflict, where the rules governing normal communication in home and school settings are at variance (see Heath 1983; and see *Educational Failure*; *Home Language and School Language*; *Black English in Education*; *Standard English and Educational Policy*).

1.5 The Linguistic Structure of Classroom Discourse

From a predominantly linguistic perspective, classrooms have had the empirical attraction that clearly structured relationships are likely to produce linguistically distinctive forms of discourse (see Coulthard 1992). Much of the resulting research has drawn heavily on speech act theory—the investigation of what is done with words, and how it is done, in circumstances where words and meanings are tied together in ways which are familiar to the participants and characteristic of that setting. A common classroom example is the likelihood that *Will you please turn to page 14*, if said by the teacher, will be heard as a directive and not as a polite request admitting the possibility of refusal. Such 'mitigating devices' are used by teachers to soften the edges of their control and make it more indirect. But that control remains pervasively evident in those particular ways of eliciting, displaying, and confirming (or disconfirming) knowledge which are characteristic of classrooms.

2. Phases of Research Activity

All research traditions carry within them a range of theoretical assumptions about language as social behavior. Before examining the variety of practices which give these assumptions life, it should be made clear that most researchers reject any notion of a single 'right' approach or set of approved procedures. While all research requires hard choices to be made about how data are to be defined and collected, the guiding principle remains one of matching techniques to aims and purposes. This is itself a difficult task, given the range of alternatives and the problem of compatibility which may arise from mixing them.

The search for appropriate techniques can usefully be considered under four phases of activity which are common to all approaches where the language used comes under close scrutiny. Initially, the choices focus upon methods of observing and recording what is said. Varying widely in technological sophistication, these usually result in recordings stored on tape. A second phase makes these accessible to detailed analysis by transcribing them according to conventions and criteria determined by the researcher's particular purposes. The act of transcription is inseparable from that next phase because what is included in the transcript, and how this material is organized, constitutes the data to be analyzed and interpreted. But in contrast to the instant coding of verbal interaction, it is possible to return to the recording and to constitute the data differently—for example, by including features of intonation or pausing which seem retrospectively to be significant. Finally, an analysis grounded in the data has to be made public and warranted, decisions having been made about the amount and type of evidence to be displayed.

These phases are now considered in greater detail.

3. Recording Classroom Talk

3.1 Naturalistic Recording and Its Problems

Classrooms are busy, noisy places with a great deal of movement and simultaneous talk. Some researchers have sought to reduce the technical problems of recording by interviewing individual students as they work, or by removing small groups to a quieter setting (see, for example, Barnes and Todd 1995). Readily audible recordings may then reveal important dimensions of individual performance without having much predictive power about normal classroom interaction. Technical developments have eased this problem. A radiomicrophone may be too costly to give to more than one participant, usually the teacher, while a single static microphone misses too much of the action. More affordable pocket-size individual recorders now allow the researcher to focus upon several individuals at once and on the evolving contexts of their talk.

It is likely that researchers with predominantly sociolinguistic or pedagogic interests will want to record normally occurring talk. And at least in comparison with such daunting alternatives as the playground, classrooms have seemed a manageable setting because so much of the talk is under the strategic direction of its most powerful participant. Where talk occurs without the teacher being present (e.g., in a small-group setting), it can still be stopped or redirected by the teacher, and its course is usually set or constrained by the teacher's agenda for the class. Moreover, where the teaching is of a more traditionally transmissional style, or where any teacher is conducting whole-class, even whole-class interactive, teaching, even temporarily so, the resulting talk presents a somewhat simplified aspect for analysis as well as for recording. Indeed, it is possible that the greater ease with which recordings can be made in such circumstances may partly explain the common researchers' view that classroom talk is excessively teacher-dominated. While the persistent pedagogical difficulties of affording students more communicative space, or of encouraging their exploratory talk, continue to exercise the minds of researchers and teachers alike, it may be that forms of classroom talk which are not teacher led are simply underrepresented in the literature because of the relative difficulty of recording them.

3.2 The 'Observer's Paradox'

A major problem of validity has been acknowledged by sociolinguists since the outset of their endeavors, namely the effects of observation on the activity being observed. Since eavesdropping is unethical, the problem can never be more than partially solved. Researchers must therefore do their ingenious best to limit the interference caused by their presence, whether by becoming accepted as a familiar non-participating observer or by adopting some appropriate auxiliary role where this does not distort the 'natural' situation unduly (see *Observer's Paradox*).

The size and obtrusiveness of the recording equipment may pose obvious problems. Although video recording no longer necessarily requires special lighting, the movements of the filmer can still be conspicuous. By comparison, what compact audio recorders lack in capacity to catch nonverbal or contextual detail, they can more than make up for in simplicity of operation, flexibility of use, and accuracy of sound track. Field notes can add important complementary data if the observer's presence is not resented. In any event, teachers and pupils can usually vouch for the normality or otherwise of events, for their awareness of disruption, and for their feelings about being recorded. Such further data are helpful in estimating how intrusive the researcher has been.

A comparable problem concerns the typicality of any particular setting in which recordings are made. It is axiomatic that any stretch of talk can only be understood in relation to its context. By the same token, questions arise about the extent to which stretches of talk may be so context specific as to be of limited general relevance. Revealing typical structures of classroom communication across various settings is a common research ambition. Alternatively, detailed studies of particular classrooms may be valued for the questions and hypotheses which they generate about other settings and for demonstrating methods of investigation which can be used elsewhere.

4. Transcribing and Analyzing Classroom Talk

4.1 Taking Account of Context

Practices and problems in making classroom recordings have their parallels at the transcription phase. In particular, researchers' working conceptions of 'context' influence their decisions about what to transcribe and how to select different kinds of data for analysis. The customary distinction between 'setting' and 'context' makes the point clear. The former term applies to location and to other 'givens' at the onset of the talk; the latter expresses the complex and dynamic interplay of forces which speakers and hearers attend to (for example, their perception of each other and of the way their utterances, gestures, hesitations, etc., are received) as the talk proceeds. In this sense, a context is talked into existence and evolves. Thus researchers' assumptions and beliefs about what is potentially 'alive' in the contexts they study can be seen to inform their collection and use of data, and partly to determine how far they wish to go in including markers of paralinguistic, nonverbal, or prosodic features rather than relying on a simple transcription of the words.

The rich redundancy of contextual meanings available to the participants also raises difficult questions about how accessible these meanings are to a researcher lacking much of their background knowledge, and about the 'commonsense' understandings of what classrooms are like on which that researcher at least implicitly relies in making sense of what is said. These questions may extend to the researcher's subsequent reliance on the reader's knowledge of classrooms to let the words exchanged by teacher and students 'speak for themselves.' They may entail some reference to 'respondent validation,' the confirmation of an account by the participants themselves (see Mehan 1979). Or, working in a different methodological tradition, the researcher may seek relatively unambiguous 'hard' indicators of meaning in, for example, the speakers' hesitations and pauses, intonation, or apparent vulnerability to interruption (see *Observer's Paradox*).

4.2 Varieties of Transcription and Analysis

Different approaches to context will now be illustrated through transcript extracts which supply varying amounts of information around the words, and so lend themselves to different forms of analysis. The order in which they are presented reflects a continuum already described: from research which assumes that a verbal record can offer a relatively unproblematical 'window' on to events, through to studies which are more oriented towards exploration of linguistic patterning.

Underlying example (2) is the view that specific accounts of classroom talk are essentially illustrative. Their credibility, like that of commentaries made upon them, derives from professional experience shared between researcher and reader. It is assumed that a plain verbal record will be 'recognized' for what it is by those who possess the relevant situational competence. Little technical sophistication is required of such transcription; here not even pausing is indicated. Interest in the passage is mainly pedagogic, to do with the conflicting views of a pupil and her teacher. The commentator (Mercer 1995) provides some preliminary information concerning the setting: a 15-year-old pupil talking with her class tutor about recent work experience in an elderly persons' social club attached to the school. Assuming that the transcript speaks for itself, he concludes (p. 51) that 'Donna is clearly rejecting her teacher's attempt to "educationalize" her work experience, to treat it as a resource for conventional educational achievement.'

Teacher	Well, you've been working now, you've been going to the frail elderly, helping them for nearly half a term now haven't you?	(1)
Donna	Yeh.	
Teacher	So I was wondering about whether you might think now might perhaps be a good time to start to write something down about it.	
Donna	Don't know, it would make it seem more like work than fun, wouldn't it? Make it more like a normal schoolday, because I enjoy it so much.	
Teacher	But for your final folder, for social sciences, it would make a really good project wouldn't it? It would look pretty good in the folder if you could put something together like that.	
Donna	I think it would change my attitude while I was there. It'd feel like I was interviewing them or something.	

The transcription conventions here are broadly literary in character; like those of a play-script but with more open punctuation. This makes the transcript easy to read, but may lose information which the participants themselves used in interpreting what was said. It therefore carries the risk of making the talk seem simpler than it was. It is therefore more usual practice to combine such everyday features as capital letters and full stops (periods) with a range of symbols specific to the technical requirements of sociolinguistic research.

There are variations within this range, but some of those commonly used are found in (2) as follows:

(...)	Words undeciphered	(2)
:	Discourse omitted as irrelevant to the issue discussed	
/	Pause of less than 2 seconds	
//	Pause of more than 2 seconds	
bold	Emphatic speech	
[	Simultaneous or interrupted speech	
(&)	Continuing speech, separated in the transcript by an interrupting speaker	

These are the conventions used by Edwards and Mercer (1987: ix–x), who describe their research purposes as being:

> ...not to produce an analysis of linguistic structure, but to provide the sort of information that is useful in analyzing how people reach common understanding with each other of what they are talking about.
>
> (Edwards and Mercer 1987: ix)

Pauses, interruptions, and the emphasizing of particular words are all well-suited to such a purpose. Indeed they can constitute valuable data for understanding various aspects of classroom talk. Whole-class teaching, for instance, tends to be fast-paced partly because teachers see pauses as entailing risks to their control of turn-taking. In a setting where teachers normally own exclusive rights over the allocation of turns at talk, interruptions are similarly exceptional. Indeed, just-perceptible pausing on the part of the teacher, in conjunction with other subtle changes of cadence and postural shifts, can function to signal a topic-boundary or a moment at which interruption becomes permissible (see Cazden (1998: 9–10) for a similar attention to pauses). Word-emphasis may also take on significance for conveying value attached to a technical term, or for identifying metastatements designed to encapsulate established knowledge. Such data can be seen to interact powerfully with pragmatic information, as in the extract (3) which comes from the first of a sequence of lessons on pendulums video-recorded in a class of 10- and 11-year-olds (see Edwards and Mercer 1987: 137–38). During this talk, the pauses appear to mark the speakers' reflection on what is being said, while the simultaneous utterances reflect their urgency. Moreover, a rhyming couplet—'The shorter the string, the faster the swing'—is given weight by the teacher is an important summarizing formula. This extract has to be lengthy because it also demonstrates the tying of meanings over extended sequences of talk.

Observing and Analyzing Classroom Talk

Participants in talk may also rely heavily upon intonation to remove ambiguities in what they hear. Towards the more linguistic end of the theoretical continuum are found researchers who, in recognition of this fact, attempt to set down on paper all those perceptual cues that participants rely on in their on-line processing (Gumperz and Berenz 1993: 92). Notable among them are Wells and his associates, whose detailed description of language development from infancy through the early years of schooling included a range of prosodic features (see Wells 1985; also *Conversation Analysis*; *Discourse*).

The database for this project came from recordings using radio-microphones, talk being sampled by means of a time-switching device which functioned without speakers being aware of it. Insight into the processes whereby growth in structural and semantic control is 'negotiated' through interactive talk depended upon close scrutiny of the children's discourse and of the meanings exchanged. Transcripts were thus heavily analytical and noted a wealth of prosodic detail as well as text and pragmatics. The absence of such features in transcriptions of classroom interaction reflects difficulties posed by the greater complexity of such contexts. This is why it is a parent–child exchange (4) which is now used to illustrate the most technically detailed form of notation (Wells 1985: 38). J is playing with the laundry as her mother washes up. The transcript displays the talk in separate columns: J's on the left, her mother's in the middle, with pragmatic notes on the right.

Although space prohibits reproduction of these transcription conventions in full, they are set out here in enough detail to raise questions about what would be gained in classroom transcriptions if similar information were included. The double-slash symbol (//) here marks the beginning or end of a 'tone-unit,' which itself may coincide with all or part of an utterance. Each tone-unit is numbered for ease of reference here, though numbering of utterances is a more common practice. A preliminary stress mark is used to denote both a prominent and a tonic syllable. Both types of syllable may also be shown in CAPS, being then preceded by two digits (1 to 5) each of which denotes a 'band' of pitch. The figure 1 marks a high, and 5 a low, pitch in relation to that speaker's normal range. Together, the two digits thus indicate the height, the direction, and the extent of pitch change for that element of the tone-unit. Upward or downward arrows show a pitch to be high or low against what is normal for the speaker; a double arrow shows extra high or low variance. Increasing speed is marked by ('accel.'), while a digit between two pairs of dots gives the length of a pause in seconds. Lastly, the symbol (v) indicates that 'the preceding word was used as a vocative, to call or hold the attention of the addressee' (Wells 1985: 177 gives the complete coding system). These details make it possible to recapture, for example, the intensifying

T:	(...) point seven three. So the shorter the string/what? What happens when you shorten the string?	T looking with Antony at his matrix of recorded timings. (3)
Antony:	The faster it gets.	
T:	The shorter the string, the faster the swing. Right. That's good isn't it?	T raising head and voice in slow, formal enunciation of the principle
	Ask Jonathan how he went/with his.	T pointing towards Jonathan (off camera).
Sharon	God I don't understand really.　⌈ They're all/ different	Sharon looking at David and Antony's matrix, speaking quietly.
T:	⌊ They're all different. So theirs is the only pendulum that's/ makes a ⌈ difference	
David:	⌊ It's just the string really.	
T:	So you don't think it's the pendulum.	
David:	It's just the string.	David gestures a string.
T:	It's the length of the ⌈ string mm (&)	T nodding. (Did David mean length?)
David:	⌊ length of the string.	
T:	(&)so that's very ⌈ interesting isn't it?	
Lucy	⌊ Say if the string's/ erm/shorter it'll go faster.	
T:	Yes.	
David:	Yeh.	
T:	We made up a little rhyme didn't we. What did we say?// The shorter	
David:	The shorter the swing. ⌈ the string the faster	T, Antony, and David recite together.
Antony and T:	the swing ⌊ the string the faster	

807

```
1  //24→LAUNdry' bag//                          [J has the laundry bag]         (4)
2  //35→LAUNdry' bag//
3  //In 14 THERE//
4  //↑' Put all THINGS in//                     [J is putting washing in the bag]
5  //↓I'm' putting 35 THINGS in//
6                                //24 NO 53 DARling (v)//
7                                //' No↑' no ↑↑ no 15 NO//
                                 ('accel.')
                                 ..4..
8  // ↓' I want to ↑↑' put those 12 THINGS//('accel.')
9                                //33 YES//
10                               //When' they're 24 WASHED
                                 you' can//
```

quality of J's mother's prohibitions which are revealed by the stress and fall–rise intonation in 6 and by the increasing speed and rising pitch of 7, with the downward sweep of its final 'no'. They also, of course, make the transcript very difficult to read.

A simpler system is briefly employed by Cazden (1998: 9), when she makes use of intonational data to identify a particular student strategy for avoiding potential interruption of an oral narrative by either teacher or peers. The strategy involves a 'sharing intonation' which is marked in the transcript by a rising arrow as, for example, (5):

> Well when I slept' over my mother's/
> the cat/
> in the middle of the night she w – /   (5)
> she went under the covers/

Some forms of analytical transcription pay more attention to the structuring of lessons treated as speech events than to prosodic detail. The pioneering work of Sinclair and Coulthard (see Coulthard 1992) drew on speech act theory to investigate how things are done with words in classrooms. By revealing organizational principles operating at the supra-sentential level, and so throwing light on how cohesion is achieved in spoken texts, their analysis proved effective in highlighting the special characteristics of teacher-led discourse. Their methodology proceeds by assigning stretches of talk, from utterance upwards, to various categories defined by function, from Act 'upwards' through Moves, Exchanges, and Transactions to the complete lesson (for a fuller commentary, see Edwards and Westgate 1994: chap. 6).

This form of analysis has proved seminal in demonstrating the extent of teachers' dominance over the marking of various boundaries within the lesson, their management of turn-taking, and their control over content. Thus Mehan's comprehensive 'grammar' of lessons included a detailed account of how students' developing competence in finding 'the seams in the essentially teacher-controlled discourse' enabled them to take occasional initiatives themselves (Mehan 1979: 139; see also Cazden 1988: 31–51). This is part of a wider competence required of students if they are to participate appropriately in classroom discourse and to adjust to the largely reactive roles assigned to them by transmissional teaching. Discourse analysis also permits some numerical measurement; Wells, for instance, has been able to quantify initiating and responding moves within his data on home and school settings. Such data have thus provided powerful leverage in opening up alternative pedagogic strategies, especially in promoting peer-to-peer exploratory talk which was the focus of much research in the early 1990s (Wells 1999).

Similar coding of talk arising in other than whole-class contexts may enable researches and teachers to evaluate the pedagogic effectiveness of small-group settings. An important dimension of that task concerns associated cognitive activity, which remains at best indirectly accessible to research. Interest however has already been shown in the additional coding of cognition, an influential example being that of Barnes and Todd (1995). They focused upon the interplay between a verbal transcript and a simultaneous commentary with 'interactional' and 'content' frames. At the level of performance, the talk was coded according to a set of 'discourse moves' (such as initiating, quantifying, contradicting, accepting) and a parallel set of 'logical processes' (to do with proposing a cause, categorizing, putting an alternative view, etc.); at a second, competence-related level, the two frames corresponded on the one hand to 'social skills' (such a supportive behavior), and on the other to 'cognitive strategies' (setting up hypothesis, using evidence, etc.) and 'reflexivity' (monitoring one's own speech and thought, showing awareness of strategies, etc.). Importantly, Barnes and Todd found the relationship between spoken language and processes of thought to be highly problematical: it certainly could not be handled on any one-to-one form–function basis. Their work had thus to retain that interpretational quality which can never be quite eradicated from even the most 'principled' and systematic of inquiries in this field. In this context, it will be interesting to follow the developing use of computers, not only as a stimulus to cooperative talk in class-rooms, but as a complementary tool for analyzing that talk (see Wegerif and Scrimshaw 1997).

4.3 Reporting Classroom Talk

At the reporting phase, similar considerations affect the amount and type of evidence to be displayed. Whether interpretation of recorded talk is considered to be self-evident to those who share the culture of the classroom, or whether the support of various transcriptional and analytical procedures is called upon, reporting has initially to be selective. Illustrative passages have to be chosen, and ways found of relating such extracts to the full range of data, so that readers can assess the validity of a given interpretation. However, even if (as Mehan insists) the entire data corpus is made potentially available for rescrutiny, problems persists concerning the extent and form of data to be provided. As at every other stage of classroom language research, there are no absolute solutions to these problems. The form of reporting adopted is similarly constrained by the form in which data were constituted, itself a response to the purposes of the research and the audience for which it is intended.

See also: Spoken Language in the Classroom; Conversation Analysis.

Bibliography

Barnes D, Todd F 1995 *Communication and Learning Revisited: Making Meaning Through Talk*. Boynton Cook, Portsmouth, NH
Bernstein B 1996 *Pedagogy, Symbolic Control and Identity: Theory, Research and Critique*. Taylor and Francis, London
Cazden C 1988 *Classroom Discourse: The Language of Teaching and Learning*. Heineman, Portsmouth, NH
Coulthard M (ed.) 1992 *Advances in Spoken Discourse Analysis*. Routledge, London and New York
Dillon J T 1994 *Using Discussion in Classrooms*. Open University Press, Buckingham, UK
Edwards A D, Westgate D P G 1994 *Investigating Classroom Talk*, 2nd edn. Falmer Press, London
Edwards D, Mercer N 1987 *Classroom Knowledge: The Development of Understanding in the Classroom*. Methuen, London
Galton M, Hargreaves L, Comber C, Wall D, Pell T 1999. Changes in patterns of teacher interaction in primary classrooms: 1976–96. *British Educational Research Journal* 25(1): 23–37
Gumperz J J, Berenz N 1993 Transcribing conversational exchanges. In: Edwards J A, Lampert M (eds.) *Talking Data: Transcription and Coding in Discourse Research*. Lawrence Erlbaum, Hillsdale, NJ
Heath S B 1983 *Ways With Words: Language, Life and Work in Communities and Classrooms*. Cambridge University Press, Cambridge, UK
Mehan H 1979 *Learning Lessons*. Harvard University Press, Cambridge, MA
Mercer N 1995 *The Guided Construction of Knowledge: Talk Amongst Teachers and Learners*. Multilingual Matters, Clevedon, UK
Stubbs M 1983 *Discourse Analysis: The Sociolinguistic Analysis of Natural Language*. Blackwell, Oxford, UK
Wegerif R, Scrimshaw P 1997 *Computers and Talk in the Primary Classroom*. Multilingual Matters, Clevedon, UK
Wells G 1985 *Language, Learning and Education*. NFER-Nelson, Windsor, UK
Wells G 1999 *Dialogic Inquiry: Towards a Sociocultural Practice and Theory of Education*. Cambridge University Press, Cambridge, UK

Reliability/Validity

E. Babbie

In social research, reliability and validity are two criteria for judging the quality of measurements. 'Validity' refers to whether the measurement technique captures the intended meaning of the variable. 'Reliability' refers to the dependability of the technique.

1. Measurement and Concepts

Measurement is a central issue in social research. Both description and explanation depend on the researcher's ability to devise and execute procedures for observing and classifying those observations in terms of variables. More specifically, this task involves the classifying of those being observed in terms of the 'attributes' comprising the 'variables' under study.

In a simple example, the gender of respondents might be measured in a survey: that is, each respondent would be identified with one of the attributes—male or female—comprising the variable, gender. The procedure for accomplishing this would be straightforward, perhaps by asking respondents to check one of two boxes: [ ] Male, [ ] Female. Because this item taps what is generally meant by the term 'gender,' it is probably a valid measure, and as such would be expected to be reliable as well.

To distinguish between validity and reliability further, consider this illustration. Imagine stepping on a bathroom scale that registered a weight of 130 pounds. Now imagine stepping repeatedly on the same scale, with the following results: 115, 140, 120, 190, etc. That scale would be judged an unreliable measuring device. By contrast, if it faithfully reported 130 every time the same person stepped on it, it would be judged reliable. Notice, however, that the scale's reliability does not guarantee its validity. If the person really weighed 110 or 210 pounds, the scale would be judged reliable but invalid.

The issues of reliability and validity apply to all social research measures. Unfortunately, most variables of interest are not as tidy as weight and gender, and thus the nature of social research variables must be examined. Most of the variables of interest to linguistics are themselves linguistic, for example, the various ways a word may be pronounced by different speakers, but many other variables may be associated with variations in language and thus be important for sociolinguistic studies.

All variables begin as 'concepts': ideas that represent experiences and thinking. Some common social science concepts would include social class, bureaucracy, alienation, kinship. Variables are concepts comprised of sets of mutually exhaustive attributes or characteristics. Thus, reviewing the list of concepts just presented, social class is a variable: comprised of attributes such as lower class, middle class, and upper class.

Bureaucracy is *not* a variable, however. It could, though, be seen as one of the attributes comprising Max Weber's variable, 'forms of social organization' (the other attributes being 'charismatic' and 'traditional').

Alienation is a variable, comprised of attributes such as low, medium, and high. Finally, kinship is not a variable per se, though 'type of kinship system' could be a variable used to describe societies; the attributes might include: patrilineal, matrilineal, egalitarian, for example.

From this perspective, measurement is a matter of identifying units of analysis with the attributes comprising the variables under study. In a linguistic survey of Canada, it might be required to measure the variable, 'language used at home,' with the attributes of that variable being 'English,' 'French,' and other languages.

The examples given above should illustrate that variables are constructed by the researcher rather than existing in nature. Consider the example of 'social class.' Though it might be comprised of the attributes, lower class, middle class, and upper class, this structure might be inappropriate to some research purposes. W. Lloyd Warner, in his examination of 'Jonesville,' distinguished lower-lower, upper-lower, lower-middle, upper-middle, lower-upper, and upper-upper classes. A Marxist analysis, on the other hand, might require attributes such as proletariat, bourgeoisie, etc.

The process of specifying the nature of variables prior to measurement is called 'conceptualization.' Choices are made among options and ambiguities are clarified.

'Operationalization,' the next step in this process, specifies the concrete procedures (operations) that will result in measurements of the variable in question. The statement of precisely how a variable will be measured and what observations will correspond to specific attributes on that variable is called the 'operational definition' of the variable.

Thus, in a survey of college students, the variable, grade point average, might be measured by asking respondents to answer the question: 'Approximately what was your grade point average as of the end of last term?' Or, alternatively, the researchers might be able to extract grade point averages from the registrar's files and add that information to the data collected by the questionnaire. The operational definition, in the latter instance, would be 'the grade point average recorded in the Registrar's student files.'

It is the operational definition of a variable—specifying what observations will be made and how those observations will be converted into attributes of the variable in question—that can be evaluated in terms of its validity and reliability. There are several aspects of each.

2. Validity

The validity of a measurement refers to the extent to which it measures what the researcher intends, or whether it actually measures something else. Asking students to report their own grade point averages, for example, might be criticized as possibly measuring what the respondents would like the researcher to think about them more than their actual scholastic achievement.

There is a basic, philosophical issue to be acknowledged before proceeding with this evaluation, however. Virtually all the variables studied by social scientists reflect concepts which were products of the mind. Their meanings are ultimately only what people agree they are. 'Social class,' for example, does not exist in nature, but only as a concept created for the purpose of organizing a set of observations regarding differential wealth, power, prestige, etc. Therefore the question of whether a particular operational definition of a variable really measures that variable rests on agreement as to the meaning of the variable in the first place, and people often differ in their use of such terms. This caveat notwithstanding, there are useful grounds upon which to judge the validity of measurements.

2.1 Face Validity

Despite some disagreements as to the meanings of concepts, there has to be some level of agreement or else people could not communicate through the use of the terms that refer to those concepts. 'Face validity' refers to the extent of agreement between a measurement and the common consensus as to what the concept in question means. Thus, despite disagreements regarding the meaning of social class, few would deny the relevance of measuring annual income in that context.

It is worth noting that annual income is an imperfect measure of social class, even of wealth. Someone with a trillion dollars in their home safe yet earning no annual income is undeniably wealthy. Or conversely, imagine someone with a substantial income but even more substantial debts: such a person might be bankrupt on balance. Still, annual income has face validity as a measure of social class, whereas a measure of, say, height would not: being able to see over other people's heads is not what is commonly meant by 'upper class.'

2.2 Criterion-related Validity

Another standard of validity involves its predictive power. Often, variables are measured in order to estimate some future behavior. Thus, a test of 'marital compatibility' might be devised in the hope of predicting whether prospective marriages would be successful or not. A study examining the extent to which the test actually correlated with the subsequent success or failure of marriages would provide a standard by which to evaluate the adequacy of the test.

Other examples where 'criterion-related validity' might easily apply could include college entrance exams as predictors of college performance, drivers' tests as predictors of driver safety, measures of political attitudes as predictors of voting behavior, etc.

2.3 Content Validity

Given that social science variables typically reference a diversity of meanings, the measurement of a variable can also be judged on the extent to which it successfully captures the different aspects of that variable.

Thus, for example, Charles Glock (1965) delineated five major dimensions of 'religiosity': belief, ritual, cognitive (knowledge), experiential, and consequential (the impact of religion in a person's life). It would be reasonable to ask, therefore, which dimensions were tapped by a particular measurement of religiosity. If a measure of religiosity that used only church attendance and praying before meals was constructed, that measurement technique could be reasonably criticized as omitting several meanings commonly associated with the term. Of course, it might be appropriate to limit the measurement, in terms of the aims of the particular study; in such a situation, it might be wiser to relabel the measurement as 'religious ritual.'

By the same token, it might be asked whether a particular measure of 'prejudice' focuses on prejudice against one or a few groups or somehow captures the idea of prejudice in general. Measures of liberalism and conservatism may tap only domestic or foreign-policy dimensions or both; similarly, liberalism and conservatism can refer strictly to politics or to morality, lifestyle, and other social issues. As a criterion of quality, content validity asks that the label assigned to a measurement cover whatever breadth of meaning is commonly associated with that term.

2.4 Construct Validity

'Construct validity' refers to how well the measurement of a particular variable articulates the place of that variable within a network of causal relationships with other variables. Whereas criterion-related validity tests the extent to which a measurement relates to other measures of the variable in question, construct validity is a matter of the measurement relating to measurements of other variables as expected on logical, theoretical grounds.

Thus, for example, a measure of alienation might be developed, based on answers to a number of questionnaire items. On theoretical grounds, there may be a number of expectations about alienated people: they might be less likely to vote, less likely to marry, and more likely to contemplate suicide than would be the case for less alienated people.

It would be reasonable to expect therefore that the measure of alienation would be negatively correlated with voting and marrying and positively correlated with reports of contemplated suicide. The failure of any one of these correlations should give cause for questioning the validity of the theoretical expectations; the failure of all should also call into question the construct validity of the measure itself.

3. Reliability

Whereas validity is a matter of measuring what it is said is being measured, reliability merely asks whether the measuring has been carried out dependably. The basic metaphor for reliability is repeated measurements of the same thing—with the same result produced each time, for example, earlier in this article the example of the same bathroom scale repeatedly, getting the same weight each time was discussed.

Unfortunately, many social science measurements do not lend themselves to such straightforward reliability testing. In a survey, for example, the same question cannot be asked repeatedly. And even if it could be, the respondent would remember his or her earlier answer and simply give it again.

Despite these difficulties, there are techniques that provide tests of reliability in social research.

3.1 Test–Retest Method

Having said that the same question cannot be asked repeatedly of the same respondent, it is nonetheless sometimes possible to repeat questions to a more limited extent. In a lengthy questionnaire, for example, it might be possible to ask the same question in different locations without drawing the respondent's attention to what is being done.

In studies that involve data collection at more than one point in time, the same question can be asked at different times, allowing an evaluation of the consistency of responses. This practice sometimes produces surprising results, however.

When Sacks and Krushat (1980) asked many of the same health and demographic questions in two surveys, three months apart, they found that only 15 percent of the respondents gave exactly the same answers. Whereas all subjects were presumably three months older, one seemed to have become five years younger. One respondent's mother aged 20 years in three months. One woman reported a missing ovary in the first survey but had evidently found it by the time of the second survey.

3.2 Split–Half Method

The test–retest method can be approximated through a somewhat different technique, if the researcher has several indicators of the variable in question. If the several indicators offer *valid* measures of the variable, then they should be correlated highly with each other. Whether they do so in fact can be taken as a test of reliability.

To give a simple example, suppose it is required to measure how 'fat' respondents are: how wide they are in relation to their height. As measures of their width, they could be asked to report the size of their waists, chests, thighs, forearms, necks, and hips. It seems obvious that any of these measures, in relation to height, offers a valid measure of how fat respondents are. In practice, however, the reports might not correlate as well as would be expected, due to the fact that people may be aware of their waistline measurements but not know the other measurements. Many of their reports, then would be estimates of less than perfect reliability.

In testing the reliability of social science indicators, the several indicators might be randomly assigned to two subsets: each providing a valid measure of the variable. All the indicators would be included in a single questionnaire. Each set of indicators would then be used to classify respondents in terms of the variable, and the two classifications would be correlated.

3.3 Standardized Measures

Since science is a cumulative enterprise, with current research growing out of and beyond the past, it is sometimes possible to choose measures that have been developed, tested, and generally accepted as reliable measures of particular variables. The US Census Bureau, for example, has established numerous definitions and measurement techniques addressing a number of demographic concepts. In addition to profiting from previous reliability testing, it is possible to compare findings with those of other studies using the same measures.

Many measures are standardized informally, by the weight of repetition among researchers addressing a particular concept. The Srole Anomia Scale is an example of this.

3.4 Coder Reliability

The question of reliability is not limited to asking questions and getting answers from respondents. Sometimes the measurement process includes the coding of textual materials, such as answers given to open-ended questions (e.g., 'What do you consider the biggest problems facing the nation today?'). To support quantitative data analysis, such answers must be converted to standardized code categories (e.g., 'crime,' 'pollution,' 'recession,' etc.). This process has two stages: (a) establishing the set of appropriate codes and (b) actually assigning textual responses (e.g., 'It's not safe to walk the streets anymore') to the appropriate code category (e.g., 'crime').

The coding of textual materials involves subjective judgments on the part of the coder(s). When more than one person does the coding, there is a danger that they will have somewhat different interpretations of the code categories and will not make comparable assignments. The easiest method for checking against this possibility is to select some subset of the materials (40 or 50 questions, for example) and have all the coders process the selected materials. You can then determine the 'intercoder reliability.'

Even if all the coding was done by one person, it would be good practice to recode some of the materials, after a suitable passage of time, to see if the interpretation is consistent.

4. Tension Between Reliability and Validity

The best measurements are those ranking high in both validity and reliability. It is worth noting in conclusion, however, that a certain tension exists between the two qualities. Increasing one often reduces the other.

Imagine a study with the aim of classifying people in terms of their religiousness. A fairly reliable measure would be represented by asking the question, 'How many times, if any, did you attend worship services during the past week?' The number of times reported would then constitute a scale of religiousness. Names might even be given to levels on the scale: 'extremely religious' for attending worship services seven or more times during the week, 'very religious' for 2 to 6 times, 'religious' for attending once, etc.

The above measure is probably a *reliable* one in that people should be able to recall accurately how many times they attended worship services during the past week. Its *validity* is subject to question, however, since attendance at worship services is only a small part of what would normally be meant by the term 'religiousness.' Moreover, one can think of reasons why a 'truly religious' person might not have attended worship services (e.g., hospitalized that week) or why nonreligious people might have attended (e.g., brought unwillingly by an insistent spouse or parents).

A more valid approach might involve unstructured, hour-long conversations with respondents, probing their beliefs about supernatural matters, their support of religious institutions, a wide range of religious practices, feelings, and behaviors regarding moral/ethical matters, etc. By the end of each interview, the researcher might be confident about gauging how religious that person really was. In any event, the interviewer would feel more confident of the judgment than if the only information available was the answers people gave to the simple question about worship services.

While the latter approach can offer more validity, it comes at a price in terms of reliability. Different interviewers, for example, might judge the same respondent differently. A respondent's inability to express complex ideas and feelings might lead to an inaccurate assessment. Many other factors conspire to make this more valid measurement technique potentially a less reliable one.

The solution to this dilemma is to use a variety of measurement techniques—varying in validity and reliability—whenever possible. These several indicators of a variable can be compared and perhaps combined in the analysis.

See also: Scaling; Social Class; Sociology of Language.

Bibliography
Babbie E 1989 *The Practice of Social Research*. Wadsworth, Belmont, CA
Burgess R 1986 *Key Variables in Social Investigation*. Routledge and Kegan Paul, London
Carmines E G, Zeller R A 1979 *Reliability and Validity Assessment*. Sage, Beverly Hills, CA
Miller D 1983 *Handbook of Research Design and Social Measurement*. Longman, New York
Sacks J, Krushat W M 1980 Reliability of the health hazard appraisal. *American Journal of Public Health* July: 730–32
Veltman C 1986 The interpretation of the language questions of the Canadian census. *Review of Canadian Sociology and Anthropology* **23**(3)

Salvage Work (Endangered Languages)
N. C. Dorian

1. Introduction
Linguistic salvage work deals, by definition, with endangered languages. The term itself indicates that the state of the language in question allows only limited opportunity to achieve a degree of documentation, that is, to 'salvage' some record of the structure of a distinctive language or dialect. General descriptive documentation goals are neatly summed up under the GDT acronym: a *g*rammar, a *d*ictionary, and a collection of *t*exts are considered (assuming a conscientious and competent researcher) to represent a language reasonably adequately in terms of the scholarly record. Sociolinguistic or anthropological linguistic documentation goals usually include, at a minimum, some account of the circumstances (in historical, political, social, and economic terms) which have made the speech variety in question precarious enough to call for salvage work.

2. Salvage Work in Descriptive Linguistics
Within descriptive linguistics a sense of the urgent need for salvage work emerged strongly, if belatedly, in areas of European settlement where indigenous peoples had been brought close to extinction by settlers' profoundly negative impact on indigenous health and subsistence modes. Many such areas were inhabited by a variety of distinctive peoples with small populations highly vulnerable to settlement pressures. Earliest settlement areas within a region suffered the worst losses (e.g., coastal eastern North America, coastal southeastern Australia). Recognition of the losses gave impetus to extensive fieldwork efforts on the part of linguistic fieldworkers. Locating last speakers of Native American languages and recording what he could of their languages occupied the American field linguist John Peabody Harrington (1884–1961) for an entire professional lifetime, for example. Few linguists have documented as many endangered languages as Harrington did, but some contemporary scholars have devoted years to documenting a variety of threatened languages in a region or a country, as have Bernd Heine in eastern Africa and R. M. W. Dixon in Australia.

3. The Evaluation Problem in Salvage Work

After locating speakers willing to serve as sources for an endangered language and beginning work, fieldworkers often face problems in evaluating the material obtained. If several speakers are available, their versions of traditional stories or their individual responses to questions can be compared, with some likelihood of identifying one or two speakers whose usage is particularly intact or conservative. If only one speaker is available, or only one proves healthy or receptive enough to take on the role of language consultant, the researcher necessarily falls back on more indirect indications of proficiency. Material gathered previously by another linguist working on the same language may provide a comparison with a current speaker's materials, though the value of this approach depends on the reliability of the predecessor's records and the proficiency and forthcomingness, in turn, of the source(s) on which he relied. In some cases there may be closely related speech forms with which the materials from the language under study can be compared. Apparent fluency is not necessarily a good indicator of an individual's usefulness as a native-speaker source. Long disuse of the language or reticence with strangers may make a proficient source hesitant in manner, while a desire to appear knowledgeable may cause an individual with very incomplete knowledge to adopt a manner of expertise and certainty. In particularly fortunate cases final speakers, who have not used their ancestral language for a long time, may begin work with poor recall but gain confidence and regain a measure of proficiency as work proceeds.

Even when final speakers prove thoroughly fluent, if no community of speakers making fairly regular use of the language remains, there is good reason to be cautious about the material obtained. The seasoned American fieldworker Mary Haas worked for example with an apparently fully fluent last speaker of the Native American language Tunica, but she took the material that she gathered from him to be only a remnant of what Tunica would have been like when it was the everyday means of communication for a community of speakers. The reasonable assumption behind her caution is that peoples' command and deployment of language resources is fundamentally social in nature and consequently maintains its full richness only in an interactive social context.

4. Sociolinguistic and Anthropological Linguistic Salvage Work

The methods and concerns of salvage work differ considerably according to whether the linguist undertaking the work has objectives primarily of a descriptive, typological, or historical sort or has, instead or as well, objectives of a sociolinguistic or anthropological linguistic sort. Descriptivists, typologists, and historical linguists work largely without reference to social context, whereas sociolinguists and anthropological linguists consider such a context an important element in their research.

4.1 Investigating Social Setting: Interplay of Language Ideologies and Language Behaviors

Anthropological linguist Lukas Tsitsipis studied imperfect renditions of the receding language Arvanitika, a form of Albanian enclaved in Greece for some 500 years, produced by terminal speakers in two communities. He found that these imperfect speakers tended to interrupt the Arvanitika narratives of older and more fluent speakers, often inserting oddly incongruent Arvanitika material such as list-like word sets or contextually inappropriate high-frequency formulaic phrases into their elders' narratives. Although it was true that the terminal speakers were not fully fluent in Arvanitika, focus on ideological and pragmatic features of the language setting revealed that it was not so much their lower proficiency as their ideological differences from their elders that led to the incoherent-seeming interruptions. In consciously disrupting fluent Arvanitika narratives, the imperfect younger speakers were reacting to the ideological and functional subordination of Arvanitika to Greek, and also to the political subordination of the Arvanitika speech communities to the surrounding Greek world. The terminal speakers had accepted a pragmatic worldview in which Greek was highly valued and Arvanitika was not, and their interruptions served to distance them both from the conservative worldview of older people who continued to use Arvanitika regularly and from the older speakers' linguistically subordinate position relative to Greek.

Tsitsipis' study of the way in which language ideology affected language use is a good example of the insistence on monitoring the interplay of language behavior and social context that informs sociolinguistic and anthropological linguistic salvage work. The process of shift from Arvanitika to Greek among younger people in the Arvanitika communities was reflected not just in the terminal speakers' lesser control of Arvanitika grammar, but also in the way they actively used what they knew of Arvanitika to disrupt the fluent language performance of their elders. Language ideology and cultural values are often implicated in choices about language transmission and acquisition, and therefore also in language maintenance and shift processes quite generally. In one village setting in Papua New Guinea, where the ancestral language had come to be associated in speakers' minds with childish, womanish, and heathenish ways, careful observational research indicated that parents were unconsciously promoting their children's acquisition of the nationally current language Tok Pisin and discouraging the acquisition of the local vernacular, Taiap, even though those same parents claimed to be surprised and disappointed that their children were not speaking their own ancestral language (Kulick 1992). Among the children and grandchildren of Gaelic-speaking fisherfolk in East Sutherland, Scotland, moving away from the home community for the sake of job opportunities often had the effect of increasing the symbolic value of the home language that the exiles had regularly heard and irregularly spoken in childhood. The experience of exile, combined in a good many cases with strong affective ties to older-generation kinfolk in the home villages, prompted a number of returned exiles to emerge as adult Gaelic speakers, imperfect in their control of Gaelic structure but loyal to the language beyond the degree usual for their age-group (Dorian 1981) (see *Language Maintenance, Shift, and Death*).

4.2 Investigating the Deployment of Linguistic Contact Phenomena in Endangered Languages

Changes in the phonological and grammatical structure of languages passing out of use are of interest to linguists for the light that they throw on processes of convergence, simplification, reduction, and outright loss during contact between languages. Apart from such matters, sociolinguists are interested in the way linguistic phenomena characteristic of language-contact settings are deployed, e.g., code-switches, borrowings, coexisting discourse markers, or cross-linguistically quoted speech. To take code-switches as an example, switches have been found to have quite various motivations. Low proficiency on the part of a speaker can lead to code-switches, but so too can high proficiency when all parties to an interaction share knowledge of the same pair (or set) of languages. Furthermore, code-switching can be a useful social compromise when a speaker wishes to avoid identifying more strongly with one language than another or wishes to avoid the connotations that use of one or the other language might have among a particular group of people or in a particular setting. Community-wide attitudes towards code-switches can be equally diverse. Unremarkable in some speech communities or social networks, code-switches are strongly disapproved of in others. In endangered-language settings, an individual aware that she represents a rapidly receding language may self-consciously try to avoid code-switches in work with a language researcher. If switching nonetheless proves frequent, evaluation of this behavior may again be difficult, since comparisons across the usage of a community of speakers are needed in order to determine whether code-switches represent a widespread and commonplace practice or whether they are appearing only late in some speakers' lives as a product of disuse of the receding language.

4.3 Sociolinguistic Salvage Work and the Speaker Community

Descriptive salvage work can sometimes be undertaken with moderate success when there is only a single source to work with, or a few scattered and isolated sources, but this is scarcely possible with sociolinguistic salvage work. The issues mentioned above, together with other context-related issues (e.g., the relative importance of topic, domain, and interlocutor in code selection; the differentiation and interplay of identities associated with the languages in a multilingual's repertory), are directly investigatable only when at least a small community of speakers continues to use the receding language. Last speakers' memories can be consulted but are seldom completely reliable on such socially sensitive matters. Sociolinguistic salvage work therefore needs to be undertaken before language shift is so far advanced as to leave only scattered elderly members of the ethnic population as speakers. Furthermore, because social context and social behaviors are humanly complex, fieldwork of this sort calls for fairly extensive familiarity with the language setting and with speakers' language behaviors. Relatively long periods of residence in the speakers' community, repeated field trips, or both, are often entailed.

Scholars disagree sharply about what the linguist's role can or should be where endangered-language research is concerned. According to one school of thought, linguists are professionally competent to document language structures but should refrain from involvement in any programs the community is undertaking to support its own language, since this lies outside their competence. Another school of thought contends that linguists assume obligations when they do research based entirely on other people's sharing of their knowledge, and that honoring such obligations makes it incumbent on linguists to acquire the skills necessary to honor community requests for language-related assistance, e.g., by producing teaching texts or user-friendly dictionaries.

See also: Anthropological Linguistics; Code-switching: Overview; Endangered Languages; Contact Languages; Language Maintenance, Shift, and Death; Reversing Language Shift.

Bibliography

Craig C G 1997 Language contact and language degeneration. In: Coulmas, F (ed.) *The Handbook of Sociolinguistics*. Blackwell, Oxford, UK

Dixon R M W 1984 *Searching for Aboriginal Languages: Memoirs of a Field Worker*. University of Queensland Press, St. Lucia, Qld

Dorian N C 1981 *Language Death: The Life Cycle of a Scottish Gaelic Dialect*. University of Pennsylvania Press, Philadelphia, PA

Dorian N C (ed.) 1989 *Investigating Obsolescence: Studies in Language Contraction and Death*. Cambridge University Press, Cambridge, UK

Grenoble L, Whaley L (eds.) 1998 *Endangered Languages: Current Issues and Future Prospects*. Cambridge University Press, Cambridge, UK

Kulick D 1992 *Language Shift and Cultural Reproduction*. Cambridge University Press, Cambridge, UK

Tsitsipis L D 1998 *A Linguistic Anthropology of Praxis and Language Shift: Arvanitika (Albanian) and Greek in Contact*. Clarendon Press, Oxford, UK

Scaling
E. Babbie

Throughout the social sciences, it often becomes necessary to measure a variable through a combination of several pieces of information, and a variety of techniques have been developed outside linguistics that can be employed profitably in language studies. First, sociolinguists need scaling techniques in order to measure the social variables they correlate with variations in language. Second, language variations themselves may often be measured most accurately through scales, rather than by relying upon single bits of data or upon intuitive summary judgments. Finally, scaling techniques rest on the linguistically interesting observation that people can seldom if ever express their attitudes validly and reliably in a single utterance, but need several utterances such as the answers to an entire set of survey questions.

1. The Logic of Composite Measures

It could be said that all social research is about the description and interrelating of variables. For example, Basil Bernstein's famous research related the variable of social class to speech codes; and other researchers have compared the speech of women with that of men. In either case, *measurement* is a fundamental element in social research: the classification of individuals (or other units of analysis) in terms of the relevant variables. Sometimes, measurement is relatively simple and straightforward, as in the case of gender, which can be determined readily through a single question. Many of the variables that interest social researchers, such as social class, authoritarianism, alienation, prejudice are not so simply measured. Such variables call for a more sophisticated measurement strategy.

In those cases where no single piece of information will represent the meaning of a complex variable *reliably* and *validly*, the solution is to construct a measure from several independent pieces of information. This is especially appropriate when the purpose is to measure a variable comprised of several attributes, representing different levels of intensity of degree. Thus, prejudice might be represented by the attributes: Extremely Prejudiced, Very Prejudiced, Somewhat Prejudiced, Slightly Prejudiced, Unprejudiced. Or, intelligence, is sometimes represented by the scores of an IQ test: 100, 101, 102, 103, etc.

The construction of composite measures is based on two assumptions: (a) that the theoretical variable under study actually represents a dimension of variation among people and (b) that there are numerous indicators of that variation. In the case of prejudice, for example, it is assumed that some people are more prejudiced, in general, than others and that there are several pieces of information attainable about people that offer clues as to how prejudiced they are.

The first assumption should not be accepted as obvious. It is not necessarily the case that those prejudiced against Jews, for example, would also be prejudiced against Blacks, against women, or, particularly, prejudiced against Arabs. Variations in prejudice against Jews, then, may occur more consistently than variations in prejudice in general. Thus, if it can be said with greater certainty that Person X is more prejudiced than person Y then one can say that Person X is more prejudiced than person Y in general.

Once the assumption is made that people do vary on the variable under study, it can be assumed further that there are several indicators of that variation. Agreeing with the statement that 'Jews tend to cheat in business' would be one indicator of antisemitism. Similarly, agreeing with the statement that 'Jews are clannish' would be another. Another possible indicator would be agreement with the statement that 'The Jews are God's Chosen People,' in this case, representing the *opposite* of antisemitism. Both positive and negative indicators of variables can be appropriate to composite measures.

There are several techniques for combining indicators into composite measures.

2. Simple Cumulative Indexes

The simplest method for creating a composite measure of a variable is to identify some list of indicators of that variable and give each subject a score equal to the number of those indicators that apply to them.

To measure levels of political activity among a sample of people possible indicators might include answers to the questions, asked in a survey questionnaire:

> 'Did you vote in the last election?'
> 'Have you ever contributed money to a political campaign?'
> 'Have you ever volunteered to work on a political campaign?'

Primarily, such indicators are selected on a *prima facie* basis, though it is often a good idea to test the empirical relationships among indicators. If voting and contributing money are both indicators of political activism, for example, it would be reasonable to expect that voters would be more likely to give money than would the nonvoters—and vice versa.

Having asked these three questions, subjects could be given one point for each 'yes' answer. The result would be a simple index ranging in scores from 0 (said 'no' to all three questions) to 3 (said 'yes' to all three).

In creating a measure such as this, the resulting index will be assumed to have the quality of *ordinality*: that those with scores of 3 are more politically active than those with scores of 2, who are more politically active than those with scores of 1, who, in turn, are more politically active than those with scores of 0.

Index scores could then be used for purposes of determining the relationship between political activism and other variables. To determine whether men or women were the more politically active, the average index scores for men and women could be calculated: if men had an average score of 2.5 and women had average scores of 1.0, it would be concluded that men were more active than women. (In lieu of such an index, comparison could be made of the percentages of men and women who vote, who have contributed money, and who have volunteered.)

Similarly, a composite index would allow the exploration of the consequences of political activism. Table 1 would suggest that politically active people are less likely to attend church than the politically less active.

Simple indexes like this one have two major weaknesses. First, the several indicators of a given variable often represent different levels of intensity. For example, volunteering to work on a political campaign seems a stronger indicator of political activism than simply voting. Yet in the simple index described above, all three indicators are treated equally. The scaling techniques to be discussed below take account of the differing intensities of indicators.

Second, while simple indexes usually represent *ordinal* measures of variables, some of the scales which will be examined seek to create *interval* measures: with equal increases of intensity separating the categories on the scale. In the political activism index above, for example, it is assumed that those with a score of 3 are more active than those scored 2; it cannot be assumed, however, that the *degree* of activism separating 3s from 2s is the same as that separating 2s from 1s and 1s from 0s. Some of the scaling techniques examined below seek to create equal-interval measures.

3. Bogardus Social Distance Scaling

E. S. Bogardus provides an excellent illustration of the different intensities represented by various indicators of a variable. Suppose that the degree to which people are willing to associate with ex-convicts is to be measured. Presumably some people would generally welcome ex-convicts back into society, perhaps feeling they had paid their debt to society, while others would be less forgiving and/or less trusting. This phenomenon is commonly referred to as the 'social distance' people desire with regard to ex-convicts.

A simple index of the social distance in this instance might be created by asking about relationships people would be willing to have with ex-convicts: buying shoes from them; sitting beside them on the subway, etc. We would simply add the number of such relationships a person would willingly accept.

It is possible, however, to create a list of relationships which, in themselves, represent differing social distances. Consider the following.

Would you be willing to have a convicted child-molester, who had served his time in prison and been released:

> ... live in your country?
> ... live in your city?
> ... live in your neighborhood?
> ... live on your block?
> ... live next door to you?
> ... marry into your immediate family?

Take a minute to answer these questions for yourself. How many did you answer 'yes.' If you answered 'yes' to at least one and fewer than all six, then you should be able to see an interesting pattern in your responses. If you said yes to only one, for example, it probably was the first one: letting the child-molester live in your country; if you said 'yes' to two, they were probably the first two items in the list. If you agreed to five of the six, on the other hand, you probably only objected to the last: marriage into your immediate family.

Table 1.

	Index of Political Activism			
	0	1	2	3
% who attended church during week ...	60	52	43	35

Imagine that these questions were asked among a sample of a thousand respondents. If each of them was assigned a score, representing the *number* of relationships agreed to, those numbers would also—in most if not all cases—reveal the answers given to each of the six questions. For example, the person with a score of 3 probably answered: yes, yes, yes, no, no, no. Such summary *scale scores*, then represent the relative *social distance* our respondents are willing to tolerate with convicted child-molesters. The same technique, of course, could be used to determine social distance with regard to groups based on religion, race, social class, nationality, etc.

The general principle illustrated in the Bogardus Social Distance Scale is that a set of attitudes may have a logical and/or empirical structure, which can be represented by a single number. This is the fundamental logic involved in all scaling.

The role of *pattern* is seen in the scoring of response patterns that seem illogical on their face. Suppose, a respondent was unwilling to let a convicted child-molester live in his or her country, city, neighborhood, block, and even next door—but agreed to have let one marry into the family. In terms of all but one of the indicators, the respondent appears to have extremely low tolerance for convicted child-molesters. Perhaps the respondent in question, however, has such an ideological commitment to letting one's children marry who they want that he or she would grimace and agree to letting the child-molester marry into the family. That response, then, would not represent tolerance toward child-molesters as much as commitment to freedom in mate-selection. In such a case, scoring the person 0 points—for no tolerance—rather than one point would seem a more accurate portrayal of their level of tolerance.

The Bogardus Social Distance scale has the quality of *ordinality*: a score of 2 represents more tolerance than a score of 1, and a score of 3 represents more tolerance than a score of 2. Ordinality is one goal of any index or scale, and the Bogardus Social Distance scale virtually assures the quality of ordinality.

Another goal—more difficult to achieve—is the creation of *equal intervals* between the scale positions. Thus it cannot be said that the distance between 0 and 1 on the Bogardus Social Distance scale is the same as the distance between 1 and 2. The achievement of equal intervals was addressed by L. L. Thurstone and his colleagues.

4. Thurstone Scaling

As seen in the case of the Bogardus Social Distance Scale, the indicators of a given variable can differ from one another in terms of *intensity*: some indicate a stronger degree than others. This phenomenon is not limited to social distance. For just about any variable, there are mild and extreme indicators of it. For example, the view that 'A woman should only be permitted to have an abortion in the case of rape or incest' represents a mild degree of anti-abortion sentiment in comparison with the view that, 'Physicians who perform abortions should be given the death penalty.'

L. L. Thurstone (1931) developed a technique for systematizing the differences in intensity that exist among the several indicators of a variable. His procedure began with the creation of a great many indicators (for example, 100), such as the two presented above. These were then presented to a panel of experts (e.g., PhD researchers specializing in studies of the variable in question) with instructions to score each item on a scale of, for example 1 to 11.

Once each panelist had scored each item, Thurstone then reviewed their scoring to identify items they had agreed on. Those items that produced disagreement among the panelists were discarded. Among those the panelists scored consistently, some were picked to represent each step on the scale: one or more items the panelists had agreed were 1s, items agreed to be 2s, etc. The resulting set of items were then administered to respondents.

Assume respondents were given a set of 11 items, one for each step in the intensity scale. Assume further that Respondent A agreed with all 11 items. In the creation of a simple index, such a person would receive a score of 11, representing an extreme case of whatever was being measured. If Respondent B disagreed with all 11, that person should receive a source of 0. Both respondents would receive those same scores on a Thurstone scale.

However, consider Respondent C, who agreed with 10 of the items, disagreeing only with the rather mild item rated 2 by the experts. In the creation of a simple index, such a respondent would receive a score of 10, representing the number of items agreed to. In Thurstone scaling, however, it would be reasoned that such a person must have idiosyncratic reasons for disagreeing with item 2, reasons that did not really reflect how they stood on the variable being measured, including misreading the item or checking the wrong box. In Thurstone scaling, Respondent C would be scored 11, based on the overall pattern of responses.

Or consider Respondent D, who agreed with only the most extreme item. Such a person would be judged to have reasons for that response that did not really reflect the variable in question—warranting a score of 0, based on the overall pattern of responses. Notice that this scoring procedure follows the same logic as discussed earlier in terms of Bogardus Social Distance scaling.

Thurstone scaling, like Bogardus scaling, results in the creation of *ordinal* scales: respondents scored 4 on the scale have a more extreme degree of the variable in question than those scored 3. In addition, however, Thurstone scales may also qualify, arguably, as *interval* scales. A simple ruler illustrates this quality of equal intervals. The *difference* in length between an object two inches long and an object three inches long is the same (one inch) as the difference between an object thirteen inches long and one that is fourteen inches long.

An interval scale, then, is one which has a standard distance between adjacent positions on the scale. On an ordinal scale of prejudice, for example, a person scored 3 would be *more* prejudiced than one scored 2 and one scored 4 would be *more* prejudiced than one scored 3. On an interval scale, the prejudice of the person scored 3 would exceed that of the one scored 2 by the same *amount* as the prejudice of the person scored 4 would exceed that of the person scored 3. Because of the manner in which they were generated—asking expert judges to rate items along an interval scale and accepting only those items the judges agreed on—Thurstone scales are sometimes described as being comprised of 'equal-appearing intervals.'

Although Thurstone scaling nicely illustrates the logical purpose of scaling in general, it is seldom used. The reason for its disuse is logistical: it is too difficult and expensive to hire a large team of expert panelists to undertake the task of scoring hundreds of potential items. Moreover, once the task has been completed and items have been selected for a scale, the passage of time will cause a change in how certain of the items are regarded by people—and, hence, what agreement or disagreement with them implies. Thus, it is necessary to repeat the difficult and expensive procedure from time to time.

5. Likert Scaling

Rensis Likert is best known for creating a questionnaire format that remains very popular among survey researchers: illustrated most commonly by the response categories 'Strongly agree,' 'Agree,' 'Disagree,' and 'Strongly disagree.' There are three main appeals to such a format. First, it is convenient to present respondents with a number of statements on a variety of topics, following each with a set of boxes to check, labeling each column of boxes with one of the response categories listed above. Second, the set of responses can be remembered easily by respondents and they can easily understand how to record their responses to specific statements.

Finally, the Likert response categories have an undeniable *ordinality* 'strongly agreeing' clearly represents more agreement than simple 'agreeing,' which represents more agreement than 'disagreeing' which, in turn, contains at least more agreement than 'strongly disagreeing.' Notice, by contrast, that responses such as 'kind of agree,' 'more or less agree,' and 'agree to some extent' are ambiguous as

Table 2.

	Responses to Item 1			
	Strongly agree	Agree	Disagree	Strongly disagree
Average scores on the large index ...	25	20	15	10

Table 3.

	Responses to Item 2			
	Strongly agree	Agree	Disagree	Strongly disagree
Average scores on the large index ...	30	28	17	13

to the relative degree of agreement they represent. It would not be possible to arrange them in order of magnitude. And even if *you* have a clear view of how they differ, there is no assurance that all respondents in a survey would regard and use the terms in that same fashion.

Likert was interested in something more than just ordinality among response categories, however. Like Thurstone, he wanted to create *interval* measures. Rather than using expert judges, however, Likert looked for evidence of an interval quality among the patterns of responses given by respondents in a study.

Likert's *item-analysis* began in a similar fashion as the creation of a simple index. Items would be selected on the basis of face validity. Then respondents were given scores based on how they answered *all* those items. For simplicity's sake, assume that all the items were worded in the same direction: agreement meant prejudice and disagreement meant tolerance, for example. Respondents would be given 3 points for every 'strongly agree,' 2 points for each 'agree,' 1 point for each 'disagree,' and no points for 'strongly disagree.' If there were 10 items under consideration, this procedure would produce an index with scores ranging from 0 to 30.

The potential interval quality of each item was assessed by calculating the average scores (on the large index) for those who strongly agreed with the item in question, those who agreed, and so forth. Consider the case in Table 2.

In this example, the 'distance' between 'strongly agree' and 'agree' would appear—at least in terms of the simple index scores—to be the same as between 'agree' and 'disagree' and so forth.

By contrast, consider the possibility in Table 3. Here, there does not appear to be much difference in the overall views of those who strongly agreed and those who agreed, nor between those who disagreed or strongly disagreed—but there is a substantial difference between agreeing and disagreeing overall. Given the fact that responses to Item 2 do not correlate well with scores on the index overall, the conclusion must be that Item 2, despite its face validity, does not provide a good measure of the variable in question.

Following a Likert item analysis, a scale might be constructed from among those items which appeared to have the quality of equal-appearing intervals. There are a number of specific techniques that might be used in the actual construction of such a scale.

6. Guttman Scaling

Guttman scaling, created by Louis Guttman, was probably the most common scaling technique used at the beginning of the 1990s. It has been widely used in sociolinguistics, especially in studies of language choice and shift, as well as of the creole continuum (see *DeCamp, David*). Like Likert scaling, it is based on an analysis of the empirical patterns to be observed in responses to items. It is more general than Likert scaling, since it can be applied to a variety of item formats—including Likert-type items.

To begin, the items considered for a Guttman scale are evaluated for intensity on the basis of how people responded. Consider two indicators of prejudice toward child-molesters: 'Do you think that child-molesters are different from other people?' and 'Do you think that all child-molesters should be executed?' Surely, more people would say yes to the first item than to the second. This is due to the fact that the first statement would have to be regarded as representing a very low level (if any) of prejudice, whereas the second is pretty extreme. Anyone who agreed to the second item would surely agree to the first as well, hence more would agree to the first one overall than to the second.

Guttman scaling would begin by examining the apparent degree of prejudice, for example, represented by each item—based only on the number who would be judged prejudiced by responses to that item. Next, responses to *pairs* of items are examined to determine whether those who agree to the harder one always (or almost always) agree to the easier one. In this fashion, a set of items would be selected appropriate to the creation of the scale.

A key to Guttman scaling lies in the scoring of response patterns. Scale scores are assigned in such a fashion as to permit the most faithful reproduction of original responses, called the *coefficient of reproducibility*. This is illustrated in Table 4.

Notice that patterns 1 through 5 are scored just as they would be in a simple cumulative index: one point for each indicator of the variable. More important, by knowing the scale score, all the specific responses could be faithfully reproduced. Knowing that a person was scored 3 for example, a '−' on Item 1 and a '+' on Items 2–4 could be predicted.

Look at Pattern 6, however. The only '+' is for Item 1, presumably the *hardest* item. In a simple index, such people would be scored 1, leading to the assumption that such people were '+' on Item 4 and

Table 4.

Item 1	Item 2	Item 3	Item 4	Pattern	Score
+	+	+	+	1	4
−	+	+	+	2	3
−	−	+	+	3	2
−	−	−	+	4	1
−	−	−	−	5	0
+	−	−	−	6	0
+	+	+	−	7	4
+	+	−	+	8	4
−	+	+	−	9	3
−	−	+	−	10	0 or 2

'−' on the rest. In each such case, then, two errors (Items 1 and 4) would arise if an attempt were made to reproduce the specific responses given by such people. By assigning a scale score of 0 in this instance, only one error would arise in reproducing the responses: guessing a '−' for Item 1.

A similar situation applies to Pattern 7. If such people were scored as 3, two errors would be made in reproducing the responses of each. Instead, by scoring them 4, only one error would be made for each such person. Patterns 8, 9, and 10 present other response patterns, indicating how each might be scored, so as to produce the fewest errors in reproducing the specific responses. Notice that in Pattern 10, either a score of 0 or 2 would produce the same number of errors (1), whereas an index score of 1 would produce two errors.

The *scalability* of a set of items is determined by calculating the *coefficient of reproducibility*. The total number of predictions that would be made (the number of cases times the number of items) is divided into the number of correct predictions that could be made on the basis of the scale scores. As a rough rule of thumb, a coefficient of 80 percent or higher is generally considered sufficient to justify the use of Guttman scale scoring instead of simple index scores.

There are numerous other techniques for creating composite measures, such as scales based on factor analysis or other such multivariate techniques. The foregoing examples should illustrate the logic of scaling techniques, however.

See also: Multidimensional Scaling; Reliability/Validity; Social Psychology; Sociology of Language.

Bibliography

Bogardus E S 1933 A social distance scale. *Sociology and Social Research* 17: 265–71
Guttman L 1944 A basis for scaling qualitative data. *American Sociological Review* 9: 139–50
Likert R 1974 A method of constructing an attitude scale. In: Maranell G M (ed.) *Scaling: A Sourcebook for Behavioral Scientists*. Aldine, Chicago, IL
McIver J P, Carmines E G 1981 *Unidimensional Scaling*. Sage, Beverly Hills, CA
Thurstone L L 1931 The measurement of social attitudes. *Journal of Abnormal and Social Psychology* 26: 249–69

Small Group Research
W. S. Bainbridge

At the dawn of human history, before agriculture had made large societies possible, every human being lived within a small group of people that hunted and gathered together, sharing all aspects of their lives. Citizens of modern societies tend to belong to several small groups simultaneously, of different kinds and with different memberships, most making only slight demands upon the individuals who comprise them. The characteristic of small groups most important for the study of language is 'solidarity,' the extent to which the individuals who belong are bound tightly together into a social unit, and modern groups tend to be much lower in solidarity than the prehistoric hunting band. Stephen Wilson identified six dimensions of solidarity that together provide a useful rubric for considering linguistic aspects of small groups: interactions, norms, status structure, goals, cohesiveness, and awareness of membership.

1. Interaction

'Interaction' is defined as the process of mutual communication between individuals, often leading to interdependence between them. Among sociologists, there is some disagreement about the way that interaction creates a social bond. Members of the school of thought called 'symbolic interactionism' believe that humans have a natural hunger for language-encoded meaning, and that this alone is sufficient to explain why individuals who have communicated extensively with each other will tend to orient themselves toward each other's perceptions and desires. Scholars in the 'exchange theory' tradition consider the words exchanged between people less important than the rewards, and they hold that a person becomes bonded to another as a result of the valuable things (including verbally communicated information as well as material goods) that have been received. Certainly, individuals who do not interact cannot be said to be members of the same small group.

'Interaction process analysis', devised by Robert F. Bales in the late 1940s, is one of a number of techniques for studying interaction rates and patterns in small groups, employing highly trained observers who identify the smallest atoms of communication, 'unit acts,' and assign them to one of a set of 12 categories (Hare 1976). The simplest of the many other such techniques is that developed by Eliot D. Chapple around 1940, who divided all interaction into just two categories, action and silence. Using a device called the 'interaction chronograph' to help with the timing and data recording, Chapple would observe two-person interactions, focusing on when each person spoke.

Bales's system of categories inspired other researchers to invent their own schemes for identifying types of communication, based either on theories or on statistical analysis of data. Timothy Leary proposed a set of 16 psychological mechanisms that could be seen in interaction, including narcissistic reflexes (boast, act proud, narcissistically exhibitionistic) and docile reflexes (act in an over-respecting manner, docilely conform). Richard D. Mann's system of 16 categories was designed to analyze 'communicative acts,' defined as single speeches or bursts of sentences within which the expressed feelings are uniform, directed by a member of the group to its leader. Three of these are in the area of authority relations: showing dependency, showing independence, and showing counterdependency.

A vast body of research has been done with these social–psychological schemes for categorizing communicative acts, much employing Bales's system or adaptations of it. One can focus either on the kinds of unit acts the group primarily produces, for example, expressing solidarity versus hostility, or on the distribution of unit acts across the individual members. Then one can study such things as the way in which a group accomplishes a set task, the balance between task accomplishment and emotional gratification, the emergence of leadership, and the processes that establish norms.

2. Norms

'Norms' are authoritative standards of behavior, principles of right action binding upon the members of a group, including rules governing proper speech. As defined by George Homans (1950: 123), a norm 'is an idea in the minds of the members of a group, an idea that can be put in the form of a statement specifying what the members or other men should do, ought to do, are expected to do, under given circumstances.' The fact that a norm can be expressed as a statement does not mean that norms are learned primarily as statements communicated verbally, nor that they are encoded in memory as strings of words. In exchange theory, norms are learned through experiencing contingencies of reward and punishment, a process that can take place without use of language, as it does among pigeons and mice in psychological experiments. The extent to which all human norms are linguistic phenomena, not those concerning speech alone, remains an open question deserving scientific attention.

Some norms are very general, established by the society as a whole to cover a wide range of circumstances. An example is the biblical commandment, 'Thou shalt not take the name of the Lord thy God in vain.' Others are very specific, belonging to only a small group of people and concerning a limited range of circumstances. As reported by Homans, a particular group of nine factory workers attaching wires to telephone switching equipment had established a norm to call a man who made more than 825 connections an hour a 'rate-buster,' and someone who made less than 825, a 'chiseler.'

2.1 Norm Standardization

Among the most enduring themes of small group research is the way an individual's behavior changes as the result of belonging to a group, which can be conceptualized as the emergence and acceptance of norms. In the 1920s, Floyd Allport did many experiments on how people performed language-related tasks, to study 'social facilitation,' an increase in performance caused by the mere presence of other people. For example, research subjects were given a piece of paper with a single word written at the top and were asked to write as many disconnected words below it as they could in the time allotted. Most of them wrote more words while working in the presence of others, but they were judged to write words of a more personal nature while alone.

In another of Allport's experiments, subjects were given either mechanical tasks (such as crossing out vowels in newspaper stories), problem-solving tasks (writing statements disproving didactic passages from ancient philosophers), and judgment tasks (such as judging the relative pleasantness of a series of odors). For part of the time they did these jobs alone, and the rest of the time they were working in the presence of other research subjects. Interestingly, results depended upon the nature of the task. Subjects crossed out vowels more rapidly when working with others than when alone, and they wrote longer arguments in the group situation. However, arguments written while alone were deemed to be of higher quality. Judgments of the pleasantness of odors were less extreme when made in a group than when alone.

The most famous experiment in this tradition was done in the 1950s by Solomon Asch. Each research subject was placed in a group of six people, unaware that the other five were confederates of the experimenter. They were shown a series of cards, each with lines drawn on it, and asked to say which of three lines was the same length as a fourth. As the session progressed the confederates began unanimously giving the wrong answer, and the real research subjects, whose turn came last, were left in the quandary whether to accede to the judgment of the majority or to disagree. Much of the time, they expressed agreement with the confederates, but interviews with the subjects revealed that they often harbored private disagreements but conformed in what they said because they wanted to avoid appearing different from the rest of the group.

When participation in a group tends to reduce the extremes of individual speech or action, processes of standardization are at work. Homans noted that individuals who interact frequently tend to become similar to each other in their behavior and attitudes. Among the examples he offered, linking speech and action, was research done in a special test room at the Western Electric Company, where women were rapidly assembling electrical relays. The work required such concentration that the women could converse with only their nearest neighbors. Analysis of output rates showed that women working next to each other had unconsciously learned to work at almost identical rates. In this case, conversation had unintentionally standardized work patterns, but frequent interaction also has the power to standardize speech itself.

In the early 1960s, social psychology experimenters reported a phenomenon they called the 'risky shift,' in which research subjects accepted greater risks when they were making decisions in groups than when they were deciding alone. Later research found that some decisions were made more cautiously by groups than by individuals. This led to the realization that a group's norms are not simply the average or sum of the wishes of the individuals who constitute the group. Under a variety of circumstances, extreme norms of one kind or another may emerge from the complex web of social interaction in groups of high solidarity.

When a group of people who work closely together is under great stress, extreme pressures toward uniformity of opinion may arise. Irving Janis has called this 'groupthink' and argued that it often leads to very bad decisions. Members limit their discussion to but a few of the many alternatives open to them, fail to admit disadvantages of the course they have chosen or advantages of courses they have not initially considered, and avoid obtaining information that might provide a more realistic basis for evaluation. They show great interest in facts and opinions that appear to support their plans, and they ignore contrary data. They fail to deliberate possible barriers to success and are unprepared to deal with them when they arise. Individuals within the group who disagree are either excluded from the discussion or voluntarily suppress their own reservations. Among the examples of groupthink analyzed by Janis are the discussions in the advisory cabinets of American presidents Kennedy and Johnson that led to an abortive invasion of Cuba and to costly prolongation of the Vietnam War.

2.2 Communication Norms

Susan Shimanoff has suggested that there are seven types of communication rules established by small groups, each specifying desired behavior for one part of the following: (a) who says; (b) what; (c) to whom; (d) when; (e) with what duration and frequency; (f) through what medium; and (g) by what decision procedure. Formally constituted committees often have elaborate rules concerning who is 'speaker' or who 'has the floor,' but almost all groups possess habits and expectations about who will speak under a specified set of circumstances. Other norms define the limits of what shall be spoken about, for example, whether obscenities are prohibited or encouraged. In a weight-control group, Overeaters Anonymous, members may talk about food in generic terms ('refined carbohydrates,' 'junk food') but are enjoined from naming particular foods ('pizza,' 'twinkies'). The person to whom an utterance is usually addressed may be the designated leader, someone who has been temporarily recognized as having the floor, an individual member with a personal interest in the topic, or the membership as a whole. Groups differ in their preferences for each of these alternatives.

Some group norms concern who speaks when and what is said when. Groups may even differ in how they talk about these timing norms. Legend has it that a joint British–American committee of the military high command in World War II fell into deadlock because their dialects of English had opposite meanings for the term *to table* a topic. For the British, *table* meant to place a topic on the agenda, while for the Americans it meant to remove it from consideration indefinitely. Groups vary in the standards they set for duration and frequency of speech. Many legislatures follow elaborate procedures for allocating debating time, and even highly informal groups discourage individuals from 'hogging the floor' or 'talking out of turn.'

Although talking is the typical medium of communication in small groups, many in business and government also employ memos or even lengthy documents, perhaps to lay the basis for oral discussion or to provide a record of positions taken and decisions made. Norms concerning the proper medium may punish persons who write their messages in an oral group, or persons who fail to write when they are expected to. Norms concerning decision procedures are the political culture of the group, specifying whether a vote should be taken and how, informally conferring decision power on a few individuals, or requiring consensus of the entire group. Decision-procedure rules may exist to modify the six other types of communication rules, for example, requiring a two-thirds vote to end a filibuster. While it is easiest to illustrate communication norms with examples from deliberative bodies that possess written rules, presumably every small group with some measure of solidarity possesses all seven kinds.

3. Status Structure

The word 'status' is often used to refer to a rank in a hierarchy, but in sociology it has a more general meaning, referring to any position in a social structure which defines a set of expectations for a person occupying it. In the USA the status of Supreme Court Judge is different from that of Senator, because they play very different roles in writing and interpreting legislation and they gain their positions through very different social processes, but the two may be of equal rank. Each status has certain rights and obligations, and satisfying the obligations attendant on a particular status is equivalent to playing the social role associated with it (see *Role Theory*). Informal small groups often lack explicit statuses, but as a group grows, a set of statuses tends to crystallize out while power differentials and division of labor become institutionalized. In modern bureaucracies, a formal structure of statuses is often outlined in an organizational chart and spelled out in detailed documents. But even in casual groups lacking any written records, members can usually say who occupies the leadership positions.

Among the most active fields for research on leadership in small groups is 'administrative science,' the study of effective and efficient management of businesses and other formal organizations. Like many other applied fields which lack clear criteria for evaluating the truth of ideas, administrative science is highly susceptible to fads, and many of its most popular notions about language and communication are based on rather shaky scientific foundations. One of the hottest continuing debates is the degree to which managers should share information and decision-making responsibilities with subordinates.

In 1960, Douglas McGregor distinguished two management philosophies he called 'theory X' and 'theory Y.' Theory X managers believe people are not to be trusted, so they keep close watch on their subordinates, avoid sharing responsibility and information with them, and are traditional authoritarian bosses. This means they tend to give detailed and complete instructions to their subordinates, setting explicit standards for performance in achieving the management-defined goals which they monitor with formal statistics. Theory Y managers, in contrast, believe their underlings can generally be trusted with responsibility, so they share more information and create a work environment in which people can best meet their own personal goals by working hard for the goals of the organization. Thus they give only general instructions, depending upon the subordinates to work out details, employing group discussion and informal verbal feedback to maintain work momentum.

Clearly, these are two competing quasipolitical ideologies—authoritarianism vs. egalitarianism—and McGregor was probably asserting his own values rather than reporting scientific findings when he claimed that theory Y was more effective. In recent years, this belief has resurfaced many times with many labels (Tubbs 1988). David Bradford and Allan R. Cohen urge managers to be 'developers,' that is, to assist their subordinates in growing as human beings and to give them considerable freedom to solve problems in their own way. Among the paradoxes of the developer approach is the belief that managers increase their own power by giving subordinates greater powers.

Theory X is comparable to Machiavellianism, the philosophy of Niccolo Machiavelli, and some researchers have used a Machiavellianism scale developed by Richard Christie to measure this untrusting style of management. Among the scale's items are several maxims concerning speech: 'Never tell anyone the real reason you did something unless it is useful to do so.' 'It is wise to flatter important people.' Machiavellians are expected to agree with these two statements, and to disagree with the proposition, 'There is no excuse for lying to someone else.' The theory X manager may not be a liar, but he does not expect other people to do what they say, and he monitors their actual behavior closely rather than trusting their words.

In contrast to these one-sided analyses, 'contingency theories' note that different styles of leadership are effective under different conditions. Paul Hersey and Kenneth Blanchard stress the importance of the degree of maturity of the followers in determining which of four kinds of management is appropriate: telling, selling, participating, and delegating. People who are both unable and unwilling to take responsibility must simply be *told* what to do. Subordinates of slightly greater maturity must be *sold*; they still need directive management but will be more fully committed to the task if they can be convinced to 'buy into' desired behaviors by the explanations of their boss. A nondirective 'participating' style will help motivate persons of moderate to high maturity, through effective two-way communication with the leader. Finally, tasks can simply be 'delegated' to fully mature subordinates who can be trusted to accomplish them without much direction, explanation, or two-way communication with the manager. This analytic scheme expands the two categories of McGregor's analysis into four, and avoids the unwarranted assumption that one is best under all conditions.

John Kotter, Leonard Schlesinger, and Vijay Sathe note that management occasionally need to change the organization they direct in a significant way, and that several tactics may be used to overcome employees' resistance, depending upon a variety of factors. When speed is essential and the managers possess considerable power, the right tactic may be coercion, but this can leave a residue of anger. Education/communication may be the right approach when resistance to change is based on lack of correct information, and once persuaded, people may actively help implementation of the change; however, this tactic is typically quite slow. Negotiation is best in situations where one group is bound to lose as a result of the change, and where they have power to resist. Tactical schemes like this are Machiavellianism of a higher order, because communication rules are treated as contingent upon the manager's analysis of the most effective way to control subordinates, not determined by invariant norms. Honesty is treated as only one of a number of good policies, the best only under certain circumstances.

4. Goals

In many cases, a group is a set of people with a common goal, but other groups may never have defined a goal, and the members of many groups may have personal goals that conflict with those of other members. Goals vary from the most specific, to the most general, what are often called values. High-solidarity groups tend to have many defined goals rather than just a few, a consensus on what the goals are rather than a disagreement, cooperative rather than competitive goals, and motives oriented toward their group rather than each member being concerned only with himself or herself. Many groups define their goals at the moment they come into being, for example, business and special interest clubs, but others experience a sometimes lengthy process of searching for goals.

Albert K. Cohen has analyzed the way 'mutual conversion' can create a group and give it distinctive goals, if a number of individuals with similar problems of social adjustment come into communication with one another. This takes place in tiny, even imperceptible steps, as one individual expresses a hope or plan and receives positive feedback in the form of similar hopes and plans from the others. Cohen believed that all human action is an ongoing series of efforts to solve problems, but he focused on the specific frustrations of lower-class adolescent boys who experienced repeated failures to meet the standards of middle-class culture, especially in school where particular kinds of verbal facility are demanded. Unable initially to express their frustrations to each other, these boys will congregate in groups and begin to share various escapades in which they explore alternative, even deviant patterns of behavior. Together, they gradually redefine conventional standards as bad and erect a new set of standards which they can successfully meet. The result is a delinquent gang (see *Subcultures and Countercultures*). Mutual conversion can occur with many other kinds of group, and Cohen's analysis sensitively describes how tentatively the parties may grope their way to a consensus.

Similarly, Richard Cloward and Lloyd Ohlin argued that youth whose attempts to achieve the goals valued by society have been thwarted may collect into delinquent gangs that seek these or other goals by deviant means. In theft or vice can provide the money and status desired by these adolescents, they will create a 'criminal' gang. But for many of them, success will be as hard to attain through crime as it was through attending school, and they will be forced to set new goals, such as violent defense of their city block against other gangs, and they will become a 'conflict' gang. If beaten in this attempt, or if the members of the adolescent group lack the strength and skill for fighting, they will become a 'retreatist' gang, descending into drug addiction or losing a sense of personal and collective goals altogether.

George Homans explained that groups exist as a means by which members can cooperatively extract resources from the environment and defend against threats. In meeting these goals, the members develop what Homans called the 'external system,' a set of social relations that allows the group to survive in its environment. As members interact, however, they come to value each other not merely as means for coping with the environment, but for their own sakes and for the social and emotional rewards they can provide each other. Thus arises the 'internal system' of the group, social relations not primarily conditioned by the external environment, often purely verbal in nature, such as pleasant conversation and joking. While the internal system can take on a life of its own, it will eventually die if the external system fails to achieve its goals.

Parallel to the different goals that groups may have are the various goals researchers pursue in studying them. Sociologists by the score have examined delinquent gangs, both because deviant behavior provides a certain journalistic excitement and because the conventional society feels gangs are a serious problem. Those who have studied psychotherapy groups typically had the goal of evaluating or promoting the particular brand of therapy, and research in business and industry sought information about how to increase profitability. The artificial groups created in social psychology laboratories contributed to the development and testing of often rather narrow theories about group dynamics.

5. Cohesiveness

'Cohesiveness' is sometimes defined as the degree to which members are attracted to their group, but a definition that has been especially productive for research is the degree to which members are tied to each other by social bonds. Sociometry (see *Sociometry*) is a set of methods for measuring the social bonds within a group, whether by simply asking each individual which others he or she especially likes or by observing which persons tend to interact most with each other. If a group is high in solidarity, its members will be connected by strong social bonds, and many researchers have used cohesiveness as a synonym for solidarity.

One language-related field of research that has made especially good use of analysis in terms of social bonds is the sociology of religion (Stark and Bainbridge 1985). A popular slogan holds that 'the family that prays together stays together,' and many studies have shown that religious belief and practice are powerfully connected to the strength and structure of social relationships. Kevin Welch assessed the role of interpersonal bonds in sustaining commitment to orthodox beliefs among members of mainline denominations in the United States, finding strong positive correlations between various measures of orthodoxy and the proportion of one's best friends who are members of one's own religious congregation. Also, the greater the number of nonchurch organizations and clubs the person belonged to, the lower his or her orthodoxy.

Members of highly cohesive religious groups are more likely than others to proselytize, to pray, and to profess their faith with confidence. Rodney Stark examined the effects social context had on religious experiences, moments when the individual believed he or she had a personal encounter with the supernatural, finding that people who had such experiences were highly concentrated among those whose closest friends were members of the same religious group. Thus, conversations with God are facilitated by communication with fellow believers; or, unusual psychological states are more likely to be defined as religious in nature if the person belongs to a cohesive group that wants to interpret them that way. But it is also true that religious groups that provide many shared spiritual experiences, whether formal rituals or informal gatherings, tend thereby to create a sense of communion and thus cohesiveness between members.

Among the best explanations of conversion to small, radical religious groups—'sects' and 'cults'—is the process of recruitment through social bonds. The model that has received the most attention was proposed by John Lofland and Rodney Stark, and it has guided many subsequent research studies. Combining social bond analysis with other factors, it has seven steps.

(a) The person must suffer enduring, acutely-felt tensions which derive from a discrepancy between the person's current life conditions and those he deeply desires.
(b) The person possesses a religious problem-solving perspective, a way of understanding life events that defines their causes in supernatural terms.
(c) Dissatisfied with the help received from a current religious group, the person defines himself as a religious seeker on a quest for a new religious group.
(d) The person encounters the sect or cult at a turning point, which may combine a period of weak social attachments with the termination of old lines of action, as may come with divorce, school graduation, or a new job.
(e) A strong emotional social bond develops with members of the radical religious group.
(f) Emotional social bonds with nonmembers are lost, weakened, or neutralized by being defined as irrelevant to the person's needs at the moment.
(g) Intensive interaction with members of the group inculcates its beliefs and turns the person into a committed member ready to recruit others to the new faith.

This analysis places great emphasis on social interaction with members of the group. An alternative theory, which has been used to explain conversion to various political creeds as well as religious faiths, postulates that converts are emotionally vulnerable to ideological appeals, because they suffer intense personal deprivations, causing unendurable frustration. The person will then encounter an ideology that explains this suffering in ways flattering to the sufferer and offers an apparent solution to the person's problems. The Lofland–Stark theory incorporates these ideas, but argues that they are not enough, and subsequent research has supported this assertion. Apparently it is not sufficient to hear 'the word.' Rather, one must develop social bonds with current believers who draw one into a small, like-minded group, and only then does one listen receptively to the word and eventually accept it. In general, membership in a group precedes acceptance of its beliefs and practices.

6. Awareness of Membership

Charles Horton Cooley wrote on *primary groups*, those characterized by intimate face-to-face association, and said membership in one 'involves the sort of sympathy and mutual identification for which *we* is the natural expression.' The 'sense of we-ness' or 'we-feeling,' as it has been called by sociologists, is a variable that is strong in some small groups but weak in others, measurable in part by members' use of the first person plural in talking about it. Another marker of significant we-feeling is the possession of a name for the group.

Names, of course, tell us much about the image members have of their own group and how they want outsiders to regard them. 'Hell's Angels' must be both terrifying and important. Members of the 'Cornbelt Lapidary and Geological Society' profess a rather specialized set of harmless interests and live in an informally defined region notable for growing corn. Churches that call themselves 'Christian Science,' 'Divine Science,' or 'Religious Science' are apparently modern creations that seek some of the prestige that science has had in recent years.

Rodney Stark studied the names adopted by novel American religious cults in different periods, finding that the proportion with innocuous, Christian-sounding names was nearly twice as high early in the century as it was after 1950. Among some of the older names that apparently provided camouflage to protect the cults from public outrage were Universal Christ Church, Liberal Catholic Church, and Congregational Church of Practical Theology, actually deviant cults in the spiritualist, theosophical, and psychic traditions, respectively. More recently, cults have been happy to be known publicly by names such as Enchanted Moon Coven or Church of Satanic Brotherhood, a sign that society is far more tolerant of religious deviance than formerly.

As Stephen Wilson explains, many social psychologists have equated awareness of membership in a group with morale, but morale has proven very difficult to measure. If one simply asks people whether they belong to a highly prestigious group, many will profess membership who do not seem really to belong. A group toward which people orient their action and which sets standards for their behavior, even if they are not in all the senses discussed here members of the group, is a 'reference group.' Actual membership in a small group involves all six of the dimensions of solidarity, not awareness alone. Calling oneself a member is not enough.

The research on small groups is vast; A. Paul Hare's 1976 bibliography lists fully 6037 publications, but he ignores most of those done by sociologists and others on natural groups in the field, concentrating instead on laboratory experimental studies. A considerable fraction of this scholarship concerns language, but few of the authors have an awareness of membership in the profession of linguistics. Nonetheless, students of language would have much to learn from examination of small group research; many of these studies should be renamed linguistic, and small group researchers would benefit from realization of the contributions that linguistics could make to their work.

See also: Social Psychology; Sociology of Language.

Bibliography

Blumberg H H, Hare A P, Kent V, Davies M F (eds.) 1983 *Small Groups and Social Interaction*. Wiley, New York
Cartwright D, Zander A (eds.) 1968 *Group Dynamics: Research and Theory*. Harper and Row, New York
Christie R, Geis F L 1970 *Studies in Machiavellianism*. Academic Press, New York
Cloward R A, Ohlin L E 1960 *Delinquency and Opportunity*. Free Press, New York
Cohen A K 1955 *Delinquent Boys*. Free Press, New York
Hare A P 1976 *Handbook of Small Group Research*. Free Press, New York
Homans G C 1950 *The Human Group*. Harcourt Brace, New York
McGregor D 1960 *The Human Side of Enterprise*. McGraw-Hill, New York
Shaw M E 1981 *Group Dynamics: The Psychology of Small Group Behavior*. McGraw-Hill, New York
Shimanoff S B 1984 Coordinating group interaction via communication rules. In: Cathcart R S, Samovar L A (eds.) *Small Group Communication: A Reader*. William C. Brown, Dubuque, IA
Stark R, Bainbridge W S 1985 *The Future of Religion*. University of California Press, Berkeley, CA
Tubbs S L 1988 *A Systems Approach to Small Group Interaction*. Random House, New York
Wilson S 1978 *Informal Groups: An Introduction*. Prentice-Hall, Englewood Cliffs, NJ

Sociometry
W. S. Bainbridge

Research frequently compares features of language in such social groups as socioeconomic classes, ethnic subcultures, and political–geographic units, yet in the modern world few social barriers are linguistically impermeable, and there is good reason to doubt the logic of dividing human beings into separate speech communities. An alternate research strategy is to map the network of social relations and communication channels that link individuals, and to measure the degrees of linguistic difference that occur at various distances across the social structure that they define. The classic method of sociometry was developed by Jacob Moreno, and a host of related techniques for measuring social relationships have been developed in recent years.

1. Measuring Social Structure

Moreno's method was designed to chart relationships in an identifiable small group, for example, the children in a particular schoolroom or the workers in a particular industrial team. The researcher might ask each of the children to write his or her name at the top of a piece of paper, and to put the numbers 1 through 4 in a column. After the number 1, the child was supposed to put the name of his or her favorite playmate among the other children in the room. After the number 2 would come the second-favorite playmate and so on until the name of four other children were listed in order of descending preference.

Research on adults typically employs several such 'sociometric' questions. The members of a work group might be asked to make one list of the fellow members they would seek out for advice on their work, and a second list of the members they most enjoy spending social time with away from work. The classical method for analyzing and displaying the data from a sociometric question is to draw a 'sociogram,' a diagram in which people are represented as dots and sociometric choices as lines connecting them. A pair of such sociograms can be seen in Figure 1, based on actual research on a small printing company, but giving pseudonyms to the seven persons whose first two sociometric choices are charted.

The actual set of social relationships represented by the sociogram is a 'social network.' A person chosen by none of the others in the group is called a 'social isolate,' while a subgroup who name each other but are not strongly connected to others in the total group constitute a 'clique.' Divisions between cliques, crossed by relatively few lines in the sociogram, are 'cleavages.' In terms of work-related advice, there are three social isolates at the printing company: Dora (secretary), Gary (pressman), and Frank (apprentice pressman), but no complete social isolates emerge in the analysis of social relations away from work. The owner, Albert, is central to communication patterns in both diagrams, as are Bob, the head pressman, Edgar, a pressman, and Connie, one of the two secretaries. A moderate cleavage appears for social relations, and the group of seven is centered on a *triad* (Albert, Bob, and Connie) and a *dyad* (Frank and Gary). During the 1980s, a host of mathematical procedures have been developed for systematically measuring these and other features of sociometric data.

2. Research Approaches

When employed in linguistic research, sociometry provides information about social structure that must be coordinated with some features of language. In principle, different features of language may be associated with different kinds of social relations. At the printing company, it would be expected that the 'mutual pairs' who choose each other for work-related advice to be very similar in their use of work-related language, such as printer's jargon. However, mutual pairs in the diagram for social relations away from work might be more similar in their use of terminology for leisure activities.

Harry Crockett and Lewis Levine used sociometry to understand variations of pronunciation of postvocalic *r* and the present participle ending *-ing*, in a small community in the Southern United States. Pairs of friends tended to be similar in their pronunciations, when compared with pairs of individuals chosen randomly from the respondents to an extensive survey. One limitation of Moreno's original methods is that they ideally require complete data from all the individuals in the group, a criterion that is very difficult to achieve with anything but the smallest groups and impossible with a random sample of a large population. By focusing on pairs of individuals, the researcher may get very much the same results as if working with a far more costly complete sociogram.

Theories can be tested with even more fragmentary sociometric data, based on individuals' replies to questions about their social relations but not attempting to coordinate data from different respondents. In a study of vernacular language loyalty in working-class sections of Belfast, Lesley Milroy and Sue Margrain (1980) were interested primarily in whether the respondent belonged to a closed, cohesive, local network, or possessed social relationships that spread out more widely both socially and geographically. Questions about the residential proximity of relatives, sharing social time with work mates, and having work mates who lived nearby distinguished persons who were tightly bound into local networks from persons more cosmopolitan in their social relations, and substantial differences of pronunciation were found between these two groups.

Potentially, any feature of language can be studied sociometrically. One of the more ambitious methodological developments is Kathleen Carley's (1986) 'frame technology' for comparing individuals' definitions of concepts. Rejecting the notion that individual differences in definitions can be captured adequately through synonym lists or other traditional methods, Carley has relied on expert systems

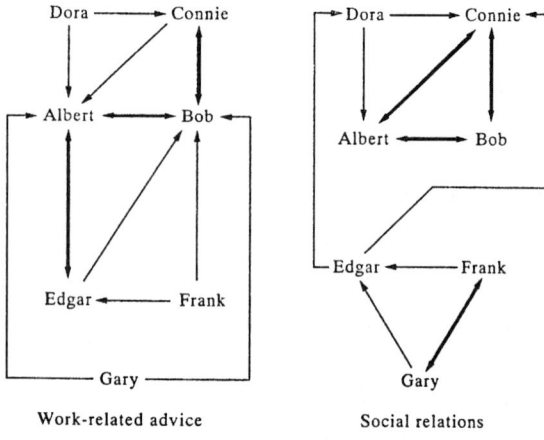

Figure 1. Sociograms of a small printing company.

techniques from the field of artificial intelligence. First, she conducted interviews with respondents, getting them to associate numerous qualities with the concept in question. The data were then put into a set of special computer programs that charted respondents' conceptual 'frames' as networks of definitional connections. Finally, measures of the similarity of respondents' frames were compared with sociometric data. In such research, the concept of network is central to all parts of the analysis, because definitions are seen as networks of concepts, shaped by the social networks revealed through sociometry.

See also: Small Group Research; Social Psychology; Sociology of Language.

Bibliography

Burt R S 1983 *Applied Network Analysis.* Sage, Beverly Hills, CA
Carley K M 1986 An approach for relating social structure to cognitive structure. *Journal of Mathematical Sociology* **12**: 137–89
Crockett H J, Levine L 1967 Friends' influences on speech. *Sociological Inquiry* **37**: 109–28
Milroy L, Margrain S 1980 Vernacular language loyalty and social network. *Language in Society* **9**: 43–70
Moreno J L 1934 *Who Shall Survive?* Nervous and Mental Disease Publishing Co., Washington, DC

Statistics in Sociolinguistics
D. Sankoff

1. Introduction

Many areas connected with sociolinguistics in which quantitative data play a role, have seen the application of statistical methods, both traditional (experimental design, sampling, estimation, hypothesis testing) and heuristic (clustering, scaling). Some of these are discussed in other entries (see *Social Psychology*; *Sociometry*; *Attitude Surveys: Question–Answer*

Process; *Scaling*; *Multidimensional Scaling*). It is within variation theory, however, where social considerations are most intimately connected to grammatical questions, that a specifically sociolinguistic protocol for statistical analysis has been developed and widely adopted. This article will survey the justifications for this approach and sketch how it has been applied to various types of linguistic problems.

2. Epistemological Concerns

Linguistics is unique among scientific disciplines in that its practitioners generally do not require statistical methodology and are not constrained by statistical criteria of validity. Linguists traditionally agreed that the grammatical structure of a language consisted, in large measure, of discrete entities or categories whose relationships and co-occurrence constraints were qualitative in nature and shared by all speakers in the speech community. These structures could then be deduced by analyzing and comparing test utterances elicited from, or intuited by, any native speaker of the language (e.g., linguists serving as their own data source), without need for any statistical apparatus.

It is only since the groundbreaking work of William Labov (see *Labov, William*) in the late 1960s that any concerted attempt has been made to investigate questions of central interest to linguistic theory using statistics (Labov 1969). He made credible to many linguists the idea that two or more different articulations of a given phonological form may occur in the same word or affix, in the same contexts, without affecting the denotational value (referential meaning) of a lexical item, or the syntactic function of an affix or particle. Which form will occur at a given point in time can only be predicted in terms of a probabilistic model, whereby the effects of the linguistic and extra-linguistic context can be ascertained with accuracy, but where the output of the analysis remains just a probability. The choice of form always contains a component of pure chance, though this is precisely delimited.

Alternation among forms also occurs at the syntactic and lexical levels, though the scope of syntactic equivalence and lexical synonymy are the subject of much debate. The distributionalist tradition of linguistics is based on the uniqueness of the form-function relationship, something variationism rejects as an unwarranted assumption. Analysts may well identify, *upon reflection*, differences in connotation among synonyms or among competing syntactic constructions, whether in isolation or in context, but there is no reason to expect these differences to be pertinent every time one of the variant forms is used. Indeed, underlying the study of syntactic variation within a framework similar to that of phonological variation is the hypothesis that for certain identifiable sets of alternations, these distinctions come into play neither in the intentions of the speaker nor in the interpretation of the interlocutor. We say that 'distinctions in referential value or grammatical function among different surface forms can be neutralized in discourse' (Sankoff 1988). This is the source of the phenomenon of 'equivalence' and the justification of the syntactic variable that have so preoccupied sociolinguists. It is the fundamental mechanism of non-phonological variation and change.

The formal models of grammatical theory have discrete structures of an algebraic, algorithmic, and/or logical nature. Such structures often involve sets of two or more alternate components, such as synonyms, paraphrases or allophones, which the analyst may determine to be carrying out identical or similar linguistic functions. By allowing a degree of randomness into the choice between such alternates, the grammatical formalisms are converted into probabilistic models of linguistic performance susceptible to statistical study (Cedergren and Sankoff 1974).

3. The Sample

Language modeled as generated by probabilistic grammars is most appropriately studied by the data of natural discourse: sustained fluent sequences of connected utterances. The construction of a sample of natural speech is very different from sampling for sociological questionnaire administration, for psychological experimentation, or for educational testing, since one generally cannot predict when or how often the linguistic phenomenon under study will occur in the flow of conversation. Hence the sample usually involves relatively few speakers (20 to 120), carefully chosen to represent the diversity of linguistic behavior within the community being studied, with a large volume of material tape-recorded from each speaker. This material is transcribed in computer-accessible form, and is systematically scanned for occurrences of the words, sounds, or grammatical structures of interest. Usually, the same data set (the 'corpus') can be used for many different studies, since it is representative of all the structures and usage of natural speech (Sankoff and Sankoff 1973).

4. The Research Question

Corpus research (see *Corpus Linguistics and Sociolinguistics*) may provide examples or counter-examples as an adjunct to theoretical arguments. But what is equally important, and often more so, are quantitative patterns of occurrence relatively inaccessible to introspection or even testing methodology. Regular, complex relationships may exist at the quantitative level among a number of structures, but upon introspection, all we can say is that they are all simply 'grammatical.' Quantitative regularities may be vaguely guessed at through introspection, but may not be characterized with anything like the precision with which intuition-based methods can establish categorical relationships.

The quantitative facts are not minor details of linguistic behavior. Universal hierarchies and co-occurrence constraints not manifested in terms of grammaticality versus ungrammaticality for a given language are nonetheless often present in clear and well-developed form in usage frequencies. The classical examples are constraint hierarchies for the expression of certain allophones (or the application of optional phonological and morphophonological rules), but it is also true of syntax, in the study of variable rule order, optional movement or deletion rules, and in preferences among semantically or functionally equivalent phrase structures.

Moreover, it is these variable aspects of grammatical structure which are always the locus of linguistic change (see *Sociolinguistics and Language Change*). Change virtually always requires a transitional period, often very lengthy, of variability, competition among structures and divergence within the speech community. The detailed nature of linguistic change and of its synchronic reflex—dialect differentiation—cannot be understood without coming to grips with quantitative relationships.

The tools for studying these relationships are necessarily very different from those used in theoretical linguistics. Frequency counts of forms in contexts are not just quantitative refinements of judgments of grammaticality and have even less to do with acceptability. Counts of 0 percent are analogous to judgments of ungrammaticality, but not identical to them. Non-occurrence does not necessarily indicate a prohibited form. It may simply be the result of a complex combination of features, which could be perfectly grammatical but unlikely to appear in any reasonably sized corpus. Conversely, intuitively ungrammatical forms may appear systematically and at a non-negligible rate in spontaneous speech through the interaction of the grammatical facility with processing constraints.

5. The Linguistic Variable

The key concept underlying variationist sociolinguistics is the 'linguistic variable.' A well-studied example is the pronunciation or deletion of syllable-final /s/ that characterizes most varieties of Caribbean Spanish. Another example, from spoken English, is the copular verb *be*, which occurs as the contracted variant (*John's a doctor, we're coming, I'm at home*) or the full variant (*John is ... we are ... I am ...*). A third example involves *th*, as in *this* and *think*, which usually have an interdental fricative pronunciation, but which are also pronounced at least occasionally by speakers of most varieties of English as stops (*dis, tink*). A fourth example is the alternation of future and periphrastic future tenses (*You will hear about it* versus *You are going to hear about it*).

6. The Model

The choice of one variant or another of a binary linguistic variable can be heavily influenced by a wide range of factors, including the phonological and syntactic context in which it occurs, the topic of conversation, the degree of situational or contextual formality, idiosyncratic tendencies of the speaker, and the identity of the hearer(s). These factors, however, usually cannot account for all the variability in the data, and so a probabilistic model is set up to evaluate their influence:

$$\log p/(1-p) = a_i + a_j + \cdots + a_k \qquad (1)$$

where p is the probability that a particular one of the two variants will be chosen and $1-p$ the probability of the other, in the context containing linguistic or extralinguistic features labeled $i, j, \ldots, k$. In this 'logistic-linear' model a_i represents the effects on the choice of variant of feature i in the context of the variable. If p represents the probability of contraction in the example of copula given above, and if feature 1 and feature 2 indicate that the sound preceding the copula is a vowel or consonant, respectively, while feature 3 and feature 4 indicate that the grammatical category following the copula is an adjective or a noun phrase, and feature 5 and feature 6 indicate informal and formal speaking styles, then a_1, a_3, and a_5 will be high (each ca. 1.0) while a_2, a_4, and a_6 will be low (each ca. -1.0). Thus the *is* in *John is the leader*, as uttered in a formal context is far less susceptible to contraction ($p=0.05$) than the *are* in *You are bad*, spoken informally ($p=0.95$).

With sociolinguistic data, it is conventional to include one feature, called the mean or corrected mean, in formula (1) for all contexts. The other features fall into disjoint 'factor groups.' Usually one or another feature from each factor group appears in every context, and no two features from the same factor group can co-occur. The mathematical structure of (1) requires us to impose some constraint on the feature effects within each factor group, such as that the sum of the effects be zero. Without this the mean cannot be estimated uniquely.

7. The Data

For statistical analysis, the speech sample is scanned for occurrences of one or the other variant of a variable, and each occurrence is recorded along with the features (or factors) present in the context. Each observed combination of contextual features is considered to define a data cell for the analysis, where the number r of occurrences of one of the variants, compared with the total occurrences n in the cell, is assumed to be a binomial random variable with parameters n and p.

Because the distribution of the data among the cells cannot be controlled when a natural speech sample is used, and because many different factors may influence the probability p, the final 'design' is often a high-dimensional array with many or even most of the possible cells empty ($n = 0$), and the data is distributed very unevenly among the others. Estimation methods based on sum-of-squares approximations such as multiple regression and analysis of variance are thus inappropriate and the parameters must be estimated using exact maximum likelihood methods. Many statistical computing packages have the capability of carrying out this type of analysis, although most of the linguistic work has made use of one or other version of the 'variable rule' program (Rand and Sankoff 1990, Robinson et al. 2001). Elimination of statistically irrelevant influences can be assured by a multiple regression type of analysis with a stepwise selection of significant factors. For example, in expressing future time in the French spoken in Montreal, if a verb is negated, this has a statistically very significant effect in reducing the use of the periphrastic future. Elevated socioeconomic status of the speaker is also a significant factor, while neither the nature of the subject of the verb nor the age of the speaker has a significant effect.

8. Detecting Heterogeneity

A major preoccupation in sociolinguistics is the degree of homogeneity of the speech community. Do all speakers in the community share a common model of type (1)—possibly involving a single parameter to account for individual differences—or might different individuals or different segments of the community each have a substantively different model of type (1)? A way of answering this question is based on a dynamic clustering procedure. An initial (random) partition into k groups of the speakers in the speech sample is made, followed by an estimation of the parameters in k versions of model (1), a separate model for each group. Speakers are then reassigned to groups according to which model they 'fit' best, using the likelihood criterion. Further iterations are carried out on the estimation and reassignment procedures until they converge. The significance of the analyses for each of $k = 2, 3 \ldots$ can be tested based on the increase in likelihood with the increase in k, compared with the number of additional parameters estimated.

Thus, in expressing an indefinite referent, Montreal French speakers fall into two groups according to how they vary between *on* 'one' and *tu* 'you.' In one group, speakers have a high rate of *on* usage in conveying proverb-like sentiments and in a certain class of syntactic construction while the other group shares the former but not the latter (syntactic) effect (Rousseau and Sankoff 1978a).

9. Implicational Scales

Data on a linguistic variable are sometimes given as a two-dimensional array, where each row represents a different speaker or speech variety and each column represents a different linguistic or sociolinguistic context. In the simplest version, each cell of the table contains a 0 or a 1, indicating which of two variants of a linguistic variable is expressed by the given speaker in the given context. The problem is to reorder the rows and columns so that every row consists of a series of 0s to the left followed by a series of 1s to the right (i.e., no 0 is to the right of a 1 in a row) and every column consists of a series of 0s at the top followed by a series of 1's on the bottom (i.e., no 0 is below a 1 in a column), as in Table 1.

If an implicational scale can be established, it represents a highly economical representation of the how the set of speakers and the set of contexts are organized in terms of this linguistic variable.

It is not always possible to arrange data into an implicational scale, so various somewhat arbitrary measures of scaling have been proposed, to assess to what extent a data set is 'scalable,' based on the minimum possible number of 'scaling errors.'

In the general case, instead of 0s and 1s, each cell contains a fraction r/n, representing the successes divided by the total trials of a binomial experiment (or the uses of one of the variants divided by the total occurrences of the variable). The problem is then to find row and column permutations (or relabelings) such that in the relabeled matrix, r/n is nondecreasing along both rows and columns, as in Table 2. This type of analysis is of interest when in most cells $r/n = 0$ or $r/n = 1$, so that all except a few 'transitional' cells correspond to the 0s and 1s of the basic analysis.

It might seem that a logistic-linear model such as (2) would not seem capable of accounting for data which form an implicational scale since p could not be 0 or 1 for any cell as long as the speaker effect a and the row effect b are finite.

$$\log p/(1 - p) = a + b \qquad (2)$$

In other words, model (2) could only give an approximate account for nonvariable behavior (i.e., when $r/n = 1$ or $r/n = 0$). In properly defined maximum likelihood estimation for data such as those in Table 2, however, the estimates for a and b in (2) remain undefined, but the estimates of p in each cell are well defined, and can take on values 0 and 1 where the data predicts nonvariable behavior (Rousseau and Sankoff 1978b). This forms the basis for an integrated logistic-linear/implicational scale analysis, including a principled basis for

Table 1. Simple implicational scale depicting variant use (0 versus 1) in 5 contexts by 6 speakers.

	context 1	context 2	context 3	context 4	context 5
speaker 1	0	0	0	0	1
speaker 2	0	0	0	0	1
speaker 3	0	0	0	1	1
speaker 4	0	0	0	1	1
speaker 5	0	1	1	1	1
speaker 6	1	1	1	1	1

Table 2. General implicational scale depicting one variant's frequency r divided by total occurrences n of the variable.

	context 1	context 2	context 3	context 4	context 5
speaker 1	0/3 = 0	0/1 = 0	0/5 = 0	1/6	2/4
speaker 2	0/10 = 0	0/3 = 0	0/3 = 0	5/12	8/9
speaker 3	0/2 = 0	0/1 = 0	0/1 = 0	6/6 = 1	10/10 = 1
speaker 4	0/7 = 0	0/4 = 0	0/2 = 0	2/2 = 1	3/3 = 1
speaker 5	0/6 = 0	3/4	8/10	6/6 = 1	6/6 = 1
speaker 6	2/7	7/8	8/9	1/1 = 1	9/9 = 1

rejecting data which cause 'scaling errors,' since these data turn out to be outliers in terms of their extremely low likelihood under a maximum likelihood analysis of the data set (Sankoff and Rousseau 1979).

10. Rare Variants

Variation theory sometimes encounters a situation, especially in syntax, where one of the two variants is extremely rare, and may not even occur once in the entire corpus at hand. This variant may well represent an important phenomenon, however, such as an incipient change or a necessary condition of some other rare contextual feature. Examples of the rare variant may only be collected through what is effectively participant observation, writing down sentences as they are heard in daily conversation, on the radio or television, or read in the written media.

We then effectively have two corpora, the conventional one containing no examples of the rare variant but sufficient examples of the usual variant distributed among a sample of contexts, and the new corpus containing exclusively examples of the rare variant, presumably in a representative sample of the contexts in which it occurs. Though it may seem somewhat counterintuitive, variable rule analysis based on formula (1) can be carried out as normal on the combined data set, as if all the occurrences originated in the same corpus (cf. Bishop 1969). The only difference is that the estimate of mean or corrected mean has no meaningful interpretation, since this would depend strongly on the (unknown) total amount of conversation from which the rare variant examples were extracted. The feature effect estimates, however, have their normal interpretation and are not affected by the dual origin of the data.

11. Multiple Variants and Rule Order

In the preceding sections, we have only discussed choice variables, which are dichotomous, although the factor groups could contain any number of factors. There are many cases, however, where a linguistic choice may be perceived as involving three or more alternatives simultaneously. Generalization of the mathematical treatment to this context offers no conceptual difficulty, only a number of complications in the formulae.

For example, consider the case of three variants A, B, and C, with probabilities p, q, and r in a given context. The logistic-linear model becomes:

$$\log(p/q) = a_i + a_j + \cdots + a_k$$
$$\log(q/r) = b_i + b_j + \cdots + b_k \qquad (3)$$
$$\log(r/p) = c_i + c_j + \cdots + c_k$$

Actually, the third equation is equivalent to the sum of the other two, and hence is redundant. In general, if there are n variants, then $n-1$ equations suffice to define the model.

When there are multiple variants, it is not always clear whether they should be considered as having been generated simultaneously, or whether certain distinctions among the variants are decided before others. This part of the classical problem of rule ordering can be studied through variable rule analysis. The other part of the problem, the question of what forms underlie what others, cannot be approached through statistical analysis of conditioned choice data.

For example, consider a hypothetical variable with four surface forms (variants 1 through 4). Mathematically speaking, there are 184 ways of generating these by different rule order schemes from a common underlying form, though many of these may be implausible. Two schemes are depicted in Fig. 1.

The first rule in scheme (a) can be analyzed by a two-variant variable rule, since we know how many times in each context the choice was made to rewrite (the number of surface occurrences of variants 2, 3, and 4) and how many times it was not (the number of occurrences of variant 1). Similarly, the choices represented by the second rule can be analyzed using the number of variant 2 versus the number of 3 and 4. And the third rule is based simply on the number of 3 versus the number of 4. In scheme (b), the two-pronged rule represents a simultaneous three-way choice between variants 1, 2, and 3, and can be analyzed using the number of variant 1 versus (2 and 4) versus 3.

The likelihood of each of the 184 schemes can be calculated as the product of the maximum likelihoods of the individual choice processes represented by its rules. We can then invoke the principle of maximum likelihood to infer the best scheme. Suppose that analysis of data showed that (b) in Fig. 1 is the most likely scheme. Then there would be at least five other schemes, such as the two in Fig. 2, which must have exactly the same likelihood, since they imply exactly the same choice processes. They differ only according to which forms underlie which others.

The implication of this equivalence for the problem of rule ordering is that this problem can be decomposed into two aspects. One is the identity of the underlying form or, more generally, which variants give rise to which other, and the second aspect is the most likely arrangement of the variants into a treelike, or hierarchical classification, of which there are only 26 different possibilities compared to the 184 schemata in the example. The data on variant occurrences in context do not bear at all on the first aspect, but do allow us to use statistical means, namely the comparison of the likelihoods of the different schemata, to infer the hierarchy. Thus only the order in which the distinctions among subsets of variants are drawn can be studied statistically, and not the question of underlying forms.

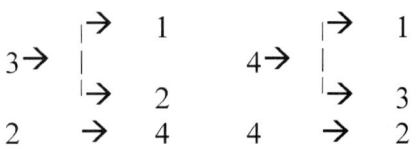

Figure 2. Two schemes with the same likelihood as scheme (b) in Fig. 1.

This methodology has been used most extensively in analyzing the variation in the pronunciation of the word-final consonants /s/, /n/, and /r/ that characterize most varieties of Caribbean Spanish (Sankoff and Rousseau 1989).

12. Discussion

Much of this article has been phrased in terms of alternations between forms that are related in some theoretical account of phonology or syntax. However, where statistical regularities are found in linguistic performance, they are important as properties of language independent of whether they are consequences of:

(a) the physiology of articulation, in phonology;
(b) processing considerations in syntax;
(c) social or biological universals, as in the competition of tense and aspect inflections with periphrastic constructions based on verbs for standing, sitting, going, etc., or in the competition of modals with verbs for volition, ability, desire, etc.;
(d) panlinguistic typological tendencies ('parameters') which may or may not be coded in some innate form on the individual level; or
(e) some punctual actualization of the individual's grammatical facility.

There are many types of causes of statistical regularity, and which one or ones are pertinent to a given linguistic pattern remains an empirical question.

See also: Sociolinguistic Variation; Sociometry; Multidimensional Scaling.

Bibliography

Bishop Y M 1969 Full contingency tables, logits and split contigency tables. *Biometrics* **25**: 119–25

Cedergren H J, Sankoff D 1974 Variable rules: Performance as a statistical reflection of competence. *Language* **50**: 333–55

Labov W 1969 Contraction, deletion, and inherent variability of the English copula. *Language* **45**: 715–62

Rand D, Sankoff D 1990 *GoldVarb: A Variable Rule Application for Macintosh*. Centre de recherches mathématiques, Université de Montréal, PQ

Robinson J, Lawrence H, Tagliamonte S 2001 *GOLDVARB 2001 for Windows*. Department of Language and Linguistic Science, University of York, UK

Rousseau P, Sankoff D 1978a A solution to the problem of grouping speakers. In: Sankoff D (ed.) *Linguistic*

```
            1 → 2             1 → 2
(a)  2 → 3        (b)  1 →
     3 → 4              └→ 3
                      2  → 4
```

Figure 1. Rule order schemes: (a) some occurrences of underlying variant 1 rewritten as 2, then some of these 2 rewritten as 3, then some 3 rewritten as 4; (b) some 1 rewritten as either 2 or 3, then some 2 rewritten as 4.

Variation: Models and Methods. Academic Press, New York

Rousseau P, Sankoff D 1978b Singularities in the analysis of binomial data. *Biometrika* **65**: 603–8

Sankoff D 1988 Sociolinguistics and syntactic variation. In: Newmeyer F (ed.) *Linguistics: The Cambridge Survey. IV: The Socio-Cultural Context*. Cambridge University Press, Cambridge, UK

Sankoff D, Rousseau P 1979 Categorical contexts and variable rules. In: Jacobson S (ed.) *Papers from the Scandinavian Symposium on Syntactic Variation*. Almqvist & Wiksell, Stockholm

Sankoff D, Rousseau P 1989 Statistical evidence for rule ordering. *Language Variation and Change* **1**: 1–18

Sankoff D, Sankoff G 1973 Sample survey methods and computer-assisted analysis in the study of grammatical variation. In: Darnell R (ed.) *Canadian Languages in their Social Context*. Linguistic Research Incorporated, Edmonton, AB

SECTION X
The Profession

Institutions and Resources

Endangered Languages Projects (An Inventory)
L. A. Grenoble and L. J. Whaley

Predictions for language loss this century range from 30–90 percent of all living languages. Alarmed by these estimates, concerned individuals and communities have responded in a variety of ways. The type of response is determined by the status of a particular endangered language (as measured in terms of number of speakers, age of speakers, existence of support materials, and so on). Of equal relevance are factors of the local-level situation, such as size and sense of community, religious and cultural traditions, and levels and amount of contact with other languages, together with the importance of government support (or lack thereof), education policies, and so on.

1. Educational Projects

Language revitalization projects are connected to formal education in a number of ways. At one end of the spectrum are those programs which teach the endangered language, to varying degrees, as a secondary subject, much the way that a foreign language is taught. The most basic programs may teach only songs, chants, or proverbs in the language so that at least some knowledge of language and culture is maintained. At the other end are total immersion programs where children are taught exclusively in the heritage language (see *Heritage Languages*). Often these programs evolve from the lower grades, where they are first implemented, to the higher grades, developing as the children themselves pass from grade to grade.

1.1 Immersion Schools

Immersion schools are possible when a language is still widely used in a speech community. In the immersion school system, primary subjects are taught in the native language. One of the most ambitious programs, the Mohawk Kahnawake Survival School (Quebec), has been in operation since 1978. The school was established by community members and directly involves parents and elders in the classroom.

Navajo, a Native American language which is still used over a wide area in the United States, is another example of an endangered language taught on an immersion basis. In the Rock Point Community School in Arizona, reading and writing are first taught in Navajo, and then in English. In the elementary school, much of the primary curriculum is taught in Navajo, with English gradually introduced as the child progresses through the school system. By the seventh and eighth grades children receive a full year of Navajo cultural instruction in Navajo, along with a quarter term's worth of writing in Navajo.

1.2 Bilingual Education Programs

In communities where the native language is no longer the dominant language, immersion school systems are often difficult to implement. Many such communities opt for teaching the native language as a second language.

For some languages, combinations of total immersion and bilingual education models are appropriate. An example is provided by Central Yup'ik, which is taught in 22 Alaskan village schools as well as three more urban schools. Where English is the dominant language, Central Yup'ik is taught for one period a day. Where Yup'ik is still dominant, it is the primary language of instruction in kindergarten through second grade. English instruction is gradually phased in, beginning with 30 minutes of instruction per day in kindergarten and building to 90 minutes per day. By the third grade, English is the main language of instruction, but Central Yup'ik language classes continue on a daily basis.

1.3 Higher Education

There are very few institutions of higher education specifically dedicated to the promotion of endangered languages. In the US, the tribal college movement began with the foundation of the Navajo Community College in 1968. The program has developed and grown so that the American Indian

Higher Education Consortium (AIHEC) lists 31 members.

Another type of program is exemplified by the Gertsen Institute, which was established in the early years of the Soviet Union in St. Petersburg (then Leningrad) as a teacher-training center for indigenous minorities of the North. Subsequently, some teacher-training has been established in Moscow and in Siberian cities (such as Yakutsk). Their efforts focus on training native speakers to return to their villages to teach in local schools. A similar effort occurs at the Central Institute of Indian Languages in Mysore, India.

2. Learning Models
2.1 The Language Nest Model

The language nest model finds its origins with the Maori of New Zealand. When, in the 1960s, the Maori realized that their children were speaking English not Maori, they began a system of language 'nests' (or Te Kohanga Reo): preschool daycare centers where Maori elders worked to create a total immersion environment in Maori language and culture for the children. The success of these daycare centers led to a demand for Maori immersion elementary and then secondary schools. The model was adopted by the Hawaiian language revitalization movement (Punana Lao) in the 1980s where it has been relatively successful.

2.2 Master–Apprentice Language Learning Program

For many seriously endangered languages, there is no longer a speaker community *per se* and creating a total immersion program is impossible. The native Californian languages provide examples, as only a handful of elders still speak each language. This prompted the master–apprentice language learning program, which aims to teach individual adult students, rather than to revitalize a large speaker base. It is based on the premise that adults can learn language informally, in much the way that children do, through listening and practicing with a native speaker. This program matches teams of one master-teacher/native speaker with an individual student; they commit to working together for approximately 20 hours per week for four months, creating an intensive learning environment. When available linguistic resources are minimal (such as having only a few native speakers), the master-apprentice language learning program has proven to be one of the most effective ways of passing on some knowledge of the language.

2.3 Higher Education

A number of programs for the study of endangered languages exist at the level of higher education. Beyond language courses affiliated with linguistics departments, some institutions specialize in the education and promotion of specific endangered languages and cultures. For example, *Studienzentrum für Keltische Sprachen und Kulturen* (the Study Center for Celtic Languages and Cultures at http://www.sksk.de/) offers courses in modern Celtic (Irish, Welsh, Breton, and Scottish Gaelish). Celtic studies are also widely taught at the universities in their own territories (e.g., Aberdeen, Belfast, Dublin, and Wales, to name just a few).

2.4 Cultural Programs

Some groups have taken a different approach and consciously rejected formal education programs. In a few cases this decision comes from a lack of resources (be it financial, linguistic, or human), but some groups argue against formal education on the grounds that it will fundamentally change the language and culture. The Tohono O'odham (in Northern Mexico and Southern Arizona in the US), for example, are committed to language use in traditional ways, such as in song, dance, and oral literature.

3. Resource Development

One of the greatest challenges facing revitalization programs is the development of pedagogical and other materials for teaching or in some way using the endangered language. Educational programs are often implemented to revitalize and preserve languages, and these require a broad range of pedagogical materials, ranging from dictionaries and reference grammars to textbooks written in the endangered language. Recent technological advances support the development of relatively inexpensive language materials for groups which have computers and Internet access. Some tools for resource development (such as fonts and software, as well as some links to support organizations) can be found at the Endangered Languages Homepage of the Linguistics Society of America. A large number of online language courses are offered; the Gaelic languages can all be studied online through a variety of programs, a possibility for a number of Native American languages as well.

The creation of resources often first requires the development of a written language. Determining the dialect upon which to base the standardized language is far from trivial. Ideally, the standardized variety will be one that is readily comprehensible to all speakers of all dialects, but when dialect variation is extensive, this may be impossible. Language planners often opt to make standard the dialect which has the greatest speaker base, or is centrally located, or has some particular historical or social prominence. The role of the linguist here is crucial, as the linguist is often in a position to answer questions of linguistic accuracy, typological consistency, or diachronic validity.

The development of orthographies (see *Orthography*) can be equally problematic. A group may turn to the alphabet used by a national language, but often this alphabet may either lack sufficient symbols to represent the endangered language's phonemes, or may have too many (or redundant) symbols. A given orthographic system may also create access to the written form of the majority language (thereby facilitating language shift).

4. Organizations

Many organizations have been developed to address issues of language documentation, revitalization, and retention. Some operate on a local level only, such as the Shuar Federation in the lowlands of Ecuador, which has been working to preserve use of the Shuar language since the 1970s. Some are more broadly based, such as the Native American Language Center, which is concerned with all of the indigenous languages of California. A number of international organizations work to support research or community language preservation efforts, or to collect and disseminate information on the status of endangered languages. In addition to these, there are a great many language-specific and regional foundations that are not listed here.

4.1 Foundation for Endangered Languages

The Foundation for Endangered Languages has specific educational and scholarly goals, seeking to raise awareness of the plight of endangered languages; to support the use of languages, through community-based programs and the monitoring of policies and political structures; to support research and education programs; and to fund the dissemination of information.

4.2 International Clearing House of Endangered Languages (ICHEL) and the UNESCO Red Book on Endangered Languages

This international organization acts as a clearing house for information on the status of endangered languages and descriptive information of many of the world's languages. The ICHEL works in conjunction with the UNESCO Red Book project; the primary goals of these projects are to conduct field work, and to create electronic corpora of published and unpublished materials (e.g., texts, word lists, and phonetic data).

4.3 Gesellschaft für bedrohte Sprachen (Society for Endangered Languages)

The society was founded in 1977 by a group of German linguists, together with linguists from the 'Endangered languages' research group of the German Society for Linguistics in Cologne. This is a non-profit organization which aims to promote the use, preservation, and documentation of endangered languages by supporting research, field work, and community efforts; by taking a proactive stance in promoting national and international cooperation between researchers; and by informing scientific and public communities about the issues of language endangerment.

4.4 Endangered Language Fund

The Endangered Language Fund, based at Yale University, provides research grants for the study of endangered languages. The fund also supports community-based efforts to preserve minority languages and supports the dissemination of information to the native communities and the scholarly world.

4.5 Terralingua

Terralingua is an internationally-based non-profit organization which is concerned with the status of minority languages in terms of not only linguistic, but also cultural and biological diversity. It is an advocacy group which supports research and the continued development of linguistic diversity, as well as studies of the interrelations between linguistic, cultural, and biological diversity.

4.6 The Native American Language Issues Institute (NALI)

NALI is a non-profit organization which was established in 1980. Its primary goals are to strengthen Native American languages and cultures while functioning as a language institute, training future educators and offering university credit for this training. It sponsors an annual institute, which aims to facilitate interaction between language practitioners and language professionals.

4.7 Aboriginal Languages of Australia

A large number of organizations in Australia are devoted to the documentation and development of the aboriginal languages. At the national level are such organizations as the Aboriginal and Torres Strait Islander Corporation of Languages (FATSIL), the Australian Indigenous Languages Framework (AILF), and Language Australia (formerly NLLIA), which is based at the Australian National University in Canberra. In addition, there are many smaller organizations, which operate on a more local level.

4.8 The Mercator Project

Mercator was established by the European Commission in 1987 to meet the address issues of minority and regional languages in the European context. Mercator is a network of three research centers, which each have related missions: the Mercator Education at the Fryske Akademy in The Netherlands studies education at all levels; Mercator Legislation at the CEIMEN foundation, Barcelona, focuses on language legislation and language in public administration; and Mercator Media at the University of Wales, Aberystwyth, works with the press and the media, including the new media.

4.9 European Bureau for Lesser-used Languages

Based in Brussels, this Bureau works to achieve the best European policies for lesser-used languages. Its goals to protect and promote the use of minority languages are achieved through linking linguistic communities with local and regional authorities in the member states of the European Union to promote the implementation of fair policies for these communities, and to increase awareness of relevant linguistic issues.

See also: Endangered Languages; Salvage Work (Endangered Languages); Reversing Language Shift; Heritage Languages.

Bibliography

Hinton L, Hale K (eds.) 2001 *The Green Book of Language Revitalization in Practice*. Academic Press, New York

Internet Resources for Sociolinguistics
A. Deumert

The rise of the Internet in the early 1990s opened up new ways of exchanging scientific information, and today the Internet provides sociolinguistic researchers with a wealth of language-related material. There are three main types of resources available: (a) mailing lists, which constitute informal channels for scientific communication; (b) websites of individuals, research institutes, academic departments, and professional associations, offering access to data bases as well as information about specific languages or areas of linguistic research; and (c) electronic journals.

1. Mailing Lists

Mailing lists enable e-mail users to broadcast (via a central list-server) e-mails to groups of other e-mail users. These lists serve as forums for questions and answers. They distribute relevant information and allow for on-line discussions of specific topics. The Linguist List (founded in 1990, http://www.linguistlist.org/) is the chief mailing list for linguists, covering all areas of linguistic research. A group of moderators ensures the academic standard of list postings. More specialized mailing lists are the CreoList (http://www.su.se/Creole/) which is dedicated to the discussion of pidgin/creole studies, and the multi-disciplinary Language-Culture List (http://www.language-culture.org/). Other mailing lists, which are of interest to sociolinguists are, for example, the Discourse Studies List (DISCOURS), the endangered languages list (ENDANGERED-LANGUAGES-L), the ethics list (ETHICS), the heritage language education list (HERITAGE), and the linguistic anthropology discussion group (LIN-GANTH). A register of mailing lists can be found on the Linguist List website, which also offers on-line access to the list's archives, information about the profession, conference announcements, dissertation abstracts, and bibliographies. Valuable links to linguistic Internet resources can be found at the Virtual Library of Linguistics (http://www.cog.brown.edu/pointers/linguistics.html).

2. Websites

2.1 Diversity on the Internet: Languages and Dialects of the World

Web-based language documentation is particularly useful for smaller, less-studied languages where the target audiences are small and conventional means of publication would have been costly. The American Indian Resources page, for example, provides access to on-line dictionaries and linguistic descriptions of American Indian languages, as well as cultural and educational material (http://www.lang.osaka-u.ac.jp/~krkvls/lang.html).

An emphasis on linguistic diversity, minority language rights, and language documentation is also characteristic of the following sites.

(a) ERIC Clearinghouse on Language and Linguistics (ERIC-CLL, http://www.cal.org/ericcll/): services and materials with a focus on language and education, including a large bibliographic database. It is operated by the Center for Applied Linguistics, Washington, USA.

(b) International Clearing House for Endangered Languages (Department of Asian and Pacific Linguistics, University of Tokyo, Japan, http://www.tooyoo.l.u-tokyo.ac.jp): databases, resources, and bibliographies on minority and endangered languages, on-line access to the UNESCO Red Book of Endangered Languages.

(c) Language Varieties Network (http://une.edu.au/langnet, University of New England, Australia): sociolinguistic descriptions of

non-standard varieties such as, for example, Geordie (Newcastle upon Tyne), Kamtok (Cameroon Pidgin English), Singlish (Singapore Colloquial English), and Aboriginal English (Australia).
(d) Rosetta Project (http://www.rosettaproject.org): publicly accessible, full-text archives of 1000+ languages. Languages are documented as follows: description (typology, history, and current status), genesis translation, glossed vernacular texts, orthographical system, Swadesh word list, phonemic inventory, and audio files. The information is collected through an open contribution model.
(e) SIL International (The Summer Institute of Linguistics, http://www.sil.org): from this page one can link to the Ethnologue, an electronic database of the world's languages. It includes information on the status of languages (official language, medium of instruction, etc.) speaker numbers, location, dialects, speaker bilingualism, linguistic affiliation, literacy, Bible translations, and alternate language names. The Ethnologue provides information about more than 6700 languages in over 200 countries.
(f) Gay language research (http://www.msu.edu/~greenm14/outil/gaybib.html). This site contains a regularly updated bibliography of sources relevant to gay language research.

Urban and regional dialectologists in North America and Europe have also begun to make use of the Internet for publication of their research, including maps and (written or acoustic) samples of the language data. Detailed background information and data files are available for the North American Linguistic Atlases (http://us.english.uga.edu). Some of the maps of the Phonological Atlas of North America (see *The Atlas of North American English*), which was produced under the leadership of William Labov, are also available on-line (http://www.ling.upenn.edu/phono_atlas/home.html). In Europe, the research institute *Deutscher Sprachatlas* (http://www.uni-marburg.de/dsa/) allows on-line access to its digitalized German dialect maps.

2.2 Corpus Linguistics and the Internet

Electronic linguistic corpora are available via the Internet for research purposes. The language data is either presented in its raw form or annotated (i.e., tagged for grammar or semantics). Michael Barlow's Corpus Linguistics page at Rice University (http://www.ruf.rice.edu/~barlow/corpus.html) provides links to corpora in several languages (including, for example, Chinese, Gaelic, Malay, Russian, etc.), as well as links to sites providing parsing software. Linguistic databases and parsing software can also be found at the Linguistic Data Consortium (http://ldc.upenn.edu). The Child Language Data Exchange System (CHILDES, http://childes.psy.cmu.edu/) gives access to its database of transcripts of first and second language learners, as well as to software for data analysis. There also exist corpora of lesser used languages such as the databases of Maori newspapers (1842–1933, http://www.nzdl.org/cgi-bin/niupepalibrary?a=p&p=about) and Hawaiian newspapers (1834–1927, http://128.171.57.100/hnp/index.shtml). The Archive of the Indigenous Languages of Latin America (AILLA, University of Texas, USA, http://www.ailla.org) holds an electronic data base of audio files and texts. The archive's focus is on naturally occurring discourse. An extensive corpus of literary texts can be found at the Project Gutenberg (http://www.gutenberg.net).

3. Electronic Journals

The advent of the Internet has changed the face of academic publishing. Many traditional journals have begun to provide electronic versions of their texts, which can be accessed with personal identification via university libraries. There also exist a number of electronic journals, which do not have a printed version, and many of these are available free of charge. An example of such an electronic journal is the *Journal for Computer Mediated Communication* (http://www.ascusc.org.jcmc/) which publishes sociolinguistically oriented articles on Internet language use. Other electronic publications of interest for sociolinguists are:

(a) *The Web Journal of Modern Language Linguistics* (http://wjmll.ncl.ac.uk).
(b) *Historical Sociolinguistics and Sociohistorical Linguistics* (http://www.leidenuniv.nl/English/staff/tieken/Internet%20journal/).
(c) *Linguistik-Online* (http://linguistik-online.com).
(d) *Electronic Journal of Communication* (http://www.cios.org/www/ejcmain.htm).
(f) *Marges Linguistiques* (http://www.marges-linguistiques.com).

4. Envoi

The network of linguistic Internet resources is continuously growing and changing. Some of the resources listed here might thus change their locations (i.e., their URLs, uniform resource locators) in the foreseeable future and new material will become available. Internet search engines, such as Google, Lycos, or Yahoo, can help to locate up-to-date mailing lists, web pages, and journals. The conventions for citing Internet sources can be found at http://www.linguistlist.org/citing.html.

See also: Corpus Linguistics and Sociolinguistics; Endangered Languages Projects; The Internet and Language; The Atlas of North American English.

Bibliography

Ackermann E, Hartman K 2001 *The Information Searcher's Guide to Searching and Researching on the Internet and the WWW*. ABF Content, Wilsonville, OR

Jones S (ed.) 1999 *Doing Internet Research: Critical Issues and Methods for Examining the Net*. Sage, Thousand Oaks, CA

Professional Associations
R. Mesthrie

This section lists some of the main sociolinguistic organizations involved in the presentation and evaluation of research via regular conferences and publications. The list is by no means exhaustive. It is better seen as a starting point.

1. American Association for Applied Linguistics (AAAL)

Many papers in the area of sociolinguistics and education are presented at AAAL. Its annual conference is held in the northern hemisphere in spring. AAAL is the largest affiliate of the *Association Internationale de Linguistique Appliquee* (AILA). Its website is: www.aaal.org

2. American Dialect Society

This society was started in 1889. Its original publication was *Dialect Notes*, now a monograph series retitled *Publications of the American Dialect Society*. It publishes the journal *American Speech* (volume 76 in 2001). Its website is: www.americandialect.org

3. Association Internationale de Linguistique Appliquee (AILA)

This is an international federation of about 35 national associations of applied linguistics founded in 1964. It hosts the World Congress of Applied Linguistics, which is organized by an affiliated member every three years. It publishes a newsletter, *AILA News*, and the journal *AILA Review* (volume 15 in 2001). Its website is: www.aila.ac

4. British Association of Applied Linguistics (BAAL)

Started in 1967, the association organizes an annual conference, at which many sociolinguistic papers are presented. It publishes a newsletter and conference proceedings. Together with AILA (of which it is an affiliate) and AAAL, the association produces the journal *Applied Linguistics* (published by Oxford University Press; volume 22 in 2001). Its website is: www.baal.org.uk

5. International Association for World Englishes (IAWE)

This society, which held its first conference in 1992, is concerned with the sociolinguistic and applied sociolinguistic aspects of the spread of English. It hosts annual conferences in different parts of the world and is associated with the journal *World Englishes* (published by Blackwell; volume 20 in 2001). Its website is: http://we.pdx.edu

6. International Pragmatics Association (IPrA)

This association covers some aspects of interest to sociolinguistics, especially intercultural communication. Based in Belgium, the association organises the International Pragmatics Conference and publishes the journal *Pragmatics*. Its website is: http://ipra-www.uia.ac.be/ipra/

7. New Ways of Analyzing Variation (in English and other languages) (NWAV(E))

This society, founded in 1971, is concerned specifically with sociolinguistic variation as studied within the quantitative paradigm. Its main focus is on North American research. The society meets annually at a North American university. It produces the journal *Language Variation and Change* (published by Cambridge University Press; volume 13 in 2001).

8. Society for Pidgin and Creole Languages (SPCL)

The society, which was started in 1989, hosts an annual conference, which coincides with the winter meetings of the Linguistic Society of America. It is associated with the *Journal of Pidgin and Creole Languages* (published by Benjamins; volume 16 in 2001).

9. Sociolinguistic Symposium (SS)

This is a loosely structured association started by British sociolinguists in 1976. It hosts a biennial conference usually held in the United Kingdom, though for the first time in 2002 the conference is being in continental Europe. All aspects of sociolinguistics are covered, with an emphasis on linguistic variation in the British context. Its website is: www.uwe.ac.uk/facults/les/research/sociling2000.html

10. International Association for Forensic Phonetics (IAFP)

This association was established in 1991 to regulate and assist the practice of speech analysis for legal purposes. It aims to ensure that practitioners are suitably qualified, to fix ethical and practical guidelines for analysis, and to promote research. It is associated with the journal *Forensic Linguistics*. Its website is: www.iafp.net

11. International Association for Language and Social Psychology

Although conferences of this group go back to 1979, the association was formally instituted in 1997. It has close links with the *Journal of Language and Social Psychology* (published by Sage; volume 20 in 2001).

12. International Association of Intercultural Communication Studies (IAICS)

The association was founded in 1991, after a series of Asian–USA conferences. Conferences are held biennially in Asian and US centers. The association's headquarters are at the Institute for Cross-Cultural Research at Trinity University in San Antonio, Texas. It runs the journal *Intercultural Communication Studies*. Its website is: www.louisville.edu/~rnstcl01/IAICS-ICS.htm

13. International Gender and Language Association (IGALA)

This association developed out of the graduate-student run Berkeley Women and Language Group into an international association in 1999. It is an interdisciplinary organization that promotes and supports research on language, gender, and sexuality. The organization hosts a biennial conference: IGALA 1 was held at Stanford University in 2000. GALA-L is the official electronic list of the association.

14. International Society for Dialectology and Geolinguistics (SIDG)

The society is concerned with the study of dialectology and geolinguistics in the international context as well as the study of minority languages and dialects. Its executive members are drawn mainly from continental Europe. The society publishes the journal *Dialectologia et Geolinguistica* (published by Edizioni dell'Orso; volume 9 in 2001) and the SIDG bulletin. It organizes an international congress of dialectology and geolinguistics at least once every three years. Its website is: www.uni-bamberg.de/~ba4es1/sidg.html

15. Societies for Endangered Languages

Many countries do not have specifically sociolinguistic associations: rather their national linguistics associations carry a heavy emphasis on sociolinguistics. This is true, for example, of the *Society for Caribbean Linguistics*; the *Linguistics Society of Southern Africa* (http://www.puk.ac.za/lssa/index.html) and the *Linguistics Society of India*. (See: *Endangered Language Projects: An Inventory*).

Likewise research centers in sociolinguistics are too numerous and scattered to be covered adequately here. However, mention must be made of a few centers and institutes that have had a major influence in sociolinguistics and applied sociolinguistics.

16. Le Centre Internationale de Recherche sur le Bilingualisme

Established in the 1960s at the University of Laval, Quebec, and re-established with a change of name (*Le Centre Internationale de Recherche en Aménagement Linguistique*), this center is a pioneer in the field of language policy and educational linguistics. It maintains a web database on language policy in countries throughout the world. Its website is: http://www.ciral.ulaval.ca

17. The Center for Applied Linguistics

This center was established in Washington, DC, in 1959 and has been closely associated with the rise of sociolinguistics and applied linguistics in the United States. It deals with a variety of issues including language policy, English as a second language, foreign language education and testing, immigrant education, and refugee affairs. Its website is: http://www.cal.org

18. The Center for Research and Documentation on World Language Problems

Based in New York, this center produces the journal *Language Problems and Language Planning* and the newsletter *Informilo por interlingvistoj*. It organizes conferences on language and communication in conjunction with the United Nations Translation Service.

19. Summer Institute of Linguistics (SIL)

This institute began in 1934 with a summer school to teach young people indigenous languages. Since then it has grown into a major organization that has come to be known for its work in Bible translation. Notwithstanding this proselytizing function, the organization has been involved in inculcating literacy, cultural awareness, teacher training, developing field methods, and theories of linguistic description. One of the most widely used books published by SIL is the *Ethnologue*, edited by Barbara F. Grimes, which is a comprehensive listing of the languages of the world country by country, with details about demographics, dialects, extent of bilingualism, and the state of Bible translation. Its website is: www.sil.org

A useful reference work on sociolinguistic and language planning organizations throughout the world is Domínguez and López (1995).

Bibliography

Domínguez F, López N 1995 *Sociolinguistic and Language Planning Organisations*. Benjamins, Amsterdam

Bendor-Samuel J 1999 Summer Institute of Linguistics. In: Spolsky B (ed.) *The Concise Encyclopedia of Educational Linguistics*. Pergamon, Oxford, UK, pp. 739–45

Paulston C B, Tucker G R (eds.) 1997 *The Early Days of Sociolinguistics-Memories and Reflections*. Summer Institute of Linguistics, Dallas, TX

Spolsky B 1999 Research centers. In: Spolsky B (ed.) *Concise Encyclopedia of Educational Linguistics*. Pergamon, Oxford, UK, pp. 734–39

Sociolinguistics Journals: A Critical Survey
N. Coupland

Reviewing the journals of any discipline is tricky territory, especially for a partisan journal editor. Listing journals as lying 'inside' or 'outside' Sociolinguistics will highlight boundary disputes, although to air these is probably the most useful ambition for this entry. Recklessly therefore, over-reliant on 12 as a conventionally round number, here is a subjective list of 'core' international sociolinguistic journals, alphabetically by title, with their 2001 volume or issue numbers and publishers:

(a) *Discourse and Society* (12), Sage
(b) *International Journal of Bilingualism* (4), Kingston Press
(c) *International Journal of the Sociology of Language* (issue 148), Mouton de Gruyter
(d) *Journal of Language and Social Psychology* (20), Sage
(e) *Journal of Multilingual and Multicultural Development* (21), Multilingual Matters
(f) *Journal of Pidgin and Creole Languages* (16), Benjamins
(g) *Journal of Sociolinguistics* (5), Blackwell Publishers
(h) *Language in Society* (30), Cambridge University Press
(i) *Language Variation and Change* (13), Cambridge University Press
(j) *Multilingua* (20), Mouton de Gruyter
(k) *Pragmatics* (11), International Pragmatics Association
(l) *Research on Language and Social Interaction* (34), Lawrence Erlbaum Associates

Of these, *Journal of Sociolinguistics* and *Language in Society* are most comprehensive in their coverage of the field, with others in the list tending towards specialist sub-fields. A secondary list comprises an array of important journals, which are listed separately for the reasons specified below:

(a) smaller scale, avowedly sociolinguistic journals such as *Current Issues in Language and Society*, *Current Issues in Language Planning* and *Sociolinguistica*;
(b) non-primarily-English language journals, such as the *Japanese Journal of Language and Society* and *Estudios de Sociolingüística* which publishes in English and Spanish, although Sociolinguistics needs to be more multilingual in its publishing;
(c) exclusively English-focused journals, such as *English World-Wide*, *World Englishes*, *American Speech*, and the more 'popular' *English Today*;
(d) general journals in Linguistics, such as *Journal of Linguistics*, *Language*, *Language Sciences*, *Lingua*, *Linguistics* and *Word*;
(e) journals in the field of Communication, such as *Human Communication Research*, *Journal of Communication*, *Language and Communication*, *Semiotica* and *Social Semiotics*;
(f) journals mainly focusing on language education or in some other sense Applied Linguistics, such as *Applied Linguistics*, *Forensic Linguistics*, *International Journal of Applied Linguistics*, *International Review of Applied Linguistics*, *Language Awareness*, *TESOL Quarterly*, and *Written Language and Literacy*;
(g) sociological, social psychological and anthropological journals, like *Anthropological Linguistics* (which would be 'core' Sociolinguistics for many), and *Annual Review of Anthropology*, *Journal of Social Issues*, *European Journal of Social Psychology* and *Sociological Inquiry*;
(h) psycholinguistic journals such as *Journal of Child Language* and *Language Learning*;

(i) nationally focused journals, such as New Zealand's *Te Reo* and *Southern African Linguistics and Applied Language Studies*;
(j) university working papers, including the University of Liverpool's very sociolinguistic *Language and Discourse*;
(k) journals in the field of discourse analysis, such as *Discourse Processes, Discourse Studies, Journal of Pragmatics* and *Text*;
(l) new journals like *Language Policy* whose first issue is due 2002;
(m) the new Internet journal *Marges Linguistiques*.

These lists point to the vast multidisciplinarity and, in many instances, genuine interdisciplinarity of Sociolinguistics. Many of the journals in the secondary list sustain much of the critical qualitative research that is becoming central to Sociolinguistics. Sociolinguistics might reasonably be characterized as 'the study of language in society and of society through linguistics.' But in that formulation 'society' is obviously shorthand for a complex, interlocking set of socio-structural, cultural, contextual, relational, and human developmental processes. Some specialist journals pick up on language as it relates to specific domains of such processes—like forensic science, aging, adolescence, health or teaching, and learning. Scholarship at these and similar interfaces is focally, not at all peripherally, sociolinguistic.

What justification is there, then, for identifying a 'core' constituency of sociolinguistic journals at all? Although not watertight, the main one is historical/institutional, in that these journals have been and are now particularly influential in giving Sociolinguistics its shape and status. More than any other journal, *Language in Society* has consolidated Sociolinguistics as a centered, coherent discipline. While it has remained open to work of many denominations, it has majored on anthropological and cultural research. It has carried analyses of minority cultural styles, texts, and events, more qualitative and interactionally focused research than quantitative surveys, and integrative theoretical work. Macro-sociological research on language has been the main domain of the *International Journal of the Sociology of Language*. It is an invaluable, substantial archive of empirical studies, often surveys, themed around specific sociolinguistic communities or languages. This is where Sociolinguistics' prioritization of global linguistic diversity is most apparent. More recently, quantitative, variationist research has *Language Variation and Change* as its home base, and variationism remains the most rigorous empirical tradition in Sociolinguistics, particularly in the United States. These three journals have gained their reputations under the guidance of some of Sociolinguistics' most inspirational figures—William Labov, Dell Hymes, and Joshua Fishman.

Other journals in the 'core' list have similarly promoted distinctive sociolinguistic traditions. For example, *Journal of Language and Social Psychology* has contributed much-needed cognitive emphases, strong empirical (often experimental) procedures, and cumulative theory-building. *Discourse and Society* is explicitly committed to ideological, sociopolitical, critical, and qualitative approaches to language. *Research on Language and Social Interaction* has supported Conversation Analysis research, extending the general traditions of Ethnmethodology and Symbolic Interactionism. *Journal of Multilingual and Multicultural Development* and *Multilingua*, self-evidently in their titles, promote multilingualism studies as well as more general Sociolinguistics. *Pragmatics* makes the 'core' list because, possibly more extensively than other journals in the wide territory of text, discourse, and social interaction, it works to integrate cognitive, social, and cultural approaches to language.

The glib but true generalization behind the list is that Sociolinguistics is admirably served by high-quality and diverse international journals. There is a clear tendency across the set towards specialization or, in the commercialist discourse, niche marketing. This is both a strength and a weakness. Any discipline will thrive on robust competition between its schools and traditions. Individual research initiatives need, at least to some extent, to fit into an architecture of pre-existing assumptions and established knowledge. Specialist journals constitute the architecture for research in their own traditions. The downside, of course, is a propensity towards insularity and dogma, and Sociolinguistics is at risk from these tendencies. Let me briefly itemize some arenas where more boundary crossing and debate is needed.

The hoary contrast between quantitative, empiricist, objectivist, survey-based research and qualitative, interpretive, insider-perspective research is all too much alive in Sociolinguistics. One unfortunate consequence is that sociolinguists interested in quantifying dialect variation and change rarely entertain discursive, richly contextualized data. Correspondingly, interactionists rarely attend to phonological nuance or to trend data across large samples. Pre-defined socio-structural categories are the *modus vivendi* for urban variationists but are targeted as naïve essentializing by constructivist discourse analysts. There are important arguments on both sides (if indeed there are only two sides here), but there is little dialog encompassing them. Similarly, cognition provides the starting point for social psychological accounts of sociolinguistic motivations, attitudes, and stereotyping. Yet Discursive Psychology, in the manner of Conversation

Analysis, is resolutely anti-cognitivist. Anthropological work, which is currently developing rich and challenging theories of performance and cultural reproduction, has little exposure in other sociolinguistic areas. A wider problem is that sociolinguistic theory is generally built in small pockets, to sub-disciplinary tolerances (see Figueroa 1994). The general, urgent point is that we need more inclusive theoretical debate within Sociolinguistics, across its own sub-traditions, and then more confident engagement by Sociolinguistics as a whole with social theory (see Coupland et al. 2001).

A forum is therefore needed where the multiple sub-traditions of Sociolinguistics can be seen, reassessed, and perhaps realigned—where new 'cores' can be bred. This was my own and Allan Bell's objective in founding the *Journal of Sociolinguistics*. Any journal's primary ambition has to be to publish work of the best quality in its field, but the *Journal of Sociolinguistics* also endeavors to sustain a metatheoretical and reflexive debate on the nature, boundaries, and future of Sociolinguistics. One element of this is a series of Dialogue contributions on 'Sociolinguistics and the community,' asking, not least, why such a vibrant, innovative and radical discipline has had so little impact to date on the communities it researches (see *Fieldwork Ethics and Community Responsibility*). Probably the greatest challenge for *all* Sociolinguistics journals, and for the discipline as a whole, is to critically monitor and then to seek to reduce the boundaries between academic Sociolinguistics and the divided worlds of language users.

Bibliography

Coupland N, Sarangi S, Candlin C N (eds.) 2001 *Sociolinguistics and Social Theory*. Longman/Pearson Education, London

Figueroa E 1994 *Sociolinguistic Metatheory*. Pergamon, Oxford, UK

Profiles of Sociolinguists

Ammon, Ulrich (1943–)

A. Deumert

Ulrich Ammon is a central figure in German and European sociolinguistics. His work includes research on dialect and sociolinguistic disadvantage in the classroom, language planning, standardization, international languages, and communication (see *International Languages*), and the variety spectrum of the German language.

Born in 1943 in Backnang, Swabia, Germany, Ammon studied German, English, and cultural anthropology at the universities of Tübingen, Göttingen, and Frankfurt and at Wesleyan University (Connecticut, USA). He completed his studies in 1971 with the state examination for teachers, and received his PhD at Tübingen in 1972. In 1971 he was appointed head of the research project 'School difficulties of dialect speakers' at the University of Tübingen, where he also worked as a lecturer until 1974. He then took up an appointment at the University of Duisburg. Since 1980 he has been professor for German linguistics at Duisburg.

Ammon's early sociolinguistic work (cf. Ammon 1973) was broadly based on Bernstein's theories of social inequality and language barriers in education (see *Bernstein, Basil*). Ammon's research showed a strong interaction of social class membership, dialect usage, and knowledge of the German standard variety in southwest Germany. The higher speakers were situated on the social scale, the better was their knowledge of the German standard language; speakers who occupied lower social positions, on the other hand, spoke the local dialect and had only limited knowledge of the (structurally dissimilar) standard variety. In the educational system, which relies on the standard language as a medium of instruction, dialect-speaking children were found to underperform when compared to their peers.

Ammon also contributed to the study of language norms, language planning, and language standardization, with a focus on the description of the national varieties of German (which as a pluricentric language has different centers of standardization; i.e., Austria, Germany, and Switzerland, cf. Ammon 1995), and the status changes of European standard languages (in particular German) vis-à-vis English. In his monograph *Die internationale Stellung der deutschen Sprache* ('The international status of the German language,' 1991a) Ammon traces the history of the demise of German as an international language of scientific communication in detail. Some years later he approached the subject once more in the book *Ist Deutsch noch internationale Wissenschaftssprache?* ('Is German still an international language of science and research?' 1998), where he discusses the impact of this development on the future educational policies in tertiary institutions.

Together with Norbert Dittmar (see *Dittmar, Norbert*) and Klaus J. Mattheier, Ammon edited the comprehensive bilingual (English-German) handbook *Sociolinguistics/Soziolinguistik* (1987/1988). He is one of the editors of the Yearbook of European Sociolinguistics, *Sociolinguistica*, which publishes papers in German, English, and French (founded 1987; co-editors of *Sociolinguistica* are Klaus J. Mattheier and Peter H. Nelde). He is (1998–2002) vice-president of the research committee on sociolinguistics, which has been established by the International Sociological Association (ISA).

Bibliography

Ammon U 1973 *Dialekt und Einheitssprache in ihrer sozialen Verflechtung. Eine emprirische Untersuchung zu einem vernachlässigten Aspekt von Sprache und sozialer Ungleichheit.* Beltz, Weinheim, Germany

Ammon U 1990 German as an international language. *International Journal of the Sociology of Language* **83**: 135–70

Ammon U 1991a *Die internationale Stellung der deutschen Sprache.* De Gruyter, Berlin

Ammon U 1991b The differentiation of the German language into national varieties of the Federal Republic of Germany (F.R.G.), German Democratic Republic (G.D.R.), Austria and Switzerland. In: Brann C M B (ed.) *Rise and Development of National European Languages.* Pergamon, Oxford, UK

Ammon U 1995 *Die deutsche Sprache in Deutschland, Österreich und der Schweiz. Das Problem nationaler Varietäten.* De Gruyter, Berlin

Ammon U 1998 *Ist Deutsch noch internationale Wissenschaftssprache? Englisch auch für die Hochschullehre in den deutschsprachigen Ländern.* De Gruyter, Berlin

Ammon U, Dittmar N, Mattheier K 1987/1988 (eds.), *Sociolinguistics: An International Handbook of the Science of Language and Society. Soziolinguistik: Ein internationales Handbuch der Wissenschaft von Sprache und Gesellschaft, 2 vols.* De Gruyter, Berlin

Ammon U 2001 English as a future language of teaching at German Universities? A question of difficult consequences, posed by the decline of German as a language of science. In: Ammon U (ed.) *The Dominance of English as a Language of Science. Effects on the Non-English Languages and Language Communities.* De Gruyter, Berlin

Bakhtin, Mikhail M. (1895–1975)
J. M. Weir

Bakhtin was born on November 16, 1895 in Orel, a provincial town south of Moscow. Although his family belonged to the nobility, Bakhtin's father owned no property and worked as a state employee in various banks. Bakhtin completed the gymnasium in Odessa, and entered the philological faculty of the city's university. In 1914 he transferred to St. Petersburg University, where he stayed until 1918. Three years later Bakhtin married Elena Okolovich while living in Vitebsk, a cultural center outside of the capital during the Civil War; husband and wife remained together until her death in 1971. From the mid-1920s Bakhtin lived in Leningrad until his arrest in 1929 on charges related to his intellectual and religious affiliations. He was subsequently exiled to a small city in Kazakhstan and, with the exception of a couple of years, he remained in the provinces until 1969 when he moved to Moscow from Saransk, where he had been teaching in the pedagogical institute. He died in Moscow on March 7, 1975.

Because the majority of his written work was not published until after 1970, and much of the earliest of that not until the latter half of the 1980s, Bakhtin's intellectual biography and reception have only recently begun to take clear shape, culminating in an international centennial conference in 1995 devoted to his life and work. Four more or less distinct periods describe the range and development of Bakhtin's thought (Clark and Holquist 1984, Morson and Emerson 1990).

His earliest and most philosophical period includes the substantial essays 'Toward a philosophy of the act,' 'Author and hero in esthetic activity,' 'The problem of content, material, and form in verbal art,' and the brief 'Art and answerability' (Bakhtin's first publication), all of which were written before 1925. These essays reflect Bakhtin's interest in Marburg neo-Kantianism and describe the ethical act and its subsequent aestheticization in terms influenced by the phenomenology of vision.

Bakhtin's second period was from 1925 to 1929 and ended with *Problems of Dostoevsky's Creative Art* (1929), a monograph proclaiming Dostoevsky inventor of a new kind of novel, the 'polyphonic' novel, in which the author grants his heroes consciousnesses liberated from authorial control. Bakhtin's well-known concept of dialogue is located in this book, but the give and take of semantic authority suggested by the term probably also emerges from the nature of Bakhtin's close relationship with other scholars (the Bakhtin circle), most notably Valentin Voloshinov (see *Voloshinov,*

Valentin Nikolavic) and Pavel Medvedev. Scholars have disputed whether the books published by Voloshinov and Medvedev in 1927–29 were not in fact the work of Bakhtin himself, though there is scant evidence to support such a contention.

The writings of the third period stretch through the 1930s and 1940s and constitute the body of texts most familiar to Western readers. Bakhtin's essays translated in *The Dialogic Imagination* (Bakhtin 1981), including 'Epic and novel,' 'Discourse in the novel,' 'Toward a prehistory of the Bildungsroman,' and 'Forms of time and chronotope,' all belong to this period. Bakhtin defended his doctoral dissertation in 1946, receiving the penultimate 'Candidate' degree after much heated debate, and the dissertation was later published as *Rabelais and His World* (Bakhtin 1968). His essay on methodology in the humanities and his reworking of the Dostoevsky monograph belong, by contrast, to the fourth and final period, when Bakhtin was in Moscow working with students devoted to his ideas, and when he finally achieved the professional recognition that had eluded him (or that he himself eluded) for the previous 35 years.

In general, Bakhtin rejects the Saussurean notion that the locus of meaning ultimately belongs to the abstract system ('langue') of language rather than to the agent's highly contextualized, historicized use of it as 'utterance.' Meaning is, thus, to be found in neither 'langue' nor 'parole,' which Bakhtin viewed as merely the cited instance of an underlying rule. He formulates his objection more provocatively: 'A code is only a technical means of transmitting information; it does not have cognitive, creative significance. A code is deliberately established, killed context' (Bakhtin 1986: 147). This is the first way that Bakhtin uses dialogue: every (spoken) utterance is by its very nature dialogic, and meaning is established through the utterance's intrinsic orientation toward other concrete utterances. Unlike the (written) sentence, an utterance can never mean the same thing twice; it is always a rejoinder to what has previously been said and an anticipation of the response it will in turn demand.

See also: Dialogism; Discourse; Voloshinov, Valentin Nikolavic.

Bibliography

Bakhtin M M 1968 (trans. Iswolsky H) *Rabelais and His World*. MIT Press, Cambridge, MA
Bakhtin M M 1981 (ed. Holquist M., trans. Emerson C, Holquist M) *The Dialogic Imagination: Four Essays by M. M. Bakhtin*. University of Texas Press, Austin, TX
Bakhtin M M 1984 (ed. and trans. Emerson C) *Problems of Dostoevsky's Poetics*. University of Minnesota Press, Minneapolis, MN
Bakhtin M M 1986 (eds. Emerson C, Holquist M, trans. McGee V W) *Speech Genres and Other Late Essays*. University of Texas Press, Austin, TX
Bakhtin M M 1990 (eds. Holquist M, Liapunov V, trans. and notes Liapunov V) *Art and Answerability: Early Philosophical Essays by M. M. Bakhtin*. University of Texas Press, Austin, TX
Bakhtin M M 1993 (trans. and notes Liapunov V) *Toward a Philosophy of the Act*. University of Texas Press, Austin, TX
Clark K, Holquist M 1984 *Mikhail Bakhtin*. Harvard University Press, Cambridge, MA
Emerson C 1997 *The First Hundred Years of Mikhail Bakhtin*. Princeton University Press, Princeton, NJ
Morson G S, Emerson C 1990 *Mikhail Bakhtin: Creation of a Prosaics*. Stanford University Press, Stanford, CA
Todorov T 1984 (trans: Godzich, W) *Mikhail Bakhtin: The Dialogic Principle*. University of Minnesota Press, Minneapolis, MN

Bamgbose, Ayo (1932–)
R. Mesthrie

Ayo Bamgbose is one of Africa's foremost sociolinguists. He was born in Nigeria and did his schooling there. He attended St. Andrews College in Oyo and later proceeded to the University College, Ibadan. Links between this university and the University of London enabled him to study for an honours degree in English in London. Between 1960 and 1963 he studied at the University of Edinburgh, where he completed his PhD on Yoruba grammar. He studied under, *inter alia*, Michael Halliday (see *Halliday, Michael Alexander Kirkwood*) and was part of the 'Edinburgh group' made up of students like Braj Kachru (see *Kachru, Braj B.*), Ruqaiya Hasan, Rodney Huddlestone, John Mountford, together with John Sinclair (on the faculty) and Robert W. Dixon (research fellow).

He taught in primary and secondary schools in Nigeria before assuming a lectureship at the University of Ibadan, rising to professor in 1968. Bamgbose's research interests are wide, spanning theoretical linguistics (the syntax and phonology of Yoruba); sociolinguistics (language, literature, and oral culture); and, necessarily in his context, attention to applied linguistics (language planning; language medium in schools; orthography; curriculum development). Amongst his many publications in these three fields, one can cite *A Grammar of Yoruba* (1966), which was the first grammar of the language based on modern linguistic theory; *Language and the Nation* (1991), which drew attention to language in the broad context of socioeconomic and political problems with particular reference to sub-Saharan Africa; and *The Novels of D.O. Fagunwa* (1974), which was the first full-length critical work on any author writing in Yoruba.

Inevitably Bamgbose has been frequently invited to lecture abroad, doing several stints as a visiting professor in the US and Germany in particular. He has nevertheless continued to develop scholarship in West Africa, by serving on a number of editorial boards of local and international journals; by holding office in important societies (e.g., West African Linguistics Society) and journals (e.g., *Journal of African Languages*); and by doing research on behalf of UNESCO. He was invited as an expert to 14 UNESCO conferences between 1971 and 1998. He was the editor-in-chief of the journal *Education and Development* between 1985 and 1987; president of the West African Linguistic Society between 1976 and 1982; the first president of the Nigerian Academy of Letters (1998); and president of the International Association of World Englishes (1999).

A full appreciation of Bamgbose's personal and scholarly qualities can be seen in this tribute from his former fellow student, Braj Kachru, in the preface to Bamgbose, Banjo and Thomas (eds.) (1995: v):

> ... over the past three decades, Ayo Bamgbose has become a guru of African linguistics, an African presence in international conferences of our profession, and a voice of wisdom and experience. He has indeed made ground-breaking contributions to diverse academic areas in his chosen discipline. These contributions have rightly been recognized by the profession nationally and internationally. While engaged in all these activities, Bamgbose has not shirked from doing equally demanding things for his continent and for all of us working in relating linguistics to the real world. In his own way, he has brought social realism and social concern to the profession to which he has devoted over four decades as a teacher, researcher, and academic administrator.

In 1990 Bamgbose was awarded the Nigerian National Order of Merit, the country's highest award for intellectual and academic achievement. He gave his valedictory lecture 'A view from the Ivory Tower' at the University of Ibadan in 1991, but remains active as a researcher, visiting lecturer and editor.

Bibliography

Bamgbose A 1966 *A Grammar of Yoruba* (West African monographs No. 5). Cambridge University Press, Cambridge, UK
Bamgbose A 1966 The assimilated low tone in Yoruba. *Lingua* **16**(1): 1–13
Bamgbose A 1967 Verbal classes in Mbe. *Afrika and Übersee* **50**: 173–93
Bamgbose A 1970 Word play in Yoruba poetry. *International Journal of American Linguistics* **36**(2): 110–16
Bamgbose A 1974 *The Novels of D. O. Fagunwa*. Ethiope Publishing Corporation, Benin, Ethiopia
Bamgbose A (ed.) 1976 *Mother Tongue Education: The West African Experience*. Hodder and Stoughton, London
Bamgbose A 1991 *Language and the Nation*. Edinburgh University Press, Edinburgh, UK
Bamgbose A, Banjo A, Thomas A (eds.) 1995 *New Englishes: A West African Perspective*. Mosuro Publishers (for the British Council), Ibadan, Nigeria

Baugh, John (1949–)
R. Mesthrie

John Baugh was born in New York and grew up in Los Angeles. He graduated with a BA from Temple University, where he majored in Speech and Rhetoric. He received his MA and PhD from the University of Pennsylvania with a dissertation on 'Linguistic Style Shifting in Black English,' supervised by William Labov (see *Labov, William*). At Penn he also came under the influence of John Fought, Dell Hymes (see *Hymes, Dell Hathaway*) and Erving Goffman (see *Goffman, Erving*). Since then, Baugh has become one of the leading scholars of African American Vernacular English (AAVE), paying attention to matters of linguistic structure, ethnography, applied linguistics, and issues of power, equity and access in US society.

One of his early contributions was 'A re-examination of the Black English copula' (1980) in which he revisited Labov's famous analysis of 1969. Baugh used an extension of Labov's original database (utilizing the data from the Harlem adolescent groups in full) and an update of the Cedergren and Sankoff (1974) program in his re-examination. With the resulting extra tokens, he was able to separate two environments that Labov had conflated out of procedural necessity, the original number of tokens for locative and adjective environments being too small for reliable statistical analysis. Baugh showed that these two environments had a differential effect: for locatives, contraction was favored over deletion; for adjectives, the reverse held. He concluded that it was more feasible to posit a zero copula in adjectival environments than a contraction rule followed by deletion. The re-analysis thus illuminates a fundamental similarity with Caribbean English Creoles and a significant difference from other American English dialects.

Baugh's teaching career began in 1975 as Lecturer in Black Studies, Linguistics, Sociology, and Anthropology at Swarthmore College. He was appointed assistant professor at the University of Texas (Austin) in 1979, being chosen to strengthen the discipline of Sociolinguistics in what was then the second most highly-rated Linguistics department in the USA. There he teamed up with the anthropologist Joel Sherzer, to produce the edited volume *Language in Use* (1984).

Baugh joined Stanford in 1990, where he holds a joint appointment as Professor of Education and Linguistics. He was director of Stanford's Teacher Education program between 1994 and 1996. The term 'Educational Linguistics' aptly sums up Baugh's commitment to applying the insights of modern Linguistics and Sociolinguistics in educational and other societal contexts with methodological rigor. He has been a vocal yet sensitive participant in the Ebonics debate (see *Ebonics and African American Vernacular English*) bringing to bear his objective knowledge of social dialectology with a commitment to understanding the viewpoint of those most in need of help within the American schooling system. Out of this concern have come two books *Out of the Mouths of Slaves: African American Language and Educational Malpractice* (1999) and *Beyond Ebonics: Linguistic Pride and Racial Prejudice* (2000a). In the latter, Baugh sifts through the volatile circumstances and evidence that triggered the debate, including the origin of Ebonics. He also considers the legal, educational, and theoretical issues that still linger as part of the quest for racial reconciliation. In related work, Baugh examines policy related to the analyses of the language of minority students, language equity and environmental change, and housing discrimination based on speech.

Baugh is a gifted lecturer, winning awards for teaching excellence at Texas and Stanford. He is a past president of the American Dialect Society (1992–4), and a past vice chair of the board of trustees for the Center for Applied Linguistics in Washington DC (1983–9), and an elected representative to the executive committee of the Linguistics Society of America (1998–).

Bibliography

Baugh J 1980 A re-examination of the Black English copula. In: Labov W (ed.) *Locating Language in Time and Space*. Academic Press, New York

Baugh J 1983 *Black Street Speech: Its History, Structure, and Survival*. University of Texas Press, Austin, TX

Baugh J 1985 Linguistic diversity and justice in America: Growing complexity in a traditional national paradox. *Urban Resources* 3(3): 31–34, 61.

Baugh J 1995 The law, linguistics, and education: Educational reform for African American language minority students. *Linguistics and Education* 7: 87–105

Baugh J 1998 Linguistic discrimination in educational contexts. In: Wodak R, Corson D (eds.) *Language Policy and Political Issues in Education* [*Encyclopedia of Language and Education, Vol. 1*]. Kluwer, Amsterdam

Baugh J 1999 *Out of the Mouths of Slaves: African American Language and Educational Malpractice*. University of Texas Press, Austin, TX

Baugh J 2000a *Beyond Ebonics: Race Relations and the Linguistic Legacy of American Slavery*. Oxford University Press, New York

Baugh J 2000b Racial identification by speech. *American Speech* 75(4): 362–4

Baugh J, Sherzer J (eds.) 1984 *Language in Use: Readings in Sociolinguistics*. Prentice-Hall, Englewood Cliffs, NJ

Cedergren H, Sankoff D 1974 Variable rules: Performance as a statistical reflection of competence. *Language* 50: 333–55

Labov W 1969 Contraction deletion and inherent variability of the English copula. *Language* 45(4): 715–62

Mufwene S, Rickford J, Bailey G, Baugh J (eds.) *African American English: Structure, History, and Use*. Routledge, London

Bernstein, Basil (1924–)

K. Rajagopalan

Basil Bernstein is a retired British sociologist with a brilliant academic career spanning several decades at the University of London. His ideas have had an impact not only on sociology but also on other areas, such as linguistics and educational theory (see *Code, Sociolinguistic*). He is best known for his distinction between 'restricted code' and 'elaborated code,' proposed in order to explain the observed linguistic differences between children of lower and middle classes. This distinction has come under scathing attack, (see *Social Class*) (often bordering on vilification) from several quarters.

1. Restricted vs. Elaborated Code

It is not at all easy to summarize Bernstein's distinction between restricted code and elaborated code for the simple reason that his ideas have evolved substantially over the years, sometimes resulting in terminological revisions. The two were initially referred to, respectively, as 'public language' and 'formal language' (Bernstein 1959). The key idea was that the children of socioeconomically underprivileged classes tend to speak in a way dependent on, and complementary to, the actual set of physical circumstances attending on the given communicative situation (public language), whereas the children of middle and upper classes had at their disposal a language (formal language) that was relatively free of the context of situation. It was argued that, since the formal language closely approximated the language privileged by the schools, these children had a head start right from the beginning (see *Home Language and School Language*).

By the mid-1960s, however, the new terminology, restricted code vs. elaborated code, replaced the old one. What had lent itself to being interpreted as a qualitative distinction between two varieties of a given language, all of a sudden seemed to point to a quantitative distinction between different manifestations of one and the same language. This gave rise to the perfectly understandable suspicion that Bernstein in effect endorsed a difference in the inherent capacities with which the children are endowed to begin with.

2. Major Influences

Bernstein's thoughts were, as he has himself acknowledged, influenced by Whorf, Sapir, Durkheim, Marx, Malinowski, Weber, Mead, Piaget, Luria, and Vygotsky, among others.

3. The Controversy in Retrospect

It seems important to register, in Bernstein's defense, that a good deal of the furore over his distinction most probably had to do with the unfortunate choice of the word 'code.' Although long familiar to sociologists, semioticians, and communication theorists, code was a fairly new term in linguistics where, thanks to the influence of Chomsky in the 1960s, the term had come to acquire the sense of a system of rules innately shared by all members of a speech community as part of their biological endowment. No wonder, then, that some of the sharpest criticisms of Bernstein's theory came from linguists of a Chomskyan persuasion.

See also: Code, Sociolinguistic; Home Language and School Language; Educational Failure; Social Class.

Bibliography

Bernstein B 1959 A public language: Some sociological implications of a linguistic form. *British Journal of Sociology* **10**: 311–26
Bernstein B 1967 Elaborated and restricted codes: An outline. In: Lieberson S (ed.) *Explorations in Sociolinguistics*, pp. 126–33
Bernstein B 1974 *Class, Codes, Control.* 4 Vols. Routledge, London
Dittmar N 1976 *Sociolinguistics.* Edward Arnold, London
Mey J 1993 *Pragmatics: An Introduction.* Blackwell, Oxford, UK
Rosen H 1974 *Language and Class: A Critical Look at the Theories of Basil Bernstein.* Falling Wall Press, Bristol, UK

Bickerton, Derek (1926–)
G. G. Gilbert

Derek Bickerton was born in Cheshire, UK. 'His father was an estate agent for Lord Leverhume and his mother was a teacher. His wife, Yvonne, who he met in Madrid where they were both living during the 1950s, is a psychologist specializing in marriage and family therapy. They have three children ...' (Byrne 1991). As well as gaining an MA in English literature in 1967 from Cambridge University and PhD from Cambridge in 1976 in linguistics, Bickerton has had a distinguished career as a writer (four novels, among many other works), journalist, EFL and linguistics professor, and creolist. Living and working for extended periods in Spain, Barbados, Ghana, Guyana, Lancaster, and Hawaii, he has also been a visiting professor and researcher at the University of Michigan, SUNY at Stony Brook, Universidade de Campinas (Brazil), Universidade Católica in São Paulo, Universidade Federale (Rio de Janeiro), University of Texas at Austin, Universiteit van Amsterdam, and the Université de Provence. In the early 1990s, he was professor of linguistics at the University of Hawaii.

In the field of creolistics, Bickerton is a skilled writer, an able linguist, and a proponent of important new ideas which convey strong claims about the nature of creole languages, first language acquisition, and the development of language over the entire historical span of the human race and its precursors. He is best known for his Language Bioprogram Hypothesis (which makes stronger and more specific claims than does Chomsky) about the nature of Universal Grammar, in its manifestation as a neurological structure, a product of biological evolution, genetically inherited, and forming an integral part of the human brain. Bickerton views creolization as the learning of a pidgin as a native language by children; the attendant extremely defective language input necessarily undergoes supplementation by the bioprogram, which is ordinarily suppressed during the course of normal (noncreole) first language acquisition. This suggests that researchers bent on linking the biological and structural (achronic) aspects of language turn their attention to creole languages. Bickerton thinks that it is the nature of the bioprogram that explains why certain creole structures (such as free morphemes, preposed to the verb, marking tense, modality, and aspect) recur so frequently, and why pidgins, which are not subject to the bioprogram, differ from each other so widely. The controversial and wide-ranging nature of claims such as these has drawn the attention of a large, general audience to Bickerton's writings. *Roots of Language* (1981) is 'the most widely cited and reviewed creole work yet produced ... [it] has received more than 200 reviews, three of which were in *Newsweek*, *The New York Times Review of Books* [*The New York Review of Books*], and *Discover*' (Byrne 1991: 3). Bickerton was the key figure in the rapid movement of creolistics to centerstage within general linguistics in the 1980s.

See also: Pidgins and Creoles: An Overview; Pidgins and Creoles: Models.

Bibliography

Bickerton D 1975 *Dynamics of a Creole System*. Cambridge University Press, Cambridge, UK
Bickerton D 1981 *Roots of Language*. Karoma, Ann Arbor, MI
Bickerton D 1990 *Language and Species*. University of Chicago Press, Chicago, IL
Black M C, Gilbert G G 1991 A reexamination of Bickerton's phylogenesis hypothesis. In: Byrne F, Huebner T (eds.) *Development and Structures of Creole Languages*. Benjamins, Amsterdam
Byrne F 1991 Introduction: Innovation and excellence within a scholarly tradition. In: Byrne F, Huebner T (eds.) *Development and Structures of Creole Languages*. Benjamins, Amsterdam [includes the most complete bibliography of Bickerton's publications available]
Byrne F, Huebner T (eds.) 1991 *Development and Structures of Creole Languages: Essays in Honor of Derek Bickerton*. Benjamins, Amsterdam
Gilbert G G 1986 The language bioprogram hypothesis: Déjà vu? In: Muysken P, Smith N (eds). *Substrata Versus Universals in Creole Genesis*. Benjamins, Amsterdam

Blommaert, Jan (1961–)

K. Maryns

Jan Blommaert is, in the first place, a multifaceted researcher. The versatility which characterizes his work manifests itself in his varied interests: through his research in the domains of language, identity, and diversity, Blommaert has come to play a key role in the current fields of pragmatics, sociolinguistics, and ethnography.

Blommaert was born in Dendermonde, Belgium on November 4, 1961. He specialized in African studies at Ghent University (1979–1983) and linguistics at the universities of Antwerp and Amsterdam (1984–1986). He received his PhD from Ghent University in 1989 with a dissertation in African studies on Kiswahili political style. From 1988 until 1991 he worked as an assistant at Ghent University and he spent the following six years of his career as research director at the Pragmatics Research Center of the University of Antwerp. In 1997, he was appointed as a professor of African linguistics and sociolinguistics at Ghent University.

Blommaert's initial work was closely tied to relations between language policy and planning in Tanzania on the one hand, and grassroots language behavior on the other. Through his concern with Kiswahili political discourse, language mixing, diversification and its impact on modern African political style, Blommaert developed an interest in the pragmatics of intercultural communication. It is in this context that Blommaert widened his concern with language politics in Africa to the pragmatics of minority politics in Belgium. Together with Jef Verschueren, Blommaert has done significant work on immigration, nationalism, and racism in Belgium, as well as on the impact of ideology in the field of migration. Blommaert is co-editor of the *Handbook of Pragmatics* (Benjamins, since 1995). A theoretical spin-off of these concerns with language politics in Africa and Belgium is his research interest in language ideologies. In 1997 *Political Linguistics* was published (co-edited with Chris Bulcaen) and in 1999 Blommaert edited a series of studies on 'Language Ideological Debates' (Mouton de Gruyter) in an attempt to formulate some ways in which sociolinguistics and history could be blended in the analysis of language-ideological processes.

Blommaert's linguistic work is deeply interlaced with ethnographic, anthropological, and sociological concerns. In fact the motivation behind most of his projects can be traced back to a longstanding interest in linguistic diversity or even 'impurity' of languages. The connection between linguistic diversity and inequality develops itself as a thread throughout Blommaert's work, one of the central objectives of which is to arrive at a better theoretical and empirical understanding of language in social life, investigating inequality as it is reflected in a materialistic view of language as a resource in people's lives. In this context Blommaert continued work on linguistic resources and inequality in narrative, as reflected in his current concerns with grassroots literacy in the Congo and narratives of African asylum seekers in Belgium. Blommaert founded an international research group sponsored by the Belgian National Science Foundation on 'Language, Power, and Identity' in which these concerns with linguistic inequality are further explored.

See also: Pragmatics and Sociolinguistics; Ideology.

Bibliography

Blommaert J (ed.) 1999 *Language Ideological Debates*. De Gruyter, Berlin
Blommaert J 1999 *State Ideology and Language in Tanzania*. Rüdiger Köppeverlag, Cologne, Germany
Blommaert J, Bulcaen C (eds.) 1997 *Political Linguistics*. Benjamins, Amsterdam

Boas, Franz (1858–1942)
R. Darnell

Franz Boas was the founder of North American anthropology as it is known in the late twentieth century. He insisted on a scope which included ethnology, linguistics, archaeology, and physical anthropology and contributed seriously to each of these subdisciplines. In practice, however, his emphasis was on the urgent salvage task of recording the languages and cultures of native North America. He eschewed the premature theoretical speculations of the classical evolutionists in favor of a diffusionist historical anthropology with a strong empiricist component.

Boas was born in Minden, Westphalia, Germany on July 9, 1858. He received his PhD from the University of Kiel in 1881 with a dissertation in physics on the color of sea water. During a year of Eskimo fieldwork in Baffin Island, his interests shifted from geography to culture. After a year at the University of Berlin, he moved to the USA. He served as associate editor of *Science*, taught at Clark University, organized anthropology exhibits at the Chicago World's Fair from 1892–95, and began a lifelong study of the Indians of the northwest coast, particularly the Kwakiutl and Tsimshian.

In 1899, he joined the faculty of Columbia University which he built into the primary center in the USA for the training of professional anthropologists. By about 1920, his first generation of students held the major positions in the discipline, which was becoming increasingly academic in its institutional base. Boas became Professor Emeritus in 1937 but continued to be active in Columbia anthropology until his death in 1942.

Boas edited the *Handbook of American Indian Languages* for the Bureau of American Ethnology. His introduction to the first volume (1911) emphasized the analytical discreteness of race, language, and culture as classificatory variables in anthropology and insisted upon deriving grammatical categories from the languages studied rather than from Indo–European theories of grammar. The *Handbook* contained brief grammatical sketches intended to be comparable in format and illustrative of methods of linguistic description.

Boas's own linguistic work was closely tied to ethnology. He proposed a shared database for linguistics and ethnology of texts in the words of native speakers. Linguistic analysis would produce texts, grammars, and dictionaries. Cultural content of the texts would be mined in relation to data observed in the field. Boas's own work, particularly on Kwakiutl and Tsimshian, exemplified the method. Generations of ethnologists trained by Boas combined linguistic work with their cultural analyses.

Boas's contributions to historical linguistics were less significant. He taught himself linguistics in order to use it in his fieldwork and never studied comparative philology in any formal way. He was ultraconservative about the demonstration of genetic relationship because he believed its effects could not be distinguished from those of borrowing. His model was historical reconstruction based on borrowing of folklore elements on the northwest coast. Consequently, he opposed the genetic reconstructions of Edward Sapir (see *Sapir, Edward*) and others of his former students.

More than any other single person, Boas was responsible for the corpus of descriptive material on native American languages and for the inclusion of linguistics within North American anthropology.

See also: Endangered Languages.

Bibliography

Boas F 1911 Introduction to the *Handbook of American Indian Languages*. Bureau of American Ethnology Bulletin **40**

Emeneau M 1943 Franz Boas as a linguist. *American Anthropological Association Memoir* **61**: 35–8

Stocking G 1968 *Race, Culture and Evolution*. Free Press, New York. [Repr. In: Stocking G (ed.) 1974 *The Shaping of American Anthropology 1883–1911: A Franz Boas Reader*. Basic Books, New York]

Bourdieu, Pierre (1930–)

C. B. Vigouroux

Pierre Bourdieu belongs to the generation of French intellectuals—including Barthes, Foucault, Lacan, Levi-Strauss, and Derrida—who were greatly interested in the structuralist thought of the 1960s. He seeks to bring together different disciplines in order to explain diverse aspects of society. The aim of his work on a range of issues such as fashion, consumer practices, museum going, the student world, etc., is to unveil the logic of domination within these social practices. Three key axes run through Bourdieu's work: theory, practice, and reflections on his own discipline.

Born in 1930 in the southern French town of Denguin (Pyrénées-Atlantiques), Bourdieu entered the prestigious *Ecole normale supérieure* at the age of 21. Having passed the agrégation (the highest competitive academic examination in France) in philosophy in 1955, he left for Algeria where he worked as an assistant lecturer at the University of Algiers. His first publications were concerned with the social transformation of Algeria (e.g., *Sociologie de l'Algérie*, 1958). Back in France he taught at the Sorbonne and for some time at the University of Lille (1961). In 1964 he was named *Directeur d'Etudes* at the *Ecole Pratique des Hautes Etudes* (now the *EHESS*). His first works on the French education system (*The Inheritors, French Students and Their Relation to Culture*, 1964 with J. C. Passeron) and on cultural practices in France (*Un art moyen*, 1965) date from this period. Bourdieu shows how the school system produces social inequalities and reproduces cultural privileges. Later, the French philosopher and sociologist Raymond Aron offered him the post of codirector of the *Centre Européen de Sociologie Historique*. Following a breakdown in relations between these two in 1968, Bourdieu set up his own research center and duly founded his own school of sociological thought. It is within this perspective that he launched his review *Actes de la recherche en sciences sociales*, in 1975, in which he wrote an impressive number of articles on various topics. In 1979 he published a major work, *La distinction*, in which he analyses the historical and social genesis of esthetic taste. Two years later he was rewarded for his work by being offered the post of chair in sociology at the highest French academic institution, the *Collège de France*. Having built up a reputation in France, Bourdieu turned his mind to the international intellectual scene (in collaboration with the Universities of Princeton and Pennsylvania in the USA). In 1981 he grouped together a collection of articles on language (*Ce que parler veut dire*), some of which had previously been published, in an original approach aiming to uncover the hidden structures of society via language.

The 1990s mark a turning point in Bourdieu's works, as social theory is transformed into social action. *La misère du monde* (1993) (a series of interviews with underprivileged groups of French society conducted by Bourdieu's team) demonstrates his desire to bring sociology to the heart of political struggles. He has been involved with numerous social causes (successive strikes in December 1995, protests by the jobless in January 1998 or support for Algerian intellectuals) and created the association 'Raisons d'agir,' along with the review 'Liber,' with the intention of opening up the social sciences to a larger public, publishing short works on diverse topics, such as the media, the intellectual world, etc.

Pierre Bourdieu's last lecture at the *Collège de France* (Spring 2001) was a personal account of his own sociological work and intellectual journey. His overall contribution, far from being restricted to the social sciences, invites us to rethink the world in which we live: whether one agrees or disagrees with Bourdieu, he remains a key intellectual figure.

See also: Symbolic Power and Language.

Bibliography

Bourdieu P 1972 *Esquisse d'une théorie de la pratique, précédé de trois études d'ethnologie kabyle*. Droz, Geneva (Eng. Trans. *Outline of a Theory of Practice*. Cambridge University Press, Cambridge, UK 1977)

Bourdieu P 1979 *La distinction. Critique sociale du jugement.* Ed. de Minuit, Paris (Eng. Trans. *Distinction. A Social Critique of the Judgment of Taste*. Harvard University Press, Cambridge, MA, 1984)

Bourdieu P 1982 *Ce que parler veut dire*. Fayard, Paris (Eng. Trans. *Language and Symbolic Power*, edited and introduced by J B. Thompson, Harvard University Press, Cambridge, MA, 1991)

Bourdieu P 1984 *Homo academicus*. Ed. de Minuit, Paris (Eng. Trans. *Homo academicus*. Polity Press, Cambridge, UK, 1988)

Bourdieu P 1989 *La noblesse d'État. Grandes écoles et esprit de corps*. Ed. de Minuit, Paris (Eng. Trans. *The State Nobility: Elite Schools in the Field of Power*. Polity Press, Cambridge, UK, 1996)

Bourdieu P 1993 *La misère du monde*. Ed. du Seuil, Paris. (Eng. Trans. *The Weight of the World: Social Suffering in Contemporary Society*. Stanford University Press, Stanford, CA, 1999)

Bright, William (1928–)

B. B. Kachru

William Bright was born in Oxnard, California. He received an AB in linguistics from the University of California at Berkeley in 1949 and a PhD in linguistics in 1955 for his study of the Karok language (published in 1957, *A Grammar of the Karok Language*). At Berkeley, Bright was initiated into the 'spirit of the Sapir tradition' (see *Sapir, Edward*) by Emeneau (see *Emeneau, Murray Barnson*) and Mary R. Haas, and later by his colleague Harry Hoijer. A Rockefeller Foundation Fellowship (1955–57) took Bright to India for teaching and research at Deccan College, Poona (now Pune). In confronting South Asia's sociolinguistic realities, Bright (1976: 271) observes that it 'was an area where the phenomena of language contact and linguistic area... and the sociolinguistic phenomena of language variation were impossible to ignore.' In India, Bright's interaction with Gumperz (see *Gumperz, John J.*) inspired him to explore the role of these sociolinguistic phenomena in language history.

Bright started his teaching career at the University of California at Los Angeles in 1959 as Assistant Professor, then Associate Professor in 1962 and Professor in 1966. He is an inspiring educator, who has trained many distinguished scholars in sociolinguistics and other branches of the linguistic sciences from Asia, Africa, Europe, and the United States. He retired to become Emeritus Professor of Linguistics and Anthropology in 1988 and is now Professor Adjoint of Linguistics in the Department of Linguistics, University of Colorado, Boulder.

Bright has held a variety of editorial positions in scholarly journals and reference volumes, including, *International Journal of American Linguistics* (1963); *Handbook of Latin American Studies* (1963–66); *Language* (1965–87); *International Encyclopedia of Linguistics* (1992); *Language in Society* (1992–99); founder-editor, *Written Languages and Literacy* (1997–); founder-editor, *Oxford Studies in Anthropological Linguistics* (1992).

Bright's peers in the profession have honored him in many ways: as the president of the Linguistic Society of America (1989), of the Society for the Study of the Indigenous Languages of the Americas (1995), and of the Dravidian Linguistic Association (1996), and as a recipient of important Fellowships (American Council of Learned Societies (1964–65) and the Guggenheim Foundation (1972)). A festschrift, *The Life of Language: Papers in Honor of William Bright* was edited by Jane H. Hill, P. J. Mistry and Lyle Campbell (1998).

Bright's scholarly work has contributed insights and fresh cross-cultural and cross-linguistic data (Amerindian and South Asian languages) to theoretical, methodological, and descriptive studies in a variety of fields: language variation; American Indian languages; language and culture; onomastics; Dravidian studies; and lexicography. Bright's other interests include writing poetry, e.g., 'Eight poems' in *Linguistic Muse* (Napoli and Rando (eds.) 1979). He also edited *Word Formations: Poems by Linguists*. A few of his many publications are cited in the bibliography.

See also: Anthropological Linguistics; Language in Society: Overview.

Bibliography

Bright W 1957 *A Grammer of the Karok Language*. University of California Publications in Lingustics (13), Berkeley, CA
Bright W 1958 An outline of colloquial Kannada. *Deccan College Monograph Series 22*; *Indian Linguistics Monograph Series 1*, Poona, India
Bright W 1966a *Sociolinguistics: Proveedings of the UCLA Sociolinguistics Conference*. Mouton, The Hague
Bright W 1966b Language, social stratification, and cognitive orientation. In: Lieberson S (ed.) *Explorations in Sociolinguistics*. (*Sociological Inquiry* **36**(2)), pp. 313–18
Bright W 1968 *A Luiseño Dictionary*. University of California Publications in Linguistics (51), Berkeley, CA
Bright W 1973 North American Indian language contact. In: Sebeok T A (ed.) *Current Trends in Linguistics X: North America*. Mouton, The Hague, pp. 713–26.
Bright W 1976 *Variation and Change in Language: Essays*. (Dil A S ed.) Stanford University Press, Stanford, CA
Bright W 1979 Eight poems. In: Napoli D J, Rando E N (eds.) *Linguistic Muse*. Linguistic Research, Edmonton, AB, pp. 53–60
Bright W 1990 *Language Variation in South Asia*. Oxford University Press, New York
Bright W 1998 The Dravidian scripts. In: Steever S (ed.) *The Dravidian Languages*. Routledge, London
Hill J H, Mistry P J, Campbell L 1998 *The Life of Language: Papers in Honor of William Bright*. De Gruyter, New York

Cameron, Deborah (1958–)

S. S. McRae

Deborah Cameron is currently Professor of Languages in Education at the Institute of Education, University of London, where she teaches MA modules on linguistic description, and on discourse and culture. Her academic career began in London in 1983, teaching English language and linguistics at what was then the Roehampton Institute. Before taking her current position at the University of London, Cameron spent eight years in the English department of Strathclyde University in Glasgow, Scotland. She started as a Senior Lecturer in their program in Literary Linguistics; in 1997 she became Professor of English Language.

Cameron's research interests are wide, and include sociolinguistics, discourse analysis, educational linguistics, media and cultural studies, language ideologies, feminist theory, and language and gender. It is for her work in the latter two areas, language and gender and feminist theory, that Cameron is best known. Among her many publications in these fields is her seminal book *Feminism and Linguistic Theory* (1992), in which she provides a critical introduction to developments in the study of language and gender. This theme is continued in *The Feminist Critique of Language* (1998), a collection of papers edited by Cameron. This collection, as well as serving as an introduction to directions and debates in feminist thinking, also looks at the historical background of feminist ideas about language. Cameron has also contributed to several collections concerned with current preoccupations in language and gender research (see Cameron 1996).

Although primarily associated with language, gender, and feminist linguistics, Cameron is also widely published in other areas. For example, in her popular book *Verbal Hygiene* (1995) she looks at attitudes towards language and the attempts made to regulate its use. More recently, Cameron has become interested in the discourse about 'communication skills.' In *Good to Talk? Living and Working in a Communication Culture* (2000) she explores the social and political implications of communication training. Cameron's most recent book, *Working with Spoken Discourse* (2001), reflects her continued interest in the analysis of talk, an area covered in an earlier publication, *Analysing Conversation*, co-authored with Talbot Taylor (1987).

See also: Gender and Language; Verbal Hygiene.

Bibliography

Cameron D 1992 *Feminism and Linguistic Theory*, 2nd edn. Macmillan, London
Cameron D 1995 *Verbal Hygiene*. Routledge, London
Cameron D 1996 The language-gender interface: Resisting co-optation. In: Bergvall V, Bing J, Freed A (eds.) *Rethinking Language and Gender Research*. Longman, London
Cameron D (ed.) 1998 *The Feminist Critique of Language*. Routledge, London
Cameron D 2000 *Good to Talk? Living and Working in a Communication Culture*. Sage Publications, London
Cameron D 2001 *Working with Spoken Discourse*. Sage Publications, London
Cameron D, Frazer E, Harvey P, Rampton B, Richardson K 1992 *Researching Language: Issues of Power and Method*. Routledge, London

Coates J, Cameron D (eds.) 1988 *Women in Their Speech Communities: New Perspectives on Language and Sex.* Longman, London

Taylor T J, Cameron D 1987 *Analysing Conversation: Rules and Units in the Structure of Talk.* Pergamon, Oxford, UK

Coates, Jennifer (1942–)
S. S. McRae

Jennifer Coates is currently Professor in English Language and Linguistics at the University of Surrey, Roehampton, London. Her academic career began in 1969, as a Research Assistant at University College, London, working on the Survey of English Usage. Following this, she was a Research Fellow in the Department of Linguistics at the University of Lancaster. In 1980 she was awarded a PhD from Lancaster for her research on the semantics of the modal auxiliaries. Three years later, Coates' thesis was published in book form, the first of many publications.

It was Coates' subsequent book, *Women, Men, and Language* (1st edn. 1986, 2nd edn. 1993), which reflected a shift towards a more sociolinguistic perspective. More specifically, it signaled the beginnings of her renowned work on language and gender. At that time, the relationship between language and gender was of minority interest. Coates carried out pioneering work in the area, focusing initially on the particularly neglected area of all-women talk. She investigated linguistic strategies used by women in their friendship groups, and found that women's communicative style tended to be cooperative, typified by solidarity-building interactive support and collaboration. A recurrent theme of Coates' work is her concern that this preference by women for a cooperative discourse style reinforces unequal power divisions between women and men, given men's apparent preference for a more competitive discourse style.

In line with current preoccupations in language and gender research, Coates' more recent work emphasizes the variable nature of masculine and feminine identities. Coates' abiding interest in narrative practices explores the role of talk in the construction of these identities, and she is currently extending the focus of this interest to include work on story-telling in men's, as well as women's, conversation. Coates' more recent work also reflects her continued interest in the cooperative nature of women's talk (see in particular Coates 1997b), and she is at present involved with Bristol University in ground-breaking research into the collaborative talk of deaf women friends.

See also: Gender and Language.

Bibliography

Coates J 1983 *The Semantics of the Modal Auxiliaries.* Croom Helm, London
Coates J 1989 Gossip revisited. In: Coates J, Cameron D (eds.) *Women in their Speech Communities: New Perspectives on Language and Sex.* Longman, London
Coates J 1993 *Women, Men, and Language*, 2nd edn. Longman, London
Coates J 1995 The language of the professions: Discourse and career. In: Mills S (ed.) *Language and Gender: Interdisciplinary Perspectives.* Longman, London
Coates J 1996 *Women Talk. Conversation Between Women Friends.* Blackwell, Oxford, UK
Coates J 1997a One-at-a-time: The organization of men's talk. In: Johnson S, Meinhof U (eds.) *Language and Masculinity.* Blackwell, Oxford, UK
Coates J 1997b The construction of a collaborative floor in women's friendly talk. In: Givon T (ed.) *Conversation: Cognitive, Communicative, and Social Perspectives.* Benjamins, Philadelphia, PA
Coates J 1998 (ed.) *Language and Gender: A Reader.* Blackwell, Oxford, UK
Coates J, Sutton-Spence R in press Deaf women friends and the collaborative floor. *Journal of Sociolinguistics*

Cooper, Robert Leon (1931–)
B. Spolsky

Trained originally as an educational psychologist, Cooper has essentially mapped the sociolinguistic aspects of educational linguistics, showing the need to incorporate social dimensions in the notion of language ability, and spelling out the place of language educational policy (which he labeled 'language acquisition planning') as a critical element in the social changes associated with language planning.

After undergraduate training at Harvard and graduate study at the University of Pennsylvania, he studied educational psychology with Thorndike and MacGinitie at Teachers College and Columbia, respectively. From 1966 to 1968, he worked with Joshua Fishman (see *Fishman, Joshua*) on the epoch-making study of bilingualism in the New Jersey *barrio*. His seminal paper 'An elaborated language testing model' drew on that experience. It was the first clear statement that language testing and teaching needed to take into account the communicative competence proposed by Dell Hymes (see *Hymes, Dell Hathaway*) rather than the rigorous but more narrowly focused notion of linguistic competence being espoused by Noam Chomsky and his followers.

Cooper then spent a year working with the pioneering Ford Foundation sponsored study of language in Ethiopia. There, alone with Charles Ferguson (see *Ferguson, Charles A.*), J. Donald Bowen and M. L. Bender, he helped trace the goals for language policy and language education in a complex multilingual society.

After teaching at Yeshiva University, Stanford University, and California State University. Cooper moved to Israel in 1972 to join Fishman again for the first major study of the spread of English. He remained in Israel, and for the rest of his academic career, he was a professor in both education and sociology at the Hebrew University, where he trained students and carried out sociolinguistic research that helped bridge the fields of sociolinguistics and education.

He coedited two key collections of papers on bilingual education in the late 1970s. In the late 1980s, he codirected a sociolinguistic survey of the Old City of Jerusalem. His magisterial *Language Planning and Social Change* (Oxford University Press) 1989 rounded out a career of research and publications that have established the key relationships between sociolinguistics and educational linguistics.

Since retirement, Cooper has been traveling and writing about travel, with a special interest in Mark Twain and the South Pacific.

Bibliography

Bender M L, Bowen J D, Cooper R L, Ferguson C A (eds.) 1976 *Language in Ethiopia*. Oxford University Press, London
Cooper R L 1968 An elaborated language testing model. *Language Learning* (Special issue No. 7): 57–72
Cooper R L 1984 A framework for the description of language spread: The case of modern Hebrew. *International Social Science Journal* **36**(1): 87–112
Cooper R L 1989 *Language Planning and Social Change*. Cambridge University Press, Cambridge, UK
Cooper R L 2000 *Around the World with Mark Twain*. Arcade Publishers, New York
Fishman J A, Cooper R L, Conrad A W 1977 *The Spread of English: The Sociology of English as an Additional Language*. Newbury House, Rowley, MA
Fishman J A, Cooper R L, Ma R 1971 *Bilingualism in the Barrio*. Research Center for the Language Sciences, Indiana University, Bloomington, IN
Spolsky B, Cooper R L (eds.) 1977 *Frontiers of Bilingual Education*. Newbury House, Rowley, MA
Spolsky B, Cooper R L 1991 *The Languages of Jerusalem*. Clarendon Press, Oxford, UK

Cummins, Jim (1949–)
C. Baker

James (Jim) Patrick Cummins was born on July 3, 1949 in Dublin, Ireland, encountering bilingual education at an Irish Gaelsciol at the age of seven. After graduating in Psychology from University College Dublin in 1970, he completed his PhD at the University at Edmonton. He then held posts at St. Patrick's College, Dublin, and the Center for the Study of Mental Retardation at the University of Alberta included investigating special needs education for bilingual children—a theme that produced an influential book in 1984 entitled *Bilingualism and Special Education: Issues in Assessment and Pedagogy*. Since 1978, he has been a Professor in the Modern Language Center at the Ontario Institute for Studies in Education in Toronto, Canada.

His voluminous writing addresses many interdisciplinary topics including cognition, cultural diversity and multiculturalism, bilingual education, the theory of bilingualism, empowering minority language children through information and communication technology (ICT), language assessment, reading instruction, immersion education, reading difficulties, mother tongue maintenance, metalinguistic

awareness, immigrant children, language proficiency, special needs children, the Ireland and Canada context, and the relationship between anglophone and francophone communities in Canada. He is particularly noted for the following:
  (a) making a distinction between Basic Interpersonal Communicative Skills and Cognitive Academic Language Proficiency (BICS and CALP);
  (b) the Separate Underlying Proficiency (SUP) model of bilingualism and the Common Underlying Proficiency (CUP) model of bilingualism;
  (c) the Thresholds Theory which posits levels of linguistic competence that a bilingual child must attain both to avoid cognitive deficits and allow the potentially beneficial aspects of becoming bilingual to influence cognitive functioning;
  (d) the Developmental Interdependence Theory which suggests that growth in a second language is much dependent on a well-developed first language;
  (e) the linguistic mismatch hypothesis;
  (f) the 'time on task' hypothesis;
  (g) the iceberg representation of language proficiency with the fusion of two languages in the cognitive systems of a child 'beneath the surface';
  (h) two dimensions of communication: cognitive demanding/undemanding; context reduced/embedded;
  (i) a theoretical framework for the empowerment of minority language students that accounts for dominant/dominated power relationships, culture, community, pedagogy, and assessment; and
  (j) the embeddedness of academic language development, and schooling generally, in a nexus of societal power relations that provides a strong argument for developing critical language awareness among students, and for minority language students to explore issues of cultural identity, critical enquiry, and knowledge generation.

Over three decades, there has been a progression from early interests in psychology, cognitive development, assessment, and psychometrics to more sociopolitical ideas. There has also grown a realization that to effect change among policy makers and politicians, among teachers and school districts, both understanding and addressing those politics is essential. Thus there has been a considerable personal involvement with policy makers and practitioners. His long association with the Californian State Education Department and the California Association for Bilingual Education (CABE) symbolizes this leadership in political activism. The involvement with CABE has meant valuable interaction with practitioners and crucial political issues such as equity, tolerance, empowerment, collaborative relationships, and critical pedagogy.

See also: Bilingual Education; Bilingualism, Societal.

Bibliography

Baker C, Hornberger N H (eds.) 2001 *A Reader on the Writings of Jim Cummins.* Multilingual Matters, Clevedon, UK

Cummins J 1984 *Bilingualism and Special Education: Issues in Assessment and Pedgogy.* Multilingual Matters, Clevedon, UK

Cummins J 2001 *Language, Power, and Pedagogy: Bilingual Children in the Crossfire.* Multilingual Matters, Clevedon, UK

Das Gupta, Jyotirindra (1933–)
L. M. Khubchandani

Jyotirindra Das Gupta (b. 1933), Professor Emeritus of Political Science, University of California, Berkeley, has worked extensively on the issues of language development and ethnicity, particularly in the context of multicultural federal polities.

Originally from East Bengal (now Bangladesh), his early education was in Calcutta; he graduated from Calcutta University in 1955. As a student activist he edited a journal, *Anvil*. Since the early 1960s, Das Gupta has been associated with the Center for South and East Asia Studies, University of California; he received his doctorate from the University of California in 1966, and retired from the same University in 1995.

Das Gupta's studies extend over nearly four decades and are wide-ranging, making a significant contribution to the field of language politics and national reconstruction. In particular they bring under a close purview the issues of languages rivalries and political integration (1970), language as a 'societal resource' and the 'decision-making' models in language planning (1972), relation of language and ethnicity in a democracy (1991), community's autonomy and institutional development in a multicultural state (1997), and India's federal design contributing to pluralism (in press).

As a member of the international project sponsored by the Ford Foundation during the late 1960s, Das Gupta worked extensively on language problems and language policies in developing countries; he jointly edited two volumes on the processes of language planning (1968, 1977). Later his focus shifted to the study of ethnicity in multicultural societies, particularly in the context of India's northeast parts.

Language plays a crucial role in the reorganization of institutions; it is inseparable from such activities as planning, propaganda, and evaluation. Das Gupta's studies have amply succeeded in dispelling the myth that language politics belongs to the realm of 'uncivil' politics. His systematic appraisal of the empirical evidence concerning decision-systems developing in the federal set-up in India convincingly shows that democratic institutions make it possible to work out language policies that contribute to pluralism—an alternative model of integration. This assessment conclusively rejects the despairing view prevailing among many political observers such as Gunnar Mrydal and Selig Harrison about the futility of democratic operations in the development of a multicultural nation.

Upholding the basic premise in Sociolinguistics that *variation* pervades all nature, including human nature, Das Gupta assumes basic compatibility between language differences and multicultural nationalism: '(these) contribute in promoting a form of nationalism that is different from the West.' He also challenges another assumption when language is usually dismissed as a 'primordial' question; primordial groups are considered to be retarding political modernization. Das Gupta argues that the very nature of language politics permits a special degree of flexibility: 'These conflicts, more often than not, have proved to be the schools of bargaining and negotiation' (1970: 269).

Das Gupta provides a wealth of material on language as an 'institution' when discussing, at length, the issues of the Assamese language policy and its conflict with tribal languages in north-east India (1997). He supports the conviction that *particularistic* loyalties (on ethnic, religious, and language issues) are not necessarily inconsistent with *national* loyalties.

Many studies in language policy-making and language planning seem to imply the *handicap* model in pursuit of development (Khubchandani 1997). Das Gupta's pathbreaking explorations in India's northeast draw our attention to the language *assets* in traditional speech communities representing rich oral cultures. This can have a significant bearing on a long-term view of the issues concerning the *quality* of human communication in a changing society.

See also: Language Planning: Models.

Bibliography

Das Gupta J 1970 *Language Conflict and National Development: Group Politics and National Language Policy in India*. University of California Press, Berkeley, CA

Das Gupta J 1991 Ethnicity, democracy, and development in India: Assam in a general perspective. In: Kohli A (ed.) *India's Democracy: An Analysis of Changing State–Society Relations*. Princeton University Press, Princeton, NJ, pp. 144–68.

Das Gupta J 1997 Community, authenticity, and autonomy: Insurgence and institutional development in India's northeast. *Journal of Asian Studies* **57**

Das Gupta J in press India's federal design and multicultural national construction. In: Kohli A (ed.) *Success of Indian Democracy*. Cambridge University Press, Cambridge, UK

Fishman J, Ferguson C A, Das Gupta J (eds.) 1968 *Language Problems of Developing Nations*. Wiley, New York

Harrison S 1960 *India. The Most Dangerous Decades*. Oxford University Press, Madras, India

Jernudd B H, Das Gupta J 1972 Towards a theory of language planning. In: Rubin J, Jernudd B H (eds.) *Can Language Be Planned? Sociolinguistic Theory and Practice for Developing Nations*. East-West Center, Honolulu, HI, pp. 195–216

Khubchandani L M 1997 *Revisualising Boundaries: A Plurilingual Ethos*. Sage, New Delhi, India

Myrdal G 1968 *Asian Drama*, Vols. 1 and 2. Pantheon, New York

Rubin J, Jernudd B H, Das Gupta J, Fishman J, Ferguson C A (eds.) 1977 *Language Planning Processes*. Mouton, The Hague

DeCamp, David (1927–79)
R. Le Page

David DeCamp was born in Michigan, USA. He completed his MA in 1949 at the University of New Mexico and his PhD in 1953 at Berkeley. An abridged version of his dissertation *The Pronunciation of English in San Francisco* was published in Orbis in 1958–59. DeCamp went to Jamaica in 1957 with his wife, Sally and three small children as Fullbright Senior Research Fellow working under

Le Page (see *Le Page, Robert*) on The Linguistic Survey of the Caribbean. DeCamp took to Jamaica like a duck to water and had two fruitful years of collaboration with Le Page, Beryl Bailey and Frederick Cassidy. He helped organize the first International Conference on Creole Language Studies at UCWI (University College, West Indies). He then joined the University of Texas at Austin in 1959, teaching in the English department. He continued to work on the recordings he had made in Jamaica for the rest of his relatively short life. From this data base came a number of papers of the Creole language of Jamaica, none perhaps better known than *Towards a Generative Analysis of a Post-Creole Continuum*. He was one of the first to apply the term 'post-creole continuum' to the language situation of Jamaica; and certainly the first to propose the adaptation of the Guttman implicational scalogram (see *Scaling*) to cope with the description of such situations in dynamic terms, providing an alternative to Labov's variable rules (see *Sociolinguistic Variation*). He labored to apply his polylectal model to his own data, working always with meticulous care, but wrote to Le Page not long before his death that he was sorry that the idea had been taken up so avidly as he had never been able to scale more than 30 percent of his Jamaica data. Nevertheless his paper has spawned legitimate work not only in creolistics but in the study of second language acquisition too (Dittmar 1980).

DeCamp was responsible for attracting other distinguished creole scholars to Texas. He was one of the co-editors of the *Bibliography of Pidgin and Creole Languages* (1975) working under Reinecke (see *Reinecke, John*) to produce the major reference work in the field. He was also an early member of the Society for Caribbean Linguistics and a regular attendee at its meetings. From 1974–76 he was Associate Director for International Programs at the Center for Applied Linguistics, and from 1973–79 had a favorite summer connection as lecturer in Linguistics at the Middle East Linguistics Institute in Tunis, while continuing to serve as professor of English, Linguistics, and Education at the University of Texas at Austin.

DeCamp's contributions were not only in Creole Studies and variation theory, but also in English, Chinese, and the teaching of English as a Second Language (TESL). In addition to a variety of Linguistics courses, he taught courses in such diverse areas as Creative Writing, Mandarin Chinese, TESL, the History of the English Language, and English Literature. In 1964 he was a Senior Linguistic Specialist in Taipei, Taiwan, advising the Chinese Ministry of Education and assisting in the preparation of materials for the teaching of English in Chinese secondary school. Between 1964 and 1966 he was Director for courses in Chinese and Japanese at Texas, and was also Principal Investigator for a research project in Chinese-English lexicography. Beginning in 1961, he also served as lecturer and linguistic consultant to 13 Peace Corps Training Projects.

When he died on October 17, 1979, DeCamp left a wife and four children, and a wealth of scholarly ideas and insights. His untimely death, I am sure, robbed us of some major published work.

See also: Pidgins and Creoles: Models.

Bibliography

DeCamp D 1958 The genesis of the old English dialects: A new hypothesis. *Language* **34**: 232–44

DeCamp D 1958–1959 The pronunciation of English in San Francisco. First Part, *Orbis* **7**: 373–91; Second Part, *Orbis* **8**: 54–77; Reprinted (abridged) in Williamson J, Burke V M (eds.) *A Various Language: Perspectives on American Dialects*. Holt, Rinehart and Winston, New York

DeCamp D 1967 African day-names in Jamaica. *Language* **43**: 139–49

DeCamp D 1972 Hypercorrection and rule generalization. *Language in Society* **1**: 87–90

DeCamp D, Hymes D 1971 Toward a generative analysis of a post-creole speech continuum. In: *Pidginisation and Creolisation of Languages*. Cambridge University Press, London

DeCamp D, Hancock I F (eds.) 1974 *Pidgins and Creoles: Current Trends and Prospects*. Georgetown University Press, Washington, DC

Dittmar N 1980 Ordering adult learners according to language abilities. In: Felix S (ed.) 1980 *Second Language Development*. Gunther Narr, Tübingen, Germany

Le Page R B, DeCamp D (eds.) 1960 *Jamaican Creole. Creole Language Studies 1*. Macmillan, London

Dittmar, Norbert (1943–)

P. Schlobinski

Norbert Dittmar is the most well known German sociolinguist, who renewed traditional German dialectology by integrating it with the variationist work of William Labov. In his work, he combines different fields of linguistics and sociology, such as formal grammar, language acquisition, rhetoric, social psychology, ethnomethodology, and discourse analysis. In practice, however, he focuses on empirical linguistics, focusing on urban varieties, second language acquisition, and German as a spoken language.

Dittmar was born in Bielefeld, Westphalia, on March 4, 1943. He studied philosophy and German as well as Slavic and Romance languages and received his PhD from the University of Konstanz with a dissertation on sociolinguistics, published in 1973 (English 1976). From 1974 to 1978 he worked at the University of Heidelberg on a research project known as 'The Heidelberg Project on Pidgin German of Foreign Workers' together with Wolfgang Klein. Since 1979 he has been a professor at the German Department of the Free University of Berlin.

During his work at the Heidelberg project he applied the so-called 'variety grammar' (which was developed by Wolfgang Klein) on syntactic features of the German language as spoken by Spanish and Italian migrants. The results were published in 1979 and have very much influenced subsequent studies on syntactic variation within the Labovian framework. Shortly after Dittmar became professor at the Free University of Berlin he started his work on the Berlin urban vernacular together with Peter Schlobinski and Inge Wachs. The project focused (a) on the description and explanation of the Berlin dialect, in particular the effect of the division of the speech community has for the socially and politically distinct subcommunities; (b) on language attitudes; and (c) on the description of the stylistic and rhetorical devices of the Berlin vernacular register which is called *Berliner Schnauze*. After the Berlin Wall was torn down, Dittmar did research in Berlin and Brandenburg regarding the question how the Berlin dialect in East and West will merge. For this research he expanded correlative sociolinguistic approaches into functional approaches. Apart from his sociolinguistic research, Dittmar has been in charge of projects on intercultural communication, second language acquisition, learner varieties, and therapeutic discourse since the beginning of the 1980s. Today, his main interest lies in the field of syntax and semantics of spoken language. Dittmar is responsible for the database of German as a spoken language at the Free University of Berlin. This database includes corpus description as well as analysis.

Dittmar's work was published in different languages. He was editor of the series *Sociolinguistics and Language Contact* (Walter de Gruyter) and is a member of the editorial board of *Linguistics* and *Linguistische Berichte*. Together with Ulrich Ammon and Klaus Mattheier he is editor of the *Handbook of Sociolinguistics* (Walter de Gruyter).

See also: Applied Linguistics and Sociolinguistics; Interlanguage; Pidgins and Creoles: An Overview.

Bibliography

Dittmar N 1976 *Sociolinguistics—A Critical Survey of Theory and Application*. Edward Arnold, London

Dittmar N, Bredel U 1999 *Die Sprachmauer. Die Verarbeitung der Wende und ihrer Folgen in Gesprächen mit Ost- und Westberlinerinnen*. Weidler Buchverlag, Berlin

Dittmar N, Klein W 1979 *Developing Grammars. The Acquisition of German by Foreign Workers*. Springer, Heidelberg, Germany

Dittmar N, Schlobinski P 1988 (eds.) *The Sociolinguistics of Urban Vernaculars. Case Studies and their Evaluation*. De Gruyter, Berlin

Dorian, Nancy (1936–)
S. Romaine

Nancy Dorian graduated from Connecticut College for Women in 1958 with a major in German. After completing her PhD in Linguistics at the University of Michigan in 1965, she joined the German Department at Bryn Mawr College in Bryn Mawr, Pennsylvania.

Her dissertation fieldwork on the Scottish Gaelic dialects spoken in the East Sutherland villages of Brora, Golspie, and Embo, ultimately led to her pioneering work on language obsolescence. In the course of conducting what she had anticipated to be a rather routine traditional dialect study under the auspices of the Gaelic Division of the Linguistic Survey of Scotland at the University of Edinburgh, Dorian was confronted with a complicated picture of variability and on-going change. Realizing that the uniqueness of the varieties of Gaelic and knowledge of the fisherfolk who spoke them were soon to disappear as the language was no longer being transmitted, she made the documentation of the dialects and local lifeways her life's work. Her 1981 monograph detailed the changes occurring in East Sutherland Gaelic in sociohistorical perspective at the same time as it laid the theoretical foundations for the study of language obsolescence. A subsequent edited volume (Dorian 1989) brought together a collection of papers from researchers working in a variety of language shift settings around the world, with invited commentaries from specialists in related fields such as creolistics, historical linguistics, and second language acquisition, to address issues from a comparative perspective.

In addition to the work in East Sutherland, Dorian also conducted fieldwork on the variety of Pennsylvania German spoken in Berks County, Pennsylvania. After disability rendered her unable to do field-work *in situ*, she continued to carry out her investigations through taped correspondence, recorded telephone conversations, and personal visits from villagers to her home in the US.

Within the field of language obsolescence Dorian is especially known for her notion of 'tip' in which language transmission abruptly ceases in seemingly sudden fashion, as well as the problem of 'personal pattern variation,' i.e., a high degree of individual variability unaccountable for in terms of the usual social factors like class, sex, region, network, etc. invoked by sociolinguistics to explain variation (Dorian 1986, 1994). Other papers have addressed a variety of methodological and theoretical issues concerning endangered languages. Since 1987 she has edited a section of the *International Journal of the Sociology of Language* entitled 'Small languages and small language communities.'

Bibliography

Dorian N C 1981 *Language Death. The Life Cycle of a Scottish Gaelic Dialect*. University of Pennsylvania Press, Philadelphia, PA

Dorian N C 1986 Abrupt transmission failure: How sudden the 'tip' to the dominant language in communities and families? In: Nikiforidou N, Van Clay M, Niepokuy M, Feder D (eds.) *Proceedings of the Twelfth Annual Meeting of the Berkeley Linguistics Society*. Berkeley Linguistics Society, Berkeley, CA

Dorian N C 1989 (ed.) *Investigating Obsolescence. Studies in Language Contraction and Death*. Cambridge University Press, Cambridge, UK

Dorian N C 1994 Varieties of variation in a small place: Social homogeneity, prestige norms, and linguistic variation. *Language* **70**: 631–96

Edwards, John Robert (1947–)
W. F. Mackey

John Robert Edwards (born in Southampton, UK, on December 3, 1947) studied in Canada at the University of Western Ontario and at McGill University (PhD in Psychology, 1974). From his basis in social psychology, he has investigated the many unexplored facets of plurilingualism, especially as they relate to ethnicity, education, identity, and nationalism. His best work is based on broad comparative studies with evident cross-disciplinary expertise. Notably, he addresses questions hitherto unheeded in the field of social psychology, as, for example, the psychological basis of the prescriptive urge, leading to a theoretical framework on which to attach the phenomenon of prescription. This has enriched his work on language academies, which may well be regarded as unique, since it constitutes an overall, interdisciplinary, descriptive, historical, and theory-oriented study.

Edwards has shown that, through group markedness, all varieties of language can possess solidarity value. The use of these varieties (including social dialects) in education can lead to a desire to purify them. Purism can become a social impulse. It promotes the acquisition of knowledge about the language, which in turns strengthens and refines attitudes toward it.

Placing himself at the intersection of social psychology and studies on nationalism, Edwards has been able to describe the mechanisms used in the construction of national identity. Appeals to the imagination engender changes in the perception of language within group identity triggering feelings of belonging. Much of the logic of language planning is calculated to touch the emotions through the promotion of value-laden opinions. Such language promotion can be a reflexion of political power.

To arrive at conclusions of such depth and scope, Edwards had to become familiar with a number of other language-related disciplines, like political philosophy, sociology, education, and linguistics for, as his work well demonstrates, language-phenomena cannot be comprehended within the paradigms of a single discipline.

That is why his publications have been able to embrace such issues as diverse as language policy, language identity, language revival, ethnicity, nationalism, prestige, and pluralism—all of which can be found within the pages of more than a dozen of his books. Notable among these are: *Multilingualism* (1994), *Language, Society, and Identity* (1985), and *Language and Disadvantage* (1979).

Much of Edwards' thought can also be found in his introductions to the many important books he has edited, like: *Language in Canada* (1998), *The Irish Language: An annotated Bibliography of Sociolinguistic Works (1772–1982)* (1983).

His skilled editorship of the Multilingual Matters Book Series has also contributed to the propagation of new knowledge in language identity, language insecurity, language planning, minority, and aboriginal languages.

Yet to appreciate the scope of his contribution to these important language-related issues one must turn to the content of more than 100 of the articles and invited lectures on sovereignty, separatism, parochialism, language stigma, sex-traits, language prestige, elaborated and restrictive codes, constructed languages, ethnic salience, Irish speakers, cross-national stereotypes, to name just these.

John Edwards is editor of the *Journal of Multilingual and Multicultural Development*, editorial advisor to a number of academic journals, a member of a dozen learned societies and a fellow of The Royal Society of Canada.

Bibliography

Edwards J R 1979 *Language and Disadvantage*. Elsevier, New York
Edwards J R (ed.) 1983 *The Irish Language: An Annotated Bibliography of Sociolinguistic Works (1772–1982)*. Garland, New York
Edwards J R 1985 *Language, Society, and Identity*. Blackwell, Oxford, UK
Edwards J R 1994 *Multilingualism*. Routledge, London
Edwards J R (ed.) 1998 *Language in Canada*. Cambridge University Press, Cambridge, UK

Emeneau, Murray Barnson (1904–)
W. Bright

Born in Lunenburg, Nova Scotia, on February 28, 1904, Emeneau is well known as an anthropologist and Indologist as well as a linguist. His doctoral degree from Yale, in 1931, was in Classics and Sanskrit; however, his postdoctoral studies with Edward Sapir (see *Sapir, Edward*) involved him in what was to become known as 'linguistic anthropology.' After carrying out three years of fieldwork with the Toda, Kota, and other Dravidian tribal peoples of south India (1935–38), he became one of the most eminent participants in the Sapirian tradition. As professor of Sanskrit and general linguistics at the University of California, Berkeley, he was founder–chair of the Department of Linguistics at that institution in 1953; since 1971, as Emeritus Professor, he has continued to work and publish prolifically.

Emeneau is famous for the breadth of his interests, which include ethnography, descriptive and historical linguistics, Sanskrit, comparative Indo–European, and Dravidian; he has done pioneering research in ethnosemantics, sociolinguistics, and oral literature. Within Indology, he has consistently pursued a vision of the integrated study of culture, language, and verbal art: he has written that his background led him to take a holistic view of India in which everything was of interest, and was fitted so far as possible into one large picture. During World War II, under military auspices, he taught Vietnamese and wrote a grammar of that language. Finally, continuing an interest in the Native American languages which he had studied with Sapir, he was responsible for initiating the Survey of California Indian Languages at Berkeley, and for inspiring several academic generations of field-workers in the area of Native American linguistics.

Emeneau is especially known for his research on the concept of the *Sprachbund* or 'linguistic area,' a geographical region in which a number of languages (apart from possible genetic relationship among them) have come to share borrowed linguistic traits. Emeneau's demonstration of the phenomenon in South Asia was, as he has said, 'essentially an injection of ethnological thinking into diachronic linguistics'; it has provided a model for studies in other parts of the world, and strongly influenced conceptions of historical relationship among languages.

See also: Areal Linguistics; Sociolinguistic Area.

Bibliography

Emeneau M B 1955 *Kolami, a Dravidian Language*. University of California Press, Berkeley, CA
Emeneau M B 1971 (ed.) *Toda Songs*. Clarendon Press, Oxford, UK
Emeneau M B 1980 *Language and Linguistic Area*. Stanford University Press, Stanford, CA
Emeneau M B 1991 A Nova Scotian becomes a linguistic Indologist. In: Koerner E F K (ed.) *First Person Singular II*. Benjamins, Amsterdam

Fairclough, Norman (1941–)
H. Janks

Norman Fairclough is the Professor of Language and Social Life at Lancaster University. He completed his undergraduate studies and Master's degree at London University and then worked for three years at

University College London. In 1996 he joined Lancaster University, where he was awarded his doctorate for his published work. He received an honorary doctorate from the University of Jyvaskyla in 1996.

He is best known for his book *Language and Power* (1989) in which he shows how language is used to maintain and reproduce existing relations of power in situated contexts. His work is important because of the ways in which he brings linguistic theory, discourse theory, and social theory together to establish connections between language, ideology, and power.

For Fairclough, language is also a means for contesting relations of domination and his sociocultural theory of language allows for human agency and creates possibilities for changing both language and social practice. He sees language as both a site of, and a stake in, social, institutional, and political struggle. In *Discourse and Social Change* (1992b) he considers the social factors that lead to the problematization of conventions, to innovation and to discursive change and he shows how such changes can conserve or transform existing relations of power. In *Critical Language Awareness* (1992a), for example, he shows the conservative force of 'appropriateness,' how it is tied to normalizing conventions and how it favors the language of socially powerful groups in the struggle for control over the sociolinguistic order.

Fairclough's work has been widely taken up because he offers both a method for critical discourse analysis and demonstrations of this method in practice. His method consists of three inter-related processes of analysis, tied to three inter-related dimensions of discourse. These three dimensions of discourse are:
(a) the object of analysis (verbal, visual, multi modal, multimedia texts);
(b) the processes by means of which the object is produced (written, spoken, designed) as well as received (read/listened to/viewed) by human subjects; and
(c) the sociohistorical conditions which govern these processes.

According to Fairclough each of these dimensions requires a different kind of analysis:
(a) text analysis (description);
(b) processing analysis (interpretation, including intertextual analysis);
(c) social analysis (explanation).

His approach enables analysts to focus on the signifiers that make up the text, to recognize the historical determination of their selection, and to understand how choices are tied to the conditions of possibility of the text's utterance.

In *Critical Discourse Analysis* (1995a), *Media Discourse* (1995b), *Discourse in Late Modernity* (1999), and *New Labour, New Language?* (2000), Fairclough applies his theory and his method of critical discourse analysis to language as social practice in both local and global contexts. He provides analyses of, amongst other things, the marketing discourse of universities, political speeches, popular television programs, speech reporting, police interviews, doctor–patient interactions, international neoliberal discourse, and the language of government.

It is in his critical discourse analysis that Fairclough's theory is grounded in practice. His leadership in the area of Critical Language Awareness and his contribution to theorizing Multiliteracies have also made an important contribution to work in education.

See also: Critical Language Awareness; Critical Sociolinguistics; Ideology.

Bibliography

Fairclough N 1989 *Language and Power*. Longman, London
Fairclough N (ed.) 1992a *Critical Language Awareness*. Longman, London
Fairclough N 1992b *Discourse and Social Change*. Polity Press, Oxford, UK
Fairclough N 1995a *Critical Discourse Analysis*. Longman, London
Fairclough N 1995b *Media Discourse*. Arnold, London
Fairclough N 2000 *New Labour, New Language?* Routledge, London
Fairclough N, Chouliaraki L 1999 *Discourse in Late Modernity*. Edinburgh University Press, Edinburgh, UK

Fasold, Ralph W. (1940–)
W. Wolfram

Ralph W. Fasold is one of the pioneers of variation studies as this subfield developed in the United States in the 1960s and 1970s. His interests in sociolinguistics and linguistics, however, are much broader than the quantitative study of systematic variability, and his sociolinguistic practice has extended from the study of variable phonetic detail to the consideration of language policy and vernacular language literacy. At the same time, his focus on linguistic structures has ranged from nominals in Thai to invariant *be* in African American Vernacular English. He is perhaps best known for authoring what are arguably the most comprehensive textbooks on sociolinguistics to appear in the latter half of the twentieth century, *The Sociolinguistics of Society* (1984) and *The Sociolinguistics of Language* (1990).

Fasold was born in Passaic, New Jersey, on April 8, 1940, and received his PhD from the University of Chicago in 1968 with a dissertation on noun compounding in Thai. In 1967, he joined the Urban Language Program at the Center for Applied Linguistics, directed at the time by his former undergraduate mentor, Roger W. Shuy. During the 1960s and early 1970s, the Center for Applied Linguistics was at the forefront of studies of urban dialectology in general and African American Vernacular English in particular. The staff conducted intensive field-initiated research studies in Washington, DC, and Detroit, Michigan, and the Center for Applied Linguistics initiated the first book series in sociolinguistics, the Urban Language Series. Fasold edited several volumes in the series (which featured Labov's *The Social Stratification of English in New York City* (1966) as its first publication), and authored *Tense Marking in Black English: A Linguistic and Social Analysis* (1972). His analysis is a paragon of exacting detail on the interaction of independent phonological and grammatical factors with social factors in the configuration of tense marking in African American Vernacular English. A less well-known but significant contribution to the study of English dialects is an unpublished paper Fasold wrote in 1969 on the vowel rotation in Detroit, Michigan, that Labov (1994: 178) acknowledges as the precursor of the widely recognized Northern Cities Vowel Shift.

In 1972, Fasold joined the faculty at Georgetown University to launch the first linguistics program in the United States with a specific PhD track in sociolinguistics. The program, funded initially by a grant from the National Science Foundation, brought together an anthropologist and psycholinguist with descriptive and applied sociolinguists to guide the first generation of PhD students concentrating in sociolinguistics. Fasold was involved in training sociolinguistic students at Georgetown for three decades, serving at various points as the Head of the Sociolinguistics Program, the Head of the Theoretical Linguistics Program, and the Department Chair.

While Fasold has maintained a continuing interest in the linguistic and social basis of systematic variability, this focus was complemented by a concern for the intersection of formal linguistics and sociolinguistics, particularly as they relate to the question of anaphora. He has also researched questions of language policy and planning, inspired by many of his international students and his lifelong concern for the application of sociolinguistic knowledge to fundamental social and educational problems. Among colleagues and students, he is known for his authentic humility and graciously affirming interactional style.

Bibliography

Fasold R W 1969 *A Sociolinguistic Study of the Pronunciation of Three Vowels in Detroit Speech.* Unpublished manuscript. Center for Applied Linguistics, Washington, DC

Fasold R W 1972 *Tense Marking in Black English: A Linguistic and Social Analysis.* Center for Applied Linguistics, Washington, DC

Fasold R W 1984 *The Sociolinguistics of Society.* Blackwell, Oxford, UK

Fasold R W 1990 *The Sociolinguistics of Language.* Blackwell, Oxford, UK

Labov W 1966 *The Social Stratification of English in New York City.* Center for Applied Linguistics, Washington, DC

Labov W 1994 *Principles of Linguistic Change: Internal Factors.* Blackwell, Malden, MA

Ferguson, Charles A. (1921–98)
J. A. Fishman

One of America's leading linguists, with an unusually broad range of well-developed interests and a highly significant number of organizational accomplishments, Charles A. Ferguson was born on July 6, 1921, in Philadelphia, Pennsylvania, a city in which he also grew up and received his elementary, secondary, and higher education (University of Pennsylvania: AB 1942 (Philosophy), AM 1943, and PhD 1945 (Oriental Studies)). Having specialized in Arabic and Bengali, Ferguson was initially employed as a linguist for Near Eastern languages by the US Department of State, Washington DC, from 1947 to 1955, and then joined Harvard University as a lecturer in linguistics and Arabic, remaining there until 1959.

In 1959, Ferguson became the founding director of the Center for Applied Linguistics, in Washington DC, a position which he maintained until 1966. Under Ferguson's leadership the Center developed from initially being under the auspices of the Modern Language Association of America into an independent institution, with a staff of approximately 100 and international stature in most of the areas of applied linguistics, a field which Ferguson and the Center firmly placed on the agenda of linguistics throughout the world.

While directing the Center, Ferguson also served as a member of the Social Science Research Council's Committee on Linguistics and Psychology (1959–61) and later became the chairman of the Council's Committee on Sociolinguistics (1964–70). In the course of half a dozen years Ferguson's leadership enabled the Committee to establish this new area of specialization as a recognized field of linguistic research and instruction, both in the USA and throughout much of the world, with journals, conferences, and research projects quickly being devoted to it. Ferguson's continued identification with sociolinguistics is evidenced by the very large number of articles and books which he has authored, coauthored, edited, and coedited in this field.

In 1967 Ferguson became Professor of Linguistics and the founding chairman of the linguistics program at Stanford University. Even in the early 2000s, linguistics at Stanford is characterized by a strong interest in many of Ferguson's areas of specialization, including not only those mentioned above but also child language, language universals, language and religion and, of course, all of the standard areas of general linguistics.

In addition to his own seminal publications, many of which have stimulated further research internationally (particularly his pioneering work on diglossia, language and religion, and on baby-talk), Ferguson has been honored by three collections of his selected papers (Dil 1971, Huebner 1996, Belknap and Haeri 1997) and by a large two-volume *Festschrift* on the occasion of his 65th birthday (Fishman et al. 1986). The latter also contains a full bibliography of his published works, articles, books, and reviews, through to 1985.

Ferguson became Emeritus Professor of Linguistics in 1986 and continued to reside near the University, in Palo Alto, CA, together with his wife and colleague, Shirley Brice Heath, and their four children. He remained active in many of the areas of interest which he had pioneered and fostered throughout an exceptionally productive and stimulating career (sociolinguistics always continuing to be among them). Several years after his death commemorative books and entire journal issues continue to be dedicated to his memory (e.g., Fishman 2001, Hudson in press) as a gentle and provocative teacher, friend, provocative researcher, and theoretician. His own unassuming account and interpretation of his life and work are presented in an account published shortly before his death (1998).

See also: Diglossia; Child Language: An Overview; Foreigner Talk.

Bibliography

Belknap K, Haeri N (eds.) 1997 *Structural Studies in Arabic Linguistics*. E. J. Brill, New York
Dil A (ed.) 1971 *Language Structure and Language Use: Essays by Charles A. Ferguson*. Stanford University Press, Stanford CA
Ferguson C A 1998 Long-term commitments and lucky events. In: Koerner E F (ed.) *First Person Singular III: Autobiographies of North American Scholars in the Language Sciences*. Benjamins, Amsterdam
Fishman J A, Tabouret-Keller A, Clyne M, Krishnamurti B, Abdulaziz M (eds.) 1986 *The Fergusonian Impact. Vol. 1: From Phonology to Society; Vol. 2: Sociolinguistics and the Sociology of Language*. Mouton de Gruyter, Berlin
Fishman J A (ed.) 2001 *Can Threatened Languages be Saved?* Multilingual Matters, Clevedon, UK
Hudson A in press Outline of a theory of diglossia. *International Journal of the Sociology of Language*
Huebner T (ed.) 1996 *Sociolinguistic Perspectives: Papers on Language in Society, 1949–1994*. Oxford University Press, New York

Firth, J. R. (1890–1960)
F. R. Palmer

J. R. Firth was Professor and Head of the Department of General Linguistics in the Department of Phonetics and Linguistics in the School of Oriental and African Studies in the University of London from 1941–56, after having served as Senior Lecturer and as Reader in that Department from 1938. The title of Professor of General Linguistics was conferred on him in 1944. He had previously been Professor of English in Lahore, India (1920–28) and from 1928–38 Senior Lecturer in the Department of

Phonetics at University College London, of which the renowned phonetician Daniel Jones was the head. During the Second World War has was in charge of short intensive training courses in Japanese, which both depended on, and influenced, his linguistic outlook. Firth's was the first and only Chair of Linguistics in Britain until 1960, but his influence is reflected in the rapid growth of the subject in the 1960s and the fact that seven members of his academic staff subsequently held chairs themselves, three of them in other universities.

Firth is probably best known for the work produced from 1948 until his death in 1960, but the work of the 'London School' includes the publications of his followers (almost all members of the department) from 1948 until the middle 1960s. His contribution can only be fully appreciated, however, in the light of his earlier works published in the years before the war. Most of his early publications, apart from two popular books *Speech* (1930) and *Tongues of Men* (1937; both reprinted in 1964), were mainly concerned with phonology, although 'The technique of semantics' ([1935] Firth 1957: 7–33) lays the foundation for his basic theory. It was in the field of phonology that he provided the greatest stimulation, with development of the theory known as 'prosodic analysis' that stemmed from his 'Sounds and prosodies' ([1948] Palmer 1970: 1–26). Most of the papers published by members of his department during the 1960s were on that topic.

A second theory with which Firth is closely associated is that of 'context of situation,' but this (and also, to some degree, prosodic analysis) are best understood in terms of his more general views on meaning. While his contemporary in the early years, Bloomfield, was suggesting that meaning was 'the weak point in language study' (Bloomfield 1935: 140), and later American linguists were to exclude it altogether, Firth was already developing his contextual theory of meaning, which is first clearly stated in 'The technique of semantics,' where ([1935] Firth 1957: 19) he speaks of meaning as 'situational relations in a context of situation' and says 'I propose to split up meaning or function into a series of component functions. Each function will be defined as the use of some language form or element in relation to some context. Meaning, that is to say, is to be regarded as a complex of contextual relations, and phonetics, grammar, lexicography, and semantics each handles its own components of the complex in its own appropriate context.'

Context of situation was 'a key concept' ([1950] Firth 1957: 181) of Firth's theory of meaning. He acknowledged that he had taken this expression from the anthropologist Malinowski, with whom he had worked in London, and whose views on meaning are best-known from his 'The problem of meaning in primitive languages,' which is a supplement to Ogden and Richards' (1923) *The Meaning of Meaning* as well as his own (1935) *Coral Gardens and Their Magic*. Malinowski's views on language derived from the difficulties he had experienced in attempting to translate the texts that he had collected, and his conclusion that they could only be understood if placed in the contexts in which they had been uttered. Written language, he suggested, was not the norm, but a far-fetched derivative function of language; language was not a 'mirror of reflected thought,' but a 'mode of action' (1923: 296). Firth felt, however, that Malinowski's context of situation was 'a bit of the social process which can be considered apart,' that it was 'an ordered series of events considered *in rebus*,' whereas his own context of situation was an abstraction, 'a schematic construct,' 'a group of related categories at a different level from grammatical categories, but rather of the same abstract nature.' The categories, he suggested, were (1):

(a) The relevant features of participants: persons, personalities.
   (i) The verbal action of the participants. (1)
   (ii) The nonverbal action of the participants.
(b) The relevant objects.
(c) The effect of the verbal action.

Firth gives just one example, which represents 'a typical Cockney event' (2):

   'Ahng gunna gi' wun fer Ber' ' (2)
   (I'm going to get one for Bert.)

'What,' Firth asks, 'is the minimum number of participants? Three? Four? Where might it happen? In a pub? Where is Bert? Outside? Or playing darts? What are the relevant objects? "Obvious!" you say. So is the convenience of the schematic construct called "context of situation"' ([1950] Firth 1957: 182). In addition to these interior relations of the context, he later suggests that there should be reference to more general frameworks such as economic, religious, and other social structures, types of discourse (monologue, narrative, etc.), personal interchanges, and types of speech function such as drills and orders together with the social techniques of flattery, deception, etc. ([1957] Palmer 1968: 178).

In his last years Firth devoted much attention to translation (there are two papers in Palmer 1968). This was, in a way, appropriate, since his theoretical views had their origins in the problems that Malinowski had faced.

Anyone who reads Firth's work will inevitably be frustrated. Much of it is programmatic and sometimes unclear and apocryphal, and there is a great deal of repetition in successive papers. Yet it is, and was, stimulating, and offered a whole generation of scholars in the UK a new insight into language study, as well as providing an alternative to the barren structuralism of his time. If some of it appears obvious today, it may be that he was ahead of his time.

See also: Malinowski, Bronislaw Kaspar; Context.

Bibliography

Firth J R 1957 *Papers in Linguistics 1934–1951*. Oxford University Press, London
Firth J R 1964 *The Tongues of Men and Speech*. Oxford University Press, London
Malinowski B 1923 The problem of meaning in primitive languages. Supplement to Ogden C K, Richards I A 1923 *The Meaning of Meaning*. Kegan Paul, London
Malinowski B 1953 *Coral Gardens and Their Magic, II*. Allen and Unwin, London
Palmer F R (ed.) 1968 *Selected Papers of J. R. Firth, 1952–1959*. Longman, London
Palmer F R 1970 (ed.) *Prosodic Analysis*. Oxford University Press, London
Robins R H 1961 John Rupert Firth. *Language* 37: 191–200
Robins R H 1963 General linguistics in Great Britain 1930–60. In: Mohrmann C, Norman F, Sommerfelt A (eds.) *Trends in Modern Linguistics*. Spectrum, Antwerp, Belgium

Fishman, Joshua A. (1926–)
B. Spolsky

Joshua Fishman is acknowledged founder of the sociology of language, a spirited advocate of bilingual education in the USA, and a sympathetic friend of all groups who strive to maintain their ancestral languages.

Born on July 18, 1926, in Philadelphia, PA, he was educated there in public schools, at Olney High School, in elementary, secondary, and tertiary level Yiddish schools and courses, and, from 1944–48, at the University of Pennsylvania, where he earned BS and MS degrees. In the summer of 1948, he studied Yiddish, the language of his home and his Jewish education, at UCLA with Max Weinreich, the doyen of Yiddish linguistics, at the same time as did the latter's son Uriel Weinreich. His first scholarly article appeared, in *Yidishe shprakh*, in 1947; in 1949 he received a prize from the Yiddish Scientific Institute for an unpublished monograph on bilingualism (subsequently published in 1951). In 1951, he married Gella Schweid; they have three sons and Yiddish has remained the home language for them, their children, and grandchildren. From 1951–54, he was educational psychologist for the Jewish Education Committee of New York, at the same time studying social psychology at Columbia University, where he gained a PhD in 1953. From 1955–58, he directed research for the College Entrance Examination Board, combining this with teaching the sociology of language (disguised as social psychology) at City College (CUNY). In 1958, he became associate professor of human relations and psychology at the University of Pennsylvania, but 2 years later moved to Yeshiva University, New York, as professor of psychology and sociology; from 1960–66, he was also Dean of the Ferkauf Graduate School of Social Sciences and Humanities. In 1966, he became Distinguished University Research Professor of Social Sciences; from 1973–75, he served as academic vice president; and, in 1988, became professor emeritus. He then began to divide the year between New York (where he has also become a Visiting Professor at New York University and at City University of New York Graduate Center, while maintaining his teaching connection with Ferkauf Graduate School of Psychology at Yeshiva University) and California (where he has become visiting Professor of Education and Linguistics at Stanford University). Four Festschriften were published in his honor by colleagues and former students on the occasion of his 65th birthday in 1991, each volume dealing with a different area of his specialization, and the Linguistic Institute of the Linguistic Society of America conducted a 4-day conference in his honor at that time.

Beginning with a number of publications on educational testing, he completed in 1964 his first major study of the sociology of language, *Language Loyalty in the United States*. A year later, *Yiddish in America* appeared. In 1968, he published three major books: *Bilingualism in the Barrio* (a pioneering study of a multilingual community), *Language Problems of Developing Nations* (the earliest major collection in language planning), and *Readings in the Sociology of Language* (a first attempt to define the new field). His prolific publication continued, amounting by now to over 900 items which have shaped and defined modern scholarly study of bilingualism and multilingualism, bilingual and minority education, the relation of language and thought, the sociology and the social history of Yiddish, language planning, language spread, language shift, language and nationalism, language and ethnicity, and (most recently) ethnic and national efforts to reverse language shift. Since its founding in 1973, he has edited the *International Journal of the Sociology of Language*. Some of his most influential works, authored or edited, are *Language and Nationalism*

(1972 [1989]), *Never Say Die!; A Thousand Years of Yiddish in Jewish Life and Letters* (1981), *Language and Ethnicity in Minority Perspective* (1989), *Yiddish: Turning to Life* (1991), *The Earliest Stage of Language Planning* (1993), *Post-Imperial English* (1995), *The Multilingual Apple: Languages in New York* (1997), and the *Handbook of Language and Ethnicity* (1999). Together with Gella Fishman he has also established the extensive five-generational 'Fishman Family Archives' at Stanford University Libraries, including his correspondence, course notes and outlines, lecture notes, manuscripts of his books, and papers and recordings/videos of his talks.

All his scholarly work with minority ethnic groups and with others engaged in the struggle to preserve their languages and traditions has been inspired by a deep and heartfelt compassion that has always sustained the markedly human tone in his most objective writings.

Bibliography

Fishman J A 1991a Bibliographical inventory (compiled by Fishman G S). In: Cooper R L, Spolsky B (eds.) *The Influence of Language on Culture and Thought: Essays in Honor of Joshua A. Fishman's Sixty-Fifth Birthday*. Mouton, Berlin

Fishman J A 1991b *Reversing Language Shift: Theory and Practice of Assistance to Threatened Languages*. Multilingual Matters, Clevedon, UK

Fishman J A 1991c *Yiddish: Turning to Life*. Benjamins, Amsterdam

Fishman J A, Rubal-Lopez A, Conrad A W (eds.) 1996 *Post-Imperial English*. Mouton de Gruyter, Berlin

Fishman J A (ed.) 1999 *Handbook of Language and Ethnic Identity*. Oxford University Press, Oxford, UK

Fishman J A (ed.) 2001 *Can Threatened Languages Be Saved? Reversing Language Shift, Revisited: A 21st Century Perspective*. Multilingual Matters Ltd., Clevedon, UK

Foucault, Michel (1926–84)

J. C. Maher

Michel Foucault, philosopher, cultural historian, and sociologist whose critical theory involved influential observations on the role of language in society, was born in Poitiers, France in 1926. He held degrees in philosophy and psychology from the *Ecole Normale Supérieure* at the Sorbonne and the University of Paris. He also held a diploma in psychopathology and was a student of the Marxist scholar, Louis Althusser. After academic appointments in Sweden and Poland, he returned to France in 1960 as chairman of the Department of Philosophy at the University of Clermont-Ferrand and then as professor at the University of Paris-Vincennes (1968–70). He held the chair as Professor of the History of Systems of Ideas at the *Collège de France* until his death in 1984.

Foucault's inaugural lecture 'Discourse in Language' at the *Collège de France* in 1970 established his reputation in France as a leading ethnomethodologist of language (see *Ethnomethodology*). In this treatise, he examined the relation between truth and description in language arguing that if one wants to be heard in society it is not enough simply to 'speak' the truth rather one must be, in some sense, within the truth and embody its regime. The prohibitions surrounding speech inexorably reveal language's links with desire and power. In his investigation of mental illness, Foucault noted how, from the Middle Ages onward, a man was considered mad if his speech could not be said to form 'part of the common discourse of man.' The language of the mentally ill was considered either inadmissible in the authentification of acts or contracts or, alternatively, 'credited with strange powers of revealing some hidden truth, of predicting the future, of revealing... what the wise were unable to perceive' (1976: 216). By examining conventional explanations and understandings of madness (likewise, criminality or homosexuality) one can see how the boundaries of the normal are created as new forms of speech emerge.

Foucault's seminal studies on the religious, therapeutic, and judicial domains emphasized the presence of a 'fellowship of discourse' for each distinct social group. In what way does the dominant discourse of a powerful group, established in an 'institutional site' (e.g., hospital, prison), control those it marginalizes? Does not every speaker, in fact, unconsciously site an interlocutor or object of discourse within a power relation as the 'questioning subject,' the 'listening subject,' or the 'seeing subject'? The function of a fellowship is to maintain and reproduce discourse in order that it may circulate within its boundaries according to strict regulations. Foucault stressed that the meanings contained in discourse cannot be based upon an *a priori* system of signification as if the world is given to people simply to decipher. Discourse is, rather, a violence that people do to things.

See also: Discourse; Power and Language.

Bibliography

Foucault M 1963 *Naissance de la Clinique*. PUF, Paris
Foucault M 1966 *Les Mots et les Choses: une archéologie des sciences humaines*. Gallimard, Paris
Foucault M 1972 Discourse in language (appendix). In: Foucault M (trans. Sheriden Smith A M) *Archaeology of Knowledge*. Tavistock, London
Foucault M 1976 *Histoire de la Folie a l'Age Classique*. Gallimard, Paris
Foucault M 1977 *Language, Counter-Memory, Practice, Selected Essays, and Interviews*. Bouchard D F (ed.) Blackwell, Oxford, UK
Hoy D (ed.) 1986 *Foucault*. Blackwell, Oxford, UK
Smart B 1985 *Michel Foucault*. Ellis Horwood, Chichester, UK

Giles, Howard (1946–)
J. Bradac

Howard Giles is the founder of the relatively new field of language and social psychology, and congruously he was the founding editor of the *Journal of Language and Social Psychology*, established in 1982. He and W. P. Robinson convened the first International Conference on Language and Social Psychology at the University of Bristol in 1979, a seminal event that spawned several more international conferences (the most recent at Cardiff, Wales in 2000) that ultimately led to the formation of the International Association for Language and Social Psychology in 1997. Giles became President of this association in 2000. Essentially, Giles's research and that of others in the field has generally focused on phenomena residing at the intersection of language, mind, and society. Thus, some of his early work examined language attitudes, focusing on hearers' evaluative reactions to communicators using different accents or dialects, a difference that often reflects membership in different social groups. Communicators exhibiting these differences are often upgraded or downgraded along the dimensions of perceived status and solidarity.

Giles was born in Cardiff, Wales, on December 22, 1946. He obtained his PhD in social psychology from the University of Bristol in 1971 and was awarded a DSc in the same field from the same institution in 1996. In 1984, he became Professor of Social Psychology and in 1987 became Head of Psychology at the University of Bristol. In 1989, he moved to the University of California, Santa Barbara where he is currently Professor of Communication and Assistant Dean of Undergraduate Studies, with appointments also in Psychology and Linguistics.

Giles may be best known for his communication accommodation theory (CAT), the roots of which can be seen in his doctoral dissertation. This theory, which was initially labeled speech accommodation theory (see *Speech Accommodation*), has evolved over the years and has stimulated a great deal of research in several fields, including linguistics, sociolinguistics, communication, and psychology. Essentially, the theory is concerned with antecedents for, and consequences of, one person's convergence to or divergence from the language style of a partner in interpersonal communication. Style refers to consistent individual or group variation in any phonological, lexical, or syntactic feature of language. Communicators may converge to the style of others in order to attain social approval or they may diverge to achieve subjective group distinctiveness. Convergence tends to produce favorable attitudes toward the converger in the mind of the person converged to, whereas divergence tends to produce unfavorable attitudes, although there are many mediating variables that can upset this general prediction. Accommodation processes have been shown to operate in the domain of nonverbal communication as well. Additionally, Giles is well known for his theoretical and research work in ethnolinguistic vitality, language and ageing, patronizing speech, and hate speech.

Giles is a fellow of six learned societies, including the British Psychological Society, the American Psychological Society, and the International Communication Association. He was the British Psychological Society's Spearman Medalist in 1978 and was recipient of that society's President's Award in 1989. In 1993, he received the inaugural Outstanding Scholar Award from the Language and Social Interaction Division of the International Communication Association.

See also: Speech Accommodation; Ethnolinguistic Vitality; Social Psychology.

Bibliography

Giles H, Coupland N 1991 *Language: Contexts and Consequences*. Open University Press, Buckingham, UK
Giles H, Powesland P F 1975 *Speech Style and Social Evaluation*. Academic Press, London
Giles H, Mulac A, Bradac J J, Johnson P 1987 Speech accommodation theory: The first decade and beyond. In:

McLaughlin M (ed.) *Communication Yearbook 10.* Sage, Newbury Park, CA

Giles H, Robinson W P (eds.) 1990 *Handbook of Language and Social Psychology.* Wiley, Chichester, UK

Robinson W P, Giles H (eds.) 2001 *The New Handbook of Language and Social Psychology.* Wiley, Chichester, UK

Ryan E B, Giles H (eds.) 1982 *Attitudes Towards Language Variation: Social and Applied Contexts.* Edward Arnold, London

Gilliéron, Jules (1854–1926)
T. Hill

Jules Louis Gilliéron, one of dialectology's most influential figures, was born at Neuveville, Neuchâtel, Switzerland, the son of a language teacher and geologist, who introduced him to field research and mapping. He qualified in Romance philology at Neuchâtel and Basel, then continued his studies with Gaston Paris at the *École normale des hautes etudes*, Paris, where he was to pass his entire professional life: maintaining himself in the earlier years as a college teacher of German. Having received his diploma for a monograph on the dialect of Vionnaz, in 1883 he became the first professor of 'Gallo-Roman dialectology' (i.e., the French dialects of France and the adjoining countries).

Gilliéron and his pupil Rousselot founded the *Revue des patois galloromans* (1887–93), for the publication of dialect monographs. In 1888 Gaston Paris called for a dialect atlas, and with his help regarding finance and publication Gilliéron undertook the project. He decided that a reliable, uniform body of data (notably lacking in the monographs) could be achieved only by means of a standard questionnaire, operated by a single nonacademic fieldworker trained by himself. For this he discovered the remarkable amateur Edmond Edmont (1849–1926), grocer and leading citizen of Saint Pol-sur-Ternoise, by Dunkirk. Edmont had achieved recognition for his local folklore collections, and in 1887 Gilliéron's *Revue* published his *Lexique saint-poloise*, a glossary complied with unusual phonetic accuracy. After training in transcription, the middle-aged enthusiast was dispatched on a three-year cycle tour of France (1897–1901), to collect data from a single informant in each of over 600 places; in 1911, aged 62, he repeated this performance for the atlas of Corsica.

The questionnaire was a list of words and phrases for translation into the dialect, yielding about 2000 singleword items of phonological, lexical, or grammatical interest: each item to appear in the atlas as a separate map. The object was to establish not merely the forms of each dialect, but also how it was surviving vis-à-vis the standard language, and the speaker's attitude to it. Accordingly, only the speaker's first, unprompted response was to be noted, with notes of interest on hesitations, etc. The maps were edited jointly by Gilliéron and Edmont, and published between 1902 and 1910 as the *Atlas linguistique de la France* (ALF).

From 1905 on, in lectures and interpretive monographs, Gilliéron developed his distinctive 'biological' view of language. Initially the ALF attached less interest at home than in, e.g., Germany, and some of Gilliéron's best known monographs were first published privately in his native village. However, his courses attracted universal scholarly attention in due course, and his writings have become classics of methodology, widely quoted in textbooks of linguistics. Gilliéron's concern was chiefly with 'intralinguistic dialectology,' i.e., the use of the geographical data to elucidate the structure and development of the language. It was naturally affected by the highly specific nature of the French language and its territory.

Gilliéron's approach has been criticized for overinterpretation of exclusively French data, while ignoring relevant facts from the wider Romance field. It is also observed that in his word histories he tacitly admits the operation of sound laws, while denying their validity in principle. Nevertheless, his achievement is probably the greatest single contribution to dialectology, and has provided the model for surveys throughout the world: in particular in the Romance, Slavonic, and Scandinavian countries, the USA, and England.

See also: Maps: Dialect and Language; Dialect and Dialectology.

Bibliography

Gilliéron J L 1918 *Généalogie des mots qui désignent l'abeille.* Champion, Paris

Gilliéron J L 1919 *La faillite de l'étymologie phonétique.* Beerstecher, Neuveville

Gilliéron J L 1921 *Pathologie et thérapeutique verbales.* Champion, Paris

Gilliéron J L, Roques M 1910 Études de géographie linguistique XII: Mots en collision, A. Le coq et le chat. *Reuve de philologie française* **24**: 278–88

Dauzat A 1922 *La géographie linguistique.* Flammarion, Paris

Goffman, Erving (1922–82)
R. L. Schmitt

Erving Goffman, a Jewish Canadian, spent three decades studying face-to-face interaction through naturalistic observation, completing 11 radically influential books and significant articles and chapters. Goffman's essays, his preferred style of presentation, influenced sociologists, anthropologists, linguists, and psychiatrists. He was not uniformly respected and his status was even varied within sociology, although his contributions to microsociology, deviance, and medical sociology were unmistakable.

Goffman's signature was controversy. His methods, theoretical persuasion, political stance, the import of his ideas, and, curiously, his personal lifestyle were religiously criticized. Attention to Goffman since his demise, however, has clarified the cornerstone of his career as *microsociological constraint* and marked much of the criticism as wrong-headed. Goffman is sometimes inappropriately described as a 'symbolic interactionist.' Symbolic interactionism emphasizes the self as a being constantly interpreting events. While for Goffman (1959: 252), the self itself was an imputation made by an audience. Goffman's intellectual roots are also often traced to the French sociologist, Emile Durkheim, but Durkheim was interested only in the constraint that was generated by the broad macrostructures within society. Goffman (1983) concluded in his Presidential Address to the American Sociological Association that the constraint that had uniquely concerned him throughout his lifetime was anchored within the 'interaction order,' i.e., a face-to-face encounter.

The dynamics of microsociological constraint was the agenda from Goffman's keynoting book, *The Presentation of Self in Everyday Life* (1959), through *Relations in Public* (1971). The dramaturgical perspective elaborated in these essays revealed how the sacredness of self morally constrained participants to ritually maintain interaction primarily through rules of courtesy and irrelevance. Rules of courtesy morally oblige persons to involve themselves in interaction and to protect the presented selves of others. Rules of irrelevance enable interactants to disattend hierarchies that would mediate against the fundamental equality demanded by the interaction order. The complexity of maintaining equality with those having deeply discredited identities was the core of Goffman's *Asylums* (1961) and *Stigma* (1963). Many concepts which are now synonymous with Goffman were developed in his 1959–1971 essays, including 'dramaturgy,' 'impression management,' 'face,' 'focused and unfocused interaction,' 'encounter,' 'strategic interaction,' 'expressions given,' 'expressions given off,' 'backstage,' 'frontstage,' 'remedial work,' 'role distance,' 'identity documents,' 'total institutions,' 'spoiled identities,' and 'secondary adjustments.'

Goffman turned to frames in his most systematic book, *Frame Analysis* (1974). The frame addresses the question, 'What is it that is going on here?' Primary frames are organizing definitions of the situation that can be understood without reference to other definitions, for example, *two lovers kiss*. Goffman's frame, however, differs from the symbolic interactionist's 'definition of the situation' because frames are given in a situation. They have a pre-existence, are always shared, usually unambiguous, and are equally 'real.'

Transformation/lamination/layered activity is the distinctive contribution of *Frame Analysis*. Goffman underscores the relational quality of reality by showing how multiple realities are interrelated. Transformations are definitions that systematically build on other definitions and encompass keys (pretend kiss between actors) and fabrications (con-man kisses widow). Goffman details various types of primary frames, keys, and fabrications and explains how primary frames and transformations are anchored in the everyday world. Paradoxically, laminations have contributed to the analysis of emergent, as well as existing, frames, including fantasy role-playing games (Fine 1983) and frame debates (Schmitt 1985).

Linguistics, ostensibly, captured Goffman's interest in *Forms of Talk*, but, for Goffman (1981: 71), 'conversation [only] constitutes an encounter of a special kind.' Goffman's views of dramaturgy and frame are suggested in his analysis of 'response cries' (whoops); the lecture; and radio talk. The import of his final book is its sociolinguistic corrective for linguistics, particularly 'conversational analysis,' a specialized branch of ethnomethodology: talk, not language or grammar, protects selves. Talk may have communicative effects but not be dialogic.

Conversation cannot be studied exclusively as oral communication or apart from context. The speaker–hearer dichotomy is inadequate because speakers switch frames. Their 'footing' shifts in various ways as they change their stance to what they say. A 'move' or unitary action, not the sentence, should be the unit of observation.

Goffman (1983) recommended that the interaction order be studied in relation to other social structures, but the memories, emotions, and meanings that concern symbolic interactionists were never mentioned. Goffman (1967: 3) remained steadfast in studying, 'Not ... men and their moments. Rather moments and their men.' Interaction orders, however, will lurk as sterile and unfulfilled enclosures until the processes that weave them together in the lives of selves, relationships, and groups are identified.

See also: Ethnomethodology; Conversation Analysis.

Bibliography

Fine G A 1983 *Shared Fantasy: Role-Playing Games as Social Worlds*. University of Chicago Press, Chicago, IL

Goffman E 1959 *The Presentation of Self in Everyday Life*. Doubleday Anchor, Garden City, NY

Goffman E 1961 *Asylums: Essays on the Social Situation of Mental Patients and Other Inmates*. Anchor Books, Garden City, NY

Goffman E 1963 *Stigma: Notes on the Management of Spoiled Identity*. Prentice-Hall, Englewood Cliffs, NJ

Goffman E 1967 *Interaction Ritual*. Doubleday Anchor, Garden City, NY

Goffman E 1971 *Relations in Public*. Basic Books, New York

Goffman E 1974 *Frame Analysis: An Essay on the Organization of Experience*. Harper and Row, New York

Goffman E 1981 *Forms of Talk*. University of Pennsylvania Press, Philadelphia, PA

Goffman E 1983 The interaction order. *American Sociological Review* **48**: 1–17

Schmitt R L 1985 Negative and positive keying in natural contexts: Preserving the transformation concept from death through conflation. *Sociological Inquiry* **55**: 383–401

Smith G W H, Waksler F C 1989 The published works of Erving Goffman. *Human Studies* **12**: 173–6

Waksler F C, Psathas G 1989 Selected books and articles about Erving Goffman and of related interest. *Human Studies* **12**: 177–81

Görlach, Manfred (1937–)

E. W. Schneider

Manfred Görlach is one of the founding fathers of 'English as a world language' as a scholarly subdiscipline, closely related to sociolinguistics. He has built a publication infrastructure for this field, stimulated much relevant research, and published widely himself (more than two dozen books, dozens of articles, and hundreds of reviews), always emphasizing sociolinguistically relevant aspects.

Born on July 12, 1937, in Berlin, in the early 1960s he was forced to interrupt his studies in this city when, having helped friends to leave the communist state after the building of the Berlin Wall, he was sentenced to a three-year confinement in an East German penitentiary for refugee smuggling. Afterwards, he taught at the University of Heidelberg, where he received his PhD in 1970 for an analysis of Middle English saints' legends. In 1984 he moved to Cologne to accept a Chair of English Linguistics which he held until his retirement.

Görlach was trained as a language historian and has continued to work in this field throughout his career. He soon became well known for two books, originally published in German—a language history adopting structuralist principles of description (1974; English translation, 1997) and an *Introduction to Early Modern English* (1978; English translation, 1991). Like two later books similar in orientation and structure (*English in Nineteenth-Century England* 1999, *Eighteenth-Century English* 2001), these volumes not only provide systematic coverage of the features of the English language of those periods, emphasizing the sociolinguistic usage conditions of dialects and sociolects and their historical and cultural background; they also illustrate this material with a rich array of sample texts which make up half of each book, texts cross-referenced to the general chapters, and thus illustrating the importance which the author places upon readers' immediate exposure to authentic texts.

Late in the 1970s Görlach became aware of the growing importance but limited scholarly coverage of varieties of English as a world language, and embarked on this topic. Along with Richard Bailey he co-edited *English as a World Language* (1982), the first classic handbook of this discipline. In 1980 he founded *English World-Wide*, the earliest international scholarly journal on this subject, and edited it until 1997. He also founded and edited a companion book series, *Varieties of English around the World*, and inspired a great many studies published there. His continuing emphasis on familiarity with source texts is reflected in a *Text Series* division, which publishes systematically compiled printed and tape-recorded text samples. He also authored a large number of articles on almost all national forms of English, typically characterized by an immense breadth of knowledge and sytematicity of description and comparison; these are put together in several collective volumes (*Englishes*, 1991, *More Englishes* 1995, *Even More Englishes* 1998, *Still More Englishes* 2002). Again, his work in this area has tended to be marked by an emphasis upon the textual basis and empirical documentation, as well as upon the historical and sociocultural factors that have shaped the sociolinguistic determinants of varieties of English around the globe.

See also: Bilingualism, Societal; English as a Foreign Language; New Englishes.

Bibliography

Görlach M 1974 *Einführung in die englische Sprachgeschichte*. Quelle & Meyer, Heidelberg, Germany

Görlach M 1978 *Einführung ins Frühneuenglische*. Quelle & Meyer, Heidelberg, Germany

Görlach M 1997 *A Linguistic History of English*. Macmillan, London

Görlach M 1991 *Introduction to Early Modern English*. Cambridge University Press, Cambridge, UK

Görlach M 1991 *Englishes. Studies in Varieties of English 1984–1988*. Benjamins, Amsterdam

Görlach M 1995 *More Englishes. New Studies in Varieties of English 1988–1994*. Benjamins, Amsterdam

Görlach M 1998 *Even More Englishes. Studies 1996–1997* Benjamins, Amsterdam

Görlach M 1999 *English in Nineteenth-Century England*. Cambridge University Press, Cambridge, UK

Görlach M 2001 *Eighteenth-Century English*. Winter, Heidelberg, Germany

Görlach M 2002 *Still More Englishes*. Benjamins, Amsterdam

Görlach M, Bailey RW 1982 *English as a World Language*. University of Michigan Press, Ann Arbor, MI

Gramsci, Antonio (1891–1937)
N. Helsloot

As a Marxist politician, Gramsci not only attached practical conclusions to linguistic theory, but also contributed to a political interpretation of linguistics itself.

He was born on the Italian island of Sardinia, where he grew up in poverty. He suffered from ill health. Though he had to work during some of his school years, he won a modest scholarship which enabled him to study philology at the University of Turin. Here he was initiated in the 'neolinguistic' school of Matteo Bartoli. The social turbulence of industrial Turin involved him in politics. He started working as a journalist and editor for the weekly paper of the Socialist Party, and became a founder and leader of the Italian Communist Party. As a member of parliament, he didn't think it appropriate to escape the increasing fascist pressure. In 1926 he was imprisoned in spite of his parliamentary inviolability. Because of the lack of medical care he became ever more ill and died in prison, some days after his official release.

As a student Gramsci furnished data for Bartoli's studies of the Sardinian dialect. Influenced by theories of linguistic radiation, he increasingly stressed the emancipatory qualities of dialects. The historical dispersion of language variants (and the implied world views) is no matter of personal choice, but Gramsci encouraged intellectuals (public speakers and writers) to further historical necessity by 'organically' taking side with rising social movements instead of sticking to established values. Thus, he criticized linguistic isolationism, like that of the Latin-speaking catholic clergy and of Mandarin-speaking Chinese leaders. He also opposed the cosmopolitanism of the Esperanto movement as not fitting in with the needs of the masses; likewise, he blamed the dominance of the Italian of Florence on the cultural hegemony of an outdated class. Gramsci argued strongly for a change, focusing on cooperation between northern industrialized Italy and the underdeveloped rural south (including Sardinia). He denied any grammaticality, correctness, or truth in language apart from the way in which it is alive in practices that are socially real and politically open. By cooperating, isolated minority languages may gain popular adherence and prestige. Linguistics should stimulate such change.

Most of Gramsci's work was written in prison and smuggled out. Editions of selected parts of his prison notebooks appeared in the years after the Second World War, when Gramsci became one of the main sources of inspiration for Italian communism. A complete edition, showing his concern with the problem of linguistic unity and the diffusion of culture, did not appear until 1975. Outside of Italy, Gramsci's reputation spread in the course of the next decade. Because of his defense of differences against enforced unity, his view of language and culture matched that of postmodern thinkers like Althusser and Foucault, and stimulated a political elaboration of anti-foundationalist theories of language.

See also: Hegemony; Power and Language; Marxist Theories of Language.

Bibliography

Gramsci A 1971 *Selections from the Prison Notebooks*. International, New York
Gramsci A 1984 Notes on language (with an introduction by Mansfield S R). *Telos* **59**: 119–50
Gramsci A 1985 *Selections from the Cultural Writings*. Lawrence and Wishart, London
Helsloot N 1989 Linguists of all countries . . . ! On Gramsci's premise of coherence. *Journal of Pragmatics* **13**: 547–66
Holub R 1992 *Antonio Gramsci: Beyond Marxism and Postmodernism*. Routledge, London
Salamini L 1981 Gramsci and Marxist sociology of language. *International Journal of the Sociology of Language* **32**: 27–44

Grierson, Sir George Abraham (1851–1941)
J. C. Wright

Sir George Abraham Grierson ICS OM KCIE FBA was the originator and compiler of the monumental *Linguistic Survey of India* (Grierson 1903–27). Completed in his 77th year, the *Survey* had been proposed to him as a work for life by Professor Robert Atkinson who, at Trinity College, Dublin, first developed in Grierson an interest in linguistics.

Grierson was born on January 7, 1851 at Glanageary, Co. Dublin. For 23 years, while an active member of the Indian Civil Service, he produced a vast series of publications bearing on the languages and orally transmitted literatures of North India, notably the Bihar dialects, the Hindi of Oudh and Braj, Kashmiri, and Gypsy Romani. His exemplary *Bihar Peasant Life* (Grierson 1885) constitutes a linguistic–geographical study of vocabulary in which the implements and procedures of an agricultural province are described and illustrated. He compiled the first extensive bio-bibliography of literature in the modern Indo-Aryan vernaculars, and conspectus accounts of their distribution and linguistic affinities.

Grierson's *Linguistic Survey of India* (1903–27) was presented to the government as intended, to enable British administrators to communicate directly with the local populace, but it was devised rather with a view to revealing the richness of modern India's vernacular cultures to a West hitherto mesmerized by India's past. In 1898, after protracted negotiations, Grierson was permitted to reside and work in Camberley, Surrey, where he was assisted for a time by the Norwegian Sten Konow who contributed much of the material relating to non-Indo-Aryan languages.

In its necessarily curtailed form, the *Survey* ensured that for every patois that could be identified, one specimen of original narrative and the translation of one standard text would be collected, along with a list of words and test sentences. The provinces of Madras and Burma, and the states of Hyderabad and Mysore declined to participate. As a result, only 179 of the 188 languages currently censused could be covered, together with 544 identified 'dialects.' Some 250 gramophone records illustrate forms of speech circa 1920. The inherent problems would have been insurmountable, but for the fact that so well-qualified a philologist and linguist was able, as a civil servant, to divert to the task some of the administrative resources of the Imperial Government and its allies. For all its inevitable faults in detail, traceable usually to the effect of political geography in predetermining linguistic groupings, Grierson's classification remains adequate for practical purposes (notably the subsequent Censuses of India) and a reference point for all research involving the languages of the Subcontinent—Mon-Khmer, Tai, Tibeto-Burman, Munda, Dravidian, and Iranian, as well as Indo-Aryan. Materials for a subsequent Ethnographical and Linguistic Survey of Burma, compiled by L. F. Taylor, were lost as a consequence of the invasion of Burma.

After completing the *Survey* in 1927, Grierson went on publishing specimens of Indo-Aryan literatures well into his eighties. He died on March 9, 1941.

See also: Dialect and Dialectology.

Bibliography

Census of India 1961, I, Pt. XI–C (i) 1969 *Inquiries into the Spoken Languages of India from Early Times to Census of India 1901*. App. I(b) Copies of Proceedings of Government Records relating to the Linguistic Survey of India by G A Grierson, Delhi, India
Grierson G A 1883–87 *Seven Grammars of the Dialects and the Subdialects of the Bihārī language*. 8 pts. Bengal Secretariat Press, Calcutta, India
Grierson G A 1885 *Bihar Peasant Life, Being a Discursive Catalogue of the Surroundings of the People of that Province*. Bengal Secretariat Press, Calcutta/Trübner & Co., London
Grierson G A 1903–27 *Linguistic Survey of India*, 11 vols. in 20. Office of the Superintendent of Government Printing, Calcutta, India
Grierson G A 1916–32 *A Dictionary of the Kāshmīrī Language. Compiled partly from Materials left by . . . Iśvara Kaula*. (Bibliotheca Indica, 229) Asiatic Society of Bengal, Calcutta, India

Randle H N 1939–42 Note on the late Sir George Grieson's manuscripts, etc. *Bulletin of the School of Oriental and African Studies* **10**: 1066

Thomas F W, Turner R L 1942 George Abraham Grierson 1851–1941. *Proceedings of the British Academy* **28**: 283–306

White E M 1936 Bibliography of the published writings of Sir George A. Grierson. *Bulletin of the School of Oriental and African Studies* **8**: 297–318

Gumperz, John J. (1922–)

N. Berenz

With more than 100 published books and articles, John J. Gumperz has been a major figure in the field of sociolinguistics for four decades. The introductory chapter to *Linguistic Diversity in South Asia* has been hailed as 'the first concise statement of sociolinguistic problems... unequaled in its grasp of the broader issues' (Dil 1971). *The Ethnography of Communication* and *Directions in Sociolinguistics* are foundational works. *Language in Social Groups* is a classic for its insights into how social groups retain their identities in complex societies.

As the founder of Interactional Sociolinguistics (see *Interactional Sociolinguistic Research Methods*), Gumperz draws on a wide variety of analytic tools—among these, implicature, speech acts, frames, network, ethnicity, and habitus—to link the macrosociological to the microconversational. His key concept, contextualization, is clearly set out in *Discourse Strategies*, which is widely used as a textbook. His chapter in *Rethinking Linguistic Relativity* reframes the Whorfian notion in terms of conversational inferencing.

Gumperz's work in institutional settings, particularly those involved in employment and education, continues to produce crucial insights into communicative practices and interpretive processes. He calls attention to minorization, the often unintentional process through which the life chances of members of particular social groups are diminished as a result of variation in cultural presuppositions and rhetorical styles. He shows that such variation contributes to communicative breakdown and may lead to pejorative stereotyping. His findings also contribute to our understanding of the process of linguistic change.

Gumperz's interest in cross-cultural communication and his concern with social justice may have its roots in his early life. As a teenager in the years leading up to World War II, Gumperz emigrated with his family from Germany to the United States. After earning a PhD (1954) at the University of Michigan, Ann Arbor, Gumperz went to India on a Cornell post-doctoral fellowship. There he carried out sociolinguistic studies on language contact and on the role of language in social stratification. Fieldwork in Norway in the 1960s broadened his interest in dialect maintenance and loss, as well as the link between language and social identity.

Gumperz recognized early on the importance of a comparative perspective, as demonstrated by his work on bilingualism and linguistic diffusion. In the 1970s Gumperz focused on the analysis of sociocultural symbolism in bilingual and ethnically mixed groups in India, Austria, the UK, and the United States. From the 1980s to the present, he established and is further developing Interactional Sociolinguistics as both a theory and a research methodology.

During his long teaching career at University of California at Berkeley (where he is now Professor Emeritus) and as a visitor at other American and European universities, Gumperz's courses and seminars introduced Interactional Sociolinguistics to scores of sociolinguists and linguistic anthropologists. He has been a Fellow of the National Science Foundation, the Guggenheim Foundation, the American Academy of Arts and Sciences, and the Max Planck Project Group in Cognitive Anthropology, among other honors. Gumperz remains actively engaged in research from which emerge new insights into the communicative complexities of our multilingual/multicultural world.

See also: Discourse in Cross-linguistic and Cross-cultural Contexts; Ethnography of Speaking; Interactional Sociolinguistic Research Methods.

Bibliography

Gumperz J J 1971 *Language in Social Groups*, Dil A (ed.), Stanford University Press, Palo Alto, CA

Gumperz J J (ed.) 1982 *Language and Social Identity*. Cambridge University Press, Cambridge, UK

Gumperz J J 1982 *Discourse Strategies*. Cambridge University Press, Cambridge, UK

Gumperz J J 1996 The linguistic and cultural relativity of conversational inference. In: Gumperz J J, Levinson S C (eds.) *Rethinking Linguistic Relativity*. Cambridge University Press, New York

Gumperz J J, Hymes D (eds.) 1964 The ethnography of communication. *American Anthropologist* **66**: 6, part 2 (special issue)

Gumperz J J, Hymes D 1986 [1972] *Directions in Sociolinguistics*. Blackwell, Oxford, UK

Hall, Robert A. Jr (1911–97)

M. Danesi

Hall contributed substantially and substantively to several areas of scientific language study, including the reconstruction of Proto-Romance (see Hall 1950, 1976, 1984), the study of pidgins and creoles (see Hall 1966) and to an appreciation of the life and thought of Leonard Bloomfield (Hall 1987a, 1990). He was also known for his caustic critique of the generative paradigm in linguistics (see Hall 1987b). In addition, Hall produced several widely read textbooks from 1948–68 (Hall 1948, 1960, 1964, 1968) with the aim of explaining the main concepts and techniques of American structuralist linguistics to a broad, general audience. He also wrote extensively on the Romance languages (especially Italian), on literary criticism, and on topics related to the teaching of foreign languages. (A bibliography of his published works 1936–87 can be found in Danesi 1987.)

Hall was born on April 4, 1911 in Raleigh, North Carolina. He graduated with a BA from Princeton University in 1931, later receiving the AM from the University of Chicago and the degree of Doctor of Letters from the University of Rome in 1934. At Princeton he majored in French and German literature. He was introduced to linguistics by Harry Hoijer while in graduate school at Chicago. Hoijer's lectures, which were based on Sapir's 1921 text *Language* (see *Sapir, Edward*), convinced Hall to change his program of study from literary criticism to linguistics. While at Chicago he also took a course on the history of the French language with T. Atkinson Jenkins. Jenkins's emphasis on the importance of *etymology* fostered in Hall an abiding interest in historical linguistics, and especially, in the reconstruction of proto-languages. This interest led him in the early 1950s to undertake extensive research on the reconstruction of Proto-Romance.

From 1937 to 1946 he held teaching positions at the University of Puerto Rico, Princeton University, and Brown University. From 1946 on he taught linguistics and Italian at Cornell University where he remained until his retirement in 1977. At Cornell he developed a close personal and professional relationship with Charles F. Hockett.

During World War II he was in charge of the US Army Italian courses at Yale University and the US Navy Pidgin English courses at Columbia University.

As a summer lecturer at the Linguistic Institutes of Indiana University and the University of Michigan he worked closely with neo-Bloomfieldian linguists. It was at the 1938 Linguistic Institute that he became intrigued by Leonard Bloomfield's ideas on applying linguistics to language teaching, although he argued with Bloomfield over the desirability of teaching grammar to school-age children (see Danesi 1987: 55). At various times in his career, Hall also held executive positions in the Linguistic Society of America, the American Association of Teachers of Italian, the Wodehouse Society, and the Linguistic Association of Canada and the United States.

Trained within the paradigm of American structuralism, Hall was always one of its main defenders, frequently emphasizing the need to be wary of turning linguistics into a theory-dominated discipline. Like other Bloomfieldians, Hall always argued that any theory should be based on the painstaking collection and analysis of data which reflect the individual and social embodiments of language. His writing style is always lucid and to the point. In his more popular writings his prose is often terse and witty. At times, his deeply rooted joviality rises to the surface in amusing ways, as when he assumed the pseudonym 'Berto Sala' for two of this works of fiction (Hall 1959, 1981). This is the Italian equivalent of his name (*Berto* = Robert, *Sala* = Hall). His overall view of the scientific linguistics enterprise can perhaps best be summed up in his own words, uttered near the start of his long and illustrious career (1948: 249): 'The contribution of linguistics is simply a part of the effort of all science in modern democratic society to find out the truth and to act upon it.' Hall died on December 2, 1997.

See also: Pidgins and Creoles: An Overview.

Bibliography

Danesi M 1987 *Robert A. Hall and American Structuralism*. Jupiter Press, Lake Bluff, IL

Hall R A 1948 *Leave Your Language Alone!* Linguistica, Ithaca, NY

Hall R A 1950 The reconstruction of Proto-Romance. *Language* **26**: 6–27

Hall R A 1959 *Cristo è andato oltre Eboli*. Lingistica, Ithaca, NY

Hall R A 1960 *Linguistics and Your Language*. Doubleday, New York

Hall R A 1964 *Introductory Linguistics*. Chilton, Philadelphia, PA

Hall R A 1966 *Pidgin and Creole Languages*. Cornell University Press, Ithaca, NY

Hall R A 1968 *An Essay on Language*. Chilton Books, Philadelphia, PA

Hall R A 1976 *Proto-Romance Phonology*. Elsevier, New York

Hall R A 1981 *Promotion and Tenure*. Linguistica, Ithaca, NY

Hall R A 1984 *Proto-Romance Morphology*. Benjamins, Amsterdam

Hall R A 1987a *Leonard Bloomfield: Essays on His Life and Work*. Benjamins, Philadelphia, PA
Hall R A 1987b *Linguistics and Pseudo-Linguistics*. Benjamins, Amsterdam
Hall R A 1990 *A Life for Language: A Biographical Memoir of Leonard Bloomfield*. Benjamins, Amsterdam
Sapir E 1921 *Language: An Introduction to the Study of Speech*. Harcourt, Brace and World, New York

Halliday, Michael Alexander Kirkwood (1925–)
J. Fine

Halliday has developed systemic function linguistic theory and its application to education at all levels.

Halliday received his BA from London University in Chinese language and literature and his PhD from Cambridge University in 1955 (published as *The Language of the Chinese 'Secret History of the Mongols'*). Halliday held professorships at University College London, 1965–70, University of Illinois, Chicago circle, 1973–75, and at University of Sydney, 1976 to his retirement in 1987. He has been visiting professor at Yale, Brown, University of California (Irvine), Nairobi, National University of Singapore, and Fellow of the Center for Advanced Studies in the Behavioral Sciences, Stanford, California.

Systemic functional linguistic theory that Halliday developed with others is concerned with the operation of texts in their contexts. Language is seen as sets of meaning resources that are selected for use in particular social contexts. Field, mode, and tenor are the variables that are at stake in contexts. Meanings at various levels of abstraction (e.g., ideology, genre, register) are studied paradigmatically to present the meaning contrasts that speakers draw from. The meaning contrasts are then worded (technically, 'realized') by the lexis and grammar of the language. The linguistic choices are grouped nto the ideational, interpersonal, and textual metafunctions.

Halliday has applied functional systemic theory to education from early language learning to university education. He has studied the intonation, vocabulary, cohesion, and grammar in first and second language teaching and learning. In these applications the emphasis is on the speaker's control over text types, the ways texts are constructed and the functions of language in social contexts. Halliday's approach to language and education has had a substantial influence on the Australian education system. His work on grammar, cohesion, and intonation is widely used in research on education, language learning, and pathology.

He is an honorary member of the Linguistic Society of America, and holds honorary doctorates from the Universities of Nancy and Birmingham.

See also: Register; Antilanguage.

Bibliography

Halliday M A K 1973 *Explorations in the Functions of Language*. Edward Arnold, London
Halliday M A K 1975 *Learning How to Mean: Explorations in the Development of Language*. Edward Arnold, London
Halliday M A K 1978 *Language as Social Semiotic*. Edward Arnold, London
Halliday M A K 1994 *An Introduction to Functional Grammar*, 2nd edn. Edward Arnold, London
Halliday M A K, Hasan R 1976 *Cohesion in English*. Longman, London
Halliday M A K, Hasan R 1989 *Language, Context, and Text: A Socio-semiotic Perspective*, 2nd edn. Deakin University Press, Geelong, Australia and Oxford University Press, Oxford, UK
Halliday M A K, Martin J R 1993 *Writing Science: Literacy and Discursive Power*. Falmer Press, London and University of Pittsburgh Press, Pittsburgh, PA
Steele R, Threadgold T 1987 *Language Topics: Essays in Honour of Michael Halliday* (2 vols.) Benjamins, Amsterdam

Haugen, Einar (1906–94)
N. Hasselmo

Einar Haugen was a leader in the development of the field of sociolinguistics during the second half of the twentieth century, while also making major contributions to the debate on linguistic structuralism and to language pedagogy, Scandinavian philology and dialectology, and Scandinavian–American cultural relations.

Haugen was born on April 19, 1906 to John and Kristine Haugen, Norwegian immigrants to the USA, and learned English as his second language. After finishing his BA at St. Olaf College in Northfield, Minnesota, in 1928, he studied under George T. Flom at Illinois, receiving his PhD in 1931 with a dissertation on Ivar Aasen's New Norwegian language. From 1931 to 1964 he served as professor of Scandinavian languages at Wisconsin, becoming Victor S. Thomas Professor of Scandinavian and Linguistics at Harvard in 1964. His many scholarly leadership positions include the presidencies of the Society for the Advancement of Scandinavian Study (1938), the Linguistic Society of America (1950), the Ninth International Congress of Linguists (1962), and the American Dialect Society (1965). Haugen was a member of the American Academy of Arts and Sciences and several Scandinavian academies. He was the recipient of fellowships from the Guggenheim Foundation, the NEH, and the Center for Advanced Study in the Behavioral Sciences, and served in a visiting or advisory capacity in Scandinavia and Japan. He was honored by the governments of Iceland, Norway, and Sweden, and held honorary degrees from St. Olaf College and the Universities of Iceland, Michigan, and Oslo.

Haugen participated actively in the debate on the nature of linguistic structuralism from the late 1930s, arguing for linguistic realism and serving as a link between European and American structuralism. With *The Norwegian Language in America* (1953) and *Bilingualism in the Americas* (1956), Haugen—with Uriel Weinreich—created a new theoretical and methodological framework for the study of bilingualism and language contact. He helped lay a new foundation for the study of language in its socioeconomic setting, and became one of the founders of the fields of sociolinguistics and contrastive linguistics. With his analysis of the problems of, and solutions to, linguistic subjugation in *Language Conflict and Language Planning* (1966), Haugen reinvigorated and gave respectability to the modern field of language planning and provided a paradigm for the now flourishing study of language policy and practice in developing countries. Linguistics owes to Haugen such concepts as 'bilingual description'—which became contrastive linguistics—'diaphone' and 'diamorph,' 'semi-communication,' 'schizoglossia,' and 'ecology of language.' In addition to his sociolinguistic work on the Scandinavian languages and specialized studies on Old Norse phonology and Norwegian dialectology, Haugen made major contributions to Scandinavian language pedogogy: several textbooks in Norwegian, a *Norwegian–English Dictionary* (1965), and *The Scandinavian Languages* (1976). Haugen also wrote on Scandinavian literature and Scandinavian–American cultural relations and served as a translator from the Norwegian.

See also: Standardization; Migrants and Migration; Bilingualism, Societal, Ecology of Language.

Bibliography

Haugen E 1953 *The Norwegian Language in America: A Study in Bilingual Behavior*, 2 vols. University of Pennsylvania Press, Philadelphia, PA
Haugen E 1956 *Bilingualism in the Americas: A Bibliography and Research Guide* (American Dialect Society, No. 26). University of Alabama Press, Alabama, AL
Haugen E 1966 *Language Conflict and Language Planning: The Case of Modern Norwegian*. Harvard University Press, Cambridge, MA
Haugen E 1972 *The Ecology of Language*. Stanford University Press, Stanford, CA
Haugen E 1976 *The Scandinavian Languages: An Introduction to their History*. Faber and Faber, London

Heath, Shirley Brice
C. B. Cazden

Shirley Brice Heath's *Ways with Words* (1983, 11th printing 1996 with postepilogue) has become an international classic. An example of research in educational anthropology, ethnography of communication, and sociolinguistics, it is arguably the most widely cited study of children's language use in and out of school. Reading of Heath's long engagement with three communities in a southeastern area of the United States—poor white, poor black, and middle-class white and black—as they sent their children to the then newly integrated public schools, one wonders how one person could become a trusted adult with multiple participant and research roles in all three groups.

Heath grew up in rural Virginia. Her grandmother ran the store in an otherwise all-black community. So from the beginning she became aware of herself as a minority, an 'other.' Close relationships with those different from herself continued through her work in the early years of the civil rights movement in

Mississippi and teaching migrant children in California. Along the way, she studied in six colleges toward BA and MA degrees, learning at different times and places: how to teach special education, reading, and English as a Second Language; and English, linguistics, Spanish, and sociology. When Heath applied for a doctorate, she was reminded again of her own marginalized identity when she was admonished to replace her southern accent with 'general American' pronunciation.

Heath received her doctorate in cultural anthropology and linguistics from Columbia University in 1970, and taught first at Winthrop College, South Carolina, where she started the research that became *Ways with Words*. After early reports of that research became known, Heath moved to the University of Pennsylvania Graduate School of Education in 1977, and then to Stanford University in 1980, where she is a professor of English and Linguistics and, by courtesy, Anthropology and Education.

On paper, these biographical details may read as a fragmented education. But the total helps to explain the range of Heath's scholarship and professional work. *Telling Tongues* (1972) is a historical study of language policy in Mexico. *The Braid of Literature* (1992) is a study of two children's literary development, co-authored with the children's mother, with extensive notes on connections to literary theory. *Language in the USA* (1981), co-edited with her sociolinguist husband Charles Ferguson (see *Ferguson, Charles A.*), is a panoramic view of a more multilingual US than its usual public image. The co-edited *Handbook for Literacy Educators* (1997) attests to her commitment to understanding student learning and the importance of all the communicative arts in education. *Identity and Inner-City Youth* (1993) is a co-edited collection that can be read as an introduction to her next book: a 10-year ethnographic and sociolinguistic study of the language and learning of adolescents in out-of-school youth organizations and enterprises around the US. She has also written more than 100 articles and chapters.

For these achievements, Heath has received many honors, including being named a MacArthur Foundation Fellow and a member of the National Academy of Education; and awarded the George and Louise Spindler Award for Scholarly Contributions to Educational Anthropology, the David Russell Research Award of the National Council of Teachers of English, and the Grawemeyer Award in Education.

See also: Narrative, Natural; Home Language and School Language.

Bibliography

Heath S B 1972 *Telling Tongues: Language Policy in Mexico: Colony to Nation*. Teachers College Press, New York
Heath S B, Ferguson C A (eds.) 1981 *Language in the USA*. Cambridge University Press, New York
Heath S B 1983/1996 *Ways with Words: Language, Life, and Work in Communication and Classrooms*. Cambridge University Press, New York (reprinted, 11th printing, 1996, with postepilogue)
Heath S B, Wolf S A 1992 *The Braid of Literature: Children's Worlds of Reading*. Harvard University Press, Cambridge, MA
Heath S B, Flood J, Lapp D (eds.) 1997 *Handbook on Research on Teaching Literacy Through the Communicative and Visual Arts*. Macmillan, New York and Prentice-Hall International, London
Heath S B, McLaughlin M W (eds.) 1993 *Identity and Innercity Youth: Beyond Ethnicity and Gender*. Teachers College Press, New York

Hesseling, Dirk Christiaan (1859–1941)
G. G. Gilbert

Dirk Hesseling was born in Amsterdam and died in Wassenaar. From 'a well-to-do merchant's family' (Muysken and Meijer 1979: vii), he enjoyed a first-rate education, with studies of Greek and Latin at Leiden, trips to the Mediterranean, and the study of Modern Greek in Paris. His doctoral thesis at Leiden was *On the Use of Wreaths among the Greeks: Selected Chapters* (in Latin). At the University of Leiden, he became '*privaatdocent*' in 1893, and was appointed to the chair of Byzantine and Modern Greek in 1907, a post which he held until 1929. His 'knowledge of languages was encyclopedic; we find references to all stages of English, French, Latin, Greek, Hebrew, Russian, German, Spanish, Portuguese, and several other languages. It is unclear, however, whether he considered himself more of a Greek scholar, or more of a creole scholar' (Muysken and Meijer 1979: viii).

Hesseling was a highly original scholar, who, throughout most of his professional life, pursued an unlikely combination of classical languages and creole languages. When one realizes, however, that his focus on Greek and Latin was on their koineization (see *Koinés*) and dispersal in space and time, it is not hard to follow his reasoning in seeing the same principles operating in the diaspora of the European colonial languages of the last 500 years, especially with regard to Dutch and English, and to Portuguese, French, and Spanish. He was a contemporary of Hugo Schuchardt (see *Schuchardt, Hugo*), and it is clear that each scholar had much to tell the other. In preparing his early published work on Afrikaans and Negerhollands, for example, Hesseling shows that he was well aware of his German colleague's studies of the Romance- and English-based creoles, publications dating from the 1880s. More than 20 years later, after Schuchardt's interests had turned primarily to other areas of linguistics (Basque and Georgian, for instance), it was Hesseling who encouraged him to publish Schumann's eighteenth-century manuscript dictionary of Saramaccan, which had been sent to Schuchardt from South America many years previously. Schuchardt, then over 70, took the occasion to express his well-considered views on the origin and development of the Saramaccan language, and on creolistics generally. Prior to John Reinecke's 1937 Yale doctoral dissertation (see *Reinecke, John E.*), this was the closest thing the world had seen to a textbook on the subject (Gilbert 1980: 90). Despite the complications of the onset of World War I (in which Austria and the Netherlands found themselves on opposing sides), Hesseling was successful in seeing the work through its publication in 1914 in Amsterdam. (Hesseling's correspondence with Schuchardt on the publication of Schumann's dictionary, and on other matters, is preserved in Graz.) Hesseling's 1899 and 1905 books, on Afrikaans and Negerhollands, were very much products of the spirit prevalent at the *fin de siècle*. As Muysken and Meijer put it:

> In a sense, Hesseling was very much between two worlds, 'at the turning point of two centuries,' to use the phrase coined by the Dutch historian Jan Romein. He was a classical scholar who much preferred spoken modern Greek and Italian to their classical ancestors. Yet he was a philologist who never got around to doing fieldwork at a time when Boas (see *Boas, Franz*) and his students were already studying the native languages of North America actively (1979: xix).

Hesseling regarded Afrikaans as a 'semi-creole,' to use the term evidently coined by Reinecke in 1937 or 1938. 'African [sic] was originally a "semi-creole patois" as you say, but the process has been brought to a stand' (letter from Hesseling to Reinecke, dated December 22, 1938, the original preserved in Honolulu, with a copy in Hesseling's hand, in Leiden). He emphasized the (until then) surprisingly strong influence, unwelcome in many white South African circles, of Malayo–Portuguese, as it had been described by Schuchardt, in the formation of Afrikaans. He was also inclined to accept broadly universalist and developmental explanations of the similarities that had been observed worldwide in the evolution of creole languages—essentially the point of view expressed in the 1880s by Coelho. Accordingly, he would have little to do with the extreme substratal position (retention of L1 structure in the lexical clothing of the European L2, in both pidgins and creoles) espoused by the French anthropologist, Lucien Adam. Although his work formed an important link in the chain of scholarship, stretching from Coelho through Valkhoff and Whinnom, that clarified the role of Portuguese in the development of modern creoles of whatever lexical base, Hesseling was clearly not the author of the monogenesis theory, namely that Portuguese Creole was the ur-creole from which most others developed (Muysken and Meijer 1979: vxi–xvii). (Most scholars agree in giving Keith Whinnom the credit for that proposal.) The fact that Hesseling wrote largely in Dutch has doubtless impeded access to his writings—most of which remain unavailable in any other language. Notwithstanding, his thorough and interesting comparisons of creole languages, and his suggestions for future research, reserve for him a distinguished place in twentieth-century creolistics.

Bibliography

Gilbert G G (ed. and transl.) 1980 *Pidgin and Creole Languages. Selected Essays by Hugo Schuchardt*. Cambridge University Press, Cambridge, UK

Gilbert G G 1981 Review of Markey T L, Roberge P T (eds.) 1979 *Language Problems and Language Planning* **5**: 309–14

Gilbert G G, Makhudu D 1987 Le continuum créole en 'Afrikaans': Une perspective non-eurocentrique. *Etudes Créoles* **10**(2): 15–24

Hesseling D C 1899 *Het Afrikaansch. Bijdrage tot de Geschiedenis der Nederlandsche Taal in Zuid-Afrika*. (Uitgegeven vanwege de Maatschappij der Nederlandsche Letterkunde te Leiden.) Brill, Leiden; 2nd rev. edn. 1923 Brill, Leiden, The Netherlands

Hesseling D C 1905 *Het Negerhollands der Deense Antillen. Bijdrage tot de Geschiedenis der Nederlandse Taal in Amerika*. Sijthoff, Leiden, The Netherlands

Hesseling D C 1934 Gemengde taal, mengeltaal, kreools en kreolisering. *De Nieuwe Taalgids* **28**: 310–22

Hesseling D C 1938 letter, dated December 22, 1938, addressed to John Reinecke. Reproduced in: Gilbert GG and Makhudu D 1987

Holm J 1988 *Pidgins and Creoles, Vol. 1: Theory and Structure*. Cambridge University Press, Cambridge, UK

Markey T L 1983 Focus on creolists (7): Dirk Christiaan Hesseling. *The Carrier Pidgin* **11**(2): 1–2

Markey T L, Roberge P T (eds. and transl.) 1979 *On the Origin and Formation of Creoles: A Miscellany of Articles, by Dirk Christiaan Hesseling*. Karoma, Ann Arbor, MI

Muysken P, Meijer G 1979 Introduction. In: Markey T L, Roberge P T (eds.) *On the Origin and Formation of Creoles: A Miscellany of Articles, by Dirk Christiaan Hesseling*. Karoma, Ann Arbor, MI

Hill, Jane (1939–)
V. Santiago-Irizarry

Jane Hassler Hill was born in Berkeley, California, on October 27, 1939. Her parents were on the faculty at UCLA. Hill attended public schools in Los Angeles.

Her roots in academia led her to a scholarly career from the outset. She graduated in 1960 with a bachelor's degree from Berkeley and the Departmental Award in anthropology. During this period of her training, she took classes with Clifford Geertz, Robert Murphy, John Rowe, Sherwood Washburn, and Seth Leacock, among other outstanding anthropologists then at Berkeley. Hill originally wanted to be an archaeologist, but the Berkeley Field School did not admit women at the time—ostensibly to avoid digging up extra latrines. David French, who had mentored her at Reed, and William Shipley at Berkeley were the first to inculcate in her an interest in the anthropology of language.

By the time she entered graduate school at UCLA, Hill had already spent two summers in Peru, participating in an ethnopharmacological expedition led by her mother and by Dermot Taylor of the UCLA Medical School. This first taste of Latin American fieldwork further shaped her career trajectory.

While doing her master's degree in linguistics at UCLA, she met her husband and professional collaborator, Kenneth C. Hill, whom she married in August of 1961; they had three children.

Hill wrote her dissertation on Cupeño grammar, a Uto-Aztecan language of southern California, and defended it in 1966. Because of an interesting coincidence, her work with a small community of the language's last indigenous speakers became her first incursion into issues of language 'death,' a topic regarding which her expertise is recognized and highly regarded. Shortly after Hill wrote her dissertation, the then-archivist of the Lowie Museum at Berkeley, Dale Valory, found a batch of field notes on Cupeño collected by one of Kroeber's students, Paul-Louis Faye. With funding from the American Philosophical Society, Hill worked on the notes, remarking upon the differences between Faye's documentation and hers. This led her to become interested in the structural effects of language attrition among members of speech communities. It also led her to her work among Nahuatl speakers since larger speech communities would facilitate statistic analysis.

Both Hill and her husband spent years researching the Mexicano Nahuatl-speaking communities in the Malinche region of Puebla and Tlaxcala, originally focusing on the structural impact of language obsolescence. But it was while doing this fieldwork that she began to move away from her roots in American structural linguistics, becoming more interested in the ways in which speakers use speech strategically and manipulate their knowledge of their local speech repertoires. She was also influenced by then emerging theoretical paradigms on the relationship between language, culture, and society: Hymes' initial elaboration of an ethnography of speaking; ethnomethodology; and, once translations of their work began to appear in the United States in the early 1980s, Bakhtin/Voloshinov (Hill 1985).

This intellectual shift led to one of Hill's first major publications, co-authored with her husband, *Speaking Mexicano* (Hill and Hill 1986). The book placed her at the forefront of new lines of inquiry in linguistic anthropology, which have significantly advanced the field in the last 20 years (Blount 1995, Grillo 1988). Eventually, Hill's interest in speakers' strategic deployment of linguistic resources led to her work on language and racism which establishes how Anglo-American speakers exploit language's indexicality by using deficient, ungrammatical, and spurious forms of Spanish (thus, 'mock' Spanish) to racialize Latinos (e.g., Hill 1993). Hill has also been working recently on historical linguistics, especially within the context of the history of the Uto-Aztecan peoples.

Hill began her teaching career at Wayne State University, where she became departmental head and active in the American Association of University Professor (AAUP) union effort. In 1983, she began teaching at the University of Arizona, where she is at present. Jane Hill was past president of the American Anthropological Association (1998–9) and is current editor of the influential journal *Language in Society*.

See also: Anthropological Linguistics; Endangered Languages.

Bibliography

Blount B (ed.) 1995 *Language, Culture, and Society*, 2nd edn. Waveland Press, Prospect Heights, IL

Grillo R D 1988 Review: Speaking Mexicano. *Man* **23**(1): 199

Hill J 1985 The grammar of consciousness and the consciousness of grammar. *American Ethnologist* **12**(4): 725–37

Hill J 1993 Hasta la vista, baby! Anglo Spanish in the American Southwest. *Critique of Anthropology* **13**(2): 145–76

Hill J, Irvine J T (eds.) 1992 *Responsibility and Evidence in Oral Discourse*. Cambridge University Press, New York

Hill J H, Hill K C 1986 *Speaking Mexicano. Dynamics of Syncretic Language in Central Mexico*. University of Arizona Press, Tucson, AZ

Hill J H, Mistry P J, Campbell L (eds.) 1998 *The Life of Language: Papers in Honor of William Bright*. Mouton de Gruyter, New York

Hymes, Dell Hathaway (1927–)

N. H. Hornberger

Dell Hathaway Hymes was born on June 7, 1927 in Portland, Oregon and attended local schools there. He earned a BA in Anthropology and Literature at Reed College (1950), and MA (1953) and PhD (1955) degrees in Linguistics at Indiana University. He taught at Harvard University (1955–60), University of California, Berkeley (1960–65), University of Pennsylvania (1965–88), and University of Virginia (1987–98, now Emeritus), with short visiting and adjunct appointments at Princeton and Johns Hopkins Universities.

Internationally recognized for his contributions in linguistics, anthropology, folklore, and education, Hymes was a founder of sociolinguistics as it emerged in the 1960s. He was a founding editor (1972–1992) of the International Journal *Language in Society*, author, and editor of various publications, all of which played determining roles in shaping and directing sociolinguistics from its beginnings to the present.

Hymes' work has had a far-reaching impact on education, specifically in the development of ethnographic and linguistic approaches to education. His book co-edited with Cazden and John and published in 1972 was the first volume to call attention to the need to examine actual classroom interaction in order to understand the role of language in learning and teaching, setting an entirely new direction for educational research which continues to the present day. Hymes' programmatic call for ethnographies of communication—for descriptions of the 'ways of speaking' of diverse speech communities—was taken up by his students and colleagues, yielding such mainstays of the educational research literature as Heath's *Ways with Words* (1983) and Philips' *Invisible Culture* (1983), among innumerable others. His theoretical formulation of communicative competence as distinct from Chomsky's linguistic competence, which he first enunciated publicly at a research conference at Yeshiva University in 1966, has been a major guide-post in second language teaching and research ever since. As Dean of the University of Pennsylvania Graduate School of Education from 1975 to 1987, Hymes founded the Educational Linguistics Programs (1976) and the Ethnography in Education Forum (1980), among the first such initiatives in the country.

Among his many awards and honors, Hymes is a Fellow of the American Association for the Advancement of Science, a Life Fellow at Clare Hall, Cambridge University, and a member of the British Academy; he has also been a Fellow at the Center for Advanced Study in the Behavioral Sciences (1957–58), a Guggenheim Fellow (1969) and a Senior Fellow of the National Endowment for the Humanities (1972–73), among others. He was a trustee of the Center for Applied Linguistics (1973–78) and served as President of the American Folklore Society (1973–74), the Council on Anthropology and Education (1978), the Consortium of Social Science Associations (1982–84), the Linguistic Society of America (1982), the American Anthropological Association (1983), and the American Association for Applied Linguistics (1986).

See also: Communicative Competence; Narrative, Natural; Ethnography of Speaking.

Bibliography

Cazden C, John V, Hymes D (eds.) 1972 *Functions of Language in the Classroom*. Teachers College Press, New York

Gumperz J, Hymes D (eds.) 1972 *Directions in Sociolinguistics: The Ethnography of Communication*. Holt, Rinehart, and Winston, New York

Heath S B 1983 *Ways with Words: Language, Life, and Work in Communities and Classrooms*. Cambridge University Press, Cambridge, UK

Hymes D H (eds.) 1964 *Language in Culture and Society: A Reader in Linguistics and Anthropology*. Harper & Row, New York

Philips S 1983 *The Invisible Culture. Communication in Community and Classroom on the Warm Springs Indian Reservation*. Longmans, New York

Jaberg, Karl (1877–1959)

T. Hill

The Swiss dialectologist Karl Jaberg created, together with J. Jud, the Linguistic and Ethnographic Atlas of Italy and Southern Switzerland, and his writings on it are a major contribution to the theory of linguistic geography. Jaberg, a Bernese, was a student and teacher at Bern University, occupying the chair of Romance studies from 1907. An early influence was a period of study at Paris with Gilliéron (see *Gilliéron, Jules*), whose method he expounded in *Sprachgeographie, Beitrag zum Verständnis des Atlas linguistique de la France* (1908). Another early influence was a field trip in the Grisons, collecting data for the Romansh dictionary, which led to his becoming a Romansh specialist, introducing this language in his courses at Bern. By 1908, Jaberg was collaborating with J. Jud, his opposite number at Zurich, on a project to survey the Italian and Rhaeto–Romance dialects of Italy and Switzerland. This project is discussed hereunder, under Jaberg's name (an entirely arbitrary placing, as both scholars contributed equally during their 30-year partnership).

The survey was intended, following Gilliéron, to capture the 'biology of language.' When each of the 2000 questionnaire items was presented to the informant for translation into the dialect, only his first response was noted, with comments on hesitations, etc., so as to record over all the dialect as such, its state of preservation, and attitudes to it. The team included the folklife specialist P. Scheuermaier, who made a survey of material culture, folklore, etc. Fieldwork began in 1908, was interrupted by World War I, and ended in 1925; funding after the war being insufficient, it was supplemented by the two scholars personally.

The eight illustrated volumes of the *Sprach- und Sachatlas Italiens und der Südschweiz* (usually abbreviated AIS, sometimes SSIS) came out between 1928 and 1943, preceded by a theoretical statement. Scheuermaier's two-volume *Bauernwerk in Italien, der italienischen und rätoromanischen Schweiz* appeared in 1945 and 1956. A place-name survey remained to be published. In 1933, Jaberg and Jud gave a series of lectures on the AIS at the Collège de France, Paris, home of Gilliéron's atlas. Jaberg's lectures were published in 1936 as Aspects *géographiques du langage*.

Dialectologists trained by Jaberg and Jud include Griera (Catalan) and Hotzenköcherle (Swiss German). In the 1930s, Jaberg was active on the coordinating board set up for the three Swiss Romance dialect dictionaries—Romansh, Italian, and French: and in 1942 he succeeded Gauchat as editor of this last, the *Glossaire de la Suisse romande*.

Jaberg's interests included the interpretation of lexical phenomena by reference to folk culture and psychology, and the study of linguistic border zones—an environment in which, through conflict between neighboring norms, specific semantic chan-ges occur, ambiguities arise, and morphological sys-tems are reconstructed. Examples can be found in *Aspects*, and in his collection of essays *Sprach-wissenschaftliche Forschungen und Erlebnisse*, published in 1937 as No. 6 in the series *Romanica helvetica*.

See also: Dialect and Dialectology.

Kachru, Braj B. (1932–)
R. V. Pandharipande

Born into a Kashmiri *Pandit* family in Shrinagar, India, and trained in the Indian and the British literary and linguistic traditions, Braj B. Kachru is a scholar in general sociolinguistics, South Asian linguistics (especially Kashmiri grammar), and the field he has made his own, 'World Englishes.' The terms 'World Englishes' and 'Indian English' summarize the *mantra* of Braj Kachru's research and define the models for analyzing, describing, and authenticating non-native 'incarnations' of the English language in diverse sociolinguistic contexts.

In the 1950s, when 'English' meant essentially British or American English, Kachru's work on Indian English, influenced by Halliday (see *Halliday, Michael Alexander Kirkwood*), and Firth (see *Firth, J. R.*), rejected the dichotomy between form and meaning. His PhD thesis, *An Analysis of Some Features of Indian English: A Study in Linguistic Method*, claimed that the goal of linguistic analysis is to relate a text to the context of situation (1982: 10) and that Indian English should therefore be analyzed in British or American cultural contexts. This approach challenged the prevailing theoretical, methodological, and pedagogical conceptualizations of English and promoted the notion 'World Englishes' (1982, 1983, 1986). His framework of three concentric circles (see *New Englishes*) provided a functional model for categorizing and differentiating all varieties of English.

Kachru's polymodel of English is based on multiple norms of acceptability, appropriateness, and intelligibility in culturally diverse contexts, which demand innovations and change in the form and function of the English language. He refers to this approach, after Firth, as the strategies of conceptualization of English. Kachru demonstrated the inadequacy of the traditional mono-model (based on the native institutionalized varieties of English) to recognize and describe the reality of the postcolonial period where English had adopted new norms of diverse cultural and linguistic identities (African English, Singaporean English, etc.) as a result of its spread in different parts of the world (see *Language Spread*).

Kachru argued against treating features of non-native varieties as deviant, viewing them as 'new/altered meaning systems' of mixed codes, which underpin the bilingual's creativity. This proposal greatly influenced the interpretation of contact literatures of Asia, Africa, etc., which can be used as tools to reconstruct underlying cultural identities. Current research on formal and functional constraints on code-mixing owes its origin to Kachru's foundational work on Hindi-English code-mixing.

Kachru's work has influenced English language education across the globe, with non-native varieties of English increasingly being recognized as valid and the notion 'cultural competence' becoming part of the English language curriculum. Recipient of many prestigious awards and recognitions (including first prize for his book *The Alchemy of English* by the English Speaking Union of the Commonwealth), Kachru continues to be a spokesman for linguistic democratization of codes through the forum of the journal *World Englishes*, thereby enhancing our understanding of the relationship between language and society.

Bibliography

Kachru B B 1982 (ed.) *The Other Tongue: English Across Cultures*. University of Illinois Press, Urbana, IL

Kachru B B 1983 *The Indianization of English: The English Language in India*. Oxford University Press, Delhi, India

Kachru B B 1986 *The Alchemy of English: The Spread, Functions, and Models of Non-Native Englishes*. Pergamon Press, Oxford, UK

Khubchandani, Lachman M. (1932–)
R. K. Agnihotri

Lachman M. Khubchandani is the only Indian scholar who has seriously examined the Indian Census data on language extensively, making significant contributions to our understanding of the sociology of language, particularly in multilingual settings. In a large number of research articles, monographs, and books published from India and abroad, he has consistently used linguistic and cultural plurality as a vantage point to examine the conflicting pressures of 'mainstreaming and development' and 'minority languages and cultures' in the lives of a variety of speech communities.

Khubchandani was born in Karachi in 1932. He graduated from Panjab University where he studied Hindi and journalism. He did his doctoral work on the acculturation of Indian Sindhi to Hindi at the University of Pennsylvania (USA) for which he received his PhD in 1963. He worked as the Professor of Indian Linguistics at Zagreb University and was later a Senior Fellow of the East-West Center, Honolulu. In India, Khubchandani is affectionately known as a one-man institution because of the amount of quality work he has produced during the past 30 years. He is currently the Director of the Center for Communication Studies, Pune, which has produced a large number of monographs on several sociolinguistic issues including language planning, language demography, multilingual education, etc. He has taught at several universities in India, Yugoslavia, Singapore, the UK, and the USA and has often been invited as a language expert on India by UNESCO and the East-West Center, Honolulu. He has been a Fellow at the Indian Institute of Advanced Study, Shimla (Himachal Pradesh, India) where some of his most insightful work was produced.

Khubchandani worked extensively on a large number of speech communities including the Hindi-Urdu-Panjabi amalgam, the Panjabi diaspora and the Sindhis. He has also worked on the role of English in India trying to show how the future of English in India can only be secure if it becomes a part of the country's multilingual fabric. Indian multilingualism is characterized by flexibility and fluidity, with variability acting as a facilitator rather than as a barrier in communication. The Indian polyglot may often acquire several languages as a matter of course and may use one language at home, one with friends, another at work, and still another for academic and religious purposes. Khubchandani (1983: 167–75) talks of multilingualism in terms of whether it is organic or structural, and whether it is homogenizing or differentiating. Indian multilingualism is at once organic and differentiating whereas the American multilingualism is organic but homogenizing. Any codification and elaboration of language that ignores grassroots-level multilingualism becoming insensitive to ethnic identities and local literacies is bound to fail.

See also: Bilingualism, Societal; Language Planning: Models.

Bibliography

Khubchandani L M 1983 *Plural Languages, Plural Cultures: Communication, Identity, and Sociopolitical Change in India*. University of Hawaii Press, Honolulu, HI

Khubchandani L M (ed.) 1988 *Language in a Plural Society*. Motilal Banarsidass, Delhi and Indian Institute of Advanced Study, Shimla, India

Khubchandani L M 1991 *Language, Culture, and Nation Building*. Indian Institute of Advanced Study, Shimla, India

Kurath, Hans (1891–1992)
T. Hill

Hans Kurath, an American Anglicist of Austrian birth, was the founder and major directing force of the North American dialect surveys. His earliest appointments (from 1920) were in German and linguistics, but from 1946 he was professor of English language and literature at the University of Michigan, Ann Arbor, where he edited, with S. M. Kuhn, the *Middle English Dictionary* (1954 ff.), himself writing its *Introduction* (1952); he also published *A Phonology and Prosody of Modern English* (1964).

During the 1920s, Kurath and others made the preparations for a survey of English in the USA and Canada, funded by the American Council of Learned Societies. It was intended to compile half-a-dozen regional atlases: Kurath being general coordinator, and also director of the first two undertaken, viz. of New England, and of the other states of the Atlantic seaboard. The survey was to be on the Swiss model, gathering, along with lexical data, related information on material culture and folk life; and in 1931 J. Jud and P. Scheuermaier came from Switzerland to instruct the first field team. This included Kurath himself, B. Bloch, who participated for 12 years and trained many fieldworkers, including the future directors of the other atlases, G. S. Lowman Jr, the most active fieldworker until his accidental death in 1941, and E. B. Atwood.

The New England survey was carried out in the 1930s, supplemented by Lowman's collection of relevant phonological data in southern England (published in 1970 as Kurath and Lowman *The Dialectal Structure of Southern English: Phonological Evidence*). In 1939, Kurath, Bloch, and Lowman published the *Handbook of the Linguistic Geography of New England*, followed by the *Linguistic Atlas of New England* itself (1939–43). Fieldwork for the *Linguistic Atlas of the Middle and South Atlantic States* began in 1933 but was interrupted by the war,

and publication as such, by editors R. I. McDavid Jr. (see *McDavid, Raven Ioor, Jr*) and R. K. O'Cain, did not commence until 1980, 19 years after Kurath's retirement. However, Kurath had drawn on the combined data of the two surveys to compile *A Word Geography of the Eastern United States* (1949), and with McDavid *The Pronunciation of English in the Atlantic States* (1961), which also utilized Lowman's data on England, and was noteworthy *inter alia* for an elegant tabular scheme, from which can be read off concurrently a dialect's system of phonemes, and their articulatory particulars. A morphological study, *A Survey of Verb Forms in the Eastern United States* (1953), was contributed by Atwood.

Unlike the traditional dialects of Europe, those of North America consist in variations that arose relatively recently in the vernacular English of settlers and immigrants. Elicitation is therefore no simple matter of translation from standard into dialect, but requires techniques for capturing data in the flow of a directed conversation, and Kurath's methodology paid great attention to this. The surveys covered both rural and urban populations, the main network of 'folk speakers' being supplemented by a less dense one of speakers from the local elite and from the intermediate strata. This scheme has been criticized as insufficiently systematic (see Pickford 1956)—mainly reflecting the differing perspectives of dialect geography and sociolinguistics. Kurath's own theoretical approach is represented in his *Studies in Area Linguistics* (1972).

Bibliography

Bailey R W 1992 Hans Kurath. *Language* **68**: 797–808
Kurath H 1972 *Studies in Area Linguistics*. Indiana University Press, Bloomington, IN
Pickford G R 1956 American linguistic geography: A sociological appraisal. *Word* **12**: 211–33

Labov, William (1927–)
D. Sankoff

William Labov has been the dominant figure in sociolinguistics since its emergence in the mid-1960s.

Having studied with Weinreich (see *Weinreich, Uriel*) at Columbia, he also taught there until 1970 before founding the sociolinguistics program at the University of Pennsylvania, which has become the Mecca for the discipline.

Through Weinreich, Labov was exposed to the most progressive view of language extant in classical linguistics, its variability and changeability across space, time, speakers, domains and contexts. With Weinreich, Labov laid down a program for the empirical study of language in the speech community in 1968, thus making the bridge between the traditional study of language and the new field of sociolinguistics.

His 1963 MA project on a sound change in progress in Martha's Vineyard and his 1964 PhD thesis on sociolinguistic stratification of New York City introduced techniques of sample surveys, natural experimentation, and quantitative analysis into sociolinguistic research. However, it was in his independent study of African American vernacular English in Harlem starting in 1965 that he made the paradigmatic breakthroughs underlying the modern field of linguistic variation theory. Labov's intent was an empirical, rigorous, and reproducible approach to language as it is actually used, a scientific linguistics. His ambivalence about the label 'sociolinguistics,' in analogy to other hyphenated domains like psycholinguistics, educational linguistics, etc., reflects his overarching project of advancing linguistic theory by grounding it in solid data and objective analyses rather than unverifiable intuitions and polemic debate, without sacrificing the creative roles of scientific insight and intricate inductive and deductive reasoning. Key components of this approach include the following:

(a) The resolution of Saussure's paradox through the notion of the linguistic variable. This is an explicit way of measurably linking the important structures of linguistic theory with time and other extralinguistic factors, through the quantitative effects of these factors on the choice among two or more different articulations of a given phonological form in a given context, involving no change in the denotational value of a lexical item, or the syntactic function of an affix.

(b) Principled sampling procedures, together with sufficient demographic, social, and linguistic characterization of the speaker within the speech community.

(c) Fieldwork methods designed to circumvent observer effects when eliciting and recording spontaneous speech samples of varying register in natural context, as well as quality control technology for speech data collected in field conditions.

(d) Scientific respect for the speech corpus, including data preservation and the principle of accountability, whereby *all* tokens in the corpus of the structure under study must be included in the analysis and calculations.

(e) Multivariate quantitative models of performance for attributing usage tendencies to linguistic and extralinguistic factors (see *Statistics in Sociolinguistics*). This work made it possible to investigate questions of central interest to linguistic theory using statistics, based on the linguistic variable.

(f) Research-based advocacy for minority speech communities. He was the first to study and 'revalorise' minority and vernacular speech forms. He fought against Bernsteinian views of working class language, against the deficit hypothesis and against elitist language attitudes in the educational establishment (see *Code, Sociolinguistic*; *Bernstein, Basil*). This linguistic activism is clear in his choice of communities to study, in his recruitment of students, in his writings, in his advocacy in the courts, and in the media.

This program, carried out by Labov, his students and disciples worldwide, has met with undeniable success. The principles of sound change he established and the universal and language-specific constraint hierarchies he discovered have had a great impact on phonology and other areas of linguistics. His studies of t/d deletion, auxiliary contraction, and others have been replicated many times and have served as models for entire research traditions in New World Spanish, Canadian French, Brazilian Portuguese, and other languages. However, despite its unwavering focus on the linguistics of spoken language, or perhaps because of it, the intellectual power of this approach (studying usage instead of intuition, and concentrating on the elucidation of linguistic structure in social and historical context rather than using predefined language features as tools for properly social science investigations), it has revolutionized many other disciplines within language science.

His Harlem work, followed up by a generation of students in the US and the Caribbean, rescued the field of creole studies from its ethnolinguistic backwater to become one of the most intellectually rigorous and socially relevant ongoing research areas.

His long-standing interest in the vowel system of American English, particularly the Northern Cities Shift (see *Chain Shifts*) and the relationships among English dialects worldwide, has profoundly changed dialectology. Based on his experience in urban speech communities, he was able to dramatically increase the social validity of survey studies, while introducing new techniques and technology to increase efficiencies and to multiply the kinds of discovery possible. This work culminated in the monumental Atlas of

North American English (see *The Atlas of North American English: Methods and Findings*), whose computer-based methods have transformed dialectology.

Labov made many contributions to the analysis of narratives (see Bamberg 1997; *Narrative, Natural*). While his deep insights into the transformation of everyday experience into narrative would be hard to rival, the example he set, and the protocols he established for the analysis of narrative discourse have inspired a proliferation of research in this area. In the study of social change, Labov's gender and class-based models of language variation and change remain fundamental for the understanding of the prestige and influence of sociodemographic groups, culturally-specific gender roles, and the modeling and quantitative dynamics of trait diffusion within the community.

Labov's role in the field is attested to by his presence as invited speaker at the large majority of the 30 annual NWAVE (New Ways of Analyzing Variation) conferences, the premier sociolinguistics meeting, since 1972. He founded and is the guiding spirit behind the major variation theory journal, *Language Variation and Change* (1988–). He was president of the Linguistics Society of America in 1979. In 1993 he became one of the very few linguists ever elected to the National Academy of Sciences of the USA. He has been awarded honorary doctorates by numerous universities worldwide. His field methods and quantitative analysis protocols are taught in sociolinguistics classes everywhere. PhD students who have studied with him include many of the top researchers in sociolinguistics and related areas today: S. Ash, J. Auger, J. Baugh (see *Baugh, John*), C. Boberg, A. Bower, S. Boyd, M. Braga, P. Cohen, B. Dayton, P. Eckert, G. Guy, N. Haeri, J. Hibaya, D. Hindle, M. Lennig, B. Lavandera, C. Linde, J. Myhill, N. Nagy, G. Nunberg, N. O'Connor, M. Oliveira, C. Paradis, P. Patrick, S. Poplack (see *Poplack, Shana*), J. Rickford (see *Rickford, John Russell*), J. Roberts, D. Schiffrin (see *Schiffrin, Deborah*), F. Tarallo, B. Wald, J. Weiner, M. Yaeger-Dror and many others, while scores of post-doctoral students and scholars on sabbatical have also worked with him.

See also: Sociolinguistic Variation; Dialect and Dialectology; Sociophonetics; Chain Shifts; Ebonics and African American Vernacular English; Narrative, Natural; Code, Sociolinguistic; The Atlas of North American English: Methods and Findings; Forensic Phonetics and Sociolinguistics; Sound Change; Sociolinguistics and Language Change; Vernacular.

Bibliography

Bamberg M (ed.) 1997 Oral versions of personal Experience: 3 decades of narrative analysis. *Journal of Narrative and Life History* **7**, Special issue (Nos. 1–4)
Guy G R, Feagin C, Schiffrin D, Baugh J (eds.) 1996 *Towards a Social Science of Language: Essays in Honor of William Labov* (2 vols.). Benjamins, Philadelphia, PA
Labov W 1966 *The Social Stratification of English in New York City*. Center for Applied Linguistics, Washington, DC
Labov W 1972a *Sociolinguistic Patterns*. University of Pennsylvania Press, Philadelphia, PA
Labov W 1972b *Language in the Inner City*. University of Pennsylvania Press, Philadelphia, PA
Labov W 1994 *Principles of Linguistic Change Vol. 1: Internal Factors. Vol. 2: Social Factors*. Blackwell, Oxford, UK
Labov W, Ash S, Boberg S in press *Atlas of North American English*. Mouton de Gruyter, Berlin
Weinrich U, Labov W, Herzog M 1968 Empirical foundations for a theory of language change. In: Lehmann W P, Malkiel Y (eds.) *Directions for Historical Linguistics*. University of Texas Press, Austin, TX

Lakoff, Robin Tolmach
J. Bennett

Robin Lakoff is widely recognized as one of the first linguists to acknowledge gender as a powerful, complex, and nuanced influence on the relation between linguistic form and social practice. Her position as feminist-sociolinguist pioneer is however logically linked to her overarching concern with connections between the institutionalization of power, discourse, and the philosophy of language.

Robin Lakoff graduated from Radcliffe College in 1964, where she majored in both classics and linguistics. She developed these joint disciplinary interests through an MA with Indiana University (1965) and a PhD in linguistics from Harvard (1967), where her dissertation laid the foundations for her first book *Abstract Syntax and Latin Complementation* (1970). Trained as a classicist and a syntactician, her work on connections between power and language often relies on rigorous and detailed analysis of the interplay between syntax, lexical choice, and conversational patterning. Lakoff held a post-doctoral fellowship in the Department of Linguistics at MIT, where she was one of a circle of linguists working with Chomsky's early work on transformational grammar, and then moved to the University of Michigan as Assistant Professor of Linguistics (1969–1972). Since 1972, Robin Lakoff has been located at the University of California, Berkeley, in the Linguistics Department.

A key difference between Lakoff and one of her renowned contemporaries in the field of gender and language, Deborah Tannen, lies in Lakoff's explicit interest in the issue of power for women. Grounded in the feminist activism of the 1970s in the USA, Lakoff wrote *Language and Woman's Place* in 1975 as an initial exploration of a then-unpopular hypothesis: the notion that gender made a difference to function and meaning in language usage. *Language and Woman's Place* illustrated that in US English, it was possible to demonstrate gender's relevance to usage of hedges, intonation patterns, tag questions, the negotiation of politeness conventions, and other linguistic elements. The book, a slim volume, sparked a wave of interest among sociolinguists in gender analysis, and offered a new route into the theorization of social power.

Lakoff has since published several books which explore the relationship between social power (channeled through race, gender, age, institutional affiliation, or professional paradigm) and individuals' pragmatic location as speakers, listeners, and interpreters of meaning. She has particularly concentrated on the language of the courtroom (*Talking Power: The Politics of Language in our Lives*) and of psychotherapy (*When Talk is Not Cheap* and *Father Knows Best: the Use and Abuse of Therapy in Freud's Case of Dora*). *The Language War* expands these interests into the discussion of news events in the US which have captured intense media attention both nationally and globally: the Anita Hill/Clarence Thomas hearings, the role of Hillary Rodman Clinton as First Lady, the Clinton sex scandal, the Eubonics controversy, and others. Lakoff's arguments chart the US media's use of language in shaping social policy, individuals' access to comprehension of the news, and public attitudes on highly-profiled events.

Bibliography

Lakoff R 1970 *Abstract Syntax and Latin Complementation.* Harvard University Press, Cambridge, MA

Lakoff R 1975 *Language and Woman's Place.* Harper and Row, New York

Lakoff R 1990 *Talking Power: The Politics of Language in our Lives.* Basic Books, New York

Lakoff R 2000 *The Language War.* University of California Press, Berkeley, CA

Lakoff R, Aftel M 1985 *When Talk is Not Cheap.* Warner Books, New York

Lakoff R, Coyne J 1993 *Father Knows Best: the Use and Abuse of Therapy in Freud's Case of Dora.* Teachers College Press, New York

Lambert, Wallace E. (1922–)
G. R. Tucker

Wallace E. Lambert was born in 1922 in Amherst, Nova Scotia although his family moved shortly thereafter to Taunton, Massachusetts where he spent his formative years. After a hiatus caused by service in the US Army during World War II, he received his BA in Psychology from Brown University (1947), his MA in Psychology from Colgate (1950), and his PhD in Psychology from the University of North Carolina (1953).

Lambert spent his entire professional career as a faculty member in the Psychology Department at McGill University which he joined in 1954. He continues this association as Professor Emeritus. By virtue of his prolific research, publication, and teaching, Lambert has had a profound and positive influence on educational policy and practice throughout the world. His early work on the relationship of bilingualism and intelligence (Peal and Lambert 1962) constituted a landmark contribution to the field. The course of inquiry into the nature of the correlates and consequences of individual bilingualism was significantly altered following the pioneering contributions by Lambert and his students. The publication of their research resulted in a 'paradigm shift' within the field.

Similarly, his early work with Gardner on the role of motivation and attitudes (Gardner and Lambert 1972) foreshadowed the development of a specialized subfield of educational linguistics—a concern with the role of individual differences in second language learning and teaching. His subsequent applied research into the effects of foreign (or second) language immersion on the cognitive, social, and educational development of English-speaking youngsters in the Province of Quebec (Lambert and Tucker 1972) likewise profoundly influenced the design and implementation of educational programs for both language minority and language majority students throughout North America (Cazabon et al. 1998). Lambert's early work led directly to an educational model referred to in the United States as Developmental Bilingual Education—that is, programs in which language minority and language majority youngsters spend some portion of the day *together* studying via one (or the other) target language to provide cross-language peer-group tutoring. This work has affected the course of subsequent (language) education for thousands of North American youngsters.

In later years, Lambert's interests focused more sharply on understanding the educational, social, and personal consequences of the increasing heterogeneity of North American society (e.g., Lambert 1992, Lambert and Taylor 1990, Taylor and Lambert 1996). As he and his colleagues pursed their research in multicultural and multilingual communities such as Detroit, Michigan or Miami, Florida, Lambert continued to argue that ethnic minorities in North America can effectively and comfortably double their cultural identity ... that 'they can have two cultures and two languages for the price of one' (Lambert 1991).

Lambert himself has often noted the important role that his family—his wife Janine Fraissinet from France, and his children Sylvie and Philippe—played in introducing him firsthand to the underlying issues of language, culture, and identity that became so prominent in his own research.

See also: Bilingual Education; Social Psychology.

Bibliography

Cazabon M T, Nicoladis E, Lambert W E 1998 *Becoming Bilingual in the Amigos Two-Way Immersion Program*. Research Report 1. Center for Research on Education, Diversity and Excellence, University of California, Santa Cruz, CA

Gardner R C, Lambert W E 1972 *Attitudes and Motivation in Second Language Learning*. Newbury House, Rowley, MA

Lambert W E 1991 And then add your two cents worth. In: Reynolds A (ed.) *Bilingualism, Multiculturalism, and Second Language Learning: Essays in Honour of W. E. Lambert*. Lawrence Erlbaum, Hillsdale, NJ

Lambert W E 1992 Challenging established views on social issues: The power and the limitations of research. *American Psychologist* **4**: 533–42

Lambert W E, Taylor D M 1990 *Coping with Ethnic and Racial Diversity in Urban America*. Praeger, New York

Lambert W E, Tucker G R 1972 *Bilingual Education of Children: The St. Lambert Experiment*. Newbury House, Rowley, MA

Peal E, Lambert W E 1962 The relation of bilingualism to intelligence. *Psychological Monographs* **546**

Taylor D M, Lambert W E 1996 The meaning of multiculturalism in culturally diverse urban America. *Journal of Social Psychology* **136**: 727–40

Le Page, Robert (1920–)
A. Tabouret-Keller

In 1950 Robert Le Page went as lecturer in English to the University College of the West Indies in Jamaica, where he met the Jamaican-American F. G. Cassidy. They formed a group, and in 1960 called a conference around their new field of *Creole language studies*. Together they published the *Dictionary of Jamaican English* (1967) which has remained a standard work. In 1964, Le Page in addition promoted the study of *The National Language Question*, which he produced for The Institute of Race Relations. Since then he has focused on a sociolinguistic approach to the study of speech via 'Acts of Identity' (see *Identity and Language*). He was particularly interested in stereotypes of *a language* as a discrete finite rule-system and their relationship to the realities of observed linguistic behavior. Le Page proposed a new framework for the definition of languages as systems inherent in the behavior of networks of individuals and as linguistic and political artifacts. To the extent that a speaker's behavior is reinforced through interaction, it may become more regular and *focused*; to the extent that he modifies it to accommodate others, it may become more variable and *diffuse*. Thus linguistic systems, both in individuals and in groups, may be considered as focused or diffuse. He was able to submit these views to a series of workshops—in 1986, 1988, 1990, and 1992—of the International Group for the Study of Language Standardization and the Vernacularization of Literacy.

Le Page was born in London on December 8, 1920. After war service in the Fleet Air Army (1940–45), he took his BA at Oxford (1945–48). His PhD dissertation (*Studies in Early English Prosody*) was accepted by Birmingham University in 1952. His time as Professor of English and Dean of the Faculty of Arts at the University of Malaya in Kuala Lumpur (1960–64) was followed by his appointment to the Chair of Language and Linguistic Science at the new University of York in England, where he was also for a time Provost of Vanbrugh College (1967–73). He finally retired in 1988, becoming Professor Emeritus and continuing to publish on linguistic topics.

See also: Identity and Language; Pidgins and Creoles: An Overview.

Bibliography

Cassidy F G, Le Page R B 1980 *Dictionary of Jamaican English*, 2nd edn. Cambridge University Press, Cambridge, UK
Le Page R B (ed.) 1960 *Jamaican Creole*. Cambridge University Press, Cambridge, UK
Le Page R B 1964 *The National Language Question*. Oxford University Press, Oxford, UK
Le Page R B 1980 The concept of 'a language.' In: Sornig K (ed.) *Festgabe für Norman Denison. Grazer Linguistische Studien* **11/12** Institut für Sprachwissenschaft: Universität Graz, Austria, pp. 174–92
Le Page R B, Tabouret-Keller A 1985 *Acts of Identity: A Creole based Approach to Language and Ethnicity*. Cambridge University Press, Cambridge, UK
Tabouret-Keller A, Le Page R B, Gardner-Chloros P, Varro G 1997 *Vernacular Literacy. A Re-Evaluation*. Oxford University Press, Oxford, UK

Lewis, E. Glyn (1920–94)
D. Brown

E. Glyn Lewis was a Welsh educationist who worked for the ministry of education in charge of bilingual education for England and Wales for a period of 20 years. His research work focused mainly on comparative perspectives of language education and policy in a wide range of countries. As a result he collaborated with a very wide network of international scholars. His work provided important comparative international research in language education.

Lewis was educated at the University of Wales and at Oxford. He taught in grammar schools and at the University of Wales, where he was director for the research project of the school council at the University of Wales, Swansea. His publications on bilingual education began in the 1950s with reports on the role of English in Welsh schools and bilingual education. He organized and reported on the International Seminar on Bilingualism held under the auspices of UNESCO in the 1960s in Aberystwyth, Wales. His network of international contacts placed him in a pivotal position to deal with bilingual education in international perspective. His contacts ranged from G. A. Senyuchenko, the Soviet scholar, to E. G. Malherbe, the South African educationist who researched bilingual education. As a consequence he developed an interest in language education in the Soviet Union which resulted in a substantial text on multilingualism in the Soviet Union (1972), the fruits of a delegation to study language education in the Soviet Union under the auspices of the British Council.

Lewis brought an historical and comparative depth to the study of bilingual education, adding understanding to the social and political circumstances that give rise to language education policy. The fruits of his long association with language education were published in a work entitled *Bilingualism and Bilingual Education: A Comparative Study* published in 1980. This work was produced while resident at the University of New Mexico where he continued his productive association with Bernard Spolsky, the noted American scholar of bilingualism. The study is an in depth analysis and comparison of bilingual education in ten countries.

He included a study of the implementation of language education amongst minority groups such as Native Americans in his study. Spolsky compliments Lewis with having made American scholarship aware of the full extent of the international research into bilingual education.

In his comparative work Lewis reports on the limitations of bilingual education and its problems and presents the research done in the 1970s in Wales on the potentially detrimental effects of what he refers to as uncoordinated bilingual education. Importantly Lewis believed in the ethical dimension of language education and his work shows an acute awareness of the social circumstances, which give rise to language education policy such as immigration, refuge, and forms of social inequality. He believed ultimately that tolerance and ethical issues in language education were more important than the scientific nature of language research.

See also: Bilingualism, Societal.

Bibliography

Lewis E G 1972 *Multilingualism in the Soviet Union*. Mouton, The Hague
Lewis E G 1974 *Linguistics and Second Language Pedagogy*. Mouton, The Hague
Lewis E G 1981 *Bilingualism and Bilingual Education*. Pergamon, Oxford, UK
Spolsky B 1980 Preface in *Bilingualism and Bilingual Education: a Comparative Study*. University of New Mexico Press, Albuquerque, NM

Malinowski, Bronislaw Kaspar (1884–1942)
A. T. Campbell

Malinowski was born in Cracow, Poland. He was the son of a well-known Slavic philologist (Lucyan Malinowski). After a PhD in physics and mathematics, he turned to anthropology, inspired, he said, by a reading of Frazer's *Golden Bough*. In 1910 he arrived at the London School of Economics, and in 1914 began anthropological fieldwork in New Guinea. Between 1915 and 1918 he did two years fieldwork on the Trobriand Islands (off Papua New Guinea). After some years teaching at the LSE he was appointed to the first Chair of Anthropology there (1927). In 1938 he went to the USA where he was appointed professor at Yale. He died in New Haven at the age of 58.

In the three great ethnographies of the Trobriand Islands (*Argonauts*, *Sexual Life*, and *Coral Gardens*), Malinowski established the tradition of intensive fieldwork, participating in the life of the society being studied, emphasizing the effort to appreciate a total view of the society and to understand matters 'from the natives' point of view.' He constantly emphasized the importance of learning and working with the indigenous language. The vivid style of writing and the colossal amount of detail have established these ethnographies as classics. The account of the *kula* ring, a complex system of formal gift giving described in *Argonauts*, is one of the most celebrated cases in anthropology.

In terms of sociological theory, Malinowski's functionalism and his ideas about 'basic needs' are pretty banal, and are only of interest as indicating an important shift in anthropology away from questions about origins and evolution which had previously been so dominant. On the other hand, his concern with language is much more fruitful. He was proud of his ability to pick up languages quickly, and, as well as insisting on the importance of conducting field research in the native language, he shows an intense concern with the processes and details of translation (*Coral Gardens*, vol. 2). He laments the lack of sound ethnolinguistic theory. Although his attempt to provide one does little with regard to phonetics, phonology, or grammar, his writing on meaning is original. In a remarkable essay (1923) appended to Ogden and Richards' *The Meaning of Meaning*, he coined the phrase 'phatic communion' (gossip, pleasantries, and so on) to make the point that language should not just be seen as a vehicle for thought through which to communicate ideas, but as a mode of action which, in this example, establishes personal bonds between people. Also in this essay he claims originality for the notion of 'context of situation' in an argument which prefigures Wittgenstein's 'the meaning of words lies in their use,' developed in *Philosophical Investigations*.

J. R. Firth wrote: 'I think it is a fair criticism to say that Malinowski's technical linguistic contribution consists of sporadic comments, immersed and perhaps lost in what is properly called his ethnographic analysis' (1957: 117). But beyond a strictly 'technical' contribution, his expertise in translating from Trobriand and his writing on meaning and translation deserve a more generous judgment.

See also: Phatic Communion; Ethnography of Speaking; Anthropological Linguistics.

Bibliography

Firth J R (ed.) 1957 *Man and Culture: An Evaluation of the Work of Bronislaw Malinowski*. Routledge and Kegan Paul, London

Kuper A 1983 *Anthropology and Anthropologists: The Modern British School*. Routledge and Kegan Paul, London

Malinowski B K 1922 *Argonauts of the Western Pacific*. Routledge, London

Malinowski B K 1923 The problem of meaning in primitive languages. In: Ogden C K, Richards I A (eds.) *The Meaning of Meaning* (suppl. 1). Harcourt Brace, New York

Malinowski B K 1929 *The Sexual Life of Savages*. Routledge, London

Malinowski B K 1935 *Coral Gardens and their Magic*, 2 vols. Allen and Unwin, London

Malinowski B K 1948 *Magic, Science and Religion, and Other Essays*, Free Press, Glencoe, IL

Malinowski B K 1967 *A Diary in the Strict Sense of the Term*. Routledge and Kegan Paul, London

Mazrui, Ali A. (1933–)
A. M. Mazrui

Ali A. Mazrui is best known for his contributions to the political sociology of language in Africa. Over the years he has regarded language as a meeting point between the world of politics and the world of culture and between his African and global concerns.

He was born in Mombasa, Kenya, on February 24, 1933. Mazrui received his PhD in political science from Oxford University, UK. He began his university career at Uganda's Makerere University in 1961, moving to the USA ten years later. In 1974 he was appointed professor at the University of Michigan. In 1991 he became the Albert Schweitzer Professor and Director of the Institute of Global Cultural Studies at the University of Binghamton. Mazrui has also held visiting professorships in several universities in five continents.

In 1979 Mazrui delivered the prestigious annual Reith Lectures of the BBC on the *African Condition*. He is also the architect of the internationally acclaimed 1986 PBS-BBC television series, *The Africans: A Triple Heritage*. He has authored over 20 books and hundreds of scholarly articles. Recipient of numerous honors and awards, Mazrui has been a fellow and office bearer of many professional organizations throughout the world.

Much of Mazrui's sociolinguistic work has focused on the role of European languages in Africa. He initially regarded European languages as allies of political liberation and facilitators of expanding intellectual horizons. His book, *Political Sociology of the English Language*, written in the 1960s but published in 1975, was deeply influenced by such linguo-optimism.

This line of sociolinguistic thinking continued after the mid-1970s—but now primarily because he regarded European languages as indispensable for the development of world culture. And yet this is a period when Mazrui was trying to strike a balance between the global and the local. In his *A World Federation of Cultures* (1976) he articulates a preferred world in which every child has to learn three languages—one global, one regional, and the third either national or subnational.

By the late 1980s Mazrui became more concerned about protecting indigenous languages than he was before, now seeing European languages as potentially corrosive forces on indigenous legacies. This imperial linguopessimism became more pronounced in the 1990s when he joined forces with Alamin M. Mazrui to produce *Power of Babel: Language and Governance in the African Experience* (1998).

Mazrui has also been fascinated by the role and impact of Kiswahili (his mother tongue) in East Africa. He has examined the role of the language in political participation, nation-building, labor unions, family life, and regional integration. He and Alamin M. Mazrui came together to produce another book, *Political Culture of Language: Swahili, Society, and the State* (1996).

Perhaps more than any other African thinker of the twentieth century, Mazrui has continuously attempted to enrich the language of social analysis with new coinages of his own such as *Afro-Saxons* (Africans who speak English as a first language), *Afrabia* (the paradoxical intimacy between Africa and Arabia), *counterpenetration* (Third World leverage in the powerful West), *romantic gloriana* (a form of cultural nationalism which glorifies national history), *lumpenmilitariat* (rough and ready soldiers capturing power) and many others.

See also: Power Differentials and Language; Nationalism and Language.

Bibliography

Kokole O H 1998 *The Global African: A Portrait of Ali A. Mazrui*. Africa World Press, Trenton NJ
Mazrui A A 1975 *Political Sociology of the English Language*. Mouton, The Hague
Mazrui A A 1976 *A World Federation of Cultures*. The Free Press, New York
Mazrui A A, Mazrui A M 1996 *Political Culture of Language: Swahili, Society, and the State*. James Currey, Oxford, UK
Mazrui A A, Mazrui A M 1998 *Power of Babel: Language and Governance in the African Experience*. University of Chicago Press, Chicago, IL

McDavid, Raven Ioor, Jr (1911–84)
T. Hill

Raven Ioor McDavid, Jr, dialect geographer and sociologist of American English, was born in 1911 at Greenville, South Carolina, and attended Furman University there. Initially a literary specialist, he was drawn to the study of American English by reading *The American Language* by H. L. Mencken, and their ensuing correspondence played a major role in his early development. From 1935 to the early 1950s, McDavid taught English and modern languages at various universities, and while he was at Southwestern University, in 1941, H. Kurath (see *Kurath, Hans*) recruited him as fieldworker for the *Linguistic Atlas of the Middle and South Atlantic States*. His work began with training by B. Bloch, was interrupted by war service (1942–47), but was resumed and completed by 1949. The atlas, edited by McDavid and R. K. O'Cain, was not published until 1980 ff.; but studies published in the interim include Kurath and McDavid's *The Pronunciation of English in the Atlantic States* (1961), to which McDavid contributed a major study of the regional and social variants of individual words.

In the 1950s, while at Western Reserve University, Cleveland, McDavid was a fieldworker for several regional atlases, viz: the Rocky Mountain States; the Upper Midwest (states west of the upper Mississippi); and the North Central States (i.e., from the Great Lakes to Kentucky)—becoming associate editor of the last, and eventually publishing its field records, with R. C. Payne, in 1977. His wife and collaborator, Virginia G. McDavid, contributed the morphological study *Verb Forms of the North Central States and Upper Midwest* (1957). During this period, U. Weinreich (see *Weinreich, Uriel*) initiated the debate on the possibility of a structural dialectology, and in 1961 McDavid reviewed the discussion in 'Structural linguistics and linguistic geography' (*Orbis* **10**: 35–46; reprinted in Kretzschmar 1979).

From 1964 to retirement in 1977, McDavid occupied a chair at the University of Chicago. The last major region not yet surveyed was the Gulf States (Texas to Florida), and the survey was set up in 1968 with McDavid and L. Pederson as directors. The survey handbook, *A Manual for Dialect Research in the Southern States* (L. Pederson et al. 1972, 1977), includes a section on 'Field procedures' by McDavid; in it, he discusses with native insight and affection the approach of the fieldworker to this distinctive culture, and stresses the importance of collecting cultural as well as dialectal data.

McDavid's wider interests lay, as he said, in 'the relationships between linguistic patterns in the American speech community and the complex of social forces in American society.' This included lexicography, in the USA a battleground between authoritarians and descriptive linguists. Accordingly, he was involved not only in the preparations for F. G. Cassidy's *American Dialect Dictionary*, but also in the controversy following the publication of *Webster's Third New International Dictionary* (1961). In 1963 Mencken's *American Language* was republished in a one-volume abridgment by McDavid, enhanced by his numerous additions and comments. Various other publications reflect his concern about the linguistic obstacles to the betterment of the poor, including the problems of 'Black English.'

See also: Dialect and Dialectology.

Bibliography

Kretzschmar W A Jr (ed.) 1979 *Dialects in Culture: Essays in General Dialectology by Raven I. McDavid*. University of Alabama Press, Birmingham, AL
McDavid R I Jr 1968 Folk speech. In: Coffin T P (ed.) *Our Living Traditions*. New York
McDavid R I Jr 1980 *Varieties of American English*. Stanford University Press, Stanford, CA
McDavid R I Jr, McDavid V G 1951 The relationship of the speech of American Negroes to the speech of whites. *American Speech* **26**: 3–17
McDavid R I Jr, Maurer D W 1964 *The American Idiom*
McDavid R I Jr, Austin M W 1966 *Communication Barriers to the Culturally Deprived*. Chicago University Press, Chicago, IL

Milroy, Lesley (1944–)
Li Wei

Lesley Milroy is Hans Kurath Collegiate Professor of Linguistics at the University of Michigan, USA. She is a sociolinguist with a broad range of interests and expertise. She has published widely on rural and urban dialectology, variation theory, the interface between phonetics/phonology and sociolinguistics, language ideology and language standardization, bilingualism, and aphasia and agrammaticism. She is, however, best known for her pioneering work in Belfast in the 1970s where she applied social network analysis to the study of linguistic variation and change.

Born in Newcastle upon Tyne, UK, Lesley Milroy was educated at the University of Manchester where she read English language and literature and obtained a First Class Honours degree in 1965 and an MA in 1967. She received a PhD from Queen's University, Belfast in 1979. She worked in Ulster Polytechnic (now University of Ulster) as a Principal Lecturer before taking up the Senior Simon Research Fellowship at the University of Manchester in 1982. She returned to her birthplace in 1983 and became Professor of Sociolinguistics in the Department of Speech, University of Newcastle upon Tyne until 1994. In 1994 she joined the University of Michigan, Ann Arbor, USA.

Lesley Milroy's work in Belfast, which was carried out in collaboration with James Milroy and others, was concerned primarily with how a stable set of linguistic norms emerges and maintains itself in a community. Lesley Milroy calls these *vernacular norms*, norms which are 'perceived as symbolizing values of solidarity and reciprocity rather than status, and are not publicly codified or recognized' (1980: 35–6). These norms contrast with middle-class norms, the ones most of us would view as being characteristic of any wide social standard.

Consequently, Milroy focused on working-class speech in three stable inner-city communities. Through participant observation and a sophisticated statistical analysis of social networks—personal relationships of various kinds that are developed over time, she was able to show that 'a closeknit network has the capacity to function as a norm enforcement mechanism; there is no reason to suppose that linguistic norms are exempted from this process. Moreover, a closeknit network structure appears to be very common... in low status communities' (ibid. p. 43). The Belfast study was a novel synthesis of Labov-type quantitative-variationist work in social dialectology (see *Sociolinguistic Variation*) and Gumperz-style interactional work in the social anthropology of language (see *Interactional Sociolinguistic Research Methods*).

While the application of the social network analysis has caught the imagination of the sociolinguistics research community at large, a major contribution of Milroy's work was her use of the ethnographic approach which produced explanations for the nature of language variation in a complex urban community of a type that could not have been revealed in any other way. Her work also demonstrates the importance of linking fieldwork methodology and data collection with the analysis and interpretation of the data and with the linguistic theory and model one aims to validate.

Since the Belfast study, Lesley Milroy has investigated sociolinguistic variation and change in a number of urban contexts, including Newcastle upon Tyne in the UK and Detroit in the USA, focusing on the role of social class, social network, and gender. She has also applied the social network model to the study of language maintenance and language shift in multilingual communities. In recent years, Milroy has attempted to develop coherent models linking the macrosocietal and microinteractional levels of sociolinguistic analyses. To this end, she has examined language ideology, language attitude, and life mode, and their influence on the speaker's language behavior. Her interest in the interactional dimension of sociolinguistics has led to her work in Conversation Analysis (see *Conversation Analysis*), which aims to deal with irregular data of various kinds, notably bilingual code-switching and aphasic conversational data. She has exploited the potential of Conversation Analysis to illuminate some key issues in interactional sociolinguistics.

Lesley Milroy has lectured worldwide and served on the editorial boards of key sociolinguistics journals and book series.

Bibliography

Lesser R, Milroy L 1993 *Linguistics and Aphasia: Psycholinguistic and Pragmatic Aspects of Intervention*. Longman, London

Milroy J, Milroy L 1998 *Authority in Language: Investigating Standard English*, 3rd edn. Routledge, London

Milroy J, Milroy L (eds.) 1993 *Real English: The Grammar of English Dialects in the British Isles*. Longman, London

Milroy L 1987a *Language and Social Networks*, 2nd edn. Blackwell, Oxford, UK

Milroy L 1987b *Observing and Analysing Natural Language*. Blackwell, Oxford, UK

Milroy L, Muysken P (eds.) 1995 *One Speaker Two Languages: Cross-disciplinary Perspectives on Code-switching*. Cambridge University Press, Cambridge, UK

Mufwene, Salikoko S. (1947–)
R. Mesthrie

Salikoko Mufwene was born in Zaire (now Democratic Republic of Congo) and educated at Lovanium University and the National University of Zaire at Lubumbashi, graduating from the latter with a *Licence en Philosophie et Lettres* (BA), *Group Philologie Anglaise* 'with highest honours.' He completed a PhD at the University of Chicago with a dissertation on semantics. Mufwene started his university teaching career in the Caribbean at UWI Mona, Jamaica in 1980. He subsequently joined the faculty at the University of Athens, Georgia. He moved to his alma mater the University of Chicago in 1991, where he has been departmental chair since 1995.

Mufwene has worked in semantics and syntax, to which he has contributed theoretical studies of English, French, Gullah, Caribbean English creoles, African American Vernacular English, and Bantu languages such as Lingala and the two languages he grew up speaking, Kikongo-Kituba and Kiyansi. He has also contributed to the fields of anthropological linguistics (see *Anthropological Linguistics*), general sociolinguistics and language contact studies. But it is to the field of creole genesis that he has made the most significant and innovative contributions. Mufwene's strengths are his intimate knowledge of several substrates, two superstrates and several creoles. A voracious reader in the creole literature in English and French, he is no mere synthesiser. Known for his original and not always popular positions, Mufwene has ensured the field of creolistics does not remain static. He has always insisted on a close scrutiny of seemingly sacred positions, as witnessed in the important 1986 paper, 'The universalist and substrate hypotheses complement one another' (the 'complementary hypothesis'). He enunciated most clearly the founder principle in creole genesis in 1996. More recently he has advocated an approach that does not take for granted a special status for pidgins and creoles, but sees them in terms of other contact phenomena, as well as of population movements in general. This work, inspired by population genetics, especially macroecology is published as *The Ecology of Language Evolution* (2001). The work has implications for Pidgin and Creole Studies, language contact generally, historical linguistics, as well as the history of American English. It proposes that creoles have evolved by the same evolutionary processes observable in the histories of noncreole languages, by competition and selection of features from a gene pool to which xenolectal features also made substantial structural contributions. The challenge is to work out what principles regulate the selections both among languages engaged in contact and among their respective features, while the prevailing language is clearly targeted by all speakers. Mufwene also argues that genetic linguistics can learn a lot from issues addressed in genetic creolistics, especially by factoring in contact in order to answer the 'actuation problem' in language diversification. The same competition-and-selection account is also used in the book to discuss mechanisms of language endangerment. In collaboration with his students, Mufwene has produced a translation of the French creolist Chaudenson's work into English, as *Creolization of Language and Culture* (2001).

Mufwene's success from humble beginnings has not gone unnoticed: he is listed in Marquis' *Who's Who in the South and Southwest* (1986) and *Who's Who of Emerging Leaders in America* (1987), as well as in *Men of Achievement* (International Biographical Centre, Cambridge, England). He has been a regular and provocative columnist for *Journal of Pidgin and Creole Languages*, a regular and incisive reviewer for many journals, and is founding editor of the Cambridge University Press series, *Approaches to Language Contact*. Amongst his hobbies are disco-dancing (Congolese, Reggae, Calypso, Salsa, Juk), travel, the cinema, and reading on population genetics, macroecology, and colonial history.

Bibliography

Chaudenson R 2001 *Creolization of Language and Culture* (trans. Mufwene S et al. of *Des îles, des hommes, des langues*). Routledge, London
Mufwene S 1986 Restrictive relativisation in Gullah. *Journal of Pidgin and Creole Languages* **1**: 1–31
Mufwene S 1988 The pragmatics of kinship terms in Kituba. *Multilingua* **7**: 441–53
Mufwene S, Dijkhoff M 1989 On the so-called 'infinitive' in Atlantic creoles. *Lingua* **77**: 297–330
Mufwene S 1996 The founder principle in creole genesis. *Diachronica* **13**: 83–134
Mufwene S 1997 Jargons, pidgins, creoles, and koinés: What are they? In: Spears A K, Winford D (eds.) *The Structure and Status of Pidgins and Creoles*. Benjamins, Amsterdam, pp. 35–70
Mufwene S, Rickford J, Bailey G, Baugh J (eds.) 1998 *African American English: Structure, History, and Use*. Routledge, London
Mufwene S 2001 *The Ecology of Language Evolution*. Cambridge University Press, Cambridge, UK

Mühlhäusler, Peter (1947–)
P. Baker

Peter Mühlhäusler is best known for his work on pidgins, particularly Tok Pisin of Papua New Guinea, but he has also published on such diverse topics as pronominal grammar, language planning, and the linguistic influence of missionary policies. However, his recent and continuing studies in language ecology could ultimately prove his most important contribution to linguistics.

Mühlhäusler was born in Freiburg, Germany, where he attended a gymnasium, but his tertiary education took place in three other countries. In 1969, he completed a BA (Hons) in Afrikaans-Dutch (with Linguistics, Gothic, Old Norse, and Medieval Literature) at Stellenbosch University, South Africa. He then wrote an MPhil thesis on *Pidginization and the Simplification of Language* at Reading University

(UK) in 1972. He completed his studies with a PhD thesis on New Guinea pidgin in 1976 (published in 1979) at the Australian National University.

After teaching at the Technical University of Berlin, he became lecturer in General Linguistics at the University of Oxford in 1979. It was during his time at Oxford that two of his most influential books were published, *Pidgin and Creole Linguistics* (1986) still widely considered to be the best single-authored volume on this topic, and *Pronouns and People* (Mühlhäusler and Harré 1990). It was also during the 1980s that he began the collaboration with Stephen Wurm and Darrell Tryon which was to lead to the massive *Atlas of Languages of Intercultural Communication in the Pacific, Asia, and the Americas*, completed a decade later (1996).

Since 1992, Mühlhäusler has been Professor of Linguistics at the University of Adelaide in South Australia. While in Australia, he has taken a growing interest in the relationship between language and environment, and is one of the pioneers of the new field of Ecolinguistics. This has already led to the publication of two books (1996, 1999) and more than a dozen articles while a third book has also been completed and is expected to appear by the end of 2001.

Mühlhäusler's greatest achievement to date has been to bring to the study of pidgins the rigor, which was formerly lacking. His influence, not only in pidgin and creole studies but far more widely, is due both to the breadth and depth of his interests and knowledge across the whole field of linguistics and to his productivity as an author, having published perhaps 200 books, articles, and book reviews over the past 20 years.

Bibliography

Brockmeier J, Harré R, Mühlhäusler P 1999 *Greenspeak.* Sage, Thousand Oaks, CA
Mühlhäusler P 1979 *Growth and Structure of the Lexicon of New Guinea Pidgin.* Australian National University, Canberra (Pacific Linguistics Series C, no. 52).
Mühlhäusler P 1986 *Pidgin and Creole Linguistics.* Blackwell, Oxford, UK
Mühlhäusler P 1996 *Language Ecology: Linguistic Imperialism and Language Change in the Pacific Region.* Routledge, London
Mühlhäusler P 1997 *Pidgin and Creole Linguistics*, 2nd edn. University of Westminster Press, London
Mühlhäusler P (forthcoming) *Language of Environment: Environment of Language.* Battlebridge, London
Mühlhäusler P, Harré R 1990 *Pronouns and People.* Blackwell, Oxford, UK
Wurm S, Mühlhäusler P, Tryon D 1996 *Atlas of Languages of Intercultural Communication in the Pacific, Asia, and the Americas.* Mouton de Gruyter, Berlin

Muysken, Pieter Cornelis (1950–)
A. Bruyn

Pieter C. Muysken's work extends into several branches of linguistics, including generative grammar and morphology alongside sociolinguistics. Broad-minded and striving for the integration of different perspectives, Muysken is involved in descriptive and theoretical linguistics, with a focus on language contact, bilingualism, second-language acquisition, code-switching, and the emergence of new languages. A central issue in his work is the diversity within and between languages, and the structural, cognitive, and sociolinguistic factors determining such diversity and its limits.

Born on April 11, 1950, Pieter Cornelis Muysken spent the first six years of his life in Bolivia and Peru, where he learned to speak not only Dutch, the language of his parents, but also English, Spanish, and Quechua. After a Dutch education, he obtained a BA in Latin American Studies and Spanish at Yale College (New Haven, Connecticut), then continued his linguistic studies at the University of Amsterdam (The Netherlands). He received his PhD in 1977, his dissertation dealing with the verb phrase in Ecuadorian Quechua.

During his fieldwork in Ecuador, Muysken discovered the Media Lengua (lit. 'half(way) language'), a socially, as well as linguistically, intermediate variety between Quechua and Spanish. Muysken (1981, 1997) attributes its origins to relexification, with Quechua stems replaced by Spanish ones with similar meanings, among Quechua speakers working in a Hispanic environment.

The existence of mixed languages such as Media Lengua aroused Muysken's interest in code-switching and -mixing. In *Bilingual Speech* (2000), he distinguishes different types of code-mixing, and explores how these may depend not only on structural-typological factors, but also on psycholinguistic and sociolinguistic aspects of different bilingual settings.

From 1976 until 1998, Muysken was attached to the Institute for General Linguistics of the University of Amsterdam, first as a lecturer, then as Professor of General Linguistics, in particular Sociolinguistics and Creole Studies. Lively and charming, he kindled the enthusiasm of scores of students, some of them continuing with dissertation projects under his direction. He was involved in the organization of several workshops on creole languages, papers from one of which appeared as *Substrata Versus Universals in Creole Genesis*, edited by him and Norval Smith (Muysken and Smith 1986). With René Appel, another colleague of many years standing, he wrote a textbook on language contact and bilingualism (Appel and Muysken 1987). He also instigated the joint enterprise *Pidgins and Creoles* (Arends et al. 1995), which contains contributions by himself and his Amsterdam colleagues and students. His interest in the study of creole languages includes the search for universals, in terms of processes as well as properties. Among the creoles he has investigated are Papiamento and Negerhollands.

After an interlude as Professor of Linguistics and Ibero-American Linguistics at Leiden University, he became Professor of General Linguistics at the University of Nijmegen in 2001. In 1998 he was awarded the Spinoza stipend of the Netherlands Organization for Scientific Research (NWO), which enabled him to set up a research program focusing on the interaction between lexicon and syntax at various levels. One of these is language contact and change; this involves a number of areal studies and the construction of a typological database. Another level is that of I(nternal)-language. It is anticipated that this will involve experimental study of the relation between syntactic and lexical processing in sign language and bilingual language use.

See also: Pidgins and Creoles: An Overview; Intertwined Languages.

Bibliography

Appel R, Muysken P 1987 *Language Contact and Bilingualism*. Arnold, London
Arends J, Muysken P, Smith N (eds.) 1995 *Pidgins and Creoles. An Introduction*. Benjamins, Amsterdam
Muysken P 1981 Halfway between Quechua and Spanish: The case for relexification. In: Highfield A, Valdman A (eds.) *Historicity and Variation in Creole Studies*. Ann Arbor, Karoma, MI, pp. 52–78
Muysken P 1997 Media Lengua. In: Thomason S G (ed.) *Contact Languages: A Wider Perspective*. Benjamins, Amsterdam, pp. 365–426
Muysken P 2000 *Bilingual Speech. A Typology of Codemixing*. Cambridge University Press, Cambridge, UK
Muysken P, Smith N (eds.) 1986 *Substrata Versus Universals in Creole Genesis*. Benjamins, Amsterdam

Myers-Scotton, Carol
S. Gross

Carol Myers-Scotton is one of the world's leading figures in code switching and language contact research. She has published scores of articles and books on subjects as diverse as the sociopragmatic motivations for code switching, the grammatical constraints governing intra-sentential code-switching, bilingualism, borrowing, creole and mixed language formation, discourse analysis, and stylistics. In all of her writings, Myers-Scotton is concerned with examining the link between language production and its underlying universal cognitive mechanisms.

Carol Myers-Scotton received her PhD in linguistics from the University of Wisconsin at Madison in 1967 with a dissertation on the syntactic and semantic restrictions of the Swahili extended verb system. After receiving her PhD, she traveled to East Africa, on numerous occasions, to conduct sociolinguistic fieldwork in the multilingual settings of Kenya, Tanzania, Zimbabwe, and Malawi. During this time, she began to focus her efforts on studying the complex code switching strategies used by the people she encountered. This fieldwork sparked a lifelong study of code switching, its social aspects, and its structural features.

In 1993, Myers-Scotton published two important books on code switching. In *Social Motivation for Code Switching: Evidence from Africa* (1993a) Myers-Scotton develops her markedness model to explain the linguistic choices that multilingual speakers make. In the markedness model, linguistic choices are seen as deriving from the speaker's desire to optimize the outcomes of an interaction. In *Duelling Languages: Grammatical Structure in Code Switching*, (1993b) she presents a formal grammar of intrasentential code switching, the matrix language frame model. Under the matrix language frame model, the language varieties that participate in code switching play different roles in building a syntactic structure. This asymmetry is played out by allowing only one participating variety as the source of the grammatical frame in a bilingual sentence, the matrix language. The role of the other variety is largely restricted to contributing singly occurring content morphemes in mixed constituents.

Since the publication of these two books, Myers-Scotton has developed two interlocking models of morpheme activation, the 4-M model and the abstract level model, which hypothesize that four different types of morphemes are activated at different levels in language production. Myers-Scotton and her associates have used these two models to explain the structural outcomes in a wide range of language contact phenomena such as creole and mixed language formation, convergence, first language attrition, and second language acquisition. In all these cases, a single universal cognitive principle underlies the seemingly disparate linguistic outcomes.

Myers-Scotton has held positions as professor of linguistics at Yale University, Michigan State University, and the University of South Carolina where she is currently the Carolina Distinguished Professor of Linguistics. She is currently writing a book for Oxford University Press on contact linguistics in which she unifies a vast body of language contact data under her theoretical models. Although her theories are controversial, Myers-Scotton is, more than any other single person, responsible for elevating the level of discourse in the field of contact linguistics by proposing a set of testable universal principles underlying bilingual language production at both the social and the structural level.

See also: Code-switching: Sociopragmatic Models; Code-switching: Structural Models.

Bibliography

Myers-Scotton C 1993a *Social Motivations for Code Switching: Evidence from Africa*. Clarendon Press, Oxford, UK

Myers-Scotton C 1993b *Duelling Languages. Grammatical Structure in Code Switching*. Clarendon Press, Oxford, UK

Myers-Scotton C 1998 A theoretical introduction to the markedness model. In: Myers-Scotton C (ed.) *Codes and Consequences*. Oxford University Press, New York

Nida, Eugene Albert (1914–)

R. E. Longacre

Nida was born in 1914 in Oklahoma City, Oklahoma, USA. He received a BA at the University of California, Los Angeles in 1936, MA in patristics in 1939 at the University of Southern California, and PhD in linguistics in 1943 at the University of Michigan; also numerous honorary degrees and awards from institutions in the USA and other countries. He was Professor of Linguistics at the Summer Institute of Linguistics (which eventually located for many years at the University of Oklahoma) 1937–53.

Nida has had a continuing involvement with agencies interested in the translation of the Christian scriptures. Besides his involvement with the early work of the Summer Institute of Linguistics in Mexico he has been Executive Secretary for Translations, American Bible Society (1943–84), consultant for the United Bible Societies (1947–90), and continues as consultant for the American Bible Society 1984 to the present. In these various capacities he has succeeded in lifting translation concerns from those of a specialist group onto the plane of broad linguistic and cultural concerns.

Nida's early linguistic interests centered around grammar, which in the 1940s and 1950s was conceived of largely as morphology. Both Nida's 1946 *Morphology* and his larger 1949 volume of the same title (both University of Michigan Press, Ann Arbor, MI) reflect shifting currents in American structural linguistics—from the process orientation of Edward Sapir (see *Sapir, Edward*) to the flat morphemes-and-their-allomorphs orientation of Zellig Harris and Bernard Bloch. Nida has never lost his interest in *words*; some of his most mature and recent work has been his exploration of the lexical resources of the Greek New Testament (see below).

Perhaps Nida's greatest contribution lies in the field of translation theory and practice. In his role as a teacher of future linguists and translators as well as in his more global role of consultant for missionary translators his influence has been profound—exceeded perhaps only by the influence exerted by the constant flow of his writings. He has done fieldwork in over 85 countries and in over 200 languages. Nida early came to emphasize dynamic and functional equivalence across languages and cultures as the key to successful translation. As linguistics has evolved during his scholarly life he has interacted with and made his own contributions to such developments as discourse analysis (textlinguistics) and sociolinguistics.

From his early 1947 work *Bible Translation* a steady stream of publication has followed. Running rather to books than articles his production has been of two sorts: (a) such general works as those already mentioned and exemplified in the bibliography; and

(b) special manuals for translators of given books of the Bible (not indicated in the bibliography). The latter have been variously authored, coauthored, and/or edited by Nida, and cover a dozen or so books of the New Testament as well as the book of Ruth. In these manuals Nida has displayed a fine sensitivity to and uncanny prescience of passages where translators of the scriptures are likely to encounter lexical problems, cultural mismatches, syntactic tangles, and problems in textual cohesion and coherence.

Nida's outstanding achievement latterly has been *The Greek Lexicon of the New Testament based on Semantic Domains* (1988). This embodies a new departure in lexicography. Here words of similar semantic domains are so grouped as to give insight into the lexical structure of the Koiné Greek (see also *Koinés*).

Nida has belonged to a number of learned societies which reflect his varied interests. Besides the American Anthropological Association, the Linguistic Society of Canada and the United States, the American Association for Applied Linguistics, and the Society of Biblical Literature, they include the Linguistic Society of America (President 1968) and the Society for Textual Scholarship (President 1987–88).

See also: Missionaries and Language; Religion and Language.

Bibliography

Louw J P, Nida E A (eds.) 1988 *The Greek Lexicon of the New Testament based on Semantic Domains*, 2 vols. United Bible Societies, New York
Nida E A 1947 *Bible Translation*. American Bible Society, New York
Nida E A 1950 *Learning a Foreign Language*. National Council of Churches, New York
Nida E A 1952 *God's Word in Man's Languages*. Harper, New York
Nida E A 1975a *Exploring Semantic Structures*. Wilhelm Fink Verlag, Munich, Germany
Nida E A 1975b *Componential Analysis of Meaning*. Mouton, The Hague
Nida E A 1983 *Style and Discourse*. United Bible Societies, Cape Town, South Africa
Nida E A Reyburn W 1981 *Meaning Across Cultures*. Orbis, Maryknoll, NY
Waard J de, Nida E A, 1986 *From One Language to Another: Functional Equivalence in Bible Translating*. Nelson, Nashville, TN

Paulston, Christina Bratt (1932–)
M. Swain

Christina Bratt Paulston was one of the earliest proponents of the application of principles derived from sociolinguistics to language teaching and to educational linguistics. She was the first to apply Dell Hymes (see *Hymes, Dell Hathaway*), notion of communicative competence to language teaching (Paulston 1974). The focus of her scholarly work proceeded from the teaching of English as a second language (Paulston 1980a) to bilingual education (Paulston 1980b, 1988, 1992) to minorities, language policy, and linguistic rights (Paulston 1994, Paulston and Peckham 1998). She has worked on the history of sociolinguistics and is currently studying the sociolinguistics of ancient Palestine.

Born in Stockholm in 1932, Paulston was educated in classics and modern languages in the gymnasium there. On graduation in 1951, she received a Kellogg Foundation scholarship to study at Carleton College, Minnesota, where she earned a BA in 1953. She went on to receive an MA in English literature at the University of Minnesota. After graduation, she taught English and French for the next five years at high schools in Clara City, Lake Woebegon, and Pine Island, all in Minnesota.

In 1960, while teaching at the American School in Tangier, Morocco, she met Rolland Paulston, her future husband. From 1963 until 1968, the new couple lived, worked, and studied in Sweden, the USA (at Columbia University), India, and Peru, each completing a PhD dissertation. In 1969, Paulston was appointed to the linguistics department at the University of Pittsburgh, where her husband had joined the school of education a year earlier. This has remained their academic home since then.

Paulson was director of the English Language Institute at the University of Pittsburgh from 1969 until 1998, and chair of the department of linguistics from 1974 until 1989. She was active in International TESOL, serving as Second Vice President and Convention Chair in 1972 and President in 1976. From 1976 until 1981 she served as a member of the Board of Trustees of the Center for Applied Linguistics.

During her career, she has published many articles and books in the areas of English as a second language, language teaching, bilingual education, teacher training, and sociolinguistics. More recently, her interests have focused on the sociology of language and gender, and historical sociolinguistics.

See also: Bilingual Education; Education and Language: Overview.

Bibliography

Paulston C B 1974 Linguistic and communicative competence. *TESOL Quarterly* **8**: 347–62
Paulston C B 1980a *English as a Second Language*. National Education Association, Washington, DC
Paulston C B 1980b *Bilingual Education: Issues and Theories*. Newbury House, Rowley, MA
Paulston C B (ed.) 1988 *International Handbook of Bilingualism and Bilingual Education*. Greenwood Press, Westport, CT
Paulston C B 1992 *Sociolinguistic Perspectives on Bilingual Education*. Multilingual Matters, Clevedon, UK
Paulston C 1994 *Linguistic Minorities in Multilingual Settings: Implications for Language Policy*. Benjamins, Amsterdam
Paulston C B, Peckham D (eds.) 1998 *Linguistic Minorities in Central and Eastern Europe*. Multilingual Matters, Clevedon, UK
Paulson C B, Tucker G R (eds.) 1997 *The Early Days of Sociolinguistics: Memories and Reflections*. Summer Institute of Linguistics, Dallas, TX

Platt, John T.
M. Görlach

John Platt was associate professor of linguistics at Monash University, Clayton, Victoria, Australia, until his untimely death in 1990. Apart from his research and teaching in various disciplines of linguistics, he was one of the leading and most stimulating scholars in the field of English as a world language, into which he brought his keen interest in his native Australian English and near-native English of Singapore and Malaysia. From the 1970s on, John Platt published a long series of articles predominantly on South East Asian Englishes, but mainly on the forms and functions of English in the city-state of Singapore, often collaborating with his wife Heidi Weber and with research students. His sociolinguistic studies of the local varieties are characterized by rigid methodology: and he was quick to see the importance of methodologies from Creolistics for New English Studies (see *New Englishes*; *Pidgins and Creoles: Models*). He was the first to use implicational scaling and to apply the concepts of 'creoloid,' 'basilect,' 'mesolect,' and 'acrolect' to Singapore English. His interest did not stop here: while including studies of literary uses of Singapore English, his research into the functions of English in the polyglot speech community quite naturally led him on to investigations of interlanguage, multilingualism, and interethnic communication. Among the publications that had—and will continue to have—the greatest impact on the study of world English, there are four that should be named. *English in Singapore and Malaysia* (Platt and Weber 1980) is an impressive, exhaustive account of the status, features, and functions of English in the region, which has not been surpassed. Almost simultaneously written, but published two years later, is his contribution on 'English in Singapore, Malaysia, and Hong Kong' in *English as a World Language* (Bailey and Görlach), which must have informed many readers, whose main interest was not in the area, on the fascinating mosaic of the three regions treated. These descriptions were complemented by the representative corpus of localized texts, which he selected and edited with excellent linguistic annotations: *Singapore and Malaysia* (Platt et al. 1983). Finally, *The New Englishes* (Platt et al. 1984) is an ambitious attempt at a cross-variational account of the similarities of New Englishes on the various levels. The forward-looking ideas in this book have not been taken up by scholars to a sufficient extent, certainly because few would have had John Platt's combination of linguistic competence that would have been indispensable to deal adequately with matters of such great complexity.

See also: Bilingualism, Societal; Contact Languages; New Englishes.

Bibliography

Bailey R W, Görlach M (eds.) 1982 *English as a World Language*. University of Michigan Press, Ann Arbor, MI
Platt J T 1982 English in Singapore, Malaysia, and Hong Kong. In: Bailey R W, Görlach M (eds.) *English as a World Language*. University of Michigan Press, Ann Arbor, MI
Platt J T, Ho M L 1993 *Dynamics of a Contact Continuum: Singaporean English*. Oxford University Press, Oxford, UK
Platt J T, Weber H 1980 *English in Singapore and Malaysia*. Oxford University Press, Kuala Lumpur, Malaysia
Platt J T, Weber H, Ho M L 1983 *Singapore and Malaysia*. (Varieties of English as a World Language Text Series 4) Benjamins, Amsterdam
Platt J T, Weber H, Ho M L 1984 *The New Englishes*. Routledge and Kegan Paul, London

Poplack, Shana
G. Van Herk

Shana Poplack was born in Detroit, Michigan. Building on the methodological innovations and minority language focus of William Labov, Shana Poplack has extended the techniques and scope of linguistic variation theory to bilingual speech patterns, comparative reconstruction of ancestral speech varieties, and prescription-praxis dialectic in the coevolution of standard and nonstandard languages.

Her 1979 dissertation (University of Pennsylvania) characterized the reduction rules affecting syllable-final consonants in Puerto Rican Spanish, and introduced a nuanced quantification of Kiparsky's functional hypothesis as it intersects with variable morphological concord. At the same time, Poplack's studies of code-switching among Puerto Ricans in New York introduced the Equivalence and Free Morpheme constraints, universal patterns of switchpoints occurring only at nonword-internal sites where word order is shared by two languages, and demonstrated that fluent code-mixing is a bilingual skill rather than a defect (see *Code-switching: Overview*).

In 1981 Poplack moved to the University of Ottawa, where she assembled, transcribed, and concordanced a 'mega-corpus' of conversations among 120 French speakers in the Canadian capital region. Studies of thousands of loanwords and switches in this corpus led her to rephrase the Free Morpheme constraint in terms of the ubiquitous process of 'nonce' borrowing, and to quantify the discourse conditions on code-switching. Over two decades, Poplack has broadened and deepened her theory of bilingual syntax in social context, and has quantitatively confirmed the predominance of nonce borrowing and equivalence-point code-switching in a range of similarly constructed bilingual corpora of typologically different language pairs.

Poplack's two wide-ranging volumes on the origins of African American Vernacular are based on evidence from elderly descendants of American slaves recorded during fieldwork in isolated communities in the Samaná peninsula (Dominican Republic) and in Nova Scotia. In these volumes, variationist analysis of Early African American English reveals widespread retention of syntactic and morphological features (including the entire tense and aspect system) from earlier British and colonial English, contrary to previous theories attributing such features to a widespread American creole.

Poplack's analyses of vernacular varieties of Spanish, French, and English are characterized by skepticism towards standard explanations of variation and change based on language simplification or external influences, in favor of historical and com-parative studies of internal evolution. This is most evident in her analyses of tense, aspect, and mood in French. In work involving large-scale multivariate analysis and systematic critical investigation of early prescriptive grammars, Poplack showed that loss of the subjunctive, advance of the periphrastic future, and the preference for conditional concord can all be traced to earlier stages of French, rather than to post-settlement contacts with English, and thus do not represent linguistic degradation.

See also: Code-switching: Overview; Ebonics and African American Vernacular English.

Bibliography

Poplack S 1980 'Sometimes I'll start a sentence in Spanish y termino en Español': Toward a typology of code-switching. *Linguistics* **18**: 581–618

Poplack S, Meechan M (eds.) 1998 Instant loans, easy conditions: The productivity of bilingual borrowing. *International Journal of Bilingualism* **2**(2): special issue

Poplack S, Turpin D 1999 Does the FUTUR have a future in (Canadian) French? *PROBUS* **11**(1): 133–64

Poplack S (ed.) 2000 *The English History of African American English*. Basil Blackwell, Oxford, UK

Poplack S, Tagliamonte S 2001 *African American English in the Diaspora*. Basil Blackwell, Oxford, UK

Quirk, Professor Sir (Charles) Randolph (1920–)
J. Roberts

When Randolph Quirk, then Professor of English Language in the University of Durham, announced his plans for a survey of British English in 1959 he cannot have foreseen the central position his work would come to occupy in language studies. At a time when linguistic theorists chose to appeal to intuition for judgment in usage, his scheme seemed particularly adventurous in its aim to draw together representative samples of a wide range of spoken and written materials. Within a few years other computerized collections were to be initiated, but the ambitions of data based surveys of usage for the latter part of the twentieth century were essentially established with the initiation of what was to become the Survey of English Usage (SEU). This uniquely combined 'corpus' study with psycholinguistic elicitation techniques, reaching beyond the corpus. Quirk was Director of the Survey, based in University College London, until 1981. He continued to play a major role in its activities during his years as Vice-Chancellor of the University of London (1981–85) and as President of the British Academy (1985–89), and he remains a central figure in the project's researches. His outstanding abilities both in scholarship and administration have ensured showers of honorary degrees, fellowships, and consultative positions. His generosity as teacher and colleague is evidenced by many fruitful collaborations over the years on innumerable books and articles, not least with Greenbaum, Leech and Svartvik on the magisterial *A Grammar of Contemporary English* (1972) and its successor *A Comprehensive Grammar of the English Language*, which was first published in 1985 but has been continually revised and updated.

Charles Randolph Quirk was born on July 12, 1920, son of the late Thomas and Amy Randolph Quirk, Lambfell, Isle of Man. After education at the Cronk y Voddy and Douglas High Schools, his undergraduate years were interrupted by service in the RAF (1940–45), and he supported himself by playing regularly in a danceband. A lectureship in English at University College London (1947–54) followed quickly upon graduation, a period broken only by a year (1951–52) as Commonwealth Fund Fellow in Yale University and the University of Michigan. During his years at Durham, first as Reader (1954–58) and afterwards as Professor (1958–60), he was still best known as a medievalist, writing articles and monographs mainly on Old and Middle English and Old Norse. His subsequent work on the structure of present-day English has always therefore been grounded upon a deep knowledge of historical scholarship. This can be seen very clearly in *The Use of English* (1962, enlarged edition 1968), a widely read book that grew out of popular talks given on the BBC World Service, and in its long-needed successor, *English in Use* (1990, with G. Stein). Although many of his publications are concerned with the technicalities of grammar, he could never be categorized as a prescriptive grammarian, despite the respect accorded his authority by those who consult his writings. Rather he shows a lively concern for what is 'appropriate language,' a phrase used by him in discussion of Dickens (inaugural lecture given in Durham, 1959), and he has communicated this concern in many lively lecturers, papers, and reviews. Some flavor of these can be gained from such collections as *The Linguist and the English Language* (1974) and *Words at Work: Lectures on Textual Structure* (1986).

Randolph Quirk first married Jean Williams (1946, marriage dissolved 1979) and has two sons. In 1984 he married Gabriele Stein, professor of English in the University of Heidelberg, with whom he has collaborated in several publications. He travels widely, often for the British Council, on whose Board he served between (1983–91). In the UK, as well as abroad, his is an important voice in deliberations on all aspects of the teaching of English, for example, EFL, speech therapy, and the teaching of Standard English in the National Curriculum.

See also: English Grammar in British Schools; Standard English and Educational Policy.

Bibliography

Crystal D, Quirk R 1964 *Systems of Prosodic and Paralinguistic Features in English*. Mouton, The Hague

Greenbaum S, Leech G, Svartvik J 1980 *Studies in English Linguistics for Randolph Quirk*. Longman, London

Quirk R 1954 *The Concessive Relation in Old English Poetry*. Yale University Press, New Haven, CT/Oxford University Press, London

Quirk R 1962 *The Use of English*. Longman, London

Quirk R 1995 *Grammatical and Lexical Variance in English*. Longman, London

Quirk R, Greenbaum S 1970 *Elicitation Experiments in English: Linguistic Studies in Use and Attitude*. Longman, London

Quirk R, Greenbaum S, Leech G, Svartvik J 1972 *A Grammar of Contemporary English*. Longman, London

Quirk R, Greenbaum S, Leech G, Svartvik J 1985 *A Comprehensive Grammar of the English Language*. Longman, London

Quirk R, Stein G 1990 *English in Use*. Longman, London

Quirk R, Greenbaum S 1990 *A Student's Grammar of the English Language*. Longman, London

Quirk R, Svartvik J 1966 *Investigating Linguistic Acceptability*. Mouton, The Hague

Quirk R, Svartvik J 1980 *A Corpus of English Conversation*. Lund Studies in English, vol. 56. Gleerups/Liber, Lund, Sweden

Quirk R, Wrenn C L 1955 *An Old English Grammar*. Methuen, London

Reinecke, John E. (1904–82)
G. G. Gilbert

Reinecke was born in Kansas, and died in Honolulu, Hawaii. He received his BA in education from Kansas State Teachers' College in 1925, moved to Hawaii in 1926, and taught at various high schools on the Big Island in 1926–35. In 1932, he married Aiko Tokimasa, with whom he collaborated in studies of Hawaiian Creole English and in the labor movement. He moved to Connecticut in 1935. He received his PhD from Yale University in race relations in 1937, and traveled in the southeastern USA. He was appointed assistant professor of sociology at the University of Hawaii 1937–38, but was not reappointed because of his liberal political views and active involvement on behalf of the labor movement. Reinecke taught at various high schools on Oahu during 1939–48. He was dismissed with revocation of his teaching certificate, because of his political views and vigorous defense of the labor movement in his writings and actions. In 1951 he was reduced to selling the local newspaper, and arrested by the FBI in August 1951 and charged with violating the Smith Act. In June 1953, he and six others ('the Hawaii Seven') were found guilty of all charges and sentenced to five years in prison and fined $5000. While the case was on appeal, he was employed as a researcher and labor negotiator by Unity House in Honolulu (1958–68). His conviction was overturned by the Ninth Circuit Court of Appeals in San Francisco in 1958. In the mid-1960s, encouraged by Stanley Tsuzaki of the University of Hawaii, he returned to the study of the sociolinguistics of pidgin/creole languages. His teaching certificate was restored in 1976 by the Hawaii State Board of Education and he was exonerated from all charges. In 1978, by special act of the Hawaii legislature, an out-of-court settlement of $250,000 was paid to Reinecke and his wife for the violation of their constitutional rights.

During his 'first' sociolinguistic period, both his MA thesis of 1935 and his dissertation of 1937 represent remarkable pieces of work. Reinecke was one of the pioneers in founding the sociology of language as a border discipline between sociology and linguistics, and was the first researcher to apply these new insights to the sociology/linguistics of pidgin/creole languages. The 1937 dissertation is still eminently worthy of publication, with annotations. Until comprehensive surveys of pidgin and creole languages and linguistics half a century later to some extent superseded it, it was regarded as the most comprehensive and ambitious work even attempted in the pidgin/creole field.

Reinecke's 'second' sociolinguistic period, from about 1965 to his death in 1982, resulted in the belated publication of his thesis, the compilation (with four collaborators) of the impressive annotated bibliography of pidgin/creole languages, and the founding and six-year editorship of the general newsletter of the field, the *Carrier Pidgin*.

He was a charismatic figure, on the Islands and elsewhere, a force to be reckoned with in the labor movement, the cultural history of Hawaii, the sociology of language, and pidgin/creole linguistics. 'John Reinecke embodied a rare combination of qualities: humanism, scholarship, and activism. The very act of studying pidgin and creole languages constitutes a form of social protest against the injustice done to their speakers. Hence, his work on behalf of the labor movement was not the only form of activism that he supported. Creole language study was the other horse pulling the cart. [For him,] labor and linguistics were thus complementary' (Gilbert 1987: ix).

See also: Pidgins and Creoles: An Overview; Pidgins and Creoles: Morphology; Pidgins and Creoles: Models.

Bibliography

Gilbert G G (ed.) 1987 *Pidgin and Creole Languages: Essays in Memory of John E. Reinecke*. University of Hawaii Press, Honolulu, HI

Hancock I 1982 Focus on creolists (1): John E. Reinecke. *The Carrier Pidgin* **10**(1): 1–2

Reinecke J E 1937 Marginal languages: A sociological survey of the Creole languages and trade jargons. (Doctoral dissertation, Yale University, New Haven, CT)

Reinecke J E 1969 *Language and Dialect in Hawaii: A Sociolinguistic History to 1935*. University of Hawaii Press, Honolulu, HI

Reinecke J E, Tsuzaki S M, DeCamp D, Hancock I F, Wood R E (eds.) 1975 *A Bibliography of Pidgin and Creole Languages*. University of Hawaii Press, Honolulu, HI

Sato C J, Reinecke A T 1987 John E. Reinecke: His life and work. In: Gilbert G G (ed.) *Pidgin and Creole Languages: Essays in Memory of John E. Reinecke*. University of Hawaii Press, Honolulu, HI

Rickford, John Russell
J. Baugh

John R. Rickford began his distinguished sociolinguistic career at the University of California at Santa Cruz, where he graduated with highest honors in 1971. He then attended the University of Pennsylvania, receiving a PhD in linguistics in 1979. Long before completing his doctoral dissertation, Rickford began to explore the historical and linguistic correlation between African American vernacular English (AAVE) and English/African-based Creoles that resided throughout North America and South America.

Early examples of his keen linguistic insight can be found in his 1975 paper, titled 'Carrying the new wave into syntax: the case of Black English BIN,' or 'The question of prior creolization in Black English' (1977). These studies, and others, defy simplistic classification of Rickford as a Creolist, sociolinguist, humanist, or educator. His scholarship, like that of his mentors William Labov and Dell Hymes, represents an array of seminal contributions that simultaneously offer precise individual discoveries at the same time that they advance general sociolinguistic principles. For example, *A Festival of Guyanese Words* (1978) offers linguistic insights into a specific speech community at the same time that it establishes firm sociolinguistic principles for data collection, interviewing, and ensuing analyses.

Rickford first developed his linguistic interest in his native Guyana, where he was born on September 16, 1949. He mingled with cane-cutters and scholars alike, noting differences in language, culture, and social opportunity. His professional resolve to bridge linguistic science with educational application was most visible during the 1997 US Ebonics controversy (see *Ebonics and African American Vernacular English*). Spawned by that controversy, he penned *Suite for Ebony and Phonics* (1997) followed thereafter by *Spoken Soul: The Story of Black English* (2000), coauthored with his son—Russell John Rickford—and winner of the exalted American Book Award. These achievements have not only advanced our collective knowledge of African American language, they hint at Rickford's broader concerns for other linguistically disenfranchised populations throughout the world.

In 1980, after teaching briefly at the University of Guyana, Rickford joined the linguistics department at Stanford University, where he continued in the footsteps of luminaries like Charles Ferguson and Joseph Greenberg, particularly regarding the empirical orientation of their collective studies of language in social context. Along with his wife, Angela Rickford, who is Professor of Education at San Jose State University, he continues to pursue advanced literacy and educational opportunities for African American students. More significantly, he does so based upon consistent and extensive sociolinguistic studies in African American communities, often through strategic collaborations with his former students and colleagues.

Another hallmark of Rickford's illustrious career is reflected by his esteem at Stanford University, where he is director of the Center for African and Afro-American Studies, serving as the Martin Luther King Jr. Centennial Professor. Through that assignment, and others as President of the Society for Pidgin and Creole Languages, he has helped to shape the future course of scientific studies of contact vernaculars, their stylistic diversity and heritage, and the educational consequences of these linguistic facts.

Rickford's collaborations and collaborators are equally noteworthy. With Suzanne Romaine he has edited *Creole Genesis, Attitudes and Discourse: Studies Celebrating Charlene Sato* (1999), while with Penelope Eckert he has edited *Style and Sociolinguistic Variation* (2001), and his forthcoming edition in collaboration with Edward Finegan is titled, *Language in the USA 2000* (in press). These substantial collaborations far exceed the speakers of African descendant that captured Rickford's attention as a young African American scholar. Unlike many American sociolinguists, whose lives were frequently shaped by the confines of American culture (diverse though that may be), Rickford is a true citizen of the world. He grew up in Guyana, and went on to be educated at London University. That global exposure and his devotion to the advancement of greater social opportunities for those who are linguistically disenfranchised represents applied linguistics at its finest.

See also: Ebonics and African American Vernacular English; Fieldwork Ethics and Community Responsibility; Sociolinguistic Variation.

Bibliography

Eckert P, Rickford J R (eds.) 2001 *Style and Sociolinguistic Variation*. Cambridge University Press, Cambridge, UK

Finegan E, Rickford J R (eds.) in press *Language in the USA 2000*. Cambridge University Press, Cambridge, UK

Rickford J R 1975 Carrying the new wave into syntax: The case of Black English BIN. In: Fasold R, Shuy R (eds.) *Analyzing Variation in Language*. Georgetown University Press, Washington, DC

Rickford J R 1977 The question of prior creolization in Black English. In: Valdman A (ed.) *Pidgin and Creole Linguistics.* Indiana University Press, Bloomington, IN

Rickford J R 1978 *A Festival of Guyanese Words.* University of Guyana Press, Georgetown, Guyana

Rickford J R 1997 Suite for ebony and phonics. *Discover* **18**(12): 82–7

Rickford J R, Rickford R J 2000 *Spoken Soul: The Story of Black English.* Wiley and Sons, New York

Rickford J R, Romaine S (eds.) 1999 *Creole Genesis, Attitudes, and Discourse: Studies Celebrating Charlene Sato.* Benjamins, Amsterdam

Romaine, Suzanne (1951–)

C. M. Sangster

Suzanne Romaine has made significant contributions to many different fields of linguistics, as a writer, editor and teacher, and, most of all, as a researcher. Both her work and her reputation can truly be said to be international. Her most important work is in the area of sociolinguistics, although she also has interests in historical linguistics. Her sociolinguistic research incorporates the areas of multilingualism, linguistic diversity, language change, language acquisition, and language contact. Romaine's other areas of interest include language and gender, corpus linguistics, pidgin and creole languages, bilingualism, and endangered languages.

Born in Massachusetts, USA, she was educated at Bryn Mawr College in Pennsylvania, where she studied German and Linguistics. After this, her graduate work was carried out in the UK, first at the University of Edinburgh, Scotland and then at the University of Birmingham, England, from which institution she received her PhD, which was about the methodology and status of sociohistorical linguistics, in 1981. After spending three years in Nijmegen, The Netherlands as a senior research scientist in Linguistic Anthropology at the Max Planck Institute for Psycholinguistics, and also as a lecturer in Linguistics at Birmingham, Romaine was appointed Merton Professor of English Language at the University of Oxford in 1984; a post she still holds.

Visiting scholarships and professorships have taken her to Toronto, Canada, and Uppsala, Sweden, and her fieldwork has been conducted on a global scale. Her work on bilingualism focused on the behavior of Punjabi speakers living in England. She has studied the language of children and adolescents both in Scotland and in Papua New Guinea and, more recently, she has worked extensively in Hawaii.

Romaine is the author of several important books; a selective bibliography is below. Her books have been translated into Italian, Spanish, and Japanese, and range from introductory textbooks such as *Language in Society* (2000), to her authoritative book *Bilingualism* (1995) to more advanced works; most recently her critically-acclaimed analysis of the loss of linguistic diversity through language death, *Vanishing Voices* (2000). She was also the editor for volume 4 (1776–1997) of the *Cambridge History of the English Language.* She continues to teach on a wide range of sociolinguistic and interdisciplinary themes and to carry out international research.

Bibliography

Romaine S 1984 *The Language of Children and Adolescents. The Acquisition of Communicative Competence.* Blackwell, Oxford, UK

Romaine S 1988 *Pidgin and Creole Languages.* Longman, London

Romaine S 1992 *Language, Education, and Development: Urban and Rural Tok Pisin in Papua New Guinea.* Oxford University Press, Oxford, UK

Romaine S 1995 *Bilingualism,* 2nd rev. edn. Blackwell, Oxford, UK

Romaine S 1999 *Communicating Gender.* Erlbaum, Mahwah, NJ

Romaine S 2000 *Language in Society. An Introduction to Sociolinguistics,* 2nd rev. edn. Oxford University Press, Oxford, UK

Romaine S, Nettle D 2000 *Vanishing Voices. The Extinction of the World's Languages.* Oxford University Press, New York

Sacks, Harvey (1935–75)

G. Psathas

Sacks was an original scholar, a profound genius whose thought spanned traditional disciplines and founded a new one, conversation analysis, thereby contributing to the systematic study of language in interaction. His efforts were oriented to the study of the organization or orderliness of language use. The sociological, linguistic, and philosophical foundations of his thought are rooted in those whose work he studied or worked with: Garfinkel and ethnomethodology, Erving Goffman and interaction analysis (see *Goffman, Erving*), Chomskyan linguistics, and Wittgenstein's ordinary language philosophy.

Sacks earned his doctorate in sociology at the University of California, Berkeley, USA (1966) an LLB at Yale Law School (1959), and a BA at Columbia College (1955). For a period of approximately 11 years, 1964–75, he lectured at the University of California, Los Angeles and Irvine. His lectures were recorded, transcribed, and then duplicated and made available to those who requested them. The tapes were not saved. His colleagues and collaborators, primarily Gail Jefferson and Emanuel Schegloff, have since been responsible for editing and preparing his lectures for publication. Sack's lectures achieved a worldwide circulation during his lifetime and since their collection and publication in 1992, have continued to influence many scholars and researchers in sociology, communication studies, and sociolinguistics.

In these and other publications, he treated such topics as: the organization of person-reference; adjacency-pairs; topic organization in conversation; pronouns as transformational operations in conversation; speaker selection preferences; sequential tyings; the presequence; preference for recipient-design or 'orientation to coparticipant' in talk; 'pro'-verbs and performatives in conversation; the organization of turn-taking; turn-allocation constraints on turn-construction; conversational openings and closings; and puns, jokes, stories, and repairs in conversation.

Two volumes now contain the bulk of his lectures (Sacks 1992). He never published a book during his lifetime, though he had planned one and had written an introduction to it.

See also: Conversation Analysis.

Bibliography

Coulter J 1976 Harvey Sacks: A preliminary appreciation. *Sociology* **10**: 507–12
Psathas G 1995 *Conversation Analysis: The Study of Talk-in-Interaction*. Sage, London
Sacks H 1963 Sociological description. *Berkeley Journal of Sociology* **8**: 1–16
Sacks H 1967 The search for help: No one to turn to. In: Schneidman E S (ed.) *Essays in Self Destruction*. Science House, New York
Sacks H 1972 An initial investigation of the usability of conversational data for doing sociology. In: Sudnow D N (ed.) *Studies in Social Interaction*. Free Press, New York
Sacks H 1972 On the analyzability of stories by children. In: Gumperz J J, Hymes D (eds.) *Directions in Sociolinguistics: The Ethnography of Communication*. Holt, Reinhart and Winston, New York
Sacks H 1972 Notes on police assessment of moral character. In: Sudnow D N (ed.) *Studies in Social Interaction*. Free Press, New York
Sacks H 1974 An analysis of the course of a joke's telling in conversation. In: Bauman R, Sherzer J F (eds.) *Explorations in the Ethnography of Speaking*. Cambridge University Press, Cambridge, UK
Sacks H 1975 Everyone has to lie. In: Blount B, Sanches M (eds.) *Sociocultural Dimensions of Language Use*. Academic Press, New York
Sacks H 1992 (ed. Jefferson G) *Lectures on Conversation*, 2 vols. Blackwell, Oxford, UK
Sacks H, Schegloff E A, Jefferson G 1974 A simplest systematics for the organization of turn-taking in conversation. *Language* **50**: 696–735
Sacks H, Schegloff E A 1979 Two preferences in the organization of reference to persons in conversation and their interaction. In: Psathas G (ed.) *Everyday Language: Studies in Ethnomethodology*. Irvington, New York
Schegloff E A 1989 Harvey Sacks—Lectures 1964–1965. Introduction/Memoir. *Human Studies* **12**: 185–209
Schegloff E A, Jefferson G, Sacks H 1977 The preference for self-correction in the organization of repair in conversation. *Language* **53**: 361–82
Silverman D 1998 *Harvey Sacks: Social Science and Conversation Analysis*. Oxford University Press, Oxford
Ten Have P 1999 *Doing Conversation Analysis*, Sage, London

Sankoff, Gillian (1943–)
C. Surek-Clark

Gillian Sankoff's contribution to sociolinguistics focuses on languages in contact using a multidisciplinary approach drawing from Linguistics, Anthropology, and Sociology. Her work advances our knowledge of the interrelationship between language and society, with special emphasis on Austronesian languages, pidgins and creoles, bilingualism, and Canadian French.

Born to English-speaking parents in Montreal, Canada, Sankoff received her academic degrees from McGill University culminating in a PhD thesis in Anthropology in 1968 titled *Social aspects of multilingualism in New Guinea*. From 1968 to 1978 she was an Assistant-Associate Professor in the Department of Anthropology at the French-speaking Université de Montréal. In the early 1970s, Sankoff held a visiting professor post in the Anthropology Department at the University of California, Berkeley, and in the summer of 1973 she was a visiting Associate Professor at the Linguistics Institute held at the University of Michigan. During 1975 Sankoff was a Fellow at the Center for Advanced Study in the Behavioral Sciences at Palo Alto, where several of her most important contributions to the field were written. In 1981 she joined the Department of Linguistics at the University of Pennsylvania where, together with William Labov, she has trained a generation of sociolinguists. A true international scholar, Sankoff has taught and carried out research in Canada, Brazil, and France lecturing in English, French, and Portuguese.

Sankoff's most important contributions to date occurred during a period of time when Chomsky's approach to language as a product of the mind strongly shaped the discipline. Her 1980 book titled *The Social Life of Language* examines the transition 'towards a view that language is structurally stamped by the fact of its use in social life' (p. xviii). Sankoff's career focuses on two communities, one situated across an ocean, and the other across an ethnic boundary in her hometown of Montreal. In the latter, she studies French–English bilingualism among the French-speaking minority population, and throughout her career she has contributed substantially to a longitudinal study carried out in collaboration with colleagues from the Université de Montréal. Working among the Buang speakers of Papua New Guinea at the beginning of her career, she was present during the transition phase in which the pidgin Tok Pisin attained the status of a national language. Sankoff observed the pidgin acquire native speakers as its creolized form emerged, shedding light on categorization and social use of language in a non-Western culture.

Most recently, Sankoff's interest focuses on language change across the lifespan of individual speakers in the Montreal population, and concurrently she is working on a book examining the evolution of New Guinea Tok Pisin over the past 100 years.

More than any other scholar of language in her generation, Gillian Sankoff is an innovator. Through her multidisciplinary work encompassing anthropology, quantitative sociolinguistics, ethnography of speaking, pidgins and creoles, and language policy she continues to illuminate important aspects of sociolinguistics.

Bibliography

Sankoff G 1980 *The Social Life of Language*. University of Pennsylvania Press, Philadelphia, PA
Sankoff G, Brown P 1976 The origins of syntax in discourse: a case-study of Tok Pisin relatives. *Language* **52**: 631–66
Sankoff G, Laberge S 1973 On the acquisition by native speakers of a language. *Kivung* **6**: 32–47

Sapir, Edward (1884–1939)
R. Darnell

Edward Sapir, unquestionably the most distinguished student of Native American languages trained by Franz Boas (see *Boas, Franz*) and cofounder with Leonard Bloomfield of an autonomous discipline of linguistics in the USA, distinguished himself in such diverse fields of anthropology as linguistics, sociolinguistics, ethnology, folklore, and culture-and-personality; he wrote poetry and literary reviews and composed music. He remains the exemplary proponent of the humanistic roots of anthropology and linguistics as well as of the inseparability of their subject matters and points of view.

Sapir was born in Lauenberg, Pomerania on January 26, 1884. His parents, Eva Siegel and Jacob David Sapir, a Jewish cantor, emigrated to New York City in 1889. While still in high school, he won a prestigious Pulitzer scholarship to Columbia University. He received a BA in 1904 and an MA in 1905 in Germanic philology. His PhD in 1909 was in anthropology and reflected the program of urgent ethnology and linguistics of Franz Boas. Sapir was the only one of Boas's students to specialize in linguistics and rapidly came to set the standards for linguistic description and theory for all of Boasian anthropology, including the work of his former teacher and mentor.

Sapir held research fellowships at the University of California in 1907–08 and at the University of Pennsylvania in 1908–10, and headed the new Division of Anthropology of the Geological Survey of Canada from 1910–25. He taught at the University of Chicago from 1925–31 and at Yale University from 1931 until his premature death on February 4, 1939.

His major linguistic fieldwork was with Wishram Chinook (1905), Takelma and Chasta Costa (1906), Yana (1907–08, 1915), Ute (1909), Southern Paiute (1910), Nootka (1910, 1913–14), Sarcee (1922), Kutchin and Ingalik (1923), Hupa (1927), and Navajo (1929). He attempted to follow the Boasian ideal of a grammar, texts, and a dictionary for each language studied. As early as 1911, in relation to the publication of his extensive grammar of Takelma in the *Handbook of American Indian Languages*, Sapir challenged the standards for linguistic description in aboriginal America set by Boas so as to include work by individuals without professional training. This was, in retrospect, Sapir's first move toward the separation of North American linguistics from its basis in anthropology and the study of the American Indian.

In 1921, Sapir published *Language: An Introduction to the Study of Speech*, which was geared to the educated layman. It remains a classic for its citation of non-Indo-European languages, appreciation of the relationship between language and culture, inclusion of humanities perspectives on language, and insistence on the beauty and elegance of linguistic form.

Independently of parallel developments in Europe, Sapir developed the concept of the phoneme, emphasizing the psychological reality of sounds for the speakers of a language. He moved toward morphophonemics, pioneered in the study of English semantics, emphasized a process model for the writing of grammar, dabbled in the construction of an international language, and returned at the end of his life to Indo-European philology with reference to the definition of the circum-Mediterranean cultural and linguistic area.

Much of his later work moved away from linguistics in the narrow sense. After his appointment at the University of Chicago in 1925, Sapir rapidly became the anthropological spokesman for the interdisciplinary social science emerging around the Chicago School of Sociology in the 1930s, particularly through his collaboration with interactional psychoanalyst Harry Stack Sullivan and political scientist Harold D. Lasswell. Sapir's theoretical writing in the period after his Rockefeller Foundation-funded move to Yale in 1931 emphasized the impact of culture on the development of personality and the creative role of the individual in culture. His Yale student, Benjamin Lee Whorf, developed Sapir's ideas about the relationship of language and culture (see also *Sapir–Whorf Hypothesis*).

Sapir's years at Yale were not entirely happy ones. He was particularly plagued by anti-Semitism and ill-health. At Chicago and Yale, however, Sapir trained a coterie of American Indian linguists. Among his most distinguished linguistic students were F. K. Li, Morris Swadesh, Stanley Newman, Mary Haas, George Trager, Benjamin Whorf (see *Whorf, Benjamin Lee*), Zellig Harris, and Charles Hockett. Sapir was a cofounder of the Linguistic Society of America in 1925 and taught at its Linguistic Institute in 1937.

See also: Whorf, Benjamin Lee; Sapir–Whorf Hypothesis.

Bibliography

Darnell R 1990 *Edward Sapir: Linguist, Anthropologist, Humanist*. University of California, Berkeley, CA
Koerner K (ed.) 1984 *Edward Sapir: Appraisals of his Life and Work*. Benjamins, Amsterdam
Mandelbaum D (ed.) 1949 *Selected Writings of Edward Sapir*. University of California, Berkeley, CA
Sapir E 1921 *Language: An Introduction to the Study of Speech*. Harcourt Brace, New York

Saville-Troike, Muriel

R. Pandharipande

As a distinguished scholar, educator, and a humanist, Muriel Saville-Troike occupies a unique position in the field of sociolinguistics. She is one of the early researchers spearheaded by Hymes (see *Hymes, Dell Hathaway*) who challenged the established paradigm of linguistic theory, which treated language as an autonomous system. In her highly acclaimed book, *The Ethnography of Communication* (1982), Saville-Troike argued for the need to include the hitherto neglected interactive and communicative functions in the theory of language. She demonstrated that the explanation for why communities differ in ways of speaking (language use), is rooted in their ethnographic make-up, i.e., in their beliefs, values, norms, and attitudes. The object of sociolinguistic investigation and description, she argued, should be the relationship between the ethnographic profiles and the linguistic structures characteristic of different speech communities. Her research provided the foundational framework for the now dominant, interdisciplinary model of language analysis in sociolinguistics called 'Ethnography of Communication' (see *Ethnography of Speaking*).

Above all, Saville-Troike is widely recognized as a humanist who has become a spokesman for the disadvantaged bilingual children of the American

Indians (Navajo and Apache) and Latinos, and has argued that their failure in the bilingual education programs was not because of their deficient potential, but rather due to the curriculum, teachers' training program, and testing methods which ignored the cultural background of the bilingual children. Likewise the alleged deficiency in the English of immigrant Spanish and Chinese children had to be evaluated in terms of the less than acceptable curriculum which was insensitive to the children's cultural background. Saville-Troike argued for the need to recognize variation in second language acquisition as a tool to reconstruct the linguistic and cultural background of the second language learner. Her most influential work in this area has been her book, *Foundations for Teaching English as a Second Language* (1976) and several subsequent textbooks and monographs, which clearly articulate the role of culture in second language acquisition.

Saville-Troike has presented a clear blueprint of the methods needed to incorporate the cultural component of the second language learner into the bilingual curriculum (*Curriculum Guide for Teachers of English in Kindergartens for Navajo Children*, and several other texts and monographs). Her bold argument for change in classroom teaching, the nature of proficiency testing, and teacher education to include the cultural component as a necessary ingredient of language learning/teaching has made her an highly influential leader in the field of bilingual education. Moreover, she actively implemented these programs through a number of administrative positions, which she has held throughout her career.

See also: Ethnography of Speaking; Discourse in Cross-linguistic and Cross-cultural Contexts.

Bibliography

Saville-Troike M 1969 *Curriculum Guide for Teachers of English in Kindergartens for Navajo Children*. Center for Applied Linguistics, Washington, DC

Saville-Troike M 1976 *Foundations for Teaching English as a Second Language*. Prentice-Hall, Englewood Cliffs, NJ

Saville-Troike M 1982 *The Ethnography of Communication*, 2nd edn. Basil Blackwell, Oxford, UK

Schegloff, Emanuel (1937–)
J. Heritage

Emanuel Schegloff is the co-originator, with the late Harvey Sacks (see *Sacks, Harvey*) and Gail Jefferson, and the leading contemporary authority of the field which has come to be known as 'conversation analysis' (CA). Educated at Harvard (BA 1958) and University of California, Berkeley (PhD 1967), Schegloff was the author of the field's first publication, 'Sequencing in conversational openings' (1968). Since that time he has published upwards of 60 research papers that have established many of the major concepts and findings that are now treated as axiomatic in the field. Schegloff has developed the field of CA through a series of fine-grained empirical studies of the details of interactional conduct. These studies have shown the truly remarkable degree to which social organization—a 'syntax' of action—inhabits the practices and behaviors that make up human social interaction. They constitute an extended demonstration of how the empirical details of human interactional conduct can be brought under precise analytic control, and have served as an inspiration to the specialty which he cofounded.

Schegloff's development of CA has involved a major reconceptualization of extant perspectives on the nature of language and social interaction, of the kinds of data which are relevant and appropriate for the study of language, and of the analytic procedures through which empirical investigation may best be forwarded. This reconceptualization is based on the recognition that social interaction is, as Schegloff puts it, 'the primordial site of human sociality,' and that the demands of social interaction are central in shaping the development and use of language. At the same time it embodies the recognition that the sociological study of interaction cannot be developed as a coherent discipline without detailed attention to the ways in which the properties of language are systematically exploited in the execution of interactional tasks.

Schegloff's papers have identified major structural axes of interaction including turn-taking (Sacks, Schegloff and Jefferson 1974), sequence organization (Schegloff 1995), repair (Schegloff, Jefferson and Sacks 1977), and turn organization (Schegloff 1996). Each of these papers establishes a domain of study by identifying fundamental choices that participants in conversation must make, and isolating elements of the functional architecture through which they are implemented. While none of these papers is intended to be definitive, and most of these areas have undergone extensive expansion over the years (whether in the form of progressive internal refinements in the empirical territory staked out, or through wholesale additions to it), the basic frameworks that were developed in the initial papers, as much as thirty years ago, have remained remarkably intact.

Schegloff's research has repeatedly and painstakingly demonstrated that behind the 'implacable familiarity' of everyday actions lie fascinating and exact orders of organization of great generality and scope. Again and again Schegloff has shown that, in social interaction, it is order rather than chaos that is the norm; precise, specific order; order that the participants use and rely on to achieve their interactional objectives. Above all, almost every paper he has written underwrites the notion that because 'language is the vehicle for living real lives,' the primary research site for CA must be the 'real life' of ordinary conversational interaction.

In the last analysis, CA constitutes the most sustained attempt yet mounted to build a natural history of human interaction; a natural history variously inflected by culture, but likely to embody a substantial mass of commonality in human interactional practices, and possibly a good measure of universality.

See also: Conversation Analysis; Discourse; Sacks, Harvey.

Bibliography

Sacks H, Schegloff E A, Jefferson G 1974 A simplest systematics for the organization of turn-taking for conversation. *Language* **50**: 696–735
Schegloff E A, Jefferson G, Sacks H 1977 The preference for self-correction in the organization of repair in conversation. *Language* **53**: 361–82
Schegloff E A 1968 Sequencing in conversational openings. *American Anthropologist* **70**: 1075–95
Schegloff E A 1995 Sequence organization. Unpublished manuscript, Department of Sociology, University of California at Los Angeles, CA
Schegloff E A 1996 Turn organization: One intersection of grammar and interaction. In: Ochs E, Thompson S, Schegloff E (eds.) *Interaction and Grammar*. Cambridge University Press, Cambridge, UK, pp. 52–133

Schiffrin, Deborah (1951–)
S. Hunt

Deborah Schiffrin is best known for her work in discourse analysis, especially interactional sociolinguistics, and, in particular, for her two books *Discourse Markers* (1987) and *Approaches to Discourse* (1994).

She received her BA and MA from Temple University, USA, in sociology. An interest in Erving Goffman's work on face-to-face interaction and, more generally, in semiotics and sociological/linguistic theory, prompted her shift to sociolinguistics. Schiffrin was awarded a PhD in linguistics from the University of Pennsylvania in 1982 for her dissertation entitled *Discourse Markers*, an analysis of interviews with seven Jewish residents of a Philadelphia neighborhood. This work was supervised by variation analyst William Labov and was later published in book form. *Discourse Markers* (1987) focuses on the use of coherence markers: the connectives *and, but, or*; the causal markers *so, because*; the temporal markers *now, then*; *well*, a marker of response; *oh*, a marker of information management; and markers of information and participation *y'know* and *I mean*.

In 1982 she was appointed to the teaching staff of the Linguistics Department at Georgetown University where she has remained to the present day. During this time she has published prolifically in discourse analysis and sociolinguistics. Her publications reflect her continuing interest in discourse markers and narrative, and include a significant number of articles which provide overviews of *discourse* analysis, *interactional sociolinguistics, conversation analysis,* and *pragmatics*. The *Handbook of Discourse Analysis* (forthcoming), with coauthors Tannen and Hamilton, continues this trend. Schiffrin is currently on the editorial boards of *Language in Society, Journal of Pragmatics, Language and Communication, Linguistic Variation and Change,* and *Discourse Studies*. She has edited books with Deborah Tannen, John Baugh and Ralph Fasold, amongst others, on topics spanning discourse analysis and language variation and change.

Approaches to Discourse (1994) provides a useful introduction to six different approaches to the analysis of discourse, focusing on the central scholars of each approach: *Speech Act Theory* (Austin and Searle); *Interactional Sociolinguistics* (Gumperz and Goffman); *Ethnography of Communication* (Hymes); *Pragmatics* (Grice); *Conversation Analysis* (Garfinkel, Sacks, Schegloff and Jefferson); and *Language Variation* theory (Labov). The first three approaches are used to analyze question–answer sequences and the remaining three to explore referring expressions, particularly existential *there is*, in an attempt to show how different approaches would bring different insights to these core concerns of discourse analysis.

More recently, Schiffrin's work has focused on Holocaust survivors' life stories and public discourse about the Holocaust in general. Her forthcoming book, *Language, Text, and Interaction* is a collection of previously published and new articles, the latter being on the discourse pragmatics of referring terms and information structure.

See also: Discourse; Speech Act Theory: An Overview.

Bibliography

Schiffrin D 1987 *Discourse Markers*. Cambridge University Press, Cambridge, UK
Schiffrin D 1994 *Approaches to Discourse*. Basil Blackwell, Oxford, UK
Schiffrin D (forthcoming) *Language, Text, and Interaction*. Cambridge University Press, Cambridge, UK
Schiffrin D, Hamilton H, Tannen D in press *Handbook of Discourse Analysis*. Basil Blackwell, Oxford, UK

Schuchardt, Hugo (1842–1927)

G. G. Gilbert

Schuchardt was born in Gotha, Germany, and died in Graz, Austria. His father was a jurist (*Staatsassessor*) in Gotha; his mother, of noble extraction, was from a family closely connected with the court of the Duke of Sachsen Gotha-Altenburg. Schuchardt studied under Diez at Bonn was *privatdozent* at Leipzig (1870), and professor at Halle (1873) and at Graz (1876–1900). A man of independent means, he remained in retirement in Graz for the last 27 years of his life, choosing to stay in the isolated southern Austrian city rather than to return to his native Germany. By all appearances, he was a hypochondriac, believing he was suffering from neurasthenia—but nevertheless living into his eighties. He never married. His house, the Villa Malvina (named after his mother), was bequeathed to the university and subsequently became the home of the Department of Romance Languages. His papers, still largely uncataloged, form an important collection in the rare book section of the university library.

Schuchardt was the first professional linguist to turn serious and detailed attention of a general and comparative nature to the topic of pidgin and creole languages as a typological genre within linguistics. Accordingly, many consider him the father of creolistics. Throughout much of his long life, he was keenly interested in geography, anthropology, and travel descriptions of all kinds. Because of real or imagined problems with his health, and his general disinclination to undergo the rigors of travel outside Europe, he was destined never to see those creole areas he studied so passionately, and was thus denied the opportunity to experience the 'trade and slave languages' at firsthand. Instead, starting about 1880, he came to rely

> on a vast network of correspondents who relayed texts and sociological background information to him in Graz. The correspondents ranged from trained professional ethnologists and linguists, to missionaries, diplomats, military men, adventurers, and travellers generally.
>
> (Gilbert 1980: 4)

The 1880s saw the publication of the bulk of his work on creoles, above all the *Kreolische Studien*, in nine parts, dealing with '*Kreolisch*' in its Portuguese, French, or English guise. An insightful manuscript, the tenth creole study 'On the Negro English of West Africa' discovered among his papers in 1983 (Gilbert 1985), was found to anticipate the creole-origin hypothesis of the genesis and development of US Black English, as it was formulated a half-century later by Melville Herskovits, T. Earl Pardoe, John Reinecke (see *Reinecke, John*), and Lorenzo Dow Turner, working independently. Early in his career, Schuchardt was inclined not to go along with the extreme universalist position (as represented, for example, by the Portuguese Creolist, Adolpho Coelho) that universal psychological or physiological laws were at work in the formation of creole languages. He tried to account for them on a case by case basis, citing substrate influences, common (chiefly societal) conditions of development, and so forth.

> Nevertheless, time and again he was struck by grammatical similarities in geographically widely separated pidgins and creoles, especially in the verb system.
>
> (Gilbert 1980: 7)

In the first 15 years of the twentieth century, two additional and highly insightful works on creole appeared: a detailed description of all that was then known about the Lingua Franca (1909) and an important essay (1914) modestly entitled '*Vorbericht*' ('*Preface*') introducing his edition (the first ever published) of C. L. Schumann's (1778) *Saramaccan Dictionary* and other texts. In these works, Schuchardt shows the increasing influence of Wilhelm von Humboldt on his thinking, especially the notion of inner and outer form. Language simplification by individuals or by speech communities is now seen to involve the automatic stripping away of the superficial to arrive at the essential, the inner form. The increased emphasis on psychological processes in the last years of Schuchardt's life indicates the narrowing of the gap between him and Coelho's speculations of the 1880s, on the one hand, and—on the other hand—Bickerton's Language Bioprogram Hypothesis (see *Bickerton, Derek*); which lay 65 years in the future.

See also: Pidgins and Creoles: An Overview.

Bibliography

Gilbert G G 1980a Introduction. In: Gilbert G G (ed. and transl.) *Pidgin and Creole Languages: Selected Essays by Hugo Schuchardt*. Cambridge University Press, Cambridge, UK

Gilbert G G (ed. and transl.) 1980b *Pidgin and Creole Languages: Selected Essays by Hugo Schuchardt*. Cambridge University Press, Cambridge, UK

Gilbert G G 1985 Hugo Schuchardt and the Atlantic Creoles: A newly discovered manuscript 'On the Negro English of West Africa.' *American Speech* **60**: 31–63

Schuchardt H 1882 Kreolische Studien I. Über das Negerportugiesche von S. Thomé. *Sitzungsberichte der kaiserlichen Akademie der Wissenschaften zu Wien (philosophisch–historische Klasse)* **101**(2): 889–917

Schuchardt H ca. 1891 Kreolische Studien X: Über das Negerenglische von Westafrika, ms

Schuchardt H 1909 Die Lingua Franca. *Zeitschrift für romanische Philologie* **33**: 441–61

Schuchardt H 1914 *Die Sprache der Saramakkaneger in Surinam*. Müller, Amsterdam

Shuy, Roger W. (1931–)
J. Kreeft Peyton

Roger W. Shuy is a pioneer in the field of sociolinguistics. His career exemplifies the highest ideals in applying linguistic knowledge to real-world issues. No one in the field of sociolinguistics (and its related field, applied linguistics) can claim a broader, more penetrating scope of inquiry and influence. Shuy has made important contributions in the fields of dialect variation, discourse analysis, education, law, literature, and medical communication, and has influenced the work of many others in these areas.

Shuy's interest in, and sensitivity to, language issues began when he was very young and growing up in Acron, Ohio. His father had a speech problem that made him difficult to understand, and as a child, Shuy often interpreted for him in conversations with others. Throughout high school and college, Shuy worked in a grocery warehouse, and while studying for a Master's degree in English at Kent State University, he worked at Firestone Tire and Rubber at night. In both of these jobs he was fascinated by the differences between his 'college boy' speech and that of his fellow workers, and he wrote an article for *American Speech* (1964) on 'Tireworker Terms.' His developing interest in dialect variation eventually led him to study with Raven I. McDavid, Jr., a leading dialectologist, and later to a number of groundbreaking studies of English dialects in Detroit and Washington, DC.

Shuy's influence in educational linguistics is profound, from the Detroit Dialect Study and the deficit/difference debates of the 1960s to the Ebonics controversy of the 1990s. He is not only a leader in public discussions of the educational implications of dialect diversity, but has also been a trailblazer in implementing practical programs for educators. In the early days of social dialectology in the 1960s, his application of linguistic knowledge to social and educational problems helped launch a national awareness about dialect diversity in the classroom. He crafted the first models for in-service programs around the country, including the workshops for teachers ordered by Judge Joiner in the celebrated Ann Arbor case (regarding instruction of speakers of African American dialect–see *Ebonics and African American Vernacular English*).

His creative research on language and the medical profession in the 1970s opened up an entirely new field of inquiry with respect to professional–client relationships. His research on language and law over the past couple of decades has led to the development of the field of forensic linguistics (see *Forensic Phonetics and Sociolinguistics*) and, more recently, to research on patients' views of the medical care they receive in the last days of their lives and to changes in provision of end-of-life medical care.

Roger Shuy has also played a prominent role in the institutional development of applied linguistics. He was largely responsible for developing the Research Division at the Center for Applied Linguistics, in Washington, DC, heading major studies on dialect diversity, classroom language, and language attitudes. He directed the first university-based sociolinguistics program in the United States at Georgetown University under a National Science Foundation grant. Over the past three decades, this program has fostered the careers of some of the most prominent sociolinguistic scholars in the field. He was also one of the initial group of people who conceived of the American Association for Applied Linguistics (AAAL), and he was a strong leader in its early development, serving as the second president in 1979.

Along with his professional and institutional roles, Shuy has had an indelible personal influence on the lives of his colleagues, students, and friends.

See also: Applied Linguistics and Sociolinguistics; Dialect and Dialectology.

Bibliography

Shuy R W 1967 *Discovering American Dialects*. National Council of Teachers of English, Champaign, IL
Shuy R W 1996 *Language Crimes: The Use and Abuse of Language Evidence in the Courtroom*. Blackwell, Oxford, UK
Shuy R W 1998a *Bureaucratic Language in Government and Business*. Georgetown University Press, Washington, DC
Shuy R W 1998b *The Language of Confession, Interrogation, and Deception*. Sage, Thousand Oaks, CA
Shuy R W, Staton J 2001 *A Few Months to Live*. Georgetown University Press, Washington, DC

Spolsky, Bernard (1932–)
R. Mesthrie

Born in New Zealand, Bernard Spolsky was educated at Wellington College and earned a BA and an MA in English from Victoria University. After a spell of high school teaching in New Zealand (where his bilingual Maori pupils set him thinking about a topic that is still central to his research), he taught at high schools in Australia and England before moving, in 1958, to Israel. In Israel, he spent a year in the army supervising foreign language teaching and two years at the Hebrew University teaching English. In 1961, he became Assistant Professor of Education at McGill University, and in 1964, having completed a PhD in Linguistics from the University of Montreal, was appointed Assistant Professor of Linguistics at Indiana University. In 1968, he moved to the University of New Mexico, where he was Professor of Linguistics, Anthropology and Elementary Education, Dean of the Graduate School, and director of the Navajo Reading Study. In 1980, he returned to Israel, being appointed Professor of English at Bar Ilan University, where he also served terms as head of the English Department and Dean of the Faculty of Humanities.

He has conducted and published research in language testing, second language learning, computers in the humanities, applied linguistics, sociolinguistics, and language policy. His first work in sociolinguistics were studies in Navajo, including Navajo language maintenance, literacy in the vernacular, and lexical borrowing. To these, he added interests in language maintenance and shift, and more recently, language policy. Spolsky's most important work is in the field of Educational Linguistics, especially in language education in multilingual settings. His book *Conditions for Second Language Learning* (1989) set out the requirements for a general theory of second language learning. It is a detailed account of 74 'conditions' (a series of typical and categorical rules or statements) covering the prerequisites for successful learning/acquisition in a variety of situations. Spolsky has published extensively, including 11 other books and numerous articles. He is the editor of *The Concise Encyclopaedia of Educational Linguistics* and a founding editor (together with Elana Shohamy) of the new journal *Language Policy*, whose first issue is due in 2002.

In professional service, he has been President of TESOL, Secretary of the American Association of Applied Linguistics, President of the Israeli Association of Applied Linguistics, Chair of the Board of Trustees of the Center for Applied Linguistics, and President of the International Language Testing Association. He has held a Guggenheim fellowship and a Mellon fellowship, and has been Adjunct Fellow and Senior Research Fellow at the National Foreign Language Center in Washington. Spolsky was honored by a festschrift in 2000 (Cooper et al. 2000).

See also: Education and Language: Overview; Language Planning: Models.

Bibliography

Cooper RL, Shohamy E, Watters J (eds.) *New Perspectives in Educational Language Policy: In Honour of Bernard Dov Spolsky*. Benjamins, Philadelphaia, PA
Spolsky B 1978 *Educational Linguistics: An Introduction*. Newbury House Publishers, Rowley, MA
Spolsky B (ed.) 1986 *Language and Education in Multilingual Settings*. Multilingual Matters Ltd., Clevedon, UK
Spolsky B 1989 *Conditions for Second Language Learning: Introduction to a General Theory*. Oxford University Press, Oxford, UK
Spolsky B 1995 *Measured Words: The Development of Objective Language Testing*. Oxford University Press, Oxford, UK
Spolsky B 1998 *Sociolinguistics* (*Oxford Introductions to Language Study*). Oxford University Press, Oxford, UK
Spolsky B (ed.) 1999 *Concise Encyclopedia of Educational Linguistics*. Elsevier, Oxford, UK

Spolsky B, Cooper R L (eds.) 1977 *Frontiers of Bilingual Education*. Newbury House Publishers, Rowley, MA

Spolsky B, Cooper R L 1991 *The Languages of Jerusalem*. Clarendon Press, Oxford, UK

Srivastava, Ravindra Nath (1936–92)
R. K. Agnihotri

Ravindra Nath Srivastava was perhaps the only Indian linguist who was trained in both the North American and Russian traditions. Though his basic interest was in the theory of language, he constantly kept in touch with empirical issues, particularly the ones that affected the underprivileged masses and minorities. He is remembered across the world for a variety of reasons. He made significant contributions in the areas of experimental phonetics, generative phonology, lexicography, applied linguistics, literacy, stylistics, translation studies, and sociolinguistics. He was an excellent teacher who taught with great dedication, clarity, and precision and whose classes students always looked forward to. He was a skillful team leader who headed several projects and departments with remarkable success, and finally, he was an extremely warm and affectionate person.

Srivastava was born in Ballia, Uttar Pradesh (North India) on July 9, 1936. He received his Master's degree in Hindi literature from Benares Hindu University, Varanasi, in 1957. Even though he subsequently earned a degree in Law, he found his real vocation when he did his Master's (1962) and PhD degrees in Linguistics (1966) from the Leningrad State University. He joined the Department of Linguistics at the University of Delhi in 1966 where he served with distinction until his death. He had undertaken (in-between) a three year stint as Professor at the Central Hindi Institute, Delhi. Even today he is remembered as one of the major architects of the Department of Linguistics, University of Delhi and the Central Hindi Institute. In 1968 he was awarded the Ford Foundation Postdoctoral Fellowship to carry out research at UCLA. During the 20 years he worked at the University of Delhi, he taught and guided research, undertook several research projects, participated in a large number of national and international seminars, and published extensively in English, Hindi, and Russian. He was the UGC National Professor for a year and was a visiting professor at different universities in the US and Italy. He was often invited as an expert consultant by various international organizations including UNESCO, Paris (1975) and the United Nations University, Tokyo (1982). It is no exaggeration to say that many of Srivastava's students hold major teaching or research positions in the discipline today.

Thanks to his wife Bina Srivastava and her editorial team, we have most of Srivastava's work available in seven volumes of *Studies in Language and Linguistics: Selected Writings of R. N. Srivastava*. The themes of these seven volumes are: literacy, stylistics, bilingualism and multilingualism, applied linguistics, Hindi linguistics, language theory and language structure, and generative phonology. All his work is situated in a dialogic relationship between theory and practice. He valued the innate linguistic potential of every human being and considered multilingualism a normal state of affairs, arguing strongly against the position that multilingualism has a debilitating effect on literacy. He showed how linguistic and cultural plurality goes hand in hand with cognitive richness. At a time when most scholars regarded only formal linguistics as linguistics proper, Srivastava constantly tried to build bridges between theory and practice.

Bibliography

Srivastava R N 1993–1999 *Studies in Language and Linguistics* (7 volumes). Kalinga Publications, Delhi, (published posthumously, Series Editor: Srivastava B), India

Verma S K, Singh D (eds.) 1996 *Perspectives on Language in Society: Papers in Memory of Prof. Srivastava* (2 Volumes). Kalinga Publications, Delhi, India

Street, Brian (1943–)
M. Prinsloo

Brian Street's work has had a shaping influence on the development of Literacy Studies over the last three decades. An anthropologist by training, he has developed a grounded and research-focused approach, concerned with the study of literacy as situated practices in specific contexts, distributed amongst co-participants and embedded within relations of culture and power.

Street's doctoral research was in the area of 'representation' of non-European societies in literature (1975) and he has continued to publish in this area. His perspective in this work is that of seeing 'representations,' (particularly notions of racism, culture, and discourse) as historically specific instances of social and cultural processes and practices, with economic, political, and ideological dimensions that can be studied. He has retained this epistemological focus in his contributions to Literacy Studies. He has confronted 'great divide' assumptions in literacy studies, which have seen literacy as a pivotal and uniform social technology that distinguishes 'modern' from 'other' cultures, and has identified the ethnocentric bias of such work. He has characterized his own work as developing an 'ideological model of literacy,' to distinguish it from what he calls the 'autonomous model of literacy' and to emphasize first, the social nature of literacy, and secondly the multiple and contested nature of literacy practices. His focus on fine-grained local accounts has made his work particularly compatible with a range of scholars from across several disciplines who have a social view of language and its functions, and they have separately and cooperatively contributed a body of work that has become known as the New Literacy Studies.

His ethnographic study of the indigenous 'maktab' literacy practices of the Cheshmehi mountain fruit-growers of north-eastern Iran (1984), together with an extended theorization of literacy as social practice established the framework for his later studies. His book *Social Literacies* (1995) confirmed and elaborated on this earlier work, extending it in various directions, including schooling, adult literacy, and social development concerns.

An edited volume of literacy studies in different cultures and societies (1993) brought together work by anthropologists and sociolinguists from Africa, Papua New Guinea, the South Pacific, Madagascar, the USA, and the UK, to show the rich cultural variation in literacy practices and to show the complex and culturally located links between literacy, identity, and power. This work demonstrated that social practices around literacy vary, but more fundamentally that what is meant by the terms literacy, reading, and writing differs across cultures. Furthermore, it is not just cross-culturally, but within different contexts in the same culture, such as the home and the workplace, and within the same activity that there can be different meanings of reading, writing, and literacy.

Street's work contributes to a broadening of the study of interaction in sociolinguistics, which has primarily been of spoken language and of face-to-face-interaction, to a focus on the multiple forms and purposes that texts and textually linked practices have in social interaction.

In the 1990s he led, contributed to, or supervised research in Literacy Studies across multiple international and local settings, including in Africa and Asia, and has led or participated in a number of funded research programs. These include the ethnographic study of the range of uses and meanings given to literacy in various contexts in South Africa during the transitional period at the end of the apartheid era (Prinsloo and Breier 1996), a study of the everyday writing practices of correspondents in Britain who contributed to the Mass-Observation Archive over decades (2000); research on academic literacies within higher education (Street, Jones and Turner 1999). His perspective on literacy practices in educational contexts stresses particular settings (universities, adult literacy classes) as embodying social practices that are in turn linked to such key concepts as nation, identity, ideology, and discourse.

Street is currently Professor of Language in Education, School of Education, King's College, London University and Adjunct Professor of Education in the Graduate School of Education at the University of Pennsylvania.

See also: Literacy; Oracy; Literacy: Research, Measurement, and Innovation.

Bibliography

Prinsloo M, Breier M 1996 *The Social Uses of Literacy: Theory and Practice in Contemporary South Africa*. Benjamins, Amsterdam

Sheridan D, Street B, Bloome D 2000 *Ordinary People Writing: Literacy Practices and Identity in the Mass-Observation Project*. Hampton Press, Cresskill, NJ

Street B 1975 *The Savage in Literature*. Routledge and Kegan Paul, London

Street B 1984 *Literacy in Theory and Practice*. Cambridge University Press, Cambridge, UK

Street B 1993 (ed.) *Cross-Cultural Approaches to Literacy*. Cambridge University Press, Cambridge, UK

Street B 1995 *Social Literacies: Critical Perspectives on Literacy in Development, Ethnography, and Education*. Longman, London

Street B, Jones C, Turner J 1999 *Student Writing in the University: Cultural and Epistemological Issues*. Benjamins, Amsterdam

Tannen, Deborah
J. Bennett

Deborah Tannen, Professor in the Department of Linguistics at Georgetown University, popularized ideas about gender differences in communication, especially communication between heterosexual American couples in the home, through *You Just Don't Understand: Men and Women in Conversation* (1990). The book argues for a notion of complex complementarity as a feature of the difference between US-based men's and women's language use: access to comprehension between men and women involves recognition of gendered communicative styles encompassing negotiation of interruption, silence, topic focus, and linguistic conventions governing the expression of aggression, desire, and cooperative intent.

Tannen has published 17 books, exploring the interaction of cultural difference and linguistic strategies used by speakers, and listeners, to achieve communication.

Conversational Style: Analyzing Talk Among Friends (1984) and *That's Not What I Meant! How Conversation Makes and Breaks Your Relations with Others* (1986) place emphasis on US based ethnic and regional difference. Many of Tannen's later publications explore gender related stylistic variation within the framework of cultural diversity: *Gender and Conversational Interaction* (1993), *Gender and Discourse* (1994), *Talking From 9 to 5: Men and Women in the Workplace* (1995), and *I Only Say This Because I Love You: How We Talk Can Make or Break Family Relationships Throughout Our Lives* (2001).

Deborah Tannen's work spans several genres. While at least two of her books have been placed on the *New York Times* bestseller list (*You Just Don't Understand* and *From 9 to 5*), and she regularly contributes to popular journals and newspapers (e.g., *Cosmopolitan, Good Housekeeping, New York Newsday, Los Angeles Times,* and *Newsweek*), she is a prolific contributor to academic sociolinguistic debates concerning approaches to understanding power and language. Her arguments move away from the notion of any predictable source of inequity, reflected through communicative style, into a preference for understanding communicative power as a flexible, interactive, diverse negotiation with linguistic strategies, individual context, and the relationship between speakers. In addition, Tannen has published poetry, short stories, and a play, *An Act of Devotion* (in *The Best American Short Plays: 1993–1994*).

See also: Gender and Language; Discourse Analysis and the Law; Conversation Analysis.

Bibliography

Tannen D 1984 *Conversational Style: Analysing Talk among Friends*. Ablex, NJ

Tannen D 1986 *That's Not What I Meant! How Conversation Makes and Breaks Your Relations with Others*. Ballantine, New York

Tannen D 1990 *You Just Don't Understand: Men and Women in Conversation*. William Morrow, New York

Tannen D 1993 *Gender and Conversational Interaction*. Oxford University Press, Oxford, UK

Tannen D 1994 *Gender and Discourse*. Oxford University Press, Oxford, UK

Tannen D 1995 *Talking From 9 to 5: Men and Women in the Workplace: Language, Sex, and Power*. Avon, New York

Tannen D 2001 *I Only Say This Because I Love You: How We Talk Can Make or Break Family Relationships Throughout Our Lives*. Random House, New York

Trudgill, Peter John (1943–)
P. Kerswill

Peter Trudgill was born in Norwich, England. He received a BA from Cambridge in 1966, a Postgraduate Diploma from Edinburgh in 1967 and a PhD in Linguistics from Edinburgh in 1971. Trudgill is one of a small number of sociolinguists who began their work in the UK in the 1970s and early 1980s, the others include Lesley Milroy (see *Milroy, Lesley*), James Milroy and Suzanne Romaine (see *Romaine, Suzanne*). Their seminal position in the UK can be judged by the fact that they (with Euan Reid and Robert Le Page) were the instigators of the Sociolinguistics Symposium in 1976, a conference series that is now the leading one in Europe in this field. While these scholars are correctly credited with introducing the 'Labovian' (see *Labov, William*) method and agenda to the UK, Trudgill has explained (Hernández Campoy 1993: 214) that he sees his intellectual roots as lying in the work of the British creolist and sociolinguist Robert Le Page (see *Le Page, Robert*), whose research is essentially in contact linguistics—a theme later taken up very strongly by Trudgill since the 1980s. Trudgill's work also places him in the tradition of British, European, and US dialectology (cf. Chambers and Trudgill 1998 and Trudgill 1983b). Trudgill is the leading proponent of what Labov has (rather awkwardly) labeled 'secular linguistics,' the study of spoken language in context for the purpose of gaining insight into language structure and change (Trudgill 1978: 11). Like Labov, he sees his own data-based work as contributing to linguistic theory, and this is as true of his Norwich study (1974; with 1988 follow-up) as it is of his much later analyses of a unique 1940s taped corpus of elderly speakers of New Zealand English (Britain and Trudgill 1999, Gordon and Trudgill 1999, Trudgill et al. 2000). The New Zealand corpus is the most significant manifestation of his interest in *dialect contact* since the publication of Trudgill (1986), which is his most substantive contribution to theorizing about language change to date. As with Trudgill (1986), many of his publications report both his original studies as well as syntheses of a wide range of other work. Notable are his publications on language and education, a field in which he had a long-running dispute with the late British sociologist Basil Bernstein (see *Bernstein, Basil*) following the publication of Trudgill (1975a, 1975b). He has also had a long-standing disagreement with the late John Honey over their differing views of the role of Standard English in British education (Trudgill 2000b). In his work oriented towards education and the sociology of language, he often adopts a liberal political stance, as in the final chapter on 'Language and humanity' in Trudgill (2000). Other work in the sociology of language includes Andersson and Trudgill (1990) and Trudgill and Tzavaras (1977). Part and parcel of dialect contact is the social psychological notion of *accommodation* (see Giles and Smith 1979; see *Speech Accommodation*); Trudgill (1986) has differentiated between short-term (immediate, context-bound) and long-term (more-or-less permanent, habitual) versions. An early expression of this idea is his study (1980) of the changing use of American pronunciation by British pop groups from the 1950s to the 1970s. Trudgill is known as a popularizer both of sociolinguistics (2000a, 1st edn. 1974) and of English dialectology (1998a). He has contributed to work on English as an international language (Trudgill and Hannah 1994, 1st edn. 1985).

See also: Sociolinguistic Variation; Sociophonetics; Koinés.

Bibliography

Andersson G, Trudgill P 1990 *Bad Language*. Blackwell, Oxford, UK

Britain D, Trudgill P 1999 Migration, new-dialect formation and sociolinguistic refunctionalisation: Reallocation as an outcome of dialect contact. *Transactions of the Philological Society* 97: 245–56

Chambers J K, Trudgill P 1998 *Dialectology*, 2nd edn. Cambridge University Press, Cambridge, UK

Giles H, Smith P 1979 Accommodation theory: Optimal levels of convergence. In: Giles H, St. Clair R (eds.) *Language and Social Psychology*. Blackwell, Oxford, UK, pp. 45–65.

Gordon E, Trudgill P 1999 Shades of things to come: Embryonic variants in New Zealand English sound changes. *English World-Wide* 20: 111–24

Hernández Campoy J M 1993 *Sociolingüística Británica: Introducción a la obra de Peter Trudgill*. Ediciones OCTAEDRO, Barcelona, Spain

Honey J 1997 *Language is Power: The Story of Standard English and its Enemies*. Faber and Faber, London

Trudgill P 1974 *The Social Differentiation of English in Norwich*. Cambridge University Press, Cambridge, UK

Trudgill P 1975a *Accent, Dialect, and the School*. Arnold, London

Trudgill P 1975b Review of Basil Bernstein (1971–5). *Class, Codes and Control* (3 vols.) *Journal of Linguistics* 11: 147–51

Trudgill P (ed.) 1978 Introduction: Sociolinguistics and sociolinguistics. In: Trudgill P (ed.) *Sociolinguistic Patterns in British English*. Arnold, London, pp. 1–18

Trudgill P 1980 Acts of conflicting identity: A sociolinguistic look at British pop songs. In: De Silva M W S (ed.) *Aspects of Linguistic Behaviour: Festschrift for R. B. Le Page*. York Papers in Linguistics 9. University of York, York, UK

Trudgill P 1983a *On Dialect: Social and Geographical Perspectives*. Blackwell, Oxford, UK

Trudgill P 1983b Sociolinguistics and linguistic value judgements: Correctness, adequacy, and aesthetics. In: Trudgill P (ed.), *On Dialect: Social and Geographical Perspectives*. Blackwell, Oxford, UK, pp. 201–26

Trudgill P 1986 *Dialects in Contact*. Blackwell, Oxford, UK

Trudgill P 1988 Norwich revisited: Recent linguistic changes in an English urban dialect. *English World-Wide* 9: 33–49

Trudgill P 1998a *The Dialects of England*, 2nd edn. Blackwell, Oxford, UK

Trudgill P 1998b Review of John Honey's *Language is Power*. *Journal of Sociolinguistics* 2: 457–61

Trudgill P 2000 *Sociolinguistics: An Introduction to Language and Society*, 3rd edn. Penguin, London

Trudgill P, Gordon E, Lewis G, Maclagan M 2000 Determinism in new-dialect formation and the genesis of New Zealand English. *Journal of Linguistics* 36: 299–318

Trudgill P, Hannah J 1994 *International English: A Guide to Varieties of Standard English*, 3rd edn. Arnold, London

Trudgill P, Tzavaras G 1977 Why Albanian-Greeks are not Albanians: Language shift in Attica and Biotia. In: Giles H (ed.) *Language, Ethnicity, and Intergroup Relations* (European Monographs in Social Psychology 13). Academic Press, London, pp. 171–84

Tucker, G. Richard (1942–)

J. Crandall

Dick Tucker was born May 3, 1942, in Scranton, Pennsylvania. He received his BA in Psychology from Williams College in 1964, and his MA and PhD in Psycholinguistics in 1965 and 1967, respectively, from McGill University in Montreal, Quebec. Upon completion of his graduate studies, Tucker worked for 18 months as a Ford Foundation Consultant to the Philippine Normal College in Manila, where he helped introduce a new specialization in Psycholinguistics into the graduate TESOL program. With Bonifacio Sibayan and Fe Otanes, he also planned and implemented that National Language Policy Survey of the Philippines which focused on the role of education in helping to develop language proficiency (Tucker 1968). He returned to McGill University in 1969, where he began a long career with a triple appointment in Psychology, Linguistics, and Football. Tucker's major research interests have focused on bilingualism, language policy, and the evaluation of innovative language education programs in diverse settings. At McGill, he and Wallace Lambert undertook what was to become a landmark longitudinal study of early immersion in a foreign language (French), the St. Lambert Experiment (Lambert and Tucker 1972). Using multiple measures, including the role of individual differences in second language acquisition in different contexts (Tucker et al. 1976), he and Lambert followed the immersion students through high school (Lambert and Tucker 1979).

During his tenure at McGill, Tucker undertook two additional Ford Foundation Consultancies with the American University of Cairo, Egypt (AUC) and the American University of Beirut, Lebanon (AUB), where he taught courses in the MATESOL program and conducted a number of studies of the language learning strategies of Arab and Hebrew students learning English (Cooper et al. 1979, Scott and Tucker 1974). While in Beirut, he also designed and implemented the English Language Policy Survey of Jordan with Clifford Prator (Harrison et al. 1975).

In 1978, Tucker left McGill to become the President of the Center for Applied Linguistics (CAL) in Washington, DC, the fourth permanent head of CAL. At CAL, he was a frequent consultant to governmental and international organizations seeking to develop effective language polices. In that role, he often called upon institutions to work to develop a language competent United State society, one in which all individuals are provided access to proficiency in English and other language (Tucker 1986), through innovative language education programs such as content-based language instruction and two-way developmental (immersion) bilingual programs (Crandall and Tucker 1990).

Tucker's tenure was co-terminous with the period of the second largest influx of refugees into the United States in the twentieth century, and under his leadership, CAL became the major national source of information and the languages and cultures of refugees from Southeast Asia, Africa, and Eastern and Central Europe.

While at CAL, Tucker maintained a courtesy adjunct professorial appointment with Georgetown University but in 1992 he left CAL to return to fulltime teaching in the Department of Modern Languages at Carnegie Mellon University in Pittsburgh, where he continues to engage in research on second language acquisition through innovative language education programs, including an ongoing study of Japanese immersion students, with Richard Donato and Janis Antonek (Donato et al. 1996). As Head of the Department, he has greatly expanded its offerings and initiated a doctoral program in Second Language Acquisition, with a focus on less commonly taught languages, such as Japanese and Chinese.

See also: Social Psychology; Bilingualism, Societal.

Bibliography

Cooper R L, Olshtain E, Tucker G R, Waterbury M 1979 The acquisition of complex English structures by adult native speakers of Arabic and Hebrew. *Language Learning* **29**: 255–75

Donato R, Antonek J, Tucker G R 1996 Monitoring and assessing a Japanese FLES program: Ambiance and achievement. *Language Learning* **46**: 497–528

Hamayan G R, Genesee F 1976 Affective, cognitive, and social factors in second language acquisition. *Canadian Modern Language Review* **32**: 115–341

Harrison W, Prator C, Tucker G R 1975 *English-Language Survey of Jordan: A Case Study in Language Planning*. Center for Applied Linguistics, Arlington, VA

Lambert W E, Tucker G R 1972 *Bilingual Education of Children*. Newbury House, Rowley, MA

Lambert W E, Tucker G R 1979 Graduates of early immersion: Retrospective views of grade 11 students and their parents. In: Obadia A (ed.) *Proceedings of the C.A.I.T. Second National Convention, Ottawa*

Scott M S, Tucker G R 1974 Error analysis and English-language strategies of Arab students. *Language Learning* **24**: 69–97

Tucker G R 1968 Psycholinguistic research in the Philippines. *Philippine Journal for Language Teaching* **5**: 29–42

Tucker G R 1986 Developing a language-competent American society. In: Tannen D (ed.) *Georgetown University Round Table on Languages and Linguistics 1985* (pp. 263–74). Georgetown University Press, Washington, DC

Valdman, Albert (1931–)

B. Spolsky

Born in Paris in 1931, Albert Valdman, without doubt one of the leading applied linguists of this generation, was educated at the University of Pennsylvania where he received a BA in Romance Languages and at Cornell University where he earned an MA and PhD in French Linguistics. In the tradition of Cornell-trained applied linguists, his first position was at the Foreign Service Institute of the US Department of State in Washington, beginning his lifelong devotion to ensuring that language teaching be based on a thorough understanding of contemporary linguistics. After a spell at the Pennsylvania State University, he joined the faculty of Indiana University in Bloomington in 1960. Appointed to the Department of French and Italian (where he still directs the graduate program in French Linguistics), he was invited by a group of linguists scattered throughout the university to put together a Department of Linguistics, which he chaired from 1963 until 1968. Now nearly 40 years on the Indiana University faculty, Valdman holds the distinguished title of Rudy Professor of French and Italian and of Linguistics and also serves as chairman of the Committee for Research and Development in Language Instruction and directs the Creole Institute. He has held visiting appointments at the University of the West Indies (Jamaica) and at the University of Nice and taught in summer institutes at Harvard University and the University of Oregon.

Valdman has held Guggenheim, NATO-NSF, Fulbright, and Senior Fulbright Research fellowships. His research and publications span a broad range of areas in applied and descriptive linguistics, including second language acquisition, foreign language teaching, pidgin and creole studies (he has had a major hand in developing research and teaching in creoles), and French linguistics (he is one of the pioneer researchers in the area of the study of French outside of France, especially in the Americas).

The author or editor of more than 40 books, Valdman co-edited the *Learner's Dictionary of Haitian Creole*, hailed as an unequaled resource for Americans who seek to learn the language. Among his major books or edited volumes are: *Trends in Language Teaching* (1964), *Le français hors de France* (1979), *Haitian Creole–French–English Dictionary* (1981), and *Bien entendu! Introduction à la phonétique française* (1993). In addition to publishing more than 200 articles and reviews in major journals in linguistics, he has been involved in the preparation of foreign language materials, including a high school French series and beginning French college textbooks. He is founder and editor of the influential journal *Studies in Second Language Acquisition* and a review editor of the *French Review*.

Valdman has made significant contributions to the profession of educational linguistics as well as to creolistics. He served eight years as secretary treasurer of the American Association for Applied Linguistics. He played a crucial role in integrating American applied linguistics into the international association, serving for six years as president of AILA, the International Association of Applied Linguistics. He has been president of the American Association of Teachers of French.

Valdman has been named Commandeur dans l'Ordre des Palmes Académiques of France, and received an honorary doctorate from the University of Neuchâtel.

See also: Interlanguage; Pidgins and Creoles: Models.

Bibliography

Lee J F, Valdman A (eds.) 2000 *Form and Meaning: Multiple Perspectives*. Heinle and Heinle, Boston, MA
Valdman A (ed.) 1966 *Trends in Language Teaching*. McGraw-Hill, New York
Valdman A (ed.) 1981 *Haitian Creole–English–French Dictionary*. Indiana University, Bloomington, IN
Valdman A 1992 *En route: Introduction au français et au monde francophone*. Prentice-Hall, Englewood Cliffs, NJ
Valdman A (ed.) 1997 *French and Creole in Louisiana*. Plenum, New York

Van Name, Addison (1835–1922)

G. G. Gilbert

Van Name was born in Chenango, near Binghamton, New York, and died in New Haven, Connecticut. 'His father owned a sawmill and was interested in the shipping on the canal' (*Dictionary of American Biography* **10**, 1936: 201). He graduated at the head of his class with a BA from Yale College in 1858. From 1859 to 1861 he traveled in Europe and studied at the universities of Halle and Tübingen. Van Name was appointed instructor in Hebrew at Yale in 1862, and librarian in 1865. In 1867 he married Julia Gibbs in Berlin; they had three children. His wife was the daughter of Josiah Willard Gibbs

(1790–1861), one of the best known American orientalists, linguists, and librarians of his day; her brother, Josiah Willard Gibbs Jr. (1839–1903), was a noted mathematician and theoretical physicist with close links to Germany and an international following.

Van Name was one of the founding members of the American Philological Association in 1869; William Dwight Whitney read his paper 'Contributions toward a grammar of the Creole dialects of Hayti and Louisiana' in his absence at the first meeting of the Association in that year.

Van Name served as head of the Yale Library for 40 years, building up its collections from 44,500 to nearly half a million volumes and manuscripts 'at a time when little money was available for books or service, but the most striking thing ... is not their number but their quality' (*Dictionary of American Biography* **10**, 1936: 202). Phelps (quoted in Schiff 1978: 534) said, in 1918, that he was 'probably the most skillful buyer of books on earth.' In 1876 Van Name was active in the formation of the American Library Association. Remarkable was his acumen in acquiring books for Yale in and about Chinese and other far (and near) eastern languages. Although his 'creole period' was relatively brief, his methods of study and his insights into the origin and development of those languages were well in advance of their time.

Van Name devoted but a short period of his life to the study of pidgin and creole languages; nevertheless, he introduced a method of study which was unusual in mid-nineteenth-century creolistics—the questioning of linguistic consultants located fortuitously at the researcher's place of residence, persons who provided linguistic data that could be supplemented and corroborated by printed materials, the aim being a comprehensive overview of a scope that no one had thought of attempting up to that time. Van Name himself states that J. J. Thomas's 1869 grammar of Trinidadian Creole French (Van Name 1869–70a: 13) first induced him to begin his own research on creole languages. He describes his local consultants as:

(a) ... 'a young man, who between the age of seven and fourteen (he is now eighteen) lived in Hayti, and has a good command of the Creole';
(b) a 'young man, ... , recently from St. Thomas ... born in Havana, but since his sixth year [he] has lived in St. Thomas, and speaks, besides the French, also the Dutch and Spanish Creole, all three with great readiness ... [and] has also visited nearly all the West India islands, and can speak from personal observation of the limits of the several dialects';
(c) two ex-slaves and a free black, two of them native speakers of Louisiana Creole French, from the vicinity of New Orleans (Van Name 1869–70b: 127).

Modern 'substratophiles' are unhappy with Van Name's emphasis on general principles of development, rather than on specific substratal influences in the formation of the creoles (e.g., Holm 1988: 24–7). Other contemporary researchers hail him as the founder of scientific creolistics (e.g., Stolz 1986: 14). Even the most critical commentators (e.g., Goodman 1964: 111–3) agree that his use of consultants, the taking into account of a variety of creoles with French, English, Portuguese, and Dutch lexical bases, and his recognition of the creole hallmark of unexpected similarities of patterning (whatever their provenience) and, at the same time, of an unusual amount of variation (a term which Van Name uses himself), guarantees him a significant place in the launching of creolistics as a science.

See also: Pidgins and Creoles: Models; Pidgins and Creoles: An Overview.

Bibliography

Goodman M F 1964 *A Comparative Study of Creole French Dialects*. Mouton, The Hague
Holm J A 1988 *Pidgins and Creoles. Vol. 1: Theory and Structure*. Cambridge University Press, Cambridge, UK
Keogh A 1936 Van Name, Addison. *Dictionary of American Biography* (*DAB*) XIX. Humphrey Milford/Oxford University Press, London, Charles Scribner's Sons, New York
Schiff J A 1978 Addison Van Name. In: *Dictionary of American Library Biography*. Libraries Unlimited Inc., Littleton, CO
Stolz T 1986 *Gibt es das kreolische Sprachwandelmodell?* Peter Lang, Frankfurt am Main, Germany
Van Name A 1869–70a Contributions toward a grammar of the Creole dialects of Hayti and Louisiana. *Transactions of the American Philological Association* **1**: 13
Van Name A 1869–70b Contributions to Creole grammar. *Transactions of the American Philological Association* **1**: 123–67

Voloshinov, Valentin Nikolavic (1895–1936)
D. Brown

V. N. Voloshinov was a Russian researcher who was part of intellectual and academic circles in Leningrad during post-revolutionary Soviet Russia. He was a close associate of M. M. Bakhtin (see *Bakhtin,*

Mikhail M.) and N. Medvedev who were semioticians working on literary criticism. Voloshinov's work on philosophy of language provided a critique of de Saussure (see *Saussurean Tradition and Sociolinguistics*), while his work on psychology provided a critique of Freud. His research concerns were for the areas of cultural inquiry explicitly not dealt with by Marxist theory (see *Marxist Theories of Language*) and his work and intellectual activity represents the critical inquiry that flourished in the newly established Soviet state until the Stalinist period of 1929. Bakhtin and Medvedev, his closest associates, were victims of Stalin. Bakhtin was sent into internal exile and only 'rehabilitated' in the 1960s and Medvedev was murdered in Stalin's purges in the 1930s. There is some doubt about the actual date and cause of Voloshinov's death but some evidence that he died of tuberculosis, which he had suffered from all his adult life.

Voloshinov's two significant works were *Marxism and the Philosophy of Language* (1973) and *Freudianism: A Marxist Critique* (1976). Both of these critiques dealt with language. The former is a systematic critique of Ferdinand de Saussure's *Course in General Linguistics*. Voloshinov's critique does not accept the distinction between langue and parole and identified and rejected the Cartesian rationalism that formed the basis of Saussure's thesis. Voloshinov considered the verbal sign a speech act which involved a speaker or writer and a listener or reader. Contrary to de Saussure, parole was an important feature of linguistic concern. His perceptions of the role of the verbal sign paralleled those of the semiotician Charles Sanders Pierce. Voloshinov believed that inner speech was like a dialogue and that linguistic understanding was intrinsic to an understanding of social psychology. His work concentrated on an understanding of reported speech as discourse as just one example of a focus for linguistic study.

Language analysis and understanding of signs was inseparable from ideology for Voloshinov. He believed that the verbal sign was a constant area of class struggle and signs consistently change their meaning socially in relation to changing social contexts. He saw the desire to stabilize the nature of meaning and control the use of signs as a consistent feature of the ideology of dominant social groups (see *Dialogism*; *Ideology*).

His work fell from any form of public attention after its initial appearance and was unknown in the West until Roman Jakobson cited his work positively in 1957, which led to its translation and reception during the 1970s. Some confusion as to the authorship of *Marxism and the Philosophy of Language* arose in the early 1970s. After an occasion to celebrate the 75th birthday of M. M. Bakhtin (the leader of the intellectual circle and its only survivor at the time), a speaker claimed that the work of his closest associates Medvedev and Voloshinov was really the work of Bakhtin. This produced a controversy known as the 'author's controversy.' However, most writers believe that, as no evidence has emerged, respect for the circumstances of the authors Medvedev and Voloshinov's difficult life circumstances and the historical period demands that we currently accept that Voloshinov was the author of this significant work.

See also: Dialogism; Ideology; Bakhtin, Mikhail M.; Critical Sociolinguistics.

Bibliography

Gardiner M 1992 *The Dialogics of Critique*. Routledge, London
Morris P 1994 *The Bakhtin Reader*. Arnold, London
Voloshinov V N 1973 *Marxism and the Philosophy of Language*. Seminar Press, New York
Voloshinov V N 1976 *Freudianism: A Marxist Critique*. Academic Press, New York

Weinreich, Uriel (1926−67)

T. Hill

When Uriel Weinreich died, aged 41, he left a record of remarkable distinction in three diverse fields: Yiddish studies, linguistic geography and sociology, and semantics. Born in Vilnius, the main center of Ashkenazic Jewish culture, he was the son of the Yiddish scholar Max Weinreich, who in 1940 took the family to the USA, joining the faculty of New York City College. Uriel Weinreich studied, and later taught, at Columbia University, graduating with a PhD in 1951 and going on to become the first Atran Professor of Yiddish studies, chairman of the linguistics department, and joint editor of *Word*.

Weinreich stimulated and contributed to modern Yiddish studies in many ways, beginning early with the textbook *College Yiddish* (1949). He founded and edited the collections of occasional papers entitled *The Field of Yiddish* (1954), and with his wife Beatrice Weinreich published the bibliography *Yiddish Language and Folklore* (1959). In his *Modern English/Yiddish, Yiddish/English Dictionary* (1968) his theories on systematic lexicography found concrete application, including the definition and application of the distinctive Yiddish register system. At the time of his death he was engaged upon the *Language and Culture Atlas of Ashkenazic Jewry*, based on data on their ancestral communities gathered from American Yiddish speakers.

Weinreich's doctoral thesis was on language contact, supervised by A. Martinet, with guidance during a year's field research in Switzerland from J. Jud and E. Dieth. Published as *Languages in Contact* (1953), it presented a systematic framework for categorizing mutual influence and mixing between languages, and quickly became a recognized basic text. The comparison of (mainly phonological) systems between dialects was already accepted practice in many surveys, though rejected by others, Weinreich's article 'Is a structural dialectology possible?' (1954a) expounded its theoretical basis, and initiated a discussion that received interesting contributions from, among others, W. G. Moulton and R. I. McDavid Jr (see *McDavid, Raven Ioor, Jr*). In the 1960s, Weinreich's attention turned to the study of linguistic variation and change at the level of idiolect and speech situation, his conclusions being presented in the article, posthumously completed by his pupil W. Labov (see *Labov, William*) and M. I. Herzog, 'Empirical foundations for a theory of language change' (Weinreich et al. 1968).

Weinreich's writings on semantics express his conviction that a valid (and necessarily complex) theory of meaning requires close study of how diverse languages meet the communicative demands made on them, within their cultures, in actual situations. Accordingly, though he had enthusiastically embraced generative linguistics as a whole, his lecture 'Explorations in semantic theory' (1964; published 1966 in *Current Trends in Linguistics*) was a critique of inadequacies in the Katz–Fodor model, which led to further debate with Katz. Regarding lexicography, Weinreich endorsed the Soviet linguists' view of it as being a distinct discipline, and contributed to it in theoretical papers, as well as in his Yiddish dictionary. His semantic and lexicographical writings were posthumously edited in Weinreich (1980).

See also: Dialect and Dialectology; Sociolinguistic Variation.

Bibliography

Malkiel Y 1967 Uriel Weinreich. *Language* **43**: 605–10
Moulton W G 1968 Structural dialectology. *Language* **44**: 451–66
Schaechter M 1971 Weinreich, Uriel. In: *Encyclopaedia Judaica, Vol. 16*, p. 406. Kether, Jerusalem
Weinreich U 1949 *College Yiddish*. YIVO, New York
Weinreich U 1953 *Languages in Contact: Findings and Problems*, Linguistic Circle of New York, **1**. Mouton, The Hague
Weinreich U 1954a Is a structural dialectology possible? *Word* **10**: 2–3
Weinreich U (ed.) 1954b *The Field of Yiddish*, 1st collection. Linguistic Circle of New York, New York
Weinreich U 1980 *On Semantics*. University of Pennsylvania Press, Philadelphia, PA
Weinreich U, Labov W, Herzog M I 1968 Empirical foundations of a theory of linguistic change. In: Lehmann W P, Malkiel Y (eds.) *Directions for Historical Linguistics*. University of Texas Press, Austin, TX

Wenker, Georg (1852–1911)
T. Hill

Wenker compiled the first dialect atlas of Germany, and founded the national dialect research center at Marburg. Graduating in Germanic philology, he became a schoolteacher in his native Düsseldorf, and in 1875 began higher degree research on the historical phonology of German dialects, using written sources. The current assumption was that the concept 'dialect' implied an area clearly delimited by linguistic boundaries, within which its specific sound changes had operated uniformly in accordance with neogrammarian principles. When his sources failed to give this clear picture, Wenker decided to clarify the matter by collecting his own data; and with this modest first step he created the method of inquiry, and the questionnaire, on which ultimately the dialect atlas of Germany would be founded. He drew up a set of 40 sentences, composed so as to illustrate phonological and morphological points, and circulated them to primary school teachers throughout the Düsseldorf district, for translation into each local dialect using ordinary German spelling conventions (a notion familiar from its application in dialect verse, etc.). The project was successful, and the results, published as *Das rheinische Platt* (Düsseldorf 1877, repr. as *Deutsche Dialektgeographie* No. 8, Marburg 1915), revealed *inter alia* the 'Uerdingen line' (*ik/ich*), which is the northernmost limit of the High German soundshift, and was the first isogloss of the 'Rhenish Fan' to be discovered.

Appointment to an assistant librarianship at Marburg University enabled Wenker to extend his survey into the Rhineland and Westphalia, then, with the support of the Prussian Academy of Sciences, to all north and central Germany, of which the atlas was published in 1881. Wenker now envisaged an atlas of all Germany, and received much scholarly support, but realized that a properly funded and staffed survey would be essential. In response to his appeal for official sponsorship, in 1887 his survey became a German state institute, with Wenker as director and two assistants, one of whom was F. Wrede; and the still outstanding southern region was surveyed. From now on collection and research were funded, but under two onerous conditions: publication of the atlas was postponed indefinitely, and Wenker himself was to abandon research and confine himself to mapmaking. By now a self-taught cartographer, Wenker selflessly accepted this burden. He had decided that each questionnaire item should be separately mapped, and, Germany being divided into three regions, he and later Wrede compiled a total of 1650 maps.

The further history of the atlas, the controversy with O. Bremer, and the theoretical achievements of the Marburg School are discussed in the article on Wrede. Wenker's own life work had shown that an indirect inquiry, intelligently framed and with a dense coverage, yields meaningful and accurate data (though this view is even now not accepted universally), and his method provided a model for numerous later surveys. His results constituted a significant contribution to the dialect boundary controversy.

See also: Dialect and Dialectology.

Bibliography

Bach A 1969 *Deutsche Mundartforschung*, 3rd edn. C. Winter, Heidelberg, Germany
Goossens J 1977 *Deutsche Dialektologie*. De Gruyter, Berlin
Schirmunski V M 1962 *Deutsche Mundartkunde*. Akademie-Verlag, Berlin

Whorf, Benjamin Lee (1897–1941)
J. H. Stam

Benjamin Lee Whorf was an amateur linguist who speculated on the relation of language to culture and thought. He is associated with the so-called 'Principle of Linguistic Relativity' or 'Sapir–Whorf Hypothesis' (see *Sapir–Whorf Hypothesis*).

Whorf was born in Winthrop, Massachusetts, April 24, 1897. His parents descended from early American settlers and his father, Harry Church Whorf, was a commercial artist, stage designer–director, and amateur geologist.

Benjamin exhibited a comparable range of curiosity as a youth and graduated from Massachusetts Institute of Technology in 1918 with a BS in Chemical Engineering. In 1919 he was hired by the Hartford Fire Insurance Company as a fire prevention engineer, then a field without academic recognition. Equally new was Hartford's notion that fire inspection and prevention could be a customer service, and Whorf became the recognized expert in this area. He ultimately became assistant secretary of the company, which generously allowed him leave to follow his linguistic and anthropological interests. He worked there until his death from cancer on July 26, 1941. He and his wife Celia Inez Peckham had three children.

An autodidact in linguistics, Whorf began to study Hebrew in 1924, inspired by Fabre d'Olivet's *La langue hébraïque restituée* (1815–16), a work that revived a kabalistic conceit which saw in Semitic sounds and characters mystical meanings. His original motivation was a desire to reconcile modern science with biblical authority: he was brought up Methodist Episcopal, had questioned the theory of evolution, and completed a lengthy manuscript on science and religion in 1925.

Whorf expanded his interests to study Aztec and then Mayan hieroglyphics. Using the collection at the Watkinson Library in Hartford, Whorf extended his pursuits to anthropology and archeology. By 1928 he was working at many other collections in the northeast; he has begun correspondence with scholars of ancient Mexican language and culture; and he published his first article, 'An Aztec account of the period of the Toltec decline.' Whorf started attending scholarly conferences and delivering papers. Although he did not accurately decipher Mayan ideograms, he correctly proposed that they were a system for writing spoken language. In 1929–30 the Social Science Research Council granted him a fellowship, which allowed him to visit Mexico and do further study of Mexican languages.

In 1931 Whorf began to study with Edward Sapir (see *Sapir, Edward*), the prominent anthropological linguist and student of Franz Boas (see *Boas, Franz*), who had come to nearby Yale University. Although he remained an amateur, Whorf now worked in the company of leading professional linguists and found particular resonance between his own ideas and those of Sapir. His study of Hopi, begun in 1932, led to his fullest formulations of the theory that different languages express different understandings of the world, the so-called 'Linguistic Relativity Principle,' particularly in 'Some verbal categories of Hopi' (1938) and 'The relation of habitual thought and behavior to language' (1941).

Whorf was a popular lecturer and wrote accessible versions of his thesis in *Technology Review*—'Science and linguistics' (1940), 'Linguistics as an exact science' (1940), 'Languages and logic' (1941)—and in the *The Theosophist*—'Language, mind, and reality' (1942).

Bibliography

Carroll J B 1956 *Language Thought and Reality: Selected Writings of Benjamin Lee Whorf*. Technology Press of Massachusetts Institute of Technology, Cambridge, MA

Williams, Glyn (1939–)
D. Brown

Glyn Williams is a Welsh sociologist who has developed a sociological critique of sociolinguistic theory and practice. His research deals with questions of language and social identity in Wales and has led to a critical appraisal of the theoretical assumptions in sociolinguistic writing. His work searches for a consistency of theory and method in the way that sociology deals with language.

Williams was born in Wales in 1939 and received his education at Brunel, completing his PhD at the University of Wales. He was appointed as a lecturer in the department of Sociology and Social Policy at the University of Wales, Bangor in the 1970s. He is currently attached to the Research Center Wales, at the University of Wales, Bangor where he is a reader.

His interest in Welsh identity began with an investigation of the Welsh émigré community in Patagonia, which resulted in the publishing of a historical study of Welsh colonization in 1975 and a bibliography on the topic in 1980, followed by a book *The Welsh in Patagonia* in 1991. He edited a book on social and cultural change in contemporary Wales in 1978.

This was followed by an edited collection on the sociology of the Welsh language in 1987. His language interest has lead to a significant theoretical text, which engages with the normative premises of much of sociolinguistics entitled: *Sociolinguistics: A Sociological Critique* (1992).

Following this, his most recent work on Language Planning has grown out of the European Commission's recent research interest in ethnic and national minorities. Williams has participated in the *Euromosaic Project*, which has funded research on ethnic minorities and minority languages within the wider European context. This resulted in a report for the European commission, done in collaboration with his colleague Deleth Morris at the University of Wales, forms the basis of his most recent publication on language planning and language use. This work contains further developments of his theoretical critique of social theory and methodology on language—for example an important short critique of Bourdieu's *Language and Symbolic Power* (1982) (see *Symbolic Power and Language*).

His interest in theory extends to a recent publication of a book on *French Discourse Analysis* (1998a). William's theoretical influences are broad, ranging from poststructuralist discourse analysis to dependency theory, the work of the Italian Marxist Antonio Gramsci (see *Gramsci, Antonio*) and critical theory. Williams identifies functionalist patterns of thinking as the central weakness in sociolinguistic writings.

He argues that language groups are a relevant feature of social organization and social inequality and that they are underestimated in conventional sociology. His work has been praised as 'exposing the often muddled treatment of minority languages within the social sciences in general and sociolinguistics in particular.' His current and future work on the role of minority language situation in Wales is likely to find a broader influence in the European context.

Bibliography

Williams G 1992 *Sociolinguistics: A Sociological Critique*. Routledge, London

Williams G 1998a *French Discourse Analysis: the Method of Post-Structuralism*. RKP, London

Williams G 1998b Language and ethnicity: the sociological perspective. In: Fishman J (ed.) *Language and Ethnicity*. Oxford University Press, Oxford, UK

Williams G, Morris D 2000 *Language Planning and Language Use: a Study of Welsh in a Global Age*. University of Wales, Cardiff, UK

Wodak, Ruth (1950–)

C. Anthonissen

Ruth Wodak is best known for her work in Critical Discourse Analysis at the University of Vienna, Austria. She is one of a number of scholars (like Fairclough, Fowler, Kress, Van Leeuwen, Van Dijk) who consider discourse as social action and who follow Halliday's (see *Halliday, Michael Alexander Kirkwood*) notion of grammar as a system developed to function optimally in communication. As professor in Applied Linguistics at the University of Vienna, and as a research professor (1999–2002) in the Austrian Academy of Sciences, she has introduced and supervised innovative research into social and political discourses of various kinds.

Wodak is the founder of an approach referred to as Discourse Sociolinguistics, that has developed analytic methods for disclosing and demystifying the ways in which language functions in establishing, sustaining, and challenging power relations. This approach follows principles set out in Critical Theory, a social theory developed by the Frankfurt School since the 1930s. It accepts the subjectivity of researchers, and it recognizes the interdependence of language and context. Thus the necessity of being explicit about the context in which texts are produced and interpreted is accepted.

As editor and co-editor of research publications on nationalistic, chauvinistic, racist, anti-Semitic, and sexist discourses Wodak has contributed to developing new insights into institutional discourse. In the latter part of the twentieth century institutions have become significant instruments for naturalizing social hierarchies through the kinds of discourses they produce and perpetuate. Wodak's interests in sociolinguistics, psycholinguistics, and discourse analysis are reflected in her investigation of political discourses, discourses in institutions such as hospitals, embassies, schools, the printed and broadcast media, Austrian and European governmental organizations, and discourses of stereotyping, prejudice, and discrimination.

Wodak was born on July 12, 1950 in London as the daughter of Austrian-Jewish exiles. The family returned to Vienna in 1953. She studied at the University of Vienna, receiving her Doctorate in Linguistics with highest distinction in 1974, and completing her Habilitation research in Sociolinguistics and Psycholinguistics in 1980. For her doctorate dissertation she was awarded the Theodor Körner Prize, and for her habilitation she was awarded the Kardinal Innitzer Prize. Continued research and development of new approaches, themes, and methods of analysis in the area of critical linguistics was rewarded in 1996 when Wodak received the prestigious Ludwig Wittgenstein Prize from the Austrian *Fonds zur Förderung der wissenschaftlichen Forschung* (Fund for Development of Scientific Research).

With the Wittgenstein prize Wodak established the Wittgenstein Research Center, 'Discourse, Politics, and Identity.' Here a team of researchers uses the discourse-historical method of critical discourse analysis for scholarly reflection on major discourses currently evolving in Europe. The projects focus on the theme of a new European identity based in the recently established European Union. The tension between supranational and national organization of established communities is being investigated. First discourses on unemployment in the EU were collected, analyzed and interpreted; second discourses on neutrality and security were considered. Currently the center's research is directed at discursive construction of alternative memories on the *Wehrmacht* and taboos around this sensitive topic.

Wodak has contributed significantly to our understanding of how social discrimination is discursively constructed and reproduced. Drawing on an enormous source of empirical data collected by researchers in Vienna she shows not only how discourse functions in establishing societal structures, but also how discourse can disclose inequality and injustice and can be applied to restructuring pathological patterns.

See also: Critical Sociolinguistics; Discourse Analysis and the Law; Ideology.

Bibliography

Muntigl P, Weiss G, Wodak R 2000 *European Union Discourses on Un/employment*. Benjamins, Amsterdam

Reisigl M, Wodak R (eds.) 2000 *The Semiotics of Racism—Approaches in Critical Discourse Analysis*. Passagen, Vienna

Reisigl M, Wodak R 2001 *Discourse and Discrimination—Rhetorics of Racism and Antisemitism*. Routledge, London

Titscher S, Wodak R, Meyer M, Vetter E 1998 *Methoden der Textanalyse: Leitfaden und Überblick*. Westdeutscher, Wiesbaden, Germany

Wodak R (ed.) 1989 *Language, Power, and Ideology*. Benjamins, Amsterdam

Wodak R 1996 *Disorders of Discourse*. Longman, London

Wodak R, Nowak P, Pelikan J, Gruber H, DeCillia R, Mitten R 1990 *Wir sind alle unschuldige Täter. Diskurshistorische Studien zum Nachkriegsantisemitismus*. Suhrkamp, Frankfurt, Germany

Wodak R, Matouschek B 1993 We are dealing with people whose origins one can clearly tell just by looking: Critical discourse analysis and the study of neoracism in contemporary Austria. *Discourse and Society* **2**(4): 225–48

Wodak R, Menz F, Mitten R, Stern F 1994 *Die Sprachen der Vergangenheiten*. Suhrkamp, Frankfurt, Germany

Wolfram, Walt (1941–)

C. T. Adger

Walt Wolfram has pioneered research on a broad range of vernacular US dialects, including African American English, Puerto Rican English, Appalachian English, Ozark English, Southern English, American Indian English, Vietnamese English, and most recently, Outer Banks and Lumbee English in North Carolina. Observing the principle of linguistic gratuity whereby 'investigators who have obtained linguistic data from members of a speech community should actively pursue positive ways [to] return linguistic favors' (Wolfram 1993: 226), he has applied sociolinguistic research findings to educational issues (e.g., Wolfram et al. 1999), in teaching, and in making his research findings accessible to the community (e.g., Wolfram and Schilling Estes 1997).

Wolfram grew up in a German-speaking, working-class community in Philadelphia. He earned a PhD at Hartford Seminary in 1969 and pursued a career in theoretical and applied sociolinguistic research at the Center for Applied Linguistics for 25 years. Concurrently, he taught at the University of the District of Columbia, returning linguistic favors to the African American community whose language he began studying as a graduate student. There he trained speech/language pathologists and broadly influenced the field regarding language diagnosis and assessment practices, and normal language behavior in African American Vernacular English (AAVE) speakers. Early in his career, Wolfram published the first descriptive linguistic volume on AAVE (Wolfram 1969). Subsequent work on this dialect has illuminated similarities to Southern English and other regional dialects, and examined the sociolinguistic significance of obscure structures such as [NP$_i$ CALL NP$_i$ V-ING] (*She calls herself saving money*).

In 1992, Wolfram became the first William C. Friday Distinguished Professor in the English Department at North Carolina State University, where he established the North Carolina Language and Life Project for study of that state's richly varied dialects. Theoretical contributions of work on Lumbee English, Ocracoke English, and Hyde County Anglo-American and African American English dialects include explanations for the development and maintenance of vernacular dialect norms based on linguistic, sociohistorical, sociolinguistic, sociopsychological, and ideological factors. He introduced the notion of endangered dialects to the language endangerment canon. Wolfram and his students have presented sociolinguistic descriptions of North Carolina dialects to schoolchildren in dialect awareness curricula, constructed a prize-winning dialect museum exhibit for the Ocracoke Preservation Society, and developed books, videos, CDs, and audiotapes that report the research for lay audiences.

Wolfram's contributions include dialect research that is broad in scope but also particular and integrative, as well as unflagging commitment to increasing public awareness of the role of vernacular dialects in society. At the same time he has served the profession in leadership (most recently as president of the Linguistic Society of America for 2001) and teaching positions beyond his institution.

See also: Dialect and Dialectology; Field Methods in Modern Dialect and Variation Studies.

Bibliography

Wolfram W 1969 *A Linguistic Description of Detroit Negro Speech*. Center for Applied Linguistics, Washington, DC

Wolfram W 1993 Ethical considerations in language awareness programs. *Issues in Applied Linguistics* **4**: 225–56

Wolfram W, Adger C T, Christian D 1999 *Dialects in Schools and Communities*. Erlbaum, Mahweh, NJ

Wolfram W, Schilling-Estes N 1997 *Hoi Toide on the Outer Banks: The Story of the Ocracoke Brogue*. The University of North Carolina Press, Chapel Hill, NC

Alphabetical List of Articles

Titles are listed in alphabetical order along with their author(s) and corresponding page number.

Academies: Dictionaries and Standards L. C. Mugglestone	615
Accent J. M. Y. Simpson	293
Adolescent Peer Group Language R. L. Taylor	297
Advertising M. L. Geis	209
Ammon, Ulrich (1943–) A. Deumert	844
Anthropological Linguistics E. Keating	5
Antilanguage P. A. Chilton	109
Applied Linguistics and Sociolinguistics D. R. Preston	691
Areal Linguistics J. M. Y. Simpson	423
Artificial Languages A. Large	616
Attitude Surveys: Question–Answer Process H. Schuman	761
Attitudes and Behavior W. S. Bainbridge	6
Audience Design A. Bell	109
Bakhtin, Mikhail M. (1895–1975) J. M. Weir	845
Bamgbose, Ayo (1932–) R. Mesthrie	846
Baugh, John (1949–) R. Mesthrie	847
Bernstein, Basil (1924–) K. Rajagopalan	848
Bickerton, Derek (1926–) G. G. Gilbert	849

Alphabetical List of Articles

Bilingual Education M. E. Brisk	696
Bilingualism and Language Acquisition C. Letts	430
Bilingualism, Individual F. Grosjean	10
Bilingualism, Societal M. H. A. Blanc	16
Black English in Education: UK M. Dalphinis	700
Blessings B. G. Szuchewycz	211
Blommaert, Jan (1961–) K. Maryns	850
Boas, Franz (1858–1942) R. Darnell	851
Borrowing J. Heath	432
Bourdieu, Pierre (1930–) C. B. Vigouroux	852
Bright, William (1928–) B. B. Kachru	853
Business Language G. Rasmussen	212
Cameron, Deborah (1958–) S. S. McRae	854
Chain Shifts G. J. Docherty & D. J. L. Watt	303
Child Language: An Overview S. Strömqvist	703
Class and Language F. Gregersen	307
Coates, Jennifer (1942–) S. S. McRae	855
Code, Sociolinguistic U. Ammon	214
Code-mixing R. Mesthrie	442
Code-switching: Discourse Models P. Auer	443
Code-switching: Overview K. M. McCormick	447

Code-switching: Sociopragmatic Models S. Gross	454
Code-switching: Structural Models R. M. Bhatt	456
Communication K. L. Berge	22
Communicative Competence A. Duranti	29
Contact Languages S. G. Thomason	461
Context U. M. Quasthoff	218
Conversation Analysis P. Drew	110
Conversational Maxims J. Thomas	116
Cooper, Robert Leon (1931–) B. Spolsky	855
Cooperative Principle J. Thomas	121
Corpus Linguistics and Sociolinguistics M. Sebba & S. D. Fligelstone. Revised by W. A. Kretzschmar Jr.	765
Critical Language Awareness J. L. Mey	541
Critical Sociolinguistics G. Kress	542
Cummins, Jim (1949–) C. Baker	856
Das Gupta, Jyotirindra (1933–) L. M. Khubchandani	857
Data Collection in Linguistics J. E. Miller & R. Cann	769
Deaf Community: Structures and Interaction J. G. Kyle	125
DeCamp, David (1927–79) R. Le Page	858
Dialect and Dialectology S. Romaine	310
Dialect Humor M. L. Apte	319
Dialogism T. A. Marshall	127

929

Alphabetical List of Articles

Diglossia A. Hudson	226
Discourse A. McHoul	133
Discourse Analysis and the Law D. Eades	231
Discourse in Cross-linguistic and Cross-cultural Contexts M. Clyne	145
Discrimination and Minority Languages T. Skutnabb-Kangas & R. Phillipson	545
Dittmar, Norbert (1943–) P. Schlobinski	859
Doctor–Patient Language M. Lacoste	152
Dorian, Nancy (1936–) S. Romaine	860
Ebonics and African American Vernacular English J. Baugh	708
Ecology of Language J. M. Y. Simpson	30
Education and Language: Overview K. Perera	710
Educational Failure J. R. Edwards	714
Edwards, John Robert (1947–) W. F. Mackey	861
Emeneau, Murray Barnson (1904–) W. Bright	862
Endangered Languages L. A. Grenoble & L. J. Whaley	465
Endangered Languages Projects (An Inventory) L. A. Grenoble & L. J. Whaley	835
English as a Foreign Language G. Abbott	467
English Grammar in British Schools A. M. Philp	723
Ethnicity and Language E. F. Kotzé	324
Ethnicity and the Crossing of Boundaries B. Rampton	321
Ethnography of Speaking G. Philipsen	154

Ethnolinguistic Vitality H. GILES	472
Ethnomethodology G. PSATHAS	160
Fairclough, Norman (1941–) H. JANKS	862
Fasold, Ralph W. (1940–) W. WOLFRAM	863
Ferguson, Charles A. (1921–98) J. A. FISHMAN	864
Field Methods in Modern Dialect and Variation Studies K. HAZEN	776
Field Methods: Ethnographic M. L. APTE	772
Fieldwork and Field Methods U. CANGER	779
Fieldwork Ethics and Community Responsibility B. JOHNSTONE	781
Firth, J. R. (1890–1960) F. R. PALMER	865
Fishman, Joshua A. (1926–) B. SPOLSKY	867
Foreigner Talk M. CLYNE	474
Forensic Phonetics and Sociolinguistics P. FOULKES & J. P. FRENCH	329
Formulaic Language F. COULMAS	233
Foucault, Michel (1926–84) J. C. MAHER	868
Gay Language W. L. LEAP	332
Gender and Language K. M. MCCORMICK	336
Gender, Education, and Language J. SWANN	735
Genre T. THREADGOLD	235
Giles, Howard (1946–) J. BRADAC	869
Gilliéron, Jules (1854–1926) T. HILL	870

Alphabetical List of Articles

Goffman, Erving (1922–82)   871
R. L. Schmitt

Görlach, Manfred (1937–)   872
E. W. Schneider

Gramsci, Antonio (1891–1937)   873
N. Helsloot

Grierson, Sir George Abraham (1851–1941)   874
J. C. Wright

Gumperz, John J. (1922–)   875
N. Berenz

Hall, Robert A. Jr (1911–97)   876
M. Danesi

Halliday, Michael Alexander Kirkwood (1925–)   877
J. Fine

Haugen, Einar (1906–94)   877
N. Hasselmo

Heath, Shirley Brice   878
C. B. Cazden

Hegemony   550
G. Mininni

Heritage Languages   619
J. Cummins

Hesseling, Dirk Christiaan (1859–1941)   879
G. G. Gilbert

Hill, Jane (1939–)   881
V. Santiago-Irizarry

Home Language and School Language   737
M. MacLure

Honorifics   552
M. Shibatani

Hymes, Dell Hathaway (1927–)   882
N. H. Hornberger

Identity and Language   165
R. Mesthrie & A. Tabouret-Keller

Ideology   559
A. Luke

Institutional Language   239
S. Sarangi

Interactional Sociolinguistic Research Methods   784
N. Berenz

Interlanguage   475
E. Tarone

International Languages U. Ammon	620
Internet Resources for Sociolinguistics A. Deumert	838
Intertwined Languages P. C. Muysken	481
Jaberg, Karl (1877–1959) T. Hill	882
Jargons P. Mühlhäusler	483
Kachru, Braj B. (1932–) R. V. Pandharipande	883
Khubchandani, Lachman M. (1932–) R. K. Agnihotri	884
Kinesics A. Kendon	169
Kinship Terminology E. L. Schusky	172
Koinés R. Mesthrie	485
Kurath, Hans (1891–1992) T. Hill	885
Labov, William (1927–) D. Sankoff	885
Lakoff, Robin Tolmach J. Bennett	887
Lambert, Wallace E. (1922–) G. R. Tucker	888
Language J. M. Y. Simpson	31
Language Adaptation and Modernization S. Bowerman	626
Language as a Social Reality T. Pateman	34
Language Change and Language Acquisition E. L. Bavin	345
Language Conflict D. P. Pattanayak	563
Language Development H. R. Dua	630
Language Diffusion Policy C. G. MacLean	634

Alphabetical List of Articles

Language Enclaves — 489
K. Mattheier

Language in Society: Overview — 36
M. L. Apte

Language in the Workplace — 177
B. Holmqvist & P. B. Andersen

Language Loyalty — 492
R. Mesthrie

Language Maintenance, Shift, and Death — 493
R. Mesthrie

Language Planning: Models — 644
A. Deumert

Language Spread — 498
R. Mesthrie

Language Transfer and Substrates — 499
T. Odlin

Le Page, Robert (1920–) — 889
A Tabouret-Keller

Lewis, E. Glyn (1920–94) — 890
D. Brown

Lingua Franca — 503
M. Barotchi

Linguicide — 567
T. Skutnabb-Kangas & R. Phillipson

Linguistic Census — 648
L. M. Khubchandani

Linguistic Habitus — 650
I. Gogolin

Linguistic Imperialism — 570
R. Phillipson & T. Skutnabb-Kangas

Literacy — 739
C. J. Daswani

Literacy: Research, Measurement, and Innovation — 787
D. Wagner

Literary Language — 243
R. Carter

Malinowski, Bronislaw Kaspar (1884–1942) — 891
A. T. Campbell

Manipulation — 574
N. Fairclough

Maps: Dialect and Language — 350
J. M. Kirk

Marxist Theories of Language G. Mininni	575
Mazrui, Ali A. (1933–) A. M. Mazrui	891
McDavid, Raven Ioor, Jr (1911–84) T. Hill	892
Media Language and Communication K. C. Schrøder	246
Medical Language J. Maclean & J. C. Maher	256
Migrants and Migration A. M. Pavlinic	504
Milroy, Lesley (1944–) Li Wei	893
Minority Languages J. M. Y. Simpson	579
Missionaries and Language P. Lewis	509
Mufwene, Salikoko S. (1947–) R. Mesthrie	894
Mühlhäusler, Peter (1947–) P. Baker	895
Multiculturalism and Language J. R. Edwards	48
Multidimensional Scaling W. C. Rau	793
Multilingual States D. D. Laitin	652
Muysken, Pieter Cornelis (1950–) A. Bruyn	896
Myers-Scotton, Carol S. Gross	897
Narrative, Natural M. Toolan	179
National Language/Official Language C. M. Eastman	657
Nationalism and Language L. Greenfeld	662
Native Speaker A. Davies	512
New Englishes B. B. Kachru	519

Alphabetical List of Articles

Nida, Eugene Albert (1914–)   898
R. E. Longacre

Observer's Paradox   802
A. Davies

Observing and Analyzing Classroom Talk   803
A. D. Edwards & D. P. G. Westgate

Oracy   746
A. M. Wilkinson

Orthography   669
M. Sebba

Paulston, Christina Bratt (1932–)   899
M. Swain

Phatic Communion   186
D. Abercrombie

Pidgins and Creoles: An Overview   524
L. Todd

Pidgins and Creoles: Models   530
J. Aitchison

Pidgins and Creoles: Morphology   536
F. C. V. Jones

Pidgins, Creoles, and Minority Dialects in Education   747
J. Siegel

Platt, John T.   900
M. Görlach

Politeness   187
G. Kasper

Politicized Language   580
A. Davies

Politics and Language   584
P. A. Chilton

Poplack, Shana   901
G. Van Herk

Power and Language   591
N. Fairclough

Power Differentials and Language   597
P. L. van den Berghe

Pragmatics and Sociolinguistics   50
J. L. Mey

Prescription in Dictionaries   672
L. C. Mugglestone

Prescriptive and Descriptive Grammar   58
C. Cullen

Professional Associations R. Mesthrie	840
Quirk, Professor Sir (Charles) Randolph (1920–) J. Roberts	901
Register W. Downes	259
Reinecke, John E. (1904–82) G. G. Gilbert	903
Reliability/Validity E. Babbie	809
Religion and Language J. F. A. Sawyer	262
Representation R. Fowler	604
Reversing Language Shift J. A. Fishman	673
Rickford, John Russell J. Baugh	904
Role Theory R. H. Turner	59
Romaine, Suzanne (1951–) C. M. Sangster	905
Sacks, Harvey (1935–75) G. Psathas	905
Salvage Work (Endangered Languages) N. C. Dorian	813
Sankoff, Gillian (1943–) C. Surek-Clark	906
Sapir, Edward (1884–1939) R. Darnell	907
Sapir–Whorf Hypothesis O. Werner	65
Saussurean Tradition and Sociolinguistics J. E. Joseph	73
Saville-Troike, Muriel R. V. Pandharipande	908
Scaling E. Babbie	816
Schegloff, Emanuel (1937–) J. Heritage	909
Schiffrin, Deborah (1951–) S. Hunt	910
	937

Alphabetical List of Articles

School Language Policies D. J. Corson	679
Schuchardt, Hugo (1842–1927) G. G. Gilbert	911
Semilingualism J. Cummins	606
Shuy, Roger W. (1931–) J. Kreeft Peyton	912
Slang: Sociology I. L. Allen	265
Small Group Research W. S. Bainbridge	821
Social Class M. W. Macy	362
Social Networks A. L. Milroy	370
Social Psychology W. S. Bainbridge	80
Socialization C. B. Cazden	87
Sociolinguistic Area J. D'Souza	538
Sociolinguistic Variation R. Mesthrie	377
Sociolinguistics and Language Change J. Milroy	389
Sociolinguistics Journals: A Critical Survey N. Coupland	842
Sociolinguistics of Sign Language C. Lucas	89
Sociology of Language W. S. Bainbridge	92
Sociometry W. S. Bainbridge	827
Sociophonetics S. Wright. Revised by C. M. Sangster	391
Sound Change J. J. Ohala	396
Speech Accommodation H. Giles	193
Speech Act Theory: An Overview K. Allan	197

Speech and Writing   270
J. E. Miller

Speech Community   105
B. B. Kachru

Speech Play   276
M. L. Apte

Spoken Language in the Classroom   749
N. Mercer

Spolsky, Bernard (1932–)   913
R. Mesthrie

Srivastava, Ravindra Nath (1936–92)   914
R. K. Agnihotri

Standard English and Educational Policy   753
M. Farr & A. Ball

Standardization   681
E. Haugen

Statistics in Sociolinguistics   828
D. Sankoff

Statistics: Principal Languages of the World (UNESCO)   683
J. M. Y. Simpson

Street, Brian (1943–)   914
M. Prinsloo

Stereotype and Social Attitudes   608
M. L. Apte

Style   280
M. Short

Subcultures and Countercultures   401
R. L. Taylor

Symbolic Power and Language   610
C. Vigouroux

Syntactic Change   407
N. Vincent

Taboo Words   283
M. L. Apte

Tannen, Deborah   916
J. Bennett

Teaching Endangered Languages   757
L. Hinton

The Atlas of North American English: Methods and Findings   412
S. Ash

The Internet and Language   287
C. Thurlow

Alphabetical List of Articles

The Linguistic Marketplace 612
I. Gogolin

Trudgill, Peter John (1943–) 916
P. Kerswill

Tucker, G. Richard (1942–) 918
J. Crandall

Urban and Rural Forms of Language 418
A. M. Hamilton

Valdman, Albert (1931–) 919
B. Spolsky

Van Name, Addison (1835–1922) 919
G. G. Gilbert

Verbal Duel 289
R. Ackerman

Verbal Hygiene 688
D. Cameron

Vernacular 420
R. Macaulay

Voloshinov, Valentin Nikolavic (1895–1936) 920
D. Brown

Weinreich, Uriel (1926–67) 921
T. Hill

Wenker, Georg (1852–1911) 922
T. Hill

Whorf, Benjamin Lee (1897–1941) 923
J. H. Stam

Williams, Glyn (1939–) 924
D. Brown

Wodak, Ruth (1950–) 925
C. Anthonissen

Wolfram, Walt (1941–) 926
C. T. Adger

List of Contributors

Contributors are listed in alphabetical order together with their affiliations. Titles of articles which they have written follow in page number order. Co-authorship is indicated by*; deceased authors are indicated by †.

ABBOTT, G. (University of Manchester, UK)
English as a Foreign Language: 467

ABERCROMBIE, D. †
Phatic Communion: 186

ACKERMAN, R. (West Hollywood, CA, USA)
Verbal Duel: 289

ADGER, C. T. (Center for Applied Linguistics, Washington, DC, USA)
Wolfram, Walt (1941–): 926

AGNIHOTRI, R. K. (Delhi, India)
Khubchandani, Lachman M. (1932–): 884; *Srivastava, Ravindra Nath (1936–92)*: 914

AITCHISON, J. (University of Oxford, UK)
Pidgins and Creoles: Models: 530

ALLAN, K. (University of Cambridge, UK)
Speech Act Theory: An Overview: 197

ALLEN, I. L. (University of Connecticut, Storrs, CT, USA)
Slang: Sociology: 265

AMMON, U. (University of Duisburg, Germany)
Code, Sociolinguistic: 214; *International Languages*: 620

ANDERSEN, P. B. (University of Aarhus, Denmark)
**Language in the Workplace*: 177

ANTHONISSEN, C. (University of the Western Cape, Bellville, South Africa)
Wodak, Ruth (1950–): 925

APTE, M. L. (Duke University, Durham, NC, USA)
Language in Society: Overview: 36; *Speech Play*: 276; *Taboo Words*: 283; *Dialect Humor*: 319; *Stereotype and Social Attitudes*: 608; *Field Methods: Ethnographic*: 772

ASH, S. (University of Pennsylvania, Philadelphia, PA, USA)
The Atlas of North American English: Methods and Findings: 412

AUER, P. (Albert-Ludwigs-Universität, Freiburg, Germany)
Code-switching: Discourse Models: 443

BABBIE, E. (Chapman College, Orange, CA, USA)
Reliability/Validity: 809; *Scaling*: 816

BAINBRIDGE, W. S. (Towson University, MD, USA)
Attitudes and Behavior: 6; *Social Psychology*: 80; *Sociology of Language*: 92; *Small Group Research*: 821; *Sociometry*: 827

List of Contributors

BAKER, C. (University of Wales, Bangor, UK)
Cummins, Jim (1949–): 856

BAKER, P. (University of Westminster, London, UK)
Mühlhäusler, Peter (1947–): 895

BALL, A. (University of Michigan, Ann Arbor, MI, USA)
*Standard English and Educational Policy: 753

BAROTCHI, M. (Sheffield, UK)
Lingua Franca: 503

BAUGH, J. (Stanford University, CA, USA)
Ebonics and African American Vernacular English: 708; *Rickford, John Russell*: 904

BAVIN, E. L. (La Trobe University, Bundoora, VIC, Australia)
Language Change and Language Acquisition: 345

BELL, A. (Auckland University of Technology, New Zealand)
Audience Design: 109

BENNETT, J. (University of Cape Town, South Africa)
Lakoff, Robin Tolmach: 887; *Tannen, Deborah*: 916

BERENZ, N. (Inter American University of Puerto Rico, San Germán, PR, USA)
Interactional Sociolinguistic Research Methods: 784; *Gumperz, John J. (1922–)*: 875

BERGE, K. L. (University of Stockholm, Sweden)
Communication: 22

BHATT, R. M. (University of Illinois at Urbana-Champaign, IL, USA)
Code-switching: Structural Models: 456

BLANC, M. H. A. (Sheepscombe, UK)
Bilingualism, Societal: 16

BOWERMAN, S. (University of Cape Town, South Africa)
Language Adaptation and Modernization: 626

BRADAC, J. (University of California, Santa Barbara, CA, USA)
Giles, Howard (1946–): 869

BRIGHT, W. (University of Colorado, Boulder, CO, USA)
Emeneau, Murray Barnson (1904–): 862

BRISK, M. E. (Boston University, MA, USA)
Bilingual Education: 696

BROWN, D. (University of Natal, Durban, South Africa)
Lewis, E. Glyn (1920–94): 890; *Voloshinov, Valentin Nikolavic (1895–1936)*: 920; *Williams, Glyn (1939–)*: 924

BRUYN, A. (Leiden University, The Netherlands)
Muysken, Pieter Cornelis (1950–): 896

CAMERON, D. (Institute of Education, London, UK)
Verbal Hygiene: 688

CAMPBELL, A. T. (University of Edinburgh, UK)
Malinowski, Bronislaw Kaspar (1884–1942): 891

CANGER, U. (University of Copenhagen, Denmark)
Fieldwork and Field Methods: 779

List of Contributors

CANN, R. (University of Edinburgh, UK)
Data Collection in Linguistics: 769

CARTER, R. (University of Nottingham, UK)
Literary Language: 243

CAZDEN, C. B. (Harvard University, Cambridge, MA, USA)
Socialization: 87; *Heath, Shirley Brice*: 878

CHILTON, P. A. (University of Warwick, UK)
Antilanguage: 109; *Politics and Language*: 584

CLYNE, M. (Monash University, Clayton, VIC, Australia)
Discourse in Cross-linguistic and Cross-cultural Contexts: 145; *Foreigner Talk*: 474

CORSON, D. J. (The Ontario Institute for Studies in Education, Toronto, ON, Canada)
School Language Policies: 679

COULMAS, F. (Chuo University, Hachioji, Japan)
Formulaic Language: 233

COUPLAND, N. (Cardiff University, UK)
Sociolinguistics Journals: A Critical Survey: 842

CRANDALL, J. (University of Maryland, Baltimore County, MD, USA)
Tucker, G. Richard (1942–): 918

CULLEN, C. (University of York, UK)
Prescriptive and Descriptive Grammar: 58

CUMMINS, J. (University of Toronto, ON, Canada)
Semilingualism: 606; *Heritage Languages*: 619

D'SOUZA, J. (Pune, India)
Sociolinguistic Area: 538

DALPHINIS, M. (Edith Cavell School, London, UK)
Black English in Education: UK: 700

DANESI, M. (Toronto, ON, Canada)
Hall, Robert A. Jr (1911–97): 876

DARNELL, R. (University of Western Ontario, London, ON, Canada)
Boas, Franz (1858–1942): 851; *Sapir, Edward (1884–1939)*: 907

DASWANI, C. J. (National Council for Educational Research and Training, New Delhi, India)
Literacy: 739

DAVIES, A. (University of Edinburgh, UK)
Native Speaker: 512; *Politicized Language*: 580; *Observer's Paradox*: 802

DEUMERT, A. (University of Heidelberg, Germany)
Language Planning: Models: 644; *Internet Resources for Sociolinguistics*: 838; *Ammon, Ulrich (1943–)*: 844

DOCHERTY, G. J. (University of Newcastle, UK)
Chain Shifts: 303

DORIAN, N. C. (Bryn Mawr College, PA, USA)
Salvage Work (Endangered Languages): 813

DOWNES, W. (University of East Anglia, Norwich, UK)
Register: 259

List of Contributors

DREW, P. (University of York, UK)
Conversation Analysis: 110

DUA, H. R. (Central Institute of Indian Languages, Mysore, India)
Language Development: 630

DURANTI, A. (University of California at Los Angeles, CA, USA)
Communicative Competence: 29

EADES, D. (University of Hawaii, Honolulu, HI, USA)
Discourse Analysis and the Law: 231

EASTMAN, C. M. †
National Language/Official Language: 657

EDWARDS, A. D. (University of Newcastle, UK)
**Observing and Analyzing Classroom Talk*: 803

EDWARDS, J. R. (St Francis Xavier University, Antigonish, NS, Canada)
Multiculturalism and Language: 48; *Educational Failure*: 714

FAIRCLOUGH, N. (Lancaster University, UK)
Manipulation: 574; *Power and Language*: 591

FARR, M. (University of Illinois, Chicago, IL, USA)
**Standard English and Educational Policy*: 753

FINE, J. (Bar-Ilan University, Ramat-Gan, Israel)
Halliday, Michael Alexander Kirkwood (1925–): 877

FISHMAN, J. A. (Stanford University, CA, USA)
Reversing Language Shift: 673; *Ferguson, Charles A. (1921–98)*: 864

FLIGELSTONE, S. D. (Lancaster University, UK)
**Corpus Linguistics and Sociolinguistics*: 765

FOULKES, P. (University of York, UK)
**Forensic Phonetics and Sociolinguistics*: 329

FOWLER, R. (University of East Anglia, Norwich, UK)
Representation: 604

FRENCH, J. P. (J. P. French Associates, York, UK)
**Forensic Phonetics and Sociolinguistics*: 329

GEIS, M. L. (Ohio State University, Columbus, OH, USA)
Advertising: 209

GILBERT, G. G. (Southern Illinois University, Carbondale, IL, USA)
Bickerton, Derek (1926–): 849; *Hesseling, Dirk Christiaan (1859–1941)*: 879; *Reinecke, John E. (1904–82)*: 903; *Schuchardt, Hugo (1842–1927)*: 911; *Van Name, Addison (1835–1922)*: 919

GILES, H. (University of California, Santa Barbara, CA, USA)
Speech Accommodation: 193; *Ethnolinguistic Vitality*: 472

GOGOLIN, I. (University of Hamburg, Germany)
The Linguistic Marketplace: 612; *Linguistic Habitus*: 650

GÖRLACH, M. (University of Cologne, Germany)
Platt, John T.: 900

GREENFELD, L. (Harvard University, Cambridge, MA, USA)
Nationalism and Language: 662

GREGERSEN, F. (University of Copenhagen, Denmark)
Class and Language: 307

GRENOBLE, L. A. (Dartmouth College, Hanover, NH, USA)
**Endangered Languages*: 465; **Endangered Languages Projects (An Inventory)*: 835

GROSJEAN, F. (University of Neuchatel, Switzerland)
Bilingualism, Individual: 10

GROSS, S. (East Tennessee State University, Johnson City, TN, USA)
Code-switching: Sociopragmatic Models: 454; *Myers-Scotton, Carol*: 897

HAMILTON, A. M. (Athens, GA, USA)
Urban and Rural Forms of Language: 418

HASSELMO, N. (University of Minnesota, Minneapolis, MN, USA)
Haugen, Einar (1906–94): 877

HAUGEN, E. †
Standardization: 681

HAZEN, K. (West Virginia University, Morgantown, WV, USA)
Field Methods in Modern Dialect and Variation Studies: 776

HEATH, J. (University of Michigan, Ann Arbor, MI, USA)
Borrowing: 432

HELSLOOT, N. (Amsterdam, The Netherlands)
Gramsci, Antonio (1891–1937): 873

HERITAGE, J. (University of California at Los Angeles, CA, USA)
Schegloff, Emanuel (1937–): 909

HILL, T. (Girvan, UK)
Gilliéron, Jules (1854–1926): 870; *Jaberg, Karl (1877–1959)*: 882; *Kurath, Hans (1891–1992)*: 885; *McDavid, Raven Ioor, Jr (1911–84)*: 892; *Weinreich, Uriel (1926–67)*: 921; *Wenker, Georg (1852–1911)*: 922

HINTON, L. (University of California, Berkeley, CA, USA)
Teaching Endangered Languages: 757

HOLMQVIST, B. (University of Aarhus, Denmark)
**Language in the Workplace*: 177

HORNBERGER, N. H. (University of Pennsylvania, Philadelphia, PA, USA)
Hymes, Dell Hathaway (1927–): 882

HUDSON, A. (University of New Mexico, Albuquerque, NM, USA)
Diglossia: 226

HUNT, S. (Rhodes University, Grahamstown, South Africa)
Schiffrin, Deborah (1951–): 910

JANKS, H. (University of the Witwatersrand, Johannesburg, South Africa)
Fairclough, Norman (1941–): 862

JOHNSTONE, B. (Carnegie Mellon University, Pittsburgh, PA, USA)
Fieldwork Ethics and Community Responsibility: 781

JONES, F. C. V. (St. Augustine's College, Raleigh, NC, USA)
Pidgins and Creoles: Morphology: 536

List of Contributors

JOSEPH, J. E. (University of Maryland, College Park, MD, USA)
Saussurean Tradition and Sociolinguistics: 73

KACHRU, B. B. (University of Illinois at Urbana-Champaign, IL, USA)
Speech Community: 105; *New Englishes*: 519; *Bright, William (1928–)*: 853

KASPER, G. (University of Hawaii at Manoa, HI, USA)
Politeness: 187

KEATING, E. (University of Texas, Austin, TX, USA)
Anthropological Linguistics: 5

KENDON, A. (Philadelphia, PA, USA)
Kinesics: 169

KERSWILL, P. (University of Reading, UK)
Trudgill, Peter John (1943–): 916

KHUBCHANDANI, L. M. (Centre for Communication Studies, Pune, India)
Linguistic Census: 648; *Das Gupta, Jyotirindra (1933–)*: 857

KIRK, J. M. (Queen's University, Belfast, UK)
Maps: Dialect and Language: 350

KOTZÉ, E. F. (University of Port Elizabeth, South Africa)
Ethnicity and Language: 324

KREEFT PEYTON, J. (Center for Applied Linguistics, Washington, DC, USA)
Shuy, Roger W. (1931–): 912

KRESS, G. (University of London, UK)
Critical Sociolinguistics: 542

KRETZSCHMAR JR., W. A. (University of Georgia, Athens, GA, USA)
**Corpus Linguistics and Sociolinguistics*: 765

KYLE, J. G. (University of Bristol, UK)
Deaf Community: Structures and Interaction: 125

LACOSTE, M. (Université Paris Nord, France)
Doctor–Patient Language: 152

LAITIN, D. D. (University of Chicago, IL, USA)
Multilingual States: 652

LARGE, A. (McGill University, Montréal, PQ, Canada)
Artificial Languages: 616

LE PAGE, R. (York, UK)
DeCamp, David (1927–79): 858

LEAP, W. L. (American University, Washington, DC, USA)
Gay Language: 332

LETTS, C. (University of Reading, UK)
Bilingualism and Language Acquisition: 430

LEWIS, P. (SIL International, Dallas, TX, USA)
Missionaries and Language: 509

LI WEI (University of Newcastle, UK)
Milroy, Lesley (1944–): 893

List of Contributors

LONGACRE, R. E. (Dallas, TX, USA)
Nida, Eugene Albert (1914–): 898

LUCAS, C. (University of Gallaudet, Washington, DC, USA)
Sociolinguistics of Sign Language: 89

LUKE, A. (University of Queensland, Brisbane, QLD, Australia)
Ideology: 559

MACAULAY, R. (Claremont, CA, USA)
Vernacular: 420

MACKEY, W. F. (Sainte-Foy, PQ, Canada)
Edwards, John Robert (1947–): 861

MACLEAN, C. G. (Pitlochry, UK)
Language Diffusion Policy: 634

MACLEAN, J. (University of Edinburgh, UK)
*Medical Language: 256

MACLURE, M. (University of East Anglia, Norwich, UK)
Home Language and School Language: 737

MACY, M. W. (Cornell University, Ithaca, NY, USA)
Social Class: 362

MAHER, J. C. (International Christian University, Tokyo, Japan)
*Medical Language: 256; *Foucault, Michel (1926–84)*: 868

MARSHALL, T. A. (University of East Anglia, Norwich, UK)
Dialogism: 127

MARYNS, K. (University of Ghent, Rozier, Belgium)
Blommaert, Jan (1961–): 850

MATTHEIER, K. (University of Heidelberg, Germany)
Language Enclaves: 489

MAZRUI, A. M. (Ohio State University, Columbus, OH, USA)
Mazrui, Ali A. (1933–): 891

MCCORMICK, K. M. (University of Cape Town, South Africa)
Gender and Language: 336; *Code-switching: Overview*: 447

MCHOUL, A. (Murdoch University, WA, Australia)
Discourse: 133

MCRAE, S. S. (The Open University, Milton Keynes, UK)
Cameron, Deborah (1958–): 854; *Coates, Jennifer (1942–)*: 855

MERCER, N. (The Open University, Milton Keynes, UK)
Spoken Language in the Classroom: 749

MESTHRIE, R. (University of Cape Town, South Africa)
*Identity and Language: 165; *Sociolinguistic Variation*: 377; *Code-mixing*: 442; *Koinés*: 485; *Language Loyalty*: 492; *Language Maintenance, Shift, and Death*: 493; *Language Spread*: 498; *Professional Associations*: 840; *Bamgbose, Ayo (1932–)*: 846; *Baugh, John (1949–)*: 847; *Mufwene, Salikoko S. (1947–)*: 894; *Spolsky, Bernard (1932–)*: 913

MEY, J. L. (Odense University, Denmark)
Pragmatics and Sociolinguistics: 50; *Critical Language Awareness*: 541

List of Contributors

MILLER, J. E. (University of Edinburgh, UK)
Speech and Writing: 270; **Data Collection in Linguistics*: 769

MILROY, A. L. (University of Newcastle, UK)
Social Networks: 370

MILROY, J. (University of Sheffield, UK)
Sociolinguistics and Language Change: 389

MININNI, G. (Università degli Studa di Bari, Italy)
Hegemony: 550; *Marxist Theories of Language*: 575

MUGGLESTONE, L. C. (University of Oxford, UK)
Academies: Dictionaries and Standards: 615; *Prescription in Dictionaries*: 672

MÜHLHÄUSLER, P. (University of Adelaide, SA, Australia)
Jargons: 483

MUYSKEN, P. C. (Katholieke Universiteit, Nijmegen, The Netherlands)
Intertwined Languages: 481

ODLIN, T. (Ohio State University, Columbus, OH, USA)
Language Transfer and Substrates: 499

OHALA, J. J. (University of California, Berkeley, CA, USA)
Sound Change: 396

PALMER, F. R. (Wokingham, UK)
Firth, J. R. (1890–1960): 865

PANDHARIPANDE, R. V. (University of Illinois at Urbana-Champaign, IL, USA)
Kachru, Braj B. (1932–): 883; *Saville-Troike, Muriel*: 908

PATEMAN, T. (University of Sussex, Brighton, UK)
Language as a Social Reality: 34

PATTANAYAK, D. P. (Mysore, India)
Language Conflict: 563

PAVLINIC A. M. (Zagreb, Croatia)
Migrants and Migration: 504

PERERA, K. (University of Manchester, UK)
Education and Language: Overview: 710

PHILIPSEN, G. (University of Washington, Seattle, WA, USA)
Ethnography of Speaking: 154

PHILLIPSON, R. (Roskilde University, Denmark)
**Discrimination and Minority Languages*: 545; **Linguicide*: 567; **Linguistic Imperialism*: 570

PHILP, A. M. (University of Glasgow, UK)
English Grammar in British Schools: 723

PRESTON, D. R. (Eastern Michigan University, Ypsilanti, MI, USA)
Applied Linguistics and Sociolinguistics: 691

PRINSLOO, M. (University of Cape Town, South Africa)
Street, Brian (1943–): 914

PSATHAS, G. (Boston University, MA, USA)
Ethnomethodology: 160; *Sacks, Harvey (1935–75)*: 905

QUASTHOFF, U. M. (University of Bielefeld, Germany)
Context: 218

RAJAGOPALAN, K. (Universidade Estadual de Campinas, Brazil)
Bernstein, Basil (1924–): 848

RAMPTON, B. (University of London, UK)
Ethnicity and the Crossing of Boundaries: 321

RASMUSSEN, G. (Odense University, Denmark)
Business Language: 212

RAU, W. C. (Illinois State University, Normal, IL, USA)
Multidimensional Scaling: 793

ROBERTS, J. (University of London, UK)
Quirk, Professor Sir (Charles) Randolph (1920–): 901

ROMAINE, S. (University of Oxford, UK)
Dialect and Dialectology: 310; *Dorian, Nancy (1936–)*: 860

SANGSTER, C. M. (University of Oxford, UK)
*Sociophonetics: 391; *Romaine, Suzanne (1951–)*: 905

SANKOFF, D. (University of Montréal, PQ, Canada)
Statistics in Sociolinguistics: 828; *Labov, William (1927–)*: 885

SANTIAGO-IRIZARRY, V. (Cornell University, Ithaca, NY, USA)
Hill, Jane (1939–): 881

SARANGI, S. (Cardiff University, UK)
Institutional Language: 239

SAWYER, J. F. A. (Lancaster University, UK)
Religion and Language: 262

SCHLOBINSKI, P. (University of Hannover, Germany)
Dittmar, Norbert (1943–): 859

SCHMITT, R. L. (Illinois State University, Normal, IL, USA)
Goffman, Erving (1922–82): 871

SCHNEIDER, E. W. (University of Regensburg, Germany)
Görlach, Manfred (1937–): 872

SCHRØDER, K. C. (Roskilde University, Denmark)
Media Language and Communication: 246

SCHUMAN, H. (University of Michigan, Ann Arbor, MI, USA)
Attitude Surveys: Question–Answer Process: 761

SCHUSKY, E. L. (Southern Illinois University, Edwardville, IL, USA)
Kinship Terminology: 172

SEBBA, M. (Lancaster University, UK)
Orthography: 669; **Corpus Linguistics and Sociolinguistics*: 765

SHIBATANI, M. (Kobe University, Nada, Kobe, Japan)
Honorifics: 552

SHORT, M. (Lancaster University, UK)
Style: 280

List of Contributors

SIEGEL, J. (University of New England, Armidale, NSW, Australia)
Pidgins, Creoles, and Minority Dialects in Education: 747

SIMPSON, J. M. Y. (State University of Ceara, Brazil)
Ecology of Language: 30; *Language*: 31; *Accent*: 293; *Areal Linguistics*: 423; *Minority Languages*: 579; *Statistics: Principal Languages of the World (UNESCO)*: 683

SKUTNABB-KANGAS, T. (Regstrup, Denmark)
**Discrimination and Minority Languages*: 545; **Linguicide*: 567; **Linguistic Imperialism*: 570

SPOLSKY, B. (Johns Hopkins University, Baltimore, MD, USA)
Cooper, Robert Leon (1931–): 855; *Fishman, Joshua A. (1926–)*: 867; *Valdman, Albert (1931–)*: 919

STAM, J. H. (Upsala College, Sussex, NJ, USA)
Whorf, Benjamin Lee (1897–1941): 923

STRÖMQVIST, S. (Gothenburg University, Sweden)
Child Language: An Overview: 703

SUREK-CLARK, C. (University of Natal, Durban, South Africa)
Sankoff, Gillian (1943–): 906

SWAIN, M. (University of Toronto, ON, Canada)
Paulston, Christina Bratt (1932–): 899

SWANN, J. (The Open University, Milton Keynes, UK)
Gender, Education, and Language: 735

SZUCHEWYCZ, B. G. (Brock University, St Catharines, ON, Canada)
Blessings: 211

TABOURET-KELLER, A. (Strasbourg, France)
**Identity and Language*: 165; *Le Page, Robert (1920–)*: 889

TARONE, E. (University of Minnesota, Minneapolis, MN, USA)
Interlanguage: 475

TAYLOR, R. L. (University of Connecticut, Storrs, CT, USA)
Adolescent Peer Group Language: 297; *Subcultures and Countercultures*: 401

THOMAS, J. (Lancaster University, UK)
Conversational Maxims: 116; *Cooperative Principle*: 121

THOMASON, S. G. (University of Michigan, Ann Arbor, MI, USA)
Contact Languages: 461

THREADGOLD, T. (University of Sydney, NSW, Australia)
Genre: 235

THURLOW, C. (Cardiff University, Wales, UK)
The Internet and Language: 287

TODD, L. (University of Ulster, Coleraine, UK)
Pidgins and Creoles: An Overview: 524

TOOLAN, M. (University of Washington, Seattle, WA, USA)
Narrative, Natural: 179

TUCKER, G. R. (Carnegie Mellon University, Pittsburgh, PA, USA)
Lambert, Wallace E. (1922–): 888

TURNER, R. H. (University of Essex, Colchester, UK)
Role Theory: 59

List of Contributors

VAN DEN BERGHE, P. L. (University of Washington, Seattle, WA, USA)
Power Differentials and Language: 597

VAN HERK, G. (University of Ottawa, ON, Canada)
Poplack, Shana: 901

VIGOUROUX, C. B. (Paris, France)
Symbolic Power and Language: 610; *Bourdieu, Pierre (1930–)*: 852

VINCENT, N. (University of Manchester, UK)
Syntactic Change: 407

WAGNER, D. (University of Pennsylvania, Philadelphia, PA, USA)
Literacy: Research, Measurement, and Innovation: 787

WATT, D. J. L. (University of York, UK)
**Chain Shifts*: 303

WEIR, J. M. (Reed College, Portland, OR, USA)
Bakhtin, Mikhail M. (1895–1975): 845

WERNER, O. (Northwestern University, Evanston, IL, USA)
Sapir–Whorf Hypothesis: 65

WESTGATE, D. P. G. (University of Newcastle, UK)
**Observing and Analyzing Classroom Talk*: 803

WHALEY, L. J. (Dartmouth College, Hanover, NH, USA)
**Endangered Languages*: 465; **Endangered Languages Projects (An Inventory)*: 835

WILKINSON, A. M. †
Oracy: 746

WOLFRAM, W. (North Carolina State University, Raleigh, NC, USA)
Fasold, Ralph W. (1940–): 863

WRIGHT, J. C. (University of London, UK)
Grierson, Sir George Abraham (1851–1941): 874

WRIGHT, S. (Northern Arizona University, Flagstaff, AZ, USA)
**Sociophonetics*: 391

Name Index

Aasen I, 682, 878
Abbott G, 471
Abdulaziz M, 489, 512, 865
Abelson R, 220, 225
Abercrombie D, 296–7
Abercrombie N, 134, 143
Abrahams R D, 157, 160, 279
Abramson P R, 104
Achebe C, 523
Ackerman F J, 95
Ackermann E, 840
Acton T, 489
Adam L, 880
Adams J M, 81–2, 86
Adams M J, 713–14
Adamson M, 242
Adamson S, 283, 503
Addison, 535
Adger C, 749, 784
Adger C T, 926
Adjémian C, 479–80
Adler L, 302
Aftel M, 239–40, 242, 888
Agar M H, 775
Agnihotri R K, 451, 453
Ainsaar S, 358, 360
Aitchison J, 328, 349–50, 390, 530–1, 534–6
Akers R, 97
Alatis J, 239, 242
Alatis J E, 218, 711, 714
Alberts M, 628, 630
Albrecht S L, 10
Alcorn D S, 10
Aleinikoff A, 581
Alexander N, 629–30
Alexiou M, 227, 230
Alfonzetti G, 444, 446
Alladina S, 712, 714
Allan K, 200, 202–4, 207
Allard R, 22, 472–3
Allen C, 409, 411
Allen D E, 137, 143
Allen H B, 319
Allen V L, 65, 723
Alleyne M C, 462, 464
Allport F, 822
Allport G W, 609
Allsop L, 92, 125, 127
Almqvist, 569
Althusser L, 79, 168, 561, 563, 587, 591, 594, 874
Althusser L L, 79, 591, 594, 868
Altieri C, 124
Altoma S J, 227, 230

Alton Walcott D, 523
Altwerger F, 608
Alvarez-Cáccamo C, 446, 670, 672
Amastae J, 453–4, 756
Ameche D, 268
Ammon U, 107, 215, 218, 499, 550, 567, 574, 620–2, 624–5, 634, 844–5, 860
Andersen E, 707–8
Andersen E S, 87–8
Andersen H, 411
Andersen P B, 178–9
Anderson B, 167–8, 657, 662, 669
Anderson B A, 101, 104
Anderson D C, 143
Anderson J, 792–3
Anderson J M, 351, 357, 360, 408
Anderson R J, 161, 165, 167, 207
Anderson S R, 207
Andersson G, 917
Andrianarivo J, 570
Androutsopoulos J, 324, 671–2
Annamalai E, 573
Ansre G, 572–3
Antonek J, 918
Anward J, 509
Apostel L, 122–4
Appel R, 326–8, 607–8, 628, 630, 897
Apresyian Y D, 71, 73
Apte M L, 42, 45–6, 65, 279, 286–7
Aramburo A J, 89, 92
Arends J, 443, 464, 481–5, 530, 535, 897
Argyle M, 135–6, 143
Aristar Dry H, 768–9
Aristotle, 76, 198, 235–6, 238, 281, 585, 617
Arndt H, 189, 190, 192
Arnold D O, 402, 406
Arnold E, 255, 480–1
Arnove R F, 572–3
Aron R, 852
Asanti M, 709–10
Asch S, 822
Ash S, 307, 319, 361, 388, 418, 887
Asher R E, 80, 104, 350, 362
Atkinson D, 473
Atkinson J M, 112, 114–16, 138, 143, 161, 164, 233, 239, 240, 242, 575
Atkinson M, 586, 591
Atkinson P, 164
Atkinson R, 874
Attridge D, 262, 324
Atwood E B, 885
Au K, 324, 756
Au K H-P, 756

953

Auer P, 322, 324, 444–6, 448, 453
Auger J, 887
Augst G, 670, 672
Aukerman F J, 95
Aulakh G, 151
Auroux S, 80
Austin G, 169
Austin J L, 6, 39, 46, 50–1, 116, 121, 135–6, 140, 143, 182, 198–202, 207, 610–11, 910
Austin M W, 893
Avoden E, 279

Babbie E, 102, 813
Bach A, 319, 923
Bach K, 202, 204, 207
Backus A, 459–60
Baetens-Beardsmore H, 16
Bailey, 693
Bailey B, 859
Bailey C-J, 315–17, 319
Bailey G, 302, 351, 353–4, 360, 413, 417, 848, 895
Bailey R, 281, 283, 350, 360, 872
Bailey R E, 243
Bailey R W, 521, 523, 873, 885, 900
Bain B, 231
Bain E, 733–4
Bain R, 733–4
Bainbridge W S, 95, 102, 104–5, 825, 827
Baker C, 16, 92, 432, 508–9, 857
Baker P, 334–5
Baker V, 473
Bakhtin M M, 6, 27, 29, 110, 127–33, 235–6, 238, 255, 260, 307, 323–4, 560, 563, 576, 845–6, 881, 920–1
Bakker P, 20, 22, 443, 462, 464, 483
Bald W, 524
Baldauf R B, 647
Baldridge L, 187, 193
Baldwin J, 331–2
Bale R F, 60, 821
Bales, 821
Bales R F, 60
Ball A F, 756
Ball M J, 231
Ball P, 82, 86
Ballachey E L, 86
Ballmer T, 201, 207
Bally C, 3, 74
Balzac, 132
Bamberg M, 887
Bamgbose A, 846–7
Banerjee J, 190, 192
Banfield A, 132–3
Banich M, 360
Banjo A, 847
Banks A, 621, 626
Banton M, 597, 604
Barbour S, 228, 230

Bardovi-Harlig K, 151
Barker V, 473
Barkhuizen G, 473
Barkin B, 608
Barlow M, 839
Barnes D, 227, 230, 679, 680, 725, 734, 752–3, 803, 805, 807, 809
Baron D, 343–5
Baron N S, 288–9, 350
Barron A, 331–2
Barth F, 497
Barthes, 852
Barthes R, 79, 129, 132–3, 135, 143, 250, 255, 560, 563
Bartoli, 873
Bartsch R, 326, 329, 518–19
Basso K, 38–9, 46, 48
Basso K H, 177
Bates B E, 431–2
Bates E, 706, 708
Bateson G, 29, 170
Bateson M C, 172
Bátori I, 219, 225
Battestini S P X, 230
Battison R, 92
Baudelaire, 611
Baudhuin E S, 287
Bauer R, 360
Bäuerle R, 225
Baugh A C, 374, 376
Baugh J, 46, 302, 310, 329, 387–8, 417, 709–10, 847–8, 887, 895, 910
Bauman R, 6, 42, 46, 143, 156–7, 160, 324, 906
Bauman Z, 323–4
Baumgardner R J, 524
Bayley R, 92, 417, 691–2, 695
Bazerman C, 237–8
Bear R, 723
Beaune C, 666, 669
Beckett, 518
Beebe, 480
Beebe L M, 190–3
Beekman J, 511–12
Begise K Y, 73
Belazi H, 457–8, 460
Belknap K, 865
Bell A, 109–10, 395–6, 844
Bell A G, 268
Bell A T, 386, 388
Bell C, 169
Bell D, 366
Bell J H, 176
Bell S C, 169
Bellot J, 467, 471
Belmore, 288
Beltramo A F, 460
Bem D J, 763, 765
Ben Yehuda E, 677, 682

Ben-Gurion D, 643
Bender M L, 227, 230, 856
Bendor-Samuel J, 842
Benesová E, 225
Bennet T L, 276
Benseler F, 29
Benskin M, 104
Benson D, 164
Benson J, 735
Benson P, 569
Bentahila A, 450–1 453, 457–8, 460
Benterrak K, 139, 143
Bentham J, 142
Benveniste E, 78–9
Bereiter, 368
Bereiter C, 513, 519, 717, 720, 722–3
Berenz N, 491–2, 786–7, 807, 809
Berg I A, 10, 100, 104
Berger P, 241–2, 365–6, 369
Berger P L, 597–8, 601, 604, 606
Bergman J, 161
Bergman M L, 191–2
Bergmann J, 161
Bergvall V, 854
Bergvall V L, 345, 736
Berk R A, 81–2, 86
Berk-Seligson S, 232–3, 450, 453
Berkeley B, 802
Berlin B, 40, 46, 71, 73
Berman R A, 703, 707, 708
Bernstein B, 50, 52, 56–7, 177, 184, 214, 216–18, 299, 302, 308–9, 353, 360–3, 366–9, 544–5, 582–3, 606, 608, 716–18, 722–3, 738, 803–4, 809, 816, 844, 848–9, 886
Bernstein C, 360–2
Berrill D, 747
Berrington S, 322, 324
Berry R, 749
Berton, 579
Besch W, 362
Bhaskar R, 34–5
Bhatia T K, 107, 211, 456–8, 460, 524
Bhatia V, 240–2
Bhatt R M, 457–60
Bhola H S, 746
Bialystok E, 519
Biber D, 769–71
Bickerton D, 19, 22, 462, 464, 530, 534–6, 693, 849–50, 912
Biddle B J, 65
Bierwisch M, 144
Billig M, 253, 255
Binet, 715
Bing J, 854
Bing J M, 345, 736
Birch D, 259–62, 283
Bird S, 670, 672
Birdsong D, 518–19

Birdwhistell R L, 169–72
Bishop G, 763–5
Bishop J, 733–4
Bishop Y M, 832–3
Bissau G, 537
Bittle W E, 73
Black M, 39, 46
Black M C, 850
Blackwell R D, 86
Blackwood E, 335–6
Blair W, 321
Blake A, 255–6
Blake W, 244
Blake W, 244–5, 255–6
Blanc H, 487, 489, 497
Blanc M H A, 16, 21–2, 517, 519
Blanchard K, 824
Blass R, 511–12
Blau J, 227, 230
Bloch B, 34, 388, 885, 892, 898
Bloch M, 583
Block J, 10, 100, 104, 407
Blom J P, 110, 444, 446, 449, 453–4, 456, 543, 545
Blommaert J, 243, 322, 324, 421, 446, 850–2
Bloom L, 219, 224–5
Bloome D, 757, 915
Bloomfield L, 1, 36, 38, 46, 76, 79, 105, 107, 286–7, 426–7, 430, 513–15, 519, 779, 866, 876, 907
Blount B, 881
Blount B G, 279, 292
Blum A, 161
Blum-Kulka S, 146–7, 150–1, 187, 190–3, 203, 206–7
Blumberg H H, 827
Blumer H, 83
Boas F, 1, 5, 36–9, 46, 170, 779, 851–2, 880, 907–8, 924
Bobda A, 330, 332
Boberg C, 307, 319, 353, 360–1, 388, 415, 417–18, 887
Boberg S, 887
Bobo L, 9, 10
Boden D, 164, 239, 241–3
Bodman J W, 190, 192
Boehme J, 665
Boer, 305
Bogardus E S, 96–7, 104, 817–18, 820
Bohannon J N, 88–9
Bokamba E G, 457, 460
Bokmål, 449
Bolinger D, 105, 107, 234–5, 581, 583
Bolle J, 481, 483
Boller F, 16
Bollobás E, 122, 124
Bolton W F, 524, 616
Bonaparte L L, 351
Bonifacio, 169
Boos F, 5, 170, 779, 880, 907, 924
Booth W C, 132

955

Borbé T, 576, 578
Boretzky N, 462, 464, 483
Borg I, 795, 801
Borker R, 302
Borker R A, 300–2
Bortoni-Ricardo S M, 372–4, 376
Bosch P, 220, 225
Boswell J, 802
Bottani N, 507–9
Bouchard D F, 869
Bourbaki N, 79
Bourdieu P, 6, 29, 35, 241–2, 541–2, 562–3, 591, 597, 610–13, 650–2, 852–3, 924
Bourhis R, 472–3
Bourhis R G, 455–6
Bourhis R Y, 473
Bowen J D, 230, 856
Bower A, 887
Bowerman M, 347, 707–8
Bowles, 366
Boxer D, 191–2
Boyd S, 887
Bradac J J, 869
Bradburn N M, 764–5
Bradford D, 824
Bradley D, 503
Braga G, 620, 626
Braga M, 887
Braine M, 219, 224–5
Braly K, 609
Brann C M B, 845
Branscombe A, 756
Braun A, 332
Breakwell G M, 86
Bréal M, 75
Breatnach R B, 497
Brecht B, 53, 57
Bredel U, 860
Breier M, 915
Breinberg P, 701
Breivik L E, 350
Bremer O, 923
Brend R M, 239
Brennan M, 231, 233
Brennenstuhl W, 201, 207
Brenzinger M, 493–5, 497
Bretherton I, 432, 708
Breton R J-L, 351, 360
Brewer, 636
Brewer W, 207
Brewster B, 591
Bridgewood M, 733–4
Briggs C, 323–4
Briggs C L, 87–8
Brigham J C, 609
Bright W, 226, 230, 647, 853–4
Brill E J, 230, 865
Brisk M E, 699

Britain D, 360, 917
Britto, 226, 229–30
Britto F, 107
Britton J, 680, 714, 725
Britton J N, 299, 302
Brock-Utne B, 569
Brockmeier J, 896
Broeder P, 707–8
Broeders A P A, 331–2
Brooks C, 131, 133
Brooks-Gunn J, 300, 302
Brown C, 71
Brown E K, 270–2, 276
Brown G, 38, 42, 46, 135–6, 138, 143, 147
Brown H R, 291
Brown J D, 254–5
Brown P, 118, 121, 151, 187–92, 199, 207, 212, 241–2, 558–9, 907
Brown R, 46, 81, 86, 174, 283, 343, 556, 559, 706, 708
Brown R W, 326, 329, 609
Brown W C, 827
Browning R, 227, 230
Bruder K A, 212
Brugmann K, 407, 411
Brumfit C, 260, 262
Brumfit C J, 472
Bruner J, 219, 224–5, 707–8, 738
Bruyn A, 530, 535
Bryant M, 279
Bryant P, 319
Bryman A, 255
Bucak S, 569–70
Büchner G, 52
Bucholtz M, 322, 324, 335, 736
Buck C D, 662, 669
Buffon, 282
Bühler K, 57
Bulcaen C, 243, 421, 851
Bullock, 724–8
Bulwer, 169
Burchfield R, 361
Burger T, 243
Burgess A, 245
Burgess D, 40, 46
Burgess R, 813
Burke V M, 859
Burkett S R, 10
Burney P, 625–6
Burns R, 310, 470
Burt, 715
Burt R S, 828
Burton, 260
Burton F, 143
Butcher A, 331–2
Butler C, 794, 801
Button G, 116, 138, 143, 161, 164
Butts R E, 124
Bybee J, 532, 536

Bybee J L, 347–50
Byrne F, 535, 849–50

Cable T, 374, 376
Cadora F J, 227, 230
Calder G, 396
Callow J, 511–12
Calvet L-J, 568–9
Cameron D, 286–7, 333, 335–6, 339, 344–5, 581–3, 689–90, 733–4, 784, 854–5
Cameron P, 287
Camillus, 131
Campbell L, 853, 854, 881
Candlin C N, 844
Caon L, 376
Capotorti F, 546, 550, 568–9, 571, 573
Caracciolo A, 551
Carbaugh D, 42, 47, 159–60
Carbaugh D C, 157, 160
Cardinal Richelieu, 681
Carew, 719
Carew R, 667
Carey W, 265, 511
Cargile A, 197
Carlen P, 143
Carley, 828
Carley K, 103
Carley K M, 828
Carlson T B, 109–10, 199, 207
Carmines E G, 813, 820
Carnap R, 58
Carrell P L, 190, 192
Carroll B J, 469, 472
Carroll J B, 37, 39, 46, 65–6, 68, 73, 606, 924
Carroll L, 512, 605
Carter R, 259–62, 282–3, 726, 731, 733–5
Carter R A, 245–6
Cartwright D, 827
Casagrande J B, 71, 73
Casey N, 138, 143
Cassidy F, 858–9
Cassidy F G, 418–19, 889–90, 893
Casson R, 71–3
Catford J C, 318–19
Cathcart R S, 827
Caton C E, 207
Cavalli-Sforza L L, 794, 796, 801
Cazabon M T, 889
Cazden C, 324, 454, 460, 803–4, 808–9, 882
Cazden C B, 87–8
Cedergren H, 44, 47, 384, 387–8, 847–8
Cedergren H J, 829, 833
Cenoz J, 473
Chadwick B A, 10
Chaffers J, 581
Chaiken S, 83, 86
Chambers J, 376, 393, 396
Chambers J C, 396

Chambers J K, 165, 168, 307, 309–11, 319, 356, 358, 360, 415, 417, 917
Chapple E D, 821
Chatman S, 246, 262, 283
Chatterjee S, 226, 230
Chaucer, 396, 667
Chaudenson R, 462, 895
Chen M, 315, 319
Cherny L, 289
Cheshire J, 197, 340, 345, 420–1, 521, 523–4, 753
Chiappelli F, 616
Chilton P, 543, 545
Chino E, 559
Chomba B, 570, 573
Chomsky N, 1, 2, 25, 30, 35–6, 46, 50–1, 67, 76, 78–9, 93, 112, 129, 133, 159–60, 165, 168, 219, 224–5, 385, 407, 458, 460, 513–14, 516, 544–5, 766, 849–50, 882, 888, 907
Chomsky N, 67, 76, 766, 856
Chouliaraki L, 545, 562–3, 863
Christian D, 419, 749, 784, 926
Christiansen J, 125–6
Christie F, 727, 734
Christie R, 7, 10, 81, 86, 824, 827
Chua B-H, 139, 143
Churchill S, 507, 509
Cicero, 169, 236, 584–5
Cichocki W, 354, 357, 360
Cicourel A, 153–4, 161, 164, 240, 242
Ciliberti B, 793
Citron S, 669
Clancy P M, 187, 192
Clark E, 705, 708
Clark E V, 347, 350, 606
Clark H, 705, 708
Clark H H, 109–10, 133, 199, 207, 350, 606
Clark K, 131, 133, 846
Clark M, 402, 406
Clarke S, 415, 417
Claudi U, 411
Clausewitz, 610
Clayman S, 161
Clegg S, 138, 143
Clément R, 473
Clinton H R, 888
Cloward R, 825
Cloward R A, 824–5, 827
Cluver A D De V, 633–4
Clyne M, 18, 22, 149, 151, 446, 454, 457, 460, 474–5, 489, 491, 512, 865
Clyne M G, 228, 230, 491
Coard B, 701–2
Coates J, 339–41, 345, 736, 855
Cobarrubias J, 519, 567, 569, 647, 662
Cochran M, 370, 376
Coelho A, 880, 911–12
Coffin T P, 893
Cohen A, 190, 193, 480

Cohen A D, 460
Cohen A K, 403, 406, 824–5, 827
Cohen A P, 784, 824
Cohen P, 403, 406, 887
Cohen P R, 207
Cohen R, 775
Cole P, 47, 121, 124, 143, 151, 208, 211, 225, 243, 765
Coleman D, 324
Coleman H, 239, 242
Coleman J S, 298, 302
Collinge N E, 360
Collins, 767
Collins J, 240, 242
Collins M, 702
Collinson W E, 683
Collison R L, 616
Collot, 288
Comber C, 809
Comrie B, 228, 230, 350, 360, 410–11, 559
Comte A, 75
Condon J C, 193
Conein B, 161
Confucius, 717
Conklin H A, 40, 46
Conklin H C, 73
Conley J, 231, 233
Connor, 325
Connor W, 48, 50
Conrad, 281, 518, 621
Conrad A W, 499, 573, 626, 856, 868
Conrad J, 480
Conrad R, 125, 127
Conrad S, 769
Cook G, 252, 255, 689–90
Cook V, 480
Cooks J, 756
Cooper A, 83, 86
Cooper C R, 756
Cooper J, 86
Cooper J F, 281
Cooper R L, 3, 230, 498–9, 626–30, 634, 645–7, 700, 855–6, 868, 913–14, 918
Cope B, 608
Coppieters R, 518–19
Coppola M, 536
Corder S P, 476, 478, 480, 695
Corkery D, 228, 230
Corliss R L, 122, 124
Cornforth M C, 577–8
Corré A D, 503–4
Corson D, 680, 848
Cortiade M, 482–3
Coseriu E, 136, 143, 355, 360
Coste D, 236–8
Coulmas F, 151, 169, 190, 192, 227, 230, 234–5, 513–14, 516, 519, 626–7, 630, 661–2, 815
Coulon A, 161
Coulter J, 136, 143, 161–2, 164, 906

Coulthard M, 42, 46, 137–8, 144, 241, 243, 713–14, 750, 753, 804, 809
Count Cosimo I, 681
Couper-Kuhlen E, 112, 115–16
Coupland J, 195–7
Coupland N, 110, 196–7, 844, 869
Couturat L, 619
Couture B, 734–5
Cowley R, 230
Cox, 702, 728, 732
Cox B, 712, 714
Coyne J, 888
Craig C, 467
Craig C G, 781, 815
Craig D, 749
Crandall, 918
Cresollius, 169
Crinson J, 732–4, 783
Crittenden K, 165
Croce, 577
Croce B, 35
Crockett H J, 828
Croft W, 410–11
Crosby F, 44, 47
Crouch I, 44, 47
Crow B K, 253, 255
Croyle R T, 83, 86
Crutchfield R S, 86
Crystal D, 248, 255, 282–3, 325, 329, 350, 360, 467–8, 471–2, 497, 519, 524, 629–30, 652, 734, 902
Culler J, 80, 182, 185
Cummings E E, 281
Cummings M J, 735
Cummins J, 21–2, 432, 508–9, 549–50, 574, 606, 608, 620, 856–7
Cunningham H, 129, 133
Currie H, 1
Cutler C, 322, 324
Cyril, 510

d'Aosta V, 17
Dabène L, 507, 509
Dahrendorf R, 364, 369
Dai Sheng, 187
Dalphinis M, 713–14
Damerow P, 218, 224–5
Danesi M, 283, 299, 302, 620, 876
Dangor A, 451, 454
Daniel S, 668
Daniels H, 754, 756
Darnell R, 47, 834, 908
Darrell Tryon, 896
Darwin, 169
Dascal M, 119, 121
Das Gupta J, 22, 489, 497, 567, 604, 634, 662, 857–8
Dauzat A, 870
Davidson D, 208, 225
Davies A, 513, 515, 747

Davies C, 320-1, 609
Davies E, 152
Davies E E, 457, 460
Davies M F, 822, 827
Davies W H, 244
Davis H, 255-6
Davis J, 92
Davis L M, 319, 351, 355-6, 360
Davy D, 248, 255, 282-3
Dayton B, 887
Deacon D, 254-5
Dean J, 194
de Beaugrande R A, 136, 143, 605-6
de Boer B, 305-6
de Bot K, 18, 22
DeCamp D, 693, 820, 858-9, 903
Decaux A, 638
De Certeau, 139
DeCillia R, 926
de Courtenay B, 77, 79
DeFleur M, 7, 10
Defoe D, 615, 681
de Fornel M, 161
DeGraff M, 464, 536
de Grève M, 509
de Groot A, 16
De Houwer A, 431-2
de Jong E J, 699
De Jorio A, 169
de Klerk V, 473
de Lauretis T, 140, 143, 237, 239
Delbrück B, 407, 411
Delph E W, 333, 335
Delpit L, 710
Delsarte, 169
D'Emilio J, 335
de Montreuil J, 665
Demuth K, 705, 708
den Besten H, 482-3
de Nebrija A, 681
Denhiere G, 225
Denison N, 448, 454, 496-7, 508-9
Derrida J, 75, 80, 852
de Saussure F, 1, 3, 25, 35-6, 73-80, 128-30,
    134-35, 166, 408, 516, 576, 886, 921
Descartes, 617
Deshpande M M, 226, 230
De Silva M W S, 917
De Sola Pool I, 583
Deuchar M, 89, 92
Deumert A, 47, 310, 630
Deutsch K W, 657
Deutsch W, 708
Deutscher I, 10
DeVito J A, 197
de Waard J, 899
Dewey J, 76
De Zulueta E, 10

Diaz R, 756-7
Dickens, 132, 283, 470, 902
Dickerson L, 691, 695
Dickerson L J H, 695
Dickerson W, 691, 695
Dieth E, 922
Digman J M, 85-6
Dijk T A van, 41, 47, 116, 134-6, 143-5, 225,
    241, 252, 255, 543, 545, 597, 925
Dijkhoff M, 895
Dil A, 865, 875
Dil A S, 498, 567, 854
Dillard J L, 46-7
Dillon J T, 804, 809
Di Luzio A, 446
Dingeldein H J, 355, 360
Dingwall R, 161
Dinkins D, 635
Dinneen D A, 208
di Pietro R J, 239, 242
Dirckx J H, 259
Dirim Y, 322, 324
Di Sciullo A, 452, 454, 457, 460
Dittmar N, 107, 218, 373, 376, 845, 849, 859-60
Dixon J, 725
Dixon J T, 804, 809
Dixon P, 591
Dixon R M W, 555, 559, 781, 813-16
Dixon R W, 846
Djilas, 365
Docherty G J, 391, 396
Doležel L, 281, 283
Domínguez F, 842
Donald J, 580
Donato R, 918
Donzelot J, 139-40, 143
Doody M A, 581, 583
Dorian N C, 467, 492, 495-8, 801, 815-16, 860-1
Dostoyevsky, 128, 132, 845
Doucet R C, 670, 672
Doughty C, 503
Doughty P S, 725, 734
Douglas M, 239, 242
Downes W, 374, 376
Downing J, 788, 793
Dow Turner L, 911
Dowty D R, 460
Doyle D P, 10
Drachman G, 350
Dreitzel H P, 30
Dressler W, 238, 391, 396, 496-7, 605-6
Dressler W U, 136, 143, 396, 497
Drew P, 114, 116, 138, 143, 161, 213-14, 233,
    239-42, 575
Dreywer P H, 710
Drummond P, 256
D'Souza D, 581, 583
D'Souza J, 539

Dua H R, 567, 631, 633–4, 660, 662
Dube N, 419
Dubois B L, 44, 47
Duchenne, 169
Duck J, 473
Ducrot O, 27, 29
Dudley P, 747
Dudov Z, 53, 57
Dufriche-Desgenettes A, 79
Duggan J J, 235
Dulong R, 161
Dumas B K, 266, 270
Duncan-Rose C, 421
Dundes A, 279, 292, 609
Durant A, 262, 324
Duranti A, 5, 6, 225, 240, 242
Durgunoglu A Y, 699
Durkacz V E, 580
Durkheim E, 34, 35, 76, 137, 166, 174, 367, 576, 849, 871
Durrell M, 353, 360
Dutcher N, 790, 793
Dwyer B, 320–1

Eades D, 233
Eakins B, 254–5
Eakins R G, 255
Eastman C, 598, 604
Eastman C M, 647, 662
Eaton R, 411
Ebaugh H R F, 64–5
Eckert P, 107, 109–10, 168, 300, 302, 306, 776, 778, 887, 904
Eckler A R, 287
Eco U, 141, 143, 230, 238, 250, 255, 560, 563
Edelman M, 581, 583
Edelsky C, 606–8
Edgerton R B, 775
Edmondson W, 137, 143, 202, 207
Edmondson W J, 192
Edmont E, 312, 319, 418–19, 870
Edwards A D, 325, 329, 712–16, 753, 803, 808–9
Edwards A L, 10
Edwards D, 752–3, 803, 806, 809
Edwards J, 48, 50, 166–8, 218, 683, 720, 722–3, 862
Edwards J R, 604, 787, 809, 861–2
Edwards V, 372, 376, 714
Efron D, 170–1
Egede H, 683
Eggan F, 174, 176
Eggins S, 239
Eggleston-Dodd, 126
Egli U, 225
Eglin P, 161, 163, 165
Ehlich K, 225
Ehrenreich B, 365, 368
Ehrenreich J, 365, 369
Eichenbaum, 182

Eide A, 546, 550
Eidheim H, 495, 497
Einstein, 799
Eisemon T E, 792–3
Eisenhower, 586
Eisenhower D, 640
Eisenstadt S N, 298, 302
Eisenstein M R, 190, 192
Ekman P, 169, 170–2
Eliade M, 265
Elias, 187
Elias N, 192
Elias-Olivares L, 453–4, 756
Elley, 724
Ellinger B, 473
Ellis S, 330, 332
Elman J, 703, 706, 708
Elman J L, 306–7
Elmer W, 357, 360
Elms F, 417
Elson B F, 231
Elwood J, 736
Elyot T, 130
Emeneau M B, 428, 430, 538–9, 852–3, 862
Emerson C, 133, 563, 845–6
Emmison M, 139, 143
Engel, 169
Engel J F, 86
Engelmann, 368, 513, 717, 720
Engelmann S, 723
Engels F, 560, 563, 570, 578
England N, 467
Engler R, 80
Enkvist N E, 280–1, 283
Epstein D, 736
Erasmus, 187
Erckenbrecht U, 578
Erickson F, 171, 755–6, 785–6
Ericsson K A, 136, 143
Erting C, 92
Ervin-Tripp S, 190, 192
Esar E, 279
Esperanto D, 618
Euler H, 622, 626
Evens M W, 71, 73
Extra G, 508–9
Eysenck, 715
Eysholdt U, 332

Fabb N, 262, 324
Fabbro F, 16
Færch C, 508–9
Faerch C, 191–2
Fagunwa D O, 847
Faiguet, 617
Fairclough N, 47, 135, 143, 242, 247, 249, 255, 283, 541–3, 545, 562–3, 582–4, 588, 591, 597, 662, 862–3, 925

Falk J S, 321
Faltis C J, 699
Fanshel D, 153–4, 197, 203, 207–8, 239
Fantel H, 287
Fantini A, 431–2
Farb P, 279
Fardon R, 699
Farr M, 754, 756
Farrar C R, 302
Farrar K, 396
Fasold R, 2, 3, 215, 218, 229, 230, 307, 309–10, 388, 418, 658, 660–2, 755–6, 904
Fasold R W, 92, 189, 192, 691, 695, 863–4
Fawcett R P, 29
Faye, 881
Faye P-L, 881
Feagin C, 887
Feder D, 861
Fehrenbacher D E, 669
Felix S, 859
Fellman J, 227, 230
Fenton A S, 361
Fenton N, 255
Ferguson, 633
Ferguson A, 567
Ferguson C, 322, 324, 439, 456, 460, 513, 519, 706, 708, 756, 904
Ferguson C A, 22, 44, 47, 87, 89, 105–7, 181, 226, 229–30, 439, 474–5, 489, 497–8, 567, 604, 630–1, 634, 647, 662, 856, 858, 864–5, 879
Ferguson C F, 484–5
Fernández M, 230
Fichte, 665
Figueroa E, 844
Fillenbaum S, 396
Fillmore, 248
Filppula M, 501–3
Fine A G, 402, 406
Fine G A, 871–2
Finegan E, 904
Firth A, 214
Firth J R, 28, 77, 80, 105, 107, 219, 317, 865–7, 883, 891
Fischer A, 361
Fischer J L, 44, 377, 388
Fischer O, 411
Fischoff E, 369
Fisher C S, 268, 270
Fisher J L, 47
Fisher S, 152, 154, 239, 242
Fishman F, 858, 865
Fishman G S, 868
Fishman J A, 2–3, 19–20, 22, 85, 93, 104, 106–7, 228–30, 325, 329, 444, 446, 489, 492, 494, 497–9, 504, 512, 519, 545–6, 550, 559, 566–7, 569, 573, 604, 621, 623, 626, 631, 633–4, 647, 658, 662, 670, 672–3, 675, 678–9, 695, 712, 714, 758–9, 843, 856, 865, 867, 868, 925

Fishman P, 592
Fisiak J, 350, 354
Fiske J, 144, 255, 248, 250–1
Fitzsimm E, 255
Flanders N A, 751, 753
Flasaquier M, 509
Fleming M, 287
Flexner S B, 266–7, 269–70, 287
Flom G T, 878
Flood J, 879
Flores S, 608
Florio J, 467
Flower R, 256
Fodor, 514
Fodor I, 647
Folb E A, 301–2
Foley W, 6
Foot H, 86
Forhan, 515
Fortes M, 174, 176
Fosheim R M, 243
Foster, 203
Foster C R, 22, 107
Foucault M, 6, 80, 134–5, 139–44, 153, 168, 237–8, 241–3, 562–3, 587–8, 591, 597, 605, 852, 868–9, 874
Fought J, 169, 172, 847
Foulkes P, 331–2, 391, 396
Fowler, 925
Fowler A, 235, 237–8
Fowler R, 185, 241, 246, 248, 255, 260, 262, 280, 283, 541–3, 545, 583, 591, 597, 600, 606
Fox J J, 156, 160
Fox M J, 572–3
Fraissinet J, 889
Francis, 353, 653
Francis D, 161
Francis I, 666
Francis I S, 282–3
Francis N, 766
Francis W N, 319, 360, 769
Frank F W, 57
Frankel R, 161
Fraser B, 187, 189, 192, 207
Fraser C, 192, 197
Frawley W, 134–5, 137–8, 143
Frazer, 283, 891
Frazer E, 784, 854
Freed A, 854
Freed A F, 345, 736
Freedle R O, 136, 143, 186
Freedman S W, 756
Freire P, 53, 57
French A, 530, 524
French D, 881
French J P, 329, 331–2
Freud, 283, 888, 921
Friday W C, 926

Fried M H, 45, 47
Fries C C, 467, 472
Friesen, 170
Frisch M, 504
Fromkin V, 58–9
Frow J, 135, 143
Fry D L, 249, 256
Frye R N, 231
Fukushima S, 190, 192
Furfey P H, 76
Furman N, 302
Furniss G, 699

Gadet F, 80, 318
Gafaranga J, 446
Gagnepain J, 29
Gair J W, 226, 230
Gal S, 19, 22, 338, 345, 444, 446, 498
Galaskiewicz J, 376
Galileo, 752
Gallagher C F, 228, 230
Gallois C, 197
Galton M, 715, 803, 809
Galtung J, 570, 573
Garcia O, 151
Gardin B, 576, 578
Gardiner M, 921
Gardner R C, 396, 695, 888–9
Gardner-Chloros P, 22, 890
Garfinkel H, 6, 111, 137, 143–4, 161–2, 164–5, 240, 243, 694, 910
Garnham A, 605–6
Garrett P, 714
Garrick D, 616
Garrod, 270
Garton A, 707–8
Garvin P, 246, 631, 634, 658–9, 662
Gass S, 192, 518
Gatbonton, 693–4
Gauchat, 883
Gaudio R, 333, 335
Gavin N T, 254–5
Gávppi J, 548
Geach, 198
Gecas, 368
Gee J P, 87–8
Geertz C, 38, 44, 47, 555, 559, 783–4, 881
Geis F L, 7, 10, 81, 86, 209, 827
Geis M L, 211
Geisler H, 355, 360
Gellner E, 662, 669
Genesee F, 918
Georgakopoulou A, 324
Gernsbacher M A, 203, 207
Gernsback, 95
Gerritsen M, 352, 360
Gertner M H, 230
Ghadessy M, 238

Giallombardo R, 94, 104
Gibbs J W, 919–20
Giddens A, 34–5, 242–3, 365
Giglioli P P, 135, 143–4, 345, 369, 567
Gilbert G G, 536, 850, 880, 903, 911–12
Gilbert M, 35
Giles H, 22, 82, 86, 195–7, 295, 297, 322, 324, 329, 455–6, 472–3, 604, 695, 719, 723, 869–70, 917
Gill S D, 265
Gilliéron J, 312, 315, 319, 418–19, 882–3, 870
Gilman, 326, 329, 556, 559
Gilmour R, 86
Gimson A C, 394, 396
Gingras R G, 696
Gintis, 366
Givón, 410
Givon T, 718, 855
Gladwin T, 30, 797, 801
Glauser B, 356–7, 361
Gleason H A, 38, 47, 66, 73
Gleitman L, 350
Glendinning S, 80
Glenn C L, 699
Glock C, 811
Glowka A W, 361
Godzich W, 29, 133
Goebl H, 350–1, 357, 360–1, 376
Goeman A C M, 357, 361
Goffman E, 6, 54, 57, 111, 141, 153, 170–1, 182, 187–8, 192, 199, 207, 221, 225, 241, 243, 557, 559, 694, 763, 765, 776, 847, 871–2, 906, 910
Gogolin I, 651–2
Goke-Pariola A,, 613, 651–2
Golding W, 605
Goldstein K, 279
Gombrich E H, 605–6
Gomez L O, 265
Goode W J, 62, 65
Goodenough W H, 70, 73, 175–6
Goodman, 26
Goodman M, 532, 536
Goodman M F, 920
Goodnow J L, 88
Goodwin C, 43, 47, 112, 116, 138, 143, 161, 171, 225, 240, 242–3, 300–1, 333
Goodwin J P, 335
Goodwin M, 161, 302
Goody J, 270, 275–6, 923
Gorbachev, 591
Gordon C, 563
Gordon D, 220, 225
Gordon E, 917
Gordon M, 402, 406
Gordon R L, 82, 86
Gorgias, 584
Görlach M, 350, 354, 360, 521, 523–4, 872–3, 900
Gospodinoff K, 322, 324
Gossen G H, 157, 160, 290, 292

Gottskalkson O, 682
Gould J, 583
Gouldner A, 366–7, 369
Grabe E, 331–2, 391, 396
Grabe W, 545
Graddol D, 350, 345, 355–6, 361, 592, 597, 751, 753
Grafman J, 16
Gramsci A, 52, 542, 550–1, 561, 563, 577, 594, 873–4, 924
Granovetter M, 374, 376
Grassmann H, 398
Gray W S, 746, 787, 793
Greatbatch D, 241, 243, 252, 255
Greaves W S, 735
Green T A, 280
Greenbaum S, 225, 524, 902
Greenberg J, 78, 168, 489, 904
Greene D, 628, 630
Greenfeld L, 99, 219, 669
Greenfield P M, 225
Grenoble L A, 467, 498, 759, 816
Grice H P, 23–4, 26, 47, 51, 116–17, 121, 123–4, 136, 143, 150–1, 187, 198–200, 208–9, 211, 221, 225, 243, 251, 764–5, 910
Grierson G A, 874
Grillo R D, 881
Grimes, 465, 467, 510, 512
Grimes B F, 841
Grimes F, 757, 759
Grimm J, 398, 401
Grin F, 20, 22
Grosjean F, 16
Grosjean J, 508–9
Grosjean M, 154
Grosz E, 237–8
Gruber H, 926
Grundy P, 569
Gu Y, 187, 189, 191–2
Gudschinsky S C, 512
Guerrero L K, 197
Guillaume G, 79
Guillorel H, 569
Gülich, 219
Gülich E, 225
Gumperz J, 6, 17, 19, 37, 40, 42–3, 69, 72–3, 106, 135, 146, 149, 158, 241, 243, 322, 324, 434, 444, 446, 449, 453–4, 483, 543, 593, 694, 754, 784, 786, 853, 875, 882, 894, 910
Gumperz J D, 143
Gumperz J J, 22, 30, 47, 73, 107, 110, 151, 160, 224–5, 302, 443, 446, 453–4, 456, 489, 545, 567, 597, 756, 782, 784, 786–7, 809, 853, 875
Gunderson K, 208
Gunnarsson B-L, 239, 243
Gunnarsson L, 376
Gupta J D, 647
Gurwitsch A, 161
Gusdorf G, 298, 302

Gusfield J, 98, 104
Guthrie G, 324, 756
Gutt E A, 511–12
Guttman L, 796, 801, 820, 859
Guy G R, 44, 47, 717, 723, 887
Guy R F, 137, 143
Gyarmathi S, 398

Haan N, 405, 407
Haarman H, 325, 329, 647
Haarmann H, 645
Haas A, 300, 302
Haas M, 814, 908
Haas M R, 853
Haas W, 230–1
Habein Y S, 227, 230
Habel C, 220, 225
Habermas J, 24, 29–30, 197–8, 208, 241–3, 562–3, 587, 591
Hacking I, 140, 143–4
Haeri N, 865, 887
Hagége C, 647
Hagen A, 720, 723
Hailu F, 230
Haiman J, 411
Haimerl E, 352, 360–1
Hajičová E, 225
Hakuta K, 16
Hale C, 289
Hale K, 466–7, 838
Hale K L, 71, 73
Hall E T, 170, 172
Hall J, 419
Hall K, 323–4, 335, 736
Hall R A, 34, 876–7
Hall R A Jr, 227, 231
Hall S, 247, 255, 323–4, 402, 407
Halle, 346
Halliday M A K, 25, 28–9, 67, 109, 135, 144, 185, 219, 225, 238, 248, 254–5, 259–62, 271–2, 276, 280, 282–3, 308, 513, 516, 519, 543, 545, 561–3, 605–6, 725, 727–8, 731–3, 735, 846, 877, 883, 925
Halmari H, 457, 460
Hamayan G R, 918
Hamers J F, 16, 21–2, 517
Hamilton A M, 419
Hamilton H, 910–1
Hancock I, 489, 600, 903
Hancock I F, 604, 859, 903
Hanks W F, 5, 6, 72
Hanley M, 388
Hannah J, 33, 34, 917
Hansegard N E, 606–8
Hansen B, 21, 92
Hansen L K, 22
Hardcastle W J, 307, 332, 392, 396
Hardman F, 727–8, 735
Hare A P 821, 826–7

Hare R M, 198, 208
Hargreaves L, 809
Harman G, 208, 225, 387
Harmon D, 569
Harnish R M, 202, 204, 207–8
Harré R, 896
Harries L, 662
Harrington J P, 813
Harris R, 35, 79, 80, 583
Harris S, 241, 243
Harris W A, 387–8
Harris Z, 898, 908
Harris Z S, 79, 134–6, 144, 583
Harrison S, 858
Harrison W, 918
Hart S, 677, 679
Hartford, 923
Hartford B, 22, 107, 151
Hartland N, 139, 144
Hartley J, 130, 133, 144, 251–2, 255
Hartman K, 840
Hartmann R, 350, 361
Hartogs R, 287
Harvey G, 667
Harwood J, 472–3
Hasan R, 219, 225, 237–8, 309–10, 726, 735, 846, 877
Haudricourt A G, 303, 305–6
Haugen E, 1, 3, 16, 30–1, 35, 494, 498, 580,
  629–30, 644–5, 647, 683, 877–8
Haugen E I, 324, 329, 657
Haugen K, 878
Hauptmeier H, 235–6, 238
Hausendorf H, 219, 222, 225
Havel V, 640
Haviland J, 555, 559
Havránek B, 244, 246
Hawkins E W, 728, 735
Hawkins J A, 411
Hawkins P, 713–14
Hayakawa S I, 659
Hayashi S, 559
Hayes A S, 172
Hazen K, 776, 778–9
Headland T N, 512
Heap J, 161
Heath C, 153, 154, 161
Heath C C, 171–2
Heath S B, 46–7, 88, 182, 184–5, 342, 345, 498,
  658, 660, 662, 713–14, 738, 754, 756, 804, 809,
  865, 878–9, 882
Hecht M, 473
Hecht M L, 197
Heidegger M, 161
Heilj P M, 29
Heine B, 409, 411–12, 497, 813
Heiss J, 65
Heller M, 107
Hellinger M, 550

Helm J, 160, 185
Helsloot N, 874
Hemingway, 470
Henderson A M, 243
Henderson C R Jr, 376
Hendricks W O, 281–3
Henley N, 45, 48, 345
Henry J, 22
Henwood K, 197
Herbert J, 272
Herbert R K, 497
Herdt G, 88
Heritage J, 111–12, 114–16, 138–9, 144, 161,
  164–5, 213–14, 239, 241–3, 252–3, 255
Hermann T, 191–2
Hernandez A C R, 10
Hernández Campoy J M, 917
Hernandez-Chavez E, 449, 453–4
Herrero Valeiro M J, 670, 672
Herring S C, 288–9
Hersey P, 824
Herskovits M, 911
Hertzler J O, 104
Herzfeld M, 241, 243
Herzog M, 779, 887
Herzog M I, 401, 922
Hess R, 717, 720, 723
Hesseling D C, 3, 879–80
Hester S, 163, 165
Hester S K, 161
Hewitt R, 322, 324
Hewlett N, 396
Hewstone M, 21–2
Hey V, 736
Heyd, 628, 629
Heyneman S P, 792–3
Hibaya J, 887
Hickmann M, 87–8
Hicks R D, 207
High, 266, 269
Highfield A, 897
Hilbert R, 84
Hilbert R A, 86
Hildebrandt R, 354, 361
Hill A, 888
Hill B, 188, 192, 558–9
Hill C P, 603–4
Hill E, 502–3
Hill J, 322, 324, 437, 442, 881
Hill J H, 853–4, 881
Hill K, 437, 442
Hill K C, 881
Hill R, 7
Hill R J, 10
Hill R K, 165
Hill S, 143
Hindelang M J, 8, 10
Hindle D, 415, 417, 887

Hinnenkamp V, 475
Hinskens F, 358, 361
Hintikka J, 225
Hinton L, 759, 838
Hippler H J, 765
Hirschi T, 8–10
Hirson A, 330–2
Hitler, 587, 625
Hjelmslev, 25, 79
Hjelmslev L, 78
Hmong, 693
Ho M L, 524, 900
Hoare Q, 563
Hobsbawm E J, 651–2
Hobson D, 255, 570
Hobson J A, 573
Hock H H, 351, 361, 401
Hockett C A, 77, 165, 168, 170, 908
Hockett C F, 36, 47, 278–9, 876
Hockey S, 361, 769
Hodge B, 135, 144, 248, 255–6, 591, 597
Hodge R, 185, 542–3, 545, 562–3, 583, 606
Hodgson R, 396
Hoffmann C, 327, 329
Hoge D R, 10
Höhne-Leska C, 270, 272, 276
Hoijer H, 38, 40, 47, 66, 73, 853, 876
Holdcroft D, 80, 123–4
Hollien H, 329–32
Holm J, 354, 361, 464, 530, 535–6, 880
Holm J A, 538, 920
Holmes J, 47, 191–2, 230, 336, 454, 507, 509, 777–8
Holmestad E, 580
Holmqvist B, 178–9
Holquist M, 131, 133, 563, 845–6
Holub R, 874
Homans G, 81, 821, 825
Homans G C, 86, 96, 822, 825, 827
Homant R, 104
Honey J, 718–19, 721–3, 917–18
Hooper B J, 350
Hopey C, 792–3
Hopkins G M, 244
Hoppenbrouwers G A J, 225
Hopper P, 409–11
Hori M, 189, 192
Hornberger N, 790, 793
Hornberger N H, 857
Horowitz, 597
Horowitz D L, 604
Horton Cooley C, 826
Horvath B, 372, 376, 387–8
Hosali P, 531, 536
Hotten J C, 267, 270
Houck C M, 360
Houlton D, 728, 735
House J, 147, 151, 190–2, 207
Householder F W, 580, 583

Houtkoop-Steenstra H, 161
Hovland C I, 82, 86
Howard D M, 330, 332
Howatt A P R, 467, 472
Hoy D, 869
Hsu F L K, 191–2
Hu H C, 189, 192
Huddleston R, 282–3
Huddlestone R, 846
Hudelson S, 608
Hudelson S J, 699
Hudson A, 230–1, 240, 865
Hudson J, 749
Hudson K, 243
Hudson R, 106–7, 262, 731, 733, 735
Hudson R A, 34
Huebner T, 693, 695, 850, 865
Hughes J, 161
Hughes J A, 164
Huisman M, 161
Huizinga J, 276, 279
Hull R, 753
Hume, 343
Hünnemeyer F, 411
Hunter I, 141, 144, 236, 238
Huspek M, 160
Husserl E, 85, 161–2
Huth E, 258–9
Huwaë R, 481, 483
Hyltenstam K, 508–9
Hyman G, 81
Hyman H H, 764–5
Hyman L M, 401
Hyman R, 86
Hymes, 146, 881, 910
Hymes D, 4, 6, 22, 29–30, 37, 41, 104–5, 106–7, 110, 135, 143, 154–5, 160, 169, 172, 237–8, 292, 324, 446, 453–4, 456, 460, 464, 475, 489, 604, 694, 754, 756, 782, 784, 859, 875, 904
Hymes D H, 30, 47, 66, 73, 182, 516, 545, 847, 856, 882, 899, 908
Hymes J, 507, 509

Ide N, 361
Ide S, 189, 192, 559
Ikle F C, 582–3
Ikuta S, 192, 559
Inez Peckham C, 923
Inglehart R, 562, 567
Innis R I, 256
Irigaray, L, 334–5
Irvine J T, 881
Isocrates, 585
Itkonen E, 35
Iwolsky H, 133

Jaburg K, 312, 319, 418–19, 882–3
Jackson B, 775

Jackson J, 157, 160
Jackson P, 335
Jacobs R A, 208
Jacobs S, 5, 90, 92
Jacobs S-E, 336
Jacobson R, 456
Jacobson S, 834
Jaeger, J J, 307
Jahangiri N, 44, 47
Jahr E H, 350
Jake J C, 458
Jake J L, 458, 460
Jakobovits L A, 57
Jakobson, 6
Jakobson R, 28, 30, 77–8, 158, 160, 261–2, 279, 921
James C, 714
James H, 281
James W, 116, 198
Jamison D T, 792–3
Janis I, 822
Janis I L, 86
Janks H, 711, 714
Janney R W, 189–90, 192
Jansen W H, 609
Janulf, P, 568–9
Jarvis S, 500–1, 503
Jauss H R, 236, 238
Jaworski A, 110
Jay T B, 287
Jayyusi L, 163, 165
Jefferson G, 6, 43, 47, 51, 111–12, 116, 137–8, 144, 161, 165, 214, 243, 906, 909–10
Jefferson T, 402, 407
Jenkins T A, 876
Jensen A, 46, 47, 715, 723
Jensen K B, 254–5
Jeppe S, 454
Jeremiás E M, 228, 231
Jernudd B, 572–3
Jernudd B H, 230, 567, 573, 632, 634, 645, 647, 662, 858
Jespersen O, 233, 235, 303–4, 306
Jilbert K, 608
Jobling M, 503
Johansen J D, 192
John V, 324, 882
John V P, 454
Johns-Lewis C, 136, 144
Johnson, 615, 672, 802, 822
Johnson E, 419
Johnson J C, 370, 376
Johnson K, 392, 396
Johnson L K, 702
Johnson M, 39, 47, 55, 57, 219, 225
Johnson M P, 10
Johnson P, 869
Johnson R, 91–2
Johnson R K, 699

Johnson S, 168, 335, 345, 644, 670, 672, 682, 736, 855
Johnson-Laird, 605–6
Johnston P, 352, 361
Johnstone B, 323–4, 784
Joiner J, 912
Jones A, 736
Jones B L, 494, 498
Jones C, 197, 401, 915
Jones D, 77, 296, 866
Jones D G, 228, 231
Jones G M, 700
Jones L, 125, 127
Jones M, 734
Jones S, 840
Jones W, 396, 401
Jönsson, 240, 243
Jönsson L, 243
Joos M, 1, 4, 415, 417
Jordon C, 756
Jorgenson M, 279
Joseph J E, 79, 80, 309–10, 583
Joshi A, 457
Joshi A K, 457, 459–60
Jourdan C, 19, 22
Joyce J, 132
Jud J, 312, 319, 416, 419, 882–3, 885, 922
Judd E, 193
Juilland A G, 303, 305–6
Juillard C, 18, 22
Jungeblut A, 790, 793
Jupp T, 152

Kachru B B, 18, 22, 105, 107, 457, 459–60, 471–2, 520–4, 567, 658, 660, 662, 846–7, 883–4
Kachru Y, 107
Kahane H, 489
Kahane R, 489
Kahn R L, 65
Kalantzis M, 606–8
Kalčik S, 301–2
Kalema J, 570, 573
Kallen J, 503
Kallen J L, 356, 361
Kalogjera D, 689–90
Kaltman H, 151
Kamei T, 559
Kamin, 715
Kannapell B, 91–2
Kapanadze L A, 270, 272–3, 276
Kaplan R B, 647
Karadzic V S, 644
Karl J, 418, 882
Karmiloff-Smith A, 708
Karpat K H, 228, 231
Karttunen L, 200, 208, 460
Kasher A, 122–4, 192
Kaspar B, 28, 186, 867
Kasper G, 146–7, 151, 190–3, 207, 508–9

Kastovsky D, 362
Katriel T, 157, 160, 190, 193
Katz D, 101, 104, 609
Katz J, 35, 36
Katz J J, 208, 514, 519
Kaufman T, 442, 462–4, 780–1
Kawasaki A, 192, 559
Kay P, 40, 46, 47, 73, 71
Keddie N, 723
Keenan E O, 121, 276
Kees W, 170, 172
Keesing R, 19, 22, 37, 47, 501–3
Keesing R M, 533, 536
Kegl J, 533, 536
Keith G, 724, 728, 732–3, 735
Kelle B, 255, 361
Keller R, 410–11
Keller R E, 34, 228, 231, 425, 430
Kelley H H, 86
Kelly B B, 360
Kelly J, 112, 115–16
Kelman H C, 659, 662
Kelman R C, 567
Kempton W, 40, 46, 47, 71
Kendall K, 334–5
Kendon A, 169–70, 172
Kennaway R, 619
Kennedy, 822
Kennedy C, 662, 680
Kennedy G, 769
Kennedy J F, 763
Kent L, 10
Kent V, 827
Keogh A, 920
Kernan K T, 279, 292
Kersta L G, 331–2
Kerswill P E, 391, 393–6
Key M R, 254–5
Khan K, 265
Khan V, 712, 714
Khubchandani L M, 18, 22, 648, 650, 858, 884–5
Kibbee D A, 569
Kiefer F, 73, 123–4, 144
Kindell G E, 512
King B, 522, 524
King Francis I, 653
King Gustav III, 681
King James, 263
King Philip V, 681
Kingman, 702, 726, 746
Kintsch W, 136, 145
Kiparsky, 1, 346, 901
Kiparsky P, 1, 4
Kirk, 354
Kirk D, 648–50
Kirk J M, 351, 357, 361
Kirkland M, 657
Kirsch I, 790, 793

Kirshenblatt-Gimblett B, 277, 279, 280, 292
Kish L, 101, 104
Kitajgorodskaja M V, 271, 276
Kitamura H, 553–4, 559
Kitayama S, 189, 193
Kjolseth R, 650
Klein W, 860
Kleinbooi H, 334–5
Kleineidam H, 625
Kleinman S, 402, 406
Kleinschmidt S, 683
Klemola J, 361
Kloss H, 106–7, 228, 231, 491–3, 498, 568–9, 645, 647–8, 650
Kluckholm C, 37, 47
Kniffka H, 332
Knight C, 396
Knoblauch H, 161
Knoop U, 362
Knott R, 680
Knudsen K, 682
Kochman R, 302
Kochman T, 46–7, 279, 291–2, 301–2, 754, 757
Köck W K, 29
Koerner E F, 865
Koerner E F K, 80, 862
Koerner K, 908
Köhler R, 361
Kohli A, 858
Kohn M, 366
Kohn M L, 366–7, 369
Kokole O H, 892
Kollat D T, 86
Komter M L, 161
König W, 350, 361
Kono R, 559
Konow S, 874
Kontra M, 569
Kontupoulos K M, 100, 104
Koopman W, 411
Korais A, 681
Köster J-P, 332
Kotter J, 824
Koubi G, 569
Kouritzin S, 568–9
Kramarae C, 45, 47, 345, 543, 545
Kramsch C, 470, 472
Krapp G P, 267, 270
Krashen S, 478, 480, 620, 700
Krashen S O, 692, 695
Krause C, 550
Krauss M, 460, 466–7, 569, 757, 759
Krech D, 81, 86
Kreeft-Peyton J, 757
Kress G, 135, 144, 185, 237, 238, 248–9, 255–6, 262, 542–3, 545, 562–3, 582–3, 591, 597, 606, 925
Kretzschmar W A, 351, 354–6, 361, 418–19
Kretzschmar W A Jr, 893

967

Krishnamurti B, 230, 489, 512, 865
Kristol I, 365
Kroch A, 407, 411
Kroeber A L, 37, 47, 173–6
Krogh E C, 255
Kroll B, 271, 276
Kroll J, 16
Kroskrity P, 323–4
Krumanae C, 45, 47
Krumbacher K, 106–7
Krushat W M, 812–3
Kruskal J B, 795, 799, 801
Kruszewski M, 77, 79
Kuam S, 219, 225
Kucera H, 766, 769
Kuhn M H, 103–4
Kuhn S M, 885
Kuhn T, 37, 47
Kuhn T S, 66, 72–3
Kulick D, 19, 22, 167–8, 333, 335–6, 345, 815–16
Kunze K, 350, 361
Künzel H, 329, 332
Künzel H J, 330–2
Kuper A, 891
Kurath H, 312–13, 318–19, 359, 378, 388, 412, 418, 885, 892–3
Kvam S, 219, 225
Kyle J, 92
Kyle J G, 89, 92, 127
Kyle J L, 125–6
Kymlicka W, 49, 50

La Barre W, 170, 172
La Piere R, 7
La Piere R T, 7, 10, 609
La Verne Masayesva J, 467
LaBerge D, 225
Laberge S, 907
Labov T, 300, 302
Labov W, 2, 4, 35–6, 41, 43–4, 46–7, 76, 142, 144, 146, 150–1, 153–4, 160, 166, 168–9, 180, 182–5, 197, 203, 207–8, 217–18, 221, 225, 237, 239, 292, 295, 297, 301–410, 319, 321, 324, 328–30, 332, 338–9, 345, 349, 352, 358, 361, 369, 371–2, 374–91, 393, 395–6, 399–401, 407, 412–15, 417–18, 420–1, 427, 430, 456, 460, 478, 480, 483, 492, 507, 543, 545, 606, 608, 691, 695, 709–10, 717–19, 722–3, 757, 777, 779, 780–2, 784, 794, 801–2, 829, 833, 839, 843, 847–8, 859, 864, 885–7, 901, 904, 907, 910, 916–17, 922
Lacan J, 79, 852
Lacoste M, 53–4, 154
Lacus C, 89–90, 92
Lade A J, 580
Lado R, 476, 480
Laertius D, 198, 207
Lafargue P, 576, 578
Lafont R, 577–8

Laing M, 353, 361
Laitin D, 627, 630, 657, 660
Laitin D D, 567, 630, 657, 662, 669
Lakoff G, 39, 44, 45, 47, 50, 55, 57, 208, 219, 220, 225
Lakoff R, 47, 50, 57, 167, 169, 187, 192–3, 208, 336, 345, 558–9, 887–8
Lakoff R T, 559
Lamb S M, 9
Lambert W, 549–50, 695, 719
Lambert W E, 393, 396, 888–9, 918
Lamgness L L, 775
Lampert M, 809
Lampert M D, 787
Lance D, 456, 460
Lance D M, 361
Landau S I, 672
Landry R, 19, 22, 472–3
Lang S, 336
Langacre R E, 237, 239
Langness L L, 775
Laponce J A, 597, 604, 599, 604
Lapp D, 879
Large A, 619
Large J A, 619
Larner M, 376
Larson M L, 511–12
Lass N, 396
Lass R, 304–5, 307, 411
Lasswell H D, 908
Lauria A, 291–2
Lavandera B, 887
Lavandera B R, 41, 47
Laver J, 332
Lavers A, 563
Lavy V, 790, 793
Law V, 503
Lawler J, 768–9
Lawrence, 281
Lawrence F, 243
Lawrence H, 833
Lawson L, 92
Lazard G, 228, 231
Leach J W, 279, 292
Leacock S, 881
Leader E, 255
Leap W, 47, 310, 335, 630
Leap W L, 333, 335–6, 495, 498
Leary T, 821
Leau L, 619
Leavis F R, 131, 133
Leboucher N, 793
Lebra T S, 189, 193
Lee B, 65, 248, 605, 908
Lee C, 756–7
Lee D, 583
Lee J F, 919
Lee J R E, 116

Lee R E, 67
Leech G, 38–9, 47, 50–1, 150–1, 187–91, 193, 225, 524, 902
Leech G N, 57, 118, 121, 281–3
Leed J, 283
Leeds-Hurwitz W, 170–2
Lees R E, 67
Lehman W, 779
Lehmann W P, 401, 412
Lehrer A, 794, 801
Leiberson S, 624, 626
Leibniz, 616–17
Leibniz R, 129
Leiter K, 162, 165
Leith R, 591
Leitner G, 254–5
Leland C G, 525, 530
LeMasters E E, 301–2
Lemert C C, 652
Lemert E, 97
Lemert E M, 97, 104
Lemon L T, 133
Lenin V I, 570, 573
Lenneberg E H, 38, 46, 518–19
Lennig M, 887
Leon R, 498
Leonard W, 795, 801
Leopold W, 431–2
LePage R, 325, 329, 388
Le Page R, 322, 324–5, 388, 859, 876, 917
Le Page R B, 17–18, 22, 166–9, 519, 662, 858–9, 889–90, 917
LePoire B, 197
Lerman P, 301–2
Lerner G, 161
Lesser R, 894
Levi J N, 497
Levin B, 272
Levin S R, 136, 144
Levine L, 827–8
LeVine R, 37, 48
Levinson S, 6, 115–16, 187–91, 199, 207, 239, 241–2, 558–9, 707–8
Levinson S C, 51, 57, 72–3, 118, 121, 135, 138, 144, 151, 192, 208, 212, 875
Levinson S L, 147, 151
Lévi-Strauss C, 79, 135, 174, 176, 852
Levy M G, 648, 650
Lewin K, 60
Lewin R, 60
Lewis D, 35–6, 225, 796, 801
Lewis E G, 700, 890
Lewis G, 225, 307, 917
Lewis M M, 302
Lewis M P, 512
Lewyckyj R, 795, 801
Leyens J P, 456
Li, 410

Li C, 401
Li F K, 908
Li W L, 494, 498
Li Wei, 16, 370, 376, 444, 446
Liang A C, 335, 736
Liapunov V, 846
Liberson S, 21
Lichtenberk F, 409, 411
Lichtenstein E H, 207
Liddell S, 92
Lidz T, 567
Lieberson S, 22, 328–9, 624, 626, 648, 650, 657, 849, 854
Lighter J, 270
Lighter J E, 266, 270
Lightfoot D, 408–12
Likert R, 819–20
Limón J, 450, 454
Lindblom B, 305–7, 400–1
Linde C, 193, 887
Lindlof T R, 255
Line M P, 29
Linell P, 29, 240, 243
Lingoes J, 801
Lingoes J C, 795–6, 801
Linnaeus C, 235
Linton R, 60
Lippi-Green R, 710
Lippmann W, 608–9
Lipset S M, 99, 104, 366
Lipski J, 457, 460, 798
Lipski J M, 794, 798–9, 801
Liska A E, 8, 10
Litowitz B E, 73
Lively P, 272
Livia A, 335
Livington E, 165
Llewellyn-Jones P, 92
Local J, 112, 115–16
Lodge D, 132–3
Lofland J, 826
Lomonosov, 668
London J, 470
Long M, 503
Longacre R E, 237, 239, 511–12
Löning P, 154
López N, 842, 892
Lo Piparo F, 551
Lord A B, 235
Louis XIII, 666
Lounsbury F, 70, 175
Lounsbury F G, 73, 175–7
Lourman G S, 388
Louw J P, 899
Love N, 36, 80, 484–5
Lowe A, 255
Lowenberg P H, 107, 489, 499, 512, 524
Lowley E G, 326, 329

Lowman G, 885
Lowth R, 724
Lowy E G, 230
Loy J, 280
Lucas C, 89–90, 92
Luckmann T, 241–2, 604, 606
Lucy J A, 40, 47, 68, 71, 73
Luick K, 303–4, 307
Luke A, 135, 144
Luke C, 140, 144
Lunt, 365
Luria, 849
Luther M, 265
Lydgate, 667
Lynch M, 161, 164, 165
Lyon J, 71
Lyons J, 34, 58–9, 157, 160, 509
Lyotard, 139

Ma R, 3, 856
Macaulay R, 388, 420–1
Macaulay R K S, 270, 272, 276
Macaulay W J, 724, 735
Macauley T B, 520
MacCabe C, 262
MacCormack W C, 454
MacDonald D A, 361
Macdonell D, 139, 144
MacDowell J, 279
Macedo D, 53, 57, 139, 144
MacGinitie, 856
Machan T W, 524
Machiavelli N, 7, 824
Mackay C, 268, 270
Mackey, 508
Mackey W F, 660–2
Maclagan M, 307, 917
MacLaury R E, 46
MacLure M, 747
Macnamara J, 350
MacRury I, 255–6
MacSwan J, 458, 460
MacWhinney B, 704, 708
Macy M, 93
Madden C, 192
Maddieson I, 400–1
Maffi L, 569–70
Mahapatra B P, 648, 650
Maher J C, 258–9
Mahootian S, 458–60
Mahshie S N, 700
Mai H, 765
Maizland H, 161
Makhudu D, 880
Makkai A, 29
Malaprop, 278
Malherbe E G, 890

Malinowski, 207, 849
Malinowski B, 73, 186, 866–7
Malinowski B K, 28, 72, 219, 891
Malkiel Y, 401, 412, 779, 922
Mallery G, 169
Mallik B, 109
Mallory J P, 442, 502–3
Maltz D N, 300–2
Manalansan M, 334, 336
Mandelbaum D, 908
Mandelbaum D G, 73, 89
Manes J, 190, 193, 491
Mann R D, 821
Manning A, 73
Manning F E, 279
Marcellesi J-B, 576, 578
Marchal A, 307
Marcus H, 83, 86
Marecek J, 254–5
Margolis J, 124
Margrain S, 828
Mario, 431
Markey T L, 880
Markowicz H, 92
Markowitz J A, 73
Markus H R, 189, 193
Marr, 560
Marr N J, 576
Martha, 166, 378
Martin J R, 237, 239, 727, 735, 877
Martin R, 237
Martin-Jones M, 516, 519, 606, 608
Martinet A, 28, 29, 79, 303, 305, 307, 922
Marx K, 363–4, 369, 560, 563, 576, 578, 849
Masica C P, 230, 351, 361, 428, 430
Massamba D, 628–30
Mateene K, 568, 570, 572–3
Matejka L, 133, 563, 578
Mather J Y, 319
Mather S, 90, 92
Matisoff J A, 212
Matouschek B, 926
Matsumoto Y, 189, 193
Matsumura K, 467
Mattheier K, 499, 845, 860
Mattheier K J, 107, 218, 491–2, 845, 860
Matthews P, 35–6
Matthews S, 360
Matthews W S, 300, 302
Matza D, 8–10
Maurer D W, 266, 269–70, 893
Mauss A, 98
Mauss A L, 70, 98, 104
Mauss M, 70, 73
Maw J, 736
Maximovich-Ambodic, 668
May K, 475
May S, 680

May W H, 801
Maybin J, 680
Mazrui A A, 891–2
Mazrui A M, 892
McArthur T, 471–2, 581, 583
McCabe A, 184–5
McCabe C, 324
McCall G J, 775
McCann C C, 473
McCarthy T, 208, 243, 563
McCarty T L, 700
McCawley, 67
McCawley J, 67
McClelland J L, 306–7
McClure J D, 498, 580
McConnell G D, 648, 650
McConnell-Ginet S, 57, 286–7, 302
McCormack W C, 22
McCormick K, 449, 451, 454
McDavid R, 76, 313, 319
McDavid R I Jr, 76, 321, 892–3, 885, 912, 922
McDavid V G, 893
McDermott R, 322, 324
McDowell J, 279
McGee V W, 846
McGregor D, 823–4, 827
McHale B, 132–3
McHoul A W, 135, 138–9, 144
McHugh P, 84, 86, 161
McIntosh A, 102, 104, 262, 319
McIver J P, 820
McKinney J C, 165
McKinnon M, 720, 723
McLaughlin B, 607–8
McLaughlin M, 869
McLaughlin M W, 879
McMahon A, 169, 166
McMahon A M, 81, 86
McNeill D, 171–2
McPartland T S, 103–4
McQuillan J, 620
McQuown N, 170
McQuown N A, 73, 66
McRae K, 657
McWhorter J H, 463–4
Mead, 849
Mead G H, 28, 60, 76, 83–4, 86
Mead M, 283–4, 287
Medevedev P N, 127, 133
Meditch A, 300, 302
Medvedev N, 846, 921
Medvedev P N, 133, 560, 563, 576
Meechan M, 901
Meeuwis M, 446
Mehan H, 722–3, 753, 804–5, 808–9
Meier C, 161
Meijer G, 879–80, 888–9
Meillet A, 74, 76, 79–80, 407, 409–10, 412

Meinhof U, 855
Meinhof U H, 167–8, 335, 345, 736
Meisel J, 474–5
Mel'čuk I A, 73
Melton J G, 402, 407
Mencken H L, 267, 270, 297, 892
Mendoza-Denton N, 777, 778
Menn L, 496, 498
Menz F, 926
Mercer N, 326, 329, 751–3, 803, 806, 809
Merleau-Ponty, 161
Merten D, 298, 300, 302–3
Merton R, 60, 403, 407
Merton R M, 60, 65
Mertz E, 88
Mesthrie R, 37, 47, 307, 310, 487, 489, 501, 503, 629–30
Metzger M, 91–2
Mey J, 135 144, 507, 543, 545, 849
Mey J L, 50, 52–8, 507, 509, 541–3, 561, 563, 575–8, 597
Meyer M, 926
Meyerhoff M, 197, 336, 737, 777–8
Meyer-Lübke W, 407, 412
Michaels E, 139, 144
Michaels L, 583–4
Milán W G, 230
Milic L T, 282–3
Miller C, 344–5
Miller D, 813
Miller J, 270–2, 276
Mills C W, 375–6, 581, 584
Mills S, 855
Milroy J, 331–2, 371, 374, 376, 391, 893, 916
Milroy L, 151, 160, 169, 339–40, 345, 371–2, 374, 376, 388–9, 442–4, 446, 448, 454, 456, 770–1, 776, 779, 781, 828, 894, 916
Minami F, 559
Minkova D, 304–5, 307
Minsky M, 220, 225
Miron M S, 801
Mishler E, 240, 243
Mishler E G, 597
Mistry P J, 853–4, 881
Mitchell C, 370
Mitchell J C, 370, 376
Mitchell S, 320–1
Mitchell T F, 134–5, 144
Mitchell-Kernan C, 279, 291–2, 301–2
Mithun M, 497–8
Mitten R, 926
Mittins W, 727, 735
Mitzka W, 319
Mohan P, 496, 498, 800–1
Mohrmann C, 867
Moll L, 756–7
Mollory J P, 502–3
Montagu A, 45, 47, 287

Montague, 28
Montague R, 220, 225
Montgomery M, 253, 255, 351, 353, 361
Montgomery M B, 361
Montreuil J, 665
Moosmüller S, 586, 591
Moravcsik J, 225
Moreno J, 60
Moreno J C, 60, 827
Moreno J L, 827–8
Moretti B, 192–3
Morgan J, 143, 207–8
Morgan J L, 121, 124, 211, 225, 243, 705, 708, 765
Morgan L H, 172–3, 175, 177
Moriel L, 335–6
Morik K, 222, 225
Morosawa A, 191, 193
Morris C, 51, 58
Morris C H, 51, 58
Morris D, 924–5
Morris P, 921
Morrison K L, 139, 144
Morson G S, 133, 845–6
Morton A Q, 281–3
Moseley C, 350, 362
Moss G, 736
Mothersill M, 35–6
Moulton W G, 351, 362, 922
Mountford J, 846
Mous M, 22, 464, 482–3
Mrydal G, 858
Msimang T, 629–30
Muecke S, 143
Mueller J E, 762, 765
Mufwene S, 302, 848, 894–5
Muhammad, 262
Muhlenberg F A, 659
Mühlhäusler P, 19, 22, 362, 474–5, 484–5, 532–3, 536, 538, 568, 570, 572–3, 895–6
Mukařovský J, 244, 246
Mulac A, 869
Mullard C, 549–50
Munroe G, 361
Muntigl P, 925
Murdock G P, 174, 177
Murphy R, 881
Murray, 430, 564
Murray L, 724
Murray S O, 333, 336
Murre J, 707–8
Musgrove F, 404–5, 407
Mussolini B, 587
Muysken P, 16, 151, 326–8, 442–3, 446, 448, 454, 456–7, 460, 464, 481–3, 485, 530, 535, 607–8, 628, 630, 880, 894, 897
Muysken P C, 896
Myers G, 252, 255
Myers K, 736

Myers-Scotton C, 442–4, 446, 448, 450, 454–60, 481–83, 661–2, 897–8
Myhill J, 887
Myrdal G, 858

Nagpal H, 563
Nagy N, 887
Napoli D J, 853–4
Nardi P M, 61, 65
Naroll R, 775
Nash W, 245–6, 259, 261–2, 278, 280, 282–3
Nataraja S, 264
Nava M, 252, 255–6
Nava O, 252, 256
Nearey T, 415, 418
Needhan R, 176
Neil D, 150–1
Nelde P, 376, 499
Nelde P H, 361, 625, 845
Nemser W, 476, 480
Nettle D, 464, 466–7, 498, 905
Neuman C A, 10
Neurath O, 58
Neustupny J, 567
Neustupny J V, 632–4
Nevalainen T, 376
Newcomb H, 128, 133, 255–6
Newman S, 908
Newmark P, 633–4
Newmeyer F, 411, 834
Newmeyer F J, 47, 287, 329, 411–12, 723
Newmeyer J, 46–7
Newton B, 318–19
Ngugi wa Thiong'o, 572–3, 661
Nice R, 563
Nichols P C, 340, 345
Nicol J, 16, 460
Nicoladis E, 889
Nida E A, 511–12, 898–9
Niederehe H-J, 80
Niepokuy M, 861
Nietzsche F W, 581, 584
Nijhof G, 542
Nikiforidou N, 861
Ninio A, 703, 708
Nixon R, 285
Noels K, 473
Nolan F, 396
Nolan F J, 329, 331–2, 393, 396
Nolen W, 192
Norberg B, 509
Nordberg B, 243
Norman F, 867
Norman J, 227, 231, 243, 341
Norman K, 753
North D, 357, 362
Nowak P, 926
Nowell E, 92

Nowell-Smith G, 563
Nunberg G, 887
Nunnally T, 361–2
Nunnally T E, 361
Nwenmely H, 713–14
Nyquist L, 44, 47

Oakes M P, 769
O'Baoill D, 628–30
O'Barr W, 231, 233, 239, 243, 545
O'Barr W M, 231
O'Cain R K, 885, 893
Ochs E, 5, 6, 87–9, 115–16, 192, 515, 519, 780, 787, 910
O'Connor N, 887
Odell L, 756
Odlin T, 442, 500–3
O'Donnell W R, 34, 282–3
O'Donohoe S, 251, 255–6
Oftedal M, 580
Ogay T, 197
Ogbu J, 755, 757, 788, 793
Ogden C K, 73, 186, 866–7, 891
Ogino T, 192, 559
Oh C-K, 208
Ohala J J, 307, 400–1
Ohlin L, 825
Ohlin L E, 827
Ohmann R, 245–6, 280, 282–3
O'Kane D J M, 361
Okara G, 523
Okolovich E, 845
Olastman J, 421
Olesky W, 146, 152
Oliveira M, 887
Olshtain E, 190, 193, 480, 918
Ó Murchú M, 228, 231
O'Neill J, 161
Ong W J, 270–1, 275–6
Onlin L E, 825, 827
Opie I, 280, 298, 302
Opie P, 280, 298, 302
Orasnu J, 302
Orr D, 635
Orr G, 501, 503
Ortiz, A, 73
Orton, 252, 262
Orton H, 314, 319
Ortony A, 29, 58
Orwell G, 583
Osgood C E, 96, 104, 794, 801
Osin L, 793
Östman J-O, 243
Ostrower A, 622, 626
O'Sullivan T, 139, 144
Otanes F, 918
Otfrid, 33
Otheguy R, 151

O'Toole M, 259–62, 283
Ozkok B, 279, 292
Ozóg A C K, 700

Padmanabha P, 650
Page R L, 889, 916–7
Pagliuca W, 536
Paikeday T M, 513–15, 519
Palmer E, 29
Palmer F R, 107, 220, 225, 860, 867
Palmer L R, 485, 489, 683
Pandit I, 458–60
Pandit P B, 18, 22, 538–9, 567
Pāṇini, 1, 264, 681
Paradis C, 887
Paradis M, 16
Pardoe T E, 911
Paris G, 870
Parisi D, 708
Park R E, 60
Parker D, 186
Parker I, 228, 231
Parker S G, 512
Parkin D, 20, 22
Parkin F, 365, 404, 407
Parmenter, 88
Parry D, 356, 362
Parsons T, 63, 161, 165, 243, 308
Partridge E, 267, 270, 287
Passeron J C, 562–3, 612, 852
Pateman T, 35–6, 58, 254, 256
Paterson R, 256
Paton J, 711, 714
Patrick P, 887
Pattanayak D P, 508–9, 567, 572–3
Paulsen F, 494, 498
Paulston C B, 1, 4, 511–12, 606, 608, 712, 714, 723, 749, 842, 899–900
Paulston R, 899
Pauwels A, 229–31
Pawley A, 234–5, 517, 519
Payne R C, 893
Peal E, 888–9
Pearce J, 734
Pêcheux M, 139, 140, 144, 561, 563
Peckham D, 899–900
Pedersen C, 682
Pederson L, 893
Pei M, 227, 231, 619–20, 625–26
Peirce C S, 51, 76, 254, 256, 921
Pelikan J, 926
Pell T, 809
Pelto G H, 775
Pelto P J, 775
Penelope J, 334, 336
Penner L, 104
Pennisi A, 352, 362
Pennycook A, 573–4

Pepicello W J, 280
Peraklya A, 112, 116
Peranteau P M, 497
Perkins R, 536
Péronnet L, 360
Perry T, 710
Peter L, 332
Peters A, 200, 234–5
Peters S, 208
Peterson C, 184–5
Peter the Great, 668
Petöfi J S, 136, 144
Petri L, 682
Petri O, 682
Pfaff C, 450, 452, 454, 457, 459, 461
Pfaff C W, 454
Pfohl S J, 104
Pham Xuan Tahi, 504
Phares G C, 497
Phelps, 920
Philip V, 653
Philips S, 321, 324, 882
Philips S U, 45, 47, 87–8, 342, 345
Philipsen G, 42, 47, 155, 157, 159–60
Phillips T, 747
Phillipson R, 488, 498–9, 523–4, 549–50, 567–70, 572–4, 625–7, 630
Philip the Fair, 666
Piaget, 849
Piaget J, 80, 184, 186
Pickford G R, 885
Pike K L, 77, 135, 144, 511–12
Pilcher W W, 286–7
Piliavan J A, 255
Pinkal M, 220–2, 225
Pinker S, 165, 169, 703, 708
Pinson K S, 665, 669
Pitt M, 510, 512
Pittam J, 197
Plato, 75–6, 236, 398, 585, 717
Platt J, 519, 521, 524, 900
Platt J T, 900
Plautus, 681
Plunkett K, 708
Plutarch, 131
Pogner K H, 214
Polinsky M, 360
Pollack M E, 207
Pollner M, 161–2, 165
Polomé E C, 603–4
Polya G, 68
Pomerantz A, 115–16, 161
Ponzio A, 575, 578
Pool I, 583
Pool J, 21–2, 567, 597, 600, 604, 657
Pop R D, 871
Pop S, 871
Pope Saint Damasas, 1

Poplack S, 16, 452, 454, 456–7, 459, 461, 887, 901
Popovskii, 669
Posey D, 570
Posner R, 179
Post B, 396
Postal P M, 208, 400–1
Poster M, 562–3
Potter D M, 663, 669
Potter J, 168–9, 253, 256, 322, 324
Poussa P, 502–3
Powesland G, 295
Powesland P, 297
Powesland P F, 723, 869
Prah K K, 630
Prator C, 918
Pratt M L, 122–4, 182, 186, 245–6, 323–4
Presser S, 8, 10, 761–2, 765
Preston D, 192, 350, 362, 417, 797
Preston D R, 360, 362, 693–6, 797, 801–2
Price G, 580
Pride J, 152, 519
Pride J B, 30, 37, 47, 230, 454, 507, 509
Priebsch R, 683
Prince A, 459, 461
Prinsloo M, 915
Propp V, 134, 144, 180
Prys Jones S, 16
Psathas G, 144, 161, 165, 872, 906
Puchner L, 788, 793
Pullen G, 125, 127
Punana Lao, 836
Putschke W, 362
Pye, 346

Quasthoff, 219, 222, 224–5
Queen Isabella, 681
Queré L, 161
Quine, 26
Quinn R P, 65
Quintilian, 169, 236
Quirk R, 219, 225, 471–2, 521, 524, 853, 901–2

Raab E, 99, 104
Rabelais, 131–3
Rabin C, 227, 230–1
Rabow J, 8, 10
Radcliffe-Brown A R, 177
Radovanovič M, 690
Rainwater L, 715, 723
Ramanujan A K, 226, 230
Ramisch H, 350, 362
Rampton B, 110, 322–4, 445–6, 854
Rampton M B H, 784
Ramsaran S, 396
Ramsey C, 91–2
Ranamål, 449
Rand D, 831, 833
Rando E N, 853–4

Rannut M, 570
Rao R, 523
Rask R, 398
Rasmussen G, 214
Rau W, 103, 795, 801
Rawls A, 165
Ray, 40, 645
Ray P S, 634, 647
Ray V F, 47
Raymond G, 242
Reagan R, 585, 640
Reardon K, 247, 256
Recanati F, 199, 208
Reddy M J, 23, 29
Redfern W, 278, 280
Redish J C, 240, 243
Reed D, 257
Reed L, 757
Rehbein J, 154
Reid E, 916
Reinecke A T, 903
Reinecke J, 859, 880, 903, 911
Reinecke J E, 903
Reis M J, 133
Reisigl M, 926
Rendsburg G A, 227, 231
Reppen R, 769
Reyburn W, 899
Reyhner J, 759
Reznikov L O, 577–8
Rice S A, 101, 104
Ricento T, 574
Richards B, 255–6
Richards I A, 186, 866–7, 891
Richards J, 235
Richards J C, 193, 514
Richardson K, 784, 854
Richelieu, 681
Richmond J, 728, 735
Rickford A, 904
Rickford J, 166, 169, 302, 376, 848, 887, 895
Rickford J R, 109–10, 709–10, 749, 782, 784, 878, 887, 904–5
Rickford R, 710
Rickford R J, 749, 904–5
Ricks C, 583–4
Riedlinger A, 3, 74
Rieger B B, 361
Rietveld A C M, 331–2
Riley D, 376
Riley R, 709
Rimmon-Kenan S, 133
Ringbom H, 500, 503, 508–9
Rintell E, 191, 193
Rissanan M, 361–2
Ritchie W, 524
Ritchie W C, 456, 460
Ritter C, 8, 10

Rivers W H R, 173–4, 177
Rivière P, 142–3
Roberge P T, 880
Roberts C, 149, 152, 242–3
Roberts I, 408–9, 412, 887
Robertson F, 468, 472
Robins R H, 34, 467, 497, 867
Robinson J, 831, 833
Robinson W P, 197, 722–3, 869–70
Roche J, 474–5
Rochefort, 337
Rodman R, 58–9
Rodney W, 570, 574
Roe P, 143
Rogers M E, 247, 256
Roget, 617
Rokeach M, 103–4
Rollinger C-R, 225
Romaine S, 16, 298, 300, 302, 345, 350, 387, 389, 467, 481, 483, 498, 516–17, 530, 604, 606, 608, 904–5, 916
Romein J, 880
Rommetveit R, 26, 28, 29
Roncek D, 795, 801
Rönnefarth H K G, 622, 626
Roosevelt F D, 636
Roques M, 870–1
Rosas A, 550
Rosch E, 39, 47
Rose T, 298, 303
Rosen H, 679, 680, 725, 849
Rosenbaum P S, 208
Rosenbaum Y, 626
Rosenberg M, 10
Rosenthal D, 473
Rosiello L, 551
Ross A, 298, 303
Ross A S C, 34
Ross J, 358, 360
Ross J R, 50, 208, 325, 329
Rosseel E, 509
Rossetti R, 504
Rossi J P, 225
Rossi-Landi F, 562–3, 578
Rothery J, 727, 735
Rothkopf E, 756
Rothstein R A, 670, 672
Roulet E, 695
Rousseau, 385
Rousseau J J, 715
Rousseau P, 831–4
Rousselot, 870
Rousselot P-J, 400–1
Rowe J, 881
Roy C, 91–2
Rubagumya C M, 711, 714
Rubal-Lopez A, 573, 868
Rubin C, 643

Rubin E, 460
Rubin J, 230, 567, 573, 634, 645, 647, 662, 858
Rudin E, 357, 360
Ruesch J, 29, 170, 172
Rugg D, 761, 765
Rumelhart D, 220, 225
Rummel R J, 799, 801
Rushdie S, 523
Rushton, 716
Russ J, 341, 345
Russell B, 50
Russell D A, 203, 238
Russell J, 887
Ryan E B, 86, 322, 324, 870
Ryckeboer H, 350, 356, 362
Ryle, 198
Ryle G, 50

Sabban A, 500, 502–3
Sabino R, 361–2
Sacks H, 6, 47, 43, 51, 111–12, 116, 137–8, 144, 161, 163–5, 213–14, 240, 243, 694, 854, 905–6, 909–10
Sacks J, 812–13
Sadock J M, 202–3, 208
Sagarin E, 287
Sahakian W S, 81, 86
Saint-Jacques B, 604
Saito M, 193
Sakiyama O, 553, 559
Salamini L, 874
Salgãdo G, 109
Salinger J D, 281
Salt J, 324
Samarin W, 265, 781
Samarin W J, 503–4
Samoilovich, 668
Samovar L A, 827
Sampson G, 35–6, 119, 121–2, 124
Samter W, 197
Samuels F, 609
Samuels J, 225
Samuels M L, 104, 305–7
Sanches M, 280, 292
Sand L, 360, 417
Sanderson S, 361
Sangster C M, 391, 396
Sankoff, 44, 384–5, 387–8, 452, 829, 831–3, 847, 906–7
Sankoff D, 388, 454, 833–4, 848
Sankoff G, 47, 834, 906–7
Santorini B, 458, 460
Sapir E, 1, 15, 34, 36, 39, 47, 65–6, 68, 76, 87, 89, 157, 170, 172, 216, 470, 583, 604–5, 717, 779, 849, 852–3, 862, 876–7, 898, 907, 924
Sapir J D, 907
Sarangi S, 239, 241–3, 284, 287, 844
Sathe V, 824
Sato C J, 903

Sattel J W, 340, 345
Saunders D, 144
Saville-Troike M, 2, 4, 512, 908–9
Savin-Williams R C, 301, 303
Scalia G, 551
Scannell P, 253, 256
Schaechter M, 922
Schaff A, 40, 47, 577–8
Schank R, 220, 225
Schank R C, 135, 144
Schatzman L, 216, 218
Scheff T, 97
Scheff T J, 97–8, 104
Scheffler H, 175
Scheffler H W, 175, 177
Scheflen A E, 171–2, 175
Schegloff E A, 6, 47, 51, 111–13, 115–16, 137–8, 144, 161, 214, 243, 906, 909–10
Schenkein J, 165
Schenkein J N, 135, 144
Schepin K I, 668
Scherer K R, 172, 192, 197
Schermer T, 92
Scheuermaier P, 883, 885
Schieffelin B, 192, 324, 87, 89
Schieffelin B B, 280, 670, 672, 787
Schiff J A, 920
Schiffman H, 228, 231, 647, 662
Schiffrin D, 43, 47, 182, 418, 887, 910–11
Schilling-Estes N, 376, 779, 926
Schiltz G, 351, 362
Schirmunski V M, 490, 923
Schleicher, 428
Schlesinger L, 824
Schleyer, 617
Schlitz, 203
Schlobinski P, 373, 376, 860
Schmidt A, 498
Schmidt J, 425
Schmidt R, 235
Schmidt R W, 193
Schmied J, 327, 329, 627, 630
Schmitt J C, 169, 172
Schmitt R L, 87, 872
Schneider D M, 175, 177, 48
Schneider E, 148, 351, 354, 361–2, 419
Schneider E W, 524
Schneidman E S, 906
Schoepfle G M, 71, 73, 775
Schön D A, 55–6, 58
Schramm W, 583
Schrøder K C, 247, 250–1, 254, 256
Schuchardt, 1, 4
Schuchardt H, 425, 536, 531, 880, 911–12
Schulz M, 545
Schulze L, 254–5
Schuman H, 8, 10, 101, 761–3, 765
Schumann C L, 880, 911

Schumann J H, 695–6
Schur E M, 98, 105
Schutz A, 137, 144, 161–2
Schütz A, 84, 86
Schwartz G, 298, 300, 303
Schwarz N, 764–5
Schwarze C, 225
Schweid G, 867
Scobbie J M, 391, 396
Scollon R, 188, 193, 781
Scollon S B K, 193, 781
Scott C T, 524
Scott J, 763, 765
Scott M S, 918
Scott R A, 61, 65
Scovel T, 480
Scrimshaw P, 809
Seaford, 170
Searle J, 39, 50–1, 135–6, 150, 198, 201–2, 204, 219–20, 225, 910
Searle J R, 48, 58, 144, 152, 208, 211
Sebba M, 444, 446, 450, 454, 481, 483, 530
Sebeok T A, 30, 76, 160, 172, 262, 559, 578, 683, 854, 871
Sechehaye A, 3, 74
Seidel G, 543, 545
Seiler R M, 165
Selby H A, 38–9, 46, 48, 177
Seligman E R A, 287
Selinker L, 192, 475, 480–1, 516
Sellers S, 340–1, 345
Selting M, 112, 115–16
Senghas A, 536
Senghor, 518
Senyuchenko G A, 890
Seuren P A M, 200, 208, 225
Seymour S, 765
Sgall P, 219, 225
Shafer R E, 714
Shaffer D R, 83, 86
Shakespeare W, 59, 282
Shapir, 604
Shapiro M, 584, 587
Shapiro M J, 597
Shapiro M L, 591
Sharrock W W, 161, 165
Shaw M E, 827
Shelley B L, 511–12
Shepard C, 193, 197
Sheridan A, 243
Sheridan D, 915
Sheriden Smith A M, 869
Sherzer J, 6, 37, 40, 42, 46, 48, 143, 156, 160, 278, 280, 310, 417, 848
Sherzer J F, 906
Shimanoff S, 823
Shimanoff S B, 827
Shin S J, 444, 446

Shipley W, 881
Shipman V, 717, 720, 723
Shklovsky V, 131, 133
Shneidman E, 144
Shohamy E, 913
Shopen T, 559
Short M, 281–3
Short M H, 283
Shultz J, 171
Shultz J J, 785–6
Shuy R, 1, 4, 634, 662, 755–7, 904, 912
Shuy R W, 37, 40, 68, 71, 92, 150, 152, 864, 912–13
Shweder R, 37, 40, 48, 68
Shweder R A, 47, 88, 71, 73
Shye S, 801
Siatkowski J, 355, 362
Sibayan B, 918
Sieber S, 62, 65
Siegel E, 907
Siegel J, 489, 749
Sigman S J, 172, 249, 256
Silver B D, 104
Silverman D, 906
Silverstein M, 482–5
Simmel G, 60, 267
Simmons J L, 775
Simon H A, 136, 143
Simpson J M Y, 80, 104, 294, 297, 580
Simpson P, 260–2
Sinclair J, 137, 144, 241, 243, 750, 753, 846
Sinclair J C, 713–14
Singh D, 914
Singh R, 454, 457, 459, 460–1, 516
Singler J V, 463–4
Sinha A K, 230
Sintow A, 335
Sjöholm K, 500, 503
Skinner, 701
Skutnabb-Kangas T, 327, 329, 508–9, 547–50, 567, 569–70, 573–4, 606, 608, 700
Slade D, 608
Slater N, 302
Slater P E, 406–7
Sledd J, 270, 755, 757
Slembrouck S, 239, 241, 243
Slevin J, 247, 256
Slobin D I, 348–50, 703–4, 707–8
Smart B, 869
Smith, 897, 903, 917
Smith A, 325, 329
Smith A D, 662, 669
Smith D, 139, 144, 161
Smith F, 709, 713–14
Smith G W H, 219, 872
Smith J H, 225, 353
Smith J J, 353, 362
Smith L E, 472, 482, 521, 523–4
Smith M, 407

977

Smith N, 443, 464, 483, 485, 530, 535, 897
Smith O, 584
Smith P, 903, 917
Smith R N, 73
Smitherman G, 301, 303, 709–10
Smolensky P, 459, 461
Smout K D, 482–3
Snoek J D, 65
Snow C, 703, 706, 708
Snow C E, 87, 89
Snyder L, 432, 708
Snyder M, 86
Socrates, 585
Solano F R, 676, 679
Sommer G, 497
Sommerfelt A, 76, 867
Sonne H, 192
Sonntag S, 567
Sonntag S K, 600, 604
Sorjonen M-J, 116
Sornig K, 190, 193, 890
Soudien C, 454
Soyinka W, 523
Spears A K, 464, 483, 895
Speech, 866
Speitel H H, 319
Spencer J, 283, 604
Spender D, 135, 144, 736
Sperber D, 118, 221, 225, 272, 667
Spindler G, 88
Spindler L, 879
Spolsky B, 227, 231, 509, 567, 700, 842, 856, 868, 890, 913–14
Spooner W, 278
Spradley J P, 775
Spratt J, 793
Sridhar, 457
Sridhar K K, 461
Sridhar S N, 459, 461
Srivastava B, 914
Srivastava R N, 914
Stalin J V, 560, 576, 591, 625, 921
Stallybrass P, 133
Stalpers J, 135, 144
Stampe, 346
Stangor C, 83, 86
Stansell C, 335
Stark R, 9–10, 84–6, 97, 105, 825–7
Starý Z, 361
Staton J, 756–7, 913
St. Clair R, 456, 917
St. Damasas I, 511
Steedman C, 345
Steele R, 262, 877
Steele S, 47, 345
Steensland L, 509
Steever S, 854
Stein D, 420–1

Stein G, 902
Steinberg D D, 57
Steiner F, 283–4, 287
Steiner P, 29
Steiner R, 307
Steinthal H, 74
Stephan C W, 80–1, 86
Stephan W G, 86
Stephanus, 667
Stephens J, 584
Stern F, 926
Stern H H, 469, 472, 515, 517
Stevenson P, 228, 230
Stewart A H, 600, 794, 801
Stewart S, 280
Stewart W, 604
Stigler J W, 88
St. Jerome, 265, 511
St. Lambert, 918
Stocking G, 852
Stockwell R P, 304–5, 307
Stokoe W C, 91–2
Stolz B A, 672
Stolz T, 920
Stone M, 392, 396, 701–2
Stouffer S, 366
Strack F, 765
Stratta L, 747
Strauss A, 216, 218
Strauss S, 225
Strawson, 26, 198
Street B, 914–15
Street B V, 793
Strevens P, 262
Strong P M, 153–4
Strong T B, 581, 584
Stross B, 157, 160
Stroud C, 606, 608
Stuart-Smith J, 396
Stubbs M, 270, 276, 711, 714, 753, 803, 809
Sturtevant W C, 30
Suci G J, 104
Sudman S, 765
Sudnow D, 165
Sudnow D N, 906
Sugito S, 629–30
Sullivan G, 335
Sullivan H S, 908
Suppes P, 225
Sutherland E, 94
Sutherland E H, 105
Sutton L, 335
Sutton L A, 736
Sutton-Smith B, 279
Sutton-Spence R, 92, 855
Svartvik J, 225, 524, 766, 902
Svetov, 669
Swadesh M, 493, 495, 498, 908

Swain M, 432, 606, 608, 699
Swales J, 204, 243
Swales J M, 258–9
Swales R, 236–7, 239
Swann J, 47, 310, 345, 592, 597, 630, 736–7, 753
Sweden E, 632
Sweet H, 303, 307
Swift J, 681
Swift K, 344–5
Syder F, 234–5, 517
Sykes G, 8
Sykes G M, 9–10
Syobo H, 467
Szwedek A, 362

Tabory M, 622, 626
Tabouret-Keller A, 17, 19, 21–2, 165–9, 322, 324–5, 329, 388, 448, 489, 512, 519, 865, 890
Taeldeman J, 361
Taeschner T, 431–2
Tagg J, 140, 144
Tagliamonte S, 833, 901
Tajfel H, 456, 518–19
Takahashi T, 190–3
Talbot, 541
Tambiah S J, 265
Tanaka, 182, 554, 754, 910, 916
Tannen D, 39, 43, 45, 48, 144, 186, 332, 754, 757, 888, 910–11, 916, 918
Tannenbaum P H, 104
Tanz C, 47, 345
Tarallo F, 887
Tarde G, 76
Tarone E, 479, 481
Tarone E E, 692–3, 696
Tawney R H, 243
Tay M, 514, 519
Taylor C, 49–50
Taylor D, 881
Taylor D M, 473, 889
Taylor E B, 73
Taylor L F, 874
Taylor T J, 80, 583, 854, 855
Tellefson J W, 326
Ten Have P, 161, 906
Ter Minasova S, 641
Terence, 681
Terman, 715
Terrell T D, 797, 801
Tesser A, 83, 86
Thadani G, 334, 336
Thakerar J N, 196–7
Thatcher M, 590
Thelander M, 509
Therborn G, 560, 563
Thernstrom S, 402, 407
Thomas, 83, 361, 888, 902
Thomas A, 360–1, 847

Thomas a Kempis, 636
Thomas A R, 357, 362
Thomas C, 888
Thomas E R, 362
Thomas F W, 875
Thomas J A, 241, 243, 920
Thomas J B, 242
Thomas V S, 878
Thomas W, 335–6
Thomason S G, 442, 462–4, 481, 483, 485, 489, 897
Thompson, 410
Thompson J B, 242, 560, 563, 597, 612–13
Thompson S, 116, 335, 910
Thomson D S, 494, 498, 580
Thomson G, 485, 489
Thomson J B, 592, 597, 611–13
Thorborn T, 645, 647
Thorlindsson T, 368–9
Thorndike, 856
Thorne B, 45, 48, 345, 737
Thornton G, 734
Thornton R, 61, 65
Threadgold T, 135, 144, 237–8, 261–2, 239, 877
Thumboo E, 523–4
Thurstone L L, 818–20
Tieken-Boon van Ostade I, 376
Tiersma P, 233
Tillery J, 360, 417
Timm L A, 229, 231
Timmins C, 396
Tiryakian E A, 165
Titscher S, 926
Titunik I R, 133, 563, 578
Todd A D, 152, 154, 239, 242
Todd F, 803–4, 808–9
Todd L, 34, 282–3, 504, 530
Todorov T, 29, 133, 846
Tollefson J, 626, 630, 647
Tollefson J W, 326, 329, 523–4
Tolstoy L N, 128
Tomaševski K, 547, 550
Tomić O M, 150, 152, 690
Toolan, 260
Torbe M, 680
Toribio A J, 460
Tough J, 738
Toukomaa P, 508–9
Trager G, 908
Trager G L, 34, 170
Traugott E C, 409–12
Treichler P A, 57
Trengove G, 283
Trew A, 583, 606
Trew T, 185, 248–9, 255–6, 542, 545, 591, 597
Trim J L M, 506, 509
Troike R, 572, 574
Trubetzkoy, 28, 79
Trubetzkoy N S, 77, 427, 429–30

979

Trudell B, 255
Trudgeon A, 396
Trudgill P, 33–4, 37, 44, 48, 166, 169, 194, 197, 286–7, 307, 311, 319, 329, 332, 339, 345, 351, 354, 356, 359–60, 362, 375–6, 386, 389, 391, 393, 396, 486, 489, 499, 695, 719, 723, 916–17
Trueba H, 324, 756
Truman H, 640
Tryon D, 896
Tryon D T, 362
Tse L, 620
Tsitsipis L, 814
Tsitsipis L D, 816
Tsunoda M, 622, 626
Tsuzaki S, 903
Tsuzaki S M, 903
Tubbs S L, 824, 827
Tucker D, 918
Tucker G, 239, 242
Tucker G R, 1, 4, 511–12, 723, 842, 888–9, 900, 918
Tucker R C, 369
Tuijnman A, 791, 793
Tulving E, 47
Turk A E, 396
Turner B S, 140, 143–4
Turner D, 144
Turner J, 915
Turner J H, 105, 161
Turner R H, 10, 65
Turner R L, 875
Turpin D, 901
Twain M, 281, 856
Tweedie F, 396
Tylor E, 169, 173
Tylor E B, 70, 73, 174, 177
Tzavaras G, 917

Ueda K, 190, 193
Uhlenbeck E M, 467, 497
Ulfilas, 511
Ullman-Margalit E, 35–6
Ullmann S, 282–3
Umiker-Sebeok J, 578
Unwin, 243, 738
Upton C, 307, 356, 360, 362
Urioste J L, 481, 483
Urwin C, 345

Vachek J, 29
Vaid J, 16
Valdman A, 22, 107, 897, 905, 919
Valencia J F, 473
Valkhoff, 880
Valli C, 90, 92
Valory D, 881
Van Clay M, 861

van den Berghe P L, 99, 597–8, 601, 604
Vanderbilt A, 187, 193
van der Leek F, 411
van der Stoel M, 548, 550
Vanderveken D, 202, 208
van de Vliert E, 65
Van Ek J A, 150, 152
Van Gennep, 283
Van Leeuwen, 238, 925
van Leeuwen T, 237–9
Van Name A, 1, 4, 535–6, 919–20
van Peer W, 283
van Reenan P T, 361
van Sturmer J R, 176
Varonis E M, 518
Varro G, 22, 890
Vedder P, 509
Veith W, 353, 362
Veltman C, 100, 105, 813
Vendler Z, 201, 208
Vendryès J, 76
Venezky R L, 788, 793
Venneman T, 421
Verdoodt A, 648, 650
Verhoeven L, 508–9, 699
Verma S K, 914
Verma V S, 650
Verne J, 102
Verner, 398
Verner K, 398
Verschueren J, 243, 322, 324, 421
Verschueren J, 850
Versteegh K, 80
Vestergaard T, 250–1, 256
Vetter E, 926
Vetterling-Braggin M, 345
Vico, 551
Viereck K, 350, 360, 362
Viereck W, 350, 357, 360–2, 523–4
Vincent N, 409, 412, 503
Vivekananda S, 510
Voegelin C F, 67, 73
Voegelin F M, 67, 73
Voloshinov V N, 25, 27, 29, 127–8, 130, 133, 139, 145, 254, 307, 310, 560–3, 578, 845–6, 881, 920–1
Volterra V, 431–2
von Bertalanffy L, 79
von der Gabelentz G, 407, 411
von Humboldt W, 65, 73–4, 216, 577, 911
von Stechow A, 225
Vossler, 577
Vygotsky, 184, 849
Vygotsky L, 6, 562–3
Vygotsky L S, 27, 577

Wachs I, 860
Wackernagel-Jolles B, 270–2, 276
Waddington C H, 79

Wade T F, 682
Wadleigh P M, 195, 197
Wagner D, 746
Wagner D A, 788–9, 791–3
Wagner K R, 225
Waksler F C, 872
Wald B, 887
Wales K, 307
Waletzky J, 180, 185
Walker P, 307, 369
Walkerdine V, 345
Wall D, 809
Wallace, 541
Wallace C, 582, 584
Wallace G, 586
Walton P, 255, 256
Wande E, 508, 509
Wang W, 315, 319
Wang W S-Y, 398, 401, 794–6, 801
Wanner E, 350
Ward C A, 21–2
Wardhaugh R, 498–9, 580
Warner, 365
Warner W L, 810
Warren-Leubecker A, 88–9
Washburn S, 881
Wasserman S, 376
Watahomigie L J, 467
Waterbury M, 918
wa Thiong'o N, 573
Watkins C, 235
Watson D R, 161
Watson G, 165
Watson K, 714
Wattel E, 357, 361–2
Watters J, 913
Watts R J, 150, 152, 189, 193
Weber, 610, 849
Weber E, 666, 669
Weber H, 519, 900
Weber H K, 524
Weber M, 103, 166, 169, 241, 243, 364, 369, 652, 810
Webster N, 644, 682
Weeks F, 468, 472
Weeks P, 161
Wegerif R, 809
Wehrle A J, 133, 563
Weijters A J M M, 225
Weiner J, 887
Weiner J E, 385, 389
Weinreich B, 921
Weinreich M, 311, 867
Weinreich U, 1, 4, 16, 22, 317, 319, 399, 401, 437, 442, 477, 480–1, 567, 776, 779, 867, 878, 885–7, 893, 921–2
Weinrich H, 136, 145
Weinstein B, 567, 657
Weis J G, 10

Weiser, 123
Weiss G, 925
Welch K, 825
Wellman, 793
Wells G, 738, 807, 808–9
Wells H G, 95, 102
Wells J, 33–4, 297
Welter H, 401
Wendell M M, 512
Wenker G, 311–12, 314, 350, 922–3
Wentworth H, 270, 287
Werner O, 70, 67, 71, 73, 775
Werry, 289
Wertsch J V, 29
West A, 734
West C, 241, 243, 341, 345
West M, 468–9, 472
West R, 472
Westerman C, 212
Westgate D P G, 713–14, 753, 803, 809
Westie F R, 7, 10
Wetherell M, 168–9, 322, 324
Whalen B, 197
Whaley L J, 467, 498, 759, 816
Wheeler S, 239, 243
Wheelock W T, 265
Whinnom K, 880
White, 574
White A, 133
White E M, 875
White M, 10
Whitney W D, 74, 77, 920
Whorf B L, 15, 37–40, 46, 65–8, 70–3, 157, 216, 248, 329, 470, 580, 583–4, 604–5, 779, 849, 908, 923–4
Whorf H C, 923
Wickham G, 140, 145
Widdowson H G, 245–6, 472
Widdowson J D A, 356, 361–2
Wieder D L, 165
Wiegand H E, 362
Wieringa S, 335–6
Wierzbicka A, 147, 150, 152, 190, 193, 202, 206, 208
Wiesinger P, 354, 362
Wignell P, 237, 239
Wikle T, 351, 360, 362, 417
Wiksell, 569
Wilder R, 320–1
Wilke T, 417
Wilkin J, 617–18
Wilkins D A, 150, 152
Wilkins L T, 403, 407
Wilkinson A M, 746–7
Willes M J, 751, 753
Williams A, 196, 197
Williams C, 329
Williams G, 308, 310, 312, 735, 924–5
Williams J, 727–8, 735, 756, 902

Williams R, 130–3, 243, 246, 551, 562–3, 708–10
Williamson D, 140, 145
Williamson J, 727–8, 735, 859
Williamson K, 353, 361–2
Willis P, 255
Willis P E, 369
Wilmott P, 371, 376
Wilson, 19, 272
Wilson D, 118, 121, 221, 225
Wilson J, 239, 243
Wilson R, 22, 434, 482–3, 488–9
Wilson S, 821–2, 826–7
Wilson T, 161
Windsor Lewis J, 332
Winford D, 464, 483, 895
Winston, 545
Winston E, 91–2
Winston P H, 225
Winter W, 355, 362
Winterbottom M, 238
Wiseman R, 197
Wish M, 795, 799, 801
Witte B, 637
Wittgenstein L, 5–6, 26, 50, 139, 145, 198, 208, 891
Wodak R, 391, 396, 543, 545, 591, 737, 848, 925–6
Woelck W, 376
Wölck W, 361
Wolf G, 35–6
Wolf H-G, 166–7, 169, 332
Wolf S A, 879
Wolfe D M, 65
Wolff K H, 267, 270
Wolfgang A, 550
Wolfram W, 44, 48, 419, 749, 776–7, 779, 782, 784, 926
Wolfson N, 182, 183, 186, 191, 193, 491
Woll B, 89, 92
Wong A, 336
Wong Fillmore L, 568, 570, 607–8
Wood D, 751, 753
Wood R E, 903
Woodward J C, 89, 92
Woodward M, 567
Woolard K, 324, 446
Woolford E, 457, 461
Wootton A, 444, 446
Wootton T, 450, 454
Wordsworth, 245
Wotton H, 582
Woyzeck, 52
Wrede F, 923

Wrenn C L, 902
Wright E O, 363, 365, 369
Wright P, 792–3
Wright S, 503
Wright S M, 396
Wrightman L S, 86
Wright Mills C, 306, 366, 581
Wunderlich D, 50, 58, 219, 225
Wundt, 283
Wundt W, 74–6, 169
Wurf E, 83, 86
Wurm S A, 22, 350–1, 362, 454, 896
Wurm S L, 896
Wyld, 719
Wynn E, 179

Yaeger M, 307
Yaeger-Dror M, 391, 396, 887
Yamamoto A, 467
Yinger J M, 401–2, 404–7
Young, 150, 693, 695
Young E P, 578
Young F, 795
Young F W, 795, 801
Young L, 152
Young M, 371, 376
Young R, 695–6
Youssef A, 417
Yule G, 42, 46, 135–6, 138, 143

Zador P, 496, 498, 800–1
Zago R, 503–4
Zamenhof L, 504, 617
Zamenhof L L, 625
Zander A, 827
Zantella A C, 757
Zapeda O, 700
Zdenek S, 376
Zeller R A, 813
Zemskaja E A, 270, 272–3, 276
Zentella A C, 757
Zernatto G, 664, 669
Zhang Q, 334, 336
Zicklin G, 405, 407
Zimmer J, 92
Zimmerman D, 161–2, 164–5, 239, 242–3, 341, 345
Znaniecki, 83
Žolkovsky A K, 73
Zurcher L A, 65, 67
Zwicky A M, 460

Subject Index

A posteriori languages 617, 618
A priori languages 616–17, 618
Abbreviations
   internet language 288, 289
   medical language 258
Ability assessment, ethnocentricity in 715, 720
Aborigines, Australian *see* Australian Aborigines
Abstract objectivists 25
Abstractness, role of language in 737–8
Abuse, verbal 290
Academic language, acquisition failure, bilinguals 432
Académie française 615, 672
Academies, standard language prescription 615–16, 672, 681
Accademia della Crusca 615, 672
Accents (social and regional) 293–7
   attitudes to 295–6
   in broadcasting 254
   and dialect 311
   differences in 293–4
   humor and 320
   in second languages
      learning 294–5
      transfer and 434
   speaker groupings 294–5
Accommodation 913–7
   attuning 196
   code-switching and 455
   complementarity 196
   in interviews 101, 194
   konéization 487, 488
   misunderstanding and 195
   and perceived competence 196
   social psychology 81
   and social support 196
Acculturation
   convergence and 194
   resistance 20
   slaves and 600
Accusations, conversation 114
Acquiescence
   distorting expression 8
   interview respondents' 101
Acquisition of language 703
   and bilingualism 430–2
   childhood 2
      early 705–7
   context in 219
   creoles 531, 533
   crosslinguistic studies 704
   discourse skills 707–8
   gender differences 342
   grammar 706–7
   imitation in 88
   immersion 88
   infancy 704–5
   Language Acquisition Device 477, 479
   and language change 345–50
   planning and 645
   Sapir–Whorf Hypothesis 70
   suppression of natural processes 346–7
   theories 703–4
   vocabulary 704, 705–6
      analysis in 705
   vs language socialization 87
Acrolects 441, 535
Acronyms
   internet language 288, 289
   in political language 586
Adaptation, language 626–30
   deliberate, factors affecting 626–7
   natural 626
   process 627–9
Address
   patterns, intercultural variation 148
   terms/means of
      cultural differences 325–6
      gender and 342–3
Adjacency pairs 222
   conversation analysis 43, 113–14, 115
Administrative science 823
Adolescence 297–8
   egocentrism 299
   and emotional expression 299
   gender differences 300
Adolescent peer group language 95, 297–303
   Black American 301–2
   childhood culture and 298
   as concealment 298, 299
   diversity 298
   functions 298–300
   gender differences 300–1, 302
   norms 299
   and status 300
   and values 299
Adstratum language 434
Advertisements, AIDA structure 251
Advertising 269
   advertising register 209
   borrowings 438–9
   cooperative principle and 210
   denotation and connotation for visual analysis 250

entailment 251
expectation 251
exploiting consumer reasoning 210–11
female voice stigmatization in TV commercials 254
generic claims 210–11
iconic/indexical/symbolic signs 250
implicit meaning 251
language 209–11
manipulation 250, 574
in media 209–10
metatextual, intertextual dimension 252
metonymy in 250
presupposition 251
reference groups and 84
rhetorical figures 250
semiotic approaches 249–50
verbal metaphors 250
visual metaphors 250

Affixes
borrowing 437
thematizing 436

Africa
colonial languages in 603
national/official languages 661

African languages
as lingua francas 603
standardization 683
in the Western Hemisphere 600

African-American Vernacular English (AAVE) see Black English, America

Afrikaans, status 601, 603

Afro-Caribbean language varieties, relationship with Standard English 712–13

After perfects 500

Age
language differences 597–8
language learning and 599
literacy and 745–6
segregation based on, and youth subcultures 298
slang use and 269–70

Agency in ideology 560

Aggression
taboo words and 286
verbal 290
males 301

Agreement, in conversation 111, 115

Air traffic control, language of 468

Airspeak 468

Alcohol consumption
attitudes to, and behavior 8
religious beliefs and 10

Alienation 363
measuring 811

Alliance française 639

Alliteration in adolescent peer group language 299

Alloglots, societal bilingualism 17

Altercasting 61

Alternating Least Squares Algorithm for Scaling (ALSCAL) 795, 796, 798, 799, 800

Alternation(s)
morphological, phonetic processes and 397
morphophonemic 397

American Association for Applied Linguistics 840

American Dialect Society 840

American English
Afro-American *see* Black English, America
and British English, comparison 311
regional factors 312–14
chain shifts 304–5, 415–17
Northern Cities Shift 304, 417
Southern Shift 305, 417
dialectology 312–17
dialects 600
phonological features 415–17
gay language 334
globalization 335
General American 293, 296
linguistic atlases 312, 351, 352, 354, 359
Atlas of North American English 412–18
as official language 659–60
pronunciation/accent 293–4, 295, 296
slang 267, 269
urban/rural language in 418–9

American languages, native
gay language in 334–5
internet resources 838, 839
kinship terminology 172, 174
recording 779
revitalization projects 835, 836, 837
standardization 683

American structuralism 1
and corpora 765–6

Amharic, spread 499

Ammon, Ulrich 844–5

Analogy, syntactic change and 410, 411

Analysis in everyday life, ethnomethodology and 161, 163–4

Anaphora, discourse 180

Anglocentrism in teaching English as a foreign language 469

Anomie
nationalism and 664
subcultures and 403

Anthropological linguistics 5–6
influences on 5–6

Anthropology
and American linguistics 36–7
cognitive, Sapir–Whorf hypothesis 70–2
cultural 37–8
definition of language 66
field methods 772–5
linguistic salvage work and 814–15

Antilanguage 109

Antonyms, questionnaires 101

Aphasia in bilinguals, testing 14–15

Applied linguistics
  missionaries and 511
  professional associations 840, 841
  sociolinguistics and 691–6
Appropriateness, language use, gender and 338, 342
Approval, impression management 84
Arabic
  Classical, Islam 510
  diglossia 227, 229
  international status 620–1, 622
  Moroccan, borrowings 436–7, 438
  standardization 683
  UNESCO statistics 684, 685–8
Areal linguistics 423–30
  borrowing 434
  genesis of areas of similarity 423–5
  Indo-European languages 426–7, 428
  wave theory 425–7, 428–9
Areas
  linguistic (Sprachbünde) 427–8, 434
    nature of 429
  sociolinguistic 538–9
Argot 94–5
Articulation, chain shifts and 305
Artificial Intelligence (AI), solutions to contextual conditions 222
Artificial languages 616–19
  characteristics 618
  international languages 625
Arvanitika 814
Arya Samaj 510
Asia, colonial languages in 603
Assimilation 397
  sociophonetic studies 393
Association of Computational Linguists Data Collection Initiative (ACL/DCI) 766
Association Internationale de Linguistique Appliquee 840
Associations, professional 840–2
Aṣṭādhyāyī (Pāṇini) 1
Atlas of North American English 412–18
  aims 412–13
  data analysis 414–15
  dialect areas established 415–17
  interviews for 414
  sampling strategy 413
  selection and recruitment of speakers 413–14
Atlases, linguistic *see* Maps, linguistic
Attitudes 7, 82–3
  ambivalent 765
  attribution theory 85
  behavior and 6–10, 83, 96
    behavior intention 8
    consistency 7–8
    justification of inconsistencies 8–9
    social support and 8, 9
  change 82–3
  expression of, social acceptability and 9

language
  matched guise study technique 88
  socialization and 88
latent process conceptions 7
measuring 7, 82
natural, ethnomethodology and 162
probability conceptions 7
public commitment and 83
surveys
  context and 763–4
  form of questions 762–3
  interviewer effects 101, 764–5
  question–answer process 101, 761–5
  question wording and 761–2
to accents 295–6
to dialect speakers 320
to sign language 91
Attribution theory 85
Audience, empirical dimension, in media language research 254
Audience Design 109–10, 386–7
Austin, John Langshaw, speech-act theory 198
Australia
  extraterritorial language promotion 636, 642–3
  heritage languages in education 711
  International Development Program 642
  language policies 680
Australian Aboriginal languages
  honorifics 555, 556
  organizations 837
  reversing language shift 677, 678
Australian Aborigines
  discourse analysis, legal contexts 233
  use of silence 233
Australian Broadcasting Commission, international services 643
Australian English as koiné 486, 488
Author, implied 261
Authority, institutional language 241
Automatic speech recognition (ASR), corpora and 768–9
Automatisms, speech formulas 234
Autonomous linguistics 35
Aviation, language of 468
Avoidance in bilingualism 12
Avoidance languages, honorifics 555, 556
Awareness of language
  grammar teaching 726, 730, 731, 732
  school courses 714
Awareness programs, language teaching 748

Babbling, infants 704
Backgrounding, in narrative 180
Bakhtin, Mikhail M. 845–6
  dialogism 127–33
Bakhtin Circle, Marxist language theories 576–7
Balkans, as linguistic area 428, 429
Bamgbose, Ayo 846–7

Bank of English, corpus linguistics 766
Basilects 420, 441, 535
Basque, reversing language shift 677, 678
Basque stick 53
Basters Hottentot 482
Baugh, John 847–8
Beautification, honorifics 555–6, 557
Behabitives 201
Behavior
  convergence 194
  field theory 81
  language and 7
  measuring 8
  medicalization 100
  naturalized 541–2
  religion and 910
  speech as 7–8
  trait theories 81
Belief systems, context in 220
Belief(s)
  ethnography and 163
  ethnomethodology and 163
  uses 163–4
Bengali, UNESCO statistics 684, 685–8
Benrath–Urdingen line 314
Berger, Peter, social class theory 365, 366
Bernstein, Basil 363, 848–9
  language and conceptualization 367, 368
  theory of elaborated and restricted codes
      366, 366–7, 367, 368, 716–17, 722, 849
  theory of families 366–7
Bhojpuri
  transplanted koinés 486–8
  Trinidad 800–1
Bias
  contagion bias 101
  in interviews 100–1, 764–5
    forced choices and 8
    interviewer bias 101
  in questionnaires 100–1
  race and 101, 764–5
  social desirability 101, 764
    distorting expression 8
  in sociology 104
Bible 510
  role in standardization of language 682
  translation, missionaries 510, 511
Bickerton, Derek 849–50
Biculturalism, bilingualism link 16
Bidialectism 748
  Standard English teaching and 712
Bilingual education 21, 508, 696–700
  endangered languages 835
  goals 696–700
  in multilingual societies 21–2
  pidgins, creoles and minority dialects in 747–9
  program models 697–8
  USA 712

Bilingualism
  academic development of bilinguals 432
  activation/deactivation procedures 12, 14
  additive 697, 748
  alloglots 17
  alternate use 11
  assimilated 653
  attitudes 151
  attrition, in children 431
  base language 12–13
  biculturalism link 16
  and bilinguality, distinction 16
  borrowing 12, 13, 14
  Canada 660
  Le Centre International de Recherche sur le
      Bilingualisme 841
  code-switching 12, 13, 145, 448, 453, 607
    in children 431
    constraints 13
    conversational 443–4
    guest words 14
    patterns 444–6
    sociopragmatic models 454–6
    structural models 456–61
  cognitive development of bilinguals 432
  competency 11
  compound bilinguals 14
  contact between languages within individual 12
  contact situations 11
  convergence 19–20
  coordinate bilinguals 14
  deactivation 12, 14
  deaf communities 89–90
  degree, in different sociolinguistic situations 430
  description 11–12
  diglossic 18, 228–9, 430
    reversing language shift and 676
  divergence and 19–20, 195
  dominance, in children 431
  dormant 11
  factors 11
  fluency 11
  foreign accents 12
  functional 661
  gender differences 337–8
  individual 10–16
  interferences (between-language deviations) 12
  interlanguage (within-language deviations) 12, 695
  internal lexicons 14
  international language 17
  interpreters 11
  and language acquisition 430–2
  language choice 12–13
  language continuum across political boundaries 17
  language learning strategies 430
  language mixing 12, 69–70
  language modes 12–13, 14
  language for special purposes 11

986

language specificity 15
language switch 14
language use in community, and child language
  acquisition 430
Latin America 602
linguistic diversity 21
linguistic minorities 11
migrants 508
mixed languages 461, 463
multilingual societies 652
native speakers 514
neurolinguistics 14–15
on-line processing 14
  models 14
origins 17
passive 495
personality change 15–16
psycholinguistics 13–14
sequential 430, 431, 432
sign language 89–90
simultaneous 430–1
societal 16–22
sociolinguistic areas 538–9
sociolinguistics 17–20
state 106
  and national/official languages 660, 661, 685–8
subordinate bilinguals 14
subtractive 698
  literacy skills 21
superposed 229
territorial 16
theoretical implications 19–20
transfer in 431–2
translators 11
types 430
unassimilated 653
Bilinguality/bilingualism distinction 16
Bilingual's grammar 456–7
Biloquialism
  school language policies 755–6
  Standard English, teaching 712
Bioprogram hypothesis, creoles 530, 534, 850
Birdwhistell, Ray L., kinesics 169, 171
Birmingham school, discourse analysis 137
Black English 369
  America 412
    adolescent peer group language 301–2
    context and 302
    as dialect 600
    ebonics and 708–10, 722
    in education 748–9
    gayspeak 334
    sociolinguistics 45–6
    and solidarity 301
    stigmatization 600
    syntax 382–4, 387
    verbal deprivation myth 717–18
    verbal dueling 291

Britain 700–2
  in African musical tradition 702
  attitudes to 702
  code-mixing 700
  creole and 700–1
  dialect studies 372
  in education 701–2
  educational expectations 701
  linguistic change 700
classroom attitudes to 701–2
code difference hypothesis 217
conflict with white English 564
copula verb deletion 718
and critical/interventional discourse analysis 142
habitual *be* 718
inferiority theory 368
oral culture 717
Blends, lexical, internet language 288
Blessings 211–12
  formula 211
  as performatives 211–12
  politeness 211, 212
  religion 211
  secular uses 212
  validation 212
Blommaert, Jan 850–1
Bloomfield, Leonard, and native languages 513–14
Boas, Franz 851–2
Bodo script 565
Body language
  Black American 301, 302
  see also Kinesics
Bogardus Social Distance Scaling 817–18
Bokmal 682
Borrowing(s) 432–42
  ad hoc 445
  adaptation
    morphological 436–7
    phonological 435
  areal linguistics 423–4
  bilingualism, individual 12, 13, 14
  code-mixing and 443
  code-switching and 433–4
  core 423–4
  diglossic 439–40
  exotic 423
  grammatical 424
  of grammatical morphemes 437
  and historical linguistics 442
  hybrid 436
  intimate, koinéization and 488
  lexical 423–4
  mechanics 435–7
  nativization 433–4, 435
  nonce 443
  phonetics/phonology 424–5
  pronunciation 435
    influence of spelling 435–6

987

role of official institutions 438–9
routines 437–8
  false 438
social and historical context 438–42
transfer and 434–5, 499
Bourdieu, Pierre 852–3
  habitus 650–1
  linguistic marketplace 612–13
  symbolic power 610–12
Brain, bilingualism and 14–15
Bright, William 853–4
British Association of Applied Linguistics 840
British Council 641–2
British National Corpus (BNC) 766
Broadcast monologues, discourse analysis 253
Broadcasting
  international, language teaching 641, 642
  news 252
  Received Pronunciation 254
  regional accents 254
Broken language *see* Jargons
Buddhism, and linguistics 265
Bullock Report (1975) (UK) 679, 723–4, 725–6
Bureaucracies, status in 823
Business and international languages 622
Business language 212–14
  business interactions and 213
  categorization 212–13
Butler English 484
Bystanders, speech acts 200

Callahuaya 482
Calques 434–5
  in pidgins and creoles 537
Cameron, Deborah 854–5
Camping 333
Canada
  bilingual education, immersion programs 697–8
  bilingualism, and national/official language 660
  censuses, language questions 100
  extraterritorial language promotion 635, 639–40
  French in, reversing language shift 676, 677–8
  Heritage Languages 619, 711–12
  language legislation 660
  multiculturalism 48–9
Canadian Broadcasting Commission, international services 640–1
Canadian International Development Assistance (CIDA) 636–7
Canadian raising 415
Canadian Shift 415
Cannibalism, linguistic 568
Capitalism, linguistic class struggle in 307
Capitalization, internet language 288, 289
Capitals, linguistic marketplace 612
Carey, William 511
Carl Duisberg Gesellshaft (CDG) 637
Carnivalization 132–3

Carolines, language variation across 794–5, 796–7
Catalan, reversing language shift 676, 677–8
Categorization
  ethnomethodology and 163
  language and 68–9
Cayuga, death 497
Censorship through media 587
Censuses
  language questions 100
  linguistic 648–50
    distortion 649
    identification of mother tongue 648, 649
    interpretation of data 648–9
    politicization of data 649–50
    social planning use 650
Center for Applied Linguistics 841
Le Centre International de Recherche sur le Bilingualisme 841
Centre for Research and Documentation on World Language Problems 841
Chain shifts 303–7
  American English 304, 305, 415–17
  Canadian English 415
  definition 303
  explanations of triggering 305–6
  Great Vowel Shift 303–4, 305
  Labov's principles 303, 304–5
  ongoing 304–6
  pull (diagonal) model 304
  push model 304
Change, linguistic
  in adolescent peer group language 299
  analogical 410, 411
  children 346
  critical period hypothesis 531
  deliberate 582–3
  dialectology 314–16
  by diffusion, sociophonetic features 393
  ethnicity and 328
  internet and 288
  language acquisition and 345–50
  and mutual intelligibility breakdown 35
  pidgins/creoles and 530–6
  propagators 348–9
  resistance 374, 378
  and school language policies 680
  social networks and 374
  sociolinguistics 377, 389–91
  sound *see* Sound changes
  statistical analysis 830
  stepping stone theory 795, 796–7
  syntactic 407–12
    generative model 408–9, 410
    grammaticalization theory 409–10
    morphology and 410
    typological approach 410, 411
Change, social, countercultures 406
Channel tunnel, language of 468

Child language 703–8
  innovations 347–8
  reduction 346, 347
  sound changes 346–7
  vowel and consonant harmony 346–7
Children
  culture 298
    Black American 301
  language change 346
  language conflicts 564
  language functions 298
  socialization
    gender differences 342
    speech play 278–9
Chinese
  diglossia 227
  international status 622
  politeness 187, 189
  UNESCO statistics 684, 685–8
  writing systems 682
    romanization 565, 682
Chinese Pidgin 461
Chinook Jargon 461, 462, 484, 525, 531
Choice, for meaning 29
Chomsky, Noam 1–2
  on native speakers 513, 514
Christianity
  and linguistics 265
  see also Missionaries
Chronotopes 131
Cities, slang 265, 267–9
Class *see* Social class
Classical languages, and language in education 711
Classification of languages, politicized language and 581
Classroom
  discourse, power relations 592
  language, gender and 735–6
  technical language 752–3
Classroom, spoken language 749–53, 803
  communication analysis for language variation fostering 721
  communicative norms 737
  cued elicitations in teacher-initiated exchanges 752
  cultural diversity and 738
  discourse analysis 750–1, 806–9
  discourse features 750
  ethnographic analyses 713, 722
  functions 749–50
  initiation-response-feedback sequence 750
  interactions, social class and understanding 737
  interruptions 806
  intonation 807, 808
  joint knowledge markers, in teacher discourse 752
  linguistic structure 804
  National Oracy Project 746–7
  naturally-occurring 804–5
  observation and analysis studies 803–9

  analysis 805–9
  cognitive activity coding 808
  communication patterning 803
  context 803, 805–6
  discourse boundary marking 808
  discourse cohesion 804
  ethnography 803, 804
  insightful observation 803–4
  linguistic structure analysis 804
  live recording 803, 804–5
  observer's paradox 805
  reporting 809
  respondent validation 805
  systematic coding 803
  on/off task talk 750
  oral communication skills 750
  pauses 806
  pragmatics 806, 807
  reconstructed recaps in teacher discourse 752
  structure 750–1
  syntactic complexity by social class 737
  teacher-initiated exchanges 750–1, 752
  teachers' questions 751–2
  teaching exchange 804
  transcription 803, 804, 805–9
  transmissional teaching and 805
  turn-taking 804, 808
  two thirds rule, in teacher talk 751
  tying of meaning 806
  verbal scaffolding 803
  word emphases 806
Clauses
  narrative 180
  spoken language 271–3
Clichés, spoken language 273
Cliques 827
Closet, language of 333
Coates, Jennifer 855
Code Michaud 666
Code-behaviour 25
Code-mixing 43, 433, 442–3, 447, 449
  Black English 700
  intertwined languages 481
  New Englishes 522
Code-switching 43, 214, 443, 447–54
  Afro-Americans 46
  alternational 444
    discourse-related 445–6
    preference-related 445
  areal linguistics 423, 427
  audience centered approach 455
  in bilingualism 12, 13, 145, 607
    children 431
    constraints 13
    guest words 14
  borrowing and, comparison 433–4
Closed Class Constraint 457
  Complaisance Constraint 459

constraints 452, 457–60
conversational 444, 447, 449–51, 453
  patterns 444–6
diglossic 447, 448, 453
discourse models 443–6
endangered-language settings 815
EQUI Constraint 459
Equivalence Constraint 457
Free Morpheme Constraint 457
Functional Head Constraint 458
in generative grammar 457–9
Government Constraint 457–8
grammatical aspects 451–2
Head Syntax Constraint 459
Hemnesberget, Norway 454–5
insertional, discourse-related 445
intra-sentential 451–3
koinéization and 488
language variation in, optimal grammars and 459–60
Linear Precedent Constraint 459
linguistic factors 451
loanwords and 447, 452
markedness 455–6
  communicative competence and 455
  significance 456
Matrix Language Frame Model 458
metaphoric 447, 454
multilingual speakers 43
New Englishes 522
in political language 586
rule-governed 452
situational 43, 444, 447, 448, 454
social factors 448–9
sociopragmatic models 454–6
Specifier Constraint 459
structural, constraints 457–60
structural models 456–61
for stylistic effect 450
Code(s)
  diglossia 229
  elaborated 56, 214, 216, 367, 368, 717, 722, 849
    and adult language/adolescent peer group language 299
  Encoding/Decoding model of mass communication 247
  linguistic 214–18
  restricted 56, 214, 215, 216, 367, 368, 717, 722, 849
    and adolescent peer group language 299
    cause of educational failure 216
    experimental situations and 369
  sociolinguistic 214–15
    deficits/differences hypothesis 217
    educational implications 216–17
    indicators 215
Coding, institutional language 240
Coercion and hegemony 551

Cognition
  coding, classroom talk 808
  development, bilingualism 432
  language and 38, 40
  place of inner speech in 27
Cognitive development, language across the curriculum policies and 713
Cognitive science 71
Cohen, A. K., subcultures 403
Coherence
  context in 219
  in discourse 136
  and ideology 595
  in texts 260
Cohesion
  context in 219
  in texts 260
Coinings, language adaptation 628
Collaboration, conversation 112
Collective conscience 551
Collins COBUILD dictionary 767
Colonial languages
  dominance 626–7
  linguistic imperialism and 570–4, 588
Colonialism 99, 597
  and borrowing 439
  imperialism and 602
  language conflicts 564
  linguistic habitus and 651
  national/official languages 660–1
  rationalization of language 656
  of settlement/of exploitation 602
  standardization and 683
Colonization
  as cause of language endangerment 466
  international languages 623
  language spread and 498–9
  symbolic power and 611
Color
  cognition 40
  terminology 40
    Sapir–Whorf Hypothesis 71
Commissives 201
Commonplaces (loci communes), formulaic speech 233
Communication 22–9
  among bilinguals 12
  authentic contexts, in second language teaching 756
  computer-mediated 179
  conduit model 23
  consensual domains 26
  context and 5
  cooperation in 23
  cross-cultural
    ethnicity in 325–6
    school literacy teaching 754, 755
  in cross-linguistic/cross-cultural discourse context 145–52

as determining language 26
dialogic model 23–4
doctor–patient language 152–4
emblematic gestures 171
feedback model 24
formulas as meta-communicative signals 234
gender differences 45
group norms 823
heteroglossia in 128
honorifics, function 558–9
information theory 22–3
international, languages of 620–6
internet 287–9
in interviewing 82
and language
  complementary phenomena 26–7
  relation between 25–7
in language 31
linguistic strategies 42–3
media 246–56
messages, as meaning potentials 28
mutual knowledge in 24
mutual relevance in context 219, 222
non-natural meaning 23
non-verbal, kinesics 169–72
perlocution in 23
phatic communion 186
power relations 24
ritual in 325–6
self-regulatory (autopoesis model) 24–5
sociocultural context 36, 40–1
solipsistic model 24–5
workplace 177
  non-verbalized 178–9
Communication acts, categorization 821
Communication skills, oral 750
Communication strategies
accommodation (foreigner talk) 146
interlanguage psycholinguistic process 477–8
second languages, elicitation research techniques 479
Communicative competence 2, 29–30, 41, 159
linguistic and cultural variation 754–5
markedness and, code-switching 455
minority-related 507
native speakers 516–17
sociolinguistics 694
Communicative functions, Prague school taxonomies 28
Communicators, credibility 82
Communities
dialect studies
  small-scale communities 372–3
  social networks 370
  working class communities 371
ethnic 325
Comparisons, implicit 500
Compensatory education 217

Competence
communicative *see* Communicative competence
linguistic
  marketplace 613
  measures of 800, 801
  native speakers 516–17
Competence-performance 25
Complements, clausal, spoken language 272
Componential analysis, Sapir–Whorf Hypothesis 70, 71
Compounding
nouns, medical terminology 257
pidgins and creoles 537
Compounds, lexical, internet language 288
Comprehension, representation and schema 605
Computational linguistics, corpora and 768–9
Computer-assisted instruction (CAI) 792
Computer-based education (CBE) 792
Computers
and linguistic maps 350, 351–2
work-place communication 179
Conceptualization
language and 367, 368
social research variables 810
Concordance/browser 768
Conditional clauses, spoken language 272, 273, 274
Conflict
language 563–7
  dialects 564–5
  language of wider communication and 566–7
  scripts 565
  speech communities 107
  standardization 565
  style 565
role 62–3
social
  language and 95, 97–9
  subcultures and 95
Congruence patterns, Halliday's theory of language 29
Connected speech, sociophonetic studies 393
Connectionism, child language acquisition 703
Connotation
in advertising 250
analysis, hazardousness of 254
Consciousness
political 307, 356, 366
self-direction and 367
Consent, in hegemony theory 550
Consonant clusters, reduction in child language 347
Constative utterances 198
Constructions, comparison of spoken and written language 273–4
Constructivism, social 168
Contact between dialects and koinés 485

Contact languages 461–4
  multilingual states 106
Content analysis 103
Content/meaning dichotomy, style and 281–2
Context(s) 218–25
  change, descriptive model needs 221
  classroom talk 803, 805–6
  context-dependency 219
  conversation 113, 115
  descriptive model 221
  in discourse 222–5
  in discourse analysis 43, 221
  felicity conditions 220
  field 260, 261
  of foreigner talk 474
  in information processing paradigms 222
  language embedded in 28
  linguistic relativity and 72–3
  in linguistic theory 218–19
  meaning and 5
  meaning in 220
  mode 260, 261
  pragmatic analysis 220–1
  primacy of text, heteroglossia and 128
  relevance 221, 222
  relevant, as mutual achievement of participants 219, 222, 224–5
  semantic analysis 219–20
  shifts in 72
  of situation 72, 220–21, 260–1, 866
  social 219
    ideology in 561
    societal pragmatics 51–2
  sociocultural 40–1
  sociolinguistics 40–1
  speaker/listener perspectives 221
  structure of 221
  tenor 260, 261
  in text 219
  theme–rheme structure in sentences 219
  variability 221
  variation, and politeness investment 191–2
Contextual sensitivity in business language use 212–13
Contrastive analysis
  theories about second language acquisition 476, 477
  transfer/transfer analysis 476
Control
  discrimination and 548–9
  through dominant language 572
Convergence 193–4, 434
  diverging as 195–6
  effects 194
  evaluation 194
  ideal 195
  koinéization and 488–9
  pidginization 533
  power and 194

  societal bilingualism 19–20
  sociolinguistic areas 538–9
Conversation
  adjacency pairs 43
  agreement 111, 115
  collaboration 112–13
  context 113, 115
  cooperation
    asymmetry 153
    in doctor–patient language 152–3
  correction 137
  deviousness 574
  discourse markers 111, 114, 115
  expressed meaning, distinction from implied 116
  gender differences 45, 340–1
  interactions, kinesics 170–1
  internet language 288–9
  invitations 112, 113, 114, 115
  laughter 111, 138
  management, use of routine formulas 234
  maxims see Maxims, conversational
  meta-communicative signals 234
  overlaps 112, 115
  phatic communion 186
  postulates, Gricean 136
  reality-maintenance role 604
  repairs 111, 112, 113, 115
  response tokens 111, 138
  sequential requirements 112, 138
  topics
    boundaries 138
    initiation and closing 111, 115
    organization 138
  turn-taking 43, 111, 112, 115, 137, 138, 148, 149
    institutional settings 240–1
    kinesics 171
    news interviews 252–3
    and power status 589
    recipient design 113, 115
  use of proper names 113
Conversation analysis 110–16, 161
  adjacency pairs 113–14, 115, 222
    insertion sequence 114
  audio-visual accomplishment of society 137
  the 'confessional' 139, 142
  conversational authenticity 139
  conversational pairs 138
  ethnomethodological 84–5, 111, 137
  extended episodes 139
  institutional discourse 115–16
    pre-allocation 138
  lack of social context 543
  lectures 139
  media language 252
  nonvocal aspects of discourse 112, 138
  origins 111
  phenomenology 137
  political discourse 589

power distribution 589
pre-sequences 115
preference organization 114–15, 138
recordings 111
sequential requirements of conversation 112–13, 138
sociolinguistics 43
solidarity 114, 115
speech perturbations 111
telephone calls 111, 138
transcriptions 111–12
troubles talk 113, 115, 138–9
written texts 139
Conversion, religious, social bonds and 825–6
Cooper, Robert Leon 855–6
Cooperation
  in communication 23
  in doctor–patient language 152–3
  girls and 300
Cooperative Principle 121–4
  and advertising 210
  Gricean 150
  and implicatures 122
  institutional setting 241
  linguistic goal-sharing 122, 123–4
  politeness 187
  real-world goal-sharing 122–3
Coppieters, R., native speakers 518
Corpora 765–9
  analyzed 769
  Association of Computational Linguists Data Collection Initiative (ACL/DCI) 766
  Bank of English 766
  British National Corpus (BNC) 766
  Brown University Corpus 766
  and *Collins COBUILD dictionary* 767
  and *hapax legomena* 767
  International Corpus of English (ICE) 766
  internet 839
  Lancaster/Oslo-Bergen Corpus 766
  lexicography and 767
  linguistic research 767–8
  London–Lund Corpus of Spoken English 766
  machine translation and 768
  parsing 768
  planning 645
  representativeness of corpus 767
  speech recognition 768–9
  speech synthesis 768–9
  static/dynamic 767
  statistical analysis 829–30
  tagged 769
  tagging 768
    Hidden Markov Model techniques 768
  texts, in data collection 770–1
  transcription 770
Corpus linguistics 765–9
  American structuralists and 765–6

Correctness
  criteria 51
  political 581, 583
Cotext 219
Council of Europe, actions on linguistic discrimination 547
Countercultures 94, 369, 401, 404–6
  origins 404–5
  and social change 406
  varieties 405–6
Courts of law
  actions on linguistic discrimination 548
  conversational authenticity analysis 139
  cross examination 241
    linguistic manipulation 574
  discourse analysis 231–2
  interpreters in 232
Cox Report (1989) (UK) 712, 727
Creativity, second languages 517–18
Credibility
  communicators' 82
  status and 82
Creoles 461, 524–30
  abrupt 462
  affix dropping 536
  in African musical tradition 702
  Black English and 700–1
  calques 537
  characteristics 525–6
  classification 527
  compounding 537
  contemporary 529–30
  decreolization 19, 441, 535
  development 462, 528–9, 533–4
    phases 536–8
  distinction from pidgins 463
  in education 747–9
  jargon 483
  and language change 530–6
  mailing list 838
  morphology 536–8
  oral literature 702
  reduplication 537
  similarities 534
  slavery and 600, 601
  social attitudes to 525
  Society for Pidgin and Creole Languages 840
  Standard English relationship with 713
  structures 462, 463
  substrate influence 502
  universal theory 531
  word-class multifunctionality 536, 537
Creolization 19, 531, 533–4, 537, 538
  bioprogram hypothesis 530, 534, 850
  koinéization and 489
  and language death 496
Crime
  defining 98

religious beliefs and 9–10
self-justification 8–9
self-reporting and 8
social class and 8
subcultures and 402–3
victimless
  definitions and 98
  religious beliefs and 10
Criminal recording, speaker identification in 330–1
Criminals
  antilanguage 109
  argot 94
Critical discourse, culture of 366
Critical discourse analysis 543, 544, 589–91
  interventional 139–40, 142
Critical language awareness 541–2
Critical linguistics
  and formal approach to discourse 135
  ideology 560, 589
  and media language 248–9
Critical sociolinguistics 542–5
  heteroglossic account need 544
  identity and 168
Cross examination, courtroom 241
Cross-linguistic influence 499–503
Crossing, language
  ethnicity and 322–3
  sociolinguistics 323
Cues, contextualizing, discourse analysis 43
Cults 95
  conversion to 825–6
  language use 95
  names 826
Cultural assets 366
Cultural capital 363, 364
  competence contribution 562
Cultural identity
  conflict with Standard English 754
  maintenance, by education in mother tongue 711
Cultural imperialism 570–1
Cultural markers 365
Cultural pluralism, school language policy 679, 711
Cultural schemata, Sapir–Whorf hypothesis and 72
Cultural superstructure, place for language and discourse 562
Cultural value systems, discourse analysis 151
Culture(s)
  Black English and, Britain 702
  context and 72–3
  countercultures 94, 369, 401, 404–6
  cross-cultural discourse *see* Discourse, cross-linguistic/cross-cultural contexts
  defining 94
  inferiority theories 368
  and knowledge of language use 41–2
  language planning and 647

and language promotion 635–6
meaning and 38–40
  theories of prototype and metaphor 39
nationalism and 663–4
power 97
relationship with language 36–48, 65, 363
see also Sapir–Whorf hypothesis
roles and 60
and speech act variations 206–7
subcultures 94–5
symbols and 37–8
theories 37
values, and stories 182
world view
  metaphors and 39
  Sapir–Whorf hypothesis 39–40, 65, 66–7
writing systems and 669–70
see also Multiculturalism
Cummins, Jim 856–7
Curriculum, hidden, societal pragmatics 53
Curses/Cursing 284, 285
  formula 211

Dahrendorf, Ralf, social class theory 364
Das Gupta, Jyotirindra 857–8
Data
  collection
    ethnography 772–5
    fieldwork 780
    informants 769, 770
    in linguistics 769–71
    literacy 790–1
    observer's paradox 802
    place of intuitions 769, 770, 771
    place of variation 769
    sociolinguistic interview 308
    spoken language, elicitation tests 770, 771
    text sampling 770
    transcription 770
    variation studies 776–8
  linguistic, statistical analysis 830–1
Dead languages 465
Deaf
  education 568–9
    sign language in 91
  language policy 91
Deaf communities
  bilingualism 89–90
  characteristics 125
  culture 126
  language contact 90
  as social structure 125–6
  status 126
  structures and interaction 125–7
Death of language 440, 493–8
  causes 493
  demographic factors 494
  linguicide 567–70

linguistics of 496–7
multidimensional scaling analysis of 800–1
DeCamp, David 858–9
Deception
   in advertising 211
   in experiments 84–5
   in political language 585
   social psychology 81
Declarations, speech acts 201
Declining languages 465
Decreolization 441, 535
Deep structure, sociological theory and 96
Defamiliarization, Formalist concept 244
Deference, honorifics 552
Deficit theory 368–9
Definition(s)
   effects on public policy 98
   methods, reduction 85
Delicacy principle, lexicon and 67
Democracy and nationalism 664
Demography, language enclaves and 491
Denotation, in analysis of advertising 250
Denotational acts 199
Deprivation, verbal, and restricted codes 217
Derivation, in pidgins and creoles 537
Derrida, Jacques 75
Description, pragmatics of 115
Descriptive grammars 48–9
Descriptive linguistics, salvage work 813
Determinism, linguistic, and Sapir–Whorf hypothesis 605
Deutsche Welle 638
Deutscher Akademischer Austauschdienst (DAAD) 637
Development of language 630–4
   characterization 630–1
   indices 632
   language features and 631–2
   measurement 633
   models 632–3
   narrative and 184–5
   parental role 738
   and planning 631, 633, 634
   process 631
   product 631
Deviance, social *see* Social deviance
Deviation, foregrounding device 244
Deviousness, linguistic manipulation and 574
Diachrony, distinction from synchrony 27
Dialectics
   Marxist 550–1
   in mental model of the world 56
Dialectology 310–19
   fieldwork 779–80
   International Society for Dialectology and Geolinguistics 841
   social 390
   and sound changes 314–16
   structuralist 317

Dialect(s) 34, 310–19
   accent and 311
   areas 358–9
   attitudes towards speakers 320
   code-switching, in political language 586
   conflicts 564–5
   continua 32
   convergence, koinéization and 488–9
   definition 319–20
   diffuseness 373
   English, non-mainstream 754
   eye 321
   geography 311–12, 317
   historical connotations 311
   humor 319–20
      accent and 320
      transcription 321
      universality 320–32
   identity and 166
   maps 312, 319, 351–2
   minority 440
      in education 747–9
   mixture of 377
   in multilingual speech communities 17
   non-standard
      courtroom witnesses 232–3
      minority groups 372
      pressures on 370
      survival 372
   North American English, phonological features 415–17
   political significance 588
   regional 310–11
      origin in trade languages 18
   rural, urbanization 373
   social 311, 316
      social network studies 370–6
   sound change and 396–7
   and standardization of language 311
   studies, field methods 776–9
   surveys 317–19
   syntax, sociolinguistics 382–4
   urban/rural 418–19
   vernacular and 420
Dialogicity in communication 27
Dialogics, polyphonic, Marxist language theories 576
Dialogism 127–33
   communication in 27–8
   and sign 127
Dialogue
   model of communication 23–4
   Socratic, carnivalization 133
Dictation, and child language development 184
Dictionaries
   prescription 672
   and standardization of language 681, 682, 683
      Academies and 615–16

995

Dictionary of the English Language (Johnson) 615–16, 672
Diffusion
   areal, statistical analysis 795
   policy 634–44
Diglossia 18, 106, 226–31
   and bilingualism *see* Bilingualism, diglossic
   borrowings 438–9
   broad 229
   categories 229
   classic 229
   code switching 447, 448, 453
   codes 229
      compartmentalization 229
   in-diglossia (*Binnendiglossie*), distinction from out-diglossia (*Aussendiglossie*) 229
   incidence 226–8
   intralanguage, distinction from interlanguage diglossia 229
   minority-related 507–8
   political 470
   reversing language shift 475, 674, 676
   style shifting 229
   typology 228–30
   varieties, low/high 420
   vehicle for written literature 226
Dimensions, personality 85
Diplomacy and international languages 622
Directives, speech acts 201
Directness
   in speech, intercultural variations 147
   speech act sets 190
Dirty words 284, 285
Disambiguation through context 220
Discernment (social indexing) 189
Discourse 133–45
   and authority/power 605
   change, centrifugal/centripetal 596–7
   child language development 707–8
   classroom *see* Classroom, spoken language
   cognitive psychology use 136
   coherence 136
   comprehension, reader protocols 136
   connected speech/writing 134
   contention and struggle 139
   context in 222–5
   contracts in 28
   critical approach (discourse as power/knowledge) 139–43
   cross-linguistic/cross-cultural contexts 145–52
      code-switching 145
      cultural value systems 151
      culture clash and breakdown/conflict 150
      fields 145–6
      intercultural variation in speech acts 146–7
      key words 145
      miscommunication 146
      non-communication 146
      non-verbal expression 146
      pragmatic rules 146–7, 150–1
      research 150–1
      rhetoric/text patterns 146
      simplification 145–6
      speech acts analysis 146, 146–7, 150
      transference 145
   data
      elicited/contrived 137
      invented 134
      naturally occurring 134, 135
   dialogical nature, ideology in 562
   disursive functioning 140
   empirical approach (discourse as conversation) 137–9
   enunciation (énonciation) 140
   felicity 140
   feminist analysis 135, 139
   focusing devices 274–5
   formal approach (discourse as text) 134, 135–7
   formations 561, 562
   functional varieties, naturalization 594
   history 134–5
   ideological investments 594, 596
   ideology 560
   institutional 115–16, 240–2, 541
      pre-allocation 138
   interactions, cross-cultural comparison 148–9
   internet language 288–9
   literary
      in narrative 132
      speech-act theories 245
   logical propositions 140
   marginal 142
   message structure 28
   monologic 128
   nonvocal aspects 138
   orders
      hegemonic structuring 594
      power relationship 588, 593
   Pierre Riviére case study 142
   political 584, 588
      rhetoric 574, 584–5
   poststructuralism 139
   power and 541
   power behind 593–5
   power in 592–3
   power relations 141, 595
   power struggle in 595–7
   power struggle over 596–7
   prescriptive/descriptive approaches 134
   properties and functions 42
   as representation of speech and thought 605
   resistance to power in 595–6
   rules 140–1
   sequential model: jobs, devices and forms 222
   sequentiality in 222–5
   sexism in 596

social class and ethnic identity, in second language texts 135–6
social psychology use 136–7
strategies 42–3
structuralist approach 139
technologization 574, 597
terminology 134–6
textual production 134
theories 139–40
  Foucault 141–2
types, politicized language and 582–3
units 140
Discourse analysis
  address patterns 148
  broadcast monologues 253
  classroom talk 750–1, 806–9
  commentary and text distinction 143
  context in 219
  downgraders 147
  ethnomethodology 694
  exchanges 804
  grammar teaching approach 727
  language play 148
  legal contexts 231–3
    courtroom 231–2
    lawyer–client interviews 233
    police interviews 233
  and literature 136
  media language 252–3
  news 252
  as official discourse 143
  pragmatics as 135
  sign language 91–2
  situational context 221
  sociolinguistics 42
  upgraders 147
Discourse markers, conversation 111, 114, 115
Discourse structure, context and 219, 222, 224–5
Discrimination
  linguistic, action against 546–8
  of minorities 607
  minority languages and 545–50
  types 545–6
Discursive capital, theory of 366–8
Dispositio, organization 236
Dissent, in hegemony theory 550
Dissimilation 397
Distinctive features, phonology 78
Dittmar, Norbert 859–60
Divergence 193, 195
  converging as 195–6
  evaluation 195
  ideal 195
  motivation for 195
  societal bilingualism 19–20
Diversity, linguistic, and societal bilingualism 21
Djuka 529
Doctor–patient language 152–4, 241, 259

dominance 153, 592, 594
expert–lay cooperation 153–4
initiative/response/acknowledgement triples 152
linguistic repression 53–4
social categorization in 153
Documentation, endangered languages 813
Domains
  consensual, in communication 26
  exclusion, effect on language adaptation 626–7
  international 621–2
  semantic, ethnoscience 40
Dominance
  discrimination and 548–9
  in doctor–patient language 153, 592, 594
  effect on language adaptation 626–7
  power and 592
  unequal encounters 592
Dominant languages 516
  acquisition, by migrants 508
  linguistic imperialism and 570
  place in education 549
  promotion 572
Dorian, Nancy 860–1
Double bind 81
Downgraders, discourse analysis 147
Dramatization, and child language development 184
Drug use
  attitudes to, and behavior 8
  religious beliefs and 10
  subcultures and 403
Durkheim, Emile
  language and conceptualization 367
  theory of families 367
Dutch
  Pennsylvania Dutch 490, 491
  use in Indonesia 599
Dyirbal, mother-in-law language 555
Dyslexia 713

Eavesdroppers, speech acts 200
Ebonics 708–10, 722
Ecology of language 30–1
Economy, linguistic 610
Education
  additive/subtractive, in multilingualism debate 549
  bilingual *see* Bilingual education
  Black English in, United Kingdom 700–2
  Canada
    French Immersion 432
    school language policies 680
  choice of language, ethnicity and 327
  cognitive deficit, societal bilingualism and 21
  computer-based 792
  cultural pluralism, school language policy need 679, 711
  deaf children 568–9
  discrimination, minority language speakers 607
  Head-start programs 56

997

ideology in 561
immigrants' children 506, 568, 569
language and 710–14
   gender and 735–7
   societal pragmatics 52–3
language use in 698–9
linguistic capital and social class 594
linguistic genocide via 569
linguistic minorities 547–8, 606
   immersion programs (language shelter programs) 607
minority languages 327, 506, 568, 571
monolingual norm 549
mother tongue in 513–14, 547–8, 549, 711
multicultural 508–9
multilingual societies 21–2
national/official languages in 658
orthography and 670
overeducation 365
pidgins, creoles and minority dialects 747–9
social class and 52, 364, 365, 366, 368
   deficit theory 368–9
standard language 718–19, 722
status of dominant language 549
theory of, symbolic interactionism and 84
working class language, differences vs deficits 716–17, 722, 737
Educational disadvantage
   biological determinism and 715
   environmental deficiency and 716
   poverty and 715
   school response 720–2
Educational failure
   caused by language mismatch attitudes 737
   language 714–23
   restricted codes and 216
Educational imperialism 570
Educational linguistics 711
Educational underachievement
   ethnicity and 738
   gender and 736, 738
   semilingualism cause 606, 607
   social class and 738
Educational wastage 789
Edwards, John Robert 861–2
Electropalatography, sociophonetics 392, 393
Elitism 566
Emancipatory linguistics 56–7
Emeneau, Murray Barnson 862
Emotions, adolescents and 299
Enclaves, language 489–92
   definition 491
   development 490–1
   objective factors in 491
Encoding/Decoding model of mass communication 247
Endangered languages 465–7, 569
   causes of endangerment 466–7

   dialect variations 836
   documentation 813
   internet resources 838
   learning models 826
   missionaries and 512
   organizations for 837–8
   orthography development 837
   professional associations 841
   projects 835–8
      educational 835–6
      resource development 836–7
   reversing language shift 673
   salvage work 813–16
   statistics 465–6
   use of linguistic contact phenomena 815
English
   Afro-American *see* Black English, America
   Afro-Caribbean language varieties relationship with Standard English 712–13
   after perfects 500
   American *see* American English
   Basic 617
   Butler 484, 531, 532
   chain shifts
      Great Vowel Shift 303–4, 305
      ongoing 304–6
   copulas, deletion 383–4, 387
   dialectology, American and British English comparison 311, 312–14
   dialects, grammar 382–4, 387
   diffusion 467–8, 519–20
   extraterritorial promotion
      by Australia 642–3
      by United Kingdom 641–2
      by United States 640–1
   gay 333, 335
   grammar, dialect variation 382–4, 387
   honorifics 554
   international status 468, 572, 573, 599, 621, 622–3
      history of 602
      science and technology 468, 622–3, 624
   language conflicts 564
   linguistic atlases 351–2
      Scotland 350
      United States 312, 351, 352, 354, 359
   medical terminology/communication 257, 258
   nativization 471, 658, 661
   negation
      dialect variations 383
      emphatic 383
   new Englishes 519–24
      as contact and interference varieties 521–2
      identificational features 521
      ideology and methodology 523
      literary creativity 522–3
      native speakers and 514, 515
      norms and models 522

subvarieties 521, 522
  users and functions 520–1
non-standard 754
Nuclear 471
Plain English movement 242
promotion of 636
pronunciation
  accents 293–7
  new Englishes 521
restricted Englishes 468
  Nuclear English 471
Scottish, pronunciation/accent 293–4, 296–7
sociolinguistic studies 371, 372, 377–89, 393–5
  /l/-vocalization 393–5
  social class 371
  Yod-coalescence 394–5
spoken/written comparison, grammatical study 727–8
Standard
  characteristics 754
  communicative competence, linguistic and cultural variation 754–5
  cross-cultural communication, school literacy teaching 754, 755
  cultural identity conflict 712–13, 755
  educational policy and 753–7
  multicultural contexts 754
  oral/written distinction 754
  power relationship 593–4
  pronunciation/accent 293
  regional variations 33
  social variables 754
  teaching 755–6
  UK teaching 712–13
standardization, proposals for Academy 615–16
teaching
  differences between UK and USA 725
  Teaching English to Speakers of Other Languages (TESOL) 467
use of
  India 598, 603
  internet 288
  League of Nations 624
  as lingua franca 468, 622
  number of speakers 467, 638
  UNESCO statistics 684, 685–8
variations 33
varieties
  contact 521–2
  inner/outer/expanding circles 468, 519–20
  intercomprehensibility 471
  interference 521–2
  learning-model 471
  natural 471
  non-mainstream 754
  restricted 468, 471
English Language Teaching (ELT) 467

English as a second/foreign language 467–72
  British Council projects 641–2
  cultural imperialism 470–1
  culture and 470–1
  as education 469–70
  extraterritorial promotion 641–2
  TENOR development 469
  USIA promotions/courses 641
English for Specific Purposes 468
Entailment, in advertising 251
Enunciation and polyphony, theory of 27–8
Epenthesis 397
Epithets, formulaic speech 234
Eponyms, medical terminology 257
Equivalence 829
  in texts 261
Error analysis 476
Esperanto 616, 617–18, 625
Ethnic groups/minorities
  integration 505
  result of late twentieth century migration 504
Ethnicism 549
Ethnicity
  differences, and oral assessment 713
  and educational underachievement 738
  endogamy and 598
  language and 45–6, 99, 166, 324–9, 598, 663
    education 327
    and human rights 326
    linguistic change and 328
    politics 327–8
    stable ethnicities 321–2
  language crossing and 322–3
  language enclaves and 490
  and nationality 663, 664
  race and 601
Ethnocentrism
  and discrimination 546
  stereotypes and 609
Ethnographic grammar 28–9
Ethnography
  classroom talk studies 803, 804
  ethnoscience 70, 71
  field methods 772–5
    field notes 773–4
    filming and photography 774–5
    informants 775
    interviews 774
    nature of data 775
    observation 773
  and kinship terminology 176
  nature and objectives 772
  of speaking 30, 154–60, 694
    cultural patterns of language use 41
    descriptive framework and categories 158–9
    social patterns and 157–8
    Standard English and 754–5
  translation 72

Ethnolects 441
　role of foreigner talk 474
Ethnolinguistic vitality 472–3
　societal bilingualism 22
Ethnologue 510, 839
Ethnomethodology 84–5, 104, 160–5
　attribution theory and 85
　conversation analysis 111, 137
　discourse analysis 694
　ethnography and 162–3
　experiments 84–5
　indexicality 162
　phenomenology and 85, 161
　pragmatics and 51
　reflexivity 162
　situational context 221
Ethnoscience 40, 70, 71
Ethnosensitivity, cross-cultural language teaching 756
Etiquette 187
European Community/Commission, modern foreign languages teaching in UK 712
European Court of Human Rights, Saami minority language case 548
Ewondo Populaire 527
Exchange theory 86, 96, 821
　norms, theory of 821
　role theory and 61
Exclamations, in adolescent peer group language 299
Exercitives 201
Expectations, in advertising 251
Experiments, deception in 84–5
Expositives 201
Expressions, free, distinction from formulas 233–4
Expressives, speech acts 201
External languages, distinction from internal languages 35
Extinct languages 465

Face
　differences, different construals of self 189
　discourse, intercultural variation 146–7, 148, 149
　institutional setting 241
　negative 188
　politeness as face-saving activity 187–8
　positive 188
　power relations 592
　threatening acts
　　avoiding 188
　　bald on record 188
Factor analysis 102, 103
Fairclough, Norman 862–3
False consciousness, theory of 99
Families
　language use in, immigrants in Canada 100
　roles in 59, 60
　social class and 367

Fanakalo (Fanagalo) 528
Fasold, Ralph W. 863–4
Feedback, social groups' goals and 824
Felicity, in discourse 140
Felicity conditions
　in advertising 251
　context in 220
　speech acts 198, 200–1
　　executive 200
　　fulfillment 200, 201
　　preparatory 200, 201
　　sincerity 201
Feminism 44
　analysis of woman's language 543
　conversational analysis input 139
　critical linguistics input 135
　genre theories 237
　and language 343–4
　language planning 646
　resistance to male domination 596
Ferguson, Charles A. 864–5
　diglossia 226–31
Ferring 494
Field, language *see* Market(place), linguistic
Field methods 780–1
　data collection 780
　ethnography 772–5
　fourth floor method 781
　interpreter for target language 780
　modern dialect and variation studies 776–9
　monolingual 780
　phonetic transcriptions 780
Fields, lexical *see* Lexical fields
Fieldwork 779–80
　data collection 780
　dialectology 779–80
　endangered languages 813–16
　first analysis 779
　informants 781
　observer's paradox 781
　transcription 779, 780
　variation studies 781
Fingerspelling 90
Finland, acquisition of English in 500, 501
Finnish, double semilingualism among speakers 606
First language 515–16
Firth, J. R. 865–7
Fishman, Joshua A. 867–8
Fixed expressions, spoken language 273
Fixed phrases 234
Flattery, management and 824
Folk taxonomy, Sapir–Whorf hypothesis 70, 71
Folklore
　esoteric–exoteric factor 609
　stereotypes 609
Foregrounding
　adult speech to children 704

literary language 244
  and text interpretation 260
Foreigner talk 146, 474–5
  contexts 474
  linguistic indices 474
  in literature 475
  reduction in 474
  relation with pidgins 474
  study methods 475
  users 474
Forensic linguistics 233
Forensic phonetics
  International Association for Forensic Phonetics 841
  sociolinguistics and 329–32
Formal language 717
  see also Code(s), elaborated
Formalism
  discourse 134, 135–7
  ideology in 560
  Russian 128
    defamiliarization 244
    on literary language 244
Formality, honorifics 557–8
Formulaic speech/language 233–5
  commonplaces (loci communes) 233
  functions 234–5
  intercultural variations 146–7
  politeness 190–1
  properties 234
  social identity indication 234
  socio-cultural knowledge incorporation 234
Formulas
  poetic 234
  ritualistic 234
  routine 234
Fossilization
  interlanguage 475, 476, 477, 479–80
  phonological, cerebral lateralization and 480
  in second language learning 695
Foucault, Michel 168, 868–9
Four-letter words 284, 285
Foyer project 696
Frame technology 828
Frames
  context in 220
  institutional language 240
  situational, context in 221
France
  extraterritorial language promotion 638–9
  linguistic atlases 312
  nationalism 666
  rationalization of language 653
Franglais 13
French
  Canada, reversing language shift 676, 677–8
  extraterritorial promotion 638–8
  international status 621, 622, 623
  nationalism and 665–6
  use of
    UNESCO statistics 684, 685–8
    worldwide 638
French Alliance 639
Frisian 494
  reversing language shift 678
Functional grammar, textual ideology in 248
Function(s)
  evaluative 180
  ideational 260
  interpersonal 260
  of language, language planning 645
  referential 180
  textual 260

Gaelic *see* Irish; Scots Gaelic
Games
  language, intercultural variation 148
  linguistic marketplace 612
Gangs 369, 403
  criminal, goals 825
Gapping, spoken language 273
Garfinkel, Harold, ethnomethodology 161, 163–4
Gastarbeiter model, of migrant workers 504
Gay language 332–6
  characteristic features 333
  defining 332–3
  diversity 334
  globalizations 334–5
  internet resources 839
  socialization 333
  world-wide emergence 334–5
Gayle 334
Ge'ez, use in Ethiopian Orthodox Church 227
Gender (sex)
  classroom language and 735–6
  differences, and oral assessment 713
  educational achievement/underachievement and 736, 738
  identity, language and 167
  language and 336–45
    International Gender and Language Association 841
  language differences 44–5, 95, 301
    in adolescent peer group language 300–1, 302
    Black American 301–2
    conversational style 340–1
    educational implications 735–7
    encoding 342–3
    gay language 334
    and language change 390
    language development 342
    language use 88, 337–40, 736
    prestige variants 386
    slang use 269
    social class variations 338–40
  literacy and 744–5

literacy rates 735–6
in mental model of the world 55
power and female–male interactions 592–3
reading and writing and 735
relations with genre 235
and self/identity 369
and use of taboo words 286
see also Feminism
Genderlects 88
Generative grammar
  code-switching in 457–9
  syntactic change 408–9
Generative Semantics, context in 219
Genocide, linguistic 567–70
Genre(s) 131–2, 235–9
  categories, rhetorically derived 237
  classifications 235–7
  cognitive schemata 236
  controlling of 582–3
  and development of writing skills 185
  in feminism 237
  framework for texts 236
  generic structure potential 237
  ideology in 560
  intertextuality 237
  kinds 236
  linguistic accounts 237–8
  link with philosophy of Natural Kinds 235
  mixed 236
  narrative grammars for, news 252
  in post-structuralism 237
  relations with gender 235
  and social contexts 260
  theories 235–7
  value systems, and representation 606
Geographical linguistics 360
Geography
  identity and 166
  linguistic 360
Geolinguistics 352–3
German
  dialect geography
    Benrath–Urdingen line 314
    Rhenish fan 314, 315
  dialectology 311–12, 314–16
  diglossia 228, 229
  extraterritorial promotion 636–8
  High German (Hochdeutsch) 314, 316
  international status 621, 622, 623
  language enclaves 490–1
  Low German (Plattdeutsch) 314, 316
  nationalism and 665
  sound shifts, areal linguistics 425
  Swiss 228, 229
  use of
    UNESCO statistics 684, 685–8
    worldwide 637, 638

Germanic languages
  dialectology 311
  second sound shift 314
Gerunds, spoken language 273
Gestalt psychology 60
Gesture(s)
  in communication 169
    cross-linguistic/cross-cultural contexts 146
  emblematic 171
  foreigner talk 475
  infant language acquisition 704
  political speeches 586
Giles, Howard 869–70
Gilliéron, Jules 870–1
Given/new information, context in 219
Glosa 617
Glossolalia 263
Glottophagie 568
Goal-sharing, Cooperative Principle 122–4
Goals
  criminal gangs' 825
  social groups' 824–5
Goethe Institute 637–8
Goffman, Erving 871–2
Görlach, Manfred 872–3
Governments, language promotion 634–44
Graded Intergenerational Dislocation Scale (GIDS) 673–5, 677–8
Graffiti 671
Grammar
  adaptation and modernization 628
  descriptive types 48–9
  development, early childhood 706–7
  generative *see* Generative grammar
  immanent 551
  prescriptive types 48–9
  social class and 362
  statistical study 829–30
  as systemic network 27
  teaching
    awareness in 726, 730, 731
    creative writing approach 723, 725–6
    discourse analysis approach 727
    discovery approach 733
    focus on ways of expressing meanings 733
    grammatical descriptions and 727
    implicit vs explicit knowledge 724–5, 731
    language-study-based approach 723, 725–6, 728
    means/strategies 732–4
    needs approach 724
    problem-solving approach 733
    role and knowledge of teacher 726–7, 729–30
    Systemic–Functional model 727
    terminology in 731–2, 733
    texts and 732, 733, 734
    traditional approach 723–4, 728–30
    United Kingdom 723–35

Grammars (works), and standardization of language 681, 682, 683
Grammatical categories, culture and 67, 69
Grammaticality
  intuitions of 35
  native speakers 514
Grammaticalization
  linguistic change and 409–10
  pidginization 532–3
Gramsci, Antonio 873–4
Graphization 629
Greek
  Ancient, international status 620
  diglossia 227, 229
  koiné 485, 681
    properties 485–6
  medical terminology 256
  standardization 681
Greenlandic, standardization 683
Greetings, conversation 113
Grice, H. P.
  Conversational Maxims 116–21
  Cooperative Principle 121–4
Grierson, Sir George Abraham 874–5
Grimm's law 398
Group identity
  intertwined languages 482
  language and 48, 165–9
    critical sociolinguistics 168
    ethnic identity 166–7
    gendered identity 167
    national identity 167
    projection model of Le Page and Tabouret-Keller 168
    regional identity 166
    social identity 166
  orthography and 669, 670
  political issues 49
Groups
  ethnolinguistic vitality 472–3
  small
    coding of talk 808
    research on 821–7
    see also Social groups
  social see Social groups
Groupthink 822
Grunts, in adolescent peer group language 299
Gullah 600
Gumperz, John J. 875
Gurmukhi script 565
Guttman Scaling 820
Guugu-Yimidhirr, honorifics 555

Habit, distorting expression 8
Habitus 612–13, 650–1
  linguistic 650–2

Haitian creoles 526–7, 528, 600, 601
  orthography 670
Hall, Robert A. Jr 876
Halliday, Michael Alexander Kirkwood 877
  sociosemiotic theory of language 28–9
Hand movements in speech 171
Hapax legomena 767
Haplology 397
Harmonization of language 629
Harmony, child language 346–7
Haugen, Einar 877–8
Hawaiian language
  creoles 462
  revitalization 836
Head Start programs 56
Heath, Shirley Brice 878–9
Hebrew
  diglossia 227, 229
  extraterritorial promotion 643–4
  in Judaism 510
  revival 487, 603, 676–7, 678, 682
  standardization 682
  teaching, *Ulpan* programs 643
Hegemony 550–1
  cultural 593
  linguistic 601–2
  linguistic matrix 551
  Marxist theory of 550
  societal pragmatics in 52
  through discrimination against minority languages 548
Heritage languages 619
  discrimination 547–58
  internet resources 838
  and language in education 711–12
  and migrants 508
  and reintegration of migrant children 506
Hesseling, Dirk Christiaan 879–80
Heteroglosses 357
Heteroglossia 128
  centrifugal/centripetal forces 128
  media language 255
  in text 560
Hidden Markov modeling (HMM), corpora tagging 768
High German (Hochdeutsch) 228
Highlighting, institutional language 240
Hill, Jane 881
Hindi
  style conflict 565
  transplanted koinés 486–7
  use in India 603, 646
Hinduism, language and 510
Hindustani, UNESCO statistics 684, 685, 688
Hiri Motu 461, 525, 527
Hiri Trade 484
Historical linguistics, borrowings 442
History of sociolinguistics 1–2, 36–7

Home languages 516
Home and school, children's language experiences 737–8
Homeland language, language enclaves and 490
Homonymy, disambiguation through context 220
Homophones, letter, internet language 288
Honorifics 552–9
  absolute system 558
  addressee 554–5, 558
  avoidance languages 555, 556
  beautification 555–6, 557
  bystander 555
  circumlocution 553–4
  class indication 557
  communicative function 558–9
  deference 552
  defining characteristic 554
  demeanour 557
  egalitarian ideology effects 557
  formality 557–8
  honorary titles 552
  honorific endings 552
  humbling forms 554, 558
  indexing function 558–9
  intercultural variation 148
  kin-terms 552, 553
  loanwords 553
  nouns 552–3
  object 554
  particles 554
  politeness 552, 558, 559
  power-based 556
  prefixes, beautification 555–6
  pronouns 552
  referent 552–4
  relative system 558
  social distance, relativity 558, 559
  social meaning 559
  solidarity-based 556–7
  subject 553–4, 558
  use 556–8
    pragmatics 552
Hospitals, language 258–9
Human rights 546–7
  linguistic 546–8, 569
    Universal Declaration of 548
Humor
  accent and 320
  code switching 450–1
  dialect 319–20
  ethnic, stereotypes and 608, 609
  speech play and 279
Hybrids, secondary *see* Jargons
Hymes, Dell Hathaway 2, 882
Hymns 263
Hypercorrection 380
  bilingualism 12
  ethnic minorities 328

social class variables 309–10
and social reality of language 35
Hyphenation, internet language 288, 289
Hypothesis testing, linguistic analysis and 794–5

Iconicity, in advertising 250
Ideal types 103–4
Idealism, discursive possibilities constraints 139
Identity
  adolescence and 298
  Black English and, Britain 702
  divergence and 195
  ethnic 321–2, 324–5
    language enclaves and 490
    modification of 322
  language and 48, 88, 107, 165–9
    critical sociolinguistics 168
    ethnic identity 166–7
    gendered identity 167
    language behavior component 217
    national identity 167
    projection model of Le Page and Tabouret-Keller 168
    regional identity 166
    social identity 166
  language enclave 491
  linguistic 563–4
  national 663, 664, 666
  orthography and 669, 670
  religious 664
  researcher's 778
  sexual, language and 33
  social construction of 168
  subcultures and 402
  variation studies 776–7
Ideology 559–63
  agency in 560
  apparatuses 561
  and coherence 595
  and critical linguistics 560, 562
  economic relations definition 560
  effect on language use 814
  in genre 560
  institutional discourse and 241–2
  interpellation 561, 595
  intertextuality 561
  language and 610–11
    inseparability 248
  language planning and 644
  linguistic salvage work and 814
  linguistic–ideological constitution of discourse 543
  and Marxism 559, 575
  in meaning 561
  as modality of power 594
  and natural narrative 185
  naturalization 542
  political formations 559
  in political language 587

power and 248, 560, 562–3, 593, 594–5
  semiosis, word as ideological phenomenon 560
  semiotic analysis 561, 576–7
  in sign 560
  social class and 559, 560
    Marxist theory 307–8
  in social context 561
  of social equality 543
  in social reality 562
  in speech situations 561
  textual 560, 561
    functional grammar and 248
Idiolects, multilingual *see* Jargons
Ido 617
Illiteracy
  by age 745–6
  by gender 744–5
  developing countries 743–4, 745–6
  multilingual societies 21
  statistics 742–6
  see also Literacy
Illocutionary acts 198, 199
  definitions 202
  direct 203
  felicity conditions 200–1, 202
  indirect 202–3
  literal/nonliteral 203
  on-record/off-record 203
  propositional content 202
Illocutionary force 198, 199
  indicating devices 202, 241
Illocutionary intentions 199, 202, 204
Illocutionary points, multiple, per utterance 203–4
Illocutionary verbs 201
Imitation, language acquisition 88
Immersion programs
  French Immersion, Canada 432
  language shelter programs 607
  revitalization of languages 835
Immigrants
  Australia, reversing language shift 678
  borrowings 441
  education 568, 569
    bilingual 698–9
  effects of monolingual habitus 651
  koinés 486–7
  language 440–1
  language assimilation 654
  loss of language 568–9
  subcultures 402
  see also Migrants
Imperialism 601–3
  colonialism and 602
  linguistic 568, 570–4, 601–2
  linguistic stratification and 99–100, 601
  nationalism and 601
Implicational scale 693

Implicatures
  additional meaning 117
  advertising 210
  context in 221
  and Cooperative Principle 122
  deviation from socially indexed politeness 189
  mechanisms 116
Implicit comparisons 500
Imposition, politeness 191
Impressions, management 84
Inclusive language 300
Indexicality
  ethnomethodology 162
  linguistic relativity 72, 73
India(n)
  attitudes to language 648–9, 649
  fluid zone 649
  language conflicts 564, 565, 566
  language policy 646
  language situation 603
  linguistic census 648–50
  national/official languages 660
  rationalization of language 656
  standardization of languages 683
  writing systems 565, 683
Indigenous languages
  discrimination 546–8
  and language in education 711
Indirectness
  in speech, intercutural variations 147, 755
  verbal dueling 291
Individualism, discursive possibilities constraints 139
Individuals
  cult of 367
  social class 364
Indo-European languages
  areal features 426–7, 428
  centum languages 426
  Proto-Indo-European, 'sonant coefficients' 74
  satem languages 426, 428
Indonesia–Australia Language Foundation (IALF) 642–3
Industrialization as cause of language endangerment 466
Inequality
  linguistic 543, 572–3
  social 543
Infants, language acquisition 704–5
Inference 43, 204–6
Inflection, in pidgins and creoles 536–7
Inflectional morphology, children's development of 705–6
Information processing paradigms, contextual conditions in 222
Information technology, work language and 179
Information theory, communication 22–3
Innateness, child language acquisition and 703
Inner speech, cognition as communication process 27

1005

Innovations
  child language 347–8
  and language change 347–8, 390
Institutional discourse 541
Institutional interactions 213
  business 213–14
Institutional language 239–43
  definition 239
Institutional settings
  conversation analysis 115–16
  discourse 54
    conversationalization 596
Instruction, language of 684, 688
Insults, verbal duel 290
Intellectuals 100
  and hegemony 551
  Russian 668
Intelligence quotients (IQs), verbal/non-verbal 216
Interaction process analysis 86, 821
Interactionism symbolic *see* Symbolic interactionalism
Interaction(s)
  institutional settings 241
  interpersonal
    kinesics 169
    regulation 170–1
  role theory 60, 61–2
  social 821
    categorization 821
  women and 301
Interdiscourse, ideology in 561
Interference 499
  otherwise see Transfer
Interjections, in adolescent peer group language 299
Interlanguage 475–81
  bilingualism 12, 695
  comparative research, speech acts 480
  and discourse analysis, in cross-linguistic/cross-cultural contexts 146
  fossilization 475, 476, 477, 479–80
  interlingual identifications 475, 476, 477, 478
  politeness strategies in 480
  psycholinguistic processes 477–8
  results of data elicitation techniques 478
  universal grammar base 478–9
  and universals 479
  variation 479
    by discourse domain 478, 479
Internal languages, distinction from external languages 35
International Association for Forensic Phonetics 841
International Association of Intercultural Communication Studies 841
International Association for Language and Social Psychology 841
International Association of World Englishes 840
International Corpus of English (ICE) 766
International Gender and Language Association 841

International languages 599, 620–6
  adoption of 618–19
  artificial 625
  asymmetrical use 622
  business communication 622
  colonization link 623
  degrees of internationality 620
  imposed language 623
  indicators 621, 624
  lingua franca use 622
  military victories 624
  modernization 625
  multilingualism 623
  in societal bilingualism 17
  and trade 623
  vs local languages 549
International Pragmatics Association 840
International Society for Dialectology and Geolinguistics 841
Internet
  contextual factors 287–8
  language and 287–9
  language change 288
  language courses, endangered languages 836
  linguistic maps 350, 351, 352
  metalanguage 289
  multilingualism and 288
  resources for sociolinguistics 838–40
  stylistic diffusion 289
Interpretation in discourse, process, Prague school theory 28
Interpreters
  bilinguals as 11
  courts of law, discourse analysis 232
Interpretive community, and shared meanings 247
Intertextuality
  in advertising 252
  in communication 27
  in ideology 561
  re-registration 259, 261
  within and among genres 237
Intertwined languages 443, 481–3
  ritual 482
Interviews
  accommodation in 101, 194
  Atlas of North American English 414
  bias in 100–1, 764–5
    forced choices and 8
  context effects on answers 763–4
  ethnography 774
  inhibiting factors 8, 82
  interaction in 241
  kinesics and 170, 171
  language and 82
  lawyer–client 233
  news 252–3
  police 233, 574

respondents' language use 101
sociolinguistic 777–8
   in sociophonetic studies 392
   techniques 308–9
technique 82, 308–9
technologization of discourse 574
variation studies 776, 777–8
Intonation
  classroom talk 807, 808
  intercultural variation 149
  and meaning 136
Intuition(s)
  in data collection 769, 770, 771
  native speakers 514
    and corpora 766, 771
  second languages 517
Inversion theory 363, 369
Invitations, conversation 112, 113, 114, 115
Irish
  diglossia 228
  reversing language shift 675, 676, 677, 678
Islam, language and 510
Isoglosses 312, 357
Isolects 315–16
Isopleths 357
Israel
  extraterritorial language promotion 643–4
  language situation 603
It-clefts, spoken language 274–5
Italian, international status 621, 622
Iterativity
  content/meaning dichotomy 281–2
  style and 281

Jaberg, Karl 882–3
Jamaica, dialectology 316–17
Japan, rationalization of language 653–4
Japanese
  honorifics 552, 553–9
  humbling forms 554
  international status 621, 623
  UNESCO statistics 684
  writing systems 682
    diglossia 227
Jargon(s) 483–5
  doctor–patient language 153
  institutional language 240
  medical 152–4
  in pidgin development 461
  political language 586
  pre-pidgin 536
  work-related 177
Javanese, honorifics 339, 552, 553
Jokes, ethnic stereotypes and 608, 609
'Joking relationships', taboo words in 286
Journalism, metatheoretical analysis of news story 237–8
Journals
  electronic 839
  sociolinguistic 842–4
Judaism
  blessings 211
  Hebrew and 510

Kachru, Braj B. 883–4
Kamtok 525–6
Kenya, national language 661
Key words in discourse, cross-linguistic/cross-cultural contexts 145
Khubchandani, Lachman M. 884–5
Kin-terms, honorifics 552, 553
Kinds, in genre 236
Kinesics 169–72
  Black American 302
  communicative code 169
  conversations 170–1
  emblematic gestures 171
  interviews 170, 171
  regulation of interactions 170–1
  self-presentation 170
  shared norms 170
  situational role 170
  in speech 171
Kingman Report (1988) (UK) 701, 726
Kinship terminology 172–7
  classificatory systems 173
  Crow–Omaha terminologies 174
  descriptive systems 173
  ecology and 174
  functional theory 174–5
  as language 173–4
  and marriage 175
  origins of study 172–3
  post-modern 176
  semantic analysis 175–6
Knowledge
  common sense, ethnomethodology and 164
  conditions of possibility, in discourse 139
  language mediation, in Marxist language theory 577
  mutual, in communication 24
  socio-cultural, and formulaic speech 234
Knowledge systems, context in 220
Kohn, Melvin 366
Koinéization 486
  processes 487–8
  relation to other linguistic processes 488–9
Koinés 485, 681
  criteria 485–6
  immigrant 486
    subordinate 486–7, 488
    superordinate 486
  modern use of term 485–6
  regional 486
Koran *see* Qur'an

Korean
  honorifics 552, 553, 554, 558
  writing systems 682–3
Krio 527
Kroeber, Alfred Louis 173
Kurath, Hans 885

Labeling, Sapir–Whorf hypothesis 65, 68, 69, 72
Labeling theory 97–8
  extreme versions 98
  mental illness 97–8
Labor
  division of 363, 367
    ethnicity and 365
  language as 562
Labov, William 2, 369, 885–7
  chain shifts 303, 304–5
  methodology 829
  narrative structure 180–1
  quantitative microsociolinguistics 691–5
  sociolinguistic variation 377–89
  sociolinguistics
    criticisms 387–8
    variable rules 384–5
  studies
    Black English syntax 382–4
    Martha's Vineyard 377–9
    New York City 379–81
  vernacular 420
Lakoff, Robin Tolmach 887–8
Lambert, Wallace E. 888–9
Language
  definitions, comparison of anthropologists and linguists 66
  use of term 31–4
Language across the curriculum, need for school policy 679
Language continuum, societal bilingualism 17
Language into Languages Teaching (LILT) 730
Language in the National Curriculum (LINC) project (1989–92) (UK) 726
Language shelter programs 607
Languages 31
  merging 32–3
  variations 33
Langue 513
  langue/parole dichotomy 25
    Bakhtin's objections 128
    Saussure on 75, 76
  social nature 75–6
  as syntagmatic and paradigmatic relations system 78–9
Latin
  diglossia 227–8
  medical terminology 256
  Pig Latin (language game) 277–8
  standardization 681
Latin America, language situations 602–3

Latino sine flexione 617
Laughter 111, 115, 138
Law, discourse analysis and 231–3
  courtroom 231–2
  lawyer–client interviews 233
  police interviews 233
Lawyer–client interviews, discourse analysis 233
Le Page, Robert B. 889–90
  projection model/group identity 167–8
Leadership
  contingency theories 824
  roles (instrumental/expressive) 60
  small groups 823
Learning
  banking concept 53
  imperfect, and language change 346
  motivation 599
    and restricted/elaborated codes 216
Learning strategies
  interlanguage psycholinguistic process 477, 478, 480
  mnemonics 478
Lects 315–16
Legislation, language
  Canada 660
  India 660
  United States 659–60
Legitimation of language 611
Lemert, Edwin 97
Lerzebuergesch 228
Lesbian language 334
Letter-writing, honorifics 554, 558
Leveling, morphological, and language change 347–8
Lewis, E. Glyn 890
Lexical fields, linguistic relativity and 71
Lexical innovation, child language 347
Lexical relations, ethnography and 71
Lexicography
  applications of corpora 767–8
  slang 266
Lexicon
  gender and 342, 344–5
  Sapir–Whorf hypothesis and 65–6
Liechtenstein, diglossia 228
Lies
  management and 824
  social psychology 81
Likert Scaling 819–20
Linearity, of signifiers 78
Lingua francas 19, 503–4, 573
  African languages as 603
  international uses 622
  pidgins as 504, 528
  and standardization of language 683
  in treaty texts 622
  types 504
Linguicide 567–70
Linguicism 549, 567, 573, 581

Linguistic Data Consortium 766
Linguistic Minorities Project (UK) 712
Linguistics
  anthropological origins, North American 36–7
  development 36–7
  society and 51–2
Listening, oracy 746–7
Literacy 739–46
  acquisition 739–40
    research in 788–9
    social and cultural differences 788
  action 726
  adult 740
  children 739–40
  definition 787–8
  design of instructional materials 792
  in developing countries 741–2, 743–4, 745–6
  functional 739, 787
  gender and 735–6
  as a global issue 742–6
  and language competence 740–1
  learning 713–14
  levels 739
  measurement 739, 788, 789–91
  missionaries' contribution 510
  mother tongue/second language issues 788–9, 790, 792
  multilingual societies 21
  multisectoral approaches 792
  National Literacy Strategy (England and Wales) 729, 732, 733, 734
  non-standard language and 712, 755
  nonmainstream groups 755
  oracy 741
  programs 787
  recognition 726
  reflection 726
  research 787–9, 791–2
    use of tchnology 791–2
  retention 789
  second language 741
  as secondary discourse 87
  socialization 87, 88
  statistics 742–6
  technology and 742
  transition to, language adaptation and 627
  see also Illiteracy
Literariness, in language 245–6
Literary criticism, sign and 131
Literary language 243–6
  contexts of reading 244–5
  Formalist theories 244
  register 261
Literary theory, context of 261
Literature
  changing signs, dialogism 130–1
  diglossia in 226
  as discourse, speech-act theory 245
  foreigner talk in 475
  literary language in 243
  sociology of 261
  style 282–3
  subcultural 95
Loanshifts, bilingualism 13
Loanwords
  bilingualism 13
  and code-switching 447, 452
  cults and 95
  honorifics 553
  spelling reform 671
Locutionary acts 199
Loss of language 568–9
  see also Death of language
Lounsbury, Floyd 175
Loyalty, language 492, 564, 566, 627
  sociometry 828
Luxembourg, diglossia 228

Ma'a 464, 482
McDavid, Raven Ioor Jr 892–3
Machiavelli, Niccolò, and lies 7
Machiavellian personality 81
Machiavellianism, management theory and 824
Mailing lists 838
Maintenance, language 493–8, 627
  bilingual education and 697, 698
  ethnic attitudes and 326
  isolation and 599
  language loyalty and 492
  status factors 494–5
Majority languages
  assimilation to 564
  suppression 564
Makeshift language see Jargons
Malapropisms 278
Malay, Bahasa (Bazaar) 525
Malay–Indonesian, UNESCO statistics 684, 685–8
Male forms, as common gender 343, 344
Malinowski, Bronislaw Kaspar 891
Management
  authoritarian vs egalitarian 823–4
  philosophies 823–4
Manipulation 574–5, 582–3
  advertising 250, 574
  deviousness 574
  institutional domains 574
  language and 54–5
  manipulatory language 54
  in political rhetoric 574, 585–6
  power and 593
  veiling 54
Maori
  reversing language shift 678
  revitalization 836

Maps
- from multidimensional scaling 795, 797–800
- linguistic 312, 360–2
  - base maps 354
  - computer-generated 351–2
  - data 354–5
  - dialect areas 312, 319, 351–2, 358–9
  - documentary maps 355
  - dual and multi-dimensional scaling maps 357–8, 779–800, 795
  - explanatory factors 359
  - internet 350, 351, 352, 839
  - interpretive maps 355–7
  - line maps 356–7
  - mapping techniques 355–8
  - properties 353–4
  - qualitative maps 355–7
  - quantitative maps 357–8
  - role and function 352–3
  - sources of information 353
  - subjects of study 359–60
  - system maps 357
  - United States 412–18
- onomasiological 317
- pronunciation 797–800
- semasiological 317

Maricon 334

Markedness
- code-switching 455–6
- gender 344
- in second language acquisition 693

Market research, reference group theory 84

Market(place), linguistic 610, 612–13

Marx, Karl 363
- inversion theory 363, 369

Marxism
- dialectic scheme of 550–1
- and ideology 559
- language theories 575–9
  - abstract objectivism 577
  - Bakhtin Circle 576–7
  - class prejudice in language 576
  - ideology in 575
  - individualistic subjectivism 577
  - linguistic praxis 577
  - material praxis models 575
  - praxematics 577
  - sign systems and social reproduction 578
  - social cognition 577
  - society link 575
  - stereotypes 577
  - world view mediated by social class 307–8
- social class theory 362, 363, 364–5
- and subcultures 403

Masoretes 264

Masquerade 333

Mass communication
- Encoding/Decoding model 247
- as sociocultural phenomenon 247–8

Mass media
- communication via 247–8
- diffusion of slang 267–8, 269
- power 593
- role in borrowing 438–9
- youth culture and 298

Matched guise technique 82, 88, 295, 393, 719

Materialism, historical 560

Matrilinearity, ethnicity and 598

Maxims, conversational 116–21
- exploiting 117–18
- flouting 117–19
- infringements 119, 120
- institutional setting 241
- misrepresentations 119
- non-observance categories 119–21
- observation 122
- optings out 119, 120
- politeness 187–8, 189
- suspensions 119, 120–1
- violations 119–20, 221

Maxims, Gricean 117
- in cross-linguistic/cross-cultural contexts 150

Mayan languages, fieldwork 780

Mazrui, Ali A. 891–2

Meaning
- aberrant, mass media 247
- associations and 103
- and culture 38–40
- defining 84
- expressed, distinction from implied 116
- ideology and 561
- implicit, in advertising 251
- negotiation, intercultural variation 149
- non-natural 23
- polyvalency, in media language 254
- potential
  - interpreted by functions 260
  - register as 259–60, 260
- signifiers 128
- social, and speech register in literature 261
- social influences on 96, 101
- social psychology 84
- survey answers and 96
- term choice and social semiotics 29
- theories of prototype and metaphor and 39

Meaning/content dichotomy, style and 281–2

Measurement
- of attitudes 82
- social research 816
  - composite measures 816–17
  - index scores 816–17
  - scaling 817–20

Media
- advertising and 209–10

communication 246–56
  ideology in 561
  politics and 574, 587
  power 593
  voices
    female 254
    sociolinguistic perspectives 253–4
  see also Mass media
Media language 246–56
  audience 246, 253
    reception processes 246
  and communication 246–56
  and critical linguistics 248–9
  discourse analysis 252–3
  ethnomethodology 252
  heteroglossia 255
  misunderstandings 254
  research, empirical audience dimension 254
  restricted/elaborated codes in 248
  as social semiotic 254
Media Lengua 464, 481–2
Medical language 240, 256–9
  hospitals 258–9
  international medical communication 258
  medical terminology 256–8
  see also Doctor–patient language
Medicalization 100
Mednyj Aleut 463–4
Mental illness, labeling theory 97–8
Mercator Project 837–8
Merton, Robert K., subcultures 403
Mesolects 441, 535
Message structure theory, Rommetveit's 28
Metafunctions, ideational, representational alternativity location 605
Metalanguage, internet 289
Metamessages 39
  gender differences 45
Metaphor(s)
  in advertising 250
  formulaic speech 234
  and meaning/culture relationship 39
  medical terminology 257–8
  in political language 591
  spatial orientation and 39
  verbal dueling 291
  in wording the world 55
Metapragmatic acts (comments) 241
Metapragmatics, child language development 87
Metatextuality, in advertising 252
Metathesis 398
Metonymy, in advertising 250
Michif 20, 443, 463–4, 482, 483
Micronesia, Carolines, language variation across 794–5, 796–7
Microsociology 85–6
Migrants, late twentieth century 504–9
  CDCC definitions 505–6

children
  educational achievement 506
  integration 506–7
  second and third generation migrants 505–6
  ethnic minorities position 504
  Gastarbeiter model 504
  integration 505
  political lever concept 507
  settlement 504
  as subclass 504
  see also Immigrants
Military slang 267
Milroy, Lesley 893–4
Minorities
  educational underachievement 607
  linguistic
    language enclaves 489–92
    semilingualism in 606
    sociocultural 489–90
    types 489–90
  linguistic denigration 581
  power structure, in cross-cultural interactions 593
  societal and educational discrimination 607
Minority languages 579–80
  attitudes to 566
  discrimination and 545–50
  education and 327, 506, 568–9, 571
    bilingual education 696–8, 699
  immigrants 440–1, 568, 569
  institutional support 494
  linguicide 568, 569
  linguicism 573
  marginalization 549
  native
    borrowing 440
    death 440
  official status 660
  rights 326
    Saami case at European Court of Human Rights 548
  status vis-à-vis dominant language 571–2
  treatment in census 649
  underdevelopment link 572
Miscommunication in cross-linguistic/cross-cultural discourse 146
Missegmentation 347
Missionaries
  Christian 265, 510
    applied linguistics 511
    Bible translation 510, 511
    and endangered languages 512
    language identification 510–11
    sociolinguistics 511
  Hindu 510
  linguistic contribution 265, 509–12
Mitigation, politeness 190
Mixed languages 20, 461, 463

Mixing of languages 442–3, 499
  bilingual situations 69–70
  intertwined languages 481–3
Mobilian Jargon 484
Modernization of language 626–30
  corpus 628–9
  international languages and 625
Monitor theory, second language acquisition 478, 692, 695
Monolingualism 571, 651
  and elitism 566
Monologic 128
Monologue
  broadcast, discourse analysis 253
  simulated dialogue in 253
Morale, social group membership and 826
Morality, attitudes to 8–9
Morgan, Lewis Henry 172–3
Moribund languages 465, 466
Morphology, inflectional, children's development of 705–6
Mother tongues 515
  education and 513–14, 547–8, 549, 568
  ethnicity and 325
  identification in census 648, 649
  influence *see* Transfer
  intergenerational transmission 673–9
  in multilingual societies 648, 649
Mother-in-law language 555
Motu, Hiri Motu 461, 525, 527
Mufwene, Salikoko S. 894–5
Muhlenberg legend 659, 660
Mühlhäusler, Peter 895–6
Multi-accentuality 129–30
Multicultural education 508–9
Multiculturalism
  Canada 48–9
  language and 48–50
  Standard English and 754
Multidimensional scaling 793–802
  algorithms 795–6
  computer-aided 794, 795
  individual speakers 800–1
  maps 796, 797–800
Multilevel generative systems *see* Jargons
Multilingual idiolect *see* Jargons
Multilingual speech communities 16, 695
  code selection 17–18
  diglossia 18
  education 21–2
  integration policy 20–1
  language planning 20–1
  language shift 18–19
  speech repertoires 17–18
Multilingual states
  language policies, political implications 652–7
  minority languages 653
  as norm 656
  post-colonial 656–7

  rationalization of language 652–4
Multilingualism 48–9
  choice of mother tongue 648, 649
  code-switching in 43
  and elitism 566
  implications 549
  India 656
  international languages 623
  internet 288
  and language acquisition 430–2
  sociolinguistic areas 538–9
  South Africa 603
  state 105–6, 656
    former Soviet Union 655–6
    and national/official languages 685–8
    political implications 657
    Switzerland 654
Muysken, Pieter Cornelis 896–7
Myers-Scotton, Carol 897–8
Myths about origin of language 264

Naga Pidgin 525
Nagari script 565, 683
Names
  personal
    influence of religion 263–4
    married women 343
    transmission of surnames 343
  proper, in conversation 113
Naming
  cults 826
  and power 611
  social groups 826
Narrative
  backgrounding in 180
  children 184–5, 707–8
  conversational, use of historic present tense 183
  diffuse 183
  discourse in 132
  embedded 183
  evaluation 181–2, 183
  evaluative function 180
  natural 179–86, 237
    political context analysis 185
  oral 180–1, 182–3
    group 183–4
  performance 182
  polyphony in 127
  referential function 180
  situated 180
  spoken 271
  structure 180–1
  tellability 180, 181
Narratology 236
National Curriculum in English (England and Wales)
  grammar 728–30, 734
  linguistic pluralism acceptance 701
  policy on Standard English 712–13

LINC (Language in the National Curriculum) project (1989–92) (UK) 726
National Curriculum in Modern Foreign Languages 712
National identity, language and 167
National languages 657–62
 bilingualism and 660, 661
 choice, new nations/former colonies 660–1
 in education 658, 680, 711
 and hegemony 551
 linguistic habitus and 651
 nationalism and 658–9
 as political concept 588
 UNESCO statistics 684
National Literacy Strategy (England and Wales) 729, 732, 733, 734
National Oracy Project (UK) 746–7
Nationalism 658
 cultural nature 663–4
 and democracy 664
 English 664, 666, 667
 French 666, 667
 German/German views 665
 history of 664
 and identity 663, 664, 666
 imperialism and 601
 and language 99, 630, 658–9
  England 666–7
  France 665–6, 667
  Germany 665
  influence on language development 666–9, 667
 language and 662–9
 language planning and, multilingual speech communities 20
 religion and 665
 romanticism and 665
 Russian 668–9
 symbolic crusade analysis and 99
Nationality
 ethnicity and 663, 664
 language and 662, 663, 664–6
 religion and 663
 tradition and 663
 United States 663
Nationism 658
 language and 658–9
 language planning and, multilingual speech communities 20
Nations 663
 constructed nature 99
 peoples and 663–4, 666–7
Native American Language Issues Institute (NALI) 837
Native languages
 American *see* American languages, native
 transfer 499
Native speakers 512–19
 bilingual 514

choice of model 514–15
competence 516–17
Coppieters' experiment 518
definition 517–18
educational issues 513–14
grammaticality 514
idealized 516
intuition 514
and new Englishes 514, 515
practical issues 514–15
psycholinguistic issues 514
racism issues 515
of second language 517–18
theoretical issues 513
Natural kinds, philosophy of, link with genre 235
Natural language
 interlanguage as 479
 modified 617
Natural language processing
 corpora and 768–9
 corpus linguistics and 765
Naturalization 541–2
 and unaccented signs 130
Navajo (Navaho)
 plant classification 68–9
 reversing language shift 677, 678
 revitalization 835
 vocabulary for 'lines' 69
Nenets 465
Neoconservatism, social class theory 365, 366
Neogrammarians, sound change 398
Neologisms
 in adolescent peer group language 299
 borrowing 438
 cults 95
 in political language 586
 Sapir–Whorf Hypothesis 68
 science fiction 95
 slang 268
 young people and 95, 299
Netlingo 287, 288
 spread and impact 289
Netspeak 287, 288–9
Networks, social 827, 828
Neurolinguistics, bilingualism 14–15
New Ways of Analyzing Variation (in English and other languages) 840
News, broadcast 252
Newspeak 583
Nida, Eugene Albert 511, 898–9
Nigerian Pidgin 529
Nominalism 26
 in philosophy of linguistics 580
Nominalization, institutional language 240
Non-communication, cross-linguistic/cross-cultural discourse 146
'Nonsense' languages 263
Normalization, speech perception 400

Norms
  adolescent peer group language 299
  emergence, and language as a social reality 35
  language planning 644–5
  shared, kinesics 170
  social *see* Social norms
  social class basis 309
  societal, code-switching and 448–9
Norwegian
  standardization 682
  written sociolects 26
Nouns
  compound, medical terminology 257
  honorifics 552–3
  strings 240
Nynorsk 682

Objectivity, representation and 604
Obscenities 284–5
  women 338
Observation
  classroom talk 803–4
  insightful 803–4
  participant
    ethnography 773
    variation studies 778
Observer's paradox 691, 802
  classroom talk 805
  field work 781
Obsolescence 409
  see also Death of language
Occidental 617
Offers, conversation 114
Official languages 657–62
  bilingual/multilingual states 105–6, 685–8
    imposition 652
  bilingualism and 106, 660, 661
  choice of 646
    new nations/former colonies 660–1
  in education 658
  literacy in 789–90
  nationism and 658
  UNESCO statistics 684
  of United Nations 622
Ol Chikki script 565
Onomasiology, dialect geography 317
Operationalization, social research 810
Oppression, linguistic, societal pragmatics 53
Optimal theory, code-switching 459–60
Oracy 746–7
  literacy and 741
    language adaptation and 627
  National Oracy Project (UK) 746–7
Oral communication skills 750
Oral narrative 180–1, 182–3
  group 183–4
Oratory, political speech devices 585
Ordinary language philosophy 50

Organic character of language 75
Origin of language, myths 264
Origins of sociolinguistics 36–7
Orok 465
Orthography/Orthographies 669–72
  adaptation and modernization 629
  education and 670
  endangered languages 837
  identity and 669, 670
  language planning and 670
  missionaries' contribution 510
  postcolonial 671
  as resistance 671
  sociolinguistic problems 670
  symbolism in 669–70
Orwell, George, politicized language 583
Overgeneralization(s)
  bilingualism 12
  child language 348
  pidginization 535
  second language learning 477
Oxford English Dictionary, prescription 672

Palatalization, sociophonetic studies 393
Pāṇini
  Aṣṭādhyāyī 1
  rules 1
Panopticism 142
Papua New Guinea, pidgins 524, 525, 527
Paradigmatic relations, Saussure on 78–9
Paradigms 561
Paradox, observer's 802, 805
Paralanguage, Black American 301
Parallelism
  foregrounding device 244
  lexical 244
  structural 244
Parody, carnivalization 133
Parole, distinction from langue 25
  Bakhtin's objections 128
  Saussure on 75, 76
Parsers, need for word-frequency statistics 767
Parsing, corpora and 768
Particles, honorifics 554
Passive voice, institutional language 240
Passives, agentless, in political language 586
Patrilinearity, ethnicity and 598
Patwa 529
Paulston, Christina Bratt 899–900
Pause-fillers 275
Pauses
  classroom talk 806
  during utterances, planning indicators 216
Pennsylvania Dutch 490, 491
Peoples, nations and 663–4, 666–7
Performance, oral narrative 182
Performative(s)
  blessings as 211–12

clauses 201
  utterances 198
Perlocutions (Perlocutionary effects) 199
  in communication 23, 574
Persian, diglossia 228
Personality
  dimensions 85
  typologies 85
Persuasion, language of 209
Peter the Great of Russia 668
Petit Nègre 526
Phatic communion 186
Phatic speech 186
Phenomenology
  conversation analysis 137
  ethnomethodology and 85, 161
Philippine languages, borrowings 437, 438
Philosophers, analytic 26
Philosophical languages, history 617
Phonemes/Phonemics
  as abstract mental sound pattern 79
  as bundles of features 78
  and signifier concept 77
Phonetics
  data collection 391–3
  experimental 392
  forensic, sociolinguistics and 329–32
  positivism in 79
  sociophonetics 391–6
Phonocentrism 75
Phonologization 393
Phonology 77, 79
  gay language 333
  variation in conversational turn-taking 115
Phrases, participial, spoken language 273–4
Pichingli 484
Pidginization 19, 524, 531–3
  distinction from creoles 463
  and language death 496
Pidgins 19, 461, 524–30
  affix dropping 536
  calques 537
  characteristics 525–6
  classification 527
  compounding 537
  contemporary 529–30
  creolization 462
  development 461, 528–9, 530
    phases 536–8
  in education 747–9
  endogenous 19
  evolution 145
  exogenous 19
  extended 532
  jargon 483
  koinés and 489
  and language change 530–6
  as lingua francas 504, 528

mailing list 838
markedness 536–7
morphology 536–8
origins 526–8
pre-pidgins 531, 532, 536
reduplication 537
relation with foreigner talk 474
sign language 90
similarities 533
slavery and 600
social attitudes to 525
Society for Pidgin and Creole Languages 840
stable 532
status 53
structures 461–2
substrate influence 502, 531, 533
trade 19, 461, 463
universals 531
word-class multifunctionality 536, 537
Pietism 665
Pig Latin 277–8
Pike, Kenneth L. 511
Pitcairnese 462
Plain English movement 242
Planning, language
  corpus 645
  deaf 91
  feminist 646
  historical and ethnographic approaches 647
  ideology and 647
  language adaptation and 627–8
  language development and 631, 633, 634
  and language in education 711–13
  models 644–7
  multilingual speech communities 20–1
  orthography 670
  politics in 587
  prestige 645
  process 644–5
    problems of rational decision-making in 645–6
  reversing language shift 676–7
  rights of ethnic minorities 326
  and school language policies 680
  social class basis 309
  status 645
Planning, social, linguistic censuses and 650
Plant classification, Navajo 69
Platt, John T. 900
Play, speech *see* Speech play
Poetic effects 244
Poetic formulas 234
Polari 334
Police interviews
  discourse analysis 233
  linguistic manipulation 574
Policespeak 468
Policies, language
  grammar teaching in United Kingdom 728–30

1015

language diffusion 634–44
minority languages in education 698–9
multilingual states 652–7
  postcolonial 656–7
schools *see* School language policies
Politeness 187–93
blessings and 211, 212
contextual variation 191–2
  Bulge Theory 191
  discourse domain and 191–2
conversational contract view 188
conversational maxim view 187
deference 188
deviation, interactional implicatures 189
different construals of self 189
face-saving 187–8
honorifics 552, 558, 559
imposition 191
indirect speech context 755
institutional setting 241
intercultural variation 146–7, 148, 149
interlanguage research 480
mitigation 190
as social indexing (discernment) 188–9
social norm view 187
social relativism in 189
solidarity strategy 188
speech act sets 190, 191
in speech acts 190–2, 589
strategic (volitional) 188
use of routine formulas 190–1
Politeness Principle 187, 189
Political beliefs, measuring 811
Political consciousness 307, 365, 366
Political correctness of language 581, 583
Politicised language 580–4
consciousness raising 581–2
deliberate changes 582–3
language classification and 581
Politics
bilingual education 698–9
and critical sociolinguistics 543
ideology in 559
interest/status 99
language and 584–91
  antithesis 586
  content 586
  conversation analysis 589
  critical approaches 587–91
  deception in 585
  descriptive approaches 584–7
  dialect-switching 586
  ethnicity and 327–8
  ideology 587
  language of politics 580
  language revivals 653, 655
  list of three 586
  manipulation 585–6

metaphor use 591
operational coding 586–7
politeness phenomena 589
politics of language 580
power aspect 584, 587, 588
rhetorical devices 585–6
semantic analysis 590
stereotypes in 590
language policies
  implications in multilingual states 652–7
  post-colonial states 656–7
multiculturalism 49
rhetoric 574, 584–5
  linguistic manipulation 574
social theory and 99
speeches, devices 585–6
Polyglossia, multilingual speech communities 18
Polyphony 127
in communication 27
Polysemy (Polysemia)
disambiguation through context 220
re-registration factor 261
Poplack, Shana 901
Popular speech 265–6
Portuguese
colonialism 602–3
international status 621, 622
UNESCO statistics 684, 685–8
Positivism 75–6, 79
Post-structuralism, genre theory 237
Power
behind discourse 593–5
change, centrifugal/centripetal 596–7
in classroom discourse 592
in cross-cultural interactions 593
culture and 97
differentials, language and 597–604
in discourse 541, 592–3, 605
  resistance to 595–6
discrimination against minority languages and 509, 549
domination link 592
and face, in discourse 592
in Foucauldian discourse theory 141–2
gender and 301, 592–3
and hegemony 550, 551
ideology and 248, 560, 562–3, 593
  as modality 594–5
language and 96–7, 541–2, 591–7, 602
  courtroom 232–3
  in ethnic relations 598–600
  minorities 507
  social class and 307
  societal pragmatics 53
linguistic habitus and 651
and manipulation 593
  linguistic 574
media 593

in mental model of the world 55
and political language 584, 587, 588
relations, in communication 24
reversing language shift and 675
signifying, of the news media 593
as social factor 541
social structure and 543
struggle in discourse 595–7
struggle over discourse 596–7
symbolic, language and 610–12
as transformative capacity 592
unequal encounters 592
and women's language 543
Pragmatic rules in cross-linguistic/cross-cultural discourse contexts 146–7, 150, 151
  interactions 148–9
Pragmatic universals, politeness 189–90
Pragmatics 50–8
  description 115
  as discourse analysis 135
  International Pragmatics Association 840
  lack of social context 543
  origins 50–1
  and philosophy of language 50–1
  situational elements and contextual indices 220–1
  societal 51–7
    conditions of language use 52
Prague School (Prague Linguistic Circle)
  polyfunctional potential of language 28
  realization of *langue* implications 79
  relevance in study of communication 28
  taxonomies of communicative functions 28
Praxematics 577
Praxis, in Marxist language theory 577
Prayer 263
Pre-aspiration, Northern Europe, wave theory and 425, 427
Prefixes, honorifics 553–4
  beautification 555–6
Prejudice
  and language 581, 719
  measuring 811
  stereotypes and 609
  variations in 816, 819, 820
Prescription, dictionaries 672
Prescriptive grammars 48–9
Prescriptivism, language maintenance role 35
Prestige
  covert 381, 386
  and hegemony 550
  language planning 645
  overt 381
  sociolinguistics 381, 386
Prestige forms (of language), sociophonetic variables use 310
Presuppositions
  in advertising 251
  and discourse analysis 43

Prisoners, argot 94–5
Prisons, antilanguage 109
Probability sampling 101–2
Professional associations 840–2
Prominence, motivated, and text interpretation 260
Promotion of language, extraterritorial 634–44
Pronouns
  honorifics 552
  personal, child language development 707
Pronunciation
  correct, and social class variables 309
  gender differences 338–9
Propaganda, politics through media 587
Propositions
  contextually-bound 220
  logical 140
Prototype theory, and meaning/culture relationship 39
Proximity, interpersonal cross-cultural context 150
Psychodrama 60
Psycholinguistics, bilingualism 13–14
Psychology, social *see* Social psychology
Psychopathology, language theory and 81
Psychotherapy, language and 81
Public language *see* Code(s), restricted
Punctuation, internet language 288
Puns 278
Purism, and borrowings 441–2

Quantitative microsociolinguistics 691–5
  Labovian paradigm 691–3, 694, 695
Queering 333
Question and answer sequences, institutional language 241
Questionnaires
  analysis, semantic differential 96
  bias in 100–1
  coding 762, 812
  repetition 812
    split-half method 812
  responses to, behavior and 7
  techniques, semantic differential 85
Questions
  context effects 763–4
  in conversation 113
  courtroom 232
  indirect, spoken language 272, 274
  open/closed, effects on responses 8, 761–3
  surveys
    form 762–3
    wording 761–2
  teachers' 751–2, 804
Quirk, Sir (Charles) Randolph 901–2
Qur'an 262–3, 510

Race 601
  interview bias and 101, 764–5

language and 45–6
  gay language 334
Race relationships, language and 597, 600–1
Racism
  acceptability, and expression of attitudes to 9
  native speakers and 515
  replaced by ethnicism 549
  symbolic 9
  see also Linguicism
Radcliffe-Brown, A. R. 174
Radio
  advertising 209
  language promotion 635, 638, 639
  language teaching, English 643
Radio Australia, teaching of English 643
Radio Canada International 640
Radio France International 639
Ramakrishna Mission 510
Rap 291
Rasta Talk 529
Rationalization of language 652–4
  and democracy 657
  and economic growth 657
  former Soviet Union 655–6
  France 653
  immigration and 654–5
  Japan 653–4
  revival movements 653, 655
  settler colonies 656
  Spain 653
  Switzerland 654
Re-registration, in literary texts 259, 261
Readability, textbooks 713–14
Reader(s)
  implied 261
  interactions with text 245–6
Reading
  and acquisition of literacy 713–14
  gender and 735
  learning 739–40
    research in 788–9
    socialization 87–8
Realism, linguistics 580
Reanalysis
  pidginization 531–2
  syntactic change 409
Reasoning skills, role of language in 737
Received Pronunciation 293, 294–5, 719
  in broadcasting 254
  in learning English as a second language 296
Recife Declaration 659
Recontextualization, institutional language 240
Recording(s)
  classroom talk 804–5
  criminal, speaker identification in 330–1
  difficult, deciphering 329–30
Reduction
  child language 346, 347

phonological
  creolization 534
  pidginization 531
Reduction (analytical technique) 85
Reduplication, in pidgins and creoles 537
Reference, context-bound phenomena 220
Reference groups 84
Reflexivity, ethnomethodology 162
Reformulations 241
Register(s)
  acquisition, through socialization 87
  casual speech 261
  honorifics 559
  in literature 259–62
  as meaning potential 259–60
  multilingual speech communities 17–18
  primary/secondary discourses 87
  representation and 605
  representation of value systems 606
  second language acquisition 692
  texts, re-registration 259, 261
  variation 87
Regraphization 629
Regularization
  language change 347–8
  pidginization 531, 532
Reinecke, John E. 903
Relative clauses, spoken language 272, 274
Relativity, linguistic *see* Sapir–Whorf Hypothesis
Relativization, transfer 501
Relevance, context 221, 222
Relexification 436, 438, 482
  pidgins 533
Reliability
  coders 812
  social research measurements 100, 809–13
    repeatability 812
Religion(s)
  authority 97
  and behavior 9–10
  beliefs about language 263–4
  bilingualism and 17
  countercultures 405
  imperialism and 571
  and language 262–5, 510
    preservation 264
  and linguistics 264–5
  measuring religiosity 811, 812–13
  nationalism and 665
  nationality and 663
  new movements 95
  sacred texts 262–3, 264–5
  social relationships and 825–6
  sociology of 95
  special languages 263
  subcultures 402, 403
  see also Missionaries; *names of specific religions*
Remedial language programs 56

Repertoire, linguistic (code; verbal) 106–7
Reported speech, in narrative 132
Representation 604–6
  discourse and 605
  institutional language 240
  lexis/transitivity options 605
  and natural kinds of language 604
  perspective and 605
  register and 605
  and Sapir–Whorf hypothesis 604, 605
  in systemic–functional linguistics 605–6
  and text interpretation 260
  and value systems 606
Representatives, speech acts 201
Repression, linguistic
  in doctor–patient language 53–4
  in media language 53
  societal pragmatics 53
Requests, conversation 114
Research
  classroom talk 804
  field methods *see* Field methods
  literacy 787–9, 791–2
  methods, social psychology 81–2
  small groups 821–7
  see also Social research
Resources, discursive 366–8
  experimental situations and 369
Reunionese 463
Revitalization of languages 653, 655
  immersion programs 835
  learning models 836
  organizations 837–8
  resource development 836–7
  schools 835
Rhetoric
  of advertising 250
  genres 237
  political 574, 584–5
    linguistic manipulation 574
    speech devices 585–6
  scientific journals 574
  topoi, genre topics 236
Rickford, John Russell 904–5
Rights
  language, ethnic minorities 326
  see also Human rights
Rites of reversal, taboo words in 286
Ritual languages, intertwined 482
Ritual(s)
  blessings 211
  communication 325–6
  formulaic speech 234 [pl
Ro 616
Role theory 59–65, 83–4, 823
  symbolic interactionism and 96
Role(s)
  adequacy 62
  allocation 61
  appropriation 61
  change 64
  conflict 62–3
  differentiation 60–1
  enactment 61–3
  language and 64–5, 83
  learning 61
  organizational 63
  person and 63–4
  sick 63
  situational, kinesics 170
  in society 63, 83–4
  strain 62–3
  structural vs interactional 60
  symbolic interactionism 83–4
  types/definitions 59–60
Romaine, Suzanne 905
Roman script 565
Romance languages, dialectology 311
Romani, Anglo-Romani 525
Romanticism, nationalism and 665
Rosetta Project 839
Rule ordering, multiple variants and, statistical analysis 832–3
Rules
  descriptive 48–9
  prescriptive 48–9
  variable, sociolinguistics 384–5
Rural speech/language 418–19
Russenorsk 531, 532
Russian
  diglossia 228
  international status 621, 623
  nationalism and 668–9
  UNESCO statistics 684

Saami
  double semilingualism 606
  minority language education, Norway 548
Sabir 527
Sacks, Harvey 905–6
  ethnomethodology 161
Sacred texts 262–3
  communication of 264–5
  preservation 264
  translation 262–3
St Jerome 511
Salvage work 813–16
  evaluation problem 814
Sampling 101–2
  natural speech 829, 830–1
Sango 525
Sankoff, Gillian 906–7
Sanskrit
  standardization 681
  writing systems, script conflicts 565
Santa Barbara School 51

Santhali script 565
Sapir, Edward 907–8
Sapir–Whorf hypothesis 39–40, 65–73, 157
  grammatical version 66
  lexical version 65–6
  and representation 604, 605
  world view 39–40, 65, 66–7
Saramaccan 529
Satire, carnivalization 133
Saussure, Ferdinand (Mongin) de 1, 73–80
  on arbitrariness of signs 77–8
  Cours de linguistique générale 74, 77
  on *langue* as a social fact 75–6
  on linearity of signifiers 78
  on primacy of spoken language 74–5
  semiology 76–7
  on syntagmatic and paradigmatic relations 78–9
  on systematicity of *langue* 79–80
Saville-Troike, Muriel 908–9
Scale and Category Grammar, influence on grammar teaching 725
Scaling 816–20
  Bogardus Social Distance 817–18
  coefficient of reproducibility and 820
  Guttman 820
  implicational scales 693, 831–2
  intensity in 818, 820
  interval measures 817, 818, 819
  item-analysis 819–20
  Likert 819–20
  multidimensional *see* Multidimensional scaling
  ordinality in 817, 818–19
  Thurstone 818–19
Scandinavian languages, standardization 682
Scheff, T. J. 97–8
Schegloff, Emanuel 909–10
Schema-usage 25
Schemata
  context in 220
  mental, neutral ideational formations 561
Schiffrin, Deborah 910–11
Schizophasia 54
Schizophrenese 54
Schizophrenia
  labeling theory 97
  language dysfunction in 54
School language policies 679–80
  and language across the curriculum 679
  and language in education 711–13
  language variety fostering 719, 720, 721
  migrant children 506, 507
  Standard English and 720, 753–7
School(s)
  failure *see* Educational failure
  and home, children's language experiences 216, 737–8
  linguistic homogenization in 651
  in reversing language shift 675

revitalization of languages 835
social class and 366
and social differentiation 300
youth subcultures 298
Schuchardt, Hugo 911–12
Science, international languages/communication in 622–3, 624
Science fiction
  language 95
  as subculture 95
  types 102–3
Scientific imperialism 571
Scientific nomenclature, sociology and 95–6
Scotland, linguistic atlas 352, 354
Scots dialects, vowel systems 317–18
Scots Gaelic
  East Sutherland 496, 497, 815, 860
  language shift 496, 497
Scottish Guidelines for English Language 730
Script theory, context in 220
Sea, language of 468
Seaspeak 468
Second languages
  creativity in 517–18
  grammatical intuitions 478
  native speakers 517–18
  speakers of, in legal contexts 232, 233
Second languages, acquisition
  bilingual education 696
  cultural dimension 518
  difficult areas 513
  interlanguage *see* Interlanguage
  language acquisition device 477, 479
  literacy 741
  markedness 693
  Monitor Model/Theory 478, 692, 695
  oral performance, monitoring 691
  social psychology of language 695
  sociolinguistics 691–6
    acculturation model 695
    fossilization 695
    networks 692
    quantitative microsociolinguistics 691–5
    variables 691–5
  sociology of language 695
  transfer and 499–503
Second languages, learning
  accent (pronunciation) 296–7
  age and 599
  contrastive analysis, transfer theory 476
  indicator of importance as international language 621
  overgeneralizations 477
  styles, intuitive/random 478
Second languages, teaching
  assumptions over correct pronunciation 797
  ethnosensitivity in cross-cultural contexts 756
  in UK (modern languages) 712

Secret languages 277–8
  intertwined languages as 482
Sects 95
  conversion to, social bonds and 825–6
  language use 95
Self
  construals, independent/interdependent 189
  defining 83–4
  discursive resources and 367
  gender and 369
  ignorance of 85
  interaction and 84
  roles 83–4
  self-conception 367
  symbolic interactionism and 83–4
Self-direction
  discursive resources and 367
  occupational 366, 367
Self-esteem, social class and 367
Self-presentation, kinesics 170
Semantic change, dialogism 130–1
Semantic differential 85, 96
Semantic relations, ethnography and 71
Semantics
  context in 219–20, 222
  determiner of language use 308
  formal, and discursive function 136
  intensional, context in 219
  intonation link 136
  lexical, context in 220
  procedural, contextual derminants 220
  propositions, context in 220
  slang 268
  structural, and representation 605
  truth-conditional, role of context 220
Semibilingualism 508
Semilingualism 606–8
  comparison with monolingual language variation 607
  double 508
Sémiologie 77
Semiosis, word as ideological phenomenon 560
Semiotics
  advertising 249–50
  Encoding/Decoding model of mass communication 247
  ideologies, analysis 561, 576–7
  langue in 76–7
  social
    ideology in 562
    media language 254
    and register 260, 262
    in texts 238
Sense
  and representation 605
  role of context 220
Sentences, spoken language 271–2
Sex *see* Gender (sex)

Sexism 95
  in discourse, resistance 596
  in language 45, 581
    replacement of 57
Sexuality, language and 333
  see also Gay language
Shift, language 493–8
  causes 493–5
  course 495–6
  demographic factors 494
  economic factors 494
  koinés and 488
  language loyalty and 492
  multilingual speech communities 18–19
  rememberers 495
  reversing 673–9
    ambivalences/difficulties 675–7
    case studies 677–8
    stages (Graded Intergenerational Dislocation Scale) 673–5, 677–8
  semi-speakers 495, 496, 497
  sociolinguistics 389–90
  status factors 494–5
  young fluent speakers 495
Shuy, Roger W. 912–13
Sick role 63
Sign language(s)
  attitudes to 91
  bilingualism 89–90
  contact phenomena 90
  discourse analysis 91–2
  language planning 91
  regional variation 89
  sociolinguistics 89–92
  use of 90–1
Significants *see* Signifiers
Signification system 25
  variation grammar form 26–7
Signifieds, in *langue* 77
Signifiers
  in *langue* 77
  linearity of 78
  of meaning 128
Signifying 291
Signing, contact 90
Sign(s)
  arbitrariness 129
    relative 77
    Saussure on 77–8
  cultural and changing meanings 130–1
  and dialogism 127
  evaluative accent 129
  iconic, in advertising 250
  in ideology 560
  indexical, in advertising 250
  in Marxist language theories 578
  multi-accentuality aspect 129–30
  Peirce's theory 250, 254

as socially/ideologically motivated structure 544
symbolic, in advertising 250
value 79
SIL International 511
Silence
Australian Aborigines' speech 233
groups, cultural variations 149–50, 755
Similes, conventional 234
Simplification
bilingualism 12
cross-linguistic/cross-cultural discourse 145–6
in foreigner talk 474
pidginization 531, 532
Situation
context of 72, 220–1, 260–1, 866
ethnomethodology 221
indirect speech acts 220–1
definition of 83
Skepticists 25–7
Slang 265–70
in adolescent peer group language 299
definitions 265–6
medical 258–9
resolutions 266
sociology 95
Slaves/Slavery
ebonics and 709
language assimilation 600
Small talk intercultural variation 148, 149
Smallest Space Analysis 796
Social bonding, creation 821
Social categorization, in doctor–patient language 153
Social class 362–70
changes 365–6, 367–8
conceptualization 810
consciousness 365, 366
crime and 8
definitions 93
divisions for research 810
and educational underachievement 738
ethnicity and 365
habitus and 651
and ideology 559, 560
individuals and 364
language and 166, 307–10, 363, 366
empirical studies 368
planning norms 309
language change 390
language variation and 93, 375–6
gender and 338–40
measuring 102
operationalizations 308
prejudices, and Marxist language theories 576
relationship with profit from education 713
reproduction 365, 366, 367
slang 265
and social networks 371, 375–6
and sociolinguistic studies 387

speech variation 93, 598
Standard English power relationship 594
and subcultures 403
syntactic complexity of speech 737
understanding of classroom interaction rules 737
Social closure 365
Social constructionism 98–9
institutional discourse and 241
Social constructivism 168
Social control, language and 582
Social deviance
amplification 403
primary/secondary 97
subcultures and 402–3
theories of causes 825
see also Labeling theory
Social dialogue, Halliday's theory of language 29
Social differences, markers 265, 266
Social differentiation, subcultures and 402, 403
Social distance relativity, honorifics and 558, 559
Social distance scaling 96, 817–18
Social facilitation 822
Social facts, languages as 35
Social groups
awareness of membership 826
categories 95–6
cohesiveness 97, 825–6
communication norms 823
divergence and 195
ethnolinguistic vitality 472–3
feelings about 826
goals 824–5
solidarity and 824
individuals and 94
meaning variations across 96
naming 826
norms 821–2
primary 826
reference groups 84, 826
negative 84
restricted codes in 214–15
risk-taking 822
social psychology 85–6
solidarity 367, 821
language and 299, 301
levels 824, 825
systems 825
'we-feeling' 826
Social identity, language and 166
Social isolate 827
Social matrix (context), language in 28
Social mobility 364, 365
Social movements
analysis of, politics and 99
symbolic crusade analysis 98, 99
nationalism and 99
Social networks 86, 370, 827, 828
density 370–1

1022

language change 390
language variation 370–6
  close-knit communities 371, 373
  gender and 339–40
  loose-knit communities 373
  small-scale communities 372–3
migrants 373
  integration index 373
  urbanization 373
multiplexity 370–1
network strength scale 371–2
restricted codes in 214–15
social class and 371, 375–6
Social norms 821–2
  adolescent peer groups and 298
  exchange theory on 821
  linguistic basis 821
  standardization 822
  subcultures and 402, 403
Social problems
  counterclutures and 404, 406
  defining 98
  social construction 98
  subcultures and 402–3
  symbolic crusades and 98
Social psychology 80–6
  attitude in 82–3
  research methods 81–2
  of speech 81–2
  structure 80–1
  symbolic interactionism and 81
Social reality
  identity conditions for a language 35
  ideology in 562
  language as 34–6
    emergence of norms 35
    hypercorrection and 35
    representation through language 248
Social relations, sociometry 827–8
Social relativism, in politeness 189
Social research
  bias in 100–1
  forced choice 8
  measurements 102, 809–10, 816
    reliability/validity 100, 809–13
    scaling 102, 103, 816–20
    sociometry 827–8
    standardization 812
  methodology, ethnomethodology and 162–3
  open/closed questions, effects on responses 8
  techniques, semantic differential 85
Social sciences, ethnomethodology and 163, 164
Social (societal) reaction theory *see* Labeling theory
Social structure, measuring 827
Social support
  accommodation and 196
  and relationship between attitudes and behavior 8, 9

Social-critical tendency 50
Socialization 87–9, 366
  acquisition of registers 87
  adolescence 298
  children
    gender differences 342
    speech play 278–9
  children's metapragmatic knowledge 87
  conflict in 564
  environmental influences 88
  and gender differences in language 88, 300, 302
  habitus 650–1
  indexicality 87
  of language, Afro-Americans 46
  language attitudes 88
  literacy 87, 88
  primary/secondary discourses 87
  reading acquisition 87–8
  resistance 88
Societal bilingualism 16–22
Society
  language in 582
    consciousness raising 581–2
    social control and 582
  theories of
    idealist/materialist 96
    language and 96
Society for Pidgin and Creole Languages 840
Sociodrama 60
Sociolects, written 26
Sociolinguistic Symposium 840
Sociolinguistics
  antecedents 1
  applications 3
  branches 2–3
  context 40–1
  critical 542–5
  culture and 37–8
  emphases 1–2
  empirical, and linguistic variation 308–9
  goals 377
  historical background 36–7
  history 1–2
  linguistic and social variation, correlation of 43–4
  linguistic stratification, paralleled in social stratification 309
  meaning and 38–40
  methodology 381–2, 386
    in sociophonetic studies 391–3
  overview 36–48
  social class in 387
  syntactic studies 382–4
  terminology 2–3
  theoretical, class in 307–8
Sociologists, language use 94
Sociology
  bias 104

1023

fragmentation 104
linguistics and 92, 94, 96, 104
microsociology 85–6
qualitative approaches 103–4
Sociology of knowledge 97
Sociology of language 2–3, 92–105
journals 93, 94
Sociometry 86, 825, 827–8
Sociophonetics 391–6
case studies 393–5
techniques 391–5
variables 392–3
Solidarity 821
adolescent peer group language and 299, 301
conversation analysis 114, 115
honorifics 556–7
mechanical 367
organic 367
Soul Talk 529
Sound changes
chain shifts 303–7
American English 304–5
Great Vowel Shift 303–4
ongoing 304–6
child language 346–7
dialectology and 314–16
Grimm's Law 398
language acquisition 346–7
language improvement and 400
method 398–9
and morphology 396–401
Neogrammarians 398
North American English 412
spread 412–13
phonetics and 400–1
reasons for 399–400
sociolinguistics 389, 390
Sounds, loss 397
South Africa
language adaptation and modernization 628, 629
language situation 603
mother tongue in education 711
Sovereignty, text feature 261
Soviet Union, as multilingual state 655–6
Spain, rationalization of language 653
Spanish
colonialism and 602–3
dialects, pronunciation maps 797–800
international status 621, 622
pronunciation 797–800
regional variations 798
reversing language shift, New York 678
standard/standardization 681
UNESCO statistics 684, 685–8
Spatial relations, child language development 706–7
Speaker identification (SID) 330–1
by lay witnesses 331–2
Speaker profiling 330

Speakers
analysis of patterns, multidimensional scaling 800–1
dominant 241
of a language
criteria 684
numbers, UNESCO study 683–8
potential 684, 685
real 684–5
Speaking
as culturally distinctive 156–7
descriptive framework 158–9
ethnography 30, 41, 154–60
Standard English and 754–5
second language processing, oral performance monitoring 691
structure 155–6
Speech
accommodation 193–7
as behavior 7–8
casual
data collection 802
register 261
colloquial, vernacular as 420
communicative competence 159
connected 393
'cross-over-pattern', lower middle class speakers 310
as culturally distinctive 156–7
deviation, primary/secondary 97
free 583
functions 157
gender differences 45, 337–40
indirect, context of situation 220–1
kinesics in 171
network 158
performance, speech formulas in 234
phatic 186
planning, function of formulas 234
prestige forms 44
second languages 692
sign-supported 91
situations, ideological interpellation in 561, 562, 595
social factors 43–4
social patterns and 157–8
as social process 128
social psychology of 81–2
structure 155–6
Speech accommodation *see* Accommodation
Speech act(s)
addressees 199–200
analysis, cross-cultural contexts 146–7, 150
Austin and 198
classification 201–2
constatives 198
dependency relationship with power 589
direct 203

direct/indirect, intercultural variation 147
directness levels 190
and discourse 207
ethnography of speaking 41
felicity conditions 198, 200–1
hierarchy 198–9
indirect 202–3
  deviousness in 574
infant understanding of 704
and intercultural pragmatics 206–7
intercultural variation 146–7
  channel 148
  honorifics 148
  linguistic creativity rules 148
  organization 147–8
  small talk 148, 149
  systems of address 148
in interlanguage comparative work 480
literal/nonliteral 203
overhearers 200
performative clauses 198, 201
politeness in 190–2, 589
  speech act sets 190, 191
ratified participants 200
as social interaction 197–8, 206
speaker's reflexive-intention 199–200
theory 197–208
  classroom discourse 804, 808
  context 219, 220–1, 222
  felicity conditions 220–1
  inferential analysis 204–6
  initiative/response pairs 152
  initiative/response/acknowledgement triples 152
  of literary discourse 245
  medical communication 152
Speech area 158
Speech communities 105–7, 157–8, 269
  bilingual 106
  characteristics 105
  differentiation 597–8
  diglossic 106
  heterogeneity, statistical studies and 831
  learners in 695
  linguistic repertoire 106–7
  monolingual 106
  new varieties 507
  rivalries and conflicts 107
  speech style and 310
  variation studies 776
Speech data, observer's paradox 802
Speech events
  ethnography 158
  ethnography of speaking 41
  functions 159
Speech exchange systems, conversation analysis 115–16
Speech field 158
Speech genres 42

Speech islands see Enclaves, language
Speech perception
  normalization 400
  sociophonetic studies 392–3
  and sound change 400–1
Speech play 276–80
  children 278–9
  cross-cultural comparison 277
  and humor 279
  linguistic characteristics 277–8
  and performance 278–9
  sociocultural contexts 277
  types 277
  verbal art and 279
Speech production
  social class and 307
  sociophonetic studies 392
Speech recognition, corpora and 768–9
Speech styles
  in adolescent peer group language 299
  attitudes towards 82
    socialization 88
  Audience Design 109–10, 386–7
  courtroom witnesses 231
  monitoring 692
  shifts 110
  social class and 93, 362, 364
  status 82
Speech synthesis, corpora and 768–9
Speeches, political, devices 585–6
Spelling
  adaptation and modernization 629
  internet language 288
  reform 670–1
  standardization 671
  variant forms 671
  see also Orthography
Spoken language
  classroom see Classroom, spoken language
  data collection, elicitation tests 770, 771
  discourse devices 274–5
    new topics 274
  evaluation 746–7
  grammatical analysis 271
  linearity 78
  narrative 271
  nature of 270–1
  primacy of, Saussure on 74–5
  properties 271
  and written language 270–6
    grammatical differences 271–5
    grammatical study 727–8
    linguistics 275–6
Spolsky, Bernard 913–14
Spoonerisms 278
Sprachbünde 427–8, 429, 434
Spread of languages 498–9, 573
Sranan 529

Srivastava, Ravindra Nath 914
Standard languages 32, 34
  and dialects 311
  European attitudes 720
  and national languages 659
  and non-standard languages, in education 712–13
  role in discrimination 546
Standardization of language 658, 681–3
  colonial and missionary influences 683
  conflicts in 565
  dictionaries 672
    role of Academies 615–6
  history 681
  institutions' role 681–2
  and modernization 628, 629
  power relationship 593–4
  process of 311
  spelling 671
  spoken language 682
  writing systems 682
State languages
  colloquial/standard form 18
  legitimate norm 19
Statistical analysis
  computerization 795
  correlation coefficients 794
  factor analysis 794
  multidimensional scaling 103, 793–802
    algorithms 795–6
    computer-aided 794, 795
    of individual speakers 800–1
    maps 795, 797–800
  regression analysis, and multidimensional scaling 794, 799, 801
  sociolinguistics 828–34
    data for 830–1
    epistemological concerns 829
    heterogeneity detection 831
    implicational scales 831–2
    sample 829, 830–1
Statistics
  endangered languages 465–6
  illiteracy 742–6
  principal languages of the world 636, 638, 683–8
    country typologies 685–8
    total number of speakers 688
Status
  adolescent peer group language and 300
  and credibility 82
  gender and 301
  language planning 645
  reversing language shift and 675
  small groups 823–4
  sociology 823–4
  subcultures and 403
Stereotypes
  in Marxist theory of language 577
  in political language 590

sociocultural 608–9
sociolinguistics 381
Stigma
  race and 600
  and subcultural boundaries 402
Stories 180
  children's 184–5
  group 183–4
  reflection of cultural presuppositions and values 182
  tellability 180, 181
Storytelling 182
Street, Brian 914–5
Structural functionalism 96
  social psychology and 81
Structuralism
  influence on grammar teaching 725
  social class 364–5
  systematicity of *langue* in 79–80
Structure, deep *see* Deep structure
Stuttering, societal effects on 97
Style(s) 280–3
  articulatory/language, symbolic value 612–13
  Audience Design 109–10, 386–7
  authorial 282
  content/form distinction 282
  continuous competence model, second language acquisition 692
  conversational, gender differences 340–1
  deviant 281
  domaine 282
  formality-related 283
  group 282
  initiative 110
  institutional language 240
  iterativity and 281
  linguistic, variation 386–7
  as linguistic choice 280–1
  literary texts 282–3
  poetic 281
  responsive 110
  second language acquisition
    observer's paradox 691
    vernacular 691
  shifting, and diglossia 229
  shifts 110
  sociolinguistics of second language acquisition 691
  speech *see* Speech style
  text 282–3
  variables
    social class and 309–10
    sociolinguistics of second language acquisition 692, 695
Stylistics 282
Stylization 110
Subclass, migrant workers as 504
Subcultures 94–5, 109, 269, 401–7
  and anomie 403

assimilation 403–4
boundaries 402
drug-based 403
ethnic 402
and identity 402
language, dictionaries 94–5
literary and artistic schools as 95
maintenance and change 403–4
origins 402–3
overlapping 402
reactions to 403
relationship to larger society 403
religious 402, 403
slang 265, 266–7, 268–70
social differentiation and 402, 403
and social norms 402, 403
social problems and 402–3
and status 403
working-class 403
youth 298
   boundaries 402, 403
see also Countercultures
Subsocieties 94
Substrate influence 499–503
koinéization and 488
pidgins 531, 533
Substrate theory, creoles 462
Substratum languages 434
Summer Institute of Linguists 841
website 839
Surinam, creoles 529
Surnames, transmission 343
Survey of English usage (Quirk) 766
Surveys
attitudes 761–5
   context effect 763–4
   form of questions 762–3
   interviewer effects 764–5
   wording of questions 761–2
coding 762, 812
'don't know' responses 8, 762
linguistic, sampling 101–2
linguistic data in 96
literacy 789–91
sociological 96
split-ballot experiments 761
   interviewer characteristic varying 761, 764
   question varying 761–2
Swahili, adaptation and modernization 627–8
Swann Report (1985) (UK) 680, 712
Swardspeak 334
Swearing 284, 285
gender differences 338
Sweden, heritage languages in education 712
Swedish, international status 622
Switzerland, as multilingual state 654
Syllables, reduction 346
Symbol systems, roles 68–9

Symbolic interactionism 60, 83, 96, 821
analysis of self 83–4
and educational theory 84
generalized other 84
influence 84
labeling theory and 97
and language 96
role theory 83–4
social psychology and 81
Symbolic power, language and 610–12
Symbolism, orthography 669–70
Symbols, culture 37–8
Synchronic linguistics, Saussure on 74
Synchrony, distinction from diachrony 27
Synonyms, supposed, responses to research questions containing 101, 761–2
Syntagmatic relations, Saussure on 78–9
Syntax
innovations, child language 347
institutional language 240
process theory, theme/rheme 28
rules, dialect variation 383–4
sociolinguistic studies 382–4
variables 385–6
Systemic linguistics, ideology in 562
Systemic Theory
ideology in narrative 185
register and 259
representation in 605–6
in teaching writing 727

Taboo
concept 283–4
words 283–7
   adolescent peer group language 299
   cross-cultural differences 285–6
   defining 294
   functions 286
   gender-specific 338
Taboos, sociolinguistic interviews 777
Tabouret-Keller, A., projection model/group identity 167–8
Tag phrases, adolescent peer group language 299
Tag questions, and restricted codes 215
Tagging 768
Tagmemics 511
Talk
classroom *see* Classroom, spoken language
coding, small groups 808
oracy 746–7
'Talking kush' 334
Talmudic script 565
Tannen, Deborah 916
Tape recordings *see* Recordings
Tarçanca 484
Tasmanian 493
Teacher training, grammar 726, 729–30
Teacher-talk 751–2

Teaching
  banking concept 53
  grammar *see* Grammar, teaching
Teaching English as a Foreign Language (TEFL)
  anglocentrism 469
  Australian initiatives 642–3
  British Council 642
  curriculum development 469–70
  history 467
  industry 468–9
  profession 468
  publishing 469
  teachers' associations 469
  testing 469
  USIA in 641
Teaching English to Speakers of Other Languages (TESOL) 467
Technical language 240
  interpretation through education 752–3
Technological nomenclature
  diffusion 96
  sociology and 95–6
Technology
  countercultures 405–6
  literacy and 742, 791–2
Teleology 399–400
Telephone calls, defining 85
Telephone conversation
  analysis of 138
  on television 253
Television
  advertising 210
  female voice stigmatization 254
  international broadcasting 635, 639
  restricted/elaborated codes in 248
  telephone conversation programs 253
Temperance Movement, symbolic crusade analysis 98
Tense, historic present, in oral narrative 183
Terminology development, language adaptation 628
Terralingua 837
Testing
  situations, validity 216
  teaching English as a foreign language 469
Tex-Mex 13
Text analysis, through rhetorical theories of genre 237
Text Encoding Initiative (TEI) 766
Text grammar, context in 219, 222
Text linguistics, formalist approach 136
Text processing, schema-theory 605
Textbooks, readability 713–14
Text(s)
  beginning-middle-end structures 236, 237
  context in 219
  contextualization 260, 261
  corpus, in data collection 770–1
  critical discourse analysis 543–4

critical sociolinguistics 543–4
dialogic/monologic distinction 128
and grammar teaching 732, 733, 734
heteroglossia 128, 560
heteroglot/monoglot distinction 128
ideological interpellation in 595
ideology in 560, 561, 595
  and functional grammar 248
interpretation 260
literacy assessment 791
Marxist language theories 576
production, as discourse 134
register 259
  re-registration 259, 261
  and sociological linguistics 259–60
register mix in 261
sampling, in data collection 770
social semiotics in 238
style analysis 282–3
voices, in narratives 128
Thai, honorifics 552, 554
Thai Boi 484
Theme–rheme
  known–new structure of context 219
  in Prague school process theory of syntax 28
Thinking, higher-order, role of language in 737–8
Thought, influence of language 66, 68
Threatened languages 465
Thurstone Scaling 818–19
Tibetan, honorifics 552, 553, 554
Titles
  gender and 343
  marriage-related 343
Tok Pisin 461, 462, 463, 524, 525–6, 532–3, 534
  adoption as official language 645
  morphology 537
Tom dee 335
Tongue twisters 277
Tourism, language and 635
Trade languages
  international languages 623
  pidgins 19, 461, 463
  polyglossia strategy 18
Tradition, nationality and 663
Transcription
  classroom talk 803, 804, 805–9
  conversation analysis 111–12
  field work 779, 780
Transfer 434–5, 499–503
  in bilingual children 431–2
  borrowing 499
  constraints 500–1
  interlanguage psycholinguistic processes 477, 480
  negative 499, 501
  positive 499, 501
  second language learning, contrastive analysis 476
  shift-induced, creole development 462
  social diffusion of transfer patterns 501–2

Transference, in cross-linguistic/cross-cultural discourse 145
Transformational Grammar, influence on grammar teaching 725
Translation
  Bible, missionaries 510, 511
  ethnographic 72
  theory, missionaries' contribution 511
Translators, bilinguals as 11
Tree Adjoining Grammar 458
Triglossia, Tanzania 572
Trinidad, Bhojpuri 800–1
Trudgill, Peter John 916–17
Truth-conditions, role of context 220
Tucker, G. Richard 918
Turkish
  diglossia 228
  standardization 682
  writing systems, conflicts 565
Turn-taking
  classroom 804, 808
  conversation 111, 112–13, 115, 137, 138
    recipient design 113, 115
  conversational analysis 43
  discourse analysis 148, 149
  institutional settings 240–1
  kinesics 171
  news interviews 252–3
  power status and 589
Typology
  diglossia 228–30
  syntactic change 410, 411

Ulfilas 511
Ulpan 643
Underprivilegedness, societal, pragmatics in 56
Understanding
  ethnomethodology and 162, 164
  indexicality and 162
UNESCO
  actions on linguistic discrimination 548
  study of principal languages of the world 683–8
United Bible Societies 511
United Kingdom, extraterritorial language promotion 641–2
United Nations
  official languages 622
  protection of minority rights 547
  working languages 622
United States
  African languages and 600
  bilingualism, assimilationist policies 712
  extraterritorial language promotion 640–1
  language legislation 659–60
  linguistic atlases 312, 351, 352, 354, 359
    Atlas of North American English 412–18
  national/official languages 659, 660
  subcultures 402

United States Information Agency/Service (USIA/USIS) 640–1
Universal Grammar
  competence 25
  influence on development of interlanguage 478–9
  second language acquisition 478–9
Universal languages, history 617
Universals
  cross-linguistic 67, 71
  and interlanguage 479
Upgraders, discourse analysis 147
Urban dialects
  attitudes to 375
  consensus model 375
  studies
    Belfast 371
    social networks 371, 375
    sociolinguistic 379–81
Urban speech/language 418–19
Usage
  correct/incorrect, prescription 672
  lexical existence guide 616
Use of language
  in bilingual child language acquisition 430
  census questions and 100
  communicative competence 29–30
  conditions of, societal pragmatics 52
  conscious and unconscious 731
  contextual sensitivity, business language 212–13
  determined by semantics 308
  in education 698–9
  effect of ideology 814
  gender and 337–40, 735–7
  implicit 215
  non-mainstream groups 754–5
  prescribed, in ritualistic formulas 234
  statistical analysis 829–30
  see also Discourse
Utterances
  as action 6
  acts 198–9
  child language development 706
  constative 198
  context, interpretation and 5
  disputed, assessment 330
  formulating, in news interviews 253
  performative 198

VARBRUL 385
Valdman, Albert 919
Validity, social research measurements 100, 809–13
  construct validity 811
  content validity 811
  criterion-related validity 811
  face validity 810–11
  predictive power 811
Values 96
  adolescent peer group language and 299

1029

content analysis 103
counterculture and 404–5
goals and 824
linguistic nature 96
power and 97
social groups and 97
Van Name, Addison 919–20
Variables
    factor analysis 102, 103
    linguistic
        sociophonetic studies 392, 393
        statistical analysis 830–1
    multidimensional scaling 103
    multiple 102–3
    social research 100, 809–10
        measurements 816
        scaling 816–20
    sociolinguistic 309, 379
        phonological 371, 374
        second language acquisition 691–5
        social class 375–6
        social network studies 371, 374
        syntactic 385–6
        types 381
    weighting 102
Variation grammar, signification system 26–7
Variation, linguistic
    field methods 781
    free 377
    gender and 336–45, 386
    hypercorrection 380
    lexical, in Norwegian's written sociolects 26
    measurement 816
    pragmalinguistic 190
    semilingualism 607
    social class and 307, 308, 387
    social networks and 370–6
    sociolinguistics 377–89
    sociophonetic variables 310
    statistical analysis 829–33
        multiple variants and rule order 832–3
        rare variants 832
    studies
        communities/individuals 776–7
        field methods 776–9
        goals 776
        interviews 776, 777–8
    style and 386–7
    syntax 382–4
Varieties of language 34
    attitudes to 719–20
        matched-guise technique 719
    fostered by school language policy 719, 720
    multilingual speech communities 17–18
    prestige differences 593
    in speech communities 507
Vatican City State Radio 636
Vedanta Society 510

Veiling of societal oppression, by means of language 54
Verbal aggression 290
Verbal art
    speech play and 279
    verbal dueling and 291
Verbal duel 289–92
    classification 290
    indirectness in 291
    as socialization process 290–1
    topics 290
    verbal art and 291
Verbalization
    explicitness 215
    implicitness 215
Verbosity, comparison with forceful and direct language 718
Verbs
    illocutionary 201
    paradigms, inflections 140
Vernacular(s) 379, 420–1
    data collection 802
    as national language 661
    variation 379
Verstehen 103
Violence, symbolic 611
Vitality, ethnolinguistic 472–3
Vivekanada, Swami 510
Vocabolario degli Accademici della Crusca 615
Vocabulary
    acquisition
        early childhood 705–6
        infants 704
        spurt in 705–6
    discriminatory language 545–6
    gay language 333
    gender differences 338
Voice of America (VoA) 640, 641
Voice parade (line-up) 331–2
Voicing, in communication 27
Volapük 617
Völkerpsychologie 75, 76
Voloshinov, Valentin Nikolavic 920–1
Vowels
    chain shifts
        American English 304–5, 415, 417
        explanations of triggering 305–6
        Great Vowel Shift 303–4
        ongoing 304–6
    merging 303, 306, 415, 417

Warfare, linguistic 568
Wave theory, areal linguistics 425–7, 428–9
    advance of wave-movements 427
Weber, Max 103–4
    social class theory 364, 365
Websites 838–9
Webster's Third New International Dictionary 672

Weinreich, Uriel 921–2
Welsh
  diglossia 228
  language shift 494
Wenker, Georg 922–3
  dialectology 311–12
Wh-clefts, spoken language 275
Whorf, Benjamin Lee 923–4
Wider communication, languages of *see* Lingua francas
Wilkins, John 617, 618
Will, human, in language production 75
Williams, Glyn 924–5
Witnesses
  courtroom, discourse analysis 232
    second language and non-standard dialect speakers 232–3
  lay, speaker identification 331–2
Wodak, Ruth 925–6
Wolfram, Walt 926
Women
  feminist analysis of language 543
  terms of address 342–3
  treatment in language 343, 344
  use of language 44–5, 336, 340–1
Word-frequency statistics, natural language processing need 767
Word play, in adolescent peer group language 299
Wording the world (language as means of seeing the world) 55–6
Words
  dirty 284–5
  four-letter 284, 285
  learning
    analysis in 705
    early childhood 100–1
    infants 704
Work-language 177–9
  and information technology 179
Working class
  child-rearing, imperative rather than argumentative mode 215
  language
    differences vs deficits, in education 716–7, 722, 737
    imperative-normative interactions 717
  social networks, restricted codes in 215
  status-oriented family structure 215

Workplace, conversation analysis 115–16
World, wording (language as means of seeing) 55–6
World languages
  English 623
  linguistic imperialism and 570
  vs local languages 549
World view(s)
  and restricted/elaborated codes 216
  Sapir–Whorf hypothesis 39–40, 65, 66–7
  social class and 307–8
Writing, learning 740
Writing (composition)
  acquisition of literacy 713
  expressive 724
  gender and 735
  skills
    different genres 185
    and grammar teaching 724
    mastering narrative 184
  teaching
    conscious and unconscious use of language 731
    discourse analysis approach 727
    register 725
    Systemic-Functional model 727
Writing systems
  adaptation and modernization 629
  conflict of 565
  reform 565
  in standardization of language 682
  symbols/symbolism in 669–70
  see also Orthography
Written language
  marginalization, formalized by Saussure 74–5
  and spoken language 270–6
    comparison of properties 271
    grammatical differences 271–5
    grammatical study 727–8
    linguistics 275–6
  transition to, language adaptation and 627
Wycliffe Bible Translators 511

Yaaku, language shift 495
Yahi 495–6
Yiddish 229
  reversing language shift 676, 677, 678
Young people, language 95
Yup'ik 81